1c

ADOBE PHOTOSHOP CS4 REVEALED

ELIZABETH EISNER REDING

ADOBE
PHOTOSHOP
CS4 REVEALED

ELIZABETH EISNER REDING

DELMAR
CENGAGE Learning™

Australia • Brazil • Japan • Korea • Mexico • Singapore • Spain • United Kingdom • United States

DELMAR
CENGAGE Learning™

Adobe Photoshop CS4 Revealed
Elizabeth Eisner Reding

Vice President, Career and Professional Editorial: Dave Garza

Director of Learning Solutions: Sandy Clark

Senior Acquisitions Editor: Jim Gish

Managing Editor: Larry Main

Product Managers: Jane Hosie-Bounar, Nicole Calisi

Editorial Assistant: Sarah Timm

Vice President Marketing, Career and Professional: Jennifer McAvey

Executive Marketing Manager: Deborah S. Yarnell

Marketing Manager: Erin Brennan

Marketing Coordinator: Jonathan Sheehan

Production Director: Wendy Troeger

Senior Content Project Manager: Kathryn B. Kucharek

Developmental Editor: Karen Stevens

Technical Editor: Susan Whalen

Art Director: Bruce Bond, Joy Kocsis

Cover Design: Lisa Kuhn, Curio Press, LLC

Cover Art: Lisa Kuhn, Curio Press, LLC

Text Designer: Ann Small

Proofreader: Kim Kosmatka

Indexer: Alexandra Nickerson

Technology Project Manager: Christopher Catalina

Production Technology Analyst: Tom Stover

For product information and technology assistance, contact us at
Cengage Learning Customer & Sales Support, 1-800-354-9706
For permission to use material from this text or product, submit all requests online at
www.cengage.com/permissions
Further permissions questions can be emailed to
permissionrequest@cengage.com

Adobe® Photoshop®, Adobe® InDesign®, Adobe® Illustrator®, Adobe® Flash®, Adobe® Dreamweaver®, Adobe® Fireworks®, and Adobe® Creative Suite® are trademarks or registered trademarks of Adobe Systems, Inc. in the United States and/or other countries. Third party products, services, company names, logos, design, titles, words, or phrases within these materials may be trademarks of their respective owners.

The Adobe Approved Certification Courseware logo is a proprietary trademark of Adobe. All rights reserved. Cengage Learning and *Adobe Photoshop CS4—Revealed* are independent from ProCert Labs, LLC and Adobe Systems Incorporated, and are not affiliated with ProCert Labs and Adobe in any manner. This publication may asssist students to prepare for an Adobe Certified Expert exam, however, neither ProCert Labs nor Adobe warrant that use of this material will ensure success in connection with any exam.

Library of Congress Control Number: 2008935174

Hardcover edition:
ISBN-13: 978-1-4354-8277-7
ISBN-10: 1-4354-8277-8

Soft cover edition:
ISBN-13: 978-1-4354-4187-3
ISBN-10: 1-4354-4187-7

Delmar
5 Maxwell Drive
Clifton Park, NY 12065-2919
USA

Cengage Learning is a leading provider of customized learning solutions with office locations around the globe, including Singapore, the United Kingdom, Australia, Mexico, Brazil, and Japan. Locate your local office at: **international.cengage.com/region**

Cengage Learning products are represented in Canada by Nelson Education, Ltd.

To learn more about Delmar, visit **www.cengage.com/delmar**

Purchase any of our products at your local college store or at our preferred online store **www.ichapters.com**

Notice to the Reader

Some of the images used in this book are royalty-free and the property of Getty Images, Inc. and Morguefile.com. The Getty images include artwork from the following royalty-free CD-ROM collections: Education Elements, Just Flowers, Portraits of Diversity, Sports and Recreation, Texture and Light, Tools of the Trade, Travel Souvenirs, Travel & Vacation Icons, and Working Bodies. Morguefile images include artwork from the following categories: Objects, Scenes, Animals, and People. Figures 17, 18, and 19 in the Appendix used with permission from Big Brothers/Big Sisters of America.

Printed in the United States of America
1 2 3 4 5 6 7 13 12 11 10 09

Revealed Series Vision

The Revealed Series is your guide to today's hottest multimedia applications. These comprehensive books teach the skills behind the application, showing you how to apply smart design principles to multimedia products such as dynamic graphics, animation, web sites, software authoring tools, and digital video.

A team of design professionals including multimedia instructors, students, authors, and editors worked together to create this series. We recognized the unique learning environment of the multimedia classroom and created a series that:

- Gives you comprehensive step-by-step instructions
- Offers in-depth explanation of the "Why" behind a skill
- Includes creative projects for additional practice
- Explains concepts clearly using full-color visuals

It was our goal to create a book that speaks directly to the multimedia and design community—one of the most rapidly growing computer fields today. We think we've done just that, with a sophisticated and instructive book design.

—The Revealed Series

Author's Vision

The Revealed Series is different from some other textbooks in that its target audience is a savvy student who wants important information and needs little hand-holding. This student has a sense of adventure, an interest in design, and a healthy dose of creativity. This person is fun to write for because he or she wants to learn.

Special thanks to the following team members:

Another 18 months, another version of the Adobe Create Suite. While it might seem unusual to some, this is what we in the computer textbook publishing biz have come to call normal. It seems as though we thrive on this hurry-up-and-wait syndrome otherwise known as a new product release. To the reader, a book magically appears on the shelf with each software revision, but to those of us "making it happen" it means not only working under ridiculous deadlines (which we're used to), but it also means working with slightly different teams with slightly different ways of doing things. Karen Stevens, Susan Whalen, Jane Hosie-Bounar and I have all worked together before on a variety of projects that have spanned more years than we care to admit. Added to the mix are Jim Gish, Sarah Timm and Tintu Thomas. The majority of us have never met face-to-face, yet once again we managed to work together in a professional manner, while defying the time-space continuum with its many time zones, cultural holidays, and countless vacation plans.

I would also like to thank my husband, Michael, who is used to my disappearing acts when I'm facing deadlines, and to Phoebe, Bix, and Jet, who know when it's time to take a break for some good old-fashioned head-scratching.

—Elizabeth Eisner Reding

Introduction to Adobe Photoshop CS4

Welcome to *Adobe Photoshop CS4—Revealed*. This book offers creative projects, concise instructions, and complete coverage of basic to advanced Photoshop skills, helping you to create polished, professional-looking artwork. Use this book both in the classroom and as your own reference guide.

This text is organized into 16 chapters, plus an appendix, "Portfolio Projects and Effects." In these chapters, you will learn many skills, including how to work with layers, make selections, adjust color techniques, use paint tools, work with filters, transform type, liquify an image, annotate and automate a Photoshop document, and create Photoshop images for the web. The appendix provides additional practice in creating projects and effects suitable for use in a design portfolio.

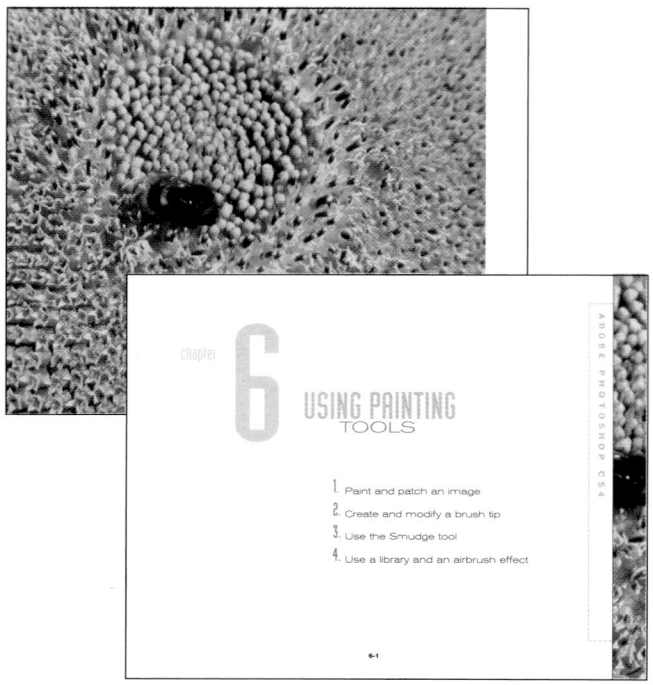

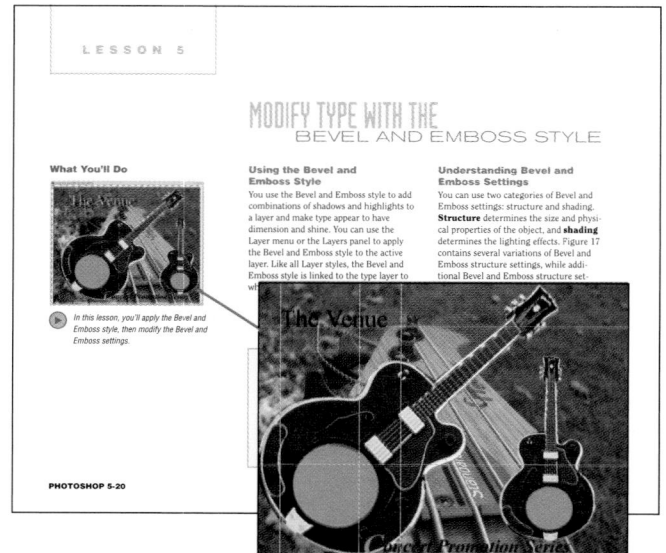

What You'll Do

A What You'll Do figure begins every lesson. This figure gives you an at-a-glance look at what you'll do in the chapter, either by showing you a file from the current project or a tool you'll be using.

Comprehensive Conceptual Lessons

Before jumping into instructions, in-depth conceptual information tells you "why" skills are applied. This book provides the "how" and "why" through the use of professional examples. Also included in the text are tips and sidebars to help you work more efficiently and creatively, or to teach you a bit about the history or design philosophy behind the skill you are using.

Step-by-Step Instructions

This book combines in-depth conceptual information with concise steps to help you learn Photoshop CS4. Each set of steps guides you through a lesson where you will create, modify, or enhance a Photoshop CS4 file. Step references to large colorful images and quick step summaries round out the lessons. The Data Files for the steps are provided on the CD at the back of this book.

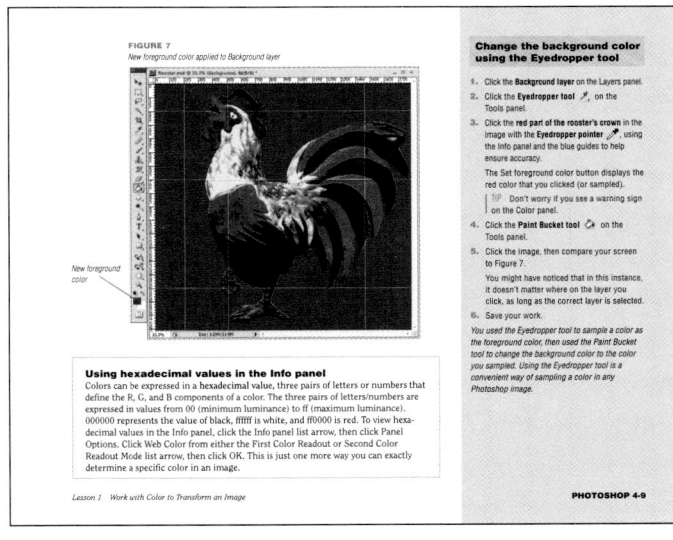

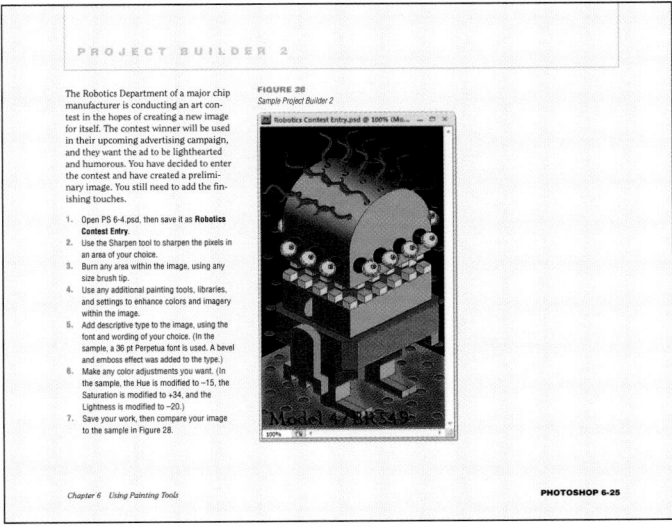

Projects

This book contains a variety of end-of-chapter materials for additional practice and reinforcement. The Skills Review contains hands-on practice exercises that mirror the progressive nature of the lesson material. The chapter concludes with four projects; two Project Builders, one Design Project, and one Portfolio Project. The Project Builders and the Design Project require you to apply the skills you've learned in the chapter. Portfolio Projects encourage students to use their resources to address and solve challenges based on the content explored in the chapter and to create portfolio-worthy projects.

What Instructor Resources Are Available with this Book?

The Instructor Resources CD-ROM is Delmar's way of putting the resources and information needed to teach and learn effectively into your hands. All the resources are available for both Macintosh and Windows operating systems.

Instructor's Manual

Available as an electronic file, the Instructor's Manual includes chapter overviews and detailed lecture topics for each chapter, with teaching tips. The Instructor's Manual is available on the Instructor Resources CD-ROM.

PowerPoint Presentations

Each chapter has a corresponding PowerPoint presentation that you can use in lectures, distribute to your students, or customize to suit your course.

Data Files for Students

To complete most of the chapters in this book, your students will need Data Files. The Data Files are available on the CD at the back of this text book. Instruct students to use the Data Files List at the end of this book. This list gives instructions on organizing files.

Solutions to Exercises

Solution Files are Data Files completed with comprehensive sample answers. Use these files to evaluate your students' work. Or distribute them electronically so students can verify their work. Sample solutions to all lessons and end-of-chapter material are provided.

Test Bank and Test Engine

ExamView is a powerful testing software package that allows instructors to create and administer printed and computer (LAN-based) exams. ExamView includes hundreds of questions that correspond to the topics covered in this text, enabling students to generate detailed study guides that include page references for further review. The computer-based and LAN-based/online testing component allows students to take exams using the EV Player and also save the instructor time by grading each exam automatically.

BRIEF CONTENTS

CHAPTER 5   PLACING TYPE IN AN IMAGE

CHAPTER 8 CREATING SPECIAL EFFECTS WITH FILTERS

CONTENTS

CONTENTS

| APPENDIX | PORTFOLIO PROJECTS AND EFFECTS |

Intended Audience

This text is designed for the beginner or intermediate student who wants to learn how to use Adobe Photoshop CS4. The book is designed to provide basic and in-depth material that not only educates but encourages the student to explore the nuances of this exciting program.

File Identification

Instead of printing a file, the owner of a Photoshop image can be identified by reading the File Info dialog box. Use the following instructions to add your name to an image:

1. Click File on the Application bar, then click File Info.
2. Click the Description tab, if necessary.
3. Click the Author text box.
4. Type your name, course number, or other identifying information.
5. Click OK.

There are no instructions with this text to use the File Info feature other than when it is introduced in Chapter 1. It is up to each user to use this feature so that his or her work can be identified.

Measurements

When measurements are shown, needed, or discussed, they are given in pixels. Use the following instructions to change the units of measurement to pixels:

1. Click Edit (Win) or Photoshop (Mac) on the Application bar, point to Preferences, then click Units & Rulers.
2. Click the Rulers list arrow, then click pixels.
3. Click OK.

You can display rulers by clicking View on the Application bar, then clicking Rulers, or by pressing [Ctrl][R] (Win) or [⌘][R] (Mac). A check mark to the left of the Rulers command indicates that the Rulers are displayed. You can hide visible rulers by clicking View on the Application bar, then clicking Rulers, or by pressing [Ctrl][R] (Win) or [⌘][R] (Mac).

Icons, Buttons, and Pointers

Symbols for icons, buttons, and pointers are shown each time they are used.

Fonts

Data and Solution Files contain a variety of fonts, and there is no guarantee that all of these fonts will be available on your computer. The fonts are identified in cases where less common fonts are used in the files. Every effort has been made to use commonly available fonts in the lessons. If any of the fonts in use are not available on your computer, please make a substitution.

Menu Commands in Tables

In tables, menu commands are abbreviated using the following format: Edit ➢ Preferences ➢ Units & Rulers. This command translates as follows: Click Edit on the Application bar, point to Preferences, then click Units & Rulers.

Skills Reference

As a bonus, a Power User Shortcuts table is included at the end of every chapter. This table contains the quickest method of completing tasks covered in the chapter. It is meant for the more experienced user, or for the user who wants to become more experienced. Tools are shown, not named.

Grading Tips

Many students have web-ready accounts where they can post their completed assignments. The instructor can access the student accounts using a browser and view the images online. Using this method, it is not necessary for the student to include his/her name on a type layer, because all of their assignments are in an individual password-protected account.

Creating a Portfolio

One method for students to submit and keep a copy of all of their work is to create a portfolio of their projects that is linked to a simple web page that can be saved on a CD-ROM. If it is necessary for students to print completed projects, work can be printed and mounted at a local copy shop; a student's name can be printed on the back of the image.

GETTING STARTED WITH ADOBE PHOTOSHOP CS4

1. Start Adobe Photoshop CS4

2. Learn how to open and save an image

3. Use organizational and management features

4. Examine the Photoshop window

5. Use the Layers and History panels

6. Learn about Photoshop by using Help

7. View and print an image

8. Close a file and exit Photoshop

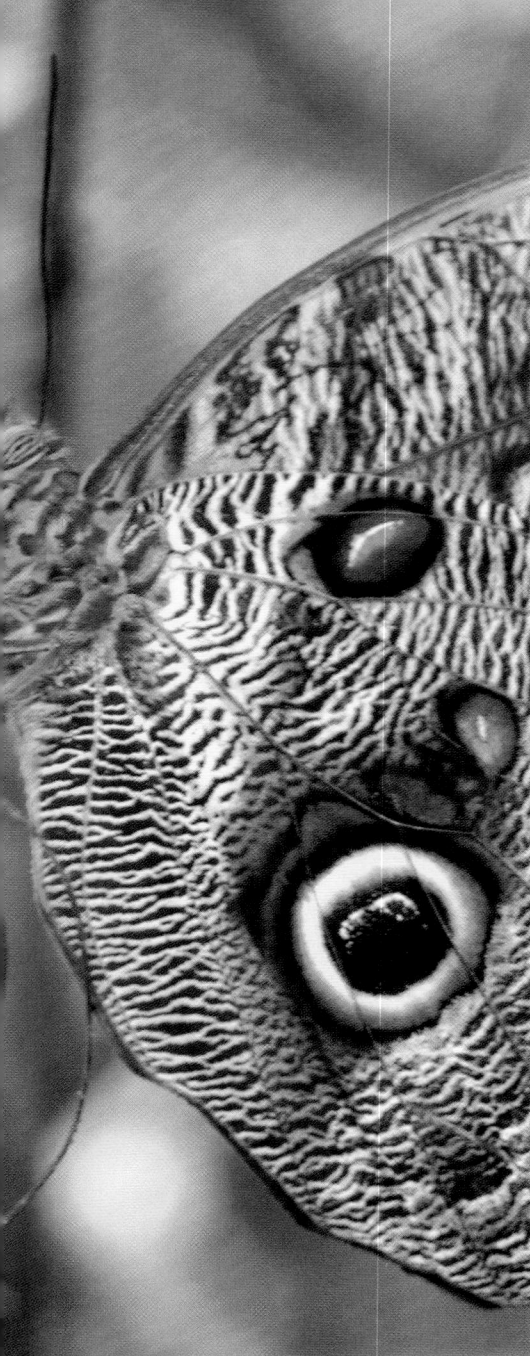

GETTING STARTED WITH
ADOBE
PHOTOSHOP CS4

Using Photoshop

Adobe Photoshop CS4 is an image-editing program that lets you create and modify digital images. 'CS' stands for Creative Suite, a complete design environment. Although Adobe makes Photoshop available as a standalone product, it also comes bundled with all of their Creative Suite options, whether your interests lie with print design, web design, or multimedia production. A **digital image** is a picture in electronic form. Using Photoshop, you can create original artwork, manipulate color images, and retouch photographs. In addition to being a robust application popular with graphics professionals, Photoshop is practical for anyone who wants to enhance existing artwork or create new masterpieces. For example, you can repair and restore damaged areas within an image, combine images, and create graphics and special effects for the web.

> **QUICK**TIP
>
> In Photoshop, a digital image may be referred to as a file, document, graphic, picture, or image.

Understanding Platform User Interfaces

Photoshop is available for both Windows and Macintosh platforms. Regardless of which platform you use, the features and commands are very similar. Some of the Windows and Macintosh keyboard commands differ in name, but they have equivalent functions. For example, the [Ctrl] and [Alt] keys are used in Windows, and the ⌘ and [option] keys are used on Macintosh computers. There are also visual differences between the Windows and Macintosh versions of Photoshop due to the user interface differences found in each platform.

Understanding Sources

Photoshop allows you to work with images from a variety of sources. You can create your own original artwork in Photoshop, use images downloaded from the web, or use images that have been scanned or created using a digital camera. Whether you create Photoshop images to print in high resolution or optimize them for multimedia presentations, web-based functions, or animation projects, Photoshop is a powerful tool for communicating your ideas visually.

Tools You'll Use

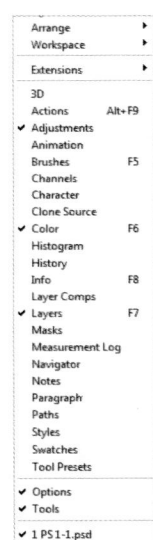

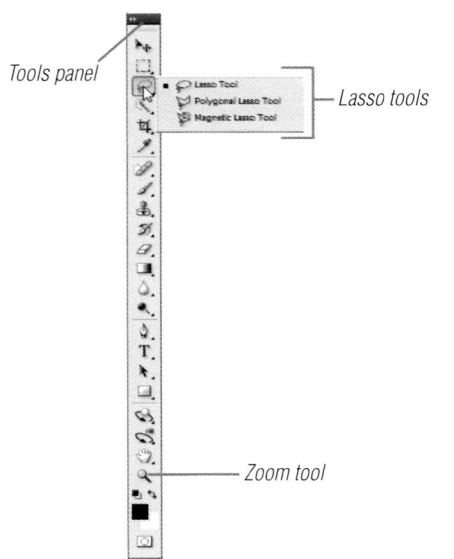

Tools panel

Lasso tools
- Lasso Tool
- Polygonal Lasso Tool
- Magnetic Lasso Tool

Zoom tool

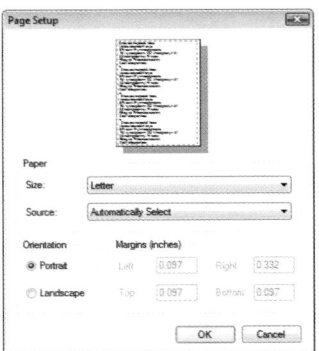

Options bar

START ADOBE
PHOTOSHOP CS4

What You'll Do

 In this lesson, you'll start Photoshop for Windows or Macintosh, then create a file.

Defining Image-Editing Software

Photoshop is an image-editing program. An **image-editing** program allows you to manipulate graphic images so that they can be reproduced by professional printers using full-color processes. Using panels, tools, menus, and a variety of techniques, you can modify a Photoshop image by rotating it, resizing it, changing its colors, or adding text to it. You can also use Photoshop to create and open different kinds of file formats, which enables you to create your own images, import them from a digital camera or scanner, or use files (in other formats) purchased from outside sources. Table 1 lists some of the graphics file formats that Photoshop can open and create.

Understanding Images

Every image is made up of very small squares, which are called **pixels**, and each pixel represents a color or shade. Pixels within an image can be added, deleted, or modified.

QUICKTIP

Photoshop files can become quite large. After a file is complete, you might want to **flatten** it, an irreversible process that combines all layers and reduces the file size.

Using Photoshop Features

Photoshop includes many tools that you can use to manipulate images and text. Within an image, you can add new items and modify existing elements, change colors, and draw shapes. For example, using the Lasso tool, you can outline a section of an image and drag the section onto another area of the image. You can also isolate a foreground or background image. You can extract all or part of a complex image from nearly any background and use it elsewhere.

QUICKTIP

You can create logos in Photoshop. A **logo** is a distinctive image that you can create by combining symbols, shapes, colors, and text. Logos give graphic identity to organizations, such as corporations, universities, and retail stores.

You can also create and format text, called **type**, in Photoshop. You can apply a variety of special effects to type; for example, you can change the appearance of type and increase or decrease the distance between characters. You can also edit type after it has been created and formatted.

Adobe Dreamweaver CS4, a web production software program included in the Design Suite, allows you to optimize, preview, and animate images. Because Dreamweaver is part of the same suite as Photoshop, you can jump seamlessly between the two programs.

Using these two programs, you can also quickly turn any graphics image into a gif animation. Photoshop and Dreamweaver let you compress file size (while optimizing image quality) to ensure that your files download quickly from a web page. Using Photoshop optimization features, you can view multiple versions of an image and select the one that best suits your needs.

Starting Photoshop and Creating a File

The specific way you start Photoshop depends on which computer platform you are using. However, when you start Photoshop in either platform, the computer displays a **splash screen**, a window that contains information about the software, and then the Photoshop window opens.

After you start Photoshop, you can create a file from scratch. You use the New dialog box to create a file. You can also use the New dialog box to set the size of the image you're about to create by typing dimensions in the Width and Height text boxes.

TABLE 1: Some Supported Graphic File Formats

file format	filename extension	file format	filename extension
3D Studio	.3ds	Photoshop PDF	.pdf
Bitmap	.bmp	PICT file	.pct, .pic, or .pict
Cineon	.cin		
Dicom	.dcm	Pixar	.pxr
Filmstrip	.flm	QuickTime	.mov or .mp4
Google Earth	.kmz		
Graphics Interchange Format	.gif	Radiance	.hdr
		RAW	varies
JPEG Picture Format	.jpg, .jpe, or .jpeg	Scitex CT	.sct
		Tagged Image Format	.tif or .tiff
PC Paintbrush	.pcx		
Photoshop	.psd	Targa	.tga or .vda
Photoshop Encapsulated PostScript	.eps	U3D	.u3d
		Wavefront	.obj

Start Photoshop (Windows)

1. Click the **Start button** ⊕ on the taskbar.

2. Point to **All Programs**, point to **Adobe Photoshop CS4,** as shown in Figure 1, then click **Adobe Photoshop CS4.**

   TIP The Adobe Photoshop CS4 program might be found in the Start menu (in the left pane) or in the Adobe folder, which is in the Program Files folder on the hard drive (Win).

3. Click **File** on the Application bar, then click **New** to open the New dialog box.

4. Double-click the number in the Width text box, type **500**, click the **Width list arrow**, then click **pixels** (if it is not already selected).

5. Double-click the number in the Height text box, type **400**, then specify a resolution of **72** pixels/inch (if necessary).

6. Click **OK**.

   TIP By default, the document window (the background of the active image) is gray. This color can be changed by right-clicking the background and then making a color selection.

7. Click the **arrow** ▶ at the bottom of the image window, point to **Show**, then click **Document Sizes** (if it is not already displayed).

You started Photoshop in Windows, then created a file with custom dimensions. Setting custom dimensions lets you specify the exact size of the image you are creating. You changed the display at the bottom of the image window so the document size is visible.

FIGURE 1
Starting Photoshop CS4 (Windows)

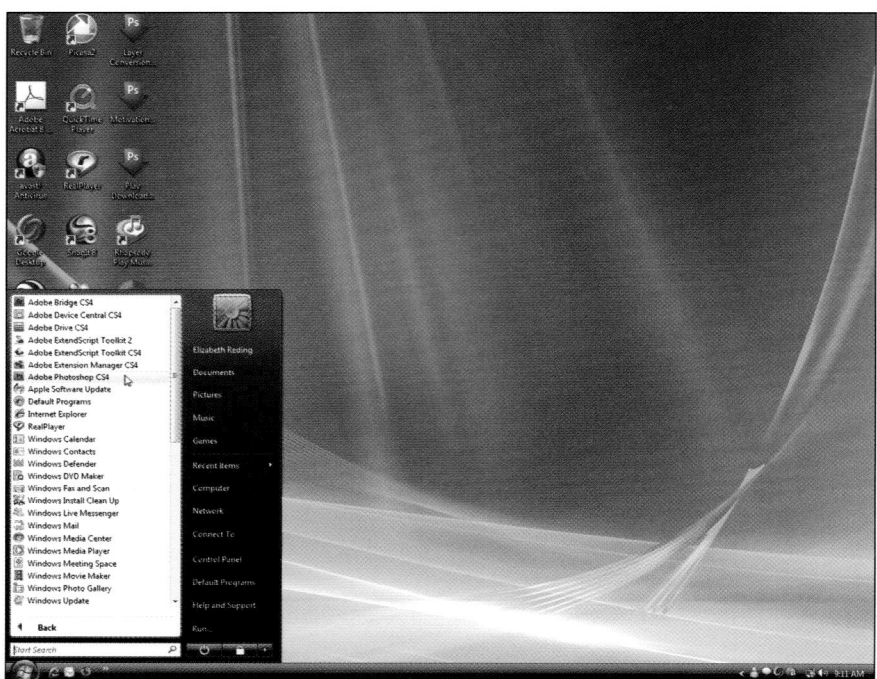

Understanding hardware requirements (Windows)

Adobe Photoshop CS4 has the following minimum system requirements:

- Processor: Intel Xeon, Xeon Dual, Centrino, or Pentium 4 processor
- Operating System: Microsoft® Windows XP SP2 or higher, or Windows Vista
- Memory: 320 MB of RAM
- Storage space: 650 MB of available hard-disk space
- Video RAM: 64 MB; Monitor with 1024 × 768 resolution
- 16-bit video card and Quick Time 7 for Multimedia features

FIGURE 2
Starting Photoshop CS4 (Macintosh)

Items as icons view

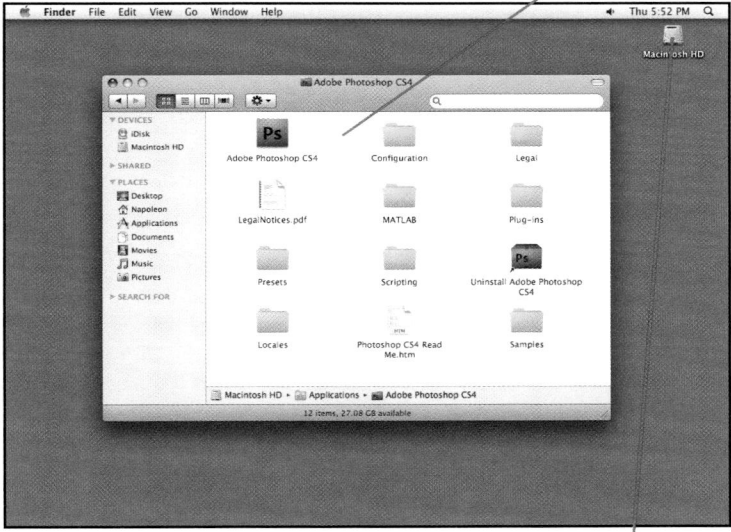

Hard drive icon

Understanding hardware requirements (Macintosh)

Adobe Photoshop CS4 has the following minimum system requirements:

- Processor: G4, G5, or Intel-based
- Operating System: Mac OS X version 10.3 through 10.5
- Memory: 320 MB of RAM (384 MB recommended)
- Storage space: 1.5 GB of available hard-disk space
- Monitor: 1024 × 768 or greater monitor resolution with 16-bit color or greater video card
- PostScript Printer PostScript Level 2, Adobe PostScript 3
- Video RAM: 64 MB
- CD-ROM Drive: CD-ROM Drive required

---

1. Double-click the **hard drive icon** on the desktop, double-click the **Applications folder**, then double-click the **Adobe Photoshop CS4 folder**. Compare your screen to Figure 2.

2. Double-click the **Adobe Photoshop CS4 program icon**.

3. Click **File** on the Application bar, then click **New**.

   TIP If the Color Settings dialog box opens, click No. If a Welcome screen opens, click Close.

4. Double-click the number in the Width text box, type **500**, click the **Width list arrow**, then click **pixels** (if necessary).

5. Double-click the number in the Height text box, type **400**, click the **Height list arrow**, click **pixels** (if necessary), then verify a resolution of **72** pixels/inch.

6. Click **OK**.

   TIP The gray document window background can be turned on by clicking Window on the Application bar, then clicking Application frame.

7. Click the **arrow** ▶ at the bottom of the image window, point to **Show**, then click **Document Sizes** (if it is not already checked).

You started Photoshop for Macintosh, then created a file with custom dimensions. You verified that the document size is visible at the bottom of the image window.

LEARN HOW TO OPEN AND
SAVE AN IMAGE

What You'll Do

 In this lesson, you'll locate and open files using the File menu and Adobe Bridge, flag and sort files, then save a file with a new name.

Opening and Saving Files

Photoshop provides several options for opening and saving a file. Often, the project you're working on determines the techniques you use for opening and saving files. For example, you might want to preserve the original version of a file while you modify a copy. You can open a file, then immediately save it with a different filename, as well as open and save files in many different file formats. When working with graphic images you can open a Photoshop file that has been saved as a bitmap (.bmp) file, then save it as a JPEG (.jpg) file to use on a web page.

Customizing How You Open Files

You can customize how you open your files by setting preferences. **Preferences** are options you can set that are based on your work habits. For example, you can use the Open Recent command on the File menu to instantly locate and open the files that you recently worked on, or you can allow others to preview your files as thumbnails. Figure 3 shows the Preferences dialog box options for handling your files.

TIP   In cases when the correct file format is not automatically determined, you can use the Open As command on the File menu (Win) or Open as Smart Object (Mac).

FIGURE 3
Preferences dialog box

Option for thumbnail preview

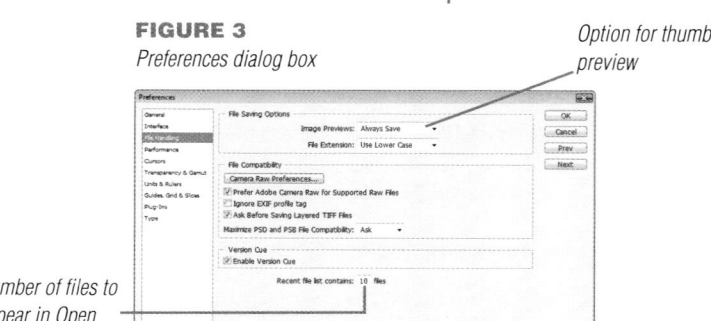

Number of files to appear in Open Recent list

Browsing Through Files

You can easily find the files you're looking for by using **Adobe Bridge**, a stand-alone application that serves as the hub for the Adobe Creative Suite. See the magnifying loupe tool in the Filmstrip view in Figure 4. You can open Adobe Bridge (or just Bridge) by clicking the Launch Bridge button on the Application bar. You can also open Bridge using the File menu in Photoshop.

When you open Bridge, a series of panels allows you to view the files on your hard drive as hierarchical files and folders. In addition to the Favorites and Folders panels in the upper-left corner of the Bridge window, there are other important areas. Directly beneath the Favorites and Folders panels is the Filter panel which allows you to review properties of images in the Content panel. In the (default) Essentials view, the Preview panel displays a window containing the Metadata and Keywords panels, which stores information about

a selected file (such as keywords) that can then be used as search parameters. You can use this tree structure to find the file you are seeking. When you locate a file, you can click its thumbnail to see information about its size, format, and creation and modification dates. (Clicking a thumbnail selects the image. You can select multiple non-contiguous images by pressing and holding [Ctrl] (Win) or ⌘ (Mac) each time you click an image.) You can select contiguous images by clicking the first image, then pressing

TIP Click a thumbnail while in Filmstrip view and the pointer changes to a Loupe tool that magnifies content. Drag the loupe over the filmstrip image to enlarge select areas. The arrowhead in the upper-left corner of the window points to the area to be magnified. Clicking the arrowhead closes the loupe.

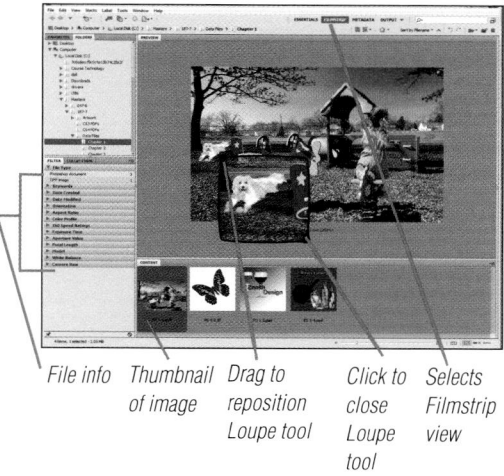

FIGURE 4
Adobe Bridge window

File info   Thumbnail   Drag to   Click to   Selects
           of image   reposition   close   Filmstrip
                       Loupe tool   Loupe   view
                                       tool

Using the Photoshop File Info dialog box

You can use the File Info dialog box to identify a file, add a caption or other text, or add a copyright notice. The Description section allows you to enter printable text, as shown in Figure 5. For example, to add your name to an image, click File on the Application bar, click File Info, then click in the Description text box. (You can move from field to field by pressing [Tab] or by clicking in individual text boxes.) Type your name, course number, or other identifying information in the Description text box, or click stars to assign a rating. You can enter additional information in the other text boxes, then save all the File Info data as a separate file that has an .xmp extension. To print selected data from the File Info dialog box, click File on the Application bar, then click Print. Click the Color Management list arrow, then click Output. Available options are listed in the right panel. To print the filename, select the Labels check box. You can also select check boxes that let you print crop marks and registration marks. If you choose, you can even add a background color or border to your image. After you select the items you want to print, click Print.

Type information to
be printed here

FIGURE 5
File Info dialog box

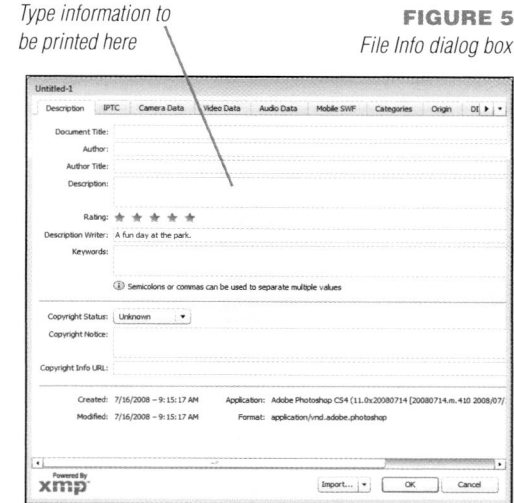

and holding [Shift] and clicking the last image in the group. You can open a file using Bridge by double-clicking its thumbnail, and find out information such as the file's format, and when it was created and edited. You can close Bridge by clicking File (Win) or Bridge CS4 (Mac) on the (Bridge) Application bar, then clicking Exit (Win) or Quit Adobe Bridge CS4 (Mac) or by clicking the window's Close button.

Understanding the Power of Bridge

In addition to allowing you to see all your images, Bridge can be used to rate (assign importance), sort (organize by name, rating, and other criteria), and label your images. Figure 4, on the previous page, contains images that are assigned a rating and shown in Filmstrip view. There are three views in Bridge (Essentials, Filmstrip, and Metadata) that are controlled by tabs to the left of the search text box. To assist in organizing your images, you can assign a color label or rating to one or more images regardless of your current view. Any number of selected images can be assigned a color label by clicking Label on the Application bar, then clicking one of the six options.

Creating a PDF Presentation

Using Bridge you can create a PDF Presentation (a presentation in the PDF file format). Such a presentation can be viewed full-screen on any computer monitor, or in Adobe Acrobat Reader as a PDF file. You can create such a presentation by opening Bridge, locating and selecting images using the file hierarchy, then clicking the Output button on the Bridge Application bar. The Output panel, shown in Figure 6, opens and displays the images you have selected. You can add images by pressing [Ctrl] (Win) or ⌘ (Mac) while clicking additional images.

FIGURE 6
Output panel in Bridge

Click to create output

Click to create PDF

Output preview

Selected thumbnails

Using Save As Versus Save

Sometimes it's more efficient to create a new image by modifying an existing one, especially if it contains elements and special effects that you want to use again. The Save As command on the File menu (in Photoshop) creates a copy of the file, prompts you to give the duplicate file a new name, and then displays the new filename in the image's title bar. You use the Save As command to name an unnamed file or to save an existing file with a new name. For example, throughout this book, you will be instructed to open your Data Files and use the Save As command. Saving your Data Files with new names keeps the original files intact in case you have to start the lesson over again or you want to repeat an exercise. When you use the Save command, you save the changes you made to the open file.

FIGURE 7
Open dialog box for Windows

Look in list arrow
displays list of
available drives

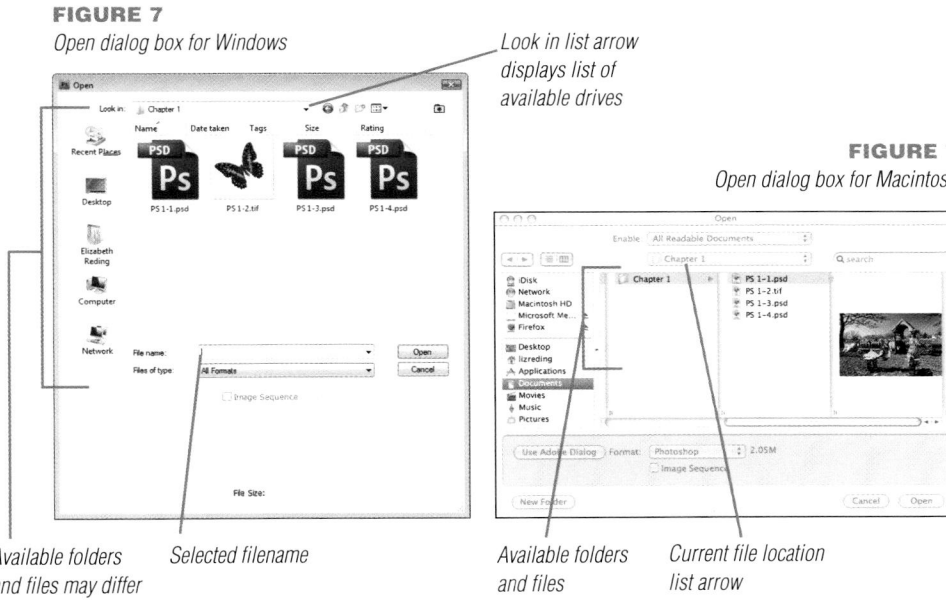

FIGURE 7
Open dialog box for Macintosh

Available folders
and files may differ
from your list

Selected filename

Available folders
and files

Current file location
list arrow

FIGURE 8
Adobe Bridge window

Essentials button

Preview of selected file
displays here

Click the Keywords
panel tab to assign
keywords to a selected
file, then click any of the
displayed keywords

Your list may
be different

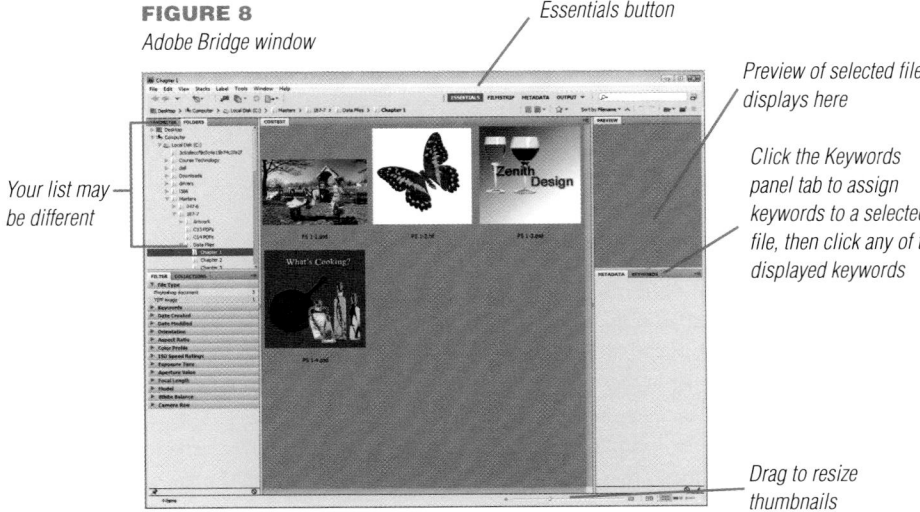

Drag to resize
thumbnails

Open a file using the Application bar

1. Click **File** on the Application bar, then click **Open**.

2. Click the **Look in list arrow** (Win) or the **Current file location list arrow** (Mac), then navigate to the drive and folder where you store your Data Files.

3. Click **PS 1-1.psd,** as shown in Figure 7, then click **Open**.

   TIP   Click Update, if you receive a message stating that some text layers need to be updated.

You used the Open command on the File menu to locate and open a file.

Open a file using the Folders panel in Adobe Bridge

1. Click the **Launch Bridge button** ![Br] on the Application bar, then click the **Folders panel tab** FOLDERS (if necessary).

2. Navigate through the hierarchical tree to the drive and folder where you store your Chapter 1 Data Files, then click the **Essentials button** if it is not already selected.

3. Drag the **slider** (at the bottom of the Bridge window) a third of the way between the Smaller thumbnail size button ▭ and the Larger thumbnail size button ▭ . Compare your screen to Figure 8.

4. Double-click the **image of a butterfly** (PS 1-2.tif). Bridge is no longer visible.

5. Close the butterfly image in Photoshop.

You used the Folders panel tab in Adobe Bridge to locate and open a file. This feature makes it easy to see which file you want to use.

Use the Save As command

1. Verify that the **PS 1-1.psd window** is active.

2. Click **File** on the Application bar, click **Save As**, then compare your Save As dialog box to Figure 9.

3. If the drive containing your Data Files is not displayed, click the **Save in list arrow** (Win) or the **Where list arrow** (Mac), then navigate to the drive and folder where you store your Chapter 1 Data Files.

4. Select the current filename in the File name text box (Win) or Save As text box (Mac) (if necessary); type **Playground**, then click **Save**.

   | TIP Click OK to close the Maximize Compatibility dialog box (if necessary).

You used the Save As command on the File menu to save the file with a new name. This command makes it possible for you to save a changed version of an image while keeping the original file intact.

Change from Tabbed to Floating Documents

1. Click the **Arrange Documents button** 🖼 ▾ on the Application bar, then click **2 Up**.

   | TIP The Arrange Documents button is a temporary change to the workspace that will be in effect for the current Photoshop session.

2. Click 🖼 ▾ , then click **Float All in Windows**. Compare your Playground image to Figure 10.

You changed the arrangement of open documents from consolidation to a 2 Up format to each image displaying in its own window.

FIGURE 9
Save As dialog box

Your list of files might be different

New filename

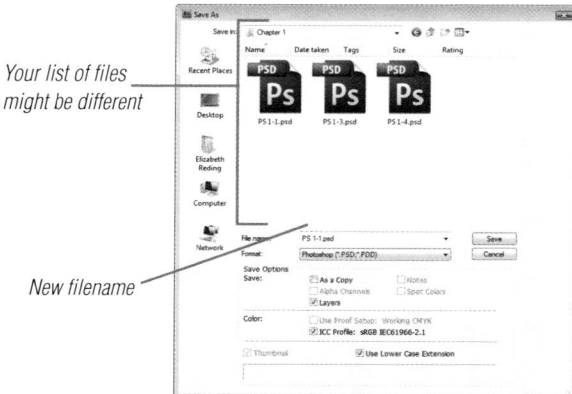

FIGURE 10
Playground image

Duplicate file has new name

Changing file formats

In addition to using the Save As command to duplicate an existing file, it is a handy way of changing one format into another. For example, you can open an image you created in a digital camera, then make modifications in the Photoshop format. To do this, open the .jpg file in Photoshop, click File on the Application bar, then click Save As. Name the file, click the Format list arrow, click Photoshop (*.psd, *.pdd) (Win) or Photoshop (Mac), then click Save. You can also change formats using Bridge by selecting the file, clicking Tools on the Application bar, pointing to Photoshop, then clicking Image Processor. Section 3 of the Image Processor dialog box lets you determine the new file format.

Getting photos from your camera

You can use Bridge to move photos from your camera into your computer by plugging your camera into your computer, opening Adobe Bridge, clicking File on the (Bridge) Application bar, then clicking Get Photos from Camera. Once you do this, the Adobe Bridge CS4 Photo Downloader dialog box opens. This dialog box lets you decide from which device you'll download images, where you want to store them, and whether or not you want to rename them, among other options.

Rated and
Approved file

FIGURE 11
Images in Adobe Bridge

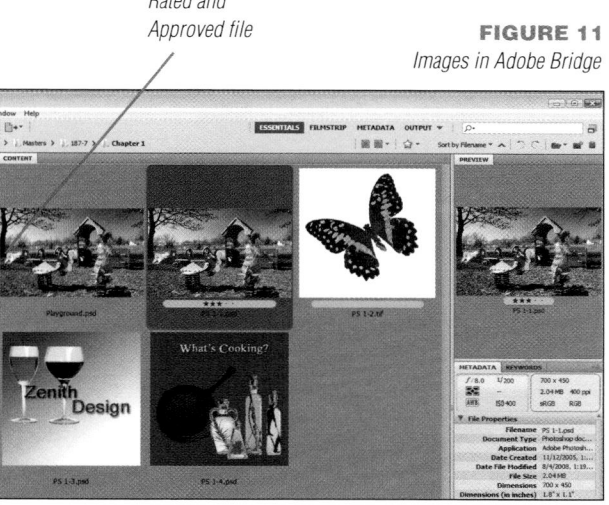

FIGURE 12
Sorted files

Rate and filter with Bridge

1. Click the **Launch Bridge button** on the Application bar.

2. Click the **Folders panel tab** if it is not already selected, then click the drive and folder where you store your Chapter 1 Data Files on the File Hierarchy tree (if necessary).

3. Click the butterfly image, file **PS 1-2.tif** to select it.

4. Press and hold **[Ctrl]** (Win) or ⌘ (Mac), click **PS 1-1.psd** (the image of the playground), then release **[Ctrl]** (Win) or ⌘ (Mac).

5. Click **Label** on the Application bar, then click **Approved**.

6. Click **PS 1-1.psd**, click **Label** on the Application bar, then click *******. See Figure 11.

7. Click **View** on the Application bar, point to **Sort**, then click **By Type**. Compare your screen to Figure 12.

   The order of the files is changed.

   TIP   You can also change the order of files (in the Content panel) using the Sort by Filename list arrow in the Filter panel. When you click the Sort by Filename list arrow, you'll see a list of sorting options. Click the option you want and the files in the Content panel will be rearranged.

8. Click **View** on the Application bar, point to **Sort**, then click **Manually**.

   TIP   You can change the Bridge view at any time, depending on the type of information you need to see.

9. Click **File** (Win) or **Adobe Bridge CS4** (Mac) on the (Bridge) Application bar, then click **Exit** or **Quit Adobe Bridge CS4** (Mac).

You labeled files using Bridge, sorted the files in a folder, then changed the sort order. When finished, you closed Bridge.

USE ORGANIZATIONAL AND
MANAGEMENT FEATURES

What You'll Do

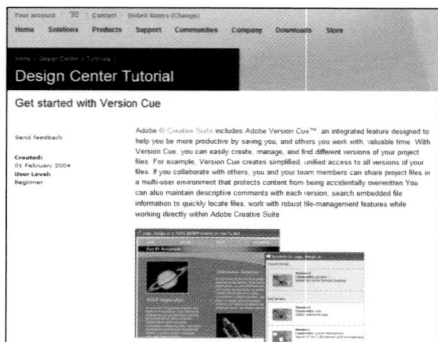

In this lesson, you'll learn how to use Version Cue and Bridge.

Learning about Version Cue

Version Cue is a file versioning and management feature of the Adobe Creative Suite that can be used to organize your work whether you work in groups or by yourself. Version Cue is accessed through Bridge. You can see Version Cue in Bridge in two different locations: the Favorites tab and the Folders tab. Figure 13 shows Version Cue in the Favorites tab of Bridge. You can also view Version Cue in the Folders tab by collapsing the Desktop, as shown in Figure 14.

Understanding Version Cue Workspaces

Regardless of where in Bridge you access it (the Favorites or Folders tab), Version Cue installs a **workspace** in which it stores projects and project files, and keeps track of file versions. The Version Cue workspace can be installed locally on your own computer and can be made public or kept private. It can also be installed on a server and can be used by many users through a network.

FIGURE 13
Favorites tab in Adobe Bridge

Your list of Favorites may differ

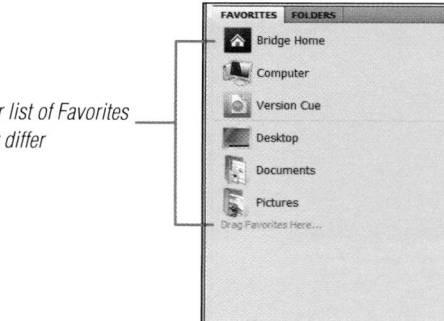

FIGURE 14
Folders tab in Adobe Bridge

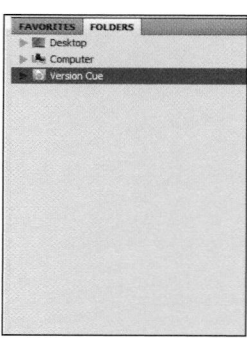

Using Version Cue's Administrative Functions

Once you log into Version Cue using Adobe Drive (shown in Figure 15), you can control who uses the workspace and how it is used with the tabs at the top of the screen. Adobe Drive, which you use to connect to Version Cue, lets you open your server, browse projects and other servers, and perform advanced tasks.

Making Use of Bridge

You've already seen how you can use Bridge to find, identify, and sort files. But did you know that you can use Bridge Center to organize, label, and open files as a group? First you select one or more files, right-click the selection (Win) or [control]-click the selection (Mac), then click Open, or Open With, to display the files in your favorite CS4 program. You can apply labels, and ratings, or sort the selected files.

QUICKTIP

You can use Bridge to stitch together panoramic photos, rename images in batches, or automate image conversions with the Tools menu. Select the file(s) in Bridge you want to modify, click Tools on the Application bar, point to Photoshop, then click a command and make option modifications.

FIGURE 15
Adobe Drive and Version Cue

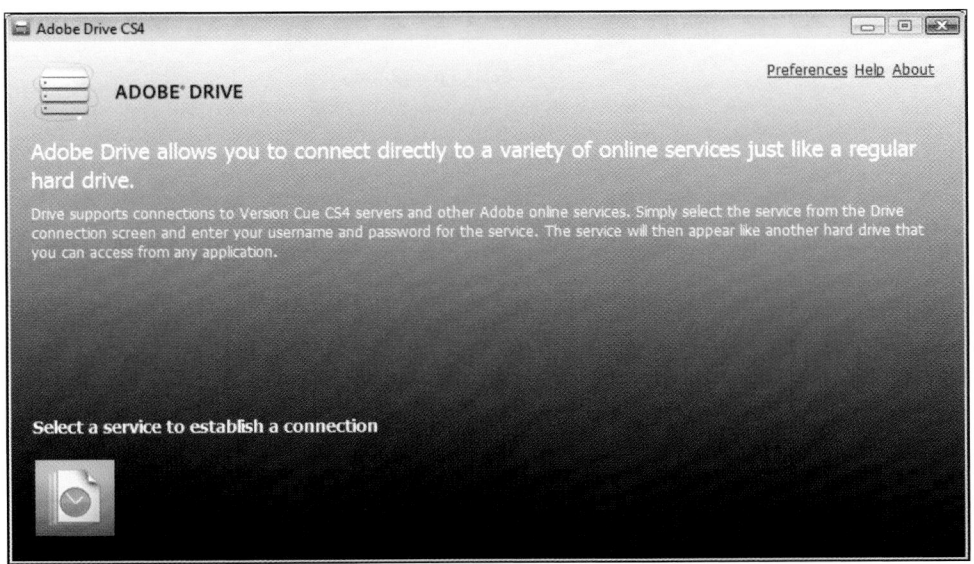

EXAMINE THE
PHOTOSHOP WINDOW

What You'll Do

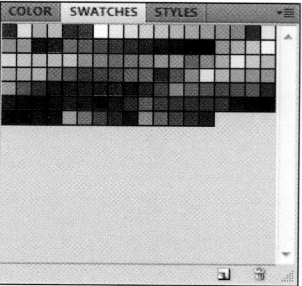

In this lesson, you'll arrange documents and change the default display, select a tool on the Tools panel, use a shortcut key to cycle through the hidden tools, select and add a tool to the Tool Preset picker, use the Window menu to show and hide panels in the workspace, and create a customized workspace.

Learning About the Workspace

The Photoshop **workspace** is the area within the Photoshop program window that includes the entire window, from the command menus at the top of your screen to the status bar (Win) at the bottom. Desktop items are visible in this area (Mac). The (Windows) workspace is shown in Figure 16.

In Windows, the area containing the menu bar (containing Photoshop commands) and the title bar (displaying the program name) is called the **Application bar**. These two areas have been combined to use space more efficiently. On the Mac, the main menus are at the top of the screen, but not on the Application bar. If the active image window is maximized, the filename of the open unnamed file is **Untitled-1**, because it has not been named. The Application bar also contains the **workspace switcher**, a Close button, and Minimize/Maximize, and Restore buttons (Win).

You can choose a menu command by clicking it or by pressing [Alt] plus the underlined letter in the menu name (Win). Some commands display shortcut keys on the right side of the menu. Shortcut keys provide an alternative way to activate menu commands. Some commands might appear dimmed, which means they are not currently available. An ellipsis after a command indicates additional choices.

DESIGNTIP **Overcoming information overload**

One of the most common experiences shared by first-time Photoshop users is information overload. There are just too many places and things to look at! When you feel your brain overheating, take a moment and sit back. Remind yourself that the active image area is the central area where you can see a composite of your work. All the tools and panels are there to help you, not to add to the confusion. The tools and features in Photoshop CS4 are designed to be easier to find and use, making any given task faster to complete.

Getting Started with Adobe Photoshop CS4

Finding Tools Everywhere

The **Tools panel** contains tools associated with frequently used Photoshop commands. The face of a tool contains a graphical representation of its function; for example, the Zoom tool shows a magnifying glass. You can place the pointer over each tool to display a tool tip, which tells you the name or function of that tool. Some tools have additional hidden tools, indicated by a small black triangle in the lower-right corner of the tool.

The **options bar**, located directly under the Application bar, displays the current settings for each tool. For example, when you click the Type tool, the default font and font size appear on the options bar, which can be changed if desired. You can move the options bar anywhere in the workspace for easier access. The options bar also contains the Tool Preset picker. This is the left-most tool on the options bar and displays the active tool. You can click the list arrow on this tool to select another tool without having to use the Tools panel. The options bar also contains the panel well, an area where you can assemble panels for quick access.

Panels, sometimes called palettes, are small windows used to verify settings and modify images. By default, panels appear in stacked groups at the right side of the window.

FIGURE 16
Workspace

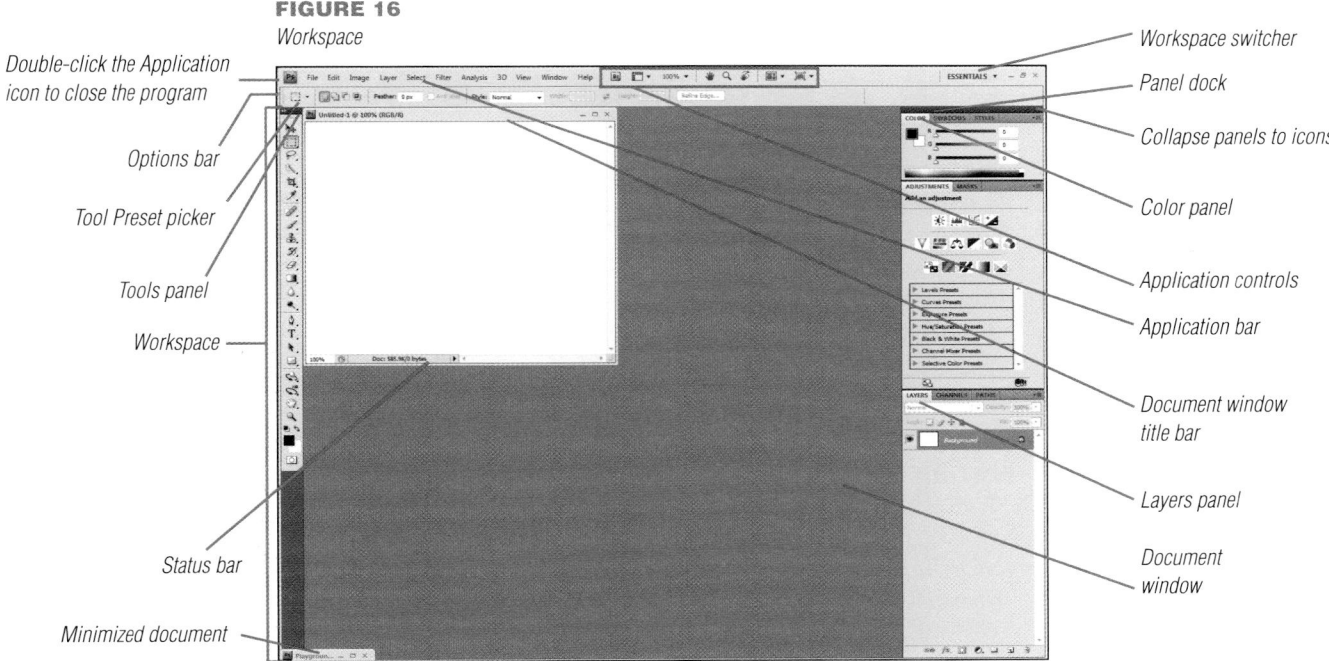

- *Double-click the Application icon to close the program*
- *Options bar*
- *Tool Preset picker*
- *Tools panel*
- *Workspace*
- *Status bar*
- *Minimized document*
- *Workspace switcher*
- *Panel dock*
- *Collapse panels to icons*
- *Color panel*
- *Application controls*
- *Application bar*
- *Document window title bar*
- *Layers panel*
- *Document window*

A collection of panels usually in a vertical orientation is called a **dock**. The dock is the dark gray bar above the collection of panels. The arrows in the dock are used to maximize and minimize the panels. You can display a panel by simply clicking the panel tab, making it the active panel. Panels can be separated and moved anywhere in the workspace by dragging their tabs to new locations. You can dock a panel by dragging its tab in or out of a dock. As you move a panel, you'll see a blue highlighted drop zone. A **drop zone** is an area where you can move a panel. You can also change the order of tabs by dragging a tab to a new location within its panel. Each panel contains a menu that you can view by clicking the list arrow in its upper-right corner.

QUICKTIP

You can reset panels to their default locations at any time by clicking Essentials on the workspace switcher. (If Essentials is not displayed, click the workspace switcher, then click Essentials.)

The **status bar** is located at the bottom of the program window (Win) or work area (Mac). It displays information, such as the file size of the active window and a description of the active tool. You can display other informa-

tion on the status bar, such as the current tool, by clicking the black triangle to view a pull-down menu with more options.

Rulers can help you precisely measure and position an object in the workspace. The rulers do not appear the first time you use Photoshop, but you can display them by clicking Rulers on the View menu.

Using Tool Shortcut Keys
Each tool has a corresponding shortcut key. For example, the shortcut key for the Type tool is T. After you know a tool's shortcut key, you can select the tool on the Tools panel by pressing its shortcut key. To select and cycle through a tool's hidden tools, you press and hold [Shift], then press the tool's shortcut key until the desired tool appears.

QUICKTIP

Tools that have assigned shortcut keys have spring-loaded keyboard shortcuts. **Spring-loaded keyboard shortcuts** let you temporarily change the active tool. If, for example, you've selected the Gradient tool and you want to move an object, press and hold V. For as long as you hold V, the Move tool will be in effect. Release the V and you're back to the Gradient tool.

Customizing Your Environment
Photoshop makes it easy for you to position elements you work with just where you want them. If you move elements around to make your environment more convenient, you can always return your workspace to its original appearance by resetting the default panel locations. Once you have your work area arranged the way you want it, you can create a customized workspace by clicking the workspace switcher on the Application bar, then clicking Save Workspace. If you want to open a named workspace, click the workspace switcher, then click the name of the workspace you want to use. In addition, Photoshop comes with many customized workspaces that are designed for specific tasks.

FIGURE 17
Keyboard Shortcuts and Menus dialog box

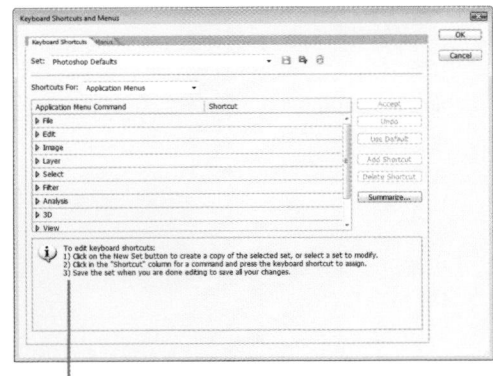

Instructions to edit shortcuts

Creating customized keyboard shortcuts
Keyboard shortcuts can make your work with Photoshop images faster and easier. In fact, once you discover the power of keyboard shortcuts, you may never use menus again. In addition to the keyboard shortcuts that are preprogrammed in Photoshop, you can create your own. To do this, click Edit on the Application bar, then click Keyboard Shortcuts. The Keyboard Shortcuts and Menus dialog box opens, as shown in Figure 17.

DESIGNTIP Composition 101

What makes one image merely okay and another terrific? While any such judgement is subjective, there are some rules governing image composition. It goes without saying that, as the artist, you have a message you're trying to deliver ... something you're trying to say to the viewer. This is true whether the medium is oil painting, photography, or Photoshop imagery.

Elements under your control in your composition are tone, sharpness, scale, and arrangement. (You may see these items classified differently elsewhere, but they amount to the same concepts.)

Tone is the brightness and contrast within an image. Using light and shadows you can shift the focus of the viewer's eye and control the mood.

Sharpness is used to direct the viewer's eye to a specific area of an image. **Scale** is the size relationship of objects to one another, and **arrangement** is how objects are positioned to one another.

Are objects in your image contributing to clarity or clutter? Are similarly-sized objects confusing the viewer? Would blurring one area of an image change the viewer's focus?

These are tools you have to influence your artistic expression. Make sure the viewer understands what you want seen.

FIGURE 18
Hidden tools

Shortcut key

Select a tool

1. Click the **Lasso tool** on the Tools panel, press and hold the mouse button until a list of hidden tools appears, then release the mouse button. See Figure 18. Note the shortcut key, L, next to the tool name.

2. Click the **Polygonal Lasso tool** on the Tools panel.

3. Press and hold **[Shift]**, press **[L]** three times to cycle through the Lasso tools, then release **[Shift]**. Did you notice how the options bar changes for each selected Lasso tool?

   TIP You can return the tools to their default setting by clicking the Click to open the Tool Preset picker list arrow on the options bar, clicking the list arrow, then clicking Reset All Tools.

You selected the Lasso tool on the Tools panel and used its shortcut key to cycle through the Lasso tools. Becoming familiar with shortcut keys can speed up your work and make you more efficient.

Learning shortcut keys

Don't worry about learning shortcut keys. As you become more familiar with Photoshop, you'll gradually pick up shortcuts for menu commands, such as saving a file, or Tools panel tools, such as the Move tool. You'll notice that as you learn to use shortcut keys, your speed while working with Photoshop will increase and you'll complete tasks with fewer mouse clicks.

Select a tool from the Tool Preset picker

1. Click the **Click to open the Tool Preset picker list arrow** ⬚ on the options bar.

   The name of a button is displayed in a tool tip, the descriptive text that appears when you point to the button. Your Tool Preset picker list will differ, and may contain no entries at all. This list can be customized by each user.

2. Deselect the **Current Tool Only check box** (if necessary). See Figure 19.

3. Double-click **Magnetic Lasso 24 pixels** in the list.

You selected the Magnetic Lasso tool using the Tool Preset picker. The Tool Preset picker makes it easy to access frequently used tools and their settings.

FIGURE 19
Using the Tool Preset picker

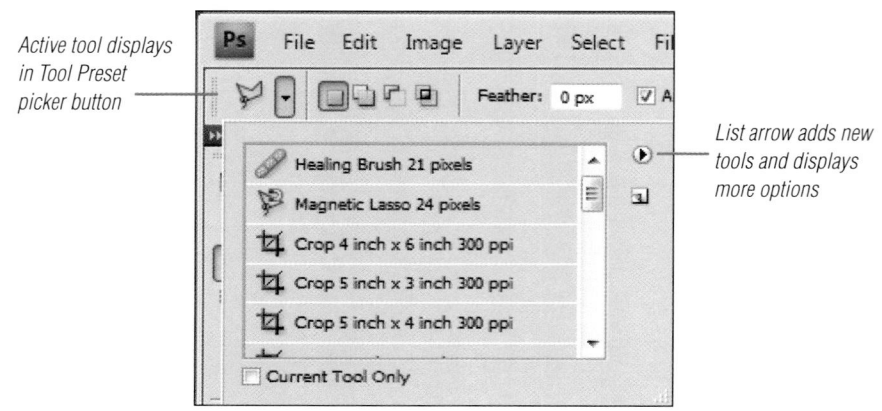

Active tool displays in Tool Preset picker button

List arrow adds new tools and displays more options

FIGURE 20
Full screen mode with Application bar

Use hand pointer to reposition image

Click to change screen modes

Using the Full Screen Mode

By default, Photoshop displays images in consolidated tabs. This means that each image is displayed within its own tab. You can choose from three other modes: Maximized Screen Mode, Full Screen Mode with Application Bar, and Full Screen Mode. And why would you want to stray from the familiar Standard Screen Mode? Perhaps your image is so large that it's difficult to see it all in Standard Mode, or perhaps you want a less cluttered screen. Maybe you just want to try something different. You can switch between modes by clicking the Change Screen Mode button (located in the Application controls area of the Application bar) or by pressing the keyboard shortcut F. When you click this button, the screen displays changes. Click the Hand tool (or press the keyboard shortcut H), and you can reposition the active image, as shown in Figure 20.

The appearance of elements in an image is important, but of equal importance is the way in which the elements are arranged. The components of any image should form a cohesive unit so that the reader is unaware of all the different parts, yet influenced by the way they work together to emphasize a message or reveal information. For example, if a large image is used, it should be easy for the reader to connect the image with any descriptive text. There should be an easily understood connection between the text and the artwork, and the reader should be able to seamlessly connect them.

FIGURE 21
Move tool added to preset picker

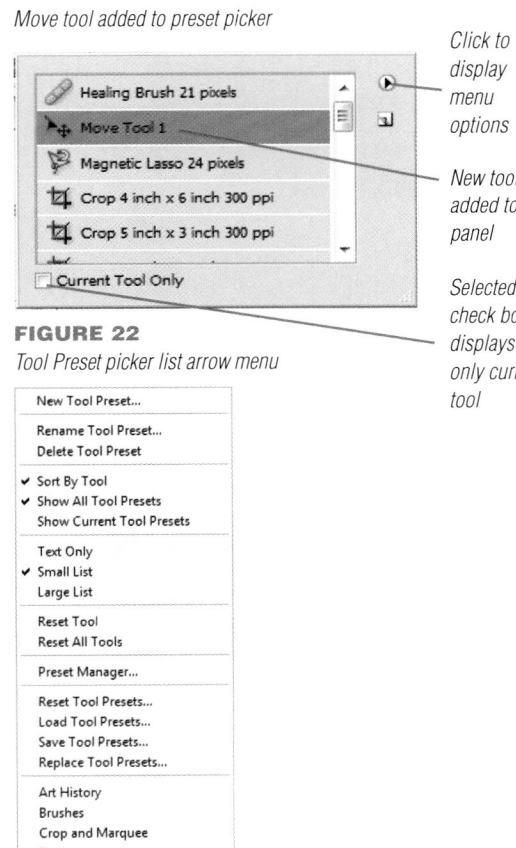

Click to display menu options

New tool added to panel

Selected check box displays only current tool

FIGURE 22
Tool Preset picker list arrow menu

Modifying a tool preset

Once you've created tool presets, you'll probably want to know how they can be deleted and renamed. To delete any tool preset, select it on the Tool Preset picker panel. Click the list arrow on the Tool Preset picker panel to view the menu, shown in Figure 22, then click Delete Tool Preset. To rename a tool preset, click the same list arrow, then click Rename Tool Preset.

Add a tool to the Tool Preset picker

1. Click the **Move tool** on the Tools panel.
2. Click the **Click to open the Tool Preset picker list arrow** on the options bar.
3. Click the **list arrow** on the Tool Preset picker.
4. Click **New Tool Preset**, then click **OK** to accept the default name (Move Tool 1). Compare your list to Figure 21.

   TIP You can display the currently selected tool alone by selecting the Current Tool Only check box.

You added the Move tool to the Tool Preset picker. Once you know how to add tools to the Tool Preset picker, you can quickly and easily customize your work environment.

Change the default display

1. Click **Edit** (Win) or **Photoshop** (Mac) on the Application bar, then click **Preferences** (Win) or point to **Preferences,** then click **Interface** (Mac).
2. Click **Interface** in the left panel (Win), click the **Open Documents in Tabs check box** to deselect it, then click **OK**.

You changed the default display so that each time you open Photoshop, each image will display in its own window rather than in tabs.

Show and hide panels

1. Click **Window** on the Application bar, then verify that **Color** has a check mark next to it, then close the menu.
2. Click the **Swatches tab** next to the Color tab to make the Swatches panel active, as shown in Figure 23.
3. Click the **Collapse to Icons arrow** to collapse the panels.
4. Click the **Expand Panels arrow** to expand the panels.
5. Click **Window** on the Application bar, then click **Swatches** to deselect it.

   TIP   You can hide all open panels by pressing [Shift], then [Tab], then show them by pressing [Shift], then [Tab] again. To hide all open panels, the options bar, and the Tools panel, press [Tab], then show them by pressing [Tab] again.

6. Click **Window** on the Application bar, then click **Swatches** to redisplay the Swatches panel.

You collapsed and expanded the panels, then used the Window menu to show and hide the Swatches panel. You might want to hide panels at times in order to enlarge your work area.

FIGURE 23
Active Swatches panel

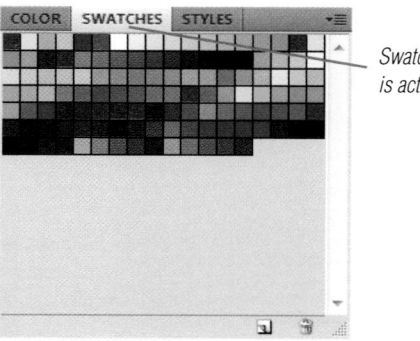

Swatches tab is active

DESIGNTIP   **Balancing objects**

The **optical center** occurs approximately three-eighths from the top of the page and is the point around which objects on the page are balanced. Once the optical center is located, objects can be positioned around it. A page can have a symmetrical or asymmetrical balance relative to an imaginary vertical line in the center of the page. In a **symmetrical balance**, objects are placed equally on either side of the vertical line. This type of layout tends toward a restful, formal design. In an **asymmetrical balance,** objects are placed unequally relative to the vertical line. Asymmetrical balance uses white space to balance the positioned objects, and is more dynamic and informal. A page with objects arranged asymmetrically tends to provide more visual interest because it is more surprising in appearance.

DESIGNTIP   **Considering ethical implications**

Because Photoshop enables you to make so many dramatic changes to images, you should consider the ethical ramifications and implications of altering images. Is it proper or appropriate to alter an image just because you have the technical expertise to do so? Are there any legal responsibilities or liabilities involved in making these alterations? Because the general public is more aware about the topic of **intellectual property** (an image or idea that is owned and retained by legal control) with the increased availability of information and content, you should make sure you have the legal right to alter an image, especially if you plan on displaying or distributing the image to others. Know who retains the rights to an image, and if necessary, make sure you have written permission for its use, alteration, and/or distribution. Not taking these precautions could be costly.

FIGURE 24
Save Workspace dialog box

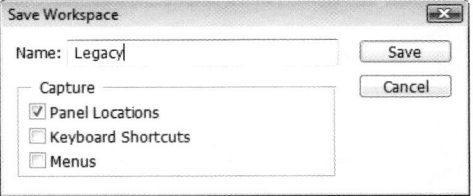

FIGURE 25
Image Size dialog box

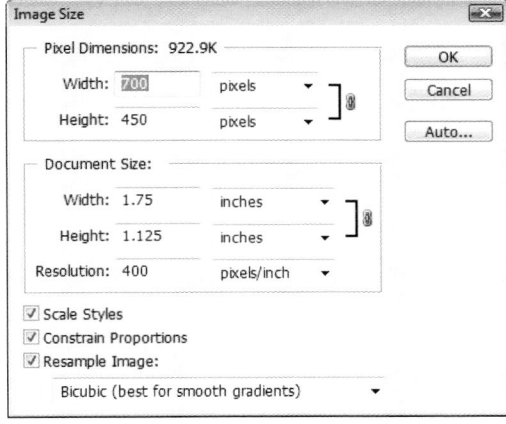

1. Click **Window** on the Application bar, click **History**, then drag the newly displayed panel in the gray space beneath the Swatches panel. (*Hint:* When you drag one panel into another, you'll see a light blue line, indicating that the new panel will dock with the existing panels.)

2. Click **Window** on the Application bar, point to **Workspace**, then click **Save Workspace**.

3. Type **Legacy** in the Name text box, then verify that only **Panel Locations** has a check mark beside it, as shown in Figure 24.

4. Click **Save**.

5. Click **Window** on the Application bar, then point to **Workspace**.

   The name of the new workspace appears on the Window menu.

   > TIP You can use the Rotate View tool on the Application bar to *non-destructively* change the orientation of the image canvas. Click the Reset View button on the options bar to restore the canvas to its original angle.

6. Click **Essentials (Default)**.

7. Click the **workspace switcher** on the Application bar, then click **Legacy**.

8. Click the **workspace switcher** on the Application bar, then click **Essentials**.

You created a customized workspace, reset the panel locations, tested the new workspace, then reset the panel locations to the default setting. Customized workspaces provide you with a work area that is always tailored to your needs.

Resizing an image

You may have created the perfect image, but the size may not be correct for your print format. Document size is a combination of the printed dimensions and pixel resolution. An image designed for a website, for example, might be too small for an image that will be printed in a newsletter. You can easily resize an image using the Image Size command on the Image menu. To use this feature, open the file you want to resize, click Image on the Application bar, then click Image Size. The Image Size dialog box, shown in Figure 25, opens. By changing the dimensions in the text boxes, you'll have your image resized in no time. Note the check mark next to Resample Image. With resampling checked, you can change the total number of pixels in the image and the print dimensions independently. With resampling off, you can change either the dimensions or the resolution; Photoshop will automatically adjust whichever value you ignore.

USE THE LAYERS AND HISTORY PANELS

What You'll Do

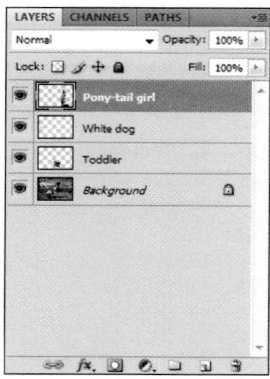

In this lesson, you'll hide and display a layer, move a layer on the Layers panel, and then undo the move by deleting the Layer Order state on the History panel.

Learning About Layers

A **layer** is a section within an image that can be manipulated independently. Layers allow you to control individual elements within an image and create great dramatic effects and variations of the same image. Layers enable you to easily manipulate individual characteristics within an image. Each Photoshop file has at least one layer, and can contain many individual layers, or groups of layers.

You can think of layers in a Photoshop image as individual sheets of clear plastic that are in a stack. It's possible for your file to quickly accumulate dozens of layers. The **Layers panel** displays all the layers in an open file. You can use the Layers panel to create, copy, delete, display, hide, merge, lock, group or reposition layers.

QUICKTIP

In Photoshop, using and understanding layers is the key to success.

Setting preferences

The Preferences dialog box contains several topics, each with its own settings: General; Interface; File Handling; Performance; Cursors; Transparency & Gamut; Units & Rulers; Guides, Grid, & Slices; Plug-Ins; Type; and Camera Raw. To open the Preferences dialog box, click Edit (Win) or Photoshop (Mac) on the Application bar, point to Preferences, then click a topic that represents the settings you want to change. If you move panels around the workspace, or make other changes to them, you can choose to retain those changes the next time you start the program. To always start a new session with default panels, click Interface on the Preferences menu, deselect the Remember Panel Locations check box, then click OK. Each time you start Photoshop, the panels will be reset to their default locations and values.

Understanding the Layers Panel

The order in which the layers appear on the Layers panel matches the order in which they appear in the image; the topmost layer in the Layers panel is the topmost layer on the image. You can make a layer active by clicking its name on the Layers panel. When a layer is active, it is highlighted on the Layers panel, and the name of the layer appears in parentheses in the image title bar. Only one layer can be active at a time. Figure 26 shows an image with its Layers panel. Do you see that this image contains six layers? Each layer can be moved or modified individually on the panel to give a different effect to the overall image. If you look at the Layers panel, you'll see that the Finger Painting text layer is dark, indicating that it is currently active.

Displaying and Hiding Layers

You can use the Layers panel to control which layers are visible in an image. You can show or hide a layer by clicking the Indicates layer visibility button next to the layer thumbnail. When a layer is hidden, you are not able to merge it with another, select it, or print it. Hiding some layers can make it easier to focus on particular areas of an image.

Using the History Panel

Photoshop records each task you complete in an image on the **History panel**. This record of events, called states, makes it easy to see what changes occurred and the tools or commands that you used to make the modifications. The History panel, shown in Figure 26, displays up to 20 states and automatically updates the list to display the most recently performed tasks. The list contains the name of the tool or command used to change the image. You can delete a state on the History panel by selecting it and dragging it to the Delete current state button. Deleting a state is equivalent to using the Undo command. You can also use the History panel to create a new image from any state.

FIGURE 26
Layers and History panels

History panel tab

History states

Layers panel tab

Make a layer active by clicking its name

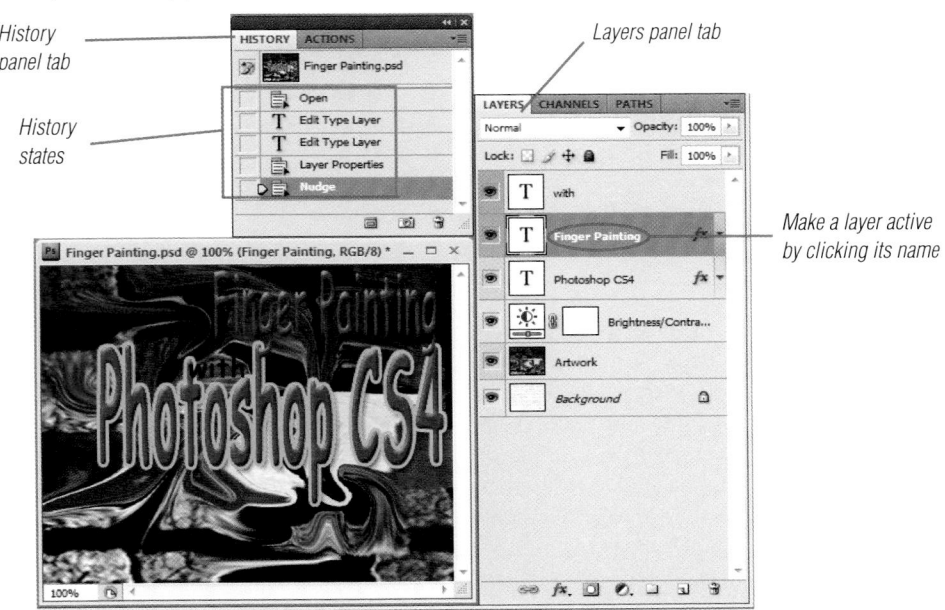

Hide and display a layer

1. Click the **Toddler layer** on the Layers panel.

   TIP Depending on the size of the window, you might only be able to see the initial characters of the layer name.

2. Verify that the **Show Transform Controls check box** on the options bar is not checked, then click the **Indicates layer visibility button** ☐ on the Toddler layer to display the image, as shown in Figure 27.

   TIP By default, transparent areas of an image have a checkerboard display on the Layers panel.

3. Click the **Indicates layer visibility button** 👁 on the Toddler layer to hide the layer.

You made the Toddler layer active on the Layers panel, then clicked the Indicates layer visibility button to display and hide a layer. Hiding layers is an important skill that can be used to remove distracting elements. Once you've finished working on a specific layer, you can display the additional layers.

FIGURE 27
Playground image

Visible Toddler layer

Indicates layer visibility button

Toddler layer

DESIGNTIP **Overcoming the fear of white space**

One design element that is often overlooked is *white space*. It's there on every page, and it doesn't seem to be doing much, does it? Take a look at a typical page in this book. Is every inch of space filled with either text or graphics? Of course not. If it were it would be impossible to read and it would be horribly ugly. The best example of the use of white space are the margins surrounding a page. This white space acts as a visual barrier—a resting place for the eyes. Without white space, the words on a page would crowd into each other, and the effect would be a cramped, cluttered, and hard to read page. Thoughtful use of white space makes it possible for you to guide the reader's eye from one location on the page to another. For many, one of the first design hurdles that must be overcome is the irresistible urge to put too much *stuff* on a page. When you are new to design, you may want to fill each page completely. Remember, less is more. Think of white space as a beautiful frame setting off an equally beautiful image.

FIGURE 28
Layer moved in Layers panel

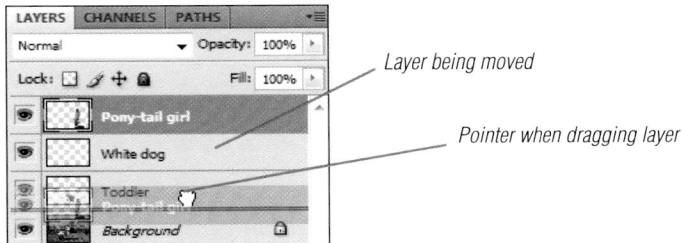

Layer being moved

Pointer when dragging layer

FIGURE 29
Result of moved layer

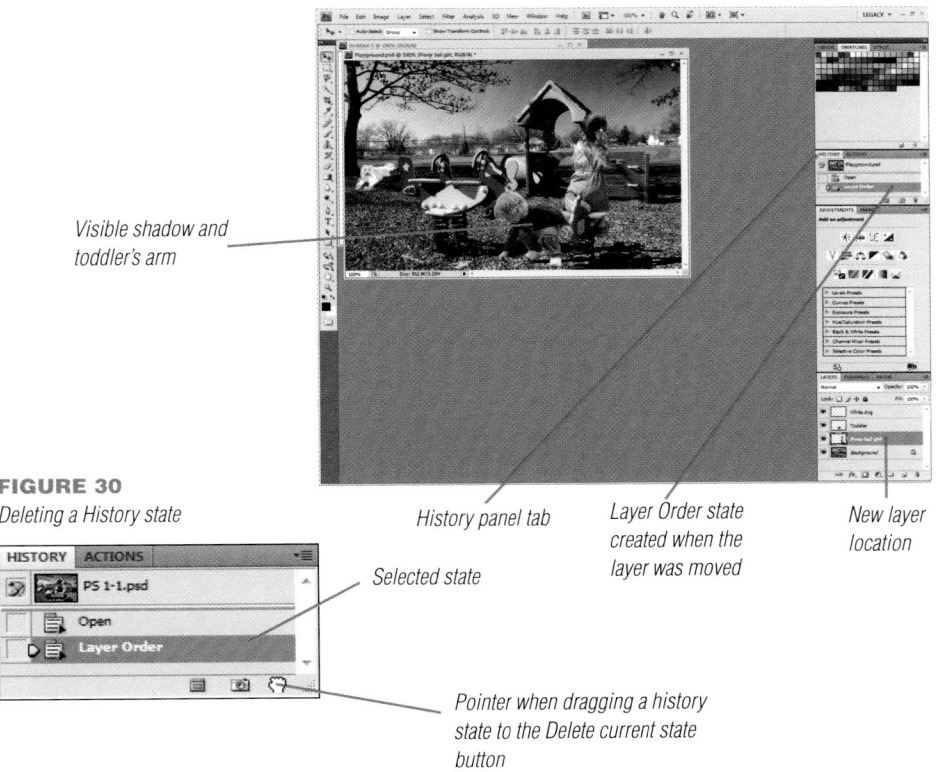

Visible shadow and
toddler's arm

FIGURE 30
Deleting a History state

History panel tab

Layer Order state
created when the
layer was moved

New layer
location

Selected state

Pointer when dragging a history
state to the Delete current state
button

Move a layer on the Layers panel and delete a state on the History panel

1. Click the **Indicates layer visibility button** on the Toddler layer on the Layers panel.

2. Click the **workspace switcher list arrow** on the Application bar, then click **Legacy**.

3. Click and drag the **Pony-tail girl layer** on the Layers panel, beneath the Toddler layer in the panel, as shown in Figure 28.

   The shadow of the toddler is now visible. See Figure 29.

4. Click **Layer Order** on the History panel, then drag it to the **Delete current state button** on the History panel, as shown in Figure 30.

   TIP Each time you close and reopen an image, the History panel is cleared.

   The shadow of the toddler is now less visible.

5. Click **File** on the Application bar, then click **Save**.

You moved the Pony-tail girl layer so it was behind the Toddler layer, then returned it to its original position by dragging the Layer Order state to the Delete current state button on the History panel. You can easily use the History panel to undo what you've done.

LEARN ABOUT PHOTOSHOP
BY USING HELP

What You'll Do

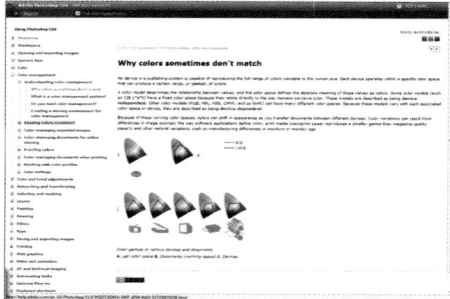

In this lesson, you'll open Help, then view and find information from the list of topics and the Search feature.

Understanding the Power of Help

Photoshop features an extensive Help system that you can use to access definitions, explanations, and useful tips. Help information is displayed in a browser window, so you must have web browser software installed on your computer to view the information; however, you do not need an Internet connection to use Photoshop Help.

Using Help Topics

The Home page of the Help window has links in the right pane that you can use to retrieve information about Photoshop commands and features. In the left pane is a list of topics from which you can choose. Help items have a plus sign (+) to the left of the

topic name. The plus sign (+) indicates that there are subtopics found within. To see the subtopics, click the plus sign (+). Topics and subtopics are links, meaning that the text is clickable. When you click any of the links, the right pane will display information (which may also contain links). The Search feature is located in a tab on the toolbar (above the left and right panes) in the form of a text box. You can search the Photoshop Help System by typing in the text box, then pressing [Enter] (Win) or [return] (Mac).

FIGURE 31
Topics in the Help window

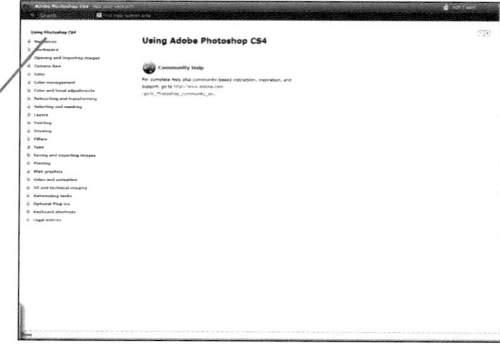

Help links

FIGURE 32

Contents section of the Help window

Choosing
Colors topic in
Contents

Subtopic

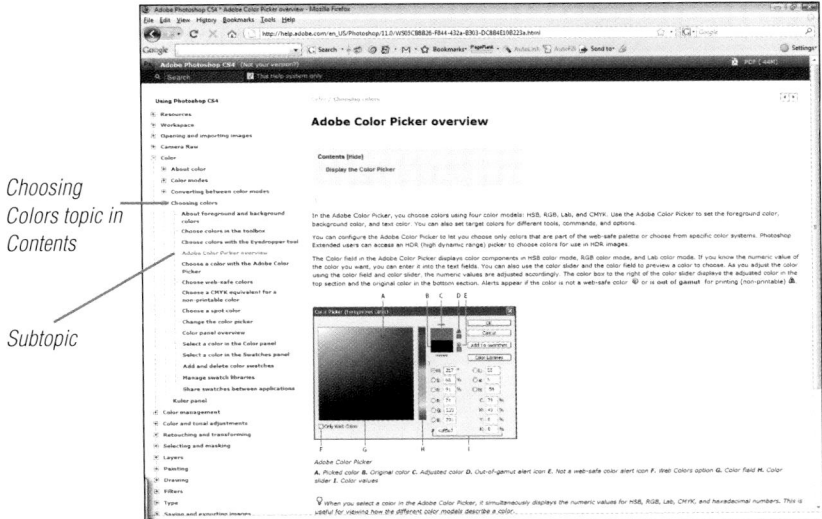

1. Click **Help** on the Application bar, then click **Photoshop Help**.

    TIP   You can also open the Help window by pressing **[F1]** (Win) or $\mathcal{H}$ **[/]** (Mac).

2. Click the **plus sign (+)** to the left of the word **Color**.

3. Click **the plus sign (+)** to the left of **Choosing colors**, then click **Adobe Color Picker overview** in the left pane. See Figure 32.

    TIP   You can maximize the window (if you want to take advantage of the full screen display).

    Bear in mind that Help is web-driven and, like any web site, can change as errors and inconsistencies are found.

You used the Photoshop Help command on the Help menu to open the Help window and view a topic in Contents.

Understanding the differences between monitor, images, and device resolution

Image resolution is determined by the number of pixels per inch (ppi) that are printed on a page. Pixel dimensions (the number of pixels along the height and width of a bitmap image) determine the amount of detail in an image, while image resolution controls the amount of space over which the pixels are printed. High resolution images show greater detail and more subtle color transitions than low resolution images. Device resolution or printer resolution is measured by the ink dots per inch (dpi) produced by printers. You can set the resolution of your computer monitor to determine the detail with which images will be displayed. Each monitor should be calibrated to describe how the monitor reproduces colors. Monitor calibration is one of the first things you should do because it determines whether your colors are being accurately represented, which in turn determines how accurately your output will match your design intentions.

Get help and support

1. Click **Help** on the Application bar, then click **Photoshop Help**.

2. Click the **link** beneath the Community Help icon (*http://www.adobe.com/go/lr_ Photoshop_community*). Compare your Help window to Figure 33.

You accessed the Community Help feature.

FIGURE 33
Community Help window

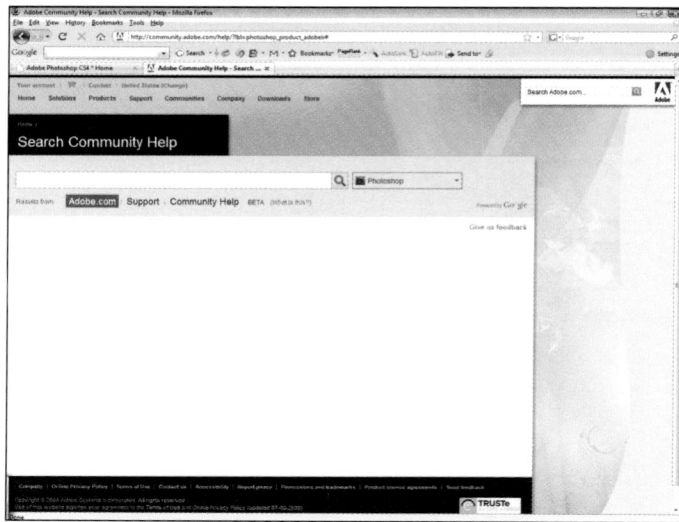

FIGURE 34
How-To Help topics

Using How-To Help features

Using Help would always be easy if you knew the name of the feature you wanted up look up. To help you find out how to complete common tasks, Photoshop has a listing of "How-To's" in the Help menu. Click Help on the Application bar, point to the How-To you'd like to read, as shown in Figure 34, then click the item about which you want more information.

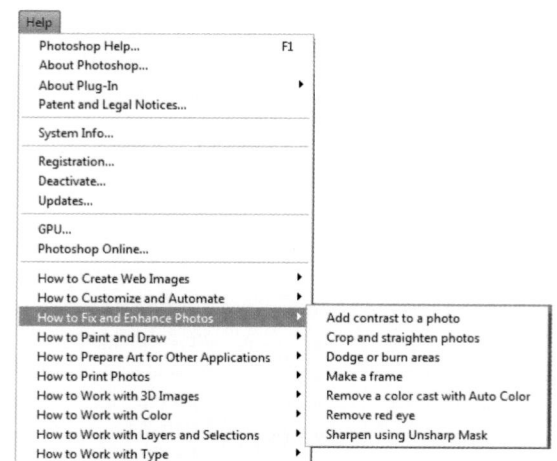

FIGURE 35

Search text box in Help

Search text box

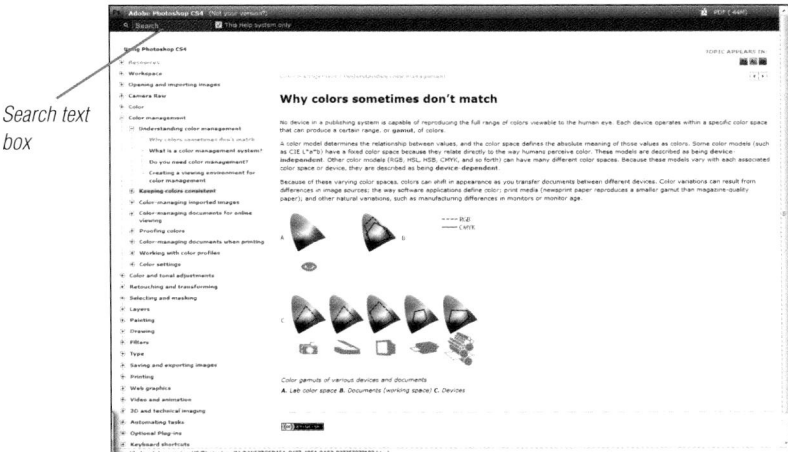

FIGURE 36

Additional keyboard shortcuts

Keys for using panels

This is not a complete list of keyboard shortcuts. This table lists only those shortcuts that are not displayed in menu commands or tool tips.

Result	Windows	Mac OS
Set options (except for Actions, Animation, Styles, Brushes, Tool Presets, and Layer Comps panels)	Alt-click New button	Option-click New button
Delete without confirmation (except for the Brushes panel)	Alt-click Delete button	Option-click Delete button
Apply value and keep text box active	Shift + Enter	Shift + Return
Load as a selection	Control-click channel, layer, or path thumbnail.	Command-click channel, layer, or path thumbnail.
Add to current selection	Control + Shift-click channel, layer, or path thumbnail.	Command + Shift-click channel, layer, or path thumbnail.
Subtract from current selection	Control + Alt-click channel, path, or layer thumbnail.	Command + Option-click channel, path, or layer thumbnail.
Intersect with current selection	Control + Shift + Alt-click channel, path, or layer thumbnail.	Command + Shift + Option-click channel, path, or layer thumbnail.
Show/Hide all panels	Tab	Tab
Show/Hide all panels except the toolbox and options bar	Shift + Tab	Shift + Tab
Highlight options bar	Select tool and press Enter	Select tool and press Return
Increase/decrease units by 10 in a pop-up menu	Shift + Up Arrow/Down Arrow	Shift + Up Arrow/Down Arrow

Find information using Search

1. Click the **Search text box** in the Help window.

2. Type **print quality**, then press **[Enter]** (Win) or **[return]** (Mac).

   TIP You can search for multiple words by inserting a space; do not use punctuation in the text box.

3. Scroll down the left pane (if necessary), click **2** or **Next** to go to the next page, scroll down (if necessary), click **Why colors sometimes don't match**, then compare your Help screen to Figure 35.

4. Click the **Close box** on your browser window or tab when you are finished reading the topic.

You entered a search term, viewed search results, then closed the Help window.

Finding hidden keyboard shortcuts

There are oodles of keyboard shortcuts in Photoshop, and not all of them are listed in menus. Figure 36 contains a table of additional keyboard shortcuts that are not available on menus or ScreenTips. You can find this help topic by searching on keyboard shortcuts.

VIEW AND PRINT
AN IMAGE

What You'll Do

 In this lesson, you'll use the Zoom tool on the Application bar and Tools panel to increase and decrease your views of the image. You'll also change the page orientation settings in the Page Setup dialog box, and print the image.

Getting a Closer Look

When you edit an image in Photoshop, it is important that you have a good view of the area that you are focusing on. Photoshop has a variety of methods that allow you to enlarge or reduce your current view. You can use the Zoom tool by clicking the image to zoom in on (magnify the view) or zoom out of (reduce the view) areas of your image. Zooming in or out enlarges or reduces your *view*, not the actual image. The maximum zoom factor is 1600%. The current zoom percentage appears in the document's title bar, on the Navigator panel, on the status bar, and on the Application bar. When the Zoom tool is selected, the options bar provides additional choices for changing your view, as shown in Figure 37. For example, the Resize Windows To Fit check box automatically resizes the window whenever you magnify or reduce the view. You can also change the zoom percentage using the Navigator panel and the status bar by typing a new value in the zoom text box.

Printing Your Image

In many cases, a professional print shop might be the best option for printing a Photoshop image to get the highest quality. Lacking a professional print shop, you can print a Photoshop image using a standard black-and-white or color printer from within Photoshop, or you can switch to Bridge and then choose to send output to a PDF or Web Gallery. The printed image will be a composite of all visible layers. The quality of your printer and paper will affect the appearance of your output. The Page Setup dialog box displays options for printing, such as paper orientation. **Orientation** is the direction in which an image appears on the page. In **portrait orientation**, the image is printed with the shorter edges of the paper at the top and bottom. In **landscape orientation**, the image is printed with the longer edges of the paper at the top and bottom.

Use the Print command when you want to print multiple copies of an image. Use the Print One Copy command to print a single copy without making dialog box selections, and use the Print dialog box when you want to handle color values using color management.

Understanding Color Handling in Printing

The Print dialog box that opens when you click Print on the File menu lets you determine how colors are output. You can click the Color Handling list arrow to choose whether to use color management, and whether Photoshop or the printing device should control this process. If you let Photoshop determine the colors, Photoshop performs any necessary conversions to color values appropriate for the selected printer. If you choose to let the printer determine the colors, the printer will convert document color values to the corresponding printer color values. In this scenario, Photoshop does not alter the color values. If no color management is selected, no color values will be changed when the image is printed.

Viewing an Image in Multiple Views

You can use the New Window command (accessed by pointing to Arrange on the Window menu) to open multiple views of the same image. You can change the zoom percentage in each view so you can spot-light the areas you want to modify, and then modify the specific area of the image in each view. Because you are working on the same image in multiple views, not in multiple versions, Photoshop automatically applies the changes you make in one view to all views. Although you can close the views you no longer need at any time, Photoshop will not save any changes until you save the file.

FIGURE 37
Zoom tool options bar

Zooms the window to the print resolution

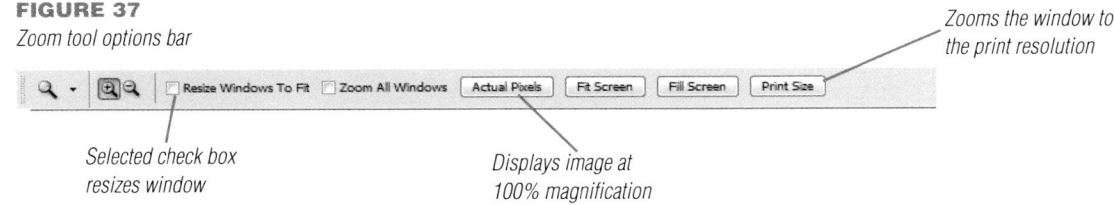

Selected check box resizes window

Displays image at 100% magnification

Choosing a Photoshop version

You may have noticed that the title bar on the images in this book say 'Adobe Photoshop CS4 Extended'. What's that about? Well, the release of the Adobe Creative Suite 4 offers two versions of Photoshop: Adobe Photoshop CS4 and Adobe Photoshop CS4 Extended. The Extended version has additional animation and measurement features and is ideal for multimedia creative professionals, film and video creative professionals, graphic and web designers who push the limits of 3D and motion, as well as those professionals in the fields of manufacturing, medicine, architecture, engineering and construction, and science and research. Photoshop CS4 is ideal for professional photographers, serious amateur photographers, graphic and web designers, and print service providers.

Use the Zoom tool

1. Click the **Indicates layer visibility button** 👁 on the Layers panel for the Toddler layer so the layer is no longer displayed.

2. Click the **Zoom tool** 🔍 on the Application bar.

   TIP You can also click the Zoom tool on the Tools panel.

3. Select the **Resize Windows To Fit check box** (if it is not already selected) on the options bar.

4. Position the **Zoom In pointer** ⊕ over the center of the image, then click the **image**.

   TIP Position the pointer over the part of the image you want to keep in view.

5. Press **[Alt]** (Win) or **[option]** (Mac), then when the Zoom Out pointer appears, click the center of the image twice with the **Zoom Out pointer** ⊖.

6. Release **[Alt]** (Win) or **[option]** (Mac), then compare your image to Figure 38.

   The zoom factor for the image is 66.7%. Your zoom factor may differ.

You selected the Zoom tool on the Tools panel and used it to zoom in to and out of the image. The Zoom tool makes it possible to see the detail in specific areas of an image, or to see the whole image at once, depending on your needs.

FIGURE 38
Reduced image

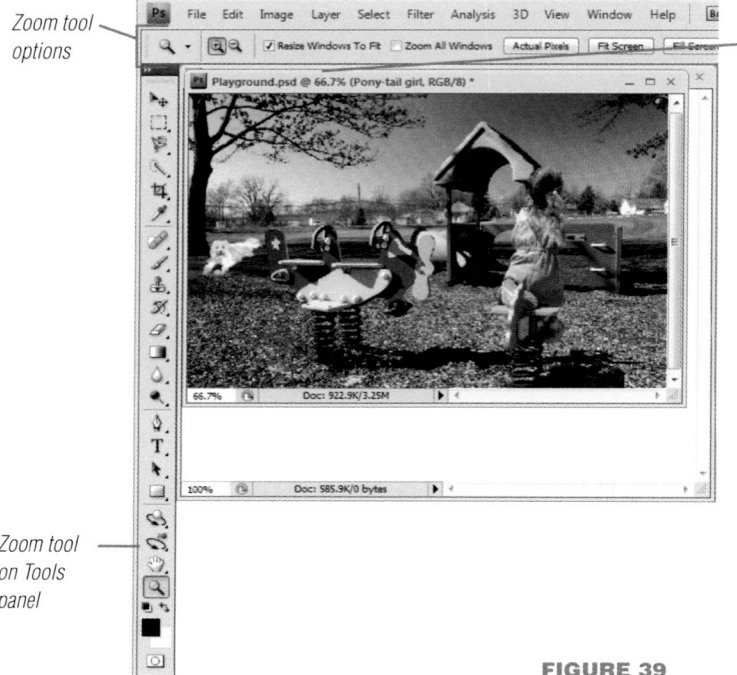

Zoom tool options

Zoom percentage changed

Zoom tool on Tools panel

Using the Navigator panel

You can change the magnification factor of an image using the Navigator panel or the Zoom tool on the Tools panel. You can open the Navigator panel by clicking Window on the Application bar, then clicking Navigator. By double-clicking the Zoom text box on the Navigator panel, you can enter a new magnification factor, then press [Enter] (Win) or [return] (Mac). The magnification factor—shown as a percentage—is displayed in the lower-left corner of the Navigator panel, as shown in Figure 39. The red border in the panel, called the Proxy Preview Area, defines the area of the image that is magnified. You can drag the Proxy Preview Area inside the Navigator panel to view other areas of the image at the current magnification factor.

FIGURE 39
Navigator panel

Viewed area of image

Getting Started with Adobe Photoshop CS4

FIGURE 40
Page Setup dialog box

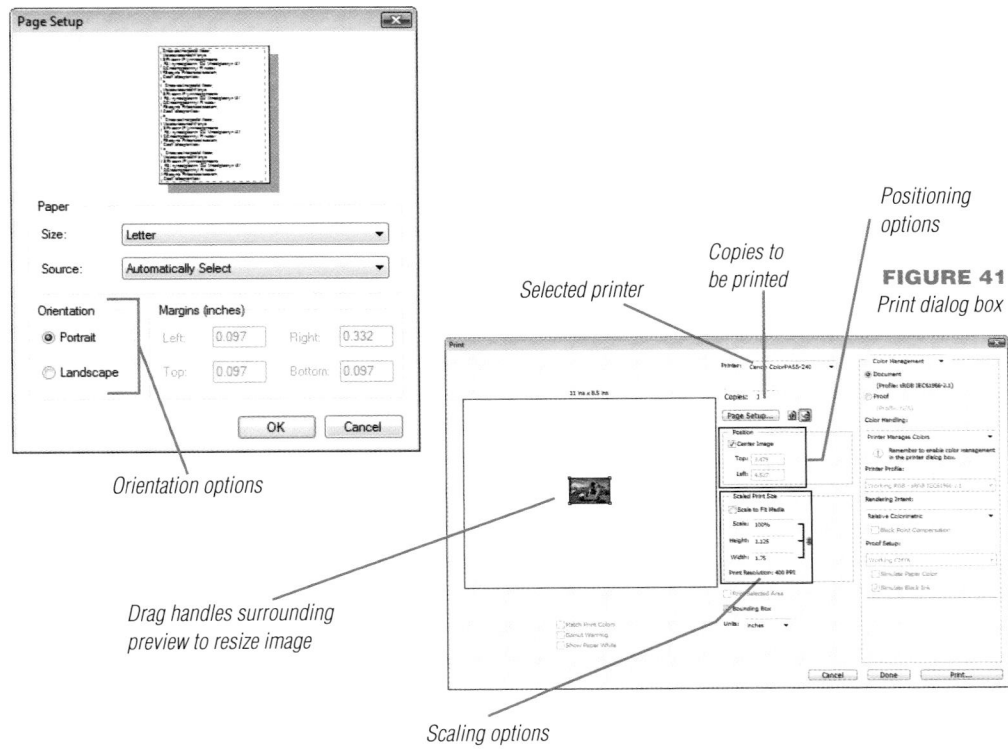

Orientation options

Drag handles surrounding
preview to resize image

Scaling options

Selected printer

Copies to
be printed

Positioning
options

FIGURE 41
Print dialog box

Modify print settings

1. Click **File** on the Application bar, then click **Page Setup** to open the Page Setup dialog box, as shown in Figure 40.

   TIP If you have not selected a printer using the Print Center, a warning box might appear (Mac).

   Page setup and print settings vary slightly in Macintosh.

2. Click the **Landscape option button** in the Orientation section (Win) or **Click the Landscape icon** (Mac), then click **OK**.

   | TIP Choose either Landscape option (Mac).

3. Click **File** on the Application bar, click **Print**, then click **Proceed** in the message box that opens. If a PostScript dialog box opens, click **OK** (Mac).

4. Make sure that **1** appears in the Copies text box, then click **Print**. See Figure 41.

   TIP You can use the handles surrounding the image preview in the Print dialog box to scale the print size.

You used the Page Setup command on the File menu to open the Page Setup dialog box, changed the page orientation, then printed the image. Changing the page orientation can make an image fit better on a printed page.

Previewing and creating a Proof Setup

You can create and save a Proof Setup, which lets you preview your image to see how it will look when printed on a specific device. This feature lets you see how colors can be interpreted by different devices. By using this feature, you can decrease the chance that the colors on the printed copy of the image will vary from what you viewed on your monitor. Create a custom proof by clicking View on the Application bar, pointing to Proof Setup, then clicking Custom. Specify the conditions in the Customize Proof Condition dialog box, then click OK. Each proof setup has the .psf extension and can be loaded by clicking View on the Application bar, pointing to Proof Setup, clicking Custom, then clicking Load.

Create a PDF with Bridge

1. Click the **Launch Bridge button** [Br] on the Application bar.

2. Click the **Folders tab** (if necessary), then click **Chapter 1** in the location where your Data Files are stored in the Folders tab (if necessary).

3. Click the **Output button** in the Bridge options bar.

4. Click the **PDF button** in the Output tab.

5. Click **Playground.psd,** hold [**Shift**], click **PS 1-4.psd** in the Content tab, then release [**Shift**].

6. Click the **Template list arrow**, click ***5 Contact Sheet**, click **Refresh Preview**, then compare your screen to Figure 1-42.

7. Scroll down the Output panel, click **Save**, locate the folder where your Data Files are stored, type **your name Chapter 1 files** in the text box, then click **Save.** You may need to click OK to close a warning box.

You launched Adobe Bridge, then generated a PDF which was printed using Adobe Acrobat.

FIGURE 42

PDF Output options in Bridge

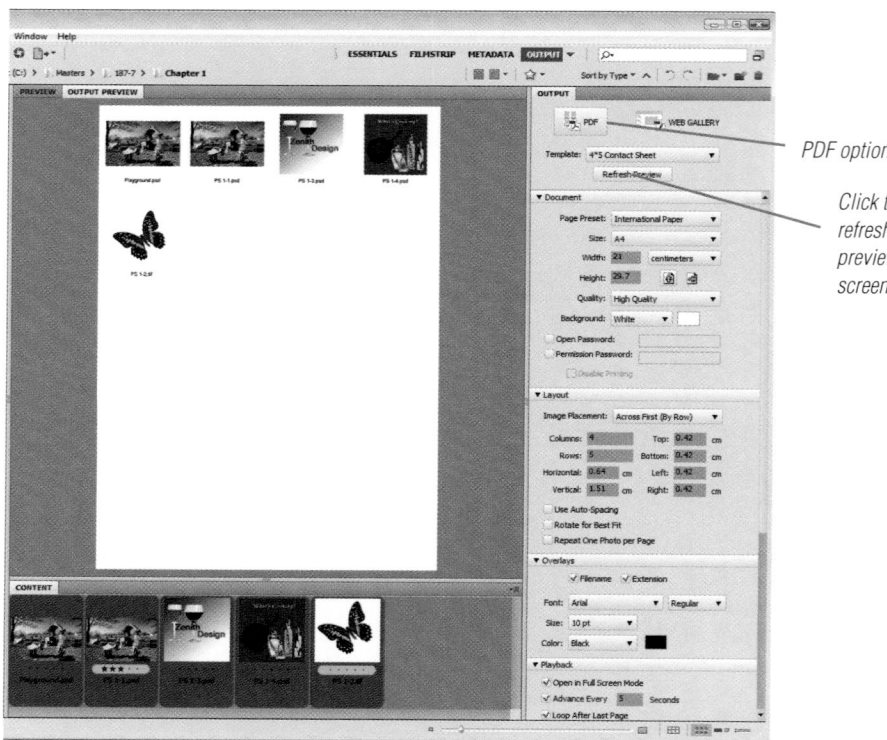

PDF option

Click to refresh preview screen

DESIGNTIP   **Using contrast to add emphasis**

Contrast is an important design principle that uses opposing elements, such as colors or lines, to produce an intensified effect in an image, page, or publication. Just as you can use a font attribute to make some text stand out from the rest, you can use contrasting elements to make certain graphic objects stand out. You can create contrast in many ways: by changing the sizes of objects; by varying object weights, such as making a line heavier surrounding an image; by altering the position of an object, such as changing the location on the page, or rotating the image so it is positioned on an angle; by drawing attention-getting shapes or a colorful box behind an object that makes it stand out (called a **matte**); or by adding carefully selected colors that emphasize an object.

FIGURE 43

Web Gallery options in Bridge

Web Gallery button

Create a Web Gallery with Bridge

1. Verify that Bridge is open.

2. Click the **Web Gallery button** in the Output tab, click **Refresh Preview**, then compare your screen to Figure 43.

3. Click the **View Slideshow button** in the Output Preview window, then click the **Play Slideshow button**.

4. Scroll down the Output panel, click the **Save to Disk option button**, click the **Browse button**, locate the folder where your Data Files are stored, then click **OK** (Win) or **Choose** (Mac).

5. Click **Save** in the Create Gallery section of the Output panel, then click **OK** when the Gallery has been created.

6. Click **File** on the Bridge menu, then click **Exit** (Win) or click **Adobe Bridge CS4**, then click **Quit Adobe Bridge CS4** (Mac).

You launched Adobe Bridge, then generated a Web Gallery.

CLOSE A FILE
AND EXIT PHOTOSHOP

What You'll Do

New...	Ctrl+N
Open...	Ctrl+O
Browse in Bridge...	Alt+Ctrl+O
Open As...	Alt+Shift+Ctrl+O
Open As Smart Object...	
Open Recent	▶
Share My Screen...	
Device Central...	
Close	Ctrl+W
Close All	Alt+Ctrl+W
Close and Go To Bridge...	Shift+Ctrl+W
Save	Ctrl+S
Save As...	Shift+Ctrl+S
Check In...	
Save for Web & Devices...	Alt+Shift+Ctrl+S
Revert	F12
Place...	
Import	▶
Export	▶
Automate	▶
Scripts	▶
File Info...	Alt+Shift+Ctrl+I
Page Setup...	Shift+Ctrl+P
Print...	Ctrl+P
Print One Copy	Alt+Shift+Ctrl+P
Exit	Ctrl+Q

 In this lesson, you'll use the Close and Exit (Win) or Quit (Mac) commands to close a file and exit Photoshop.

Concluding Your Work Session

At the end of your work session, you might have opened several files; you now need to decide which ones you want to save.

QUICKTIP

If you share a computer with other people, it's a good idea to reset Photoshop's preferences back to their default settings. You can do so when you start Photoshop by clicking Window on the Application bar, pointing to Workspace, then clicking Essentials (Default).

Closing Versus Exiting

When you are finished working on an image, you need to save and close it. You can close one file at a time, or close all open files at the same time by exiting the program. Closing a file leaves Photoshop open, which allows you to open or create another file. Exiting Photoshop closes the file, closes Photoshop, and returns you to the desktop, where you can choose to open another program or shut down the computer. Photoshop will prompt you to save any changes before it closes the files. If you do not modify a new or existing file, Photoshop will close it automatically when you exit.

QUICKTIP

To close all open files, click File on the Application bar, then click Close All.

Using Adobe online

Periodically, when you start Photoshop, an Update dialog box might appear, prompting you to search for updates or new information on the Adobe website. If you click Yes, Photoshop will automatically notify you that a download is available; however, you do not have to select it. You can also obtain information about Photoshop from the Adobe Photoshop website (*www.adobe.com/products/photoshop/main.html*), where you can link to downloads, tips, training, galleries, examples, and other support topics.

FIGURE 44
Closing a file using the File menu

Workspace switcher

Close command

Exit command

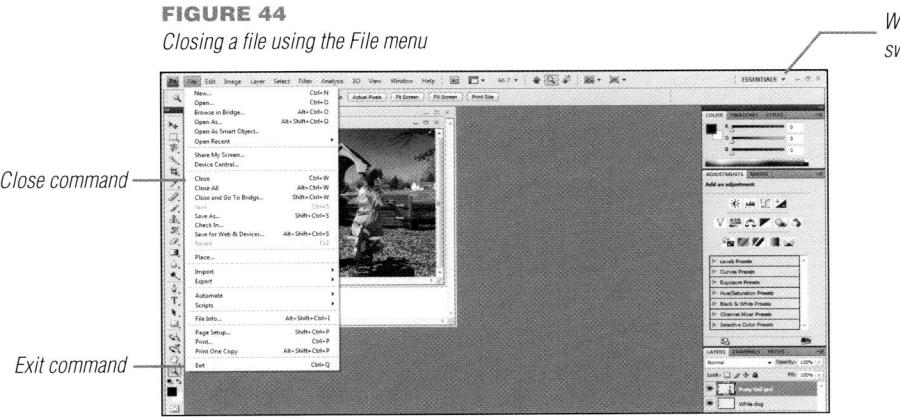

DESIGNTIP   **Using a scanner and a digital camera**

If you have a scanner, you can import print images, such as those taken from photographs, magazines, or line drawings, into Photoshop. Remember that images taken from magazines are owned by others, and that you need permission to distribute them. There are many types of scanners, including flatbed or single-sheet feed. You can also use a digital camera to create your own images. A digital camera captures images as digital files and stores them on some form of electronic medium, such as a SmartMedia card or memory stick. After you upload the images from your camera to your computer, you can work with images in Photoshop.

You can open a scanned or uploaded image (which usually has a .jpg extension or another graphics file format) by clicking File on the Application bar, then clicking Open. All Formats is the default file type, so you should be able to see all available image files in the Open dialog box. Locate the folder containing your scanned or digital camera images, click the file you want to open, then click Open. A scanned or digital camera image contains all its imagery in a single layer. You can add layers to the image, but you can only save these new layers if you save the image as a Photoshop image (with the extension .psd).

Close a file and exit Photoshop

1. Click the **workspace switcher**, then click **Essentials**.

2. Click **File** on the Application bar, then compare your screen to Figure 44.

3. Click **Close**.

   TIP   You can close an open file (without closing Photoshop) by clicking the Close button in the image window. Photoshop will prompt you to save any unsaved changes before closing the file.

4. If asked to save your work, click **Yes** (Win) or **Save** (Mac).

5. Click **File** on the Application bar, then click **Exit** (Win) or click **Photoshop** on the Application bar, then click **Quit Photoshop** (Mac).

   TIP   To exit Photoshop and close an open file, click the Close button in the program window. Photoshop will prompt you to save any unsaved changes before closing.

6. If asked to save your work (the untitled file), click **No**.

You closed the current file and exited the program by using the Close and Exit (Win) or Quit (Mac) commands.

Power User Shortcuts

Key: Menu items are indicated by ➤ between the menu name and its command. Blue bold letters are shortcuts for selecting tools on the Tools panel.

to do this:	use this method:
Close a file	[Ctrl][W] (Win) ⌘[W] (Mac)
Create a new file	[Ctrl][N] (Win), ⌘[N] (Mac)
Create a workspace	Window ➤ Workspace ➤ Save Workspace
Drag a layer	✍
Exit Photoshop	[Ctrl][Q] (Win), ⌘[Q] (Mac)
Hide a layer	👁
Lasso tool	◯ or L
Modify workspace display	ESSENTIALS ▾
Open a file	[Ctrl][O] (Win), ⌘[O] (Mac)
Launch Bridge	▶Br
Open Help	[F1] (Win), ⌘ [/] (Mac)
Open Preferences dialog box	[Ctrl][K] (Win) ⌘[K] (Mac)
Page Setup	[Shift][Ctrl][P] (Win) [Shift]⌘[P] (Mac)
Print File	File ➤ Print or, [Ctrl][P] (Win) ⌘[P] (Mac)

to do this:	use this method:
Reset preferences to default settings	[Shift][Alt][Ctrl] (Win) [Shift] option ⌘ (Mac)
Save a file	[Ctrl][S] (Win) ⌘[S] (Mac)
Show a layer	☐
Show hidden lasso tools	[Shift] L
Show History panel	🕒
Show or hide all open panels	[Shift][Tab]
Show or hide all open panels, the options bar, and the Tools panel	[Tab]
Show or hide Swatches panel	Window ➤ Swatches
Use Save As	[Shift][Ctrl][S] (Win) [Shift]⌘[S] (Mac)
Zoom in	🔍 [Ctrl][+] (Win), ⌘[+] (Mac)
Zoom out	[Alt] 🔍 (Win) [Ctrl][-] (Win), ⌘[−] (Mac)
Zoom tool	🔍 or Z

Start Adobe Photoshop CS4.

1. Start Photoshop.
2. Create a new image that is 500 × 500 pixels, accept the default resolution, then name and save it as **Review**.

Open and save an image.

1. Open PS 1-3.psd from the drive and folder where you store your Data Files, and if prompted, update the text layers.
2. Save it as **Zenith Design Logo**.

Use organizational and management features.

1. Open Adobe Bridge.
2. Click the Folders tab, then locate the folder that contains your Data Files.
3. Close Adobe Bridge.

Examine the Photoshop window.

1. Locate the image title bar and the current zoom percentage.
2. Locate the menu you use to open an image.
3. View the Tools panel, the options bar, and the panels that are showing.
4. Click the Move tool on the Tools panel, then view the Move tool options on the options bar.
5. Create, save and display a customized workspace (based on Essentials) called History and Layers that captures panel locations and displays the History panel above the Layers panel.

Use the Layers and History panels.

1. Drag the Wine Glasses layer so it is above the Zenith layer, then use the History panel to undo the state.

2. Drag the Wine Glasses layer above the Zenith layer again.
3. Use the Indicates layer visibility button to hide the Wine Glasses layer.
4. Make the Wine Glasses layer visible again.
5. Hide the Zenith layer.
6. Show the Zenith layer.
7. Show the Tag Line layer.

Learn about Photoshop by using Help.

1. Open the Adobe Photoshop CS4 Help window.
2. Using the Index, find information about resetting to the default workspace.

3. Print the information you find.
4. Close the Help window.

View and print an image.

1. Make sure that all the layers are visible in the Layers panel.
2. Click the Zoom tool, then make sure the setting is selected to resize the window to fit.

3. Zoom in on the wine glasses twice.
4. Zoom out to the original perspective.
5. Print one copy of the image.
6. Save your work.

Close a file and exit Photoshop.

1. Compare your screen to Figure 45, then close the Zenith Design Logo file.

2. Close the Review file.
3. Exit (Win) or Quit (Mac) Photoshop.

FIGURE 45
Completed Skills Review

Getting Started with Adobe Photoshop CS4

As a new Photoshop user, you are comforted knowing that Photoshop's Help system provides definitions, explanations, procedures, and other helpful information. It also includes examples and demonstrations to show how Photoshop features work. You use the Help system to learn about image size and resolution.

1. Open the Photoshop Help window.
2. Click the Workspace topic in the topics list.
3. Click the Panels and menus subtopic, in the left pane, then click Enter values in panels, dialog boxes, and the options bar topic.
4. Click the Display context menus topic, then read this topic.
5. Click the Opening and importing images topic in the left pane.
6. Click the Image size and resolution topic in the left pane, then click About monitor resolution. Print out this topic, then compare your screen to the sample shown in Figure 46.

FIGURE 46
Sample Project Builder 1

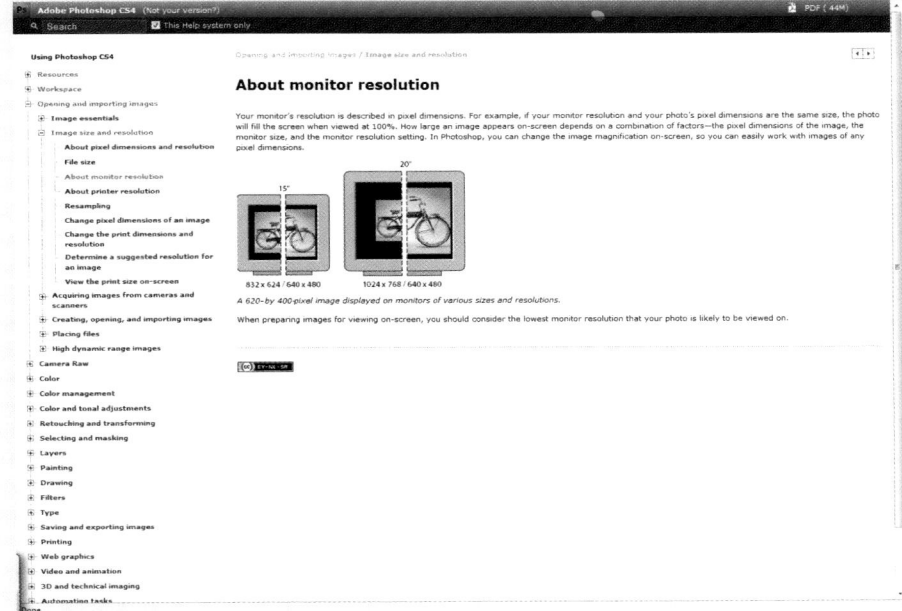

Kitchen Experience, your local specialty cooking shop, has just added herb-infused oils to its product line. They have hired you to draft a flyer that features these new products. You use Photoshop to create this flyer.

1. Open PS 1-4.psd, then save it as **Cooking**.
2. Display the Essentials workspace (if necessary).
3. Make the Measuring Spoons layer visible.
4. Drag the Oils layer so the content appears behind the Skillet layer content.
5. Drag the Measuring Spoons layer above the Skillet layer.
6. Save the file, then compare your image to the sample shown in Figure 47.

FIGURE 47
Sample Project Builder 2

Getting Started with Adobe Photoshop CS4

As an avid, albeit novice Photoshop user, you have grasped the importance of how layers affect your image. With a little practice, you can examine a single-layer image and guess which objects might display on their own layers. Now, you're ready to examine the images created by Photoshop experts and critique them on their use of layers.

1. Connect to the Internet, and use your browser to find interesting artwork located on at least two websites.
2. Download a single-layer image (in its native format) from each website.
3. Start Photoshop, then open the downloaded images.
4. Save one image as **Critique-1** and the other as **Critique-2** in the Photoshop format (use the .psd extension).
5. Analyze each image for its potential use of layers.

6. Open the File Info dialog box for Critique-1.psd, then type in the Description section your speculation as to the number of layers there might be in the image, their possible order on the Layers panel, and how moving the layers would affect the image.
7. Close the dialog box.
8. Compare your image to the sample shown in Figure 48, then close the files.

FIGURE 48
Sample Design Project

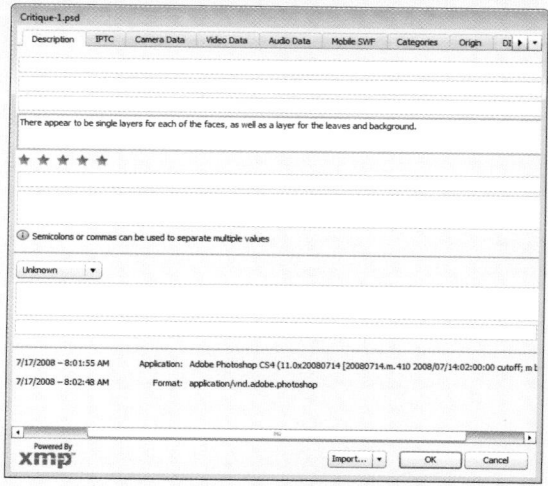

Getting Started with Adobe Photoshop CS4

You are preparing to work on a series of design projects to enhance your portfolio. You decide to see what information on digital imaging is available on the Adobe website. You also want to increase your familiarity with the Adobe website so that you can take advantage of product information and support, user tips and feedback, and become a more skilled Photoshop user.

1. Connect to the Internet and go to the Adobe website at *www.adobe.com.*
2. Point to Products, then find the link for the Photoshop family, as shown in Figure 49.
3. Use the links on the web page to search for information about digital imaging options.
4. Print the relevant page(s).
5. Start Photoshop and open the Photoshop Help window.

6. Search for information about Adjusting the Monitor Display, then print the relevant page(s).
7. Evaluate the information in the documents, and then compare any significant differences.

FIGURE 49
Completed Portfolio Project

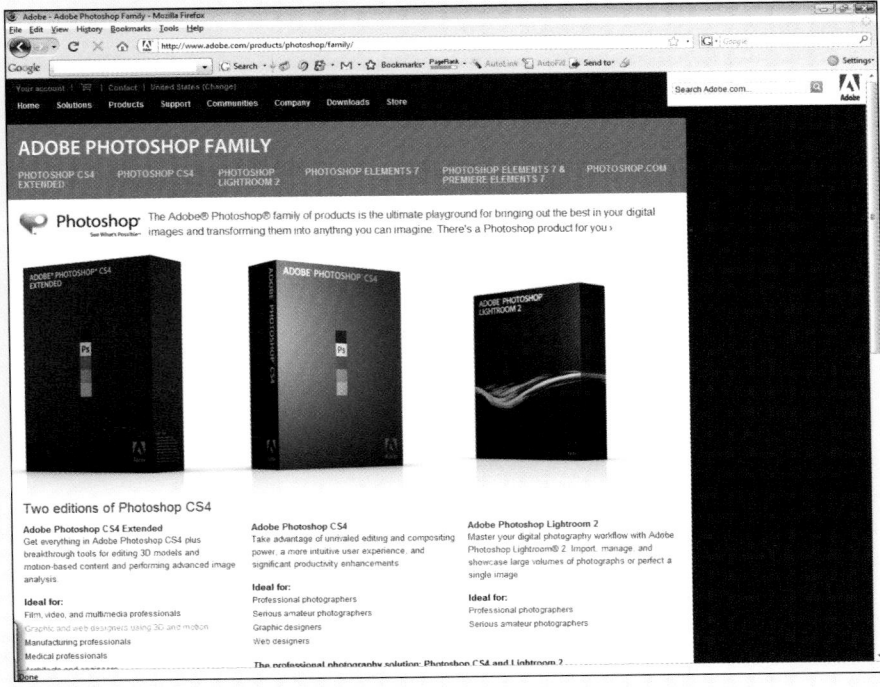

2

WORKING
WITH LAYERS

1. Examine and convert layers

2. Add and delete layers

3. Add a selection from one image to another

4. Organize layers with layer groups and colors

Layers Are Everything

You can use Photoshop to create sophisticated images in part because a Photoshop image can contain multiple layers. Each object created in Photoshop can exist on its own individual layer, making it easy to control the position and quality of each layer in the stack. Depending on your computer's resources, you can have a maximum of 8000 layers in each Photoshop image with each layer containing as much or as little detail as necessary.

> QUICKTIP
>
> The transparent areas in a layer do not increase file size.

Understanding the Importance of Layers

Layers make it possible to manipulate the tiniest detail within your image, which gives you tremendous flexibility when you make changes. By placing objects, effects, styles, and type on separate layers, you can modify them individually *without* affecting other layers. The advantage to using multiple layers is that you can isolate effects and images on one layer without affecting the others. The disadvantage of using multiple layers is that your file size might become very large. However, once your image is finished, you can dramatically reduce its file size by combining all the layers into one.

Using Layers to Modify an Image

You can add, delete, and move layers in your image. You can also drag a portion of an image, called a **selection**, from one Photoshop image to another. When you do this, a new layer is automatically created. Copying layers from one image to another makes it easy to transfer a complicated effect, a simple image, or a piece of type. You can also hide and display each layer, or change its opacity. **Opacity** is the ability to see through a layer so that layers beneath it are visible. The more opacity a layer has, the less see-through (transparent) it is. You can continuously change the overall appearance of your image by changing the order of your layers, until you achieve just the look you want.

Tools You'll Use

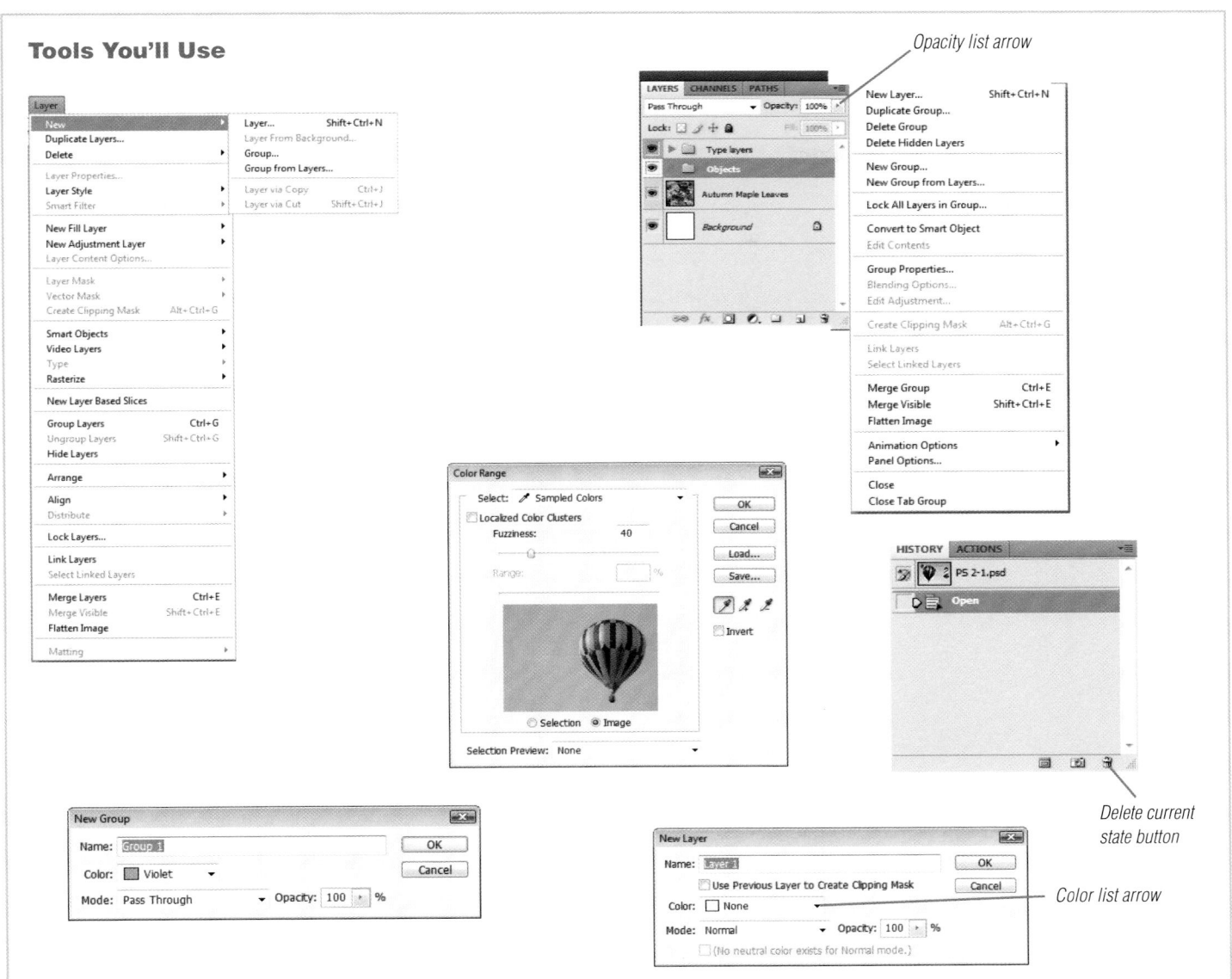

Opacity list arrow

Delete current state button

Color list arrow

2-3

EXAMINE AND
CONVERT LAYERS

What You'll Do

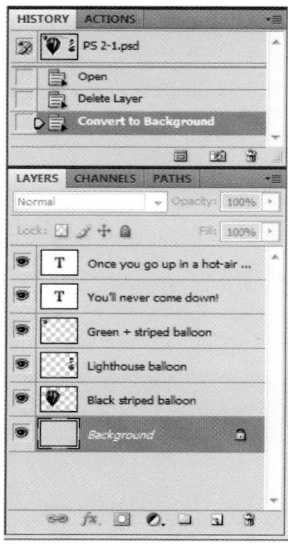

 In this lesson, you'll use the Layers panel to delete a Background layer and the Layer menu to create a Background layer from an image layer.

Learning About the Layers Panel

The **Layers panel** lists all the layers within a Photoshop file and makes it possible for you to manipulate one or more layers. By default, this panel is located in the lower-right corner of the screen, but it can be moved to a new location by dragging the panel's tab. In some cases, the entire name of the layer might not appear on the panel. If a layer name is too long, an ellipsis appears, indicating that part of the name is hidden from view. You can view a layer's entire name by holding the pointer over the name until the full name appears. The **layer thumbnail** appears to the left of the layer name and contains a miniature picture of the layer's content, as shown in Figure 1. To the left of the layer thumbnail, you can add color, which you can use to easily identify layers. The Layers panel also contains common buttons, such as the Delete layer button and the Create new layer button.

Recognizing Layer Types

The Layers panel includes several types of layers: Background, type, adjustment, and image (non-type). The Background layer—whose name appears in italics—is always at the bottom of the stack. Type layers—layers that contain text—contain the type layer icon in the layer thumbnail, and image layers display a thumbnail of their contents. Adjustment layers, which make changes to layers, have a variety of thumbnails, depending on the kind of adjustment. Along with dragging selections from one Photoshop image to another, you can also drag objects created in other applications, such as Adobe

Dreamweaver, Adobe InDesign, or Adobe Flash, onto a Photoshop image, which creates a layer containing the object you dragged from the other program window.

Organizing Layers

One of the benefits of using layers is that you can create different design effects by rearranging their order. Figure 2 contains the same layers as Figure 1, but they are arranged differently. Did you notice that the yellow-striped balloon is partially obscured by the black-striped balloon and the lighthouse balloon? This reorganization was created by dragging the layer containing the yellow balloon below the Black striped balloon layer and by dragging the Lighthouse balloon layer above Layer 2 on the Layers panel. When organizing layers, you may find it helpful to resize the Layers panel so you can see more layers within the image.

FIGURE 1
Image with multiple layers

Layers panel list arrow

Type layer thumbnail

Image layer thumbnail

Position mouse over layer name to display full title

FIGURE 2
Layers rearranged

Guide

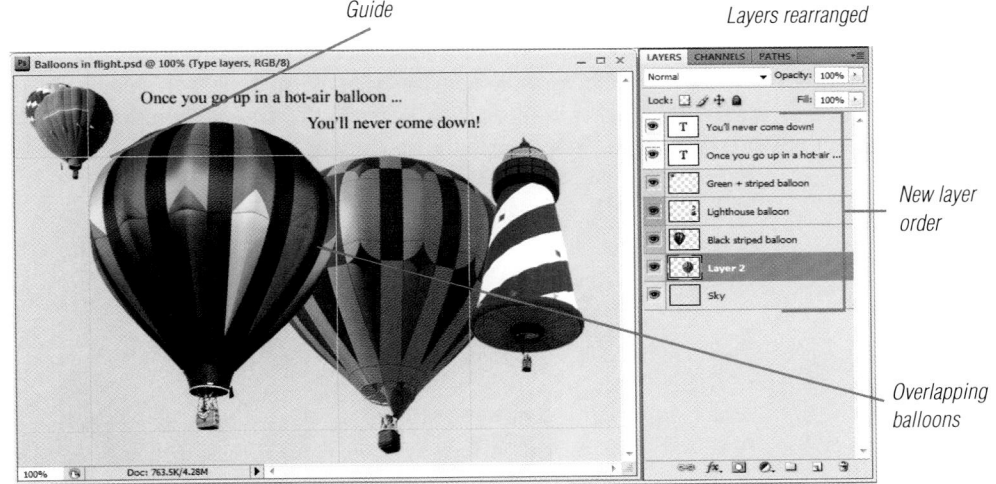

New layer order

Overlapping balloons

Converting Layers

When you open an image created with a digital camera, you'll notice that the entire image appears in the Background layer. The Background layer of any image is the initial layer and is always located at the bottom of the stack. You cannot change its position in the stack, nor can you change its opacity or lighten or darken its colors. You can, however, convert a Background layer into an image layer (non-type layer), and you can convert an image layer into a Background layer. You need to modify the image layer *before* converting it to a Background layer. You might want to convert a Background layer into an image layer so that you can use the full range of editing tools on the layer content. You might want to convert an image layer into a Background layer after you have made all your changes and want it to be the bottom layer in the stack.

QUICKTIP

Before converting an image layer to a Background layer, you must first delete the existing Background layer. You can delete a Background layer by selecting it on the Layers panel, then dragging it to the Delete layer button on the Layers panel.

Using rulers and changing units of measurement

You can display horizontal and vertical rulers to help you better position elements. To display or hide rulers, click View on the Application bar, then click Rulers. (A check mark to the left of the Rulers command indicates that the rulers are displayed.) In addition to displaying or hiding rulers, you can also choose from various units of measurement. Your choices include pixels, inches, centimeters, millimeters, points, picas, and percentages. Pixels, for example, display more tick marks and can make it easier to make tiny adjustments. You can change the units of measurement by clicking Edit [Win] or Photoshop [Mac] on the Application bar, pointing to Preferences, then clicking Units & Rulers. In the Preferences dialog box, click the Rulers list arrow, click the units you want to use, then click OK. The easiest way to change units of measurement, however, is shown in Figure 3. Once the rulers are displayed, right-click (Win) or [Ctrl]-click (Mac) either the vertical or horizontal ruler, then click the unit of measurement you want. When displayed, the Info panel, displays the current coordinates in your image. Regardless of the units of measurement in use, the X/Y coordinates are displayed in the Info panel.

FIGURE 3
Changing units of measurement

Right-click (Win) or [Ctrl]-click (Mac) to display measurement choices

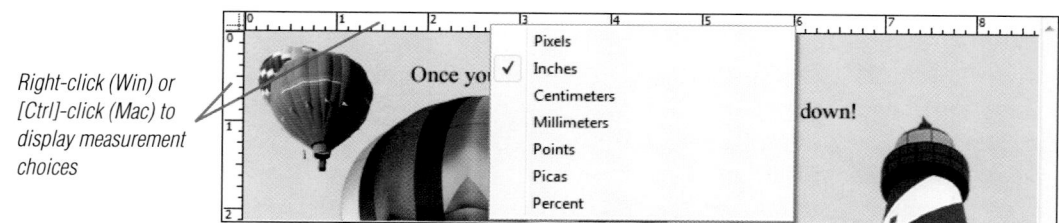

Working with Layers

Yout title bar may
differ (Mac)

FIGURE 4
Warning box

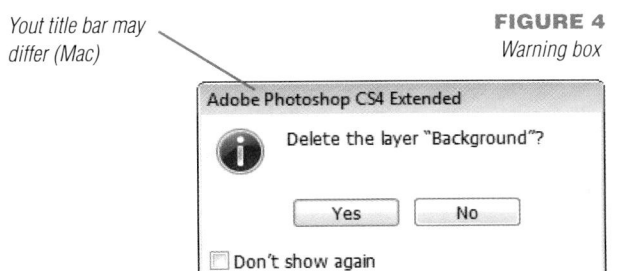

Adobe Photoshop CS4 Extended

Delete the layer "Background"?

Yes   No

☐ Don't show again

FIGURE 5
Background layer deleted

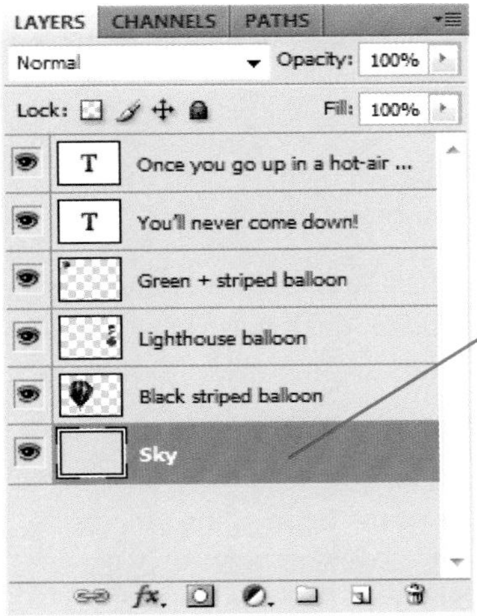

LAYERS CHANNELS PATHS

Normal   Opacity: 100%

Lock: ☐ ✎ ✛ ☐   Fill: 100%

👁 T   Once you go up in a hot-air ...

👁 T   You'll never come down!

👁 ▨ Green + striped balloon

👁 ▨ Lighthouse balloon

👁 ♠ Black striped balloon

👁 ☐ Sky

Background layer
no longer present

FIGURE 6
New Background layer added to Layers panel

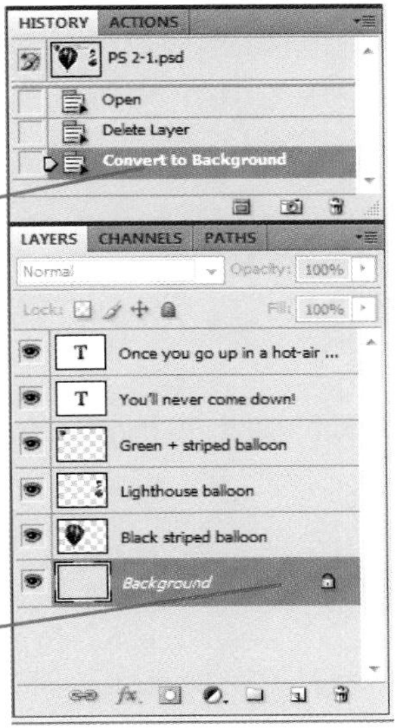

HISTORY ACTIONS

📷 PS 2-1.psd

     Open

     Delete Layer

▷   Convert to Background

History state
indicating layer
conversion

LAYERS CHANNELS PATHS

Normal   Opacity: 100%

Lock: ☐ ✎ ✛ ☐   Fill: 100%

👁 T   Once you go up in a hot-air ...

👁 T   You'll never come down!

👁 ▨ Green + striped balloon

👁 ▨ Lighthouse balloon

👁 ♠ Black striped balloon

👁 ☐ Background

New
Background
layer

Convert an image layer into a Background layer

1. Open PS 2-1.psd from the drive and folder where you store your Data Files, then save it as **Balloons in flight**.

   TIP   If you receive a warning box about maximum compatibility, or a message stating that some of the text layers need to be updated before they can be used for vector-based output, and/or a warning box about maximum compatibility, click Update and/or click OK.

2. Click **View** on the Application bar, click **Rulers** if your rulers are not visible, then make sure that the rulers are displayed in pixels.

   TIP   If you are unsure which units of measurement are used, right-click (Win) or [Ctrl]-click (Mac) one of the rulers, then verify that Pixels is selected, or click Pixels (if necessary).

3. Click the **workspace switcher** on the Application bar, then click **History and Layers** (created in the Skills Review in Chapter 1).

4. On the Layers panel, scroll down, click the **Background layer**, then click the **Delete layer button** 🗑 .

5. Click **Yes** in the dialog box, as shown in Figure 4, then compare your Layers panel to Figure 5.

6. Click **Layer** on the Application bar, point to **New**, then click **Background From Layer**.
   The Sky layer has been converted into the Background layer. Did you notice that in addition to the image layer being converted to the Background layer that a state now appears on the History panel that says Convert to Background? See Figure 6.

7. Save your work.

You displayed the rulers and switched to a previously created workspace, deleted the Background layer of an image, then converted an image layer into the Background layer. You can convert any layer into the Background layer, as long as you first delete the existing Background layer.

ADD AND DELETE LAYERS

What You'll Do

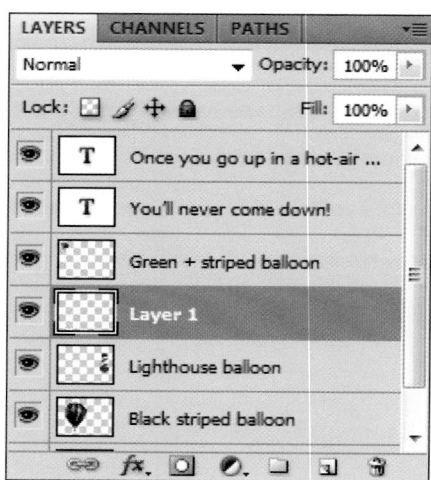

In this lesson, you'll create a new layer using the New command on the Layer menu, delete a layer, and create a new layer using buttons on the Layers panel.

Adding Layers to an Image

Because it's so important to make use of multiple layers, Photoshop makes it easy to add and delete layers. You can create layers in three ways:

- Use the New command on the Layer menu.
- Use the New Layer command on the Layers panel menu.
- Click the Create a new layer button on the Layers panel.

QUICKTIP

See Table 1 for tips on navigating the Layers panel.

Objects on new layers have a default opacity setting of 100%, which means that objects on lower layers are not visible. Each layer

Merging layers

You can combine multiple image layers into a single layer using the merging process. Merging layers is useful when you want to combine multiple layers in order to make specific edits permanent. (This merging process is different from flattening in that it's selective. Flattening merges *all* visible layers.) In order for layers to be merged, they must be visible and next to each other on the Layers panel. You can merge all visible layers within an image, or just the ones you select. Type layers cannot be merged until they are **rasterized** (turned into a bitmapped image layer), or converted into uneditable text. To merge two layers, make sure that they are next to each other and that the Indicates layer visibility button is visible on each layer, then click the layer in the higher position on the Layers panel. Click Layer on the Application bar, then click Merge Down. The active layer and the layer immediately beneath it will be combined into a single layer. To merge all visible layers, click the Layers panel list arrow, then click Merge Visible. Most layer commands that are available on the Layer menu, such as Merge Down, are also available using the Layers panel list arrow.

has the Normal (default) blending mode applied to it. (A **blending mode** is a feature that affects a layer's underlying pixels, and is used to lighten or darken colors.)

Naming a Layer

Photoshop automatically assigns a sequential number to each new layer name, but you can rename a layer at any time. So, if you have four named layers and add a new layer, the default name of the new layer will be Layer 1. Although calling a layer "Layer 12" is fine, you might want to use a more descriptive name so it is easier to distinguish one layer from another. If you use the New command on the Layer menu, you can name the layer when you create it. You can rename a layer at any time by using either of these methods:

■ Click the Layers panel list arrow, click Layer Properties, type the name in the Name text box, then click OK.
■ Double-click the name on the Layers panel, type the new name, then press [Enter] (Win) or [return] (Mac).

Deleting Layers from an Image

You might want to delete an unused or unnecessary layer. You can use any of four methods to delete a layer:

■ Click the name on the Layers panel, click the Layers panel list arrow, then click Delete Layer, as shown in Figure 7.
■ Click the name on the Layers panel, click the Delete layer button on the Layers panel, then click Yes in the warning box.
■ Click the name on the Layers panel, press and hold [Alt] (Win) or [option] (Mac), then click the Delete layer button on the Layers panel.
■ Drag the layer name on the Layers panel to the Delete layer button on the Layers panel.
■ Right-click a layer (Win) or [Ctrl]-click a layer (Mac).

You should be certain that you no longer need a layer before you delete it. If you delete a layer by accident, you can restore it during the current editing session by deleting the Delete Layer state on the History panel.

QUICKTIP

Photoshop always numbers layers sequentially, no matter how many layers you add or delete.

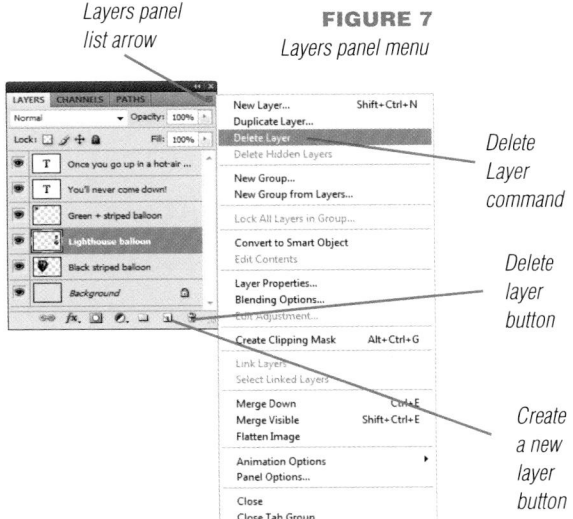

Layers panel list arrow

FIGURE 7
Layers panel menu

Delete Layer command

Delete layer button

Create a new layer button

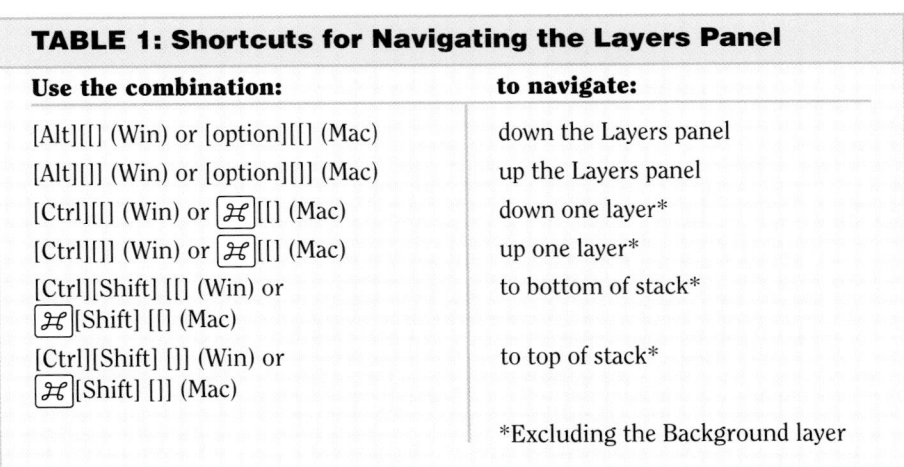

TABLE 1: Shortcuts for Navigating the Layers Panel

Use the combination:	to navigate:
[Alt][[] (Win) or [option][[] (Mac)	down the Layers panel
[Alt][]] (Win) or [option][]] (Mac)	up the Layers panel
[Ctrl][[] (Win) or ⌘[[] (Mac)	down one layer*
[Ctrl][]] (Win) or ⌘[]] (Mac)	up one layer*
[Ctrl][Shift] [[] (Win) or ⌘[Shift] [[] (Mac)	to bottom of stack*
[Ctrl][Shift] []] (Win) or ⌘[Shift] []] (Mac)	to top of stack*
	*Excluding the Background layer

Add a layer using the Layer menu

1. Click the **Lighthouse balloon layer** on the Layers panel.

2. Click **Layer** on the Application bar, point to **New**, then click **Layer** to open the New Layer dialog box, as shown in Figure 8.

    A new layer will be added above the active layer.

    TIP You can change the layer name in the New Layer dialog box before it appears on the Layers panel.

3. Click **OK**.

    The New Layer dialog box closes and the new layer appears above the Lighthouse balloon layer on the Layers panel. The New Layer state is added to the History panel. See Figure 9.

    You created a new layer above the Lighthouse balloon layer using the New command on the Layer menu. The layer does not yet contain any content.

FIGURE 8
New Layer dialog box

FIGURE 9
New layer in Layers panel

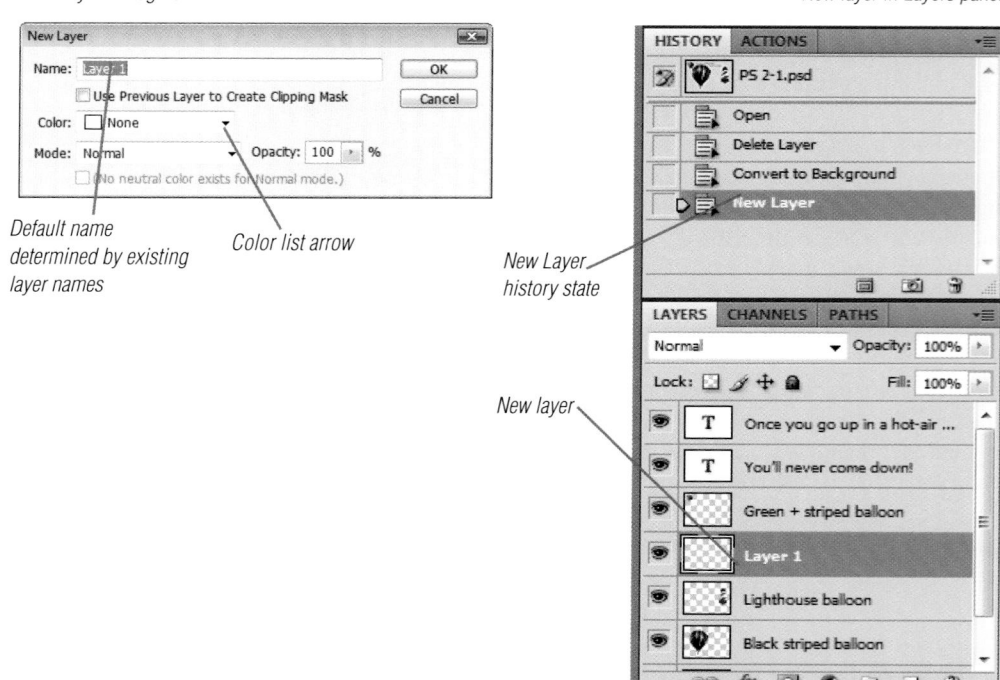

Default name
determined by existing
layer names

Color list arrow

New Layer
history state

New layer

Inserting a layer beneath the active layer

When you add a layer to an image either by using the Layer menu or clicking the Create a new layer button on the Layers panel, the new layer is inserted above the active layer. But there might be times when you want to insert the new layer beneath, or in back of, the active layer. You can do so easily, by pressing [Ctrl] (Win) or ⌘ (Mac) while clicking the Create a new layer button on the Layers panel.

FIGURE 10
New layer with default settings

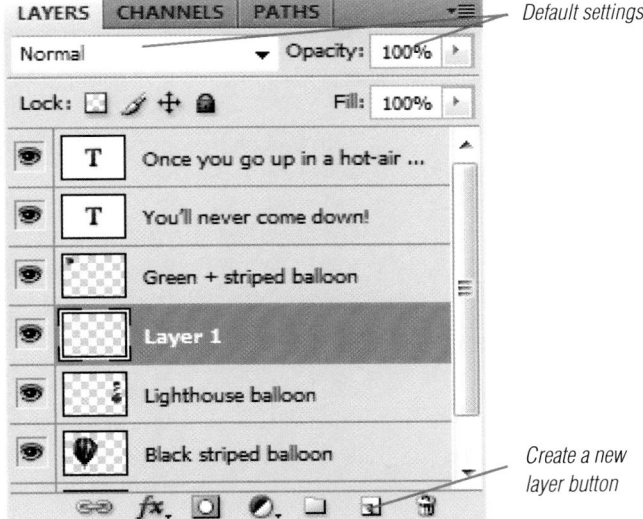

Default settings

Create a new layer button

Right-clicking for everyone (Mac)

Mac users, are you feeling left out because you can't right-click? If so, you'll welcome this news: anyone (yes, even Mac users!) can right-click simply by replacing the mouse that came with your computer with any two-button mouse that uses a USB connector. OS X was designed to recognize secondary clicks without having to add software. Once you've switched mice, just plug and play! You can then right-click using the (Win) instructions in the steps.

Delete a layer

1. Position the **Layer selection pointer** 👆 over Layer 1 on the Layers panel.

2. Drag **Layer 1** to the **Delete layer button** 🗑 on the Layers panel.

   TIP   You can also delete the layer by dragging the New Layer state on the History panel to the Delete current state button.

3. If the Delete the layer "Layer 1" dialog box opens, click the **Don't show again check box**, then click **Yes**.

   TIP   Many dialog boxes let you turn off this reminder feature by selecting the Don't show again check box. Selecting these check boxes can improve your efficiency.

You used the Delete layer button on the Layers panel to delete a layer.

Add a layer using the Layers panel

1. Click the **Lightouse balloon layer** on the Layers panel, if it is not already selected.

2. Click the **Create a new layer button** 🔲 on the Layers panel, then compare your Layers panel to Figure 10.

3. Save your work.

You used the Create a new layer button on the Layers panel to add a new layer.

ADD A SELECTION FROM ONE
IMAGE TO ANOTHER

What You'll Do

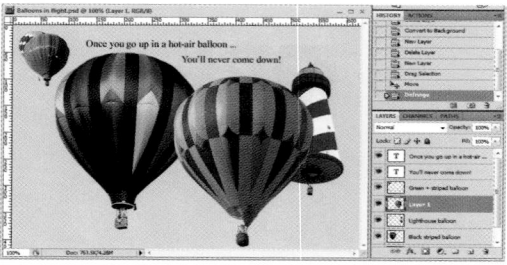

 In this lesson, you'll use the Invert check box in the Color Range dialog box to make a selection, drag the selection to another image, and remove the fringe from a selection using the Defringe command.

Understanding Selections

Often the Photoshop file you want to create involves using an image or part of an image from another file. To use an image or part of an image, you must first select it. Photoshop refers to this as "making a selection." A selection is an area of an image surrounded by a **marquee**, a dashed line that encloses the area you want to edit or move to another image, as shown in Figure 11. You can drag a marquee around a selection using four marquee tools: Rectangular Marquee, Elliptical Marquee, Single Row Marquee, and Single Column Marquee. Table 2 displays the four marquee tools and other selection tools. You can set options for each tool on the options bar when the tool you want to use is active.

Understanding the Extract and Color Range Commands

In addition to using selection tools, Photoshop provides other methods for incorporating imagery from other files. The **Extract command**, located on the Filter menu, separates an image from a background or surrounding imagery. You can use the **Color Range command**, located on the Select menu, to select a particular color contained in an existing image. Depending on the area you want, you can use the Color Range dialog box to extract a portion of an image.

Cropping an image

You might find an image that you really like, except that it contains a particular portion that you don't need. You can exclude, or **crop**, certain parts of an image by using the Crop tool on the Tools panel. Cropping hides areas of an image from view *without* decreasing resolution quality. To crop an image, click the Crop tool on the Tools panel, drag the pointer around the area you *want to keep*, then press [Enter] (Win) or [return] (Mac).

For example, you can select the Invert check box to choose one color and then select the portion of the image that is every color *except* that one. After you select all the imagery you want from another image, you can drag it into your open file.

Making a Selection and Moving a Selection

You can use a variety of methods and tools to make a selection, which can then be used as a specific part of a layer or as the entire layer. You use selections to isolate an area you want to alter. For example, you can use the Magnetic Lasso tool to select complex shapes by clicking the starting point, tracing an approximate outline, then clicking the ending point. Later, you can use the Crop tool to trim areas from a selection. When you use the Move tool to drag a selection to the destination image, Photoshop places the selection in a new layer above the previously active layer.

Defringing Layer Contents

Sometimes when you make a selection, then move it into another image, the newly selected image can contain unwanted pixels that give the appearance of a fringe, or halo. You can remove this effect using a Matting command called Defringe. This command is available on the Layer menu and allows you to replace fringe pixels with the colors of other nearby pixels. You can determine a width for replacement pixels between 1 and 200. It's magic!

FIGURE 11
Marquee selections

— *Area selected using the Rectangular Marquee tool*

— *Specific element selected using the Magnetic Lasso tool*

TABLE 2: Selection Tools

tool	tool name	tool	tool name
▢.	Rectangular Marquee tool	◯.	Lasso tool
◯	Elliptical Marquee tool	◸	Polygonal Lasso tool
▭	Single Row Marquee tool	◉	Magnetic Lasso tool
▯	Single Column Marquee tool	◿.	Eraser tool
▸.	Crop tool	◿	Background Eraser tool
✳	Magic Wand tool	◿	Magic Eraser tool

Make a color range selection

1. Open PS 2-2.psd from the drive and folder where you store your Data Files, save it as **Yellow striped balloon**, click the **title bar**, then drag the **window** to an empty area of the workspace so that you can see both images.

   TIP   When more than one file is open, each has its own set of rulers. The ruler on the inactive file appears dimmed.

2. With the Yellow striped balloon image selected, click **Select** on the Application bar, then click **Color Range**.

   TIP   If the background color is solid, you can select the Invert check box to pick only the pixels in the image area.

3. Click the **Image option button**, then type **150** in the Fuzziness text box (or drag the **slider** all the way to the right until you see **150**).

4. Position the **Eyedropper pointer** 🖋 in the **blue background** of the image in the Color Range dialog box, then click the **background**.

5. Select the **Invert check box**. Compare the settings in your dialog box to Figure 12.

6. Click **OK**, then compare your Yellow striped balloon.psd image to Figure 13.

You opened a file and used the Color Range dialog box to select the image pixels by selecting the image's inverted colors. Selecting the inverse is an important skill in making selections.

FIGURE 12
Color Range dialog box

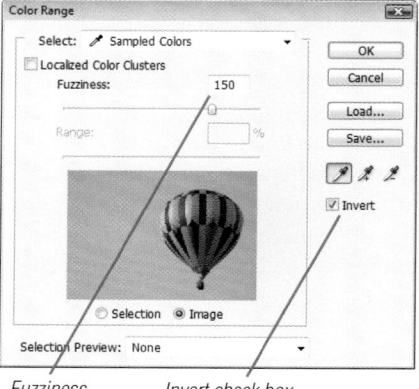

Fuzziness
text box   Invert check box

FIGURE 13
Marquee surrounding selection

Marquee surrounds
everything that is the
inverse of the blue
background

Using the Place command

You can add an image from another image to a layer using the Place command. Place an image in a Photoshop layer by clicking File on the Application bar, then clicking Place. The placed artwork appears *flattened* inside a bounding box at the center of the Photoshop image. The artwork maintains its original aspect ratio; however, if the artwork is larger than the Photoshop image, it is resized to fit. The Place command works well if you want to insert a multi-layered image in another image. (If all you want is a specific layer from an image, you should just drag the layer you want into an image and not use the Place command.)

FIGURE 14

Yellow striped balloon image dragged to Balloons in flight image

Slight fringe
surrounds object

Document sizes
selected

FIGURE 15

New layer defringed

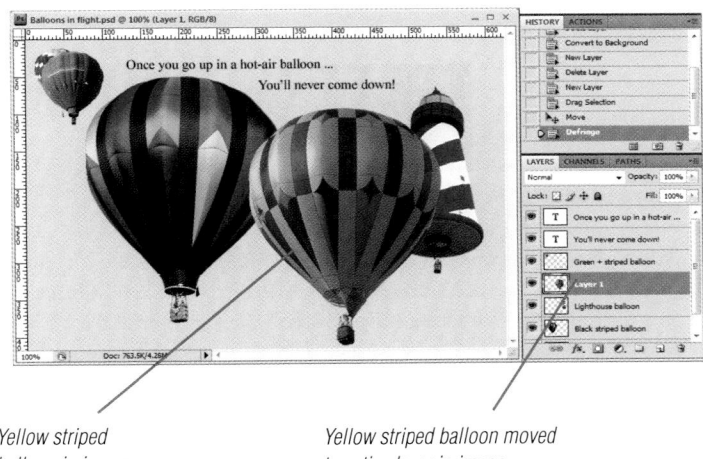

Yellow striped
balloon in image

Yellow striped balloon moved
to active layer in image

Move a selection to another image

1. Click the **Move tool** ⊹ on the Tools panel.

2. Position the **Move tool pointer** ⊹ anywhere over the selection in the Yellow striped balloon image.

3. Drag the **selection** to the Balloons in flight image, then release the mouse button.

   The Yellow striped balloon image moves to the Balloons in flight file appearing on Layer 1.

4. If necessary, use the **Move tool pointer** ⊹ to drag the yellow-striped balloon to the approximate location shown in Figure 14.

5. Click the **triangle** ▶ in the document window status bar, point to **Show**, then verify that Document Sizes is selected.

You dragged a selection from one image to another. You verified that the document size is displayed in the window.

Defringe the selection

1. With Layer 1 selected, click **Layer** on the Application bar, point to **Matting** then click **Defringe**. Defringing a selection gets rid of the halo effect that sometimes occurs when objects are dragged from one image to another.

2. Type **2** in the Width text box, then click **OK**.

3. Save your work.

4. Close **Yellow striped ballon.psd**, then compare the Balloons in flight image to Figure 15.

You removed the fringe from a selection.

ORGANIZE LAYERS WITH
LAYER GROUPS AND COLORS

What You'll Do

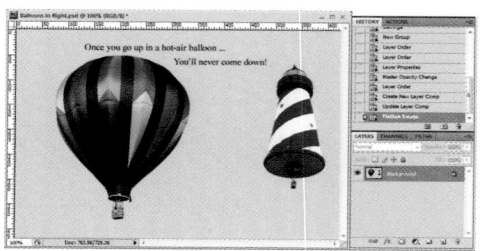

 In this lesson, you'll use the Layers panel menu to create, name, and color a layer group, and then add layers to it. You'll add finishing touches to the image, save it as a copy, then flatten it.

Understanding Layer Groups

A **layer group** is a Photoshop feature that allows you to organize your layers on the Layers panel. A layer group contains individual layers. For example, you can create a layer group that contains all the type layers in your image. To create a layer group, you click the Layers panel list arrow, then click New Group. As with layers, it is helpful to choose a descriptive name for a layer group.

QUICKTIP

You can press [Ctrl][G] (Win) or $\mathcal{H}$ [G] (Mac) to place the selected layer in a layer group.

Organizing Layers into Groups

After you create a layer group, you simply drag layers on the Layers panel directly on top of the layer group. You can remove layers from a layer group by dragging them out of the layer group to a new location on the Layers panel or by deleting them. Some changes made to a layer group, such as blending mode or opacity changes, affect every layer in the layer group. You can choose to expand or collapse layer groups, depending on the amount of information you need to see. Expanding a layer group

Duplicating a layer

When you add a new layer by clicking the Create a new layer button on the Layers panel, the new layer contains default settings. However, you might want to create a new layer that has the same settings as an existing layer. You can do so by duplicating an existing layer to create a copy of that layer and its settings. Duplicating a layer is also a good way to preserve your modifications, because you can modify the duplicate layer and not worry about losing your original work. To create a duplicate layer, select the layer you want to copy, click the Layers panel list arrow, click Duplicate Layer, then click OK. The new layer will appear above the original.

shows all of the layers in the layer group, and collapsing a layer group hides all of the layers in a layer group. You can expand or collapse a layer group by clicking the triangle to the left of the layer group icon. Figure 16 shows one expanded layer group and one collapsed layer group.

Adding Color to a Layer

If your image has relatively few layers, it's easy to locate the layers. However, if your image contains many layers, you might need some help in organizing them. You can organize layers by color-coding them, which makes it easy to find the layer or the group

you want, regardless of its location on the Layers panel. For example, you can put all type layers in red or put the layers associated with a particular portion of an image in blue. To color the Background layer, you must first convert it to a regular layer.

QUICKTIP

You can also color-code a layer group without losing the color-coding you applied to individual layers.

Flattening an Image

After you make all the necessary modifications to your image, you can greatly reduce

the file size by flattening the image. **Flattening** merges all visible layers into a single Background layer and discards all hidden layers. Make sure that all layers that you want to display are visible before you flatten the image. Because flattening removes an image's individual layers, it's a good idea to make a copy of the original image *before* it is flattened. The status bar displays the file's current size and the size it will be when flattened. If you work on a Macintosh, you'll find this information in the lower-left corner of the document window.

FIGURE 16
Layer groups

Right-pointing triangle indicates
collapsed layer group

Down-pointing triangle indicates
expanded layer group

Different colors used within a
layer group

Layer group icon

Individual layers
in layer group are indented

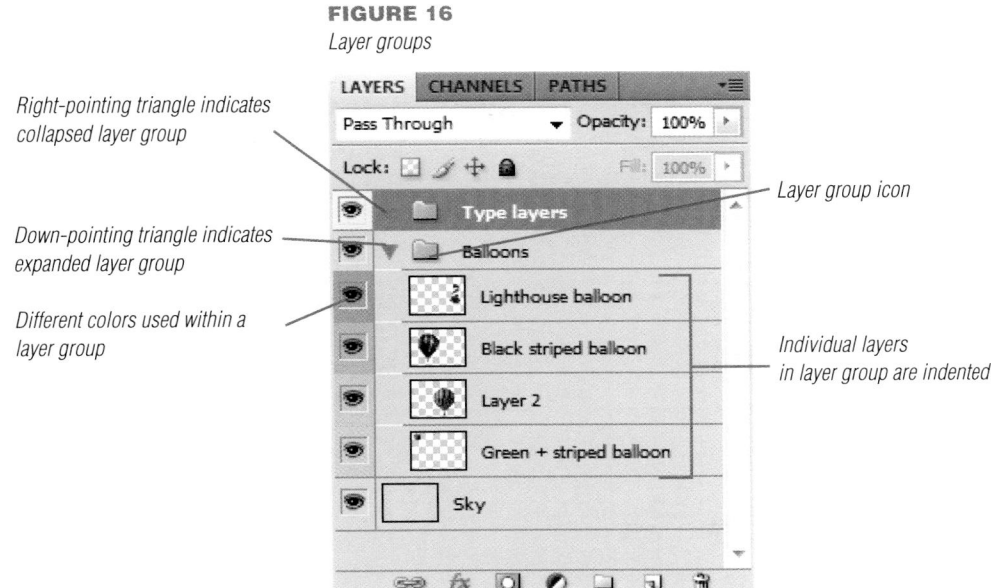

Understanding Layer Comps

The ability to create a **layer comp**, a variation on the arrangement and visibility of existing layers, is a powerful tool that can make your work more organized. You can create a layer comp by clicking the Layer Comps button on the vertical dock (if it's visible), or by clicking Window on the Application bar, then clicking Layer Comps. Clicking the Create New Layer Comp button on the panel opens the New Layer Comp dialog box, shown in Figure 17, which allows you to name the layer comp and set parameters.

Using Layer Comps

Multiple layer comps, shown in Figure 18, make it easy to switch back and forth between variations on an image theme. Say, for example, that you want to show a client multiple arrangements of layers. The layer comp is an ideal tool for this.

FIGURE 17
New Layer Comp dialog box

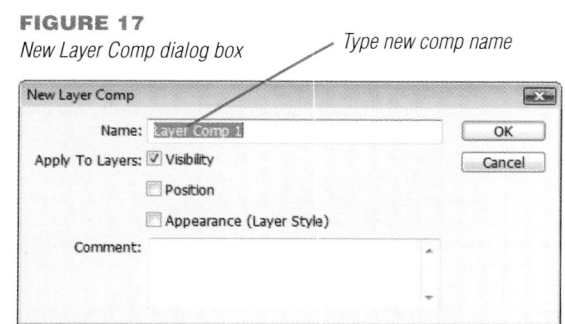

Type new comp name

FIGURE 18
Multiple Layer Comps in image

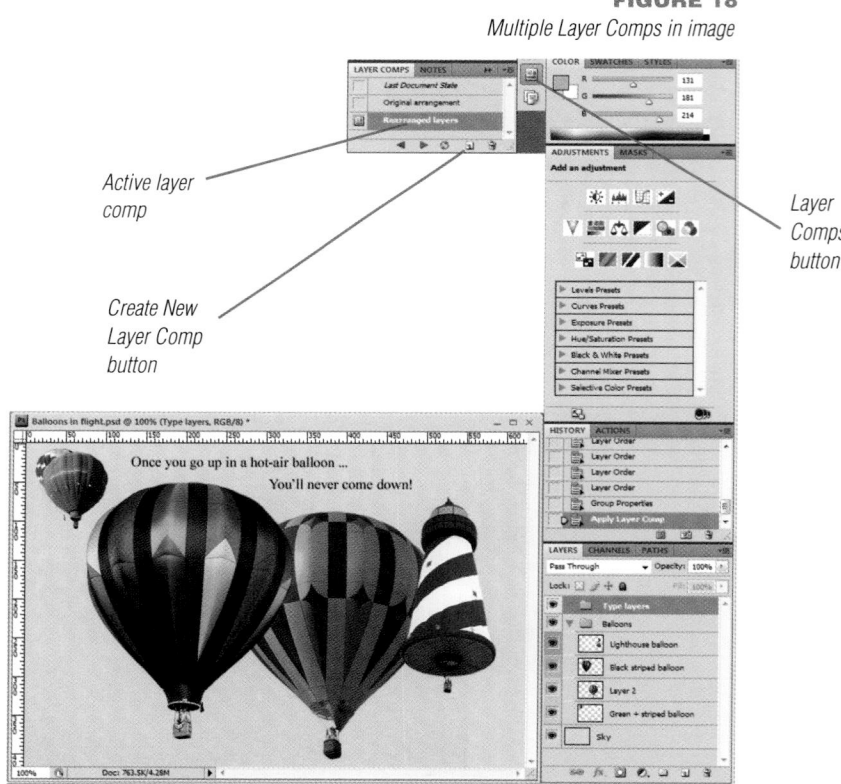

Active layer comp

Create New Layer Comp button

Layer Comps button

FIGURE 19
New Group dialog box

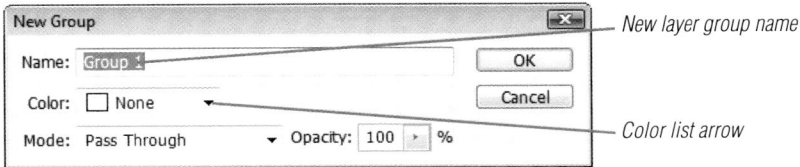

New layer group name

Color list arrow

FIGURE 20
New layer group in Layers panel

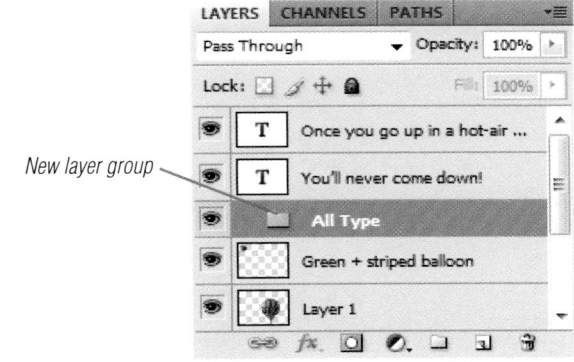

New layer group

FIGURE 21
Layers added to the All Type layer group

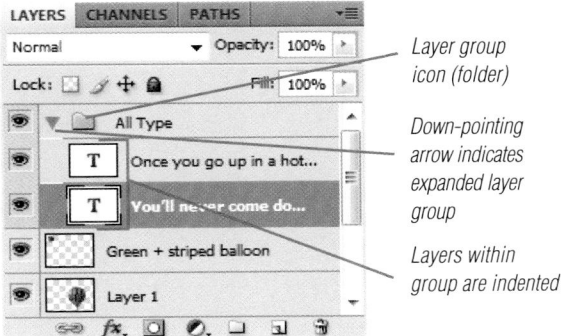

Layer group icon (folder)

Down-pointing arrow indicates expanded layer group

Layers within group are indented

Lesson 4   Organize Layers with Layer Groups and Colors

Create a layer group

1. Click the **Green + striped balloon layer**, click the **Layers panel list arrow** ▾☰, then click **New Group**.

   The New Group dialog box opens, as shown in Figure 19.

   TIP Photoshop automatically places a new layer group above the active layer.

2. Type **All Type** in the Name text box.

3. Click the **Color list arrow**, click **Green**, then click **OK**.

   The New Group dialog box closes. Compare your Layers panel to Figure 20.

You used the Layers panel menu to create a layer group, then named and applied a color to it. This new group will contain all the type layers in the image.

Move layers to the layer group

1. Click the **Once you go up in a hot-air balloon layer** on the Layers panel, then drag it on to the **All Type layer group**.

2. Click the **You'll never come down! layer**, drag it on to the **All Type layer group**, then compare your Layers panel to Figure 21.

   TIP If the You'll never come down! layer is not below the Once you go up in a hot-air balloon layer, move the layers to match Figure 21.

3. Click the **triangle** ▽ to the left of the layer group icon (folder) to collapse the layer group.

You created a layer group, then moved two layers into that layer group. Creating layer groups is a great organization tool, especially in complex images with many layers.

Rename a layer and adjust opacity

1. Double-click **Layer 1**, type **Yellow striped bal-loon**, then press **[Enter]** (Win) or **[return]** (Mac).

2. Double-click the **Opacity text box** on the Layers panel, type **85**, then press **[Enter]** (Win) or **[return]** (Mac).

3. Drag the **Yellow striped balloon layer** beneath the Lighthouse balloon layer, then compare your image to Figure 22.

4. Save your work.

You renamed the new layer, adjusted opacity, and rearranged layers.

Create layer comps

1. Click **Window** on the Application bar, then click **Layer Comps**.

2. Click the **Create New Layer Comp button** 🔲 on the Layer Comps panel.

3. Type **Green off/Yellow off** in the Name text box, as shown in Figure 23, then click **OK**.

4. Click the **Indicates layer visibility button** 👁 on the Green + striped balloon layer and the Yellow striped balloon layer.

5. Click the **Update Layer Comp button** 🔄 on the Layer Comps panel. Compare your Layer Comps panel to Figure 24.

6. Save your work, then click the **Layer Comps button** on the vertical dock to close the Layer Comps panel.

You created a Layer Comp in an existing image.

FIGURE 22
Finished image

Overlapping balloon layers

Lower opacity allows pixels on lower layers to show through

Renamed and moved layer

FIGURE 23
New Layer Comp dialog box

New Layer Comp name

FIGURE 24
Layer Comps panel

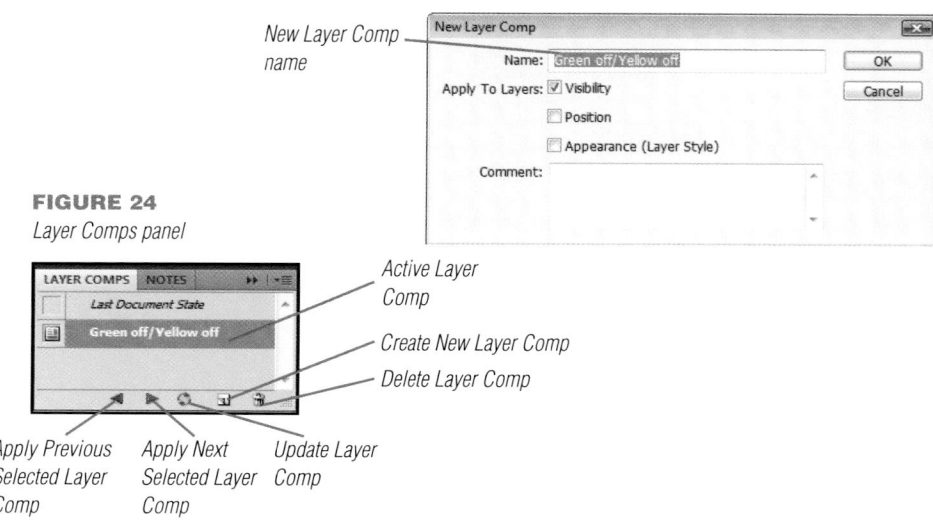

Active Layer Comp

Create New Layer Comp

Delete Layer Comp

Apply Previous Selected Layer Comp

Apply Next Selected Layer Comp

Update Layer Comp

FIGURE 25
Save As dialog box

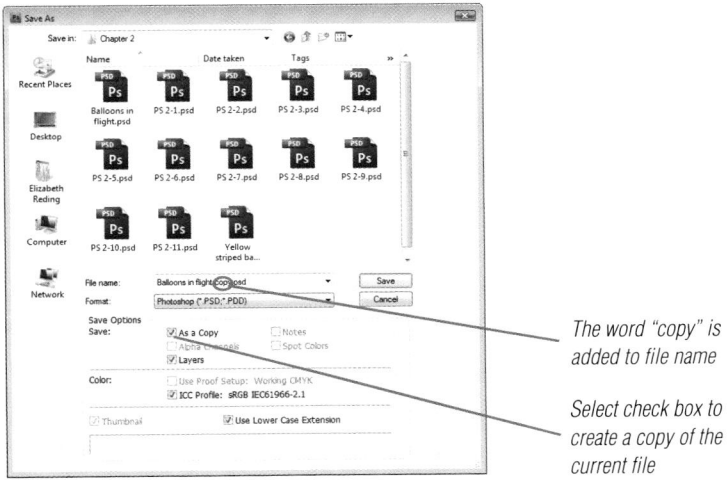

The word "copy" is added to file name

Select check box to create a copy of the current file

FIGURE 26
Flattened image layer

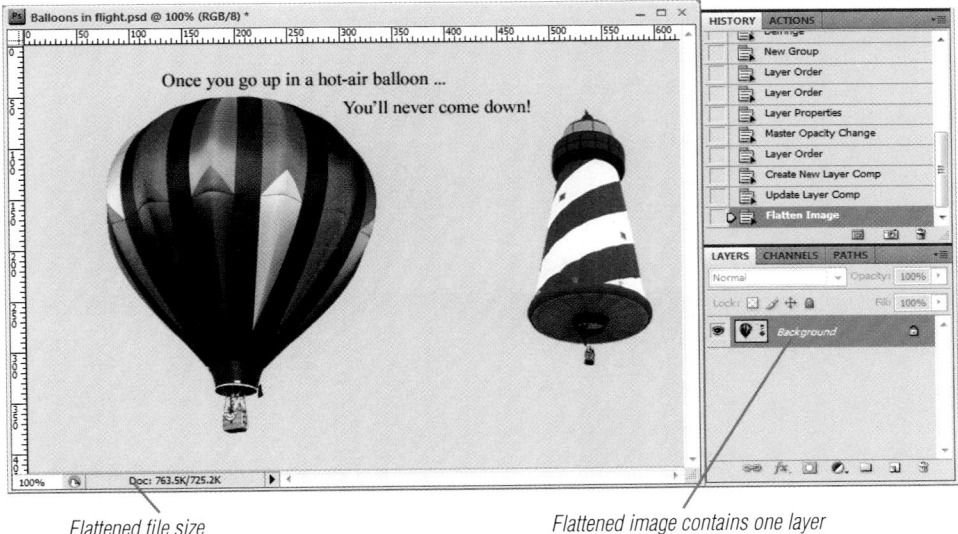

Flattened file size

Flattened image contains one layer

Flatten an image

1. Click **File** on the Application bar, then click **Save As**.

2. Click the **As a Copy check box** to add a check mark, then compare your dialog box to Figure 25.

   TIP   If "copy" does not display in the File name text box, click this text box and type copy to add it to the name.

3. Click **Save**.

   Photoshop saves and closes a copy of the file containing all the layers and effects.

4. Click **Layer** on the Application bar, then click **Flatten Image**.

5. Click **OK** in the warning box, if necessary, then save your work.

6. Compare your Layers panel to Figure 26.

7. Click the **workspace switcher** on the Application bar, then click **Essentials**.

8. Close all open images, then exit Photoshop.

You saved the file as a copy, and then flattened the image. The image now has a single layer.

Power User Shortcuts

to do this:	use this method:
Adjust layer opacity	Click Opacity list arrow on Layers panel, drag opacity slider or Double-click Opacity text box, type a percentage
Change measurements	Right-click (Win) or [Ctrl]-click (Mac) ruler
Color a layer	Click Layers panel list arrow, Layer Properties, Color list arrow
Create a layer comp	Click Create New Layer Comps button on the Layer Comps panel ⬜
Create a layer group	▾≡ , New Group
Delete a layer	🗑
Defringe a selection	Layer ➤ Matting ➤ Defringe

to do this:	use this method:
Flatten an image	Layer ➤ Flatten Image
Use the Move tool	▸⊕ or V
Make a New Background layer from existing layer	Layer ➤ New ➤ Background From Layer
Make a New layer	Layer ➤ New ➤ Layer or ⬜
Rename a layer	Double-click layer name, type new name
Select color range	Select ➤ Color Range
Show/Hide Rulers	View ➤ Rulers [Ctrl][R] (Win) ⌘[R] (Mac)
Update a layer comp	↻

Key: Menu items are indicated by ➤ between the menu name and its command. Blue bold letters are shortcuts for selecting tools on the Tools panel.

Working with Layers

Examine and convert layers.

1. Start Photoshop.
2. Open PS 2-3.psd from the drive and folder where you store your Data Files, update any text layers if necessary, then save it as **Music Store**.
3. Make sure the rulers appear and that pixels are the unit of measurement.
4. Delete the Background layer.
5. Verify that the Rainbow blend layer is active, then convert the image layer to a Background layer.
6. Save your work.

Add and delete layers.

1. Make Layer 2 active.
2. Create a new layer above this layer using the Layer menu.
3. Accept the default name (Layer 4), and change the color of the layer to Red.
4. Delete Layer 4.
5. Make Layer 2 active (if it is not already the active layer), then create a new layer using the Create a new layer button on the Layers panel.
6. Save your work.

Add a selection from one image to another.

1. Open PS 2-4.psd.
2. Reposition this image of a horn by dragging the window to the right of the Music Store image.
3. Open the Color Range dialog box. (*Hint*: Use the Select menu.)
4. Verify that the Image option button is selected, the Invert check box is selected, then set the Fuzziness to 0.
5. Sample the white background in the preview window in the dialog box, then close the dialog box.
6. Use the Move tool to drag the selection into the Music Store image.
7. Position the selection so that the upper-left edge of the instrument matches the sample shown in Figure 27.
8. Defringe the horn selection (in the Music Store image) using a 3 pixel width.
9. Close PS 2-4.psd.
10. Drag Layer 4 above Layer 3.
11. Rename Layer 4 **Horn**.
12. Change the opacity for the Horn layer to 55%.
13. Drag the Horn layer so it is beneath Layer 2.
14. Hide Layer 1.
15. Hide the rulers.
16. Save your work.

Organize layers with layer groups and colors.

1. Create a Layer Group called **Type Layers** and assign the color yellow to the group.
2. Drag the following layers into the Type Layers folder: Allegro, Music Store, Layer 2.
3. Delete Layer 2, then collapse the Layer Group folder.
4. Move the Notes layer beneath the Horn layer.
5. Create a layer comp called **Notes layer on**.
6. Update the layer comp.
7. Hide the Notes layer.
8. Create a new layer comp called **Notes layer off**, then update the layer comp.
9. Display the previous layer comp, save your work, then close the tab group. (*Hint:* Click the Layer Comps list arrow, then click Close Tab Group.)
10. Save a copy of the Music Store file using the default naming scheme (add 'copy' to the end of the existing filename).
11. Flatten the original image. (*Hint*: Be sure to discard hidden layers.)
12. Save your work, then compare your image to Figure 27.

FIGURE 27
Completed Skills Review

PHOTOSHOP 2-24

A credit union is developing a hotline for members to use to help abate credit card fraud as soon as it occurs. They're going to distribute ten thousand refrigerator magnets over the next three weeks. As part of their effort to build community awareness of the project, they've sponsored a contest for the magnet design. You decide to enter the contest.

1. Open PS 2-5.psd, then save it as **Combat Fraud**. The Palatino Linotype font is used in this file. Please make a substitution if this font is not available on your computer.
2. Open PS 2-6.psd, use the Color Range dialog box or any selection tool on the Tools panel to select the cell phone image, then drag it to the Outlaw Fraud image.
3. Rename the newly created layer **Cell Phone** if necessary, then apply a color to the layer on the Layers panel. Make sure the Cell Phone layer is beneath the type layers.
4. Convert the Background layer to an image layer, then rename it **Banner**.
5. Change the opacity of the Banner layer to any setting you like.
6. Defringe the Cell Phone layer using the pixel width of your choice.
7. Save your work, close PS 2-6.psd, then compare your image to the sample shown in Figure 28.

FIGURE 28
Completed Project Builder 1

Your local 4-H chapter wants to promote its upcoming fair and has hired you to create a promotional billboard commemorating this event. The Board of Directors decides that the billboard should be humorous.

1. Open PS 2-7.psd, then save it as **4H Billboard**. Substitute any missing fonts.
2. Open PS 2-8.psd, use the Color Range dialog box or any selection tool on the Tools panel to create a marquee around the llama, then drag the selection to the 4-H Billboard image.
3. Name the new layer **Llama**.
4. Change the opacity of the Llama layer to 90% and defringe the layer containing the llama.
5. Save your work, then compare your image to the sample shown in Figure 29.

FIGURE 29
Completed Project Builder 2

A friend of yours has designed a new heat-absorbing coffee cup for take-out orders. She is going to present the prototype to a prospective vendor, but first needs to print a brochure. She's asked you to design an eye-catching cover.

1. Open PS 2-9.psd, update the text layers if necessary, then save it as **Coffee Cover**. The Garamond font is used in this file. Please make a substitution if this font is not available on your computer.
2. Open PS 2-10.psd, then drag the entire image to Coffee Cover.
3. Close PS 2-10.psd.
4. Rename Layer 1 with the name **Mocha**.
5. Delete the Background layer and convert the Mocha layer into a new Background layer.
6. Reposition the layer objects so they look like the sample. (*Hint*: You might have to reorganize the layers in the stack so all layers are visible.)
7. Create a layer group above Layer 2, name it **Hot Shot Text**, apply a color of your choice to the layer group, then drag the type layers to it.
8. Save your work, then compare your image to Figure 30.

FIGURE 30
Completed Design Project

Harvest Market, a line of natural food stores, and the trucking associations in your state have formed a coalition to deliver fresh fruit and vegetables to food banks and other food distribution programs. The truckers want to promote the project by displaying a sign on their trucks. Your task is to create a design that will become the Harvest Market logo. Keep in mind that the design will be seen from a distance.

1. Open PS 2-11.psd, then save it as **Harvest Market**. Update the text layers as necessary.

2. Obtain at least two images of different-sized produce. You can obtain images by using what is available on your computer, scanning print media, or connecting to the Internet and downloading images.

3. Open one of the produce files, select it, then drag or copy it to the Harvest Market image. (*Hint*: Experiment with some of the other selection tools. Note that some tools require you to copy and paste the image after you select it.)

4. Repeat step 3, then close the two produce image files.

5. Set the opacity of the Market layer to 80%.

6. Arrange the layers so that smaller images appear on top of the larger ones. (You can move layers to any location in the image you choose.)

7. Create a layer group for the type layers, and apply a color to it.

8. You can delete any layers you feel do not add to the image. (In the sample image, the Veggies layer has been deleted.)

9. Save your work, then compare your image to Figure 31.

10. What are the advantages and disadvantages of using multiple images? How would you assess the ease and efficiency of the selection techniques you've learned? Which styles did you apply to the type layers, and why?

FIGURE 31
Completed Portfolio Project

chapter

3

MAKING
SELECTIONS

1. Make a selection using shapes

2. Modify a marquee

3. Select using color and modify a selection

4. Add a vignette effect to a selection

ADOBE PHOTOSHOP CS4

3-1

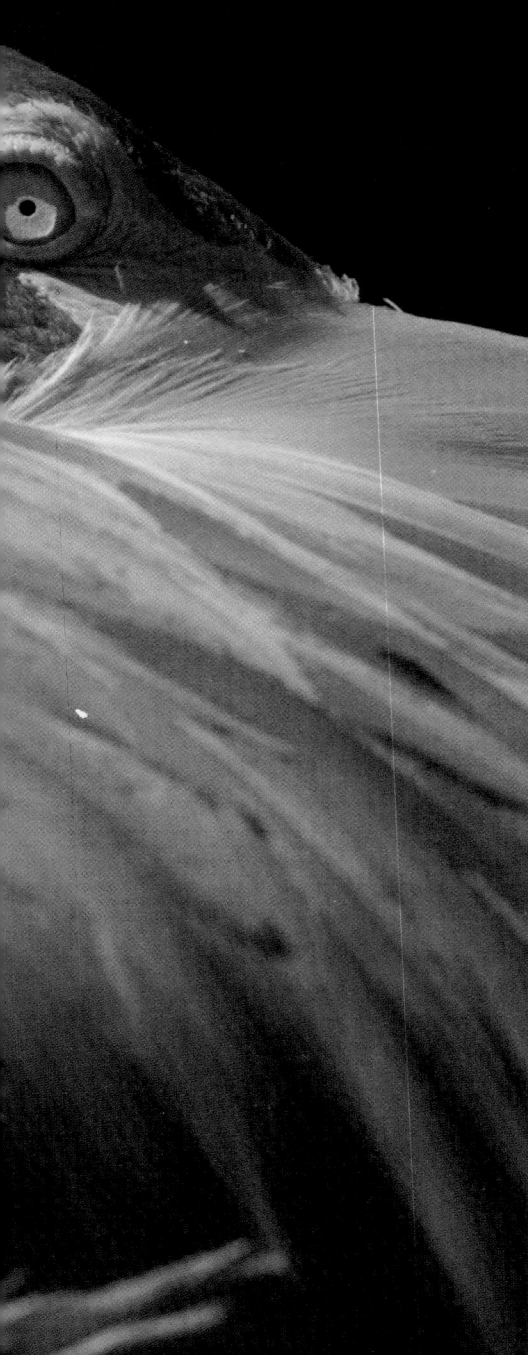

Combining Images

Most Photoshop images are created using a technique called **compositing**—combining images from different sources. These sources include other Photoshop images, royalty-free images, pictures taken with digital cameras, and scanned artwork. How you get all those images into your Photoshop images is an art unto itself. You can include additional images by using tools on the Tools panel and menu commands. And to work with all these images, you need to know how to select them—or exactly the parts you want to work with.

Understanding Selection Tools

The two basic methods you can use to make selections are using a tool or using color. You can use three free-form tools to create your own unique selections, four fixed area tools to create circular or rectangular selections, and a wand tool to make selections using color. In addition, you can use menu commands to increase or decrease selections that you made with these tools, or make selections based on color.

Understanding Which Selection Tool to Use

With so many tools available, how do you know which one to use? After you become familiar with the different selection options, you'll learn how to look at images and evaluate selection opportunities. With experience, you'll learn how to identify edges that can be used to isolate imagery, and how to spot colors that can be used to isolate a specific object.

Combining Imagery

After you decide on an object that you want to place in a Photoshop image, you can add the object to another image by cutting, copying, and pasting, dragging and dropping objects using the Move tool, or using the **Clipboard**, the temporary storage area provided by your operating system.

Tools You'll Use

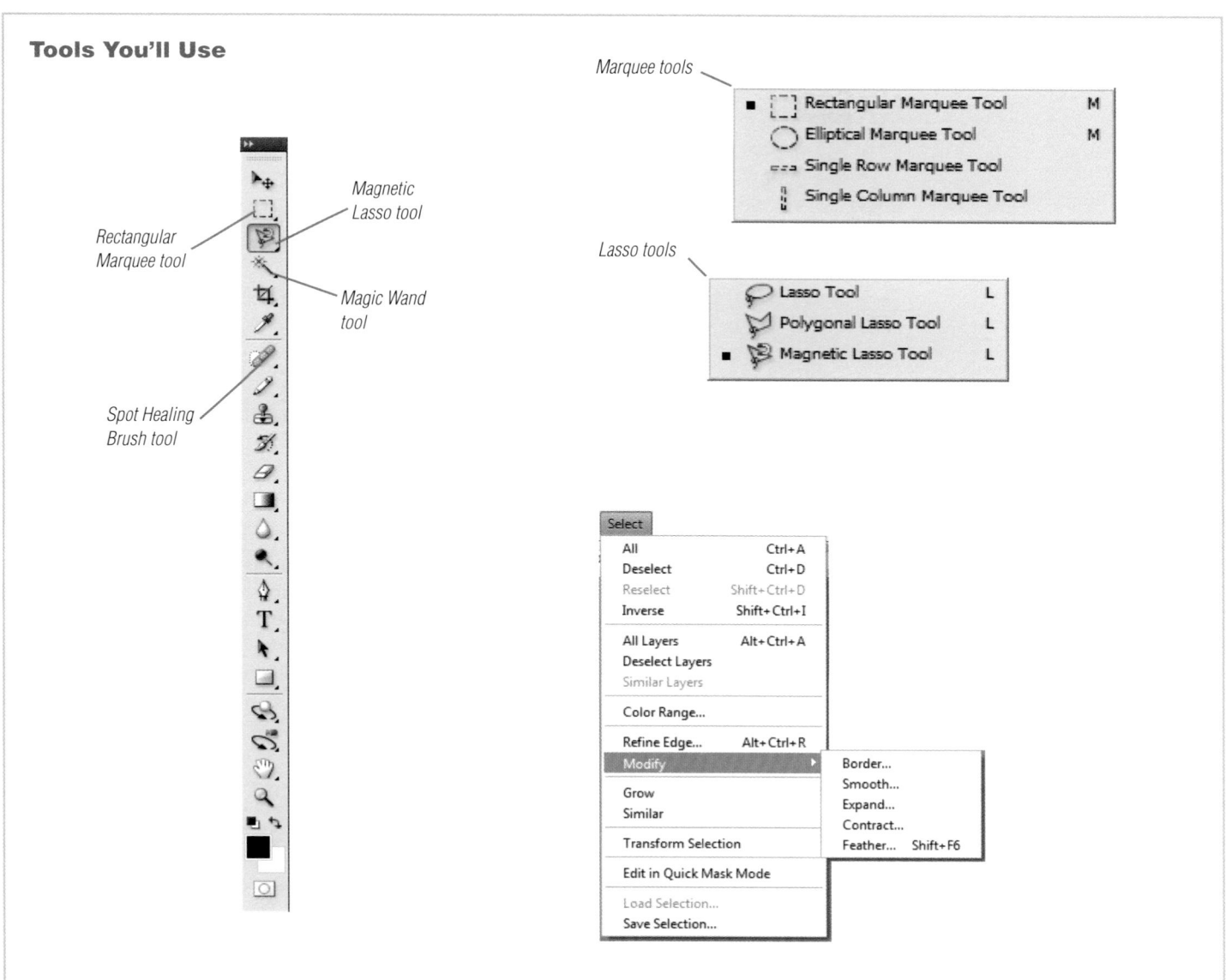

Rectangular
Marquee tool

Magnetic
Lasso tool

Magic Wand
tool

Spot Healing
Brush tool

Marquee tools

■	Rectangular Marquee Tool	M
	Elliptical Marquee Tool	M
	Single Row Marquee Tool	
	Single Column Marquee Tool	

Lasso tools

	Lasso Tool	L
	Polygonal Lasso Tool	L
■	Magnetic Lasso Tool	L

Select	
All	Ctrl+A
Deselect	Ctrl+D
Reselect	Shift+Ctrl+D
Inverse	Shift+Ctrl+I
All Layers	Alt+Ctrl+A
Deselect Layers	
Similar Layers	
Color Range...	
Refine Edge...	Alt+Ctrl+R
Modify ▶	
Grow	
Similar	
Transform Selection	
Edit in Quick Mask Mode	
Load Selection...	
Save Selection...	

Border...	
Smooth...	
Expand...	
Contract...	
Feather...	Shift+F6

MAKE A SELECTION
USING SHAPES

What You'll Do

▶ *In this lesson, you'll make selections using a marquee tool and a lasso tool, position a selection with the Move tool, deselect a selection, and drag a complex selection into another image.*

Selecting by Shape

The Photoshop selection tools make it easy to select objects that are rectangular or elliptical in nature. It would be a boring world if every image we wanted fell into one of those categories, so fortunately, they don't. While some objects are round or square, most are unusual in shape. Making selections can sometimes be a painstaking process because many objects don't have clearly defined edges. To select an object by shape, you need to click the appropriate tool on the Tools panel, then drag the pointer around the object. The selected area is defined by a **marquee**, or series of dotted lines, as shown in Figure 1.

Creating a Selection

Drawing a rectangular marquee is easier than drawing an elliptical marquee, but with practice, you'll be able to create both types of marquees easily. Table 1 lists the tools you can use to make selections using

shapes. Figure 2 shows a marquee surrounding an irregular shape.

QUICKTIP

A marquee is sometimes referred to as *marching ants* because the dots within the marquee appear to be moving.

Using Fastening Points

Each time you click one of the marquee tools, a fastening point is added to the image. A **fastening point** is an anchor within the marquee. When the marquee pointer reaches the initial fastening point (after making its way around the image), a very small circle appears on the pointer, indicating that you have reached the starting point. Clicking the pointer when this circle appears closes the marquee. Some fastening points, such as those in a circular marquee, are not visible, while others, such as those created by the Polygonal or Magnetic Lasso tools, are visible.

Selecting, Deselecting, and Reselecting

After a selection is made, you can move, copy, transform, or make adjustments to it. A selection stays selected until you unselect, or **deselect**, it. You can deselect a selection by clicking Select on the Application bar, then clicking Deselect. You can reselect a deselected object by clicking Select on the Application bar, then clicking Reselect.

QUICKTIP

You can select the entire image by clicking Select on the Application bar, then clicking All.

FIGURE 1
Elliptical Marquee tool used to create marquee

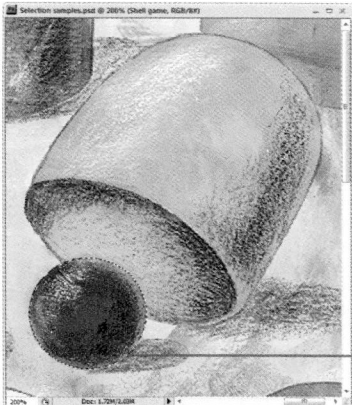

Elliptical Marquee
tool surrounds
object

QUICKTIP

Correcting a Selection Error

At some point, you'll spend a lot of time making a complex selection only to realize that the wrong layer was active. Remember the History panel? Every action you do is automatically recorded, and you can use the selection state to retrace your steps and recoup the time spent. Your fix may be as simple as selecting the proper History state and changing the active layer in the Layers panel.

FIGURE 2
Marquee surrounding irregular shape

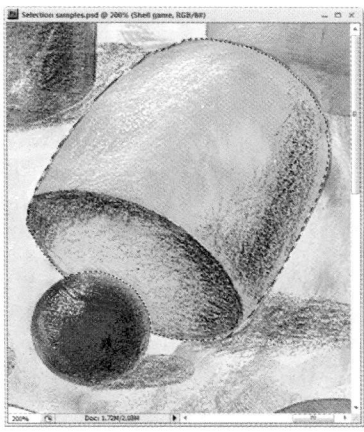

TABLE 1: Selection Tools by Shape

tool	button	effect
Rectangular Marquee tool		Creates a rectangular selection. Press [Shift] while dragging to create a square.
Elliptical Marquee tool		Creates an elliptical selection. Press [Shift] while dragging to create a circle.
Single Row Marquee tool		Creates a 1-pixel-wide row selection.
Single Column Marquee tool		Creates a 1-pixel-wide column selection.
Lasso tool		Creates a freehand selection.
Polygonal Lasso tool		Creates straight line selections. Press [Alt] (Win) or [option] (Mac) to create freehand segments.
Magnetic Lasso tool		Creates selections that snap to an edge of an object. Press [Alt] (Win) or [option] (Mac) to alternate between freehand and magnetic line segments.

Placing a Selection

You can place a selection in a Photoshop image in many ways. You can copy or cut a selection, then paste it to a different location in the same image or to a different image. You can also use the Move tool to drag a selection to a new location.

Using Guides

Guides are non-printing horizontal and vertical lines that you can display on top of an image to help you position a selection. You can create an unlimited number of horizontal and vertical guides. You create a guide by displaying the rulers, positioning the pointer on either ruler, then clicking and dragging the guide into position. Figure 3 shows the creation of a horizontal guide in a file that contains two existing guides. You delete a guide by selecting the Move tool on the Tools panel, positioning the pointer over the guide, then clicking and dragging it back

to its ruler. If the Snap feature is enabled, as you drag an object toward a guide, the object will be pulled toward the guide. To turn on the Snap feature, click View on the Application bar, then click Snap. A check mark appears to the left of the command if the feature is enabled.

FIGURE 3
Creating guides in image

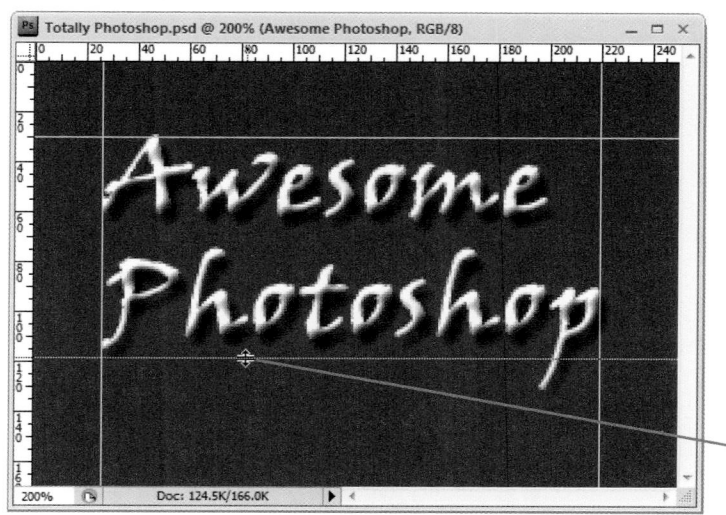

Dragging a guide to a new location

FIGURE 4

Rectangular Marquee tool selection

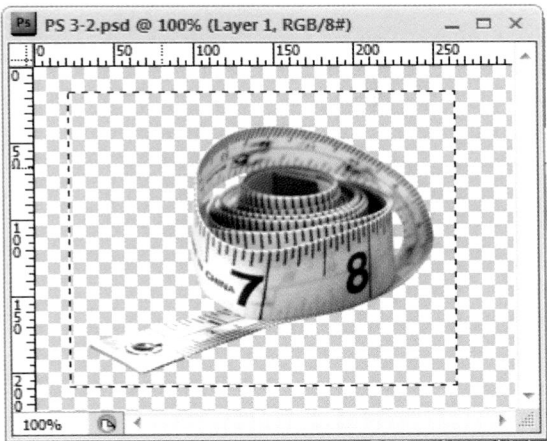

TABLE 2: Working with a Selection

if you want to:	then do this:
Move a selection (an image) using the mouse	Position the ⊕ over the selection, then drag the marquee and its contents
Copy a selection to the Clipboard	Activate image containing the selection, click Edit ➤ Copy
Cut a selection to the Clipboard	Activate image containing the selection, click Edit ➤ Cut
Paste a selection from the Clipboard	Activate image where you want the selection, click Edit ➤ Paste
Delete a selection	Make selection, then press [Delete] (Win) or [delete] (Mac)
Deselect a selection	Press [Ctrl][D] (Win) or ⌘[D] (Mac)

Create a selection with the Rectangular Marquee tool

1. Start Photoshop, open PS 3-1.psd from the drive and folder where you store your Data Files, save it as **Sewing Box**, then click **OK** if the Maximize compatibility dialog box displays.
2. Click the **workspace switcher** on the Application bar, click **Analysis**, click the **Layers tab**, then display the rulers (if necessary) in pixels.
3. Open PS 3-2.psd, then display the rulers in pixels for this image (if necessary).
4. Click the **Rectangular Marquee tool** ⬚ on the Tools panel.
5. Make sure the value in the Feather text box on the options bar is **0 px**.

    Feathering determines the amount of blur between the selection and the pixels surrounding it.
6. Drag the **Marquee pointer** ✛ to select the tape measure from approximately **20 H/20 V** to **260 H/210 V**. See Figure 4.

    The first measurement refers to the horizontal ruler (H); the second measurement refers to the vertical ruler (V).

    | TIP   You can also use the X/Y coordinates displayed in the Info panel.
7. Click the **Move tool** ⬆ on the Tools panel, then drag the selection to any location in the Sewing Box image.

    The selection now appears in the Sewing Box image on a new layer (Layer 1).

    | TIP   Table 2 describes methods you can use to work with selections in an image.

Using the Rectangular Marquee tool, you created a selection in an image, then you dragged that selection into another image. This left the original image intact, and created a copy of the selection in the destination image.

Position a selection with the Move tool

1. Verify that the **Move tool** ▶✛ is selected on the Tools panel, and display the rulers (if necessary).

2. If you do not see guides in the Sewing Box image, click **View** on the Application bar, point to **Show**, then click **Guides**.

3. Drag the **tape measure** so that the top-right corner snaps to the ruler guides at approximately **1030 H/250 V**. Compare your image to Figure 5.

   Did you feel the snap to effect as you positioned the selection within the guides? This feature makes it easy to properly position objects within an image.

   TIP   If you didn't feel the image snap to the guides, click View on the Application bar, point to Snap To, then click Guides.

4. Rename Layer 1 **Tape Measure**.

You used the Move tool to reposition a selection in an existing image, then you renamed the layer.

FIGURE 5
Rectangular selection in image

Tape measure

Using Smart Guides

Wouldn't it be great to be able to see a vertical or horizontal guide as you move an object? Using Smart Guides, you can do just that. Smart Guides are turned on by clicking View on the Application bar, pointing to Show, then clicking Smart Guides. Once this feature is turned on, horizontal and vertical purple guidelines appear automatically when you draw a shape or move an object. This feature allows you to align layer content as you move it.

Making Selections

FIGURE 6
Deselect command

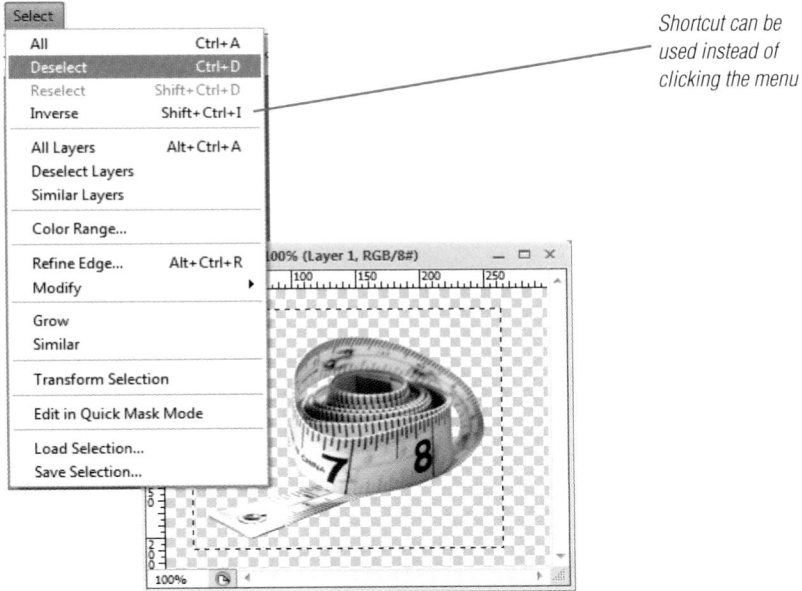

Shortcut can be used instead of clicking the menu

1. Click **Window** on the Application bar, then click **PS 3-2.psd**.

   TIP   If you can see the window of the image you want anywhere on the screen, you can just click it to make it active instead of using the Window menu.

2. Click **Select** on the Application bar, then click **Deselect**, as shown in Figure 6.

You hid the active layer, then used the Deselect command on the Select menu to deselect the object you had moved into this image. When you deselect a selection, the marquee no longer surrounds it.

FIGURE 7
Save Selection dialog box

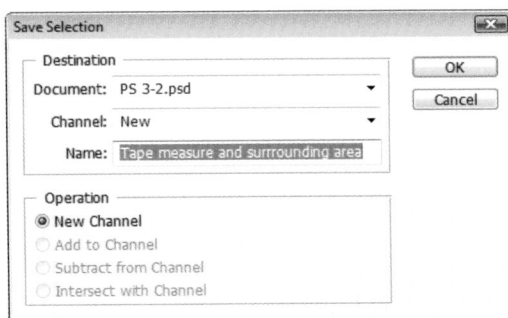

Saving and loading a selection

Any selection can be saved independently of the surrounding image, so that if you want to use it again in the image, you can do so without having to retrace it using one of the marquee tools. Once a selection is made, you can save it in the image by clicking Select on the Application bar, then clicking Save Selection. The Save Selection dialog box opens, as shown in Figure 7; be sure to give the selection a meaningful name. When you want to load a saved selection, click Select on the Application bar, then click Load Selection. Click the Channel list arrow, click the named selection, then click OK.

Create a selection with the Magnetic Lasso tool

1. Click the **Magnetic Lasso tool** on the Tools panel, then change the settings on the options bar so that they are the same as those shown in Figure 8. Table 3 describes Magnetic Lasso tool settings.

2. Open PS 3-3.psd from the drive and folder where you store your Data Files.

3. Click the **Magnetic Lasso tool pointer** once anywhere on the edge of the pin cushion, to create your first fastening point.

   TIP   If you click a spot that is not at the edge of the pin cushion, press [Esc] (Win) or ⌘ [Z] (Mac) to undo the action, then start again.

4. Drag the **Magnetic Lasso tool pointer** slowly around the pin cushion (clicking at the top of each pin may be helpful) until it is almost entirely selected, then click directly over the initial fastening point. See Figure 9.

   Don't worry about all the nooks and crannies surrounding the pin cushion: the Magnetic Lasso tool will select those automatically. You will see a small circle next to the pointer when it is directly over the initial fastening point, indicating that you are closing the selection. The individual segments turn into a marquee.

   TIP   If you feel that the Magnetic Lasso tool is missing some major details while you're tracing, you can insert additional fastening points by clicking the pointer while dragging. For example, click the mouse button at a location where you want to change the selection shape.

   You created a selection with the Magnetic Lasso tool.

FIGURE 8
Options for the Magnetic Lasso tool

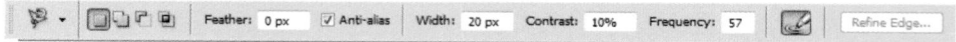

FIGURE 9
Creating a selection with the Magnetic Lasso tool

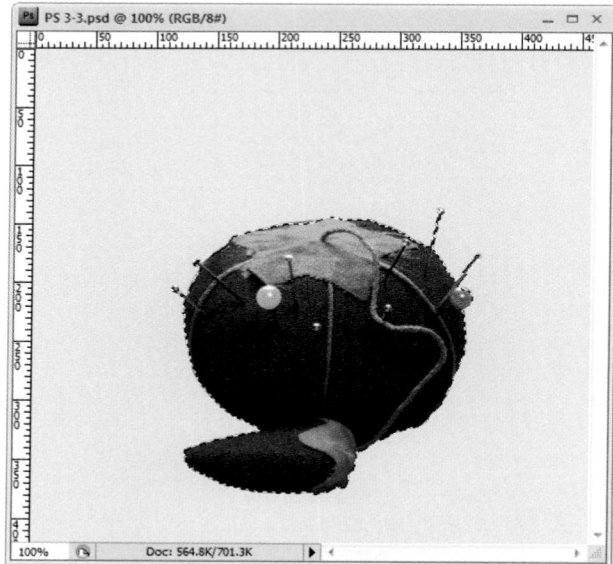

Mastering the art of selections

You might feel that it is difficult when you first start making selections. Making selections is a skill, and like most skills, it takes a lot of practice to become proficient. In addition to practice, make sure that you're comfortable in your work area, that your hands are steady, and that your mouse is working well. A non-optical mouse that is dirty will make selecting an onerous task, so make sure your mouse is well cared for and is functioning correctly.

FIGURE 10
Selection copied into image

Defringing the layer reduces the amount of the original background that appears; your results will vary

Complex selection includes only object, no background

TABLE 3: Magnetic Lasso Tool Settings

setting	description
Feather	The amount of blur between the selection and the pixels surrounding it. This setting is measured in pixels and can be a value between 0 and 250.
Anti-alias	The smoothness of the selection, achieved by softening the color transition between edge and background pixels.
Width	The interior width by detecting an edge from the pointer. This setting is measured in pixels and can have a value from 1 to 40.
Contrast	The tool's sensitivity. This setting can be a value between 1 percent and 100 percent: higher values detect high-contrast edges.
Frequency	The rate at which fastening points are applied. This setting can be a value between 0 and 100: higher values insert more fastening points.

Lesson 1   Make a Selection Using Shapes

Move a complex selection to an existing image

1. Click the **Move tool** on the Tools panel.

   TIP   You can also click the Click to open the Tool Preset picker list arrow on the options bar, then double-click the Move tool.

2. Use the **Move tool pointer** to drag the pin cushion selection to the Sewing Box image.

   The selection appears on a new layer (Layer 1).

3. Drag the object so that the left edge of the pin cushion snaps to the guide at approximately **600 Y** and the top of the pin cushion snaps to the guide at **200 X** using the coordinates on the info panel.

4. Use the Layer menu to defringe the new Layer 1 at a width of **1** pixel.

5. Close the PS 3-3.psd image without saving your changes.

6. Rename the new layer **Pin Cushion** in the Sewing Box image.

7. Save your work, then compare your image to Figure 10.

8. Click **Window** on the Application bar, then click **PS 3-2.psd.**

9. Close the PS 3-2.psd image without saving your changes.

You dragged a complex selection into an existing Photoshop image. You positioned the object using ruler guides and renamed a layer. You also defringed a selection to eliminate its white border.

MODIFY A MARQUEE

What You'll Do

In this lesson, you'll move and enlarge a marquee, drag a selection into a Photoshop image, then position a selection using ruler guides.

Changing the Size of a Marquee

Not all objects are easy to select. Sometimes, when you make a selection, you might need to change the size or shape of the marquee.

The options bar contains selection buttons that help you add to and subtract from a marquee, or intersect with a selection. The marquee in Figure 11 was modified into the one shown in Figure 12 by clicking the Add to selection button. After the Add to selection button is active, you can draw an additional marquee (directly adjacent to the selection), and it will be added to the current marquee.

One method you can use to increase the size of a marquee is the Grow command. After you make a selection, you can increase the marquee size by clicking Select on the Application bar, then by clicking Grow. The Grow command selects pixels adjacent to the marquee that have colors similar to those specified by the Magic Wand tool. The Similar command selects both adjacent and non-adjacent pixels.

QUICKTIP
While the Grow command selects adjacent pixels that have similar colors, the Expand command increases a selection by a specific number of pixels.

Modifying a Marquee

While a selection is active, you can modify the marquee by expanding or contracting it, smoothing out its edges, or enlarging it to add a border around the selection. These four commands, Expand, Contract, Smooth, and Border, are sub-menus of the Modify command, which is found on the Select menu. For example, you might want to enlarge your selection. Using the Expand command, you can increase the size of the selection, as shown in Figure 13.

Moving a Marquee

After you create a marquee, you can move the marquee to another location in the same image or to another image entirely. You might want to move a marquee if you've drawn it in the wrong image or the wrong location. Sometimes it's easier to draw a marquee elsewhere on the page, and then move it to the desired location.

QUICKTIP

You can always hide and display layers as necessary to facilitate making a selection.

FIGURE 12
Selection with additions

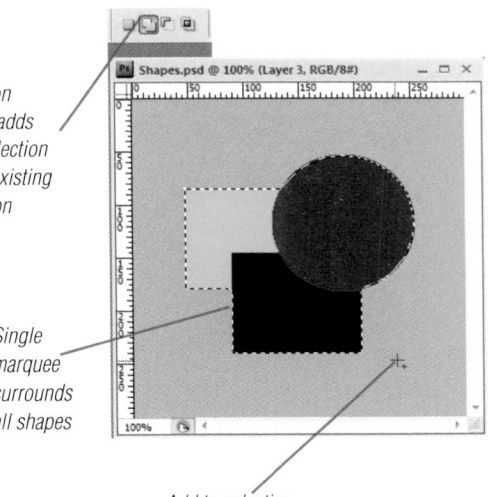

Add to selection button adds new selection to the existing selection

Single marquee surrounds all shapes

Add to selection pointer

FIGURE 11
New selection

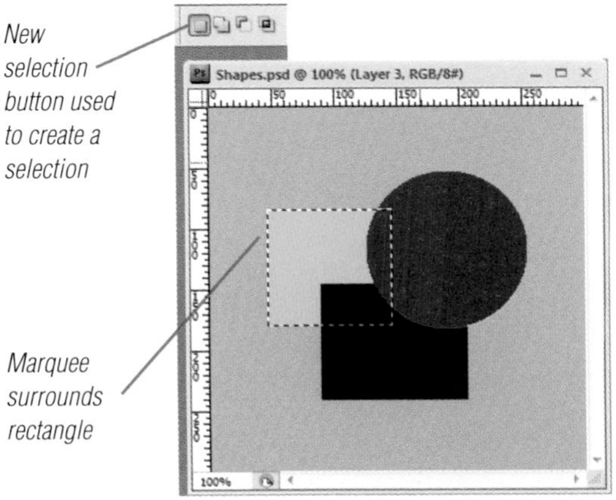

New selection button used to create a selection

Marquee surrounds rectangle

Using the Quick Selection Tool

The Quick Selection tool lets you paint-to-select an object from the interior using a resizeable brush. As you paint the object, the selection grows. Using the Auto-Enhance check box, rough edges and blockiness are automatically reduced to give you a perfect selection. As with other selection tools, the Quick Selection tool has options to add and subtract from your selection.

FIGURE 13
Expanded selection

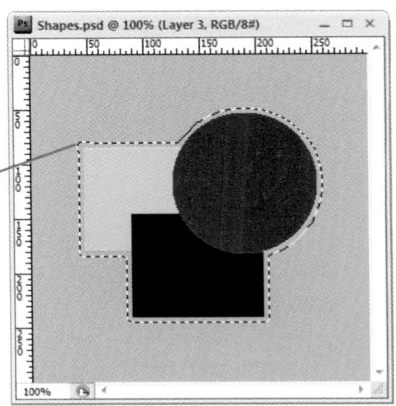

Marquee expanded by 5 pixels

Adding and subtracting from a selection

Of course knowing how to make a selection is important, but it's just as important to know how to make alterations in an existing selection. Sometimes it's almost impossible to create that perfect marquee on the first try. Perhaps your hand moved while you were tracing, or you just got distracted. Using the Add to selection, Subtract from selection, and Intersect with selection buttons (which appear with all selection tools), you can alter an existing marquee without having to start from scratch.

Move and enlarge a marquee

1. Open PS 3-4.psd from the drive and folder where you store your Data Files. Change the zoom factor to **200%**.

2. Click the **Elliptical Marquee tool** ◯ on the Tools panel.

   TIP The Elliptical Marquee tool might be hidden under the Rectangular Marquee tool.

3. Click the **New selection button** ▣ on the options bar (if it is not already selected).

4. Drag the **Marquee pointer** ✛ to select the area from approximately **150 X/50 Y** to **200 X/130 Y**. Compare your image to Figure 14.

5. Position the **pointer** ▷ in the center of the selection.

6. Drag the **Move pointer** ▶ so the marquee covers the thimble, at approximately **100 X/100 Y**, as shown in Figure 15.

   TIP You can also nudge a selection to move it, by pressing the arrow keys. Each time you press an arrow key, the selection moves one pixel in the direction of the arrow.

7. Click the **Magic Wand tool** ✦ on the Tools panel, then enter a Tolerance of **16**, and select the **Anti-alias** and **Contiguous checkboxes**.

8. Click **Select** on the Application bar, then click **Similar**.

9. Click **Select** on the Application bar, point to **Modify**, then click **Expand**.

10. Type **1** in the Expand By text box of the Expand Selection dialog box, then click **OK**.

11. Deselect the selection.

You created a marquee, then dragged the marquee to reposition it. You then enlarged a selection marquee by using the Similar and Expand commands.

FIGURE 14
Selection in image

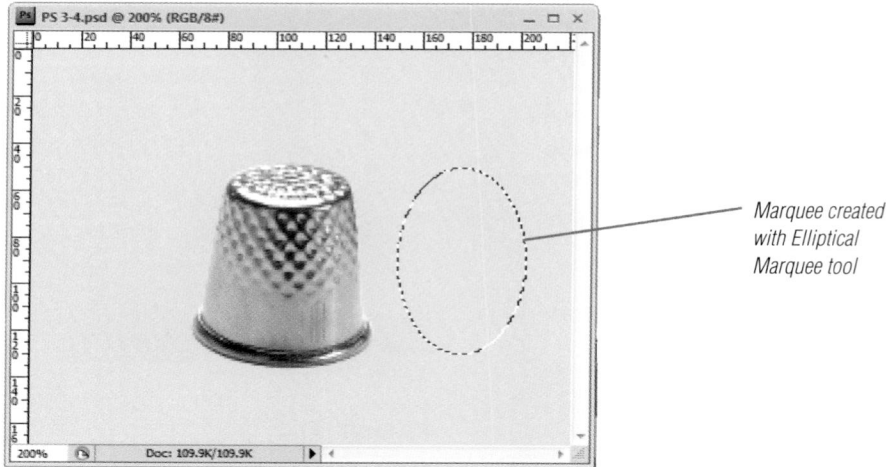

Marquee created with Elliptical Marquee tool

FIGURE 15
Moved selection

New marquee location

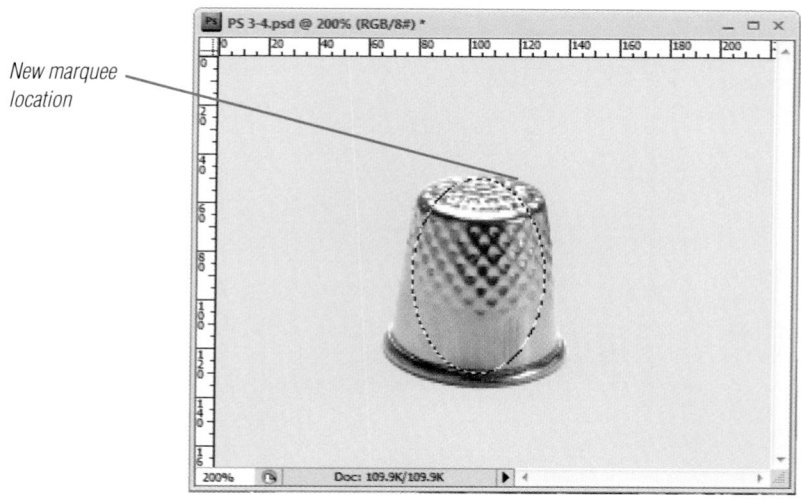

FIGURE 16
Quick Selection tool settings

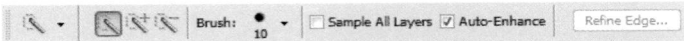

FIGURE 17
Selection in file

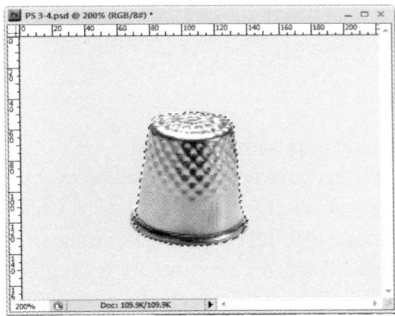

FIGURE 18
Selection moved to the Sewing Box image

1. Click the **Quick Selection tool** , on the Tools panel, then adjust your settings using Figure 16.

   TIP If you need to change the Brush settings, click Brush list arrow on the options bar, then drag the sliders so the settings are 10 px diameter, 0% hardness, 1% spacing, 0° angle, 100% roundness, and Pen Pressure size.

2. Position the pointer in the **center of the thimble,** then slowly drag the pointer to the outer edges until the object is selected. See Figure 17.

   TIP Sometimes making a selection is easy, sometimes . . . not so much. Time and practice will hone your selection skills. It will get easier.

3. Click the **Move tool** on the Tools panel.

4. Position the **Move pointer** over the selection, then drag the **thimble** to the Sewing Box image.

5. Drag the **thimble** so that it is to the left of the pin cushion and snaps to the vertical guide at approximately **600 X/550Y**.

6. Defringe the thimble using a setting of **1** pixel.

7. Rename the new layer **Thimble**.

8. Save your work on the sewing box image, then compare your image to Figure 18.

9. Make **PS 3-4.psd** active.

10. Close PS 3-4.psd without saving your changes.

You selected an object using the Quick Selection tool, then you dragged the selection into an existing image.

SELECT USING COLOR AND
MODIFY A SELECTION

What You'll Do

In this lesson, you'll make selections using both the Color Range command and the Magic Wand tool. You'll also flip a selection, then fix an image using the Healing Brush tool.

Selecting with Color

Selections based on color can be easy to make, especially when the background of an image is different from the image itself. High contrast between colors is an ideal condition for making selections based on color. You can make selections using color with the Color Range command on the Select menu, or you can use the Magic Wand tool on the Tools panel.

Using the Magic Wand Tool

When you select the Magic Wand tool, the following options are available on the options bar, as shown in Figure 19:

- The four selection buttons.
- The Tolerance setting, which allows you to specify whether similar pixels will be selected. This setting has a value from 0 to 255, and the lower the value, the closer in color the selected pixels will be.
- The Anti-alias check box, which softens the selection's appearance.
- The Contiguous check box, which lets you select pixels that are next to one another.
- The Sample All Layers check box, which lets you select pixels from multiple layers at once.

Knowing which selection tool to use

The hardest part of making a selection might be determining which selection tool to use. How are you supposed to know if you should use a marquee tool or a lasso tool? The first question you need to ask yourself is, "What do I want to select?" Becoming proficient in making selections means that you need to assess the qualities of the object you want to select, and then decide which method to use. Ask yourself: Does the object have a definable shape? Does it have an identifiable edge? Are there common colors that can be used to create a selection?

Using the Color Range Command

You can use the Color Range command to make the same selections as with the Magic Wand tool. When you use the Color Range command, the Color Range dialog box opens. This dialog box lets you use the pointer to identify which colors you want to use to make a selection. You can also select the Invert check box to *exclude* the chosen color from the selection. The **fuzziness** setting is similar to tolerance, in that the lower the value, the closer in color pixels must be to be selected.

QUICKTIP

Unlike the Magic Wand tool, the Color Range command does not give you the option of excluding contiguous pixels.

Transforming a Selection

After you place a selection in a Photoshop image, you can change its size and other qualities by clicking Edit on the Application bar, pointing to Transform, then clicking any of the commands on the submenu. After you select certain commands, small squares called **handles** surround the selection. To complete the command, you drag a handle until the image has the look you want, then press [Enter] (Win) or [return] (Mac). You can also use the Transform submenu to flip a selection horizontally or vertically.

Understanding the Healing Brush Tool

If you place a selection then notice that the image has a few imperfections, you can fix the image. You can fix imperfections such as dirt, scratches, bulging veins on skin, or wrinkles on a face using the Healing Brush tool on the Tools panel.

QUICKTIP

When correcting someone's portrait, make sure your subject looks the way he or she *thinks* they look. That's not always possible, but strive to get as close as you can to their ideal!

Using the Healing Brush Tool

This tool lets you sample an area, then paint over the imperfections. What is the result? The less-than-desirable pixels seem to disappear into the surrounding image. In addition to matching the sampled pixels, the Healing Brush tool also matches the texture, lighting, and shading of the sample. This is why the painted pixels blend so effortlessly into the existing image. Corrections can be painted using broad strokes, or using clicks of the mouse.

QUICKTIP

To take a sample, press and hold [Alt] (Win) or [option] (Mac) while dragging the pointer over the area you want to duplicate.

FIGURE 19
Options for the Magic Wand tool

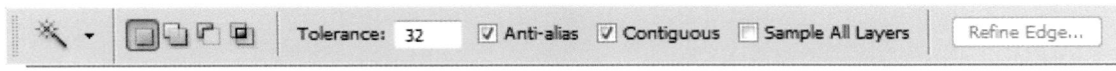

Select using color range

1. Open PS 3-5.psd from the drive and folder where you store your Data Files.

2. Click **Select** on the Application bar, then click **Color Range**.

3. Click the **Image option button** (if it is not already selected).

4. Click the **Invert check box** to add a check mark (if necessary).

5. Verify that your settings match those shown in Figure 20, click anywhere in the background area surrounding the sample image, then click **OK**.

   The Color Range dialog box closes and the spool of thread in the image is selected.

6. Click the **Move tool** ⊕ on the Tools panel.

7. Drag the selection into Sewing Box.psd, then position the selection as shown in Figure 21.

8. Rename the new layer **Thread**.

9. Defringe the spool of thread using a setting of **1** pixel.

10. Activate **PS 3-5.psd**, then close this file without saving any changes.

You made a selection within an image using the Color Range command on the Select menu, and dragged the selection to an existing image.

FIGURE 20
Completed Color Range dialog box

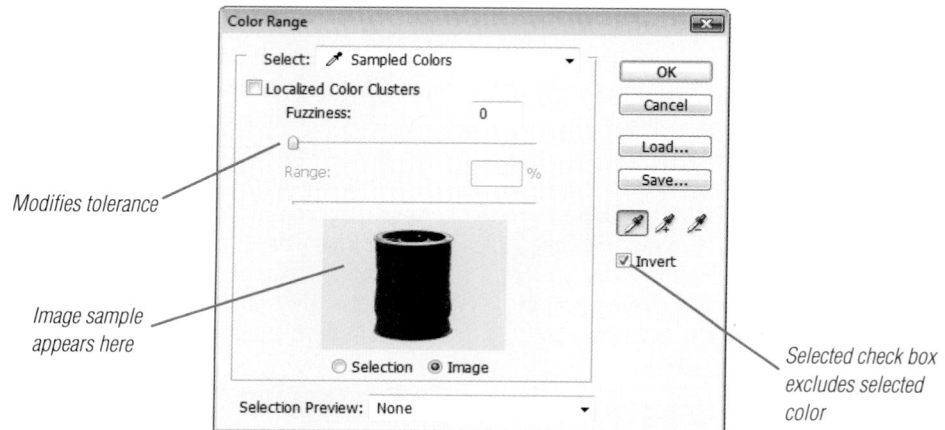

Modifies tolerance

Image sample appears here

Selected check box excludes selected color

FIGURE 21
Selection in image

FIGURE 22

Magic Wand tool settings

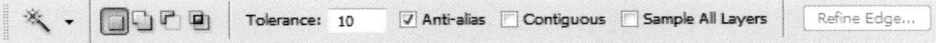

FIGURE 23

Selected area

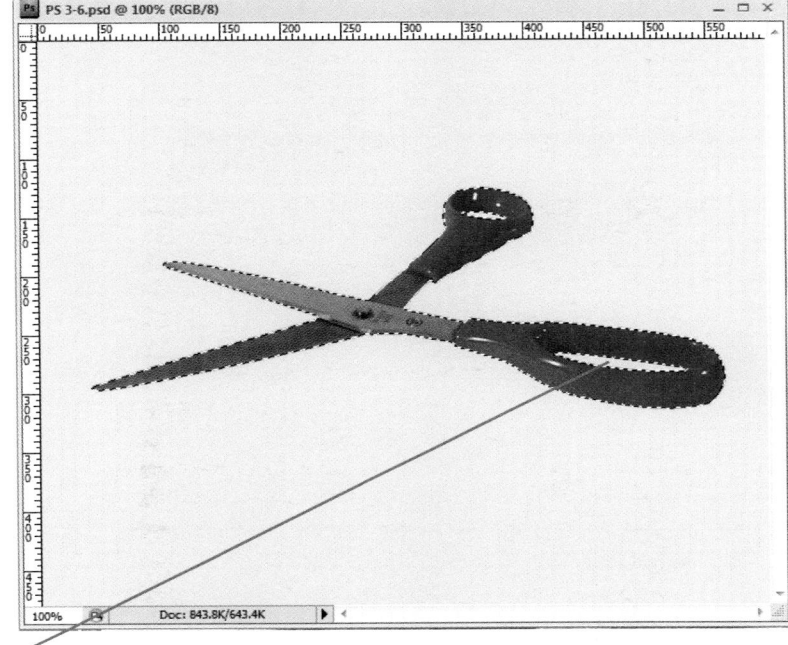

Selection excludes background color

1. Open PS 3-6.psd from the drive and folder where you store your Data Files.

2. Click the **Magic Wand tool** ✺ on the Tools panel.

3. Change the settings on the options bar to match those shown in Figure 22.

4. Click anywhere in the background area of the image (such as **50 X/50 Y**).

   TIP Had you selected the Contiguous check box, the pixels within the handles *would not* have been selected. The Contiguous check box is a powerful feature of the Magic Wand tool.

5. Click **Select** on the Application bar, then click **Inverse**. Compare your selection to Figure 23.

6. Click the **Move tool** ▸+ on the Tools panel, then drag the selection into Sewing Box.psd.

You made a selection using the Magic Wand tool, then dragged it into an existing image. The Magic Wand tool is just one more way you can make a selection. One advantage of using the Magic Wand tool (versus the Color Range tool) is the Contiguous check box, which lets you choose pixels that are next to one another.

Flip a selection

1. Click **Edit** on the Application bar, point to **Transform**, then click **Flip Horizontal**.

2. Rename Layer 1 as **Scissors**.

3. Defringe **Scissors** using a **1** pixel setting.

4. Drag the flipped selection with the **Move tool pointer** ▶₊ so it is positioned as shown in Figure 24.

5. Make **PS 3-6.psd** the active file, then close PS 3-6.psd without saving your changes.

6. Save your work.

You flipped and repositioned a selection. Sometimes it's helpful to flip an object to help direct the viewer's eye to a desired focal point.

FIGURE 24
Flipped and positioned selection

Getting rid of red eye

When digital photos of your favorite people have that annoying red eye, what do you do? You use the Red Eye tool to eliminate this effect. To do this, select the Red Eye tool (which is grouped on the Tools panel with the Spot Healing Brush tool, the Healing Brush tool, and the Patch tool), then either click a red area of an eye or draw a selection over a red eye. When you release the mouse button, the red eye effect is removed.

FIGURE 25
Healing Brush tool options

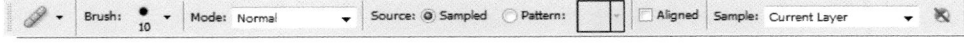

FIGURE 26
Healed area

Crack removed
from image

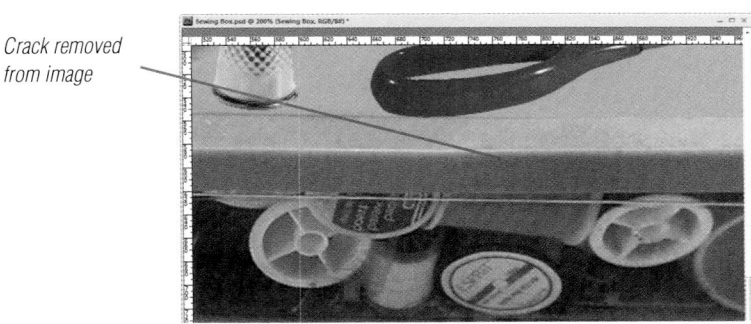

FIGURE 27
Image after using the Healing Brush

Lesson 3   Select Using Color and Modify a Selection

1. Click the **Sewing Box layer** on the Layers panel, then click the **Zoom tool** 🔍 on the Tools panel.

2. Click the image with the **Zoom tool pointer** ⊕ above the pink spool of thread (in the box) at **750 X/600 Y** until the zoom factor is **200%** and you can see the crack in the lid of the box.

3. Click the **Healing Brush tool** 🖌 on the Tools panel. Change the settings on the options bar to match those shown in Figure 25.

    TIP   If you need to change the Brush settings, click the Brush list arrow on the options bar, then drag the sliders so the settings are 10 px diameter, 0% hardness, 1% spacing, 0° angle, 100% roundness, and Pen Pressure size.

4. Press and hold **[Alt]** (Win) or **[option]** (Mac), click next to the crack at any location on the green lid, such as **700 X/580 Y**, then release **[Alt]** (Win) or **[option]** (Mac).

    You sampled an area of the box that is not cracked so that you can use the Healing Brush tool to paint a damaged area with the sample.

5. Click the crack (at approximately **720 X/580 Y**).

6. Repeat steps 4 and 5, each time choosing a new source location, then clicking at a parallel location on the crack.

    Compare the repaired area to Figure 26.

7. Click the **Zoom tool** 🔍 on the Tools panel press and hold **[Alt]** (Win) or **[option]** (Mac), click the center of the image with the **Zoom tool pointer** ⊖ until the zoom factor is **66.67%**, then release **[Alt]** (Win) or **[option]** (Mac).

8. Save your work, then compare your image to Figure 27.

You used the Healing Brush tool to fix an imperfection in an image.

ADD A VIGNETTE EFFECT
TO A SELECTION

What You'll Do

In this lesson, you'll create a vignette effect, using a layer mask and feathering.

Understanding Vignettes

Traditionally, a **vignette** is a picture or portrait whose border fades into the surrounding color at its edges. You can use a vignette effect to give an image an old-world appearance. You can also use a vignette effect to tone down an overwhelming background. You can create a vignette effect in Photoshop by creating a mask with a blurred edge. A **mask** lets you protect or modify a particular area and is created using a marquee.

Creating a Vignette

A **vignette effect** uses feathering to fade a marquee shape. The **feather** setting blurs the area between the selection and the surrounding pixels, which creates a distinctive fade at the edge of the selection. You can create a vignette effect by using a marquee or lasso tool to create a marquee in an image layer. After the selection is created, you can modify the feather setting (a 10- or 20-pixel setting creates a nice fade) to increase the blur effect on the outside edge of the selection.

Getting that Healing feeling

The Spot Healing Brush tool works in much the same way as the Healing Brush tool in that it removes blemishes and other imperfections. Unlike the Healing Brush tool, the Spot Healing Brush tool does not require you to take a sample. When using the Spot Healing Brush tool, you must choose whether you want to use a proximity match type (which uses pixels around the edge of the selection as a patch) or a create texture type (which uses all the pixels in the selection to create a texture that is used to fix the area). You also have the option of sampling all the visible layers or only the active layer.

FIGURE 28
Marquee in image

FIGURE 29
Layers panel

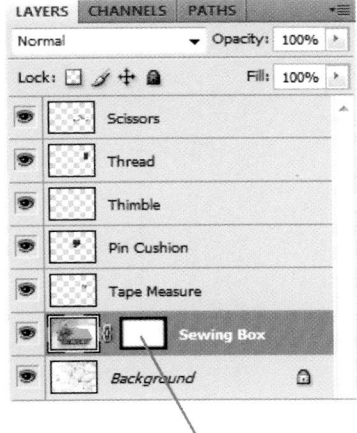

Feathered mask creates
vignette effect

FIGURE 30
Vignette in image

Vignette effect
fades border

Create a vignette

1. Verify that the **Sewing Box layer** is selected.

2. Click the **Rectangular Marquee tool** on the Tools panel.

3. Change the **Feather setting** on the options bar to **20px**.

4. Create a selection with the **Marquee pointer** from **50 X/50 Y** to **1200 X/800 Y**, as shown in Figure 28.

5. Click **Layer** on the Application bar, point to **Layer Mask**, then click **Reveal Selection**.

   The vignette effect is added to the layer.

   Compare your Layers panel to Figure 29.

6. Click **View** on the Application bar, then click **Rulers** to hide them.

7. Click **View** on the Application bar, then click **Clear Guides**.

8. Save your work, then compare your image to Figure 30.

9. Close the Sewing Box image, select **Essentials** from the workspace switcher, then exit Photoshop.

You created a vignette effect by adding a feathered layer mask. You also rearranged layers and defringed a selection. Once the image was finished, you hid the rulers and cleared the guides.

Power User Shortcuts

to do this:	use this method:
Copy selection	Click Edit ➤ Copy or [Ctrl][C] (Win) or 〘⌘〙[C] (Mac)
Create vignette effect	Marquee or Lasso tool, create selection, click Layer ➤ Layer Mask ➤ Reveal Selection
Cut selection	Click Edit ➤ Cut or [Ctrl][X] (Win) or 〘⌘〙[X] (Mac)
Deselect object	Select ➤ Deselect or [Ctrl][D] (Win) or 〘⌘〙[D] (Mac)
Elliptical Marquee tool	◯ or [Shift] M
Flip image	Edit ➤ Transform ➤ Flip Horizontal
Grow selection	Select ➤ Grow
Increase selection	Select ➤ Similar
Lasso tool	♀. or [Shift] L
Magnetic Lasso tool	🖉 or [Shift] L
Move tool	⊹ or V

to do this:	use this method:
Move selection marquee	Position pointer in selection, drag ⊹ to new location
Paste selection	Edit ➤ Paste or [Ctrl][V] (Win) or 〘⌘〙[V] (Mac)
Polygonal Lasso tool	🖅 or [Shift] L
Rectangular Marquee tool	⬚ or [Shift] M
Reselect a deselected object	Select ➤ Reselect, or [Shift][Ctrl][D] (Win) or [Shift]〘⌘〙[D] (Mac)
Select all objects	Select ➤ All, or [Ctrl][A] (Win) or 〘⌘〙[A] (Mac)
Select using color range	Select ➤ Color Range, click sample area
Select using Magic Wand tool	🪄 or W, then click image
Select using Quick Selection tool	🖌 or [Shift] W, then drag pointer over image
Single Column Marquee tool	▯
Single Row Marquee tool	▭

Key: Menu items are indicated by ➤ between the menu name and its command. Blue bold letters are shortcuts for selecting tools on the Tools panel.

Make a selection using shapes.

1. Open PS 3-7.psd from the drive and folder where you store your Data Files, substitute any missing fonts, then save it as **Cool cats**.
2. Open PS 3-8.tif.
3. Display the rulers in each image window (if necessary), switch to the Analysis workspace, then display the Layers panel.
4. Use the Rectangular Marquee tool to select the entire image in PS 3-8.tif. (*Hint*: Reset the Feather setting to 0 pixels, if necessary.)
5. Deselect the selection.
6. Use the Magnetic Lasso tool to create a selection surrounding only the Block cat in the image. (*Hint*: You can use the Zoom tool to make the image larger.)
7. Drag the selection into the Cool cats image, positioning it so the right side of the cat is at 490 X, and the bottom of the right paw is at 450 Y.
8. Save your work.
9. Close PS 3-8.tif without saving any changes.

Modify a marquee.

1. Open PS 3-9.tif.
2. Change the settings on the Magic Wand tool to Tolerance = 5, and make sure that the Contiguous check box is selected.
3. Use the Elliptical Marquee tool to create a marquee from 100 X/50 Y to 200 X/100 Y, using a setting of 0 in the Feather text box.
4. Use the Grow command on the Select menu.
5. Use the Inverse command on the Select menu.

6. Drag the selection into the Cool cats image, positioning it so the upper-left corner of the selection is near 0 X/0 Y.
7. Defringe the new layer using a width of 2 pixels.
8. Save your work.
9. Close PS 3-9.tif without saving any changes.

Select using color and modify a selection.

1. Open PS 3-10.tif.
2. Use the Color Range dialog box to select only the kitten.
3. Drag the selection into the Cool cats image.
4. Flip the kitten image (in the Cool cats image) horizontally.

FIGURE 31
Completed Skills Review project

5. Position the kitten image so the bottom right snaps to the ruler guides at 230 X/450 Y.
6. Defringe the kitten using a width of 2 pixels.
7. Save your work.
8. Close PS 3-10.tif without saving any changes.

Add a vignette effect to a selection.

1. Use a 15-pixel feather setting and the Backdrop layer to create an elliptical selection surrounding the contents of the Cool cats image.
2. Add a layer mask that reveals the selection.
3. Hide the rulers and guides, then switch to the Essentials workspace.
4. Save your work.
5. Compare your image to Figure 31.

As a professional photographer, you often take photos of people for use in various publications. You recently took a photograph of a woman that will be used in a marketing brochure. The client is happy with the overall picture, but wants the facial lines smoothed out. You decide to use the Healing Brush tool to ensure that the client is happy with the final product.

1. Open PS 3-11.psd, then save it as **Portrait**.
2. Make a copy of the Original layer using the default name, or the name of your choice.
3. Use the Original copy layer and the Healing Brush tool to smooth the appearance of facial lines in this image. (*Hint*: You may have greater success if you use short strokes with the Healing Brush tool than if you paint long strokes.)
4. Create a vignette effect on the Original copy layer that reveals the selection using an elliptical marquee.
5. Reorder the layers (if necessary), so that the vignette effect is visible.
6. Save your work, then compare your image to the sample shown in Figure 32.

FIGURE 32
Completed Project Builder 1

The St. Louis Athletic Association, which sponsors the St. Louis Marathon, is holding a contest for artwork to announce the upcoming race. Submissions can be created on paper or computer-generated. You feel you have a good chance at winning this contest, using Photoshop as your tool.

1. Open PS 3-12.psd, then save it as **Marathon Contest**.
2. Locate at least two pieces of appropriate artwork—either on your hard disk, in a royalty-free collection, or from scanned images—that you can use in this file.
3. Use any appropriate methods to select imagery from the artwork.
4. After the selections have been made, copy each selection into Marathon Contest.
5. Arrange the images into a design that you think will be eye-catching and attractive.
6. Deselect the selections in the files you are no longer using, and close them without saving the changes.
7. Add a vignette effect to the Backdrop layer.
8. Display the type layers if they are hidden.
9. Defringe any layers, as necessary.
10. Save your work, then compare your screen to the sample shown in Figure 33.

FIGURE 33
Completed Project Builder 2

You are aware that there will be an opening in your firm's design department. Before you can be considered for the job, you need to increase your Photoshop compositing knowledge and experience. You have decided to teach yourself, using informational sources on the Internet and images that can be scanned or purchased.

1. Connect to the Internet and use your browser and favorite search engine to find information on image compositing. (Make a record of the site you found so you can use it for future reference, if necessary.)
2. Create a new Photoshop image, using the dimensions of your choice, then save it as **Sample Compositing**.
3. Locate at least two pieces of artwork—either on your hard disk, in a royalty-free collection, or from scanned images—that you can use. (The images can contain people, plants, animals, or inanimate objects.)
4. Select the images in the artwork, then copy each into the Sample Compositing image, using the method of your choice.
5. Rename each of the layers using meaningful names.
6. Apply a color to each new layer.
7. Arrange the images in a pleasing design. (*Hint*: Remember that you can flip any image, if necessary.)

8. Deselect the selections in the artwork, then close the files without saving the changes.
9. If desired, create a background layer for the image.
10. If necessary, add a vignette effect to a layer.

11. Defringe any images as you see necessary.
12. Save your work, then compare your screen to the sample shown in Figure 34.

FIGURE 34
Completed Design Project

At your design firm, a Fortune 500 client plans to start a 24-hour cable sports network called Total Sportz that will cover any nonprofessional sporting event. You have been asked to create some preliminary designs for the network, using images from multiple sources.

1. Open PS 3-13.psd, then save it as **Total Sportz**. (*Hint*: Click Update to close the warning box regarding missing fonts, if necessary.)
2. Locate several pieces of sports-related artwork—either on your hard disk, in a royalty-free collection, or from scanned images. Remember that the images should not show professional sports figures, if possible.
3. Select imagery from the artwork and move it into the Total Sportz image.
4. Arrange the images in an interesting design. (*Hint*: Remember that you can flip any image, if necessary.)
5. Change each layer name to describe the sport in the layer image.
6. Deselect the selections in the files that you used, then close the files without saving the changes.

7. If necessary, add a vignette effect to a layer and/or adjust opacity.
8. Defringe any images (if necessary).

9. Save your work, then compare your image to the sample shown in Figure 35.

FIGURE 35
Completed Portfolio Project

INCORPORATING COLOR
TECHNIQUES

1. Work with color to transform an image

2. Use the Color Picker and the Swatches panel

3. Place a border around an image

4. Blend colors using the Gradient tool

5. Add color to a grayscale image

6. Use filters, opacity, and blending modes

7. Match colors

Using Color

Color can make or break an image. Sometimes colors can draw us into an image; other times they can repel us. We all know which colors we like, but when it comes to creating an image, it is helpful to have some knowledge of color theory and be familiar with color terminology.

Understanding how Photoshop measures, displays, and prints color can be valuable when you create new images or modify existing images. Some colors you choose might be difficult for a professional printer to reproduce or might look muddy when printed. As you become more experienced using color, you will learn which colors reproduce well and which ones do not.

Understanding Color Modes and Color Models

Photoshop displays and prints images using specific color modes. A **mode** is the amount of color data that can be stored in a given file format, based on an established model. A **model** determines how pigments combine to produce resulting colors. This is the way your computer or printer associates a name or number with colors. Photoshop uses standard color models as the basis for its color modes.

Displaying and Printing Images

An image displayed on your monitor, such as an icon on your desktop, is a **bitmap**, a geometric arrangement of different color dots on a rectangular grid. Each dot, called a **pixel**, represents a color or shade. Bitmapped images are *resolution-dependent* and can lose detail—often demonstrated by a jagged appearance—when highly magnified. When printed, images with high resolutions tend to show more detail and subtler color transitions than low-resolution images.

Tools You'll Use

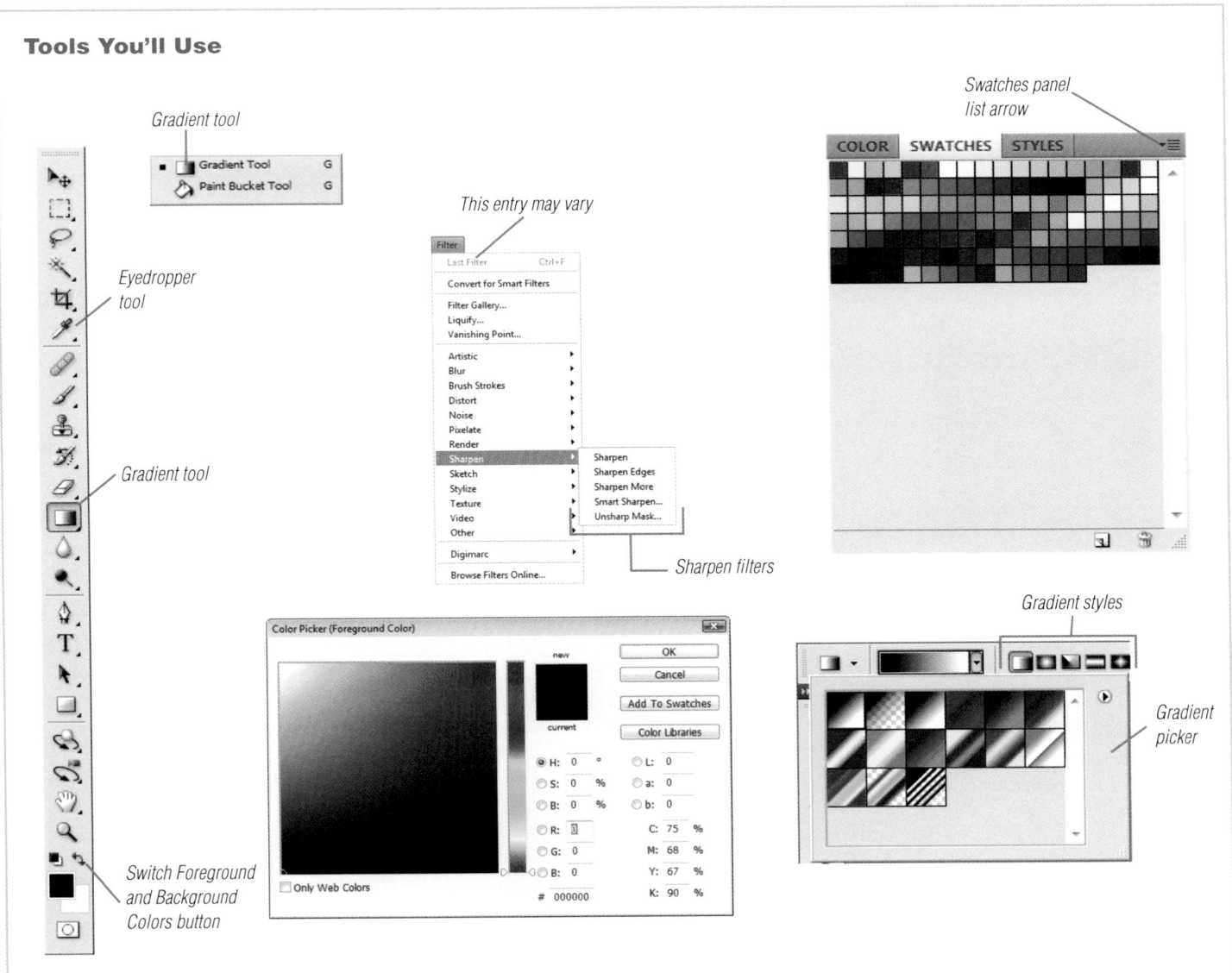

Gradient tool

Eyedropper tool

Gradient tool

Switch Foreground and Background Colors button

This entry may vary

Sharpen filters

Swatches panel list arrow

Gradient styles

Gradient picker

WORK WITH COLOR TO
TRANSFORM AN IMAGE

What You'll Do

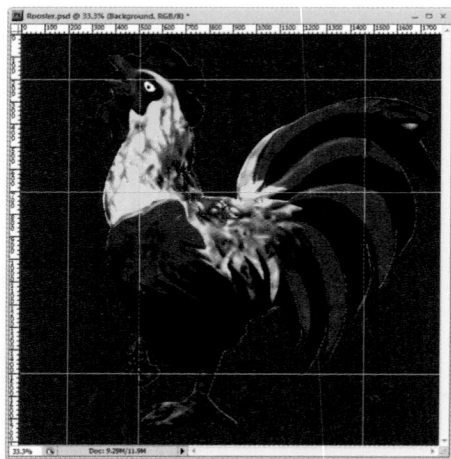

 In this lesson, you'll use the Color panel, the Paint Bucket tool, and the Eyedropper tool to change the background color of an image.

Learning About Color Models

Photoshop reproduces colors using models of color modes. The range of displayed colors, or **gamut**, for each model available in Photoshop is shown in Figure 1. The shape of each color gamut indicates the range of colors it can display. If a color is out of gamut, it is beyond the color space that your monitor can display or that your printer can print. You select the color mode from the Mode command on the Image menu. The available Photoshop color models include Lab, HSB, RGB, CMYK, Bitmap, and Grayscale.

QUICKTIP

A color mode is used to determine which color model will be used to display and print an image.

DESIGNTIP **Understanding the psychology of color**

Have you ever wondered why some colors make you react a certain way? You might have noticed that some colors affect you differently than others. Color is such an important part of our lives, and in Photoshop, it's key. Specific colors are often used in print and web pages to evoke the following responses:

- Blue tends to instill a feeling of safety and stability and is often used by financial services.
- Certain shades of green can generate a soft, calming feeling, while others suggest youthfulness and growth.
- Red commands attention and can be used as a call to action; it can also distract a reader's attention from other content.
- White evokes the feeling of purity and innocence, looks cool and fresh, and is often used to suggest luxury.
- Black conveys feelings of power and strength, but can also suggest darkness and negativity.

Lab Model

The Lab model is based on one luminance (lightness) component and two chromatic components (from green to red, and from blue to yellow). Using the Lab model has distinct advantages: you have the largest number of colors available to you and the greatest precision with which to create them. You can also create all the colors contained by other color models, which are limited in their respective color ranges. The Lab model is device-independent—the colors will not vary, regardless of the hardware. Use this model when working with photo CD images so that you can independently edit the luminance and color values.

HSB Model

Based on the human perception of color, the HSB (Hue, Saturation, Brightness) model has three fundamental characteristics: hue, saturation, and brightness. The color reflected from or transmitted through an object is called **hue**. Expressed as a degree (between 0° and 360°), each hue is identified by a color name (such as red or green). **Saturation** (or *chroma*) is the strength or purity of the color, representing the amount of gray in proportion to hue. Saturation is measured as a percentage from 0% (gray) to 100% (fully saturated). **Brightness** is the measurement of relative lightness or darkness of a color and is measured as a percentage from 0% (black) to 100% (white). Although you can use the HSB model to define a color on the Color panel or in the Color Picker dialog box, Photoshop *does not* offer HSB mode as a choice for creating or editing images.

RGB Mode

Photoshop uses color modes to determine how to display and print an image. Each mode is based on established models used in color reproduction. Most colors in the visible spectrum can be represented by mixing various proportions and intensities of red, green, and blue (RGB) colored light. RGB colors are additive colors. **Additive colors** are used for lighting, video, and computer monitors; color is created by light passing through red, green, and blue phosphors. When the values of red, green, and blue are zero, the result is black; when the values are all 255, the result is white. Photoshop assigns each component of the RGB mode an intensity value. Your colors can vary from monitor to monitor even if you are using the exact RGB values on different computers.

FIGURE 1
Photoshop color gamuts

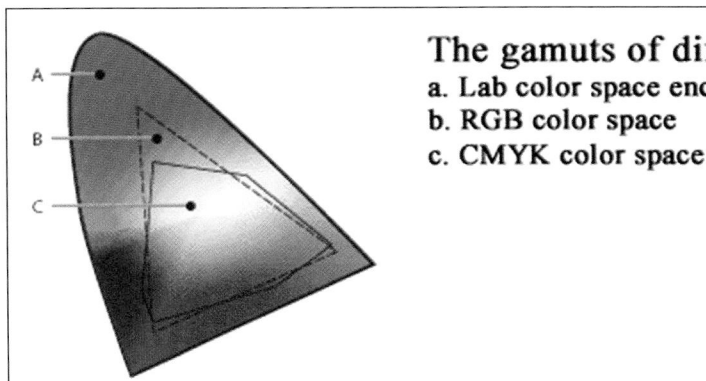

The gamuts of different color spaces
a. Lab color space encompasses all visible colors
b. RGB color space
c. CMYK color space

CMYK Mode

The light-absorbing quality of ink printed on paper is the basis of the CMYK (Cyan, Magenta, Yellow, Black) mode. Unlike the RGB mode—in which components are *combined* to create new colors—the CMYK mode is based on colors being partially *absorbed* as the ink hits the paper and being partially *reflected* back to your eyes. CMYK colors are **subtractive colors**—the *absence* of cyan, magenta, yellow, and black creates white. Subtractive (CMYK) and additive (RGB) colors are complementary colors; a pair from one model creates a color in the other. When combined, cyan, magenta, and yellow absorb all color and produce black. The CMYK mode—in which the lightest colors are assigned the highest percentages of ink colors—is used in four-color process printing. Converting an RGB image into a CMYK image produces a **color separation** (the commercial printing process of separating colors for use with different inks). Note, however, that because your monitor uses RGB mode, you will not see the exact colors until you print the image, and even then the colors can vary depending on the printer and offset press.

Understanding the Bitmap and Grayscale Modes

In addition to the RGB and CMYK modes, Photoshop provides two specialized color modes: bitmap and grayscale. The **bitmap mode** uses black or white color values to represent image pixels, and is a good choice for images with subtle color gradations, such as photographs or painted images. The **grayscale mode** uses up to 256 shades of gray, assigning a brightness value from 0 (black) to 255 (white) to each pixel. Displayed colors can vary from monitor to monitor even if you use identical color settings on different computers.

Changing Foreground and Background Colors

In Photoshop, the **foreground color** is black by default and is used to paint, fill, and apply a border to a selection. The **background color** is white by default and is used to make **gradient fills** (gradual blends of multiple colors) and fill in areas of an image that have been erased. You can change foreground and background colors using the Color panel, the Swatches panel, the Color Picker, or the Eyedropper tool. One method of changing foreground and background colors is **sampling**, in which an existing color is used. You can restore the default colors by clicking the Default Foreground and Background Colors button on the Tools panel, shown in Figure 2. You can apply a color to the background of a layer using the Paint Bucket tool. When you click an image with the Paint Bucket Tool, the current foreground color on the Tools panel fills the active layer.

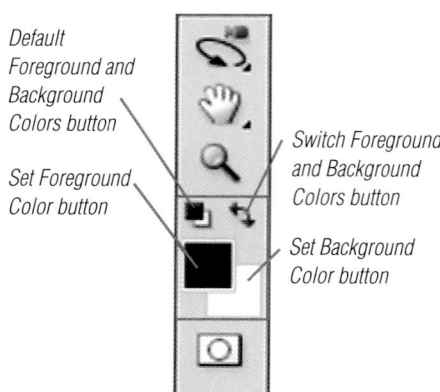

FIGURE 2
Foreground and background color buttons

Default Foreground and Background Colors button

Set Foreground Color button

Switch Foreground and Background Colors button

Set Background Color button

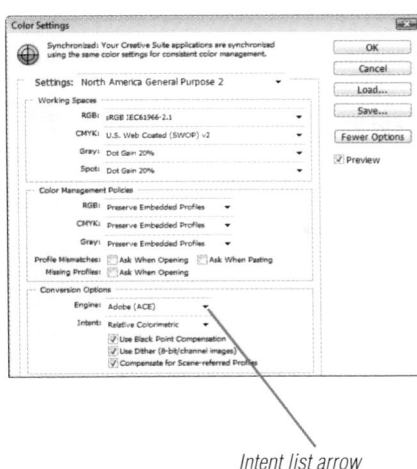

Intent list arrow

Creating a rendering intent

The use of a **rendering intent** determines how colors are converted by a color management system. A **color management system** is used to keep colors looking consistent as they move between devices. Colors are defined and interpreted using a **profile**. You can create a rendering intent by clicking Edit on the Application bar, then clicking Color Settings. Click the More Options button in the Color Settings dialog box, click the Intent list arrow shown in Figure 4, then click one of the four options. Since a gamut is the range of color that a color system can display or print, the rendering intent is constantly evaluating the color gamut and deciding whether or not the colors need adjusting. So, colors that fall inside the destination gamut may not be changed, or they may be adjusted when translated to a smaller color gamut.

Set the default foreground and background colors

1. Start Photoshop, open PS 4-1.psd from the drive and folder where you save your Data Files, then save it as **Rooster**.

   TIP   Whenever the Photoshop Format Options dialog box appears, click OK to maximize compatibility.

2. Click the **Default Foreground and Background Colors button** 🔳 on the Tools panel.

   TIP   If you accidently click the Set foreground color button, the Color Picker (Foreground Color) dialog box opens.

3. Change the status bar so the document sizes display (if necessary).

   TIP   Document sizes will not display in the status bar if the image window is too small. Drag the lower-right corner of the image window to expand the window and display the menu button and document sizes.

4. Display the rulers in pixels (if necessary), show the guides (if necessary), then compare your screen to Figure 3.

   TIP   You can right-click (Win) or [control]-click (Mac) one of the rulers to choose Pixels, Inches, Centimeters, Millimeters, Points, Picas, or Percent as a unit of measurement, instead of using the Rulers and Units Preferences dialog box.

You set the default foreground and background colors and displayed rulers in pixels.

Change the background color using the Color panel

1. Click the **Background layer** on the Layers panel.

2. Display the History and Layers workspace.

3. Click the **Color panel tab** COLOR (if necessary).

4. Drag each color slider on the Color panel until you reach the values shown in Figure 5.

   The active color changes to the new color. Did you notice that this image is using the RGB mode?

   > TIP   You can also double-click each component's text box on the Color panel and type the color values.

5. Click the **Paint Bucket tool** ⬙ on the Tools panel.

   > TIP   If the Paint Bucket tool is not visible on the Tools panel, click the Gradient tool on the Tools panel, press and hold the mouse button until the list of hidden tools opens, then click the Paint Bucket tool.

6. Click the image with the **Paint Bucket pointer** ⬙.

7. Drag the **Paint Bucket state** on the History panel onto the **Delete current state button** 🗑.

   > TIP   You can also undo the last action by clicking Edit on the menu bar, then clicking Undo Paint Bucket.

You set new values in the Color panel, used the Paint Bucket tool to change the background to that color, then undid the change. You can change colors on the Color panel by dragging the sliders or by typing values in the color text boxes.

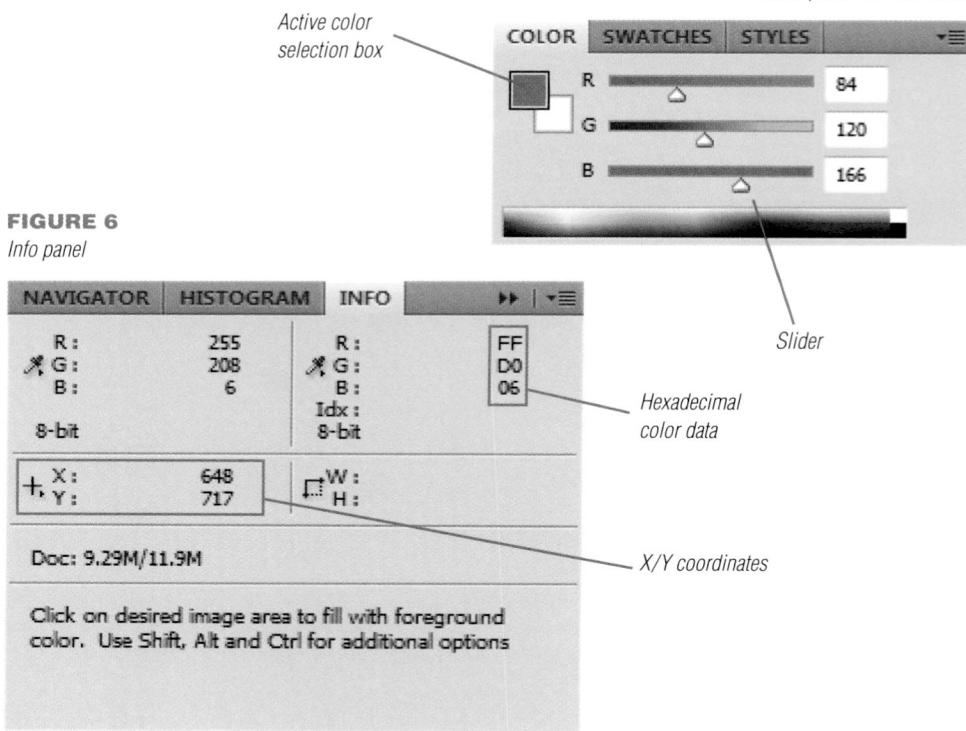

FIGURE 5
Color panel with new color

Active color selection box

Slider

Hexadecimal color data

FIGURE 6
Info panel

X/Y coordinates

Using ruler coordinates

Photoshop rulers run along the top and left sides of the document window. Each point on an image has a horizontal and vertical location. These two numbers, called X and Y coordinates, appear on the Info panel (which is located in the tab group with the Navigator and Histogram panels) as shown in Figure 6. The X coordinate refers to the horizontal location, and the Y coordinate refers to the vertical location. You can use one or both sets of guides to identify coordinates of a location, such as a color you want to sample. If you have difficulty seeing the ruler markings, you can increase the size of the image; the greater the zoom factor, the more detailed the measurement hashes.

FIGURE 7
New foreground color applied to Background layer

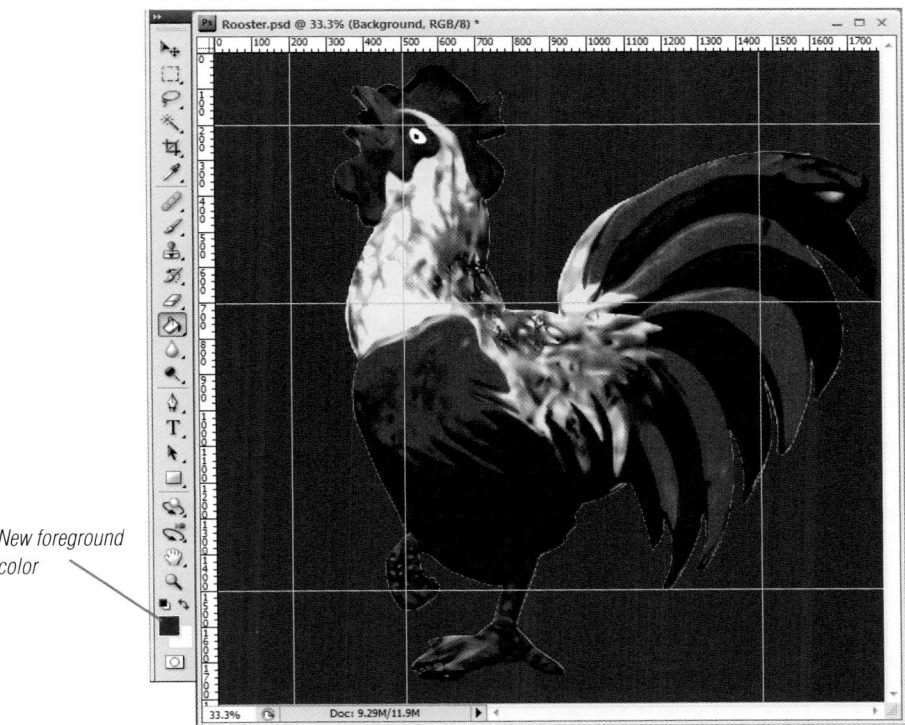

New foreground
color

Using hexadecimal values in the Info panel

Colors can be expressed in a **hexadecimal value**, three pairs of letters or numbers that define the R, G, and B components of a color. The three pairs of letters/numbers are expressed in values from 00 (minimum luminance) to ff (maximum luminance). 000000 represents the value of black, ffffff is white, and ff0000 is red. To view hexadecimal values in the Info panel, click the Info panel list arrow, then click Panel Options. Click Web Color from either the First Color Readout or Second Color Readout Mode list arrow, then click OK. This is just one more way you can exactly determine a specific color in an image.

Change the background color using the Eyedropper tool

1. Click the **Background layer** on the Layers panel.

2. Click the **Eyedropper tool** 🖋 on the Tools panel.

3. Click the **red part of the rooster's crown** in the image with the **Eyedropper pointer** 🖋, using the Info panel and the blue guides to help ensure accuracy.

   The Set foreground color button displays the red color that you clicked (or sampled).

   | TIP Don't worry if you see a warning sign on the Color panel.

4. Click the **Paint Bucket tool** 🪣 on the Tools panel.

5. Click the image, then compare your screen to Figure 7.

   You might have noticed that in this instance, it doesn't matter where on the layer you click, as long as the correct layer is selected.

6. Save your work.

You used the Eyedropper tool to sample a color as the foreground color, then used the Paint Bucket tool to change the background color to the color you sampled. Using the Eyedropper tool is a convenient way of sampling a color in any Photoshop image.

USE THE COLOR PICKER AND
THE SWATCHES PANEL

What You'll Do

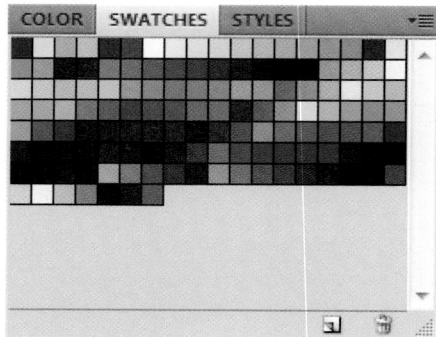

 In this lesson, you'll use the Color Picker and the Swatches panel to select new colors, then you'll add a new color to the background and to the Swatches panel. You'll also learn how to access and download color themes from kuler.

Making Selections from the Color Picker

Depending on the color model you are using, you can select colors using the **Color Picker**, a feature that lets you choose a color from a color spectrum or numerically define a custom color. You can change colors in the Color Picker dialog box by using the following methods:

- Drag the sliders along the vertical color bar.
- Click inside the vertical color bar.
- Click a color in the Color field.
- Enter a value in any of the text boxes.

Figure 8 shows a color in the Color Picker dialog box. A circular marker indicates the active color. The color slider displays the range of color levels available for the active color component. The adjustments you make by dragging or clicking a new color are reflected in the text boxes; when you choose a new color, the previous color appears below the new color in the preview area.

Using kuler to coordinate colors

Kuler, by Adobe Labs, is a web-hosted application from which you can download pre-coordinated color themes or design your own. These collections can be saved in your own Mykuler space or shared with others. Use kuler as a fast, effective way of ensuring that your use of color is consistent and harmonious. If you decide to select an existing kuler theme, you'll find that there are thousands from which to choose. Kuler themes can be seen by clicking the Window menu, pointing to Extensions, then clicking Kuler. You can also access kuler through your browser at *kuler.adobe.com*, using the kuler desktop (which requires the installation of Adobe AIR), or from Adobe Illustrator (CS4 or higher). When you pass the mouse over any paint chip in the kuler website, the colors in the theme expand. Click the theme name, and the colors display in the paint chips at the top of the window.

Using the Swatches Panel

You can also change colors using the Swatches panel. The **Swatches panel** is a visual display of colors you can choose from, as shown in Figure 9. You can add your own colors to the panel by sampling a color from an image, and you can also delete colors. When you add a swatch to the Swatches panel, Photoshop assigns a default name that has a sequential number, or you can name the swatch whatever you like. Photoshop places new swatches in the first available space at the end of the panel. You can view swatch names by clicking the Swatches panel list arrow, then clicking Small List. You can restore the default Swatches panel by clicking the Swatches panel list arrow, clicking Reset Swatches, then clicking OK.

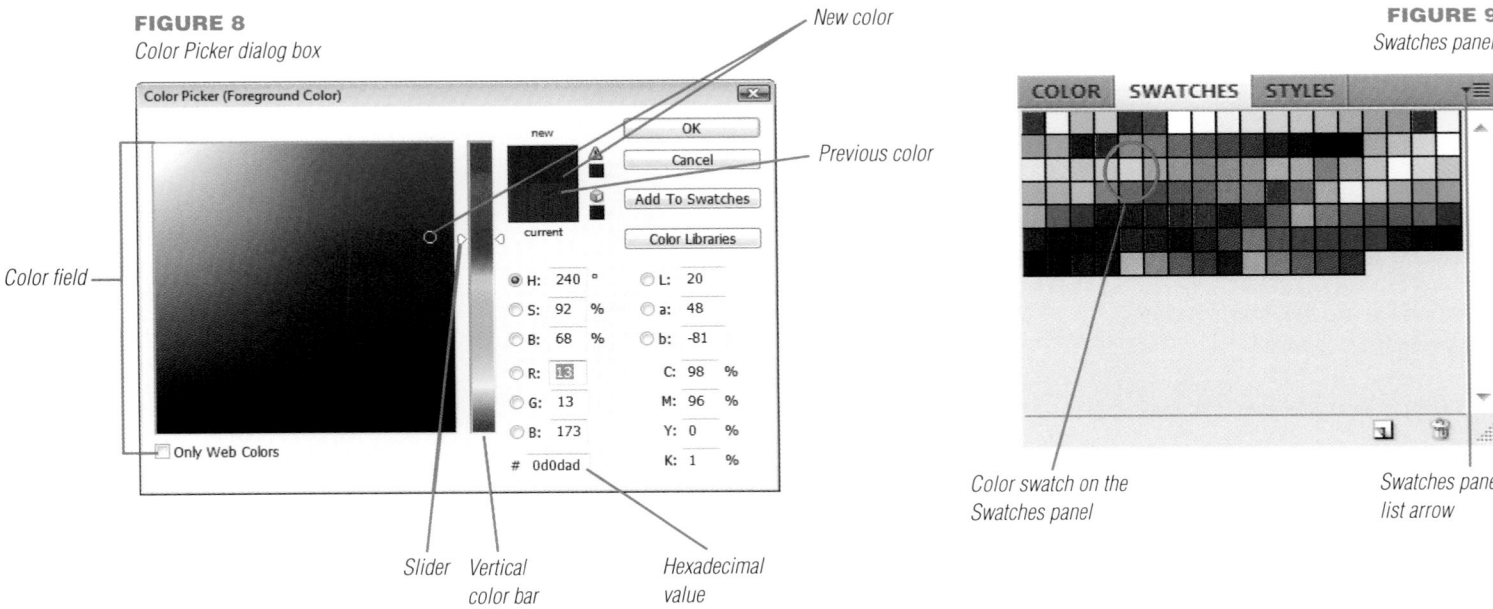

FIGURE 8
Color Picker dialog box

New color

Previous color

Color field

Slider Vertical
color bar

Hexadecimal
value

FIGURE 9
Swatches panel

Color swatch on the
Swatches panel

Swatches panel
list arrow

Downloading a kuler theme

Once you've logged into kuler, you can download a theme as an Adobe Swatch Exchange (ASE) file. Click the download button, select a name and location for the downloaded file, then click Save. You can add a kuler theme to your color panel by clicking the Swatches panel option button, then clicking Load Swatches. The new colors will display at the end of the Swatches panel.

Select a color using the Color Picker dialog box

1. Click the **Set foreground color button** on the Tools panel, then verify that the H: option button is selected in the Color Picker dialog box.

2. Click the **R: option button**.

3. Click the **bottom-right corner** of the Color field (purple), as shown in Figure 10.

   TIP If the Warning: out-of-gamut for printing indicator appears next to the color, then this color exceeds the printable range.

4. Click **OK**.

You opened the Color Picker dialog box, selected a different color mode, and then selected a new color.

Select a color using the Swatches panel

1. Click the **Swatches panel tab** [SWATCHES].

2. Click the **second swatch from the left in the first row** (RGB Yellow), as shown in Figure 11.

   Did you notice that the foreground color on the Tools panel changed to a light, bright yellow?

3. Click the **Paint Bucket tool** on the Tools panel (if it is not already selected).

4. Click the image with the **Paint Bucket pointer**, then compare your screen to Figure 12.

You opened the Swatches panel, selected a color, and then used the Paint Bucket tool to change the background to that color.

FIGURE 10
Color Picker dialog box

New color

Out-of-gamut indicator

Click to add a color to the Swatches panel

Your values might vary

Click here for new color   Previous color

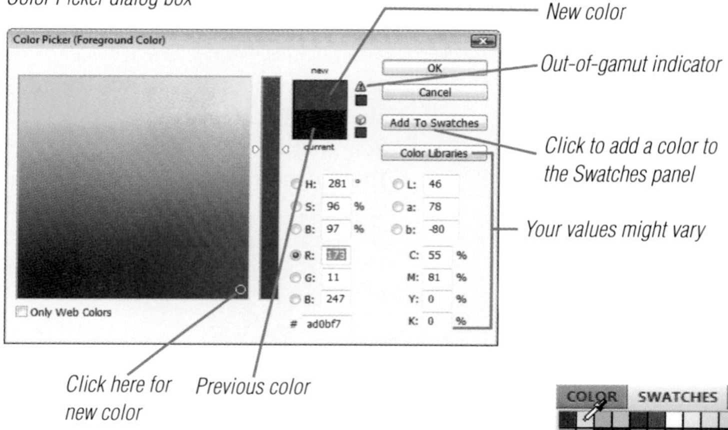

FIGURE 11
Swatches panel

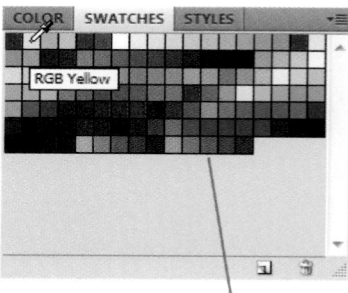

Your swatches on the last row might vary

FIGURE 12
New foreground color applied to Background layer

FIGURE 13
Swatch added to Swatches panel

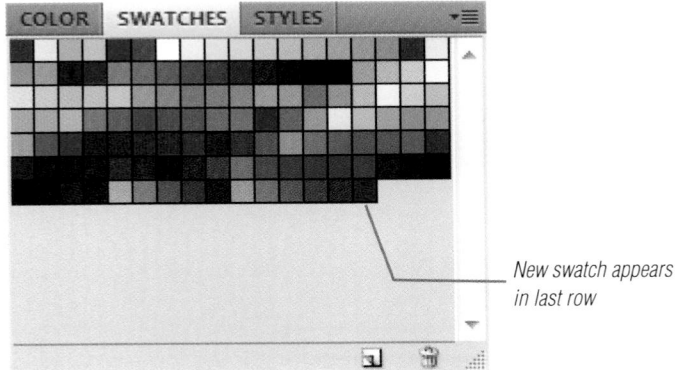

New swatch appears
in last row

1. Click the **Eyedropper tool** 🖋 on the Tools panel.

2. Click **above and to the left of the rooster's eye** at coordinates **500 X/200 Y**.

   TIP   Use the Zoom tool whenever necessary to enlarge/decrease your workspace so you can better see what you're working on.

3. Click the **empty area to the right of the last swatch** in the bottom row of the Swatches panel with the **Paint Bucket pointer** 🪣.

4. Type **Rooster eye surround** in the Name text box.

5. Click **OK** in the Color Swatch Name dialog box.

   TIP   To delete a color from the Swatches panel, press [Alt] (Win) or [option] (Mac), position the pointer over a swatch, then click the swatch.

6. Save your work, then compare the new swatch on your Swatches panel to Figure 13.

You used the Eyedropper tool to sample a color, and then added the color to the Swatches panel, and gave it a descriptive name. Adding swatches to the Swatches panel makes it easy to reuse frequently used colors.

Maintaining your focus

Adobe Photoshop is probably unlike any other program you've used before. In other programs, there's a central area on the screen where you focus your attention. In Photoshop, there's the workspace containing your document, but you've probably already figured out that if you don't have the correct layer selected in the Layer's panel, things won't quite work out as you expected. In addition, you have to make sure you've got the right tool selected in the Tools panel. You also need to keep an eye on the History panel. As you work on your image, it might feel a lot like negotiating a shopping mall parking lot on the day before a holiday: you've got to be looking in a lot of places at once.

Use kuler from a web browser

1. Open your favorite browser, then type **kuler.adobe.com** in the URL text box.

2. Click the **Sign In link**, then type your **Adobe ID** and **password**. (If you don't have an Adobe ID, click the Register link and follow the instructions.)

3. Click the **Newest link**, then compare your results with Figure 14. (Your color results will be different.)

4. Type **wine olives** in the Search text box, press **[Enter]** (Win) or **[return]** (Mac). The swatch shown in Figure 15 will display.

5. Click the **Download this theme as an Adobe Swatch Exchange file button** [icon], find the location where you save your Data Files in the Select location for download by kuler.adobe.com dialog box, then click **Save**.

6. Sign Out from kuler, then activate Photoshop.

7. Click the **Swatches list arrow**, then click **Load Swatches**.

8. Find the location where you save your Data Files, click the **Files of type list arrow** (Win), click **Swatch Exchange (*.ASE)**, click **Wine, Olives and Cheese**, then click **Load**.

You searched the kuler website and downloaded a color theme to your Photoshop Swatches panel.

FIGURE 14
Kuler website

Color chip for active theme: the displayed theme will vary

Indicates the current user

Click to download the active theme

Active color theme is expanded

Hover pointer over a theme to expand it

FIGURE 15
Theme in kuler

FIGURE 16
Kuler panel

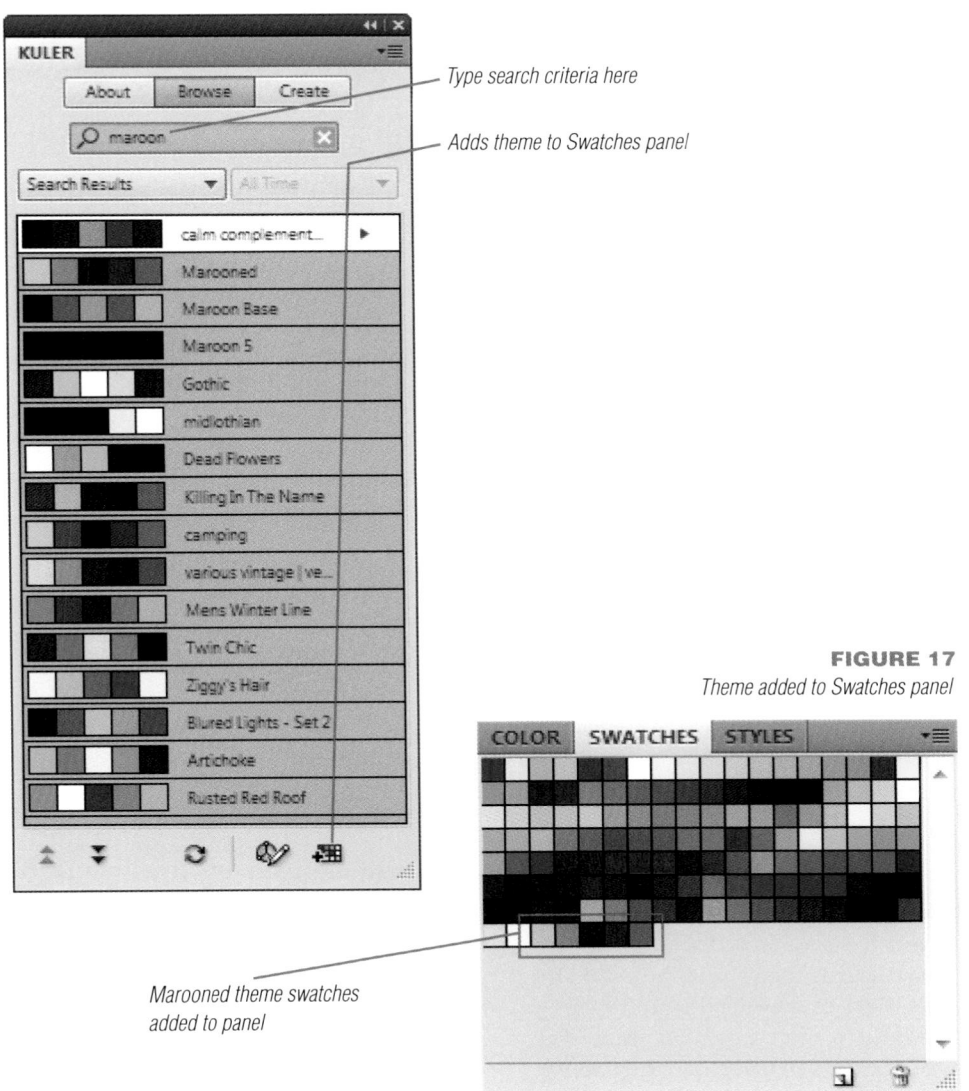

Type search criteria here

Adds theme to Swatches panel

Marooned theme swatches
added to panel

FIGURE 17
Theme added to Swatches panel

Use kuler from Photoshop

1. Click **Window** on the Application bar, point to **Extensions**, then click **Kuler**.

2. Click the **Search text box** , type **maroon**, then press **[Enter]** (Win) or **[return]** (Mac). Compare your kuler panel to Figure 16.

   TIP   Your kuler panel may differ as themes change frequently.

3. Click the **Marooned** theme, then click the **Add selected theme to swatches button** . Compare your Swatches panel to Figure 17.

4. Close the kuler panel.

You opened kuler in Photoshop, then added a color theme to the Swatches panel.

PLACE A BORDER AROUND AN IMAGE

What You'll Do

In this lesson, you'll apply a downloaded color and add a border to an image.

Emphasizing an Image

You can emphasize an image by placing a border around its edges. This process is called **stroking the edges**. The default color of the border is the current foreground color on the Tools panel. You can change the width, color, location, and blending mode of a border using the Stroke dialog box. The default stroke width is the setting last applied; you can apply a width from 1 to 16 pixels. The location option buttons in the dialog box determine where the border will be placed. If you want to change the location of the stroke, you must first delete the previously applied stroke, or Photoshop will apply the new border over the existing one.

Locking Transparent Pixels

As you modify layers, you can lock some properties to protect their contents. The ability to lock—or protect—elements within a layer is controlled from within the Layers panel, as shown in Figure 18. It's a good idea to lock transparent pixels when you add borders so that stray marks will

not be included in the stroke. You can lock the following layer properties:

- Transparency: Limits editing capabilities to areas in a layer that are opaque.
- Image: Makes it impossible to modify layer pixels using painting tools.
- Position: Prevents pixels within a layer from being moved.

QUICKTIP

You can lock transparency or image pixels only in a layer containing an image, not in one containing type.

FIGURE 18
Layers panel locking options

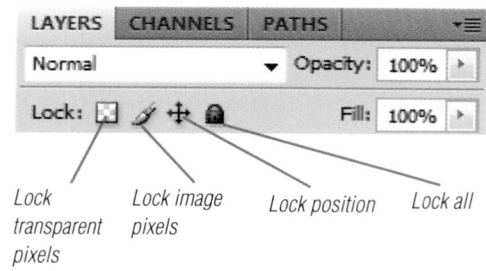

Lock transparent pixels

Lock image pixels

Lock position

Lock all

Incorporating Color Techniques

FIGURE 19
Locking transparent pixels

Lock transparent pixels button

Lock icon

FIGURE 20
Stroke dialog box

Your default stroke width might vary

Changes stroke color

Location options

FIGURE 21
Border added to image

Border

1. Click the **Indicates layer visibility button** 👁 on the Background layer on the Layers panel.

   TIP You can click the Indicates layer visibility button to hide distracting layers.

2. Click the **Default Foreground and Background Colors button** ▣.

   The foreground color will become the default border color.

3. Click the **Rooster layer** on the Layers panel.

4. Click the **Lock transparent pixels button** ⊠ on the Layers panel. See Figure 19.

   The border will be applied only to the pixels on the edge of the rooster.

5. Click **Edit** on the menu bar, then click **Stroke** to open the Stroke dialog box. See Figure 20.

6. Type **5** in the Width text box, click the **Inside option button**, then click **OK**.

   TIP Determining the correct border location can be confusing. Try different settings until you achieve the look you want.

7. Click the **Indicates layer visibility button** ☐ on the Background layer on the Layers panel.

8. Activate the Background layer on the Layers panel, click the newly-added tan-colored box in the Swatches panel (255 R, 211 G, 114 B), click the **Paint Bucket tool** ◇ on the Tools panel, then click the image.

9. Save your work, then compare your image to Figure 21.

You hid a layer, changed the foreground color to black, locked transparent pixels, then used the Stroke dialog box to apply a border to the image.

BLEND COLORS USING THE GRADIENT TOOL

What You'll Do

In this lesson, you'll create a gradient fill from a sampled color and a swatch, then apply it to the background.

Understanding Gradients

A **gradient fill**, or simply **gradient**, is a blend of colors used to fill a selection of a layer or an entire layer. A gradient's appearance is determined by its beginning and ending points, and its length, direction, and angle. Gradients allow you to create dramatic effects, using existing color combinations or your own colors. The Gradient picker, as shown in Figure 22, offers multi-color gradient fills and a few that use the current foreground or background colors on the Tools panel.

FIGURE 22
Gradient picker

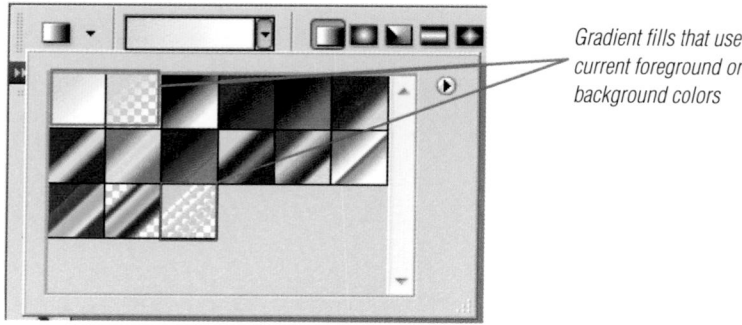

Gradient fills that use current foreground or background colors

Using the Gradient Tool

You use the Gradient tool to create gradients in images. When you choose the Gradient tool, five gradient styles become available on the options bar. These styles—Linear, Radial, Angle, Reflected, and Diamond—are shown in Figure 23. In each example, the gradient was drawn from 50 X/50 Y to 100 X/100 Y.

Customizing Gradients

Using the **gradient presets**—predesigned gradient fills that are displayed in the Gradient picker—is a great way to learn how to use gradients. But as you become more familiar with Photoshop, you might want to venture into the world of the unknown and create your own gradient designs. You can create your own designs by modifying an existing gradient using the Gradient Editor. You can open the Gradient Editor, shown in Figure 24, by clicking the selected gradient pattern that appears on the options bar. After it's open, you can use it to make the following modifications:

- Create a new gradient from an existing gradient.
- Modify an existing gradient.
- Add intermediate colors to a gradient.
- Create a blend between more than two colors.
- Adjust the opacity values.
- Determine the placement of the midpoint.

FIGURE 23
Sample gradients

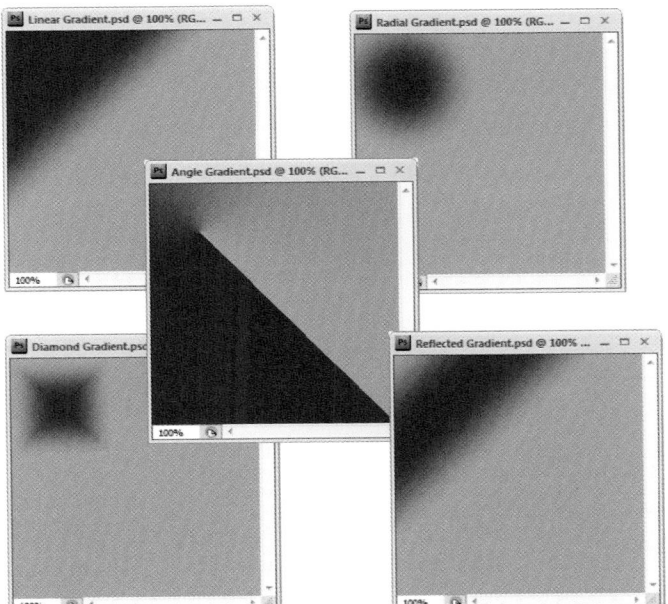

FIGURE 24
Gradient Editor dialog box

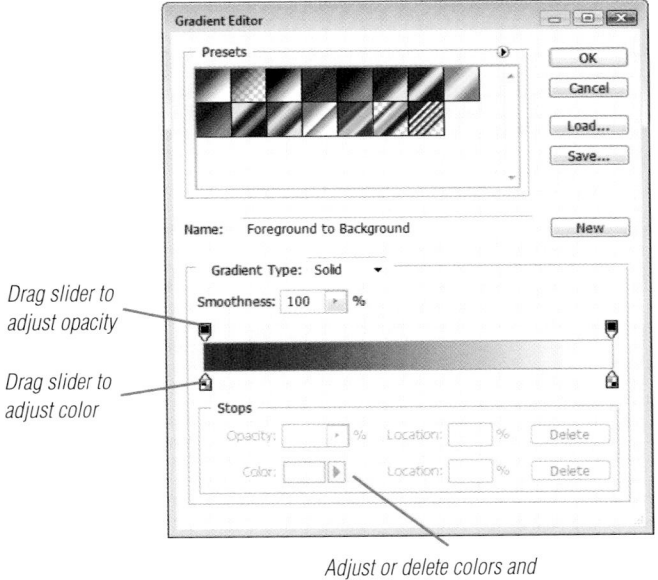

Drag slider to adjust opacity

Drag slider to adjust color

Adjust or delete colors and opacity values

Create a gradient from a sample color

1. Verify that the **Eyedropper tool** is selected.

2. Click the **yellow neck** in the image at coordinates **500 X/600 Y**.

   TIP To accurately select the coordinates, adjust the zoom factor as necessary.

3. Click the **Switch Foreground and Background Colors button** on the Tools panel.

4. Click the **Maroon swatch** (R=180 G=25 B=29) on the Swatches panel (one of the new swatches you added) with the **Eyedropper pointer**.

5. Click the **Indicates layer visibility button** on the Rooster layer, as shown in Figure 25.

6. Click the **Paint Bucket tool** on the Tools panel, then press and hold the mouse button until the list of hidden tools opens.

7. Click the **Gradient tool** on the Tools panel, then click the **Angle Gradient button** on the options bar (if it is not already selected).

8. Click the **Click to open Gradient picker list arrow** on the options bar, then click **Foreground to Background** (the first gradient fill in the first row), as shown in Figure 26.

You sampled a color on the image to set the background color, changed the foreground color using an existing swatch, selected the Gradient tool, and then chose a gradient fill and style.

FIGURE 25
Rooster layer hidden

Maroon swatch

Rooster layer is hidden

Background layer is active

Click to open Gradient picker list arrow

FIGURE 26
Gradient picker

Foreground to Background (Current foreground and background colors)

Gradient styles

Gradient picker

FIGURE 27
Gradient fill applied to Background layer

1. Click the **Click to open Gradient picker list arrow** to close the Gradient picker.

   TIP You can also close the Gradient picker by pressing [Esc] (Win) or [esc] (Mac).

2. Drag the **Gradient pointer** -+- from **1430 X/200 Y** to **200 X/1500 Y** using the Info panel and the guides to help you create the gradient in the work area.

3. Click the **Indicates layer visibility button** on the Rooster layer.

   The Rooster layer appears against the new background, as shown in Figure 27.

   TIP It is a good practice to save your work early and often in the creation process, especially before making significant changes or printing.

4. Save your work.

You applied the gradient fill to the background. You can create dramatic effects using the gradient fill in combination with foreground and background colors.

Collaborating with ConnectNow

Adobe has created a tool to help you collaborate with others: ConnectNow. This online tool lets you share information and collaborate with others. Using screen sharing, chat, shared notes, audio, and video, you can more effectively manage your workflow and get your work done. Open ConnectNow from within Photoshop by clicking File on the Application bar, then clicking Share My Screen or type *www.adobe.com/acom/connect-now* in your favorite browser. Once you have logged into Adobe ConnectNow, you can invite participants, share your computer screen, and upload files. ConnectNow uses the metaphor of a meeting, into which you invite participants and use pod tools to interact. When you are finished, you click the End Meeting command from the Meeting menu. You can use the Connections panel in Photoshop by clicking Window on the Application bar, pointing to Extensions, then clicking Connections to log in and check for updates.

ADD COLOR TO A
GRAYSCALE IMAGE

What You'll Do

 In this lesson, you'll convert an image to grayscale, change the color mode, then colorize a grayscale image using the Hue/Saturation dialog box.

Colorizing Options

Grayscale images can contain up to 256 shades of gray, assigning a brightness value from 0 (black) to 255 (white) to each pixel. Since the earliest days of photography, people have been tinting grayscale images with color to create a certain mood or emphasize an image in a way that purely realistic colors could not. To capture this effect in Photoshop, you convert an image to the Grayscale mode, then choose the color mode you want to work in before you continue. When you apply a color to a grayscale image, each pixel becomes a shade of that particular color instead of gray.

Converting Grayscale and Color Modes

When you convert a color image to grayscale, the light and dark values—called the **luminosity**—remain, while the color information is deleted. When you change from grayscale to a color mode, the foreground and background colors on the Tools panel change from black and white to the previously selected colors.

Converting a color image to black and white

Using the Black & White command, you can easily convert a color image to black and white. This feature lets you quickly make the color to black and white conversion while maintaining full control over how individual colors are converted. Tones can also be applied to the grayscale by applying color tones (the numeric values for each color). To use this feature, click Image on the menu bar, point to Adjustments, then click Black & White. The Black & White command can also be applied as an Adjustment layer.

Tweaking Adjustments

Once you have made your color mode conversion to grayscale, you may want to make some adjustments. You can fine-tune the Brightness/Contrast, filters, and blending modes in a grayscale image.

Colorizing a Grayscale Image

In order for a grayscale image to be colorized, you must change the color mode to one that accommodates color. After you change the color mode, and then adjust settings in the Hue/Saturation dialog box, Photoshop determines the colorization range based on the hue of the currently selected foreground color. If you want a different colorization range, you need to change the foreground color.

FIGURE 28
Gradient Map dialog box

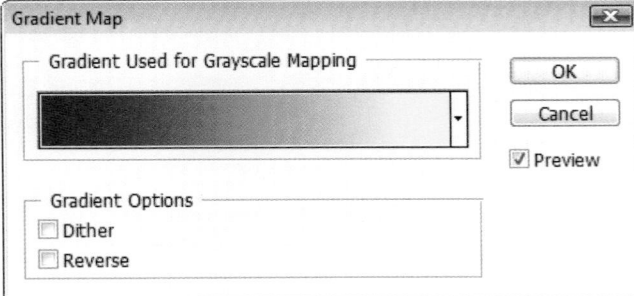

Applying a gradient effect

You can also use the Gradient Map to apply a colored gradient effect to a grayscale image. The Gradient Map uses gradient fills (the same ones displayed in the Gradient picker) to colorize the image, which can produce some stunning effects. You use the Gradient Map dialog box, shown in Figure 28, to apply a gradient effect to a grayscale image. You can access the Gradient Map dialog box using the Adjustments command on the Image menu.

Change the color mode

1. Open PS 4-2.psd from the drive and folder where you store your Data Files, save it as **Rooster Colorized**, then turn off the rulers if they are displayed.

2. Click **Image** on the Application bar, point to **Mode**, then click **Grayscale**.

3. Click **Flatten** in the warning box, then click **Discard**.

   The color mode of the image is changed to grayscale, and the image is flattened so there is only a single layer. All the color information in the image has been discarded.

4. Click **Image** on the Application bar, point to **Mode**, then click **RGB Color**.

   The color mode is changed back to RGB color, although there is still no color in the image. Compare your screen to Figure 29.

You converted the image to Grayscale, which discarded the existing color information. Then you changed the color mode to RGB color.

FIGURE 29
Image with RGB mode

Mode changed
to RGB

Converting color images to grayscale

Like everything else in Photoshop, there is more than one way of converting a color image into one that is black and white. Changing the color mode to grayscale is the quickest method. You can also make this conversion through desaturation by clicking Image on the menu bar, pointing to Adjustments, then clicking Black & White, or Desaturate. Converting to Grayscale mode generally results in losing contrast, as does the desaturation method, while using the Black & White method retains the contrast of the original image.

Incorporating Color Techniques

FIGURE 30

Hue/Saturation dialog box

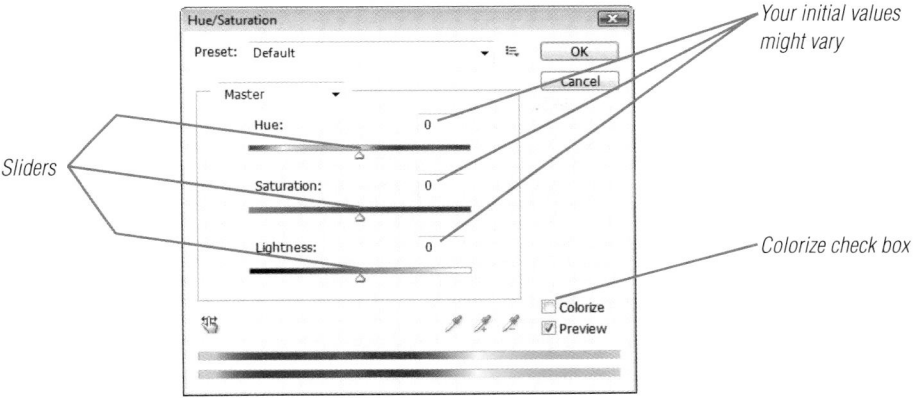

Sliders

Your initial values might vary

Colorize check box

FIGURE 31

Colorized image

1. Click **Image** on the Application bar, point to **Adjustments**, then click **Hue/Saturation** to open the Hue/Saturation dialog box, as shown in Figure 30.

2. Click the **Colorize check box** in the Hue/Saturation dialog box to add a check mark.

3. Drag the **Hue slider** until the text box displays **240**.

   TIP   You can also type values in the text boxes in the Hue/Saturation dialog box. Negative numbers must be preceded by a minus sign or a hyphen. Positive numbers can be preceded by an optional plus sign (+).

4. Drag the **Saturation slider** until the text box displays **55**.

5. Drag the **Lightness slider** until the text box displays **-15**.

6. Click **OK**.

7. Save your work, then compare your screen to Figure 31.

You colorized a grayscale image by adjusting settings in the Hue/Saturation dialog box.

Understanding the Hue/Saturation dialog box

The Hue/Saturation dialog box is an important tool in the world of color enhancement. Useful for both color and grayscale images, the saturation slider can be used to boost a range of colors. By clicking the Edit list arrow, you can isolate which colors (all, cyan, blue, magenta, red, yellow, or green) you want to modify. Using this tool requires patience and experimentation, but gives you great control over the colors in your image.

USE FILTERS, OPACITY,
AND BLENDING MODES

What You'll Do

 In this lesson, you'll adjust the brightness and contrast in the Rooster colorized image, apply a Sharpen filter, and adjust the opacity of the lines applied by the filter. You'll also adjust the color balance of the Rooster image.

Manipulating an Image

As you work in Photoshop, you might realize that some images have fundamental problems that need correcting, while others just need to be further enhanced. For example, you might need to adjust an image's contrast and sharpness, or you might want to colorize an otherwise dull image. You can use a variety of techniques to change the way an image looks. For example, you have learned how to use the Adjustments command on the Image menu to modify hue and saturation, but you can also use this command to adjust brightness and contrast, color balance, and a host of other visual effects.

Understanding Filters

Filters are Photoshop commands that can significantly alter an image's appearance. Experimenting with Photoshop's filters is a fun way to completely change the look of an image. For example, the Watercolor filter gives the illusion that your image was

Fixing blurry scanned images

An unfortunate result of scanning a picture is that the image can become blurry. You can fix this, however, using the Unsharp Mask filter. This filter both sharpens and smoothes the image by increasing the contrast along element edges. Here's how it works: the smoothing effect removes stray marks, and the sharpening effect emphasizes contrasting neighboring pixels. Most scanners come with their own Unsharp Masks built into the TWAIN driver, but using Photoshop, you have access to a more powerful version of this filter. You can use Photoshop's Unsharp Mask to control the sharpening process by adjusting key settings. In most cases, your scanner's Unsharp Mask might not give you this flexibility. Regardless of the technical aspects, the result is a sharper image. You can apply the Unsharp Mask by clicking Filter on the menu bar, pointing to Sharpen, then clicking Unsharp Mask.

painted using traditional watercolors. Sharpen filters can appear to add definition to the entire image, or just the edges. Compare the different Sharpen filters applied in Figure 32. The **Sharpen More filter** increases the contrast of adjacent pixels and can focus a blurry image. Be careful not to overuse sharpening tools (or any filter), because you can create high-contrast lines or add graininess in color or brightness.

Choosing Blending Modes

A **blending mode** controls how pixels are made either darker or lighter based on underlying colors. Photoshop provides a variety of blending modes, listed in Table 1, to combine the color of the pixels in the current layer with those in layer(s) beneath it. You can see a list of blending modes by clicking the Add a layer style button on the Layers panel.

Understanding Blending Mode Components

You should consider the following underlying colors when planning a blending mode: **base color**, which is the original color of the image; **blend color**, which is the color you apply with a paint or edit tool; and **resulting color**, which is the color that is created as a result of applying the blend color.

Softening Filter Effects

Opacity can soften the line that the filter creates, but it doesn't affect the opacity of the entire layer. After a filter has been applied, you can modify the opacity and apply a blending mode using the Layers panel or the Fade dialog box. You can open the Fade dialog box by clicking Edit on the menu bar, then clicking the Fade command.

QUICKTIP
The Fade command appears only after a filter has been applied. When available, the command name includes the name of the applied filter.

Balancing Colors

As you adjust settings, such as hue and saturation, you might create unwanted imbalances in your image. You can adjust colors to correct or improve an image's appearance. For example, you can decrease a color by increasing the amount of its opposite color. You use the Color Balance dialog box to balance the color in an image.

FIGURE 32
Sharpen filters

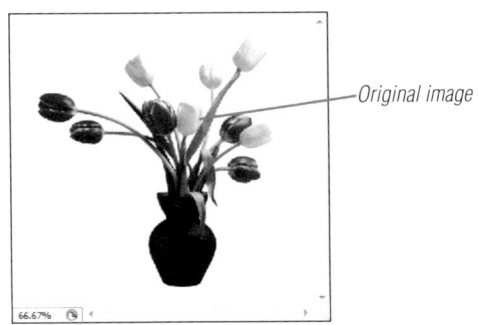

Original image

Sharpen filter applied

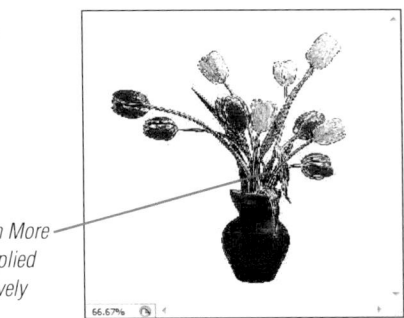

Sharpen More filter applied excessively

TABLE 1: Blending Modes

blending mode	description
Dissolve, Behind, and Clear modes	Dissolve mode creates a grainy, mottled appearance. The Behind mode paints on the transparent part of the layer—the lower the opacity, the grainier the image. The Clear mode paints individual pixels. All modes are available only when the Lock transparent pixels check box is *not* selected.
Multiply and Screen modes	Multiply mode creates semitransparent shadow effects. This mode assesses the information in each channel, then multiplies the value of the base color by the blend color. The resulting color is always *darker* than the base color. The Screen mode multiplies the value of the inverse of the blend and base colors. After it is applied, the resulting color is always *lighter* than the base color.
Overlay mode	Dark and light values (luminosity) are preserved, dark base colors are multiplied (darkened), and light areas are screened (lightened).
Soft Light and Hard Light modes	Soft Light lightens a light base color and darkens a dark base color. The Hard Light blending mode creates a similar effect, but provides greater contrast between the base and blend colors.
Color Dodge and Color Burn modes	Color Dodge mode brightens the base color to reflect the blend color. The Color Burn mode darkens the base color to reflect the blend color.
Darken and Lighten modes	Darken mode selects a new resulting color based on whichever color is darker—the base color or the blend color. The Lighten mode selects a new resulting color based on the lighter of the two colors.
Difference and Exclusion modes	The Difference mode subtracts the value of the blend color from the value of the base color, or vice versa, depending on which color has the greater brightness value. The Exclusion mode creates an effect similar to that of the Difference mode, but with less contrast between the blend and base colors.
Color and Luminosity modes	The Color mode creates a resulting color with the luminance of the base color, and the hue and saturation of the blend color. The Luminosity mode creates a resulting color with the hue and saturation of the base color, and the luminance of the blend color.
Hue and Saturation modes	The Hue mode creates a resulting color with the luminance of the base color and the hue of the blend color. The Saturation mode creates a resulting color with the luminance of the base color and the saturation of the blend color.

FIGURE 33
Brightness/Contrast dialog box

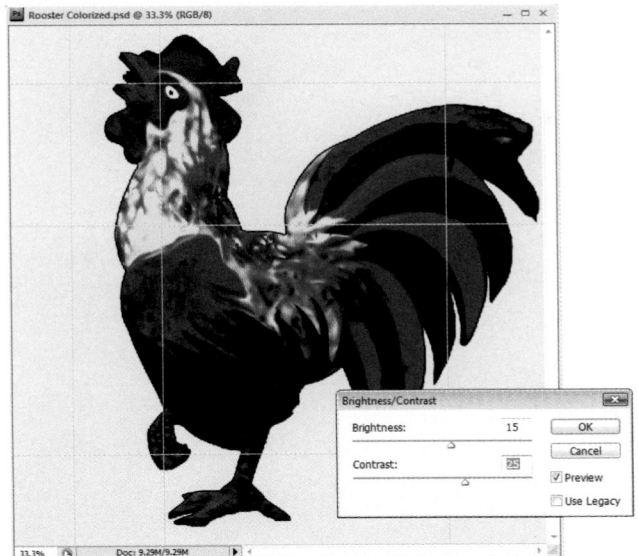

FIGURE 34
Shadows/Highlights dialog box

1. Click **Image** on the Application bar, point to **Adjustments**, then click **Brightness/Contrast** to open the Brightness/Contrast dialog box.

2. Drag the **Brightness slider** until **15** appears in the Brightness text box.

3. Drag the **Contrast slider** until **25** appears in the Contrast text box. Compare your screen to Figure 33.

4. Click **OK**.

You adjusted settings in the Brightness/Contrast dialog box. The image now looks much brighter, with a higher degree of contrast, which obscures some of the finer detail in the image.

Correcting shadows and highlights

The ability to correct shadows and highlights will delight photographers everywhere. This image correction feature (opened by clicking Image on the Application bar, pointing to Adjustments, then clicking Shadows/Highlights) lets you modify overall lighting and make subtle adjustments. Figure 34 shows the Shadows/Highlights dialog box with the Show More Options check box selected. Check out this one-stop shopping for shadow and highlight adjustments!

Work with a filter, a blending mode, and an opacity setting

1. Click **Filter** on the Application bar, point to **Sharpen**, then click **Sharpen More**.

   The border and other features of the image are intensified.

2. Click **Edit** on the Application bar, then click **Fade Sharpen More** to open the Fade dialog box, as shown in Figure 35.

3. Drag the **Opacity slider** until **45** appears in the Opacity text box.

   The opacity setting softened the lines applied by the Sharpen More filter.

4. Click the **Mode list arrow**, then click **Dissolve**.

   The Dissolve setting blends the surrounding pixels.

5. Click **OK**.

6. Save your work, then compare your image to Figure 36.

You applied the Sharpen More filter, then adjusted the opacity and changed the color mode in the Fade dialog box. The border in the image looks crisper than before, with a greater level of detail.

FIGURE 35
Fade dialog box

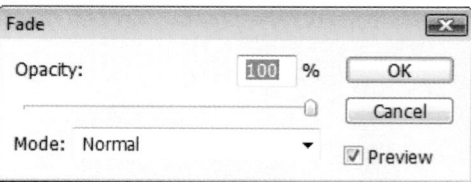

FIGURE 36
Image settings adjusted

FIGURE 37
Color Balance dialog box

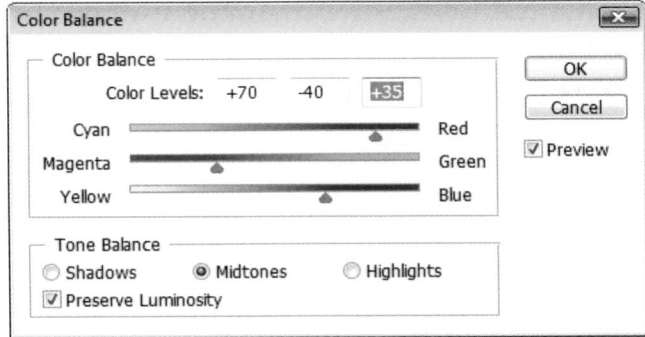

Adjust color balance

1. Switch to the Rooster image, with the Background layer active.

    The image you worked with earlier in this chapter becomes active.

2. Click **Image** on the Application bar, point to **Adjustments**, then click **Color Balance**.

3. Drag the **Cyan-Red slider** until **+70** appears in the first text box.

4. Drag the **Magenta-Green slider** until **–40** appears in the middle text box.

5. Drag the **Yellow-Blue slider** until **+35** appears in the last text box, as shown in Figure 37.

    Subtle changes were made in the color balance in the image.

6. Click **OK**.

7. Save your work, then compare your image to Figure 38.

You balanced the colors in the Rooster image by adjusting settings in the Color Balance dialog box.

FIGURE 38
Image with colors balanced

LESSON 7

MATCH COLORS

What You'll Do

In this lesson, you'll make selections in source and target images, then use the Match Color command to replace the target color.

Finding the Right Color

If it hasn't happened already, at some point you'll be working on an image and wish you could grab a color from another image to use in this one. Just as you can use the Eyedropper tool to sample any color in the current image for the foreground and background, you can sample a color from any other image to use in the current one. Perhaps the skin tones in one image look washed out: you can use the Match Color command to replace those tones with skin tone colors from another image. Or maybe the jacket color in one image would look better using a color in another image.

Using Selections to Match Colors

Remember that this is Photoshop, where everything is about layers and selections.

To replace a color in one image with one you've matched from another, you work with—you guessed it—layers and selections.

Suppose you've located the perfect color in another image. The image you are working with is the **target**, and the image that contains your perfect color is the **source**. By activating the layer on which the color lies in the source image, and making a selection around the color, you can have Photoshop match the color in the source and replace a color in the target. To accomplish this, you use the Match Color command, which is available by pointing to Adjustments on the Image menu.

FIGURE 39
Selection in source image

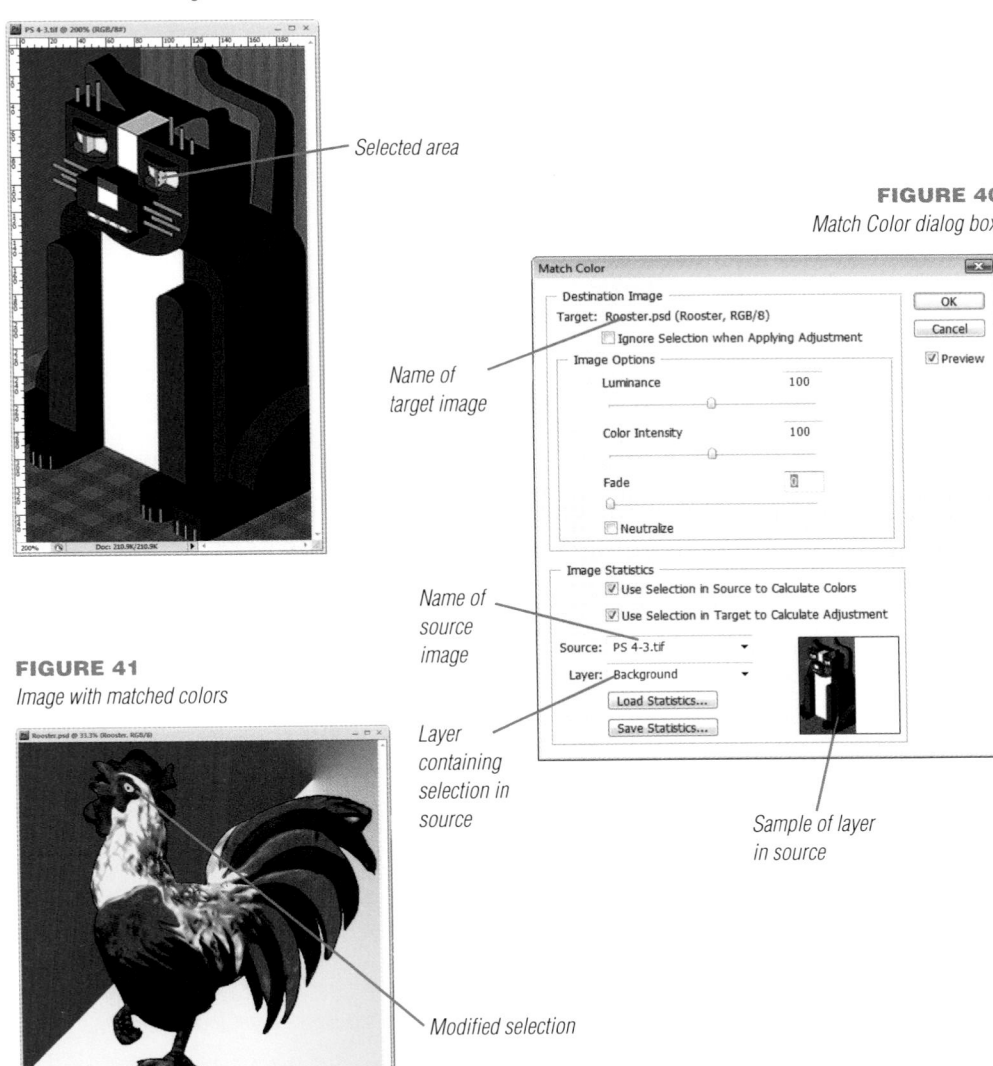

Selected area

FIGURE 40
Match Color dialog box

Name of
target image

Name of
source
image

FIGURE 41
Image with matched colors

Layer
containing
selection in
source

Sample of layer
in source

Modified selection

1. Click the **Rooster layer** on the Layers panel, then zoom (once) into the eye of the rooster.

2. Click the **Magic Wand tool** ✹ on the Tools panel.

3. Verify that the **Anti-alias** and **Contiguous check boxes** on the options bar are selected, then set the **Tolerance** to **10**.

4. Click the image with the **Magic Wand pointer** ✹ on the white of the eye at approximately **550 X/210 Y**.

5. Open PS 4-3.tif from the drive and folder where you store your Data Files, zoom into the image (if necessary), change the tolerance to **40**, then click the **light green part of the cat's eye** (at **100 X/95 Y**) with the **Magic Wand pointer** ✹. Compare your selection to Figure 39.

6. Activate the **Rooster image**, click **Image** on the Application bar, point to **Adjustments**, then click **Match Color**.

7. Click the **Source list arrow**, then click **PS 4-3.tif**. Compare your settings to Figure 40.

8. Click **OK**.

9. Deselect the selection, turn off the rulers and the guides, save your work, then compare your image to Figure 41.

10. Close all open images, display the Essentials workspace then exit Photoshop.

You used the Match Color dialog box to replace a color in one image with a color from another image. The Match Color dialog box makes it easy to sample colors from other images, giving you even more options for incorporating color into an image.

Power User Shortcuts

to do this:	use this method:
Apply a sharpen filter	Filter ➢ Sharpen
Balance colors	Image ➢ Adjustments ➢ Color Balance
Change color mode	Image ➢ Mode
Choose a background color from the Swatches panel	[Ctrl]Color swatch (Win) [⌘]Color swatch (Mac)
Delete a swatch from the Swatches panel	[Alt], click swatch (Win) [option], click swatch (Mac)
Eyedropper tool	⌖. or I
Fill with background color	[Shift][Backspace] (Win) [⌘][delete] (Mac)
Fill with foreground color	[Alt][Backspace] (Win) option [delete] (Mac)
Gradient tool	▦
Guide pointer	╫ or ╪
Hide a layer	👁

to do this:	use this method:
Hide or show rulers	[Ctrl][R] (Win) [⌘][R] (Mac)
Hide or show the Color panel	[F6] (Win) COLOR
Lock transparent pixels check box on/off	[/]
Make Swatches panel active	SWATCHES
Paint Bucket tool	▱ or G
Return background and foreground colors to default	◪ or D
Show a layer	▢
Show hidden Paint Bucket/ Gradient tools	[Shift] G
Switch between open files	[Ctrl][Tab] (Win) [control][tab] (Mac)
Switch foreground and background colors	↰ or X

Key: Menu items are indicated by ➢ between the menu name and its command. Blue bold letters are shortcuts for selecting tools on the Tools panel.

Work with color to transform an image.

1. Start Photoshop.
2. Open PS 4-4.psd from the drive and folder where you store your Data Files, then save it as **Firetruck**.
3. Make sure the rulers display in pixels, and that the default foreground and background colors display.
4. Use the Eyedropper tool to sample the red color at 90 X/165 Y using the guides to help.
5. Use the Paint Bucket tool to apply the new foreground color to the Background layer.
6. Undo your last step using either the Edit menu or the History panel. (*Hint:* You can switch to another workspace that displays the necessary panels.)
7. Switch the foreground and background colors.
8. Save your work.

Use the Color Picker and the Swatches panel.

1. Use the Set foreground color button to open the Color Picker dialog box.
2. Click the R:, G:, and B: option buttons, one at a time. Note how the color panel changes.
3. With the B: option button selected, click the panel in the upper-left corner, then click OK.
4. Switch the foreground and background colors.
5. Add the foreground color (red) to the Swatches panel using a meaningful name of your choice.

Place a border around an image.

1. Make Layer 1 active (if it is not already active).
2. Revert to the default foreground and background colors.

3. Create a border by applying a 2-pixel outside stroke to the firetruck.
4. Save your work.

Blend colors using the Gradient tool.

1. Change the foreground color to the sixth swatch from the right in the top row of the Swatches panel (35% Gray). (Your swatch location may vary.)
2. Switch foreground and background colors.
3. Use the new red swatch that you added previously as the foreground color.
4. Make the Background layer active.
5. Use the Gradient tool, apply the Angle Gradient with its default settings, then using the guides to help, drag the pointer from 145 X/70 Y to 35 X/165 Y.
6. Save your work, and turn off the rulers display.

Add color to a grayscale image.

1. Open PS 4-5.psd, then save it as **Firetruck Colorized**.
2. Change the color mode to RGB Color.
3. Open the Hue/Saturation dialog box, then select the Colorize check box.
4. Drag the sliders so the text boxes show the following values: 155, 56, and -30, then click OK.
5. Save your work.

Use filters, opacity, and blending modes.

1. Use the Sharpen filter to sharpen the image.
2. Open the Fade Sharpen dialog box by using the Edit menu, change the opacity to 40%,

change the mode to Hard Light, then save your work.
3. Open the Color Balance dialog box.
4. Change the color level settings so the text boxes show the following values: +61, -15, and +20.
5. Turn off the rulers display (if necessary).
6. Save your work.

Match colors.

1. Open PS 4-6.tif, then use the Magic Wand tool to select the light yellow in the cat's eye.
2. Select the white areas of the firetruck cab in Firetruck.psd. (*Hint:* You can press [Shift] and click on multiple areas using the Magic Wand tool.)
3. Use the Match Color dialog box to change the white in Layer 1 of the firetruck image to yellow (in the cat's eye). Compare your images to Figure 42. (The brightness of your colors may vary.)
4. Save your work.
5. Exit Photoshop.

FIGURE 42
Completed Skills Review

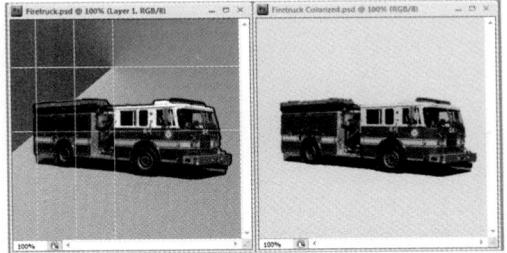

You are finally able to leave your current job and pursue your lifelong dream of opening a furniture repair and restoration business. While you're waiting for the laser stripper and refinisher to arrive, you start to work on a sign design.

1. Open PS 4-7.psd, substitute any missing fonts, then save it as **Furniture Fixer**.
2. Move the objects to any location to achieve a layout you think looks attractive and eye-catching.
3. Sample the blue pliers in the tool belt, then switch the foreground and background colors.
4. Sample the red tape measure in the tool belt.
5. Use any Gradient tool to create an interesting effect on the Background layer.
6. Save the image, then compare your screen to the sample shown in Figure 43.

FIGURE 43

Completed Project Builder 1

Incorporating Color Techniques

You're painting the swing set at the PB&J Preschool, when you notice a staff member struggling to create a flyer for the school. Although the basic flyer is complete, it doesn't convey the high energy of the school. You offer to help, and soon find yourself in charge of creating an exciting background for the image.

1. Open PS 4-8.psd, update layers as needed, then save it as **Preschool**.
2. Apply a foreground color of your choice to the Background layer.
3. Add a new layer above the Background layer, then select a background color and apply a gradient you have not used before to the layer. (*Hint*: Remember that you can immediately undo a gradient that you don't want.)
4. Add the foreground and background colors to the Swatches panel.
5. Apply a Sharpen filter to the Boy at blackboard layer and adjust the opacity of the filter.
6. Save your work.
7. Compare your screen to the sample shown in Figure 44.

FIGURE 44
Completed Project Builder 2

Incorporating Color Techniques

A local Top 40 morning radio show recently conducted a survey about chocolate, and discovered that only one in seven people knew about its health benefits. Now everyone is talking about chocolate. An interior designer wants to incorporate chocolates into her fall decorating theme, and has asked you to create a poster. You decide to highlight as many varieties as possible.

1. Open PS 4-9.psd, then save it as **Chocolate**.
2. If you choose, you can add any appropriate images that have been scanned or captured using a digital camera.
3. Activate the Background layer, then sample colors from the image for foreground and background colors. (*Hint*: Try to sample unusual colors, to widen your design horizons.)
4. Add the sampled colors to the Swatches panel.
5. Display the rulers, then move the existing guides to indicate the coordinates of the colors you sampled.
6. Create a gradient fill by using both the foreground and background colors and the gradient style of your choice.
7. Defringe the Chocolate layer, if necessary.
8. Hide the rulers, save your work, then compare your image to the sample shown in Figure 45.

FIGURE 45
Completed Design Project

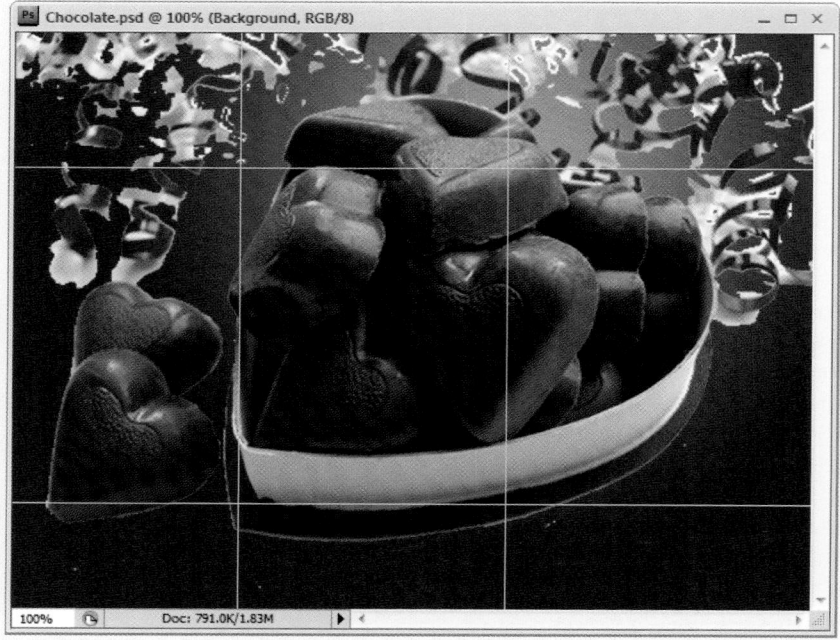

Incorporating Color Techniques

An educational toy and game store has hired you to design a poster announcing this year's Most Unusual Hobby contest. After reviewing the photos from last year's awards ceremony, you decide to build a poster using the winner of the Handicrafts Award. You'll use your knowledge of Photoshop color modes to convert the color mode, adjust color in the image, and add an interesting background.

1. Open PS 4-10.psd, then save it as **Rubberband**.
2. Convert the image to Grayscale mode. (*Hint*: When Photoshop prompts you to flatten the layers, click Don't Flatten.)
3. Convert the image to RGB Color mode. (*Hint*: When Photoshop prompts you to flatten the layers, click Don't Flatten.)
4. Colorize the image and adjust the Hue, Saturation, and Lightness settings as desired.
5. Adjust Brightness/Contrast settings as desired.
6. Adjust Color Balance settings as desired.
7. Sample the image to create a new foreground color, then add a color of your choice as the background color.
8. Apply any two Sharpen filters and adjust the opacity for one of them.
9. Add a reflected gradient to the Background layer that follows the path of one of the main bands on the ball.

10. Save your work, then compare your image to the sample shown in Figure 46.
11. Be prepared to discuss the color-correcting methods you used and why you chose them.

FIGURE 46
Completed Portfolio Project

chapter

5

PLACING TYPE IN
AN IMAGE

1. Learn about type and how it is created

2. Change spacing and adjust baseline shift

3. Use the Drop Shadow style

4. Apply anti-aliasing to type

5. Modify type with the Bevel and Emboss style

6. Apply special effects to type using filters

7. Create text on a path

Learning About Type

Text plays an important design role when combined with images for posters, magazine and newspaper advertisements, and other graphics materials that need to communicate detailed information. In Photoshop, text is referred to as **type**. You can use type to express the ideas conveyed in a file's imagery or to deliver an additional message. You can manipulate type in many ways to reflect or reinforce the meaning behind an image. As in other programs, type has its own unique characteristics in Photoshop. For example, you can change its appearance by using different fonts (also called typefaces) and colors.

Understanding the Purpose of Type

Type is typically used along with imagery to deliver a message quickly and with flare. Because type is used sparingly (often there's not a lot of room for it), its appearance is very important; color and imagery are frequently used to *complement* or *reinforce* the message within the text. Type should be limited, direct, and to the point. It should be large enough for easy reading, but should not overwhelm or distract from the central image. For example, a vibrant and daring advertisement should contain just enough type to interest the reader, without demanding too much reading.

Getting the Most Out of Type

Words can express an idea, but the appearance of the type is what drives the point home. After you decide on the content you want to use and create the type, you can experiment with its appearance by changing its **font** (characters with a similar appearance), size, and color. You can also apply special effects that make it stand out, or appear to pop off the page.

Tools You'll Use

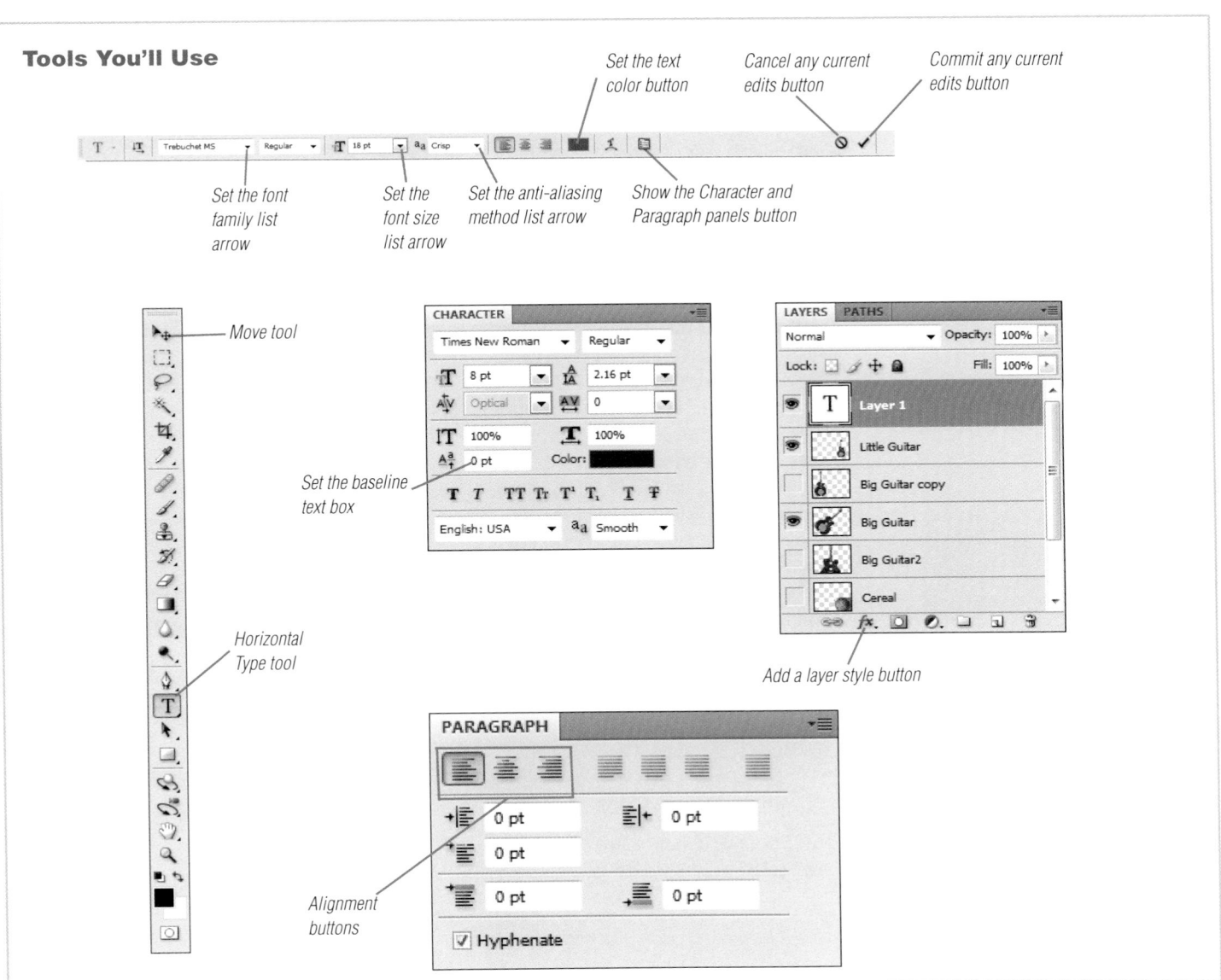

Set the text color button

Cancel any current edits button

Commit any current edits button

Set the font family list arrow

Set the font size list arrow

Set the anti-aliasing method list arrow

Show the Character and Paragraph panels button

Move tool

Horizontal Type tool

Set the baseline text box

Add a layer style button

Alignment buttons

LEARN ABOUT TYPE AND
HOW IT IS CREATED

What You'll Do

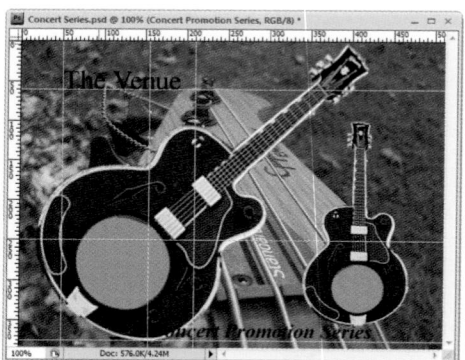

In this lesson, you'll create a type layer, then change the alignment, font family, size, and color of the type.

Introducing Type Types

Outline type is mathematically defined, which means that it can be scaled to any size without losing its sharp, smooth edges. Some programs, such as Adobe Illustrator, create outline type, also known as **vector fonts**. **Bitmap type** is composed of pixels, and, like images, can develop jagged edges when enlarged. The type you create in Photoshop is initially outline type, but it is converted into bitmap type when you apply special filters. Using the type tools and the options bar, you can create horizontal or vertical type and modify font size and alignment. You use the Color Picker dialog box to change type color. When you create type in Photoshop, it is automatically placed on a new type layer on the Layers panel.

QUICKTIP
Keeping type on separate layers makes it much easier to modify and change positions within the image.

Getting to Know Font Families

Each **font family** represents a complete set of characters, letters, and symbols for a particular typeface. Font families are generally divided into three categories: serif, sans serif, and symbol. Characters in **serif fonts** have a tail, or stroke, at the end of some characters. These tails make it easier for the eye to recognize words. For this reason, serif fonts are generally used in text passages. **Sans serif fonts** do not have tails and are commonly used in headlines.

TIP The Verdana typeface was designed primarily for use on a computer screen.

Symbol fonts are used to display unique characters (such as $, ÷, or ™). Table 1 lists some commonly used serif and sans serif fonts. After you select the Horizontal Type tool, you can change font families using the options bar.

Measuring Type Size

The size of each character within a font is measured in **points**. **PostScript**, a programming language that optimizes printed text and graphics, was introduced by Adobe in 1985. In PostScript measurement, one inch is equivalent to 72 points or six picas. Therefore, one pica is equivalent to 12 points. In traditional measurement, one inch is equivalent to 72.27 points. The default Photoshop type size is 12 points. In Photoshop, you have the option of using PostScript or traditional character measurement.

Acquiring Fonts

Your computer has many fonts installed on it, but no matter how many fonts you have, you probably can use more. Fonts can be purchased from private companies, individual designers, computer stores, or catalog companies. Fonts are delivered on CD, DVD, or over the Internet. Using your browser and your favorite search engine, you can locate websites where you can purchase or download fonts. Many websites offer specialty fonts, such as the website shown in Figure 1. Other websites offer these fonts free of charge or for a nominal fee.

TABLE 1: Commonly Used Serif and Sans Serif Fonts

serif fonts	sample	sans serif fonts	sample
Lucida Handwriting	*Adobe Photoshop*	Arial	Adobe Photoshop
Rockwell	Adobe Photoshop	Bauhaus	Adobe Photoshop
Times New Roman	Adobe Photoshop	Century Gothic	Adobe Photoshop

FIGURE 1
Font website

Courtesy of Fonts.com - http://fonts.com/

Create and modify type

1. Start Photoshop, open PS 5-1.psd from the drive and folder where you store your Data Files, update the layers (if necessary), then save the file as **Concert Series**.

2. Display the document size in the status bar, the rulers in pixels (if they are not already displayed), and change the workspace to **Typography**.

   TIP You can quickly toggle the rulers on and off by pressing [Ctrl][R] (Win) or ⌘[R] (Mac).

3. Click the **Default Foreground and Background Colors button** 🔳 on the Tools panel.

4. Click the **Horizontal Type tool** T. on the Tools panel.

5. Click the **Set the font family list arrow** on the options bar, click **Arial** (a sans serif font), click the **Set the font style list arrow**, then click **Italic**.

   TIP If Arial is not available, make a reasonable substitution.

6. Click the **Set the font size list arrow** on the options bar, then click **6 pt** (if it is not already selected).

7. Click the image with the **Horizontal Type pointer** 🫙 at approximately **155 X/375 Y**, then type **Concert Promotion Series** as shown in Figure 2.

You created a type layer by using the Horizontal Type tool on the Tools panel and modified the font family and font size.

FIGURE 2
New type in image

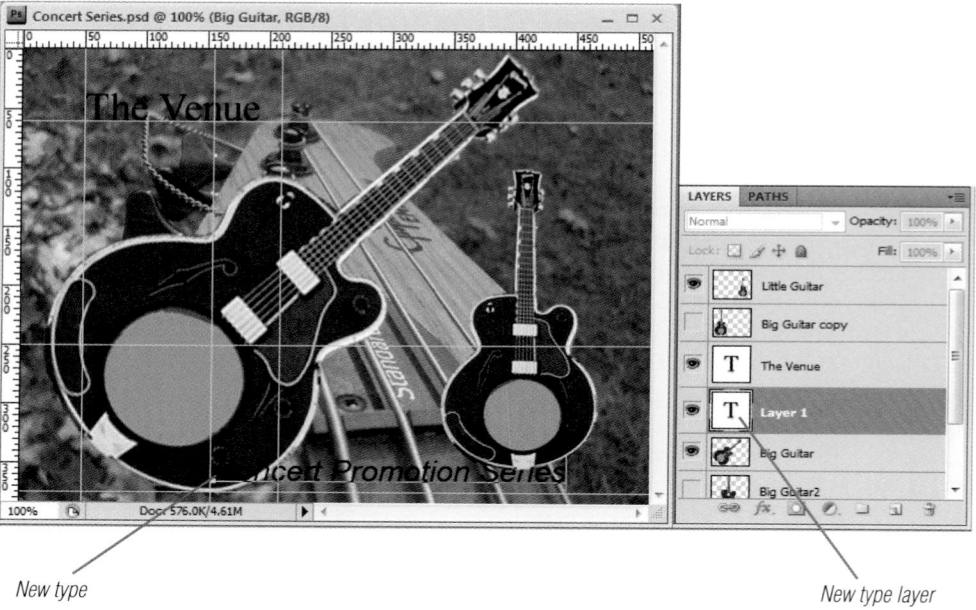

New type

New type layer

Using the active layer panel background (Macintosh)
Icons used in Macintosh to identify type layers are similar to those found in Windows. In Macintosh, the active layer has the same Type and Layer style buttons. The active layer's background color is the same color as the color used to highlight a selected item. (In Windows, the active layer's background color is a dark cyan blue.)

FIGURE 3

Type with new color

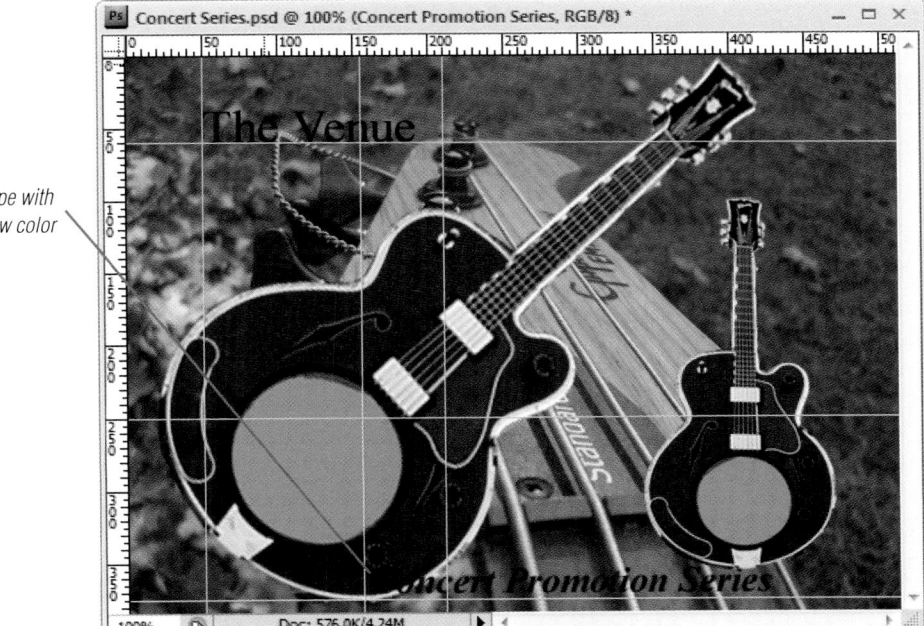

Type with
new color

1. Press **[Ctrl][A]** (Win) or ⌘**[A]** (Mac) to select all the text.

2. Click the **Set the font family list arrow** on the options bar, scroll down, then click **Times New Roman**.

   TIP   Click in the Set the font family text box and you can select a different font by typing the first few characters of the font name. Scroll through the fonts by clicking in the Set the font family text box, then pressing the [UpArrow] or [DownArrow].

3. Click the **Set the font style list arrow**, then click **Bold Italic**.

4. Click the **Set the text color button** ▬ on the options bar.

   TIP   Drag the Set text color dialog box out of the way if it blocks your view of the image.

   As you position the pointer over the image, the pointer automatically becomes an Eyedropper pointer.

5. Click the image with the **Eyedropper pointer** 🖋 anywhere in the blue area at the top of the large guitar at approximately **155 X/175 Y**.

   The new color is now the active color in the Set text color dialog box.

6. Click **OK** in the Select text color dialog box.

7. Click the **Commit any current edits button** ✓ on the options bar.

   Clicking the Commit any current edits button accepts your changes and makes them permanent in the image.

8. Save your work, then compare your image to Figure 3.

You changed the font family, modified the color of the type by using an existing image color, and committed the current edits.

Using the Swatches panel to change type color

You can also use the Swatches panel to change type color. Select the type, then click a color on the Swatches panel. The new color that you click will appear in the Set foreground color button on the Tools panel and will be applied to type that is currently selected.

CHANGE SPACING AND
ADJUST BASELINE SHIFT

What You'll Do

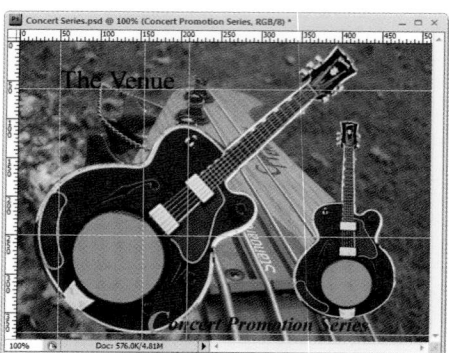

 In this lesson, you'll adjust the spacing between characters and change the baseline of type.

Adjusting Spacing

Competition for readers on the visual landscape is fierce. To get and maintain an edge over other designers, Photoshop provides tools that let you make adjustments to your type, offering you the opportunity to make your type more distinctive. These adjustments might not be very dramatic, but they can influence readers in subtle ways. For example, type that is too small and difficult to read might make the reader impatient (at the very least), and he or she might not even look at the image (at the very worst). You can make finite adjustments, called **type spacing**, to the space between characters and between lines of type. Adjusting type spacing affects the ease with which words are read.

Understanding Character and Line Spacing

Fonts in desktop publishing and word processing programs use proportional spacing, whereas typewriters use monotype spacing. In **monotype spacing**, each character occupies the same amount of space. This means that wide characters such as "o" and "w" take up the same real estate on the page as narrow ones such as "i" and "l". In **proportional spacing**, each character can take up a different amount of space, depending on its width. **Kerning** controls the amount of space between characters and can affect several characters, a word, or an entire paragraph. **Tracking** inserts a *uniform* amount of space between selected characters. Figure 4 shows an example of type before and after it has been kerned.

The second line of text takes up less room and has less space between its characters, making it easier to read. You can also change the amount of space, called **leading**, between lines of type, to add or decrease the distance between lines of text.

Using the Character Panel

The **Character panel**, shown in Figure 5, helps you manually or automatically control type properties such as kerning, tracking, and leading. You open the Character panel from the options bar and the Dock.

Adjusting the Baseline Shift

Type rests on an invisible line called a **baseline**. Using the Character panel, you can adjust the **baseline shift**, the vertical distance that type moves from its baseline. You can add interest to type by changing the baseline shift. Negative adjustments to the baseline move characters *below* the baseline, while positive adjustments move characters *above* the baseline.

QUICKTIP

Clicking the Set the text color button on either the options bar or the Character panel opens the Select text color dialog box.

FIGURE 4
Kerned characters

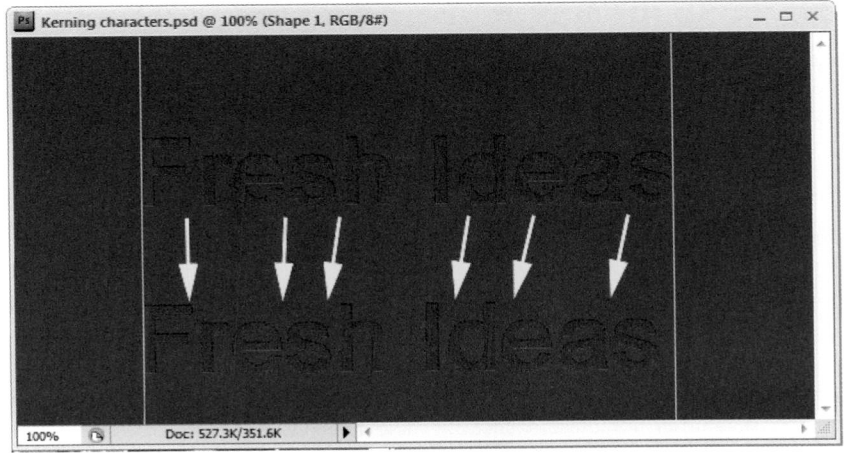

FIGURE 5
Character panel

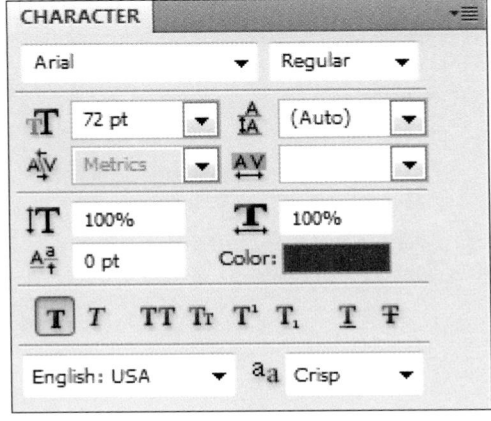

Kern characters

1. Click the **Concert Promotion Series type layer** on the Layers panel (if it is not already selected).

2. Click the **Horizontal Type tool** T. on the Tools panel.

3. Click between "r" and "i" in the word "Series."

4. Click the **Set the kerning between two characters list arrow** A͢V on the Character panel, then click **–25**.

   The spacing between the two characters decreases.

   TIP   You can close the Character panel by clicking the list arrow in the upper-right corner of its title bar then clicking the Close command. You can also open and close the Character panel by clicking the Character button on the vertical dock.

5. Click between "i" and "o" in the word "Promotion."

6. Click A͢V , then click **–25**, as shown in Figure 6.

7. Click the **Commit any current edits button** ✔ on the options bar.

You modified the kerning between characters by using the Character panel.

FIGURE 6
Kerned type

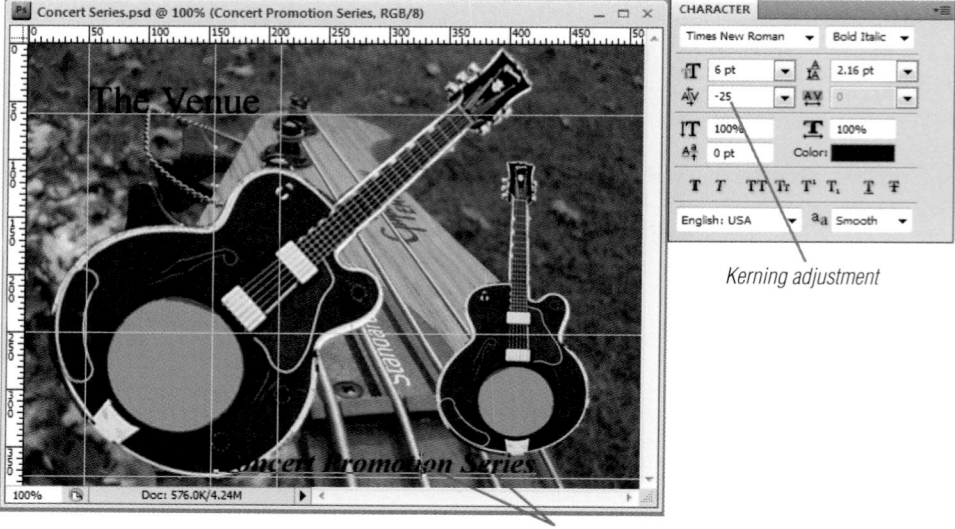

Kerning adjustment

Kerned type

Correcting spelling errors

Are you concerned that your gorgeous image will be ruined by misspelled words? Photoshop understands your pain and has included a spelling checker to make sure you are never plagued by incorrect spellings. If you want, the spelling checker will check the type on the current layer, or all the layers in the image. First, make sure the correct dictionary for your language is selected. English: USA is the default, but you can choose another language by clicking the Set the language on selected characters for hyphenation and spelling list arrow at the bottom of the Character panel. To check spelling, click Edit on the Application bar, then click Check Spelling. The spelling checker will automatically stop at each word not already appearing in the dictionary. One or more suggestions might be offered, which you can either accept or reject.

FIGURE 7
Select text color dialog box

Your color field may differ (Mac)

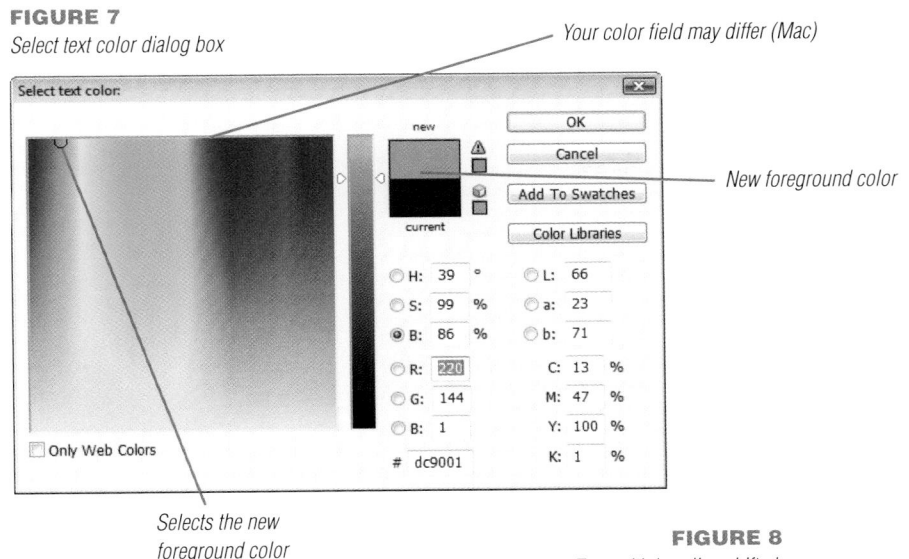

New foreground color

Selects the new
foreground color

FIGURE 8
Type with baseline shifted

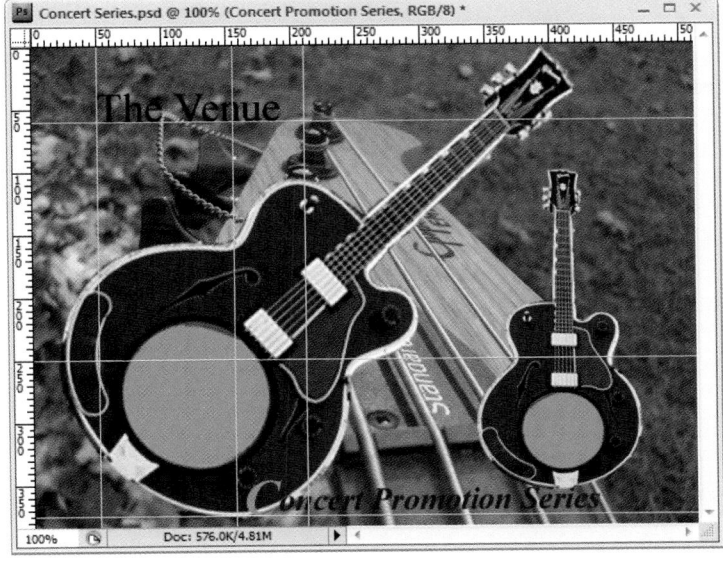

Lesson 2   Change Spacing and Adjust Baseline Shift

1. Use the **Horizontal Type pointer** 𝐈 to select the "C" in "Concert".

2. Click the **Set the text color button** ▬ on the options bar.

3. Click anywhere in the gold area in the center of either guitar, such as **100 X/250 Y**, compare your Select text color dialog box to Figure 7, then click **OK**.

4. Double-click **6** in the Set the font size text box on the Character panel, type **10**, double-click **0** in the Set the baseline shift text box on the Character panel, then type **–1**.

5. Click the **Commit any current edits button** ✔ on the options bar.

6. Save your work, then compare your screen to Figure 8.

You changed the type color, then adjusted the baseline of the first character in a word, to make the first character stand out.

USE THE DROP
SHADOW STYLE

What You'll Do

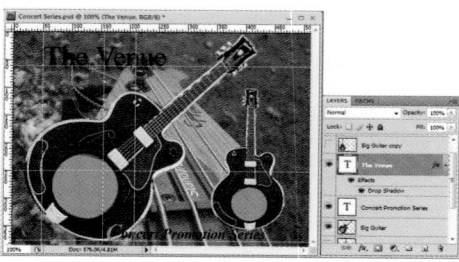

In this lesson, you'll apply the drop shadow style to a type layer, then modify drop shadow settings.

Adding Effects to Type

Layer styles (effects which can be applied to a type or image layer) can greatly enhance the appearance of type and improve its effectiveness. A type layer is indicated by the appearance of the T icon in the layer's thumbnail box. When a layer style is applied to any layer, the Indicates layer effects icon (*fx*) appears in that layer when it is active. The Layers panel is a great source of information. You can see which effects have been applied to a layer by clicking the arrow to the left of the Indicates layer effects icon on the Layers panel if the layer is active or inactive. Figure 9 shows a layer that has two type layer styles applied to it. Layer styles are linked to the contents of a layer, which means that if a type layer is moved or modified, the layer's style will still be applied to the type.

Using the Drop Shadow

One method of placing emphasis on type is to add a drop shadow to it. A **drop shadow** creates an illusion that another colored layer of identical text is behind the selected type. The drop shadow default color is black, but it can be changed to another color using the Color Picker dialog box, or any of the other methods for changing color.

Applying a Style

You can apply a style, such as a drop shadow, to the active layer, by clicking Layer on the Application bar, pointing to Layer Style, then clicking a style.

The settings in the Layer Style dialog box are "sticky," meaning that they display the settings that you last used. An alternative method to using the Application bar is to select the layer that you want to apply the style to, click the Add a layer style button on the Layers panel, then click a style. Regardless of which method you use, the Layer Style dialog box opens. You use this dialog box to add all kinds of effects to type. Depending on which style you've chosen, the Layer Style dialog box displays options appropriate to that style.

QUICKTIP
You can apply styles to objects as well as to type.

Controlling a Drop Shadow

You can control many aspects of a drop shadow's appearance, including its angle, its distance behind the type, and the amount of blur it contains. The **angle** determines where the shadow falls relative to the text, and the **distance** determines how far the shadow falls from the text. The **spread** determines the width of the shadow text,

and the **size** determines the clarity of the shadow. Figure 10 shows samples of two different drop shadow effects. The first line of type uses the default background color (black), has an angle of 160 degrees, a distance of 10 pixels, a spread of 0%, and a size of five pixels. The second line of type uses a purple background color, has an angle of 120 degrees, a distance of 20 pixels, a spread of 10%, and a size of five pixels. As you modify the drop shadow, the preview window displays the changes.

FIGURE 9
Effects in a type layer

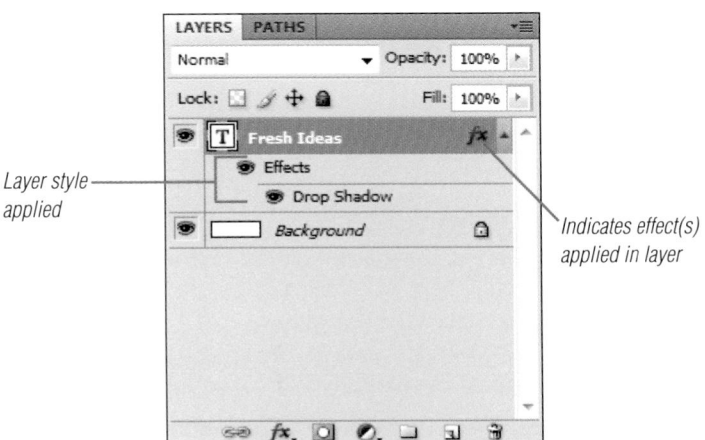

Layer style applied

Indicates effect(s) applied in layer

FIGURE 10
Sample drop shadows

Add a drop shadow

1. Click the **layer thumbnail** on The Venue type layer.

2. Double-click **8** in the Set the font size text box in the Character panel, type **12**, then press **[Enter]** (Win) or **[return]** (Mac).

3. Click the **Add a layer style button** *fx.* on the Layers panel.

   > TIP You can make your life easier by creating your own styles. Do you apply the stroke effect often? You can create your own stroke style by clicking the Add a layer style button on the Layers panel, clicking Stroke, entering your settings, then clicking New Style.

4. Click **Drop Shadow**.

5. Compare your Layer Style dialog box to Figure 11.

   The default drop shadow settings are applied to the type. Table 2 describes the drop shadow settings.

   > TIP You can also open the Layer Style dialog box by double-clicking a layer on the Layers panel.

You created a drop shadow by using the Add a layer style button on the Layers panel and the Layer Style dialog box.

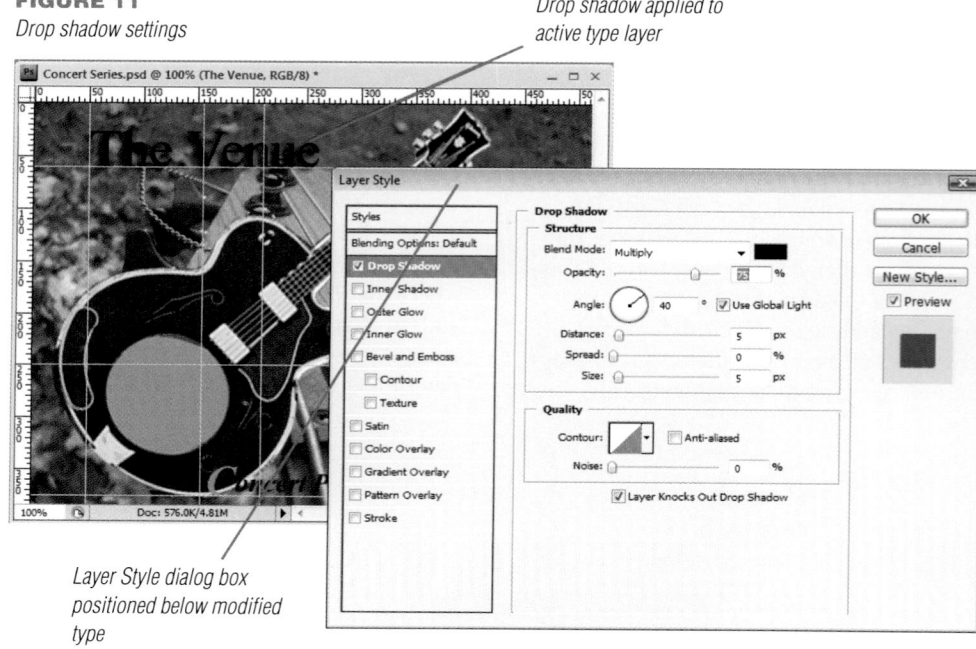

FIGURE 11
Drop shadow settings

Drop shadow applied to active type layer

Layer Style dialog box positioned below modified type

TABLE 2: Drop Shadow Settings

setting	scale	explanation
Angle	0–360 degrees	At 0 degrees, the shadow appears on the baseline of the original text. At 90 degrees, the shadow appears directly below the original text.
Distance	0–30,000 pixels	A larger pixel size increases the distance from which the shadow text falls relative to the original text.
Spread	0–100%	A larger percentage increases the width of the shadow text.
Size	0–250 pixels	A larger pixel size increases the blur of the shadow text.

FIGURE 12
Layer Style dialog box

Angle text box ⟶

Distance text box ⟶

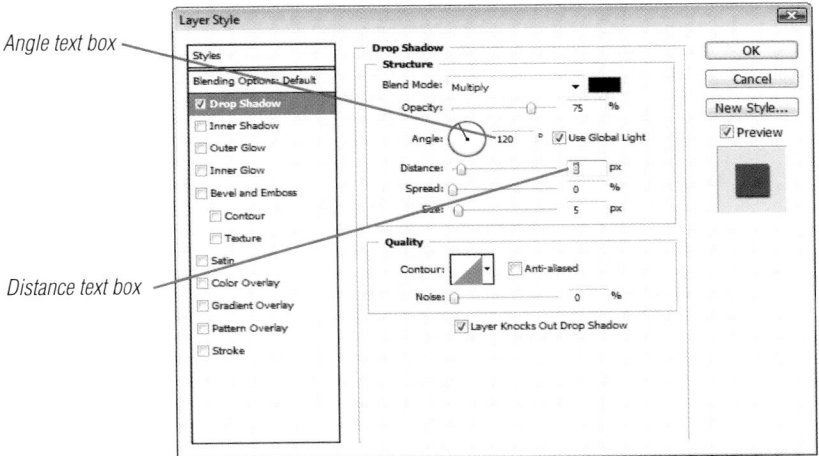

FIGURE 13
Drop shadow added to type layer

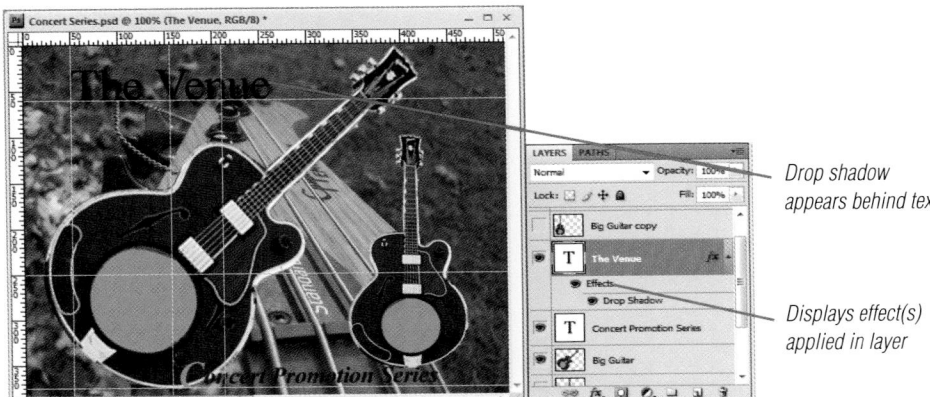

Drop shadow
appears behind text

Displays effect(s)
applied in layer

Modify drop shadow settings

1. Double-click the number in the Angle text box, then type **120**.

   Each style in the Layer Style dialog box shows different options in the center section. These options are displayed as you click each style (in the Styles pane).

   TIP   You can also set the angle by dragging the dial slider in the Layer Style dialog box.

2. Double-click the number in the Distance text box, then type **8**. See Figure 12.

   TIP   You can create your own layer style in the Layer Style dialog box, by selecting style settings, clicking New Style, typing a new name or accepting the default, then clicking OK. The new style appears as a preset in the Styles list of the Layer Style dialog box.

3. Click **OK**, then compare your screen to Figure 13.

4. Click the **list arrow to the right of the Indicates layer effects icon** ▲ on The Venue layer to collapse the list.

5. Save your work.

You used the Layer Style dialog box to modify the settings for the drop shadow.

Lesson 3   Use the Drop Shadow Style

APPLY ANTI-ALIASING
TO TYPE

What You'll Do

In this lesson, you'll view the effects of the anti-aliasing feature, then use the History panel to return the type to its original state.

Eliminating the "Jaggies"

In the good old days of dot-matrix printers, jagged edges were obvious in many print ads. You can still see these jagged edges in designs produced on less sophisticated printers. To prevent the jagged edges (sometimes called "jaggies") that often accompany bitmap type, Photoshop offers an anti-aliasing feature. **Anti-aliasing** partially fills in pixel edges with additional colors, resulting in smooth-edge type and an increased number of colors in the image. Anti-aliasing is useful for improving the display of large type in print media; however, this can cause a file to become large.

Knowing When to Apply Anti-Aliasing

As a rule, type that has a point size greater than 12 should have some anti-aliasing method applied. Sometimes, smaller type sizes can become blurry or muddy when anti-aliasing is used. As part of the process, anti-aliasing adds intermediate colors to your image in an effort to reduce the jagged edges. As a designer, you need to weigh these three factors (type size, file size, and image quality) when determining if you should apply anti-aliasing.

Understanding Anti-Aliasing

Anti-aliasing improves the display of type against the background. You can use five anti-aliasing methods: None, Sharp, Crisp, Strong, and Smooth. An example of each method is shown in Figure 14. The **None** setting applies no anti-aliasing, and can result in type that has jagged edges.

The **Sharp** setting displays type with the best possible resolution. The **Crisp** setting gives type more definition and makes type appear sharper. The **Strong** setting makes type appear heavier, much like the bold attribute. The **Smooth** setting gives type more rounded edges.

FIGURE 14
Anti-aliasing effects

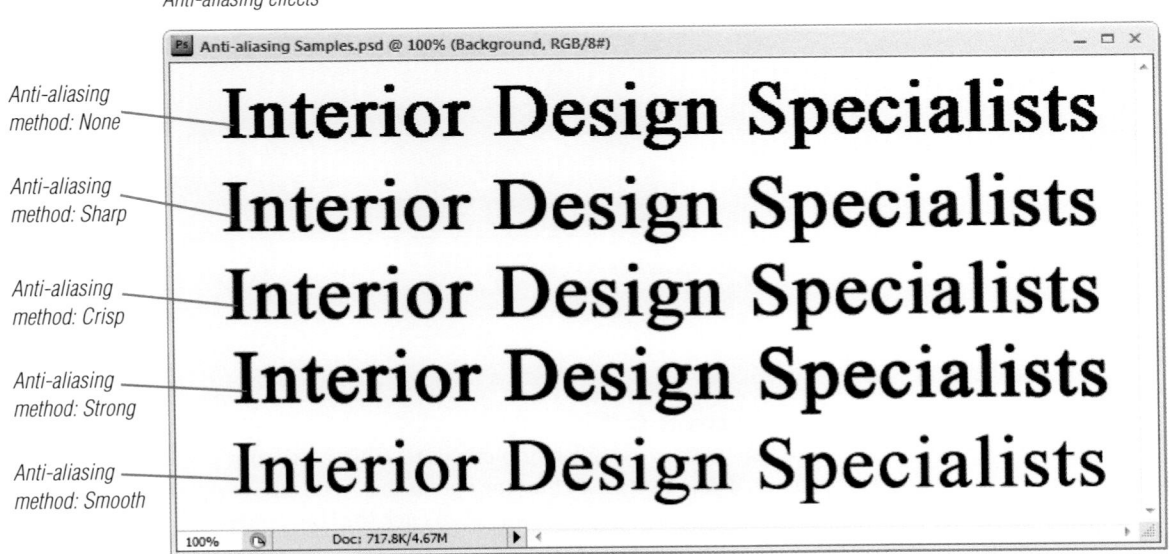

Anti-aliasing method: None

Anti-aliasing method: Sharp

Anti-aliasing method: Crisp

Anti-aliasing method: Strong

Anti-aliasing method: Smooth

Apply anti-aliasing

1. Double-click the **layer thumbnail** on The Venue layer.

2. Click the **Set the anti-aliasing method list arrow** aa Sharp ▾ on the options bar.

   TIP   You've probably noticed that some items, such as the Set the anti-aliasing method list arrow, the Set the text color button, and the Set the kerning between two characters list arrow are duplicated on the options bar and the Character panel. So which should you use? Whichever one you feel most comfortable using. These tasks are performed identically regardless of the feature's origin.

3. Click **Strong**, then compare your work to Figure 15.

4. Click the **Commit any current edits button** ✔ on the options bar.

You applied the Strong anti-aliasing setting to see how the setting affected the appearance of type.

FIGURE 15
Effect of Strong anti-aliasing

Type appearance altered

Different strokes for different folks

You're probably already aware that you can use different methods to achieve the same goals in Photoshop. For instance, if you want to see the type options bar, you can either double-click a type layer thumbnail or single-click it, then click the Horizontal Type tool. The method you use determines what you'll see in the History panel. Using the double-clicking method, a change in the anti-aliasing method will result in the following history state 'Edit Type Layer'. Using the single-clicking method to change to the anti-alias method to Crisp results in an 'Anti Alias Crisp' history state.

Placing Type in an Image

FIGURE 16

Deleting a state from the History panel

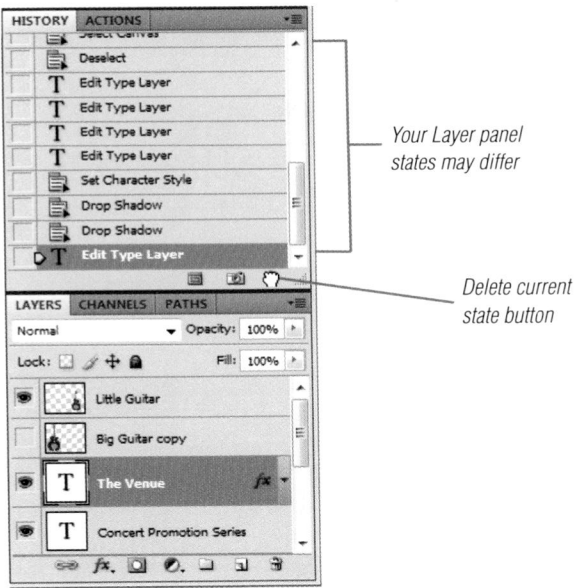

Your Layer panel states may differ

Delete current state button

Undo anti-aliasing

1. Click the **workspace switcher** on the Application bar, then click **History and Layers**.

   The History panel is now visible.

2. Click the **Edit Type Layer state** listed at the bottom of the History panel, then drag it to the **Delete current state button** 🗑 , as shown in Figure 16.

   | TIP   Various methods of undoing actions are reviewed in Table 3.

3. Return the display to the **Typography** workspace.

4. Save your work.

You deleted a state in the History panel to return the type to its original appearance. The History panel offers an easy way of undoing previous steps.

TABLE 3: Undoing Actions

method	description	keyboard shortcut
Undo	Edit ➤ Undo	[Ctrl][Z] (Win) ⌘[Z] (Mac)
Step Backward	Click Edit on the Application bar, then click Step Backward	[Alt][Ctrl][Z] (Win) [option]⌘[Z] (Mac)
History panel	Drag state to the Delete current state button on the History panel, or click the Delete current state button on the History panel	[Alt] 🗑 (Win) [option] 🗑 (Mac) 🗑

Lesson 4   Apply Anti-Aliasing to Type

PHOTOSHOP 5-19

MODIFY TYPE WITH THE
BEVEL AND EMBOSS STYLE

What You'll Do

In this lesson, you'll apply the Bevel and Emboss style, then modify the Bevel and Emboss settings.

Using the Bevel and Emboss Style

You use the Bevel and Emboss style to add combinations of shadows and highlights to a layer and make type appear to have dimension and shine. You can use the Layer menu or the Layers panel to apply the Bevel and Emboss style to the active layer. Like all Layer styles, the Bevel and Emboss style is linked to the type layer to which it is applied.

Understanding Bevel and Emboss Settings

You can use two categories of Bevel and Emboss settings: structure and shading. **Structure** determines the size and physical properties of the object, and **shading** determines the lighting effects. Figure 17 contains several variations of Bevel and Emboss structure settings, while additional Bevel and Emboss structure settings are listed in Table 4. The shading

Filling type with imagery

You can use the imagery from a layer in one file as the fill pattern for another image's type layer. To create this effect, open a multi-layer file that contains the imagery you want to use (the source), then open the file that contains the type you want to fill (the target). In the source file, activate the layer containing the imagery you want to use, use the Select menu to select all, then use the Edit menu to copy the selection. In the target file, press [Ctrl] (Win) or ⌘ (Mac) while clicking the type layer to which the imagery will be applied, then click Paste Into on the Edit menu. The imagery will appear within the type.

used in the Bevel and Emboss style determines how and where light is projected on the type. You can control a variety of settings, including the angle, altitude, and gloss contour, to create a unique appearance. The **Angle** setting determines where the shadow falls relative to the text, and the **Altitude** setting affects the amount of visible dimension. For example, an altitude of 0 degrees looks flat, while a setting of 90 degrees has a more three-dimensional appearance. The **Gloss Contour** setting determines the pattern with which light is reflected, and the **Highlight Mode** and **Shadow Mode** settings determine how pigments are combined. When the Use Global Light check box is selected, *all the type* in the image will be affected by your changes.

FIGURE 17
Bevel and Emboss style samples

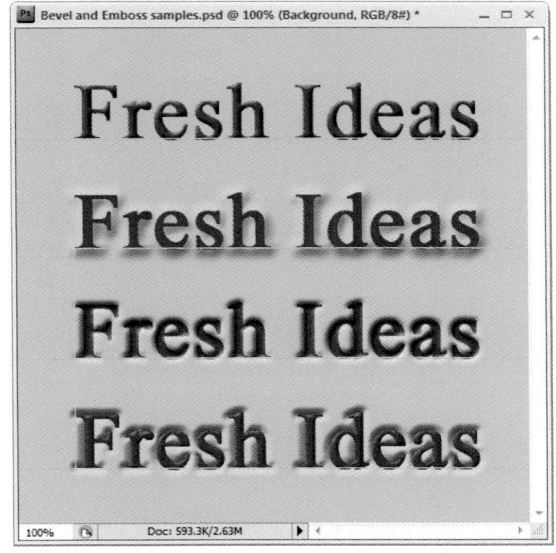

TABLE 4: Bevel and Emboss Structure Settings

sample	style	technique	direction	size	soften
1	Inner Bevel	Smooth	Up	5	1
2	Outer Bevel	Chisel Hard	Up	5	8
3	Emboss	Smooth	Down	10	3
4	Pillow Emboss	Chisel Soft	Up	10	3

Lesson 5   Modify Type with the Bevel and Emboss Style

Add the Bevel and Emboss style with the Layer menu

1. Verify that **The Venue layer** is the active layer, then use any Zoom tool so the image is viewed at a zoom level of 200%.

2. Click the **Set the text color button** ▬ on the options bar, click the silver area in the large guitar (at approximately **70 X/330 Y**), then click **OK**.

3. Click **Layer** on the Application bar, point to **Layer Style**, click **Bevel and Emboss**, then click **Bevel and Emboss** in the Styles column (if it is not already selected).

4. Review the Layer Style dialog box shown in Figure 18, then move the Layer Style dialog box (if necessary), so you can see "The Venue" type.

You applied the Bevel and Emboss style by using the Layer menu. This gave the text a more three-dimensional look.

FIGURE 18
Layer Style dialog box

Angle text box

When selected, changes will affect all type layers

Altitude text box

Warping type

You can add dimension and style to your type by using the Warp Text feature. After you select the type layer you want to warp, click the Horizontal Type tool on the Tools panel. Click the Create warped text button on the options bar to open the Warp Text dialog box. If a warning box opens telling you that your request cannot be completed because the type layer uses a faux bold style, click the Toggle the Character and Paragraph panels button on the options bar, click the Character panel list arrow, click Faux Bold to deselect it, then click the Create warped text button again. You can click the Style list arrow to select from 15 available styles. After you select a style, you can modify its appearance by dragging the Bend, Horizontal Distortion, and Vertical Distortion sliders.

FIGURE 19

Bevel and Emboss style applied to type

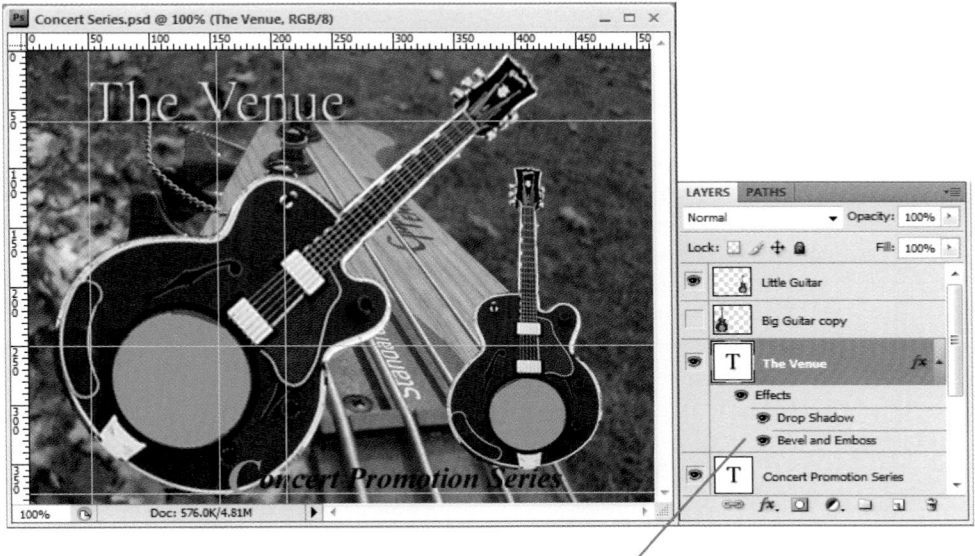

Bevel and Emboss
style applied to layer

1. Double-click the number in the Angle text box, then type **165**.

   You can use the Layer Style dialog box to change the structure by adjusting style, technique, direction, size, and soften settings.

2. Double-click the **Altitude text box**, then type **20**.

3. Click **OK**, reduce the zoom level to 100%, expand The Venue layer in the Layers panel, then compare your type to Figure 19.

4. Save your work.

You modified the default settings for the Bevel and Emboss style. Experimenting with different settings is crucial to achieve the effect you want.

APPLY SPECIAL EFFECTS TO
TYPE USING FILTERS

What You'll Do

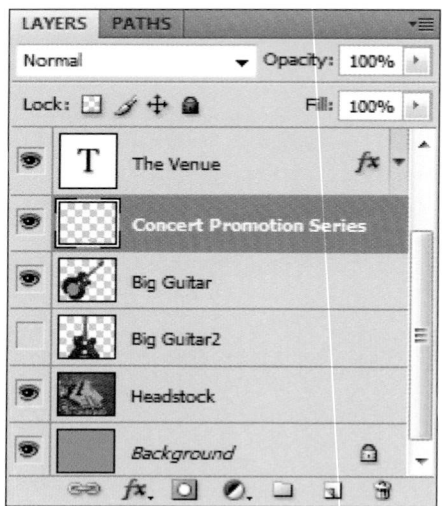

In this lesson, you'll rasterize a type layer, then apply a filter to it to change its appearance.

Understanding Filters

Like an image layer, a type layer can have one or more filters applied to it to achieve special effects and make your text look unique. Some filter dialog boxes have preview windows that let you see the results of the particular filter before it is applied to the layer. Other filters must be applied to the layer before you can see the results. Before a filter can be applied to a type layer, the type layer must first be **rasterized**, or converted to an image layer. After it is rasterized, the type characters *can no longer be edited* because it is composed of pixels, just like artwork. When a type layer is rasterized, the T icon in the layer thumbnail becomes an image thumbnail while the Effects icons remain on the type layer.

Creating Special Effects

Filters enable you to apply a variety of special effects to type, as shown in Figure 20. Notice that none of the original type layers on the Layers panel in Figure 20 display the T icon in the layer thumbnail because the layers have all been rasterized.

QUICKTIP

Because you cannot edit type after it has been rasterized, you should save your original type by making a copy of the layer *before* you rasterize it, then hide it from view.

Producing Distortions

Distort filters let you create waves or curves in type. Some of the types of distortions you can produce include Glass, Pinch, Ripple, Shear, Spherize, Twirl, Wave, and Zigzag. These effects are sometimes used as the basis of a corporate logo. The Twirl dialog box, shown in Figure 21, lets you determine the amount of twirl effect you want to apply. By dragging the Angle slider, you control how much twirl effect is added to a layer. Most filter dialog boxes have Zoom In and Zoom Out buttons that make it easy to see the effects of the filter.

Using Textures and Relief

Many filters let you create the appearance of textures and **relief** (the height of ridges within an object). One of the Stylize filters, Wind, applies lines throughout the type, making it appear shredded. The Wind dialog box, shown in Figure 22, lets you determine the kind of wind and its direction. The Texture filter lets you choose the type of texture you want to apply to a layer: Brick, Burlap, Canvas, or Sandstone.

Blurring Imagery

The Gaussian Blur filter softens the appearance of type by blurring its edge pixels. You can control the amount of blur applied to the type by entering high or low values in the Gaussian Blur dialog box. The higher the blur value, the blurrier the effect.

QUICKTIP

Be careful: too much blur applied to type can make it unreadable.

Colored pencil filter

Fresco filter

Gaussian blur filter

FIGURE 20
Sample filters applied to type

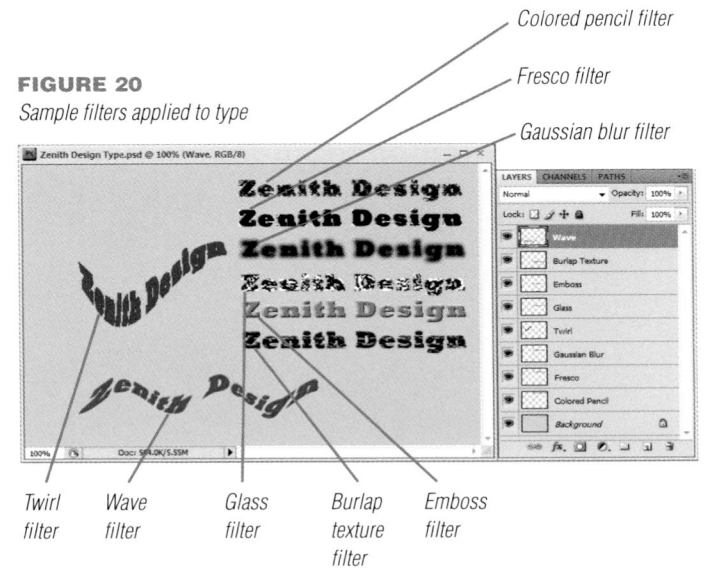

Twirl filter · Wave filter · Glass filter · Burlap texture filter · Emboss filter

FIGURE 21
Twirl dialog box

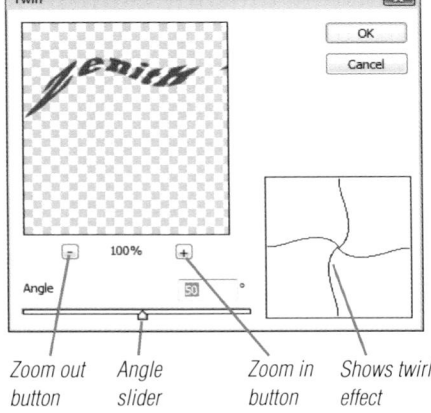

Zoom out button · Angle slider · Zoom in button · Shows twirl effect

FIGURE 22
Wind dialog box

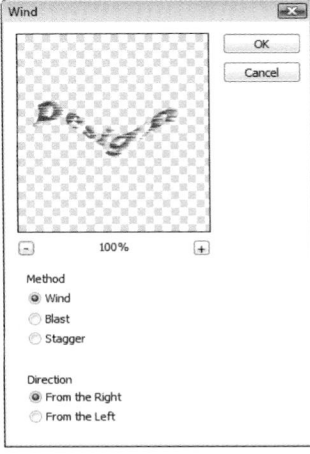

Rasterize a type layer

1. Click the **Concert Promotion Series** layer on the Layers panel.

2. Click **Filter** on the Application bar, point to **Noise**, then click **Dust & Scratches**.

3. Click **OK** to rasterize the type and close the warning box shown in Figure 23.

   TIP   You can also rasterize a type layer by clicking Layer on the Application bar, pointing to Rasterize, then clicking Type.

   The Dust & Scratches dialog box opens.

You rasterized a type layer in preparation for filter application.

Adobe Photoshop CS4 Extended

This type layer must be rasterized before proceeding. Its text will no longer be editable. Rasterize the type?

OK   Cancel

DESIGNTIP   Using multiple filters

Sometimes, adding one filter doesn't achieve the effect you had in mind. You can use multiple filters to create a unique effect. Before you try your hand at filters, though, it's a good idea to make a copy of the original layer. That way, if things don't turn out as you planned, you can always start over. You don't even have to write down which filters you used, because you can always look at the History panel to review which filters you applied.

FIGURE 24
Dust & Scratches dialog box

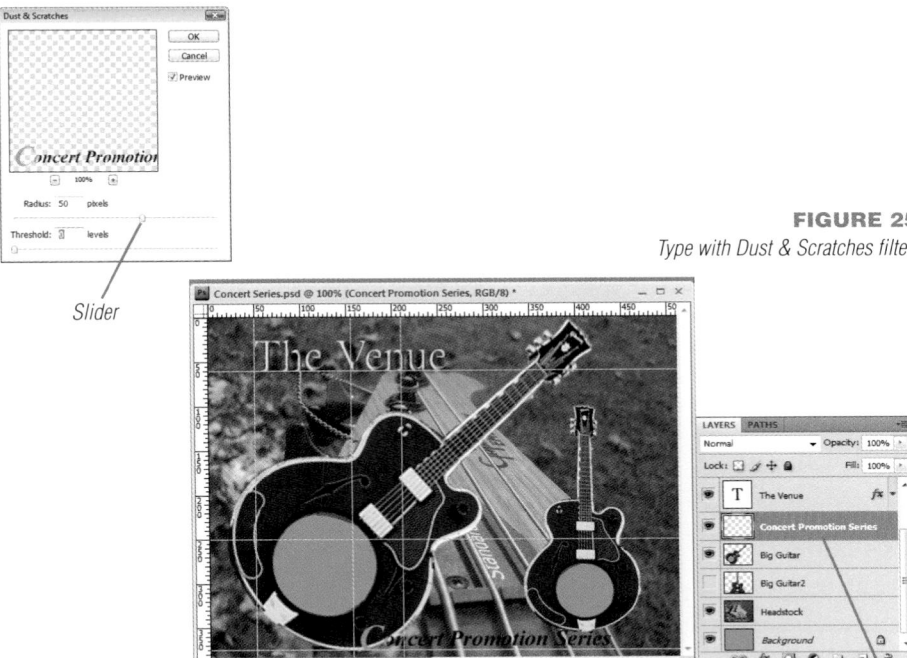

Slider

FIGURE 25
Type with Dust & Scratches filter

No longer a type layer

Modify filter settings

1. Drag the default background patterns in the preview window of the dialog box to position the type so at least part of the type is visible.

2. Drag the sliders in the Dust & Scratches dialog box until **50** appears in the Radius pixels text box, and **0** appears in the Threshold levels text box, as shown in Figure 24.

3. Click **OK**.

4. Save your work. Compare your modified type to Figure 25.

You modified the Dust & Scratches filter settings to modify the appearance of the layer.

Creating a neon glow

Want to create a really cool effect that takes absolutely no time at all, and works on both type and objects? You can create a neon glow that appears to surround an object. You can apply the Neon Glow filter (one of the Artistic filters) to any flattened image. This effect works best by starting with any imagery—either type or objects—that has a solid color background. Flatten the image so there's only a Background layer. Click the Magic Wand tool on the Tools panel, then click the solid color (in the background). Click Filter on the Application bar, point to Artistic, then click Neon Glow. Adjust the glow size, the glow brightness, and color, if you wish, then click OK. (An example of this technique is used in the Design Project at the end of this chapter.)

CREATE TEXT
ON A PATH

What You'll Do

In this lesson, you'll create a shape, then add type to it.

Understanding Text on a Path

Although it is possible to create some cool type effects by adding layer styles such as bevel, emboss, and drop shadow, you can also create some awesome warped text. Suppose you want type to conform to a shape, such as an oval or a free-form you've drawn? No problem—just create the shape and add the text!

Creating Text on a Path

You start by creating a shape using one of the Photoshop shape tools on the Tools panel, and then adding type to that shape (which is called a path). Add type to a shape by clicking the Horizontal Type tool. When the pointer nears the path, you'll see that it changes to the Type tool pointer. Click the path when the Type tool pointer displays and begin typing. You can change fonts, font sizes, add styles, and any other interesting effects you've learned to apply with type. As you will see, the type is on a path!

> **QUICK**TIP
>
> Don't worry when you see the outline of the path on the screen. The path won't print, only the type will.

FIGURE 26
Type on a path

Path does
not display
when image
is printed

Create a path and add type

1. Click the **Rectangle tool** ⬜ on the Tools panel.
2. Click the **Ellipse tool** ⬭ on the options bar.
3. Click the **Paths button** 🔲 on the options bar.
4. Drag the **Paths pointer** +⊗ to create a circular path within the gold circle on the large guitar from **100 X/250 Y** while holding [Shift].
5. Click the **Horizontal Type tool** T, on the Tools panel.
6. Change the font to **Arial**, use the Bold font style, set the font size to **8** pt, then verify that the **Left align text button** is selected.

   TIP You can change to any point size by typing the number in the Set the font size text box.

7. Click the **Horizontal Type pointer** ⌖ at approximately **90 X/270 Y** on the left edge of the ellipse.
8. Change the font color by sampling the blue at the top of the large guitar then type **The Venue**.
9. Commit any current edits.
10. Hide the rulers and guides, return to the **Essentials** workspace, and save your work. Compare your image to Figure 26.
11. Close the Concert Series.psd file and exit Photoshop.

You created a path using a shape tool, then added type to it.

Power User Shortcuts

to do this:	use this method:
Apply anti-alias method	a_a Sharp ▾
Apply Bevel and Emboss style	*fx.* , Bevel and Emboss
Apply blur filter to type	Filter ➤ Blur ➤ Gaussian Blur
Apply Drop Shadow style	*fx.* , Drop Shadow
Cancel any current edits	🚫
Change font family	Times New Roman ▾
Change font size	T 6 pt ▾
Change type color	▬▬
Close type effects	▼
Commit current edits	✓
Display/hide rulers	[Ctrl][R] (Win) or ⌘[R] (Mac)
Erase a History state	Select state, drag to 🗑

to do this:	use this method:
Horizontal Type tool	T, or T
Kern characters	A̲V Metrics ▾
Move tool	⊹ or V
Open Character panel	🗒
Save image changes	[Ctrl][S] (Win) or ⌘[S] (Mac)
See type effects (active layer)	▼
See type effects (inactive layer)	▼
Select all text	[Ctrl][A] (Win) or ⌘[A] (Mac)
Shift baseline of type	IT 100%
Warp type	�

Key: Menu items are indicated by ➤ between the menu name and its command. Blue bold letters are shortcuts for selecting tools on the Tools panel.

Learn about type and how it is created.

1. Open PS 5-2.psd from the drive and folder where you store your Data Files, then save it as **ZD-Logo**.
2. Display the rulers with pixels.
3. Use the Horizontal Type tool to create a type layer that starts at 45 X/95 Y.
4. Use a black 35 pt Lucida Sans font or substitute another font.
5. Type **Zenith**.
6. Use the Horizontal Type tool and a 16 pt type size to create a type layer at 70 X/180 Y, then type **Always the best**.
7. Save your work.

Change spacing and adjust baseline shift.

1. Use the Horizontal Type tool to create a new type layer at 205 X/95 Y.
2. Use a 35 pt Myriad font.
3. Type **Design**.
4. Select the Design type.
5. Change the type color to the color used in the lower-left background.
6. Change the type size of the Z and D to 50 pts.
7. Adjust the baseline shift of the Z and D to –5.
8. Save your work.

Use the Drop Shadow style.

1. Activate the Zenith type layer.
2. Apply the Drop Shadow style.
3. In the Layer Style dialog box, set the angle to 150°, then close the Layer Style dialog box.
4. Save your work.

Apply anti-aliasing to type.

1. Activate the Zenith type layer.
2. Change the Anti-Alias method to Smooth (if necessary).
3. Save your work.

Modify type with the Bevel and Emboss style.

1. Activate the Design type layer.
2. Apply the Bevel and Emboss style.
3. In the Layer Style dialog box, set the style to Inner Bevel.
4. Set the angle to 150° and the altitude to 30°.
5. Close the Layer Style dialog box.
6. Activate the Zenith type layer.
7. Apply the Bevel and Emboss style.
8. Set the style to Inner Bevel.
9. Verify that the angle is set to 150° and the altitude is set to 30°.
10. Close the Layer Style dialog box.
11. Save your work.

Apply special effects to type using filters.

1. Apply a 1.0 pixel Gaussian Blur effect to the "Always the best" layer.
2. Save your work.

Create text on a path.

1. Use the Ellipse tool to draw an ellipse from approximately 200 X/120 Y to 370 X/185 Y.
2. Click the line with the Horizontal Type tool at 210 X/130 Y.
3. Type **Founded in 1957** using the second color swatch in the first row of the Swatches panel (RGB Yellow), in a 16 pt Arial font.
4. Change the anti-aliasing method to Crisp.
5. Change the opacity of the type (using the Opacity slider in the Layers panel) on the path to 45%.
6. Turn off the ruler display.
7. Save your work, then compare your image to Figure 27.

FIGURE 27
Completed Skills Review Project

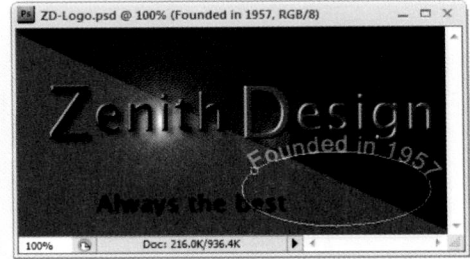

Placing Type in an Image

A local flower shop, Beautiful Blooms, asks you to design its color advertisement for the trade magazine, *Florists United*. You have already started on the image, and need to add some type.

1. Open PS 5-3.psd, then save it as **Beautiful Blooms Ad**.
2. Click the Horizontal Type tool, then type **Beautiful Blooms** using a 55 pt Impact font in black.
3. Create a catchy phrase of your choice, using a 24 pt Verdana font.
4. Apply a drop shadow style to the name of the flower shop using the following settings: Multiply blend mode, 75% Opacity, 30%, 5 pixel distance, 0° spread, and 5 pixel size.
5. Apply a Bevel and Emboss style to the catch phrase using the following settings: Inner Bevel style, Smooth technique, 100% depth, Up direction, 5 pixel size, 0 pixel soften, 30° angle, 30° altitude, and using global light.
6. Compare your image to the sample in Figure 28.
7. Save your work.

FIGURE 28

Sample Project Builder 1

You are a junior art director for an advertising agency. You have been working on an ad that promotes milk and milk products. You have started the project, but still have a few details to finish up before it is complete.

1. Open PS 5-4.psd, then save it as **Milk Promotion**.
2. Create a shape using any shape tool, then use the shape as a text path and type a snappy phrase of your choosing on the shape.
3. Use a 24 pt Arial font in the style and color of your choice for the catch phrase type layer. (If necessary, substitute another font.)
4. Create a Bevel and Emboss style on the type layer, setting the angle to 100° and the altitude to 30°.
5. Compare your image to the sample in Figure 29.
6. Save your work.

FIGURE 29
Sample Project Builder 2

You are a freelance designer. A local clothing store, Attitude, is expanding and has hired you to work on an advertisement. You have already created the file, and inserted the necessary type layers. Before you proceed, you decide to explore the Internet to find information on using type to create an effective design.

1. Connect to the Internet and use your browser to find information about typography. (Make a record of the site you found so you can use it for future reference, if necessary.)
2. Find information about using type as an effective design element.
3. Open PS 5-5.psd, update the layers (if necessary), then save the file as **Attitude**.
4. Modify the existing type by changing fonts, font colors, and font sizes.
5. Edit the type, if necessary, to make it shorter and clearer.
6. Rearrange the position of the type to create an effective design.
7. Add a Bevel and Emboss style using your choice of settings, then compare your image to the sample in Figure 30. (The fonts Mistral and Trebuchet MS are used in this image. Make substitutions if you don't have these fonts on your computer.)
8. Save your work.

FIGURE 30
Sample Design Project

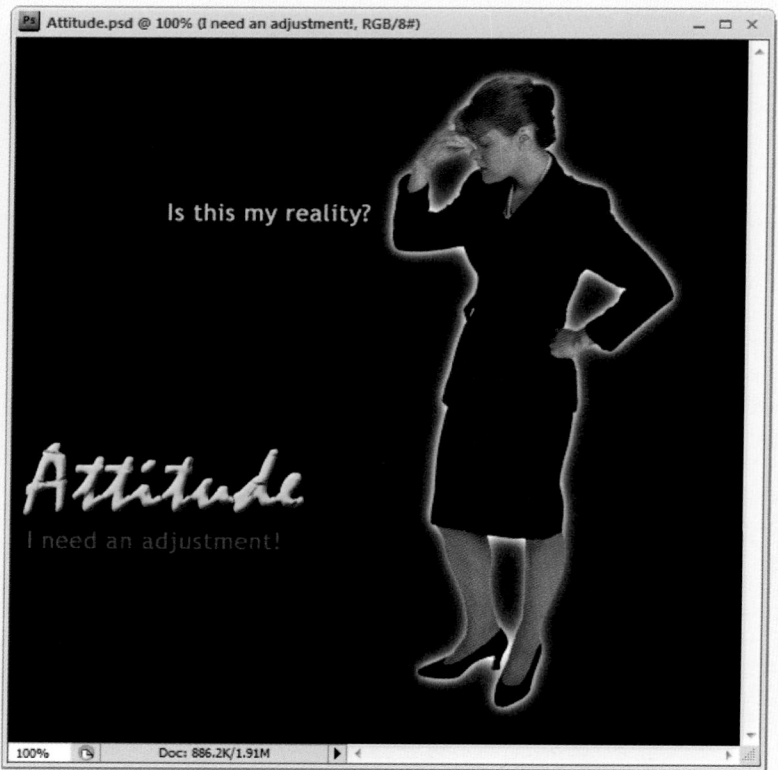

You have been hired by your community to create an advertising campaign that promotes tourism. Decide what aspect of the community you want to emphasize. Locate appropriate imagery (already existing on your hard drive, on the web, your own creation, or using a scanner), then add type to create a meaningful Photoshop image.

1. Create an image with the dimensions 550 pixels × 550 pixels.
2. Save this file as **Community Promotion**.
3. Locate appropriate imagery of your community on your hard drive, from a digital camera, or a scanner.
4. Add at least two layers of type in the image, using multiple font sizes. (Use any fonts available on your computer. You can use multiple fonts if you want.)
5. Add a Bevel and Emboss style to at least one type layer, and add a drop shadow to at least one layer. (*Hint*: You can add both effects to the same layer.)
6. Position type layers to create an effective design.
7. Compare your image to the sample in Figure 31.
8. Save your work.

FIGURE 31
Sample Portfolio Project

Placing Type in an Image

chapter

6

USING PAINTING
TOOLS

1. Paint and patch an image

2. Create and modify a brush tip

3. Use the Smudge tool

4. Use a library and an airbrush effect

6 USING PAINTING
TOOLS

Painting Pixels

In addition to the color-enhancing techniques you've already learned, Photoshop has a variety of painting tools that allow you to modify colors. Unlike the tools an oil painter might use to *apply* pigment to a canvas, such as a brush or a palette knife, these virtual painting tools let you *change* existing colors and pixels.

Understanding Painting Tools

In most cases, you use a painting tool by selecting it, then choosing a brush tip. Just like a real brush, the brush size and shape determines how colors are affected. You paint the image by applying the brush tip to an image, which is similar to the way pigment is applied to a real brush and then painted on a canvas. In Photoshop, the results of the painting process can be deeper, richer colors, bleached or blurred colors, or filter-like effects in specific areas. You can select the size and shape of a brush tip, and control the point at which the brush stroke fades.

Learning About Brush Libraries

Brushes that are used with painting tools are stored within a brush library. Each **brush library** contains a variety of brush tips that you can use, rename, delete, or customize. After you select a tool, you can select a brush tip from the default brush library, which is automatically available from the Brush Preset picker list arrow. Photoshop comes with the following additional brush libraries:

- Assorted Brushes
- Basic Brushes
- Calligraphic Brushes
- Drop Shadow Brushes
- Dry Media Brushes
- Faux Finish Brushes
- Natural Brushes
- Natural Brushes 2
- Special Effect Brushes
- Square Brushes
- Thick Heavy Brushes
- Wet Media Brushes

Tools You'll Use

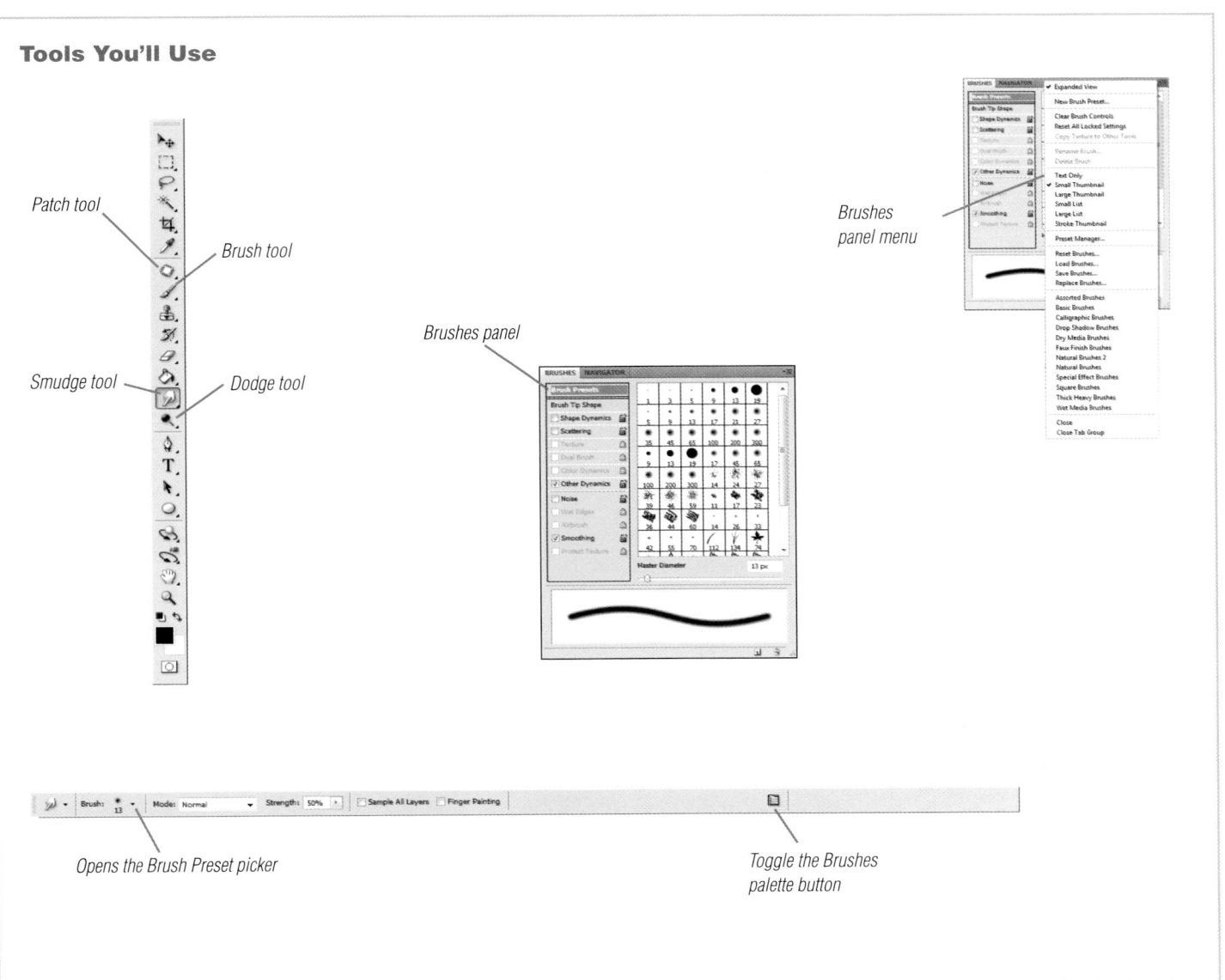

Patch tool

Brush tool

Smudge tool

Dodge tool

Brushes panel

Brushes panel menu

Opens the Brush Preset picker

Toggle the Brushes palette button

PAINT AND
PATCH AN IMAGE

What You'll Do

In this lesson, you'll use the Sharpen tool to give pixels more definition, the Burn tool to darken specific areas, then use fade settings to paint an area. You'll also use the Patch tool to hide unnecessary imagery.

Using Painting Tools

As you've probably realized, you can use many different methods to achieve similar effects in Photoshop. No one method is necessarily better than another. Like a mask that hides a specific area, Photoshop painting tools can be used to enhance specific areas of a layer. You can use the painting tools, shown in Table 1, to create the effects shown in Figure 1. Unlike a mask that is applied to a defined area within a layer, or a filter that is applied to an entire layer, the effects of painting tools are applied to whatever areas the pointer contacts. In some ways, Photoshop painting tools function very similarly to real painting brushes; in others, they go far beyond traditional tools to let you achieve some incredible effects.

Understanding Fade Options

When you dip a real brush in paint and then stroke the brush across canvas, the brush stroke begins to fade as more of the pigment is left on the canvas than on the brush. This effect can be duplicated in Photoshop using fade options. Fade options are brush

settings that determine how and when colors fade toward the end of brush strokes. Fade option settings are measured in steps. A **step** is equivalent to one mark of the brush tip and can be any value from 1–9999. The larger the step value, the longer the fade. You can set fade options for most of the painting tools using the Size Jitter Control option on several of the Brush Tip Shape options within the Brushes panel.

QUICKTIP

To picture a brush fade, imagine a skid mark left by a tire. The mark starts out strong and bold, then fades out gradually or quickly, depending on conditions. This effect is analogous to a brush fade.

Learning About the Patch Tool

Photoshop offers many tools to work with damaged or unwanted imagery. One such tool is the Patch tool. Although this is not a painting tool, you might find as you work in Photoshop, you have to combine a variety of tool strategies to achieve the effect you want. The Patch tool is located on the

Tools panel and is grouped with the Healing Brush tool and Spot Healing Brush tool. You can use this tool to cover a selected area with pixels from another area, or a pattern. Both the Patch tool and the Healing Brush tool match the texture, lighting, and shading of the sampled pixels so your repaired area will look seamless. The Healing Brush tool, however, also matches the transparency of the pixels.

QUICKTIP

As you drag a selection made with the Patch tool, look at the selection and you'll see what the pixels will be replaced with.

Using the Patch Tool

The Patch tool provides a quick and easy way to repair or remove an area within an image. You can use the Patch tool in the following ways:

- Select the area you want to fix, click the Source option button on the options bar, then drag the selection over the area you want to replicate.
- Select the area you want replicated, click the Destination option button on the options bar, then drag the selection over the area you want to fix.

QUICKTIP

There's not necessarily one "right tool" for any given job; there might be several methods of completing a task.

Eliminating Red Eye

The red eye effect is the appearance of red eyes in photos due to the use of a flash. It is more evident in people, and animals, with light-colored eyes. The effect can be eliminated using the Red Eye tool. Select the tool (grouped on the Tools panel with the Patch tool, the Healing Brush tool, and the Spot Healing Brush tool), then click in the red eye area. The Pupil Size list arrow lets you increase or decrease the area affected, and the Darken Amount list arrow sets the darkness of the correction.

FIGURE 1
Painting samples

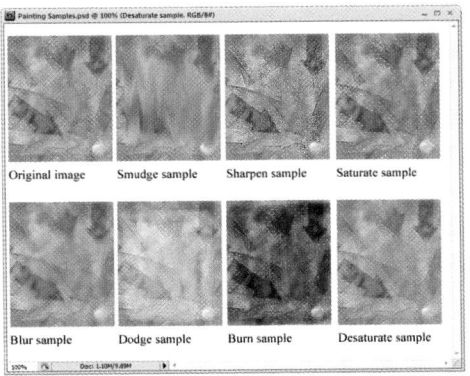

TABLE 1: Painting Tools

tool	button	effect
Smudge tool		Smears colors across an image as if you dragged your finger across wet ink. (Grouped with the Blur tool.)
Sharpen tool		Increases contrast between pixels, giving a sharp, crisp look. (Grouped with the Blur tool.)
Blur tool		Decreases contrast between pixels, giving a soft, blurred look.
Dodge tool		Lightens underlying pixels, giving a lighter, underexposed appearance.
Burn tool		Darkens underlying pixels, giving a richer, overexposed appearance. (Grouped with the Dodge tool.)
Sponge tool		Increases or decreases the purity of a color by saturating or desaturating the color. (Grouped with the Dodge tool.)

Use the Sharpen tool

1. Start Photoshop, open PS 6-1.psd from the drive and folder where you store your Data Files, then save it as **CyberArt**.

2. Display the guides, the rulers in pixels (if they are not already displayed), and make sure the document size displays in the status bar.

3. Use the workspace switcher to display the **Painting workspace**.

4. Click the **Sharpen tool** △ on the Tools panel.

   TIP Look under the Blur tool if the Sharpen tool is hidden.

5. Click **Brush Presets** in the Brushes panel (if necessary), scroll up the list, then click **19 (Hard Round 19 pixels)**.

   TIP You can also click the Click to open the Brush Preset picker list arrow on the options bar to select brushes.

6. Drag the **Brush pointer** ◯ from **20 X/20 Y** to **530 X/20 Y**, to sharpen across the top area of the image.

7. Press and hold **[Shift]**, click the image in the lower-right corner at **530 X/530 Y**, then release **[Shift]**.

   TIP Instead of dragging to create a line from point to point, you can click a starting point, press and hold [Shift], click an ending point, then release [Shift] to create a perfectly straight line.

8. Press and hold **[Shift]**, click the image in the lower-left corner at **20 X/530 Y**, then release **[Shift]**.

9. Press and hold **[Shift]**, click the image in the upper-left corner at **20 X/20 Y**, then release **[Shift]**. Compare your image to Figure 2.

You used the Sharpen tool to focus on the pixels around the perimeter of the image. The affected pixels now appear sharper and crisper.

FIGURE 2
Results of Sharpen tool

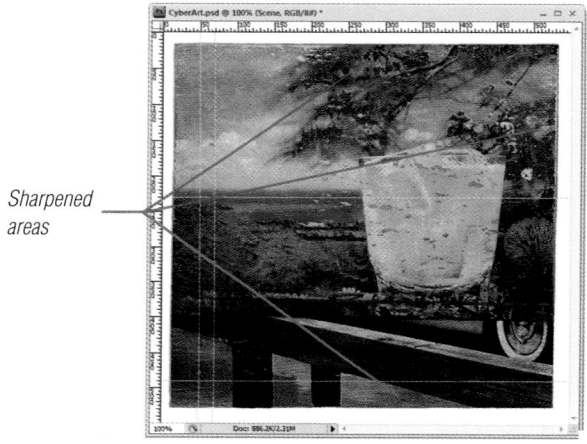

Sharpened areas

FIGURE 3
Red eyes – before and after

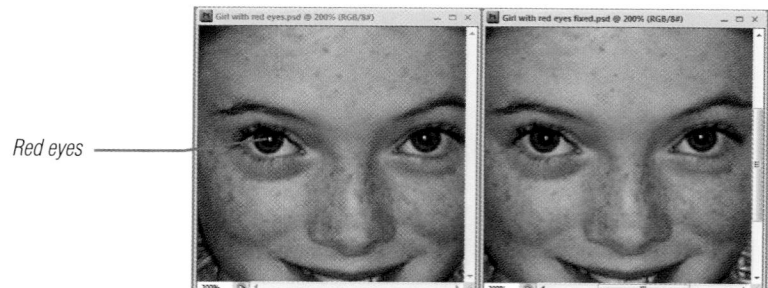

Red eyes

Getting rid of red eye

What do you do with that picture of your niece's doggie that looks so cute but has annoying red eye? You use the Red Eye tool, that's what! Hidden in with the Patch tool and the Healing Brush tool, you can select the Red Eye tool and drag it over any red eye in an image and the eye will be magically corrected. If necessary, you can adjust the pupil size in the Options bar. Figure 3 shows an image before (on the left) and after red eye correction.

FIGURE 4

Results of Burn tool

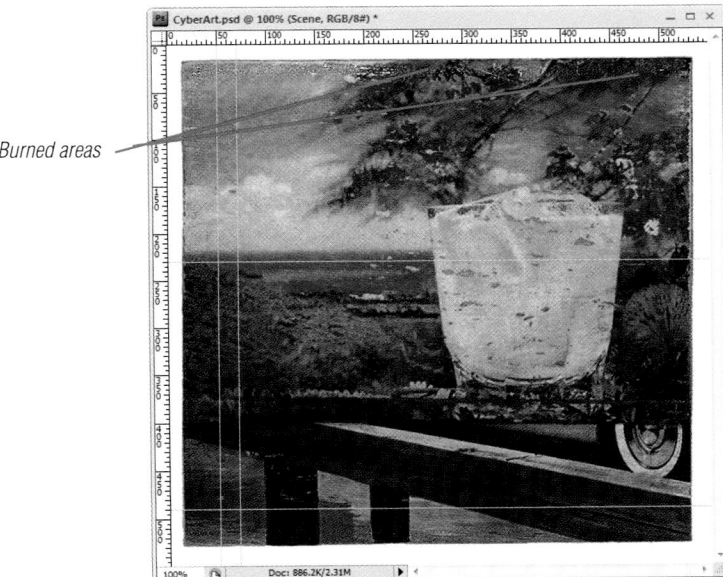

Burned areas

1. Click the **Burn tool** 🖑 on the Tools panel.

    TIP   Look under the Dodge tool if the Burn tool is hidden.

2. Click ⟨Brush: ⬚⟩ **27 (Soft Round 27 pixels)** on the Brushes panel.

    TIP   You can change any brush tip size at any time. Press []] to increase the brush tip or [[] to decrease the brush tip in increments of 5.

3. Drag the **Brush pointer** ⬡ from **20 X/25 Y** to **550 X/25 Y**.

    Did you notice that the area you painted became darker? It looks as though the edges are burned.

4. Drag the **Brush pointer** ⬡ back and forth throughout the upper-right corner from **400 X/25 Y** to **530 X/120 Y**. Compare your image to Figure 4.

You used the Burn tool to tone down the pixels in the upper-right corner of the image. This technique increases the darker tones, changing the mood of the image.

Painting with a pattern

Suppose you have an area within an image that you want to replicate on a new or existing layer. You can paint an existing pattern using the desired area and the Pattern Stamp tool. To create this effect, select the Rectangular Marquee tool using a 0 pixel feather setting, then drag the outline around an area in your image. With this area outlined, click Edit on the Application bar, click Define Pattern, type a name in the Name text box, then click OK. Deselect the marquee, click the Pattern Stamp tool on the Tools panel (hidden under the Clone Stamp tool), click the Click to open Pattern picker list arrow on the options bar, then click the new pattern. Each time you click the pointer on a layer, the new pattern will be applied. You can delete a custom pattern by right-clicking the pattern swatch in the Pattern picker, then clicking Delete Pattern.

Set fade options and paint an area

1. Click the **Eyedropper tool** 🔍 on the Tools panel.

2. Use the **Eyedropper pointer** 🖊 to click the image at **50 X/490 Y**, as shown in Figure 5.

3. Click the **Brush tool** 🖌 on the Tools panel.

4. Click **19 (Hard Round 19 pixels)** on the Brushes panel.

   TIP   You can also open the Brushes panel by clicking the Brushes button 🖫 on the dock, if it is displayed.

5. Click **Shape Dynamics** on the Brushes panel, then adjust your settings using Figure 6 as a guide.

   Available fade options and their locations on the Brushes panel are described in Table 2.

   TIP   Click the option Brush Tip Shape on the Brushes panel to see the option settings. Selecting an option's check box turns the option on, but doesn't display the settings.

6. Press and hold **[Shift]**, drag the **Brush pointer** ◯ from **25 X/25 Y** to **525 X/25 Y**, then release **[Shift]**.

7. Use the **Brush pointer** ◯ to click the image at **25 X/40 Y**, press and hold **[Shift]**, click the image at **25 X/520 Y**, then release **[Shift]**, as shown in Figure 7.

You modified the fade options, then painted areas using the Brush tool.

FIGURE 5
Location to sample

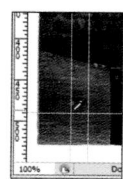

FIGURE 7
Areas painted with fade

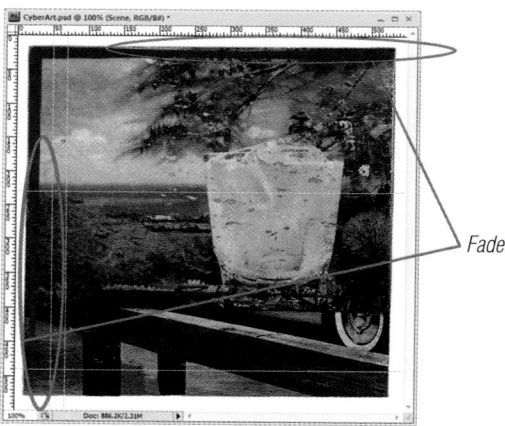

Faded area

FIGURE 6
Brushes panel

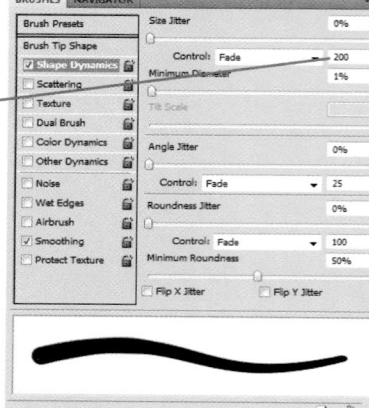

Indicates how many steps it takes for fade to occur

TABLE 2: Fade Options

option	on Brushes panel	description
Size Jitter	Shape Dynamics	Decreases the brush stroke size toward the end of the stroke.
Opacity Jitter	Other Dynamics	Decreases the brush stroke opacity toward the end of the stroke.
Foreground/ Background Jitter	Color Dynamics	Causes the foreground color to shift to the background color toward the end of the stroke. Available in the following tools: Brush 🖌 and Pencil ✏ .

FIGURE 8
Marquee surrounding source area

Selection to be patched

FIGURE 9
Results of Patch tool

The location of your
young girl may vary

1. Click the **Patch tool** on the Tools panel.

   TIP   Look under the Healing Brush tool if the Patch tool is hidden.

2. Drag the **Patch tool pointer** around the periphery of the glass, being sure to complete the loop so you create the selection as shown in Figure 8.

3. Click the **Source option button** on the options bar, if it is not already selected.

4. Drag the selection so that the outline of the left edge of the glass (the outline source) is at approximately **60 X/170 Y**.

   The selection is replaced with imagery from the location that you defined with the selection. As you drag, you'll see the pixels that will be replacing the selection. When finished, the horizon should be aligned.

   TIP   You can reverse steps using the History panel, then retry until you're satisfied with the results.

5. Click **Select** on the Application bar, then click **Deselect**.

6. Click the **Young girl** on the Layers panel and display the layer.

7. Click the **Move tool** on the Tools panel, then press the arrow keys as needed until the right side of the young girl covers any remnants of the glass. Compare your image to Figure 9.

   Selecting and patching are difficult skills to master. Your results might differ.

8. Click the **Scene layer** on the Layers panel.

9. Save your work.

You used the Patch tool to cover an area within an image. The tool makes it possible to correct flaws within an image using existing imagery.

Lesson 1   Paint and Patch an Image

PHOTOSHOP 6-9

CREATE AND MODIFY
A BRUSH TIP

What You'll Do

In this lesson, you'll create a brush tip and modify its settings, then you'll use it to paint a border. This new brush tip will be wide and have a distinctive shape that adds an element of mystery to the image.

Understanding Brush Tips

You use brush tips to change the size and pattern of the brush used to apply color. Brushes are stored within libraries. In addition to the default brushes that are available from the Brush Preset picker list, you can also select a brush tip from one of 12 brush libraries. You can access these additional libraries, shown in Figure 10, by clicking the Brush Preset picker list arrow on the options bar, then clicking the menu list arrow.

Learning About Brush Tip Modifications

You can adjust the many brush tip settings that help determine the shape of a brush. One factor that influences the shape of a brush stroke is jitter. **Jitter** is the randomness of dynamic elements such as size, angle, roundness, hue, saturation, brightness, opacity, and flow. The number beneath the brush tip indicates the diameter, and the image of the tip changes as its values are modified. Figure 11 shows

some of the types of modifications that you can make to a brush tip using the Brushes palette. The shape of the brush tip pointer reflects the shape of the brush tip. As you change the brush tip, its pointer also changes.

FIGURE 10
Brush tip libraries

Click to open menu

Brush Preset picker list arrow

Creates a new brush

Available libraries

Using Painting Tools

Creating a Brush Tip

You can create your own brush tip by clicking the Brushes panel list arrow, then clicking New Brush Preset to open the Brush Name dialog box, where you can type a descriptive name in the Name text box. All the options on the Brushes panel are available to you as you adjust the settings. As you select settings, a sample appears at the bottom of the panel. You can delete the current brush tip by clicking the Brush Preset picker list arrow, clicking Delete Brush, then clicking OK in the warning box. You can also right-click (Win) or [Ctrl]-click (Mac) a brush tip on the Brushes panel, then click Delete Brush.

FIGURE 11
Brush Presets in the Brushes panel

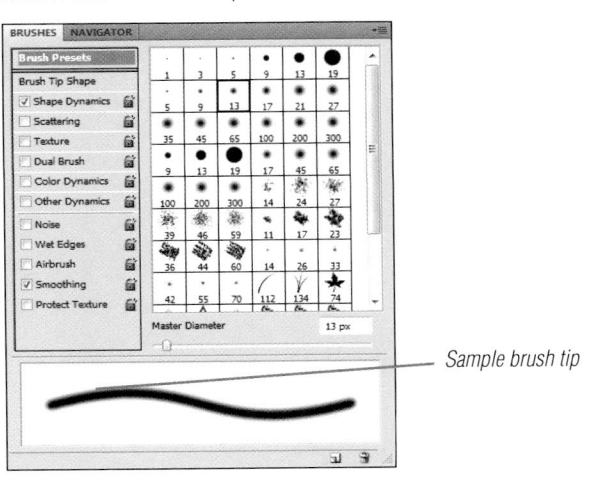

Sample brush tip

FIGURE 12
Tinted image

After tinting has been applied

Original grayscale image

Applying a tint

You can use brush tips to apply a tint to a grayscale image. By changing the mode of a grayscale image to RGB color, you can use painting tools to tint an image. After you change the image mode, create a new layer, click the Mode list arrow in the New Layer dialog box, click Color, select colors from the Swatches panel, then apply tints to the new layer. See Figure 12 for an example.

Create a brush tip

1. Click the **Brush tool** ✐. on the Tools panel.

2. Click the **list arrow** ▾≡ to the right of the Brushes panel, then click **Clear Brush Controls**.

3. Click the **Brushes panel list arrow** ▾≡ again, then click **New Brush Preset**.

4. Type **Custom oval brush tip** to replace the current name, then click **OK**.

   TIP A newly added brush tip generally is added in brush tip size order in the Brushes panel.

   The new brush tip appears on the options bar or by opening the Brushes panel and scrolling to the bottom.

5. Click **Brush Tip Shape** on the Brushes panel, then adjust your settings using Figure 13 as a guide.

   TIP If you have a pen tablet installed on your computer, you may periodically see a floating icon ▱ indicating that your tablet can be used to make entries.

You cleared the current brush settings, and then created a brush tip using the Brushes panel. You modified its settings to create a custom brush tip for painting a border.

FIGURE 13
Brush Tip Shape settings

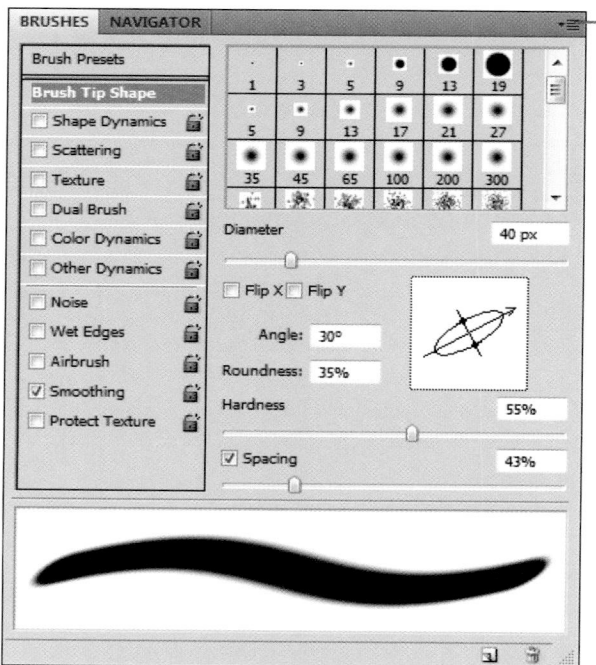

Brushes panel
list arrow

FIGURE 14
Painted image

CyberArt.psd @ 100% (Young girl, RGB/8#)

Effects of the custom brush tip

100%   Doc: 886.2K/2.31M

1. Click the **Mode list arrow** on the options bar, then click **Multiply**.

   TIP   The Multiply blend mode creates semi-transparent shadow effects and multiplies the value of the base color by the blend color.

2. Double-click the **Opacity text box**, then type **75**.

3. Click **Shape Dynamics** on the Brushes panel.

4. Click the **Control list arrow** under the Size Jitter section, then click **Fade**.

5. Type **400** in the text box to the right of the Control list arrow.

6. Use the **Brush pointer** ⬭ to click the image near the upper-right corner at **515 X/25 Y**, press and hold **[Shift]**, click the image near the lower-right corner at **515 X/515 Y**, then release **[Shift]**.

7. Save your work, then compare your image to Figure 14.

Using the newly created brush tip, you painted an area of the image. You also made adjustments to the opacity and fade settings to make the brush stroke more dramatic.

USE THE SMUDGE TOOL

What You'll Do

In this lesson, you'll smudge pixels to create a surreal effect in an image.

Blurring Colors

You can create the same finger-painted look in your Photoshop image that you did as a kid using paints in a pot. Using the Smudge tool, you can create the effect of dragging your finger through wet paint. Like the Brush tool, the Smudge tool has many brush tips that you can select from the Brushes panel, or you can create a brush tip of your own.

> **QUICK**TIP
>
> You can use the Smudge tool to minimize defects in an image.

Smudging Options

Figure 15 shows an original image and three examples of Smudge tool effects. In each example, the same brush tip is used with different options on the options bar. If you select the Smudge tool with the default settings, your smudge effect will be similar to the image shown in the upper-right corner of Figure 15.

Using Painting Tools

Using Finger Painting

The image in the lower-right corner of Figure 15 shows the effect with the Finger Painting check box selected *prior* to the smudge stroke. The image in the upper-right corner did not have the Finger Painting check box selected. The image in the lower-left corner had the Finger Painting option off, but had the Use All Layers check box selected. The Use All Layers check box enables your smudge stroke to affect all the layers beneath the current layer.

FIGURE 15
Smudge samples

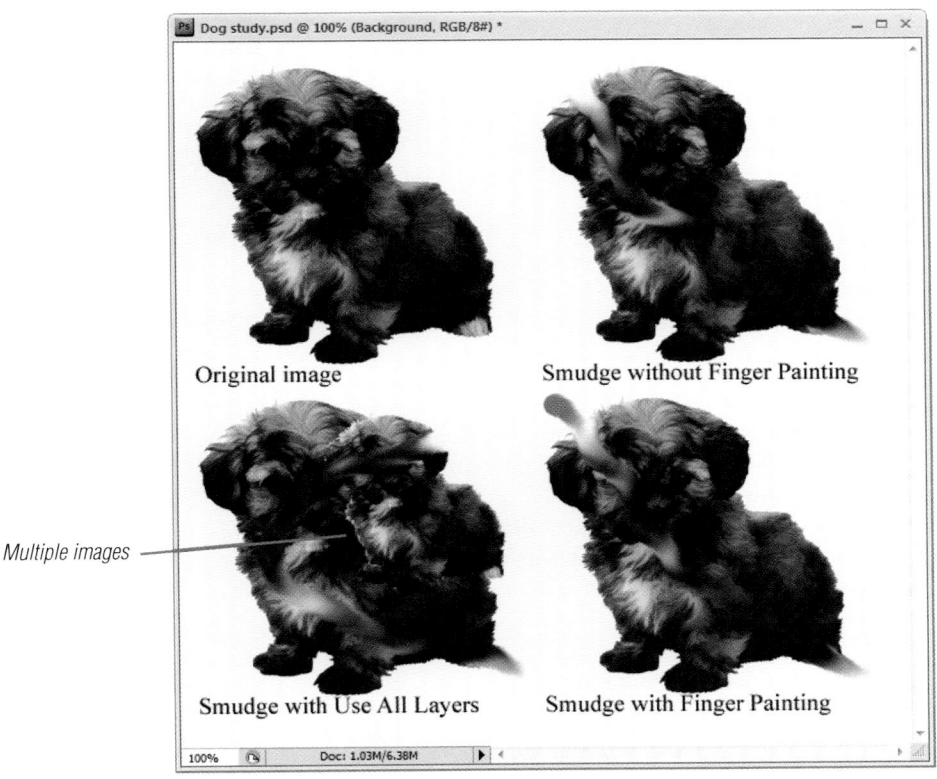

Multiple images

Modify smudge settings

1. Click the **Smudge tool** 🖑 on the Tools panel.

   TIP Look for the Smudge tool under the Sharpen tool.

2. Click **Brush Presets** on the Brushes panel.

3. Click **46 (Spatter 46 pixels)**.

   TIP This brush tip is located in the middle of the list.

4. Select the **Finger Painting check box** on the options bar (if it is not already selected).

5. Make sure your settings match those shown in Figure 16.

You modified the existing smudge settings to prepare to smudge the image.

FIGURE 16
Smudge tool options bar

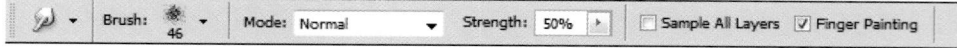

FIGURE 17
Pen tablet

Using a graphics tablet

If you really want to see Photoshop take off when you use brush tools, try using a graphics tablet. Although you can find a pen tablet for as little as $50, this nifty high-end item might set you back several thousand dollars, but you'll love what you get in return.

Figure 17 shows the Wacom Cintiq 21UX graphics tablet, with a cordless, battery-free pen and a 21.3" high-resolution display. The dynamically adjustable stand makes it possible to rotate, incline, or use the display on your lap. (You can learn more about the product at *www.wacom.com*.) The benefits of using a graphics tablet include the following:

- Multiple levels of pressure sensitivity
- Use of pressure-sensitive tools already included in Photoshop
- Programmable menu buttons, touch strips, and a contoured grip pen
- The ability to move even faster than when you use shortcut keys

And as an added bonus, you'll probably experience fewer problems with repetitive stress injuries.

FIGURE 18
Smudged area

Unchanged imagery

FIGURE 19A
Original image

FIGURE 19B
Painted image

Smudge an image

1. Verify that the **Scene layer** is active.
2. Drag the **Smudge tool pointer** (zigzagging from right to left) from **0 X/400 Y** to **530 X/530 Y**.

   Dragging the pointer back and forth as you move from left to right creates an interesting smudge effect. The degree and effect of your smudging will vary.

   An area on the current layer is smudged. Did you notice that the young girl layer is unchanged?
3. Save your work, then compare your image to Figure 18.

You used the Smudge tool to smear the pixels in the bottom third of the image. That area now has a dreamy quality.

Turning a photo into a "painting"
You can create a painting-like appearance using a photographic image and a few simple Photoshop brush tools. Take an image, like the one shown in Figure 19A, and make any necessary color adjustments. Define the entire image as a pattern by clicking Edit on the Application bar, clicking Define Pattern, typing a name, then clicking OK. Click the Pattern Stamp tool, click the Create new fill or adjustment layer button on the Layers panel, then click Solid Color. Choose white from the Color Picker, then lower the opacity so you can see the image. Create another new layer, then use the Pattern Stamp tool and the new pattern you created to paint over the existing image. Figure 19B shows the same image after the painting treatment.

USE A LIBRARY AND AN
AIRBRUSH EFFECT

What You'll Do

 In this lesson, you'll sample an area of the image, then use brush tips from a library to create additional effects. You'll also use an airbrush effect to apply gradual tones.

Learning About the Airbrush Effect

You might have heard of professional photographers using an airbrush to minimize or eliminate flaws in faces or objects. In Photoshop, the effect simulates the photographer's technique by applying gradual tones to an image. Airbrushing creates a diffused effect on the edges of pixels. The airbrush effect is located on the options bar and on the Brushes panel. You can apply the airbrush effect with any brush tip size, using the Brush tool, History Brush tool, Dodge tool, Burn tool, and Sponge tool. The **flow** setting determines how much paint is sprayed while the mouse button is held.

> QUICKTIP
>
> When using the airbrush effect, you can accumulate color by holding the mouse button without dragging.

Restoring pixel data

You can use the History Brush tool to restore painted pixels. The History Brush tool makes a copy of previous pixel data, and then lets you paint with that data, making this tool another good source for undoing painting errors. The Art History Brush tool also lets you re-create imagery using pixel data, but with more stylized effects. This tool has many more options than the History Brush tool, including Style, Area, and Tolerance. Style controls the shape of the paint stroke. Area controls the area covered by the brush tip (a higher area value covers a larger area). Tolerance controls the region where the paint stroke is applied, based on color tolerance. A greater spacing value causes paint strokes to occur in areas that differ in color from the original area. Some of the Art History Brush tool options are shown in Figure 20.

Using Brush Tip Libraries

Photoshop comes with 12 brush libraries that can replace or be appended to the current list of brushes. All the libraries are stored in a folder called Brushes. Each of the libraries is stored in its own file (having the extension .abr). The Load dialog box, from which additional libraries are loaded, is shown in Figure 21. When you use the Load Brushes command (found by clicking the Brushes panel list arrow), the brush tips are added to the end of the brushes list. When you click the name of a brush tip library from the Brush Preset picker list, you are given the option of replacing the existing brush tips with the contents of the library, or appending the brush tips to the existing list.

> **QUICK**TIP
> You can restore the default brush tip settings by clicking the list arrow on the Brushes panel, clicking Reset Brushes, then clicking OK.

Managing the Preset Manager

The **Preset Manager** is a Photoshop feature that allows you to manage libraries of preset brushes, swatches, gradients, styles, patterns, contours, custom shapes, and tools. You can display the Preset Manager by clicking Edit on the Application bar, and then clicking Preset Manager. Options for the Preset Manager are shown in Figure 22. You can delete or rename individual elements for each type of library. Changes that you make in the Preset Manager dialog box are reflected on the corresponding panels.

FIGURE 21
Load dialog box

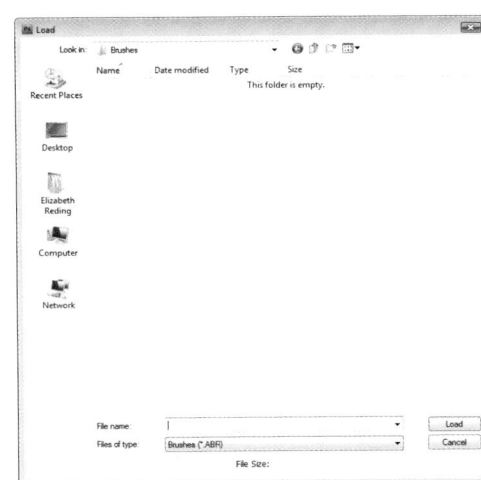

FIGURE 20
Art History Brush tool options

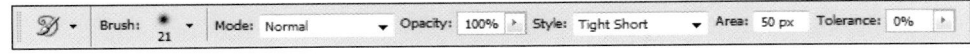

FIGURE 22
Preset Manager dialog box

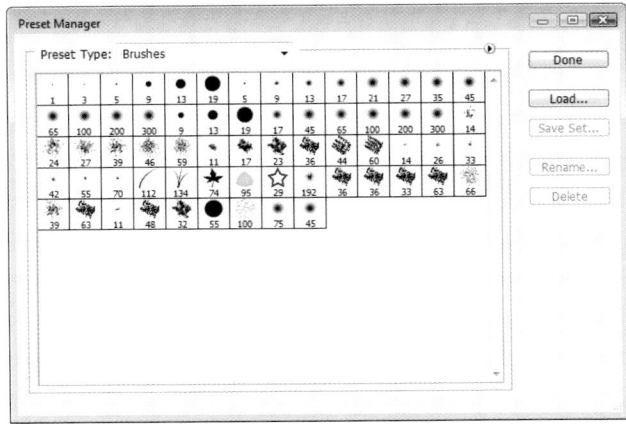

Load a brush library

1. Click the **Eyedropper tool** on the Tools panel.

2. Use the **Eyedropper pointer** to click the image at **50 X/230 Y** (at the intersection of the guides).

3. Click the **Brush tool** on the Tools panel.

4. Click the **Brushes list arrow** ▾≡ , then click **Faux Finish Brushes**, as shown in Figure 23.

   TIP   This brush library is located in the Brushes folder. The Brushes folder is located in /Program Files/Adobe/Adobe Photoshop CS4/Presets/Brushes (Win) and the Presets folder in the Adobe Photoshop CS4 folder in Applications (Mac).

5. Click **Append**.

6. Scroll to the bottom of the list of brush tips, then click **75 (Veining Feather 1)** near the bottom of the list.

   The active brush tip is from the Faux Finish Brushes library.

You sampled a specific location in the image, then loaded the Faux Finish Brushes library. You selected a brush tip from this new library, which you will use to paint an area.

FIGURE 23
Load Brushes command

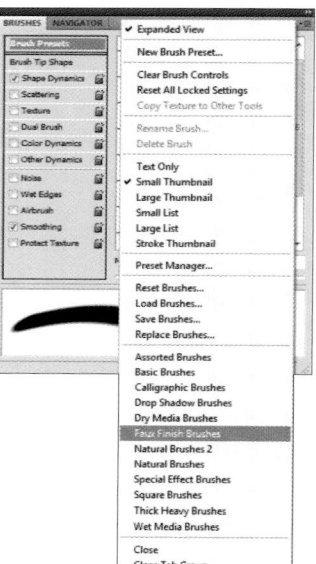

Added benefits of using a pen tablet in Photoshop CS4

If you are using a pen tablet in Photoshop CS4, you'll find that you have more options than ever for image fine-tuning. Using your pen and tablet in conjunction with Photoshop CS4, you'll find that:

- A pressure-sensitive pen and tablet can be used to selectively apply adjustments to a layer mask using the presets in the Adjustments panel.
- By adjusting the intensity setting of your pen, you can use the Dodge, Burn, and Sponge tools with a higher degree of accuracy.
- You'll be able to get into hard-to-reach places by changing the Shape Dynamics setting to Pen Pressure.
- In OpenGL-enabled documents, you can use your pen in combination with the Rotate View tool (grouped with the Hand tool in the Tools panel or on the Application bar) to spin your image canvas.
- You can easily pan your image using your pen.

FIGURE 24

Brush tool options

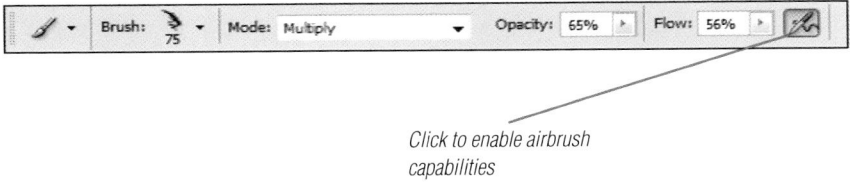

Click to enable airbrush
capabilities

FIGURE 25

Results of Airbrush option and style

Airbrushed effect; your
results may differ

1. Click the **Set to enable airbrush capabilities button** 🖌 on the options bar.
2. Change the settings on the options bar so they match those shown in Figure 24.
3. Drag the **Brush pointer** 🖋 back and forth over the areas of the image containing the sky (from approximately **30 X/50 Y** to **150 X/200 Y**).
4. Hide the rulers.
5. Clear the guides.
6. Click the **Young girl layer** on the Layers panel.
7. Click the **Add a layer style button** *fx.* on the Layers panel.
8. Click **Bevel and Emboss,** then click **OK** to accept the existing settings.
9. Save your work, restore the **Essentials** work-space, then compare your image to Figure 25.
10. Close the image and exit Photoshop.

You used an airbrush effect to paint the sky in the image. You applied the Bevel and Emboss style to a layer to add finishing touches.

Power User Shortcuts

to do this:	use this method:
Apply tint to grayscale image	Image ➤ Mode ➤ RGB Color, choose paint tool, then apply color from Swatches panel
Blur an image	⬦.
Burn an image	🖐 or [Shift] O
Create a brush tip	✎ , ▼≡ , click New Brush Preset
Define a pattern	Edit ➤ Define Pattern, type name, click OK
Delete brush tip	▼≡ , then click Delete Brush
Dodge an image	🔍 or [Shift] O
Load brush library	Click painting tool ▼≡ , in Brushes panel, click Load Brushes in Brushes panel, choose a library, then click Load

to do this:	use this method:
Paint a straight line	Press and hold [Shift] while dragging pointer
Paint an image	🖌 or [Shift] B
Patch a selection	⟳ or [Shift] J
Restore default brushes	▼≡ , click Reset Brushes in Brushes panel
Select Fade options	✎ , then click Shape Dynamics
Sharpen an image	△
Smudge an image	✍

Key: Menu items are indicated by ➤ between the menu name and its command. Bold blue letters are shortcuts for selecting tools on the Tools panel.

Using Painting Tools

Paint and patch an image.

1. Open PS 6-2.psd from the drive and folder where you store your Data Files, then save it as **The Maze**.
2. Display the rulers in pixels.
3. Select the Sharpen tool.
4. Select brush tip 27 (Soft Round 27 pixels).
5. Drag the pointer back and forth over the maze walls along the right edge of the image, as shown in Figure 26; start at 740 X/20 Y and finish at 840 X/540 Y.
6. Select the Burn tool.
7. Select brush tip 19 (Hard Round 19 pixels).
8. Drag the pointer back and forth over the two (middle) dark red arrows.
9. Sample the image at the ball's shadow (located at 50 X/100 Y) with the Eyedropper tool.
10. Select the Brush tool, then use brush tip 17 (Soft Round 17 pixels).
11. Toggle the Brushes panel (if necessary), choose Shape Dynamics, set the Control to Fade, adjust the Size Jitter Fade to 700 steps, then drag the pointer over the inside perimeter of the entire image. (You can perform this action several times.)
12. Select the Patch tool.
13. Select the far-left red arrow (located at 150 X/350 Y) by outlining it with the Patch tool.
14. Select the Destination option button.
15. Drag the selection up and to the right, to the cubicle located at approximately 500 X/140 Y.
16. Deselect the selection.
17. Save your work.

Create and modify a brush tip.

1. Create a brush called **25 Pixel Sample** using the Brush tool and Brushes panel.
2. Change the existing settings (using the Brush Tip Shape area on the Brushes panel) to the following: Diameter = 25 pixels, Hardness = 15%, Spacing = 65%, Angle = 15 degrees, and Roundness = 80%.
3. Use the new brush and the current foreground color to fill in the remaining white space surrounding the perimeter of the image.
4. Save your work.

Use the Smudge tool.

1. Select the Smudge tool.
2. Select brush tip 24 (Spatter 24 pixels).
3. Verify that the Finger Painting check box is selected.
4. Use the Normal mode and 70% strength settings.
5. Drag the pointer in a jagged line from the top left to the bottom right of the image.
6. Save your work.

Use a library and an airbrush effect.

1. Use the Eyedropper tool to sample the aqua arrow in the lower-right corner of the image.
2. Select the Brush tool and apply the airbrush effect.

3. Replace the existing brushes with the Calligraphic Brushes library.
4. Select brush tip 45 (Soft Round 45) towards the end of the list.
5. Drag the pointer over the aqua arrow.
6. Hide the rulers.
7. Create three type layers, using the text shown in Figure 26. The type layers were created using a black 35 pt Poor Richard font; use a different font if this one is not available on your computer. The first layer should read "Help Me," the second should read "Find," and the third should read "My Way Home."
8. Save your work.
9. Compare your image to Figure 26. The appearance of your image might differ.

FIGURE 26
Completed Skills Review project

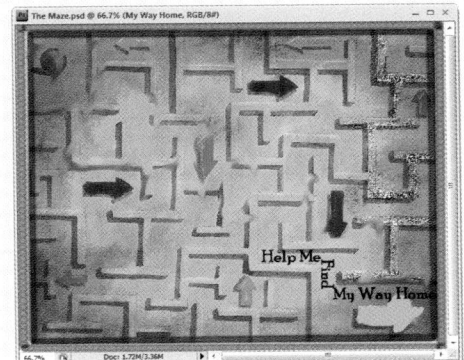

A national bank has hired you to create artwork for its new home loan division. The bank wants this artwork to be original. They have instructed you to go wild, and make this ad look like a work of art. You have created a suitable image, but want to add some artistic touches.

1. Open PS 6-3.psd, then save it as **Bank Artwork**.
2. Use the Burn tool and any brush tip you think is appropriate to accentuate the money and the hand that is holding it.
3. Sample a dark brown area within the image (an area on the coat sleeve of the outstretched arm, located at 420 X/180 Y, was used in the sample).
4. Use a painting tool and brush tip of your choice (brush tip 27 is used in the sample) to paint areas within the suits. (*Hint*: In the sample, the suit lapels are painted.)
5. Create a brush tip using a size and shape of your choice, and give the brush tip a descriptive name.
6. Use any painting tool and any color to create a border that surrounds the image. Use the Fade options of your choice.
7. Use the Smudge tool and the settings of your choice to create an interesting effect in the image. (In the sample, the Smudge tool is used on the shaking hands.)
8. Add a library of your choice, and apply an effect using the Burn tool and the airbrush effect. (Brush tip 43 from the Drop Shadow library is used in the sample.)
9. Make any color adjustments you want. (*Hint*: The Brightness was changed to –26, and the Contrast was changed to +15 in the sample.)

10. Add a type layer using the wording of your choice and any desired effects. (A 75 pt Perpetua font is used on an elliptical path in the sample.)
11. Save your work, then compare your image to the sample in Figure 27.

FIGURE 27
Sample Project Builder 1

The Robotics Department of a major chip manufacturer is conducting an art contest in the hopes of creating a new image for itself. The contest winner will be used in their upcoming advertising campaign, and they want the ad to be lighthearted and humorous. You have decided to enter the contest and have created a preliminary image. You still need to add the finishing touches.

1. Open PS 6-4.psd, then save it as **Robotics Contest Entry**.
2. Use the Sharpen tool to sharpen the pixels in an area of your choice.
3. Burn any area within the image, using any size brush tip.
4. Use any additional painting tools, libraries, and settings to enhance colors and imagery within the image.
5. Add descriptive type to the image, using the font and wording of your choice. (In the sample, a 36 pt Perpetua font is used. A bevel and emboss effect was added to the type.)
6. Make any color adjustments you want. (In the sample, the Hue is modified to −15, the Saturation is modified to +34, and the Lightness is modified to −20.)
7. Save your work, then compare your image to the sample in Figure 28.

FIGURE 28
Sample Project Builder 2

Using Painting Tools

You have been hired by a local art gallery, Expressions, to teach a course that describes how Photoshop can be used to create impressionistic artwork. This gallery specializes in offbeat, avant-garde art, and wants you to inspire the attendees to see the possibilities of this important software program. They hired you because you have a reputation for creating daring artwork. As you prepare your lecture, you decide to explore the Internet to see what information already exists.

1. Connect to the Internet and use your browser and favorite search engine to find information about digital artwork. (Make a record of the site you found so you can use it for future reference, if necessary.)
2. Identify and print a page containing an interesting piece of artwork that you feel could be created in Photoshop.

3. Using your word processor, create a document called **Art Course**. A sample document is shown in Figure 29. (*Tip*: You can capture your image, then paste it in your document by pressing [Print Scrn], then [Ctrl][V] in your word processor (Win) or pressing [Ctrl] [⌘] [shift][4] , then [⌘][V] (Mac).)

FIGURE 29
Sample Design Project

4. In the document, analyze the image, pointing out which effects could be created in Photoshop, and which Photoshop tools and features you would use to achieve these effects.
5. Save your work.

Courtesy of Fred Casselman - http://www.earthecho.com/sun/ni13.html

A local car dealer has hired you to create a poster that can be used in magazine ads and highway billboards. The dealership's only requirement is that an automobile be featured within the artwork. You can use any appropriate imagery (already existing on your hard drive, from the web, or your own creation, using a scanner or a digital camera), then compile the artwork and use Photoshop's painting tools to create daring effects. You should create a tag line for the image. You do not need to add a name for the dealership; it will be added at a later date.

1. Start Photoshop and create an image with any dimensions.
2. Save this file as **Dealership Ad**.
3. Make selections and create a composite image.
4. Use any painting tools and settings to create interesting effects.
5. Add at least one layer of type and an effect in the image. Use any fonts available on your computer. (The font shown in the sample is 136 pt Informal Roman.)
6. Make color adjustments.
7. Save your work, then compare your image to the sample in Figure 30.

FIGURE 30
Sample Portfolio Project

Using Painting Tools

chapter

7

WORKING WITH SPECIAL
LAYER FUNCTIONS

1. Use a layer mask with a selection

2. Work with layer masks and layer content

3. Control pixels to blend colors

4. Eliminate a layer mask

5. Use an adjustment layer

6. Create a clipping mask

Designing with Layers

Photoshop is rich with tools and techniques for creating and enhancing images. After the imagery is in place, you can hide and modify objects to create special effects. When used in conjunction with other relatively simple techniques, such as merging layers or duplicating layers, the results can be dramatic.

Making Non-destructive Changes to a Layer

If you want to alter a layer, the easiest thing to do is to select the layer and then make the changes. But if you do that, the layer is changed forever, and once you end the current Photoshop session, there is no going back. Adjustment layers make it possible to alter a layer non-destructively, so you *can* go back and revise (or reverse) your changes.

Modifying Specific Areas Within a Layer

You can use special layer features to modify the entire image or a single layer of an image. For example, suppose that you have an image with objects in multiple layers. Perhaps you want to include certain elements from each layer, but you also want to hide some imagery in the finished image. You can *define* the precise area you want to manipulate in each layer, and then accurately adjust its appearance to exactly what you want, without permanently altering the original image. You can turn your changes on or off, align images, blend and adjust color, and combine elements to enhance your image.

Tools You'll Use

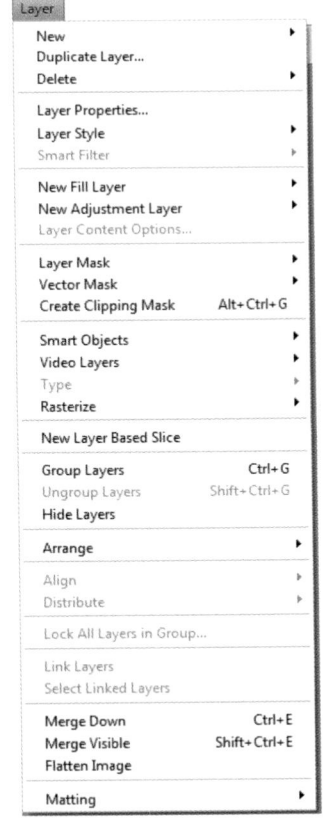

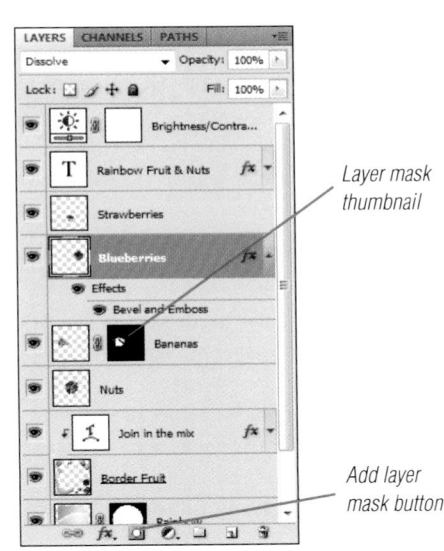

Layer mask thumbnail

Add layer mask button

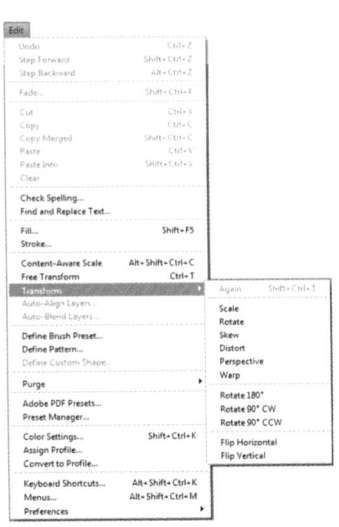

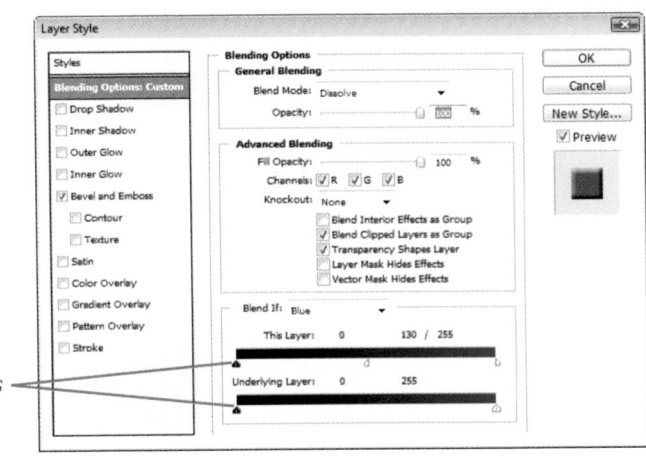

Blending sliders

USE A LAYER MASK WITH
A SELECTION

What You'll Do

In this lesson, you'll use the Elliptical Marquee tool to make a selection and create a layer mask on the Market layer and on the Bananas layer. You'll select the Brush tool and a brush tip, and then paint on the layer mask to hide pixels.

About Layer Masks

You can hide or reveal a selection within a layer by using a layer mask. A **layer mask** can cover an entire layer or specific areas within a layer. When a layer contains a mask, a layer mask thumbnail appears on the Layers panel to the left of the layer name. As you hide or reveal portions of a layer, the layer mask thumbnail mirrors the changes you make to the object. Some Photoshop features are permanent after you implement them. Masks, however, are extremely flexible—you can hide their effect when you view the image, or change them at will. Because you alter the mask and not the image, no actual pixels are harmed in the creation of your image. You can add an unlimited number of masks to an image, but only one mask to each layer. You can also continue to edit the layer without affecting the layer mask.

QUICKTIP

You can think of a mask as a type of temporary eraser. When you erase pixels from an image, they're gone. A mask can be used to cover pixels—either temporarily or permanently. You can also think of a mask as a cropping tool that offers flexible shapes.

Creating a Layer Mask

You can use tools on the Tools panel to create the area you want to mask. You can apply a mask to the selection, or you can apply the mask to everything except the selection. You can also feather a selection (control the softness of its edges) by typing pixel values in the Feather text box on the options bar.

QUICKTIP

The term "mask" has its origin in printing. Traditionally, a mask was opaque material or tape used to block off an area of the artwork that you did not want to print.

Using the Masks Panel

Once you have created an area to be masked, you can create and refine the masked area using the Masks panel. This panel can be found in both the Essentials and Color and Tone workspaces, and is grouped with the Adjustments panel. It provides a central area where you can create and control a mask. Using the Masks panel, you can adjust the mask density and feathering *non-destructively*. (Non-destructive changes are those that can be reversed even after the image has been closed.)

Painting a Layer Mask

After you add a layer mask to a layer, you can reshape it with the Brush tool and a specific brush size, or tip. Photoshop offers dozens of brush tips, so you can paint just the area you want. For example, you can create a smooth transition between the hidden and visible areas using a soft-edged brush. Here are some important facts about painting a layer mask:

- When you paint the image with a black foreground, the size of the mask *increases*, and each brush stroke hides pixels on the image layer. *Paint with black to hide pixels.*
- When you paint an object using white as the foreground color, the size of the mask *decreases*, and each brush stroke restores pixels of the layer object. *Paint with white to reveal pixels.*

In Figure 1, the School Bus layer contains a layer mask. The area where the bus intersects with the camera has been painted in black so that the bus appears to be driving through the lens of the camera.

Correcting and Updating a Mask

If you need to make a slight correction to an area, you can just switch the foreground and background colors and paint over the mistake. The layer mask thumbnail on the Layers panel automatically updates itself to reflect changes you make to the mask.

FIGURE 1
Example of a layer mask

Masks panel

Selected mask

Layer thumbnail

Layer mask

Create a layer mask using the Layer menu

1. Start Photoshop, open PS 7-1.psd from the drive and folder where you store your Data Files, then save it as **Produce Market**.

   TIP If you see a message stating that some text layers need to be updated before they can be used for vector-based output, click Update (Mac).

2. Click the **Default Foreground and Background Colors button** ![icon] on the Tools panel.

3. Display the guides, and the rulers in pixels (if necessary), and verify that the Essentials workspace is displayed.

4. Verify that the **Market layer** is the active layer.

5. Click the **Elliptical Marquee tool** ⬭ on the Tools panel.

   TIP Look under the Rectangular Marquee tool if the Elliptical Marquee tool is hidden.

6. Change the Feather setting to **5 px** (if this is not the current setting).

7. Drag the **Marquee pointer** ┼ from **30 X/20 Y** to **550 X/540 Y**, to create a marquee that includes the text, bananas, and blueberries using the guides, then compare your image to Figure 2.

8. Click **Layer** on the Application bar, point to **Layer Mask**, then click **Reveal Selection**.

   TIP You can deselect a marquee by clicking Select on the Application bar, then clicking Deselect; by clicking in another area of the image with the marquee tool that you are using; or by right-clicking the object, then clicking Deselect in the shortcut menu.

You used the Elliptical Marquee tool to create a selection, and created a layer mask on the Market layer using the Layer Mask command on the Layer menu.

FIGURE 2
Elliptical selection on the Market layer

Elliptical marquee selection

Creating a selection from a Quick Mask

Once you have created a selection, you can click the Edit in Quick Mask Mode button ![icon] on the Tools panel to create a mask that can be saved as a selection. When you click the Edit in Quick Mask Mode button, a red overlay displays. Use any painting tools to form a shape in and around the selection. When your mask is finished, click the Edit in Standard Mode button on the Tools panel, and the shape will be outlined by a marquee. You can then save the selection for future use, or use any other Photoshop tools and effects on it.

FIGURE 3
Elliptical selection on the Bananas layer

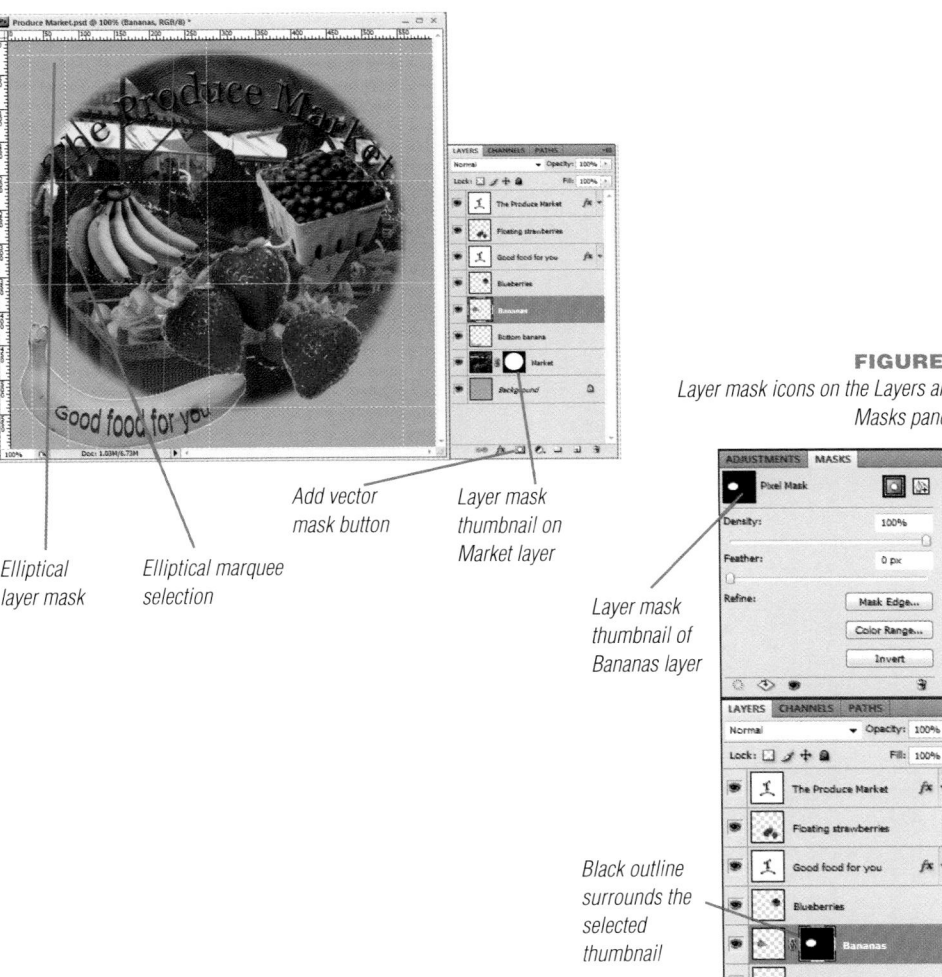

Add vector
mask button

Layer mask
thumbnail on
Market layer

Elliptical
layer mask

Elliptical marquee
selection

FIGURE 4
*Layer mask icons on the Layers and
Masks panels*

Layer mask
thumbnail of
Bananas layer

Black outline
surrounds the
selected
thumbnail

Create a layer mask using the Masks panel

1. Click the **Bananas layer** on the Layers panel.

2. Drag the **Marquee pointer** ┼ from approximately **80 X/210 Y** to **280 X/360 Y** (to surround the bunch of bananas), as shown in Figure 3.

3. Click the **Masks tab** MASKS to make it active.

4. Click the **Add a pixel mask button** 🔲 on the Masks panel.

   The lower-left edge of the Bananas layer is partially obscured by the layer mask. The layer mask thumbnail appears to the right of the layer thumbnail in the Layers panel and appears at the top of the Masks panel. Once the mask is created, the Masks panel options are available (and no longer dimmed).

   TIP You can also create a layer mask by clicking the Add layer mask button in the Layers panel. If you use this method, you can press and hold [Alt] (Win) or [option] (Mac) while clicking the Add layer mask button to add a mask that *hides* the selection, rather than reveals it.

5. Verify that the **layer mask thumbnail** on the Bananas layer is active, then compare your Layers panel to Figure 4.

   TIP You can tell whether the layer mask or the layer object is active by the outline surrounding the thumbnail and by its appearance in the Masks panel.

You used the Elliptical Marquee tool to create a selection, and then used the Select the pixel mask button on the Masks panel to create a layer mask on the Bananas layer.

Paint a layer mask

1. Click the **Zoom tool** 🔍 on the Application bar.

2. Select the **Resize Windows To Fit check box** on the options bar.

3. Click the **bananas** at approximately **150 X/300 Y** with the **Zoom pointer** ⊕ until the bananas are centered and the zoom factor is **200%**.

4. Click the **Brush tool** ✎ on the Tools panel.

5. Click the **Click to open the Brush Preset picker list arrow** on the options bar, then double-click the **Hard Round 9 pixels brush tip**.

6. Change the Painting Mode on the options bar to **Normal** and the Opacity to **100%** (if necessary).

7. Verify that **Black** is the foreground color and **White** is the background color. (*Hint*: You may have to switch foreground and background colors.)

   TIP Learning to paint a layer mask can be challenging. It's important to make sure the correct layer (and thumbnail) is active before you start painting, to know whether you're adding to or subtracting from the mask, and to set your foreground and background colors correctly.

8. Drag the **Brush pointer** ⭕ along the far-left banana until it is completely hidden. Compare your screen to Figure 5.

   As you painted, the shape of the mask thumbnail changed in both the Masks and Layers panels.

   TIP Select a different brush tip if the brush is too big or too small.

You used the Zoom tool to keep a specific portion of the image in view as you increased the zoom percentage, selected a brush tip, and painted pixels on the layer mask to hide a banana.

FIGURE 5
Layer mask painted

Painted area

FIGURE 6
Refine Mask dialog box

Modify the layer mask

1. Drag the **Brush pointer** ◯ along the right edge of the object, until the far-right banana is no longer visible and you revealed more produce from the Market layer.

   TIP As you paint, a new History state is created each time you release the mouse button.

2. Click the **Mask Edge button** in the Masks panel.

   The Refine Mask dialog box opens with the On White box selected, as shown in Figure 6. You can use this feature to see if you missed any areas that need to be painted away.

3. Click **OK** to close Refine Mask dialog box, then use the brush pointer to paint away any omissions.

4. Click the **Zoom tool** 🔍 on the Application bar.

5. Press **[Alt]** (Win) or **[option]** (Mac), click at **150 X/300 Y** with the **Zoom pointer** 🔍 until the zoom factor is **100%**, then release **[Alt]** (Win) or **[option]** (Mac).

6. Save your work, then compare your screen to Figure 7.

You painted pixels to hide the far-right banana, then reset the zoom percentage to 100%.

FIGURE 7
Modified layer mask

Editing a layer mask versus editing a layer

Modifying a layer mask can be tricky because you have to make sure that you've selected the layer mask and not the layer thumbnail. Even though the active thumbnail is surrounded by an outline, it can be difficult to see. To make sure whether the layer mask or layer thumbnail is selected, click each one so you can see the difference, then make sure the one you want is selected. You'll know if you've selected the wrong item as soon as you start painting!

WORK WITH LAYER MASKS
AND LAYER CONTENT

What You'll Do

In this lesson, you'll select three layers simultaneously, align the images on three layers, and then deselect the layers. You'll also scale and horizontally flip the strawberries on the Floating strawberries layer.

Understanding Layers and Their Masks

The ability to repeatedly alter the appearance of an image without ever disturbing the actual pixels on the layer makes a layer mask a powerful editing tool. By default, Photoshop links the mask to the layer. This means that if you move the layer, the mask moves as well.

Understanding the Link Icon

The link icon automatically appears when you create a layer mask. When you create a layer mask, the link icon appears *between* the layer thumbnail and the layer mask thumbnail, indicating that the layer and the layer mask are linked together. To unlink the layer mask from its layer, you click the link icon. The Unlink Mask state displays in the History panel. You can re-link a mask to its layer by clicking the space between the layer and mask thumbnails. The Link Mask state displays in the History panel.

Selecting Multiple Layers

You can select more than one layer on the Layers panel to allow multiple layers to behave as one. Selecting multiple layers in

Photoshop is analogous to grouping objects in other programs. You select multiple layers or layer sets by clicking a layer on the Layers panel. To select contiguous layers (layers that are next to one another on the Layers panel), press and hold [Shift] while clicking additional layers on the Layers panel. To select non-contiguous layers, press and hold [Ctrl] (Win) or [⌘] (Mac) while clicking additional layers on the Layers panel. When selecting multiple layers make sure that you click the layer, *not the layer mask*. You can make multiple selections that include the active layer and any other layers on the Layers panel, even if they are in different layer sets. You can select entire layer sets along with a single layer or with other layer sets.

QUICKTIP

When you move multiple selections of layers, the relocation of layers affects the objects' appearance in your image, as well as the layers' position on the Layers panel. This means that you can link two layers and then align them in your image. You can also select two non-contiguous layers and then move them simultaneously as a unit to the top of the Layers panel where they will become contiguous.

Working with Layers

After you select multiple layers, you can perform actions that affect the selection such as moving their content as a single unit in your image. To deselect multiple layers, click any layer (within the selection) on the Layers panel with [Ctrl] for each layer you want to deselect. When you deselect each layer, each one returns to its independent state. You can also turn off a layer's display while it is part of a selection of layers by clicking the layer's Indicates layer visibility button.

Aligning Selected Layers

Suppose you have several type layers in your image and need to align them by their left edges. Rather than individually moving and aligning numerous layers, you can precisely position selected layers in your image. You can align the content in the image by first selecting layers on the Layers panel, then choosing one of six subcommands from the Align command on the Layer menu. Photoshop aligns layers relative to each other or to a selection border. So, if you have four type layers and want to align them by their left edges, Photoshop will align them relative to the far-left pixels in those layers only, not to any other (nonselected) layers on the Layers panel or to other content in your image.

Distributing Selected Layers

To distribute (evenly space) the content on layers in your image, you must first select three or more layers, verify that their opacity settings are 50% or greater, and then select one of the six options from the Distribute command on the Layer menu. Photoshop spaces out the content in your image relative to pixels in the selected layers. For example, imagine an image that is 700 pixels wide and has four type layers that are 30 pixels wide each and span a range between 100 X and 400 Y. If you select the four type layers and click the Horizontal Centers command on the Distribute Layers menu, Photoshop will distribute them evenly, but only between 100 X and 400 Y. To distribute the type layers evenly across the width of your entire image, you must first move the left and right layers to the left and right edges of your image, respectively.

Transforming Objects

You can **transform** (change the shape, size, perspective, or rotation) of an object or objects on a layer, using one of 11 transform commands on the Edit menu. When you use some of the transform commands, eight selection handles surround the contents of the active layer. When you choose any transform command, a transform box appears around the object you are transforming. A **transform box** is a rectangle that surrounds an image and contains handles that can be used to change dimensions. You can pull the handles with the pointer to start transforming the object. After you transform an object, you can apply the changes by clicking the Commit transform (Return) button on the options bar, or by pressing [Enter] (Win) or [return] (Mac). You can use transform commands individually or in a chain. After you choose your initial transform command, you can try out as many others as you like before you apply the changes by pressing [Enter] (Win) or [return] (Mac). If you attempt another command (something other than another transform command) before pressing [Enter] (Win) or [return] (Mac), a warning box will appear. Click Apply to accept the transformation you made to the layer.

Select and align layers

1. Verify that the **Bananas layer** on the Layers panel is active.

2. Press and hold **[Ctrl]** (Win) or ⌘ (Mac), click the **Floating strawberries layer** on the Layers panel, then release **[Ctrl]** (Win) or ⌘ (Mac).

3. Press and hold **[Ctrl]** (Win) or ⌘ (Mac), click the **Blueberries layer** on the Layers panel, release **[Ctrl]** (Win) or ⌘ (Mac), then compare your Layers panel to Figure 8.

4. Click **Layer** on the Application bar, point to **Align**, then click **Vertical Centers**.

   The centers of the Blueberries and Floating strawberries layers are aligned with the center of the Bananas layer. Compare your image to Figure 9.

5. Press and hold **[Ctrl]** (Win) or ⌘ (Mac), click the **Floating strawberries layer** and the **Blueberries layer** on the Layers panel, then release **[Ctrl]** (Win) or ⌘ (Mac).

   The additional objects are no longer selected, yet all retain their new locations.

You selected three layers on the Layers panel, aligned the objects on those layers by their vertical centers using the Align Vertical Centers command on the Layer menu, then you deselected the layers.

Grouping layers

You can quickly turn multiple selected layers into a group. Select as many layers as you'd like—even if they are not contiguous, click Layer on the Application bar, then click Group Layers. Each of the selected layers will be placed in a Group (which looks like a layer set) in the Layers panel. You can ungroup the layers by selecting the group in the Layers panel, clicking Layer on the Application bar, then clicking Ungroup Layers.

FIGURE 8
Blueberries layer and Floating strawberries layer selected with Bananas layer

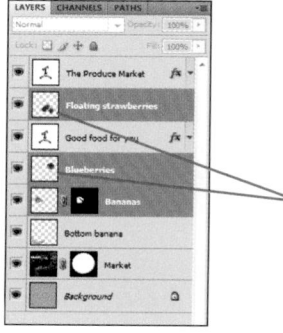

Layers selected with Bananas layer

FIGURE 9
Aligned layers

Center pixel of blueberries and floating strawberries layers aligned with center pixel of bananas layer

FIGURE 10
Floating strawberries layer scaled

Drag handle to
resize

FIGURE 11
Floating strawberries layer transformed

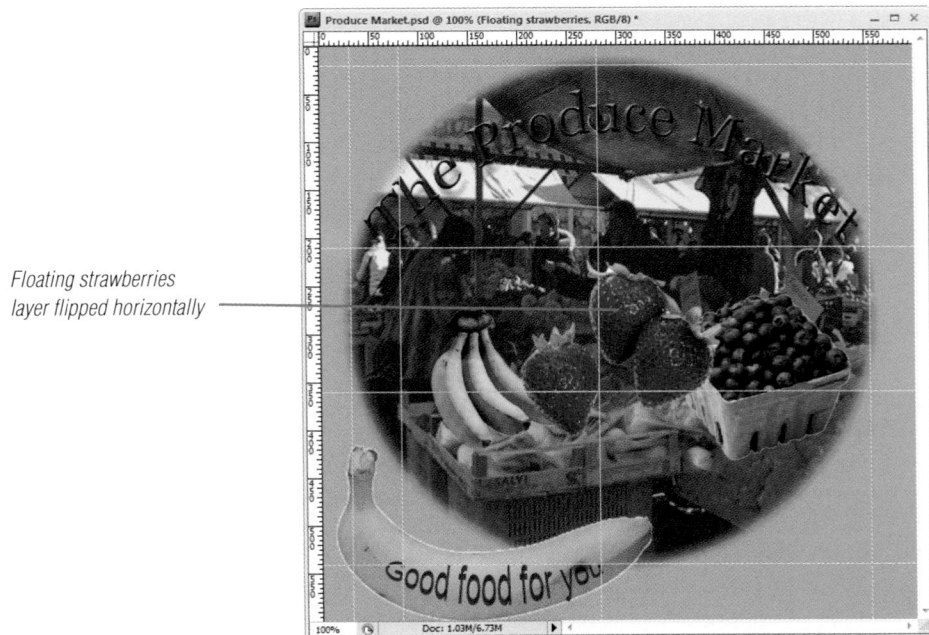

Floating strawberries
layer flipped horizontally

Transform a layer using Scale

1. Click the **Floating strawberries layer** on the Layers panel.

2. Click **Edit** on the Application bar, point to **Transform**, then click **Scale**.

3. Position the **Scaling pointer** over the **bottom-right sizing handle** using the ruler pixel measurements at approximately **495 X/465 Y**, drag to **400 X/405 Y** up and to the left, as shown in Figure 10, then release the mouse button.

4. Click the **Commit transform (Return) button** ✔ on the options bar.

    The strawberries image is reduced.

You resized the Floating strawberries layer using the Scale command. This command makes it easy to resize an object while maintaining its proportions.

Transform a layer using Flip Horizontal

1. Verify that the **Floating strawberries layer** is the active layer.

2. Click **Edit** on the Application bar, point to **Transform**, then click **Flip Horizontal**.

3. View the transformation.

4. Save your work, then compare your image to Figure 11.

You horizontally flipped the Floating strawberries layer using the Flip Horizontal command. You can use this command to change the orientation of an object on a layer.

CONTROL PIXELS
TO BLEND COLORS

What You'll Do

 In this lesson, you'll apply styles to layers using the Layer Style dialog box. You'll also work with blending modes to blend pixels on various layers.

Blending Pixels

You can control the colors and form of your image by blending pixels on one layer with pixels on another layer. You can control *which* pixels from the active layer are blended with pixels from lower layers on the Layers panel. You can control how the pixels are blended by specifying which color pixels you want to change. If you set the Blend If color to Red, then all pixels on the layer that are red will be blended based on your new settings. Blending options are found in the Layer Style dialog box. You can control *how* these pixels are blended by choosing a color as the Blend If color, and using the This Layer and Underlying Layer sliders. The **Blend If** color determines the color range for the pixels you want to blend. You use the **This Layer** sliders to specify the range of pixels that will be blended on the active layer. You use the **Underlying Layer** sliders to specify the range of pixels that will be blended on all the lower—but still visible—layers. The color channels available depend on the color mode. For example, an RGB image will have Red, Green, and Blue color channels available.

> **QUICK**TIP
> Color channels contain information about the colors in an image.

Using duplicate layers to blend pixels

You can create interesting effects by duplicating layers. To duplicate a layer, click the layer you want to duplicate to activate it, click the Layers panel list arrow, click Duplicate Layer, then click OK. The duplicate layer is given the same name as the active layer with "copy" attached to it. (You can also create a duplicate layer by dragging the layer to the Create a new layer button on the Layers panel.) You can modify the duplicate layer by applying effects or masks to it. In addition, you can alter an image's appearance by moving the original and duplicate layers to different positions on the Layers panel.

Using Color Sliders

The colors that are outside the pixel range you set with the color sliders will not be visible, and the boundary between the visible and invisible pixels will be sharp and hard. You can soften the boundary by adjusting the slider position and creating a gradual transition between the visible and invisible pixels. Normally, you determine the last visible color pixel by adjusting its slider position, just as you can set opacity by dragging a slider on the Layers panel. Photoshop also allows you to split the color slider in two. When you move the slider halves apart, you create a span of pixels for the visible boundary. Figure 12 shows two objects before they are blended and Figure 13 shows the two objects after they are blended. Do you see how the blended pixels conform to the shape of the underlying pixels?

FIGURE 12
Pixels before they are blended

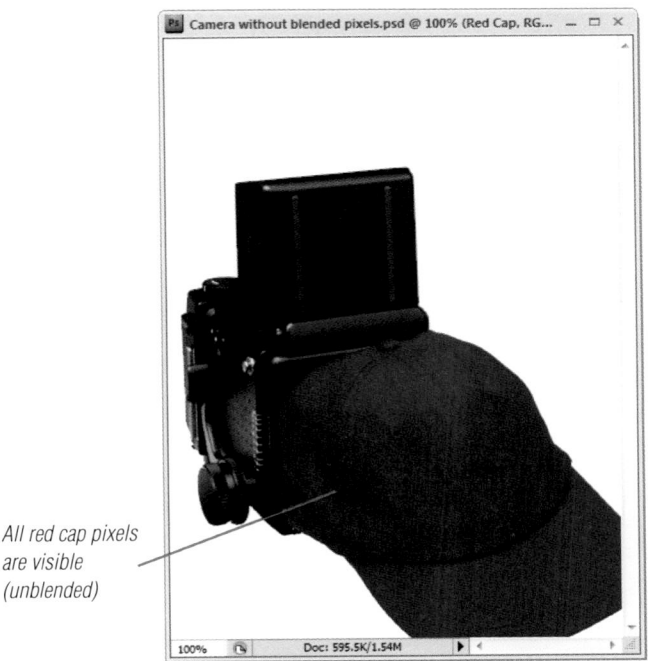

All red cap pixels are visible (unblended)

FIGURE 13
Pixels after they are blended

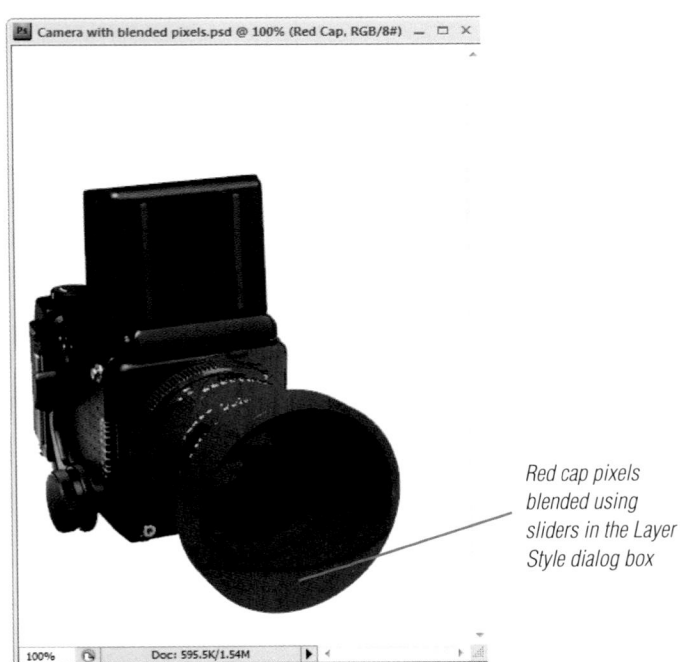

Red cap pixels blended using sliders in the Layer Style dialog box

Blend pixels with a color range

1. Double-click the **Floating strawberries thumbnail** on the Layers panel to open the Layer Style dialog box.

   | TIP   Move the Layer Style dialog box if it obscures your view of the strawberries.

2. Click to highlight the **Blending Options: Default bar** at the top of the list (if it is not already selected).

3. Select the **Drop Shadow check box**.

4. Click the **Blend If list arrow**, then click **Red**.

5. Drag the right (white) **This Layer slider** to **240**, as shown in Figure 14.

   | TIP   Slider position determines the number of visible pixels for the color channel you've selected.

6. Click **OK**, then view the fade-out effect on the Strawberries layer.

   | TIP   If you want to really observe the fade-out effect, display the History panel, then delete the last state and redo steps 4 through 6.

You opened the Layer Style dialog box for the Floating strawberries layer, applied the Drop Shadow style, selected Red as the Blend If color, and then adjusted the This Layer slider to change the range of visible pixels. The result is that you blended pixels on the Floating strawberries layer so that red pixels outside a specific range will not be visible.

FIGURE 14
Layer Style dialog box

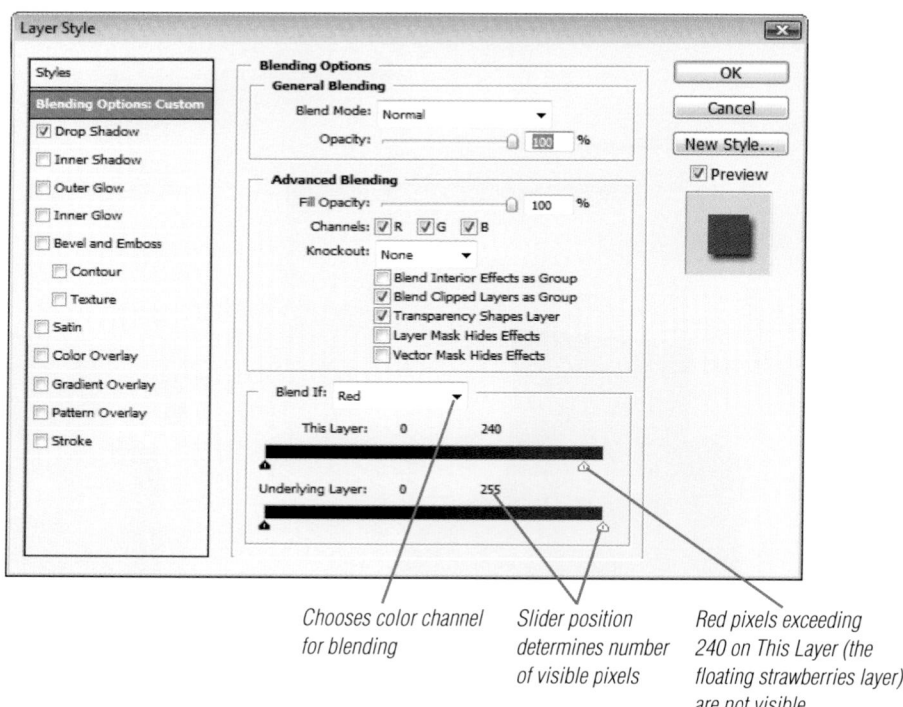

Chooses color channel for blending

Slider position determines number of visible pixels

Red pixels exceeding 240 on This Layer (the floating strawberries layer) are not visible

FIGURE 15
Transition range for visible pixels

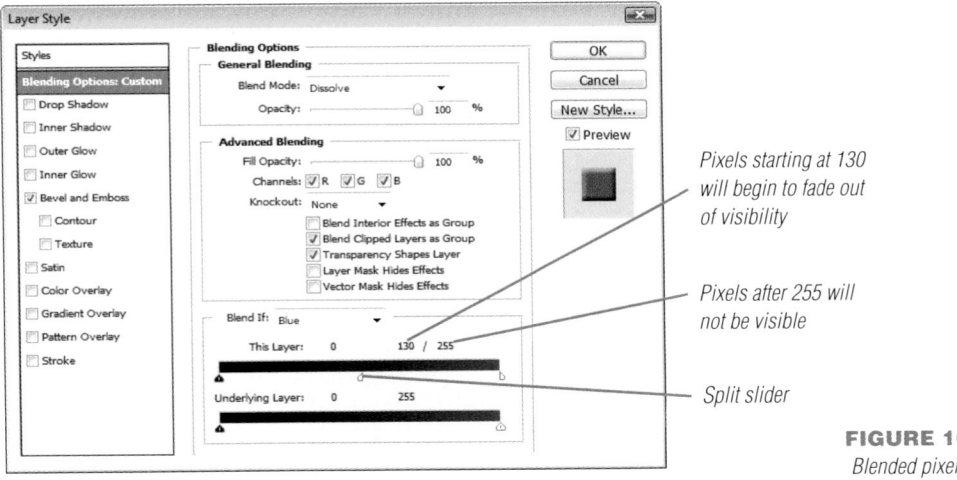

Pixels starting at 130 will begin to fade out of visibility

Pixels after 255 will not be visible

Split slider

FIGURE 16
Blended pixels

Blended areas

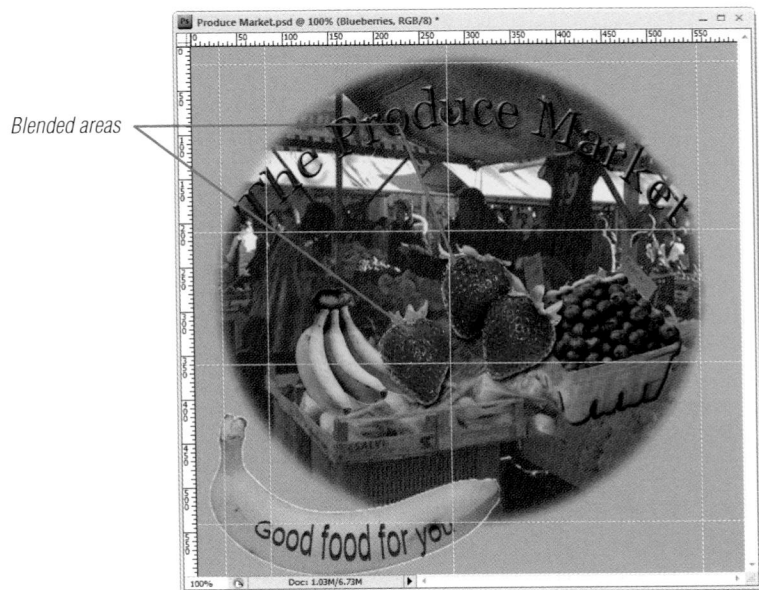

Split sliders to select a color range

1. Double-click the **Blueberries thumbnail** on the Layers panel to open the Layer Style dialog box.

2. Click to highlight the **Blending Options: Default bar** at the top of the list (if necessary), then click the **Bevel and Emboss check box**.

3. Click the **Blend Mode list arrow**, then click **Dissolve**.

4. Click the **Blend If list arrow**, then click **Blue**.

5. Press and hold **[Alt]** (Win) or **[option]** (Mac), click the right **This Layer slider**, drag the left half of the **Right slider** to **130**, then release **[Alt]** (Win) or **[option]** (Mac).

   | TIP   Pressing [Alt] (Win) or [option] (Mac) splits the slider into two halves.

6. Compare your dialog box to Figure 15, then click **OK**.

7. Save your work, then compare your image to Figure 16.

You opened the Layer Style dialog box for the Blueberries layer, applied the Bevel and Emboss style to the layer and changed the blending mode to Dissolve, specifying the blue pixels as the color to blend. To fine-tune the blend, you split the right This Layer slider and set a range of pixels that smoothed the transition between visible and invisible pixels.

ELIMINATE
A LAYER MASK

What You'll Do

In this lesson, you'll use the Layer menu to temporarily disable a layer mask, and discard a layer mask using the Layers panel.

Disposing of Layer Masks

As you have seen, layer masks enable you to radically change an image's appearance. However, you might not want to keep every layer mask you create, or you might want to turn the layer mask on or off, or you might want to apply the layer mask to the layer and move on to another activity. You can enable or disable the layer mask (turn it on or off), or remove it from the Layers panel by deleting it from the layer entirely or by permanently applying it to the layer.

Disabling a Layer Mask

Photoshop allows you to temporarily disable a layer mask from a layer to view the layer without the mask. When you disable a layer mask, Photoshop indicates that the layer mask is still in place, but not currently visible, by displaying a red X over the layer mask thumbnail in both the Layers and Masks panels, as shown in Figure 17. Temporarily disabling a layer mask has many advantages. For example, you can create duplicate layers and layer masks, apply different styles and effects to them, and then enable and disable (show and hide) layer masks individually until you decide which mask gives you the look you want.

> **QUICK**TIP
>
> The command available for a layer mask changes depending on whether the layer is visible or not. If the layer mask is enabled, the Layer Mask Disable command is active on the Layer menu. If the layer mask is disabled, the Layer Mask Enable command is active.

Removing Layer Masks

If you are certain that you don't want a layer mask, you can permanently remove it. Before you do so, Photoshop gives you two options:

- You can apply the mask to the layer so that it becomes a permanent part of the layer.
- You can discard the mask and its effect completely.

QUICKTIP

Each layer mask increases the file size, so it's a good idea to perform some routine maintenance as you finalize your image. Remove any unnecessary, unwanted layer masks, and then apply the layer masks you want to keep.

If you apply the mask, the layer will retain the *appearance* of the mask effect, but it will no longer contain the actual layer mask. If you discard the mask entirely, you delete the effects you created with the layer mask, and return the layer to its original state.

QUICKTIP

You can select a layer mask by pressing [Ctrl][\] (Win) or ⌘[\] (Mac) and select the layer thumbnail by pressing [Ctrl][~] (Win) or ⌘[~] (Mac).

FIGURE 17
Layer mask disabled

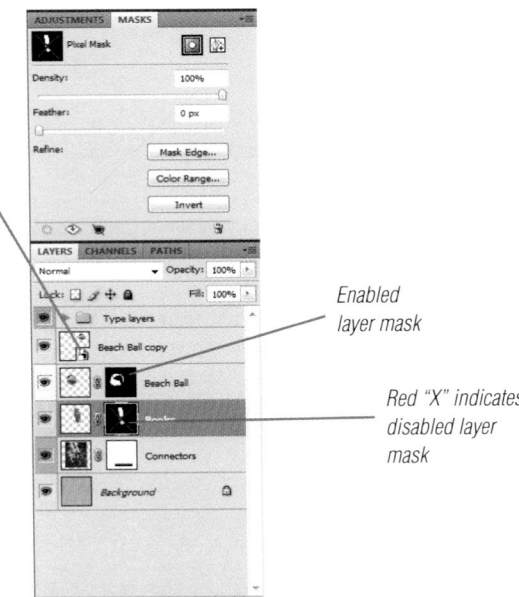

Smart Object thumbnail

Enabled layer mask

Red "X" indicates disabled layer mask

Working with Smart Objects

Just as multiple layers can be selected, you can combine multiple objects into a Smart Object. This combination, which has a visible indicator in the lower-right corner of the layer thumbnail, makes it possible to *non-destructively* scale, rotate, and warp layers without losing image quality. Once the layers you want to combine are selected, you can create a Smart Object by clicking Layer on the Application bar, pointing to Smart Objects, then clicking Group into New Smart Object; or by clicking the Layers panel list arrow, then clicking Convert to Smart Object.

Disable and enable a layer mask

1. Click **Window** on the Application bar, point to **Workspace**, then click **History and Layers**.

2. Click the **Bananas layer** on the Layers panel.

3. Click **Layer** on the Application bar, point to **Layer Mask**, then click **Disable**. See Figure 18.

    When you disable the mask, the bananas are fully displayed.

    > TIP   You can also disable a layer mask by pressing [Shift] and then clicking the layer mask thumbnail, and then enable it by pressing [Shift] and clicking the layer mask thumbnail again.

4. Drag the **Disable Layer Mask history state** to the **Delete current state button** 🗑 on the History panel.

    Deleting the Disable Layer Mask history state causes the remasking of the bananas.

    > TIP   Before you remove a layer mask, verify that the layer mask, not just the layer, is active. Otherwise, if you use the Delete layer button on the Layers panel to remove the mask, you will delete the layer, not the layer mask.

You disabled the layer mask on the Bananas layer, using commands on the Layer menu, and deleted the Disable Layer Mask history state using the History panel.

FIGURE 18
Layer mask disabled

Original view of bananas
without the layer mask

Disabled layer mask

FIGURE 19
Warning box

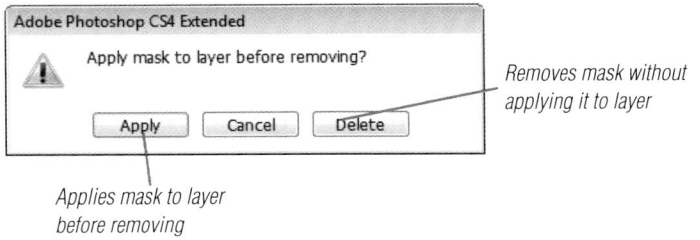

Removes mask without
applying it to layer

Applies mask to layer
before removing

FIGURE 20
Market layer with layer mask removed

Layer mask
reverts to
original
appearance

Layer mask
removed

Remove a layer mask

1. Click the **layer mask thumbnail** on the Market layer on the Layers panel.

2. Click the **Masks tab** `MASKS` to activate the Masks panel.

3. Click the **Delete layer button** 🗑 on the Layers panel, then compare your warning box to Figure 19.

4. Click **Delete** to remove the mask without first applying it to the Market layer. Compare your screen to Figure 20.

   TIP You can use the Delete Mask button 🗑 in the Masks panel to delete the mask *without* seeing the warning box.

5. Click **Edit** on the Application bar, then click **Undo Delete Layer Mask**.

6. Save your work.

You used the Delete layer button on the Layers panel to delete a layer mask, chose the Delete option in the warning box to remove the mask without applying it to the Market layer, and then used the Edit menu to undo the action to restore the layer mask on the Market layer.

USE AN ADJUSTMENT LAYER

What You'll Do

 In this lesson, you'll create an adjustment layer, choose Brightness/Contrast as the type of adjustment layer, adjust brightness and contrast settings for the layer, and then use the Layers panel to change the blending mode of the adjustment layer.

Understanding Adjustment Layers

An **adjustment layer** is a special layer that acts as a color filter for a single layer or for all the layers beneath it. Just as you can use a layer mask to edit the layer content without permanently deleting pixels on the image, you can create an adjustment layer to adjust color and tone. If you were to make changes directly on the original layer, the changes would be irreversible. (You could use the Undo feature or the History panel to undo your changes, but only in the current Photoshop session.) However, the color changes you make to the adjustment layer exist only in the adjustment layer.

Creating an Adjustment Layer

You can create an adjustment layer by selecting the layer you want to adjust, then clicking the button for the preset in the Adjustments panel; by using the Layer menu to click a new adjustment layer command; or by clicking the Create new fill or adjustment layer button on the Layers panel. When you create an adjustment layer, it affects all the layers beneath it, by default, but you can change this setting so that it affects only the selected layer. When creating color adjustments, you must specify which one you want to use. Color adjustment presets that can be made directly on a layer or by using an adjustment layer are described in Table 1. (Also included in Table 1 are preset symbols used in the Adjustments panel.)

QUICKTIP

If you use the Create new fill or adjustment layer button on the Layers panel, you'll see three additional menu items: Solid Color, Gradient, and Pattern. You can use these commands to create fill layers, which fill a layer with a solid color.

Modifying an Adjustment Layer

You can change the adjustment layer settings by double-clicking the layer thumbnail on the adjustment layer. Photoshop identifies the type of adjustment layer on the Layers panel by including the type of adjustment layer in the layer name.

QUICKTIP

When you double-click an adjustment layer thumbnail, its settings display in the Adjustments panel.

TABLE 1: Color Adjustments

symbol	color adjustment	description	symbol	color adjustment	description
	Black & White	Converts a color image to grayscale while controlling how individual colors are converted, and applies color tones such as a sepia effect.		Match Color	Changes the brightness, color saturation, and color balance in an image.
	Brightness/Contrast	Makes simple adjustments to a tonal range.		Photo Filter	Similar to the practice of adding a color filter to a camera lens to adjust the color balance and color temperature.
	Channel Mixer	Modifies a color channel, using a mix of current color channels.		Posterize	Specifies the number of tonal levels for each channel.
	Color Balance	Changes the overall mixture of color.		Replace Color	Replaces specific colors using a mask.
	Curves	Makes adjustments to an entire tonal range, using three variables: highlights, shadows, and midtones.		Selective Color	Increases or decreases the number of process colors in each of the additive and subtractive primary color components.
	Equalize	Redistributes brightness values of pixels so that they evenly represent the entire range of brightness levels. (Available on the Image > Adjustments menu.)		Shadows/ Highlights	Corrects images with silhouetted images due to strong backlighting, as well as brightening up areas of shadow in an otherwise well-lit image. (Available on the Image > Adjustments menu.)
	Exposure	Controls the tone.			
	Gradient Map	Maps the equivalent grayscale range of an image to colors of a specific gradient fill.			
	Hue/Saturation	Changes position on the color wheel (hue) or purity of a color (saturation).		Threshold	Converts images to high contrast, black-and white images.
	Invert	Converts an image's brightness values to the inverse values on the 256-step color-values scale.		Variations	Adjusts the color balance, contrast, and saturation of an image, and shows alternative thumbnails. (Available on the Image > Adjustments menu.)
	Levels	Sets highlights and shadows by increasing the tonal range of pixels, while preserving the color balance.		Vibrance	Controls the color.

Create and set an adjustment layer

1. Click the **The Produce Market layer** on the Layers panel.

2. Display the **Essentials** workspace.

3. Click the **Brightness/ Contrast** button ☀ in the Adjustments panel. Compare your Adjustments panel to Figure 21.

   TIP You can also create a new adjustment layer by clicking the Create new fill or adjustment layer button on the Layers panel, then selecting a color adjustment or by clicking Layer on the Application bar, pointing to New Adjustment Layer, then clicking the type of adjustment you want.

4. Type **−15** in the Brightness text box.

5. Type **30** in the Contrast text box. Compare your Layers panel to Figure 22.

   Did you notice that the new adjustment layer appears on the Layers panel above the The Produce Market layer? The new layer is named Brightness/Contrast 1 because you chose Brightness/Contrast as the type of color adjustment.

You used the Adjustments panel to create a Brightness/Contrast adjustment layer on the The Produce Market layer, then adjusted the brightness and contrast settings.

Understanding Adjustment panel controls

The Adjustments panel, in Figure 23, is grouped with the Masks panel, and allows you to apply 15 preset adjustment levels. Presets are grouped by theme. The top four presets (Brightness/Contrast, Levels, Curves, and Exposure) are tonal controls; the next six presets (Vibrance, Hue/Saturation, Color Balance, Black & White, Photo Filter, and Channel Mixer) are color controls, and the remaining five presets are creative/advanced controls (Invert, Posterize, Threshold, Gradient Map, and Selective Color).

FIGURE 21
New adjustment layer

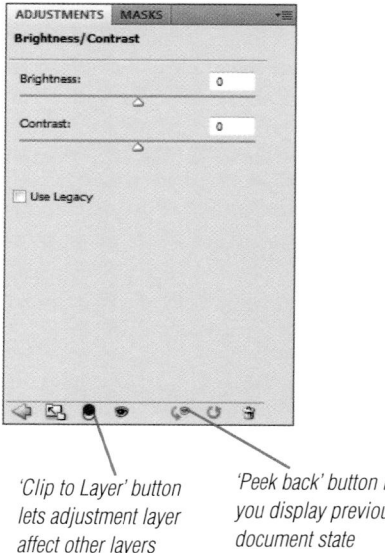

'Clip to Layer' button lets adjustment layer affect other layers

'Peek back' button lets you display previous document state

FIGURE 22
Adjustment layer in Layers panel

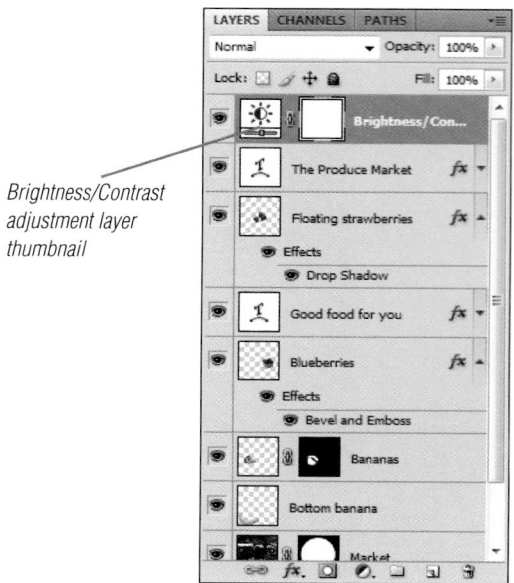

Brightness/Contrast adjustment layer thumbnail

FIGURE 23
Adjustments panel

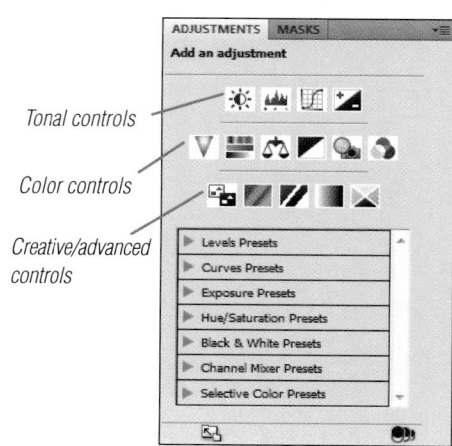

Tonal controls

Color controls

Creative/advanced controls

Working with Special Layer Functions

FIGURE 24

Result of adjustment layer

Set the blending mode for the layer list arrow

Layer thumbnail for adjustment layer

Modifying an adjustment layer

What if you've created an adjustment layer that affects all the layers beneath it, and then you decide you want it to only affect the previous layer? Do you have to delete this adjustment layer and start over? Certainly not. To toggle an adjustment layer between applying to all the layers beneath it and only the layer immediately beneath it, position the pointer between the adjustment layer and the layer beneath it. Press [Alt] (Win) and [option] (Mac), then click between the two layers. So, when you see an adjustment layer that is *inset* (not aligned with all the other layers) it applies only to the layer immediately beneath it.

Set the blending mode

1. Make sure that the **Brightness/Contrast 1** layer is the active layer.

   TIP If you choose, you can rename an adjustment layer by double-clicking its name in the Layers panel, typing the new name, then pressing [Enter] (Win) or [return] (Mac).

2. Click the **Set the blending mode for the layer list arrow** on the Layers panel, then click **Soft Light**.

   TIP You can use as many adjustment layers as you want, but you must create them one at a time. At first glance, this might strike you as a disadvantage, but when you're working on an image, you'll find it to be very helpful. By adding one or more adjustment layers, you can experiment with a variety of colors and tones, then hide and show each one to determine the one that best suits your needs. Adjustment layers can also contain layer masks, which allow you to fine-tune your alterations by painting just the adjustment layer mask. When you are positive that the changes in your adjustment layers should be permanent, you can merge them with any *visible* layers in the image, including linked layers. You cannot, however, merge one adjustment layer with another adjustment layer. Merging adjustment layers reduces file size and ensures that your adjustments will be permanent.

3. Save your work, then compare your image to Figure 24.

You changed the blending mode for the adjustment layer to Soft Light, using the Layers panel.

CREATE A
CLIPPING MASK

What You'll Do

In this lesson, you'll create a clipping mask, adjust the opacity of the base layer, remove and restore the clipping mask, then flatten the image.

Understanding Clipping Masks

A **clipping mask** (sometimes called a *clipping group*) is a group of two or more contiguous layers that are linked for the purpose of masking. Clipping masks are useful when you want one layer to act as the mask for other layers, or if you want an adjustment layer to affect only the layer directly beneath it. The bottom layer in a clipping mask is called the **base layer**, and it serves as the group's mask. For example, you can use a type layer as the base of a clipping mask so that a pattern appears through the text on the base layer, as shown in Figure 25. (On the left side of the figure is the imagery used as the pattern in the type.) The properties of the base layer determine the opacity and visible imagery of a clipping mask. You can, however, adjust the opacity of the individual layers in a clipping mask.

QUICKTIP
You can merge layers in a clipping mask with an adjustment layer, as long as the layers are visible.

Creating a Clipping Mask

To create a clipping mask, you need at least two layers: one to create the shape of the mask, and the other to supply the content for the mask. You can use a type or an image layer to create the clipping mask shape, and when the shape is the way you want it, you can position the pointer between the two layers, then press [Alt] (Win) or [option] (Mac). The pointer changes to two circles with a left-pointing arrowhead. Simply click the line between the layers to create the clipping mask. You can tell if a clipping mask exists by looking at the Layers panel. A clipping mask is indicated when one or more layers are indented and appear with a down arrow icon, and the base layer is underlined.

QUICK TIP

Not all clipping mask effects are so dramatic. You can use a clipping mask to add depth and texture to imagery.

Removing a Clipping Mask

When you create a clipping mask, the layers in the clipping mask are grouped together. To remove a clipping mask, press and hold [Alt] (Win) or [option] (Mac), position the clipping mask pointer over the line separating the grouped layers on the Layers panel, then click the mouse. You can also select the mask layer, click Layer on the Application bar, and then click Release Clipping Mask.

FIGURE 25
Result of clipping group

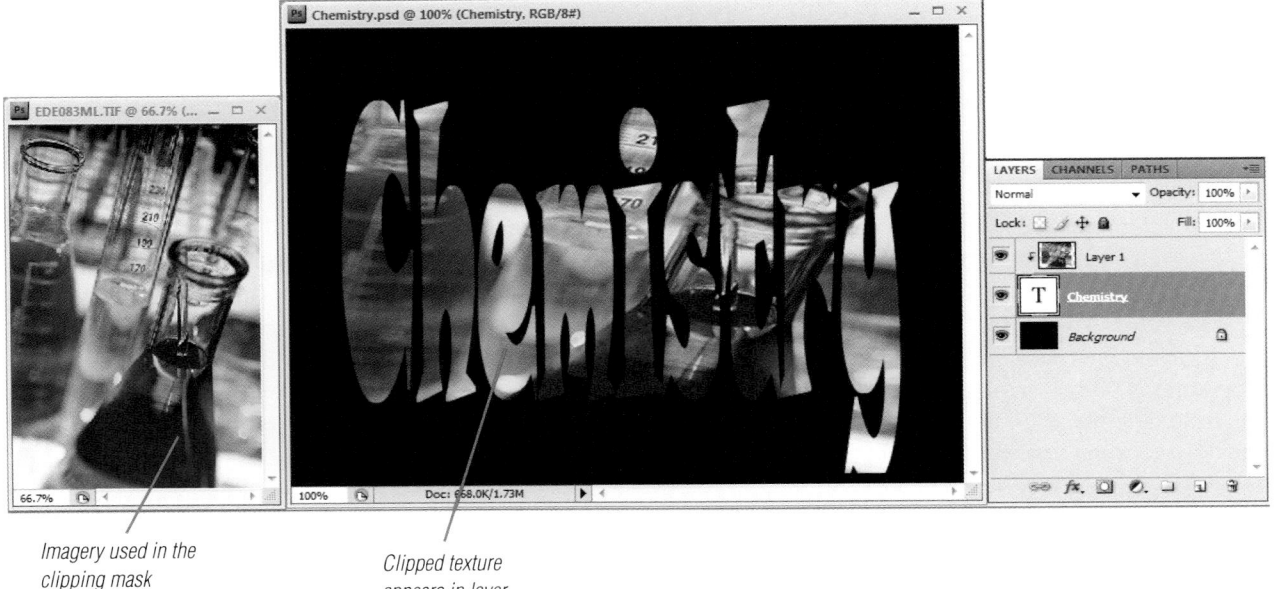

Imagery used in the
clipping mask

Clipped texture
appears in layer

Create a clipping mask

1. Click the **Good food for you layer** on the Layers panel to make it the active layer.

2. Drag the **active layer** below the **Bananas layer** on the Layers panel.

3. Press and hold **[Alt]** (Win) or **[option]** (Mac), then point with the **Clipping mask pointer** ◄🖑 to the line between the Bottom Banana and the Good food for you layers. Compare your Layers panel to Figure 26.

4. Click the line between the two layers with the **Clipping mask pointer** ◄🖑, then release **[Alt]** (Win) or **[option]** (Mac).

   The Good food for you (member) is filled with the image from the Bottom banana layer (base).

5. Verify that the clipping icon (a small downward pointing arrow) appears in the Good food for you layer, then compare your Layers panel to Figure 27.

6. Make sure the **Good food for you layer** is active, click the **Opacity list arrow** on the Layers panel, drag the slider to **100%**, then press **[Enter]** (Win) or **[return]** (Mac).

You created a clipping mask, using the Bottom banana layer as the base and the Good food for you layer as a member of the clipping mask to make the banana peel appear as the fill of the Good food for you layer, and then you adjusted the opacity of the Good food for you layer.

FIGURE 26
Creating a clipping group

FIGURE 27
Clipping group on Layers panel

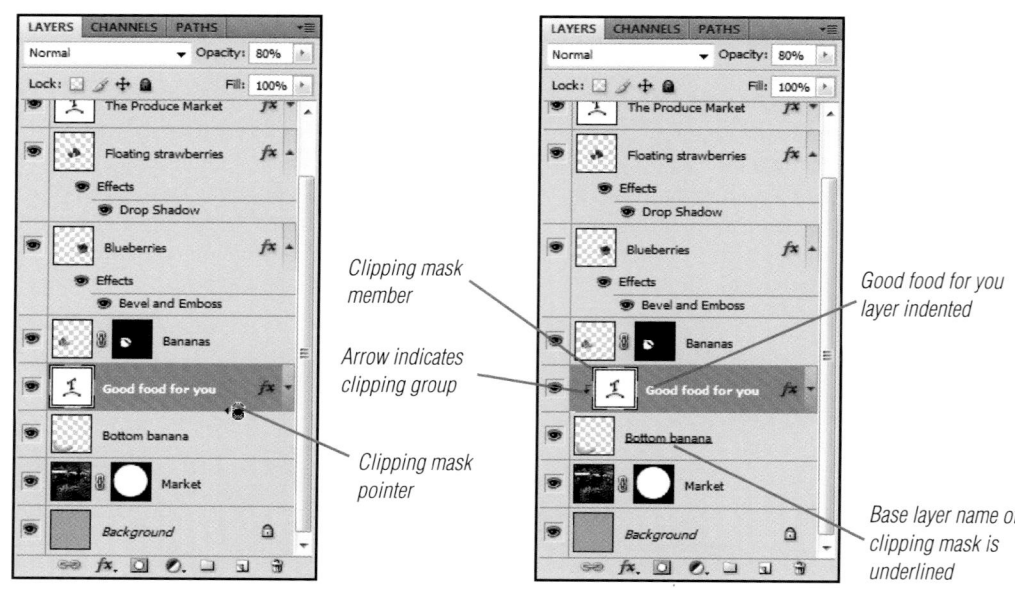

Clipping mask member

Arrow indicates clipping group

Clipping mask pointer

Good food for you layer indented

Base layer name of clipping mask is underlined

Creating 3D files in Photoshop

The Photoshop Extended version of Photoshop CS4 allows you to open and work with 3D files created in programs like Adobe Acrobat 3D Version 8, 3d Studio Max, Alias, Maya, and Google Earth. Photoshop puts 3D models on a separate layer that you can move or scale, change the lighting, or change rendering modes. Although you must have a 3D authoring program to actually edit the 3D model, you can add multiple 3D layers to an image, combine a 3D layer with a 2D layer, or convert a 3D layer into a 2D layer or Smart Object. Textures within a 3D file appear as separate layers in Photoshop and can be edited using any painting or adjustment tools. With Photoshop CS4 Extended you can paint directly on 3D models, and edit, enhance, and manipulate 3D images without using dialog boxes. 2D images can be wrapped around common 3D geometric shapes (such as cylinders and spheres) and you can convert gradient maps to 3D objects.

FIGURE 28
Finished product

*Good food for you
layer text filled in
with banana texture*

1. Click the **Good food for you layer** on the Layers panel (if necessary).

2. Hide the rulers and guides.

3. Defringe the Bottom banana layer using two pixels.

4. Click the **Good food for you layer** in the Layers panel, click **Layer** on the Application bar, then click **Release Clipping Mask**.

5. Click **Edit** on the Application bar, then click **Undo Release Clipping Mask**. Compare your screen to Figure 28.

6. Click **File** on the Application bar, click **Save As**, using the name given, select the **As a Copy check box**, then click **Save**.

   The text **copy** is inserted after the original filename.

7. Click **Layer** on the Application bar, then click **Flatten Image**.

8. Save your work, then close the file and exit Photoshop.

You removed the clipping mask by using the Release Clipping Mask command on the Layer menu, restored the clipping mask by using the Undo command on the Edit menu, saved a copy of the image, and then flattened the file.

Power User Shortcuts

to do this:	use this method:
Activate layer mask	Press and hold [Ctrl][\] (Win) or ⌘[\] (Mac)
Add an adjustment layer	*(icon)*
Align linked layers by vertical centers	Layer ➢ Align ➢ Vertical Centers
Blend pixels on a layer	Double-click a layer thumbnail, click Blend; If list arrow, choose color, drag This Layer and Underlying Layer sliders
Brush tool	*(icon)* or B
Change brush tip	Select Brush tool, right-click, then select brush tip
Create a clipping mask	Press and hold [Alt] (Win) or option -click (Mac), move the pointer to the line between two layers, then click
Create a layer/vector mask	*(icon)*
Create a layer mask that hides the selection	Press and hold [Alt] (Win) or option -click (Mac) ➢ *(icon)*

to do this:	use this method:
Create a layer mask that reveals the selection	Layer ➢ Layer Mask ➢ Reveal Selection
Delete layer	*(icon)*
Disable layer mask	Layer ➢ Layer Mask ➢ Disable
Previous or Next brush tip in Brushes panel	[,] or [.]
Remove a clipping mask	Click a layer in the group ➢ Layer ➢ Release Clipping Mask
Remove a link	Click *(icon)*
Scale a layer	Edit ➢ Transform ➢ Scale
Rotate a layer 90° to the left	Edit ➢ Transform ➢ Rotate 90° CCW
Select first or last brush tip in Brushes panel	[Shift][,] or [Shift][.]

Key: Menu items are indicated by ➢ between the menu name and its command. Blue bold letters are shortcuts for selecting tools on the Tools panel.

Working with Special Layer Functions

Use a layer mask with a selection.

1. Start Photoshop, open PS 7-2.psd from the drive and folder where you store your Data Files, then save it as **Stripes**.
2. Make sure the rulers are displayed in pixels.
3. Change the zoom factor to 150% or 200%, to enlarge your view of the image.
4. Create a type layer title in black with the text "See Stripes?" above the Zebra layer and add the drop shadow layer style (using default settings). (*Hint*: A 30 pt Segoe Print font is shown in the sample. Use any other font on your computer if this font is not available.)
5. Make the Zebra layer active, then select the Elliptical Marquee tool.
6. Change the Feather setting on the options bar to 5 pixels.
7. Create a marquee selection from 35 X/35 Y to 235 X/360 Y. (*Hint*: Feel free to add guides, if necessary.)
8. Use the Masks panel to add a layer mask.
9. Save your work.

Work with layer masks and layer content.

1. Select the Brush tool.
2. Hide the type layer.
3. Change the existing brush tip to Soft Round 9 pixels.
4. Change the Painting mode to Normal, and the flow and opacity to 100% (if those are not the current settings).
5. Use the default foreground and background colors to paint the area from 20 X/70 Y to

65 X/290 Y. (*Hint*: Make sure the layer mask thumbnail is selected and that white is the foreground color and black is the background color.)
6. Display the type layer.
7. Make the Fern layer active.
8. Unlink the Background layer.
9. Rotate the fern so that its left edge barely touches the zebra's nose.
10. Save your work.

Control pixels to blend colors.

1. Double-click the Fern layer thumbnail.
2. Using green as the Blend If color, drag the right This Layer slider to 200.
3. Split the right This Layer slider, drag the right half to 240, then click OK. (*Hint*: Click OK to close the Layer Style dialog box after step 2, *before* splitting the slider. You may have to reopen the dialog box.)
4. Save your work.

Eliminate a layer mask.

1. Click the layer mask thumbnail on the Zebra layer.
2. Use the Layer menu to disable the layer mask.
3. Use the Layer menu to enable the layer mask.
4. Save your work.

Use an adjustment layer.

1. Make the Fern layer active.
2. Using the Layer menu, create a Color Balance adjustment layer called **Modifications**.
3. Make sure the Midtones option button is selected, drag the Cyan/Red, Magenta/Green,

and Yellow/Blue sliders to +36, +12, and –19, respectively.
4. Create a Brightness/Contrast adjustment layer, above the Modifications layer.
5. Change the Brightness to –25 and the Contrast to +20.
6. Hide the Modifications layer.
7. Hide the Brightness/Contrast layer.
8. Display both adjustment layers.
9. Save your work.

Create a clipping mask.

1. Make the Background layer active.
2. Create a clipping mask (with the Background layer as the base layer) that includes the type layer. (*Hint*: Move the type layer to a new location, if necessary.)
3. Include the Zebra layer in the clipping mask.
4. Save your work, then compare your image to Figure 29.

FIGURE 29
Completed Skills Review

Your cousin has recently purchased a beauty shop and wants to increase the number of manicure customers. She's hired you to create an eye-catching image that can be used in print ads. You decided to take an ordinary image and use your knowledge of masks and adjustment layers to make the image look striking.

1. Open PS 7-3.psd, then save it as **Manicure**.
2. Duplicate the Polishes layer, then name the new layer Red Polish.
3. On the Red Polish layer, select the red nail polish bottle and cap, then delete everything else in the layer. (*Hint*: You can do this by deleting a selection.)
4. Hide the Red Polish layer, then make the Polishes layer active.
5. Create a layer mask that hides the red polish, then brush in the remaining items on the Polishes layer.
6. Use any tools at your disposal to fix the area where the red polish (on the Polishes layer) has been masked.
7. Display the Red Polish layer.
8. Move the Red Polish layer below the Polishes layer in the Layers panel (if necessary).
9. Use the existing layer mask to hide the white polish (with the blue cap).
10. Position the red polish bottle so it appears where the white polish bottle was visible.
11. Use any tools necessary to fix areas you want to improve, such as the Blur tool to soften the edges of polish bottles.

12. Add an adjustment layer to the Red Polish layer that makes the polish color violet. (*Hint*: In the sample, a Hue/Saturation adjustment layer was used with the following settings: Hue: −45, Saturation: +35, and Lightness: −5.)
13. Add one or two brief type layers, and apply layer styles to at least one of them. (*Hint*: In the sample, the type used is a 60 pt Edwardian Script ITC and a 50 pt Perpetua font.)

FIGURE 30
Sample Project Builder 1

14. Save a copy of the file as **Manicure copy**, then flatten the original image.
15. Save your work, then compare your image to the sample in Figure 30.

In exchange for free concert tickets, you have volunteered to work on the cleanup crew for an outdoor concert facility. After the second concert, the promoter asks you to design a poster to inspire concert-goers to throw trash in the trash barrels. You decide to create a Photoshop image that contains several unique illusions. Using any city or locale other than your own as a theme, you'll use your Photoshop skills to create and paint layer masks in an image that conveys a cleanup message.

1. Obtain the following images: a landscape, a sign, one large inanimate object, and two or more smaller objects that evoke a city or locale of your choice. You can use images that are available on your computer, scan print media, or use a digital camera. (*Hint*: Try to obtain images that fit your theme.)
2. Open the images you obtained, then create a new Photoshop image and save it as **Cleanup**.
3. Drag the landscape to the Cleanup image above the Background layer, then delete the Background layer.
4. Drag the large object image to the Cleanup image above the landscape layer.
5. Transform the large object as necessary to prepare it to be partially buried in the land-scape. (*Hint*: The tower layer in the sample has been rotated and resized.)
6. Apply a layer mask to the large object, then paint the layer mask to reshape the mask and partially obscure the object.

7. Drag the sign image to the Cleanup image, and then place it below the large object layer.
8. Create a type layer for the sign layer with a message (humor optional), link the layers, then transform the layers as needed to fit in the image. (*Hint*: The sign layer and type layer in the sample have been skewed.)
9. Drag other images as desired to the Cleanup image, and add styles to them or transform them as necessary.

10. Create other type layers (humor optional) as desired, and apply a style to at least one layer. (*Hint*: The title layer in the sample has drop shadow and outer glow styles applied to it. A 14 pt, Arial Narrow font is used in the sign, and a 35 and 24 pt Arial Black is used in the title.)
11. Add an adjustment layer to the landscape layer, and to any other layer that would benefit from it.
12. Save a copy of your file as **Cleanup copy**, then flatten the original image.
13. Save your work, then compare your image to the sample in Figure 31.

FIGURE 31
Sample Project Builder 2

As the publishing director for a large accounting firm, you've been asked to design a banner for the new International Monetary Division website. They've asked that you include a flag, paper currency, and coinage of a country of your choice. You decide to use techniques to create an interesting collage of those three items.

1. Obtain several images of paper currency and coins, and a flag from a country (or countries) of your choice. You can use the images that are available on your computer, scan print media, or connect to the Internet and download images. (*Hint*: Try to obtain at least two denominations of both paper and coin.)

2. Create a new image in Photoshop and save it as **Currency**.

3. Open the paper money image files, then drag the paper money images to the currency image above the Background layer.

4. Transform the paper money layers as desired. (*Hint*: The paper money layers in the sample have been rotated and skewed.)

5. Add layer masks as desired.

6. Add an adjustment layer to the paper money layer, and apply at least one color adjustment. (*Hint*: The paper money layers in the sample have a Brightness/Contrast adjustment applied to them.)

7. Open the flag file, then drag the flag image to the Currency image, and position it to appear on top of the paper money layers, then resize it and adjust opacity, as necessary.

8. Apply a Curves adjustment to the flag.

9. Open the coin image files, drag the coin images to the Currency image, duplicate the coin layers as desired, position them above the flag layer, then apply at least one transformation and one layer style to them.

(*Hint*: The coins in the sample have a Drop Shadow style and have been rotated.)

10. Blend the pixels for two of the coin layers.

11. Save a copy of the file as **Currency copy**, flatten the original image, then close the other files.

12. Save your work, then compare your image to the sample in Figure 32.

FIGURE 32
Sample Design Project

Working with Special Layer Functions

Lost Horizons, a tragically hip coffee-house, is hosting a regional multimedia Poetry Slam contest. You have teamed up with the Surreal Poetry Enclave, an eclectic poetry group. The contest consists of the poetry group reading poetry while you create a visual interpretation using two preselected images and as many elective images as you want. First, though, you must submit an entry design. Find a poem for inspiration, design the interpretation, obtain images, and write some creative copy (tag line or slogan) to be used in the design.

1. Obtain images for your interpretative design. The images you must include are a picture frame and a background image; the other pieces are up to you. You can use the images that are available on your computer, scan print media, or connect to the Internet and download images.
2. Create a new Photoshop image, then save it as **Poetry Poster**.
3. Open the background image file, drag the background image to the Poetry Poster image above the Background layer.
4. Open the picture frame image file, drag it to the Poetry Poster image above the Background layer, transform it as necessary, then apply styles to it if desired. (*Hint*: The frame in the sample has been skewed.)

5. Open the image files that will go in or on the picture frame, drag them to the Poetry Poster image, then transform them as necessary.
6. Arrange the image layers on the Layers panel in the configuration you want, and apply styles to them if you think they will enhance the image.
7. Apply a layer mask to two or more of the image layers.
8. Create a clipping mask using two or more of the image layers. (*Hint*: The clipping mask in the sample consists of the frame layer as the base and the Lantern and Alarm clock layers as members.)
9. Create type layers as desired and apply styles to them. (*Hint*: The type layer in the sample has an Outer Glow style applied to it.)

10. Close the image files, save your work, then compare your image to the sample in Figure 33.
11. Be prepared to discuss the creative ways you can use clipping masks.

FIGURE 33
Sample Portfolio Project

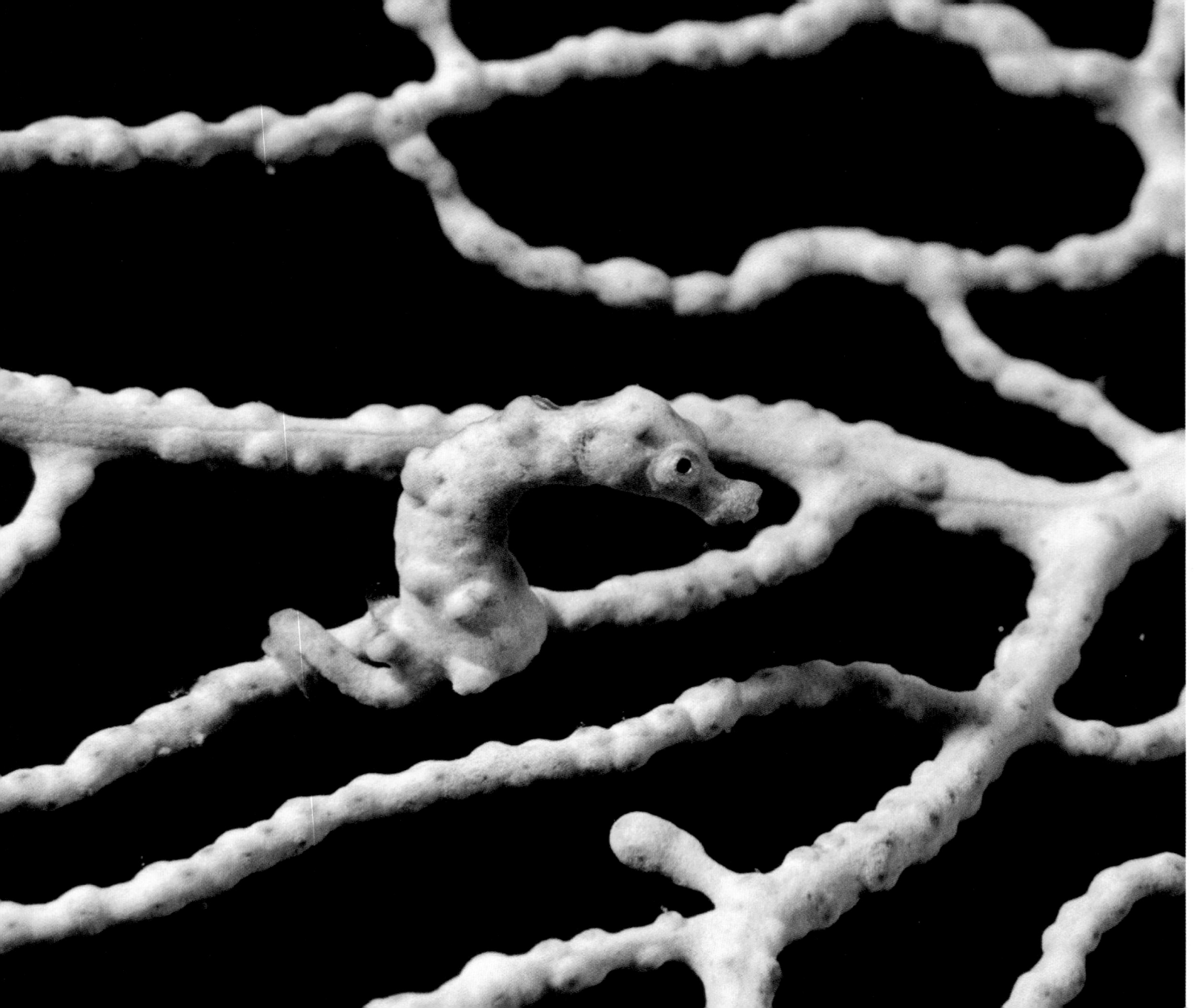

8

CREATING SPECIAL
EFFECTS WITH
FILTERS

1. Learn about filters and how to apply them

2. Create an effect with an Artistic filter

3. Add unique effects with Stylize filters

4. Alter images with Distort and Noise filters

5. Alter lighting with a Render filter

6. Use Vanishing Point

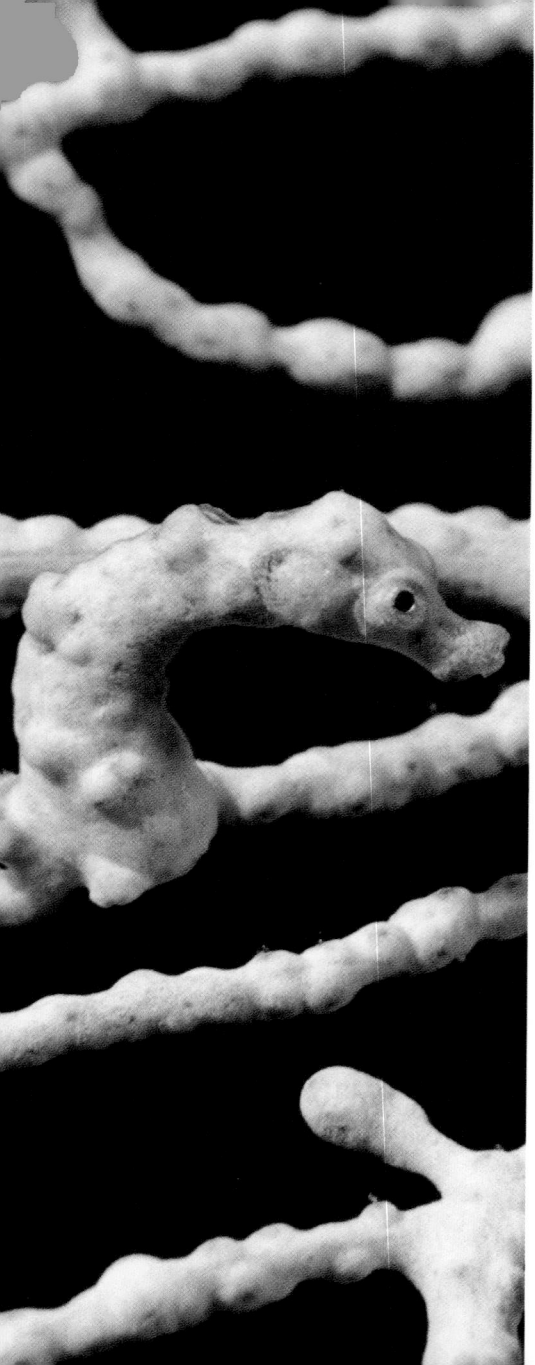

8 CREATING SPECIAL
EFFECTS WITH
FILTERS

Understanding Filters

You've already seen some of the filters that Photoshop offers. Filters modify the look of an image by altering pixels in a particular pattern or format, across a layer or a selection. This results in a unique, customized appearance. You use filters to apply special effects, such as realistic textures, distortions, changes in lighting, and blurring. Although you can use several types of filters and options, and can apply them to multiple layers in an image, the most important thing to remember when using filters is subtlety.

Applying Filters

You can apply filters to any layer (except the Background layer) using commands on the Filter menu. Most filters have their own dialog box, where you can adjust filter settings and preview the effect before applying it. The preview window in the dialog box allows you to evaluate the precise effect of the filter on your selection. You can zoom in and out, and pan the image in the dialog box to get a good look before making a final decision. Other filters—those whose menu command is not followed by an ellipsis (...) —apply their effects instantly as soon as you click the command.

> **QUICK**TIP
>
> Does your computer have enough RAM? You'll know for sure when you start using filters because they are very memory-intensive.

Tools You'll Use

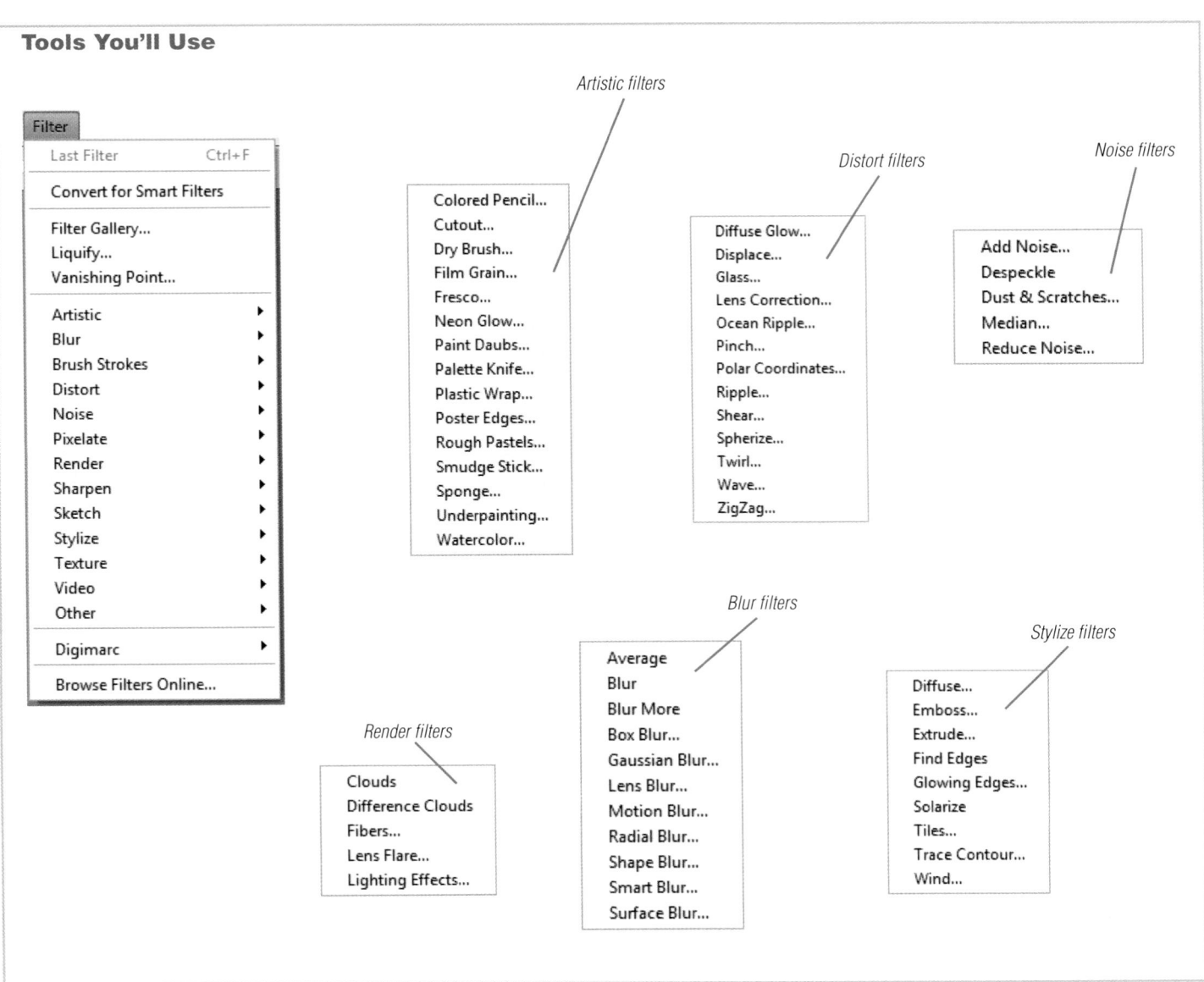

Filter

Last Filter	Ctrl+F
Convert for Smart Filters	
Filter Gallery...	
Liquify...	
Vanishing Point...	
Artistic	▶
Blur	▶
Brush Strokes	▶
Distort	▶
Noise	▶
Pixelate	▶
Render	▶
Sharpen	▶
Sketch	▶
Stylize	▶
Texture	▶
Video	▶
Other	▶
Digimarc	▶
Browse Filters Online...	

Artistic filters

Colored Pencil...
Cutout...
Dry Brush...
Film Grain...
Fresco...
Neon Glow...
Paint Daubs...
Palette Knife...
Plastic Wrap...
Poster Edges...
Rough Pastels...
Smudge Stick...
Sponge...
Underpainting...
Watercolor...

Distort filters

Diffuse Glow...
Displace...
Glass...
Lens Correction...
Ocean Ripple...
Pinch...
Polar Coordinates...
Ripple...
Shear...
Spherize...
Twirl...
Wave...
ZigZag...

Noise filters

Add Noise...
Despeckle
Dust & Scratches...
Median...
Reduce Noise...

Render filters

Clouds
Difference Clouds
Fibers...
Lens Flare...
Lighting Effects...

Blur filters

Average
Blur
Blur More
Box Blur...
Gaussian Blur...
Lens Blur...
Motion Blur...
Radial Blur...
Shape Blur...
Smart Blur...
Surface Blur...

Stylize filters

Diffuse...
Emboss...
Extrude...
Find Edges
Glowing Edges...
Solarize
Tiles...
Trace Contour...
Wind...

LEARN ABOUT FILTERS AND
HOW TO APPLY THEM

What You'll Do

In this lesson, you'll apply the Motion Blur filter to the Red bar layer and convert a layer into a Smart Object.

Understanding the Filter Menu

The Filter menu sorts filters into categories and subcategories. Many filters are memory-intensive, so depending on the capabilities of your computer, you might need to wait several seconds while Photoshop applies the effect. Using filters might slow down your computer's performance. Figure 1 shows samples of several filters.

Learning About Filters

You can read about filters all day long, but until you apply one yourself, it's all academic. When you do, here are a few tips to keep in mind.

- Distort filters can completely reshape an image; they are highly resource-demanding.
- Photoshop applies most of the Pixelate filters as soon as you click the command, without opening a dialog box.

- Digimarc filters notify users that the image is copyright-protected.

QUICKTIP

Some imported files may require rasterizing before they can be used in Photoshop. These files have vector artwork. During rasterization, the mathematically defined lines and curves of vector art are converted into pixels or bits of a bitmap image.

Applying a Filter

You can apply a filter by clicking its category and name under the Filter menu. When you click a Filter menu name, a dialog box opens displaying a sample of each filter in the category. You can also apply one or more filters using the Filter Gallery.

FIGURE 1

Examples of filters

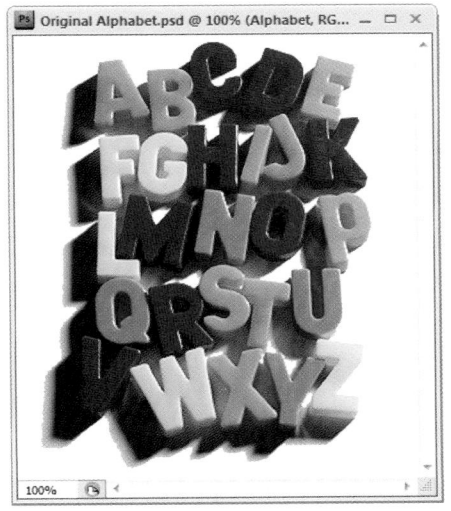

Original Alphabet.psd @ 100% (Alphabet, RG...)

Blur-Motion Blur.psd @ 100% (Alphabet, RG...)

Artistic-Neon Glow.psd @ 100% (RGB/8#)

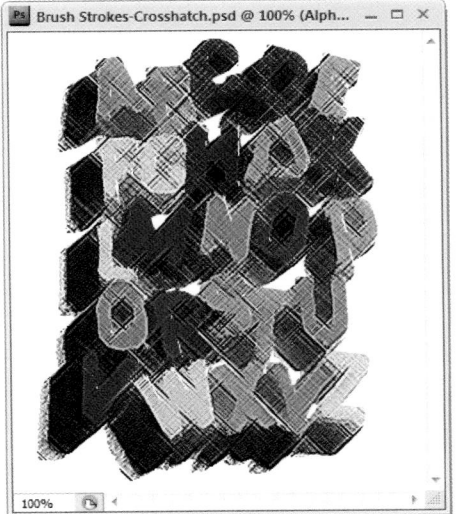

Brush Strokes-Crosshatch.psd @ 100% (Alph...)

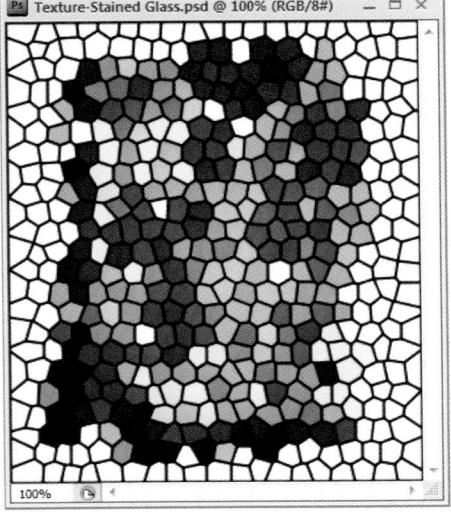

Texture-Stained Glass.psd @ 100% (RGB/8#)

Distort-Twirl.psd @ 100% (Alphabet, RGB/8#)

You will be amazed by how many filters there are, how much they can do for an image, and just how much fun they can be. Table 1 describes each filter category.

Understanding the Filter Gallery

The **Filter Gallery** is a feature that lets you see the effects of each filter *before* its application. You can also use the Filter Gallery to apply filters (either individually, or in groups), rearrange filters, and change individual filter settings. The Filter Gallery is opened by clicking Filter on the Application bar, then clicking Filter Gallery. In Figure 2, the Mosaic Tiles filter (in the Texture category) is applied to the active layer, which has been enlarged for easier viewing in the preview window.

FIGURE 2
Filter Gallery dialog box

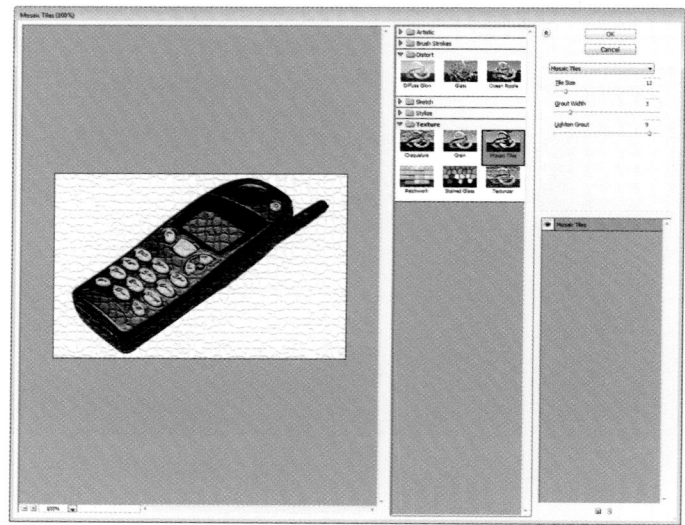

TABLE 1: Filter Categories

category	use	category	use
Artistic	Replicates traditional fine arts effects.	Sharpen	Refocuses blurry objects by increasing contrast in adjacent pixels.
Blur	Simulates an object in motion; can use to retouch photographs.	Sketch	Applies a texture, or simulates a fine arts hard-drawn effect.
Brush Strokes	Mimics fine arts brushwork and ink effects.		
Distort	Reshapes an image.	Stylize	Produces a painted or impressionistic effect.
Noise	Gives an aged look; can use to retouch photographs.	Texture	Gives the appearance of depth or substance.
		Video	Restricts color use to those that are acceptable for television reproduction and smooth video images.
Pixelate	Adds small honeycomb shapes based on similar colors.		
		Other	Creates unique filters, modifies masks, or makes quick color adjustments.
Render	Transforms three-dimensional shapes; simulates light reflections.	Digimarc	Embeds a digital watermark that stores copyright information.

FIGURE 3
Current Layers panel

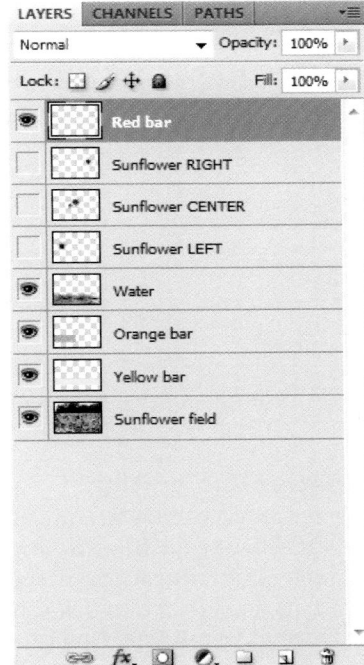

Learning about Motion filters

When you apply a Blur filter, keep in mind how you want your object to appear—as if it's moving. Blur filters smooth the transitions between different colors. The effect of the Blur More filter is four times stronger than the Blur filter. The Gaussian Blur filter produces more of a hazy effect. The direction of the blur is determined by the Angle setting—a straight horizontal path has an angle set to zero. The Motion Blur filter simulates taking a picture of an object in motion, and the Radial Blur filter simulates zooming or rotation. You can use the Smart Blur filter to set exactly how the filter will blur the image.

Open a Blur filter

1. Start Photoshop, display the **Essentials** workspace (if necessary), open PS 8-1.psd from the drive and folder where you store your Data Files, then save it as **Sunflowers**.

2. Click the **Default Foreground and Background Colors button** ▉ on the Tools panel to display the default settings (if necessary).

   TIP It's a good habit to check Photoshop settings and display the rulers before you begin your work if you'll need these features.

3. Click the **Indicates layer visibility button** 👁 on the Sunflower LEFT layer on the Layers panel.

4. Click the **Indicates layer visibility button** 👁 on the Sunflower RIGHT layer on the Layers panel.

5. Click the **Indicates layer visibility button** 👁 on the Sunflower CENTER layer on the Layers panel.

6. Click the **Red bar layer** on the Layers panel to make it active. Compare your Layers panel to Figure 3.

7. Use the **Zoom tool** 🔍 on the Application bar to increase the magnification to 200%.

8. Click **Filter** on the Application bar, point to **Blur**, then click **Motion Blur**.

   TIP The last filter applied to a layer appears at the top of the Filter menu.

You set default foreground and background colors, hid three layers, then opened the Motion Blur dialog box.

Apply a Blur filter

1. Position the **red bar** in the preview window with the **Hand pointer** 🖐, reduce or enlarge the image with the buttons beneath the preview window so it displays in the center.

   The red bar image is repositioned from the lower area to the center of the preview window.

2. Verify that **0** is in the Angle text box.

   | TIP   In this case, increasing the angle results in a thicker bar.

3. Type **100** in the Distance text box, then compare your dialog box to Figure 4.

   | TIP   You can also adjust the settings in the Motion Blur dialog box by dragging the Angle radius slider and Distance slider.

4. Click **OK**.

   The Motion Blur filter is applied to the Red bar layer.

You repositioned the Red bar layer in the preview window and then applied a Motion Blur filter to the layer.

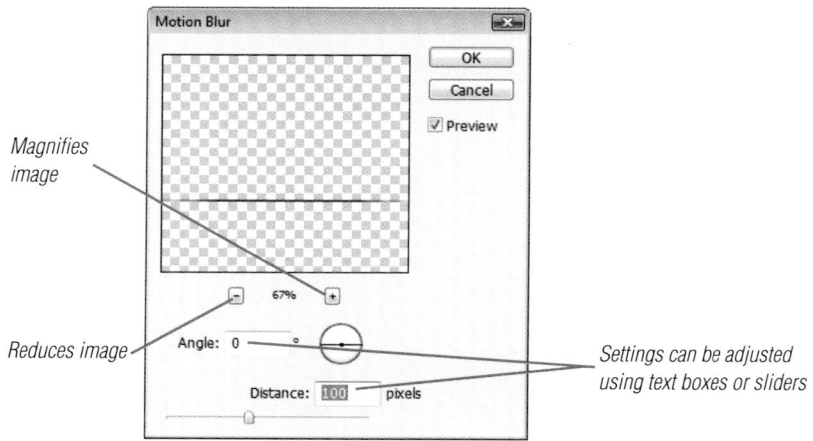

FIGURE 4
Motion Blur dialog box

Magnifies image

Reduces image

Settings can be adjusted using text boxes or sliders

Destructive vs. nondestructive editing

In the early days of Photoshop (i.e., a few years ago), any editing change you made was *destructive*, in that it permanently altered the pixels in your image. There was no going back, except of course if you made duplicate layers of everything you ever did. *Nondestructive* editing, as the name implies, means that you can go back and re-edit what used to be a permanent change to pixels. An example of nondestructive editing is the application of adjustment layers versus applying an adjustment to a layer and hoping that you never have to remove or change it.

Reducing blur with the Smart Sharpen Filter

You can use the Smart Sharpen Filter to remove or reduce blurriness. This filter can be used to remove blur effects in images created by Gaussian Blur, Lens Blur, or Motion Blur filters. The Smart Sharpen Filter is available by clicking Filter on the Application bar, pointing to Sharpen, then clicking Smart Sharpen. Using the Smart Sharpen dialog box, you can change the amount as a percentage and the radius in pixels of the settings. You can choose the type of blur to be removed from the image.

FIGURE 5
Motion Blur filter applied to layer

*Effect of Motion
Blur filter*

*Smart Object
in layer*

Using Smart Filters

Smart Objects, one or more objects on one or more layers that have been modified so that they can be scaled, rotated, or warped without losing image quality, can have filters applied to them. These filters are called Smart Filters. **Smart Filters** can be adjusted, removed, or hidden, and are nondestructive. Any filter, with the exception of Extract, Liquify, Pattern Maker, and Vanishing Point, can be applied as a Smart Filter. You won't find the Smart Filter command on the Filter menu; simply apply a filter to a Smart Object and it will be applied as a Smart Filter. Once the filter is applied, the Smart Filter appears in the Layers panel. Double-clicking the filter on the Layers panel opens the Filter Gallery, enabling you to modify or change the existing filter.

Create a Smart Object

1. Click the **Indicates layer visibility button** on the Sunflower RIGHT layer on the Layers panel.

2. Click the **Indicates layer visibility button** on the Sunflower CENTER layer on the Layers panel.

3. Click the **Indicates layer visibility button** on the Sunflower LEFT layer on the Layers panel.

4. Click the **Sunflower RIGHT layer** on the Layers panel.

   TIP Any layer can be turned into a Smart Object. Before you apply any filters to a layer, convert it to a Smart Object to give you full editing capabilities over your filter selections.

5. Click **Layer** on the Application bar, point to **Smart Objects**, then click **Convert to Smart Object**.

6. Save your work, then compare your image and Layers panel to Figure 5.

You restored the visibility of three layers and converted one of the layers into a Smart Object. The ability to turn layers on and off while working on an image means you can decrease distracting elements and concentrate on specific objects.

CREATE AN EFFECT WITH
AN ARTISTIC FILTER

What You'll Do

In this lesson, you'll apply the Poster Edges filter from the Artistic category to the Sunflower RIGHT layer and adjust the contrast and brightness of the layer.

Learning About Artistic Filters

You can dramatically alter an image by using Artistic filters. **Artistic filters** are often used for special effects in television commercials and other multimedia venues.

Taking Advantage of Smart Filters

Just as you can convert an object on a layer into a Smart Object to make your edits nondestructive, you can perform a similar operation to give the application of filters the same power. So, while you can apply a filter directly to a layer, you can just as easily apply a Smart Filter. If the active layer is not already a Smart Object, you can apply a Smart Filter on-the-fly

using the Convert for Smart Filters command on the Filter menu.

> QUICKTIP A Smart Filter is nothing more than a filter that is applied to a Smart Object.

Using Artistic Filters

There are 15 Artistic filters. Figure 6 shows examples of some of the Artistic filters. The following list contains the names of each of the Artistic filters and their effects.

- Colored Pencil has a colored pencil effect and retains important edges.
- Cutout allows high-contrast images to appear in silhouette and has the effect of using several layers of colored paper.

Learning about third-party plug-ins

A **plug-in** is any external program that adds features and functionality to another program while working from within that program. Plug-ins enable you to obtain and work in additional file types and formats, add dazzling special effects, or provide efficient shortcut modules. You can purchase Photoshop plug-ins from third-party companies, or download them from freeware sites. To locate Photoshop plug-ins, you can use your favorite Internet search engine, or search for plug-ins on Adobe's website: *www.adobe.com*.

- Dry Brush simplifies an image by reducing its range of colors.
- Film Grain applies even color variations throughout an object.
- Fresco paints an image with short, rounded dabs of color.
- Neon Glow adds a glow effect to selected objects.
- Paint Daubs gives an image a painterly effect.
- Palette Knife reduces the level of detail in an image, revealing underlying texture.

- Plastic Wrap accentuates surface details and makes the contents of a layer appear to be covered in plastic.
- Poster Edges reduces the number of colors in an image.
- Rough Pastels makes an image look as if it is stroked with colored pastel chalk on a textured background.
- Smudge Stick softens an image by smudging or smearing darker areas.
- Sponge creates highly textured areas, making an object look like it was painted with a sponge.

- Underpainting paints the image on a textured background.
- Watercolor simplifies the appearance of an object, making it look like it was painted with watercolors.

Adjusting Filter Effects

You can change the appearance of a filter by using any of the functions listed under the Adjustments command on the Image menu. For example, you can modify the color balance or the brightness/contrast of a layer before or after you apply a filter to it.

FIGURE 6

Examples of Artistic filters

Apply a Smart Filter (Artistic filter) with the Filter Gallery

1. Click **Filter** on the Application bar, click **Filter Gallery**, then move and enlarge the image so that it is visible in the preview window (if necessary).

   The Filter Gallery displays thumbnails of each filter as you expand each category, so you can see a quick overview of what effects are available.

   > TIP The settings available for a filter in the Filter Gallery are the same as those in the individual dialog box that opens when you click the category name in the menu.

2. Click the **triangle to the left of the Artistic folder** ▶, then click **Poster Edges**.

3. Type **5** in the Edge Thickness text box.

   The Edge Thickness determines the settings of the edges within the image.

4. Type **5** in the Edge Intensity text box.

   The Edge Intensity setting gives the edges more definition.

5. Type **3** in the Posterization text box, then compare your dialog box to Figure 7.

   The Posterization setting controls the number of unique colors the filter will reproduce in the image.

6. Click **OK**, then compare your image and Layers panel to Figure 8.

Using the Filter Gallery, you applied the Poster Edges filter to the Sunflower RIGHT layer. The far right sunflower now looks less realistic than the flowers next to it, and has poster effects.

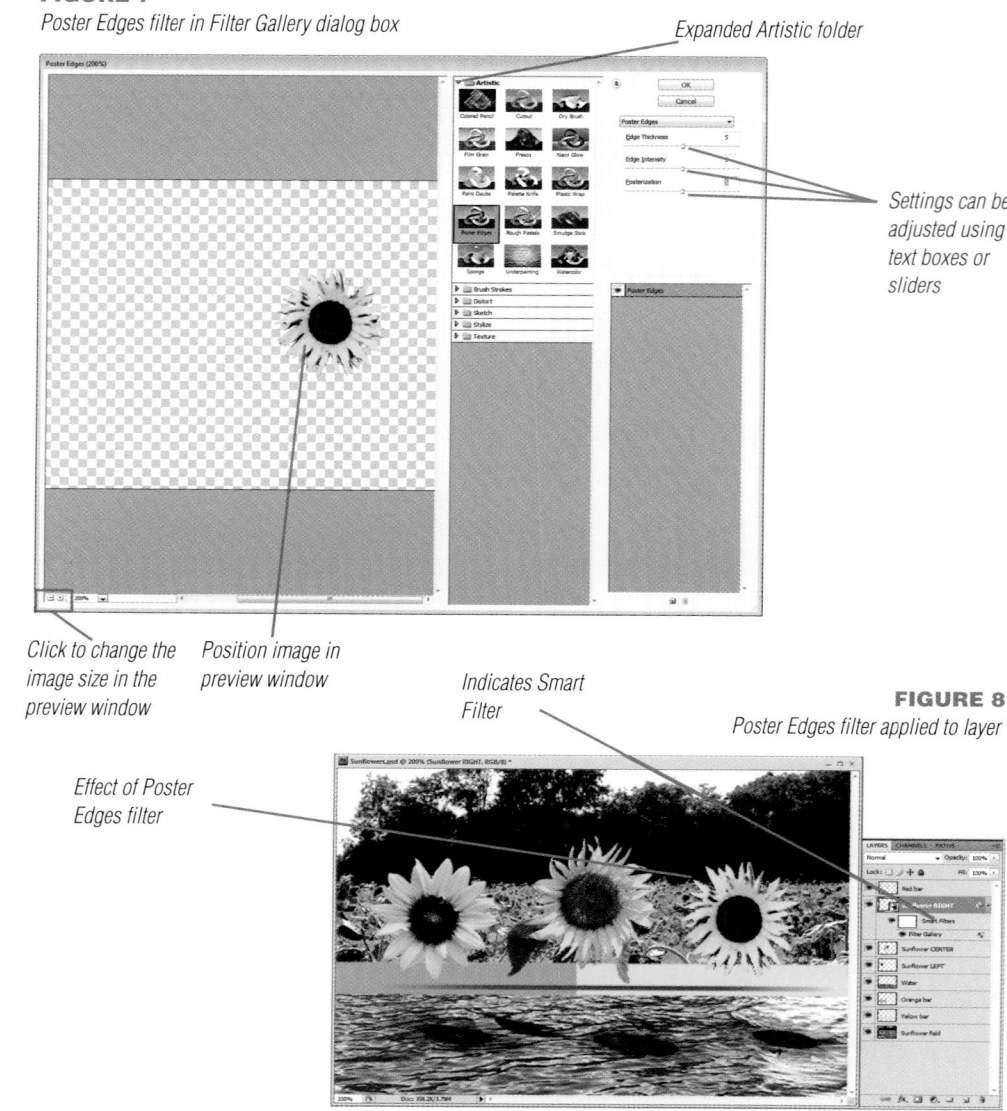

FIGURE 7
Poster Edges filter in Filter Gallery dialog box

Expanded Artistic folder

Settings can be adjusted using text boxes or sliders

Click to change the image size in the preview window

Position image in preview window

Indicates Smart Filter

Effect of Poster Edges filter

FIGURE 8
Poster Edges filter applied to layer

FIGURE 9
Image adjusted

Brightness and contrast
adjusted on layer

1. Click the **Brightness/Contrast button** 🔆 on the Adjustments panel.

    The effects of the adjustment layer will be limited to the active layer.

2. Type **20** in the Brightness text box.

3. Type **15** in the Contrast text box.

4. Double-click the **Filter Gallery effect** under the Sunflower RIGHT layer on the Layers panel.

5. Click **OK** if a warning box opens.

    This warning box indicates that Smart Filters stacked on top of this filter will not preview while this filter is being edited and will be applied after committing the filter parameters.

6. Click **Watercolor** in the Artistic category, then click **OK**.

7. Save your work, then compare your image to Figure 9.

You adjusted the brightness and contrast of the Sunflower RIGHT layer and changed the existing filter type.

ADD UNIQUE EFFECTS
WITH STYLIZE FILTERS

What You'll Do

In this lesson, you'll apply a solarize filter to the Sunflower field layer and a Wind filter to the Orange bar layer. You'll also apply the Poster Edges filter to two layers using the Filter Gallery.

Learning About Stylize Filters

Stylize filters produce a painted or impressionistic effect by displacing pixels and heightening the contrast within an image. Figure 10 shows several Stylize filters. Several commonly used Stylize filters and their effects are listed below:

- The Diffuse filter breaks up the image so that it looks less focused. The Darken Only option replaces light pixels with dark pixels, and the Lighten Only option replaces dark pixels with light pixels.
- The Wind filter conveys directed motion.
- The Extrude filter converts the image into pyramids or blocks.

Applying a Filter to a Selection

Instead of applying a filter to an entire layer, you can specify a particular area of a layer to which you want to apply a filter. You need to first define the area by using a marquee tool, and then apply the desired filter. If you want to apply a filter to a layer that contains a mask, be sure to select the layer name, not the layer mask thumbnail.

Detecting a watermark

Before you can embed a watermark, you must first register with Digimarc Corporation. When Photoshop detects a watermark in an image, it displays the copyright image © in the image file's title bar. To check if an image has a watermark, make the layer active, click Filter on the Application bar, point to Digimarc, then click Read Watermark.

FIGURE 10
Examples of Stylize filters

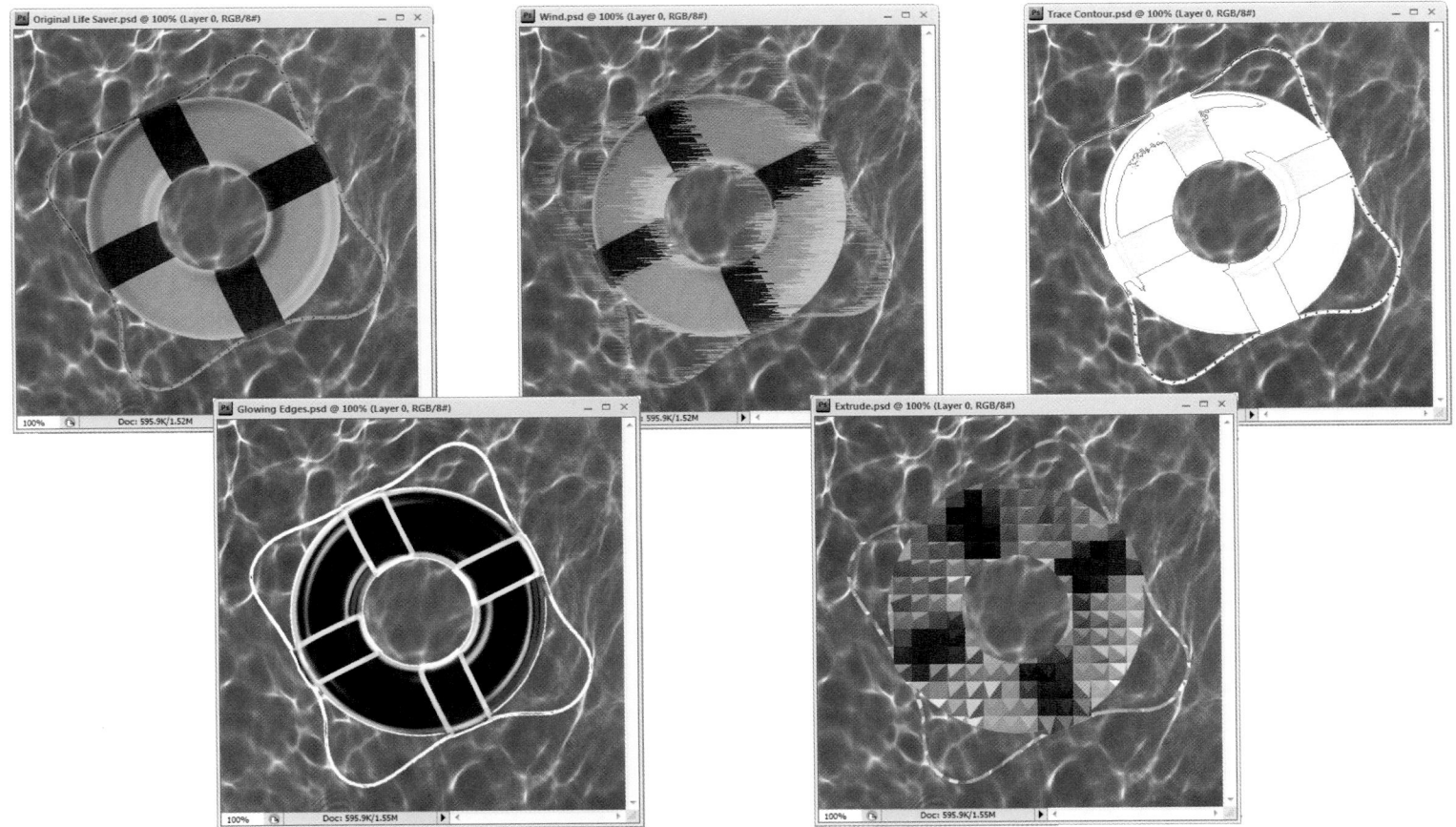

Browsing filters online

You might notice that at the bottom of the Filter menu is the option to Browse Filters Online. When you click this option, your browser will open and go to an Adobe website that contains links for filter downloads. You can also use your favorite browser to locate sites that offer Photoshop filters that are either available for free or for a small fee. (Some filters are available as plug-ins.)

Apply a Stylize filter

1. Click the **Sunflower field layer** on the Layers panel.

2. Click **Filter** on the Application bar, point to **Stylize** as shown in Figure 11, then click **Solarize**.

   TIP In addition to just looking interesting, the Solarize filter can be used to reduce shadows and make an image more equalized. In this effect, dark areas appear lighter and light areas appear darker.

3. Compare your image to Figure 12.

You applied the Solarize filter to the Sunflower field layer.

FIGURE 11
Stylize options on the Filter menu

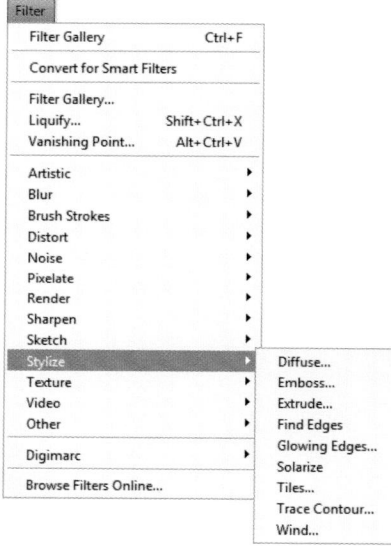

FIGURE 12
Effect of Solarize filter

Pixels appear darker

Using filters to reduce file size

If you apply a filter to a small area, you can view the effect while conserving your computer's resources. For example, you can test several filters on a small area and then decide which one you want to apply to one or more layers. Alternatively, you can apply a filter to a large portion of a layer, such as applying a slight Motion Blur filter to a grassy background. Your viewers will not notice an appreciable difference when they look at the grass, but by applying the filter, you reduce the number of green colors Photoshop must save in the image, which reduces the size of the file.

FIGURE 13
Elliptical Marquee selection

Marquee surrounds
the box

FIGURE 14
Wind dialog box

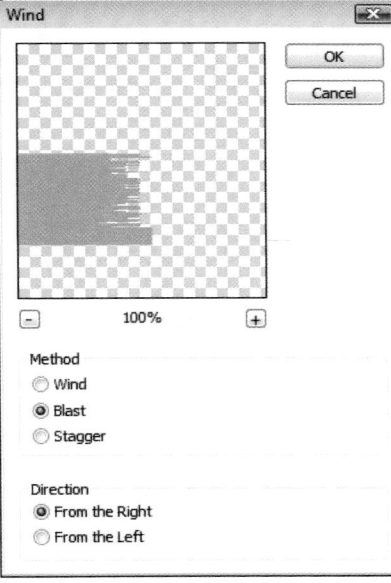

FIGURE 15
Effect of Wind filter

Wind filter applied
to orange bar

1. Click the **Orange bar layer** on the Layers panel.

2. Click the **Rectangular Marquee tool** ⬚. on the Tools panel.

3. Change the Feather setting to **0 px** (if it is not already set to 0).

4. Draw a rectangle around an area that includes the right side of the bar (from approximately **140 X/140 Y** to **250 X/225 Y**) using the **Marquee pointer** +, as shown in Figure 13.

5. Click **Filter** on the Application bar, point to **Stylize**, then click **Wind**.

6. Click the **Blast option button** in the Method section of the Wind dialog box.

7. Click the **From the Right option button** in the Direction section of the Wind dialog box (if it is not already selected), then compare your dialog box to Figure 14.

8. Click **OK**.

9. Deselect the marquee, then compare your image to Figure 15.

You used the Rectangular Marquee tool to select a specific area on the Orange bar layer, then applied the Wind filter to the selection.

Use the Filter Gallery to apply a previously used filter

1. Click the **Sunflower CENTER layer** on the Layers panel.

2. Click **Filter** on the Application bar, then click **Filter Gallery**. Compare your Filter Gallery dialog box to Figure 16.

   TIP When the Filter Gallery opens, the filter that was last applied using the Filter Gallery is selected by default.

3. Click **OK**.

   The filter last applied using the Filter Gallery is applied to the active layer.

You applied the Poster Edges filter to a layer using the Filter Gallery.

FIGURE 16
Last filter applied on Filter Gallery

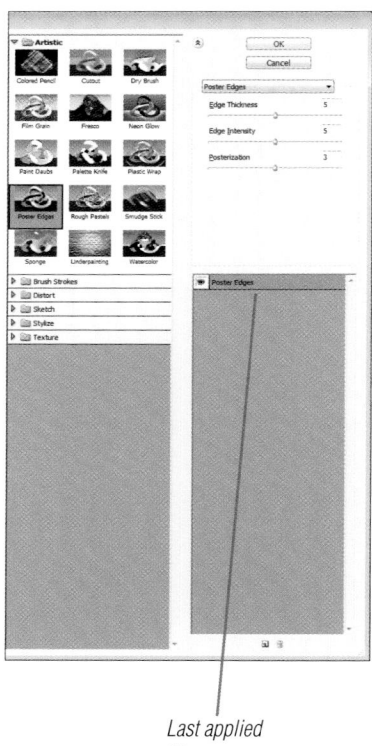

Last applied filter

FIGURE 17
Combining filters

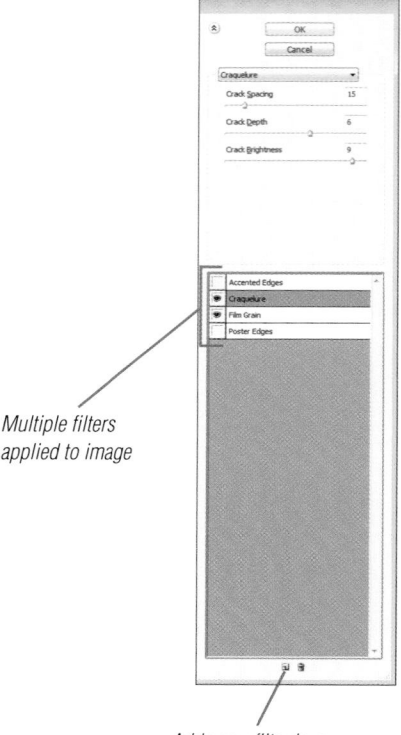

Multiple filters applied to image

Adds new filter layer

Using the Filter Gallery to combine effects

The Filter Gallery offers more than just another way of applying a single filter. Using this feature, you can apply multiple filters. And using the same principles as on the Layers panel, you can rearrange the filter layers and control their visibility. Figure 17 shows an image to which four different filters have been applied, but only the effects of two are visible. Each time you apply, reorder, or turn off one of the filters, the preview image is updated, so you'll always know how your image is being modified.

Creating Special Effects with Filters

FIGURE 18
Solarize filter applied to multiple layers

*Solarize filter
applied to all
Sunflowers layers*

1. Click the **Sunflower LEFT layer** on the Layers panel.

2. Click **Filter** on the Application bar, then click the first instance of **Filter Gallery**.

   The Sunflower LEFT and Sunflower CENTER layers have the same filter applied.

3. Save your work, then compare your image to Figure 18.

You used the last filter applied on the Filter Gallery to apply the Poster Edges filter to the Sunflower LEFT layer and the Sunflower CENTER layer.

Getting some perspective with Vanishing Point

In the real world, perspective changes as you move towards and away from objects. If you use Photoshop to stretch the top of a skyscraper, to maintain proper perspective the modified shape should change so it appears to get taller and narrower. Using a grid, the Vanishing Point filter lets you do this by defining the area of any angle you want to modify so you can wrap objects around corners having multiple planes and into the distance while maintaining the correct perspective. The sky's the limit! The Vanishing Point feature is opened by clicking Filter on the Application bar, then clicking Vanishing Point.

ALTER IMAGES WITH DISTORT
AND NOISE FILTERS

What You'll Do

 In this lesson, you'll apply the Twirl filter to the Water layer and the Noise filter to the Yellow bar layer.

Understanding Distort and Noise Filters

Distort filters use the most memory, yet even a minimal setting can produce dramatic results. They can create a 3D effect or reshape an object. The Diffuse Glow filter mutes an image, similar to how classic film cinematographers layered cheesecloth or smeared Vaseline on the lens of a movie camera when filming leading ladies. Others, such as the Ocean Ripple, Glass, Wave, and Ripple filters make an object appear as if it is under or in water. The Twirl filter applies a circular effect to a layer. By adjusting the angle of the twirl, you can make images look as if they are moving or spinning. Figure 19 shows the diversity of the Distort filters.

Noise filters give an image an appearance of texture. You can apply them to an image layer or to the Background layer. If you want to apply a Noise filter to a type layer, you must rasterize the type layer to convert it to an image layer. You can apply effects to the rasterized type layer; however, you can no longer edit the text.

Optimizing Memory in Photoshop

Many of the dynamic features in Photoshop are memory-intensive, particularly layer masks and filters. In addition to significantly increasing file size, they require a significant quantity of your computer memory to take effect. Part of the fun of working in Photoshop is experimenting with different styles and effects; however, doing so can quickly consume enough memory to diminish Photoshop's performance, or can cause you to not be able to work in other programs while Photoshop is running. You can offset some of the resource loss by freeing up memory as you work in Photoshop, and by adjusting settings in the Preferences dialog box.

Understanding Memory Usage

Every time you change your image, Photoshop stores the previous state in its buffer, which requires memory. You can control some of the memory that Photoshop uses by reducing the number of states available on the History panel.

To change the number of states, point to Preferences on the Edit menu (Win) or Photoshop menu (Mac), select Performance, then enter a number in the History States text box. You can also liberate the memory used to store Undo commands, History states, and items on the clipboard by clicking Edit on the Application bar, pointing to Purge, then clicking the area you want to purge. It's a good idea to use the Purge command after you've tried out several effects during a session, but be aware that you cannot undo the Purge command. For example, if you purge the History states, they will no longer appear on the History panel.

Controlling Memory Usage

Factors such as how much memory your computer has, the average size file you work with, and your need to multitask (have other programs open) can determine how Photoshop uses the memory currently allotted to it. To change your memory settings, click Edit (Win) or Photoshop (Mac) on the Application bar, point to Preferences, then click Performance. Make the desired change in the Let Photoshop Use text box (in the Memory Usage section), then click OK. You should carefully consider your program needs before changing the default settings. For additional tips on managing resources, visit Adobe's Photoshop Help and Support website: *www.adobe.com/support/photoshop*.

FIGURE 19
Examples of Distort filters

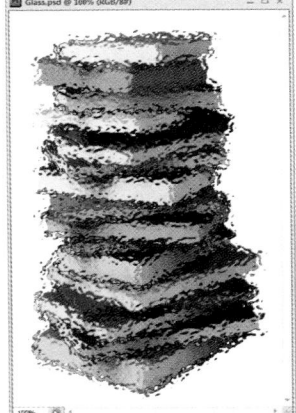

Lesson 4   Alter Images with Distort and Noise Filters

Apply a Twirl filter

1. Click the **Water layer** on the Layers panel.

2. Click **Filter** on the Application bar, point to **Distort**, then click **Twirl**.

3. Drag the **Angle slider** to **225**, as shown in Figure 20.

   ▎TIP   The selection is rotated more sharply in the center of the selection than at the edges.

4. Click **OK**.

5. Click the **Red bar layer** on the Layers panel, drag it beneath the Water layer, then compare your image to Figure 21.

You applied a Twirl filter to the Water layer. You moved the Red bar layer beneath the water to complete the effect.

FIGURE 20
Twirl dialog box

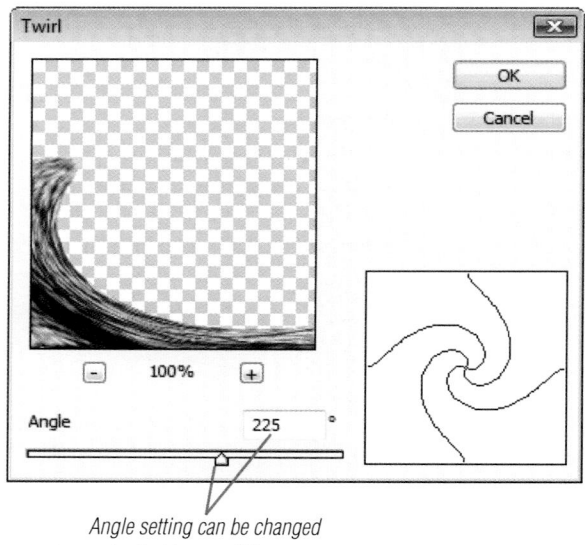

Angle setting can be changed
using text box or slider

FIGURE 21
Twirl filter applied to Water layer

Effect of
Twirl filter

Correction lens distortion

Some distortions occur as a result of the camera lens. You can use the Lens Correction filter to counteract barrel (convex appearance), pincushion (concave appearance), and perspective distortions. You can also correct for chromatic aberrations and lens vignetting. These distortions can occur as a result of the focal length or f-stop in use. The Lens Correction filter can also be used to rotate an image or fix perspectives caused by camera tilt. Click Filter on the Application bar, point to Distort, and then click Lens Correction.

Creating Special Effects with Filters

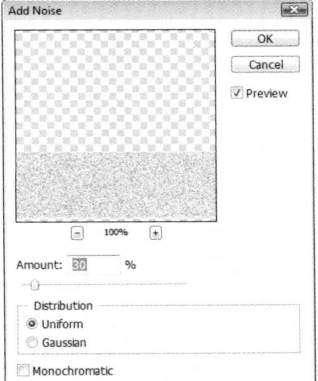

Effect of Add
Noise filter

Apply a Noise filter

1. Click the **Yellow bar layer** on the Layers panel.

2. Click **Filter** on the Application bar, point to **Noise**, then click **Add Noise**.

3. Drag the **Amount slider** to **30** (or type the value in the text box), then compare your dialog box to Figure 22.

   TIP The Uniform setting distributes color values using random numbers between 0 and a specified value, while the Gaussian setting distributes color values along a bell-shaped curve for a speckled effect.

4. Click **OK**.

   Flecks of noise are visible in the layer.

5. Save your work, then compare your image to Figure 23.

You applied a Noise filter to the active layer.

FIGURE 24
Reduce Noise dialog box

Reducing noise

While some images look better when you've added some noise, others can benefit from a little noise reduction. You can quiet things down using the Reduce Noise dialog box shown in Figure 24. Here you can adjust the strength, details, and color noise, and can also sharpen the image.

ALTER LIGHTING WITH
A RENDER FILTER

What You'll Do

 In this lesson, you'll add a lighting effect to the Sunflower LEFT layer, add text, save a copy of the file, then flatten the original image.

Understanding Lighting Effects

The Lighting Effects filter in the **Render** category of the Filter menu allows you to set an atmosphere or highlight elements in your image. You can select the style and type of light, adjust its properties, and texturize it. The preview window displays an ellipse that shows the light settings and allows you to position the light relative to your image, so that it looks like the light in the image is coming from a specific source. You can drag the handles on each circle, ellipse, or bar to change the direction and distance of the light sources. Figure 25 shows how you can position the light using the Soft Spotlight style.

Adjusting Light by Setting the Style and Light Type

You can choose from over a dozen lighting styles, including spotlights, floodlights, and full lighting, as shown in Figure 25. After you select a style, you choose the type of light—Directional, Omni, or

Spotlight—and set its intensity and focus. Directional lighting washes the surface with a constant light source, Omni casts light from the center, and Spotlight directs light outward from a single point. As shown in Figure 26, you can adjust the brightness of the light by using the Intensity slider. You can use the Focus slider to adjust the size of the beam of light filling the ellipse. The light source begins where the radius touches the edge of the ellipse. The Light type color swatch lets you modify the color of the light. You can also create custom lighting schemes and save them for use in other images. Custom lighting schemes will appear in the Style list.

Adjusting Surrounding Light Conditions

You can adjust the surrounding light conditions using the Gloss, Material, Exposure, or Ambience properties, as shown in Figure 26. The Gloss property controls the amount of surface reflection on the lighted surfaces. The Material property controls the parts of an image that reflect the light source color. The Exposure property lightens or darkens the ellipse (the area displaying the light source). The Ambience property controls the balance between the light source and the overall light in an image. The Properties color swatch changes the ambient light around the spotlight.

Adding Texture to Light

The Texture Channel allows you to add 3D effects to the lighting filter. The Texture Channel controls how light reflects off an image. If a channel is selected and the 'White is High' check box is also selected, white parts of the channel will be raised. To use this option, you select one of the three RGB color channels, then drag the Height slider to the relief setting you want. You

can also choose whether the black or white areas appear highest in the relief. Figure 27 shows a lighting effect texture with black colors highest.

QUICKTIP

You can add additional light sources by dragging the light bulb icon onto the preview window, and then adjusting each new light source that you add.

FIGURE 25
Lighting Effects dialog box

FIGURE 27
Texture added to lighting effect

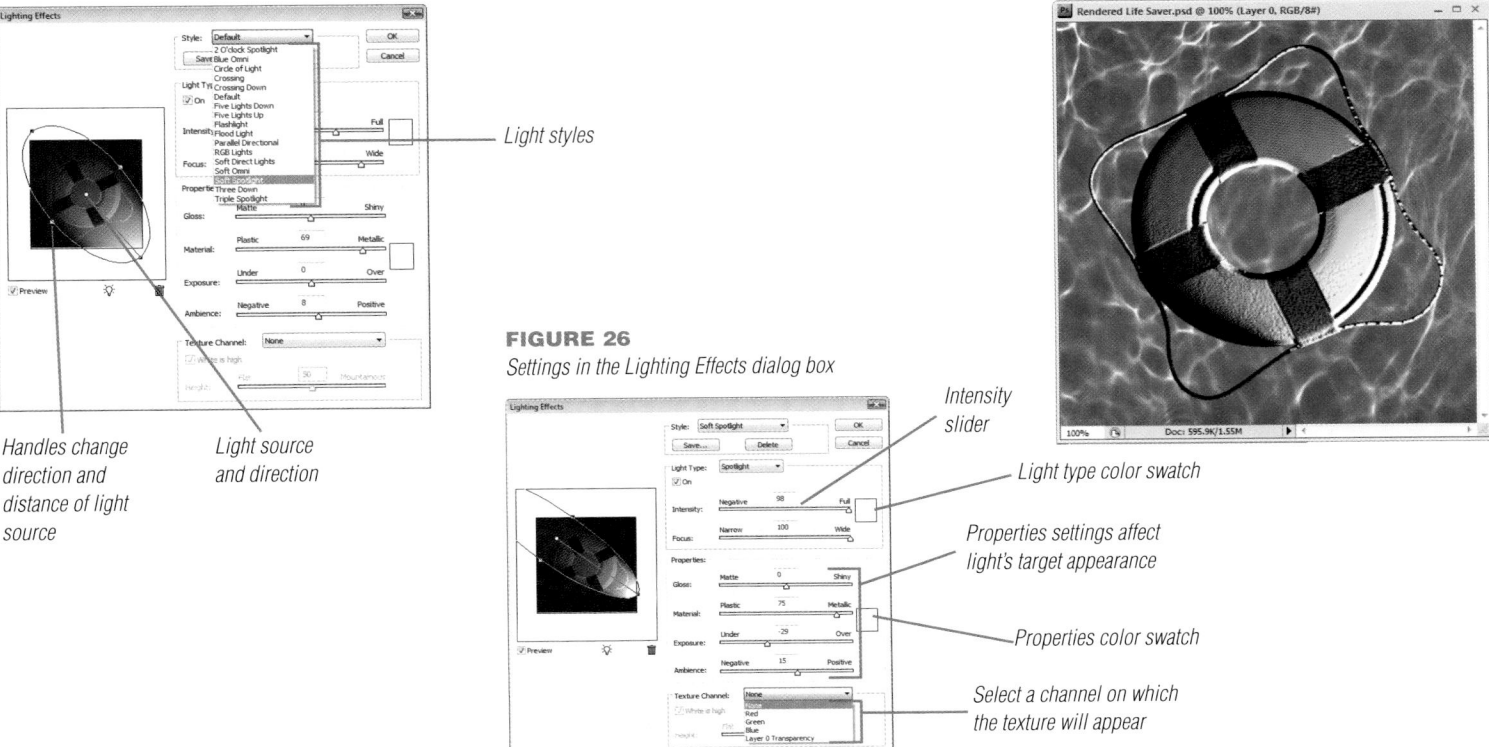

Light styles

Handles change direction and distance of light source

Light source and direction

FIGURE 26
Settings in the Lighting Effects dialog box

Intensity slider

Light type color swatch

Properties settings affect light's target appearance

Properties color swatch

Select a channel on which the texture will appear

Select lighting settings

1. Click the **Sunflower LEFT layer** on the Layers panel.

2. Click **Filter** on the Application bar, point to **Render**, then click **Lighting Effects**.

3. Click the **Style list arrow**, then click **Flashlight**.

   The preview window displays the newly selected style.

4. Click the **Light type list arrow**, then click **Omni** (if it is not already selected).

5. Verify that the **On check box** is selected.

   The preview window shows the settings for the Flashlight light source.

6. Drag the **center handle** of the flashlight so it is directly over the sunflower in the preview box.

   As you drag the ellipse handle, the preview window automatically displays the change in the lighting direction and distance.

7. Drag any **one of the handles** on the edge of the flashlight so the spotlight is larger than the sunflower (if necessary).

8. Adjust the **slider settings** as shown in Figure 28 in the Lighting Effects dialog box.

   | TIP   Lighting effects must include at least one light source.

You selected a lighting style and type, then changed the direction and distance of the lighting.

FIGURE 28
Light direction and source repositioned

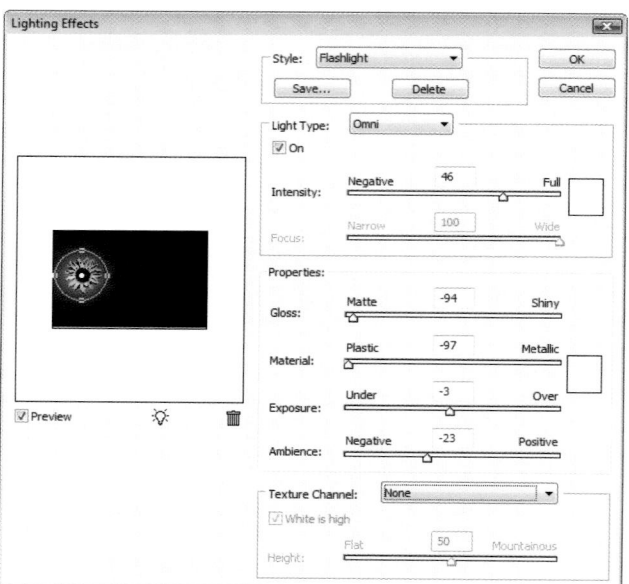

Using Analysis and Measurement Tools

One of the menus tucked between Filter and View on the Application bar is the Analysis menu. This group of commands lets you select many options, such as changing the measurement scale, selecting data points, selecting the Ruler Tool (which help you position images or elements, and calculates the distance between any two points). The Count Tool lets you manually count items. You can record measurements, and place a scale marker at the top or bottom of the image. Recorded measurements are displayed in the Measurement Log panel (which appears behind the Animation [Timeline] panel) and can be opened by clicking Window on the Application bar, then clicking Measurement Log.

FIGURE 29
Lighting Effects filter applied to Sunflower LEFT

FIGURE 30
Type layer in flattened file

Apply a lighting effect

1. Click **OK**.

   The light appears brightest in the center of the flower.

   > TIP When there are multiple sources of light, you can delete a light source ellipse by dragging its center point over the Delete icon in the Lighting Effects dialog box.

2. Compare your image to Figure 29. Your results may vary, depending on your settings in the Lighting Effects dialog box.

You applied a lighting effect to the Sunflower LEFT layer.

Apply finishing touches

1. Use a 36-point black Impact font to create a type layer at approximately 210 H/ 220 V that says **Sunflower Grill**.

2. Save a copy of this file using the default naming scheme, flatten the file, then compare your image to Figure 30.

3. Save your work.

You added a type layer to the image, then saved a copy and flattened the file.

Creating custom lighting effects

As you modify a style in the Lighting Effects dialog box, you can save the settings as a new style with a unique name. To create a custom style, choose your settings, then click the Save button beneath the Style list arrow. Enter a new name in the Save As dialog box, then click OK. The new style name will appear in the Style list. You can delete an entry by selecting it from the Style list, then clicking the Delete button.

USE VANISHING POINT
TO ADD PERSPECTIVE

What You'll Do

In this lesson, you'll use Vanishing Point to apply a Photoshop image to the perspective created in another image.

Understanding Vanishing Point

Vanishing Point, which is found in the Filter menu, allows you to create planes which can visually adjust for perspective caused by width, height, and depth. With Vanishing Point, matching perspective is made easy. (Without this feature, you can fuss with the Transform commands to try to create the illusion of perspective. You'll work very hard and may not be very happy with the results.) From within Vanishing Point, you can create an unlimited number of planes from which you can copy and clone objects around corners.

Creating Planes

You may find it helpful to use this feature on a newly created empty layer. That way, if you make a mistake, your original image will still be intact. Once you've opened Vanishing Point, you create an initial plane from which others can be drawn.

Each plane is surrounded by a light blue line, and while any image can have multiple planes, only one plane can be active at a time in editing mode. The active plane is indicated by a displayed grid. Figure 31 shows the Vanishing Point window, and an object containing two drawn planes. As you draw each plane (using tools in the Vanishing Point window), the grid color lets you know if your perspective is realistic. A red grid indicates that the drawn perspective is not possible. A yellow grid indicates that the perspective is unlikely.

Pasting One Image into Another

Using the Clipboard, you can copy an image which can then be pasted and manipulated in Vanishing Point. When imagery is initially pasted into Vanishing Point, it floats at the top until you pull it within the planes you have created. Figure 32 shows imagery that has been pulled onto the planes of a gift box.

Getting that Healing Feeling

Vanishing Point tools are located in the upper-left corner of the dialog box. You can use the Transform tool to flip images and the Stamp tool and Brush tool to paint over pixels.

QUICK TIP

You can use Vanishing Point and create a grid even if you don't have an image in which to paste it. If you don't have an image in which to paste a graphic, create a new layer or open a new file, open Vanishing Point, create a grid, then paste your graphic.

FIGURE 31
Vanishing Point window

Tools

FIGURE 32
Image applied to multiple planes

Outline of inactive plane

Handle of grid on active plane

TABLE 2: Vanishing Point tools

tool	name	used to
	Edit Plane tool	Selects, edits, moves, and resizes planes.
	Create Plane tool	Defines a plane, adjusts its size and shape, and tears off a new plane.
	Marquee tool	Makes square or rectangular selections, and moves and clones selections.
	Stamp tool	Paints with a sample of the image.
	Brush tool	Paints with a selected color in a plane.
	Transform tool	Scales, rotates, and moves a floating selection using handles.
	Eyedropper tool	Selects a color for painting when you click in the preview image.
	Measure tool	Measures distances and angles of an item in a plane.
	Hand tool	Repositions the image in the preview window.
	Zoom tool	Magnifies/reduces the image in the preview window.

Prepare to use Vanishing Point

1. Select the entire flattened image.
2. Copy the selection to the Clipboard.
3. Open PS 8-2.psd from the drive and folder where you store your Data Files, then save it as **Sunflower Grill-VP**.
4. Create a new layer.
5. Click **Filter** on the Application bar, then click **Vanishing Point**.
6. If necessary, select the **Create Plane tool** 📐.
7. Click point 1 in the building, click point 2, click point 3, then click point 4 using Figure 33 as a guide.

You selected the contents of a flattened image, copied it to the Clipboard, opened Vanishing Point, then created an initial plane.

Create an additional plane

1. Click the **Create Plane tool** 📐.
2. Position the pointer over the right center handle, as shown in Figure 34.
3. Drag the grid along the long edge of the building, stopping at the extension towards the building's right edge.
4. With the **Edit Plane tool** 📐, **[Ctrl]-drag** (Win) or ⌘**-drag** (Mac) the **right-most** handles so they cover the top four floors of the building, as shown in Figure 35.

You created an additional plane in Vanishing Point, then adjusted the points in the plane to include a specific area in an image.

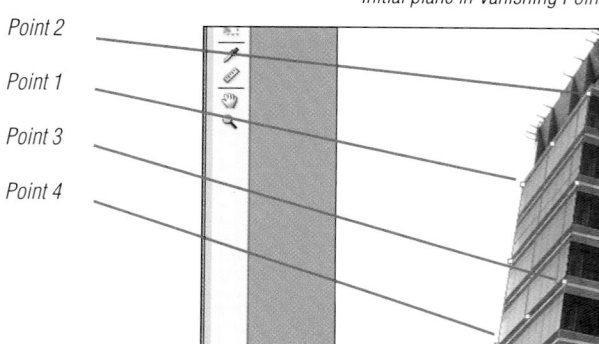

FIGURE 33
Initial plane in Vanishing Point

Point 2
Point 1
Point 3
Point 4

FIGURE 34
Preparing to create new plane

Drag handle to create new plane

FIGURE 35
Grid covering 4 top floors of building

Your results may differ

Creating Special Effects with Filters

FIGURE 36

Pasted contents floating in Vanishing Point

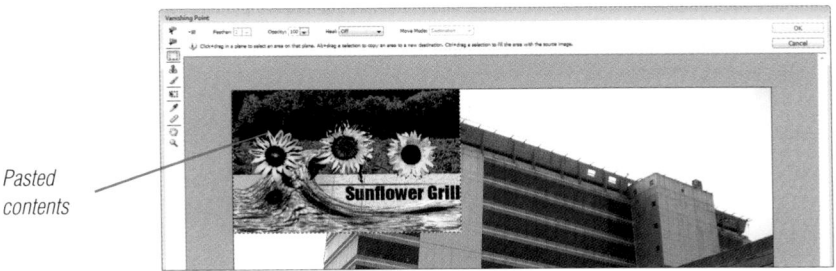

Pasted
contents

FIGURE 37

Clipboard contents in grid

FIGURE 38

Repositioned Clipboard contents

1. Paste the copied image.

   The contents of the Clipboard is copied into Vanishing Point, as shown in Figure 36.

2. Position the pointer over the pasted selection, then drag the pointer ▶ over the left side of the grid until you feel it pop into place, as shown in Figure 37.

3. Drag the pointer ▶ until the image fills the grid and the type displays. (*Hint*: If you need to reposition the pasted object, click it again with the pointer.)

4. Click **OK** to close Vanishing Point.

5. Save your work, then compare your image to Figure 38. (Your zoom factor and results may differ.)

6. Close the file, then exit Photoshop.

You pasted the contents of the Clipboard into Vanishing Point, then adjusted the image within the grid.

Power User Shortcuts

to do this:	use this method:
Apply a filter	Filter ➤ Filter category ➤ Filter name
Apply last filter	[Ctrl][F] (Win) or ⌘ [F] (Mac)
Apply last filter, but set new options	[Ctrl][Alt][F] (Win) or ⌘ option [F] (Mac)
Ascend one layer at a time on the Layers panel	[Alt][]] (Win) or option []] (Mac)

to do this:	use this method:
Descend one layer at a time on the Layers panel	[Alt][[] (Win) or option [[] (Mac)
Fades effect of previous filter	[Ctrl][Shift][F] (Win) or ⌘ [Shift][F] (Mac)
Open Filter Gallery	Filter ➤ Filter Gallery
Open Vanishing Point	Filter ➤ Vanishing Point

Key: Menu items are indicated by ➤ between the menu name and its command.

Creating Special Effects with Filters

Learn about filters and how to apply them.

1. Start Photoshop, open PS 8-3.psd from the drive and folder where you store your Data Files, then save it as **B&B Poster**.
2. Make the Dunes layer active.
3. Use the Elliptical Marquee tool to draw an ellipse around the bend in the driftwood limb.
4. Apply a Gaussian Blur filter (Blur category) with the following setting: Radius = 1.0 pixels. Remember to deselect the selection when you are finished.
5. Create four separate type layers with the text **Fish**, **Swim**, **Hike**, and **Relax**, and arrange them vertically starting from below the bend in the tree limb down over the tree trunk on the left side of the image. (*Hint*: A 36 pt Pure Yellow Copperplate Gothic Bold is used in the sample.)
6. Save your work.

Create an effect with an Artistic filter.

1. Make the B&B layer active, then convert the layer into a Smart Object.
2. Apply a Film Grain filter (Artistic category) with the following settings: Grain = 3, Highlight Area = 1, Intensity = 10.
3. Save your work.

Add unique effects with Stylize filters.

1. Make the Trout layer active.
2. Apply a Glowing Edges filter (Stylize category), with the following settings: Edge Width = 2,

Edge Brightness = 2, Smoothness = 3.
3. Transform the Trout layer by resizing and rotating the trout so that it appears to be jumping, then drag it behind the Fish type layer.
4. Save your work.

Alter images with Distort and Noise filters.

1. Make the Swim type layer active.
2. Apply a Ripple filter (Distort category) with the following settings: Amount = 55%, Size = Medium. (*Hint*: Click OK to rasterize the layer.)
3. Make the Relax type layer active.
4. Recolor the type to the following settings: R = 227, G = 4, B = 178.
5. Apply an Add Noise filter (Noise category) with the following settings: Amount = 25%, Distribution = Uniform, Monochromatic = Selected.
6. Save your work.

Alter lighting with a Render filter.

1. Make the Dunes layer active.
2. Apply Lighting Effects (Render category) with the following settings: Style = Crossing, type = Spotlight.
3. Use the following Lighting Effects settings: Intensity = 28, Focus = 100, Gloss = 0, Material = -100, Exposure = 0, Ambience = 11. (Your results may vary.)
4. Save your work as a copy using the default naming, flatten this file, then save your work.

Use Vanishing Point to add perspective.

1. Use the Image menu to change the image size to have a width of 3".
2. Select the contents of the flattened file, then copy it into the Clipboard.
3. Open PS 8-4.psd from the drive and folder where you store your Data Files, then save it as **Billboard**.
4. Create a new layer, then open Vanishing Point.
5. Create a realistic plane in the billboard, then paste the Clipboard contents into the image.
6. Center the B&B poster image in the sign, then return to Photoshop. (*Hint*: It's okay if Fish, Swim, Hike, Relax do not all display in the sign as the image and billboard have different dimensions.)
7. Save your work, close the flattened file *without saving the changes*, then compare your image to Figure 39.

FIGURE 39
Completed Skills Review

Theatre in the Park, an outdoor production company, is adding Shakespeare's comedies to their summer repertoire. The company has convinced several rollerbladers to wear sandwich boards promoting the event as they blade downtown during the noon hour. You've volunteered to design the board for the Bard. You can use the title from any Shakespearian comedy in the sign.

1. Obtain the following images that reflect the production: a park, an image related to Shakespeare, and any other images that reflect a summer theater production. You can use the images that are available on your computer, scanned images, or images from a digital camera.
2. Create a new Photoshop image with the dimensions 630 × 450 pixels, then save it as **Play**.
3. Drag or copy the Park image to the Play image above the Background layer, apply at least one filter to it, then rename the Background layer. (*Hint*: The Park layer in the sample has a Render category Lighting Effects filter applied to it.)
4. Drag the Shakespeare image to the Play image above the Park layer, and modify it as desired. (*Hint*: The face in the sample has an opacity setting of 64%, and has been rotated.)

5. Create a sign announcing the play, and apply at least one style and filter to it. (*Hint*: The sign in the sample was created using the Rectangle tool, and has the Drop Shadow, Satin, and Bevel and Emboss styles, and a Texture category Craquelure filter applied to it.)
6. Create type layers as desired, and apply at least one style or filter to them. (*Hint*: A 23 pt Myriad Pro font is used in the sample.)

7. Drag or copy the remaining images to the Play image, close the image files, then transform them or apply at least one style or filter to them.
8. Save your work, then compare your image to the sample in Figure 40.

FIGURE 40
Sample Project Builder 1

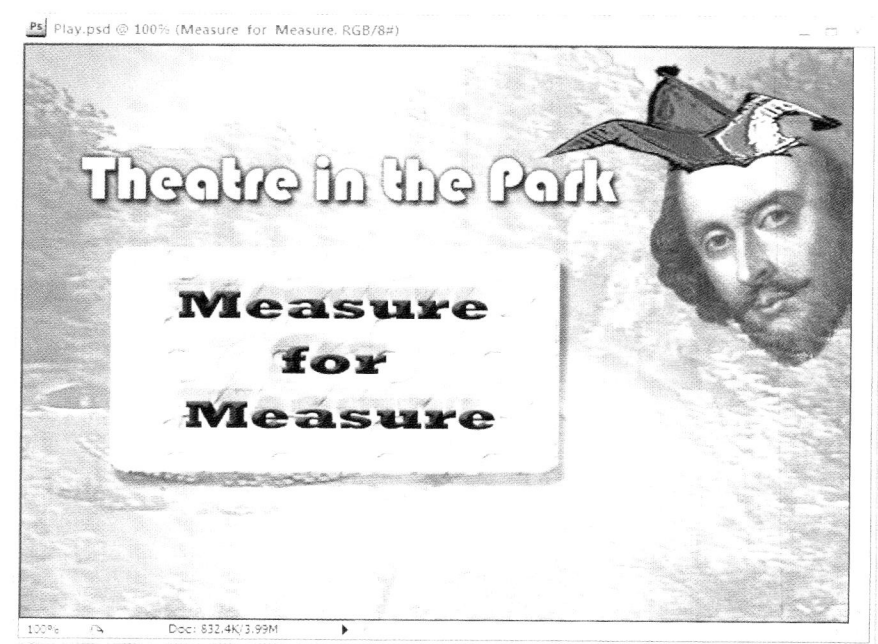

Creating Special Effects with Filters

Local musical instrument shops in your town are producing a classic jazz and blues event. Last year, the poster displayed sponsor logos and never conveyed the feel of the genre. This year, they've decided not to include sponsor logos, and have asked you to design a poster that focuses attention on the music itself. Use your Photoshop skills to express the sponsors' intent.

1. Obtain images for the design, including at least one with one or more instrument that will dominate the image. You can use the images that are available on your computer, scanned images, or images from a digital camera.
2. Create a new Photoshop image of any dimension, then save it as **Jazz and Blues**.
3. Open the main instrument file, drag it to the Jazz and Blues image above the Background layer, then remove the Background layer.
4. Open the remaining image files, drag or copy them to the Jazz and Blues image, then close the image files.

5. Apply filters and styles and transform the other image layers as desired. (*Hint*: The Keyboard layer was converted into a Smart Object and has a Color Overlay layer applied to it.)
6. Create type layers as desired and apply filters or styles to them. (*Hint*: The Jazz Title type layer has a 43.83 pt Times New Roman font with the Drop Shadow, Inner Shadow, Bevel and Emboss, and Gradient Overlay

styles applied to it. The text in the lower-left corner has a 9.98 pt Century Gothic font.)
7. Save your work, then compare your image to the sample in Figure 41.

FIGURE 41
Sample Project Builder 2

Destined Nations, a local travel agency, is looking to hire a freelance graphic artist to design their marketing pieces. Rather than peruse portfolios, they are holding a contest to select a poster design. Each entrant is given the same image to modify as they see fit. As an incentive to get the very best entries, they're offering an all-expense paid week vacation to the winner. You like vacations, so you decide to enter the contest.

1. Obtain at least one image for the vacation destination design. You can use the images that are available on your computer, scanned images, or images from a digital camera.
2. Open PS 8-5.psd, then save it as **Shield**.
3. Verify that the Shield layer is active, open the Lighting Effects dialog box, then choose a lighting style.
4. Continue working in the Lighting Effects dialog box. Change the Light type color swatch to yellow. (*Hint*: To change color, click the color swatch.)
5. Place at least two other spotlights around the preview window using different colored lights. (*Hint*: To add a spotlight, drag the light bulb icon to the preview window.) Close the Lighting Effects dialog box and view the image.
6. Apply a subtle texture to the Shield layer. (*Hint*: The Shield layer in the sample has the Smudge Stick Artistic filter applied to it.)
7. Delete the large center circle from the Shield layer. (*Hint*: To delete the circle quickly, select

the Elliptical Marquee tool, draw a selection around the circle, then press [Delete], or you can apply a layer mask and paint the circle.)
8. Delete the triangles from the Shield layer. (*Hint*: To delete the triangles quickly, select the Polygonal Lasso tool, draw a selection around the edges of the triangles, then press [Delete], or you can apply a layer mask and paint the triangles.)
9. Create a new layer at the bottom of the Layers panel, and then fill it in black.
10. Create a new layer above the black layer and name it **Blur**.
11. Use a Lasso tool or any other shape tool to create a shape that fills the left side of the layer, then apply a fill color to the selection.

FIGURE 42
Sample Design Project

12. Apply at least one Blur filter to the Blur layer.
13. Transform the shield so that it has dimension, then move it to the left side of the window. (*Hint*: The Shield layer in the sample has been distorted.)
14. Add type layers as desired and apply styles or filters to them. (*Hint*: The Acapulco layer in the sample has a border applied by clicking the Rasterize command on the Layer menu, and then using the Stroke command on the Edit menu. The your ultimate playground! layer in the sample is a 36 pt Monotype Corsiva.)
15. Open the image files, drag or copy them to the Shield image, close the image files, then apply filters or styles to them.
16. Save your work, then compare your image to the sample in Figure 42.

You have been asked to put together a presentation on traditional and modern dance styles from around the world. Choose a dance style and use your Photoshop skills to create a title slide that conveys the feel of that style.

1. Obtain at least three images that reflect the style of dance you've chosen. You can use the images that are available on your computer, scanned images, images from a digital camera, or images downloaded from the Internet. Try to select images that you can transform and to which you can add styles and apply filters. Make sure that one image can be used as a background.
2. Create a new Photoshop image, then save it as **Dance**.
3. Drag or copy the background to the Dance image above the Background layer, then rename the Background layer and apply a fill color as desired.
4. Drag an image to the Dance image, transform it as desired, then apply a filter to it. (*Hint*: The Swan layer [dancer in lower-left corner] in the sample has an Artistic category Plastic Wrap filter applied to it.)
5. Drag or copy the remaining images, transform as needed, and apply at least one style or filter to them. (*Hint*: The Large Ballerina layer has a layer mask applied to it, and the Shoes layer has the Distort category Diffuse Glow filter applied to it.)
6. Create type layers as desired, and apply at least one style or filter to them. (*Hint*: The Dancing type layer was created in a separate image using an image as a member of a clipping mask, then a variety of effects was applied to it. The Start when you're young type layer in the sample uses a 20 pt Kalinga font with Outer and Inner Glow layer styles applied.)
7. Be prepared to discuss the effects you generate when you add filters to styles and vice versa.
8. Save your work, then compare your image to the sample in Figure 43.

FIGURE 43
Sample Portfolio Project

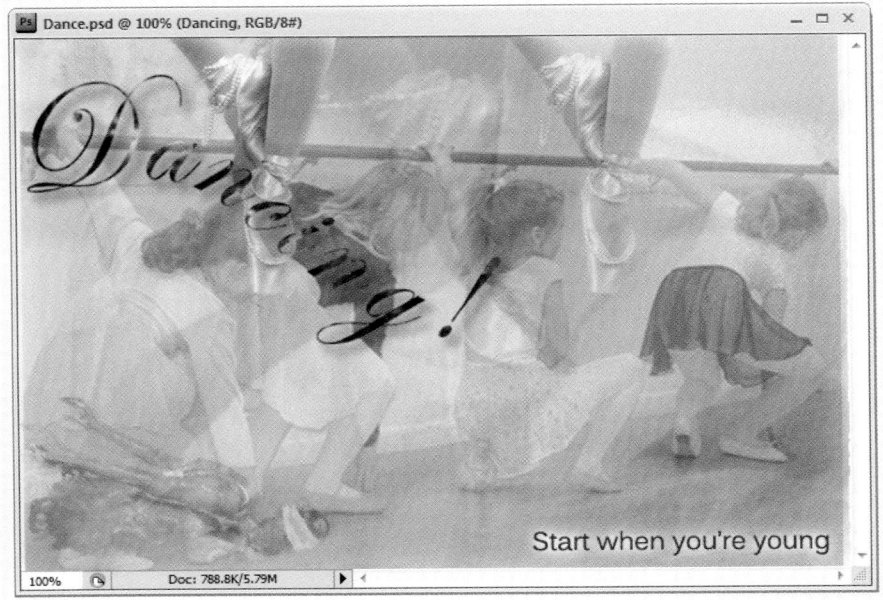

CHAPTER

9

ENHANCING SPECIFIC
SELECTIONS

1. Create an alpha channel

2. Isolate an object

3. Erase areas in an image to enhance appearance

4. Use the Clone Stamp tool to make repairs

5. Use the Magic Wand tool to select objects

6. Learn how to create snapshots

7. Create multiple-image layouts

Modifying Objects

As you have most likely figured out by now, a great part of the power of Photoshop resides in its ability to isolate graphics and text objects and make changes to them. This chapter focuses on several of the techniques used to isolate graphics objects and then make changes that enhance their appearance.

Using Channels

Nearly every image you open or create in Photoshop is separated into **channels**. Photoshop uses channels to house the color information for each layer and layer mask in your image. The number of color information channels depends on the color mode of the image. You can also create specific channels for layer masks.

Photoshop creates default channels based on the image mode, but you can create additional channels to gain more control of an image.

Fixing Imperfections

From time to time, you'll probably work with flawed images. Flawed images are not necessarily "bad," they just might contain imagery that does not fit your needs. Photoshop offers several ways to repair an image's imperfections. You can use the following methods—or combinations of these methods—to fix areas within an image that are less than ideal:

- Isolate areas using the Extract feature.
- Erase areas using a variety of eraser tools.
- Take a sample and then paint that sample over an area using the Clone Stamp tool.

Creating Snapshots

The Snapshot command lets you make a temporary copy of any state of an image. The snapshot is added to the top of the History panel and lets you work on a new version of the image. Snapshots are like the states found on the History panel but offer a few more advantages:

- You can name a snapshot to make it easy to identify and manage.
- You can compare changes to images easily. For example, you can take a snapshot before and after changing the color of a selection.
- You can recover your work easily. If your experimentation with an image doesn't satisfy your needs, you can select the snapshot to undo all the steps from the experiment.

Using Automation Features

After you complete an image that you want to share, you can create an image that contains various sizes of the same image, or several different images. Using a multiple-image layout, for example, makes it possible to print images in a variety of sizes and shapes on a single sheet. Another example is a contact sheet, a file that displays thumbnail views of a selection of images, so that you can easily catalog and preview them without opening each individual file.

Tools You'll Use

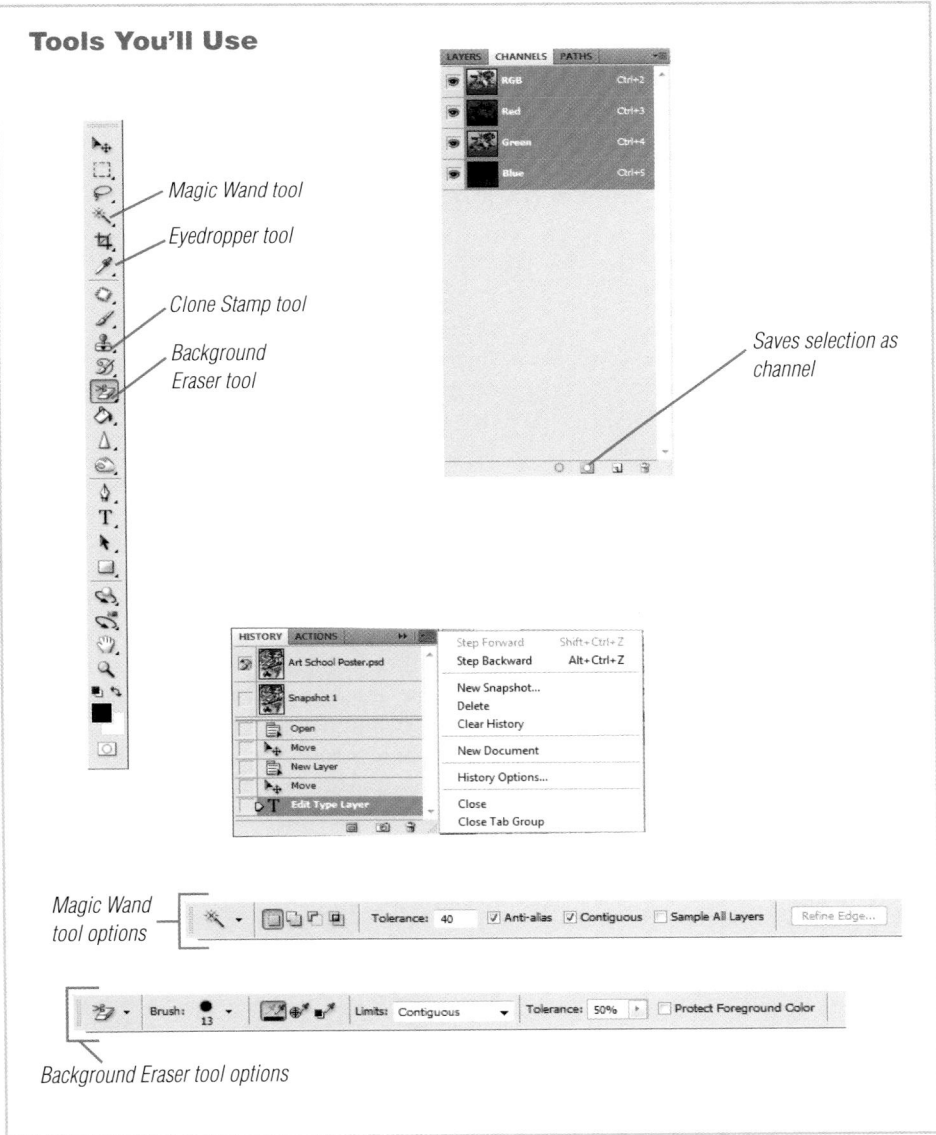

Magic Wand tool

Eyedropper tool

Clone Stamp tool

Background Eraser tool

Saves selection as channel

Magic Wand tool options

Background Eraser tool options

What You'll Do

In this lesson, you'll view the colors in the default color mode on the Channels panel. You'll also create a selection, save it as an alpha channel, and then change the color of the alpha channel.

Defining Channels

Photoshop automatically creates channel information in a new image and uses channels to store color information about images. Channels are created at the same time the image is created, and the number of channels is determined by the image mode. For example, a CMYK image has at least four channels (one each for cyan, magenta, yellow, and black), whereas an RGB image has three channels (one each for red, green, and blue). Every Photoshop image has at least one channel, and can have a maximum of 24 color channels. The color channels contained in an image are known as **default channels**, which Photoshop creates automatically. You can add specific color information by adding an **alpha channel** or a **spot channel**. You use an alpha channel to create and store masks, which let you manipulate, isolate, and protect parts of an image. A spot channel contains information about special pre-mixed inks used in CMYK color printing. The default number of channels is determined by the color mode you select in the New dialog box that opens when you create

a new file, as shown in Figure 1. You can add channels to images displayed in all color modes, except the bitmap modes.

Understanding Alpha Channels

You create alpha channels on the Channels panel. You can create an alpha channel that masks all or specific areas of a layer. For example, you can create a selection and then convert it into an alpha channel. Photoshop superimposes the color in an alpha channel onto the image; however, an alpha channel might appear in grayscale on the Channels panel thumbnail. You can use alpha channels to preserve a selection, to experiment with, to use later, to create special effects, such as screens or shadows, or to save and reuse in other images. Photoshop supports the following formats for saving an alpha channel: PSD, PDF, PICT, TIFF, and Raw. If you use other formats, you might lose some channel information. You can copy the alpha channel to other images and instantly apply the same information. Alpha channels do not print— they will not be visible in print media.

Understanding the Channels Panel

The Channels panel lists all the default channels contained in a layer and manages all the image's channels. To access this panel, click the Channels tab next to the Layers tab, as shown in Figure 2. The top channel is a **composite channel**—a combination of all the other default channels. The additional default channels, based on the existing color mode, are shown below the composite channel, followed by spot color channels, and finally by the alpha channels.

Channels have many of the same properties as layers. You can hide channels in the same way as you hide layers, by clicking a button in the column to the left of the thumbnail on the Channels panel. Each channel has a thumbnail that mirrors the changes you make to the image's layers. You can also change the order of channels by dragging them up or down on the Channels panel.

The thumbnails on the Channels panel might appear in grayscale. To view the channels in their actual color, click

Edit (Win) or Photoshop (Mac) on the Application bar, point to Preferences, click Interface, select the Show Channels in Color check box, then click OK. The default channels will appear in the color mode colors; an alpha channel will appear in the color selected in the Channel Options dialog box. You open the Channel Options dialog box by double-clicking the alpha channel on the Channels panel.

FIGURE 1
New dialog box

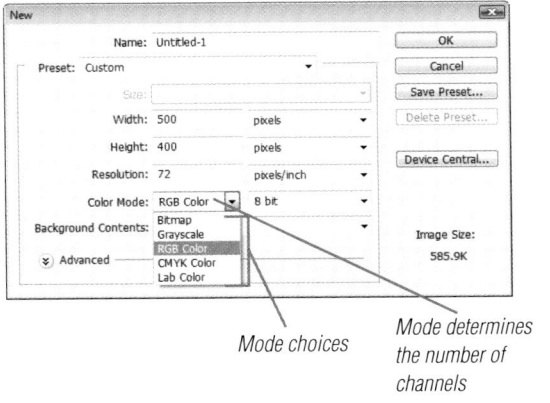

Mode choices

Mode determines the number of channels

FIGURE 2
Channels on the Channels panel

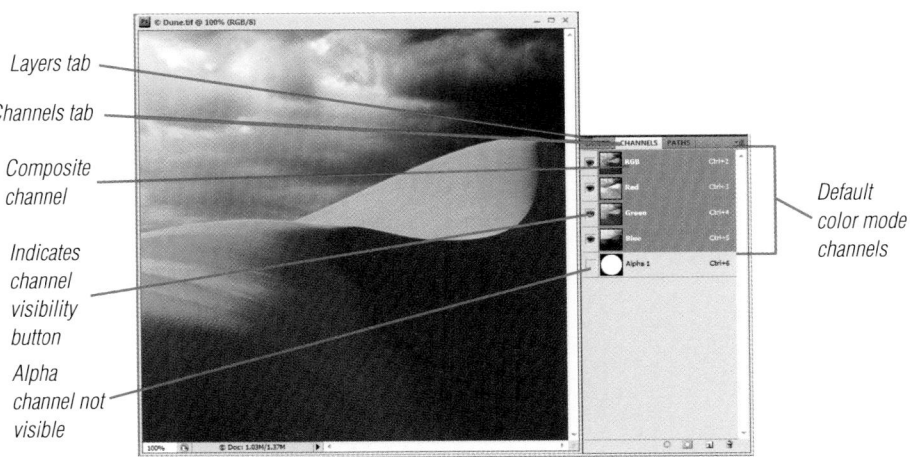

Layers tab

Channels tab

Composite channel

Indicates channel visibility button

Alpha channel not visible

Default color mode channels

View the Channels panel

1. Start Photoshop, open PS 9-1.psd from the drive and folder where you store your Data Files, update the text layer (if necessary), then save it as **Market Fresh**.

2. Click the **Default Foreground and Background Colors button** on the Tools panel to display the default settings (if necessary).

3. Verify that the **Essentials** workspace is displayed.

4. Display the rulers in pixels, change the zoom factor to **100%**, then make sure you can see the guide at 685V.

5. Click **Edit** (Win) or **Photoshop** (Mac) on the Application bar, point to **Preferences**, click **Interface**, verify that there is a check mark in the **Show Channels in Color check box**, then click **OK** to verify that the default color channels are displayed in color.

6. Click the **Channels tab** CHANNELS next to the Layers tab on the Layers panel, then compare your Channels panel to Figure 3.

   The Channels panel is active and displays the four channels for RGB color mode: RGB (composite), Red, Green, and Blue.

You opened the Channels panel, and verified that colors are displayed in the default color channels. This allows you to see the actual colors contained in each channel when working with images.

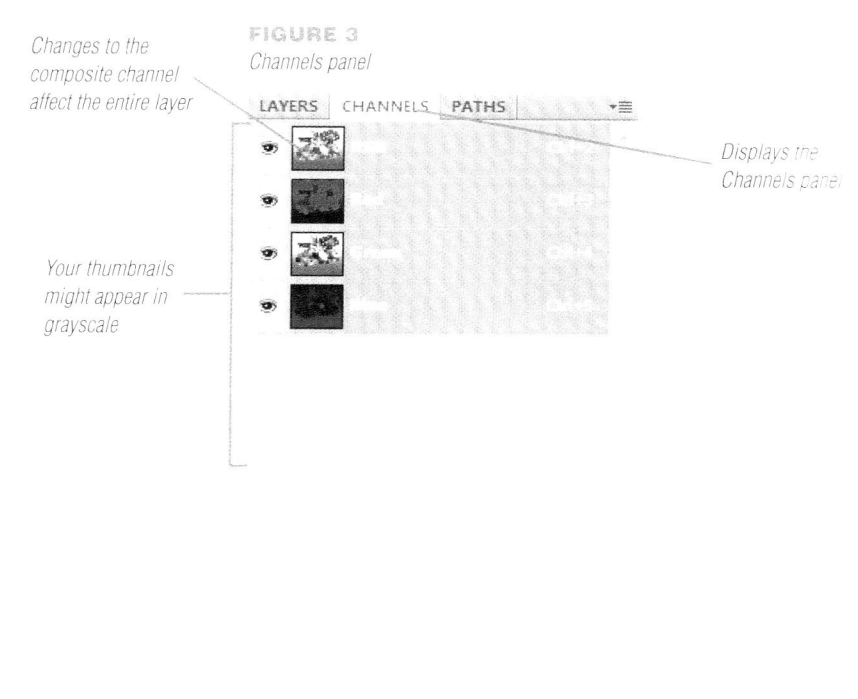

FIGURE 3
Channels panel

Changes to the composite channel affect the entire layer

Displays the Channels panel

Your thumbnails might appear in grayscale

Changing alpha channel colors

You can change the color that the alpha channel displays (to alter the appearance of the image) by picking a color in the Channel Options dialog box. To open the Channel Options dialog box, double-click the alpha channel (which appears at the bottom of the Channels panel once it is created), click the color box, select a color in the Select color channel dialog box, then click OK. Click an option button in the Channel Options dialog box to choose whether the color indicates masked areas, selected areas, or a spot color, then click OK.

FIGURE 4
Selection created

Elliptical marquee   Save selection as
                                      a channel button

FIGURE 5
Alpha channel created

Alpha 1 channel

Create an alpha channel from a selection

1. Click the **Elliptical Marquee tool** ⬭ on the Tools panel, then set the Feather setting on the options bar to **0 px** (if it is not already set to 0).

2. Drag the **Marquee pointer** ┼ from approximately **10 X/10 Y** to **685 X/590 Y**, then compare your image to Figure 4.

3. Click the **Save selection as channel button** ◻ on the Channels panel.

4. Double-click the **Alpha 1 thumbnail** on the Channels panel, then click the **color box** in the Channel Options dialog box.

5. Verify that the **R option button** is selected in the Select channel color dialog box (R=255, G=0, B=0), then click **OK**.

6. Verify that the opacity setting is **50%** and that the **Masked Areas option button** is selected, then click **OK**.

7. On the Channels panel, click the **RGB channel**, then click the **Indicates channel visibility button** ☐ for the Alpha 1 channel to view the alpha channel.

   The combination of the red alpha channel color overlaying blue produces the rose color at the bottom of the image.

8. Click **Select** on the Application bar, click **Deselect**, then compare your image to Figure 5.

9. Save your work.

You used the Elliptical Marquee tool to create a selection and then saved the selection as an alpha channel. You also verified the alpha channel color and reviewed the results by viewing the alpha channel.

In this lesson, you'll create a duplicate layer, and use tools to extract the kiwi from the Fruit and Vegetables layer so that you can adjust its color. You'll also adjust the color of the kiwi by applying a Gradient Map to it.

Using Your Photoshop Knowledge

The goal in isolating an object is to use your knowledge of Photoshop tools to pick the best tool to select an object, then place the selection on its own layer so you can perform any additional tasks on it. Easier said than done.

Isolating Objects

You can use a variety of Photoshop tools to isolate a foreground object from its background. Using any of the tools at your disposal, you can define the object you want to extract, even if its edge is vaguely defined. When you extract an object from a layer, Photoshop deletes the non-extracted

Using the Extract plug-in on a complex object

The Extract feature is an Adobe plug-in that is used not only to isolate objects, but to *filter out* background imagery. It's great for objects that you want to look blurry, in motion, or translucent. (You can find this plug-in on the web by using your favorite browser and search engine and searching for *Photoshop CS4 Extract plug-in*.) Let's say you want to extract a woman who has bushy hair—the kind with strands you can see through. Use a larger brush tip and trace on the outside edge of the object you want to extract. If your object has a well-defined edge (even in only a few places), turn on the Smart Highlighting feature. This feature highlights just the edge. It ignores the current brush size and applies a highlight wide enough to cover the edge. In our example, only the woman and her hair will be extracted, not the pieces of sky between individual strands of hair. If you are going to be working with images that involve complex selections, consider adding this plug-in to your tools repertoire.

portion of the image's background to underlying transparency. It's always a good idea to first copy the original layer and then extract an object from the duplicate layer. This preserves the original layer, which you can use as a reference, and helps you to avoid losing any of the original image information. After you extract an image, you can modify the extracted object layer as you wish.

FIGURE 6
Outlined content in the Extract dialog box

FIGURE 7
Results of complex extraction

Understanding the Extract plug-In

You isolate objects using tools in the Extract dialog box. You first trace the edge of the object you want to extract with the Edge Highlighter tool, then you select everything inside of the edge with the Fill tool. In the example shown in Figure 6, the woman and her hair will be extracted, not the pieces of background between individual strands of hair. Figure 7 shows the result. It takes practice to become proficient at using the Edge Highlighter tool. If you do not draw a continuous edge around the object, Photoshop might not fill in the area accurately. You can edit portions of the edge as often as necessary. Depending on the size of the brush tip you select, the dimensions of your extracted object will vary.

Isolate an object

1. Click the **Layers tab** LAYERS on the Layers panel.

2. Click the **Fruit and Vegetables layer** on the Layers panel, click the **Layers panel list arrow** ▾≡ , then click **Duplicate Layer**.

3. Type **Kiwi** in the As text box. then click **OK** to close the Duplicate Layer dialog box.

   The new layer appears above the Fruit and Vegetables layer on the Layers panel, and is now the active layer.

4. Click the **Channels tab** CHANNELS , click the **Indicates layer visibility button**   for any channel that is not visible, then click the **Layers tab** LAYERS .

5. Click the **Indicates layer visibility button** ☞ for the Fruit and Vegetables layer, so the layer is not visible.

6. Click the **Zoom tool** 🔍 on the Application bar, then click the **center of the kiwi** three times.

7. Click the **Magnetic Lasso tool** ⭦ on the Tools panel.

8. Verify that the feather setting is 0, drag the **pointer** ⭦ around the inner edge of the kiwi, avoiding the celery leaf (if possible), then compare your screen to Figure 8.

   The kiwi is selected.

You created and named a duplicate layer of the Fruit and Vegetables layer, then used the Magnetic Lasso tool to outline the kiwi.

FIGURE 8
Selection in image

Selection

Enhancing Specific Selections

FIGURE 9
Layer containing the extracted object

FIGURE 11
Extracted object with a Gradient Map applied

Gradient Map adjustment
on the extracted object

Lesson 2   Isolate an Object

FIGURE 10
Sample gradients

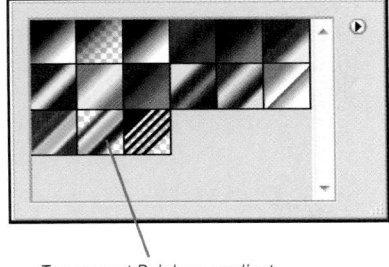

Transparent Rainbow gradient

What You'll Do

In this lesson, you'll use the Background
Eraser tool to delete pixels on the Fruit and
Vegetables layer, then adjust the brightness
and contrast of the isolated object.

Learning How to Erase Areas

As you have learned, you can discard
pixels by selecting and then inverting the
selection. But there may be times when
you want to simply erase an area *without*
making a selection. Photoshop provides
three eraser tools that can accommodate
all your expunging needs. Figure 12
shows samples of the effects of each eraser
tool. The specific use for each eraser tool
is reflected in its options bar, as shown
in Figure 13.

Understanding Eraser Tools

The **Eraser tool** has the opposite function
of a brush. Instead of brushing *on* pixel
color, you drag it *off*. When you erase a layer
that has a layer beneath it, and the Lock
transparent pixels button is not selected,
you'll expose the color on the underlying
layer when you erase. If there is no underlying layer, you'll expose transparency. If the
Lock transparent pixels button *is* selected,
you'll expose the current background color
on the Tools panel, regardless of the color
of an underlying layer.

Setting options for eraser tools

Each eraser tool has its own options bar. You can select the brush mode for the Eraser
tool, and the brush tip and size for both the Eraser tool and Background Eraser tool.
Depending on the tool, you can also set the **tolerance**—how close a pixel color must
be to another color to be erased with the tool. The lower the tolerance, the closer the
color must be to the selection. You can also specify the opacity of the eraser strength.
A 100% opacity erases pixels to complete transparency. To set options, click an eraser
tool on the Tools panel, then change the tolerance and opacity settings using the text
boxes and list arrows on the options bar.

The **Magic Eraser tool** grabs similarly colored pixels based on the tool settings, and then exposes background color in the same way as the Eraser tool. However, instead of dragging the eraser, you click the areas you want to change. The Magic Eraser tool erases all pixels on the current layer that are close in color value to where you first click or just those pixels that are contiguous to that area.

The **Background Eraser tool** contains small crosshairs in the brush tip. When you click, the tool selects a color in the crosshairs, then erases that particular color anywhere within the brush tip size. The Background Eraser tool exposes the color of the layer beneath it, or it exposes transparency if there is no layer beneath it. You can preserve objects in the foreground,

while eliminating the background (it works best with a large brush tip size). The Background Eraser tool will sample the background colors of the current layer as you drag the tool in your image—you can watch the current background color change on the Tools panel.

FIGURE 12

Examples of eraser tools

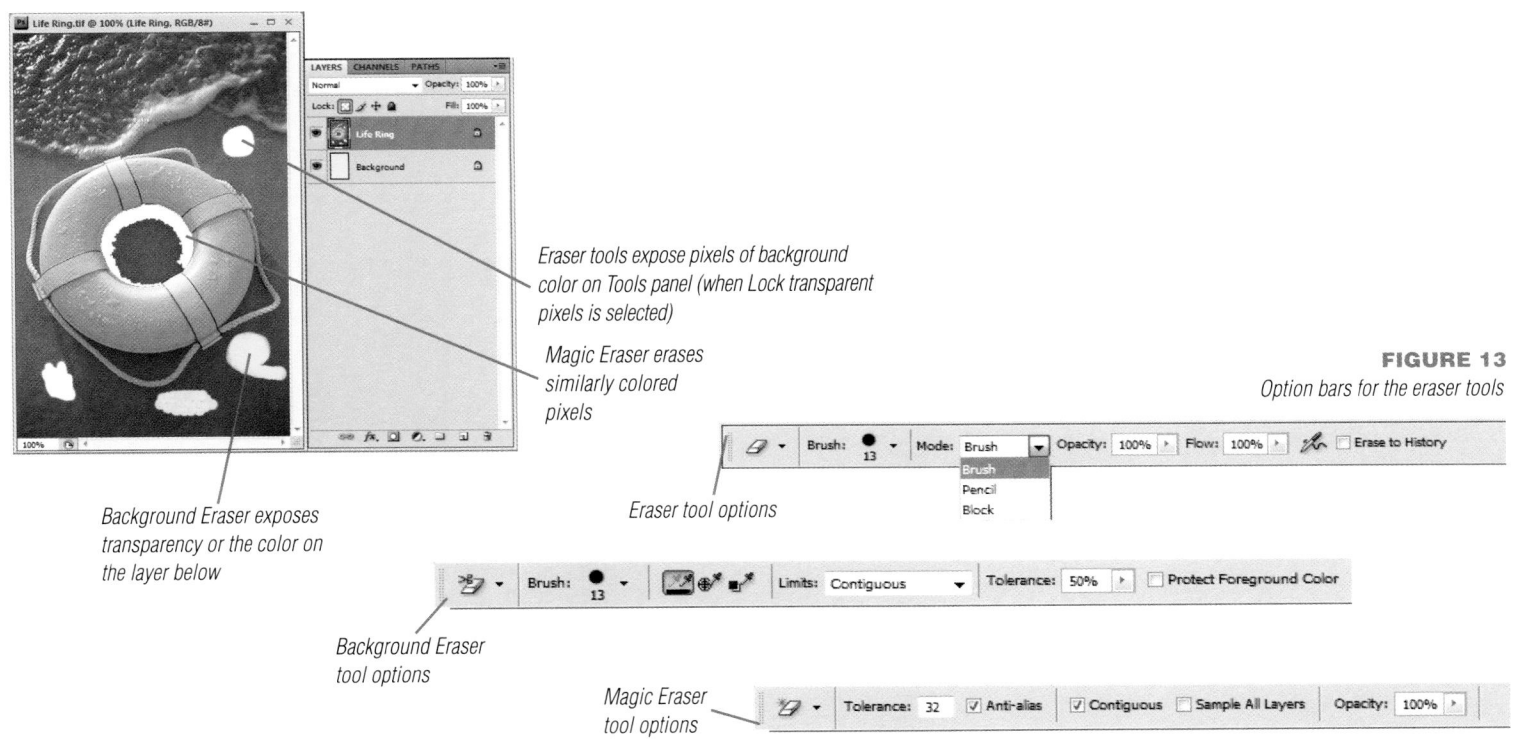

Eraser tools expose pixels of background color on Tools panel (when Lock transparent pixels is selected)

Magic Eraser erases similarly colored pixels

FIGURE 13

Option bars for the eraser tools

Eraser tool options

Background Eraser exposes transparency or the color on the layer below

Background Eraser tool options

Magic Eraser tool options

Use the Background Eraser tool

1. Click the **Indicates layer visibility button** 👁 on the Kiwi layer to hide the layer.

2. Click the **Fruit and Vegetables layer** to make it the active layer.

3. Click the **Zoom tool** 🔍 on the Application bar.

4. Click the **center of the kiwi** with the **Zoom pointer** ⊕ until the zoom factor is **300%**.

5. Click the **Background Eraser tool** 🖌 on the Tools panel.

   TIP Look under the Eraser tool if the Background Eraser tool is hidden. To cycle through the eraser tools, press and hold [Shift], then press [E].

6. Click the **Click to open the Brush Preset picker list arrow** on the options bar, set the Diameter to **5 px**, the Hardness to **100%**, and the Spacing to **15%** as shown in Figure 14.

7. Press **[Enter]** (Win) or **[return]** (Mac).

8. Keeping the crosshairs of the **Brush tip pointer** ⊕ on the kiwi, drag the brush tip over the **kiwi** until it is completely erased, as shown in Figure 15.

You hid the Kiwi layer, zoomed in on the Fruit and Vegetables layer, selected a brush tip for the Background Eraser tool, and erased the kiwi on the Fruit and Vegetables layer.

FIGURE 14
Brush Preset picker

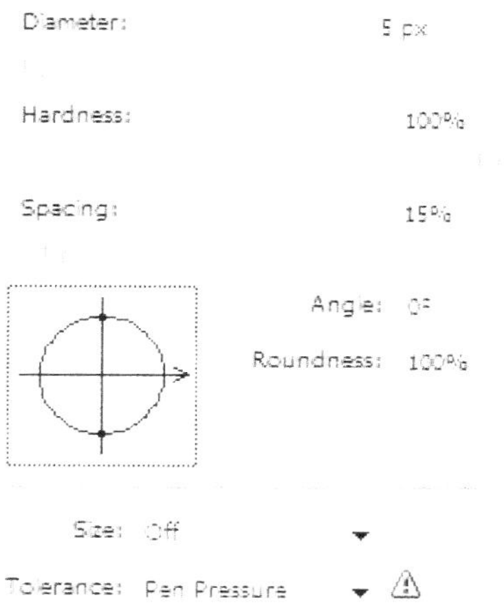

Diameter:	5 px
Hardness:	100%
Spacing:	15%
Angle:	0°
Roundness:	100%
Size:	Off
Tolerance:	Pen Pressure

FIGURE 15
Selection erased on layer

Erased area exposes pixels on Background layer

FIGURE 16

Object adjusted in image

Equalize adjustment applied to Kiwi layer

Equalize brightness and contrast

1. Click the **Kiwi layer** on the Layers panel, then make the Kiwi layer visible.

2. Click the **Zoom tool** 🔍 on the Application bar.

3. Press and hold **[Alt]** (Win) or **[option]** (Mac), click the center of the kiwi with the **Zoom pointer** 🔍 until the zoom factor is **100%**, then release **[Alt]** (Win) or **[option]** (Mac).

4. Click **Image** on the Application bar, point to **Adjustments**, then click **Equalize**.

   The Equalize command evens out the brightness and contrast values in the kiwi.

5. Save your work, then compare your image to Figure 16.

You adjusted the color of the kiwi by equalizing the colors, then viewed the color-adjusted image.

Redistributing brightness values

The Equalize command changes the brightness values of an image's pixels so they more evenly display the entire range of brightness levels. Photoshop changes the brightest and darkest values by remapping them so that the brightest values appear as white and the darkest values appear as black, then it redistributes the intermediate pixel values evenly throughout the grayscale. You can use this command to "tone down" an image that is too bright. Conversely, you could use it on a dark image that you want to make lighter.

What You'll Do

In this lesson, you'll use the Clone Stamp tool to sample an undamaged portion of an image and use it to cover up a flaw on the image.

Touching Up a Damaged Area

Let's face it, many of the images you'll want to work with will have a visual flaw of some kind, such as a scratch, or an object obscuring what would otherwise be a great shot. While you cannot go back in time and move something out of the way, you can often use the Clone Stamp tool to remove an object or cover up a flaw.

Using the Clone Stamp Tool

The Clone Stamp tool can copy a sample (a pixel selection) in an image, and then paste it over what you want to cover up. The size of the sample taken with the Clone Stamp tool depends on the brush tip size you choose on the Brushes panel. Figure 17 shows the Clone Stamp tool in action. In addition to using the Clone Stamp tool to touch up images, you can use it to copy one image onto another. Using the Clone Stamp tool to copy an image differs from copying an image because you have extensive control over how much of the cloned area you expose and at what opacity.

FIGURE 17
Clone Stamp tool in action

Object to be deleted

Sampled area

Sampled area applied twice to hide portions of the object

FIGURE 18

Comparing images

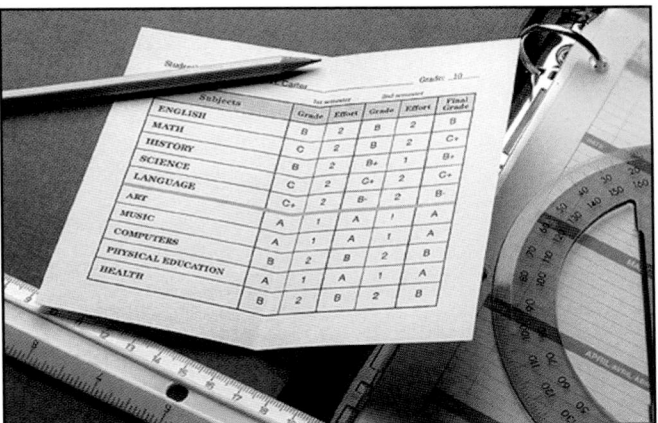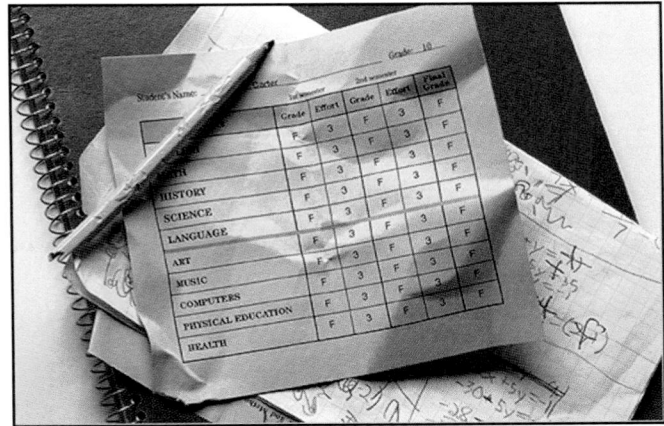

DESIGNTIP   **Perfecting your analytical skills**

An important step in making an adjustment to any image is to examine it critically and figure out what is wrong. An area that you select for fixing does not necessarily have to look bad or appear wrong. An image might be "wrong" because it simply does not convey the right meaning or mood. Compare the two images in Figure 18. They contain basically the same elements but express entirely different ideas. The figure on the left conveys a more positive image than the one on the right; clearly the grades are better for the student on the left, however, this is also reflected in the lighter colored paper, which is in pristine condition. The elements that you choose for your content should depend on what you want to convey. For example, if you want to convey a positive mood, using the elements in the image on the right would be inappropriate for your image. Choosing the right content in the beginning can save you a lot of time in the end. It is much easier and quicker to reach a destination if you know where you are going before you begin the journey.

Sample an area to clone

1. Click the **Fruit and Vegetables layer** on the Layers panel.

2. Click the **Zoom tool** 🔍 on the Application bar.

3. Click the **center of the far-left tomato** with the **Zoom pointer** ⊕ until the zoom factor is **300%** so you can clearly see the fly.

4. Click the **Clone Stamp tool** 🖆 on the Tools panel.

5. Click the **Click to open the Brush Preset picker list arrow** on the options bar, then double-click the **Hard Round 13 pixels brush tip**.

6. Verify that the Opacity setting on the options bar is **100%**.

7. Position the **Brush pointer** ◯ at approximately **60 X/400 Y**, as shown in Figure 19.

8. Press **[Alt]** (Win) or **[option]** (Mac), click once, then release **[Alt]** (Win) or **[option]** (Mac).

    The sample is collected and is ready to be applied to the fly.

You selected the Fruit and Vegetables layer, set the zoom percentage, selected a brush tip for the Clone Stamp tool, and sampled an undamaged portion of the tomato.

FIGURE 19
Defining the area to be sampled

Ps Market Fresh.psd @ 300% (Fruit and Vegetables, RGB

Area to be hidden by sample

Area to be sampled

Using the Clone Source panel

You can open the Clone Source panel using the Window command on the Application bar or a button on the options bar when the Clone Stamp tool is active. Use the Clone Source panel to set up to five sample sources for use with the Clone Stamp tools or Healing Brush tools. The sample source can be displayed as an overlay so you can clone the source at a specific location. You can also rotate or scale the sample source at a specific size and orientation.

FIGURE 20

Clone Stamp tool positioned over defect

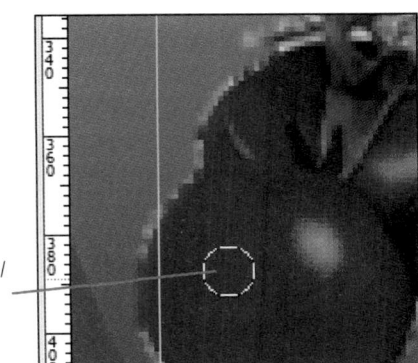

Clone Stamp tool
positioned over
the fly

1. Position the **Brush pointer** ○ *directly* over the fly, as shown in Figure 20.

2. Click the **fly.**

   TIP Select a different brush size if your brush is too small or too large, and then reapply the stamp.

3. Click the **Zoom tool** 🔍 on the Application bar.

4. Press and hold **[Alt]** (Win) or **[option]** (Mac), click the **center of the tomato** with the **Zoom pointer** 🔍 until the zoom factor is **100%**, then release **[Alt]** (Win) or **[option]** (Mac).

5. Save your work, then compare your image to Figure 21.

You fixed the damaged area of the tomato by covering up the fly.

FIGURE 21

Corrected image

Using pressure-sensitive tablets

For specialized painting that gives you maximum control when you create an image, you can purchase a pressure-sensitive stylus or tablet. A pressure-sensitive device mimics the force you'd use with an actual brush; you paint softer when you press lightly and paint darker when you press harder. You can set the stylus or tablet pressure for the Magnetic Lasso, Freeform Pen, Pencil, Brush, Eraser, Clone Stamp, Pattern Stamp, History Brush, Art History Brush, Smudge, Blur, Sharpen, Dodge, Burn, and Sponge tools. Also affected by pen pressure are the magnetic pen feature and the airbrush feature. To access the magnetic pen, select the Freeform Pen tool, then click the Magnetic checkbox. To use the Airbrush feature, click the Brush, Clone Stamp, History Brush, Eraser, or Dodge tools, then click the Set to enable airbrush capabilities button on the options bar.

What You'll Do

In this lesson, you'll open a new image, use the Magic Wand tool to select an image in the new image, and move it to the Market Fresh image. You'll also readjust the Eyedropper tool sample size, reselect and move the image so you can compare the selection difference, then delete the incomplete layer and position the complete layer in the Market Fresh image.

Understanding the Magic Wand Tool

You can use the Magic Wand tool to select an object by selecting the color range of the object. The **Magic Wand tool** lets you choose pixels that are similar to the ones where you first click in an image. You can control how the Magic Wand tool behaves by specifying tolerance settings and whether or not you want to select only contiguous pixels on the options bar. The Magic Wand tool options bar is shown in Figure 22.

Learning About Tolerance

The tolerance setting determines the range of colors you can select with the Magic Wand tool. For example, if you select a low tolerance and then click an image of the sky, you will only select a narrow range of blue pixels and probably not the entire sky. However, if you set a higher tolerance, you can expand the range of blue pixels selected by the Magic Wand tool. Each time you click the Magic Wand tool, you can choose from one of four buttons on the options bar to select a new

area, add to the existing area (the effect is cumulative; the more you click, the more you add), subtract from the existing area, or intersect with the existing area.

You can also press and hold [Shift] and repeatedly click to add pixels to your selection, or press and hold [Alt] (Win) or [option] (Mac), then click to subtract pixels from your selection.

Using the Eyedropper Tool and the Magic Wand Tool

The Contiguous and Tolerance settings are not the only determinants that establish the pixel area selected by the Magic Wand tool. The area that the Magic Wand tool selects also has an intrinsic relationship with the settings for the Eyedropper tool. The sample size, or number of pixels used by the Eyedropper tool to determine the color it picks up, affects the area selected by the Magic Wand tool. To understand this, you need to first examine the Eyedropper tool settings.

Understanding Sample Size

When the Eyedropper tool sample size is set to Point Sample, it picks up the one pixel where you click on the image. When the sample size is set to 3 by 3 Average, the Eyedropper tool picks up the color values of the nine pixels that surround the pixel where you click the image and averages them. The sample area increases exponentially to 25 pixels for the 5 by 5 Average setting. The sample size of the Eyedropper tool influences the area selected by the Magic Wand tool. Figure 23 shows how different Eyedropper tool sample sizes change the Magic Wand tool selections, even when you sample an image at the same coordinates and use the same tolerance setting. As you become familiar with the Magic Wand tool, it's a good idea to verify or change the Eyedropper tool sample size as needed, in addition to changing the tolerance setting.

FIGURE 22
Magic Wand tool options

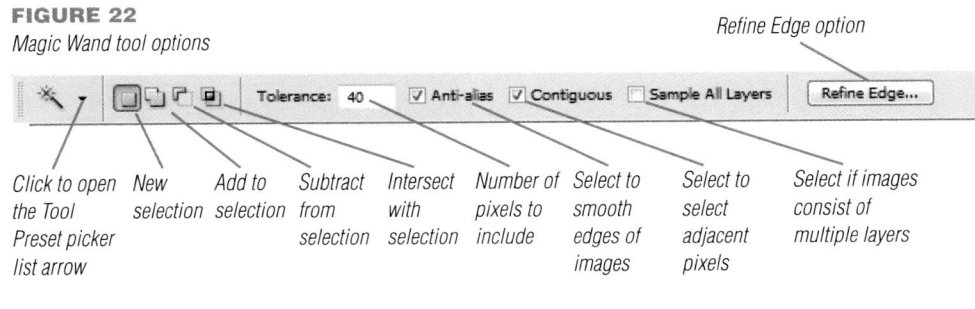

Refine Edge option

Click to open the Tool Preset picker list arrow — New selection — Add to selection — Subtract from selection — Intersect with selection — Number of pixels to include — Select to smooth edges of images — Select to select adjacent pixels — Select if images consist of multiple layers

FIGURE 23
Selection affected by Eyedropper tool sample size

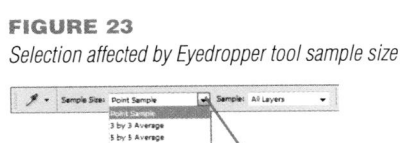

The sample size affects the number of pixels selected

Fewer pixels selected using Point Sample with Magic Wand

More pixels selected using 5 by 5 Average sample with Magic Wand

Using the Refine Edge option

The Refine Edge button is on the options bar of a variety of tools, including the Magic Wand tool. It lets you improve the quality of a selection's edges and allows you to view the selection against different backgrounds, making editing easier. Once you've made a selection, click Refine Edge. Using the Refine Edge dialog box, you can make adjustments in the Radius (which determines the size of the region around the selection), Contrast (which sharpens selection edges), Smooth (which reduces irregular areas), Feather (which creates a soft-edged transition), and Contract/Expand (which shrinks or enlarges the selection).

Select an object using the Magic Wand tool

1. Verify that the **Fruit and Vegetables layer** is the active layer.

2. Open PS 9-2.psd from the drive and folder where you store your Data Files, then save it as **Peppermint.psd**.

3. Drag the **Peppermint.psd window** to the right side of the workspace. and resize your windows so that they look similar to those shown in Figure 24.

4. Click the **Eyedropper tool** ✐, on the Tools panel, then set the Sample Size to **5 by 5 Average** on the options bar.

5. Click the **Magic Wand tool** ✨ on the Tools panel.

6. Type **50** in the Tolerance text box on the options bar, then press **[Enter]** (Win) or **[return]** (Mac).

7. Deselect the **Contiguous check box** (if it is selected).

   > TIP If the Contiguous check box is selected, you'll select only the adjoining pixels that share the same color values.

8. In the Peppermint window, click the **bottom-left leaf** at approximately **20 X/175 Y** to select the peppermint plant, as shown in Figure 25.

9. Click the **Move tool** ▸⊹ on the Tools panel.

10. Position the **Move pointer** ▸⊹ over the **bottom-left leaf**, drag the **plant** in front of the lower orange quarter (and in front of the apples) in the Market Fresh image, then compare your image to Figure 26.

You opened a new file, set the Eyedropper tool sample size to a different selection setting, used the Magic Wand tool to select the Peppermint image you opened, then moved the selected image into the Market Fresh image.

FIGURE 24
New image opened and positioned

FIGURE 26
Selected object moved to current image

FIGURE 25
Selection indicated by marquee

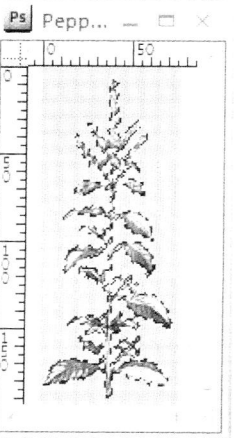

FIGURE 27
Comparison of selections

Selection made
with 5 by 5
Average sample
size captures
more pixels

Selection made with
Point Sample size
captures fewer pixels

FIGURE 28
Selection positioned in image

1. Click **Window** on the Application bar, then click **Peppermint.psd**.

2. Click **Select** on the Application bar, then click **Deselect**.

3. Repeat Steps 4 through 10 in the previous steps, but this time, set the sample size for the Eyedropper tool to **Point Sample** in Step 4 and drag the plant above the green apple in Step 10.

4. Verify that the **Show Transform Controls check box** is selected on the options bar, then compare the two plants in the Market Fresh image, as shown in Figure 27.

   TIP   You can see the difference in the plants more easily if you hide and then display the Apples layer. Your results may vary from the sample.

5. Delete **Layer 2** on the Layers panel.

6. Verify that the **Move tool** is selected and **Layer 1** (with the Peppermint plant) is active, click the **top of the peppermint plant** with the **Move pointer** ▶⊹, then drag it so it is centered behind the far left tomato at approximately **70 X/200 Y**.

7. Hide the rulers, deselect the **Show Transform Controls check box,** save your work, then compare your image to Figure 28.

You changed the Eyedropper tool sample size to its smallest setting, reselected the plant, moved it to the Market Fresh image, deleted one new layer, then repositioned the peppermint plant image.

What You'll Do

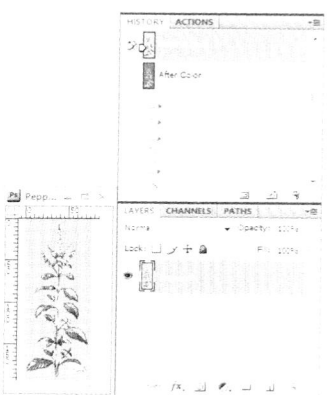

In this lesson, you'll create a snapshot on the History panel, edit an image, then use the snapshot to view the image as it existed prior to making changes.

Understanding Snapshots

As mentioned earlier in this chapter, it is a good work habit to make a copy of an original layer to help you avoid losing any of the original image information. Creating a snapshot is like creating that new copy. The History panel can only record a maximum of 20 tasks, or states, that you perform. When the History panel reaches its limit, it starts deleting the oldest states to make room for new states. You can create a **snapshot**, a temporary copy of your image that contains the history states made to that point. It's a good idea to take a snapshot of the History panel image before you begin an editing session and after you've made crucial changes because you can use snapshots to revert to or review your image from an earlier stage of development. You can create multiple snapshots in an image, and you can switch between snapshots as necessary.

Creating a Snapshot

To create a snapshot, you can click the Create new snapshot button on the History panel, or click the History panel list arrow and then click New Snapshot, as shown in Figure 29. Each new snapshot is numbered consecutively; snapshots appear in order at the top of the History panel. If you create a snapshot by clicking the New Snapshot command, you can name the snapshot in the Name text box in the New Snapshot dialog box. Otherwise, you can rename an existing snapshot in the same way that you rename a layer on the Layers panel: double-click the snapshot, then edit the name once the existing name is highlighted. You can create a snapshot based on the entire image, merged layers, or just the current layer. A snapshot of the entire image includes all layers in the current image. A snapshot of merged layers combines all the layers in the current image on a single layer, and a snapshot of the current layer includes only the layer active at the time you took the snapshot. Figure 30 shows the New Snapshot dialog box.

Changing Snapshot Options

By default, Photoshop automatically creates a snapshot of an image when you open it.

To change the default snapshot option, click the History panel list arrow, click History Options, then select one of the check boxes shown in Figure 31. You can open files faster by deselecting the Automatically Create First Snapshot check box.

QUICKTIP

Photoshop does not save snapshots when you close a file.

FIGURE 29

Snapshot commands on the History panel

FIGURE 30

New Snapshot dialog box

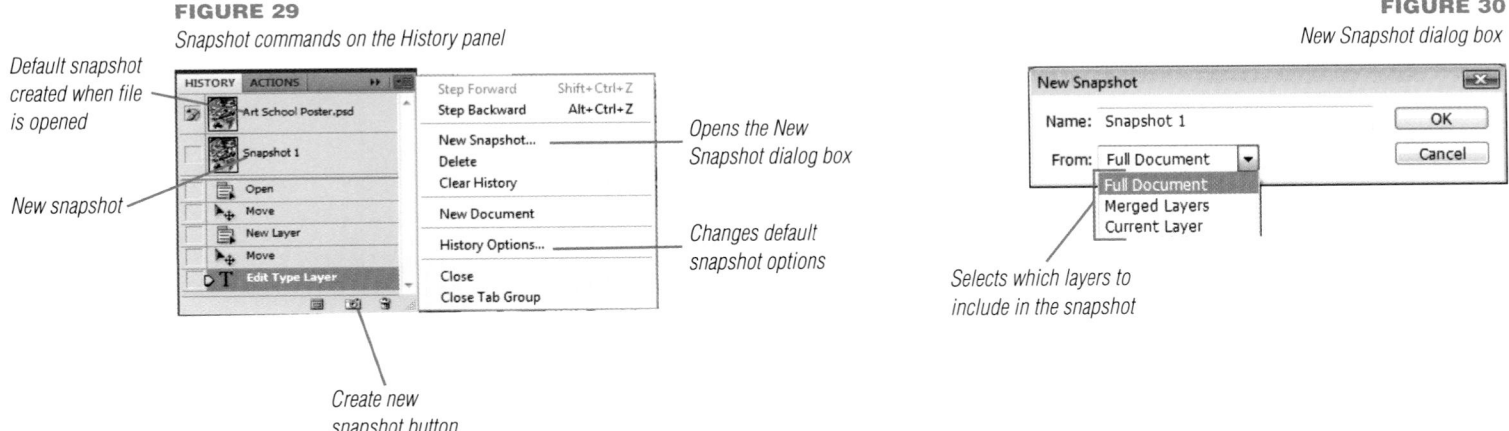

Default snapshot created when file is opened

New snapshot

Opens the New Snapshot dialog box

Changes default snapshot options

Create new snapshot button

Selects which layers to include in the snapshot

FIGURE 31

History Options dialog box

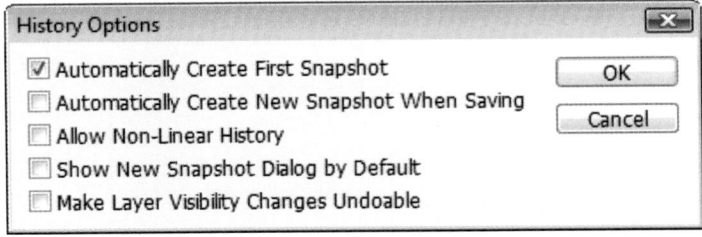

Create a snapshot

1. Deselect any selections in Peppermint.psd.

2. Click the **Invert button** 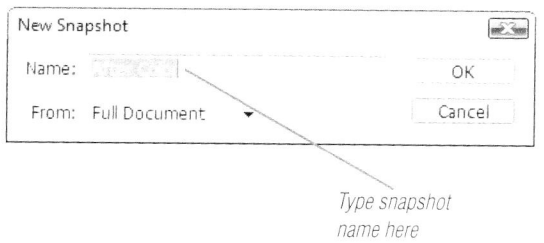 on the Adjustments panel, then compare your screen to Figure 32.

3. Change the workspace to **History and Layers**.

4. Click the **History panel list arrow** ▼≡, then click **New Snapshot**.

5. Type **After Color** in the Name text box, as shown in Figure 33.

6. Click **OK**.

   The newly named snapshot appears on the History panel beneath the snapshot Photoshop created when you opened the image.

You deselected the selection in the Peppermint image, inverted the color in the image, then created and named a new snapshot.

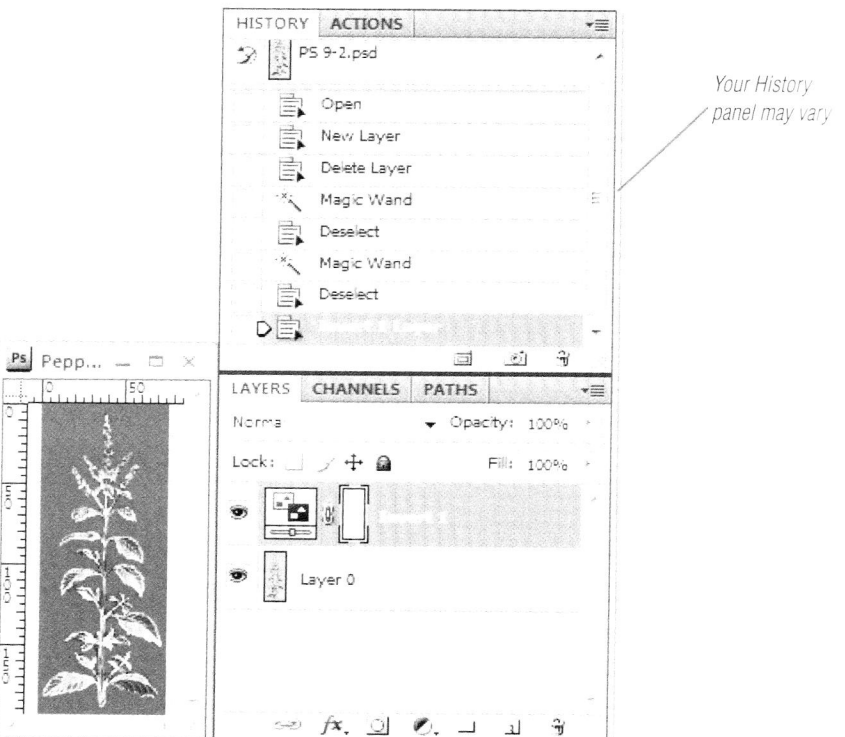

FIGURE 32
Inverted image

Your History panel may vary

FIGURE 33
New Snapshot dialog box

Type snapshot name here

FIGURE 34
Original snapshot view

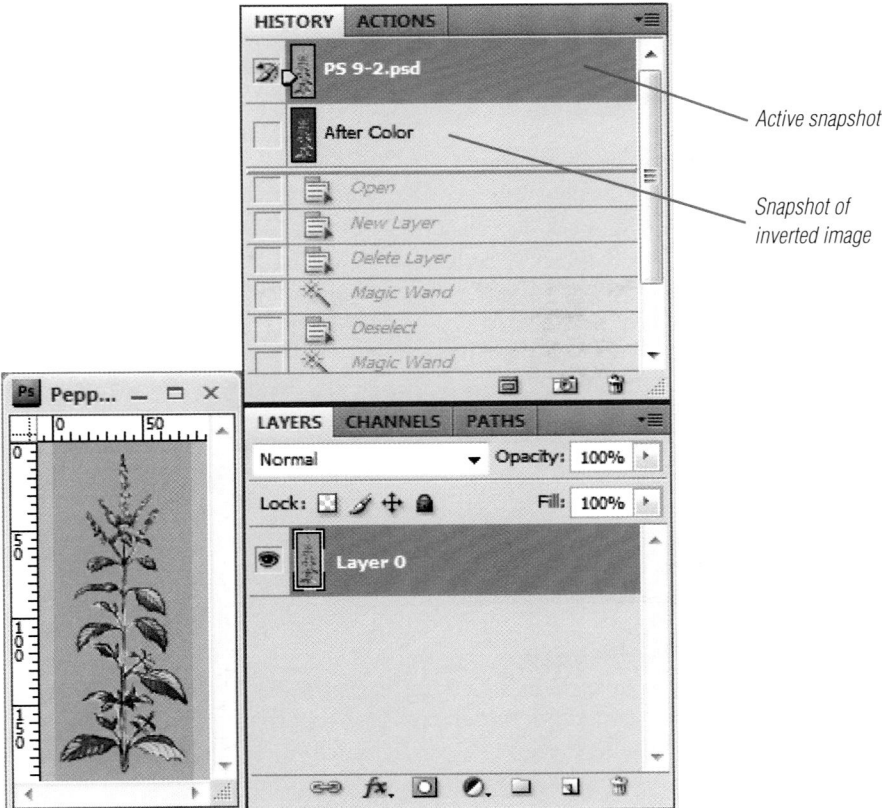

Active snapshot

Snapshot of
inverted image

1. Scroll up (if necessary), click the **PS 9-2.psd snapshot** on the History panel, then compare your image to Figure 34.

   The image returns to its original color.

2. Click the **After Color snapshot** on the History panel.

3. Reset the panels to the **Essentials** workspace.

4. Close Peppermint.psd, save any changes.

You used the snapshot to view the image as it was before you made changes.

LAYOUTS

In this lesson, you'll create a picture package of the current image and then create a folder containing a contact sheet of images.

Understanding a Picture Package

With all the choices available for creating different variations of your images, you might get the idea that keeping track of all these choices is time-consuming or difficult. Not so; to facilitate the task, Adobe Bridge lets you generate multiple-image layouts. **Multiple-image layouts** are useful when you need to gather one or more Photoshop images in a variety of sizes for a variety of uses. For example, if you create an advertisement, you might want to have multiple image layouts for printing in different publications. Can you imagine what would be involved to create this type of arrangement of images manually? For each duplicate image, you'd have to create a layer, resize it, then position it correctly on the page. A lot of work! You can generate a single layout, also known as a **picture package**, which contains multiple images in a single file, as shown in Figure 35. The picture package option lets you choose from eight possible predesigned layouts of the same image, plus a custom layout, and then arranges them in a single printable image.

Creating a Web Gallery

You can display your image files on a website by creating a Web Photo Gallery. A Web Photo Gallery contains a thumbnail index page of all files you choose. To create a Web Photo Gallery, open Bridge, click the Output tab in the Application bar and the Web Gallery button in the Output panel. Click the Folders tab and the location of the files you want to include, then click Refresh Preview in the Output panel to see the gallery display in Bridge, or click the Preview in Browser to see the images in your browser.

Assembling a Contact Sheet

Previewing and cataloging several related images could be a time-consuming and difficult chore, but Bridge makes it easy. It allows you to assemble a maximum of 30 thumbnail images in a specific folder, called a **contact sheet**, as shown in Figure 36. If the folder used to compile the contact sheet contains more than 30 files, Bridge automatically creates new sheets so that all the images appear.

FIGURE 35

Sample picture package

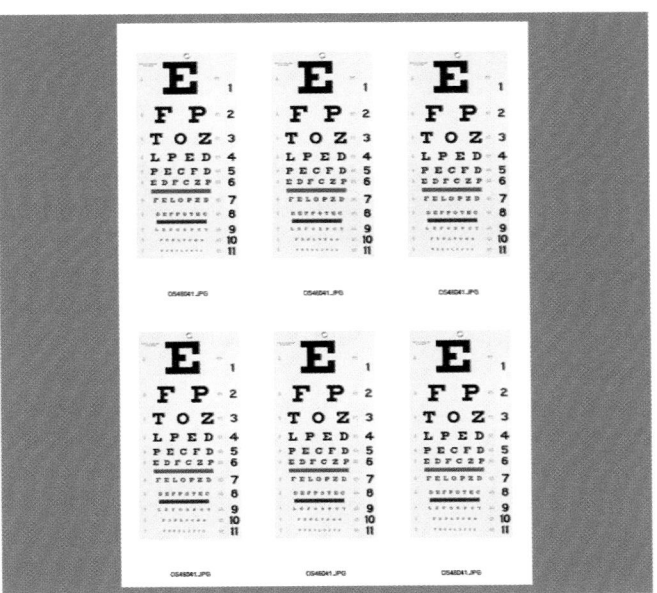

FIGURE 36

Sample contact sheet

Create a Multi-image layout

1. Click the **Launch Bridge button** ▶Br on the Application bar.

2. Click the **Folders tab** FOLDERS if necessary.

3. Click the Folder where you store your Data Files, use the Content tab slider to locate the Market Fresh file, then click **Market Fresh.psd**.

4. Click **Output** at the top of the Bridge window, click the **PDF button** in the Output panel (if necessary), then click the **Repeat One Photo per Page check box** in the Layout section, and compare your settings to those shown in Figure 37, then click the **Refresh Preview** button.

5. Scroll down to the **Watermark section** of the Output panel, click the **View PDF After Save checkbox**, then click **Save**.

6. Save the multi-image layout in the location where you store your Chapter 9 Data Files, as **Picture Package.pdf**, then close the file.

You opened Adobe Bridge to create a multi-image layout, selected a layout for a picture package, then created and saved a layout using the Market Fresh image.

FIGURE 37
Multi-image settings in Adobe Bridge

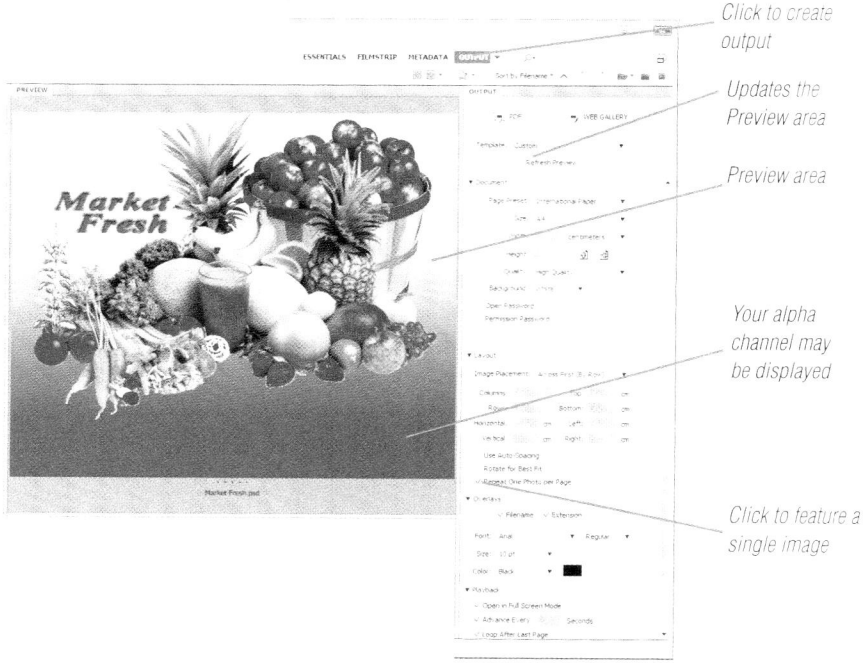

Click to create output

Updates the Preview area

Preview area

Your alpha channel may be displayed

Click to feature a single image

FIGURE 38
Layout section of the Output panel

▼ Layout

Image Placement:	Across First (By Row)	▼
Columns: **4**	Top: **0.42**	cm
Rows: **5**	Bottom: **0.42**	cm
Horizontal: **0.64** cm	Left: **0.42**	cm
Vertical: **1.51** cm	Right: **0.42**	cm

Use Auto-Spacing
Rotate for Best Fit
✓ Repeat One Photo per Page

Customizing a Layout

With so many layout options available, you might think it would be impossible to customize any further. Well, you'd be wrong. Using the Layout section of the Output panel, shown in Figure 38, you can change the number of columns and rows, the amount of space in the margins, and rotate the page for the best fit.

Enhancing Specific Selections

FIGURE 39
Contact Sheet settings

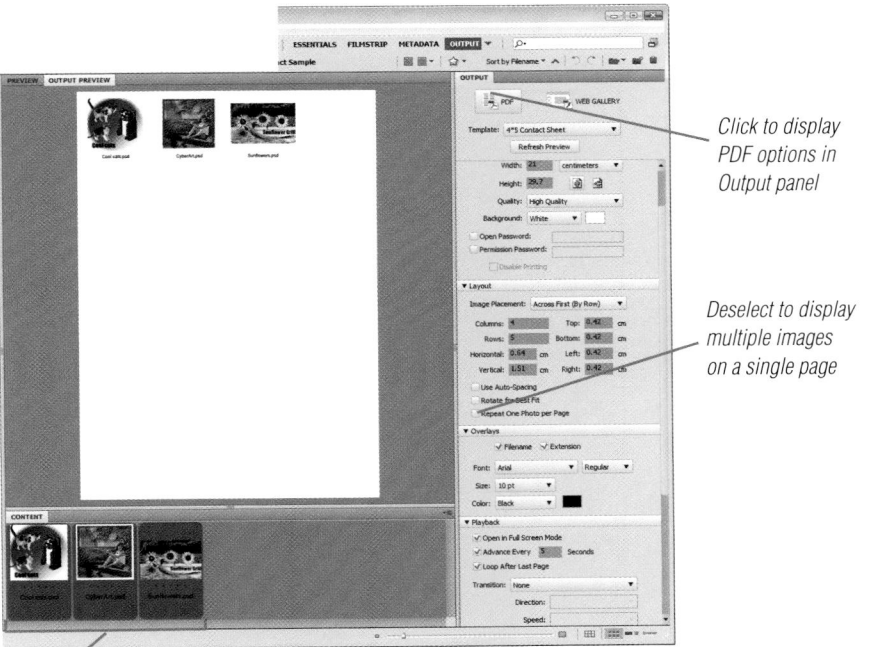

Click to display PDF options in Output panel

Deselect to display multiple images on a single page

Selected images in Content panel: your images will differ

1. Create a folder on your computer that contains copies of at least three Photoshop images you have created, then name the folder **Contact Sample**.

2. Click the **Folders tab** in Adobe Bridge, click the **Contact Sample folder**, then click the **PDF button** in the Output panel.

3. Select the files in the Contact Sample folder in the Content tab (use [Shift] to select multiple files), and use the settings in the Output panel shown in Figure 39, then click **Refresh Preview**.

   Photoshop opens the files and places them in a new file to which you can assign a meaningful name.

4. Scroll down to the Watermark section of the Output panel, click **Save**, type the name **ContactSheet-001.pdf**, click **Save**, then close the file and exit Bridge and Photoshop.

You created a folder and placed images in it, and then used Adobe Bridge to select files from which you created a contact sheet of the images.

Automating Photoshop

Photoshop offers several automation options. You can also use the Automate command (on the File menu) to create batches, crop and straighten crooked images, change color modes conditionally, fit an image to a specified size (without distorting the image), and merge multiple images to create panoramas. You may notice that there is some duplication between Photoshop and Bridge. For example, you can use the Photomerge command in Bridge by clicking the Tools menu, pointing to Photoshop, then clicking Photomerge.

to do this:	use this method:		to do this:	use this method:
Clone Stamp tool	or S		Eraser tools	E
Create a snapshot			Magic Wand tool	or W
Duplicate selection and move 1 pixel:	Press and hold [Ctrl][Alt] (Win) or ⌘ [option] (Mac), then press		Move selection 1 pixel:	
Left	←		Left	←
Right	→		Right	→
Up	↑		Up	↑
Down	↓		Down	↓
Move selection 10 pixels:	Press and hold [Shift] (Win) or ⌘ [shift] (Mac),then press			
Left	←			
Right	→			
Up	↑			
Down	↓			

Key: Blue bold letters are shortcuts for selecting tools on the Tools panel.

Create an alpha channel.

1. Open PS 9-3.psd from the drive and folder where you store your Data Files, then save it as **Tools**.
2. Make sure the rulers appear in pixels, then enlarge the image to 200%.
3. Display the Channels panel.
4. Select the Rectangular Marquee tool, then change the Feather to **25** on the options bar.
5. Create a selection from 70 X/50 Y to 400 X/270 Y (use the guides as a reference).
6. Save the selection, using your choice of name, on the Channels panel, then display the Alpha 1 channel.
7. Deselect the selection.
8. Open the Channel Options dialog box, select a blue color swatch of your choice at 50% Opacity, then close the Select channel color dialog box and the Channel Options dialog box.
9. Hide the Alpha 1 channel.
10. Save your work.

Isolate an object.

1. Display the Layers panel.
2. Duplicate the Tools layer, then name it **Red Tape**.
3. Use the Elliptical Marquee tool to surround the outer edge of the roll of red tape.
4. Select the inverse of the selection, then delete the selection.
5. Use the Elliptical Marquee tool to select the interior (hole) of the roll of red tape.
6. Delete the selection, then deselect the selection.
7. Save your work.

Erase areas in an image to enhance appearance.

1. Hide the Red Tape layer.
2. Make the Tools layer active.
3. Enlarge your view of the red tape.
4. Using the Background Eraser tool, erase the roll of red tape.
5. Make the Red Tape layer active.
6. Adjust the Color Balance settings on the Red Tape layer to +75, −57, and −10, so that the adjustment affects only the Red Tape layer. (*Hint*: Click the Color Balance button on the Adjustments panel.)
7. Save your work.

Use the Clone Stamp tool to make repairs.

1. Make the Tools layer active.
2. Select the Clone Stamp tool on the Tools panel.
3. Use the Hard Round 5 pixels brush tip. (*Hint*: Use the Brush Preset picker.)
4. Sample the area at 345 X/50 Y by pressing [Alt] (Win) or [option] (Mac) and clicking over the wire cutters.
5. Click the red dot (at approximately 310 X/85 Y) to remove this imperfection.
6. Save your work.

Use the Magic Wand tool to select objects.

1. Open PS 9-4.psd, then save it as **Wrench**.
2. Select the Magic Wand tool, deselect the Contiguous check box (if it is selected), then set the Tolerance to 0.
3. Click the wrench image anywhere on the white background.

4. Select the inverse of the selection.
5. Move the selection to the Tools image.
6. Move the top of the handle of the wrench to approximately 270 X/150 Y.
7. Deselect the selection, then close Wrench.psd.

Learn how to create snapshots.

1. Use the History panel list arrow to create a new snapshot.
2. Name the snapshot **New**.
3. Save your work, zoom out to 100% magnification, hide the rulers, then compare your image to Figure 40.

Create multiple-image layouts.

1. Use Bridge to create a 3 column, 4 row sheet containing the Tools image.
2. Save the file as **Picture Package-Tools** and close it.
3. Create a folder called Contact Sample 2 with image files to use for a 4 column, 4 row contact sheet.
4. Save this file as ContactSheet-002, then close it.
5. Close Bridge.

FIGURE 40
Completed Skills Review

Science Discovery, a traveling educational show for children, is planning a piece on earth science. For the first segment, the puppets will teach about different shapes, starting with spheres. You're going to design the spot graphic that will link users to the Science Discovery web page.

1. Obtain the following images for the graphic: a background that contains one or more round objects, at least two images that contain spheres whose content you can select, and any other images as desired. You'll use two of the sphere images for a clipping group.
2. Create a new Photoshop image, then save it as **Spheroid**.
3. Apply a color or style to the Background layer, or use any of the techniques you learned in this chapter to select and drag the image that will be the background to the Spheroid image, then apply at least one style to it. (*Hint*: An Adjustment layer is applied to the grapes.)
4. Use any of the techniques you learned in this chapter to select and drag the image that will be the base of the clipping group to the Spheroid image above the Background layer, and modify it as desired. (*Hint*: The tennis ball in the sample is the base image and has been duplicated.)
5. Use any of the techniques you learned in this chapter to select and drag an image that will be the target of a clipping mask to the Spheroid image, and modify it as necessary. (*Hint*: The golf balls in the sample are the target image.)

6. Create a clipping mask using the two images, then modify the result as desired. (*Hint*: The tennis ball has been copied to another layer, which was adjusted to a lower opacity setting and moved above the clipping mask to create the illusion that the golf balls are inside it.)
7. Create an alpha channel and ensure that it is visible in the image. (*Hint*: The tennis ball has a selected area alpha channel applied to it.)

FIGURE 41
Completed Project Builder 1

8. Create type layers as desired, and apply at least one style or filter to at least one of the type layers. (*Hint*: The Nature's perfect snack type has a Dissolve blending mode, and the Drop Shadow and Gradient Overlay styles applied to it.)
9. Drag or copy any remaining images to the Spheroid image, transform them or apply at least one style or filter to them, then close the image files.
10. Save your work, then compare your image to the sample in Figure 41.

Enhancing Specific Selections

Several resort hotels want to accommodate the unique vacation needs of their younger guests. They're going to give each child under 12 a bag of equipment, books, games, and other items that match their interests. Your job is to design the cover of the information booklet that will be included in the package.

1. Obtain images for the cover that are centered on a beach vacation theme. Include images whose content you can select or extract, and any other images as desired. You can use scanned images or images that are available on your computer, or you can connect to the Internet and download images. You'll need a background image and at least one layer to serve as the focal point.

2. Create a new Photoshop image, then save it as **Perfect Oasis**.

3. Apply a color or style to the Background layer, or use any of the techniques you learned in this chapter to select and drag the image that will be the background to the Perfect Oasis image.

4. Use any of the techniques you learned in this chapter to select and drag the image that will be the focal point of the Perfect Oasis image. (*Hint*: In the sample shown, the image of the boy and girl has a layer mask applied to it, and has been copied to another layer that has an elliptical marquee

with Drop Shadow and Bevel and Emboss styles applied to it.)

5. Open the surrounding image files, then use any of the techniques you learned in this chapter to select and drag the images to the Perfect Oasis image.

6. Add layer masks, transform, or apply filters or styles to the images as desired. (*Hint*: In the sample, the image of the boy and girl has been enhanced and has a layer mask; the surf also has been enhanced.)

7. Create type layers as desired and apply filters or styles to at least one of them. (*Hint*: The Could be right in your own backyard type has Drop Shadow, Bevel and Emboss, and Gradient Overlay styles applied to it.)

8. Create a layer set called **Title**, add a color to the layer set, and then add the type layers to it.

9. Save your work, close the image files, then compare your image to the sample in Figure 42.

FIGURE 42
Completed Project Builder 2

You're the senior graphics engineer at a 3D software simulation company and have just hired a few new graphic designers. Some of the work at your company involves reverse engineering, a process that your new artists will need to understand and capture visually. To better orient them to the practice, you've asked them to deconstruct a Photoshop image on the web, and then reinterpret the image using the techniques they identified. Before you assemble the staff, you want to walk through the process yourself.

1. Connect to the Internet, and use your browser to find information containing digital artwork that contains images and type that appears to have styles or filters applied. (Make a record of the site you found so you can use it for future reference, if necessary.)
2. Create a new Photoshop image and save it as **My Vision**.
3. Create a type layer named **Techniques**, then on the layer, type the skills and features that you believe were used to create the appearance of each letter and its background image. In addition to addressing the specifics for each letter, be sure to include the following general analyses:
   - Identify the light source for the image, and how light is handled for each letter and its background.
   - Discuss the relationship between the styles applied to the type and the styles or filters applied to the background image.
   - Evaluate any seemingly conflicting or unidentifiable techniques.
4. Complete your analyses and print the image.
5. Hide the Techniques layer, then obtain images to use for your own interpretation of the digital artwork. You can use scanned images or images that are available on your computer, or download images from the Internet.

6. Place the images in your image, create type layers for the letters, and then apply the techniques you identified. Compare your image to the sample shown in Figure 43.
7. Create a snapshot, then update the Techniques layer as necessary, print the image so that the Techniques layer prints clearly, then compare your before and after analyses. (*Hint*: Hide distracting layers if necessary.)
8. Hide the Techniques layer, make the other layers active, then save your work.

FIGURE 43
Design Project Website

After years of lackluster advertising campaigns, you've decided to combine the talent of local photographers and your Photoshop skills to create new artwork for a local beach. You know that this is a grand public relations opportunity not to be missed. You decide to design a poster and a companion bumper sticker that highlights the beach. You can use any appropriate images of your choice in the design.

1. Obtain images for the poster and bumper sticker. Include those whose content you can select or extract, and any other images as desired. You can use scanned images, or images that are available on your computer, or connect to the Internet and download images. You'll need a background image that might or might not include the animal, at least one small image (such as a snack, toy, or flower) to accompany the animal, and as many other images as desired.

2. Create a new Photoshop image and save it as **Beach Poster**.

3. Drag or copy the background to the Beach Poster image above the Background layer, then delete the Background layer, if necessary.

4. Select the animal in its image file, then copy the image to a new layer in the Beach Poster file. (*Hint*: The horses were selected using the Quick Selection tool.)

5. Duplicate the animal layer if desired, and apply filters or styles to it. (*Hint*: The horses

were selected, then copied.)

6. Create type layers for the bumper sticker as desired, include something unique about the species you selected, and apply at least one style or filter to them. (*Hint*: The background of the bumper sticker was created with the Rectangle tool and has Drop Shadow and Stroke effects applied to it, the heart was created with the Custom Shape tool, and the cut corners were created with the Eraser tool.)

7. Drag or copy the small image, transform it as needed, and then apply at least one style or filter to it. (*Hint*: The type has been scaled, rotated, and background erased.)

8. Drag or copy other images as desired, then apply filters or styles to them.

9. Be prepared to discuss the effects you can generate when you select an image, copy it, and apply different opacity settings, filters, or styles to each copy.

10. Save your work, then compare your image to the sample in Figure 44.

FIGURE 44
Completed Portfolio Project

ADJUSTING
COLORS

1. Correct and adjust color

2. Enhance colors by altering saturation

3. Modify color channels using levels

4. Create color samplers with the Info panel

Enhancing Color

Photoshop places several color-enhancing tools at your disposal. By changing tonal values, these tools make it possible to change the mood or "personality" of a color. **Tonal values**, also called **color levels**, are the numeric values of an individual color and are crucial if you ever need to duplicate a color. For example, when you select a specific shade in a paint store that requires custom mixing, a recipe that contains the tonal values is used to create the color.

Using Tools to Adjust Colors

You can use color adjustment tools to make an image that is flat or dull appear to come to life. You can mute distracting colors to call attention to a central image. You can choose from several adjustment tools to achieve the same results, so the method you use depends on which one you *prefer*, not on which one is *better*.

Reproducing Colors

Accurate color reproduction is an important reason to learn about color measurement and modification. Because colors vary from monitor to monitor, and can be altered during the output process, you can specify exactly how you want them to look. Professional printers know how to take your Photoshop settings and adapt them to get the colors that match your specifications. Color levels, depicted in a **histogram** (a graph that represents the frequency distribution—for example, the number of times a particular pixel color occurs), can be modified by making adjustments in the input and output levels. When working with color levels, moving the input sliders toward the center of the histogram increases the tonal range, resulting in increased contrast in the image. Moving the output sliders toward the center decreases the tonal range, resulting in decreased contrast.

You can make color adjustments directly on a layer, or by using an adjustment layer. Directly applying a color adjustment affects only the layer to which it is applied. Applying a color adjustment using an adjustment layer affects all visible layers beneath it.

Tools You'll Use

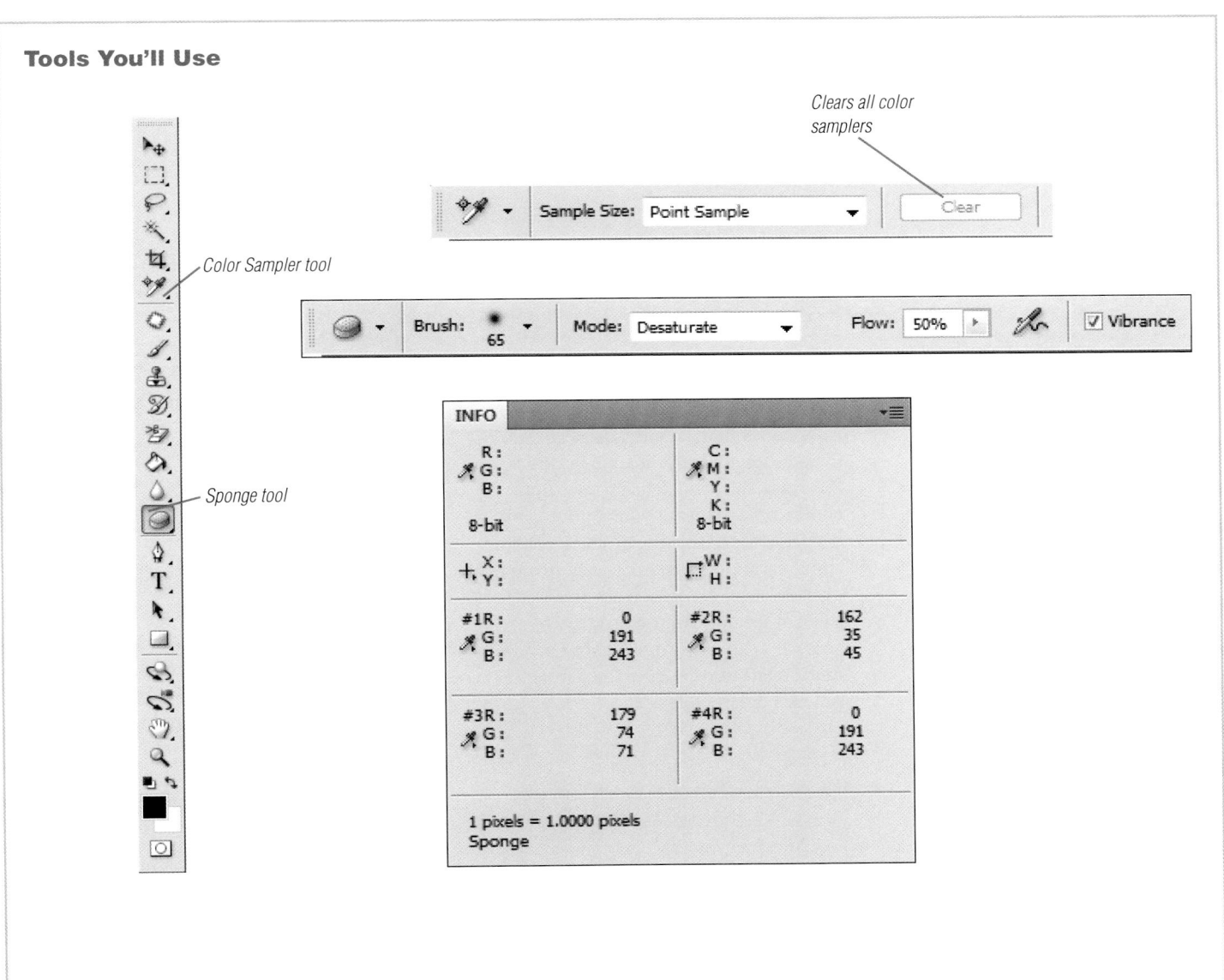

Clears all color samplers

Color Sampler tool

Sample Size: Point Sample   Clear

Brush: 65   Mode: Desaturate   Flow: 50%   ☑ Vibrance

Sponge tool

INFO

R:		C:	
G:		M:	
B:		Y:	
		K:	
8-bit		8-bit	

| X: | | W: | |
| Y: | | H: | |

#1R:	0	#2R:	162
G:	191	G:	35
B:	243	B:	45

#3R:	179	#4R:	0
G:	74	G:	191
B:	71	B:	243

1 pixels = 1.0000 pixels
Sponge

10-3

ADJUST COLOR

What You'll Do

In this lesson, you'll modify settings for color balance and curves to make dull colors look more vivid.

Making Color Corrections

Learning to recognize which colors need correction is one of the hardest skills to develop. Adjusting colors can be very difficult because, while there is a science to color correction, you must also consider the aesthetics of your image. Beauty is in the eye of the beholder, and you must choose how you want your work to look and feel. Add to this the problem of reconciling hardware differences, where *my* red may look very different from *your* red, and you can see how color management can become a can of worms. A **color management system** reconciles the differences between different devices.

Most color corrections can be made by clicking the appropriate button on the Adjustments panel, or by using a dialog box that is opened by clicking the Image menu on the Application bar, then clicking Adjustments.

Using a Color Management System

Photoshop has a way to deal with hardware discrepancies: the device profile. A **profile** (also called an ICC profile) can be created for specific devices and embedded in an image, and is used to define how colors are interpreted by a specific device. ICC stands for International Color Consortium. You can create a profile by clicking Edit on the Application bar, then clicking Color Settings. Use the list arrows in the Working Spaces section. An image's working space tells the color management system how RGB or CMYK values are interpreted. You don't have to use profiles, but you can assign a specific profile by selecting the ICC Profile check box (Win) or the Embed Color Profile check box (Mac) in the Save As dialog box. Doing so embeds the profile in the working space of an image. Assigning an ICC profile is different from converting to an ICC profile. Converting occurs during output preparation, when you can select color management options in the Adobe PDF Options dialog box.

PHOTOSHOP 10-4

Balancing Colors

You can **balance colors** by adding and subtracting tonal values from those already existing in a layer. You do this to correct oversaturated or undersaturated color and to remove color casts from an image. The Color Balance dialog box or Adjustments panel contains three sliders: one for Cyan-Red, one for Magenta-Green and one for Yellow-Blue. You can adjust colors by dragging each of these sliders or by typing in values in the Color Levels text boxes. You can also use the Color Balance dialog box to adjust the color balance of shadows or highlights by clicking the Shadows or Highlights option buttons.

QUICKTIP

Color cast is a situation in which one color dominates an image to an unrealistic or undesirable degree, such as the yellowing of a photograph.

Modifying Curves

Using the Curves Adjustments panel or dialog box, you can alter the output tonal value of any pixel input. Instead of just being able to make adjustments using three variables (highlights, shadows, and midtones), you can change as many as 16 points along the 0–255 scale in the Curves dialog box. The horizontal axis in the Curves dialog box represents the original intensity values of the pixels (the Input levels), and the vertical axis represents the modified color values (the Output levels). The default curve appears as a diagonal line that shares the same input and output values. Each point on the line represents each pixel. You add curves to the line to adjust the tonal values.

Analyzing Colors

When you look at an image, ask yourself, "What's wrong with this picture?" Does the image need more blue than yellow? Preserve your work by creating an adjustment layer, then try adjusting the color sliders, and see how the image changes. Then try modifying the curves. Much of the color correction process involves experimentation—with you, the artist, learning and applying the subtleties of shading and contrast.

FIGURE 1

Variations dialog box

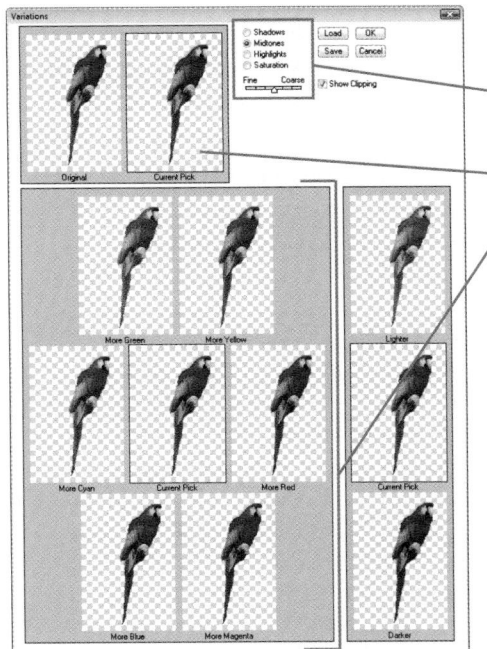

Additional adjustment options

Current selection

Color variations

Using Variations to adjust color

You can make color adjustments by viewing thumbnails of color variations on your current image. You can see a variety of thumbnails that show you some specific results of color correction. Start by clicking the layer you want to adjust. Click Image on the Application bar, point to Adjustments, then click Variations. The Variations dialog box, as shown in Figure 1, will open, showing your current layer with its settings, and thumbnails of the same layer with lighter, darker, or more of the individual colors from the Color Balance dialog box. This tool lets you see what a layer would look like if it had more of a particular color, *without* making any modifications to the actual image. You can use the Variations dialog box as a tool to help you develop your color correction skills.

Modify color balance settings

1. Start Photoshop, open PS 10-1.psd from the drive and folder where you store your Data Files, update the text layers (if necessary), then save the file as **Scarlet Macaws**.

2. Click the **Default Foreground and Background Colors button** on the Tools panel (if necessary).

3. Display the **Color and Tone** workspace.

   TIP Some workspaces, such as Color and Tone, have the option of displaying additional information. You can display this additional information by clicking the list arrow in the top panel, then clicking Expanded View. Use the display that best meets your needs.

4. Click the **Large Macaw layer** on the Layers panel.

5. Click the **Color Balance button** on the Adjustments panel.

6. Drag the **sliders** so that the Midtones settings in the Color Levels text boxes are **60** for Cyan/Red, **−40** for Magenta/Green, and **−50** for Yellow/Blue, verify that the Preserve Luminosity check box is selected, then click the **Return to adjustment list button**.

7. Compare your image to Figure 2.

You modified the color balance settings by using the sliders. As you drag the sliders, you can see changes in the image on the active layer.

FIGURE 2
Color balanced layer

Intensified reds, magentas, and yellows

Using the Auto Adjustments commands

You can make color adjustments by clicking Image on the Application bar and using one of the Auto Adjustments commands. You can use three Auto Adjustments commands (Auto Tone, Auto Contrast, and Auto Color) to make color adjustments automatically without any additional input. The Auto Tone command adjusts the intensity levels of shadows and highlights by identifying the lightest and darkest pixel in each color channel and then redistributing the pixel's values across that range. You can use the Auto Contrast command to make simple adjustments to the contrast and mixture of colors in an RGB image; it works by analyzing the distribution of colors in the composite image, not in the individual color channels. The Auto Color command adjusts the contrast and color mixtures using the image itself to make the adjustment, resulting in neutralized midtones.

FIGURE 3
Curves graph in Adjustments panel

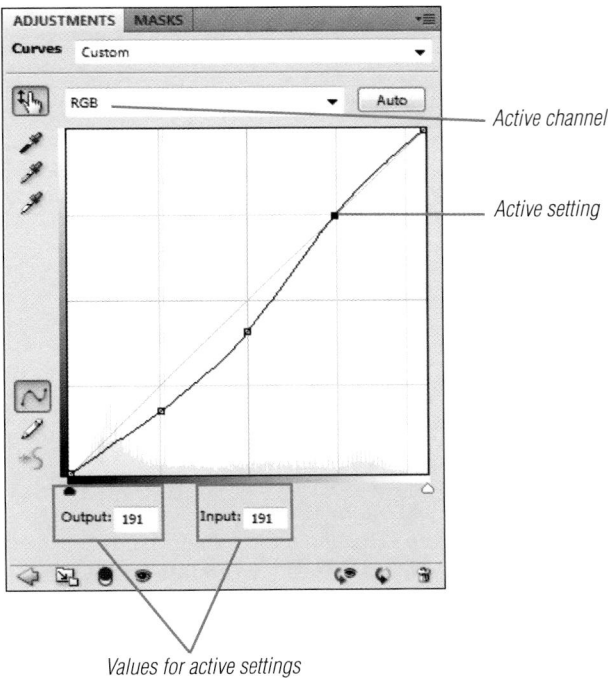

Active channel

Active setting

Values for active settings

FIGURE 4
Image with modified curves

Using the Color Settings dialog box

You can use the Color Settings dialog box to save common color management controls, such as working spaces, color management policies, conversion options, and advanced controls. You might want to create a custom color setting, for example, to match a specific proofing setup used by a commercial printer. To open the Color Settings dialog box, click Edit on the Application bar, then click Color Settings. In most cases, it's best to use preset color settings that have been tested by Adobe Systems unless you are knowledgeable about color management. If you do make changes, you can save them as a preset using the Color Settings dialog box.

Modify curves

1. Click the **Large Macaw layer**, then click the **Curves button** on the Adjustments panel.

2. Click the **center of the graph** at the point on the line where the input and output values both equal **128**.

   TIP When you position the pointer over the Curves graph, input and output values display beneath the graph.

3. Drag the point down so that the input value equals **128** and the output value equals **104**.

   TIP This is not an exact science. Don't worry if you can't get the input and output values to be exactly as stated in the steps.

   Did you notice that the image's colors change as you drag the line? If you use the Curves dialog box, you can see the changes if the preview check box is checked.

4. Click the **point where the curve intersects the right vertical gridline** (input value equals approximately **191**, and output value equals approximately **178**).

   TIP The point that you click in the Curves dialog box is called the **active setting**.

5. Drag the **active setting** up as needed until the input and output values both equal **191**, as shown in Figure 3.

   TIP After you select the active setting, you can also change its location by changing the values in the Input and Output boxes.

6. Click the **Return to adjustment list button**.

7. Save your work, then compare your screen to Figure 4.

You modified curves settings by using Curves on the Adjustments panel.

What You'll Do

In this lesson, you'll modify the appearance of an image by altering color saturation.

Understanding Saturation

Saturation is the purity of a particular color. A higher saturation level indicates a color that is more intense. To understand saturation, imagine that you are trying to lighten a can of blue paint. For example, if you add some gray paint, you decrease the purity and the intensity of the original color or desaturate it. Photoshop provides two methods of modifying color saturation: the Hue/Saturation dialog box and the Sponge tool.

Using the Sponge Tool

The Sponge tool is located on the Tools panel, and is used to increase or decrease the color saturation of a specific area within a layer. Settings for the Sponge tool are located on the options bar and include settings for the brush size, whether you want the sponge to saturate or desaturate, and how quickly you want the color to flow into or from the Sponge tool.

You can reset the active tool to its default settings by right-clicking the tool on the options bar, then clicking the Reset tool.

Using the Hue/Saturation Dialog Box

Hue is the amount of color that is reflected from or transmitted through an object. Hue is assigned a measurement (between 0 and 360 degrees) that is taken from a standard color wheel. In conversation, hue is the name of the color, such as red, blue, or gold and described in terms of its tints or shades, such as yellow-green or blue-green. Adjusting hue and saturation is similar to making modifications to color balance. You can make these adjustments by using the Hue, Saturation, and Lightness sliders, which are located in the Hue/Saturation dialog box. When modifying saturation levels using the Hue/Saturation dialog box, you have the option of adjusting the entire color range, or preset color ranges. The available preset color ranges are shown in Figure 5. To choose any one of these color ranges, click the Edit list arrow in the Hue/Saturation setting on the Adjustments panel *before* modifying any of the sliders.

Using Saturation to Convert a Color Layer to Grayscale

Have you ever wondered how an image could contain both a color and a grayscale object, as shown in Figure 6? You can easily create this effect using the Hue/Saturation setting on the Adjustments panel. This image was created by clicking the layer containing the ice chest, clicking the Hue/Saturation button on the Adjustments panel, then changing the Saturation setting to –100.

FIGURE 5

Preset color ranges in the Hue/Saturation setting on the Adjustments panel

Select colors to be changed

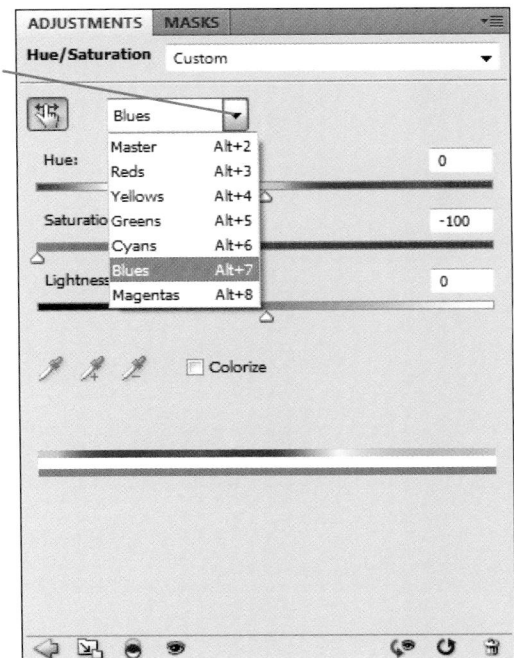

FIGURE 6

Grayscale layer

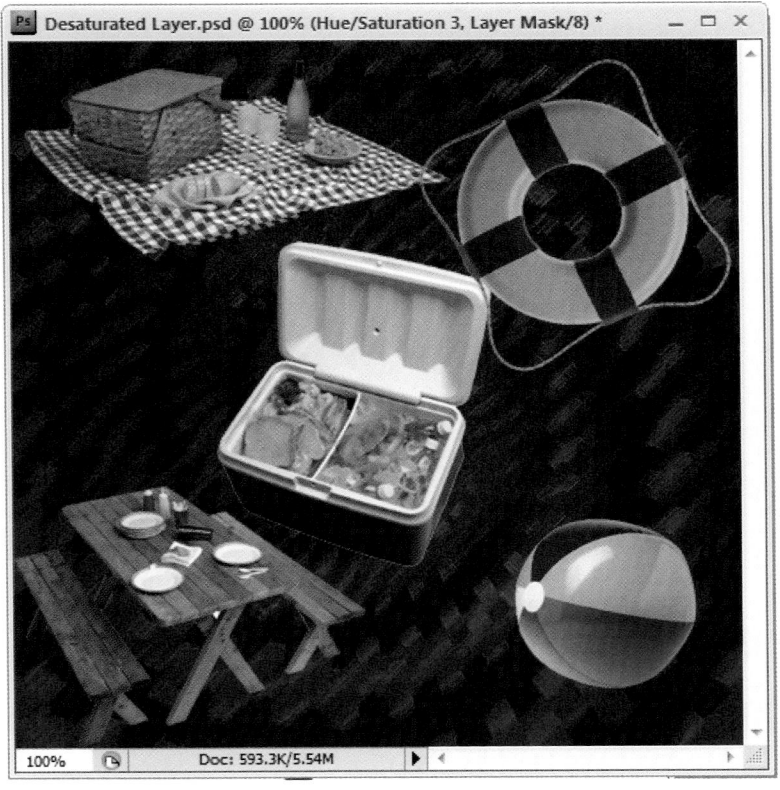

Saturate a color range

1. Click the **Small Macaw 1 layer** on the Layers panel to make it active, then make the layer visible.
2. Click the **Indicates layer visibility button** 👁 on the Large Macaw layer to hide it.
3. Click the **Hue/Saturation button** 🔅 on the Adjustments panel.

   TIP When making color adjustments, you can use the preset buttons on the Adjustments panel, or use the Adjustments command on the Image menu.

4. Click the **Edit list arrow**, then click **Blues**.
5. Drag the **Saturation slider** to **+40**.
6. Click the **Edit list arrow**, then click **Yellows**.
7. Drag the **Saturation slider** to **+30**.

   The image's blues and yellows are intensified.

8. Click the **Return to adjustment list button** ↵, then compare your image to Figure 7.

You changed the saturation of two preset color ranges. As you altered the saturation, the richness of the colors became more defined.

Getting more color data using HDR images

High Dynamic Range images, which use 32 bits per channel, allow real-world levels of illumination to be represented. The level of detail afforded by using 32 bits per channel means that imagery is more realistic and better able to simulate light conditions and a wider range of color values. You can create an HDR image using multiple photographs, each captured at a different exposure. In Photoshop, you can create HDR images from multiple photographs by clicking File on the Application bar, pointing to Automate, then clicking Merge To HDR command.

FIGURE 7
Modified blues and yellows

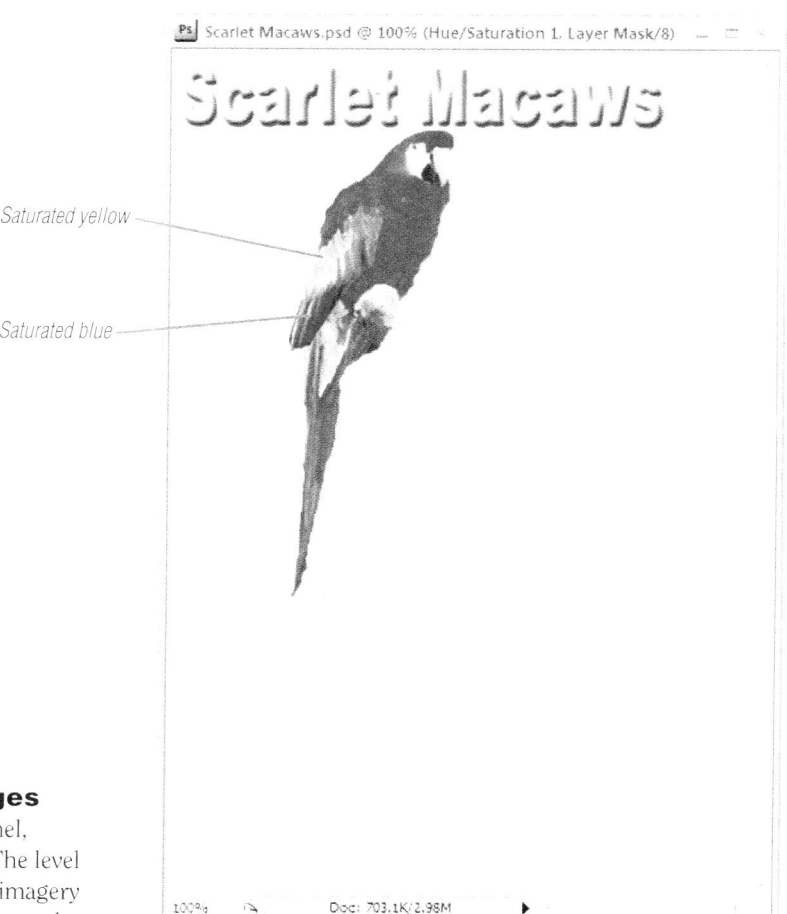

Saturated yellow

Saturated blue

FIGURE 8
Reds saturated with the Sponge tool

Saturated red areas

1. Click the **Small Macaw 1 layer** to make it active.

2. Click the **Sponge tool** ⊜ on the Tools panel.

   TIP   The Sponge tool is grouped with the Dodge tool and the Burn tool on the Tools panel.

3. Click the **Click to open the Brush Preset picker list arrow** ⬚, then double-click the **Hard Round 13 pixels brush tip**.

4. Click the **Mode list arrow** on the options bar, click **Saturate**, then set the Flow to **100%**.

5. Click and drag the pointer over the **red areas** (head, body, and tail feathers) of the parrot.

   The red color in the saturated area is brighter.

6. Save your work, then compare your screen to Figure 8.

You used the Sponge tool to saturate specific areas in an image. The Sponge tool lets you saturate spot areas rather than an entire color on a layer.

Correcting faulty exposures

The Exposure adjustment feature lets you correct for under- or over-exposure in images. By making adjustments to the black points (which can result in an image being too dark) or the white points (which can result in an image appearing too light), you can make corrections that will make an image's exposure settings just right. You can make exposure adjustments by clicking Image on the Application bar, pointing to Adjustments, then clicking Exposure, or by clicking the Exposure button on the Adjustments panel.

What You'll Do

In this lesson, you'll use levels to make color adjustments.

Making Color and Tonal Adjustments

You can make color adjustments using the Levels button on the Adjustments panel or the Levels dialog box (which can be opened by clicking Image on the Application bar, pointing to Adjustments, then clicking Levels). This feature lets you make modifications across a tonal range, using the composite color channel or individual channels. The Levels setting takes the form of a histogram and displays light and dark color values on a linear scale. The plotted data indicates the total number of pixels for a given tonal value.

There is no "ideal" histogram shape. The image's character and tone determine the shape of the histogram. Some images will be lighter and their histogram will be bunched on the right; some will be darker and their histogram will be bunched on the left. When working with the Levels setting, three triangular sliders appear beneath the histogram representing shadows, midtones, and highlights. Three text boxes appear for input levels (one box each for the input shadows, midtones, and highlights). Two text boxes appear for output levels (one for output shadows and one for highlights).

Correcting Shadows and Highlights

You can modify the settings for shadows and highlights independently. By moving the output shadows slider to the right, you can decrease contrast and *lighten* the image on an individual layer. You can decrease contrast and *darken* an image by moving the output highlights slider to the left in the Levels setting.

Adjusting Colors

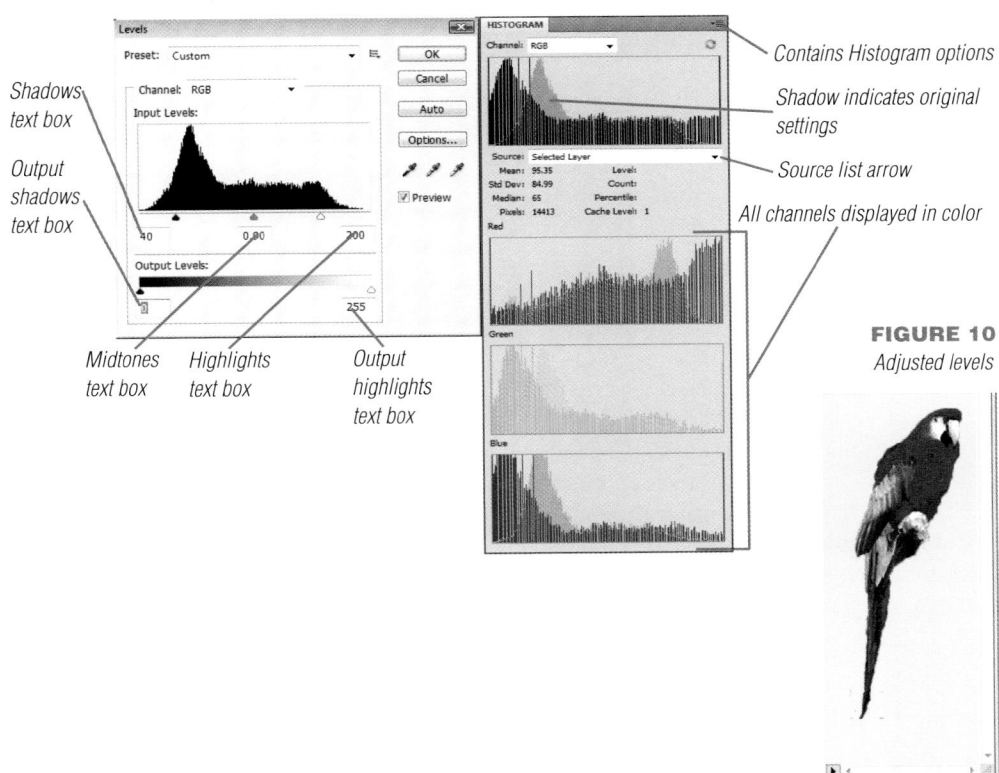

FIGURE 9
Levels dialog box and Histogram panel

Shadows text box

Output shadows text box

Midtones text box

Highlights text box

Output highlights text box

Contains Histogram options

Shadow indicates original settings

Source list arrow

All channels displayed in color

FIGURE 10
Adjusted levels

Understanding the Histogram panel

Using the Histogram panel, you can watch as you adjust color settings such as levels, curves, color balance, and hue/saturation. When the Histogram panel opens, you'll see the compact view: a single chart containing a composite channel for the image. You can view all the channels in color using the menu options on the list arrow on the panel. As you make color adjustments, the Histogram panel is updated. In addition to the modifications, the original settings are displayed as a light-colored shadow. This makes it easy to see how the settings have changed.

Adjust color using the Levels setting

1. Click the **Small Macaw 2 layer** on the Layers panel to make it active, then make the layer visible.

2. Click the **Indicates layer visibility button** 👁 on the Small Macaw 1 layer to hide it.

3. Drag the **Histogram panel tab** `HISTOGRAM` out of the dock (to the left of its current location).

4. Click the **Histogram panel list arrow** ▾☰, then click **Expanded View** (if it is not already expanded).

5. Click the **Histogram panel list arrow** ▾☰, then click **All Channels View**.

6. Click the **Histogram panel list arrow** ▾☰, verify that the **Show Statistics** and **Show Channels in Color commands** contain check marks, then click RGB in the Channels list arrow (if necessary).

7. Click the **Small Macaw 2 layer**, click the **Source list arrow** on the Histogram panel, then click **Selected Layer**.

8. Click **Image** on the Application bar, point to **Adjustments**, then click **Levels** to open the Levels dialog box. Type **40** in the Shadows text box, press **[Tab]**, type **.90** in the Midtones text box, press **[Tab]**, then type **200** in the Highlights text box. See Figure 9.

9. Click **OK**, reset the **Color and Tone** workspace, then compare your work to Figure 10.

10. Save your work.

You modified levels for shadows, midtones, and highlights. You were also able to see how these changes were visible on the Histogram panel.

In this lesson, you'll take multiple color samples and use the Info panel to store color information.

Sampling Colors

In the past, you've used the Eyedropper pointer to take a sample of an existing color. By taking the sample, you were able to use the color as a background or a font color. This method is easy and quick, but it limited you to one color sample at a time. Photoshop has an additional feature, the **Color Sampler tool**, that makes it possible to sample—and store—up to four distinct color samplers.

The color samplers are saved with the image in which they are created.

Using Color Samplers

You can apply each of the four color samplers to an image or use the samplers to make color adjustments. Each time you click the Color Sampler tool, a color

reading is taken and the number 1, 2, 3, or 4 appears on the image, depending on how many samplers you have already taken. See Figure 11. A color sampler includes all visible layers and is dynamic. This means that if you hide a layer from which a sampler was taken, the next visible layer will contain a sampler that has the same coordinates of the hidden layer, but the sampler will have the color reading of the visible layer.

Using the Info Panel

The Info panel is grouped with the Actions and Histogram panels in the Color and Tone workspace. The top-left quadrant displays actual color values for the current color mode. For example, if the current mode is RGB, then RGB values are displayed. The Info panel also displays CMYK values, X and Y coordinates of the current pointer location, and the width and height of a selection (if applicable).

as shown in Figure 12. When a color sampler is created, the Info panel expands to show the color measurement information from that sample. Figure 13 shows an Info panel containing four color samplers. After you have established your color samplers but no longer want them to be displayed, click the Info panel list arrow, then deselect Color Samplers. You can display hidden color samplers by clicking the Info panel list arrow, then clicking Color Samplers.

Manipulating Color Samplers

Color samplers, like most Photoshop features, are designed to accommodate change. Each color sampler can be moved by dragging the sampler icon to a new location. After the sampler is moved to its new location, its color value information is updated on the Info panel. You can individually delete any of the samplers by selecting the Color Sampler tool, holding

[Alt] (Win) or [option] (Mac), then clicking the sampler you want to delete. You can also delete all the samplers by clicking the Clear button on the options bar.

FIGURE 11
Color samplers

Color samplers

FIGURE 12
Information displayed in the Info panel

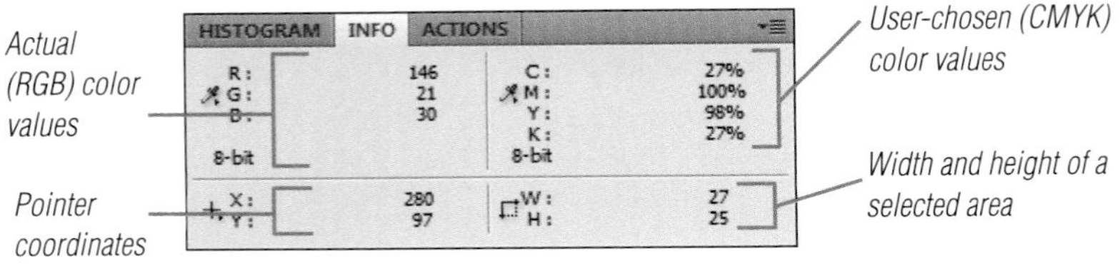

Actual (RGB) color values

Pointer coordinates

User-chosen (CMYK) color values

Width and height of a selected area

FIGURE 13
Info panel with color samplers

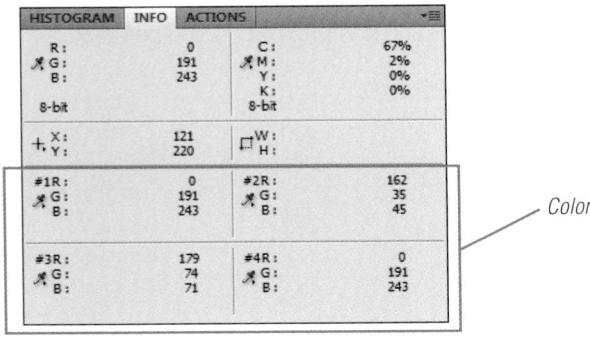

Color samplers

Create color samplers

1. Click the **Indicates layer visibility button** for the Large Macaw and Small Macaw 1 layers on the Layers panel, so that all layers in the image are visible.

2. Display the rulers in pixels (if they are not already displayed).

3. Click the **Info panel tab** INFO to display the Info panel (if it is not displayed).

4. Click the **Color Sampler tool** on the Tools panel.

   > TIP   The Color Sampler tool is grouped with the Eyedropper tool, the Ruler tool, the Note tool, and the Count tool on the Tools panel.

5. Using Figure 14 as a guide, click the image in four locations.

6. Click the **Info panel list arrow**, then click **Color Samplers** to hide the color samplers.

7. Click the **Info panel list arrow**, then click **Color Samplers** to display the color samplers.

8. Hide the rulers.

You sampled specific areas in the image, stored that color data on the Info panel, then hid and revealed the color samplers.

FIGURE 14
Color samplers in image

Sample 1 is the yellow background

Sample 2 is the yellow feather

Sample 4 is the brighter yellow feather

Sample 3 is the red tail feather

Creating a spot color channel

Printing a Photoshop image can be a costly process, especially if a spot color is used. A **spot color** is one that can't easily be re-created by a printer, such as a specific color used in a client's logo. By creating a spot color channel, you can make it easier for your printer to create the ink for a difficult color, assure yourself of accurate color reproduction, and save yourself high printing costs. If you use this feature, you won't have to provide your printer with substitution colors: the spot color contains all of the necessary information. You can create a spot color channel by displaying the Channels panel, clicking the Channels panel list arrow, then clicking New Spot Channel. Create a meaningful name for the new spot channel, click the Color box, click the Color Libraries button in the Select spot color dialog box, click the Book list arrow located at the top of the Color Libraries dialog box, click a color-matching system, then click a color from the list. You can also create a custom color by clicking the Picker button in the Custom Libraries dialog box. If you have created a color sampler, you can use this information to create the custom color for the spot color channel. Click OK to close the Color Libraries dialog box, then click OK to close the New Spot Channel dialog box.

FIGURE 15

Unsharp Mask dialog box

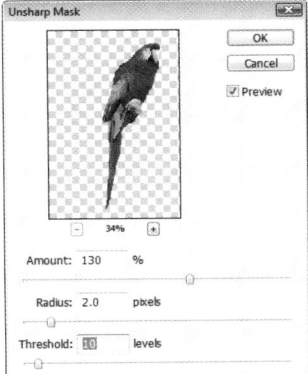

FIGURE 17

Lighting effect applied

Unsharp Mask changes the
appearance of the Large
Parrot layer

Your background colors
may vary

Lighting effect changes
the appearance of the
Backdrop layer

FIGURE 16

Lighting Effects dialog box

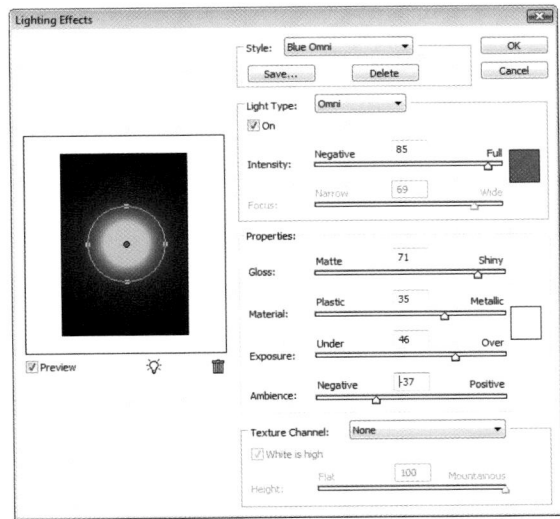

Apply a color sampler and filter and add a lighting effect

1. Make the **Large Macaw layer** active.

2. Click **Filter** on the Application bar, point to **Sharpen**, then click **Unsharp Mask**.

   You are now ready to put the finishing touches on your color-corrected image.

3. Adjust your settings in the Unsharp Mask dialog box as necessary so they match those shown in Figure 15, then click **OK**.

   These settings emphasize the edges and create the illusion of a sharper image.

4. Make the **Backdrop layer** active.

5. Click **Filter** on the Application bar, point to **Render**, then click **Lighting Effects**.

6. Adjust your settings in the Lighting Effects dialog box so they match those shown in Figure 16, then click **OK**.

7. Double-click the **Scarlet Macaws layer thumbnail**, then click **Set the text color box** on the options bar.

8. Type the R, G, and B values in sample 3 on the Info panel in the R, G, and B text boxes in the Select text color dialog box, click **OK**, then click the **Commit any current edits button** ✔ on the options bar.

9. Save your work, hide the color samplers, then compare your screen to Figure 17.

10. Close the Scarlet Macaws image, then exit Photoshop.

You added the Unsharp Mask and Lighting Effects filters to make the objects stand out more dramatically against the background. You also changed the type color using the values from a sampled color.

to do this:	use this method:
Adjust color with thumbnails	Window ➤ Adjustments panel ➤ Variations
Adjust saturation	🔲 on Adjustments panel
Balance colors	🔲 on Adjustments panel
Choose color range	Click Edit list arrow in Hue/Saturation dialog box, click color range
Convert color layer to grayscale	🔲 or ◢ on Adjustments panel
Create color sampler	Click ✎, click image using 🔲
Create spot color channel	Click CHANNELS, click ▾☰, New Spot Channel
Delete color sampler	Click ✎, press [Alt] (Win) or option (Mac), click sampler using 🔲

to do this:	use this method:
Modify curves	🔲 on Adjustments panel
Modify levels	🔲 on Adjustments panel
Move color sampler	Press [Ctrl] (Win) or ⌘ (Mac), then click sampler with 🔲
Open Histogram panel	HISTOGRAM
Open Info panel	INFO
Saturate with Sponge tool	🔲 or O
Show/Hide color samplers	Click INFO, click ▾☰ ➤ Color Samplers

Key: Menu items are indicated by ➤ between the menu name and its command. Blue bold letters are shortcuts for selecting tools on the Tools panel.

Correct and adjust color.

1. Start Photoshop.
2. Open PS 10-2.psd from the drive and folder where your Data Files are stored, then save it as **Big Bird**.
3. Make the Bird layer active (if it is not already active), then display the Color and Tone workspace.
4. Display the Color Balance adjustment settings.
5. Change the Magenta-Green setting to +62, then return to the adjustment list.
6. Display the Curves adjustment settings.
7. Click the point where the Input and Output both equal 64.
8. Drag the curve up so that the Output equals 128 while the Input remains at 64, then return to the adjustment list.
9. Save your work.

Enhance colors by altering saturation.

1. Display the Hue/Saturation settings.
2. Edit the Greens color range.
3. Change the Hue to –70 and the Saturation to –15, then return to the adjustment list.
4. Use the Sponge tool to further saturate the green, light blue, and dark blue areas of the bird.
5. Save your work.

Modify color channels using levels.

1. Display the Levels adjustment settings.
2. Modify the Blue channel Input Levels to 95, 1.60, 185.
3. Modify the Red channel Output Levels to 0, 2, 200.
4. Return to the adjustment list and save your work.

FIGURE 18
Completed Skills Review

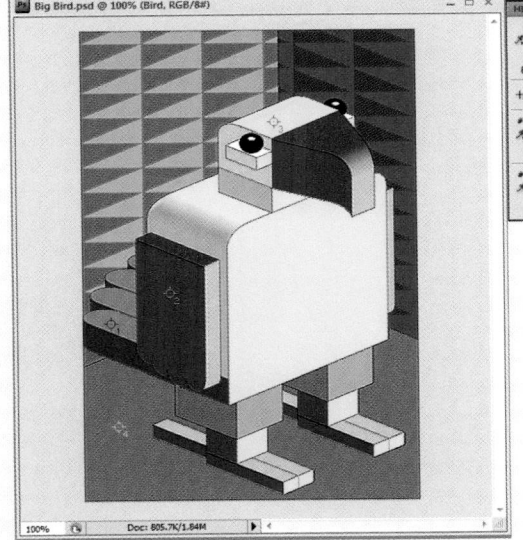

Create color samplers with the Info panel.

1. Click the Color Sampler tool.
2. Display the Info panel.
3. Create samplers for the following areas: the light blue feathers, the red wing, the yellow head, and the tan floor.
4. Compare your image to the sample shown in Figure 18.
5. Hide the color samplers.
6. Save your work.

The Artworks Gallery has commissioned you to create a promotional poster for an upcoming art show called Moods and Metaphors, which will be held during September of this year. The only guidance they have provided is that they want a piece that looks moody and evocative. You have already created a basic design, and you want to use color adjustments to heighten the mood.

1. Open PS 10-3.psd, then save it as **Gallery Poster**.
2. Make the Backdrop layer active (if necessary).
3. Display the Curves settings and adjust your settings so they match those shown in Figure 19.
4. Make the Shadow Man layer active.
5. Display the Hue/Saturation settings and change the Saturation setting to +60.
6. Create two color samplers: one using the color of the man's tie, and the other using the yellow under the spotlight.
7. Create two type layers: one for the date and location of the art show and one for expressive language that encourages people to come to the show, then position them appropriately in the image. Use either of the colors in the samplers for the font colors. For example, you can enter the color sampler RGB values in the Color Picker dialog box to create that color. (*Hint*: You can use any font and font size you want. The font used in the sample is Bernhard MT Condensed; the font size

is 85 pt for the Hurry . . . Don't miss it! layer and 36 pt for the Date and location layer.)
8. Hide the samplers.
9. Apply the following colors to the layer thumbnails: Hurry . . . Don't miss it! = Red, Date and location = Green. (*Hint*: Make these modifications using the Layer Properties command.)
10. Apply any styles to the type you feel are appropriate. (*Hint*: The Bevel and Emboss style is applied to the Hurry . . . Don't miss it! type layer in the sample. The Outer Glow and the Inner Glow styles are applied to the Date and location layer in the sample.)
11. Apply any lighting effect you feel adds to the theme of the show. (*Hint*: The Flood Light style and Spotlight light type are applied to the Backdrop layer in the sample.)
12. Save your work, then compare your image to the sample in Figure 20.

FIGURE 19
Curves adjustment panel

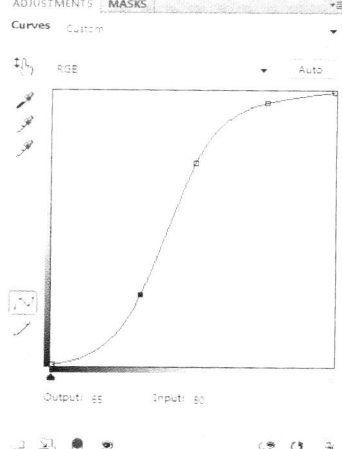

FIGURE 20
Completed Project Builder 1

Adjusting Colors

A new, unnamed e-commerce company has hired you to create an advertisement for their upcoming debut. While they are leaving the design to you, the only type they want in the imagery is "Find your inner self." They want this ad to be a teaser; more descriptive type will be added in the future. This is a cutting-edge company, and they want something really striking.

1. Open PS 10-4.psd, then save it as **Heads Up**.
2. Make the Backdrop layer active if it is not already active.
3. Use the Levels settings to modify the Input Levels of the RGB color settings. (*Hint*: The settings used in the sample are 82, 1.46, 200.)
4. Make the Head layer active.
5. Use the Hue/Saturation settings to modify the Head layer. (*Hint*: The settings used in the sample are Hue = –25, Saturation = +30, Lightness = –5.)
6. Create a color sampler for the color of the head, then hide the sampler.
7. Create a type layer for the image, then position it appropriately. (*Hint*: You can use any font, font size, and color you want. The font used in the sample is a blue OCRA Extended; the font size is 72 pt.)

8. Apply the color Yellow to the type layer thumbnail.
9. Apply any styles to the type you feel are appropriate. (*Hint*: The Drop Shadow and Bevel and Emboss styles are applied to the type layer in the sample.)

FIGURE 21
Sample Project Builder 2

10. Apply any filter you feel adds to the image. (*Hint*: The Lens Flare filter is applied to the Head layer in the sample.)
11. Save your work, then compare your image to the sample in Figure 21.

A friend of yours is a textile artist; she creates artwork that is turned into materials for clothing, curtains, and bedding. She has turned to you because of your Photoshop expertise and wants your advice on how she can jazz up her current project. You love the design, but think the colors need correction so they'll look more dynamic. Before you proceed, you decide to explore the Internet to find information on how Photoshop color correction techniques can be used to create an effective design.

1. Connect to the Internet, and use your browser to find information about adjusting colors in Photoshop. (Make a record of the site you found so you can use it for future reference, if necessary.)
2. Read about color correction and take notes on any information that will help you incorporate new ideas into the image.
3. Open PS 10-5.psd, then save the file as **Puzzle Pieces**.
4. Use the skills you have learned to correct or adjust one or more of the colors in this image.
5. Create two color samplers from colors used in the image.
6. Apply any filter you feel enhances the image. (*Hint*: The Smudge Stick filter is applied to the Yellow Pieces layer in the sample. The Texture Craquelure filter is applied to the Blue Pieces layer.)

7. Save your work, then compare your image to the sample in Figure 22.

FIGURE 22
Sample Design Project

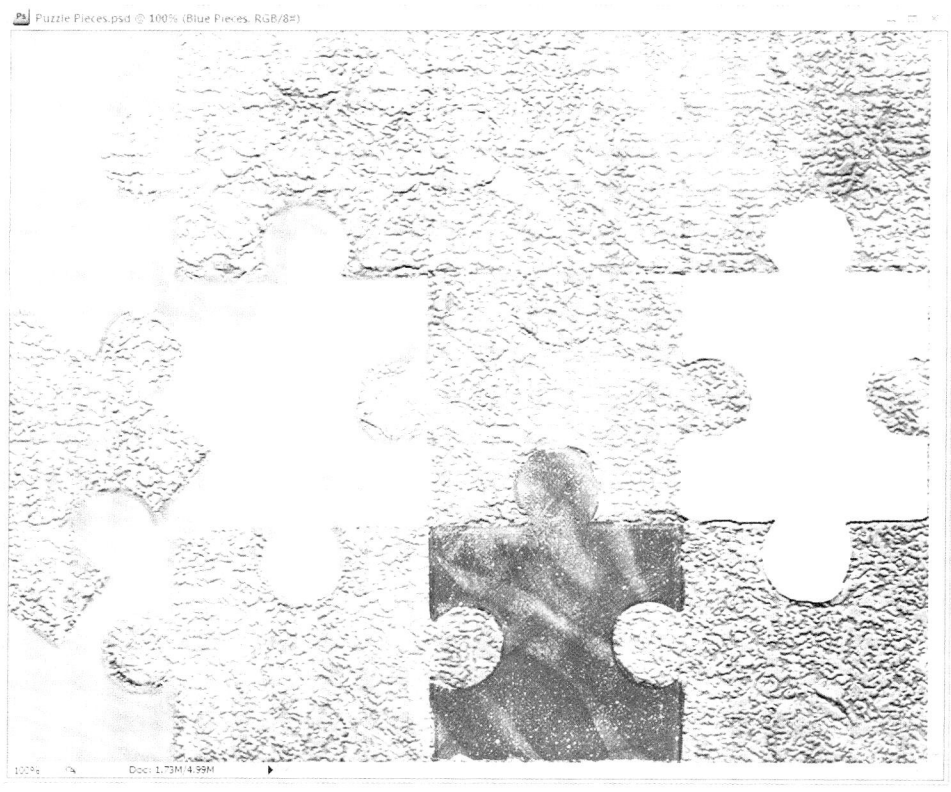

Each year, your company, OnTarget, has an art contest, and the winning entry is used as the cover of the Annual Report. OnTarget encourages employees to enter the contest. You decide to use your Photoshop skills to craft a winning entry. The OnTarget logo will be added once a winner of the contest has been selected.

1. Create an image with the dimensions 500 × 650 pixels.
2. Locate several pieces of artwork to use in the design. These can be located on your computer, from scanned images, or on the Internet. Remember that the images can show anything, but you want to show the flexibility of Photoshop and the range of your skills.
3. Save this file as **Annual Report Cover**.
4. Use any skills you have learned to correct or adjust the colors in this image.
5. Create a color sampler for at least two colors in the image, then hide the samplers.

6. Create one or two type layers for the name of the image (OnTarget Annual Report), then position the layer(s) appropriately in the image. Use your choice of font colors. (*Hint*: You can use any font and font size you want. The font used in the sample is Tempus Sans ITC; the font size is 110 pt in the title and 48 pt in the subtitle.)

FIGURE 23
Sample Portfolio Project

7. Add any necessary effects to the type layer(s).
8. If necessary, apply any filters you feel add to the image.
9. If desired, apply sampled colors within the image.
10. Save the image, then compare your image to the sample in Figure 23.

chapter

11

USING CLIPPING MASKS,
PATHS, & SHAPES

ADOBE PHOTOSHOP CS4

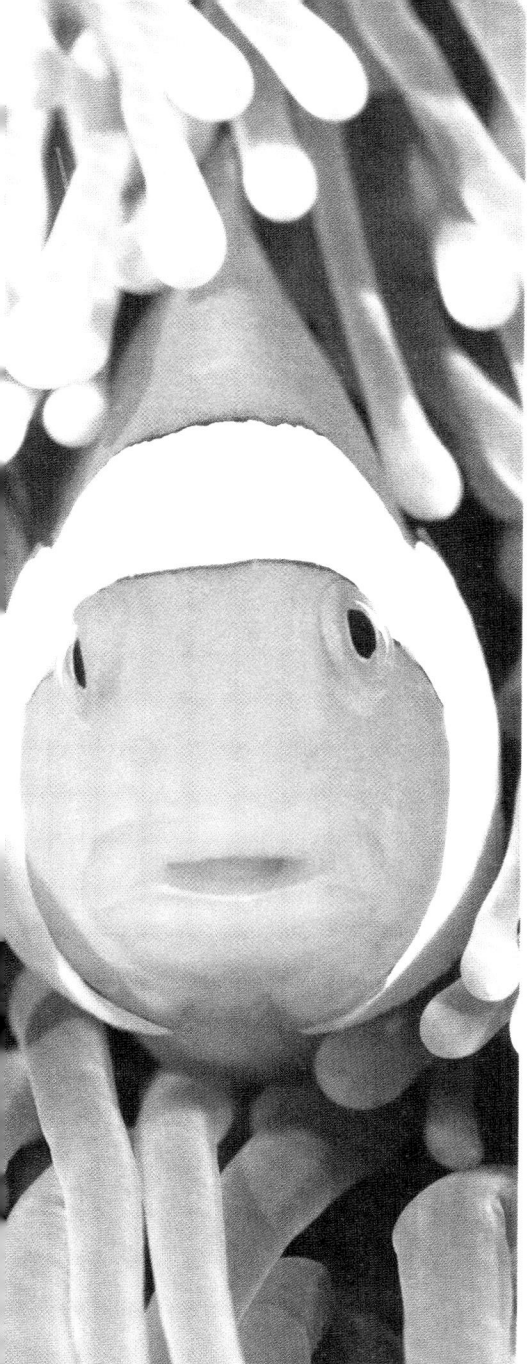

Working with Shapes

Photoshop provides several tools that help add stylistic elements, such as shapes, to your work. You can add either a shape or a rasterized shape to an image. A **shape** is simply a vector object that keeps its crisp appearance when it is resized, edited, moved, reshaped, or copied. A **rasterized shape** is converted into a bitmapped object that cannot be moved or copied; the advantage is that it can occupy a small file size, if compressed. The disadvantage is that a bitmapped object is resolution dependent. You can add either kind of shape as a predesigned shape, such as an ellipse, circle, or rectangle, or you can create a unique shape using a pen tool.

Defining Clipping Masks and Paths

A **clipping mask** (also called a **clipping group**) creates an effect in which the bottommost layer acts as a mask for all other layers in the group. You can use a **path** to turn an area defined within an object into a separate individual object—like an individual layer. A **path** is defined as one or more straight or curved line segments connected by **anchor points**, small squares similar to fastening points. Paths can be either open or closed. An **open path**, such as a line, has two distinct **endpoints**, anchor points at each end of the open path. A **closed path**, such as a circle, is one continuous path without endpoints. A **path component** consists of one or more anchor points joined by line segments. You can use another type of path called a **clipping path**, to extract a Photoshop object from within a layer, place it in another program (such as QuarkXPress or Adobe Illustrator), and retain its transparent background.

A shape and path are basically the same: the shape tools allow you to use an existing path instead of having to create one by hand. A path has a hard edge and is vector-based.

Creating Paths

Using a path, you can manipulate images on a layer. Each path is stored on the **Paths panel**. You can create a path using the Pen tool or the Freeform Pen tool. Each **pen tool** lets you draw a path by placing anchor points along the edge of another image, or wherever you need them, to draw a specific shape. As you place anchor points, line segments automatically fall between them. The **Freeform Pen tool** acts just like a traditional pen or pencil. Just draw with it, and it automatically places *both* the anchor points and line segments wherever necessary to achieve the shape you want. With these tools, you can create freeform shapes or use existing edges within an image by tracing on top of it. After you create a path, you can use the **Path Selection tool** to select the entire path, or the **Direct Selection tool** to select and manipulate individual anchor points and segments to reshape the path. Unlike selections, multiple paths can be saved using the Paths panel. When first created, a path is called a **work path**. The work path is temporary, but becomes a permanent part of your image when you name it. Paths, like layers, can be named, viewed, deleted, and duplicated.

Tools You'll Use

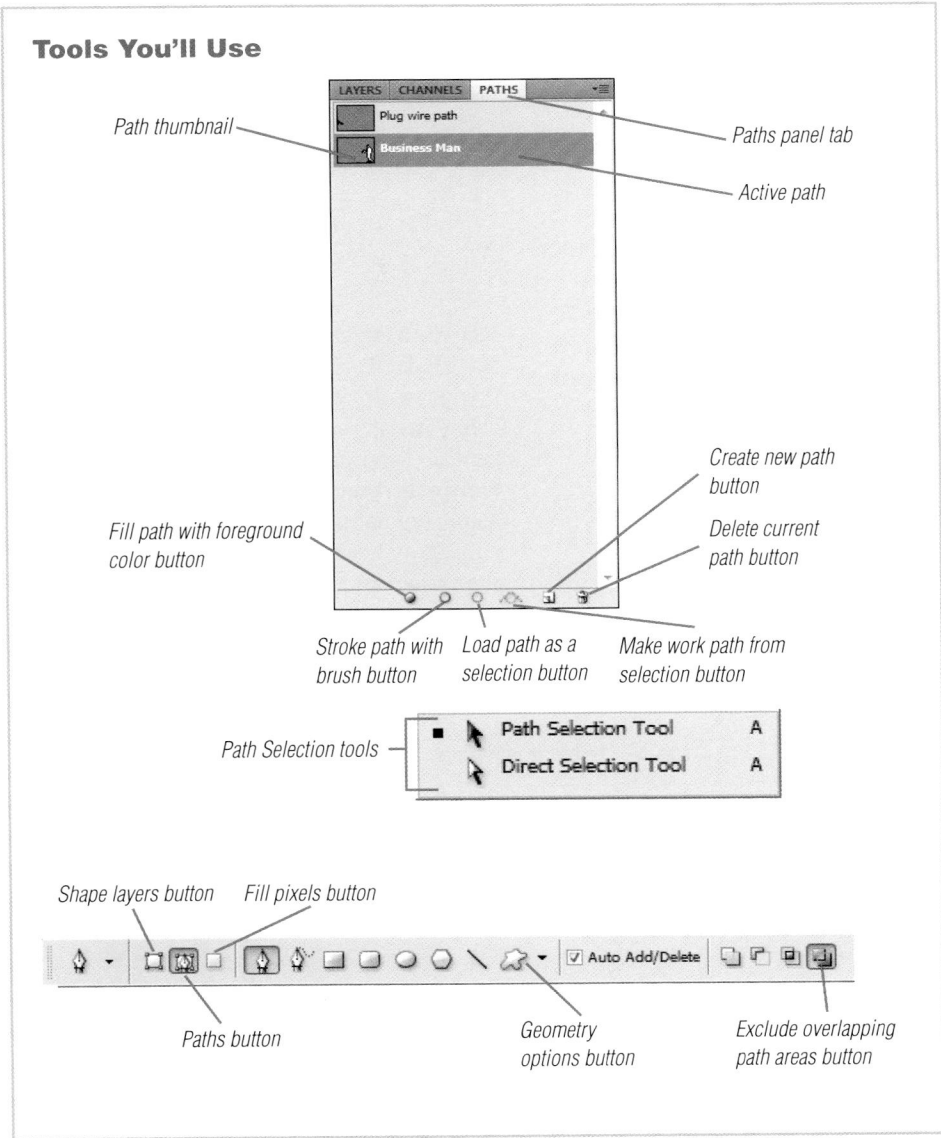

Path thumbnail

Paths panel tab

Active path

Create new path button

Delete current path button

Fill path with foreground color button

Stroke path with brush button

Load path as a selection button

Make work path from selection button

Path Selection tools

| | Path Selection Tool | A |
| Direct Selection Tool | A |

Shape layers button

Fill pixels button

Paths button

Geometry options button

Exclude overlapping path areas button

Auto Add/Delete

What You'll Do

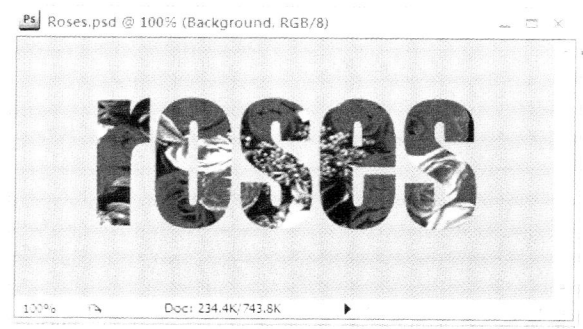

In this lesson, you'll rasterize a type layer, then use a clipping group as a mask for imagery already in an image. You'll also use the Transform command to alter an object's appearance.

Understanding the Clipping Mask Effect

If you want to display type in one layer using an interesting image or pattern in another layer as the fill for the type, then look no further. You can create this effect using a clipping mask (also called a clipping group). With a clipping group, you can isolate an area and make images outside the area transparent. This works very well with type, and can be used with a variety of images. Figure 1 shows an example of this effect in which type acts as a mask for imagery. In this effect, the (rasterized type) layer becomes a mask for the imagery. The image of the roses is *masked* by the text. For this effect to work, the layer that is being masked (the imagery, in this case) *must* be positioned above the mask layer (in this case, the type layer) on the Layers panel.

FIGURE 1
Sample clipping group effect

Rasterizing Text and Shape Layers

To use type or a shape in a clipping mask, the type or shape layer must first be rasterized, or changed from vector graphics into a normal object layer. Rasterizing changes the vector graphic into a bitmapped object, one that is made up of a fixed number of colored pixels. **Vector graphics** are made up of lines and curves defined by mathematical objects called vectors. The advantage to using vector graphics for shapes is that they can be resized and moved without losing image quality.

QUICKTIP

Bitmapped images contain a fixed number of pixels; as a consequence, they can appear jagged and lose detail when resized.

Using Transform Commands

Before you create a clipping mask, you might want to use one of the transform commands on the Edit menu to reshape layer contents so the shapes conform to the imagery that will be displayed. The transform commands are described in Table 1. Samples of the transform commands are shown in Figure 2. When a transform command is selected, a **bounding box** is displayed around the object. The bounding box contains **handles** that you can drag to modify the selection. A **reference point** is located in the center of the bounding box. This is the point around which the transform command takes place.

QUICKTIP

You can change the location of the reference point by dragging the point to a new location within the bounding box.

FIGURE 2

Sample transformations

TABLE 1: Transform Commands

command	use
Scale	Changes the image size. Press [Shift] while dragging to scale proportionally. Press [Alt] (Win) or [option] (Mac) to scale from the reference point.
Rotate	Allows rotation of an image 360°. Press [Shift] to rotate in increments of 15°.
Skew	Stretches an image horizontally or vertically, but cannot exceed the image boundary.
Distort	Stretches an image horizontally or vertically, and can exceed the image boundary.
Perspective	Changes opposite sides of an image equally, and can be used to make an oval appear circular, or change a rectangle into a trapezoid.
Rotate 180°	Rotates image 180° clockwise.
Rotate 90° CW	Rotates image 90° clockwise.
Rotate 90° CCW	Rotates image 90° counterclockwise.
Flip Horizontal	Produces a mirror image along the vertical axis.
Flip Vertical	Produces a mirror image along the horizontal axis.

Transform a type layer for use in a clipping mask

1. Open PS 11-1.psd from the drive and folder where you store your Data Files, update the text layers, then save the file as **Stamps**.

   The STAMPS type layer is active.

2. Click **Layer** on the Application bar, point to **Rasterize**, then click **Type**.

   The STAMPS layer is no longer a type layer, as shown in Figure 3.

3. Click the **Move tool** ⊕ on the Tools panel (if necessary).

4. Click **Edit** on the Application bar, point to **Transform**, then click **Skew**.

5. Type **-15** in the Set horizontal skew text box on the options bar, as shown in Figure 4, so the type is slanted.

   TIP   You can also drag the handles surrounding the object until the skew effect looks just right.

6. Click the **Commit transform (Return) button** ✓ on the options bar.

7. Turn off the guides if they are displayed, and then compare your image to Figure 5.

   TIP   There are two methods you can use to turn off the display of guides: you can hide them (using the Show command on the View menu) or clear them (using the Clear command on the View menu). Hiding the guides means you can display them at a later date, while clearing them means they will no longer exist in your document. Unless you know that you'll never need the guides again, it's a good idea to hide them.

You rasterized the existing type layer, then altered its shape using the Skew command and the Set horizontal skew by entering the value in the text box on the options bar. This transformation slanted the image.

FIGURE 3
Rasterized layer

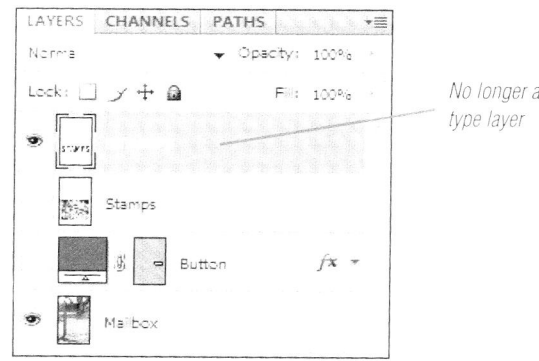

No longer a type layer

FIGURE 4
Skew options bar

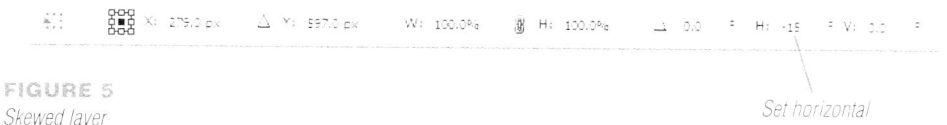

Set horizontal skew text box

FIGURE 5
Skewed layer

FIGURE 6

Preparing to create the clipping group

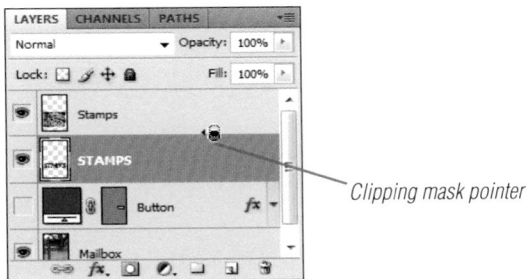

Clipping mask pointer

FIGURE 8

Layers and History panels

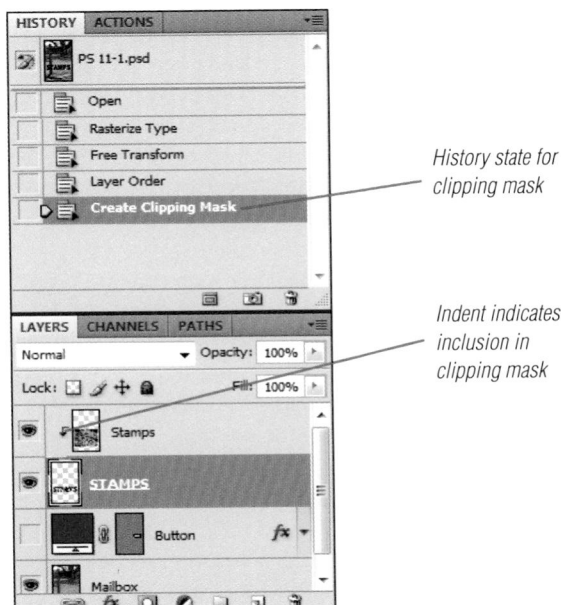

History state for
clipping mask

Indent indicates
inclusion in
clipping mask

FIGURE 7

Effect of clipping mask

Stamps background
visible through text

1. Drag the **STAMPS layer** beneath the Stamps layer.

   TIP   Having multiple layers with the same or similar names is not a problem for Photoshop. To help out, try varying layer names or using upper and lowercase letters.

2. Click the **Indicates layer visibility button** on the Stamps layer on the Layers panel.

   The Stamps layer will serve as the fill for the clipping mask.

   TIP   It's a good idea to first position the layer that will act as a mask *above* the layer containing the pattern so that you can adjust its size and shape. After the size and shape are the way you want them, reposition the mask layer *beneath* the pattern layer.

3. Use the workspace switcher to display the **History and Layers** workspace (created in Chapter 1).

4. Point to the **horizontal line** between the STAMPS and Stamps layers, press and hold **[Alt]** (Win) or **[option]** (Mac), then click, as shown in Figure 6.

5. Release **[Alt]** (Win) or **[option]** (Mac).

   The clipping mask is created. The stamps background becomes visible through the text.

6. Save your work, then compare your image to Figure 7 and the Layers panel to Figure 8.

7. Restore the **Essentials** workspace.

You created a clipping mask using the STAMPS and Stamps layers. This effect lets you use the imagery in one layer as the fill for an object in another layer.

Lesson 1   *Use a Clipping Group as a Mask*

What You'll Do

In this lesson, you'll create and name a path, expand the path to give it a wider, more curved appearance, then fill it with the foreground color.

Using Pen and Shape Tools

You have seen how you can use a clipping mask to create a mask effect. You can also create a path to serve as a mask by using any of the shape tools—the Pen tool, the Freeform Pen tool, or the Magnetic Pen tool. You can modify a path using any of the following Pen and Path Selection tools: the Add Anchor Point tool, Delete Anchor Point tool, Convert Point tool, Direct Selection tool, and the Path Selection tool. Table 2 describes some of these tools and their functions. When you select a pen tool, you can choose to create a shape layer or a path by choosing the appropriate option on the options bar.

Creating a Path

Unlike temporary selections, paths you create are saved with the image they were created in and stored on the Paths panel. Although you can't print paths unless they are filled or stroked, you can always display a path and make modifications to it. You can create a path based on an existing object, or you can create your own shape

with a pen tool. To create a closed path, you must position the pointer on top of the first anchor point. A small circle appears next to the pointer, indicating that the path will be closed when the pointer is clicked. Figure 9 shows an image of a young woman and the Paths panel containing four paths. The active path (Starfish 1) displays the starfish in the lower-right corner. Like the Layers panel, each path thumbnail displays a representation of its path. You can click a thumbnail on the Paths panel to see a specific path. The way that you create a path depends on the tool you choose to work with. The Pen tool requires that you click using the pointer each time you want to add a smooth (curved) or corner anchor point, whereas the Freeform Pen tool only requires you to click once to begin creating the path, and places the anchor points for you as you drag the pointer.

Modifying a Path

After you establish a path, you can modify it and convert it into a selection. For example, you can add more curves to an existing path, widen it, or fill a path with the foreground color. Before you can modify an unselected path, you must select it with the Direct Selection tool. When you do so, you can manipulate its individual anchor points without affecting the entire path. Moving an anchor point automatically forces the two line segments on either side of the anchor point to shrink or grow, depending on which direction you move the anchor point. You can also click individual line segments and move them to new locations. If you are working with a curved path, you can shorten or elongate the direction handles associated with each smooth point to adjust the

amount of curve or length of the corresponding line segment.

Other methods for modifying a path include adding anchor points, deleting anchor points, and converting corner anchor points into smooth anchor points, or vice versa. Adding anchor points splits an existing line segment into two, giving you more sides to your object. Deleting an anchor point does the reverse. Deleting anchor points is helpful when you have a bumpy path that is the result of too many anchors. Converting corner points into smooth points can give your drawing a softer appearance; converting smooth

points into corner points can give your drawing a sharper appearance.

QUICKTIP

Each time you click and drag using the Add Anchor pointer, you are adding smooth anchor points. You use two direction handles attached to each anchor point to control the length, shape, and slope of the curved segment.

QUICKTIP

You can press [Alt] (Win) or [option] (Mac) while you click a path thumbnail to view the path and select it at the same time.

FIGURE 9
Multiple paths for the same image

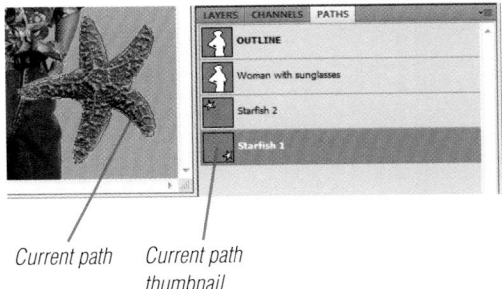

Current path   Current path
                thumbnail

TABLE 2: Pen Tools

tool	button	use
Pen tool		Creates curved or straight line segments, connected by anchor points.
Freeform Pen tool		Creates unique shapes by placing anchor points at each change of direction.
Magnetic Pen tool	☑ Magnetic	Selecting the Magnetic check box on the options bar lets the Freeform Pen tool find an object's edge.
Add Anchor Point tool		Adds an anchor point to an existing path or shape.
Delete Anchor Point tool		Removes an anchor point from an existing path or shape.
Convert Point tool		Converts a smooth point to a corner point and a corner point to a smooth point.

Lesson 2   Use Pen Tools to Create and Modify a Path

Create a path

1. Click the **Indicates layer visibility button** 👁 on the STAMPS layer on the Layers panel so that it is no longer visible.

2. Click the **Mailbox layer** on the Layers panel.

   Hiding layers makes it easier to work on a specific area of the image.

3. Click the **Freeform Pen tool** 〽 on the Tools panel.

4. Click the **Paths button** 🔲 on the options bar (if it is not already selected).

5. Click the **Geometry options list arrow** on the options bar, then adjust the settings so that your entire options bar matches Figure 10.

6. Use the **Freeform Pen tool pointer** ⛁ to trace *the vertical and horizontal posts* that hold the mailbox.

7. Click when you reach the starting point and the small 'O' appears in the pointer.

8. Click the **Paths panel tab** `PATHS`.

9. Double-click the **Work Path layer** on the Paths panel.

10. Type **Post path** in the Name text box.

11. Click **OK**, then compare your path and Paths panel to Figure 11.

You created a path using the Freeform Pen tool, then named the path in the Paths panel.

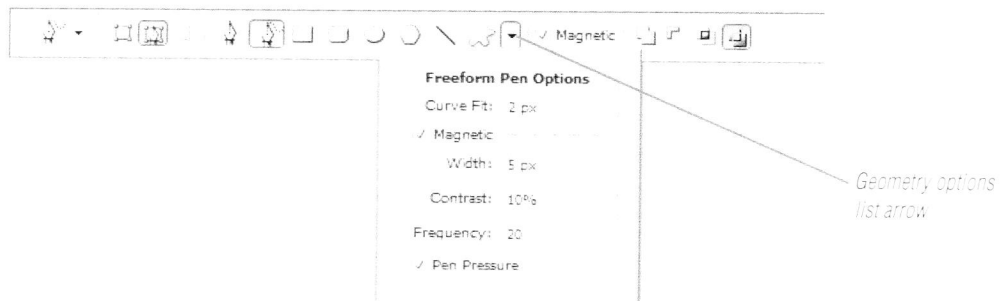

FIGURE 10
Freeform Pen tool settings

Freeform Pen Options
Curve Fit: 2 px
✓ Magnetic
Width: 5 px
Contrast: 10%
Frequency: 20
✓ Pen Pressure

Geometry options list arrow

FIGURE 11
Path and Paths panel

Path formed around post

New path name

FIGURE 12
Points added to path

FIGURE 14
Modified path

FIGURE 13
Fill Path dialog box

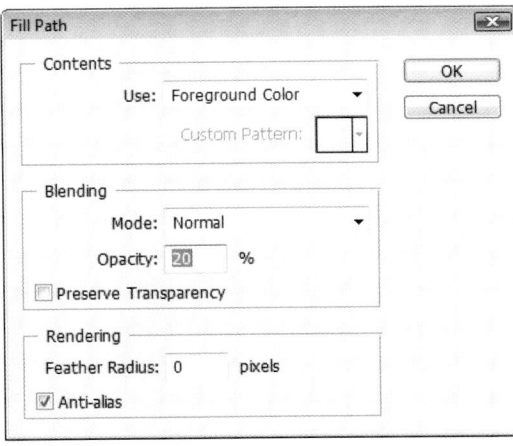

1. Zoom into the mailbox so the zoom factor is **200%**, then click the **Add Anchor Point tool** ₳⁺ on the Tools panel.

2. Click a **point near the curve at the top of the mailbox**, then drag a **handle** so the curve conforms to the left side of the mailbox, using Figure 12 as a guide.

   As you drag the new anchor points, direction handles appear, indicating that you have added smooth points instead of corner points. You can drag any of these points so they conform to the shape you want for the path.

3. Zoom out to the 100% magnification, then click the **Eyedropper tool** 🖉 on the Tools panel.

4. Click the **mailbox** to sample its color.

5. Click the **Paths list arrow** ≡ on the Paths panel, click **Fill Path**, modify the settings in the Fill Path dialog box using Figure 13 as a guide, then click **OK**.

   TIP   The Mailbox layer on the Layers panel must be selected or the Fill Path option on the Paths panel will not be available.

6. Deselect the path by clicking a blank area of the Paths panel.

7. Save your work, then compare your image to Figure 14.

You modified an existing path, then filled it with a color from a color existing in the image.

SHAPES

What You'll Do

In this lesson, you'll create two shapes, then modify and add a style to a shape layer.

Using Shape Tools

You might find that the imagery you are working with is not enough, and you need to create your own shapes. There are six shape tools on the Tools panel for creating shapes. A shape can occupy its own layer, called a **shape layer**. When you select a shape or pen tool, three buttons appear on the options bar to let you specify whether you want your shape to be on a new or existing shape layer, be a new work path, or be rasterized and filled with a color. Shapes and paths contain **vector data**, meaning that they will not lose their crisp appearance if resized or reshaped. You can create a rasterized shape using the Fill pixels button, but you cannot resize or reshape the rasterized shape.

Creating Rasterized Shapes

You cannot create a rasterized shape on a vector-based layer, such as a type or shape layer. So, to create a rasterized shape, you must first select or create a non-vector-based layer, select the shape you desire, then click the Fill pixels button on the options bar. You can change the blending mode to alter how the shape affects existing pixels in the image. You can change the opacity setting to make the shape more transparent or opaque. You can use the anti-aliasing option to blend the pixels on the shape's edge with the surrounding pixels. If you want to make changes to the content of a shape's blending mode, opacity, and anti-aliasing, you must make these changes *before* creating the rasterized shape; since the rasterization process converts the detail of the shape to an object layer. After you rasterize the shape, you can make changes to blending mode and opacity to the *layer* containing the shape.

Creating Shapes

A path and a shape are essentially the same, in that you edit them using the same tools. For example, you can modify a path and a shape using the Direct Selection tool. When selected, the anchor points are white or hollow, and can then be moved to alter the appearance of the shape or path. When you click a shape or path with the Path Selection tool, the anchor points become solid. In this case, the entire path is selected, and the individual components cannot be moved: the path or shape is moved as a single unit. A shape can be created on its own layer and can be filled with a color. Multiple shapes can also be added to a single layer, and you can specify how overlapping shapes interact.

(Painting tools are used when individual pixels are edited, such as by changing a pixel's color on a rasterized shape.)

Embellishing Shapes

You can apply other features such as the Drop Shadow and the Bevel and Emboss style, or filters, to shapes. Figure 15 shows the Layers panel of an image containing two layer shapes. The top layer (in Yellow) has the Bevel and Emboss style applied to it.

QUICKTIP

When you first create a shape, it is automatically filled with the current foreground color.

FIGURE 15
Shape layers on Layers panel

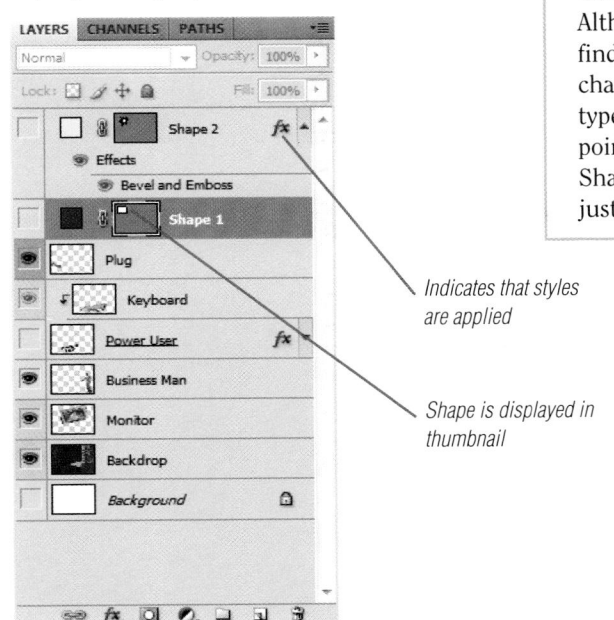

Indicates that styles are applied

Shape is displayed in thumbnail

Creating custom shapes

Although Photoshop comes with many interesting custom shapes, you still may not find the one you're looking for. If that's the case, consider creating your own using characters found within any symbol fonts installed on your computer. First create a type layer using the symbol of your choosing, then click Layer on the Application bar, point to Type, and click the Convert to Shape command. Use the Define Custom Shape command on the Edit menu to create your own custom shape. The shape you just created now appears at the bottom of the panel containing custom shapes.

Create a shape

1. Click the **Rectangle tool** ⌐ on the Tools panel.

2. Click the **Shape layers button** 🔲 on the options bar.

3. Make sure the Style picker list arrow displays the Default Style (None) ⌐ N⌐.

4. Display the rulers in pixels and display the guides.

5. Verify that the **Mailbox layer** is active.

6. Drag the **Marquee pointer** ╋ from approximately **0 X/510 Y** to **555 X/685 Y** using the guides to draw the rectangle. Compare your Paths panel to Figure 16.

7. Compare your image to Figure 17.

   The shape is added to the image, and the Rectangle tool is still active.

You created a new shape layer, using the Rectangle tool. The new shape was created on its own layer.

FIGURE 16
Path created by shape

FIGURE 17
Shape in image

New shape

Export a path into another program

As a designer, you might find yourself working with other programs, such as Adobe Illustrator, or QuarkXPress. Many of the techniques you have learned, such as working with paths, can be used in all these programs. For example, you can create a path in Photoshop, then export it to another program. Before you can export a path, it must be created and named. To export the path, click File on the Application bar, point to Export, then click Paths to Illustrator (Win) or Write to Illustrator (Mac). The Paths list arrow (Win) or Write list arrow (Mac) in the Export Paths dialog box lets you determine which paths are exported. You can export all paths or one specific path. After you choose the path(s) that you want to export, choose a name and location for the path, then click Save.

FIGURE 18

Additional shape in image

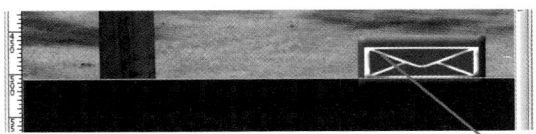

FIGURE 19

Styles added to custom shape   New shape

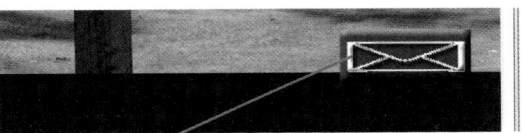

*Custom shape with Drop Shadow
and Bevel and Emboss styles*

FIGURE 20

Style added to shape

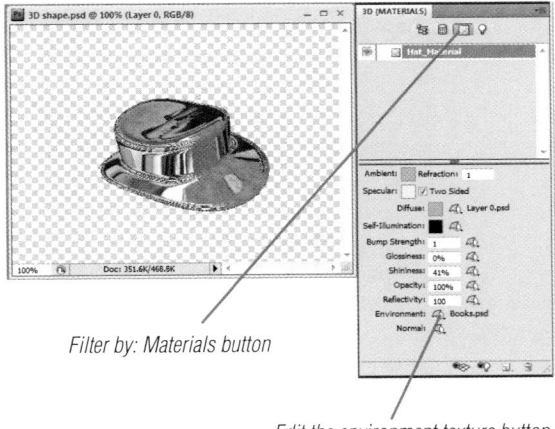

Filter by: Materials button

Edit the environment texture button

Creating realistic 3D shapes

Using the Advanced 3D workspace and your knowledge of shapes, you can create and rotate realistic 3D shapes that show naturalistic reflection. To do this, create an RGB file, then fill the layer with any pattern. Display the Advanced 3D workspace, click the 3D menu on the Application bar, point to New Shape from Layer, then click one of the shapes listed, such as the Hat. The image in the layer (the fill pattern) is wrapped around the 3D shape. Click the 3D Rotate tool in the Tools panel, position the pointer over the shape, then drag the shape to reposition it. Take note of the lifelike shadows and highlights as you reposition the shape. Using the 3D panel, you can treat the contents of a graphics file as a texture and wrap it around a shape, as shown in Figure 20. To do this, click the Filter By: Materials button in the 3D panel, click the Edit the environment texture button, then click Load Texture. Click a file, then click Open. The original layer will automatically be converted into a Smart Object. (You may see a warning box if your video card does not meet the requirements necessary for 3D rendering.)

Create and modify a custom shape

1. Click the **Layers panel tab** LAYERS , then select and make the **Button layer** visible.

2. Click the **Custom Shape tool button** on the options bar.

3. Click the **Click to open Custom Shape picker list arrow** →·, then double-click **Envelope 2** (the first shape from the right in the second row).

4. Drag the **Marquee pointer** + over the flat surface of the button from approximately **390 X/470 Y** to **510 X/505 Y**.

5. Display the **Swatches panel**, click **white swatch** on the Swatches panel, then click **OK** to close the Pick a solid color dialog box. Compare your image to Figure 18.

6. Verify that the **Shape 2 mask thumbnail** on the Layers panel is selected.

7. Click the **Add a layer style button** *fx.* on the Layers panel.

8. Click the **Drop Shadow**, click **Bevel and Emboss**, then click **OK** to accept the current settings.

9. Save your work, turn off the guides and rulers, then compare your image to Figure 19.

You created an additional shape layer, changed the color of the shape, then applied a style to the shape.

SELECTIONS

What You'll Do

In this lesson, you'll convert a selection into a path, then apply a stroke to the path.

Converting a Selection into a Path

You can convert a selection into a path so that you can take advantage of clipping paths and other path features, using a button on the Paths panel. First, create your selection using any technique you prefer, such as the Magic Wand tool, lasso tools, or marquee tools. After the marquee surrounds the selection, press and hold

Customizing print options

Because a monitor is an RGB device and a printer uses the CMYK model to print colors even a well-calibrated monitor will never match the colors of your printer. Therefore, professional printers use standardized color systems such as Pantone or Toyo.

In the course of working with an image, you may need to print a hard copy. In order to get the output you want, you can set options in the Page Setup dialog box. To open this dialog box, click File on the Application bar, then click Page Setup. The relationship of the length to the width of the printed page is called **orientation**. A printed page with the dimensions 8½" W × 11" L is called **portrait orientation**. A printed page with dimensions 11" W × 8 ½" L is called **landscape orientation**.

For additional printing options, click File on the Application bar, click Print, then in the Print dialog box click the Output from the list arrow at the top of the dialog box (that has Color Management as the default selection). Here you can gain increased control over the way your image prints. For example, pages printed for commercial uses might often need to be trimmed after they are printed. The trim guidelines are called **crop marks**. These marks can be printed at the corners, center of each edge, or both. You can select the Corner Crop Marks check box and/or Center Crop Marks check box to print these marks on your image.

[Alt] (Win) or [option] (Mac), then click the Make work path from selection button on the Paths panel, as shown in Figure 21.

Converting a Path into a Selection

You also can convert a path into a selection. You can do this by selecting a path on the Paths panel, then clicking the Load path as a selection button on the Paths panel.

Choosing the Right Method

Are you totally confused about which method to use to make selections? You might have felt equally at sea after learning about all your paint tool choices. Well, as with painting, you need to experiment to find the method that works best for you. As you gain experience with Photoshop techniques, your comfort level—and personal confidence—will grow, and you'll learn which methods are *right for you*.

FIGURE 21
Path created by selection

FIGURE 22
Skewing a layer

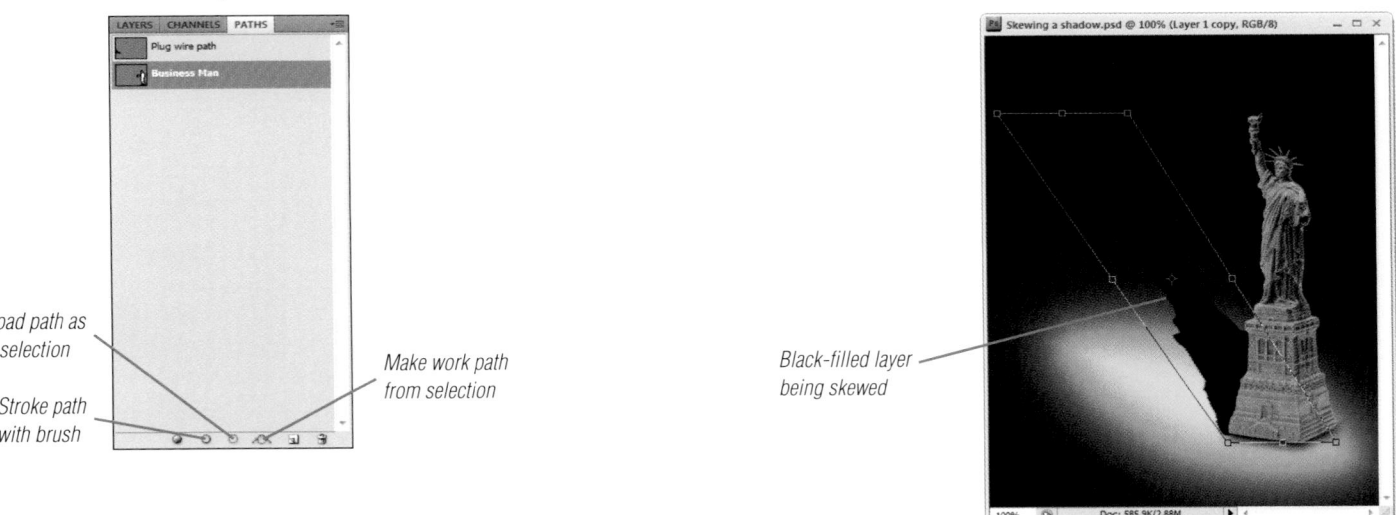

Load path as a selection

Stroke path with brush

Make work path from selection

Black-filled layer being skewed

Using the Transform command to create a shadow

You've already experienced using the Transform command to change the existing shape of an object or type. You can also use this command to simulate a shadow. To do so, you simply duplicate a layer, then fill the copy of the layer with black by changing the background color to black, then press [X] to swap foreground and background colors. Make the black copy the active layer, then use the Transform command to skew the object. Figure 22 shows an example of this technique.

Convert a selection into a path

1. Display the **STAMPS layer** and the **Stamps layer**.

2. Click the **STAMPS layer** on the Layers panel.

3. Click the **Magic Wand tool** ✳ on the Tools panel, and verify that the Contiguous checkbox is selected.

4. Click anywhere in the **burgundy color** behind the word STAMPS.

5. If necessary, click the **Add to selection button** ⊡ on the options bar, click the open area in the **A,** click the open area in the letter **P**, click **Select** on the Application bar, then click **Inverse**. Compare your image to Figure 23.

6. Click the **Paths panel tab** `PATHS`.

7. Press and hold [**Alt**] (Win) or [**option**] (Mac), click the **Make work path from selection button** ◌ on the Paths panel, then release [**Alt**] (Win) or [**option**] (Mac).

   TIP Pressing [Alt] (Win) or [option] (Mac) causes the Make Work Path dialog box to open. You can use this to change the Tolerance setting. If you don't press and hold this key, the current tolerance setting is used.

8. Type **1.0** in the Tolerance text box, then click **OK**.

9. Double-click **Work Path** on the Paths panel.

10. Type **Stamps path** in the Name text box of the Save Path dialog box, then click **OK**. Compare your Paths panel to Figure 24.

You created a selection using the Magic Wand tool, then converted it into a path using the Make work path from selection button on the Paths panel.

FIGURE 23
Selection in image

Selected object

FIGURE 24
Selection converted into path

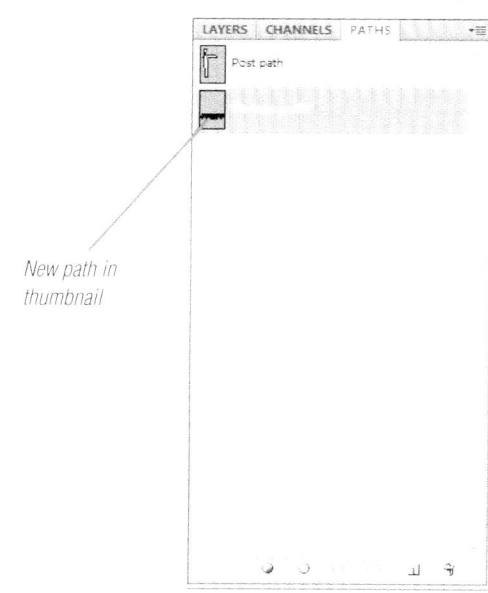

New path in thumbnail

FIGURE 25
Stroked path

New stroked path in thumbnail

FIGURE 27
Completed image

FIGURE 26
Layers panel

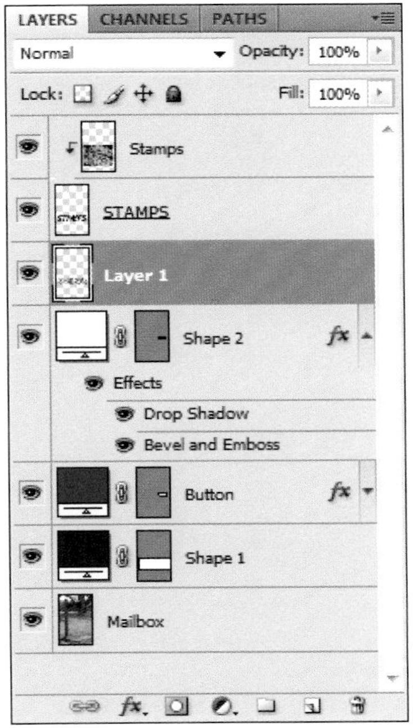

1. Click the **Eyedropper tool** on the Tools panel.

2. Click the **black swatch** on the Swatches panel.

3. Activate the **Shape 2 layer** on the Layers panel, then create a new layer above it.

4. Click the **Stamps path** on the Paths panel, then click **Brush tool** on the Tools panel, and select the **Hard Round 9 pixels brush size** with 100% opacity (if necessary).

   TIP   You can select a path as a *selection* (rather than as a path) by holding [Ctrl] (Win) or ⌘ (Mac) while clicking the name of the path. When you do this, marching ants surround the path, which indicate that it's a *selection*.

5. Click the **Paths list arrow** on the Paths panel, click **Stroke Path**, click the **Tool list arrow** in the Stroke Path dialog box, click **Brush** (if necessary), then click **OK**.

6. Click anywhere on the **Paths panel** to deselect the path, then compare your panel to Figure 25.

7. Click the **Layers panel tab** LAYERS , then compare your Layers panel to Figure 26.

8. Save your work, then compare your image to Figure 27.

9. Close the file and exit Photoshop.

You stroked a path, using a color from the Swatches panel and a command from the Paths list arrow.

Key: Menu items are indicated by ➤ between the menu name and its command. Blue bold letters are shortcuts for selecting tools on the Tools panel.

to do this:	use this method:
Add an anchor point	✒️⁺
Change perspective	Edit ➤ Transform ➤ Perspective
Convert a selection into a path	⌒
Convert a point	⌐
Create a clipping group	Press and hold [Alt] (Win) or option (Mac), position pointer between layers, then click using ◄ 🖤
Create a custom shape	⌒ or [Shift] U
Create a line	＼ or [Shift] U
Create a new shape layer	⎕
Create a new work path	⊠
Create a polygon	⬠ or [Shift] U
Create a rectangle	⌐ or [Shift] U
Create a rounded rectangle	⌐ or [Shift] U
Create an ellipse	◡ or [Shift] U
Delete an anchor point	✒️⁻

to do this:	use this method:
Deselect a path	Click an empty space on Paths panel
Distort a selection	Edit ➤ Transform ➤ Distort
Draw freeform shapes	✒️ or [Shift] P
Draw paths	✒️ or [Shift] P
Draw along the object's edge	Click the Magnetic check box
Export a path	File ➤ Export ➤ Paths to Illustrator
Fill a layer with background color	[Ctrl][Shift][Backspace] (Win) or [shift][⌘][delete] (Mac)
Flip a selection	Edit ➤ Transform ➤ Flip Horizontal or Flip Vertical
Load path as a selection	◌
Repeat last transform command	Edit ➤ Transform ➤ Again or [Shift][Ctrl][T] (Win) or [shift][⌘][T] (Mac)
Rotate a selection	Edit ➤ Transform ➤ Rotate
Scale a selection	Edit ➤ Transform ➤ Scale
Skew a selection	Edit ➤ Transform ➤ Skew
Stroke a path	◌

Using Clipping Masks, Paths, & Shapes

Use a clipping group as a mask.

1. Open PS 11-2.psd from the drive and folder where you store your Data Files, then save it as **Mathematics**. (Substitute a font available on your computer for the Mathematics type layer, if necessary. The font used in the sample is a 72 pt Arial.)
2. Rasterize the Mathematics type layer, then click the Move tool on the Tools panel.
3. Transform the rasterized type layer by distorting it, using Figure 28 as a guide.
4. Drag the Mathematics layer beneath the Symbols layer on the Layers panel.
5. Create a clipping group with the Mathematics and Symbols layers.
6. Apply the Bevel and Emboss style (using the existing settings) to the Mathematics layer.
7. Save your work.

Use pen tools to create and modify a path.

1. Make the Man layer active.
2. Click the Freeform Pen tool on the Tools panel.
3. Click the Paths button and verify that the Magnetic check box is selected.
4. Open the Paths panel.
5. Trace the figure, *not the shadow*.
6. Change the name of the Work Path to **Figure path**.
7. Use the Eyedropper tool on the Tools panel to sample Pure Yellow Green using the Swatches panel.
8. Fill the path with the Foreground Color using 100% opacity.

9. Deselect the Figure path on the Paths panel.
10. Save your work.

Work with shapes.

1. Activate the Layers panel, then make the Megaphone layer active.
2. Use the Eyedropper tool to sample the RGB Red swatch on the Swatches panel.
3. Click the Custom Shape tool on the Tools panel.
4. Click the Shape layers button on the options bar.
5. Open the Custom Shape picker on the options bar, then select the Scissors 2 custom shape.
6. Create the shape from 200 X/50 Y to 330 X/220 Y.
7. Apply a Bevel and Emboss style (using the existing settings) to the Shape 1 layer.
8. Save your work.

Convert paths and selections.

1. Make the Megaphone layer active.
2. Hide the Backdrop, Mathematics, and Shape 1 layers.
3. Use the Magnetic Lasso tool to select the megaphone. (*Hint*: Try using a 0-pixel Feather, a 5-pixel Width, and 10% Edge Contrast.)

4. Display the Paths panel, then make a path from the selection.
5. Change the name of the Work Path to **Megaphone path**.
6. Use the Eyedropper tool to sample the Dark Violet Magenta swatch on the Swatches panel, then fill the megaphone path with this color.
7. Deselect the path, display the Layers panel, then show all layers.
8. Clear the guides, hide the rulers, then adjust the contrast of the Symbols layer to +42.
9. Apply a Radial Blur filter, using the Spin method with Good quality and the Amount = 10, to the Backdrop layer.
10. Apply a 100% Spherize filter (Distort Filter) to the Backdrop layer.
11. Save your work, then compare your image to Figure 28.

FIGURE 28
Completed Skills Review

Using Clipping Masks, Paths, & Shapes

A cable manufacturer wants to improve its lackluster image—especially after a scandal that occurred earlier in the year. The company has hired you to create a dynamic image of one of its bestselling products, which they plan to use in an image advertising campaign. You have been provided with a picture of the product, and your job is to create a more exciting image suitable for print ads.

1. Open PS 11-3.psd, then save it as **Power Plug**.
2. Duplicate the Power Plug layer.
3. Add a type layer (using any font available on your computer) that says Power Plug. (In the sample, a 146.82 pt Cooper font is used.)
4. Rasterize the type layer.
5. Transform the rasterized type layer, using a method of your choosing.
6. Apply any layer styles. (In the sample, a contoured Bevel and Emboss style and Drop Shadow is applied.)
7. Move the rasterized layer below the Power Plug copy layer, then create a clipping mask.
8. Adjust the Saturation of the Power Plug copy layer to +90.

9. Create an adjustment layer that changes the Yellow/Blue Color Balance of the Power Plug copy layer to +65.
10. Create an adjustment layer that changes the Color Balance of the (original) Power Plug layer so that the text is more visible. (In the sample, the color levels of the midtones are −80, +80, −80.)
11. Modify the Opacity of the Power Plug layer to 85%.
12. Save your work, then compare your image to the sample in Figure 29.

FIGURE 29
Sample Project Builder 1

Using Clipping Masks, Paths, & Shapes

The National Initiative to Promote Reading has asked you to come up with a preliminary design for their upcoming season. They have provided you with an initial image you can use, as well as the promise of a fat paycheck if you can finish the project within the day. You can use any additional imagery to complete this task.

1. Open PS 11-4.psd, then save it as **Booklovers**.
2. Locate at least one piece of appropriate artwork—either on your computer, in a royalty-free collection, or from scanned images—that you can use in this image.
3. Use any appropriate methods to select imagery from the artwork.
4. After the selections have been made, copy them into Booklovers.
5. Transform any imagery (if necessary).
6. Use your skills to create at least two paths in the image.
7. Add any special effects to a layer, such as a style or a vignette.
8. Add descriptive type to the image, using the font and wording of your choice. (In the sample, an 80 pt Onyx font is used.) You can rasterize the type and create a mask (if necessary).
9. Make any color adjustments, or add filters, (if necessary).
10. Save your work, then compare your image to the sample in Figure 30.

FIGURE 30
Sample Project Builder 2

Using Clipping Masks, Paths, & Shapes

You can pick up some great design tips and tricks from the Internet. Because you are relatively new to using Photoshop shapes, you decide to see what information you can find about shapes on the Web. Your goal is not only to increase your knowledge of shapes and paths, but to create attractive artwork.

1. Connect to the Internet and use your browser to find information about using paths and shapes in Photoshop. (Make a record of the site you found so you can use it for future reference, if necessary.)
2. Create a new Photoshop image, using the dimensions of your choice, then save it as **Shape Experimentation**.
3. Use paths and shapes to create an attractive image.
4. Create an attractive background, using any of your Photoshop skills.
5. Create at least two paths, using any shapes you want.
6. Add any special effects to the paths.
7. Make any color adjustments, or add filters, (if necessary).
8. If you want, add a type layer, using any fonts available on your computer. (In the sample, an Caslon Pro font of varying size is used.)
9. Save your work, then compare your image to the sample in Figure 31.

FIGURE 31
Sample Design Project

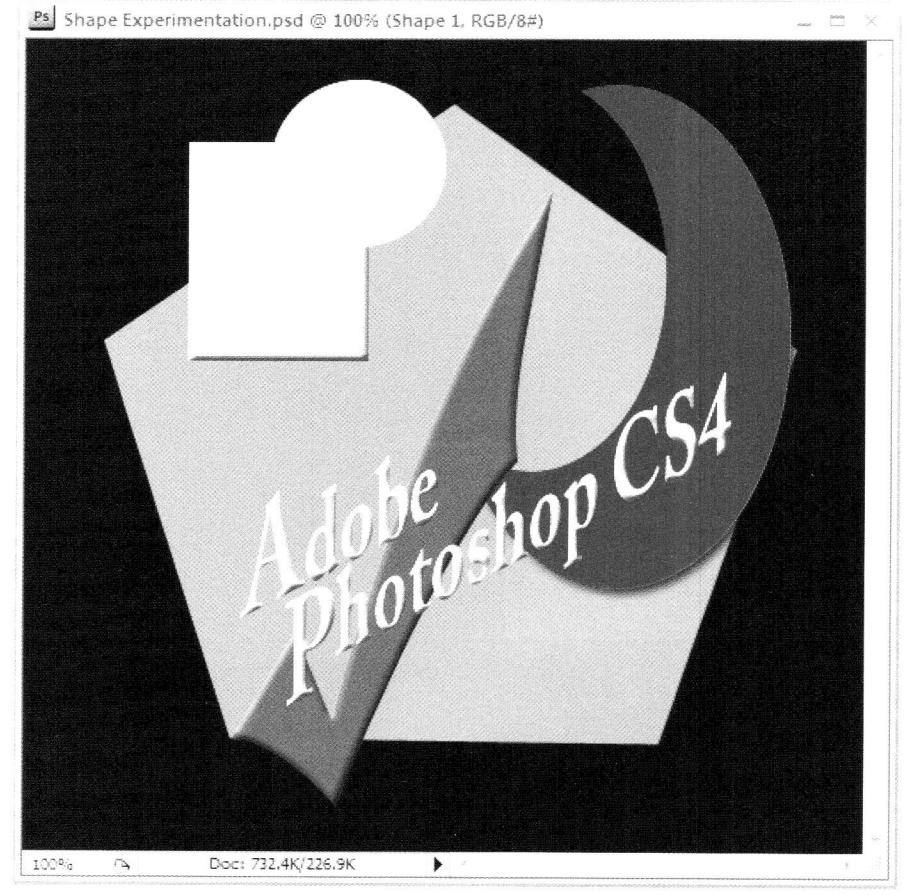

Using Clipping Masks, Paths, & Shapes

A Photoshop design contest, sponsored by a high-powered advertising agency, has you motivated. You have decided to submit the winning entry. Your entry must be completely original, and can use any imagery available to you.

1. Start Photoshop and create an image with any dimensions you want.
2. Save this file as **Contest Winner**.
3. Locate several pieces of artwork—either on your computer, in a royalty-free collection, or from scanned images. Although the images can show anything, remember that you want to show positive imagery so that the judges will select it.
4. Select imagery from the artwork and move it into Contest Winner.
5. Use your knowledge of shapes and paths to create interesting effects.
6. Add text to the image, and use any transform commands to enhance the text.
7. Add any filter effects if you decide they will make your image more dramatic. (In the sample, the Spatter filter was applied to the Computer layer.)
8. Make any color adjustments (if necessary).
9. Add type in any font available on your computer. (A 60 pt Britannic Bold font is shown in the sample. The following styles have been applied: Drop Shadow and Bevel and Emboss.)

10. Save your work, then compare your image to the sample in Figure 32.

FIGURE 32
Sample Portfolio Project

chapter

12

TRANSFORMING
TYPE

1. Modify type using a bounding box

2. Create warped type with a unique shape

3. Screen back type with imagery

4. Create a faded type effect

Working with Type

Type is usually not the primary focus of a Photoshop image, but it can be an important element when conveying a message. You have already learned how to create type and to embellish it using styles, such as the Drop Shadow and the Bevel and Emboss styles, and filters, such as the Twirl and Wind filters. You can further enhance type using techniques such as transforming or warping.

Transforming and Warping Type

When you want to modify text in an image, you can simply select the type layer, select the Horizontal Type tool, then make changes using the options bar. You can also modify type by dragging the handles on the type's bounding box. A **bounding box** (or transform controls box) is a rectangle that surrounds type and contains handles that are used to change the dimensions. Many of the Photoshop features that can be used to modify images can also be used to modify type layers. For example, type can be modified using all the transform commands on the Edit menu except Perspective and Distort. For more stylized type, you can use the Create warped text button to create exciting shapes by changing the dimensions. **Warping** makes it possible to distort type so that it conforms to a shape. Some of the distortions available through the warp feature are Arc, Arch, Bulge, Flag, Fish, and Twist. You do not need to rasterize type to use the warp text feature, so you can edit the type as necessary after you have warped it.

If you want to use the Perspective or Distort commands, or you want to apply a filter to type or create a clipping mask, you must first rasterize the type.

Using Type to Create Special Effects

In addition to adding styles to type, you can also create effects with your type and the imagery within your image. One popular effect is **fading type**, where the type appears to originate in darkness and then gradually gets brighter, or vice versa. You can use the Gradient tool to fade type. The **screening back** effect displays imagery through the layer that contains type. One way to create the screened back effect is to convert a type layer into a shape layer, add a mask, and then adjust the levels of the shape layer. As with graphic objects, adding special effects to type changes the mood, style, and message of the content. You'll probably want to experiment with all your choices to strike just the right note for a particular project.

Tools You'll Use

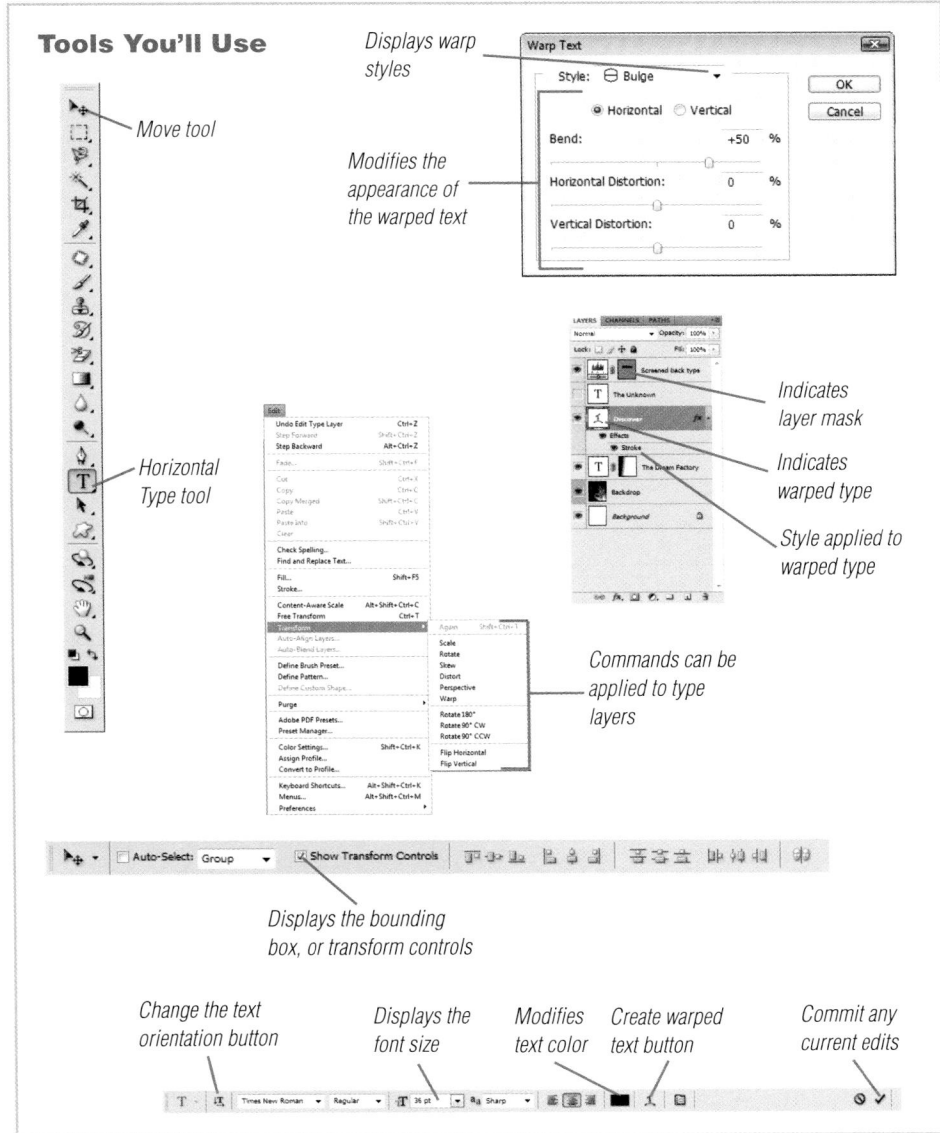

Displays warp styles

Modifies the appearance of the warped text

Move tool

Horizontal Type tool

Indicates layer mask

Indicates warped type

Style applied to warped type

Commands can be applied to type layers

Displays the bounding box, or transform controls

Change the text orientation button

Displays the font size

Modifies text color

Create warped text button

Commit any current edits

In this lesson, you'll change the dimensions of type using a bounding box.

Selecting the Bounding Box

A bounding box, such as the one shown in Figure 1, is a tool you can use to control the size and proportions of existing type. You can display the bounding box by clicking the Move tool on the Tools panel, then selecting the Show Transform Controls check box on the options bar. After the transform controls (also known as the bounding box) feature is turned on, it will appear around type whenever a type layer is selected. As soon as you click a handle on the bounding box, the dotted lines of the box become solid, as shown in Figure 2. At the center of the bounding box (by default) is the **reference point**, the location from which distortions and transformations are measured.

You can resize the bounding box to visually change type size instead of specifying point sizes on the options bar.

FIGURE 1
Bounding box around type

Handle

Bounding box

Reference point

FIGURE 2
Resizing the bounding box

Preparing to resize the bounding box

Outline becomes solid when clicked

Changing the Bounding Box

When the bounding box around type is selected, the options bar displays additional tools for transforming type. Table 1 describes the bounding box options in detail. You can change the size of the bounding box by placing the pointer over a handle. When you do this, the pointer changes to reflect the direction in which you can pull the box. When you resize a bounding box, the type within it reflows to conform to its new shape. As you can see from the table, some of these tools are buttons and some are text boxes.

QUICKTIP

You can use the text boxes on the Transform Controls option bar to make entries or to visually inspect the results of your changes.

TABLE 1: Transform Control Tools

tool	button	use
Reference point location button		The black dot determines the location of the reference point. Change the reference point by clicking any white dot on the button.
Set horizontal position of reference point text box	X: 249.1 px	Allows you to reassign the horizontal location of the reference point.
Use relative positioning for reference point button	△	Determines the point you want used as a reference.
Set vertical position of reference point text box	Y: 194.8 px	Allows you to reassign the vertical location of the reference point.
Set horizontal scale text box	W: 80%	Determines the percentage of left-to-right scaling.
Maintain aspect ratio button		Keeps the current proportions of the contents within the bounding box.
Set vertical scale text box	H: 156.3%	Determines the percentage of top-to-bottom scaling.
Set rotation text box	∠ 0.0 °	Determines the angle the bounding box will be rotated.
Set horizontal skew text box	H: 0.0 °	Determines the angle of horizontal distortion.
Set vertical skew text box	V: 0.0 °	Determines the angle of vertical distortion.
Switch between free transform and warp modes button		Toggles between manual entry of scaling and warp styles.
Cancel transform (Esc) button		Returns to the image without carrying out transformations.
Commit transform (Return) button	✔	Returns to the image after carrying out transformations.

Display a bounding box

1. Open PS 12-1.psd from the drive and folder where you store your Data Files, update the text layers as needed, then save the file as **Happy Hound**.

   > TIP The fonts in this file are various point sizes of Times New Roman and Arial. Please substitute another font if these are not available on your computer.

2. Display the rulers in pixels and display the **Typography workspace**.

3. Click the **Happy Hound layer** on the Layers panel.

4. Click the **Move tool** ⊕ on the Tools panel (if it is not already selected).

5. Click the **Show Transform Controls check box** on the options bar. Compare your image to Figure 3.

   Transform control handles surround the bounding box. When you place the pointer on or near a handle, you can transform the shape of a bounding box. Table 2 describes the pointers you can use to transform a bounding box.

You displayed the bounding box of a text selection to make it easier to adjust the size and shape of the layer contents. Resizing a bounding box is the easiest way to change the appearance of an object or type layer.

FIGURE 3
Displayed bounding box

Selected check box indicates that bounding box is displayed

Move tool selected

Bounding box surrounds active type layer

TABLE 2: Transform Pointers

pointer	use to
↗	Resize bounding box; drag upper-right and lower-left handles.
↖	Resize bounding box; drag upper-left and lower-right handles.
↔	Resize bounding box; drag middle-left and middle-right handles.
↕	Resize bounding box; drag upper-center and lower-center handles.
↰	Rotate bounding box; appears below the lower-right handle.
↱	Rotate bounding box; appears below the lower-left handle.
↲	Rotate bounding box; appears above the upper-right handle.
↳	Rotate bounding box; appears above the upper-left handle.
↺	Rotate bounding box; appears to the left of the middle-left handle.
⤸	Rotate bounding box; appears below the lower-center handle.
▶	Skew type. Press and hold [Ctrl] (Win) or ⌘ (Mac) while dragging a handle.

FIGURE 4
Modified bounding box

Enlarged type and
bounding box

FIGURE 5
Bounding box before modification

Bounding box (and
text it contains takes
up less room)

FIGURE 6
Transform settings

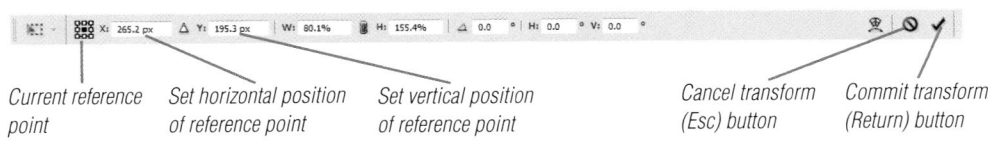

Current reference   Set horizontal position   Set vertical position   Cancel transform   Commit transform
point   of reference point   of reference point   (Esc) button   (Return) button

1. Drag the **top-center handle** ‡ with the Resizing pointer until you see that the Set vertical position of reference point text box (Y:) displays approximately **195 px**. Compare your bounding box to Figure 4.

   TIP   When you begin dragging the resizing handles, the option bar changes to display the bounding box transform tools. You can also type values in these text boxes.

2. Drag the **right-center handle** ↔ until the Set horizontal scale text box (W:) displays approximately **80%**.

3. Compare your bounding box to Figure 5 and your options bar to Figure 6. Your settings might differ.

   TIP   You can use the Transform commands (Rotate, Scale, Skew, Distort, Perspective, and Warp) with any of the resizing pointers to distort a bounding box using an angle other than 90°.

4. Click the **Commit transform (Return) button** ✔ on the options bar.

5. Save your work.

Using the bounding box, you modified the type by scaling disproportionately.

DESIGNTIP   **Thinking out side the (bounding) box**

You're probably used to thinking in terms of font size: 10pt, 12pt, etc. Once you understand how to resize type using the bounding box, you'll realize that the rigid font size you apply from a list arrow is just a starting point. You really can have *any size* font you want!

In this lesson, you'll warp text, then enhance the text with color and a layer style.

Warping Type

Have you ever wondered how designers create those ultra-cool wavy lines of text? They're probably using the Create warped text feature, which gives you unlimited freedom to create unique text shapes. You can distort a type layer beyond the limits of stretching a bounding box by using the Create warped text feature. You can choose from 15 warped text styles. These styles are shown in Figure 7. You can warp type horizontally or vertically.

FIGURE 7
Warp text styles

Default setting — None
Arc
Arc Lower
Arc Upper

Bulge
Shell Lower
Shell Upper

Flag
Wave
Fish
Rise

Fisheye
Inflate
Squeeze
Twist

Adding Panache to Warped Text

After you select a warp text style, you can further modify the type using the Bend, Horizontal Distortion, and Vertical Distortion sliders in the Warp Text dialog box. These settings and what they do are described in Table 3. A sample of warped text is shown in Figure 8. You adjust the warped style by using the sliders shown in Figure 9.

QUICKTIP

You cannot use the Distort and Perspective transform commands on non-rasterized type; however, you can achieve similar results by warping type.

Combining Your Skills

By this time, you've learned that many Photoshop features can be applied to more than one type of Photoshop object. The same is true for warped text. For example, after you warp text, you can apply a style to it, such as the Bevel and Emboss style, or a filter. You can also use the Stroke style to really make the text pop.

FIGURE 8
Sample of warped type

Bounding box surrounds warped type

FIGURE 9
Warp Text dialog box

Current style

Selects a new style

Options are displayed when style other than 'None' is selected

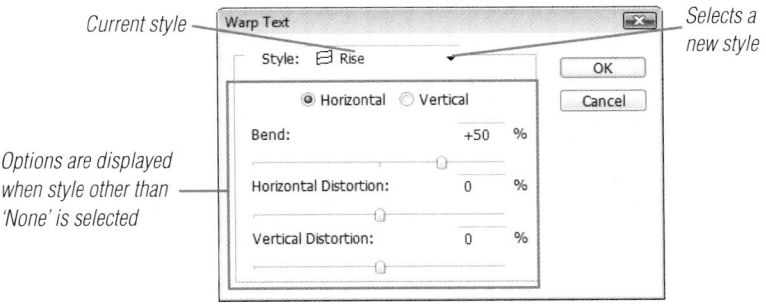

TABLE 3: Warped Type Settings

setting	use
Horizontal	Determines the left-to-right direction of the warp style.
Vertical	Determines the top-to-bottom direction of the warp style.
Bend	Determines which side of the type will be affected.
Horizontal Distortion	Determines if the left or right side of the type will be warped.
Vertical Distortion	Determines if the top or bottom of the type will be warped.

Create warped text

1. Click the **Gourmet Bones Edition layer** on the Layers panel.

2. Zoom into the image until the magnification factor is **100%**.

3. Double-click the **Gourmet Bones Edition layer thumbnail** T on the Layers panel.

4. Click the **Set the font size list arrow** on the options bar, then click **12 pt**.

5. Click the **Create warped text button** on the options bar.

6. Click the **Style list arrow** in the Warp Text dialog box, then click **Arc Upper**.

7. Verify that the **Horizontal option button** is selected.

8. Change the settings for the **Bend**, **Horizontal Distortion**, and **Vertical Distortion text boxes** so that they match those shown in Figure 10.

9. Click **OK** to close the Warp Text dialog box, commit any current edits, then compare your type to Figure 11.

10. Use the **Move tool** on the Tools panel to drag or nudge the type so it is centered over the logo of the bones as shown in Figure 12.

    TIP You can also use the (keyboard) arrow keys to nudge objects when the Move tool is active.

You transformed existing type into a unique shape using the Create warped text button. This feature lets you make type a much more dynamic element in your designs.

FIGURE 10
Warp Text dialog box

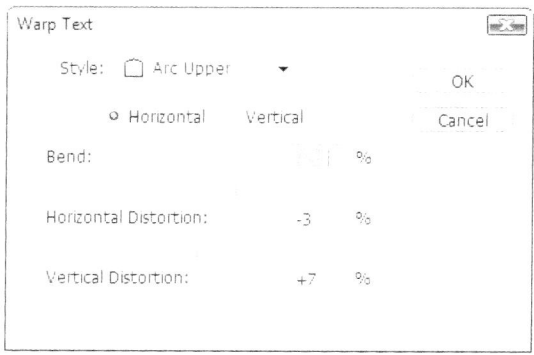

FIGURE 11
Warped type

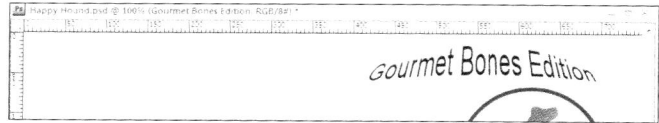

FIGURE 12
Moved type

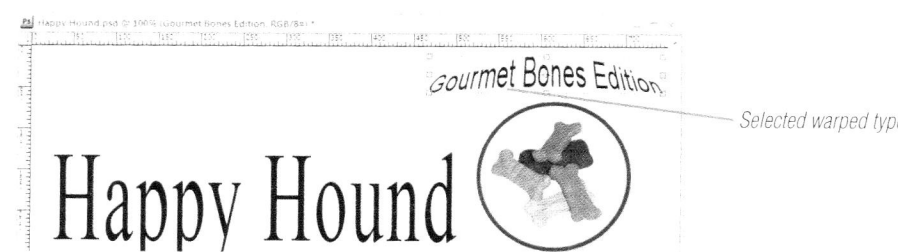

Selected warped type

FIGURE 13
Sampled area

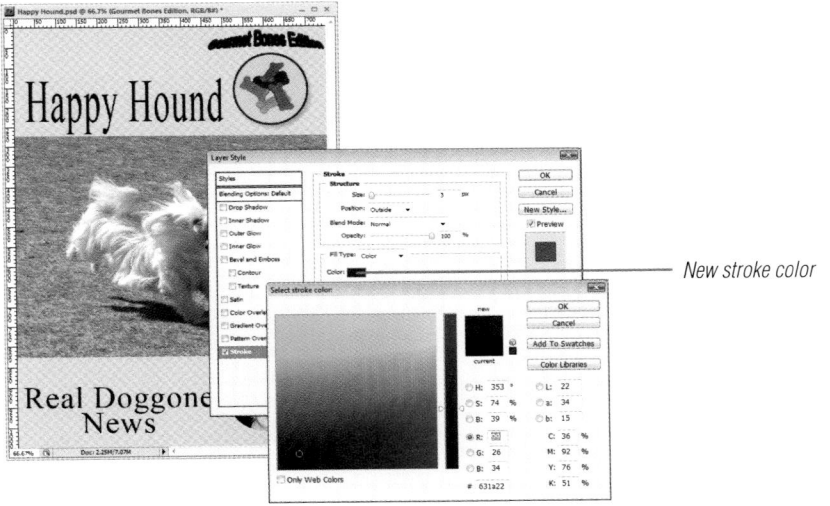

New stroke color

FIGURE 14
New color applied to warped type

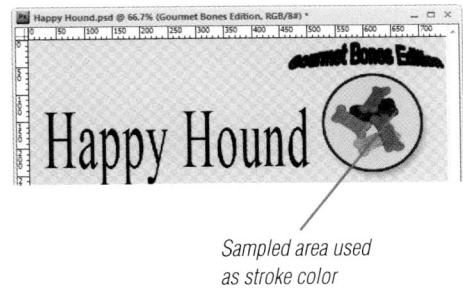

Sampled area used
as stroke color

FIGURE 15
Layers panel

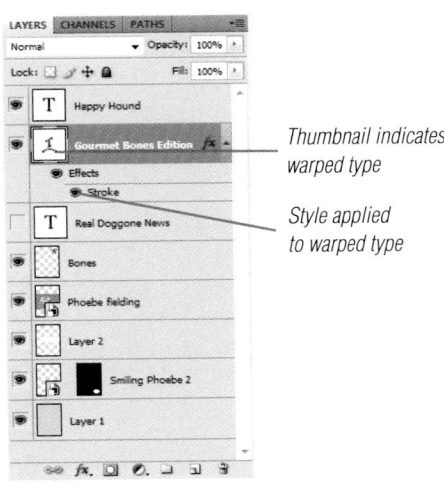

Thumbnail indicates
warped type

Style applied
to warped type

Enhance warped text with effects

1. Zoom out until the magnification level is at **66.7%**.

2. Click the **Add a layer style button** *fx.* on the Layers panel, then move the Layer Style dialog box so the warped type is visible (if necessary).

3. Click **Stroke**.

4. Click the **Set color of stroke button** in the Layer Style dialog box.

5. Verify that the **Only Web Colors check box** is not selected, then click the image anywhere on the **maroon bone** (at approximately **650 X/130 Y**), as shown in Figure 13.

6. Click **OK** to close the Select stroke color dialog box.

7. In the Layer Style dialog box, make sure the Size is set to **3 px** and the Position is set to **Outside**, click **OK**, then turn off the bounding box display (if necessary).

8. Save your work, then compare your image to Figure 14 and the Layers panel to Figure 15.

You added a Stroke style to the warped text and changed the color of the stroke using a color already present in the image.

Lesson 2 Create Warped Type with a Unique Shape

In this lesson, you'll convert type to a shape layer using the Convert to Shape command, then adjust the levels to create a screened back effect.

Screening Type

Using many of the techniques you already know, you can create the illusion that type appears to fade into the imagery below it. This is known as **screening back** or **screening** type. You can create a screened back effect in many ways. One method is to adjust the opacity of a type layer until you can see imagery behind it. Another method is to convert a type layer into a shape layer, which adds a vector mask, then adjust the levels of the shape layer until you achieve the look you desire. A **vector mask** makes a shape's edges appear neat and defined on a layer. As part of this screening back process, the type assumes the shape of its mask. Figure 16 shows a sample of screened back type. Notice that the layer imagery beneath the type layer is visible.

FIGURE 16
Screened back type

Image visible beneath screened back text

Screened back text

Creating the Screened Back Effect

Before converting a type layer, it's a good idea to duplicate the layer. That way, if you are not satisfied with the results, you can easily start from scratch with the original type layer. After the duplicate layer is created, you can convert it into a shape layer, using the Layer menu. After the layer is converted, make sure the original layer is hidden. Using the Levels setting in the Adjustments panel, you can increase or decrease the midtones and shadows levels, as shown in Figure 17, to create different effects in the screened back type.

Adding Finishing Touches

Adding effects to a layer can give your screened back type a more textured or three-dimensional look. For example, you can add the Bevel and Emboss style to a screened back shape layer, as shown in Figure 18. Here, the Bevel and Emboss style serves to accentuate the type. You can also add filter effects such as noise or lighting to make the text look more dramatic.

FIGURE 17
Levels setting in Adjustments panel

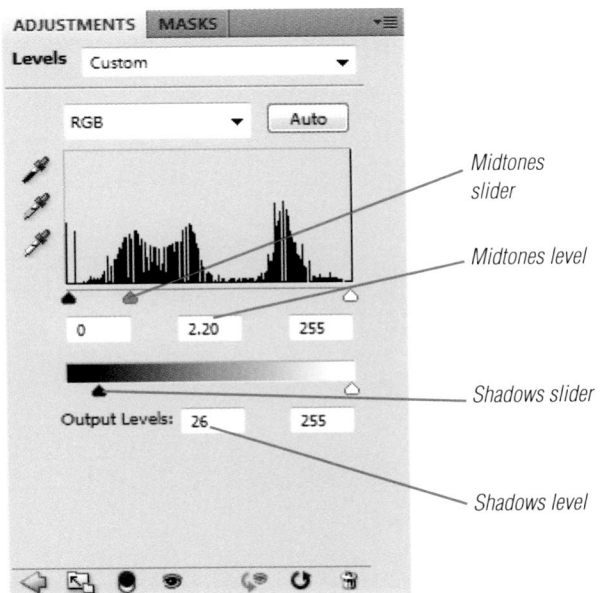

Midtones slider

Midtones level

Shadows slider

Shadows level

FIGURE 18
Screened back type with Bevel and Emboss style

Lesson 3   Screen Back Type with Imagery

Convert a type layer to a shape layer

1. Click the **Real Doggone News layer** on the Layers panel.

2. Click the **Layers panel list arrow** ⋅≡.

3. Click **Duplicate Layer**.

   TIP   When duplicating a layer, you have the option of keeping the duplicate in the current image, placing it in another image that is currently open, or in a new image, by clicking the Document list arrow in the Duplicate Layer dialog box, then clicking another filename or New.

4. Type **Screened back type** in the As text box, then click **OK**.

5. Click the **Indicates layer visibility button** 👁 on the Real Doggone News layer on the Layers panel, then compare your Layers panel to Figure 19.

6. Use the workspace switcher to display the **History and Layers workspace** (created in Chapter 1).

7. Click **Layer** on the Application bar, point to **Type**, then click **Convert to Shape**, as shown in Figure 20.

   The type layer is converted to a shape layer. Figure 21 shows the Layers panel (with the converted type layer state and vector mask thumbnail) and the History panel (with the Convert to Shape state).

In preparation for screening back type, you created a duplicate layer, then hid the original from view. You then converted the duplicate layer into a shape layer.

FIGURE 19
Duplicate layer

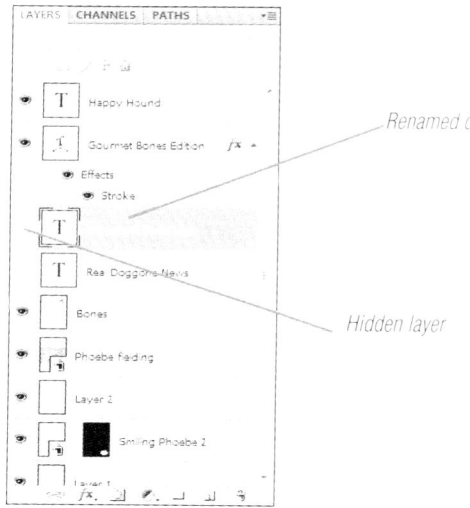

Renamed duplicate layer

Hidden layer

FIGURE 20
Layer menu

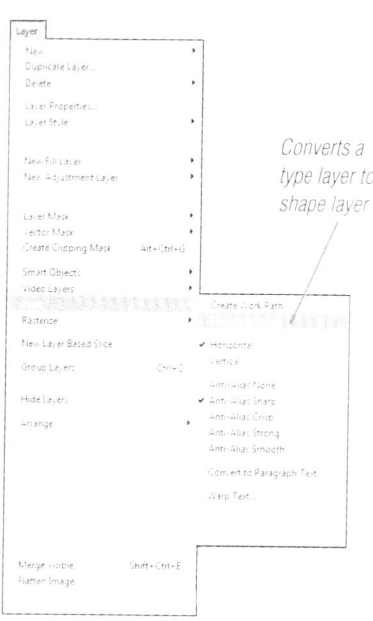

Converts a type layer to a shape layer

FIGURE 21
History and Layers panel

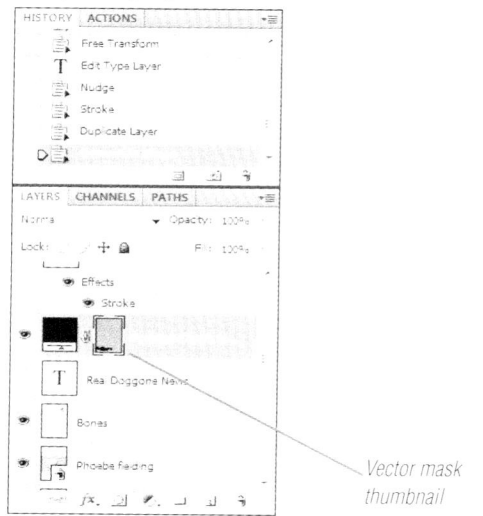

Vector mask thumbnail

FIGURE 22

Levels setting in Adjustments panel

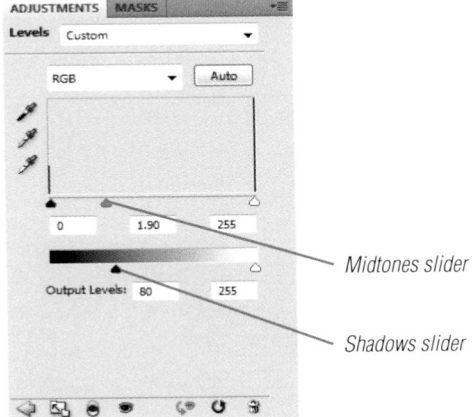

Midtones slider

Shadows slider

FIGURE 23

Screened back type

Screened
back layer

1. Click the **Levels button** 📊 on the Adjustments panel, then click the **This adjustment affects all the layers below (click to clip to layer) button** 🌑.

2. Drag the **Input Levels midtones slider** to the left, until the middle Input Levels text box reads approximately **1.90**.

   The content of the layer is now less transparent.

3. Drag the **Output Levels shadows slider** to the right until the left Output Levels text box reads **80** as shown in Figure 22.

   The content of the layer now looks lighter.

4. Click the **Return to adjustment list button** ◁ on the Adjustments panel.

5. Click **Layer 1** on the Layers panel.

6. Save your work, then compare your image to Figure 23.

7. Display the **Essentials workspace**.

You modified the midtones and shadows levels on the shape layer to make the text less transparent. You adjusted the Output Levels shadows slider to make the pixels that make up the text appear brighter.

Lesson 3 Screen Back Type with Imagery

What You'll Do

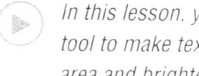 *In this lesson, you'll use the Gradient tool to make text appear faded in one area and brighter in another. You'll also apply a lighting filter.*

Creating a Fade Effect

In addition to being able to change the font, size, color, and shape of your text, you might want to create the illusion that type is fading away in order to add an element of mystery to your masterpiece. You can create this effect using a type layer, a layer mask, and the Gradient tool. You can apply this effect to part of a type layer, if you want the text to look as if it's fading in or out, or to the entire layer.

Type does not have to be rasterized to create the fade effect.

Creating semitransparent type

You can use blending options to create what appears to be semitransparent type. To do this, create a type layer and apply any layer styles you want. The Satin style, for example, can be used to darken the type, and the Pattern Overlay style can be used to create a patterned effect. In the Layer Style dialog box, drag the Set opacity of effect slider to the left and watch the preview until you get the amount of transparency you like. Any background images behind the type will appear as the fill of the type.

Adding Styles to Type

You may have noticed the rather colorful Styles panel included in the Typography workspace as well as the Essentials, Painting, and Web workspaces, although its location varies. You can apply these (preset) styles to any layer, much as you can use the (adjustable) layer styles button on the Layers panel.

FIGURE 24
White chrome type effect

Using the Gradient Tool

Before you can apply the fade effect, you need to create a layer mask for the type layer. You create the layer mask by clicking the Add layer mask button on the Layers panel. Then, you click the Gradient tool on the Tools panel. You can experiment with different types of gradient styles, but to create simple fading type, make sure

Linear Gradient is selected on the options bar, click the Click to open Gradient picker list arrow, then click the Black, White button on the Gradient panel.

Creating white chrome type

By now, you've come to realize that not only can you create cool type by warping and fading it, you can also apply other techniques to create a variety of unique effects. For instance, you can give type the illusion of white chrome, and even add color to the chrome effect. To create this effect, start with black type in a large point size. Add a drop shadow, switch the foreground color to white, then fill the type with the new foreground color by pressing [Alt][Backspace] (Win) or [option][delete] (Mac). Add an Inner Shadow style, then the Satin style (with a low Distance setting). See the top of Figure 24. To add color to the effect (at the bottom of Figure 24), modify the Hue/Saturation setting and the Curves setting.

Create a fade effect

1. Click the **Phoebe fielding layer** on the Layers panel.

2. Click the **Horizontal Type tool** T, on the Tools panel, click above the **dog's tail** at approximately **100 X/360 Y**, set the font to **Arial** or **Arial Black**, the font size to **48 pt**, the alignment to **Left align text**, then type **Times** as shown in Figure 25.

3. Click the **Commit any current edits button** ✓ on the options bar.

4. Click the **Add layer mask button** 🔘 on the Layers panel.

5. Click the **Gradient tool** 🔲 on the Tools panel.

   TIP The Gradient tool might be hidden under the Paint Bucket tool on the Tools panel.

6. Click the **Linear Gradient style** 🔲 on the options bar (if necessary).

7. Click the **Click to open Gradient picker list arrow** on the options bar.

8. Double-click the **Black, White style** (top row, third from left), then adjust the settings on your options bar to match Figure 26.

9. Verify that the **layer mask** is selected, press and hold **[Shift]**, drag the **Gradient pointer** ┼ from the bottom of the Times text letter 'm' halfway up in the letter 'm', then release **[Shift]**. Compare your text to Figure 27.

10. Save your work.

You added a layer mask and a gradient to create a faded type effect.

FIGURE 25
New type in image

New type layer

FIGURE 26
Options for the Gradient tool

Black, White gradient   *Linear Gradient*   *Reverse check box reverses the direction of the fade*

FIGURE 27
Faded text in image

Bottom half of type is faded

FIGURE 28
Styles panel

FIGURE 29
Lighting effect

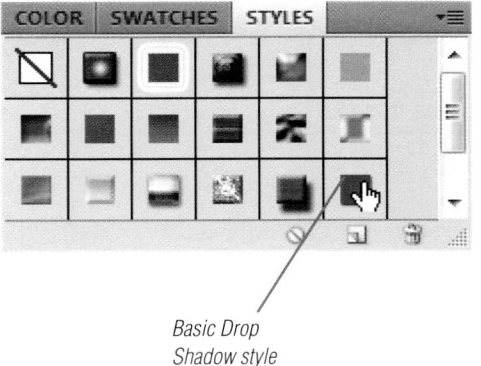

Basic Drop
Shadow style

Apply a style to type

1. Click the **Happy Hound layer** on the Layers panel.

2. Click the **Basic Drop Shadow box** in the Styles panel, as shown in Figure 28.

You applied a preset style to type using the Styles panel.

Add a lighting effect

1. Click the **Smiling Phoebe 2 layer** on the Layers panel.

   Make sure the layer thumbnail is selected, not the mask thumbnail.

2. Click **Filter** on the Application bar, point to **Render**, then click **Lighting Effects**.

3. Make sure that the **Default style** and **Omni Light type** are selected, and that the light source is directly above the dog's left ear (in the black area), then click **OK**.

4. Hide the rulers, save your work, then compare your image to Figure 29.

5. Close the image, then exit Photoshop.

You added a lighting filter to give the image a more polished appearance.

Warping objects

You can warp any rasterized object by clicking Edit on the Application bar, pointing to Transform, then clicking Warp. When you do this, a grid displays around the object. Clicking and dragging any of the points on the grid allows you to transform the shape of the object. Once you have selected this command, the options bar displays the Warp list arrow. You can use a custom shape, in which you drag the handles that surround the object, or you can select a shape from the list to use to warp the object.

Lesson 4   Create a Faded Type Effect

to do this:	use this method:
Adjust color levels	⚎ on Adjustments panel
Change warp type color	Double-click $\mathcal{T}$, click ▉
Commit a transformation	✔
Convert type to a shape	Layer ➤ Type ➤ Convert to Shape
Create faded type	⬛ , ◢ , ◢ , click to open Gradient picker list, then drag pointer over type
Create warped type	Double-click T , click $\mathcal{T}$
Display a bounding box	⊹ or V, select ☐ Show Transform Controls

to do this:	use this method:
Scale a bounding box	Press [Shift] while dragging handle. click ✔
Screen back type	Duplicate layer, hide original layer, convert type to shape, then adjust Levels
Select Gradient tool	◢ or [Shift] G
Skew a bounding box	Press [Ctrl] (Win) or ⌘ (Mac) while dragging handle, ✔
Stroke a type layer	fx. , Stroke, Set color of stroke button
Turn off bounding box display	⊹ or V, deselect ☐ Show Transform Controls

Key: Menu items are indicated by ➤ *between the menu name and its command. Blue bold letters are shortcuts for selecting tools on the Tools panel.*

Modify type using a bounding box.

1. Open PS 12-2.psd, update the text layers (if necessary), then save it as **Charge Card**.
2. Substitute a font available on your computer (if necessary). (*Hint*: The fonts used in the sample are a 36 pt and 48 pt Courier New.)
3. Display the rulers in pixels and make sure the guides are showing.
4. Select the Move tool (if it is not already selected), and make sure that the Show Transform Controls check box is selected.
5. Make the Ace Shopper layer active, drag the bounding box to the left so that the left edge of the A is just to the left of the guide at 155 X, then drag the top-middle handle of the bounding box to 290 Y.
6. Use the Transform command on the Edit menu to skew the text by dragging the upper-right handle of the bounding box to 420 X.
7. Commit the transformations, then save your work.

Create warped type with a unique shape.

1. Double-click the layer thumbnail on the Photoshop type layer on the Layers panel.
2. Change the font size to 72 pt.
3. Commit the transformation, then drag the type's bounding box so that the bottom-left corner is at 135 X/150 Y. (*Hint*: this may take more than one step to complete.)
4. Open the Warp Text dialog box.
5. Change the Warp Text style to Arch.

6. Click the Horizontal option button (if it is not already selected).
7. Change the Bend setting to +42, the Horizontal Distortion setting to +42, and the Vertical Distortion setting to 0, then close the Warp Text dialog box.
8. Move the type so that the bottom-right corner of the bounding box is at 545 X/150 Y.
9. Change the type color using the Swatches panel (Dark Violet Magenta).
10. Apply the default Drop Shadow and Bevel and Emboss styles to the Photoshop type layer, then save your work.

Screen back type with imagery.

1. Make the CHARGE layer active.
2. Increase the font size to 80 pt.
3. Move the CHARGE layer so the bottom-left corner is at 90 X/275 Y.
4. Duplicate this layer, calling the new layer **Screened back type**.
5. Hide the CHARGE layer.

FIGURE 30
Completed Skills Review

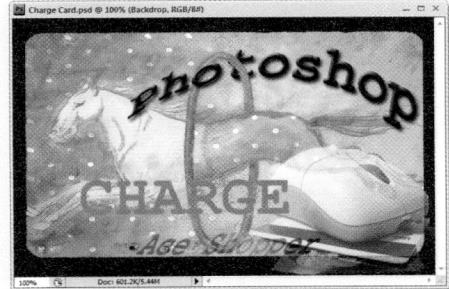

6. Convert the Screened back type layer to a shape layer.
7. Add a (clipped) Levels Adjustment layer that modifies the Midtones Input level to 0.45 and the Output levels shadow slider to 136, then close the Adjustment layer.
8. Make the Backdrop layer active, then use the Sponge tool to saturate the part of the image that is behind the text CHARGE.
9. Save your work.

Create a faded type effect.

1. Make the Ace Shopper layer active, then add a mask to this layer.
2. Select the Gradient tool, set the opacity to 70%, select the Linear Gradient style, then select Black, White on the Gradient picker.
3. Drag a straight line the length of the text, starting at approximately 155 X/315 Y and ending at the right edge of the image.
4. Clear the guides, then hide the rulers.
5. Add the Add Noise filter with a 50% Uniform Distribution to the Background layer.
6. Save your work, then compare your image to Figure 30.

You have been asked to create cover art for a new pop-psychology book entitled *Dueling Personalities: Outer Struggles*. The author has created some initial artwork that she wants on the cover. You can use any of your Photoshop skills to enhance this image, but you particularly want to transform the type to convey the mood and theme of the book.

1. Open PS 12-3.psd, then save it as **Dueling Personalities**.
2. Create two type layers: **Dueling Personalities** and **Outer Struggles**. (*Hint*: You can use any font available on your computer. In the sample, a 72 pt and 60 pt Trebuchet MS font is shown.)
3. Position the type layers appropriately.
4. Make sure the Show Transform Controls check box is selected.
5. Warp the Dueling Personalities type, using the Rise style and the settings of your choice in the Warp Text dialog box.
6. Use the bounding box to enlarge the warped text.
7. Duplicate the Outer Struggles type layer, choosing a suitable name for the duplicate layer.
8. Convert the copied layer to a shape, then change the levels using the settings of your choice. (In the sample, the Midtones input level is 2.26, and the Output shadows level is 20.)
9. Hide the original type layer.

10. Add a new type layer using the text and font of your choice in an appropriate location on the image.
11. Use the bounding box to scale the type layer to a smaller size.
12. Create a mask on this new layer.
13. Use the Gradient tool and the new type layer to create a fade effect.

FIGURE 31
Sample Project Builder 1

14. Change any font colors, and add any enhancing effects to the type layers.
15. Add any filter effects or color adjustments that you determine are necessary to complete the image. (In the sample, the Brightness is adjusted to −15, and the Contrast is adjusted to +15 using an Adjustment Layer.)
16. Save your work, then compare your image to the sample in Figure 31.

You work for Creativity, a graphic design firm that works almost exclusively with the high-tech business sector. As the newest member of the creative team, you have been assigned the design of the cover for the upcoming Annual Report. You have seen the Annual Reports for previous years, and they always feature dramatic, exciting designs. You have already started on the initial design, but need to complete the project.

1. Open PS 12-4.psd, then save it as **Creativity**.
2. Create a new layer containing just the dice. (*Hint*: You can duplicate the Backdrop layer, then use any of your Photoshop skills to isolate the dice in their own layer. Possible alternatives include creating a mask or erasing pixels.)
3. Modify the Backdrop layer so that only the pattern is displayed.
4. Create type layers for text appropriate for an annual report. (*Hint*: You can use any font available on your computer. In the sample, a Georgia font is shown.)
5. Position the type layers appropriately.
6. Warp at least one of the type layers, using the style and settings of your choice. (*Hint*: In the sample, the Bulge style was used.)
7. Enlarge or skew at least one type layer.
8. Create a screened back effect using one of the type layers and the settings of your choice. (In the sample, the Midtones input level is 2.26, and the Output shadows level is 20.)

9. Create a fade effect using one of the type layers.
10. Change any font colors (if necessary), then add any enhancing effects to the type layers.
11. Add any filter effects or color adjustments (using the existing and newly created and modified layers) that you determine are necessary. In the sample, the Brightness is adjusted to

+25, and the Contrast is adjusted to +10. The area underneath the dice in the Backdrop layer was saturated using the Sponge tool, and the default Lighting Effects filter was applied to the Backdrop layer.
12. Save your work, then compare your image to the sample in Figure 32.

FIGURE 32
Sample Project Builder 2

You have been asked to design an advertisement for your favorite television station. Before you begin, you decide to see what information you can find about type enhancements on the Internet. You intend to use the information you find to improve your skills and create a dramatic image. Be prepared to discuss the design elements used in this project. (*Hint*: If you don't have a favorite television station, invent call letters that you can use in this exercise.)

1. Connect to the Internet and use your browser to find information about transforming type in Photoshop. (Make a record of the site you found so you can use it for future reference, if necessary.)
2. Create a new Photoshop image, using the dimensions of your choice, then save it as **Television Station Ad**.
3. Create a type layer, using any color for the layer, any font available on your computer, and any text you want. (In the sample, an Onyx font is used.)
4. Create a warped type effect, using any style and settings of your choice. (In the sample, the Arc style is used.)
5. Create an attractive background, using any of your Photoshop skills or any imagery available to you. You can use scanned or digital camera images, purchased imagery,

or any images available on your computer.
6. Create any necessary additional type layers.
7. Resize any fonts, if necessary, using the bounding box.
8. Add any special effects to the type layers.

FIGURE 33
Sample Design Project

9. If necessary, make color adjustments or add filters.
10. Save your work, then compare your image to the sample in Figure 33.

You are a member of a fan club devoted to your favorite musical group. The fan club is holding a contest to choose a cover design for the band's new CD. You decide to put your expert Photoshop skills to work on this project. After the design is complete, take time to consider what you did, why you did it, and how your efforts contributed to the overall design of the image.

1. Create a Photoshop image using the dimensions of your choice, then save it as **CD Cover Artwork**.
2. Locate several pieces of artwork—either on your computer, in a royalty-free collection, or from scanned images. Although the images can show anything, you want to show positive imagery in keeping with the band's message.
3. Select imagery from the artwork and move it into CD Cover Artwork.
4. Create a warped type effect using any style and settings of your choice. (In the sample, the Viner Hand ITC font is used.)
5. Create any necessary additional type layers.
6. Resize any fonts, if necessary, using the bounding box.
7. Add any special effects to the type layers.
8. If necessary, make color adjustments or add filters.
9. Use at least one of the transformation skills you learned in this chapter to enhance the text.
10. Add any filter effects, if you decide they will make your image more dramatic. (In the sample, the Wind filter is applied to a layer.)

11. Make any color adjustments you feel would improve the look of the image.
12. Save your work, then compare your image to the sample in Figure 34.

FIGURE 34
Sample Portfolio Project

Transforming Type

LIQUIFYING
AN IMAGE

1. Use the Liquify tools to distort an image

2. Learn how to freeze and thaw areas

3. Use the mesh feature as you distort an image

13 LIQUIFYING
AN IMAGE

Distorting Images

If you want to have some fun with an image, try your hand at the Liquify feature. Like the Smudge tool and the distort filters, you can use it to distort an image. But unlike those tools, the Liquify feature gives you much more control over the finished product. This feature contains ten distinct tools that you can use to create distortion effects.

Using the Liquify Feature

The Liquify feature lets you make an image look as if parts of it have melted. You can apply the eight Liquify distortions with a brush, and like other brush-based Photoshop tools, you can modify both the brush size and pressure to give you just

the effect you want. You can use the two non-distortion Liquify tools to freeze and thaw areas within the image. Freezing protects an area from editing and possible editing errors, whereas thawing a frozen area allows it to be edited. With these two tools, you can protect specific areas from Liquify distortions, and can determine with great accuracy which areas are affected.

Using Common Sense

Because the effects of the Liquify feature are so dramatic, you should take the proper precautions to preserve your original work. You can work on a copy of the original image, or create duplicate layers to ensure that you can always get back to your starting point.

Tools You'll Use

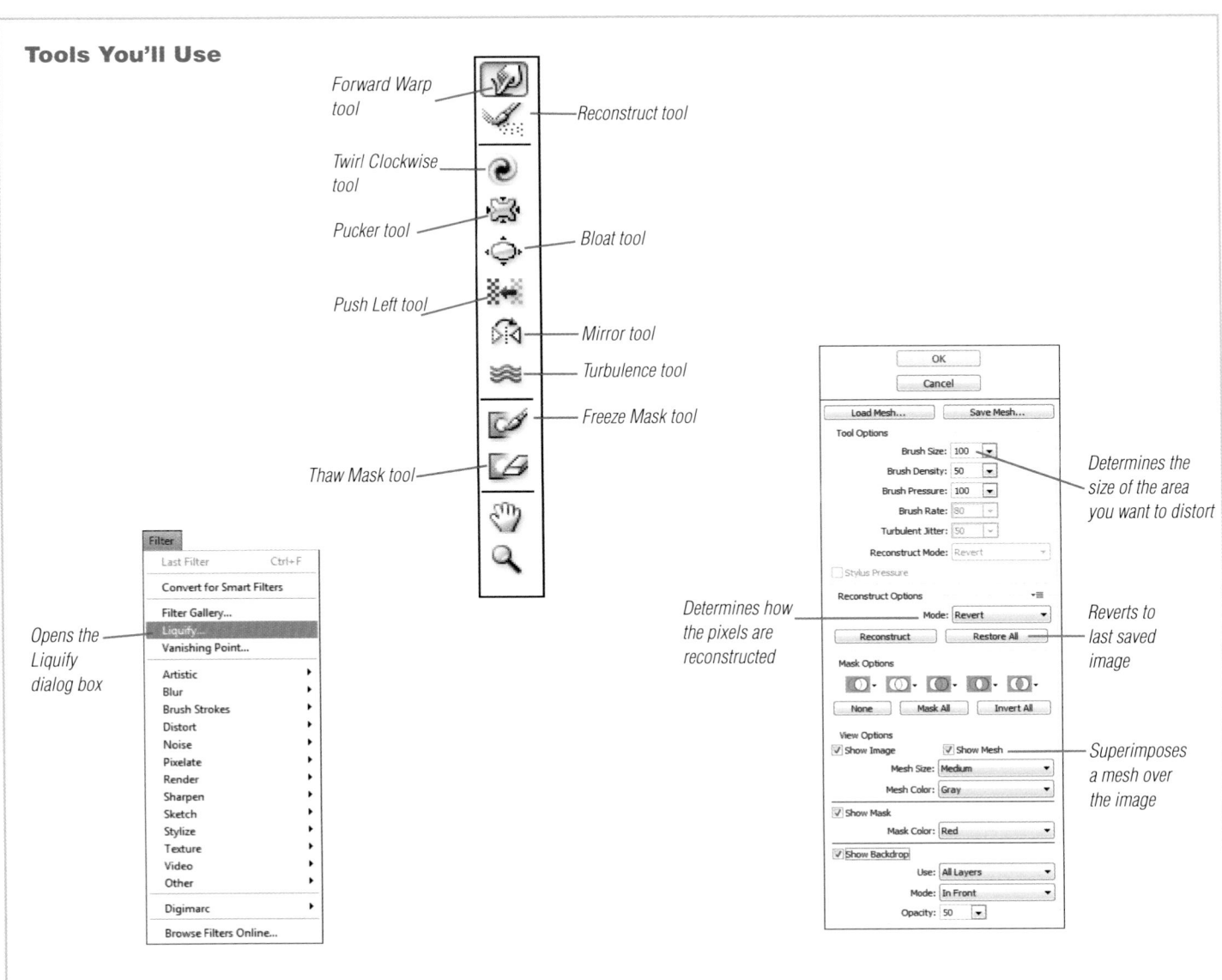

Forward Warp tool

Reconstruct tool

Twirl Clockwise tool

Pucker tool

Bloat tool

Push Left tool

Mirror tool

Turbulence tool

Freeze Mask tool

Thaw Mask tool

Filter

Last Filter	Ctrl+F
Convert for Smart Filters	
Filter Gallery...	
Liquify...	
Vanishing Point...	
Artistic	▶
Blur	▶
Brush Strokes	▶
Distort	▶
Noise	▶
Pixelate	▶
Render	▶
Sharpen	▶
Sketch	▶
Stylize	▶
Texture	▶
Video	▶
Other	▶
Digimarc	▶
Browse Filters Online...	

Opens the Liquify dialog box

OK

Cancel

Load Mesh...   Save Mesh...

Tool Options

Brush Size: 100
Brush Density: 50
Brush Pressure: 100
Brush Rate: 80
Turbulent Jitter: 50
Reconstruct Mode: Revert

Stylus Pressure

Determines the size of the area you want to distort

Reconstruct Options

Mode: Revert

Reconstruct   Restore All

Determines how the pixels are reconstructed

Reverts to last saved image

Mask Options

None   Mask All   Invert All

View Options

☑ Show Image   ☑ Show Mesh

Mesh Size: Medium
Mesh Color: Gray

Superimposes a mesh over the image

☑ Show Mask

Mask Color: Red

☑ Show Backdrop

Use: All Layers
Mode: In Front
Opacity: 50

USE THE LIQUIFY TOOLS
TO DISTORT AN IMAGE

What You'll Do

▶ *In this lesson, you'll use the Forward Warp tool in the Liquify dialog box to create distortions.*

Using the Liquify Dialog Box

With the **Liquify feature**, you can apply distortions to any rasterized layer. When you use the Liquify command, the contents of the active layer appear in a large preview window in the Liquify dialog box. The distortion tools—used to apply the Liquify effects—are displayed on the left side of the dialog box; the tool settings are displayed on the right side. Unlike other tools that you use in the image window, you can only access the Liquify tools from the Liquify dialog box. (The Liquify feature is similar to the Vanishing Point feature in this respect.) In this dialog box, you can create eight different types of distortions.

> **QUICK**TIP
>
> As you apply distortions, the effects are immediately visible in the preview window of the Liquify dialog box.

Exploring the Possibilities

Compare Figures 1 (the original image) and 2 (the distorted image). As you can see from the altered image, you can use this feature to make drastic changes in an image. The following Liquify tools were used for the distorted image:

- The Twirl Clockwise tool was used repeatedly on the top book.
- The Pucker tool was used on the third book eight times. (The Pucker tool pulls the pixels toward the center of the brush tip.)
- The Bloat tool was used repeatedly on the second book. (The Bloat tool pushes pixels away from the center of the brush tip, which can create a more subtle effect.)

You can use distortions to create wild effects or to make subtle mood changes within an image. You can also use the Liquify tools to endow a person with instant weight gain—or weight loss!

Going Wild with Distortions

Of course, you can create wild, crazy distortions using the Liquify feature, and it is a lot of fun. As you can see from Figure 2, you can create some rather bizarre effects using these tools, but you can also use the distortion tools very conservatively to just correct a flaw or tweak an image.

FIGURE 1
Undistorted image in Liquify dialog box

Twirl Clockwise tool
Pucker tool
Bloat tool

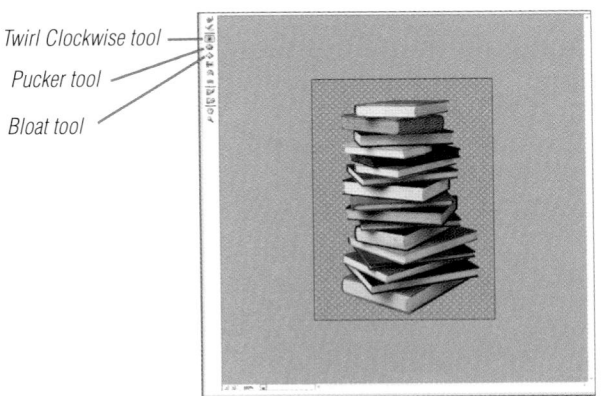

FIGURE 2
Distortion samples

Effect of the Twirl Clockwise tool
Effect of the Pucker tool
Effect of Bloat tool

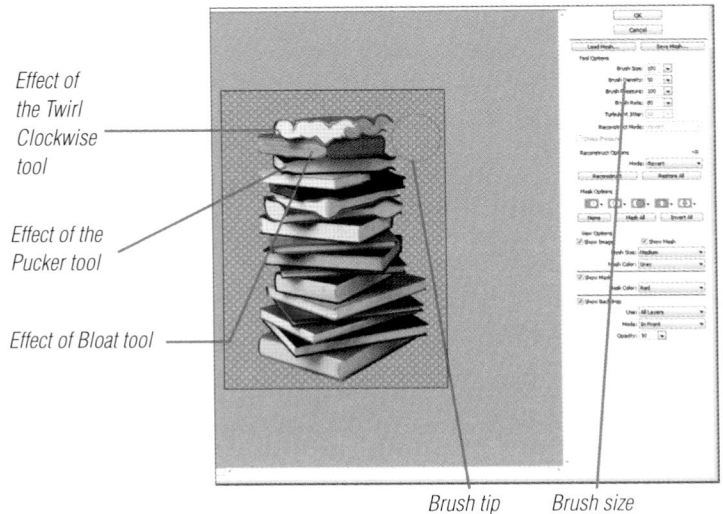

Brush tip   Brush size

Open the Liquify dialog box and modify the brush size

1. Open PS 13-1.psd from the drive and folder where you store your Data Files, then save the file as **Las Vegas**.

2. Click **Filter** on the Application bar, then click **Liquify**.

3. Click the **Zoom tool** 🔍 in the Liquify dialog box, then click the center of the image.

4. Make sure the following check boxes are *not* selected: **Show Mesh**, **Show Mask**, and **Show Backdrop**.

5. Click the **Forward Warp tool** 〰️ in the Liquify dialog box.

   The Liquify tools are described in Table 1.

6. Double-click the **Brush Size text box**, type **125**, then press **[Enter]** (Win) or **[return]** (Mac).

   TIP You can adjust the brush size by typing a value between 1 and 600 in the text box, pressing **[[]** to decrease by 2 or **[]]** to increase by 2, or by clicking the Brush Size list arrow, then dragging the slider to a new value.

7. Adjust your settings in the Liquify dialog box so that they match those shown in Figure 3.

   TIP The Stylus Pressure check box option will appear dimmed if you do not have a graphics tablet attached to your computer.

You opened the Liquify dialog box, then chose the Forward Warp tool and a brush size.

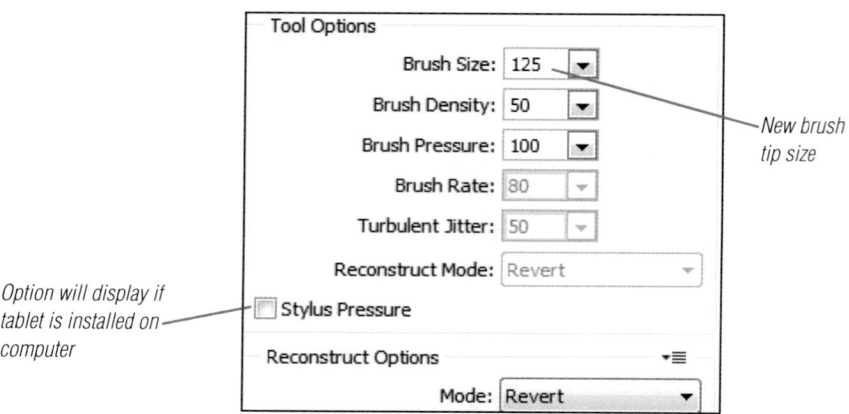

FIGURE 3
Choosing a brush size

New brush tip size

Option will display if tablet is installed on computer

TABLE 1: Liquify Tools

tool	button	use
Forward Warp tool	〰️	Pushes pixels forward during dragging.
Reconstruct tool	✎	Unpaints recently distorted pixels completely or partially.
Twirl Clockwise tool	◉	Rotates pixels clockwise during dragging. (Hold [Alt] to twirl counter-clockwise.)
Pucker tool	▩	Moves pixels toward the center of the active brush tip.
Bloat tool	◇	Moves pixels away from the center of the active brush tip.
Push Left tool	▓	Moves pixels perpendicular to the brush stroke.
Mirror tool	▩	Copies pixels to the brush area.
Turbulence tool	≈	Randomly scrambles pixels.
Freeze Mask tool	✎	Protects an area from distortion.
Thaw Mask tool	✎	Makes a frozen area available for distortions.

FIGURE 4
Positioned pointer

Forward Warp
tool brush
tip pointer

FIGURE 5
Enlarged globe

Enlarged globe is
distorted

FIGURE 6
Effect of Forward Warp tool

Your results will be different

Lesson 1   Use the Liquify Tools to Distort an Image

Use the Forward Warp tool

1. Position the **Forward Warp tool pointer** ⊕ over the gold circle in the Paris balloon, as shown in Figure 4.

   TIP   Your results may vary slightly from those shown in the figures in this book.

2. Drag the **gold circle** up so it stretches the top of the globe, as shown in Figure 5.

   TIP   You can return an image to its previous appearance by clicking Restore All in the Reconstruction Options section of the Liquify dialog box. The Reconstruct button undoes each action of the brush, much like the Undo command or History panel.

3. Use the **Forward Warp tool pointer** ⊕ in different locations of the **gold circle** to create an enlarged balloon effect.

4. Click **OK** to close the Liquify dialog box.

5. Save your work, then compare your image to Figure 6.

You used the Forward Warp tool to distort the pixels of the balloon in an image. By dragging, you pushed the pixels forward, giving the balloon a larger, distorted appearance.

LEARN HOW TO FREEZE
AND THAW AREAS

What You'll Do

In this lesson, you'll freeze an area of an image, make distortions, then thaw the areas so that they can be edited.

Controlling Distortion Areas

Like storing food in the freezer to protect it from spoiling, you can **freeze** areas within an image so that the Liquify tools leave them unaffected. Using the Liquify dialog box, you can protect areas within an image, then **thaw** them—or return them to a state that can be edited—and make necessary distortions. You control which areas are distorted by using the Freeze Mask and Thaw Mask tools in the Liquify dialog box.

Freezing Image Areas

You can selectively freeze areas by painting them with a pointer. The View Options section in the Liquify dialog box lets you display frozen areas in the preview window. By default, frozen areas are painted in red, but you can change this color to make it more visible. For example, Figure 7 shows an image that has not yet been distorted. If you froze areas of this image using the default red color, they would not be visible because of the colors in this image.

QUICKTIP
To isolate the exact areas you want to freeze, try painting a larger area, then using the Thaw Mask tool to eliminate unwanted frozen areas.

Reconstructing Distortions

No matter how careful you are, you will most likely either create a distortion you don't like, or need to do some sort of damage control. Unlike typical Photoshop states, individual distortions you make using the Liquify feature do not appear on the History panel, and therefore cannot be undone. You can, however, use the History panel to delete the effects of an entire **Liquify session**. When you delete a Liquify state from the History panel, your image is restored to its original condition. In order to correct or delete the effects of a liquify tool during a Liquify session you need to use a reconstruction method. However, how distortions are reconstructed is determined by the mode used. If you want to reconstruct, you can do so by using one of five different reconstruction modes in the Liquify dialog box. Each mode affects the way pixels are

Liquifying an Image

reconstructed, relative to frozen areas in the image. This allows you to redo the changes in new and innovative ways.

Undergoing Reconstruction

Figure 8 shows several reconstructed areas as well as a frozen area painted in blue.

Using the Reconstruct tool and the Stiff mode, the tail feathers of the chicken were restored to their original condition. The Rigid mode was used on the feet, and the beak was reconstructed using the Loose mode. You can use several methods to reconstruct an image:

- Click Restore All in the Liquify dialog box.
- Choose the Revert mode, then click Reconstruct in the Liquify dialog box.

- Click the Reconstruct tool, choose the Revert mode, then drag the brush over distorted areas in the Liquify dialog box.
- Click the Cancel button in the Liquify dialog box.
- Make distortions in the Liquify dialog box, then drag the Liquify state to the Delete current state button on the History panel.

FIGURE 7
Original image

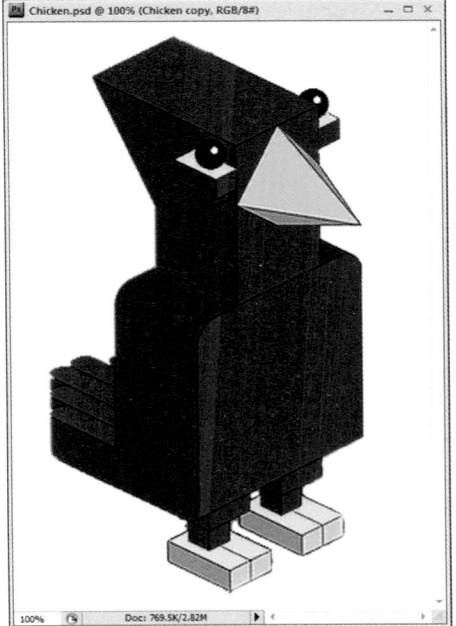

FIGURE 8
Frozen areas and distortions in preview window

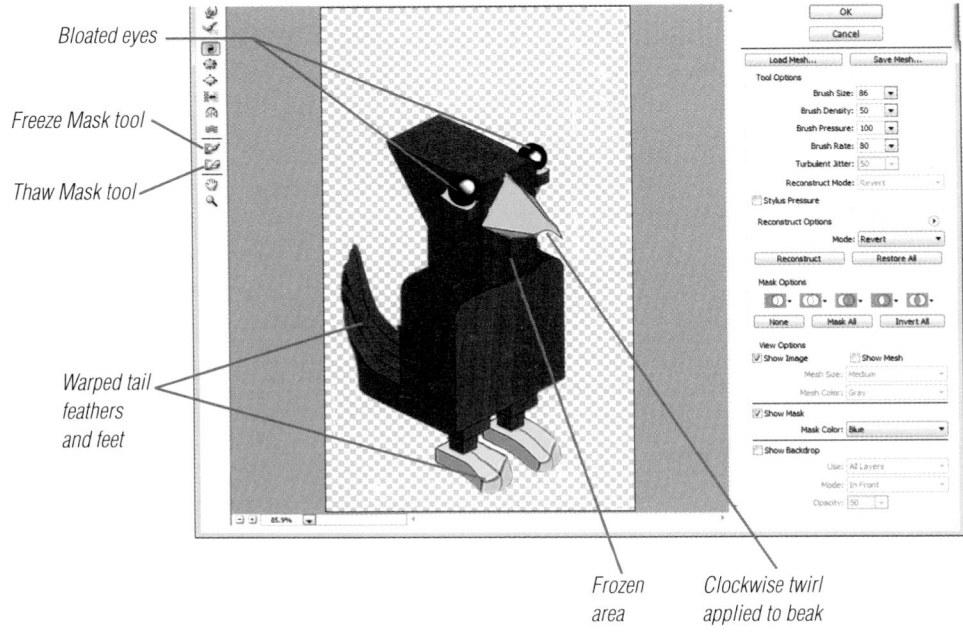

Bloated eyes

Freeze Mask tool

Thaw Mask tool

Warped tail feathers and feet

Frozen area

Clockwise twirl applied to beak

Freeze areas in an image

1. Click **Filter** on the Application bar, then click **Liquify**.

2. Use the **Zoom tool** 🔍 in the Liquify dialog box to magnify the image.

   > TIP Use the Zoom tool in the Liquify dialog box as needed to increase the size of objects you're working on. Use the Hand tool to reposition objects for better visibility.

3. Click the **Freeze Mask tool** in the Liquify dialog box.

4. Double-click the **Brush Size text box**, type **20**, then press **[Enter]** (Win) or **[return]** (Mac).

5. Click the **Show Mask check box**, click the **Mask Color list arrow**, then click **Red** (if it is not already selected). Compare your Liquify dialog box settings to Figure 9 and make any necessary adjustments.

6. Drag the **Freeze pointer** ⊕ around the perimeter of the top of the Eiffel Tower, using Figure 10 as a guide. (Don't worry if your results differ.)

   Table 2 describes the reconstruction modes available in the Liquify dialog box.

   You modified Liquify settings, then froze an area within the image by using the Freeze Mask tool. Freezing the areas protects them from any Liquify effects you apply going forward.

FIGURE 9
Liquify settings

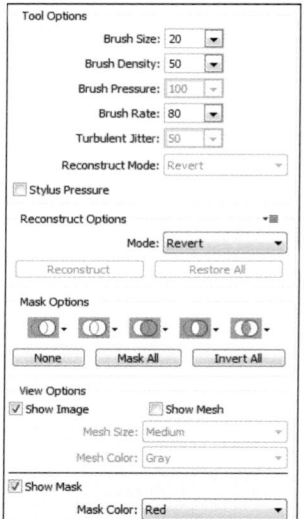

FIGURE 10
Frozen area

Red area is frozen

TABLE 2: Reconstruction Modes

mode	use
Revert	Changes areas back to their appearance before the dialog box was opened.
Rigid	Maintains right angles in the pixel grid during reconstruction.
Stiff	Provides continuity between frozen and unfrozen areas during reconstruction.
Smooth	Smoothes continuous distortions over frozen areas during reconstruction.
Loose	Smoothes continuous distortions similar to the Smooth mode but provides greater continuity between distortions in frozen and unfrozen areas.

FIGURE 11
Distortions in image

Distortion
applied to spire

FIGURE 12
Distortions applied

Mail truck is
reduced

FIGURE 13
History panel

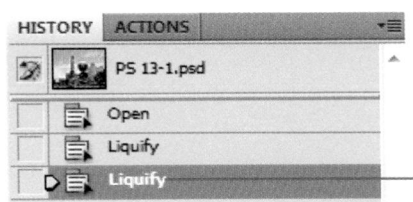

State indicates most
recent distortions

Distort unprotected areas of an image

1. Click the **Pucker tool** in the Liquify dialog box.
2. Change the brush size to **100**.
3. Position the center of the **Pucker pointer** ⊕ over the **US Postal truck**, then press and hold the mouse button until the truck is noticeably smaller.
4. Click the **Bloat tool** in the Liquify dialog box.
5. Center the **Bloat pointer** ⊕ over the center of the **top of the Eiffel Tower**, then press and hold the mouse button until the tip increases in size and fills the frozen area.
6. Compare your image to Figure 11.
7. Click **None** in the Mask Options section to remove the mask.
8. Click **OK**, then display the **History and Layers workspace**.

   The distortions are applied to the image.
9. Save your work, compare your image to Figure 12 and the History panel to Figure 13.
10. Display the **Essentials workspace**.

After distorting two areas, you removed the frozen mask and displayed two different workspaces.

USE THE MESH FEATURE AS
YOU DISTORT AN IMAGE

What You'll Do

In this lesson, you'll use the mesh feature to assist you when making distortions.

Using the Mesh Feature

The **mesh** is a series of horizontal and vertical gridlines superimposed on the preview window. You can easily see the effects of your distortions while working in an image by turning on the mesh. Although this feature is not necessary to create distortions, it can be helpful for seeing how much distortion you have added. The mesh can be controlled using the View Options section in the Liquify dialog box, shown in Figure 14. A magnified and distorted image, with the default medium-size, blue mesh displayed, is shown in Figure 15.

> QUICKTIP
>
> Distortions on the gridlines look similar to isobars on a thermal map or elevations on a topographic map.

Changing the Mesh Display

You can modify the appearance of the mesh so that it is displayed in another color or contains larger or smaller gridlines. You may want to use large gridlines if your changes are so dramatic that the use of smaller gridlines would be distracting. As shown in Figure 16, you can use the large gridlines to see where the distortions occur. If the mesh color and the colors in the image are similar, you may want to change the mesh color. For example, a yellow mesh displayed on an image with a yellow background would be invisible. A red mesh against a white background, as shown in Figure 16, is more noticeable.

Visualizing the Distortions

When the mesh feature is on and clearly visible, take a look at the gridlines as you make your distortions. Note where the gridlines have been adjusted and if symmetrical objects have equally symmetrical distortions. For example, distortions of a rectangular skyscraper can be controlled so that they are equivalent on all visible sides. If symmetry is what you want, the mesh feature gives you one method of checking your results.

Getting a Better View of Distortions

The active layer is always shown in the Liquify dialog box, but you might find it helpful to distort imagery with its companion layers visible. You can do this in two ways. One way is by selecting the Show Backdrop check box in the Liquify dialog box, and selecting which layer (or all layers) you want to be visible with the selected layer. You can then adjust the opacity of the backdrop layer(s) to make the layer(s) more visible. This technique distorts only the layer selected on the Layers panel. The other way is by merging visible layers: Click the highest layer on the Layers panel, click the Layers panel list arrow, then click Merge Visible. When you open the merged layers in the Liquify dialog box, all the imagery will be visible and can be altered by distortions. One way of ensuring that you can get back to your original layers—in case things don't turn out quite as you planned—is by making copies of the layers you want to combine before you merge the layers.

QUICKTIP

You can always turn off the mesh feature if it is distracting.

FIGURE 14

Mesh display options

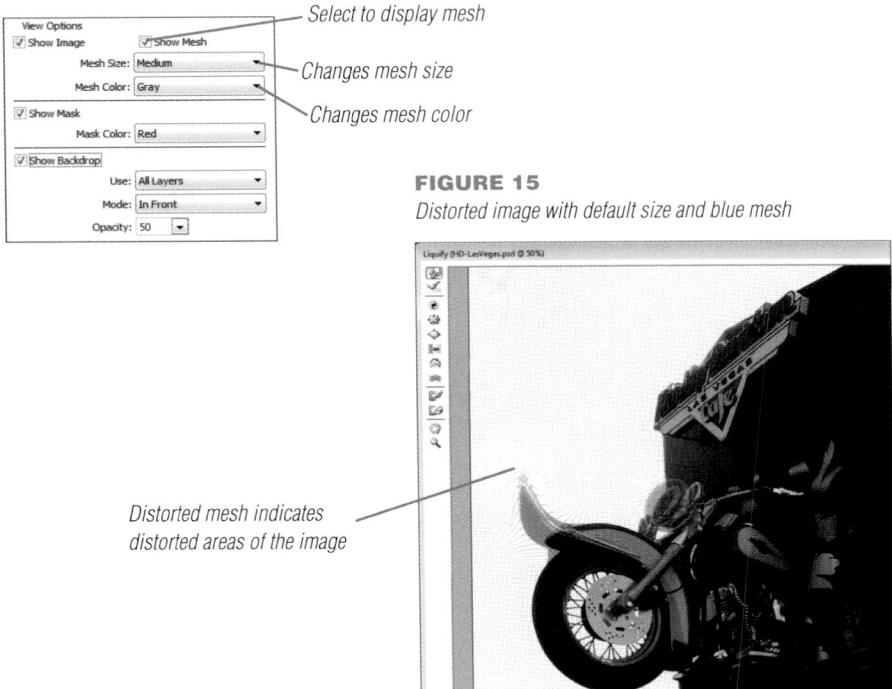

Select to display mesh

Changes mesh size

Changes mesh color

Distorted mesh indicates distorted areas of the image

FIGURE 15

Distorted image with default size and blue mesh

FIGURE 16

Distorted image with large red mesh

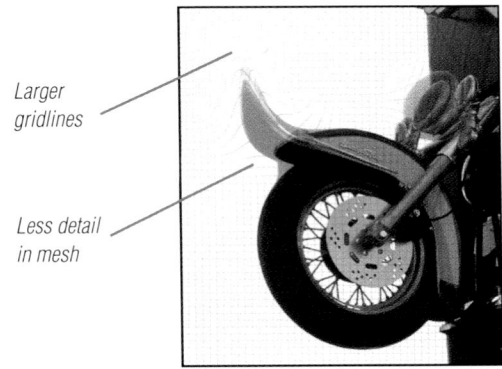

Larger gridlines

Less detail in mesh

Turn on the mesh

1. Click **Filter** on the Application bar, then click **Liquify**.

2. Use the **Zoom tool** 🔍 in the Liquify dialog box to magnify the image.

3. Click the **Bloat tool** ⟡ in the Liquify dialog box, then verify that the brush size is **100**.

4. Select the **Show Mesh check box.**

5. Click the **Mesh Color list arrow**, then click **Red**.

6. Verify that the **Mesh Size** is set to **Medium** and the **Show Backdrop check box** is selected Compare your image and settings to Figure 17, then make any adjustments necessary so that your settings match those shown in the figure.

You turned on the mesh and changed the mesh color and verified the setting of the mesh size.

FIGURE 17

Medium red mesh over an image

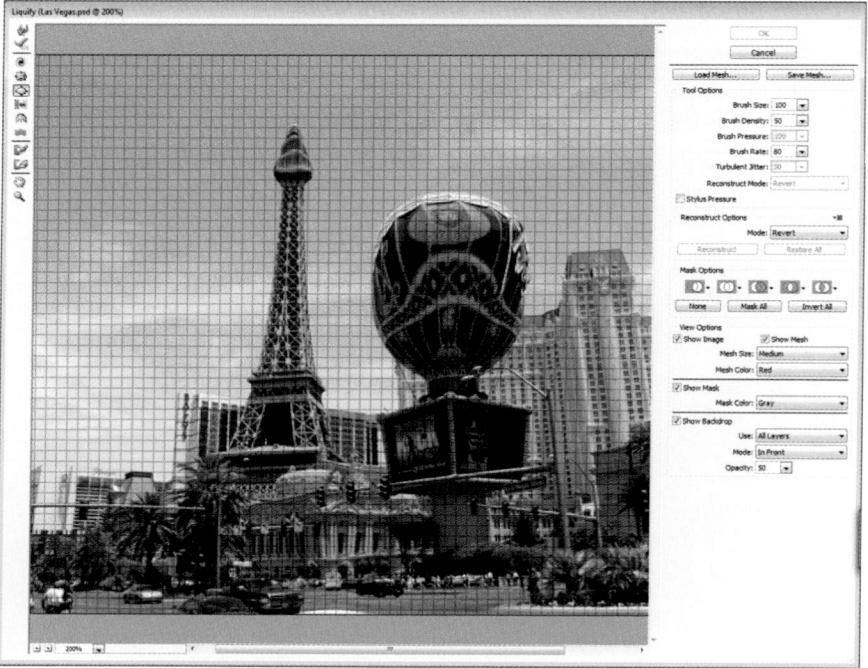

FIGURE 18
Warped Eiffel Tower and marquee

This mesh is undistorted as the balloon's distortion was created in a previous Liquify session

Distorted mesh

Spikes on marquee

FIGURE 19
Distortions applied to image

Distort an image with the mesh feature activated

1. Position the **Bloat pointer** ⊕ over the middle of the center of the Eiffel Tower, press and hold the mouse button until you see the mesh being distorted, then release the mouse button.

2. Click the **Forward Warp tool** 🖉 in the Liquify dialog box, then change the brush size to **25**.

3. Click the **Mesh Size list arrow**, then click **Large**.

   The gridlines appear larger.

4. Drag the **Forward Warp pointer** ⊕ in the top edge of the **Paris marquee** (the two framed screens beneath the Paris balloon) so that it forms spikes using medium horizontal strokes, as shown in Figure 18.

5. Click the **Show Mesh check box** to turn off the mesh.

6. Click **OK**.

7. Save your work, then compare your image to Figure 19.

8. Close the image, then exit Photoshop.

You added new distortions to the image and modified the mesh size. After viewing the distortions with the larger mesh, you turned off the mesh and viewed the image.

Power User Shortcuts

to do this:	use this method:
Bloat an area	Filter ➢ Liquify, ◌ or B
Change freeze color	Filter ➢ Liquify, Mask Color list arrow
Change mesh color	Filter ➢ Liquify, select Show Mesh check box, click the Mesh Color list arrow
Change mesh size	Filter ➢ Liquify, select Show Mesh check box, click the Mesh Size list arrow
Change brush size	Filter ➢ Liquify, [100 ▸] or [[] or []]
Freeze pixels	Filter ➢ Liquify, ✍ or F
Open Liquify dialog box	Filter ➢ Liquify or [Shift][Ctrl][X] (Win) or [⌘] [shift][X] (Mac)
Pucker an area	Filter ➢ Liquify, ⬢ or S
Reconstruct pixels in an area	Filter ➢ Liquify, ✎ or R

to do this:	use this method:
Reflect pixels in an area	Filter ➢ Liquify, 🔁 or M
Return image to prewarp state	Click Restore All in Liquify dialog box, click Cancel in Liquify dialog box, or drag state to 🗑 on the History panel
Shift pixels in an area	Filter ➢ Liquify, ✣ or O
Thaw frozen pixels	Filter ➢ Liquify, ✎ or D
Turn mesh on/off	Filter ➢ Liquify, select Show Mesh check box
Turn Backdrop on/off	Filter ➢ Liquify, select Show Backdrop check box
Twirl an area clockwise	Filter ➢ Liquify, ◉ or C
Warp an area	Filter ➢ Liquify, ✎ or W

Key: Menu items are indicated by ➢ between the menu name and its command. Blue bold letters are shortcuts for selecting tools in the dialog box.

Use the Liquify tools to distort an image.

1. Open PS 13-2.psd, then save it as **Blurred Vision**.
2. Open the Liquify dialog box.
3. Change the Brush Size to 65.
4. Select the Twirl Clockwise tool.
5. Twirl the F in Line 2.
6. Twirl the P in Line 2.
7. Close the Liquify dialog box, then save your work.

Learn how to freeze and thaw areas.

1. Open the Liquify dialog box.
2. Turn on the Show Mask feature, then change the Mask Color to Green.
3. Use the Freeze Mask tool to freeze the O in the middle of Line 3.
4. Select the Bloat tool.
5. Bloat each remaining letter in Line 3.

6. Use the Thaw Mask tool to thaw the frozen areas.
7. Click OK, then save your work.

Use the mesh feature as you distort an image.

1. Open the Liquify dialog box.
2. Turn on the Show Mesh feature.
3. Change the Mesh Color to Blue.
4. Change the Mesh Size to Large.
5. Select the Pucker tool, then change the Brush Size to 135.
6. Pucker the E on Line 1 and the number 7.
7. Use the Bloat tool and a 150 Brush Size to distort the green bar (between lines 6 and 7) and the red bar (between lines 8 and 9). Then distort the letter P in line 4.
8. Close the Liquify dialog box, save your work, then compare your image to Figure 20.

FIGURE 20
Completed Skills Review

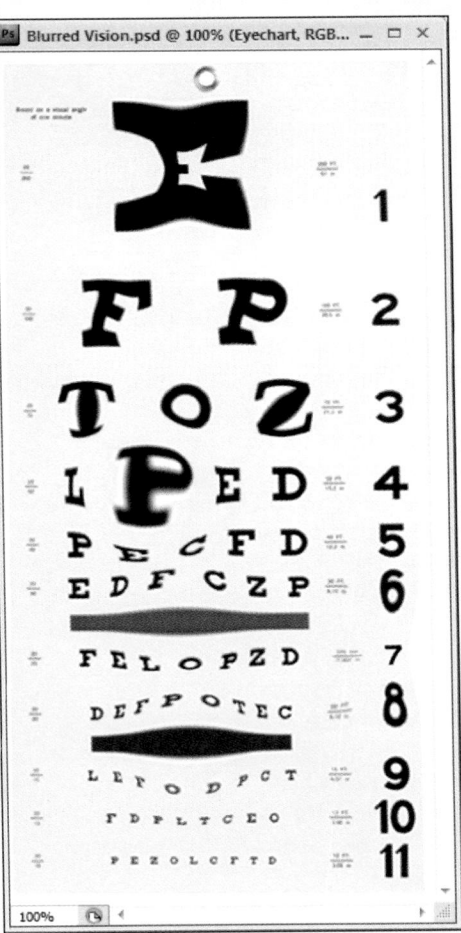

Liquifying an Image

Your lifelong dream to open a restaurant is about to come true. In fact, even though you haven't found a location, you've already chosen a name: the Shooting Star Restaurant. Fortunately, you can use your Photoshop skills to save some money by designing your own promotional advertisements. You've created the initial background art, but need to complete the image.

1. Open PS 13-3.psd, then save it as **Shooting Star**.
2. Activate the Shooting Star layer, then open the Liquify dialog box.
3. Display the mesh in a size and color you think are appropriate.
4. Change the freeze mask color to Red (if necessary).
5. Use the brush size of your choice to freeze the face in the lower-left corner.
6. Use the Twirl Clockwise tool and a Brush Size of 25 to distort the bright shooting star.
7. Use the Bloat tool with a Brush Size of 250 to distort the shooting star.
8. Turn off the mesh, then click OK to close the Liquify dialog box.
9. Add a type layer that says **Shooting Star Restaurant**. (*Hint*: You can use any color and any font available on your computer. In the sample, a Poor Richard font is shown.)
10. Use the bounding box to change the size of the text.
11. Warp the type layer using the style and the settings of your choice. (*Hint*: Do not rasterize the type layer.)
12. Apply the type effects of your choice to the text.
13. Make any color adjustments you feel are necessary. (*Hint*: In the sample, the Levels were adjusted so that the input midtones are .69.)
14. Add any filter effects that you determine are necessary to enhance the image. (In the sample, the Lens Flare filter was set at 105mm Prime at 90% Brightness and positioned over the shooting star.)
15. Save your work, then compare your image to the sample in Figure 21.

FIGURE 21
Sample Project Builder 1

Liquifying an Image

Your friend is a film photographer and doesn't understand the power of Photoshop and digital photography. His birthday is coming soon, and you think it is a great opportunity to show him how useful Photoshop can be and to have a little fun with him. One of the things you like best about your friend is his great sense of humor. You decide to use the Liquify tools to distort a photo of him so it looks like a caricature.

1. Open PS 13-4.psd, then save it as **Buddy Boy**.
2. Locate at least one piece of appropriate artwork—either a scanned image of a friend, an image on your computer, or an image from a royalty-free collection—that you can use in this file.
3. Use any appropriate methods to select imagery from the artwork.
4. After the selections have been made, copy each selection into Buddy Boy.
5. Transform any imagery, if necessary.
6. Change the colors of the gradient fill in the Backdrop layer to suit the colors in your friend's image.
7. Open the Liquify dialog box.
8. Display any size mesh in any color you find helpful.
9. Change the freeze mask color to a color you find helpful.
10. Use the brush size of your choice to freeze an area within the image. (*Hint*: In the example,

the face was protected while the hair was enlarged and brushed back.)
11. Use any distortion tool in any brush size of your choice to distort an area near the frozen area.
12. Thaw the frozen areas.
13. Use any additional distortion techniques to modify the image and distort the physical characteristics, as a caricaturist would do.

FIGURE 22
Sample Project Builder 2

14. Turn off the mesh, then click OK to close the Liquify dialog box.
15. Add a type layer with a clever title for your friend. You can position it in any location you choose.
16. Save your work, then compare your image to the sample in Figure 22.

Liquifying an Image

You really love the Photoshop Liquify feature and want to see other samples of how this tool can be used. You decide to look on the Internet, find a sample, then cast a critical eye on the results.

1. Connect to the Internet and use your browser to find information about the Liquify feature in Photoshop. (Make a record of the site you found so you can use it for future reference, if necessary.) You might find an image similar to a liquified image such as the sample shown in Figure 23.

2. Ask yourself the following questions about a specific image to which the Liquify feature has been applied.
   - Do you like this image? If so, why?
   - Does the distortion prevent you from determining what the image is?
   - In your opinion, does the distortion make the image more or less effective?
   - How was the distortion created?
   - After seeing this sample, what is your opinion as to the overall effectiveness of the Liquify feature? How can it best be used?

3. Be prepared to discuss your answers to these questions either in writing, in a group discussion, or in a presentation format.

FIGURE 23
Sample Design Project

You have been asked to give a presentation to a group of students who are interested in taking computer design classes. The presentation should include general topics, such as layers, type, and making selections, and can also include more exotic features, such as Liquify. Make it clear that the Liquify feature can be used on people, objects, or abstract images. Create an image that you can use in your presentation.

1. Create a new Photoshop image with any dimensions.
2. Save the file as **Photoshop Presentation**.
3. Locate several pieces of artwork—either on your computer, in a royalty-free collection, or from scanned images. Remember that the images can show anything, but you want to demonstrate the flexibility of Photoshop and the range of your skills.
4. Select imagery from the artwork and move it into Photoshop Presentation.
5. Open the Liquify dialog box.
6. Display any size mesh in any color you find helpful.
7. Use the Freeze Mask tool and the brush size of your choice to isolate areas that you don't want to distort.
8. Use any distortion tool in any brush size of your choice to distort an area in the image.
9. Thaw the frozen areas.
10. Use any additional distortion techniques to modify the image.
11. Turn off the mesh, then click OK to close the Liquify dialog box.
12. Use any transformation skills to enhance the image.
13. Add any filter effects, if you decide they will make your image more dramatic. (In the sample, the Fresco filter was applied to the Abstract layer.)
14. Make any necessary color adjustments.
15. Add at least one type layer in any font available on your computer. (A Constantia font is shown in the sample.)
16. Use your knowledge of special effects and the bounding box to enhance the type layer. (The following effects have been applied: Flag-style warped text, Drop Shadow style, Stroke style, and Bevel and Emboss style.)
17. Save your work, then compare your image to the sample in Figure 24.

FIGURE 24
Sample Portfolio Project

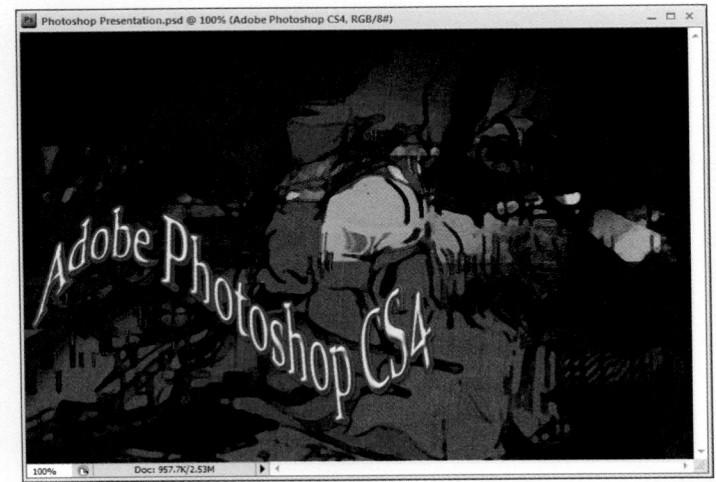

chapter 14

PERFORMING IMAGE SURGERY

1. Delete unnecessary imagery

2. Correct colors in an image

3. Tweak an image

Understanding the Realities

By now you've realized that working with Photoshop is not always about creating cool effects and exciting images. Sometimes, your main task is problem-solving. For example, you don't always have access to perfect images. If you did, you wouldn't need the arsenal of tools that Photoshop provides. Often, we find ourselves with images that need some "help." Perhaps the colors in an image are washed out, or maybe the image would be perfect except for one element that you don't want or need.

Assessing the Situation

In some situations, there may be many obvious ways to achieve the look you want in an image. A smart Photoshop user knows what tools are available, evaluates an image to see what is needed, then decides which methods are best to fix the problem areas in the image.

Applying Knowledge and Making Decisions

People who can apply their Photoshop knowledge effectively are in demand in today's job market. The ability to assess which tools are needed in the first place is as much a part of Photoshop expertise as knowing how to use the tools. You can approach the same design problem in many ways; your job is to determine which approach to take in order to make an image look right. And it is up to you to determine what "right" is. By the time your image is finished, you may feel as if it has undergone major surgery.

QUICKTIP

Image surgery often goes unappreciated. You may spend a lot of time cleaning up edges and eliminating "dirt" and "smudges"—defects that often are noticeable in an image only when they've been neglected!

Tools You'll Use

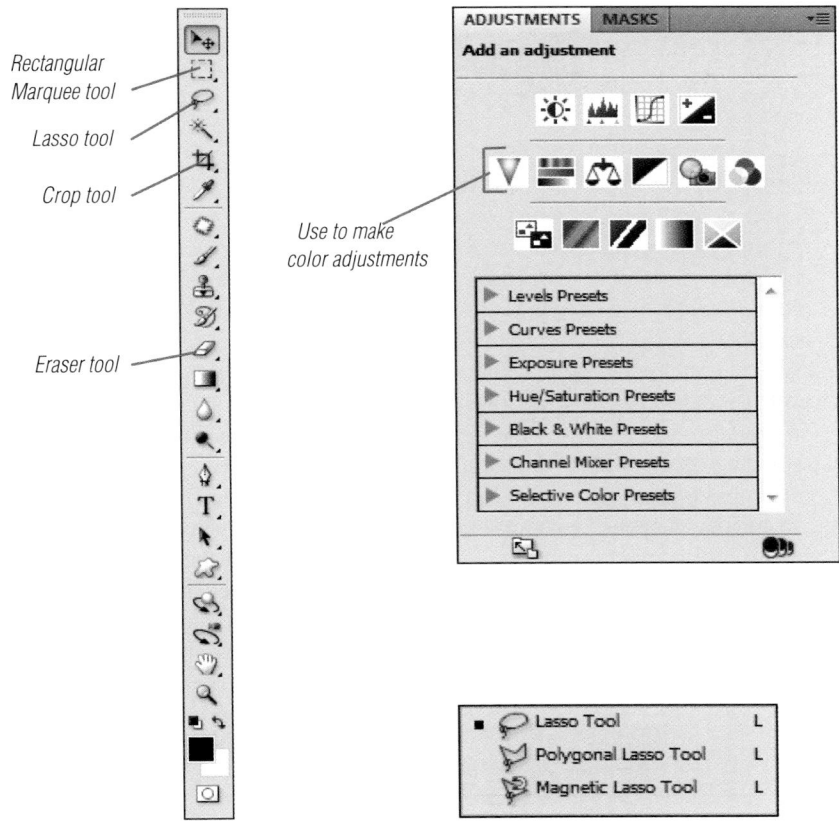

Rectangular
Marquee tool

Lasso tool

Crop tool

Use to make
color adjustments

Eraser tool

DELETE UNNECESSARY IMAGERY

What You'll Do

In this lesson, you'll use your skills and a variety of tools to conceal unwanted imagery. You'll also add a new layer from a selection and add a layer mask.

Evaluating the Possibilities

Now that you have some experience creating and editing images, your assessment abilities have probably sharpened. You are more accustomed to deciding what imagery is useful for a particular project. You may also find that you've begun looking at images in terms of their potential usefulness for other projects. You might, for example, see a great element in one image and think, "That object has a crisp edge. I could isolate it using the Magnetic Lasso tool and use it for this other project."

QUICKTIP

Don't be surprised when a simple touch-up job that you thought would take a few minutes actually takes hours. Sometimes a seemingly simple effect is the one that requires the most work.

Performing Surgery

Removing unwanted imagery can be time-consuming and frustrating, but it can also be extremely gratifying (after you're finished). It's detailed, demanding, and sometimes complicated work. For example, Figures 1 and 2 show the same image *before* and *after* it underwent the following alterations:

- The .tif file was saved as a Photoshop .psd file.
- Selection tools were used to create separate layers for the background, the backdrop, and the candles.
- The candles layer was duplicated, as insurance—just in case it became necessary to start over. See the Layers panel in Figure 3.
- The backdrop color was changed from black to pure blue violet.
- The candles on the left and right sides were eliminated by using eraser tools.
- Extraneous "dirt" and "smudges" were eliminated by using eraser tools.
- Contrast was added to the candles by using an adjustment layer.
- The Liquify feature was used to extend the individual flames and to smooth out the candle holder at the bottom of the image.
- The Noise filter was applied to the Backdrop layer, to give it more texture and dimension.

Understanding the Alternatives

Could these effects be achieved using other methods? Of course. For example, the bottom of the image was modified using the Forward Warp tool in the Liquify dialog box, but a similar effect could have been created using a painting tool such as the Smudge tool. The effect of the Noise filter could also have been created using the Grain filter. How many different ways can you think of to get the imagery from Figure 1 into the separate layers shown in Figure 2? It's possible that you can create these effects in many ways. For example, you might want to use the Magnetic Lasso tool to select areas with clearly defined edges, then zoom in and use the Eraser tool to clean up dirt and smudges. Or you just may decide to keep it simple and use the Rectangular Marquee tool to copy and paste pixels from one area to another.

Preparing for Surgery

Even if you think you've got it all figured out, sometimes things do not go the way you planned. Doesn't it make sense to take the time to prepare for a worst-case scenario when using Photoshop? Of course. You can easily protect yourself against losing hours of work by building in some safety nets as you work. For example, you can duplicate your original image (or images) just in case things go awry. By creating a copy, you'll never have to complain that your original work was ruined. You can also save interim copies of your image at strategic stages of your work. Above all, make sure you plan your steps. To do this, perform a few trial runs on a practice image before starting on the *real* project. Until you get comfortable reading the states on the History panel, write down what steps you took and what settings you used. Careful planning will pay off.

FIGURE 1
Original TIFF file

FIGURE 2
Modified image

Flames extended using the Liquify feature's Forward Warp tool

Noise filter added to new background color to give texture

Eraser tool used to delete candles and eliminate smudges

FIGURE 3
Layers panel of modified image

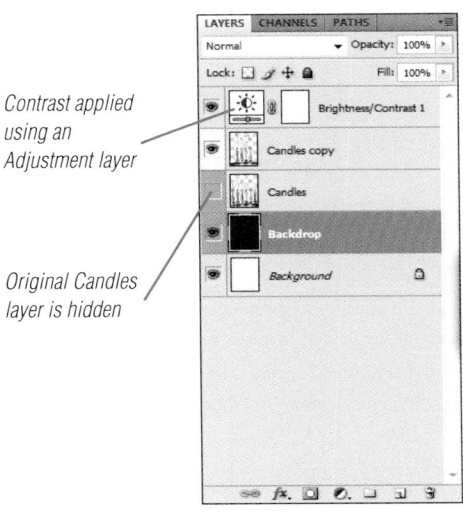

Contrast applied using an Adjustment layer

Original Candles layer is hidden

Lesson 1   Delete Unnecessary Imagery

Prepare the image for surgery

1. Open PS 14-1.jpg from the drive and folder where you store your Data Files.

2. Use the **Format list arrow** in the Save As dialog box to change the file from a JPG to the **Photoshop (*.PSD, *.PDD)** format, then save the file as **Swimmers.psd**.

3. Change the workspace to **History and Layers** (created in Chapter 1).

4. Click **Layer** on the Application bar, point to **New**, then click **Layer From Background**.

5. Type **Swimmers** in the Name text box.

6. Click the **Color list arrow** in the New Layer dialog box, click **Green**, then click **OK**.

7. Drag the **Swimmers layer** on the Layers panel to the **Create a new layer button** .

   A copy of the Swimmers layer (named Swimmers copy) is created. Compare your image and History and Layers panels to Figure 4.

8. Click the **Swimmers layer** on the Layers panel.

9. Click the **Indicates layer visibility button** 👁 on the Swimmers copy layer.

   Table 1 reviews some of the many possible selection methods you can use to remove unwanted imagery.

You saved a .jpg file in the Photoshop PSD format, converted a Background layer into an image layer, then made a copy of the image layer.

FIGURE 4
Duplicated layer

New file format

Copied layer

TABLE 1: Image Removal Methods

tool	name	method
🖎	Magnetic Lasso tool	Trace an object along its edge, then click Edit ≻ Clear.
✳	Magic Wand tool	Select by color, then click Edit ≻ Clear.
🖌	Clone Stamp tool	Press and hold [Alt] (Win) or [option] (Mac), click sample area, release [Alt] (Win) or [option] (Mac), then click areas you want to remove.
⬚	Rectangular Marquee tool	Select area, select Move tool, press and hold [Alt] (Win) or [option] (Mac), drag selection to new location.
◯	Elliptical Marquee tool	Select area, select Move tool, press and hold [Alt] (Win) or [option] (Mac), drag selection to new location.
▱	Eraser tool	Drag over pixels to be removed.
◇	Patch tool	Select source/destination, then drag to destination/source.

FIGURE 5
Selection in image

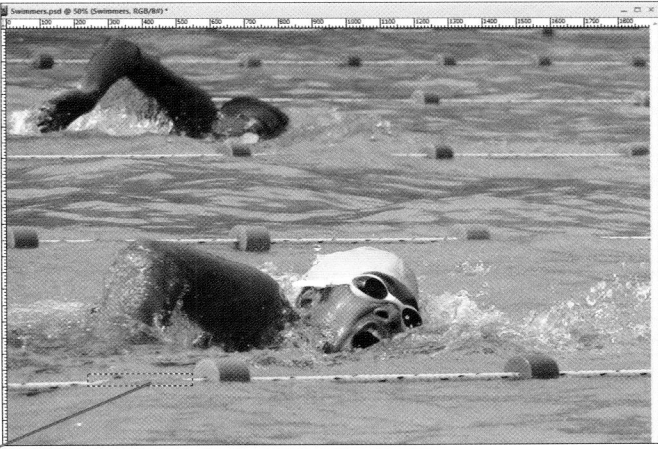

Imagery surrounded
by marquee

FIGURE 6
Cleared selection

Area with
deleted pixels

Lesson 1   Delete Unnecessary Imagery

1. Verify that the rulers are displayed in pixels, then click the **Zoom tool** 🔍 on the Application bar.

   TIP   Make sure the Resize Windows To Fit check box on the options bar is selected.

2. Click the **lowest-left piece of yellow rope** until the zoom level is 50%.

3. Click the **Rectangular Marquee tool** ▢ on the Tools panel, then change the Feather setting to **0 px**, if necessary.

4. Drag the **Rectangular Marquee pointer** ✛ around the rectangular section of yellow rope to the left of the orange buoy (from approximately **220 X/1070 Y** to **540 X/1100 Y**).

   Compare your selection to Figure 5.

5. Click **Edit** on the Application bar, then click **Clear**.

   TIP   You can also use the Eraser tool to delete the rope hidden by the water, although it would be difficult to erase all the nooks and crannies. You can also choose to cover these pixels rather then remove them.

6. Click **Select** on the Application bar, then click **Deselect**.

   Compare your image to Figure 6.

   TIP   You can also cut a selection by clicking Edit on the Application bar, then clicking Cut, which allows you to paste the selection elsewhere by clicking Edit on the Application bar, then clicking Paste.

You used the Zoom tool to get a closer look at an image, then used the Rectangular Marquee tool to eliminate unwanted imagery.

Duplicate imagery

1. Verify that the **Rectangular Marquee tool** ⊡ is selected.

2. Select a rectangular area of rope that is clearly visible above the water from approximately **1000 X/1050 Y** to **1350 X/1100 Y**. Compare your selection to Figure 7.

3. Press and hold **[Ctrl][Alt]** (Win) or ⌘ **[option]** (Mac), drag the selection to the area displaying the deleted pixels, then release **[Ctrl][Alt]** (Win) or ⌘ **[option]** (Mac).

   The selection is duplicated over the deleted pixels.

   TIP   Pressing and holding [Ctrl] [Alt] (Win) or ⌘ [option] (Mac) lets you temporarily convert the current tool to the Move tool.

4. Click **Select** on the Application bar, then click **Deselect**.

5. Use any Photoshop tools, such as the Clone Stamp tool, to fill in any missing areas until you are satisfied with the results.

   Compare your screen to Figure 8.

   TIP   You can use pixels from anywhere in the image.

6. Display the **Essentials workspace**.

You selected areas within the image and then duplicated them to cover deleted imagery and make the image look more natural.

FIGURE 7
Selected area

FIGURE 8
Image with duplicated pixels

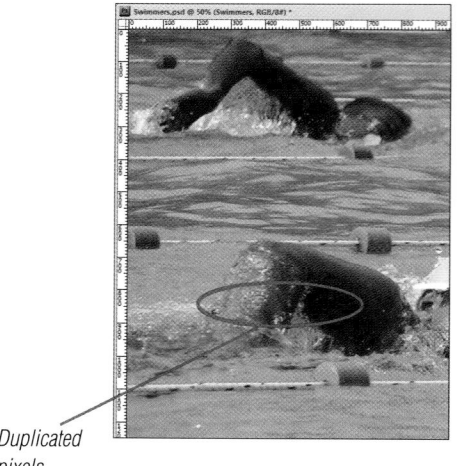

Duplicated
pixels

DESIGNTIP   **Fooling the eye**

You can fool the eye when you replace pixels in an image. Even if the replacement pixels are not completely accurate, the eye can be tricked into thinking that the image looks reasonable. For example, you can duplicate ground and sky pixels, and most viewers will accept them as looking "right." However, the reverse is not necessarily true. If you remove something from an image but leave some pixels behind, viewers are likely to think that something is wrong. For example, if you erase the figure of a woman from an image, but you neglect to eliminate all the pixels for the woman's hair, the reader's eye would probably recognize the incongruity. Remnants of dangling hair would almost certainly bring into question the accuracy of the image.

FIGURE 9
Image with new layer and mask

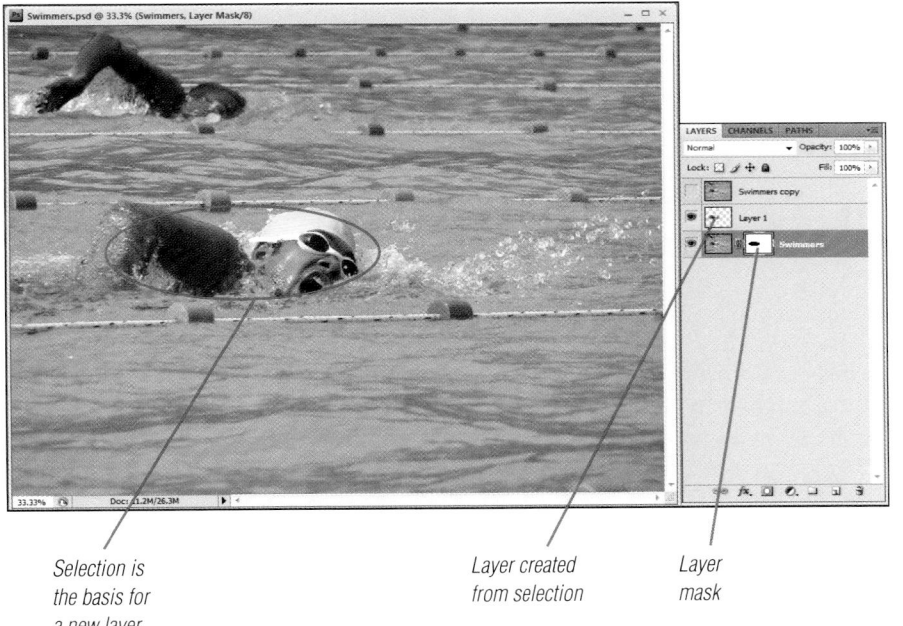

Selection is
the basis for
a new layer

Layer created
from selection

Layer
mask

Correcting color

You can make color corrections on a layer in a number of ways. One option is to make your corrections directly on the original layer. Another option is to make a copy of the original layer *before* making the corrections on the layer. You can also make your corrections using adjustment layers, and then merge the layers down when you are satisfied with the results. You can add an adjustment layer to the current layer by clicking Layer on the Application bar, pointing to New Adjustment Layer, then clicking the type of adjustment you want to make, or by clicking a preset button on the Adjustments panel.

Create a layer from a selection

1. Click the **Elliptical Marquee tool** ⬭ on the Tools panel, then verify that the Feather setting is set to **0 px**.

2. Drag the **Marquee pointer** ✛ around the swimmer with the yellow cap from approximately **200 X/660 Y** to **1300 X/1070 Y**.

3. Click **Layer** on the Application bar, point to **New**, then click **Layer via Copy**.

    A new layer containing the selection is created and is the active layer.

4. Click the **Swimmers layer** on the Layers panel.

5. Drag the **Marquee pointer** ✛ around the swimmer with the yellow cap but slightly smaller than the oval used in Step 2 from approximately **250 X/670 Y** to **1260 X/1050 Y**.

6. Click **Layer** on the Application bar, point to **Layer Mask**, then click **Hide Selection**.

    A layer mask is placed over the selection on the Swimmers layer. The mask will be used to conceal pixels while highlighting the image of the swimmer.

7. Hide the rulers.

8. Click the **Zoom tool** 🔍 on the Application bar.

9. Press and hold **[Alt]** (Win) or **[option]** (Mac), click the image until the zoom level is **33.3%**, then release **[Alt]** (Win) or **[option]** (Mac).

10. Save your work, then compare your image to Figure 9.

You created a new layer from a selection, then created a layer mask from a selection.

CORRECT COLORS IN
AN IMAGE

What You'll Do

In this lesson, you'll make color adjustments to a specific layer.

Revitalizing an Image

You may find that you are working with an image that looks fine except that it seems washed out or just leaves you in the doldrums. You may be able to spice up such an image by adjusting the color settings. By modifying the color balance, for example, you can increase the red tones while decreasing the green and blue tones to make the image look more realistic and dramatic. After you select the layer that you want to adjust, you can make color-correcting adjustments by displaying the Adjustments panel, then clicking the type of color adjustment you want to make.

Making Color Adjustments

So, the image you're working with seems to need *something*, but you're not quite sure what. Until you become comfortable making color corrections, do everything in your power to provide yourself with a safety net. Create duplicate layers and use adjustment layers instead of making corrections directly on the original layer. Before you begin, take a long look at the image and ask yourself, "What's lacking?" Is the problem composition, or is it truly a color problem? Do the colors appear washed out rather than vibrant and true to life? Is the color deficiency really a problem, or does the image's appearance support what you're trying to accomplish?

Assessing the Mood

Color can be a big factor in establishing mood in an image. For example, if you are trying to create a sad mood, increasing the blue and green tones may be more effective than modifying specific imagery. If you decide that your image does need color correction, start slowly. Try balancing the color and see if that gives you the effect you want. Keep experimenting with the various color correction options until you find the method that works for you.

FIGURE 10

Hue/Saturation Adjustments panel

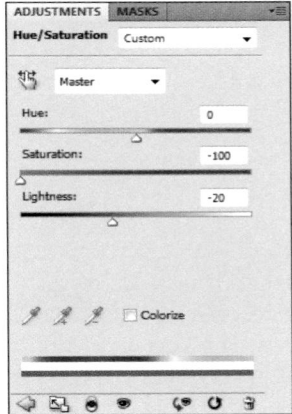

FIGURE 11

Brightness/Contrast Adjustments panel

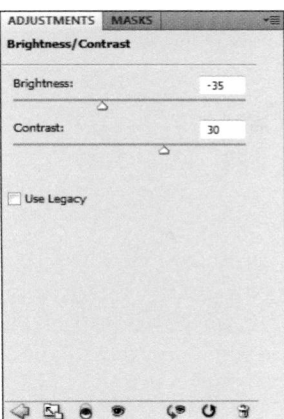

FIGURE 12

Color corrected image

Adjusted pixels
created from
selection

FIGURE 13

Layers panel

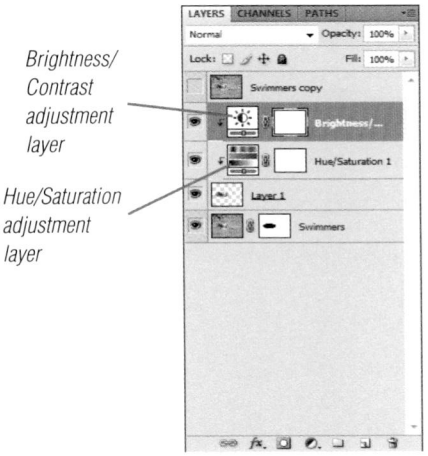

Brightness/
Contrast
adjustment
layer

Hue/Saturation
adjustment
layer

Correct colors

1. Click **Layer 1** on the Layers panel.
2. Click the **Hue/Saturation button** on the Adjustments panel.
3. Click the **This adjustment affects all layers below (click to clip to layer) button** on the Adjustments panel.
4. Change the settings in the Hue/Saturation dialog box so that they match those shown in Figure 10, then click the **Return to adjustment list button** on the Adjustments panel.
5. Click the **Brightness/Contrast button** on the Adjustments panel.
6. Click on the Adjustments panel.
7. Change the settings so that they match those shown in Figure 11, then click on the Adjustments panel.
8. Save your work, then compare your image to Figure 12 and your Layers panel to Figure 13.

You adjusted the hue/saturation and brightness/ contrast in the layer created from a selection, making the image of the swimmer's face stand out. You made color adjustments using adjustment layers, which you grouped with Layer 1.

Lesson 2   Correct Colors in an Image

TWEAK AN IMAGE

What You'll Do

 In this lesson, you'll crop out unnecessary imagery. You'll also add a layer style to enhance the image, and draw attention away from the background.

Evaluating What's Next

Every image has its own unique problems, and you'll probably run into a few final challenges when coordinating an image to work with other elements in a final publication or finished product. The last step in preparing an image for production is to decide what final fixes are necessary so that it serves its intended purpose.

Cropping an Image

Sometimes an image contains more content than is necessary. In the image of the swimmers, there's too much water. Of course, *you* have to determine the central focus of the image and what it is you want the reader to see. Is the subject of the image the water, or the swimmers? If your image suffers from too much of the wrong imagery, you can help your reader by getting rid of the unnecessary and possibly distracting imagery. This type of deletion not only removes imagery, but changes the size and shape of the image. You can make this type of change using the Crop tool on the Tools panel. When you make a selection within an image, you can use cropped area settings (the Shield check box and the Opacity list arrow) on the options bar to see how the image will appear after it has been cropped.

Adding Layer Styles

Image layers can also benefit from the same layer styles that can be applied to type layers, such as a Drop Shadow.

FIGURE 14
Cropped area in image

Darker area will be deleted during cropping

Dotted line indicates new boundaries

FIGURE 15
Completed image

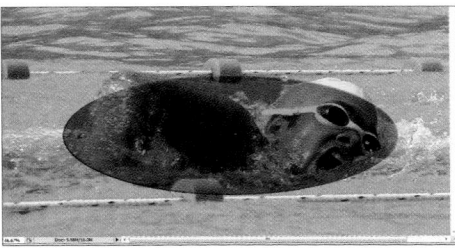

FIGURE 16
Layers panel for completed image

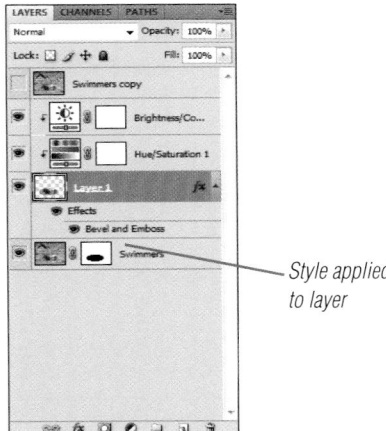

Style applied to layer

Crop the image

1. Display the rulers in pixels.
2. Click the **Crop tool** 🔲 on the Tools panel.
3. Drag the **Crop pointer** 🔲 in a rectangular area surrounding the two swimmers from approximately **0 X/0 Y** to **1620 X/1200 Y**.

   The area that will be cropped from the image appears darker, as shown in Figure 14.
4. Click the **Commit current crop operation button** ✔ on the options bar.

   The cropped imagery is discarded.
5. Hide the rulers, then resize the image so it fits your screen.
6. Click **Layer 1** on the Layers panel.
7. Click the **Add a layer style button** *fx.* on the Layers panel.
8. Click **Bevel and Emboss**, accept the existing settings, then click **OK**.
9. Save your work, then compare your image to Figure 15 and your Layers panel to Figure 16.
10. Close the image file and exit Photoshop.

You cropped the image, then applied the Bevel and Emboss style to the layer created from a selection.

Rotate and pan-and-zoom a canvas

Perhaps you need to rotate an image from its current axis in order to paint or draw on it. If this is the case, you can click the Rotate View tool on the Application bar, then drag any corner of the image. The Rotate View tool allows you to rotate a canvas *non-destructively*: it does not transform the image. As you drag, a compass displays in the center of the image which indicates how much rotation you have added to the original image. (The amount of rotation is also shown in the Rotation Angle text box in the options bar.) If you are using Photoshop Extended, you can use the *pan and zoom feature*. If you have a graphics card and your computer has OpenGL enabled (in Preferences), you can zoom in and out by holding the Zoom tool (rather than just clicking) without loss of resolution. You can pan by holding the [spacebar] while pressing the Zoom tool.

Power User Shortcuts

to do this:	use this method:
Add layer style	*fx.*, click style(s)
Clear selection	[Delete] (Win) or [delete] (Mac)
Clone an area	♨. or [Shift] S, press and hold [Alt] (Win) or option (Mac), click sample area, release [Alt] (Win) or option (Mac), then click areas you want cloned
Create an adjustment layer	Layer ➤ New Adjustment Layer ➤ type of adjustment
Create layer from selection	[Ctrl][J] (Win) or ⌘[J] (Mac)
Crop an image	⊄.
Cut selection	Edit ➤ Cut or [Ctrl][X] (Win) or ⌘[X] (Mac)
Deselect selection	Select ➤ Deselect or [Ctrl][D] (Win) or ⌘[D] (Mac)

to do this:	use this method:
Duplicate a layer	Drag layer to ⬐
Duplicate a selection and move it to a new location	⬚. or ◯ or [Shift] M, create selection, press and hold [Ctrl][Alt] (Win) or ⌘ option (Mac), then drag selection to new location
Erase pixels	⊘. or [Shift] E, drag pointer over pixels to be removed
Magnify an area	🔍 or Z, then click image
Paste selection	Edit ➤ Paste or [Ctrl][V] (Win) or ⌘[V] (Mac)
Select a complex object	🔖 or [Shift] L
Select and delete by color	⚒ or W, then click Edit ➤ Clear

Key: Menu items are indicated by ➤ between the menu name and its command. Blue bold letters are shortcuts for selecting tools on the Tools panel.

Delete unnecessary imagery.

1. Open PS 14-2.psd from the drive and folder where you store your Data Files, then save it as **Paradise Lost**.
2. Zoom in on the metronome.
3. Use the tool of your choice to select as much of the metronome as possible *without* selecting the toy boat or telephone. (*Hint*: You can use the Add to selection button on the options bar, or you can make multiple selections.)
4. Clear the metronome selection from the image.
5. Deselect the selection.
6. Use the Eraser tool and any size brush tip to get rid of any remaining metronome pixels.
7. Create a selection around the telephone and its cord using the tool of your choice. (*Hint*: You can use multiple selections to select this object.)
8. Clear the selection. (*Hint*: You will repair the defects created by this step later.)
9. Deselect the selection.
10. Use the Eraser tool and any size brush tip to get rid of any remaining telephone pixels.
11. Sample the red color of the toy boat image near the damaged area on the shell of the boat.
12. Use the Brush tool and any size brush tip to repair the damaged toy boat (where the telephone was removed).
13. Zoom out to the original magnification.
14. Save your work.

Correct colors in an image.

1. Make the Whistle layer active and visible.
2. Create a Color Balance adjustment layer that is clipped to the Whistle layer.
3. Correct the Cyan/Red level to +73, and the Magenta/Green level to −57.
4. Create a Brightness/Contrast adjustment layer that is clipped to the previous layer.
5. Change the Brightness slider to −10 and the Contrast slider to +15.
6. Use the bounding box feature to rotate the whistle, then nudge the object up using the sample in Figure 17 as a guide.
7. Make the Toy Boat layer active.
8. Create a Hue/Saturation adjustment layer that is clipped to the Toy Boat layer.
9. Change the Hue slider to +45 and the Saturation slider to +60.
10. Save your work.

Tweak an image.

1. Hide the Background layer.
2. Make the Push Pins layer active.
3. Use the tool of your choice, such as the Clone Stamp tool or the Magnetic Lasso tool and the Patch tool, to remove the two shadows above and below of the body of the whistle using Figure 17 as a guide. (*Hint*: You can magnify the area, if necessary.)

4. Apply the Ocean Ripple (Distort) filter using the following settings: Ripple Size = 3, Ripple Magnitude = 6.
5. Display the Background layer.
6. Change the opacity of the Push Pins layer to 60%.
7. Apply the Drop Shadow style to the Toy Boat layer using the default settings.
8. Make the Push Pins layer active.
9. Use the Horizontal Type tool to create a red type layer in the upper-right corner of the image that says Paradise Lost. (In the sample, a Matura MT Script Capitals font is used.)
10. Add the following styles to the type: Drop Shadow, Stroke, and Bevel and Emboss.
11. Save your work, then compare your image to the sample in Figure 17.

FIGURE 17
Completed Skills Review project

An exclusive women's clothing shop, First Class Woman, has hired you to revamp its image by creating the first in a series of advertisements. First Class Woman has been known for some time as a stuffy clothing store that sells pricey designer originals to the over-60 set. The time has come to expand its customer base to include women between the ages of 30 and 60. Their advertising agency recommended you, having seen samples of your work. They want you to inject some humor into your creation. They have provided you with some whimsical images they want to see in the ad.

1. Open PS 14-3.psd, then save it as **First Class Woman**.
2. Separate each of the items in the Glasses, Necklace, Bags layer into their own layers. (*Hint*: You can use the selection method(s) of your choice.)
3. Rename the layers using appropriate names.
4. Apply colors to each renamed thumbnail on the Layers panel.
5. Rearrange the objects as you see fit.
6. Turn on the Show Transform Controls feature. Use a bounding box to resize the glasses, bags, or neckace, if you choose.
7. Make the Fan layer active and visible, then transform the size of the fan so it is smaller. (*Hint*: Click Edit on the Application bar, point to Transform, then use the Scale command.)

8. Make a duplicate of the Glasses layer, accepting the default name.
9. Hide the original Glasses layer.
10. Use the Liquify feature on the duplicate Glasses layer using your choice of effects.
11. Add at least one adjustment layer, as you feel necessary. (*Hint*: In the sample, the Brightness was adjusted to –8, and the Contrast was adjusted to +35 in the Bags layer. In the Necklace layer, the following color balance adjustments were made: Cyan/Red level to +53, the Magenta/Green level to –65, and the Yellow/Blue level to –49. In the Roses layer, the Brightness was adjusted to –55, and the Contrast to –1.)

FIGURE 18
Sample Project Builder 1

12. Add a type layer that says **First Class Woman**. (*Hint*: You can use any color and any font available on your computer. In the sample, a 48 pt Snap ITC font is shown.)
13. Warp the type layer using the style and the settings of your choice.
14. Apply the styles of your choice to the text.
15. Adjust the opacity of the Roses layer using any setting you feel is appropriate.
16. Add any filter effects you want. (In the sample, the Smudge Stick filter is applied to the Roses layer, and the Lens Flare filter is applied to the Glasses copy layer.)
17. Save your work, then compare your image to the sample in Figure 18.

Your local chamber of commerce has asked you to volunteer your services and design a new advertisement for the upcoming membership drive. The theme of this year's membership drive is "The Keys to the City." They have supplied you with an initial image, but the rest is up to you.

1. Open PS 14-4.psd, then save it as **Membership Drive**.
2. Convert the Background layer into an image layer.
3. Rename the layer using any name you want, then apply a color to the thumbnail.
4. Create a new layer, then convert it into a Background layer.
5. Locate at least one piece of appropriate artwork—either a scanned image, an image on your computer, one from a digital camera, or an image from a royalty-free collection—that you can use in this image.
6. Use any appropriate methods to select imagery from the artwork.
7. After the selections have been made, copy them into Membership Drive.
8. Transform any imagery you feel will improve the finished product.
9. Use any method to eliminate some of the keys in the image. (In the sample, the third key from the bottom is eliminated.)

10. Add a type layer using the text and style of your choice to create a catch phrase for the ad. (*Hint*: You can use any color and any font available on your computer. In the sample, a Perpetua font in various sizes is shown.)
11. Add another type layer that contains the chamber of commerce name. (*Hint*: You can use the name of the town in which you live.)

FIGURE 19
Sample Project Builder 2

12. Add additional type layers, if desired.
13. Add an adjustment layer to at least one of the layers.
14. Modify the layer containing the keys using any method(s) you want. (In the sample, the Opacity is lowered to 86%, and the Tiles filter is applied.)
15. Save your work, then compare your image to the sample in Figure 19.

DESIGN PROJECT

You have seen how you can use Photoshop to take ordinary photographs and manipulate them into exciting artistic creations. You can use the web to find imagery created by many new and exciting artists who specialize in photo manipulation. To broaden your understanding of Photoshop, you decide to closely examine an artistic work, then *deconstruct it* to speculate as to how it was accomplished.

1. Connect to the Internet and use your browser to find digital artwork. (Make a record of the site you found so you can use it for future reference, if necessary.)
2. Click the links for the images until you find one that strikes you as interesting. A sample image is shown in Figure 20.
3. Examine the image, then ask yourself the following questions:
   - What images would you need to create this montage? In what format would you need them (electronic file, hard-copy image, or photograph)?
   - What techniques would you use to create this effect?
   - Do you like this image? If so, why?
4. Be prepared to discuss your answers to these questions, either in writing, in a group discussion, or in a presentation format.
5. Using your favorite word processor, create a document called **Digital Art Analysis** that records your observations.

FIGURE 20
Sample Design Project

Final Project

Digital Art Analysis

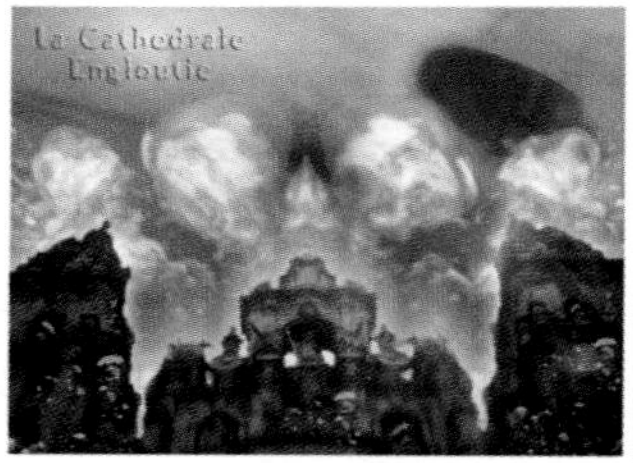

This image was created by artist Anairam Zeravia and was located on the morguefile.com Web site.

This is an excellent example of compositing, as only a few of the images is recognizable in terms of the actual origin of the imagery. To create this montage, the images would need to be in electronic form. If this is not possible, any photograph or paper copy images could be scanned and then manipulated in Photoshop. The following imagery would be needed to reconstruct the displayed image: an at least two buildings, one or more clouds, and several dark objects.

- Most of the images are probably from color photographs, any many have been altered, either using opacity settings or color adjustments.
- Using different layers, the artist probably used different filters and/or the liquify feature.
- Opacity adjustments appear to be used throughout this composite image, and color

Morguefile: (c) 2006 anairam_zeravla. http://www.morguefile.com/archive/?display=134637

You are about to graduate from The Art League, a local, independently-owned institution that trains artists in the use of all art media. Because of your talent, you have been asked to create next year's poster for the school.

1. Develop a design concept for the poster.
2. Create a new Photoshop image with your choice of dimensions.
3. Save this file as **Art School Poster**.
4. Locate several pieces of artwork—either on your hard disk, in a royalty-free collection, from a digital camera, or from scanned images. The images can show anything that is art-related and can be part of other images.
5. Create a layer for each image, then name each layer and apply a color to each layer thumbnail.
6. Transform any imagery you feel will enhance the design.

7. Add a type layer using a style and color of your choosing that contains a phrase you like. (*Hint*: You can use any font available on your computer. A Papyrus font in various sizes is used in the sample.)

8. Add an adjustment layer to at least one of the layers.
9. Add any filter effects, if you decide they will make your image more dramatic.
10. Save your work, then compare your image to the sample in Figure 21.

FIGURE 21
Sample Portfolio Project

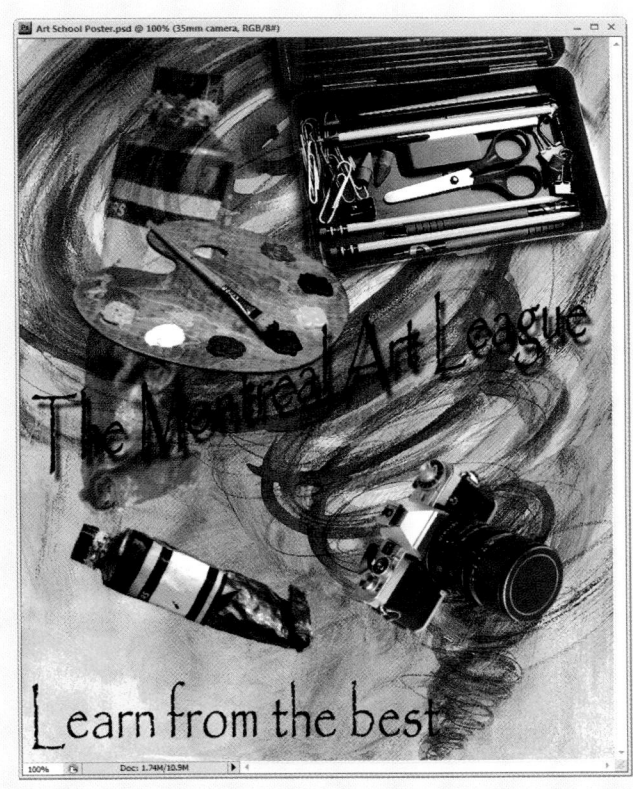

15

ANNOTATING AND AUTOMATING AN IMAGE

1. Add annotations to an image

2. Create an action

3. Modify an action

4. Use a default action and create a droplet

chapter **15** ANNOTATING AND AUTOMATING AN IMAGE

Creating Notes

Have you ever wished you could paste a sticky note on an image, to jot down an idea or include a message to someone who will be reviewing the design? Well, in Photoshop you can, using notes.

Communicating Directly to Your Audience

By creating written **notes**, you can communicate directly to anyone viewing your image. You can place written comments—electronic sticky notes—right in the file. Once a note is in place, anyone opening your image in Photoshop can double-click the note icon and read your comments.

Using Automation

Have you ever performed a repetitive task in Photoshop? Suppose you create an image with several type layers containing different fonts, and then you decide that each of those type layers should use the same font family. To make this change, you would have to perform the following steps on each type layer:

- Select the layer.
- Double-click the layer thumbnail.
- Click the Set the font family list arrow.
- Click the font you want.
- Click the Commit any current edits button.

Wouldn't it be nice if there were a way to speed up commonly performed tasks like this one? That's where automation, courtesy of the Actions feature, comes in. Using this feature you can record these five steps as one action. Then, rather than having to repeat each of the steps, you just play the action.

> **QUICK**TIP
>
> Many programs have a feature that records and then can play back repetitive tasks. Other programs call this feature a macro, script, or behavior.

Tools You'll Use

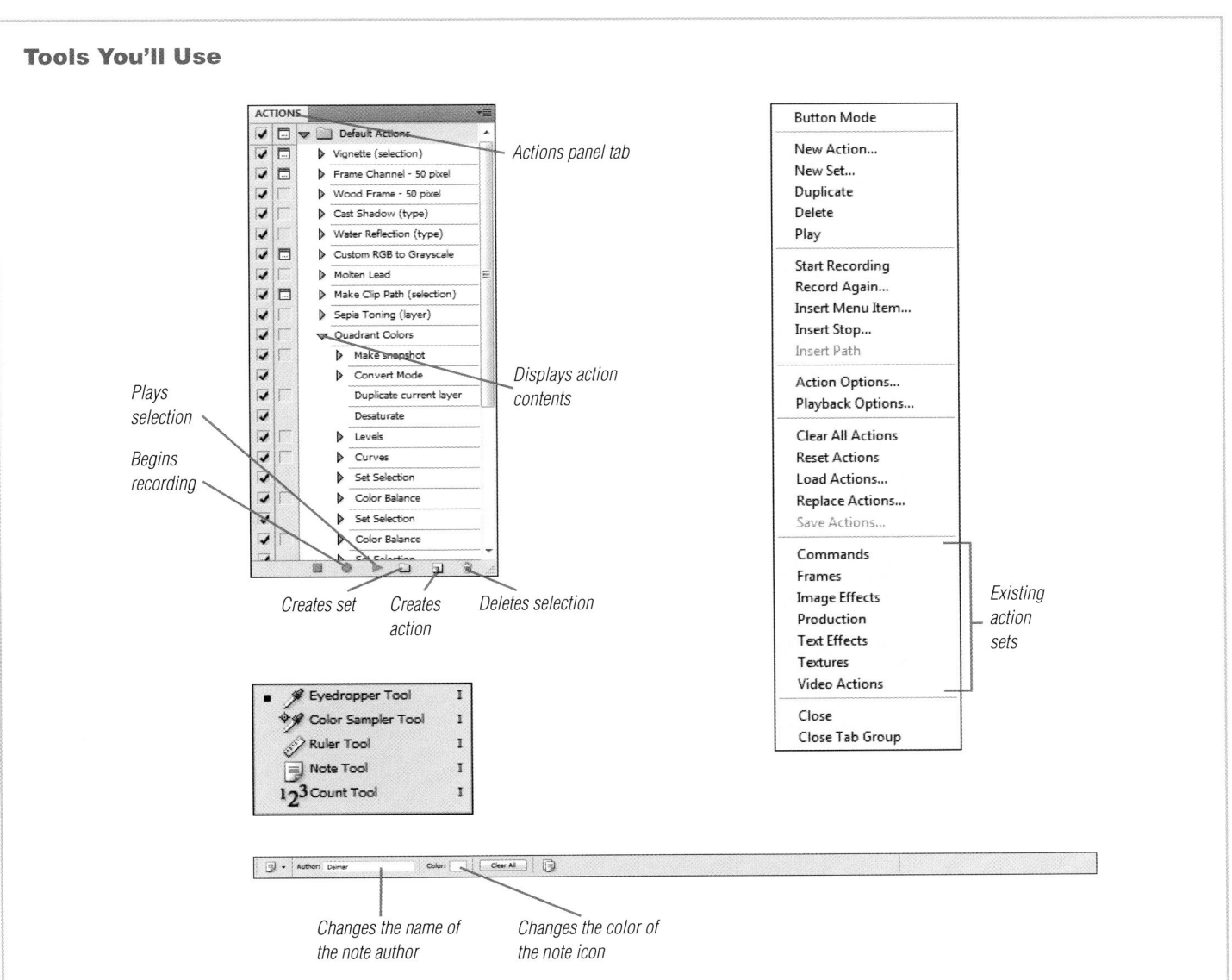

ADD ANNOTATIONS TO
AN IMAGE

What You'll Do

 In this lesson, you'll create a note.

Creating an Annotation

Annotations are similar to the yellow sticky notes you might attach to a printout. You can create a annotation by clicking the Note tool on the Tools panel (in the Eyedropper group), clicking in the image where you want the note to appear, then typing the contents. Each note within a file has an icon that appears on the image in the work area, as shown in Figure 1, while the contents of the note displays in the Notes panel.

Reading Notes

To open a closed note, double-click the note icon. You can also right-click (Win) or [control]-click (Mac) the note icon, then click Open Note, as shown in Figure 1. You can move the note within the image by dragging the note's icon.

> **QUICK**TIP
>
> You can differentiate between active and inactive notes by the appearance of the note icons. The icon for an inactive note has a solid color, while the icon for an active note displays a pencil.

Using the Notes Panel

The contents of a note displays in the Notes panel, which can be opened by double-clicking a note icon, clicking the Show or hide the notes panel button on the Note tool options bar, or clicking Notes on the Window menu. Scroll bars display in the Notes panel if the contents exceed the window display, although you can resize the Notes panel by dragging any of the edges (Win) or the bottom edge (Mac) to the desired dimension. The status bar (at the bottom of the Notes panel) contains left and right arrows that let you navigate all the notes within an image, a counter to tell you which note is currently active, and a trash can that lets you delete the active note.

> **QUICK**TIP
>
> You can delete a selected note by clicking the Delete note button in the Notes panel, pressing [Delete], or by right-clicking the note (Win) or [control]-clicking the note (Mac), then clicking Delete Note.

Personalizing a Note

By default, the note icon is a pale yellow color. You can change this color by clicking the Note color box on the options bar. When the Select note color dialog box opens, you can use any method to change the color, such as sampling an area within an existing image. You can also change the author of the note by selecting the contents in the Name of author for notes text box, typing the information you want, then pressing [Enter] (Win) or [return] (Mac).

The font size of the note can be changed using the Type section of the Preferences command in the Edit menu (Win) or Photoshop menu (Mac).

FIGURE 1
Open note in an image

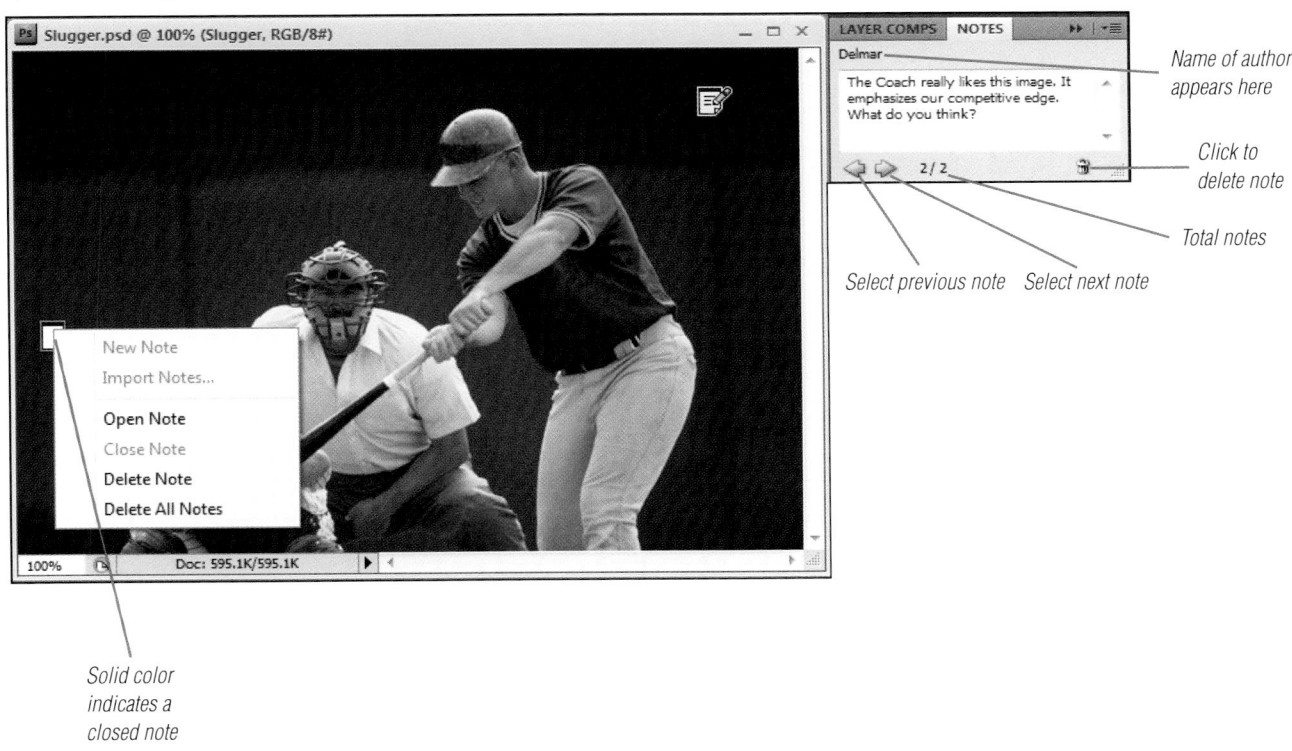

Name of author appears here

Click to delete note

Total notes

Select previous note   Select next note

Solid color indicates a closed note

Create a note

1. Open PS 15-1.psd from the drive and folder where you store your Data Files, update the text layers (if necessary), save the file as **Hawaiian Vacation**, then turn off any displayed guides (if necessary).

2. Click the **Note tool** 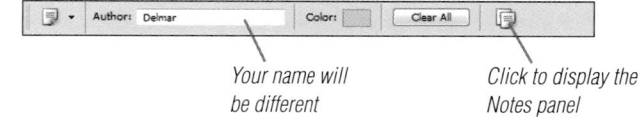 on the Tools panel.

3. If your name does not appear in the Name of author for notes text box on the options bar, select the contents of the text box, type **Your Name**, then press **[Enter]** (Win) or **[return]** (Mac).

4. Click the **Swatches panel tab** SWATCHES, click the **Note color box** on the options bar, then click **RGB Cyan** (the fourth swatch from the left in the first row) on the Swatches panel.

5. Click **OK**. Compare your options bar to Figure 2. The Note color box is cyan.

6. Display the rulers in pixels, then click in the water above the far left button at approximately **30 X/220 Y**.

7. Type the text shown in Figure 3.

8. Click the **Show or hide the notes panel button** in the Note tool options bar, then compare your image to Figure 4.

You used the Note tool to create a note within an image. You specified an author for the note, and you changed the color of the note icon using the Swatches panel. Notes are a great way to transmit information about an image.

FIGURE 2
Options for the Note tool

Your name will
be different

Click to display the
Notes panel

FIGURE 3
Note annotation in image

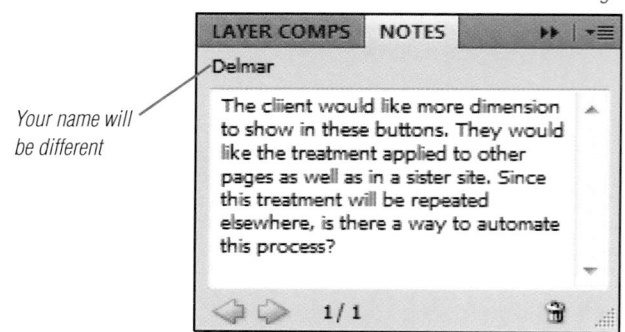

Your name will
be different

FIGURE 4
Note icon

Open note
icon

FIGURE 5
Notes panel contents

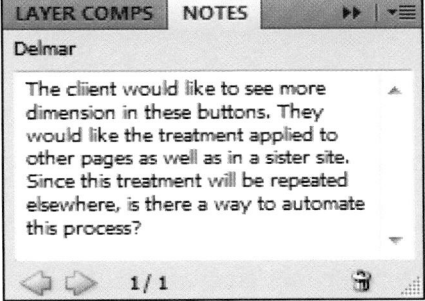

FIGURE 6
Note icon in image

Modify a note annotation

1. Click the **Show or hide the notes panel button** in the Note tool options bar.
2. Click to the **left of 'more'** in the first line of the note, type **to see**, select **to show (and its trailing space)**, then press **[Delete]**.

    Compare your note to Figure 5.
3. Click the image in the **shaded mountain** to the right of the island (beneath the 'n').
4. Type **The client may want to find another image for the next advertising cycle**.
5. Click the **Select previous note button** .

    The first note displays in the Notes panel.
6. Click the **Select next note button** in the Notes panel.
7. Click the **Delete note button** in the Notes panel, then click **Yes** to delete the note.

    One note remains in the image.
8. Save your work, then compare your image to Figure 6.

You modified an existing note, added a new note, viewed each of the notes using buttons in the Notes panel, then deleted the second note.

CREATE AN ACTION

What You'll Do

In this lesson, you'll create an action that applies a style to a layer by creating a snapshot that is used to restore your file to its original condition, then you'll record steps using the Actions panel.

Simplifying Common Tasks

Suppose you are responsible for maintaining the ad slicks for all your company's products (and there are a lot of them). What would you do if the company decided to change their image designs so that each existing product advertisement is shown with Drop Shadow and Inner Shadow styles? (Resigning your position is *not* an option.) Instead, you can create an action to speed up this monumental task.

Understanding Actions

Most tasks that you perform using a button or menu command can be recorded as an action. Each action can contain one or more steps and can also contain a **stop**, which lets you complete a command that can't be recorded (for example, the use of a painting tool). Actions can be stored in sets, which are saved as .atn files and are typically named by the category of actions they contain. For example, you can create multiple type-related actions, then store them in a set named Type Actions. You access actions from the Actions panel, which is normally grouped with the History panel. You can view actions in List Mode or in Button Mode on the Actions panel. The **List Mode**, the default, makes it possible to view the details within each action. The **Button Mode** displays each action without details.

QUICKTIP

The act of creating an action is not recorded on the History panel; however, the steps you record to define a new action are recorded on the History panel.

Knowing Your Options

You use commonly recognizable media player buttons to operate an action. These buttons are located at the bottom of the Actions panel and let you play, record and stop, as well as move forward and backward in an action.

QUICKTIP

The Actions panel displays in the Automation workspace.

Recording an Action

When recording is active, the red Recording button on the Actions panel appears. The action set also opens as soon as you begin recording to show all the individual actions in the set.

QUICKTIP

To test your actions, first you can create a snapshot of your image. Then you work on an action, make any changes, or record new steps. Use the snapshot to restore the image to its original state. After the image is restored, you can play the action to verify that the steps work.

Playing Back Actions

You can modify how actions are played back using the Playback Options dialog box, as shown in Figure 7. The playback options are described in Table 1. You can open the Playback Options dialog box by clicking the Actions panel list arrow, then clicking Playback Options. The Accelerated, Step by Step, and Pause For options control the speed at which the steps are performed.

QUICKTIP

An action creates internal automation, while **a script** (or scripting) creates external automation from an outside source. JavaScript, for example, lets you write Photoshop scripts that run on Windows or Mac OS.

FIGURE 7
Playback Options dialog box

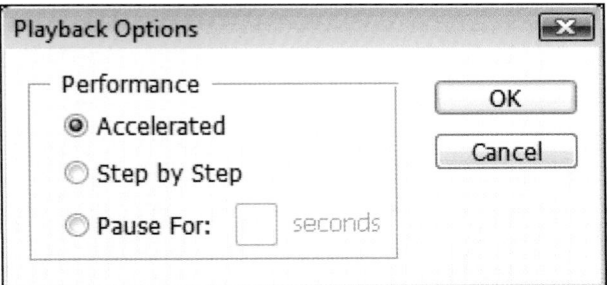

TABLE 1: Action Playback Options

option	description
Accelerated	Plays all steps within an action, then makes all changes.
Step by Step	Completes each step in an action and redraws the image before advancing to the next step.
Pause For	Lets you specify the number of seconds that should occur between steps in an action.

Create an action

1. Display the **Automation** workspace.

2. Click **Window** on the Application bar, click **History** to display the History panel, then click the **Create new snapshot button** 📷.

3. Drag the **History panel tab** `HISTORY` out of the Actions panel group so it appears separately to the left of the Actions panel.

   > TIP By default, the History panel window is small. Enlarge it by dragging the bottom edge.

4. Verify that the **triangle** to the left of the Default Actions set on the Actions panel is facing to the right and that the set is closed. Compare your panel to Figure 8.

   > TIP You can toggle the button mode on and off by clicking the list arrow on the Actions panel, then clicking Button Mode.

   You can click the triangle next to a *set* to show or hide the actions in it. You can also click the triangle next to an *action* to show or hide the steps in it.

   > TIP When you create an action in the Default Actions set, or in any set, the action is available in all your Photoshop images.

5. Click the **Create new action button** 🔲 on the Actions panel. The New Action dialog box opens.

6. Type **Button Drop Shadow** in the Name text box.

7. Click the **Color list arrow**, click **Violet**, then compare your dialog box to Figure 9.

8. Click **Record**. Did you notice that the red Recording button is displayed on the Actions panel and all default actions opened? See Figure 10.

You created a snapshot to make it possible to easily test the new action. You used the Create new action button on the Actions panel to create an action called Button Drop Shadow.

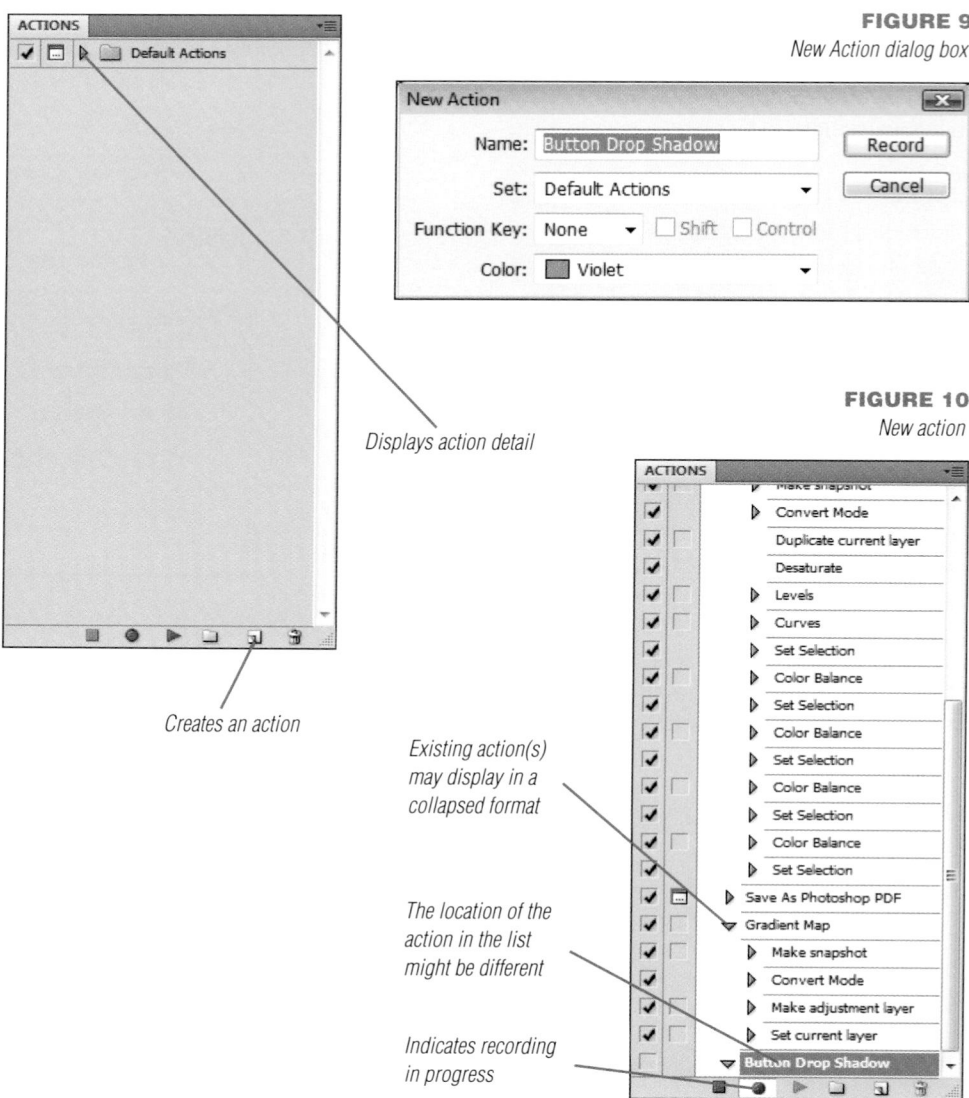

FIGURE 8
Actions panel with detail hidden

FIGURE 9
New Action dialog box

Displays action detail

Creates an action

FIGURE 10
New action

Existing action(s) may display in a collapsed format

The location of the action in the list might be different

Indicates recording in progress

Annotating and Automating an Image

FIGURE 11
Layer Style dialog box

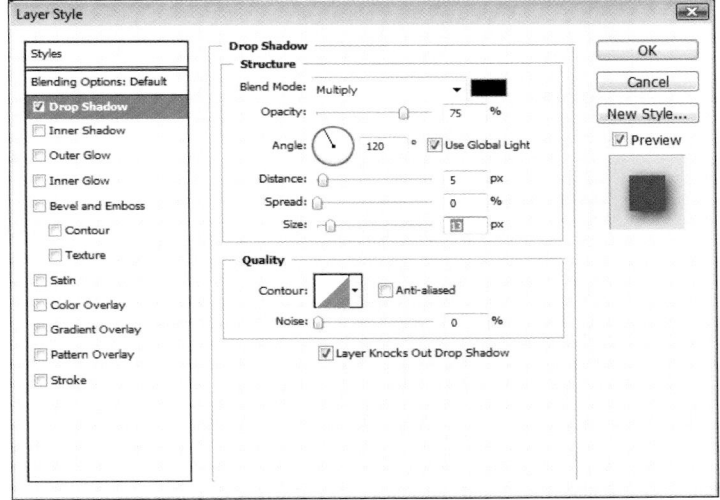

FIGURE 13
Modified image

Drop shadow
behind buttons

FIGURE 12
Selected action

Record an action

1. Click the **Button layer** on the Layers panel (if it is not already selected).

2. Click the **Add a layer style button** *fx.* on the Layers panel, click **Drop Shadow**, then change your Layer Style dialog box settings so they match those shown in Figure 11.

3. Click **OK**.

4. Click the **Stop playing/recording button** on the Actions panel.

5. Click the **Button Drop Shadow action** on the Actions panel. See Figure 12.

6. Scroll to the top of the History panel (if necessary), then click **Snapshot 1**.

   The Button layer returns to its original appearance.

7. With the **Button Drop Shadow action** still selected, click the **Play selection button** on the Actions panel.

8. Save your work, then compare your screen to Figure 13.

You recorded steps for the Button Drop Shadow action. After the recording was complete, you used a snapshot to restore the image to its original state, \then you played the action to test it. Testing is an important step in creating an action.

MODIFY AN
ACTION

What You'll Do

In this lesson, you'll modify the recently created action by adding new steps to it.

Getting It Right

Few of us get everything right the first time we try to do something. After you create an action, you might think of other steps that you want to include, such as changing the order of some or all of the steps, or altering an option. The beauty of Photoshop actions is that you can make modifications and additions to them with little effort.

Revising an Action

You can modify an existing action by clicking the step that is just above where you want the new step(s) to appear. Click the Begin recording button on the Actions panel, record your steps (just as you did when you initially created the action), then click the Stop playing/recording button when you're finished. The new steps are inserted after the selected step.

> QUICKTIP
>
> Because users may not know how to resume playback after encountering a stop, it's a good idea to include a helpful tip that tells them to click the Play selection button after encountering the stop.

Changing the Actions Panel View

In addition to dragging the borders to change the shape of the Actions panel, you can also change the way the steps are displayed. By default, actions are displayed in a list; the steps appear as a list below each action included in them. Figure 14 shows the actions in the Default Actions set in a list in which all the detail is accessible but hidden. (Remember that you can display the detail for each action by clicking the triangle next to the action, to expand it.)

Working in Button Mode

In Button Mode, each action is displayed as a button—without the additional detail found in the list format. Each button is displayed in the color selected when the action was created and the Play button is not displayed. In Button Mode, all you need to do to play an action is to click the button. Figure 15 shows the same actions in Button Mode. You can toggle between these two modes by clicking the Actions panel list arrow, then clicking Button Mode, as shown in Figure 16.

FIGURE 14
Actions displayed in a list

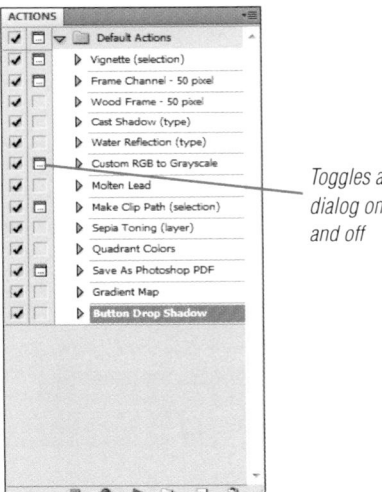

Toggles a
dialog on
and off

FIGURE 15
Actions displayed in Button Mode

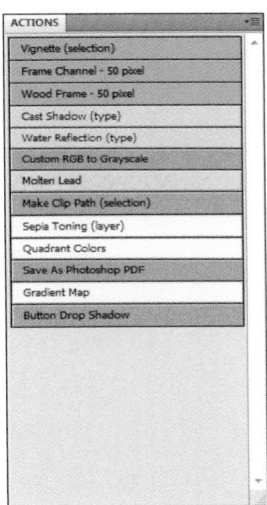

FIGURE 16
Actions panel menu

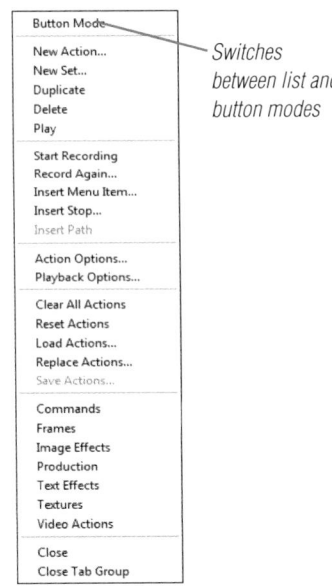

Switches
between list and
button modes

Understanding a stop

In addition to containing any Photoshop task, an action can include a stop, which is a command that interrupts playback to allow you to perform other operations—particularly those that cannot be recorded in an action, or those that might change each time you play the action. You insert a stop by clicking the step *just above* where you want the pause to take place. Click the Actions panel list arrow, then click Insert Stop. The Record Stop dialog box opens, allowing you to enter a text message that appears when the action is stopped, as shown in Figure 17. You select the Allow Continue check box to include a Continue button in the message that appears when the action is stopped. You can resume the action by clicking this button. An action that contains a dialog box—such as an action that contains a stop—displays a toggle dialog on/off icon to the left of the action name on the Actions panel. This icon indicates a **modal control**, which means that dialog boxes are *used* in the action, but are not displayed. When the action is resumed, the tasks begin where they were interrupted. You can resume the action by clicking the Play selection button on the Actions panel.

FIGURE 17
Record Stop dialog box

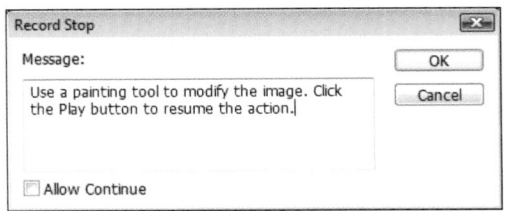

Add steps to an action

1. Verify that the **Button layer** is active on the Layers panel.
2. Click the **Set Layer Styles of current layer step** (the first step) in the Button Drop Shadow action on the Actions panel.
3. Click the **Begin recording button** ⬤ on the Actions panel.
4. Click **Image** on the Application bar, point to **Adjustments**, then click **Brightness/Contrast**. Change the settings in your dialog box to match the settings in Figure 18.
5. Click **OK**.
6. Click the **Stop playing/recording button** ▪ on the Actions panel. Compare your Actions panel to Figure 19.

   The Button Drop Shadow action has a new step added to it.
7. Click **Snapshot 1** on the History panel.
8. Click the **Button Drop Shadow action** on the Actions panel, then click the **Play selection button** ▶ on the Actions panel. Compare your screen to Figure 20.

You added a new step (which modified the brightness/contrast) to the Button Drop Shadow action. You then tested the modified action by using a snapshot and playing the action.

FIGURE 18
Brightness/Contrast dialog box

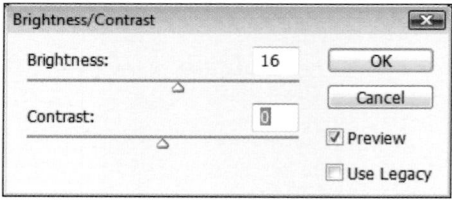

FIGURE 19
New steps added to the Button Drop Shadow action

FIGURE 20
Result of modified action

Annotating and Automating an Image

FIGURE 21
Modified image

Automating with data sets

You can use the Photoshop Variables feature to combine text and images into a graphic template. Imagine a Photoshop image that contains placeholders for the name of a car, it's make and model, price, and an image of the car. Use as many layers as you like to put all the graphic elements needed to finish the completed files, such as .jpgs for each car, in a single folder, click Image on the Application bar, point to Variables, then click Define. Use the Variables dialog box to assign variables for text and graphic layers, and use a text editor to create a document containing variables separated by commas. To create the data sets, click Image on the Application bar, point to Variables, point to Data Sets, then click Import. You can export the data sets as individual files by clicking File on the Application bar, pointing to Export, then clicking Data Sets as Files. Once you've made any changes to the individual files, you can use the Image Processor in Bridge to create flattened copies.

Add steps and modify an action

1. Click the **Brightness/Contrast step** on the Actions panel (the second step in the Button Drop Shadow action).
2. Click the **Begin recording button** ⬤ on the Actions panel.
3. Click the **Add a layer style button** *fx*. on the Layers panel.
4. Click **Bevel and Emboss**, then click **OK** to accept the existing settings.
5. Click the **Stop playing/recording button** 🔳 on the Actions panel.

   The new step is added to the existing action. Table 2 describes other ways to modify actions.
6. Click **Snapshot 1** on the History panel.
7. Click the **Button Drop Shadow action** on the Actions panel, then click the **Play selection button** ▶ on the Actions panel.
8. Save your work, then compare your image to Figure 21.

You added the Bevel and Emboss style to an action, then you tested the action.

TABLE 2: Methods for Modifying an Action

modification type	method
Rearrange steps	Move an existing step by dragging the step to a new location in the action.
Add new commands	Click the step above or below where you want the new step to appear, then click ▶ .
Rerecord existing commands	Click the step you want to recreate, click ▾≡, then click Record Again.
Duplicate existing commands	Click the step you want to duplicate, click ▾≡, then click Duplicate.
Delete actions	Click the action you want to delete, then click 🗑 .
Delete a step in an action	Click the step you want to delete, then click 🗑 .
Change options in an action	Click the step that has options you want to change, click ▾≡, then click Action Options or Playback Options.

USE A DEFAULT ACTION
AND CREATE A DROPLET

What You'll Do

In this lesson, you'll use actions from other sets and create a droplet.

Taking Advantage of Actions

Photoshop actions can really help your session by automating tedious tasks. You can add a default action to any action you've created. A **default action** is an action that is prerecorded and tested, and comes with Photoshop. You can incorporate some of these nifty actions that come with Photoshop into those you create.

Identifying Default Actions

The default actions that come with Photoshop are Vignette, Frame Channel, Wood Frame, Cast Shadow, Water Reflection, Custom RGB to Grayscale, Molten Lead, Make Clip Path (selection), Sepia Toning (layer), Quadrant Colors, Save As Photoshop PDF, and Gradient Map. In addition, there are seven action sets that come with Photoshop: Commands, Frames, Image Effects, Production, Text Effects, Textures, and Video Actions. You can load any of these action sets by clicking the Actions panel list arrow, then clicking the name of the set you want to load.

Using Default Actions

You can incorporate any of the default actions that come with Photoshop—or those you get from other sources—into a new action by playing the action in the process of recording a new one. Each time an existing action is played, a new snapshot is created on the History panel, so don't be surprised when you see additional snapshots that you never created. To incorporate an existing action into a new action, first select the step that is *above* where you want the new action to occur. Begin recording your action, then scroll through the Actions panel and play the action you want to include. When the action has completed all steps, you can continue recording other steps or click the Stop playing/ recording button if you are done. That's it: all of the steps in the default action will be performed when you play your new action.

Loading Sets

In addition to the Default Actions, the seven additional sets of actions are listed at the bottom of the Actions panel menu.

If you store actions from other sources on your computer you can load those actions by clicking the Actions panel list arrow, clicking Load Actions, then choosing the action you want from the Load dialog box. The default sets that come with Photoshop are stored in the Actions folder that is in the Presets folder of the Adobe Photoshop CS4 folder.

QUICKTIP

If you want to save actions to distribute to others, you must first put them in a set. You create a set by clicking the Create new set button on the Actions panel (just like creating a Layer set). Place the action or actions in a set, select the set, click the Actions panel list arrow, then click Save Actions.

Understanding a Droplet

A **droplet** is a stand-alone action in the form of an icon. You can drag one or more closed Photoshop files onto a droplet icon to perform the action on the file or files. You can store droplets on the hard drive on your computer, place them on your desktop, or distribute them to others using other storage media. Figure 22 shows an example of a droplet on the desktop. Droplets let you further automate repetitive tasks.

Creating a Droplet

You create a droplet by using the Automate command on the File menu, an existing action, and the Create Droplet dialog box. In the Create Droplet dialog box, you use the Set list arrow to choose the set that

contains the action you want to use to create the droplet, then use the Action list arrow to choose the action. Finally, you can choose the location on your computer where you'll store the droplet.

QUICKTIP

When placed on the desktop, a droplet has a unique down-arrow icon filled with the Photoshop logo. The droplet name appears below the icon.

FIGURE 22
A droplet on the desktop

Photoshop droplet

Icons on your desktop will be different

Automating using batches

There may be times when you might need to perform the same action on multiple files. Rather than dragging each image onto a droplet, one at a time, you can combine all of the images into a batch. A **batch** is a group of images designated to have the same action performed on them simultaneously. You can create a batch using all of the files in one specific folder or using all of the Photoshop images that are currently open. When you have opened or organized the files you want to include in a batch, click File on the Application bar, point to Automate, then click Batch. The Batch dialog box opens, offering you options similar to those used for creating droplets. You can also use Adobe Bridge as a source of creating batches by clicking Tools on the Adobe Bridge menu bar, pointing to Photoshop, then clicking Batch.

Include a default action within an action

1. Verify that the **Set Layer Styles of current layer step** at the bottom of the Actions panel is active (the last step in the Button Drop Shadow action).

   TIP If your Actions panel becomes too messy, you can clear it by clicking the Actions panel list arrow, then clicking Clear All Actions. To restore the Default Actions set, click the Actions panel list arrow, then click Reset Actions.

2. Verify that the **Button layer** is active in the Layers panel.

3. Click the **Begin recording button** ⦿ on the Actions panel.

4. Scroll to the top of the Actions panel, then click the **Cast Shadow (type) action**, as shown in Figure 23.

You prepared to insert the Cast Shadow default action into the Button Drop Shadow action. If this action had been applied to a type layer, the type would have been rasterized before the effect could be applied.

FIGURE 23

Action to be added to the Button Drop Shadow action

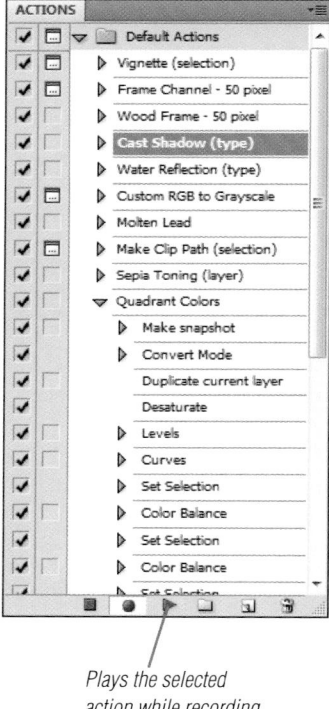

Plays the selected action while recording

FIGURE 24

Example of a website that offers Photoshop Actions

Courtesy of http://www.visual-blast.com/

Finding actions on the web

Actions can be fun to design, and the more practice you get, the more you'll want to make use of them. But no matter how good you are, time is at a premium for most of us. You can find great actions on the web—and many of them are free! Figure 24 shows one example of a website that offers free actions. Just connect to the web, open your browser and favorite search engine, and search on the text "Photoshop Actions."

FIGURE 25

*Cast Shadow action in the Button Drop
Shadow action*

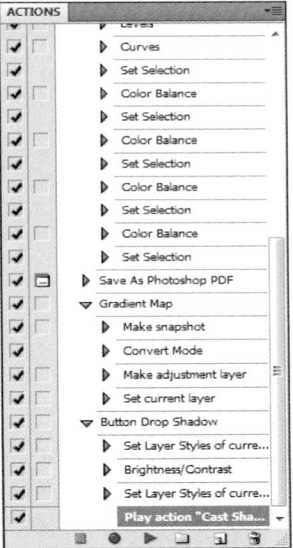

FIGURE 26

Modified Layers panel

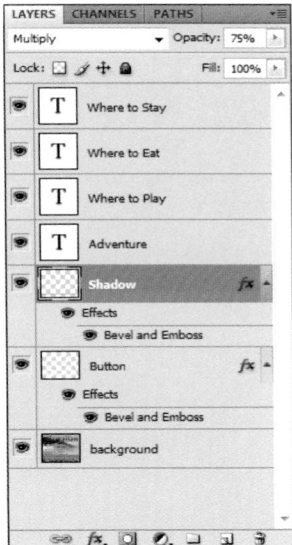

Play an existing action in a new action

1. Click the **Play selection button** ▶ on the Actions panel.

2. Click the **Stop playing/recording button** ▪ on the Actions panel. A new layer is created in the Layers panel. Compare your Actions panel to Figure 25.

3. Click **Snapshot 1** on the History panel.

   TIP Some default actions create a snapshot as their initial step. For this reason, you might see multiple snapshots on the History panel.

4. Click the **Button Drop Shadow action** on the Actions panel.

5. Click the **Play selection button** ▶ on the Actions panel.

6. Save your work, then compare your Layers panel to Figure 26.

   The Cast Shadow action added a reflection beneath the buttons.

You included the Cast Shadow action in the Button Drop Shadow action. You used the snapshot to revert to the image's original appearance and replayed the action, which modified the image.

Understanding scripts and actions

Like an action, a script is a series of commands that manipulates objects in Photoshop and the other programs of the Creative Suite. While individual actions are tremendous time-savers, you can use Photoshop Scripts to save even more time performing repetitive tasks. A script has the following advantages over an action in that it can:

- contain conditional logic, giving it the ability to make decisions based on content.
- perform actions that involve multiple applications, such as those programs found in the Creative Suite.
- open, save, and rename files.
- be copied from one computer to another. An action would have to be recreated or turned into a droplet.
- use variable file paths to locate and open a file.

You can manage scripts within Photoshop using the Script Events Manager, which is accessed by clicking File on the Application bar, pointing to Scripts, then clicking Script Events Manager.

Create a droplet

1. Click **File** on the Application bar, point to **Automate**, then click **Create Droplet**.

2. Click **Choose** in the Create Droplet dialog box.

   The Save dialog box opens.

3. Type **Button Drop Shadow-Cast Shadow** in the File name text box (Win) or Save As text box (Mac) in the Save dialog box.

4. Click the **Save in list arrow** (Win) or **Places panel** (Mac), then click **Desktop**, as shown in Figure 27.

   TIP You can create a droplet and save it anywhere on your computer by clicking the Save in list arrow (Win) or Places panel (Mac), and clicking the location where you want to store the file.

5. Click **Save**.

6. Click the **Action list arrow** in the Create Droplet dialog box, then click **Button Drop Shadow** (if it is not already selected). Compare your dialog box settings to Figure 28.

7. Click **OK**.

You created a droplet using the Button Drop Shadow action and saved it to the desktop for easy access.

FIGURE 27
Save dialog box

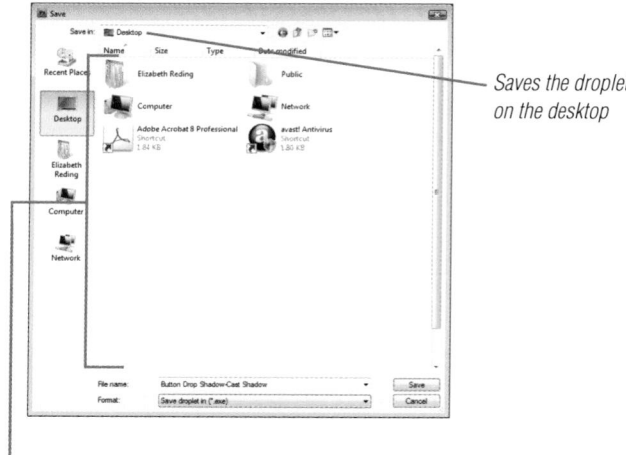

Saves the droplet on the desktop

Your list will be different

FIGURE 28
Create Droplet dialog box

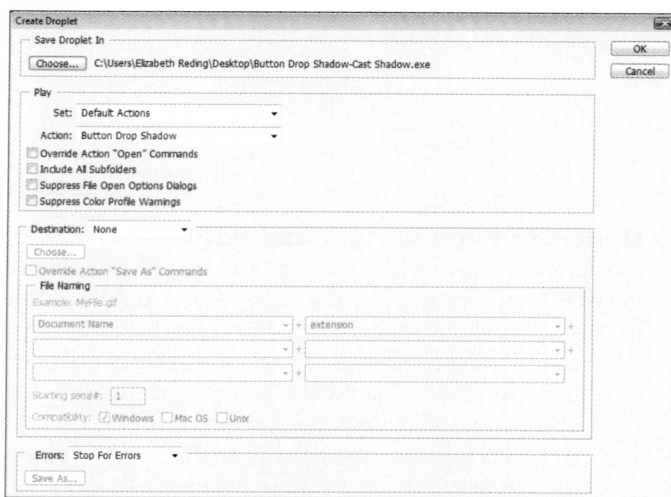

FIGURE 29
Droplet on desktop

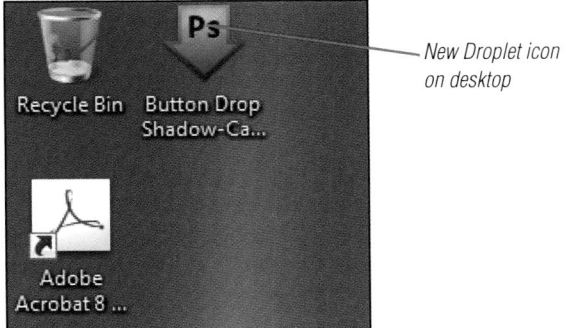

New Droplet icon
on desktop

FIGURE 30
Image updated by droplet

Run a droplet

1. Minimize all open windows so the desktop is visible, then compare your desktop to Figure 29.

2. Maximize the Photoshop window.

3. Click **Snapshot 1** on the History panel.

4. Save your work, close the Hawaiian Vacation image, then minimize Photoshop (Win) or Hide Photoshop (Mac).

   > TIP When Photoshop is *not* running, activating a droplet automatically launches the program.

5. Locate the closed Hawaiian Vacation image on your computer, using the file management program of your choice, then adjust the windows so you can see the Hawaiian Vacation file and the droplet icon on the desktop.

6. Drag the **Hawaiian Vacation file** onto the droplet icon on the desktop.

   The Photoshop window is restored, the Hawaiian Vacation image opens, and the action is replayed.

   > TIP Sometimes a file automatically closes after a droplet has been applied. To see the applied droplet, you must reopen the file.

7. Display the **Essentials workspace**, save your work, then compare your screen to Figure 30.

8. Close the file and exit Photoshop, then drag the **droplet** to the location where you store your Data Files.

You returned the image to its original appearance by using Snapshot 1 on the History panel, and closed the file. Then you tested the droplet by dragging the Hawaiian Vacation file onto the droplet.

Power User Shortcuts

to do this:	use this method:	to do this:	use this method:
Apply droplet	Drag closed Photoshop file onto droplet	Expand action detail	▷
Change author display	▤ or [Shift] I, then type name in Name of author for notes text box	Open a closed note	Double-click note icon
		Play an action	▶
Change Note icon color	▤ or [Shift] I, click Note color color box, choose color, then click OK	Record an action	●, then perform tasks
Close an open note	Click ▤	Record an action from another set	●, click existing action in another set, click ▶, then click ▪
Collapse action detail	▼	Return Actions panel to original size and location	Workspace Switcher➤ Automation
Create a batch	File ➤ Automate ➤ Batch		
Create a droplet	File ➤ Automate ➤ Create Droplet	Revert image to original appearance using a snapshot	HISTORY, click snapshot
Create a note	▤ or [Shift] I, then click where you want the note to appear		
		Stop recording	▪
Create a snapshot	▦ on the History panel	Toggle Actions panel between List and Button Modes	▾≡, then click Button Mode
Create an action	▣ on the Actions panel, select options, then click ●		
		Select next note	➪
Delete a note	Select note, press [Delete] (Win), or click ▤	Select previous note	⬅

Key: Menu items are indicated by ➤ between the menu name and its command. Blue bold letters are shortcuts for selecting tools on the Tools panel.

Annotating and Automating an Image

Add annotations to an image.

1. Open PS 15-2.psd from the drive and folder where you store your Data Files, then save it as **Team Players**.
2. Select the Note tool.
3. Enter your name as the Author of the note (if necessary).
4. Change the Note color to Pure Magenta (the second box from the right in the fifth row of the Swatches panel).
5. Display the rulers (if necessary).
6. Click the image at 30 X/650 Y, then type the following: **This will make a great motivational poster for our department**.
7. Close the note.
8. Hide the rulers, then save your work.

Create an action.

1. Make the A Source of Strength and Stability layer active (if it is not already active).
2. Display the Automation workspace and the History panel, and create a new snapshot using the History panel, then display the Actions panel.
3. Collapse the Default Actions set (if necessary).
4. Create a new action using the Actions panel.
5. Name the new action **Motivation**, and apply the color Yellow to it.
6. Record the action using the following steps:
   a. Make the Team Players layer active.
   b. Change the font in this layer to an 85 pt Impact (or another font available on your computer).
   c. Stop recording.

7. Click Snapshot 1 on the History panel to restore the original appearance of the image.
8. Replay the Motivation action.
9. Save your work.

Modify an action.

1. Select Set current text layer of the Motivation action at the bottom of the Actions panel.
2. Begin recording the following steps:
   a. Make the A Source of Strength and Stability layer active.
   b. Change the font in this layer to a 36 pt Impact (or another font available on your computer).
   c. Make the Team Players layer active.
   d. Add the default Bevel and Emboss style with Contour to the layer.
   e. Stop recording.
3. Click Snapshot 1 on the History panel to restore the original appearance of the image.
4. Replay the Motivation action.
5. Save your work.

Use a default action and create a droplet.

1. Make the A Source of Strength and Stability layer active.
2. Select the Set Layer Styles of current layer step (the last step in the Motivation action).
3. Begin recording the following steps:
   a. Make the Team Players layer active.
   b. Play the Water Reflection (type) action in Default Actions. (Substitute another action if this one is not available.)
   c. Stop recording.

4. Click Snapshot 1 on the History panel to restore the original appearance of the image.
5. Replay the Motivation action.
6. Restore Snapshot 1, then save your changes.
7. Create a droplet on the desktop called **Motivation** using the Motivation action, save your work, then exit Photoshop.
8. Drag the Team Players file onto the Motivation droplet. See Figure 31.
9. Drag the droplet to the location where you store your Data Files.

FIGURE 31
Completed Skills Review project

As the newest member of the Game Corporation design team, you have noticed that some of your fellow designers perform many repetitive tasks and could really benefit from using actions. One of these repetitive tasks is taking a single-layer image, creating a layer from the Background layer, creating a new layer, then turning the new layer into the Background layer. This way, they can preserve the Background layer while modifying the image that was on the existing Background layer. You want to make their lives easier, so you decide to create an action that completes this task. To circulate the action among your co-workers, you decide to create a droplet for this action that you can e-mail or post to the network. (*Hint:* There are a variety of steps in a varied sequence you can take to create this action.)

1. Open PS 15-3.psd, then save it as **New Layers**.
2. Create a snapshot of the current image using the default name.
3. Hide any displayed action details (if necessary).
4. Write down the steps you will need to perform to create this action. (You can use a word processor or a sheet of paper, or you can use the Notes panel in Photoshop.)
5. Create a new action in the Default Actions set called **New Layers**.

6. Apply the Orange color to the action.
7. Record the necessary steps to complete the action.
8. Use the snapshot to return the image to its original condition.
9. Play the action to verify that it works as you expected.
10. If the action does not perform as expected, make any necessary modifications to it.

FIGURE 32
Sample Project Builder 1

11. Save your work, then compare your screen, Layers panel, and Actions panel to the sample in Figure 32.
12. Create a droplet for the action named **New Layers**, then save it in the drive and folder where you store your Data Files.

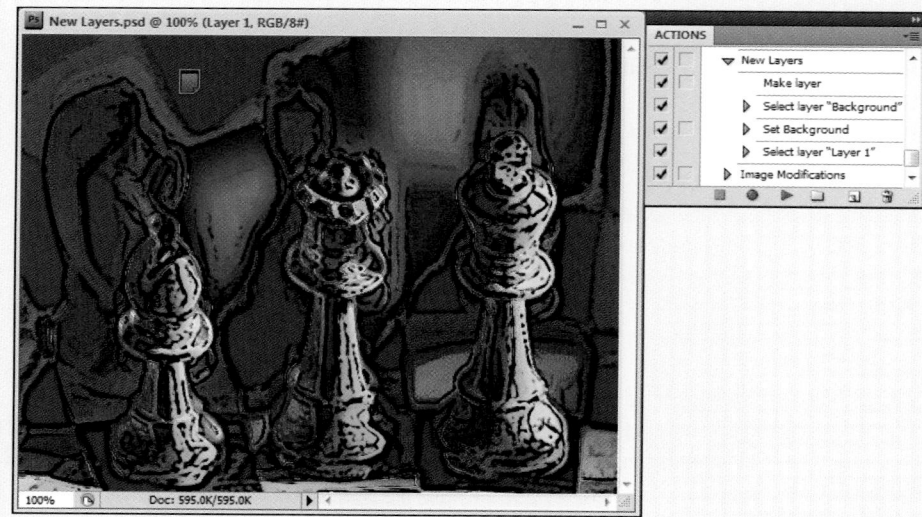

Annotating and Automating an Image

An anniversary is coming up for some friends of your family. You and your twin have decided to collaborate on a gift, even though you live at opposite sides of the country. You each have a great photo of the couple that you'd like to modify in the same way, using Photoshop. Because your twin has a slow Internet connection, you decide to create a droplet (which is significantly smaller in size than a completed Photoshop image), then e-mail the droplet so that your twin can apply it to the photo. The droplet can be used to apply your proposed modifications to the picture.

1. Open PS 15-4.psd, then save it as **Anniversary Gift**.
2. Create a snapshot of the current image using the default name.
3. After examining the image, decide what changes you want to make. Write down the steps you will need to perform to create this action, including any stops. (*Hint*: You can use any of your Photoshop skills and any Photoshop features. It is recommended that you create a layer from the Background layer, then create a new layer to be used as the Background layer. Include any necessary color corrections in adjustment layers.)
4. Create a new action in the Default Actions set called **Image Modifications**.
5. Apply the red color to the action (for the Button Mode).

6. Record the steps you wrote down. (*Hint*: In the sample, a 48 pt Trebuchet MS font is used. You do not have to include a type layer, but if you do, use any font available on your computer.)
7. Use the snapshot to return the image to its original condition.
8. Play the action to verify that it works as you expected.

FIGURE 33
Sample Project Builder 2

9. If the action does not perform as expected, make any necessary corrections to it.
10. Save your work, then compare your image, Layers panel, and Actions panel to the sample in Figure 33.
11. Create a droplet for the new action called **Gift Image**, and save it to the drive and folder where you store your Data Files.

The Internet is a great resource for actions and droplets. You can find many actions that incorporate sophisticated design concepts. Some websites let you download actions for free, while others might charge a subscription fee. As you perfect your skills using actions, you decide to scour the web and see what cool actions you can find.

1. Connect to the Internet and use your browser to find Photoshop actions. (Make a record of the site you found so you can use it for future reference, if necessary.)
2. Download an action that you want to try.
3. Create a new Photoshop image called **Action Sample** using any dimensions.
4. Supply any imagery and/or type layers by using any electronic images you can acquire through Internet purchase, from your hard disk, or by using a scanner. Use any fonts available on your computer.
5. Duplicate the image and type layers to preserve your original image.
6. Create a note anywhere on the image, indicating the source of the action (include the URL).
7. Create a snapshot of the image.
8. Load and play the action in the image. If necessary, click Continue or OK to accept any messages or settings in dialog boxes that open.
9. Create a droplet called **Play Downloaded Action**.

10. Save your work to the drive and folder where you store your Data Files, then compare your screen (and the partial view of the downloaded action) to the sample in Figure 34.
11. Review the design features used in your downloaded action.

FIGURE 34
Sample Design Project

Creating an interesting design can be a challenge. As a motivational exercise, the head of your department has asked you to create an image to inspire a positive working environment using Photoshop actions, along with your raw creativity and imagination. You can choose any topic for the artwork, work with any existing or scanned imagery, and use any new or existing actions. As you determine what actions to create, think about why a series of tasks is worthy of an action. How will automating a task benefit you, your co-workers, and your organization? Think efficiency; think quality.

1. Create a new Photoshop image with any dimensions.
2. Save this file as **Game Plan**.
3. Locate artwork—either on your computer, in a royalty-free collection, or from scanned images.
4. Sketch a rough draft of your layout.
5. Add any necessary type layers using any fonts available on your computer. (*Hint*: In the sample, a Comic Sans MS font is used.)
6. Create a note that lists the actions you used. (*Hint*: You can use actions created in this chapter, or you can create one or more new actions, if necessary.)

7. Write down the steps that were used in any new actions. Review the following questions: Why did you create the actions that you did? What factors determined that a task should be converted into an action?

8. Be prepared to prove that the actions work correctly.
9. Save your work, then compare your image, Layers panel, and Actions panel to the sample in Figure 35.

FIGURE 35
Sample Portfolio Project

chapter **16**

CREATING IMAGES FOR THE WEB

1. Learn about web features

2. Optimize images for web use

3. Create a button for a web page

4. Create slices in an image

5. Create and play basic animation

6. Add tweening and frame delay

7. Modify video in Photoshop

8. Use Camera Raw features

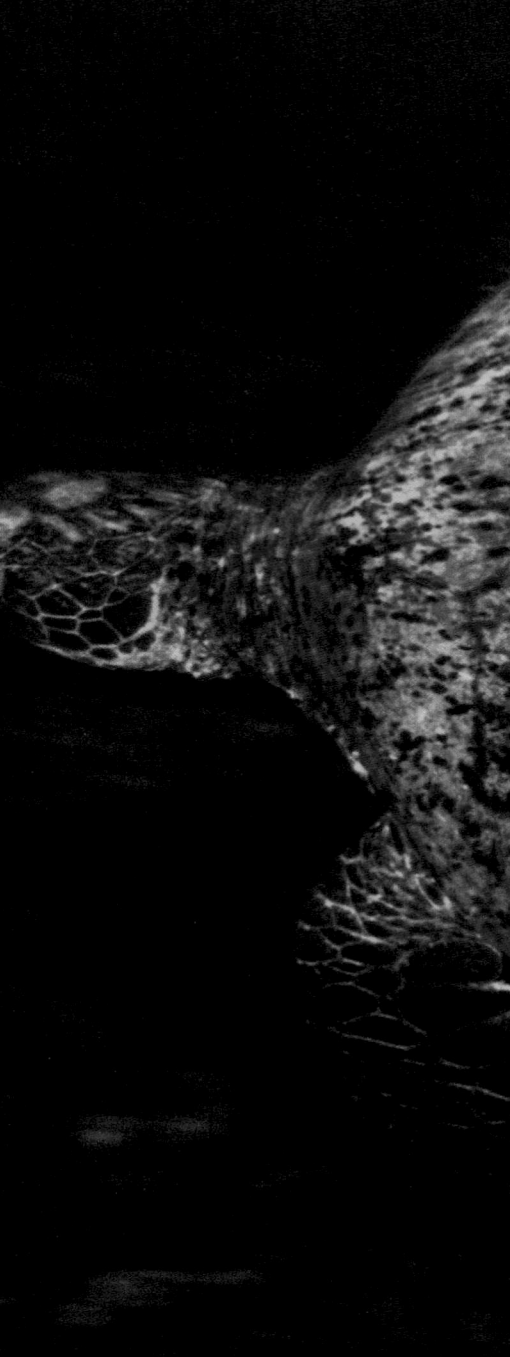

Using Photoshop for the Web
In addition to creating exciting images that can be professionally printed, you can use the tools in Photoshop to create images for use on the web. Once you have a Photoshop image, you can use additional web-specific tools and features to add the dimension and functionality required by today's web audience.

Understanding Web Graphics
Images and graphics can be tailored specifically for the web by creating buttons and other features unique to web pages. Using Photoshop, you can combine impressive graphics with interactive functionality to create an outstanding website.

> **QUICK**TIP
> Photoshop provides the capabilities for dividing one image into smaller, more manageable parts, and for creating more efficient web-ready files.

Extending Skills to Video
Photoshop Extended and QuickTime can be used to play and modify video. Almost any Photoshop skill you can apply to images can be applied to video clips.

Fine-Tuning Images with Camera Raw
Images that you take with your own digital camera can be tweaked using Adobe Bridge and the Camera Raw dialog box. You can use the Camera Raw dialog box to adjust images in RAW format (as well as those in JPG and TIFF formats) while preserving all the original image data.

Tools You'll Use

Slice tool

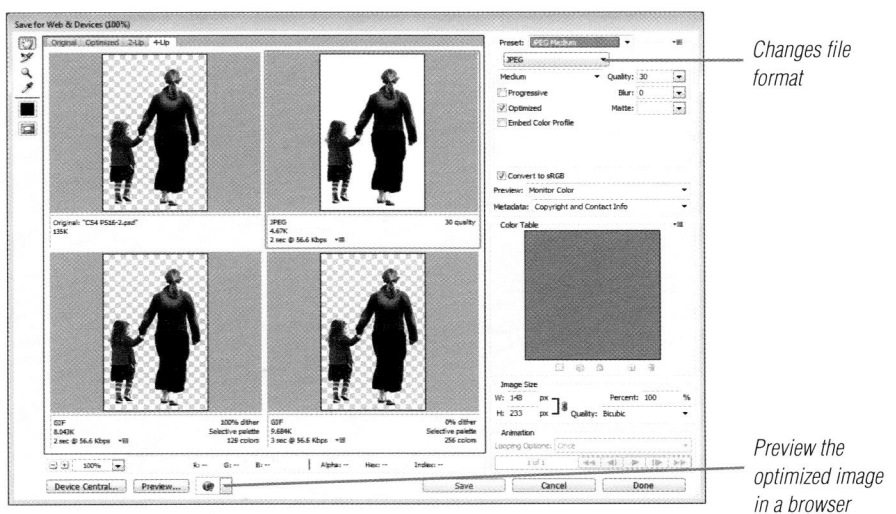

Changes file format

Preview the optimized image in a browser

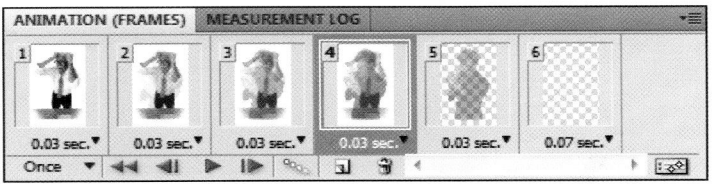

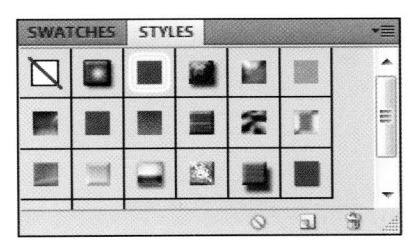

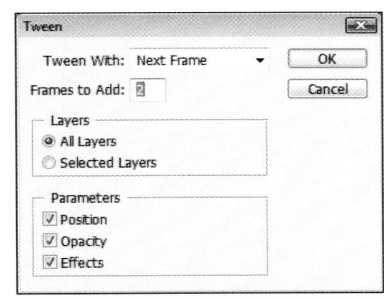

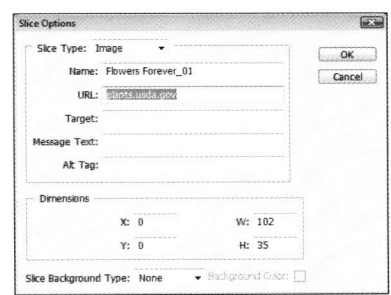

LEARN ABOUT
WEB FEATURES

What You'll Do

In this lesson, you'll open and rename a
file in Photoshop, create slices and then
turn off the display of the slices.

Using Photoshop to Create Web Documents

Using Photoshop to create web documents is
similar to creating any other image, except
that there are new features that you will use.
These new features include **slices** (subsec-
tions of an image to which you can assign
additional functionality) and the Animation
panel. The Animation panel does exactly
what it's name suggests: it is used to apply
movement to layers in an image.

> QUICKTIP
>
> Photoshop contains a web-specific workspace (called Web)
> that contains panels you're likely to use when creating
> documents for the web.

Previewing Files for the Web

You can add many sophisticated web
effects to the files you create in Photoshop,
such as slices and animation, as shown in
Figure 1. To insert and view them in a web
page, you need to follow the procedures
dictated by your HTML editor. HTML
(Hypertext Markup Language) is the
language used for creating web pages. You
can preview most web effects directly in
Photoshop. You can preview your files in

your browser by clicking the Preview the optimized image in a browser button in the Save For Web & Devices dialog box.

Creating Navigational and Interactive Functionality

You can divide an image you create for a website into many smaller sections, or slices. You use a **slice** to assign special features, such as links and animation, to specific areas within an image. **Links** allow you to direct the reader to sites specifically related to a particular topic. An image sequence, or **animation**, simulates an object moving on a web page. You can create an animation by making slight changes to several images, and then adjusting the timing between their appearances. When you convert an image to HTML, slices become cells in an HTML table, and animations become files in object folders.

FIGURE 1
Image with web features

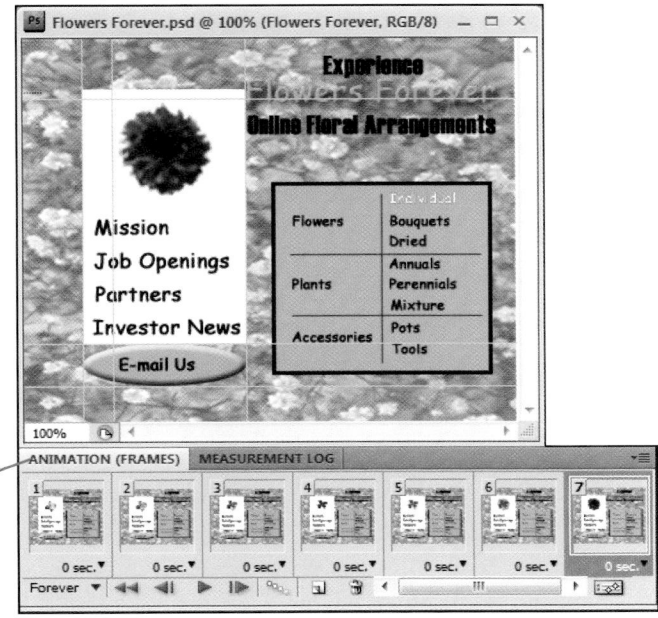

Creates the appearance of animation

View Slices

1. Start Photoshop, open PS 16-1.psd from the drive and folder where you store your Data Files, then save it as **Europa Market**.

   TIP Update the text layers if you see a message box stating that some text layers need to be updated before they can be used for vector-based output.

2. Click the **Default Foreground and Background Colors button** 🔳 on the Tools panel.

3. Verify that the rulers display in pixels.

4. Click the **Slice tool** ✂ on the Tools panel.

   TIP The Slice tool is grouped with the Crop tool and the Slice Select tool.

5. Display the **Web** workspace.

6. Use the **Zoom tool** 🔍 on the Application bar to change the magnification level to 200% (selecting the Resize Windows to Fit check box, if necessary).

7. Click **Window** on the Application bar, then click **Animation**.
   The Animation panel and the slices in the Europa Market image are visible. Compare your screen to Figure 2.

You opened an image in Photoshop, then displayed the document slices and the Animation panel.

FIGURE 2
Image with slices and Animation panel

Individual
slice

Magnification
level

Animation
panel

Creating Images for the Web

FIGURE 3
Slices turned off

*Your magnification
level may differ*

1. Click **View** on the Application bar, point to **Show** then deselect **Slices**.

2. Click the **Fit Screen button** [Fit Screen] on the options bar.

   The size of the document may change (depending on the size of your monitor and your resolution setting) after clicking the Fit Screen button. This button is just one more tool you can use to create your ideal work environment.

3. Verify that the guides are displayed, then compare your image to Figure 3.

You adjusted your view of the image, turned off the display of the Slices, then verified that the guides are displayed.

OPTIMIZE IMAGES
FOR WEB USE

What You'll Do

In this lesson, you'll optimize an image for the web in Photoshop. Then you'll modify the optimized image and add it to an existing file.

Understanding Optimization

You can create an awesome image in Photoshop and merge and flatten layers conscientiously, but still end up with a file so large that no one will wait for it to download from the web. An **optimized** file is as beautiful as a non-optimized file; it's just a fraction of its original size.

Optimizing a File

When you optimize a file, you save it in a format that balances the need for detail and accurate color against file size. Photoshop allows you to compare an image in the following common web formats:

- JPEG (Joint Photographic Experts Group)
- GIF (Graphics Interchange Format)
- PNG (Portable Network Graphics)
- WBMP (a Bitmap format used for mobile devices, such as cell phones)

In Photoshop, the Save For Web & Devices dialog box has four view tabs: Original, Optimized, 2-Up, and 4-Up. See Figure 4. The Original view displays the graphic without any optimization. The Optimized, 2-Up, and 4-Up views display the image in its original format, as well as other file formats. You can change the file format being displayed by selecting one of the windows in the dialog box, then clicking the Optimized file format list arrow.

Exporting an image

You can export an image with transparency in Photoshop by saving your file in either a PNG or GIF format, then converting the image's background layer to an image layer. Select any elements in the layer you want as transparent, delete them from the layer, then save your changes.

QUICKTIP

You can also use the Photoshop Save As command on the File menu to quickly save a file in a different graphics format by using Photoshop's default settings. Using the Save As command, however, will *not* preserve web features such as slices, links, or animations.

Understanding Compression

GIF, JPEG, and PNG compression create compressed files without losing substantial components. Figuring out when to use which format can be challenging. Often, the decision may rest on whether color or image detail is most important. JPEG files are compressed by discarding image pixels; GIF and PNG files are compressed by limiting colors. GIF is an 8-bit format (the maximum number of colors a GIF file can contain is 256) that supports one transparent color; JPEG does not support transparent color. Having a transparent color is useful if you want to create a fade-out or superimposed effect. Because the JPEG format discards, or *loses*, data when it compresses a file, it is known as **lossy**. GIF and PNG formats are **lossless**—they compress solid color areas but maintain detail.

FIGURE 4
Optimizing files in Photoshop

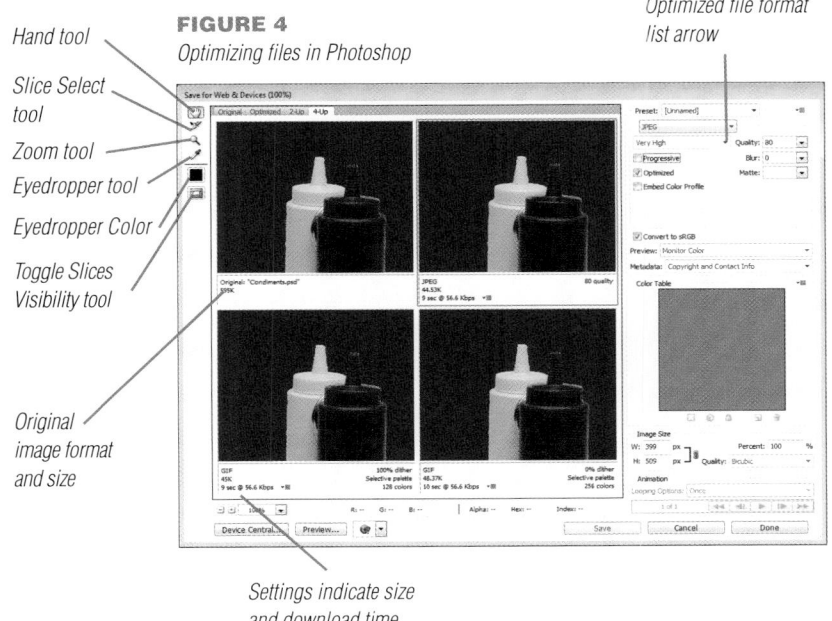

Hand tool
Slice Select tool
Zoom tool
Eyedropper tool
Eyedropper Color
Toggle Slices Visibility tool
Original image format and size
Optimized file format list arrow
Settings indicate size and download time

FIGURE 5
Comparing file formats

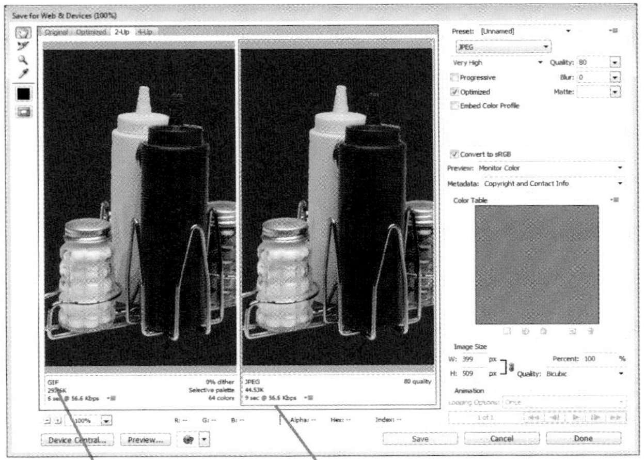

GIF (64 no dither) optimization
JPEG (high) optimization

Comparing Image Types

Figure 5 compares optimization of a photograph with a solid color background optimized in both GIF and JPEG formats. If you look closely, you'll see that the GIF colors look streaky and appear to be broken-up, while the JPEG colors appear crisp and seamless. Table 1 lists optimization format considerations. Because you cannot assume that other users will have access to the latest software and hardware, it's a good idea to compare files saved under different formats and optimization settings, and preview them in different browsers and on different computers. Yes, this can be time-consuming, but you'll end up with images that look great in all web browsers.

FIGURE 6
Adobe Device Central CS4

TABLE 1: Optimization Format Considerations

format	file format	use with
JPEG (very common)	All 24-bit (works best with 16 M colors)	Photographs, solid colors, soft edges
GIF (very common)	8-bit (256 colors)	Detailed drawings, sharp edges (logos, vector graphics), animation
PNG (less common)	24-bit (16 M colors)	Detailed drawings, logos, bitmap graphics
WBMP (less common)	1-bit (2 colors)	Cell phones and other mobile devices

Using Adobe Device Central CS4

Adobe Device Central CS4 is designed to give more flexibility to those professionals who create content for mobile phones and other consumer electronic devices. You can use the window shown in Figure 6 to obtain detailed specifications needed to design content for consumer electronic devices you may not have at your fingertips. You can then use the Emulator tab to preview your content on those same devices. This feature lets you increase your range of consumer electronic devices and can be updated to keep pace with new products, as well as manufacturer updates and improvements to existing products.

FIGURE 7
Save For Web & Devices dialog box

Outline surrounds selected format

List arrow changes format

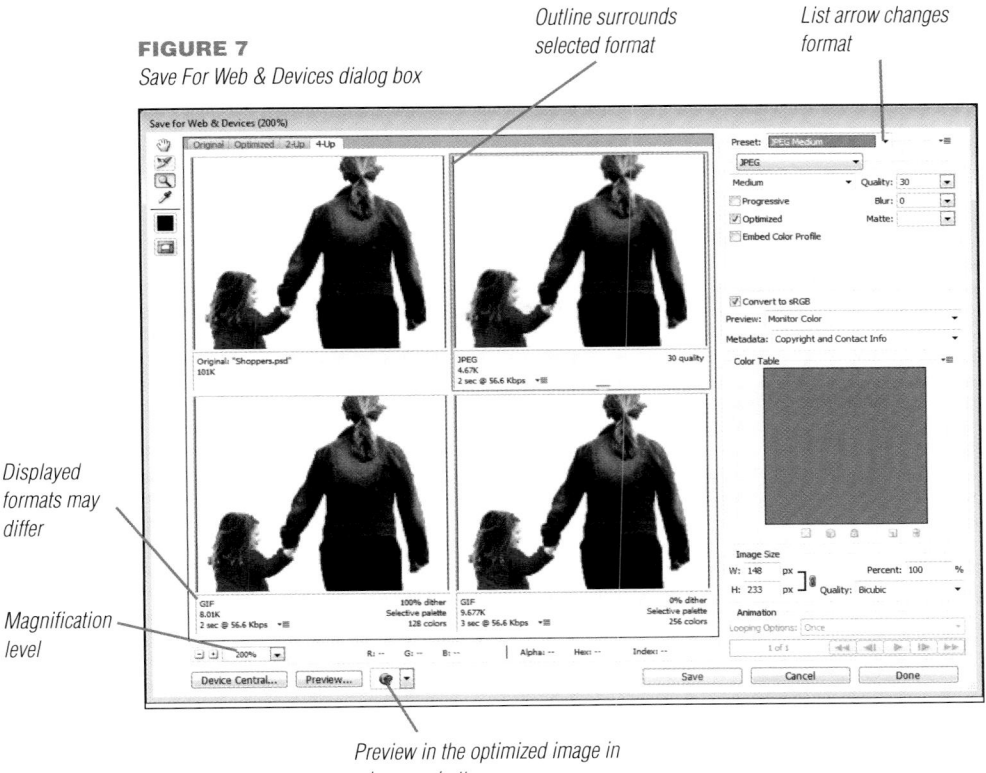

Displayed formats may differ

Magnification level

Preview in the optimized image in a browser button

Using Transparency and Matte options

When using the Save for Web & Devices command, you can determine how the Transparency and Matte options are optimized within an image. Using both of these tools in a variety of combinations, you can blend fully or partially transparent pixels with a color from the Color Picker or Matte menu.

Prepare to optimize an image

1. Open PS 16-2.psd from the drive and folder where you store your Data Files, then save it as **Shoppers** in the folder where you store your Data Files.

2. Click **File** on the Application bar, then click **Save for Web & Devices**.

3. Click the **4-Up tab**.

4. Click the **Zoom tool** 🔍 on the left side of the Save For Web & Devices dialog box.

   TIP   You can use the Hand tool to reposition the image.

5. Click the **top-right image** until all four images are enlarged to **200%**.

   TIP   The zoom level is displayed in the lower-left corner of the Save For Web & Devices dialog box. You can also click the Zoom Level list arrow and select a magnification.

6. Click the **Preset list arrow**, click **JPEG Medium**, then compare your dialog box to Figure 7.

   The Save button saves a file in the selected format, the Cancel button resets the settings and closes the dialog box, and the Done button remembers the current settings and closes the dialog box.

   TIP   To complete optimization of the file, you can click the desired format in the dialog box, click Save, enter a new name (if necessary) in the Save Optimized As dialog box, then click Save.

You opened a file, then used the Save for Web & Devices command on the File menu to open the Save For Web & Devices dialog box. You observed the differences between possible formats.

Lesson 2   Optimize Images for Web Use

PHOTOSHOP 16-11

Complete image optimization

1. Click the **Preset list arrow**, then click **GIF 128 Dithered**. Compare your image to Figure 8.

   TIP   The Preset list arrow contains 12 predesigned settings, while the Optimized file format list arrow lets you create your own unique settings with any options you choose.

2. Click **Save**.

3. Navigate to the folder where you store your Data Files, verify that **Shoppers** is in the File name text box (Win) or the Save As text box (Mac), then click **Save**.

   TIP   Click OK if a warning box displays.

   The optimized file is similar in color quality, but approximately one-tenth the size of the original file (118 KB vs. 11.3 KB).

   TIP   The optimized file is saved in the designated file format and folder. If your optimized file had spaces in its name, you would notice that the spaces in the optimized file name were replaced with hyphens.

4. Close the Shoppers.psd file without saving any changes.

You optimized a file, and then saved the optimized file. When you optimize a file, a copy of the file is saved, and no changes are made to the original.

FIGURE 8
Image optimized

Outline surrounds selected format

Click to select a predesigned format

List arrow changes format

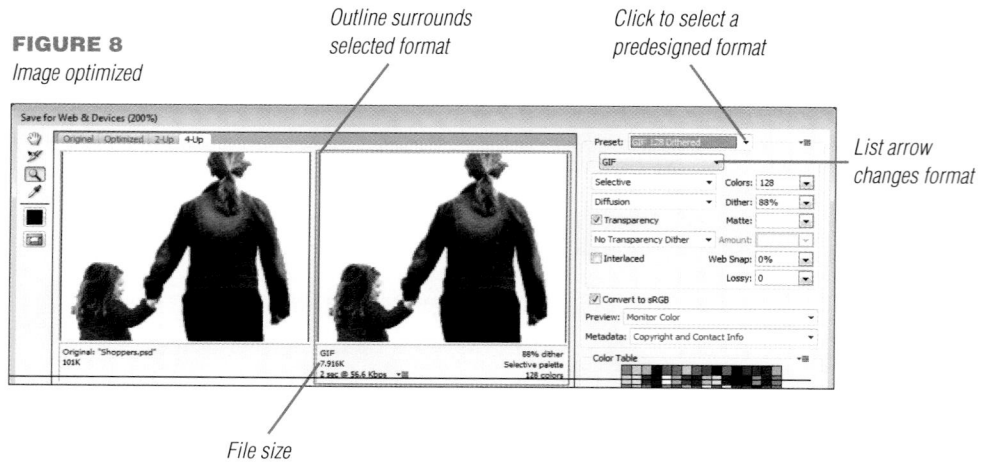

File size

Using High Dynamic Range (HDR) images

HDR images are used in motion pictures, special effects, 3D work, and high-end photography. An HDR image is one that stores pixel values that span the whole tonal range. HDR images store linear values, meaning that the value of each pixel is proportional to the amount of light measured by the camera. Each HDR image stores 32-bits per color channel, and is coded using floating point numbers. In Photoshop, an HDR image is converted to an 8-bit/channel or 16-bit/channel image mode. You can use the HDR Conversion dialog box to adjust the brightness and contrast using one of the following methods: Exposure and Gamma, Highlight Compression, Equalize Histogram, or Local Adaptation.

FIGURE 9
Optimized file moved to image

GIF image
in document

1. Verify that the Europa Market.psd is active, then select the **Shoppers layer**.

2. Open Shoppers.gif.

3. Click **Select** on the Application bar, click **Color Range**, then verify that the **Image option button** is selected and that the Fuzziness text box is set to **0**.

4. Click the **white background** of the image in the Color Range dialog box, select the **Invert check box**, then click **OK**.

5. Click the **Move tool** ▸⊕ on the Tools panel, verify that the **Show Transform Controls check box** is *not* selected, then use the **Move pointer** ▸⊱ to drag the selection to the Europa Market image.

6. Drag the **Shoppers** so the top of the woman's head is below the "R" in Market, and below the guideline at 150Y.

7. Defringe the contents of Layer 2 using a setting of 2 pixels.

8. Click the **Layers panel list arrow** ▾☰ , then click **Layer Properties**.

9. Type **2 Shoppers** in the Name text box, then click **OK**.

10. Close the Shoppers.gif file, save your work, then compare your screen to Figure 9.

You opened an optimized file, selected the file and dragged it into the Europa Market image, defringed the image, then renamed the layer. The optimized file will be easier for a viewer to load in any browser.

CREATE A BUTTON FOR
A WEB PAGE

What You'll Do

In this lesson, you'll create and name a layer, then create a button to use in a web page. You'll add type to the button, apply a style, and then link the type and button layers so they can be used as a single object in a web page.

Learning About Buttons

A **button** is a graphical interface element that helps visitors navigate through and interact with a website with ease. Photoshop provides several ways for you to create buttons. You can create your own shape, apply a preformatted button style, or import a button you've already created. You can also assign a variety of actions to a button so that the button completes the required task when clicked or moused-over by someone viewing the site in a browser.

Creating a Button

You can create a button by drawing a shape with a shape tool, such as a rectangle, on a layer. After you create the shape, you can stylize it by applying a color or style, and then add text that will explain what will happen when it's clicked.

Saving a file for the web

Before you can use Photoshop files on the web, you must first convert them to the HTML format. Photoshop uses default settings when you save optimized images for the web. You can specify the output settings for HTML format, your HTML editor, and the way image files, background files, and slices are named and saved. To change the output settings in Photoshop, click the Preset list arrow in the Save For Web & Devices dialog box, select a file and compression type, then click the file format and compression quality list arrows to 'dial-in' the exact settings you want. To change a file to the HTML format, open the file in the Save for Web & Devices dialog box, click the Save as type list arrow, click one of the HTML options, then click Save.

Applying a Button Style

You can choose from the many pre-designed Photoshop button styles on the Styles panel, or you can create your own.

To apply a style to a button, you must first select a style, then create a button shape. Before creating the button, draw a shape for the button (using the Rectangle tool, for example) double-click one of the button styles on the Styles panel, which appear as thumbnails, or click a style name from the Set style for new layer list arrow on the options bar. Figure 10 shows the button styles on the Styles panel. You can also modify a button with a style already applied to it by first selecting the button and then choosing a new style from the Styles panel.

FIGURE 10
Button styles

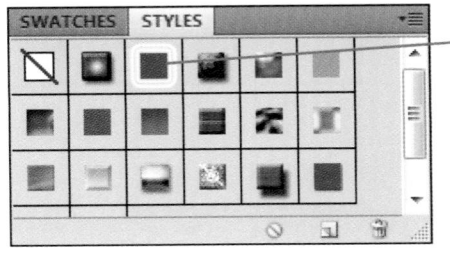

Style thumbnail

Changing a web image using Variables

When designing a web page, you may want to experiment with a variety of text samples (such as text on a button) or with different imagery for different occasions. You can do this in Photoshop using Variables. This feature lets you define many data sets, each containing different text or pixel information. You can then insert each data set and easily make changes to your web page. You define data sets by clicking Image on the Application bar, pointing to Variables, then clicking Define. Each data set is defined for a specific layer, which is selected from the Layer list arrow in the Variables dialog box. You can also view existing data sets for the active file by clicking Next in the Variables dialog box. Once the data sets are defined, you can quickly switch between them by clicking Image on the Application bar, then clicking Apply Data Set. This dialog box lets you apply a specific data set by clicking its name.

Create a button

1. Click the **Zoom tool** 🔍 on the Application bar.

2. Click the **Fit Screen button** [Fit Screen] on the options bar.

3. Verify that the **2 Shoppers layer** on the Layers panel is selected.

4. Click the **Create a new layer button** 🖺 on the Layers panel.

   A new layer, Layer 2, appears above the 2 Shoppers layer, and beneath the Type Layers set.

5. Double-click the name **Layer 2** on the Layers panel, type **QuickGift Button**, then press **[Enter]** (Win) or **[return]** (Mac).

6. Click the **Rounded Rectangle tool** 🔲 on the Tools panel.

7. If necessary, click the **Shape layers button** 🔲 on the options bar.

   | TIP   The Rounded Rectangle tool is grouped with the Rectangle tool.

8. Click the **Click to open Style picker list arrow** ◻▯ on the options bar, click the **list arrow**, click **Buttons**, then click **Append**.

9. Using the guides as a reference to create a shape beneath the word A in A Spot of Tea, drag the **Marquee pointer** ╋ from approximately **60 X/320 Y** to **185 X/350 Y**.

10. Click the **Click to open Style picker button** ◻▯, scroll to the bottom of the list, then click **Star Glow**, as shown in Figure 11.

    You created the shape that will be used for a button.

You verified settings, created a new layer, selected the Rounded Rectangle tool, selected a button style on the options bar, and then created a button.

FIGURE 11
Button style list

List arrow displays style panel

FIGURE 12

Button created in image

Add type to a button

1. Click the **Horizontal Type tool** T. on the Tools panel.

2. Click the **button shape** at approximately **70 X/335 Y**.

3. Click the **Set the text color box** on the options bar, sample the red in the existing type, then click **OK**.

4. Click the **Set the font family list arrow** on the options bar, then click **Arial**.

5. Click the **Set the font size list arrow** on the options bar, then click **18 pt**.

6. Type **QuickGift**, then commit the current edits.

7. Right-click the **QuickGift layer**, then click **Convert to Smart Object**.

   The Smart Object and button shape layers are linked.

8. Click the **Move tool** on the Tools panel, then center the type on the button.

9. Save your work, then compare your work to Figure 12.

You added type to a button, and then converted the QuickGift type layer to a Smart Object.

CREATE SLICES IN
AN IMAGE

What You'll Do

In this lesson, you'll view the existing slices in the Europa Market image, create slices around the Shopping and Dining type, resize a slice, and assign a web address to the slice. You'll also create a new slice from the 2 Shoppers layer on the Layers panel.

Understanding Slices

You not only have the ability to work with images in layers, but you can also divide an image into unlimited smaller sections, or slices. Photoshop uses slices to determine the appearance of special effects in a web page. A **slice** is a rectangular section of an image that you can use to apply features, such as rollovers and links, and can be created automatically or by using any marquee tool or the Slice tool.

Using Slices

There are two kinds of slices: a **user-slice**, which you create, and an **auto-slice**, which is created in response to your user-slice. You can use the Slice tool to create a slice by dragging the pointer around an area. Every time you create a slice,

Photoshop automatically creates at least one auto-slice, which fills in the area around the newly created slice. Photoshop automatically numbers user- and auto-slices and updates the numbering according to the location of the new user-slice. User-slices have a solid line border, auto-slices have a dotted line border, and any selected slices have a yellow border. A selected user-slice contains a bounding box and sizing handles. You can resize a slice by dragging a handle to a new location, just as you would resize any object.

Learning About Slice Components

By default, a slice consists of the following components:

- A colored line that helps you identify the slice type
- An overlay that dims the appearance of the unselected slices
- A number that helps you identify each individual slice
- A symbol that helps you determine the type of slice

QUICKTIP

When two slices overlap, a subslice is automatically created.

Adjusting Slice Attributes

You can adjust slice attributes by clicking Guides, Grid & Slices under the Preferences command. Figure 13 shows slice preferences. You can choose how to display slice lines and line color.

FIGURE 13
Preferences dialog box

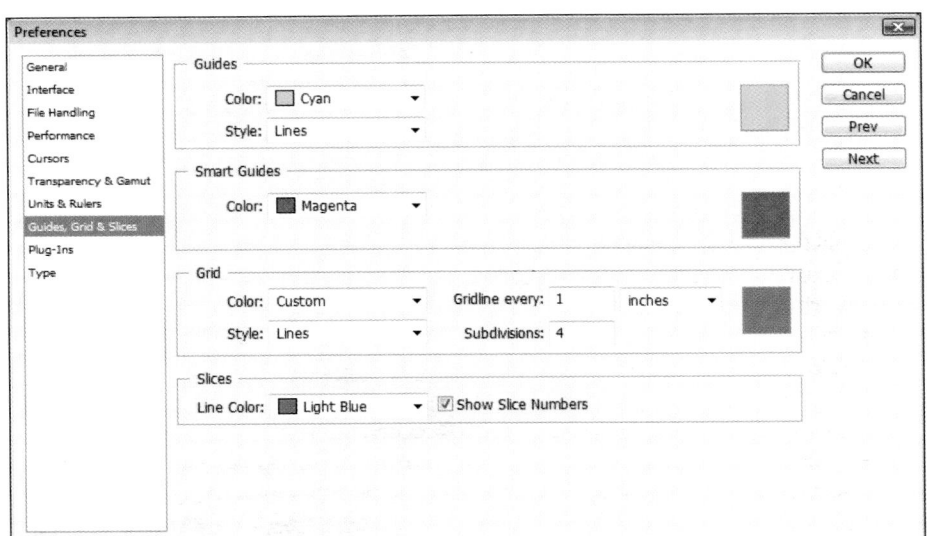

Slice numbering changes as you add or delete slices. Each user-slice contains a symbol indicating if it is an image slice or a layer-based slice, if the slice is linked, or if it includes a rollover effect. See Table 2 for a description of the symbols used to identify user-slices.

QUICKTIP

It doesn't matter which layer, if any, is active when you create slices using the Slice tool or any of the marquee tools.

Using a Layer-Based Slice

In addition to drawing a slice using the Slice tool, you can use the New Layer-Based Slice command on the Layer menu to create a slice from a layer on the Layers panel. This is an easy way of creating a slice *without* having to draw an outline.

Creating a Layer-Based Slice

Creating a layer-based slice automatically surrounds the image on the layer with a slice, which can be useful if you want to create a slice quickly or if you want a large slice. Photoshop updates the slice whenever you modify the layer or its content. For example, the slice automatically adjusts if you move its corresponding layer on the Layers panel, or you erase pixels on the layer. In Figure 14, the active slice is an Image slice.

QUICKTIP

To delete a layer-based slice, user-slice, or auto-slice, select the slice, then press [Delete] (Win) or [delete] (Mac).

TABLE 2: User-Slice Symbols

symbol	used to identify
 ⊠	Image slice
✦	Layer-based slice
⊠	No image slice

Using the Slice Options Dialog Box

The Slice Options dialog box is used to set options such as content type, name, and URL for a specific slice. You open this dialog box by double-clicking a slice with the Slice Select tool. You use the list arrows in the Slice Options dialog box to assign individual settings, features, and effects to the slices you've created in your image. For example,

you could set a slice to initiate an action, such as displaying the linked file in a new browser window, or displaying the linked file in the same frame using the Target field.

Assigning a Web Address to a Slice

You can assign a web page to a selected slice by typing its Uniform Resource Locater (URL) in the URL text box. The URL is the

web page's address that appears in the Address box in your browser. You can designate how that web page will be displayed in your browser by choosing one of the options on the Target list.

FIGURE 14
Sliced image

User-slice

Selected slice

Auto-slice

Create a slice using the Slice tool

1. Click the **Zoom tool** 🔍 on the Application bar.

2. Click the image of the **Shopping text** until the zoom percentage is **200%**.

3. Click the **Slice tool** ✂ on the Tools panel.

   The existing slices in the image are visible.

   TIP You can also create a slice by creating a selection with any marquee tool, clicking Select on the Application bar, then clicking Create Slice from Selection.

4. Drag the **Slice pointer** ✂ around the **Shopping type** (from approximately **30 X/125 Y** to **185 X/150 Y**).

5. Drag the **Slice pointer** ✂ around the **Dining type** (from approximately **30 X/225 Y** to **120 X/250 Y**), fit the image to the screen, then compare your slices to Figure 15.

You viewed the existing slices in the Europa Market image and created two user-based slices, one for the Shopping text and one for the Dining text.

FIGURE 15
New slices added to image

Newly added slice

Selected slice

Slice numbering automatically changes with each modification (your numbers might be different)

1. Click the **2 Shoppers** on the Layers panel.

2. Click **Layer** on the Application bar, click **New Layer-Based Slice**, then compare your screen to Figure 16.

A new slice surrounds the 2 Shoppers layer object. Slice numbering automatically changes with each modification so your numbers might be different.

> TIP   You can also create a layer-based slice by right-clicking the layer, and then clicking New Layer-Based Slice.

You made the 2 Shoppers layer active on the Layers panel, then created a slice based on this layer.

FIGURE 16
New layer-based slice

Layer-based slice does not display sizing handles

Resize a slice

1. Click the **Slice Select tool** 🔪 on the Tools panel.

2. Click the **Dining slice**.

3. Drag the **right-middle sizing handle** ↔ to **185 X**, compare your slice to Figure 17, then release the mouse button.

   > TIP Because layer-based slices are fitted to pixels on the layer, they will not display sizing handles when selected.

You resized the Dining slice.

FIGURE 17
Resized slice

Drag handle to new position

FIGURE 18

URL assigned to slice

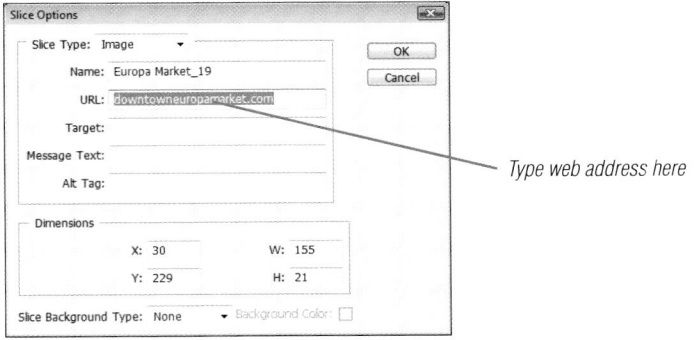

Type web address here

Assign a web address to a slice

1. Double-click the **Dining slice** with the **Slice Select tool** 🔪 .

   The Slice Options dialog box opens when you double-click a slice with the Slice Select tool.

2. Type **downtowneuropamarket.com** in the URL text box, then compare your Slice Options dialog box to Figure 18.

   | TIP   Your slice numbers might vary.

3. Click **OK** to close the Slice Options dialog box.

4. Click an area outside of the slice to deselect the Dining slice, then compare your image to Figure 19.

   TIP   To hide slices in your image, click View on the Application bar, point to Show, then click Slices.

5. Save your work, then close Europa Market.psd.

You assigned a web address to a slice using the Slice Options dialog box, then deselected the slice.

FIGURE 19
Slice with URL assigned

CREATE AND PLAY
BASIC ANIMATION

What You'll Do

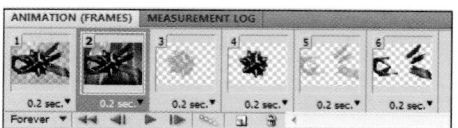

In this lesson, you'll create basic animation by creating animation frames. For each newly created frame, you'll modify layers by hiding and showing them, and changing their opacity. You'll also play and preview the animation, to test your work.

Understanding Animation

You can use nearly any type of graphics image to create interesting animation effects. You can move objects in your image or overlap them so that they blend into one another. Once you place the images that you want to animate in an image, you can determine when and how you want the animation to play.

Creating Animation on the Animation Panel

Remember that animation is nothing more than a series of still images displayed rapidly to give the illusion of motion. The Animation panel displays a thumbnail of the animation image in each frame. A **frame** is an individual image that is used in animation. When you create a frame on the Animation panel, you create a duplicate of the current frame, and can then modify it as desired. The layers that are visible on the Layers panel appear in the selected frame, and thus, in the animation. Here's all that's involved in creating a simple animation:

- Place images on layers in the image.
- Hide all but one layer.
- Duplicate the frame, turn off the displayed layer, then turn on the layer you want to see.

Animating Images

If you look at the Layers panel in Figure 20, you'll see that there are images on two layers. The Animation panel contains two frames: one for each of the layers. When frame 1 is selected, the man appears in the image; when frame 2 is selected, the woman appears. When the animation is played, the images of the man and woman alternate.

Moving and Deleting Frames

To move a frame to a different spot, click the frame on the Animation panel, and drag it to a new location. To select contiguous frames, press and hold [Shift], and then click the frames you want to include. To select noncontiguous frames, press and hold [Ctrl] (Win) or [⌘] (Mac), and then click the frames you want to include. You can delete a frame by clicking it on the Animation panel, then dragging it to the Deletes selected frames button on the Animation panel.

Looping the Animation

You can set the number of times the animation plays by clicking the Selects looping options list arrow on the Animation panel, then clicking Once, Forever, or Other. When you select Other, the Set Loop Count dialog box opens, where you can enter the loop number you want.

Previewing the Animation

When you're ready to preview an animation, you have a few choices:

- You can use the buttons on the bottom of the Animation panel. When you click the Plays/stops animation button, the animation plays.
- You can preview and test the animation in your browser by clicking the Preview the optimized image in a browser button in the Save for Web & Devices dialog box.

QUICKTIP
You can change the size of the Animation panel thumbnails by clicking the panel list arrow, clicking Panel Options, clicking a thumbnail size, and then clicking OK. You can select a different-sized thumbnail for each panel.

FIGURE 20
Sample of basic animation

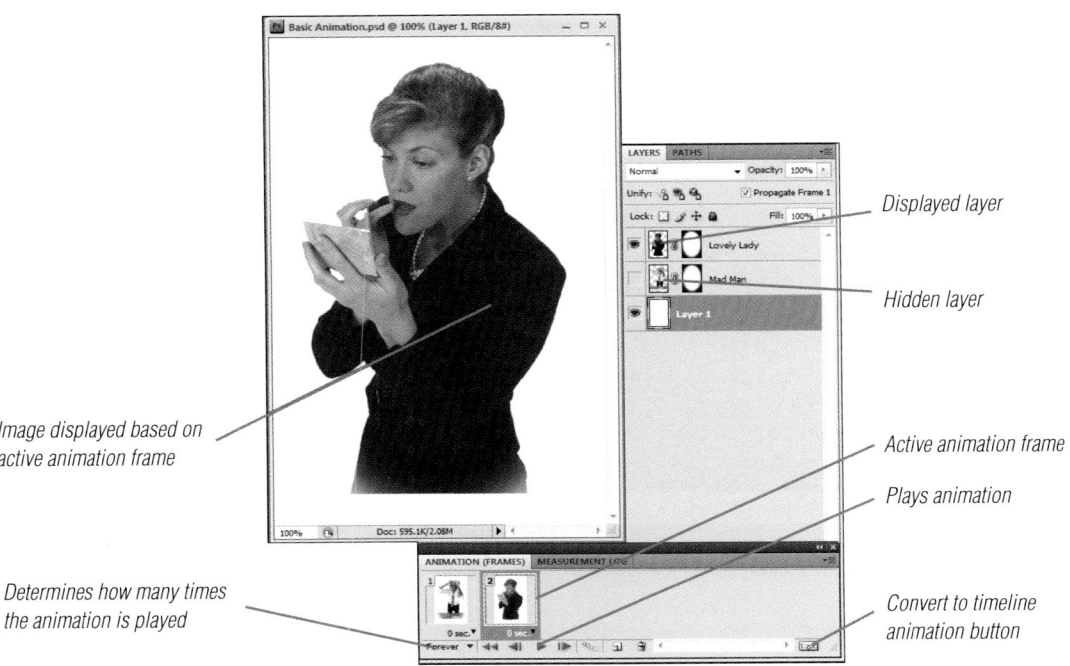

Displayed layer

Hidden layer

Image displayed based on active animation frame

Active animation frame

Plays animation

Determines how many times the animation is played

Convert to timeline animation button

Converting Animation Frames to a Timeline

By default, the Animation panel displays frames, but you can change the display so it shows a timeline. You can change the display by clicking the Convert to timeline animation button in the lower-right corner of the Animation (Frames) panel. (Change back to displaying frames by clicking the Convert to frame animation button when the timeline is displayed.) Figure 21 shows the Animation (Timeline) panel. As you drag the bars for each of the layers in the animation, the image updates to show the effect of your changes.

QUICKTIP

If the Animation panel displays the timeline, the Convert to frame animation button displays. The Convert to timeline animation button displays in the Animation (Frames) panel.

FIGURE 21
Animation (Timeline) panel

Convert to frame animation button

FIGURE 22
Zoomify Export dialog box

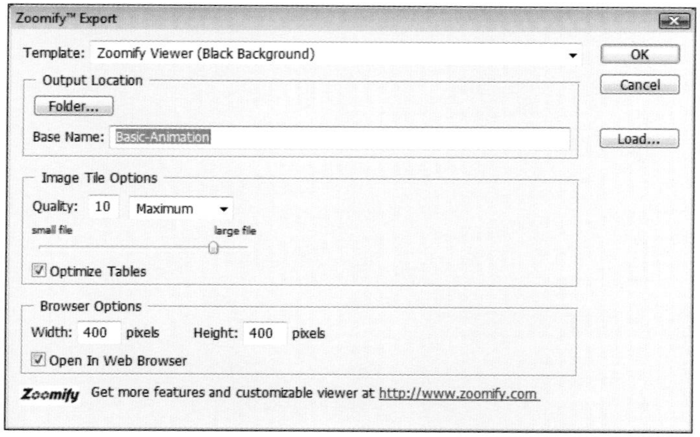

Exporting to Zoomify™

Using the Export to Zoomify feature, you can post your high-resolution images on the web so viewers can pan and zoom them in more detail. Using this feature, your image will download in the same time as an equivalent size JPEG file. Figure 22 shows the Zoomify Export dialog box which you can open by clicking File on the Application bar, point to Export, then click Zoomify.

FIGURE 23
Frames created on Animation panel

Indicates state
has an animation

Opacity setting of
newly created
animation frame

New animation frame

FIGURE 24
Completed animation frames

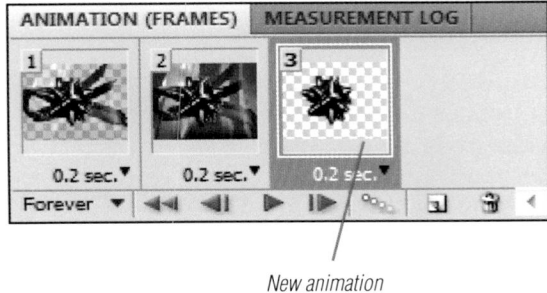

New animation
frame

Create and duplicate animation frames

1. Open PS 16-3.psd from the drive and folder where you store your Data Files, then save it as **Package Morph**.

2. Click **Window** on the Application bar, then click **Animation** to open the Animation panel (if it is not already open) and display the rulers in pixels.

3. Adjust the opacity setting of the Paper layer to **50%** on the Layers panel.

4. Click the **Duplicates selected frames button** on the Animation panel.

   A new Animation frame is created and is now the active frame.

5. Adjust the opacity setting of the Paper layer to **100%**, then compare your Animation panel to Figure 23.

6. Click the **Duplicates selected frames button** on the Animation panel.

7. Click the **Indicates layer visibility button** on the Paper layer on the Layers panel.

8. Click the **Indicates layer visibility button** on the Ribbons layer on the Layers panel to hide this layer.

9. Click the **Bow layer** to make it active.

   The content from the Bow layer appears in frame 3 of the Animation panel. See Figure 24.

You created an animation frame, duplicated existing frames, and adjusted the opacity of the frames. Duplicating frames with different levels of opacity creates an animated effect when viewed in a browser.

Adjust animation frames

1. Set the opacity setting of the Bow layer to **50%**.
2. Click the **Duplicates selected frames button** on the Animation panel, then adjust the opacity setting of the Bow layer to **100%**.
3. Click the **Duplicates selected frames button** on the Animation panel.
   You have now created five frames.
4. Click the **Indicates layer visibility button** on the Bow layer to hide it.
5. Click the **Ribbons layer** on the Layers panel to make it active, then click the **Indicates layer visibility button** on the Layers panel for this layer.
6. Adjust the opacity setting to **50%**.
7. Click the **Duplicates selected frames button** on the Animation panel, then adjust the opacity setting of the Ribbons layer to **100%**. Compare your screen to Figure 25.

You adjusted the opacity of frames using the Layers panel. The adjustment of frame settings lets you simulate movement when the animation is played.

FIGURE 25
Completed animation frames

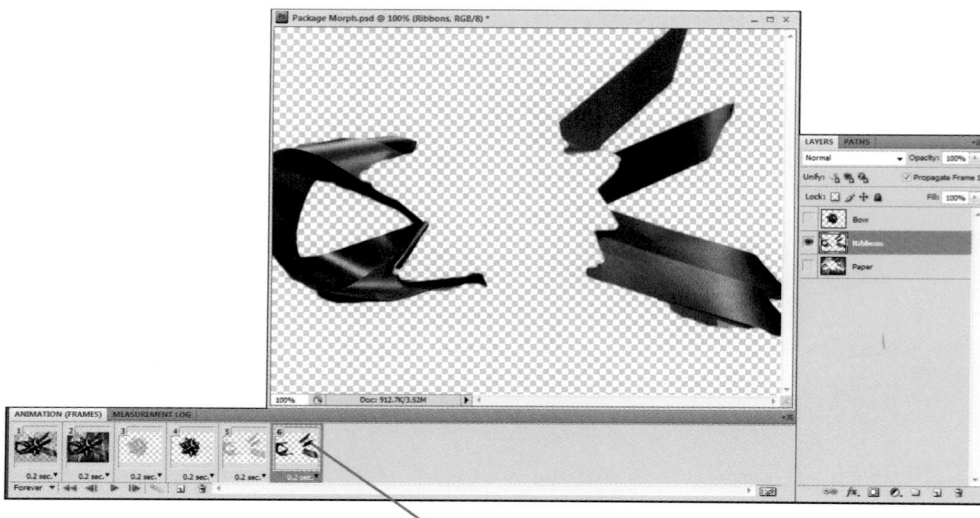

New animation frame

Using video layers in Photoshop Extended

If you have QuickTime 7.1 or higher installed on your computer, you can use Photoshop Extended to edit individual frames of video and image sequence files. You can also edit and paint on video, apply filters, masks, transformations, layer styles, and blending modes. When you open a video file in Photoshop Extended, the frames are contained within a video layer (indicated by a filmstrip icon in the Layers panel). You can create a video layer in an active document by displaying the Animation panel in Timeline mode, clicking Layer on the Application bar, pointing to Video Layers, then clicking New Video Layer from File.

FIGURE 26
Animation displayed in browser

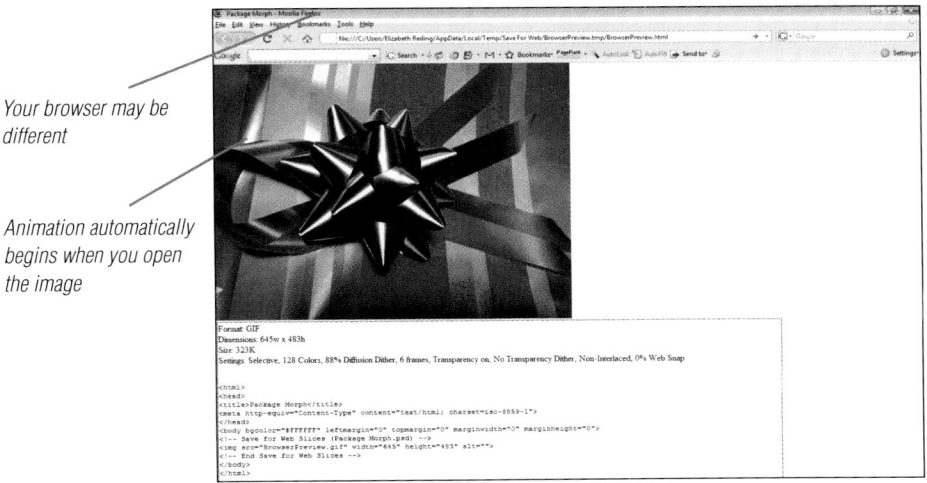

Your browser may be different

Animation automatically begins when you open the image

Play animation in the image and browser

1. Verify that **Forever** displays in the Selects looping options text box, click the **first frame** in the Animation panel, then click the **Plays/stops animation button** ▶ on the Animation panel.

   The Plays/stops animation button changes its appearance depending on the current state of the animation. See Table 3 for a description of the buttons on the Animation panel.

2. Click the **Plays/stops animation button** ■ on the Animation panel.

   The animation stops, displaying the currently active frame.

3. Save your work.

4. Click **File** on the Application bar, click **Save for Web & Devices**, then click the **Preview the optimized image in a browser button** (at the bottom of the dialog box to the right of the Preview button) then compare your preview to Figure 26.

   TIP   The first time you use this feature you will have to add a browser.

5. Close your browser, then click **Cancel** in the Save for Web & Devices dialog box.

   TIP   The animation might play differently in your browser, which is why it is important to preview your files on as many different systems as possible.

You played the animation in your image, then viewed it in a browser.

TABLE 3: Animation Tools

tool	tool name	description
▼	Selects looping options	Determines how many times the animation plays
◀◀	Selects first frame	Makes the first frame on the panel active
◀❙	Selects previous frame	Makes the previous frame on the panel active
▶	Plays animation	Plays the animation
■	Stops animation	Stops the animation
❙▶	Selects next frame	Makes the next frame to the right on the panel active
°°°°	Tweens animation frames	Creates frames in slight increments
🗐	Duplicates selected frames	Creates a duplicate of selected frames
🗑	Deletes selected frames	Disposes of selected frames

ADD TWEENING AND FRAME DELAY

What You'll Do

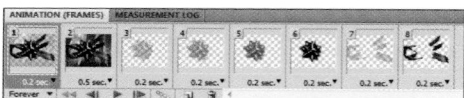

 In this lesson, you'll add tweening to animation and adjust the frame delay for a frame on the Animation panel.

Understanding Tweening

To create animation, you assemble a series of frames, then play them quickly to create the illusion of continuous motion. Each frame represents a major action point. Sometimes the variance between actions creates erratic or rough motion. To blend the motion *in between* the frames, you can tween your animation. **Tweening** adds frames that change the action in slight increments from one frame to the next. The origin of this term predates computer animation, when an artist known as an *inbetweener* hand-drew each frame that linked major action frames (at 24 frames per second!), and thus the term tweening was born.

Using Tweening on the Animation Panel

You can add tweening to a frame by clicking the Tweens animation frames button on the Animation panel, and then entering the number of in-between frames you want in the Tween dialog box. You can choose whether you want the tweening to affect all layers or just the selected layer, and if you want the image to change position or opacity. You can also specify the frame on which you want the tweening to start, and specify the number of frames to add in between the frames (you can add up to 100 frames in a single tween). Figure 27 shows a two-frame animation after four tween frames were added. The opacity of the man is 100% in the first frame and 0% in the last frame. Adding five tween frames causes the two images to blend into each other smoothly, or **morph** (metamorphose).

> **QUICK**TIP
> You can select contiguous frames and apply the same tweening settings to them simultaneously.

Understanding Frame Delays

When you create frames on the Animation panel, Photoshop automatically sets the **frame delay**, the length of time that each frame appears. You can set the delay time in whole or partial seconds by clicking the Selects frame delay time list arrow below each frame. You can set the frame delay you want for each frame, or you can select several frames and apply the same frame delay to them.

Setting Frame Delays

To change the delay for a single frame, click a frame, click the Selects frame delay time list arrow, then click a time. To change the delay for contiguous frames, press and hold [Shift], click the frames you want to include, and then click the Selects frame delay time list arrow on *any* of the selected frames. To change the delay for noncontiguous frames, press and hold [Ctrl] (Win) or ⌘ (Mac), click the frames you want to include, then click the Selects frame delay time list arrow on any of the selected frames.

FIGURE 27
Animation panel

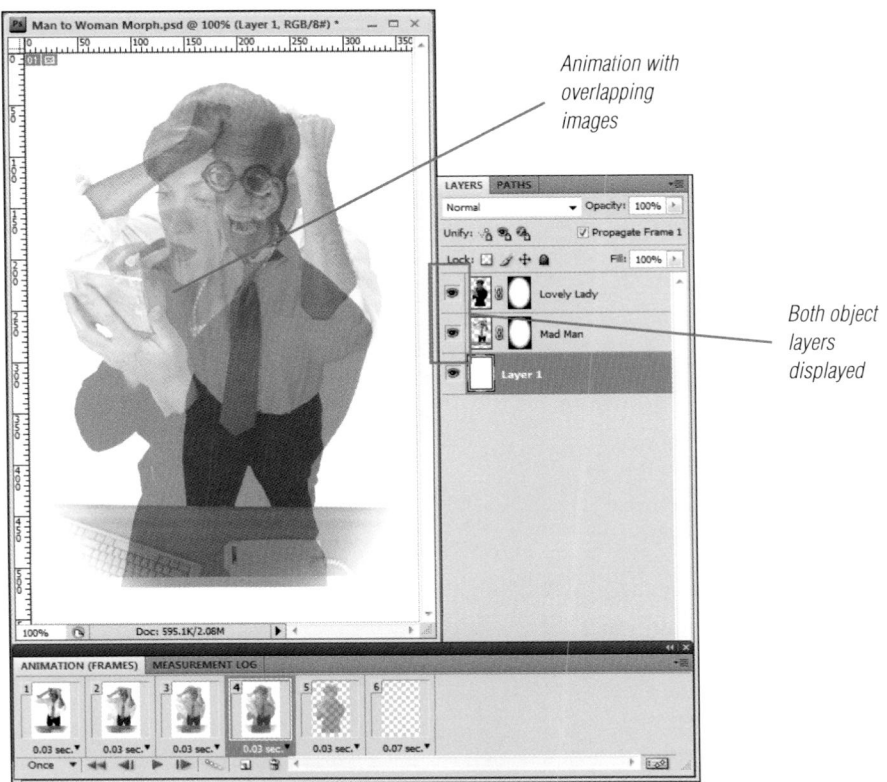

Animation with overlapping images

Both object layers displayed

Correcting pixel aspect ratio in video

This feature automatically corrects the ratio of pixels displayed for the monitor in use. Without this correction, pixels viewed in a 16:9 monitor (such as a widescreen TV) would look squashed in a 4:3 monitor (typical rectangular TV). Use the Pixel Aspect Ratio Correction command to turn off the scaling correction and view the image as it looks on a computer (square pixel) monitor. Photoshop automatically converts and scales the image to the pixel aspect ratio of the non-square pixel document. Images brought in from Adobe Illustrator will also be properly scaled. You can assign a pixel aspect ratio to a document by clicking View on the Application bar, pointing to Pixel Aspect Ratio, then selecting a pixel aspect ratio. When you have selected a pixel aspect ratio, the Pixel Aspect Ratio Correction option will be checked on the View menu.

Tween animation frames

1. Click **frame 3** on the Animation panel.

2. Click the **Tweens animation frames button** ⌇ on the Animation panel.

3. Adjust the settings in your Tween dialog box so that they match those shown in Figure 28.

4. Click **OK**.

   Two additional frames are added after frame 3.

5. Click the **Plays/stops animation button** ▶ on the Animation panel, then view the animation.

6. Click the **Plays/stops animation button** ■ on the Animation panel, then compare your panel to Figure 29, which now has eight frames.

You used the Tweens animation frames button on the Animation panel to insert two new frames, then played the animation to view the results. Did you notice that the overall effect is smoother and more fluid motion?

FIGURE 28
Tween dialog box

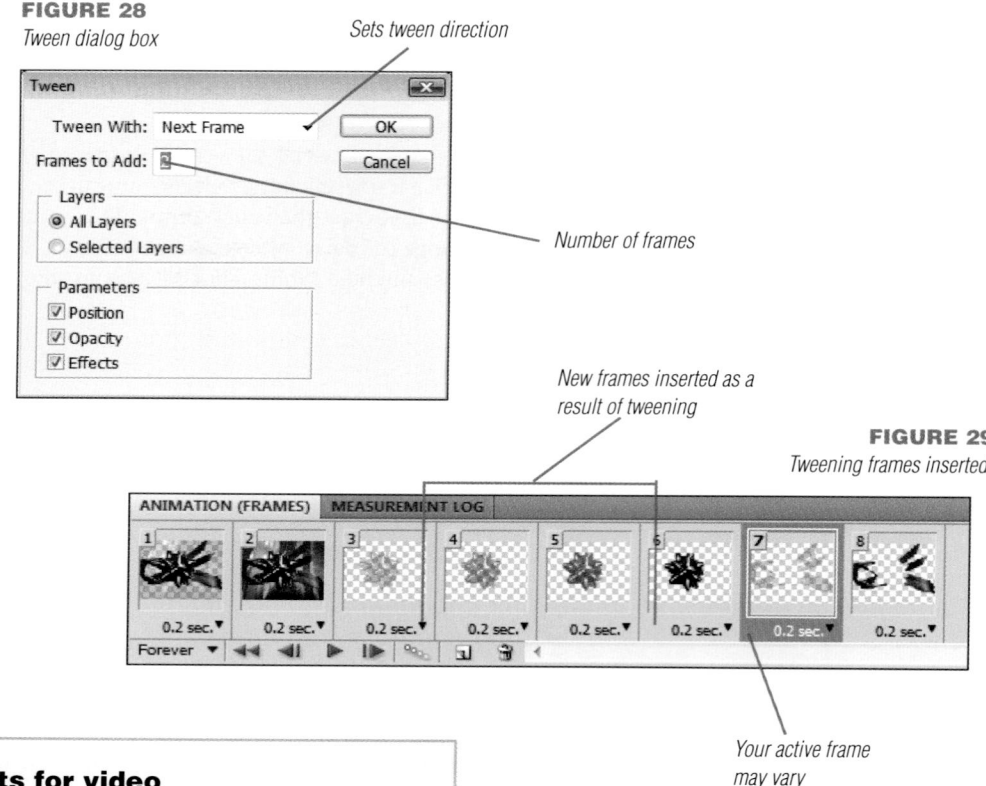

Sets tween direction

Number of frames

New frames inserted as a result of tweening

FIGURE 29
Tweening frames inserted

Your active frame may vary

Previewing Photoshop documents for video

When you're working on a Photoshop image that you plan to include in a digital video or video presentation, you can use the Video Preview plug-in (included with Photoshop) to see real-time results as you work. Because the images you create in Photoshop are made up of square pixels, and video editing programs usually convert these to non-square pixels for video encoding, distortion can result when you import an image into a video editing program. But with Video Preview, you can check for distortion and make changes before finalizing your image. When the Video Preview plug-in is installed, and your computer is connected to a video monitor via FireWire, you can access Video Preview by clicking File on the Application bar, pointing to Export, then clicking Video Preview. This command also lets you adjust the aspect ratio as necessary for different viewing systems, such as NTSC, PAL, or HDTV.

FIGURE 30

Frame delay menu

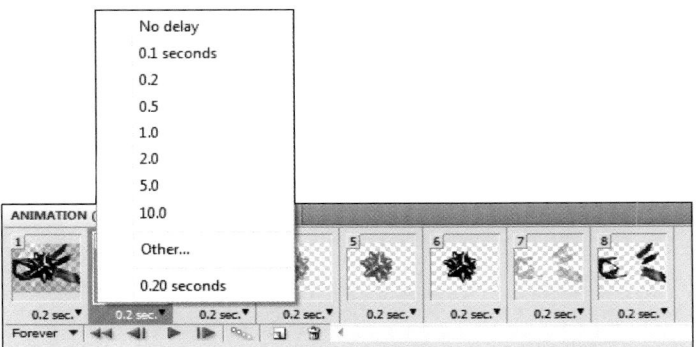

FIGURE 31

Frame delay in Animation panel

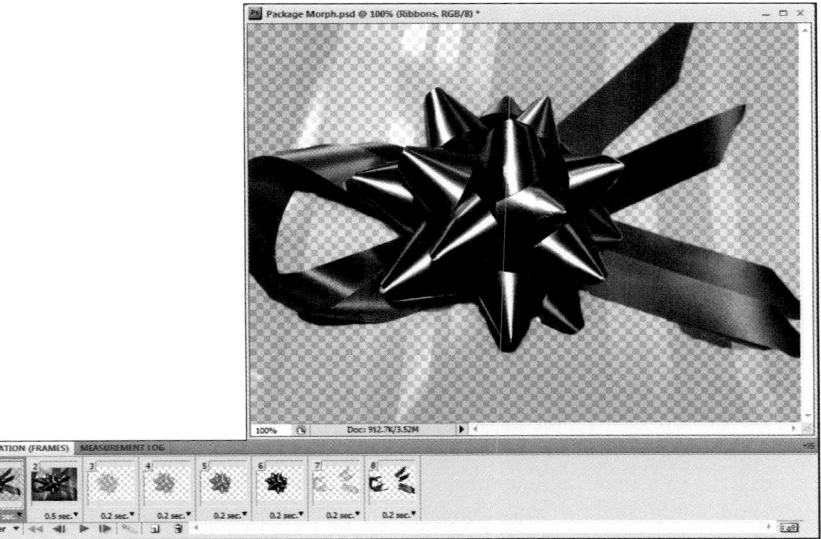

1. Click **frame 2** on the Animation panel.
2. Click the **Selects frame delay time list arrow** 0.2 sec. ▼ at the bottom of the selected frame.
3. Compare your frame delay menu to Figure 30, then click **0.5**.

   The frame delay for frame 2 changes to 0.5.
4. Click the **Plays/stops animation button** on the Animation panel, then view the animation.
5. Click the **Plays/stops animation button** on the Animation panel.
6. Open the **Save for Web & Devices dialog box**, then click the **Preview the optimized image in a browser button** .
7. Close your browser.
8. Save your work, then compare your image and Animation panel to Figure 31.
9. Close the Animation panel, then close the image.

You fine-tuned your animation by changing the frame delay for frame 2, then previewed the animation in your browser. It's important to preview animations in multiple web browsers on as many computers and operating systems as you can manage, so that you can see your work as others will view it.

MODIFY VIDEO IN
PHOTOSHOP

What You'll Do

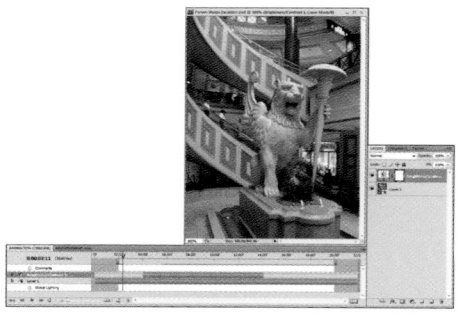

In this lesson, you'll open a video file and save it in a Photoshop format. You'll rotate the frame, apply several effects, and change the starting and ending points of the video sequence.

Playing Video

It might surprise you to know that you can play video using Photoshop Extended (with QuickTime 7.1 or higher installed), but then again, you might have guessed that it was possible after creating animation sequences using individual frames, since video is the natural next step after working with individual images.

QUICKTIP
You can create your own video sequences using most digital cameras. You may have to modify your camera settings or flip a switch on the camera body.

Working with Video

When you open a video file in Photoshop Extended, individual frames are contained in a video layer, and the layer appears in the Layers panel with a special filmstrip icon, shown in Figure 32. You can use your existing Photoshop skills (such as creating and editing adjustment layers, adjusting opacity, making selections, adding masks, painting, and cloning) on the video layer.

Table 4 lists the movie file extensions that can be opened in Photoshop Extended.

Frame Versus Timeline in the Animation Panel

Although the Animation panel has two modes (frame and timeline), you use the timeline mode when working with video. The timeline mode tools at the bottom of the Animation panel, shown in Figure 33, allow you to navigate the sequence. In addition to the tools in the Animation panel, you can use the spacebar to start and stop playing the animation. The Frame mode shows frame duration and layer animation properties; timeline mode shows frame duration and keyframed layer properties.

QUICKTIP
If you convert a video sequence from timeline to frame animation, you will be left with a single frame in the Animation panel.

Enhancing Video

Changes you can make to layers in a Photoshop image can also be applied to video layers. For example, you can apply adjustment layers to lighten or darken the overall look of a video sequence. Such enhancements can be used throughout a video sequence or can be controlled so that they only affect specific areas of the time-line. Figure 34 shows several adjustment layers, although only the Levels adjustment layer affects the entire sequence.

FIGURE 32

Filmstrip icon in Layers panel

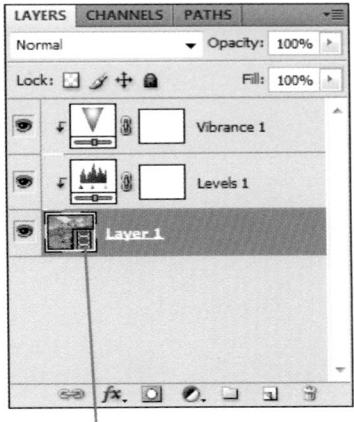

Filmstrip icon in thumbnail

FIGURE 33

Animation panel

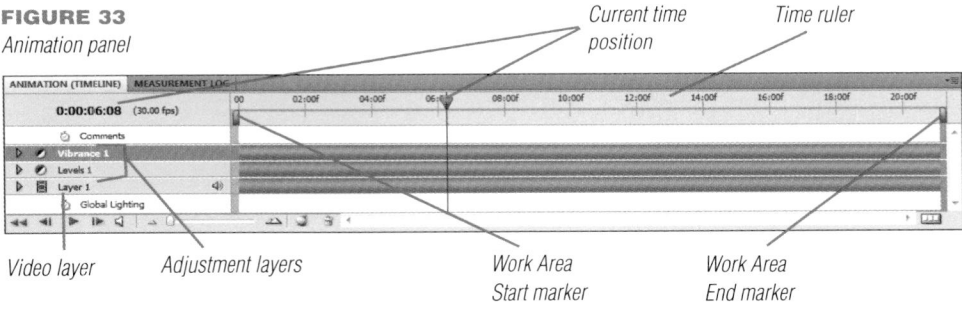

Current time position

Time ruler

Video layer   *Adjustment layers*

Work Area Start marker

Work Area End marker

FIGURE 34

Animation panel with adjustment layers

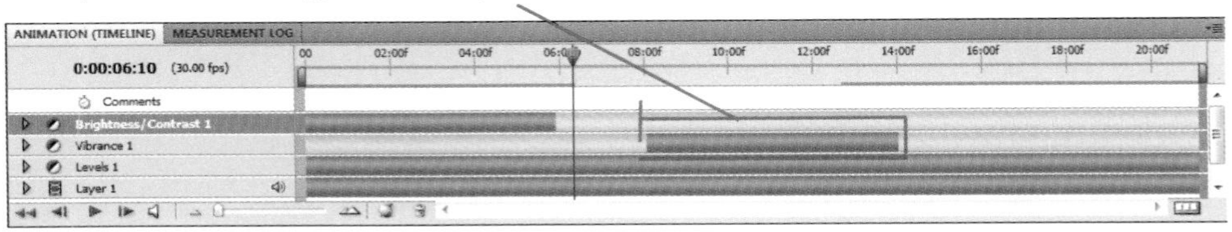

Adjustment level affecting part of video sequence

TABLE 4: Usable Movie File Types in Photoshop Extended

name	stands for	additional information
AVI	Audio Video Interleave	Developed by Microsoft
FLV	Flash video	Streaming video files
MOV	QuickTime format	Developed for Mac. Can be uploaded toYouTube without additional conversion
MPEG-1	Moving Pictures Expert Group	Used on the web for short video and animation files
MPEG-2 (with encoder)		Used for higher resolution video, digital television and DVDs
MPEG-4		Used for compression of AV data and CD distribution

Apply an adjustment layer

1. Open PS 16-4.avi from the drive and folder where you store your Data files, then save it as **Forum Shops Escalator.psd**.

   TIP When you save a video file in Photoshop, the file format is changed to .psd, which can be edited in many Adobe video programs.

2. Click **Image** on the Application bar, point to **Image Rotation**, click **90° CW**, then click **Convert** to transform the video layer into a Smart Object layer.

   The image is rotated, and the filmstrip icon on the thumbnail in the Layers panel is changed to a Smart Object. See Figure 35.

3. Switch to the **Essentials workspace**, display the Animations panel, then click the **Brightness/Contrast button** on the Adjustments panel.

4. Change the Brightness to **10** and the Contrast to **10**, then click the **Return to Adjustment list button** on the Adjustments panel.

5. Click the **Play button** on the Animation panel.

6. When you are finished watching the video, click the **Stop button** , then compare your work to Figure 36.

   TIP In addition to using the familiar DVD buttons in the Animation panel, you can also press the spacebar (on the keyboard) to start and stop video playback.

You saved a movie file in the Photoshop format, rotated the image, added an adjustment layer, then played the video.

FIGURE 35
Rotated image with Smart Object

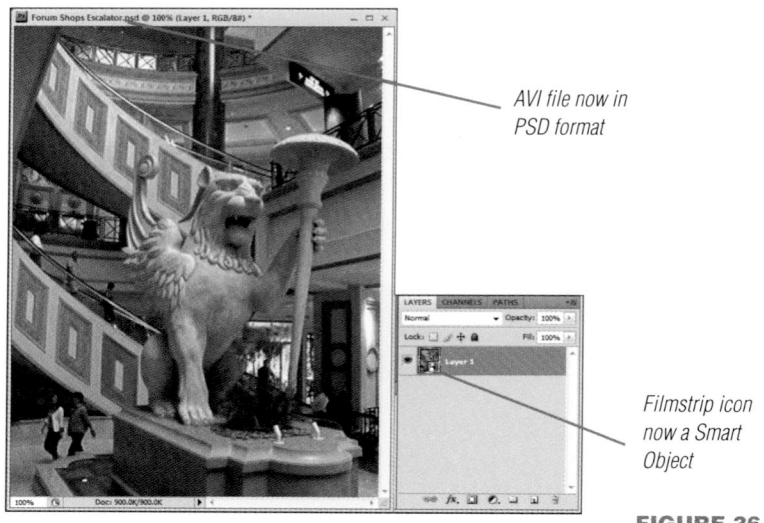

AVI file now in PSD format

Filmstrip icon now a Smart Object

FIGURE 36
Adjustment layer in video sequence

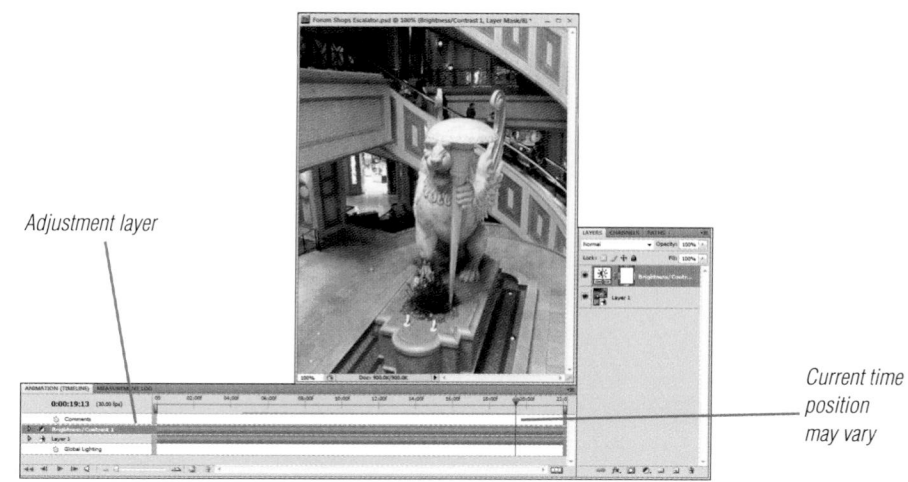

Adjustment layer

Current time position may vary

FIGURE 37
Modifying starting point of Adjustment layer

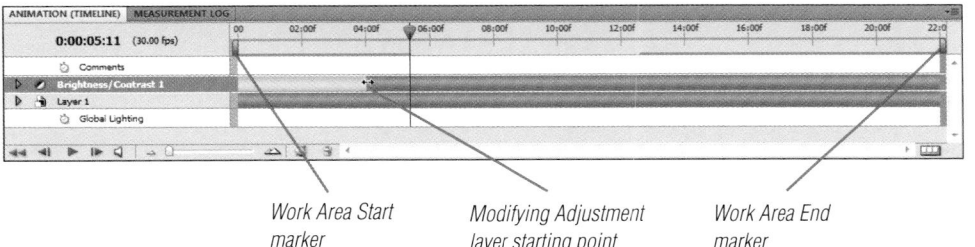

Work Area Start marker   Modifying Adjustment layer starting point   Work Area End marker

FIGURE 38
Modified video settings

Modify video settings

1. Make Layer 1 the active layer.

2. Drag the **Starting point of the Brightness/ Contrast 1 layer** to approximately **4:00f** on the time ruler, as shown in Figure 37.

3. Drag the **Ending point of the Brightness/ Contrast layer** to approximately **14:00f** on the time ruler.

4. Drag the **Work Area Start marker** to approximately **2:00f** on the time ruler.

5. Drag the **Work Area End marker** to approximately **20:00f** on the time ruler.

6. Press the **spacebar** on the keyboard to play the video, then press the **spacebar** when you are finished watching.

7. Save your work, compare your Animation panel to Figure 38, then close the file.

You modified the starting and ending point of an Adjustment layer, changed the position of the work area markers on the time ruler, then played the video sequence.

Using Video Document Presets for video

When you open a new document in Photoshop, you're presented with a blizzard of choices, and these choices extend to video. You can see the Video presets that are available by clicking File on the Application bar, then clicking New. Click the Preset list arrow, then click Film & Video. Click the Size list arrow and you'll see all the size presets that are available.

USE CAMERA
RAW FEATURES

What You'll Do

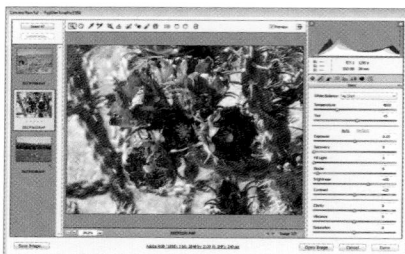

▶ In this lesson, you'll learn how to use the Camera Raw dialog box to make adjustments to images in the Raw, TIFF, and JPEG formats.

Using Raw Data from Digital Cameras

When you consider all the elements you'll need to get your website up and running, you'll probably want to use your own camera as a source of imagery. If you're a digital camera photographer, or have access to digital photos, you'll appreciate the ability to use images in the 16-bit Camera Raw format because it contains so much controllable data. Sure, the files are twice the size, but the resolution contains 65,000 data points (versus the 256 data points in an 8-bit image). Once an image with raw data is opened, the Camera Raw interface appears. This interface contains magnification and color correction options.

FIGURE 39
Camera Raw dialog box

Camera description

Camera raw Image

Buttons cancel, save changes, or open Photoshop

Creating Images for the Web

The Camera RAW dialog box shown in Figure 39 contains three buttons in the lower-right corner: Open Image, Cancel, and Done, and one button in the lower-left corner: Save Image. The Open Image button applies changes and opens the image. The Save Image button converts and saves an image. The Done button applies the changes and closes the dialog box without opening the image. The Cancel button closes the dialog box without accepting any changes. In addition to files in the RAW format, JPEG and TIFF digital images can also be opened using the Camera Raw dialog box, enabling you to take advantage of the same powerful setting options. To do this, right-click the image in Adobe Bridge, then click Open in Camera Raw.

Don't be alarmed if you see a caution icon in the Camera Raw dialog box. This icon indicates that the preview image has been generated from a camera raw image.

Modifying Camera Raw Images

An image in the camera raw format can be opened using the File menu or Adobe Bridge, but the image initially opens in the Camera Raw dialog box rather than in the Photoshop window. This dialog box creates a sidecar XMP file that contains metadata and accompanies the camera raw file. An image that has been modified using the Camera Raw plug-in is accompanied by an icon in Bridge, as shown in Figure 40.

QUICKTIP
You can synchronize image settings from one to many images in Camera Raw by selecting an image (in Filmstrip View), clicking the Synchronize button at the top of the Filmstrip pane, then clicking the Synchronize button.

Using Camera Raw Settings and Preferences

The Camera Raw file format is similar to a digital negative. It contains all the information a camera has about a specific image. It is also similar to the TIFF format in that it does not discard any color information, yet it is smaller than an uncompressed TIFF. Camera Raw settings can be saved (up to 100 settings) and then applied to a specific camera or for specific lighting conditions. The Apply Camera Raw Settings menu allows you to save current settings and add them to the Settings menu, as well as modify settings for Exposure, Shadows, Brightness, Contrast, and Saturation.

QUICKTIP
You can use Adobe Bridge to copy and paste Camera Raw settings from one image to another. To do this, open Adobe Bridge, select a file, click Edit on the Application bar, point to Develop Settings, then click Copy Camera Raw Settings. Once this is complete, select one or more (other) Raw images in Bridge, click Edit on the Application bar, point to Develop Settings, then click Paste Camera Raw Settings.

FIGURE 40
Raw image in Adobe Bridge

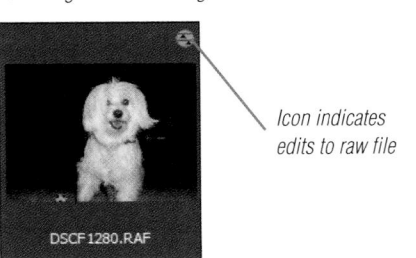

Icon indicates edits to raw file

Using Camera Raw adjustment settings
Because the Camera Raw format for each digital camera is different, you can adjust the Camera Raw settings to recreate the colors in a photo more accurately. Using the Camera Calibration button located in the Image Adjustment tabs, you can select a profile: ACR 4.4 (the built-in camera profile for Photoshop CS4). Use the Hue and Saturation sliders to adjust the red, green, and blue in the image. Camera Raw adjustments made to the original image are always preserved, so you can adjust them repeatedly if necessary. The adjustment settings are stored within the Camera Raw database file or in a sidecar XMP file that accompanies the original Camera Raw image in a location of your choosing.

Understanding the Camera Raw Dialog Box

When you open multiple camera raw images, the Camera Raw dialog box displays a filmstrip, as shown in Figure 41. The left panel of the dialog box, which only appears when multiple images are open, displays camera raw, TIFF, or JPEG files opened in the Camera Raw dialog box. The center panel displays the view controls, the selected image, zoom levels, and navigation arrows. The right panel displays a histogram for the active image, the image adjustment tabs, and adjustment sliders.

QUICKTIP

Open multiple camera raw images by selecting image thumbnails in Adobe Bridge, pressing and holding [Shift] right-clicking, then clicking Open in Camera Raw.

FIGURE 41

Multiple open images in Camera Raw dialog box

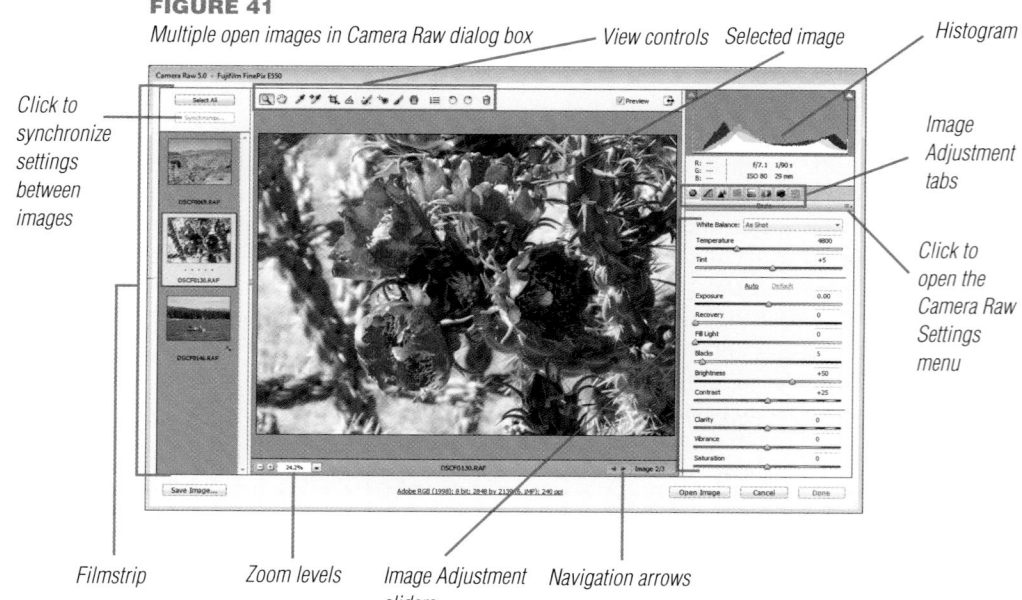

Click to synchronize settings between images

View controls *Selected image* *Histogram*

Image Adjustment tabs

Click to open the Camera Raw Settings menu

Filmstrip *Zoom levels* *Image Adjustment sliders* *Navigation arrows*

Using the Digital Negative format (DNG)

Adobe DNG (Digital Negative format) is an archival format for camera raw files that contains the raw image data created within a digital camera, as well as the metadata that define what that data means. This format is designed to provide compatibility among the increasing number of Camera Raw file formats. The following Saving options are available:

• Compressed (lossless), which applies a lossless compression to the DNG file.
• Convert to Linear Image, which stores the image data in an interpolated format.
• Embed Original Raw File, which stores the entire original camera raw image data in the DNG file, and JPEG Preview, which specifies whether to embed a JPEG preview in the DNG file.

Export Camera Raw settings

The settings you created and stored in the Camera Raw database can be exported to a sidecar XMP file, embedded in a DNG file, or can be used to update JPEG previews embedded in DNG files. To export Camera Raw settings, open the files in the Camera Raw dialog box, switch to the Filmstrip view if necessary, then select the thumbnail(s) whose settings you want to export. Open the Camera Raw Settings menu in the Camera Raw dialog box, then click Export Settings to XMP. An XMP file will be created in the folder where the Raw image is located.

Modifying Images in the Camera Raw Dialog Box

You can make many image modifications right in the Camera Raw dialog box. Some of the tools should look familiar to you, as you've already seen or used them in Photoshop. Figure 42 identifies unfamiliar view control tools as well as the additional tools that are displayed when the Retouch tool is selected. Using the Retouch tool, you can heal or clone defective areas of an image *before* bringing it into Photoshop.

You can make changes to colors using tabs in the Image Adjustments area in the right panel. Adjustments you can make include the following:

- Basic: adjusts white balance, color saturation, and tonality.
- Tone Curve: fine-tunes tonality using a Parametric curve and a Point curve.
- HSL/Grayscale: fine-tunes colors using Hue, Saturation, and Luminance adjustments, as shown in Figure 43.
- Split Toning: lets you color monochrome images or create special effects with color images.

- Detail: Sharpens images or reduces noise.
- Lens Corrections: compensates for chromatic aberration and vignetting caused by a camera lens.
- Camera Calibration: corrects a color cast in shadows and adjusts non-neutral colors to compensate for the differences between camera behavior and the Camera Raw profile for your particular camera model.
- Presets: lets you save and apply sets of image adjustment settings.

FIGURE 42
Camera Raw view controls

Open preferences dialog button

White Balance tool   *Straighten tool*   *Retouch tool*   *Toggle full screen mode*

FIGURE 43
HSL/Grayscale Adjustment tab

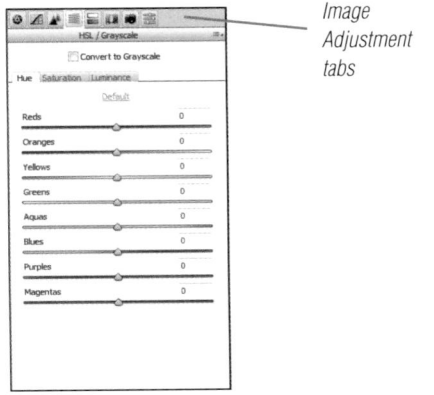

Image Adjustment tabs

FIGURE 44
Camera Raw Preferences dialog box

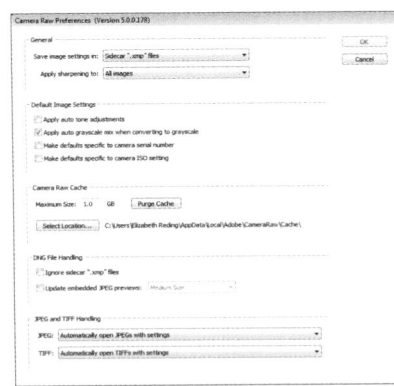

Changing Camera Raw Preferences

To change the preferences in the Camera Raw dialog box, click Edit in the Adobe Bridge Application bar, then click Camera Raw Preferences, or click the Open preferences dialog button in the view controls area of the Camera Raw dialog box. The Camera Raw Preferences dialog box lets you determine how image settings will be saved, and how default image settings are handled. See Figure 44.

Power User Shortcuts

to do this:	use this method:
Create a slice	✂ or [Shift][C]
Cycle shape tools	[Shift][U]
Deselect slices	[Ctrl][D] (Win) ⌘[D] (Mac)
Hide/show rulers	[Ctrl][R] (Win) ⌘[R] (Mac)
Preview in browser	🌐 or your browser button

to do this:	use this method:
Save for Web & Devices	[Ctrl][Shift][Alt][S] (Win) ⌘[Shift] option [S] (Mac)
Select a slice	✂
Show Animation panel	[F11] (Win)
Start animation playback	▶
Stop animation playback	■

Key: Menu items are indicated by ➤ between the menu name and its command. Blue bold letters are shortcuts for selecting tools on the Tools panel.

Learn about web features.

1. Start Photoshop, open PS 16-5.psd from the drive and folder where you store your Data Files, then save it as **Optimal Dolphin**.
2. Set the background and foreground colors to their default values.
3. Fit the image on the screen.

Optimize images for web use.

1. Open the Save For Web & Devices dialog box.
2. Display the 4-Up tab, then zoom in or out of the image (if necessary).
3. Verify the settings of the image to the right of the original image as GIF 64 Dithered.
4. Save the file as **Optimal-Dolphin-GIF.gif** to the drive and folder where you store your Data Files.
5. Open the Save for Web & Devices dialog box, click the first GIF image after the original image, change the settings to JPEG High, then compare your image to Figure 45.
6. Use the Save button to save the file as **Optimal-Dolphin-JPG.jpg**.
7. Close Optimal Dolphin *without* saving changes.

FIGURE 45
Completed Skills Review 1

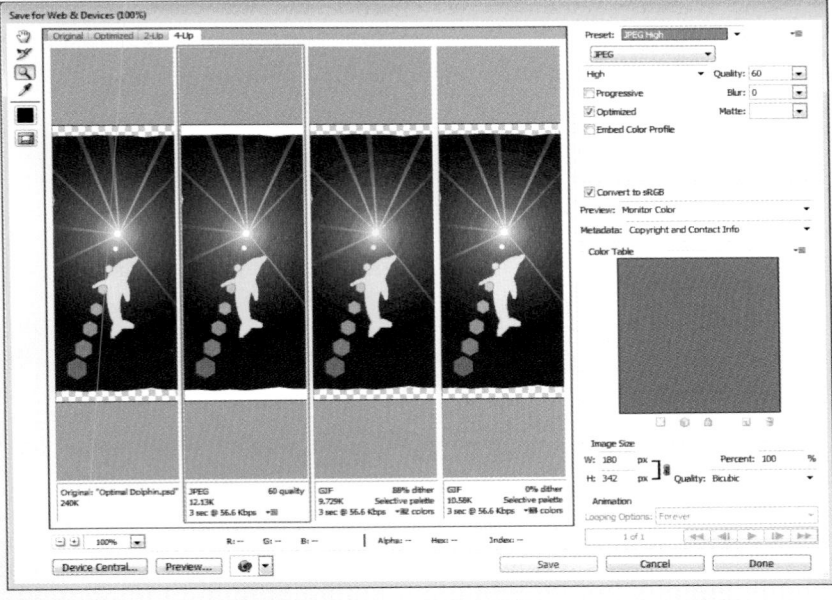

Create a button for a web page.

1. Open PS 16-6.psd, then save it as **Canine-Nation**.
2. If prompted, update the text layers.
3. Set the background and foreground colors to the default.
4. Fit the image on the screen, and display the rulers and slices (if necessary).
5. Select the Rounded Rectangle tool.
6. Activate the Board layer.
7. Select the Woodgrain style, then use the guides to help you draw a button from 15 X/340 Y to 135 X/390 Y.
8. Select the Type tool.
9. Click the image within the button type **Rescue** (use a White, Bold 18 pt Arial font), then center the text within the button.
10. Save your work.

Create slices in an image.

1. Draw a slice for the Train button from 15 X/150 Y to 135 X/200 Y.
2. Draw a slice for the Groom button from 15 X/210 Y to 135 X/260 Y.
3. Draw a slice for the Board button from 15 X/275 Y to 135 X/325 Y.
4. Draw a slice for the Rescue button from 15 X/340 Y to 135 X/390 Y.
5. Resize the Jack Russell slice (the image of the dog in the top-right portion of the image) so that the top is 90 Y and the bottom is 320 Y.
6. Type the following (fictitious) URL for the Jack Russell slice: **http://www.caninenation. com/breed/jackrussell_faq.html**.
7. Hide the slices and rulers.
8. Save your work, compare your image to Figure 46, then close Canine-Nation.

FIGURE 46
Completed Skills Review 2

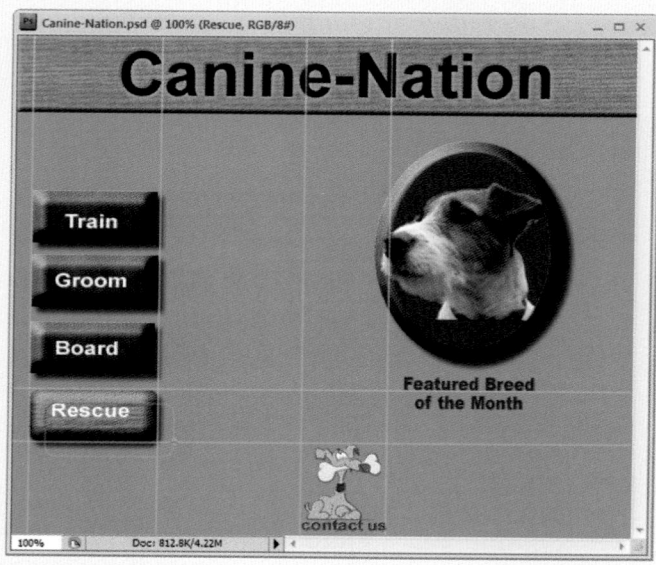

Create and play basic animation.

1. Open PS 16-7.psd, then save it as **The Old Soft Shoe**.
2. Display the rulers (if necessary).
3. Display the Animation panel, duplicate frame 1, make the Cat Forward layer active, then drag the Cat Forward image to approximately 250 X.
4. Duplicate frame 2, then hide the Cat Forward layer and make the Cat Dancing layer visible.
5. Duplicate frame 3, then hide the Cat Dancing layer and make the Cat Forward layer visible.
6. Duplicate frame 4, hide the Cat Forward layer, make the Cat Dancing layer visible, then change the Opacity setting of the Cat Dancing layer to 0%.
7. Play the animation.
8. Save your work, then hide the rulers, if necessary.

Add tweening and frame delay.

1. Tween frame 2 using the previous frame and adding two frames.
2. Tween frame 5 using the previous frame and adding one frame.
3. Tween frame 6 using the previous frame and adding five frames.
4. Set the looping option to Forever, than play the animation.
5. Set the frame delay for frames 1, 4, 6, and 7 to 0.2 seconds.
6. Play the animation.
7. Preview the animation in your browser.
8. Save your work, then compare your image to Figure 47.

FIGURE 47
Completed Skills Review 3

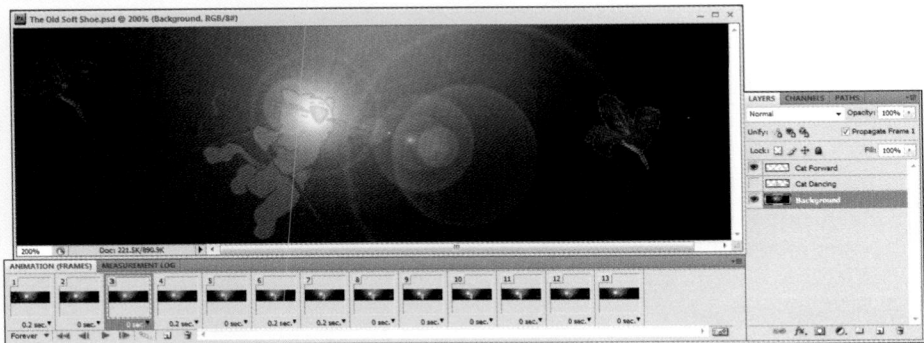

Modify Video in Photoshop.

1. Open **PS 16-8.avi**, then save it as **Wind Trancer sculpture**.

2. Convert the video layer into a Smart Object.

3. Add a Color Balance adjustment layer using the following midtone settings:
   Cyan-Red: +41
   Magenta-Green: +37
   Yellow-Blue: +22

4. Clip the adjustment layer to the existing layer.

5. Add a Brightness/Contrast adjustment layer using a Brightness of −29 and a Contrast of +30.

6. Clip this adjustment layer to the existing layer, then compare your image to Figure 48.

FIGURE 48
Partially completed Skills Review 4

7. Change the starting point of the Color Balance 1 layer to approximately 9:00f.

8. Change the ending point of the Color Balance 1 layer to approximately 18:00f.

9. Change the starting point of the Brightness/ Contrast 1 layer to approximately 3:00f.

10. Change the ending point of the Brightness/ Contrast 1 layer to approximately 12:00f.

11. Play the video.

12. Decrease the work area by approximately one second at the beginning and ending of the video sequence.

13. Save your work, play the video, then compare your screen to Figure 49.

FIGURE 49
Completed Skills Review 4

A local long-distance runners group is sponsoring a cross-country run for charity. The event will offer short cross-country races for all ages and fitness levels. You've volunteered to use your skills to design an animation for their web page that encourages even the slowest runners to join in the fun.

1. Obtain the following images for the animation: one object that conveys the idea of movement and an obstacle it moves over, around, or toward. You can also obtain a background and any other images, as desired. You can draw your own images, use the images that are available on your computer, scan print media, create images using a digital camera, or connect to the Internet and download images.

2. Create a new Photoshop image and save it as **Xtream Charity**.

3. Apply a color or style to the Background layer. (*Hint*: The Background layer in the sample has a Pattern Overlay style applied to it.)

4. Add frames to the Animation panel. Make one a motion animation and the other a fade-out effect.

5. Tween each animation and add frame delays as necessary.

6. Preview the animation in your image and in your browser.

7. Save your work, then compare your screen to the sample shown in Figure 50.

FIGURE 50
Sample Project Builder

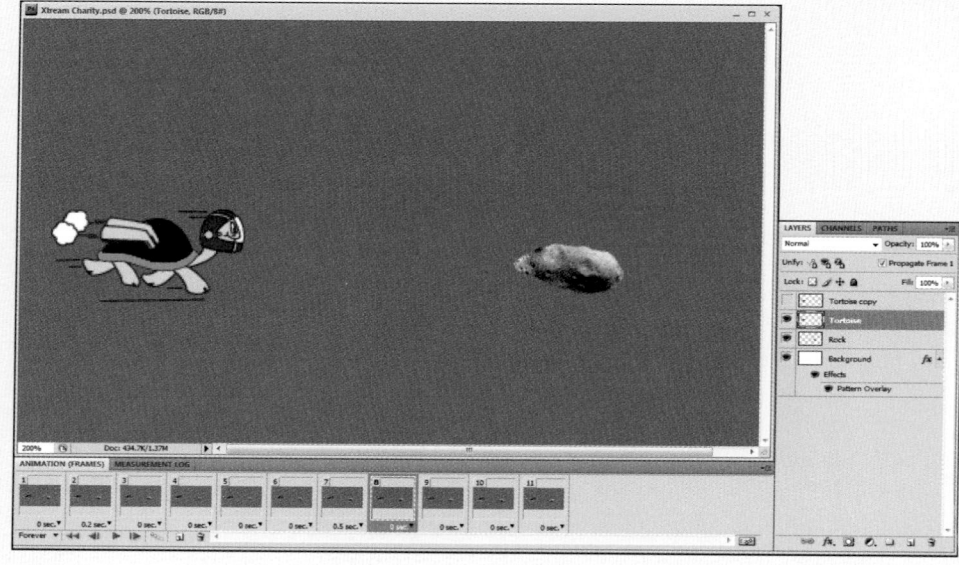

You've just been elected to the board of directors of a community access TV station. Each board member is expected to serve on at least one committee. You've chosen the Community Involvement Committee, and have been asked to design a snappy, numeric countdown animation that will introduce public service announcements.

1. Obtain images appropriate for a countdown. You can draw your own numbers, use the images that are available on your computer, scan print media, create images using a digital camera, or connect to the Internet and download images. You must include at least one other image, and can include any additional images, as desired.

2. Create a new Photoshop image, then save it as **Countdown**.

3. Apply a color or style to the Background layer, add images as desired, and apply effects to them. (*Hint*: The Background layer in the sample has a Pattern Overlay style applied to it.)

4. Create at least three type layers with numbers for a countdown, and apply styles or filters to them as desired. (*Hint*: Each number in the sample has a duplicate with different opacities.)

5. Create an animation that makes the numbers move across the image and fade into one another.

6. Duplicate the last number so that it changes appearance at least twice.

7. Tween each animation and add frame delays as necessary.

8. Preview the animation in your image and in your browser.

9. Save Countdown as **Countdown Browser**, then adjust tweening and frame delays so that it plays perfectly in your browser.

10. Save your work, then compare your screen to the sample shown in Figure 51.

FIGURE 51
Sample Project Builder 2

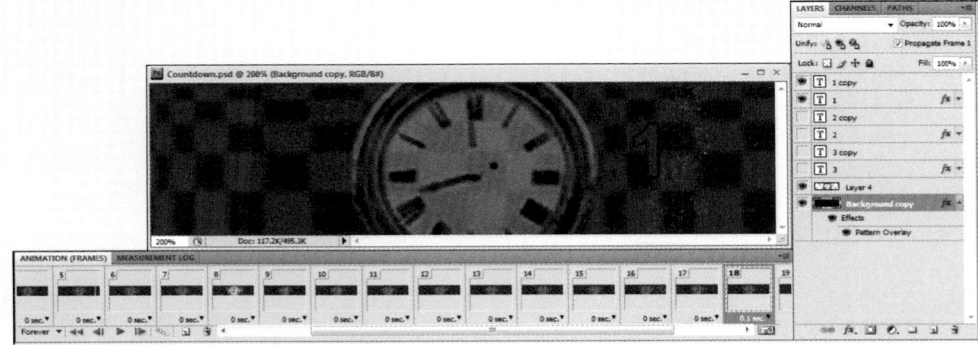

DESIGN PROJECT

After your first experience with creating your own animation, you and your friends are hooked. You want to peruse the full range of animation on the web. You decide to study one aspect of web animation. Your first stop will be to check out the latest in animated banner ads.

1. Connect to the Internet and use your browser to find sites containing downloadable animation. (Make a record of the site you found so you can use it for future reference, if necessary.) A sample site is shown in Figure 52.
2. Create a new Photoshop image and save it as **Banners et al**.
3. Identify an animation that interests you by scrolling down the page or linking to one of the sites listed on the page.
4. Create a type layer named **Animation Techniques**, then type the animation techniques and Photoshop skills and features that you believe were used to create the appearance of the animation.
5. Be sure to add the following points to the Animation Techniques layer:
   - Identify how many different animations are active throughout the sequence and at any one time.

   - Identify instances of tweening and frame delay.
   - Give examples of techniques unknown to you.
6. When your analysis is complete, print the image.
7. Hide the Animation Techniques layer, then obtain images to use for your own interpretation of the animation. You can use the images that are available on your computer, scan print media, or download images from the Internet.

8. Place the images in your image, create type layers as needed, and then apply the animation techniques you identified.
9. Update the Animation Techniques layer as necessary, print the image so that the Animation Techniques layer prints clearly, then compare your before and after analyses. (*Hint*: Hide distracting layers.)
10. Hide the Animation Techniques layer, make the other layers active, then save your work.

FIGURE 52
Sample Design Project

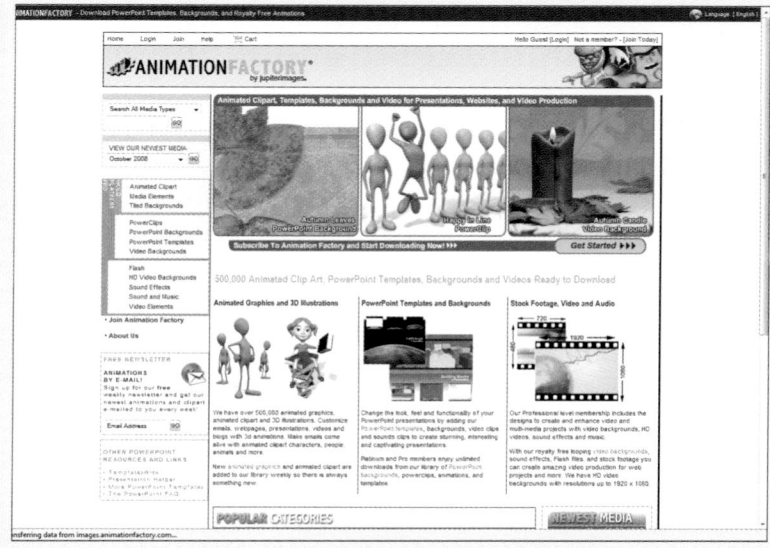

Courtesy of Jupiterimages Corporation - http://www.animationfactory.com/en/

You and your team handle new product presentations for Never Too Late (NTL), an online message service that sends daily reminders to clients. NTL is teaming with an automated home electronics company to offer a new home-based service. They're going to provide an automatic wake-up call that turns on a client's computer, plays a wake-up message until the client responds, and then lists the day's important activities. You want to demonstrate a prototype that shows off the product at your next staff meeting. This prototype will transform a black-and-white line drawing into a color image as part of the wake-up call feature. You'll add appropriate sounds later.

1. Obtain images for the wake-up call. One image should be a black-and-white image that you can easily transform to color. You can draw your own images, use the images that are available on your computer, scan print media, create images using a digital camera, or connect to the Internet and download images.
2. Create a new Photoshop image, then save it as **Wake Up**.
3. Apply a color or style to the Background layer, add other images as desired, and apply effects to them. (*Hint*: The sample has three color layers that alternate as the background, two of which have gradients applied to them.)
4. Place the images in the file. (*Hint*: The black-and-white line art is a cartoon line drawing that was filled in to colorize it. You can color a similar image by choosing background colors on the Tools panel, selecting the Eraser tool, and then clicking the Lock transparent pixels button on the Layers panel.)
5. Create at least one type layer as desired and at least one other image or background.

FIGURE 53
Sample Portfolio Project

6. Create an animation for the state you created.
7. Tween each animation, and add frame delays as necessary.
8. Preview the animation in your image and in your browser.
9. Save your work, then compare your screen to the sample shown in Figure 53.

appendix

PORTFOLIO PROJECTS
AND EFFECTS

1. Create a pencil sketch from a photo

2. Create a montage effect with blocks

3. Simulate a slide mount

4. Create a reflection effect

5. Fake a motion blur

6. Improve a photo

7. Animate warped type

8. Fix photographic defects

PORTFOLIO PROJECTS
AND EFFECTS

Introduction

Now that you've got all kinds of Photoshop skills under your belt, you're ready to discover real-world opportunities to use these skills and have some fun, too. This appendix presents seven projects that you can complete at your own pace using your own design choices. Rather than guiding you through each step, these projects suggest strategies and methods for achieving the finished product. As you complete these projects, you'll build on the knowledge you already have, and even learn a few new Photoshop tricks along the way.

Getting the Most from the Projects

Of the seven projects in this appendix, three are effects—smaller, mini-projects that you can use within other images. For example, the reflected object effect shown in Figure 1 could stand on its own or be used as a component in a larger image. The pulsing type and motion blur projects seen in Figures 2 and 3 could each easily be used in a web page. (You'll create each of these effects later in this appendix.) Any of the techniques shown in this appendix could be increased or reduced. How much a technique is used depends entirely on what sort of effect you're going for and the results you see.

FIGURE 1
Sample 1

Using Multiple Skills

Like most real-life projects, the image in Figure 2 makes use of many different Photoshop skills. Look at the figure, then see how many tasks from the following list you can identify:

- Warped type
- Composite images
- Button images with type
- Type resized using its bounding box

Viewing Animation

It would be great to be able to see an animation on a static page, wouldn't it? Well, short of that, the effect shown in Figure 3 is achieved by turning on all the layers in the image so you can see approximately what the animation will look like when viewed in a browser.

FIGURE 2
Sample 2

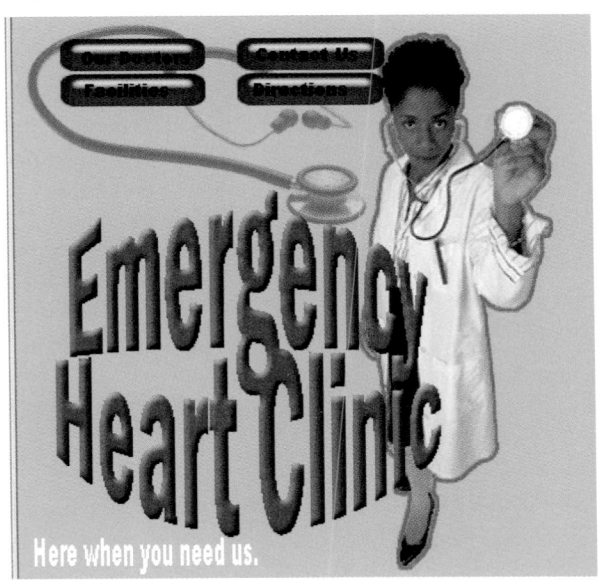

FIGURE 3
Sample 3

CREATE A PENCIL SKETCH
FROM A PHOTO

Skills You'll Use

In this lesson, you'll do the following:
- Save a digital image as a Photoshop file.
- Change the color mode.
- Duplicate and invert a layer.
- Change the blending mode.
- Apply a filter.
- Use the History Brush to restore color.

Creating a Unique Look

How about this? Take an ordinary photo, and give it a look that's not realistic at all. You can do this by duplicating a layer here and there, changing the color mode, applying a filter, and then selectively restoring color. How much you restore is entirely up to you!

> **QUICK**TIP
>
> As you work through each exercise, carefully examine the History panel of the completed project. It may help you understand the steps that were taken to achieve the final product.

Preparing for Magic

Figure 4 contains an ordinary portrait photo, but watch what happens. First, you turn this color image to grayscale mode (discarding the color information), then duplicate the existing background layer. Next, you invert the duplicate layer. This process (which you achieve by clicking Image on the Application bar, pointing to Adjustments, then clicking Invert) flips

the colors or tones of the active layer, so whatever is dark becomes light. Change the Blending Mode to Color Dodge. Don't panic: it looks like your image has disappeared, doesn't it? But apply a Gaussian Blur and a pencil-like sketch will be visible. Pretty cool, huh?

Using the History Brush Tool

You might be satisfied with the image the way it is, but wait—there's more! To add a little more pizzazz, you can selectively reapply some color. First, flatten the image, then change the mode back to RGB color. Now we're going to see some magic! Select the History Brush tool from the toolbox and selectively paint areas in the image. In Figure 5, for example, the face and hair are painted, but you could paint any areas you want.

> **QUICK**TIP
>
> The History Brush tool is a source of earlier pixel data, but can only be used within a single image.

FIGURE 4

Project 1 – Beginning

FIGURE 5

Project 1 – Completed

FIGURE 6

Project 1 – Portfolio Sample

Project 1   Create a Pencil Sketch from a Photo

1. Open PS APP-1.jpg from the drive and folder where you store your Data Files, then save it as **Colorized Pencil Sketch.psd**.

2. Use the following suggestions to guide you through completing the project:

   - Change the image mode to Grayscale.

   - Duplicate the background layer, then rename the duplicate.

   - Invert the new layer (click Image on the Application bar, point to Adjustments, then click Invert or click the Invert button on the Adjustments panel), then use the Layer Style dialog box to change the blending mode to Color Dodge.

   - Add a Gaussian Blur filter. (A setting of 4 pixels is used in the sample.)

   - Flatten the image, then change the mode to RGB Color.

   - Create a new layer, then set the blending mode to Multiply.

   - Use the History Brush to paint the woman's face, hair, and neck. (*Hint*: The image will look almost blank up to this point.)

3. Save your work, then compare your image to Figure 5.

   Figure 6 shows how this image might be used in a marketing piece to promote a product. In this example, type was added to promote the name of a photography studio.

You saved a digital image as a Photoshop file, changed the image mode, applied a filter, flattened the image, then used the History Brush to selectively restore color to the image.

CREATE A MONTAGE
EFFECT WITH BLOCKS

Skills You'll Use

In this lesson, you'll do the following:
- Save a digital image as a Photoshop file.
- Add a background layer.
- Resize imagery.
- Create layers from selections.
- Add layer styles.

Keeping It Simple

Sometimes all it takes to make an image stand out is a simple technique executed with artistic flair. Take, for example, the image shown in Figure 7. This is a nice photograph as is, but with a little Photoshop sleight-of-hand, you can really make it pop.

> **QUICK**TIP
>
> Most Photoshop tasks are easy to accomplish but may take longer than you think.

Getting Boxy

The boxy effect you see in Figure 8 is not difficult to create. Once you've added a background layer and resized the initial image (in this case, the quaint shop),

the real fun begins. Make the layer containing the actual image active, then randomly pick a spot and draw a rectangle with the Rectangular Marquee tool. Create a layer from the selection using the Layer via Copy command, then add a drop shadow to the layer. Then, to add to the effect, move the layer (the one you created from the selection) so it's slightly offset from the original. Repeat this process in different parts of the image until you're satisfied with the results. As you can see from the completed image, this effect was repeated eight times (resulting in eight new layers). Now, that wasn't hard, was it?

> **QUICK**TIP
>
> You could automate this process by creating an action for these repetitive steps.

FIGURE 7
Project 2 – Beginning

FIGURE 8
Project 2 – Completed

FIGURE 9
Project 2 – Portfolio Sample

Project 2   Create a Montage Effect with Blocks

Create a block montage effect

1. Open PS APP-2.jpg from the drive and folder where you store your Data Files, then save it as **Shopping.psd**.

2. Use the following suggestions to guide you through completing the project:

   ■ Create a new background layer using the color of your choice. (A medium brown is shown in the sample.)

   ■ Resize the original layer so it appears to be framed by the background layer.

   ■ Make a rectangular selection, create a layer from the selection, add a drop shadow or outer glow effect, then move the layer.

   ■ Repeat the process of creating a drop-shadowed or outer glowed, offset layer from a selection until you've achieved the look you want.

   TIP   You can easily copy formatting from one layer to another by selecting the layer containing the formatting you want to duplicate, press and hold [Alt] while dragging the formatting effect(s) to the layer where you want to apply the formatting.

3. Save your work, then compare your image to Figure 8.

   Figure 9 shows how this image could be used in a promotional poster.

You saved a digital image as a Photoshop file, added a new background layer, resized an object, created layers from selections, then added layer styles.

SIMULATE
A SLIDE MOUNT

Skills You'll Use

In this lesson, you'll do the following:
- Use a digital image in a Photoshop file.
- Draw a shape.
- Delete a selection.
- Add a drop shadow.
- Add type.
- Merge layers.
- Resize and skew or rotate a shape.

Creating an Illusion

You've probably seen photos that look like slides in a magazine or an ad somewhere, and asked "How'd they do that?" The illusion is actually very easy to create, using a few simple Photoshop tricks. Just draw a shape, add some text, and pop in an image.

Simulating a Slide

To create the effect of a slide, you create a new layer, change the foreground color to gray, then draw a rounded rectangle shape. (You don't want to draw a shape layer or a path, you want to fill pixels.) Draw a horizontal marquee within the rounded rectangle (this is where the slide image would appear), rasterize the shape, then delete the selection to 'punch a hole' in the slide. Add a drop shadow to the object, and your slide is finished. You can add text to the

slide to make it look more realistic. When your slide looks just right, merge all the appropriate layers into a single slide layer.

> **QUICK**TIP
>
> You'll probably want to duplicate your blank slide so it'll be easier to use over and over. No point in reinventing the wheel!

Adding the Image to the Slide

The individual photos in Figure 10 will work fine for the individual slide images. Make sure you've got enough slide blanks, then select each photo and drag it into the slide image. Each photo will have to be resized to fit the hole in each slide, and you may want to skew the slides to make them look scattered, rather than perfectly aligned. This gives the slides a more realistic look.

FIGURE 10

Project 3 – Beginning

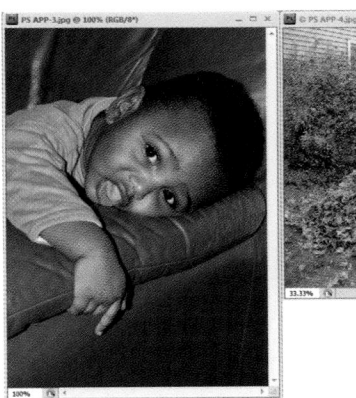

FIGURE 11

Project 3 – Completed

FIGURE 12

Project 3 – Portfolio Sample

Project 3   Simulate a Slide Mount

Create a slide mount effect

1. Open PS APP-3.jpg and PS APP-4.jpg from the drive and folder where you store your Data Files.

2. Open a new Photoshop image with the dimensions 450 X 225 pixels, then save it as **Slide Mount.psd**.

3. Use the following suggestions to guide you through completing the project:

   ■ Create a rounded-rectangular shape in a shade of gray.

   ■ Knock out a rectangle in the middle of the shape.

   ■ Add a drop shadow to the shape.

   ■ Add text to the image, then merge the layers so the slide is a single layer.

   ■ Copy the slide layer (you may want to make multiple copies, depending on your overall design goal).

   ■ Insert an image in the rectangular knock-out.

   ■ Rotate or skew the slide (if that is the look you want to achieve).

4. Save your work, then compare your image to Figure 11.

   TIP   The image on the right was converted into a Smart Object, then enhanced with the Sharpen filter.

   Figure 12 shows an example of how the slides could be used in a corporate advertisement.

You created a new Photoshop image, opened two digital image files to use in the new image, created a shape that looks like a slide, knocked out a rectangle in the slide, added type to the shape, inserted an image in the shape, and rotated or skewed it to make it look more realistic. You repeated this process for all the images you wanted to present as "slides."

CREATE A
REFLECTION EFFECT

Skills You'll Use

In this lesson, you'll do the following:

- Save a Photoshop image using a new name.
- Duplicate a layer.
- Flip and reposition an image.
- Apply a blur filter and a distort filter.
- Apply a mask and gradient.
- Adjust midtones.

Understanding Illusion

So much of what we do in Photoshop involves creating an illusion. As you saw in the previous project, you can create an image that looks like a photographic slide by using what you know about how real slides look to trick the eye. In this project, you trick the eye again—by making an object look as if it were reflected in rippling water. The beauty of Photoshop layers is that you can easily duplicate objects, then manipulate the images within selected layers. Once a layer is duplicated, it can be flipped, and then 'doctored' to display the ephemeral qualities that it might have by being reflected in a pool of water. Figure 13 shows objects against a background, and Figure 14 shows those same objects after a reflection effect was created.

Creating a Reflection

You can begin creating the reflection effect by duplicating the Tools layer. Flip the duplicate vertically, and then drag it beneath the original. (The duplicate will serve as the reflected object.) Since a reflected object should not be a mirror-image, apply a Motion Blur filter, then apply a Ripple filter to give it that 'watery' look.

Applying a Fade

To give the reflection a faded look, apply a mask, then apply a gradient to the mask. You can give depth to the surface on which the object sits, by creating a marquee on the background layer, then adjusting the midtones in the Levels dialog box. *Voila!*

FIGURE 13

Project 4 – Beginning

Create a reflection effect

1. Open PS APP-5.psd from the drive and folder where you store your Data Files, then save it as **Reflected Object Effect.psd**.

2. Use the following suggestions to guide you through completing the project:

   - Duplicate the Tools layer.

   - Flip the image vertically on the duplicate layer.

   - Reposition the duplicate layer so it appears to be *beneath* the original layer.

   - Apply a Motion Blur filter to the duplicate layer.

   - Apply a Ripple filter to the duplicate layer.

   - Add a rectangular layer mask to the duplicate layer, then draw a linear gradient from the top of the reflection to the bottom of the image.

   - Select the Rectangular Marquee tool, then set the feather setting to 5 px.

   - With the Background layer active, draw a marquee around the bottom half of the image.

   - Open the Levels dialog box, then modify the midtones (the center slider) setting to darken the selection. (In the sample, the midtones are adjusted to .70.)

3. Save your work, then compare your image to Figure 14.

You saved a Photoshop file using a new name, duplicated and flipped an image, applied two filters, created a layer mask, then added a gradient and modified the midtones in the Levels dialog box.

FIGURE 14

Project 4 – Completed

FAKE A MOTION
BLUR

Skills You'll Use

In this lesson, you'll do the following:
- Save a Photoshop image using a new name.
- Rasterize a type layer.
- Create multiple type layers by duplicating and editing a single layer.
- Apply a motion blur filter.
- Make frames from each layer.
- Add movement and time delays to an animation sequence.

Deciding What's Possible

Using a little imagination, you can create interesting animations for your website. You've seen words fly in from the side in what looks like a blur, right? This type of moving text is often used to call attention to a special event or important information, because it's more likely to catch a viewer's eye than static type. You can create this effect, often called a motion blur, using a few simple tools in Photoshop.

Dividing and Conquering

You start with a simple line of type, as shown in Figure 15, which you can rasterize and duplicate. Then you apply the motion blur filter to the duplicate layer. This is the layer that's going to simulate the movement. The next step is to separate each blurred word onto its own layer. (If your sanity is important to you, you'll probably want to do some layer renaming.) With the duplicate layer active, draw a

marquee around a single word, then click Layer on the Application bar, point to New, then click Layer via Cut. (This step puts the selected object on its own layer.) Repeat this process until you have separated all the words—blurred and clear—as you want them. Moving the blurred words slightly left or right will make your animation more convincing.

> **QUICK**TIP
> The Layer via Cut command is similar to the Layer via Copy command, except that the source layer is modified.

Animating the Layers

Now the animation fun begins. Make frames from layers and reorder the layers (if necessary), then turn on and off layers for each frame depending on the effect you want. Move any layers that will add to the effect of movement, add time delays, then play the animation.

FIGURE 15
Project 5 – Beginning

FIGURE 16
Project 5 – Completed

Fake a motion blur

1. Open PS APP-6.psd from the drive and folder where you store your Data Files, then save it as **Motion Blur Effect.psd**.

2. Use the following suggestions to guide you through completing the project:

   ■ Rasterize the type layer.

   ■ Duplicate the type layer.

   ■ Add a motion blur filter to the duplicate layer. (In the sample, a setting of 50 pixels and a 0° angle is used.)

   ■ Separate each blurred word from the duplicate layer.

   ■ Separate each clear word from the original layer.

   ■ Open the Animation panel, if it is not already displayed.

   ■ Make frames from the layers.

   ■ Turn on and off layers for each frame as necessary. Position the type so that the blurred type appears first, then the sharp type appears in a slightly different location, creating the illusion of movement.

   ■ Add time delays.

   ■ Play the animation in Photoshop and in a browser.

3. Save your work, then compare your image to Figure 16.

You saved a Photoshop file using a new name, rasterized and duplicated a type layer, added a motion blur filter, then separated each word onto its own layer. Using the Animation panel, you made frames from the layers, turned the layers on and off, added time delays, then played the animation.

IMPROVE
A PHOTO

Skills You'll Use

In this lesson, you'll do the following:
- Save a digital image as a Photoshop file.
- Paint areas to make them brighter.
- Use Liquify to move pixels.

Dieting with Photoshop

This is better than cosmetic surgery—much faster and certainly much cheaper! Suppose you have a photo, like the one in Figure 17. Handsome guy, right? But he could stand some improvement. His teeth look a little dingy, and let's face it, there's a little too much to love here. But you can fix that!

Improving on Reality

You can whiten dingy teeth by simply painting them white, right? Sure, but that's not always the most effective technique—in fact, this can make someone look ridiculous. Impossibly white teeth can look unrealistic. A better approach is either to sample a brighter area of the existing teeth, or to find a brighter off-white that looks believable.

QUICKTIP

Remember that real-life objects are rarely made up of solid colors. That means that no one's teeth are completely one color. Look closely, and you'll see greens and blues in your teeth. This means that when coloring objects in Photoshop, you may need to mix colors rather than using only one shade.

Pushing Pixels

When you look at Figure 18, you can see what a difference these changes can make. Using the Liquify feature, pixels were pushed to slim the waist and neck areas. A mask was placed over the man's beard so it wouldn't get distorted when the neck pixels were moved.

QUICKTIP

To move pixels with greater control, use the Push Left tool in the Liquify feature.

FIGURE 17
Project 6 – Beginning

FIGURE 19
Project 6 – Portfolio Sample

FIGURE 18
Project 6 – Completed

Teeth
whitened

Neck
thinner

Waist
thinner

Improve a photo

1. Open PS APP-7.jpg from the drive and folder where you store your Data Files, then save it as **Improved Image.psd**.

2. Use the following suggestions to guide you through completing the project:

   ■ Duplicate the original image, so that you can work on each area in a different layer.

   ■ Zoom into the teeth, select a small brush size, then paint the teeth.

   ■ Choose a lighter off-white, then paint the teeth. (In the sample, the foreground color was changed to R=234, G=231, B=216.)

   ■ Use the Liquify feature to reduce the waist and neck areas.

   ■ Add any necessary adjustment layers for color correction.

   TIP   The image was converted into a Smart Object, then enhanced with the Sharpen More filter.

3. Save your work, then compare your image to Figure 18.

   Figure 19 shows an example of how this improved photo could be used in an advertisement.

You saved a digital image as a Photoshop file, brightened teeth by painting them, and used the Liquify feature to make the image more flattering.

ANIMATE WARPED
TYPE

Skills You'll Use

In this lesson, you'll do the following:
- Warp a type layer.
- Modify the warped type layer.
- Add frames to animation.
- Set time delays to animation.

Text with a Pulse

One of the simplest animations you can create with type is a pulsing effect. Similar to creating a motion blur with type, this effect can be used to call attention to information in a web page, but instead of text appearing to fly in from off-screen, it can seem to pulse or vibrate on its own.

Warping Type

To create this effect, you simply warp multiple frames of identical text in different ways. Start by warping a type layer. Modify the warp settings so each frame is different. Add and tween frames until you have a sufficient number to simulate movement. Add some time delays and you're ready to play the animation.

FIGURE 20

Project 7 – Completed

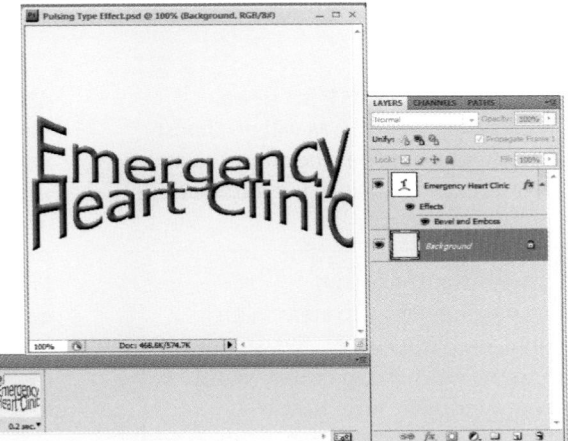

1. Open PS APP-8.psd from the drive and folder where you store your Data Files, then save it as **Pulsing Type Effect.psd**.

2. Use the following suggestions to guide you through completing the project:

   ■ Apply a warp to the type layer.

   ■ Open the Animation panel (if it is not already displayed), then create an additional frame.

   ■ Modify the warp for the new frame.

   ■ Tween the two frames.

   ■ Create additional frames as necessary, modifying the warp in each. In the sample, a Bulge style warp is used with different bend settings for each frame.

   ■ Add tweening and frame delays to smooth the animation effect.

   ■ Play the animation in a browser.

3. Save your work, then compare your image to Figure 20.

You saved a Photoshop file with a different name, then warped a type layer. Using the Animation panel, you added frames, modified the warp settings in each frame, tweened frames, added time delays, then played the animation.

FIX PHOTOGRAPHIC
DEFECTS

Skills You'll Use

In this lesson, you'll do the following:

- Duplicate an image.
- Clean dirt with the Spot Healing Brush tool.
- Eliminate the red eye effect.
- Brighten teeth.
- Add a vignette effect.
- Add a new layer.

Not-So-Perfect Pictures

Our new digital cameras will do almost everything for us, but they won't clean a dirty face, and they may not automatically get rid of red eye.

Isolating Defects

Figuring out problem areas in a photograph can be a challenge. If you're lucky, however, it can be easy. A dirty face, stained outfit, or misplaced blob is easily identified, but composition errors can be harder to spot.

> **QUICK**TIP
>
> It's easy to become fixated on every word and every pixel in your image. It is possible that no one else will notice something you consider a major problem. Learn to let go!

Defining Problems

Part of the problem in identifying problems in images is that we form irrational attachments to our artwork. An ugly sign in an otherwise beautiful image is not a reflection on you. And with Photoshop, you can improve on those defects. It's very difficult to look objectively at your work, but that skill is as essential as learning what Photoshop tool to use in a given situation.

FIGURE 21
Project 8 – Beginning

FIGURE 22
Project 8 – Completed

FIGURE 23
Project 8 – Portfolio Sample

Project 8   Fix Photographic Defects

1. Open PS APP-9.jpg from the drive and folder where you store your Data Files, then save it as **Happy Dog.psd**.

2. Use the following suggestions to guide you through completing the project:

   - Duplicate the original image so that you can work on each area in a different layer.

   - Zoom into the dog's face, then use the Spot Healing Brush tool (or Healing Brush tool) to clean the area around the mouth and under each eye.

   - Use the Red Eye tool to eliminate the red eye effect.

   - Use a light color to whiten the dog's teeth. (The 20% Gray swatch was used in the sample.)

   - Add a vignette effect. (The sample vignette has a 30 px feather.)

   - Add a layer that lies beneath the vignette. (The sample Layer 1 is filled with the swatch Pale Warm Brown.)

3. Save your work, then compare your image to Figure 22.

   Figure 23 shows an example of how this improved photo could be used for promotional purposes.

You saved a digital image as a Photoshop file, used the Spot Healing Brush tool to clean dirt, painted teeth to make them appear brighter, created a vignette effect, then added a layer filled with a complementary color.

ACE Certification Grid for Adobe Photoshop CS4

Topic Area	Objectives	Chapter(s)
1.0 General knowledge	1.1 Describe how to arrange panels and save workspaces. (Includes: arranging and docking panels, customizing menus and shortcuts, and saving workspaces.)	1 (p. 16-23)
	1.2 Describe how to use tabbed documents and the application frame. (Includes: window management (not panel/workspace management), includes screen modes, canvas rotation, n-up views.)	1 (p. 12, 20-23) 14 (p. 13)
	1.3 Describe options for changing the document view and zoom level. (Includes: GPU-assisted pan and zoom techniques.)	1 (p. 34-36) 14 (p. 13)
	1.4 Given a scenario, describe the best way to resize an image. (Includes: Canvas Size dialog box, Image Size dialog box, resampling options, Free Transform, Options bar, resolution concepts.)	1 (p. 23, 29) 12 (p. 4-7)
	1.5 Add metadata to an image in Adobe Photoshop.	1 (p. 9-10)
	1.6 Explain the advantages of and when you would use 32-bit, 16-bit, and 8-bit images.	16 (p. 10, 12, 40)
	1.7 Explain the advantages of different file format choices when saving a Photoshop document. (Includes: file formats, compression methods, color support.)	16 (p. 40-42)
2.0 Correcting, painting, and retouching	2.1 Explain how to correct tonal range and color in Photoshop by using the Adjustments panel. (Includes: setting black point and white point, using Curves/Levels, Hue/Saturation vs. Vibrance, Auto Color, new Curves interface, Selective Color, new color correction UI)	10 (p. 6-13)
	2.2 Given a painting tool, adjust options appropriately and paint on a layer. (Includes: Brush tool, Pencil tool, blending modes, Options bar.)	6 (p. 4-21)
	2.3 Create, edit, and save a custom brush.	6 (p. 10-13)
	2.4 Given a scenario, explain which retouching tool would be most effective. (Includes: Healing, Spot healing, Patch tools and options, Clone Source panel.)	6 (p. 4-21)
	2.5 Create and use gradients and patterns.	9 (p. 8-11)
	2.6 Explain how to use filters and the Filter Gallery.	8 (p. 12, 2-27)
3.0 Working with selections	3.1 Given a scenario, create a selection using the appropriate tool. (Includes: Quick Selection, Lasso tools, Magic Wand, Marquee tool, Color Range, luminosity shortcut.)	2 (p. 12-15) 3 (p. 4-19)
	3.2 Save and load selections.	3 (p. 9)
	3.3 Move and transform selections.	3 (p. 12-14)
	3.4 Modify and preview a selection using Refine Edge.	9 (p. 21)

CERTIFICATION GRID

Topic Area	Objectives	Chapter(s)
4.0 Creating and using layers	4.1 Create and arrange layers and layer groups.	1 (p. 24-27) 2 (p. 10, 16-19)
	4.2 Given a scenario, select, align, and distribute multiple layers in an image.	7 (p. 10-13)
	4.3 Explain the uses of layer comps, and compare to layer groups.	2 (p. 16-20)
	4.4 Given a scenario, explain the use of layer Blending Options.	7 (p. 14-17)
	4.5 Create and edit layer effects.	5 (p. 12-15, 24-27)
	4.6 Create and edit layer styles.	5 (p. 12-15 20-22)
	4.7 Explain how to convert an image to black and white with the most control.	4 (p. 22)
5.0 Working with masks and channels	5.1 Explain the uses of masks and channels.	7 (p. 6-20) 9 (p. 4-7)
	5.2 Given a scenario, use the Masks panel and painting tools to create and edit a layer mask.	7 (p. 4-9)
	5.3 Create, view, and edit channels.	9 (p. 4-7)
	5.4 Explain the difference between a layer mask and a vector mask.	7 (p. 4-12) 12 (p. 12)
	5.5 Explain why you would use a clipping mask.	7 (p. 26-29) 11 (p. 2-7)
	5.6 Convert to or from a selection, a channel, a layer mask, a vector mask, and a Quick Mask.	7 (p. 23, 28) 9 (p. 4) 11 (p. 8-9) 12 (p. 12-13)
6.0 Working with vector tools	6.1 Create shape layers and paths using the Pen and Shape tools.	11 (p. 8-19)
	6.2 Explain the advantages of using vector drawing tools versus pixel-based tools.	11 (p. 2-5, 12)
	6.3 Given a scenario, manage paths using the Paths panel.	11 (p. 8-11)
	6.4 Given a scenario, alter the properties of type.	12 (p. 4-19)

Topic Area	Objectives	Chapter(s)
7.0 Using Camera Raw and Bridge	7.1 Describe the advantages of using Adobe Camera Raw to process digital camera raw files.	16 (p. 40-42)
	7.2 Given a Camera Raw adjustment setting, explain the purpose of that setting.	16 (p. 40-42)
	7.3 Export files from Camera Raw.	16 (p. 42)
	7.4 Given a scenario, import files directly from a camera using Bridge. (Includes: Adobe Photo Downloader options.)	1 (p.13)
	7.5 Given a scenario, describe the best way to apply one image's adjustments to many others. (Includes: Synchronize in Camera Raw, or copy and paste settings in Bridge.)	16 (p. 41-42)
	7.6 Apply keywords and metadata to images by using Bridge. (Includes: Keywords panel, Metadata panel, and metadata templates.)	1 (p. 9-10)
	7.7 Given a scenario, find a specific group of files out of a large collection in Bridge.	1 (p. 9-10)
8.0 Automating tasks	8.1 Create and use actions.	15 (p. 8-19)
	8.2 Create and use a batch action.	15 (p. 16)
	8.3 List and describe the automation features in Photoshop.	1 (p. 15) 9 (p. 28-31)
	8.4 Given a scenario, describe the best way to process a large number of images through Photoshop.	9 (p. 31) 15 (p. 16)
	8.5 Describe the difference between actions and scripting.	15 (p. 19)
	8.6 Create variables.	16 (p. 15)
9.0 Working with filters	9.1 Describe the process and components of Photoshop color management. (Includes: profiles, working spaces, rendering intents, settings.)	4 (p. 7) 10 (p. 4, 7, 13)
	9.2 Configure the Color Settings dialog box.	10 (p. 7, 13)
	9.3 Given a scenario, describe the proper color conversion to apply. (Scenarios include: To CMYK for prepress, to a different color space for Web or video.)	10 (p. 4-7)
	9.4 Given a scenario about a color management problem, describe the proper action to take.	10 (p. 4-7)
	9.5 Discuss the relationship between color gamut and rendering intents.	4 (p. 7)
	9.6 Explain the purpose and use of the Proof Setup command.	1 (p. 35)

Topic Area	Objectives	Chapter(s)
10.0 Advanced knowledge	10.1 Given a scenario, create and edit a Smart Object. (Scenarios include: create from Camera Raw files, imported vector objects, and layers.)	7 (p. 19, 28) 11 (p. 15)
	10.2 Create and edit Smart Filters.	8 (p. 9, 12-13)
	10.3 Given a scenario, use Vanishing Point to edit in perspective.	8 (p. 28-31)
	10.4 Explain how to use features that handle images moving to and from video workflows. (Includes: Pixel aspect ratio, document presets, Video Preview.)	16 (p. 32-34, 39)
	10.5 Create, edit, and convert an HDR image.	10 (p. 10)
	10.6 Describe how to use Photomerge to create a panorama.	14 (p. 13)
11.0 Create output for print	11.1 Given a scenario, describe how to set up the Print dialog box.	1 (p. 32-37)
	11.2 Using the Print dialog, position an image at a given size and location on a sheet of paper.	1 (p. 35)
	11.3 Configure the Print dialog for color-managed output to a high-quality inkjet printer. (Includes: set the correct Color Management options, understand the relationship of Photoshop to the printer driver.)	1 (p. 9, 35)
	11.4 Given a scenario, prepare an image for use in a printed Adobe InDesign document. (Includes: flattened CMYK, layered RGB with layer comps, Photoshop PDF with vector layers.)	1 (p. 32-37) 2 (p. 17, 18, 21)
	11.5 Set up the Print dialog box to proof one device on another.	1 (p. 35)
12.0 Creating output for Web and mobile devices	12.1 Given a scenario, choose the appropriate Save for Web options for a Web graphic. (Includes: file format, transparency, and metadata inclusion.)	16 (p. 4-11, 41)
	12.2 Explain the options in the Save for Web and Devices dialog box.	16 (p. 8-13)
	12.3 Explain how to create an animated Web image.	16 (p. 26-35)
	12.4 Create and upload a complete Web gallery.	1 (p. 37)
	12.5 Explain how to create a sliced Web image.	16 (p. 18-25)
	12.6 Explain how to preview content for a device using Device Central.	16 (p. 10)

Data Files List

Chapter	Data File Supplied	Student Creates File	Used in
Chapter 1	PS 1-1.psd PS 1-2.tif		Lessons 2–8
		Review.psd	Skills Review
	PS 1-3.psd		Skills Review
	PS 1-4.psd		Project Builder 2
		Critique-1.psd Critique-2.psd	Design Project
Chapter 2	PS 2-1.psd PS 2-2.psd		Lessons 1–4
	PS 2-3.psd PS 2-4.psd		Skills Review
	PS 2-5.psd PS 2-6.psd		Project Builder 1
	PS 2-7.psd PS 2-8.psd		Project Builder 2
	PS 2-9.psd PS 2-10.psd		Design Project
	PS 2-11.psd		Portfolio Project
Chapter 3	PS 3-1.psd PS 3-2.psd PS 3-3.psd PS 3-4.psd PS 3-5.psd PS 3-6.psd		Lessons 1–4
	PS 3-7.psd PS 3-8.tif PS 3-9.tif PS 3-10.tif		Skills Review
	PS 3-11.psd		Project Builder 1
	PS 3-12.psd		Project Builder 2
		Sample Compositing.psd	Design Project
	PS 3-13.psd		Portfolio Project

Chapter	Data File Supplied	Student Creates File	Used in
Chapter 4	PS 4-1.psd		Lessons 1–4, 6-7
	PS 4-2.psd		Lessons 5–6
	PS 4-3.tif		Lesson 7
	PS 4-4.psd PS 4-5.psd PS 4-6.tif		Skills Review
	PS 4-7.psd		Project Builder 1
	PS 4-8.psd		Project Builder 2
	PS 4-9.psd		Design Project
	PS 4-10.psd		Portfolio Project
Chapter 5	PS 5-1.psd		Lessons 1–7
	PS 5-2.psd		Skills Review
	PS 5-3.psd		Project Builder 1
	PS 5-4.psd		Project Builder 2
	PS 5-5.psd		Design Project
		Community Promotion.psd	Portfolio Project
Chapter 6	PS 6-1.psd		Lessons 1–4
	PS 6-2.psd		Skills Review
	PS 6-3.psd		Project Builder 1
	PS 6-4.psd		Project Builder 2
		Art Course.doc	Design Project
		Dealership Ad.psd	Portfolio Project
Chapter 7	PS 7-1.psd		Lessons 1–6
	PS 7-2.psd		Skills Review
	PS 7-3.psd		Project Builder 1
		Cleanup.psd Cleanup copy.psd	Project Builder 2
		Currency.psd Currency copy.psd	Design Project
		Poetry Poster.psd	Portfolio Project

Chapter	Data File Supplied	Student Creates File	Used in
Chapter 8	PS 8-1.psd		Lessons 1–6
	PS 8-2.psd		Lesson 6
	PS 8-3.psd PS 8-4.psd		Skills Review
		Play.psd	Project Builder 1
		Jazz and Blues.psd	Project Builder 2
	PS 8-5.psd		Design Project
		Dance.psd	Portfolio Project
Chapter 9	PS 9-1.psd		Lessons 1–7
	PS 9-2.psd		Lessons 5–6
		Picture Package.pdf /Contact Sample ContactSheet-001.pdf	Lesson 7
	PS 9-3.psd PS 9-4.psd	Picture Package-Tools.pdf /Contact Sample 2 ContactSheet-002.pdf	Skills Review
		Spheroid.psd	Project Builder 1
		Perfect Oasis.psd	Project Builder 2
		My Vision.psd	Design Project
		Beach Poster.psd	Portfolio Project
Chapter 10	PS 10-1.psd		Lessons 1–4
	PS 10-2.psd		Skills Review
	PS 10-3.psd		Project Builder 1
	PS 10-4.psd		Project Builder 2
	PS 10-5.psd		Design Project
		Annual Report Cover.psd	Portfolio Project
Chapter 11	PS 11-1.psd		Lessons 1–4
	PS 11-2.psd		Skills Review
	PS 11-3.psd		Project Builder 1
	PS 11-4.psd		Project Builder 2
		Shape Experimentation.psd	Design Project
		Contest Winner.psd	Portfolio Project

Chapter	Data File Supplied	Student Creates File	Used in
Chapter 12	PS 12-1.psd		Lessons 1–4
	PS 12-2.psd		Skills Review
	PS 12-3.psd		Project Builder 1
	PS 12-4.psd		Project Builder 2
		Television Station Ad.psd	Design Project
		CD Cover Artwork.psd	Portfolio Project
Chapter 13	PS 13-1.psd		Lessons 1–3
	PS 13-2.psd		Skills Review
	PS 13-3.psd		Project Builder 1
	PS 13-4.psd		Project Builder 2
		Photoshop Presentation.psd	Portfolio Project
Chapter 14	PS 14-1.jpg		Lessons 1–3
	PS 14-2.psd		Skills Review
	PS 14-3.psd		Project Builder 1
	PS 14-4.psd		Project Builder 2
		Digital Art Analysis.doc	Design Project
		Art School Poster.psd	Portfolio Project
Chapter 15	PS 15-1.psd		Lessons 1–4
	PS 15-2.psd		Skills Review
	PS 15-3.psd		Project Builder 1
	PS 15-4.psd		Project Builder 2
		Action Sample.psd (downloaded action - varies) Play Downloaded Action.exe	Design Project
		Game Plan.psd	Portfolio Project

Chapter	Data File Supplied	Student Creates File	Used in
Chapter 16	PS 16-1.psd		Lessons 1–6
	PS 16-2.psd		Lesson 2
	PS 16-3.psd		Lesson 5
	PS 16-4.avi		Lesson 7
	PS 16-5.psd PS 16-6.psd PS 16-7.psd		Skills Review
	PS 16-8.avi		
		Xtream Charity.psd	Project Builder 1
		Countdown.psd Countdown Browser.psd	Project Builder 2
		Banners et al.psd	Design Project
		Wake Up.psd	Portfolio Project
Appendix	PS APP-1.jpg		Project 1
	PS APP-2.jpg		Project 2
	PS APP-3.jpg PS APP-4.jpg		Project 3
	PS APP-5.psd		Project 4
	PS APP-6.psd		Project 5
	PS APP-7.jpg		Project 6
	PS APP-8.psd		Project 7
	PS APP-9.jpg		Project 8

Action
A series of tasks that you record and save to play back later as a single command.

Active layer
The layer highlighted on the Layers panel. The active layer's name appears in parentheses in the image window title bar.

Active setting
In the Curves dialog box, the point that you click and drag to change the input and output values.

Additive colors
A color system in which, when the values of R, G, and B are 0, the result is black; when the values are all 255, the result is white.

Adjustment layer
An additional layer for which you can specify individual color adjustments. The adjustment layer allows you to temporarily alter a layer before making the adjustment permanent.

Adjustment panel
Visible panel that makes creation of adjustment layers easy.

Adobe Bridge
A stand-alone application that serves as the hub for the Adobe Create Suite. It can be used for file management tasks such as opening, viewing, sorting, and rating files.

Adobe Device Central
Gives flexibility to those who create content for mobile phones and other consumer electronic devices. The Emulator tab allows you to preview your content on a variety of devices.

Alpha channel
Specific color information added to a default channel. Also called a *spot channel*.

Altitude
A Bevel and Emboss setting that affects the amount of visible dimension.

Ambience property
Controls the balance between the light source and the overall light in an image.

Anchor points
Small square handles, similar to fastening points, that connect straight or curved line segments.

Angle
In the Layer Style dialog box, the setting that determines where a drop shadow falls relative to the text.

Animation
The illusion of motion, created by placing a series of images in the same location and adjusting the timing between their appearances.

Animation panel
Panel that is used to display and edit frames and video (in Timeline mode).

Annotation
A written note embedded in a Photoshop file.

Anti-aliasing
Partially fills in pixel edges, resulting in smooth-edge type. This feature lets your type maintain its crisp appearance and is especially useful for large type.

Application bar
The area containing the menu bar (containing Photoshop commands), additional buttons, and the title bar (displaying the program name).

Arrangement
How objects are positioned relative to one another.

Artistic filters
Used to replicate natural or traditional media effects.

Asymmetrical balance
When objects are placed unequally on either side of an imaginary vertical line in the center of the page.

Auto-slice
A slice created by Photoshop. An auto-slice has a dotted-line border.

Background color
Used to make gradient fills and to fill in areas of an image that have been erased. The default background color is white.

Background Eraser tool
Used to selectively remove pixels from an image, just as you would use a pencil

eraser to remove unwanted written marks. The erased areas become transparent.

Balance colors
Process of adding and subtracting colors from those already existing in a layer.

Base color
The original color of an image.

Base layer
The bottom layer in a clipping group, which serves as the group's mask.

Baseline
An invisible line on which type rests.

Baseline shift
The distance type appears from its original position.

Batch
A group of files designated to have the same action performed on them simultaneously.

Bitmap
A geometric arrangement of different color dots on a rectangular grid.

Bitmap mode
Uses black or white color values to represent image pixels; a good choice for images with subtle color gradations, such as photographs or painted images.

Bitmap type
Type that may develop jagged edges when enlarged.

Blend color
The color applied to the base color when a blending mode is applied to a layer.

Blend If color
Determines the color range for the pixels you want to blend.

Blending mode
Affects the layer's underlying pixels or base color. Used to darken or lighten colors, depending on the colors in use.

Blur filters
Used to soften a selection or image.

Bounding box
A rectangle with handles that appears around an object or type and can be used to change dimensions, also called a *transform controls box*.

Bridge
See Adobe Bridge.

Brightness
The measurement of relative lightness or darkness of a color (measured as a percentage from 0% [black] to 100% [white]).

Brush library
Contains a variety of brush tips that you can use, rename, delete, or customize.

Brush Strokes filters
Used to mimic fine arts effects such as a brush and ink stroke.

Button
A graphical interface that helps visitors navigate and interact with a website easily.

Button mode
Optional action display in which each action available in Photoshop is displayed as a button—without additional detail.

Camera Raw
Allows you to use digital data directly from a digital camera. The file extension that you see will vary with each digital camera manufacturer.

Channels
Used to store information about the color elements contained in each channel.

Channels panel
Lists all channel information. The top channel is a composite channel—a combination of all the default channels. You can hide channels in the same manner that you hide layers: click the Indicates layer visibility button.

Character panel
Helps you control type properties. The Toggle the Character and Paragraph panel button is located on the options bar when you select a Type tool.

Clipboard
Temporary storage area, provided by your operating system, for cut and copied data.

Clipping mask (Clipping group)
A group of two or more contiguous layers linked for the purposes of masking. Effect used to display the image or pattern from one layer into the shape of another layer.

Clipping path
Used when you need to extract a Photoshop object from within a layer, then place it in another program (such as QuarkXPress or Adobe Illustrator), while retaining its transparent background.

Closed path
One continuous path without endpoints, such as a circle.

CMYK image
An image using the CMYK color system, containing at least four channels (one each for cyan, magenta, yellow, and black).

Color cast
A situation in which one color dominates an image to an unrealistic or undesirable degree.

Color channel
An area where color information is stored. Every Photoshop image has at least one channel and can have a maximum of 24 color channels.

Color management system
Keeps colors looking consistent as they move between devices.

Color mode
Used to determine how to display and print an image. Each mode is based on established models used in color reproduction.

Color Picker
A feature that lets you choose a color from a color spectrum.

Color Range command
Used to select a particular color contained in an existing image.

Color Sampler tool
Feature that samples—and stores—up to four distinct color samplers. This feature is used when you want to save specific color settings for future use.

Color separation
Result of converting an RGB image into a CMYK image; the commercial printing process of separating colors for use with different inks.

Composite channel
The top channel on the Channels panel that is a combination of all the default channels.

Compositing
Combining images from sources such as other Photoshop images, royalty-free images, pictures taken from digital cameras, and scanned artwork.

ConnectNow
An Adobe tool that allows for online collaboration with others.

Contact sheet
Compilation of a maximum of 30 thumbnail images (per sheet) from a specific folder.

Contiguous
Items that are next to one another.

Crisp
Anti-aliasing setting that gives type more definition and makes it appear sharper.

Crop
To exclude part of an image. Cropping hides areas of an image without losing resolution quality.

Crop marks
Page notations that indicate where trimming will occur and can be printed at the corners, center of each edge, or both.

Darken Only option
Replaces light pixels with darker pixels.

Default action
An action that is prerecorded and tested, and comes with Photoshop.

Default channels
The color channels automatically contained in an image.

Defringe command
Replaces fringe pixels with the colors of other nearby pixels.

Deselect
A command that removes the marquee from an area so it is no longer selected.

Destructive editing
Changes to pixels that are irreversible and *cannot be undone* once the current Photoshop session has ended.

Diffuse filter
Used to make layer contents look less focused.

Digimarc filter
Embeds into an image a digital watermark that stores copyright information.

Digital camera
A camera that captures images on electronic media (rather than film). Its images are in a standard digital format and can be downloaded for computer use.

Digital image
A picture in electronic form. It may be referred to as a file, document, picture, or image.

Digital Negative Format
An archival format for camera raw files that contains the raw image data created within a digital camera as well as its defining metadata. Also called *Adobe DNG*.

Direct Selection tool
Used to select and manipulate individual anchor points and segments to reshape a path.

Distance
Determines how far a shadow falls from the text. This setting is used by the Drop Shadow and Bevel and Emboss styles.

Distort filters
Create three-dimensional or other reshaping effects. Some of the types of distortions you can produce include Glass, Pinch, Ripple, Shear, Spherize, Twirl, Wave, and ZigZag.

Dithering
Occurs when a web browser attempts to display colors that are not included in its native color palette.

Dock
A collection of panels or buttons surrounded by a dark gray bar. The arrows in the dock are used to maximize and minimize the panels.

Droplet
A stand-alone action in the form of an icon.

Drop Shadow
A style that adds what looks like a colored layer of identical text behind the selected type. The default shadow color is black.

Drop Zone
A blue outline area that indicates where a panel can be moved.

Endpoints
Anchor points at each end of an open path.

Eraser tool
Has the opposite function of a brush in that it eliminates pixels on a layer.

Exposure property
Lightens or darkens the lighting effects ellipse.

Extract feature
Used to isolate a foreground object from its background. This (plug-in) feature requires a separate installation, and may not be installed on your computer.

Extrude filters
Used to convert an image into pyramids or blocks.

Fade options
Brush settings that determine how and when brushes fade toward the end of their strokes.

Fading type
An effect in which the type appears to originate in darkness and then gradually gets brighter, or vice versa.

Fastening point
An anchor within the marquee. When the marquee pointer reaches the initial fastening point, a small circle appears on the pointer, indicating that you have reached the starting point.

Feather
A method used to control the softness of a selection's edges by blurring the area between the selection and the surrounding pixels.

Filter Gallery
A feature that lets you see the effects of each filter before applying it.

Filters
Used to alter the look of an image and give it a special, customized appearance by applying special effects, such as distortions, changes in lighting, and blurring.

Flattening
Merges all visible layers into one layer, named the Background layer, and deletes all hidden layers, greatly reducing file size.

Flow
Brush tip setting that determines how much paint is sprayed while the mouse button is held.

Font
Characters with a similar appearance.

Font family
Represents a complete set of characters, letters, and symbols for a particular typeface. Font families are generally divided into three categories: serif, sans serif, and symbol.

Foreground color
Used to paint, fill, and stroke selections. The default foreground color is black.

Frame
An individual image that is used in animation.

Frame delay
In an animation sequence,the length of time that each frame appears.

Freeform Pen tool
Acts like a traditional pen or pencil, and automatically places *both* the anchor points and line segments wherever necessary to achieve the shape you want.

Freeze
To protect areas within an image from being affected by Liquify tools.

Fuzziness
Similar to tolerance, in that the lower the value, the closer the color pixels must be to be selected.

Gamut
The range of displayed colors in a color model.

Gloss Contour
A Bevel and Emboss setting that determines the pattern with which light is reflected.

Gloss property
Controls the amount of surface reflectance on the lighted surfaces.

Gradient fill
A type of fill in which colors appear to blend into one another. A gradient's appearance is determined by its beginning and ending points. Photoshop contains five gradient fill styles.

Gradient presets
Predesigned gradient fills that are displayed in the Gradient picker.

Graphics tablet
An optional hardware peripheral that enables use of pressure-sensitive tools, create programmable menu buttons, and maneuver faster in Photoshop.

Grayscale image
Can contain up to 256 shades of gray. Pixels can have brightness values from 0 (black) to white (255).

Grayscale mode
Uses up to 256 shades of gray, assigning a brightness value from 0 (black) to 255 (white) to each pixel.

Guides
Horizontal and vertical lines that you create to help you align objects. Guides appear as light blue lines.

Handles
Small boxes that appear along the perimeter of a selected object and are used to change the size of an image.

HDR (High Dynamic Range) Image
An image that is used in motion pictures, special effects, 3D work, and high-end photography, and stores pixel values that span the whole tonal range.

Hexadecimal values
Sets of three pairs of letters or numbers that are used to define the R, G, and B components of a color.

Highlight Mode
A Bevel and Emboss setting that determines how pigments are combined.

Histogram
A graph that displays the frequency distribution of colors and is used to make adjustments in the input and output levels.

History panel
Contains a record of each action performed during a Photoshop session. Up to 1000 levels of Undo are available through the History panel (20 levels by default).

Hotspot
Area within an object that is assigned a URL. This area can then be clicked to jump to the associated web address.

HTML
Hypertext Markup Language (HTML) is the language used for creating web pages.

Hue
The color reflected from/transmitted through an object and expressed as a degree (between 0° and 360°). Each hue is identified by a color name (such as red or green).

ICC profile
Created for specific devices and embedded in an image, and used to define how colors are interpreted by a specific device. ICC stands for International Color Consortium.

Image-editing program
Used to manipulate graphic images that can be reproduced by professional printers using full-color processes.

Image map
An area composed of multiple hotspots; can be circular, rectangular, or polygonal.

Intellectual property
An image or idea that is owned and retained by legal control.

Jitter
The randomness of dynamic brush tip elements such as size, angle, roundness, hue, saturation, brightness, opacity, and flow.

Kerning
Controlling the amount of space between two characters.

Keyboard shortcuts
Combinations of keys that can be used to work faster and more efficiently.

Kuler
A web-hosted application that lets you create, save, share, and download color-coordinated themes for use in images. It can be accessed from a browser, the desktop, or Adobe products such as Photoshop or Illustrator.

Landscape orientation
An image with the long edge of the paper at the top and bottom.

Layer
A section within an image on which objects can be stored. The advantage: Individual effects can be isolated and manipulated without affecting the rest of the image. The disadvantage: Layers can increase the size of your file.

Layer comp
A variation on the arrangement and visibility of existing layers within an image; an organizational tool.

Layer group
An organizing tool you use to group layers on the Layers panel.

Layer mask
Can cover an entire layer or specific areas within a layer. When a layer contains a mask, an additional thumbnail appears on the Layers panel.

Layers panel
Displays all the layers within an active image. You can use the Layers panel to create, delete, merge, copy, or reposition layers.

Layer style
An effect that can be applied to a type or image layer.

Layer thumbnail
Contains a miniature picture of the layer's content, and appears to the left of the layer name on the Layers panel.

Leading
The amount of vertical space between lines of type.

Libraries
Storage units for brushes.

Lighten Only option
Replaces dark pixels with light pixels.

Lighting Effects filter
Applies lighting effects to an image.

Link
Clickable text, graphic, or object that hyperlinks to a specific website and opens that website in a browser window.

Liquify feature
Applies distortions to layers using distinct tools in the Liquify dialog box.

Liquify session
The period of time from when you open the Liquify dialog box to when you close it.

List mode
The default display of actions in which all action detail can be viewed.

Logo
A distinctive image used to identify a company, project, or organization. You can create a logo by combining symbols, shapes, colors, and text.

Lossless
A file-compression format in which no data is discarded.

Lossy
A file format that discards data during the compression process.

Luminosity
The remaining light and dark values that result when a color image is converted to grayscale.

Magic Eraser tool
Used to erase areas in an image that have similar-colored pixels.

Magic Wand tool
Used to choose pixels that are similar to the ones where you first click in an image.

Marquee
A series of dotted lines indicating a selected area that can be edited or dragged into another image.

Mask
A feature that lets you protect or modify a particular area; created using a marquee.

Match Color command
Allows you to replace one color with another.

Material property
Controls parts of an image that reflect the light source color.

Matte
A colorful box placed behind an object that makes the object stand out.

Menu bar
Contains menus from which you can choose Photoshop commands.

Merging layers
Process of combining multiple image layers into one layer.

Mesh
A series of horizontal and vertical gridlines that are superimposed in the Liquify preview window.

Modal control
Dialog boxes that are used in an action, and are indicated by an icon on the Actions panel.

Mode
Represents the amount of color data that can be stored in a given file format, and determines the color model used to display and print an image.

Model
Determines how pigments combine to produce resulting colors; determined by the color mode.

Monitor calibration
A process that displays printed colors accurately on your monitor.

Monotype spacing
Spacing in which each character occupies the same amount of space.

Morph
To blend multiple images in the animation process. Short for *metamorphosis*.

Motion Blur filter
Adjusts the angle of the blur, as well as the distance the blur appears to travel.

Multiple-image layout
Layout (generated in Adobe Bridge) that features more than one image.

Noise filters
Used to add or remove pixels with randomly distributed color levels.

Non-destructive editing
Alterations to an image that are *not* permanent and can be edited.

None
Anti-aliasing setting that applies no anti-aliasing, resulting in jagged edges.

Normal blend mode
The default blending mode.

Opacity
Determines the percentage of transparency. Whereas a layer with 100% opacity will obstruct objects in the layers beneath it, a layer with 1% opacity will appear nearly transparent.

Open path
A path that comprises two distinct endpoints, such as an individual line.

Optical center
The point around which objects on the page are balanced; occurs approximately $3/8^{ths}$ from the top of the page.

Optimized image
An image whose file size has been reduced without sacrificing image quality.

Options bar
Displays the settings for the active tool. The options bar is located directly under the Application bar, but can be moved anywhere in the workspace for easier access.

Orientation
Direction an image appears on the page: portrait or landscape.

Other filters
Allow you to create your own filters, modify masks, or make quick color adjustments.

Outline type
Type that is mathematically defined and can be scaled to any size without its edges losing their smooth appearance. (Also known as a *vector font.*)

Out-of-gamut indicator
Indicates that the current color falls beyond the accurate print or display range.

Panels
Floating windows that can be moved and are used to modify objects. Panels contain named tabs, which can be separated and moved to another group. Each panel contains a menu that can be viewed by clicking the list arrow in its upper-right corner.

Panel well
An area where you can assemble panels for quick access.

Path
One or more straight or curved line segments connected by anchor points used to turn the area defined within an object into an individual object.

Path component
One or more anchor points joined by line segments.

Path Selection tool
Used to select an entire path.

Paths panel
Storage area for paths.

Pen tool
Used to draw a path by placing anchor points along the edge of another image or wherever you need them to draw a specific shape.

Picture package
Shows multiple copies of a single image in various sizes, similar to a portrait studio sheet of photos.

Pixel
Each dot in a bitmapped image that represents a color or shade.

Pixel aspect ratio
A scaling correction feature that automatically corrects the ratio of pixels displayed for the monitor in use. Prevents pixels viewed in a 16:9 monitor (such as a widescreen TV) from looking squashed in a 4:3 monitor (nearly-rectangular TV).

Pixelate filters
Used to sharply define a selection.

Plug-ins
Additional programs—created by Adobe and other developers—that expand the functionality of Photoshop.

Points
Unit of measurement for font sizes. Traditionally, one inch is equivalent to 72.27 points. The default Photoshop type size is 12 points.

Portrait orientation
An image with the short edge of the paper at the top and bottom.

PostScript
A programming language created by Adobe that optimizes printed text and graphics.

Preferences
Used to control the Photoshop environment using your specifications.

Preset Manager
Allows you to manage libraries of preset brushes, swatches, gradients, styles, patterns, contours, and custom shapes.

Profile
Defines and interprets colors for a color management system.

Properties color swatch
Changes the ambient light around the lighting spotlight.

Proportional spacing
The text spacing in which each character takes up a different amount of space, based on its width.

Quick Selection tool
Tool that lets you paint to make a selection from the interior using a brush tip, reducing rough edges and blockiness.

Radial Blur filter
Adjusts the amount of blur and the blur method (Spin or Zoom).

Rasterize
Converts a type layer to an image layer.

Rasterized shape
A shape that is converted into a bitmapped object. It cannot be moved or copied and has a much smaller file size.

Red Eye effect
Photographic effect in which eyes within photographs look red.

Reference point
Center of the object from which distortions and transformations are measured.

Refine Edge option
Button found on the options bar of a variety of tools that allows you to improve the size and edges of a selection.

Relief
The height of ridges within an object.

Render filters
Transform three-dimensional shapes and simulated light reflections in an image.

Rendering intent
The way in which a color-management system handles color conversion from one color space to another.

Resolution
Number of pixels per inch.

Resulting color
The outcome of the blend color applied to the base color.

RGB image
Image that contains three color channels (one each for red, green, and blue).

Rulers
Onscreen markers that help you precisely measure and position an object. Rulers can be displayed using the View menu.

Sampling
A method of changing foreground and background colors by copying existing colors from an image.

Sans serif fonts
Fonts that do not have tails or strokes at the end of characters; commonly used in headlines.

Saturation
The strength or purity of the color, representing the amount of gray in proportion to hue (measured as a percentage from 0% [gray], to 100% [fully saturated]). Also known as *chroma*.

Save As
A command that lets you create a copy of the open file using a new name.

Scale
The size relationship of objects to one another.

Scanner
An electronic device that converts print material into an electronic file.

Screening back
An illusory effect in which type appears to fade into the imagery below it. Also known as *screening*.

Script
Creates external automation of Photoshop from an outside source, such as JavaScript. Also called *scripting*.

Selection
An area in an image that is surrounded by a selection marquee and can then be manipulated.

Serif fonts
Fonts that have a tail, or stroke, at the end of some characters. These tails make it

easier for the eye to recognize words; therefore, serif fonts are generally used in text passages.

Shading
Bevel and Emboss setting that determines lighting effects.

Sharpness
An element of composition that draws the viewer's eye to a specific area.

Shadow Mode
Bevel and Emboss setting that determines how pigments are combined.

Shape
A vector object that keeps its crisp appearance when it is resized and, like a path, can be edited.

Shape layer
A clipping path or shape that can occupy its own layer.

Sharp
Anti-aliasing setting that displays type with the best possible resolution.

Sharpen More filter
Increases the contrast of adjacent pixels and can focus blurry images.

Size
Determines the clarity of a drop shadow.

Sketch filters
Used to apply a texture or create a hand-drawn effect.

Slice
A specific area within an image to which you can assign special features, such as a link, or animation.

Smart Blur filter
Adjusts the quality, radius, and threshold of a blur.

Smart Guides
A feature that displays vertical or horizontal guides that appear automatically when you draw a shape or move an object and are helpful in its positioning.

Smart Filter
A filter applied to a Smart Object and allows for nondestructive editing of the filter(s).

Smart Object
A combination of objects that has a visible indicator in the bottom-right corner of the layer thumbnail. Makes it possible to scale, rotate, and wrap layers without losing image quality.

Smooth
Anti-aliasing setting that gives type more rounded edges.

Snapshot
A temporary copy of an image that contains the history states made up to that point. You can create multiple snapshots of an image, and you can switch between snapshots.

Source
The image containing the color that will be matched.

Splash screen
A window that displays information about the software you are using.

Spot channel
Designed to provide a channel for additional inks, also called a spot color channel. A spot channel is added to an image using the Channels panel.

Spot color
A method of defining a difficult or unique color that couldn't otherwise be easily re-created by a printer.

Spread
Determines the width of drop shadow text.

Spring-loaded keyboard shortcuts
Shortcut keyboard combinations that *temporarily* change the active tool.

State
An entry on the History panel, or the individual steps in an action in the Actions panel.

Status bar
The area located at the bottom of the program window (Win) or the image window (Mac) that displays information such as the file size of the active window and a description of the active tool.

Step
Measurement of fade options that can be any value from 1–9999, and equivalent to one mark of the brush tip.

Stop
In an action, a command that interrupts playback or includes an informative text

message for the user, so that other operations can be performed.

Stroking the edges
The process of making a selection or layer stand out by formatting it with a border.

Strong
Anti-aliasing setting that makes type appear heavier, much like the bold attribute.

Structure
A Bevel and Emboss setting that determines the size and physical properties of the object.

Style
Eighteen predesigned styles that can be applied to buttons.

Stylize filters
Used to produce a painted or impressionistic effect.

Subtractive colors
A color system in which the full combination of cyan, magenta, and yellow absorb all color and produce black.

Swatches panel
Contains available colors that can be selected for use as a foreground or background color. You can also add your own colors to the Swatches panel.

Symbol fonts
Used to display unique characters (such as $, ÷, or ™).

Symmetrical balance
When objects are placed equally on either side of an imaginary vertical line in the center of the page.

Target
When sampling a color, the image that will receive the matched color.

Texture filters
Used to give the appearance of depth or substance.

Thaw
To remove protection from a protected area in an image so it can be affected by Liquify tools.

This Layer slider
Used to specify the range of pixels that will be blended on the active layer.

Threshold
The Normal mode when working with bitmapped images. The threshold is the starting point for applying other blending modes.

Thumbnail
Contains a miniature picture of the layer's content, appears to the left of the layer name, and can be turned on or off.

Title bar
Displays the program name and filename of the open image. The title bar also contains buttons for minimizing, maximizing, and closing the image.

Tolerance
The range of pixels that determines which pixels will be selected. The lower the tolerance, the closer the color is to the selection. The setting can have a value from 0–255.

Tonal values
Numeric values of an individual color that can be used to duplicate a color. Also called *color levels*.

Tone
The brightness and contrast within an image.

Tools panel
Contains tools for frequently used commands. On the face of a tool is a graphic representation of its function. Place the pointer over each button to display a ScreenTip, which tells you the name or function of that button.

Tracking
The insertion of a uniform amount of space between characters.

Transform
To change the shape, size, perspective, or rotation of an object or objects on a layer.

Transform box
A rectangle that surrounds an image and contains handles that can be used to change dimensions. Also called a *bounding box*.

Tweening
The process of selecting multiple frames, then inserting transitional frames between them. This effect makes frames appear to blend into one another and gives the animation a more fluid appearance.

Twirl filter
Applies a circular effect.

Type
Text, or a layer containing text. Each character is measured in points. In PostScript measurement, one inch is equivalent to 72 points. In traditional measurement, one inch is equivalent to 72.27 points.

Type spacing
Adjustments you can make to the space between characters and between lines of type.

Underlying Layer slider
Used to specify the range of pixels that will be blended on lower visible layers.

URL
Uniform Resource Locator, a web address.

User-slice
A slice created by you. A user-slice has a solid-line border.

Vanishing Point filter
Used to maintain perspective as you drag objects around corners and into the distance.

Vector data
A shape or path that will not lose its crisp appearance if resized or reshaped.

Vector font
Fonts that are vector-based type outlines, which means that they are mathematically defined shapes.

Vector graphic
Image made up of lines and curves defined by mathematical objects.

Vector mask
Makes a shape's edges appear neat and defined on a layer.

Version Cue
A file versioning and management feature of the Adobe Creative Suite.

Video filters
Used to restrict colors to those acceptable for television reproduction and smooth video images.

Vignette
A feature in which the border of a picture or portrait fades into the surrounding color at its edges.

Vignette effect
A feature that uses feathering to fade a marquee shape.

Warping type
A feature that lets you create distortions that conform to a variety of shapes.

Web Photo Gallery
Contains a thumbnail index page of all exported images, the actual JPEG images, and any included links.

Web-safe colors
The 216 colors that can be displayed on the web without dithering.

Wind filter
Conveys the feeling of direction and motion on the layer to which it is applied.

Work path
A path when it is first created, but not yet named.

Working space
Tells the color management system how RGB and CMYK values are interpreted.

Workspace
The entire window, from the Application bar at the top of the window, to the status bar at the bottom border of the program window.

Workspace switcher
Button on the Application bar that lets you switch between defined workspaces.

Written annotation
Text similar to a sticky note that is attached to a file.

correcting, 3–17, 3–21, 9–2
faulty exposures, correcting,
10–11
fixing in photos,
APP–18—APP–19
removing, 3–22
Info panel
color samplers, 10–14—10–17
hexadecimal values, 4–9
information overload, overcoming,
1–16
intellectual property, 1–22
Invert color adjustment, 7–23
isolating objects, 9–8—9–11
enhancing extracted objects,
9–11

jitter, 6–10
JPEG format, 16–9, 16–10
Jutter option, 6–8

kerning, 5–8, 5–10
keyboard shortcuts
customized, 1–18
hidden, finding, 1–31
learning shortcut keys, 1–19
navigating Layers panel, 2–9
spring-loaded, 1–18
Keywords panel, Bridge, 1–9
kuler
coordinating colors, 4–10
downloading theme, 4–11
from Photoshop, 4–15
from web browser, 4–14
Kuler panel, 4–25

Lab model, 4–4, 4–5
landscape orientation, 1–32, 11–16
Lasso tool, 3–5
layer(s), 1–24, 2–1—2–24,
7–1—7–31
active. *See* active layers
adding images from another
image, 2–14
adding to images, 2–8—2–9,
2–10, 2–11
adjusting content, 12–15
adjustment. *See* adjustment
layers
animation, APP–12
base, 7–26
blending pixels, 7–14—7–17
clipping masks. *See* clipping
masks
color, 2–17
color, adjustments, 10–2
color, converting to grayscale,
10–9
converting, 2–6, 2–7
creating from selections, 14–9
defringing layer contents,
2–13, 2–15
deleting, 2–9, 2–11
designing with layers, 7–2
displaying, 1–25, 1–26
duplicate, blending pixels using,
7–14
duplicating, 2–16
editing, 7–9
grouping, 7–12
hiding, 1–25, 1–26

hiding panels, 1–25, 1–26
importance, 2–2
layer masks. *See* layer mask(s)
link icon, 7–10
merging, 2–8
modifying images, 2–2
modifying specific areas, 7–2
moving multiple selections, 7–10
moving on Layers panel, 1–27
naming, 2–9, 2–20
non-destructive changes, 7–2
number, 2–2
opacity, 2–2, 2–20
organizing, 2–5
rasterized, 2–8
rasterizing, 11–5
renaming, 2–20
selected. *See* selected layers
selecting multiple layers, 7–10
selections, 2–2
shape, 11–12
styles. *See* drop shadows; layer
style(s)
type (text). *See* type layers
types, 2–4—2–5
using imagery from one layer as
fill pattern for another image's
type layer, 5–20
video, 16–30
layer comps, 2–18, 2–20
Layer Comps panel, 2–20
layer groups, 2–16—2–17, 2–19
creating, 2–19
organizing layers into,
2–16—2–17, 2–19

PSYCHOLOGY

Science and Application

PSYCHOLOGY
Science and Application

Mark G. McGee
Brain Sciences Laboratories and
University of Colorado School of Medicine, Denver

David W. Wilson
Phillips University

WEST PUBLISHING COMPANY
St. Paul   New York   Los Angeles   San Francisco

Library of Congress Cataloging in Publication Data

McGee, Mark G.
    Psychology: science and application.

    Bibliography: p.
    Includes index.
    1. Psychology.   2. Psychology, Experimental.
3. Psychology, Applied.   I. Wilson, David W.   II. Title.
BF121.M426   1984   150   83–23441
ISBN 0–314–77927–2

COPYEDITING: Jo-Anne Naples
ARTWORK: House of Graphics
COMPOSITION: The Clarinda Company
COVER: Morris Louis *Point of Tranquility,* Hirshhorn Museum and Sculpture Garden, Smithsonian Institution. Photo by John Tennant.

To our parents
Theodore and Martha
Bill and Norma

To our wives
Ellen and Ruth Ann

To our children
Alyson, Katy, and Maureen
Jessica and Jocelyn

— Acknowledgments

Page 97, Figure 4–15. From "Plasticity in Sensory-Motor Systems," by Richard Held. Copyright © 1965 by Scientific American, Inc. All rights reserved. Page 115, Table 5–2. From "Prevalence of Sleep Disorders and Sleep Behaviors in Children and Adolescents," by John F. Simonds and Humberto Parraga. In *Journal of American Academy of Child Psychiatry,* 1982, *21,* p. 385. Copyright © 1982 by American Academy of Child Psychiatry. Reprinted by permission of the publisher and author. Page 116, Figure 5–6. Charles Waller Design. Page 167, Figure 7–3. From John P. Houston: *Fundamentals of Learning and Memory* 2nd Ed., Copyright © 1981 by Academic Press, Inc. Adapted by permission of Academic Press, Inc. and the author. Page 179, Table 7–3. From Geoffrey R. Loftus and Elizabeth F. Loftus: *Human Memory: The processing of information.* Copyright © 1979 by Lawrence Erlbaum Associates, Inc. Reprinted by permission. Page 179, Figure 7–9. From "Interference and Forgetting" by Benton J. Underwood, 1957, Psychological Review, *64,* p. 53. Copyright 1957 by the American Psychological Association. Adapted by permission of the author. Page 180, Table 7–4. From Geoffrey R. Loftus and Elizabeth F. Loftus: *Human Memory: The processing of information.* Copyright © 1979 by Lawrence Erlbaum Associates, Inc. Reprinted by permission. Page 181, Figure 7–10. From "Mood and Memory" by Gordon H. Bower, 1981, *American Psychologist, 36,* p. 132. Copyright 1981 by the American Psychological Association. Adapted by permission of the author. Page 197, Figure 8–1. From *The Developing Person: A Life-Span Approach* by Helen L. Bee and Sandra K. Mitchell. Copyright © 1980 by Helen Bee Douglas and Sandra K. Mitchell. Reprinted by permission of Harper and Row, Publishers, Inc. and the University of Iowa Press. Based on data from M. E. Smith's "An investigation of the development of the sentence and the extent of vocabulary in young children," *University of Iowa Studies in child welfare,* 1926, *3* (5). Page 198, Figure 8–2. Reproduced from Berko, J. "The Child's Learning of English Morphology," In W. Meyer, Readings in the Psychology of Childhood and Adolescence, *Word,* 14 (1958) p. 154. Johnson Reprint Corporation. New York, N.Y. Page 198, Table 8–1. Reprinted from Psychology Today Magazine. Copyright © 1972 American Psychological Association. Page 207, Figure 8–6. From Cognition by Margaret Matlin. Copyright © 1983 by CBS College Publishing. Reprinted by permission of Holt, Rinehart and Winston, CBS College Publishing. Page 209, Table 8–2. Bourne/Dominowski/Loftus, Cognitive Processes, © 1979, pp. 233, 268. Adapted by permission of Prentice-Hall, Inc. Englewood Cliffs, NJ. Page 210, Table 8–3. Bourne/Dominowski/Loftus, Cognitive Processes, © 1979, pp. 233, 268. Adapted by permission of Prentice-Hall, Inc. Englewood Cliffs, NJ. Page 221, copyright 1983 Time Inc. All rights reserved. Reprinted by permission from Time. Page 232, Figure 9–6. From "The influence of complexity and novelty in visual figures on orienting responses" by Daniel E. Berlyne, 1958, *Journal of Experimental Psychology, 55,* p. 291. Copyright 1958 by the American Psychological Association. Adapted with permission of the publisher. Page 233, Table 9–2. Reprinted from Psychology Today Magazine. Copyright © 1978 American Psychological Association. Page 243, Figure 9–10. Illustration provided by David C. Raskin, Department of Psychology, University of Utah. Page 309-311, Figure 12–6. From "The Omni-Mensa I.Q. Test," by Scott Morris. In *Omni,* July 1981, pp. 96–98. Reprinted by permission. Mensa is an organization whose members have scored at or above the 98th percentile of the general population on any standardized I.Q. Test. Page 320, Figure 12–11. From "Twins Nature Twice Told Tale," by Thomas J. Bouchard, Jr. In *Encyclopaedia Britannica,* 1983 Yearbook, p. 69. Reprinted by permission. Page 336, Figure 13–2. From Robert M. Liebert and Michael D. Spiegler: *Personality: Strategies and Issues,* 4th ed. Copyright © The Dorsey Press, 1970, 1974, 1978, and 1982. Reprinted with permission. Page 337, Table 13–1. From Robert M. Liebert and Michael D. Spiegler: *Personality: Strategies and Issues,* 4th ed. Copyright © 1970, 1974, 1978, and 1982. Reprinted with permission. Page 341, Figure 13–4. Adapted from Eysenck, H. J. and Rachman, S. *Causes and Cures of neurosis,* San Diego, CA, Robert R. Knapp, Publisher, Copyright, 1965. All rights reserved. Page 351, Table 13–2. From Robert M. Liebert and Michael D. Spiegler: *Personality: Strategies and Issues,* 4th ed. Copyright © The Dorsey Press, 1970, 1974, 1978, and 1982. Adapted with permission. Page 356, Table 13–4. From Introduction to Personality 3rd Ed. by Walter Mischel. Copyright © 1981 by CBS College Publishing. Reprinted by permission of Holt, Rinehart and Winston, CBS College Publishing. Page 358, Table 13–5. Donn Byrne, An Introduction to Personality: Research, Theory, and Applications, 2nd Ed., © 1974, pp. 88-91. Adapted by permission of Prentice-Hall, Inc., Englewood Cliffs, NJ. Page 367, Table 14–1. From Phillip Shaver and Caren Rubenstein, "Childhood attachment experience and adult loneliness," pp. 42–73 in *Review of personality and social psychology* (Vol. 1), ed. by L. Wheeler, Copyright © 1980 by Sage Publications, Inc. Reprinted by permission of Sage Publications, Inc. and the authors. Page 368, Table 14–2. From Phillip Shaver and Caren Rubenstein, "Childhood attachment experience and adult loneliness," pp. 42–73 in *Review of personality and social psychology* (Vol. 1), ed. by L. Wheeler, Copyright © 1980 by Sage Publications, Inc. Reprinted by permission of Sage Publications, Inc. and the authors. Page 370, Table 14–3. Reprinted with permission from the authors and the *Journal of Psychosomatic Research, II,* T. H. Holmes an R. H. Rahe, "The Social Readjustment Rating Scale", Copyright 1967, Pergamon Press, Ltd. Page 372, Figure 14–4. From Hans Selye: *The Stress of Life,* revised ed. Copyright © 1976 by McGraw-Hill. Adapted with permission. Page 379, Table 14–4. From Meyer Friedman and Ray H. Rosenman: *Type A behavior and your heart.* Copyright © 1974 by Meyer Friedman. Adapted by permission of Alfred A. Knopf, Inc. Page 393, David Sue, Derald Wing Sue, and Stanley Sue: *Understanding Abnormal Behavior,* Copyright © 1981, Houghton Mifflin Company, used by permission. Page 394, Table 15–2. Irwin G. Sarason, Barbara R. Sarason, *Abnormal Psychology: Problem of Maladaptive Behavior* 3rd Ed., © 1980, p. 159. Reprinted by permission of Prentice-Hall, Inc., Englewood Cliffs, New Jersey. Page 394. From Gerald C. Davison and John M. Neale: *Abnormal Psychology,* 3rd ed. Copyright © 1982 by John Wiley and Sons, Inc. Reprinted with permission. Page 396. Copyright 1981 by Field Newspaper Syndicate. Reprinted by permission of Field Newspaper Syndicate and Ann Landers. Page 397. David Sue, Derald Wing Sue, and Stanley Sue: Understanding Abnormal Behavior, Copyright © 1981, Houghton Mifflin Company, used by permission. Page 397, Table 15–3. David Sue, Derald Wing Sue,

and Stanley Sue: Understanding Abnormal Behavior, Copyright © 1981, Houghton Mifflin Company, used by permission. Page 402. From Abnormal Psychology and Modern Life, 6th Edition by James C. Coleman, et. al. Copyright © 1980, 1976, 1972 by Scott, Foresman and Co. Reprinted by permission. Page 404, Figure 15–6. From the book, Control Your Depression by Peter M. Lewinsohn; Ricardo F. Munoz; Mary Ann Youngren; Antonette M. Zeiss, © 1978 by Peter M. Lewinsohn. Published by Prentice-Hall, Inc., Englewood Cliffs, NJ 07632. Page 405, Table 15–4. Reprinted with permission from: Beck, Rush, Shaw and Emery, Cognitive Therapy of Depression. Copyright 1979, Aaron T. Beck, A. John Rush, Brian F. Shaw, and Gary Emery. Page 406–407. From Abnormal Psychology and Modern Life, 6th Edition by James C. Coleman, et. al. Copyright © 1980, 1976, 1972 by Scott, Foresman and Co. Reprinted by permission. Page 410, Table 15–5. Leonard Goodstein, James Calhoun, Understanding Abnormal Behavior, Description, Explanation, Management, © 1982, Addison Wesley Publishing Co., Inc., Reading, MA.; page 296, Table 10.1. Reprinted by permission. Page 411. From Abnormal Psychology, and Modern Life, 6th Edition by James C. Coleman, et. al. Copyright © 1980, 1976, 1972 by Scott, Foresman and Co. Reprinted by permission. Page 417. Reprinted with permission of author and publisher from: Cautela, J. R. Covert Sensitization. Psychological Reports, 1967, 20, 461–462. Page 421. From Marshall Duke and Stephen Nowicki, Jr.: *Abnormal Psychology: perspectives on being different.* Copyright © 1979 by Wadsworth Publishing Co., Inc. Reprinted with permission. Page 422. From Marshall Duke and Stephen Nowicki, Jr.: *Abnormal psychology: perspectives on being different.* Copyright © 1979 by Wadsworth Publishing Co., Inc. Reprinted with permission. Page 424. From Gerald C. Davison and John M. Neale: *Abnormal Psychology,* 3rd ed. Copyright © 1982 by John Wiley and Sons, Inc. Reprinted with permission. Page 424–425. From David C. Rimm and John W. Somervill: *Abnormal Psychology.* Copyright © 1977 by Academic Press, Inc. Reprinted by permission. Page 427, Figure 16–5. From "Relative efficacy of desensitization and modeling approaches for inducing behavioral, affective, and attitudinal changes" by Albert Bandura, Edward B. Blanchard, and Brunhilde Ritter, 1969, *Journal of Personality and Social Psychology, 13,* p. 179. Copyright 1969 by the American Psychological Association. Reprinted by permission of the authors. Page 429, Table 16–1. From Albert Ellis and Robert A. Harper: *A new guide to rational living.* Copyright © 1975 by Institute for Rational Living, Inc. Reprinted by permission of Albert Ellis. Page 429. From David C. Rimm and John C. Masters: *Behavior Therapy,* 2nd ed. Copyright © 1979 by Academic Press, Inc. Reprinted with permission. Page 432. From Charles P. Barnard and Ramon Garrido Corrales, The Theory and Technique of Family Therapy, 1979. Courtesy of Charles C. Thomas, Publisher, Springfield, Illinois. Page 439. From David C. Rimm and John W. Somervill: *Abnormal psychology.* Copyright © 1977 by Academic Press, Inc. Reprinted with permission. Page 449. Copyright 1980 by Field Newspaper Syndicate. Reprinted by permission of Field Newspaper Syndicate and Ann Landers. 449–450, Table 17–1. From Human Sexuality, Fourth Edition by James Leslie McCary and Stephen P. McCary. © 1982 by S. P. McCary and L. P. McCary. Reprinted by permission of Wadsworth Publishing Company, Belmont, CA. 94002. Page 451, Figure 17–1. Reprinted from Biology: Today and Tomorrow by Jack A. Ward and Howard R. Hetzel. Copyright © 1980 by West Publishing Company. All rights reserved. Page 452, Figure 17–2. Reprinted from Biology: Today and Tomorrow by Jack A. Ward and Howard R. Hetzel. Copyright © 1980 by West Publishing Company. All rights reserved. Page 456, Table 17–2. From "Sex role stereotypes: A current appraisal" by Inge K. Broverman, Susan Raymond Vogel, Frank E. Clarkson, Donald M. Broverman and Paul S. Rosenkrantz, 1972, *Journal of Social Issues, 28,* p. 63. Copyright by the Society for the Psychological Study of Social Issues. Reprinted by permission of the Society for the Psychological Study of Social Issues and the authors. Page 459, Table 17–3. From Janet S. Hyde: *Human Sexuality,* 2nd ed. Copyright © 1982 by McGraw-Hill. Reprinted by permission. Page 462, Figure 17–8. From Robert A. Baron and Donn Byrne, Social Psychology: Understanding Human Interaction, Third Edition. Copyright © 1981 by Allyn and Bacon, Inc. Reprinted with permission. Page 482, Figure 18–3. From Robert A. Baron and Donn Byrne, Social Psychology: Understanding Human Interaction, Third Edition. Copyright © 1981 by Allyn and Bacon, Inc. Reprinted with permission. Page 488, Figure 18–5. From "Effects of need for cognition on message evaluation, recall, and persuasion" by John T. Cacioppo, Richard E. Petty, and Katherine Morris, 1983, *Journal of Personality and Social Psychology, 45,* p. 409. Copyright 1983 by the American Psychological Association. Adapted by permission. Page 489, Figure 18–6. From Robert A. Baron and Donn Byrne, Social Psychology: Understanding Human Interaction, Third Edition. Copyright © 1981 by Allyn and Bacon, Inc. Reprinted by permission. Page 513. used by permission of the Associated Press. Page 516, Figure 19–3. From the book, Personal Space by Robert Sommer © 1969 by Prentice-Hall, Inc. Published by Prentice-Hall, Inc., Englewood Cliffs, NJ 07632. Page 521, Figure 19–6. From "Density, perceived choice, and response to controllable and uncontrollable outcomes" by Judith Rodin, 1976, *Journal of Experimental Social Psychology, 12,* p. 575. Copyright © 1976 by Academic Press, Inc. Reprinted by permission of the publisher and author. Page 523, Figure 19–8. From "Effects of noise and perceived control on ongoing and subsequent aggressive behavior" by Edward Donnerstein and David W. Wilson, 1976, *Journal of Personality and Social Psychology, 34,* p. 777. Copyright 1976 by the American Psychological Association. Adapted with permission of the authors. Page 524, Figure 19–10. From Robert A. Baron: *Human agression.* Copyright © 1977 by Plenum Press. Reprinted by permission of publisher and author. Page 525, Figure 19–11. From "Ambient temperature and the occurrence of collective violence: The "long, hot, summer" revisited" by Robert A. Baron and Victoria M. Ransberger, 1978, Journal of *Personality and Social Psychology, 36,* p. 354. Copyright 1978 by the American Psychological Association. Adapted by permission of the authors. Page 527, Figure 19–12. From "Reducing the stress of high-density living: An architecural intervention" by Andrew Baum and Glenn E. Davis, 1980, *Journal of Personality and Social Psychology,* 38, p. 475. Copyright 1980 by the American Psychological Association. Reprinted by permission of the authors.

— Photo Credits

1 Hirshhorn Museum and Sculpture Garden, Smithsonain Institution. 3 Jeff Albertson, Stock, Boston. 11 The Bettmann Archive. 12 The Granger Collection, New York. 23 Lester V. Bergman & Associates. 28 Dr. E. R. Lewis, Electronic Research Lab, University of California, Berkeley (from Lewis, Leexi Everhart, 1969). 34 The Bettmann Archive. 44 (left) courtesy of Roy Kurasia. 44 (right) courtesy of David W. Shucard. 51 David Farr. 74 Black Star. 77 T. D. Lovering, Stock, Boston. 82 Leonard Lee Rue III, Monkmeyer Press Photo Service. 83 (bottom three) David Farr. 85 (top left) T. D. Lovering, Stock, Boston. 85 (top right) David Farr. 86 Wide World Photos, Inc. 87 Museum of Art, Carnegie Institute, Pittsburgh; Museum Purchase: Director's Discretionary Fund, 1974. 88 (top) Scientific American, April 1959, page 58; photo by William Vandivert. 89 © George Gerster, Photo Researchers, Inc. 90 (bottom left & right) David Farr. 91 T. D. Lovering, Stock, Boston. 95 Al Fenn, LIFE Magazine © Time, Inc. 105 Jean-Claude Lejeune, Stock, Boston. 108 (top) David Farr. 108 (bottom) © Joseph Szabo, Photo Researchers, Inc. 111 Wide World Photos. 122 Both photos courtesy of Sleep Disorders Center, Stanford University School of Medicine. 119 The New-York Historical Society. 120 Ginger Wall, TIME Magazine. 125 Jean-Claude Lejeune, Stock, Boston. 131 Elizabeth Crews, Stock, Boston. 135 Historical Pictures Service, Chicago. 137 Photo courtesy of Professor Ben Harris, Vassar College (taken from Watson's 1919 film). 139 The Granger Collection, New York. 140 (left top & bottom) Nina Leen, LIFE Magazine © 1971, Time, Inc. 144 courtesy Yerkes Primate Research Center, Emory University. 147 Magnum Photos. 149–150 From Howard H. Kendler's *Basic Psychology* (3rd Ed.) Menlo Park, California, W. A. Benjamin, Inc. Originally photographed by Meyer Hiebowitz of The New York Times of research conducted by Drs. R. Pierrel and J. G. Sherman. 157 Mark McGee. 160 photo by Norma Morris. 163 Stock, Boston 166 Both photos, United Press International. 176 From Geoffrey R. Loftus and Elizabeth F. Loftus: *Human Memory: The processing of information.* Copyright © 1979 by Lawrence Erlbaum Associates, Inc. Reprinted by permission. 177 From "Semantic integration of verbal information into a visual memory" by Elizabeth F. Loftus, David G. Miller, and Helen J. Burns, 1978, *Journal of Experimental Psychology, 4,* p. 20. Copyright 1978 by the American Psychological Association. Reprinted by permission of the author. 182 All photos from

(Continued Following Subject Index)

— CONTENTS IN BRIEF —

— CONTENTS —

—CHAPTER 6—
Conditioning and Learning 131

—CHAPTER 7—
Memory and Information Processing 163

━CHAPTER 11━
Life-Span Development 267

━CHAPTER 12━
Intelligence and the Measurement of Individual Differences 299

━CHAPTER 13━
Personality Theories and Assessment 331

━CHAPTER 14━
Stress and Coping 363

═══CHAPTER 15═══
Abnormal Behavior 387

═══CHAPTER 16═══
Treatment of Abnormal Behavior 415

━ CHAPTER 17 ━
Human Sexuality 447

━ CHAPTER 18 ━
Social Psychology 475

— PREFACE —

To Students and Instructors

The purpose of this book is to introduce the field of psychology in an *accurate, useful,* and *interesting* manner. To achieve accuracy, we emphasize that psychology is a science. In part, this means presenting material throughout the book that is solidly based in published research findings. It also means that the book must be thorough in its explanation of theories, principles, and concepts. We have presented many important studies in enough detail so that students can appreciate how psychologists conceptualize a problem and conduct research to test their hypotheses. Accuracy is enhanced by the presentation of diverse perspectives. The book is comprehensive in the range of material and the depth of material covered. It presents an up-to-date picture of the field, highlighting the many currently popular issues and areas of research.

The strategies we have just described certainly have helped us achieve accuracy but being accurate really isn't enough. It is also important to us that the book be useful. To achieve this goal we emphasize that psychology is an applied discipline. Our emphasis on the application of scientific psychology is reflected in more than just a chapter on "Applied Psychology." Throughout the book, we point out the relevance of the material to the lives of the students. We demonstrate how psychological knowledge may be used to promote human welfare and solve everyday problems in living. We also attempt to show how such knowledge may be used to enhance self-knowledge and self-improvement. We believe that psychology has much to say about our understanding and management of many real-world phenomena. We hope you agree that we have effectively captured that theme. In part, the usefulness and relevance of psychology is reflected by the structured format of an "Application" at the end of each major section of each chapter. In addition to the Applied Psy-

chology chapter, the chapters on Stress and Coping, Human Sexuality, and Environmental Psychology also are particularly helpful in making this point. But we would like to emphasize that the applied nature of the discipline is evident and highlighted throughout the book.

Even if a book is accurate and useful, students will have difficulty enjoying it if the material is too complex, too confusing, or too "dry." Our goal has been to avoid these problems and present the field of psychology in a manner that students will find interesting. Our approach has been to use a personal writing style with language that is straightforward, clear, and familiar. An uncluttered and easily understandable presentation has been one of our highest priorities. A book is also made interesting by its content, of course. Above and beyond the applied focus, we present numerous real-life examples and case histories that will hopefully add to the interest value of the book. Finally, to help make the book enjoyable we have included a number of features specifically designed to facilitate interest in addition to usefulness and efficient learning. A brief introduction to these features will allow you to better appreciate their purpose and significance.

A list of *Chapter Objectives* at the beginning of each chapter poses to students a number of questions to keep in mind while reading. A *Chapter Outline* of the material allows students to immediately survey the topics included and begin reading with a sense of the chapter's organization in mind. A chapter *Introduction* gives students an immediate glimpse into the nature of the material through the presentation of a non-fictitious example of the chapter's topic in action. Each chapter consists of either two or three major sections and each section ends with an *Application,* the significance of which we have already described. Each chapter concludes with an *On the Horizon* section. Here, we point out ways in which psychological research and knowledge or recent developments or trends in the field may likely affect students' lives in the future. A point by point *Summary* at the end of each chapter allows students to review the material read. *Important Terms and Concepts* appear throughout each chapter in boldface type. They also appear at the end of each chapter to facilitate the students' rehearsal of the material read. Terms are precisely defined within the text as well as in a glossary at the end of the book. Italic type is used for emphasis and to highlight new terms with particular relevance to psychology but which may be less important than boldface terms. *Suggestions for Further Reading,* usually other books which expand upon the topics covered, are provided in annotated format at the end of each chapter. In addition to these eight standard features, the chapters also contain many *photographs, tables,* and *figures,* which serve to organize and illustrate the text material. Also, some of the chapters contain *Personal Profiles* of selected individuals who have made important contributions to the discipline of psychology. These give students insight into the background and personal history of some of the people whose research they are studying. Finally, *case histories* are incorporated throughout the text.

The text is supplemented by a *Study Guide* and *Instructor's Manual* prepared by M. Aaron Roy. The material in the Study Guide is designed to help students master the material presented in the text. For each of the 20 text chapters there is a corresponding chapter in the Study Guide, each consisting of four features: a chapter preview, a matching self-test, a fill-in-the-blank self-test, and a multiple-choice self-test. The Instructor's Manual consists of chapter summaries, answers to chapter objectives, and test questions covering all the material in the book, including Application and On the Horizon sections.

We wish to express our gratitude to the many people who made this book possible. First we thank the psychologists who read and criticized draft copies of each chapter. Their helpful suggestions have been incorporated throughout the book. To the following reviewers we offer our sincere appreciation for their time, effort, and expertise:

Paul R. Abramson
University of California, Los Angeles

John Best
Eastern Illinois University

Nancy S. Breland
Trenton State College, New Jersey

Larry T. Brown
Oklahoma State University

Dudley Campbell
Los Angeles Pierce College

Roderick S. Carman
University of Wyoming

Garvin Chastain
Boise State University

Nathan T. Clark
University of Illinois, at Chicago

Edward S. Cobb
Bronx Community College

Terry Cozad
University of Denver

Jerry P. Dodson
Boise State University

David Fitzpatrick
California State University, Los Angeles

William C. Gordon
University of New Mexico

Christine Harris
Chaffey College, California

Richard H. Haude
University of Akron

Bruce F. Hertz
Velencia Community College, Florida

Steve Hinkle
Miami University, Ohio

John C. Jahnke
Miami University, Ohio

William A. Johnston
Utah State University

Phillip S. Jones
Lyndon State College, Vermont

Marc S. Lewis
University of Texas, Austin

Edward Lovinger
University of Nevada, Las Vegas

Kenneth O. McGraw
University of Mississippi

Robert C. Mathews
Louisiana State University

Terry Maul
San Bernardino Valley College, California

Martin M. Oper
Erie Community College

Jay G. Riggs
Eastern Kentucky University

M. Aaron Roy
Ashland College, Ohio

Steve M. Smith
Texas A & M University

David G. Thomas
Brain Sciences Laboratories, Denver

Joe M. Tinnin
Richland College, Texas

Marty Weaver
Eastfield College, Texas

Karen P. Williams
George Mason University, Virginia

Allen B. Wolach
Illinois Institute of Technology

Carol Woodward
Moorpark College, California

Mike Zeller
Mankato State University, Minnesota

We are particularly indebted to Dennis Coon for his comments and advice. Special thanks are also extended to Professor Howard H. Kendler for his contribution to the first draft of Chapter 6. We wish to thank Terry Cozad and Dr. Paul Wellman for their contributions to the first drafts of Chapter 2 and the Statistics Appendix, respectively. We are greatly appreciative as well for the helpfulness of Dr. Allan Mirsky with respect to issues in Chapter 15. Special thanks also go to Dr. Ed Jorden and Dr. David Shucard who were supportive and helpful in more ways than can be mentioned.

We are extremely grateful to the numerous individuals who helped in the many phases of manuscript preparation. They are Judy Lairsmith, Barb Benton, Carol Ellis, Murel Denny, Joan Drumright, Bethany Bice, and Maureen Brady.

In addition, we owe a great deal of gratitude to the staff of West Publishing Company for their superb efforts and professionalism in bringing this book to fruition. Specifically we wish to thank Carole Grumney for her work on the study guide and instructor's manual, Jeanne Hoene for her work in marketing, and William Stryker for designing the book and for his tireless round-the-clock efforts during the final months prior to publication. Most of all, we thank Clyde Perlee, Editor-in-Chief, for making it all happen and putting it all together. For his confidence in us from the very outset and for his guidance and encouragement, we are forever grateful.

Finally, to Ellen McGee and Ruth Ann Wilson, we owe more than just thanks. Not only were they involved in every phase of writing this book, they never complained when all they heard about was "the book." To them, our on-the-spot critics and reviewers, we owe much.

Mark G. McGee
David W. Wilson

— CHAPTER 1 —

INTRODUCTION TO PSYCHOLOGY

INTRODUCTION TO PSYCHOLOGY

— CHAPTER OBJECTIVES —

To achieve the objectives of this chapter, you should be able to answer the questions listed here. You should also be able to define the important terms and concepts listed at the end of the chapter.

1. What is psychology?
2. What makes psychology a science? What makes it a discipline?
3. List the methods that psychologists use for collecting, analyzing, and interpreting new knowledge about behavior.
4. Of what value are case-history, correlational, and experimental research approaches? What are the limitations of each?
5. Which specialty areas currently characterize the discipline of psychology?
6. Where do psychologists work? What are the educational requirements for becoming a psychologist? What are the future employment opportunities for psychologists?

— CHAPTER OUTLINE —

The Science of Psychology
Psychology is the science of human and animal behavior. As a scientific field of study, it encompasses the research methods and techniques necessary for collecting, analyzing, and interpreting new knowledge about behavior.

Research Methods
Ethical Guidelines for Psychological Research
Application: An Illustrative Example—Does Marijuana Affect Memory?

The Discipline of Psychology
As an academic discipline, psychology is a major field of study in colleges and universities.

Early Schools of Psychology
Specialty Areas in Psychology
Where Psychologists Work
Careers in Psychology
Plan of This Book
Application: Getting the Most out of This Book

On the Horizon: Psychology, the Future, and You

PSYCHOLOGY IS . . .

Although many people believe otherwise, psychology embraces more than just the study and treatment of abnormal behavior (see Figure 1–1). The following examples show how broad the field is:

— Psychologists study differences in the brains of men and women. The fact is that women excel at certain tasks, men at others. Although there are no agreed-on differences in the physical size of the brains of the two sexes, scientists have found evidence that males' brains may function differently than females' brains (see chapter 2).

— Psychologists study machines that think. The use of machines, including computers, to simulate human behavior appears to have no limits. For example, devices that allow the blind to "see" are being built (see chapters 3 and 8).

— Psychologists study sleep and dreams. New knowledge is enabling some of the more than 50 million Americans who suffer from a variety of sleep disturbances to be treated (see chapter 5).

— Psychologists study animal and human learning. Just as rats can learn to press a bar for food, humans can learn to alter their brain waves, lower their heart rate and blood pressure, and eliminate bad habits (see chapter 6).

— Psychologists study remembering and forgetting. In the not-too-distant future, memory modification specialists may be able to help people alter their memories on command (see chapter 7).

— Psychologists study human intelligence. Although most people are of average intelligence, intellectual functioning ranges from the level of mental re-

Figure 1–1.
Mental hospital ward.

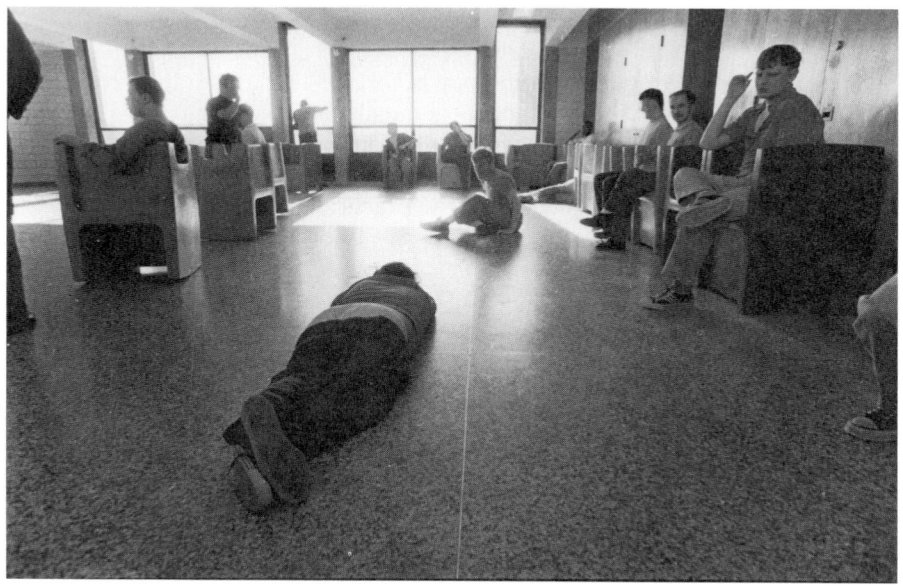

tardation to the level of genius. Although genetic engineering is controversial today, it may one day be used to prevent some forms of mental retardation (see chapter 12).

– Psychologists study stress and coping. The negative effects of stress may be prevented when people learn ways of coping with it (see chapter 14).

– Psychologists study abnormal behavior and ways of treating it (see chapters 15 and 16).

– Psychologists study human sexuality. Many unusual forms of sexual behavior exist (see chapter 17).

– Psychologists study group behavior. Numerous factors influence why people like, help, and hurt others (see chapter 18).

– Psychologists use their knowledge to solve problems facing professionals in other disciplines, such as medicine, law, and education (see chapter 20).

How do psychologists investigate so many phenomena? We will address the question in this section of the chapter. First, however, we should point out that the topics just mentioned are but a few of the ones that psychologists investigate. Among others are the working of the brain, extrasensory perception, drugs, language development in infants, thinking, problem solving, emotion and motivation, love, social development, personality, creativity, abnormality, crowding in urban areas, personnel selection, educational testing, aging, and death. The vast scope of psychology may at first surprise you, but we hope that it also excites you. Let's begin with a definition of *psychology* and a brief description of what this chapter is about.

Psychology is the science of human and animal behavior; it is also an academic discipline and a profession (Kasschau, Johnson, & Russo, 1975).

As a *scientific field of study*, psychology consists of the research methods and techniques necessary for collecting, analyzing, and interpreting new knowledge about behavior. Broadly speaking, psychologists conduct two types of research, basic and applied. *Basic research* is aimed at accumulating knowledge purely for its own sake. *Applied research* is aimed at using research findings to solve practical problems or to improve the quality of human life. In the first section of the chapter, we will describe various approaches for conducting both kinds of research.

As an *academic discipline*, psychology is a major field of study in colleges and universities. In the second section of the chapter, we will trace its development as an independent field and provide an overview of its many specialty areas.

As a *profession*, psychology involves the practical application of knowledge gained through scientific inquiry. Psychologist George Miller, in his 1969 presidential address to the *American Psychological Association* (APA), argued that psychologists' knowledge can and should be used by everyone. According to Miller (1969), the greatest challenge to psychologists should be the determination of how best to "give psychology away." Psychology is a useful science, capable of promoting human welfare. Thus, throughout the book, we will describe the many ways in which it can be applied to everyday problems.

As will become apparent, psychologists study many species of animals, including rats, cats, pigeons, monkeys, and selected populations of humans, ranging from newborn infants to the elderly. Regardless of the topic under investigation or the subjects studied, psychologists who do scientific research use systematic methods of observation to answer questions about behavior.

Research Methods

The New College Edition of the *American Heritage Dictionary* defines **science** as the "observation, identification, description, experimental investigation, and theoretical explanation of natural phenomena." In Latin, *science* means "knowledge." To advance knowledge, psychologists use the **scientific method,** which involves two steps: conducting observations and experiments and interpreting the information obtained from them. The method relies on *empirical data*—information that can be observed and measured. A variety of techniques are used to collect and interpret information. In fact, applications of the scientific method vary in as many ways as there are types of problems and disciplines (Christensen, 1980).

As we will see in later chapters, psychologists study behavior in many ways. They also use a variety of research methods, all of which employ systematic observation or experimentation. Let's examine some approaches used to collect, analyze, and interpret new psychological knowledge.

— Case Histories

One of the oldest methods for investigating psychological phenomena is the **case-history approach,** which looks into a person's past in an attempt to reconstruct life events. Although perhaps the weakest investigative method, it can provide useful insight into human behavior. Following is the case history of a patient diagnosed by psychologists as suffering from *schizophrenia* (described in detail in chapter 15), a mental disorder characterized by profound disturbances in behavior and mental processes:

There was no family history of mental illness in the case of F. C. He had been an average scholar but introspective

and solitary at school, with no liking for games and no hobbies. . . . In the year following his demobilization from the army he was admitted to a mental hospital, aged 23 years.

In the hospital at first he lay in bed with an occasional vacant smile, and refused food. . . . He complained of hearing buzzing noises . . . and voices which he could sometimes understand but whose messages he could not remember. . . . He expressed the belief that the doctors and nurses could manipulate their shadows, and that there was another person in his bed. Later he complained of tasting soap in his mouth and of receiving poison from the post beside his bed. Often he could not be engaged in conversation, sat vacantly by the hour and had both to be taken to his meals and pressed to eat. At times he was incontinent, chewed the end of his tie and hoarded rubbish. For weeks on end he would be in a state of stupor or near to it. . . . Then a period of excitement would intervene, when for days or weeks on end he would be hyperactive and talk a great deal in a disjointed and usually incoherent way. At these times he would strike out impulsively at the nursing staff. On occasion he clowned in a crude way and would walk on his hands. (quoted in Calhoun, 1977, p. 295)

Case histories provide a rich source of **hypotheses**—tentative explanations used to account for observed phenomena—that can be tested by controlled studies. Therein lies the strength of the case-history approach. The weaknesses, however, outweigh the strengths. For example, case histories are open to a variety of interpretations. The first sentence of the case history just presented provides a good illustration. That there was "no family history of mental illness" might well be true; however, even if true, the fact is misleading in that it is not representative for other schizophrenic patients. The aggregate of family histories of patients with schizophrenia (and other mental disorders) shows that the illness does tend to run in families, at least to some extent.

Another weakness of the case-history approach is that the data are obtained *retrospectively*—by looking into the person's past. The reconstruction of history is subject to the bias of the person doing it. It is always possible to criticize the *validity* or accuracy of data obtained from case histories because people tend to include certain life events and selectively exclude others. Often, facts that are unusual and that support the expected outcome tend to be included. For example, it could be argued that many young people are introspective and solitary at school, with no liking for games or hobbies. Whether this aspect of F. C. had anything to do with his breakdown is an empirical question, and there are insufficient empirical data to answer it.

Case histories thus are not the best way of obtaining facts or testing hypotheses about psychological phenomena. Although they provide a starting point for investigation, their data are unique, open to a variety of interpretations, and difficult to validate because they are obtained retrospectively.

— Correlational Research

The **correlational-research approach** provides a systematic way of investigating relationships among variables. A **variable** is any phenomenon that can be quantified and therefore measured in some way. The investigator begins by observing and measuring variables of interest, such as performance on psychology examinations. Correlational analysis yields a **correlation coefficient,** which is a mathematical expression of the degree of relationship between two variables. We performed such an analysis on test scores obtained by students who took a midterm and a final examination in one of our introductory psychology courses. The question of interest to us was whether there would be any relationship between students' scores on the two tests. Using the formula provided in the appendix to this book we calculated the correlation coefficient as .85. The possible values of correlation coefficients range from +1.00 (a perfect positive correlation) to −1.00 (a perfect negative correlation). A correlation that falls between 0 and +.99 indicates an imperfect positive relationship; one that falls between 0 and −.99 indicates an imperfect negative relationship. Thus, the observed correlation of .85 expresses a strong, but imperfect, positive correlation (or degree of relationship) between students' scores on the two tests. Students who obtained high scores on the midterm exam tended to obtain high scores on the final; students who obtained low scores on the midterm tended to obtain low scores on the final.

Correlational analysis, an important tool for studying relationships among variables, may use data from various sources. Let's examine some typical sources.

Observation. Much psychological data comes from observing behaviors of interest. The observation may take place either in natural, real-life settings or in con- trived, controlled settings. When it occurs in natural settings, it is referred to as **naturalistic observation**. An example of naturalistic observation is provided by the pioneering research of Jane Goodall, who for many years lived among and observed chimpanzees in East Africa (Goodall, 1971).

Another example of naturalistic observation is provided by Roger Barker (1968), who for several years lived among and observed the residents of Oskaloosa, Kansas. Barker observed the influence on behavior of *behavior settings,* such as weddings, public meetings, picnics, and baseball games; he found that the regularity of behavior within particular settings is greater than the regularity of behavior across settings. (For example, people behave differently at weddings than at picnics.) Barker's studies, which provide a clear demonstration that behavior varies by setting, suggest the importance of observing behavior in natural settings.

Observation that takes place in contrived or controlled settings, such as laboratories, hospitals, or schools, is referred to as **nonnaturalistic observation.** A general problem with both observational methods is that the presence of the observer may alter the behavior being observed, although this is more likely to be a problem in contrived situations. We can assume, however, that if the observer does interfere, the data obtained may be *biased*. For instance, Jane Goodall's presence at first caused the chimpanzees to be anxious and to behave in unnatural ways. Eventually, though, her presence went unnoticed and the chimps' behavior became more natural.

To prevent bias that may occur as the result of the observer's presence, behavior may be observed unobtrusively. **Unobtrusive observation** makes use of data that the observed subjects need not be aware of. Many natural behaviors can be studied unobtrusively. For example, the popularity of exhibits at the Museum of Science and Industry in Chicago was assessed by noting the amount of wear on the floor tiles in front of each exhibit. The amount of alcohol consumption in a supposedly dry town was determined by counting discarded liquor and wine bottles in trash cans. The racial attitudes of college students were assessed by noting the degree to which black and white students sat together in lecture halls. These and other examples are provided in a book on unobtrusive measures by Webb, Campbell, Schwartz, and Sechrest (1966).

Structured interviews, surveys, and questionnaires. Many psychological phenomena are difficult to study by either direct or unobtrusive observation.

In such cases, structured interviews, surveys, and questionnaires provide information about subjects' opinions, beliefs, and behaviors. In each method, usually subjects answer a prearranged set of questions. For example, the first systematic data on human sexuality, (see Chapter 17) came from large-scale survey studies carried out by Alfred Kinsey and his co-workers (1948, 1953).

Today, surveys are commonly used to obtain data on population characteristics, political attitudes, and consumer preferences. Some examples are the United States Census and the Gallup and Harris polls.

Tests. A quantitative means for measuring psychological variables such as intelligence, attitudes, interests, and abilities is provided by **psychometric tests.** Such tests were first widely used to select military recruits during World War I. They can be administered individually or to large groups of persons (see chapter 12). Thus they provide a way of collecting data from many individuals with minimum cost and equipment.

— Experimental Research

The case-history approach provides an important starting point in psychological investigations, and correlational research can uncover relationships among variables of interest. The **experimental-research approach**, however, is an even more powerful method of investigation because it allows the researcher to exercise precise control over conditions that might affect observed or measured relationships among variables.

Research design. As with correlational research, experimental research begins with a research plan, or design. The **research design** includes detailed specification of the procedures to be followed, the subjects to be studied, the hypotheses to be tested, the ways in which the data will be analyzed, and the conclusions that can be reasonably drawn from the data obtained. If you examine an article in a psychological journal, you'll notice that it contains various parts; these parts correspond to the elements of a research design. Generally, the articles include descriptions of the method, subjects, procedures, and results.

Independent variables. Experimental research differs from other types of research in that variables are carefully controlled and manipulated so that cause-effect relationships between them can be identified.

Independent variables (IVs) are the variables that the investigator manipulates, independent of other controlled variables, in order to determine effects of the manipulation. They are synonymous with the *causes* of some behavioral effect. For example, the independent variable in an experiment designed to study the effects of marijuana on memory might be the amount of marijuana consumed; the experimenter could manipulate this amount. The behavior settings described by Roger Barker can also be considered independent variables. (Barker observed the effects of different settings on behavior.) In some studies, age, sex, and other personal characteristics are considered independent variables.

Dependent variables. The purpose of an experiment is to observe and measure effects on the **dependent variables** (DVs). These variables are the behaviors of interest, which may or may not change when the independent variables are manipulated. Variations in the dependent variables are assumed to be caused by manipulations of the independent variables and therefore to depend on them. The dependent variables are synonymous with the behavioral *effects*.

Extraneous variables. Experiments are valid only to the extent that variations in the dependent variables cannot be attributed to **extraneous variables**—other, uncontrolled variables. The experimenter strives to control, or hold constant, all extraneous variables.

Experimental and control groups. Minimizing the effects of extraneous variables can be accomplished by **randomization,** which involves the random assignment of subjects to experimental and control groups. The **experimental group** is exposed to manipulation of the independent variables; the **control group** is not. The two groups are treated exactly the same in every other possible way. This controls extraneous variables by equalizing their effects across both groups. Also, if subjects have an equal chance of being assigned to either the control group or the experimental group, any of the personal characteristics that might affect behavior are eliminated from the experiment. Under such carefully controlled conditions, observed variations in the dependent variables (such as performance differences on a memory test) can be attributed to the deliberate manipulation of the independent variables (such as the amount of marijuana consumed). Cause-effect relationships are investigated in this manner.

Ethical Guidelines for Psychological Research

The hypothetical marijuana experiment just mentioned raises a question relevant to all psychological research: What ethical principles govern research with human subjects? The issue may be more than academic, since many students are called upon to participate in psychological research. Indeed, college students provide an important pool of human research volunteers. You may therefore be relieved to learn that the American Psychological Association has issued a list of ethical principles (Ethical principles, 1981) to be followed by psychologists, psychology students, and other researchers who are supervised by psychologists.

The first and most important is that psychological researchers have an ethical obligation to protect the dignity and welfare of research subjects. In designing a study, the researchers must stringently safeguard the rights of participants by:

– Protecting participants from physical and mental harm or discomfort.
– Establishing beforehand a fair, clear agreement that states the investigator's and participant's obligations and responsibilities.
– Providing participants with an explanation, as soon as possible, for any deception required by the study.
– Allowing participants to decline participation or withdraw from the study at any time.
– After the data are collected, informing the participants about the nature of the study.
– Protecting confidentiality—that is, keeping information confidential unless the participants agree in advance to its release.

— APPLICATION —

AN ILLUSTRATIVE EXAMPLE—DOES MARIJUANA AFFECT MEMORY?

At this point, an example may help you remember important differences among the case-history, correlational, and experimental-research approaches. Let's look at the relationship between marijuana and memory. The single most consistently reported behavioral effect of marijuana in humans is an alteration in memory functioning (Miller & Branconnier, 1983). How might this relationship be studied? To determine whether marijuana has an effect on memory, the investigator could proceed in a variety of ways. A nonexperimental-research approach might involve inspecting records or perhaps obtaining information from persons known to have either a history of marijuana use or problems with memory. Another such approach might involve the search for a relationship between marijuana use and memory failure or for brain damage that could be linked with memory deficits. An experimental approach, on the other hand, might involve the administration of tetrahydrocannabinol (THC), the active ingredient in marijuana, to an experimental group of subjects but not to a control group in order to examine marijuana's effects on memory.

— Nonexperimental-Research Approaches

Schaeffer, Andrysiak, and Ungerleider (1981) reported results that provide an example of a nonexperimental-research approach. These researchers observed a group of long-term heavy users of marijuana on a Caribbean island. The marijuana was used for religious reasons. According to the reports, marijuana symbolized the sacrament of communion—"the Green Herb of the Bible." The investigators examined 10 subjects—7 men and 3 women—ranging in age from 25 to 36 years. The subjects reported using between 2 and 4 ounces per day of a marijuana-tobacco mixture of equal proportions. The average duration of use was 7.4 years. All 10 subjects were active in daily work, mostly agriculture and business, and had been leading spiritually oriented lives since joining the religious group. It was not possible to examine a comparable control group, as all group members continuously smoked the mixture. In fact, they smoked throughout their waking hours, even while taking the various tests, including memory tests, administered by the investigators. Test scores obtained from the 10 volunteers were compared with published standards. The volunteers' scores were all in the superior-to-very-superior range of intellectual functioning.

Does marijuana affect memory? One might conclude from the study that it does not. Indeed, one might conclude that instead it makes people intelligent. Neither conclusion is warranted, however, because it is not possible to identify cause-effect relationships using nonexperimental-research approaches. Several problems of interpretation exist. For example, it is not known whether the 10 volunteers were a random (representative) sample of the religious group or of the general population. Also, the investigators were unable to study a control group.

Campbell, Evans, Thomson, and Williams (1971) did make use of a control group in studying marijuana users. These researchers compared brain x-rays for a group of 10 long-term marijuana users who had histories of consistent marijuana smoking over a period of from 3-11 years and a control group of 13 nonusers. Although they did not conduct a correlational analysis, the investigators found a *relationship* between chronic marijuana use and brain atrophy—a wasting away of brain tissue. Evidence of brain atrophy was found in the x-rays of the users but not in the x-rays of the nonusers.

Does marijuana use, then, cause brain damage? It is not possible to specify a precise cause-effect relationship even though a control group was included. As in the study reported by Schaeffer and colleagues (1981), the results are open to a variety of interpretations. For instance, the investigators failed to rule out the possibility that brain atrophy was due to something other than marijuana. In fact, the marijuana users had all used other drugs extensively, including LSD and amphetamines. Thus, the brain damage found in the x-rays of the marijuana users may have been caused by any of these drugs or, possibly, by other unknown factors.

— Experimental-Research Approach

Darley, Tinklenberg, Roth, Hollister, and Atkinson (1973) experimentally examined the effects of marijuana on memory. Male college students who volun-

teered for the experiment were assigned to one of two groups. Each subject was given either a 20 milligram oral dose of THC in the form of a brownie or a placebo brownie that contained no THC but was represented by the experimenter as containing an unknown amount of it. All subjects were given brownies of the same size; only the dosage level of THC was different. After ingesting the brownie, each subject was asked to perform a number of memory tasks. For example, in one task, the subjects were given 10 lists of 20 words each and were asked to memorize as many of the words as possible during a fixed period of time. Recall of the memorized words was then tested. Results indicated that the percentage of words recalled varied as a function of THC dosage. Subjects who received no THC showed the highest recall, those who received 20 milligrams showed the lowest.

This study experimentally demonstrated the effects of THC on memory and, by implication, the effects of marijuana on memory. The investigators varied only the dosage level of THC administered to the subjects; all other variables were held constant. For example, the laboratory instructions and the time allowed for memorizing the word lists were *controlled variables*—variables that might have affected the experimental outcome had they not been held constant for all subjects. The administration of different dosages of THC served as an *independent variable* in this study. The investigators wanted to determine the effect of THC dosage on memory. The THC dosage was an independent variable because the investigators chose to manipulate it independently from other variables, which were controlled. The phenomenon of interest to the investigators—percentage of words recalled after a memorization session—was a *dependent variable* because variations in it were assumed to be caused by manipulations of the independent variable and therefore to be dependent upon it. Thus, by holding all other variables constant and manipulating only the THC dosage, the investigators were able to observe an *experimental outcome,* or cause-effect relationship.

— Interpretation of Research Findings

The studies just discussed raise a number of important issues about the interpretation of research findings. First is the issue of *statistical significance.* Various statistical procedures are used to evaluate the *probability* that the results obtained in a study occurred because of the experimental manipulation rather than by chance. Statistical significance, discussed in more detail in the appendix to the book, provides a way of expressing this probability. Whether the results of a study are statistically significant will depend, in part, on the magnitude of difference in the dependent variable for the groups of subjects studied. The number (N) of subjects studied also affects statistical significance. The total number of subjects studied by Darley and his colleagues was adequate (N = 48). Also, because of the magnitude of the difference in the percentage of words recalled (between the groups receiving 0 and 20 milligrams of THC), the difference in memory performance was statistically significant.

Randomization is a second issue relevant to the interpretation of research findings. As mentioned earlier, it involves the random assignment of subjects to groups; that is, subjects have an equal chance of being assigned to each of the groups in a study. In the study reported by Darley and colleagues, whether a subject received a brownie containing 0 or 20 milligrams of the THC was randomly determined. To have done otherwise could have caused problems in interpreting the experimental results. For example, suppose that some of the subjects had a history of marijuana use and others did not. If the subjects had not been randomly assigned to the drug and placebo groups, one group might have included more heavy marijuana users than the other group. Any resulting differences between experimental groups might therefore have been due to prior marijuana use, not to the dosage of THC ingested. The influence of prior marijuana use would have been *confounded with* the influence of THC dosage. The investigators would have been unable to distinguish the effect of one from the other. Randomization ensured that the variable of prior marijuana use was randomly distributed across the two groups, thus

having no possible impact on any differences in the dependent variable between groups.

Replication (repetition) is a third important issue because it adds to our confidence in the reliability of research findings. *Reliability* is a statistical term that refers to the likelihood of obtaining the same results if the experiment is repeated using the same or similar procedures. For instance, follow-up investigations could be designed to replicate the THC and memory experiment. The evidence from a replication study would either confirm or reject the hypothesis that THC impedes the memorization and recall of word lists.

Our confidence in the findings reported by Darley and his colleagues would be enhanced if a *baseline measure* of memory and recall had been obtained from subjects prior to the experimental manipulation. Such a measure was obtained, which provided data about the percentage of words recalled when subjects were not under the influence of THC. Prior to intoxication, recall of words memorized was identical for the marijuana and placebo groups. As for information processed during intoxication, however, marijuana-intoxicated subjects showed poorer recall than placebo subjects.

The inclusion of additional control groups would also bolster our confidence in the findings reported by Darnley and his colleagues. For example, a third group of subjects, for comparison with the marijuana and placebo group, could have participated in the memorization and recall tasks without having eaten any brownies. Control groups and baseline measures in any experiment are valuable because they provide a standard against which to compare the effects of the manipulated independent variable. Other types of research designs, which incorporate still other types of control, will be introduced in our discussions of research findings throughout the book.

— THE DISCIPLINE OF PSYCHOLOGY —

Early Schools of Psychology

Little more than a century ago, psychology was a minor branch of philosophy. Then, in the late 1800s, two laboratories devoted to psychological research were established, one in Germany and the other in the United States. The pioneers responsible for developing these laboratories, Wilhelm Wundt and William James, deserve much of the credit for the birth of psychology as an independent discipline. With his emphasis on laboratory experimentation, Wundt turned psychology into a science. James interpreted the new science, teaching and writing about it in a way that gave it wide meaning and social relevance. Both were influential in starting

WILHELM WUNDT (1832–1920)

Wilhelm Wundt was born on August 16, 1832, in a small village near Heidelberg, Germany. Wundt was the son of a Lutheran pastor. He grew up with few friends, playing little and daydreaming a lot. As a boy, he lived and studied with a private tutor until it was time to enter high school. His first year away at school, at the age of 12, was disastrous. His habitual daydreaming, lack of friends, and occasionally brutal teachers undoubtedly contributed to his failure. After wasting another year at school, Wundt moved back to Heidelberg, continued his studies, and received his MD from the University there in 1856. Wundt moved again in 1875, this time to the University of Leipzig, where, for the next 45 years, he taught and did his most important work. In 1879, he established the first psychological laboratory in the world.

Wundt is considered the first person to make psychology a major interest and therefore is viewed as the first psychologist. He is also the recognized father of experimental psychology. In addition to being the first psychologist, Wundt offered the first formal course in psychology, edited the first experimental journal in psychology, and was a prolific writer in the field. He is credited with about 500 publications totaling close to 60,000 printed pages. (It would take more than 3 years, at 50 pages a day, to read all Wundt's works.) When James McKeen Cattell, a student from the United States, presented Wundt with an American typewriter, a rival German psychologist grumbled that it was an evil gift, enabling Wundt to write twice as many books as would have been possible without it (Fancher, 1979).

independent schools of psychology—groups of psychologists who associated themselves with these early leaders.

— Structuralism

Using a method called *introspection* (which means self-examination and contemplation of one's own feelings and thoughts), Wundt set out to systematically explore the private world of *consciousness*. It was his conviction that the central problem facing psychology was analyzing the elements, or structures, of conscious experience. From subjects' reports about their experiences, he and his followers concluded that consciousness consists of three elements—sensations, images, and feelings. Wundt's school of psychology became known as **structuralism,** the study of how the elements of human consciousness form the structure of the mind. Wundt's laboratory attracted students from around the world; they came to study psychology and to conduct psychological research. Many of these students later returned to their homelands, where they set up laboratories modeled after Wundt's.

— Functionalism

While Wundt was busy in Germany studying the basic elements of conscious experience, others were beginning to disagree with his approach. Wundt's critics believed it more important to understand how the mind functions. **Functionalism** is the name given to the school of psychology whose advocates studied those aspects of the mind, such as learning and intelligence, that help organisms adapt to the environment (Chaplin & Krawiec, 1979). The functionalists believed in the importance of studying conscious experience, as did the structuralists, but they argued that consciousness is an ongoing and ever-changing stream of mental events that cannot be split into discrete elements. William James was one of the people who contributed most to the development of this school of psychology in the United States.

— Behaviorism

A new school of psychology, known as **behaviorism,** soon developed to challenge both structuralism and functionalism. Behaviorism was led by an energetic young American psychologist, John B. Watson (whose work is discussed in chapter 6). Watson's group revolted against the idea that consciousness was psychol-

William James (1842–1910)

William James, who was born in 1842 in New York, has come to be known as the father of American psychology. He and his brother, Henry, a noted novelist, were encouraged intellectually by their father, who sent them to Europe to broaden their knowledge. After an unsuccessful attempt to become an artist, William James enrolled at Harvard University in 1861 to study chemistry. Drifting from chemistry into the study of physiology, anatomy, and biology, James entered the Harvard medical school—despite the fact that the practice of medicine was not altogether appealing to him. After trips to the Amazon and Europe, James completed his studies, taking his medical degree in 1869. He then accepted a position at Harvard and began teaching physiology. Although he never received formal training in psychology, James offered his first course on the subject in 1875. Three years later, he signed a contract to write a volume on psychology, which he promised to deliver in 2 years; 10 years later, he published a giant, two-volume work, *The Principles of Psychology.*

After 1890, James became increasingly interested in philosophy. He took a pessimistic view of psychology as a laboratory science, once remarking to a colleague that psychology was a "nasty little subject." Although he served as president of the American Psychological Association from 1894 to 1904, at this stage in his career James was strictly a philosopher. He is, in fact, considered by many to be America's greatest philosopher. Despite his brief tenure as a psychologist, James's impact on the struggling science was immense. Not only was *The Principles of Psychology* a major work of the time, but with his book *Pragmatism* James laid the foundation for functionalism (which emphasized the adaptive utility of behavior rather than merely its description). Before he died, in 1910, William James had been successful in a number of careers. More importantly, he had established psychology as a practical science, giving it wide meaning and social relevance.

ogy's central problem. The *behaviorists,* as psychologists who aligned themselves with this movement were called, opposed the analysis of conscious experience by introspection. They were interested in neither the structure nor the function of the mind; their concern was only behaviors that could be observed and measured. They advocated the study of *observable behavior* by objective experimental procedures. Watson (1913) argued that psychology is the "science of behavior" and that there is no justification for studying such concepts as mind or consciousness or feelings.

Behaviorism dominated American psychology for many years. Gradually, however, the domain of psychology expanded beyond the limits of behaviorism to a consideration once again of conscious experience. Today, psychologists regard behavior as a very general, global term that encompasses the overt actions of organisms as well as physiological activity and mental processes such as attending, thinking, remembering, wanting, wishing, expecting, and fantasizing.

The diverse ways in which behavior is studied today are suggested by various other schools of thought that emerged during the early years of the 20th century. These schools and the many current approaches to the study of human and animal behavior are discussed in subsequent chapters. From this brief historical introduction, however, we can see that psychology, since 1879, has undergone explosive growth. With the upsurge of various schools, knowledge began pouring in from several fronts. The inevitable result was specialization.

Specialty Areas in Psychology

One way of grasping the diversity of areas currently attracting the attention of psychologists is to list the special-interest groups, or *divisions,* within the American Psychological Association (see Table 1–1). As we can see, there are divisions of psychologists devoted to social issues, the arts, the military, law, engineering, consumer behavior, philosophical issues, religious issues, women, children, physical health, hypnosis, and drugs—to name just a few. New divisions develop periodically with the expansion of interests and the growth of new areas in which psychological knowledge is applied.

A second way of grasping the diversity of psychology is to consider various *specialty areas,* as illustrated in Figure 1–2. Let's briefly examine each of these areas.

Table 1–1.

Divisions in the American Psychological Association.

—General Psychology
—Teaching of Psychology
—Experimental Psychology
—Evaluation and Measurement
—Physiological and Comparative Psychology
—Developmental Psychology
—Personality and Social Psychology
—Society for the Psychological Study of Social Issues
—Psychology and the Arts
—Clinical Psychology
—Consulting Psychology
—Industrial and Organizational Psychology
—Educational Psychology
—School Psychology
—Counseling Psychology
—Psychologists in Public Service
—Military Psychology
—Adult Development and Aging
—Society of Engineering and Applied Psychologists
—Rehabilitation Psychology

—Consumer Psychology
—Theoretical and Philosophical Psychology
—Experimental Analysis of Behavior
—History of Psychology
—Community Psychology
—Psychopharmacology
—Psychotherapy
—Psychological Hypnosis
—State Psychological Association Affairs
—Humanistic Psychology
—Mental Retardation
—Population and Environmental Psychology
—Psychology of Women
—Psychologists Interested in Religious Issues
—Child, Youth, and Family Services
—Health Psychology
—Psychoanalysis
—Clinical Neuropsychology
—Psychology and the Law
—Psychologists in Independent Practice

Figure 1–2.

Specialty areas in psychology.

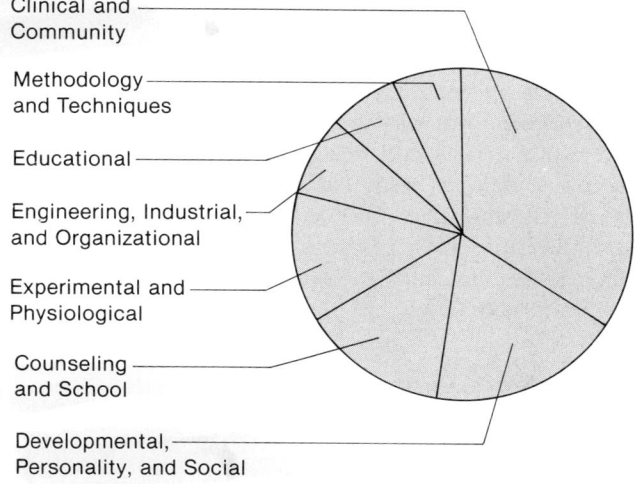

DOCTORAL DEGREE

MASTERS DEGREE

Clinical and Community Psychology

Hospitals, universities, institutions, communities, and private practices are common work settings for *clinical* and *community psychologists*. They do research and apply psychological knowledge to the treatment of psychological disorders. They are interested in understanding and treating such problems as depression, anxiety, and phobias, as well as many other disorders that will be discussed in later chapters.

Developmental, Personality, and Social Psychology

An overlapping number of interests are shared by developmental, personality, and social psychologists. For example, *developmental psychologists* study infants, children, adolescents, and adults—human growth and development from the beginning of life until death. They apply knowledge about human development to children in special school programs, to preschool children, and to programs for the elderly.

Personality psychologists, most of whom work in teaching or research settings, focus on individual differences in behavior. Personality research is utilized in various applied areas, including clinical, counseling, and school psychology.

Social psychologists study the interactions of individuals and how people influence one another, including such areas as aggression, prejudice, attraction, attitudes, and group behavior. They apply their knowledge to problems in business, industry, schools, the community, and other social settings.

Counseling and School Psychology

Counseling psychologists draw heavily on the fields of developmental, educational, personality, and social psychology. *School psychologists* work in school settings as academic and career counselors. Today, high schools without school psychologists are unusual, and an increasing number of elementary schools now employ them. Counseling and school psychologists perform a variety of functions. For example, they help people who have problems in personal, marital, social, educational, and vocational development and adjustment.

Experimental and Physiological Psychology

Sensation, perception, learning, and motivation are some of the concerns of experimental psychologists, who conduct basic and applied research in a variety of areas. They study seeing, hearing, feeling, perceiving, learning, and wanting. Knowledge gained in these areas forms a basis for understanding the complex processes of knowing, thinking, judging, and problem solving. More than two-thirds of all experimental psychologists work in research settings in colleges and universities or research institutions.

Physiological psychologists study the biological bases of behavior. For example, they examine the role of the brain in behaviors ranging from eating and sex to reading and problem solving. They work primarily in research settings.

Engineering, Industrial, and Organizational Psychology

The study of people at work is the specialty of engineering, industrial, and organizational psychologists. *Engineering psychologists* are concerned with the human factor in production and with optimizing human-machine relations. They do applied research in designing airplanes, automobiles, and machinery for the government and for businesses. *Industrial psychologists* play an important role in personnel selection and placement and in the development and evaluation of training programs for workers. *Organizational psychologists* deal with problems that face private organizations and government agencies, including leadership, morale, and the work environment. Industrial and organizational psychologists study the factors that influence job satisfaction, productivity, and consumer behavior.

Educational Psychology

Research on teaching and learning is the domain of *educational psychologists*. These psychologists develop educational tests and design programs for the gifted and for children with learning disabilities. Although most educational psychologists teach and do research at universities, their research applications span psychological testing and measurement, counseling, and school psychology.

Methodology and Techniques

A minority of psychologists develop the methods and techniques for acquiring and applying psychological knowledge. For example, the subspecialty of *psychometrics* is concerned with test development and the measurement of intellectual abilities and personality. Tests developed by psychometricians are used in clinical, counseling, and school settings, and in business and industry.

— Emerging Specialty Areas

Three areas in which psychologists have become increasingly involved are the environment, law, and medicine. *Environmental psychologists* work in school, industrial, and government settings; they design work environments and study the effects on behavior of crowding, noise, and air pollution. *Forensic psychologists* work with law-enforcement officials; they are involved in crime prevention, jury selection, and the design of rehabilitation programs. *Health psychologists* design wellness programs for employees. They also study the relationship of stress to high blood pressure, ulcers, cancer, and heart attacks, and they help patients adjust to various injuries and diseases.

These are just a sample of the many specialty areas in psychology and of the many activities performed by psychologists.

Where Psychologists Work

Another way to illustrate the diversity of psychology is to describe the settings in which psychologists work. As shown in Figure 1–3, a majority of psychologists work in university, college, and other eduactional settings where they can counsel students, teach and conduct both basic and applied research. More than 25 percent of all psychologists employed by colleges and universities also do some outside consulting work (Super & Super, 1978). In fact, the proportion of psychologists doing basic research in colleges and universities has been declining in recent years and will probably continue to decline as college enrollments level off and as competition for government financial support for research increases. However, an increasing proportion of psychologists will find employment in such work settings as hospitals, community centers, private practice, business and industry, research organizations, and government agencies (see Figure 1–3).

Careers in Psychology

Psychology's diversity is also revealed by the variety of career possibilities open to people with bachelor's, master's, and doctoral degrees in psychology. The myth that you can do little with a bachelor's degree

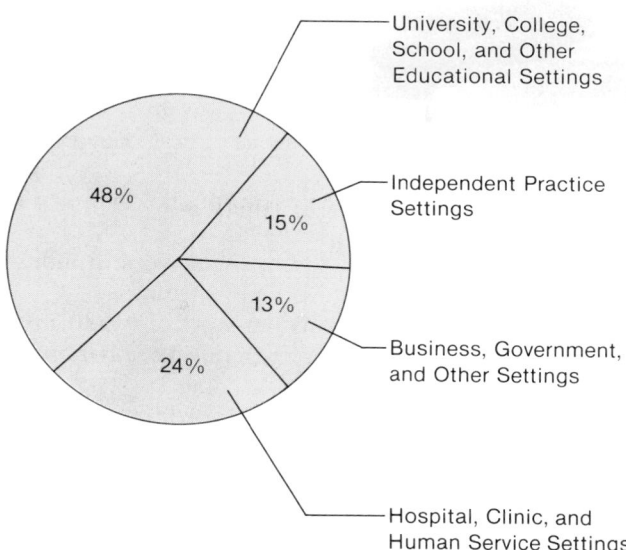

Figure 1–3.

Where psychologists work. As shown here, a majority of psychologists (about 48%) work in university, college, and other educational settings. About 24% work in hospital clinic, and human service settings; 15% in independent practice settings; and 13% in business, government, and other settings. (Based on data from Stapp & Fulcher, 1981.)

(BA or BS) in psychology except seek additional education may take time to dispel (Matthews, 1983). Although undergraduate education in psychology is considered to be nonprofessional in nature, a variety of job opportunities are available to those with a bachelor's degree in psychology, especially those with supporting course work in such fields as business, computer science, education, management, and marketing.

Students often think only of mental hospitals as places of employment for psychologists. A bachelor's degree in psychology can, however, lead to work in many interesting and challenging positions. A few examples are listed here.

— Psychiatric assistants work in private and state mental hospitals and schools for the mentally retarded. They administer routine tests and provide patient care under the supervision of staff psychologists and psychiatrists.
— Probation officers work with police and prison officials in supervising the activities of juveniles who are judged delinquent.
— Vocational rehabilitation workers counsel people with handicaps and help prepare them for new vocations.

– Research assistants help collect and analyze data. They work on projects in government agencies, hospitals, universities, and businesses.

– Newspaper and magazine specialists in psychology work in positions ranging from technical copy editor to newspaper reporter.

– Advertising copywriters probe public interest in products and write advertisements.

– Management and personnel trainees work in industrial, organizational, and government settings.

– Volunteer service coordinators work in youth programs and scouting. They are responsible for training and supervising the activities of volunteers.

– Day-care workers supervise and coordinate the activities of preschool children.

– Sales representatives work in many industries. Publishers of psychology textbooks, for example, employ people with a background in psychology as sales representatives on college campuses.

These are only a few of the opportunities open to psychology majors. Additional opportunities, described by Fretz and Stang (1982), are available to students who earn a master's degree (MA or MS) in psychology, which takes an additional 2 or 3 years of course work beyond the bachelor's degree level. Positions include those just mentioned as well as the following: group leader in a psychiatric ward; academic counselor at a high school, college, or university; supervisor of personnel; and teacher at a junior college. The master's level psychologist may find employment in a variety of clinical, industrial, and school settings.

Depending on the area of specialization, a person with a doctoral degree may pursue university teaching and research, consulting, private practice, or a variety of other lines of work. The doctor of philosophy (PhD) degree usually involves between 4 and 6 years of course work and supervised training beyond the bachelor's degree. In contrast to psychiatrists, who are medical doctors with MD degrees, psychologists with PhD degrees receive extensive training in research. To get the degree, they are required to conduct an original research project and write a doctoral dissertation. The doctor of psychology (PsyD) degree involves the same amount of course work and supervised training as does the PhD; however, it places less emphasis on research experience and more on practical clinical experience.

Educational requirements for psychologists have changed over recent decades to keep pace with the demands imposed by our changing times. Perhaps the best sources of current information about requirements are the colleges and universities that offer training programs and degrees in psychology. In addition, the APA publishes a booklet, *Careers in Psychology,* that you can obtain by contacting the Publication Sales Department, American Psychological Association, 1200 Seventeenth Street NW, Washington, DC 20036. The booklet provides details on selected types of work available to students who earn bachelor's, masters, and doctoral degrees in psychology.

Plan of This Book

Perhaps the best way to view the diversity of psychology is to simply browse through this book and note the variety of topics covered in upcoming chapters. For an overview, look at the brief table of contents in Table 1–2. As you can see, in chapter 2 we explore the biological foundations of behavior. In chapters 3 and 4 we examine sensation (what we hear, see, taste, touch, and smell) and perception (the process by which meaning

Table 1–2.
Brief Table of Contents.

is given to sensations). In chapter 5 we view the nature of consciousness and the altered states of consciousness induced by sleep, dreams, drugs, hypnosis, and meditation. In chapter 6 we deal with the fundamentals of animal and human learning. In chapters 7 and 8 we focus on the complex processes of human memory, language, and thought. In chapter 9 we cover motivation and emotion. In chapters 10 and 11 we examine developmental changes that occur during the prenatal period, infancy, childhood, adolescence, adulthood, and old age. In chapter 12 we view the many factors that influence the development of individual differences in human intelligence. In chapters 13 through 16 personality and abnormality are our topics of concern. In chapters 17 and 18 we examine human sexuality and social psychology. In chapters 19 and 20, the final two chapters of the book, we look at current developments in environmental and applied psychology. This brief overview gives not only the plan of this book but also an idea of the range of topics currently attracting the attention of psychologists.

— APPLICATION —
GETTING THE MOST OUT OF THIS BOOK

Each chapter in this book consists of two or three major sections, and each section is followed by an Application. Some Applications provide an example of how information in the preceding section can be used to understand or manage real-world problems and issues. Others are designed to show how one or more theories or principles can be used for self-improvement or to enhance self-knowledge. The first Application in this chapter, for example, described how psychologists might examine the effect of marijuana on memory. The present Application describes features, in addition to the Applications, that appear in each chapter.

– *Chapter Objectives*. Each chapter begins with a list of Chapter Objectives, which pose questions to keep in mind while reading. When you finish reading each chapter, you should be able to answer the questions.
– *Chapter Outline*. Following the Chapter Objectives is a Chapter Outline that enables you to survey the topics to be covered and to begin your reading with a sense of the chapter's organization. (For a detailed outline of the contents of each chapter, see the Table of Contents at the front of the book.) There are four levels of headings in most chapters; they are meant to help you grasp the outline and organization of the chapter.
– *Introduction*. An Introduction opens each chapter. It gives an immediate glimpse of the nature of the chapter's topic by presenting an example. All chapter Introductions are real accounts of the chapter's topic in action. They are designed to show the potential real-life relevance of the topic.

– *Figures and Tables*. Throughout each chapter, figures and tables serve to organize and illustrate the material. Their captions expand on the topics discussed in the text.
– *Personal Profiles*. Some chapters contain Personal Profiles, such as those on Wilhelm Wundt and William James in this chapter. These profiles are of individuals who have made important contributions to psychology. They are written to give insight into the background and personal history of some of the people whose research you are studying.
– *On the Horizon*. An "On the Horizon" section concludes each chapter. Each one provides an example of how current psychological research or recent developments or trends in the field may affect people's lives in the coming years.
– *Summary*. A point-by-point Summary allows you to review the material presented in each chapter.
– *Important Terms and Concepts*. Each chapter has a number of important terms and concepts that are set off in boldface type and that are precisely defined within the text as well as in the Glossary at the end of the book. These key terms are listed at the end of each chapter to allow you to rehearse and recite the material read. Italic type is used within the chapters for emphasis and, more importantly, to highlight new terms that are particularly relevant to psychology but that are less important than the boldface terms.
– *Suggestions for Further Reading*. At the end of each chapter is an annotated list of suggested readings. It consists of books and articles that expand on the topics discussed. In addition, throughout each chapter, refer-

ences to other sources of information are given, using the author-date method of citation. Authors' names are followed by the year of the publication. If there is no author, the first few words of the reference appear as the text citation. This method of citing sources enables you to locate the full reference easily in the alphabetical reference list provided at the end of the text. Many citations are to research published in the journals of the American Psychological Association: *American Psychologist, Behavioral Neuroscience, Contemporary Psychology, Journal of Abnormal Psychology, Journal of Applied Psychology, Journal of Comparative Psychology, Journal of Consulting and Clinical Psychology, Journal of Counseling Psychology, Developmental Psychology, Journal of Educational Psychology, Journal of Experimental Psychology, Journal of Personality and Social Psychology, Professional Psychology: Research and Practice, Psychological Bulletin,* and *Psychological Review.* Other citations are to material published in non-APA journals, books, and magazines.

We have already referenced several sources of information, but consider this specific example: Siegel and Pallak (1983) recently announced the marriage of the American Psychological Association and the popular magazine *Psychology Today.* The full entry in the reference list at the end of the book looks like this: Siegel, M., & Pallak, M. S. (1983, May). PT and APA: A perfect marriage. *APA Monitor,* p. 5. The references give the authors' names, the year (and, where appropriate, the month) of publication, the article title, the journal or book title, the volume number (where appropriate), and the page numbers (where appropriate). With this information, you can look up any of the citations referenced in the text. APA publications and many of the other books, journals, and magazines cited in this book are available in most college libraries.

PSYCHOLOGY, THE FUTURE, AND YOU

The growth of psychology in the United States parallels the growth of the American Psychological Association. In 1920, there were approximately 400 members in the APA. This number increased to about 2,500 by 1940, 7,500 by 1950, 18,000 by 1960, and 45,000 by 1980; it stands at about 55,000 today (see Figure 1–4), making the APA one of the largest professional organizations in the United States. The continuing rapid growth of psychology suggests that the prospects for psychologists are good.

What are these prospects? Will psychology continue to enjoy the rapid growth and popular support in future decades that it experienced in its first 100 years of development?

These questions were asked of a panel of nine prominent psychologists, and their responses are the subject of an article "Psychology and the Future," published in *American Psychologist* (Wertheimer et al., 1978). A sampling of the responses indicates the following. First, students preparing for the practice of psychology will increasingly seek the PsyD degree, the professional degree that emphasizes practical application rather than basic research. Second, psychology will be more responsive to everyday problems in living, such as pollution, crowding, energy shortages, urban decay, crime, and international conflict. Consequently, it will receive more federal financial support to the extent that it can contribute to the solution of such problems. Third, the discipline of psychology is likely to become still more fractionated in the decades ahead, as new specialty areas arise to meet the needs of our rapidly changing society. Finally, the future will bring a merging of the professional and scientific orientations in psychology. The trend toward an increase in applied research and a decrease in basic research without practical applications is already evident and should continue to characterize the discipline of psychology in the years ahead.

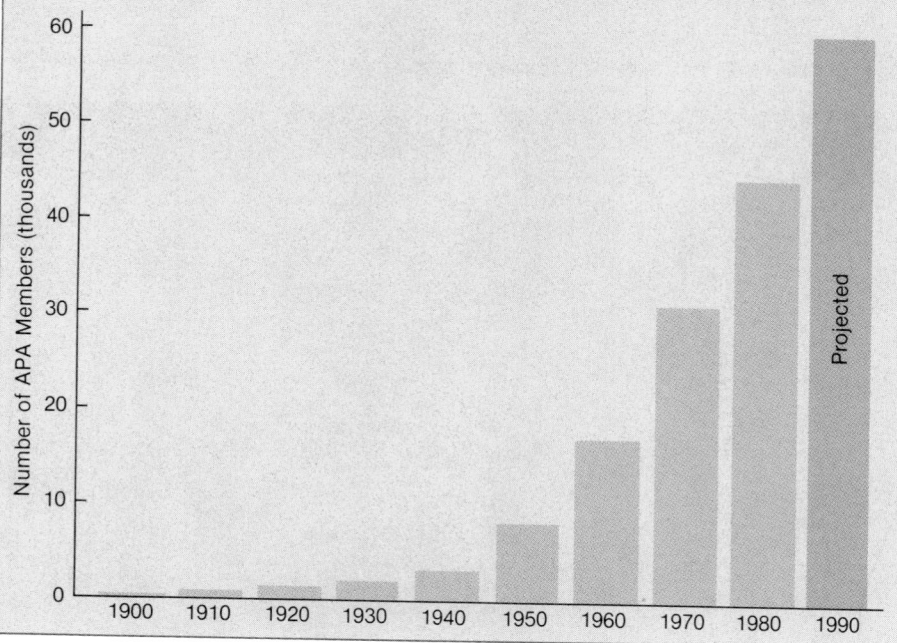

Figure 1–4.
Growth (and projected growth) of APA membership since 1900. Based on data adapted from Hilgard (1978) and Siegel & Pallak (1983).

How might these trends affect you? Even if you take no further course work in psychology, this first course is likely to be of some benefit to you. For example, currently available psychological knowledge bears on a wide range of concerns that students today face. Can you alter bad habits? Is it possible to improve your memory? Can you better manage your time? Should you contact a therapist if you have a personal problem? Is it possible to control test anxiety? How can you test your own IQ? What are your career alternatives? Can diet affect your mood? Can marijuana make you sterile? How do psychoactive drugs alter your consciousness? Can dreams be controlled? Can you become a more relaxed person through the use of meditation and other self-control techniques? Is it possible to manage stress and prevent heart disease? These are but a few of the questions that we will address in this book. Thus, even if this is the first and last psychology textbook you ever read, it should help prepare you for the future.

It is also true that psychology is likely to affect your life in the future whether you read on or stop here. Psychologists are researching the frontiers of human behavior. All of us will be affected by a greater understanding of such puzzles as: How does the brain work? What causes mental disorders? How can they be treated and prevented? Why do some parents abuse their children? Can drug addiction be prevented? Will the blind one day see without eyes? Will genetic counseling lead to the prevention of birth defects? What steps can be taken to reduce the threat of nuclear war? Answers to the most puzzling questions about human behavior are not yet known. As noted by Siegel and Pallak (1983), however, every social issue, large or small, arises from the way human beings behave. The next 19 chapters are designed to give you some insight into psychology—both the science and its applications.

— SUMMARY —

1. Psychology is the study of human and animal behavior.

2. It is a scientific field of study, an academic discipline, and a profession.

3. As a scientific field of study, it consists of the research methods and techniques necessary for collecting, analyzing, and interpreting new knowledge about behavior.

4. As an academic discipline, it is a major field of study in colleges and universities.

5. As a profession, it involves the practical application of knowledge gained through scientific inquiry.

6. The scientific method involves the conduct of observations and experiments and the interpretation of information obtained from them.

7. Case-history, correlational, and experimental-research approaches provide contrasting and unique ways of collecting, analyzing, and interpreting data relevant to the study of psychological phenomena. Each approach has certain strengths and weaknesses.

8. Psychological research is guided by a considered judgment by the individual psychologist about how best to contribute to psychological science while maintaining respect and concern for the dignity and welfare of the subjects who participate. Having made the decision to conduct psychological research, the psychologist must consider the approach and techniques that are most suitable for the problem under investigation.

9. Two pioneers in psychology, Wilhelm Wundt and William James, deserve much of the credit for the development of psychology as an independent science and discipline. Wundt turned psychology into a science. James interpreted the new science, teaching and writing about it in a way that gave it wide meaning and social relevance.

10. Early schools of psychology are structuralism, functionalism, and behaviorism. Today, psychology includes a diverse array of perspectives, theories, models, and methods.

11. Specialty areas in psychology currently include clinical and community psychology; developmental, personality, and social psychology; counseling and school psychology; experimental and physiological psychology; engineering, industrial, and organizational psychology; educational psychology; and methodology and techniques.

12. Career opportunities and specialty areas in psychology have broadened to meet the challenges presented by everyday problems in living. Psychology as a science and profession will meet with success in future decades to the extent that it is responsive to these challenges. The trend toward an increase in applied research and a decrease in basic research without practical applications is already evident and should continue to characterize the discipline of psychology in the years ahead.

— IMPORTANT TERMS AND CONCEPTS —

Psychology	Naturalistic Observation	Extraneous Variables
Science	Nonnaturalistic Observation	Randomization
Scientific Method	Unobtrusive Observation	Experimental Group
Case-history Approach	Psychometric Tests	Control Group
Hypotheses	Experimental-Research Approach	Structuralism
Correlational-Research Approach	Research Design	Functionalism
Variable	Independent Variables (IVs)	Behaviorism
Correlation Coefficient	Dependent Variables (DVs)	

— SUGGESTIONS FOR FURTHER READING —

Careers in psychology. (1980). Washington, DC: American Psychological Association. Recommended reading for students who think they may want to major in psychology or who want to learn more about career options for psychologists. Updated versions of this booklet are available through the Publication Sales Department, American Psychological Association, 1200 Seventeenth St. NW, Washington, DC 20036.

Christensen, L. B. (1980). *Experimental methodology* (2nd ed.). Boston: Allyn & Bacon. A nicely written book on methodology that provides examples for the beginning student of how to design and carry out a research project and write up the results in a manner consistent with APA format.

Fretz, B. R., and Stang, D. J. (1982). *Preparing for graduate study in psychology: Not for seniors only!* Washington, DC: American Psychological Association. Recommended reading for students who plan to go to graduate school.

Roy, M. A. (1984). *Study guide to accompany Psychology: Science and Applications.* St. Paul, MN: West. The supple-mental study guide designed to help you master the material presented in the text and pass your introductory psychology course with flying colors.

Super, D. & Super, C. (1978). *Opportunities in psychology.* Skokie, IL: VGM Career Horizons. A delightful paperback volume dealing with opportunities and careers in psychology.

Wood, G. (1977). *Fundamentals of psychological research* (2nd ed.). Boston: Little, Brown. For the student who wishes to go beyond our brief treatment of research methods, we recommend Wood's introductory book on psychological research.

BIOLOGICAL FOUNDATIONS OF BEHAVIOR

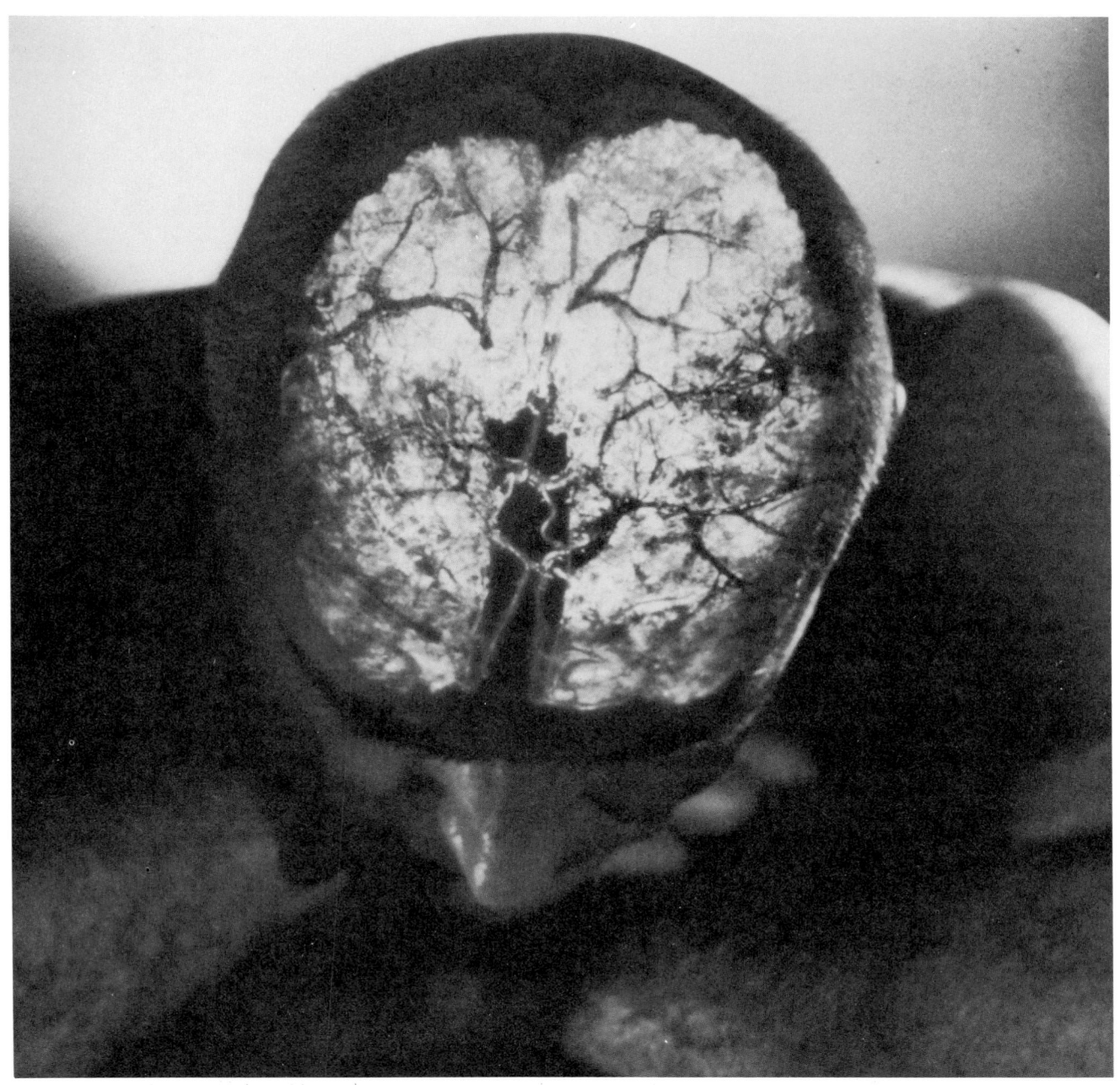

BIOLOGICAL FOUNDATIONS OF BEHAVIOR

— CHAPTER OBJECTIVES —

To achieve the objectives of this chapter, you should be able to answer the questions listed here. You should also be able to define the important terms and concepts listed at the end of the chapter.

1. What are the basic components of the neuron, or nerve cell? How do neurons transmit information to one another?

2. How is the nervous system organized?

3. What are neurotransmitters? Why are they important? What effects do they have on behavior?

4. List the major cortical areas and their functions.

5. What techniques are available for studying brain function?

6. What is known about specialization of function in the two cerebral hemispheres? What types of studies are conducted to answer this question?

— CHAPTER OUTLINE —

The Nervous System
The individual nerve cell, or neuron, is the building block of the nervous system.

Neurons and the Transmission of Nerve Impulses
Organization of the Nervous System
Application: Brain Neurotransmitters and Behavior

The Brain and Behavior
Complex processes—thinking, feeling, learning, and remembering—may one day be understood in terms of patterns of communication among the neurons of the brain.

Cortical Areas and Their Functions
Techniques for Studying Brain Function
Specialization of Function in the Two Cerebral Hemispheres
Application: ESB Works in Humans Too

On the Horizon: Brain Implants

SOME EFFECTS OF DISCONNECTING THE TWO SIDES OF THE BRAIN

She watched as Carl left the hospital. For the first time in 10 years, he was free of seizures. . . . The surgeons had literally split Carl's brain in two. She wondered which brain listened when she talked to him, which brain laughed when she told him a joke, and which brain took credit for beating her at checkers. Through the weeks, he carried on as usual: he dressed himself, went for walks, answered the phone, and read a novel. Their friends did not notice anything different about him. She was much relieved.

One morning, she entered the bedroom as he was dressing. Standing quietly in the doorway, she watched a strange spectacle. One of Carl's hands was pulling his pants up while his other hand was pulling them down. After several ups and downs, one hand finally succeeded in pulling the pants up. . . .

She forgot about this incident until one afternoon when they were in the kitchen. They were disagreeing about what to have for lunch. Suddenly, Carl grabbed her shoulder with his left hand and began to shake her violently. She was afraid and knew he was not joking. As his left hand continued to shake her, she saw that his right hand was trying to stop his left hand. The shaking stopped as the right hand gained control over the left. A few minutes later they were conversing normally, as if nothing had happened. . . . She could not help thinking that sometimes Carl's right brain did not know what his left brain was doing. (Plotnik & Mollenauer, 1978, p. 197)

Carl is one of many patients who have undergone brain surgery to alleviate severe epileptic seizures (Gazzaniga, 1970). As described later in this chapter, the purpose of the split-brain operation is to disconnect the two sides of the brain, thereby preventing a seizure that begins in one hemisphere from spreading to the other hemisphere. By studying split-brain patients, who have had the connecting fibers cut, it is possible to examine each hemisphere of the brain independently and to determine the functions for which each is specialized.

This chapter is about the human nervous system and how it works. Many techniques have been used to study nervous system–behavior relationships, as we will soon see. But first we will examine the organization of the nervous system, including the all-important brain.

— THE NERVOUS SYSTEM —

Let's reflect for a moment on the events associated with such a seemingly simple behavior as picking up this book, opening it to this page, and beginning to read.

First, a thought must have taken form within your brain, prompting a desire to read the book. Next came the order to reach over to the book, grasp and lift it, and open its pages. The subtlety of one simple activity of the human hand exceeds the complexities of the most sophisticated computer; so does the visual perception involved in recognizing a few letters on a printed page. Yet picking up the book and seeing some words are minor accomplishments compared with the far more remarkable feat of thinking about the book and formulating the plan to read it. (Paraphrased from Synder, 1982, p. 172)

How can we explain the wondrous events associated with picking up a book and reading it? The explanation lies within the **nervous system,** a cellular network that processes input from the sense organs (the eyes, for example) and regulates information flow to the muscles and body organs. How does the nervous system translate sensory input into information the brain can interpret? How does the brain communicate this information to other parts of the body? Answers to these questions are found in the behavior of individual nerve cells, called **neurons.** As the basic units of the nervous system, neurons specialize in transmitting and receiving information.

Later, we will examine the overall organization of the nervous system. But first let's become more familiar with neurons and how they communicate.

Neurons and the Transmission of Nerve Impulses

The nervous system is composed of about 100 billion nerve cells, or neurons, as well as *glial cells,* whose number is also large. Glial cells surround and support networks of neurons, insulate the neurons from one another, and provide the neurons with nutrients.

Although no two neurons are identical in form, most have certain features in common. A diagram of a typical neuron is shown in Figure 2–1. Like glial cells, all neurons have a nucleus, or *cell body,* where metabolism takes place. Unlike glial cells, however, neurons have dendrites and axons—fibers that extend from the cell body. **Dendrites** are short fibers that branch out around the cell body. Their function is to receive messages from other neurons and carry them to the cell body. **Axons** are nerve fibers that extend from the cell body and transmit messages to other neurons or to the muscles and body organs. Dendrites tend to cluster like tree branches around the cell body; axons may be very short or as long as 3 feet. Many of them are coated with a white fatty substance called the *myelin sheath,* which insulates them and speeds the transmission of neural messages.

— Nerve Impulses

The electrical activity that travels down the axon when the cell body is stimulated is called the **nerve impulse.** The activity can be measured and recorded with special equipment. For example, thin wires or fluid-filled glass tubes, called *microelectrodes,* can be inserted into the axon. As a nerve impulse travels past an electrode, electrical activity is detected and recorded on an oscilloscope (see Figure 2–2).

Figure 2–1.
A typical nerve cell, or neuron. Stimulation of the dendrites or cell body initiates an action potential in the form of electrical activity that travels along the axon to the terminal buttons. This activity constitutes the nerve impulse.

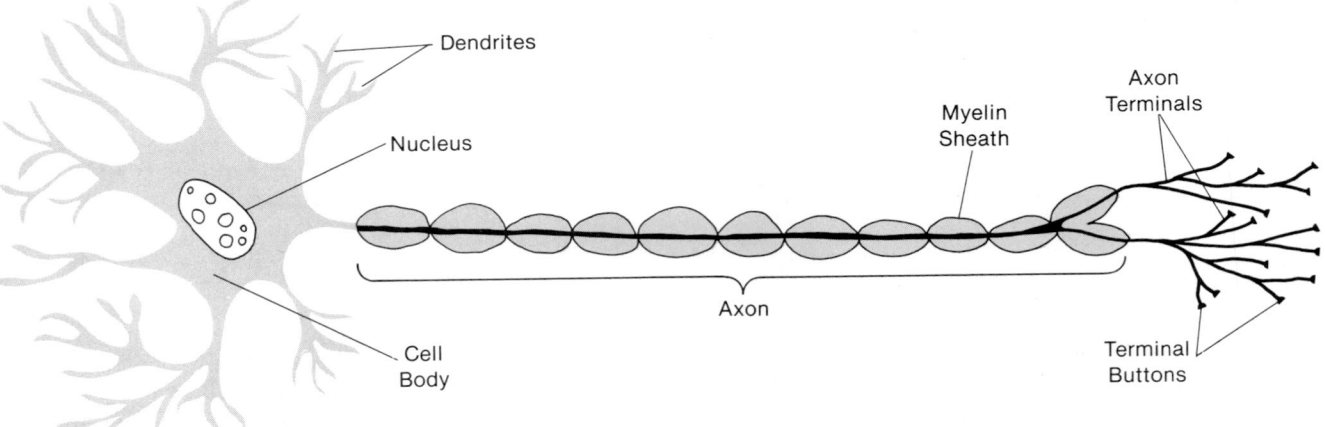

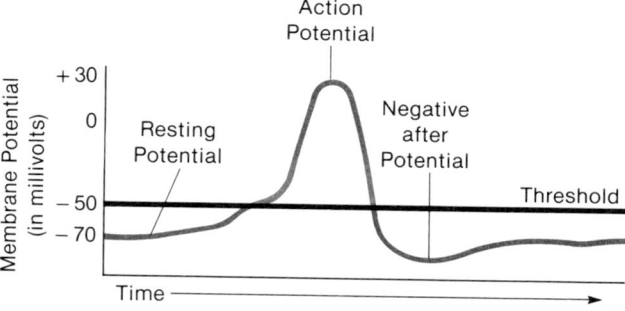

Figure 2–2.

Action potential. Stimulation of a nerve cell initiates an action potential when sodium ions are allowed to enter the cell. Potassium ions flow out, thus causing a reversal in the cell's electrical potential.

Let's examine in detail the transmission of impulses. Each neuron is filled with a fluid that contains electrically charged particles, called *ions.* A similar fluid surrounds the neuron. The surrounding fluid is about 10 times richer in *sodium ions* than is the fluid inside the neuron. In contrast, the fluid inside is about 10 times richer in *potassium ions* than is the outside fluid (Stevens, 1979). In a resting state (when the neuron is not firing an impulse) the cell allows potassium ions to enter through tiny pores in the cell membrane, but it keeps out sodium ions. The result is a small difference in electrical potential across the cell membrane, called the *resting potential.*

A nerve impulse begins when a neuron is stimulated either by another neuron or by a stimulus from outside the body. (A *stimulus* is any form of physical energy to which an organism is capable of responding.) The stimulus produces a rapid change in the cell membrane at the point of stimulation. Sodium ions are allowed to enter the cell while potassium ions flow out. This causes a reversal in electrical potential, known as the cell's *action potential* (see Figure 2–2). The action potential travels along the length of the axon in much the same way that a spark travels along the fuse of a firecracker. This activity constitutes the nerve impulse. The exchange of sodium and potassium ions along the axon is accomplished by a mechanism known as the *sodium-potassium pump.* The typical neuron has about 1 million such pumps and the capacity to move more than 200 million ions per second (Iversen, 1979).

After an action potential, the cell returns to its original resting potential by restoring the concentration of potassium and sodium ions inside and outside itself.

For a fraction of a second following an action potential, however, the neuron cannot fire another impulse no matter how intense the stimulus. This period is called the *absolute refractory period.* For a fraction of a second following the absolute refractory period, the neuron can fire another impulse, but stronger-than-normal stimulation is required. This period is called the *relative refractory period.* Once the neuron returns to its resting state, nerve impulses can be initiated normally.

All neurons have a *threshold value* that must be reached before an action potential occurs. A very weak stimulus will not cause an action potential. If, however, the intensity of a stimulus exceeds a neuron's threshold, then an action potential will occur. The stimulus causes either a full-strength action potential or none at all. This is referred to as the *all-or-none law of action potentials.* As the law suggests, the stimulus intensity is unrelated to the size of the action potential.

If the size of an action potential is not influenced by the intensity of a stimulus, how can neurons convey information about differences among stimuli? First, stimulus intensity can be coded by the rate of nerve impulses. Although the action potential for any given neuron travels at the same velocity, there is a wide range in the rate at which different neurons fire nerve impulses. Heavily myelinated neurons are capable of firing 1,000 impulses per second, although most fire at a rate of from 1 per second to several hundred per second (Stevens, 1979). Second, the intensity of a stimulus is related to the number of neurons that fire. For example, if someone slaps you on the back, many more neurons will be stimulated than if you are lightly tapped on the shoulder. Thus, some stimuli in the environment are experienced as being more intense than others because they exceed the firing thresholds of more neurons than do other, less intense stimuli.

— Synaptic Transmission

For the nervous system to function as a unit, each neuron must be able to communicate with other neurons. How do nerve impulses get from one neuron to another? The axon provides a pathway for nerve impulses leaving the neuron's cell body. Tiny fibers, which have enlarged tips called *terminal buttons,* branch at the end of each axon. A nerve impulse is transmitted from one neuron to the next at the junction, known as a **synapse,** between the terminal buttons and dendrites or cell bodies of adjacent neurons (see Figure 2–3). There, the impulse is relayed by chemicals,

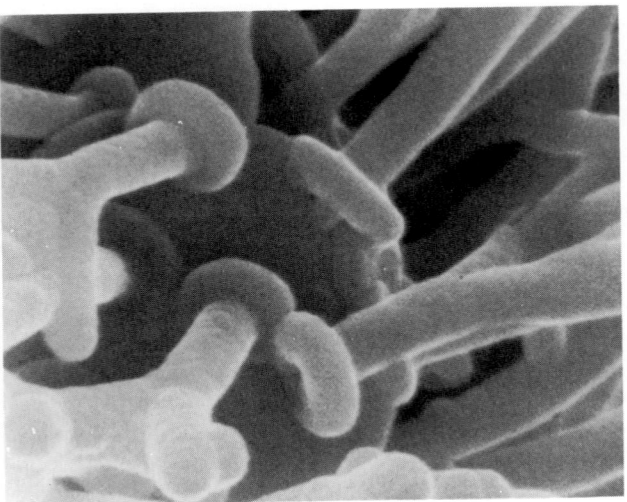

Figure 2–3.
Photograph showing tiny nerve fibers with terminal buttons.

Figure 2–4.
Synaptic transmission. When the nerve impulse reaches the terminal buttons, it causes neurotransmitters to be released into the synaptic cleft. The chemical substances attach to receptor sites on the dendrites or cell body of an adjacent neuron; the electrical potential of the receiving neuron is thereby altered thus initiating another action potential.

called **neurotransmitters,** which are released from the terminal buttons and activate the next neuron. Some important features of the synapse are shown in Figure 2–4.

Synaptic transmission, then, is an electrochemical process, which begins when a nerve impulse arrives at a dendrite, altering the resting potential of the cell body. When the cell's threshold is reached, a new nerve impulse is triggered and travels along the axon to the terminal buttons. The terminal buttons contain many small pockets, called *synaptic vesicles,* each of which can hold several thousand molecules of a chemical transmitter. When the nerve impulse reaches the terminal buttons, it causes neurotransmitters to be released into the *synaptic cleft,* or gap, that separates the two neurons. The chemical then diffuses across the synaptic cleft and attaches to receptor sites on the dendrites or cell body of an adjacent neuron. This event usually alters the electrical potential of the receiving neuron. If the threshold of that neuron is reached, the whole chain of events is repeated.

At least two types of synapses occur between neurons. *Excitatory synapses,* as just described, move neurons toward their firing thresholds. *Inhibitory synapses* move neurons away from their firing thresholds. Although it has been known for many years that synaptic transmission in both instances is a chemical process,

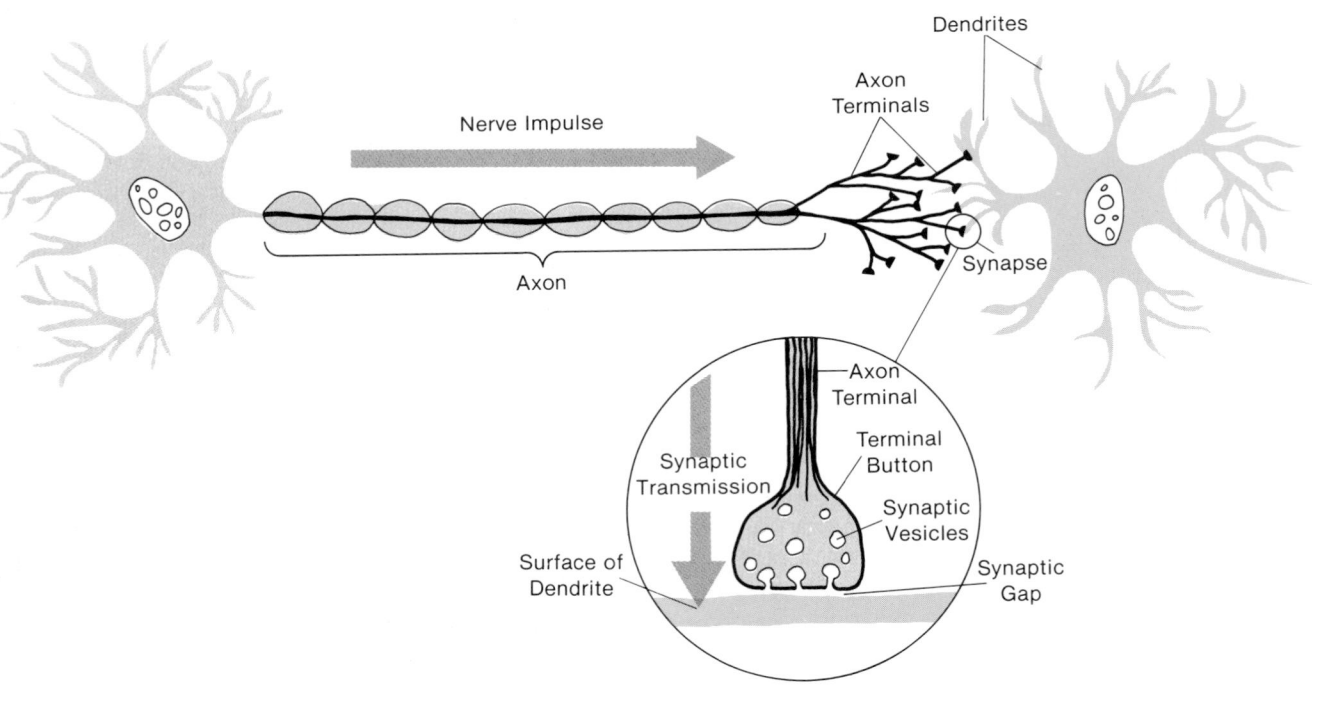

Nerve Impulse

Dendrites

Axon Terminals

Axon

Synapse

Synaptic Transmission

Axon Terminal

Terminal Button

Synaptic Vesicles

Surface of Dendrite

Synaptic Gap

the mystery surrounding the number of possible neurotransmitter chemicals is far from solved. Nonetheless, research on these chemical messengers is progressing rapidly. As we will indicate in the application section later in the chapter, this research has profound practical implications for understanding human behavior.

Organization of the Nervous System

The nervous system is far more complex than is implied by the simple strings of neurons just described. Single neurons may connect with thousands of others throughout the nervous system. Moreover, **nerves,** consisting of bundled groups of axons, branch out to all parts of the body. How can this tangle of cells and fibers be broken down into parts relevant to behavior? The process begins with a distinction between the peripheral and central nervous systems (see Table 2–1). The **central nervous system** consists of the brain and the spinal cord. The **peripheral nervous system** consists of all neural tissue that connects the brain and spinal cord with other parts of the body.

— The Brain

The soft, convoluted (folded) mass of neural tissue located within the skull is the **brain.** The portions of the brain that appear whitish (*white matter*) consist of myelinated nerve tissue; those that appear grayish (*gray matter*) consist of unmyelinated nerve tissue and cell bodies. This structure of the central nervous system governs and coordinates physical movements and such mental activities as sensation, perception, awareness, learning, memory, language, thought, and emotion.

The human brain is the most complex interconnected physical structure known—more complicated by far than the largest computer. It has been estimated that it contains as many neurons as there are stars in

Table 2–1.
Organization of the nervous system.

CENTRAL NERVOUS SYSTEM	PERIPHERAL NERVOUS SYSTEM
Brain	Somatic nervous system
Forebrain	Autonomic nervous system
Midbrain	Sympathetic system
Hindbrain	Parasympathetic system

our galaxy—somewhere between 10 billion and 100 billion. Since the typical neuron may have anywhere from 1,000 to 10,000 synapses, it is likely that the number of synapses in the brain is on the order of 100 trillion (Hubel, 1979). After considering the number of interactions among neurons in the brain, Snyder (1982) concluded that even with the newest technology, a comparable computer would fill a 10-story building—covering an area the size of Texas, or approximately 267,000 square miles.

Although much remains to be learned, many interesting facts are known about how the human brain develops. For example, nearly all of the neurons present in the fully mature adult brain are present at birth, when the nerve cells lose their ability to divide. The brain continues to grow in weight, however, from about 350 grams at birth to about 1,400 grams (approximately 3 pounds) at maturity. This continued growth in brain weight is due mainly to the increase in the size of individual cells, the buildup of myelin around the axons of nerve cells, and the proliferation of glial cells, which by adulthood are about 10 times as numerous as neurons.

Although much is known about brain development, how neurons make specific connections that create various parts of the brain remains largely a mystery. Also, we are only beginning to understand how different parts of the brain function. Two interrelated branches of *neurobiology* (the science of the nervous system) attempt to address these issues. *Neuroanatomy* seeks to describe the particular brain parts, or structures, and their organization. *Neurophysiology* seeks to describe how the various parts of the brain operate, or function. For convenience, neuroanatomists divide the brain into three major parts—the hindbrain, the midbrain, and the forebrain. These structures of the human brain are shown in Figure 2–5.

The forebrain. The largest division of the human brain is the **forebrain,** which consists of numerous structures, such as the cerebrum, the limbic system, the hypothalamus, and the thalamus.

The **cerebrum** is the largest portion of the forebrain; it consists of two *cerebral hemispheres,* the right and the left, and the *cerebral cortex,* or outer layer. The grayish cerebral cortex is made up of unmyelinated axons and cell bodies. It is the portion of the brain that has evolved most recently and is more highly developed in humans than in any other animal. Its size may be larger than one might first imagine. If one were to spread out this convoluted portion of the

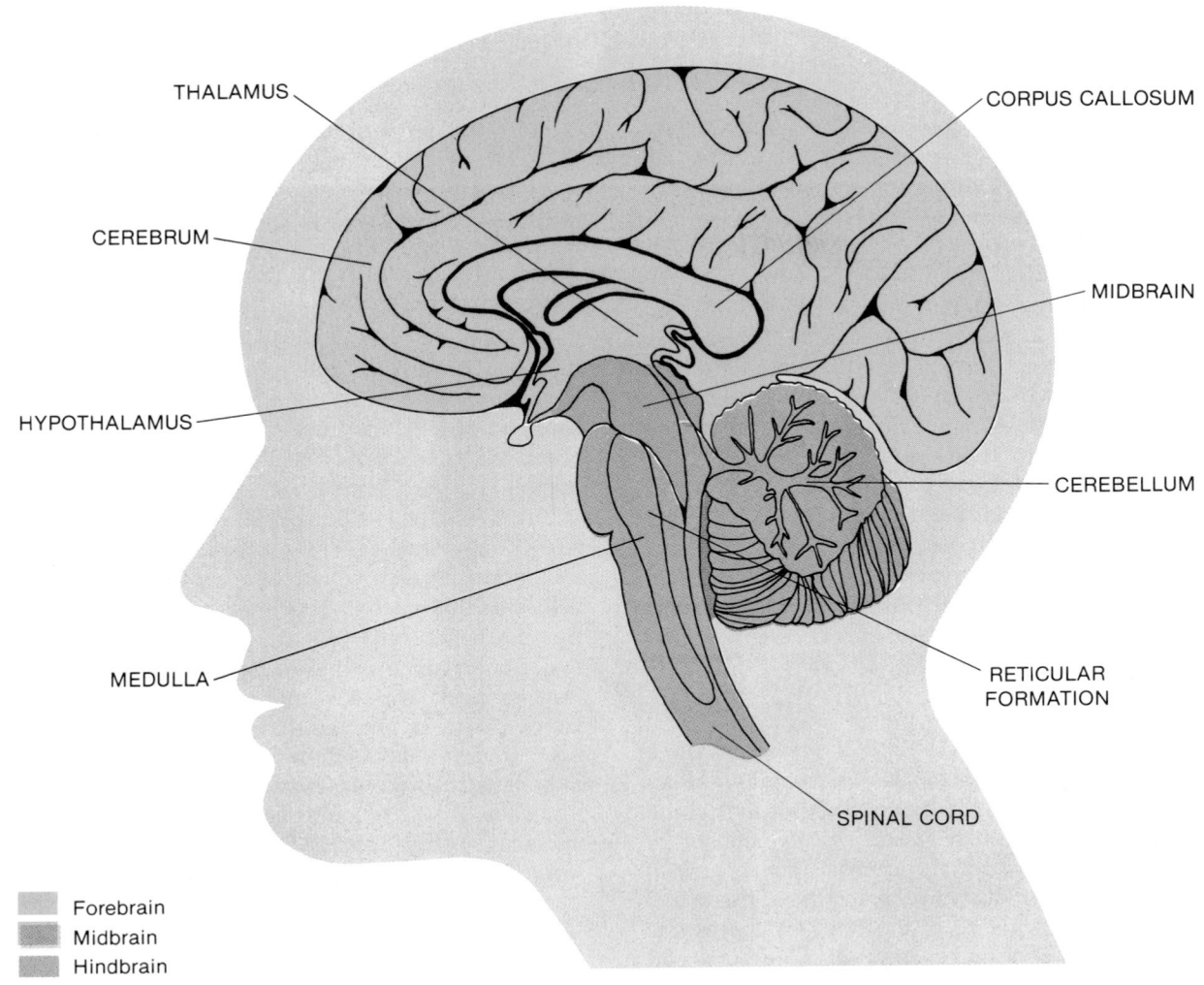

THALAMUS

CEREBRUM

HYPOTHALAMUS

MEDULLA

CORPUS CALLOSUM

MIDBRAIN

CEREBELLUM

RETICULAR FORMATION

SPINAL CORD

Forebrain
Midbrain
Hindbrain

Figure 2–5.
Major structures of the human brain. (Adapted from Coon, 1983.)

brain, as if uncrumpling a piece of paper, it would cover an area of about 2 square feet. The *gyri,* or rounded portions of brain tissue (shown in Figure 2–5), allow a large surface area of cortex to fit inside a small skull. Notice also the numerous *sulci,* the narrow folds between the gyri. One of them runs down the middle of the cerebrum from front to back and divides the cerebrum into the right and left cerebral hemispheres. The **corpus callosum** is the bundle of nerve fibers that connects the right and left hemispheres and provides a pathway for communication between them. It is primarily the corpus callosum that

allows one hemisphere to know what the other is doing (as was discussed in the chapter introduction). As we will see later in this chapter, the two hemispheres of the cerebral cortex are believed to be specialized for different functions. Their specialization gives rise to the popular right brain–left brain concept.

The **limbic system** (not shown in Figure 2–5) is an interconnected series of brain structures involved in emotional behavior, sexual behavior, aggression, and memory formation. One portion of this system is the **hypothalamus,** the part of the forebrain involved in regulating hunger, rage, thirst, sleep, and sex. The

thalamus, also part of the limbic system, relays nerve impulses from the sense organs to the cerebral cortex.

The midbrain. A second major division of the human brain, the **midbrain,** contains densely packed neurons that are involved primarily in controlling eye movements and relaying visual and auditory information to higher brain centers. The **reticular activating system,** which extends through the midbrain and sends nerve fibers into the forebrain, is a brain structure involved in arousal, attention, and the sleep-waking cycle.

The hindbrain. The part of the brain believed to have evolved first is the **hindbrain.** It is involved in controlling digestion, blood flow, and breathing—functions considered to be automatic and necessary for survival. The **medulla** is the portion of the hindbrain responsible for regulating heartbeat, breathing, body temperature, digestion, blood pressure, and swallowing. A second portion of the hindbrain, called the **cerebellum,** governs body balance and coordination.

— The Spinal Cord

The portion of the central nervous system that connects the brain to various parts of the peripheral nervous system is the **spinal cord.** Nerve fibers within the spinal cord provide the pathway for nerve impulses transmitted from the brain to the muscles and body organs and from the sense organs to the brain.

Although all neurons transmit information, different types of neurons specialize in carrying messages either to or from the central nervous system. **Sensory neurons,** also called *afferent neurons,* are nerve fibers that carry nerve impulses from the sense organs to the spinal cord and brain. They receive their messages from specialized receptor cells located in the eyes, ears, nose, tongue, skin, muscles, and joints. (Chapter 3 provides a detailed account of how these specialized receptors translate physical stimulation in the environment into nerve impulses.) **Motor neurons,** also called *efferent neurons,* are nerve fibers that carry nerve impulses from the brain and spinal cord to other parts of the body. These neurons bring messages from the central nervous system to the muscles that control body movement and to the muscles that control the functioning of various body organs, including the heart, the eyes, and the bladder. A helpful way to remember these specialized neurons and the functions

they serve is through the SAME acronym: *Sensory = Afferent; Motor = Efferent.*

The simplest set of connections between neurons is found in the spinal cord, where sensory neurons connect directly with motor neurons. The well-known *knee-jerk reflex* is an example of a behavior carried out without the brain's help. (A *reflex* is an automatic, unlearned response to a stimulus.) The neural pathway of the knee-jerk reflex, called the *reflex arc,* is illustrated in Figure 2–6.

To experience this reflex, sit on a table, cross your legs, and tap your knee, just below the kneecap, with a rubber hammer or other solid object. Your leg will jerk uncontrollably. Stimulation from the tap causes sensory neurons to carry an impulse from the knee to the spinal cord. In the spinal cord, the sensory neu-

Figure 2–6.

Neural pathway in the knee-jerk reflex.

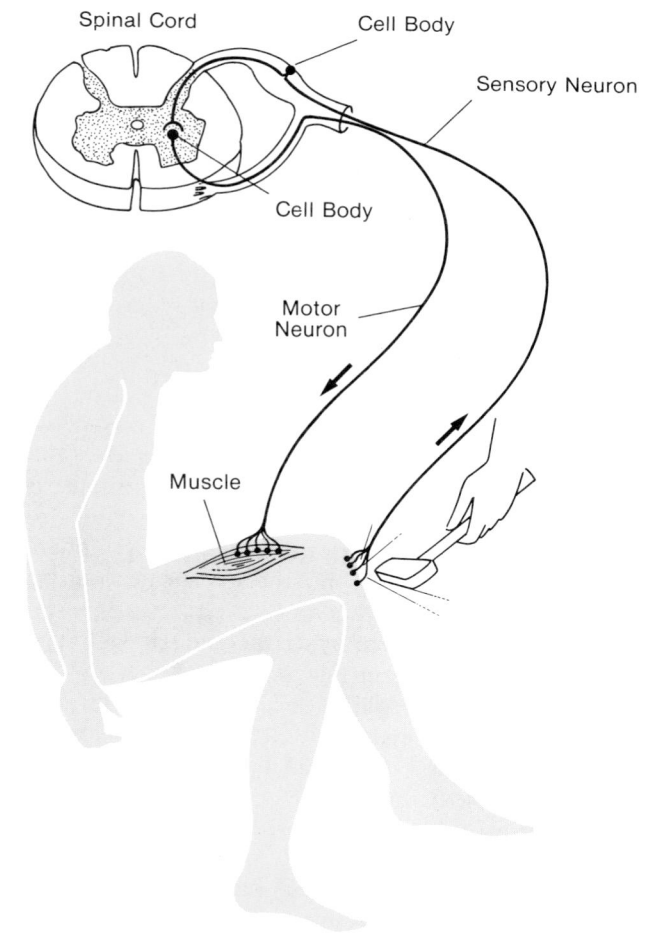

rons connect with motor neurons that lead from the spinal cord back to the the thigh muscles, thereby completing the sensory-motor (reflex) arc. This type of simple behavior pattern does not involve the brain; only the spinal cord and sensory and motor neurons are involved.

Although simple reflexes, such as the knee-jerk reflex, may involve only sensory and motor neurons, more complex reflexes involve another type of neuron. These neurons are called **interneurons** (sometimes referred to as *association neurons*) because they connect and integrate the activities of sensory and motor neurons. Interneurons carry messages between sensory and motor neurons within the brain and spinal cord. They are not required for the knee-jerk reflex to occur; however, it is only when nerve impulses reach the brain—via nerve fibers leading from the interneurons—that you become aware that your knee has been tapped.

The importance of neurons that lead from the spinal cord to the brain has been demonstrated in studies of *paraplegics*—people whose spinal cords have been injured or severed. Such people are paralyzed below the point of injury and are thus unable to move their legs voluntarily. Reflexes that involve only sensory and motor neurons in the spinal cord remain intact below the point of injury. The knee-jerk reflex, for example, can be caused by tapping the knee of a paraplegic. Because interneurons leading to the brain have been severed, however, the person will be unable to feel the leg moving.

— The Peripheral Nervous System

As mentioned earlier, the *peripheral nervous system* consists of nerve fibers that carry nerve impulses outward from the spinal cord and brain to the muscles and organs of the body and inward from sensory receptors to the spinal cord and brain. The peripheral nervous system is divided into the somatic nervous system and the autonomic nervous system.

The **somatic nervous system** is the part of the peripheral nervous system that consists of sensory neurons that lead to the spinal cord and brain from receptors in the sense organs and of motor neurons that lead from the brain and spinal cord to the skeletal muscles that move the body.

The **autonomic nervous system** is the part of the peripheral nervous system that controls body functions normally considered to be automatic, or involuntary, such as the heartbeat and the operations of the smooth muscles of the stomach, the intestines, the blood vessels, and various other internal organs. *Smooth muscles* are so named because they appear to be smooth, not *striated* (as are the skeletal muscles in the arms and legs). Thus, one important distinction to be made between the two parts of the peripheral nervous system is that the somatic system controls the striate muscles and the autonomic system controls the smooth muscles.

As shown in Figure 2–7, the autonomic system can be subdivided into the sympathetic and parasympathetic systems. Although many organs of the body receive input from both the sympathetic and parasympathetic systems, these two divisions of the autonomic nervous system differ in both structure and function.

The **sympathetic system** plays a dominant role in preparing the body to react during times of emergency or stress by speeding up the heart, dilating the pupils, and slowing down digestion. It also diverts blood from the internal organs to the skeletal muscles to prepare them for action. It can be said that the sympathetic system is especially useful in preparing the body for fight or flight (see chapter 14).

The **parasympathetic system** is the part of the autonomic nervous system that is most active during periods when the body is relaxed. As Figure 2–7 shows, it affects many of the same organs as does the sympathetic system. The two systems, however, tend to act in opposing ways. For example, the sympathetic system causes the heart rate to increase, whereas the parasympathetic system causes the heart rate to slow. Because of the physiological processes that each system initiates, sympathetic arousal is associated with nervous tension, whereas parasympathetic arousal is associated with calmness. These two parts of the autonomic nervous system maintain an internal balance so that normal body functions occur smoothly.

— The Endocrine System

The central and peripheral nervous systems are not the only mechanisms that regulate body functions. The nervous system works closely with the **endocrine system,** which consists of numerous *glands,* located in different parts of the body, that release chemicals into the bloodstream (see Figure 2–8). The chemicals, called **hormones,** which are produced in the glands of the endocrine system, travel through the bloodstream and affect a wide range of physiological activities and behaviors.

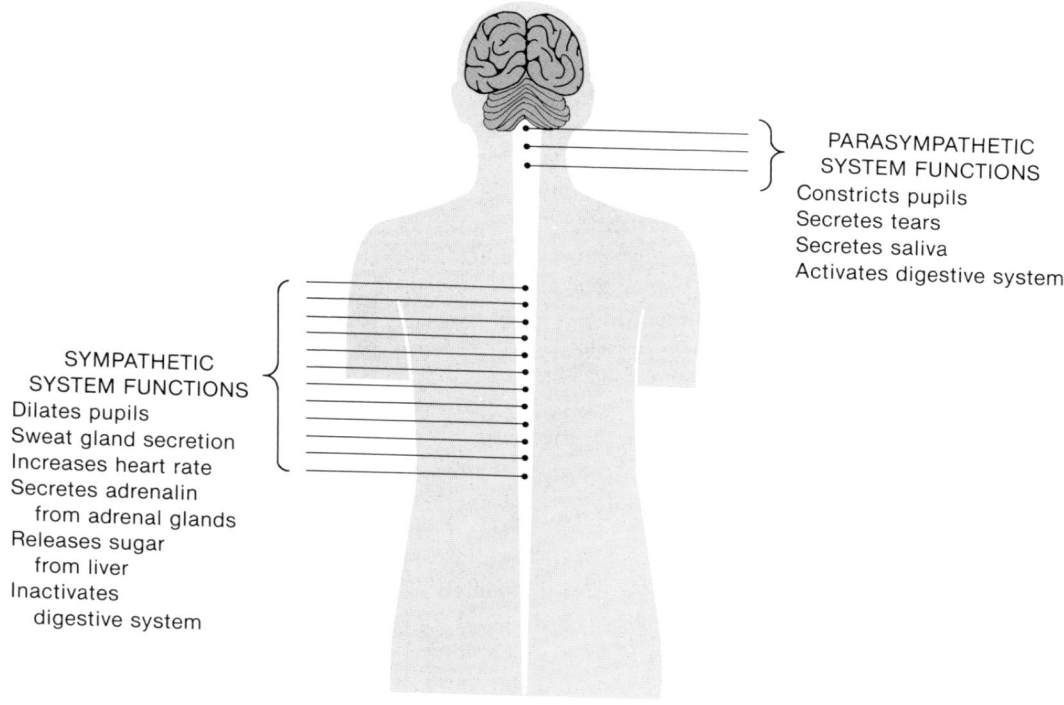

Figure 2-7.
Functions of the sympathetic and parasympathetic systems of the autonomic nervous system.

PARASYMPATHETIC
SYSTEM FUNCTIONS
Constricts pupils
Secretes tears
Secretes saliva
Activates digestive system

SYMPATHETIC
SYSTEM FUNCTIONS
Dilates pupils
Sweat gland secretion
Increases heart rate
Secretes adrenalin
    from adrenal glands
Releases sugar
    from liver
Inactivates
    digestive system

Because hormones are released into the blood, their effects on behavior are slower than those of the nervous system. Nonetheless, these chemical messengers are as critical as neurons to the overall functioning of the organism. Let's take a close look at the vital pituitary and adrenal glands.

The pituitary gland.   Located in the brain, the **pituitary gland** is called the master gland of the endocrine system because it controls the other glands. It produces and releases at least eight hormones, but we will examine only a few of them. One of the most important is the *antidiuretic hormone (ADH)*. This substance is actually manufactured in the hypothalamus and transported to the pituitary by way of nerve axons. It acts on the kidneys, causing them to decrease the amount of water that is drawn from body tissue and passed to the kidneys. Normally, the hypothalamus causes the pituitary to release ADH at a relatively slow rate. However, when the body is hydrated (from excessive water intake), the release of ADH stops completely. In this case, the amount of urine excreted is vastly increased. *Oxytocin* is another important hormone released by the hypothalamus and transported to the pituitary. It acts on the smooth muscles and is

Figure 2-8.
The endocrine system.

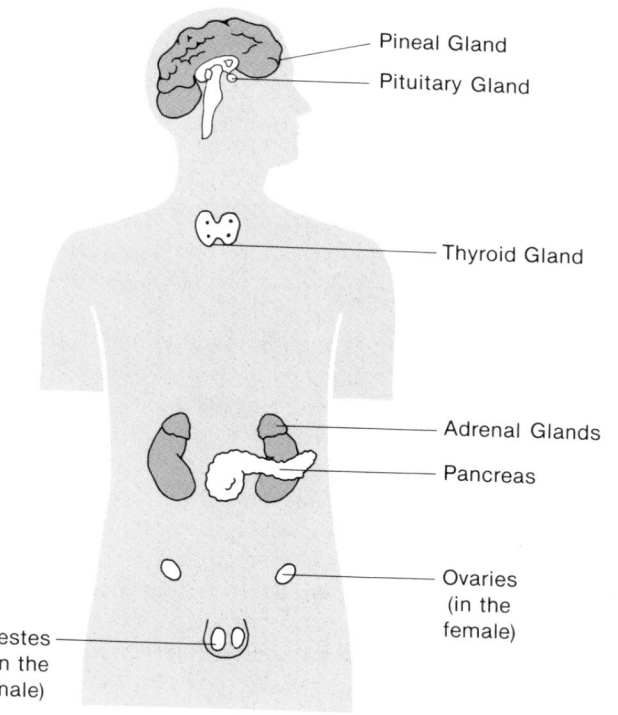

Pineal Gland
Pituitary Gland
Thyroid Gland
Adrenal Glands
Pancreas
Ovaries
(in the
female)
Testes
(in the
male)

important in a variety of body functions, such as contracting the uterus during childbirth and producing milk in the mammary glands. (Oxytocin is also believed to play a role in memory; see chapter 7.)

Certain hormones are transported from the hypothalamus to the pituitary gland by way of tiny blood vessels. These hormones stimulate the pituitary to release several additional hormones. Three such hormones act on the *gonads,* or sex glands (see chapter 17). Another is a *growth hormone,* which affects the growth of the body, including bone and soft-tissue development. Too little of this hormone can produce a dwarf; too much can produce a giant (see Figure 2–9).

The adrenal glands. Located above the kidneys, the **adrenal glands** secrete various hormones, including sex hormones (see chapter 17) and those that help the body cope with stress (see chapter 14). Two hormones released from the *adrenal medulla* (the inner portion of these glands) are *epinephrine* (also called *adrenaline*) and *norepinephrine* (also called *noradrenaline*). These hormones work in conjunction with the sympathetic part of the autonomic nervous system. As will be discussed in chapter 14, they act to prepare the body for emergency action by making the heart beat faster, increasing blood pressure, and directing blood away from the digestive tract and to the muscles of the body. In addition, they are of critical importance in synaptic transmission.

Figure 2–9.
Dwarf and giant.

BRAIN NEUROTRANSMITTERS AND BEHAVIOR

Epinephrine was the first clearly identified neurotransmitter. The landmark discovery was made by T. R. Elliott in 1905, when he was a graduate student (Kalat, 1981). At first, Elliott's breakthrough was not readily accepted, because most scientists believed that nerve impulses were transmitted electrically. Now, it is known that neural transmission is a chemical and an electrical process. The number of known chemical neurotransmitters has grown to over 30 in recent years (Iversen, 1979). There may, in fact, be well over 100 of them (Snyder, 1982). Why has there been such a flurry of research on these chemicals? As noted by Snyder (1982),

"Of all aspects of brain functioning, it is this one that we can most easily modify medically" (p. 180).

The many possible applications of research on neurotransmitters are suggested by what is already known about their effects on behavior. For example, one of the best-understood neurotransmitters is *acetylcholine* (*ACh*), which is involved in the transmission of nerve impulses between motor neurons and skeletal muscles. Substances that interfere with the action of ACh produce paralysis. For example, certain nerve gasses developed for chemical warfare cause ACh to accumulate in the synaptic cleft, eventually making synaptic transmission impossible. The poisonous venom of the black widow spider produces a similar effect. Other substances block the action of ACh. *Curare,* for instance, is a substance once used by South American Indians to poison arrow tips. The Indians found that a small amount of curare was enough to completely paralyze an attacker (Evarts, 1979). Another poisonous substance, *botulin,* can develop in improperly canned foods. Ingestion of the poisoned foods can be fatal if the smooth muscles that regulate breathing become paralyzed.

ACh may also affect the formation and maintenance of memories (for review, see chapter 7 and McGaugh, 1983b). This hypothesis is supported by research with patients suffering from *Alzheimer's disease,* a condition associated with memory loss during the later years of life. Six independent groups of researchers have now reported that the brains of some patients with Alzheimer's disease contain significantly decreased concentrations of *choline,* the enzyme that makes ACh (Kolata, 1981). Would choline supplements provide an effective treatment or possible prevention of memory impairments in patients with the disease? Studies designed to answer this question are currently underway. For example, Richard Wurtman and his colleagues have demonstrated that the administration of choline increases synthesis of ACh in the brain (cf. Blusztajn & Wurtman, 1983; Wurtman, 1982). Moreover, their research indicates that *lecithin* (the food constituent found predominantly in egg yolks, soybeans, and liver, which provides a rich source of choline in adult diets) also increases brain levels of the neurotransmitter ACh. However, whether Alzheimer's disease will one day be treated nutritionally by choline supplements remains speculative—especially since structural abnormalities also appear in the brains of victims. Nonetheless, it can be concluded from available evidence that Ach plays an active and complex role in human behavior.

Neurotransmitters that are believed to inhibit pain are among the most exciting chemical messengers discovered in recent years. Some neurons in the brain appear to have specific receptor sites for pain-relieving drugs, such as morphine, as well as for two recently discovered classes of naturally produced brain opiates, the *endorphins* and *enkephalins.* Like morphine, these neurotransmitters are believed to inhibit pain. Researchers now suspect that the key to the centuries-old use of acupuncture may be provided at least in part by an understanding of these brain chemicals. **Acupuncture,** a pain-blocking technique developed in China, involves the insertion of thin needles into certain body areas. Although the technique has been used for several hundred years and has been found to work for many people, the Chinese explanation of it is largely metaphysical. Recent studies, though, suggest that acupuncture works by triggering the release of endorphins or enkephalins in the brain and spinal cord (Watkins & Mayer, 1982). It has also been suggested that the pain associated with running may likewise stimulate the production of the natural brain opiates. Regular runners commonly report the feeling of euphoria after running—which may explain why many runners become addicted to the sport.

In addition to their role in inhibiting pain, it is likely that the brain's natural opiates influence emotional behavior and mood states. It has long been known, for instance, that opium (the drug from which morphine is derived) relieves not only pain but also anxiety and depression and promotes a sense of well-being. (See chapter 5 for further elaboration of this topic.) It is now believed that certain disorders, such as depression and schizophrenia, are in some cases related to chemical imbalances in the brain. (The application of neurotransmitter research to the treatment of such disorders is reserved for discussion in chapter 15.)

— THE BRAIN AND BEHAVIOR —

Cortical Areas and Their Functions

Figure 2–10 shows that the brain is divided into four major sections, or *lobes.* The central fissure divides the *frontal lobe* from the *parietal lobe.* The lateral fissure divides the *temporal lobe* from the frontal and parietal lobes. The *occipital lobe,* not bordered by a major fissure, is located at the rear of the brain. As we will see, these areas of the cerebral cortex have different functions.

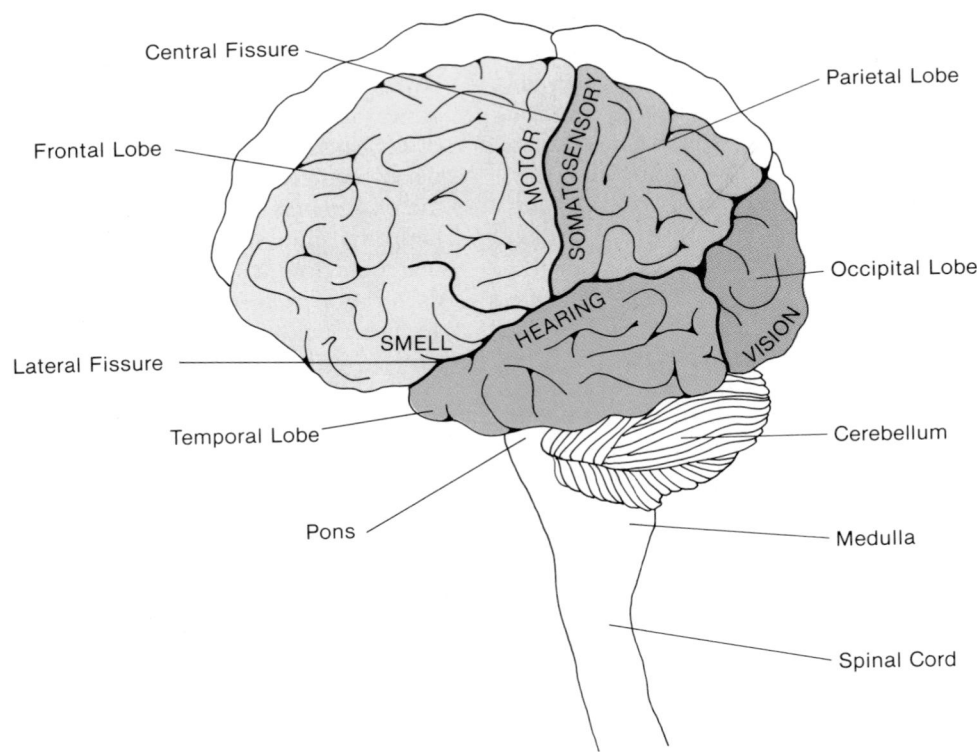

Figure 2-10.
Cortical areas are divided into four major sections, or lobes.

— Motor Cortex

Voluntary movements of the body are controlled by the **motor cortex** of the frontal lobe. A large portion of the motor cortex is devoted to the face (including the lips and tongue), the hands, and body areas that require fine muscular control. Movements of the right side of the body are controlled by the left motor cortex, and left-body movements are controlled by the right motor cortex.

— Somatosensory Cortex

The **somatosensory cortex** of the parietal lobe is involved in the senses of touch, heat, cold, and pain, as well as in body movement. When this area is stimulated electrically (a procedure described later), it gives rise to sensory experiences, as though a part of the body were being touched or moved. For example, nerve cells in the somatosensory cortex respond to both finger movement and differences in surface textures (Darian-Smith, Sugitani, Heywood, Karita, &

Goodwin, 1982). An injury or disease that affects the somatosensory cortex usually disturbs sensations but rarely causes their complete loss. A person with such an injury may be unable to make fine distinctions between similar temperatures but will still be able to distinguish between hot and cold.

— Auditory Cortex

The area of the temporal lobe that is specialized for receiving and responding to sound stimuli is the **auditory cortex** (see Figure 2-10). Some neurons in this area of the brain respond only to high-pitched sounds; others respond only to low-pitched sounds (Carlson, 1981).

— Visual Cortex

The portion of the occipital lobe that is highly specialized for receiving and responding to visual stimuli is the **visual cortex** (see Figure 2-10). When light strikes the eye, neural activity is initiated. As can be seen in Figure 2–11, the neural message is transmitted along nerve fibers in the *optic nerve,* through the *optic chiasm,* and into the visual cortex of the occipital lobe. The **optic chiasm** is the point at which the optic nerves from both eyes meet and cross. Neural messages from the right side of each eye are relayed to the right occipital lobe; those from the left side of each eye end up in the left occipital lobe. In this way, roughly half of the nerve fibers in each eye connect with each hemisphere. These pathways are diagrammed in Figure 2–11.

Figure 2–11.
Neural pathways for vision. Neural messages are transmitted along nerve fibers in the optic nerve, through the optic chiasm, to the visual cortex of the occipital lobe.

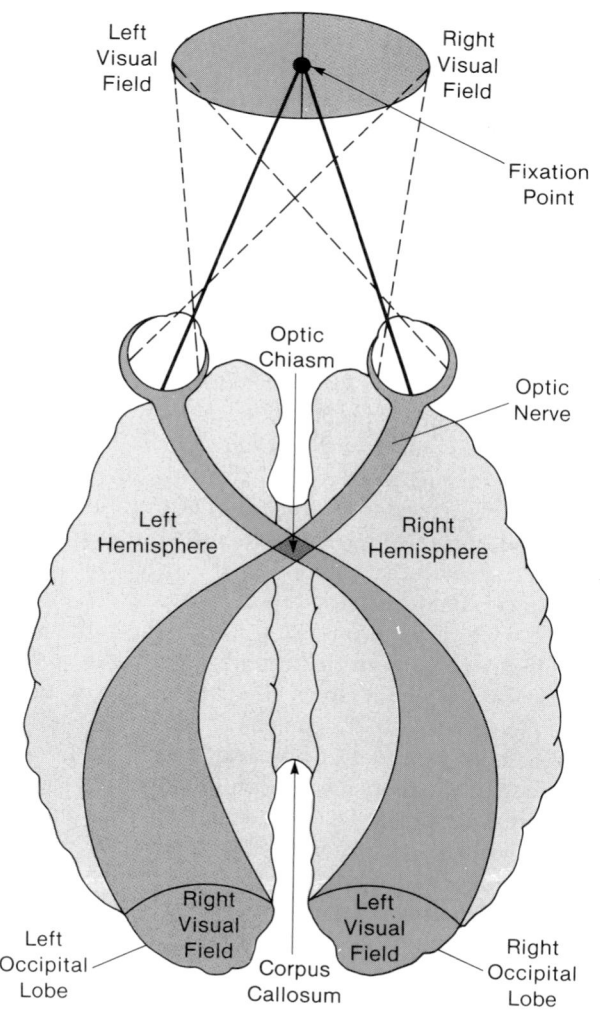

If, during the course of surgery, the visual areas of the brain are electrically stimulated, patients report seeing flashes of light. Similarly, if the visual cortex is damaged, loss of vision is likely.

— Association Areas

Portions of each of the lobes of the cerebral cortex are known as the **association areas.** Together, these areas are involved in thinking and problem solving and are responsible for organizing, storing, processing, and integrating information from the senses.

Techniques for Studying Brain Function

A fundamental question at this point is: How are the functions of specific brain areas identified? A variety of approaches are used to study brain and behavior relationships. They include techniques that utilize lesions and ablations, clinical observations, radiation, electrical stimulation, electrical recordings, and behavioral testing.

— Lesion and Ablation Techniques

The oldest techniques for studying brain function are lesioning and ablation. A **lesion** is an intentional injury of a particular area of the brain. **Ablation** is the removal of a particular part of the brain. Much of what we know about brain function comes from lesion and ablation studies. Lesions made in specific areas of the rat hypothalamus, for example, cause extreme overeating and obesity. Lesions made in an adjacent area of the hypothalamus can cause a rat to stop eating unless it is force-fed (cf. Teitelbaum & Epstein, 1962; see also chapter 9). Results from animal studies may one day lead to a better understanding of eating disorders in humans. One particularly devastating eating disorder, called *bulimia,* involves an uncontrollable urge to overeat. Victims gorge on food and then violently purge themselves by vomiting to avoid gaining weight. Another eating disorder is *anorexia nervosa,* a lack of appetite leading to self-imposed starvation. The latest research suggests that both disorders may have a physiological basis in the brain (cf. Seligmann, 1983). (A more detailed discussion of eating disorders is provided in chapter 9.)

— Clinical Observations

For obvious ethical reasons, most lesion and ablation studies have been conducted on laboratory animals. In humans, however, such studies are possible with patients who have suffered accidental brain damage. Any resulting loss of function can then be observed.

It might be expected that damage to the visual area from, say, a blow to the back of the head would result in partial or complete blindness. Indeed, when the rear portion of the brain is removed, the result is blindness—in humans as well as in various experimental animals. It is still a mystery, however, how a blow to the head can, on rare occasions, restore sight. Such was the case of Joseph Sardler who saw his five-year old daughter, Tammy, for the first time after stumbling and falling headlong down his basement stairs. Sardler, who had been blind for six years prior to the fall, struck his head against the wall during his tumble and regained his sight.

It is far more common for blows to the head to be associated with signs of brain damage, such as memory loss. Boxing may be particularly dangerous because the boxer's goal is to inflict shock on the brain of the opponent until the opponent loses consciousness. Although boxing's specific effects are unknown, a study that examined 40 ex-boxers found a significant relationship between the number of bouts fought and the extent of brain injury (Ross, Cole, Thompson, & Kim, 1983).

Specific effects of brain damage are sometimes evident in persons who have sustained head wounds. One instructive example is the case of James Brady, who was shot during the assassination attempt on Ronald Reagan in March 1981. A bullet tore through Brady's right cerebral hemisphere, cutting a swath from the frontal lobe to a point just above the ear (Clark & Lindsay, 1981). With his left hemisphere largely spared, Brady is able to speak, read, and write, although with some difficulty. Damage in the right hemisphere crippled the left side of his body and impaired his control over emotions. After the shooting, Brady had difficulty suppressing such reactions as laughing and crying and would frequently burst into sobs. He has gradually learned to suppress emotional outbursts by using deep-breathing and related exercises.

The consequences of brain damage may be serious and far-ranging. For example, tumors—abnormal growths of brain tissue—have been implicated in bizarre, aggressive acts of violence. Consider the case of Charles Whitman. In the summer of 1966, Whitman climbed to the top of a University of Texas tower. From there he shot and killed 13 people and wounded 31 others before he was killed by police officers. An autopsy of Whitman's brain revealed a tumor pressing against the amygdala, a part of the limbic system involved in emotional response. When an animal's amygdala is stimulated, the animal shows signs of fear, fleeing, and rage (Nolte, 1981). Was Whitman's tumor the cause of his bizarre outburst of aggression? Although we will never know the answer to this question, the case of Charles Whitman suggests the range and severity of the consequences that may result from brain damage.

Even though lesion and ablation studies are informative, they cannot be relied on exclusively. Every behavior depends on interconnecting networks of neurons in the brain. When one particular part of a network is damaged, it is possible for the entire network to be affected, at least to some extent. When parts of the brain are experimentally damaged, everything in the immediate area, including brain cells and tissue, may also become damaged. Thus, neurons that are responsible for carrying information to other parts of the brain and nervous system may be adversely affected. When this occurs, it is almost impossible to assign the effects of damage to any particular part of the brain. Therefore, other techniques must be used to determine the exact function of particular brain sites.

— Radiation Techniques

An exciting technique for studying brain function is a recently developed modification in x-ray technology called positron emission tomography, or PET. The **PET scanning technique** involves injecting subjects with a radioactive substance and monitoring its action within the brain using a special sensor (Snyder, 1982). When a radioactive sugar substance injected into a subject's bloodstream reaches the brain, the sensor detects the presence of positrons (atomic particles emitted by the substance). The greatest numbers of positrons are emitted by the brain areas that are the most active while the subject is performing various tasks. The sensor detects the amount of positrons emitted and translates the information into a color-coded map of the brain's response. The PET scanning technique thus allows researchers to observe brain functioning and to locate specific areas involved in various physical and mental activities. The technique has great potential for diagnosing some forms of mental disorder (see chapter 15).

— Stimulation Techniques

Electrical stimulation of the brain (ESB) involves inserting into the brain a tiny electrode through which a weak electric current is passed. Specific brain sites can be activated, and any resulting behavior can then be observed. The first such studies were reported in 1870 by Fritsch and Hitzig (cited in Kalat, 1981), who electrically stimulated the cerebral cortex of a dog. As noted by Kalat, depending on the exact point stimulated, the dog moved different parts of its body—its head or legs, for example. The investigators also succeeded in making the dog wag its tail.

In a landmark experiment, Olds and Milner (1954) implanted permanent electrodes into the brains of rats. The electrodes allowed ESB to be delivered while the rats walked about in their cages (see Figure 2–12). Experimentation soon showed that the animals would move to any spot in a cage if they received electrical stimulation to the limbic system when they got there. It appeared that the rats were actively seeking the brain stimulation. To further test this hypothesis, Olds and Milner placed individual rats in a cage with a lever at one end. Each time a rat pressed the lever, it received a brief brain stimulation. When parts of the hypothalamus were stimulated, the animals pressed over and over again. A hungry rat would often ignore available food in favor of the pleasure of stimulating itself electrically. "Some rats stimulated their brains more than 2000 times per hour for 24 consecutive hours!" (Olds, 1972, p. 298).

Delgado (1963) demonstrated that ESB could be used to inhibit aggressive behavior in a large, aggressive male monkey named Ali. Ali was known to frequently attack Elsa, one of two small female monkeys who lived in the same cage as Ali. An electrode was implanted into Ali's brain, and the cage in which the monkeys lived was equipped with a lever for pressing. When the lever was pressed, Ali received a brief electrical current. The stimulation tended to immediately halt Ali's aggressive attacks. Not only did Elsa learn to press the lever to ward off her attacker, she also learned that she could tease Ali. Elsa would look straight at Ali and make threatening faces (behaviors that evoke retaliation in monkeys) and then stop his attack by pressing the lever.

Electrical stimulation techniques such as those described here have been put to practical use with human patients. An upcoming application section will describe some of the uses.

Figure 2–12.

A rat receives brief electrical stimulation of the brain each time it presses the lever. Some animals have been seen to stimulate themselves as often as 5,000 times an hour.

— Recording Techniques

Another means for studying brain-behavior relationships involves recording electrical activity in the brain. Typically, an electrode is placed near or in direct contact with the brain site being studied. As mentioned previously, for example, **microelectrodes** (thin electrodes usually made of glass or wire) can be inserted into the cell body of a neuron to measure the electrical activity of a single nerve cell. Studies using this technique are described in chapter 3.

Electrodes can also be placed on the scalp and connected to a recording device, called an *electroencephalograph,* that plots the brain's electrical activity on a piece of paper. The **electroencephalogram (EEG)** provides a continuous record of electrical activity from neurons that underlie the scalp electrodes. The EEG has been quite useful in studying brain activity during sleep (see chapter 5) and for diagnosing a variety of disorders, such as epilepsy, the condition briefly mentioned in the chapter introduction. Notice the difference in EEG recordings obtained from a normal sub-

Normal Adult EEG

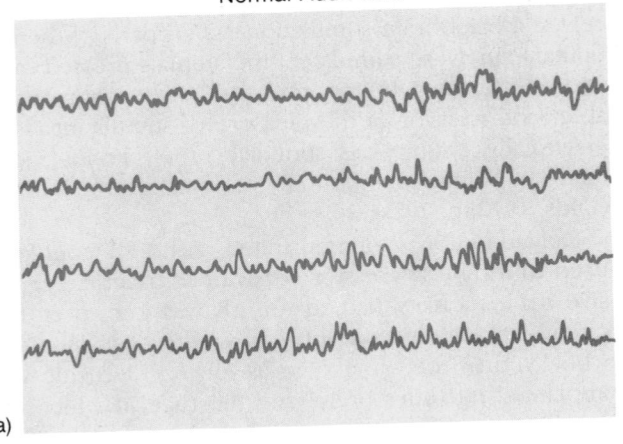

(a)

Epileptic Adult EEG (during seizure)

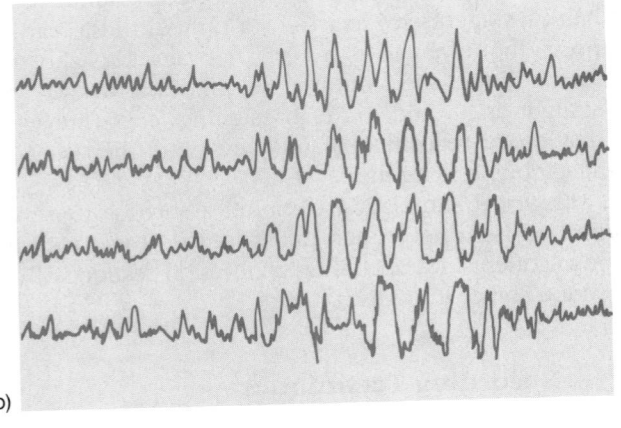

(b)

Figure 2–13.
EEG recordings from subjects: (a) normal and (b) epileptic.

ject (Figure 2–13a) and from a subject with epilepsy (Figure 2–13b).

Suppose that an investigator wants to record the brain's response to a specific stimulus, such as a tone, a light, or a word. This can be accomplished using the **evoked-potential technique,** which provides a record of the brain's electrical activity following a specific stimulus. Typically, the stimulus is presented to the subject 20 to 30 times, and the brain's response is recorded with scalp electrodes. A computer is used to average the brain's response to the stimulus. Electrical activity unrelated to the stimulus will average to zero. The pattern of electrical activity caused by the stimulus is called an *evoked potential.*

Like the EEG, the evoked-potential technique has many applications. One such application has been de-

veloped by David Shucard and his colleagues. Shucard, Shucard, and Thomas (1977), for example, demonstrated that the amplitude of evoked potentials recorded from the cerebral hemispheres to pairs of tones was related to differential hemispheric engagement in ongoing cognitive activity. Their technique is called the *two-tone probe technique* because evoked potentials are recorded to tone pairs presented over headphones while subjects perform tasks that are hypothesized to differentially involved areas of the right and left cerebral hemispheres. Since the tones remain constant across different tasks the subjects perform, any hemispheric differences in evoked potentials recorded to the tones can be attributed to differences in hemispheric activation due to the task rather than to the tones.

Results from the first study using the technique (reported in 1977), showed that when adult subjects were presented verbal information they produced higher amplitude evoked potentials recorded from the left hemisphere to the probe tones. Conversely, when the same subjects were presented musical information they produced higher amplitude evoked potentials recorded from the right hemisphere to the probe tones. No differences in hemisphere responding were found during a baseline condition in which pairs of probe tones were superimposed on background noise. Another study using the technique found that the pattern of evoked-potential activity for the right and left hemispheres of children with reading disabilities was opposite to that of age-matched control children with normal reading skills (Shucard, Cummins, & McGee, 1984).

Recording techniques such as those described here offer great promise for the development and refinement of diagnostic tests to help identify children with learning disabilities (cf. Hillyard & Kutas, 1983).

— Behavioral Techniques

A variety of other techniques are used to measure brain functioning. Included are dichotic-listening and tachistoscopic techniques (Bryden, 1982).

In the **dichotic-listening technique,** two different spoken messages (words, for example) are simultaneously presented, one to each ear, over headphones. Subjects are asked to attend to both messages and to recall later as much of both of them as possible. Subjects tend to recall words presented to the right ear more accurately than words presented to the left ear. Input to the right ear is transmitted to auditory areas of the left cerebral hemisphere. Consequently, the finding has typically been interpreted as reflecting a greater left-hemisphere specialization for speech.

The **tachistoscopic technique** allows the study of brain functioning by testing a subject's recall of visual information presented simultaneously to each eye. Typically, a slide projector is used to project information on a screen. If you look again at Figure 2–11, you will see that stimuli presented in either the right or left visual field will be transmitted to the contralateral (opposite) hemisphere. The subject's eyes must be focused straight ahead on a fixed point on the screen, and the stimulus must be presented on the screen for no longer than 200 milliseconds; otherwise involuntary eye movements make the stimulus available to both eyes (Sergent, 1983). The tachistoscopic technique has been used in numerous studies to determine which hemisphere processes visual information more efficiently.

Specialization of Function in the Two Cerebral Hemispheres

Cerebral specialization of function is the hypothesis that the two cerebral hemispheres are specialized for different higher mental functions. As noted by Geschwind (1979):

> That the human brain is not fully symmetrical in its functioning could be guessed from at least one observation of daily experience: most of the human population favors the right hand, which is controlled by the left side of the brain. Linguistic abilities also reside mainly on the left side. For these reasons the left cerebral hemisphere was once said to be the dominant one and the right side of the brain was thought to be subservient. In recent years this concept has been revised as it has become apparent that each hemisphere has its own specialized talents. Those for which the right cortex is dominant include some features of aptitudes for music and for the recognition of complex visual patterns. (p. 108)

How is cerebral specialization of function studied? How do we know that areas of the right cerebral hemisphere are specialized for certain functions and that areas of the left are specialized for other functions? Let's examine results from some studies using techniques previously described.

— Split-Brain Studies

In the early 1960s, a surgical technique was devised to alleviate severe seizures in patients suffering from **epilepsy,** that, as mentioned in the chapter introduction, is a disorder caused by abnormal activity of neurons in the brain. During an epileptic episode, the abnormal activity, which begins in one area of the brain, spreads to other areas, sometimes causing a seizure. There are several types of epileptic seizures, some more serious than others. In a *grand mal seizure,* for example, the hyperactivity of brain neurons causes the person to lose consciousness and fall to the ground, the limbs rigid. Often, anticonvulsant drugs can prevent seizures; however, some people do not respond to drug therapy. For example, in Carl's case (see chapter introduction) the corpus callosum was cut to prevent the abnormal activity from spreading from one hemisphere to the other. The **split-brain technique,** which involves severing the thick band of neural tissue that connects the two cerebral hemispheres, has been used successfully as a last resort to reduce the frequency and severity of epileptic seizures (Gazzaniga, 1970).

Normally, the right and left hemispheres of the brain communicate with one another via some 200 million interconnecting nerve fibers. Surprisingly, patients who have had the split-brain operation are usually able to function normally in their daily routine. Most of them go undetected in a casual conversation and even in an entire routine medical examination (Sperry, 1982).

Systematic studies of split-brain patients have unlocked some of the mysteries of how the brain works. There remains a controversy concerning right-hemisphere language in split-brain patients: whether it exists at all and, if so, to what extent (for example, see Gazzaniga, 1983; Levy, 1983b). Nonetheless, it has been apparent from the earliest split-brain studies that the right hemisphere is not mentally retarded, as once believed; it just lacks the words necessary to inform investigators of its specialized abilities. Today it is widely recognized that areas of the left hemisphere are specialized for verbal, analytic, speech, and language functions, whereas areas of the right hemisphere are specialized for nonverbal, nonanalytic, visual-spatial functions—"the kind in which a single picture or mental image is worth a thousand words" (Sperry, 1982, p. 1225). Let's consider in more detail the split-brain research that led to these conclusions. (It was for this line of research that Roger Sperry was awarded the Nobel Prize in 1981).

Figure 2–14 illustrates a situation typically used for testing split-brain subjects. The subject's eyes are focused on a point straight ahead on a screen. Using the tachistoscopic technique described earlier, a word, such as *spoon,* is flashed for one-tenth of a second on the left side of the screen (see Figure 2–14a). The visual information is then relayed via the optic pathways to the right hemisphere of the brain (which controls the left side of the body). As a result, the subject can pick up the spoon with the left hand if asked to do so. However, when asked what was flashed on the screen, the subject cannot say, because language is served primarily by areas of the left hemisphere, not the right hemisphere (which received the message). In addition, since sensory input from the left hand goes to the right hemisphere, the subject is unable to tell the experimenter what the left hand was doing. This occurs because the speech area of the left hemisphere has been disconnected from the right hemisphere. It is important, however, to remember that if the image is flashed on the screen for longer than 200 milliseconds (or one-fifth of a second), then the subject's natural eye movements will allow the information to reach both hemispheres. (This is why the deficiencies caused by severing the corpus callosum are not noticeable to the casual observer.)

There is further support for the notion that language is served by the left hemisphere and that the two hemispheres do not communicate when the corpus cal-

losum has been severed. In the situation shown in Figure 2–14b, the words *oil* and *well* are flashed on the screen in such a way that the message oil is relayed to the right hemisphere and the message well is relayed to the left hemisphere. When asked what word was seen, split-brain subjects answer "well," the word transmitted to the left hemisphere. When asked what kind of well was seen, several different guesses are offered—ink well, wishing well, and so on. The subject guesses oil well only by chance. Tests with other words that are split up, such as *hat band* or *suit case,* show similar results.

Figure 2–14c illustrates another situation in which a word, such as car, is flashed on the left side of the screen in such a way that the word is relayed to the right hemisphere. When subjects are asked to write the word with the left hand, they can do so correctly. When asked what the left hand wrote, however, they can only guess. They cannot say what was written because of the lack of communication between the speech-producing left hemisphere and the right hemisphere, which was involved in both seeing and writing the word. As noted by Sperry (1982):

The speaking hemisphere in these patients could tell us directly in its own words that it knew nothing of the inner experience involved in test performances correctly carried out by the mute partner hemisphere. Lateralization of brain functions could be inferred not only from the defi-

Figure 2–14.
Procedure for testing split-brain subjects (after Gazzaniga, 1983 and Nebes & Sperry, 1971). See text for further explanation.

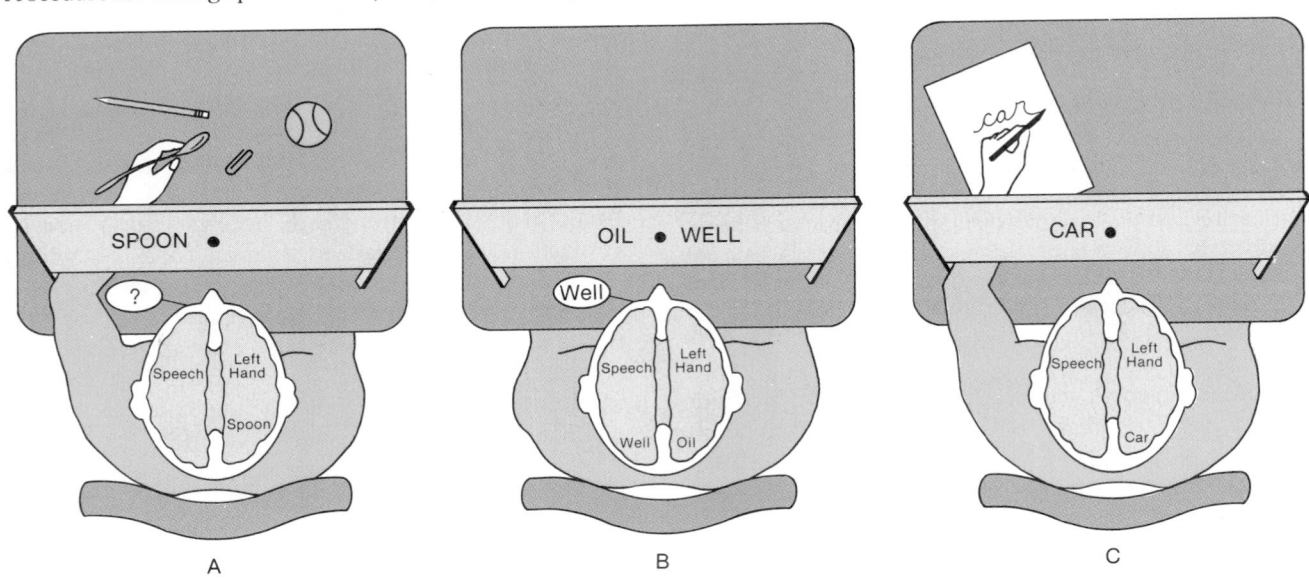

A   B   C

ciency or absence of function on one side but also from its concurrent presence on the other. (p. 1224)

The evidence from studies of split-brain subjects suggests that severing the corpus callosum creates two independent minds, or spheres of consciousness, within the same brain. That the human brain is not fully symmetrical in its functioning is a conclusion supported also by clinical observations and studies of normal persons.

— Clinical Observations

Several investigations of patients with brain lesions have demonstrated that visual-spatial abilities are more impaired by right than by left cerebral injury (Kimura, 1967). Similarly, it has been demonstrated that patients who have suffered the loss of the left temporal lobe show impaired memory for verbal information but no significant impairments on tasks that require memory for visual-spatial information, such as faces (Milner, Taylor, & Sperry, 1968).

— Studies of Neurologically Normal Persons

Other evidence for right brain–left brain differences comes from studies of normal persons. Language function was the first mental process found to be *asymmetrically* represented in the human brain, and it remains the best-documented case of cerebral specialization of function (Nebes, 1974). A right-ear (left-hemisphere) advantage for processing easy-to-verbalize stimuli, such as numbers, words, and letters, has been found in numerous dichotic-listening studies. For example, Kimura (1961) demonstrated that when pairs of contrasting digits were presented simultaneously to both ears, those presented to the right ear were more accurately reported. Conversely, a left-ear, or right-hemisphere, advantage for processing difficult-to-verbalize stimuli, such as melodies and abstract patterns of sound, has also been demonstrated. Tachistoscopic studies of normal subjects have shown a similar asymmetry between the left and right hemispheres for processing verbal and nonverbal information (Kimura, 1966).

Studies such as these further support the conclusion that areas of the right hemisphere are specialized for nonverbal information processing and areas of the left hemisphere are specialized for verbal information pro-

cessing. It is important to emphasize, however, that the difference in competencies of the two sides of the brain is not static. The relative degree to which the right and left hemispheres of the brain participate in complex mental activity is likely to vary from moment to moment and from task to task (Levy, 1983a). Also, general conclusions about cerebral specialization do not apply uniformly to all persons. As we will see, important differences in brain organization may exist between males and females and between right- and left-handers.

Sex-related differences in cerebral specialization of function. Articles in popular magazines suggest that there is currently no hotter issue in psychology than the study of differences in the brains of males and females (Gelman 1981; Goleman, 1978; Johmann, 1983; Konner, 1982). Indeed, there appear to be differences between males and females in precisely those intellectual abilities previously associated with opposite sides of the brain (cf. McGlone, 1980; Wittig & Petersen, 1979). Females in general perform better than males on various tasks requiring verbal or language abilities. Males in general perform better than females on various tasks requiring spatial abilities, such as the visual-spatial mental rotation skills required in engineering and architecture.

Is there a biological basis for differences in ability between the sexes? Are male-female differences in spatial and verbal abilities due to learning and differences in experience? Unfortunately, the available evidence is insufficient to draw any firm conclusions. We will examine some of this evidence in chapter 12.) Here we will only briefly look into some studies that suggest that males' brains are organized differently than are females' brains.

Some studies have found that females performing various verbal and spatial tasks tend to rely on both hemispheres (rather than one) more than do males. They are thus said to be more *bilateral* than males in their cerebral specialization of function (see, for example, Bryden, 1982; McGlone, 1980). Studies of clinical patients support this view. Observations of brain-damaged patients who have sustained injury to one or the other cerebral hemisphere show that females have a better chance of recovery than do males (Inglis & Lawson, 1981). If the left hemisphere is damaged, for example, females more often than males show recovery of lost language skills. Presumably, this is because the females' right hemisphere is more readily able than the males' right hemisphere to serve language functions.

Another finding that supports the view that females' brains are more bilaterally organized is that, on the average, the corpus callosum may be larger and more bulbous in females' brains than in males' (Lacoste-Utamsing & Holloway, 1981). It is not possible to conclude, however, that observed sex-related structural differences in the brain play a causal role in male-female differences in ability. Differences could result instead from different learning experiences while growing up. For this reason, some researchers are now investigating whether male and female babies differ in cerebral specialization of function.

Recent studies in Shucard's laboratory have involved recording evoked potentials over the right and left cerebral hemispheres while infants are presented with verbal and musical information (see, for example, Shucard, Shucard, Cummins, & Campos, 1981). Using the two-tone probe technique described earlier, Shucard and his colleagues found that the brains of female babies may function differently from those of male babies. The difference may explain why girls begin to talk earlier than boys. Three-month-old female babies who listened to music and to recorded passages of fairy tales tended to use areas of the left hemisphere more than those of the right. Three-month-old male babies, in contrast, tended to use areas of the right hemisphere more than the left. (See Figure 2–15.)

It seems safe to conclude from available clinical and experimental research that the brains of males and females are not organized in exactly the same manner. One remaining question, among many, however, is whether brain differences between the sexes play a causal role in determining male-female ability differences.

Handedness and cerebral specialization of function. The majority of both males and females in the general population (about 90 percent) are right-handed, and this situation is unlikely to change in the near future. From inspection of historical records, Coren and Porac (1977) concluded that the proportion of humans who show a preference for use of the right hand has remained relatively unchanged for more than 50 centuries. About 7 to 8 percent of the people show strong left-hand preference, and a small minority show mixed preference (McGee & Cozad, 1980). This lopsided prevalence of right-handedness may reflect the

Figure 2–15.
Evoked-potential study of brain lateralization: (left) three-month-old infant participant and (right) the laboratory equipment necessary to record the subject's brain electrical activity. Experimenters monitor the subject's record produced on chart paper and observe her and and her mother's behavior on a TV screen.

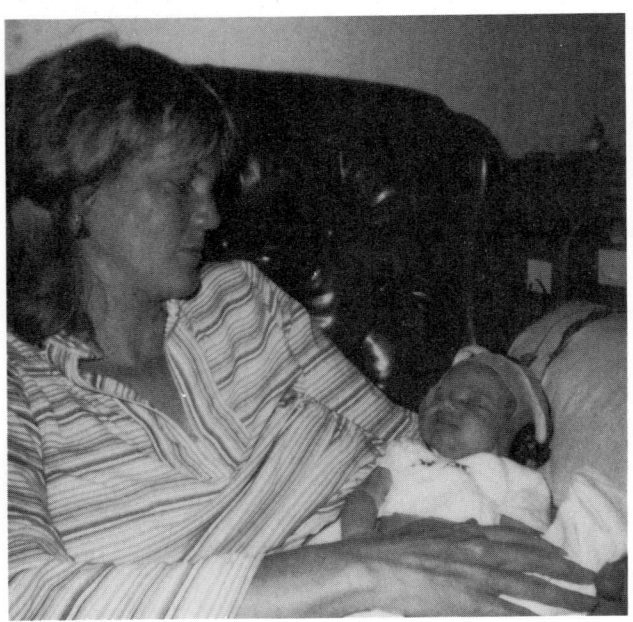

left brain's dominance for language function (Corballis, 1980). Indeed, it is true that about 97 percent of all right-handers show left-hemisphere specialization for language. Among left-handers, however, the picture is somewhat more complicated. Although we might expect left-handers to have language represented in the opposite (right) hemisphere, only about 25 percent show this pattern (Delis, Knight, & Simpson, 1983); 60 percent of left-handers show left-hemisphere specialization for language; and the remaining 15 percent tend to show bilateral language representation (Herron, 1979).

Left-handers have long been recognized as being somehow different from right-handers in cerebral specialization of function, although the differences are not well understood at the present time. In general, studies have failed to find an association between left-handedness and cognitive deficit (e.g., Newcombe & Ratcliff, 1973). Moreover, left-handedness may confer an advantage in certain areas of intellectual performance. For example, since the left hand is controlled by the right side of the brain, where visual-spatial and perhaps drawing abilities are represented, left-handers may have an advantage over right-handers in performing these skilled activities.

There is some evidence to support this view. First, there is a disproportionately high percentage of left-handers among students enrolled in schools of architecture (Peterson & Lansky, 1974), and architecture is a profession requiring a high level of mechanical and visual-spatial aptitude. Second, many great artists (among them Michelangelo, Leonardo da Vinci, and Pablo Picasso) have been left-handed (Hardyck & Petrinovich, 1977). Finally, perhaps the most important advantage of being left-handed shows up when there is brain damage. Left-handers, like females, are more bilateral in their cerebral representation of both verbal and spatial functions. Consequently, they have a better chance than their right-handed counterparts to recover from the effects of injury to either side of the brain (cf. Herron, 1979).

— APPLICATION —
ESB WORKS IN HUMANS TOO

Olds and Milner's (1954) discovery that rats seemed to experience pleasure from electric current delivered to certain portions of the brain raises an interesting question: Can human behavior be controlled with electrical stimulation of the brain? For obvious ethical reasons, psychologists have not experimented on human subjects to find out. However, ESB has been used for legitimate medical and therapeutic purposes.

ESB has been used most often in attempts to surgically treat patients who have epilepsy. As mentioned earlier, epilepsy is a disorder caused by abnormal activity of nerve cells in the brain. The focus of abnormality is sometimes restricted to a small group of neurons, and in such cases the section of the brain causing the problem can be removed surgically. Patients are typically given a local anesthetic for the opening of the skull, but they remain awake during surgery. The surgeon uses an electrode to stimulate specific areas of the cerebral cortex. (There is no pain associated with the procedure, since the brain does not contain pain receptors.) During the course of the surgery, the patient might be observed to involuntarily clench a fist or jerk an arm or leg. Eventually, the surgeon may stimulate an area that makes the patient feel as though a seizure is about to begin. Once this area has been located, that section of the brain can be surgically removed, usually without any harmful side-effects. For patients who do not respond favorably to medication, surgery of this kind is generally successful in eliminating the epileptic seizures. Sometimes, however, the abnormality is widespread in one hemisphere of the brain. The split-brain operation was first devised to treat such cases (see chapter introduction).

ESB has also been used in treating patients with chronic pain. Dworetzky (1982) described the case of C.N., a man who underwent surgery to relieve pain in his lower extremities caused by a back injury. The surgeon placed a radio receiver in C.N.'s chest cavity and ran wires from the radio up through the patient's neck to his brain, where small electrodes were implanted. By pressing a button on a transmitter, C.N. can activate the radio, thereby sending a small amount of electric current to his brain. The electrical stimulation causes the release of endorphins, the neurotransmitter chemicals that are important in pain control. Now, whenever C.N. feels pain in his lower extremities, "he takes out his transmitter, presses the button, and the pain goes away almost magically for hours and sometimes days" (Dworetzky, 1982, p. 71).

ESB has also been used to treat patients with *narcolepsy*, a sleep disorder that causes people to fall asleep at inappropriate times (see chapter 5). One patient with narcolepsy had an electrode permanently implanted in his brain and attached to a portable control device. Whenever the man felt himself starting to fall asleep, he could quickly press a button on the device. This would stimulate a part of his brain that would arouse him. "If he failed to press it in time, one of his friends could go over to press it and turn him back on again" (Kalat, 1981, p. 30).

Many studies have confirmed the now-classic results reported by Olds and Milner concerning the effectiveness of ESB. Stimulation of the proper brain area can evoke eating, drinking, terror, rage, anxiety, sexual desire, sleeping, memories, speech, tears, and euphoria. Happily, ESB testing with humans has been limited to situations involving extraordinary medical need (Coon, 1983).

BRAIN IMPLANTS

Unlike glial cells and other cells that are able to regenerate themselves, brain neurons that die have been irreplaceable—until recently, that is. Researchers have found that in some cases damaged brain cells can be coaxed to regenerate by the implantation of new cells. In one particularly compelling application, Labbe, Firl, Mufson, and Stein (1983) found that learning impairments caused by damage to the frontal cortex are significantly reduced by implantation of brain cells at the lesion site. Their subjects were rats whose frontal cortexes were surgically removed. The frontal cortex is involved in tasks that require learning and memory. Eight rats received implants of frontal-cortex tissue obtained from 3-week-old rat fetuses. Six rats received implants of cerebellar tissue. A control group of seven rats had their frontal cortexes removed but did not receive implants. After implantation, all of the rats began training on a maze task that required them to alternate right and left turns in the correct order to receive water at the end of the maze. Eight rats that had not been operated on showed the best performance on the maze task. Rats receiving frontal-cortex implants performed significantly better than did the lesion group that did not receive implants; they also outperformed the group given cerebellar tissue. Most encouraging, perhaps, was the finding that the brain's capacity for recovery from injury is greater than was previously believed. After the maze-learning sessions were completed, several of the animals were further studied to determine whether the grafts had made connections with existing tissue. The grafts were clearly visible only in those rats that had been implanted with frontal-cortex tissue.

What are the potential human applications of brain-tissue implants? According to researcher Richard Wyatt (cf. Young, 1983), an immediate application once the basic research in animals is done would be in the disorders that produce relatively discrete brain damage. Such would be the case in persons with *Parkinson's disease,* a progressive nervous-system disorder characterized by muscular tremor, slowing of movement, partial facial paralysis, and weakness. Impaired motor function in Parkinson's patients results from the loss of a small number of brain cells, perhaps 2,000 to 3,000. In a series of experiments in rats, Wyatt and his colleagues treated rats with fetal-cell implants to relieve symptoms resembling Parkinson's disease in humans. Several months after the implant operations, the implanted cells were examined. The researchers observed that the grafts of tissue had grown and thrived. Electrodes placed into the cells demonstrated that the neurons were capable of firing normally. Moreover, the implanted cells produced *dopamine,* a chemical neurotransmitter lacking in the brain-damaged rats and in Parkinson's patients.

Although brain implants are in the experimental stage today, some researchers believe that they will lead to a cure for Parkinson's disease within 5 to 10 years. Eventually, it may also become possible to repair the spinal cords of paraplegics and regenerate parts of the extensively damaged brains of patients with various disorders, such as stroke, multiple sclerosis, Huntington's chorea, and Alzheimer's disease (Brain healing, 1983).

The implications of brain-implant research are as frightening as they are exciting. One difficult ethical question involves the donor. In rat studies, the donors of brain tissue are normal rat fetuses whose fetal cells are capable of growth and of ready adaptation to a new environment. In humans, as noted by Wyatt, the major question is: What will be the source of the donor tissue? (Young, 1983). Although the obvious source of human implants would be aborted fetuses, researchers hoping to avoid controversy are looking for alternatives. In the case of Parkinson's disease, it may be possible to implant dopamine-secreting cells taken from the patient's own adrenal glands (Brain healing, 1983). Since Parkinson's disease is associated with decreased concentrations of dopamine in the brain, the transplanted dopamine-

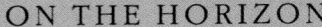
producing cells could prevent the effects of the disease. Such experiments in rats have produced favorable results. Whether similar success can be achieved in human brain implants is a problem that awaits further research.

Another equally exciting alternative is the application of recombinant DNA research in genetics to the search for neurotransmitters (cf. Bloom, 1983). Because everything that brain cells make is on instruc-

tion from their genes, recombinant DNA technology may allow researchers to find the genetic blueprints for all the key substances in the brain cells. By following those blueprints, once discovered, it is hoped that presently available cloning procedures could be used to produce dopamine-secreting cells in Parkinson's patients. Widespread application of such techniques to the treatment of human brain disorders is on the horizon.

— SUMMARY —

1. There are two different types of cells that comprise the nervous system: glial cells and nerve cells, or neurons.

2. Glial cells provide the physical framework that supports the system of neurons.

3. Neurons are the basic communicative unit of the nervous system.

4. The major parts of the neuron are (a) the cell body, which contains the nucleus; (b) numerous dendrites, which receive information for the neuron; and (c) axons, which extend from the cell body and carry the neural impulse from one neuron to another.

5. The neuron transmits information by means of the electrochemical action potential. An electrical potential is set up by means of electrically charged ions of sodium and potassium flowing in and out of the cell when the cell is stimulated. At the junction between neurons, called the synapse, chemical transmitter substances, or neurotransmitters, flow across the junction to stimulate nearby neurons and complete the transfer of information.

6. Differences in stimulus intensity are conveyed from one neuron to another by changes in frequency of the action potential and the number of neurons stimulated.

7. There are three basic types of neurons: sensory (or afferent) neurons, motor (or efferent) neurons, and interneurons, which connect afferent and efferent neurons.

8. The nervous system can be subdivided into the central and peripheral nervous systems.

9. The central nervous system consists of the brain and spinal cord.

10. The peripheral nervous system consists of the somatic and the autonomic systems.

11. The autonomic system is subdivided into the sympathetic and parasympathetic parts.

12. The endocrine system consists of numerous glands that release hormones into the bloodstream. The endocrine system and the nervous system together provide for communication between different parts of the body.

13. The brain consists of three main parts: the hindbrain, the midbrain, and the forebrain.

14. Parts of the forebrain control the glands and are responsible for speech, emotions, and mental processes.

15. The midbrain is responsible for orienting the body, as in the head turning in the direction of a light or sound. Parts of this portion of the brain are primarily involved in controlling eye movements and relaying visual and auditory information to higher brain centers.

16. The hindbrain is the division of the brain involved in controlling automatic body functions, including digestion, blood flow, and breathing.

17. The techniques used in studying how the brain functions include lesion and ablation techniques, clin-

ical observations, radiation techniques, electrical stimulation, electrical recordings, and behavioral testing.

18. Cerebral specialization of function is the hypothesis that certain higher mental functions, such as language, depend on specialized regions in the brain.

19. When the corpus callosum (the band of neural tissue connecting the two cerebral hemispheres) is severed, significant differences between the functioning of the two hemispheres can be observed. In a majority of right-handed adults, the left hemisphere is dominant in serving language and verbal functions and the right hemisphere is dominant in serving nonverbal, visual-spatial functions.

— IMPORTANT TERMS AND CONCEPTS —

Nervous System
Neurons
Dendrites
Axons
Nerve Impulse
Synapse
Neurotransmitters
Synaptic Transmission
Nerves
Central Nervous System
Peripheral Nervous System
Brain
Forebrain
Cerebrum
Corpus Callosum
Limbic System
Hypothalamus
Thalamus

Midbrain
Reticular Activating System
Hindbrain
Medulla
Cerebellum
Spinal Cord
Sensory Neurons
Motor Neurons
Interneurons
Somatic Nervous System
Autonomic Nervous System
Sympathetic System
Parasympathetic System
Endocrine System
Hormones
Pituitary Gland
Adrenal Glands
Acupuncture

Motor Cortex
Somatosensory Cortex
Auditory Cortex
Visual Cortex
Optic Chiasm
Association Areas
Lesion
Ablation
PET Scanning Technique
Electrical Stimulation of the Brain (ESB)
Microelectrodes
Electroencephalogram (EEG)
Evoked-potential Technique
Dichotic-listening Technique
Tachistoscopic Technique
Cerebral Specialization of Function
Epilepsy
Split-brain Technique

— SUGGESTIONS FOR FURTHER READING —

The Brain. (1979). San Francisco: W. H. Freeman. Originally 11 separate articles in the September 1979 issue of Scientific American; topics include the development of the brain, specializations of the human brain, and disorders of the human brain.

Gazzaniga, M. S. (1970). The bisected brain. New York: Appleton-Century-Crofts. A presentation of the details of split-brain research and a description of interesting case studies.

Herron, J. (Ed.). (1979). Neuropsychology of left-handedness. New York: Academic Press. A description of everything from the prevalence of left-handedness in artists to anatomical differences of the two sides of the brain in right-and left-handers.

Plotnik, B., & Mollenauer, S. (1978). Brain and behavior. San Francisco: Canfield Press. An entertaining and readable introduction to physiological psychology.

Rosenzweig, M. R., & Leiman, A. L. (1982). Physiological psychology. Lexington, MA: D. C. Heath. Designed for courses in physiological psychology, biological psychology, and behavioral neuroscience. A description of recent research covering many of the aspects of physiological psychology discussed in this chapter.

Springer, S. P., & Deutsch, G. (1981). Left brain, right brain. San Francisco: W. H. Freeman. A popular paperback that provides an insightful discussion of the many myths and controversies surrounding the concept of cerebral specialization of function.

— CHAPTER 3 —

SENSATION

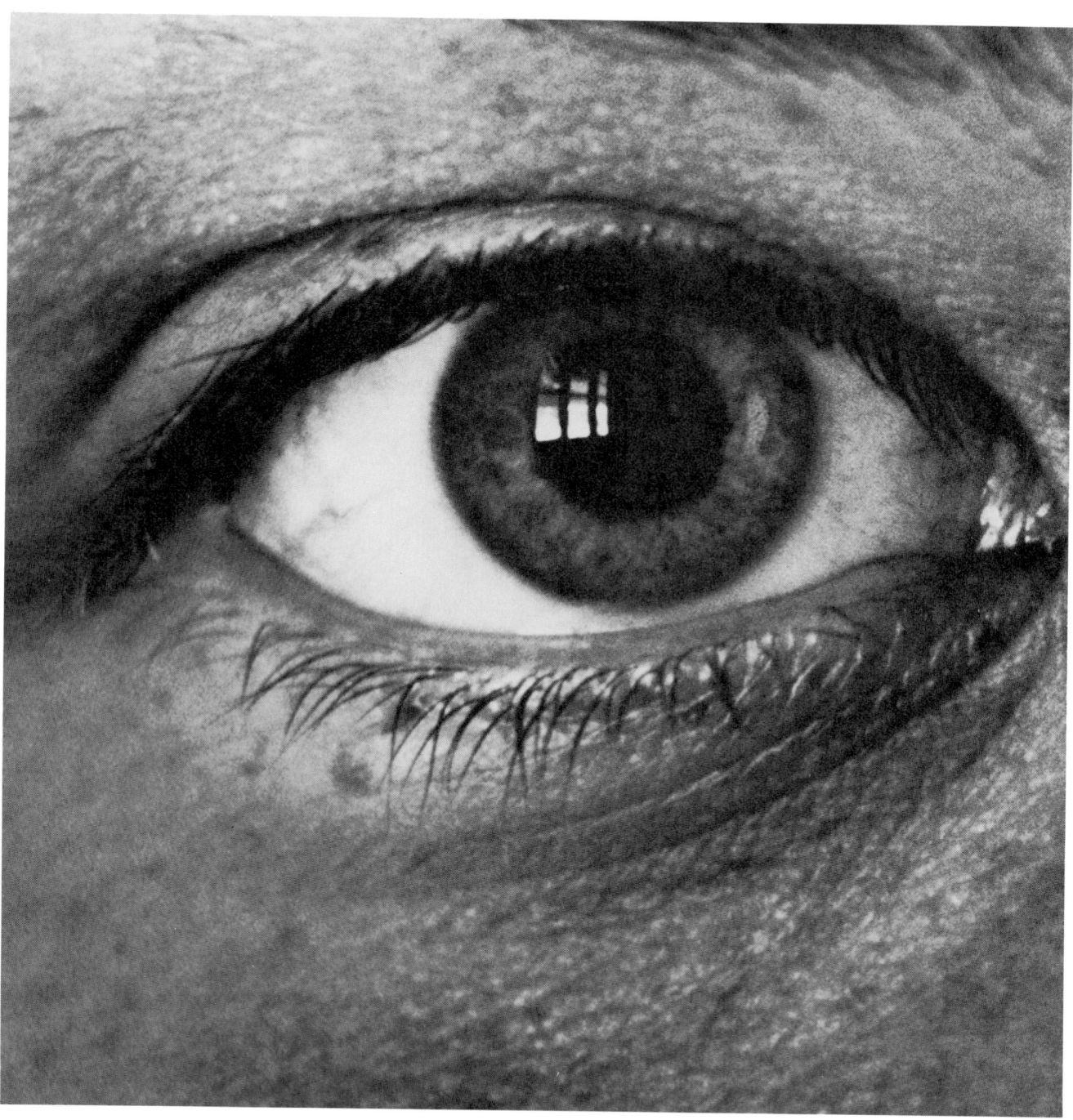

SENSATION

— CHAPTER OBJECTIVES —

To achieve the objectives of this chapter, you should be able to answer the questions listed here. You should also be able to define the important terms and concepts listed at the end of the chapter.

1. What is sensation? List the physical stimuli to which the human sense organs are sensitive.
2. Which common processes characterize the major sensory systems?
3. How is light energy translated into visual sensations?
4. What roles do the photoreceptive cells play in producing color sensations?
5. How can we account for auditory sensations and for our capacity to experience the diversity of sounds comprising the audible spectrum?
6. What are the physical energies that give rise to the sensations of smell, taste, and touch?

— CHAPTER OUTLINE —

The Measurement of Sensitivity
Psychophysical methods are used to test the sensitivity of sensory systems.

Signal Detection Theory
Application: Subliminal Stimulation

The Visual System
The visual system translates light energy into visual sensations.

Light: The Stimulus for Vision
The Structure and Function of the Human Eye Color Vision
Application: Measuring Visual Acuity

The Other Senses
Hearing, smelling, tasting, and feeling sensations are also produced by physical energy.

The Auditory System
Smell and Taste: The Chemical Senses
The Skin Senses
The Body Senses
Application: Seeing with the Skin Senses

On the Horizon: Seeing without Eyes

STIMULATION, ABOVE AND BELOW THE LIMEN

A shopper in a department store picks up a scarf, glances furtively about, crumples it up and shoves it into her pocket. Then come second thoughts. She fishes out the scarf, smooths it again and returns it to the counter. Another victory for honesty? Not quite. Credit for the would-be shoplifter's change of heart really belongs to what the store's managers call their "little black box," a kind of electronic conscience.

Basically a sound mixer like those used by disco deejays, the box mingles bland music with subliminal anti-theft messages ("I am honest. I will not steal"). Repeated rapidly—9,000 times an hour—and at very low volume, the words are barely audible to shoppers and employees. They do register in some deep recess of the brain and apparently influence behavior. (Secret voices, 1979, p. 71)

The use of subliminal messages, as described, raises some intriguing questions. To what physical stimuli are humans sensitive? What are the limits of our sensory capacities? Do subliminal messages really affect behavior?

You probably already have some notion of what the term *subliminal* means. The word comes from the Latin words *sub,* meaning "below," and *limen,* meaning "threshold." Some of the earliest research in psychology was aimed at testing sensory limits, or finding the thresholds for various senses. This research gave rise to the branch of psychology known as *psychophysics.* In the first section of this chapter, we will discuss some of the findings of psychophysics, including what they tell us about subliminal stimulation.

In the remainder of the chapter, we will move above the limen to investigate each of the major sensory systems. Your brain, like all other brains, resides in a house of total silence and darkness. Yet, you are continuously bombarded by physical stimuli: Light, sound, heat, pressure, and chemicals surround you with stimulation.

The brain's only connection to the physical world is through the sense organs, each of which is distinct and highly selective in the stimuli to which it responds. Yet, at the same time, all sensory systems have certain commonalities. Each is designed to respond most readily to a particular type of physical stimulation. Also, the path from stimulus to sensation can be traced in a similar way for each. It begins when *receptor cells* in a sense organ are activated by physical stimuli. Next, the receptor cells translate physical energy into neural energy, which is the only language interpretable by the nervous system. Finally, the message is transmitted, in the form of nerve impulses, to the brain. The type of sensation experienced—visual, auditory, and so on—depends on the specific area of the brain that receives the impulses. Each sensory system, then, combines this entire chain of events to convert an external stimulus into the psychological experience we call sensation. Before we explore the various sensory systems themselves, let's begin with a brief look at psychophysics.

Psychophysics is one of the original areas of study in psychology. Its goal is to relate characteristics of physical stimuli to characteristics of the sensations they produce. A *physical stimulus* is any form of energy to which an organism is capable of responding. **Sensation** describes the response of sensory systems, such as vision or hearing, to physical stimuli. Much early research conducted by psychophysicists focused on discovering the minimum stimulus intensity required to produce a sensation. This value is called the **absolute threshold.** Actually, there is no abrupt point at which stimuli are suddenly intense enough to be detected. Consequently, psychologists have defined the absolute threshold as the intensity at which a stimulus is detected on 50 percent of its presentations.

In concrete terms, the approximate absolute thresholds for human sensation are impressive. For vision, the absolute threshold is roughly equal in intensity to the light from a candle flame, seen at 30 miles on a clear, dark night. For hearing, the stimulus intensity is roughly the tick of a wristwatch, under quiet conditions, at 20 feet. For taste, an example of the absolute threshold is 1 teaspoon of sugar in 2 gallons of water. For touch, it is the wing of a bee falling on the cheek from a distance of 1 centimeter (Galanter, 1962). Geldard (1972) reported that the human system for smell can detect mercaptan, the scent made by skunks, at concentrations as low as 1 part mercaptan to 50 trillion parts air.

Signal Detection Theory

Historically, psychophysicists were concerned with measuring sensitivity under ideal conditions. In reality, stimuli often must be detected against a background of distracting "noise." Consider, for instance, the radar-screen operator who must decide whether a spot of light is a missile or one of the hundreds of meaningless flashes occurring each hour. **Signal detection theory** was developed to investigate such situations.

This approach abandons the idea of an absolute threshold and focuses on measuring subjects' ability to detect stimuli when the stimuli are presented against background noise (Green & Birdsall, 1978).

Let's say that you are a subject in an experiment in which you are asked to indicate with a yes or no whether you hear an auditory signal. The signal is a very quiet tone that must be detected against a background of random sounds (noise) in the room. Any given trial may produce one of four outcomes:

1. *Hit.* A hit is correct; the signal is presented and the subject says yes.
2. *Miss.* A miss is incorrect; the signal is presented but the subject says no.
3. *False alarm.* A false alarm is incorrect; the signal is absent, but the subject says yes.
4. *Correct rejection.* In a correct rejection, no signal is presented and the subject says no.

By analyzing such responses, signal detection theorists determine how detectable a stimulus is, or how sensitive subjects are to it. *Sensitivity* to signals of a particular intensity can range from very low to very high. However, signal detection theorists tell us that it is not enough to know if a person is sensitive to a signal. We must also know what criteria the person uses to decide whether or not to report the signal. For example, two radar operators with equal sensitivity to signals might differ in their willingness to sound an alarm. Similarly, one operator might exceed the other in the desire to avoid a false alarm. Their criteria for detecting a signal therefore differ.

Changing an observer's criteria alters the number of hits, misses, false alarms, and correct rejections made. It does not, however, change the underlying sensitivity. The criteria a person uses are affected by how probable the signal is and by other factors, such as the cost of misses or false alarms. Thus, by using signal detection theory, it becomes possible to test the sensitivity of sensory systems apart from the observer's bias in responding (Goldstein, 1980).

— APPLICATION —
SUBLIMINAL STIMULATION

As hinted by the chapter introduction, public concern has recently focused on whether human behavior is affected by subliminal messages broadcast over loudspeakers, whether people are being influenced by invisible suggestions to "eat popcorn" flashed during films, and the like (Brody, 1982). As signal detection theory suggests, this may be a false concern. Unless a stimulus is detectable to some degree, it can have no effect on behavior. But if a person is sensitive to a stimulus, then it is not subliminal.

To clarify the distinction, assume that a person claims to be unable to hear a test signal. Classical psychophysicists would describe the signal as subliminal. However, if the person is told to simply guess when the "inaudible" message is or is not present, the person will respond with a greater than chance level of detections. Whatever the person might say, he or she is, in fact, sensitive to the signal. This does not mean, however, that the "inaudible" message will have greater impact on the person's behavior than a clearly

audible signal would. In fact, one point that psychophysical research makes is that weaker, less intense stimulation is less likely to produce a sensation than is stronger, more intense stimulation. That is, weak stimuli exert less influence on behavior than do strong stimuli. To return to the example in the chapter introduction, a *loud* antitheft message ("the employees of this store thank you for your honesty") could have a greater impact on shoppers than would a barely audible subliminal message.

Let's turn now from sensory sensitivity to a discussion of each of the major sensory systems. We will begin with vision, the sense that provides most of our information about people, objects, and events in the environment. We will then explore the other senses: hearing, smell, taste, and touch.

— THE VISUAL SYSTEM —

The delicacy of the eyes is truly amazing. So too is their role in transforming light into images. Even more awe-inspiring, perhaps, is the realization that vision provides our closest link to the external world. How does the miracle of vision occur? The answer lies in the **visual system,** which includes all parts of the nervous system that process information from the eyes. Actually, the visual system consists of many subsystems (Wolfe, 1983). We will expore the more important of them as we trace the conversion of light energy into visual sensations.

Light: The Stimulus for Vision

Most visual sensations are produced by light energy *reflected* from the surface of objects. Other visual sensations arise when light energy is *emitted,* or released, from luminous objects, such as the sun, a light bulb, or a firefly. In either case, light is a form of physical energy transferred by radiation. However, the eyes are sensitive to only a narrow range of such energies. For example, electromagnetic (radiant) energy emitted by the sun travels in waves of various lengths. At one end of the *electromagnetic spectrum* (see Figure 3–1 in the color insert) are short waves, which are invisible to the human eye. These waves include gamma rays, x-rays, and ultraviolet rays. At the other end of the spectrum are invisible long waves, including infrared rays and radio waves such as radar, TV, FM, AM, and AC circuits.

Electromagnetic energies to which the human visual system responds are called *light waves.* The various light waves make up the **visual spectrum** (see Figure 3–1). The length of light waves is measured in *nanometers* (1 nanometer equals 1-billionth of a meter). Visible light waves range in length from about 400 to 750 nanometers (or about 16- to 32-millionths of an inch). In contrast, invisible radio waves are thousands of meters in length, and invisible gamma rays are only about 10-trillionths of a meter long.

The position of light waves in the visual spectrum—that is, their *wavelength*—is a major determinant of color sensations. Very short light waves produce the sensation of violet, whereas long-wavelength light is seen as red. Later, we will return to the topic of color vision to see how such sensations arise, but first we need to examine the more basic optical and visual systems of the human eye.

The Structure and Function of the Human Eye

Of all the instruments made by man, none resembles a part of the body more than a camera does the eye. Yet this is not by design. A camera is no more a copy of an eye than the wing of a bird is a copy of that of an insect. Each is the product of an independent evolution; and if this has brought the camera and the eye together, it is not because one has mimicked the other, but because both have had to meet the same problems, and frequently have done so in much the same way. This is the type of phenomenon that biologists call convergent evolution, yet peculiar in that one evolution is organic, the other technological. (Wald, 1972, p. 94)

The human eye and a typical camera share many similarities, as well as important differences. A survey of both can be helpful for describing the eye's structure and function.

— Focus Control: The Cornea, Lens, and Ciliary Muscles

Figure 3–2 shows the structure of the human eye. As light enters the eye, it passes first through the **cornea,** the eye's transparent outer surface and initial focusing device. Next, the light rays bend as they pass through the **lens.** This elastic structure allows the eye to change focus and maintain clear images of objects at various distances. Focusing occurs when the **ciliary muscles,** which are attached to the lens, relax or contract to change the shape and thickness of the lens. When the muscles relax, the lens flattens somewhat, because of pressure from the *vitreous humor,* or fluid, in the eyeball. Under this condition, distant objects should be in sharp focus. When the muscles contract, the lens reverts to its natural, bulging shape, so that closer objects can be focused.

As a person ages, the lens loses some of its elasticity and does not thicken as much when the ciliary muscles contract. As a result, nearby objects may no longer be properly focused without the aid of artificial lenses. Despite this limitation, the human eye is capable of focusing feats that are impossible to accomplish with a camera. If you have ever taken a blurry photograph, you know that it was probably because you accidentally moved the camera while tripping the shutter. The same is not true of the visual system. We are capable of continuous fine-focusing adjustments, even while jumping up and down or jogging at a fast pace.

— Aperture Control: The Pupil and Iris

Between the cornea and the lens in the human eye is an *aperture,* or adjustable opening, similar to that in cameras. The aperture in the eye is called the **pupil.** The diameter of the pupil is regulated by the **iris,** a colored muscle that surrounds the pupil. (The color of an eye comes from the color of the iris.) The iris performs a function similar to that of the diaphragm of a camera. In dim light, it retracts to allow more light to

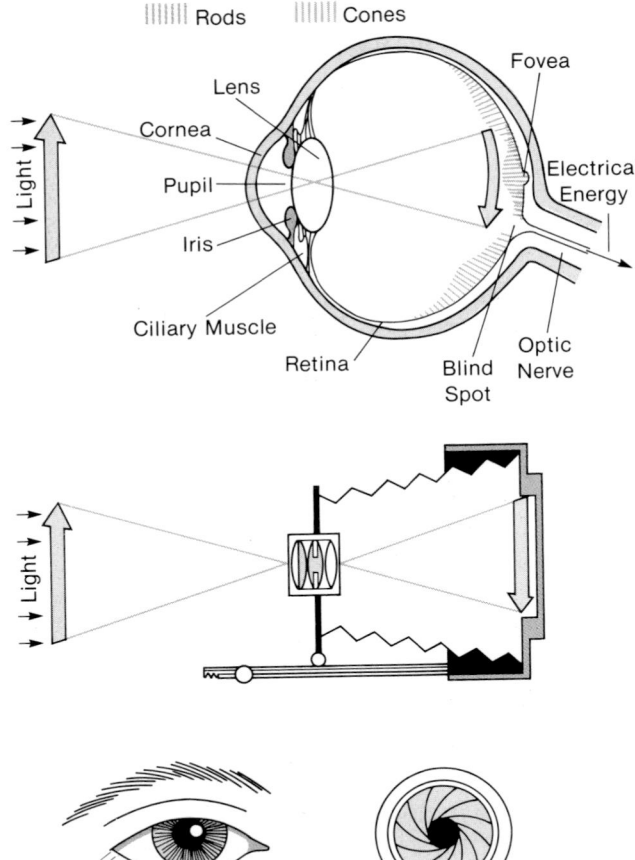

Figure 3–2.

A simplified representation of the human eye and its similarity to a camera. Both the eye and the camera have a lens for focusing an inverted image on a light-sensitive surface. Both possess an aperture that adjusts to various intensities of light. (See text for further description.)

enter the eye. In bright light, the opposite occurs; the iris narrows the pupil to reduce entering light. In short, the visual system adjusts to changing light stimuli with iris movements, which dilate or contract the pupils.

— Photosensitivity: The Retina

When you focus a camera, the lens moves closer or farther from the film. In the eye, the distance between the lens and the back of the eye is fixed, which is why lens shape and pupil aperture must be used for focusing. In a camera, the focused image falls on a light-sensitive film. In the eye, the focused image falls on the **retina,** the photosensitive surface at the back of the eye. Film consists of crystals of silver bromide embedded in gelatin, whereas the retina is made up of light-sensitive *photoreceptive cells* (or photoreceptors). These cells convert projected light patterns into corresponding patterns of neural activity.

Rods and cones. There are two main types of photoreceptive cells in the retinas of most vertebrates, including humans. These cells, which are named for their distinctive shape, are called **rods** and **cones.** Both consist of an inner segment that is similar to an ordinary nerve cell (see chapter 2) and a rod- or cone-shaped outer segment that is sensitive to light (Wald, 1972). Research conducted during the past 7 decades indicates that the rods and cones differ in function as well as structure.

One important functional difference between these receptors is their sensitivity to color. The cones, numbering more than 6 million in the human retina, are somewhat like color film; they are responsible for color sensations. On the other hand, the more than 100 million rods in the human retina act like black-and-white film in that they produce only black and white sensations. Although the rods may contribute to color vision (McKee, McCann, & Benton, 1977), the cones are primarily responsible for color sensations. Basically, the rods are "color-blind." (More will be said about this later.)

As you can see in Figure 3–2, the rods and cones differ in their distribution across the retina. The cones are heavily concentrated in and near the **fovea,** a tiny depression roughly at the center of the retina. The rods, on the other hand, are completely absent from the fovea; they are found mainly in the periphery of the retina. This distribution of rods and cones apparently serves a worthwhile function. For example, **visual acuity,** the ability to form fine, sharply-focused images of objects, is best served by the cones. When you move an object to the center of your field of vision

to inspect it closely, its image falls on the fovea, where visual acuity is greatest.

Images of objects that fall toward the edge of the retina, where the rods are located, are less sharply distinguished. As shown in Figure 3–2, one area of the retina contains neither rods nor cones. This area is insensitive to light and is known, appropriately, as the **blind spot.** It causes a gap in the visual field that normally goes unnoticed. There is, however, a way of demonstrating that images that fall on this area of the retina are indeed invisible (see Figure 3–3).

The rod and cone receptors also differ in their sensitivity to changes in light intensity. Just as the length of light waves varies, so does their height. That is, they also vary in *intensity,* or amount of radiant energy per unit of time. Intensity, as we will see later, is a major determinant of brightness. The cones respond to bright, high-intensity light and are largely responsible for daylight vision. The rods respond to low light intensities and are most active at night and in reduced lighting conditions. Vision in dim light, such as starlight or moonlight, often involves only the rods and is characteristically *achromatic* (colorless). The reason we experience few color sensations in dim light is that there is not enough intensity to stimulate the cones.

Several lines of evidence amplify the functional differences between the rods and cones. For example, the retinas of bats, owls, and other animals that are active at night contain mostly rods. The retinas of pigeons, chickens, and other animals that are active mainly during the day contain mostly cones. In humans, who are active during both night and day, a division of labor between the rods and cones has evolved. The presence of both types of receptors allows us to function in an incredible range of light-intensity conditions. For example, the ratio between the stimulus energy transmitted by a single candle flame, viewed at great distance, and the glare of the midday sun on a snow-covered ski slope is about 1 to

Figure 3–3.

Blind spot illustration. The back of the eye is covered with receptors except for the point where the optic nerve fibers leave the eye, creating a *blind spot.* To apply a stimulus to this point close your right eye and with the cross in front of your left eye, look at the cross. Now, move the book slowly back and forth; until it is about a foot from your eye. When the circle disappears, its image has fallen on the blind spot.

1 trillion. How does the visual system accommodate such a large variety of light intensities?

Visual adaptation. The answer to this question is found in research on *visual adaptation.* One type of visual adaptation, known as **dark adaptation,** is an increased sensitivity to light that occurs during exposure to darkness. Dark adaptation takes place when you shift from conditions of bright light to those of dim light, as, for example, when you enter a darkened movie theater. After your eyes become dark adapted, you can see objects and people to which you were blind moments before, even though the lighting remains dim. On leaving the movie theater and stepping into the sunlight, the opposite effect, called *light adaptation,* occurs. Your eyes gradually become less sensitive to the sun's blinding brightness.

Dark adaptation has been studied in the laboratory by researchers who ask subjects to look at a bright light until their eyes become light adapted. When the subjects are then exposed to total darkness, their eyes become increasingly sensitive to light flashes of lower intensities. The absolute threshold, as measured in response to light flashes, decreases as time spent in the dark increases. A sharp break in sensitivity between the cones and the rods, called the *rod-cone break,* takes place after a period of between 7 and 10 minutes in the dark (see Figure 3–4). The cones become dark adapted first; they are followed by the rods, which become maximally sensitive after about 40 minutes.

Experiments on dark adaptation show beyond doubt that the ability to see in the dark is due largely to the function of the rods (Cornsweet, 1970). Conversely, in bright light, the cones dominate vision; and although the rods do not actually stop functioning altogether, as brightness increases their relative contribution to vision falls to so low a level as to be almost negligible (Wald, 1972).

Although most people can adapt to dim light conditions, several factors affect one's ability to see in the dark. For example, one factor is vitamin A deficiency. Vitamin A plays a critical role in the production of the photochemical pigment found in the rods. This is why the vitamin is commonly prescribed for night blindness. It is probably also why eating carrots, which contain vitamin A, has long been associated with maintaining good eyesight.

Another factor that can affect one's ability to see in the dark is the ingestion of alcohol. If you drink only a few ounces of alcohol, it takes 30 to 50 percent longer than normal for your rods to recover their dark

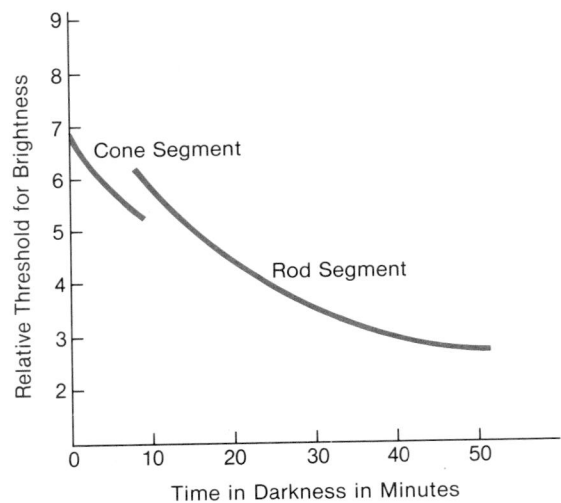

Figure 3–4.

Dark adaptation. Note that the curve has one segment for the cones and one for the rods which take over from the cones after 7–10 minutes in darkness. The rods become maximally sensitive after about 40 minutes.

adaptation following exposure to a bright light, such as the glare from headlights of an oncoming automobile (Dworetzky, 1982). The effect of alcohol on dark adaptation suggests one good reason, among many, that drinking and driving do not mix.

Transduction: The eye and the brain. The rod and the cone visual receptor cells form the rear layer of the retina. In front of them lies another layer of cells, called the *bipolar cells,* whose dendrites connect with the rods and cones. A third layer of the retina is formed by *ganglion cells,* whose axons weave over the outer surface of the retina, converging at the *optic nerve.* The optic nerve connects the eye with the brain (see chapter 2).

Figure 3–5 shows that light entering the eye must pass through the cornea, the lens, and the vitreous humor before reaching the retina. Having traveled this far, light passes through the layers of ganglion and bipolar cells before reaching the rearward-facing rods and cones. There, light energy is translated into nerve impulses in a process called **transduction.** In this process, electromagnetic (light) energy is absorbed by photosensitive pigments found in the rods and cones. Its absorption causes a chemical reaction in which the pigment molecules change shape. The photochemical

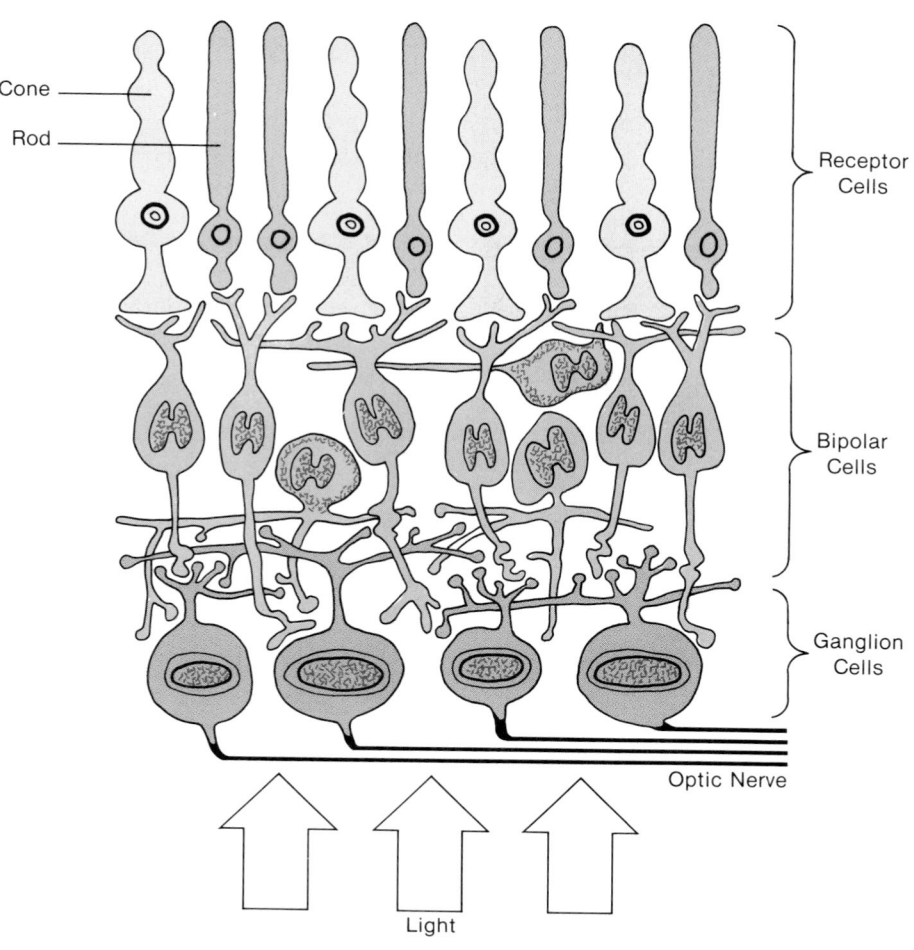

Cone

Rod

Receptor Cells

Bipolar Cells

Ganglion Cells

Optic Nerve

Light

Figure 3–5.

The retina. Light travels through a complex network of cells before reaching the rods and cones. Here, light energy is translated into electrical energy in a process called transduction.

reaction stimulates a release of electrical energy in the form of nerve impulses. Impulses generated in the rods and cones activate the bipolar cells and then the ganglion cells. Axons from the ganglion cells exit the eyes through the optic nerve, which leads to the visual areas of the brain.

Brain mechanisms of vision. How does the brain process visual information? Among the most exciting discoveries in recent years is the pioneering, Nobel prize-winning research reported by Harvard University professors David H. Hubel and Torsten N. Wiesel. Thanks to their experiments, it is now known that a complicated hierarchy of cells in the visual cor-

tex of the brain processes sensory information. Collectively, these cells are called **feature detectors** because they specialize in detecting specific features, or patterns, of visual stimulation.

Hubel and Wiesel (1959, 1979) have accumulated convincing evidence for three types of feature detectors in the visual cortex. First, there are *simple cells*. These cells respond to the particular orientation and location of a visual stimulus. Second, there are *complex cells*. These cells respond to movement of a visual stimulus. In addition, they preserve and respond to information about stimulus orientation and location that is passed on from the simple cells. Third, there are *hypercomplex* cells, but in far fewer numbers than either simple or complex cells. These cells respond to the length of a visual stimulus while preserving information about stimulus orientation. Still other cells in the visual cortex are expert at detecting specific patterns and shapes (DeValois & DeValois, 1980). All the evidence so far suggests:

1. Neural impulses initiated by visual stimuli stimulate a hierarchy of cells in the visual cortex. The functions of these cells range from relatively simple to increasingly complex.
2. Nerve impulses form a *sensory code* that represents properties or features of stimuli. The code is processed in a hierarchical manner by simple, complex, and hypercomplex cells.
3. Simple cells activate a smaller number of complex cells, which in turn converge on and activate a yet smaller number of hypercomplex cells.
4. The three types of cells, which respond differentially to specific features of visual stimulation, may represent the biological building blocks for complex perceptions.

The method used by Hubel and Wiesel in their pioneering studies of the visual cortex of monkeys and cats is quite straightforward (see Figure 3–6a). A tiny *microelectrode* is inserted near or into a cell somewhere in the visual system. Then, different patterns of light are projected onto the retina, and the electrical response of the cell is measured. Hubel and Wiesel recorded single-cell responses from the visual cortex when the retina was stimulated by a small rectangular bar of light. Figure 3–6b shows the varying responses of simple cells to the light as its orientation was systematically changed. When the light was presented horizontally, there was no response. When the light was tilted, a weak response was recorded. When the light was presented vertically, the simple cells responded strongly.

Using procedures similar to those described here and illustrated in Figure 3–6, Hubel and Wiesel demonstrated that visual information processing results from the specialized response of cortical cells to the orientation, movement, and length of visual stimuli. In short, they established that there are mechanisms in the brain specifically responsible for processing visual stimuli. As noted by Hubel (1972):

One cannot expect to "explain" vision . . . from a knowledge of the behavior of a single set of cells. . . . We are now studying how still "higher" structures build on the

information they receive from these cortical cells, rearranging it to produce an even greater complexity of response. (p. 156)

In conclusion, there are at least three steps involved in turning light into visual sensations. First, physical (light) energy stimulates receptor cells in the retina. Next, the receptor cells transduce light energy into nerve impulses. Finally, specialized cells in the brain organize and interpret patterns of nerve impulses—messages sent from the receptor cells. Although much has been learned, questions remain concerning how visual information striking the retina is transduced from photochemical energy into neural energy. A related question that has intrigued investigators for centuries, and one for which some answers are available, concerns how the visual system transduces light energy into sensations of color.

Color Vision

During the 1660s, Isaac Newton discovered that light, when passed through a prism, breaks into bands of different colors. The light bands thus created consist of the colors of a rainbow (see Figure 3–7 in the color insert). Short wavelengths of light, between 380 and 450 nanometers, produce violet; longer wavelengths, between 650 and 700 nanometers, produce red. The sensations blue, green, yellow, and orange are produced by light waves of intermediate lengths. Thus, quantitative changes in a physical stimulus, the length of light waves, lead to qualitative changes in color sensations. Violet does not look "shorter" than red; rather, it looks qualitatively different. Under controlled laboratory conditions, the number of color qualities that can be discriminated by adults with normal color vision ranges into the millions. How is it possible for us to experience so many colors? This diversity arises from the fact that color varies on three psychological dimensions: hue, brightness, and saturation.

— The Dimensions of Color

Hue refers to the name given to a particular color—for example, red, green, yellow, blue. As mentioned earlier, color, or hue, is determined by a light wave's *length*. Newton discovered this when he observed that sunlight passing through a prism would form a full spectrum of hues. Newton also observed that the colors of the spectrum leaving the prism could be recom-

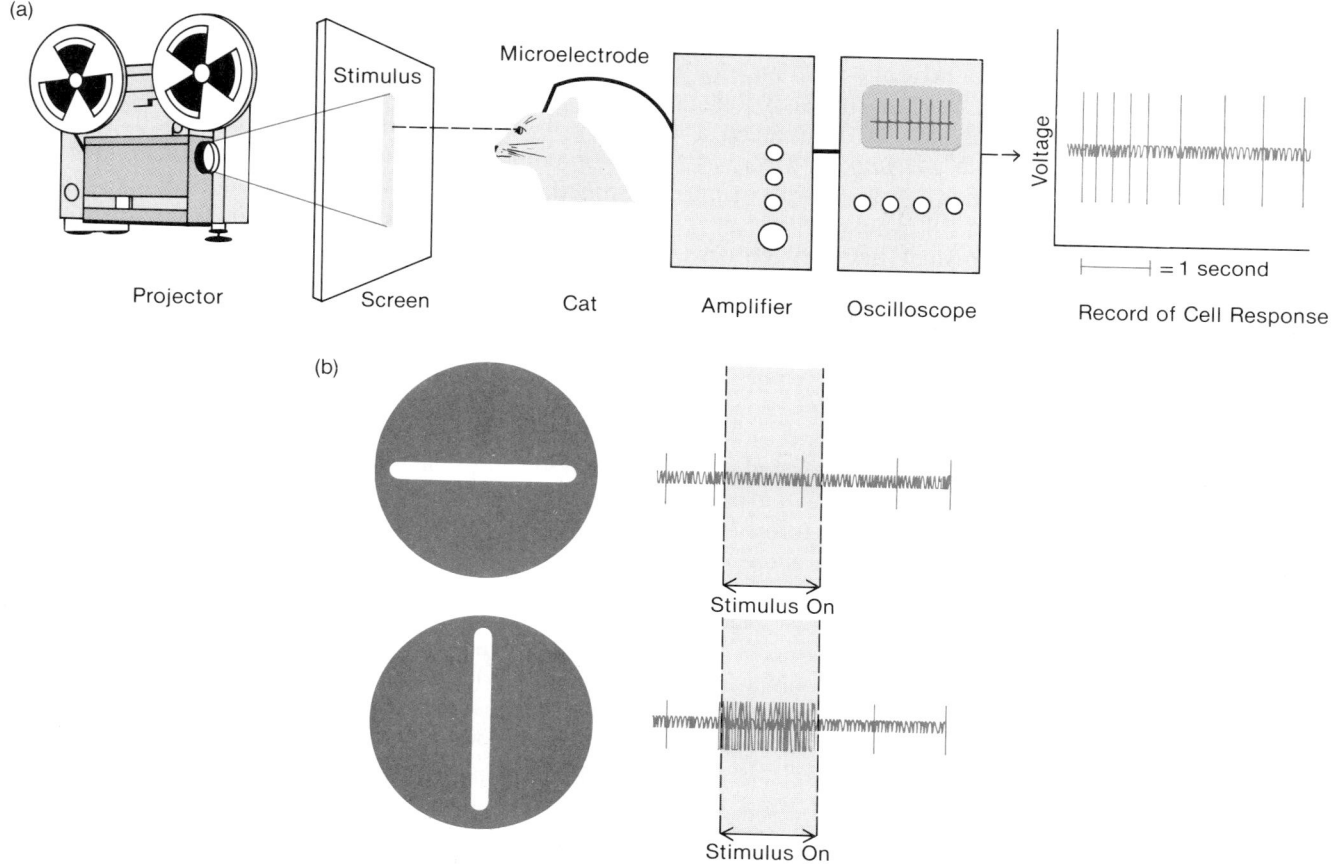

Figure 3–6.

Hubel and Wiesel technique (a) and results (b). Simple cortical cells show varying responses to a bar of light whose orientation is systematically changed. A horizontal bar of light produces no response but a vertical bar produces a strong response.

bined, with a lens, to recreate the white light that entered the prism. He correctly concluded that sunlight is made up of the spectral hues, each differing in wavelength.

Brightness refers to how light or bright a color appears. It is determined by light-wave *amplitude,* or intensity. Increasing amplitude, which is a physical property of the light wave, increases brightness. In addition to amplitude, wavelength can also influence the sensation of brightness. Some colors (for example, yellow) may appear brighter than others, even though the amplitude of the compared wavelengths may be identical.

Saturation, which refers to a color's degree of purity, is determined principally by the *complexity* of the light wave. A single wavelength will result in the most highly saturated color. A saturated color will be purer than one consisting of several wavelengths. Thus, light waves consisting of many wavelengths will be more complex, less pure, and therefore less saturated. *Achromatic sensations* (white, gray, black), which are made up of many wavelengths, are unsaturated and have no hue. All three dimensions of color—hue, brightness, and saturation—are represented in the *color solid* shown in Figure 3–8 in the color insert.

— Theories of Color Vision

How are light waves of different intensities and wavelengths translated into sensations of color? You may recall from our earlier discussion that retinal photoreceptive cells differ in their color sensitivity. The cones, not the rods, are primarily responsible for color vision.

Trichromatic theory. According to one theory, human color vision is produced by three types of retinal cone cells, each most sensitive to a different color. This **trichromatic** (three-color) **theory** was first proposed in 1802 by the English physicist Thomas Young. Later, it was refined by Hermann von Helmholtz, a German physiologist. The *Young-Helmholtz theory* is still widely accepted because it is consistent with many of the facts of color vision and color mixture.

The existence of three **physical primary colors** lends support to the trichromatic color theory. Red, green, and blue have long been referred to as primary colors because by mixing red, green, and blue wavelengths of light in different proportions, it is possible to create all the colors of the visual spectrum. For example, a mixture of red and green wavelengths of light produces yellow. Combining different wavelengths of emitted light is called *additive mixture;* it is the principle used to produce color television pictures. You would soon be frustrated, however, if you attempted the additive mixture of paints. Red, green, and blue paint, when mixed together, produce black (see Figure 3–9 in the color insert), because paint pigments absorb most wavelengths of light, reflecting only a few. For this reason, the mixture of paint pigments or other light-absorbing substances is called *subtractive mixture.* Understandably, subtractive mixture follows different rules than does additive mixture. Mixing red and green pigments, for instance, produces brown.

The trichromatic theory explains color mixing by proposing that there are three cone types corresponding to the physical primary colors red, blue, and green. This idea is directly supported by laboratory studies. In such studies, individual cone cells are stimulated with various wavelengths of light, and their electrical responses are measured. Experiments reported by MacNichol (1964) and Nobel Prize winner George Wald (1972) verify that there are at least three types of cones. One type is maximally sensitive to long-wavelength (red) light. The second responds most to medium wavelengths (green). The third is most sensitive to short wavelengths (blue or violet). Activation of the three cone types in various degrees produces an almost infinite variety of color sensations.

The trichromatic theory of color vision seems, almost indisputably, to explain color processing at the receptor level (that is, in the retina). However, the theory is not consistent with all the facts of color vision. A chief limitation is its failure to explain certain types of *color blindness,* especially the inability to discriminate red from green. People who are unable to see red also have color blindness for green. Since the trichromatic theory holds that yellow is a mixture of red and green, red-green color-blind individuals should be unable to see yellow—but they do.

Opponent-process theory. A second theory of color vision, proposed by Ewald Hering in 1878 and refined by Hurvich and Jameson (1957), assumes the existence of three color receptor systems instead of the three cone types proposed by the Young-Helmholtz theory. Hering argued that there are red-green receptors, blue-yellow receptors, and black-white receptors.

According to the **opponent-process theory,** each receptor system contains photoreceptive cells that are activated by light waves of different lengths. In the red-green receptor system, for example, some cells are "excited" by red wavelengths of light and "inhibited" by green wavelengths of light. This same system contains cells that are excited by green wavelengths and inhibited by red wavelengths. Hering envisioned the same *opponent process* for blue-yellow receptors and for black-white receptors. He also speculated that the receptors within each system oppose one another while at the same time interacting with the receptor cells of the other systems in a complementary fashion.

It makes sense from the opponent-process view of color vision that red and green cannot exist together in the same color; neither can yellow and blue. Reddish greens and greenish reds are nonexistent, as are yellowish blues and bluish yellows. As noted by Hering, people who have trouble seeing blue also have difficulty seeing yellow. Likewise, people who are unable to see red also have color blindness for green, which suggests a malfunctioning of the red-green receptor system. Consequently, red-green color blindness viewed in this way does not imply the blindness for yellow that would be predicted from the simpler three-color theory described by Young and Helmholtz.

Hering's theory is also consistent with what is known about **afterimages,** sensory impressions that persist after removal of the stimulus that caused them. To illustrate the point that the color receptor systems proposed by Hering are linked in opposing fashion, look at the center of the red square shown in Figure 3–10 in the color insert for about 1 minute. Then, look immediately at a white wall or a piece of white paper and quickly blink your eyes a few times. You should see a green afterimage, called a *negative afterimage,* because green is the opposing color of red. Staring at a green stimulus will produce a red afterimage, as predicted from Hering's theory. The negative afterimages for blue and yellow are similarly paired.

The opponent-process theory of color vision explains some phenomena, such as color blindness and negative afterimages, better than does the simpler three-color theory. In addition, the *lateral geniculate body,* a way station for visual information moving toward the cortex, seems to analyze visual information in the fashion proposed by the opponent-process theory. As mentioned earlier, however, the three-color theory appears to explain activity in the retina. Thus, both theories may be correct at particular levels of the visual system. Perhaps both theories eventually will be combined to more fully explain human color vision.

— APPLICATION —

MEASURING VISUAL ACUITY

So far we have focused on the normal functioning of the visual system. Problems do sometimes arise, however, in the form of visual defects. Such problems can be detected with tests designed to measure visual acuity. Two familiar tests of acuity are the *Snellen eye chart* and the *Landolt rings test,* shown in Figure 3–11. These are sometimes called 20/20 tests because visual acuity measurements are usually reported as ratios. People with normal vision see stimuli such as the Snellen letters or the Landolt rings clearly at 20 feet. Thus, they have 20/20 vision. A person who has 20/50 vision sees clearly at 20 feet what a person with normal vision can see at 50 feet. Conversely, a person who has 20/10 vision sees clearly at 20 feet what a person with normal vision sees at 10 feet.

There are a variety of defects in visual acuity that can be detected. Two common visual defects are *nearsightedness* and *farsightedness;* each can be corrected with properly prescribed artificial lenses. Both defects are due to abnormalities in the overall shape of the cornea, the lens, or the entire eye. Figure 3–12 illustrates the effects of corrective lenses on nearsightedness and farsightedness. In nearsightedness, or *myopia,* an abnormally long eyeball causes images to be focused on a point short of the retinal surface. Objects in the distance appear blurry, although close objects are seen clearly. In farsightedness, or *hyperopia,* an abnormally short eyeball causes images to be deflected to a point beyond the retinal surface. Images close to the eye cannot be focused properly, although objects far away are seen clearly.

Another type of visual defect is *color blindness.* As mentioned earlier, normal color vision depends on three types of cones or cone systems, each sensitive to light waves of different lengths. When all three systems work properly, individuals have normal color vision and are called *trichromats.*

Partial color blindness is associated with a lack of one of the three chemical pigments normally found in the cones or a malfunction in one of the opponent-receptor systems. Affected persons are called *dichromats.* A dichromat can perceive some colors, but the

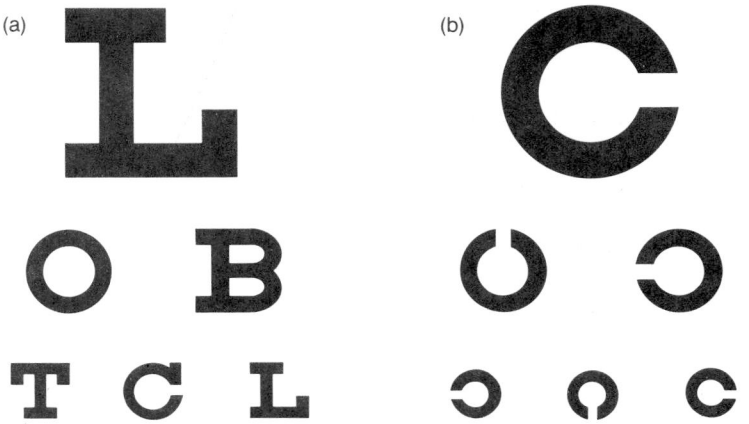

(a)

(b)

Figure 3–11.

Tests of visual acuity: (a) Snellen letters and (b) Landolt rings.

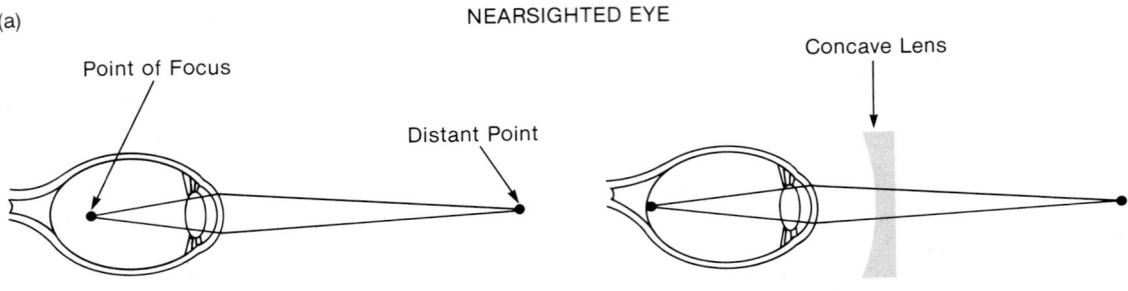

(a) NEARSIGHTED EYE

Point of Focus

Distant Point

Concave Lens

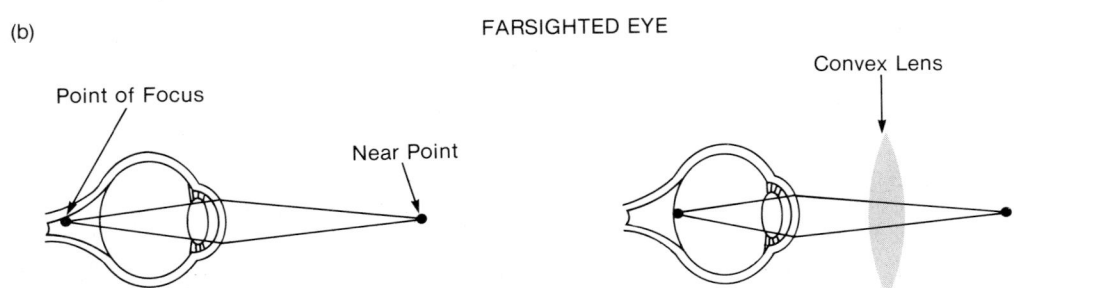

(b) FARSIGHTED EYE

Point of Focus

Near Point

Convex Lens

Figure 3–12.

Normal vision, nearsightedness, and farsightedness. In nearsightedness, the eyeball is longer than normal and light rays are focused in front of the retina. In farsightedness, the eyeball is shorter than normal and light rays are focused in back of the retina. Corrective lenses are designed to adjust the point of focus.

range of color experiences is decreased. Inability to distinguish red and green is the most common form of dichromatism. This type of color blindness affects about 8 percent of all males and less than 1 percent of all females. According to the opponent-process theory of color vision, described earlier, people with red-green color blindness have a defect in the red-green color receptor system. Similarly, people with the less common blue-yellow color blindness have a defect in the blue-yellow color receptor system.

People who are completely color-blind, called *monochromats,* see only shades of gray and white.

Such people presumably are missing either all three cone systems or both opponent-process color systems. Monochromatism is a rare condition, occurring in about 10 persons out of 1 million. Those who are completely color-blind are also sensitive to bright lights, possibly because they use rod vision in both dim and bright light conditions (Goldstein, 1980).

Are you color-blind? You can test yourself to determine if you have normal color vision. One test of color blindness is provided in Figure 3–13 in the color insert.

— THE OTHER SENSES —

The Auditory System

Even in our era of technological wonders, the performances of our most amazing machines are still put in the shade by the sense organs of the human body. Consider the accomplishments of the ear. It is so sensitive that it can almost hear the random rain of air molecules bouncing against the eardrum. Yet in spite of its extraordinary sensitivity the ear can withstand the pounding of sound waves strong enough to set the body vibrating. (Békésy, 1972, p. 232)

— Hearing

The sense of hearing, **audition,** is the product of mechanical energy, or pressure changes in the molecules of air. Changes in air pressure move in all directions from vibrating objects, much like the ripples produced by a stone thrown into a pond. Except for vibrations applied directly to the skull, these air-pressure changes, called *sound waves,* provide the physical stimulus for everything that we hear.

The simplest kind of sound wave is the sine wave. A *sine wave* is produced when a single vibrating object, such as a tuning fork, moves back and forth, displacing air molecules surrounding it (see Figure 3–14). Sounds produced by sine waves are called *pure tones.* Some musical instruments, such as the flute, can be made to produce sounds that are close to pure tones. We generally hear sounds that are not pure, however, since true sine waves are produced only with special laboratory equipment. Our everyday auditory experience depends on *complex sound waves,* which may take on an infinite variety of forms. Some are *periodic complex sound waves,* composed of several sine waves that are multiples of one another. Others are *aperiodic complex sound waves,* composed of a variety of waves that are irregular in amplitude and frequency. Aperiodic sound waves produce what we call *noise,* the auditory result of hearing many inharmonious frequencies. *White noise* is the hissing sound produced when all the frequencies in the audible spectrum are combined. (The *audible spectrum* is the range of auditory stimuli to which the human ear is sensitive.) White noise is analogous to white light, which contains all wavelengths of the visible spectrum.

Our ability to perceive a vast number of sounds in the audible spectrum arises from the fact that sound varies on three psychological dimensions: pitch, loudness, and timbre.

Pitch and sound-wave frequency. The psychological experience that accompanies variations in *sound-wave frequency* is referred to as **pitch.** High-frequency sound waves produce high-pitched sounds; sound waves that are low in frequency produce low-pitched sounds. Frequency of sound waves is usually expressed in Hertz (Hz), the number of cycles (or complete waves) per second (see Figure 3–14). Sounds made on a piano range in frequency from about 30 to 4,000 Hz, whereas those made on a tuba range from about 45 to 320 Hz. Humans are most sensitive to sounds that fall within a range of frequencies used in speech, from about 500 to 3,000 Hz. The ear is least sensitive at the low frequencies. Its sensitivity for a tone of 100 cycles per second is 1,000 times lower than for one at 1,000 cycles per second (Békésy, 1972). This relative insensitivity to sounds of lower frequency is useful and adaptive. Think how distracting and annoying it would be to hear all the vibrations of the head that are produced by the shock of each step we take when walking.

We are capable of detecting sounds with frequencies that range from 20 to 20,000 Hz—the same range that a good stereo system is designed to reproduce. This is the range of the audible spectrum for humans. As the limits of the spectrum indicate, many sounds are too high pitched for humans to detect. Most dog whistles, for instance, produce sounds that exceed human sensory capacity. Dogs and cats can hear sounds with frequencies as high as 40,000 or 50,000 Hz.

Loudness and sound-wave amplitude. The psychological experience of **loudness** corresponds to variations in *sound-wave amplitude.* Turning up the volume of a stereo system amplifies vibrations from the speakers. The more intense the vibrations, the higher the amplitude. The higher the amplitude, the greater the loudness. Loudness is determined also by sound-wave frequency. Low-frequency sounds require greater amplitude to seem as loud as sound waves of

Figure 3–14.

Sound waves. The distance between successive peaks of a sine wave is the wavelength. In measuring characteristics of sound, in contrast with light, wavelength is referred to as frequency. The frequency of a sound wave, which is commonly measured in Hertz (Hz), is the number of cycles or alternations between peaks and troughs in a specified period of time. One Hz is equal to one cycle of pressure change per second. The height of successive peaks of a sine wave is the amplitude, which provides a measure of sound intensity. Frequency and amplitude are two principal ways of characterizing and defining a given sound wave.

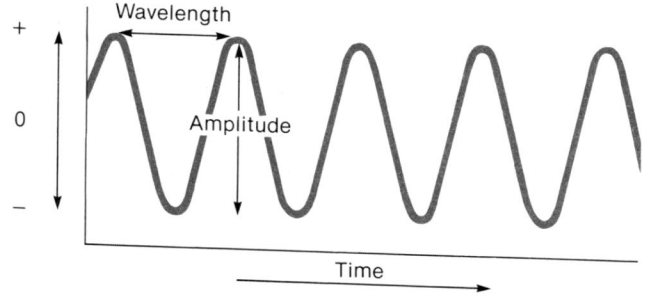

higher frequency. Loudness, or sound intensity, is commonly measured in *decibels* (dB) (in honor of Alexander Graham Bell) to indicate *sound-pressure level*. In decibels, a just noticeable whisper would be about 20 dB; the sound of a rock band at close range would be about 110 dB.

The kinds of noises we hear every day can be damaging (see Figure 3–15). The noise level of a motorcycle, for example, can be around 100 dB. This is loud enough to damage some people's hearing in less than 1 hour. Rock concerts, discos, and some of the new stereo headsets can go up to 135 dB, about the same level as a jet engine. Exposure to such loud noises for extended periods of time can damage the tiny cells in the inner ear that are responsible for converting sounds into electrical signals to the brain.

One symptom of hearing damage, called *tinnitus* (pronounced tin-NYE-tus), is a ringing, buzzing, or tingling sensation in the ears. A survey conducted in England showed that between 0.5 and 1.0 percent of the population have tinnitus severely enough to interfere with work or sleep. If this provides an accurate estimate for the United States, it corresponds to approximately 1 to 2 million people (McFadden & Wightman, 1983). If you are bothered by an occasional ringing in your ears, or know someone who is, you might be comforted to know that tinnitus is a sign of hearing damage, not of insanity (as many people seem to believe) (Dunkle, 1982).

Timbre and sound-wave complexity. The psychological experience that accompanies variations in

Figure 3–15.
Decibel levels of some ordinary sounds.

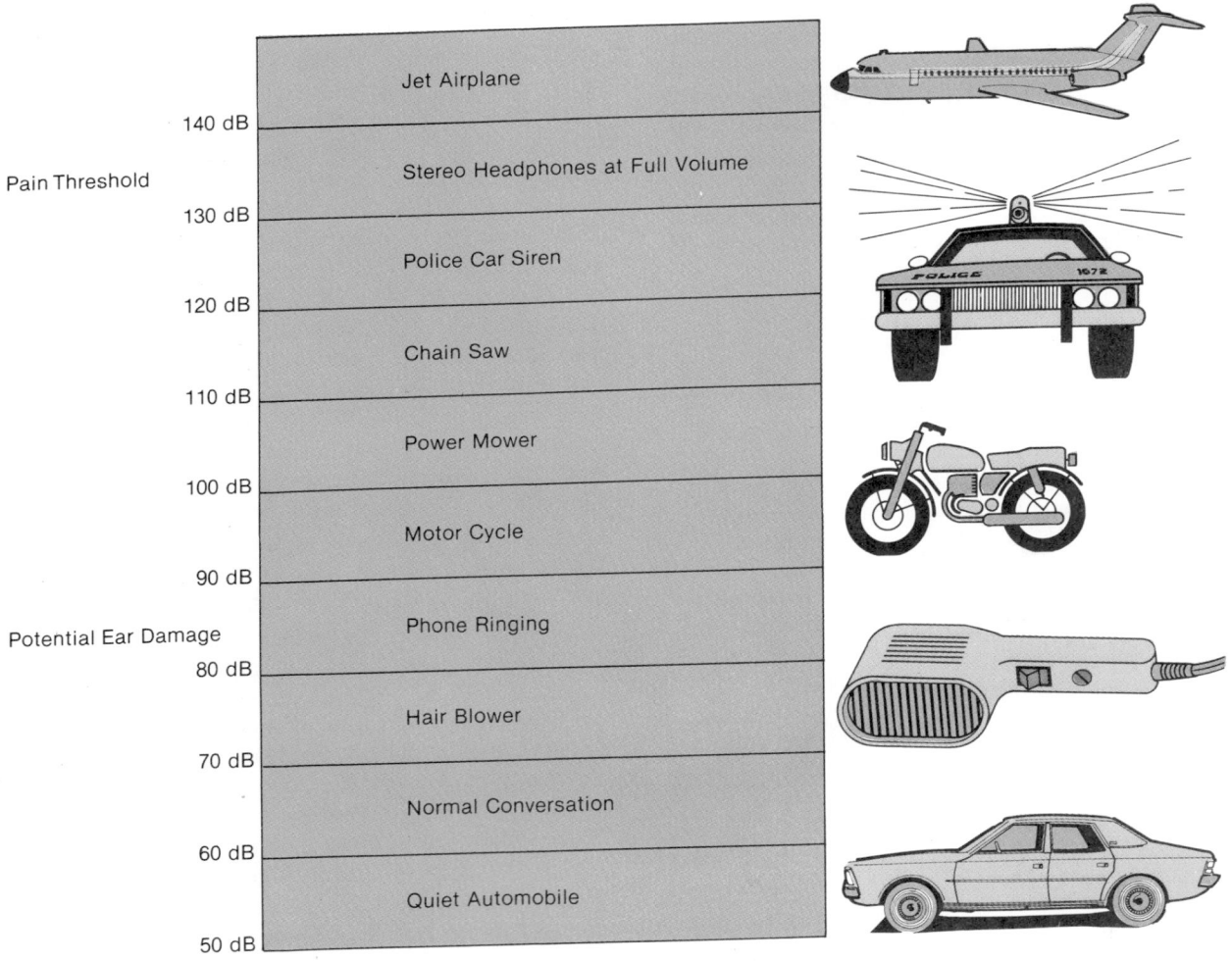

SENSATION
66

sound-wave complexity is referred to as **timbre.** As mentioned earlier, most sounds that we hear are not pure tones consisting of a single frequency. Rather, they are complex in the sense that they are composed of many different frequencies. Periodic sound waves consist of a *fundamental tone frequency,* or pure tone, plus higher frequencies, called *overtones* or *harmonics.* Such overtones produce a distinctive quality, or *timbre,* of sounds. When two musical instruments are made to sound the same note, say middle C, they differ in their perceived voice, or timbre, because each instrument, although producing the same fundamental tone, amplifies certain overtones while suppressing others.

— Structure and Function of the Human Ear

A diagram of the structure of the human ear is shown in Figure 3–16. For convenience, the three major parts of the ear—the outer ear, the middle ear, and the inner ear—are shown together. Let's briefly consider the functional characteristics of these structural parts of the ear.

The outer ear. The pinna and the auditory canal comprise the *outer ear.* In addition to being a convenient place to hang earrings, the *pinna,* which is the visible external portion of the ear, serves as a funnel that channels sound waves into the head. The sound waves pass through the *auditory canal,* which serves as a resonator to amplify the intensity of the waves entering the ear. Sound waves entering the outer ear exert pressure against the eardrum, a thin membrane technically referred to as the *tympanic membrane,* causing it to vibrate.

Unless the tympanic membrane remains properly pressurized, normal hearing will be adversely affected. Flying at high altitudes can cause rapid changes in the external pressure on the eardrum. Swallowing, yawning, and chewing gum help equalize the pressure on the eardrum because they allow air to pass from the back of the mouth through the *eustachian tube.* The air thereby enters the middle ear, where it presses on the eardrum from the inside, thus equalizing the pressure on the eardrum.

The middle ear. Three bony structures, named for their shapes, comprise the *middle ear.* The *malleus* (Latin for "hammer") is connected directly to the eardrum. The *incus* (Latin for "anvil") is attached to the malleus at one end and to the *stapes* (Latin for "stirrup") at the other end. These hinged structures, collectively known as the *ossicles,* vibrate in synchrony with sound waves entering the outer ear. Vibration of the stapes then moves the *oval window,* a membrane that leads into the inner ear.

Figure 3–16.

Structure of the human ear. (See text for description.)

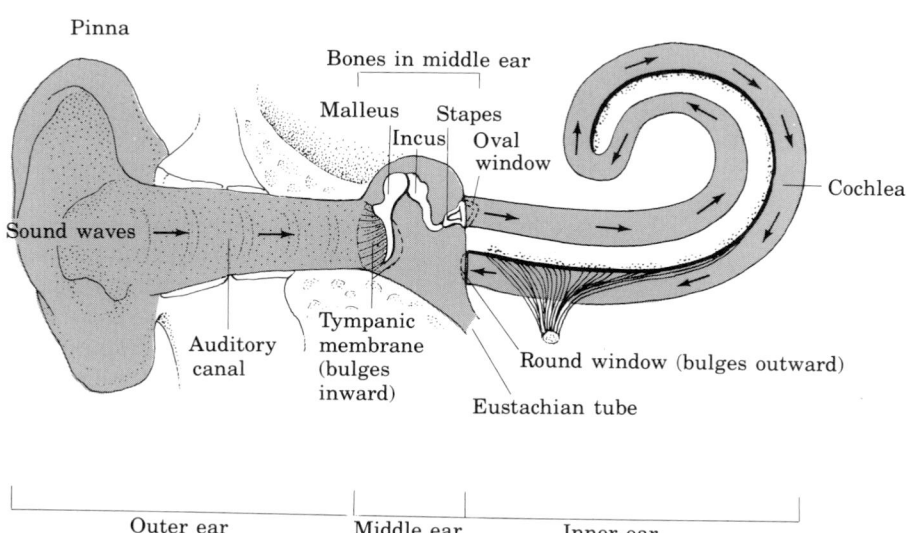

The inner ear. The primary structure of the *inner ear* is the *cochlea,* a structure shaped like a snail shell, which is filled with fluid and contains the auditory receptors. Vibrations transmitted by the middle ear cause cyclic changes in pressure against the fluid inside the cochlea. Pressure waves in the *cochlear fluid* cause displacement of the *basilar membrane,* a thin, elastic tissue in the cochlea. The displacement of this membrane causes the *organ of Corti,* which rests on the basilar membrane, to vibrate. The organ of Corti contains the actual receptors for hearing—tiny *hair cells* (Hudspeth, 1983).

Transduction: The ear and the brain. Physical (sound) energy entering the outer ear causes vibrations in the middle ear that in turn stimulate the auditory receptors. It is at the location of these receptors, hair cells in the organ of Corti, that physical energy is translated into nerve impulses in the process called *transduction.* Transduction occurs when the hair cells (which number approximately 30,000) move in response to vibrations of the basilar membrane. Movement of these tiny hair cells stimulates the thousands of nerve cells to which they are connected, thereby generating electrochemical impulses. This energy is transmitted out of the cochlea along nerve fibers that funnel into the auditory nerve. The *auditory nerve* provides the pathway through which auditory messages, in the form of nerve impulses, are sent to the brain.

Experiments reported by George von Békésy demonstrate how the basilar membrane vibrates in response to sounds of various frequencies and how this vibration affects the hair cells. Because of Békésy's research, it is now believed that sounds differing in pitch, loudness, and timbre produce different patterns of vibrations in the basilar membrane (Békésy, 1960). Additionally, it is believed that these patterns of vibrations result in different nerve-impulse patterns that are differentially interpreted in the auditory cortex of the brain (see chapter 2). There are currently several theories that help explain how this process works.

— Theories of Hearing

According to the **place theory of pitch,** for example, particular areas of the basilar membrane are responsive to particular sound frequencies. This idea was first proposed by Hermann von Helmholtz, whose theory of color vision was described earlier. Experiments conducted by Békésy, for which he won the Nobel Prize

in 1961, proved Helmholtz correct, at least to some extent. Békésy's microscopic observations of the cochlea in guinea pigs (and some taken from human cadavers) showed a correspondence between sound frequency and the place at which the basilar membrane is maximally stimulated. High frequencies from a vibrating stimulus caused a wavelike motion of the basilar membrane, with a peak close to the oval window; low frequencies stimulated regions of the basilar membrane close to the tip of the cochlea.

Simply stated, the place theory says that the experience of pitch depends on the precise place at which the basilar membrane is maximally displaced. There is one problem with the theory, however. When sound frequency is low, it causes a wavelike motion of the basilar membrane that has no particular peak. Thus, all the hair cells are stimulated equally. This holds true for sound frequencies below about 4,000 cycles per second.

An alternate theory, called the **frequency theory of pitch,** helps explain the reception of low-frequency sounds. According to this theory, the rate (rather than the place) at which the hair cells are stimulated determines pitch. The frequency theory, proposed by Rutherford (1886, cited in Goldstein, 1980), is based on the discovery that low-frequency sounds between 20 and 1,000 cycles per second tend to vibrate the basilar membrane at the same frequency as the stimulus and to produce nerve impulses of the same frequency. Thus, according to the theory, the experience of pitch is determined by the frequency of auditory nerve impulses. The lower the frequency, the lower the pitch. There is a complication, however, in that frequency theory does not adequately explain sounds above 1,000 Hz. The reason is that single neurons are incapable of firing more than about 1,000 times per second (see chapter 2).

The **volley theory of pitch** helps explain the transduction of low-frequency sounds between 1,000 and 4,000 cycles per second. According to this theory, nerve impulse frequencies above 1,000 per second are generated by groups of neurons, each firing in turn. No single group fires more than 1,000 times per second. But by dividing the work, the groups combine to produce a higher overall impulse frequency. This principle was recognized by American soldiers in the Revolutionary War, who confronted their enemy in rows. By loading and reloading one after another, the rows of soldiers could produce more frequent and continuous *volleys* of gunfire than could one row alone. This principle explains how two neurons, each firing at a rate of 1,000 impulses per second but alternating in their firing, could produce a combined firing rate of 2,000 impulses per second.

Research has shown that frequency theory, even with the incorporation of the volley principle, adequately explains the transduction of pitch for frequencies up to only about 4,000 cycles per second. The place theory of pitch seems to provide an adequate explanation for all but low-frequency sounds. For years, experts tended to adhere to one theory or another. Today, it is recognized that all three theories—place, frequency, and volley—must be combined to explain human hearing.

Smell and Taste: The Chemical Senses

Smell and taste are sometimes referred to as the **chemical senses** because chemical substances provide the physical stimulus for each. Chemical stimulation of receptor cells initiates transduction (wherein physical energy is translated into electrical energy) and

transmission of nerve impulses to the smell and taste centers of the brain (see chapter 2).

— Smell

The sense of smell, or **olfaction,** provides information about chemical substances in the air around us. A diagram of the structure of the olfactory system is shown in Figure 3–17. The nostrils provide passageways through which the chemical stimuli for smell enter the nose. These stimuli contact hairshaped *receptor cells* located in the upper part of each *nasal cavity.* When contacted by chemical stimuli at one end, these receptor cells generate nerve impulses at the other end. Olfactory nerve impulses travel along nerve fibers to the *olfactory bulb* and from there along the *olfactory nerve tract* to a number of areas in the brain. These areas include the amygdala, the hippocampus, and the hypothalamus (where feeding, drinking, and reproductive behaviors are regulated). Unlike vision and hearing, which terminate at well-defined areas in the brain, no one area has yet been located for the sense of smell. However, an area in the frontal lobe of the ce-

Figure 3–17.
The olfactory system.

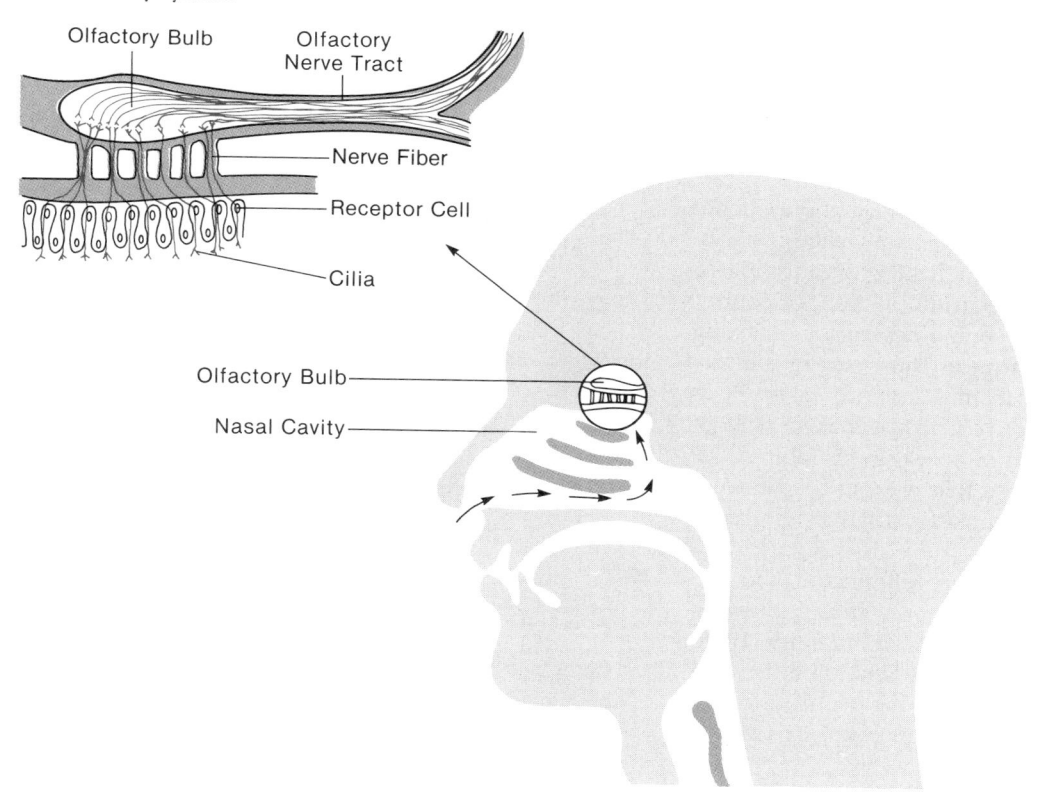

rebral cortex has been identified as being perhaps most important (Goldstein, 1980).

For humans, the sense of smell is something of a luxury, being for all practical purposes unnecessary for survival. It does, however, offer some protection by enabling us to detect the telltale smoke of an otherwise invisible fire or the telltale odor of spoiled food. For most animals, smell is important for both survival and communication. The olfactory organs in dogs, for example, are much larger than those in humans. This knowledge has been put to good use by customs officials. For years they have used the keen sense of smell of trained dogs to detect heroin, marijuana, and other drugs in unopened packages.

In many animals, smell provides the dominant means of communication. Some animals, for example, release chemicals called *pheromones,* which cause specific and predictable reactions in other animals of the same species. Honeybees are capable of releasing an alarm pheromone (isopental acetate) that signals other bees to attack objects in the vicinity of their hive. Chemicals that control sexual behavior are perhaps among the most potent pheromones. The pheromone bombykol is released by the female silkworm moth to attract a male and trigger a sequence of behaviors necessary for mating. Although a single female has only about 0.01 micrograms of this pheromone, this tiny amount is enough to attract about 1 million males (Goldstein, 1980).

— Taste

The sense of **taste** provides information about chemical substances entering the organism's digestive system. Its function is simple. It helps the organism keep out substances that may be harmful. Smell, of course, provides a preliminary screening device for detecting substances that may be harmful. Thus, part of the recognition of foods comes from sensations of smell as well as taste. Have you ever pinched your nostrils, hoping to eliminate the flavor of some undesirable food? You have probably observed that without the sense of smell, your ability to taste most food flavors is greatly diminished.

When the effects of smell are eliminated, the primary taste qualities are *sweet, sour, salt,* and *bitter.* These four basic taste qualities were first identified over 2,000 years ago by Aristotle, and they are still viewed today as the basic ones. What are the mechanisms that determine these taste qualities? To answer this question, we must look to the surface of the tongue and the structure of the *taste system* (see Figure 3–18).

The surface of the tongue contains ridges and valleys. Embedded in them are *taste buds.* There are about 10,000 taste buds in the human tongue, all of which are made up of tiny spindle-shaped receptor cells. Stimulation of the taste receptor cells generates neural impulses that are transmitted along nerve fibers leaving the taste bud. These fibers form a pathway from the tongue to the medulla, near the base of the

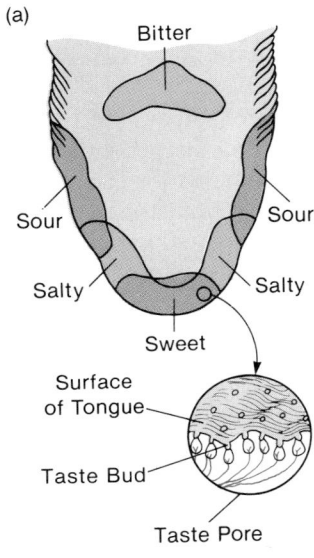

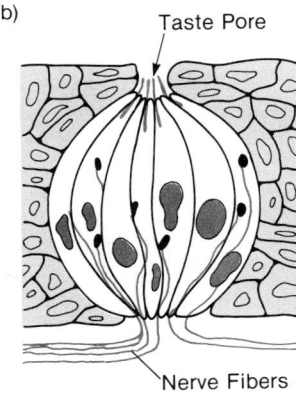

Figure 3–18.
The human tongue. (a) Areas most sensitive to the four primary taste qualities. (b) A magnified view of a taste bud.

brain, then to the thalamus and the parietal cortex (see chapter 2).

Microelectrode studies of rats and hamsters show that individual taste receptor cells vary in their response to the four basic taste stimuli. Some cells are excited by sweet-tasting substances; others are inhibited. Some cells respond only to sour stimuli, others only to bitter, and so on. These findings are consistent with the subjective reports provided by student volunteers who have reliably identified sweet, sour, salt, and bitter as basic taste qualities. The findings also suggest that the brain mechanisms of taste depend on individual receptor cells and groups of cells that respond differently to different taste stimuli (Goldstein, 1980). As in the case for olfaction, the precise cortical mechanisms for taste are not yet known.

The Skin Senses

The **skin senses** produce a broad range of sensations, all of which provide (through the skin) information to the organism about physical stimuli in the environment. As noted by Goldstein (1980), touch is just one of the sensations we experience through the skin. Stimulation of the skin can also cause us to feel pressure, pain, itchiness, warmth, cold, tickling, and vibration. This large array of sensations has led to the suggestion that there are many more senses than just vision, hearing, smell, taste, and touch.

In a series of influential papers written during the 1890s, Max von Frey proposed that there were four primary skin senses: *pressure* (touch), *pain, cold,* and *warmth.* Today, it is known that there are distinct types of nerve endings within the skin that play different roles in our "touching" experiences. Although it has not been possible to show a consistent correspondence between specific types of skin receptors and types of sensations, it is now accepted that certain areas of the skin react only to pressure, to pain, to warmth, or to cold. Because these qualities of experience can be mapped separately on the skin, we regard them as basic skin senses. Attempts to map other sensations, such as tickling, itchiness, vibration, and so on, have not successfully identified separate responsive spots on the skin. Instead, these other sensations overlap with the basic skin senses. For instance, a tickle is experienced when *pressure spots* are touched gently but in rapid succession. An itch is experienced when *pain spots* are gently and repeatedly stimulated.

The Body Senses

The sense of **kinesthesis** informs us of body movement. Receptors for this sense are neurons that branch off from the central nervous system and terminate in muscles, joints, and tendons throughout the body. *Kinesthetic receptor cells* in the muscles serve to automatically control muscle movements and to inform us when our muscles are flexed. Receptors in the joints and tendons are sensitive to body movement. Stimulation of these receptors is initiated by changes in posture, walking, running, climbing, grasping, manipulating, lying, sitting, and so on. The kinesthetic receptors converge with nerve fibers in the skin that lead through the spinal cord to the brain. Patterns of kinesthetic nerve impulses are believed to be transmitted to several areas of the brain. As with the senses of hearing, smell, taste, and touch, little is yet known about how the brain interprets these patterns.

Kinesthesis monitors body parts in relation to one another and to external objects in the environment. The **vestibular sense,** by comparison, governs body orientation and position in three-dimensional space with respect to gravity. Thus, it monitors the motion of the body as a whole. The vestibular sense is responsible for controlling body balance and position and is sometimes referred to as the *equilibratory sense.*

The vestibular organs are located in the inner ear (see Figure 3–19). Three *semicircular canals,* filled with fluid and positioned at right angles to each other, are maximally sensitive to changes in rotations of the body, especially the head. Movement of the head, for example, causes the fluid in the semicircular canals to move, thus exerting pressure on tiny hair cells in the *ampulla* at the base of each canal. (These hair cells are similar to those located in the organ of Corti.) Stimulation of the hair cells results in the transmission of nerve impulses to the brain through a nonauditory branch of the auditory nerve.

Position of the body in space and knowledge of the "upright" with respect to gravity is maintained by the *vestibular sacs,* located below the ampulla between the semicircular canals and the cochlea. As in the semicircular canals, there are hair cells located in the vestibular sacs that are stimulated when the head is tilted. These receptor cells detect stimuli that help us maintain an upright position.

Have you ever suffered from vestibular disturbance? The most common sensations produced by an upset in

Figure 3–19.
The inner ear. (a) A highlight of the inner ear. (b) An enlargement of the vestibular organ.

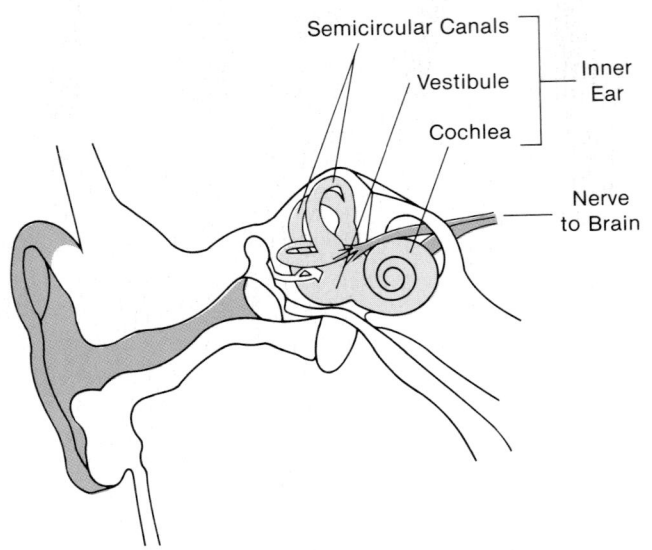

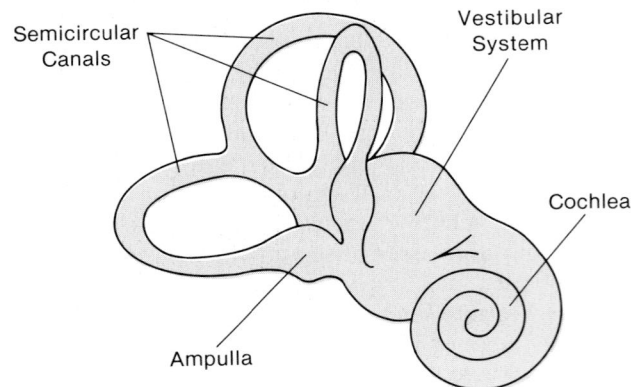

the vestibular system are dizziness and nausea resulting from motion sickness. Airsickness, carsickness,
seasickness, and spacesickness are examples of such
disturbance. Each is caused by abrupt and continuous
movement of the body in situations where the individual has no control over the motion.

Vertigo is a term used to describe sensations of dizziness and lightheadedness. On the ground, vertigo
tends to upset physical balance. In the air, a pilot affected by vertigo does not know which way is up or
down. The fluids in the pilot's vestibular canals, which
under normal conditions indicate by gravitational force
which way is down, have been disturbed. Sudden
changes in altitude while flying, loss of visual reference
with respect to the ground and horizon, and a disturbance of gravitational pull on muscles, joints, and the
vestibular organs all contribute to vertigo.

Pilots fight vertigo by closing their eyes for a few
seconds, then concentrating on the airplane's instruments, believing them, and maintaining them in normal positions. In a moving vehicle, either in the air or
on the ground, you can combat motion sickness by
imagining, with your eyes closed, that you are fixing
your gaze on a stable object. Relaxation techniques,
such as slowly tensing and loosening muscles, can also
help (see chapters 6 and 14), as can slow, deep breathing with the mouth open (Fromer, 1983).

--- APPLICATION ---

SEEING WITH THE SKIN SENSES

Our most efficient sense becomes our dominant mode
for knowing the world. For sighted people, vision is
the dominant sense. For the blind, the dominant sense
may be touch. Descartes acknowledged this possibility
centuries ago when he proposed that a blind person,
by tapping objects with a stick, uses touch to build up
mental images of the outside world. Descartes hypothesized, "If you take men born blind, who have made
use of such sensation all their lives, you will find that

they feel things with such perfect exactness . . . one
might almost say that they see with their hands"
(quoted in Hechinger, 1981, p. 39).

The ability of the blind to read Braille by moving
their fingers over patterns of raised dots and blank
spaces is an extraordinary example of how one can
"see" with the skin senses. Braille was invented in
1824 by the blind Frenchman Louis Braille and has
been used ever since as a means of seeing with the

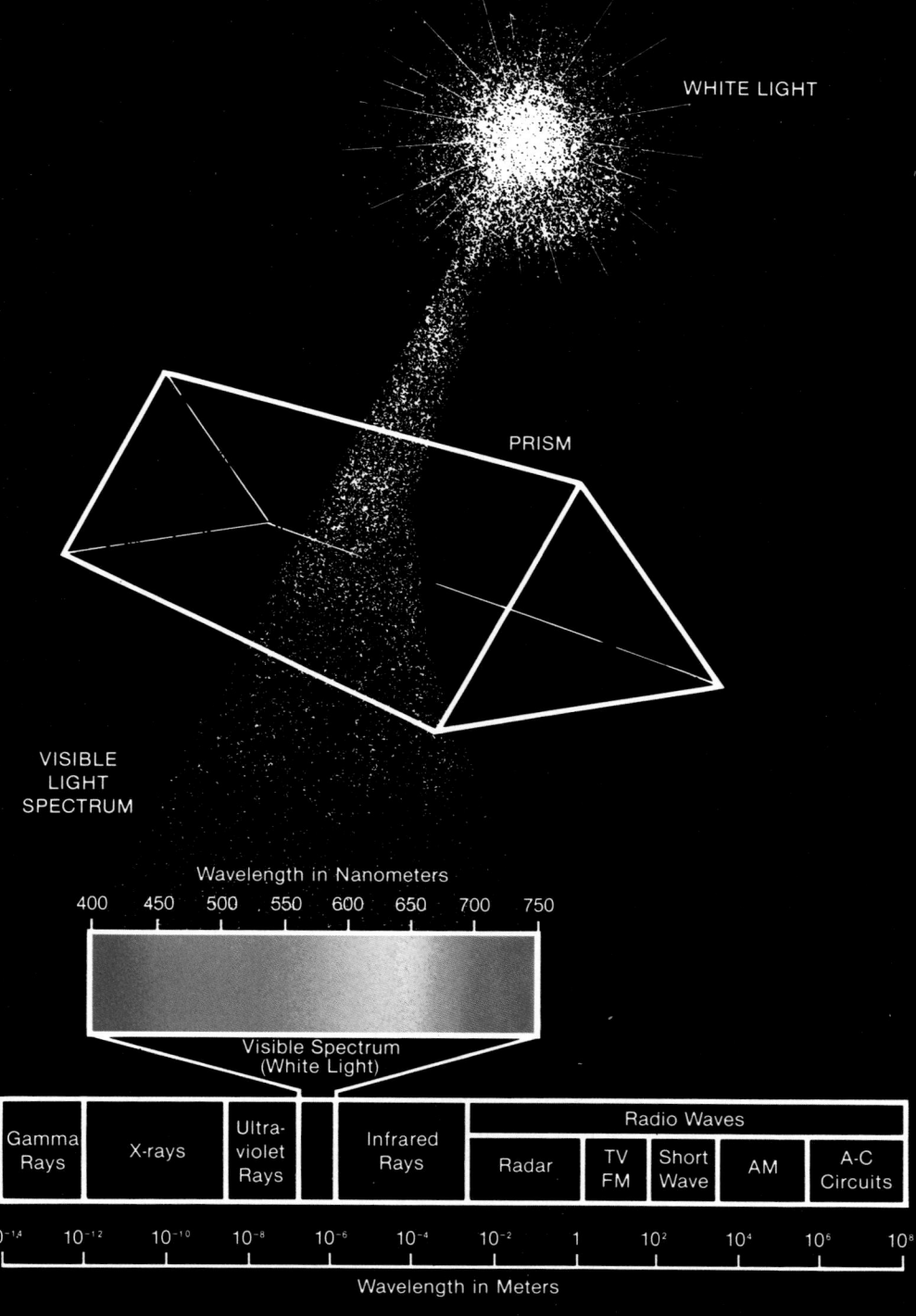

Figure 3–1.

The electromagnetic spectrum. Electromagnetic (radiant) energy travels in waves through space at approximately 186,000 miles per second. These waves can be measured by their length. Wavelength is obtained mathematically by dividing speed by frequency. The small portion of the entire electromagnetic spectrum that is visible to the human eye is what we call light, or the visual spectrum (see enlarged portion of the electromagnetic spectrum). The shortest light waves visible to the human eye are about 400 nanometers and are perceived as violet or dark colors. The longest light waves are about 750 nanometers and are perceived as red.

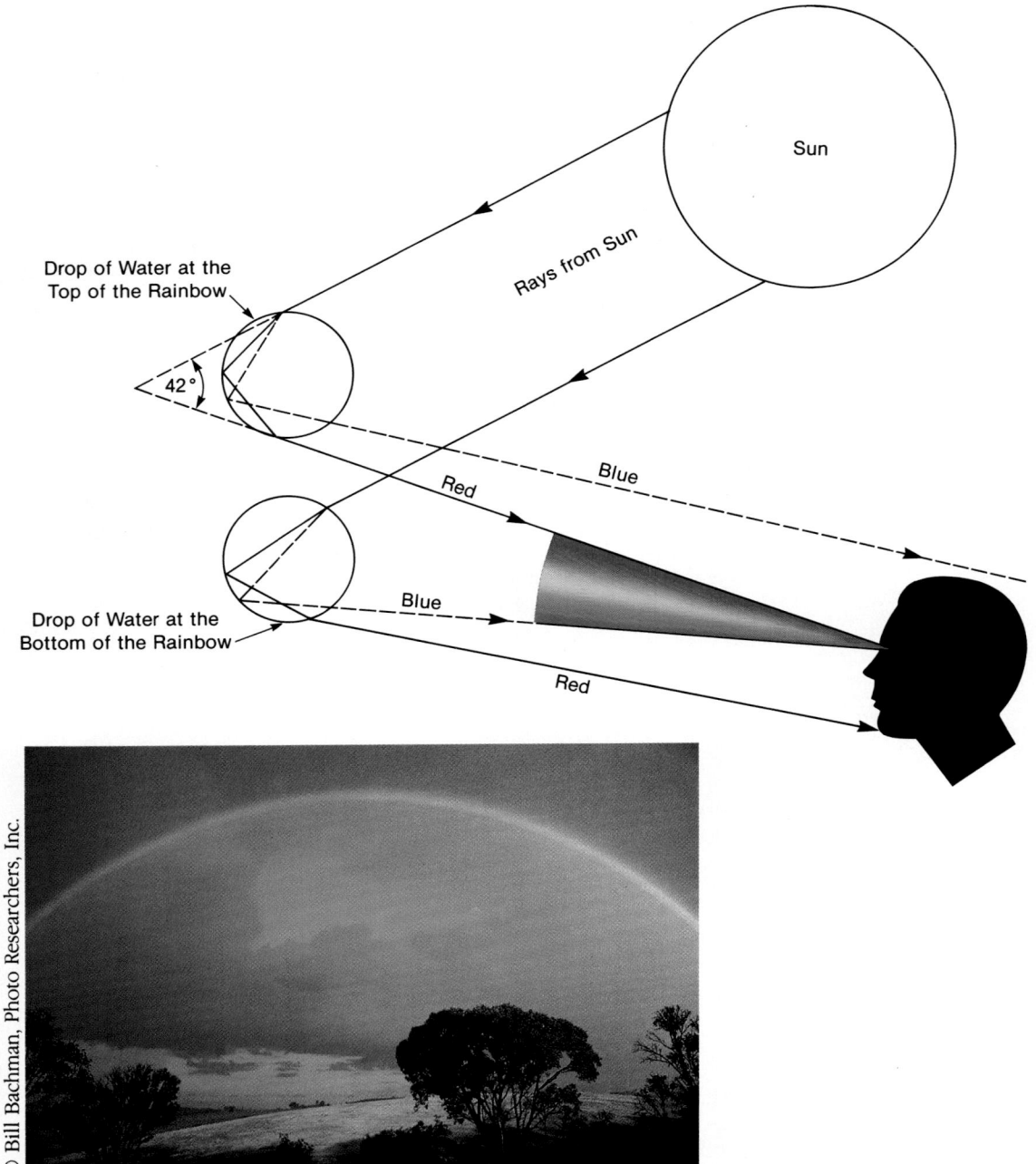

Figure 3–7.

How we see rainbows. Just as Isaac Newton produced the colors of the visible spectrum by passing white light through a prism, nature produces the colors of the rainbow by passing white light through tiny drops of rain that act like little prisms. White light entering a raindrop is separated into all of the spectral colors. If you consider the relationship between the rays of light and the observer's eye, you will notice that the raindrop at the top of the rainbow refracts the blue and red rays so that the blue ray passes over the observer's head and the red ray enters the observer's eye. The lower raindrop does the opposite; the red ray passes below the observer, and the blue ray enters the observer's eye. This relationship between the angle of the rays from the sun that enter the raindrops and the ray refracted from the raindrops that enter the observer's eye, which must be 42 degrees, helps explain why red is always seen at the top of the rainbow and blue at the bottom, with the other colors in between (after Goldstein, 1980).

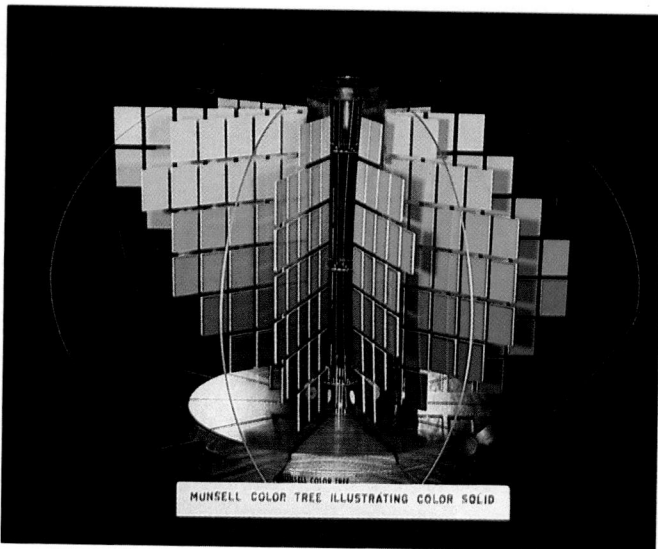

Figure 3–8.

Color solid. Hue is represented by the circumference, brightness by the vertical axis, and saturation by horizontal axis or radius. Munsell Color, 2441 N. Calvert St. Baltimore, MD 21218.

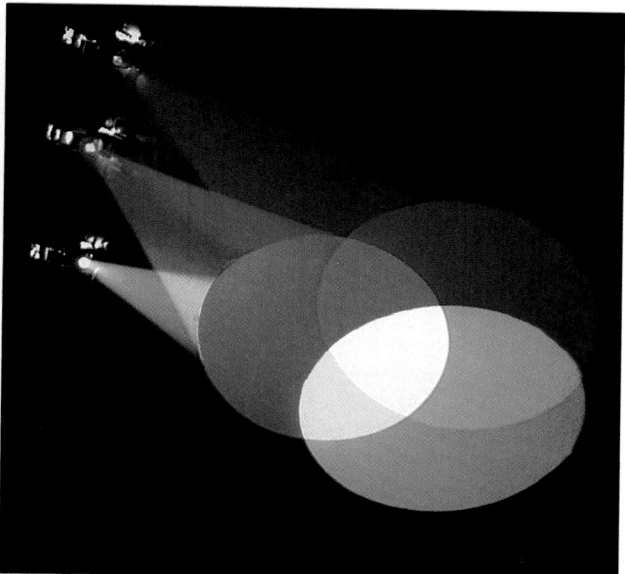

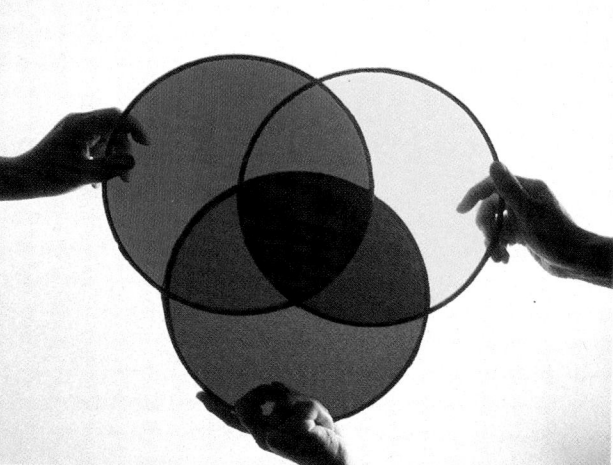

Figure 3–9.

Color mixture. Additive mixture: White light is produced by mixing red, green, and blue wavelengths of light. Subtractive mixture: Black is produced by mixing red, green, and blue paint pigment because paint pigments absorb most wavelengths of light. (See text for explanation.) Fritz Goro, LIFE Magazine, © 1944 Time, Inc.

Figure 3–10.

Red square. Stare at the center of the red square. Then look at a white wall or piece of paper and blink your eyes. The green afterimage that most people see is called a negative afterimage because green is the opposing color of red. Consistent with the opponent-process theory of color vision, staring at green will produce a red afterimage. The afterimages for blue and yellow are similarly paired.

ARE YOU COLOR BLIND?

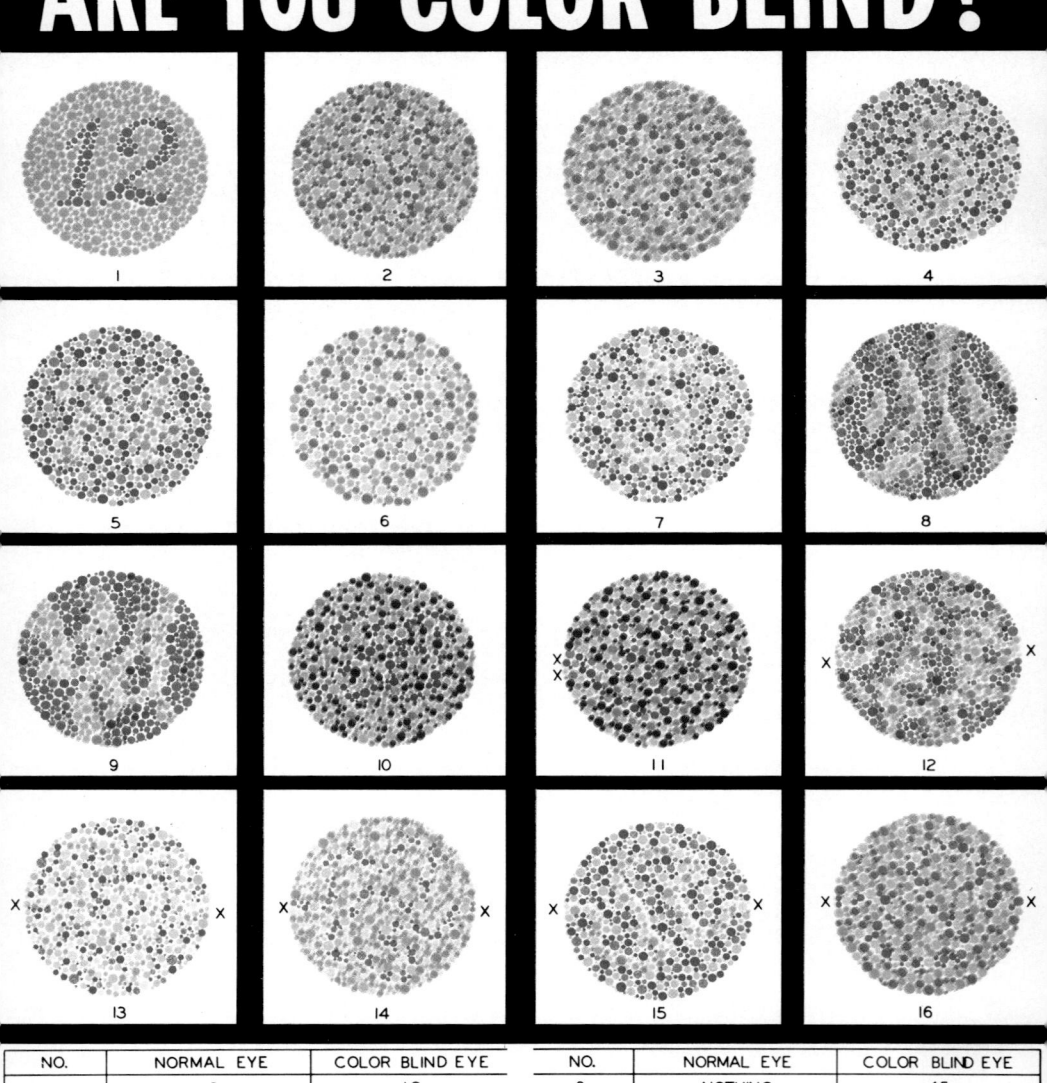

NO.	NORMAL EYE	COLOR BLIND EYE
1	12	12
2	8	3
3	29	70
4	5	2
5	74	21
6	45	NOTHING
7	5	NOTHING
8	NOTHING	5

NO.	NORMAL EYE	COLOR BLIND EYE
9	NOTHING	45
10	26	2 OR 6
11	2 LINES X TO X	LINE X TO X
12	NOTHING	LINE X TO X
13	LINE X TO X	NOTHING
14	LINE X TO X	NOTHING
15	LINE X TO X	NOTHING
16	LINE X TO X	LINE X TO X

Figure 3–13.

A test for color blindness. A color blind person would have difficulty detecting numbers and designs superimposed on backgrounds containing other colored dots.

skin. Braille characters of the alphabet consist of one to six dots. In addition to characters for each letter of the alphabet, there are characters for numbers, punctuation marks, and other aspects of written language.

The reading rate for experienced Braille readers varies from about 104 words per minute, on the average, to over 125 words per minute for experts. The blind often achieve rapid reading speeds through the use of various strategies. For example, with experience, familiar words are recognized more quickly than unfamiliar ones and familiar material is read faster than unfamiliar material. Also, Braille readers who become familiar with idiosyncratic spelling patterns (knowing, for example, that the letter *q* is always followed by the letter *u*) will tend to read more quickly and accurately than those who are unfamiliar with such rules. These strategies in reading Braille make it possible for experienced blind readers to identify the meanings of words and phrases before they have touched all the characters (Goldstein, 1980).

SEEING WITHOUT EYES

Seeing with the skin has also been made possible by means of a mechanical substitution system developed by Paul Bach-y-Rita (1972) and co-workers. A television camera controlled by the blind person translates images into electrical signals which in turn activate tiny vibrators in the back of the chair in which the person is seated. With training, blind people can learn to interpret patterns of vibrations as representing objects and their relative locations. A remarkable demonstration is reflected in the following statement, made by a blind person experienced in using the system: "That is Betty; she is wearing her hair down today and does not have her glasses on. Her mouth is open, and she is moving her right hand from her left side to the back of her head" (quoted in Goldstein, 1980, p. 208).

A more recent version of the mechanical substitution device, weighing only 5 pounds, is entirely portable. A small, 10-inch square box with over a thousand vibrators is worn around the waist. A tiny television camera is mounted on a pair of glasses worn by the blind person. The electrical circuitry and batteries are incorporated in a vest. Blind students who have worn the system (see Figure 3–20) have been able to find and retrieve objects in a room, read meters, and use oscilloscopes. One blind technician using the system learned to assemble microcircuits (Hechinger, 1981).

Although technological refinements are required, the challenge facing researchers during the years ahead will be to develop a more affordable mechanical substitution device that someday may be widely used by the blind to navigate through their environment.

Figure 3–20.

A portable system used by the blind to see with the skin senses.

— SUMMARY —

1. Sensation is the response of a sensory organ to some form of physical energy.

2. The field of psychophysics is concerned with the objective measurement of sensitivity. Its goal is to relate characteristics of physical stimuli to characteristics of the sensations they produce.

3. Visual sensations are the product of light energy of various wavelengths reflected from surfaces in the environment or emitted from luminous objects.

4. Light entering the eye must pass through the cornea, the lens, and the vitreous humor, or fluid in the eyeball, before it reaches the complex layers of ganglion and bipolar cells and, finally, the rod and cone photoreceptive cells. There, light energy is transformed into electrochemical energy in a process called transduction.

5. Electrochemical energy in the form of nerve impulses is transmitted along the optic nerve to the areas of the cerebral cortex where vision is represented.

6. The rods and cones, located in the retina of the eye, are differentially sensitive to achromatic sensations (white, black, and gray) and chromatic colors (red, green, blue, and so on).

7. Quantitative changes in the length of light waves lead to qualitative changes in color sensations.

8. The great number of color discriminations that can be made by people with normal color vision arises from the fact that color varies on three psychological dimensions—hue, brightness, and saturation.

9. Auditory sensations are the product of mechanical energy, or pressure changes in the molecules of air that surround vibrating objects.

10. Our ability to perceive an amazing range of sounds in the audible spectrum arises from the fact that sound varies on three psychological dimensions: pitch, loudness, and timbre.

11. Smell and taste are sometimes referred to as the chemical senses because the physical stimulus for each is provided by chemical substances.

12. Physical stimulation of receptor cells initiates the process of transduction, wherein physical (chemical) energy is transformed into electrochemical energy that can be transmitted as nerve impulses to smell and taste centers of the brain.

13. Four primary skin senses are pressure, pain, cold, and warmth.

14. In addition to the variety of skin receptor cells that are maximally sensitive to the four skin senses, there are kinesthetic receptor cells located in the muscles, joints, and tendons throughout the body. These receptor cells serve to automatically control muscle and body movements.

15. Whereas the sense of kinesthesis monitors body parts in relation to one another and to external objects in the environment, the vestibular sense governs body orientation and position in three-dimensional space with respect to gravity and monitors the motion of the body as a whole.

— IMPORTANT TERMS AND CONCEPTS —

Psychophysics
Sensation
Absolute Threshold
Signal Detection Theory
Visual System
Visual Spectrum
Cornea
Lens
Ciliary Muscles
Pupil
Iris
Retina
Rods
Cones

Fovea
Visual Acuity
Blind Spot
Dark Adaptation
Transduction
Feature Detectors
Hue
Brightness
Saturation
Trichromatic Theory
Physical Primary Colors
Opponent-Process Theory
Afterimages

Audition
Pitch
Loudness
Timbre
Place Theory of Pitch
Frequency Theory of Pitch
Volley Theory of Pitch
Chemical Senses
Olfaction
Taste
Skin Senses
Kinesthesis
Vestibular Sense

Boynton, R. M. (1979). *Human color vision.* New York: Holt, Rinehart and Winston. A well-balanced presentation of concepts from physics, physiology, and psychology for the nonspecialist. The book presents classical material on human color vision, the physics of light, the structure of the eye, visual receptors, and other topics covered in this chapter.

Goldstein, E. B. (1980). *Sensation and perception.* Belmont, CA: Wadsworth. An introductory textbook that is broad in coverage and easy to read.

Gregory, R. L. (1977). *Eye and brain* (3rd ed.). New York: McGraw-Hill. Available in most public libraries and bookstores, this popular paperback is fun to read and is packed with facts and illustrations about the visual system.

Levine, M. W., & Shefner, J. M. (1981). *Fundamentals of sensation and perception.* Reading, MA: Addison-Wesley. This textbook provides an extended coverage of most of the topics included in Chapters 3 and 4.

Marr, D. (1982). *Vision.* San Francisco: W. H. Freeman. A textbook that focuses on the visual system.

Melzack, R. (1973). *The puzzle of pain.* New York: Basic Books. An entertaining, easy-to-read book on the sensation of pain.

— CHAPTER 4 —

PERCEPTION

PERCEPTION

To achieve the objectives of this chapter, you should be able to answer the questions listed here. You should also be able to define the important terms and concepts listed at the end of the chapter.

1. What is perception?
2. How does the brain organize sensations into meaningful perceptions?
3. What are the processes involved in perceptual organization and in form, depth, size, and movement perception?
4. How have psychologists learned about perceptual processes through the study of perceptual illusions?
5. What can newborn babies see? How can depth and form perception in human infants be tested?
6. What effect does visual deprivation have on perceptual development?

Perceptual Processes
Perception is the term used to describe the brain's interpretation of information made available through the sense organs.

Gestalt Psychology: Perceptual Organization and Form Perception
Depth Perception
Perception of Size
Perception of Movement and Motion
Application: Movement in Cinema and Television

Perceptual Development
Perception depends on biological mechanisms and learning.

Infant Perceptual Development
Experience and Perceptual Development
Application: Attention and Perception

On the Horizon: Extrasensory Perception

READING RECORDS AND RECORDING SENSATIONS

Have you read any good records lately? Arthur Lintgen, a Philadelphia physician, cannot explain his bizarre talent. But he has it: the ability to "read" the grooves on a phonograph record and identify the music on it. Lintgen simply holds a disc flat in front of him—with the label and other identifying marks covered, of course—and turns it slightly this way and that, peering along its grooves through his thick glasses. After a few seconds he calmly announces, as the case may be, "Stravinsky's *Rite of Spring*," or "Strauss's *Alpine Symphony*," or "Janacek's *Sinfoniette*." Performing for the television crew from *That's Incredible,* Lintgen scored 20 correct guesses out of 20 in a demonstration set up by Stimson Carrow, a musicologist from Temple University.

How does Lintgen "read" records? Lintgen's explanation is simple. All phonograph grooves, he says, vary minutely in their spacing and contour depending on the dynamics and frequency of the music on them. Grooves containing soft passages look black or dark gray. As the music gets louder or more complicated, the grooves turn silvery. (Paraphrased from Read any, 1982, p. 84)

Lintgen has apparently learned to recognize the subtle patterns of light reflected from bands of recorded music—much as a checkout clerk in a supermarket might recognize some of the zebra codes imprinted on food containers. As astounding as Lintgen's feat may seem, it is no more amazing than our routine ability to recognize faces, voices, and other complex patterns. Similar skills are shown by the scientists who can read the history of a tree from its growth rings or the mechanic who can tell which part of an engine is malfunctioning by listening carefully. Such abilities at first seem to require unusual talent. But, in fact, they reflect interest, experience, and perceptual learning.

Reading phonograph records, then, is a strange but not altogether unrepresentative example of human perception. **Perception** is the term we use to describe the brain's interpretation of sensory information (Hochberg, 1978). Our examination of sensation in chapter 3 indicated that each sense organ is a specialized receiver of a particular kind of physical energy. Information received by the sense organs in transduced into nerve impulses. But nerve impulses themselves bear no resemblance to objects and people in the surrounding environment. Somehow the brain interprets and gives meaning to the impulses sent to it by the sense organs. This is the process we call perception.

In this chapter, we will focus on processes that underlie visual perception. We have chosen to emphasize vision because of its importance and because so much more is known about it than about other perceptual systems. A century-long program of psychological research has led to a fairly clear picture of the processes involved in the visual perception of form, depth, movement, and size. After addressing these topics, we will investigate how perception develops.

Gestalt Psychology: Perceptual Organization and Form Perception

How does the brain organize sensations into meaningful perceptions? The founders of **Gestalt psychology**—Max Wertheimer, Wolfgang Köhler, and Kurt Koffka—believed that perception depends on the brain's tendency to organize pieces of sensory information into wholes whose significance differs from the mere sum of the parts. *Gestalt* is a German word that means "pattern," and the Gestalt psychologists studied perception in terms of patterns, or the whole perception. The following tale may help illustrate this point:

One day, an elephant appeared in the main square of a town where all the inhabitants were blind. No one in the town knew what the animal was, so the king sent out his three wisest men, all blind, to find out. One blind man, who touched only the leg of the elephant, reported that the beast was like a column. The second, who touched only the trunk, said the beast was like a huge trumpet. The third, who touched only the ear, said the beast was wide and flat, like a rug. By investigating only one part of the animal's body, the wise men lacked a sense of the whole. They lacked perception. (Paraphrased from Hechinger, 1981, p. 43)

To repeat, then, Gestalt psychologists believe that the brain organizes sensory information in ways that go beyond individual sensations (Wertheimer, 1938). Much evidence for this view comes from what these psychologists have learned about *principles of perceptual organization* (Kubovy & Pomerantz, 1982). These principles include figure and ground, grouping, contour, and context.

— Figure and Ground

The fact that most seen objects tend to stand out from a background of one kind or another is referred to as the **principle of figure and ground.** The figure tends to be seen as being in front of the ground (or the ground appears to be located behind the figure). The figure tends to have a distinctive shape, whereas the ground does not. Nonetheless, it is the whole pattern—the figure and the ground—that helps give meaning to our perceptions. For example, as you read the words on this page, they appear as black figures against a white background. It is only with effort that a "white" word can be perceived against a black background (see Figure 4–1a).

Figure-ground relationships, such as the one shown in Figure 4–1a, illustrate that the same stimulus pattern can be perceptually organized by the brain in different ways. A figure can sometimes become a background, and vice versa. For a further illustration of this point, look at the rest of Figure 4–1. Figure 4–1b can be perceived as either a white vase on a dark background or two shaded faces looking at each other in front of a white background. Figure 4–1c is a reversible pattern that can be perceived either as a pretty young lady or an unattractive old woman. In each of these reversible figure-ground patterns it is possible to perceive only one of the figures at a time.

— Grouping

In addition to the principle of figure and ground, Gestalt psychologists identified several *principles of grouping,* which help explain how we organize incoming stimuli. The **principle of perceptual grouping** refers to the tendency to perceive stimuli as meaningful wholes or patterns. We see complex patterns of stimuli as unitary forms or objects because of such grouping. In general, we tend to organize subsets of stimuli into meaningful forms on the basis of similarity, proximity, continuation, and closure.

The **principle of similarity** states that objects or stimuli of like appearance are grouped together. Look at Figure 4–2a. Typically, people perceive the dots as either vertical columns of circles, horizontal rows of circles, or both. However, when some of the circles are changed to squares, most people then perceive vertical columns of circles alternating with vertical columns of squares (see Figure 4–2b). Thus, similar objects tend to be grouped.

Perceptual grouping can also occur because of proximity, or nearness. The **principle of proximity** states that objects or stimuli that are near each other appear to be grouped together. Look at Figure 4–2c. Typically, the dots are perceived as horizontal rows of circles be-

Figure 4–1

Reversible figure-ground relationships: (a) A word in white against a black background, (b) Reversible face-vase, (c) Reversible wife and mother-in-law figure.

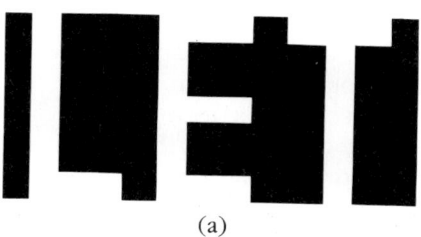

(a)

(b)

(c)

Figure 4–2

Principles of perceptual grouping: (a) and (b) principle of similarity, (c) and (d) principle of proximity, (e) principle of continuation, (f) principle of closure. (See text for description.)

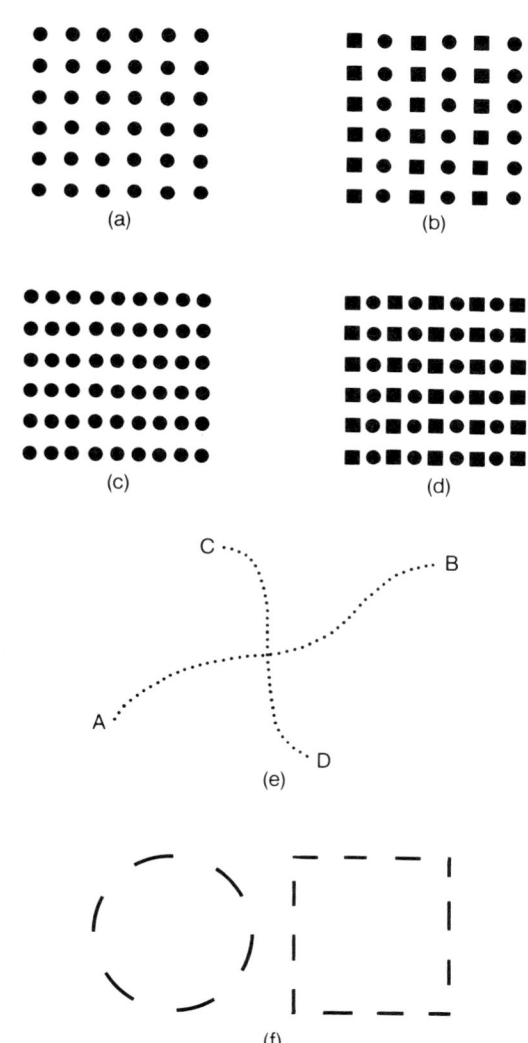

cause they are nearer horizontally than vertically. Even when some of the circles are changed to squares (as in Figure 4–2d), most people perceive horizontal rows. In this case, proximity has a stronger influence than similarity on our perception.

The **principle of continuation** states that lines and contours tend to be seen as following the smoothest path. Lines that start in one direction will be perceived as continuing that way. An illustration of this principle is provided in Figure 4–2e. When we look at the dots, we perceive them as curved lines. The dots that begin at Point A and end at Point B seem to belong together, as do the dots between Points C and D. Even though the curved lines cross and have dots in common, it is only with effort that we can perceive an angled line between, for example, Points C and B or A and D.

The **principle of closure** states that we tend to perceive a complete object even though parts of it may be obscured or missing. Figure 4–2f illustrates this principle. We see the form on the left as a circle and the form in the middle as a square. What do we see in the form at the right?

— Contours in Form Perception

Contours are also important in organizing perceptions because they give shape, and thus meaning, to objects in our visual world. A **contour** is the boundary between a figure and its ground. Contours are typically formed by marked differences in brightness or color between figure and ground. Too much or too little light can easily affect our ability to perceive figure-ground differences. When contours are diminished, as in *camouflage*, objects become difficult to see because they blend into the background. By using natural camouflage, many animals are able to avoid predators. Their coloration allows them to blend into the surrounding habitat (see Figure 4–3).

Sometimes the boundaries that give shape to an object are subjective. As can be seen from an inspection of Figure 4–4, the contours of the upright triangle are incomplete; yet a triangle contour results from the surrounding configuration. For this reason, such perceptions are called *subjective contours* (Kanizsa, 1976). Prove the subjectivity to yourself by covering the black circles in Figure 4–4. When the circles are covered,

Figure 4–3
Natural camouflage makes the animal in this photograph difficult to see.

Figure 4–4

Subjective contours. Cover the black circles and the white triangle disappears. (After Kaniza, 1976.)

the subjective contours that form the upright triangle disappear. This illustration supports the point made by Gestalt psychologists that the perception of parts of a stimulus depends on the whole configuration being perceived.

— Context in Form Perception

The setting in which an object appears is its **context.** Our perceptions are highly influenced by context. For example, read the following lines:

Read this line: **A B C**

Now read this line: **12 13 14**

As noted by Silverman (1982) most people read the first line as a group of letters and the second as a group of numbers. Look carefully at the letter B and the number 13. They are identical, but you probably read one as a letter and the other as a number because of the context in which each appeared. The same pattern of lines in a different context takes on a different meaning and even a different appearance. Contexts are learned through experience. Past experience with the alphabet and number systems provides an *adaptation level* for the psychological dimensions of stimuli. We learn through experience that certain stimuli go together because of context, and we adapt our perceptions to our expectations. Thus the whole configuration, or context, in which a stimulus appears can influence our perception of the parts of the stimulus.

— Shape Constancy

Learning also helps explain why we tend to see forms and shapes as unchanging, even as the angle from which they are viewed changes. The **principle of shape constancy** states that an object's apparent physical shape remains unchanged even though the object's image on the retina changes shape as the viewing angle varies (Goldstein, 1980). For example, if you view a square "Do Not Enter" sign from different angles while walking past it, the sign will retain its squareness, even though its retinal image changes dramatically (see Figure 4–5). When the sign is viewed at an angle, the outer border forms a trapezoidal image on the retina and the dark circular area casts an ellip-

Figure 4–5

Shape constancy. There is a strong tendency to see correct physical shapes even with the viewing angle changed.

(a)

(b)

(c)

tical shape. When the sign is viewed straight on, the retinal image of its border is square and the retinal shape of its dark area is circular. If perception of the sign depended only on retinal images, its shape would appear to change continually as the viewing angle changed. Because of past experience in viewing signs and because of familiarity with the shapes and contours of objects in the environment, however, there is a strong tendency to see the correct physical shapes of objects, no matter what their orientation.

Depth Perception

Our remarkable ability to judge accurately how far objects are from us or from each other is referred to as **depth perception.** It is difficult to imagine what it would be like to live without the ability to judge distance and depth; the perceptual world would be restricted to two dimensions—height and width—rather than three. As noted by Gardner (1983), creating depth from flat surfaces is a psychological tour de force. How is it that we perceive three dimensions solely on the basis of images on the two-dimensional surface of the retina? The answer lies in depth perception, a complex process by which the brain organizes and gives meaning to sensory input. Research has identified the cues we use to make inferences about three-dimensional objects on the basis of two-dimensional retinal images (Haber, 1978). Let's examine **binocular depth cues** (depth cues that require the use of both eyes) and **monocular depth cues** (depth cues that require the use of only one eye).

— Binocular Depth Cues

Vision with both eyes, called **stereoscopic vision,** provides valuable information about depth because each eye receives a slightly different view of the world. That the two eyes scan objects at slightly different angles can be seen clearly if first one eye, then the other, is closed. Near objects (your index finger held up in front of you, for instance) appear to shift back and forth relative to more distant objects (such as the trunk of a tree). This occurs because the retinal images formed by the near object and the more distant object differ, their angles being different. We call this difference in retinal images **binocular disparity.** The binocular disparity of distant objects is less than that of near objects. Thus, this difference in disparity provides information about the depth and distance of objects.

The degree of disparity in retinal images can be measured with a stereoscope, an instrument used for presenting pictures separately to the two eyes. Photographs are presented to subjects in pairs; the photos are taken by two cameras that are separated by the distance between the eyes. Such photos provide the disparity registered by the brain in normal stereoscopic vision (Gregory, 1977). Through experimentation with instruments such as the stereoscope, researchers have learned that stereoscopic vision functions only for comparatively near objects. "We are effectively one-eyed for distances greater than perhaps 100 meters" (Gregory, 1977, p. 67)

— Monocular Depth Cues

Because binocular disparity, by definition, requires two eyes, we might ask what it would be like to be sighted in only one eye. Without binocular disparity, which is perhaps our most important cue for depth, is it possible to perceive depth from two-dimensional retinal images? The answer, happily, is yes. The reason is that several additional depth cues, called monocular depth cues, operate on each eye separately. Let's look briefly at each.

Linear perspective. If you stand between railroad tracks and look into the distance, the separation between the railroad tracks will appear to decrease until the tracks seem to meet at the horizon (see Figure 4–6a). This example illustrates what is meant by the **principle of linear perspective,** which states that parallel lines appear to converge in the distance and that distant objects appear to be closer together than near objects.

Aerial perspective. On a clear day, it has been said, you can see forever. The **principle of aerial perspective,** also called the principle of clearness, states that clearly seen objects appear closer than they actually are and that unclear objects appear farther away than they actually are. Imagine that you are standing on a hilltop looking toward some mountains. Distant peaks typically appear closer on clear days and farther away on hazy days.

Interposition. When one object obstructs the view of another object, generally the object that is entirely in view will appear to be the closer of the two (see Figure 4–6b), according to the **principle of interposition.** Imagine, for example, the perceptual ef-

Figure 4–6a
Monocular depth cue—Principle of linear perspective. Parallel tracks appear closer together at the horizon.

Figure 4–6b
Monocular depth cue—principle of interposition, or overlap. (See text for description.)

Figure 4–6c
Monocular depth cue—texture gradients. Surfaces appear coarse in the foreground and less detailed in the background.

fect of sliding one playing card partially in front of another.

Texture gradients. An additional cue to depth perception is provided by texture gradients. The **principle of texture gradients** states that the texture of near objects in the visual field will appear to be coarse and detailed, whereas the texture of distant objects will appear to be finer and less detailed (see Figure 4–6c). A look down a cobblestone street will provide a good example of this effect.

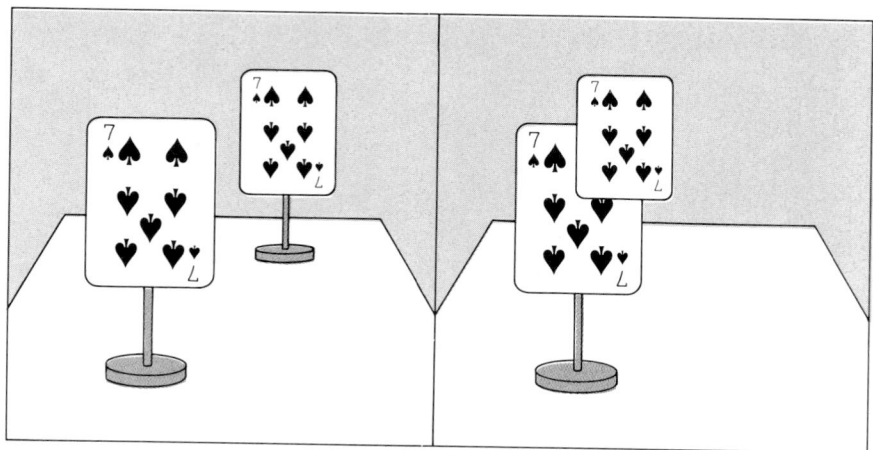

Light and shadow. When light creates shadows on objects, the shadowed, darker areas will appear farther away and the lighted surfaces will appear closer, according to the **principle of light and shadow.** This occurs because we normally expect light to come from above. The importance of shadows can be illustrated by looking at the picture shown in Figure 4–6d, turned upside down. The upside-down buildings take on the appearance of skyscrapers. Areas that before looked like shadows now appear to be the black-painted roofs of tall buildings. Because we assume that the light is coming from above, experience tells us that the dark areas of the buildings cannot possibly be shadows and therefore must be the tops of the buildings.

Relative size. Objects in the background of the visual field appear farther away and thus smaller, according to the **principle of relative size.**

Pictorial depth. The monocular cues described here are sometimes referred to as *pictorial depth cues.* Using these cues, artists have for centuries successfully portrayed three-dimensional depth on two-dimensional surfaces. The picture shown in Figure 4–7 provides an example. Notice the use of linear perspective. Lines that are parallel in the foreground of the picture converge in the distance. The details of the buildings in the foreground are clearer than those of the buildings in the background. Buildings that overlap and thus obstruct the view of other buildings appear to be

nearer than buildings whose view is obstructed. The texture of the squares in the foreground is coarse and detailed, whereas the texture of the squares in the background is finer and less detailed. Light and shadow provide additional depth cues; light surfaces appear closer than shadowed surfaces. Finally, the relatively smaller image size of buildings in the background adds to the perception of depth in this two-dimensional picture.

Motion parallax. A final monocular depth cue does not appear in still photographs or paintings. When you move through space, as in walking or riding in an automobile, or when you move your head, the images of nearby objects appear to move farther than do the images of more distant objects. This difference in apparent movement, called **motion parallax,** is an added source of depth perception in many situations.

— Accommodation and Convergence

The binocular and monocular depth cues considered thus far depend on visual information projected onto the retina. Two additional cues—accommodation and convergence—supply information about depth and distance from the eye muscles rather than from images. **Accommodation** refers to the changes in lens shape that the eye makes to focus objects at various distances. **Convergence** refers to the way the eyes look inward and outward to focus on near and far objects. When you focus on a nearby object, the

Figure 4–6d
Monocular depth cue—light and shadows. Turn the book upside down and the buildings in this picture take on the appearance of skyscrapers. (See text for description.)

Figure 4–7

A street with various buildings (ca. 1500, artist unknown). The use of pictorial depth cues allows the artist to portray three-dimensional depth on a two dimensional surface.

lens of the eye bulges because of the action of the attached ciliary muscles (see chapter 3) and the eyes converge, or look inward. As the object is moved farther away, the lens flattens and the eyes diverge so the lines of sight become parallel. The important point is that accommodation and convergence provide helpful depth cues as we learn that focusing movements and the position of the eyes are related to the distance of seen objects. Research has shown, however, that these cues provide depth information only for objects within about 10 feet of the observer (Goldstein, 1980).

Perception of Size

Familiarity with objects allows us to perceive their actual size, even when depth cues are unavailable or the objects are far away. The **principle of size constancy** states that an object's perceived size remains constant regardless of the object's distance from the observer (Goldstein, 1980). In everyday experience, size constancy is the rule rather than the exception, because depth cues are available and we have strong expectations about the sizes of objects we encounter. There are situations, however, in which ambiguous

depth cues may cause *perceptual illusions of size*. An **illusion** is a distortion in perception that contradicts objective reality. Psychologists have learned a great deal about perceptual processes from studying illusions. For example, over 30 years ago, Adelbert Ames cleverly demonstrated that size constancy may be distorted by context.

— The Ames Room Illusion

Figure 4–8a shows an apparatus, now called the Ames room, that Ames constructed to study the influence of context on perception (Ittelson, 1952). Because of the way the room is constructed, the heights of three equally tall people in it appear to differ, thus creating the *Ames room illusion*. What causes this illusion? Looking at the photograph of the observer's view of the Ames room, we note that the shape of the windows on the back wall makes the room look normal. But, in fact, as shown in the diagram (see Figure 4–8b), the room is shaped so that the left corner is nearly twice as far from the observer as the right corner. The shorter distance to the man on the right enlarges his *visual angle* (the size of his image on the retina), whereas the greater distance to the man on the left makes the latter's visual angle smaller. This is the key

Figure 4–8

The Ames Room. (See text for description.)

(a)

(b)

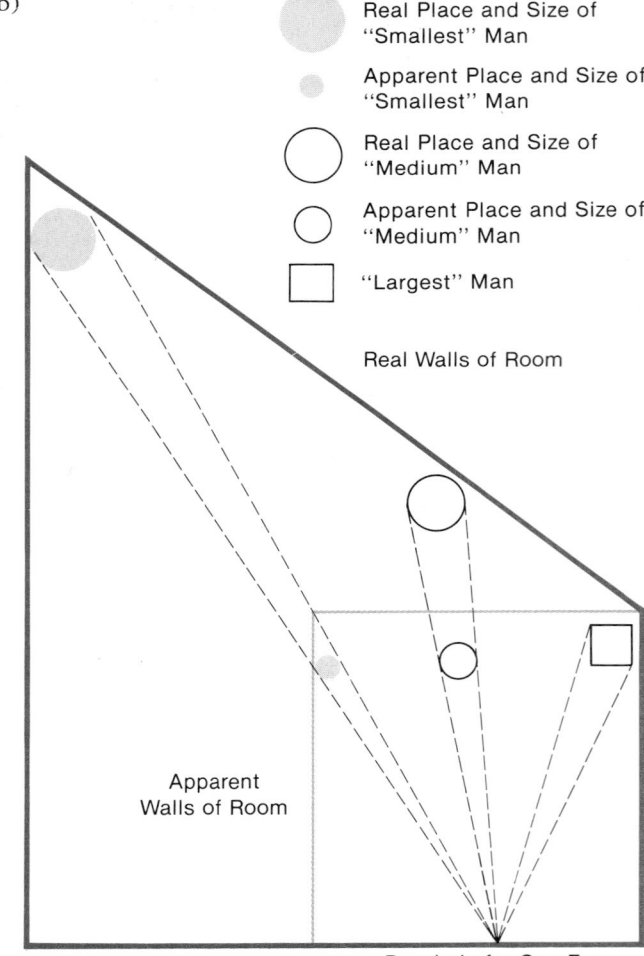

Real Place and Size of
"Smallest" Man

Apparent Place and Size of
"Smallest" Man

Real Place and Size of
"Medium" Man

Apparent Place and Size of
"Medium" Man

"Largest" Man

Real Walls of Room

Apparent
Walls of Room

Peephole for One Eye

to understanding the Ames room illusion. We think that we are looking at a perfectly normal room, so we assume that the men are equally distant. Consequently, we rely solely on information concerning the visual angle of each man. The man on the left, being farthest away from the observer and having the smallest visual angle, is perceived as being the shortest. Here, then, is an instance in which observers can be fooled, or their perceptions distorted, by alterations in depth cues and physical context.

— The Moon Illusion

There are few sights more beautiful than a full moon on the horizon (see Figure 4–9). The moon at that point can look truly gigantic; its size at its zenith, high in the sky, seems tiny by comparison. We call this the *moon illusion*—a distortion in perception that, like the Ames room illusion, can be understood in terms of depth perception (Baird, 1982; Baird & Wagner, 1982).

In the Ames room demonstration, men of equal height appear to differ in height because of their distance from the observer. In the moon illusion, we have a slightly different situation. The moon's physical distance from the earth and its image size remain virtually constant throughout the night. If the moon's retinal image and its distance are constant, then the moon's visual angle is also constant. Why, then, does the horizon moon appear larger than the zenith moon?

Figure 4–9

The moon illusion. Why does the horizon moon appear larger than the Zenith moon? See the text for the explanation.

Many theories have been offered to explain the moon illusion. The *apparent distance theory,* proposed by the astronomer Ptolemy over 1,600 years ago, provides a remarkably accurate explanation. Ptolemy reasoned that the horizon moon looks larger than the zenith moon because there are more depth cues present when one views the horizon moon. These cues are provided by terrain stretching between the viewer and the horizon. To demonstrate that the horizon moon appears larger because of such cues, Lloyd Kaufman and Irwin Rock (1962) examined observers' perceptions under two conditions. First, observers were asked to view the horizon moon over the terrain. They reported that the horizon moon was over 1.3 times larger than the zenith moon. Then they were asked to report on the size of the horizon moon as they viewed the moon through a peephole in a piece of cardboard. (This condition served to mask the terrain between the

observer and the moon.) In the absence of depth cues (linear and aerial perspective and interposition, for example), the moon illusion vanished.

Another way of thinking about the moon illusion is in terms of figure and ground. We view the horizon moon as a figure against the sky. We see less of the sky when we look at the horizon moon than when we look at the zenith moon. A smaller background makes an object look larger. (A football helmet on an infant's head looks larger than it does on the head of a professional football player.) Thus the smaller background of sky at the horizon makes the horizon moon appear larger than the zenith moon (Restle, 1970).

— Other Illusions of Size

In the *Müller-Lyer illusion* (shown in Figure 4–10a), two line segments of equal length appear to be differ-

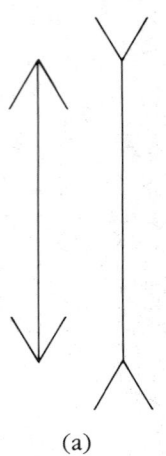

(a)

(b)

Figure 4–10
Müller-Lyer illusion. (a) two lines of equal length appear to be different lengths when V's and arrowheads are added to them.

ent lengths when *Vs* and arrowheads are added to them. Why does the line on the right look longer than the line on the left? Gregory (1977) attributed this illusion to what he called *misapplied size constancy*. Normally, an object's size is perceived as constant regardless of how far the object is from the observer. According to Gregory, the mechanism that allows us to maintain stable three-dimensional perceptions of size can sometimes create illusions when applied to objects viewed in two dimensions. To illustrate this point,

compare the left and right lines in Figure 4–10a to the left and right pictures in Figure 4–10b. The Müller-Lyer line on the left (Figure 4–10a) corresponds to the outside corner of the building (Figure 4–10b). Since the outside corner of a three-dimensional building appears closer than the inside corner of a room, we tend to perceive the Müller-Lyer line on the left as being closer, and therefore shorter, than the line on the right. Stated in other terms, our perceptual system responds to expectations about *depth information* obtained through experience with the three-dimensional world, and it misapplies the information to two-dimensional lines, as shown in Figure 4–10a.

Gregory's explanation of the Müller-Lyer illusion applies also to the *Ponzo illusion,* in which two identical horizontal lines appear to differ in length when shown against a background that contains depth cues. In the photo of the railroad tracks (see Figure 4–11), the overwhelmingly powerful depth cue is linear perspective. The line on the top appears to be farther away and is therefore perceived as longer than the bottom, closer line. Even though the lines are the same physical length (measure them yourself), their perceptual length is very different.

Perception of Movement and Motion

Real motion refers to a change in an object's position in space. As the object changes position, cues for *motion perception* are made available to the visual system. One such cue involves changes in the angle at which light from a moving object strikes the retina. Another cue comes from the continuous stimulation of receptor cells in the retina, as the moving object covers portions of the immobile background in the visual field. The ability to perceive moving objects is essential for survival. Each day, we avoid disaster by responding appropriately to moving objects in the environment; for example, we may jump out of an automobile's path or steer a bicycle clear of an oncoming truck.

Movement can be perceived when the eyes are stationary, as when a person stands on a street corner and watches the traffic go by. In this case, the image of moving objects passes across the retina and stimulates a series of receptor cells, or *movement detectors.* Movement can also be perceived when the eyes follow a moving object, as when a person visually tracks a tennis ball. In this case, the image of the object remains relatively stationary on the retina, but the object is still perceived as moving because of certain cues present in the environment. How is movement perceived in the two situations described?

One explanation for motion perception has been provided by Gregory (1977), who described two movement-signaling systems: the image-retina system and the eye-head system. The *image-retina system* is responsible for detecting the movement of objects when the eyes are stationary. Information concerning movement is provided by sequential firing of receptor

Figure 4–11

Ponzo illusion. Two identical horizontal lines appear to differ in length when shown against a background that contains depth cues.

cells as the object's image moves across the retina. The *eye-head system* is responsible for detecting moving objects that are followed with the eyes when the object's retinal image remains stationary. Here, information concerning movement is provided by signals from muscles that surround the eyes and move the head and by the vestibular sense.

— Apparent Motion

As we will see, movement perception does not depend solely on the real physical movement of objects in the environment. Stimulation of retinal receptors and eye muscles by moving objects provides only a partial explanation for movement perception. It is possible, for instance, to perceive movement in the absence of any real motion. Movement perceived without the physical motion of objects is called **apparent motion.** To clarify this point, let's contrast the perception of real movement with the perception of three types of apparent movement: autokinetic, induced, and stroboscopic.

Autokinetic movement. The simplest way to create the *illusion* of movement is to view a spot of light in total darkness. You can experiment on your own by observing the glowing end of a lighted cigarette placed on an ashtray at the far end of a completely dark room. If you view the spot of light from the cigarette for a minute or two, the light will appear to wander around in an erratic manner, swooping in one direction and then another. The movement that you observe is paradoxical; that is, the spot of light appears to move and yet not change its position (Gregory, 1977). We call this effect **autokinetic movement** because movement is perceived in the absence of real movement. This particular illusion results from signals provided by muscles that surround the eye and by tiny, uncontrollable head movements.

Induced movement. Another way to create illusory movement is to project a spot of light on a larger, movable background. If the background is moved to the left, the spot of light appears to move to the right, even though the light remains stationary. This type of apparent motion is called **induced movement.** In the situation described, induced movement is based on our assumption that smaller objects move and that larger, background objects remain stationary.

Stroboscopic movement. An illusion of movement can be created between two stationary lights. Here, one light is flashed on and off; then, after a brief lapse in time, another light is flashed on and off. Movement perceived between two stationary lights is called **stroboscopic movement;** it is similar to the movement perceived in motion pictures, in which a series of still pictures are flashed one after another.

— APPLICATION —
MOVEMENT IN CINEMA AND TELEVISION

In a classic experiment on stroboscopic movement, Max Wertheimer provided a foundation for the development of motion pictures. Wertheimer used a stroboscope to investigate apparent movement created by the successive exposure of still pictures. First, one vertical line was exposed to the observer; then, another line, 1 centimeter from the first, was exposed briefly. Wertheimer found that if the time interval between the flashed lines was between about 30 and 200 milliseconds, observers reported that a single line appeared to move from one position to the other. Wertheimer referred to this apparent movement as the *phi phenomenon.*

Wertheimer's (1912) experiment (cited in Goldstein, 1980) demonstrates that the perception of one line flashing on and off plus the perception of another line flashing on and off can combine perceptually to produce movement in the space between them. The movement perceived by the observer, called stroboscopic movement, is *apparent movement,* not *real movement.*

The most familiar example of the stroboscopic effect is the appearance of movement created by cinema and television. Experiments conducted by Wertheimer and his colleagues showed that the time interval between still pictures must be short to facilitate the illusion of smooth movement. Movement in old black-and-white films sometimes appears jerky because only 16 still pictures, or frames, per second were used. Modern films flash up to 24 pictures per second, and television presents about 30 per second. At 24 pictures per second, the time interval between pictures is 42 milliseconds. The individual frames in movies are usually very similar to each other, thereby facilitating the perception of smooth stroboscopic movement (Goldstein, 1980).

— PERCEPTUAL DEVELOPMENT —

Now that you know something about how perception works, consider how perception develops. As indicated in chapter 3, experiments on brain mechanisms of vision have identified cells called feature detectors, which are located in the visual cortex. Some cells respond to the orientation of a visual stimulus; other cells specialize in detecting movement, length, pattern, and shape of visual stimuli. Such evidence strongly supports the view that perception has a biological basis. But perception is also affected by learning and experience. Earlier in this chapter we demonstrated, for example, that the same pattern of lines ("13") takes on different meaning and appearance depending on the context in which it is perceived.

Direct experience is the best teacher of many perceptual skills. The next time you have an opportunity, sit in a quiet park, close your eyes, and listen carefully to the birds chirping and singing. Unless you are specially trained, you will likely have difficulty distinguishing one bird song from another or identifying the different birds on the basis of their songs' melodies. To do so would require **perceptual learning.** Such learning involves the ability to extract information from stimuli in the environment as a result of practice, training, or experience (Gibson, 1966; see also chapter introduction). (We will have more to say about perceptual learning in a moment.)

It should become apparent as we proceed that the key to understanding perceptual development lies in the continuous interaction that occurs between the person and the environment. Nevertheless, the question of whether human perceptual abilities are *innate* (due to nature) or *learned* (due to nurture) has been argued by philosophers for centuries. Today, psychologists are less preoccupied with the question of how much nature and nurture contribute to perception than with discovering how nature and nurture interact to influence the course of perceptual development. For this reason, we will explore some of the research that has attempted to address this question. The conclusion to be drawn from such research is that biological mechanisms provide a necessary foundation for perceptual development and that perceptual learning is required if perceptual capacities are to develop normally.

Infant Perceptual Development

How much can a newborn see? For centuries it was commonly believed that the infant's visual world was a blur. William James described the world of the newborn as "buzzing confusion." Experiments in infant perceptual development, however, allow us to conclude that babies are, in fact, born with a highly developed visual system.

A recent examination of the eyes from a normal, full-term infant who died accidentally at 8 days of age reveals that the human retina is probably not fully functional at birth (Abramov et al., 1982). Nonetheless, newborns are capable of a variety of interesting visual feats. Let's take a look at some research findings concerning the perceptual capacities of young babies.

Research has shown that newborns a few hours old can follow a moving light and that infants will momentarily stop sucking on a nipple if they see a light move (Haith, 1980). Also, newborns show signs of boredom when the same stimulus is repeated, such as when a yellow ball is presented 15 or so times in succession. In order to regain the infant's attention, it is necessary only to present a different color ball. This observation suggests that infants can perceive *changes* in stimuli. By clever manipulation of stimulus characteristics, psychologists have determined that infants can distinguish between colors and that they have color preferences. For instance, infants seem to show a marked preference for the color red. Also, even though visual acuity is by no means fully developed at birth, most newborns are capable of focusing on objects that are about 8 inches away. By 4 months of age, an infant's ability to focus on objects at different distances is fully developed and comparable to that of an adult.

Moving beyond visual acuity, what about the development of other perceptual capacities? Some researchers have examined the development of form and depth perception in human infants.

— Form Perception in Human Infants: Visual Scanning Studies

If infants could tell us what they perceive, many problems facing researchers in infant perceptual development would be solved. Psychologists have devised experiments, however, that allow inferences to be made about what infants can see. Phillip Salapatek (1975), for example, measured *visual scanning* in 1- and 2-month-old infants by filming their eye movements as they were shown triangles and other geometric objects. As illustrated in Figure 4–12, 1-month-old infants tend to look at one peak of a triangle. By 2 months of age, infants are more likely to scan the entire triangle. Similar results are obtained when infants are shown pictures of faces. Infants at 1 month of age demonstrate little interest in the pictures or tend to focus on limited portions of them. By 2 months of age, however, infants begin to visually scan the details of the faces (Maurer & Salapatek, 1976).

R. L. Fantz observed babies' eye movements while the babies were shown a variety of forms, including pictures of faces. When shown two pictures, one of a face with normally arranged features and the other with its features reorganized (see Figure 4–13), newborns looked about equally often at the two faces. By 4 months of age, babies preferred to look at the picture of a normal face; they spent about twice as much time scanning a facelike picture than a jumbled picture of the same perceptual features (Fantz, Fagan, & Miranda, 1975).

— Depth Perception in Human Infants: Visual Cliff Studies

A debate has raged among psychologists over whether the human infant can perceive depth innately or whether experience and the opportunity to learn about depth are necessary for perception of the third dimension. In hopes of resolving the debate, Eleanor Gibson, Richard Walk, and co-workers at Cornell Uni-

Figure 4–13

Pictures of faces similar to those used by Fantz and his colleagues to study eye movements in young infants.

versity designed one of the most elegant psychological experiments ever conducted. The apparatus they used to study depth perception in infants (shown in Figure 4–14) consists of a board laid across a large sheet of heavy glass, which is supported a few feet above the floor. On one side of the board, a sheet of patterned material is placed flush against the undersurface of the glass. On the other side, a sheet of the same patterned material is laid on the floor, thus simulating a *visual cliff.*

Gibson and Walk (1973) reported results obtained from testing 36 infants, ranging in age from 6 to 14 months. Each infant was placed on the center board. Then, the mother called the infant to her, first from the cliff side, then from the shallow side. All of the 27 infants who moved off the board (9 did not move off it) crawled out onto the shallow side at least once. Only 3 crept toward the cliff, onto the glass suspended above the floor. Many of the infants crawled away from the mother when she called to them from the cliff side. Others cried when she stood there, because they could not come to her without crossing an apparent chasm. The experiment thus demonstrated that most human infants can discern depth as soon as they can crawl.

Unfortunately, it is not possible to conclude from the Gibson and Walk study that human depth perception is innate, since the infants were at least 6 months of age and could have learned a fear of heights. Recognizing this problem, Gibson and Walk observed the visual cliff behavior of chicks, turtles, rats, lambs, kids, pigs, kittens, and dogs. Chicks, for example, can be reared in the dark and tested at an age of less than 24 hours. When placed on the bridge or center board of

Figure 4–12

Visual scanning as measured by eye movements in human infants. Eye movements of a typical 1-month-old (left) and those of a typical 2-month-old.

1-Month-Old	2-Month-Old

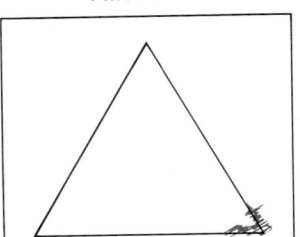 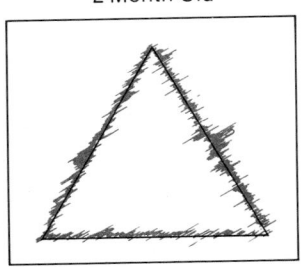

Figure 4–14

An apparatus used by Gibson and Walk to study the development of depth perception. The visual cliff.

the visual cliff, the chicks never made a mistake, always hopping to the shallow side. Kids and lambs, as soon as they could stand (at 1 day of age), also chose the shallow side (Gibson & Walk, 1973).

Experience and Perceptual Development

Many theorists have concluded from visual cliff studies such as those reported by Gibson and Walk that hu-

man infants are innately afraid of heights. However, recent experiments conducted by Joseph Campos and his colleagues have challenged this conclusion. Their studies suggest that fear of heights in infancy is not necessarily innate. Rather, learning and experience may be more important in the development of depth perception than previously believed. These researchers found that infants do not show much avoidance of the deep side of a visual cliff until after they begin to move about on their own. Studies comparing human infants of the same age have revealed that it is loco-motor infants—those capable of *self-produced movement*—who show wariness of heights. As determined from measures of heart rate, prelocomotor infants tend not to show fear of the deep side of the visual cliff (Campos, Svejda, Campos, & Bertenthal, 1982).

— Importance of Self-Produced Movement

The strongest evidence for the role of self-produced movement in perceptual development comes from a series of studies reported by Richard Held and Alan Hein. Held and Hein (1963) raised 20 kittens in darkness. The kittens were then placed two at a time in an apparatus called the kitten carousel (see Figure 4–15). In this study, the kittens' visual experience was kept the same, but their experience with self-produced movement was varied experimentally. This was accomplished by placing one kitten in a body harness that allowed it to walk in a circular path within the carousel. A second kitten was suspended above the floor in a gondola attached to the actively moving kitten. The passively moving kitten, carried in the gondola, received essentially the same visual stimulation as the actively moving kitten because an unvarying pattern of vertical stripes was placed on the wall and center post of the apparatus. Only the actively moving kitten, however, experienced self-produced movement.

The kitten carousel experiments conducted by Held and Hein and their co-workers yielded clear and consistent findings: Kittens that experience self-produced movement show normal perceptual development. After these actively moving kittens spend an average of about 30 hours in the apparatus, they avoid the deep side of the visual cliff. Furthermore, they blink when faced with an approaching object, and they extend their forepaws before contacting a solid surface to which they are lowered. In comparison, the kittens prevented from actively moving within the carousel show none of these behaviors. Happily, the deprived kittens acquire these perceptual capacities after being allowed to move about freely for several days.

— Importance of Visual Stimulation: Deprivation Studies

Visual stimulation, like self-produced movement, is essential for normal development of perceptual capacities. This fact is revealed by studies concerning the ef-

fects of *visual deprivation* on animals. Here, animals reared under normal laboratory conditions are compared to animals reared in the dark, and thus deprived of visual stimulation, from birth. One of the first such studies was reported by Riesen (1947), who reared two chimpanzees in the dark from birth until they were tested at 16 months of age. In comparison with chimpanzees reared under normal laboratory conditions, the dark-reared chimps behaved in most respects as if they were blind.

In a classic experiment reported by Blakemore and Cooper (1970), kittens were reared in the dark for the first 2 weeks of life. Thereafter, they were placed in an apparatus similar to that used by Held and Hein. The kittens remained in the dark except for 5 hours each day in the lighted apparatus. As noted by Blakemore and Cooper, the kittens did not seem upset by the monotony of their surroundings; they sat for long periods inspecting the walls of the apparatus. The results from this experiment are unequivocal. Tests conducted after 5 months of severely restricted visual experience detected several defects in perceptual development. The deprived kittens' head movements were jerky, the kittens tried to paw moving objects that were across the room, and they bumped into things.

The Blakemore and Cooper study and similar experiments led many researchers to conclude that experience and learning are essential for perceptual capacities to develop normally. It was not until later that a flaw in this type of experiment was discovered. Being reared mainly in the dark does not simply prevent animals from learning; it also impairs the development of their visual system. The animals' poor depth perception, which originally seemed to be due to a lack of learning and experience, was more likely caused by damage to cells in the visual system.

One attempt to demonstrate the adverse effect of visual deprivation on brain-cell growth and perceptual development was reported by Hirsch and Spinelli (1970, 1971). These investigators fitted kittens with goggles that presented them with vertical, horizontal, or diagonal stripes. After initial periods of exposure to the stripes, the goggles were removed. At that time, the kittens responded only to things in the same orientation as the stripes to which they had been exposed. In these experiments, single-cell recordings were obtained from the visual cortex, using procedures similar to those made popular by Hubel and Wiesel (see chapter 3). Cells in the visual cortex of kittens previously exposed to horizontal lines responded best to horizontal lines during testing. Similarly, cells in kittens reared

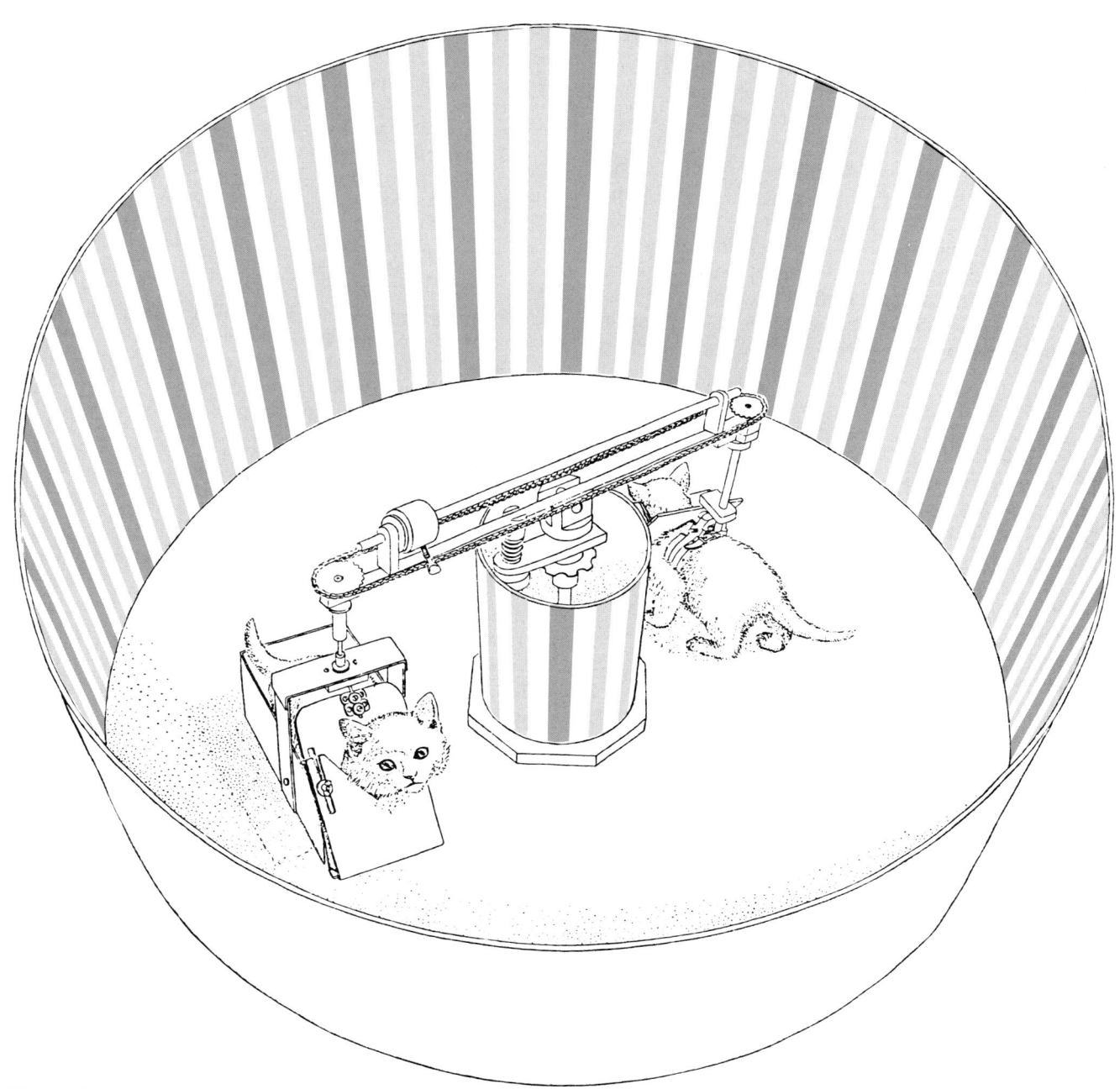

Figure 4–15
Kitten carousel designed by Held and Hein to study the role
of self-produced movement in perceptual development.

with vertical-line patterns responded best to vertical lines.

Other investigators have found striking differences between the brains of rats reared in enriched, complex environments and those of rats reared in isolation (Ro-senzweig, Bennett, & Diamond, 1973). For example, regions of the visual cortex were heavier and thicker in rats reared for 30 days in environments that provided a rich variety of stimuli, such as toys to play with, than in rats reared in standard laboratory cages. Such studies show that the number of interconnections of various types of central nervous system neurons depends, to a significant degree, on the organism's experience during development (Greenough & Green, 1981).

Studies of laboratory animals, now replicated by numerous investigators, argue strongly that visual experience is crucial for the development of a normally functioning visual system. We must, of course, be cautious in generalizing from laboratory animals to humans. Still, it seems possible that those who are born blind or who lose their sight in the first years of life may suffer lasting harm because of early visual deprivation.

— Effects of Restored Vision

For centuries, philosophers and psychologists have been interested in persons who were born blind and who later recovered all or part of their sight. Such case studies, it is argued, provide a natural and practical means of studying the effects of visual deprivation on perceptual development in humans.

Gregory (1977) described S. B., a 53-year-old man who was blind from the age of 10 months until he underwent a corneal transplant operation that restored his vision. When examined 48 days after the operation, S. B. was found to have distortions in depth perception. For example, when looking down from a window 35 feet above the ground, S. B. thought that he could safely lower himself to the ground by hanging from the window ledge. Seeing the same window from the ground, however, provided sufficient visual information for him to realize the impossibility of his planned action.

In another case study, reported by Valvo (1968—cited in Goldstein, 1980), a man blinded at age 6 had his vision surgically restored at age 35. An excerpt from the man's diary indicates the slowness of his recovery:

My first visual impression after years of blindness was vague and confused. I remember that I saw an indistinct shape moving back and forth, and I understood later that it was the surgeon's hand and that a glimmering in this shape was a ring. The first nine months were quite disappointing: to me, the world was only a mosaic of meaningless patches. Then little by little, I started improving. Only after about a year did I feel ready for the first step toward independence and dare to remove the guide from my seeing-eye dog. A few weeks later I decided to give up the dog altogether and go around by myself. I acquired an evergrowing confidence so that, although I was scared by traffic in the beginning, I am now able to walk fast and avoid people and obstacles. As far as stairs are concerned, I do not see the differences in depth, but only in color, and understanding what they are, I do not stumble.

I am aware of the presence of persons at about 20 feet and I can recognize details at about three or four feet. I can read print but handwriting is more difficult. I know that true seeing is different but I am happy to have what I have now and be able to recognize the face of my mother and to see, for the first time, the features of my wife and children. (Goldstein, 1980, p. 312)

Results from the two case studies described here, as well as those from numerous other studies of restored vision in humans, suggest that recovery from blindness is a slow and tedious process that requires experience and long periods of training. Indeed, complete recovery never occurred in many cases. Some people reportedly gave up and reverted to a life of blindness. Even when recovery was relatively successful, the patients commonly reported unhappiness and depression. For example, S. B. became more and more depressed following his operation, eventually withdrawing from active life. The great difficulty in adjusting to sighted life is also revealed in the following excerpt from the diary of the man studied by Valvo:

Paradoxically, when my sight started improving I began to feel depressed. I often experienced periods of crying, without knowing the reason, maybe because of striving so intensely for vision. In the evening I preferred to rest in a dark room. Some days I felt confused: I did not know whether to touch or to look. . .

Recovery of vision has been a long and hard road for me, like entering a strange world. In these moments of depression I sometimes wondered if I was happier before. (Goldstein, 1980, p. 313)

ATTENTION AND PERCEPTION

Sightless individuals are masters at perceptual learning. By learning to perceive the differences in sound echoes made by people and objects in the environment, for example, the blind often learn to hear depth and judge distance with apparent ease. Because of their visual handicap, they learn to extract meaning from tactile, auditory, and other information sources that sighted people do not ordinarily use. This fact helps illustrate that perception is highly selective. Every waking moment we are bombarded by an amount of stimulation that far exceeds our perceptual capacities. Somehow, we select certain sights, sounds, smells, and other sensations for processing and ignore others. This process, which allows us to selectively focus on some stimuli and filter out others, is called **attention.**

Imagine being at a noisy party. You are trying to converse with someone you just met. It is difficult to hear the person because of distracting music and several other conversations going on around you. It is impossible to listen to everything at once, so you concentrate your full attention on your conversational partner. Then, someone in a nearby group mentions your name. You are suddenly aware that you are being talked about. As you strain to listen, your attention shifts from your partner to the other conversation. This *cocktail party phenomenon,* as it is called, demonstrates the selective nature of perception. It is impossible to pay attention to both conversations at the same time, so you block out one, focusing your attention on the conversation that is of greater interest. Attention, then, is of practical value, since it allows us to focus on the stimuli that are most important to us.

Advertisers have long been concerned with identifying factors responsible for gaining attention. It is now generally recognized that certain characteristics of stimuli, such as *intensity, novelty, movement,* and *repetition,* influence perceptual selectivity. The louder a sound, the brighter a light, the bigger an advertisement, the more likely each is to draw attention. Have you ever noticed that television commercials often seem louder in volume than the programs they interrupt? In general, when two stimuli are competing for attention, the one that is more intense will attract attention first. Stimuli that are novel also tend to draw attention. Advertisers are creative in presenting new or novel ads to gain and hold attention. Attention is also directed toward stimuli that move. The illusion of movement can be produced by blinking neon signs, which attract attention more readily than do signs that do not "move." Finally, advertisers use repetition almost to the point of irritation. They know that stimuli repeated again and again are more likely to gain attention than are unrepeated stimuli.

In addition to the characteristics of stimuli, certain characteristics of people, such as *motives* and *needs* are important in determining which stimuli gain attention. If you are hungry, your attention is naturally directed toward food. If you are thinking of buying a car, automobile advertisements and the cars others are driving will no doubt catch your attention. Aware of the fact that sex is a powerful attention-getter, advertisers appeal to the motives and needs of men by using attractive, sometimes seductive females to advertise their products. And everything from mouthwashes to designer jeans promise to increase one's chances of finding a mate and fulfilling the need for sexual gratification.

Many factors serve to direct attention. Those described here are but a few of the influences that determine which of a multitude of competing stimuli will be selected for attention. Attention, in turn, is of great practical value, since it allows us to monitor incoming stimuli and focus on those that are the most interesting, relevant, or important.

EXTRASENSORY PERCEPTION

This chapter has emphasized perceptual processes based on information from one or another of the senses. We might now ask: Are there perceptions that occur without normal sensory stimulation? **Extrasensory perception (ESP)** is the term for perceptions that purportedly do not depend on normal sensory input. You may have wondered if ESP exists or how it operates if it does exist. Almost everyone has had at least one seemingly unexplainable psychic experience (Boom times, 1974). For example, an old friend may be suddenly remembered, and just as suddenly the telephone rings and the friend is on the line. Are such experiences mere coincidence? This and related questions have generated over 70 years of research by *parapsychologists*—researchers interested in phenomena that cannot be explained by accepted psychological principles. Research on ESP will likely continue during the years ahead. Whether any breakthroughs will occur soon remains an open question. No definitive answers have emerged yet. Although the outcome of this research cannot be predicted, we should be informed about the types of phenomena that parapsychologists study and about some of the criticisms of parapsychological research.

Parapsychologists have investigated three principal types of ESP: clairvoyance, telepathy, and precognition. *Clairvoyance* is the purported ability to perceive objects and events from information that does not affect the senses (e.g., at a distance or through physical barriers). *Telepathy* is the purported ability to read another person's thoughts. *Precognition* is the purported ability to perceive future events. Strong desires to achieve each of these feats probably account, to some extent, for a widespread willingness to believe that certain people possess such powers. Although many claims have been made by psychics, and many people believe them, psychologists, for the most part, remain skeptical about the existence of ESP.

Examples of poorly conducted parapsychological research abound and are often widely reported. A case in point is the sensational study of psychic Uri Geller, reported by Puthoff and Targ (1974). An experiment on clairvoyance, typical of their studies, suggests one of the ways in which parapsychological research is conducted. Someone not associated with the experiment entered a room, placed an object into a can chosen at random from 10 cans, and left the room. The experimenters then entered the room with Geller. Neither Geller nor the experimenters supposedly knew which can contained the object. Puthoff and Targ claim that Geller correctly identified the can.

Such results seem to verify the existence of paranormal abilities. However, Puthoff and Targ have been severely criticized for the unscientific nature of their testing of Geller. As one critic notes, hundreds of other tests of Geller were never reported: "Instead, tests with favorable results were selected, in spite of their poor control and heavily biased ambiguity, to be published as genuine scientific results despite strenuous objections from more serious and careful scientists" (Randi, 1980, p. 143).

Not all parapsychological research is as sloppy as Puthoff and Targ's testing of Geller. Many parapsychological experiments, in fact, appear to be elegant, controlled, and difficult to challenge. Why, then, do many psychologists continue to question them? Some of the major objections are as follows:

1. People who claim to have ESP may be using deception or trickery to mislead well-meaning researchers. Geller, for example, repeatedly has been caught cheating and using simple stage magic (Randi, 1980). Several other famous psychics have also been caught in the act of deliberate cheating (Diaconis, 1978). There have been many cases of known fraud (Hansel, 1980). It would be wise to include an experienced stage magician in any team of researchers seriously interested in investigating the paranormal. The magician might easily detect trickery that trusting scientists would miss.

2. Since the mechanisms by which ESP occurs, or is purported to occur, remain unspecified, it is often impossible to design adequate control groups for parapsychological experiments. For this and other reasons, many critics regard ESP as outside the scope of scientific inquiry (Gardner, 1981).

3. In many cases, positive results in ESP studies are obtained only by after-the-fact reanalysis of the data. Suppose, for instance, that a subject in a telepathy experiment fails to guess the order in which a series of cards are turned up by a person concentrating on them in a separate room. The investigator might discover that the subject's guesses match cards two ahead of the original series and then declare this as evidence of precognition instead of clairvoyance. With sufficient manipulation and reinterpretation, almost any set of data can be made to seemingly support ESP.

4. Perhaps the severest criticism of ESP is that tests of it cannot be replicated (Marks & Kammann, 1979). Parapsychologists sometimes respond that other researchers did not have the same gifted subjects that they did or that subjects have good days and bad days. Critics simply assume that positive results are due to chance.

Questions about ESP persist, and sincere research efforts are likely to continue in the coming years. Perhaps future research will resolve the long-standing debate about the legitimacy of ESP. In the meantime, it would be wise to keep in mind the problems listed here and to be especially cautious in interpreting claims reported in the popular press (McClenon, 1982).

— SUMMARY —

1. Perception is the term used to describe the brain's interpretation of sensory information—information that is made available to the brain through each of the sense organs.

2. Gestalt psychologists believe that perception results when the brain organizes sensory information in ways that go beyond the individual elements of sensation.

3. Much of the evidence for the Gestalt view of perception comes from what psychologists have learned about various principles of perceptual organization and the perceptual processes involved in form, depth, size, and movement perception.

4. Psychologists have learned much about perceptual processes from studies of perceptual illusions—distorted perceptions that contradict objective reality.

5. The key to understanding perceptual development lies in the interaction between nature and nurture.

6. Perceptual learning involves the ability to extract information from stimuli as a result of practice, training, or experience.

7. Perceptual development in human infants follows a predictable course. Contrary to popular belief, it is now known that babies are born with a highly developed visual system.

8. Perceptual capacities of a limited range are present in the newborn.

9. The maintenance and further normal development of the perceptual capacities present at birth depend in large part on experience and visual stimulation during early periods of development.

10. Visual deprivation can lead to degeneration in the visual system, as measured by changes in brain-cell growth and activity.

11. Attention is the process that allows us to focus on some stimuli while filtering out others.

12. Types of extrasensory perception (ESP) that have been studied include clairvoyance (the purported ability to perceive objects and events from information that does not affect the senses directly), telepathy (the purported ability to receive information from other people's thoughts), and precognition (the purported ability to perceive future events).

— IMPORTANT TERMS AND CONCEPTS —

Perception
Gestalt Psychology
Principle of Figure and Ground
Principle of Perceptual Grouping
Principle of Similarity
Principle of Proximity
Principle of Continuation
Principle of Closure
Contour
Context
Principle of Shape Constancy
Depth Perception

Binocular Depth Cues
Monocular Depth Cues
Stereoscopic Vision
Binocular Disparity
Principle of Linear Perspective
Principle of Aerial Perspective
Principle of Interposition
Principle of Texture Gradients
Principle of Light and Shadow
Principle of Relative Size
Motion Parallax
Accommodation

Convergence
Principle of Size Constancy
Illusion
Real Motion
Apparent Motion
Autokinetic Movement
Induced Movement
Stroboscopic Movement
Perceptual Learning
Attention
Extrasensory Perception (ESP)

Gibson, J. J. (1950). *The perception of the visual world.* Boston: Houghton Mifflin. This book and Gibson's more recent books *(The senses considered as perceptual systems, 1966;* and *The ecological approach to visual perception, 1979)* provide a set of resources on the psychology of perception.

Gregory, R. L. (1970). *The intelligent eye.* New York: McGraw-Hill. A fun, easy-to-read paperback available in most libraries and bookstores. The book provides a nice introduction to a variety of fascinating topics relevant to the psychology of perception. (Refer also to *Eye and brain,* a book written by the same author and referenced in the suggested reading list for chapter 3.)

Hochberg, J. E. (1978). *Perception* (2nd ed.). Englewood Cliffs, NJ: Prentice-Hall. A textbook that covers most of the material discussed in this chapter. The book focuses on the experimental research findings that provide the foundation for a psychology of perception.

Marks, D., & Kammann, R. (1980). *The psychology of the psychic.* Buffalo, NY: Prometheus Books. Explodes the Geller myths and critically examines ESP experiments.

Panati, C. (Ed.). (1976). *The Geller papers: Scientific observations on the paranormal powers of Uri Geller.* Boston: Houghton Mifflin. Replete with photographs, diagrams, and charts, this edited volume contains the scientific reports on Uri Geller's paranormal powers observed in laboratories in the United States and five other countries.

Robinson, J. D. (1972). *The psychology of visual illusion.* London: Hutchinson. A detailed examination of visual illusions described in this chapter.

— CHAPTER 5 —

STATES OF CONSCIOUSNESS

STATES OF CONSCIOUSNESS

— CHAPTER OBJECTIVES —

To achieve the objectives of this chapter, you should be able to answer the questions listed here. You should also be able to define the important terms and concepts listed at the end of the chapter.

1. To what does the term consciousness refer?
2. How is hypnosis done? What is it like to be hypnotized?
3. How is it possible to study sleep and dream states? What is known about the stages of sleep?
4. How is waking consciousness altered by sleep, dreams, and drugs?
5. What do the most widely used consciousness-altering drugs have in common?
6. What techniques are available as alternatives to drugs for achieving control over mental and physiological processes?

— CHAPTER OUTLINE —

The Nature of Consciousness
Consciousness refers to an awareness of both the external environment and internal events, such as fantasies and daydreams.

Modes and Levels of Consciousness
Hypnosis and Consciousness
Application: Hypnosis as a Clinical
    Tool
Sleep and Dreams
Sleep and dream states are considered altered states of consciousness.
Sleep
Dreams
Application: Diagnosis and Treatment
    of Sleep Disorders
Drug-Induced Alterations in Consciousness
Consciousness can be altered by the use of psychoactive drugs.
Narcotics
Sedatives
Stimulants
Hallucinogens
Application: Self-Regulation with Med-
    itation

On the Horizon: Consciousness, Physiology, and Longevity

FROM THE DEPTHS OF CONSCIOUSNESS

The woman didn't pay much attention to the tall man who knocked on her door. He was there to see her husband, so she returned to the kitchen. Moments later she heard gunshots. She ran to the front porch and found her husband mortally wounded. The blood streaming from his body blotted out her memory: she couldn't describe the killer who had looked her in the eye. Two weeks later, frustrated Los Angeles police persuaded the widow to be hypnotized. Working slowly, Lt. Richard King told her to imagine that she was watching a documentary of the murder, and then to "freeze the frame" just as she opened the door. With that cue, the woman managed to give a detailed description of an Ichabod Crane look-alike who, as it turned out, was a junkie already under arrest on a drug charge. (The trials of hypnosis, 1981, p. 96)

A similar incident took place in 1976 in Chowchilla, California (Terr, 1982). There, you may recall, three gunmen kidnapped school bus driver Ed Ray and 26 children, transferred them to a truck, and then buried the truck in a rock quarry. During the kidnapping, Ray saw the license plate of the gunmen's car, but after he and the children escaped, he was too frightened and upset to remember the license number. On this occasion, too, the police decided to try hypnosis. Ray was asked by the hypnotist to visualize the scene as though it were on television. In due course, Ray was asked about the elusive license number, which he promptly provided. Shortly thereafter, the gunmen were arrested.

Did hypnosis really jog the memories of these witnesses? Can all crime victims or eyewitnesses be hypnotized? What can and cannot be achieved through hypnosis? The answers to such questions require an examination of both ordinary consciousness and hypnosis. These topics are discussed in the first section of this chapter. The next section focuses on sleep and dreams to see why they, like hypnosis, are considered altered states of consciousness. Finally, in the third section, drug-altered consciousness is discussed.

— THE NATURE OF CONSCIOUSNESS —

Consciousness refers to an immediate awareness of both the external environment and internal events, such as thoughts, fantasies, and daydreams. Specific states of consciousness vary with respect to content, sensory impressions, alertness, attention, and volition. During *waking consciousness,* for instance, we recall the past, plan for the future, make decisions, perform voluntary actions, and selectively attend to our surroundings. The quality of consciousness can be changed significantly by hypnosis, sleep and dreams, drugs, and meditation—to give but a few examples. Before examining such altered states, let's further consider consciousness in general.

Modes and Levels of Consciousness

It is useful to distinguish between two basic modes of consciousness, the passive and the active. *Passive consciousness* (see Figure 5–1) is characterized by open

Figure 5–1.

Passive consciousness: College student listening to music.

awareness of surroundings, relaxed enjoyment of day-dreaming, and similar states, such as when listening to music. *Active consciousness* (see Figure 5–2) is associated with productive mental activities, such as planning, decision making, and initiating actions (Hilgard, 1980).

Psychologists and other theorists have found it useful to identify several *levels* of consciousness (e.g., Freud, 1938). The **conscious** level contains thoughts and memories of which we are fully aware. It excludes **nonconscious** information, such as hormone changes or electrical brain patterns, which are not normally a part of our awareness. Information found at the **preconscious** level may be brought to awareness, but otherwise it remains out of consciousness. For example, your memories of your first day at college will remain at the preconscious level until you stop to think of them. The **unconscious** level contains memories, feelings, and impulses that are difficult to bring to awareness. Such information, however, may become available through dreams, hypnosis, and other special means.

Hypnosis and Consciousness

Hypnotic phenomena have long been used as evidence for the existence of an unconscious level of awareness. As hypnosis researcher Ernest Hilgard (1980) comments, By its very nature, hypnotism deals with alterations in conscious experience and in the interplay between voluntary and involuntary control. In **hypnosis,** an altered state of awareness (sometimes called a trance) is induced by suggestions made by another person or, in *self-hypnosis,* by the subjects themselves.

Hypnotic procedures date to the 1700s, when a Viennese physician, Friedrich Anton Mesmer, became adept at "curing" aches and pains by "mesmerizing" his patients into a trance by passing magnets over their bodies. Mesmer's system of healing, called *animal magnetism,* rapidly gained a wide following. To treat more patients, Mesmer built a large circular vat, similar to today's hot tub but with an odd assortment of substances mixed into the water. Patients sat around the vat holding the ends of iron rods that extended from it. Meanwhile, Mesmer, dressed in a violet robe, circled the vat, waved a wand, and spoke strangely. Although the medical community pronounced Mesmer an unwitting fraud, elements of his technique, later

Figure 5–2.

Active consciousness: College student taking an examination.

called *hypnosis,* transcended their shady origin. Today, hypnosis has achieved respectability in its use to probe psychological problems and to relieve pain (Smith, 1973).

— How Is Hypnosis Done?

Not all theorists agree that hypnosis is a unique altered state of consciousness. Critic T. X. Barber, for example, has demonstrated that many of the unusual feats attributed to hypnosis can be obtained through simple suggestion—no trance need be induced (Barber, Spanos, & Chaves, 1974). Nevertheless, there does appear to be a fair degree of agreement that hypnosis involves relaxation, suggestion, restriction of attention, and intense concentration (Hilgard, 1980). To induce such changes, hypnotists use a wide range of procedures. As noted by Tart (1975), all hypnotists commonly encourage their subjects (1) to focus attention on what is being said, (2) to relax and feel tired, (3) to accept suggestions, and (4) to use vivid imagination. The hypnotist may dangle a watch or some other object in front of the subject or may rely on verbal suggestions alone. If you were being hypnotized, you might be asked to: "Relax. Relax your eyes, your arms, your legs. Relax your jaw. Release the tension from your body. Your eyes are becoming heavy; they are tired; it is difficult for you to keep them open. You feel warm all over. Your body is relaxed. Relax. Sleep. Sleep, deep sleep."

— Who Can Be Hypnotized?

Although not everyone can be hypnotized, "susceptible" people can be identified by the *Stanford Hypnotic Susceptibility Scale,* developed at Stanford University. Separate scales are available for children and adults. Questions on these scales and procedures for administering them have been provided by Morgan and Hilgard (1979a, 1979b).

There are wide individual differences in hypnotizability. Although about 8 out of 10 persons can be hypnotized, only a small percentage are highly responsive. Those who are typically have a good imagination, an openness to suggestion, and a willingness to seek new experiences.

— The Experience of Being Hypnotized

Just as only some people can be hypnotized, personal hypnotic experiences vary. Here is a description of one person's hypnotic experience:

> I recently got hypnotized to find out what it feels like. The "trance state" was not anything like what I expected. At all times I was completely aware of everything that was going on in the room, of street noises, and of my own thoughts. There was no sense of being "asleep," or "controlled." I was completely relaxed and had my eyes closed, but I felt as if I could get up and walk out any time I wanted to. (Smith, 1973, pp. 6–7)

The subject felt as if he could do as he pleased, but in fact he continued to do what the hypnotist suggested. Investigations of hypnosis over the past few decades help clarify this seeming paradox (Hilgard, Atkinson, & Atkinson, 1979). First, when deeply hypnotized, the subject generally sits passively, initiating no activity. He or she quietly waits for the hypnotist to suggest what to do. Second, the subject's attention becomes more selective. If told to concentrate on a particular past event, the subject is able to do so while ignoring competing thoughts. Third, the subject tends to accept altered consciousness uncritically, with a willingness to comply with the hypnotist's requests. Fourth, the subject is able to act out experiences and may thereby recall "forgotten" details of prior events. For example, under hypnosis, subjects have, at times, provided detailed descriptions of suspected killers (see chapter introduction).

— APPLICATION —
HYPNOSIS AS A CLINICAL TOOL

Long associated with the mystical, the bizarre, and the occult, hypnosis has gained respectability during recent decades as a potentially useful clinical tool. For example, as suggested by the chapter introduction, hypnosis is being used increasingly by police to help crime victims recall "unconscious" memories. This use of hypnosis in solving crimes, however, is not without its opponents (Loftus & Loftus, 1980). Several states have banned hypnotic questioning. Recently, for example, the California Supreme Court barred virtually all witnesses who had been hypnotized from giving evidence in court (A ban on hypnosis, 1982). According to the ruling, hypnotized people are highly susceptible to suggestion and may therefore produce "pseudomemories" that they later believe are true. (More information on this issue is presented in chapter 7.)

The memory controversy notwithstanding, hypnotic procedures have found increasing clinical use (Wadden & Anderton, 1982). The practice of *hypnotherapy*, as it is called, is growing in popularity. Hilgard and Hilgard (1975) have described a midwestern obstetrician who prefers hypnosis to chemical anesthetics during childbirth. The physician used chemical anesthesia for only 186 out of 1,000 births. In the remaining instances, the babies were delivered, some by cesarean section, by mothers who were given verbal instructions, under hypnosis, to feel no pain. Hypnosis has been used also as a means for relieving pain in terminal cancer patients and as an alternative to chemical anesthesia in surgery (Newton, 1983). Although clinical studies of hypnotherapy do not always agree, it is becoming more widely accepted among experts that the benefits of hypnosis depend on a person's hypnotizability (Hilgard, 1982). Only about 10 percent of patients are suitably hypnotizable for major surgery, for example.

The advantages of hypnosis over other therapies, at least in some cases, is straightforward. First, hypnosis is not harmful or addictive, as are some drugs. And with hypnosis, tolerance and physical dependence do not develop, as they do with many pain-relieving drugs. (See the section of this chapter on drug-induced alterations in consciousness.) Second, hypnosis can be inexpensive. For patients who are properly trained in self-hypnosis, treatment is free. Some asthma patients, for example, use self-hypnosis to relieve attacks by concentrating on thoughts of breathing cool, fresh air (Spiegel & Spiegel, 1978). Finally, trained patients have used self-hypnosis to reduce everyday tension and stress, to bolster self-confidence, to sleep easier, and to study and work more effectively (Hilgard & Hilgard, 1975). Although hypnosis has many limitations, its overall usefulness is readily apparent.

— SLEEP AND DREAMS —

Sleep

The necessity of sleep is shown by the failure of scientists to find anyone who never sleeps. According to Dement (1976), the record is held by two healthy Australians who sleep less than three hours a night. Although it is impossible to say exactly how much sleep is needed, we do know that individual sleep requirements vary and that sleep needs change throughout life. (For a review, see Goleman, 1982.) At one time, "experts" recommended that newborns sleep at least 21 hours per day. Today, it is recognized that some infants may, indeed, sleep 20 or more hours per day, but others may need only half that amount. During an infant's first year, total sleep time declines from an average of 16 hours to 13 hours per night. Adolescents tend to sleep between 10 and 11 hours per night; adults report an average of between 7 and 8 hours (Dement, 1976). Many adults can be classified as "larks" (early to bed, early to rise) or "owls" (late to bed, late to rise) (Webb, 1975). However, no clear-cut personality differences have been found between short and long sleepers (Webb & Friel, 1971).

— The Function of Sleep

Sleep consumes one-third of the average person's lifetime. Yet, why we sleep remains a mystery. As noted by Hartmann (1973), "In sleep research, as in other areas of scientific inquiry, *why* is often the first question asked and the last question answered or left unanswered." Current scientific explanations of sleep fall into three broad categories: the **energy conservation theory,** the **behavioral adaptive theory,** and the **biological rhythm theory.** According to the first theory, sleep serves as a restorative period each day—a time when organisms are forced to conserve energy. In contrast, the behavioral adaptive theory emphasizes that the sleep patterns of each species were shaped over hundreds of years by environmental pressures

(Webb & Cartwright, 1978). Still other scientists believe that sleep represents a natural rhythm governed by the body's biological clock. Thus, the pattern of waking and sleeping each day is similar to other daily cycles, involving body temperature, hunger, blood sugar, hormone levels, and the like. Daily cycles such as these are called **circadian rhythms,** a term from the Latin *circa diem,* meaning "about a day" (Takahashi & Zatz, 1982). From this perspective, sleep is an unlearned, evolved, and adaptive natural body rhythm (Webb & Cartwright, 1978).

— Sleep Deprivation

Theories such as those just described provide only a partial explanation for sleep. To further probe why we sleep, many investigators have conducted experiments on *sleep deprivation*. For example, in January 1959, sleep researchers observed New York disk jockey Peter Tripp as he stayed awake for 200 consecutive hours to raise funds for the March of Dimes (see Figure 5–3). Tripp made daily broadcasts from a glass booth on

Figure 5–3.

Peter Tripp, a New York disk jockey, after being awake for 200 hours.

Times Square. For several days his performance was unimpaired.

> In the last days of the marathon, however, a dramatic change occurred. The disk jockey developed an acute paranoid psychosis during the nighttime hours, accompanied at times by auditory hallucinations. He believed that unknown adversaries were attempting to slip drugs into his food and beverages in order to put him to sleep. (Dement, 1976, p. 8)

By the end of his 200th hour "awakeathon," Tripp was no longer able to distinguish his waking nightmares from reality.

Negative side-effects from sleep deprivation are not inevitable, however, as the case of Randy Gardner demonstrates. In January 1965, at age 17, Gardner attempted to set a world record for prolonged wakefulness. He succeeded in staying awake for 264 hours. At the end of his 11-day vigil, before going to sleep, Gardner held a press conference in which he

> conducted himself in an absolutely impeccable fashion. Asked how he was able to stay awake for eleven days, he answered lightly, "It's just mind over matter." (Dement, 1976, p. 12)

Sleep deprivation studies have begun to answer at least some questions regarding sleep needs and the effects of prolonged wakefulness. A few of the conclusions offered by Dement (1976) are:

— The crucial factor in surmounting sleep loss is probably physical fitness. There is almost no degree of sleepiness that cannot be overcome by engaging in vigorous physical exercise.
— Auditory and visual hallucinations, will occur in some sleep-deprived subjects but not others.
— The amount of sleep required to catch-up after prolonged wakefulness is about the same as for a normal night's sleep.

As an example of the last point, Randy Gardner slept only 14 hours and 40 minutes after his 11-day marathon. When he awoke, researchers found him to be essentially recovered (Dement, 1976).

Have you ever considered trying to get by on less sleep? The famous painter Salvador Dali reportedly cut down on sleep by napping in a chair while holding a spoon over a tin plate. At the moment of sleep onset the spoon would drop and awaken him. Dali claimed to be completely refreshed by these brief interludes

(Dement, 1976). Unfortunately, sleep research suggests that this technique would be of little use to the majority of individuals.

Other, more practical techniques for reducing sleep time are available, however. Napoleon, for instance, reportedly slept only 4 hours a night by taking 10-minute catnaps during the day to restore his energy. Thomas Edison similarly reduced his nighttime sleep. Some people who meditate daily, at regular intervals, report needing less sleep at night. The application at the end of this chapter describes some appropriate meditation techniques.

As mentioned earlier, individual sleep needs vary. Insisting that all people sleep 8 hours per night is like demanding that everyone wear the same size shirt. According to sleep researcher Wilse Webb (Goleman, 1982), people should discover their natural sleep length and stick to it. *Natural sleep length* is when you go to bed sleepy and wake up rested. To find it, Webb recommends going to bed at 5:00 in the morning and getting up at 7:00 so you can observe the symptoms of insufficient sleep. Then, a week later, sleep 4 hours one night and see how you feel. Let yourself sleep 2 hours longer one night each week until you wake spontaneously and aren't tired during the day. That's your natural sleep length.

— The Measurement of Sleep

The mystery of sleep has begun to yield to laboratory measurements of the electrical activity of the brain, the muscles, and the eyes (see Figure 5–4).

As described in chapter 2, electrodes placed on the scalp detect voltage changes, which provide a record of brain activity called the EEG, or *electroencephalogram*. Surface electrodes placed near the chin provide a record of muscle activity called the **electromyogram (EMG).** A record of eye movements, called the **electrooculogram (EOG),** is derived from electrodes placed near the eyes. These three measures produce distinct patterns of electrical activity that give an objective picture of sleep states.

Two kinds of sleep. Using the EEG, EMG, and EOG, sleep researchers have identified some basic facts about normal sleep. The first of these is that there appear to be *two distinctly different states of sleep:* **REM** (rapid-eye-movement) **sleep,** in which dreams commonly occur, and **NREM** (non-rapid-eye-movement) **sleep.** "Any prolonged sleep period consists of a regular alternation between these states, which are as different from one another as both are from wakefulness" (Dement, 1979, p. 420). How do REM and NREM sleep differ?

During NREM sleep:

– The EEG shows that the brain is relatively inactive.
– The EMG shows that the body is highly active, with body movements, reflexes, and other muscular activity evident.
– The EOG reveals a minimum of eye movement.

Figure 5–4.
On the left is a sleep subject with electrodes in place for recording EEG and eye movements. On the right, the experimenter monitors the record produced on chart paper.

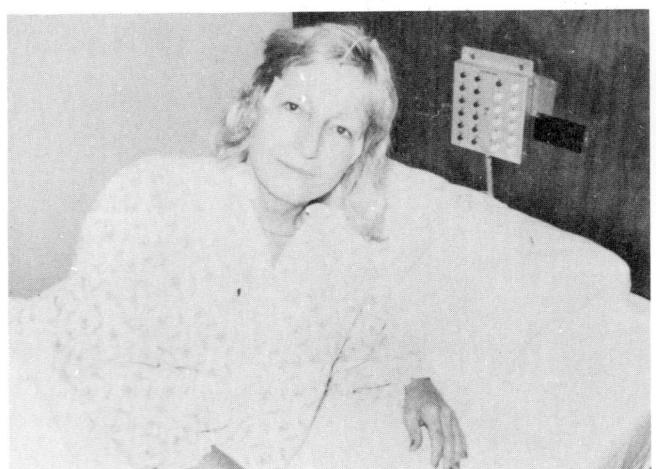

During REM sleep:

- The EEG shows that the brain is "awake" and furiously active.
- The EMG shows that the body is so immobile as to appear paralyzed.
- The EOG detects wakinglike eye movements, as when a person is actively scanning the environment. (For review, see Morrison, 1983.)

Stages of sleep. Interestingly, it is during REM sleep that most dreams occur. Volunteer subjects awakened during REM sleep tend to report detailed dream images. Subjects awakened during NREM periods more commonly report nondreamlike thoughts. In a moment we will return to dreams, but first let's consider a second important fact about sleep: *There are five sleep stages that characterize a typical night's sleep.*

The normal adult enters *Stage 1* sleep from wakefulness. This first stage of sleep, NREM state, is characterized by irregular, low-amplitude brain wave activity (see Figure 5–5). During *Stage 2,* also NREM state, brain wave *spindles,* or short, fast bursts of activity, appear. *Stage 3* and *Stage 4* are marked by slow brain wave activity, called *delta waves.* During these deep NREM stages it is difficult to awaken the sleeper. Adults normally progress from waking to Stage 1, then through Stages 2, 3, 4, and back to Stage 2 before entering the first REM period.

A typical night's sleep involves a cyclical shift between NREM and REM states. The progression from Stage 1 through Stage 4 and back to Stage 2 lasts about 60 minutes and is followed by a short, 10-minute period of REM sleep. The 70-minute period, consisting on one NREM period and one REM period, makes a *sleep cycle.* The next sleep cycle lasts somewhat longer, about 110 minutes, and is followed by a third cycle, which lasts about 120 minutes. Subsequent cycles tend to be briefer, averaging about 90 minutes. Five sleep cycles make up an average night's sleep, about three-fourths of which is spent in NREM sleep (Dement, 1979).

Research findings from sleep laboratories suggest some additional important facts about sleep cycles. To summarize:

- The periods of NREM and REM sleep described here represent a general pattern, from which many people normally deviate.

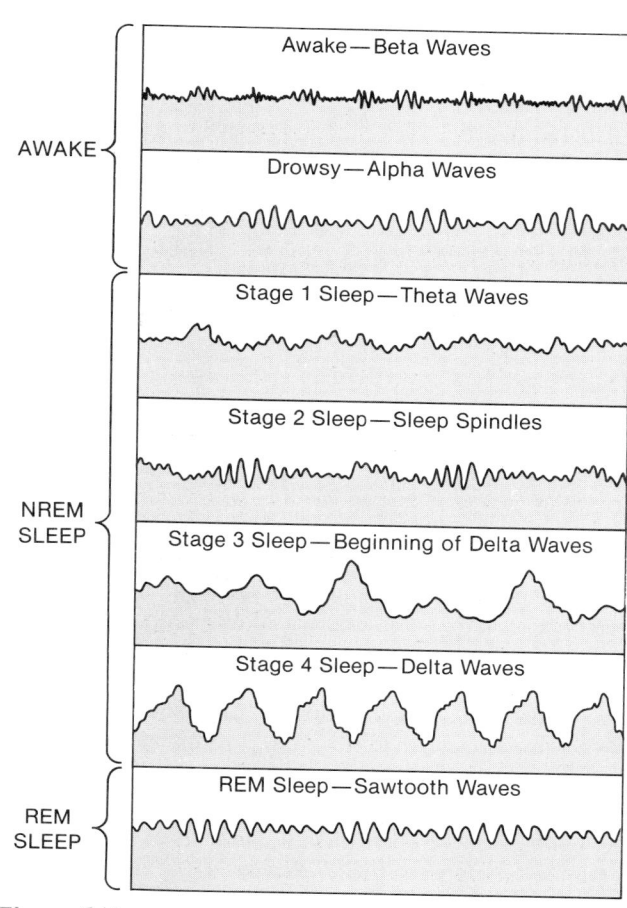

Figure 5–5.

Stages of sleep. Changes in EEG activity from waking through successive stages of sleep are shown.

- Most adults enter NREM Stage 1 sleep from wakefulness. Infants may go directly into REM sleep.
- Stages 3 and 4 of deep sleep tend to disappear toward morning, as REM periods grow somewhat longer.
- Older adults tend to sleep lighter, with less time spent in Stage 4.
- Of a normal night's sleep, Stages 1, 2, 3, 4, and REM account for approximately 4, 52, 5, 12, and 25 percent, respectively, for young adult females. The young adult male percentages are approximately 4, 46, 6, 15, and 28 percent, respectively. (For review, see Salamy, 1976.)

Dreams

As stated earlier, REM sleep is characterized by intense visual imagery—"mental pictures," the stuff of *dreams.*

During NREM sleep, however, mental activity is more thoughtlike or verbal. These facts were ascertained by Eugene Aserinsky (Aserinsky & Kleitman, 1953), who also discovered REM sleep. Aserinsky suspected that rapid eye movements might signal the onset of dreams. To find out if this was so, he awakened sleepers during REM and NREM periods and questioned them about their mental activity. Aserinsky found, and others have confirmed, that about 80 to 85 percent of REM awakenings result in dream reports. Dreamlike thoughts are rarely reported by subjects awakened during NREM sleep (Berger, 1969).

Dreaming tends to occur throughout REM sleep, but it becomes more vivid 10 minutes or more after REM period has begun (Foulkes, 1966, 1978). Contrary to popular belief, it is now well established from dream research that: (1) Even though some people are unable to recall their dreams, all people dream. (2) Dreams occur throughout the night at approximately 90-minute intervals that coincide with REM sleep. (3) Dreams last more than a second, and each dream lasts a little longer than the previous one. The first dream each night may last about 10 minutes, the last dream as long as 50 minutes. (For review, see Kiester, 1980.)

— The Importance of Dreaming

How important is dreaming for psychological health? To answer this question, William Dement conducted experiments in which subjects were awakened each time they entered REM sleep. In one particular study (Dement, 1960), subjects were awakened from REM sleep on 5 consecutive nights. Three interesting findings emerged. First, as the experiment proceeded, it became necessary to awaken subjects more frequently to prevent them from dreaming—a fact suggesting that *dream deprivation* increases the need to dream. Second, dream deprivation leads to REM *rebound*. After dream deprivation, when subjects slept without interruption, their average time spent in REM sleep increased sharply, by 37 percent.

Such results have been interpreted as indicating that a certain amount of dreaming is a necessity. Just how much of a necessity remains an open question, however. Bearing on this question, a third provocative finding from Dement's dream deprivation study was that subjects suffered from a variety of psychological disturbances, such as anxiety, irritability, and poor concentration, during their waking hours. In a subsequent study, Dement found that when dream deprivation was prolonged for 15 to 16 nights, behavior became even more disturbed. More recent studies, however, have failed to replicate the association between dream deprivation and serious personality disruption (e.g., Webb, 1975).

— The Interpretation of Dreams

Humans, it seems, have always been interested in understanding and interpreting their dreams. The first documented attempt can be traced to Aristotle's book *Concerning Dreams and Their Interpretation.* More recently, Sigmund Freud published, in 1913, *The Interpretation of Dreams,* in which he set out to prove that there exists a psychological technique by which dreams may be interpreted and sensibly related to waking personality (see Table 5–1).

According to Freud, a dream could be described in terms of its *manifest content,* or visible "surface," and its deeper *latent content,* or hidden meaning. Freud believed that by probing a person's images and mental associations, he could expose a dream's latent content. Unfortunately, Freud's belief that dreams function to gratify forbidden wishes, drives, or impulses has been difficult to test experimentally. More recent theories that attempt to explain the *function* of dreams are subject to the same criticism. Perhaps for this reason, investigators have turned from the why of dreaming to a description of dream content.

Table 5–1.

Dream interpretation according to Sigmund Freud. (From Coon, 1983. p. 162).

Common Freudian dream interpretations and their symbols:

1. Parents—emperors, empresses, kings, queens
2. Children (brothers and sisters)—small animals
3. Birth—water
4. Death—journey
5. Nakedness—clothes, uniforms
6. Male genitals—sticks, umbrellas, poles, trees, anything elongated, pointed weapons of all sorts
7. Erection—balloons, airplanes, zeppelins, dreamer himself flying
8. Male sexual symbols—reptiles, fishes, serpent, hand or foot
9. Female genitalia—pits, hollow caves, jars, bottles, doors, ships, chests
10. Breasts—apples, peaches, other fruit
11. Intercourse—mounting a ladder or stairs, entering a room, walking down a hall or into a tunnel, horseback riding, and so forth.

Interesting findings on dream content have been reported by Hall and Van de Castle (1966), who have analyzed dream logs recorded by college students. Content analyses of more than 1,000 dreams suggest the following:

– Color appears in about one-third of all dreams.
– Dreams tend to be about failure and misfortune more often than success.
– About 95 percent of all dreams involve two or more people.
– More often than not, people in dreams tend to be familiar to the dreamer.
– Only rarely do movie stars or popular sports figures appear in dreams.

Interesting gender differences have also been found in dream content. Men tend to dream more often of other men, whereas women dream of the two sexes more equally. Women's dreams tend to have more characters, more friendly interpersonal interactions, and more home and family themes than do men's dreams. Men's dreams, on the other hand, tend to have aggression, hostility, and achievement striving as their themes more often than do women's dreams. These differences in the dream content of college men and women have been described by Hall and Van de Castle (1966) and more recently by Hall, Domhoff, Blick, and Weesner (1982).

— APPLICATION —
DIAGNOSIS AND TREATMENT OF SLEEP DISORDERS

The study and treatment of sleep disorders is a fast-growing clinical discipline. Much has been learned since the early 1900s, when chewing gum was advertised and recommended for a restful night's sleep. With our burgeoning scientific knowledge of normal sleep, it is becoming increasingly possible to study, diagnose, and treat sleep disturbances (Simonds & Parraga, 1982) (see Table 5–2). Such disturbances affect an estimated 50 million Americans, who sleep too little, sleep too much, or have serious problems when they sleep.

— Nightmares and Night Terrors

It happens early in the night, usually during the first two or three hours of sleep. The person sits up in bed suddenly, talks incoherently, and may get up and move around wildly. He appears to be terrified of something unseen—and his pulse rate and respiratory rate may have doubled. (Hartmann, 1981, p. 14)

Only recently have researchers been able to distinguish nightmares from night terrors (Carlson, White, & Turkat, 1982). **Nightmares** are bad dreams that generally occur toward morning during REM sleep. **Night terrors,** as exemplified in the quotation, occur early

in the night during NREM Stage 4 (see Figure 5–6). After a night terror, the sufferer returns to sleep without waking fully and the next morning remembers ei-

Table 5–2.
Prevalence of sleep disorders and sleep behaviors in children and adolescents.

SLEEP DISORDERS AND SLEEP BEHAVIORS	PERCENT SUBJECTS WITH AT LEAST 1 EPISODE	PERCENT SUBJECTS WITH AT LEAST WEEKLY EPISODES
Sleeptalking	44.34	12.7
Restless sleeper	34.63	27.6
Snoring	31.07	7.5
Nightmares	16.51	1.7
Grinding teeth	15.21	7.5
Fearful of dark	14.88	10.1
Bed-wetting	11.65	4.3
Need for security object	11.65	10.7
Insistence on sleeping with others	10.36	5.2
Sleepwalking	10.03	2.3
Drowsy during daytime	9.06	4.9
Bedtime rituals	8.7	7.5
Fearful going to sleep	8.41	3.6
Irresistible sleepiness	6.1	2.3
Night terrors	2.66	1.3

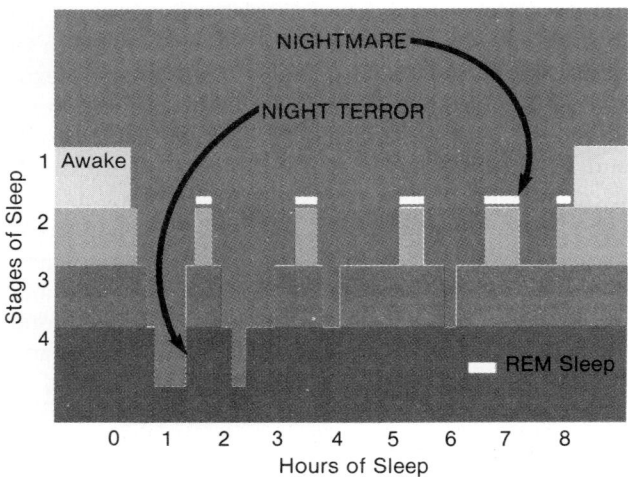

Figure 5–6.

Sleep cycles that occur during a typical night's sleep. Night terrors occur early in the night, often within an hour or so of falling asleep, during Stage 4 sleep. Nightmares occur toward morning, during REM sleep.

ther nothing or only a vague image of the episode. Following a nightmare, the sleeper clearly remembers dreaming and that the dream was intense and frightening.

Sleepwalking, or **somnambulism** and sleeptalking, which generally occur during NREM sleep, often accompany night terrors but not nightmares. Both nightmares and night terrors are more common in children than adults. About one-fourth of all 3-to-8-year-old children suffer from one or the other problem. Terrors may be associated with stress and may worsen if the person has bottled up anger or rage. They may sometimes begin after a psychological trauma, such as losing a parent by death or divorce. In many instances time is a sufficient cure for both night terrors and somnambulism.

— Insomnia

One of the most prevalent sleep disorders, **insomnia** refers to sleeping too little or being unable to fall asleep. In a questionnaire study of more than 700,000 adults over 30 years of age, 6 percent of the men and 14 percent of the women reported suffering from insomnia often or fairly often (Kripke & Simons, 1976). As noted by Dement (1979), the average physician spends about 3 minutes on this complaint and usually treats it by writing a prescription for sleep medication.

Most sleep experts agree that barbiturates (sedative drugs, described later in this chapter) and other sleeping pills, such as Seconal and Nembutal, initially enhance sleep. But within a few weeks, total sleep time declines, compelling the patient to increase the dosage. Doing so eventually leads to drug tolerance and dependence. (See the section of this chapter on drug-induced alterations in consciousness.) *Drug-dependence insomnia* is not uncommon among people who habitually use sleep medications or other drugs, including alcohol and tranquilizers. As a general rule, most regularly used drugs will impair sleep and lead to REM deprivation.

Withdrawal from sleep medications is often complicated by intensified insomnia or by REM rebound that disturbs sleep. Some sleep experts have noted that convulsions and nightmares may occur after abrupt withdrawal from certain drugs (Dement, 1979). Other experts, such as Anthony Kales (Clark, Gosnell, Shapiro, & Hager, 1981), believe that the best treatment of insomnia is largely behavioral. On the assumption that from 60 to 80 percent of insomniacs have faulty sleep habits, behavioral therapists try to change the patient's behavior. Some recommended behavioral changes for the insomniac are: (1) Do not read in bed. (2) Do not stay in bed if you remain sleepless for 10 minutes at night. (3) Sleep for a maximum of 7 to 8 hours at night. (4) Get up when you wake up. (5) Rule out daytime napping.

— Hypersomnia

Excessive daytime sleepiness (EDS) is **hypersomnia.** It most often involves complaints of sleeping too much or of continuous fatigue. Sadly, a majority of EDS patients who consult physicians either remain undiagnosed or are misdiagnosed as suffering from depression, hypoglycemia (low blood sugar), or hypothyroidism (underactivity of the thyroid gland) (Dement, 1979). In fact, the most common causes of excessive sleepiness are sleep apnea and narcolepsy.

Sleep apnea. An inability to breathe and sleep at the same time is involved in **sleep apnea.** In its commonest form, it is caused by an obstruction of the upper airway passages. Apnea, which means "without breath," occurs in patients who complain of sleeping too much (hypersomniacs), as well as in those who complain of sleeping too little (insomniacs). Most people suffering from it (about two-thirds) experience hypersomnia (Dement, 1976). Excessive daytime sleepiness is understandable, since apnea patients awaken as many as 500 times during the night in their repeated attempts to breathe. Strangely, most apnea patients are unaware of their illness and of the hundreds of nightly wakings (Dement, 1976).

Severe sleep apnea, in which the sleeper may have five or more attacks an hour, afflicts about 1 million Americans, mostly overweight men. It may also be common among infants. **Sudden infant death syndrome (SIDS),** commonly known as crib death, kills between 7,000 and 10,000 children between 1 and 12 months of age in the United States annually (Clark et al., 1981; Naeye, 1980). It is now thought to result from apnea, at least in some cases (Getts & Hill, 1982; Naeye,1980).

Although the cause of sleep apnea remains unknown, effective treatments are available. For infants suspected of apnea, electronic bedside monitors can be used to sound an alarm when breathing stops. In adults, the most effective permanent treatment for apnea is a *tracheotomy,* a surgical procedure that allows the patient to breathe through a tube inserted into the trachea. The tube's valve is opened by the patient before sleep to allow direct breathing; closing the valve upon waking enables the patient to breathe and talk normally.

Narcolepsy. The sleep disorder known as **narcolepsy** is characterized by excessive daytime drowsiness (hypersomnia) and *cataplexy,* a loss of muscle control. In addition to sleeping at normal times, narcoleptic patients fall asleep at the most inappropriate moments—while making love or driving a car, for instance (Browman, Sampson, Gujavarty, & Mitler, 1982; Dement, 1979). One narcoleptic patient described how he was forced to lie helpless and speechless while fellow employees forced a spoon down his throat, be-

cause they had confused his collapse with an epileptic convulsion. When the person regained control, he had a lacerated throat (from a case reported by Dement, 1979, p. 422).

Narcolepsy may develop at any age, but in most cases onset occurs during adolescence. Children of a narcoleptic parent have a 1-in-20 risk of someday also being narcoleptic, which suggests that the disorder may be genetic.

Treatment for narcolepsy consists of life-style changes and prescribed medications. Helpful changes include a regular bedtime and regular naps throughout the day. However, a cure has not yet been found. Many patients with narcolepsy are partially or completely disabled by age 40.

— Sleep Disorders in Perspective

Sleep disorders such as apnea and narcolepsy are serious, disabling conditions that often go undiagnosed. Awareness of them is therefore valuable. These and other sleep disorders often cause considerable emotional stress within affected families. A growing number of sleep disorder and research centers are now available for diagnosis and treatment of sleep disturbances. Their services may also be helpful for less severe disorders, including *bruxism* (teeth-grinding) and *enuresis* (bedwetting), as well as night terrors and somnambulism (described earlier). For example, bruxism, which may cause facial discomfort, is treated by rubber guards worn over the teeth at night. In the case of bedwetting, training techniques for bladder control are now available (see chapter 6). And although somnambulism will usually be outgrown, parents are encouraged to take certain safety precautions to protect the child from harm.

— DRUG-INDUCED ALTERATIONS IN CONSCIOUSNESS —

Consciousness-altering drugs have been used for centuries by people of all cultures (Schlaadt & Shannon, 1982). Before we turn to a survey of such drugs, a general introduction is in order.

To begin with, drugs can be dichotomized as *licit* or *illicit.* **Licit drugs** are legal and sanctioned by a partic-

ular culture. **Illicit drugs** are legally or socially prohibited, often because of their undesirable or dangerous side-effects. We should point out, however, that whether a drug is legal or illegal tells us nothing about the drug's potential impact, be it personal, social, or societal. Legal drugs, such as caffeine, alcohol, and nicotine, have become so widely accepted and used in Western cultures that we do not readily think of them as mind-altering or addictive. Everyone knows, for example, that the stimulating lift delivered by a cup of coffee comes from caffeine, which drug researcher Solomon Snyder refers to as "the most widely used psychoactive substance on Earth" (Marx, 1981, p. 1408). Other licit drugs, including the thousands of prescription and nonprescription drugs that Americans spend billions on annually, are legally promoted and advertised even though the medical value of most of them is questionable.

The negative, emotional term *drug abuse* is usually associated with illicit drugs. However, the misuse of *licit* drugs can cause just as much harm as illicit drug abuse. It is therefore important to recognize that although nearly everyone uses drugs, not everyone abuses drugs. *Drug use* refers to both licit and illicit drug consumption. *Drug abuse* is characterized by individual dysfunction and societal harm resulting from drug use. The relative risks and social consequences of

— *Experimental use* is the short-term trial of one or more drugs, motivated primarily by curiosity or a desire to experience an altered mood state.
— *Recreational use* occurs among friends or acquaintances who voluntarily share an experience that they define as acceptable and pleasurable.
— *Circumstantial use* is generally motivated by the user's perceived need to cope with a specific personal or vocational problem situation. Examples are the use of stimulants at work and the use of drugs to relieve tension or boredom.
— *Intensive use* occurs at least daily and is motivated by a perceived need to achieve relief or maintain a level of performance.
— *Compulsive use* involves an intense, high-frequency pattern and a high degree of dependence, such as that seen with chronic alcoholics, heroin dependents, and compulsive barbiturate users. (Paraphrased from President's Commission on Mental Health, 1978, pp. 2109–2110.)

The overwhelming majority of drug use is experimental, recreational, or circumstantial. "To classify all psychoactive drug use as misuse or 'abuse' is the same as equating light or moderate use of alcohol with the problems associated with alcoholism" (President's Commission on Mental Health, 1978, p. 2110).

Whether drug use leads to misuse depends on *tolerance* and *dependence*. **Tolerance** exists when a drug becomes less effective due to repeated use. With tolerance, larger and more frequent doses are required to produce the desired effect. Dependence, which also results from increased use of a drug, may be either physical or psychological (Falk, Schuster, Bigelow, & Woods, 1982). In **Physical dependence,** bodily processes are modified so that continued use of the drug is required to prevent uncomfortable *withdrawal symptoms*. **Psychological dependence** is defined as compulsive use of a drug to produce pleasure or avoid emotional discomfort (Cotman & McGaugh, 1980). Tolerance and dependence may be associated with both illicit and licit drugs.

Two additional points on drugs are in order. First, all drugs can be classified into four main groups, according to their effect on the central nervous system. The groups are *narcotics, sedatives, stimulants,* and *hallucinogens* (or psychedelics). Drugs in each category have noticeably different effects on consciousness:

A second point to keep in mind is that drug effects are highly individual: The effects of a drug depend on the dosage, the form in which the drug is taken and the route by which it enters the body. Many effects also vary with the frequency with which the drug is taken. . . . The effects of psychoactive drugs also differ according to the expectations of the user, the setting or circumstances in which the drug is taken and the history and personality of the user. (Dyke & Byck, 1982, p. 132)

With these introductory comments made, we are now ready to discuss those drugs most widely used for their effects on consciousness.

Narcotics

Narcotic drugs numb the senses and with prolonged use become addictive. They produce an intoxication euphoria that is heightened when the drug is injected into the bloodstream. One of the more commonly available narcotic drugs is *opium*, a derivative of the poppy plant. Opium is an illicit substance today in the United States. During the second half of the 19th century, however, opium and other narcotic drugs were sold legally in drugstores and were popularly used for a variety of purposes (see Figure 5–7). *Morphine*, a narcotic drug refined from opium, was used extensively to treat the wounded during the Civil War. A re-

DR. McMUNN'S
ELIXIR OF OPIUM.
AN INVALUABLE DISCOVERY IN THE PREPARATION OF OPIUM.

The following testimonial, recently received, embraces several interesting and very important facts connected with the administration of the Elixir of Opium; and it is believed the views expressed by Dr. Webb will accord with the experience of every Physician who may adopt the use of this truly valuable remedial agent in his practice.

Messrs. A. B. & D. Sands:
Hempstead, L. I., July 7, 1846.

GENTLEMEN,—I regret that urgent and unavoidable engagements have prevented me from answering yours before, requesting my opinion of McMunn's Elixir of Opium, or any facts with respect to its operation in my practice. I have frequently witnessed its effects in cases which resisted every other remedy; and I might cite a number of instances in which it seemed to act like a charm in allaying the most dangerous symptoms when other means had been tried in vain. I have been in the habit of using it more or less in my practice, ever since it was first presented to public use, and I know of no substitute for it in all those cases in which it is desirable to allay nervous irritability, either as an anodyne or soporific, without producing all the unpleasant consequences incident to the narcotic property of Opium. A case occurred recently, in which the use of Morphine was followed by a state resembling catalepsy. The patient remained insensible for five hours after taking a moderate dose, with a complete suspension of sensorial power or volition, without my discovering the causes; but as the effects of the Morphine subsided, the pains for which it was given returned with such severity that the dose was repeated, and the same results followed. I substituted the Elixir, and she was perfectly free from all unpleasant symptoms afterwards, and completely relieved.

Another case, in which every other form of Opium had been tried before I was called, was relieved by McMunn's Elixir. The patient was a lady, who had been vomiting incessantly for two or three days. She cautioned me not to prescribe any preparation of Opium, insisting that it would make her worse. I ventured, however, to try it without her knowledge, and she was at once relieved, falling into a delightful slumber, without feeling any other than the desired effect, so that as an anti-emetic it is invaluable. I might add a variety of other cases, but the opinions expressed in this testimonial you have already adduced are sufficient to convince the most skeptical, that, when judiciously administered, it is superior to all other articles in use for particular conditions.

Very respectfully yours,
EDWIN WEBB, M.D.

A. B. & D. Sands:
New York, 9th Mo., (Sept.) 30, 1846.

GENTLEMEN,—I give you the result of my experience with Dr. McMunn's Elixir of Opium, in a severe case of Hooping-cough, as requoted by you. Having recently had several cases under treatment, I was induced to try the Elixir combined with a weak solution of Hydrocyanic Acid. I administered to a child one year old, one drop of the mixture on a lump of sugar, three or four times a day, and the effect exceeded any thing I ever saw; the spasms were almost immediately allayed in a most decided manner, at the same time it promoted free and easy expectoration. I consider this combination a most valuable medicine in the treatment of Hooping-cough.

Yours respectfully,
C. T. COLLINS, M.D.

Dr. J. B. McMUNN:
Dr. Mitchell's trials of the Elixir of Opium in the Hospitals.
New York, February 8th, 1837.

Figure 5–7.
Advertisement announcing the over-the-counter sale of narcotics in the United States during the middle of the 19th century.

ported 45,000 soldiers became dependent on it as a result (Brecher, 1972). Morphine is still prescribed today, primarily for pain relief. However, its medical use is severely restricted because of the high risk of physical dependence.

The euphoric effects of narcotic drugs such as morphine afford considerable relief to patients suffering from pain, tension, or anxiety. Anxieties and feelings of inferiority vanish while a person is on morphine, and perceptions of reality are rosy—until the pleasurable drug effects wear off. Larger doses are required as tolerance develops. The potential for addiction and abuse of narcotic drugs is great, because both tolerance and dependence develop rapidly. *Heroin,* for example, which is much stronger than the opium from

which it is derived, can produce a 10-fold increase in tolerance after repeated use for only 2 or 3 weeks (Cotman & McGaugh, 1980).

Medical treatment for physical narcotic dependence is generally considered to be relatively simple. Quitting heroin, for instance, results in an acute *withdrawal reaction* that first becomes apparent several hours after the last injection, reaching a peak in 2 or 3 days and lasting about a week. "The signs of heroin abstinence are highly characteristic and include tearing, nasal discharge, yawning, chills, fever, vomiting, muscular aches, and diarrhea" (Cotman & McGaugh, 1980, p. 746). Medical treatment generally lasts throughout the withdrawal period. Psychological dependence, related to anxiety-reducing and pleasurable effects of the drug, can last a lifetime. Many addicted patients continue to take the drug in spite of their conscious admission that it causes extreme physical, social, and psychological damage.

Sedatives

Sedative drugs have a calming or tranquilizing effect; they act as *general depressants* on the central nervous system. Commonly used sedatives include *alcohol* and synthetic *barbiturate* sleeping pills such as Seconal, Nembutal, and Tuinal.

— Barbiturates

A class of sedative drugs, *barbiturates* differ in their pharmacologic action. However, in small dosages, all commonly produce a euphoric lift and disinhibition—the feeling one might experience after a cocktail or two. In high dosages these drugs impair motor coordination and produce stupor and severe respiratory depression (Cotman & McGaugh, 1980). Barbiturate sleeping pills reduce REM sleep (Ray, 1983). Their continued use thus disrupts normal sleep, and they may be physically addictive.

The allure of barbiturates is summarized by the drug expert Dr. Sidney Cohen in testimony before a U.S. Senate investigating committee:

For the youngsters barbiturates are a more reliable high and less detectable than "pot." They are less strenuous than LSD, less "freaky" than amphetamines, and less expensive than heroin. A school boy can "drop a red" and spend the day in a dreamy, floating state of awayness untroubled by reality. It is drunkenness without the odor of alcohol. (Quoted by Kimble, Garmezy, & Zigler, 1980, p. 114)

Physical dependence is more difficult to produce on barbiturates than on narcotic drugs. However, once dependence is established, barbiturate withdrawal symptoms are far more dangerous. Upon removal of the drug, patients generally show signs of restlessness, agitation, unpleasant hallucinations, tremors, and suicidal tendencies. Gradually decreasing the daily dosage tends to minimize the severity of these symptoms (Cotman & McGaugh, 1980).

— Alcohol

A licit drug, *alcohol* acts as a sedative, or central nervous system depressant. Drinking small amounts, such as 2 ounces of 90-proof whiskey (0.05 percent blood alcohol), results in relaxation and loss of inhibition. Six ounces of 90-proof whiskey (approximately 0.15 percent blood alcohol level) affects motor areas of the brain. The drinker staggers, slurs speech, and may become overconfident and impulsive. Ten ounces of 90-proof whisky (0.25 percent blood alcohol level) affects emotional centers of the brain. Sensations become distorted, and the drinker shows signs of drowsiness and may fall asleep. Sixteen ounces of 90-proof whiskey (0.4 percent blood alcohol level) affects the sensory areas of the cerebellum. The drinker shows clear signs of being in a stupor. Twenty-four ounces of 90-proof whiskey (0.6 percent blood alcohol level) affects perceptual areas of the brain. The drinker is likely to lose conscious control over movements; only breathing and heartbeat remain. Thirty-two ounces of 90-proof whiskey (0.8 percent blood alcohol level) affects the entire brain; heartbeat and respiration stop, and the end result is death (Cohen, 1970—cited in Coon, 1983).

The problem of alcohol misuse. For the true alcoholic, no stimulus seems aversive enough to deter persistent consumption of alcohol. The urge to drink can dominate the alcoholic personality despite loss of friends, job, family, and public reputation. Yet, alcohol misuse remains the number 1 drug problem in developed nations. Over 100 million people in the United States alone use alcohol, and an estimated 12 to 15 million of them have a severe drinking problem. A most troublesome statistic is the increased incidence of alcohol abuse among adolescents. Chafetz (1979), for example, suggests that about 20 percent of young people between 14 and 17 years of age are problem drinkers. How do you know if you have a drinking problem? Table 5–3 lists some early warning signs and signals.

Table 5–3.
Early warning signs and signals not to be ignored in the course of the development of a drinking problem. (From Coon, 1983. p. 142).

Early Warnings

You are beginning to feel guilty about your drinking.

You drink more than you used to and tend to gulp your drinks.

You try to have a few extra drinks before or after drinking with others.

You have begun to drink at certain times or to get through certain situations.

You drink to relieve feelings of boredom, depression, anxiety, or inadequacy.

You are sensitive when others mention your drinking.

You have had memory blackouts or have passed out while drinking.

Signals Not to Be Ignored

There are times when you *need* a drink.

You drink in the morning to overcome a hangover from previous drinking.

You promise to drink less and are lying about your drinking.

You often regret what you have said or done while drinking.

You have begun to drink alone.

You have weekend drinking bouts and Monday hangovers.

You have lost time at work or school due to drinking.

You are noticeably drunk on important occasions.

Your relationship to family and friends has changed due to your drinking.

Despite the fact that alcohol use is regarded by many to be rewarding and gratifying, it is associated with severe social and health problems. Consider the following facts about alcohol-related problems, provided by the President's Commission on Mental Health (1978, p. 2084):

— In the last 30 years there has been a marked shift from tavern drinking to drinking in homes and other private places.
— By some accountings, deaths from alcohol problems rank third in number, after heart diseases and cancer.
— Alcohol misuse plays a significant role in death from a number of chronic diseases, as well as in homicide, suicide, and accidents of all kinds.
— About 38 percent of patients in state mental hospitals have a primary diagnosis of alcoholism.
— Drivers with blood alcohol levels of .10 percent or

higher (the legal driving impairment level in many jurisdictions) are involved in from 35 to 59 percent of highway fatalities.

– The social costs generated by alcohol-related problems are astronomical, estimated as high as $42.75 billion for 1975.

Stimulants

Stimulant drugs are a class of drugs that stimulate or arouse the central nervous system. The most widely used stimulants are the licit drug substances found in coffee and tobacco. *Caffeine* is the active drug in coffee. It is also an ingredient in many soft drinks. *Nicotine* is the active drug in tobacco (McMorrow & Foxx, 1983). Caffeine and nicotine are considered to be mild central nervous system stimulants, or uppers. Their effect on consciousness is to produce a psychological lift. Because the use of these drugs is legal and commonplace, we do not readily think of them as being capable of producing alterations in consciousness. Excessive use of caffeine and nicotine, however, leads to tolerance and both physical and psychological dependence.

— Amphetamines

Stimulant drugs that produce central nervous system stimulation, euphoria, and heightened activity are classed as *amphetamines*. Benzedrine, Dexedrine, and Preludin are examples. They are prescribed for a variety of reasons: to combat fatigue, to suppress appetite in the treatment of obesity, and to prevent sleep. Unfortunately, a person can easily slip into addiction, with tolerance leading to dependence, as illustrated by the remarks of country and western singer Johnny Cash:

> With all the traveling I had to do, and upon reaching a city tired and weary, those pills could pep me up and make me really feel like doing a show. . . .
>
> Before I really got hooked, I would realize what was happening and I'd think, "What am I doing to myself?" I think back now to interviews where questions would be coming, and I couldn't think of the answers. . . . And I'd realize it was the pills. They regulated my mind and began to take control. . . .
>
> My friends made a joke out of my "nervousness." I had a twitch in the neck, the back, the face. My eyes dilated. I couldn't stand still. I twisted, turned, contorted, and popped my neck bones. It often felt like someone had a fist between my shoulder blades, twisting the muscle and bones, stretching my nerves, torturing them to the breaking point. (Quoted by Cotman & McGaugh, 1980, p. 748)

The most dangerous of the amphetamines is methedrine, or speed, which, when injected intravenously, is an upper that produces an ecstatic high. The initial flash experienced by the user has been described as a feeling similar to sexual orgasm, and there may be a sense of having extreme mental physical power (Cotman & McGaugh, 1980). Injecting a higher than accustomed dose may cause restlessness, uncoordination of thought and actions, insomnia, nervousness, irritability, and psychotic symptoms. The "speed freak" requires larger and more frequent administrations of the drug. Injections every few hours for several days become a pattern of misuse that results in hyperactivity and going without food or sleep. Eventually, exhaustion and collapse lead to what is sometimes called *amphetamine psychosis,* a state characterized by paranoid delusional thinking.

Two facts about the use of amphetamines are particularly disturbing. First, their misuse, and the consequent development of tolerance and dependence, is on the increase—predominantly among adolescents. Second, misuse of amphetamines too often develops from initially innocent use of prescribed medications. Not all people who develop tolerance and dependence on prescribed drugs survive the experience, as Johnny Cash did.

— Cocaine

Like the other drugs discussed in this section, *cocaine* acts as a central nervous system stimulant. It is found in the leaves of two South American species of the coca shrub. The coca leaves of one species are harvested for legal export to the United States, where the cocaine is extracted for medical use. You may be surprised to learn that after the cocaine has been removed, the remaining portions of the coca leaf are used as flavoring in the world's most popular soft drink, Coca-Cola.

Growing popularity of cocaine. Although archaeological findings in Ecuador indicate that human experience with cocaine dates back at least 5,000 years, its recreational use in America is a recent phenomenon (see Figure 5–8). Available statistics suggest that about 2 million Americans used cocaine in 1976. A 1979 report by the White House Strategy Council on

Figure 5–8.
A Manhattan freelance artist sniffs cocaine during his lunch break.

Drug Abuse indicates that this figure increased to 10 million during 1978 (Dyke & Byck, 1982).

Street-grade cocaine consists of 10 to 85 percent cocaine that is mixed with various other substances, such as amphetamines, simple carbohydrates, or anesthetics. The white powder mixture can be sold on the street illicitly for between $100 and $145 per gram. Estimates of the retail sales of cocaine in 1980 are between $27 billion and $32 billion, ranking the cocaine industry seventh in volume of domestic sales by comparison to industrial corporations and placing it between the Ford Motor Company and the Gulf Oil Corporation in retail sales (Dyke & Byck, 1982).

Effects of cocaine on consciousness. When ground into powder and arranged into several lines or rows, small amounts of cocaine, between 25 and 100 milligrams, can be inhaled, or snorted, into the nostrils through a straw or a rolled piece of paper or dollar bill and are quickly absorbed into the bloodstream. *Intranasal ingestion* in this manner produces a sense of euphoria and clarity of thought that peaks within a

few minutes and may last for only 30 minutes. From 45 to 60 minutes after the ingestion of a 100-milligram dose, about one-third of the laboratory subjects studied in one investigation experienced anxiety, depression, fatigue, and a strong desire for more cocaine—a finding that appears to be consistent across investigations (Dyke & Byck, 1982).

One of the first systematic attempts to document the effects of cocaine was made by Sigmund Freud. In his *Cocaine Papers,* Freud (1885/1974) described how the drug relieved his depression and gave him the energy to continue his work. Freud also noted an absence of craving for the further use of cocaine after the first and subsequent uses of the drug.

Freud's belief that cocaine is not addictive is at odds with more recent investigations. Medically speaking, a drug is addictive if tolerance (a need for increased doses to obtain the same effect) develops and if physical dependence (a need for repeated doses to prevent withdrawal symptoms) occurs. Since cocaine users can take the same dose repeatedly and achieve the same effect, the drug is not physically addictive according to this definition. It is now recognized, however, that cocaine use can lead to severe psychological dependence (Siegel, 1982).

Hallucinogens

Sometimes referred to as *psychedelics,* the **hallucinogens** are a class of drugs that produce alterations in perception, thinking, and emotion. In sufficiently large doses, many will produce *hallucinations* and vivid sensory changes in color or form perception. Drugs that produce hallucinations include *mescaline,* from the peyote cactus plant, and *psilocybin,* from the Aztec mushroom. The most commonly used hallucinogens are *LSD, PCP,* and *marijuana,* the effects of which we will now briefly review.

— LSD

Lysergic acid diethylamide (LSD) is the most powerful of the hallucinogenic drugs. It has been used by 1 in 20 Americans over the age of 12. Usage among young adults has been reported to be as high as 17.3 percent (President's Commission on Mental Health, 1978).

Only small oral dosages of LSD are required to cause hallucinations and marked changes in mood and judgment. Overdoses of LSD predispose people to acute psychotic episodes that may last from 8 to 10 hours. The symptoms that characterize these episodes appear to mimic some of the symptoms of extreme forms of mental disorders. For example, even though physical dependence on LSD does not occur, users have reported disturbing delayed visual hallucinations, called flashbacks. These may appear days, weeks, or months after the last use of the drug (Stanton, Mintz, & Franklin, 1976).

— PCP

The most abused illicit street drug in the United States today is *phencyclidine* (PCP), otherwise known as angel dust. Small doses of PCP can alter consciousness so dramatically that users become dissociated from their surroundings, insensitive to pain, and uninhibited in their actions. A monograph published in 1978 by the National Institute of Drug Abuse provides some startling accounts about the effects of PCP. Consider the following descriptions:

A young man smokes some PCP and proceeds to rob a gas station at gunpoint. A juvenile smokes PCP and rapes his baby sister. . . . A police officer encounters a young man who may have ingested an analog of PCP. The man, naked and unarmed, reportedly becomes combative and assaultive and is shot to death by the officer. Two lovers are smoking PCP alone in their bedroom; within a few minutes one of them is bleeding to death from a knife wound which may or may not have been self-inflicted. A middle-aged woman takes some cocaine which has been adulterated with PCP and tries to rob a bank armed only with a broom which she manipulates as if it were a gun. (Quoted by Kimble et al., 1980, p. 114)

— Marijuana

More commonly called "pot" or "grass," *marijuana* is a mildly hallucinogenic substance. It is derived from the hemp plant *(Cannabis sativa),* native to Jamaica, Mexico, Africa, India, and the Middle East. Its cultivation is also a burgeoning industry in the United States (Morganthau et al., 1982).

Marijuana's active ingredient, tetrahydrocannabinol (THC), is concentrated in the resin at the flowering tops. Marijuana users smoke or eat the plant's leaves to achieve the desired effects. The potency of marijuana varies with the plant strain and the growing conditions, but a preparation containing 2 percent THC is considered to be quite potent (Cotman & McGaugh, 1980). Hash, or *hashish,* is derived from the same plant and also contains THC, but in a 2- to 10-fold higher amount.

Anecdotal descriptions of marijuana's psychological effects suggest that it induces a dreamy, euphoric state of altered consciousness, sometimes characterized by detachment, uncontrollable laughter and gaiety. Antisocial, aggressive behavior is rare. Perceptual distortions in which distances are judged incorrectly and time is overestimated may occur with large dosages (Cotman & McGaugh, 1980). Although marijuana is mild in comparison with other hallucinogens, excessive dosages of it may produce visual or auditory hallucinations.

What are we to conclude from existing knowledge about the use of marijuana? Consider the following: Between 40 and 50 million Americans have tried marijuana, and approximately 15 million regard themselves as regular users. Increased usage of marijuana has led to its decriminalization in several states; however, possession of even small amounts of marijuana is a misdemeanor in most states, and possession of larger amounts with an intent to sell is a felony (Oakes,

Table 5–4.

A 1982 Newsweek Poll on attitudes toward marijuana.

A Newsweek Poll on Pot					
Opposition to legalizing marijuana is growing again, but majorities of Americans also believe that use of the drug is increasing (58 percent) and that it probably can't be eliminated (65 percent).					

Do you think the use of marijuana should be made legal?

	1972	1977	1980	1982
Yes	15%	28%	25%	20%
No	81%	66%	70%	74%
No opinion	4%	6%	5%	6%

Do you think the growing of small amounts of marijuana for personal use should be treated as a criminal offense?

Yes	No	No opinion
53%	40%	7%

Do you think that the growing of marijuana for sale to others should be treated as a criminal offense?

Yes	No	No opinion
85%	12%	3%

In general, do you think the government spends too much money and effort combating marijuana use, too little—or is the government's effort just about right?

Too much	23%
Too little	31%
About right	24%
Don't know	22%

What proportion of your friends and acquaintances occasionally smokes marijuana?

None	43%
Hardly any	22%
Somewhat fewer than half	11%
About half	10%
More than half	7%
Almost all	4%
Don't know	3%

What proportion of your friends and acquaintances regularly smokes marijuana?

None	53%
Hardly any	20%
Somewhat fewer than half	11%
About half	7%
More than half	4%
Almost all	1%
Don't know	4%

Do you think that marijuana use is increasing, decreasing or remaining about the same?

Increasing	58%	Decreasing	8%
About the same	24%	Don't know	10%

For this Newsweek Poll. The Gallup Organization telephoned 785 adults on Oct. 13 and 14. The margin of error is plus or minus 4 percentage points. (The Newsweek Poll © 1982 Newsweek, Inc.)

Robert Morris—Newsweek

1980). A 1982 Newsweek Poll shows that the percentage of Americans who oppose marijuana's legalization has risen by eight points, to 74 percent, since 1977 (see Table 5–4). Nevertheless, the fact remains that the use of marijuana is on the increase (Maugh, 1982).

The final word on the dangers associated with marijuana use is not in yet. Common sense tells us that continued use of any substance to achieve an altered state of consciousness or to escape life's problems can lead to psychological dependence, even if the risk of physical dependence is minimal. Although a study by Schaeffer and others (1981) provided evidence for the lack of negative effects associated with long-term marijuana use, a newer report, issued in 1982 by the National Academy of Sciences, concluded that marijuana has some potentially harmful effects that justify serious concern (Maugh, 1982). (The report, *Marijuana and Health,* was prepared by a panel of 22 scientists; it was published by and is available through National Academy Press, Washington, DC.)

— APPLICATION —

SELF-REGULATION WITH MEDITATION

A variety of *self-regulation* techniques that seem to provide sensible alternatives to drugs for achieving control over mental and physiological processes are now available. (For review, see Shapiro, 1982.) One such technique, known as **meditation,** dates at least to the 13th century. For 7 centuries since then, meditation has been practiced by people around the world. Those who are successful report achieving heightened powers of concentration, an altered sense of consciousness, and personal enlightenment. In a typical meditative self-regulation technique, the beginner is instructed to spend a few minutes daily sitting motionless in a quiet place with eyes closed (see Figure 5–9). Powers of concentration and self-control are fostered by repeated counting of breaths, from 1 to 10, while thus seated. More experienced meditators merely focus on their breathing while dispelling from awareness all other competing distractions.

Transcendental meditation, or TM, is a popular Westernized form of meditation and self-regulation. There is, of course, no evidence for claims by some TM instructors that meditators achieve supernatural powers that enable them to walk through walls and levitate. But there is evidence that TM practice does alter body processes and subjective feelings, producing relaxation and a sense of well-being (Benson, 1975).

Even though personal reports obtained from those who practice TM may be exaggerated, it does seem that meditation has no harmful side-effects, as do drugs, and that it can be beneficial in controlling psychological stress (Hoffman et al., 1982). As with other forms of self-regulation, body changes measured while subjects are practicing TM include lowered heart rate, breathing, and oxygen consumption. These physiological changes tend to be the reverse of what is observed in subjects during stress (Wallace & Benson, 1972).

TM is easily mastered. Instructors emphasize the importance of the *mantra,* a special word or sound that is chosen for each person and that is to be repeated over and over during the breathing and relaxation exercise (Maharishi Mahesh Yogi, 1963). Some instructors prefer the use of a *yantra,* a visual pattern on which to focus one's concentration, or a *koan,* a paradox to contemplate.

Figure 5–9.
Person meditating.

A simple technique recommended for beginning meditation was demonstrated in a study by Maupin (1965). College students were instructed to spend a few minutes twice each day sitting on the floor in a quiet room, with back straight and head tilted forward slightly. While sitting, students were to let their breathing become relaxed and natural, setting its own pace and depth. They were to focus attention on the breathing—the movements of the abdomen, not the nose or throat—and to turn everything else aside. At the end of a two-week session, students who responded to the experience reported changes in consciousness that included improved concentration and detachment from worries and problems in everyday living.

A technique known as **progressive relaxation,** which uses procedures similar to those just described, is being applied increasingly in therapy to improve self-regulation. Designed by Edmond Jacobson (1938), this technique involves learning how to alternately tense and relax body muscles. People who master the *relaxation response* show decreases in muscle tension, heart rate, blood pressure, and breathing rate (Benson, 1975). After several months of daily practice with progressive relaxation, people have reported achieving deep levels of relaxation and a sense of self-control. Some of the most useful applications of this technique are described in later chapters.

CONSCIOUSNESS, PHYSIOLOGY, AND LONGEVITY

Research on self-regulation techniques such as meditation shows that people can, to a degree, exert control of "mind over body." What implications does this fact have for the future? Let's focus for a moment on transcendental meditation, described in the preceding application. The TM program has taught a relatively uniform type of meditation to over 2 million people during the last 20 years (Orme-Johnson, Dillbeck, Wallace, & Landrith, 1982). This form of meditation, therefore, has been readily available for study. Subjectively, practitioners of TM report achieving a state of consciousness called *pure awareness,* marked by inner wakefulness, expansion, and inner silence. Objectively, the state of pure awareness is defined by variations in physiological activity that correspond to deep physical rest. Thus, pure awareness has been described by Maharishi Mahesh Yogi (1978), the founder of the TM technique, as a state of stress-free functioning of mind and body.

A series of reports suggest that this state, however attained, may slow the process of biological aging and increase longevity. For example, Wallace, Dillbeck, Jacobe, and Harrington (1982) administered Morgan's *Adult Growth Examination* to a group of 84 subjects with an average age of 53 years. This scale uses measures of auditory threshold, vision, and blood pressure as indicators of biological age. The average biological age of the 33 short-term TM subjects (those who had practiced the TM program less than 5 years) was 5.0 years less than for subjects in the general population. The average biological age of the 40 long-term TM subjects (those who had practiced TM for more than 5 years) was 12.0 years less than for subjects in the general population. The

11 control subjects showed an average biological age that was only 2.6 years less than that of the general population. Differences between groups were independent of differences in exercise and diet.

This study indicates that meditation may affect basic physiological mechanisms in a direction opposite to those that usually characterize aging. Long-term meditators showed significantly younger biological ages. A number of additional studies using different methods also suggest that the TM technique may influence longevity. For example, Jevning (1981) reported studies that showed a marked increase of brain blood flow during TM. Since brain blood flow may decrease with aging, the fact that it increases during meditation suggests a mechanism by which meditation might slow biological aging.

Various studied suggest that the immune system is the body's principal means of defense against disease, including cancer. One theory concerning the spread of cancer within the body proposes that the immune system normally rejects beginning clones of malignant cancer cells (Van Boxel, 1981). Currently, it is believed that both aging and psychological stress (see chapter 14) may affect the efficiency of the immune system in warding off diseases such as cancer. (For review, see Garfield, 1983.) Since meditative techniques can bring about physiological changes opposite to those produced by psychological stress, it would be helpful to develop a further understanding of their effects on immune system functioning. This knowledge, in turn, might shed light on how self-regulation of consciousness can be used to forestall biological aging and increase longevity.

— SUMMARY —

1. In contemporary psychology, consciousness refers to a variety of mental states that are not easily defined and that have only recently been subjected to systematic investigation.

2. Passive consciousness is characterized by open awareness, relaxed enjoyment associated with daydreaming, and receptive states. It may appear as when we passively listen to music, for example.

3. Active consciousness is characterized by productive mental states, as when we make plans for the future and initiate activities that lead to the fulfillment of plans.

4. Theorists following in the footsteps of Sigmund Freud have found it useful to distinguish among four levels of consciousness: conscious, nonconscious, preconscious, and unconscious.

5. Hypnosis, first practiced during the 1700s by Friedrich Anton Mesmer, is characterized by relaxation, suggestibility, restriction of attention, and intense concentration. Hypnosis is widely, and questionably, used to help crime victims recall memories. It has therapeutic value in cancer treatment and as an alternative to chemical anesthesia in surgery.

6. Sleep and dreaming represent altered states of consciousness. Although many questions about the function of sleep remain unanswered, part of the mystery surrounding the nature of sleep has yielded to objective measurement techniques developed and refined during the past three decades.

7. Relatively recent research has revealed that there are two distinctly different states of sleep: rapid-eye movement (REM) sleep and non-rapid-eye-movement (NREM) sleep. Also, there are five sleep stages, or cycles, that characterize an average night's sleep.

8. About 80 to 85 percent of awakenings during REM sleep result in dream reports. Dreams are rarely reported by subjects awakening during NREM sleep.

9. Dream deprivation studies have shown how vital dreaming is to a good night's sleep. Subjects prevented from dreaming show an increased need to dream. During the waking hours after dream deprivation, subjects may exhibit a variety of disturbances, such as anxiety, irritability, and difficulty in concentration.

10. The study and treatment of sleep disorders, including insomnia, sleep apnea, narcolepsy, and other, less severe sleep disturbances, is one of the newest and fastest growing clinical disciplines.

11. Drug-induced alterations in consciousness provide escape to users, either by lifting them to a new psychological high or by relieving the physical or psychological discomforts associated with everyday problems in living.

12. The drugs most widely used for their effects on consciousness include (1) narcotic or opiate drugs, such as opium, morphine, and heroin; (2) general depressants or sedatives, such as barbiturates and alcohol; (3) stimulants, such as nicotine, caffeine, amphetamines, and cocaine; and (4) hallucinogens, such as LSD, PCP, marijuana, and hashish.

13. A variety of self-regulation techniques seem to offer sensible alternatives to drugs for achieving control over mental and physiological processes. Two techniques that have been reported to lead to enhanced health, happiness, and control over psychological stress are relaxation and meditation.

— IMPORTANT TERMS AND CONCEPTS —

Consciousness
Conscious
Nonconscious
Preconscious
Unconscious
Hypnosis
Energy Conservation Theory of Sleep
Behavioral Adaptive Theory of Sleep
Biological Rhythm Theory of Sleep
Circadian Rhythms
Electromyogram (EMG)

Electrooculogram (EOG)
REM Sleep
NREM Sleep
Nightmares
Night Terrors
Somnambulism
Insomnia
Hypersomnia
Sleep Apnea
Sudden Infant Death Syndrome (SIDS)
Narcolepsy

Licit Drugs
Illicit Drugs
Tolerance
Physical Dependence
Psychological Dependence
Narcotic Drugs
Sedative Drugs
Stimulant Drugs
Hallucinogens
Meditation
Progressive Relaxation

SUGGESTIONS FOR FURTHER READING

Barber, T. X., Spanos, N. P., & Chaves, J. F. (1974). *Hypnosis, imagination, and human potentialities*. Elmsford, N.Y.: Pergamon Press. A critical look at hypnosis.

Benson, H. (1976). *The relaxation response*. New York: Avon Books. Some reasons that this could be the most important book of your life are on the opening page, which explains that the relaxation response (1) relieves fatigue and helps you cope with your anxieties; (2) relieves the stress that can lead to high blood pressure; (3) reduces the tendency to smoke, drink, or "turn on" with drugs; (4) can be used to help you sleep; (5) conserves the body's store of energy; (6) makes you more alert; (7) can be learned without classes and in your own home; (8) can be used anywhere, even on your way to work or class; and (9) has no dangerous side-effects. Available in most bookstores.

Dement, W. C. (1976). *Some must watch while some must sleep*. Stanford, CA: Stanford Alumni Association. A delightful, easy-to-read paperback that covers most of the material on sleep and dreaming discussed in this chapter.

Ornstein, R. E. (Ed.). (1974). *The nature of human consciousness*. New York: Viking Press. A multiple-author book of readings that provides a detailed background for topics covered in the first part of this chapter as well as other topics relevant to the study of consciousness.

Ray, O. S. (1983). *Drugs, society and human behavior* (3rd ed.). St. Louis, MO: C. V. Mosby. A broad, fascinating overview of topics related to this chapter's discussion of drug-induced alterations in consciousness.

Smith, S. (1973). *ESP and hypnosis*. New York: Macmillan. Traces the fascinating history of hypnosis from its shady origins during Mesmer's day to its present status of quasi respectability and its promising future as a clinical tool.

Tart, C. T. (1975) *States of consciousness*. New York: E. P. Dutton. A book that covers much of the material on states of consciousness discussed in this chapter.

- CHAPTER 6 -

CONDITIONING AND LEARNING

CONDITIONING AND LEARNING

— CHAPTER OBJECTIVES —

To achieve the objectives of this chapter, you should be able to answer the questions listed here. You should also be able to define the terms and concepts listed at the end of the chapter.

1. What is learning?
2. List the essential characteristics of classical (respondent) conditioning.
3. What are the basic features of instrumental (operant) conditioning?
4. In what ways are classical and instrumental conditioning different? In what ways are they similar?
5. What are the differences between primary and secondary reinforcers? Between positive and negative reinforcement? How does partial reinforcement affect learning?
6. What distinguishes cognitive learning from associative learning?

— CHAPTER OUTLINE —

Classical and Instrumental Conditioning
Conditioning is a process by which learned behaviors are acquired.

Classical (Respondent) Conditioning
Instrumental (Operant) Conditioning
Application: Extinction of Conditioned Responses

Principles of Learning and the Interaction of Classical and Instrumental Conditioning
Classical and instrumental conditioning interact during learning and are often jointly responsible for the development of learned responses.

Operant Conditioning of Respondent Behavior
Principle of Reinforcement
Reinforcement Schedules
Stimulus Control of Behavior
Aversive Control of Behavior
Application: Behavior Modification and Self-Control Techniques

Cognitive Learning
Not all learning can be explained by conditioning. Cognitive learning involves processes that are more complex than those involved in the conditioning of associations between stimuli and responses.

Latent Learning
Insight Learning
Application: Learning Through Observation

On the Horizon: Behavioral Technology in the Coming Years

PATHOLOGICAL GAMBLING

As a college student, Charlie K. watched a friend win $18,000 at the racetrack one afternoon. Charlie never forgot that big win. Soon, everything else became secondary to gambling. Charlie was married and divorced twice; he changed jobs so often he had difficulty remembering where he worked. The only place Charlie wanted to be was at the track. During his 20 years as a pathological gambler, Charlie focused his whole being on getting money for more gambling. One of Charlie's favorite scams was to make a small purchase, such as a $2 sandwich, and pay for it with a worthless $10 check. By repeating the scam, Charlie could get enough cash to return to the racetrack. To Charlie, pulling off his scam became as exhilarating as the gambling itself.

It's no wonder that pathological gambling can be extremely destructive. Professionals estimate that each compulsive gambler disrupts the lives of 10 to 17 others, including relatives, creditors, and co-workers. The average pathological gambler bets twice what he or she makes and costs society approximately $40,000 per year. Arrests of gamblers for forgery, fraud, embezzlement, and income tax evasion are not uncommon. And even though 90 percent of those who gamble lose, an estimated 6 million to 9 million gamblers in the United States believe they are immune to the odds. (Paraphrased from Greene, 1982)

Pathological gambling is a topic of considerable interest to psychologists who study learning. Many behaviors—ranging from the bizarre and deviant to the most routine—can best be understood through an appreciation of learning principles. Indeed, Charlie's addiction to gambling can be explained, to a large degree, by the learning principles covered in this chapter, which surveys two major perspectives on learning: associative, stimulus-response approaches and cognitive approaches.

Associative, stimulus-response approaches view learning as a connection between stimuli (events that are sensed) and responses. Two examples of such learning that we will discuss are classical (respondent) conditioning and instrumental (operant) conditioning. In contrast, *cognitive approaches* emphasize more mental (cognitive) activities, such as thinking, reasoning, and remembering; examples in this chapter include latent learning, insight learning, and observational learning. Both approaches generally define **learning** as any relatively permanent change in behavior that can be attributed to experience or practice.

— CLASSICAL AND INSTRUMENTAL CONDITIONING —

Classical (Respondent) Conditioning

A basic form of learning is **classical (respondent) conditioning.** It takes place when a neutral stimulus is paired with a stimulus that elicits a reflex response.

If this pairing is repeated, the previously neutral stimulus will also begin to elicit the response. To understand this effect more fully, you should know that a **reflex** is an unlearned reaction to a specific stimulus. **Respondent (reflex) behavior** includes human and animal responses that are *elicited* (drawn out) by stimuli in the environment. Table 6–1 offers some examples of reflex behaviors and their stimuli. The pupillary reflex occurs when the pupils of the eyes contract or dilate in response to changes in light. The salivary reflex occurs when the mouth waters at the taste of food. A gust of cold air raises goose bumps on the skin. Onion juice can elicit teardrops in the eye. Each of these behaviors is an example of a reflex. In general, classical conditioning begins with reflex behavior, and it is complete when a neutral stimulus alone is capable of eliciting the reflex response.

— Pavlov's Contribution to the Psychology of Learning

Much of what we know about classical conditioning was formulated early in this century by the Nobel Prize winning Russian physiologist Ivan P. Pavlov. Pavlov (1927) was studying digestion in dogs when he noticed, quite by accident, that the dogs often salivated when he approached them with food. Pavlov knew that the taste of food elicits the salivary reflex; however, he thought it was curious for a dog to salivate at the mere sight of food. To test his hypothesis that any stimulus preceding food would cause a dog to salivate, Pavlov paired a tone with the presentation of food. After only

Table 6–1.

Examples of reflex behaviors and the stimulus-response relationships involved in them.

STIMULUS		RESPONSE	REFLEX
Light	→	Contraction	Pupillary
Food in mouth	→	Salivation	Salivary
Cold air	→	Goose flesh	Goose flesh
Onion juice	→	Teardrops in eye	Tearing

a few such pairings, the dog indeed began to salivate to the tone. Let's further explore this interesting result.

Figure 6–1 shows an experimental chamber and laboratory equipped with an observation window and instrumentation. A hungry dog is led into a soundproof room and placed in a comfortable harness. A tube is then attached to one of the dog's salivary glands through a small opening made in the dog's cheek. When the dog responds, saliva flows through the tube into a glass cylinder, allowing the experimenter to determine how much the dog has salivated.

Before conditioning, some preliminary training is required. First, the dog is allowed to stand in the lab-

Figure 6–1.

A laboratory for studying classical conditioning. The dog is in a soundproof room; the experimenter, in an adjacent area, observes the dog's behavior. The dog's responses are recorded with automatic electronic equipment.

oratory room with the harness on to get used to it. Second, a stimulus tone is sounded. Initially, the tone is a *neutral stimulus*. (It does not elicit salivation.) The dog typically orients itself toward the sound and pays attention but does nothing more. This *orienting reflex*, as Pavlov called it, is a tendency to pay attention to any novel stimulus. If a neutral stimulus, such as a tone, is presented repeatedly without anything else happening, the orienting reflex will gradually disappear—an effect known as **habituation.** Habituation is actually a simple form of learning because it involves a change in behavior. The dog ceases to respond to a repeated stimulus. (In a similar manner, the dog habituates—gets used to—the laboratory setting, the harness, and the tube stuck in its cheek, so that during the conditioning procedure the dog stands quietly.) Finally, some food, usually in the form of meat powder, is delivered automatically to the dish in front of the dog. The dog, if hungry, begins to salivate. These events, which take place prior to conditioning, can be represented by

$$S^{tone} \rightarrow R^{orientation}$$
$$S^{food} \rightarrow R^{salivation}$$

As you can see, the tone elicits an orientation response, but not salivation. The tone stimulus is therefore not connected with, or associated with, the salivation response, whereas the food stimulus is.

Now classical conditioning can begin. The tone is sounded, and a fraction of a second later food is given to the dog. Each pairing of the tone with food is called a *trial*. If the pairing of the tone and the food is repeated from 10 to 20 times, the sound of the tone alone will produce a salivation response. The tone, initially a neutral stimulus, has acquired the ability to elicit salivation.

The **law of classical (respondent) conditioning** states that when two stimuli are paired, and one elicits a reflex response, a new reflex is created in which the previously neutral stimulus comes to elicit the original reflex response. To better understand this law, we need names for the elements involved.

The stimulus that initially brings forth the reflex is called an **unconditioned stimulus (UCS);** it is any stimulus that elicits an unconditioned response. An **unconditioned response (UCR)** is any response elicited by an unconditioned stimulus. (The term *unconditioned* means "not learned.") In Pavlov's experiment, then, food was the UCS and salivation the UCR. After a number of conditioning trials, a neutral stimulus became capable of eliciting salivation. At that point,

the *neutral stimulus* (the tone) had become a **conditioned stimulus (CS),** which is any stimulus that elicits a conditioned response. A **conditioned response (CR)** is any response elicited by a conditioned stimulus. (The term *conditioned* indicates that the association between the stimulus and the response is learned.) Before we continue with conditioning, let's get better acquainted with the man who discovered it.

— PERSONAL PROFILE —

IVAN P. PAVLOV (1849–1936)

Ivan P. Pavlov, a man of contrasts, lived an interesting and fruitful life. Privately, he was impractical, absent-minded, and notoriously careless with money. Despite his near poverty, Pavlov often forgot to pick up his paychecks. Because of this and other financial misadventures, Pavlov's wife rarely let him carry more than pocket change. In the laboratory, Pavlov was strikingly different. There, he was energetic, vigilant, and often tyrannical. He supposedly once fired a worker who arrived late because he had been trying to avoid the street battles of the Russian Revolution.

Pavlov's work won him the Nobel Prize in 1904. His fame for discovering one of the most basic units of learning, the conditioned reflex, is worldwide. His work has even inspired a newspaper cartoon that bears his name. More notably, an estimated 6,000 experiments have been conducted using Pavlov's conditioning procedures. It is no wonder that he is considered one of psychology's greatest pioneers (Fancher, 1979).

Acquisition of Classically Conditioned Responses

Let's examine Pavlov's procedure in detail. The dog learns to associate the conditioned stimulus (tone) with the conditioned response (salivation) during the *acquisition stage* of conditioning. Acquisition can be quantified, or measured, in two simple ways. First, the *amplitude,* or amount, of salivation gradually increases with each learning trial—until a limit is reached. Second, *latency,* or the time elapsed from the onset of the tone to the beginning of salivation, gradually decreases during conditioning, until a limit is reached.

Timing and Conditioning

As we have seen, classical conditioning depends on pairing a CS with a UCS. Until fairly recently, it was thought that *temporal contiguity,* or close timing, of the CS and UCS was the key ingredient for classical conditioning (Hulse, Egeth, & Deese, 1980). Over the years, this idea has been examined in laboratory experiments using relationships between the CS and UCS. To illustrate the five most common arrangements (shown in Figure 6–2), we will use Pavlov's experiment again.

In the *standard pairing procedure,* the CS (tone) begins one-half second before the UCS (food); it is left on until the dog salivates (R). In delayed conditioning, or the *delayed pairing procedure,* the tone is presented for a short time and then is turned off before food is presented. *Simultaneous conditioning,* as the term suggests, involves presenting the tone and the food together. *Backward conditioning* involves presenting the food first, taking it away, and then sounding the tone (Hilgard & Bower, 1975).

Classical conditioning typically occurs most rapidly with the standard pairing procedure. In comparison, simultaneous and backward pairings often fail to produce conditioning. Such findings again suggest that timing is the all-important factor in classical conditioning. However, this conclusion has been challenged by Robert Rescorla (1967), who argues that the presence of a *predictive contingency,* or relationship, between the CS and UCS is more crucial than timing. That is, the CS *predicts* the UCS and therefore imparts information to the learner. In one clever experiment, Rescorla pitted timing against predictability. To prevent the CS from predicting the UCS, even though it preceded it, Rescorla separated the CS and UCS by random time intervals. In this situation, there was no evi-

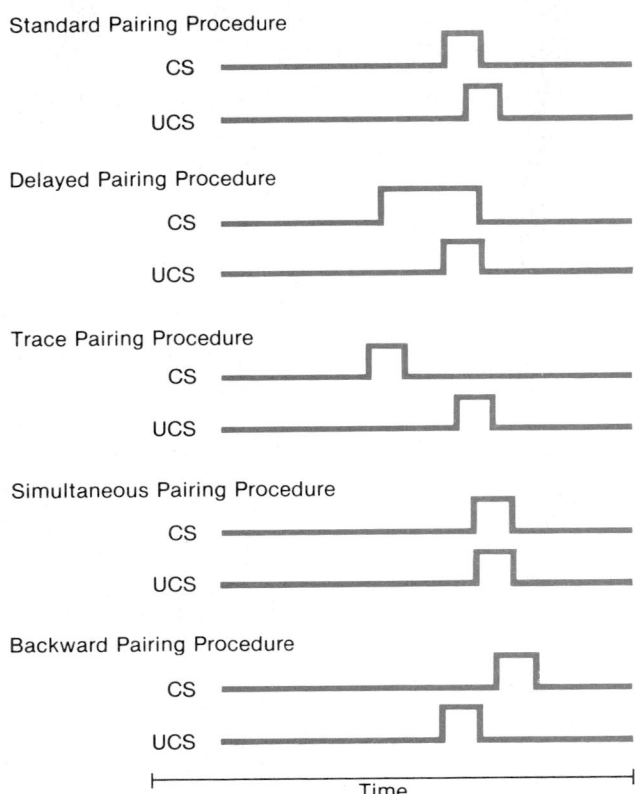

Figure 6–2.
Schematic drawing of some common CS-UCS pairing procedures. The upward inflections of the lines indicate the onset of the CS and UCS; the downward deflections indicate the termination of the CS and UCS.

dence of conditioning—a result that clearly favors the predictive contingency theory. (For a recent review, see Rescorla & Holland, 1982.)

Watson's Interpretation of Learning

America's foremost proponent of classical conditioning early in this century was John B. Watson. Watson attributed *all* learning, both animal and human, to classical conditioning. In one of the most cited experiments in psychology, Watson and Rayner (1920) described how emotional responses such as fear may be conditioned. Their subject was a normal 9-month-old infant named Albert B. In initial testing, Albert was shown a white rat, a dog, a monkey, and other objects. At no time did he display fear of any of the animals or objects. Next, to determine whether fear could be conditioned, a loud sound, made by striking a hammer against a steel bar, was presented to Albert. The laboratory notes are as follows:

> [An experimenter], stationed back of the child, struck the steel bar a sharp blow. The child started violently, his breathing was checked and the arms were raised in a characteristic manner. On the second stimulation the same thing occurred, and in addition the lips began to pucker and tremble. On the third stimulation the child broke into a sudden crying fit. This is the first time an emotional situation in the laboratory has produced any fear or even crying in Albert. (Watson & Rayner, 1920, p. 2)

Watson and Rayner hoped that this experiment would answer several questions. First, could they condition fear of an animal by pairing the animal with a loud, startling noise? Second, if fear developed, would it generalize (transfer) to other animals and objects? Third, if the fear failed to die out (extinguish) in time, what laboratory methods could be devised to remove it?

Although later experiments have been unsuccessful in duplicating this study's results (Harris, 1979; Samelson, 1980), from Watson's perspective the experiment was a smashing success. Presentation of a neutral stimulus (a white rat) just before an unconditioned stimulus (the loud noise) resulted in a conditioned emotional response (fear, as evidenced by crying). On the eighth conditioning trial, at the instant when the white rat was presented alone, Albert cried out, turned sharply, fell over on his left side, and then began to crawl away rapidly. Later, Albert's fear reaction generalized to other objects. More than a month after conditioning, Albert showed signs of fear when he saw a Santa Claus mask, a fur coat, and a rabbit (see Figure 6–3). Unfortunately, Albert left the experiment before having his cpnditioned fear respnses removed (Harris, 1979).

Instrumental (Operant) Conditioning

As we have seen, respondent (reflex) behavior is involuntary, elicited by particular stimuli. The learner is relatively passive because responses occur automatically. Also, respondent conditioning is based on the pairing of two *stimuli,* as in Pavlov's pairing of a tone with a food stimulus.

Instrumental (operant) conditioning differs in several ways from respondent conditioning. *Operant behavior* occurs whenever an organism actively "operates" on its environment; that is, it emits responses to which the environment reacts. In this sense, the response is *instrumental* in bringing about some effect. Thus, learning involving such behavior is called instrumental, or operant, conditioning. According to the **law of instrumental (operant) conditioning,** if an op-

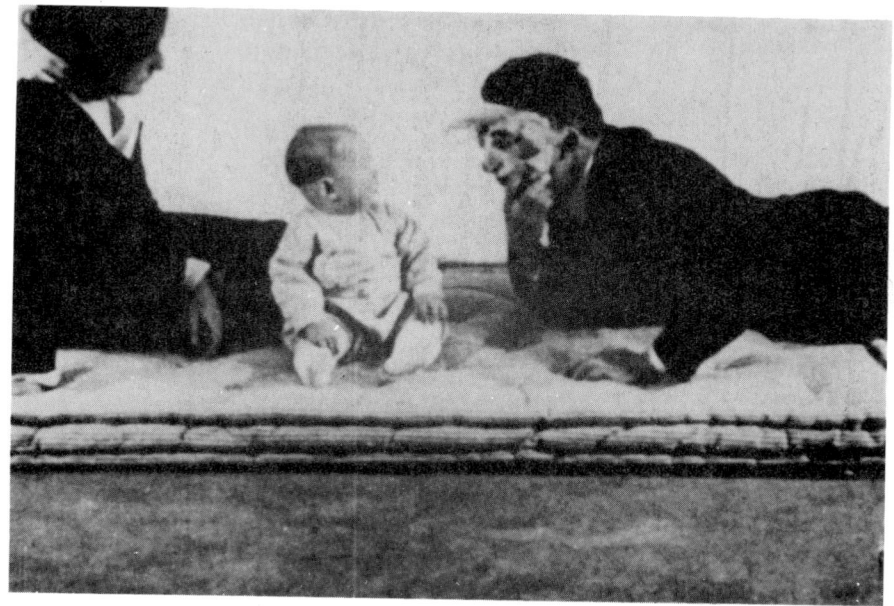

Figure 6–3.
Watson, Rayner, and Albert B.

erant response (R) is followed by a reinforcing stimulus (S^R) (sometimes also called a reinforcer or a reward), then the probability of the response occurring again is increased. The basic elements of instrumental (operant) learning can be represented as

$$R \rightarrow S^R$$

This diagram shows that what is learned in instrumental (operant) conditioning is an association between a response and a stimulus *consequence*. When such events or consequences strengthen responses that precede them, **reinforcement** has occurred. Also important is the stimulus present before a reinforced response is made. This stimulus is called the **discriminative stimulus (S^D).** Operant conditioning is thus more fully represented as

$$S^D \rightarrow R \rightarrow S^R$$

The discriminative stimulus (S^D) sets the occasion for reinforcement; it provides a *cue,* or *signal,* which indicates that if the response (R) is made, it is likely to be followed by a particular reinforcing stimulus (S^R). Similarly, the organism learns that if the response is made in the absence of the S^D, then reinforcement is unlikely to follow. The reinforcement is thus said to be *contingent* (or dependent) on the response being made under particular stimulus conditions. This means that behavior can be controlled by arrangements of the contingencies between operant responses and their consequences. Thus, the idea that *behavior is a function of its consequences* lies at the core of instrumental (operant) conditioning. This fact can be seen clearly in the work of pioneer researcher E. L. Thorndike.

— Thorndike's Contribution to the Psychology of Learning

E. L. Thorndike was one of the first American psychologists to study instrumental learning. He observed that a hungry cat confined in a "puzzle box" (see Figure 6–4) would meow, howl, and scratch in an attempt to reach a tempting morsel of fish placed just outside the door of the box. To be released, the cat had to unlatch the door with its paw. Given enough time, the cat would learn to make this response because it was instrumental in producing food. The cat would do so, according to Thorndike, by trial and error with accidental success.

Thorndike's (1911) puzzle-box experiments offered a model of learning that differed markedly from Pav-

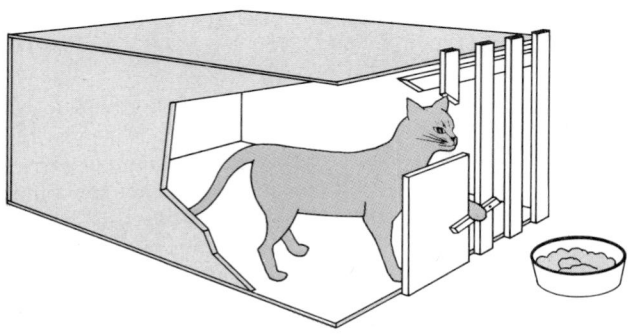

Figure 6–4.
A puzzle box used by Thorndike to study animal learning.

lov's. Thorndike found that after a few successful instrumental conditioning trials, the cat spent less energy meowing and scratching the cage. Eventually, the cat learned to immediately unlatch the door, thereby gaining access to the food.

Thorndike's careful observations led him to conclude that animals solve problems not by reasoning or by instinct but rather by the gradual "stamping-in" of an association between the stimulus (door latch) and response (pawing the latch). His *law of effect* stated that the gradual stamping-in of a stimulus-response connection depended on the effects that followed a response.

— Skinner's Contribution to the Psychology of Learning

In the 1930s, B. F. Skinner revolutionized the study of learning by redesigning and simplifying Thorndike's puzzle box into what is now commonly referred to as the Skinner box. The typical apparatus (shown in Figure 6–5) includes a device, such as a bar or lever, for pressing. Bar pressing, then, is an operant response the subject is required to make to obtain a reinforcing stimulus (S^R), such as a food pellet (delivered by a special mechanism). Modern Skinner boxes can be programmed so experimenters can be away from their subjects for hours at a time. This also frees the subjects to respond at any time. Whereas instrumental conditioning is a *discrete-trial procedure* (e.g., the cat must be put back into the puzzle box after each escape), operant conditioning is characterized by a *free-responding procedure*—the organism being allowed to respond at its own rate.

B. F. Skinner (1904–   )

B. F. Skinner is among the most famous and controversial of contemporary psychologists. He received a PhD in psychology from Harvard University in 1931 and 7 years later published his first and perhaps most important book, *The Behavior of Organisms* (Skinner, 1938). In 1948, after having spent a few years working at the University of Minnesota and Indiana University, Skinner returned to Harvard and remained there.

While his research with animals continued, Skinner grew interested in applying operant conditioning to practical problems. For example, during World War II, he helped demonstrate that pigeons could guide missiles by pecking on a screen inside them. Although a 1944 demonstration of the system went flawlessly, the project was abandoned by the Air Force. Another of Skinner's controversial projects was called the baby-tender. This crib-sized chamber had sound-absorbing walls, so the baby would not be disturbed and a large picture window. When Skinner's daughter Deborah came home shortly after birth,

> she went directly into this comfortable space and began to enjoy its advantages. She wore only a diaper. Completely free to move about, she was soon pushing up, rolling over, and crawling. She breathed warm, moist, filtered air, and her skin was never waterlogged with sweat or urine. . . . When she was still quite young, she could grasp and pull a ring hanging from the ceiling of the baby-tender to sound a whistle, and grasp and turn a T-bar to spin a pinwheel of brightly colored pennants. (Skinner, 1979, p. 30)

As people began to hear about the baby-tender by word of mouth, many supposed that Skinner and his wife, Eve, were experimenting with Deborah as if she were a rat or pigeon. In a letter to one of his critics, Skinner replied:

> I hope to be able to put a number of these apparatuses in homes under normal conditions and compare the development of the babies with others raised in traditional fashion. . . . If, as many people have claimed, the first year is extraordinarily important in the determination of character and personality, then by all means let us control the conditions of this year as far as possible in order to discover the important variables. (Skinner, 1979, p. 31)

The reaction to Skinner' baby-tender was mild in comparison to criticism of his utopian novel, *Walden Two* (Skinner, 1948b). *Walden Two* describes a society in which children are conditioned from birth to be cooperative, intelligent, and happy. In another controversial best seller, *Beyond Freedom and Dignity,* Skinner (1971) argued again that an ideal society can be achieved only through behavioral engineering. At the 90th annual convention of the American Psychological Association, Skinner (1982) reiterated his conviction that society can be deliberately designed for the welfare of its inhabitants.

Skinner's fame is indicated by his inclusion in the 1970 edition of *The 100 Most Important People in the World* and by a 1975 survey that showed him to be the best-known scientist in America. Skinner's impact on psychology has been profound. Potentially more important will be his effect on society in general.

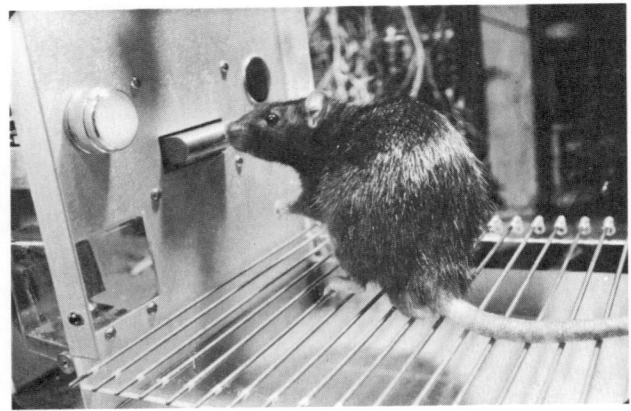

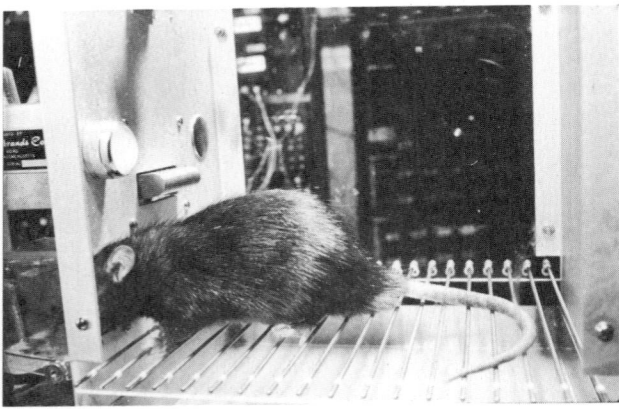

Figure 6–5.
A conditioned rat in a Skinner box pressing a lever to obtain food.

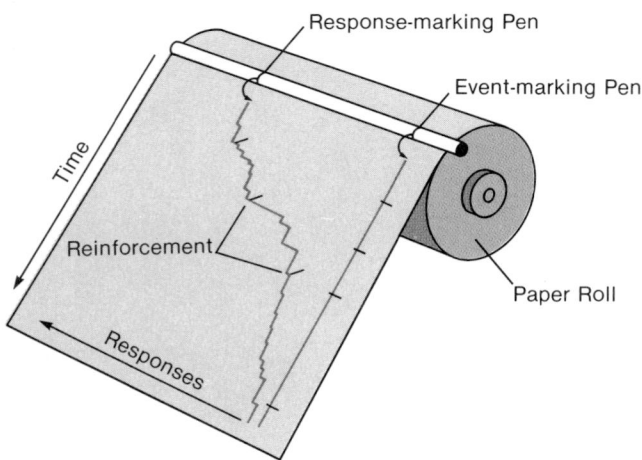

Figure 6–6.
Cumulative recorder. For each response by the animal, the pen steps up a fixed amount. When no responses are being made, the pen moves in a straight line across the paper. Since the paper is moving at a fixed rate, the slope of the cumulative curve indicates the rate of responding.

dure produces a cumulative record of the organism's responses (Skinner, 1972).

Figure 6–7 illustrates operant conditioning through three different phases: operant level, conditioning, and

Figure 6–7.
A cumulative record showing the operant level, conditioning, and extinction of an individual rat's barpressing response. The rate of responding prior to conditioning is low; it increases dramatically during conditioning and decreases during extinction to the initial operant level of responding.

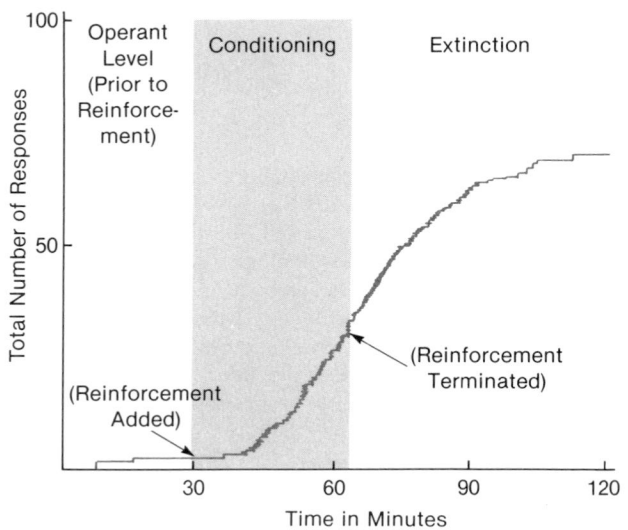

— Acquisition of Operantly Conditioned Responses

Let's examine in some detail the fundamentals of the procedure used by Skinner. In operant conditioning, behavior is most often measured in terms of rate of responding. Consider a Skinner box with the bar always available. One rat presses the bar 120 times during a period of 60 seconds; another rat presses it only 60 times. The first rat is responding at a higher rate. **Rate of responding** is found by dividing the number of responses by a constant unit of time. Let's use 60 seconds as a unit of time. The first rat in the example has a rate of 2 and the second a rate of 1. Rate of responding can be shown graphically by equipment that records the barpresses on a moving sheet of paper (Figure 6–6). With each barpress, the pen moves upward, raising the line a notch. This recording proce-

extinction. Before conditioning, when a hungry rat is placed in a Skinner box for the first time, it rarely presses the bar. *Operant level* is the rate of responding prior to any known conditioning and prior to receiving food (see Figure 6–7). When food does reinforce bar pressing, the rate of responding increases. This phase is called *operant conditioning*. The process by which learned behaviors may be eliminated is the topic of the following application.

EXTINCTION OF CONDITIONED RESPONSES

Respondent and operant conditioning produce relatively permanent changes in behavior. Nevertheless, conditioned responses may be weakened, or eliminated altogether, by a process known as **extinction.** How does this process work? When an operant response is no longer reinforced, the rate of responding gradually decreases. As shown in Figure 6–7, if food reinforcement is withdrawn, the high rate of responding achieved during operant conditioning will return to its initial low level. To put it in human terms, during extinction the rat learns that pressing the bar is a waste of energy. Children learn in the same way. If crying in a grocery store results in increased parental attention, a child is likely to cry more often (assuming that attention is reinforcing). To eliminate such crying, parents may decide to ignore the child's cries. Eventually, this may decrease the crying. But conditioned responses do not always extinguish easily or quickly. After reinforcement is withdrawn, the response may at first be emitted more forcefully than before. For instance, when food pellets are no longer made available for bar pressing, rats tend to exaggerate the response by pressing the bar more frequently and with greater strength than before. Similarly, a child whose crying is not reinforced will likely cry louder and longer and perhaps throw a tantrum or two before the response disappears completely.

Classically conditioned responses may be extinguished also. As you might guess, extinction in this case takes place when the conditioned stimulus occurs repeatedly without the unconditioned stimulus. Pavlov discovered that a conditioned response persists only if the CS and UCS are paired at least occasionally. As Pavlov also noticed, the effects of extinction may be temporary. A dog whose salivation response to a tone has been extinguished will once again salivate when the tone is sounded later. Pavlov aptly described this phenomenon as **spontaneous recovery**—the spontaneous, although brief, recurrence of a response following extinction. You have probably experienced the extinction of classically conditioned responses yourself. For example, as a child, you may have had a fear of dark rooms that you no longer experience today. Over the years, the classically conditioned fear was extinguished. Why? Because the conditioned stimulus (dark room) occurred repeatedly without being paired with unconditioned (frightening) stimuli. Of course, it takes only an occasional pairing of conditioned and unconditioned stimuli to maintain a response. Seeing a frightening movie, for instance, can reactivate the fear response, but it usually disappears again with time.

As the experiment with Albert B. suggests, fear responses can be learned through classical (respondent) conditioning. Such responses are common among children. Although most childhood fears are considered normal and gradually decline, others may become excessive and disruptive. Such exaggerated fears, especially when they are directed to one situation or object, are called *phobias* (see chapter 15). Fears of dogs, heights, elevators, snakes, and public speaking are common phobias. The most frequent childhood phobia is *school phobia,* marked by strong fears about attending school. The phobia may be acquired when a previously neutral stimulus, such as the school building or classroom, acquires fear-arousing properties by being paired with an unconditioned stimulus, such as being physically abused by other students, being criticized in front of the class by the teacher, or receiving failing grades.

How can phobias be reduced? One technique, *systematic desensitization,* has successfully lessened fears by teaching patients responses that are incompatible with fear (Ross, 1980). In the case of a school phobia, attending school would be paired repeatedly with a relaxation response (see chapter 5) to *countercondition* the fear. For example, the child would learn to relax while imagining feared situations, such as standing at the bus stop, riding the bus to school, approaching the school building, and entering the classroom. (The child must confront situations that are increasingly fear arousing.) If, after several sessions, the child is able to remain relaxed while imagining the feared situations, the psychologist and the child might actually carry out the actions described. The child's relaxation is incompatible with the fear of attending school and gradually replaces it. Using systematic desensitization techniques, Kennedy (1965) successfully treated 50 students who had school phobias.

Conditioning principles have also been used to treat a variety of other disorders, which will be discussed in chapter 16. For an immediate appreciation of the possibilities, let's consider a final example here. Bed-wetting, or *enuresis,* is a common problem among children. It has long been recognized that this disorder results from a failure of cues from the bladder (unconditioned stimulus) to elicit the appropriate unconditioned response of waking and then urinating. Mowrer and Mowrer (1938) developed an ingenious device to condition a waking response prior to urination. An alarm, activated by a liquid-sensitive bed pad, serves as an unconditioned stimulus to wake the child who is urinating. Cues from a full bladder (initially neutral stimuli), which precede the alarm, eventually elicit waking before urination. The treatment of enuresis by the application of the principles of classical conditioning may involve operant conditioning principles as well. For instance, the child may be reinforced for dry nights. Together these techniques provide an effective means for control of urination, and the resulting behavior change permits a dry night's sleep.

— PRINCIPLES OF LEARNING AND THE INTERACTION OF CLASSICAL AND INSTRUMENTAL CONDITIONING —

The two types of learning discussed so far, classical and instrumental conditioning, were once regarded as entirely separate learning processes. Classical (respondent) conditioning was viewed as a change in the capacity of a stimulus to elicit a response, whereas instrumental (operant) conditioning was viewed as a change in the rate of a response because of its consequences. Accordingly, classical conditioning was regarded as being limited to reflex responses controlled by the autonomic nervous system—heart rate, blood pressure, vasodilation and vasoconstriction, intestinal contractions, salivation, and so on. That is, in classical (respondent) conditioning, the organism responds to a stimulus. In contrast, instrumental conditioning was regarded as being limited to skeletal muscles under voluntary control—finger, hand, leg, mouth, tongue, and so on. In instrumental (operant) conditioning, the organism operates on the environment. A comparison of classical and instrumental conditioning from this point of view is shown in Table 6–2.

More recent developments in the study of learning have led theorists to conclude that respondent and operant conditioning frequently occur together in producing complex behavior. Consider, for example, a child who is bitten by a large dog. From a classical conditioning perspective, the unconditioned stimulus of pain from the bite elicits an unconditioned emotional response, fear. In the future, the sight of the dog becomes a conditioned stimulus for fear. If the child runs home, thus escaping from the fear-producing sight of the dog, this operant running response will be *reinforced by fear reduction.* Thus, to understand the child's running at the sight of a dog, both types of learning must be considered.

Operant Conditioning of Respondent Behavior

Of the various lines of evidence that support the view that both respondent and operant conditioning are involved in complex learning, one of the most interesting is the operant conditioning of involuntary respon-

Table 6–2.

Comparison of classical (respondent) conditioning and operant (instrumental) conditioning.

	CLASSICAL (RESPONDENT) CONDITIONING	INSTRUMENTAL (OPERANT) CONDITIONING
Behavior	Involuntary, reflex behavior	Voluntary behavior
Response	Response elicited	Response emitted
Conditioning procedure	Pairing two stimuli (CS and UCS)	Pairing stimulus and response
Paradigm	CS $\longrightarrow$ CR UCS $\longrightarrow$ UCR	$R \rightarrow S^R$

dent behavior. The first studies on this topic were initiated by Neal Miller and his associates. For example, Miller and DiCara (1967) showed that it was possible, by using rewards, to condition heart-rate changes in rats. Such results imply that operant conditioning of autonomic responses is theoretically possible. Thus, just as an organism can be trained to change its rate of bar pressing, it can be trained to modify its autonomic reactions.

Results from such research make it clear that respondent and operant conditioning can no longer be regarded as entirely separate. More importantly, this research has potential clinical application. Evidence has been accumulating that some people may be able to learn to control their own internal involuntary behavior through the technique popularly known as *biofeedback* (Miller, 1978). By receiving feedback concerning biological functions, some subjects have learned to alter their brain waves and lower their heart rate and blood pressure. Such results would seem to offer hope for treating and possibly preventing hypertension, headaches, and other reactions to stress (Wallis, 1983). In chapter 14 we will describe how biofeedback has been used to treat some patients with stress-related disorders. There is, however, an ongoing debate over the clinical value of biofeedback. As noted by Simkins (1982):

It is . . . quite conceivable that we are expecting too much from biofeedback. As an example, although biofeedback may have some limited value in the control of hypertension, it is doubtful that clinically significant reductions in

blood pressure will be accomplished without the patient beginning an exercise program, changing diet, and reducing weight, and/or reducing smoking. This would entail that many patients embrace a major change in their lifestyle. A few biofeedback training sessions per week are not going to solve their problem. (p. 15)

Despite the controversy over the utility of biofeedback, the results from basic research on operant conditioning of respondent behavior continue to provide evidence for an interaction between respondent and operant conditioning. With this possibility introduced, let's now consider in greater detail some of the important principles of learning involved in both classically and instrumentally conditioned responses.

Principle of Reinforcement

Recall that operant level is the rate of responding prior to conditioning. Technically speaking, a *reinforcer* is any stimulus that increases or maintains the rate of responding above operant level. There are two basic types of reinforcers or reinforcing stimuli: **unconditioned (primary) reinforcing stimuli (S^R)** have the ability to reinforce without prior learning, whereas **conditioned (secondary) reinforcing stimuli (S^r)** are learned and reinforce because of their prior association with a primary reinforcing stimulus. Examples of unconditioned reinforcers are food, water, and sleep. Through experience, almost any stimulus can become a conditioned reinforcer: "The voice of a dog's master, ineffectual at first, comes to reinforce the dog's behavior. Stock market quotations, at first dull lists of numbers, come to reinforce an investor's behavior" (Reynolds, 1975, p. 57). Praise and money for doing a task well are additional examples of conditioned reinforcing stimuli. Money is a conditioned reinforcer because it makes it possible to obtain certain unconditioned reinforcers, such as food (see Figure 6–8).

Unconditioned and conditioned reinforcers can be positive or negative. **Positive reinforcers (S^{R+}, S^{r+})** are stimuli whose *presentation* is reinforcing. **Negative reinforcers (S^{R-}, S^{r-})** are stimuli whose *withdrawal,* or removal, is reinforcing. Regardless of whether reinforcers are positive or negative, their effect is the same: to increase the probability of a response. Some examples of unconditioned, conditioned, positive, and negative reinforcers are given in Table 6–3. Let's examine these examples closely. A hungry baby cries and is fed. The probability of the baby's crying when hungry increases because crying results in a predictable consequence—receiving food, which is an *unconditioned positive reinforcing stimulus.* A rat presses a bar and terminates a mild electric shock. Bar pressing is reinforced because it results in shock termination, which is an *unconditioned negative reinforcing stimulus.* A college student works part-time and obtains money to buy food, clothing, and shelter. Working results in a predictable consequence—earning money, which is a *conditioned positive reinforcing stimulus.* A rat presses a bar and turns off a buzzer previously paired with shock. Bar pressing results in a predictable consequence—termination of a buzzer, which is a *conditioned negative reinforcing stimulus* because it was paired with shock. As these examples suggest, there are many ways in which operantly conditioned responses are learned.

Sometimes responses increase in probability not because they cause a reinforcing consequence but because they accidentally precede reinforcement. Behavior that is learned and maintained in this manner is called **superstitious behavior.** For example, a student may insist on sitting at a particular desk, writing with a favorite pen, and wearing certain clothes while taking an examination. Why does the student do so? Probably because each of these superstitious behaviors, when emitted in the past, was accidentally linked to a favorable outcome—a high score on an examination.

Would you believe that pigeons, too, are capable of superstitious behavior? Skinner (1948a) demonstrated such behavior in pigeons by giving them food on a regular schedule, regardless of what they were doing when the food was delivered. Before long, each pigeon developed its own superstitious behavior. Just before food was to be delivered, one pigeon turned in circles, another hopped, a third bobbed its head, and so on. The pigeons, not unlike the student in our example, behaved as if they thought their responses caused the reinforcing consequences.

Reinforcement Schedules

What determines the rate of responding? One important variable is the schedule of reinforcement. A *schedule of reinforcement* is a pattern of reinforcements and

Figure 6–8.
Chimp-O-Mat, from which chimpanzees learn to use "money."

Table 6–3.

Examples of conditioned and unconditioned positive and negative reinforces. The effect on response probability is always to increase it.

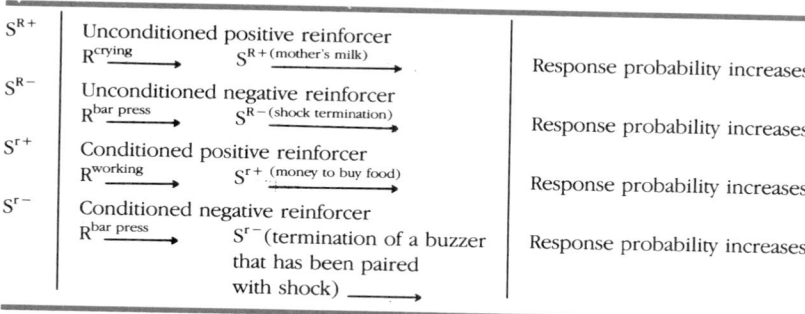

S^{R+}	Unconditioned positive reinforcer $R^{crying} \longrightarrow S^{R+\,(mother's\,milk)} \longrightarrow$	Response probability increases
S^{R-}	Unconditioned negative reinforcer $R^{bar\,press} \longrightarrow S^{R-\,(shock\,termination)}$	Response probability increases
S^{r+}	Conditioned positive reinforcer $R^{working} \longrightarrow S^{r+\,(money\,to\,buy\,food)}$	Response probability increases
S^{r-}	Conditioned negative reinforcer $R^{bar\,press} \longrightarrow S^{r-}$ (termination of a buzzer that has been paired with shock)	Response probability increases

nonreinforcements. A **continuous reinforcement schedule,** for instance, reinforces each response emitted. In **continuous nonreinforcement schedules,** on the other hand, responses receive no reinforcement. In everyday life, reinforcement and nonreinforcement are much more likely to be intermittent than continuous. Much of the research on the effects of intermittent **partial reinforcement schedules** has used pigeons as subjects because they can maintain a high rate of key pecking in a Skinner box (see Figure 6–9). On the basis of such research, Skinner distinguished two main classes of intermittent reinforce-

Figure 6–9.

An operant conditioning situation used to investigate the effects of different schedules of partial reinforcement on behavior.

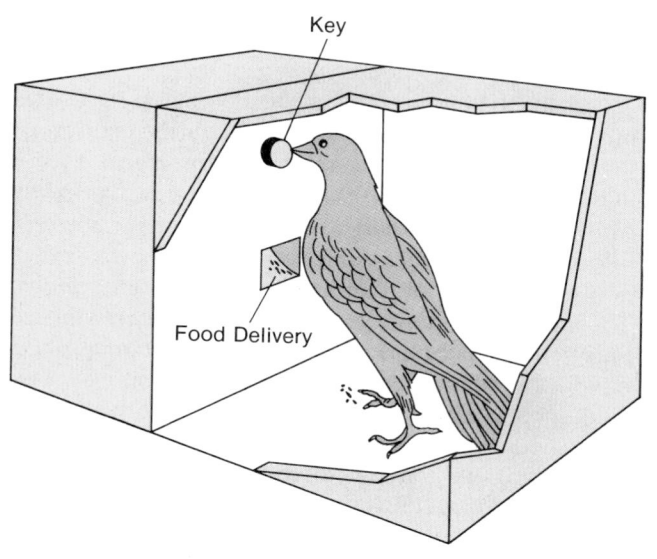

Key

Food Delivery

ment: interval schedules and ratio schedules (see, for example, Ferster & Skinner, 1957).

In a **fixed-interval (FI) schedule,** reinforcement is given after fixed time periods. For example, in an FI 5-minute schedule, the first response that occurs after a lapse of 5 minutes is reinforced. Thereafter, the subject is reinforced for the first response it makes after each 5-minute interval. Figure 6–10a shows the typical cumulative record of a pigeon operating on a fixed-interval schedule of reinforcement.

An organism will adjust to a fixed-interval schedule of reinforcement by responding slowly after a reinforcer is given and at a higher rate just before the next reinforcer is due. If the interval is short, the rate will be higher and more even. This is true not only of responses emitted by rats and pigeons but also of those emitted by children and adults. The study behavior of college students is maintained by grade cards given out twice per year, at the end of each academic semester. A salaried worker's behavior is maintained by paychecks given at regular intervals. Practically speaking, a child who is just beginning piano lessons should be reinforced with praise at short intervals throughout each session rather than at the close of a practice session. When reinforcement comes at short intervals, it tends to sustain more persistent effort.

In a **variable-interval (VI) schedule,** the subject is reinforced after time periods that vary in length. In a VI 5-minute schedule, for example, a response is reinforced once every 5 minutes on the average. That is, the interval between reinforcements may be as long as 10 minutes or as short as a few seconds, but it averages 5 minutes. Not knowing exactly when reinforcement will be presented, the organism is less likely to slow down after each reinforcer (Figure 6–10b).

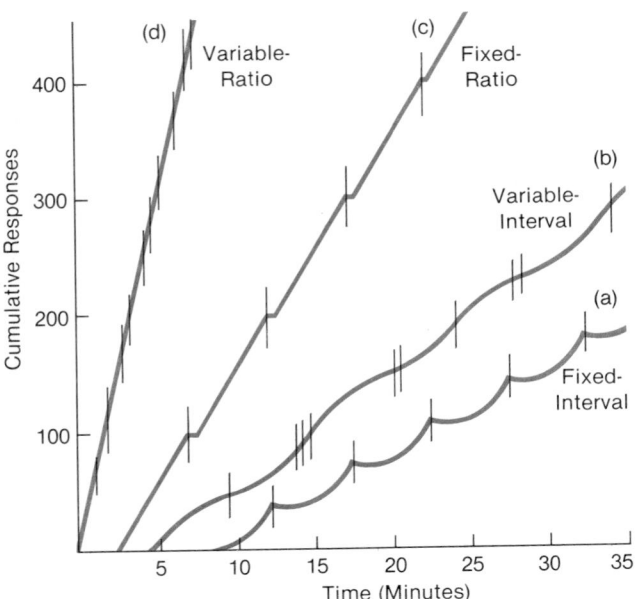

Figure 6–10.

The precise effect of intermittent or partial reinforcement depends on the nature of the particular schedule. There are four basic schedules of partial reinforcement: (a) fixed-interval (FI), (b) variable-interval (VI), (c) fixed-ratio (FR), and (d) variable-ratio (VR). Cumulative response curves for each of these schedules are shown here. The vertical lines marked "R" mean "reinforcement."

College students should perhaps be reinforced on a variable-interval schedule rather than on a fixed-interval schedule. Reinforcement at fixed intervals (e.g., a test every 6 weeks) produces a high rate of study behavior before each test and a low rate following each test. You may have found that your study behavior evens out when your professor gives you pop quizzes on a variable-interval schedule.

An entirely different way to schedule partial reinforcement is to use a *ratio schedule,* in which reinforcers are given after the organism has made a certain number of responses. The subject may, for example, receive reinforcement after every 5 responses (a 5:1 ratio) or after every 100 responses (a 100:1 ratio). Because the subject must make a certain number of responses before receiving a reinforcer, ratio schedules encourage high rates of responding.

Something like a **fixed-ratio (FR) schedule** (Figure 6–10c) was once used with piecework in the garment industry. A shirtmaker was paid, say, according to the number of buttons sewed on. The more buttons sewed on, the more money received. This practice resulted in increased productivity, but it also increased payroll expenses. To limit costs, some employers shifted the ratio upward and demanded more work for the same pay. Employees were under constant pressure to produce in order to maintain the same income. This was one of several problems that led to the formation of labor unions in the United States.

In a **variable-ratio (VR) schedule,** the ratio of responses to reinforcers varies. In a VR 48:1 schedule, for example, the number of nonreinforced responses may vary from 0 to 200. On the average, however, every 48th response will be reinforced. Not knowing how many responses are required for reinforcement, the organism produces constant, high rates of sustained responding (Figure 6–10d). Pigeons have been trained on VR schedules to peck for several hours at a rate of 5 times per second (Kendler, 1974).

Many human behaviors are maintained by ratio schedules. In slot-machine gambling, for instance, reinforcement occurs intermittently and unpredictably (Figure 6–11). The gambler who makes a large number of responses, however, is assured of an occasional win. The chronic gambler is not unlike the pigeon in a Skinner box. Both emit high rates of responding as a function of particular intermittent reinforcement. This may be why, for some people, gambling becomes the type of addictive, maladaptive behavior described in the chapter introduction. Intermittent reinforcement, of course, also sustains constructive behavior. Students who labor through 4 years of college course work and writers and others who strive to do their best maintain their behavior on intermittent reinforcement schedules. Delayed gratification is necessary in many professions.

Perhaps the most dramatic effect of partial reinforcement can be seen after conditioning, during extinction. Behaviors maintained on partial reinforcement schedules show much greater persistence, or *resistance to extinction,* than do those maintained by continuous reinforcement (Nation & Woods, 1980). This phenomenon is known as the **partial reinforcement effect.** To put it another way, a response reinforced every time (continuous reinforcement) can be extinguished rapidly by withholding the reinforcer. For example, putting coins into a food vending machine will be extinguished immediately if the food (reinforcer) is not forthcoming. In contrast, intermittently reinforced responses extinguish less rapidly.

Figure 6–11.
The slot machine (one-armed bandit) is a dispenser of partial reinforcement.

Stimulus Control of Behavior

The principles discussed so far illustrate how behavior can be controlled by its consequences. At the same time, behavior is controlled by stimuli present at the time of reinforcement. As mentioned earlier, in operant conditioning, the stimulus present during reinforcement is known as the S^D (discriminative stimulus). The stimulus present at times of nonreinforcement is labeled S^Δ, (Δ is the Greek letter for *delta*). An S^D sets the occasion for reinforced responding, whereas an S^Δ sets the occasion for nonreinforced responding. Discriminative cues exert powerful control over behavior. Say, for example, that a child often cries at the grocery store in the presence of his mother, because she reinforces the crying with attention or candy. In contrast, the child rarely cries while at the store with his father, because the father does not reinforce crying. Here, the mother is an S^D for crying and the father is an S^Δ. When responses are controlled by such environmental cues, behavior is said to be under stimulus control.

— Stimulus Generalization

Whenever a new behavior is acquired through conditioning, there will inevitably be some *generalization*. Infants beginning to talk receive ecstatic approval when they respond to the sight of their mother with "ma-ma." But imagine the embarrassment when a 15-month-old child calls every passing woman "ma-ma." **Stimulus generalization,** which may occur in both respondent and operant conditioning, is the tendency for stimuli other than the one originally conditioned to evoke the conditioned response. Numerous laboratory experiments demonstrate this effect (c.f., Bower & Hilgard, 1980). For example, in operant conditioning experiments, pigeons have been trained to peck at a key illuminated with a green light. Later, the key is lighted with different colors. The pigeons still peck, but at a decreasing rate as the color of each test stimulus grows more different from that used during conditioning. The symmetrically shaped curve shown in Figure 6–12 is called a *generalization gradient*. It can be observed in similar testing of many different responses and organisms.

— Stimulus Discrimination

Learning often requires **stimulus discrimination**—that is, the ability to make distinctions among stimuli and to respond in a particular way to a specific stimulus. As a result of studying for many hours, for example, students learn to discriminate among stimulus alternatives on multiple-choice examinations. Some of

Pavlov's most interesting research involved investigating the ability of dogs to discriminate between stimuli. In one particularly illustrative experiment, a dog was conditioned to salivate to the presentation of a circle but not to the presentation of an ellipse (Figure 6–13). As the ellipse was gradually changed to look more like the circle, the dog's ability to discriminate broke down, and the dog became agitated and aggressive. Similar behaviors can be observed in humans who are required to perform beyond the limit of their discriminative capacity.

In operant conditioning, a discrimination can be established by **differential reinforcement**—that is, by reinforcing some responses but not others. For example, if we want to know whether a pigeon can tell the difference between red and orange, we can arrange for the pecking key in a Skinner box to be red for some time periods and orange for others. Reinforcement will occur only if the red key is pecked. Typically, the cumulative record will show that the pigeon responds at a higher rate to the red key than to the orange key. If the two keys differ only in hue, not in brightness or shape, we can conclude that the pigeon is capable of discriminating between red and orange. This method has shown that pigeons can tell the difference between red and orange but that dogs cannot.

— Shaping Complex Chains of Behavior

The foregoing discussion leads us to shaping—another psychological technique for changing behavior. In **shaping,** a desired behavior is achieved by reinforcing small steps, or successive approximations, to the final behavior rather than directly reinforcing the desired response itself. By careful reinforcement of correct responses and no reinforcement of incorrect ones, behavior can be shaped, or molded.

Shaping techniques have been used to teach animals unusual tricks that consist of complex chains of behav-

Figure 6–12.
Gradient of generalization for a group of pigeons trained to peck at a button illuminated with a green light and then presented with test buttons of several other colors. The closer the test stimulus is to the training stimulus, the greater the frequency of responding.

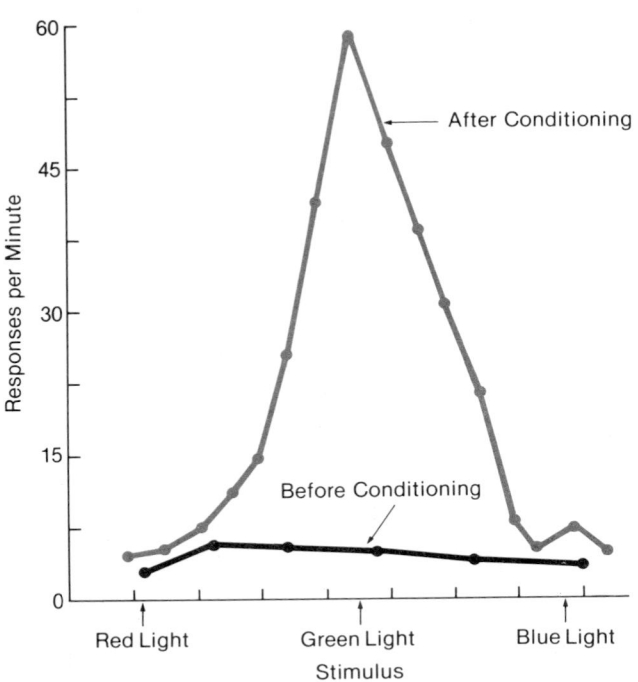

Figure 6–13.
Pairs of stimuli used in Pavlov's laboratory to produce experimental neurosis in dogs.

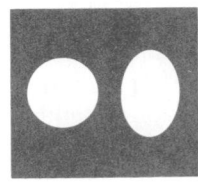 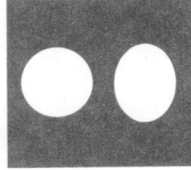 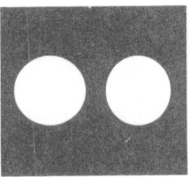

ior. A **chain of behavior** is a series of responses in which each response produces a reinforcer, which then serves as the cue (or discriminative stimulus) for the next response in the chain. The photographs in Figure 6–14 illustrate a complex chain of responses acquired by Barnabus, a male rat. When a light flashes at the lower left of the cage, Barnabus scampers up a pathway to a landing (1), where he crosses a moat (2) to the bottom of a ladder. He climbs the ladder (3) to a second platform. There, with his teeth and paws, he hauls in a chain attached to a small red car. He then climbs in the car and pedals away (4). When the car reaches a stairway, Barnabus gets out, runs upstairs (5) to reach a third platform, and squeezes through a glass tube (6). He then enters an elevator. As it descends, he yanks a chain that raises the flag of his university (7). When he reaches the bottom of the cage, he presses a bar. A buzzer sounds, and Barnabus is free to eat all the food he can (8) during a 1-minute period (Kendler, 1974).

If you would like to train a pet dog using procedures like those used to train Barnabus, the first step

Figure 6–14. (continued on the next page.)
Demonstration of shaping. Barnabus, the rat in these photographs, is able to execute this complex chain of responses in under 2 minutes.

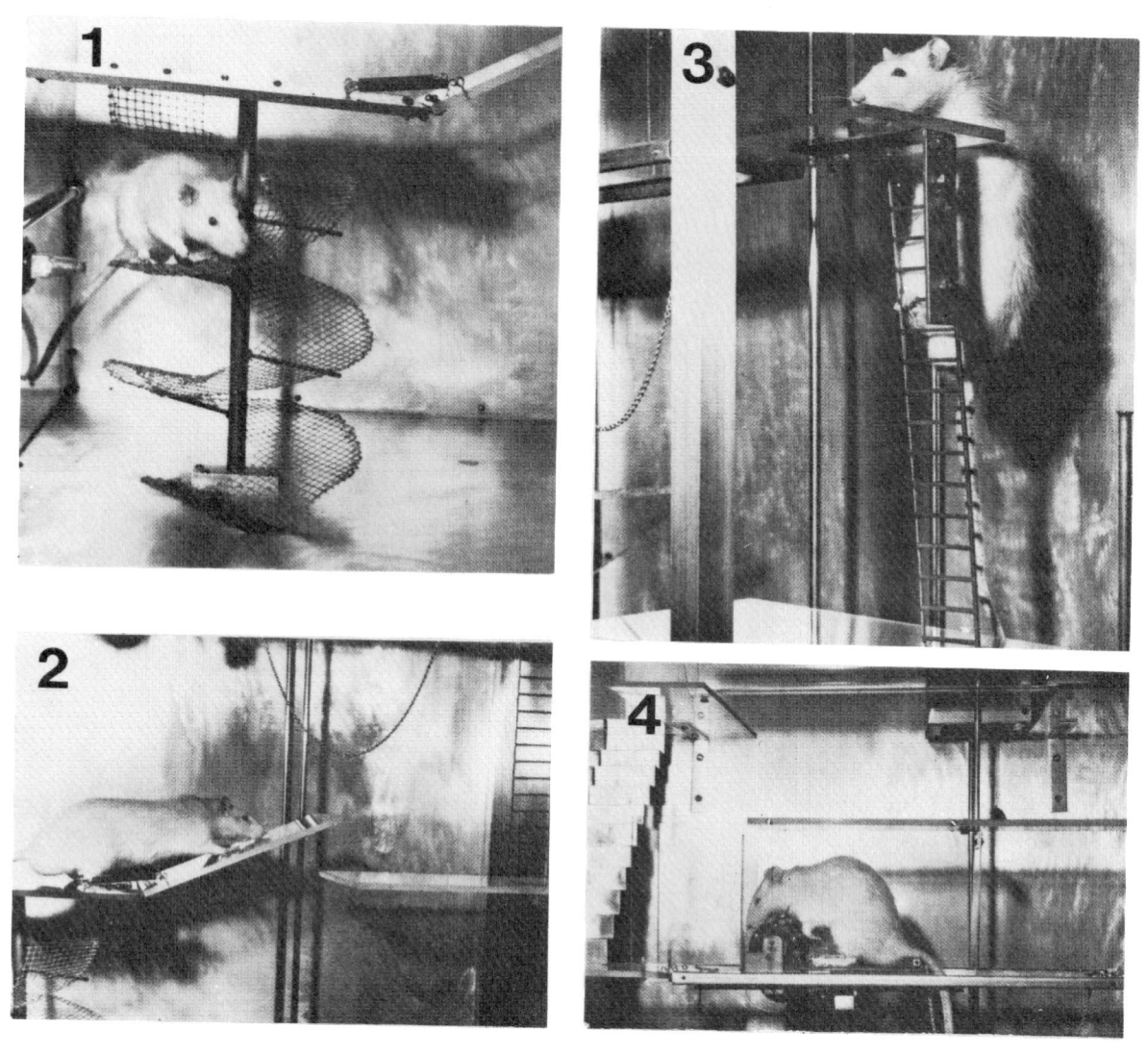

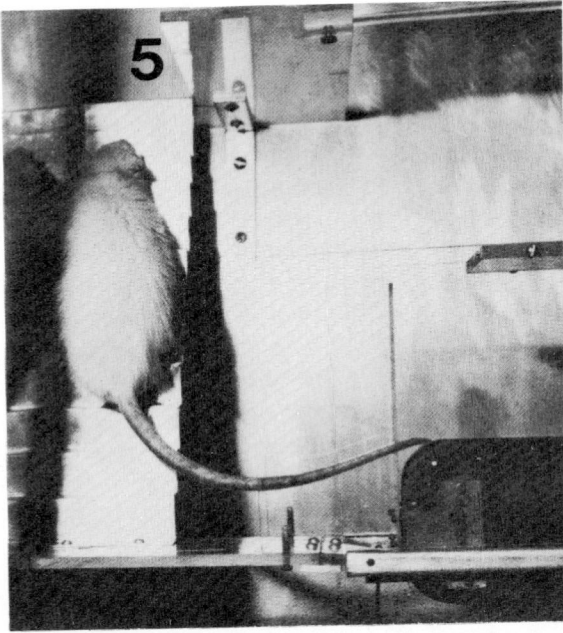

is to purchase a whistle. Preliminary conditioning requires that the whistle be sounded only at meals, just prior to feeding. At first, food should be offered with each whistle (continuous reinforcement). Then a partial reinforcement schedule should be introduced. After such training, the whistle will serve as a conditioned (secondary) reinforcer that can be used to shape the dog's behavior. Thus, if you want the dog to heel (walk at your side), you provide reinforcement by sounding the whistle each time the dog approaches or follows you. By reinforcing correct responses and not reinforcing incorrect ones (differential reinforcement), you will condition the dog to heel. This procedure

may be hastened by putting the dog on a leash, so that heeling is forced to occur early in training.

Shaping also works with humans. Kazdin (1975) cites a case history reported by Isaacs, Thomas, and Goldiamond (1960) to illustrate this point.

A schizophrenic who had been mute for 19 years joined a group therapy session but remained silent, impassive, and withdrawn. At one session, a therapist accidentally dropped a package of chewing gum and noticed that the patient's eyes followed the gum. The therapist decided to use successive approximations to increase the patient's verbal behavior. During the first 2 weeks of private sessions, the therapist held up a stick of gum and waited for the patient to move his eyes toward it. If he did, he received the gum. During the 3rd and 4th weeks, the patient was required to move his eyes, move his lips, and, eventually, make a sound before receiving the gum. In the 5th and 6th weeks, the therapist made receiving the gum contingent on vocalizations progressively approximating "gum." At the end of the 6th week, the patient suddenly said, "Gum, please." Soon after, this supposedly mute patient answered questions regarding his name and age. (Paraphrased from Kazdin, 1975, p. 38.)

— Biological Constraints on Shaping Learned Behaviors

Shaping is not limited to operant behaviors. In a clever experiment, Brown and Jenkins (1968) freely gave pigeons food, without regard for their actions. Each time a light came on, food was made available, thus establishing a connection between the light and food. Although key pecking was not required for receiving food, the pigeons began pecking at the lighted key. Brown and Jenkins observed that the pigeons pecked at the key without prior shaping or reinforcement. They called this phenomenon **autoshaping,** because learning appeared automatically, without response-contingent reinforcement. Autoshaping, which has been demonstrated repeatedly, suggests that, for pigeons, key pecking may be a reflex response. If so, it constitutes a *species-specific response* (a response that is relatively fixed and universal for a given species). Thus, humans talk, dogs circle before reclining, and pigeons, it seems, peck at any conspicuous target when food is present.

In some instances, species-specific behaviors can interfere with learning. Two psychologists, Keller Breland and Marion Breland (1966), were among the first to notice this problem. They had been successfully using operant conditioning to teach animals, ranging from pigs to porpoises, to perform stunts for commercials and for paying audiences (see Figure 6–15). However, they occasionally had tremendous difficulties. In one instance, they failed in attempts to get a pig to put tokens in a piggy bank. Instead of doing so, the pig tossed the tokens in the air, snuffing, snorting, and rooting. In another case, a chicken was taught to hit a toy baseball on a pinball type machine. When it did, it was supposed to run to first base. Instead, it attempted to field the ball (or so it seemed) by pecking furiously at it.

What is the explanation for the "misbehavior" of the Brelands' pigs and chickens? In each case, an innate,

Figure 6–15.

Porpoises trained by the shaping of operant responses.

species-specific response interfered with the training. As Figure 6–15 shows, animals are often capable of learning complex and unusual food-getting behaviors. Nevertheless, genetically based responses and their consequences can keep reinforcement from controlling behavior.

This idea can be carried a step further by consideration of the principle of **preparedness.** According to Seligman (1970), an organism may be prepared, contraprepared, or unprepared to learn a specific response. *Prepared responses* are easy to learn because they reflect innate predispositions (such as a pigeon's pecking for food). *Contraprepared responses* are difficult to learn because they conflict with species-specific behaviors. *Unprepared responses,* such as a rat pressing a bar, are neither prepared nor contraprepared. Although shaping is a powerful technique for controlling behavior, it is now recognized that there are often biological constraints on learning that cannot be ignored.

Aversive Control of Behavior

The time has come to consider the other side of the behavioral coin, so to speak. It is important to recognize that behavior is also controlled by aversive events or punishment. In **punishment,** after an operant response, an aversive (negative) event is presented or a positive event is removed. Technically, punishment reduces, at least temporarily, the frequency of the response that is being punished. This use of the term *punishment* differs from its everyday use; that is, so called punishment can sometimes actually be reinforcing. Although it can be assumed that most children find punishment aversive, children who crave attention may learn to obtain it by misbehaving. Thus, what parents consider punishment may actually reinforce a child's attention-seeking behavior. Therefore, psychologists define an event as punishment only if it reduces the probability of a preceding response.

It is also important not to confuse punishment with negative reinforcement. Recall that both positive and negative reinforcing stimuli *increase* response probability. As just stated, punishing stimuli *decrease* response probability. Negative reinforcement occurs whenever an organism escapes from an aversive event. For example, turning down (or off) an obnoxiously loud television upon entering a room is reinforcing. Avoidance of aversive events, such as oncoming traffic when walking across streets, is also reinforcing.

Escape and Avoidance Conditioning

Adverse control of behavior is illustrated by experiments on escape and avoidance conditioning. Consider an experiment utilizing a Skinner box with an electric floor grid. The grid delivers a mild shock to the paws of a rat placed inside. The shock is terminated only when the rat presses the bar. When first shocked, the rat will exhibit a wide variety of behaviors, such as crouching, leaping, squealing, urinating, and defecating. Sooner or later, the rat will accidentally press the bar and terminate the shock. The rat learns to escape shock in much the same way that it learns to press the bar for food. This kind of conditioning is known as **escape training,** because it involves learning to make a response that leads to the withdrawal of an aversive stimulus. Thus, in the example here, bar pressing brings about escape from the shock.

Avoidance training involves learning to make a response that prevents the onset of an aversive stimulus. In avoidance training, a signal (for example, a tone) precedes the onset of the shock. During the first trials, when the tone precedes the shock, the rat learns only to press the bar when it is shocked. Within a few trials, however, it learns to press the bar at the onset of the tone, thereby avoiding the shock. In escape conditioning, the rat is shocked on all trials; bar pressing results only in *escaping* the shock. In avoidance conditioning, the rat is more fortunate. By making the appropriate response, it can completely *avoid* shock.

Escape and avoidance learning, which involve both respondent and operant conditioning, occur quite often in everyday life. For example, if a dentists's drilling becomes intolerable, you may emit an operant response such as yelling, whereupon a considerate dentist will allow you to "escape" (give you a rest), which is reinforcing. In addition, respondent conditioning occurs when a neutral stimulus (the noise of the dentist's drill) is paired with the unconditioned stimulus (pain). Once you are in the chair, escape is only a temporary relief from pain, however, which might explain why so many adults avoid regular dental checkups and dislike the sound of dental drills.

Learned Helplessness

In both escape and avoidance conditioning, organisms have at least some control over aversive stimuli. What happens when reinforcement or punishment occurs independently of responses made by an organism? This question, addressed by Steven F. Maier and Martin E. P. Seligman, has important implications for us, since we frequently encounter events over which we have little or no control.

Maier and Seligman (1976) examined the behavioral consequences of exposure to uncontrollable aversive events. In one experiment, three groups of dogs were placed in a two-compartment shuttle box with electrified floor grids. One group of dogs received no shock. The second group received mild electric shocks that could be escaped by the pressing of a panel in the shuttle box. The third group of dogs received inescapable electric shocks. (The latter two groups of dogs received the same degree of shock, because shocks for both groups were controlled by the actions of the dogs in the second group.)

Maier and Seligman next returned each dog to the shuttle box for testing. This time, all the dogs could escape the shocks by jumping to the opposite side of the shuttle box. At the onset of shock, dogs in the first two groups ran about frantically, until they accidentally scrambled over the barrier to the safe side of the shuttle box. Within a few trials, these dogs became efficient at escaping the shocks. However, the dogs in the third group, who earlier had no control over shock, behaved quite differently. Typically, they first ran about frantically, but then they stopped moving and passively whined. On succeeding trials, these dogs failed to learn escape behavior; instead, they sat passively and accepted the shocks. Maier and Seligman have referred to this phenomenon as learned helplessness.

Learned helplessness results from exposure to aversive stimuli that cannot be controlled and leads to failure to respond appropriately in a new situation. It is now recognized as a possible explanation for maladaptive human behaviors. For example, Seligman (1975) sees his laboratory studies of learned helplessness in animals as a model for understanding depression and other human clinical disorders (see chapter 15).

— Punishment: An Evaluation of Its Effects

Although there is a vast literature on the topic of punishment, we can conclude from available research that the effects of punishment on behavior are complex and that the role of punishment in human learning is unsettled (Axelrod & Apsche, 1983; Johnston, 1972; Parke, 1974). Here, we would like to focus on an aspect of punishment that is of practical concern: the use of physical punishment in child rearing.

Spanking children in an attempt to reduce or eliminate undesirable behavior is both commonplace and controversial. One reason for the popularity of physical punishment is that such punishment is readily available. Positive reinforcement requires that an appropriate response be emitted by the child before it can be rewarded by the parent. In contrast, punishment in the form of hitting, slapping, or snapping does not. "Put more bluntly, a parent's hand is always at the ready and its sting on a handy part of the child's body is almost always an effective stimulus which, at least temporarily, disrupts the ongoing annoying behavior" (Ross, 1980, p. 51). Thus, a second reason that physical punishment is a common parental behavior is that it is reinforced by the child's response. A child's irritating behavior is an aversive stimulus. Hitting the child is likely to disrupt the behavior, thus terminating the aversive stimulus and resulting in negative reinforcement of the parent's delivery of physical punishment.

"Since immediate and consistent reinforcement greatly strengthens a response, this circumstance probably accounts for the fact that punishment is the most frequent mode used by adults to influence the behavior of children" (Ross, 1980, p. 51).

Although the immediate effect of punishment may be to suppress a child's annoying behavior, in the long run physical punishment is believed by psychologists to be counterproductive. For one thing, the use of spanking to punish a behavior, such as stealing candy, under one set of conditions (such as when the parent is present) is not likely to eliminate that behavior under other conditions (such as when the parent is absent). In other words, spankings may suppress misbehavior as long as the person who does the spanking is present. But when that person is absent or when the child leaves home to go to school, generalized forms of the punished behavior (such as stealing other objects) may emerge or may become more frequent than before. In addition, the person who does the punishing (conditioned stimulus) becomes paired, through respondent conditioning, with physical pain (unconditioned stimulus). The punisher may then elicit not only fear but also avoidance or escape responses. Avoiding a punitive parent by lying or escaping (including running away from home) is not uncommon among children. The reason is that such behaviors, when emitted by the child, are reinforced through operant conditioning. Recall your own childhood experiences. Did lying to your parents ever save you from impending punishment?

Our evaluation would be incomplete without mention of the positive role of punishment in learning. Punishment can, under some conditions, aid the learner. The child who touches a hot burner on the kitchen stove, for example, is severely punished. The child learns never to purposely touch the burner again when it is hot. The systematic use of punishment in child rearing may also have benefits. If a parent's administration of punishment is prompt, consistent, and contingent on the child's undesirable behavior, the punishment can impart information concerning socially acceptable behavior. Verbal admonitions, for example, will be most beneficial when presented with suggestions of acceptable alternate responses. It is also valuable to follow up with positive reinforcement of the desirable response when it is emitted by the child. Thus, a strong no is sometimes in order: "No, do not pull the doggie's tail! Love the doggie. That's right. You are being so gentle."

BEHAVIOR MODIFICATION AND SELF-CONTROL TECHNIQUES

The principles of learning described in this chapter have been applied in hospital and clinical settings to change undesirable behaviors. In general, techniques for modifying and controlling behavior are termed **behavior modification** (Craighead, Kazdin, & Mahoney, 1981). During the 1960s and 1970s, mental health professionals increasingly turned to training non-professionals, especially parents, as agents of behavior modification. For example, parents have been trained to decrease their children's stealing, hair pulling, and fear of riding a school bus. Additionally, they have been trained to increase their children's cooperative behavior during shopping trips and their desirable interactions with brothers and sisters (Moreland, Schwebel, Beck, & Wells, 1982).

In addition to training parents as therapists, mental health professionals have been increasingly successful in training individual clients to modify and control their own behavior, a type of behavior modification known as **self-control** (Kazdin, 1975). According to Kazdin and other learning theorists, self-control is presumably learned in much the same way that other behaviors are. As Skinner (1953) noted, we control our own behavior with a variety of techniques resembling those a behavior therapist might use. Let's examine several techniques for developing self-control.

To begin with, we may exert control over our own behavior by changing the *stimulus conditions,* or cues, that occasion a response. For the student who has difficulty studying, this may involve establishing stimulus control over study behavior. For example, rather than trying to study in bed (which cues behaviors such as sleeping), the student selects a particular setting, such as a quiet corner in the library, and a time of day for studying. With consistent studying at this place and time, the setting will come to exert strong control over study behavior. Henceforth, all the student has to do is go to the chosen setting and studying will tend to occur.

As a second means of self-control, a person can provide *self-reinforcement* or *self-punishment* for behaving in certain ways. A student who wants to develop self-control of study behavior may decide to make reinforcing or punishing consequences contingent on the be-

havior. Thus, if a schedule of studying is maintained during weekdays, the student administers self-reinforcement by not studying on the weekend and by going to the movies. If the schedule is not maintained, however, the student administers self-punishment by not going to the movies and studying instead.

The effectiveness of self-reinforcement is shown by a study in which male college students overcame difficulties in meeting and dating females. Each subject selected responses, such as sitting next to a female student in class, asking one for a date, or expressing affection, and then administered himself points for doing so. At the end of this experiment, and at the last check 9 months later, the subjects showed reduced anxiety and increased socializing with females (Rehm & Marston, 1968).

The effectiveness of self-punishment is shown by a study in which clients were trained to administer aversive consequences to themselves to control overeating. As described by Kazdin (1975), clients were asked to write a list of the most aversive consequences of eating they could think of, such as being rejected socially, having trouble attracting a mate, and incurring heart disease. Clients then were to imagine and recite the aversive consequences prior to eating a rich dessert, for instance. Prior thinking about the aversive consequences, which normally are of little concern until after overeating, helped clients exert control over their eating behavior. Self-punishment is usually combined with techniques such as stimulus control to suppress behaviors. Imagine how this method might be applied to the smoker who wishes to stop.

We can also achieve self-control through *alternate response training.* In this case, alternate responses are substituted for undesirable behaviors. Kazdin (1975) described a study, reported by Watson, Tharp, and Krisberg (1972), that demonstrates how alternate response training can be accomplished. In this particular case, the training was used to control the persistent scratching of a 21-year-old woman who suffered from itchy rashes on her arms, legs, and hands. At first, during Plan 1, the woman simply recorded the daily number of times she scratched. This led to a brief, but temporary, decrease in scratching. The therapist then asked the woman to substitute an alternate response for scratching (Plan 2). She was to stroke herself instead of scratching. This led gradually to a decrease in the number of instances of scratching. During this phase of treatment, the woman awarded herself points when she stroked instead of scratched. In the last treatment phase (Plan 3), she was instructed to substitute patting for both stroking and scratching. The program dramatically decreased the woman's scratching behavior. You may wonder whether such effects are lasting. For this woman, scratching returned, but only twice during the year and a half following treatment. Each time, the woman again successfully eliminated this undesirable behavior with alternate response training. Perhaps you can think of ways to apply this technique in eliminating other habits, such as swearing or fingernail biting.

In alternate response training, clients frequently are taught to control anxiety by emitting an incompatible relaxation response instead. Deep relaxation may be achieved for this purpose by alternately tensing and relaxing muscles or by meditating (see chapters 5 and 14). Once relaxation is learned, it can be used as a self-control technique in any situation that provokes anxiety, including childbirth, public speaking, interviewing for a job, or performing in sports (Kazdin, 1975).

There are, of course, limitations to self-control. First, you are your own client. As a result, you alone have control over the contingent behaviors, and it is possible that you will not adhere to them. The student who decides to go to a movie despite failing to maintain a study schedule is an example. Second, not everyone is capable of using self-control techniques to alter behavior; one example is a person who uncontrollably abuses alcohol. Thus, for some people and for some problems, professional help may be warranted.

— COGNITIVE LEARNING —

Not all learning can be adequately explained by simple stimulus-response associations. **Cognitive learning** involves consideration of the mental (cognitive) processes, such as thinking, reasoning, and remembering, that intervene between the stimulus and response. At one time, scientists believed that rats learn to negotiate a maze by making a robotlike series of correct turns to reach a morsel of grain. In recent experiments, however, psychologists have shown that some animals actually form categories, construct intricate mental maps of their world, and follow a process of reasoning that cannot be explained by basic conditioning. One experiment, for example, was designed to determine whether pigeons can form categories. In it, the pigeons were taught to peck at a key when they saw a photographic slide of a person. For each correct peck, they were rewarded with food. Then they were shown slides of objects they had never seen before; here, the food reward was withheld. After this initial training, the birds were shown more than 1,000 slides, some containing people and others showing objects. The birds passed their test with flying colors. Regardless of whether the slide contained one person or many, and no matter what the people looked like, the birds pecked correctly. Apparently, they had come to recognize the concept of *people*. (c.f. Begley, Carey, & Grant, 1982).

Latent Learning

Edward C. Tolman was among the first investigators to question stimulus-response, association theory. Tolman (1932; 1948) tried to replace reinforcement theory with a theory emphasizing cognitive aspects of behavior. He and his associates conducted a series of experiments that strongly support the notion that organisms can learn without being reinforced. To account for this possibility, Tolman proposed the concept of **latent learning**—learning that is not immediately revealed by any obvious change in behavior. Latent learning occurs when learners develop mental (cognitive) expectations about the relationships among stimuli. In a classic experiment, Tolman and his colleagues demonstrated that rats can learn a maze without any food reward. They permitted rats to explore a maze over a 10-day trial period, without giving them food at the end of the maze. A control group of rats received food at the end of each maze. The control group showed decreases in running time and error scores in the maze performance; the unfed (experimental) group did not. When food was given on the 11th trial day to the unfed rats, however, their time and error scores quickly fell to the same low level as the control group's. In fact, the experimental group of rats achieved the same level of learning in less time than did the rats that were reinforced with food from the start of the experiment. The experimental group of rats benefited by their exploratory behavior, forming what Tolman referred to as *cognitive maps,* or mental pictures, of the maze. However, their learning was not visible or apparent; it remained *latent* until food (reinforcement) was introduced into the situation. In Tolman's view, the rats were able to learn about the maze without reinforcement, but this learning did not become obvious until they were reinforced.

Numerous experiments (e.g., Olton, 1979) have provided evidence that rats may be capable of developing the cognitive maps described by Tolman and his associates. Such experiments suggest that rats not only de-

velop these cognitive maps but that they can remember them and later recall the locations at which they have been fed. These experiments demonstrate that, to some extent, animals share the human ability to reflect on recent experience. But exactly how animals think without language remains a baffling question (Terrace, 1982).

Insight Learning

The complex nature of learning is further illustrated by the work of Wolfgang Köhler (1925), the German Gestalt psychologist (see chapter 4). In one of Köhler's experiments, which investigated the problem-solving ability of chimpanzees, a bunch of bananas was hung from the top of a cage out of a chimpanzee's reach. Also inside the cage were boxes on which the chimp could stand to grasp the bananas. Köhler's chimpanzees would initially jump for the food repeatedly, without success. Eventually, jumping would give way to restless pacing (Figure 6–16). Sultan, Köhler's most in-

Figure 6–16.
Demonstration of insight learning. A chimpanzee is in a cage where a bunch of bananas is hanging out of reach. Several boxes are scattered around. After trying unsuccessfully to reach the bananas by jumping, the animal paces restlessly for a while, then suddenly stacks the boxes beneath the bananas, climbs up, and grabs the fruit.

telligent chimpanzee, paced restlessly up and down, then suddenly stood still in front of the boxes, as if to study the problem. He then seized a box, tipped it toward the bananas, climbed on it, and, springing upwards with all his force, tore down the bananas (Köhler, 1925).

Köhler called this type of learning **insight learning** to indicate that it results from a sudden perception, or grasp, of a problem that leads to a solution. Thus, instead of perceiving the boxes and bananas as isolated objects, the chimpanzee suddenly perceived the boxes as a tool for reaching the bananas.

Experiments conducted by Köhler and others (e.g., Birch, 1945) demonstrated that insight learning is not totally independent of past experience. In one study, several chimpanzees were tempted with food that was outside their cages, just beyond their reach. Sticks that could be used to gather in the food were placed near the chimps. Only one of several chimpanzees solved this problem—the one that had had experience playing with sticks. The other chimpanzees were then given sticks to play with. When these chimps were retested, they solved the problem with ease, raking in the food with the sticks. Their *experience* with the sticks enabled them to use the sticks in an insightful manner.

Insight such as that described by Köhler also occurs in human learning. A child may learn the multiplication table by rote memorization and only later recognize that multiplication is essentially addition or that there are meaningful patterns among the numbers. In the 9s table, for instance, the sum of the digits in the answers is always 9, as in the case of $9 \times 5 = 45$ (Bigge, 1964). Insight learning, in this sense, involves a sudden perception from which a new meaningful relationship emerges.

— APPLICATION —

LEARNING THROUGH OBSERVATION

Experiments investigating insight learning and latent learning have played an important role in fostering the idea that organisms learn a great deal through observation without being directly reinforced. Learning of this type, which Albert Bandura (1977b) refers to as **observational learning,** is accomplished by observing the behavior of others. Observational learning often occurs without reinforcement, and, as with latent learning, it may not be revealed by any obvious change in behavior at the time of learning. For example, a young girl who observes her mother bottle feeding a younger sister may retain this information and later attempt to imitate the mother's behavior (Figure 6–17). (In this figure, the girl is also attempting to imitate the facial sucking expression of her "baby.")

The powerful impact of observational learning was demonstrated initially in a classic experiment conducted by Bandura, Ross, and Ross (1963). Children viewed a movie in which an adult attacked a large blow-up doll with a hammer. The experimenters then put the children in a similar situation and noted the number of imitative responses they made. These children displayed twice as many physical and verbal aggressive responses directed toward the doll as did the

Figure 6–17.

A 4-year-old girl imitates her mother's behavior and the facial sucking expression of her "baby."

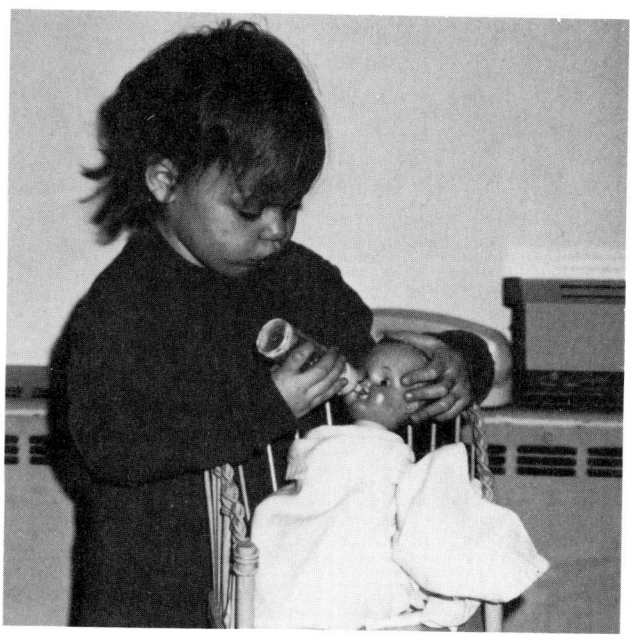

children in a control group, who had viewed the behavior of a nonaggressive model.

Basic research on observational learning, which will be discussed in more detail in chapter 18, suggests some important applications. For example, recall our earlier discussion of punishment. There, we stated that punishment in the form of verbal admonition can be beneficial in curbing a child's undesirable activities if it is paired with positive reinforcement of an acceptable alternate response. In addition, parents should be aware of the strong influence they exert on their children's behavior merely by behaving as they would like the child to behave. Children who observe a parent engage in spanking, for example, are likely to learn that it is acceptable to hit people if they misbehave and that spanking is what parents are supposed to do to their children. Indeed, much social learning is fostered by exposure to real-life models (such as parents, teachers, and peers) who exhibit behaviors that may be imitated by others (Fairchild & Erwin, 1977).

Observational learning and the other types of cognitive learning described in this brief section contribute to many areas of psychology and provide a foundation for topics that we will explore in subsequent chapters.

BEHAVIORAL TECHNOLOGY IN THE COMING YEARS

B. F. Skinner's (1938) experimental analysis of behavior is now applied in laboratories throughout the world. Advances in our understanding of operant and respondent conditioning, as well as in cognitive learning (including types not yet discussed), have had diverse applications. The psychological principles covered in this chapter alone suggest that techniques are available for resolving significant personal, social, and, perhaps, world problems. Already, we have the basic knowledge needed to make constructive changes in a variety of settings. For example, behavior modification has been successfully applied in mental institutions, hospitals, prisons, homes for delinquent youth, schools, and day-care facilities. Use of behavior modification in such settings arouses minimum controversy because its goals are widely accepted as worthwhile. These goals include alleviating bizarre behavior, rehabilitating criminals, returning individuals to self-sufficient living, ameliorating learning problems, accelerating academic performance, and developing social skills. Achieving such goals through carefully designed programs has created the early stages of a *behavioral technology*. "Yet, a technology devoted primarily to the amelioration of problems is only in its germinal stage of development. . . . When behavioral programs are applied to prevent problems, the technological advances will be more evident" (Kazdin, 1975, p. 249).

"Technology is the systematic application of tested scientific principles to pragmatic, real-life tasks and problems" (Willems, 1974, p. 151). In no area has behavioral technology had greater impact than in education, especially through the development of programmed instruction (Kazdin, 1981). **Programmed instruction** is a procedure that provides the student with immediate feedback, and therefore reinforcement, for each response that is to be learned. It is based on laboratory studies that suggest that learning proceeds best when *knowledge of results* is provided immediately following a correct response. This principle is too often ignored in traditional classrooms. It may be a full week or more before students receive their test scores, for example. In contrast, programmed instruction is designed to give students immediate feedback (and thus reinforcement) for correct answers. Learning is scheduled (programmed) to proceed by small steps, which bring about ever-closer approximations to a desired level of mastery.

One advantage of programmed learning is that students progress at their own pace, advancing only after previous information is understood. A second advantage is that teachers receive continuous feedback about the success of the program and about student achievement. Programmed records show correct and incorrect responses and the number of students missing each item. If many students find an item difficult, it can be altered or additional learning steps can be included. In self-paced courses using programmed materials, students move at their own pace through successive units of material, and they are tested as many times as necessary to guarantee mastery of the material, with no penalty for failure. Each test is graded immediately on completion, thus providing students with immediate knowledge of results.

The technology of programmed instruction has been expanded in recent years by the use of computers. *Computer-assisted instruction* (CAI) has been used successfully in teaching children to read (Atkinson, 1974) (see Figure 6–18). In addition, CAI systems have been developed for teaching graduate students enrolled in science courses (Ragosta, 1979). Taken together, programmed and computer-assisted instruction continue to provide a striking demonstration of the practical value of behavioral technology.

Can behavioral technology help solve or prevent social and world problems? As Skinner (1974) noted, "The major problems facing the world today can be solved only if we improve our understanding of human behavior" (p. 6). We must also probe the

Figure 6–18.

A student at a computer-assisted instructional system terminal. The audio headset and the typewriter enable the student to enter into a conversation with the computer.

consequences of wider use of behavioral technology within society. The use of behavioral principles to achieve social goals will likely affect each of us (Willems, 1974). But what are our goals? Who will decide? Seeking agreement is one of our challenges.

Future applications of behavioral technology will require extensive basic research beyond that presently available. And as psychologists continue to find better solutions to social problems, there will be an increasing need to convince the public of their usefulness. Air pollution, crime, overcrowding, depletion of limited natural resources, and the threat of world nuclear war are but a few of the problems facing us. Allowed to go unchecked, any one of these problems could be disastrous. The question posed to psychologists by Skinner (1982), "Why are we not acting to save the world?" demands serious consideration. In the years ahead, we will all be challenged to go well beyond present applications to discover new ways of preventing the social and world problems that face us.

— SUMMARY —

1. Learning is a relatively permanent change in behavior that can be attributed to experience or practice.

2. In classical (respondent) conditioning, a neutral stimulus is paired with an unconditioned stimulus that elicits an unconditioned response. After repeated pairings of the two stimuli, the neutral stimulus becomes a conditioned stimulus because it is by itself capable of eliciting the response. A conditioned response can be extinguished by presenting the conditioned stimulus in the absence of the unconditioned stimulus.

3. Basic phenomena in conditioning are spontaneous recovery (the reappearance of an extinguished conditioned response after the passage of time), stimulus generalization (the ability of stimuli similar to the conditioned stimulus to elicit the conditioned response), and conditioned discrimination (the application of acquisition and extinction methods to training an organism to respond to one stimulus but not to a similar one).

4. In instrumental conditioning, reinforcement occurs only after the subject makes an appropriate response (e.g., opening the door of a puzzle box).

5. In operant conditioning, behavior is measured in terms of rate of responding, which is computed by dividing the number of responses by a constant unit of time. The rate of responding before conditioning takes place is known as the operant level of that response.

6. A major variable that determines the rate of responding is the schedule of reinforcement. In a continuous reinforcement schedule, there is a 1:1 correspondence between responses and reinforcers. In an intermittent schedule, reinforcement occurs only after some responses, not after others.

7. The principles of learning described in this chapter illustrate the numerous ways behavior can be controlled by arrangements of the contingencies between behavioral responses and reinforcing stimuli.

8. Positive reinforcement consists of presenting positive primary (unconditioned) reinforcers (e.g., food) or positive secondary (conditioned) reinforcers (e.g., money). Negative reinforcement consists of terminating aversive stimuli (e.g., shock). Both positive and negative reinforcement increase the rate of reinforced responses.

9. Aversive control of behavior may result from the use of punishment. A punishing stimulus, operationally defined, is one that, when delivered immediately after a specific response, will decrease the probability of occurrence of that response for a given period of time.

10. Behavior can be shaped into new and complex forms by differential reinforcement of successive approximations to a desired form of behavior. Principles utilized in shaping are generalization, differential reinforcement, and chaining of behavior segments.

11. Models of learning that correspond to a cognitive approach are latent learning, insight learning, and observational learning. Whereas traditional theorists emphasize the importance of stimulus-response relationships in learning, cognitive psychologists emphasize the importance of complex mental (cognitive) processes, such as thinking, reasoning, and remembering.

12. The application of learning principles via behavior modification and programmed instruction demonstrates that laboratory research can be applied to the treatment of dysfunctional behavior and to problems in education.

— IMPORTANT TERMS AND CONCEPTS —

Learning
Classical (Respondent) Conditioning
Reflex
Respondent (Reflex) Behavior
Habituation
Law of Classical (Respondent) Conditioning
Unconditioned Stimulus (UCS)
Unconditioned Response (UCR)
Conditioned Stimulus (CS)

Conditioned Response (CR)
Law of Instrumental (Operant) Conditioning
Reinforcement
Discriminative Stimulus (S^D)
Rate of Responding
Extinction
Spontaneous Recovery
Unconditioned (Primary) Reinforcing Stimuli (S^R)

Conditioned (Secondary) Reinforcing Stimuli (S^r)
Positive Reinforcers (S^{R+}, S^{r+})
Negative Reinforcers (S^{R-}, S^{r-})
Superstitious Behavior
Continuous Reinforcement Schedule
Continuous Nonreinforcement Schedules
Partial Reinforcement Schedules
Fixed-Interval (FI) Schedules

Variable-Interval (VI) Schedules
Fixed-Ratio (FR) Schedules
Variable-Ratio (VR) Schedules
Partial Reinforcement Effect
Stimulus Generalization
Stimulus Discrimination
Differential Reinforcement

Shaping
Chain of Behavior
Autoshaping
Preparedness
Punishment
Escape Training
Avoidance Training
Learned Helplessness

Behavior Modification
Self-Control
Cognitive Learning
Latent Learning
Insight Learning
Observational Learning
Programmed Instruction

— SUGGESTIONS FOR FURTHER READING —

Bower, G. H., & Hilgard, E. R. (1980). *Theories of learning* (5th ed.). Englewood Cliffs, NJ: Prentice-Hall. A review of the major theories of learning.

Hill, W. F. (1977). *Learning: A survey of psychological interpretations* (3rd ed.). New York: Crowell. An elementary and effective treatment of theories of learning.

Hulse, S. H., Egeth, H., & Deese, J. (1980). *The psychology of learning* (5th ed.). New York: McGraw-Hill. An elementary treatment of the psychology of learning. Introductory chapters cover the basic problems of conditioning and reinforcement; subsequent chapters deal with more complex forms of learning.

Kazdin, A. E. (1975). *Behavior modification in applied settings.* Homewood, IL: Dorsey. An interesting and readable introduction to behavior modification techniques in applied settings.

Skinner, B. F. (1948). *Walden two.* New York: Macmillan. A controversial best seller that describes a utopian society in which reinforcement is used as a means of social control and the use of punishment is unnecessary.

Skinner, B. F. (1971) *Beyond freedom and dignity.* New York: Knopf. An interesting and controversial book that seeks to apply the principles of operant conditioning to social planning for the betterment of humanity.

CHAPTER 7 =

MEMORY AND INFORMATION PROCESSING

— CHAPTER —

MEMORY AND INFORMATION PROCESSING

— CHAPTER OBJECTIVES —

To achieve the objectives of this chapter you should be able to answer the questions listed here. You should also be able to define the important terms and concepts listed at the end of the chapter.

1. What are the core distinctions between sensory memory, short-term memory, and long-term memory? How is information processed through these three systems?
2. What is the dual memory view? Describe the evidence for it. What is the competing position?
3. In what way is memory more a process of reconstruction than of recollection? What are the implications of this for eyewitness testimony?
4. Why do we sometimes forget information we have learned? Is all information in long-term memory permanently stored? Explain.
5. How can memory be improved? What are mnemonic devices? How do they work?
6. What is the SQ3R method? Why does it help improve memory?

— CHAPTER OUTLINE —

The Nature of Memory
Information is stored in memory in different ways.

Information Processing and Memory
The Structure of Memory
Short-Term and Long-Term Memory: One or Two Memory Systems?
The Fallibility of Reconstruction
Application: Eyewitness Testimony—Psychology Goes to Court

Forgetting
Why do we forget? A number of theories have been proposed.

Theories of Forgetting
Application: The Problem of Getting "Permanent" Information out of Memory

Improving Memory
If you are willing to put forth the time and effort, you can improve your memory.

Organization and Memory
Elaboration and Encoding: The Role of Meaning
The Role of Context in Memory
Additional Memory Aids
Application: The SQ3R Method—Remembering What You've Read

On the Horizon: Memory Control

THE FRAILTIES OF HUMAN MEMORY

You should be able to tell the difference between a real penny and a fake, you might think. After all, you have seen so many pennies over the years that the task would appear to be a simple one. But look at the drawings in Figure 7–1. Which is the correct reproduction of a penny?

Fewer than half the subjects studied by Nickerson and Adams (1979) were able to identify the correct drawing. (The answer is given at the bottom of the page following Figure 7–1.)

As this example illustrates, human memory is not as reliable as we might like to think it is. This fact becomes especially troubling with regard to eyewitness testimony. In one particularly striking case, Father Bernard Pagano (Figure 7–2), a Roman Catholic priest, stood trial for a series of armed robberies in 1979 (Rodgers, 1982). Seven witnesses identified Father Pagano as the criminal. However, the trial ended abruptly when another man, Ronald Clouser (Figure 7–2), confessed to the robberies.

There is a world of difference between faulty memory for pennies and faulty eyewitness memories. On numerous occasions, imperfect memories of eyewitnesses have caused innocent people to spend months or years in prison for crimes they did not commit. Nevertheless, both examples make the same basic point: Sometimes our memories can fail, and often they are fraught with distortions.

Later in this chapter we will explore some of the reasons for memory failures such as forgetting names, faces, appointments, and other information. These memory problems are common and often distressing. Yet, people are also capable of remarkable memory feats. Indeed, it is difficult to imagine life

Figure 7–1.

Which is the real penny? (See bottom of next page for answer.) (Adapted from Nickerson & Adams, 1979, p. 297.)

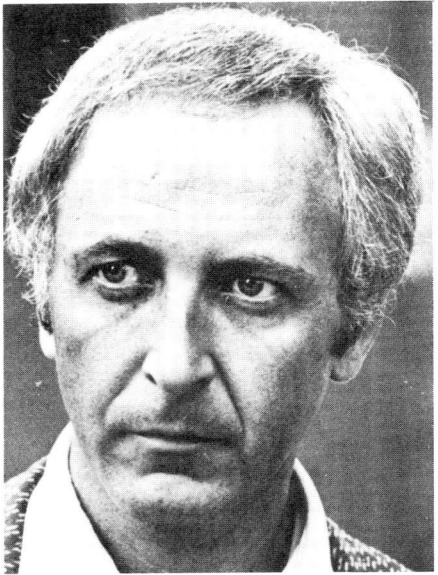

Figure 7–2.
Father Bernard Pagano (left) eventually was cleared of charges for armed robberies actually committed by Ronald Clouser (right).

without the capacity to remember what has happened. Without memory we would be unable to learn, carry on a conversation, or read a book. As Mc-Gaugh (1983b) put it, "Our abilities to talk, think, plan, dream, hate, and love are all based on memory" (p. 161).

In this chapter we will first focus on how memory works, so we can answer such questions as: How do we get information into memory? How is it stored there? How do we get it out? In the second section we will shift our focus to forgetting, answering such questions as: What is the nature of forgetting? What are some of the reasons memory often fails? Finally, in the third section, we will address the issue of how to improve memory.

— THE NATURE OF MEMORY —

As we investigate memory, it is useful to separate its *processes* from its *structure* (Wingfield & Byrnes, 1981). *Memory processes* are the mental activities we perform to put information into memory, to keep it there, and to make use of it later. *Structure* is the nature of memory storage itself—how information is represented in memory, how long it lasts, and how it is organized.

The correct drawing of the penny in Figure 7–1 is A. Many of the subjects studied by Nickerson and Adams (1979) chose B, E, or I. Did you?

Information Processing and Memory

Memory processes can be divided into at least three categories: encoding, storage, and retrieval. Perhaps we can best appreciate each of them if we think of individuals as information-processing systems. The **information-processing model** of memory suggests that, much like the operation of a computer, information is first put into memory (encoding), then stored (storage), and later recovered (retrieval) (Klatzky, 1980).

To understand the information-processing model, simply imagine what is involved when you study for an exam, take the exam, and perform well on it. What does it take to accomplish this feat? The first step is **encoding,** or putting information into memory. During encoding, you transform a sensory input (such as seeing the written material you are studying) into a form, or *memory code,* that can be further processed. Next, you retain the information between the time you study it and the time you take the exam. Hence, some **storage** process holds the information in memory. (More technically, storage is the persistence of information in memory.) Finally, when you take the exam, you retrieve the information from memory. Thus, **retrieval** involves the use of stored information. Poor performance on the exam because of the inability to remember what was studied can result from a breakdown in any of the three processes. As Klatzky (1980) observes, you may not have encoded the information properly, the information may have been lost from storage, or you could have been unable to retrieve the information even though it was encoded and stored.

The Structure of Memory

What form does information take when it is stored in memory? That is, what is the *structure* of memory? Many theorists view the overall memory system as a series of separate stores, or "boxes," through which information is processed (e.g., Atkinson & Shiffrin, 1971). Figure 7–3 is a model of memory that combines the ideas of several theorists (Houston, 1981). It distinguishes between three types of memory: sensory, short-term, and long-term. Each system retains information for different periods of time and is subject to different causes of forgetting, each appears to use different kinds of memory codes, and each has different limitations on the amount of information it can hold (Wingfield & Byrnes, 1981). According to the model, incoming information is first stored in sensory memory. If attended to and not lost, it enters short-term memory. There it can be maintained by **rehearsal,** or conscious repetition of the material. Rehearsal also transfers information to long-term memory; information that is not transferred is forgotten. Once information has entered long-term memory, retrieval brings it back into short-term memory. Let's examine the memory structures in more detail and trace the flow of information through them.

— Sensory Memory

To begin, let's imagine looking up a telephone number. The information first enters memory through a sense organ (see chapter 3), in this case the eyes. For this reason, the first information storage area is called **sensory memory.** It can hold virtually all the information reaching a sense organ (Loftus & Loftus, 1976). Information stored there, however, fades quickly, usu-

Figure 7–3.

A model of memory incorporating three separate structures, or stores, of memory. Incoming information first enters sensory memory. If attended to, it enters short-term memory; otherwise, it is forgotten. As long as the information in short-term memory is rehearsed, it will remain there; if not rehearsed, it will be forgotten. Rehearsal also provides the mechanism by which the information is transferred to long-term memory. When information from long-term memory is retrieved, it enters short-term memory. Information in long-term memory can be forgotten for a variety of reasons. (Adapted from Houston, 1981, p. 340.)

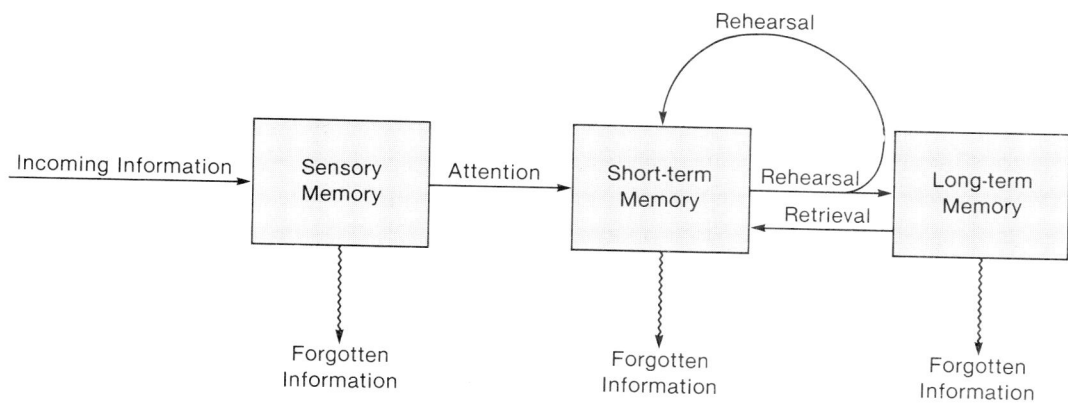

ally within a second or so. Unless it is transferred to short-term memory, it will be lost.

There are several different sensory memories, one for each of the senses (Loftus & Loftus, 1976). For example, information entering through the eyes passes into a visual sensory memory, or **iconic store.** Information entering through the ears is first held in a sound-oriented sensory memory, or **echoic store.** An example of echoic store (acoustic sensory storage) is the ability to answer a spoken question after first not comprehending it. For a split second the listener is bewildered and may ask, "What did you say?" Then, suddenly, the listener "hears" the question and answers before the speaker has a chance to repeat it. Similarly, when someone looks away from a picture, the image persists momentarily (but not as long as a sound image, or echo, lasts) (Loftus, 1980). For example, look briefly at the letters and numbers in Figure 7–4. Now look away and try to recall what you saw. For a moment, you will hold a complete visual sensory image of what you saw, but it will soon fade. The items that you will remember will be transferred into short-term memory. The rest of them will be lost.

Besides simply fading, information in sensory memory can also be replaced by new information (Klatzky, 1980). In fact, this is what generally happens; old information is constantly being replaced by new information. Imagine what would happen if this were not the case. If you first looked at Figure 7–4 and then looked at a different pattern, you would see overlapping visual images. Keep in mind that new information entering a sensory pathway replaces only information in that sensory system. Your image of Figure 7–4, for example, would not be disrupted if it were followed by a sound, because the sound would be stored in a different sensory system.

Information in sensory memory is stored there only a second or so, but during that short time a very basic function is being served (Klatzky, 1980). At a given moment, we are able to select the information that we want to attend to and process further. Usually, we choose the information that we consider the most important and meaningful. This useful information is then moved into short-term memory.

Short-Term Memory

Given what has just been described, it seems logical to state that **short-term memory** is the part of memory that holds the contents of our attention (Loftus, 1980). Whatever we are attending to right now is in short-term memory. It will remain there as long as we are thinking about it. When we look up a phone number and repeat it as we dial it, the number is placed in short-term memory. As Loftus (1980) observes, what we keep in short-term memory is essentially a matter of personal interest. What interests us and is important to us will hold our attention and will be in short-term memory at any given moment. If we do not consciously attend to the information in short-term memory, that information will be forgotten within 15 to 20 seconds. Consider a phone number you have just looked up. If you don't keep attending to it by rehearsing it, it will fade or be replaced in short-term memory by other information. Perhaps you have experienced looking up a number, closing the book, and starting to dial the number—only to forget it before you had completely dialed it. If so, you probably were not rehearsing the number.

The capacity of short-term memory. How much can short-term memory hold? This can be tested by a *memory span procedure* (Loftus & Loftus, 1976). Simply read someone a string of numbers, such as 8422, and ask the person to repeat as many numbers as possible. Then keep increasing the lengths of subsequent strings. As they are increased, the individual will begin to make errors. The *capacity* of short-term memory is defined by the maximum number of items the individual can repeat perfectly. If you try the memory span procedure, you should find that most people can retain only about 7 digits in short-term memory. In fact, short-term memory can hold about 7 of *anything,* not just single digits. Miller (1956) described this phenomenon as the "magical number seven, plus or minus two," because short-term memory capacity tends to range from 5 to 9 items. Miller noted that these items did not have to be single bits of information. He proposed that short-term memory can hold 7 ± 2 "chunks." A **chunk** is any meaningful unit of information. Thus, digits, letters, words, and even proverbs (such as "Look before you leap") are all chunks.

Figure 7–4.
A typical display for testing visual sensory memory.

5	M	7	P
1	X	T	4
B	3	2	W

The principle, then, is that short-term memory can store about seven chunks, regardless of what those chunks might be (Loftus & Loftus, 1976).

The importance of chunks is that when information is meaningfully organized, a sizable amount of it can be stored in short-term memory. Therefore, to improve short-term memory, we should organize information into larger chunks. Our language already does this for letters and words. Let's consider, though, what happens when letters are neither related nor organized into meaningful units. The following sequence of 17 letters, for example, is beyond short-term memory capacity:

KOOEROFEUOPEALBYL

If you were asked to look at this sequence briefly and then repeat it, you would probably find it impossible to recall all 17 letters. After all, 17 chunks is far beyond the short-term memory capacity. But what if you chunk the letters into meaningful units? If you rearrange the series of letters, you will find that they spell "Look before you leap." Even though this proverb contains 17 letters, those letters have now been grouped into 4 words. Each word, viewed alone, is a meaningful unit or chunk, and 4 chunks, of course, is easily within the short-term memory capacity. But you can also view the 4 words together as a meaningful unit—a proverb. In this sense, then, you have reduced 17 chunks to only 1. Similarly, note how difficult it would be to repeat in correct order the following sequence of letters as they are presently grouped:

C-IAFB-II-BMTW-A

But what if the letters were grouped differently, as:

CIA-FBI-IBM-TWA

Now the letters form 4 chunks, which are easy to repeat.

Digits present a more difficult problem in that they are not as easy to group. But they can be grouped if you can find an effective recoding scheme. You can store in short-term memory only about 7 *unrelated* digits. However, you can recall many more digits if you *recode* them into larger units, or chunks. Remembering the following sequence of numbers, for example, is made difficult by the fact that they represent 17 unrelated chunks:

24816361224481632

But if you grouped the numbers into 3 meaningful

chunks, remembering all 17 numbers would be a much easier task:

(2-4-8-16)(3-6-12-24)(4-8-16-32)

Recoding the string of numbers as 3 chunks requires that you discover some rule by which to form a meaningful unit. In this case, the first chunk is defined as a set of 4 numbers, beginning with 2, in which each successive number is the previous number multiplied by 2. The other chunks are similarly defined.

In recoding information into larger chunks, you are relying on existing stored knowledge (in long-term memory) to help you group or categorize the information. The extent of your ability to effectively chunk material depends on how much useful knowledge already stored in memory you can retrieve as an aid in categorizing. For example, in this instance, a person who does not understand multiplication will not discover the necessary rules and will therefore be unable to store all 17 numbers in short-term memory.

Keep in mind that we cannot increase the capacity of short-term memory per se, but we can increase the amount of material in each chunk. As we have seen, to do this, we must come up with some type of system for grouping material into larger chunks. With repsect to digits, creating such a system is generally difficult, although certainly not impossible (Ericsson, Chase, & Faloon, 1980). Most digit strings, unlike the earlier example, are difficult to recode into familiar or meaningful units. This fact presents a problem in everyday life when we must deal with strings of digits in excess of our short-term memory capacity. Consider telephone numbers. Without the area code, a telephone number is relatively easy to store in short-term memory because it consists of 7 numbers. Adding the area code, however, raises the total number of *unrelated* digits to 10, a number that exceeds short-term memory capacity. It is possible, of course, that we may be able to find a way to chunk some part of the number (e.g., the area code may already be a familiar and meaningful unit). But if not, we invariably find ourselves needing to look at the number as we dial it. Given that the telephone dial has letters as well as numbers on it, our task will be made much easier if we "translate" the telephone "numbers" into "words" (Matlin, 1983). Remembering (SUE)ANN-TRIP is much easier than remembering (783)266-8747.

Another problem of short-term memory capacity can arise with respect to zip codes. As Matlin (1983) has pointed out, the American public has not reacted favorably to the implementation of 9-digit zip codes. Zip codes of 5 digits are well within short-term memory capacity; we can look up a number and easily repeat it or write it down without looking at it anymore. Zip codes of 9 digits, on the other hand, are at the upper limit of our short-term memory capacity. Most people find that they are not as easy to remember as the five-digit ones.

You can see that you don't have to be a memory expert to improve your short-term memory. But no matter how you organize information, short-term memory still has a limited capacity. This means that once capacity is reached, adding a new item will result in losing an old one—an effect called **displacement.** In fact, displacement seems to be the major cause of forgetting in short-term memory. For example, if you just learned someone's name 20 seconds ago and now can't recall it (something that happens to all of us occasionally), it may be that you forgot the name because of the interference caused by new material entering short-term memory. Because of the limited capacity of short-term memory, new information can displace old information. To prevent such an occurrence, it is necessary to rehearse the name. This rehearsal helps maintain and strengthen the information in short-term memory (Atkinson & Shiffrin, 1971). Another explanation of short-term memory forgetting, though, is that unless you rehearse the information, it fades, or decays, as time passes. If this is true, then even in the absence of any new, interfering information or rehearsal, information in short-term memory will still be lost. Support for both displacement and decay as causes of short-term memory forgetting does indeed exist (Reitman, 1974). With respect to either cause, the prevention is rehearsal of the material. As we will see later, with enough rehearsal, the information can perhaps be processed further, into long-term memory.

How is short-term memory information encoded? In sensory memory, the original stimulus is reflected directly, or in its original form, so that information in echoic store is auditory and information in iconic store is visual. Research has shown, however, that information in short-term memory is stored mainly in auditory form, that is, by the way it sounds. The conclusion that short-term storage is auditory stems from the fact that errors made in memory span tests tend to be *acoustic* (e.g., Conrad, 1964; Wickelgren, 1965). Consider Wickelgren's (1965) study as an example. He presented subjects with an 8-item list of random digits and letters (such as 5G2RN34Z) and asked them to recall the list. Of interest are the kinds

of errors made. When subjects incorrectly substituted one item for another, the incorrect choice tended to be acoustically similar to the correct one. For example, if the Z at the end of the list was not correctly recalled, subjects were likely to have substituted a T, V, C, B, or some other letter (or even the number 3) that had the same "ee" sound as Z. In effect, such errors are made because the digits or letters *sound similar.*

Some researchers believe that part of the time we also code information in short-term memory according to the way it looks (Posner & Keele, 1967). Such a visual code, or *image,* for verbal information is apparently very fragile, however, and we soon replace it with an acoustic code (Matlin, 1983). In other words, we end up remembering the way the information sounded, not the way it looked. The acoustic code seems to be dominant in short-term memory, but it applies mainly to letters, words, and symbols. The visual code becomes more important when we store nonverbal items, such as pictures, that are difficult to describe and thus difficult to encode acoustically (Smith, 1983). Short-term memory codes for other senses, such as touch and smell, seem to exist, and researchers also believe that semantic codes exist in short-term memory. (Semantic codes are codes related to meaning.) For example, Shulman (1972) found that when subjects viewed a list of words and immediately afterward were required to identify whether a given word (called a probe word) was among those in the list, they tended to make errors related to the meanings of the words. They were much more likely to say that the probe word was a member of the list when it was a synonym of a word in the list than when it was unrelated to the list words. It seems, then, that at times we store information in short-term memory not only according to how it looks and sounds but also according to its meaning.

Retrieving short-term memory information. Some psychologists believe that retrieval of information from short-term memory is based on a sequential, item-by-item search. Sternberg (1966, 1969) deduced this by varying the amount of information in short-term memory and seeing how much time it took subjects to recall a single item. If each item in short-term memory is examined in sequence, then the more items there are, the longer the search should take. This is what seems to happen. To retrieve information from short-term memory, we apparently make an exhaustive search. That is, we look through all items in short-term memory to see if the one we are seeking is there. According to Sternberg, we do not carry out a self-terminating search, in which we quit once the desired item is found. This idea of retrieving something from short-term memory by doing an exhaustive, item-by-item search of what is stored there may not seem intuitively correct. Why would we search through all the items one at a time when, by definition, we are conscious of all material in short-term memory and thus have direct access to it? Why not examine all the contents of short-term memory simultaneously (through what is called parallel processing) and simply retrieve what we are looking for? Despite Sternberg's findings, psychologists are still debating the nature of the short-term memory retrieval process. Whatever the answer eventually arrived at, though, it is clear that the retrieval process is rapid. Even if we must do an item-by-item exhaustive search of short-term memory in order to retrieve information, the process is so rapid that we are unaware of it.

Short-term memory is important for two reasons. First, it represents what we usually call consciousness (Atkinson & Shriffin, 1971). (See chapter 5.) Whenever we engage in conscious thought, we are using short-term memory. Second, it provides the gateway through which information passes into long-term memory (Loftus, 1980).

— Long-Term Memory

The largest part of the memory system, **long-term memory,** stores information for indefinite periods, from only a few minutes to several decades or more. For example, it may hold both a recent conversation and vivid childhood memories. In many respects, long-term memory is like a library (Loftus, 1980). A lot of information is stored there, new information is periodically added, and the amount of information that can be stored is almost unlimited. Without long-term memory, we would be unable to profit from experience or to communicate. We would have no newspapers, schools, books, television, or learning.

The major question about long-term memory is: How does information make the crucial leap from short-term memory to long-term memory? As already noted, information is maintained in short-term memory by repetition, or rehearsal. Rehearsal also acts to transfer information from short-term memory to long-term memory. For example, if you look up a phone number, you can rehearse it to keep it in short-term memory as you dial. If you rehearse it enough, you may also transfer it to long-term memory, so it can be

retrieved later. Rehearsal does not, however, necessarily produce a long-term memory (Houston, 1981). That is, for information to move from short-term memory to long-term memory, it must be rehearsed, but it is possible to rehearse information in short-term memory without transferring it to long-term memory. In general, the longer an item is maintained in short-term memory by rehearsal, the more likely it is to be placed in long-term storage (Houston, 1981).

Even when information is stored in long-term memory, some amount of forgetting occurs. Research has shown, though, that greater rehearsal slows the loss of a long-term memory (Rundus, Loftus, & Atkinson, 1970). (See Figure 7–5.)

It is equally true, however, that the type of rehearsal is important (Craik & Lockhart, 1972). Simple repetition, or **maintenance rehearsal,** may be enough to transfer something like a phone number from short-term memory to long-term memory. However, retention of the information in long-term memory can be enhanced through various mental operations (Loftus & Loftus, 1976). For example, we can embellish, or elaborate on, information we want to remember (noting, for instance, that a telephone number has the same digits as a familiar zip code); we can form images and use memory aids or strategies; and we can organize the new information so it connects with a body of information we have already stored in long-term memory. The type of rehearsal in which information is pro-

Figure 7–5.

The more often material is rehearsed, the more likely it is to be recalled later. (Adapted from Rundus, Loftus, & Atkinson, 1970, p. 685.)

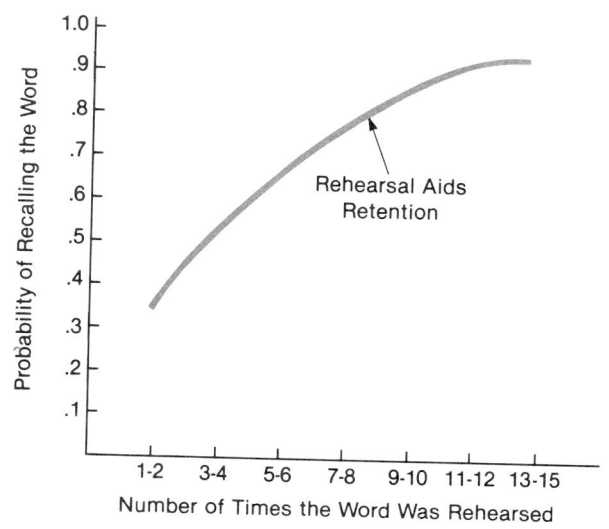

cessed in some meaningful way is often referred to as **elaborative rehearsal.** A later section of this chapter ("Improving Memory") will detail how to make use of elaborative rehearsal.

Encoding, storage, and retrieval of long-term memory information. As noted earlier, short-term memory can be encoded in several forms, the most basic being acoustic. What about long-term memory? Long-term memory is most often encoded by *meaning.* For example, after having a conversation, you are likely to recall the meaning of what was said, not the word-for-word exchange. Likewise, if you see the word *car,* you will later be more likely to think you saw a word such as *auto* or *Buick* (semantically related words) than to think you saw a word such as *tar* (which sounds like *car* but is not related in meaning) (Loftus & Loftus, 1976). Such findings suggest that for long-term memory the dominant code is semantic.

Some information in long-term memory is coded by the way it looks. For example, the ability to recognize people we know suggests the use of a visual code. Tastes and smells are similarly coded in long-term memory. It is also clear that we store at least some information in long-term memory acoustically (Nelson & Rothbart, 1972). How else could we explain our ability to remember the sound of a loved one's voice?

Long-term memory is an immense warehouse of information. With so much stored, there must be some organization. Otherwise, finding or remembering any particular bit of information would be difficult or impossible. Indeed, long-term memories seem to be categorized much like library materials (Loftus, 1980). We are able to get from one item of information to related items because they are associated in storage. Such associations become evident when we try to answer this sort of question: What were you doing on August 23, 1980? To answer, we would probably look for some easily recalled information related to that date or to one close to it, such as an anniversary or birthday. Then we could work forward or backward to it. Any information we can recall that is associated with the date provides a cue for remembering what we did that day. Fortunately, items in long-term memory seem to be linked in intricate networks of related information.

To appreciate how information is organized in long-term memory, try the following demonstration, suggested by Houston (1981). Read the list of words in Table 7–1. Then, without looking at the list, immediately write down as many of the words as you can, in any order. Now look at your responses. You probably

Table 7–1.
Word list for use in experiment on clustering.

Jupiter
robin
two
sparrow
Saturn
ten
rose
twenty
canary
tulip
Mars
six
finch
mum
Pluto
fifteen
lark
orchid
daisy
Venus

grouped, or organized, some of the items according to categories. For example, you may have recalled two or more birds together or several flowers together. This tendency to organize items during recall has been termed subjective organization (Tulving, 1962), or **clustering.** It shows that as we store words in long-term memory, we tend to organize them in a meaningful way. In one study, students in their last semester of college were asked to list the names of faculty members (Rubin & Olson, 1980). As might be expected, they tended to list together faculty members from the same department. In other words, names were clustered according to department.

Clustering in recall also shows that we rely on cues to retrieve information from long-term memory. For example, the category *birds* could serve as a cue for retrieving *robin,* which could then serve as a cue for retrieving *sparrow,* and so on. **Retrieval cues** help us check different parts of long-term memory while searching for a particular item of information. Just about anything can serve as a retrieval cue, including a sight, a smell, or a word (Loftus, 1980). Whatever the cue, the effect (we hope) is to lead us to the information we desire. For example, the cue *pet* might bring forth memories of cats, dogs, and other animals. The cue *dog* might then elicit an image of a particular dog, which might then elicit the dog's name and other memories.

Most researchers believe that information is relatively permanently stored in long-term memory. Yet, it is not always easy to retrieve information. Just as it can be forgotten from short-term memory, it can also be forgotten from long-term memory. Explanations for the loss of long-term memories are given later in this chapter.

Measuring retrieval. Retrieval from long-term memory is measured mainly in two ways: recall and recognition (Hall, 1983). **Recall** involves retrieving or reproducing information; it is usually guided by retrieval cues. Suppose, for example, that someone has asked you to remember what a former classmate looked like. Or suppose you are taking an essay examination. Such tasks require that you recall specific information. **Recognition,** on the other hand, involves the correct identification of some specific item of information and the rejection of other alternatives. When errors in recognition occur, it is usually because the target (correct) item and the alternatives are very similar. Recognition tasks include identifying the correct answer on a multiple-choice exam or identifying a former classmate's picture in a yearbook.

As mentioned earlier, it is sometimes difficult to recall information without the aid of retrieval cues. For example, you might find it easier to recall a list that included the words *bomb, theft,* and *lawyer* if you were given general retrieval cues such as *weapons, crimes,* and *professions* than if you were not given those cues (Tulving & Pearlstone, 1966).

Most people believe that recognition is easier than recall, and experimental research supports this notion (Loftus & Loftus, 1976). You might have trouble *recalling* the names of all your high school classmates, but if you were shown a list of 10,000 names, you would probably do a surprisingly good job of *recognizing* familiar names. In a sense, recognition tests provide built-in retrieval cues because the correct information is already supplied; it just has to be properly identified.

Short-Term and Long-Term Memory: One or Two Memory Systems?

As indicated, information in short-term memory is stored only briefly, whereas that in long-term memory can last for many years. Also, short-term memory capacity is quite limited, whereas long-term memory capacity is essentially unlimited. Furthermore, the dominant encoding form appears to be different for the two types of memory. Such findings suggest that short-term memory and long-term memory are two distinct memory systems. But compelling as the evidence seems, some researchers have raised questions about this **dual memory theory.** In light of this doubt, we will examine additional evidence supporting the distinction between short-term memory and long-term memory.

— A Dual Memory

Electroconvulsive therapy (discussed in more detail in chapter 16) is a treatment for depression that involves delivery of electric shocks to the brain. A major side-effect of such therapy is memory loss. More specifically, patients often forget anything learned just before the shock, a condition called **retrograde amnesia.** However, if the shock is delayed long enough for the new information to be transferred to long-term memory, the shock is less likely to disrupt recall. Similarly, a severe blow to the head may impair recall of the accident and of the events immediately preceding it. Such findings clearly support the distinction between short-term memory and long-term memory, suggesting that short-term memory of information is more easily lost than long-term memory. Apparently, information in short-term memory must have time to be transferred into long-term memory before any disruption occurs or it will not be recalled later. During the transfer period, the memory presumably becomes solidified and durable—a process called **consolidation.** Memories formed long before a disruption remain because they are already consolidated.

Nearly all research on retrograde amnesia has involved physical "insults" to the brain, such as accidental injury or electroconvulsive therapy. Loftus and Burns (1982) found, however, that "mental shock" can also produce retrograde amnesia. Some of their subjects viewed a film of a bank robbery in which a young boy is shot in the face. Compared to subjects who watched a nonviolent version of the same film (no shooting), the mentally shocked group showed poorer retention of the details of the film. According to Loftus and Burns (1982), these results may indicate that "mental shock disrupts the lingering processing necessary for full storage of information in memory" (p. 321). The implication of this finding is that people who witness an emotionally traumatic event, such as a crime, accident, or fire, may have poorer than usual recall for events immediately preceding it. Loftus and Burns (1982) note that many people, including judges, believe that the reliability of witnesses' memories is increased in the case of violent crimes. But according to the evidence just described, it seems otherwise.

Anterograde amnesia also supports the dual memory view. In this condition, memory for new events is impaired, but older information is recalled normally (Hirst, 1982). This type of amnesia can be produced by removing part of the hippocampus, a small area located in the forebrain, and part of the limbic system (see chapter 2). The operation, which was once used to control epilepsy, is no longer performed, because it limits the ability to form new long-term memories.

In one striking case, a man, "H. M.," continued to have normal short-term memory after the operation (Milner, Corkin, & Teuber, 1968). He also retained knowledge acquired before the operation. However, he could no longer transfer information from short-term memory to long-term memory. Although his early memories were intact, he was unable to learn anything new. For example, when his parents moved, he continued to go to the old house. He also could not remember people he had met following the operation. In addition to emphasizing the importance of long-term memory, this fascinating case history provides further evidence for the dual memory theory. Whatever mechanism is responsible for transferring the information from short-term memory to long-term memory was apparently destroyed in H. M.

The value of the distinction between short-term memory and long-term memory is further revealed in the following situation. Subjects are presented with a list of words, one at a time. They are then allowed to engage in **free recall**—recall in any order. When the procedure is repeated, the result is what you see in Figure 7–6. The words toward the middle of the list are the least likely to be recalled. The words at the end of the list are the most likely to be recalled, a phenomenon termed the **recency effect.** The first part of the list is more likely to be recalled than the middle part— a phenomenon referred to as the **primacy effect**— but not as likely as the words at the end.

Although not all psychologists agree on this point (Glenberg, Bradley, Kraus, & Renzaglia, 1983), the typical explanation of the recency effect is that it occurs because items at the end of the list are still in short-term memory at the time of recall. After first recalling these items, the subject next remembers items from

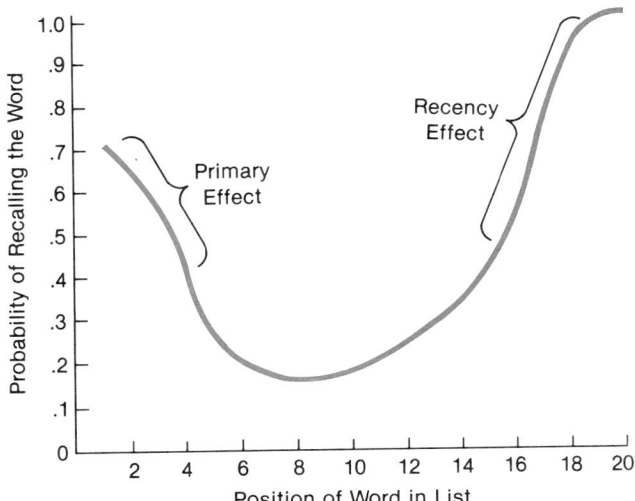

Figure 7–6.

Results similar to those obtained in many free-recall experiments.

the first part of the list, which were transferred to long-term memory. The first few items have the best chance of getting into long-term memory because they get the most attention and rehearsal. Middle items get only partial attention because the subject is trying to remember earlier ones as well.

— The Levels-of-Processing View

It is clear that many findings are consistent with the dual memory theory. Some psychologists, however, have suggested that memory should not be conceptualized as a series of boxes. Instead, they have proposed a **levels-of-processing view,** in which memory is conceptualized as one system with multiple levels of processing (Craik & Lockhart, 1972; Craik & Tulving, 1975; Craik, 1979). From this perspective, information processing can be thought of as occurring at different levels of a hierarchy. Memory is said to be a function of how deeply and elaborately information is processed. At the shallowest level, information is processed in terms of its physical features, such as visual or acoustic properties. At deeper levels, the processing is in terms of the semantic properties of the information. Semantic processing may result in a more elaborate or distinctive form of encoding (Craik, 1979). When we semantically enrich, or elaborate on, information, we give meaning to it, relate it to information we already have stored, form images of it, and so on.

According to this view, as we give greater depth to

processing, we remember information for longer periods of time. With shallow processing, memory is weak and forgetting is rapid. Craik and Tulving (1975) tested these ideas by having subjects rate words according to their physical structure (e.g., "Is the word printed in capital letters?"), their acoustic properties (e.g., "Does the word rhyme with weight?"), and their semantic aspects (e.g., "Would the word fit in the following sentence?"). Presumably, analyzing or processing a word in terms of its meaning involves greater depth than does processing it in terms of its structure or sound. As predicted, on both recall and recognition tests, subjects retained the words better after deep processing (semantic analysis) than after shallow processing (structural or sound analysis).

Although research suggests that there is merit to the levels-of-processing view (e.g., Bradshaw & Anderson, 1982; Glover, Plake, & Zimmer, 1982; Lammens & d'Ydewalle, 1983), the evidence generally tends to support the dual memory theory. Perhaps the best approach will one day incorporate the ideas of both views (Craik, 1979). One could argue, for example, that information in short-term memory is more likely to be transferred to long-term memory when it is processed in a deep rather than a shallow manner. This notion, of course, is consistent with the distinction made earlier between maintenance and elaborative rehearsal.

The Fallibility of Reconstruction

As discussed earlier, a very basic way in which we recover memories is by reconstructing past events. And, of course, our memories often serve us well in this regard. Unfortunately, however, when we cannot remember every fact about some event, we tend to fill in our memories with things that may have been true. This process, called **refabrication,** is the building of a memory from bits and pieces of truth. Loftus and Loftus (1976) have observed that a little untruth is likely to accompany most everyday reports of facts, not just recollections of long past events. Once this happens, they argue, the refabrication becomes a memory. Thus, the refabrication seems real itself, and it is virtually impossible to distinguish it from a real memory.

In a classic study, Bartlett (1932) gave students an American Indian folk tale to read. One student read a story, then told it to another, who in turn told it to another, and so on. Bartlett found that the students' reconstructions became increasingly shorter with repetition (a process called *leveling*) and that selected features of the story became dominant (a process called *sharpening*). The story also changed as subjects used more familiar words to recall its essential meaning. These tendencies can be seen in the example of an original sentence, "One night two young men from Egulac went down to the river to hunt seals," which became, after a few repetitions, "Two Indians were out fishing" (cf. Loftus & Loftus, 1976). Interestingly, most subjects were unaware that they were making such changes.

Bartlett's subjects, then, distorted their "memories" to fit their preconceptions, or already existing ways of thinking about things. Bartlett viewed memory as more a process of *reconstruction* than of *recollection*. He proposed that we remember by organizing present experiences within the framework of past experience. As Norman (1976) notes, one consequence of such organizing is that we often remember what we expected to perceive, rather than what we actually did perceive. Consider, in this regard, a study by Bruner and Postman (cited in Buckhout, 1974). Subjects were briefly shown an array of playing cards and asked how many aces of spades there were. Most subjects reported seeing three aces of spades. Actually, there were five, two of which were colored red instead of the more familiar black. Obviously, subjects expected black aces of spaces and did not waste time looking carefully at the whole display. Thus, what we ultimately recall about something may very much depend on what we expect to see.

— APPLICATION —

EYEWITNESS TESTIMONY—PSYCHOLOGY GOES TO COURT

Perhaps the most disturbing implications of the reconstructive nature of memory pertain to eyewitness testimony (see the chapter introduction). Both real-life examples and psychological research suggest that errors are sometimes made by eyewitnesses (Buckhout, 1974; Levine & Tapp, 1982; Loftus, 1979). As time passes, following a crime or accident, forgetting becomes more likely. Moreover, eyewitnesses are exposed to new information, which may affect their memory of the original event (Loftus, 1979). Figure 7–7 illustrates this point. It shows the basic results of an experiment by Loftus and Palmer (1974). Put yourself in just such a situation. First you see a car accident. Later someone asks you, "About how fast were the cars going when they *smashed* into each other?" The implication of the question, of course, is that the cars must have been traveling at a high rate of speed, or at least at a speed higher than if the question had included the word *hit* rather than *smashed*. Your resulting "memory" of the accident is, in effect, an integration of the details of the original event with the information to which you were later exposed. You recall the accident as being severer in nature than it really was. Consider the ramifications of such a finding. In reading the newspaper or in being questioned by lawyers or the police, your memory for some event may actually be distorted. Loftus (1979) suggests that interrogators should do whatever they can to avoid introducing external information into a witness's memory.

The susceptibility to external information provided in questioning was further illustrated in another study by Loftus (1975). In this case, subjects saw a filmed accident involving a car that ran a stop sign. If early questioning after the film had merely alluded to the stop sign, subjects in later questioning were much more likely to say that they did in fact see the stop sign (53 percent) than if the earlier questioning had not mentioned it (35 percent). In other words, a mere mention of something can apparently enhance the chance that you will recall seeing it.

In some cases, external information encountered through questioning or any other means conflicts with one's original memory of an event. In other cases, it does not. When conflicts do occur, compromise sometimes seems to occur in our memories (Loftus, 1979). A study by Loftus (1977) illustrates this point well. In the experiment, subjects viewed a series of color slides depicting an auto-pedestrian accident. The plot centered around two cars. One of them, a red Datsun, turned at an intersection and knocked down a pedestrian who was crossing the street. In the meantime, another car, green in color, went through the intersection without stopping. In later questioning, some subjects were presented with incorrect, misleading information. It was implied to them that the car that drove through the intersection was blue instead of green. Other subjects received no color information in their questioning. When asked to pick the color of the car, the subjects who were misinformed were likely to pick the color blue or bluish-green. The other subjects were likely to pick the color green. The introduction of false and misleading information, then, actually led subjects to remember seeing something that did not exist—a blue or bluish-green car.

Compromise in one's memories is sometimes not as easy (Loftus, 1979). If you saw a car speed through a stop sign, and someone later suggested that what you really saw was a yield sign, compromise would be difficult or impossible. The conflict presented by the information would force you to settle on one memory or the other. Just such a situation was studied by Loftus, Miller, and Burns (1978). Again, in this experi-

Figure 7–7.
When original information is integrated with external information, the resulting memory can be quite different from what actually took place. (From Loftus & Loftus, 1976, p. 161.)

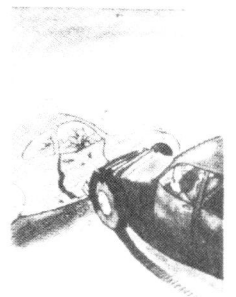

Original
information

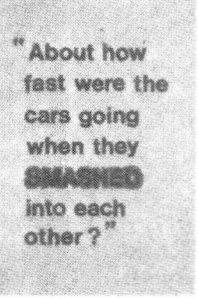

External
information

The "memory"

ment, subjects viewed color slides of an auto-pedestrian accident. But this time they saw at the intersection either a stop sign or a yield sign (Figure 7–8). In later questioning, some subjects were asked, "Did another car pass the red Datsun while it was stopped at the stop sign?" Other subjects were asked the same question but with *stop sign* replaced by *yield sign.* In other words, some subjects were questioned in such a way that they received conflicting and inaccurate information with respect to what they had witnessed (Table 7–2). Other subjects received consistent and accurate information. When asked to identify whether they had seen a stop sign or a yield sign, 75 percent of the subjects who received accurate information responded correctly. However, only 41 percent of the subjects who were given inaccurate information responded correctly. So again the nature of the questioning led some subjects to recall seeing a nonexistent object.

These studies clearly show the fallibility of eyewitness accounts. Misinformation presented after witnessed events can either supplement or alter original memories of the events. Perhaps one way to avoid such distortions is to warn people about the effects of misinformation. Recent evidence, in fact, suggests that a warning just prior to the presentation of the misinformation makes people resistant to it (Greene, Flynn, & Loftus, 1982). Apparently, forewarned subjects scrutinize the information more carefully.

Loftus (1980) has observed that "few things, outside a smoking pistol, carry as much weight with a jury as

Figure 7–8.

In the experiment on eyewitness testimony by Loftus, Miller, and Burns (1978, p. 20) some subjects saw the top slide, showing the stop sign; other subjects saw the bottom slide, showing the yield sign.

SIGN ACTUALLY WITNESSED

SIGN IMPLIED
IN
QUESTIONING

Consistent Information = Accurate Responding ("I saw a stop sign")	Inconsistent Information = Inaccurate Responding ("I saw a stop sign")
Inconsistent Information = Inaccurate Responding ("I saw a yield sign")	Consistent Information = Accurate Responding ("I saw a yield sign")

Table 7–2.
In the study by Loftus, Miller, and Burns (1978), subjects tended to correctly identify whether they had earlier seen a stop sign or a yield sign if the intervening questioning conveyed consistent and accurate information (e.g., if they had seen a stop sign and the questioning referred to a stop sign). If the questioning conveyed inaccurate and inconsistent information (e.g., they had seen a stop sign and the questioning referred to a yield sign), the subjects tended to respond incorrectly when identifying which type of sign they had seen.

the testimony of an actual witness" (p. 161). Many times a defendant is convicted on no other basis than the testimony of eyewitnesses. But as Loftus (1980) notes, even with its shortcomings, it would be wrong to exclude all eyewitness testimony, since very often it is the only evidence available and it is often correct. Loftus suggests, instead, that jurors should be made to understand the dangers of eyewitness testimony. A psychologist could testify as an expert witness to explain how human memory operates and to apply research findings to the particular situation. Ideally, memory research would have the effect of enlightening all those concerned. Whether psychology should go to court, however, and whether expert psychological testimony can actually improve jurors' ability to evaluate eyewitness testimony are topics currently being debated (McCloskey & Egeth, 1983a, 1983b; Loftus 1983a, 1983b).

— FORGETTING —

Even with some distortions, memory can legitimately be said to serve us remarkably well. Unfortunately, it is also true that memory sometimes fails us. Forgetting can be both embarrassing and frustrating. Why do we forget?

Theories of Forgetting

Psychologists have proposed a number of theories to explain why long-term memories are forgotten. Although their accounts conflict somewhat, each contributes to our understanding of forgetting.

— Interference Theory

One widely held theory is that we forget information when something else we have learned blocks, or interferes with, recall. There are actually two kinds of interference: proactive and retroactive. In **proactive interference** something previously learned interferes with our ability to recall newly learned material. We may find it difficult, for example, to remember a friend's new phone number because of interference from having learned the old number.

Proactive interference can be demonstrated experimentally with the design in Table 7–3. The experimental group learns Information B prior to learning Information A and shows proactive interference when trying to recall A. The control group, which learns only Information A before recalling it, has better recall for A than does the experimental group (Loftus & Loftus, 1976).

You might consider doing your own experiment on proactive interference; it should produce results generally consistent with findings reported by Underwood

Table 7–3.

Basic experimental design for demonstrating proactive interference. (From Loftus & Loftus, 1976, p. 76.)

GROUP	FIRST TASK	SECOND TASK	RETENTION MEASURE
EXPERIMENTAL GROUP	LEARNS INFORMATION B	LEARNS INFORMATION A	RECALLS INFORMATION A
CONTROL GROUP	(NO PRIOR LEARNING)	LEARNS INFORMATION A	RECALLS INFORMATION A

(1957). Learn a list of 10 nonsense syllables (e.g., DAX, FYP, GREZ) and 24 hours later try to recall them. You will probably forget only about 20 percent of this first list. Now continue to learn a new list each day for a total of 20 days, each time trying to recall the list 24 hours later. You should find a sharp rise in errors. Underwood reported that subjects forget about 80 percent of the items from the 20th list. In general, proactive interference increases as the amount of previously learned material increases (Figure 7–9). In addition, the greater the similarity between old and new material, the greater the interference; and the more rehearsing of the old material relative to the new material, the greater the interference (Wingfield & Byrnes, 1981).

If you are taking a chemistry course, the more information you commit to memory, the greater the likelihood of interference with your new learning. To lessen proactive interference, you may have to spend

Figure 7–9.

Proactive interference increases (recall decreases) as the number of previously learned lists increases. (Adapted from Underwood, 1957, p. 53.)

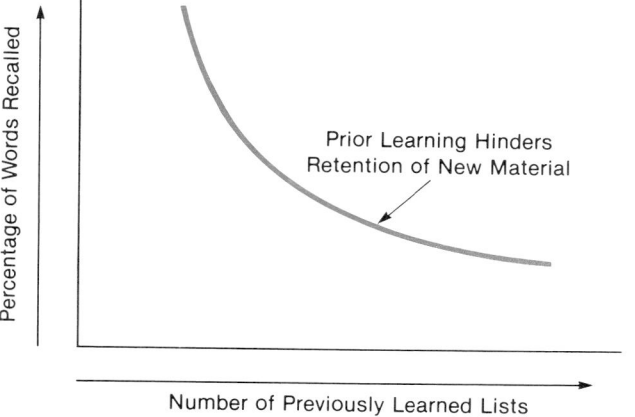

extra time studying new material. You also can try to look for ways that the new knowledge builds upon or differs from what you previously learned. Adding to the store of knowledge does not invariably impair retrieval of newer material, but proactive interference remains a major factor in many cases of forgetting (Houston, 1981).

Retroactive interference refers to the fact that learning additional information interferes with recall of information learned earlier. It can be demonstrated experimentally with the design in Table 7–4. The experimental group learns and recalls Information A, but prior to recall it also learns Information B. The control group also learns A, but it does not learn any new material before recalling A (Loftus & Loftus, 1976). Between learning and testing, control group subjects do an irrelevant task to keep them from rehearsing Information A. They may, for example, count backwards or work on simple mathematical problems. Retroactive interference is revealed when the experimental group recalls Information A more poorly than the control group. Usually, the harder it is to learn Information B, the greater the interference.

As an example of retroactive interference, think of how difficult it is to remember an old phone number or an old license plate number. Or perhaps you find the first few lectures in a history class crystal clear and have no difficulty remembering them. Then, as the lectures progress, you find it increasingly difficult to recall earlier characters, dates, countries, and events (Wingfield & Byrnes, 1981). It seems safe to say that retroactive interference occurs in our lives in many ways.

Several factors affect retroactive interference (Wingfield & Byrnes, 1981). First, the more similar new learning is to old, the greater the interference. Second, the more the new material is practiced, relative to the previously learned material, the greater the interference. Third, the greater the rehearsal of the original

Table 7–4.

Basic experimental design for demonstrating retroactive interference. (From Loftus & Loftus, 1976, p. 76.)

GROUP	FIRST TASK	SECOND TASK	RETENTION MEASURE
EXPERIMENTAL GROUP	LEARNS INFORMATION A	LEARNS INFORMATION B	RECALLS INFORMATION A
CONTROL GROUP	LEARNS INFORMATION A	(NO NEW LEARNING)	RECALLS INFORMATION A

material, the less retroactive interference there is (Slamecka, 1960). You can help reduce this type of interference and forgetting by taking the time to rehearse and practice what you have already learned. As you are studying for various classes, occasionally review earlier material. Interference as a cause of forgetting is a fact of life, and the only way to deal with it is through such a tactic.

— Decay Theory

All memory involves changes in the brain; that is, some memory "traces," or changes in neural tissue, must record information. Presumably, such traces may fade or decay from disuse. This, in essence, is the **decay theory** of forgetting. If information is not used or rehearsed, forgetting will occur in time. According to decay theory, you may no longer remember an old phone number because the memory trace faded away. Although decay theory is intuitively appealing, its usefulness as an explanation of forgetting can be questioned (Houston, 1981).

For decay theory to be tested, interfering activities must not occur between learning and recall. Otherwise, any observed forgetting might be due to interference, not decay. So far, it has been virtually impossible to "turn off" an individual to prevent exposure to interfering thoughts after learning. Decay may very well account for some forgetting, but its isolation from interference effects has not yet been achieved.

— Retrieval Failure

Have you ever been unable to remember something, try as you might, only to have it pop into your mind sometime later? The **retrieval failure** hypothesis posits that "forgotten" information is temporarily inaccessible because an appropriate retrieval cue is lacking. In this sense, then, forgetting is much like being un-

able to find a misplaced book in a library. The book (or memory) is there but not retrievable at the moment.

The effectiveness of retrieval cues in facilitating recall can be seen in a study by Tulving and Pearlstone (1966), which we alluded to earlier. Subjects were given a list of category names, such as *weapons, crimes,* and *professions.* Listed with each category name were items fitting into the category, such as *cannon, treason,* and *engineer.* Subjects were asked to memorize these specific items. Later, they were asked to recall as many items as they could. Some subjects had been provided with the category names; others had not. In one of the experimental conditions, involving a list of 48 items, those who had been provided with category names, which served as retrieval cues, were able to recall about 36 words. The others could recall only about 19 words. When the latter subjects were then given the category names, their recall jumped to about 32 words. Presumably, the other 13 words had been stored in memory but were unretrievable without the help of cues. An important point in all this is that seemingly lost information can often be recovered, at least to some extent. When you try to jog your memory, you may use a few initial details as retrieval cues for further information, and eventually you retrieve the full memory.

Context-dependent memory. Interestingly, the context in which something is learned can serve as a retrieval cue. In other words, recall is enhanced when testing occurs under the same conditions as learning did (Smith, 1979; Smith, Glenberg, & Bjork, 1978). In a study reported by Smith (1979), all subjects studied a list of 80 words in a distinctively decorated room. The next day all subjects were given an unannounced recall test for the word list. Some subjects were tested in the original room (same-context group); others were tested in a different room (different-context group). Average recall for the same-context group was much better than for the different-context group. Altering context, then, impaired memory performance.

It would seem, therefore, that students would do better if they took exams under conditions similar to those of their study environment. It might even be logical to suggest that performance would be better if tests were given at home rather than in the classroom—a strategy the academic world is unlikely to accept soon. But don't despair. Taking exams in the classroom even after studying elsewhere need not be a problem, according to other results from Smith's (1979) research. A third group of subjects also had different rooms for learning and testing. But before their recall test, they were given special instructions in an effort to reinstate their memory of the first room. For example, they were to list the things they could remember seeing in the first room. They were also to spend a few minutes thinking about the room and trying to use their memory of it to help them recall the words they learned there. Interestingly enough, average recall for this group was just as high as for the same-context subjects. Even though the third group was not actually in the original room, the learning context was effectively reinstated through imagination and thought.

To make use of Smith's findings, the next time you take an exam, mentally reconstruct the environment in which you studied. Note, though, that context seems to affect recall only, not recognition (Smith, Glenberg, & Bjork, 1978). Recognition tests are already replete with retrieval cues, thereby rendering contextual cues less relevant. Nevertheless, you undoubtedly have your share of essay exams, so keep this strategy in mind. Finally, in a more recent study, Smith (1982) found that changed-context forgetting can be alleviated by studying in a variety of settings rather than a single environment. Apparently, learning new material in many different settings makes one less likely to use or rely on contextual cues for recall. Thus, your test performance in class should theoretically be enhanced (at least for recall items) if you study in many different places rather than just your room or apartment.

State-dependent memory. Context can change internally as well as externally. Thus retention is improved when one's mood or "state" is the same on occasions of learning and testing (Bower, 1981). For instance, sober subjects may be unable to remember what happened to them while they were intoxicated, but if they are asked the same questions when they are again inebriated, their memory is better (Weingartner, Adefris, Eich, & Murphy, 1976).

Bower (1981) has labeled improved recall when moods during learning and testing are similar as "mood-state-dependent-memory." He has shown that the effect applies to word lists (Figure 7–10), personal experiences recorded in a daily diary, and childhood experiences. Furthermore, when reminiscing about the past, individuals seem especially likely to remember events and experiences consistent with their current mood (Clark & Teasdale, 1982; Snyder & White, 1982; Natale & Hantas, 1982). Feelings of elation lead to recall of pleasant events, whereas feelings of depression lead to recall of unpleasant ones. According to Bower (1981), an emotion can become associated in memory with a particular event or fact much as a house lived in as a child can be associated in memory with a particular pet. Just as thinking of the house may serve as a retrieval cue for memory of the pet, so can a particular emotional state act as a retrieval cue for events associated with that particular emotion.

The TOT phenomenon. At times, you have probably felt that although you couldn't remember some fact, it was on the tip of your tongue and would surface with the right retrieval cue. This **tip-of-the-tongue (TOT) phenomenon** has been studied by psychologists. In one study (Brown & McNeill, 1966), the subjects' task was to come up with the words whose definitions were provided. The words being

Figure 7–10.

When subjects learn a list of words while in a happy mood, their later recall of those words is best when they are again in a happy mood; when they learn while in a sad mood, recall is best when they are in a sad mood. (Adapted from Bower, 1981, p. 132.)

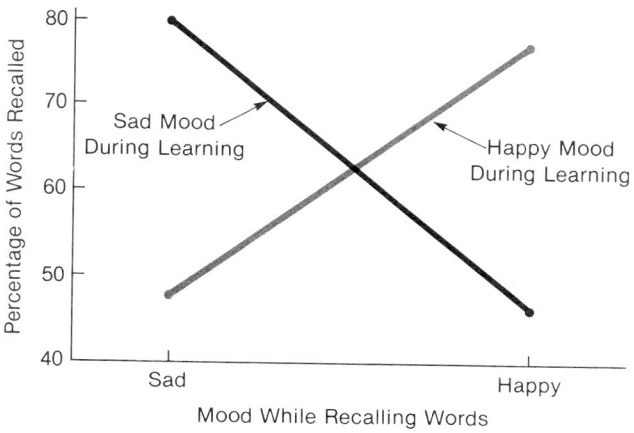

looked for were uncommon ones, like *sextant* and *sampan*. Even when subjects couldn't think of the word, they often believed that it was on the tip of their tongue (a TOT state). In trying to retrieve the word, they often thought of words that sounded similar to the correct one or had a similar meaning. In 57 percent of the cases, subjects could even correctly identify the initial letter of the word. In the same percentage of cases, they could identify the precise number of syllables. All of this suggests that recall and recognition are not the only ways in which we express what we know. Apparently, we can also express knowledge of stored information through a "feeling of knowing" (Schacter, 1983). In addition, this suggests that remembering may occur a little at a time (Loftus, 1980).

Bit-by-bit retrieval also occurs when we recognize a face and are sure we know the person's name but can't recall it (a TOT state) (Loftus, 1980). To retrieve the name, we may find ourselves first trying to recall the person's profession or where we had seen the person before (Yarmey, 1973). To get the name itself, we may search for its initial letter or number of syllables. In short, while we are in a TOT state, anything related to the name or word we are trying to recall (e.g., another name or word, a sound, or an event) will aid in the retrieval process. In other words, the name or word we are trying to recall is linked by many associations or pathways to yet other words, sounds, events, and information we have stored in memory (Loftus, 1980; Anderson, 1983). If a given word is associated with some event, then thinking of the event may help us recall the word. If you see a face and can't think of the

person's name, you might try thinking of other things you know about the person. Once you do this, the name might readily come to mind. Can you identify the individuals shown in Figure 7–11?

Motivated Forgetting

Perhaps you have observed that people seem to remember more of the good or happy events of their lives than the bad or sad events. Forgetting something because we want to is known as **motivated forgetting.** Although it is not yet a well-understood process, psychologists are increasingly recognizing that people do sometimes try to forget things (Geiselman, Bjork, & Fishman, 1983; Kihlstrom, 1983). The idea, though, has been around for a long time. Freud (1920/1955), for instance, suggested that we unconsciously push unacceptable, anxiety-provoking thoughts out of awareness so we do not have to confront them directly. He referred to this process as *repression* (see also chapter 14). For example, feelings of hatred toward one's father may be repressed because they would elicit anxiety.

Evidence for repression comes mainly from patients undergoing psychotherapy. Firm experimental support for repression is lacking because subjects must be exposed to some highly traumatic event, which is unethical. In addition, it is difficult to know when forgetting is unconsciously motivated. Do all memory failures brought on by painful, threatening, or embarrassing material reflect an unconscious desire to forget? Maybe so, but it is difficult to be certain. Remembering a dentist appointment after it is too late to keep it may re-

Figure 7–11.

Who are these people? Did it take you a while to think of their names? What kinds of retrieval cues did you use? (Look below the figure for the names.)

Nancy Lopez

Hank Aaron

Gloria Steinem

flect repression, but it also may reflect a conscious effort to forget the appointment. Or, perhaps, there was simply distraction by other matters, and, after it was too late, some retrieval cue elicited the memory.

Even with such difficulties, it seems reasonable to believe that at least some forgetting occurs to prevent anxiety, threat, pain, embarrassment, and other negative feelings. In addition, forgetting can also be motivated by a desire to enhance self-esteem (Loftus, 1980). For example, people seem to remember themselves as having received higher pay and as having donated more to charity than objective records indicate (Cannell & Kahn, 1968). We tend to see ourselves more favorably, it seems, than we actually are.

— Storage Failure

Some apparent forgetting is due to the fact that desired information was never stored in the first place. It may be that the information was too brief to get encoded and stored, or it may not have been noticed, or it may not have been attended to long enough to be placed in long-term memory (Loftus, 1980). As an example of this sort of memory failure, we need look no further than the chapter introduction and the example of the penny. Why would people have difficulty retrieving from memory information about the details of a penny? Probably because the details of the penny never got stored (Loftus, 1980). Although the penny itself is meaningful, details such as the location of the word *Liberty* are not. We simply have no need to remember them, and few of us ever attend to them or commit them to memory. We might be surprised at how little we know about other common objects as well. As Loftus (1980) notes, our memories are imprecise and incomplete for objects such as telephone dials or dollar bills. If you doubt this, try to draw one of these objects accurately.

— APPLICATION —
THE PROBLEM OF GETTING "PERMANENT" INFORMATION OUT OF MEMORY

We have suggested that long-term memory is a relatively permanent storehouse of knowledge. Furthermore, the concepts of interference, retrieval failure, and motivated forgetting suggest that memories, once stored, could last forever. Forgetting may be a problem of gaining access to them. If we could be sure that memories really are permanent, perhaps special techniques could be devised to retrieve them. Let's examine some evidence described by Loftus and Loftus (1980) on the controversial issue of memory permanence.

— Brain Stimulation

Strong support for memory permanence would appear to come from the work of brain surgeon Wilder Penfield (e.g., Penfield & Perot, 1963). In operations on epileptic patients (see chapter 2), Penfield discovered that long-forgotten events are vividly recalled during electrical stimulation of certain regions of the cortex of the brain. One young woman whose temporal lobe was stimulated remembered various sounds and events from her past, such as a woman calling her son and the sights and sounds of a circus. From such observations, Penfield concluded that memories are highly stable and that the brain contains a complete record of past experience.

Loftus and Loftus (1980) have observed that Penfield's results may not be as impressive as they first seem. Only 40 out of 1,132 patients reported memories in response to brain stimulation. More importantly, even in these cases, there is a distinct possibility that the patients were refabricating memories that did not correspond to real experiences. For instance, in one case a patient recalled being somewhere she had never been. Rather than reliving experiences, then, Penfield's patients may have had false memories based in part on real memories and in part on thoughts or ideas that existed just before and during brain stimulation.

— Hypnosis

A technique long viewed as being capable of retrieving buried memories is hypnosis. For more than 20 years, law agencies have used hypnosis abundantly as an aid in criminal investigations (see chapter 5). The assumption, again, seems to be that memories are permanent and that they can be recovered. Loftus and Loftus (1980) report, however, that there is no evidence to support the view that hypnotically induced memories are any more accurate or complete than ordinary waking memories. (See also Sheehan & Tilden, 1983). It is true that hypnotized subjects who are asked to relive former experiences often produce an abundance of recollections. It is also true that many of their recollections are fabrications. The hypnotic subject may want to please the questioner and may therefore simply lie during hypnosis. Particularly revealing are experiments showing that hypnotized subjects will confidently recall events not only from the past but also from the future (Rubenstein & Newman, 1954). Thus, according to Loftus and Loftus (1980), there is little evidence for the idea that memories are permanent and retrievable through hypnosis.

In further support of this conclusion, Sanders and Simmons (1983) recently asked, "Does hypnosis enhance eyewitness accuracy?" and answered with a resounding No. These researchers studied the effects of hypnosis on the accuracy of eyewitnesses in recognizing a thief in a lineup and in recalling details related to the crime. In the latter case, subjects were asked several leading questions that implied that an affirmative answer was correct (e.g., "Did you see the package tucked under the arm of the victim?"). Compared to a control group of nonhypnotized individuals, subjects who were hypnotized subsequent to viewing the videotaped crime were actually less accurate on both the recognition and recall tasks. The major source of their reduced accuracy apparently was their heightened susceptibility to misleading implications such as those in the recall questions. Another misleading implication was provided about the lineup in which subjects had to identify the actual thief. Compared to control subjects, hypnotized subjects were more prone to incorrectly identifying as the thief someone else in the lineup wearing the distinctive jacket originally observed on the thief. Furthermore, they were less likely to identify the actual thief when he was not wearing the distinctive jacket. The much-heralded notion that hypnotic induction provides direct access to true, accurate, and permanently stored memories received no credence in this study.

— Psychoanalysis

Freud's concept of repression was mentioned earlier. According to Freud, repressed memories can be released or brought to consciousness by appropriate therapeutic methods *(psychoanalysis),* which will be examined in detail in chapter 16. As seen before, evidence for repression comes mainly from clinical patients. As Loftus and Loftus (1980) note, though, it has been argued that subjects who supposedly report on previously lost memories may in fact be guessing, fantasizing, or offering pure fictions. It is often difficult or impossible to verify the accuracy of such "memories."

In sum, it simply does not seem that all memories are potentially recoverable. Other work described by Loftus and Loftus (1980) further suggests the impermanence of memories. For example, the study described earlier, in which some subjects came to believe they had seen a stop sign instead of a yield sign (or vice-versa) implies that the misleading information actually may have banished the original information from memory. Some investigators have argued that in such cases the original memories, rather than no longer existing, simply have not been elicited by the appropriate retrieval cues (Bekerian & Bowers, 1983). Nevertheless, our best conclusion at this point is that not all memories are permanently stored. The implications of this conclusion for police investigations, courtroom testimony, and therapy seem particularly evident.

— IMPROVING MEMORY —

Fortunately, there are a number of helpful strategies for improving long-term memory, several of which we have already examined. Their relevance for improving memory has sometimes been implicit, sometimes explicit. At this point, it should be valuable to review them briefly and to look at some additional techniques.

Organization and Memory

The key to effective retrieval from long-term memory is organization. Just as it is easier to find organized rather than unorganized items in a wallet or desk drawer, it is easier to retrieve organized rather than unorganized material in memory. The organization of information aids in retrieval presumably by making the memory search from item to item more efficient. Anyone can increase the capacity to store and retrieve information simply by organizing information more effectively. Bower and Clark (1969) had subjects learn 12 different lists of 10 unrelated words. For each list, some subjects made up a story linking the words together. Subjects in a control group studied the lists without the aid of this technique. When later tested for recall of the 120 words, those subjects who used the story strategy recalled over 90 percent of the words, a performance level dramatically greater than the 13 percent level achieved by control subjects.

These subjects were using one of the many memory-aiding techniques called **mnemonic devices** (*mnemonic* is from the Greek word *mnema,* meaning "memory"). Mnemonics are really organizational devices. They help us organize new material by relating it to existing, well-learned information. And the better the material is organized, the better the recall for it later.

The strategy of making up a story that links items to be remembered is called the **narrative-chaining method.** It is particularly effective when several lists of items have to be remembered (cf. Loftus, 1980). The strategy calls for the items to be woven into a story so they are somehow tied together. If you have several distinct lists of information you want to remember, you should make up that many different stories. The narrative-chaining method has been shown to be far superior to ordinary rote memorization, in which subjects try to remember without aid (Loftus, 1980). Organization, of course, applies to more than simple word lists. Anytime you are faced with remembering a lot of information, such as from a lecture or a book, try to impose some organization on it. As you study, one way to impose structure and organization is to make an outline of the material. You will find such a strategy quite valuable.

A number of other specific mnemonic devices help us organize information. Many of them are commonly used in everyday life. One popular strategy for remembering a list of words, called the first-letter technique, is to compose a word or sentence using the first letter of each of the words you want to remember. For example, it is easy to remember the colors of the rainbow—red, orange, yellow, green, blue, indigo, and violet—by remembering the name ROY G. BIV. Matlin (1983) suggests the sentence, "My Very Earnest Mother Just Showed Us Nine Planets" as a mnemonic device for remembering the order of the planets. Remember-

ing an ordered list of single letters may also be important, for example, in music. A beginning guitarist might recall the notes of the six strings by remembering the sentence, "Eat A Darn Good Breakfast Every (Morning)."

Rhymes are also effective mnemonic devices (Matlin, 1983). All of us no doubt find ourselves occasionally repeating "*i* before *e* except after *c*" as we are trying, for example, to decide between *receive* and *recieve.* Probably even more common is our resort to the rhyme "Thirty days hath September" in order to figure out how many days there are in a particular month.

— Imagery, Encoding, and Mnemonics

A number of other mnemonic devices rely on the use of **imagery,** or forming a mental representation of something that is not physically present (Matlin, 1983). With imagery, one uses a mental image to link the items to be remembered. The image seems to connect things in memory by establishing a meaningful link between them. Let's say, for example, that you want to remember a word pair, bread and milk, from a shopping list. One of the most effective strategies for encoding such material in long-term memory is to form a mental image linking the two words. Thus you might imagine milk pouring onto a soggy loaf of bread.

Although imagery is an effective device, researchers have found that some people are more adept at it than others (Swann & Miller, 1982). John Conrad of Boulder, Colorado, seems to have developed the art of imagery to perfection (Singular, 1982). As a restaurant waiter, Conrad can take orders from numerous customers without writing them down. He once handled a table of 19 complete dinner orders without error. Although he uses a variety of strategies, imagery is an important key to his success. Conrad begins by associating the entree with the customer's face. In an easy case, he might think that a person looks like a turkey only to have that person actually order a turkey sandwich. Let's look at how imagery plays a role in several well-known mnemonic devices.

Method of loci. A mnemonic device that involves associating new information with a series of specific physical locations (or loci, which is Latin for "places") that are already firmly established in memory is known as the **method of loci.** For example, Luria (1968) studied a man, referred to as "S," who exhibited an extraordinary memory. To remember a series of items,

S used the method of loci and mental imagery. To begin with, he simply imagined himself walking along a familiar street. While on this mental walk, S would visualize the specific items in specific locations (e.g., a pencil next to a fence). When he later wanted to recall the items, all he had to do was go on his imaginary walk. As he "arrived" at each location, the image associated with that location, and therefore the item he wanted to remember, would be elicited.

You might try this method yourself (see Loftus, 1980). Begin by memorizing a series of mental snapshots or locations that are familiar to you, such as those you pass each morning while walking or driving to school. Then imagine that you want to remember this list of grocery items: cheese, bacon, peas, popcorn, and oranges. Next form a visual image of each item in a specific location. You might imagine the cheese melting all over your mailbox, the bacon hanging over the first stop sign you see, the peas rolling down the sidewalk in front of the local elementary school, the popcorn popping out of the chimney of a house, and the oranges bouncing down the steps of a campus building. Simply picture each item in its location for a few seconds. Later, when you want to recall the items, just take your "mental walk" to school and you will be able to note what you placed in each location.

Keyword method.   Imagery is also evident in the **keyword method.** This mnemonic device is especially useful in learning foreign language vocabularies (Atkinson, 1975). The first step in using the method is to find a "keyword" in the foreign word to be learned.

This keyword is "an English word that sounds like some part of the foreign word" (Atkinson, 1975, p. 821). Take the Spanish word *caballo* as an example. This word, meaning "horse," is pronounced "cob-eye-yo." A reasonable keyword for learning *caballo,* then, would be *eye.* Similarly, in learning the Spanish word *pato,* meaning "duck" and pronounced "pot-o," you could use *pot* as the keyword (Figure 7–12). In the second step of the keyword method, you form a mental image of the keyword interacting with the foreign word's English equivalent. As Atkinson suggests, in learning *caballo,* you could imagine a horse kicking a giant eye; for *pato,* you could imagine a duck with a pot covering its head (see Figure 7–12 for an alternative). Later, to recall the English translation for one of these words, you simply think of the keyword. The image of it interacting with the English translation will be elicited, and you will have the answer you are looking for.

Bower and Hilgard (1981) suggest that we are likely to see an increase in curriculums that use mnemonics in foreign-language vocabulary learning. The keyword method has, in fact, been shown to facilitate the learning of a wide range of foreign languages, including Spanish, Russian, Latin, French, and German (Atkinson, 1975; Pressley, Levin, & Delaney, 1982). The method can also be used to aid in recalling state capitals (Levin, Shriberg, Miller, McCormick, & Levin, 1980), to associate the names of individuals with their accomplishments (Shriberg, Levin, McCormick, & Pressley, 1982), and to link technical terms with definitions (Jones & Hall, 1982). The method is thus clearly relevant to college course work.

Figure 7–12.
Examples of the use of imagery in associating Spanish words with corresponding English ones. (Adapted from Atkinson, 1975, p. 822.)

CABALLO — (eye) — HORSE

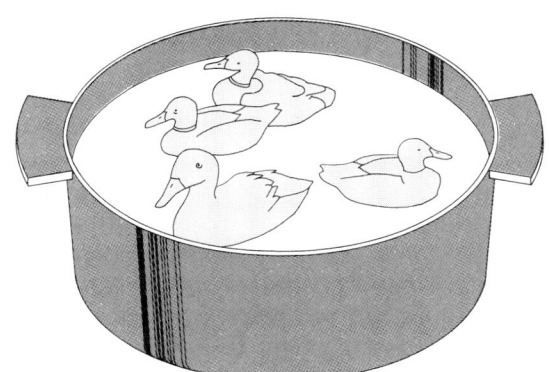

PATO — (pot) — DUCK

Elaboration and Encoding: The Role of Meaning

It is worth mentioning again that an efficient strategy for encoding material is to elaborate on it or give it meaning. The more you can relate new information to what you already know, the better your chances of recalling it. What you are doing, in essence, is establishing connections between different items of information, which adds to the number of retrieval cues. When studying a textbook, for instance, you shouldn't simply try to commit information to memory as if it were a grocery list. Considerable research has shown that your recall will be improved if you make an effort to comprehend what is presented. Elaborating on material and giving greater meaning to it seems to describe what successful learners do (Wingfield & Byrnes, 1981).

In relating new information to already existing knowledge, a particularly effective strategy is to relate the new information to yourself and your own experiences (Bower & Gilligan, 1979). In reading about the concept of motivated forgetting, for example, ask yourself if you have ever forgotten something intentionally. Having done this, you have made yourself a retrieval cue. Thinking of your personal experiences in this regard will lead to memories of what you learned about motivated forgetting.

The Role of Context in Memory

We have already seen that learning contexts can be powerful retrieval cues for improving memory. When the external context is unavailable, an equally effective strategy is to re-create the context mentally. This is true whether you're trying to recall information from a textbook, the name of your childhood family doctor, or the names of high school classmates. For example, in trying to retrieve the name of a high school classmate, you could mentally re-create the context by imagining various high school classes and activities. The name you are looking for might very well come to mind (Williams & Hollan, 1981).

Additional Memory Aids

There are several additional strategies for improving memory, all of which relate to how you can study most effectively for your classes. One strategy is to keep in mind that *distributed practice* is generally more efficient than *massed practice*. Try studying for your psychology class in a number of different short sessions rather than one long session. With a shorter session involving less material, you may find it easier to organize the material and relate it to what you already know. Furthermore, your attention to the material will likely be greater.

Another fundamental strategy is to practice retrieval. There is no better testimony to the importance of this strategy than the experience of remembering the correct answer on a test after you turn in the exam. The retrieval process may have failed you because you did not practice the task of retrieving information (Ellis, 1972). To prevent this problem, spend a considerable amount of your studying time summarizing to yourself what you have read and formulating and answering questions. In other words, repeat to yourself what you have learned. In a study by Gates (cited in Coon, 1983), it was found that students who evidenced the best memory for what they had read were those who spent only 20 percent of their time reading and the other 80 percent reciting. In practicing retrieval, you are rehearsing the very process you will be required to engage in at test time.

Finally, if you want to enhance your likelihood of retaining information, pay attention to it. When you let your attention wander, you may not remember what you just read or what someone said. Anything that increases your attention should help memory. Generally, we are most attentive to that which interests us. If you are not already very interested in some particular material you are to learn and remember, devise strategies for becoming interested in it. Finding ways of relating the material to your own life is one approach you might try.

THE SQ3R METHOD—REMEMBERING WHAT YOU'VE READ

Organizing and giving meaning to information, as well as practicing retrieval, can be achieved with a well-known study technique called the SQ3R method (Robinson, 1970). The first SQ3R step is to *survey* the assignment. Don't read everything yet; simply examine the material to find out the main ideas and the general nature of what is being covered. Look at the headings, boldface terms, summaries or reviews, and so on. You are now prepared to read effectively; you have a framework for organizing the material.

In the second step, turn each topic heading of the text into a *question*. By doing so, you are determining precisely what information is to be gleaned from the material. Formulating questions gives you a sense of purpose as you are reading; you know what to look for. In short, this strategy forces you to focus on the content and increases your interest. As you are being more attentive to what you are reading, you will also be comprehending it better.

In the third step, *read* the material. With your questions in hand, your reading will be of an active, information-seeking nature. Read only from one topic heading to the next; then proceed to the next step. In the fourth step, *recite* answers to the questions you asked yourself. In other words, after you have turned a heading into a question and then read that particular section, stop and recite. Answer the questions you have formulated by saying the answers to yourself or writing them down. Try to answer without referring to the text. If you find you are unable to do so, go back over the material. Once you have found the answers, you are ready to read to the next heading, repeating the process just described. After you have read the entire chapter, *review* by again reciting answers to your questions.

In sum, the five steps—*survey*, *question*, *read*, *recite*, and *review*—accomplish a number of things that help facilitate memory. First, you read with a sense of how the material is organized and how one item of information relates to another. Second, by being an active reader, you closely attend to what you are reading. Third, you elaborate on the material and give meaning to it. And fourth, you practice retrieval. Consider learning and using the SQ3R method; research has shown that it works (Robinson, 1970).

MEMORY CONTROL

The control of the past depends above all on the training of memory. . . . [It is] necessary to remember that events happened in the desired manner. And if it is necessary to rearrange one's memories or to tamper with written records, then it is necessary to forget that one has done so. The trick of doing this can be learned like any other mental technique (Orwell, 1949, p. 176)

While pointing out this quote from George Orwell's *1984*, psychologist Elizabeth Loftus (1980) has offered some interesting thoughts about the future and the issue of memory control. Orwell wrote his classic novel more than 30 years ago. The year 1984 has arrived even if the Orwellian vision of memory control has not. But perhaps Orwell's 1984 isn't that far away. If any single fact stands out in this chapter, it is that memory is easily altered. Loftus believes that this fact offers some intriguing possibilities for the future. She suggests that people might someday be able to go to "memory doctors" in order to have their memories modified. The therapeutic possibilities could be unlimited. Every so often, you might go to a local memory clinic to have some especially troublesome memory modified. The memory might be causing you grief, depression, low self-esteem, or unhappiness. But whatever the problem, the memory doctor would alter the memory that presumably led to those feelings.

Is such an idea unrealistic? It may seem so, but we have seen in this chapter that memories can be modified, at least to some extent. Perhaps someday the altering of an individual's memories through psychological intervention will be a common occurrence. Since first suggesting the idea of memory clinics, Loftus (1982) has noted that some therapists are in fact using a form of memory restructuring with clients. Loftus tells of an individual who had experienced a very unhappy childhood and who was now plagued with low self-esteem. Through hypnotic suggestion, her therapist "inserted into her mind memories of happy experiences with a loving

father" (Loftus, 1982, p. 149). This woman's new "memory" of a happy and loving childhood is reported to have given her increased feelings of self-worth. Only time will tell whether the technique of giving people new memories will become a standard therapeutic tool.

If the common use of effective and reliable psychological control of memory is not far off, perhaps much the same can be said of chemical control. Already, strides are being made in our understanding of the chemistry of memory, as pointed out in chapter 2. Particularly intriguing is the work being done with the hormone *vasopressin*. Research shows that vasopressin administered in the form of a nasal spray significantly enhances learning and memory in human subjects (e.g., Weingartner et al., 1981). Weingartner and his colleagues (1981) even report that vasopressin can at least partially reverse the retrograde amnesia that follows electroconvulsive therapy. According to these researchers, another important use of vasopressin may be in lessening the memory impairments evident in individuals with Alzheimer's disease (see chapter 2). Other researchers have reported that vasopressin can apparently help an individual regain memories that were lost dur to factors such as car accidents or alcoholism (Oliveros et al., 1978).

Maybe memory doctors of the future will be able to help you improve your memory through regular doses of vasopressin. Maybe you will be able to get a dose of vasopressin when you want to sharpen your memory of some special occasion. Perhaps vasopressin will prove valuable in reversing memory loss that sometimes occurs in elderly people (Burke & Light, 1981). The general availability of vasopressin, however, may still be a long way off. At this point, the hormone is being used only experimentally as scientists try to gain a better understanding of how it works.

Rather than wanting to improve memory, you may

be more interested sometimes in forgetting something. You may have witnessed an event that was so unpleasant or depressing that you do not want it permanently etched in your brain (for example, a war-related or disaster-related memory). In such a case, you may want to go to a memory doctor for a chemical treatment to wipe away the memory. Recent research suggests that the hormone *oxytocin* may have effects that are generally the opposite of those of vasopressin (McGaugh, 1983a). Research shows that oxytocin injections impair memory retention in animals. As researchers learn more about these chemicals and others, the possibilities for applying them to benefit human beings become increasingly more realistic.

═══ SUMMARY ═══

1. The information-processing model of memory suggests three distinct memory processes: encoding, storage, and retrieval. Encoding refers to putting information into memory. Storage refers to holding information in memory. Retrieval involves recovery and use of stored information.

2. Many theorists believe that there are three separate memory "stores" through which information is processed. The first is sensory memory. Information stored here fades quickly. If it is attended to, it enters short-term memory, where it can be maintained indefinitely through rehearsal.

3. We can hold 5 to 9 chunks in short-term memory at any given time. Information in short-term memory seems to be stored primarily in acoustic form. Considerable evidence suggests that retrieval from short-term memory is a sequential, exhaustive search process, in which all items are examined. Despite the evidence, however, the nature of the retrieval process is still being debated.

4. Long-term memory has an unlimited capacity and holds information for an indefinite period of time. Information gets transferred from short-term memory to long-term memory through rehearsal.

5. Long-term memory information is stored primarily according to meaning. Retrieval from long-term memory seems to rely on the use of cues. Retrieval cues are effective because related items of information are associated in storage.

6. The notion that short-term memory and long-term memory are really two separate systems is supported by several lines of evidence. Clinical findings relating to retrograde and anterograde amnesia suggest two separate systems. Free-recall evidence also suggests a dual memory. In contrast to the dual memory view is the levels-of-processing view, which proposes that memory is not a discrete series of phases but rather is a hierarchy of processing levels through which information is passed.

7. Recovering memories by reconstruction is a fundamental, but not always accurate, process. When we can't remember every single fact about some event, we tend to fill in with things that may have been true. Much of our reconstruction is based on what we expected to perceive rather than on what we actually did perceive.

8. Research on eyewitness testimony provides evidence of the reconstructive nature of memory. Eyewitnesses' memories can be dramatically influenced by information exposure following the viewing of a crime or accident.

9. Theories of why we forget information in long-term memory are varied in nature. Interference theory proposes that we forget when something else we have learned prevents a particular item of information from being remembered. Decay theory suggests that memory traces simply fade or decay with disuse. The retrieval failure explanation posits that when we forget something, the information is only temporarily inaccessible; given the appropriate retrieval cue, it may be successfully retrieved. Another theory suggests that we sometimes forget information because we want to. Some forgetting can perhaps be best explained by suggesting that the information was never stored in memory to begin with.

10. The notions of interference, retrieval failure, and motivated forgetting suggest the possibility that our memories, once stored, remain forever. Such a belief

has its basis in work and theorizing related to brain stimulation, hypnosis, and psychoanalysis. Considerable evidence, however, suggests that not all memories are necessarily still stored.

11. A number of techniques have been suggested for improving long-term memory. The key to effective retrieval is organization. Memory aids known as mnemonic devices help us organize new material by relating it to existing well-learned information.

12. Several mnemonic devices rely on the use of imagery, which connects items in memory by establishing a meaningful link between them. The method of loci and the keyword method are among the techniques that utilize imagery.

13. Memory can also be improved through the use of elaboration or giving meaning to material by relating it to what is already known. Recall is improved by exerting effort to comprehend what is presented.

14. Retrieval from long-term memory can be enhanced by restoring the original context in which learning occurred. An equally effective strategy is to re-create the context mentally. Additional effective strategies include distributing one's studying time, practicing retrieval, and increasing attention and interest.

15. The SQ3R study method facilitates organizing and comprehending when reading and encourages practicing retrieval. The five steps of the method are survey, question, read, recite, and review.

16. Memory doctors of the future may be able to help us enhance positive memories and wipe away unpleasant ones. Already, some therapists are using memory restructuring in working with clients who have problems such as low self-esteem. Chemical control of memories may also be a viable technique of the future. Considerable evidence suggests that the hormone vasopressin, for example, significantly enhances human learning and memory. The potential for applying this hormone to a variety of memory-related problems is enormous. The hormone oxytocin seems to have effects that are generally the opposite of those of vasopressin.

— IMPORTANT TERMS AND CONCEPTS —

Information-Processing Model
Encoding
Storage
Retrieval
Rehearsal
Sensory Memory
Iconic Store
Echoic Store
Short-Term Memory
Chunk
Displacement
Long-Term Memory
Maintenance Rehearsal

Elaborative Rehearsal
Clustering
Retrieval Cues
Recall
Recognition
Dual Memory Theory
Retrograde Amnesia
Consolidation
Anterograde Amnesia
Free Recall
Recency Effect
Primacy Effect
Levels-of-Processing View

Refabrication
Proactive Interference
Retroactive Interference
Decay Theory
Retrieval Failure
Tip-of-the-Tongue (TOT) Phenomenon
Motivated Forgetting
Mnemonic Devices
Narrative-Chaining Method
Imagery
Method of Loci
Keyword Method

— SUGGESTIONS FOR FURTHER READING —

Loftus, E. F. (1979). *Eyewitness testimony.* Cambridge, MA: Harvard University Press. A fascinating book detailing research on the reliability of eyewitness accounts and applying memory research to real-life problems.

Loftus, E. F. (1980). *Memory.* Reading, MA: Addison-Wesley. A highly readable, engaging, brief introduction to how we remember and why we forget. The discussion of how memory is affected by stress, drugs, brain injuries, sexual intercourse, and old age is particularly interesting.

Matlin, M. (1983). *Cognition.* New York: Holt, Rinehart and Winston. An interesting discussion of memory, including many real-life examples and applications and intriguing demonstrations for the student.

Neisser, U. (1982). *Memory observed: Remembering in natural contexts.* San Francisco: W. H. Freeman. A fascinating collection of readings on many topics, among them eyewitness testimony and mnemonic devices.

Robinson, F. P. (1970). *Effective study* (4th ed.). New York: Harper & Row. An excellent source for more about the SQ3R method and other effective study strategies.

Wingfield, A., & Byrnes, D. L. (1981). *The psychology of human memory.* New York: Academic Press. A good, solid introduction to the field of memory. Contains some interesting material dealing with memory research on applied problems.

CHAPTER 8
LANGUAGE AND THOUGHT

LANGUAGE AND THOUGHT

— CHAPTER OBJECTIVES —

To achieve the objectives of this chapter, you should be able to answer the questions listed here. You should also be able to define the important terms and concepts listed at the end of the chapter.

1. How does language develop as the child grows? What are some of the important features of each stage of development?
2. How can we account for the child's acquisition of language? How do theories of language acquisition differ?
3. What evidence exists that language and thought are or are not related?
4. What are concepts? What is their significance in everyday life? What affects the learning of concepts?
5. List the stages of problem solving. What is involved in each stage?
6. Name some factors that can inhibit effective problem solving.

— CHAPTER OUTLINE —

Language
Language development occurs in the same sequence for children of all cultures. How it is acquired is a matter of debate.

The Development of Language
Theories of Language Acquisition
Language and Chimpanzees
Relationship between Language and Thought
Application: Facilitating Language Development in Young Children

Thought
Forming concepts and solving problems are what we do when we think.

Concept Formation
Problem Solving
Application: Some Tips on Solving Problems

On the Horizon: Programming Intelligent Computers

THE STORY OF GENIE

From infancy until adolescence, Genie's mentally disturbed father kept her imprisoned, alone in a small bedroom. By day, Genie was harnessed to a potty chair; at night, she was restrained in a sleeping bag and wire mesh cage. When Genie made sounds, her father beat her. No one spoke to Genie during her long isolation. The father made only barking and growling sounds at her. Family members (the father, a nearly blind mother, and a son) rarely conversed; and when they did, they kept quiet for fear of enraging the father, who had an intolerance for noise. The only language Genie may have heard was her father's swearing when he was angry.

When Genie was 13½ years old, her mother, abused and living in fear herself, managed to leave home with Genie. Ultimately, Genie got the treatment and help she needed, including help with learning language. But, at her age, was it too late? Gradually, Genie learned to understand a number of words and to say them herself. For several years, however, she spoke only in one-word utterances. Then she slowly began constructing sentences of two, three, and more words. Soon she was able to create, on her own, totally new utterances, not just imitations of others'.

Despite the evidence that Genie was acquiring language, it was clear that her learning was far from complete. Four years after her first sentences, she was still using abbreviated and simplistic speech, devoid of questions and proper grammar. She did not show the rapid increase in language performance that characterizes most children. Although we can say that Genie now has language, her language is far from normal (Curtiss, 1977).

Genie's story is tragic and intriguing. For those interested in language development, her achievements raise many questions. How is language learned? Is there a critical period for acquiring language, after which it cannot be learned at all, or only with great difficulty? Was Genie exposed to language too late in life to ever fully learn it? Psychologists have much to say about such questions, as this chapter will show. Although much remains to be learned, Genie has contributed greatly to efforts at understanding language and its origins.

For reasons that will soon become apparent, this chapter is about language and thought. Before addressing these issues, though, we need to define some terms. First, we can define **language** as an arbitrary system of symbols that allows individuals to understand and communicate an infinite variety of messages (Brown, 1965). Language is more than just communication, though. Most animals, whether birds or honeybees, have some type of signaling communication system (Wilson, 1972). Language can be distinguished from this kind of communication in that it is used creatively. We learn to arrange the sounds of our language in numerous and varied ways to form an infinite variety of distinctive messages.

It will become evident as we progress that language is closely related to other mental processes, such as thinking and problem solving. In fact, it has been said that "language is the basic tool with which humans think" (Ellis, 1972, p. 172). There is no higher-level human function than the mental activity we call thinking. We can define **thinking** as an inherent ability to mentally manipulate symbols and concepts in order to organize information, make plans, solve problems, and make decisions.

We begin this chapter with a consideration of how language develops, how it is acquired, and how it is related to thought processes. We then address the process called thinking by focusing on concept learning, problem solving, and some of the difficulties faced in each.

— LANGUAGE —

The Development of Language

First, we will describe how language is acquired; we will follow the description with theories of language acquisition. Language development, which seems to follow the same sequence in all cultures, occurs in three basic stages: the prelinguistic stage, the first-words stage, and the first-sentences stage (Bee & Mitchell, 1980).

— The Prelinguistic Stage: The Emergence of Phonemes

Encompassing approximately the first 10 to 12 months of life, when language skills do not yet exist, is the **prelinguistic stage.** Development in this stage progresses through phases of crying, cooing, and babbling.

An infant's essential first task is to learn the specific sounds of the language. The basic sounds of any language are known as **phonemes.** Humans can produce about 100 distinguishable phonemes. Languages vary greatly in the number of phonemes used, but no language uses all the phonemes that humans can utter. English uses about 45 phonemes, which correspond roughly to the letters of the alphabet. Sounds produced by certain letter combinations, such as *sh* and *th,* are also phonemes. Most phonemes have no meaning by themselves. They must be combined with other phonemes to make a meaningful unit—something that occurs in the next stage of language development.

Not until about a month of age does the infant begin to make sounds other than crying, sneezing, and coughing. The most common first language sound is a vowellike cooing, in which the /u/ phoneme occurs frequently (Santrock, 1983). At about 6 months of age,

the infant begins using more varied sounds, including such consonants as *b* and *d.* The unsystematic use of a wide variety of speechlike sounds is known as **babbling.** Babbling infants often produce repetitious strings of alternating vowels and consonants, such as "babababa." Rather than attempted communication, babbling appears to be a type of vocal play (Clarke-Stewart & Koch, 1983). The beginning of something like speech is apparent, however, in the baby's use of changing pitch patterns and speechlike rhythms (Bee & Mitchell, 1980).

Interestingly, babbling may have no direct relationship to the child's acquisition of words and sentences (McNeill, 1970). Supportive of this is the fact that babbling includes many sounds that adults do not make. Early in the babbling phase, infants tend to utter almost every phoneme (Dworetzky, 1981). But by the end of the phase, they mainly use only phonemes of their native language. Through listening to the speech of those around them, infants gradually learn and imitate the phonemes they hear. It is also true, however, that babies of deaf parents go through the same sequence of early vocalization development as do babies of hearing parents, even though they are rarely exposed to language (Lenneberg, 1967). Furthermore, all babies seem to begin babbling at about the same age (Dworetzky, 1981). In sum, the evidence suggests that experience and learning play no role in the emergence of babbling. It is, instead, a maturational development.

Even though young children show early evidence of distinguishing between phonemes, their ability to articulate some phonemes may lag behind their recognition of them (Kuczaj, 1983). The following example illustrates the point (cf. Alexander, Roodin, & Gorman, 1980):

When Erika was three, she pronounced her name "Ewika." If someone repeated "Ewika?," she would protest, "No, Ewika!" "Is it Erika, then?" "Yes, you siwwy, Ewika!" (Glucksberg & Danks, 1975, pp. 125–126)

Erika substituted a sound she could pronounce for several she couldn't. Also, she could detect differences in the sounds of spoken phonemes even though she couldn't pronounce those differences herself.

— The First-Words Stage: The Emergence of Morphemes

An exciting time for parents is when their child says the first words, typically between 12 and 18 months of age. It is particularly delightful when the words refer to mother or father, as they often do. With these first words, the child systematically joins phonemes to express meaning. In linguistic terminology, the child begins to utter **morphemes,** the smallest meaningful units in a language. Most, but not all, morphemes are words. They may also be prefixes (e.g., *un, non,* and *ex*) and suffixes (e.g., *ed, ly,* and *ing*). Learning all the morphemes and how to use them correctly takes place gradually over a period of years.

Much research has focused on the words children first use. In addition to designations for mother and father, children first seem to learn words that refer to or name something (Nelson, 1973). Typically, the words relate to such things as food, toys, body parts, animals, and household items. Such early words might include *ball, milk,* and *doggie.* Most of the early words are concrete nouns and verbs (Moskowitz, 1978). Least common are words having only a grammatical function, such as *what, where,* and *if.*

The single-word phase of the first-word stage is also referred to as the *holophrastic stage.* Such a label signifies that the child's single words often communicate an entire idea, thought, or sentence. When this is the case, the words are known as **holophrases.** *Papa* may mean "Papa is home from work!" or it may mean "Papa is in the bathroom." At this stage, the child has not yet learned to combine words into sentences. But to more fully communicate, the child combines words with facial expressions, gestures, and tone of voice. Listeners, in turn, use these cues, in combination with context, to understand what the child means. This provides a good illustration of how children can understand much more than they can speak (Clark & Hecht, 1983).

The young child's vocabulary growth is slow at first.

The average age for achieving the first 10 words is about 15 months. But after this period, there is a rapid gain in vocabulary development (Nelson, 1973). Nelson reported an average age of about 19 months for achieving a 50-word vocabulary, an acquisition rate of about 11 new words per month. Beyond the first 50 words, vocabulary development seems to be very rapid, as evidenced in a study conducted in 1926 by Smith (cited in Bee & Mitchell, 1980). Figure 8–1 shows the rate of vocabulary growth found in that study for the first 3 years of life. As we can see, a very large rise in vocabulary development occurs between the ages of 18 months and 2 years. Vocabulary growth continues to be rapid thereafter.

Another good example of gradual language acquisition is the development of rules governing pluralization. Berko (1958) studied this aspect of morphology with children aged 4 to 7. The children were shown pictures of objects and were given names describing the objects. Some of the names were nonsense words. Figure 8–2 gives an example involving the nonsense name *wug.* When children had to give the plural of *wug,* they had no difficulty answering *wugs.* In general, they could correctly pluralize nonsense names as long as the sound required was either /s/ (as in book*s*) or /z/ (as in gun*s* or wug*s*) (Alexander, Roodin, & Gorman, 1980). They did have trouble, though, in correctly applying the /əz/ sound (as in glass*es*). It appears that by age 4 children have mastered the first two plurali-

Figure 8–1.

The increase in vocabulary size during the first 3 years of life. (Based on data from Smith, 1926; adapted from Bee & Mitchell, 1980, p. 254.)

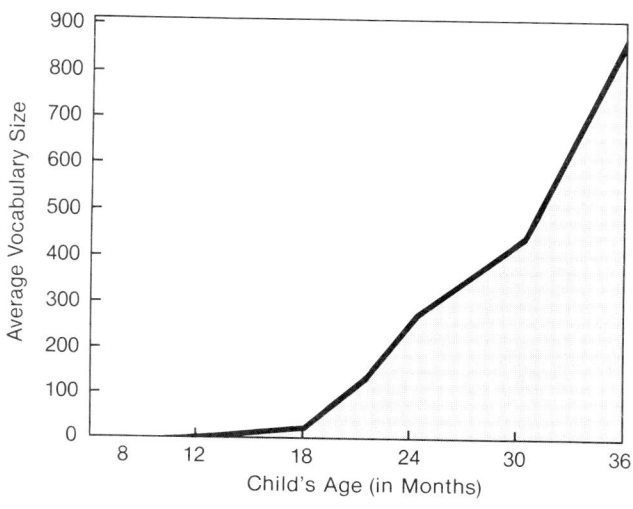

THIS IS A WUG.

NOW THERE IS ANOTHER ONE.
THERE ARE TWO OF THEM.
THERE ARE TWO _____.

Figure 8–2.
In Berko's (1958) study of language rule acquisition, children were presented tasks such as this one. The "wugs" example was part of the test for acquisition of the rules governing pluralization. (From Berko, 1958, p. 154.)

zation rules, but not until about age 8 do they master the third rule (Alexander, Roodin, & Gorman, 1980).

— The First-Sentences Stage: The Emergence of Syntax

A particularly important stage in developing adultlike speech is the stage when the child is able to combine words into sentences. At about 20 months of age, the child begins putting words together in an orderly fashion (Alexander, Roodin, & Gorman, 1980). (Compare this to how long it took Genie, in the chapter introduction, to form her first word pairs.) Gradually, the child begins using increasingly longer and more complex sentences. In doing so, the child begins to demonstrate a knowledge of **syntax,** the rules for combining words into sentences. Rules of syntax, in conjunction with rules relating to phonemes and morphemes, are called **grammar.**

The child's earliest sentences are short and simple, typically including only two or three words (Bee & Mitchell, 1980). Whatever is needed to convey meaning—mainly nouns and verbs—is used, but less informative words, such as articles, auxiliary verbs, conjunctions, and prepositions, are all missing. Also deleted are the less critical grammatical markers, such as *s* for plural, *ed* or *ing* for verb endings, and the possessive markers. These markers, which are added to words to

change their meaning, are called **inflections.** Along with the small, less informative words just described, they constitute **grammatical morphemes.** The child's sentences at this stage are often referred to as **telegraphic speech** (Brown, 1973) because the child talks in the kind of shorthand used in telegrams. Even the child's imitation of speech is telegraphic.

The following conversation between a 2-year-old and her mother illustrates telegraphic sentences. The sentences on the right show the morphemes missing in the child's telegraphic speech.

JOCELYN: Where Papa? (Where *is* Papa?)
MOTHER: Papa's at work.
JOCELYN: Papa work? (Papa *is at* work?)
MOTHER: Yes, he's over at the office.
JOCELYN: Papa work office. (Papa *is* work*ing at the* office.)

It is important to recognize that, though the child's telegraphic words are simple, their underlying meanings are varied and complex. Even with two-word sentences, the child is able to communicate a variety of relationships. Table 8–1 provides some relevant samples from Slobin (1972).

To understand a child's telegraphic sentences, the context in which the child is speaking must be considered. As indicated by the examples in Table 8–1, the child expresses different meanings with exactly the

Table 8–1
The types of relationships described by children's telegraphic sentences (left) and examples of the telegraphic sentences (right). (From Slobin, 1972, p. 73.)

RELATIONSHIP	SENTENCE
Identification	See doggie.
Location	Book there.
Repetition	More milk.
Nonexistence	Allgone thing.
Negation	Not wolf.
Possession	My candy.
Attribution	Big car.
Agent-action	Mama walk.
Agent-object	Mama book (meaning "Mama read book").
Action-location	Sit chair.
Action–direct object	Hit you.
Action–indirect object	Give papa.
Action–instrument	Cut knife.
Question	Where ball?

same form of word construction. But in different contexts, the same word combination can mean different things. A young child studied by Bloom (1973) said "Mommy sock" on two distinct occasions—once when she found her mother's sock and once when she was being dressed by her mother. So the same words conveyed *possession* ("Mommy's sock") and an *agent-object* relationship ("Mommy is putting on the sock").

The absence of various grammatical morphemes generally continues for up to about a year. Once the morphemes appear, the child over the next several years gradually moves closer to adultlike sentences. There appears to be an order in which grammatical morphemes are added (de Villiers & de Villiers, 1973). For example, plurals and the prepositions *in* and *on* seem to emerge very early; irregular verbs (such as *went* and *fell*) occur somewhat later; and articles (*a* and *the*), possessives (*'s*), and auxiliary verbs (*am, is, be,* etc.) occur even later, and in the order given here.

One of the most interesting phenomena to occur at this stage in the child's language development is known as **overregularization**—the tendency for children to take grammatical rules they have discovered and inappropriately generalize them to instances where they do not apply. For example, a child might discover the rule of adding *ed* to form a past tense and might overregularize by saying "Daddy *goed*" instead of "Daddy *went*." The 3- or 4-year-old child seems especially likely to exhibit this type of overregularization. As Kuczaj (1978) discovered, 5- and 6-year-olds are less likely to make this particular error. Interestingly, though, they begin to exhibit a different type of overregularization—adding *ed* to the past tense of irregular verbs, for example: *wented, maded,* and *ated.* By the age of 7, this tendency has disappeared in most children. Yet another type of overregularization displayed by young children is evident in plurals, such as *mans* or *foots.* As Dworetzky (1981) points out, overregularization errors do not suggest that the child is regressing. Rather, they demonstrate how rapidly children acquire the general rules of grammar. The exceptions to the rules are learned a little later.

More on syntax.   We have indicated that the child demonstrates a knowledge of syntax in constructing sentences. But what exactly does the child learn? For one thing, the child learns rules governing the construction and interrelationships of phrases within the sentences. For example, three rules seem to be used repeatedly in understanding and creating sentences (Miller, 1981):

– *Rule 1:* A sentence consists of a noun phrase plus a verb phrase.
– *Rule 2:* A noun phrase consists of an article plus a noun.
– *Rule 3:* A verb phrase consists of a verb plus a noun phrase.

Numerous sentences could be constructed with these three rules. A description of a sentence in terms of such rules is called a *phrase structure.* Using the rules, Figure 8–3 shows the phrase structure of the sentence "The dog ate a bone."

The three rules described here are only a small fraction of all the rules needed for a complete syntax. Generating a complete set of rules is theoretically possible, but it has yet to be done (Miller, 1981). Even if all such rules have not been recorded, language users nevertheless employ the rules every day in writing and speaking.

The most fundamental rule in constructing sentences seems to be that a verb phrase follows a noun phrase. The importance of this rule is illustrated when the rule is violated. For example, "Ate a bone the dog" is not an acceptable sentence and is not as easy to comprehend as a grammatically correct sentence. The fact that we have a syntax, and that most of us follow it, is what allows us to communicate with one another. However, a simple list of phrase structure rules would not explain everything we know about creating and understanding sentences. We also seem to recognize

Figure 8–3.

The phrase structure for the sentence "The dog ate a bone."

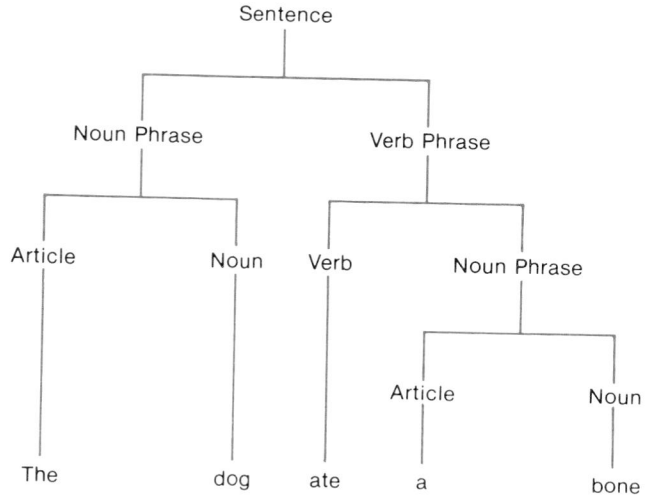

that the same underlying meaning can be expressed in many different sentence forms. Noam Chomsky (1957, 1965) has made just such a point by distinguishing between surface structure and deep structure.

The **surface structure** of a sentence refers to the actual words and their organization within that sentence. The **deep structure,** on the other hand, refers to the underlying meaning of the sentence, or what the speaker intends to convey. In Chomsky's terms, a single deep structure can be expressed by many different surface structures. "The boy caught the ball" and "The ball was caught by the boy" express the same deep structure with different surface structures.

Chomsky suggests that we learn syntactic rules, called **transformation rules,** which explain how a single underlying meaning can be expressed in different surface forms. Such rules show how we can take a basic idea and express it in a passive or active sentence, a question, a negative statement, and so on. The importance of transformation rules, then, lies in the fact that they specify how various types of sentences are related to one another despite their differing phrase structures.

Ambiguous sentences are sentences that have more than one plausible deep structure. The sentence "They are flying planes" could be about planes or about people; within this single surface structure, there are two possible deep structures. Even with such ambiguities, however, we are usually able to discover the deep structures. This suggests that in comprehending language, we do much more than just interpret words and their grammatical relationships; we also use context as a cue to aid comprehension (Reed, 1982).

A final note on syntax. Although people are generally aware that syntactic rules exist, they typically cannot specify them (Howard, 1983). Most of us know when we hear bad grammar or improper English, which suggests that we do know something about the rules of grammar. If you heard someone say "Went we today work to," you'd know right away that something was wrong. Psychologists realize, though, that one's *competence* to identify grammatically correct sentences may differ from one's everyday *performance* in speaking and writing. We may have competence, but we do not always use it.

Theories of Language Acquisition

We are now ready to examine the whys of language development. Why do young children learn to speak?

Several theories have been offered by psychologists and linguists (those who study language). Debate over the issue has been intense.

Social Learning Theory: The Role of Imitation

Social learning theorists such as Bandura (1977) argue that *imitation* (see Chapter 6) plays a primary role in language acquisition. Bandura believes that not only is a child's vocabulary learned through imitation, so are the more complex grammatical rules. Critics contend, however, that imitation cannot adequately account for a child's creative constructions such as "all-gone sticky" or "I maded a house." It is argued that such constructions are not products of observational learning. Critics of the social learning approach also note that even when adult models supply young children with appropriate grammatical sentences, the children's imitations of those sentences represent conversions to much simpler grammatical forms. All in all, then, many language theorists believe that while imitation helps explain some aspects of language such as vocabulary learning, it does not account for the complex aspects of language, such as the development of grammar.

Reinforcement Theory

The *reinforcement* (see chapter 6) explanation of language acquisition holds that adults shape the child's language by giving and withholding reinforcement. According to Skinner (1957), the child who utters the "correct" sound, word, or sentence is reinforced. Also, adults presumably require ever-closer approximations to correct, adultlike speech before giving reinforcement. Theoretically, then, the child is gradually pressured to learn adultlike speech in order to obtain reinforcement.

Does this describe what adults do? Do they use reinforcement in shaping a child's language? As with imitation, it is difficult to deny that reinforcement plays at least some role in language acquisition (Schell & Hall, 1983). A child probably learns many words by receiving some type of reinforcement, such as approval or attention, for uttering those words. In many cases, a word is reinforced by some tangible reward—as when the child says "water" and then receives a drink of water. Learning a language, though, involves much more than just learning single words; as we have seen, it also involves learning rules for generating novel sentences.

Here, it seems, reinforcement theory has not fared well in explaining the development of language.

If reinforcement theory truly provided a valid explanation of grammar acquisition, we would find that parents reward their children when grammatical sentences are uttered but withhold rewards otherwise. As Bandura (1977a) notes, however, "adults are more inclined to approve the factual accuracy than the grammatical correctness of children's utterances" (p. 174). In other words, children do not appear to be significantly pressured by their parents to improve sentence quality. Whether a child's utterance gets reinforced seems to have little to do with whether that utterance was well-formed (Foss & Hakes, 1978). An additional argument against reinforcement theory is that language acquisition occurs too rapidly to be accounted for by reinforcement principles (Bandura, 1977a). Finally, critics have suggested that reinforcement, like imitation, cannot account for the creative nature of early language nor can it account for the regular sequence in which language develops regardless of culture (Lerner & Hultsch, 1983). In sum, reinforcement theory does not successfully explain the complex aspects of language development.

— Innate Theory

Given the inadequacy of the social learning and reinforcement theories of language development, many psychologists and linguists have turned to an innate theory proposed by Chomsky (1957, 1965). Chomsky's **innateness hypothesis** suggests that children have a genetic potential for creating and understanding language—a "language acquisition device" that contains the basic elements or structures of language. Recall Chomsky's distinction between surface and deep structures and the idea of transformation rules. According to Chomsky, children are innately equipped to focus on transformations in order to learn the rules for changing deep structure into various surface structures.

Several lines of evidence make the innate language acquisition device plausible (Bee & Mitchell, 1980). First, the brain must be sufficiently developed for language to emerge. This suggests the importance of biological maturation in language development. Second, children the world over seem to go through similar early grammatical stages. This suggests a common biological mechanism for language learning. Third, linguists have found that all languages share a number of important features—a division between nouns and

verbs, a way of expressing the negative, and so on. Chomsky believes that the human brain is programmed to enable a person hearing language sounds to sort those sounds into various categories, such as words, questions, and negatives, and then to apply a system of rules to the sounds to create totally new sentences. A further support for the innateness hypothesis is that congenitally deaf children who have not been exposed to any adults using sign language appear to begin creating sign language on their own (Goldin-Meadow & Feldman, 1977).

If there is indeed an innate language acquisition device that begins to take effect once the brain is sufficiently developed, it might be that there is a *critical period* for language development (see chapter 11). Lenneberg (1967) has suggested that such a critical period does indeed exist. He has argued that from a physiological point of view, the optimal time for language learning is about ages 2 to 12. Furthermore, the earlier in this period that language is learned, the easier the learning presumably is. After this period, learning a first language is thought to be extremely difficult or impossible (see Colombo, 1982). Genie's language handicap (see chapter introduction) provides convincing evidence for a critical period in language development and lends support to innate theory.

From the perspective of innate theory, language learning is not a matter of learning a string of reinforced words. To the contrary, it is a process of acquiring complex rules of grammar. Gradually, through a process of testing, discarding, and revising ideas regarding appropriate grammatical constructions, the child acquires transformation rules that approximate those of the adult. Because the emphasis is on acquiring rules of grammar, it is easy to see why children's language can be so creative. When children speak, they presumably apply the rules they think are appropriate. As this gradual rule acquisition takes place, then, many creative and novel constructions such as "bye bye not" and "all-gone sticky" inevitably occur.

In sum, although the creative nature of the child's language causes problems for the reinforcement approach as well as the imitation approach, it is easily accounted for by the innateness hypothesis. The research goes on, and so does the debate between theorists of each perspective (Moerk, 1983). Perhaps all the theories described here are necessary to fully account for language development. Nevertheless, with respect to children's development of grammar, it is reasonable to conclude, at least for the present, that the innate theory is better supported than either the social learning or reinforcement theory.

Language and Chimpanzees

The intriguing idea of being able to talk to animals has launched numerous efforts to teach animals language. Chimpanzees have been the most frequent subjects of these efforts. The earliest studies attempted to teach chimpanzees to speak as humans do (Kellogg & Kellogg, 1933; Hayes & Hayes, 1951). Even with extensive training, however, the chimps were unable to talk. (See Benjamin & Bruce, 1982, for a historical overview of the Kelloggs' work.)

In the 1960s, Gardner and Gardner (1969) renewed efforts to teach language to chimps. Apes, they reasoned, may not have the vocal apparatus necessary for speech. But chimps do use their hands a great deal. The Gardners therefore wondered if chimps could learn a nonvocal language, such as American Sign Language (ASL)—a language of the deaf used extensively in North America. In 1966, the Gardners began to teach ASL to a female chimp named Washoe (see Figure 8–4).

Washoe was an impressive student. After 21 months of training, she had learned 34 signs. Her vocabulary eventually expanded to more than 160 signs (Fouts & Rigby, 1977). Washoe was not limited to using signs just for individual words; she also learned to construct simple sentences—many of which she presumably invented on her own. For example, when she wanted to

be tickled, she signed "gimme tickle." When she wanted the refrigerator opened, she signed "open food drink." (Her teachers, incidentally, had used the signs "cold" and "box" when referring to the refrigerator.) Washoe even used ASL to "swear" at other animals. She once called a rhesus money a "dirty monkey" (Fouts & Rigby, 1977).

Instead of using ASL, the Premacks (e.g., Premack, 1971; Premack & Premack, 1972) developed a system whereby words, in the form of colored plastic shapes, are attached to a magnetic board. One of the Premacks' chimps, Sarah, mastered more than 100 such "words." Sarah communicates in sentences by arranging the symbols on the magnetic board. Lana, a chimp studied by Rumbaugh (1977), "types" sentences by pushing various buttons on a computerlike keyboard. Each of the buttons represents a different word. Research by Patterson (e.g., 1978) with a female gorilla named Koko suggests that this species may be even more efficient than chimps in using sign language. Koko has mastered nearly 400 signs, can create sentences, and, like Washoe, often appears to create novel phrases.

Although the evidence to date seems to suggest that apes can create at least simple humanlike sentences, not all researchers are convinced. After studying Nim Chimsky, a chimp named after linguist Noam Chomsky, Terrace and his colleagues at Columbia University concluded that apes use signs merely to get rewards (Terrace, 1979; Terrace, Petitto, Sanders, & Bever, 1979). In

Figure 8–4.
Washoe signing.

other words, the chimps simply may be conditioned to make certain signs, without any awareness of what they mean.

At present, Terrace agrees that apes can acquire a large vocabulary. However, he believes that they are incapable of creating genuine sentences. What may appear to be original, creative sentences may only be imitations of signs made by the human trainer. In the future, the possibility of imitation must be ruled out if one wants to conclude that chimps can, in fact, construct their own sentences. Although Terrace accepts that chimps may turn out to be capable of using language, he currently considers language a uniquely human phenomenon. He is not alone in taking this position. (See, for example, Sebeok & Umiker-Sebeok, 1979.)

Research on language-learning chimpanzees continues, as does the controversy (Rubinstein & Slife, 1982). Whether language separates humans from other species remains to be definitively demonstrated.

Relationship between Language and Thought

The Arabic language includes numerous words for camel; in English, there is only one. The Eskimos have many words for different types of snow; in English, snow is snow. The Hanunoo people in the Philippine Islands have 92 different words to describe varieties of rice. Given such differences in language, psychologists and linguists have long wondered whether language affects how we perceive and think (Bourne, Dominowski, & Loftus, 1979). Does the Arab villager perceive differences among camels that English-speaking people cannot see? To what extent, if any, does language control perception and understanding of the world around us?

— Linguistic Relativity

That language does indeed affect how we think and how we perceive the world is the **linguistic relativity hypothesis** (Whorf, 1956). Thought is presumed to be relative to the particular language used. To support this view, Whorf observed that languages often have several words to describe phenomena that English describes with a single word. As mentioned, for example, Eskimos use many words to describe different types of snow. Other languages have only one word for snow or just a few. For English-speaking peo-

ple, it doesn't matter if snow is falling, on the ground, slushy, dry, or whatever—it is simply snow. Eskimos have a name for each variety but no single term for snow in general.

Whorf suggested that because Eskimos have more words for describing snow, they are better able to perceive differences in snow than are speakers of languages with fewer categories. Although this argument was once widely accepted, it is now generally believed that vocabulary differences between languages do not necessarily alter how speakers view the world (Bourne, Dominowski, & Loftus, 1979). English-speaking people, in other words, can perceive the same differences in snow that Eskimos can; they just don't need words for each type of snow. Snow is very important to the Eskimos; hence, they have many names for it. The perception of different types of snow came first, followed by the invention of words for each type; the existence of words does not alter perceptions.

Particularly problematic for the linguistic relativity hypothesis is a lack of experimental research support. If Whorf's hypothesis were true, for instance, language differences would alter the perception of colors. Research suggests the contrary, however. For example, Rosch (1974) studied the Dani, a Stone Age agricultural people who live in New Guinea. Unlike the numerous color names used by English-speaking people, the Dani have only two color terms: *mili* for dark and cold hues and *mola* for bright and warm hues. Despite this limitation in category names, Rosch found that the Dani were fully able to perceive differences among all 11 basic colors (black, white, red, yellow, green, blue, brown, purple, pink, orange, and gray). Limited language did not limit their color perception. On balance, research suggests that thinking and perception are not greatly affected by language.

— Other Language and Thought Relationships

Despite evidence against the linguistic relativity hypothesis, some language-thought links do seem to exist. Thinking about a particular topic may not depend on having an appropriate vocabulary, but having such a vocabulary can certainly facilitate thinking and communicating about the subject. Undoubtedly, you can think about baseball without having a large sports vocabulary. But if you do have a good baseball vocabulary, you may notice things during a game that less baseball-wise individuals do not. For example, you may be able to make finer discriminations concerning the game, including such events as a forced out, a suicide squeeze, an infield fly rule, a balk, a wild pitch, a passed ball, a ground-rule double, and a fielder's choice. Having such terms in your vocabulary allows you to better understand the game, think about it, and talk about it with others.

Language also affects problem-solving ability. To the extent we are able to verbalize just exactly what the problem is, finding the solution becomes an easier task. Although language apparently does facilitate thought and problem solving, *spoken language* does not seem to be essential for either. For example, Ellis (1972) notes that deaf children, who are deficient in spoken language, are nevertheless able to understand many concepts. Obviously, many of these children have learned to communicate with symbol systems other than spoken language. Such language systems seem to facilitate their thinking and problem solving much as conventional language does for others.

Yet another way in which language may affect the way we perceive, remember, or think about the world can be seen in studies of verbal labeling. One study showed that labeling affected how ambiguous figures were remembered and reproduced (Carmichael, Hogan, & Walter, 1932). That is, subjects' memories for various figures depended greatly on the labels assigned to the figure. When the figure originally seen was O—O, and was labeled "eyeglasses," subjects' later reproductions tended to look like eyeglasses. If the figure was labeled "dumbbells," the reproductions tended to look like dumbbells. You might also recall from chapter 7 that language can lead people to believe that they have seen or heard things that in fact never existed. In sum, language does seem to play an important role in the way we perceive, remember, and think about the objects and events around us. The exact nature of this relationship, though, does not seem to be quite as Whorf envisioned it.

— Language Disorders: Aphasias

A good way to learn more about the relationship of language to thought is to study **aphasias**—language disorders caused by brain injuries (e.g., from a gunshot wound or a stroke). Aphasia victims are known as *aphasics*. Nearly all aphasias result from injury to the left hemisphere of the brain (Slobin, 1979; see also chapter 2). Two major types of aphasia can be distinguished in part by the location of the brain injury: anterior and posterior.

Anterior aphasia, or **Broca's aphasia,** results from

injury to the anterior, or front, part of the brain. Broca was the man who first reported in the 1860s that language function is localized there. *Broca's area* (see Figure 8–5) is adjacent to a part of the cortex that controls the muscles used in speech. Individuals with Broca's anterior aphasia have difficulty speaking, but they have no difficulty comprehending either spoken or written language. Their speech is halting and labored, and they have difficulty pronouncing words correctly. In addition, Broca's aphasics do not speak grammatically. Their speech is likely to include only the essential words, mostly nouns. There is a loss of syntax, but vocabulary seems to be intact (Slobin, 1979). Even though grammar is disturbed, word order is generally maintained. For this reason, the speech of Broca's aphasics often makes sense. And, as indicated, these aphasics generally do not seem to have difficulty comprehending language. Thus, there is generally no impairment in their abilities to think and reason. This observation suggests that language is not essential for complex thought.

An apparent dissociation between language and thought is evident in the second major type of aphasia as well, but in a different way. *Posterior aphasia,* or **Wernicke's aphasia,** results from injury to the posterior, or back, part of the brain, Wernicke was a German physician who first described and localized it, in

Figure 8–5.

Drawing of brain showing location of Broca's area and Wernicke's area. In generating language, meaningful information from Wernicke's area is transferred through the arcuate fasciculus to Broca's area. There a program for the sequencing of muscle actions necessary for vocalization is evoked. That program is then transferred to the face area of the motor cortex, which activates the appropriate muscles of the mouth, lips, tongue, larynx, and so on to produce the spoken word. (Adapted from Geschwind, 1979, p. 209.)

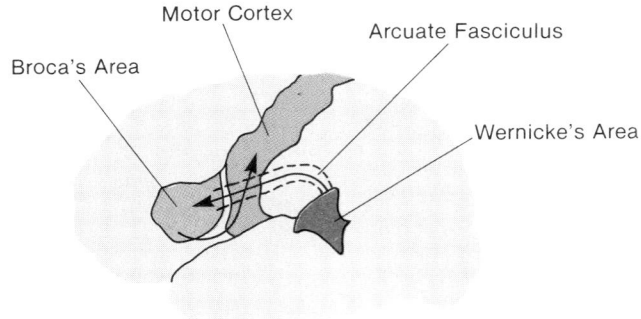

Motor Cortex

Arcuate Fasciculus

Broca's Area

Wernicke's Area

1875, shortly after Broca's discovery. The location of *Wernicke's area* is shown in Figure 8–5.

In patients with Wernicke's aphasia, comprehension of speech is seriously impaired (Slobin, 1979). Such patients do not understand the meaning of words. Unlike Broca's aphasics, their syntax seems intact. These individuals speak rapidly, enunciate clearly, and use correct grammar, but their speech is filled with pronouns and is almost meaningless. As an example, consider the following comment from a patient who was asked to describe a picture showing two boys stealing cookies behind a woman's back: "Mother is away here working her work to get her better, but when she's looking the two boys looking in the other part. She's working another time" (Geschwind, 1979, p. 209).

In contrast to Broca's aphasics, Wernicke's aphasics speak fluently, but their thinking appears to be disturbed. Their language comprehension is impaired; consequently, their thought is also impaired. Together, the two types of aphasias help us realize that even though thought and language are related, there is no necessary link between the two.

An understanding of the aphasias helps us see how the brain produces and understands language. Wernicke's area is responsible for both interpreting incoming information and producing meaningful sentences (Geschwind, 1979). The information is then transferred to Broca's area through a bundle of interconnecting nerve fibers called the *arcuate fasciculus* (see Figure 8–5). Broca's area is responsible for coordinating the particular sequence of muscle actions necessary to produce spoken words.

— APPLICATION —

FACILITATING LANGUAGE DEVELOPMENT IN YOUNG CHILDREN

Even though children do not learn language solely through imitation and reinforcement, parents can still serve as facilitators of language development. Researchers have suggested or discovered a number of useful strategies parents can adopt. They include the following (adapted from Bee & Mitchell, 1980, and Turner & Helms, 1983):

1. *Talk to your children as much as possible.* In their early years, children who are talked to the most develop language the fastest. The more words children hear, the more they have to work with.

2. *Talk with children at their level.* Young children pay more attention to simple speech than to complex speech. Hearing understandable speech allows children to learn the rules of language and use language creatively.

3. *Expand on children's remarks when talking with them.* If a child says "Mommy sock" in reference to ownership, the parent might say, "This is Mommy's sock." In other words, the parent adds all the grammatical elements that are missing in the child's sentence to expand correct language use (Hoff-Ginsberg & Shatz, 1982).

4. *Provide opportunities in which children can actively use verbal skills.* Practicing language is a good way of refining and sharpening it. Have children tell stories. As they learn to read, have them read aloud. In short, give children something to talk about. Ask them questions. Provide them with toys or books or other materials they find interesting and want to talk about.

5. *Be a good speech model for children.* Imitation is not the most important factor in language development, but children can nevertheless learn some things through imitation. Do not speak too fast. Enunciate words correctly. If you don't want "ain't" to be a part of the child's vocabulary, don't use that word in the child's presence. Children often utter cute mispronunciations or create cute sentences. Resist the temptation to use the same errors when replying to the child.

6. *Encourage good listening and attention skills.* Children will not improve their articulation skills, even with a good speech model, if they don't listen effectively. To help sharpen children's listening skills, engage them in games in which they must attend to the sounds around them.

7. *Encourage words as a substitute for action.* Sometimes words speak louder than action. When a child is physically trying to take a toy away from a playmate, say to the child, "Ask her if you can play with the toy

for a while, and maybe she will give it to you." Substituting words for actions can help children develop self-expression.

8. *Do not criticize children's words or inexact terminology.* There is nothing wrong with correcting children's speech errors, but avoid being critical. Remember that language acquisition is a complex task and that children will make many errors along the way. Be a facilitator, not a squelcher.

THOUGHT

All humans think. Even though thinking is a covert activity, we become aware of it by witnessing what people say and do. From such observations it has been suggested that thinking encompasses at least three broad categories of mental, or cognitive, activity: concept formation, problem solving, and decision making (Ellis, Bennett, Daniel, & Rickert, 1979). In forming concepts, we collect, categorize, and organize information. This allows efficient use of information to achieve a goal or solve a problem. After information is organized and possible problem solutions are identified, a course of action must be decided on. In the following section, we will describe concept formation and problem solving. Although we will not formally discuss decision making, its importance as a component of thinking will become evident.

Concept Formation

A **concept** is a verbal or nonverbal symbol representing a class or group of objects or events having common properties (Houston, 1981). Each time you see a dog, you do not have to view it as completely unique and in a category by itself. That's because you have learned the concept *dog. Dog* is a concept because it stands for a large number of objects, each of which has a number of characteristics in common with all the others (Houston, 1981). *House, building,* and *magazine* are also concepts for the same reason. In fact, given the definition of a concept, it is clear that most words stand for concepts; however, not all concepts are associated with words. Young children, for example, can possess the concept *dog* or *adult* before knowing the appropriate word. Thus, concepts can be nonverbal as well as verbal.

Concepts lend a certain sense of stability and regularity to our interactions with our environment (Ellis, 1972). With concepts, the world is not a random collection of unrelated items that must be responded to as if each were totally novel and unique. Having knowledge organized into categories also aids memory (see chapter 7). It can be said, then, that concepts "are a fundamental aspect of our knowledge, and they constitute the cornerstone of many of our cognitive activities" (Wessells, 1982, p. 198).

By forming concepts, we are able to apply general rules to specific situations. Our knowledge of the concept *professor* or *minister* guides our behavior in the presence of a person fitting the category. Our knowledge of the concept *poisonous snakes* allows us to avoid several types of dangerous snakes. In part, then, concept formation is a process of generalizing a response across similar stimuli (see chapter 6). There is an obvious advantage in discriminating between groups of stimuli: "If we failed to distinguish between wolves and sheep, between pastors and criminals, or between food preservatives and poisons, we would probably not live to tell about it" (Wessells, 1982, p. 199).

Of particular relevance in studying concept learning is the notion that concepts have two critical features—attributes and rules (Ellis, 1972). *Attributes* are features of stimuli that are relevant to the concept. Whiteness is the relevant attribute for the concept *white;* roundness is the relevant attribute for the concept *circle.* Simple concepts, such as *circle,* may be defined by the value of one dimension (e.g., roundness).

Psychologists believe that individuals learn concepts by a process of *hypothesis testing,* wherein they make guesses as to what the relevant attribute is. Given a number of choices, an individual may try an irrelevant hypothesis that leads to an incorrect response. Upon doing so, the individual may sample a new hypothesis, continuing until one leads to continuous correct responding (Tumblin & Gholson, 1981). Try your hand at discovering the relevant attribute in the concept-learning task shown in Figure 8–6. What you see there

		Answers
1.	☺	Yes
2.	☺	Yes
3.	☹	No
4.	☺	No
5.	☹	No
6.	☹	Yes
7.	☺	No
8.	☹	Yes

Figure 8–6.

Study these faces one by one until you think you have figured out what the concept is. Each face may or may not be an example of the concept. If it is, the answer indicated next to the face is yes. There is one relevant attribute that describes the concept in question. Other attributes, which are not related to the particular concept, are irrelevant. You must ignore them if you are to learn the concept. Check the bottom of page 208 for the answer. (From Matlin, 1983, p. 180.)

is a simplified version of the type of task psychologists use in studying concept learning.

In everyday life, concept learning is typically more complicated than the examples thus far described. Many concepts—such as *living things, justice, patience, freedom, integrity, animals,* and *economy cars*—have more than one dimension. In learning the concept *sports car,* for example, we would have to consider the dimensions of speed, handling, and style (Houston, 1981). Multidimensional concept learning is basically rule learning (Bourne, 1970). That is, attributes can be combined to define a conceptual rule. When you have learned the rule, you have learned the concept, and generalization is possible. For example, having learned the rule that the concept *sports car* is defined by a car being fast and stylish and having good handling, you

can quickly and accurately decide whether any particular car is, in fact, a sports car (Houston, 1981).

There are actually a number of rules for combining conceptual attributes (Haygood & Bourne, 1965). One, the **conjunctive rule,** is based on *and* relationships. It states that both Attribute A and Attribute B must be present to define the concept. For example, the concept *good quality* can be defined only if both material and workmanship are first class (Neisser & Weene, 1962). Conjunctive rules can also apply to more than two dimensions. A conjunctive rule for the sports-car concept would be any car that is fast and has good handling and is stylish. A **disjunctive rule** uses the logical relation *or*; it states that a concept is defined if either Attribute A or Attribute B is present. The concept *person,* for example, is defined by either a male or a female. (We will soon return to the issue of rules to examine an alternate approach to learning complex concepts.)

As might be judged from some of the examples of complex concepts, not all concepts are precise and well defined. To the contrary, many—such as *integrity, freedom,* and *cancer-causing substances*—may be quite vague (Wessells, 1982). However, we repeatedly refine these concepts as we gain more experience and new knowledge. Consider the concept *bird,* for example. For some people, the concept may be defined primarily by the attribute *can fly.* But for those more knowledgeable about birds, *can fly* is an irrelevant attribute. Not all birds fly (e.g., penguins), and some animals that fly (e.g., bats) are not birds. The process of refining concepts through increased experience and knowledge describes what happens during formal education. The importance of developing concepts, of course, is that such learning directly affects our ability to think about particular topics and communicate with others about them.

With this background, let's now consider some of the factors that influence concept learning.

— Factors Affecting Concept Formation

One factor important in concept learning is the types of examples or instances of the concept to which we are exposed. These examples can be either *positive* (actual instances or examples of the concept) or *negative* (not instances of the concept). Ellis (1972) concludes that in everyday life we are more likely to encounter positive instances of a concept. We are therefore more accustomed to such instances, tend to prefer them, and actually learn faster from them than from negative instances (Wessells, 1982).

Another element of concept learning is *relevant versus irrelevant attributes*. As the number of irrelevant attributes in a conceptual task increases, so does the difficulty of the task. Clearly, it is more difficult for the learner to discover what the relevant feature is when many irrelevant cues must be ignored. A young child, after learning to identify a particular animal as a dog, may start referring to all four-legged animals as dogs (Clark & Clark, 1977). Learning the concept *dog* is made difficult by the fact that numerous irrelevant features associated with dogs must be ignored, including the dog's having four legs, a tail, and the ability to bite. In contrast to dealing with the concept *dog,* it should be much easier for the child to discover the relevant attribute of the concept *ball,* because there are fewer irrelevant attributes, such as color and size, associated with it.

A third important factor is the *abstractness versus concreteness* of a concept. Young children have more difficulty learning abstract concepts, such as *circle* or *rectangle,* than they do learning concrete concepts, such as *house* or *dog.* Finally, conceptual rules also affect the ease of concept learning (Bourne, 1970). Concepts described by the conjunctive rule, described earlier, are the easiest to learn, followed by concepts described by the disjunctive rule.

The most difficult concepts to learn, and the least common in everyday life, are **relational concepts.** With such concepts, classification is based on how an object is related to something else on some attribute dimension (such as location or size) rather than on the basis of the presence or absence of the attribute. Two of the concepts many kindergartners learn, *left* and *right,* are relational. *Large* and *small* and *north* and *south* are also relational concepts.

As Houston (1981) observed, some concepts are more perceptual than logical or rule-bound. It may be that in such cases, rather than learning a verbal rule to define the concept, we form some sort of internal picture, or *prototype,* of the concept (Rosch, 1978). For example, you may have a triangle prototype. Whenever you encounter a given pattern, you can decide if it is a triangle by comparing its shape to your internal image of what an ideal triangle looks like. Houston (1981) suggests that many concepts—for example, *chicken*—are better defined by prototypes than by logical rules. In deciding whether a strange bird is a chicken, you would probably compare its overall appearance with your prototype of a chicken. You would not think of logical rules that define chickenness and base your decision on those rules.

Although we do use prototypes, at the same time we also can use logical rules to render decision making more efficient. A chicken prototype may allow us to decide, in most cases, whether a bird is in fact a chicken. But we might also be using a logical rule such as "chickens usually have red wattles, but not always" (Houston, 1981). Using such a rule will help reconcile any difference between our ideal prototype and the particular bird we are considering. We might employ the same strategy in judging whether a particular plant is poison ivy. On the one hand, our poison ivy prototype helps us make this decision, but we may also have to rely on conceptual rules in order to make a definite decision. In other words, we will have to remember that (1) "a poison ivy vine has three-leaf clusters," (2) "each leaf is pointed and has toothed edges," and (3) "the stems for the three leaves are red at the base" (Moates & Schumacher, 1980, p. 209).

— Applying Principles of Concept Formation

As indicated, acquiring and refining concepts is a continuing process especially relevant to formal learning. How might we improve concept learning in the classroom? Ellis (1972) has a few suggestions. He suggests, for example, that for you to fully understand a concept (e.g., *classical conditioning*), you must think of extra examples of the concept, beyond those offered by the instructor. Doing so will help sharpen and refine the concept. It will also give you practice in retrieving information, which will be important at examination time. The problem in basing understanding on only one example is that you may be attending to some nonessential feature of the concept. The best thing to do is to try to select examples that cover the entire range of the concept. This will help ensure that you consider all of its relevant features.

Highlighting the relevant features of concepts is, of course, an important task for teachers. The essential features of a concept need to be made more distinctive than the irrelevant features (Ellis, 1972). You can accomplish this task yourself by verbalizing the important features of concepts. That is, try to define the concept in your own words. You can also highlight relevant attributes by considering both positive and negative instances of the concept (e.g., by comparing

---

The concept in Figure 8–6 is *rounded eyebrows.*

examples of classical conditioning to examples of operant conditioning). By comparing the instances, you will appreciate the relevant features more than if you concentrate only on positive examples.

Problem Solving

Life seems to present a never-ending succession of problems to be solved. The problems vary, of course, in difficulty and importance. All problems present us with the same basic task, however—that of discovering how to achieve some goal. While some problems require considerable mental effort, in many cases, problem-solving efforts amount to searching memory for solutions that have been effective in the past for similar problems. As we will see later, though, habitual solution strategies may inhibit problem solving in situations requiring a new or fresh approach.

Table 8–2 offers some examples of the types of tasks often used in studying problem solving in the laboratory (Bourne, Dominowski, & Loftus, 1979). As you try to solve them, evaluate the steps you are taking in light of the following discussion. Table 8–3 and Figure 8–7 give the solutions to the problems in Table 8–2.

— Stages of Problem Solving

Psychologists find it useful to view problem solving as a series of definable stages: preparation, production, and judgment (or evaluation) (Bourne, Dominowski, & Loftus, 1979). We will also consider an additional phase of the problem-solving process known as incubation. While incubation is not a necessary part of problem solving, it is believed to often be an important one.

Preparation. During the preparation stage, we study a problem and arrive at some understanding or interpretation of it. It can help considerably when problems can be solved with already existing solution methods. Research shows, for example, that experts solve problems much more efficiently when this is the case (Larkin, McDermott, Simon, & Simon, 1980). How much time and effort are devoted to the preparation stage depends greatly, then, on both the type of problem and the problem solver. An expert at solving a particular type of problem will generally spend much less time in this stage than will a novice.

It is important to recognize that the ease of finding

Table 8–2

Some examples of tasks used in studying problem solving. From Bourne/Dominowski/Loftus, COGNITIVE PROCESSES, © 1979, p. 233. Adapted by permission of Prentice-Hall, Inc., Englewood Cliffs, NJ.

---

1. ANAGRAMS
Rearrange the letters in each set to make an English word:

> EFCTA
> IAENV
> BODUT
> LIVAN
> IKCTH

2. MATCHING PROBLEM
Sitting at a bar, from left to right, are George, Bill, Tom, and Jack. Based on the information below, figure out who owns the Cadillac.
a. George has a blue shirt.
b. The man with a red shirt owns a VW.
c. Jack owns a Buick.
d. Tom is next to the man with a green shirt.
e. Bill is next to the man who owns a Cadillac.
f. The man with a white shirt is next to the Buick owner.
g. The Ford owner is furthest away from the Buick owner.

3. HOBBITS AND ORCS
Three hobbits and three orcs stand on one side of a river. On their side of the river is a boat which will hold up to two creatures. The problem is to transport all six creatures to the other side of the river. However, if orcs ever outnumber hobbits, orcs will eat the hobbits. How should they get across?

4. TWO-STRING PROBLEM
Two strings hang from the ceiling in a large, bare room. The strings are too far apart to allow a person to hold one and walk to the other. On the floor are a book of matches, a small screwdriver, and a few pieces of cotton. How could the strings be tied together?

5. PYRAMID PUZZLE
Place a piece of paper on a table and draw three circles on it, labeling them A, B, and C. On Circle A stack four coins—from top to bottom, dime, penny, nickel, quarter. The task: Moving only one coin at a time, moving only the top coin in any stack, and moving a coin only from one circle to another, get the coins stacked in exactly the same way on Circle C. Important restriction: A coin may never be stacked on top of a smaller coin (e.g., the nickel cannot be placed on top of the dime, etc.).

Solutions for Problems 1, 2, 4, and 5 appear in Table 8–3. The solution for Problem 3 appears in Figure 8–7.

solutions is affected greatly by how one initially structures the problem. Consider the following example:

Two train stations are fifty miles apart. At 2 P.M. one Saturday afternoon two trains start toward each other, one from each station. Just as the trains pull out of the stations, a bird springs into the air in front of the first train and flies

Figure 8–7.

The solution for Problem 3 in Table 8-2. The diagram illustrates the locations of hobbits ■ orcs ● and the boat ▲ in successive states of transition. In State 1, all hobbits, orcs, and the boat are on one side of the river (reflected in the fact that all are above the line). In State 2, a hobbit, an orc, and the boat have gone to the other side of the river (noted by the boat, one hobbit, and one orc on the other side of the line). State 3 reflects the fact that a hobbit has taken the boat back across the river. The rest of the diagram continues in the same way. (Adapted from Anderson, 1980, p. 270.)

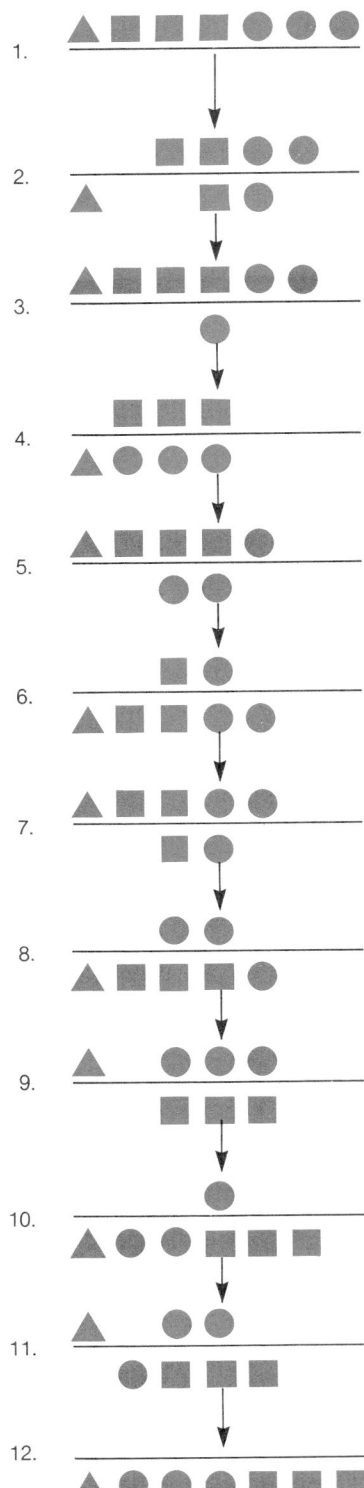

ahead to the front of the second train. When the bird reaches the second train it turns back and flies toward the first train. The bird continues to do this until the trains meet.

If both trains travel at the rate of twenty-five miles per hour and the bird flies at a hundred miles an hour, how many miles will the bird have flown before the trains meet? (Posner, 1973, pp. 150–151)

If you view the problem in terms of the *distance* the bird travels, calculating the length of all the trips is difficult (Posner, 1973). If, instead, you view the problem in terms of *time,* the solution is much easier. In this case, the question is: How much time did the bird spend in the air? The two trains are approaching each other at 50 miles per hour (25 miles per hour each) and so will travel the 50-mile distance in 1 hour. Since the bird flies at 100 miles an hour, it will cover 100 miles in that time. How the problem is viewed, then, greatly determines the ease of finding a solution.

Table 8–3.

Solutions to Problems 1, 2, 4 and 5 in Table 8–2. From Bourne/Dominowski/Loftus, COGNITIVE PROCESSES, © 1979, p. 268. Adapted by permission of Prentice-Hall, Inc. Englewood Cliffs, NJ.

1. ANAGRAMS   Answers are *facet, naive, doubt, anvil, thick.*

2. MATCHING PROBLEM   Tom owns the Cadillac.

PERSON	SHIRT COLOR	CAR
George	Blue	Ford
Bill	Red	VW
Tom	White	Cadillac
Jack	Green	Buick

3. HOBBITS AND ORCS   See Figure 8–7 for solution.

4. TWO-STRING PROBLEM   Tie the screwdriver to the end of one string and set it swinging. Walk to the other string, grasp it, and wait for the swinging string to come over. The two strings may then be tied together.

5. PYRAMID PUZZLE   (In the answer, 10-A means move the dime to Circle A, etc.) 10-B, 1-C, 10-C, 5-B, 10-A, 1-B, 10-B, 25-C, 10-C, 1-A, 10-A, 5-C, 10-B, 1-C, 10-C.

Production. In the production stage, we generate one or more potential solutions to the problem, rejecting those that do not appear feasible. In some cases, rather complex solution strategies are needed. Two general classes of such strategies have been noted: algorithms and heuristics (Bourne, Dominowski, & Loftus, 1979).

Algorithms are solution methods that, if correctly applied, guarantee a solution, even if we do not understand how they work. A formula for determining the area of a shape, such as a rectangle, is an algorithm. Correct use of the formula guarantees a correct solution. An algorithm can also be used in solving anagrams like those in Table 8–2. If you devise a strategy for producing all possible orders of the letters in an anagram, you will ultimately solve it.

The anagrams example makes it clear, however, that while algorithms can be quite useful, they can also be time consuming. And besides this, algorithms do not always exist for a particular problem. In other words, there are not always clear and simple rules that, if followed, will always lead to a solution (Houston, 1981).

It is for these very reasons that problem solving is often not of the algorithmic variety. We also, and perhaps typically, use heuristics. **Heuristics** are rules of thumb, or educated guesses, with respect to the best ways of solving a problem. They increase our chances of success and may lead to quick solutions, but they may also lead to no solution at all. Preparing for a test by studying only lecture notes, ignoring the reading material, is a heuristic (Wessells, 1982). This unadvisable strategy may or may not lead to success on the exam. Studying the notes certainly increases the chances of doing well on the exam, but it does not guarantee that outcome. You would be using a heuristic in making educated guesses about how to get someone to like you (Houston, 1981). There is no clear algorithm for solving this problem, but you can make educated guesses as to what you might do.

Three particular heuristics seem to be especially important. One, called a **planning process,** entails simplifying the problem by ignoring some of the details surrounding it. Solving the more restricted problem will be easier and ultimately may help in solving the entire problem. Again in solving an anagram, you could use a planning process by simply ignoring some of the letters and trying to think of words that contain the remaining letters (Bourne, Dominowski, & Loftus, 1979). If you think about this strategy for a moment, you can see that it may or may not be helpful and applicable when considering the complete problem.

Another important heuristic is known as **means-end analysis.** This strategy involves taking only those steps that will reduce the difference between the given state and the desired state or goal. Many people commonly use this strategy to solve problems, whether they realize it or not. Consider the problem of how to keep warm outside during the winter (Wessells, 1982). The existing state is coldness, and the desired state is warmth. Using a means-end analysis, the individual takes whatever steps are necessary and available to achieve the desired goal, perhaps adding clothing, building a fire, or finding shelter from the wind. At the same time, the person avoids actions that increase the differences between the existing and the desired states, such as removing clothing.

We should note, however, that in some cases, rigidly applying a means-end analysis can be inefficient and can inhibit problem solving. If you study the solution to the pyramid-puzzle problem (see Table 8–3), you will see that this is the case (Bourne, Dominowski, & Loftus, 1979).

As part of a means-end analysis, it is sometimes helpful to break down a problem into secondary goals, or *subgoals,* that are more easily solved than the overall problem. Each subgoal can, in turn, be broken down into further subgoals. Rather than ignoring part of the relevant information, as in the planning process, this strategy defines smaller, more directly solvable tasks. When these tasks are solved, they resolve the entire problem. The overall problem does not seem terribly complex and overwhelming this way, which heightens the motivation to tackle it.

The reverse of means-end analysis is an important heuristic, called **working backward.** This strategy involves working from the desired state or goal toward the existing state (Bourne, Dominowski, & Loftus, 1979). You might do this in playing chess or in solving mathematical proofs. Since you are always in direct contact with the goal, this strategy has the advantage of keeping you out of a lot of blind alleys (Houston, 1981). Consider the following as an example:

> Suppose that you want to trace a route from New York to San Francisco on a road map. You could start in New York and work your way west. But, because you will not be able to predict what is ahead, you may end up on a detour to Des Moines. However, if you start in San Francisco, and work backward toward New York you may be able to avoid some of these "dead ends." (Houston, 1981, p. 465–466)

The strategy of working backward is helpful only to the extent that you are able to make it back to the initial state. The most efficient strategy is generally a combination of working forward and working backward (Bourne, Dominowski, & Loftus, 1979).

Judgment. In the judgment stage, the problem solver evaluates the adequacy of potential solutions. How does each solution compare with the solution criteria generated in the preparation stage? If it is determined that a match exists, the problem is solved. If not, more work is needed.

Incubation. Some theorists believe that a fourth step may also be involved in the problem-solving process. This stage, called **incubation,** refers to a period in which the problem solver does not actively work on an unsolved problem that was begun earlier. Is it possible that taking time off from a problem is better than continuing to work on it? You may have had the experience of forgetting about a problem while attending to other matters, only to have the solution come to you out of the blue. Many artists, mathematicians, and scientists have reported experiencing such a phenomenon (Moates & Schumacher, 1980).

Why might the incubation effect occur? There are several plausible reasons (Bourne, Dominowski, & Loftus, 1979). One is that you may overcome mental fatigue by ignoring the problem for a while. Furthermore, the rest period may give you a chance to shed inappropriate ways of thinking about the problem. Finally, the rest period allows the dissipation of the frustration that tends to build up as you unsuccessfully work on a problem. Although the idea of incubation is intuitively appealing, research findings are mixed. Sometimes incubation seems to help; sometimes it does not.

— Problems in Solving Problems

As you are well aware, problem solving sometimes fails. Just as previous experience can aid our problem solving efforts, it can also hinder them. This can be seen in two phenomena, known as set and functional fixity (Moates & Schumacher, 1980).

Set. The tendency to always approach a problem the same way is known as **set.** It is a style of problem solving characterized by continued use of familiar or habitual types of solutions (Moates & Schumacher, 1980). The problem of set is evident in a study by Luchins (1942). Subjects in that study were given volume-measuring problems in which they were to suppose the existence of a supply of water and three water jars of specified size. Using paper and pencil, the subjects were to figure out how to obtain quantities of water. Table 8–4 lists the sizes of jars and the amounts of water to be obtained for seven different problems. On the first five problems, it was possible to obtain the requested amount of water by using the same formula each time: Goal = Jar B − Jar A − 2 (Jar C). In other words, fill Jar B, fill Jar A once from it, and fill Jar C twice; what remains in Jar B will be the amount desired. For Problem 6, this formula could once again be used, but a much simpler formula existed: Goal = Jar A − Jar C. That is, fill Jar A, and out of it, fill Jar C. Jar A will then contain the proper amount. Likewise, Problem 7 can be solved by either the longer formula or the simpler one. Despite these easier solutions for Problems 6 and 7, subjects who first solved Problems 1 through 5 tended to use the formula they had used previously, not the simpler one. In contrast, control subjects, who did not work on the first five problems, were not victimized by this problem-solving set and almost always used the simpler solution on Problems 6 and 7. Clearly, the phenomenon of set can blind us to fresh and new ways of exploring problems (Moates & Schumacher, 1980).

Functional fixity. Sometimes the solution to a problem eludes us because of a phenomenon known

Table 8–4.

The Luchins (1942) water-jar problem.

PROBLEM	JAR SIZE (IN QUARTS)			QUARTS OF WATER TO BE OBTAINED
	Jar A	*Jar B*	*Jar C*	
1	21	127	3	100
2	14	163	25	99
3	18	43	10	5
4	9	42	6	21
5	20	59	4	31
6	23	49	3	20
7	15	39	3	18

as **functional fixity**—the tendency to perceive objects as having only the uses for which they were originally designed. The result is that anytime a new and creative use of a common object is required, functional fixity may interfere with problem solving.

To appreciate how easily one can focus on the usual purpose of an object, consider a study by Duncker (1945). Given only a candle, some matches, and a box of tacks, as shown in Figure 8–8, try solving the following problem: Find a way of attaching the candle to the wall so that it burns properly. Can you do it? Duncker's subjects had difficulty with this task. According to Duncker, the solution, shown in Figure 8–9, is to empty the box of tacks, tack the box to the wall, and then use it as a base for holding the candle.

With the tacks in the box, it apparently is difficult to restructure one's perception of the function of the box and to envision it for purposes other than holding tacks. This is evident in the fact that control subjects, who were given the tacks and the box as separate objects, were much more likely to find the solution. Particularly striking are the results obtained by Adamson (1952): Only 41 percent of the subjects given a box containing tacks solved the candle problem, but 86 percent of the subjects given an empty box did so.

It is clear that both set and functional fixity can impede effective problem solving. Although previous experience is helpful for many, or even most, kinds of problems, when new ways of approaching a problem are required, previous experience can blind us and inhibit us (Moates & Schumacher, 1980).

Figure 8–8.

Duncker's candle problem. Using only the objects shown, how can you mount the candle on the wall in such a way that it will burn properly?

Figure 8–9.

The solution to Duncker's candle problem.

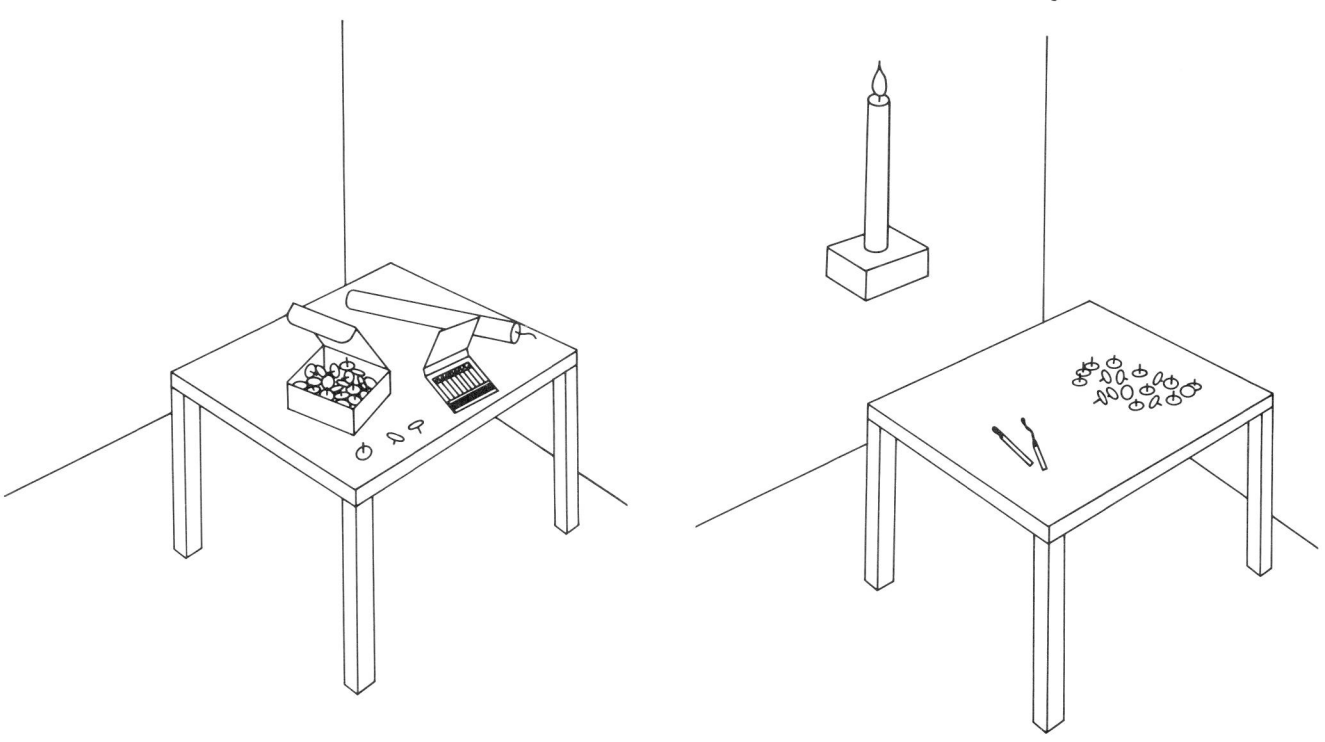

SOME TIPS ON SOLVING PROBLEMS

Now that we have examined the nature of problem solving, perhaps it would be beneficial to describe some practical problem-solving aids offered by Moates and Schumacher (1980):

1. *Broaden your knowledge.* Approach a problem with as much knowledge and preparation as you can. The more resources you have available, the better.

2. *Look for new ways of structuring the problem.* Remember that how you view a problem is critical to finding a solution. Thus, it is helpful to look for alternate ways of conceptualizing or structuring the problem.

3. *Describe the problem to someone.* By simply verbalizing the problem, you might discover some errors in your thinking or some faulty assumptions that you didn't realize you were making.

4. *Set the problem aside.* As is clear from our discussion, incubation might help. It certainly can't hurt. Getting away from the problem for a while might allow you to divorce yourself from old and unsuccessful approaches, and you might return to the problem with a new conceptualization.

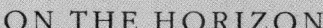

PROGRAMMING INTELLIGENT COMPUTERS

In this computer age, computer technology seems to expand almost daily. One outgrowth of this technology is a science known as **artificial intelligence.** Its goal is to program computers to behave intelligently, such as in conversing with human beings, playing chess, and solving problems. It is intriguing to think about what the future might hold with respect to computers and human behavior. One of the many practical reasons for making computers intelligent is that they could help us in our problem-solving efforts by taking over many routine mental chores and by helping with more complex tasks, such as medical diagnosis (Blois, 1983; Johnson, 1983; McMullin, 1983b).

Artificial intelligence has, in fact, already made its breakthrough into the practice of medical diagnosis. As Stengel (1982) notes, the technology is still years away from widespread use, but it is now being utilized in a few hospitals. The idea is not to take decision making away from doctors but to have the computer help them in their calculations. Artificial intelligence in medicine is the result of programming that attempts to imitate the thought processes of physicians who are making diagnoses. But the computer serves as more than just a memory bank ready to spit out a diagnosis when given a list of symptoms. Its diagnosis programs work with uncertainty factors, as would a physician making a diagnosis. They are designed to consider all available evidence that might support or question a particular diagnosis. This allows the physician to return to the computer and ask how it weighed the relevant information and arrived at its recommendation (Stengel, 1982).

The subtlety in computer reasoning and logic that has just been described is possible only because programmers spent hundreds of hours with physicians, trying to understand the thought processes that led to particular diagnoses (Stengel, 1982). It is true, as Stengel points out, that diagnosis is not an exact science, and physicians given the same set of symptoms sometimes disagree on a diagnosis. Even so, the computer programs already seem to be functioning well, compared to human performance (Blois, 1980). Not surprisingly, some physicians are still cautious about the use of computers (Yu, 1983). There does seem to be consensus, though, that consultation by diagnostic computers may soon be quite prevalent. The computer has certain advantages that make it a potentially excellent aid to problem solving of this kind (McMullin, 1983a). One of the main ones is that it has "an infallible memory for past cases and an encyclopedic knowledge of symptoms and diseases" (Stengel, 1982, p. 71).

What the future holds with respect to artificial intelligence is limited only by our understanding of human memory, language, and thought. Perhaps it will be possible in future years to see a computer therapist. Or how about a computer tutor that could help you diagnose why you are making mistakes in your mathematical problem solving? Progress is already being made in this latter area (Brown & Burton, 1978). With the current rapid decline in the costs of computers, perhaps we are not too far away from seeing widespread uses of intelligent computer tutors that can help people solve a variety of problems (Reed, 1982). It may be that the future holds in store some rather mind-boggling feats.

═ SUMMARY ═

1. A girl named Genie was isolated and not spoken to for most of her first 13½ years of life. Subsequent attempts to teach her language were only partially successful.

2. Language is an arbitrary system of symbols that allows individuals to understand and communicate an infinite variety of messages.

3. Language is closely related to other mental processes, such as thought and problem solving. Thinking can be defined as an inherent ability to mentally manipulate symbols and concepts in order to organize information, make plans, solve problems, and make decisions.

4. The development of language seems to occur in the same sequence for children of all cultures. In the prelinguistic state, the child progresses through crying, cooing, and babbling.

5. The child's first words are often holophrastic in nature, and early sentences are telegraphic. Gradually, though, the child begins to make adultlike sentences.

6. A knowledge of syntax is evident in our use of phrase structure rules. But we also learn transformation rules by which we are able to express a single underlying meaning (deep structure) in different surface forms (surface structures).

7. Various theories of language acquisition have been proposed. Although imitation plays some role, there are many arguments against it as a major explanation of language acquisition.

8. The notion of reinforcement also does not adequately account for language learning.

9. An innateness hypothesis, which holds that the child comes into the world already programmed in some way to learn language, is favorably viewed by many psychologists and linguists.

10. Recent research has questioned earlier findings that chimpanzees are capable of constructing original, creative sentences. What have appeared to be creative constructions may only have been imitations of sentences signed by human trainers.

11. Linguistic relativity is the hypothesis that language determines how one thinks and how one perceives the world. Support for the hypothesis is lacking.

12. Language and thought are related in some ways, however. Language seems to facilitate problem solving, but at the same time it does not appear essential for complex mental processes.

13. Although language does have some important influences on our thought processes, language disorders known as aphasia illustrate how thought and language can be dissociated. Broca's aphasia seems to result in thought without language, whereas Wernicke's aphasia seems to result in language without thought.

14. Parents can do many things to facilitate their children's language development, including talking to children as much as possible, talking to them at their level, serving as good speech models, encouraging good listening and attention skills, and providing opportunities for the children to utilize their verbal skills.

15. Concepts play a significant role in our thinking. They make thinking more efficient by allowing us to fit new objects and events into categories we have already formed.

16. In solving problems, we go through a series of definable stages: preparation, production, and judgment. A fourth stage, called incubation, may also accompany problem solving.

17. Previous experience can help us find solutions to problems, but it can also hinder us. This is suggested by two phenomena, known as set and functional fixity. Set is the tendency to always approach a problem the same way. Functional fixity is the tendency to perceive objects as having only the uses for which they were originally designed.

18. The following problem solving aids have been suggested: (1) broaden your knowledge, (2) look for new ways of structuring the problem, (3) describe the problem to someone, and (4) set the problem aside.

19. The science of artificial intelligence has already had an impact on the practice of medical diagnosis. Programs for diagnosis that attempt to imitate physicians' thought processes have been written. Although some physicians are still cautious about the use of computers, the programs thus far developed seem to function well, compared to human performance.

IMPORTANT TERMS AND CONCEPTS

Language
Thinking
Prelinguistic Stage
Phonemes
Babbling
Morphemes
Holophrases
Syntax
Grammar
Inflections
Grammatical Morphemes
Telegraphic Speech

Overregularization
Surface Structure
Deep Structure
Transformation Rules
Ambiguous Sentences
Innateness Hypothesis
Linguistic Relativity Hypothesis
Aphasias
Broca's Aphasia
Wernicke's Aphasia
Concept
Conjunctive Rule

Disjunctive Rule
Relational Concepts
Algorithms
Heuristics
Planning Process
Means-end Analysis
Working Backward
Incubation
Set
Functional Fixity
Artificial Intelligence

SUGGESTIONS FOR FURTHER READING

Curtiss, S. (1977). *Genie: A psycholinguistic study of a modern-day "wild-child."* New York: Academic Press. A detailed examination of the efforts made and the progress achieved in teaching language to a girl who was isolated and not spoken to for most of her first 13½ years of life.

Matlin, M. (1983). *Cognition.* New York: Holt, Rinehart and Winston. A good, solid introduction to concept formation and problem solving as well as other aspects of thought, including reasoning and decision making.

Miller, G. A. (1981). *Language and speech.* San Francisco: W. H. Freeman. A brief and pleasant introduction to the topic of language for the beginning student.

Slobin, D. I. (1979). *Psycholinguistics* (2nd ed.). Glenview, IL: Scott, Foresman. An engaging introduction to the psychology of language.

Terrace, H. S. (1979). *Nim.* New York: Knopf. A fascinating and personal account of the triumphs and disappointments in teaching sign language to a chimpanzee named Nim.

Wicklegren, W. E. (1974). *How to solve problems: Elements of a theory of problems and problem solving.* San Francisco: W. H. Freeman. A good source of material on the nature of problems and how we can solve them.

— CHAPTER 9 —
MOTIVATION AND EMOTION

MOTIVATION AND EMOTION

— CHAPTER OBJECTIVES —

To achieve the objectives of this chapter, you should be able to answer the questions listed here. You should also be able to define the important terms and concepts listed at the end of the chapter.

1. How do each of the major theories of motivation account for behavior?
2. What factors explain the biological motives of hunger, thirst, and sex? Describe some of the problems and theories associated with obesity.
3. What are stimulus-seeking motives? What evidence supports the existence of such motives? How can they best be explained?
4. What are acquired motives? In what ways are needs for affiliation and achievement expressed?
5. What are emotions? How are they expressed?
6. How do the various theories of emotion explain the subjective experience of emotion? How do emotions affect us?

— CHAPTER OUTLINE —

Theories of Motivation
Psychologists disagree about what motivates behavior and propose various theories to account for motivation.

Instinct Theory
Drive Theory
Incentive Theory
Arousal Theory
Cognitive Theories
Competence and Control
Application: Intrinsic Motivation, Rewards, and Threats

Types of Motives
Some motives are biologically based; others seem to be innate but not tied to any biological need; still others seem to be learned.

Biological Motives
Stimulus-Seeking Motives
Acquired Motives
Application: Achievement Motivation and Achievement Behavior

Emotion
Emotions are strong feelings accompanied by physiological activity and observable body expressions, especially facial expressions.

Defining Emotions
How Do Emotions Occur?
How Emotions Affect Us
Application: Lie Detectors

On the Horizon: Anorexia Nervosa

THE "SUBWAY SAMARITAN"

As the subway roared into the 14th Street station to take him to his sparsely furnished Harlem walk-up, Reginald Andrews, 29, was deep in thought. Except for occasional work unloading produce, the father of eight had been unemployed for a year, and he was not optimistic about the job interview he had had that morning at Jamac Frozen Foods, a Manhattan food-delivery company.

Suddenly someone else's troubles grabbed Andrews' attention. Trying to board the train, David Schnair, 75, blind from an injury suffered in combat in World War II, was tapping a metal cane to identify an open door. But when he mistook a space between two cars for a door, he toppled onto the track. The train was about to pull out. "My mind left Jamac and Christmas for the kids," recalled Andrews. "I knew what I had to do."

Andrews jumped under the train and dragged Schnair, bleeding from a gash in his head, to a narrow cubbyhole beneath the platform out of the way of the wheels. The train began moving, but then screeched to a halt when a screaming bystander implored the conductor to stop the train. Andrews and Schnair huddled in the crawl space until the power was cut off and they could be hoisted to safety. (*Time,* "Soul of a Hero," January 3, 1983, p. 53)

The study of motivation is a search for the underlying whys of behavior. Why, for instance, would a person risk injury to help someone in distress, as Reginald Andrews did? According to Batson and Coke (1981), some people help because they are *altruistically* motivated; that is, they empathize with the victim's suffering and seek to relieve it. For others, helping is *egoistically* motivated; that is, they help to relieve their own discomfort, not the victim's. It is apparent, then, that the same act may have various underlying motives (cf. Davis, 1983a). That fact is a challenge to psychologists who study motivation.

This chapter discusses both motivation and emotion. As we have just seen, the two are often interrelated—for example, when an emotion, such as empathy, provides the motivation for an altruistic act. Although closely related, emotion and motivation are separable. An **emotion** consists of a *feeling*—accompanied by *internal body reactions* in the brain, nervous system, and internal organs—and *observable expressions*, especially those of the face (Izard, 1977). **Motivation,** on the other hand, is any force acting on or within an organism that initiates and directs behavior as well as governing its intensity (Petri, 1981).

With this information as a foundation, we will first focus on theories of motivation. Then we will examine several specific motives, such as hunger and achievement motivation. Finally, we will explore the nature of emotions and their relationship to motivation.

Instinct Theory

In the early part of this century, the term *instinct* was virtually a household word. An **instinct** is an innate, unlearned, goal-directed, species-specific behavior. Various early psychological theorists, among them Sigmund Freud (see chapter 13), assumed that much human behavior is instinctual. William McDougall (1908) identified a number of principal human instincts (listed in Table 9–1, along with their presumed corresponding emotions).

A major problem with early instinct theory was that the list of proposed instincts grew quite large. The temptation to explain behavior by inventing new instincts soon rendered the explanations meaningless (Cofer, 1972). However, instinct theory is not dead, having been revitalized in more recent times by **ethologists**—those who study the behavior of animals in their natural habitat.

— Modern Instinct Theory of the Ethologists

Ethologists postulate that behind each instinctive act is a reservoir of *reaction-specific energy,* which motivates the act (Arkes & Garske, 1982). In order for an instinctive act to occur, a specific *sign stimulus* must be present. If that stimulus is not present, the discharge of instinctual energy is inhibited by an *innate releasing mechanism.* This mechanism acts like a lock that can be opened only with the proper key, the key being the

Table 9–1.

Principal instincts proposed by McDougall, along with presumed corresponding emotions.

INSTINCT	CORRESPONDING EMOTION
Flight	Fear
Repulsion	Disgust
Curiosity	Wonder
Pugnacity	Anger
Self-abasement	Negative self-feeling or subjection
Self-assertion	Positive self-feeling or elation
Parenting	Tenderness

appropriate sign stimulus (Petri, 1981). The stickleback fish, studied by Tinbergen (1951), provides an example (cf. Arkes & Garske, 1982). During mating periods, the male stickleback exhibits an instinctive *territoriality,* in that it defends a specific area by attacking other male sticklebacks. The sign stimulus responsible for triggering an attack is the red underside of another male stickleback.

Ethologists assume that reaction-specific energy builds up if instinctive behaviors are not carried out (Arkes & Garske, 1982). The longer the buildup, the less intense the stimulus needs to be to trigger the innate releasing mechanism. A male stickleback, for example, may go some time without needing to defend his territory. If so, a stimulus that isn't quite red may be adequate to activate the innate releasing mechanism and initiate territorial defense.

A specific type of instinctive activity that has received much attention from ethologists is **imprinting** (Lorenz, 1952). It occurs when an animal, such as a duckling, becomes socially attached to and follows the first moving object (normally the mother) it sees shortly after birth (Beck, 1983). We will have more to say about imprinting in chapter 11; for now we will note that it seems to occur only during a brief critical period that varies for each animal species.

An extension to humans? Some ethologists believe that certain human instincts may also exist. At least one ethologist, for example, claims that human territoriality is instinctive (Ardrey, 1966). (See chapter 19 for a full discussion of human territoriality and a noninstinctive view.) Other ethologists, such as Lorenz (1966), have attributed human aggression to reaction-specific energies (see chapter 18 for an alternate view). Some psychologists have even suggested that imprinting occurs in humans. As we will see in chapter 11, theorists such as Bowlby (1969) believe that human infants form a bond of social attachment to their caregivers during a critical period after birth.

Most contemporary psychologists are skeptical that instincts fully explain behaviors as diverse as aggression and attachment. Nevertheless, instinct theories should not be ignored. It is certainly possible that at least some behaviors are genetically programmed (Petri, 1981).

Recently, a field known as *sociobiology* has emerged; the biological basis for social behaviors is its focus. For example, E. O. Wilson (1975) has observed that members of many animal species readily risk their lives to defend fellow animals, especially offspring and relatives. Such altruism is also evident in animals' food-sharing. Sociobiologists assume that altruism and similar social behaviors evolved because they are adaptive and help animals survive. Wilson speculates that human altruism, illustrated in the chapter introduction by Reginald Andrews's heroic rescue, may also be under genetic control. To date, however, there is no evidence that specific genes determine altruistic acts or other social behaviors. Many scientists prefer the view that humans inherit a potential for learning social behaviors (cf. Mussen & Eisenberg-Berg, 1977).

The sociobiological view of human social behavior is new, speculative, and enormously controversial (Arkes & Garske, 1982). It is also receiving considerable attention from both biologists and psychologists (see Cunningham, 1981; Ridley & Dawkins, 1981). Perhaps the most important statements from sociobiologists are still forthcoming.

Drive Theory

By the 1930s, drive had replaced instinct as the dominant motivational concept. Drives are assumed to result from specific biological needs for food, water, and the like (Bolles, 1975). To survive, organisms must meet various biological requirements. The body attempts to maintain an optimal physiological balance, a tendency known as **homeostasis. Needs** are any physiological deviations from homeostatic balance. They give rise to psychological tensions known as **drives.**

Drives impel (motivate) organisms to behave in a manner that reduces underlying needs. The goal of drives is to maintain homeostatic balance. An organism needing food, for example, experiences a drive that activates food-seeking. Similarly, a water deficiency activates the thirst drive, which impels the organism to seek water.

According to theorist Clark Hull (1943), eating, drinking, and similar actions bring about *drive-reduction,* which is reinforcing. Consequently, such behaviors are repeated when needs recur. The essentials of this model are illustrated in Figure 9–1. The drive model usefully accounts for biological motives, but other concepts must be added to compensate for its inadequacies.

Incentive Theory

The drive concept suggests that internal conditions impel organisms to engage in particular behaviors. **Incentives,** on the other hand, are external objects or stimuli to which organisms are attracted (Bolles, 1975). To put it another way, there seems to be something more to motivation than just the push of internal drives. The motivating pull of external stimuli, or incentives, must also be taken into account.

As Bolles (1975) suggests, drives and incentives complement each other as explanations of motivated behavior. Motivation can, in fact, be best understood in many cases as an interaction of drives and incentives. Eating, for example, may be motivated in part by a physiological deficit that induces a food-seeking drive. But the food itself may also serve as an incentive for eating. Furthermore, drives and incentives can affect one another. For instance, the greater one's need for food, the more attractive food will be. In other words, food will have greater incentive value. On the other hand, the incentive of the sight or smell of food can also elicit a drive and motivate eating. No doubt you have had the experience of not being hungry, only to become hungry when offered a piece of cake or pie. The effect of incentives, then, is to exert pull on drives and motivate the organism to approach the incentive object.

Figure 9–1.

Sequence of events posited by the drive-reduction theory of motivation.

Arousal Theory

One weakness of drive theory is its inability to explain why individuals often actively seek increases in stimulation or arousal. Clearly, we do not limit our behavior to acts that reduce stimulation, as drive theory implies (Weiner, 1980). We also engage in activities that increase stimulation. We read thrilling books, we go to amusement parks, we explore the unknowns of space, and so on. Such activities have not escaped the attention of psychologists, who view arousal as important for understanding motivation.

Arousal theory proposes that individuals seek an optimal level of arousal. With too little stimulation, they engage in activities that increase arousal. If stimulation is too great, they attempt to reduce it. By arousal, we mean physiological arousal, the activation of the nervous system. Any number of things, of course, can increase arousal—fear or anxiety, exposure to a loud noise, riding a roller coaster, watching a violent movie, or taking such drugs as caffeine, for example. In their research, arousal theorists have often focused on specific elements of stimuli that affect arousal. It appears, for example, that the more intense, complex, meaningful, and novel a stimulus is, the more arousing it is.

Cognitive Theories

That individuals are motivated to evaluate the consistency or accuracy of their knowledge about the world or themselves is the assumption of **cognitive theories** of motivation (Buck, 1976). Most theories of this type are closely associated with social psychology (see chapter 18) and will be discussed only briefly here.

— Social-Comparison Theory

Leon Festinger (1950, 1954) proposed that humans are motivated to evaluate the correctness of their opinions and appraisals of their abilities. Often, such evaluations cannot be made objectively. For example, one cannot evaluate a political candidate by looking in a book. Festinger suggests that when objective yardsticks are unavailable, people evaluate their opinions and abilities by comparing them with those of other people—an idea known as **social-comparison theory.** Comparison with similar others provides the most useful information. For example, if similar others think as we do, it validates our thinking and gives us a sense of correctness.

— Cognitive-Consistency Theories

That people have a need for consistency in their thoughts is maintained by **cognitive-consistency theories.** When such consistency is lacking, people presumably alter their cognitions or their behavior in an attempt to achieve consistency. For example, a person with the cognitions "I smoke" and "Smoking leads to cancer" would be expected to either quit smoking or decide that smoking isn't really harmful. In chapter 18, we will offer several examples of consistency theories. For now, we will say simply that behavior is often motivated by the need for consistency.

Competence and Control

A number of motivation theories emphasize that we strive for competence (Buck, 1976; Petri, 1981). The drive to achieve a sense of control—a belief that we can affect the world around us—seems to motivate many of our actions. Various theorists have dealt with the ideas of competence and control, but using differing terminology. Several theorists have suggested that individuals strive toward full functioning, or actualization. We will begin our examination of competence theories by focusing on actualization.

— Self-Actualization

As we will see in more detail in chapter 13, Carl Rogers (e.g., 1951, 1961) believes that all humans are innately motivated to achieve **self-actualization,** a state characterized by wholeness, full functioning, and the expression of all of one's capacities. That is, we are motivated to become everything we can become as we strive to enhance and better ourselves. Abraham Maslow (e.g., 1970, 1971) also proposed that humans strive to achieve full potential. However, although Maslow considered self-actualization to be the ultimate goal, he believed that other motives must first be satisfied.

Maslow's hierarchy of needs. Maslow conceived of human motivation as a **hierarchy of needs,** ranging from basic biological motives to the ultimate motive of self-actualization (see Figure 9–2). He saw our lives as centering around the movement up this

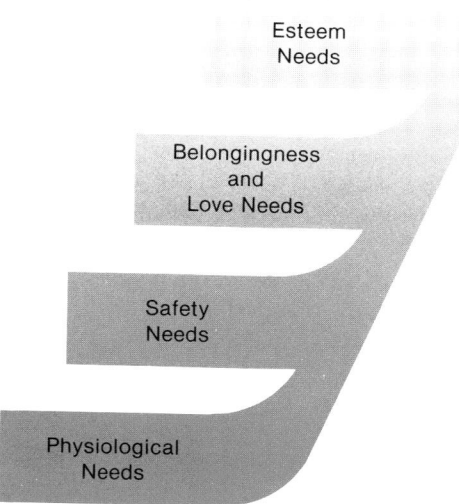

Self-actualization
Needs

Esteem
Needs

Belongingness
and
Love Needs

Safety
Needs

Physiological
Needs

Figure 9–2.

Maslow's hierarchy of needs.

hierarchy; he noted that we first satisfy the stronger, more basic, lower-level needs before striving for higher-level needs. However, if the lower-level needs are even partially satisfied, the higher-level needs can be partially active (cf. Petri, 1981).

As Figure 9–2 shows, one is first motivated to fulfill basic *physiological needs,* such as hunger and thirst. Fortunately, those needs are adequately met for most people. If they are not, higher-level needs will be of little or no motivational importance; malnourished people are rarely concerned with self-actualization. When physiological needs are met, individuals are then motivated to satisfy *safety needs;* at this level, people look for stability and security in life. Again, when such needs are threatened or not met, higher-level needs are less important. At the next level, *belongingness and love needs* motivate people to seek affectionate relationships with others. Such needs might be fulfilled through marriage, friendship, or close family relationships. Fulfillment of these needs allows the next level—*esteem needs*—to influence behavior. Here, people are concerned with achieving high self-regard; they want to feel competent and independent and to have a sense of worth. They also want to be recognized and appreciated by others.

— PERSONAL PROFILE —

ABRAHAM MASLOW (1908–1970)

Abraham Maslow was born in Brooklyn, New York, in 1908. As the only Jewish boy in his neighborhood, he was unhappy and felt socially isolated. Books and education became his companions. Following high school, he began studying law, at his father's urging, but soon found he did not like it. Much to his father's bewilderment, Maslow preferred to study everything.

A turning point in Maslow's life was his marriage, at age 20. From the marriage he derived a sense of belongingness and love as well as purpose and direction. After taking psychology courses as an undergraduate, Maslow began to see behaviorism as the answer to the world's problems. A later disenchantment with behaviorism was directly related to the birth of his first child. Two of Maslow's comments describe his new feelings on the subject: "I'd say that anyone who had a baby couldn't be a behaviorist" and "It's [behaviorism] useless at home with your kids and wife and friends." Later, moved by the events of World War II, Maslow turned to developing a psychology that dealt with the best of human nature, with human ideals and potentials.

Maslow spent most of his academic career as professor and chairman of the psychology department at Brandeis University. His awards and honors were numerous. He died in 1970 at the age of 62. (Massey, 1981; Schultz, 1981b)

Satisfaction of the first four levels of needs allows the emergence of *self-actualization needs*. Here, behavior is no longer dominated and influenced by lower-level deficiencies. Instead, people try to become everything they are capable of becoming.

— Competence and Intrinsic Motivation

Robert White (1959) has suggested that much of our behavior is motivated by a striving for *competence*, the ability to deal effectively with our surroundings. White termed this striving **effectance motivation.** The effectance motive leads us to attend to, explore, and manipulate the environment.

In a theory similar to White's, Edward Deci (1975; Deci & Ryan, 1980) emphasizes that our behavior is motivated by intrinsic needs for competence, self-de-termination, and the feeling that we control our environment. We can say, then, that **intrinsic motivation** refers to performing activities for their own sake, not for extrinsic (external) rewards. In other words, intrinsically motivated activities are themselves rewarding and enjoyable.

Needs for competence and self-determination are thought to motivate two general classes of behaviors. One class includes behaviors that place the individual in reasonably challenging situations. Being bored, for example, will lead the person to find a situation in which creativity and resourcefulness can be used. The second class includes behaviors meant to conquer challenging situations. Presumably, by overcoming challenges we achieve a sense of competence and control.

— APPLICATION —
INTRINSIC MOTIVATION, REWARDS, AND THREATS

Reading mystery stories, solving puzzles, and a multitude of other intrinsically motivating activities are done simply for enjoyment. Evidence suggests, however, that intrinsic motivation can be undermined by extrinsic reasons for performing an activity (Deci & Ryan, 1980; Deci, Betley, Kahle, Abrams, & Porac, 1981; Fazio, 1981; Earn, 1982). Much research has assessed the effects of receiving a reward for an otherwise intrinsically motivating task. Unless such rewards reflect one's ability or competence, getting them seems to lower intrinsic motivation (Rosenfield, Folger, & Adelman, 1980; Vallerand, 1983).

One explanation for this observation is that when people have both an intrinsic explanation for their behavior ("I like this activity") and an extrinsic one ("I can get a reward for doing this"), they often choose the latter (Wilson & Lassiter, 1982). Accordingly, intrinsic interest is lessened. Consider child rearing and discipline as an example. An overuse of external rewards for activities children find interesting may undermine the children's intrinsic motivation. Also, an abundance of external rewards for sharing and for being honest, kind, and so on may reduce the frequency of such behaviors when parental surveillance is absent. Powerful external reasons for helping someone, such as being paid for doing so, have also been shown to lessen the intrinsic motivation for helping in college students (Kunda & Schwartz, 1983). Being paid undermines one's sense of moral obligation to help others in need and leads to the perception that helping was done for the money rather than because the behavior itself was positively valued. The consequence, of course, is that in the absence of any possible reward, future acts of spontaneous helpfulness become less likely. The implication seems to be that when we use rewards to get others to engage in desirable activities, we should use those rewards judiciously and moderately.

We have described what can happen when extrinsic reasons are provided for performing attractive activities. What happens when there are extrinsic reasons for not performing an unattractive activity? For example, what happens when students are told that they will be severely punished for cheating on a test? Wilson and Lassiter (1982) argue that students then have two plausible explanations for not cheating. One is "I didn't want to cheat"; the other is "I would have been punished if I had cheated." Is it possible that students who choose the second reason will be more likely to cheat when punishment is absent, since they have discounted any intrinsic motivation for not cheating? In support of this possibility, Wilson and Lassiter (1982) found that college students warned not to cheat in one situation were later more likely than nonthreatened students to cheat in a different situation.

It seems that to keep people from cheating or engaging in other undesirable behaviors, it is best to use extrinsic constraints moderately. Such constraints should be strong enough to forestall the negative behavior but not so strong that people will perceive their good behavior as being due entirely to extrinsic factors.

TYPES OF MOTIVES

It is now time to move beyond general theoretical perspectives to a variety of specific motives. We have chosen to classify such motives as *biological, stimulus-seeking,* and *acquired.*

Biological Motives

It is evident that much animal and human behavior is motivated by biological needs. We must eat, drink, and avoid injurious stimuli, or we will die. Sexual behavior also has a biological basis, but (as we will see later) it differs somewhat from other biologically based behaviors. **Biological motives** are motives related to survival of the individual or the species. We will examine three such motives here: hunger, thirst, and sex.

Hunger

As indicated in chapter 2, the part of the brain known as the hypothalamus is responsible for regulating a number of basic behaviors, including eating. With respect to eating, the hypothalamus actually has two tasks (Petri, 1981). One is to regulate the intervals between meals; the other is to control body weight over longer time periods.

How is eating initiated and suppressed on a day-to-day, meal-to-meal basis? Much early work on this question focused on specific areas of the hypothalamus, such as the *ventromedial hypothalamus (VMH)*. Damage to this particular area causes extreme overeating, a condition known as **hyperphagia.** (Figure 9–3 shows a normal rat on the left and a hyperphagic rat on the right.) The fat rats eventually grow two to three times heavier than normal and stabilize there (Arkes & Garske, 1982). Overeating caused by damage to the VMH suggests that the VMH is normally responsible for suppressing or inhibiting eating.

Another brain area, the *lateral hypothalamus (LH),* also is involved in hunger. Damage to this area stops the animal from eating, which leads researchers to believe that the LH normally initiates eating (Petri, 1981). According to the popular **glucostatic theory,** the hypothalamus regulates eating by monitoring glucose (blood-sugar) levels. Presumably, the hypothalamus has glucose-sensitive cells, called *glucoreceptors,* that monitor blood-glucose levels. When the glucose level is too low, the body's energy needs are not met, hunger occurs, and eating is initiated. When the glucose level is too high, eating is inhibited.

The brain apparently is not the only glucose-sensitive organ. It has also been suggested that the duo-

Figure 9–3.

A hyperphagic rat, such as the one on the right, can grow two to three times heavier than normal.

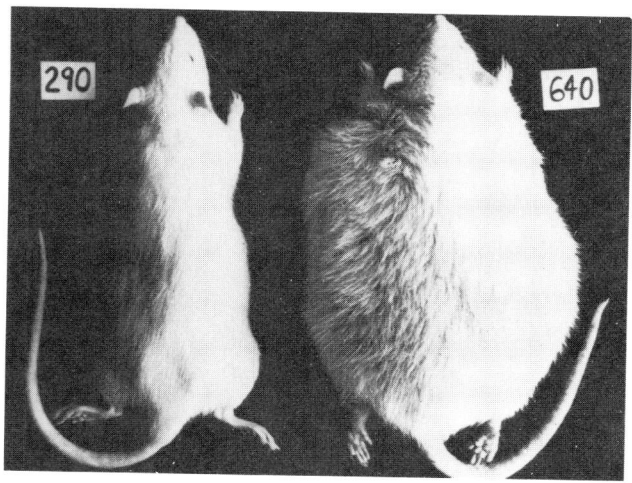

denum (upper small intestine) and liver contain glucoreceptors (Arkes & Garske, 1982; Petri, 1981). In addition, *stretch receptors* in the stomach wall relay information to the brain that the stomach is full, thus limiting the amount of food eaten (Petri, 1981). Finally, hormones have been implicated as possible satiety signals (Beck, 1983).

You have no doubt observed that despite minor fluctuations, your body weight tends to remain remarkably stable. According to many researchers, eating is regulated in such a way that body fat remains fairly stable. According to one theory, known as **set-point theory,** the body has a normal weight, or set-point, which the hypothalamus works to maintain by monitoring stored fat (Nisbett, 1972). Presumably, both the VMH and the LH are involved in regulating the set-point.

As indicated, damage to the VMH leads to overeating, but eventually the organism stabilizes at a new, higher weight. It may be, then, that such damage raises the body's set-point (Keesey & Powley, 1975). On the other hand, damage to the LH, which suppresses eating, may lower the body's set-point. Rats with LH lesions who quit eating will die unless they are force-fed. As these rats recover and begin eating on their own, however, they stabilize at a lower weight.

There is more to eating than maintaining homeostasis, or a set-point. Think of all the times when eating is motivated by incentives—the sight or smell of food, for example. Or consider the fact that eating is often determined as much by the time of day as by internal hunger pangs. Most of us also have learned to associate certain settings, such as parties, with eating. Thus we eat or overeat in those settings, regardless of whether there is a physiological need. The obvious complexity of eating is perhaps best illustrated by the problem of obesity.

— The Problem of Obesity

Although definitions vary, **obesity** can be defined as a condition in which body weight exceeds the ideal weight for one's height by 20 percent or more (Maloney & Klykylo, 1983). Although obesity knows no age boundaries, it is more prevalent in adults than in children or adolescents. One estimate holds that 30 percent of all U.S. adults are obese (see Figure 9–4).

Every year, Americans spend billions of dollars trying to fight overweight. Their good intentions are well founded, as obesity is a serious problem (Brownell, 1982). It is known to increase the risk of such diseases as hypertension (chronic high blood pressure) and diabetes. Furthermore, the obese are viewed more negatively than are normal-weight individuals and are often discriminated against. Obese people are often unhappy, and evidence suggests that their unhappiness is typically a consequence of obesity, not a cause of it.

Unfortunately, taking off weight is not as easy as putting it on. Why this is so will become clear as we explore a number of theories and explanations of overeating.

Responsiveness to external cues. One theory is that obesity occurs in individuals who are responsive to external cues, such as the sights, smells, or tastes of food. Research shows that such responsiveness can lead to overeating in the presence of food. Of course, not all externally responsive people become obese

Figure 9–4.
The problem of obesity is a common one, particularly in adults.

(Rodin, 1981). Nevertheless, if your experience tells you that your eating is greatly affected by such factors as the smell and sight of food or the time of day, you would be wise to avoid such cues. Don't cook big, lavish meals; don't leave food or high-calorie snacks in view; don't wear a watch. Perhaps you can think of other useful strategies.

Set-point theory. Obese people are biologically programmed to have elevated set-points, according to set-point theory. Nisbett (1972) believes that set-points are determined by the number of fat cells in the body. One study found that obese people had three times as many fat cells as nonobese people (Knittle & Hirsch, 1968). Whatever a person's set-point, the body defends it against change. If the body's fat stores are too low relative to the set-point, the hypothalamus activates compensatory mechanisms. Not only is the person motivated to seek food, but the body's metabolic rate is slowed so energy reserves are used more sparingly. Calories are burned at a slower rate, making it possible for the person to maintain weight on a meager diet. This fact helps explain why dieting can be so difficult. Bennett and Gurin (1982) describe the set-point as a "tireless opponent" of the dieter.

Set-point theory helps explain the origins of obesity; the number of fat cells is thought to be fixed at birth by heredity. Some researchers believe that overfeeding during infancy may also affect the set-point. In either case, the number of fat cells is believed to be largely determined by age 2 (Knittle, 1975).

Overeating seems primarily to increase the size of fat cells. Dieting causes the cells to shrink but does not reduce their number. The obese person who loses weight has numerous empty fat cells waiting to be replenished, which makes weight gains easy. Indeed, for most people, losing weight is a battle, because the body acts as if its fat cells are chronically starved. These facts may explain why a permanent change in eating habits is usually required to keep excess weight off (Mahoney & Mahoney, 1976).

Restrained eaters. A number of studies point to the conclusion that individuals who consciously restrain their eating—that is, chronic dieters—risk becoming overweight (or more obese if they are already obese). The effects of dietary restraint have been studied extensively by Herman and his associates (e.g., Herman & Mack, 1975; Hibscher & Herman, 1977). In one study, for example, subjects were classified as having either high or low restraint. As part of a purported taste experiment, subjects either ate nothing or had one or two milkshakes. Next, they were allowed to eat as much ice cream as they wanted. As Figure 9–5 shows, low-restraint subjects ate less ice cream after first consuming milkshakes. High-restraint subjects, in contrast, ate more ice cream after consuming one or two milkshakes. Apparently, for dieters, eating is governed by self-control. However, when dieters believe that they have already overeaten, they seem to lose their motivation to limit food intake. Once they lose control, they abandon all restraints and actually eat more than unrestrained eaters.

Belief that one has already overeaten is not the only thing that can disrupt a restrained eater's self-control. Strong emotional states, such as anxiety and depression, can also have this effect. Whereas unrestrained eaters (both obese and nonobese) decrease eating in response to anxiety and depression, restrained eaters (both obese and nonobese) increase eating (Baucom & Aiken, 1981).

We are left with this conclusion: Dieting may enhance one's chances of overeating and becoming overweight or obese. In basic terms, the problem of the chronic dieter who has lost self-control is that the person no longer monitors or regulates eating. Anything

Figure 9–5.

For low-restraint subjects, preloading led to less eating; for high-restraint subjects, preloading led to more eating. (Based on data from Herman & Mack, 1975, p. 655.)

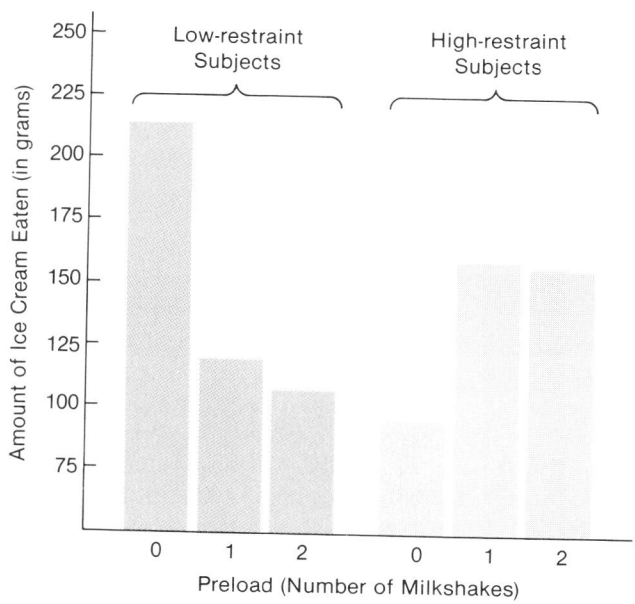

that would help such individuals regulate their eating would be beneficial. Researchers are currently studying the problem (Kirschenbaum & Tomarken, 1982).

Consequences of obesity. Becoming obese is just part of the problem. As Rodin (1981) suggests, a number of consequences of obesity serve to maintain the obesity, thereby making it difficult for a person to lose weight. For example, obesity directly affects the body's *basal metabolism rate,* the minimum amount of energy the body uses at rest to sustain its vital functions. Fatness, unfortunately, lowers the metabolic rate. Because an obese body does not burn up energy as fast as a nonobese body, it takes fewer calories to maintain obesity than to produce it. Also given that dieting may promote the maintenance of overweight, it is easy to appreciate why dieting can be so frustrating.

Considerable research suggests that inactivity is related to obesity (Thompson, Jarvie, Lahey, & Cureton, 1982). However, it is generally believed that the sedentary life-style is a consequence rather than a cause of the obesity. For the obese person, exercise may be difficult and unrewarding. Furthermore, the lack of exercise and activity consumes fewer calories and lowers the metabolic rate.

Looked at from a more positive point of view, exercise can benefit a person by consuming calories, reducing blood pressure, increasing self-esteem, offsetting the lowered metabolism that comes with dieting, and suppressing appetite (Brownell, 1982). In addition to these benefits, sustained exercise may be one of the few factors that can lower a person's set-point (Bennett & Gurin, 1982). In sum, exercise seems critical in any effort to control body weight.

Some conclusions about obesity. The theories and data discussed here suggest a rather dismal outlook for the overweight person who wants to lose weight. But the situation is not as hopeless as it would appear. Many obese people do lose weight. In fact, many do it on their own (Schachter, 1982). Others seek professional help or the social support of other individuals with the same problem. The presented theories suggest a number of things the obese person can do to help conquer a weight problem. They include the following: Keep active physically with a regular program of exercise. Avoid a diet of fattening foods. Minimize external cues that might elicit eating. Be prepared for the problems that dieting brings. Be aware that self-regulation and self-control are necessary. Be patient; losing weight is neither easy nor fast. In short, losing weight and keeping it off usually means adopting a new life-style.

— Thirst

Another important biological motive is thirst. Clearly, at times we drink liquids even though we have no water deficit. We may do so, for example, when we want to be sociable. True thirst reflects the operation of a physiologically regulated motive that ensures survival. In fact, in terms of survival, water deprivation is much more serious than food deprivation. Humans can survive without food for weeks; they can live without water only a few days (Beck, 1983).

When you feel thirsty, you seek water. What are the physiological mechanisms involved? Cannon (1918) suggested that salivation is reduced when the body's supply of water is diminished. This produces the discomfort of a dry throat, which can be relieved by drinking. Dryness of the mouth can motivate drinking; it is now believed, however, that such dryness is neither a primary nor an essential factor in the regulation of thirst (Arkes & Garske, 1982; Petri, 1981).

At least two mechanisms seem to regulate drinking. Each controls different aspects of water balance (Petri, 1981). One mechanism regulates *intracellular thirst,* which is triggered by water loss within the body cells. A theory is that receptors in the hypothalamus, known as *osmoreceptors,* detect reductions in the volume of cells caused by water loss. Such loss occurs through a process called **osmosis,** in which water diffuses from the cell because of increased sodium, or salt, concentration in the surrounding fluid. Increased sodium concentration could occur from a water deficit or from an increase in salt intake, such as through eating salty foods. In either case, cells become dehydrated. The hypothalamus relays that information to the cortex, which then initiates drinking. In addition, the hypothalamus signals the pituitary gland to secrete the hormone vasopressin (also called antidiuretic hormone, or ADH). The effect of vasopressin is to increase water absorption by the kidneys. Thus the body increases both water intake and water conservation.

A different thirst mechanism deals with *extracellular thirst,* which is triggered by water loss from the spaces between cells and in the blood. This type of thirst might occur because of insufficient water intake, excessive perspiration, blood loss, diarrhea, or vomiting. Whatever the cause, when there is a water deficit, there is a loss in both the volume of blood and the volume of the fluids surrounding the cells. In such cases, thirst is triggered by a reduced volume of *extracellular fluid*. Petri (1981) notes that this "explains why a common cry of the wounded on the battlefield is for water" (p. 97). Blood loss triggers thirst, despite the fact that it does not change the body's sodium concentration.

The loss of extracellular fluids results in a drop in blood pressure. It is believed that receptors sensitive to this change are located in the heart and large veins. They respond to reduced blood pressure by triggering the release of ADH by the pituitary and the secretion of a substance known as *renin* by the kidneys. We have already seen that ADH acts to increase water absorption by the kidneys. Renin has the same effect, so the two work together to increase blood volume (Petri, 1981).

— Sex

Unlike hunger and thirst, sexual motivation involves no body deficit (Cofer, 1972). And whereas eating and drinking work to restore deficits, sexual behavior is a matter of using up energy. Furthermore, although eating and drinking are necessary for individual survival, sex is not. To account for such peculiarities, Baron and Byrne (1981) have analyzed sexual motivation with respect to external stimulation, physiological processes, beliefs and expectations, emotions and attitudes, and fantasy and imagination. We will follow their framework here.

In both animals and humans, a number of external cues lead to sexual arousal; among them are tactual cues. In humans, whether touching takes the form of hand-holding or genital stimulation, it can serve as a stimulus for sexual arousal and sexual pleasure. Olfactory cues are also important, at least in animals. Depending on the species, either the females or the males secrete chemical substances known as *sex pheromones* (see also chapter 3), which attract members of the opposite sex and lead to courtship and copulation (Shorey, 1977). Whether smell has a similar effect on human sexual motivation is unclear at present. Visual cues, however, are definitely significant in human sexual motivation. Simply seeing someone perceived as sexually attractive can be arousing.

We cannot fully understand sexual motivation without considering its physiological aspects. In many animal species, sexual behavior is highly governed by sex hormones and is therefore periodic. Whereas mature males of such species are always hormonally ready to mate, females are not (Cofer, 1972). The females are sexually receptive only when in heat—the time during which successful fertilization of ova is most likely. The female's fertility, or estrous, cycle is governed by changes in the level of female sex hormones, known as *estrogens*. Thus sexual behavior is governed by the female's hormonal state. The importance of hormones in lower animals can also be seen in the fact that male sexual behavior declines after castration. Removal of the testes eliminates the male's principal source of *testosterone*, the major hormone in the class of male hormones called *androgens*.

The situation with humans (as well as with some species of monkeys and apes) is somewhat different. First of all, sexual maturation and sexual interest emerge at puberty, when there is an upsurge in sex-hormone levels. The sex hormones produce reproductive fertility and a continual state of sexual readiness. Sexual interest and activity are not periodic in humans. They can occur at any time. Female estrogen levels vary throughout the menstrual cycle, but without apparent effect on sexual motivation.

The main source of sexual interest for both males and females seems to be the male sex hormones, the androgens, which are present in both sexes (Hyde, 1982). Although the androgen level tends to remain relatively stable, a reduction can lead to reduced sexual interest and activity. In human males, for example, castration or illness may have this result. It has also been documented, however, that castration may cause only a slow decrease in sexual behavior, which suggests the important role of experience and learning in maintaining sexual interest (Hyde, 1982).

These facts indicate that although hormones are important, they have less impact on human sexual behavior than on the sexual behavior of other animals. However, thought processes are more important to human sexual behavior than to the sexual behavior of other animals (Baron & Byrne, 1981). In fact, imagination may be one of the strongest sources of human sexual arousal. Beliefs and expectations also greatly affect human sexual behavior. Unfortunately, many beliefs about sex are inaccurate, usually the result of inadequate education. Moreover, sexual myths often give rise to negative emotions, such as guilt and shame, which may cause avoidance of certain sexual activities (Baron & Byrne, 1981).

Sexual motivation is a complex matter, determined by a myriad of factors. Many of the points we have made here will be expanded upon in chapter 17, where we further explore human sexuality.

Stimulus-Seeking Motives

The biological motives, such as hunger and thirst, are closely related to specific bodily needs and their associated drives. Biological motives, then, fit the drive-reduction model of motivation. Other motives, however, do not. Although sexual motivation is classified as biological, it is clearly at odds with the drive-reduction model. No bodily need is met, and the organism seeks an initial increase in stimulation rather than a decrease. Other behaviors, such as exploration, manipulation, and curiosity, follow the same pattern. In short, we engage in many activities that appear to have as their goal the seeking of stimulation. Such **stimulus-seeking motives** do not appear to be directly related to physiological needs; yet they do not seem to be learned either.

Stimulus-seeking motives are perhaps best explained by the theory of optimal level of arousal, described earlier. White (1959) and Deci (1975), however, would interpret the stimulus-seeking motives in terms of the desire to achieve competence and control over the environment.

— Exploration and Stimulus-Seeking

The desire to seek stimulation expresses itself in numerous ways. Children, for instance, seem to find the exploration of novel stimuli to be *intrinsically motivating*. That is, the activity itself is inherently rewarding. Seeking novel stimulation is evident even in infants, who tend to gaze first at the most complex stimuli in an array of patterns (Berlyne, 1958b; Fantz, 1958). A preference for more complex stimuli is also evident in adults. Berlyne (1958a) showed adult subjects the stimuli reproduced in Figure 9–6. He found that the more complex stimuli were preferred, as measured by subjects' attention and the time spent looking at the stimuli. In general, it seems that novel, complex, challenging, and entertaining stimuli are most likely to evoke exploration and manipulation (Pittman, Emery, & Boggiano, 1982).

The phenomena of exploration, manipulation, and stimulus-seeking are often collectively labeled *curiosity*. In both animals and humans, curiosity has an essential adaptive purpose. Without it, organisms would possess much less information about their environment, which would lessen the chances of their survival. The desire to explore and learn about one's environment is not equally present in all humans, however. A sense of alienation that results from feelings of uninvolvement and powerlessness may lead individuals to show less curiosity than they might otherwise show (Maddi, Hoover, & Kobasa, 1982).

Sensory deprivation. The importance of stimulation can also be seen in research on sensory deprivation in humans. In research described by Heron (1957), college students were paid $20 a day to lie on a cot for the entire day (a full 24 hours)—which may sound easy. The students, however, were also confined to a partially sound-deadened room, in which they wore translucent plastic visors to prevent pattern vision and gloves with cardboard cuffs to restrict touch. The sensory deprivation thus created was quite aver-

Figure 9–6.
Berlyne manipulated complexity in a number of different ways, as illustrated here. In each case, subjects attended more to the complex figures on the right than to the simpler figures on the left. (Adapted from Berlyne, 1958a, p. 291.)

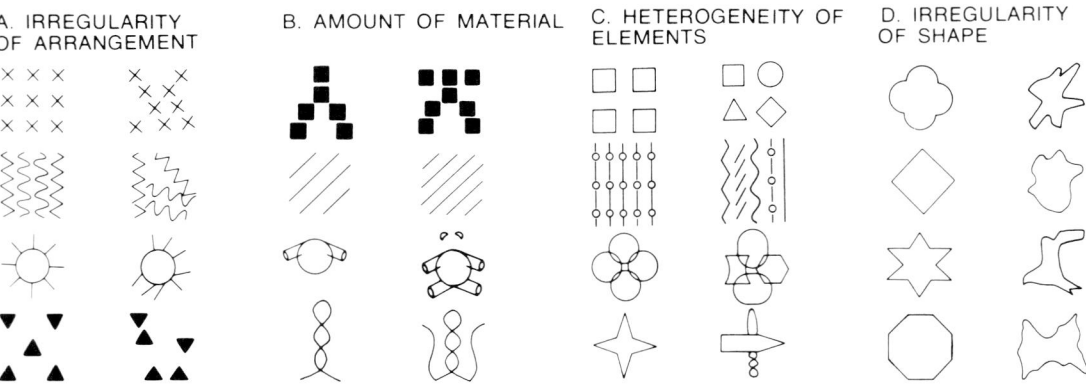

sive. Few subjects were able to tolerate the situation; most became bored, restless, and irritable and were in need of stimulation (Buck, 1976). Some subjects even reported hallucinations—seeing, feeling, or hearing things that weren't there.

— Sensation-Seekers

Earlier we referred to the fact that not all individuals exhibit equally high levels of exploratory and stimulus-seeking behavior. Recognizing this, Marvin Zuckerman (1979; Zuckerman, Buchsbaum, & Murphy, 1980) has developed a scale called the *Sensation-Seeking Scale,* which identifies people high in sensation-seeking (i.e., with a high optimal level of arousal) versus those low in sensation-seeking. Table 9–2 is a shortened version of the test that makes up this scale (Zuckerman,

1978a). If you take the test, you can get a rough idea of whether you are a high sensation-seeker. It may be informative for you to know that males generally score higher than females on the scale (Zuckerman, 1978b).

Zuckerman hypothesized that high scorers have a higher level of optimal arousal than do low scorers. Consequently, high scorers should be more motivated than low scorers to seek out stimulation in a variety of contexts. Although the optimal-level-of-arousal theory is by no means a proved explanation of sensation-seeking (Carrol, Zuckerman, & Vogel, 1982), research continues to test its validity.

According to Zuckerman, high and low scorers differ in four basic ways:

1. *Thrill and adventure seeking.* High scorers express a desire to seek excitement in risky and adventurous

Table 9–2.

Test of sensation-seeking. (From Marvin Zuckerman, 1978a, p. 46.)

ARE YOU A HIGH OR A LOW SENSATION-SEEKER?

To test your own sensation-seeking tendencies, try this shortened version of one of Marvin Zuckerman's earlier scales. For each of the 13 items, circle the choice, A or B, that best describes your likes or dislikes or the way you feel. Instructions for scoring appear at the end of the test.

1. A. I would like a job that requires a lot of traveling.
   B. I would prefer a job in one location.
2. A. I am invigorated by a brisk, cold day.
   B. I can't wait to get indoors on a cold day.
3. A. I get bored seeing the same old faces.
   B. I like the comfortable familiarity of everyday friends.
4. A. I would prefer living in an ideal society in which everyone is safe, secure, and happy.
   B. I would have preferred living in the unsettled days of our history.
5. A. I sometimes like to do things that are a little frightening.
   B. A sensible person avoids activities that are dangerous.
6. A. I would not like to be hypnotized.
   B. I would like to have the experience of being hypnotized.
7. A. The most important goal of life is to live it to the fullest and experience as much as possible.
   B. The most important goal of life is to find peace and happiness.
8. A. I would like to try parachute-jumping.
   B. I would never want to try jumping out of a plane, with or without a parachute.

9. A. I enter cold water gradually, giving myself time to get used to it.
   B. I like to dive or jump right into the ocean or a cold pool.
10. A. When I go on a vacation, I prefer the comfort of a good room and bed.
    B. When I go on a vacation, I prefer the change of camping out.
11. A. I prefer people who are emotionally expressive even if they are a bit unstable.
    B. I prefer people who are calm and even-tempered.
12. A. A good painting should shock or jolt the senses.
    B. A good painting should give one a feeling of peace and security.
13. A. People who ride motorcycles must have some kind of unconscious need to hurt themselves.
    B. I would like to drive or ride a motorcycle.

Scoring

Count one point for each of the following items that you have circled: 1A, 2A, 3A, 4B, 5A, 6B, 7A, 8A, 9B, 10B, 11A, 12A, 13B. Add up your total and compare it with the norms below.

0–3   Very low on sensation-seeking
4–5   Low
6–9   Average
10–11 High
12–13 Very high

Although the test gives some indication of a person's rating, it is not a highly reliable measure. One reason is, of course, that the test has been abbreviated. Another is that the norms are based largely on the scores of college students who have taken the test. As people get older, their scores on sensation-seeking tend to go down.

activities, such as parachute jumping or fast driving—a desire they often carry out (Zuckerman & Neeb, 1980; Zuckerman, 1983).

2. *Experience seeking.* High scorers seek excitement by adopting a nonconventional life-style. They may seek unusual friends, travel frequently, or take drugs.

3. *Disinhibition.* High scorers tend to be socially disinhibited. They are characterized by social drinking, gambling, and the need for sexual variety.

4. *Boredom susceptibility.* High scorers have a low tolerance for experiences that are constant or repetitious. They do not like routine work or predictable, boring people.

Acquired Motives

We turn now to **acquired motives,** which are thought to be based on learning and experience. A number of such motives have been proposed, including the need for social approval, the need to achieve, the need to dominate others, the need to affiliate, the need for recognition, and the need for nurturance (see, for example, Murray, 1938). Here we focus on two particular needs that have received considerable attention from researchers: the need for affiliation and the need to achieve. These needs are purely psychological, not physical. Researchers interested in acquired motives tend to use the words *needs* and *motives* synonymously, and we will do so here.

— Need for Affiliation

Some people easily and frequently initiate conversations with strangers; others prefer to keep to themselves. Those who prefer social contact are said to have a strong **need for affiliation (*n* Aff).** They are more likely than others to seek social contact and to try to make new friends (Crouse & Mehrabian, 1977).

Regardless of our level of *n* Aff, certain situations may alter our desire to be with others. Being a newcomer at college, for instance, may enhance the desire to seek affiliation. Furthermore, the desire to affiliate often arises during significant events or when we are fearful (Schachter, 1959; Shaver & Klinnert, 1982). At such times, we seem to seek contact with others so that we can talk, reduce our anxieties, compare ideas, and confirm that our perceptions and feelings are appropriate (social comparison) (Byrne & Kelly, 1981). Cer-

tain factors also noticeably lessen the desire for affiliation. For example, embarrassment may be heightened by the presence of others, which leads us to avoid affiliation (Fish, Karabenick, & Heath, 1978).

— Need for Achievement

Another significant human motive is the **need for achievement (*n* Ach)**—the need to strive for success and excellence (Byrne & Kelly, 1981). Because of the diversity in learning experiences, it should not be surprising to find that people differ greatly in this motive.

Measuring the achievement motive. The most popular means for assessing achievement motivation has been the *Thematic Apperception Test (TAT)* (see also chapter 13). For *n* Ach to be measured with the TAT, subjects are shown ambiguous pictures of people and are asked to create stories to go with the pictures, answering certain questions in their stories (McClelland, Atkinson, Clark, & Lowell, 1953). The more achievement-related themes contained in the TAT stories (e.g., someone working toward a goal), the higher the subject's presumed *n* Ach.

Development of achievement motivation. Early research suggested that two important factors foster achievement motivation: independence training and achievement training. Children with high *n* Ach scores had parents who expected them to display independence at an early age and to do things well (Byrne & Kelley, 1981). A recent study, though, suggests that such parental expectations foster achievement motivation only in middle-class boys (McClelland & Pilon, 1983). When children of both sexes from lower- and middle-class families were considered, two other parental practices appeared to be of greater importance: scheduling of feeding and severity of toilet-training. Although more research is needed, something about strictness in these practices apparently contributes to the development of *n* Ach. In addition to such factors, a number of other experiences during school or adult life may encourage the development of *n* Ach.

Characteristics of high achievers. Much research has focused on the effects of being low or high in *n* Ach. For example, a positive relationship exists between n Ach and IQ and n Ach and school grades (Byrne & Kelley, 1981). However, because of their concern with achieving success, those high in n Ach are also more likely to cheat than are those low in n Ach (Johnson, 1981). Researchers have also examined relationships between n Ach and risk-taking. It appears that individuals high in n Ach prefer tasks that are challenging but not so difficult that failure is likely (Byrne & Kelley, 1981).

As Byrne & Kelly note, those high in n Ach are also typically concerned with using time efficiently and planning ahead. They are therefore better able than others to delay immediate gratification in order to obtain greater rewards at a later time (Mischel, 1961).

What about women?   To date, most studies have explored male achievement motivation. We should not jump to the conclusion, however, that women are not also motivated to achieve. Although some gender differences have been found, men and women do not seem to differ consistently in their level of n Ach (Spence & Helmreich, 1978). They may differ, however, in the kinds of activities and goals they choose as a focus for their achievement needs (Deaux, 1976). Learning experiences—what our parents teach us, what we read, and what we watch on television—can influence our ideas about what achievement means.

One hindrance to achievement is **fear of success,** a learned motive to avoid success for fear of its negative consequences. This idea, proposed by Horner (e.g., 1972), was first thought to apply primarily to women. It has been theorized that many women learn to avoid success because they anticipate negative consequences, such as social rejection or a loss of femininity, if they do succeed. Researchers realize now, though, that men also exhibit fear of success (Popp & Muhs, 1982). In fact, it appears that there is no difference between men and women in fear of success (Condry & Dyer, 1976; Miron Zuckerman & Wheeler, 1975). Both are motivated to avoid success and will indeed avoid it if they perceive its consequences to be unpleasant (Deaux, 1976). This outcome is particularly likely when activities are out of the gender role.

— APPLICATION —

ACHIEVEMENT MOTIVATION AND ACHIEVEMENT BEHAVIOR

Spence and Helmreich (1978) have constructed a measure of achievement motivation called the *Work and Family Orientation Questionnaire.* The questionnaire assesses three major components of achievement motivation: (1) mastery—a preference for difficult, challenging tasks; (2) work orientation—positive attitudes toward hard work; and (3) competitiveness—enjoyment of interpersonal competition and of surpassing others. The higher one's standing on the three dimensions, the higher one's overall achievement motivation.

Spence, Helmreich, and colleagues have related the three dimensions to real-life achievement. For example, their studies have examined grade-point averages of undergraduate students (Helmreich & Spence, 1978), mean income levels of male business-school alumni (Sanders, 1978), and eminence of doctorate-level scientists (assessed by references to their work in the *Science Citation Index*) (Helmreich, Beane, Lucker, & Spence, 1978; Helmreich, Spence, Beane, Lucker, & Matthews, 1980). Generally, it was found that high scorers on work and mastery consistently achieved higher incomes, greater eminence, and higher grade-point averages than did low scorers. Low scorers on competitiveness, on the other hand, performed better than did high scorers. This was especially true for those who were otherwise well motivated (high in work and mastery). Only for those who were not highly motivated in terms of work and mastery did being highly competitive confer a slight advantage.

It is intriguing that competitiveness limits high achievement. Our society seems to promote a competition ethic, which assumes that being competitive is essential for success (Riskind & Wilson, 1982). Clearly, competition has its place, but it does not seem to be as valuable as society proclaims. Why competitiveness limits achievement is, for the moment, unknown. Nevertheless, it is worth remembering that an emphasis on work and challenges leads to achievement.

What is emotion? How does it occur? How do we know which emotion we are experiencing? How does emotion affect behavior? Each of us has some common-sense ideas about the answers to these questions. Psychologists, in turn, have also proposed answers, none of which is, as yet, definitive. Before we examine the psychology of emotion, let's again consider how emotion and motivation are connected.

Emotion and motivation are closely related. Some theorists, in fact, view emotions as the principal motivational system in human behavior (e.g., Izard, 1977). We noted in the chapter introduction, for example, that emotions of distress and empathy can provide the motivation for helping behavior. Analogously, anger may motivate aggressive behavior. To reverse the relationship, motives may also produce emotions. Sexual motivation, for example, may lead to such emotions as joy or guilt, depending on how it is expressed.

Defining Emotions

Experiencing an emotion produces a subjective feeling or awareness of emotion, reflected in such statements as "I feel happy." Izard (1977) suggests that everyone experiences 10 fundamental emotions: interest-excitement, joy, surprise, distress, anger, disgust, contempt, fear, shame, and guilt. According to Izard, we experience other emotions too, but they seem to reflect combinations of the 10 basic emotions. For example, anxiety might be thought of as a combination of fear plus two or more of the following: distress, anger, shame, guilt, and interest-excitement (Izard, 1977).

Emotion is also defined by body changes. A number of these changes reflect autonomic nervous system (ANS) activity (see chapter 2). When we experience an emotion, the sympathetic branch of the ANS becomes more active in an attempt to prepare us for emergency action, such as fight or flight. Whether we experience anger, fear, or other emotions, the physiological reactions are similar. As chapter 2 explained, the sympathetic branch increases heart rate, respiration, blood flow to the muscles, blood sugar release by the liver, adrenaline secretion by the adrenal glands, and blood pressure. Other effects include inhibition of digestion, dry mouth caused by decreased salivation, dilation of

the pupils of the eyes to let in more light, and decreased electrical resistance of the skin, which is known as the galvanic skin response, or GSR. The GSR reflects the fact that during emotion the sweat glands increase their activity.

Following emotional arousal, the changes just described are counteracted by the parasympathetic branch of the ANS, which works to restore and conserve the body's energy reserves and maintain homeostatic balance. Among its effects are reduced heart rate, increased salivation, and resumption of normal digestive processes. It is possible, of course, for the body to remain physiologically aroused for long periods of time. As we will discover later (see chapter 14), prolonged emotion can sometimes damage the body.

Physiological arousal does not necessarily cause emotion, but certainly it accompanies it. Perhaps because it is easy to notice a pounding heart or sweaty palms, theorists have emphasized body changes when discussing emotion. Izard (1977), however, notes the occurrence of other body activity—activity that we do not typically think about during an emotion. According to Izard, before we become aware of an emotion, various brain structures send neural messages to the skin and muscles of the face, producing a facial expression. Izard argues that we do not become aware of the facial activity itself; all we notice is the overall feeling of the emotion. Nevertheless, as we will see later, Izard believes that facial activity plays a crucial role in emotional experience.

Specific facial expressions, such as the smile associated with joy or the frown with anger are among the body's outward, visible signs of emotion. Emotions are outwardly expressed in other ways too, but these expressions are more open to interpretation than are facial expressions. Crying, for example, is a response we associate with emotions as disparate as distress and joy (Patrusky, 1981). Eye contact is another rough indicator of emotion. A lot of eye contact by another person leads us to assume that the person is experiencing a positive emotion; avoidance of eye contact leads us to assume a negative emotion, such as guilt or depression (Baron & Byrne, 1981).

Posture is another way in which emotions can express themselves through the body, although there is no evidence that all of the emotions can be distinguished from one another on this basis. Nevertheless, depression seems to be one emotion associated with a particular postural cue, namely a slumped-over body posture (Riskind & Gotay, 1982). Verbal behavior also seems to vary somewhat with emotion. Depression, for example, is associated with a reduction in the normal range of loudness, pitch, and length of utterance (LaFrance & Mayo, 1978). Anxiety seems to be associated with stuttering, word omissions, repetition, and slips of the tongue.

Of the various outward signs of emotion, facial expressions provide observers with the best clue as to the emotion being experienced. Also, as we will see later, according to some theories, facial expressions are even more important to the person experiencing the emotion than they are to the observer.

How Do Emotions Occur?

Psychologists have long debated how we know we are experiencing an emotion or, more particularly, a specific emotion, such as fear or anger. Let's examine a few of their thoughts on this issue.

The James-Lange Theory

Common sense may dictate that a stimulus that we know represents a potential danger, such as seeing a wild grizzly bear, causes us to experience fear. The fear in turn causes physiological arousal, which prepares us for fight or flight. If we are like most mortals, we flee. This commonsense view bears little resemblance to some of the theories of emotion that have been offered.

William James (1884), the American philosopher-psychologist, offered a theory of emotion that has come to be known as the James-Lange theory. Lange (1885/1922) was a Danish physiologist who expressed ideas very similar to those of James. The James-Lange theory proposes an interesting twist on the commonsense theory of emotion. According to the theory, the experience of emotion occurs in this sequence: stimulus → internal body changes → subjective experience of emotion. The theory recognizes that when we experience an emotion, internal body changes (caused by the actions of the sympathetic branch of the ANS) occur. Beyond this, the perception of body changes leads to the subjective experience of an emotion.

For the preceding to be true, there has to be some means by which we detect one emotion versus an-other. How do we know, for example, that we are experiencing joy rather than anger? The James-Lange theory suggests that we differentiate emotions by the pattern of body changes, which is different for each emotion. As our earlier discussion noted, this aspect of the theory is not supported by the available evidence, a point made by Cannon (1927) in his critique of the James-Lange theory. The same pattern of body changes seems to occur for all the emotions. Nevertheless, the James-Lange theory has had an important influence on the study of emotion. Part of the theory was later salvaged by Stanley Schachter, as we will now see.

Schachter's Cognitive-Physiological Theory

In recognizing both the virtues and the liabilities of the James-Lange theory, Schachter (1964) sought to explain how the same pattern of physiological changes could accompany all emotions when, at the same time, we are able to distinguish various emotions subjectively. His answer was that first we are physiologically aroused in response to some stimulus and then we label that arousal in a manner consistent with our circumstances. In effect, Schachter added a cognitive, or thinking, component to the physiological component of emotions. The cognitive component is what allows us to evaluate or interpret arousal. As Schachter (1964) points out, the physiological arousal elicited by meeting a figure with a gun in a dark alley would likely be labeled as fear because of our knowledge of dark alleys and guns.

A classic study by Schachter and Singer (1962) illustrates the predictions made in Schachter's theory. In the study, subjects received an injection of epinephrine, which produces strong autonomic arousal—increased heart rate, for example. Some of the subjects were correctly informed about the signs of this arousal—pounding heart, hand tremors, and warm, flushed face. Other subjects were misinformed about the signs; they were told that their feet would get numb, they would itch in various places, and they would perhaps get a headache. Still other subjects were left ignorant about the possible side-effects of the injection.

According to Schachter, the correctly informed subjects had a ready explanation for their arousal—the injection. The uninformed and misinformed subjects, in contrast, were highly aroused but didn't know why. Under such circumstances, Schachter suggests, subjects look to situational cues to explain or interpret their arousal. To test this prediction, following the injection,

Schachter placed an associate (or stooge) in the room with each subject. The stooge intentionally acted either euphoric or angry during the 20 minutes spent in the room with the subject. The euphoria-anger manipulation provided situational cues that the subjects could use to label the arousal they were experiencing.

As expected, the informed subjects were much less likely to be influenced by the stooge than were the other subjects. With the euphoric stooge, informed subjects reported being less happy than did other subjects, and with the angry stooge, they showed less anger than did other subjects. The misinformed and uninformed subjects tended to rely on the stooge's actions to label their arousal. When the stooge was angry, they were angry; when he was happy, they were happy.

It seems, then, that in inferring our emotional states, we rely not only on our body's state of arousal but also on external cues, such as the behavior of others. Schachter's theory has not been without its critics, however. Controversy exists, for example, regarding replication of Schachter and Singer's findings (Marshall & Zimbardo, 1979; Maslach, 1979; Schachter & Singer, 1979). One reviewer (Reisenzein, 1983) concluded the following with respect to Schachter's theory: "There is no convincing evidence for Schachter's claim that arousal is a necessary condition for an emotional state, nor for the suggestion that emotion states may result from a labeling of unexplained arousal" (p. 239). According to Reisenzein, the case for arousal in emotion has been overstated. Despite the criticisms, however, Schachter's theory has had widespread appeal and application and is likely to continue being an influential theory and source of ideas regarding the nature of emotions. The advantage of Schachter's theory over the James-Lange theory is that it easily explains how we are able to distinguish between various emotions. In Schachter's view, the same physiological arousal can be labeled as fear, anger, joy, or any other emotion, depending on situational cues and the resulting cognitions.

— Lazarus's Cognitive-Appraisal Theory

Richard Lazarus (e.g., 1968) maintains that emotions arise from the evaluations we make of environmental stimuli. In his terminology, we cognitively appraise these stimuli in order to assess their significance and relevance for us. For Lazarus, such "cognitive activity is a necessary as well as sufficient condition of emotion" (Lazarus, 1982, p. 1019). Physiological changes may in-

deed be part of the emotional experience, but as we can see from his statement, Lazarus views emotions as resulting only from thought.

As an example, consider the different appraisals that students might make when told that there will be a pop quiz. An unprepared student may evaluate the news as a threat and may therefore experience fear. A prepared student may evaluate the news as a challenge and may therefore experience interest and excitement. As we will see in chapter 14, Lazarus's view has much to say about how we can cope with anxiety and stressful situations. The key is to change our cognitive appraisal of the situations. As our cognitions change, so do our emotional reactions.

— Izard's Differential-Emotions Theory

Carroll Izard (e.g., 1977) has proposed a view that he refers to as differential-emotions theory. Izard believes that the 10 basic emotions listed earlier result from facial feedback to the brain that is made conscious as a specific emotional feeling. He adds that a number of different events can initiate emotions. A sudden and unexpected event can cause surprise, personal insults can cause anger, violating a moral code can cause guilt, and so on. These varied events cause emotions to occur in the form of particular patterns of facial-muscle activity (specific facial expressions). Through innate neural programs, the brain gets feedback about the facial expression and transforms that feedback into a conscious feeling of a specific emotion. Thus, although other physiological changes are the same for various emotions, facial-muscle activity varies. It is such variability, according to Izard, that allows us to perceive different emotions.

What evidence is there that facial feedback and facial expression do, in fact, influence emotional experience? What evidence is there that facial expressions are innate rather than learned? Let's examine both questions.

The facial-feedback hypothesis. Facial expressions regulate emotional experiences, according to the **facial feedback hypothesis** (Buck, 1980). Laird (1974) had subjects frown or smile. He found that smiling subjects reported a more positive mood and judged cartoons as more humorous than did frowning subjects. In a study by Ekman, Friesen, and Ancoli (1980), spontaneous facial expressions were elicited by showing subjects films intended to elicit positive or negative affect. Not only did specific facial expressions correspond to specific felt emotions (a smiling face led to a feeling of positive affect), but the intensity of the felt emotion even varied with the facial expressions. For example, some types of smiles led to more intense happiness than did other types of smiles.

These studies and others (e.g., Miron Zuckerman, Klorman, Larrance, & Spiegel, 1981), suggest a one-to-one correspondence between felt emotion and specific facial expressions. Facial expressions appear to do more than just provide a read-out for observers to use in judging someone's emotional state. They also provide the source of one's own emotional experience.

The innateness of facial expressions. If it is true that facial expressions lead to felt emotions via built-in genetic programs, it should be true that all people, from all cultures, will display the same facial expressions for the same emotions. In assessing the universality or innateness of facial expressions, the work of Paul Ekman and his colleagues (Ekman & Friesen, 1975), is particularly relevant. Crucial to exploring this hypothesis, of course, is finding people who have had no contact with our culture. Otherwise, their expressions could perhaps be learned. Ekman and Friesen solved the problem by going to remote areas of New Guinea and asking subjects to demonstrate by facial expressions how they would feel in certain situations, such as when their child has died. The expressions they displayed for the emotions of happiness, sadness, anger, and disgust were recognizable and familiar to Western observers.

Despite the apparent fact that facial expressions are unlearned, it is possible for learning to play a role in determining when certain emotions are expressed. Ekman (1973) has noted in this regard that cultures vary in what he calls **display rules**—"norms regarding the expected management of facial appearance" (Ekman, 1973, p. 176). In a particular situation, what is appropriate in one culture may not be in another.

The universality of facial expressions is also evident in Ekman and Friesen's finding about the recognition of emotions. Figure 9–7 shows the extent of agreement about the particular emotion being expressed. The observers, who were from five countries, seemed to recognize happiness and the other emotions regardless of their nationality. In addition, even subjects in remote areas of New Guinea and Western Iran have been able to recognize expressions as signs of particular emotions.

The convincing evidence for the innateness of emotional expressions is further supported by Izard's finding that facial expressions of emotions are evident even in infants (Trotter, 1983). Infants express joy, anger, interest, disgust, surprise, distress, sadness, and fear (in the same fashion as adults do) by the time they are approximately 8 months old. In fact, most of these emotions are expressed much sooner than that. Facial expressions of contempt and guilt typically appear by age 2.

How Emotions Affect Us

Emotions affect us in a variety of ways. As examples, let's consider emotional effects on the body and on perception, cognition, actions, and sexual behavior (Izard, 1977).

In addition to the body changes already described, emotions associated with stress can wreak havoc on the body, creating such health problems as ulcers, migraine headaches, hypertension, and other disorders (see chapter 14). With respect to perception, Izard (1977) cites several examples of how emotion can influence us. A distressed or sad person may misperceive the remarks of others as critical. A fearful person may view the world with tunnel vision and see only that which is feared. A joyful person may see the world through rose-colored glasses. Isen and Shalker (1982), for example, found that subjects in a positive mood perceived pictures of scenery as more pleasant than did control subjects (neutral mood), who in turn perceived them as more pleasant than did subjects in a negative mood. Thinking, memory, and imagination seem to be similarly affected (Izard, 1977). An angry person may think only angry thoughts. A depressed person may think only depressing or negative thoughts. In fact, as noted in chapter 7, people seem especially likely to remember events and experiences that are consistent with the emotions they are experiencing.

Emotions heavily influence our actions also. Positive emotions cause liking for others. Guilt motivates us to atone for our sins. Depression may lead to inactivity and possibly to suicide. Interest and excitement over some issue or topic may motivate us to increase our knowledge. Disgust over the same topic may lead us to reject it. Negative emotions, such as those created by failure, may lead us to desire more personal space, or a greater distance from others (see chapter 19). A fearful person may not go anywhere near the feared objects. The fear may be so intense the person may not even leave the house. Shame or shyness may motivate a person to hide and to avoid other people.

Figure 9–7.

When observers from five nations judged the emotions being displayed in the photographs, agreement was high in most cases. (From Ekman & Friesen, 1975, p. 25.)

Percentage of Observers in Agreement as to Emotion Shown in Photograph					
	UNITED STATES	BRAZIL	CHILE	ARGENTINA	JAPAN
Fear	85	67	68	54	66
Disgust	92	97	92	92	90
Happiness	97	95	95	98	100
Anger	67	90	94	90	90

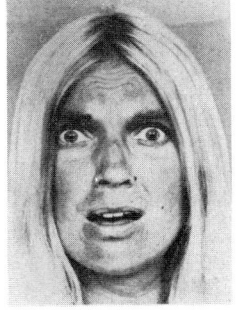

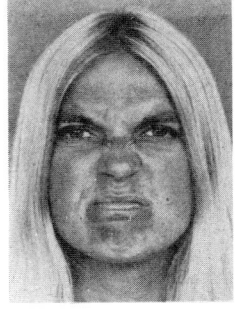

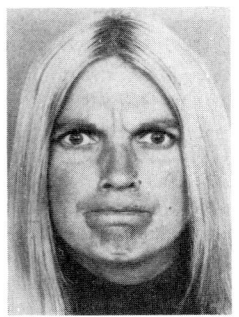

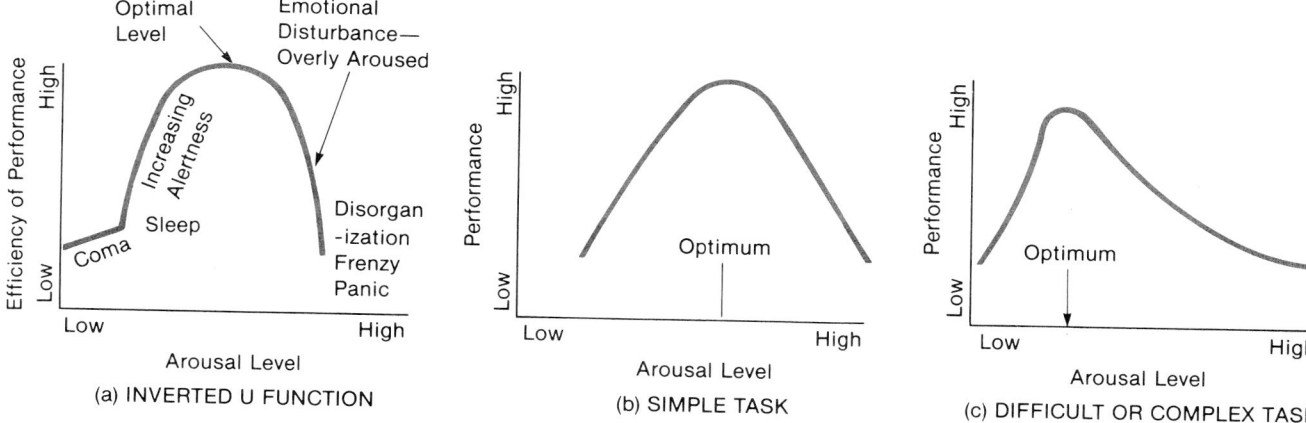

Figure 9–8.

The graph on the left shows the relationship between arousal and performance. There is an optimal level of arousal; greater or lesser arousal results in poorer performance. As the middle and right-hand graphs show, however, what that optimal level is depends on the complexity of the task. The greater the complexity, the lower the optimal level, a principle known as the Yerkes-Dodson law.

Consistent with arousal theory, discussed earlier in the chapter, strong emotional arousal can lead to disorganized and ineffective task performance. As shown in the left-hand graph of Figure 9–8, up to some point, increases in arousal facilitate behavioral efficiency by making a person increasingly alert and attentive (Hebb, 1955). However, beyond some optimal level, further increases in arousal lead only to confusion, reduced awareness, divided attention, and disorganized and poor behavioral performance (Lindsley, 1952).

There is more to the story, however. The inverted U-shaped relationship between arousal and performance shown on the left in Figure 9–8 depends on the complexity of the task one is engaging in. This is illustrated in the middle and right-hand graphs in the figure, where the optimal level of arousal for a simple task is shown to be higher than it is for a complex task. Stated in other terms, for relatively simple tasks, the optimal level of arousal is an intermediate level; for more complex or difficult tasks, the optimal level is low. These principles define what is known as the

Yerkes-Dodson law, which states that the more difficult a task is, the lower the optimal level of arousal (Beck, 1983). Thus, although a little arousal is good, too much can be detrimental to task performance, such as test-taking. If you have a tendency to become extremely anxious when taking tests, perhaps the best strategy is to be well prepared and to develop good test-taking skills (Kirkland & Hollandsworth, 1980). Doing so will tend to keep your anxiety at a low level.

Finally, emotion is intertwined with sexual motivation. As Izard (1977) points out, when sexual motivation interacts with the emotions of anger and contempt, rape may be a result. Shame, guilt, and fear may lead to the avoidance of certain types of sexual activity or even to the inability to have an orgasm. Guilt, anxiety, and embarrassment may lead to the avoidance of contraceptive devices (see chapter 17).

These examples are only a sampling of the ways emotions affect us. They do illustrate, however, that the

═══ APPLICATION ═══

LIE DETECTORS

The lie detector, or, more accurately, the **polygraph,** is an instrument that measures a number of body

changes associated with emotion. It is often used to assess the truthfulness of an individual's verbal responses to questions. Body changes usually measured by the polygraph include breathing rate, blood pressure, and galvanic skin response (GSR). Figure 9–9 shows a typical polygraph test. The GSR is measured by electrodes attached to the examinee's fingertips. Sensors around the chest and abdomen record respiration. Blood pressure is measured by means of a cuff attached to the examinee's arm. Pens on the polygraph record on a moving strip of paper each of the body reactions as the examinee responds to questions.

Traditionally, the polygraph has been used by law-enforcement officials to probe leads and verify facts in criminal investigations. Recently, however, polygraph testing has invaded private industry. Each year, hundreds of thousands of individuals are given the test either when applying for jobs or during employment in an effort to detect employee theft (Beach, 1980; Meyer, 1982). Meyer (1982) has observed that the polygraph "has become a common fixture in American society, almost to an Orwellian degree" (p. 24). That statement seems particularly appropriate in light of recent efforts by the U.S. Department of Defense to expand its polygraph testing to include the thousands of civilian and military employees who deal with classified information (Mervis, 1983).

We saw earlier that emotions are associated with a number of specific body changes. Presumably, the presence of such changes shows that a person is in a highly emotional state. We have all undoubtedly experienced the racing heart and sweaty palms that accompany lying and guilt. Does that mean, then, that when the polygraph shows that we are highly emotional, we are lying? Not necessarily. The same body reactions associated with lying also accompany other emotions, such as anxiety. While taking a polygraph test, we could tell the truth but show heightened emotional arousal caused by anxiety. If we do, we may be accused of deception.

The lie detector is incapable of detecting the specific emotion of guilt (Lykken, 1981). Furthermore, as David Lykken, a critic of polygraph testing, notes, even if a lie detector could detect that emotion, it wouldn't matter. People do not always feel guilty when they lie, and at times people feel guilty while telling the truth. In effect, the lie detector doesn't really measure lying. What it measures is unspecified, general emotional arousal, nothing else (Lykken, 1981). To appreciate the implications, let's examine the nature of the questioning in a polygraph test. One common format, called the Lie Control Test (Lykken, 1981), entails two types of questions. The first type involves questions that are relevant

Figure 9–9.
The typical set-up for a polygraph examination.

or critical (such as "Did you rob the Sunny Lane Grocery Store the night of June 2, 1983?"). The second type involves questions which are more general and of the following nature: "Have you ever, in your life, taken from someone something that didn't belong to you?" It is assumed that a person innocent of a crime will still lie in response to control questions for fear of appearing to be the kind of person who would commit a crime. It is also assumed that most people at some time in their lives have taken something that wasn't theirs. Presumably, then, innocent subjects will respond more emotionally to control questions than to relevant questions. In contrast, subjects who are lying about the crime are expected to respond more emotionally to the relevant questions than the control questions. Figure 9–10 shows polygraph results from such a questioning format.

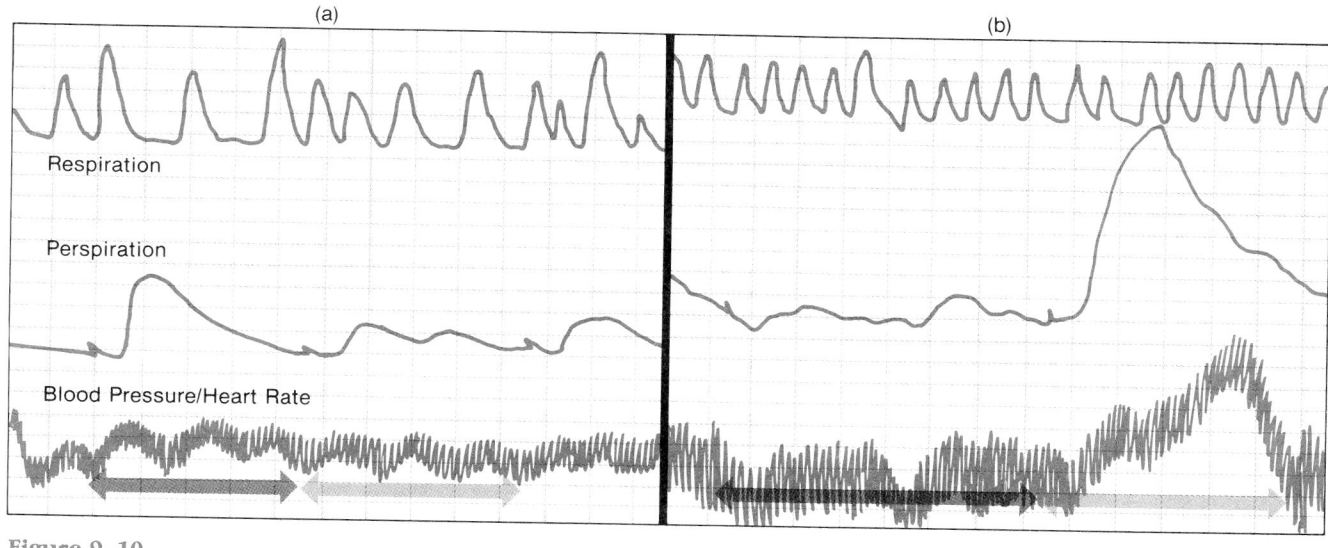

Figure 9–10.

The left polygraph record (a) shows the results from a subject considered to be truthful. Her physiological reactions were stronger to the control question (black arrow), which she answered with no, than to the relevant question (brown arrow), which she answered with yes. The right side (b) shows the results from a subject considered to be guilty because his physiological reactions were less strong to the control question (answered no) than to the relevant question (answered yes). (See Meyer, 1982.)

Suppose that a truthful subject answers a control question truthfully and shows low emotional arousal. At the same time, this person responds strongly to the relevant questions, not from lying but because the content of the questions arouses an emotion such as anxiety or sadness (Horvath, 1977; Waid & Orne, 1982). Being asked about a serious crime, even when you are being truthful, can be arousing—much more arousing than being asked about your general behavior over a lifetime. You might even feel indignant at being asked about possible involvement in a serious crime, and this will be arousing (Lykken, 1981). Even if you lie when answering the control question, your response may not exceed the arousal elicited by the relevant question. In short, you could be innocent but still appear guilty according to the polygraph. Unfortunately, such errors occur often—more often than do errors finding guilty people innocent (Lykken, 1981). Furthermore, not all guilty subjects are detected by polygraphs. Guilty subjects don't necessarily find relevant ques-

tions more threatening and arousing than control questions. Besides, a guilty person (or an innocent one, for that matter) could resort to taking tranquilizers, which lower arousal (Waid & Orne, 1982).

Clearly, the validity of the polygraph is questionable. Examiners generally set the accuracy rate at 90 percent or higher (Lykken, 1981). But well-conducted, definitive validity studies are lacking, and the claim of 90 percent accuracy is unfounded. The actual accuracy rates appear to be much lower. For example, in a study by Horvath (1977), although 77 percent of the guilty subjects were correctly detected from their polygraph records, only 51 percent of the innocent subjects were correctly classified as innocent. In other words, half the innocent subjects were considered deceptive.

Beyond validity problems, many people view the polygraph as an invasion of privacy. You have the right to refuse a polygraph test, but many people discover that refusal often is equated with guilt and may result in losing a job or the chance for a job.

ANOREXIA NERVOSA

An eating disorder involving self-starvation and severe weight loss, **anorexia nervosa,** is rapidly increasing in the United States. The disorder (see Figure 9–11) occurs primarily in adolescent or young-adult females (Bemis, 1978), but it may affect males as well. Anorexia nervosa is currently receiving considerable attention from medical and psychological researchers, and it is hoped that the future will bring solutions to the problem. Today, the prognosis for complete recovery is not good (Franken, 1982). Many treated anorexic patients suffer relapses and require further treatment. Many others die as a result of the disorder.

In a number of cases of anorexia, the individual also has episodes of **bulimia**—intense, recurrent episodes of excessive eating (binge-eating), followed by depression, self-deprecating thoughts, and weight-reducing efforts. Such efforts include self-induced vomiting and a severely restricted diet (Halmi, 1983). Bulimia also occurs without anorexia, and it too seems to be on the rise (Casper, 1983; Mintz, 1982).

Researchers are looking at many possible causes of anorexia nervosa. Some are seeking biological causes, such as genetic or hormonal problems. For example, lower levels of hormones known as *catecholamines* have been associated with anorexia (Franken, 1982). Whether the lowered levels are a cause or a result of anorexia remains to be determined. It is nevertheless interesting to note that catecholamine deficiency is also associated with depression (see chapter 15) and that depression is often linked to anorexia nervosa (Hendren, 1983).

Other researchers believe that our preoccupation with thinness is at fault; this belief suggests the importance of learning and experience. For the anorexic, any fat at all is perceived as too much, which leads to excessive dieting. Particularly notable here is the fact that "anorexia nervosa appears to be reaching epidemic proportions in upper socioeconomic level girls" (Maloney & Klykylo, 1983, p. 99)—the individuals who are probably the most

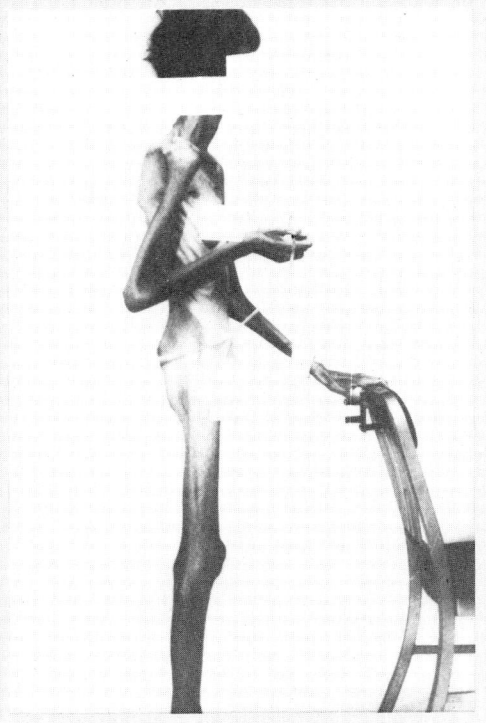

Figure 9–11.
A severely ill anorexic.

concerned with having a thin appearance. Another factor in anorexic patients is their distorted body images. They tend to see themselves as overweight even when, by all other accounts, they are grotesquely emaciated (Bemis, 1978).

The families of anorexics have not gone unnoticed (Franken, 1982). One theory is that the anorexic has a dominant mother and turns to dieting and starvation as part of an intense struggle for self-control. Other theorists contend that the entire family unit is at fault, that the family is characterized by disturbed relationships and interactions involving overprotectiveness, rigidity, and poor conflict management. Not eating becomes a way of dealing with

the power struggle that seems to characterize many of these families.

To reiterate, there are as yet no definitive statements about the causes of anorexia nervosa. The search has really just begun. Even more uncertainty exists with respect to treatment. Most researchers, however, seem to agree that the parents as well as the patient should be involved in therapy (Anyan & Schowalter, 1983; Halmi, 1983; Liebman, Sargent, & Silver, 1983; Maloney & Klykylo, 1983; Harper,

1983). Other forms of individual treatment (described in chapter 16), such as operant-conditioning, systematic-desensitization, and cognitive-behavioral therapy, have been used in conjunction with family therapy. Drugs, too, are often used in treatment. The problem, however, is that "very few controlled treatment studies have been done" (Halmi, 1983, p. 120). Much remains to be learned about which treatments are most effective. Perhaps a solution for anorexia nervosa is already on the horizon.

═══ SUMMARY ═══

1. Motivation can be thought of as the forces acting on or within an organism that initiate and direct behavior as well as governing its intensity.

2. Instincts were once considered by many psychologists to explain all behavior. In recent times, they have reappeared in the work of ethologists, many of whom argue that both animals and humans are governed by instincts.

3. Drive theory assumes that behavior is motivated by biological needs. Incentive theory emphasizes the role of external stimuli in motivating behavior. Arousal theory suggests that organisms sometimes seek stimulation to maintain an optimal level of arousal.

4. Cognitive theories of motivation emphasize that we are motivated to evaluate the accuracy and consistency of our knowledge about the world and ourselves. Other theories focus on our striving toward competence and control.

5. Extrinsic rewards and threats can affect the intrinsic interest one has in some activity.

6. Biological motives relate to the survival of the individual or the species. Hunger is one such motive. Research shows that short-term regulation of eating may result from changes in glucose levels. Long-term regulation of body weight is probably controlled by some system that monitors the body's fat content.

7. Research on obesity has focused on external responsiveness, set-point, restraint, and the consequences of obesity.

8. Two mechanisms appear to be involved in thirst motivation. One of them senses water loss within the

body cells; the other detects water loss from the spaces between the cells and in the blood.

9. Sexual motivation is influenced by a number of factors, including external stimulation, emotion and attitudes, fantasy and imagination, and physiological processes, beliefs, and expectancies.

10. Stimulus-seeking motives include exploration, manipulation, and stimulation-seeking. Arousal theory seems to account for such motives, as do hypothesized needs for competence and self-determination.

11. Acquired motives include needs for affiliation and for achievement. Although the affiliation motive varies by individual, it also seems to be greatly affected by situation.

12. Achievement motivation seems to be highly influenced by independence training and achievement training, as well as by early experiences with feeding and toilet-training. People with high achievement motivation are moderate risk-takers and are able to delay gratification successfully.

13. Scores on the components of achievement motivation known as mastery and work orientation are positively related to achievement behaviors; competitiveness scores are negatively related to such behaviors.

14. Emotions are characterized by both subjective feelings and body changes (including sympathetic arousal and neural activity from face-brain feedback). Outwardly, emotions express themselves most reliably in facial changes.

15. Theories of how emotions occur include the James-Lange theory, Schachter's cognitive-physiological

theory, Lazarus's cognitive-appraisal theory, and Izard's differential-emotions theory.

16. Considerable support exists for the facial-feedback hypothesis, which states that facial expressions and facial feedback regulate emotional experience. Considerable evidence also suggests that facial expressions are innate.

17. Emotions affect the body, perception, cognition, actions, and sexual motivation.

18. The polygraph, or lie detector, measures general emotional arousal, not lying. The validity of the polygraph is questionable.

19. Anorexia nervosa is an eating disorder characterized by self-starvation and severe weight loss.

— IMPORTANT TERMS AND CONCEPTS —

Emotion
Motivation
Instinct
Ethologists
Imprinting
Homeostasis
Needs
Drives
Incentives
Arousal Theory
Cognitive Theories
Social-comparison Theory

Cognitive-consistency Theories
Self-actualization
Hierarchy of Needs
Effectance Motivation
Intrinsic Motivation
Biological Motives
Hyperphagia
Glucostatic Theory
Set-point Theory
Obesity
Osmosis

Stimulus-seeking Motives
Acquired Motives
Need for Affiliation (*n* Aff)
Need for Achievement (*n* Ach)
Fear of Success
Facial-feedback Hypothesis
Display Rules
Yerkes-Dodson Law
Polygraph
Anorexia Nervosa
Bulimia

— SUGGESTIONS FOR FURTHER READING —

Arkes, H. R., & Garske, J. P. (1982). *Psychological theories of motivation* (2nd ed.). Monterey, CA: Brooks/Cole. A readable introduction to the full range of motivational theories, from biological bases of motivation to social motivation.

Buss, A. H. (1980). *Self-consciousness and social anxiety*. San Francisco: W. H. Freeman. A brief but interesting analysis of four kinds of social anxiety—embarrassment, shame, audience anxiety, and shyness—including many everyday examples.

Deci, E. L. (1975). *Intrinsic motivation*. New York: Plenum Publishing. A highly readable, excellent discussion of motivation based on the human needs to be competent and self-determining with respect to the environment.

Franken, R. E. (1982). *Human motivation*. Monterey, CA: Brooks/Cole. Topics (including many discussed in this chapter) such as hunger and eating, sexual behavior, stress, addiction, aggression, and altruism examined from the biological, learning, and cognitive points of view.

Izard, C. E. (1977). *Human emotions*. New York: Plenum Publishing. A high-level, scholarly treatment of emotions, containing material on theories and expressions of emotion. The beginning student may find most interesting the discussion of specific emotions, such as joy, grief, shame, shyness, and guilt.

Lykken, D. T. (1981). *A tremor in the blood*. New York: McGraw-Hill. One of the most vocal critics of the lie detector presenting his case. A highly informative and interesting book.

– CHAPTER 10 –

EARLY DEVELOPMENT

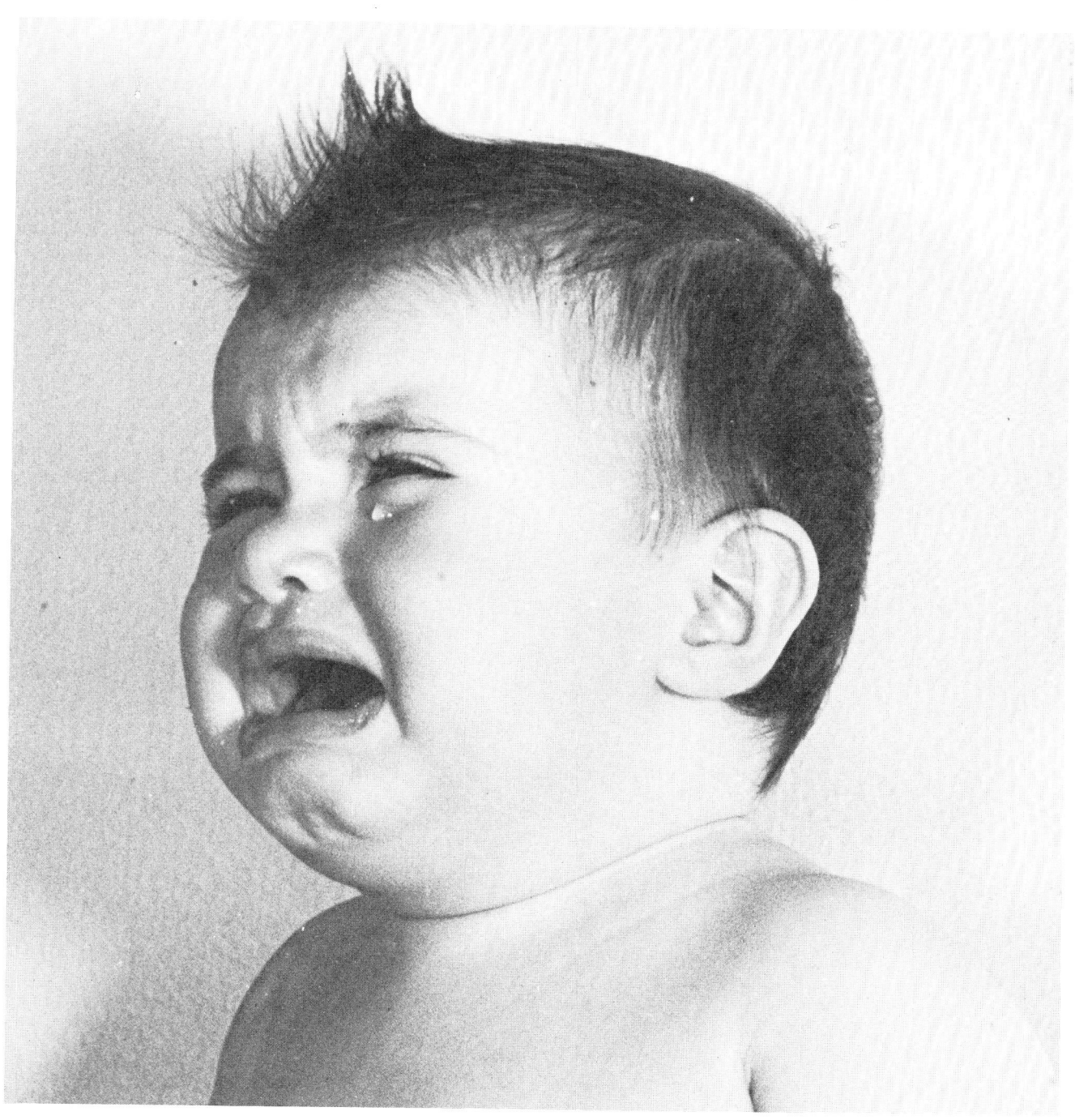

EARLY DEVELOPMENT

— CHAPTER OBJECTIVES —

To achieve the objectives of this chapter, you should be able to answer the questions listed here. You should also be able to define the important terms and concepts listed at the end of the chapter.

1. What is development? How do psychologists study it?

2. What are the goals of developmental psychology?

3. What are three major phases of prenatal development? What behaviors characterize each phase?

4. To what extent do factors such as diet, drug use, and general health affect the prenatal environment and the unborn baby's development?

5. What are the capacities of the newborn? What types of stimulation are most likely to aid the developing infant?

6. How do complications during birth relate to later difficulties in development? What prenatal screening procedures are available for early diagnosis, and possible prevention, of developmental and birth complications?

— CHAPTER OUTLINE —

Prenatal Growth and Development
Development begins at conception.

The Beginning of Life
Phases of Prenatal Development
Application: Factors That Influence the Prenatal Environment

The World of the Newborn
The newborn enters the world equipped with a growing body and rapidly expanding motor, sensory, and mental capacities.

The Newborn Baby
Developmental and Birth Complications
Application: Diagnosing Developmental and Birth Complications

On the Horizon: Genetic Counseling and the Prevention of Developmental and Birth
Complications

A BABY IS BORN

What follows is one family's story. It began with a routine blood sample taken in the office of Pat's obstetrician. The tests showed that there was a 95 percent chance that her baby would be born with severe underdevelopment of the brain.

Two months before the baby was due, Pat underwent more tests. The tests revealed that the baby's head was abnormally small because it was missing much of its brain. Infants in that condition usually die within hours of birth, although some have survived as long as 18 months. "You don't want to see a baby live in such a state," says Pat. "But how do you hope that your own baby will die?"

The delivery was difficult and painful. Afterward, in the recovery room, a nurse brought Pat's baby to her wrapped in a hospital blanket. The baby had died, but Pat had made the doctor promise to show the baby to her after the delivery. Pat saw the face only as a blur. She remembers that except for the head, there were no deformities. "I felt good that I had seen it."

Several months ago—for the first time in about a year—Pat and her husband, Tony, started talking about having another child. Their doctor advised them that they have a 95 percent chance of conceiving a normal baby.

"If I get up enough nerve to get pregnant again," Pat told him, "I'll be back here. I can't imagine going through nine months expecting to have a healthy baby and then suddenly waking up to a stillborn. That would have been ten times harder." (Paraphrased from Chedd, 1981, pp. 35–36)

Most pregnancies proceed without complications, and most babies are born normal and healthy. On occasion, however, and possibly more frequently than you might imagine, prenatal or birth complications alter the course of development. Defects may be minor, or so serious that they threaten the life of the baby. (Later in this chapter we will return to the case of Pat and Tony and describe some of the tests used by doctors to diagnose the health of the unborn baby.)

Such problems are but one of the many topics of interest to *developmental psychologists*. Mussen, Conger, and Kagan (1979) have defined **developmental psychology** as the scientific study of the determinants of human growth and development, the underlying processes of change, and the hows and whys of alterations in behavior.

To elaborate on what is meant by developmental psychology, let's consider its three major goals. One goal is the description, measurement, and explanation of universal, age-related changes in behavior, such as learning to walk or talk. A second goal is the description, measurement, and explanation of individual differences in behavior during particular developmental periods. A third goal is the description, measurement, and explanation of malformations or disruptions in development (Mussen et al., 1979). In other words, developmental psychologists are concerned with normal and abnormal changes in behavior with increasing age and with individual differences in behavior at various points in life. This chapter examines the baby's development during the **prenatal period,** the 9 months of growth that precede birth (see Figure 10–1). We will follow development from a fertilized egg to a healthy, normal baby. As we do, it should become clear that we cannot fully understand human development without examining the phases of prenatal growth. More

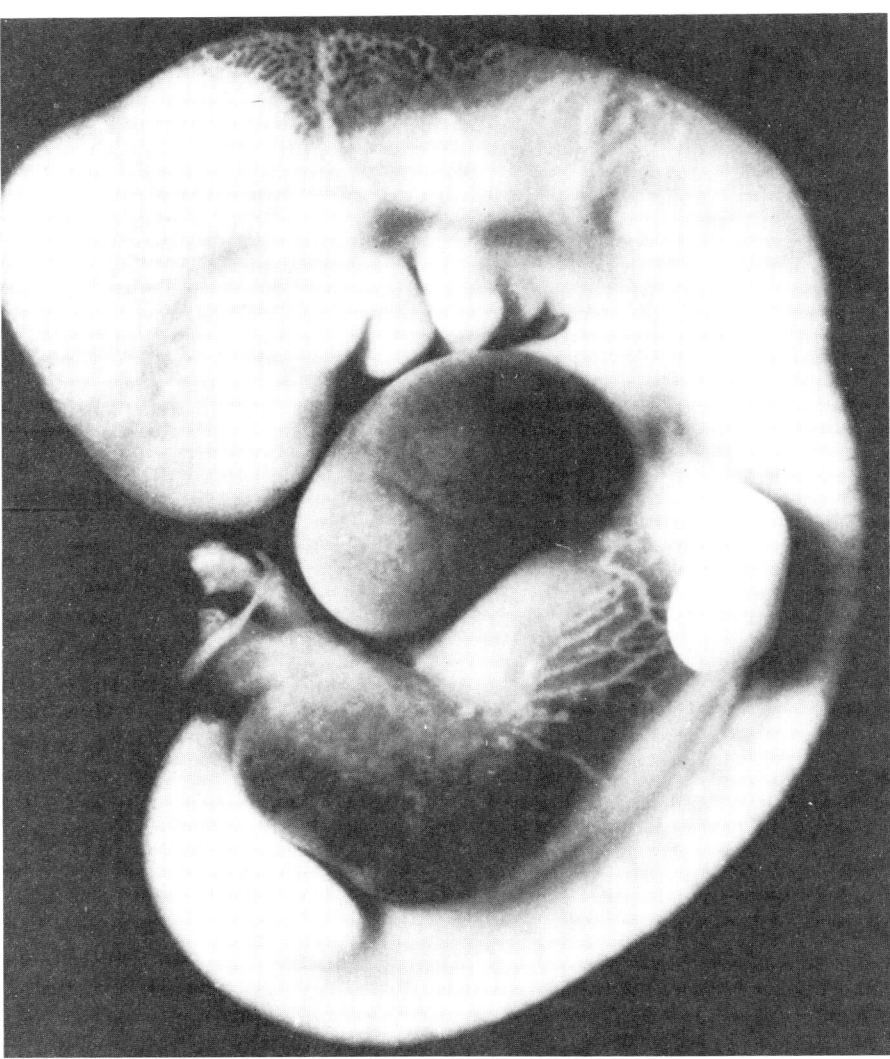

Figure 10–1.
The human embryo at 5 weeks of age.

changes take place prenatally than in any other comparable period of life (Hall, Perlmutter, & Lamb, 1982).

In this chapter, it will also become evident that, by the moment of birth, much that will distinguish individuals for the rest of their lives already has happened. The baby's *heredity*, transmitted from the mother and father and fully determined at conception, guarantees that the baby will be a unique individual. But heredity alone does not specify exactly how the baby will look, function, or behave. From the moment of conception on, the baby's *environment* interacts with heredity. As we progress through the chapter, we will see that the key to understanding human development is the continuous *interaction*, from conception to death, of hereditary and environmental influences. Thus, in addition to examining normal prenatal development, we will explore some of the factors known to affect the prenatal environment: for example, the woman's diet during pregnancy, her physical and emotional condition, and her use of medicines and drugs.

Other important topics covered here are the world of the newborn—including early hearing, visual, motor, and vocal development—and developmental and birth complications. Human development, of course, stretches far beyond infancy. Thus, the chapter following this one will continue the survey of development. In chapter 12 we will examine the relative influence of heredity and environment in determining individual differences in intellectual development.

— PRENATAL GROWTH AND DEVELOPMENT —

Events that occur before birth are of great importance in determining the course of later physical and psychological development. (For review, see Stechler & Halton, 1982.) Consequently, we would like to trace the phases of prenatal development and describe factors that can influence the quality of the prenatal environment.

The Beginning of Life

Although the question of exactly when a human life begins remains unresolved in the legal world, by definition human development begins at conception. **Conception** occurs when a female's egg cell (or *ovum*) and a male's sperm cell are united. The fertilization of egg by sperm creates the first cell, or *zygote,* of the new generation. Within the zygote are threadlike structures, called *chromosomes,* that carry the hereditary instructions needed to form a new individual. In a suitable environment, the zygote undergoes *cell division.* Also called *mitosis,* this is the process by which 1 cell splits into 2 genetically similar cells. Under normal conditions, the 1st cell divides into 2 cells, then into 4 cells, 8, 16, 32, and so on. The hereditary instructions carried on the chromosomes of the sperm and egg cells trigger an amazing 9-month-long series of pre-birth developmental changes. (Figure 10–2.)

Phases of Prenatal Development

Prenatal development, from conception to birth, consists of three phases. The first phase, called the period of the ovum, lasts for about 2 weeks. The second, or embryo, phase lasts from the 2nd through the 8th week. The third phase, called the period of the fetus, extends from the 8th week of gestation to birth. We will highlight the most important characteristics of each of these milestones in prenatal growth.

— The Period of the Ovum (1–14 Days)

Also called the egg phase or germinal period, the **period of the ovum** lasts from fertilization until the zygote is firmly implanted in the uterine wall. At this time, the fertilized egg makes a 3- to 7-day trip down the Fallopian tube to the uterus. The ovum's first division into 2 cells usually occurs 24 to 36 hours after fertilization. Within another few hours, a second division occurs, producing 4 cells. Development is under way. The major event of this period is the implantation in the uterine wall of the free-floating but developing zygote (or *blastocyst,* as it is called). Implantation takes about 10 to 14 days. If the blastocyst is successfully embedded in the womb, an outer layer of cells forms nutrient material for the developing embryo. A second layer forms the *placenta* and *umbilicus.* The inner cluster of cells becomes the embryo itself.

— The Period of the Embryo (15–56 Days)

The embryo phase, or **period of the embryo,** is characterized by 6 weeks of rapid development. By day 18, the embryo begins to take some shape; the head and body are discernible. By the end of the 3rd week, a prim-

Figure 10–2.
Prenatal development prior to birth.

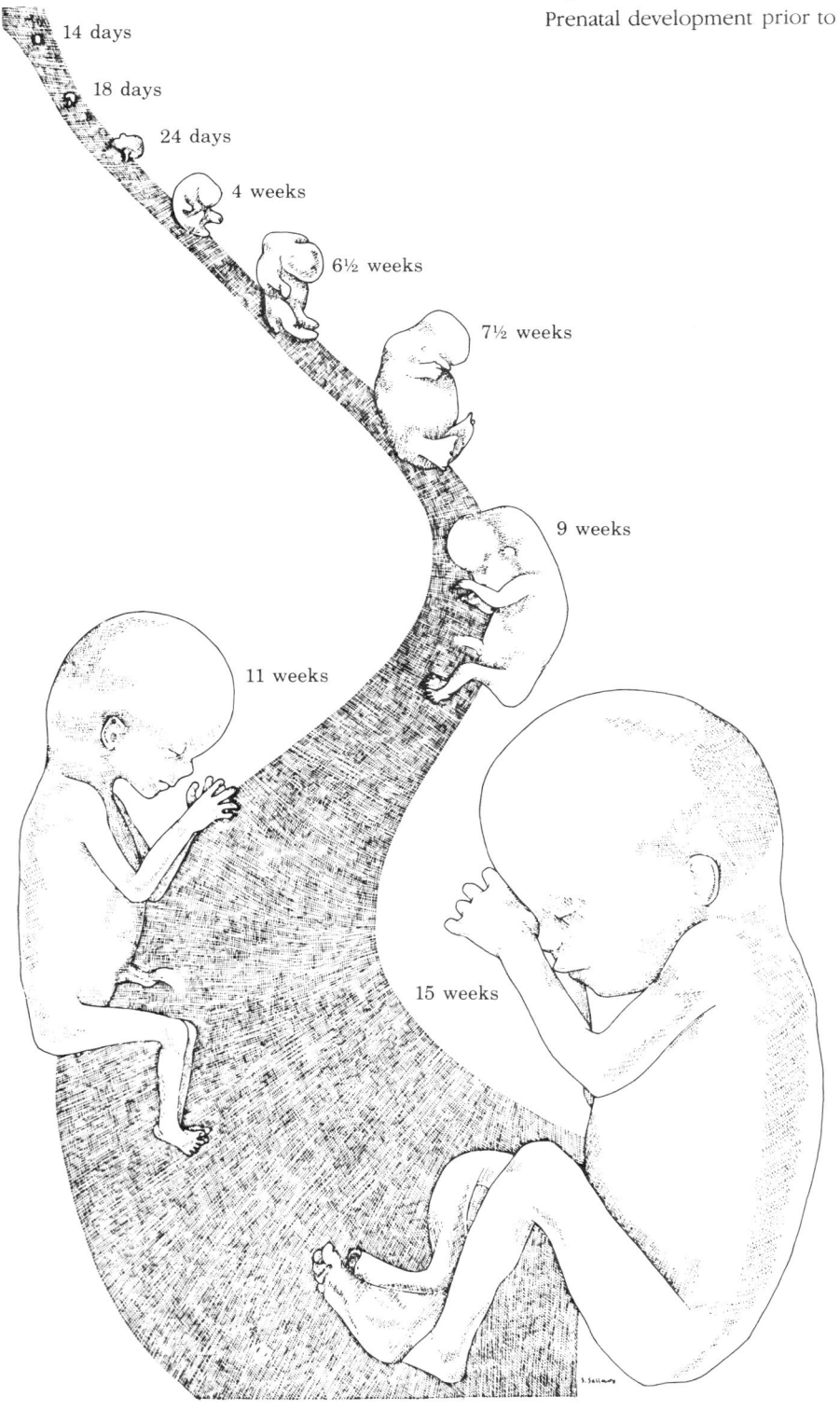

14 days

18 days

24 days

4 weeks

6½ weeks

7½ weeks

9 weeks

11 weeks

15 weeks

itive heart develops and begins to beat. (A 5-week-old human embryo is shown in Figure 10–1.)

By the end of the 2nd month, the embryo is about 1 inch long. The face, mouth, ears, and eyes have begun to take form; the arms, legs, hands, and feet have also appeared. The sex organs are just beginning to form. Internal organs such as the lungs, kidneys, and liver have begun to function to some degree. The nervous system is developing rapidly. These events suggest that the embryo phase is a particularly *critical* or *sensitive developmental period*—a fact amplified in the later discussion of the prenatal environment.

The Period of the Fetus (57–280 Days)

Marked by the development of bone cells, the **period of the fetus** extends from the end of the 8th week until birth. By the end of week 12, the fetus is about 3 inches long. Major organ systems, including respiration, digestion, and excretion, have begun to function. The sex of the fetus becomes apparent. By the end of 16 weeks, motor behavior becomes more complex, and the woman is able to feel fetal movements. During weeks 16 to 32, the fetus increases in length to about 16 inches and in weight to about 4 pounds. At full term, or 40 weeks, the average newborn is about 20 inches long and weighs between 7 and 8 pounds (Mussen et al., 1979).

═ APPLICATION ═
FACTORS THAT INFLUENCE THE PRENATAL ENVIRONMENT

Recent research suggests that the quality of the environment in which the fetus grows may substantially influence both prenatal and postnatal development. The following discussion covers some of the major factors affecting prenatal development.

Diet During Pregnancy

Both clinical and experimental research suggest a link between the pregnant woman's diet and fetal development (Stechler & Halton, 1982). For example, diets deficient in calcium, iodine, and various vitamins, including B, C, and D, are associated with higher-than-average rates of fetal malformations and mental retardation in infants (Kaplan, 1972). Laboratory studies of animals have shown that protein-deficient diets may irreversibly reduce brain weight and the number of brain cells (Winick, 1976). Studies by Bresler, Ellison, and Zamenhof (1975) demonstrated that female rats born to protein-deficient mother rats later gave birth to offspring that were underweight and learning disabled. This was true even for the baby rats who later, as adults, received adequate diets during their own pregnancies. The reason? Rats born to malnourished mothers may later be unable to form normal placentas or prenatal environments.

The results of animal studies suggest that poor maternal nutrition during pregnancy may damage not only the offspring but also the offspring's offspring. Too little direct experimental evidence exists to say exactly how or to what extent these findings may apply to humans. Nevertheless, it would seem prudent for prospective mothers to heed their message. Additional evidence pertaining to the relationship between undernourishment and intellectual development is reviewed in chapter 12.

Emotional State During Pregnancy

A woman's emotional state during pregnancy may indirectly affect the health of her unborn child (Stechler & Halton, 1982). There are, of course, no direct connections between the nervous systems of the pregnant woman and the fetus. Despite this, specific hormones, such as adrenaline, that are released into the woman's bloodstream at times of emotional stress may cross the *placental barrier* to the fetal bloodstream. A variety of emotional states, such as rage, fear, and anxiety, activate the woman's autonomic nervous system and release various hormones into her bloodstream. The hormones can apparently irritate the developing fetus. Emotional stress during pregnancy is related to more difficult labor and delivery, an increased probability of premature birth, and lower birth weight (Mussen, Conger, & Kagan, 1980).

Use of Medicines and Drugs During Pregnancy

It has long been recognized that certain medicines or drugs taken by pregnant women may affect fetal development. Today, as knowledge grows about the negative effects of drug use during pregnancy, most physicians advise pregnant women to take as little medication as possible. During the 1960s, widespread use of the sedative *thalidomide* during the early weeks of pregnancy produced thousands of babies with severely deformed arms and legs. More recently, it has been suggested in various court cases that women who took the antimiscarriage drug *stilbestrol* during early pregnancy had daughters who developed vaginal or uterine cancer as young adults (Mussen et al., 1980).

Some more commonly used drug substances may also adversely affect fetal growth and development. Heavy cigarette smokers who continue to smoke throughout pregnancy tend to give birth to infants who have a lower-than-average birth weight. Sontag and Wallace (1935) were the first to report that the fetal heart rate increases as the pregnant woman smokes, and cigarette smoking by pregnant women has now been linked to oxygen deprivation in the fetus. (For review, see Stechler & Halton, 1982.)

Alcohol consumption during pregnancy can also harm the fetus. Jones and Smith (1973) identified a condition in newborn infants called **fetal alcohol syndrome;** it is associated with chronic heavy drinking by pregnant women. Symptoms of the syndrome include retarded physical and mental development, premature birth, congenital eye and ear problems, and sleep disturbances. A review of the evidence by Abel (1980) suggests that fetal alcohol syndrome is not associated with moderate drinking. Nonetheless, when a pregnant woman drinks, her unborn baby does, too. "Almost everything a pregnant woman eats, drinks, injects or inhales reaches her baby through the placenta" (O'Connell, 1977, p. 18).

Increased drug addiction among young women has led to a greater incidence of damaged and addicted newborns. Alcohol, for example, may be detected in the blood and breath of newborns with fetal alcohol syndrome. Infants born to heroin addicts suffer severe withdrawal symptoms, including tremors, convulsions, and vomiting, which may last up to 6 months after birth (Mussen et al., 1980). Babies born to narcotic-addicted mothers are also at high risk for a variety of psychological disturbances (Householder, Hatcher, Burns, & Chasnoff, 1982).

The effects of drugs on prenatal development have only recently been systematically investigated. The following advice, given by Virginia Apgar, neatly summarizes the upshot of these investigations: "A woman who is pregnant, or thinks she could possibly be pregnant, should not take any drugs whatsoever unless absolutely essential—and then only when prescribed by a physician who is aware of the pregnancy" (Apgar & Beck, 1974; quoted in Mussen et al., 1979).

Other Factors Influencing the Prenatal Environment

In addition to a pregnant woman's diet, emotional state, and use of drugs, there are other factors that influence the prenatal environment. Among them are exposure to radiation and maternal diseases.

Exposure to radiation, from x-ray examination or radiation therapy, should be avoided by pregnant women. Radiation exposure between conception and implantation is thought to destroy the fertilized ovum in nearly all cases, thus ending the pregnancy. The risk of fetal malformations is highest when radiation exposure occurs during the period of the embryo (Mussen et al., 1979).

Maternal diseases during pregnancy may also lead to fetal malformations. Numerous viral diseases can be dangerous early in pregnancy. They include, but are not limited to, hepatitis, chicken pox, and rubella. Rubella, or German measles, is one of the most seriously disruptive diseases early in pregnancy. About one-half of all babies born to mothers who had rubella during the 1st month of pregnancy suffer *birth defects* (described later in this chapter). The number of affected babies drops to 22 percent for infections during the 2nd month of pregnancy, to 6 percent for 3rd-month infections, and only a small percentage thereafter (Mussen et al., 1980). Affected babies may suffer a variety of symptoms, including deafness, blindness, and mental retardation (see chapter 12).

— THE WORLD OF THE NEWBORN —

At one time, it was commonly believed that newborn babies were passive, inert, and unaware. Now research into the **neonatal period,** which encompasses the 1st month of life, has greatly expanded our view of the newborn. What is the newborn baby's world like? Is it "buzzing confusion," as William James once suggested? Today we know that the newborn enters the world with surprisingly sophisticated sensory and reflex capacities. To understand the newborn's world, we will explore some milestones of early hearing, vision, speech, and motor development.

The Newborn Baby

In most ways, all newborn infants are physically alike. They have many behavioral similarities, too. The average newborn in the delivery room, for example, will react to a loud noise but will tune it out if it is repeated. This change, which is a simple form of learning called *habituation* (see chapter 6), seems to be universal among babies. That infants are able to suppress obnoxious, aversive stimulation is impressive. As an illustration, consider the following case history of a newborn undergoing hospital tests of heart-rate and brain-wave activity:

> He [the newborn infant] was brought into the room for a cardiogram and an electroencephalogram or brain-wave test. The rubber bands were tightly placed around his scalp like a headband, and around his wrists. Both were constricting enough to cause swelling of his flesh on either side of the bands and must have been painful. The infant screamed for a few seconds, then quieted abruptly. He kept his arms and legs pulled up into a fetal position and remained motionless throughout the rest of the testing period. He seemed asleep except that his extremities were tightly flexed. A series of bright lights and sharp noises seemed barely to disturb him. All those in the room said, "See, he's asleep!" When the stimulation ceased, however, and the tightly constricting bands were removed, he immediately roused and cried lustily for fifteen minutes. (Brazelton, 1979, pp. 25–26)

How do we account for the newborn's lack of crying during such ordeals? One explanation is that newborns make an involuntary sleep response to shut out disturbing stimuli. This reaction allows them to withstand various disturbances and insults from the outside world.

The Newborn's Sensory Reactions and Reflex Behaviors

As mentioned earlier, a loud noise will startle the newborn, but reactions to a repeated sound are suppressed. Interestingly, however, presenting a slightly different loud noise will again startle the newborn. Reactions such as these suggest that babies can hear and differentiate various sounds during the 1st week of life.

At birth, infants are active visual explorers, capable of reacting to light (Haith & Goodman, 1982). They will shut their eyes tightly and keep them shut after being exposed to a bright white light. But they will look intently at a red or soft yellow object dangled before them (Brazelton, 1979). The newborn is able to follow such objects visually, moving the eyes and head from side to side, as well as up and down, if necessary. As noted by Brazelton, visual responses of this kind can be observed in newborns still in the delivery room.

Can the newborn see more than just colored lights? Tiffany Field and her associates reported on an experiment in which babies averaging 36 hours of age discriminated among a live model's happy, sad, and surprised facial expressions (Field, Woodson, Greenberg, & Cohen, 1982). Sample photographs of the model's expressions and a newborn's reactions are shown in Figure 10–3. Findings similar to these have been reported by other investigators (e.g., Meltzoff & Moore, 1977, 1983). Contrary to what most of us have been taught, research shows conclusively that newborn infants can see in some detail (Haith, 1980; also, see chapter 4).

Newborn infants tested 1 or 2 days after birth also demonstrate a capacity to detect differences in *smell* and *taste* (cf. Cowart, 1981).

Newborns also react significantly to *touch,* as demonstrated by a number of reflexes. For example, when the sole of a baby's foot is pricked, the normal response is a *withdrawal reflex.* A *rooting reflex* can be elicited by tickling the side of the newborn's mouth

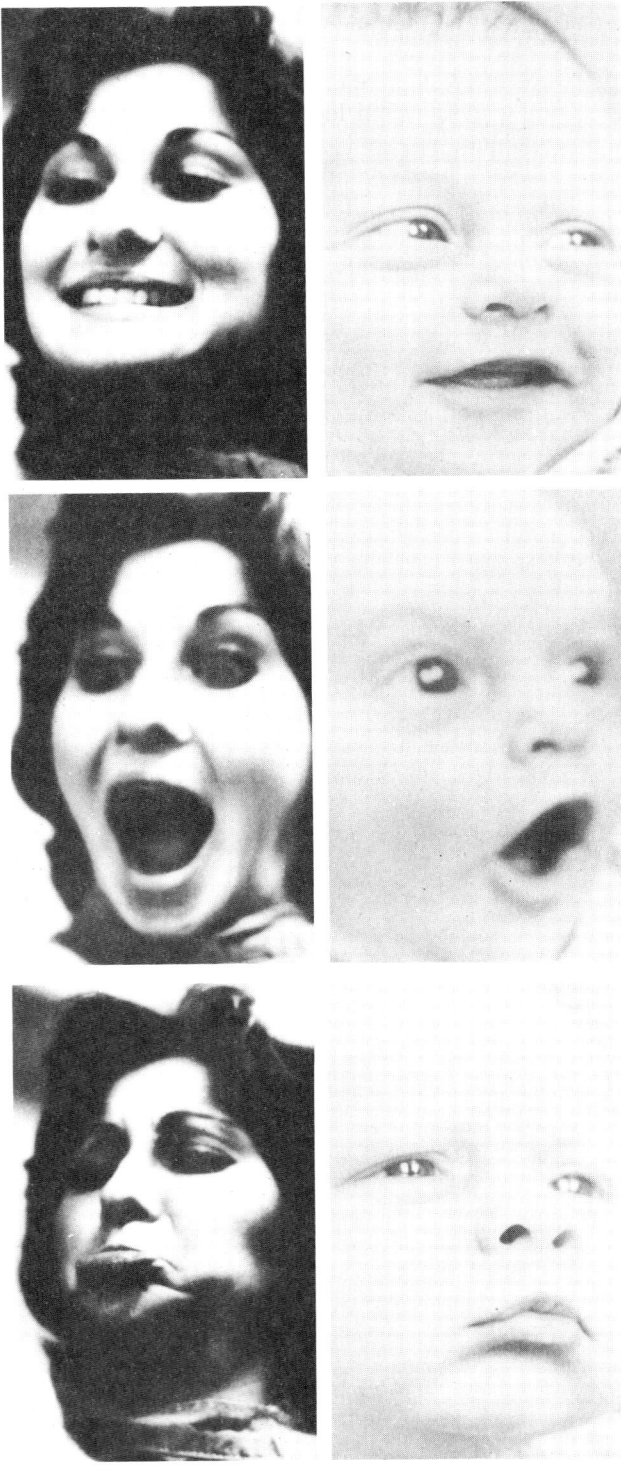

Figure 10–3.
Psychologist Tiffany Field with newborn.

with a finger. The infant turns his or her head in the direction of the finger and attempts to suck. Another interesting reponse in newborns is the *Moro reflex,* elicited by sudden changes in head position or, sometimes, by other surprise stimuli. In the Moro reflex, newborns cry briefly, then bring their arms together while flexing the body. This reflex begins to disappear at 3 to 4 months of age, and by 6 months it is nearly impossible to detect. Persistence of the Moro reflex beyond about 10 months of age indicates possible central nervous system damage (Mussen et al., 1980).

— Motor Development

A very important development during the first year and a half of life is the orderly emergence of active movement skills, a sequence of behaviors called **motor development** (see Figure 10–4). Most infants proceed from rolling over and sitting without support to standing, creeping, and walking alone by the age of 13 or 14 months. Even though the *rate* of motor development varies for individual babies, its *order* is similar for children of all cultures.

— Vocalization and the Influence of Early Stimulation

Cooing, babbling, and other vocal sounds are also universal during infancy. Although the *rate* at which babies develop speech varies somewhat, the *sequence* remains basically the same for children everywhere (see Chapter 8).

The cooing that infants engage in during the first 6 weeks after birth is an innate, unlearned response. However, environmental stimulation can affect the frequency and type of speech sounds made by infants. For example, when parents and their infants engage often in vocal play, the infants vocalize more and with greater variety than do infants from homes where vocal play is infrequent (Mussen et al., 1979). The impact of environment and experience on early language development was demonstrated in a study comparing Indian infants in rural Guatemala to infants in the United States. The U.S. infants were frequently included in vocal play, whereas the Guatemalan babies were spoken to less often. (Guatemalan Indians do not believe in the value of verbal play with infants.) The U.S. infants studied vocalized about 25 percent of the time they were awake, compared to less than 10 percent for the Guatemalan infants (Kagan & Klein, 1973).

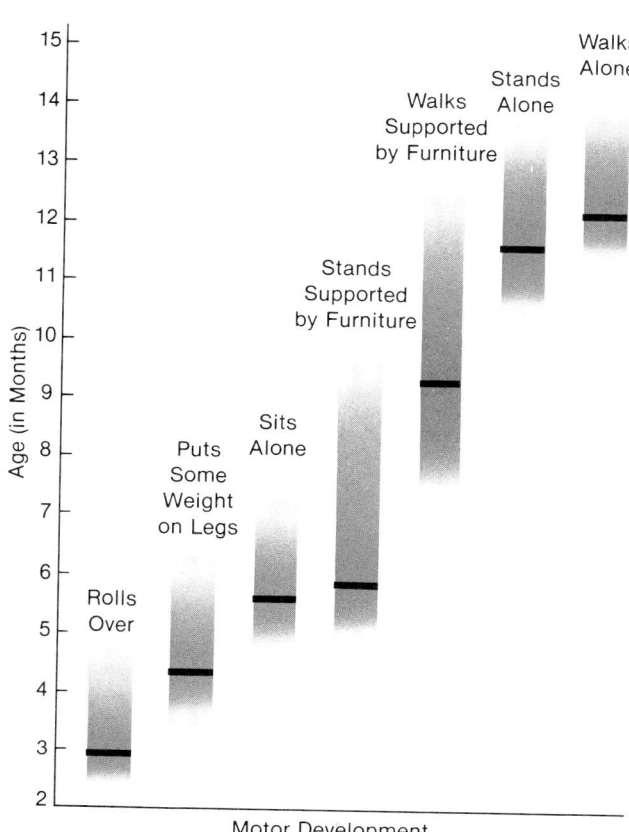

Age (in Months)

Rolls
Over

Puts
Some
Weight
on Legs

Sits
Alone

Stands
Supported
by Furniture

Walks
Supported
by Furniture

Stands
Alone

Walks
Alone

Motor Development

Figure 10—4.
Motor development.

— Behavioral States and Differences in Temperament

In contrast to the universal developmental patterns just discussed, the individual behavior patterns of newborns are often strikingly different. Brazelton's (1973) *Neonatal Behavioral Assessment Scale* distinguishes six **behavioral states,** or levels of alertness and consciousness. The two *sleep states* are:

1. *Deep sleep.* The baby will have eyes closed, regular breathing, and no spontaneous movement, except an occasional startle (or jerky) movement.
2. *Light sleep.* Eyes are closed but may be moving under the lids, breathing is irregular, and baby may make sucking movements or noises while still sleeping.

The four *awake states* are:

1. *Drowsy.* The baby is in a semisleeping state; eyes may be open or closed.
2. *Alert.* The baby has a bright look and focuses atten-

tion on source of stimulation, such as mother or father; baby is quiet in motor activity.
3. *Active.* Eyes are open; there is considerable motor activity, with arms and legs moving in and out; baby reacts to environment.
4. *Crying.* Intense crying, which is difficult to break through.

There are differences among infants in the amount of time spent in each of the behavioral states described by Brazelton. Accordingly, in his book *Infants and Mothers: Differences in Development,* Brazelton details differences among *average babies, quiet babies,* and *active babies* and prescribes optimal ways of interacting with each (Brazelton, 1979).

Like Brazelton, Alexander Thomas and his colleagues have identified and described differences in temperament among babies. **Temperament** refers to the newborn's predispositions in mood and behavior. These predispositions tend to remain fairly stable during the course of early development and appear to be related to later childhood personality (Thomas, Chess, & Birch, 1968). Three major dimensions of temperament found in more recent studies are activity level, responsiveness, and irritability. (For review, see Hubert, Wachs, Peters-Martin, & Gandour, 1982.)

Activity level refers to the fact that some newborns are extremely active, whereas others move more slowly. Such differences can be observed as early as the first days of life. The second characteristic of temperament, *responsiveness,* refers to the fact that some babies seem to enjoy being hugged and cuddled, but others stiffen and resist handling. Parents often have difficulty accepting an unresponsive baby. "They may falsely infer that their baby dislikes them or that they are inadequate parents." (Hall et al., 1982, p. 122) The third characteristic of temperament is the newborn's *irritability,* or mood. Some babies sleep and eat on a regular schedule and seldom cry. Other babies seem to cry on a regular schedule and seldom sleep (Figure 10–5). Temperamental differences such as those just described may directly affect parents. Osofsky and Connors (1979) found that parents often develop a style of relating to the baby and an opinion of the baby's personality within days after birth.

Developmental and Birth Complications

The majority of newborns are born healthy and develop normally. And although maturation-paced simi-

Figure 10–5.

The newborn's way of
expressing feelings.

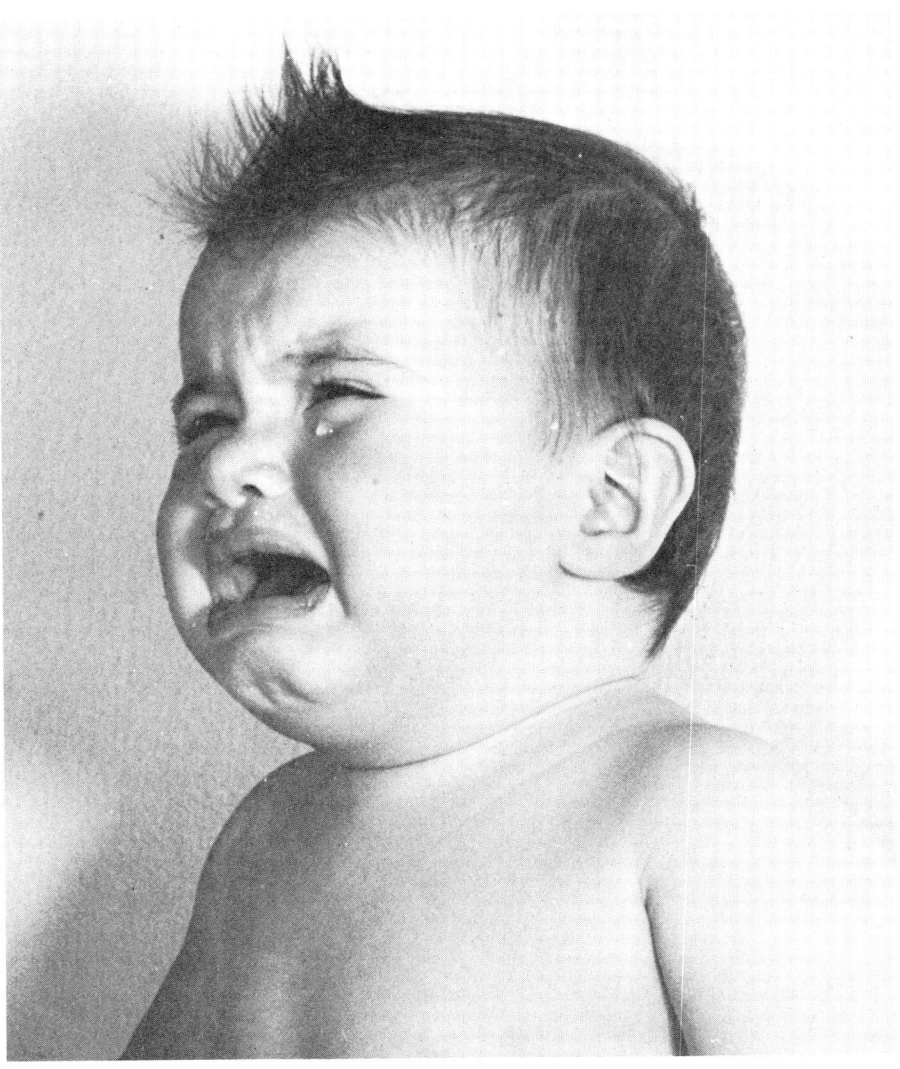

larities are the rule, we have seen that all newborns
are different. Nowhere else does this seem more evident than in newborns with birth defects. Prenatal and
birth complications that retard normal development
are the nation's most serious child health problem. According to the National Foundation/March of Dimes
(O'Connell, 1977), in the United States, more than
250,000 infants each year are born with some type of
birth defect—a rate of 1 birth in every 12. Although
many infants with birth defects die shortly after birth
(see the chapter introduction), more than 1 billion infants, children, and adults are hospitalized annually for
treatment. In the United States, birth defects afflict approximately 4 million persons with diabetes, 580,000

with blindness, 350,000 with heart defects, 300,000
with impaired hearing, 170,000 with impaired speech,
millions more with defects of nervous, endocrine, and
other systems, and many with mental retardation (see
chapter 12). Clearly, it behooves us to know something
about such problems.

In general, a **birth defect** is an abnormality of structure, function, or metabolism. *Structural* defects affect
the body's physical shape or size, as when a body part
is missing or duplicated. *Functional* defects involve
one or more body parts not working properly. With
inborn errors of metabolism, the body is unable to
convert certain chemicals into others. In a majority of
cases, birth defects have both genetic and environmen-

tal causes. In the remaining pages of this chapter, we will examine a variety of birth complications and their causes. We will then conclude by describing advances in prenatal screening and genetic counseling that are improving early diagnosis and prevention of birth defects.

Genetic and Chromosomal Abnormalities

The **Lesch-Nyhan syndrome,** named after the two investigators who first studied it, in 1965, presents a fascinating example of abnormal behavior with genetic causation. It is a genetic disorder that affects mostly males. Children with this condition exhibit spastic movements, abnormal posture, difficulty with speech, and self-destructive behavior. As described by Lerner and Libby (1976):

> In one case, when restraints were removed, the child generally appeared terrified. His hands would go directly to his mouth and he would begin tearing the flesh, screaming all the time. Lip tissue is invariably bitten away in Lesch-Nyhan patients, unless the teeth are removed. Some children have learned to lacerate themselves with braces or catch themselves in the spokes of wheelchairs. (p. 206)

Phenylketonuria (PKU), another major genetic disorder, is capable of causing mental retardation. The discovery that PKU involves a defect in enzyme production led to the development of a screening test for newborns, that is now routinely performed in most U.S. hospitals. Once diagnosed, in many cases of PKU, mental retardation can be prevented by simple dietary regulation. The PKU infant is placed on a restricted, low-protein diet and is taken off milk products, fish, most meats, peanut butter, eggs, and other high-protein foods. A prescription powder, which resembles milk when mixed with water, is also given.

Cretinism is a problem that can be either genetic or environmental. It results from an insufficiency of the thyroid gland hormone thyroxine. Cretinism causes severe mental retardation, but thyroid hormone therapy soon after birth reverses the effects of the condition. Unfortunately, early detection is not always possible. Cretinism may also result from iodine deficiencies in the pregnant woman's diet. However, this possibility has been greatly reduced by the use of iodized table salt.

Chromosomal abnormalities also can have a serious effect on development. **Down's syndrome,** for example, noticeably retards mental development. This disorder was first described in 1866 by an English physician, Langdon Down. It was discovered nearly 100 years later that people with Down's syndrome have 47 chromosomes, rather than the normal 46 (Stine, 1977). Advances in human genetics and *karyotype analysis*—a method for displaying the chromosome pairs from a cell—made this discovery possible (see Figure 10–6).

We now know that about 95 percent of all Down's syndrome individuals have a trisomy 21 condition. That is, they have three instead of two chromosomes in Group 21 (as shown in Figure 10–6). About one-

Figure 10–6.

A karyotype of chromosome pairings from a girl with Down's syndrome. Note the extra chromosome in group 21.

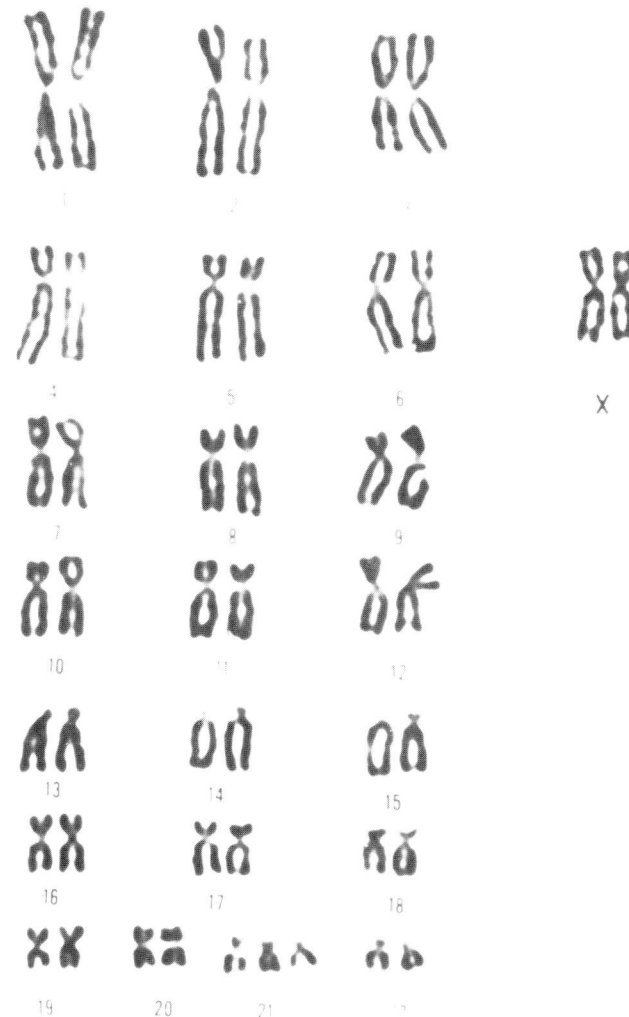

fourth of the trisomy 21 cases have been traced to faulty cell division within the father's sperm (Hall et al., 1982). The remaining cases are believed to be related to faulty egg cell division. The chances of producing a child with Down's syndrome through an error in the cell divisions that produce sperm and eggs increases with the parents' age. For example, the approximate risk, per pregnancy, for women under the age of 29 is 1 in 3,000. For women over age 45, the risk increases to about 1 in 40.

In physical appearance, a Down's syndrome child is characterized by short stature, a rounded head, a protruding lower lip, ears that are round and small, and thick, short hands with stubby fingers (see Figure 10–7). Additionally, a fold of skin over each eye gives the appearance that the eyes are slanted. This feature led Langdon Down to assume, falsely, that these children had something in common with the Mongolian race. The term *mongolism* is often incorrectly used to describe this disorder.

— Hemorrhaging and Anoxia

In addition to chromosomal and genetic abnormalities, there are a variety of birth complications that can have lifelong consequences. Two such complications are fetal hemorrhaging and anoxia.

Hemorrhaging refers to the breaking of blood vessels in the brain. It may be caused by excessive pressure on the head of the fetus during prolonged labor and delivery (Mussen et al., 1979). Hemorrhaging can affect the oxygen supply to the brain. The resulting damage to nerve cells can later cause psychological defects and, in extreme cases, death.

Anoxia refers to a lack of oxygen. It may occur if the newborn fails to breathe normally after the mother ceases to supply oxygen or if hemorrhaging occurs. In either instance, the result may again be damaged brain cells. Oxygen deprivation during birth is more likely to damage the brain stem than the cerebral cortex. Anoxia is therefore likely to cause defects in motor be-

Figure 10–7.
A young boy with Down's syndrome.

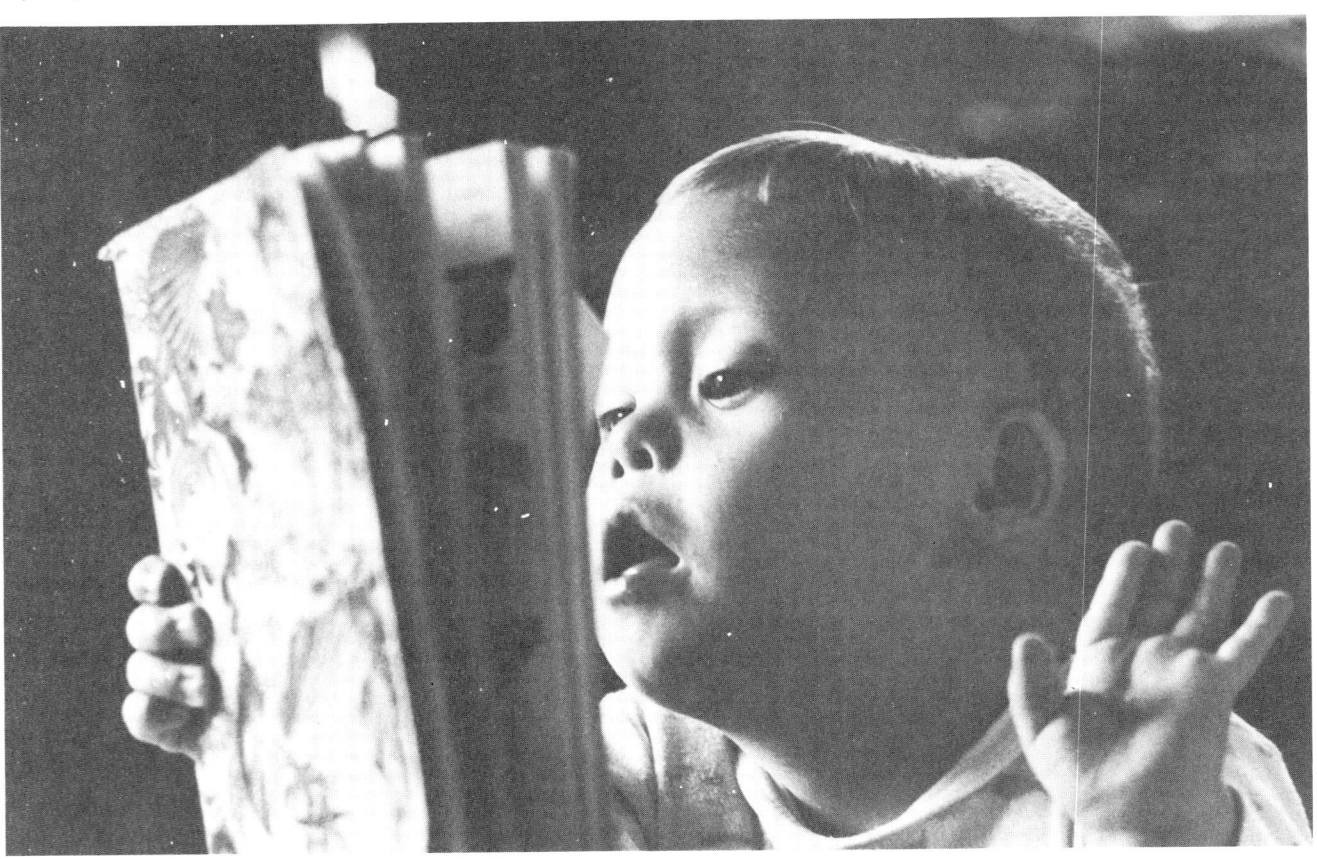

havior. Hemorrhaging, on the other hand, is likely to impair intellectual development.

Symptoms of brain-stem damage include varying degrees of paralysis in the arms and legs and, in some cases, an inability to speak coherently. *Cerebral palsy* is a general term used to describe a variety of motor deficits associated with brain cell damage. For about one-third of cerebral palsy patients there is evidence of anoxia at birth (Mussen et al., 1979).

While gross brain damage from severe anoxia has been related to later intellectual and motor impairment, less is known about the effects of mild oxygen deprivation during birth. *Minimal brain damage,* which can result from mild anoxia, may lead to *hyperkinesis*—a childhood pattern characterized by heightened activity (hyperactivity); it may also lead to *impulsivity*—a tendency to act and make decisions quickly, with little reflection or concern for consequences. Happily, studies comparing mildly anoxic and normal children have found that differences reported during infancy tend to decrease with age. There is presently no firm evidence of permanent intellectual or motor impairment due to mild oxygen deprivation during birth (Mussen et al., 1980).

— Prematurity

A serious, and common, birth complication is **prematurity,** defined medically by preterm birth (gestational age of 37 weeks or less) and by low birth weight (less than 2,500 grams, or about 5.5 pounds) (Kopp & Parmelee, 1979). Approximately 1 of every 10 babies in the United States is born prematurely (see Figure 10-8). In 1979, about 242,000 babies were born preterm, and more than 18,000 of them weighed less than 1,000 grams (Fincher, 1982). The chance of death soon after birth is markedly increased for premature babies, usually because of breathing difficulties (Koops & Harmon, 1980). Prematurity has also been related to various problems, including a higher than normal incidence of cerebral palsy, hyperkinesis, lower measured intelligence, and learning disabilities during the early school years (Caputo & Mandell, 1970).

A growing concern about such effects has spurred much recent research on prematurity (Friedman & Sigman, 1981). Fortunately for those born prematurely, the news is not all negative. For instance, Rawlings, Reynolds, Stewart, and Strang (1971) point out that disabilities caused by prematurity are by no means inevitable; they are just more likely than in full-term births. Thus, 87 percent of a group of infants who weighed

less than 4.5 pounds at birth were apparently normal. Other research has assessed the fate of premature infants reared in incubators for the first weeks of life. Those removed routinely for feeding, fondling, and bathing weighed more and were more developmentally advanced than those isolated in incubators and treated in a hands-off manner (Scarr-Salapatek & Williams, 1973). A more recent study suggests that behavioral problems of premature babies may result more from illness and prolonged hospitalization than from prematurity itself (Holmes et al., 1982).

Undoubtedly, as knowledge about how to care for premature infants grows, so too will their chances for survival and optimal development. A better understanding of beneficial parent-infant interactions is especially important (Crawford, 1982). Already, sophisticated hospital care is available in a growing number of specialized nurseries for the premature. Recent advances have contributed to a dramatic decrease in deaths of premature infants and an equally dramatic improvement in their likelihood of normal development (Fincher, 1982).

Figure 10–8.
A premature newborn.

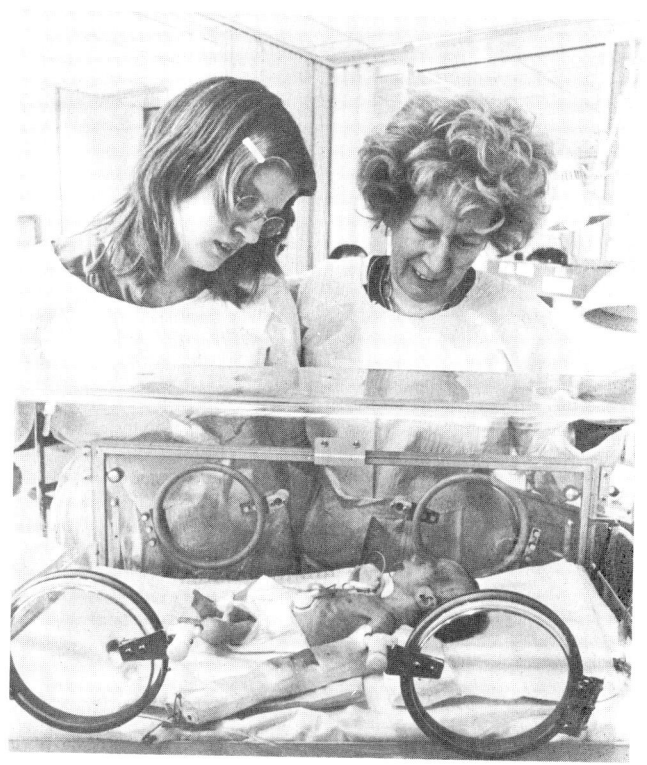

DIAGNOSING DEVELOPMENTAL AND BIRTH COMPLICATIONS

Over the past 30 years, **amniocentesis** has become increasingly important in prenatal care. In this technique (see Figures 10–9a and 10–9b), fetal cells for analysis are obtained from *amniotic fluid* (the fluid that bathes the developing fetus) drawn from the woman's womb (Fuchs, 1980). With this procedure, genetic and chromosomal abnormalities, such as Lesch-Nyhan syndrome and Down's Syndrome, can be detected. The optimal time for amniocentesis is the 14th to 16th weeks of pregnancy. This period is best because withdrawal of the required 10 to 20 milliliters of fluid poses less danger to the fetus than it would earlier. In addition, there is an adequate number of cells for chromosomal analysis.

Amniocentesis presents maternal and fetal risks ranging from hemorrhaging to infection and trauma. Although the risks are minimal when the procedure is done within the optimal time period, some investigators have noted that removing large amounts of amniotic fluid, even during the optimal period, may impair mental development (Stine, 1977). The seriousness of such potential damage has not yet been thoroughly documented or investigated.

A relatively recent innovation in prenatal diagnosis involves the use of mechanical energy in the form of sound waves, known as **ultrasound,** that are applied to the woman's abdomen. As the sound waves are reflected back, they can be assembled on a screen to form an image of the unborn baby (Wicks & Howe, 1983). This image is used to locate the placenta and fetal head prior to amniocentesis.

One of the newest techniques for detecting birth defects is called **AFP screening.** This procedure measures the amount of the chemical alphafetoprotein (AFP) in the pregnant woman's blood (Chedd, 1981). The simple blood test, which is given in the 16th to 18th weeks of pregnancy, can often eliminate the need for amniocentesis. If high levels of AFP are found in the blood, then both ultrasound and amniocentesis tests can be used to help confirm the diagnosis of abnormality. Pat (whose case was described in the chapter introduction) underwent both AFP screening and ultrasound tests, which showed that her baby would likely be born with severe underdevelopment of the brain.

Figure 10–9.
A photograph showing a woman undergoing amniocentesis (a), and a diagram illustrating the withdrawal of amniotic fluid (b).

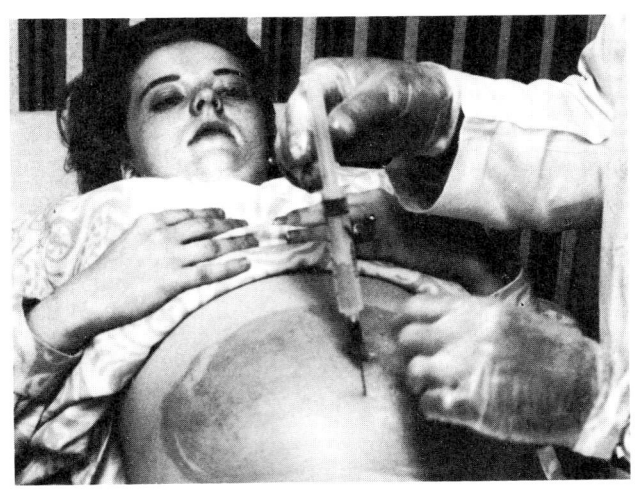

(a)

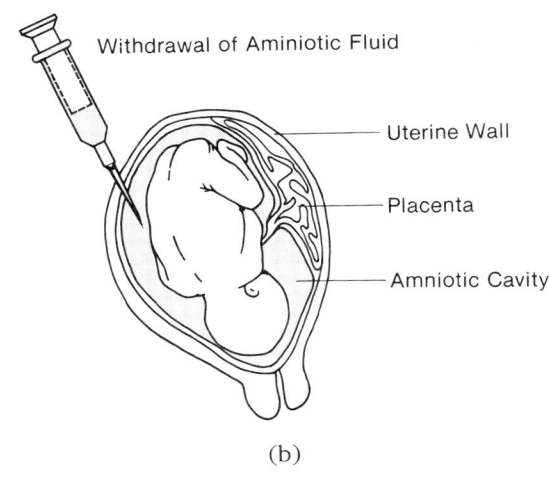

Withdrawal of Aminiotic Fluid

— Uterine Wall

— Placenta

— Amniotic Cavity

(b)

GENETIC COUNSELING AND THE PREVENTION OF DEVELOPMENTAL AND BIRTH COMPLICATIONS

Prospective parents are increasingly drawing on screening procedures to diagnose prenatal and birth complications. As prenatal screening becomes more popular, there should be a corresponding increase in the popularity of **genetic counseling,** a form of counseling aimed at helping people cope with and prevent the occurrence of genetic abnormalities. Genetic counselors offer advice both before and after a diagnosis is made. Unfortunately, many people are unaware that such counseling is available. Estimates suggest that less than 5 percent of the people who could benefit from genetic counseling have talked with a counselor. In a survey of parents of PKU children, Frankel (1973—cited in Stine, 1977) found that 61 percent did not know the disease was inherited, 58 percent did not understand the importance of early diagnosis, 56 percent were unaware that special diet might help the child, and 56 percent never received professional counseling. These results are surprising given that PKU screening at birth is so common.

As noted earlier, amniocentesis and other prenatal screening can provide information concerning the health of an unborn baby. Prospective parents thus have an option of seeking an abortion early in pregnancy rather than possibly having a malformed or mentally retarded child (Cates, 1982). Most people do not object to the use of prenatal screening to detect suspected abnormalities. However, many prospective parents object—on emotional, moral, ethical, or religious grounds—to the available alternatives when it is likely that the child will have a birth defect. In genetic counseling, the emphasis is on information that will help parents and family understand, choose intelligently, take action, and make the best possible adjustment (cf. Reed, 1980).

Good genetic counseling begins with an exact diagnosis. Beyond this, the successful counselor must (1) help the consultee, or patient, feel at ease, (2) ascertain that the person understands what has been said (most adults will say they understand, even if they don't), and (3) make certain that the person is aware of the alternatives and their consequences. Within this framework, Stine (1977) has described two counseling strategies: nondirective and directive. The major difference between the two is whether the counselor actively participates in decision making. In the *nondirective* approach, facts are presented in an unbiased manner, and responsibility for decision making is placed in the hands of the consultee. In *directive* counseling, a particular decision may be strongly urged.

Knowing that prenatal screening procedures are not 100 percent reliable, many counselors take a cautious, nondirective approach. For example, Stine (1977) described a case of a woman with strong religious convictions who had a child with *Tay-Sachs disease*. This genetic disorder first causes mental deterioration and then death, usually between 3 and 5 years of age. When the woman accidentally became pregnant again, she sought prenatal screening. Several tests seem to show conclusively that the child had the disease. After consultation, the family decided on abortion. The aborted fetus was completely normal. In light of such cases, nondirective counseling strategies tend to be preferred.

Who seeks genetic counseling? First, there are parents who have a child with a birth defect. These people want to know the chance of having another afflicted child. Forwarned about the odds, parents who decide to conceive also know that diagnostic tests will be available. If the tests show that the fetus is abnormal, the parents can decide whether to continue the pregnancy or end it. Many parents decide to give birth to a baby with a chromosomal or genetic abnormality. Knowing about the baby's condition in advance prepares them emotionally for the added care and expense that may be required.

A second group who seek genetic counseling are people who worry about possible abnormality in

their offspring. Many of them have experienced a spontaneous abortion, a stillbirth, or infertility that has led them to ask why these problems occur. Those who fear that they may carry a genetic disease can be tested and, in some cases, informed about the risk of abnormality in their offspring. If the probability of giving birth to a baby with a specific disorder is high, they may decide to prevent a pregnancy from occurring in the first place. Adoption and artificial insemination are among their options. In many cases, however, prospective parents who fear that they may be carriers of a genetic disorder can be tested and reassured that their concerns are unwarranted.

Prenatal screening raises a number of ethical and legal questions for prospective parents: Who should be born? Does the fetus have a right, independent of its parents, to be born? Alternatively, does the fetus have a right not to be born? These questions are now before the courts. In several cases, parents have successfully filed suit to recover the costs of raising a child who, they argued, was born because of negligence on the part of a physician or laboratory. In 1980, the California Court of Appeals ruled that a child with a genetic defect could sue not only a neg-

ligent physician or laboratory but also the parents, claiming to have been "wrongfully born." The decision stated that the child suffered because of the negligence of others (Chedd, 1981).

During the decades ahead, as the prenatal detection of disorders becomes even more common than it is today, will more and more people with birth defects claim that they were wrongfully born? As one court argued in rejecting a wrongful life suit in 1978: "The implications of such a proposition are staggering. Would claims be honored . . . for less than a perfect birth? And by what standard and by whom would perfection be defined?" (Chedd, 1981, p. 41).

Ethical and legal questions such as those raised here intensify the need for personal and family genetic counseling. This need will only increase in the years ahead. Further information about genetic counseling and birth defects, as well as a listing of diagnostic and counseling centers, can be obtained from the National Foundation/March of Dimes, 1275 Mamaroneck Avenue, White Plains, NY 10605, or the National Genetic Foundation, 250 West 57th Street, New York, NY 10019.

━ SUMMARY ━

1. Developmental psychologists are concerned with the description, measurement, and explanation of normal and abnormal changes in behavior with increasing age. They are also interested in individual differences in behavior during particular developmental periods.

2. Developmental psychology studies the determinants of human growth and development, the underlying processes of change, and the hows and whys of alterations in behavior.

3. The key to understanding human development lies in the continuous interaction, from conception to death, of hereditary factors and environmental influences.

4. Three phases of prenatal development are the period of the ovum, the period of the embryo, and the period of the fetus.

5. Events during the prenatal period are of great importance in determining the future course of physical and psychological development of the child.

6. A number of factors have been found to have an important influence on the quality of the prenatal environment. They include the pregnant woman's diet, use of drugs and medications, and general health status.

7. A majority of newborns are healthy, and most show a normal pattern of maturation-paced similarities in hearing, visual, motor, and vocal development.

8. Individual differences in development are evident in normal babies. Alterations in development are evident in fetuses and newborns with developmental and birth complications.

9. During recent years, a number of procedures have been used increasingly to diagnose prenatal abnormalities in development. These prenatal procedures include amniocentesis, ultrasound, and AFP screening.

10. Genetic counseling services are now widely available to parents who have a child with a birth defect and to people who are concerned about the possibility of abnormality in their offspring.

━ IMPORTANT TERMS AND CONCEPTS ━

Developmental Psychology
Prenatal Period
Conception
Period of the Ovum
Period of the Embryo
Period of the Fetus
Fetal Alcohol Syndrome
Neonatal Period

Motor Development
Behavioral States
Temperament
Birth Defect
Lesch-Nyhan Syndrome
Phenylketonuria (PKU)
Cretinism
Down's Syndrome

Hemorrhaging
Anoxia
Prematurity
Amniocentesis
Ultrasound
AFP Screening
Genetic Counseling

━ SUGGESTIONS FOR FURTHER READING ━

Brazelton, T. B. (1979). *Infants and mothers: Differences in development.* New York: Dell. A best-selling paperback now in its 10th printing. This book presents the developmental characteristics of three types of infants—the active baby, the average baby, and the quiet baby. The message is that no single pattern of infant behavior is normal; rather, parents learn to live with the baby they give birth to by learning to respond to the child's strengths and weaknesses.

Fenlon, A., McPherson, E., & Dorchak, L. (1979). *Getting ready for childbirth.* Englewood Cliffs, NJ: Prentice-Hall. A practical guide for expectant parents.

Hall, E., Perlmutter, M., & Lamb, M. E. (1982). *Child psychology today.* New York: Random House. A topic-oriented account of human development that is presented in a highly readable and interesting textbook format.

Mussen, P. H., Conger, J. J., Kagan, J., & Huston, A. C. (1984). *Child development and personality (6th ed.).* New York: Harper & Row. A best-selling introductory textbook on child development that provides a thorough, scientific, and up-to-date review of existing knowledge and expanded coverage of many of the topics discussed in this chapter.

Nilsson, L. (1977). *A child is born.* New York: Dell. Now in its 11th printing, this best seller provides a guide for expectant parents and a series of photographs that beautifully illustrate the drama of life before birth.

Stine, G. J. (1977). *Biosocial genetics.* New York: Macmillan. Topics on human heredity and social issues in a case-problem format that assumes no prior training in genetics. Principles of genetics are applied directly to case situations, thereby enabling the reader to learn the social, ethical, and legal implications of genetic research.

– CHAPTER 11 –

LIFE-SPAN DEVELOPMENT

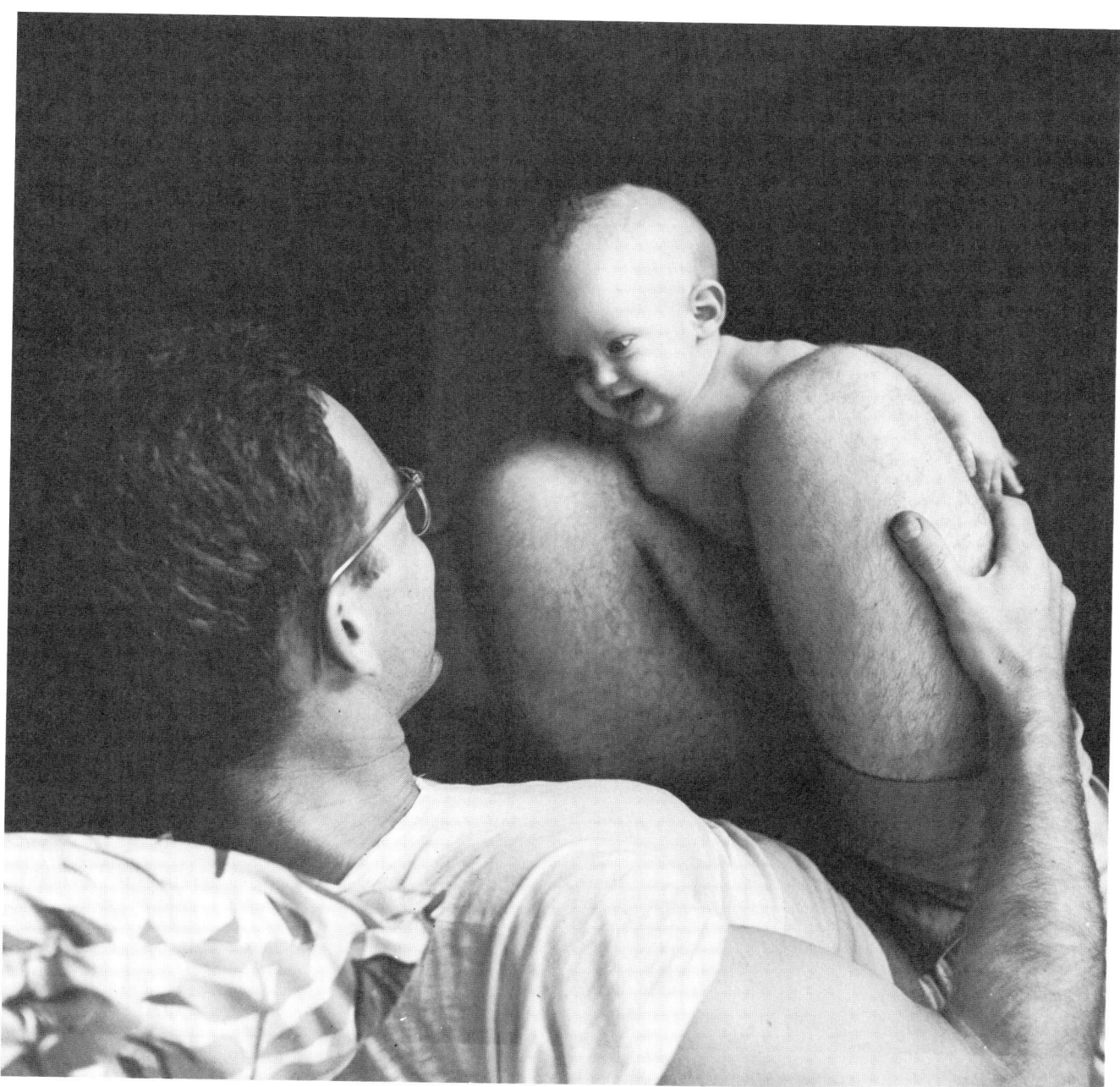

LIFE-SPAN DEVELOPMENT

— CHAPTER OBJECTIVES —

To achieve the objectives of this chapter, you should be able to answer the questions listed here. You should also be able to define the important terms and concepts listed at the end of the chapter.

1. Why do psychologists study cognitive development in infants and children? How is such development studied?
2. How does the special bond of attachment between infant and care-giver develop? What are the consequences of early attachment for later development?
3. Describe the course of physical development during adolescence. How do boys and girls differ with respect to the rate of maturation and physical development?
4. What developmental tasks characterize the transition from childhood to adulthood?
5. What developmental tasks characterize adulthood and later maturity?
6. Describe Erikson's stages of psychosocial development. What can parents do to meet their children's needs at each stage of psychosocial development?

— CHAPTER OUTLINE —

Infancy and Childhood
The periods of infancy and childhood provide a foundation of special importance for later development.

Developmental Tasks of Infancy and Childhood
Cognitive Development
Psychosocial Development
Social Attachments
Families, Children, and Social Change
Application: Child-Rearing Practices I: Styles of Parenting

Adolescence
During adolescence, the developing person experiences an almost unprecedented rate of biological maturation.

Maturation and Physical Development During Adolescence
Developmental Tasks of Adolescence
Application: Child-Rearing Practices
   II: Fostering Moral Judgment
   Development

Adulthood and Later Maturity
Development is a lifelong process.

Early Adulthood
Middle Age
Later Maturity
Application: Charting Life-Span
   Development

On the Horizon: Death and Dying

THE PARENT'S ROLE
IN CHILD DEVELOPMENT

One morning Sharon wakes up wet, hungry, or perhaps just lonely, and cries. Nothing happens. She cries again. Still no response. She continues crying for several minutes, but no one comes. Finally, she falls asleep, exhausted. On the same morning another infant, Toby, awakes. She, too, is wet, hungry, or lonely, and cries. Within seconds she has the attention of a warm hand, a smiling face, and the food or dry diaper she needs. Sharon's world is unresponsive; her behavior has no effect. Toby's world is highly responsive; her behavior gets results almost immediately. Now, what is the lesson each child is taught by her respective experience? Sharon learns that making an effort to affect one's condition is useless. Things happen or they don't; what she does is unimportant. Toby learns that her efforts are worthwhile. What happens depends, in part, upon what she does. (Chance, 1982, p. 58)

Babies, like adults, get bored. It's one of the main reasons a baby cries. Unfortunately a baby can do little to provide stimulation since it is helpless. The cry of distress or boredom means "pick me up—hold me—cuddle me—show me things—make the environment change." This is frequently the reason a baby stops crying when he is picked up. Don't feel you are spoiling your baby if this happens. I know many parents are told that if you pick a baby up and he stops crying you will be encouraging him to cry—that's nonsense. When the boredom stops the baby is happy and stops crying. If you let the baby cry and cry—he will eventually go to sleep. When this occurs repeatedly, the child learns to go off to sleep as a means of relieving tension and stress. He learns through his helplessness and the lack of responsiveness of others that it's hopeless to try and he gives up easily. Eventually this baby gives up trying altogether. This is a learned pattern that we call learned helplessness [see chapter 6] and persists into childhood and even adult life. Studies have shown that depression in adult life is related to this kind of early parent-child relationship. (Salk, 1982, p. 7)

Do you agree with Salk's view of crying babies? Or is parental responsiveness just another name for permissiveness? What kind of child do you think Toby will be? The contrast between Sharon and Toby along with Salk's comments illustrate some of the variations to be found in parenting styles, which is one of the topics we will explore in this chapter.

Contrary to what you might think, it is often possible to collect clear-cut empirical data bearing on basic child-rearing issues. It might be argued, for instance, that Toby is sure to become a crybaby who howls to get whatever she wants. However, studies show just the opposite. In one study, mother-child interactions during the child's first year of life were observed. Mothers differed greatly in how often they responded to their baby's cries, ranging from 96 percent of the time to only 3 percent. Did the babies of highly responsive mothers become spoiled? On the contrary. Babies who could control their environment by crying soon learned to use other means to get what they needed; they also learned to do things for themselves (Bell & Ainsworth, 1972).

This chapter describes how infants develop into adults. Throughout, it relies on research, like that just described, concerning factors of importance in psychological growth. Development is a never-ending process, extending from infancy and childhood through adolescence and into adulthood and old age (see Table 11–1). At each *life-span stage,* the individual faces certain developmental tasks, or skills, that must be mastered. One such task in infancy that we will investigate is the formation of social attachments to others. In addition, we will describe the rapid cognitive and psychosocial development of infancy and childhood. Later, we will look at how changes in American families are affecting development. Then, we will examine the physical changes and developmental tasks of adolescence. Finally, we will consider the developmental tasks of early adulthood, middle age, and later maturity.

Let's begin, appropriately, with development during infancy.

Table 11–1.

Life-span stages of human development.

STAGES OF THE LIFE-SPAN	APPROXIMATE AGE SPANS
Prenatal period	9 months prior to birth
Neonatal period	Birth to about 1 month
Infancy	1 month to 1.5 years
Early childhood	1.5 to 5 years
Late childhood	5 to 13 years
Adolescence	13 to 18 years
Early adulthood	18 to 35 years
Middle age	35 to 65 years
Later maturity	65 years to death

— INFANCY AND CHILDHOOD —

Infants are the most studied subjects in developmental psychology. **Infancy,** which means "incapable of talking," extends from the end of the neonatal period (one month of age) to 18 months of age. The next period, **early childhood,** lasts until the beginning of the school years, or roughly age 5. **Late childhood** follows, extending to the beginning of the teenage years. As will soon be apparent, researchers in human development have made it increasingly clear that infancy and childhood provide a foundation of special importance for later development.

Developmental Tasks of Infancy and Childhood

Each stage of life is characterized by developmental tasks whose mastery prepares the individual to master the tasks of later stages. Havighurst (1972) defined **developmental tasks** as behavior skills that characterize different stages of development. Some tasks, such as learning to walk, are governed by biological *maturation.* (In the broadest sense, maturation involves orderly, sequential changes in behavioral capacities that are due to physical growth.) Other tasks, such as mastering reading and writing, are learned. Hence they are greatly influenced by people and events in the social environment.

Some important developmental tasks that must be mastered by infants and children are provided in Table 11–2. Learning to crawl precedes learning to walk; learning to talk prepares the child to acquire basic skills in reading, writing, and calculation. To better understand a number of specific developmental tasks, we will explore the child's early cognitive development, psychosocial development, and social attachments.

Table 11–2.

Developmental tasks required of the infant and developing child.

Infancy and Early Childhood
Learning to walk and talk
Achieving bowel and bladder control
Developing an awareness of gender
Learning to relate emotionally to others
Learning to distinguish right from wrong

Middle Childhood
Developing physical skills
Learning to get along with age-mates and others
Learning sex role
Developing skills in reading, writing, and calculating
Developing values

(Adapted from Hurlock, 1980)

Cognitive Development

One 4-year-old girl's favorite birthday present was an electric train. After the train was set up, the child's mother said, "Later we'll get some little trees and houses and telephone poles and glue them down on the board." The little girl's eyes glowed. "Now?" she asked. "No, later," repeated her mother. The 4-year-old accepted the postponement gracefully, but in less than 15 minutes she came into the kitchen, where her mother was preparing lunch. "Is it later enough yet?" she asked. (Paraphrased from Hall et al., 1982, p. 285)

Learning the concept of time is an example of the changing ways in which children think about the world. In his pioneering studies, the late Jean Piaget confirmed that younger children think differently than do older children. Piaget elegantly described the development of thought—from the newborn's inability to distinguish self from others to the first signs of logical and abstract thinking in adolescence. Before we examine his theory, a little background might be helpful.

The term **cognition** comes from a Latin word meaning "coming to know." You might say that *cognitive development* is the process by which infants come to know their world and acquire knowledge. Historically, the study of how they come to know falls into two opposing philosophical camps. **Empiricism** views experience as the source of all knowledge. Thus, the mind at birth is seen as a *tabula rasa,* or blank slate, to be written on by experience. **Rationalism** is the view that the source of all knowledge, the intellect, is present at birth. Extreme empiricists, or environmen-

talists, attribute all knowledge to *nurture* (external influences). Extreme rationalists, or hereditarians, attribute all knowledge to *nature* (internal hereditary influences).

The *interactionist view* of knowledge attainment is more in keeping with present thought (Thomas, 1982). It also characterizes Piaget's theory. According to this view, innate building blocks of knowledge are present at birth. Through interactions with the environment, these primitive thought structures are molded and reorganized during successive stages of development.

Much current research on cognitive development either continues Piaget's work or challenges it. For this reason, we would like to focus on the basic concepts of Piaget's theory and on some of the major cognitive developmental tasks it identifies. For a detailed description of Piaget's theory, see Flavell (1977) or Wadsworth (1979).

— Piaget's Theory of Cognitive Development

In Piaget's view, the building blocks of knowledge, called *schemata,* are present at birth. They underlie the patterns of action that infants use to interact with objects in their environment. According to Piaget, infants gain knowledge through action—by feeling, tasting, and handling objects around them. Schemata, then, are cognitive structures that organize patterns of action and relate means (for example, sucking, grasping, reaching) with ends (for example, receiving food).

Cognition develops as schemata become more complex through the complementary processes of assimilation and accommodation. **Assimilation** is the process of modifying new information to make it fit existing schemata, or knowledge. Through assimilation, children use what they already know to do something new or to understand new experiences. **Accommodation** is the process of changing existing mental structures to make them correspond with new information. Through accommodation, children acquire new ways of doing things. Thus, when a child encounters an object or stimulus, the child understands it in terms of current cognitive structures (assimilation), or the child's cognitive structures are changed by the experience (accommodation). Both processes continue throughout life. For example, people in the United States have been asked to convert a number of measures to the metric system, a difficult task for many adults. Will we have to worry about getting a speeding ticket for driving 80 kilometers per hour on a freeway? Should we wear a sweater or coat outdoors at 30°C? In essence, learning the metric system requires that we restructure existing schemata through accommodation (Hall et al., 1982).

— Stages of Cognitive Development

According to Piaget's theory, cognitive development occurs in four stages, each marked by assimilation and accommodation. The stages are (1) sensorimotor, (2) preoperational, (3) concrete operational, and (4) formal operational. Table 11–3 shows the average age ranges and characteristics for the stages. During each stage, certain measurable cognitive skills are mastered. Their mastery indicates advances in the child's information-processing abilities. The critical feature of Piaget's **Stage theory of cognitive development** is not the age at which a stage is attained but the fact that all children proceed through the stages in the same order. The skills of one stage are impossible to master without first having mastered the skills of the preceding stage.

Sensorimotor stage (birth to 2 years). During the first 2 years of life, the infant acquires knowledge mainly through *sensory perception* and *motor action*. Piaget refers to this period as the **sensorimotor stage.** At this time, the infants are preverbal, and their knowledge is body centered, or *egocentric*. At first, the infants rely exclusively on "prewired" reflex schemata, such as sucking and grasping, to guide responses. Then their actions gradually become more sophisticated through assimilation and accommodation. Although their knowledge is at first body centered, infants soon begin to interact with the world and relate external objects to the body.

An important developmental task during this period is mastering **object permanence,** an awareness that objects and people continue to exist even when they are not directly perceived. Infants do not at first realize that objects and people have permanence. For example, an infant who reaches for a toy elephant will no longer attempt to do so if the toy is covered by a screen (see Figure 11–1). The infant turns away and appears uninterested, presumably because the toy no longer exists. "Out of sight, out of mind," as Piaget would say.

Sometime before the end of the sensorimotor stage, infants develop the concept of object permanence. Older infants seem to know that an object exists even when it is not in view. They make repeated attempts to find hidden objects and may become upset if these attempts fail. Object permanence signals the transition from the sensorimotor stage to the next, more advanced stage.

Holland (1975) has provided several practical suggestions for stimulating children as they progress through Piaget's cognitive stages. During the sensorimotor stage, Holland advises, we should play actively with the infant and encourage exploration in the use of all the senses, especially touching, smelling, and manipulating objects. The game of peekaboo, he suggests, is a good way to establish object permanence.

Preoperational stage (2 to 7 years). Cognition that occurs between the approximate ages of 2 and 7 years is still egocentric, or body centered. However, sometime around 1.5 years of age, children begin to use language and to think symbolically. Piaget refers to

Table 11–3.
Piaget's stage theory of cognitive development.

APPROXIMATE AGE SPAN	STAGE OF COGNITIVE DEVELOPMENT	CHARACTERISTICS
Birth to 2 years	Sensorimotor stage	Preverbal period during which infant acquires knowledge through sensory perception and motor action.
2–7 years	Preoperational stage	Child begins to use language and to think symbolically, but cognitive operations are not yet logical.
7–12 years	Concrete operational stage	Thought becomes logical, but only when applied to concrete objects and situations.
12 years to adult	Formal operational stage	Thought becomes systematic and abstract. Various solutions to a problem and possible consequences of an action can be considered in abstract terms.

Figure 11–1.

Illustration of the concept of object permanence. (See text for explanation.)

this period as the **preoperational stage,** because thought operations are not yet logical.

Piaget described two substages of preoperational thought: preconceptual and intuitive. The preconceptual substage occurs between 2 and 4 years of age and the intuitive substage between 4 and 7 years of age. During the period of *preconceptual thought,* children become better able to relate external objects to the body. Gradually, they are able to identify broad classes of objects, such as houses, dogs, and people, presumably because they develop schemata for each. At the same time, they have difficulty discriminating between objects within the same class. Thus, young children can remain convinced that there is only one Santa Claus even after seeing several different Santas on the same day.

During the *intuitive* period, visual impressions still dominate children's thought. Although there is an increasing use of language and symbolic thought, children do not yet comprehend the rules and operations necessary for logic. Piaget illustrated intuitive thought with tasks that measure what he referred to as **conservation**—the ability to recognize that an object's amount, length, number, volume, and area remain the same despite changes in the object's appearance (see Figure 11–2).

During the past 20 years, there have been over 200 articles published on conservation (Siegler, 1983). These articles suggest that conservation develops with age. For example, it seems obvious to adults that the

amount, or mass, of a lump of clay does not change when its shape is changed or when it is divided into parts. A child who does not yet understand the *conservation of substance,* however, will describe an elongated piece of clay as being larger than a rounded, short piece. The preoperational child will describe an

Figure 11–2.

Conservation of liquid.

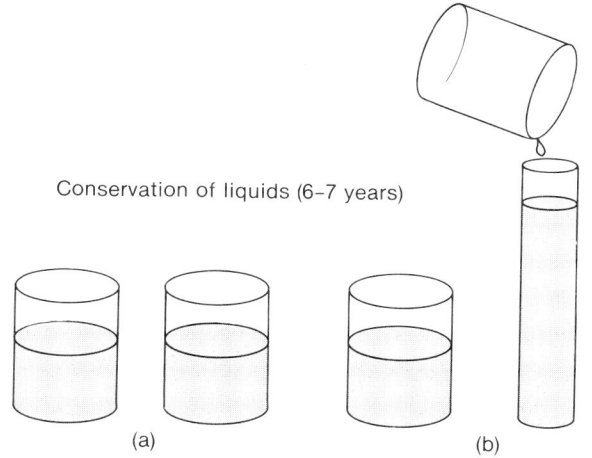

Conservation of liquids (6–7 years)

(a)

Two glasses are filled with the same amount of water. The subject sees that they contain an equal amount.

(b)

The water of one glass is poured into a tall glass. The subject is asked if each glass contains the same amount of water.

elongated piece of clay that has been cut into five pieces as consisting of more clay than one that has not been divided. Similarly, prior to the development of conservation of number, a child will describe a broken cookie as being "more" than an unbroken cookie. If the child argues for more than one cookie, he or she will be easily satisfied when handed one cookie broken into pieces!

Holland (1975) also has provided suggestions about how to interact with preoperational children. To get a point across, concrete examples, which rely on the use of the senses, are better than abstract words. For example, the concept of conservation will be learned more easily by children who are allowed the opportunity to explore their environment and to manipulate substances such as bread dough, liquid, clay, and blocks.

Concrete operational stage (7 to 12 years).

Transition from the preoperational stage to the **concrete operational stage** is shown by mastery of conservation tasks such as those described earlier. Thought becomes logical, but only when applied to concrete objects and situations. Piaget described four rules of logic that are necessary for conservation and for solving increasingly complex problems: (1) identity, (2) associativity, (3) reversibility, and (4) combinativity. To understand the importance of each, consider again the conservation of substance problem described above.

The rule of *identity* suggests that the amount of clay remains the same even when cut into pieces because nothing has been added and nothing has been taken away. The rule of *associativity* suggests that there are multiple ways of achieving the same ends. (This rule is less related to the conservation of substance than to other conservation tasks.) The rule of *reversibility* suggests that because the clay ball can be shaped and reshaped to look the same, the amount must be the same regardless of shape. The rule of *combinativity* suggests that the elongated piece of clay has more in one dimension and less in another; therefore, changes in shape compensate for one another. Although rather general, the four rules of logical thought enter into the solution of various problems requiring conservation.

Holland (1975) suggests that adults continue to use concrete examples, rather than abstract explanations, in discussions with children who are in the concrete operational stage of thought. Although such children are beginning to think abstractly, there will be a de-

gree of inconsistency in their ability to deal effectively with concepts of time, volume, quantity, and space.

Formal operational stage (12 years to adult).

To solve conservation problems, children in the concrete operational stage use logic based on concrete operations. That is, they experiment by thinking of various solutions, but not in an abstract or systematic way. During the **formal operational stage,** adolescents are more likely to solve problems by first forming several hypotheses, which they then systematically test. Doing so requires considering the consequences of various hypothetical possibilities. Hence, Piaget defines *formal operational thought* as the ability to consider all the hypothetical possibilities for solving a particular problem and then to proceed to confirm or deny them. Various solutions and possible consequences of an action can be considered in abstract terms.

Although formal operational thought is possible from about age 12 on, not all adolescents or adults think in this fashion. Many factors interact to determine whether individual cognitive potential will develop to the fullest degree. Thus, a 10-year-old may display formal operational thought, whereas some adults may never consider all the hypothetical possibilities in solving a problem. More generally, it bears repeating that children reach the different stages of cognitive development at various ages. In that case, can training accelerate children's progress through Piaget's cognitive stages? Piaget himself was not much interested in the issue, often referring to it as the "American question." Nevertheless, research has demonstrated that training can facilitate development of conservation of number and length (e.g., Gelman, 1969).

— Piaget's Theory in Action

Coon (1983) has suggested an exercise for thinking about Piaget's four stages of cognitive development that may help you remember them. Imagine yourself playing a game of Monopoly with children. During the sensorimotor stage, infants would put the houses, hotels, and dice in their mouths. During the preoperational stage, children would make up their own rules; they would be unable to understand and follow instructions. During the concrete operational stage, children would play by the rules but would be incapable of the abstract reasoning required for financial transactions such as arranging loans and mortgages. With children who are capable of formal operational

JEAN PIAGET (1896–1980)

Jean Piaget was born in 1896 in Neuchâtel, Switzerland. His first scientific article, published when he was 10 years old, marked the beginning of a long and productive academic career. During subsequent years his curiosity about mollusks (shellfish) led to so many publications on the subject that he was offered a job at a natural history museum in Geneva. He declined the offer, however, because he had not yet graduated from high school. Instead, he pursued further study at the University of Neuchâtel, where he received his doctoral degree in biology at the age of 21.

Shortly thereafter, Piaget headed for Paris, where he met and worked with Théodore Simon, who, with Alfred Binet, had developed the first widely used intelligence tests (see chapter 12). It was there that Piaget began his pioneering studies on cognitive development. After carrying out an assignment to administer a series of intelligence tests to grade-school children in Paris, Piaget's curiosity led him to question children about the reasons underlying both their correct and incorrect answers. His observation that children of different ages appeared to think differently provided the foundation for his theory of cognitive development.

Piaget returned to Geneva in 1921 and continued his studies of child psychology and of how children think and learn. He did so with vigor for nearly 60 years, until his death at the age of 84. During that period, Piaget published more than 100 articles and 40 books on child psychology, in addition to numerous publications in education and philosophy (Miller, 1983). Piaget has been hailed as one of the most influential psychologists of this century, if not of all time (Leo, 1980).

thought, be careful. They no longer play the game mechanically; complex transactions are now possible.

Psychosocial Development

Whereas Piaget dealt with cognitive changes, Erik Erikson (1963) has evolved an elaborate stage theory of psychosocial development. **Psychosocial development** refers to lifelong changes in the individual's psychological and social interactions with others and with society as a whole. Erikson's theory is that the indivdual develops through eight stages, from infancy to old age. At each stage, a conflict must be resolved, and the conflicts are closely tied to social relationships. A complete list of Erikson's stages will be provided later in this chapter. For now, we will consider only the first four stages.

According to Erikson, infants first face a conflict of *trust versus mistrust*. Infants' relationships during their 1st year with their primary care-givers are critical for establishing basic trust. Infants whose needs are met, whose discomforts are removed, and who are cuddled and loved (like Sharon in the chapter introduction) will develop this basic trust. Consistent and predictable care is required, however. Infants who are left to cry and who receive inconsistent, unpredictable care will develop a basic mistrust. This outcome leads to an attitude of fear and suspicion toward other people and the world in general.

The second stage in Erikson's theory concerns *autonomy versus doubt*. Interactions with parents during the 2nd and 3rd years are especially critical for establishing autonomy. A sense of autonomy is fostered by parents who recognize new skills and who allow the children to explore and develop at their own pace. Such children will take pride in their growing ability to master both motor and intellectual skills, such as walking and talking. Children reared by parents who are overcritical or who punish bed-wetting and other accidents, such as spilling or breaking things, are likely to develop a sense of shame and doubt.

The next psychosocial stage involves *initiative versus guilt*. During the 3rd through the 5th years, children develop a sense of purpose and direction. Confidence in their ability to initiate activities will result if parents respond positively to them. Children who consistently hear the message that they are bad or stupid will come to believe it. This message leads to a negative self-concept and guilt over self-initiated activities.

During the 6th through the 11th years, in Erikson's fourth stage, a conflict develops over *industry versus inferiority*. A sense of industry is fostered in children who are rewarded at home and in school for efforts to create and to make things. Children who learn that they are capable of producing something worthwhile achieve a sense of self-worth and accomplishment. Children who are criticized for their efforts and who do not discover their potential for productive work achieve only a feeling of inferiority.

It bears repeating that, according to Erikson, the conflicts described here must be resolved by the developing individual. In this sense, the conflicts are developmental tasks that must be mastered. Mastering the tasks of infancy and childhood provides a foundation for mastering the tasks of adolescence, adulthood, and old age. This foundation is strengthened by and through social interactions with parents, siblings, and peers, or age-mates. Through the gradual process of **socialization,** individuals acquire behaviors, beliefs, standards, and motives that are valued by families, peers, and the larger community (cf. Maccoby, 1980; Mussen et al., 1979; Parke & Asher, 1983).

Social Attachments

A major element of all children's socialization and social development is their attachment to a primary caregiver. For human babies, **attachment** refers to the early love bond that develops between infant and caregivers, usually both parents (Hall et al., 1982). How important is infant attachment? The answer is revealed by the tale of Frederick II, the 13th-century ruler of Sicily. Believing that people are born with an innate language, Frederick arranged an experiment to learn what the language was. Several children were reared in isolation and total silence so that their first words would reveal the true natural language. Instead of speaking, however, all the children died. They could not survive without the touching, the joyful faces, and the loving words of their care-givers (Gardner, 1973).

An important implication of Frederick's tale is that the period shortly after birth is critical in a baby's development. The existence of *critical periods of development* is supported by studies of *imprinting* in animals (Lorenz & Leyhausen, 1973; see also chapter 9). In geese, for example, imprinting occurs when a gosling first hatches. Konrad Lorenz demonstrated that during the first 24 hours of life baby geese become

imprinted on the first moving object they see. Normally, that object is the mother, so the bird becomes imprinted on her. Imprinting, then, refers to a social attachment in animals that develops quickly, completely, and only during an early critical period.

The critical period for imprinting geese lasts from hatching to about 36 hours. It occurs most readily within the first 13 hours of life. Studies by Lorenz and others illustrate that baby geese will follow and become imprinted on nearly any moving object, including human beings, but only during this critical period (see Figure 11–3).

Critical periods of development, sometimes referred to as *sensitive periods* or *optimal periods,* are times when the organization of certain behaviors is most easily affected by environmental events. For ex-

Figure 11–3.

Demonstration by Konrad Lorenz of imprinting in baby geese.

ample, throughout the prenatal growth period, the developing human is highly vulnerable to damage from environmental insults, such as drugs, alcohol, radiation, and maternal disease (as discussed in chapter 10). Poor maternal nutrition during pregnancy or undernourishment during the first 18 months after birth can irreversibly damage brain development. There also appear to be critical periods for developing depth perception (see chapter 4) and language skills (see chapter 8). Is there a critical period for forming social attachments in human babies? Let's examine some evidence.

The death of the babies in Frederick's tale has a second implication—that early experiences can have lasting effects on development. This idea is supported by studies of *bonding* in humans. Some theorists have suggested that the bond, or social attachment, between human babies and their care-givers (see Figure 11-4) develops during a critical period after birth in the same way that imprinting occurs for baby geese. For example, Klaus and Kennell (1982) reported on studies demonstrating that physical, skin-to-skin contact soon after birth encourages human bonding. In one study, after giving birth, some mothers in the hospital were allowed to spend extra time with their infants. The mothers in a control group were permitted contact with their infants only for the usual brief time periods. Klaus and Kennell found that the extra-contact mothers showed stronger attachment to their infants. When observed 1 month later and 1, 2, and 5 years later, these mothers stayed closer to their children, soothed and touched them more, and made more eye contact with them.

As convincing as this study might seem, new research challenges the claim that newborn infants and their mothers must have skin-to-skin contact during the first hours of life (cf. Emde & Harmon, 1982). Although some mothers apparently feel closer to their babies after extra contact, it is not necessarily true that brief separations after normal birth impair infant-mother bonding. Attachment, in the broad sense, takes time to develop.

How does attachment develop? What effect does early attachment have on later development? Let's take a look at the fascinating research bearing on these questions.

Figure 11-4.
Bonding in humans is exemplified by the touching between parent and child.

The Development of Attachment

The first comprehensive attachment theory was offered by the eminent English psychoanalyst John Bowlby (1958). In recent years, a number of American psychologists have extended his work; most notable are Mary Ainsworth and her colleagues (Ainsworth, Blehar, Waters, & Wall, 1978). Like Bowlby, Ainsworth described four phases of attachment, three of which occur in the infant's first year: (1) the initial, preattachment phase; (2) the phase of attachment-in-the-making; and (3) the phase of clear-cut attachment. The fourth and final phase, involving "goal-corrected partnerships," begins toward the end of the third year or later.

Preattachment begins at birth and ends when the infant can discriminate the principal care-giver from others. At first, the infant is unable to tell one person from another and hence responds similarly to everyone. However, the infant is equipped at birth with innate signaling behaviors, such as crying, smiling, and vocalizing. These appear at 2 to 3 months of age and combine with actions such as sucking and grasping to aid in food seeking and attachment. As noted by Emde, Gaensbauer, and Harmon (1976):

> From a physiological point of view, the survival value [of these behaviors] consists of a built-in message system geared to arouse a caretaker about urgent needs. From a psychological point of view, the survival value consists of a facilitation of attachment bonds. (p. 143)

The second phase, *attachment-in-the-making,* begins when infants can distinguish their primary care-givers from others. During this phase, infants can also discriminate between one familiar person and another. They alter the way they direct proximity-seeking actions, such as smiling or grasping, toward different figures. Likewise, these figures may differ in how easily they can end the infants' attachment behaviors, such as crying. As noted by Ainsworth et al. (1978), "During this phase the baby's repertoire of active attachment behaviors becomes expanded—for example, with the emergence of coordinated reaching" (p. 24).

The third phase, *clear-cut attachment,* is identified by Bowlby (1969) as maintenance of proximity to a discriminated care-giver figure by means of locomotion as well as signals. As this definition implies, infants during this phase are more active than before in seeking nearness to and contact with their care-givers. At this time the infants' behaviors first become goal oriented, and behavior patterns that maintain care-giver contact are established. Goal-oriented attachment can be observed in most infants between 6 and 12 months of age. Its onset coincides roughly with Piaget's (1936/1952) final phase of sensorimotor development, when individuals and objects begin to have permanence for the infant.

The development of a goal-corrected partnership marks the fourth phase of attachment (Ainsworth et al., 1978; Bowlby, 1969). Here children are able to make inferences about a primary care-giver's point of view, feelings, motives, goals, and plans. When this level of attachment is reached, it can be said that the care-giver and child have formed a flexible, goal-oriented partnership. They influence one another's behavior (Bell, 1979).

Consequences of Attachment for Later Development

The early attachment between the care-giver and infant, in Bowlby's view, must be lasting and satisfactory for the child to develop normally. Accordingly, a child is more likely to learn from a care-giver who provides a feeling of friendship and security. This positive attitude is lacking for deprived children. The effects of *maternal deprivation* (separation from mother) and *social deprivation* (lack of social stimulation) are especially severe and potentially irreversible if they occur for prolonged periods during the first 2 years of life. Such deprivation may impair development or the ability to form relationships later in life.

Infants reared in orphanages sometimes show retarded physical, mental, social, and emotional development. Studies of such infants suggest that poor or inconsistent care-giving is often the underlying cause (Hunt, 1979). The first such studies were done by René Spitz (1945, 1950), who found that institutionalized infants had elevated death rates, retarded physical and social development, and various emotional immaturities. Many were apathetic, withdrawn, and severely depressed. Spitz referred to these symptoms of maternal and social deprivation as *hospitalism.*

In the early 1950s, Spitz's studies of hospitalism spurred the change from orphanage to foster home care in the United States. These and related studies also led to a flood of human and animal experiments regarding attachment and separation during infancy. (For review, see Emde & Harmon, 1982; Joffe & Vaughn, 1982). Let's take a look at some of the classic studies in this area.

Attachment and separation in infant monkeys. How does maternal deprivation affect the social and emotional development of infant monkeys? An answer was provided in pioneering studies by Harry F. Harlow and his associates at the Primate Laboratory of the University of Wisconsin. In these studies, monkeys were reared in social isolation during periods when attachment to their mothers and peers would normally develop; the monkeys thus deprived later failed to show normal mating and care-taking skills (Harlow, 1958, 1971).

In Harlow's initial studies of attachment and separation, infant monkeys were separated from their mothers a few hours after birth and placed with *surrogate* mothers made of either wire or cloth (see Figure 11–5). The newborn monkeys were put in individual cages, each with equal access to a cloth and a wire surrogate mother. Half the infants received their milk from one "mother" and half from the other. In each case, the milk was furnished by a nursing bottle installed in the mother's "breast" (Harlow, 1973).

Harlow's findings were astounding. The surrogate mothers proved to be *physiologically equivalent.* That is, the monkey infants drank the same amount of milk from each mother and gained the same amount of weight. However, the mothers were not *psychologically equivalent.* Both groups of infants spent far more time clinging to their cloth mothers than to their wire mothers. As noted by Harlow (1973), these results attest to the importance of bodily contact and the im-

mediate comfort it supplies in forming the infant's attachment for its mother.

In later studies, Harlow and his colleagues designed an experiment to determine whether infant monkeys would seek contact comfort when they were emotionally distressed. The monkeys were confronted with a mechanical bear beating a drum. This fear test showed that an infant faced with a strange object quickly learned to seek comfort from the cloth mother rather than the wire mother. The infant would cling to the cloth mother, rubbing its body against hers, and then would look at the previously terrifying toy bear without the slightest sign of alarm (Harlow, 1973).

Many studies suggest that maternal separation may affect young animals physically as well as psychologically. Reite (1978a, 1978b), for example, found that the psychological stress of maternal separation altered the heart rate, body temperature, and sleep patterns of infant rhesus monkeys. Such findings suggest that normal development in rhesus monkeys begins with a secure attachment to the mother. In humans, this attachment provides the basis for confidence in a safe base for exploration.

Some research supports the hypothesis that secure infant–care-giver attachment leads to normal peer attachments and to normal social-emotional development in adulthood. For example, Harlow's studies showed that infant monkeys reared with their natural

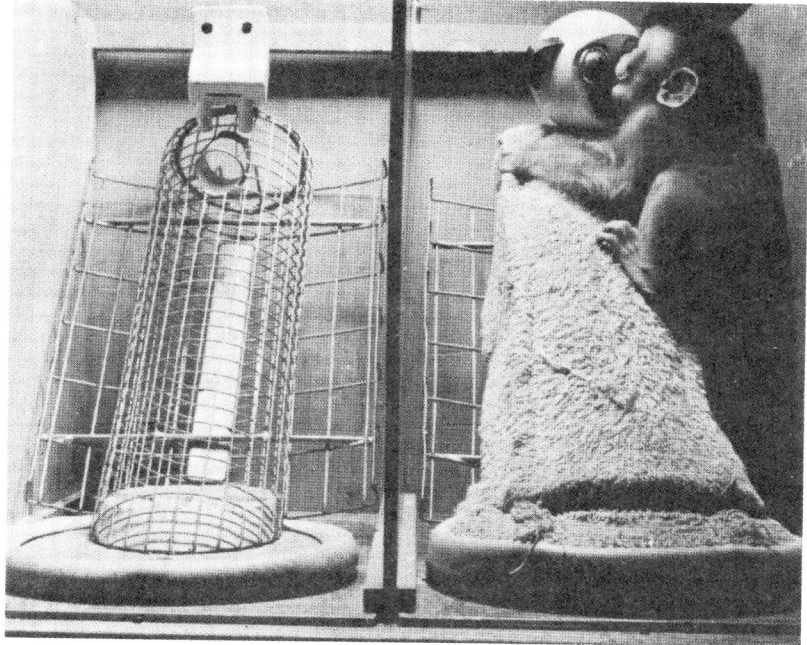

Figure 11–5.

Cloth and wire mother surrogates used to test the preference of infant monkeys.

mothers but deprived of peer relations do not learn to play with their age-mates, and they become aggressive later in life. This research suggests that young monkeys, through social interactions with peers, gradually develop the skills needed to form later attachments to mates and offspring and to function competently as adults.

Attachment and separation in human infants. Human mother-infant separation has also been studied. The quality of infant attachment has been measured by the reactions of infants to several types of separation, such as being left alone in a room with a stranger.

Many investigators have now studied infant attachment and separation using the *strange situation procedure,* which consists of the following events. First, the mother brings the infant into a laboratory playroom, places the infant on a chair surrounded by toys, and then walks to a chair at the opposite side of the room. Shortly afterwards, a stranger enters, sits quietly for a while, and then attempts to play with the child. At that point, the mother leaves the room. The mother then returns and engages the infant in play while the stranger leaves the room. Next, the mother leaves the infant alone for several minutes. The stranger returns to the room, and, finally, the mother returns. Throughout the sequence, an experimenter observes the infant through a one-way mirror and records the infant's crying, attempts to gain the mother's attention, level of play, and other behaviors of interest.

Several studies using the strange situation procedure found that infants typically responded in one of three ways when they were reunited with their mothers after a brief separation. A majority of infants wanted to be close to their mothers; these infants were described as having a *secure attachment.* Another group of infants sought contact but at the same time resisted it; they were described as having an *ambivalent attachment.* A third group of infants did not seek contact at all; they were described as *avoidant infants.* Mothers of avoidant infants showed less evidence of promoting physical contact with their infants than did mothers of securely attached infants. (For review, see Ainsworth et al., 1978.)

Psychologists are becoming increasingly interested in attachment in human infants. One reason is that a number of studies indicate that security of attachment often affects later behavior. For example, Hazen and Durrett (1982) found that 30-to-40-month-old children who had been securely attached at 12 months explored more widely than did children who were not

securely attached. Secure attachment also seems to affect the development of peer attachments (Matas, Arend, & Sroufe, 1978).

The most important factor underlying secure attachment appears to be the amount of stimulation and attention that the care-giver gives the child. That is, secure attachment is fostered by responses to the child's crying and by social interaction initiated by the care-giver (Schaffer & Emerson, 1964; see also chapter introduction). The quality of care-giving, of course, reaches far beyond the topic of attachment. In the next section we will explore a broader range of topics concerned with social and emotional development.

Families, Children, and Social Change

The future of any society depends in large part on the rearing of healthy and competent children. In the United States, the family is the prime source of a child's socialization and basic sense of self-worth. And even though the family has undergone rapid change in recent years, there is evidence that it remains capable of fulfilling these vital societal functions (Conger, 1981). Nonetheless, researchers have begun to examine the effects on children of the changing American family. What are some of the changes? The following facts are paraphrased from The President's Commission on Mental Health, 1978, pp. 564–565:

– Divorce ends 40 percent of the marriages.
– Unknown numbers of marriages are dissolved by desertion.
– The number of single-parent families, mostly poor and headed by women, is increasing rapidly. In 1975, one in every six children under 18 years of age was living in a single-parent family, a percentage double that of 1950. One-quarter of all school-age children do not live with their biological fathers.
– Adults are increasingly unavailable to children. Since 1950, the proportion of working mothers with school-age children has doubled, from 26 percent to 51 percent; the proportion of working mothers with pre-school children has tripled, from 11 percent to 37 percent.
– The number of children born to unmarried women is increasing. In 1960, about 1 out of every 20 women giving birth was unmarried. Today, the ratio is about 1 out of every 8. Most unwed mothers are young, and their babies are often underweight and frail at birth.
– The feminist movement is dramatically altering the

roles of both women and men—at home, at work, and in the community.

What are the implications of these changes for child development? In the remaining pages of this section we will explore the American family in more detail and discuss some research that bears on this question.

— Working Mothers

At present, more than half of all mothers with school-age children and more than a third of mothers with children under age 3 work outside the home. During recent years, there has been a sharp and continuing increase in the percentage of mothers who work outside the home. Currently, the fastest-growing segment of the workforce is mothers of children under the age of 3 (Zigler & Muenchow, 1983). The growing percentage of working mothers of preschool children has increased the demand for day-care services. Despite the fact that over 50 percent of mothers with children work outside the home, licensed day-care facilities exist for only an estimated 10 percent of the children who need them. By 1990 there will be an estimated 24.3 million preschool children in the United States, an increase of 36 percent over the 1979 figure. It is estimated that by 1990 at least 1 million more day-care spaces and 1.6 million more child-care workers will be needed. This represents a two-thirds increase over current needs (Edelman, 1981).

The large number of children receiving substitute care has raised serious questions about the effects of such care. A traditional belief in our society is that mothers must stay at home if their children are to develop properly. As noted by Claire Etaugh (1980), this belief has been strengthened by studies of the long-term effects of maternal deprivation (reviewed earlier). Recent research, however, suggests that the issue is complicated and that maternal employment per se is not harmful to children (Etaugh, 1980). The effects of day-care depend on the *quality of care* the child receives while the mother is working and the *quality and quantity of interactions* between the mother and child when they are together. In general, research reveals little, if any, evidence that maternal employment affects children negatively. For example, from a comprehensive study of the effects of infant day-care on psychological development, Jerome Kagan and his colleagues concluded that attendance at a day-care center staffed by competent adults during the first 2.5 years of a child's life does not seem to sculpt a psychological

profile much different from the one created by total home rearing (Kagan, Kearsley, & Zelazo, 1978).

One reason that maternal employment has little apparent negative effect may be that working mothers often compensate for being absent. Compensation of this sort is most successful when the mother focuses on the child's needs rather than overcompensating out of a sense of guilt (L. W. Hoffman, 1974, 1979). Working mothers who resent their jobs or who stay home but are unsatisfied in the role of homemaker may negatively affect their children. The most adequate mothers seem to be those who are satisfied in their roles. In short, if the mother's attitude toward her role as homemaker or outside worker is positive, the child will be better off than if her attitude is negative.

Many women wonder what effects their choice to work at an outside job or to remain at home will have on their families. As noted by Nye (n.d.), several years of research have disclosed both advantages and disadvantages for mothers employed outside the home. Whether such employment is a good decision for a particular woman depends on her answers to three questions: (1) Is she satisfied with her situation? (2) Is she managing it without undue stress? (3) Are her children well cared for?

— Separation and Divorce

Divorce has become a fact of American life; there are roughly 1 million divorces each year. Public awareness of the problem of marital discord has been heightened by popular books and movies, which themselves reflect the turmoil found in an increasing number of American families. For example, as noted by Emery (1982), the Academy Award winner for best motion picture in 1980 depicted the problems of marital separation, divorce, and child custody *(Kramer vs. Kramer)*; the 1981 winner portrayed family conflict in a two-parent household *(Ordinary People)*.

In a review of research on separation and divorce, Emery (1982) reported figures that suggest a 79 percent increase in the number of single-parent families between 1970 and 1980. The result is that a growing number of children are being reared in single-parent homes. What are the effects on children of marital turmoil, separation, and divorce? Are children of divorce disadvantaged in comparison to children from intact homes?

Research on the effects of divorce provides both good and bad news. For example, the first year following divorce tends to be very stressful for most families.

The household is disorganized, discipline is inconsistent, and the quality and quantity of parent-child interactions tend to diminish (Hetherington, Cox, & Cox, 1982). Loneliness and a sense of isolation are serious problems facing the single parent who lacks social contact with other adults and who feels locked into the dual role of care-giver and economic provider. There is some evidence that if the single parent begins to work at about the time of separation and divorce or during the first year following divorce, there will be an increased incidence of behavior problems in the children. There seems to be no negative effect on the children, however, if a mother employed prior to the divorce continues to work after it (President's Commission on Mental Health, 1978).

Research findings are consistent in showing that children in single-parent homes function at least as well as children in unhappy, conflict-ridden intact families. One study compared 1,800 adolescent boys and girls from mother-only, mother-and-stepfather, father-and-stepmother, and intact families. The study found no differences in children's social development as indicated by scores on a personality inventory, school grades, numbers of friends, attitudes toward school, and participation in extracurricular activities. In short, it appears that divorce does not by itself have overriding negative effects on children. In fact, most divorces occur after a long period of parental strife that results in the mutual decision that the marriage is intolerable and that all parties would be better off after divorce. "In these cases, where the alternatives for children are a conflict-ridden two-parent family or a calm one-parent family, divorce is often the better alternative" (President's Commission on Mental Health, 1978, p. 581).

As noted by Hetherington (n.d.), parental conflict, either in marriage or after divorce, is a major cause of problems for children. The children who suffer most are those in families where the conflict continues after divorce. Thus, the current view is that parental conflict, not divorce, hurts children. Children adjust best to divorce when they have loving relationships with both parents. Nonetheless, it is not possible at the present time to generalize about the effects of joint custody or its advantages or disadvantages in comparison with sole custody (Clingempeel & Reppucci, 1982).

— The Father's Role

A clear majority of children reared in single-parent families live with their mothers. Only about 10 percent

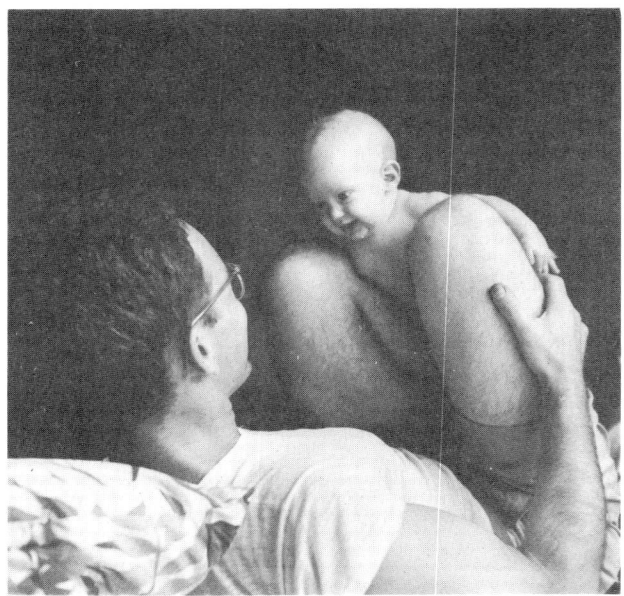

Figure 11–6.
The father-child relationship is extremely important to the childs development and psychological well-being.

live with their fathers, but the proportion has tripled since 1960 (Hetherington, 1979). The number of single-parent families headed by fathers continues to increase. As noted by Lamb (1979):

> Not long ago, men in our culture neither sought nor assumed active responsibility for the rearing of their children. This was especially true during the children's earlier years: Infant care was clearly perceived as the province of women. Today, however, increasing numbers of men appear eager to play an active and important role in child rearing. (p. 938)

Very little information is available on the impact on children of being reared solely by the father, even though there is a rapidly growing literature on the father's role in child development (cf. Biller, 1982; Lamb, 1981). Much of the available literature has examined the relationships of divorced fathers to their children. The literature can be summarized as follows. First, there is very little carry-over between pre- and postseparation father-child interactions. For example, some fathers find limited, brief contacts with their children intolerable and therefore withdraw from the children. On the other hand, many father-child relationships improve following divorce (Hetherington, 1979). Second, the effects of divorce on children depend largely on the parents' attitudes. As noted by Hetherington (1979), frequent contact with the father and continued mutual support between father and child are associated with positive adjustment, especially among boys.

Finally, there is growing awareness that the father is not only an economic provider but also a significant contributor to his children's development and psychological well-being. See Figure 11-6.

— APPLICATION —
CHILD-REARING PRACTICES I: STYLES OF PARENTING

Various trends in child-rearing practices have come and gone over the years. During the early years of this century, experts warned that thumb sucking and masturbation permanently damaged children. Beginning in the 1930s, interest shifted, and parents were advised that feeding on a fixed schedule and toilet training during the first year were essential for proper child rearing. Further, they were warned not to spoil babies by picking them up each time they cried. Consider the following declaration by one such expert, the father of behaviorism (see chapter 6), John B. Watson (1928):

> There is a sensible way of treating children. Treat them as though they were young adults. Dress them, bathe them with care and circumspection. Let your behavior always be objective and kindly firm. Never hug or kiss them. Never let them sit on your lap. If you must, kiss them once on the forehead when they say goodnight. Shake hands with them in the morning. Give them a pat on the head if they have made an extraordinary good job of a difficult task. Try it out. In a week's time you will find how easy it is to be perfectly objective with your child and at the same time kindly. You will be utterly ashamed of the mawkish, sentimental way you have been handling it. (Quoted in Kimble et al., 1980, p. 374)

Watsonian behaviorism viewed child rearing as a struggle between parent and child in which the child was never allowed to gain the upper hand. A more permissive attitude toward children prevailed during the 1940s and 1950s. Parents became more responsive to their children's needs. Thumb sucking and masturbation were not to be interfered with, and parents were advised to delay weaning and toilet training until the child was ready.

A lesson to be learned from the ever-changing child-rearing trends is that children are adaptable. They have, in fact, flourished under a wide variety of child-rearing conditions. The most important ingredient in child rearing is a caring, loving mother figure or father figure (or both) who enjoys the child's company and willingly spends time to help the child grow up.

Although specific child-rearing techniques do not predict later development, certain types of parent-child relationships are more likely than others to result in happy, confident, self-reliant children. Some research on the topic is available. Baumrind (1967), for example, investigated child-rearing practices of parents whose 3- and 4-year-old children had been classified on the basis of home and nursery school behavior as being (1) mature and competent, (2) moderately self-reliant and self-controlled but apprehensive in new situations, and (3) immature and dependent on adults. Parents' child-rearing practices were ascertained by interviews and observations of parent-child interactions. Parent-child relationships were rated on several dimensions, including:

— *Maturity demands:* the amount of pressure that parents exerted on children to perform at their level of ability.
— *Parent-child communication:* the extent to which parents reasoned with children and considered their opinions and feelings.
— *Parental nurturance:* the extent to which parents showed warmth and compassion toward children and expressed pleasure in their accomplishments.

The results of this study suggest the kinds of parent-child relationships that foster social competence in children. The mature and competent children in Group 1 had parents who were rated highly on all three dimensions (maturity demands, parent-child communication, and parental nurturance). These parents tended to clearly communicate their attitudes about appropriate behavior to their children while also respecting the children's opinions. The parents of the moderately self-reliant children (Group 2) tended to be rather low in warmth and compassion and unable or unwilling to communicate their attitudes effectively or to consider the feelings and opinions of their children. The parents of the immature and dependent children (Group 3) showed warmth and compassion toward their children, but they tended to exert less pressure on them to perform at their level of ability and they spent less time communicating with them.

— ADOLESCENCE —

The term **adolescence** comes from a Latin word meaning "to grow into maturity." This developmental stage, which extends from the end of childhood to the beginning of adulthood and spans the teenage years, has long been considered a difficult period. Aristotle commented over 2,300 years ago that adolescents "are passionate, irascible, and apt to be carried away by their impulses" (Conger, 1979, p. 4).

In the early years of this century, contemporary scientific investigation of adolescence by psychologists began when G. Stanley Hall (1904) published a two-volume book, *Adolescence*. Hall was the first person in America to earn a PhD in psychology. He was also the founder of the American Psychological Association and the father of the study of adolescence in the United States (Conger, 1977). In this section we will follow Hall's inspiration by examining adolescence and its developmental tasks.

Maturation and Physical Development During Adolescence

Adolescence begins in biology and ends in culture. On the one hand, maturational processes lead to the rapid acceleration of physical growth, changing bodily dimensions, hormonal changes and increased sexual drive, the development of primary and secondary sex characteristics, and further growth and differentiation of cognitive ability. These biological developments and the individual's need to adapt to them give adolescence certain universal qualities and separate it from earlier periods of development. (Mussen et al., 1979, p. 427)

Additionally, the adolescent faces

so many socialization demands—for independence, changing relationships, with peers and adults, sexual adjustment, education and vocational preparation. (Mussen et al., 1979, p. 426)

To better understand adolescence, let's begin with biology, returning later to socialization demands.

— Puberty

Also called *pubescence,* the term **puberty** refers to the biologically determined phase of adolescence when sexual maturation becomes apparent.

In girls, puberty brings a gradual enlargement of such organs as the ovaries, uterus, and vagina, the appearance of pubic hair, and *menarche*—the first menstrual period (Greif & Ulman, 1982). The beginning of breast development is usually the first observable sign of puberty in girls. Menarche occurs late in puberty relative to changes in breast size, pubic hair distribution, and height; it tends to occur after the spurt in height has begun to slow down (Marshall & Tanner, 1969).

As shown in Table 11–4, the average age at menarche is quite variable cross-culturally, ranging from 12.5 years to as high as 18.8 years of age. This broad range, as well as individual differences in age at menarche within cultures, is due to differences in general health and nutrition, heredity, sampling differences across studies, and other factors. It has long been believed that the average age at menarche has been declining steadily. This supposed trend has led to the popular view that earlier menarche is responsible for increased teenage sexuality and pregnancies. A reanalysis of menarche studies, however, led Bullough

Table 11–4.

Average age at menarche for different populations.

POPULATION OR LOCATION	MEDIAN AGE, YEARS
Florence, Italy	12.5
California, U.S.	12.8
Moscow, U.S.S.R.	13.0
Tel Aviv, Israel	13.0
London, U.K.	13.1
France	13.5
New Guinea (Bundi)	18.8

(Adapted from Lerner and Spanier, 1980)

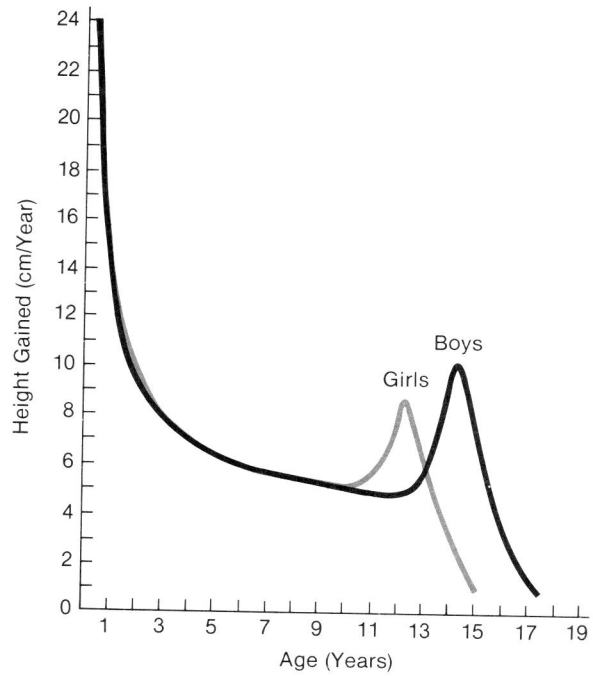

Figure 11–7.

Growth curves typical of the average boy and girl.

(1981) to conclude that the reported decline from 17 years of age in the 19th century to under 13 years of age in the United States today was based on misinformation and sampling error. There has indeed been a decline in age at menarche in the United States since the 19th century, but the actual figures—13 or 14 years of age then and under 13 now—is much less than was once assumed.

In boys, puberty is characterized by gradual enlargement of the testes and, at about the same time or shortly thereafter, the appearance of pubic hair. An acceleration in the growth of the penis occurs nearly simultaneously with the beginning of a growth spurt in height. Other maturation-paced changes include the beginning growth of facial and body hair, about 2 years after the appearance of pubic hair, and the lowering of the voice, usually fairly late in puberty (Marshall & Tanner, 1970).

— Adolescent Growth Spurt

As noted, the onset of puberty and sexual maturation is accompanied by a *growth spurt,* or accelerated rate of increase in height. Growth curves typical of the average boy and girl are illustrated in Figure 11–7. In normal girls, the growth spurt may begin as early as 7.5 years of age or as late as 11.5 years. The average adolescent girl experiences a rapid acceleration in growth at about age 11; rate of growth reaches a peak at about age 12. Slow growth continues until about age 16.

In normal boys, the growth spurt in height occurs later than in girls, supporting the popular belief that girls mature faster than boys by about 2 years. For the average boy, the spurt begins at about age 13, although it may begin as early as 10.5 years; rate of growth

reaches a peak at about age 14. Slow growth continue until age 18 or beyond.

— Individual Differences in Physical Development

The sequence of developmental changes discussed here represents typical, or average, boys and girls. There is wide variation in the onset of puberty and sexual maturation among perfectly normal adolescents reared under similar environmental conditions. Statistically, half of all boys and girls mature more rapidly than the average boy or girl, and half mature more slowly. In normal girls, the range in ages at menarche is from 9 to 17 years. Breast development may begin as early as age 8 or as late as age 13. In normal boys, penis growth may be complete as early as 13.5 years of age or as late as 17 years of age. (For review, see Chumlea, 1982; Mussen et al., 1979). Figure 11–8 illustrates the dramatic differences in maturation that occur among normal adolescents. Differing degrees of maturity are shown for three normal girls, all 12.75 years of age, and three normal boys, all 14.75 years of age.

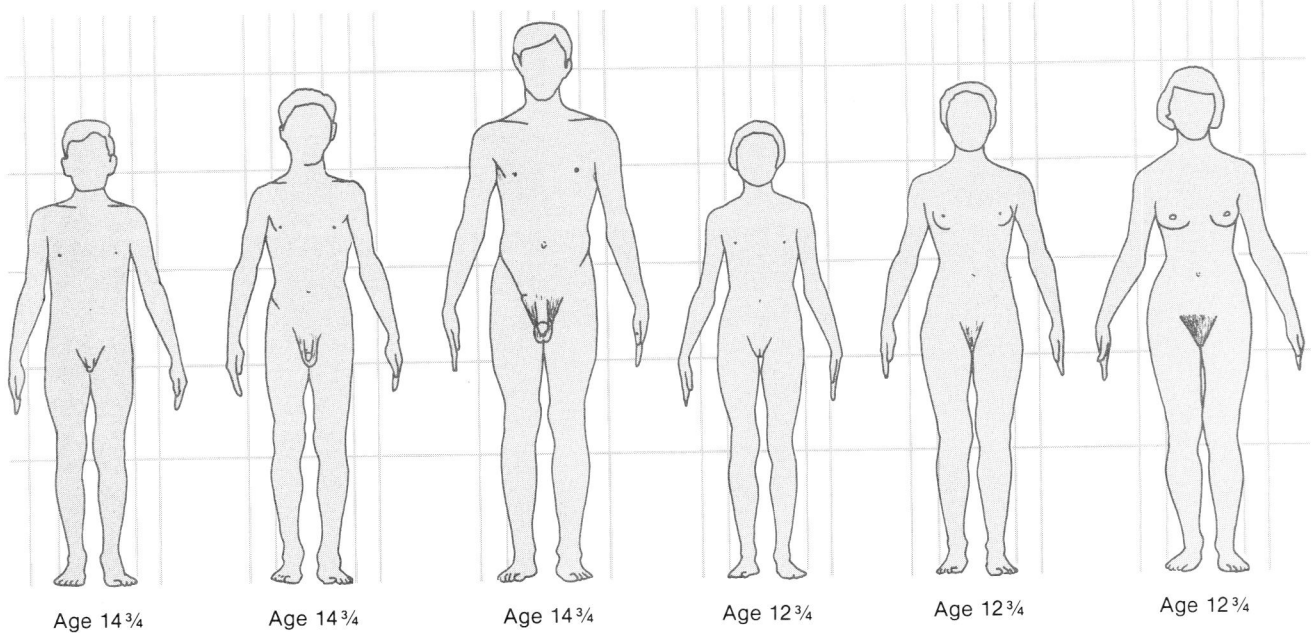

Age 14¾   Age 14¾   Age 14¾   Age 12¾   Age 12¾   Age 12¾

Figure 11–8.
Individual differences in physical development among normal adolescents.

Developmental Tasks of Adolescence

A number of developmental tasks must be accomplished if the adolescent is to become truly adult, not just physically mature (Table 11–5). "The fact that in today's changing world these tasks may be more complex [than previously] and that both parent and child have fewer consistent blueprints to guide them in their accomplishment does not fundamentally alter the situation" (Mussen et al., 1979, p. 442).

— Adjustment to Physical Changes

One developmental task that is not easily mastered by all adolescents is adjustment to the physical changes that occur during puberty. This task involves accepting one's physique and using one's body effectively in physical activities. A question that numerous researchers have addressed is how *early versus late maturation* affects psychological development. For example, a review of studies by Greif and Ulman (1982) shows that a girl's age at the time of menarche influences the psychological impact of menarche. According to the re-

sults of one large-scale study, boys who were late maturing (as measured by skeletal age) engaged in more attention-getting behaviors and were more restless and bossy than were early-maturing boys. They were also less attractive in physical appearance and less poised. Early-maturing boys were more reserved, self-confident, and able to engage in socially appropriate behavior. Developmental differences for girls were not nearly as large as for boys. But early-maturing girls had a more positive self-concept and a more accepting, relaxed, and secure view of themselves than did late-maturing girls (Jones & Mussen, 1958).

Table 11–5.
Developmental tasks of adolescence.

Accepting a masculine or feminine role
Developing new relations with age-mates of both sexes
Achieving independence
Preparing for an occupation
Achieving socially responsible behavior

(Adapted from Hurlock, 1980)

Achieving Independence from Parents

If adolescents are to become adult, they must gradually achieve emotional independence from parents. Before this developmental task can be accomplished, however, adolescents must have some idea of who they are, where they are going, and what the likelihood is of getting there (Conger, 1979). In Erik Erikson's view, developing a sense of *role identity versus role confusion* is the challenge facing adolescents. Those who earlier developed trust, autonomy, initiative, and industry will likely arrive at a sense of identity, which allows planning for the future. Those burdened with mistrust, doubt, guilt, and inferiority will likely experience role confusion, an identity crisis involving not knowing who one is or where one belongs. "An adolescent's failure to resolve the conflict between continuing dependence and the newer demands [and privileges] of independence will lead to difficulties in most other areas as well" (Mussen et al., 1979, p. 443).

Developing Mature Peer Relationships

The development of mature relationships with same-sex peers (age-mates) is very important in the psychological development of most adolescents. Peer rela-

tionships serve as models for later adult relationships in social and vocational settings. Close peer relationships are especially important during adolescence because ties with parents begin to lessen and greater independence is sought.

Adolescence is a period of intense desire for increased socialization with peers. Yet, it is often a period of intense loneliness. Perhaps at no other time of life is there a stronger need to share doubts, confusing emotions, and dreams for the future (Mussen et al., 1979). Peer acceptance and having one or more close friends may be of crucial importance. (See Figure 11-9.)

The adolescent's need for acceptance and belonging leads naturally to conformity to peer-group standards, fashions, and fads. Parents may wonder why their adolescents demand designer jeans or why only certain kinds of music, hairstyles, language, foods, recreational activities, hobbies, and television programs are acceptable. As noted by Conger (1979), to the parent these preferences may seem arbitrary and trivial; to the adolescent, however, they are essential badges of belonging.

Parents should perhaps take comfort in such relatively harmless and superficial expressions of independence. Although peers do tend to have a stronger influence than parents on adolescent tastes, parents usually have a stronger influence on beliefs, values, and life goals (Conger, 1979). However, adolescents

Figure 11–9.

Peer acceptance among adolescents is very important in the development of mature relationships.

rejected by parents may be unable to satisfy their need for independence superficially, which results in more harmful attempts to gain peer acceptance and establish an identity.

Of all the tasks of adolescence, perhaps the most challenging is the development of mature heterosexual relationships. Teenage boys and girls have much in common in their concerns about sexuality. Most of all, they want to fit in and be liked by their opposite-sex age-mates. They also want to know about such practical matters as masturbation, sexual intercourse, venereal disease, conception, pregnancy, and birth control (Conger, 1979).

Adolescents today display a greater openness about sex and an increasing tendency to regard decisions about sexual behavior as a purely private concern. This trend appears to reflect in part a growing disenchantment with parental values and with established social standards. Changing adolescent attitudes about sex are clearly reflected in behavior. Most disturbing is the continuing increase in adolescent pregnancies during recent years. Consider some of the facts:

– About 570,000 American children are born annually to teenagers, at an estimated annual cost of $8.3 billion in welfare and related expenditures (Edelman, 1981).
– Over 1 million 15-to-19-year-old girls in the United States become pregnant each year; this figure represents about 10 percent of the entire age group. Two-thirds of the pregnancies are conceived outside marriage.
– Between 55 and 75 percent of unmarried girls having intercourse use no contraceptive device in their first experience, and only a minority consistently use such a device thereafter (Conger, 1979).

The epidemic of adolescent pregnancies is a fact of life that has serious consequences. More than 25 percent of adolescent pregnancies are terminated by induced abortion, 10 percent result in within-marriage births of children who were conceived premaritally, more than 20 percent result in babies born to unwed mothers, and about 14 percent lead to miscarriages. Even among the 27 percent of adolescent pregnancies that occur within marriage each year, complications are more frequent than for women in their 20s and early 30s. For example, low-birthweight babies are more than twice as common among adolescents than among older women. Also, the risk of maternal death is significantly higher among adolescents. Finally, babies of younger adolescents are two to three times more likely to die in the first year, and the younger the mother the greater the risk (Conger, 1979).

— Development of Social Responsibility and Morals

Children inevitably encounter situations that require a knowledge of right and wrong, good and bad. The development of morality occurs gradually during childhood and adolescence. (For review, see Carroll & Rest, 1982.) Broadly stated, desiring and accepting social responsibility are developmental tasks that involve a philosophy of life and a system of values to guide behavior. They are a crucial step from adolescence to mature adulthood. How do morals develop?

One of the most comprehensive series of investigations of moral judgment development has been conducted by Lawrence Kohlberg, a professor of psychology at Harvard University. Kohlberg and his colleagues (e.g., Colby, Kohlberg, Gibbs, & Lieberman, 1983) have concluded that children tend to progress through six stages of moral development. Their ability to progress from one stage to the next depends largely on corresponding progress in cognitive development (Krebs & Gillmore, 1982). Let's take a close look at each of Kohlberg's stages.

During the early preschool years, behavior is governed primarily by whatever the child wants at a particular moment. However, with the onset of concrete operational thinking (discussed earlier), the child enters what Kohlberg describes as the first of two **preconventional stages of moral development.** During Stage 1, the child develops a sense of good and bad. During Stage 2, the child learns to conform in order to obtain rewards in return for good behavior.

Conventional stages of moral development tend to become dominant during the development of formal operational thought. During Stage 3, for instance, moral thought is likely to involve behavior that pleases or helps others. In Stage 4, it is expanded to include an awareness of authority, fixed rules, doing one's duty, and maintaining the social order for its own sake.

Postconventional stages of moral development are possible only with the development of formal operational thought. During the first postconventional stage, Stage 5, there is an increasing orientation toward

moral internalization—learning to conform to rules even when there is an opportunity to transgress and a lack of surveillance or social sanctions. In Stage 6, post-conventional moral thought and judgment reaches its most advanced form. Morality at this level is characterized by moral principles that have validity and application apart from the authority of those who hold them. Thus, for example, a person may obey the traffic speed limit, not out of fear of getting caught but out of recognition of the limits of safety.

Kohlberg emphasizes the ordered nature of the six stages, the need to achieve and master lower stages before moving on to more advanced stages. As with Piaget's stages of cognitive development, however, there are individual differences in the age at which any given stage is reached. Furthermore, a particular person may not progress beyond any given stage. We noted earlier that not all adults reach formal operational thought. Even fewer, according to Kohlberg, reach a postconventional stage of moral development. Postconventional morality (Stages 5 and 6) was characteristic of about 20 percent of Kohlberg's adult subjects, but only 5 to 10 percent of the subjects consistently operated in Stage 6. Since all of Kohlberg's Stage 6 subjects were capable of formal operational thought, Kohlberg reasoned that reaching an appropriate cognitive stage is necessary but not sufficient for attaining the corresponding moral stage.

To measure moral development, Kohlberg devised a *Moral Judgment Scale,* which consists of stories posing hypothetical moral conflicts or dilemmas. Solutions to the conflicts or dilemmas, according to Kohlberg, provide an index of the quality of abstractness of a person's answers and suggest the person's level of *moral maturity.* Let's consider one such story.

> In Europe a woman was near death from a special kind of cancer. There was one drug that the doctors thought might save her. It was a form of radium that a druggist in the same town had recently discovered. The drug was expensive to make, but the druggist was charging ten times what the drug cost to make. He paid $200.00 for the radium and charged $2000.00 for a small dose of the drug. The sick woman's husband, Heinz, went to everyone he knew to borrow the money, but he could only get together $1000.00. He told the druggist that his wife was dying and asked him to sell it cheaper or let him pay later. But the druggist said, "No, I discovered the drug and I'm going to make money from it." So Heinz got desperate and began

to think about breaking into the man's store to steal the drug for his wife. (Rest, 1972, p. 3)

Should Heinz steal the drug? Typical answers to the ethical conflict posed by Heinz's dilemma—corresponding to Stages 1, 4, and 6—are described here:

– Stage 1 is characterized by a punishment and obedience orientation; it is limited to concern with consequences as opposed to intentions. Children who favored stealing typically offered as the reason: "If his wife dies, he will get into trouble." Those not in favor of stealing typically offered as the reason: "If you steal the drug, then you'll get caught and get sent to jail."
– Stage 4 is characterized by conformity to authority and acceptance of societal standards. A typical reason offered by children in Stage 4 is: "Even though stealing the drug was for a noble cause, there is a violation of a basic biblical commandment when the property of another person is taken."
– Stage 6 is characterized by moral internalization of principles used to guide one's actions and thoughts, even though these principles may contradict accepted or popular norms. A typical response might be: "Heinz would fail to live up to the dictates of his own conscience if he did not exhaust every alternative in trying to save his wife's life."

Kohlberg's is the most researched theory of how moral reasoning develops. Nonetheless, it has been criticized as being far too simple. For example, children in the preconventional stages of moral development may be able to say how they would solve a particular moral dilemma. But whether their verbal responses are accurate indications of how they would act in a given situation cannot be assumed. Another criticism of Kohlberg's theory is that it may be culturally biased. Although the description of conventional stages of moral development captures the flavor of American adolescents' moral development, adults in many nonindustralized societies do not use Stages 3 and 4 (Simpson, 1974). Most criticism has been directed toward Kohlberg's postconventional stages of moral development. Kohlberg himself has questioned whether Stages 5 and 6 can effectively be separated. Nonetheless, a 20-year longitudinal study of moral judgment development found that subjects tended to proceed through the developmental stages proposed by Kohlberg's theory (Colby et al., 1983).

CHILD-REARING PRACTICES II:
FOSTERING MORAL JUDGMENT DEVELOPMENT

What factors determine whether a child or developing adolescent is likely to have a strong conscience that will guide behavior in situations requiring a knowledge of right and wrong? Undoubtedly, many factors are involved, but probably the most important one is the role played by parents (Conger, 1979).

Research has described how different types of parents have different effects on moral development (cf. M. L. Hoffman, 1975; 1979). *Power-assertive parents* attempt to influence the child's behavior by the use of physical punishment or by relying on the child's fear of punishment. Their children tend to achieve weak moral development. Power-assertive parents are *authoritarian* in their style of parenting (Baumrind, 1968). They tell the adolescent what is right and wrong and feel no obligation to explain why. They emphasize obedience to authority as an absolute virtue. Children reared by power-assertive, authoritarian parents tend to emerge from adolescence as adults lacking in self-confidence and self-esteem. Their behavior is less likely to be guided by internalized moral standards (conscience) than by external rewards and punishments (Conger, 1979).

In contrast, *non-power-assertive parents* attempt to influence the child's behavior with techniques that rely on the child's inner resources, such as love, respect, shame, and guilt. Their children tend to develop mature consciences. Non-power-assertive parents treat the child as a potentially responsible person. In addition to pointing out the differences between behaviors that are right and wrong, the parents explain why each behavior may be harmful to the child or to others. According to Baumrind (1968), such parents are *authoritative,* not authoritarian, in their style of parenting. They attempt to control the child's activities by providing direction, guidance, and logical reasons for behav-

ing in certain ways. Such parents are perceived as being rational and reasonable, and they tend to promote the development of internalized moral standards. This description by a 16-year-old girl is typical of such parents:

> I guess the thing I think is great about my parents, compared to those of a lot of kids, is that they really listen. And they realize that eventually I'm going to have to live my own life. . . . A lot of the time when I explain what I want to do, they'll go along with it. Sometimes, they'll warn me of the consequences I'll have to face if I'm wrong, or just give me advice. And sometimes, they just plain tell me no. But when they do, they explain why, and that makes it easier to take. (Conger, 1979, p. 49)

Available research suggests that the internalization of moral standards is fostered by a delicate balance of parental discipline and affection. A summary of findings from many studies reviewed by Martin Hoffman (1979) leads to the following conclusions. First, moral internalization may be fostered by disciplinary techniques that point up the harmful consequences of the child's behavior for others. Second, affection is important in fostering moral internalization because it helps create an environment in which the child will likely be more receptive to discipline. A close, affectionate relationship with parents enhances the child's sense of emotional security, which in turn makes the child willing to accept the parents' judgment of what is right and wrong and secure enough to be open to the needs and rights of others. Third, although discipline and affection tend to foster internalization of morals, discipline based on punishment alone—physical punishment, withdrawal of privileges, or the threat of either one—seems to foster a morality based on fear of external consequences.

— ADULTHOOD AND LATER MATURITY —

It is not easy to say exactly when adolescence ends and adulthood begins. In some societies, puberty marks

the transition from childhood to adulthood. In American culture, the question of when an adolescent becomes an adult is not at all clear. Keniston (1970— cited by Conger, 1977) proposed a new stage of life, called *youth,* to encompass the years during the late teens and early 20s, when so many young people are caught in an ambiguous period of development between adolescence and adulthood. In past decades, a majority of young people went to work at 17 or 18 years of age, before or after graduating from high school. Today, an increasing number of adolescents postpone full adult status for longer and longer periods of time, either because of extended careers as students or because of rootless unemployment (Conger, 1977). Nonetheless, life-span developmental psychologists have found it useful to distinguish the stages of adolescence and adulthood in terms of behaviors that are unique to each stage. An overview of developmental tasks during the periods of early adulthood, middle age, and later maturity is the focus of the remainder of this chapter.

Early Adulthood

Havighurst (1972) defined **early adulthood** as the period of development extending from 18 to 35 years of age. This period (as other life stages is characterized by a number of developmental tasks. The tasks of early adulthood include selecting and learning to live with a marriage partner, starting a family and rearing children, getting started in an occupational career, and taking on civic responsibility (see Table 11–6).

In Erikson's (1963) view, the challenge facing the older adolescent and young adult is that of developing a sense of *intimacy versus isolation.* Intimacy involves the ability to form close and mature relationships with peers—relationships that involve more than sexual attraction. In the broadest sense, for example, intimacy may develop between persons of the same sex who

Table 11–6.

Developmental tasks of early adulthood.

Getting started in an occupation
Taking on civic responsibility
Finding a congenial social group
Developing intimacy

(Adapted from Hurlock, 1980)

share intense, meaningful experiences. The older adolescent or young adult who is incapable of forming mature, intimate relationships with others, either in friendship or in marriage, will likely experience a sense of isolation, of being alone with no one to care for.

Middle Age

Extending from age 35 to age 65, **middle age** is a period during which the maturing adult becomes concerned about doing something useful in life. The period includes transitions in the worlds of work, marriage, child bearing and child rearing, and community participation (Newman, 1982). The general concerns of middle age are suggested by the developmental tasks outlined by Havighurst (1972): achieving adult civic and social responsibility, establishing and maintaining satisfactory performance in an occupation, developing appropriate leisure-time activities, guiding the next generation, relating successfully to one's spouse, and accepting and adjusting to one's own aging and to one's aging parents (see Table 11–7). As with the developmental tasks that characterize other life-span stages, the tasks of middle age may differ from individual to individual. For example, although not all adults marry and have children, the tasks described by Havighurst do indicate the general concerns of maturing individuals.

Erikson (1963) observed that the proper concern of the mature middle-age adult involves *generativity versus self-absorption.* Generativity is primarily a concern with establishing and guiding the next generation. In this regard, Conger (1977) has noted:

> The middle-age adult who can gain satisfaction from using his experience, resources, security, and his position in society and his family—in short, his maturity—in caring for

Table 11–7.

Developmental tasks of middle age.

Achieving social responsibility
Establishing and maintaining an income
Assisting children to become responsible adults
Developing recreational activities
Adjusting to physiological changes of middle age
Deepening sensitivity to needs of others

(Adapted from Hurlock, 1980)

others (whether his own adolescent young, his parents, or those of any age in the larger society that are often in desperate need of care) has perhaps the best insurance against the approaching fall and winter of life. (p. 248)

In Erikson's view, individuals who are incapable of establishing a sense of generativity are likely to fall into a state of self-absorption, where their personal needs and comforts are of predominant concern.

Later Maturity

The psychology of adult development and aging has shown explosive growth in recent years. One of the most active areas of research is concerned with the growth and decline of intellectual abilities with age (Birren, Cunningham, & Yamamoto, 1983), a topic reserved for chapter 12. Before concluding this chapter, let's briefly consider some of the developmental tasks that face the elderly.

During **later maturity,** from age 65 on, the developing individual is confronted with the demands of old age and of new challenges in coping with life. (See Figure 11–10.) Bernice Neugarten's research (for review, see Neugarten, 1982) suggests that health, adjustment, and successful aging later in life depend on the amount of choice the older person has. Self-absorbed people who have few hobbies and who prefer their rocking chairs to a neighbor's company may be happy and well adjusted if they have chosen that mode of existence. Even happy, older adults, however, face certain tasks that characterize this period of life. Adjusting to decreasing physical strength, declining health, retirement, reduced income, establishing satisfactory living arrangements and relationships with people of the same age, and coping with the death of a spouse are some of the concerns of the elderly (see Table 11–8).

Table 11–8.
Developmental tasks of later maturity.

Adjusting to physical aging
Adjusting to retirement
Adjusting to death of loved ones
Meeting social and civic obligations
Maintaining satisfactory physical living arrangements

(Adapted from Hurlock, 1980)

ERIK ERIKSON (1902–   )

Erik Erikson was born near Frankfurt, Germany, to Danish parents. In a recent interview published in *Psychology Today,* Erikson recalls some of the crises he experienced as an adolescent (Hall, 1983). The man who coined the term *identity crisis* could not decide what he wanted to do when he grew up. As an artist during his young adult years, he remained unhappy with his life. In Erikson's view, artists were people with some talent and nowhere to go. Settling in Vienna, he worked as a tutor in a family that was friendly with the family of Sigmund Freud. It was through this association that Erikson became familiar with Freud's ideas about personality development (see chapter 13).

During the late 1920s, Erikson accepted a teaching appointment at an American school in Vienna and undertook psychoanalytic training with Freud's daughter, Anna; he graduated as a psychoanalyst in 1933. In the same year, Erikson and his wife, an American artist of Canadian descent, came to the United States to practice and teach in Boston. Erikson has remained in the United States and during the years since his arrival has held academic and clinical appointments at Yale, Berkeley, and Harvard. In 1961, he was appointed professor of human development at Harvard, where he worked until his retirement, in 1970.

Figure 11–10.

The grandparent-grandchild relationship can be a very enriching and stabilizing one for the elderly person and the child.

The challenge of old age, in Erikson's (1963) view, is *integrity versus despair*. A sense of integrity is derived from an individual's overall satisfaction with life. The individual who sees life as a series of missed opportunities is likely to experience despair over the realization that it is too late to start over. A life history characterized by personal trust, autonomy, initiative, identity, intimacy, and generativity will lead naturally in the later years to a sense of integrity and an acceptance of life's inevitable outcome.

— APPLICATION —

CHARTING LIFE-SPAN DEVELOPMENT

As alluded to earlier, Erikson's theory of life-span psychosocial development may be useful in guiding child-rearing practices and suggesting behavioral strategies that can optimize the individual's chances for successful mastery of developmental tasks (Erikson, 1963). In Erikson's view, the tasks, or conflicts, that characterize life-span stages are accompanied by basic virtues, which appear to emerge from generation to generation. *Drive* and *hope* emerge from basic trust, *self-control* and *willpower* from autonomy, *purpose* and *direction* from initiative, *competence* from industry, *fidelity* from role identity, *affiliation* and *love* from intimacy, *production* and *care* from generativity, and, in later adulthood, *wisdom* from integrity. Table 11–9 shows the ages, stages, and basic virtues proposed by Erikson, along with the developing person's needs and appropriate parental behaviors for meeting those needs at each stage.

Table 11–9.

Life-span developmental chart.

AGE	BASIC VIRTURE	ERIKSON'S STAGES	CHILD'S NEEDS	PARENT'S APPROPRIATE RESPONSES
1	Drive and Hope	Trust versus mistrust	Child needs to be fed, to be dressed, to have diapers changed, to be talked to, to be bathed, to be hugged and loved.	Parent responds to the child's needs, attempting to satisfy them.
2–3	Self-control and Willpower	Autonomy versus doubt	Child needs to play, to walk, to talk, to feed self, to move about with some freedom, to control urine and bowels, to have a sense of self-control.	Parent encourages child's freedom but seeks to protect child against injury.
4–5	Purpose and Direction	Initiative versus guilt	Child needs to develop muscles and sense of mastery of them. Child needs someone to talk with.	Parent provides opportunities for making friends and provides appropriate play materials, such as swings, art materials, and books. Parent talks with child.
6–12	Competence	Industry versus inferiority	Child needs to have many experiences, to develop skills and competence, to have opportunities for friendship, to have relationships with adults other than parents.	Parent provides opportunities for new experiences and allows play time.
13–18	Fidelity	Role identity versus role confusion	Young person needs to accept and control sexual and aggressive drives and to move gradually toward independence from parents.	Parent provides financial and emotional support, but allows young person to move toward independence.
Early adulthood (18–35)	Affiliation and Love	Intimacy versus isolation	Person needs intimacy with another person. Person needs to work.	
Middle age (35–65)	Production and Care	Generativity versus self-absorption	Person needs to help establish the next generation. Usually this need is fulfilled through creative work, or the rearing of one's children.	
Later maturity (65–)	Wisdom	Integrity versus despair	Person needs to accept life's inevitable outcome.	

SOURCE: Adapted from Erikson (1963) and Parrott (1978).

DEATH AND DYING

All evidence substantiates the fact that the U.S. population continues to age. As of July 1983, for the first time in history, there were more Americans over age 65 (27.4 million) than teenagers (26.5 million) (Wallis, 1983). In 1970, approximately 10 percent of the 200 million Americans were over age 65; only 1 in 30 Americans was over 65 in 1900. Recent projections are that if the present trend continues, by the year 2020, 1 person out of every 5 will be over age 65 (Eisdorfer, 1983). Until recently, the Census Bureau had never reported the number of Americans over age 100 because there were so few. A 1983 report, however, showed that in mid-1982 there were 32,000 people in the United States who were over 100 years old (Schreiner, 1983).

As the number of adults increases, more of us must deal with parents, friends, and relatives who, although afflicted with injuries or illness, are being sustained by improved medical technology. How to deal psychologically with death is a task of increasing concern. Let's consider the case of Karen Ann Quinlan, who, in April 1975, at the age of 21, was found unconscious in the bedroom of a friend's home, apparently the victim of drugs and alcohol.

For more than a year, Karen lay in a coma in the intensive care unit of the New Jersey hospital near her home. Machines "breathed" for her and pumped blood through her veins. She was fed intravenously. What to do about her became a dilemma that called into question the very meaning of human existence. Would turning off the respirator constitute an act of mercy? Karen herself was in no distress, but her parents obviously were. Theologians, lawyers, doctors, and judges argued the matter while the Quinlans agonized. Eventually, convinced that there was no hope of recovery, they made their own decision. The respirator was turned off, and the young woman was removed to a nursing home. Here, it was expected, nature would take its course.

And nature did—in an unusual fashion. Although she never regained consciousness, Karen Quinlan continued to "live," breathing on her own, her heart still beating, yet hardly "human." Lying motionless in a fetal position, legs drawn up underneath her, hands joined as if in prayer, the physical body of Karen Ann Quinlan survived. But the real Karen Ann Quinlan—the person with feelings and thoughts, the ability to recognize others and make decisions—had long been dead. (Paraphrased from Dempsey & Zimbardo, 1978, p. 177)

This story provocatively illustrates the difference between *biological death,* which occurs when all vital organs cease to function, and *psychological death,* which occurs with the loss of ability to experience feelings and thoughts, to recognize others, and to make decisions. The story also heightens our awareness of the psychological needs of the dying and of those who are left behind. We are learning more and more about death and dying, and current research and knowledge in this area should be useful to all of us as we deal with the deaths of others, then with our own deaths.

Perhaps of greatest value will be our expanding knowledge of dying itself. In this regard, Elizabeth Kübler-Ross (1969, 1974) has identified five phases through which dying people pass:

1. *Denial,* or refusal to accept the fact that one is dying.
2. *Anger,* the phase when one protests the fact of death and wonders, "Why me?" A sense of unfairness and injustice is often manifested by open hostility toward doctors, nurses, and loved ones.
3. *Bargaining,* the phase during which one recognizes the inevitability of death and bargains for time.
4. *Depression,* the phase characterized by expressions of self-pity, sorrow, and grief.
5. *Acceptance,* which one experiences under optimal conditions. The preceding phases have been

worked through successfully, and death is met with peace and tranquility.

The psychological needs of the dying and of their survivors are the focus of Kübler-Ross's (1969) book *On Death and Dying*. Kübler-Ross's pioneering effort to understand dying has broadened awareness that death is a fact of life, a natural part of the life cycle. Her work, however, has raised more questions about death and dying than it has answered. Further research into the subject will undoubtedly lead not only to increased awareness about death but, more importantly, to an expanded knowledge of the death process. Also, psychological research on dying should lead to further development of programs for the dying and for those who must live daily with a close friend or relative who is terminally ill. In support of such programs, Congress passed a bill that could bring millions more in federal funds to the approximately 800 hospices across the country (Cunningham, 1983). The term **hospices** refers to centers for the care of people who

are terminally ill. It also refers to communities or professionals and volunteers who provide support for patients and their families, both at the centers and in the patients' homes (DuBois, 1980).

The new law means that Medicare will pay for hospice services such as physical, occupational, and speech therapy, nurse and physician services, medication, and short-term social services in the home, as well as inpatient care. To receive money for hospice services, a person must have a life expectancy of 6 months or less. Although *bereavement counseling* (the counseling of the family after the patient's death) will not be covered, counseling prior to the patient's death will be. Also covered will be relief services that give family members a rest from the stress of caring for a patient (Cunningham, 1983). So far, there is little research on the effects of hospice care on the dying and their families. Nonetheless, the hospice movement, which originated in its modern form in England, is catching on in the United States.

1. Each life-span stage of development—infancy, childhood, adolescence, and adulthood—is characterized by developmental tasks, or behavior skills, that must be mastered before the individual can master the tasks of later stages of development.

2. Psychologists have devoted much time and energy to the study of cognitive development in an effort to understand how knowledge is attained.

3. Jean Piaget's stage theory of cognition describes how knowledge is acquired during successive stages of mental development.

4. Four stages proposed by Piaget are the sensori-motor stage, which extends from birth to 2 years of age; the preoperational stage, which extends from 2 to 7 years of age; the concrete operational stage, which extends from 7 to 12 years of age; and the formal operational stage, which extends from 12 years of age to adulthood.

5. Erik Erikson has proposed a stage theory of psychosocial development, which emphasizes the importance of the developing individual's interactions with society.

6. According to Erikson's psychosocial theory, the individual develops through eight stages, from infancy to old age. Each stage has its own conflict to be resolved. The failure to resolve the conflict at any stage can lead to difficulty in mastering the developmental tasks of subsequent stages.

7. No process is more basic or more important to normal social development than the child's attachment to the primary care-giver. In human babies, attachment refers to the early love bond that develops between care-giver and infant.

8. Many studies point to deficient or inconsistent care-giving or disturbances in the development of attachment to a care-giver as underlying causes of retarded physical, cognitive, and social development in human infants.

9. The American family is undergoing substantial changes in its traditional functions and basic structure. There has been a sharp and continuing increase in the number of working mothers during recent years. Marital separation and divorce are common. About one-sixth of all children in America are presently being reared in single-parent families. Such changes have led to widespread concern about the effects on children of substitute day-care, separation, and divorce.

10. There is some evidence about the types of parent-child relationships that are most likely to produce happy, confident, and self-reliant children.

11. Adolescent development is characterized by rapid physical and psychological change.

12. Adjustment to the physical changes of puberty is a developmental task that is not easily mastered by all adolescents.

13. Adolescents who are to become adult, not just physically mature, must gradually achieve emotional independence from parents. In addition, they must develop mature relationships with same-sex and opposite-sex peers and must achieve a sense of social responsibility and morality.

14. The study of human values has a long history. Lawrence Kohlberg's developmental approach suggests that moral judgment tends to develop in a series of stages and that a child's ability to progress from one stage to the next depends in large part on corresponding progress in cognitive development.

15. Postconventional stages of moral development, unlike earlier stages, are characterized by moral internalization. That is, the person learns to conform to rules when faced with temptation in the absence of surveillance and social sanctions.

16. Moral judgment development can be assessed objectively. The Moral Judgment Scale, for instance, consists of hypothetical ethical conflicts, the solutions to which provide an index of the abstractness of a person's answers. The level of abstractness, in turn, suggests the level of the person's moral maturity.

17. Available research suggests that the internalization of moral standards is fostered by a delicate balance of parental discipline and affection.

18. Developmental tasks of early adulthood range from selecting a marriage partner to starting a family and rearing children, getting started in an occupation, and taking on civic responsibility.

19. Developmental tasks of middle age range from maintaining satisfactory performance in an occupational career to developing appropriate leisure-time activities, guiding the next generation, relating successfully to one's spouse, and accepting one's own aging.

20. Developmental tasks of later maturity include adjusting to decreasing physical strength, declining health, retirement, reduced income, and ultimately, death.

— IMPORTANT TERMS AND CONCEPTS —

Infancy
Early Childhood
Late Childhood
Developmental Tasks
Cognition
Empiricism
Rationalism
Assimilation
Accommodation
Stage Theory of Cognitive Development
Sensorimotor Stage
Object Permanence

Preoperational Stage
Conservation
Concrete Operational Stage
Formal Operational Stage
Psychosocial Development
Socialization
Attachment
Critical Periods
Adolescence
Puberty
Preconventional Stages of Moral Development

Conventional Stages of Moral Development
Postconventional Stages of Moral Development
Moral Internalization
Early Adulthood
Middle Age
Later Maturity
Hospices

— SUGGESTIONS FOR FURTHER READING —

Bowlby, J. (1969) *Attachment and loss: Vol. 1. Attachment; (1973) Attachment and loss: Vol. 2. Separation: Anxiety and anger; (1980) Attachment and loss: Vol. 3. Loss: Sadness and depression.* New York: Basic Books. The world's leading authority on attachment and loss provides a trilogy on the subject.

Byrne, D., & Fisher, W. A. (Eds.). (1983). *Adolescents, sex, and contraception.* Hillsdale, NJ: Erlbaum. This book deals with the problem of the noncontraceptive sexual behavior of adolescents, the reasons for that behavior, and possible solutions to the problem.

Conger, J. J., & Petersen, A. C. (1983). *Adolescence and youth: Psychological development in a changing world* (3rd ed.). New York: Harper & Row. A scholarly, well-balanced, and up-to-date integration of the scientific literature relevant to adolescent development, including an expanded coverage of topics discussed in this chapter.

Lamb, M. R. (Ed.). (1981). *The role of the father in child development* (2nd ed.). New York: Wiley. This edited volume contains thought-provoking, insightfully written chapters contributed by numerous psychologists on the father's role in children's social development.

Maccoby, E. E. (1980). *Social development: Psychological growth and the parent-child relationship.* New York: Harcourt Brace Jovanovich. Already hailed as a classic, this book takes the process of socialization within the family as its major theme and focuses on parent-child interactions during the first decade of the child's life.

Mussen, P. H. (Ed.). (1983). *Handbook of child psychology* (4th ed.). New York: Wiley. This four volume work consists of chapters contributed by 90 of the world's most outstanding authorities in the field of child development. Volume 1, edited by W. Kessen, covers history, theory and methods. Volume 2, edited by J. J. Campos and M. M. Haith, covers infancy and developmental psychobiology. Volume 3, edited by J. H. Flavell and E. M. Markham, covers cognitive development. Volume 4, edited by E. M. Hetherington, deals with socialization, personality, and social development. Together these volumes provide a comprehensive and current reference of the study and practice of child development.

— CHAPTER 12 —

INTELLIGENCE AND THE MEASUREMENT OF INDIVIDUAL DIFFERENCES

INTELLIGENCE AND THE MEASUREMENT OF INDIVIDUAL DIFFERENCES

━━ CHAPTER OBJECTIVES ━━

To achieve the objectives of this chapter, you should be able to answer the questions listed here. You should also be able to define the important terms and concepts listed at the end of the chapter.

1. What is intelligence? How is it measured?
2. List the characteristics of good psychological tests.
3. How can the range of individual differences in intelligence best be described?
4. How do psychologists define and diagnose mental retardation?
5. What is genius? How does it differ from giftedness and creativity?
6. To what extent are individual differences in intellectual development due to genetics versus environment? What methods are available to answer this question?

━━ CHAPTER OUTLINE ━━

Measurement of Human Intelligence
Among the capabilities of human beings, intelligence is the most widely studied and, in recent years, by far the most controversial.

History of Mental Testing
Types of Mental Tests
Characteristics of Good Psychological Tests
Testing for Intelligence over the Life-Span
Application: Testing Your Own IQ

Distribution of IQ Scores
Most people are of average intelligence; however, intellectual functioning ranges from mental retardation to genius.

Mental Retardation
Genius, Giftedness, and Creativity
Application: Identifying Creative Talent

Genetic and Environmental Determinants of Intellectual Development
Heredity sets a limit on intellectual development. Quality of environmental rearing conditions determines the range of possible outcomes.

Human Behavioral Genetics
Controversies in Behavioral Genetics
Family Configuration and Intellectual Development
Environmental Enrichment Programs and Intellectual Development
Application: Enrichment through Nutrition

On the Horizon: Engineering Human Intelligence

AUTISTIC SAVANTS—A PUZZLE UNSOLVED

Charles and Ann have extraordinary capabilities in making calendar calculations. Almost instantly, Charles can figure out on what day of the week a date fell 2,000 years ago or will fall 2,000 years in the future. Ann can name the months during 1998 in which the 7th day will fall on a Wednesday. When Arthur is asked how much 4,234 times 6,427 is, the boy responds slowly but without hesitation, "27,211,918." Julie can sing any specified musical note and identify any note that is played, an ability known as perfect pitch. She knows nearly every song ever written. Michael can solve a scrambled Rubik's cube in less than 40 seconds. Solving the cube, which was designed by Professor Rubik to challenge architecture students, is impossible for many people. There are more than 43 quintillion possible arrangements on the cube (cf. Restak, 1982; Rimland, 1978).

Despite their peculiar talents, all of the children described have a disorder that renders them retarded in many other areas of mental functioning. They are among the 10 percent of all autistic children who perform certain mental feats resembling those of geniuses. It is for this curious combination of retardation and genius that they are called **autistic savants.** *Autism* is a term applied to children who are noncommunicative and often totally self-absorbed and who escape reality through daydreams or fantasy. *Savant* is a French term that means "a person of exceptional learning."

Bernard Rimland, a psychologist whose own son, Mark, is autistic, has spent much of his career attempting to understand autistic savants. Despite his and others' inquiries, it remains largely a mystery how autistic savants achieve their extraordinary abilities. Only during the last decade have we begun to learn enough about brain function to speculate about possible explanations.

In this chapter, we will explore a number of questions raised by autistic savants. Does human intelligence consist of one general ability or various specific mental abilities? How can intelligence be measured? Why are some people mentally retarded and others mentally gifted? How is it that some people are retarded in some areas and gifted in others? How can we account for the extraordinary accomplishments of recognized geniuses? Are the talents of gifted people inherited or acquired through learning? Is it possible to determine the relative influence of heredity versus environment on intellectual development? These questions, which have intrigued psychologists for nearly a century, are the topics of this chapter.

═ MEASUREMENT OF HUMAN INTELLIGENCE ═

How should we define human **intelligence?** Students' definitions are often remarkably similar to those offered by psychologists. Before reading further, try jotting down your own definition. Now consider the one proposed by Alfred Binet, whose work we will soon describe:

> To judge well, to comprehend well, to reason well, these are the essential activities of intelligence. A person may be a moron or an imbecile if he is lacking in judgment; but with good judgment he can never be either. (Quoted in Willerman, 1979, p. 84)

Binet's definition assumes a basic ability that he called judgment and that others have called good sense, practical sense, or the ability to adapt to circumstances. Students frequently choose the same terms to define human intelligence, and their description of intelligence is similar to that proposed by David Wechsler (1958), whose work we will also discuss. According to Wechsler, intelligence is the capacity of the individual to act purposefully, to think rationally, and to deal effectively with the environment.

Psychologists do not always agree on how to define human intelligence. Some believe it is a general ability that enters into all mental functioning. Others question whether there is such a thing as general intelligence and argue that intelligence tests sample a number of relatively separate mental abilities. For example, Charles Spearman (1927) introduced *factor analysis* to settle the issue—a statistical method for determining the minimum number of constructs (factors) necessary to account for the interrelationships among a group of tests. Using the technique Spearman found evidence for a general factor of intelligence that he called "g". Other researchers (e.g., Thurstone, 1938) failed to find a general factor that explains performance on different tests and instead found evidence for a number of statistically independent primary mental abilities. In support of Thurstone's hypothesis, it seems also that the specific and highly focused abilities of autistic savants provide evidence for the existence of relatively independent mental abilities. Thus, a useful model includes a general ability called intelligence plus specific mental abilities that are relatively independent of one another. It will be helpful to keep this model in mind as we proceed.

History of Mental Testing

The first systematic study of human intelligence began only about a century ago, when Francis Galton devised a series of methods to measure sensory and motor functioning (vision, hearing, reaction time, and so on). During the late 1800s, he used these measures in his laboratory in London to assess the physical and mental characteristics of large numbers of individuals (see Figure 12–1). An American psychologist, James McKeen Cattell, expanded Galton's measures and coined the term *mental test.* However, a major setback to the mental testing movement came when studies failed to show a relationship between performance on Cattell's tests of intelligence and real-life behavior, such as school performance.

At about the same time, Alfred Binet (pronounced Ba-Nay), in France, was beginning to develop another approach to the measurement of intelligence. Binet proposed that intelligence could be assessed by measuring memory, imagery, imagination, attention, comprehension, suggestibility, aesthetic appreciation, will power, moral sentiments as well as motor skill. With

Figure 12–1.
Handbill of 1884 announcing Galton's laboratory. (Source: Courtesy of the Galton Laboratory, University College, London.)

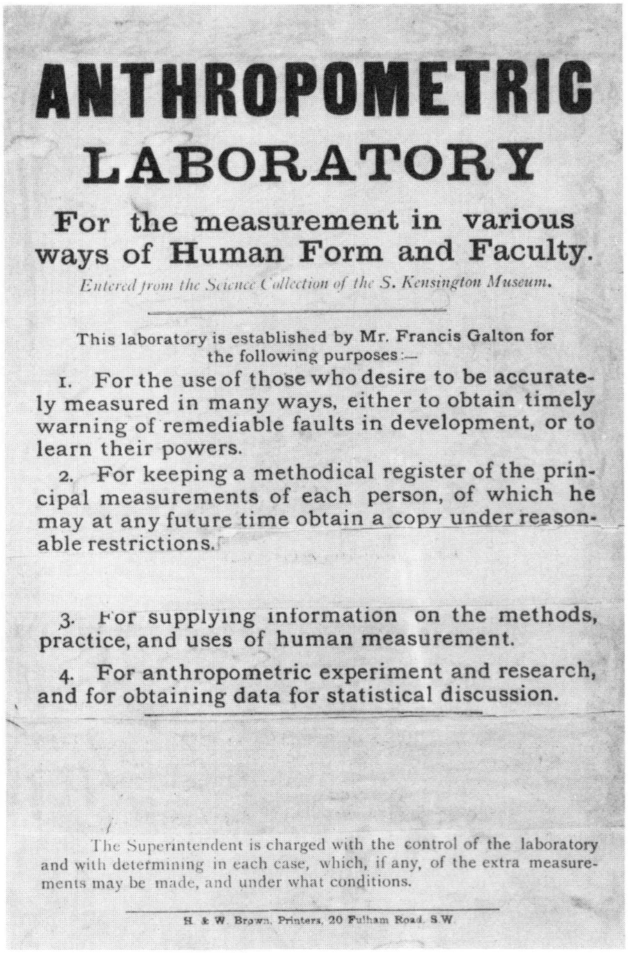

ANTHROPOMETRIC
LABORATORY

For the measurement in various ways of Human Form and Faculty.

Entered from the Science Collection of the S. Kensington Museum.

This laboratory is established by Mr. Francis Galton for the following purposes:—

1. For the use of those who desire to be accurately measured in many ways, either to obtain timely warning of remediable faults in development, or to learn their powers.

2. For keeping a methodical register of the principal measurements of each person, of which he may at any future time obtain a copy under reasonable restrictions.

3. For supplying information on the methods, practice, and uses of human measurement.

4. For anthropometric experiment and research, and for obtaining data for statistical discussion.

The Superintendent is charged with the control of the laboratory and with determining in each case, which, if any, of the extra measurements may be made, and under what conditions.

H. & W. Brown, Printers, 20 Fulham Road, S.W.

Théodore Simon, Binet developed a test of these abilities that would identify objectively which children in French public schools could benefit from normal schooling and which needed special instruction (Binet & Simon, 1905/1979).

— Stanford-Binet Intelligence Scale

Binet's work did not go unnoticed. In the United States, a professor at Stanford University, Lewis Terman (1916), translated the Binet test into what now is known as the *Stanford-Binet Intelligence Test* (Terman & Merrill, 1960; see also Figure 12–2). As on the Binet-Simon test, items on the Stanford-Binet test were *age-standardized*. That is, they were grouped by age level, each being placed at an age where approximately 75

Figure 12–2.

Stanford-Binet Intelligence Test being administered to a child.

percent of the children passed. Recognition of age-related differences in ability and the use of age-standardized items led to the familiar **intelligence quotient (IQ)**—an index of intelligence based on the relationship between *mental age (MA)* and *chronological age (CA)*. IQ is computed by dividing MA by CA. The resulting quotient is multiplied by 100 to eliminate the decimal point. Thus:

$$IQ = \frac{MA}{CA} \times 100$$

When MA equals CA, IQ is 100, which is the average IQ score. Scores above 100 indicate above-average performance; scores below it indicate below-average performance.

— Wechsler Intelligence Scales

Since the denominator of the IQ equation is chronological age, adults who continued to answer the same number of items correctly would obtain decreasing IQs. (MA would remain the same and CA would increase, thereby reducing the IQ.) Wechsler's (1958) solution was to introduce the concept of **deviation IQ,** an IQ defined by one's relative standing among others of the same age. Using the concept of deviation IQ, Wechsler constructed several of the most widely used intelligence tests. Each assesses a broad range of abilities for different age groups. Best known are the *Wechsler Adult Intelligence Scale (WAIS)* and the *Wechsler Intelligence Scale for Children (WISC)*. The WAIS was first published in 1955. The current version, published in revised form in 1981 and referred to as the WAIS-R, consists of 11 subtests, 6 of which are grouped into a *Verbal Scale* and 5 into a *Performance Scale* (Wechsler, 1981). Brief descriptions of their content are provided in Table 12–1.

Although the Wechsler tests measure various elements of intelligence, Wechsler believed that a global index of intellectual capacity can be obtained from scores on the subtests. Thus, the Wechsler tests provide a *verbal IQ,* a *performance IQ,* and a *full-scale IQ* (the average of the verbal and performance IQs).

Types of Mental Tests

The Stanford-Binet and Wechsler tests share one major limitation: Each must be individually administered.

Table 12–1.

WAIS-R subtests. (After Wechsler, 1981.)

The Verbal Scale of the WAIS-R consists of the following subtests:

1. INFORMATION. This subtest consists of questions that cover a wide variety of information that individuals have presumably had an opportunity to acquire simply by living in our culture. Specialized or academic knowledge is avoided.

2. DIGIT SPAN. The subject is required to listen to and then repeat a series of digits given orally by the examiner. The easiest item consists of 3 digits; the most difficult has 9.

3. VOCABULARY. This subtest consists of words of increasing difficulty presented orally and visually. The subject is required to provide a definition of each.

4. ARITHMETIC. This subtest consists of problems in elementary-school arithmetic. Each problem is orally presented, and the subject is asked to solve the problem without the use of paper and pencil.

5. COMPREHENSION. This subtest consists of items that present problems for the subject to explain.

6. SIMILARITIES. This subtest consists of items requiring the subject to say in what way two things are alike, for example, an orange and a banana.

The Performance Scale of the WAIS-R consists of the following subtests:

7. PICTURE COMPLETION. This subtest consists of cards, each containing a picture from which some part is missing. The subject is asked to identify the missing part.

8. PICTURE ARRANGEMENT. This subtest consists of sets of cards. Each card has a picture on it; when the cards of a set are placed in the proper order, they tell a story. The subject is given 1 set of cards at a time and asked to arrange the cards so that they tell the story.

9. BLOCK DESIGN. This subtest consists of blocks that must be assembled to reproduce designs of increasing complexity.

10. OBJECT ASSEMBLY. Cutout pieces of an object are to be assembled to make a flat picture of the object.

11. DIGIT SYMBOL. The subject is required to substitute symbols for digits on an answer sheet during a limited time period.

With the advent of World War I, the armed forces needed large-scale testing of recruits. Necessity led to the creation of group tests of intelligence by a committee of psychologists, including Lewis Terman of Stanford University. Two tests, the *Army Alpha* and the *Army Beta,* were devised for use with English-speaking and non-English-speaking individuals, respectively. Group tests have been used by psychologists to screen large numbers of individuals in relatively short periods of time. However, individually administered intelli-gence tests are still widely used and even preferred in certain (for example, clinical) settings.

Refinements in group-testing methods made it possible to create batteries of tests that measure a wide range of achievements and aptitudes. **Achievement tests** are designed to measure what individuals have learned in the past. Teachers at all levels give achievement tests to assess student learning. Along with other information, achievement scores are used for educational counseling and the evaluation of instructional programs.

Aptitude tests are designed to measure the capacity to learn particular skills or subject matter. Some psychologists use the term *aptitude* almost interchangeably with *ability* and *intelligence.* Perhaps you have taken a familiar aptitude test: the *Scholastic Aptitude Test (SAT),* or college entrance exam. If so, you know that aptitude tests often include elements of achievement or prior learning. It is difficult to measure aptitude without drawing on at least some existing knowledge or skills.

Characteristics of Good Psychological Tests

What are the characteristics of good psychological tests? How are we to determine whether a particular test is useful and will yield meaningful results? We can assess the merits of any psychological test by considering its reliability, validity, and standardization.

— Reliability

The consistency of scores obtained when the same people take the same test on different occasions is **test reliability.** An intelligence test would be unreliable and therefore useless if a person taking it obtained greatly discrepant scores from one occasion to another.

Three methods are commonly used to determine a test's reliability. In the *test-retest method,* a group of individuals takes the same test on two occasions, and scores from both sessions are compared. As illustrated in Figure 12–3, the more reliable the test, the more stable the scores will be from one testing session to the next. In the *alternate-forms method,* scores on two versions of the same test are compared. Each version is composed of different items, randomly selected from a pool of items of comparable content and difficulty. In the *split-half method,* scores on half of a test

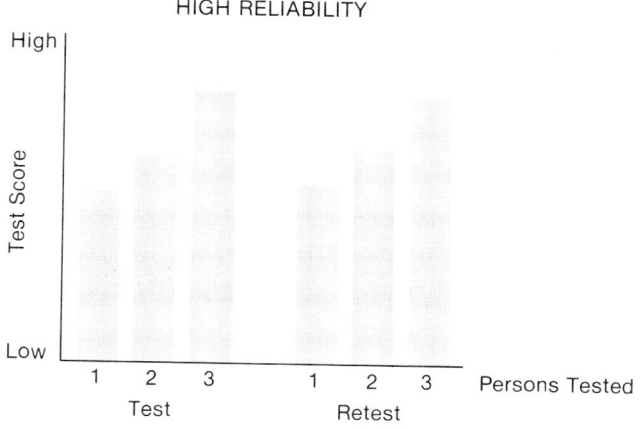

HIGH RELIABILITY

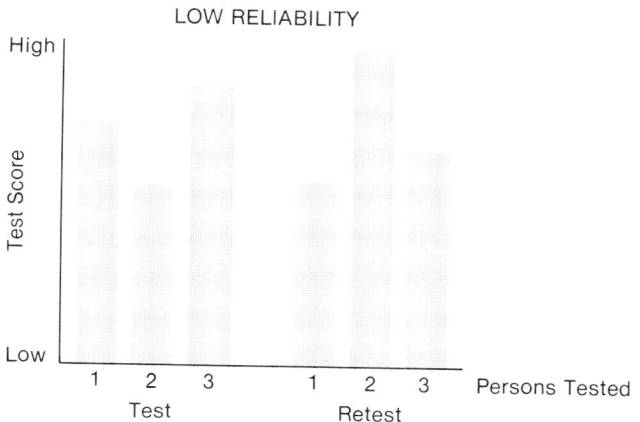

LOW RELIABILITY

Figure 12–3.
Concept of reliability.

are compared with scores on the other half of the test (for example, the odd- versus even-numbered items). The correlation coefficient, or index of similarity, between odd and even items on the WAIS was found to be .97, indicating high reliability (Wechsler, 1955).

— Validity

A second characteristic of good psychological tests is **test validity.** A valid test is one that measures what it claims to measure. Three types of validity are content validity, criterion-related validity, and construct validity. **Content validation** involves examining a test's content (the test items) to determine whether the test fairly represents the abilities being measured. For your examinations in introductory psychology to be content-valid, their questions should fairly represent the textbook and lecture material. If the exams include questions on economics or history, you have every right to be unhappy.

Criterion-related validation is established by determining how well a test predicts some specific behavior. It is most commonly applied to aptitude tests. Take the Scholastic Aptitude Test as an example (see Figure 12–4). A high degree of relationship between SAT scores (the predictor) and grade-point averages (the criterion) would provide evidence that the SAT is a valid predictor of academic achievement (at least as measured by grades). There is much controversy over this issue. In chapter 20 we will explore the controversy and describe situations in which tests have been most useful for predicting real-life behavior.

Construct validation demonstrates the extent to which a test is capable of measuring a psychological trait, or *construct,* such as human intelligence. **Traits**

Figure 12–4.
Concept of validity. (Dots represent persons taking SAT.)

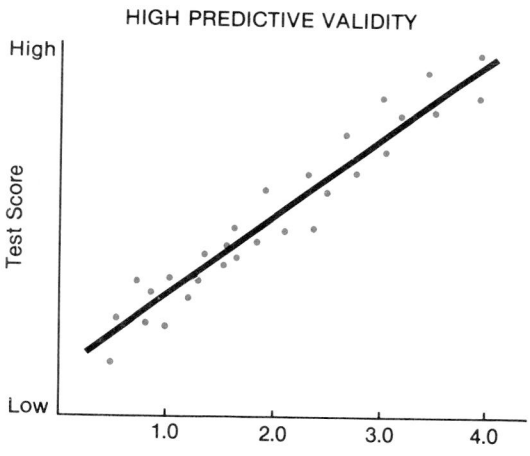

HIGH PREDICTIVE VALIDITY

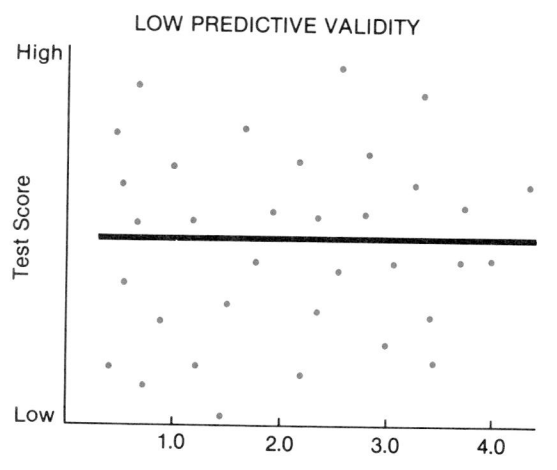

LOW PREDICTIVE VALIDITY

are defined as relatively enduring characteristics of individuals that remain fairly stable over the life-span (Anastasi, 1983; Tyler, 1965). Construct validation is difficult because intelligence, like other human traits, cannot be observed or directly measured; it must instead be estimated by intelligence testing. It is critically important, therefore, to emphasize that IQ and intelligence are not synonomous. Intelligence is a psychological trait that we try to estimate; IQ represents a score on a test and is not intelligence per se. In this sense, IQ provides only one measure of the intelligence construct.

— Standardization

To be useful, a psychological test must be standardized as well as reliable and valid. **Standardization** is the administration of a test to a large *standardization, or norm group,* which represents the population in which the test is to be used. Standardization allows meaningful comparisons of individual test scores with those obtained by others in the norm group.

The adequacy of test standardization increases as the size and representativeness of the norm group increase. The original Binet scale was poorly standardized, covering only 300 children. The 1937 revised Stanford-Binet test was standardized on over 3,000 U.S.-born white children. To better represent the entire U.S. population, nearly 4,500 individuals were included in the norm group for the 1960 revision of the Stanford-Binet test. To further remove bias, in 1972, the test was standardized with samples of English-speaking Americans of different ancestries (Terman & Merrill, 1973). In comparison, the WAIS standardization sample consisted of 1,700 individuals, including an equal proportion of men and women between the ages of 16 and 64. The sample was chosen with exceptional care to ensure that the entire U.S. population was fairly represented (cf. Wechsler, 1955; 1981).

— Normal Probability Distribution

Test developers often make a special effort to ensure that the test scores of a large sample of individuals will yield a symmetrical, bell-shaped curve, commonly referred to as the **normal probability distribution,** or normal curve. The normal curve is a mathematical ideal; yet it provides a surprisingly good description of numerous characteristics in nature. Take, for instance, the measured heights of people. Some people are very tall, others are very short, and most are intermediate, or of average height. When many heights are collected,

they closely match the normal curve. Similarly, the normal curve provides a good description of many psychological characteristics. This is true of IQ scores for a large group of individuals. A few individuals obtain very high or very low IQ scores; the majority score in the average range. The range, or distribution, of individual differences in such scores is shown in Figure 12–5.

The two most important statistics for describing a distribution of test scores are the mean and the standard deviation. The *mean* is the average score, found by adding all scores and dividing the total by the number of scores. The *standard deviation* is a measure of how widely scores are spread around the mean (see appendix). Knowing that a test is standardized with a mean of 100 and a standard deviation of 15 allows us to compare test scores for different individuals. Take, for example, an individual who obtains an IQ score of 115. We know that the person's score falls one standard deviation above the mean of 100. The information provided in Figure 12–5 shows that this places the score at approximately the 84th percentile; that is, 84 percent of the population scores at or below that level and 16 percent scores above it. (Again, for a more detailed presentation of statistics, see the appendix.)

Testing for Intelligence over the Life-Span

The Stanford-Binet and Wechsler scales are standardized, acceptably reliable, and valid tests of intelligence. Since the development of these and other intelligence tests, there has been considerable research concerning

Figure 12–5.

Concept of standardization: The normal probability distribution.

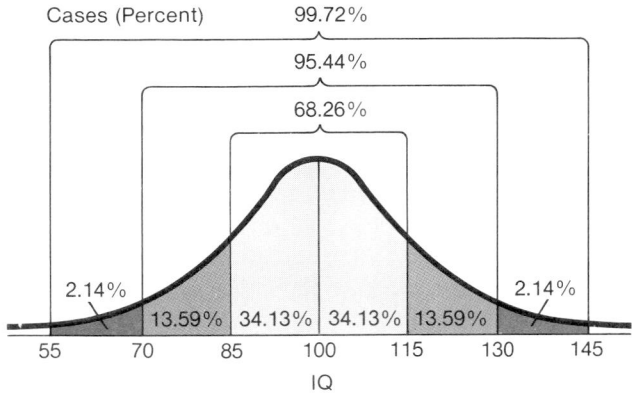

the stability of IQ over the life-span. Also of interest is the relationship between infant and adult intelligence and the rise and decline of particular mental abilities. To conclude this section, we would like to briefly address each of these topics.

— Stability and Change in IQs

Using deviation IQs, we can ask: Does a person's position in the distribution of IQs remain relatively stable at different ages? The best evidence on this question comes from the Berkeley Growth Study (Bayley & Schaefer, 1964). In the study, 61 individuals born between 1928 and 1929 were tested repeatedly from infancy through adulthood. The researchers found essentially no relationship between test scores obtained in the first 6 months of life and IQ at age 18. It was not until the ages of 18 to 24 months that any appreciable relationship was observed between early and later IQ. By the ages of 5 to 7, early IQ became highly predictive of IQ at ages 17 and 18. The Berkeley Growth Study and other studies confirming these findings indicate that children's IQs at the beginning of formal education do predict their IQs at the end of high school.

— The Special Case of Infant Intelligence

You may question why infant IQs do not correlate highly with later IQs. Probably the best explanation is that tests of infant intelligence tend to assess sensorimotor skills rather than the mental abilities tested on IQ tests. Since sensorimotor development and IQ scores are unrelated in school-age children (Knobloch & Pasamanick, 1974), it is not surprising to find low correlations between infant tests and later IQs.

To better measure intellectual processes in infants, Arnold Gesell and co-workers (1940) described tests for age levels ranging from 1 month to 2 years. The tests are divided into four categories: motor development, adaptive skills, language use, and personal-social

development. Gesell's tests determine the infant's level of development and thus yield a **developmental quotient (DQ).** Performance on Gesell's tests tends to be related to later IQ-test performance.

— Growth of Intellectual Abilities

As noted previously, a significant advance in mental testing was Binet's insight that children's intelligence increases with age. Binet unexpectedly observed that his two daughters scored higher on his tests as they became older. When the Binet scales were first used in France, test scores were found to peak at about age 16. Some research indicates that intelligence-test scores peak at about age 20 and then begin to decline gradually. (For review, see Horn, 1982.) However, other research challenges the belief that intelligence (as opposed to IQ) declines with age (Baltes & Schaie, 1976).

Most early studies of age-related changes in IQ used **cross-sectional research designs.** In this type of study, individuals of various ages, representing a cross-section of the population, are tested at the same time. Because older and younger people differ in experience and in exposure to cultural and educational opportunities, results from such studies may be inaccurate. Any observed changes in IQ could reflect aging, experience, or both. Studies using **longitudinal research designs** have consistently found little or no decline in intellectual abilities with age (Baltes, 1968). This type of research involves periodic retesting of the same individuals, as in the Berkeley Growth Study. Although longitudinal research is difficult because it spans so many years, it tends to yield more accurate results than does cross-sectional research.

In summary, cross-sectional data indicate an IQ decline with age, whereas longitudinal data indicate little or no decline with age. It should be noted, however, that when individuals in their 80s and 90s have been studied, modest declines in abilities have been found (Jarvik, Eisdorfer, & Blum, 1973).

=== APPLICATION ===

TESTING YOUR OWN IQ

You can estimate your own IQ using the test provided in Figure 12–6 (pages 309–311). The test was prepared for *Omni* magazine by representatives of *Mensa,* the international high-IQ society. Mensa's criterion for membership is an IQ-test score in the upper 2 percent of the general population—that is, at or above the 98th percentile (Morris, 1981). This criterion corresponds to a score of 133 on the Wechsler Adult Intelligence Scale, or 1250 on the Scholastic Aptitude Test.

If you decide to take the test, fill in the answer sheet with your chosen answers. Here are the instructions.

1. Allow a limit of 30 minutes to make your score comparable to those of the Mensa sample.
2. Take the test alone and without help.
3. Provide only one answer to each item.

Answers to the test are provided at the end of the chapter along with a distribution of scores that shows how the 88 Mensa members who took the test scored and guidelines for converting your raw score into a rough estimate of your IQ. Your score on the test will not qualify you for membership in Mensa, but it should indicate whether you would be likely to do well on an official standardized IQ-test. Procedures for applying for Mensa membership may be obtained by writing to Mensa, Department D, 1701 West Third Street, Brooklyn, New York 11223.

— DISTRIBUTION OF IQ SCORES —

Mental Retardation

Historically, mentally retarded individuals have been the victims of injurious myths, fears, and prejudices. Lack of understanding has often led to cruel treatment, including sterilization, infanticide, and unnecessary institutionalization. Until the early years of this century, the mentally retarded were commonly believed to be immoral and devil-possessed. Today, there is a growing recognition that retarded individuals are people whose role in life is determined largely by the quality of care and training society provides.

— Definition, Diagnosis, and Classification

The American Association of Mental Deficiency (AAMD) defines **mental retardation** as significantly subaverage intellectual functioning existing concurrently with deficits in adaptive behavior and manifested during the developmental period (Grossman, 1977). Let's consider the AAMD's definition in further detail.

Intellectual functioning. Table 12–2 provides both obsolete and currently accepted classifications of mental retardation based on various IQ scores. The traditional cutoff IQ in the AAMD's definition is 70. On that basis alone, about 2.3 percent of the population is considered mentally retarded. Note, however, the wide range of intellectual functioning, from an IQ of 70 to an IQ of below 20. Of the entire mentally retarded population, most individuals (about 80 percent) are mildly retarded, 12 percent are moderately retarded, 7 percent are severely retarded, and 1 percent are profoundly retarded (American Psychiatric Association, APA, 1980).

The updated edition of the AAMD's *Manual on Terminology and Classification in Mental Retardation* (Grossman, 1981) gives less weight to IQ than in the past. More emphasis is now placed on adaptive behavior, social and developmental history, and functioning in a variety of social settings.

Adaptive behavior. The various duties and social roles appropriate to each age are referred to as **adaptive behavior.** The person's routine level of function-

Table 12–2.

Obsolete and currently accepted classifications of mental retardation based upon levels of measured intelligence.

IQ RANGE	CURRENT CLASSIFICATION	OBSOLETE TERMINOLOGY
50–70	Mild retardation	Moron
35–49	Moderate retardation	Imbecile
20–34	Severe retardation	Idiot
Below 20	Profound retardation	Idiot

Source: American Psychiatric Association (APA, 1980).

Figure 12–6.

IQ self-test. (Continued on page, 310 and 311)

THE OMNI-MENSA I. Q. TEST

By Scot Morris

(Reprinted from *Omni*, July, 1981, pp. 96–98.)

Our readers love to test themselves. After we published "The World's Hardest I.Q. Test" in April 1979, so many of you sent in answer sheets—about 25,000 at last count—that the California society scoring the test was overwhelmed by the volume and fell several months behind in processing. We apologize again for the inconvenience this caused you.

The results of that test are now in, and we couldn't be prouder. Among the first 20,000 persons whose answer sheets were scored, the average I.Q. was 137. An I.Q. of just 133 on a standardized test puts you above 98 percent of the general population and makes you eligible for membership in Mensa, the high-I.Q. society. Well over half of you scored above the Mensa qualification level.

Ten percent of the *Omni* readers who entered had I.Q.'s of 154 or higher. Two percent of you scored above 163, the cutoff for membership in the Four Sigma Society, makers of the test. Four hundred *Omni* respondents qualified for membership in this elite club. Twenty of you had I.Q.'s in the intellectual stratosphere, above 171.

The volume of response more than confirmed the popularity of this I.Q. feature. We have decided to try it again, this time with the help of Mensa, and with a test that readers may score themselves.

Mensa is an international society with more than 42,000 members in the United States alone. Each year about 35,000 people try to qualify for membership and 15,000 succeed.

Other than their ability to get high scores on "intelligence tests" (which may measure nothing more significant than test-taking skills), Mensa members have little in common. The society has no restrictions on race, religion, sex, and age (there are currently three members who are four years of age and several in their nineties).

With the help of Alice Fixx, public relations director for Mensa, we prepared a preliminary test consisting of 46 items similar to those found in standardized intelligence tests. Marvin Grosswirth, a past chairman, helped organize a session of the New York City Mensa, at which 88 members kindly took this test.

After scoring the test (each scored another's paper), we went over it item by item. Members were asked to criticize or praise the items, point out ambiguities, suggest alternate interpretations, or judge items too difficult or too easy. As a result of this session 7 items were discarded, leaving the 39 items presented here.

We did not impose a time limit on the Mensa testees, but we asked them to work as fast as they could and to raise their hands when they were finished. A tally indicated that most took about 35 minutes to complete the 46-item test. For this 39-item test, allow a limit of 30 minutes to make your score comparable to those of the Mensa sample.

Scores on this test are not recognized for membership in Mensa, but they can indicate whether you would be likely to do well on an official test. Good luck!

THE OMNI–MENSA I.Q. TEST
Time limit: 30 minutes.

1. What number follows logically in this series?
   2, 3, 5, 9, 17 _____

2. In the group of words below, underline the two words that are most nearly opposite in meaning.
   [Example: heavy, large, flat, light, bright]
   punish, vex, pinch, ignore, pacify, determine

3. Figure out the rule that is used to determine the prices below and find the price of the last item.

Watch	$46
Bracelet	$ 4
Earrings	$10
Chain	$ 6
Ring	$?

4. Study the four drawings in the top row. Which of the four drawings in the bottom row should appear next in the series?

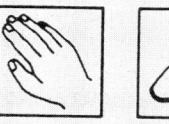   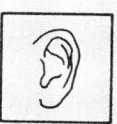

   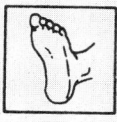

(a)　　　　(b)　　　　(c)　　　　(d)

5. The arrows represent a simple code. What common English word do they spell?

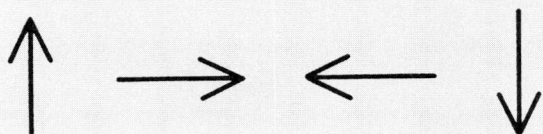

6. In the square below, a rule applies both from top to bottom and from left to right. Find the rule and figure out the missing number.

Example: 2 7 9
          5 4 9
          7 11 18

          6 2 4
          2 ? 0
          4 0 4

7. Which drawing in the bottom row logically comes next in the series that is shown in the top row?

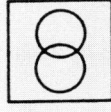 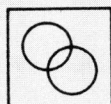 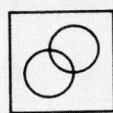 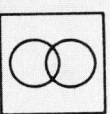

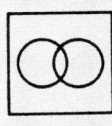 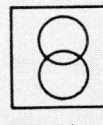 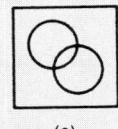 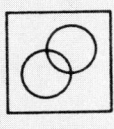

   (a)   (b)   (c)   (d)

8. Complete this analogy by writing one word on the lines, ending with the printed letter.
Lend is to borrow as harmony is to _ _ _ _ _ _ D.

9. Underline the two words in parentheses that have the same relation as the two words in the first phrase:
Island is to water as (without, hypotenuse, center, diagonal, perimeter).

10. If Doris turns either left or right at the stop sign, she will run out of gas before reaching a service station. She has already gone too far past a service station to turn around and return to it. She does not see a service station ahead of her. Therefore:

(a) Doris may run out of gas.
(b) Doris will run out of gas.
(c) Doris should not have taken this route.

11. Find the number that logically completes this series.
1, 2, 6, 12, 36 _____

12. Which building logically is next in the series?

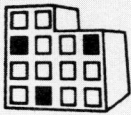  

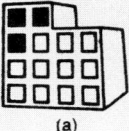 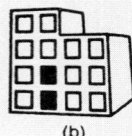 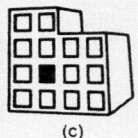

   (a)   (b)   (c)

13. M is above N and O.
N is above O and below P.

Therefore:

(a) M is not above O and P.
(b) O is above N.
(c) P is above O.
(d) O is above P.

14. In the group of words below, underline the two words that are most similar in meaning.
Example: mat, linoleum, floor, rug
beam, lump, wood, ray, chuckle, sliver

15. Which figure in the lower row should appear next in the series of figures in the upper row?

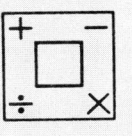 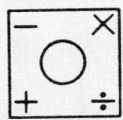  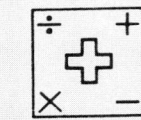

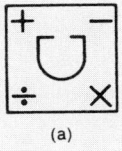 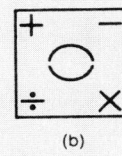 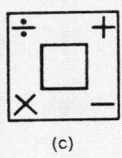 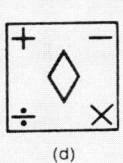

   (a)   (b)   (c)   (d)

16. If $A \times B = 24$, $B \times C = 24$, $B \times D = 48$, and $C \times D = 32$, what then does $A \times B \times C \times D$ equal?
(a) 480 (b) 744 (c) 768 (d) 824

17. Complete the top series with one of the lettered figures.

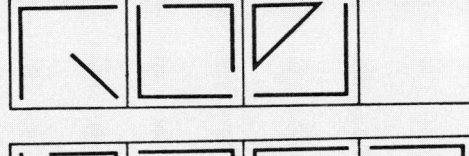

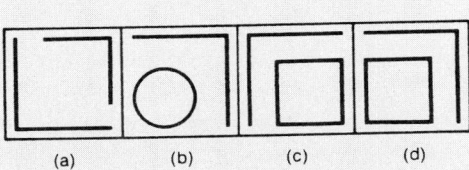

   (a)   (b)   (c)   (d)

18. "Don't throw good money after bad" means:
(a) Take your loss and walk away from it.
(b) Don't gamble; think of the future.
(c) Don't invest in a losing proposition.
(d) Don't borrow to gamble.

19. Sam, Fred, Steve, and Joe are weight lifters. Joe can outlift Steve, and Fred can outlift Joe. Steve can outlift Sam. Therefore:
(a) Both Sam and Fred can outlift Joe.
(b) Joe can outlift Sam but can't outlift Steve.
(c) Joe can outlift Sam by more than he can outlift Steve.
(d) None of the above is true.

20. Select the two figures in the following series that represent mirror images of each other.

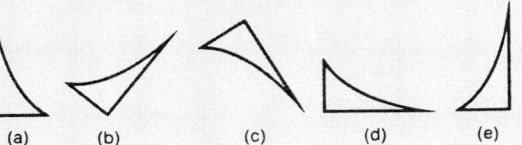

   (a)   (b)   (c)   (d)   (e)

21. Determine what process was followed in arriving at the prices below and find the price of the last item.

Skirt	$50
Tie	$30
Raincoat	$80
Sweater	$70
Blouse	$?

22. Which plate in the bottom row belongs next in the series in the top row?

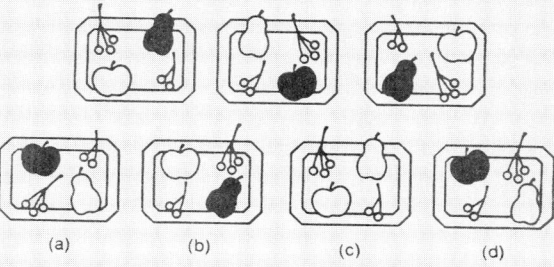

(a)   (b)   (c)   (d)

23. What number logically comes next in this series?
7, 12, 27, 72 _____

24. The old saying "The good is the enemy of the best" most nearly means:
(a) If you are good, you will best your enemy.
(b) Be good to your best enemy.
(c) Don't accept less than your best.
(d) The good struggle against the best.

25.

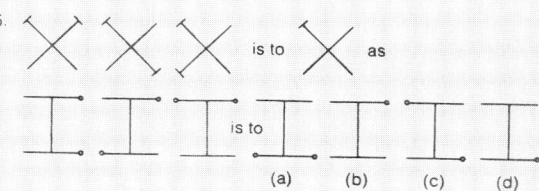

is to __ as __

is to

(a)   (b)   (c)   (d)

26. Alex, Allan, Carol, Celia, and Sharon took intelligence tests. Celia scored higher than Carol, but Allan scored higher than Celia. Carol outscored Alex, but Allan outscored Carol. Sharon scored lower than Allan. Therefore:
(a) Celia scored higher than Alex but lower than Carol.
(b) Both Alex and Allan outscored Celia.
(c) Sharon scored higher than Carol.
(d) Celia outscored Alex by more than she outscored Carol.
(e) None of the above is definitely true.

27. What number follows logically in this series?
9, 12, 21, 48 _____ (a) 69 (b) 70 (c) 129 (d) 144

28. Which one of the lettered diagrams in the bottom row can be turned over or rotated to become the same as the diagram below?

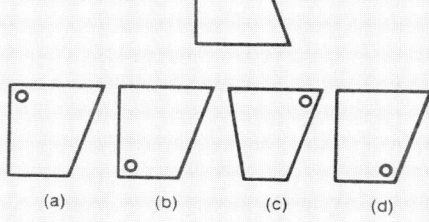

(a)   (b)   (c)   (d)

29. In the group of words below, underline the two words that are most nearly alike in meaning.
tale, novel, volume, story, book

30. If Barbara's daughter is my daughter's mother, what relationship am I to Barbara?
(a) Her grandmother
(b) Her mother
(c) Her daughter
(d) Her granddaughter
(e) I am Barbara.

31. In a row of four houses, the Whites live next to the Carsons, but not next to the Reeds. If the Reeds do not live next to the Lanes, who are the Lanes' next-door neighbors?
(a) The Whites
(b) The Carsons
(c) Both the Whites and the Carsons
(d) Impossible to tell

32. Wall is to window as face is to:
(a) skin
(b) hair
(c) eye
(d) teeth

33. Select the two figures in the following series that represent mirror images of each other.

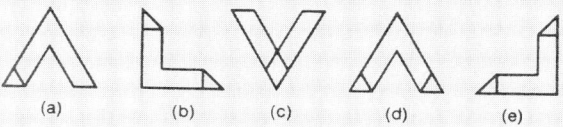

(a)   (b)   (c)   (d)   (e)

34. What is the next number in this series?
21, 20, 18, 15, 11 _____

35. Underline the two words in parentheses that have the same relation as the two words in the first phrase:
Eyelid is to eye as (window, glass, view, curtain, lash).

36. Complete the following analogy by writing one word on the lines, ending with the printed letter.
Skull is to brain as shell is to _ _ _ K.

37. Complete this diagram:

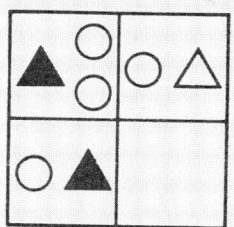

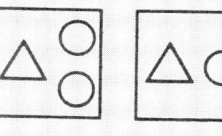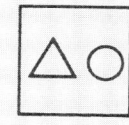

(a)   (b)   (c)   (d)

38. "A stream cannot rise higher than its source" means:
(a) You decline after achieving your highest level.
(b) Streams of knowledge can't come from high sources.
(c) Your stream of consciousness is highly resourceful.
(d) Your stream of achievement is limited by your background.

39. Underline the two words in parentheses that have the same relation as the two words in the first phrase.
Hat is to head as (spout, kettle, handle, copper, lid).

DISTRIBUTION OF IQ SCORES

ing is used to determine social competence. An example of adaptive behavior for young children includes dressing oneself. For adults, examples include the ability to perform skilled work and live independently. Social incompetence, however, is not sufficient for a diagnosis of mental retardation. Many socially incompetent individuals, such as criminals, are not mentally retarded.

Age of onset. A third criterion used to diagnose mental retardation is onset before the age of 18. When the clinical symptoms develop for the first time after the age of 18, the typical diagnosis is *dementia,* to denote mental deterioration rather than mental retardation.

Today, more than 6 million Americans—about twice as many males as females—have been diagnosed as mentally retarded (Haywood, Meyers, & Switzky, 1982). Each year, an estimated 100,000 children are born who will be diagnosed as mentally retarded sometime during their lives. About one-third of all mentally retarded persons have multiple handicaps, including emotional disturbance, although mental retardation should not be confused with other handicapping disorders (Reiss, 1982; Reiss, Levitan, & McNally, 1982).

Because the majority of mentally retarded persons are mildly or moderately retarded, the number in institutions has never exceeded about 200,000 and has decreased rapidly in recent years. Increasingly, mentally retarded persons live in their own homes with parents or other relatives, in foster homes, or independently. Many hold jobs, and a majority participate in family life, move fairly freely in their own communities, and attend school during their school-age years (Haywood et al., 1982).

— Two Broad Classes of Mental Retardation

There is a common misconception that all mentally retarded people have the same disorder. Actually, there are more than 200 different etiologies, or causes, of mental retardation. The criteria discussed earlier—intellectual functioning, adaptive behavior, and age of onset—although useful for diagnosis and classification, tell us little about the causes of mental retardation. Causal factors may be biological, environmental, or both. It would be difficult to discuss individually each known cause; however, in this section we will consider two broad classes of mental retardation—organic retar-

dation and cultural-familial retardation (Zigler, 1967; see also Figure 12–7).

Organic retardation. About 25 percent of all cases of mental retardation are due to some known biological defect, most commonly chromosomal and genetic abnormalities (see chapter 10). Such cases are therefore referred to as **organic retardation.**

Organic retardation is usually diagnosed at birth or shortly after. The severity of intellectual impairment can be moderate to profound. This class of retardation occurs about equally among children from all social classes. Its incidence is apparently unrelated to parents' income, occupation, or educational level; and there is no increased likelihood of mental retardation in other family members, unless the biological condition is genetic.

Cultural-familial retardation. A term used to describe nearly 75 percent of all cases, including all cases not due to some known biological disorder, is **cultural-familial retardation.** As the term implies, such cases are thought to be related to cultural disadvantage or to factors related to one's family, or both. Individuals classified as having this type of retardation, unlike those with organic disorders, are most often mildly retarded, having IQs above 50. They are often from families in which parents, siblings, or other relatives are similarly retarded. The problem occurs with greatest frequency among children from lower social

Figure 12–7.

Two broad classes of mental retardation. (After Zigler, 1967.)

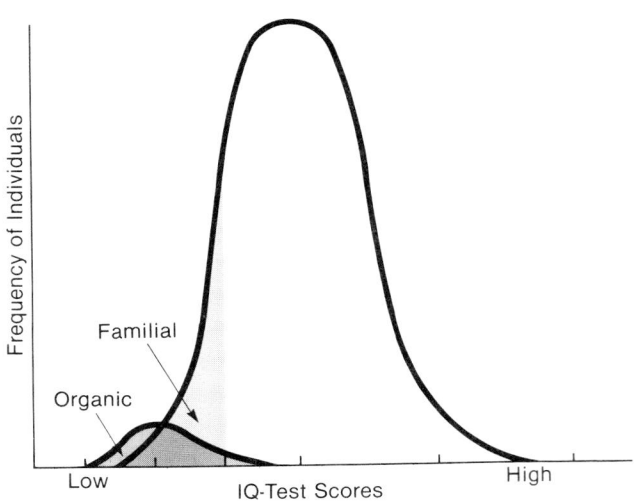

classes, although the specific reason is unclear (APA, 1980).

Although the precise cause of cultural-familial retardation is unknown, evidence increasingly implicates both genetic and environmental factors interacting on intellectual development. We will turn to a discussion of those influences in the final section of this chapter, but first let's consider the treatment and prevention of mental retardation.

— Treatment and Prevention

For specific organic abnormalities, such as Down's syndrome (see chapter 10), mental retardation generally is chronic and the prognosis (likelihood of recovery) is poor. In certain other types of organic retardation, such as PKU (see chapter 10), the biological abnormality may be treated, thereby preventing severe mental retardation. With our rapidly expanding biological knowledge, it is reasonable to hope that the treatment and prevention of other types of organic retardation will become possible.

In mild forms of cultural-familial retardation without known cause, the prognosis is more favorable than for most forms of organic retardation. As suggested earlier, cultural-familial retardation may be associated with psychosocial deprivation. Thus, when such deprivation is lessened, the chance for normal development increases. Later in this chapter, we will review enrichment programs designed to reverse the retarding effects of poor nutrition and insufficient social and intellectual stimulation.

Genius, Giftedness, and Creativity

Newspapers occasionally print stories about intellectually gifted young people, who typically score in the upper IQ range. Take, for example, the young English boy shown at age 4 in Figure 12–8. The boy, who taught himself to read at age 2, was tested by child psychologists, who found his IQ to be 170. Consider also Jay Luo, who recently completed a degree in mathematics at Boise State University of Idaho. As a 12-year-old, Jay became the youngest college graduate in U.S. history (He's a college grad, 1982).

For a historical example of a gifted person, consider Francis Galton, whose life has been detailed in a biography by Pearson (1914). Here is a letter (quoted in Willerman, 1979, p. 340) written by Galton to his older sister on the day before his 5th birthday:

Figure 12–8.

Young genius. Four-year-old Richard James is shown at his books in England. Richard, son of a school caretaker, was recently checked by child psychologists and advised that he had an IQ of 170. He taught himself to read at age 2 and also tutors his 15-year-old sister.

My Dear Adele,

I am 4 years old and I can read any English book. I can say all the Latin Substantive and Adjective and active verbs besides 52 lines of Latin poetry. I can cast up any sum in addition and can multiply by 2, 3, 4, 5, 6, 7, 8, (9), 10, (11).

I can also say the pence table. I read French a little and I know the clock.

Francis Galton
Febuary (sic) 15, 1827

Commenting on the letter, psychologist Lewis Terman (1917—cited in Willerman, 1979) noted that the only misspelling is in the month and that the numbers 9

SIR FRANCIS GALTON (1822–1911)

Francis Galton was born near Birmingham, England, on February 16, 1822. By the age of 2½, he could read and write; by age 5 he could read any English book and some Latin and was proficient at basic math. At 6 he could quote from the *Iliad* and *Odyssey,* and a year later he was reading Shakespeare and Pope for fun. When he was older, Galton's parents, fearing that the family fortune was insufficient to afford him a life of leisure, sent him away for medical training. After a year of on-the-job training, Galton enrolled in a medical school; but shortly thereafter he began pursuing an arts degree at Cambridge University. As a result of intense academic competition, Galton suffered an emotional breakdown, although he returned to take a nonhonors degree in 1843.

For the next several years, Galton lived the life of the idle rich, traveling widely and amusing himself with occasional adventures. In 1859, Galton's interests took a major change with the publication of Charles Darwin's book *On the Origin of Species.* Although the theory of evolution dealt primarily with lower animals, Galton quickly grasped its significance for humans. He proposed that psychological or mental abilities, like physical characteristics, are inherited. Proof for this position came from the family genealogies of eminent men. Studying a dozen separate groups, including statesmen, scientists, artists, and military leaders, he found in them a greater proportion of eminent relatives than in the general population.

Galton was responsible for a number of innovations, including the first workable system of classifying and identifying fingerprints. In his book *Inquiries into Human Faculty and its Development* (1883) and his other publications, he introduced numerous terms and concepts that are now part of our everyday vocabulary in psychology. For example, he described the first use of self-report questionnaires, he introduced the phrase *nature and nurture,* he developed the statistical measure of correlation, and he described the first use of twin studies to examine genetic and environmental influences on intelligence. Galton's pioneering work distinguished him as the founder of behavioral genetics, a field of study discussed later in the chapter.

and 11 are in parentheses because the young Galton had scratched out one of the numbers and pasted paper over the other. Terman concluded on the basis of the letter and other evidence that Galton's childhood IQ must have been close to 200. (See Personal Profile.)

Studies of Geniuses

Current definitions of **genius,** reviewed by Albert (1975), emphasize the following points. First, genius is based on evidence of public achievement. Second, the person's ideas must solve some practical problem and result in a major shift in thinking. Third, there must be widespread agreement among qualified peers that the person is a genius.

The three-part definition of genius is based on public and observable behavioral acts. It is obvious, then, that there can be no hidden geniuses. Furthermore, the definition differentiates geniuses from individuals who score well on intelligence tests but whose achievements go unnoticed. Thus, genius differs from giftedness: All geniuses are recognized as being intellectually gifted; however, not all intellectually gifted individuals become geniuses.

Giftedness

Although not everyone with a high IQ is a genius, it has long been believed that the intellectually gifted are somehow different. To explore this possibility, Lewis Terman and his colleagues began, in 1920, a longitudinal study of giftedness that continues today. **Giftedness** is a term reserved for the most intellectually capable individuals in the general population.

Terman's goals in the study were threefold. First, he wanted to study the academic and career accomplishments of intellectually gifted children to discover whether these children differed from children in general. Second, he wanted to follow the children into young adulthood to determine whether they would maintain their early intellectual giftedness. Third, it occurred to him that if the sample were followed into later maturity, a great deal could be learned about what contributes to coping styles and to satisfaction in life.

Working within the California public school system, Terman identified 1,470 children with IQs of 135 or over (Sears, 1977). Since 1920, there have been numerous results reported from follow-up studies of the original sample. The children in Terman's initial study have been tested and retested on several occasions, and their children and their children's children are still being studied. The third follow-up study, reported by Terman and Oden (1959) nearly 35 years after the original data were collected, appraised the intellectual and vocational accomplishments of participants. The authors concluded:

That the superior child, with few exceptions, becomes the able adult, superior in nearly every respect to the generality. . . . More than 85% of the group entered college and almost 70% graduated. The latter figure is about ten times as high as for a random group of comparable age. Graduation honors and elections to Phi Beta Kappa were at least three times as numerous as in the typical senior class. . . .

Additional evidence of the productivity and versatility . . . is found in their publications and patents. Nearly 2000 scientific and technical papers and articles and some 60 books and monographs in the sciences, literature, arts, and humanities have been published. Patents granted amount to at least 230. Other writings include 33 novels, about 375 short stories, novelettes, and plays; 60 or more essays, critiques, and sketches; 265 miscellaneous articles on a variety of subjects. These figures on publications do not include the hundreds of publications by journalists that classify as news stories, editorials, or newspaper columns, nor do they include the hundreds, if not thousands, of radio, television, or motion picture scripts. (Quoted in Willerman, 1979, p. 331)

Creativity

Is high IQ all-important in high accomplishment? An increasing number of psychologists and educators recognize that creative ability is not synonymous with intelligence measured by IQ tests. It is now believed that *creative thinking* is at least as important as academic intelligence for outstanding achievement in a variety of fields. Although only vaguely defined, **creativity** can be considered a quality of thought that leads to novel and unexpected problem solving.

Guilford (1959) identified two separate abilities that characterize creative thinking: divergent thinking and convergent thinking. **Divergent thinking** involves examining alternate solutions to a problem or coming up with new solutions. It is the kind of thinking that goes off in different directions. **Convergent thinking** involves an ability to narrow the possibilities, to converge on and choose the one best solution. Problem solving in everyday life often involves both divergent and convergent thinking. Standardized IQ tests typically use multiple-choice questions, which require only convergent thinking; they are inadequate as measures of divergent-thinking ability (Frederiksen, Ward, & Carlson, 1980).

Research on creativity is exemplified by studies conducted by Donald MacKinnon and his associates at the University of California's Institute of Personality Assessment and Research (IPAR). Since 1950, researchers at IPAR have studied the intellectual and personality characteristics of creative professionals. The typical procedure has been to select members of a particular field who are nominated by peers for their outstanding creative accomplishments. Selected individuals are then compared with persons in the same profession who have not made significant creative contributions.

The IPAR researchers defined true creative accomplishment in terms of three conditions (see, for example, MacKinnon, 1965). First, the accomplishment must involve an idea that is novel or statistically infrequent. Second, it must solve a major problem or accomplish a recognizable goal. Finally, it must involve sustaining an original insight through its full development. From this point of view, creativity is an extended process, characterized by originality of insight, adaptiveness, and realization of a goal.

Studies conducted by IPAR researchers have revealed significant differences in the personality traits of creative and noncreative individuals. Let's look at a summary description of the creative person, especially of the creative architect, as revealed in a profile from the California Personality Inventory:

> He is dominant; possessed of those qualities and attributes which underlie and lead to the achievement of social status; poised, spontaneous, and self-confident in personal and social interaction; not of an especially sociable or participative temperament; intelligent, outspoken, sharp-witted, demanding, aggressive, and self-centered; persuasive and verbally fluent, self-confident and self-assured; and relatively uninhibited in expressing his worries and complaints.
>
> He is relatively free from conventional restraints and inhibition, not preoccupied with the impression which he makes on others and thus perhaps capable of great independence and autonomy, and relatively ready to recognize and admit self-views that are unusual and unconventional.
>
> He is strongly motivated to achieve in situations in which independence in thought and action are called for. But, unlike his less creative colleagues, he is less inclined to strive for achievement in settings where conforming behavior is expected or required. In efficiency and steadiness

of intellectual effort, however, he does not differ from his fellow workers. (MacKinnon, 1965, p. 291)

— Predicting Creativity and Identifying the Academically Gifted

MacKinnon's approach is *retrospective* in that he located highly creative individuals on the basis of their past histories to determine whether they had distinctive characteristics. A second research approach to creativity is *prospective* in design. That is, it attempts to identify creative talent before such talent expresses itself. This approach is best exemplified by the continuing work of J. P. Guilford.

Guilford (1959) developed numerous tests of divergent thinking in the hope that test scores could be used to predict later creative accomplishments. One such test is Guilford's Plot Titles Test, which requires an individual to write as many titles for a story as possible within a specific period of time. Typically, an individual receives two scores, one based on quantity of titles provided and the other based on quality—that is, the cleverness or statistical infrequency of the titles. One of Guilford's stories describes a missionary who, having been captured by a tribe of cannibals, is confronted with the ultimatum of marrying the village princess or being boiled alive. He chooses the latter. Examples of nonclever, commonplace titles are "African Death," "The Missionary," and "The Princess." Examples of clever titles are "Potluck Dinner," "Stewed Parson", "Guess Who's Coming to Dinner", "Goil or Boil", "A Mate Worse than Death", "Chaste in Haste", and "A Hot Price for Freedom." Can you think of other titles?

Studies are currently underway to determine whether performance on divergent-thinking tests predicts later creative accomplishment. Despite years of use, it is not at all clear whether such tests actually measure creative thinking. A cautious conclusion drawn by Barron and Harrington (1981) is that some divergent-thinking tests, administered under certain conditions and scored by certain sets of criteria, do measure abilities related to creative accomplishment.

Although predicting creativity has proved difficult, some psychologists have been successful in identifying students who are gifted in specific academic areas and in fostering their talents and abilities (Fox, 1981). The Study of Mathematically Precocious Youth (SMPY), initiated in 1971 by Julian Stanley at Johns Hopkins University, provides one example of such efforts (Stanley, Keating, & Fox, 1974). SMPY researchers sought 7th- and 8th-grade students who scored exceptionally well on standardized math tests, such as the math portion of the Scholastic Aptitude Test. In this way, SMPY researchers have been able to help teachers recognize superior talent and foster it. SMPY's most precocious subject entered college as a full-time student at age 11, after completing the 6th grade at a public elementary school. He began his university studies with courses such as Calculus III. At age 13, he had completed four full college semesters, with As in all courses except French III and one credit in bowling (in which he got Bs) (Stanley, 1976).

— Factors That Block the Development of Creative Thinking

Can creative thinking be fostered? Efforts to answer this question have been more successful in identifying factors that block the development of creativity (see, for example, Torrance, 1962, 1965). One such factor seems to be the attempts teachers and parents sometimes make to eliminate fantasies from children's play. Actually, such fantasies, including imaginative role playing, telling fantastic stories, and drawing unusual pictures, are a healthy and normal part of cognitive development. Restricting children's curiosity is another problem. To develop creative thinking, it is important that children explore and manipulate objects and ideas within the limits of safety. Yet another impediment to creativity is overemphasis on sex roles. As noted by Torrance, in our society, the independence and autonomy involved in creative thinking have a distinctly masculine character; however, the high degree of sensitivity involved has a distinctly feminine character. Thus, the highly creative boy may be considered more effeminate than his male peers, and the highly creative girl may be regarded as more masculine than her female peers.

Factors such as these can easily stifle creative talent. Consider the case history of Gary, a 15-year-old boy who is both highly intelligent and creatively gifted. From the time Gary was a toddler, he was unique. A pencil was not just for writing. Food was not just for eating. Gary was never satisfied with a simple answer to a question. Consequently, for Gary, school was a disaster. The teachers could not cope with his unconventional ways of thinking. He was labeled a weirdo, and before long, his drive, initiative, and creativity were crushed. Today, he wants to be like everyone else. He wouldn't dare write a poem or paint a picture (Hochman, 1976).

— GENETIC AND ENVIRONMENTAL DETERMINANTS OF INTELLECTUAL DEVELOPMENT —

What factors determine intellectual development? Have you ever wondered why the trait we call human intelligence varies so widely? Why are some people intellectually gifted and others intellectually retarded? Even more perplexing, how can we begin to understand autistic savants (see chapter introduction)? These questions are difficult but not unanswerable.

Human Behavioral Genetics

Our perspective on the questions just raised is influenced by recent advances in **human behavioral genetics,** a rapidly growing field of study that examines the contribution of heredity to behavior (Fuller & Simmel, 1983; Henderson, 1982; Plomin, 1983). The relative influence of heredity versus environment in determining intellectual development is one of the oldest and most controversial issues in the behavioral sciences (Plomin, DeFries, & McClearn, 1980). The remainder of this chapter broadly traces the history of human behavioral genetics, summarizes research on genetic and environmental determinants of intellectual development, and explores some relevant recent controversies.

— Brief History of Behavioral Genetics

It is tempting to speculate whether, if Charles Darwin had followed his youthful interest in becoming a clergyman, he would have won so exalted a place in the history of science (Bingham, 1982). Darwin had hopes of becoming a physician also, but he gave up medicine and accepted the position of naturalist aboard the *HMS Beagle,* a British survey ship, in 1831. During a voyage to the Galapagos Islands, young Darwin made compelling observations of 14 species of finch; from his observations, he concluded that species evolve one from the other. Several years later, Darwin published an abstract of his theory of evolution, entitled *On the Origin of Species by Means of Natural Selection, or the Preservation of Favoured Races in the Struggle for Life* and now recognized as one of the most influential books ever written (Darwin, 1859/1967). Darwin's major contribution to the theory of evolution is the principle of **natural selection,** which can be summarized as follows:

1. Individuals differ in various characteristics.
2. Such differences are determined in part by heredity.
3. Whenever characteristics are associated with differences in fitness (that is, the relative success of offspring in surviving to reproduce), the characteristics of the more fit individuals will increasingly occur in succeeding generations.

One of Darwin's strongest admirers was his cousin Francis Galton. Galton extended the principle of natural selection and championed the idea that mental characteristics are inherited. In his book *Hereditary Genius* he proposed to show that a man's natural attributes are derived by inheritance. He argued that it would be not only possible but practical to produce a highly gifted race of men by judicious marriages during several consecutive generations (Galton, 1869). Galton's controversial notion of *eugenics* (selective breeding for desirable characteristics) is explored further in the "On the Horizon" section at the end of this chapter.

The mechanism for heredity was not understood until 1865, when Gregor Mendel reported his experimental work with pea plants. In 1905, the term *genetics* was coined, and 4 years later the term *gene* was proposed to describe the elements that transmit genetic information. At the same time, geneticists made a fundamental distinction: A person's **genotype** is the unique set of genes inherited; in contrast, **phenotype** refers to the outward, visible expression of traits affected by the genes (Plomin et al., 1980). This distinction makes it clear that observable traits are not perfect indicators of genotypes. For instance, two individuals might have the same genotype for height; yet one might be taller because of better nutrition.

Individual differences in traits such as height and intelligence can be readily measured. Although limitations are imposed on both by genotypes, there is a range of outcomes (phenotypes) that depend on the quality of the environment in which the traits develop. In 1963, Irving Gottesman introduced the concept of **reaction range** to describe the phenotypic variations induced by the interaction of nature and nurture. In general, the growth of traits such as height or intelligence is suppressed by rearing in a *restricted environment*—an environment characterized by poor nutrition or by deprivations such as social isolation or emotional abuse. In contrast, enriched environments are more likely to enable individuals to achieve their full genotypic growth potential. By *enriched environment,* we mean an environment characterized by above-average conditions, including proper nutrition, educational opportunities, a stimulating home life, and so on. Let's examine some of the ways in which such influences are studied.

— Methods of Human Behavioral Genetics

Several methods of human behavioral genetics provide means for studying the relative influence of genetic versus environmental factors on intellectual development. Of the various research designs available, twin, adoption, and family studies have proved the most useful.

Twin studies. Based on the study of one-egg, *monozygotic* twins and two-egg, *dizygotic* twins, the *twin-study method* provides a powerful way of examining the relative influence of heredity and environment in humans. The reason? Monozygotic (MZ) twins have identical genes; hence, any differences between them in IQ or other characteristics are presumably due to differences in their environments. Dizygotic (DZ) twins, sometimes referred to as *fraternal twins,* are no more alike genetically than other siblings; on the average, they have 50 percent of their genes in common. By comparing the similarities in IQ's of MZ twins with those of DZ twins, we are able to investigate the influences of genetics and environment. A trait caused entirely by heredity should result in a high degree of similarity between MZ twins, even those raised in radically different environments. The IQ *correlation* (a statistical index of similarity) between MZ twins theoretically is 1.00 if only heredity is operating. For DZ twins, the IQ correlation theoretically is .50.

Adoption studies.   On February 9, 1979, James Springer and James Lewis were reunited in Lima, Ohio. Springer and Lewis are identical twins who were adopted weeks after birth by different families and who lived apart for 39 years. Upon discovering the "Jim twins," psychologist Thomas Bouchard invited them to the University of Minnesota for a week of extensive psychological and medical testing. The twins consented, thus becoming the first of more than 30 pairs of identical twins to participate in the Minnesota Study of Twins Reared Apart (Bouchard, Heston, Eckert, Keyes, & Resnick, 1981). In-depth interviews with the "Jim twins" revealed a puzzling mixture of similarities and differences (see Figure 12–9).

MZ twins reared apart are rare, and the Minnesota project is one of only four studies of such twins. The studies are important, because MZ twins reared apart provide a powerful means for determining the influence of heredity on behavior. Similarities between identical twins reared apart must be due to their identical genotypes. The correlation of IQs for identical twins reared apart thus offers a direct estimate of the relative influence of heredity on intelligence (Bouchard, 1983).

Adoption-study methods also have involved adopted siblings. The study of children adopted shortly after birth who grow up in adoptive homes with adoptive siblings presents a natural experiment opposite to that provided by identical twins reared apart. Adoptive siblings share a common family environment but are unrelated genetically. A trait caused entirely by genetics

Figure 12–9.

The "Jim twins." The rate of twin births in the United States is approximately one in 83 deliveries. About one-third of the conceptions that produce twins result in same-sex dizygotic twins, one-third in opposite-sex dizygotic twins, and the remaining one-third in monozygotic twins. Shown here are Jim Lewis and Jim Springer, identical twins separated as infants and reunited 39 years later. Research has revealed some bizarre similarities between the two men. Besides having the same first name, both had first wives named Linda, second wives named Betty, and first-born sons with the same first and middle names, James Alan Lewis and James Allan Springer (cf. Powledge, 1983).

should result in a zero correlation between genetically unrelated individuals. Similarities in IQ between adoptive siblings reared together must be due to similarities in their environment. The correlation of IQs for adoptive siblings thus offers a direct estimate of the relative influence of environment on intellectual development.

Family studies. To further estimate the relative contributions of heredity and environment, in *family-study methods,* similarities between parents and their children and among brothers and sisters are examined. Family members, who are genetically similar, should show greater similarity in such traits as intelligence than should individuals who are unrelated genetically. Thus, family resemblance is necessary, although not sufficient, evidence for demonstrating the influence of heredity on behavior.

— Summary of Results from Twin, Adoption, and Family Studies

Bouchard and McGue (1981) summarized 111 studies from the world literature on family resemblances in measured intelligence. Figure 12–10 shows the degree of similarity in IQ between selected relatives reared together and apart. Looking at Figure 12–10, you can see that the IQs of identical twins are more similar than for fraternal twins. The correlation for identical twins reared together is .86; for fraternal twins reared together it is .60. Identical twins reared apart show greater similarity in intelligence than do fraternal twins or ordinary brothers and sisters reared together. Moreover, the correlation for identical twins raised in different homes (.72) is much higher than that for genetically unrelated adoptive siblings reared together (.32).

Using the concept of heritability, we can summarize what is known about the relative importance of heredity and environment in causing individual differences in IQ. **Heritability** is a statistical measure of the contribution of heredity to observed variations of a trait for a given population in a certain environment. The heritability statistic provides an estimate of the proportion of the observed variation in a trait, such as intelligence, that is due to genetic differences among individuals. As described earlier, the IQ correlation of identical twins reared apart provides a direct estimate of the influence of heredity on a trait. Conversely, the IQ correlation of unrelated individuals reared together provides a direct estimate of the influence of environment on a trait. The results presented in Figure 12–10,

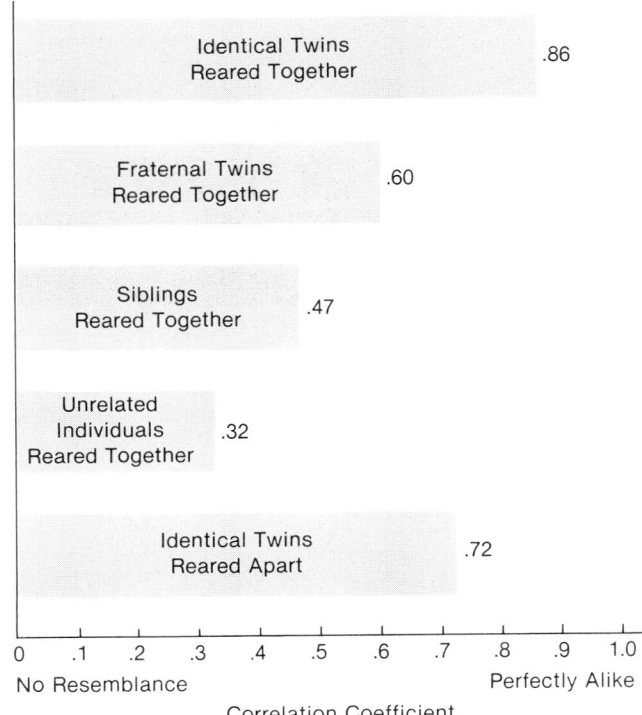

Figure 12–10.
IQ correlations for individuals differing in degree of genetic relatedness. (From Bouchard, 1983.)

as well as other lines of evidence not discussed here, "suggest that approximately 70 percent of the variation in intelligence among individuals is due to genetic factors and 30 percent to environmental factors and error of measurement" (Bouchard, 1983, p. 77).

Thus, to conclude that the trait of intelligence is influenced solely by heredity or environment is incorrect. Evidence exists for the relative influence of both. In fact, the strongest evidence for the influence of environment in producing differences in intelligence among individuals comes from research on twins reared together and apart. Monozygotic twins, who are 100 percent similar genetically, do not show 100 percent similarity on tests of intelligence.

Controversies in Behavioral Genetics

America's foremost proponent of the hereditarian view of human intelligence is Arthur Jensen. His pioneering and controversial research has focused on the measurement of individual differences in cognitive abilities, genetic and environmental determinants of intellectual development, and causes of group differences in academic achievement. Jensen's often cited 1969 *Harvard Educational Review* article, "How Much Can We Boost IQ and Scholastic Achievement?" claimed that, on the basis of IQ tests, whites are brighter than blacks and only about 25 percent of the 15-point IQ difference between American whites and blacks is due to environmental and cultural differences (the rest being due to genetics). In the article, Jensen defended three major hereditarian arguments. The first was that IQ tests measure a general mental ability of social relevance. The second was that individual differences in intelligence are due mainly to heredity. (At the time he wrote his article, Jensen estimated the heritability of IQ to be about 80 percent.) Finally, Jensen provided evidence of social-class and racial-ethnic differences in IQ and argued that such group differences represent genetic deficits that cannot be overcome by a few hours a day of compensatory education. Since 1969, Jensen has written prolifically on the topic of racial differences in intelligence. In his recent books, *Straight Talk about Mental Tests* (1981), *Educability and Group Differences* (1973), and *Bias in Mental Testing* (1980), he has extended his ideas on intelligence into one of the greatest controversies in the history of the behavioral sciences.

— IQ and Socioeconomic Status

Is socioeconomic status related to measured intelligence? If we define a person's **socioeconomic status (SES)** using the sociological variables of income, education, and occupation, then SES and IQ do appear to be related. (For review, see Scarr, 1981; White, 1982.) A positive relationship, one in which higher occupational status is related to higher intelligence-test scores, is a well-documented finding (Tyler, 1965). This relationship is reflected in the data (shown in Table 12–3) collected by Harrell and Harrell (1945). Average IQ-test scores obtained on the Army General Classification Test by more than 18,000 white enlisted men during World War II are shown by civilian occupation. Test scores increase with the social prestige of the various occupations.

To explain such results, Harvard psychologist Richard Herrnstein (1973) suggested that the relationship between occupational status and intelligence-test scores is rational and necessary in an advanced technological society. Accordingly, the ties among IQ, oc-

Table 12–3.

IQ and SES: Average scores on the Army General Classification Test obtained by men in various occupations.

OCCUPATION	APPROXIMATE MEAN IQ SCORE
Accountant	128
Engineer	127
Teacher	123
Pharmacist	121
Salesman	115
Sales clerk	109
Mechanic	106
Bartender	102
Truck driver	96
Lumberjack	95
Miner	91

Source: Adapted from Harrell and Harrell, 1945.

cupation, and social standing make practical sense because the intellectual demands of engineering, for example, exceed those of ditch digging.

A contrary position has been asserted by David McClelland, also of Harvard University. In an article entitled "Testing for Competence Rather than for Intelligence," McClelland (1973) asserts that coming from a high-SES family helps people get into college and into certain occupations. This is particularly true, he believes, because entry into the professions requires a college degree and admission to college requires mastery of the "word-game skills" used in scholastic aptitude tests. Many youths from low-SES backgrounds do not have the verbal skills to do well on such tests. Therefore, their test scores are low and they are barred from professional positions. McClelland believes, however, that many of these individuals are quite intelligent and that the apparent correlations among SES, IQ, and occupation are spurious.

— Racial-Ethnic Differences in IQ

Loehlin, Lindzey, and Spuhler (1975) examined the role of genetic and environmental factors in determining *racial-ethnic differences* in cognitive ability. Their review, like that of Jensen's, showed a significant IQ difference between U.S. blacks and whites—15 IQ points on the average. Although an IQ difference of approximately this magnitude has been found in numerous studies, there is considerable controversy over its cause. If the heritability of intelligence is 70 percent, it might be reasonable to assume, as some investigators have, that approximately 70 percent (or 10.5 points) of the black-white IQ difference is due to genetic differences between the groups. However, meaningful heritability estimates assume equal environments—an assumption that clearly does not hold for blacks and whites in the United States. In other words, differences in average test scores could be caused purely by environment. Even if the differences were genetic, though, they would not preclude the favorable effects of living in an enriched environment. For example, Scarr and Weinberg (1976) used the adoption-study method to investigate IQ-test performance of 130 black children adopted into middle-to-upper-middle-class white families. The black children showed an average IQ of 106, considerably above the level that would have been expected if they had been reared in their biological families.

Most available research on racial-ethnic differences in intelligence has focused on black-white differences. New research, however, shows that the Japanese outperform both U.S. blacks and U.S. whites in intelligence tests. In a study reported by Richard Lynn (1982), the Japanese showed an average IQ score of 111, compared with the average U.S. score of 100. Lynn concluded that about 10 percent of Japan's population has an IQ level higher than 130, whereas only 2 percent of Americans achieve that level. Differences may be due to genetics, or increased educational opportunities in Japan during the years since World War II may account for the higher test performance of Japanese children. One Japanese child psychologist acknowledged that Japanese children are more used to taking tests than other children are and that their higher national IQ may be related to the "examination hell" inflicted on Japanese students (Mohs, 1982). Studies comparing the two groups found that Japanese children attend school an average of 240 days a year, compared to 178 for Americans, and that Japanese first-graders put in an average of 233 minutes a week on their lesson after school, compared to 79 minutes for American first-graders (Garfinkel, 1983).

— Sex-Related Differences in Mental Abilities

Many recent studies have shown a difference in spatial, mathematical, and verbal abilities between males and females (cf. Benbow & Stanley, 1982; Maccoby & Jacklin, 1974; Wittig & Petersen, 1979). Males, in general, show higher performance than females on various types of tasks that require spatial ability. Such tests measure the abstract reasoning required in higher mathematics (e.g., geometry) and the sense of direction required for reading maps and flying airplanes through 3-dimensional space (McGee, 1979a; Potegal, 1982). The sex difference in spatial ability is pronounced on tasks that require 3-dimensional mental rotation and visualization (see Figure 12–11a). There is no evidence, however, for a sex difference on 2-dimensional (see Figure 12–11b) tests of spatial ability (McGee, Cozad, & Pate, 1982).

In general, females show higher performance than males on various types of tasks that require verbal ability (Hyde, 1981). Tests of verbal ability measure the fluency required in the rapid production of different ideas and the comprehension required in vocabulary tests. A difference between the sexes in verbal abilities (as well as in spatial and mathematical abilities) is one of the most persistent and well-documented findings in the abilities literature.

That sex-related cognitive differences exist is not disputed; the controversy concerns why they exist. Some investigators favor a biological explanation (see chapter 2); others argue that socialization fosters attitudes that influence performance on tests (cf. McGee, 1979b). The fact is that we cannot state with any precision the relative contribution of these factors. The conclusion to be drawn from available studies is that genetic factors that influence hormone production and brain development interact with environmental factors to influence sex differences in intellectual development. As noted by Nash (1979), such differences do not emerge to any significant degree until puberty. Thus, environmental effects may be explained, in part, by role conflicts:

> It becomes apparent to them (children) that their talents are either congruent or incongruent with their gender. For example, if a girl discovers she has superior quantitative and spatial abilities, she may wish she were a boy so that she could express her aptitudes with less sex-role conflict. Similarly, if a boy feels he has feminine capabilities or traits, he may wish he were a girl so that he could express those parts of himself without "deviating" from society's rigid masculine standards. (Nash, 1979, p. 291)

Family Configuration and Intellectual Development

Is it possible that family makeup affects intelligence? The most popular current theory of family effects on

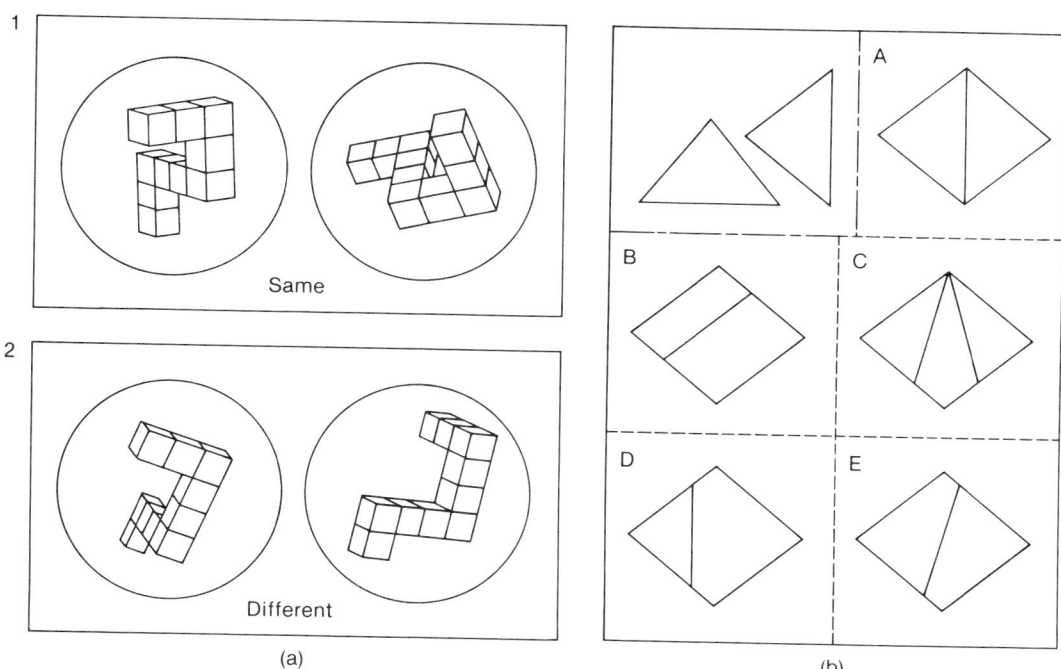

Figure 12-11.

Spatial ability test items: (a) 3-dimensional; (b) 2-dimensional. For the 3-dimensional test item, the subject is required to determine if the picture of blocks on the right is the same or different as the picture on the left after the picture on the left has been rotated. For the 2-dimensional test item, the subject is required to determine which of the alternative patterns (A, B, C, D, or E) is the same as the stimulus pattern after it has been pieced together (without rotating the pieces in 3-dimensions).

intellectual development has been advanced by Robert Zajonc (pronounced Zy-ence), professor of psychology at the University of Michigan. Zajonc (1983) argued that variations in **family configuration,** defined by family size, birth order, and sibling spacing, have a major influence on the development of intelligence. Let's consider the theory.

— Theory of Family Configuration

As noted by Zajonc and Markus (1975), intellectual development within the family context depends on the cumulative effects of the intellectual environment. Accordingly, the basic idea of the theory is that different family configurations constitute different intellectual environments. The *value of the intellectual environment (VIE)* for any family is considered to be the average of all the members' independent contributions.

Family configuration theory can be illustrated by simplified examples in which each parent's contribution to the VIE is 100 arbitrary units. The newborn child's contribution is 0. The VIE for a family consisting of two parents and a newborn child, as illustrated in the first example in Table 12–4, is 67 (100 + 100 +

0 ÷ 3). Suppose that the secondborn child in the family arrives at a time when the firstborn's intellectual level (or contribution) has reached 40. As illustrated in the second example in Table 12–4, the VIE of the family decreases from 67 to 60 (100 + 100 + 40 + 0 ÷ 4). Suppose that a third child is born (see the third example in Table 12–4) when the intellectual level of the firstborn is at 50 and the level of the secondborn is at 30. The family's VIE will be reduced to 56 (100 + 100 + 50 + 30 + 0 ÷ 5).

These hypothetical examples illustrate a significant consequence predicted by family configuration theory—that the value of the intellectual environment declines with increased family size. Zajonc's (1975) *Psychology Today* article, entitled "Dumber by the Dozen," advised that to have brighter children, keep them few and far between. It concluded that the brightest children come from the smallest families, and within any given family size, the children that come along early tend to have higher IQs.

Zajonc has compiled an impressive amount of data from numerous studies of large numbers of individuals to support the family configuration theory. These data were derived from different tests of intellectual

Table 12–4.

Hypothetical values of intellectual environment (VIE) as a function of changing family configurations.

EXAMPLE	FAMILY CONFIGURATION	CONTRIBUTIONS TO THE INTELLECTUAL ENVIRONMENT BY FAMILY MEMBERS					FAMILY VIE
		Mother	*Father*	*Firstborn*	*Secondborn*	*Thirdborn*	
1	3-person family	100	100	0	—	—	67
2	4-person family	100	100	40	0	—	60
3	5-person family	100	100	50	30	0	56

Source: Adapted from Zajonc, 1975.

performance and different countries. They indicate that intellectual level generally declines with increasing family size and birth order. The best evidence for these effects comes from a study by Lillian Belmont and Francis Marolla (1973), who examined the relationship of family size and birth order to intelligence-test performance in a sample of 386,114 Dutch people.

— Evaluation of the Family Configuration Theory

The purported consequences for intellectual development of birth order and family size have aroused much public interest. Some psychologists, however, have bitterly opposed Zajonc's theory on the ground that it does not account adequately for individual differences in intelligence observed within families (e.g., Page & Grandon, 1979).

Furthermore, most data presented to support the theory have come from cross-sectional studies using test scores of individuals from *different* families. It would be of obvious value, at this point, to test the theory on a large sample of individuals *within* families. With the exception of one family study by Berbaum and Moreland (1980), other studies have failed to support the theory (e.g., Brackbill & Nichols, 1982; Galbraith, 1982; Grotevant, Scarr, & Weinberg, 1977; Velandia, Grandon, & Page, 1978). Clearly a longitudinal study of families is required to clarify the adequacy of family configuration theory.

Environmental Enrichment Programs and Intellectual Development

A great deal of time, effort, and taxpayers' dollars have been invested in recent years to determine whether environmental enrichment can enhance the intellectual development of culturally disadvantaged children. Studies of environmental enrichment typically examine the effects of training programs on IQ-test performance. The best studies assess performance before and after enrichments and at follow-ups a year or more later. Additionally, they involve subjects who are randomly assigned to experimental and control groups. Studies that meet these criteria have demonstrated that culturally disadvantaged children participating in early enrichment programs do show improvements in IQ-test scores. The increases, however, tend to be short-lived.

Consider, for example, the results from three preschool enrichment programs reviewed by Karnes (1973). Subjects in each study were 4-year-olds from low-income families. As illustrated in Figure 12–12, gains in IQ were substantial during the first year in each program. During the second year, children who continued to participate (the Bereiter-Engelmann group) showed continued improvement. The two other groups, who went on to public-school kindergarten, showed slight declines in test performance. After first grade in public school, children in the Bereiter-Engelmann group also showed a decline in mean IQ. By third grade, scores were only six or seven points above initial levels—considerably less than gains found after 1 year in the program.

Karnes concluded from these results that one year of preschool programming, no matter how immediately effective, does not equip disadvantaged children to maintain performance in the kindergarten setting. Despite this criticism there have been widespread attempts to initiate preschool enrichment programs for children from culturally disadvantaged environments. Probably one of the most widely known such programs is Project Head Start.

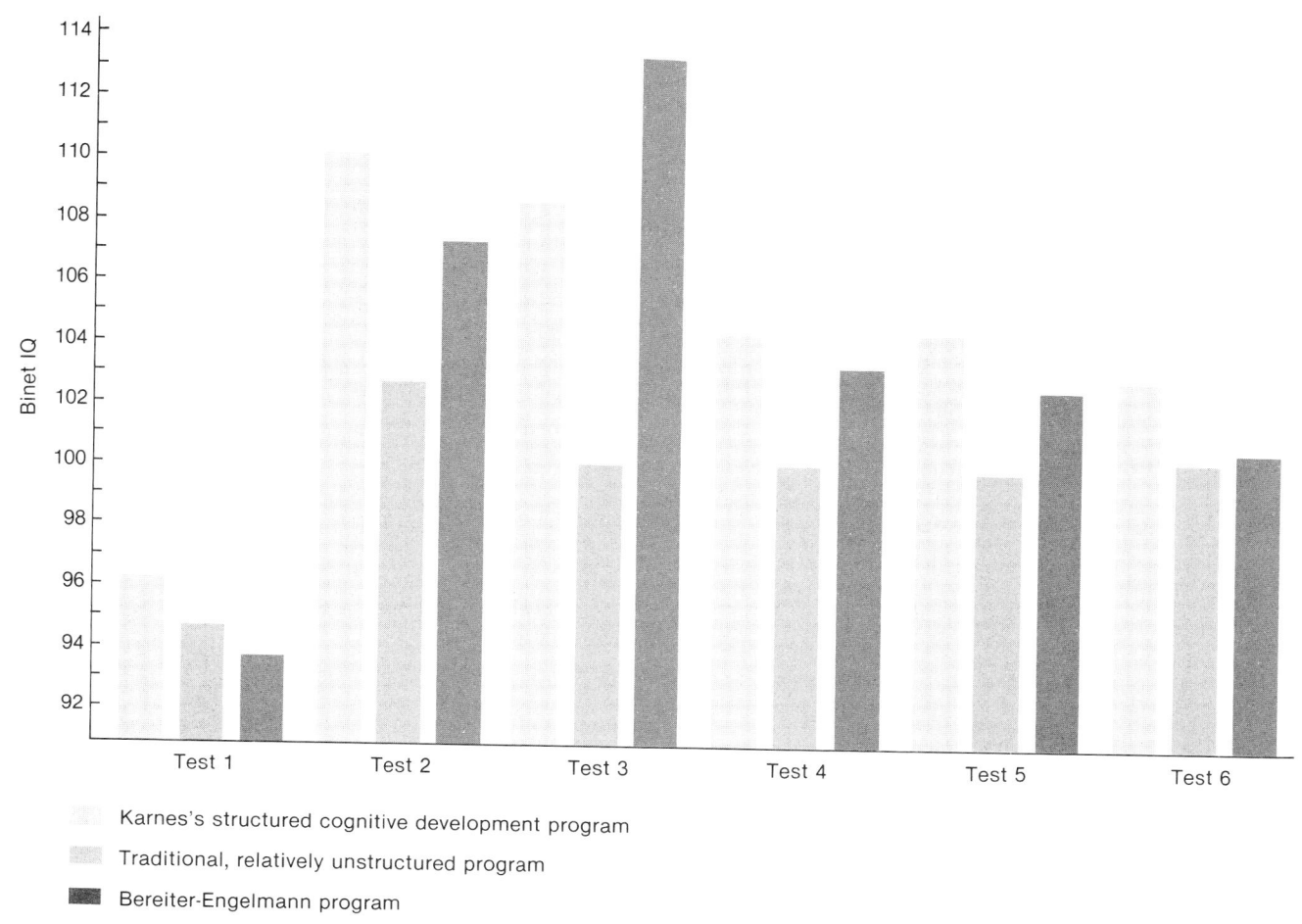

Figure 12–12.

Results from three preschool enrichment programs. (After Karnes, 1973.)

— The Head Start Program

In the beginning, **Project Head Start** was an 8-week summer program for disadvantaged children who were about to enter public school (cf. Zigler, Abelson, Trickett, & Seitz, 1982). Today, it is an all-year program that serves about 350,000 preschool children each year. It is a half-day program for about two-thirds of the children and a full-day education and day-care program for the remaining one-third.

Preliminary evaluations of the Head Start effort were positive; children showed substantial gains in measured IQ. Enthusiasm for the program subsided considerably, however, as later reports indicated that the IQ gains disappeared soon after participating children entered public school (cf. Hodges & Cooper, 1981). If IQ gains had been the only criterion by which the

project's success was determined, federal funding for it would have ended several years ago. However, the goals of Head Start are broader in scope. They include fostering children's social and emotional development, meeting their health and nutritional needs, involving parents and the larger community in those purposes, and improving later social and school competence.

When the program's effectiveness is evaluated with these broader goals in mind, we find that Project Head Start children are better adjusted socially and emotionally than control children, that they do show somewhat higher scores on academic achievement tests, and that they have had the advantage of being screened, diagnosed, and treated for various health-related problems. As a result, they are physically healthier than control children. Also, community activity centered around family health and education is fostered to a greater level in Head Start communiites than in communities that do not have Head Start centers (cf. Zigler & Valentine, 1979).

— Early Enrichment Programs: Summary and Evaluation

The measured effectiveness of early enrichment programs for the culturally disadvantaged depends in large part on the goals that such programs set out to achieve. When an increase in measured intelligence is abandoned as the only goal of intervention, then enthusiasm for the enriching effects of early intervention seems justified. Lasting success in meeting the broader goals is especially evidenced in the programs that begin early in the children's lives and last for several years.

The strongest support for lasting positive effects of preschool enrichment programs for children from low-income families comes from a recent follow-up study of eight separate research projects initiated during the 1960s (Darlington, Royce, Snipper, Murray, & Lazar, 1980; see also Lazar & Darlington, 1982). Follow-up results on IQ-test performance replicated those from numerous previous investigations. Substantial gains in test performance tapered down to smaller but statistically significant effects 3 and 4 years after preschool intervention and thereafter vanished. The most significant findings, however, concerned the effects of early enrichment on direct measures of school success. Children who participated in a preschool enrichment program were more likely to progress normally through school than were children with no preschool experience. The failure rate, as determined by being held back a grade or by being placed in a special-education class, was 24 percent for the program participants and 45 percent for the control children. These pooled results from several independent projects provide compelling evidence for the effectiveness of early enrichment programs in improving later school competence.

— APPLICATION —
ENRICHMENT THROUGH NUTRITION

Although it is far too early to proclaim that you are what you eat, many recent studies have attempted to determine whether undernutrition leads to intellectual deficits (cf. Winick, 1979). This question is difficult to answer, because poor nutrition is often accompanied by low family income and impoverished rearing conditions. Although findings have been conflicting, a study conducted in Colombia by McKay, Sinisterra, McKay, Gomez, and Lloreda (1978) demonstrated the benefit of intervening to reverse the negative effects of malnutrition. At various ages during the preschool years, groups of chronically malnourished children from Colombian families of low socioeconomic status began receiving supplements in nutrition, health care, and education. By school age, the gap in intellectual functioning between the treated children and a group of privileged children in the same city had narrowed. The younger the children were on entering the program, the more favorable were the results. Cognitive gains were still evident a year after the experiment ended.

Can the world's food shortage and its devastating effects be prevented? Coca-Cola chief executive John Paul Austin has a radical but simple solution to the world's nutritional problems: Soft drinks now sold widely in Brazil and Mexico that contain up to one-third of an adult's entire daily vitamin and mineral needs and 10 percent of an adult's protein needs (Loeb, 1979). According to Austin, the entire world's starving population can be simply and cheaply fed with the soft drink. The drink, called Sampson, currently comes in orange or mango flavor, but it can be given any flavor (and color).

Sampson is made from a protein-potent residue left over from cheese manufacturing; the residue normally is dumped as waste into streams, which it pollutes by providing food for algae. Austin plans to test the effects of Sampson thoroughly in severely improverished areas of the world, then gradually introduce the drink to the United States. Already, Sampson has been tested in five Atlanta, Georgia elementary schools, where it was given to ghetto children with a record of poor school performance. Children who were fed the food supplement every school-day morning for 4 months showed improvements in academic achievement; they also stopped sleeping in class, their attention spans increased, and their truancy rate declined.

Below are test answers, some explanations, and the number (in parentheses) of Mensa members, out of a sample of 88, who answered each item correctly.

1. 33. Each increment is double the previous increment. (72)

2. vex. pacify. Although other words have antithetical meanings, these two are considered most nearly opposite. (63)

3. $36. The price is determined by the initial letter of each item and then multiplied by two. $2 for an item beginning with A, $4 for one starting with B, etc. (45)

4. b. Human things are alternated right and left. Although this item was missed by most Mensans, once it was explained, there was virtually no argument about the answer. (32)

5. NEWS. The arrows represent North, East, West, and South. (35)

6. 2. In rows, the left number minus the middle number equals the right number. In the columns, the top number minus the middle equals the bottom number. (76)

7. a. The figure rotates counterclockwise by increments increasing one-eighth turn in each successive drawing: The second drawing has rotated one-eighth turn counterclockwise; the third has rotated an additional quarter-turn; the fourth has rotated an additional three-eighths turn. The correct answer, a, shows the figure rotated an additional four-eights (one-half) turn. (37)

8. Discord. (77)

9. Center, perimeter. (73)

10. a. (75)

11. 72. Each succeeding number is alternately multiplied by two or three. (72)

12. a. The black window in the far left column goes down one square each time before it starts again at the top; the black window in the middle goes up on square each time; the black window in the second horizontal row moves left one square each time. (38)

13. c. (72)

14. Beam, ray. (62)

15. d. The center figure is always solid; the symbols in the corners are moving counterclockwise. (65)

16. c. (67)

17. d. The right angle is moving counterclockwise. The changing figure increases the number of its line segments by one in each succeeding square. (64)

18. a. (66)

19. c. (60)

20. a, e. (83)

21. $60. The price of each is determined by the number of letters in the word, multiplied by ten. (55)

22. a. The apple and pear alternate black and white and are moving counterclockwise. The two bunches of cherries are moving clockwise. (79)

23. 207. Each succeeding interval is multiplied by three. (50)

24. c. (65)

25. b. The second dot moves clockwise and is "hidden" in the fourth drawing. (74)

26. d. (52)

27. c. Each increment is multiplied by three. (74)

28. b. (81)

29. Tale, story. (73)

30. c. (59)

31. a. (66)

32. c. This item was the "easiest" on the test. Still, one Mensan missed it. (87)

33. b, e. (83)

34. 6. Each number is reduced by a number that is increased by one with each succeeding term. (85)

35. Curtain, window. (77)

36. Yolk. (41)

37. a. Each square is exactly like its diagonal counterpart, except the color of the triangle changes black to white or white to black. (81)

38. d. (77)

39. Lid, kettle. (73)

For the 88 Mensa members who took the test the range of scores was from 13 to 36. The mean score was 28.91, and the median score was 29. Although your score on the test cannot be used to qualify you for membership in Mensa, it is possible to convert your score into a rough estimate of your IQ using the guidelines provided by Morris (1981).

Mensa IQ-Test Score	Probable IQ Range
20-23	125-131
24-29	132-139
29-33	140-147
34 and above	148 and above

ENGINEERING HUMAN INTELLIGENCE

Although numerous articles appearing recently in scientific and popular journals have discussed the moral and ethical aspects of *artificial insemination* with donor semen, little is known about its scope or its current methods. Articles by Foss (1982) and by Curie-Cohen and colleagues (Curie-Cohen, Luttrell, & Shapiro, 1979) suggest that the procedure is more common than expected.

In a survey of more than 700 physicians, the Curie-Cohen group obtained responses from 379 physicians who had performed artificial insemination, accounting for approximately 3,576 births by this means in 1977. From estimates made from this survey, it was concluded that between 6,000 and 10,000 children are born annually in the United States as a result of the procedure. The primary reason given by physicians for administering artificial insemination was infertility of the husband. About 33 percent of the responding physicians indicated that they had inseminated women whose husbands feared transmitting a genetic disease; and despite societal pressures, about 10 percent of the inseminations were for single women.

In coming years, we should have a chance to witness the results of a controversial artificial insemination program begun by Robert K. Graham, a wealthy California optometrist (Superkids?, 1980). Graham has been collecting and storing sperm from Nobel Prize winning scientists. Graham's project, first revealed in the *Mensa Bulletin* in 1980, offers Nobel sperm to young women who have high IQs and are healthy, under 35 years of age, and, preferably, married to sterile men.

So far, only one sperm donor has revealed himself to the press. He is William Shockley, who won the prize for his co-invention of the transistor in 1956 and has since become a vocal proponent of racially tinged eugenics. Graham has shipped sperm to several unidentified women. On April 21, 1982, the project's director announced the birth of its first child, a healthy, 9-pound baby girl. The baby's father was identified as an eminent mathematician and the mother as a member of Mensa (Elite sperm bank, 1982).

Are the offspring of participants in Graham's project likely to become superkids? The next decade should tell the story. The use of artificial insemination for the purpose of engineering human intelligence is likely to remain controversial, however, because the benefits and risks remain largely unknown. Most Nobel laureates are far along in age, and (as discussed in chapter 10) new evidence suggests that the incidence of Down's syndrome births increases not only with the mother's age but with the father's age as well. Also, there is no guarantee that high-IQ people produce better children or a happier society. As suggested by Daniel Callahan, director of the Institute of Society, Ethics and the Life Sciences, Graham's project assumes that brighter is better; but it is not the mentally retarded people in our world who produce wars and destruction (Superkids?, 1980).

SUMMARY

1. A French psychologist, Alfred Binet, is credited with developing the first widely used test of intelligence. His work provided the foundation for conceiving the intelligence quotient (IQ) as a ratio of mental age to chronological age. His test, in revised form, is known today as the Stanford-Binet Intelligence Scale.

2. Advances in psychological testing during this century are reflected in the widespread development and use of both individual and group tests of general intellectual ability and the development of tests to assess aptitudes and achievements in a variety of specific areas.

3. For a psychological test to be considered worthwhile, it must be reliable, valid, and standardized on a norm group. A test is reliable if there is consistency in test scores obtained by the same persons when they are reexamined on different occasions. A test is valid if it measures what it is supposed to measure. Standardization allows accurate and objective test-score interpretations.

4. The range of intellectual functioning is reflected in the wide distribution of intelligence-test scores from 0 to over 200.

5. Low scores on intelligence tests are indications of mental retardation. IQ-test scores are used in conjunction with scores on adaptive behavior scales to determine the level of social competence for a given person. Adaptive behavior refers to the capacity of the individual to perform various age-appropriate social roles.

6. There are two broad classes of mental retardation. Organic retardation encompasses about 25 percent of the cases for which there is a known biological abnormality. Cultural-familial retardation encompasses the remaining 75 percent of the cases for which a precise cause is unknown.

7. Very high IQ scores are associated with genius and giftedness. The determination of genius is based on novel achievements that solve important practical problems and high IQ. Creativity is associated to some degree with IQ, but not all high-IQ individuals are creative thinkers. Creativity is defined as a quality of thinking that leads to novel and unsuspected ways of solving problems.

8. Intellectual and cognitive development are determined by both hereditary and environmental factors. Methods of behavioral genetic research provide a means for examining the relative impact on intellectual development of both sources of influence.

9. Evidence for the relative importance of heredity is provided by studies examining the correlations (degrees of similarity) of IQ-test scores between individuals differing in degree of genetic relatedness. Very similar IQ scores are observed between genetically identical twins. Little similarity is found between genetically unrelated individuals. An intermediate degree of similarity is found between siblings, parents and offspring, and fraternal twins.

10. Current areas of controversy in behavioral genetics include the work of Arthur Jensen, intelligence and social class, racial-ethnic differences in intelligence, and sex-related differences in cognitive abilities.

11. Evidence exists for the relative importance of environmental rearing conditions. The strongest evidence for the impact of environment on intellectual development comes from behavioral genetic research on twins reared together and apart. Monozygotic twins, who are 100 percent similar genetically, do not show 100 percent similarity on tests of intelligence. Also, adoption and family studies have demonstrated the influence of family environment on intellectual development.

12. The most popular current theory of family effects on intellectual development is family configuration theory. The effects of birth order, family size, and age spacing between siblings are described by family configuration theorists to show how individual differences in intellectual growth emerge within the social context of the family.

13. Culturally disadvantaged children who participate in enrichment programs show improvements in IQ-test scores in comparison with children in control groups. The increases, however, tend to be rather short-lived. The length and timing of intervention seem to be especially important in long-lasting environmental enrichment effects.

— IMPORTANT TERMS AND CONCEPTS —

Autistic Savants
Intelligence
Intelligence Quotient (IQ)
Deviation IQ
Achievement Tests
Aptitude Tests
Test Reliability
Test Validity
Content Validation
Criterion-related Validation
Construct Validation
Traits

Standardization
Normal Probability Distribution
Developmental Quotient (DQ)
Cross-sectional Research Designs
Longitudinal Research Designs
Mental Retardation
Adaptive Behavior
Organic Retardation
Cultural-familial Retardation
Genius
Giftedness
Creativity

Divergent Thinking
Convergent Thinking
Human Behavioral Genetics
Natural Selection
Genotype
Phenotype
Reaction Range
Heritability
Socioeconomic Status (SES)
Family Configuration
Project Head Start

— SUGGESTIONS FOR FURTHER READING —

Albert, R. S. (Ed.). (1983). *Genius and eminence*. New York: Pergamon Press. An up-to-date review of research findings in the areas of genius, giftedness, and creative behavior.

Anastasi, A. (1982). *Psychological testing* (5th ed.). New York: Macmillan. An accurate evaluation of psychological tests and the correct interpretation and use of their results.

Eysenck, H. J. (1979). *Check your own IQ*. New York: Bell. A book that enables you to estimate your IQ. Answers to all test questions and explanations of how they were obtained are given at the end of the book, together with tables for converting scores into intelligence quotients. The book also provides a brief history of intelligence testing and a discussion of whether intelligence is inherited or acquired.

Plomin, R., DeFries, J. C., & McClearn, G. E. (1980). *Behavioral genetics*. San Francisco: W. H. Freeman. A soft-cover primer and readable introduction to the field of behavioral genetics.

Raudsepp, E. (1981). *How creative are you?* New York: G. P. Putnan's Sons (Perigee Books). A fun-to-read paperbook useful for measuring and expanding your creative potential.

Willerman, L. (1979). *The psychology of individual and group differences*. San Francisco: W. H. Freeman. A thorough and readable introduction to the scientific study of individual and group differences in intelligence and personality.

— CHAPTER 13 —

PERSONALITY THEORIES AND ASSESSMENT

— CHAPTER 13 —

PERSONALITY THEORIES AND ASSESSMENT

— CHAPTER OBJECTIVES —

To achieve the objectives of this chapter, you should be able to answer the questions listed here. You should also be able to define the important terms and concepts listed at the end of the chapter.

1. What is personality? How is it defined?
2. List the essential features of the five major approaches to studying personality.
3. Name some criticisms of the five approaches.
4. What are some of the major personality-assessment devices?
5. How do personality-assessment techniques relate to personality theories?
6. What are some problems associated with personality assessment?

— CHAPTER OUTLINE —

Personality Theories
Psychologists have devised many theories to interpret and explain personality.

Psychoanalytic Approach
Trait Approach
Humanistic Approach
Cognitive Approach
Behavioral Approach
Application: Locus of Control—Personality in Action

Personality Assessment
Each theoretical approach offers some means for measuring personality.

Psychoanalytic Approach
Trait Approach
Humanistic and Cognitive Approaches
Behavioral Approach
Application: The MMPI in Personnel Selection

On the Horizon: Personality Assessment in the Courtroom

THE THREE FACES OF EVE

Time and again, Chris Sizemore (see Figure 13–1) has seen her personality change (Steinbach, 1982). In fact, she has experienced 22 distinct personalities—in 3s. In each series of 3, a single personality would dominate temporarily, then relinquish control to a 2nd personality. The change would be evidenced in memory losses or blackouts. The 1st personality would have no knowledge of the 2nd, and the 1st and 2nd personalities would be unaware of the 3rd. However, the 3rd would know everything about the other 2. Ultimately, the 3 personalities would die, only to be replaced by 3 .more.

What Sizemore experienced for most of her life is a disorder known as multiple personality. Her experience was made famous by the book *The Three Faces of Eve,* written by her first psychotherapists (Thigpen & Cleckley, 1957), and by an Oscar-winning movie of the same name. During Sizemore's initial therapy, 3 separate and coexisting personalities became apparent, each with its own characteristics and memories. One of the personalities, Eve White, was a naive and reserved wife and mother. The 2nd personality, Eve Black, was more flamboyant. She was aware of the 1st personality, but she rejected Eve White's husband and child. The third personality, Jane, was more mature and appeared at first to be capable of leading a normal life. It was not to be. Over the next 20 years, Sizemore continued to experience frightening

Figure 13–1.

Chris Sizemore in front of *Three Faces of Eve* painting.

personality changes and to undergo psychiatric treatment. She also survived a number of suicide attempts.

Today, Sizemore believes that her separate personalities represented an attempt on her part to cope with anxiety. Her first personality change apparently occurred at the age of 2. She recalls the following experience:

> My mother had cut her arm badly and there was a lot of blood. I thought she was going to die. She told me, "Go get Daddy," but I ran over to the bed and stuck my head under a pillow. I could feel this strange weakness in my body as I vacated and somebody else took over. Then I watched this little girl go get my father. It wasn't me, I was watching another little girl emerge. (Steinbach, 1982, p. 22)

Shortly before this accident, young Chris had also witnessed the violent deaths of two men.

In 1974, 45 years after the terrified real Chris Sizemore hid her head under the pillow, the last of the multiple personalities disappeared. The real Chris Sizemore returned, and today she continues to be free of the problem (Steinbach, 1982).

Multiple personality will be discussed in greater detail in chapter 15, which covers abnormal behavior. For now, the story of *Eve* raises many important questions about personality. What is personality? Can it be described or measured? What is its structure? How does it develop? Can it change? What is the link between personality and behavior? How can similarities and differences in personality be explained? These are all questions of interest to the personality psychologist.

In everyday language, the term *personality* often refers to social adroitness or effectiveness (Mischel, 1981). We might say that someone has a charming personality, a good or bad personality, or perhaps even no personality at all. At other times, we employ the term *personality* to describe people by their most prominent characteristics, as in shy personality or aggressive personality. These common usages, however, differ from what psychologists mean by the term. In general, psychologists define **personality** as the personal characteristics that account for consistent and enduring patterns of response to various situations (Pervin, 1980). This definition recognizes that people differ in a variety of characteristics and in their interpretations of and responses to situations. In this sense, each personality is unique and distinctive. The definition also recognizes that personality is enduring, consistent, and stable over time. Its third point is that although people differ in many ways, they are also similar; personality represents characteristics common to all people.

Each personality theory emphasizes these points to a different degree, as each makes different assumptions about human behavior. Ultimately, the personality theories are theories of behavior, because they attempt to explain why we think, feel, and behave as we do.

— PERSONALITY THEORIES —

We will now examine five theoretical views of personality: psychoanalytic, trait, humanistic, cognitive, and behavioral.

Psychoanalytic Approach

Developed by Sigmund Freud (e.g., 1933/1964, 1924/1952), **psychoanalytic theory** was the first modern personality theory. Freud's fame is such that the terms *ego, id, Freudian slip,* and *Oedipus conflict* have become part of our everyday language. Within psychology, the theory is known for its emphasis on unconscious motives, instincts for sex and aggression, and early-childhood experiences as forces that direct and influence behavior.

— Major Assumptions

Psychoanalytic theory is guided by the *principle of psychic determinism;* that is, it assumes that all behavior is motivated, has meaning, and is purposeful (Rotter & Hochreich, 1975). Freud saw not only bizarre behavior but also everyday behavior (such as dreams, slips of the tongue, and memory losses) as having meaning and motives. Have you ever forgotten someone's name while trying to introduce the person to someone else? Freud's explanation might be that you wanted to forget, perhaps because you harbored some hostility toward the person. Freud's theory also assumes that people are *unconsciously motivated*—that they are not always aware of the true motives underlying their behavior.

— Processes of Personality: Energy and Instincts

For Freud, all psychological activities use psychic energy. This energy, he proposed, derives from biological instincts of two types: life (Eros) and death (Thanatos). The *life instincts* are associated with survival needs, such as hunger, thirst, sex, and maternal attachment. Freud referred to the energy from the life instincts as the **libido.** Because Freud emphasized sex, the libido is often equated with sexual energy. The *death instincts* are associated with destructive impulses, such as aggression and suicidal tendencies. These

instincts have as their goal returning the organism to an inorganic state. But because the death instincts are often blocked by the life instincts, the individual may deal with the conflict by redirecting the death instinct toward others in aggression, physical assault, murder, war, and so on. In fact, witnessing the carnage of World War I was what prompted Freud to propose the notion of a death instinct (cf. Byrne & Kelley, 1981). (For more information, see the discussion of aggression in chapter 18.)

— Personality Structure

According to Freud, behavior is governed by three interacting systems—the id, the ego, and the superego. The three systems must work together harmoniously or the individual will be said to be maladjusted or not functioning normally (Rotter & Hochreich, 1975). As Byrne and Kelley (1981) observe, in Freud's theory everything results from compromises among our primitive desires (id), the constraints of reality (ego), and our acquired moral code (superego).

Id. The part of the personality from which the instincts and instinctual energy are derived is the **id.** It functions according to the *pleasure principle,* which means that it desires gratification and tension reduction. The id's objective is to avoid pain and to gain immediate pleasure. That is why, Freud believed, infants cry as soon as a need arises that they cannot satisfy. But the id operates in adults too. In Freud's thinking, the id pushes us to obtain life's pleasures at any cost and regardless of any rules or constraints that might dictate otherwise.

However, an unrestrained id soon runs into problems. The id says, "I want it and I want it now." From a more realistic point of view, though, the desire may be inappropriate (e.g., a desire to hurt someone), the circumstances for expressing the desire may be inappropriate (e.g., the desire to have sexual intercourse in public), or the desire may be appropriate but require postponement (e.g., a young child may want to be fed but may have to wait until a parent is free to do the feeding).

For the young child, postponing needs and delaying gratification are difficult tasks. Inevitably, though, the tolerance of such delays is necessary. A capacity for delaying gratification comes with the infant's increasing awareness of an external world and the development of the ego. It is with the emergence of the ego that we develop a mechanism whereby we are able to control the id's basic and primitive desires throughout our lives.

Ego. The part of the personality that functions in accordance with objective reality is the **ego.** It operates according to the *reality principle,* which means that its goal is to postpone the discharge of tension until there is a realistic possibility of satisfying the need. The ego is operating when a child waits until dinnertime to satisfy hunger instead of eating mud or crayons, as the id might dictate. In contrast to the id, the ego is able to reason and plan. Working from an objective and realistic base, the ego serves as mediator and arbitrator—trying to find a balance among the id's desires, the realities of the external world, and the values imposed by the superego.

Superego. If people are to behave responsibly, they must adhere to social norms, rules, and laws—even when no one is present to administer disapproval or punishment. In the 3rd or 4th year of life, children begin to judge and control their behavior independently of immediate threat or reward. Their growing self-control reflects the functioning of the **superego**—the part of the personality that represents the cultural values adopted by the child through the process of identification with the parents. Essentially, the superego acts as an internalized parent, or conscience, that evaluates and restrains behavior.

In well-adjusted individuals, the id, ego, and superego work together in harmony. As Rotter and Hochreich (1975) observe, the id seeks immediate gratification of needs, the superego seeks perfection in meeting its moral standards, and the ego seeks to balance the needs of the id and the superego realistically. According to Freud's theory, the amount of psychic energy available for psychological functioning is limited. Thus, if one of the three systems gains energy or strength, the other two are weakened. For example, if the superego becomes too strong, or overdeveloped, the id and ego will be de-energized; the resulting behavior will be unrealistically good, or rigidly inhibited (Rotter & Hochreich, 1975). A final complication in Freud's theory is that the three structures can operate both consciously and unconsciously; the result sometimes is unconscious clashes among the structures.

In sum, personality is a three-part structure that is partly conscious and partly unconscious (as illustrated in Figure 13–2) and that is marked by constant internal conflicts. The ego is involved in most of these conflicts, since it must find a means of reconciling the needs of the id and the superego as well as the requirements of the outside world. Some of the possible intrapsychic conflicts are presented in Table 13–1. The result of such conflicts is *anxiety.* Freud proposed that we deal with anxiety in a number of ways (which he called defense mechanisms). We will examine this matter in detail in chapter 14.

Psychosexual Stages of Personality Development

An important aspect of Freud's theory is his suggestion that the first 5 years of life have a decisive effect on the development of the adult personality. Freud's ideas in this regard form a theory of *psychosexual development.* The basic idea behind the theory is that children pass through a series of *psychosexual stages.* During each of these stages, instinctual sexual energy (libido) is focused on a particular body area, or *erogenous zone.* It is in this erogenous zone that the child seeks pleasure or satisfaction (the "sexual" part of the term *psycho-*

Figure 13–2.

The relationship of Freudian personality structures to levels of awareness. All of the id, most of the superego, and much of the ego operate at the unconscious level of awareness. Both the ego and the superego are partly conscious and thus are in contact with external reality. Preconscious material is now unconscious but can become conscious (e.g., knowledge that may be on the tip of the tongue). (From Liebert & Spiegler, 1982, p. 94.)

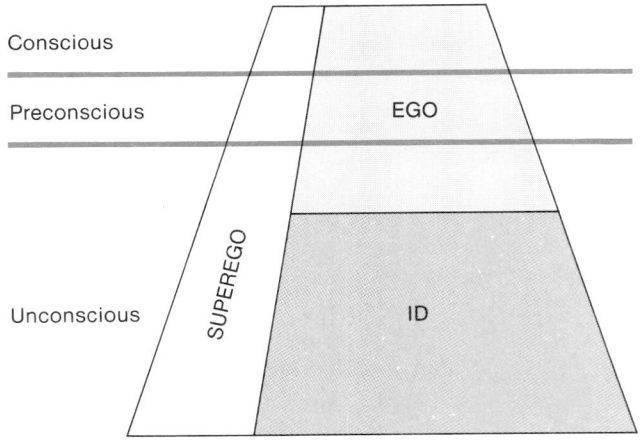

PERSONALITY THEORIES AND ASSESSMENT

336

Table 13–1.

Possible conflicts among the aspects of personality. (From Liebert & Spiegler, 1982, p. 102.)

Conflict	Example
Id versus ego	Choosing between a small immediate reward and a larger reward that requires some period of waiting (i.e., delay of gratification).
Id versus superego	Deciding whether to return the difference when you are overpaid or undercharged.
Ego versus superego	Choosing between acting in a realistic way (e.g., telling a white lie) and adhering to a potentially costly or unrealistic standard (e.g., always telling the truth).
Id and ego versus superego	Deciding whether to retaliate against the attack of a weak opponent or to turn the other cheek.
Id and superego versus ego	Deciding whether to act in a realistic way that conflicts with both your desires and your moral convictions (e.g., the decision faced by devout Roman Catholics as to the use of contraceptive devices).
Ego and superego versus id	Choosing whether to act on the impulse to steal something you want and cannot afford. The ego would presumably become increasingly involved in such a conflict as the probability of being apprehended increased.

sexual can be translated to mean "pleasurable"). As the child develops, the preferred area of pleasure changes. Regardless of the stage or erogenous zone, however, conflicts occur and have to be adequately dealt with. At each stage, the libido energizes behaviors associated with the particular erogenous zone. The unrestrained expression of these behaviors (eating, elimination, sex play) is unacceptable to others, which creates conflicts. Also, for normal development, the libido must be freed from one erogenous zone (through resolution of the conflict) so that it can energize a new zone in the next stage (Liebert & Spiegler, 1982).

Freud theorized that, to move from one stage to the next, children must receive neither too little nor too much gratification. If children are frustrated or over-indulged, they may be reluctant to move on to a new stage. The result is **fixation,** wherein some of the libido is permanently invested in a particular psychosexual stage (Liebert & Spiegler, 1982).

As Liebert and Spiegler (1982) point out, some of the libido is inevitably fixated at each psychosexual stage. However, if much of it is fixated at an early stage, adult personality may be dominated by the modes of obtaining satisfaction used in that stage—which is why Freud believed that adult personality is relatively set by about the age of 5. Psychosexual conflicts and their resolution during the first three Freudian stages are crucial in personality development. Let's now consider the stages.

Oral stage. During the first year of life, when the infant interacts with the world mainly through eating, the **oral stage** occurs. At this time, Freud believed, the sexual instinct seeks expression through oral stimulation. The infant finds oral pleasure in eating as well as in putting things in the mouth, sucking, and biting. If weaning is handled poorly, the infant may find it difficult to give up oral pleasures, and the libido will become fixated at this stage.

The oral stage is sometimes viewed as consisting of two phases. The first phase, *oral eroticism,* involves the pleasurable stimulation of the mouth through sucking or putting things in the mouth. An adult fixated at this stage is likely to be excessively concerned with oral activities—eating, drinking, smoking, kissing, and so on. The adult personality of an infant who was excessively gratified at this stage will be characterized by excessive optimism and dependence. The second oral phase, *oral sadism,* begins with the eruption of teeth, when for the first time the infant may view the mother with hatred as well as love. Fixation at this phase leads to excessive pessimism, hostility, and aggression. The adult is likely to be argumentative and sarcastic.

Anal stage. Usually, during the 2nd year of life, after weaning has taken place, the libido changes its focus from the oral to the anal region, creating the **anal stage.** Whereas conflict revolved around weaning in the oral stage, it centers on toilet-training in the anal stage. The conflict arises because of the demands that parents place on the child to develop self-control over defecation. For the child, these demands conflict with the pleasurable release of tension associated with elimination whenever and wherever it is desired.

An inability to meet the parents' increasing, and perhaps harsh, toilet-training demands may lead the child to cope with the frustration of toilet-training in one of two ways. One option is to retain the feces and refuse any demands to use the toilet. Such a strategy is thought to form the basis, through fixation, for an adult personality characterized by compulsiveness— the *anal-retentive personality*. Compulsive individuals are overly tidy and orderly; they are also thought to be stubborn and stingy.

Another option the child may use if toilet-training is not going well is to defecate when and where it is forbidden (by the parents) to do so. Fixation at this point forms the basis for an adult *anal-aggressive personality,* characterized by such hostile and sadistic behavior as cruelty, destructiveness, and temper tantrums.

Phallic stage. Between 3 and 5 years of age, the child's libido focuses on the genitals. During this **phallic stage,** pleasure presumably comes from masturbation, sex play, and other genital stimulation. At this stage, Freud believed, the child experiences an unconscious longing for affection and sexual contact with the parent of the opposite sex. At the same time comes the child's growing realization that the parents have a sexual relationship (Ryckman, 1982). This realization leads to the child's desire to eliminate the parent of the same sex, who in effect is a rival for the other parent's affections. The conflict at this stage lies in the fact that the impulse to possess one parent and eliminate the other is at odds with what is socially acceptable. Freud referred to this phenomenon as the **Oedipus complex,** a name borrowed from the Greek myth in which Oedipus unwittingly kills his father and commits incest with his mother.

Let's examine the development of the Oedipus conflict for boys and then for girls. Although the boy desires his mother and resents his father, he also fears that his father will harm his genitals. Freud referred to this unconscious fear as *castration anxiety*. To reduce his anxiety, the boy represses his sexual feelings toward his mother and identifies with and emulates his father. (Freud termed this phenomenon *identification with the aggressor*.) As a result, the child is able to possess his mother vicariously, take on his father's values, and form a superego in the process.

In contrast to the boy's situation, the girl discovers during the Oedipus period that males have penises, and she feels an undercurrent of disappointment that Freud termed *penis envy*. The desire to have a penis leads the girl to unconsciously desire her father, who does have a penis, and to resent her rival mother. Eventually, the girl identifies with her mother and thus vicariously possesses her father. The female Oedipus complex is sometimes called the *Electra complex*. (In Greek mythology, Electra persuaded her brother to murder their hated mother.) Again, identification with the parent of the same sex fosters the emergence of the superego, as the child internalizes parental and social standards.

Freud believed that adult attitudes toward the opposite sex hinge on the Oedipus complex. Poorly or insufficiently resolved Oedipus conflicts theoretically lead to lingering castration anxiety and penis envy in the adult. Adult men who are fixated in this stage respond to severe castration anxiety by behaving in a reckless and self-assured manner as they try to prove that they are real men (Ryckman, 1982). The penis is overvalued, and the men show excessive vanity and exhibitionism. The primary motive of women fixated in this stage is penis envy. Such women always strive for superiority over men—in Freudian theory.

Latency period. At around the age of 5, following the resolution of the Oedipus complex, the child enters a phase known as the **latency period.** Latency is not actually a psychosexual stage, since there is a repression of sexual impulses until puberty—again, according to Freud.

Genital stage. Sexual urges are renewed during adolescence, when the individual enters the **genital stage.** Again, the libido is focused on the genitals, but the individual's sexual instincts turn from self-gratification to the desire to mate with and display affection for someone of the opposite sex. During this stage (which lasts through adulthood), the individual is expected to become fully socialized—that is, to work, marry, and raise a family (Rotter & Hochreich, 1975). Presumably the ability to live a well-adjusted life is enhanced if one reaches the genital stage without serious fixations at earlier stages. According to Freud, those who do carry fixations into adulthood often become maladjusted.

— Neoanalytic Approaches

Freud's many followers developed theories that retain a number of his ideas while differing from his theory in important respects. Most of these *neoanalytic approaches* de-emphasize the biological and sexual determinants of behavior and pay more attention to the social environment. This emphasis is especially evident in the views of Erik Erikson and Alfred Adler.

SIGMUND FREUD (1856–1939)

Sigmund Freud was born in 1856 in the small town of Freiberg, Moravia (Czechoslovakia). He was one of eight children in a relatively poor Jewish family. When Freud was born, his father was 40 years old and his mother only 20. The father was rather strict, and Freud recalled, as an adult, having childhood hostility toward him. Freud's mother, on the other hand, was loving and protective. Freud felt a passionate sexual attraction to her, a situation that set the stage for his later ideas about the Oedipus complex.

Freud showed extremely high intelligence from an early age, and his parents fostered it in every way possible. Freud entered high school a year earlier than was usual and was at the head of his class most of the time. In addition to Hebrew and German, he mastered Latin, Greek, French, English, Italian, and Spanish. Freud eventually chose medicine as a career because he believed that it would enable him to do scientific research. However, a brief research career in neurology ended when a lack of funds forced him to abandon it for a clinical practice.

Freud's interest in what became psychoanalysis developed in 1884. With the publication of such widely circulated books as *Studies on Hysteria, The Interpretation of Dreams, The Psychopathology of Everyday Life,* and *A General Introduction to Psychoanalysis,* Freud made his mark as the father of psychoanalysis.

When the Nazis invaded Austria in 1938, Freud was forced to flee to England. He died there on September 23, 1939, of cancer of the mouth and jaw. (It is reported that he smoked 20 cigars a day.) Freud's impact on modern thinking has been so great that almost no aspect of the social sciences and humanities has been untouched by his theory (Deese, 1972; Fancher, 1979; Rychlak, 1981; Schultz, 1981a).

Erikson. The views of Erikson were discussed in chapter 11. Here, we wish to emphasize the relationship of Erikson's theory to Freud's. In contrast to Freud's *psychosexual stages,* Erikson (e.g., 1963, 1968) proposed a sequence of *psychosocial stages* that reach from infancy into adulthood. According to Erikson, at each of these stages, different relationships and different social events require us to adapt and resolve specific crises. How we deal with each crisis determines how well adjusted we will be as adults. (For example, recall from chapter 11 that the psychosocial crisis at the first stage of life is one of trust versus mistrust; how the crisis is resolved determines whether we later have a basic trust or mistrust in our dealings with others.) In stark contrast to Freud's emphasis on instinctual influences, Erikson clearly prefers to emphasize the social influences on people's lives. (Because this discussion of Erikson is brief, we urge you to return to chapter 11 for a review of his theory.)

Adler. Another psychoanalyst to depart from Freud's sexual emphasis was Adler (e.g., 1927, 1930). His approach, called *individual psychology,* emphasized that each of us begins life totally helpless and dependent. Adler saw life as a struggle against feelings of inferiority. We are motivated to strive for superiority, and our behavior can be seen as a reflection of this desire. In Adler's view, each of us has a *style of life,* our own particular way of seeking a sense of superiority. Some life-styles are adaptive and constructive; relationships with others are characterized by social interest, concern for others' welfare, and cooperation. Maladaptive or destructive life-styles, however, lead people to have little concern for others and to want to compete with and dominate others.

— Evaluation of Psychoanalytic Approach

There is no denying Freud's importance to psychology, psychiatry, and humanity in general. Within the helping professions, he has many followers (cf. Silverman, 1976; Silverman & Fishel, 1981). Freudian theory nevertheless has not gone unchallenged (cf. Schultz, 1981b). One criticism is that the theory is based on unverified data. Indeed, Freud made no attempt to verify the experiences reported to him by his patients. These experiences, of course, were used to construct and support his theory. Others' attempts to find empirical support for Freud's theory have met with only modest success. Part of the problem is that many of the major constructs of the theory are ambiguous or poorly defined. In order to empirically verify such constructs as the unconscious, the Oedipus complex, or the superego, it is necessary to know precisely what they mean.

Many of Freud's basic assumptions have also been questioned (Schultz, 1981b). Some theorists believe that Freud too strongly emphasized biological determinants of behavior—that there is much more to human motivation than sex and aggression. Others believe that Freud concentrated too much on the disturbed people, ignoring well-adjusted and mature individuals. We will see that such criticisms have formed the foundation for alternate conceptualizations of human personality.

Trait Approach

The view of personality in terms of how people differ is known as the **trait approach.** A *trait* is any distinct, consistent personal quality (see chapter 12). The psychologist's task is to discover which traits differentiate people and to learn the origins of the traits and how they relate to each other and to behavior. Traits can be thought of as continuous. Thus, individuals can be classified in terms of the relative amount of a given characteristic they display, such as dependency or honesty (Mischel, 1981).

The trait approach assumes that people differ in their reactions to identical stimulus events. If criticized by an employer, for example, some people will consistently respond with anger, some with guilt, some with acceptance, and so on (see Figure 13–3). The essence of traits, then, is consistent differences in personal behavior or characteristics. Traits are said to direct action and motivate people to behave as they do. Trait theorists believe that by knowing a person's traits, they can predict the person's behavior in a variety of situations.

Several major trait theories have been proposed. Among them are those of Raymond Cattell and Hans Eysenck.

— Cattell

Surface traits and source traits are what Cattell (1950, 1965) distinguishes between. *Surface traits* consist of visible response patterns, including such dimensions as assertive-indecisive and talkative-silent. They reflect overt manifestations of various underlying source traits. *Source traits,* then, are the more basic variables that underlie surface behavior. In Cattell's scheme, they include such dimensions as dominant-submissive, radical-conservative, self-sufficient–group-dependent, relaxed-tense, emotionally stable–emotionally unstable, and reserved-outgoing. To identify source traits, Cattell used the mathematical technique of *factor analysis,* which (in simplistic terms) examines groups of

Figure 13–3.
According to the trait approach, different people respond in different ways to the same stimulus (such as criticism from an employer). (Adapted from Mischel, 1981, p. 19.)

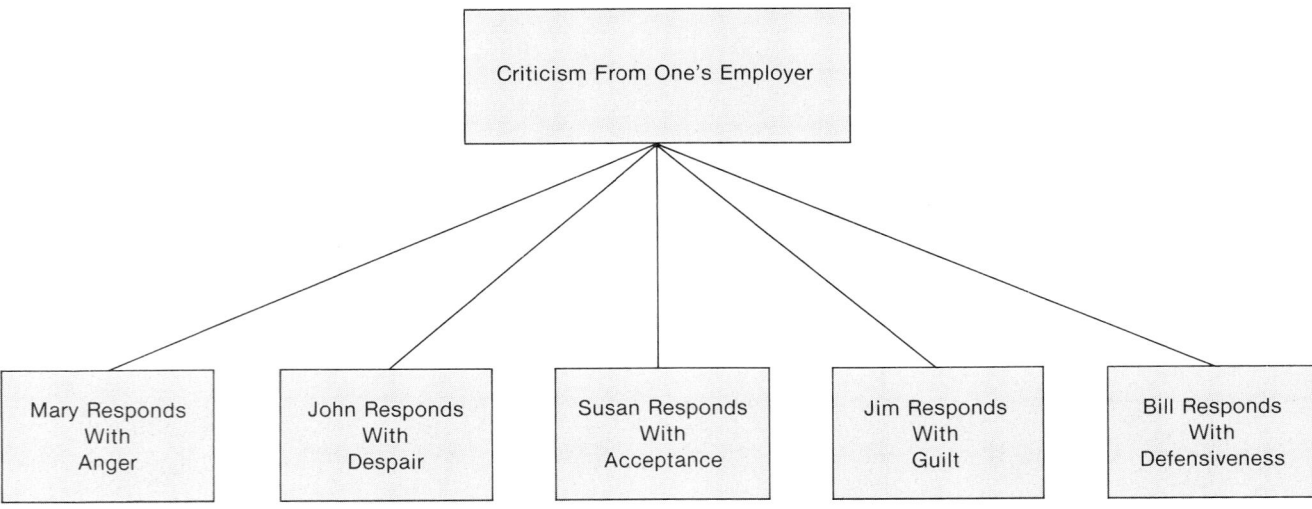

correlations to determine when a set of behaviors is so interrelated that the behaviors must reflect a single underlying factor. In Cattell's work, source traits represent such factors. Later in the chapter, we will examine Cattell's measure of personality, the 16 Personality Factor Inventory (16 PF), which provides rankings on 16 source traits. For Cattell, these traits represent personality in its entirety.

— Eysenck

Perhaps the most influential trait theorist of all is Eysenck (e.g., 1965, 1970, 1975). His approach, like Cattell's, uses factor analysis first to identify traits, or factors, that reflect a number of interrelated responses and then to identify even more basic traits or factors. Eysenck calls these basic dimensions *types,* because they encompass a group of lesser traits. For example, Eysenck has found that the traits of sociability, impulsiveness, activity, liveliness, and excitability can be grouped together as the *extroverted personality type.* Each of these traits encompasses a particular set of behaviors. Eysenck's scheme, then, begins with specific responses and builds more inclusive categories until reaching the concept of type.

Eysenck (1970) has proposed that the two major dimensions of personality are introversion-extroversion and stability-instability. The *introversion-extroversion dimension* describes people as varying in the extent to which they are quiet, reserved, and introspective **(introversion)** versus sociable, outgoing, and impulsive **(extroversion).** The *stability-instability dimension* describes people as varying in the extent to which they are stable, calm, carefree, even-tempered, and reliable **(stability)** versus moody, touchy, anxious, and restless **(instability).**

Figure 13–4 illustrates Eysenck's (1975) conception of individual personality as lying within one of four quadrants created by the two dimensions just described. Although Eysenck (1975) has noted that extremes are rare, he considers psychological disorders (see chapter 15) and criminality the result of extremes on the two dimensions. Specifically, he believes that people who evidence both high emotionality (instability) and high introversion tend to exhibit such psychological problems as severe anxiety. High emotionality combined with high extroversion tends to encourage criminality.

Eysenck contends that introverts behave differently from extroverts because they are characterized by higher levels of physiological arousal than are extro-

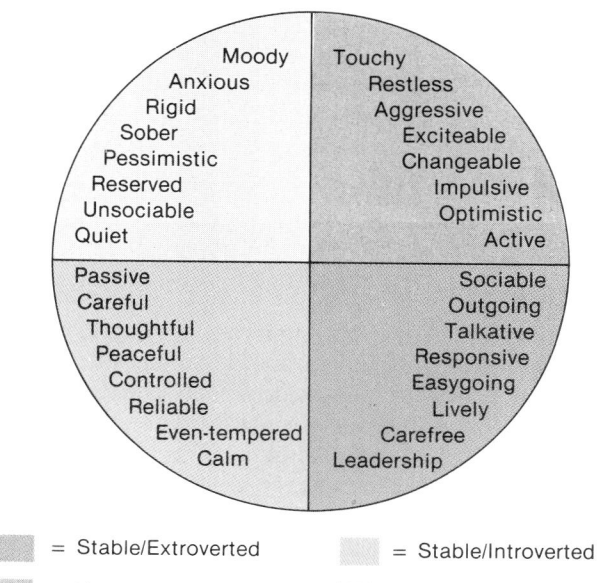

= Stable/Extroverted   = Stable/Introverted

= Unstable/Extroverted   = Unstable/Introverted

Figure 13–4.
The two major dimensions of personality suggested by Eysenck. An individual personality can fall into any one of the four quadrants and will be characterized by the traits shown within each quadrant. (From Eysenck & Rachman, 1965, p. 16.)

verts. When stimulated, introverts respond more strongly (physiologically) than extroverts because of their higher level of arousal. Furthermore, extroverts require a higher level of stimulation than introverts in order to maintain the same level of arousal (cf. Geen, 1976). In a somewhat paradoxical fashion, then, we have the following situation:

> Introverts, being more sensitive to stimulation than extroverts, must keep their level of the stimulation controlled so that they are not overwhelmed and placed under stress by it. Thus they avoid excessive social stimulation, seek out quiet places, and maintain a reserved attitude. The extrovert, being less sensitive, requires fairly high levels of stimulation in order to maintain a normal level of activation. The extrovert therefore makes friends, goes to parties, and avoids prolonged isolation. (Geen, 1976, p. 260)

In accord with the preceding, one recent study (Campbell & Hawley, 1982) found that extroverts prefer library study locations that provide relatively high noise levels and stimulating opportunities to socialize. Introverts, on the other hand, prefer to study where the number of people and the amount of external stimulation are minimized. Analogously, elderly nursing-home residents classified as extroverts have been found to participate in programs characterized as high-activity, interpersonal events. Elderly introverts, on the other hand, are more often involved in low-activity, noninterpersonal events (Quattrochi-Tubin & Jason, 1983).

— Evaluation of Trait Approach

As we have seen, the trait approach assumes that traits influence behaviors across a wide variety of settings. Critics point out that people are not always consistent—not always anxious, not always aggressive, not always sociable, and so on. Trait theorists generally have not viewed such inconsistency as detracting from the usefulness of the trait approach. In other words, they have interpreted behavior as being generally consistent despite some inconsistencies.

Behavioral theorists have long argued that there is too much inconsistency in behavior to warrant a trait approach (e.g., Mischel, 1968). A child may be aggressive at school, for example, but not at home. A husband may be dependent on his wife but not on his co-workers. A student may be outgoing in one class but not in another. In other words, behavior is highly dependent on the situation one is in. In predicting behavior, the behavioral theorists consider the specific circumstances one is in; the trait theorists consider one's trait. If the trait does not in fact influence behavior across all situations, critics want trait theorists to tell us exactly when the traits will be influential and when they will not. We will examine this issue again in our discussion of behavioral theories.

Despite the limitations of the trait approach, it is to the credit of trait psychologists that they have uncovered many important predictors of behavior. It is indeed accurate to say that in spite of the criticisms, trait theory is alive and well today in modern personality theorizing and research (Byrne & Kelley, 1981).

Humanistic Approach

Contrasting sharply with the psychoanalytic and behavioristic approaches is the **humanistic approach** to personality. It views both of the other approaches as limited and demeaning (Schultz, 1981b). Schultz (1981b) suggests that, in contrast to psychoanalytic theorists, humanistic psychologists believe that we must study human strengths and virtues, learning what people are like at their best, not at their worst. Humanistic psychologists also see behaviorism as being too narrow and sterile in its objective focus on overt behavior. To the humanists, people are more than conditioned, robotlike organisms who react mechanically to stimuli.

The humanistic approach, represented by such theorists as Carl Rogers and Abraham Maslow, emphasizes human virtues and aspirations, conscious experience, free will, and the fulfillment of personal potential (Schultz, 1981b). Humanistic theories assume that humans are born with a capacity for psychological growth that is the basis for all behavior. They see the individual as basically good and naturally interested in seeking positive goals.

— Rogers

The basic assumption of Rogers's *self theory* (e.g., 1951, 1959) is that all humans are innately motivated to achieve *self-actualization,* the tendency to become everything that they can become (see chapter 9). For Rogers, personality (and thus behavior) is the individual's attempts to achieve self-actualization within the world as that person views it. To understand someone's behavior, we must view the world from that person's point of view.

According to Rogers, all people develop a **self-concept**—an image of who they are, should be, and might like to be. Rogers believes that infants differentiate between the environment and the self early on; that is, they distinguish between "I" or "me" experiences and "not me" experiences. A self-concept emerges from such experiences and influences further perceptions and behavior. The basis of the influence is a tendency to maintain organization and consistency in one's self-concept.

In Rogers's view, self-concept is formed by evaluating experiences positively or negatively. One way to evaluate an experience is by how it *feels*—its direct *organismic feeling.* If, as a child, you once hit another child, you may have evaluated the experience positively if it felt good. But another source of evaluation is what others say about the experience. Perhaps your parents told you that you were a bad child because you hit the other child. If so, you may have given the action a positive organismic evaluation while negatively evaluating it in terms of your parents' reaction.

Suppose that, as a child, you treated your baby brother kindly, you felt good about it (an organismic evaluation), and your parents approved of your behavior. The result was probably a positively evaluated self-experience, such as "I like my brother." In Rogers's terms, your organismic experience was *congruent* (consistent) with your self-experience. This circumstance allowed you to accurately perceive your own behavior and its evaluation.

Problems arise when there is an *incongruity* between one's true organismic experience and the associated self-experience. Such problems occur because individuals tend to seek *positive regard* from others (i.e., to be evaluated positively by them). However, there are often *conditions of worth* attached to positive regard. In other words, individuals learn to act in prescribed ways to win approval. But in doing so, they begin to apply conditions of worth to themselves, so that some experiences are distorted, excluded, or rejected—even if they are organismically valid. To reduce incongruity, individuals may misperceive reality so that it fits the self-concept. Each time this occurs, however, the self-concept becomes less accurate, which leads to further distortions. Eventually, incongruity may lead to psychological maladjustment.

Rogers's approach to the treatment and prevention of maladaptive behavior is to establish an atmosphere of *unconditional positive regard* (see chapter 16). In such an atmosphere, no conditions of worth are applied. The person and the person's experiences are accepted as unconditionally valid. The resulting sense of safety allows the person to gradually accept denied and distorted experiences and rebuild an accurate and fully functioning self-image—while the person strives for self-actualization. As might be predicted, Rogers considers positive and unconditional regard from parents and others to be especially important early in life.

Maslow

Like Rogers, Maslow (1970) believed that people are basically good, in the sense that all people have an inherent tendency toward self-actualization (see chapter 9). Maladjustment occurs when this basic human impulse is interfered with. In other words, our striving toward optimal adjustment and complete psychological development and growth is impeded when we are unable to achieve all that we are capable of achieving.

Maslow (e.g., 1971) is well known for his study of individuals he believed to have achieved self-actualization. His research suggests that self-actualizing people have a number of distinguishing characteristics, including the following (Maslow, 1971). They take pride in bringing an end to injustices. They work for, reward, and encourage all that is good and virtuous. They do

not seek out honor, fame, or glory. They are attracted to situations that present a challenge. They are able to look objectively at the facts of a situation, freeing themselves from illusions. They believe that everyone should have the chance to achieve the fullest potential. They enjoy knowing and having contact with admirable people. They accept and welcome responsibility. They enjoy and practice efficiency in what they do.

Maslow studied historical figures as well as his contemporaries. Examples of some people he considered to be self-actualized are Abraham Lincoln, Thomas Jefferson, Albert Einstein, and Eleanor Roosevelt. Not everyone, of course, is a Lincoln or an Einstein. In fact, Maslow believed that few of us achieve full self-actualization. His research led him to conclude that less than 1 percent of the general population can be considered self-actualized. This conclusion, however, does not detract from the important point that each of us has the potential to become self-actualized and that, presumably, we are constantly working toward that goal.

Evaluation of Humanistic Approach

The humanistic position has been criticized on a number of grounds (Liebert & Spiegler, 1982). One criticism is that the approach limits itself to the person's present, conscious, subjective experiences. Doing so excludes any influences beyond the person's immediate awareness and makes past experiences on which the person is not presently concentrating seem unimportant. Another criticism is that humanists offer a narrow and simplistic view of personality. With their emphasis on such key concepts as self-actualization, humanists tend to dismiss many other psychological processes. Perhaps the most important criticism of the humanistic approaches is that they describe rather than explain personality and behavior. To say that a person behaves a certain way because of a self-actualizing tendency does not really explain the behavior unless one also accounts for the existence of the self-actualizing tendency.

On a more positive note, let us reiterate that the humanists offer an optimistic and positive view of human nature that may be badly needed. Maslow in particular demonstrated a primary concern with psychologically well-adjusted and mature individuals. The need for such an approach is underscored by the enormous influence Maslow has had on the field of psychology despite his theory's relative lack of detailed development and the lack of empirical research (Smith & Vetter, 1982).

Cognitive Approach

As we know, cognitions are thoughts and ideas that we have about the world around us. The **cognitive approach** to personality is concerned with how thoughts and beliefs affect people's behavior. How we respond is determined by our perspectives and our unique interpretations of various situations. Other personality theories also emphasize cognition, but the cognitive approach, represented by George Kelly, focuses exclusively on conscious mental activities (Schultz, 1981b).

— Kelly

Kelly's (1955) theory focuses solely on the ways in which we process information to predict and control events in our lives. In Kelly's view, we continually form hypotheses about the world, test them, and revise them if they do not work. In doing so, we create what Kelly called **personal constructs** to predict events. It is these constructs, or expectations, that guide behavior. Thus, Kelly defined *personality* as an individual's set of personal constructs that define reality for that person. One construct might be that making connections is essential for success in business. We would expect the person with that construct to behave in such a way as to meet other businesspersons. If the person believes that such behavior is, in fact, contributing to success, this particular construct is *validated* for the person.

In Kelly's thinking, the focus of the personality psychologist should be viewing and understanding the world from the subject's perspective. Such an approach necessitates our knowing precisely what a given individual's personal constructs are. Kelly devised a test, called the Role Construct Repertory (REP) Test, for measuring personal constructs. With this test, it is possible to detect some of the individual's specific world views. It may become evident, for example, that the person tends to distinguish between people in terms of their kindness or hostility. This particular dimension (kindness-hostility) may be an important construct for the individual.

According to Kelly, difficulties ensue when one's construct system is inflexible or especially overly narrow and restrictive. For instance, an individual may interpret and anticipate events through only a few broadly applied constructs. With such limited ways of construing the world, the person may often show inappropriate or maladaptive behavior. Consider this construct: People are cold and uncaring, and it is best not to get too close to others. A person holding such a construct would likely behave toward others in a superficial, distant manner. Such behavior, in turn, would likely elicit similar reactions from others. The construct itself would be validated, in that others would behave as expected. But in the final analysis, the individual's constructs and behavior would be considered generally inappropriate and ineffective.

Fortunately, we need not be locked into our personal constructs. Kelly believes that individuals can develop new constructs, replace old ones, and in general, find more appropriate ways of interpreting the world. A reorganized and less narrow construct system allows the individual to behave in flexible and adaptive ways. Kelly's therapeutic approach in this vein is called *constructive alternativism*. It involves getting the individual to experiment with new and altered construct systems. The person develops a revised set of constructs, tries them out, and then evaluates them.

— Evaluation of Cognitive Approach

Smith and Vetter (1982) have pointed out several problems as well as virtues with Kelly's theory. One problem is that it deals exclusively with cognitive determinants of behavior and essentially ignores emotional or irrational influences. Another is that Kelly was not clear about the development or precise functioning of constructs. We don't have explicit statements, for example, about how constructs are learned or how and why they vary over time or from one person to another. Given a number of constructs, we don't know how to predict which will govern behavior in a particular situation. If you think of a person as both inconsiderate and interesting, which construct is relevant in guiding your interactions with that person?

To his credit, Kelly has provided us with an innovative and potentially useful alternative to the traditional personality theories, which typically focus on motivational variables such as unconscious motivation or self-actualization. The theory itself has never had a large-scale impact. However, Kelly's emphasis on cognitive processes has perhaps helped encourage later theorists to take cognitive factors into account.

Behavioral Approach

As the name implies, the **behavioral approach** to personality focuses on behavior and on the environmental conditions that influence it. For the behavioral theorist, personality is not a hypothetical internal structure, such as a set of traits. Rather, it is the sum total of the individual's behavior, which is determined primarily by social learning. One person, for example, may have learned to deal with anger by behaving aggressively. Another may have a history of reinforcement for constructive patterns of behavior in the face of anger. Consistencies in behavior can be interpreted, therefore, as cases of generalized learning.

The behavioral approach deals with personal inconsistencies by suggesting that behavior changes to fit the circumstances, an idea termed **behavioral specificity** (see Figure 13–5). In fact, the general view of the behavioral psychologist is that when consistency does occur, it is usually within a given situation. For example, a child may be consistently aggressive at school (where aggression may be rewarded) but not at home (where aggression may not be rewarded). The situation clearly controls the behavior. Or, stated another way, the behavior is said to be situation-specific. This view of personality stands in contrast to the assumption of cross-situational consistency made by the other approaches we have examined, particularly the psychoanalytic and trait approaches.

Two new trends within the behavioral approach have occurred in recent years (Liebert & Spiegler, 1982). One is that some theorists now take a **cognitive-behavioral approach,** emphasizing the study of covert as well as overt behaviors. *Covert behaviors,* such as thoughts and mental images, are internal, private events that are not directly observable. *Overt behaviors* are external and observable. Cognitive-behavioral theories examine the relationship between covert and overt behaviors. A second trend is the growing recognition that person variables, or individual differences, must be examined along with external circumstances for behavior to be fully understood.

In sum, then, all behavioral psychologists are interested in measurable behavior and in the importance of environmental influences on behavior. They also place high value on using experimental research and scientific methods to test hypotheses. Behavioral theories differ mainly in the learning processes they emphasize, the degree to which cognition, or thinking, plays a role in learning, and the emphasis they put on person var-

Figure 13–5.

According to the behavioral approach, behavior changes as the situation changes. Criticism may elicit a variety of responses from the same person, depending on who it comes from. (Adapted from Mischel, 1981, p. 91.)

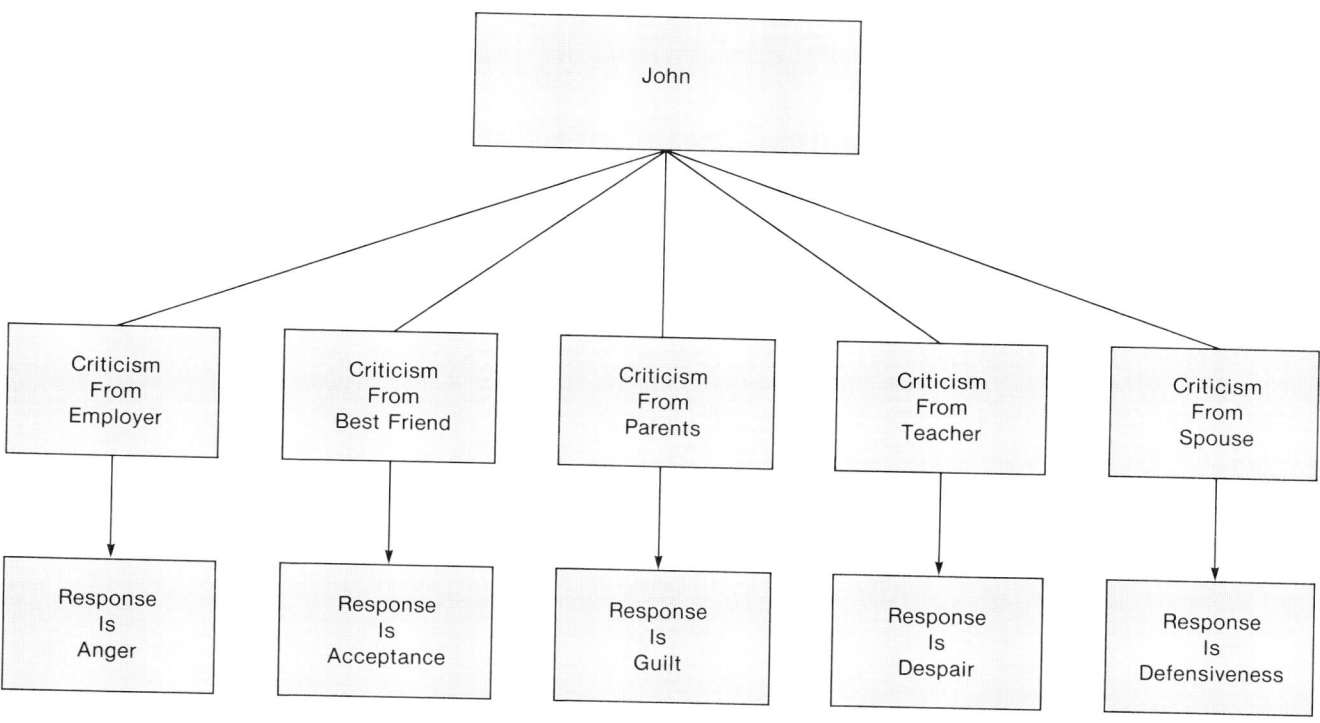

iables. We will now examine several individual approaches, including the behavioral theories of B. F. Skinner, Albert Bandura, Julian Rotter, and Walter Mischel.

— Skinner

The operant-conditioning principles (reinforcement, punishment, etc.) of Skinner were discussed in chapter 6, so we will concentrate here on the relevance of operant conditioning to personality. Rather than invoking unobservable constructs, such as ego or trait, to explain behavior, Skinner urges us to observe how behavior relates to its consequences and then to describe these relationships. This approach, termed a **functional analysis of behavior,** analyzes the cause-effect, or functional, relationships between behavior and the environment. Behavior, then, is a function of reinforcement, shaping, extinction, punishment, and so on.

Skinner's view of personality contrasts sharply with that of the trait theorists. Trait theorists assume that people have within themselves the causes of behavior. Some people are aggressive, for example, because they have the trait of hostility. Skinner would argue instead that such people have simply been previously rewarded for displaying aggressive behavior. Thus, operant conditioning (rather than an internal trait) causes their aggressiveness. In general, Skinner challenges the idea that behavior is caused by internal factors, such as unconscious impulses, traits, self-actualizing tendencies, or cognitions. To understand behavior or personality, Skinner examines external influences, particularly the consequences of behavior, and rejects covert mental events, viewing them as scientifically irrelevant.

— Bandura

Skinner pays too little attention to cognitive, or symbolic, processes, according to Bandura (e.g., 1977b). Bandura (1977b) suggests, for example, that people are not "much affected by response consequences if they are unaware of what is being reinforced. Sudden increases in appropriate behavior upon discovery of the reinforcement contingency is indicative of the acquisition of insight" (p. 165). Furthermore, what one *believes* the consequences to be is more important than what they actually are. In Bandura's (1977b) words, "The widely accepted dictum that behavior is governed by its consequences fares better for anticipated than for actual consequences" (p. 166). Our be-

havior, then, is thought to be regulated and maintained by rules called **expectancies**—anticipations about the consequences of various actions. Typically, what we believe to be the consequences and the actual consequences are the same. But there can be a discrepancy, since as Bandura notes, anticipated consequences are based in part on what we observe happen to others, what we are told, and so on.

It is clear, then, that Bandura places a heavy emphasis on cognitive processes. With this in mind, let's examine two important concepts in Bandura's theory—an approach he calls *social learning theory,* because behavior or personality is learned in a social context.

Observational learning. Bandura is best known for the concept of *observational learning*. As indicated in chapter 6, Bandura has shown that people can learn without obvious reward and even without practice. All that is necessary for learning to occur is observation of a model's behavior. Since no direct reinforcement is involved in observational learning, cognitive processes are considered paramount. The model's behavior is attended to and then encoded in memory in some symbolic form (perhaps a verbal representation or a visual image of the model's behavior). The knowledge is thus stored and available to later retrieve and guide behavior. As Bavelas (1978) observes, these are all cognitive operations. Learning, in Bandura's view, requires "someone who thinks" (Bavelas, 1978).

Whether the model's behavior is in fact later imitated depends in part on the observer's ability to perform the behavior and on the anticipated consequences, which as we already suggested, can be partly inferred from the observed consequences to the model. If the model is rewarded, imitation is more likely than if the model is not rewarded or is punished. In other words, we don't just mimic others' behavior in some sort of reflexive, nonthinking manner. We evaluate the model's behavior and its outcomes. If we value those outcomes and find them self-satisfying, we are much more likely to perform the modeled behavior ourselves than if we do not value the outcomes. The observer also evaluates the characteristics of the model. A high-status model, for example, is more likely to be imitated than a low-status model.

For Bandura, then, personality develops not only through operant conditioning but also through observational learning. The observation of models is thought to influence such important behaviors as the capacity for delaying gratification (see chapter 14), maladaptive behaviors such as anxiety and fears (chapter 15), gender roles (chapter 17), and aggression and prosocial behavior (chapter 18).

Self-regulation. Bandura (1977b) also emphasizes **self-regulation**—our ability to exercise influence over our own behavior. One important aspect of this is the process of **self-reinforcement**, whereby we reinforce ourselves for attaining personal goals or standards. Behavior, then, is not governed solely through external reinforcers. We first establish what we believe to be acceptable standards for expecting reinforcement. Upon behaving in a particular manner, we reward or punish ourselves depending on whether we have or have not met those standards. The reward may be something tangible or it may simply be self-praise. The punishment may be in the form of self-criticism. The importance of self-reinforcement in regulating and maintaining behavior is especially evident when you consider behaviors, such as writing a textbook, that must be sustained despite little external reinforcement (until the book is completed).

According to Bandura, we are in a continuous process of setting internal standards for our behavior and then evaluating our performance against those standards. Our standards may be learned from observing others' behavior and they may be based on our own past experiences and accomplishments. The standards, of course, can change. If we repeatedly fail to meet our goals, we may be frustrated and find it necessary to lower them. Alternatively, we may also find it more challenging and personally satisfying to raise our standards. But whatever the standards are, how well we meet them can greatly affect our expectations for meeting them in the future. We may be convinced that a certain behavior will lead to certain outcomes but we may have little confidence in being able to perform that behavior. Meeting one's standards builds confidence and fosters what Bandura (1977b) calls an efficacy expectation—"the conviction that one can successfully execute the behavior required to produce the outcomes" (p. 79). In other words, **self-efficacy** is the perceived ability to cope with specific situations (Bandura, 1977a, 1982).

Having realistic standards seems necessary, then, in fostering a sense of self-worth and the belief that one can deal effectively with life's situations. High self-efficacy motivates us to intensify our efforts and to persevere in working toward desired goals (Bandura & Cervone, 1983). Repeatedly not meeting unrealistically high standards, however, may lead to discouragement and abandonment of one's efforts to achieve a goal.

We have seen that for Bandura, personality or behavior is a function of both the external environment and cognitive processes. In his thinking, people are influenced by their environment, but they also influence it by choosing how to behave. Bandura calls this interaction **reciprocal determinism**. He believes that people actively seek outcomes that will maximize their rewards, both external and internal (e.g., self-praise). As Pervin (1980) describes it, in reciprocal determinism, people first place a value on certain outcomes and then identify the situations that might produce them. They next judge their own ability to perform effectively in those situations and decide which situations to enter and how to behave in them. Finally, they use feedback information to judge their decisions and to form further discriminations, expectations, and decisions.

— Rotter and Mischel

Rotter (1954; Rotter, Chance, & Phares, 1972) is another social-learning theorist who emphasizes cognition. In his theory, the probability that a behavior will occur is a function of the individual's expectancies regarding outcomes of making a response and the subjective values placed on those outcomes. Consider as an example the question of whether a student is likely to study hard for an exam. In Rotter's terms, the answer is yes if the student expects studying to lead to good grades, approval, and recognition and if such outcomes are valued. Both expectancies and subjective values are presumably learned.

In addition to believing that expectancies pertain to specific situations, Rotter also suggests that **generalized expectancies** exist. Such expectancies are applied broadly and are, in a sense, like learned traits.

One example of a generalized expectancy is known as the **locus of control** (Rotter, 1966). It refers to whether an individual believes in *internal control* (that reinforcements are due to one's own efforts) or *external control* (that reinforcements are due to luck, chance, fate, or powerful others). Such generalized expectancies predict behavior mainly in new or ambiguous situations (Phares, 1978). Nevertheless, they can predict a wide range of behaviors. We will look at the locus-of-control dimension in more detail in the upcoming application section.

In Rotter's theory, both the situation and the person are relevant in predicting behavior. This view is also exemplified in Mischel's (1973, 1981) *cognitive social-learning theory*. In addition to acknowledging that behavior can be influenced by situations, the theory states a number of ways in which differences in people affect behavior. It is recognized that situations evoke, maintain, and modify behavior only through the information they provide. The "person" is the mediating variable between these situations and the ultimate responses. Because of our unique learning histories, we may have differing ways of perceiving, organizing, and interpreting the specific events around us. That is, we differ in how we process the information available to us. The impact of a situation, then, hinges greatly on cognitive variables. Mischel focuses on how person (cognitive) variables help us understand an individual's construction or interpretation of a situation. These person variables are only "studied in relation to the specific conditions that evoke, maintain, and modify them" (Mischel, 1973, p. 265). Mischel does not view these person variables as global traits that allow us to predict a person's behavior across a wide range of situations. What these variables do illustrate is that the influence of situations on behavior cannot be analyzed without also examining how people evaluate and interpret those situations. The situations themselves are an important component of the analysis since different situations elicit differing cognitions (for example, expectancies). Let's now examine the five person variables proposed by Mischel (1973):

1. *Competencies.* People vary in their abilities to generate particular cognitions and behaviors. They differ in what they know and what they can do. Some may have high intelligence, good problem-solving skills, and so on; others may not.
2. *Encoding strategies and personal constructs.* People differ in how they categorize a particular situation — the meaning or label they apply to it. They differ in how they construe themselves and others.
3. *Behavior-outcome and stimulus-outcome expectancies.* People have different expectations about the effects of various behaviors and stimuli.
4. *Subjective values of outcomes.* People place different values on outcomes.
5. *Self-regulatory systems and plans.* People differ in their standards for self-reward and self-punishment, and in their self-instructions and plans for carrying out complex sequences of behavior.

— Interactionism

Should we study individual differences or situational influences to best understand behavior? On the one hand, we have approaches that emphasize individual differences in internal characteristics and the importance of the person, such as the psychoanalytic and trait views. On the other hand, we have approaches that emphasize external or situational factors, such as Skinner's behavioral view. Which are better—person or situation approaches? Recent theorizing suggests that this question is no longer useful. Many personality psychologists now advocate **interactionism,** the study of both individual differences and situation variables and of how they interact. This approach is reflected in the views of Rotter and Mischel. Interactionism will probably be the guiding framework for most personality work in the years to come, as is already evidenced by a number of discussions of the issue (e.g., Magnusson & Endler, 1977; Pervin & Lewis, 1978). The field of personality psychology is adopting an increasingly interactionist approach (Sarason, Smith, & Diener, 1975).

— Evaluation of Behavioral Approach

Behavioral approaches have been criticized for many reasons. Some critics contend that they put undue emphasis on learning, unfairly excluding hereditary influences and biological differences. Others argue that they give too little attention to such psychological dispositions as traits and to people's subjective views of the environment (Liebert & Spiegler, 1982). It is exactly this kind of criticism that has led cognitive-behavioral theorists, such as Bandura and Mischel, to examine how environmental influences interact with cognition and individual differences. Such an approach may offer one of the broadest and most comprehensive views of personality. Although the cognitive-behavioral theorists have met one major criticism, the radical behaviorists, such as Skinner (1974), consider thoughts to be the effects of our various experiences, not the causes of behavior.

LOCUS OF CONTROL—PERSONALITY IN ACTION

In discussing Rotter's theory, we referred to the concept of locus of control. This personality dimension can be viewed as a continuum with varying degrees of internality or externality. However, we will speak simply of internals and externals, since scores on the *Locus of Control Scale* (the I-E Scale) are often grouped by the highest (the externals) and the lowest (the internals). The 29 items on the I-E Scale require subjects to choose between two statements similar to the following:

People have little control over the bad things that happen in life.
People can overcome any obstacle in life if they try.

One's locus of control affects many aspects of one's behavior. For example, evidence suggests that internals try to control outcomes and events more actively than do externals (cf. Phares, 1976, 1978). This is because internals believe that they can influence events. Internal husbands, for example, are more assertive than ex-

ternal husbands in trying to achieve favorable outcomes in marital conflicts (Doherty & Ryder, 1979).

Internal employees tend to be more motivated than external employees as long as they believe that their efforts on the job will be followed by rewards (Spector, 1982). Internal students show greater academic achievement than do external students (Findley & Cooper, 1983). Other findings suggest that internals seek and use information to control their environment more actively than do externals. For example, Seeman (1963) found that internal prisoners knew more than external prisoners about such things as parole regulations. Another study of inmates found that internals were better than externals at obtaining time away from the institution and improvements in living conditions (Wright, Holman, Steele, & Silverstein, 1980).

A significant finding concerning locus of control is that internals are more active than externals in guarding their health through dental hygiene, vaccinations, physical-fitness activities, and the use of auto seatbelts (Strickland, 1977) (see Figure 13–6). Because they en-

Figure 13–6.

Internals are more likely than externals to engage in these types of practices.

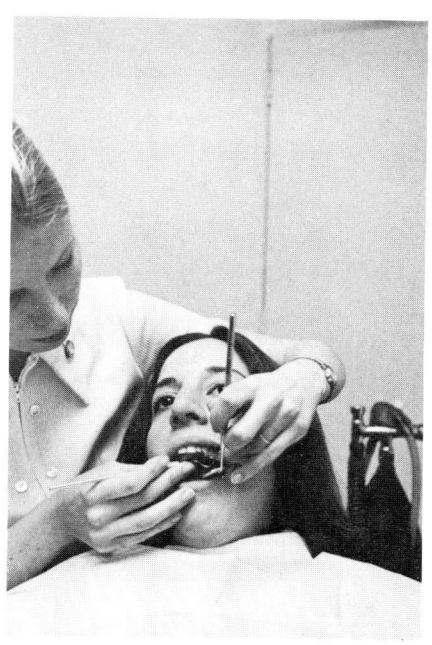
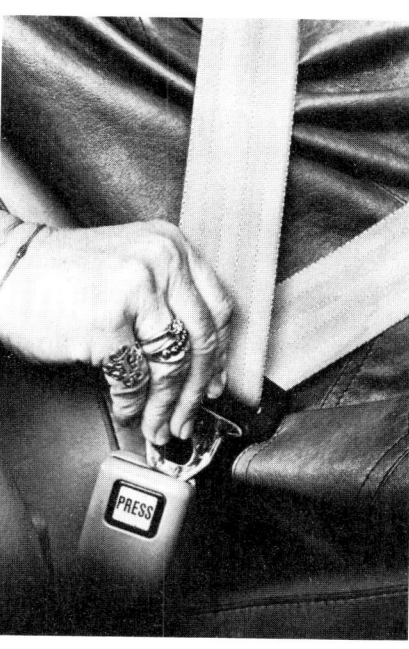

gage in more precautionary health practices, internals experience less physical illness than do externals (Strickland, 1977); and when internals do become ill, they follow the prescribed treatment more fully. Thus, an internal locus of control contributes to better coping with illness than does an external locus. As several researchers recently put it, "Persons who believe that their own behavior affects their health . . . have more positive attitudes toward self-treatment and active involvement in their own care" (Wallston et al., 1983, p. 381).

Lau (1982) found that belief in self-control over health is related to early health habits involving self-care and medical professionals. Practicing a variety of health habits as a child seems to foster the belief in adulthood that it actually does help to take care of oneself and to see a doctor. Parents might be well advised, for this reason alone, to make sure that their children practice good health habits (Lau, 1982). These habits include regular medical checkups and vaccinations as well as brushing teeth, getting exercise, sleeping enough, and eating well. Such habits contribute greatly to later health-promoting beliefs.

— PERSONALITY ASSESSMENT —

Personality theories have little merit unless they spell out how personality can be measured or assessed. Assessment procedures depend on the theory or general approach from which they derive.

Psychoanalytic Approach

As we have seen, the psychoanalytic position is that much of the structure and functioning of an individual's personality are at an unconscious level. How does one get at this hidden material? Since people are presumably unaware of the unconscious influences on their behavior, it is necessary to find methods of indirectly measuring these aspects of personality. In therapeutic settings, psychoanalytically oriented therapists have traditionally relied on dream interpretation as one of the most powerful means for assessing unconscious events. (This aspect of Freud's approach was discussed in chapter 5.) More formal assessment devices, known as **projective techniques,** have also been developed to probe unconscious impulses and attitudes.

— Projective Techniques

The *projective hypothesis* is the basis for projective techniques. The hypothesis states that "the person's response to an ambiguous or vague stimulus is a reflection (i.e., projection) of his or her own needs and feelings" (Feshbach & Weiner, 1982, p. 300). Projective techniques, then, are highly unstructured and give the subject considerable freedom of response. A variety of projective techniques exist. Let's look at two specific examples.

The Rorschach. Developed by a Swiss psychiatrist, Hermann Rorschach, the Rorschach Inkblot technique (or simply the Rorschach) consists of a set of 10 inkblots similar to the inkblot shown in Figure 13–7.

Figure 13–7.
Inkblot similar to inkblots used by Rorschach.

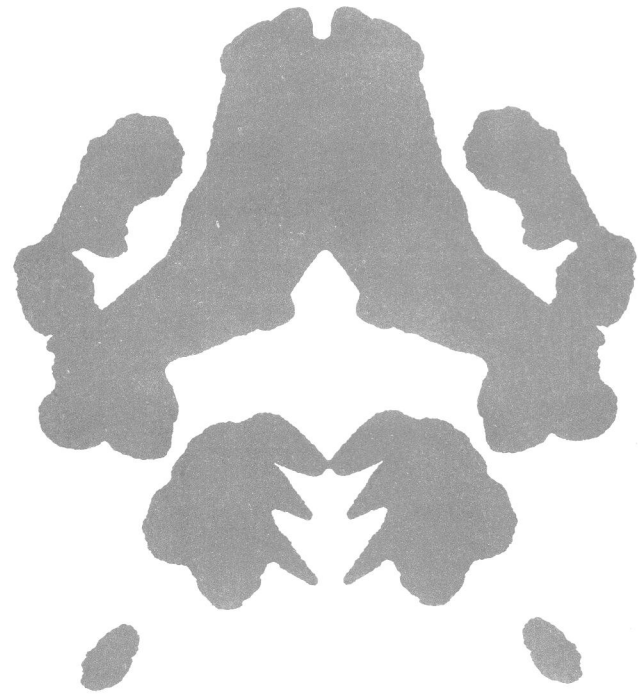

Table 13–2.

Sample responses on the Rorschach and possible interpretations of them. (Adapted from Liebert & Spiegler, 1982, p. 132.)

RESPONSE OR TYPE OF RESPONSE	POSSIBLE INTERPRETATION*
Entire blot used for concept	Ability to organize and integrate material
Small part, which is easily marked off from rest of blot	Need to be exact and accurate
Response that many people give	Need to be conventional
Response that few people give and that fits blot well	Superior intelligence
"Looks like a house cat"	Passivity and dependence
"It's a man or woman"	Problem with sexual identity

*Interpretations would be made only if the type of response occurred a number of times, not just once.

Figure 13–8.

A scene similar to scenes used in the TAT.

The basic task of subjects is for them to say what they see in the inkblot, elaborating on what the inkblot resembles. But beyond the question of what is seen, the examiner is also concerned with such issues as where in the inkblot something is seen or what specific features of the inkblot led a subject to see it. In this way, insight into mental content, perceptions, and emotions emerges. Although the interpretation of Rorschach responses is complex, we have provided several sample interpretations in Table 13–2 to suggest how meaning is given to subjects' responses.

The Thematic Apperception Test. Developed by Henry Murray, the Thematic Apperception Test (TAT) is probably the most widely used projective test. (Recall from chapter 9 that the TAT is often used in measuring achievement motivation.) As indicated in chapter 9, the TAT consists of a series of cards (29 of them), each showing an ambiguous scene similar to that appearing in Figure 13–8. The task is to make up a story about each card, indicating what is happening in the picture, what the outcome will be, and so on. It is assumed that the subjects will unknowingly reveal their personality structure through their responses. In other words, the subjects' fantasies with respect to the stories are assumed to reflect such underlying motives as the needs for affiliation, achievement, aggression, and dependency. Another assumption is that whatever is expressed in fantasy is also expressed in behavior. Pervin (1980) notes that the validity of both assumptions is questionable. He points out, for example, that although a particular fantasy may be associated with a related behavior, it may also be a substitute for it. With respect to a strong need for aggression, for example, one person may both fantasize aggression in a TAT story and exhibit it overtly; another person may fantasize aggression but refrain from overt exhibitions of it.

Critique. One of the problems with the Rorschach and the TAT is that "neither test has a universally accepted, standardized scoring or interpretation" (Feshbach & Weiner, 1982, p. 304). Generally speaking, evidence for the reliability and validity of projective techniques is lacking (Fehr, 1983). (Refer to chapter 12 for a discussion of reliability and validity.) Despite these problems, though, projective techniques continue to be used by many personality and clinical psychologists. Fehr (1983) suggests that supporters of such techniques believe that the tests are useful for those who are skilled in interpreting them. Besides this, the techniques have been around for a long time, and that alone may contribute to their widespread use in research and clinical settings.

Trait Approach

The trait approach to assessment must deal with the fact that traits are not directly observable. To measure them, personality psychologists have relied on various *self-report inventories*. Responses to such inventories are assumed to reflect or signify the underlying traits.

— Self-Report Inventories

All self-report inventories contain a large number of statements regarding feelings, thoughts, and behaviors to which subjects are to respond in some manner (e.g., agree or disagree). The statements are of the following type:

I often get depressed for no apparent reason.
My sleep is often restless.
Generally speaking, it is safest to trust no one.

Such tests are widely used in personality research and in clinical settings for diagnostic screening. Some self-report inventories are designed to measure personality in its entirety; others are designed to measure only one particular aspect of personality, such as locus of control. Our discussion here will focus on several comprehensive tests. First, however, we will consider ways in which self-report inventories can be constructed.

Construction of self-report inventories. Some self-report inventories use a *content-validation* approach (see chapter 12). They include statements that presumably reflect the trait being measured. (For example, "It is important for me to get approval from others" would reflect a need for approval.) A problem with such statements is that unless they are subtle, respondents may respond dishonestly in order to create a favorable impression.

An alternate testing approach is known as *criterion keying*. In this case, the selected statements are those that will be answered differently by subjects who have or do not have a particular trait. The content of the statements is therefore irrelevant. If, for example, depressed psychiatric patients consistently agreed with the statement "I sometimes read the newspaper" and normal subjects disagreed, the statement could be included on a depression scale. The Minnesota Multiphasic Personality Inventory (MMPI), to be described shortly, uses criterion keying.

Finally, test development may employ factor analysis, a technique described earlier. Although it is a complex procedure, factor analysis begins simply, with a large variety of statements administered to a large number of subjects (cf. Pervin, 1980). Statements to which many subjects respond similarly are related and are said to form a cluster, or factor. Statements within any given factor are highly related to one another and not highly related to statements in the other factors. A factor presumably represents an important characteristic or trait, and all the statements within the factor measure that trait. Cattell's 16 Personality Factor Inventory was developed with this approach.

Cattell's 16 Personality Factor Inventory. Cattell's measure of personality in its entirety is the 16 Personality Factor Inventory (16 PF). It has 187 statements, such as "I get jealous very easily." Subjects respond with one of three choices: yes, occasionally, and no. There is no attempt to disguise the purpose of the test. To guard against faking, subjects are told to answer as honestly as possible. Subjects receive scores on 16 personality dimensions corresponding to Cattell's source traits (referred to earlier). The scores are plotted on a profile sheet, which shows the individual's pattern of scores across the 16 dimensions. Cattell advocates an objective scoring system, one in which the individual's profile is statistically compared with profiles obtained from large groups of subjects. The characteristics of profiles are described in detail in a test manual.

The reliability of the 16 PF has been described as reasonable and adequate (Fehr, 1983; Pervin, 1980). The validity of the test comes mainly from the nature of its construction. That is, factor analysis presumably can identify those traits that do, in fact, distinguish people. The appearance of validity is also enhanced by the fact that many of Cattell's factors correspond to those obtained from studies using different procedures.

The Minnesota Multiphasic Personality Inventory. The most often used personality questionnaire is the Minnesota Multiphasic Personality Inventory (MMPI). It contains 550 statements that deal with a wide range of matters, such as general health, fears, family relationships, attitudes, and moods (Greene 1980). The inventory has 4 validity scales and 10 basic clinical scales. The purpose of the validity scales is to gauge the validity of answers on the clinical scales. A high score on one of the validity scales, for example, the Lie Scale, indicates that the subject is trying to be presented in a favorable light. On the clinical scales, subjects respond with true, false, or cannot say to statements such as "At times I am full of energy" or "I enjoy social gatherings just to be with people." The clinical scales measure the 10 basic dimensions of personality shown in Table 13–3.

The MMPI was constructed as an aid in diagnosing psychiatric patients. To obtain a clinical diagnosis, the pattern of scores across the 10 clinical scales is examined. Interpretation of this pattern, or profile, of scores is greatly aided by atlases that describe typical personalities with such profiles (e.g., Gilberstadt & Duker, 1965).

Although the MMPI is still used as a diagnostic tool in clinical settings, it is also widely used as a device for measuring normal personality traits and studying their effects on behavior.

Table 13–3.

The clinical scales of the MMPI and interpretations of high scores on each scale.

MMPI CLINICAL SCALE	INTERPRETATION OF HIGH SCORE
Hypochondriasis	Many physical complaints, fearful of illness
Depression	Depressed, despondent, distressed
Hysteria	Immature, egocentric, demanding
Psychopathic deviate	Antisocial tendencies, rebellious, nonconforming
Masculinity/femininity	Effeminate
Paranoia	Suspicious, guarded, worrisome
Psychasthenia	Fearful, anxious, worrisome, agitated
Schizophrenia	Withdrawn, unusual, bizarre in thinking
Hypomania	Hyperactive, energetic, impulsive
Social introversion/extroversion	Introverted, shy, self-effacing

In either case, the MMPI seems relatively effective in predicting long-range behavior. Liebert and Spiegler (1982) have offered several relevant examples of its effectiveness. In one study (Hathaway & Monachesi, 1952), future delinquent behavior (2 years after MMPI testing) was reliably predicted by a combination of subjects' scores from the psychopathic-deviate and hypomania scales. The hypomania scale has also proved effective in predicting how far graduate students in business will have advanced in their field and how high their incomes will be 10 years after testing (Harrell, 1972).

Generally speaking, the MMPI has proved valuable. Thousands of studies have used it, and its validity seems to be adequately documented. Its reliability, however, seems to be acceptable only over short periods of time (Feshbach & Weiner, 1982). The lack of long-term stability in MMPI scores may hold only for those individuals who exhibit, over time, fluctuations in psychological disturbance (Feshbach & Weiner, 1982). As a device for assessing normal personality in individuals who exhibit no psychological disturbance, the reliability issue may be less of a concern.

The California Psychological Inventory. Another criterion-keyed assessment device is the California Psychological Inventory (CPI). In contrast to the MMPI, it was designed for use with normal populations. The scales of the CPI measure to what degree individuals possess "personality characteristics that are important determinants of the ability of people to function in a world in which social interactional skills are critical" (Fehr, 1983, p. 265). More specifically, the 480 statements of the inventory measure 15 dimensions, including self-acceptance, responsibility, flexibility, self-control, sociability, and tolerance. The validity of the CPI appears to be good (Fehr, 1983).

Critique. Some critics argue that questionnaire responses are susceptible to biases. Subjects may respond to qualities other than statement content or may consistently respond in one way or another to statements (Pervin, 1980). For example, some people display *acquiescence,* the tendency to agree with statements regardless of their content. Subjects may also respond to statements in terms of their relative *social desirability.* That is, a person may respond so as to appear to have a socially acceptable personality characteristic. Such tendencies are called **response sets.**

As Pervin (1980) points out, all the self-report inventories attempt to deal with the response-set problem. For example, instructions encourage subjects to be honest. Furthermore, where relevant, statements are generally created in such a way that the trait being measured is reflected in yes responses for half the statements and no responses for the remainder. This avoids the possibility, then, that a person's high score on the trait is merely reflecting a tendency to acquiesce. Other strategies for dealing with response sets exist; they include validity scales, such as those in the MMPI. Although there is some disagreement about the impact of response sets on self-report inventories (Block, 1965), it seems wise to assume that they may exist and then to proceed to construct personality tests that avoid them.

Humanistic and Cognitive Approaches

Both the humanistic and the cognitive approaches attempt to assess people's subjective experiences and the meanings that people give them. As we might expect, these approaches favor self-report measures. Assessments of the subjects' interpretations of the world are deemed of utmost significance. Even though both approaches focus on subjective experience, they try whenever possible to make objective measurements. This is evident, for example, in George Kelly's REP Test for assessing personal constructs. The task in the REP Test is to list the individuals of significance in a subject's life. After the names have been placed in groups of three, the subject, through a comparison process, indicates how any two of the three are alike and how they differ from the third. From this information, the examiner gains a quantifiable assessment of the number and kind of constructs the subject uses in construing the world. It may turn out, for example, that a subject uses a limited number of constructs in organizing events, which limits the subject's flexibility in relating to others.

Objective measurement is also evident in assessment devices commonly used by humanistic psychologists. We now turn to several examples of this type of measurement.

— Interviews

Although psychologists of all theoretical orientations use interviews, humanistic psychologists find interviews particularly relevant in exploring subjects' unique interpretations of, perceptions of, and meanings for events. There are many types of interviews. The type that allows the greatest assessment of subjects' unique subjective experiences is open in format. In other words, there are no established questions, and the interviewer can move in any direction, exploring whatever issues seem to be of special significance to subjects. In the interview, the assessor can find out how subjects view themselves and how they describe themselves in specific relationships, such as with family members or co-workers (Gatchel & Mears, 1982).

A problem with the open format is that quantitative comparisons of subjects or of a single subject over time (as in the progress of therapy) may be difficult. A solution to this problem is **content analysis.** In this procedure, categories of verbal behavior that can be reliably rated by scorers are established. One category, for example, might be sexual conflict. Independent raters would be asked to examine what a subject said and to indicate how many times sexual conflict was mentioned (Gatchel & Mears, 1982).

Although interviews can provide an abundance of information about people, they are not without problems. Rarely is an interview just a verbal exchange (Pervin, 1980). What the subject says may be influenced in subtle ways by the appearance and manner of the interviewer. As a measurement device, then, the interview is subject to error and bias. It is nevertheless a major method of assessment for the humanistic psychologist. It is a flexible tool that allows the clinician considerable latitude in examining various features of clients' behavior (Gatchel & Mears, 1982).

Measures of Self-Concept

More structured methods than interviews also exist. One such method is the *Q-sort technique,* in which subjects are asked to select from a variety of statements those that apply to them most and least.

Subjects are given a pile of cards, each of which has printed on it a statement such as "I often feel guilty" or "I feel helpless." The subjects sort the cards into piles that reflect their determination of the extent to which the statements are accurate characterizations of themselves. At one end of the continuum are the statements "most characteristic of me"; at the other end are the statements "least characteristic of me."

After sorting the cards according to how they feel about themselves (i.e., what is true), subjects are asked to sort the same cards according to what they would like to be. This provides the assessor with an indication of the congruence of each subject's self-concept. As in the case of interview data, the clinician can also determine how subjects change their views of themselves over the course of therapy.

Critique

It is obvious that cognitive and humanistic psychologists place great emphasis on self-report data. In fact, they have been criticized for relying too greatly on such reports (cf. Liebert & Spiegler, 1982). Self-report techniques assume that people are both willing and able to describe their subjective experiences accurately. In general, however, it can be said that the effectiveness and validity of this assessment approach "is limited to the extent that people are reticent to be fully open about their subjective experiences" (Liebert & Spiegler, 1982, p. 409).

Behavioral Approach

In contrast to the other approaches described, the behavioral approach is direct in its assessment. It seems to be saying: If you want to know about someone's behavior, measure it directly. Don't make inferences about it by looking at responses to some ambiguous stimulus or statements on a questionnaire. If you want to know if someone is aggressive, put the individual in a particular situation or a variety of situations and see if aggression occurs.

A researcher who is interested in anxiety, as Paul (1966) was, will observe it directly. In studying anxiety in public speakers, Paul did not ask subjects how they felt. Rather he focused on their overt behaviors as they delivered speeches in front of audiences. Their behavioral indicators of anxiety included pacing, trembling, swallowing, perspiring, and not making eye contact.

Although the behavioral approach emphasizes direct assessment, it does not exclude the option of measuring behavior through self-reports. However, though self-reports are deemed more useful than data obtained through projective devices, they are considered less satisfactory than direct observation. In contrast to trait psychologists, behavioral psychologists would not assume that subjects' self-reports reflected some underlying trait. An example of a self-report questionnaire used by behavioral psychologists is the Fear Survey Schedule (Geer, 1965). In this questionnaire, subjects indicate the extent of fear elicited by a variety of specific situations, such as public speaking, and a variety of objects, such as animals.

The behavioral emphasis in assessing personality is on linking specific responses to specific situations. After some target behavior is identified as being of special interest, the behavioral psychologist attempts to ascertain the situational factors that might be responsible for eliciting or maintaining the behavior. Beyond that, emphasis is placed on determining how the environment can be altered to either increase or decrease the target behavior, whichever is appropriate.

The behavioral assessor believes that cross-situational consistency in a target behavior cannot be assumed unless the situations are similar in nature. Therefore, it is necessary to assess a given behavior in whatever situations are of concern. Aggression in the home by a 10-year-old boy may, for example, be a target behavior of interest. In assessing the behavior, it would be necessary first of all to define objectively what was meant by aggression and then to determine the specific factors within the home that might be eliciting and reinforcing the behavior. Certain alterations might then be made and their effect on the boy's aggression observed.

Some behavioral theorists also emphasize the importance of cognitive, or mental, activities, such as expectancies. Yet, here again, direct self-report is emphasized as a means of measuring such constructs. In other words, you simply ask subjects to report their expectation of a certain outcome occurring.

As noted earlier, Bandura believes that the expectation of self-efficacy is of considerable importance. Self-efficacy can be assessed by asking subjects to indicate the degree of confidence that they have in being able to carry out a particular task. Table 13–4 shows how Bandura and Reese (as cited by Mischel, 1981) measured self-efficacy in heart-attack victims. The investigators wanted to know how self-efficacy might be involved in the recovery of these patients. As we can see in Table 13–4, the tasks were potentially stressful. For

each one, the patient was to indicate the confidence level for being able to perform it.

— Critique

There seems to be something meaningful and advantageous in the behavioral assessor's emphasis on linking specific situations and responses. If you want to know about a person's anxiety level, you observe anxiety in particular situations. Any inferences made about the person's anxiety in other situations has to take into consideration whether those situations are comparable to the ones in which anxiety has already been ob-

Table 13–4.

A measure of self-efficacy. (From Mischel, 1981, p. 220; based on work by Bandura & Reese.)

Listed below are situations that can arouse anxiety, annoyance, and anger. Imagine the feelings you might have in each situation, such as your heart beating faster and your muscles tensing. Indicate whether you could tolerate now the emotional strain caused by each of the situations.

Under the column marked *Can Do,* check (√) the tasks or activities you expect you could do *now*.

For the tasks you check under *Can Do,* indicate in the column marked *Confidence* how confident you are that you could do the task. Rate your degree of confidence using a number from 10 to 100 on the scale below:

10	20	30	40	50	60	70	80	90	100

Quite Uncertain	Moderately Certain	Certain

	Can Do	Confidence
Attend a social gathering at which there is no one you know.	——	——
At a social gathering, approach a group of strangers, introduce yourself, and join in the conversation.	——	——
At a social gathering, discuss a controversial topic (politics, religion, philosophy of life, etc.) with people whose views differ greatly from yours.	——	——
Be served by a salesperson, receptionist, or waiter whose behavior you find irritating.	——	——
Complain about poor service to an unsympathetic sales or repair person.	——	——
When complaining about bad service, insist on seeing the manager if you are not satisfied.	——	——
In a public place, ask a stranger to stop doing something that annoys you, such as cutting in line, talking in a movie, or smoking in a no-smoking area.	——	——
Ask neighbors to correct a problem for which they are responsible, such as making noise at night or not controlling children or pets.	——	——
At work, reprimand an uncooperative subordinate.	——	——

served. This strategy is quite different from assessment strategies such as projective testing.

The behavioral-assessment approach is open to several criticisms, however (Feshbach & Weiner, 1982). First, with respect to any given target behavior (e.g., anxiety), there is no standard for how one observes it or even for what precisely is observed (e.g., which behaviors are most relevant as indicators of anxiety and which are irrelevant). Second, there is the problem that while being observed, a subject may alter behavior because of the presence of the observer. This is not unlike the problem faced by trait assessors, whose subjects may attempt to present certain images. One solution for the behavior assessor is to keep subjects unaware of which target behaviors are being observed or even that any behavior is being monitored.

— APPLICATION —
THE MMPI IN PERSONNEL SELECTION

As noted earlier, the MMPI was developed as a tool for assessing psychological disturbance and making psychiatric diagnoses. It and other, similar tests have also been widely used for a purpose not originally intended—personnel selection. The idea, of course, has been to screen out applicants who may have some type of emotional disturbance. What are the problems inherent in such personality testing? Lamberth, Rappaport, and Rappaport (1978) have suggested several that we will consider. Besides the problem of confidentiality and the fact that untrained people may be involved in the administration of the tests, there are the additional problems of accuracy and privacy.

With respect to accuracy, Mischel (1981) suggests that MMPI results be viewed with caution. The correlation between one's test results and actual behavior may be modest. As Mischel observes, the MMPI might be of greatest value in making gross screening decisions about whether people need further testing before being given some type of sensitive job. The MMPI is not so accurate that we should use it indiscriminately or as the sole device in predicting specific and important behaviors that a person may or may not display.

The question of privacy has also been debated. Most people do not like to reveal very personal information if they think that that information might be used against them in a job decision. How does such a concern weigh against the fact that certain stressful types of jobs require people who evidence a strong sense of responsibility and who are free of any psychological disturbances? The need to find such individuals and the fact that the MMPI is at least a fairly reliable indicator of psychological disturbance in job applicants has facilitated the use of the MMPI for this precise purpose (Liebert & Spiegler, 1982).

The conflict between the right to privacy and the need for screening out certain individuals for particular jobs came to a head in 1977. As Liebert and Spiegler (1982) relate it, five men sued officials in Jersey City, New Jersey, in connection with psychological testing of the emotional fitness of would-be fire fighters. Their complaint was that the tests constituted an invasion of privacy. In 1978, Senior Judge James A. Coolahan issued his opinion on the case. The judge ruled that despite his belief that the psychological testing was indeed an invasion of privacy, the interests of the state in selecting well-adjusted fire fighters was of greater importance. It was his opinion that the use of such testing for screening applicants was justified given the important role that psychological factors play in fire fighting. His decision was upheld by the Circuit Court of Appeals in Philadelphia in 1979.

PERSONALITY ASSESSMENT IN THE COURTROOM

The use of personality tests in mental-health, industrial, and educational settings is routine. A relatively new use—to select jury members—may affect all of us in the coming years (Andrews, 1982). Over the last decade or so, psychologists have more and more often aided lawyers in the selection of jury members (cf. Schulman, Shaver, Colman, Emrich, & Christie, 1973; Bermant, 1975; Saks, 1976; Tapp, 1981). For example, Schulman and his colleagues (1973) helped defense attorneys choose the jury for the Harrisburg Seven conspiracy trial, in which the defendants were accused of plotting to raid draft boards, blow up heating tunnels in Washington, DC, and kidnap Henry Kissinger.

In such situations, the problem for psychologists is to determine what type of person would make a good juror—that is, a juror who would favor the defendant or at least be impartial. To accomplish this goal, psychologists determine the juror characteristics that are relevant to the case at hand. They may find, for example, that religion or race is related to attitudes toward the defendant. With such information, lawyers can assess which types of people would make good jurors.

In another approach to jury selection, psychologists may draw on existing psychological research that suggests some relationship between a variable and its impact on juror behavior. For instance, the personality trait of **authoritarianism** is typified by resistance to change, prejudice, a hostile attitude toward those who have violated the conventional values of society, and submission to authority (Adorno, Frenkel-Brunswick, Levinson, & Sanford, 1950). (Table 13–5 gives a full listing of the characteristics thought to define the authoritarian person.) Simulated, or mock, jury trials have shown that authoritarianism affects jurors' decisions. This knowledge was used in jury selection in two conspiracy cases— one in Gainesville, Florida, against the Vietnam Veterans against the War and the other in the Wounded Knee conspiracy case against Russell Means and Dennis Banks of the American Indian Movement (cf. Bermant, 1975).

In the Wounded Knee trial, several psychologists assessed potential jurors' authoritarianism by scoring their apparent attitudes toward authority (cf. Bermant, 1975). One method they used was to examine responses that people made as the judge questioned

Table 13–5.

Characteristics that are thought to define the authoritarian person. (Adapted from Byrne, 1974, pp. 88–91.)

1. *Conventionalism.* A rigid adherence to middle-class values as a function of external social pressure, not because of personal conviction.

2. *Authoritarian submission.* A submissive, uncritical attitude toward authority figures of one's in-group, which may include one's family, church, nation, and so on.

3. *Authoritarian aggression.* The tendency to be on the lookout for and to condemn, reject, and punish people who violate conventional values (i.e., the aggression is directed toward members of one's out-group, which may include Jews, communists, sex offenders, etc.).

4. *Destruction and cynicism.* A generalized hostility and a cynical attitude toward human nature.

5. *Power and toughness.* A preoccupation with power, strength, and leadership.

6. *Superstition and stereotypy.* The tendencies to believe in mystical determinants of one's fate and to categorize things rigidly or to see them in terms of black and white.

7. *Anti-intraception.* A distrust of tender feelings; tough-mindedness.

8. *Projectivity.* The disposition to believe that wild and dangerous things go on in the world; the tendency to project onto the external world one's internal problems—taboo impulses, fears, weaknesses, and so on.

9. *Sex.* An exaggerated concern with sexual goings-on; the desire to punish those who violate sexual standards and to censor sexual materials; the projection of sexual excesses onto others.

them about their qualifications. Were they overly deferential, for instance? How did they respond to questions about the law? Nonverbal cues were also noted. If a potential juror adopted a closed posture and always directed attention to the judge, this indicated a high probability of deference to authority, which could mean deference to government prosecutors. In such cases, the psychologists recommended to defense lawyers that the person be excluded from the jury.

The psychologists involved in the Wounded Knee trial were using behavioral-assessment techniques. Other psychologists have applied the questionnaire approach to jury selection. Kirby and Lamberth (1974), for instance, developed a short oral authoritarianism scale that could be used during the evaluation phase of the jury trial. In several mock trials conducted by Kirby and Lamberth, high scorers on the authoritarianism scale proved more likely than low scorers to make a decision early and then not change it on hearing further evidence. (See also Werner, Kagehiro, & Strube, 1982.) Also, high scorers were more lenient toward a defendant similar to themselves than to a dissimilar one. Similarity had no effect on the decisions of low scorers. With the aid of such personality-assessment techniques, psy-

chologists may come to play an increasingly important role in jury selection.

Do you find scientific jury selection objectionable? Etzioni (1974), a prominent sociologist, believes that such jury selection procedures threaten the integrity of the jury system (cf. Saks, 1976). However, if scientific jury selection proves successful in some cases, its use is likely to continue. Under standard courtroom procedures, both sides in a trial are allowed to exclude from the jury persons believed to be biased against their side. Thus, the whole process could work more effectively if both sides had the help of social scientists. The jurors chosen would be the neutral people, whose attitudes and personality would play a minimal role in determining the outcome of the trial (Saks, 1976).

The other side of the argument is that, in reality, only one side in a trial is likely to have access to scientific help. Thus far, it seems that only the wealthy and celebrated have been able to secure these services. In future years, maybe it will be mainly the prosecutors who will have access to social scientists. As Saks (1976) has observed, this does not demonstrate an evil inherent in scientific jury selection. Rather, it points to a basic inequity in the courts. Clearly, the issue is open to debate.

1. Personality psychologists study the factors that make people different and the same.

2. Freud's psychoanalytic theory emphasizes unconscious motivation and the role played by biological instincts (especially sex and aggression) in determining behavior. The neoanalytic approaches of Erikson and Adler deemphasize the biological and sexual determinants of behavior and put more emphasis on environmental factors, especially the role played by the individual's social situation.

3. Trait theories conceptualize personality in terms of traits, or characteristics, that make people different from others. The basis of the trait approach is that people can be expected to consistently differ in their behavior when faced with the same stimulus events. Two trait theorists, Cattell and Eysenck, have used factor analysis in deriving the basic traits that they consider important in determining behavior. Cattell believes that there are 16 such underlying traits; Eysenck believes that the two basic dimensions of personality are introversion-extroversion and stability-instability.

4. Humanistic and cognitive theories stress the importance of an individual's unique perception of the world. Humanistic theories deemphasize biological needs in the development of personality and assume that individuals are born with a capacity for psychological growth. Rogers assumes that all humans are innately motivated to achieve self-actualization within the world as they view it. According to Rogers, a person can be fully functioning and adjusted only when there is a congruency between the person's self-experience and organismic experience. Kelly believed that behavior is determined by personal constructs, or ways of predicting the world.

5. Behavioral theories focus on behavior and the environmental conditions that influence it. They assume that behavior is determined primarily through learning that takes place in a social context. They view behavior as situation-specific rather than as consistent from situation to situation. Skinner's operant-conditioning approach is one example of a behavioral theory.

6. Bandura also believes that behavior is learned, but he thinks that Skinner pays too little attention to cognitive, or symbolic, processes. Bandura's social-learning theory emphasizes the importance of observational learning and self-regulation. People learn not only through the consequences of their behavior but also through observation of others' behavior. Furthermore, people are able to influence their own behavior rather than reacting to external influences in a mechanical way.

7. Rotter also emphasizes the role of cognitions in explaining personality. In his theory, behavior is a function of both the expectation of certain outcomes in response to the behavior and the perceived values of those outcomes. Rotter and Mischel recognize that both the situation and the person affect behavior. Mischel proposed a number of important person variables, including competencies, encoding strategies and personal constructs, expectations, subjective values of outcomes, and self-regulatory systems and plans.

8. Research on locus of control suggests that internals try to control outcomes and events more actively than do externals. This is evidenced in numerous ways, including job-related behaviors, academic achievement, and self-control over health.

9. Each theoretical approach must specify means for assessing personality. Psychoanalytic approaches, which place a heavy emphasis on unconscious factors, utilize indirect methods of assessment known as projective techniques. With such techniques, such as the Rorschach Inkblots and the TAT, individuals are assumed to project their feelings, desires, and needs onto the ambiguous stimuli (e.g., the inkblots).

10. Trait approaches rely heavily on the use of self-report inventories, which yield signs of underlying dispositions. Among the most widely used inventories are the Cattell 16 Personality Factor Inventory, the Minnesota Multiphasic Personality Inventory, and the California Psychological Inventory.

11. Humanistic assessment and cognitive assessment involve trying to understand another person's subjective experience from that person's perspective. Most assessment techniques in this approach use self-report measures, including interviews. Since self-concept is an important variable in the humanistic approach, a number of measures of self-concept are also used.

12. Behavioral theorists emphasize the importance of observing behavior as it occurs in specified situations. Behavioral assessment identifies specific target behaviors, the situational or environmental factors that elicit and maintain these behaviors, and the environmental factors that can be manipulated to alter the behaviors. More cognitive-oriented theorists, such as Bandura, also emphasize the assessment of cognitive activities (e.g. expectations).

13. The MMPI has also been used as a screening device in personnel selection. This particular use of the instrument has raised many questions, including those involving the accuracy of results and invasion of privacy.

14. A relatively new use of personality tests is as an aid in selecting jurors. In a number of trials, psychologists have helped lawyers by assessing potential jurors' authoritarianism, a personality trait that affects juror decision making. This has been accomplished through both behavioral assessments and questionnaires. Although scientific jury selection has been intensely debated, its use is likely to increase in the coming years.

━━ IMPORTANT TERMS AND CONCEPTS ━━

Personality
Psychoanalytic Theory
Libido
Id
Ego
Superego
Fixation
Oral Stage
Anal Stage
Phallic Stage
Oedipus Complex (Electra Complex)
Latency Period
Genital Stage

Trait Approach
Introversion
Extroversion
Stability
Instability
Humanistic Approach
Self-concept
Cognitive Approach
Personal Constructs
Behavioral Approach
Behavioral Specificity
Cognitive-behavioral Approach
Functional Analysis of Behavior

Expectancies
Self-regulation
Self-reinforcement
Self-efficacy
Reciprocal Determinism
Generalized Expectancies
Locus of Control
Interactionism
Projective Techniques
Response Sets
Content Analysis
Authoritarianism

━━ SUGGESTIONS FOR FURTHER READING ━━

Hall, C. S., & Lindzey, G. (1978). *Theories of personality* (3rd ed.). New York: Wiley. The classic comprehensive textbook on personality theories, written at a fairly difficult level, but an excellent scholarly source of information on most theories.

London, H., & Exner, J. E., Jr. (1978). *Dimensions of personality*. New York: Wiley. A high-level but excellent source of research about individual differences on such personality dimensions as authoritarianism, introversion-extroversion, and locus of control.

Mischel, W. (1981). *Introduction to personality* (3rd ed.). New York: Holt, Rinehart and Winston. An introduction to the major personality theories and assessment techniques, including a section on personality development and such basic processes as defense and self-control. Good material on Mischel's own social learning position and the issue of interactionism is also here.

Pervin, L. A. (1978). *Current controversies and issues in personality*. New York: Wiley. A very readable discussion of the issue of personal dispositions, situationism, and interactionism as applied to such topics as gender differences, altruism, and aggression.

Pervin, L. A. (1980). *Personality: Theory, assessment, and research* (3rd ed.). New York: Wiley. As the title suggests, a fairly high-level textbook introducing not only the major schools of thought but also their implications for personality assessment and research.

Phares, E. J. (1976). *Locus of control in personality*. Morristown, NJ: General Learning Press. A relatively brief, well-written review of the locus-of-control literature by one of the experts in the area.

- CHAPTER 14 -

STRESS AND COPING

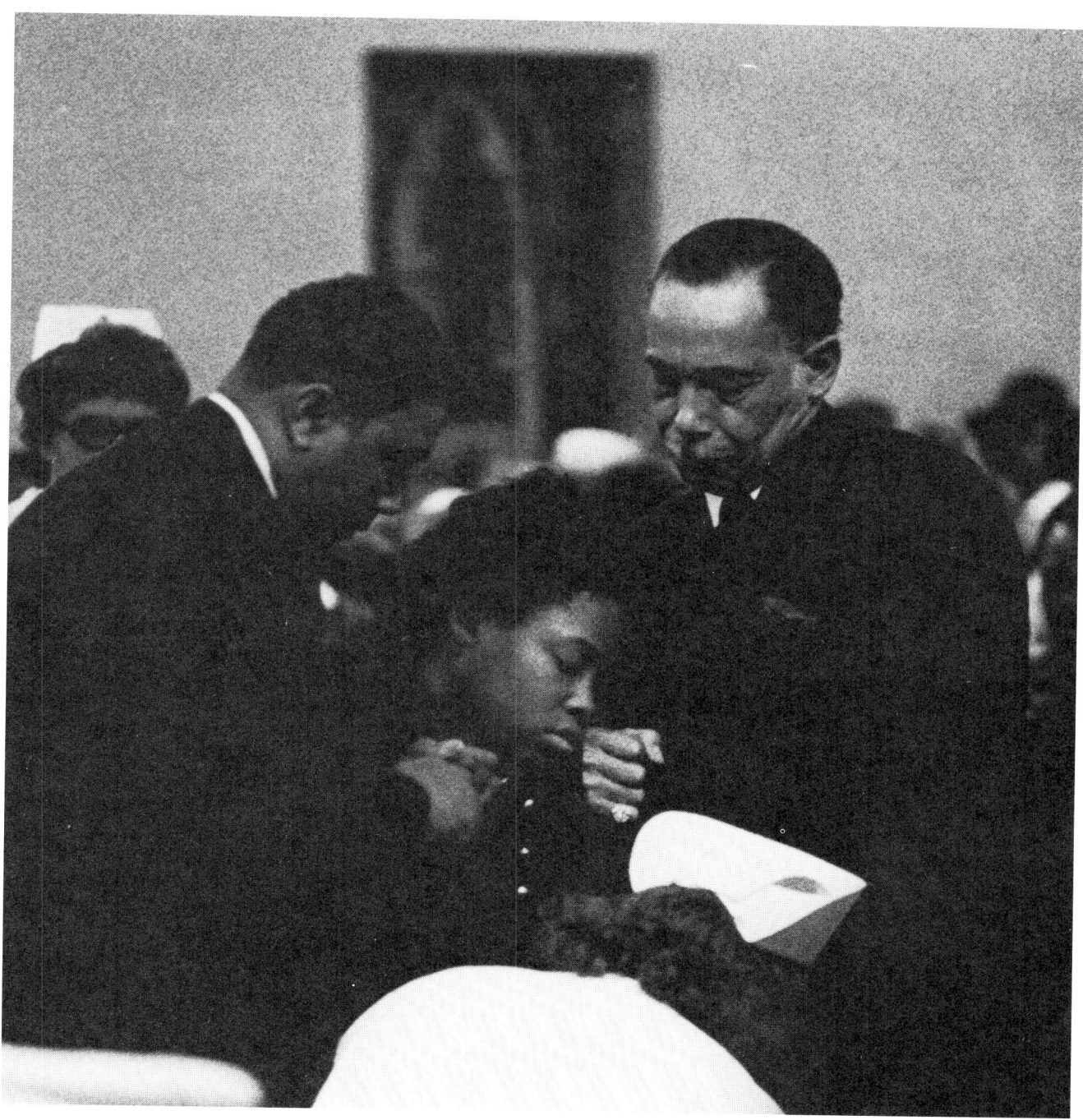

STRESS AND COPING

━ CHAPTER OBJECTIVES ━

To achieve the objectives of this chapter, you should be able to answer the questions listed here. You should also be able to define the important terms and concepts listed at the end of the chapter.

1. How can frustration lead to stress? What is conflict? In what ways might one experience conflict?
2. How does pressure produce stress? What role do life events play in producing stress?
3. What is the general adaptation syndrome? How does it help us understand the occurrence of stress-related disorders?
4. List some common psychosomatic reactions.
5. What is the role of cognitive appraisal in managing stress? Why do predictability and perceived control affect the severity of stress and the ability to cope with it?
6. How are social support, personality, and defense mechanisms involved in coping with stress?

━ CHAPTER OUTLINE ━

Sources of Stress
Stress arises out of demands on a person; it can stem from a variety of sources.

Frustration
Conflict
Pressure
Life Events
Environmental Stressors
Application: Managing the Frustration of a Delay

Physiological Effects of Stress
Stress can produce a multitude of physiological effects, such as peptic ulcers and hypertension.

General Adaptation Syndrome
Psychosomatic Disorders
General Health
Application: Relaxation and Biofeedback

Coping with Stress
The negative effects of stress can be prevented by learning ways to cope with it.

Cognitive Appraisal
Predictability
Perceived Control
Social Supports
Personality and Health
Defense Mechanisms
Application: Breaking Type A Habits

On the Horizon: Community Stress Checks—Three Mile Island and Beyond

LIFE'S LITTLE HASSLES

You've misplaced something. You're worried about your physical appearance. You have too many things to do. You're stuck in a traffic jam. You've had an argument with a co-worker. Sound familiar? Psychologist Richard Lazarus believes that such everyday annoyances may have a greater effect on moods and health than do major misfortunes. Lazarus (1981) had 100 middle-aged persons complete several questionnaires over the course of a year. Among the questionnaires was a 117-item "hassle checklist." Each month, participants marked the hassles that occurred and rated their frequency and severity. At the beginning and end of the year, participants completed a health questionnaire. A separate psychological questionnaire asked how often the individual had such problems as headaches, bad dreams, and worries. Another questionnaire assessed monthly fluctuations in mood (anger, excitement, boredom, and loneliness, for example). Finally, participants indicated at the beginning and end of the year what major life events they had experienced (e.g., death of a spouse or divorce).

As Lazarus expected, little hassles better predicted psychological and physical health than did major life events. The more frequent and intense the hassles, the poorer the overall mental and physical health of the individual. Major life events did have a long-term effect, but hassles appeared to have a much greater impact on mental and physical health in the short-run.

Petty everyday annoyances, then, can potentially make us candidates for psychological and physical problems (see also DeLongis, Coyne, Dakof, Folkman, & Lazarus, 1982). The hassles reported most frequently vary by group. A group of white middle-class, middle-aged men and women studied by Lazarus reported such hassles as weight problems, poor health of a family member, home maintenance problems, and rising prices. Your own hassles may differ from these, but which ones you experience are not as important as their frequency, duration, and intensity and how you react to them. The less effective you are at coping with the hassles, the more damaging they are.

As this information suggests, the chapter is about stress. In addition to the stresses just described, stress is also associated with important life events, such as major illness in the family, losing a job, or failing a course in school. Some psychologists believe that even pleasant events, such as getting married or promoted, can also be stressful. Whether pleasant or unpleasant, all stressful events require *adjustment* or *adaptation*.

When we cope with stressful situations, our adjustment is said to be successful. When we do not cope, some form of maladjustment, such as physical health problems, anxiety, or depression (see chapter 15), may result. All of us experience stress, but most of us find ways of coping with it.

Some stress is necessary to keep us alert and motivated (Rathus & Nevid, 1983). Indeed, any physical or mental effort and any problem solving or decision making involves some degree of stress. Stress is not something that can, or should, be entirely avoided. As Selye (1974) noted, "Complete freedom from stress is death" (p. 20). It has been observed that humans function best at moderate levels of stress—a "healthy tension" (Rathus & Nevid, 1983). Stress that is too intense or prolonged, however, can overtax our ability to adjust and adapt, producing harmful physical and psychological effects.

Formally defined, **stress** is a physical and psychological condition experienced whenever environmental demands are placed on an organism. In our discussion of stress, we will also have many occasions to speak of **anxiety,** an emotion that accompanies stress and that is characterized by unpleasant feelings of apprehension. This chapter deals first with various sources of stress, then with its physiological effects, and finally with factors that affect coping ability, including some specific coping strategies.

— SOURCES OF STRESS —

Stress arises when demands, called **stressors,** are imposed on a person. We will first examine two major stressors—frustration and conflict—and then look at several others, including pressure, life events, and environmental stressors.

Frustration

The blocking of any goal-directed behavior can be defined as **frustration.** Many frustrations are minor, but others are perceived as real threats to well-being. In any case, the effect is the same: Frustrations prevent the satisfaction of some need or desire. A child who cannot have a desired ice cream is frustrated. A worker who does not get a highly sought raise is frustrated. A student who does not get an expected and hoped for grade is frustrated.

— Sources of Frustration

The number of specific frustrations is almost limitless. We can list, however, some of the commonly encountered ones. Coleman (1979) offers delays, lack of resources, losses, failures, and loneliness as frustrations that often cause special difficulty.

Delays. As we know, delays are unavoidable. Waiting in traffic (see Figure 14–1), delaying marriage, spending years studying for a career, and waiting for enough money to buy some valued object are common examples. Psychologist Walter Mischel of Columbia University has studied such delayed gratification extensively (Mischel, 1981). Mischel investigated the ef-

fects of being offered a small immediate reward that would have to be forsaken in order to get an even bigger reward later. His research identified several strategies for managing delay-caused frustration. We will examine some of them in an upcoming "Application" section.

Lack of resources. Most people are at least occasionally dissatisfied with what they have, especially when having more would lead to a desired goal. A person might, for example, feel a lack of the personal resources—education, skills, or experience—needed to obtain a certain job.

Losses. Losing something valued is frustrating in that it may lessen the chances of achieving some goal. Losing money, time, or friendship, for example, may have this effect.

Failures. We all experience an occasional failure in our lives, no matter who we are or what we are trying to accomplish. In a sense, failure is in the eye of the beholder; subjectively, a person need only define a situation as a failure to experience frustration.

Loneliness. One of the major frustrations seems to be loneliness (Peplau & Perlman, 1982). It can occur at any age, but the highest levels are among 18-to-25-year-olds (Peplau, 1982), many of whom are moving away from parents to live independently.

Loneliness is a feeling of distress or unhappiness about the absence of social contact or close relationships. Table 14–1 gives some specific reasons for feeling lonely (Shaver & Rubenstein, 1980). Table 14–2

Figure 14–1.
Delays of this sort can be particularly frustrating.

shows the feelings that often accompany loneliness. The results come from a large sample of U.S. adults (Shaver & Rubenstein, 1980).

Peplau (1982) has noted that people whose work or residence keeps them socially isolated are more susceptible than others to loneliness. Furthermore, certain personal qualities, such as unattractiveness, aloofness, and unusualness, discourage the formation of

Table 14–1.
Specific reasons for feeling lonely.

BEING UNATTACHED	ALIENATION	BEING ALONE	FORCED ISOLATION	DISLOCATION
Having no spouse	Feeling different	Coming home to an empty house	Being housebound	Being far from home
Having no sexual partner	Being misunderstood	Being alone	Being hospitalized	In new job or school
Breaking up with spouse or lover	Not being needed		Having no transportation	Moving too often
	Having no close friends			Traveling often

From Shaver, P. & Rubenstein, C., "Childhood attachment experience and adult loneliness," pp. 42–73 in *Review of personality and social psychology* (Vol. 1), ed. by L. Wheeler. Copyright © 1980 by Sage Publications, Inc. Reprinted by permission of Sage Publications, Inc. and the authors.

Table 14–2.

Feelings people have when lonely.

DESPERATION	DEPRESSION	IMPATIENT BOREDOM	SELF-DEPRECATION
Desperate	Sad	Impatient	Unattractive
Panicked	Depressed	Bored	Down on self
Helpless	Empty	Desire to be elsewhere	Stupid
Afraid	Isolated	Uneasy	Ashamed
Without hope	Sorry for self	Angry	Insecure
Abandoned	Melancholy	Unable to concentrate	
Vulnerable	Alienated		
	Longing to be with one special person		

From Shaver, P. & Rubenstein, C., "Childhood attachment experience and adult loneliness," pp. 42–73 in *Review of personality and social psychology* (Vol. 1), ed. by L. Wheeler. Copyright © 1980 by Sage Publications, Inc. Reprinted by permission of Sage Publications, Inc. and the authors.

lasting relationships. Research has shown too that shyness and poor social skills are related to loneliness (Cheek & Busch, 1981; Jones, 1982; Jones, Hobbs, & Hockenbury, 1982; Solano, Batten, & Parish, 1982).

Conflict

In and of itself, conflict can be considered a major source of stress, but it is also a cause of frustration. **Conflict** exists whenever a person has incompatible or opposing goals. The frustration comes from being unable to satisfy all the goals. Whatever goal the person decides to satisfy, there will be frustration, most likely preceded by turmoil, doubt, and vacillation. Four major types of conflict described by researchers are approach-avoidance, double approach-avoidance, approach-approach, and avoidance-avoidance.

— Approach-Avoidance Conflicts

When a person is motivated to both approach and avoid the same goal, an **approach-avoidance conflict** exists. You may want to remain in school but may think you should quit because you can't do the work. You may want to ask someone for a date but may be too shy to do so. You may want to go to the dentist but may fear the pain of the drill. Such conflicts can cause a great deal of stress as you waver back and forth trying to come to a decision.

A particularly useful concept in understanding approach-avoidance conflicts is **goal gradients,** which describe the strength of the tendency to approach or avoid some goal object at various distances from the

goal (Miller, 1944). Figure 14–2 shows the goal gradient for approaching a goal in comparison to the goal gradient for avoiding the goal. The avoidance gradient is the steeper one. The result is that when we are far from a goal, our tendency to approach it is stronger than our tendency to avoid it. As we approach the goal, however, the gradients cross; the avoidance tendency then becomes stronger than the approach tendency, and we retreat from the goal. As we retreat, of course,

Figure 14–2.

As one approaches a goal, the tendency to both approach and avoid it increases. The avoidance gradient, however, is steeper than the approach gradient. As one gets close to the goal, the tendency to avoid it becomes stronger than the tendency to approach it. Far from the goal, the opposite holds.

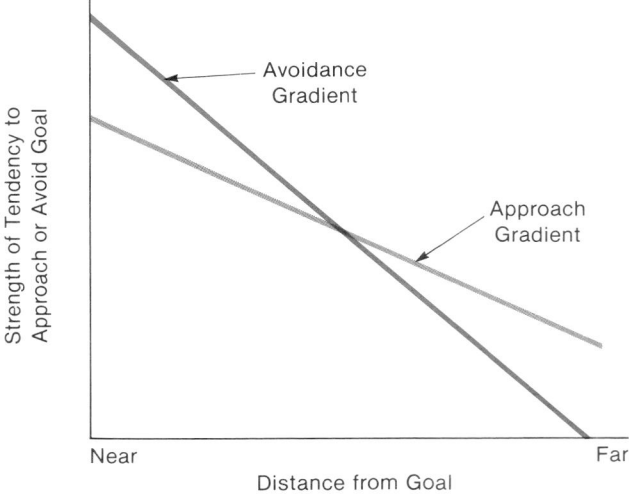

we get to a point where the approach tendency is again the stronger one; we then approach the goal once more, only to ultimately retreat again.

The situation may seem familiar to you. Perhaps you experienced this type of conflict in trying to decide whether to approach one of your instructors about a problem. Or perhaps you wanted to ask for a raise and then retreated from the manager's door just as you were ready to knock. Life is filled with such conflicts. We eventually resolve many of them, but not without a great deal of worry and anxiety. Others may present such a problem that we need to seek professional help.

— Double Approach-Avoidance Conflicts

A more complex conflict is the **double approach-avoidance conflict,** in which a person is motivated to both approach and avoid two different goals. (Even more complex are multiple approach-avoidance conflicts.) As an example, consider what happens when you are faced with choosing between two colleges, both of which have positive and negative characteristics. You want to attend College A because it is small, but you hesitate because it is also expensive. You want to attend College B because it is less expensive, but you don't like the fact that it is a large school.

— Approach-Approach Conflicts

When we are motivated to approach each of two (or more) equally desirable alternatives, but must choose one, an **approach-approach conflict** exists. Generally, such conflicts cause little distress and are easily resolved. The reason is that although we must choose one alternative now, we can often obtain the other at a later time (Coleman, 1979). Still, stressful approach-approach conflicts can exist—for example, indecision about which of several highly desirable careers to pursue.

— Avoidance-Avoidance Conflicts

When we are motivated to avoid each of two (or more) equally unattractive choices, but must choose one, an **avoidance-avoidance conflict** exists. In this situation, avoiding unpleasant consequences is impossible; the choice is just a matter of the lesser of two evils. As a student, you might have to choose between studying for a course you don't like or failing it. As a employee, you might have to choose between working at a job you don't like or quitting it and risking your income.

Such conflicts tend to involve a great deal of vacillation and hesitation. Moving closer to one of the unattractive choices increases our discomfort and leads us to retreat (Goodstein & Lanyon, 1979). This retreat brings us closer to the other unattractive alternative, and we retreat in the opposite direction. In effect, we find both goals equally punishing, so we unhappily vacillate between them.

A common solution to avoidance-avoidance conflicts is to search for a way to avoid both of the unattractive goals (Derlega & Janda, 1978; Goodstein & Lanyon, 1979). You could, for example, avoid studying for the disliked course and direct your efforts toward trying to drop the course and still graduate. Many times, of course, it is impossible to find such alternatives. As Goodstein and Lanyon (1979) observe, it is just such unavoidable and seemingly unresolvable conflicts that can cause problems such as anxiety, physical ailments, or sleeplessness.

Pressure

Another common source of stress is pressure. If you are a conscientious college student, you no doubt know about it. Pressure can have both internal and external origins. Coleman (1979) suggests that we often get caught up in the "tyranny of the should": We should get along with all people; we should show more self-control; we should do much better than we are doing. Unrealistic assumptions of this sort generate a great deal of pressure. Common external pressures include community problems, work, financial pressures, and family, marriage, and other relationships (Coleman, 1979). Such pressures complicate lives and increase stress.

Life Events

In the chapter introduction, we noted that major life events seem to produce stress. We get married or divorced; there is a death in the family; we buy a new home or get promoted at work. According to some stress researchers, all such events involve a change in life circumstances, which requires an adjustment to new demands. As indicated earlier, many psychologists believe that any change, whether pleasant or unpleasant, is stressful. Getting married, getting a raise or promotion, and taking a vacation, then, can be stressful, just as can a death in the family, getting fired, or getting divorced.

In recent years, researchers have developed a scale to quantify stress in terms of life changes (Holmes & Rahe, 1967). The Social Readjustment Rating Scale (SRRS), shown in Table 14–3, lists 43 common life events, ranging from death of a spouse (most stressful) to minor legal violations (least stressful). The events on the scale vary in perceived severity and time required for adjustment. The effects of life events are expressed in life-change units (LCUs). The more stressful an event, the higher its LCU value.

A person tested with the SRRS receives a score for the total amount of recent change. Research has shown that as life changes increase, so does the risk of illness within the next 2 years. More specifically, it has been found that individuals who scored 300 (LCUs) or above on the SRRS (for the past year) had a 79 percent risk of developing a major illness within the next 2 years (see Holmes & Masuda, 1974).

Some researchers, however, believe that stress is more closely related to negative life events than to positive ones (Johnson & Sarason, 1979); in other words, negative life changes predict illness better than do positive life changes or a combined life-change score. Researchers also have found that life events perceived as uncontrollable are more strongly associated with stress and illness than are controllable events (Stern, McCants, & Pettine, 1982). We will have more to say a little later about the negative effects of a lack of perceived control over one's environment.

Environmental Stressors

A number of aspects of the physical environment are stress-producing; among them are noise, heat, crowding, and urban settings (e.g., Holahan, 1982). In chapter 19, we will devote considerable attention to these and related topics. For now, we can say that such environmental stressors require personal adaptation to reduce stress and its damaging effects. For instance, a student in a crowded dormitory could study at the library as often as possible. Otherwise, dislike of others in the dorm, illness, and negative feelings could occur.

Table 14–3.

The Social Readjustment Rating Scale. (From Holmes & Rahe, 1967, p. 216.)

RANK	LIFE EVENT	VALUE	RANK	LIFE EVENT	VALUE
1	Death of spouse	100	23	Son or daughter leaving home	29
2	Divorce	73	24	Trouble with in-laws	29
3	Marital separation	65	25	Outstanding personal achievement	28
4	Jail term	63	26	Wife beginning or stopping work	26
5	Death of close family member	63	27	Beginning or ending school	26
6	Personal injury or illness	53	28	Change in living conditions	25
7	Marriage	50	29	Revision of personal habits	24
8	Fired at work	47	30	Trouble with boss	23
9	Marital reconciliation	45	31	Change in work hours or conditions	20
10	Retirement	45	32	Change in residence	20
11	Change in health of family member	44	33	Change in schools	20
12	Pregnancy	40	34	Change in recreation	19
13	Sex difficulties	39	35	Change in church activities	19
14	Gain of new family member	39	36	Change in social activities	18
15	Business readjustment	39	37	Loan for lesser purchase (car, TV, ect.)	17
16	Change in financial state	38	38	Change in sleeping habits	16
17	Death of close friend	37	39	Change in number of family get-togethers	15
18	Change to different line of work	36	40	Change in eating habits	15
19	Change in number of arguments with spouse	35	41	Vacation	13
20	Loan for major purchase (home, etc.)	31	42	Christmas	12
21	Foreclosure of mortgage or loan	30	43	Minor violations of the law	11
22	Change in responsibilities at work	29			

MANAGING THE FRUSTRATION OF A DELAY

We noted earlier that delays can be frustrating. What strategies help make them more tolerable? Mischel has researched this issue extensively (e.g., Mischel, 1974, 1981). In one study (Mischel & Ebbesen, 1970), pre-school children were shown two objects (e.g., food treats), one more preferred than the other. To obtain the more-preferred object, each child had to wait alone in a room until the experimenter returned. Children who summoned the experimenter (instead of waiting) could have the less-preferred object immediately but could not get the more-preferred object. For one group of children, neither reward was in sight during the wait. For another group, both rewards were in full view. A third group had only the more desirable reward in sight. A fourth group had only the less desirable reward in sight. Which children were best able to avoid summoning the experimenter, thus receiving the desired reward? Those for whom no rewards were visible (see Figure 14–3).

Mischel (1981) reports that the children apparently managed their aversive wait by converting it into a more pleasant, nonwaiting situation. They devised elaborate self-distraction techniques so they could spend their time doing something other than merely waiting and anticipating. They avoided looking at the rewards, talked to themselves, sang, and invented games that involved using their hands and feet. One child even chose sleep over waiting.

According to Mischel, diverting attention from delayed rewards is a key to tolerating delays. (Of course, one still must maintain behavior directed toward achieving the goal.) Not thinking about delayed goals makes sense if you consider denial of a reward aversive. Anything that enhances attention to the reward merely increases discomfort. As Mischel observes, it is difficult to wait for a meal when you can see it and smell it. The same applies to other rewards for which we must endure the passing of time.

Effective self-control, then, may necessitate our being able to transform the aversive into the pleasant while we still engage in the activity necessary to obtain the preferred reward (Mischel, 1981). With this information, perhaps we can now understand how the frus-

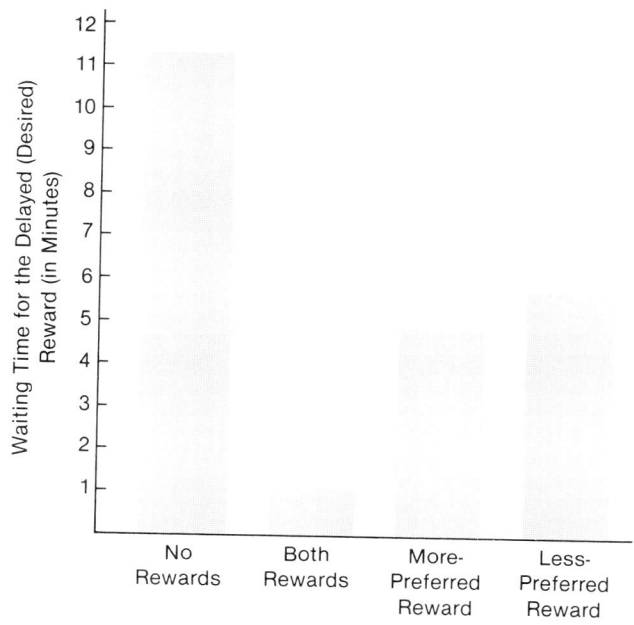

Figure 14–3.

Children had the least difficulty waiting for a delayed (desired) reward when neither the desired nor the less-preferred rewards were visible. (Based on data from Mischel & Ebbesen, 1970, p. 333.)

tration of delays can be best endured. Mischel (1981) points out that self-distraction can also be a good strategy for reducing the effects of unavoidable stressors, such as unpleasant medical examinations. In fact, cognitively transforming the aversive into the pleasant seems to work for a variety of stressors. In one study, surgical patients were helped to reinterpret their threatening ordeal (Langer, Janis, & Wolfer, —cited in Mischel, 1981). They were encouraged, for example, to define the hospital experience as an escape from pressure and a vacation. This technique seemed to help the patients cope with their stressful circumstances.

Thus far, we have emphasized the psychological component of stress, including the feelings, thoughts, and behaviors related to various stressors. Stress also has a physiological component, which includes a variety of changes in such body processes as heart rate, respiration, endocrine secretions, and sweat-gland activity (see chapter 2). But this is only the tip of the iceberg, as we are about to see.

General Adaptation Syndrome

Hans Selye, a pioneer in the study of stress, noticed as a young medical student that regardless of the particular stressor, the body's responses to this demand for adjustment were always the same. As Selye (1980) notes, whether it's a game of chess, a kiss, pneumonia, or a broken finger, the body's reaction is identical.

Selye termed this nonvarying pattern of physical reactions to a stressor the **general adaptation syndrome (GAS).** The syndrome consists of three stages: alarm reaction, resistance, and exhaustion. In the first stage, *alarm reaction,* the body works to defend itself against the threatening stimulus (the fight-or-flight reaction referred to in chapter 9). Sympathetic nervous-

Figure 14–4.
The body's level of resistance to stressors over the course of the General Adaptation Syndrome. During the alarm stage, resistance drops below normal. As adaptation begins, resistance rises above normal. Eventually, in exhaustion, resistance once more falls below normal. (Adapted from Selye, 1976, p. 111.)

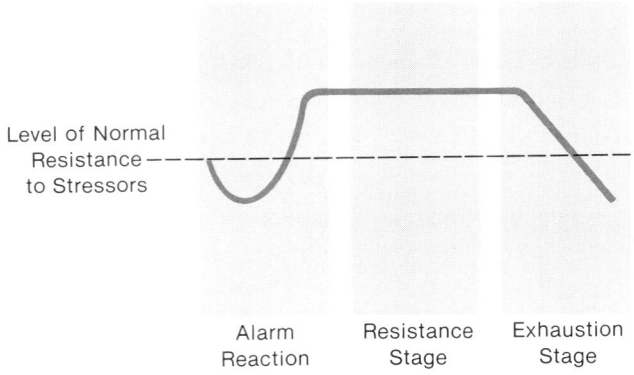

Level of Normal
Resistance
to Stressors

Alarm
Reaction

Resistance
Stage

Exhaustion
Stage

system activity is the hallmark of the alarm reaction; it includes increased heart rate and respiration and adrenaline secretion (changes outlined in chapter 9). During this stage, resistance to stress is diminished and below normal (see Figure 14–4).

As the body continues its adaptation to the stressor, it enters the second stage, *resistance.* The reactions of the first stage have essentially disappeared. But although resistance to the stressor is increased (Figure 14–4), resistance to other stressors is lowered (Selye, 1980). In Selye's thinking, adaptation energy is finite. If the stressor is prolonged and severe, the body eventually enters the third stage, *exhaustion.* At this point, resistance weakens, symptoms of the alarm reaction reappear, and "diseases of adaptation" (such as heart disease or ulcers) appear. Ultimately, even death may occur.

Psychosomatic Disorders

Sometimes stress continues over a long period of time. For example, one's job or one's marriage may be stressful. The resulting heightened physiological activity may lead to tissue damage in some body systems (Coleman, 1979). Organic disorders of this type that develop in response to stress and anxiety are called **psychosomatic disorders.** Three of the most common forms of psychosomatic disorders are peptic ulcers, migraine and tension headaches, and hypertension.

— Peptic Ulcers

A hole, or lesion, in the lining of the stomach or duodenum is a **peptic ulcer.** Not all such ulcers are due to stress, but many are. When a person experiences stress and the accompanying anxiety, the stomach secretes an excess amount of acid. It is this acid that does the damage (Rimm & Somervill, 1977; Wolf, 1982).

The link between stress and ulcers was demonstrated with rats in a study by Weiss (1972). All the rats in Weiss's study received electric shocks, but some of them heard a tone precisely 10 seconds before each shock. For these rats, the shocks were predictable. The other rats heard tones that were unrelated to the timing of the shocks. The latter rats developed severe ulcerations. Other work by Weiss suggests that control, as well as predictability, is important. Some rats were given control over their shocks; upon hearing a warning signal, they could behave in ways that would prevent the shock. These rats developed significantly fewer ulcers than did rats who were given identical shocks but who were not in control of them. As we will see later, it is now well documented that the less control and predictability present, the greater the stress. And, as we have just seen, the greater the stress, the greater the likelihood of ulceration.

— Migraine and Tension Headaches

Although headaches can have organic causes, most are thought to be due to stress. **Migraine headaches** are intense, recurrent headaches that are characterized by a deep, throbbing pain (Rimm & Somervill, 1977). Most migraines occur on only one side of the head. The pain is thought to be due to the dilation (expansion) of the cranial arteries. Coleman (1979) observes that (1) the onset of a migraine headache is accompanied by dilation of the cranial arteries, (2) the diminishing of the pain is associated with the return of the arteries to their normal size, and (3) experimentally induced stressors such as frustrations or anxiety-arousing interviews cause vascular dilation for migraine sufferers but not for other people.

In contrast to migraine headaches, the more common **tension headaches** involve a sensation of tightness or pressure and a dull but steady pain around the entire head (Blanchard & Andrasik, 1982). Whereas the migraine headache has a vascular origin, the tension headache has a muscular origin (Rimm & Somervill, 1977). We will examine some treatments for both types of headaches in the next "Application" section.

— Hypertension

Anytime we experience stress, our blood pressure increases. When the stress abates, so does our blood pressure. Under chronically stressful conditions, however, our blood pressure may also become chronically high, a condition known as **hypertension.** Not all cases of high blood pressure are due to stress; often, factors such as kidney disease, diet, or weight play a role. Most of the time, though, stress is the major causal factor (Coleman, 1979). Some researchers believe that the stress-related emotions of anger and hostility may underlie chronic high blood pressure (Dia-

mond, 1982). At least some afflicted individuals seem to be hostile and resentful, yet in conflict about overtly expressing anger. However, not everyone fitting this description develops high blood pressure.

General Health

Many researchers are interested not only in psychosomatic disorders but in the link between stress and general health. Constant adaptation to stress may lower resistance to disease, thereby increasing its likelihood (Gottschalk, 1983; Gottschalk, Welch, & Weiss, 1983). Earlier, we noted that research with the SRRS has shown that as major life changes accumulate, the risk of illness from any cause increases. Here, we would like to explore related findings.

In a study reported by Holmes and Masuda (1974), naval personnel provided health-change data after 6 months at sea. High-risk subjects—those with the highest LCUs—consistently reported more illnesses each month of the 6-month cruise period than did low-risk subjects. Furthermore, their illnesses were more serious.

In their overview of the relevant research, Johnson and Sarason (1979) observe that life stress has been related to such health problems as sudden cardiac arrest (and death), heart attack, pregnancy and birth complications, serious chronic illnesses such as tuberculosis and diabetes, and an assortment of less serious physical conditions. They conclude that the research supports the hypothesis "that rather than being related to specific disorders, life stress serves to increase one's overall susceptibility to illness" (Johnson & Sarason, 1979, p. 207). They add that life stress is also related to various indexes of mental health. Depression, for example, has been found to be positively related to significant life-event changes (cf. Anisman & Zacharko, 1982).

The potential link between life stress and cancer has also received considerable attention (Cooper, 1982; Sklar & Anisman, 1981). For example, Jacobs and Charles (1980) found that, in children, the year preceding the detection of cancer included significant life changes, such as personal injury or change in health of a family member. The incidence of cancer was especially prevalent among individuals who had lost an important emotional relationship.

Although the life stress–illness relationship is best documented for men, it seems also to hold for women

(Stewart & Salt, 1981). For women, however, the type of stress and personal life-style are important factors. In the Stewart and Salt (1981) study of normal adult women, work-related stress was associated with illness; family-related stress was not. Also, the life stress–illness relationship was strongest among work-centered women.

Research on life stress and illness is not without problems. For one thing, we need more research using a *prospective design,* one in which individuals first give information on their recent life changes and 6 months to a year later are questioned about changes in their health. In other words, the research question is: Can we predict future health on the basis of current knowledge of a person's life stress? The prospective studies that have been done suggest that we can. By and large, though, our knowledge in this area has come from research using a *retrospective design,* one in which subjects recall past events and health changes. One of the problems with such an approach is that subjects may not recall either type of information with complete accuracy (Monroe, 1982).

Finally, we know little about individual differences in the effects of life stress on illness. Some people who experience high life stress succumb to illness later on; others do not. A simple score on the SRRS, in other words, is not enormously predictive of a given individual's future health changes. We need to know more about the person in making predictions about future illness. Our understanding of what else we need to know is just beginning to unfold. One important factor uncovered to date is the personality trait known as hardiness. We will examine this characteristic in detail later. In general, we might suggest that if a person with high life stress has resources available for coping with that stress, such as family and friends who can be relied on for emotional support, the effects of the stress may be attenuated considerably. That coping strategies can indeed ameliorate stress will become apparent shortly.

— APPLICATION —
RELAXATION AND BIOFEEDBACK

There seems to be no doubt that stress can be harmful to physical health. One strategy for coping with stress and preventing stress-related disorders is to learn techniques for voluntarily controlling body processes. Two such techniques are relaxation and biofeedback.

An effective way to relax is through a series of exercises developed by Jacobson (1938), whose technique is known as *progressive muscle relaxation* (see chapter 5). The idea behind the technique is to learn how to sense body tenseness and how to voluntarily control it (Williams & Long, 1983). Jacobson's technique involves alternately tensing and relaxing each of the muscle groups in the body. The result is a deep relaxation with a lessening of both physical and mental tension. Martin and Poland (1980) suggest that although progressive relaxation can be self-taught, better results might be achieved with the help of a professional who is experienced in teaching relaxation.

Several recent studies show that relaxation is indeed helpful. It effectively improves at least some types of headaches (Blanchard & Andrasik, 1982), reduces blood pressure (Glasgow, Gaarder, & Engel, 1982; Engel, Glasgow, & Gaarder, 1983), and reduces anxiety and the self-reported physical symptoms of anxiety (Kappes, 1983).

In **biofeedback,** information about normally imperceptible body functions such as blood pressure or heart rate is routed back to the individual in an easily perceived form, such as a tone or light (Martin & Poland, 1980). Even though we are not normally aware of these biological processes, biofeedback assumes we can learn to control them when we are provided with feedback about them (see chapter 6). That people can control such processes has been shown; exactly how or why they can do it is not presently understood (Martin & Poland, 1980). Despite this, several clinical applications of biofeedback have been successful.

Headache is one of the stress-related disorders that has been treated by biofeedback. For tension headaches, subjects are typically trained to relax the forehead muscle with the aid of electromyographic (EMG) biofeedback (see Figure 14–5). This particular use of biofeedback, then, can be viewed as a form of relaxation training (Qualls & Sheehan, 1981).

Figure 14–5.
Biofeedback is often used as a technique for training people to relax.

For EMG biofeedback, electrodes attached to the forehead register minute electric potentials from muscles, amplify them, and convert them to an auditory or visual signal (Martin & Poland, 1980). As tension in the muscles changes, so does signal intensity. Blanchard and Andrasik (1982) report that, across a number of studies, the average rate of improvement in tension-headache patients treated by EMG biofeedback was about 61 percent. This rate was approximately the same for relaxation training alone and for EMG biofeedback combined with relaxation. All of the approaches were much more effective than no treatment at all.

One apparently successful biofeedback approach to treating migraine headaches has been to teach patients to voluntarily increase their finger temperature. The effects of the strategy are increased blood flow to the periphery of the body and general relaxation (Rice &

Blanchard, 1982). Another approach teaches migraine sufferers to constrict cranial blood vessels by decreasing blood-pulse magnitude (Martin & Poland, 1980). Blanchard and Andrasik (1982) report that both approaches appear to hold promise as effective treatments (see, for example, Knapp, 1982).

Biofeedback has also been used in the treatment of high blood pressure. Lustman and Sowa (1983), for example, found that EMG biofeedback was effective in this regard. Increased heart rate, one of the hallmarks of anxiety and stress, has been treated by biofeedback. Although achieving voluntary control of heart rate certainly seems possible (Martin & Poland, 1980), Rice and Blanchard (1982) argue that, to date, there is only minimal support for the effectiveness of heart rate biofeedback in reducing anxiety.

It is too early to assess the ultimate usefulness of relaxation and biofeedback techniques, since they re-

STRESS AND COPING

375

main experimental (Raczynski, Thompson, & Sturgis, 1982; Simkins, 1982). At the very least, though, they offer some hope to people who find it difficult to cope with the effects of stress. However, reducing stress requires other techniques, some of which will be described in the next section.

— COPING WITH STRESS —

In this section, we will devote our attention to strategies for managing stress and factors that affect coping ability.

Cognitive Appraisal

Reactions to a potentially stressful event depend greatly on how it is evaluated (Coyne & Lazarus, 1980). Such evaluations, called **cognitive appraisals,** reflect the fact that what one person sees as threatening may not be a threat to someone else. Furthermore, cognitively reappraising a stressful event can make it less threatening. We can see, then, that the cognitive appraisal of events influences how we cope with them.

The impact of cognitive appraisals can be seen in a series of studies by Lazarus and his colleagues. In one study (Speisman, Lazarus, Mordkoff, & Davison, 1964), male subjects watched a stress-inducing film about a puberty ritual in an Australian tribe. Depending on which sound track accompanied the film, subjects heard either (1) about the great suffering the boy in the film was experiencing, (2) about the benefits of the ritual rather than the suffering involved, or (3) a detached, scientific perspective on the ritual. Control subjects saw the film but did not hear an accompanying sound track.

Subjects who heard the sound track emphasizing the boy's suffering showed far greater signs of physiological stress than did control subjects. Subjects who heard either of the other two sound tracks, on the other hand, showed slightly less stress than did control subjects. The point is this: By reappraising some stressful event as nonthreatening, we can reduce the stress that it produces. Cognitive reappraisal can therefore be a very useful coping technique.

Predictability

A number of findings indicate that both humans and animals would rather receive a predictable aversive stimulus than one that is unannounced. Predictability seems to reduce the severity of stressful events, allowing us to better deal with them. It also lessens negative consequences, such as performance declines and negative feelings (Burger & Arkin, 1980; Cohen, 1980).

Why is predictability so beneficial? One explanation, called the *safety signal hypothesis,* suggests that unpredictable events are more stressful because they offer no safe periods during which one can relax (Seligman, 1968). The individual is therefore chronically anxious.

Another explanation of the benefits of predictability is that more attention is directed toward unpredictable events than toward predictable ones (Matthews, Scheier, Brunson, & Carducci, 1980). It has been argued that individuals experiencing predictable stress habituate, or adapt, more quickly than do those experiencing unpredictable stress, because they attend less to the aversive stimulus. According to this view, "it is the slowed habituation brought on by heightened attention that causes unpredictable stressors to have more severe negative consequences" (Matthews, Scheier, Brunson, & Carducci, 1980, p. 534).

Mischel (1981) observes that even when people cannot control an aversive future outcome (such as by escaping from it), they seem to prefer to know something about it. The greater their knowledge about it, the less anxious they are. It might be expected, for example, that a person facing major surgery would experience less distress if provided with a thorough explanation of what was to take place.

Perceived Control

A feeling of control over a stressor also seems effective in lessening its negative effects. There is abundant evidence that people strongly value and are reluctant to relinquish the perception that they can control the events around them (Rothbaum, Weisz, & Snyder, 1982). **Perceived control** can be defined as the belief that one has the ability to influence the aversiveness of an event (Thompson, 1981). Control doesn't have to be exercised for it to be effective. It doesn't even have to be real. What is important is that the control be perceived.

As indicated, people seem to prefer having control over stressful events. Pervin (1963) found that when subjects had the choice between giving themselves an electric shock or letting the experimenter do it, they preferred to do it themselves. As Geen (1976) notes, "let me do it myself" is a common plea when we are faced with painful tasks, such as removing a splinter.

Above and beyond preferring control, actually having control or perceived control is beneficial in many ways. For example, it seems that pain tolerance is enhanced. A number of studies substantiate the importance of control in showing that stress aftereffects follow uncontrollable, but not controllable, stressors. This is true, for example, for noise (Glass & Singer, 1972; Gardner, 1978) and crowding (Sherrod, 1974). Exposure to uncontrollable noise has been shown to lead to such negative effects as lessened tolerance for frustration, less efficient task performance (Glass & Singer, 1972), and decreased sensitivity toward others (Sherrod & Downs, 1974; Donnerstein & Wilson, 1976).

— Why Does Control Affect Stress?

Control lessens anxiety in anticipating a stressor and increases tolerance of it, apparently by giving a message about future outcomes (Thompson, 1981). Having control means one can limit maximum future danger. People with control know that the situation will not become so aversive that they cannot handle it; control can be applied before then.

Other theories are needed to account for the aftereffects of stress. It may be that perceived control, or a lack of it, reflects on one's self-image. As Thompson (1981) points out, a number of theories suggest that a lack of control leads to feelings of anger, incompetence, helplessness, and futility (deCharms, 1968; Brehm, 1966; Seligman, 1975). These reactions may explain why people who are exposed to uncontrollable events lose motivation and experience decreases in performance.

Social Supports

Many of the stressful situations we encounter can be made less stressful through the emotional support of others, such as family and friends (Aneshensel & Stone, 1982; Sarason, 1981; Sarason, Levine, Basham, & Sarason, 1983). Not having such support increases the severity of a given stressor, leaving us less able to cope with it. Coleman (1979) observes that having surgery, going through a divorce, or experiencing the death of a loved one may be more stressful when one feels alone and isolated than if there are others who can be counted on for emotional support (see Figure 14–6).

Figure 14–6.

A stressful event can be coped with more effectively if one can rely on others for emotional support.

A number of research findings point to the importance of social support. One study, for example, found that mothers who had abused and neglected their children were far more isolated from other people than were mothers who had not mistreated their children (Salzinger, Kaplan, & Artemyeff, 1983). A reviewer summarized the research in the following way: "Emotional support is repeatedly cited in the literature as a correlate of emotional health. Coping with depression, transition to parenthood, work stress, recovery from car accidents, and the aging process are all related to having a confidant" (Leavy, 1983, p. 3). It is worth pointing out also that, in many cases, just believing that you have others you can count on (perceived social support) can be as beneficial as actually having the support and using it (Procidano & Heller, 1983).

As Sarason (1981) has observed, Bowlby's (1969, 1973) review of the literature suggests that people are happiest and function most efficiently when they believe that trusted people are ready and willing to come to their aid in times of need. Having this social support helps them cope with crises and adjust to change (Sarason, 1981).

Personality and Health

Personality may play a critical role in how people respond to stressful situations. Two important personality characteristics are hardiness and Type A behavior.

— Hardiness

As we have indicated, leading a stressful life can be a health hazard. Yet, many highly stressed individuals remain healthy. What is it about such people that enables them to avoid illness? Kobasa (1979) has suggested that those who experience high degrees of stress without feeling ill have a personality structure best characterized by the term **hardiness.** In contrast to highly stressed persons who do become ill, hardy individuals seem to be characterized by (1) the belief that they can *control* the events of their lives, (2) the ability to feel *committed* to the activities of their lives, and (3) the anticipation of change as an exciting *challenge* to further development.

Kobasa's theorizing was supported in her study of two groups of middle- and upper-level executives who had gone through comparably stressful life events during the 3 previous years (Kobasa, 1979). Members of

one group had suffered high stress without falling ill; members of the other group reported becoming sick after their encounter with stressful life events. As expected, high stress–low illness executives showed greater hardiness. They had a strong commitment to self, a vigorous attitude toward the environment, a sense of meaningfulness, and a belief that they were in control of the events of their lives. Kobasa (1982) found further support for the stress-resistant nature of commitment in a sample of lawyers. Both of these studies, however, were retrospective and therefore do not allow one to conclude that personality causes stress resistance. After all, it is possible that the personality characteristics resulted from the illness or the stress or the interaction of the two. Still, a recent prospective study of middle- and upper-level managers (Kobasa, Maddi, & Kahn, 1982) supported the idea that hardiness—commitment, control, and challenge—does function to break the stressful events–illness link. Yet another study by Kobasa and her colleagues (Kobasa, Maddi, & Puccetti, 1982) found that hardiness combined with exercise provides an even greater buffer against illness. Future research should point out how such characteristics as hardiness can be developed.

— Type A Behavior Pattern

An excessive competitive drive, a strong need to achieve success, aggressiveness, impatience, and a sense of time urgency mark the **Type A behavior pattern** (Friedman & Rosenman, 1974; Glass, 1977). They also lead to a greater likelihood of heart attacks than does an absence of such characteristics (Type B behavior). As Baron and Byrne (1981) note, the stereotypical Type A is a hard-driving businessperson who is always under pressure and fighting to meet deadlines. But in reality anyone can be a Type A person, headed for heart disease. Perhaps you can appreciate the nature of the Type A person by examining the listing of Type A characteristics in Table 14–4. Do you think you lean more toward being Type A or Type B?

Psychological research has strongly supported the many hypothesized differences between Type As and Type Bs (Matthews, 1982). For example, Type As respond more aggressively to frustration than do Type Bs (Carver & Glass, 1978). Type As are not, however, more aggressive than Type Bs when they are not frustrated. Carver and Glass (1978) argue that frustration poses a threat to the Type A's sense of mastery and control over the environment. Aggression reflects an attempt to regain that control. The sense of time ur-

Table 14–4.

Type A characteristics.

You may be a Type A person if you:

—Seem to be harboring feelings of aggression or hostility.

—Tend to talk, eat, move, and walk rapidly.

—Feel and exhibit an impatience with the rate at which most events take place.

—Often try to think of or do two or more things simultaneously.

—Find it difficult to refrain from directing a conversation toward those subjects of particular interest to you.

—Tend to feel guilty when you relax and do absolutely nothing.

—Tend to not observe or appreciate the beauty of your surroundings.

—Tend to be preoccupied with *having* things rather than *becoming* something.

—Try to schedule more and more in less and less time.

—Feel compelled to "challenge" other Type A individuals.

—Have nervous gestures or habits such as fist clenching or teeth grinding.

—Believe that your successes are due to your ability to do things faster than others.

—Tend to evaluate your own and others' activities in terms of "numbers."

(Adapted from Friedman & Rosenman, 1974, pp. 82–85.)

gency of Type As is also well documented. Type As tend to arrive early for appointments (Gastorf, 1980), they perceive time as passing more quickly than Type Bs do, and they work more quickly to complete time-limited tasks (Yarnold & Grimm, 1982).

Other differences between Type As and Type Bs, summarized by Baron and Byrne (1981), include the following. Type As get less sleep each night than do Type Bs, presumably because they want to get more accomplished. Type As work hard even without a deadline, whereas Type Bs seem to need a deadline before they will put forth extra effort. Type As focus their attention on the task at hand and ignore distractions. Type As complain less than Type Bs about hard work, and they claim to be less tired when a job is completed.

How can we make sense of the Type A behavior pattern? Competitive achievement striving, a sense of time urgency, and an easily aroused hostility may all reflect the Type A individual's continual struggle to control the environment (Brunson & Matthews, 1981). According to Glass (1977), this struggle leads Type As, when confronted by a threat, to increase their efforts at control (see also Rhodewalt & Davison, 1983). But if such efforts meet with repeated failure, Type As give up and

appear helpless (Brunson & Matthews, 1981; Fazio, Cooper, Dayson, & Johnson, 1981).

How does Type A behavior get translated, physically, into a heart attack? We really don't know for sure yet, but several intriguing possibilities have been offered. One is that Type A individuals may display a damaging hyperreactivity of the autonomic nervous system in response to competition, time urgency, and loss of control (Goldband, 1980; Houston, 1983). Recent medical research further supports the idea that the Type A behavior–coronary disease link is due to overreactivity of specific body responses (Williams et al., 1982). Williams and his colleagues studied blood pressure, blood flow to muscle, and the levels of five hormones in Type A and Type B subjects. These responses were measured while subjects performed mental arithmetic and reaction-time tasks. Type As showed greater physiological reaction (such as excessive secretions of testosterone and epinephrine) to each of the tasks than did Type Bs. These physiological responses, in turn, are specifically linked to coronary problems and ultimately to an increased risk of heart attack.

Type A behavior may also be linked to other health problems. It has been found that individuals high in Type A behavior and low in hardiness are particularly susceptible to the variety of illnesses that can result from stressful life events (Kobasa, Maddi, & Zola, 1983).

Defense Mechanisms

Although people deal with conflict and stress in numerous ways, Freud believed **defense mechanisms** to be particularly important in this regard (see chapter 13). He thought that they were unconscious psychological processes used by people to protect themselves against anxiety through distorting reality. Let's examine the specifics of some of these mechanisms.

— Denial

The defense mechanism whereby we pretend that some unpleasant reality does not exist is **denial.** For example, a close family member may be dying, but we refuse to acknowledge it. We may have a serious health problem, but we deny that it is a real threat to us. There may be a problem in our marriage, but we avoid facing it, pretending that it doesn't exist.

— Repression

The defense mechanism of **repression** involves keeping out of our consciousness threatening and unacceptable thoughts. We may repress unacceptable or inappropriate sexual or aggressive feelings, for example, so that we do not have to become aware of them. By keeping such feelings blocked from consciousness, we are able to avoid the stress and anxiety that would otherwise occur.

— Reaction Formation

The defense mechanism wherein we substitute in awareness a socially acceptable desire opposite to one that is socially unacceptable is **reaction formation.** The substitute behavior is always extreme or excessive. For example, a mother who has unacceptable negative feelings toward her baby may behave in an excessively loving and overprotective manner toward the child (Goodstein & Lanyon, 1979). Showering the child with love and affection protects the mother from the anxiety that negative feelings would cause.

— Rationalization

The defense mechanism that involves finding "logical" and acceptable reasons to justify behavior is **rationalization.** By using rationalization, we can find good cause in just about anything we do, regardless of how unacceptable or inappropriate it may at first seem to us or to others. The anxiety that might otherwise be associated with not returning a phone call, not studying for an exam, lying to someone, or failing at something important to us can be reduced through rationalization.

You are no doubt familiar with Aesop's sour-grapes fable. A fox couldn't reach a bunch of grapes and so decided that he didn't really want them because they were sour anyway. All of us sometimes use the sour-grapes type of rationalization when we must cope with our frustrations and failures. If we can't have something we want, we decide we really don't want it after all. Along with the sour-grapes approach, we may also use the sweet-lemon type of rationalization, in which we decide that what we do have is perfectly adequate. If we can't get the job we've been seeking, we may decide not only that we didn't want the job anyway (sour grapes) but that the job we now have is just fine (sweet lemon).

— Projection

The defense mechanism in which we project our own unacceptable thoughts or behavior onto other people or blame them for our faults is **projection.** A husband who feels guilty over having an extramarital affair may blame his wife for his behavior (Coleman, 1979). Our unacceptable feelings of hostility toward someone may be dealt with by our decision that the other person is actually hostile toward us. Projection allows us to reduce the anxiety caused by our unacceptable feelings, thoughts, and behaviors.

Projection seems to be found more often than normal in persons who have rigid moral codes (Goodstein & Lanyon, 1979). Such persons are extremely sensitive to, and threatened by, departures from morality. To avoid recognizing any evidence of their own immorality, they direct their sensitivity toward others. Other people are perceived as having sinful and immoral thoughts and motives.

— Regression

The defense mechanism in which long-outgrown behaviors are used to lessen a threat or anxiety is **regression.** It is commonly viewed as one possible reaction to frustration. A young child who feels threatened by a new baby in the family may revert to bedwetting in order to once again gain parental attention (Coleman, 1979). When faced with a severely threatening situation, it is sometimes easiest and most satisfying to simply regress to outgrown, less mature ways of behaving (see Figure 14–7).

— Compensation

The defense mechanism of **compensation** involves counteracting an undesirable characteristic that makes a person feel anxious and inadequate by exaggerating an opposing trait. Extremely shy people may become overbearing and intimidating. Those who have doubts about their sexual competence may try to seduce as many people as possible (Derlega & Janda, 1978). Such compensations are attempts to deal with the stress and anxiety caused by inadequacies.

— Summing Up

All the defense mechanisms described can be normal and useful techniques for dealing with the stress and

Figure 14–7.
The display of behaviors that have long been outgrown characterizes regression.

anxiety caused by failures, feelings of incompetence, unacceptable thoughts and impulses, and so on. Typically, our approach to such problems is to be somewhat defensive about them but at the same time try to solve them in a direct, constructive manner. For example, we may search for ways to overcome our inadequacies. Defense mechanisms become a problem only when they are our only strategies for dealing with stress and anxiety. In the long run, although defensive strategies help us feel better and cushion the blows of life's problems, they do not help solve the problems. Thus, as the sole strategies for handling stress, they are ultimately ineffective. They serve to distort reality, not to confront it head-on.

— APPLICATION —
BREAKING TYPE A HABITS

As we noted earlier, Type A individuals lead a high-pressure life-style that makes them ripe for heart attacks. According to Richard Suinn of Colorado State University (Suinn, 1976), these individuals are very resistant to change because of the way they respond to stress. In effect, they deal with stress by pushing themselves even harder than before, trying to do more and more and thus causing even more stress.

Fortunately, something can be done to help the Type A person get out of this vicious cycle. Suinn suggests several strategies for changing Type A habits. The first is to *learn to relax*. It doesn't matter what one does to relax, as long as an effort is made to take the time to do it. The problem with many Type A individuals is that they never take that time. For them, leisure time too often means "I'm not getting anything accomplished."

A second strategy is to *retrain reactions*. The typical Type A person reacts to pressure and deadlines with tension and considerable stress. Suinn suggests that Type As can combat this tendency by mentally rehearsing a different reaction. They can get relaxed and simply imagine themselves in a situation that typically makes them tense. With practice, they will be able to imagine such scenes without feeling tense at all. The idea is that the effects of such mental rehearsal will transfer to the real events when they occur.

A third strategy is to *take control of the environment*. One of the Type A tendencies is to try to accomplish more and more in less and less time. According to Suinn, a poorly managed environment can contribute to the stress caused by such a tendency. If you are a Type A, try to avoid an environment in which you are constantly rushed. Allow sufficient time between appointments. Try to avoid unnecessary interruptions.

Don't try to do more than is humanly possible and realistic, even if this means having to turn down requests from others to do even more. Allow time to do things well. Avoid an environment that is so pressure-packed and hectic that there is little time for thinking things through.

A fourth strategy is to *slow down*. Typical Type A persons are impatient and dissatisfied with the pace of events in their lives. If you are like this, one effective strategy for counteracting the tendency is to make yourself take it easy. It may be difficult at first, but whether you're eating, talking, or walking, remember that the quality of an event isn't always measured by how fast it gets done.

Suinn's (1976) research suggests that after using the preceding strategies, Type As report more control over stress, and even their cholesterol and blood-pressure levels drop. The latter factors, of course, are thought to be related to heart disease. As Suinn suggests, if the Type A individual is willing to put forth the effort, a dangerous life-style can be made less risky (see also Suinn, 1982; Levenkron, Cohen, Mueller, & Fisher, 1983).

COMMUNITY STRESS CHECKS—THREE MILE ISLAND AND BEYOND

You are probably aware of the accident that took place at the nuclear power station on Three Mile Island in Pennsylvania in March 1979 (see Figure 14–8). You may not be aware, however, of the great deal of stress that this accident caused residents living in the surrounding communities. The residents realized, of course, that if a meltdown had occurred at the plant, many of them could have lost their lives. Fortunately, instead of a massive release of ra-dioactive material, most of the radiation was contained.

Despite the fact that the reactor was controlled and the worst did not happen, psychological studies have shown that the Three Mile Island accident and continuing fears of possible radiation damage and future accidents have produced chronic stress for many nearby residents (Baum, Fleming, & Singer, 1982; Cunningham, 1982; Davidson, Baum, & Col-

Figure 14–8.

The nuclear accident at Three Mile Island represented an acutely stressful event for the residents living nearby.

lins, 1982; Fleming, Baum, Gisriel, & Gatchel, 1982). At the very least, the incident has not been easily forgotten. In January 1982, a United States Court of Appeals ruled that before an undamaged reactor on the island could start up again, the effect that a re-start might have on the psychological health of nearby residents must be considered. To put it an-other way, the Nuclear Regulatory Commission (NRC) was ordered to file a psychological impact statement, which is analogous to the environmental impact statements submitted before new atomic power plants are licensed (Cunningham, 1982). Even if it were determined that stress among residents would be likely, the crucial issue would be: How much is too much? How negative must the emo-tional impact be before a decision is made not to al-low operations?

All of this was made moot, however, in April 1983, when the Supreme Court overturned the ruling of the federal appeals court (Cunningham, 1983b). The Court ruled that the possible psychological stress on nearby residents of the Three Mile Island plant does not have to be considered in determining whether to restart the undamaged unit. Interestingly, though, the decision did keep open the possibility that, in some future cases, potential psychological harm would have to be considered (Cunningham, 1983a). The new ruling suggests that a psychological impact statement may be required when the government is planning some action that will significantly change the physical environment, not just pose a risk of such change, as in the Three Mile Island case.

Many of us will undoubtedly be affected by psy-chological impact statements in the coming years, perhaps in cases dealing with massive pesticide spraying or the dumping of toxic chemicals. No doubt, psychologists and other experts will help document and predict potential stress effects. How-ever, in the case of restarting the Three Mile Island plant, Cunningham (1982) has noted that "NRC engi-neers reacted with outright derision to suggestions that residents' reactions to restarting the plant could be predicted" (p. 52). The big question of the future may be how sensitive decision-makers are to the psychological impact of various environmental risks. The attitude that if it's psychological, it's not real may permeate the thinking of many people (Cun-ningham, 1982). But if community stress checks do become a common practice of the future, the effort certainly will be aided by the knowledge and tools of psychologists.

1. Daily hassles are an important source of stress and seem to predict psychological and physical health better than do major life events. In general, stress arises from a variety of sources. Frustration is one such source. It can be due to delays, lack of resources, losses, failure, or loneliness.

2. Conflict, which is also a source of stress, can be of several types. An approach-avoidance conflict involves strong tendencies to both approach and avoid the same goal. In a double approach-avoidance conflict, each of two or more goals has both positive and negative features. Approach-approach conflicts involve competiton between two or more desirable alternatives. Avoidance-avoidance conflicts involve the presence of two or more equally unattractive choices in a situation where one must be chosen.

3. Another common source of stress is pressure, which can stem from inner or outer sources. We may put pressure on ourselves, or it may come from others. Stress can also be induced through major life events. Such events involve a change in life circumstances and thus require one to adjust to them. Environmental stressors such as noise and crowding are also stress-producing. Unless an individual successfully adapts to such stressors, negative effects can be expected to occur.

4. The most effective strategy for managing an aversive waiting period and delaying gratification is to divert one's attention from the delayed rewards.

5. An important component of the stress reaction is its physiological effects. Selye has observed that there is a general pattern of physical reactions that seems to occur regardless of the source of the stress. He referred to this as the general adaptation syndrome. If the stressor isn't eliminated and stress is experienced over a long period of time, the syndrome is maintained and physical problems may ensue.

6. Stress-related pathological changes or organic disorders are called psychosomatic disorders. Among the most common body reactions to prolonged stress are migraine and tension headaches, hypertension, and peptic ulcers.

7. Much research has focused on how stress affects general health. As life stress increases, so does the risk of illness. This relationship is thought to exist because stress lowers the body's natural resistance to disease. Although the life stress–illness relationship is well documented, it is not a strong relationship and is affected by other factors.

8. Progressive muscle relaxation and biofeedback have been found useful in controlling body processes and in helping cope with such physical problems as headaches and high blood pressure.

9. People deal with stress in a variety of ways. Their reactions depend very much on their cognitive appraisal of the stress. If they do not perceive a situation as threatening, they will be better able to cope with it.

10. Both predictability and perceived control also affect stress tolerance. The better able we are to predict the occurrence of a stressor, the less its perceived severity. Having perceived control, whether it is actually used or not, also increases stress tolerance. Other work on coping with stress points to the importance of having social supports in helping manage stress.

11. Some individuals seem better equipped than others to deal with stress. Such individuals, characterized by the term hardiness, have a sense of control over their lives, feel committed to their activities, and see change as an exciting challenge. These hardy individuals also appear to be able to experience life stress without succumbing to illness. Another personality characteristic, the Type A behavior pattern, also seems to affect health, but in a negative way. Those who display a sense of time urgency, hostility, impatience, and competitive striving are at a great risk of succumbing to coronary heart disease.

12. Common strategies for defending against the anxiety caused by stress are the defense mechanisms of denial, repression, reaction formation, rationalization, projection, regression, and compensation.

13. Suinn suggests that Type A individuals learn to relax, retrain their reactions, take control of their environment, and slow down.

14. Community stress checks may become common in the future when the government is planning actions that will significantly alter the physical environment.

— IMPORTANT TERMS AND CONCEPTS —

Stress

Anxiety

Stressors

Frustration

Conflict

Approach-avoidance Conflict

Goal Gradients

Double Approach-avoidance Conflict

Approach-approach Conflict

Avoidance-avoidance Conflict

General Adaptation Syndrome (GAS)

Psychosomatic Disorders

Peptic Ulcer

Migraine Headaches

Tension Headaches

Hypertension

Biofeedback

Cognitive Appraisals

Perceived Control

Hardiness

Type A Behavior Pattern

Defense Mechanisms

Denial

Repression

Reaction Formation

Rationalization

Projection

Regression

Compensation

— SUGGESTIONS FOR FURTHER READING —

Beech, H. R., Burns, L. E., & Sheffield, B. F. (1982). *A behavioral approach to the management of stress: A practical guide to techniques*. Chichester, England: Wiley. Practical ideas for coping with stress, including relaxation techniques and biofeedback.

Coleman, J. C. (1979). *Contemporary psychology and effective behavior* (4th ed.). Glenview, IL: Scott, Foresman. A book that deals with problems of adjustment, it is a good place to get a general introduction to the concept of stress.

Friedman, M., & Rosenman, R. H. (1974). *Type A behavior and your heart*. New York: Knopf. A popular introduction to the Type A personality, exploring some possible antecedents and addressing ways to reengineer life-styles.

Geen, R. G. (1976). *Personality: The skein of behavior*. Saint Louis, MO: C. V. Mosby. An advanced-level book containing a wealth of experimental findings relevant to the topics of stress, anxiety, defense, and conflict.

Kutash, I. L., & Schlesinger, L. B. (Eds.). (1980). *Handbook on stress and anxiety*. San Francisco: Jossey-Bass. An advanced-level volume containing material on numerous sources of stress as well as treatment of stress disorders.

Selye, H. (1974). *Stress without distress*. New York: Lippincott. An insightful look into stress by the foremost authority on the subject, the late Hans Selye.

— CHAPTER 15 —

ABNORMAL BEHAVIOR

ABNORMAL BEHAVIOR

— CHAPTER OBJECTIVES —

To achieve the objectives of this chapter, you should be able to answer the questions listed here. You should also be able to define the important terms and concepts listed at the end of the chapter.

1. What is abnormal behavior?
2. List some advantages and disadvantages in classifying abnormal behavior into specific categories.
3. What are the most useful current models of abnormality?
4. How do the models of abnormality differ in their explanations of mental disorders?
5. Name the major characteristics of each of the categories of abnormal behavior.
6. What are some of the specific factors that have been cited as causes of the different psychological disorders?

— CHAPTER OUTLINE —

Classifying and Conceptualizing Abnormal Behavior
Developing a reliable classification system and explaining abnormality are important tasks.

Issues in Classification
Models of Abnormality
Application: Interpreting Abnormality from Different Perspectives

Categories of Abnormal Behavior
Abnormality takes many forms and varies considerably in severity.

Anxiety Disorders
Somatoform Disorders
Dissociative Disorders
Affective Disorders
Schizophrenic Disorders
Personality Disorders
Application: Warning Signs for Student Suicide

On the Horizon: Diagnosing Abnormal Behavior with the PET Scanner

SCHIZOPHRENIA
AND THE GENAIN QUADRUPLETS

For more than two decades, researchers have been studying the Genain quadruplets—Nora, Iris, Myra, and Hester—who are shown in Figure 15–1 (Hamer, 1982). The interest in these sisters is due to the fact that all of them have been diagnosed as schizophrenic. Schizophrenia is often considered the severest form of mental breakdown, involving, as it does, major disturbances in perception, thought, and emotion and a loss of contact with reality, among other symptoms. As Hamer (1982) points out, for those interested in the causes of schizophrenia, the Genains are an important source of information. Since all of them exhibit schizophrenic symptoms, and since they are genetically identical, it appears that genetics may be the underlying cause of their disorder. The sisters also differ considerably in the severity of their disorder, however, which suggests the importance of environmental influences. Iris and Myra seem to be the least troubled.

This fact has even shown up in PET scans (see chapter 2) done on the quadruplets (see Hamer, 1982). According to one interpretation of the PET data, Nora and Hester exhibit the greatest abnormality in brain functioning; their frontal lobes burn less energy than do Iris's or Myra's (the use of the PET scanner in diagnosing schizophrenia is still a controversial issue—see the "On the Horizon" section at the end of this chapter). Given that the frontal lobes play an important role in thinking and emotion, the fact that they are less active in Nora and Hester may help explain why these two sisters are the most severely afflicted of the quadruplets. What still needs to be explained, of

Figure 15–1.

The Genain quadruplets.

course, is why such differences exist. One hypothesis is that Nora (the first-born) and Hester (the lastborn) experienced the most traumatic births of the four sisters, suffering greater brain damage in the process. In sum, the Genain quadruplets provide suggestive evidence that schizophrenia may be determined or influenced by both genetic and nongenetic factors.

Schizophrenia represents just one of many problems comprising this chapter's central topic: the study of abnormal behavior. By **abnormal behavior** we mean any behavior that has undesirable consequences for the individual or for others. Behavior is abnormal, then, when it is maladaptive and self-defeating—that is, when it impairs optimal functioning, causes personal distress, or causes others distress or harm (Coleman, Butcher, & Carson, 1980). At least some abnormal behaviors are strange or bizarre. But many ordinary behaviors are also maladaptive. Consider, for example, students who become so anxious when taking tests that their performance suffers.

Note that we do not define *abnormal behavior* in terms of its statistical frequency in the general population. Some maladaptive behaviors are, in fact, rare or infrequent. However, infrequency alone does not mean that a behavior is maladaptive. Refusing to travel by airplane or needing to read in bed for 2 hours before falling asleep may be infrequent behaviors, but they are not necessarily maladaptive (Sarason & Sarason, 1980). They would be considered maladaptive only if they caused the individuals (or those around them) distress or interfered with their daily functioning. Likewise, behaviors aren't necessarily adaptive just because they occur frequently.

In the first section of this chapter, we will examine some of the issues and problems associated with classifying abnormal behavior. We will also examine a number of ways of conceptualizing abnormality. In the second section, we will look into various types of abnormal behavior and their possible causes.

— CLASSIFYING AND CONCEPTUALIZING ABNORMAL BEHAVIOR —

Issues in Classification

In any science, there must be a *classification system* whereby observations are organized into reasonably similar groups (Goodstein & Calhoun, 1982). In psychology, the classification of abnormal behavior allows clinicians and researchers to communicate efficiently about the behavior. Moreover, classifications suggest possible causes of problems, behaviors that might be expected, possible treatment methods, and probable outcomes.

Classification systems for abnormal behavior have been repeatedly revised to reflect new knowledge and viewpoints. Classification is still in flux, though, partly because it is somewhat arbitrary (Sarason & Sarason,

1980). When, for example, does normal depression become severe enough to be a depressive disorder? When does apprehensiveness become an anxiety disorder? In these and other cases, there is no precise point for separating normality from abnormality or one category of abnormal behavior from another. Ultimately, normality and abnormality are best thought of as being on a continuum. Thus, although constructing categories is useful, the categories themselves are somewhat arbitrary.

The value of any classification system lies in its *reliability* (Goodstein & Calhoun, 1982)—that is, the likelihood that the behavior an individual exhibits will be correctly classified. Unfortunately, at present there is more likely to be agreement about general categories (e.g., whether or not an individual is schizophrenic) than about specific disorders (e.g., what type of schizophrenia it is). As long as personal judgment is involved in classifying abnormality, this lack of agreement is going to be a problem. Consequently, some unreliabilility can be expected unless clinical assessment becomes highly standardized and less open to bias (Sarason & Sarason, 1980). Standardization has been the goal in recent efforts at improving classification systems, and it is reflected most notably in the development of DSM-III, which we will now examine briefly.

— DSM-III

Currently, the most widely used system for classifying abnormal behavior is the third edition of the American Psychiatric Association's *Diagnostic and Statistical Manual of Mental Disorders* (DSM-III) (APA, 1980). We will follow the DSM-III categories when we look into various disorders later in this chapter. Table 15–1 lists the categories we will be using.

DSM-III is a set of guidelines for categorizing disorders on the basis of symptoms, or behaviors. Earlier systems based diagnoses on the causes of disorders rather than their symptoms. Often, this approach rendered the diagnoses unreliable because it involved too much speculation about those causes. DSM-III has improved classification by providing detailed descriptions of each disorder. Whenever possible, it also lists potential causes of disorders, typical ages of onset, sex ratios, and prevalence in the general population. Theoretically, DSM-III's shift in emphasis should improve reliability, but only time will tell if it does.

— The Labeling Problem

Surely, progress toward a full understanding of maladaptive behavior would be impeded without a classification system such as DSM-III. At the same time, though, we must recognize the dangers of *labeling*. Simply making a diagnosis can have harmful effects. Coleman, Butcher, and Carson (1980) have pointed out several problems in this regard. First, we run into problems when we expect all people in a category to behave in precisely the same way. However, once a person is labeled, there may be a tendency to no longer question that label—to assume that it does, in fact, accurately describe the person, when it may not. Prejudgments regarding what a client is like or should be like can then affect decisions such as what treatments to employ. An incorrect label may therefore slow recovery.

Table 15–1.

Selected DSM-III Categories

ANXIETY DISORDERS
  Generalized anxiety disorder
  Phobic disorder
    Agoraphobia
    Social phobia
    Simple phobia
  Obsessive-compulsive disorder

SOMATOFORM DISORDERS
  Hypochondriasis
  Conversion disorder

DISSOCIATIVE DISORDERS
  Psychogenic amnesia
  Psychogenic fugue
  Multiple personality

AFFECTIVE DISORDERS
  Major affective disorders
    Major depressive disorder
    Bipolar disorder
  Other specific affective disorders

SCHIZOPHRENIC DISORDERS
  Disorganized schizophrenia
  Catatonic schizophrenia
  Paranoid schizophrenia
  Undifferentiated schizophrenia

PERSONALITY DISORDERS
  Paranoid
  Schizoid
  Schizotypal
  Histrionic
  Narcissistic
  Antisocial
  Borderline
  Avoidant
  Dependent
  Compulsive
  Passive-aggressive

Beyond this, the client may begin to accept a label or identity and change to fit it. This is the problem of the *self-fulfilling prophecy,* whereby one behaves as seems to be expected (see also chapter 18). For example, a person diagnosed as schizophrenic might display disturbed behavior in part because of the labeling. A closely related problem is the tendency for both clients and clinicians to view the label as a name for the person rather than the person's behavior. This tendency can lead to the lifelong stigma of being an ex-mental patient.

All of this suggests that although labels may be helpful, they should be used judiciously. We should not lose sight of the fact that their basic function is to help researchers and clinicians describe and organize information relating to the various mental disorders.

Models of Abnormality

Research on, treatment for, and explanations for abnormal behavior can be thought of as falling into one of several broad conceptual frameworks: biological, psychoanalytic, behavioral, cognitive, humanistic, family-interaction, and sociocultural models. A brief description of each follows.

— Biological Model

Also sometimes referred to as the *medical model,* the **biological model of abnormality** views abnormal behavior as resulting from some organic or biological impairment. This model, long considered an important and viable approach to understanding abnormality, is the basis of much current research in abnormal psychology. For example, as we will see later, some investigators are now examining the genetic and biochemical bases of such disorders as schizophrenia and depression.

— Psychoanalytic Model

The **psychoanalytic model of abnormality** is that mental disorders represent substitute expressions of repressed unconscious impulses. Freud (see chapter 13) believed that these impulses, primarily sexual in nature, had their origin in early childhood. When the repression is not totally effective and the impulse threatens to express itself, a less threatening symptom (maladaptive behavior) arises in its place.

— Behavioral Model

The **behavioral model of abnormality** suggests that maladaptive behavior can be attributed to faulty learning processes. Behavioral psychologists use such concepts as classical and operant conditioning, reinforcement, generalization, discrimination, modeling, and shaping (see chapter 6) to explain the behavior. For example, classical conditioning, while usually *adaptive,* can also be *maladaptive,* as when we develop irrational fears or phobias. As an example, you may recall from chapter 6 the story of Albert, who was classically

conditioned to fear a white rat. Such fears or other maladaptive behaviors may also be acquired by reinforcement or by observational learning. An implication of the behavioral model is that maladaptive behavior can be unlearned and adaptive behavior can be learned to replace it.

— Cognitive Model

The underlying premise of the **cognitive model of abnormality** is that our response to some event depends largely on how we think about the event. In other words, maladaptive behavior can result from the assumptions we make, our interpretations of experiences, and the dialogue we carry on within ourselves. Cognitive-oriented theorists emphasize that problems occur when self-statements and other cognitions are distorted, irrational, illogical, negative, pessimistic, and self-critical.

— Humanistic Model

The central theme of the **humanistic model of abnormality,** represented by Rogers and Maslow (see chapter 13), is that people strive for personal growth and are motivated to fulfill their potentials. Presumably, psychological disorders arise when these basic tendencies are interfered with. The key problem, from Rogers's point of view, is that people may acquire a self-concept that is at odds with their innermost desires and needs. To avoid rejection and to gain the approval of significant figures in their lives, these people may deny their real selves and become something different from what they would like to be. The result is the inability to achieve self-actualization, which leads to unhappiness and maladaptive behavior.

— Family Interaction Model

Abnormal behavior results from faulty or disturbed relationships among family members, according to the **family interaction model of abnormality.** Poor communication patterns within the family may be one problem. As will be discussed later, Bateson (1960) has suggested that disturbed communication patterns contribute to the development of schizophrenia. Other investigators have focused on specific parental behaviors, such as whether the parents are rejecting or loving in interactions with their children.

Figure 15–7.

Fragmentation and body image diffusion are reflected in these spontaneous self portraits by a schizophrenic patient undergoing therapy. Christine W. Wang, ATR Director, Graduated Art Therapy Program, Goucher College, Towson, Maryland.

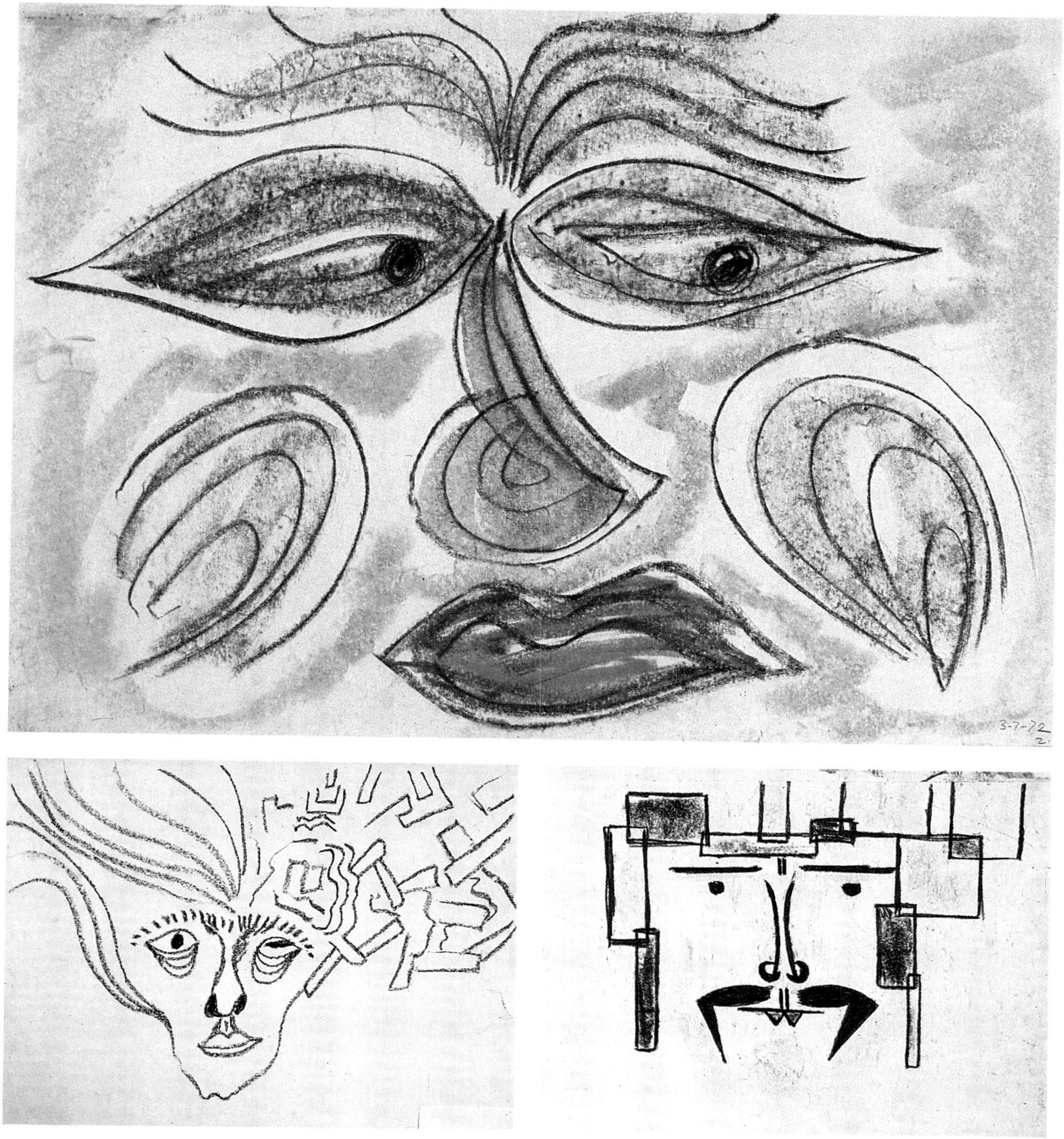

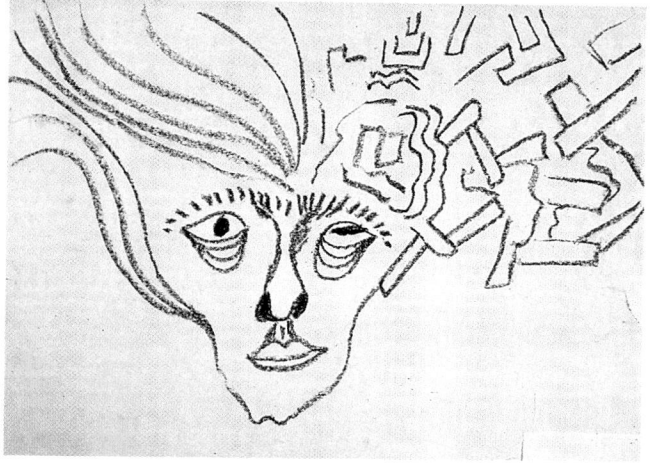

Figure 15–18.

The paintings shown here were done by Louis Wain (1860–1939), a well-known artist who suffered from schizophrenia during the latter part of his life. The paintings reveal how Wain's mental state increasingly deteriorated. The distortions of perception which characterize schizophrenia are evident as the cats changed over time from realistic to fragmented and almost unrecognizable as Wain's condition worsened. Derek Bayes, LIFE Magazine, © 1964 Time, Inc.

Figure 15–10.
A PET scanner. Copyright 1980 by Newsweek, Inc. All rights reserved.

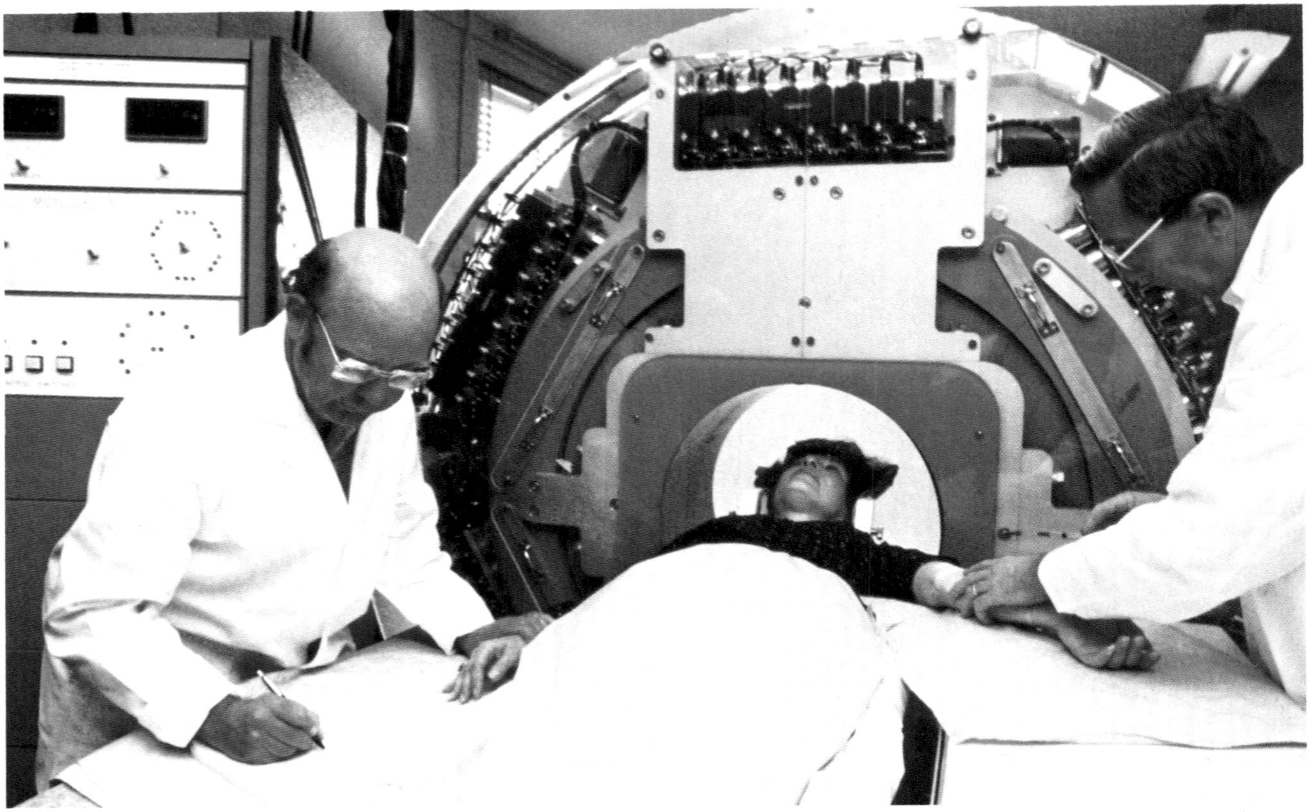

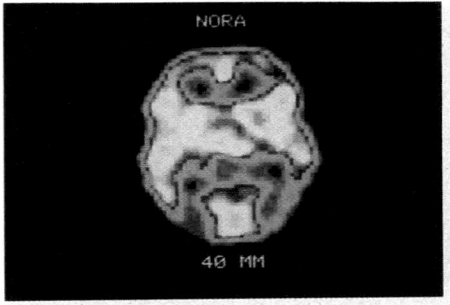

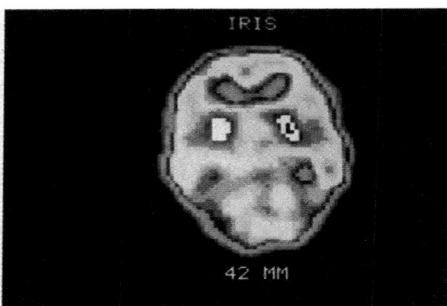

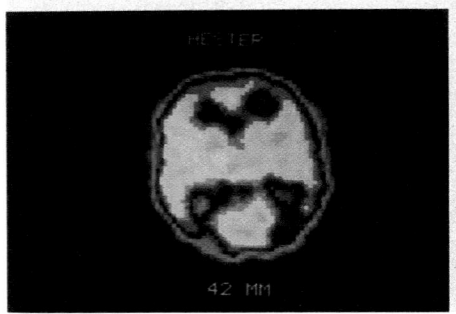

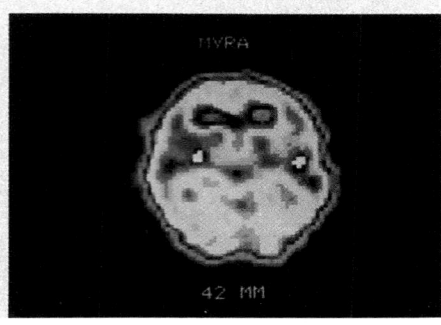

Figure 15–11.
PET scans of the Genain sisters show that little glucose is being consumed (low activity indicated by blue and green) in the frontal lobes (at top of each scan) of Nora and Hester. The orange spots on the scans of Iris and Myra indicate a more normal use of energy. Courtesy Allan F. Mirsky.

Sociocultural Model

The causes of abnormality lie in the larger society rather than in the individual or family, according to the **sociocultural model of abnormality.** Theorists of this persuasion point to factors such as poverty, discrimination, and illiteracy as potential sources of maladaptive behavior. When people who are not equipped to cope with these factors attempt to respond to societal pressures and mistreatment, they develop abnormal behavior (Rathus & Nevid, 1983).

As we look into the various mental disorders, we will examine a number of possible causes of each. We will not necessarily apply all the models to each disorder, but the models do provide an overview of alternate perspectives. Whenever one or more of them is particularly relevant to our understanding of a given disorder, we will point that out. Before we look at the disorders, it may be instructive to consider how some of the models would compare in dealing with a particular case.

— APPLICATION —

INTERPRETING ABNORMALITY FROM DIFFERENT PERSPECTIVES

The following example compares psychoanalytic, behavioral, cognitive, and humanistic views.

> George, a 24-year-old college student, came in for counseling, complaining of an inability to attend lectures. George revealed that he felt anxious when women were present. He described himself as shy and said he had only limited contact with women. His anxiety towards them had increased following an attempt to have sexual intercourse with the only woman that he had ever dated and the discovery that he was impotent. This heterosexual anxiety increased to the point where George stopped attending classes and remained in his dormitory room so that he would not have to have any contact with females. (Sue, Sue, & Sue, 1981, p. 83)

As Sue, Sue, and Sue (1981) point out, George's behavior can be interpreted in a variety of ways, depending on one's theoretical perspective. From a psychoanalytic point of view, his anxiety and impotence are signs of an unconscious conflict. For example, George may have strong sexual feelings for his mother, which will cause enormous anxiety unless the ego finds some way to defend against it. Given that all women may symbolize his mother, the ego prevents George from being overcome with anxiety by preventing any sexual activity at all.

The behavior-oriented theorist does not view George's anxiety and impotence as symptoms or signs of some internal conflict. Instead, the behaviorist sees the anxiety and impotence themselves as the basic problems and assumes that they arose through faulty learning. George's report of shyness and little contact with women suggests to the behaviorist that George has inadequate social skills. From a classical-conditioning perspective, the anxiety caused by being unable to interact with women is paired with women and leads to anxiety in their presence and avoidance of them. In operant-conditioning terms, the anxiety caused by inadequate social skills gets reinforced when George fails to interact effectively with women.

From a cognitive point of view, George's anxiety and impotence are a result of his distorted and irrational thinking. He may be telling himself such things as "I am worthless" and "No woman is going to be satisfied with me." These negative thoughts cause George considerable anxiety, and as a result he avoids all heterosexual situations.

The humanistic perspective accounts for George's problems by suggesting the following. On the one hand, George wants to fulfill normal sexual desires and to express the feelings that he really has; on the other hand, he is inhibited from doing so because part of his self-concept (learned in interactions with important others) tells him that it is bad or immoral to express these feelings. He is therefore experiencing an internal conflict; he is torn between what he is and what he would like to be. Being with women or thoughts of being with them arouse his anxiety because they make him feel guilty; he feels that he is a bad person if he has sexual feelings. To avoid sexual feelings and the subsequent feelings of guilt, George avoids women altogether.

In our review of mental disorders listed in DSM-III, we will examine the following major types of disorders: anxiety, somatoform, dissociative, affective, schizophrenic, and personality.

Anxiety Disorders

We have encountered the concept of anxiety before, particularly as the emotion that accompanies stress. *Anxiety* is best described as a vague, diffuse, and unpleasant feeling of apprehension (Sarason & Sarason, 1980). Its aversiveness often motivates people to try to avoid it. Table 15–2 lists some ways that highly anxious individuals describe themselves.

The central feature in **anxiety disorders** is either a high level of anxiety or the disruptive consequences of trying to avoid it or defend against it (Coleman, Butcher, & Carson, 1980). This category includes generalized anxiety disorders, phobic disorders, and obsessive-compulsive disorders. These disorders have affected from 2 to 4 percent of the general population at some time (APA, 1980).

— Generalized Anxiety Disorder

The individual with a **generalized anxiety disorder** displays a chronically high level of anxiety (at least 1 month in duration) but is unaware of its source. The anxiety is not due to any specific stressor or recent life

Table 15–2.
High levels of anxiety tend to lead to these types of self-descriptions. (From Sarason & Sarason, 1980, p. 159.)

1. I am often bothered by the thumping of my heart.
2. Little annoyances get on my nerves and irritate me.
3. I often become suddenly scared for no good reason.
4. I worry continuously and that gets me down.
5. I frequently get spells of complete exhaustion and fatigue.
6. It is always hard for me to make up my mind.
7. I always seem to be dreading something.
8. I feel nervous and high strung all the time.
9. I often feel I can't overcome my difficulties.
10. I feel constantly under strain.

experience and therefore is often referred to as free-floating anxiety. It is exhibited most notably in the following ways (APA, 1980):

1. *Motor tension.* The individual complains of an inability to relax and exhibits jumpiness and tenseness.
2. *Autonomic hyperactivity.* The individual may experience a number of physical symptoms, such as a racing or pounding heart, cold and clammy hands, lightheadedness, and an upset stomach.
3. *Apprehensive expectation.* The individual tends to worry excessively about the future.
4. *Vigilance.* The individual tends to be constantly on guard against unspecified possible threats or dangers.

The following case history of a generalized anxiety disorder illustrates these characteristics well.

> The patient, a twenty-four-year-old mechanic, had been referred for psychotherapy by his physician, whom he had consulted because of dizziness and difficulties in falling asleep. He was quite visibly distressed during the entire initial interview, gulping before he spoke, sweating, and continually fidgeting in his chair. His repeated requests for water to slake a seemingly unquenchable thirst were another indication of this extreme nervousness. Although he first related his physical concerns, a more general picture of pervasive anxiety soon emerged. He reported that he nearly always felt tense. He was apprehensive of possible disasters that could befall him as he worked and interacted with other people. He reported a long history of difficulties in interpersonal relationships, which had led to his being fired from several jobs. As he put it, "I really like people and try to get along with them, but it seems like I fly off the handle too easily. Little things they do upset me too much. I just can't cope unless everything is going exactly right." (Davison & Neale, 1982, p. 166)

Anxiety is also central to the other anxiety disorders, but in them, avoidance mechanisms alleviate the threat somewhat (Coleman, Butcher, & Carson, 1980). In generalized anxiety disorders, such mechanisms seem not to exist, so feelings of anxiety may be marked and free-floating.

Causes. From a biological perspective, it may be that some people inherit a type of nervous system that is more easily aroused than that of others (Rathus &

Nevid, 1983). Evidence for the role of genetics comes from the **concordance rate,** or degree of similarity between related individuals. The concordance rate for generalized anxiety disorder among identical (monozygotic) twins is 49 percent; among fraternal (dizygotic) twins it is 4 percent (Slater & Shields, 1969). These figures indicate that heredity is involved in the disorder. However, it is not the only factor, since in some cases only one identical twin in a pair may display the problem.

Psychological explanations of generalized anxiety vary greatly. The psychoanalytic model emphasizes unconscious forbidden impulses that threaten the ego's ability to maintain control. From the behavioral viewpoint, modeling (see chapter 6) may underlie anxiety. For example, a child who observes an anxious parent may become anxious as an adult. As another possibility, Wolpe (1958) proposed that generalized anxiety may be caused by an intense unconditioned stimulus (see chapter 6) or a lack of distinct environmental stimuli during conditioning (cf. Sue, Sue, & Sue, 1981). Either condition can attach anxiety to a broad range of stimuli. From a cognitive view, generalized anxiety stems from unrealistic appraisals of situations and overestimation of their danger. Further, Ellis (e.g., Ellis & Harper, 1975) suggests that anxiety is caused by perfectionistic and irrational expectations. Finally, Rogers's (1961) humanistic view holds that anxiety results when individuals view themselves as inadequate—chiefly because of a discrepancy between artificial standards and their true selves.

— Phobic Disorder

A **phobia** is an irrational, persistent fear of some specific object, activity, or situation in which no real danger exists or the danger is unrealistically magnified. Most of us have fears. We may, for example, be afraid of snakes, heights, or darkness (see chapter 6). In the case of phobias, however, the fears are sufficiently exaggerated to interfere with routine activities. A phobic individual may go to great lengths to avoid the feared stimulus, even though such behavior may be quite disruptive. When approaching the feared object or situation, the phobic individual is overcome with anxiety that ranges from a mild feeling of uneasiness to a full-blown anxiety attack (Coleman, Butcher, & Carson, 1980).

DSM-III subdivides the phobic disorders into three types: agoraphobia, social phobia, and simple phobia. Agoraphobia is the most general type and the severest. It is also the most common basis for seeking treatment. Both social and simple phobias generally involve more specific, circumscribed stimuli. Simple phobia, although less often treated, is the most common type in the general population. Let's look more closely at each disorder.

Agoraphobia is a marked fear of open spaces and unfamiliar settings. As Chambless (1982) observes, "agoraphobics tend to fear any situation where an easy retreat to safe territory is not possible" (p. 2). Settings that are commonly avoided include crowds, tunnels, elevators, bridges, and public transportation (see Figure 15–2). Agoraphobics often demand that a family

Figure 15–2.

Being in, or even thinking about being in, a crowd setting like this causes the agoraphobic considerable anxiety.

member or friend accompany them whenever they leave home. As fears begin to dominate the person's life, normal activities become increasingly constricted. In extreme cases, such individuals may be house-bound, unable even to walk down the street. The agoraphobic's intensity of fear is illustrated by a woman who was invited by a neighbor to drive to a newly opened shopping center. She comments:

> I didn't know how to tell her that there isn't a chance in the world that I'd go to that shopping center or any other place outside our neighborhood. She must have seen how upset I got, but I was shaking like a leaf even more inside. I imagined myself in the crowd, getting lost, or passing out. I was terrified. (Sarason & Sarason, 1980, p. 165)

Social phobia is a persistent irrational fear of situations in which the individual may be scrutinized by others or may behave in a manner that will be humiliating or embarrassing. Examples of such phobias are "speaking or performing in public, using public lavatories, eating in public, and writing in the presence of others" (APA, 1980, p. 227). The disruptive nature of a social phobia is illustrated in the following letter to advice columnist Ann Landers. Note the individual's distress.

> Dear Ann Landers: I've read so much about phobias, but never have I seen an article concerning mine. It is the inability to eat around people. I feel like an animal sometimes because I have to hide in corners or bathrooms to eat. . . .
>
> I've tried to explain my fears to some people, but no one knows how to help me. I just want to die. I'm begging you to check your resources and let me know what can be done about this problem. You're my last hope.
> —Carol. (Reprinted by permission of Ann Landers and Field Newspaper Syndicate)

Simple phobia is a persistent irrational fear of any object or situation other than those already described. Simple phobias are also called specific phobias because the feared stimulus is relatively circumscribed. They sometimes involve animals (e.g., Costello, 1982), particularly dogs, snakes, insects, and mice (APA, 1980). *Claustrophobia* (fear of closed spaces) and *acrophobia* (fear of heights) are other common simple phobias.

Causes. From the psychoanalytic point of view, phobias occur when unconscious conflicts are displaced onto an external object or situation. For exam-

ple, a man with repressed ideas of stabbing his wife might develop a phobia for knives because they make him anxious. The behaviorists propose that phobias are often the result of conditioning. That is, a phobia about some object may develop after an especially painful or traumatic experience with that object (Davison & Neale, 1982). Thus, a person who has a serious car accident may develop an intense fear of driving. Also, Bandura (1969) has suggested that many fears are learned by observing others who fear particular objects or situations. The cognitive model suggests that phobics have distorted thinking. For example, an individual with a phobia of elevators may think, "If I go into an elevator, it might get stuck and I might suffocate" (Sarason & Sarason, 1980).

— Obsessive-Compulsive Disorder

Individuals with an **obsessive-compulsive disorder** are compelled to think thoughts they do not want to think or to engage in some act they do not want to perform (Coleman, Butcher, & Carson, 1980). An **obsession** is a recurrent and persistent idea, thought, or impulse that comes involuntarily. A **compulsion** is a repetitive behavior that the individual feels compelled to perform to prevent intolerable anxiety. Everyone has probably experienced minor obsessions, such as having a certain tune repeat itself over and over in the mind or being unable to stop thinking about some person or event. In the case of obsessive disorders, the obsessions are much more persistent, distressing, disruptive, and senseless to the individual.

According to DSM-III, the most common obsessions are thoughts of violence (such as killing someone), contamination (for example, getting a disease from shaking hands with someone), and doubt (for instance, wondering if one has done something, such as having hurt someone in a traffic accident) (APA, 1980). Especially common are obsessions about committing immoral acts, such as a daughter obsessed with the idea of pushing her mother down a staircase. Such obsessions are typically not carried out in action, but they can nevertheless continue to torment the individual (Coleman, Butcher, & Carson, 1980).

Just as with obsessions, most of us have also experienced some compulsive behaviors. They are usually, but not always, associated with an obsession. We check and recheck locked doors or make sure we step over cracks in the sidewalk. But with the obsessive-compulsive disorder, the compulsiveness is more extreme. Individuals with this disorder feel it necessary to perform the act even though they consider it senseless and do not want to do it. The disorder can vary greatly in its severity. Davison and Neale (1982) discuss an extreme case of excessive hand washing; one of their patients washed her hands more than 500 times a day despite the painful sores it caused. Engaging in such compulsive acts provides a release of tension for the individual. Resisting the compulsion brings anxiety. According to DSM-III, the most common compulsions are hand washing, counting, checking, and touching (also see Figure 15–3). Table 15–3 gives some clinical examples of both obsessions and compulsions. In addition, the following case history shows the nature of an obsessive-compulsive disorder.

A 15-year-old boy had a two-year history of compulsive behaviors, involving 16 repetitions of the following behaviors: opening and closing a door, touching glasses before drinking from them, walking around each tree in front of his house before going to school. These compulsive acts produced a great deal of discomfort in the boy. His schoolmates ridiculed him and his parents were upset because his rituals prevented him from reaching school at the appropriate time. An interview with the boy revealed that his compulsive behaviors were associated with the onset of masturbation, an act that the boy considered "dirty," although he was unable to refrain from it. It was when he

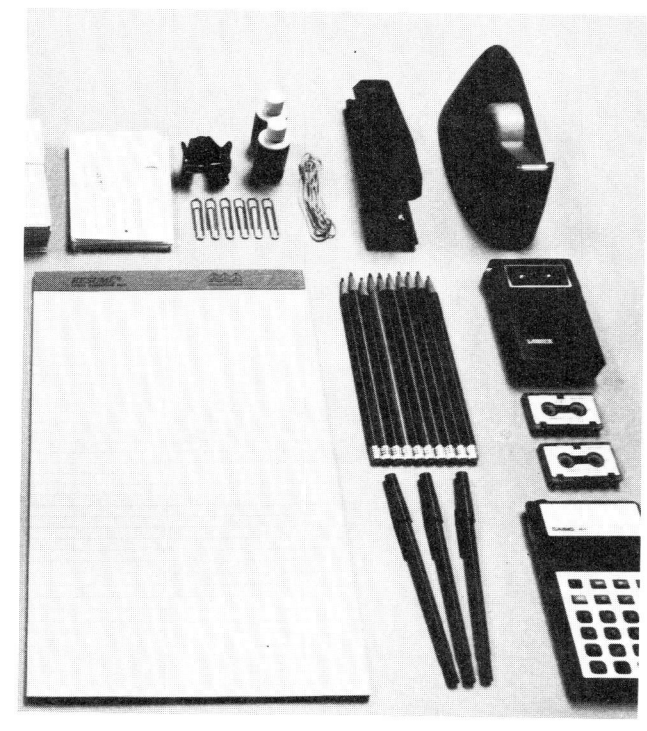

Figure 15–3.

A frequently reported compulsion is one of orderliness.

Table 15–3.

Examples of obsessions and compulsions. (From Sue, Sue, & Sue, 1981, p. 175; sources: Boersma, Den Hengst, Dekker, & Emmelkamp (1976), Rachman, Marks, & Hodgson (1973), Roper, Rachman, & Marks (1975), and Stern, Lipsedge, & Marks (1973).)

AGE	SEX	DURATION OF OBSESSION IN YEARS	CONTENT OF OBSESSION
21	M	6	Teeth decaying, particles between teeth
42	M	16	Women's buttocks, own eye movements
55	F	35	Fetuses lying in street, killing babies, people buried alive
24	M	16	Worry about touching vomit
21	F	9	Strangling people

AGE	SEX	DURATION OF COMPULSIONS IN YEARS	COMPULSIVE RITUALS
47	F	23	Handwashing and housecleaning; contact with dirt, toilet, or floor triggers about 100 hand washings per day
20	F	13	Severe checking ritual—checking 160 times to see if window is closed; also compulsion to read license numbers of cars and numbers on manhole covers
21	M	2	Intense fear of contamination after touching library books or money; Hand washing 25 times a day and rumination about how many people had already handled objects

began to masturbate that the first of his compulsive behaviors (touching a glass 16 times before drinking from it) developed. (Sue, Sue, & Sue, 1981, p. 177)

Causes. The psychoanalytic view is that obsessions replace a threatening conflict (usually sexual) with something that is less threatening (Sue, Sue, & Sue, 1981). Because the substitute thought is less disturbing, it prevents the ego defenses from being overwhelmed. Similarly, compulsive acts are viewed as attempts to cancel or atone for threatening or forbidden impulses. In contrast, the behavioral perspective suggests that many obsessions and compulsions occur because they are reinforced by a reduction in anxiety. The cognitive view emphasizes that obsessive-compulsives give themselves commands to perform specific acts and make arbitrary rules that they must follow (Sarason & Sarason, 1980). Disordered thought is thus seen as the principal problem.

Somatoform Disorders

In the **somatoform** (*soma* means "body") **disorders,** physical symptoms exist without any known organic or physiological basis. These disorders can be contrasted with psychosomatic disorders (see chapter 14), in which real tissue damage occurs. Two examples of somatoform disorders are hypochondriasis and conversion disorder.

— Hypochondriasis

A preoccupation with the fear of having a serious disease characterizes **hypochondriasis.** The individual has numerous physical complaints and an exaggerated, morbid concern with health. Most of us are concerned with our physical well-being, but hypochondriacal individuals have unrealistic fears of disease that persist despite medical reassurance. Many hypochondriacal people are very up-to-date on medical literature and do considerable self-diagnosis. It is important to recognize that these people are not faking. They have symptoms and feel them, but they go one step beyond and exaggerate their significance. They sincerely view their symptoms as indicative of a serious disease.

Causes. From a biological perspective, hypochondriacal people may have a higher-than-normal arousal

level that results in increased sensitivity to internal stimuli such as pain and body functionings (Sue, Sue, & Sue, 1981). The psychoanalytic view suggests that these individuals experience an unconscious conflict or unacceptable impulse that is converted into a more acceptable physical complaint to keep the threatening material from entering awareness and causing intense anxiety (Barsky & Klerman, 1983). The behavioral model proposes that hypochondriasis allows a person to avoid responsibilities and stress and at the same time receive sympathy and attention from others (Coleman, Butcher, & Carson, 1980). In other words, the individual's behavior is reinforced.

— Conversion Disorder

The central feature of a **conversion disorder** is a loss or alteration in physical functioning that has no physical basis and is not under voluntary control. The dominant view today is that the individual with this disorder develops physical symptoms as a defense against encountering stressful situations.

During World Wars I and II, conversion disorders were common among combat soldiers (Coleman, Butcher, & Carson, 1980) (see Figure 15–4). For these men, the war was a highly threatening approach-avoidance conflict (see chapter 14). They wanted to obey orders and do their duty, but they did not want to be killed or severely injured. Conversion symptoms such as paralyzed legs allowed the soldiers to avoid combat without directly defying orders. The symptoms in conversion disroders may be sensory, motor, or visceral. In wartime military settings, they are often related to duties. For example, night fliers tend to develop night blindness, and day fliers are prone to failing day vision.

A good example of a conversion disorder is a case discussed by Viscott (1972) and noted by Goodstein and Calhoun (1982). A girl named Charlotte was brought to a hospital by her boyfriend because she claimed to be unable to move her feet. The two of them had been traveling from her home to a distant city. Before they had left, Charlotte had had an upsetting confrontation with her mother about moving away with her boyfriend. Charlotte later told a doctor: "She thinks just because I'm going North with a man means I'm a tramp. . . . She wants me to get married. . . . She says if I didn't get married I should consider myself a slut." Thus, although Charlotte wanted to make the move, she also knew that it meant bad things to her mother. Interestingly, her symptom was paralysis

Figure 15–4
Severe stress, such as that associated with war, can sometimes lead to a conversion disorder.

of the feet. This, of course, kept her from traveling and symbolized her inner conflict (Goodstein & Calhoun, 1982).

Causes. The psychoanalytic position is that a conflict or forbidden impulse is turned into a physical symptom. For example, someone experiencing a conflict over masturbation might develop paralysis of the hands (Sue, Sue, & Sue, 1981). The behavioral position suggests several possible factors in conversion disorders. First, as indicated in our examples, the conversion symptoms are reinforced by a reduction in anxiety. Second, the person is able to avoid stressful and unpleasant situations and responsibilities. Third, as in hypochondriasis, the symptoms are reinforced by the attention and sympathy accorded the individual. Finally, it is likely that the person has learned the symptoms by observing someone who actually has the illness.

Dissociative Disorders

A separation or alteration between an individual and the individual's normal consciousness, identity, or motor behavior is involved in **dissociative disorders** (APA, 1980). The specifics of this definition can be illustrated in three examples of such disorders, all of which are relatively rare: psychogenic (psychologically induced) amnesia, psychogenic fugue, and multiple personality.

— Psychogenic Amnesia

The most common dissociative disorder is **psychogenic amnesia,** which involves extensive but selective memory losses (Sarason & Sarason, 1980). Although some memory losses have organic causes, such as brain injury, psychogenic amnesia has psychological causes (hence the word *psychogenic*). The most common type of recall disturbance is *localized amnesia* (APA, 1980). In such a case, the individual is unable to recall anything that occurred during a specific period of time, typically the first few hours following some extremely disturbing event. A survivor of a car accident in which all the other members of the immediate family were killed may not be able to recall events that occurred between the time of the accident and several days after it (APA, 1980). In the less common *selective amnesia,* individuals may not recall specific people, objects, or events from a specific time period even though they can recall other material from that time period. Thus, the accident survivor may recall making funeral arrangements but may not recall conversations with family members that took place during the same time. Even less common are *generalized amnesia,* the failure to remember anything at all about one's past, and *continuous amnesia,* the failure to recall events from a particular point in the past up to and including the present.

During amnesia, disorientation and purposeless wandering may occur. In psychogenic amnesia, there may be a sudden failure to recall important personal events, including one's personal identity. However, there is no purposeful travel to a distant locale and no assumption of a new identity, as there is with psychogenic fugue (which we will explore next).

— Psychogenic Fugue

A loss of memory, a sudden move away from home and work, the assumption of a new identity, and no memory for the former identity are the characteristics of **psychogenic fugue.** The individual gives up customary life and habits and, at the distant place, establishes a new life as a presumably different person (Sarason & Sarason, 1980). The person's travel appears to be more purposeful than that seen in psychogenic amnesia. The fugue state typically ends when the person suddenly "wakes up" and is distressed at being in strange surroundings. When the fugue state ends, the person usually has no recollection of what happened during the fugue (Sarason & Sarason, 1980).

— Multiple Personality

A rare and fascinating dissociative disorder known as **multiple personality** involves the presence of two or more distinct personalities within a single person (Davison & Neale, 1982). (Remember the case of Chris Sizemore—*The Three Faces of Eve*—from chapter 13.)

In this type of disorder, each personality may have its own memories and own behaviors, and each may be unaware of the others. Or there may be one-way amnesia, such that one personality is aware of the others but not vice versa. A recently documented case of multiple personality is that of a man named Charles. In 1982, Charles was found wandering in a shopping mall in Florida. Months of treatment revealed 27 personalities.

Another interesting case is that of William Milligan, who, in 1978, was acquitted of rape on the basis of having multiple personalities. Milligan assumed at least 9 different personalities, 2 of which were female. Adelena, a lesbian, was thought to be the one that committed the rapes (Sarason & Sarason, 1980).

— Causes

From the psychoanalytic view, dissociative disorders represent an attempt by the ego to keep unacceptable impulses (typically sexual) from the consciousness. The impulses are trying to express themselves; and when the usual defense mechanism of repression is not enough to inhibit them, a severer step is taken: The impulse is completely erased from consciousness (Davison & Neale, 1982). In the case of multiple personality, this occurs through a dissociation, or splitting off, of one part of the personality from another in such a way that part of the personality is banished from awareness. In psychogenic amnesia and fugue, the unacceptable or threatening material is dealt with through repression of the individual's identity and even the acquisition of a new one.

Learning theorists suggest that stress avoidance is the main factor in dissociative disorders. Events that might trigger dissociation include the threat of physical injury or death, abandonment by one's spouse, marital quarrels, personal rejections, military conflict, or natural disaster (APA, 1980). In each case, the individual is faced with an intolerable, traumatic, or extremely painful situation. The pattern is basically that of conversion disorders except that instead of avoiding the situation by getting sick, the individual leaves the stressful situation by blocking out thoughts about it (Coleman, Butcher, & Carson, 1980).

Affective Disorders

As country singer Merle Haggard suggests in one of his songs, it is normal for people to get the blues or feel depressed occasionally. Normal depressions typically result from some recent stressful experience, such as the death of a loved one, separation, divorce, or financial loss. As Goodstein and Calhoun (1982) observe, less dramatic events, such as forced retirement or graduation from college, may also trigger depression. Even positive events, such as giving birth, can be depressing (see, for example, O'Hara, Rehm, & Campbell, 1982). New mothers and some new fathers may undergo a brief *postpartum depression* (see Figure 15–5), perhaps because of the difference in what they anticipated (total bliss) and what actually exists (happiness combined with frustration and fatigue). Cutrona (1982) suggests that the depression is due to stressful events occurring during pregnancy and at the time of delivery and to a lack of adequate social support.

When we experience depression, we feel sad, discouraged, pessimistic, and hopeless about changing things. Fortunately, such temporary depressions tend to come and go. For most of us, they are not extreme and do not require the help of a mental health professional. However, when depression persists for months or occurs for no apparent reason, it can be destructive,

Figure 15–5.
New mothers may suffer from temporary postpartum depression.

and professional help may be required (Goodstein & Calhoun, 1982). Depression is the most prevalent mental health problem in the United States. More than 1½ million Americans are currently being treated for it. Unfortunately, three to five times that number may need treatment but aren't getting it (see Goodstein & Calhoun, 1982).

DSM-III defines **affective disorder** as a major disturbance of mood or emotions. The disorder may involve *depression* and usually does, but it may also involve *mania,* a state of elation, excitement, and confidence. Mania rarely occurs alone; it usually is in combination with periods of depression. Again, all of us experience, to some extent, the alternating lows of depression and highs of mania. Such states are considered affective disorders, however, only if they are severe enough to affect our daily functioning and cause us great subjective distress.

The affective disorders are divided into *major affective disorders* and *other affective disorders* (APA, 1980). Since the disorders in the latter category are simply less severe than those in the former, we will examine the major affective disorders only. DSM-III delineates two basic types of major affective disorders: **major depressive disorder,** a persistent and pronounced dysphoric (unhappy) mood state, and **bipolar disorder,** a persistent mood disturbance in which both depressive and manic symptoms are prominent. *Manic* (from *mania*) refers to a highly excited or irritable mood state.

— Major Depressive Disorder

The most common major affective disorder is the major depressive disorder. It resembles the everyday, normal depression that we all experience, but it is much more serious, disruptive, and persistent. The depressed mood state is characterized in part by feelings of sadness, hopelessness, and worthlessness. The individual may also withdraw from others, exhibit no interest in normally pleasurable activities, be unable to concentrate, and show disturbances in sleep or appetite. In some cases, the depressed person may be agitated and unable to sit still. In other cases, movements may be slowed and the person may speak very little. Thoughts of death or suicide are also common in this disorder.

Even within the major depressive disorder, there can be great variability in severity. The severer the case, the more prominent the symptoms. In severe forms of the disorder, delusions and hallucinations may occur. **Delusions** are thoughts that have no basis in reality. Commonly, the delusions are of being persecuted for wrongdoings or inadequacies or of having a serious illness or body disturbance. **Hallucinations**—sensory experiences in the absence of any external stimulation—may involve voices that criticize and ridicule the person for various sins and faults. The following example of a 47-year-old depressed male patient illustrates fairly typical reactions of a rather severe form of major depressive disorder (Th. = Therapist; Pt. = Patient):

Th.: What seems to be the trouble?

Pt.: . . . There's just no way out of it . . . nothing but blind alleys . . . I have no appetite . . . nothing matters anymore . . . it's hopeless . . . everything is hopeless.

Th.: Can you tell me how your trouble started?

Pt.: I don't know . . . it seems like I have a lead weight in my stomach . . . I feel different . . . I am not like other people . . . my health is ruined . . . I wish I were dead.

Th.: Your health is ruined?

Pt.: . . . Yes, my brain is being eaten away, I shouldn't have done it . . . If I had any willpower I would kill myself . . . I don't deserve to live . . . I have ruined everything . . . and it's all my fault.

Th.: It's all your fault?

Pt.: Yes . . . I have been unfaithful to my wife and now I am being punished . . . my health is ruined . . . there's no use going on . . . (sigh) . . . I have ruined everything . . . my family . . . and now myself . . . I bring misfortune to everyone . . . I am a moral leper . . . a serpent in the Garden of Eden . . . why don't I die . . . why don't you give me a pill and end it all before I bring a catastrophe on everyone . . . No one can help me . . . It's hopeless . . . I know that . . . it's hopeless. (Coleman, Butcher, & Carson, 1980, p. 374)

As indicated earlier, in some cases of depression (diagnosed under the category of other affective disorders), many of the symptoms just described are present but are less severe and persistent in form and less disruptive to the person's life. Also, the individual in such cases experiences no delusions or hallucinations.

— Bipolar Disorder

In contrast to the persistent depression of the major depressive disorder, the bipolar disorder involves an alternation between depression and periods of mania. In a period of mania, the individual is extremely elated and euphoric, impatient and easily irritated, very active physically, and very talkative, with an almost endless chain of rapidly changing thoughts and ideas (a flight of ideas). The person has an inflated self-esteem and abundant energy and shows a decreased need for sleep. Commonly, the individual becomes involved in activities that have a good chance of producing negative consequences. Although a diagnosis of bipolar disorder implies at least one manic and one depressive episode, many individuals display primarily one or the other emotional state.

Goodstein and Calhoun (1982) suggest that a good illustration of a typical case of bipolar disorder comes from McNeil (1967). This is the case of Joe A., who, overnight, devised a plan for a nationwide telephone dating service. When the business failed, Joe initially worked even harder, sleeping and eating less than normal. Finally, in an agitated state, Joe was taken to the local mental hospital by police. Here is a sample of Joe's speech to the police officers who brought him in. Note how quickly Joe jumps from one thought to another and how disorganized and incoherent his speech is.

You've got to be decisive! decisive! decisive! No shilly-shallying! Sweat! Yea, sweat with a goal! Push, push, push, and you can push over a mountain! Two mountains, maybe. It's not luck! Hell, if it wasn't for bad luck I wouldn't have any luck at all! Be there firstest with the mostest! My guts and your blood! That's the system! I know, you know, he, she, or it knows it's the only way to travel! Get'em off balance, baby, and the rest is leverage! Use your head and save your heels! What's this deal? Who are these guys? Have you got a telephone and a secretary I can have instanter if not sooner? What I need is office space and the old LDO [long-distance operator]. (McNeil, 1967, p. 147)

As in the case of depression, the severity of mania can vary greatly. In severe manic episodes, the individuals clearly lose touch with reality and all of the manic symptoms are exaggerated. Such people are extremely excited and agitated, very incoherent, and sometimes violent, and they have delusions and hallucinations. They may believe that they have a special relationship to God, or they may hear God's voice explaining that they have a special mission to perform.

A less severe and less disruptive form of the more serious bipolar disorder sometimes occurs (diagnosed under the category other affective disorders). Mood swings from depression to mania still occur, but each mood state is less extreme than what has been described. Furthermore, there may be periods of no mood disturbance at all. Finally, there are no delusions or hallucinations.

— Causes

Because they constitute a major mental health problem, the affective disorders have been the subject of much research and theorizing. A sampling of proposed explanations for such disorders follows.

Biological model. One possible explanation of affective disorders is that they reflect a hereditary predisposition. Studies of families, twins, and adoptions do, in fact, suggest that both bipolar disorder and unipolar disorder (depression only) have a genetic component (Schlesser & Altshuler, 1983). The influence of genetics seems to be more pronounced, however, in bipolar disorder. The twin studies find essentially that the concordance rate for affective disorders is higher for identical twins than for fraternal twins. For either fraternal or identical twins, however, the concordance rate is higher for bipolar disorder than for unipolar disorder (Goodstein & Calhoun, 1982). Genetics, of course, does not fully explain the occurrence of these disorders. Heredity may provide only the predisposition. Whether the disorders actually develop may then depend on other factors.

Other theorists taking a biological approach have focused on biochemical factors, namely the role played by neurotransmitters (see chapter 2). One theory, known as the **catecholamine hypothesis,** suggests that depression results from low levels of catecholamines (a group of neurotransmitters), particularly norepinephrine. Mania, on the other hand, is thought to result from an excess of these neurotransmitters. Yet another theory, the **serotonin hypothesis,** suggests that depression results from low levels of the neurotransmitter serotonin. It may be that some cases of depression are due to a deficiency of norepinephrine and others are due to a deficiency of serotonin (Davison & Neale, 1982).

Anisman and Zacharko (1982) suggest that norepinephrine, serotonin, and dopamine (another of the catecholamines) are depleted when an individual is unable to cope effectively with environmental demands or stressors. The investigators believe, then, that stress causes depression and does so by causing significant neurochemical change, namely a depletion of certain neurotransmitters. At this point, it is premature to conclude that a deficiency of neurotransmitters is always due to stress, and it may be even more prema-

ture to conclude that stress is a definite cause of depression (Beck & Harrison, 1982).

The issue of stress aside, some support does exist for both the catecholamine and serotonin hypotheses. To give one example, Swedish researchers have reported that depressed people with unusually low serotonin levels are 10 times more likely to commit suicide than are those with high levels of serotonin (Begley, 1983). However, in such research, it is often unclear whether chemical abnormalities are a cause or an effect of the observed disorder. Nevertheless, it is of interest to note that drugs which are effective in alleviating depression have been shown to increase the levels of norepinephrine and serotonin at key synaptic sites (see chapter 16).

There are also a number of psychological explanations for affective disorders. Most address the problem of depression (see, for example, Billings & Moos, 1982), so that will be our focus here.

Psychoanalytic model. One psychoanalytic view is that depression has its origin in early childhood when a child experiences a real, imagined, or feared loss of a significant person. Because the loss arouses considerable anxiety, it is pushed out of consciousness. Later on, however, it can cause depression when other significant losses that are symbolic of the early loss occur.

Depression has also been interpreted by psychoanalysts as the turning inward of unconscious aggressive impulses that were threatening to become conscious. Since such impulses would arouse great anxiety if directly expressed, they are redirected toward the self (Newman & Hirt, 1983).

Behavioral model. Behavioral or learning theorists view depression as resulting from too little positive reinforcement (Lewinsohn, Muñoz, Youngren, & Zeiss, 1978). Depressed people are thought to receive insufficient love, praise, status, and other rewards that would make them feel good. In effect, such individuals are on an extended extinction schedule; as positive reinforcement diminishes, depression increases. The problem can even worsen as time goes on. Ultimately, no one wants to be around the depressed person, which gives the individual an even lower rate of positive reinforcement. Thus, not only is the depression maintained this way, it is perhaps intensified. Furthermore, as Lewinsohn and his colleagues (1978) note, once depression sets in, the individual is even less motivated to engage in the activities that would ordinarily lead to positive outcomes. This lessened activity causes even greater depression which, in turn, leads to even less activity, and so on. The depressed individual is caught in a vicious cycle (Figure 15–6).

Cognitive model. According to the cognitive view, depression is due to the fact that people often think in a distorted, irrational, and negative way. Events that might have any number of plausible interpretations are interpreted in a negative, self-critical way (see Table 15–4). A husband whose wife has just deserted him may conclude that she left him because he is an unlovable person (Beck, 1976). This type of thinking is typical of depressed individuals. Aaron Beck (1967) refers to it as **overgeneralization.** Individuals who overgeneralize reach a general conclusion about their ability or worth on the basis of only one event. Students may be overgeneralizing when they do poorly on one exam in one course and then conclude that they are complete failures and will never amount to anything in life.

According to Beck (1967), depressed persons have negative ways of thinking about their experiences, themselves, and the future. Events are misinterpreted and their meaning exaggerated. It is not the events in life (such as rejection or defeat) that trigger depression but rather the way one thinks about them. Beck suggests that negative and overgeneralized interpretations derive from the person's sense of loss when unrealistic expectations are not met. If you establish unrealistically high goals for achievement at work or in social

relationships and you do not match those goals, the door is open for self-criticism and such statements as "I'm not good enough; I'll never succeed." Depressed individuals magnify their personal faults and overlook their positive qualities. That depressed individuals are indeed characterized by the type of cognitive patterns discussed by Beck has been documented in a number of studies (e.g., Hamilton & Abramson, 1983; Nekanda-Trepka, Bishop, & Blackburn, 1983).

Another cognitive theory, proposed by Seligman (1975; Abramson, Seligman, & Teasdale, 1978; Abramson, Garber, & Seligman, 1980), is the notion of learned helplessness (see chapter 6). The theory proposes that depression may be due in part to the feeling of helplessness and the impact it has on self-esteem. People who view a state of helplessness as *externally caused, specific, and temporary* may be angry and frustrated but are not likely to develop depression or think negatively about themselves. This would be the case, for example, if your car had a flat tire while you were driving to work. You would be more likely to experience depression if you were to view your helplessness as *internally caused, global (applying to all circumstances), and stable (lasting or recurrent).* Repeatedly not getting a raise at work, for example, might be attributed to personal inadequacy. A number of such failures might lead one to think of oneself as generally inadequate, which would result in a negative self-image and depression. Although support for this model has been somewhat mixed, recent evidence suggests that internal, stable, and global attributions are related to depression (Metalsky, Abramson, Seligman, Semmel, & Peterson, 1982; Raps, Peterson, Reinhard, Abramson, & Seligman, 1982).

Schizophrenic Disorders

Spectroautorotation . . . relaudation . . . circlingology. Although these words may make no sense to you, they made much sense to a patient diagnosed as schizophrenic (cf. Sarason & Sarason, 1980). Whereas the affective disorders involve mainly mood dysfunction, the schizophrenic disorders (see chapter introduction) are disorders primarily of perception and thought.

The **schizophrenic disorders** are a group of disorders involving disturbances in thought and perceptual processes, inappropriate affect, or emotion, disturbances in motor activity, withdrawal from social relationships, and loss of contact with reality. The term *schizophrenia* was coined by the Swiss psychiatrist Eu-

Figure 15–6.

The vicious cycle of depression. (From CONTROL YOUR DEPRESSION by Peter M. Lewinsohn, Ricardo F. Muñoz, Mary Ann Youngren, & Antonette M. Zeiss, © 1978 by Peter M. Lewinsohn, published by Prentice-Hall, Inc., Englewood Cliffs, NJ 07632.)

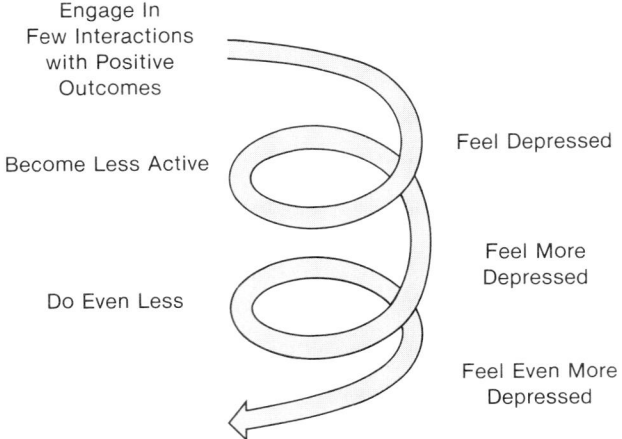

Engage In Few Interactions with Positive Outcomes

Become Less Active

Do Even Less

Feel Depressed

Feel More Depressed

Feel Even More Depressed

Table 15–4.

In these 2 examples, a particular event led to unpleasant feelings, negative cognitions, and depression. As you can see, the negative interpretations of the events were not the only plausible ones. (From Beck, Rush, Shaw, & Emery, 1979, p.165.)

This example is from a medical records librarian with a 6-year history of depression.

EVENT	FEELINGS	COGNITIONS	OTHER POSSIBLE INTERPRETATIONS
The charge nurse in the coronary care unit was curt and said "I hate medical records" when I went to collect charts for the record review committee.	Sadness Slight anger Loneliness	She doesn't like me.	The charge nurse is generally unhappy. Hating medical records is not the same as hating me; she actually hates paper work. She is under a lot of pressure for unknown reasons. She is foolish to hate records; they are her only defense in a lawsuit.

This example is from a 24-year-old nurse recently discharged from the hospital for severe depression.

EVENT	FEELINGS	COGNITIONS	OTHER POSSIBLE INTERPRETATIONS
While at a party Jim asked me "How are you feeling?" shortly after I was discharged from the hospital.	Anxious	Jim thinks I am a basket case. I must really look bad for him to be concerned.	He really cares about me. He noticed that I look better than before I went into the hospital and wants to know if feel better too.

gene Bleuler in 1911 and refers to the splitting or fragmentation of the mind's functions—thought, perception, and emotion (see Figure 15–7 in the color section). At any particular point in time, approximately 2 million Americans suffer from some form of schizophrenia, making this mental disorder the most commonly diagnosed one in the United States. Of the patients admitted to mental hospitals each year, about one-fourth are diagnosed as schizophrenic, and overall the schizophrenic disorders account for nearly half the mental-hospital population.

— Characteristics of Schizophrenia

It is important to distinguish between *process schizophrenia* and *reactive schizophrenia* (Shean, 1978). In the process type, the onset of symptoms is gradual and the individual has an early and long history of poor adjustment, withdrawal from others, emotional blunt-

ing, and other symptoms. The prognosis for improvement is not good in these cases. In the reactive type, the onset of symptoms is sudden and seems to follow a highly traumatic or stressful event. The individual's early background is one of good adjustment and few abnormal symptoms. The prognosis for improvement for reactive schizophrenia is much better than it is for process schizophrenia. Let's take a look now at some of the specific characteristics of the schizophrenic disorders. As we examine them, bear in mind that symptoms vary greatly across individuals as well as over time.

Thought. One of the hallmarks of the schizophrenic disorders is bizarre, disorganized, and illogical thinking. The schizophrenic's associations of ideas may be so loose and disconnected that it may be hard to follow or communicate with the person. It is as if the individual has a personal and unique way of communicating, understandable to no one else. This is apparent, for example, in the schizophrenic's use of *neologisms* (newly-coined words, such as *relaudation*).

The content of schizophrenic thinking is delusional. Schizophrenics may believe, for example, that others are spying on them *(delusions of persecution),* that they are being controlled by some external force *(delusions of control),* that their thoughts are being broadcast to others *(thought-broadcasting),* or that they are some famous and important individual, such as Napoleon *(delusions of grandeur).*

Perception. Schizophrenics not only think differently than others, they perceive the world differently (see Figure 15–8 in the color section). This is apparent in the hallucinations that markedly characterize the disorder. These hallucinations are usually auditory in form. Schizophrenics may believe that they hear voices that often make insulting comments about their thoughts or behaviors.

Emotion. In the schizophrenic, emotion, or affect, is characterized by blunting, flattening, or inappropriateness. The blunting is seen in the lessened intensity of expressed emotions. The flattening is evident in the lack of any emotional expression, such as in the voice or face. Inappropriateness occurs when the situation and the expressed emotion are inconsistent. For example, the schizophrenic may laugh and smile when it is more appropriate to express sadness, for example, at a funeral.

Motor activity. In some cases, the schizophrenic may adopt an unusual or bizarre posture and maintain it for long periods of time. In other cases, the schizophrenic may be very agitated, excited, and difficult to control.

— Types of Schizophrenia

As suggested, schizophrenics vary in the types of symptoms they display. Clinicians and researchers have found it useful to distinguish between several subtypes of schizophrenia. DSM-III divides the schizophrenic disorders into four main categories: disorganized, catatonic, paranoid, and undifferentiated.

Disorganized schizophrenia. Marked incoherence and flat, incongruous, or silly affect characterize **disorganized schizophrenia.** Delusions and hallucinations that have no coherent theme are common. Individuals with this type of schizophrenia often show

a childish disregard for social conventions (Sarason & Sarason, 1980). For example, they may resist wearing clothes or eat all their food with their fingers. Their behavior seems aimless, and their emotional responses are inappropriate to the circumstances. Quite common are grimacing, giggling, silly mannerisms, unexplainable gestures, and extreme social withdrawal. In general, the terms *odd* and *bizarre* describe many of the characteristics seen in this disorder.

Catatonic schizophrenia. The major symptom in **catatonic schizophrenia** is disturbance in motor activity of either an excited or a stuporous type. The excited or agitated catatonic shows extreme excitement by endlessly talking and shouting. Violence is not uncommon in such individuals. In the stuporous type (withdrawal reaction), the individual may stay rigidly motionless and mute for hours or days, lost in delusions and hallucinations. Some catatonics show a waxy flexibility, maintaining bizarre and uncomfortable postures in which they are placed (see Figure 15–9). More often, however, catatonics are negativistic and respond to requests by doing nothing or by doing the opposite of what is asked.

Paranoid schizophrenia. The primary disturbance of **paranoid schizophrenia** is in thought patterns. Particularly characteristic are delusions and persistent, extreme suspiciousness. Persecutory delusions are the most common, but delusions of control and of grandeur may also occur. Along with delusions, individuals may experience auditory hallucinations, such as the accusing and critical voices of their enemies. Related to these delusions are *ideas of reference:* "Paranoid schizophrenics believe that overheard conversations, newspaper articles, and TV and radio broadcasts are meant for them personally" (Goodstein & Calhoun, 1982, p. 332).

The following excerpt is from a conversation between a doctor and a patient diagnosed as a chronic paranoid schizophrenic. Note the illogical, delusional thinking of the patient.

Dr.: What are you doing here?
Pt.: Well, I've been sent here to thwart the Russians. I'm the only one in the world who knows how to deal with them. They got their spies all around here though to get me, but I'm smarter than any of them.
Dr.: What are you going to do to thwart the Russians?
Pt.: I'm organizing.
Dr.: Whom are you going to organize?

Figure 15–9.
A catatonic schizophrenic.

Pt.: Everybody. I'm the only man in the world who can do that, but they're trying to get me. But I'm going to use my atomic bomb media to blow them up.

Dr.: You must be a terribly important person then.

Pt.: Well, of course.

Dr.: What do you call yourself?

Pt.: You used to know me as Franklin D. Roosevelt.

Dr.: Isn't he dead?

Pt.: Sure he's dead, but I'm alive.

Dr.: But you're Franklin D. Roosevelt?

Pt.: His spirit. He, God, and I figured this out. And now I'm going to make a race of healthy people. My agents are lining them up. Say, who are you?

Dr.: I'm a doctor here.

Pt.: You don't look like a doctor. You look like a Russian to me.

Dr.: How can you tell a Russian from one of your agents?

Pt.: I read eyes. I get all my signs from eyes. I look into your eyes and get all my signs from them. (Coleman, Butcher, & Carson, 1980, p. 407)

Undifferentiated schizophrenia. An individual who is definitely schizophrenic but does not meet the criteria for the preceding categories (or who meets the criteria for more than one) is categorized as suffering from **undifferentiated schizophrenia.** Symptoms include incoherence, prominent delusions, hallucinations, and grossly disorganized behavior.

— Causes

Biological model. A number of attempts have been made to link the schizophrenic disorders with biological factors such as heredity and biochemistry (see chapter introduction). With regard to heredity, some researchers have concluded that there must be a genetic component to schizophrenia since there is a high incidence of schizophrenia in the families of schizophrenic patients (Coleman, Butcher, & Carson, 1980). Furthermore, research has shown that schizophrenia concordance rates for identical twins are higher than for fraternal twins (Gottesman & Shields, 1976; Sarason & Sarason, 1980). Some researchers have found concordance rates for identical twins to be in excess of 60 percent. The average concordance rate of schizophrenia is about 50 percent for identical twins, 9 percent for fraternal twins, and 8 percent for nontwin siblings (Goodstein & Calhoun, 1982). Because the concordance rate for identical twins is not 100 percent, genetics appears to be only a partial factor. It is usually assumed that heredity may produce a predisposition for schizophrenia, but its actual development depends on environmental factors, such as exposure to various stressors.

As convincing as this evidence is, one could argue that similarity between twins in the diagnosis of schizophrenia is due not to genetics but to the similar environments in which the twins are raised. To help resolve this question, it is necessary to turn to adoption studies. These studies support the role of genetics even more than the twin studies do. For example, it appears that a child with at least one schizophrenic parent stands a good chance of also being diagnosed as schizophrenic, regardless of whether the child is raised by the schizophrenic parents or by normal (adoptive) parents (Rathus & Nevid, 1983). Children born to normal parents, on the other hand, are not likely to be diagnosed as schizophrenic, whether they are raised by their normal parents or by schizophrenic (adoptive) parents.

Other researchers have looked for a biochemical cause for schizophrenia. Perhaps the most prominent biochemical theory today is the **dopamine hypothesis,** which attributes schizophrenia to an excess of the neurotransmitter dopamine (Deutsch & Davis, 1983). Apparently, when unusually high levels of dopamine exist, the neurons' rate of firing speeds up (Goodstein & Calhoun, 1982).

Indirect support for the dopamine hypothesis comes from the fact that amphetamines produce schizophreniclike behavior and worsen schizophrenic symptoms (Goodstein & Calhoun, 1982). This is noteworthy because amphetamines release dopamine into the synapses between neurons. Also, the effectiveness of various antischizophrenic drugs (the neuroleptics—see chapter 16) is highly correlated with the extent to which they block dopamine action at synaptic receptor sites (Coleman, Butcher, & Carson, 1980). Whether schizophrenics have higher levels of dopamine in their brains than other people do remains to be determined.

Psychoanalytic model. The psychoanalytic position is that schizophrenia represents a regression to an early phase of the oral stage, where the ego, id, and superego still are not highly differentiated. Presumably, the id's unacceptable sexual and aggressive impulses seek expression and thus cause the person anxiety. The person seeks protection from that anxiety, regressing to a stage where the reality-oriented ego does not exist, where contact with reality is lost.

Behavioral model. While acknowledging the role that genetics may play in schizophrenia, behavioral theorists argue that many of the schizophrenic symptoms may be due to learning. Operant conditioning is the type of learning most often implicated in this regard. It may be, for example, that delusions, hallucinations, social withdrawal, and other schizophrenic symptoms have been reinforced in the past, whereas nonschizophrenic behaviors have not (Rimm & Somervill, 1977). Similarly, one could argue that classical conditioning and observational learning account for many of the symptoms. The learning theory argument, then, is that schizophrenic behavior is learned in the same way that any other behavior is learned.

The best evidence for the learning view of schizophrenia is indirect but compelling (Rimm & Somervill, 1977). Although it is difficult to be certain that learning can explain the origin of schizophrenic symptoms, there is good evidence that these symptoms can be modified using learning principles. One demonstration is a reinforcement program called the token economy (discussed in chapter 16), which has proved effective in alleviating such schizophrenic symptoms as unresponsiveness to others and the environment (Ayllon & Azrin, 1965). Meichenbaum (1969) found that he could increase the frequency of coherent speech by schizophrenics by rewarding such speech whenever it occurred. Another compelling finding noted by Rimm and Somervill is that a schizophrenic patient and her broom became inseparable after the patient was reinforced for carrying the broom (Ayllon, Haughton, & Hughes, 1965). Keep in mind, however, that although such findings are important in their implications for treatment of schizophrenia, they do not necessarily suggest that learning accounts for the origins of the symptoms.

Family interaction model. With respect to the schizophrenic disorders, the family interaction approach has received considerable attention. One view is that schizophrenia results from faulty parent-child relationships. *Schizophrenogenic mother* (the mother-son relationship has received the most theoretical attention) is the name often used for a mother who produces schizophrenia in her child by behaving in a cold, overprotective, rejecting, and insensitive manner.

Another family pattern implicated in schizophrenia is the **double-bind pattern,** in which parents give their children incompatible and contradictory messages (Bateson, 1960). The children are then caught in a double-bind. For example, when a child responds with affection to the father's own display of affection, the father may act coldly and reject the child. It is believed that such behavior on the part of parents may cause a child to withdraw from others and to deal with the situation by retreating into a world of bizarre behavior and distorted thinking.

Although both of these family-oriented theories have been popular, the empirical evidence does not suggest that the family factors they present are highly influential. Other theorists have focused on families in which the child receives little nurturance and care because of discord between the parents, but again, strong supportive evidence is lacking.

Sociocultural model. The sociocultural explanation of schizophrenia is that it is a result of low socioeconomic status. It has been shown, in fact, that in urban areas, schizophrenia is most frequently diagnosed at the lowest socioeconomic levels (Goodstein & Calhoun, 1982). The poor education and general lack of rewards and opportunities associated with low socioeconomic status are thought to cause people a great deal of stress, one outcome of which may be schizophrenia.

Some researchers, however, believe that low social standing does not necessarily cause mental disorders. To the contrary, there is some support for the **social-drift hypothesis.** This hypothesis states that individuals with mental disorders lose jobs, families, and good housing; thus, at the time of admission for treatment, their socioeconomic status—which is determined by these factors—is identified as lower class. The data on the matter are conflicting, however, so it is not clear at present what the relationship between schizophrenia and social drift really is (Goodstein & Calhoun, 1982).

Personality Disorders

According to DSM-III, **personality disorders** are inflexible and maladaptive patterns of relating to and interacting with others. In other words, such disorders are defined by the presence of *maladaptive personality traits*. Personality disorders can be disruptive to both social and occupational functioning, and although they may cause the affected person subjective distress, it is others who are more likely to be distressed. Those who come into contact with the disordered person may be victims of unethical behavior, may find it difficult to get along with the individual, and so on. In general, though, the severity of these disorders varies greatly. Some individuals may function reasonably well and cause others only mild distress; other individuals may be so disruptive to society that incarceration is required (Munsinger, 1983).

— Common Features of the Personality Disorders

Although a number of specific types of personality disorders can be distinguished, they all have much in common (Coleman, Butcher, & Carson, 1980). Most prominent is the difficulty in establishing positive interpersonal relationships. Individuals with personality disorders are known for being demanding of others and for shunning responsibility for their actions—feeling guiltless about their unethical behavior and blaming others for their own faults and troubles. These individuals seem not to profit from their past mistakes and problems, since the maladaptive pattern of behavior occurs repeatedly. Not surprisingly, these people typically have little interest in changing their ways by seeking therapy. Finally, personality disorders reflect lifelong patterns of maladaptive behavior that commonly originated during adolescence.

Types of Personality Disorders

As shown in Table 15–5, personality disorders can be examined in three clusters (APA, 1980):

1. *Paranoid, schizoid, and schizotypal disorders.* In these disorders, individuals seem odd or different.
2. *Histrionic, narcissistic, antisocial, and borderline disorders.* In these disorders, individuals tend to be dramatic, emotional, or erratic.
3. *Avoidant, dependent, compulsive, and passive-aggressive disorders.* In these disorders, individuals often exhibit anxiety.

The personality disorders are among the most difficult for clinicians to diagnose. Some of the characteristics given in Table 15–5 to describe the various personality disorders can also be used to describe other disorders, such as schizophrenia or the anxiety disorders. The exact nature and severity of these characteristics varies, however, across the disorders, allowing a specific diagnosis to be made. (It is also worth noting that these same characteristics can be found to a milder extent in many normal individuals.)

Causes

The causes of personality disorders have been difficult for researchers to pinpoint. Several hypotheses have been advanced, however.

Biological model. At least in the case of antisocial personality, it may be that a certain type of nervous system is a predisposing factor. For example, it has been hypothesized that psychopaths—those diagnosed as having an antisocial personality—have an autonomic nervous system that functions at a low level of arousal. One consequence is that these individuals may be impulsive, stimulus-seeking, and intolerant of discipline in order to increase their level of stimulation and thus their level of physiological arousal. Another consequence is that since they respond to external stimuli with less reactivity or arousal, they may react less strongly than others to fear- and anxiety-arousing situations. Therefore, during socialization, they may be less prone to being conditioned to fear certain situations or less likely to feel anxious or guilty about engaging in negative and undesirable behavior.

Family interaction model. Another proposed explanation of antisocial personality characteristics is that they derive from a faulty family environment. To the extent that a child suffers neglect and emotional deprivation in the family, there is little opportunity for that child to learn socially appropriate behavior or the importance of close and meaningful relationships (Sue, Sue, & Sue, 1981). Not only may there be an absence of a positive model in the family, there may be a parent (especially a father) who models antisocial behavior. The fact that not all children exposed to such family disturbances develop an antisocial personality suggests that other factors are important as well.

Sociocultural model. From the sociocultural perspective, antisocial personality is believed to be most likely to occur in lower socioeconomic groups

Table 15–5.

Major features of personality disorders. (From Goodstein & Calhoun, 1982, p. 296.)

PARANOID	Suspicious in the extreme; hostile
SCHIZOID	Completely withdrawn and emotionless
SCHIZOTYPAL	Showing mild schizophrenic tendencies
HISTRIONIC	Overly dramatic and temperamental
NARCISSISTIC	Self-centered, needing to be admired
ANTISOCIAL	Amoral, cold, but superficially charming
BORDERLINE	Unstable, constantly switching from low to high mood
AVOIDANT	Hypersensitive to rejection, withdrawn
DEPENDENT	Unwilling to make decisions
COMPULSIVE	Perfectionistic, rigid, aloof
PASSIVE-AGGRESSIVE	Deliberately forgetful, resentful

(Coleman, Butcher, & Carson, 1980). Such environments might foster an antisocial personality to the extent that they teach people destructive behavior, negative attitudes toward middle-class society, lawlessness, and a lack of concern for others and for ethical behavior.

— APPLICATION —
WARNING SIGNS FOR STUDENT SUICIDE

At least 200,000 Americans attempt suicide every year; 1 in 10 succeeds (Davison & Neale, 1982). An additional problem is the psychological aftermath of suicide for the many individuals close to the suicide victim who survive the person's death (Calhoun, Selby, & Selby, 1982). In an earlier discussion, we alluded to the possibility that suicidal behavior—thoughts, threats, or attempts—is always a possibility with individuals who are depressed. Contrary to stereotypes, this possibility extends to college students, for whom suicide is a common cause of death.

It has been estimated that each year approximately 10,000 American college students attempt suicide, a rate higher than that of their noncollege counterparts (Davison & Neale, 1982). College students confront many stressors, including heavy course loads, jobs to maintain in addition to schoolwork, pressure from parents to excel, and career decisions to make. All of this may make it difficult for some students to cope, and suicide may be perceived as the only way out.

Although three times more female than male students attempt suicide, male students are more likely to succeed, presumably because they tend to use such violent means as gunshots (Goodstein & Calhoun, 1982). It is also of interest that most suicide attempts by college students occur at the beginning and end of the school quarter or semester, when the level of stress is probably at its greatest (Coleman, Butcher, & Carson, 1980).

Given the extent and seriousness of the problem, it would be useful if we could spot the signals of possible suicide. Coleman, Butcher, and Carson (1980) offer the following suggestions about the warning signs of suicide:

A change in a student's mood and behavior is a significant warning of possible suicide. Characteristically, the student becomes depressed and withdrawn, undergoes a marked decline in self-esteem, and shows deterioration in habits of personal hygiene. This is accompanied by a profound loss of interest in studies. Often he or she stops attending classes and stays at home most of the day. Usually the student's distress is communicated to at least one other person, often in the form of a veiled suicide warning. A significant number of students who attempt suicide leave suicide notes.

When college students attempt suicide, one of the first explanations to occur to those around them is that they may have been doing poorly in school. As a group, however, they are superior students, and while they tend to expect a great deal of themselves in terms of academic achievement and to exhibit scholastic anxieties, grades, academic competition, and pressure over examinations are not regarded as significant precipitating stresses. Also, while many lose interest in their studies prior to the onset of suicidal behavior and their grades get lower, the loss of interest appears to be associated with depression and withdrawal caused by other problems. Moreover, when academic failure does appear to trigger suicidal behavior—in a minority of cases—the actual cause of the behavior is generally considered to be loss of self-esteem and failure to live up to parental expectations, rather than the academic failure itself.

For most suicidal students, both male and female, the major precipitating stressor appears to be either the failure to establish, or the loss of, a close interpersonal relationship. Often the breakup of a romance is the key precipitating factor. It has also been noted that there are significantly more suicide attempts and suicides by students from families where there has been separation, divorce, or the death of a parent. A particularly important precipitating factor among college males appears to be the existence of a close emotional involvement with a parent that is threatened when the student becomes involved with another person in college and tries to break this "parental knot."

Although most colleges and universities have mental health facilities to assist distressed students, few suicidal students seek professional help. Thus, it is of vital importance for those around a suicidal person to notice the warning signs and try to obtain assistance. (p. 581)

DIAGNOSING ABNORMAL BEHAVIOR WITH THE PET SCANNER

Diagnosing abnormal behavior can be time-consuming and not completely reliable. For at least some disorders, it may become common in the future to use a new technique that should make diagnosing both easier and more precise.

This latest diagnostic tool, the PET scanner (see Figure 15–10 in the color section, chapter 2, and this chapter's introduction), resembles somewhat an airplane engine with a hollow core (Toufexis, 1981). The PET scanner enables researchers to observe the chemical processes occurring in any cross section of the body. For example, it can reveal in what location and with what intensity the brain is using energy. In effect, the PET scanner allows the researcher to map the brain's activity.

Fascinating inroads are being made into the study of the brain, and the future looks promising for use of the PET scanner in diagnosing certain disorders. Researchers are using PET scans to study the brains of people with schizophrenia and bipolar disorder, for example. To the extent that numerous individuals with one of these disorders show a distinctive pattern of biochemical activity, diagnosis will be a much more exact and easier process (Toufexis, 1981). In other words, to diagnose a potential case of schizophrenia, one would simply look for the pattern that had in the past characterized individuals with that diagnosis. An advantage of the PET procedure is that it takes only a few hours to complete.

Some early evidence from PET scans has indicated that, in schizophrenia, the frontal lobes of the brain consume glucose at a very low rate (Toufexis, 1981; Landis, 1980). Figure 15–11 in the color section shows PET scans from the Genain sisters (who were discussed in the chapter introduction). Nora's and Hester's frontal lobes appear blue and green, which indicates a low consumption of glucose (Hamer, 1982). The orange spots on the scans of Iris and Myra indicate a more normal use of energy. (You may recall that Iris and Myra seem to be less severely afflicted by schizophrenia than are the other two Genain sisters.) Figure 15–12 in the color sec-

tion shows a PET scan of a normal individual which you can examine for comparison purposes. In contrast to what happens in schizophrenia, glucose appears to burn at a very rapid rate during the manic phase in bipolar disorders (Landis, 1980).

These findings are intriguing and, we hope, ultimately beneficial. However, the technology of diagnosing abnormal behavior with PET scanners is just emerging. At this point, it is difficult to predict what their ultimate utility will be. The scanners will likely remain an additional diagnostic tool, not the sole tool. Even at that, according to Dr. Allan Mirsky of the National Institute of Mental Health, the use of the PET scanner in diagnosing schizophrenia is still very much a controversial and complicated issue (Mirsky, 1983). Mirsky points out that there is no general agreement on the proper and best way of analyzing PET scan data for diagnosing schizophrenia. In other words, what exactly does one look for on the scans that is truly indicative of the disorder? Researchers are currently debating this issue. As in a case in point, consider once again, the PET scans of the Genains. As we saw, one interpretation of the scans suggests that Nora and Hester exhibit the least effective and most abnormal functioning of the frontal lobes (what is called hypofrontaility, referring to depressed glucose use in the frontal lobes). But there is more than one way to assess hypofrontality. A different analysis of the Genains' PET data than what we have seen has led to the conclusion that Myra and Iris show the greatest hypofrontality (Buchsbaum et al., 1984). This is the reverse, of course, of what we have been discussing. While it appears that any interpretation of the PET data shows the Genains to have abnormal brain functionings, there is obviously considerable controversy regarding the methods used in examing such data. In fact, it is not just the frontal lobes that have been found to show decreased activity in schizophrenics, suggesting that it may prove useful to examine various areas of the brain (Asher, 1983). Our point in this: diagnosing schizophrenia through PET scans is promising but still a very rough technique (Mirsky, 1984). As Mirsky suggests, it is very much a frontier area. The PET scans of the Genains may someday be able to tell us something definitive about these women and the differences between them but we are not at that point yet.

In sum, the PET scanner as a diagnostic instrument remains a speculative and nondefinitive phenomenon. In no way is it yet a standard technique but rather one that holds potential for the future.

SUMMARY

1. Abnormal behavior is any behavior that is maladaptive in the sense that it results in undesirable consequences for the individual or others.

2. Many efforts have been made to develop a useful and reliable system for classifying abnormal behavior. The latest system, DSM-III, categorizes abnormality in terms of the symptoms displayed. One advantage of classification systems is that clinicians can communicate with each other in common terms. A given classification suggests possible causes of the problem, behaviors that might be expected, possible treatment methods, and probable outcomes.

3. A problem in diagnosing abnormality is that the individual is labeled as abnormal, and such labels have a way of sticking. Once the individual is labeled, others may have difficulty viewing that person objectively. Prejudgments about what a client is like or should be like, based on the label, can affect decisions such as which treatment to employ. In addition, the individual may come to accept the label and begin behaving in accordance with it, because the behavior seems to be expected.

4. Prominent contemporary models of abnormality include the biological, psychoanalytic, behavioral, cognitive, humanistic, family-interaction, and sociocultural models. The biological model views abnormal behavior as having an organic basis. The psychoanalytic model sees mental disorders as substituted expressions of repressed unconscious impulses. The behavioral perspective attributes maladaptive behavior to faulty learning processes. The cognitive perspective emphasizes the role that negative cognitions or self-statements play in the development of maladaptive behavior. The humanistic perspective sees abnormal behavior as a result of a stifling of the tendency to seek self-actualization. The family-interaction model holds that abnormal behavior grows out of faulty or disturbed relationships with family members. The sociocultural model attributes abnormality to the larger society in factors such as poverty and discrimination.

5. In anxiety disorders, anxiety (or the person's attempts to avoid it or defend against it) is the central feature. Included among the anxiety disorders are generalized anxiety disorders, phobic disorders, and obsessive-compulsive disorders.

6. In somatoform disorders, physical symptoms exist but without any known organic or physiological basis. Two examples of such disorders are hypochondriasis and conversion disorder.

7. Dissociative disorders involve a separation or alteration between the individual and the individual's consciousness, identity, or motor behavior. Examples are psychogenic amnesia, psychogenic fugue, and multiple personality.

8. Affective disorders involve primarily a disturbance of mood—at extreme and inappropriate levels. One type, the major depressive disorder, involves a persistent and pronounced dysphoric mood state. Bipolar disorder involves both depressive and manic episodes.

9. Schizophrenic disorders are disorders primarily of perception and thought. They are also characterized by inappropriate affect, or emotion, disturbances in motor activity, withdrawal from social relationships, and loss of contact with reality. Several subgroups exist, including disorganized, catatonic, paranoid, and undifferentiated schizophrenia.

10. Personality disorders are inflexible and maladaptive patterns of relating to and interacting with others. The most prominent characteristic is difficulty in establishing positive interpersonal relationships. Affected

persons are also known for being demanding and for shunning responsibility for their actions—feeling guiltless when engaging in unethical behavior and blaming others for their own faults and troubles. Such individuals also show consistency in their maladaptive behavior, with no apparent learning from previous troubles.

11. Suicide is always a possibility with depressed individuals. It is a common cause of death among college students. It is important for those around a suicidal person to be on the lookout for warning signs of suicide.

12. The PET scanner provides a new technique that should make diagnosing mental disorders both easier and more precise. Its ultimate utility remains to be determined, but research thus far suggests that disorders such as schizophrenia do show distinctive PET patterns.

═══ IMPORTANT TERMS AND CONCEPTS ═══

Abnormal Behavior
DSM-III
Biological Model of Abnormality (Medical Model)
Psychoanalytic Model of Abnormality
Behavioral Model of Abnormality
Cognitive Model of Abnormality
Humanistic Model of Abnormality
Family Interaction Model of Abnormality
Sociocultural Model of Abnormality
Anxiety Disorders
Generalized Anxiety Disorder
Concordance Rate
Phobia
Agoraphobia

Social Phobia
Simple Phobia
Obsessive-compulsive Disorder
Obsession
Compulsion
Somatoform Disorders
Hypochondriasis
Conversion Disorder
Dissociative Disorders
Psychogenic Amnesia
Psychogenic Fugue
Multiple Personality
Affective Disorder
Major Depressive Disorder
Bipolar Disorder

Delusions
Hallucinations
Catecholamine Hypothesis
Serotonin Hypothesis
Overgeneralization
Schizophrenic Disorders
Disorganized Schizophrenia
Catatonic Schizophrenia
Paranoid Schizophrenia
Undifferentiated Schizophrenia
Dopamine Hypothesis
Double-bind Pattern
Social-drift Hypothesis
Personality Disorders

═══ SUGGESTIONS FOR FURTHER READING ═══

Coleman, J. C., Butcher, J. N., & Carson, R. C. (1984). *Abnormal psychology and modern life* (7th ed.). Glenview, IL: Scott, Foresman. A readable, comprehensive, and eclectic introduction to the field.

Kazdin, A. E., Bellack, A. S., & Hersen, M. (Eds.). (1980). *New perspectives in abnormal psychology*. New York: Oxford University Press. A collection of scholarly reviews by experts in the field. Included are papers dealing with models of abnormality, history, classification, causes of abnormality, specific dysfunctional behaviors such as affective disorders and schizophrenia, and treatment methods.

Kesey, K. (1962). *One flew over the cuckoo's nest*. New York: Viking Press. A fictional account of the world of abnormality from the patient's viewpoint. The book explores mental disorder and its treatment.

Neale, J. M., Davison, G. C., & Price, K. P. (1978). *Contemporary readings in psychopathology* (2nd ed.). New York: Wiley. A good assortment of essays, reviews, and research papers covering diagnosis, a multitude of behavior disorders, and therapy.

Shean, G. (1978). *Schizophrenia: An introduction to research and theory*. Cambridge, MA: Winthrop Publishing. A detailed exposure to schizophrenia, containing case histories and good coverage of theories of schizophrenia.

Spitzer, R. L., Skodol, A. E., Gibbon, M., & Williams, J. B. W. (1983). *Psychopathology: A case book*. New York: McGraw-Hill. Using the diagnostic categories of DSM-III, this book presents numerous fascinating case histories, each followed by a discussion relating to issues of diagnosis, cause, treatment, and prognosis.

— CHAPTER 16 —

TREATMENT OF
ABNORMAL BEHAVIOR

TREATMENT OF ABNORMAL BEHAVIOR

— CHAPTER OBJECTIVES —

To achieve the objectives of this chapter, you should be able to answer the questions listed here. You should also be able to define the important terms and concepts listed at the end of the chapter.

1. What are the core principles of the various psychological therapies?
2. What basic differences distinguish the psychoanalytic, humanistic, and behavioral approaches?
3. How do the behavioral and cognitive-behavioral approaches differ?
4. What are medical therapies? When are they used?
5. Is therapy generally effective? Are some therapies more effective than others?
6. What processes do psychotherapies have in common?

— CHAPTER OUTLINE —

Psychological Therapies
A variety of psychological approaches are used to treat abnormal behavior.

Freudian Psychoanalysis
Humanistic Therapies
Behavioral Therapies
Cognitive-Behavioral Therapies
Group Therapy
Application: On Selecting a Therapist

Medical Therapies
Some cases call for medical treatment rather than psychological therapy.

Chemical Therapy
Electroconvulsive Therapy
Psychosurgery
Application: Drug Therapy in Action

General Evaluation of Therapies
How do the various therapies compare in effectiveness? Are they better than no treatment at all?

Methodological Issues in Evaluating Therapies
An Evaluation of Psychological Therapies
An Evaluation of Medical Therapies
Application: "You're On The Air"—The New Radio Psychologists

On the Horizon: The Future of Psychotherapy

A HELPFUL DOSE OF DISGUST

You are walking into a bar. You decide to have a glass of beer. You are now walking toward the bar. As you are approaching the bar you have a funny feeling in the pit of your stomach. Your stomach feels all queasy and nauseous. Some liquid comes up your throat and it is very sour. You try to swallow it back down, but as you do this, food particles start coming up your throat to your mouth. You are now reaching the bar and you order a beer. As the bartender is pouring the beer, puke comes into your mouth. You try to keep your mouth closed and swallow it down. You reach for the glass of beer to wash it down. As soon as your hand touches the glass, you can't hold it down any longer. You have to open your mouth and you puke. It goes all over your hand, all over the glass and the beer. You can see it floating around in the beer. Snots and mucous come out of your nose. Your shirt and pants are all full of vomit. The bartender has some on his shirt. You notice people looking at you. You get sick again and you vomit some more and more. You turn away from the beer and immediately you start to feel better. As you run out of the bar, you start to feel better and better. When you get out into clean fresh air you feel wonderful. You go home and clean yourself up. (Cautela, 1967, pp. 461–462)

If the preceding strikes you as aversive and disgusting, it has had its intended effect. The passage is part of a treatment program for alcoholics developed by Cautela (1967). In a technique called **covert sensitization,** clients imagine highly aversive events in order to reduce their attraction to troublesome behaviors, such as sexual deviancy, overeating, cigarette smoking, and alcohol abuse. Covert sensitization is one of many treatments collectively referred to as *behavioral therapy*—a topic we will return to later.

The wide array of therapies developed by psychologists directly reflects psychologists' diverse views of personality and abnormal behavior. Each viewpoint offers a different prescription for altering behavior. For example, covert sensitization conditions a new response to a selected stimulus. Therefore, therapists who believe that undesirable behavior is learned are likely to use covert sensitization to change it. On the other hand, therapists who believe that such behavior is caused by unconscious conflicts (as in psychoanalytic theory) are more concerned with resolving the conflicts than with unlearning. Prior to the 20th century, abnormality was often attributed to supernatural causes, and treatment took the form of exorcism rituals, punishment, and even execution—techniques designed to drive demons and spirits from afflicted individuals (see Figure 16–1). In short, methods of treatment typically reflect theories of how maladaptive behavior develops. Some therapists, however, are *eclectic*, which means that they use a variety of methods to treat the same problem or different problems (e.g., Lazarus, 1976).

Psychological treatment is an important topic. Large numbers of people have received or will receive professional treatment for psychological problems. The settings are public or private mental hospitals, community mental health centers, private practitioners' offices, and university student health centers. The problems range from mild to severe, including such difficulties as test anxiety, poor interpersonal relationships, sexual maladjustment, phobias,

Figure 16–1.
Dealing with mental disorders by burning the victim to death.

and depression. Therapists may be clinical or counseling psychologists, psychiatrists, or one of several other types of therapists.

This chapter will provide an understanding of the issues and concepts inherent in treating problem behavior. The discussion begins with psychological therapies; it then considers medical therapies; it concludes with a general evaluation of various therapeutic approaches.

— PSYCHOLOGICAL THERAPIES —

The first therapies to be discussed all have one thing in common. Their approach is psychological rather than physical or medical. Each one pairs a therapist with a client; the two communicate in an attempt to alter the client's disordered feelings, beliefs, or actions—a process called **psychotherapy.** As already indicated, not all psychotherapists agree on how maladaptive behavior should be treated. Furthermore, they tend to disagree on the basic problem and its origin. They even disagree on the focus of treatment—the client's feelings, thinking, or behavior, for example.

Freudian Psychoanalysis

Freud believed that many maladaptive behaviors reflect repressed (unconscious) impulses and internal conflicts (see chapter 15). The anxiety-arousing nature of such impulses and conflicts often keeps them from the individual's awareness, but it may not prevent their indirect expression as various symptoms. Thus, the goal of Freudian **psychoanalysis** is to help the patient gain insight into and become aware of buried conflicts and impulses. Presumably, better self-understanding allows an emotional release that serves to defuse the anxiety associated with previously unconscious material.

Since we do not normally become aware of unconscious desires and conflicts, Freud used several strategies to bring this material to the surface. The most basic strategy is **free association.** In this technique, patients are told to say anything that comes to mind, regardless of how meaningless, embarrassing, or illogical it may seem. Free association is done with the patient relaxed and in a reclining position so as to facilitate the remembering of the hidden material (see Figure 16–2). The psychoanalyst's task in listening to the patient free-associate is to find meaning in what is said and relationships between the patient's statements and problems. During free association, unconscious material is said to surface only in disguised or symbolic form. Thus, the therapist must see through the disguise and uncover its true meaning.

Freud observed that during free association patients are often unwilling to discuss or explore certain topics. He believed that such **resistances** reflect unconscious efforts to repress sensitive topics, thereby protecting the person from anxiety. The psychoanalyst views such areas of resistance as precisely those that need to be explored in therapy.

Freud also thought that unconscious material surfaces in disguised form in dreams. Therefore, in psychoanalysis, the therapist analyzes the content of the patient's dreams. (Return to chapter 5 for a review of Freud's view of dream content.) As with resistances, Freud believed that the disguised nature of dream content is an unconscious attempt to protect the person from anxiety that would occur if the material were more directly expressed.

Freud believed that patients are naturally defensive about recognizing the true meanings of their dreams and free associations. Consequently, the therapist must actively help the patient see the meaning of unconscious material. This is done through **interpretation,** in which the psychoanalyst identifies for patients their defenses, repressed conflicts, and wishes. By interpreting the true meaning of symptoms, resistances, and dreams, the analyst explains how symptoms relate to unconscious material. Because Freudian theory emphasizes the importance of early childhood, many such

Figure 16–2.
Freud's famous couch.

interpretations relate conflicts and maladaptive behavior to childhood experiences. The goal of psychoanalysis is for the patient to face these interpretations, understand them, and realize that the repressed material can now be expressed without anxiety.

According to Freud, one of the most important avenues to self-insight is **transference.** This phenomenon refers to the fact that, during therapy, patients may display attitudes toward and feelings for the therapist that are similar to those aimed at important people earlier in life, primarily their parents. Transference is thus thought to give insight into unconscious conflicts, many of which have their origin in early childhood and are at the heart of the patients' current problems (Bernstein & Nietzel, 1980). The therapist uses the transference to reveal to patients both their feelings and the origins of those feelings.

In Freudian psychoanalysis, patients' problems are dealt with indirectly. Problem resolution relies on the gaining of insight and self-understanding. In behavioral therapies, on the other hand, changing maladaptive behavior is the focus of treatment. This distinction will become clearer a little later.

— Evaluation of Freudian Psychoanalysis

Psychoanalysis is subject to many criticisms. First, it is nearly impossible to test Freudian concepts empirically. For example, how are we to know for sure that the unconscious has indeed been uncovered in psychoanalysis? Also, how are we to know for sure that transference has in fact taken place? Research suggests that even therapists themselves have difficulty agreeing on whether transference has occurred (Luborsky, Graff, Pulver, & Curtis, 1973). Second, psychoanalysis is both time-consuming and expensive. Four or five sessions a week may be required, and therapy often continues for as long as 5 years. Fees of $60 per hour and more are not unusual (Gallatin, 1982). Thus, psychoanalysis appears to require affluent clients. Ideally, clients should also be highly verbal and average or above average in intelligence. Critics contend that there are less expensive and equally effective alternate therapies.

In general, evidence on the effectiveness of psychoanalysis comes from clinical studies that often lack control groups. Even the few well-controlled studies have produced contradictory findings. For example, in one study, psychoanalytically oriented therapy proved less effective than behavioral therapy in treating stage fright (Paul, 1966). Yet, in another study (Sloane, Staples, Cristol, Yorkston, & Whipple, 1975), behavioral therapy was only slightly superior for treating a variety of problems.

Unfortunately, definitive studies of long-term psychoanalysis are unlikely to be done, principally because of the length and complexity of treatment (Lichtenstein, 1980). At present, it can be said that psychoanalysis has not consistently proved less effective than other therapies; neither, however, has it proved more effective (Mahoney, 1980; Fisher & Greenberg, 1977). It is, however, better than no treatment at all for patients who are not experiencing severe debilitation, such as in schizophrenia (Fisher & Greenberg, 1977; also cf. Sloan, Staples, Cristol, Yorkston, & Whipple, 1975).

Humanistic Therapies

Freudian psychoanalysis and humanistic therapies share the view that individuals must gain insight into their problems before improvement can be achieved. Beyond that point, they part company, viewing the underlying roots of behavior much differently. For the psychoanalyst, behavior is a result of unconscious, instinctual forces and people's attempts to control them. For the humanistic therapist, people are inherently good and naturally strive for personal growth if their environments do not inhibit that growth. Humanistic therapy, then, becomes a matter of structuring environments and therapeutic relationships in which people can realize their potentials and work toward self-enhancement. Let's examine two humanistic approaches, both of which focus on facilitating clients' awareness of feelings, desires, and experiences.

— Client-Centered Therapy

We can recall from earlier chapters that, according to Carl Rogers, maladjustment and unhappiness result when our basic tendency to self-actualize is interrupted. Such interruptions occur when we deny our real selves by denying our feelings and distorting our experiences. We do this to maintain a self-concept that is acceptable to others but that is false or unacceptable to us. Rogers's (1961) therapeutic approach is a direct extension of his theories of personality and maladjustment. His **client-centered therapy** aims to establish a warm, accepting, and nonjudgmental atmosphere. In such an atmosphere, individuals can explore their true feelings and desires, rather than denying them, and can become more self-accepting.

To facilitate self-acceptance, according to Rogers, certain therapist behaviors are necessary. The most important behavior is the therapist's display of **unconditional positive regard.** That is, the therapist maintains a totally accepting and nonjudgmental attitude toward anything the client feels or expresses. Through such unconditional acceptance, clients can come to accept themselves and develop positive self-regard. To do so, they must feel free to say anything or be anything, without being judged negatively for it. Rogers also believes that the therapist must show an ability to see the client's world as the client sees it. In other words, the therapist must have *empathetic understanding* of the client's experiences and feelings.

All of the preceding is aimed at allowing the client's natural tendencies for self-growth and actualization to reemerge. Rogers assumes that when clients engage in self-exploration and talk about themselves honestly, they will begin to make healthy changes in their self-images and behavior. The responsibility for doing so, however, is squarely on the shoulders of the client. The client-centered therapist is warm and accepting, not probing and interpreting.

The excerpt that follows is an example of how client-centered therapy might proceed. The therapist reflects what the client seems to be feeling but does not direct the conversation.

> *Client:* I really feel bad today . . . just terrible.
> *Therapist:* You're feeling pretty bad.
> *Client:* Yeah, I'm angry and that's made me feel bad, especially when I can't do anything about it. I just have to live with it and shut up.
> *Therapist:* You're very angry and feel like there's nothing you can safely do with your feelings.
> *Client:* Uh-huh. I mean . . . if I yell at my wife, she gets hurt. If I don't say anything to her, I feel tense.
> *Therapist:* You're between a rock and a hard place—no matter what you do, you'll wind up feeling bad.
> *Client:* I mean she chews ice all day and all night. I feel stupid saying this. It's petty, I know. But when I sit there and try to concentrate, I hear all these slurping and crunching noises. I can't stand it . . . and I yell. She feels hurt—I feel bad—like I shouldn't have said anything.
> *Therapist:* So when you finally say something, you feel bad afterward.
> *Client:* Yeah, I can't say anything to her without getting mad and saying more than I should. And then I cause more trouble than it's worth. (Duke & Nowicki, 1979, p. 565)

Gestalt Therapy

Another humanistic approach was developed by the late Frederick (Fritz) Perls (1969, 1973). Perls's **Gestalt therapy** attempts to deal with problems by helping clients achieve full awareness of their experiences and needs. As should be evident from previous references to the Gestalt school of psychology (see chapter 4), *Gestalt* in Perls's therapy refers to an emphasis on the awareness of all of one's entire experiences. Perls held that maladaptive behavior stems from being unaware of or being afraid to express various aspects of the self—especially conflicting needs, unacceptable feelings, and inconsistencies. In Perls's thinking, a defensive and unaccepting attitude toward all that one is lies at the heart of maladjustment.

The basic strategy in Gestalt therapy is to focus on the here-and-now, not the past. Its immediate goal is to enhance clients' awareness and acceptance of present needs and experiences. Self-understanding, personal growth, and self-actualization are the ultimate goals. Awareness and acceptance are considered the necessary and sufficient conditions for change and for more adaptive behavior. Perls (1973) suggested that the maladjusted person simply hasn't seen the obvious. To become happy and adjusted, he believed, we need to become better aware of what we experience and feel moment by moment. We need not probe the unconscious; what we seek is already at the surface. Consider the example that follows (Perls, 1973). If you have a fight with someone and become angry, you may feel like taking revenge. If you find this need for revenge unacceptable, you may defensively deny it. Nevertheless, the internal conflict generated still persists. In Perls's thinking, you need to recognize and accept your desire for revenge.

In Gestalt therapy, the therapist attempts to create situations in which the client faces unpleasant experiences that have been avoided. Much emphasis is placed on verbally expressing whatever is felt at the moment. The client is also encouraged to recognize body language. A client may say one thing while physically expressing something different, perhaps through hand gestures or a wrinkled brow. Presumably, recognizing what one is experiencing physically can serve as an aid to better understanding and self-acceptance.

The following excerpt from a Gestalt therapy session offers an example of how such therapy might proceed:

> *Client:* You know, I wanted to talk today about my mother. She always was a problem for me as long as I remember. She used to . . .
> *Therapist:* Tell me how you feel about your mother now.
> *Client:* Now? I haven't seen her in a week so I'm not too angry. When I was with her . . .
> *Therapist:* Right now, at this moment how do you feel about her?
> *Client:* I guess I'm not too angry with her right now. When I think of some of our arguments I get a little angry.
> *Therapist:* You say you are not angry, yet look at your hands; they are clenched into fists.
> *Client:* Yes?
> *Therapist:* Relax them—open them up. How do you feel?
> *Client:* I feel like I want to close them again—they don't feel comfortable being open.
> *Therapist:* So acting as if you aren't angry doesn't make the anger go away. Just opening your fists doesn't make them not tense.
> *Client:* You mean I *am* angry at her even now? (Duke & Nowicki, 1979, p. 568)

Evaluation of Humanistic Therapies

Given that unconditional positive regard and empathetic understanding are not the province solely of professional therapists, the client-centered approach has found widespread application. For example, even mental-health volunteers can learn to apply these behaviors in interactions with clients. With respect to the course of therapy, the client-centered approach tends to be much briefer than psychoanalysis and in this sense is more cost-effective. Like psychoanalysis, however, it may be inappropriate for individuals with severe psychological disorders.

Unfortunately, client-centered therapy cannot be easily evaluated, because support for its effectiveness has not been well-documented (cf. Lichtenstein, 1980). Likewise, there are no data with which to evaluate the effectiveness of Gestalt therapy. It is a cost-effective approach in that it is often short-term and often practiced in groups (Lichtenstein, 1980). As with psychoanalysis and client-centered therapy, Gestalt therapy seems best suited for verbal individuals whose disorders are not severe.

Behavioral Therapies

In contrast to insight therapies, **behavioral therapies** attempt to alter problem behaviors directly. This is done through the use of scientific principles of learning such as reinforcement, extinction, shaping, and modeling (see chapter 6). Behavioral therapists consider behaviors themselves the problem, not underlying instincts, conflicts, or motives. If a client is highly anxious, the behavioral therapist uses learning principles in an attempt to reduce the anxiety. In general, behavioral therapists assume that maladaptive behavior is learned. Hence, it can be unlearned, or more adaptive behavior can be learned in its place.

Behavioral therapy is often used synonymously with *behavior modification*. However, we will use only *behavioral therapy* because many people mistakenly associate behavior modification with all forms of therapy—including drug therapy, electroconvulsive therapy, and psychosurgery (Spiegler, 1983). As we will see later, none of the therapies just mentioned are behavioral. Let's examine now several behavioral approaches.

— Counterconditioning

A number of behavioral-therapy techniques are based on **counterconditioning,** in which one response to a stimulus is substituted for another (Davison & Neale, 1982).

Systematic desensitization. One of the most widely used counterconditioning techniques is *systematic desensitization* (see chapter 6). This technique, developed by Wolpe (1958), involves substituting relaxation for such maladaptive responses as anxiety or fear. While working with people who had fears, Wolpe found that such people could gradually learn to approach feared objects or situations if they simultaneously engaged in an anxiety-inhibiting behavior. One such behavior is deep muscle relaxation (Jacobson, 1938). The first step in systematic desensitization, then, is to teach clients how to relax (see Figure 16–3). The next step is to pair relaxation with stimuli that ordinarily elicit anxiety in varying degrees.

To accomplish the pairing, Wolpe found it most useful to simply have clients imagine anxiety-arousing stimuli. They begin with the mildest anxiety-arousing stimulus, for example, being in the same building with

Figure 16–3.

These clients are learning how to relax as part of the systematic desensitization procedure.

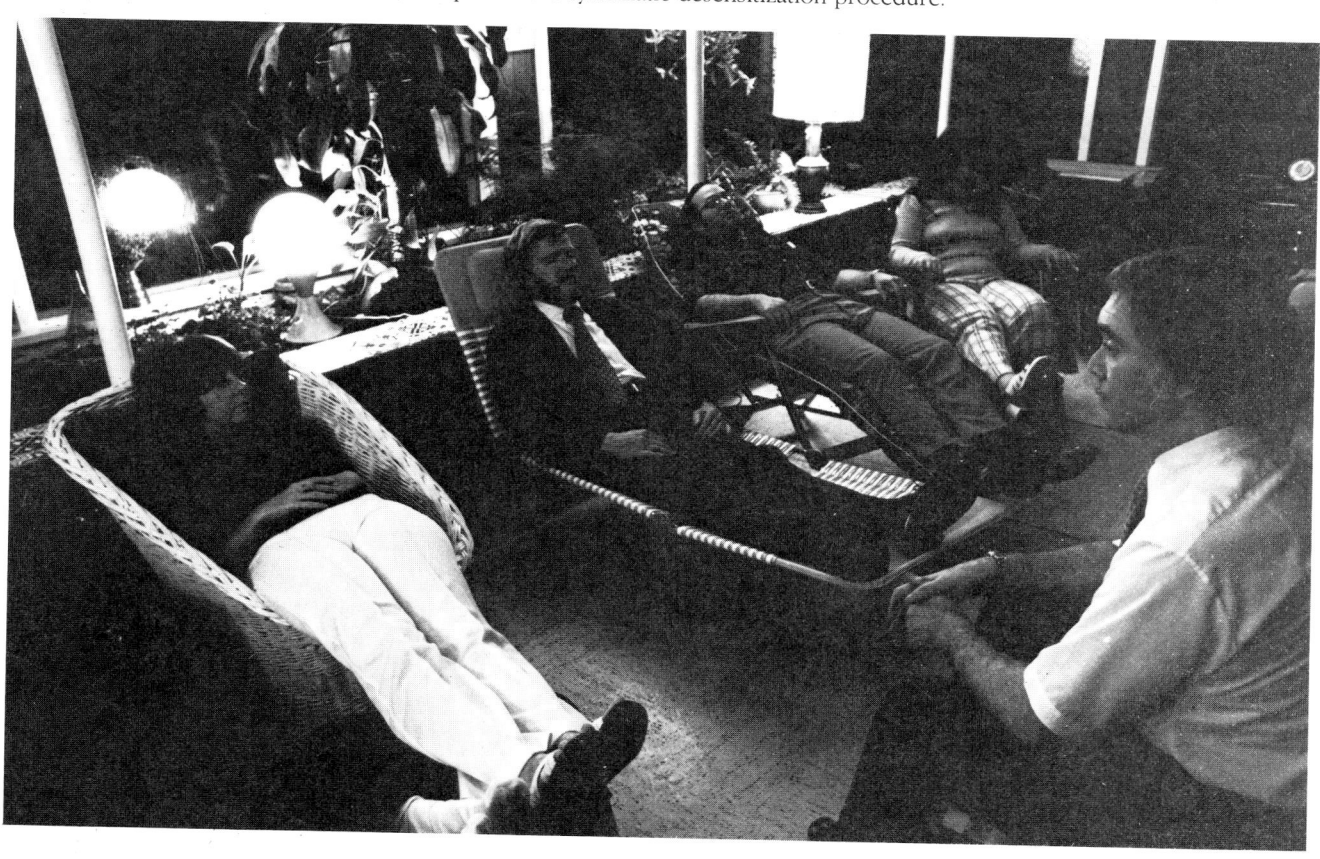

a caged snake. When they can think about the first stimulus without anxiety, they then imagine a second, more threatening stimulus, for example, being in the same room with a caged snake. Gradually, they work through a list of stronger and stronger anxiety-arousing stimuli, called a hierarchy of fears. Ultimately, the strongest anxiety-arousing stimulus, for example, handling a snake, can be imagined without anxiety.

As we can see, the essence of systematic desensitization is pairing an anxiety-arousing stimulus with relaxation. In this way relaxation will replace anxiety as a response to the stimulus. Even though the client only imagines the stressful scene, evidence indicates that a similar reduction of anxiety occurs in real-life situations (Davison & Neale, 1982).

Systematic desensitization has been applied to the treatment of a wide variety of problems. Irrational fears of objects and situations (phobias), various obsessions and compulsions, social withdrawal, test anxiety, and sexual difficulties are just some of the problems that have been successfully treated with this technique (Duke & Nowicki, 1979).

The following excerpt illustrates how systematic desensitization may be applied.

The thirty-five-year-old substitute mail carrier who consulted us . . . was debilitated by fears of criticism in general and of evaluations of his mail-sorting performance in particular. As a consequence, his everyday activities were severely constricted. . . . After agreeing that a reduction in his unrealistic fears would be beneficial, the client was taught over several sessions to relax all the muscles of his body while in a reclining chair. A list of anxiety-provoking scenes was also drawn up in consultation with the client.

– You are saying "Good morning" to your boss.
– You are standing in front of your sorting bin in the post office, and your supervisor asks why you are so slow.
– You are only halfway through your route, and it is already 2:00 p.m. As you are delivering Mrs. Mackenzie's mail, she opens her screen door and complains about how late you are.
-- Your wife criticizes you for bringing home the wrong kind of bread.
– The officer at the bridge toll gate appears impatient as you fumble in your pocket for the correct change.

These and other scenes were arranged in an *anxiety hierarchy*, from least to most fear-evoking. Desensitization proper began with the client being instructed first to relax

deeply as he had been taught. Then he was to imagine the easiest item, remaining as relaxed as possible. When he had learned to confront this image without becoming anxious, he went on to the next scene, and so on. After ten sessions the man was able to imagine the most distressing scene in the hierarchy without feeling anxious, and gradually his tensions in real life became markedly less. (Davison & Neale, 1982, p. 57)

Assertion training. When a given fear, such as asking someone for a date, has some rational basis, assertion training may be more appropriate than desensitization for alleviating anxiety (Rimm, 1977). The anxious person may be aware, for example, of a lack of skill in such situations. **Assertion training** is a technique by which a therapist attempts to increase a client's ability to express both negative and positive feelings and to do so in an honest, socially appropriate manner (Rimm, 1977; Rimm & Masters, 1979). As Rimm and Masters (1979) note, one benefit of such training is that the client has a "greater feeling of well being" (p. 63). In other words, the client is now assertive in situations that once led only to anxiety. A second benefit of enhanced assertiveness is the client's increased ability to achieve social and material rewards leading to a greater satisfaction with life.

Assertion training is carried out mainly through *behavior rehearsal*—the practicing of more assertive behavior. In counterconditioning terms, anxiety is replaced with assertion. Rimm (1977) notes that although assertion training is often used for timid individuals, it also has potential value for individuals who blow up and verbally or physically abuse others. The problem in many such cases, Rimm believes, is that people keep their anger and resentment bottled up too long and then express it explosively. Assertion training can help people express anger and resentment appropriately— before it becomes uncontrollable.

The following dialogue, between a therapist and a client who has trouble refusing unreasonable requests, uses behavior rehearsal. The process exemplified is continued until both therapist and client are satisfied with the client's response of little or no anxiety.

1. *(Assessment) Therapist:* "OK, now pretend I'm this acquaintance of yours, Bill, and I ask to borrow your car. What do you usually say?" *Client:* "Well, I guess I would say, 'Yeah, OK.' "
2. *(Feedback to client) Therapist:* "Your eye contact was good, but you gave right in, although you didn't want to."
3. *(Modeling an assertive response by the therapist)*

Therapist: "Why not try something like this: 'Bill, I would loan you my car, but I need it myself because I've got some errands to run.' "

4. *(Client rehearsal) Therapist:* "Let's see you practice something like that. I'll be Bill: 'I'd like to borrow your car today.' " *Client:* "Bill, I wish I could, but I need it myself. I've got some shopping to do."

5. *(Feedback and additional assessment) Therapist:* "That was very good. You were direct, but tactful. How anxious did you feel?" *Client:* "Not very anxious at all . . . well, maybe a little bit . . . I'm not used to saying no."

6. *(Additional rehearsal) Therapist:* "OK, let's try it again." (Rimm, 1977, pp. 467–468)

Aversive conditioning. A third form of counterconditioning, **aversive conditioning,** seeks to make negative feelings the response to a particular stimulus. Typically, such feelings replace the socially maladaptive pleasant feelings associated with smoking, drinking, gambling, and so on (Spiegler, 1983). We have, then, a reversal of the situation found in desensitization. Rather that a positive response replacing a negative one, a negative response (such as pain or disgust) replaces a positive one. An example of this process was given at the beginning of the chapter; in the example, covert sensitization was used to discourage drinking. Covert sensitization may be useful in treating sexual deviance; however, its effectiveness in treating alcoholism, smoking, and obesity has not been adequately demonstrated (Little & Curran, 1978). More direct forms of aversion therapy also exist. For example, emetics (drugs that cause nausea) and electric shock have been used to treat alcoholism (Cannon & Baker, 1981; Cannon, Baker, & Wehl, 1981). The idea, of course, is to associate the smell and taste of alcohol with unpleasant feelings.

— Operant Conditioning

Chapter 6 introduced the principles of operant conditioning. The same general principles (reinforcement, punishment, shaping, and so on) have been used by behavioral therapists to treat a variety of behavior disorders. Let's consider several examples.

Reinforcement and shaping. The guiding rule of operant conditioning is that if you want to increase the frequency of a behavior, reinforce it. In therapeutic settings, this principle has broad application. One group of therapists (Bachrach, Erwin, & Mohr, 1965) used positive reinforcement to increase eating for a person who had anorexia nervosa (see chapter 9). Other therapists have used reinforcement and shaping to initiate speech in a patient who had been mute during 19 years of hospitalization (Isaacs, Thomas, & Goldiamond, 1960). Reinforcement and shaping have also proved effective for teaching retarded individuals certain self-help skills.

Perhaps the best-known therapeutic application of reinforcement is the **token economy,** a procedure by which tokens (e.g., plastic chips) are used to reinforce adaptive behaviors, usually in an institutional setting. The tokens that are earned can be exchanged for specific rewards, such as food or recreational privileges (Bernstein & Nietzel, 1980). The advantage of using tokens as reinforcers is that they can be given immediately after the desired behavior occurs. The first token economy was established in a psychiatric institution by Ayllon and Azrin (1965). Many patients in such institutions do not take care of themselves (in such ways as not brushing their teeth), do not complete the jobs they are asked to do (such as making their beds), do not go to dinner when they are supposed to, and so on. Token economies, in which such desirable behaviors as self-care and completing work assignments are reinforced, have significantly increased these behaviors.

Because of their success in psychiatric institutions, token-economy procedures have been applied in other settings as well. For example, they have been used in classrooms to control disruptive behavior and as an aid to learning. They have also been used to control delinquent and antisocial behavior (Bernstein & Nietzel, 1980).

Withholding rewards (extinction). Sometimes conditioning principles are used to decrease the frequency of socially inappropriate or maladaptive behaviors. The operant conditioner would recommend, for example, that a child's aggression, temper tantrums, or disruptive behavior not be rewarded. In many cases, the reward that maintains such behavior is attention from others. If this is so, simply ignoring the behavior when it occurs may reduce its frequency. Another option is to institute a time-out procedure. In this case, the child is temporarily removed from the environment in which rewards for the inappropriate behavior are available. The general rule, then, is that if you can identify the rewards that maintain a maladaptive behavior and remove those rewards, the behavior will decrease in frequency. At the same time, it is beneficial to reward more adaptive behaviors that replace it.

Satiation. Operant techniques do not rely exclusively on the giving and withholding of reinforcers. Consider Ayllon's (1963) description of a hospitalized schizophrenic woman who hoarded towels (20 to 30 at any given time) in her room. Ayllon reports that behavioral treatment consisted of simply giving the patient an extra towel whenever she was in her room and never removing any of them. When the number of towels exceeded 600, the patient asked that they be removed. No further hoarding was evident even a year later. The principle in operation here is known as **satiation;** it means that a reinforcer is no longer reinforcing when it occurs with such high regularity or frequency that it is no longer associated with a state of deprivation. Food is an effective reinforcer as long as we are hungry; money is an effective reinforcer as long as we think we don't have enough of it. Eventually, the towel hoarder had so many towels that the act of collecting them was no longer reinforcing.

Punishment. As a technique for reducing the frequency of inappropriate behavior, punishment has both proponents and opponents. Opponents say that it is unethical, or they worry about possible negative consequences, such as negative feelings about the punisher. Some researchers, however, argue that with respect to aggression or other disruptive behavior in children and retarded individuals, punishment may be the most efficient technique (Fleece, O'Brien, & Drabman, 1982). Reducing aggression by ignoring it or by reinforcing behavior incompatible with it can often take a great deal of time. In the meantime, someone may be severely hurt. Fleece and his colleagues (1982) note that punishment (e.g., electric shock) has been used to rapidly suppress the aggression of retarded and psychologically disturbed children. They also report a study in which the biting behavior of a 2½-year-old child was significantly reduced by the application of an aversive (bad-tasting) liquid to the child's mouth whenever biting was attempted.

— Modeling

Given the importance of modeling in learning (Bandura, 1977b), it is not surprising that behavioral therapists have used it to help individuals develop more useful and adaptive ways of behaving. Modeling has been successfully used, for example, to teach individuals fundamental social skills and more assertive behavior (Rosenthal & Bandura, 1978). It has also been widely used in the treatment of phobias. By watching a model approach a feared object, the client is able to learn vicariously that no aversive consequences occur as a result of the action. Bandura uses the term **vicarious extinction** to refer to this learning process.

Modeling can be carried out either live or symbolically, such as by viewing a film. In treating phobias, the therapist and client often construct a hierarchy of fears, as in systematic desensitization. The therapist then models the desired behavior, beginning with the least-feared behavior and gradually working up to the most-feared.

A particularly useful adjunct to modeling is *guided participation*. The therapist-model demonstrates one of the desired behaviors on the hierarchy and then encourages the client to immediately perform the same behavior. Thus, the client not only witnesses the model's actions but also is guided by the therapist in imitating those actions. Live modeling with guided participation has been effective in reducing snake phobias in adults (see Figure 16–4; Bandura, Blanchard, & Ritter, 1969). It has been shown to be not only more effective than no treatment but also more effective than simply viewing filmed models as they interact with snakes and more effective than systematic desensitization. Figure 16–5 illustrates the effects of these procedures on subjects' success in completing a series of behaviors ranging from approaching a snake to letting the snake lie in their laps while they held their hands at their sides.

Self-efficacy. While on the topic of modeling, it is relevant to again mention *perceived self-efficacy* (Bandura, 1977b, 1978, 1982). In chapter 13, self-efficacy referred to the belief that one has the ability to cope with specific situations. According to Bandura, an increase in perceived self-efficacy may underlie all successful treatment approaches. Presumably, such perception would be best encouraged by methods that give the person direct, compelling experiences of success (Mischel, 1981). This observation may explain why participant modeling has been found to be superior to modeling alone in treating phobias (Bandura, Adams, & Beyer, 1977).

In a similar vein, Biran and Wilson (1981) found that a guided exposure technique was particularly effective in increasing subjects' perceived self-efficacy and ability to cope with phobic situations in daily life. In this approach, subjects were requested to attempt increasingly difficult encounters with feared situations, first with the help of the therapist and then alone. Such a strategy proved more effective than did a cognitive re-

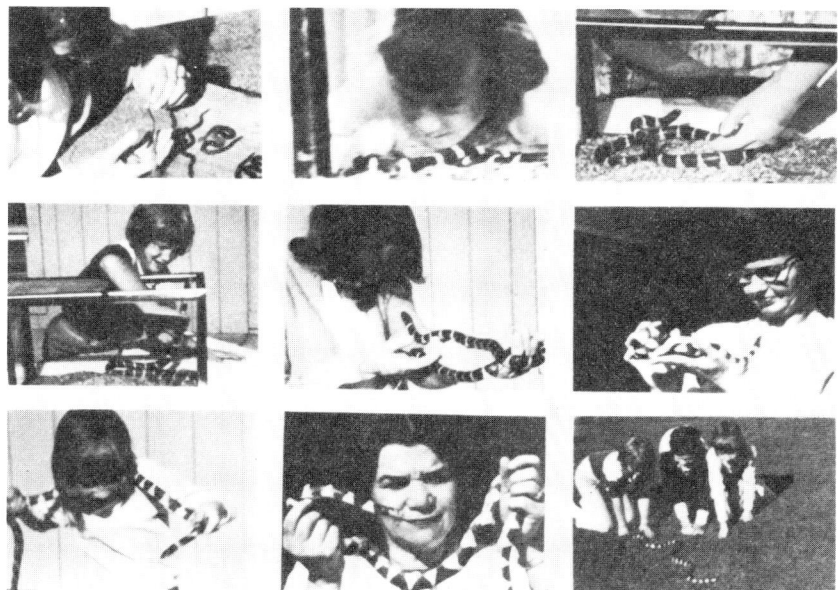

Figure 16-4.
Bandura and his colleagues have found modeling to be an effective technique for reducing snake phobias. Here, a model is demonstrating progressively greater fear-arousing interactions with a king snake.

structuring approach, in which the therapist focused on subjects' maladaptive ways of thinking about phobic situations. As Goldfried and Robins (1982) put it, "Performance accomplishments provide the most dependable information for efficacy expectancies" (p. 364). At present, it appears that the more effective a treatment is, the better it is in increasing clients' efficacy expectations (Liebert & Spiegler, 1982).

— Evaluation of Behavioral Therapies

Probably no other approaches have been so thoroughly evaluated as the behavioral therapies. Much of the evaluation has matched specific behavioral-therapy methods with specific problems. For example, it appears that behavioral approaches such as desensitization and modeling are superior to nonbehavioral approaches in treating phobias and anxiety (cf. Lichtenstein, 1980; see also Klein, Zitrin, Woerner, & Ross, 1983, for an alternate view). Likewise, token-economy programs seem to be effective in fostering adaptive behaviors in institutionalized mental patients as well as in certain other subject populations. Some evidence indicates that token economies are superior to nonbehavioral approaches in promoting later community adjustment for institutionalized individuals (Paul & Lentz, 1977).

Generally speaking, the effectiveness of all of the behavioral-therapy approaches discussed has at least some empirical support (cf. Rimm & Masters, 1979).

Figure 16-5.
Mean number of snake-approach responses before and after various treatments. (From Bandura, Blanchard, & Ritter, 1969, p. 183.)

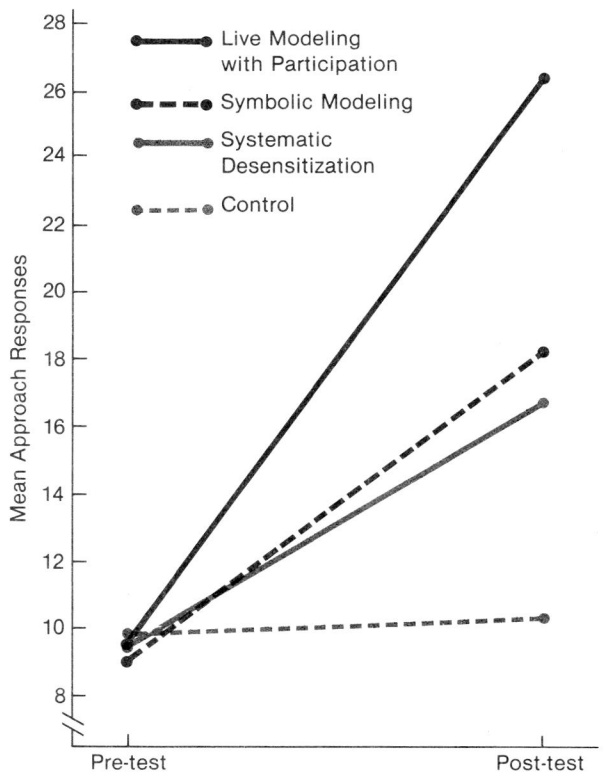

Such techniques seem to be superior to nonbehavioral approaches in some cases; overall, though, little research has been done to compare behavioral and nonbehavioral methods. In much of the behavioral-therapy research, subjects have been college students with specific problems, such as phobias. Critics sometimes point out that subjects who are recruited and who may not feel debilitated by their problems may differ from the usual clients who seek therapy. In fact, some evidence (e.g., Sloane, Staples, Cristol, Yorkston, & Whipple, 1975) does exist that with more typical clients, who often have diffuse and complex problems, behavioral therapy is no more effective than other treatment approaches (cf. Lichtenstein, 1980).

Psychoanalytic advocates have criticized behavioral therapy for failing to treat the underlying emotional conflicts that presumably lead to specific symptoms. These critics contend that if symptoms are eliminated without their cause being removed, the individual will merely express the problem or conflict in other ways—a phenomenon known as **symptom substitution.** Behavioral therapists, however, respond that symptom substitution is rare. Indeed, evidence of its occurrence is difficult to find (Kazdin, 1982).

As with client-centered therapy, the principles of behavioral therapy can be learned and put to use by a number of people: nurses or psychiatric aides working in mental hospitals, parents dealing with their children at home, teachers with their students in the classroom, and so on (Lichtenstein, 1980). Also, the range of clients amenable to behavioral therapy seems larger than with the other therapies. Behavioral therapy tends to involve more action and fewer words, which is perhaps why it is better than other therapies in dealing with patients with chronic mental disorders, and aggressive children (Lichtenstein, 1980).

Cognitive-Behavioral Therapies

Many behavioral therapists have realized that changes in behavior, even those brought about by altered environmental conditions, are mediated by altered thoughts or cognitions. That is, what we tell ourselves—our beliefs and expectations and especially the meanings we place on events—greatly affect behavior. As Spiegler (1983) suggests, "A central premise of cognitive-behavioral therapies is that *the way we view or interpret events in our environment influences how we behave*" (p. 261). **Cognitive-behavioral therapies** emphasize techniques that directly alter troublesome cognitions (for example, the self-statement "I am a failure"). Because such cognitions are often faulty, irrational, or pessimistic, it is assumed that changing them will lead directly to more adaptive overt behavior. Cognitive-behavioral therapists may also attempt to alter overt behavior, but their concern is with how doing so affects the person's thought processes. Two examples will be used to illustrate cognitive-behavioral therapies: Ellis's rational-emotive therapy and Beck's cognitive therapy.

— Rational-Emotive Therapy

According to Albert Ellis (e.g., 1977), psychological problems result from misperceptions and mistaken cognitions. Emotional disturbances are due not simply to external events but rather to our perceptions of those events. Ellis has focused specifically on irrational beliefs as the essence of emotional disorders. The following gives a flavor of his view:

> We feel anxious or depressed because we strongly convince ourselves that it is not only unfortunate and inconvenient but that *it is terrible and catastrophic* when we fail at a major task or are rejected by a significant person. And we feel hostile because we vigorously believe that people who behave unfairly not only *had better not* but *absolutely should not* act the way they indubitably do and that it is *utterly insufferable* when they frustrate us. (Ellis, 1977, p. 273)

The goal of **rational-emotive therapy (RET)** is to help clients shed their irrational beliefs so that they can behave logically and rationally and experience appropriate and adaptive emotions. Table 16–1 shows some irrational beliefs that Ellis finds crucial in emotional disturbances. The irrationality lies in the fact that the beliefs do not accurately reflect reality.

The basic therapeutic technique that Ellis advocates is active, direct confrontation (Ellis, 1977). The goal is to reeducate clients by pointing out their irrational and illogical ways of thinking and by demonstrating how self-defeating thought processes cause and maintain unhappiness (Patterson, 1980). Beyond this, the therapist teaches clients how to think in new, more logical ways. The essence of RET, then, is to challenge and dispute the client's belief system.

Ellis also believes that various behavioral techniques help clients change unrealistic assumptions and false

Table 16-1.
Ellis believes that these irrational beliefs lie at the heart of maladjustment and unhappiness. (From Ellis & Harper, 1975, pp. 88–186.)

1. You must have love or approval from all the people you find significant.
2. You must prove thoroughly competent, adequate, and achieving.
3. When people act obnoxiously and unfairly, you should blame them, and see them as bad, wicked, or rotten individuals.
4. You have to view things as awful, terrible, horrible, and catastrophic when you get seriously frustrated, treated unfairly, or rejected.
5. Emotional misery comes from external pressures and you have little ability to control or change your feelings.
6. If something seems dangerous or fearsome, you must preoccupy yourself with it and make yourself anxious about it.
7. You can more easily avoid facing many life difficulties and self-responsibilities than undertake more rewarding forms of self-discipline.
8. Your past remains all-important and because something once strongly influenced your life, it has to keep determining your feelings and behavior today.
9. People and things should turn out better than they do and you must view it as awful and horrible if you do not find good solutions to life's grim realities.
10. You can achieve maximum human happiness by inertia and inaction or by passively and uncommittedly "enjoying yourself."

beliefs. In particular, he suggests homework assignments. For example, clients may be asked to spend time each day disputing their irrational beliefs and then giving themselves some reward. Or they may be asked to apply for a job, to visit (rather than avoid) a nagging in-law, or to ask for a date. Such activities are intended to help clients develop new assumptions and new ways of looking at various activities and events. In Ellis's approach, then, behavioral and cognitive changes complement each other.

In the following example of RET, a 39-year-old woman is seeing a therapist because of her anxiety over being in public places, especially in restaurants (Rimm & Masters, 1979). On the day prior to the session, she experienced extreme anxiety while in a restaurant. She thought that she couldn't finish her meal, and she worried that she might even faint, which she believed would be terrible because it would make her appear worthless and incompetent. The therapist has worked at persuading her that fainting does not diminish one's worth as a human. Let's pick up the session

from there and see how rational-emotive therapy works.

Therapist: Okay, if you and I agree that just because you passed out and people around you don't approve doesn't have any bearing on your worth, tell me how it is terrible?
Client: Well . . . people *should* be able to handle themselves!
Therapist: Guess what, Helen . . . you just *musturbated*.
Client: (Looks shocked, then laughs) What do you mean?
Therapist: You said people *should* do such and such . . . like, people *must* do such and such . . . that's where the term *musturbation* comes from. The thing is this: As children we are taught we *should* do this, or we *must* do that, or we *shouldn't* do this. And we grow up accepting this without ever thinking about it logically. The reality is that the "shoulds" and "musts" are the rules that other people hand down to us, and we grow up accepting them as if they are absolute truth, which they most assuredly aren't.
Client: You mean it is perfectly okay to, you know, pass out in a restaurant?
Therapist: Sure!
Client: But . . . now I'm confused . . . I know I wouldn't *like* it to happen.
Therapist: I can certainly understand that. It would be unpleasant, awkward, inconvenient. But it is illogical and irrational to think that it would be terrible, or that you shouldn't or that it somehow bears on your worth as a person. Thinking this way is also very self-defeating.
Client: What do you mean?
Therapist: Well, suppose one of your friends calls you up and invites you back to that restaurant. If you start telling yourself, "I might panic and pass out and people might make fun of me and that would be terrible," you are going to *make* yourself uptight. And you might find you are dreading going to the restaurant, and you probably won't enjoy the meal very much.
Client: Well, that *is* what usually happens.
Therapist: But it doesn't have to be that way. That is the really important thing. Remember the *A-B-C*'s. The way you feel, your reaction, C, depends on what you *choose* to believe or think, or say to yourself, at *B*. A could be anything. Like your friend inviting you to meet her at the restaurant. Or noticing you are tense when the meal is being served.
Client: Well, what *should* I think, Doctor?
Therapist: That was a musturbation! Can you state that in a more rational way?
Client: (Laughs) Hmmm . . . let's see. What would be a . . . healthy . . . thing to think?
Therapist: Let's role-play it. I'll be your friend calling you up to invite you to the restaurant. Then you say aloud the thoughts that you might think that would be, well, healthy, to use your word. (Rimm & Masters, 1979, pp. 384–385)

Cognitive Therapy

An approach very similar to rational-emotive therapy is Beck's (1976) **cognitive therapy**—a strategy that emphasizes the importance of undoing negative thinking and faulty reasoning to overcome emotional disorders. Cognitive therapy was developed to treat depression. In Beck's (1976) view, the cognitive approach for counteracting depression consists of enabling patients to see themselves as winners rather than losers, as masterful rather than helpless. Clients are encouraged, through pointed but friendly questioning, to see that their assumptions are ideas that can be examined, rather than indisputable facts. Presumably, recognizing the incongruity of these faulty assumptions helps clients change their negative thinking.

The excerpts that follow illustrate Beck's work with a woman who had recently attempted suicide. At the time of the interview, the woman still wanted to commit suicide, believing that she had nothing to live for because her husband was unfaithful. Following the interview, the woman was more cheerful and no longer suicidal. She eventually divorced her husband and began leading a more stable life.

> *Therapist:* Why do you want to end your life?
> *Patient:* Without Raymond, I am nothing . . . I can't be happy without Raymond . . . But I can't save our marriage.
> *Therapist:* What has your marriage been like?
> *Patient:* It has been miserable from the very beginning . . . Raymond has always been unfaithful . . . I have hardly seen him in the past five years.
> *Therapist:* You say you can't be happy without Raymond . . . Have you found yourself happy when you are with Raymond?
> *Patient:* No, we fight all the time and I feel worse.
> *Therapist:* You say you are nothing without Raymond. Before you met Raymond, did you feel you were nothing?
> *Patient:* No, I felt I was somebody.
> *Therapist:* If you were somebody before you knew Raymond, why do you need him to be somebody now?
> *Patient:* (Puzzled) Hmm . . . (Beck, 1976, pp. 289–290)

At this point the conversation shifted to marriage and the woman's prospects if she ended her marriage. It concluded this way:

> *Therapist:* Do you have a *real marriage?*
> *Patient:* I guess not.
> *Therapist:* If you don't have a real marriage, what do you actually lose if you decide to end the marriage?
> *Patient:* (Long pause) Nothing, I guess. (Beck, 1976, p. 291)

As Beck and his colleagues (Beck, Rush, Shaw, & Emery, 1979) have pointed out, the thrust of the therapy was to get the woman to see that a break-up with Raymond was not really a loss, since their relationship was already nonexistent, and that she did have other options. Furthermore, the therapist tried to make a dent in the woman's apparent formula of "Unless I am loved, I am nothing" (Beck, Rush, Shaw, & Emery, 1979).

Cognitive therapy does not rely on persuading clients that their thinking is faulty. Instead, it encourages clients to test their ideas to find out if they can be empirically supported. By performing real-life experiments and gathering information about themselves, clients may find out that their thinking is distorted and overly pessimistic. Clients who are depressed and who believe that they are thought of and responded to negatively by everyone they meet may be asked to keep a daily log of all of their interactions. If they discover that they are actually thought of and responded to positively by at least some people, they can begin to re-evaluate the mistaken belief that they are social misfits.

The basic idea, then, is to give clients experiences that will provide positive feedback about themselves and allow them to disconfirm their false beliefs, thereby enhancing their feeling of self-worth. Beck, Rush, Shaw, and Emery (1979) describe the situation of a depressed graduate student who believed that her English professor considered her a reject. Her basis for believing this was a grade of C and two pages of critical comments on a recent essay she had written. In a reality-testing experiment suggested by the therapist, the student called the professor and learned two interesting facts: (1) that the average class grade was a C and (2) that the professor believed that although she did need some improvement in her style, the content of her essay was promising. This information prompted the student to get some tutoring instead of withdrawing from the course or from school, and her emotional state showed considerable improvement. She no longer considered herself a reject; she saw that she simply needed improvement in her writing style.

Sometimes depressed clients complain that they gain absolutely no satisfaction from life—their perception being that "I never enjoy anything anymore" (Beck, 1976). In such cases, the therapist may have the patient systematically record the events of each day and the degree of satisfaction and sense of mastery achieved from each event. As Beck (1976) notes, "We have found that, as the patients realize the number of actual experiences of mastery or pleasure, they begin to feel a more enduring sense of satisfaction" (p. 298).

A sense of mastery and pleasure is often instilled through a series of graded task assignments. The least difficult task is assigned and completed first; it is followed by increasingly difficult tasks. As the tasks are completed, the client gradually sheds the belief that "I am worthless and can accomplish nothing." Such a belief often arises from the fact that the depressed person is doing nothing because of the mistaken belief that all is unconquerable. As each small task is completed, even greater satisfaction can be fostered by following it with some type of self-reward.

— Evaluation of Cognitive-Behavioral Therapies

Although the cognitive-behavioral therapies are not behavioral therapies per se, they are becoming increasingly accepted by behavioral therapists. Thus far, however, even though the evidence looks promising, the techniques are too new for a definitive assessment of their effectiveness. Although each of the cognitive-behavioral therapies has some empirical support (see, for example, Rush, 1983; Smith, 1982; and Wise & Haynes, 1983), none of them (including approaches we did not discuss) presently has an exceptionally strong empirical base (Rimm & Masters, 1979). With respect to RET, even though a number of studies suggest that it is effective, there is no evidence that changing irrational beliefs is the specific factor responsible for improvement (Smith, 1982). Much the same kind of problem exists with respect to Beck's approach. That is, it is not certain which aspect of the therapy is responsible for the beneficial effects (Rush, 1983). Nevertheless, Rush (1983) concludes "that this therapy is effective for some types of depressions" (p. 124). In particular, he suggests that "one might speculate that depressions that are characterized by an abundance of negative cognitive distortions are particularly likely to benefit from cognitive therapy" (p. 121).

Especially enlightening is Miller and Berman's recent (1983) review of 48 studies involving cognitive-behavioral therapies. These authors conclude that

1. Cognitive-behavioral treatment is better than no treatment.
2. Cognitive-behavioral treatment has not been shown to be better than any other therapy.
3. The effectiveness of cognitive-behavioral therapies

seems to be due as much to the behavioral component as to the cognitive component of the treatment.
4. There is no evidence that cognitive-behavioral therapies are the best treatment for disorders such as depression. This point, of course, contradicts the claims of cognitive therapists such as Rush.

Group Therapy

Several people are treated simultaneously in **group therapy.** An advantage of this approach is that it makes efficient use of the therapist's time. But there are also other good reasons for conducting group therapy. When people with similar problems come together for treatment, they can give one another special support and understanding. Groups also offer the opportunity to acquire new skills from others who are learning to deal effectively with problems. Social situations provide ample opportunities for people to discover their hostility, irrational beliefs, or negative self-concept. Such issues can then be dealt with in a safe environment before new ways of feeling, thinking, and behaving in the outside world are tried out.

The therapies already discussed, although generally used as individual therapies, can certainly be used in a group format. Additionally, some therapeutic approaches are specifically designed for group therapy; such approaches are based on the belief that people's problems are best dealt with in a group setting. Let's turn now to several examples.

— Psychodrama

In the 1920s, Jacob Moreno, a Viennese psychiatrist, made an interesting observation. When he had children act out stories rather than merely read them or listen to them, the children seemed to display greater understanding and to show more emotional intensity. Out of this observation grew an approach known as psychodrama.

In **psychodrama,** individuals gain insight into problems by acting out feelings with respect to emotionally significant events or situations as if they were in a play. It is assumed that such spontaneous and unrehearsed role-playing among a group of "actors" helps individuals express emotions, thoughts, and conflicts that would be too threatening to express in a more traditional verbal exchange between client and therapist. Presumably, then, the individual gains a better understanding of both motives and behavior.

— Family and Marital Therapy

In an approach known as **family therapy,** family members are treated as a group rather than individually (Lecker, 1976). The need for family therapy often arises when it becomes evident that what seemed at first to be only one person's problem is actually a problem of the entire family. Consequently, family members are encouraged to work as a group to improve communication and cooperation. The importance of the family system in understanding the problems of any family member is made clear in the following example, provided by Barnard and Corrales (1979):

Imagine a Saturday morning in the Arbor family. Mr. Arbor is reading the paper in the family room. Mrs. Arbor goes into her daughter's room and discovers that the room is a mess. Susie, the daughter, is fifteen years old. Mother gets very angry and proceeds to scold Susie, who fights back. As father hears the fight, his "guts" begin to churn; he then pops two tablets into his "Rolaid stomach." Before the quarrel gets too far underway, Mr. Arbor decides to leave for a round of golf—escape of some kind is his usual reaction to any overt conflict in the family. He leaves with a vague realization that, somehow, his wife's outburst may be partially related to the marital conflicts and tensions that have been smoldering for years. Mother, too, feels guilty because the vehemence of her anger does not match the event (the messy room); she may subconsciously sense her overreaction as an overflow of the unresolved tension in the marital relationship.

Furthermore, Mrs. Arbor becomes angry when she realizes that once again Father has escaped the emotional field. She resents having to shoulder the full brunt of the disciplinarian role, silently saying to herself, "Why do I have to be the bad person all the time? Why can't he shoulder the family leadership sometimes? Every time it gets hot around here, he abandons me." Susie, on the other hand, although primarily aware of the present intrusion into her personal boundaries, has sensed the underlying but unresolved tension between her parents. So she, too, feels somewhat victimized by being made the dumping ground of the marital relationship. However, more significant than the resentment, she feels the insecurity of living in a situation in which her intimate world (her family) is sitting on so shaky a foundation as her parents' brittle marriage. She also resents Father's rarely coming to her aid, as well as his being so emotionally unavailable.

What started as a simple quarrel over a messy room is based on a complex and powerful set of emotional links that affected every member in that family. (pp. 4–5)

In effect, then, problems that have their origin within family interactions need to be resolved within the family group as a whole. Chapter 9 indicated that family treatment is often encouraged in cases of anorexia nervosa. Given that family conflicts of various sorts may lie at the heart of this disorder, improvement may be unlikely unless the entire family is involved in therapy. In general, the goals of the family therapist are to improve lines of communication, to clarify expectations that family members have of each other, and to aid family members in working toward more mutually satisfying and fulfilling interactions (Atwater, 1983).

These goals also apply to **marital therapy,** the form of family therapy involving treatment for couples having marital problems (see Figure 16–6). If a couple's unhappiness has its roots in the couple's relationship and interactions, it is almost fruitless for only one of the two people to receive therapy. Therapy involving both can improve communication and enhance understanding of the roles that each person plays and how they influence each other's behavior. Consider the following exchange between a husband and wife the night before the husband was to take a real estate agents' exam (Stuart, 1980):

June: Bill, would you please help me get dinner on the table?

Bill: Why don't you have some understanding once in a while? Can't you see I'm up to my ears in landlord and tenant rights?

June: You've had six months to study for that exam. If you'd watched ten fewer football games, you would have been ready for it by now. I've worked all day and I need some help from you now, exam or not.

Bill: *(Storms out of the kitchen, grabs his coat, and heads for the door.)* I've got to get out of here or I'll go batty!

June: You can get out of here all right—and you can stay out, too! (pp.68–69)

As Stewart (1980) points out, Bill might describe this interaction in terms of how June first blew up at him, leading him to say he was leaving and prompting her to say he should stay out. June, on the other hand, might see it as a case in which Bill accused her of bothering him, to which she responded that he shouldn't have put off his studying until the last minute and that she needs some of his time, leading him to storm out of the house. Each of them, however, forgot to mention an important point. Bill didn't mention that he prompted June's blow-up by accusing her of having no understanding. June didn't mention that she asked

Figure 16–6.
One of the goals of marital therapists is to help couples communicate effectively with each other.

for Bill's help at what was, for him, a very inconvenient and tense time. When a therapist points out such omissions, couples begin to see how often they view the same event differently. They also learn that neither of their interpretations reflects the entire truth. As the therapist fills in the story for them, they can better see how each of them prompts and maintains the actions of the other (Stuart, 1980).

— Evaluation of Group Therapy

In evaluating the therapies specifically designed as group approaches, we must note that little evidence as to their effectiveness is available. With regard to psychodrama, there is no evidence at all with which to evaluate it. Research on family and marital therapy "is still in its infancy" (Gurman & Kniskern, 1978, p. 819). Definitive statements as to whether one approach to these therapies is better than another or whether the therapies are better than no treatment at all cannot yet be made. However, echoing our earlier comments, we can say that the evidence does suggest that when only one spouse gets therapy for marital problems, the outcome is much less successful than when both spouses receive therapy (Gurman & Kniskern, 1978).

— APPLICATION —
ON SELECTING A THERAPIST

In this section, we would like to discuss some issues that you might consider if you ever seek out a therapist, either for yourself or for someone else. Choosing a psychotherapist can be a difficult task, given the many different disciplines that offer therapy services. Therapists who are *psychologists* have either a doctorate (PhD or PsyD) or a master's degree (MA or MS) in clinical or counseling psychology. They are trained to deal with diverse problems. Typically they are prepared to use a variety of therapeutic approaches, although they may specialize in only one—for instance, behavioral therapy.

Psychiatrists are another type of psychotherapist. They are physicians (MDs) who have specialized in the treatment of mental disorders. Their training in psychology is secondary to their medical training. They are much more likely than psychologists to work with severely disturbed people, such as those with a diagnosis of schizophrenia or bipolar disorder. This specialization stems mainly from the fact that severely disturbed people are typically in need of some type of medical therapy, such as drugs, which the psychiatrist is qualified to prescribe and administer. Most psychiatrists tend to be psychoanalytically oriented. Several well-known exceptions include Joseph Wolpe, known for his work in behavioral therapy, and Aaron Beck, known for his cognitive-therapy approach.

Psychoanalysts are psychotherapists who specialize in psychoanalysis. They are usually psychiatrists but need not be. What allows them to be called psychoanalysts is training at a psychoanalytic institute.

Psychiatric social workers hold a master's degree (MSW) in social work. These therapists are commonly employed in psychiatric settings, working alongside psychiatrists, or in social agencies, working with families in the community. Some, however, are in independent practice. They are qualified to practice psychotherapy with both individuals and groups and usually have an academic background in sociology and psychology.

Pastoral counselors also practice psychotherapy. They are clergy who have had training in working with people who have emotional and behavioral problems.

This description of psychotherapists is not exhaustive, but it includes the types of psychotherapists you are most likely to encounter. Most therapists use a number of approaches and are experienced in dealing with a wide range of problems, so it is generally not necessary to let the particular problem dictate the choice of therapist. A therapist who cannot help you can always refer you to someone else. You might keep in mind, however, that many therapists do specialize in certain therapeutic approaches, such as psychoanalysis or behavioral therapy. If you think you would prefer a certain approach or would find some approach unattractive, take that into account in your choice of therapist.

How do you locate a therapist? Most college students can see a therapist at the university student health center. Your own school likely employs one or more psychologists or psychiatrists to help students with problems. Beyond that possibility, a good place to start your search is to ask people you trust to recommend a therapist. For example, ask your minister, teacher, or physician for recommendations. Talk with those you know who have gone to a therapist and get their suggestions. The yellow pages in telephone directories also list local mental-health professionals. You can find listings there of therapists in private practice as well as of mental-health agencies, such as community mental-health centers and private mental hospitals and clinics. You can also write to professional organizations, such as the American Psychological Association, the American Psychiatric Association, and state psychological associations, for listings of qualified and licensed therapists in your area.

It is a good idea to find out as much as possible about the therapist before beginning therapy (this discussion draws upon many of the ideas proposed by Linehan—edited in Spiegler, 1983). If you can't do this without setting up an appointment, view your initial session with the therapist as a get-acquainted time without any firm commitment to continuing the therapy. This is the time for you to ask questions and to find out what therapy would be like with this person. Only if you think that you would be comfortable with and have confidence in the therapist should you continue.

Try to leave the first session with answers to the following questions: Does the therapist think therapy will help you? What treatment approach will the therapist use? Are the therapist's values compatible with your own? Do you and the therapist share the same goals as to what therapy should accomplish? How long will treatment last? What are the therapist's fees? Does the therapist charge according to income? Does your health insurance cover fees paid to the therapist? Above all, what are the therapist's qualifications? Don't hesitate to ask. A competent and qualified therapist won't be offended. Find out if the therapist is certified or licensed to practice.

If you are not satisfied with the information you get, or if you are uncomfortable with the therapist in any way, seek another therapist. If you actually do begin therapy but are frustrated with your progress or are uncomfortable with the therapist, discuss it. Let your feelings be known. The two of you may be able to establish new goals or a different approach. If progress appears to be unlikely, discuss with the therapist the possibility of consulting someone else about your problem. You need never think that you must stay with a therapist once you have started .

— MEDICAL THERAPIES —

In some cases, especially when a mental disorder is severe or does not respond to psychological therapy, **medical therapies** may be used. These therapies involve physical alteration or manipulation of the body for the purpose of treating maladaptive behavior; they include chemical therapy, electroconvulsive therapy, and psychosurgery.

Chemical Therapy

One major medical approach is **chemical therapy**— the use of drugs to treat maladaptive behavior. This form of therapy is relatively recent (since the 1950s). Nevertheless, it is now a widespread and much-used strategy. As Duke and Nowicki (1979) have observed, chemical therapy has had an enormous effect on the treatment of mental disorders. Many individuals who might otherwise be hospitalized are able to remain at home and lead fairly normal lives while taking daily doses of medication. Within mental hospitals, patients are easier to work with because of drug therapy. What are the drugs behind such changes? What are their effects?

Drugs are often classified according to their therapeutic application. We will examine here four categories (see Table 16–2): Neuroleptics, anxiolytics, antidepressants, and antimanics (Breuning & Poling, 1982).

— Neuroleptics

The class of drugs used to treat and control extreme psychological disturbances, such as hallucinations, severe agitation, and confusion, is called **neuroleptics.** Also known as major tranquilizers, these drugs are most often used to treat schizophrenia. Perhaps the best-known of the neuroleptics is chlorpromazine

Table 16–2.

Classification of some of the drugs used in the treatment of mental disorders. (Trade names are in parentheses.)

NEUROLEPTICS	ANXIOLYTICS	ANTIDEPRESSANTS	ANTIMANICS
Phenothiazines	*Benzodiazepines*	*Tricyclics*	*Lithium carbonate*
Chlorpromazine (Thorazine)	Chlordiazepoxide (Librium)	Imipramine (Tofranil)	
Fluphenazine (Prolixin)	Diazepam (Valium)	Amitriptyline (Elavil)	
Thioridazine (Mellaril)	*Glycerol derivatives*	*MAO inhibitors*	
Trifluoperazine (Stelazine)	Meprobamate (Miltown, Equanil, Trelman)	Phenelzine (Nardil)	
Butyrophenones		Tranylcypromine (Parnate)	
Haloperidol (Haldol)			
Thioxanthenes			
Chlorprothixene (Taractan)			

(Thorazine), a drug in the group of neuroleptics known as *phenothiazines*. According to a recent report, one of the most potent neuroleptics is haloperidol (Haldol) (Turkington, 1983). Haloperidol is not a phenothiazine; it is in a group of neuroleptics known as *butyrophenones*.

Pharmacologically, neuroleptics are known to block the activity of dopamine receptors. Recall from chapter 15 the dopamine hypothesis, which suggests that schizophrenia is caused by an excess of dopamine. Given that neuroleptics block dopamine activity, their benefits are understandable. Their action provides further support for the role of dopamine in schizophrenia—as does the fact that large doses of amphetamines, which increase dopamine activity in the brain, worsen the symptoms of schizophrenics (see chapter 15).

— Anxiolytics

Also known as minor tranquilizers or antianxiety agents, the **anxiolytics** are used to treat such chronic problems as mild anxiety and tension, insomnia, and night terrors (Breuning & Poling, 1982). They may also be used to help alleviate the stress associated with traumatic events such as divorce. Anxiolytics are the most widely prescribed drugs today. You are probably familiar with the trade names of some of them: Librium, Valium, and Miltown.

One of the major groups of the anxiolytics is the *benzodiazepines,* among which are chlordiazepoxide (Librium) and diazepam (Valium). Another major group is the *glycerol derivatives,* the most important of which is meprobamate (Equanil, Miltown, Trelman). All of these drugs make the user feel more relaxed and less anxious. Duke and Nowicki (1979) note that heavy use of these drugs can lead to physical dependence. Indeed, withdrawal symptoms, including convulsions and hallucinations, can occur when the drugs are discontinued after prolonged usage.

— Antidepressants

The drugs used to treat severe depression and its symptoms, such as sadness, guilt, thoughts of suicide, and inactivity, are the **antidepressants.** These drugs elevate one's mood and greatly alter the listed symptoms.

There are two major groups of antidepressants: the *tricyclics* and the *monoamine oxidase (MAO) inhibitors.* The MAO inhibitors are considered less effective and more toxic than the tricyclics and are therefore less frequently used (Breuning & Poling, 1982). One of the most commonly used antidepressant tricyclics is imipramine (Tofranil). Another well-known tricyclic is amitriptyline (Elanil).

Zitrin and her colleagues (Zitrin, Klein, Woerner, & Ross, 1983) argue that the antidepressant label associated with tricyclics and MAO inhibitors is unfortunate because these drugs also alleviate severe anxiety attacks and panic attacks. This effect has been observed in the treatment of both agoraphobia and school phobia (Zitrin, Klein, Woerner, & Ross, 1983; Rabiner & Klein, 1969; Klein, Zitrin, & Woerner, 1977; Klein, 1982). However, as Liebowitz and Klein (1981) note, although imipramine blocks panic attacks in agoraphobics, the phobic avoidance pattern and the accompanying anxiety in anticipating the phobic situation are still evident. Other forms of therapy are therefore warranted and necessary at this point.

The last several years have witnessed the appearance of a new generation of antidepressants (Kelwala, Stanley, & Gershon, 1983). These drugs include trimipramine, amoxapine, malprotiline, and trazodone. Feighner (1983) notes that the traditional tricyclics and MAO inhibitors have a slow onset of action, have numerous side-effects, and can be lethal in overdoses. Thus far, there seems to be no convincing evidence that the new antidepressants are any faster to act, but for some at least, the side-effects may be more benign (Dominguez, 1983; Zarifian & Rigal, 1982).

Like the earlier antidepressants, these new drugs inhibit the reuptake of either norepinephrine or serotonin, or both, into presynaptic nerve endings after being released into the synapse (Breuning & Poling, 1982). The consequence of this action is that the effects of the released transmitter are augmented because of a higher-than-normal level at the synapse (Linnoila, Karoum, Rosenthal, & Potter, 1983). This ties in, of course, with the catecholamine and serotonin theories of depression (see chapter 15), which suggest that depression is caused by a deficiency of these neurotransmitters at key synaptic sites.

— Antimanics

Although depression occurs most often by itself, it can also occur in conjunction with periods of mania (see chapter 15). **Antimanics** are the drugs used in treating the mania associated with bipolar disorder. The only known effective antimanic in use today is lithium carbonate. One explanation of its effectiveness is that the drug reduces the production of norepinephrine. As

Breuning and Poling (1982) note, some evidence indicates that lithium carbonate decreases the release of norepinephrine while enhancing its reuptake into the presynaptic neuron. At the synapse, then, there should be a decreased level of norepinephrine. Chapter 15 noted that one theory of mania is that it results from an excess of norepinephrine.

Electroconvulsive Therapy

The form of medical therapy in which a brief electric current (approximately 70 to 130 volts) is passed through the brain as a method of treating depression is known as **electroconvulsive therapy (ECT),** or electroshock (see Figure 16–7). ECT has a bad reputation among the general public and is a generally misunderstood procedure. Indicative of the negative attitude toward ECT was the vote taken in 1982 in Berkeley, California, to ban the therapy in that city. A California superior-court judge later ordered an end to the ban after the legality of the vote was challenged by the Northern California Psychiatric Society (Cunningham, 1983c).

In severe depressions in which suicidal thoughts are prominent, antidepressants may not act fast enough. In such cases, ECT seems to be the preferred form of treatment, since quick improvement in mood occurs. The sinister reputation of ECT may stem in part from the lack of a definitive understanding of how it works. There is some evidence that ECT affects the levels of neurotransmitters in the same way that antidepressants do (Linnoila, Karoum, Rosenthal, & Potter, 1983).

One of the concerns about ECT is its potential side-

Figure 16–7.
Electroconvulsive therapy has been shown to be an effective treatment for severe depression.

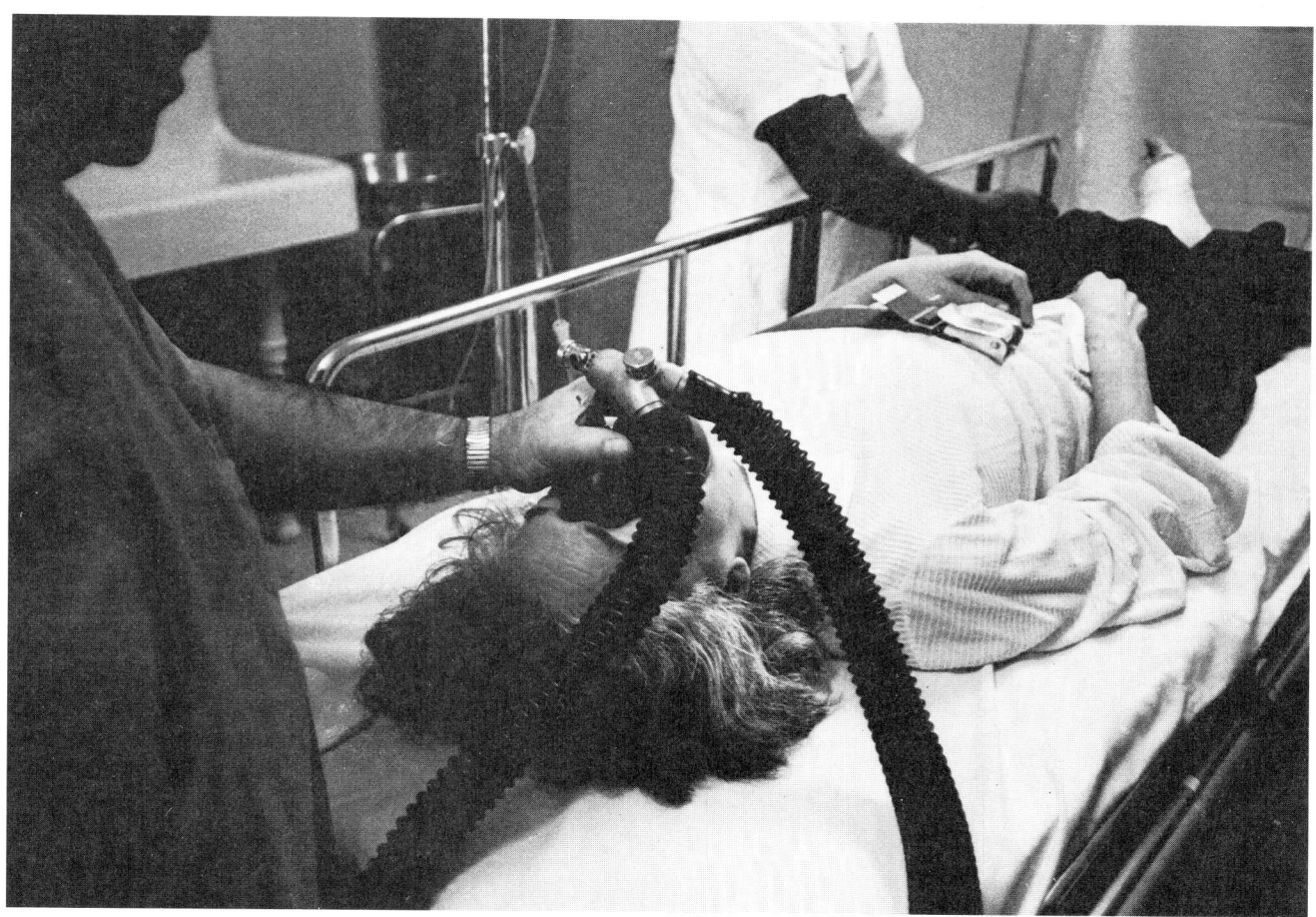

MEDICAL THERAPIES
437

effects. Memory impairment, sometimes short-term in nature and sometimes lasting for months or years, occurs in some cases. The possibility of such impairment can be lessened considerably, however, when the electric current is limited to only one side of the brain. All in all, ECT seems to be a relatively safe procedure, and it is effective in treating severe cases of depression. Any risks involved have to be weighed against the advantages. Although not used as frequently as it was before the advent of drug therapy, it may be a much-needed adjunct when depression is severe and unresponsive to other forms of treatment.

Psychosurgery

Given potential side-effects such as memory loss, it is certainly reasonable to view ECT ethically as an extreme procedure—one to be used only if absolutely necessary. An even more extreme medical therapy is **psychosurgery**—any form of surgery in which part of the brain is removed or made nonfunctional for the purpose of treating severe psychological disorders, such as schizophrenia or severe depression. If you have read the novel or seen the movie *One Flew over*

the Cuckoo's Nest (Kesey, 1962), you are probably familiar with the example of psychosurgery called *lobotomy*. You may recall that McMurphy (played by Jack Nicholson in the movie—see Figure 16–8) was given a lobotomy in an effort to control his violent behavior. Such surgery involves destroying parts of the brain that connect the frontal lobes with other parts of the brain involved in emotions.

After the 1950s, when drug therapies came on the scene, interest in lobotomies decreased greatly. But even without drugs, lobotomies are ethically questionable. Their effectiveness has never been demonstrated, they can produce side-effects such as listlessness, they can sometimes cause death, and their effects are irreversible.

Today, psychosurgery is still in existence, but it has become much more sophisticated and precise. No longer are large areas of brain tissue destroyed, as was the case in the early lobotomies. In modern forms of psychosurgery, specific and relatively small areas of the brain are destroyed by means of an electrical impulse (Valenstein, 1973). Even the newer forms of psychosurgery, however, are limited to only the severest cases— in those in which patients present a danger to themselves or others and in which all other forms of treatment have been tried without success.

Figure 16–8.

In the movie *One Flew over the Cuckoo's Nest,* McMurphy (played by Jack Nicholson) was given a lobotomy in an effort to control his violent behavior.

— APPLICATION —
DRUG THERAPY IN ACTION

This section provides a case history of a patient who was treated with one of the medical therapies. The account illustrates the use of drug therapy in a severe case of bipolar disorder. Lithium carbonate, in combination with a neuroleptic (chlorpromazine, or Thorazine), was used during the patient's hospitalization. Following discharge, the lithium was continued and an antidepressant (amitriptyline, or Elavil) was also administered for a subsequent depression episode. Dunner and Somervill (1977) note that the use of multiple drugs in controlling severe bipolar disorder is common.

A 30-year-old housewife was brought to the hospital by her husband for evaluation. Over a 2-week period she had begun staying up late at night writing a book about world peace. Although of modest means, she had bought an expensive new car and several hundred dollars' worth of clothes, and had scheduled a world tour to publicize her book. Her mood was euphoric and she spoke rapidly. She had a history of being hospitalized for depression beginning at age 22 while in college and again at the age of 27 following a suicide attempt. Her father had been an alcoholic and his sister had committed suicide during a depressive episode.

She was admitted to the hospital and treated with lithium carbonate and chlorpromazine. Over a 1-week period she began to sleep normally, had a reduction in her speed of speech, and was able to restore her relationship with her husband. She returned to her normal mood state after three weeks of treatment and was discharged. Lithium carbonate was continued; the chlorpromazine had been discontinued a week prior to discharge. A month later she again became depressed and amitriptyline was added to the lithium carbonate treatment. Her depressive symptoms improved with continued outpatient treatment over a 3-month period. During the enusing five years she was maintained with lithium carbonate and had no recurrence of symptoms. (Dunner & Somervill, 1977, p. 598)

— GENERAL EVALUATION OF THERAPIES —

Earlier, data regarding the usefulness and effectiveness of various therapies were presented. The time has come for a broader evaluation. Investigators have drawn informative general conclusions about the effectiveness of both psychological and medical therapies, which will be considered shortly. But first, several methodological issues must be addressed. Awareness of these issues will help us understand how the effectiveness of a therapy can be validly assessed.

Methodological Issues in Evaluating Therapies

Proponents of various approaches routinely assert that successes are due to specific features of their favorite therapy. Such assertions, however, cannot be accepted on faith; they must be empirically evaluated, and other explanations must be considered. Let's briefly examine some of the issues that Lichtenstein (1980) has raised with respect to evaluating therapies.

One major possiblity is that a therapy produces only an apparent change rather than a real one. For example, there is a tendency for both therapist and client to magnify problems at the outset to justify treatment. Later, they may tend to minimize problems to justify terminating the therapy. This combination can make it seem that real change occurred when it did not. Suppose, though, that real change does occur. We still cannot conclude that the therapy was responsible for the change. It may be, for example, that some significant event (marriage, for instance) that coincided with the therapy caused the client's improvement. Just growing older and perhaps a little wiser might also explain the change.

The solution to the problem of eliminating rival explanations is to conduct *controlled research*. One research strategy is to compare a no-treatment control group with a group receiving therapy (treatment group). If the two groups are identical in all ways except exposure to therapy and if the treatment group shows greater improvement, we can conclude that the change was real and was caused by the therapy.

This strategy, however, does not rule out all rival hypotheses. Although therapy may be the factor causing improvement, it is not clear what aspect of the therapy is responsible. For example, the improvement may result from some quality of the therapist rather than from the specific therapeutic procedure. Furthermore, it may be that the improvement is due to some process common to all helping situations. As various writers have pointed out (Frank, 1973; Lichtenstein, 1980; Cross, Sheehan, & Khan, 1982), such processes include having a sympathetic listener and receiving a credible explanation for one's problem. The results of such factors include a feeling of hope, an expectation of improvement, and a lessened demoralization with respect to one's situation.

In order to rule out common processes as rival hypotheses, it is necessary to compare a treatment group to an *attention-placebo group*. The latter group is given the same amount of attention as the treatment group. The clients in the placebo group discuss their problem with a sympathetic listener, but they do not receive the specific therapy considered important in the treatment group. Having an attention-placebo group helps resolve the question of whether improvement in the treatment group is only a placebo effect. The **placebo effect** is any improvement in the client that is due to the elements of hope and expectation of improvement rather than to specific therapeutic procedures. Theoretically, expectations and hopes would be present in both the treatment group and the attention-placebo group. The advantage, then, of having an attention-placebo group is this: If the treatment group fares comparatively better, improvement is due to something specific to the therapy rather than to common processes.

An alternate approach for ruling out common processes is to simply observe a group that is given a different treatment (an alternative-treatment group). For example, one could compare client-centered therapy and behavioral therapy. Since the therapies have common processes, such as a sympathetic listener, any differences in the improvement of clients have to be due to procedures inherent in each approach.

Ideally, psychotherapy research would compare a treatment group with an attention-placebo group (or an alternative-treatment group) and a no-treatment group (see, for example, Paul, 1966). Such a research design tells us whether a given treatment is better than nothing and whether something specific to the treatment is helpful (over and above what it has in common with the attention-placebo or alternative-treatment group).

Evaluation problems also apply to medical therapies. For instance, when drug treatment seems to be effective, we must ask if the benefits were due to drug action alone or to clients' expectations that they would get better (a placebo effect). To eliminate the second possibility, drug research often includes along with the drug-treatment group a group that receives a placebo (sugar pill), which has no pharmacological effect. Merely comparing a drug-treatment group to a no-treatment group leaves open the possibility that a placebo effect is responsible for any observed improvement. The placebo group in drug-therapy research is comparable to the attention-placebo group in nondrug research. Thus, the ideal research design would include a drug group, a placebo group, and a no-treatment group. Furthermore, since the therapist's expectations may bias the results, the study should use the *double-blind method,* in which neither the subjects nor the therapists know who received the drug and who received the placebo.

An Evaluation of Psychological Therapies

The preceding discussion raises three pertinent questions: Is psychotherapy more effective than no treatment at all? Does psychotherapy offer any benefits above and beyond what might be gained by an attention-placebo group? Is one type of psychotherapy better than another? The following discussion offers some answers. However, it cannot overlook the specific findings already stated (for example, that the effectiveness of Gestalt therapy has not been adequately demonstrated).

A number of recent reviews of psychotherapy research lead to the conclusion that therapy is effective (Bergin & Lambert, 1978; Luborsky, Singer, & Luborsky, 1975; Smith & Glass, 1977; Tramontana, 1980; Shapiro & Shapiro, 1982; Landman & Dawes, 1982). We can be most confident in stating that psychotherapy is better than no treatment at all. So if you, a friend, or a relative has a problem, don't think that seeing a therapist is futile. Therapy does help.

Is therapy more effective than placebo treatment?

We'll let several reviewers speak for themselves: "When groups that received therapy were directly compared with groups administered placebo treatment, therapy emerges as superior" (Landman & Dawes, 1982, p. 511). True, placebo treatment appeared to result in some improvement over no treatment, but it certainly did not fully account for the greater improvements seen in therapy or treatment groups. This finding is further supported by a review that examined only cognitive-behavioral therapies. Miller and Berman (1983) found that such therapies produce greater improvement than that seen in either no-treatment or attention-placebo groups. A similar conclusion was reached by Dush, Hirt, and Schroeder (1983), prompting them to say that "it appears to be timely to go beyond polemic debates over whether therapy works toward more specific analyses of the determinants of its effectiveness" (p. 418). In sum, researchers now seem to be comfortable with the notion that psychotherapy is more effective than ministrations by a sympathetic listener.

We might now ask if there is any evidence that some therapies are better than others? Here, we find much confusion and debate. For the most part, reviews of the literature suggest that psychotherapies are roughly equivalent in their effectiveness (Smith & Glass, 1977; Shapiro & Shapiro, 1982). If there is any qualification to be made, it is that the behavioral and cognitive therapies may be modestly superior to other approaches (Shapiro & Shapiro, 1982; Bergin & Lambert, 1978). But even on this point there are tremendous differences of opinion. Many of the reviews and individual studies suggest equivalency in the effectiveness of behavioral and nonbehavioral approaches (Smith & Glass, 1977; Klein, Zitrin, Woerner, & Ross, 1983; Cross, Sheehan, & Khan, 1982). Also, as noted earlier, one review (Miller & Berman, 1983) found cognitive-behavioral approaches to be no better than other psychotherapies. Given this state of affairs, it would be premature at this point to say that any approach is definitely better than others.

If we assume that psychotherapies tend to have uniformly positive results, why should this be so, given their disparate procedures? The honest answer is that we really don't know yet. Apparently, such procedures are better than just listening to, discussing, and giving a rationale for the client's problem. But it appears that the specific procedures used may not make much difference. Klein and his colleagues (Klein, Zitrin, Woerner, & Ross, 1983) echo the point that all of the various therapies do more than just arouse helpful expectan-

cies and combat demoralization. Regardless of format, these researchers suggest, each therapy persuades clients to confront feared situations and to behave in more adaptive ways. In other words, clients are persuaded to put themselves into real-life situations outside of therapy that will result in successful experiences and more adaptive behavior. If, regardless of the approach, a client can be induced to take some type of remedial action, the chances for improvement seem to be enhanced.

To return to an earlier point, it may be that all effective approaches engender strong feelings of perceived self-efficacy (Bandura, 1977b). Clearly, our basic task for the future should be to learn more about what in the therapeutic relationship helps clients change (see, for example, Schaffer, 1982). As Garfield (1983) recently put it, "We need desperately to discover the variables that are actually therapeutic in psychotherapy" (p. 42).

An Evaluation of Medical Therapies

As already suggested, the effectiveness of drug therapy is well documented for many disorders. Klerman (1983), a psychiatrist, suggests that evidence for the efficacy of drug therapy appears to be more conclusive than that for psychotherapy. Perhaps not all psychologists would agree. Just because drugs are effective doesn't mean that they are always the preferred treatment or the only sensible treatment. Those psychotherapists (including psychiatrists) who believe that many mental disorders have psychological origins either doubt the value of drugs or recommend them only if psychotherapy proves ineffective. (Most psychotherapists recognize that some disorders, such as bipolar disorder, are not highly responsive to psychotherapy alone.) On the other hand, many biologically oriented psychiatrists do not see value in psychotherapy and prefer drug therapy (Klerman, 1983). A third group consists of therapists who recommend or use a combination of psychotherapy and drug therapy. Obviously, evidence from well-controlled studies is needed to determine the efficacy of medical approaches in comparison to that of psychotherapy alone or of a combination of approaches.

Let's first consider the efficacy of the neuroleptics. As we have seen, these drugs have been widely used in treating the schizophrenic disorders (see Hollon & Beck, 1978). In one study (Cole, 1964), the phenothiazines (one of the groups of neuroleptics) were found to be more effective than a placebo, psychotherapy, or general hospital care in lessening schizophrenic symptoms. Furthermore, adding psychoanalytic psychotherapy to the drug treatment did not give any benefit over and above the effects of the drug alone. Although most psychotherapists would readily admit, at minimum, that drugs are needed in treating schizophrenic disorders, they would not necessarily agree that psychotherapy is useless. Behavioral therapists, especially, hold that learning principles are useful for improving schizophrenics' adjustment (see the earlier discussion of token economies).

There seems to be a widespread belief that the anxiolytics, or antianxiety drugs, are overprescribed. General practitioners routinely prescribe them to outpatients experiencing anxiety, tension, and nervousness. Not only can the drugs be addicting, but additionally, their ability to alleviate anxiety may be only temporary. They do not solve problems, and they do not seem to result in complete and lasting improvement (Lahey & Ciminero, 1980). The primary value of such drugs may be in the early stages of psychotherapy, when anxiety is often highest. As an additional consideration, Dunner and Somervill (1977) argue that "the placebo effect in anxious patients is generally quite large" (p. 600). They believe that the evidence for the effectiveness of antianxiety drugs over and above that of a placebo is unconvincing.

There seems to be little doubt as to the efficacy of the antidepressants, as judged from numerous well-controlled studies (Klerman, 1983). Nevertheless, one study comparing cognitive-behavioral therapy to drug therapy (imipramine) found the cognitive-behavioral therapy to be more effective in treating depression (Rush, Beck, Kovacs, & Hollon, 1977). A study comparing psychotherapy and amitriptyline found that both treatments were more effective than no treatment (the control group), but even better was a combination of the two treatments (Weissman et al., 1979). Apparently, although a drug works to alleviate such symptoms as sleep disturbance, somatic complaints, and poor appetite, psychotherapy can help alleviate such symptoms as depressed mood, suicidal thoughts, and feelings of guilt (Klerman, 1983). In Klerman's (1983) words,

"Drugs have a positive effect on psychotherapy in that the symptom relief, produced more readily by drugs, rendered the patient more accessible to psychotherapy" (p. 99).

Finally, the efficacy of the antimanic drug lithium in treating bipolar disorder has been well-established in a number of controlled studies (Klerman, 1983). It is effective not only in treating the disorder but also in preventing its recurrence. Although psychotherapy as a sole strategy in treating bipolar disorder does not seem warranted, there is growing evidence that a combined drug-psychotherapy strategy may be optimal (Klerman, 1983).

The effectiveness of another medical therapy, electroconvulsive therapy, seems to be well documented, at least with respect to severe depression. In contrast to no treatment or treatment with antidepressants, ECT has been shown to lead to a greater reduction in depressive symptoms (Dunner & Somervill, 1977). Although antidepressants may require 10 or more days to take effect, improvement occurs by the 3rd or 4th day after ECT (Munsinger, 1983). Antidepressants may, however, remain important for patients receiving ECT. Abrams (1976) suggests that patients given antidepressants following ECT treatment experience fewer relapses. He believes that the use of antidepressants is essential because the relapse rate following ECT for depression ranges from 25 percent to 50 percent within a 6-month period.

As Munsinger (1983) suggests, ECT is often the most appropriate or useful treatment. This is true when there are suicidal tendencies, when antidepressants cannot be prescribed (such as when the patient has glaucoma), or when antidepressants do not seem to be working. ECT is a fast and effective treatment, but its possible side-effect of memory loss must not be overlooked. It seems clear that the appropriate strategy in a case of severe depression would be to try antidepressants first (unless suicide seems imminent) and then to use ECT only if the patient does not improve. Finally, the effectiveness of psychosurgery techniques is not well substantiated. These techniques are usually considered a last resort because they are irreversible.

"YOU'RE ON THE AIR"—THE NEW RADIO PSYCHOLOGISTS

While evaluating the work of therapists, we might also consider another medium in which the helper–help-seeker relationship takes place—the radio talk show. Although we don't have the data with which to evaluate the effectiveness of radio psychologists, we can certainly consider some pros and cons of what they do.

On a typical day, a caller on Dr. Toni Grant's call-in radio talk show explained that he was increasingly withdrawing from those around him. Other callers told Dr. Grant of their obsessive-compulsive behaviors, their depressions, their phobias, and their many other problems. Dr. Grant is one of a growing list of therapists who offer advice over the radio to listeners looking for hope, support, encouragement, and, of course, advice.

According to the guidelines of the American Psychological Association, giving advice over the air is legitimate and ethical as long as good professional judgment is used. However, diagnosing and conducting psychotherapy over the airwaves are considered unethical. (It would be unethical, for example, to tell a caller, after a 2-minute conversation, that she had a bipolar disorder.) Because of the fine line between giving advice and doing psychotherapy, many psychologists and other therapists have been quick to criticize the radio psychologists (see Rice, 1981).

Critics contend that it is impossible for a therapist, in just a short phone conversation, to understand a caller's problem and background well enough to give sound advice. They also worry that when advice is given with respect to a given caller's problem, other listeners may inappropriately apply that advice to their own situation. In general, the critics contend that making accurate diagnoses and judgments and giving sound advice can be done only in the context of a traditional client-therapist relationship. In short, they believe that hasty judgment and advice may be worse than no advice at all. Furthermore, they ask, how does the therapist know if the advice was properly followed or what its effect was? What if the advice was followed but it failed? What happens then?

What are the arguments for radio psychology, or radio therapy? In one sense, radio therapy can be thought of as an important public service—a way of educating the public about theories, principles, and research findings in psychology. As Rice (1981) observes, some people have little access to or awareness of information about mental health. The radio psychologists are filling a gap in that respect. Listeners may discover what is in fact a problem and what is not; they may learn that a variety of treatment methods exist for dealing with various problems; they may learn that it is acceptable and appropriate to seek help for one's problems. Perhaps, above all, listeners have an opportunity to discover that they are not the only ones in the world with a problem, that many others find themselves in the same situation. If all of these things help foster the desire to cope or the perceived ability to cope, with or without the help of a therapist, then something may indeed be gained from radio psychology.

In the final analysis, radio psychologists must exercise good judgment. If a caller's problem is limited or specific, helpful recommendations can, perhaps, reasonably be given. In other cases, the problem may be too complex, or too little information may be available. If so, it may be inappropriate for the therapist to offer a specific remedy. Instead, the therapist should perhaps do nothing more than put the problem in perspective for the caller. At the same time, of course, the therapist should function as a sympathetic and understanding listener, which is all many callers are seeking (Rice, 1981). In many cases, the best approach for the therapist may be to listen, offer encouragement, and suggest that the caller seek direct contact with a therapist.

The debate between the proponents and opponents of radio psychology will likely continue. If you have listened to such programs, perhaps you already know where you stand on the issue. Do you think these programs serve a useful function in helping people resolve their problems? Whether they do or not, radio psychology seems destined to be around for some time. Shows like Dr. Grant's are becoming increasingly popular with the public.

THE FUTURE OF PSYCHOTHERAPY

In this chapter, we have seen what the field of psychotherapy is like right now—its theories, methods, and research findings. But what about its future? What is on the horizon? To find answers to this question, Prochaska and Norcross (1982) recently polled a panel of 36 experts.

It is critical for therapists, policy makers, and prospective students to be alerted to possible trends in the discipline. Such information helps those in the mental-health industry plan for the future by pointing out human-resource needs, critical research areas, the kinds of clinical training programs that are needed, and the types of therapeutic services that will need to be made available.

From the Prochaska and Norcross (1982) poll, it appears "that self-change approaches will increase dramatically during the 1980s" (p. 625). That is, the experts believe that we will witness a strong emphasis on therapeutic techniques that stress self-reliance. This is especially interesting in light of recent arguments by Schachter (1982) that self-cures for such problems as smoking and overeating are common. The psychotherapy community will perhaps be taking a closer look at what clients can do for themselves in their own natural environments—the strategies that seem to work and the strategies that seem not to work.

The panel of experts also agreed that over the next 10 years, psychotherapy will become more cognitive-behavioral in orientation, a trend already under way (Garfield, 1981). The experts further characterized future psychotherapy as being briefer and as focusing on the client's present circumstances rather than past history. Long-term psychoanalytic, aversive-conditioning, and client-centered approaches were seen as likely to decrease in popularity. Psychoanalytic therapy and any other long-term approaches that are not cost-effective may indeed find it tough going when both clients and therapists are looking for affordable approaches.

It is of interest to note that the panel predicted a marked increase in family and marital therapy. This may reflect their recognition of the strong need for such therapy given the currently high divorce rate and changing family patterns (see chapter 11). The panel members also predicted increases in the numbers of female and minority therapists, increased services to underserved populations, and increased specialization of therapists (see also Anderson, Parenté, & Gordon, 1981).

Rather pessimistically, the panelists predicted more malpractice suits, too few positions for new therapists, no real increases in funding for clinical research and training, and no headway in surpassing psychiatrists as the dominant force in psychotherapy. Interestingly, they thought that drug therapy would increase at the expense of psychotherapy.

Bernstein and Nietzel (1980) have offered their own prognostications, several of which we will note. For one thing, they echo the point about specialization—that therapists will increasingly prepare themselves for specialty areas such as drug abuse, geriatrics, and rural mental health. Finally, noting that various therapies seem to be essentially equivalent in their effectiveness, Bernstein and Nietzel suggest that brand-name approaches to psychotherapy—such as Gestalt therapy or behavioral therapy—will fall by the wayside.

1. Psychologists have developed a diverse array of treatments for abnormal behavior. Such diversity reflects psychologists' equally diverse views of personality and abnormal behavior; each view leads to a different prescription for how to best alter behavior.

2. Psychological therapies attempt to alter the client's disordered feelings, beliefs, or actions.

3. The general goal of Freudian psychoanalysis is to make the individual aware of unconscious impulses and conflicts that have been repressed. This is accomplished through the use of free association, dream analysis, interpretation, and analysis of transference.

4. Client-centered therapy, a type of humanistic therapy, involves constructing a warm and responsive atmosphere in which the client feels free to say anything. The goal is to help clients accept themselves and have positive self-regard. The main strategy for establishing this receptive environment is unconditional positive regard.

5. Gestalt therapy, another humanistic therapy, attempts to deal with problems by helping clients achieve awareness of all of their experiences and needs. Self-awareness and acceptance are considered the necessary and sufficient conditions for change and more adaptive behavior.

6. Behavioral therapies have as their direct goal the alteration of the problem behaviors themselves. One such therapy, systematic desensitization, involves substituting relaxation for responses such as anxiety or fear. In assertion training, the client learns to express feelings in an honest and socially appropriate manner. Aversive conditioning, another behavioral method, attempts to establish negative feelings as the response to a stimulus that elicits socially inappropriate or maladaptive positive feelings. Covert sensitization, for example, involves associating imagined highly aversive events with a particular stimulus.

7. A number of behavioral-therapy methods involve operant conditioning and use the principles of reinforcement, shaping, extinction, satiation, and punishment.

8. Modeling is another behavioral-therapy method that has proved particularly helpful in the treatment of various phobias (e.g., snake phobias). Learning by observing how others act in the absence of aversive consequences is known as vicarious extinction.

9. Cognitive-behavioral approaches emphasize the importance of overt behavior as well as the effects of thoughts on behavior. In Ellis's rational-emotive therapy, the goal is to stop the client's irrational thoughts. In addition to disputing those beliefs in therapy, the rational-emotive therapist uses behaviorally oriented techniques to bring about changes in thoughts and overt behavior.

10. Beck's cognitive therapy states that emotional disorders occur because the person thinks negatively. In therapy, this negative reasoning is undone. The approach also emphasizes the importance of using behavioral methods in inducing cognitive change.

11. Any of the methods previously discussed can be used in groups. Still other methods were specifically designed as group therapies. Psychodrama is one such method. In it, individuals gain insights by acting out their feelings with respect to emotionally significant events or situations, as if they were in a play. In family therapy, the group consists of a single family. Family members are encouraged to work together to improve communication, cooperation, and sharing. Marital therapy is designed for couples having marital problems. Marital therapists, like family therapists, focus on improving the lines of communication, clarifying expectations, and helping each individual experience more mutually satisfying and fulfilling interactions.

12. When selecting a therapist, it is wise to find out as much as possible about the therapist before making any commitment to a therapy program. One should find out what therapy would be like with the person by asking about issues such as fees, type of therapy to be used, length of treatment, and the therapist's qualifications. One must be comfortable with the therapist.

13. Medical therapies treat maladaptive behavior through the use of some type of physical treatment or manipulation of the body. One such method is chemical therapy, or the use of drugs, namely neuroleptics, anxiolytics, antidepressants, and antimanics. Electroconvulsive therapy (ECT) involves passing a brief electric current through the brain. Psychosurgery as a medical therapy is used infrequently today. It consists of removing or making nonfunctional certain parts of the brain in an effort to treat severe psychological disorders.

14. In evaluating the effectiveness of any therapy, it is important to eliminate rival hypotheses that might explain the success of the therapy. No real change may have occurred. Even if a change did occur, the success may have been due to the therapist or to processes common to all helping situations rather than to the therapy. In order to rule out these rival hypotheses,

proper control groups must be used in research.

15. Most reviewers agree that psychotherapy is more effective than no treatment or placebo treatment. Generally speaking, there do not seem to be any significant differences between the various types of therapy. Some evidence suggests that behavioral and cognitive-behavioral approaches are superior.

16. The effectiveness of drug therapy and ECT seems to be well-established. Some evidence indicates that ECT is more effective than drug treatment. Psychosurgery is considered an extreme and controversial treatment, and its effectiveness is not well substantiated.

17. Radio talk shows in which psychologists dispense advice to callers are growing in popularity. Critics voice concerns about hasty advice and the inability to make accurate judgments about callers' problems in just a short telephone conversation. Proponents of talk shows see them as an important educational device.

18. A recent poll of 36 experts revealed several possible future trends in the field of psychotherapy, including a strong emphasis on therapeutic techniques that stress self-reliance; a greater movement toward the cognitive-behavioral orientation; briefer psychotherapy; a greater focus on clients' present circumstances; a decreased use of long-term psychoanalytic, aversive-conditioning, and client-centered approaches; an increase in the use of family and marital therapy; and an increase in specialization.

═ IMPORTANT TERMS AND CONCEPTS ═

Covert Sensitization
Psychotherapy
Psychoanalysis
Free Association
Resistances
Interpretation
Transference
Client-centered Therapy
Unconditional Positive Regard
Gestalt Therapy
Behavioral Therapies
Counterconditioning

Assertion Training
Aversive Conditioning
Token Economy
Satiation
Vicarious Extinction
Symptom Substitution
Cognitive-behavioral Therapies
Rational-emotive Therapy (RET)
Cognitive Therapy
Group Therapy
Psychodrama

Family Therapy
Marital Therapy
Medical Therapies
Chemical Therapy
Neuroleptics
Anxiolytics
Antidepressants
Antimanics
Electroconvulsive Therapy (ECT)
Psychosurgery
Placebo Effect

═ SUGGESTIONS FOR FURTHER READING ═

Beck, A. T. (1976). *Cognitive therapy and the emotional disorders*. New York: International Universities Press. A highly readable book in which Aaron Beck presents his rationale for cognitive therapy and shows how the theory is applied to depression and other disorders.

Corey, G. C. (1977). *Theory and practice of counseling and psychotherapy*. Monterey, CA: Brooks/Cole. A relatively brief but excellent overview of the major therapeutic approaches that compares and contrasts the approaches and discusses some basic issues in therapy, including ethical issues.

Lichtenstein, E. (1980). *Psychotherapy: Approaches and applications*. Monterey, CA: Brooks/Cole. An excellent discussion and analysis of three major approaches —psychoanalytic, humanistic, and behavioral therapy —including much material on evaluations of the approaches and an interesting discussion of social, economic, and political influences on psychotherapy.

Martin, R. A., & Poland, E. Y. (1980). *Learning to change: A self-management approach to adjustment*. New York: McGraw-Hill. A very interesting discussion and guide regarding how learning principles can be used in the self-management of adjustment problems.

Rogers, C. R. (1961). *On becoming a person: A therapist's view of psychotherapy*. Boston: Houghton Mifflin. A good introduction to the rationale and approach of Carl Rogers.

Spiegler, M. D. (1983). *Contemporary behavioral therapy*. Palo Alto, CA: Mayfield Publishing. An up-to-date, well-written overview of the behavioral therapies, including numerous case studies and exercises.

- CHAPTER 17 -
HUMAN SEXUALITY

— CHAPTER 17 —

HUMAN SEXUALITY

— CHAPTER OBJECTIVES —

To achieve the objectives of this chapter, you should be able to answer the questions listed here. You should also be able to define the important terms and concepts listed at the end of the chapter.

1. From a biological perspective, what is involved in gender development?
2. What role does socialization play in gender development?
3. How is the survey approach used to study sexual behavior? What is the nature of current sexual practices and attitudes? How have they changed from earlier times?
4. Why is sexual behavior also studied through direct observation and experiments? What is known about the physiology of sexual response? What has experimentation taught us about pornography?
5. List the most common variations in sexual behavior. What have psychological studies revealed about homosexuality?
6. What are the major sexual dysfunctions of men and women? What are some of the origins of such dysfunctions? How can the dysfunctions be treated?

— CHAPTER OUTLINE —

Development of Gender
Gender development depends on both biology and socialization.

Biological Differences
Gender Roles
Application: Gender Roles and Sexuality

Researching Human Sexual Behavior
A variety of methods are used to study human sexuality.

Surveys of Sexual Behavior and Attitudes Toward Sex
Physiology of Sexual Behavior: Laboratory Observations of the Sexual-Response Cycle
Experimental Studies of Sexual Behavior
Application: Adolescent Sex and the Problem of Contraception

Sexual Variations, Sexual Dysfunctions, and Homosexuality
Many forms of sexual behavior exist.

Variations in Sexual Behavior
Homosexuality
Sexual Dysfunctions
Application: Preventing Sexual Dysfunctions

On the Horizon: Society's Reactions to the Rape Victim

"DEAR ANN LANDERS"

DEAR ANN LANDERS: You stated in your column recently that the executive who exposed himself to two neighborhood females was "mentally ill." Will you please explain?

Does this mean that all people who have the desire to display their bodies are ill in the same way? What about folks who frequent nudist camps? And the ones who like swimming in the nude? And the nude dancers—both male and female?

Are these people sick? If so, where can they get help? Please print this letter, Ann. It is very important that I get answers to these questions, and there is nowhere I can go but to you. Wondering in USA.

DEAR USA: The executive who exposed himself to the neighborhood girls is indeed sick. The poor fellow needs psychiatric help. This illness is called exhibitionism. The man is intensely insecure about his sexuality and gets his jollies from the startled reactions of females who come upon the sight of him unexpectedly. It reassures him that he is male.

Nudists and strippers and people who enjoy swimming in the buff run the gamut from free spirits to nature-lovers. They may be a little far-out, but they are not necessarily in need of a head doctor. There's a big difference between showing off a good body and flashing one's genitals. (Reprinted by permission of Ann Landers and Field Newspaper Syndicate)

Concerns and questions about human sexuality are so pervasive that many people seek information from "nonexperts" such as advice columnist Ann Landers. Indeed, many of the letters in advice columns deal with such topics as premarital sex, homosexuality, rape, and masturbation.

Sexuality is one of the more important aspects of human nature; perhaps no other aspect gets discussed so often. Despite widespread interest in the topic, many people reach adulthood with little accurate information about it. Often, they accumulate an alarming number of false beliefs, or myths, about sexual behavior (McCary & McCary, 1982). (Table 17–1 lists a number of the more common sexual myths.) The resulting confusion and misunderstanding can create crippling apprehension and unnecessary bad feelings.

Table 17–1.

Commonly held myths about sexual behavior. (From McCary & McCary, 1982, pp. 30–34.)

1. Simultaneous orgasms are more satisfactory than those experienced separately and are, moreover, necessary for sexual compatibility.

2. Sexologists are in agreement that there is a distinct difference between a vaginal and a clitoral orgasm.

3. During menstruation, women should not engage in sports; nor should they take a bath or shower or shampoo their hair.

4. The absence of the hymen proves that a girl is not a virgin.

5. A large penis is of great importance to a woman's sexual gratification.

6. The man with a large penis is more sexually potent than the man with a small penis.
(continued next page)

Table 17–1. (continued)

7. Each individual is allotted just so many sexual experiences; when they are used up, sexual activity is finished for that person.

8. Blacks have a greater sex drive than whites.

9. Alcohol is a sexual stimulant.

10. Sterilization reduces the sex drive of a man or woman.

11. Castration always destroys the sex drive completely.

12. Menopause or hysterectomy terminates a woman's sex life.

13. Sexual desire and ability decrease markedly after the age of 40 to 50.

14. A poor sexual adjustment in marriage inevitably spells its doom.

15. A couple must have simultaneous climaxes if conception is to occur.

16. Homosexuals are a menace to society.

17. People are either totally homosexual or totally heterosexual.

18. Oral-genital sex between a man and a woman indicates homosexual tendencies.

19. Frequent masturbation has been known to lead to lunacy.

20. Masturbation can cause a number of physical problems, including warts, hair on the palms of the hands, pimples, acne, and, ultimately, impotence.

21. Masturbation is a practice restricted almost exclusively to men.

22. Women who have strong sex drives, climax easily, and are capable of multiple orgasms are nymphomaniacs.

23. The virginity of the woman is an important factor in the success of a marriage.

24. Today's young adults are going wild sexually.

25. Sex education has no place in our schools because it is a communist plot to destroy the country from within and because it leads to sexual acting-out behavior, a rise in promiscuity, an increase in premarital pregnancy, and so on.

Whether or not you believe any of the myths listed here, it is the authors' hope that this chapter will be enlightening. Before we begin, we should note our use of the term **gender** rather than *sex* in referring to the state of being male or female. The more ambiguous term *sex* is typically used to refer not only to gender but also to sexual behavior or reproduction (Hyde, 1982).

— DEVELOPMENT OF GENDER —

This chapter is about the many ramifications of being male or female. You may think that becoming a man or woman is relatively straightforward. But the determination of gender is not always a simple either-or matter. What does it mean to be male or female? What factors determine gender? How does gender develop?

Biological Differences

In part, being a male or a female is dependent on biology. We are all aware, certainly, that males and females differ in their sexual and reproductive organs, or **primary sexual characteristics.** In males, these organs include the penis, testes, and scrotum; in females, they include the ovaries, uterus, and vagina (see Figures 17–1 and 17–2). What causes these differing structures to develop? At the moment of conception, genetic materials from each parent combine to begin a process called **prenatal sexual differentiation** (Masters, Johnson, & Kolodny, 1982). This process is what leads to specific physical diffferences between males and females.

The sexual differentiation that occurs during the *prenatal period* (see chapter 10) is controlled essentially by biological forces—genetic and hormonal mechanisms. Genetically, embryos that become females receive an X chromosome from each parent; embryos that become males receive an X chromosome from their mother and a Y chromosome from their father (Nass, Libby, & Fisher, 1981). Genetic sex (XX or XY chromosomes) is determined at the moment of conception and remains the same throughout life.

Regardless of the specific genetic makeup, all embryos are anatomically identical in the first few weeks of development (Masters, Johnson & Kolodny, 1982). During this period, the **gonads** (reproductive glands) are *undifferentiated*. They have the potential to differentiate into either testes (male gonads) or ovaries (female gonads). Whether testes or ovaries develop depends on the presence or absence of a Y chromosome. If a Y chromosome is present, it causes a chemical substance to be produced; that substance starts the transformation of the undifferentiated gonads into testes. The transformation occurs at about the 7th week after conception. If the chemical substance is not present (because there is no Y chromosome), the undifferentiated gonads will develop into ovaries, at about the 12th week after conception.

Figure 17–1.
Primary sexual characteristics of the male. (From Ward & Hetzel, 1984, p. 223.)

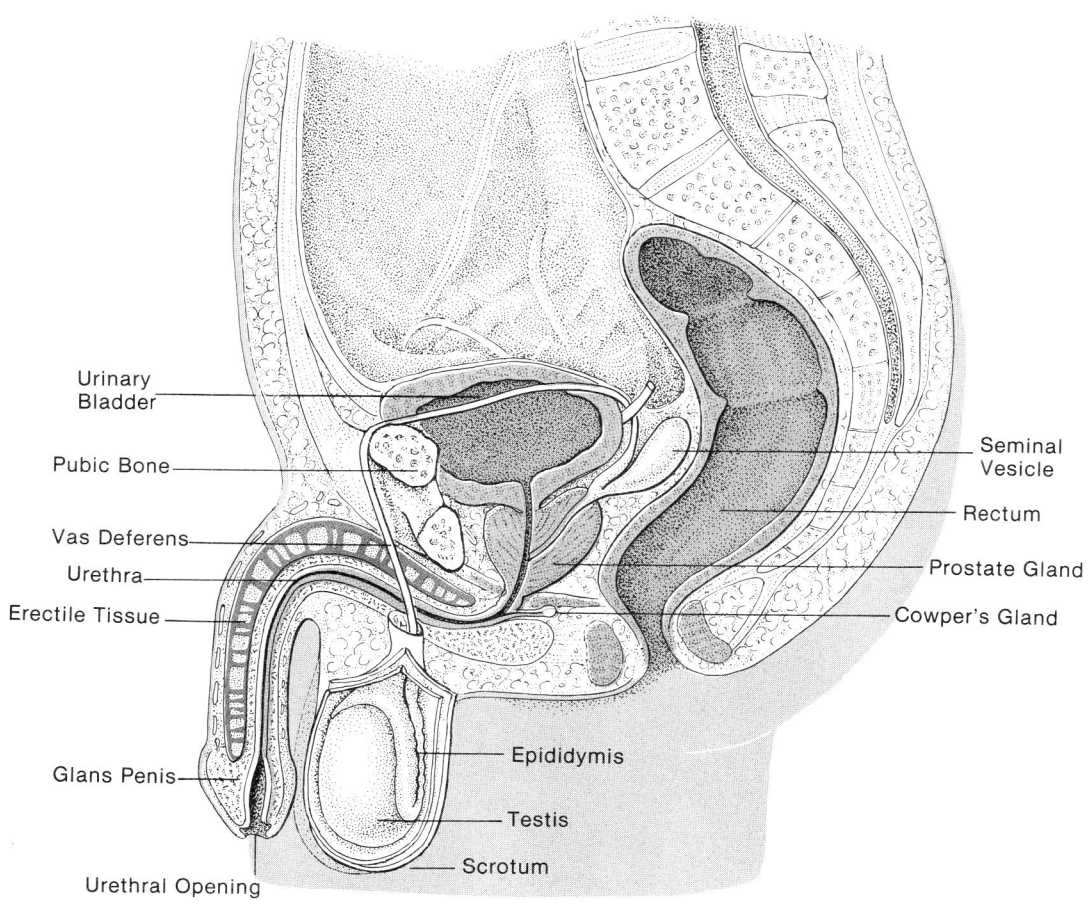

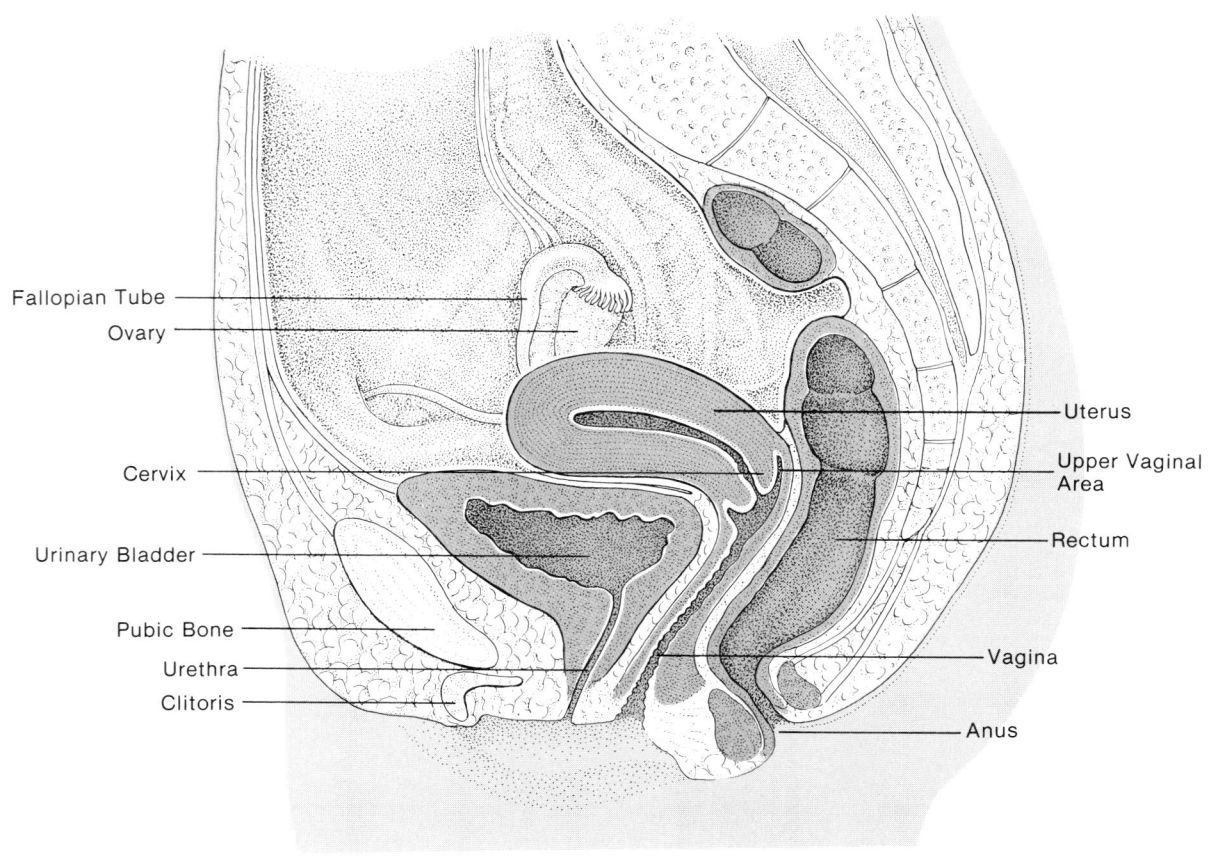

Fallopian Tube

Ovary

Cervix

Urinary Bladder

Pubic Bone

Urethra

Clitoris

Uterus

Upper Vaginal Area

Rectum

Vagina

Anus

Figure 17–2.
Primary sexual characteristics of the female. (From Ward & Hetzel, 1984, p. 230.)

After this development, sexual differentiation is controlled basically by hormones (see chapter 2). Given the importance of hormones during the prenatal period, it is clear that gender is determined by more than genetic sex. In fact, even with XY chromosomes, anatomic development will be female rather than male if an insufficient level of male hormones is produced (Masters, Johnson & Kolodny, 1982). Let's examine hormonal influences in detail.

By the 8th week after conception, the testes in the male embryo begin producing male hormones known as **androgens,** which cause masculinization. The most important androgen is **testosterone,** which triggers further male sexual differentiation by stimulating the development of internal and external male sex structures (see Fig 17–3). At the same time, another chemical substance produced by the testes works to retard the growth of structures that would otherwise form female internal sex organs.

Female sexual differentiation, in contrast, is not de-

pendent on hormones (Masters, Johnson & Kolodny, 1982). If the level of androgens is low, female sex structures will develop. Generally speaking, by the 14th week of development, there is a distinct difference in the internal and external structures of male and female fetuses. At 6 to 7 weeks, they were identical.

Both males and females produce androgens. As noted, in males the main source of androgens is the testes. However, the adrenal gland (see chapter 2) also produces these hormones. In females the adrenal gland is the major source of androgens, and the ovaries also produce some of these hormones. The level of androgens in females is low, however—and insufficient to alter the course of gender development.

Hormonal influences on gender development emerge once again at puberty. In males there is an increased level of testosterone, mainly from the testes but also from the adrenal gland. In females the level of female hormones, known as **estrogens,** increases. The source of estrogens in females is the ovaries. (The

Figure 17–3.

Stages of prenatal sexual differentiation (external structures).

BEFORE THE 6TH WEEK—UNDIFFERENTIATED

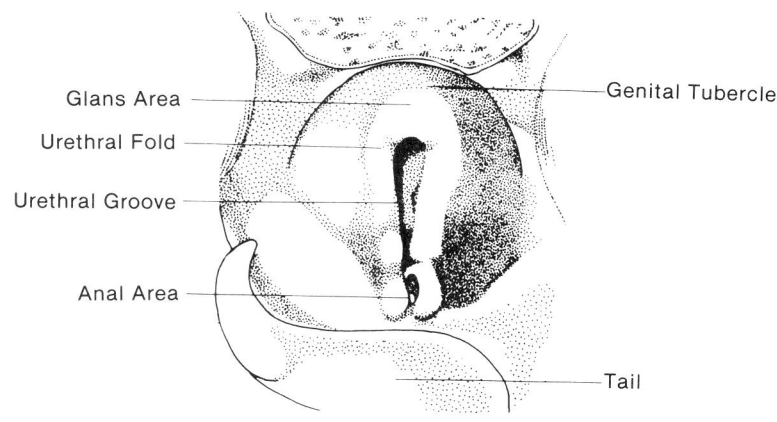

Glans Area — Genital Tubercle
Urethral Fold
Urethral Groove
Anal Area
— Tail

7TH TO 8TH WEEK

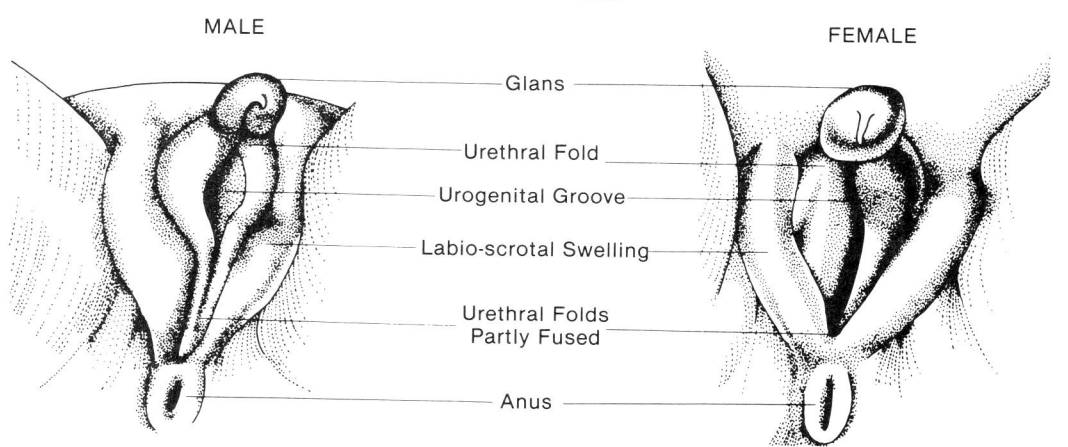

MALE   FEMALE

Glans
Urethral Fold
Urogenital Groove
Labio-scrotal Swelling
Urethral Folds Partly Fused
Anus

12TH WEEK—FULLY DEVELOPED

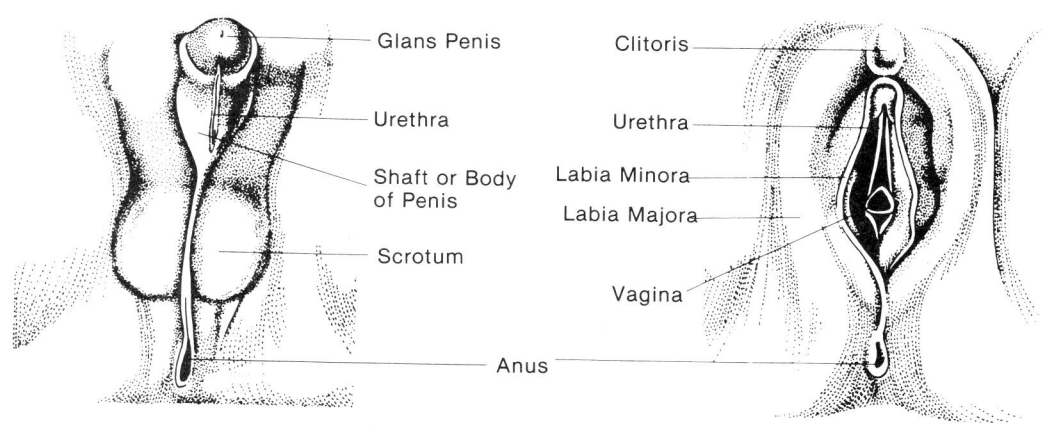

Glans Penis   Clitoris
Urethra   Urethra
Shaft or Body of Penis   Labia Minora
    Labia Majora
Scrotum   Vagina
Anus

The source of estrogens in females is the ovaries. (The testes in males also produce estrogens, but the function of these hormones in males, if any, is not known.) As is true with males, some of the changes that occur in females at puberty are due to androgens secreted by the adrenal gland. These changes, discussed in chapter 11, have traditionally been termed **secondary sexual characteristics,** and they signal the readiness for reproduction.

The biological development of gender has much to do with the development of **gender identity,** one's personal sense of maleness or femaleness. More than biology is involved, however. To see this, let's examine what happens when there are abnormal developments in prenatal sexual differentiation.

John Money, a medical psychologist, has made the important observation that to determine an individual's gender, one must examine the following (see Money & Ehrhardt, 1972):

1. *Genetic sex* (XX chromosome in the female, XY in the male).
2. *Hormonal sex* (estrogens in the female, androgens in the male).
3. *Gonadal sex* (ovaries in the female, testes in the male).
4. *Genital sex,* or the nature of the external sex organs (clitoris and vaginal opening in the female, penis and scrotum in the male).
5. Nature of the *internal reproductive organs* (uterus and vagina in the female, prostate and seminal vesicles in the male).

Gender assignment on the basis of these criteria is generally straightforward, since these aspects of sex are typically consistent. Because of abnormalities in prenatal development and differentiation, however, rare inconsistencies can occur. When they do, the individual is called a **hermaphrodite.** Money's studies of such individuals have provided a great deal of information about how gender identity develops.

The gender of a hermaphrodite is biologically, indistinct. Several different forms of hermaphroditism have been identified. In one of them, the *adrenogenital syndrome,* the basic problem is that, during the course of prenatal development, a genetic female with normally developed ovaries also develops external genitals that are male in appearance. The cause is a malfunctioning adrenal gland that produces an overabundance of androgens. A common result is that these individuals are identified at birth as males.

In another syndrome, the prenatal development of a genetic male is feminized because of an abnormal insensitivity to the body's production of testosterone. The result is that, at birth, the external genitals suggest a female and the individual is identified as such.

Money's studies of hermaphrodites illustrate the enormous complexity of gender. How should gender be determined? Perhaps it would be appropriate to consider none of the criteria outlined here and instead to base gender assignment on each individual's personal determination of gender (i.e., gender identity). Probably no one would agree more with this strategy than Dr. Renée Richards (see Figure 17–4), who underwent a sex-change operation in order to become a woman. Dr. Richards is a **transsexual**—a person who is psychologically uncomfortable with the anatomical sex. (We will examine transsexualism in more detail later in the chapter.) Genetically a male, Dr. Richards has had difficulty convincing those in the world of tennis that she is a woman, even though she now has female genitals and considers herself to be a woman.

Although gender is certainly biologically determined, Money considers learning experiences to be more crucial in determining gender identity. This conclusion stems from Money's studies of hermaphrodites. His essential finding is that two identical hermaphrodites can develop different gender identities simply by being assigned either the male or the female label and then being reared in that fashion (along with being given hormone therapy and undergoing surgery to correct the appearance of the external genitals). Money's emphasis on the importance of one's environment, in contrast to biology, is not accepted by all researchers, however. Perhaps the most reasonable conclusion to draw is that gender development is due to the interaction of biology and environment (Masters, Johnson, & Kolodny, 1982).

Gender Roles

Clearly, gender identity is due only partly to biology. Another necessary consideration is the way in which males and females are socialized. Early in life, we are taught a **gender role**—our society's expectations about how individuals of a particular gender are to behave. It is this role that is said to be appropriate behavior.

Gender roles are actually *stereotypes,* or fixed ways of thinking about a particular group of people (see

Figure 17–4.

Dr. Richard Raskin (left), an eye surgeon and successful tennis champion, became Dr. Renée Richards (right) after a sex-change operation.

also chapter 18). What are males and females supposedly like? Table 17–2 provides one answer to this question. In a study of gender-role stereotypes, Broverman and her colleagues (Broverman, Vogel, Broverman, Clarkson, & Rosenkrantz, 1972) found that positively valued masculine traits revolved around the general characteristic of competence. Positively valued feminine traits reflected the general characteristic of warmth-expressiveness. By studying the traits in Table 17–2, we can begin to appreciate the different perceptions of what men and women are like.

Stereotypes regarding how we should behave contribute to the formation of our gender identity. We learn to behave in ways that are expected of us, and we may feel that we should not or cannot behave in ways that are inconsistent with our gender role. In that sense, gender roles can sometimes be limiting and constricting, keeping us from desired activities that we are capable of performing. We may believe that others will approve of us and reward us only when we behave in accordance with our gender role. Gender roles may keep men from showing emotion or keep women from being assertive. They may hinder both men and women from exploring certain types of career possibilities.

There is no doubt that men and women do differ in accordance with traditional stereotypes, but only to a degree (Maccoby & Jacklin, 1974). The differences are not nearly as great, either in number or size, as the stereotypes would lead us to believe (Deaux, 1976). When male-female differences, such as in aggression, do exist, how are we to explain them? Are they due to biology or to *socialization* (the learning of gender roles)? According to some theorists, such as Money (1977), although both factors are influential, socialization is more important in shaping gender identity and personality traits.

Gender roles are communicated in many ways. The

Table 17–2.

Stereotypical gender role traits. (From Broverman, Vogel, Broverman, Clarkson, & Rosenkrantz, 1972, p. 63.)

Competency Cluster (Masculine Pole More Desirable)

FEMININE	MASCULINE
Not at all aggressive	Very aggressive
Not at all independent	Very independent
Very emotional	Not at all emotional
Does not hide emotions at all	Almost always hides emotions
Very subjective	Very objective
Very easily influenced	Not at all easily influenced
Very submissive	Very dominant
Dislikes math and science very much	Likes math and science very much
Very excitable in a minor crisis	Not at all excitable in a minor crisis
Very passive	Very active
Not at all competitive	Very competitive
Very illogical	Very logical
Very home-oriented	Very worldly
Not at all skilled in business	Very skilled in business
Very sneaky	Very direct
Does not know the way of the world	Knows the way of the world
Feelings easily hurt	Feelings not easily hurt
Not at all adventurous	Very adventurous
Has difficulty making decisions	Can make decisions easily
Cries very easily	Never cries
Almost never acts as a leader	Almost always acts as a leader
Not at all self-confident	Very self-confident
Very uncomfortable about being aggressive	Not at all uncomfortable about being aggressive
Not at all ambitious	Very ambitious
Unable to separate feelings from ideas	Easily able to separate feelings from ideas
Very dependent	Not at all dependent
Very conceited about appearance	Never conceited about appearance
Thinks women are always superior to men	Thinks men are always superior to women
Does not talk freely about sex with men	Talks freely about sex with men

Warmth-Expressiveness Cluster (Feminine Pole More Desirable)

FEMININE	MASCULINE
Does not use harsh language at all	Uses very harsh language
Very talkative	Not at all talkative
Very tactful	Very blunt
Very gentle	Very rough
Very aware of feelings of others	Not at all aware of feelings of others
Very religious	Not at all religious
Very interested in own appearance	Not at all interested in own appearance
Very neat in habits	Very sloppy in habits
Very quiet	Very loud
Very strong need for security	Very little need for security
Enjoys art and literature	Does not enjoy art and literature at all

teaching of how to be a male or how to be a female begins literally at birth and continues thereafter (see Figure 17–5). With a blue room for boys and a pink room for girls, we begin communicating early on our belief that boys and girls are different, that we expect them to behave differently, and that we intend to treat them differently. Much gender-role learning occurs through the messages that parents and others communicate to children. For example, boys may be given toy trucks, guns, and tools; girls may be given dolls, toy dishes, purses, makeup, and miniature mops and brooms. When children engage in what is considered appropriate behavior, they are reinforced. When they do not, they may be punished. Consider aggression as an example. Boys are encouraged to be tough and are reinforced for behaving aggressively; any "sissy" behavior is disapproved of. Girls, on the other hand, are discouraged from behaving aggressively, told it isn't ladylike, and perhaps punished for doing it (Maccoby & Jacklin, 1974). Although biological explanations of greater male aggression do exist (aggression is increased by increases in androgens, and males have more androgens than females), social learning also provides a compelling explanation of this particular gender difference.

Expectations regarding gender differences are also

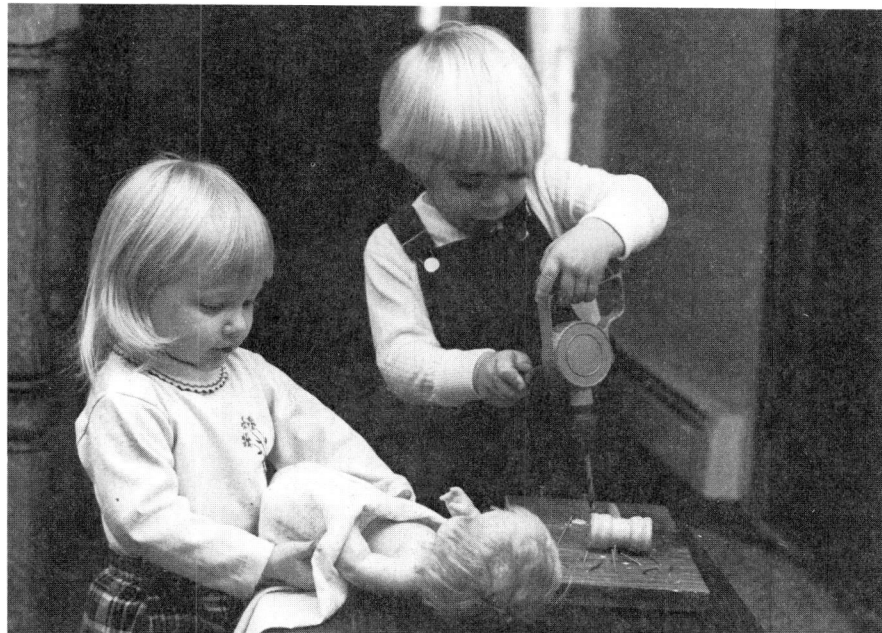

Figure 17–5.
The learning of gender roles begins at a very early age.

communicated with respect to achievement in school. It is known, for example, that parents believe mathematics is more important for boys than girls and are more likely to encourage boys than girls to continue in math (Parsons, Adler, & Kaczala, 1982). The expectation, then, is that boys should do better than girls in such courses. Perhaps that expectation helps contribute to the greater spatial and mathematical ability of males and the greater verbal ability of females (see chapter 12). If boys are expected to perform well in math and science, they will be steered in that direction, even to the point of being given toys (such as construction sets) that require spatial skills (Myers, 1983).

Children also learn gender roles through observing others. They notice, for example, that most plumbers, doctors, carpenters, and astronauts are men and that most teachers, nurses, and secretaries are women. The message is that only certain types of activities are appropriate for each gender. Outstanding and well-publicized exceptions to these general patterns, such as the first female American astronaut to go into outer space (see Figure 17–6), help highlight the fact that activities need not be restricted by gender.

Observational learning occurs in other ways too—in real life as well as on television (Myers, 1983). Men are shown behaving aggressively, withholding the expres-sion of feelings, and playing the role of the assertive and powerful authority figure. Women are shown behaving more passively and more emotionally. A consequence is that people may behave in a manner consistent with the roles they see portrayed around them (Myers, 1983).

Figure 17–6.
Astronaut Sally Ride.

GENDER ROLES AND SEXUALITY

Gender roles and sexuality are closely related. As a result, conforming to traditional gender roles might affect sexual relationships in several ways. One relevant traditional male-role characteristic is the desire to achieve and be successful (Mahoney, 1983). This means, of course, that men are likely to want to achieve sexual goals—a certain number of conquests, being competent sexual performers, or whatever.

Other traditional aspects of the male stereotype are aggressiveness and power or control. Each of these stereotyped characteristics may lead men to believe that they must be responsible for initiating sex and perhaps must even be aggressive or rough in lovemaking (Hyde, 1982; Mahoney, 1983). Women, on the other hand, may believe that they should play a passive role and not initiate lovemaking. The traditional man may, in fact, feel threatened if the woman does not conform to this feminine stereotype and instead tries to assume some control in the sexual relationship. One consequence of the male-in-charge, passive-female relationship is that the man is always expected to know what his partner will find pleasurable (even though he doesn't), and the woman, not being in control, may not communicate her desires adequately. The man may also be affronted if the woman implies in any way that he is not sexually knowledgeable. The result can be a sexual relationship that is less than optimally satisfying to both partners.

Another gender-role stereotype is that the men are always ready for sex and are easy to arouse, whereas women are difficult to arouse (Hyde, 1982; Strong & Reynolds, 1982). A man may even question his masculinity if he does not become highly aroused by every attractive woman who passes by. The woman who believes that she is not supposed to be easily aroused may avoid becoming aroused or may try not to show it when she is. If she does become easily or highly aroused, she (or the man) may believe that she is not feminine or has loose morals.

Finally, part of the male gender role is not expressing emotion. The carry-over of this to the sexual relationship may mean that the man will believe that he should be interested only in the physical aspects of the sexual relationship rather than in any emotional commitment (Hyde, 1982). The man may refrain from being tender or expressing his feelings to his partner for fear he will not be perceived as strong and masculine. Again, the relationship suffers because of the rigidity of gender-role behavior.

Traditional gender roles are, of course, satisfying to many individuals. If they are mutually satisfactory, they will not be likely to cause difficulties in relationships. But to the extent that traditional roles limit the potential of a relationship, they are inappropriate and maladaptive (Strong & Reynolds, 1982). There is evidence, in fact, that many individuals today are shedding the inflexibility of the traditional gender roles and adopting more flexible ways of behaving—ways in which behavior is defined as appropriate for a person, not for a man or a woman.

RESEARCHING HUMAN SEXUAL BEHAVIOR —

Surveys of Sexual Behavior and Attitudes Toward Sex

Much of what is known about human sexual behavior has come from survey research, which was pioneered by Alfred Kinsey. Kinsey and his associates conducted individual interviews with 5,300 men and 5,940 women and reported the results in two volumes, *Sexual Behavior in the Human Male* (Kinsey, Pomeroy, & Martin, 1948), and *Sexual Behavior in the Human Female* (Kinsey, Pomeroy, Martin, & Gebhard, 1953).

Since Kinsey's reports, a number of other large-scale surveys have been conducted. One of the most ambitious and widely cited surveys is Hunt's *Sexual Behavior in the 1970s* (Hunt, 1974), which is based on questionnaire responses from 982 men and 1,044 women. Hunt's survey represents an attempt to collect more recent data that could be compared with Kinsey's. In fact, any comparison of sexual behavior in the 1940s and more recent times must rely for the most part on the Kinsey and Hunt reports. Unfortunately, both surveys have some problems (Rathus & Nevid, 1983). Perhaps the biggest is that neither sample accurately represents the nation's population. In Kinsey's sample, certain groups, such as rural dwellers and the poorly educated, were underrepresented. Hunt's respondents probably had more liberal attitudes and behavior than the average American; only 20 percent of the originally identified sample agreed to participate. Although it is important to recognize such limitations, the surveys are nevertheless informative and provide an important avenue for gaining insight into sexual behavior.

— Sexual Behaviors

In our description of American sexual behavior and attitudes toward sex, we will be examining two types of reported findings—incidence and frequency. *Incidence* refers to the percentage of individuals who have engaged in a particular behavior, regardless of the number of times. *Frequency* refers to how often they engage in the behavior.

Masturbation. Self-stimulation of the genitals is **masturbation.** It is a common practice among both males and females, married and unmarried. The Kinsey and Hunt surveys reveal that nearly all (about 95 percent) adult men and approximately two-thirds of adult women have masturbated to orgasm. (**Orgasm** is the climax of sexual arousal, the pleasurable release of sexual tension.) Comparing the two surveys, we find that the incidence of masturbation has not increased, but the age at which individuals first engage in it seems to have decreased.

Petting. Physical, sexual contact between individuals that does not include sexual intercourse is **petting.** The behavior includes kissing and hugging and, in the case of heavy petting, genital stimulation (including oral-genital contact). Almost all males and females, married or unmarried, have engaged in one form of petting or another. Oral-genital contact has been the most slowly accepted form of petting, but even this seems to be rather widely accepted now as a normal sexual outlet (McCary & McCary, 1982). Like masturbation, petting seems to be occurring at an earlier age (Hunt, 1974).

Premarital intercourse. A double standard of morality has long existed with regard to premarital intercourse as an acceptable sexual behavior. This standard has held that premarital sex is all right for men but not for women. Of course, that standard raises an interesting question: With whom are men supposed to have sex? The double standard is clearly visible in the Kinsey survey. As you can see in Table 17–3, in a comparison of the Kinsey and Hunt surveys, the incidence of premarital sex increased for both men and women—but more for women. Other surveys support these findings.

Marital intercourse. The frequency of marital intercourse has increased in every age group according to estimates by both men and women in the Kinsey and Hunt studies. These surveys, as well as others, also suggest that the frequency of **coitus** (another term for sexual intercourse) decreases with age. One of the most significant changes in marital sex indicated by the Kinsey and Hunt surveys is an increase in the incidence of oral sex. In the Hunt survey, 90 percent of the married couples under age 25 reported having practiced both **fellatio** (oral stimulation of the male genitals) and **cunnilingus** (oral stimulation of the female genitals).

Extramarital intercourse. Sexual relations between a married person and someone other than that person's spouse is *extramarital intercourse*. The Kinsey and Hunt surveys suggest that nearly half of all married men and about one-fifth of all married women

Table 17–3.
Percentage of males and females who had engaged in premarital sex, according to Kinsey and Hunt surveys. (From Hyde, 1982, p. 268.)

	KINSEY (1948, 1953)	HUNT (1974)
Males (by age 25)	71	97
Females (by age 25)	33	67

have engaged in extramarital sex. Thompson (1983) reports, however, that 11 surveys published since 1970 suggest that "the figure for married women is rapidly approaching the same level" (p. 18) as that for married men. If we look at age groups, we find that the only significant increase in extramarital sex from the Kinsey surveys to the Hunt survey is for women under age 25. Perhaps this is due to their rejection of the double standard; they may believe that if extramarital sex is acceptable for men, it is also acceptable for women (Hyde, 1982).

— Sexual Attitudes

Attitudes toward various aspects of sexual behavior have been assessed in several studies. With regard to masturbation, attitudes seem to have shifted greatly. In the early years of this century, the common view of masturbation was that it caused an assortment of ills ranging from acne to sterility to mental problems. Attitudes today are much more positive, although many college students still seem to believe that masturbation is harmful (Abramson & Mosher, 1975). The view to-

day among authorities on human sexuality is that masturbation is harmless. The only negative effects might be the anxiety and guilt caused by the belief that the behavior is wrong or harmful.

Attitudes toward premarital sex have also become more positive in recent years. Traditionally, the majority of Americans have been in favor of abstinence until marriage; some have adopted a double-standard approach, in which it is acceptable for men, but not women, to engage in premarital sex. Hunt's survey, however, reveals a much different story (see Figure 17–7). The new attitude seems to be that premarital sex is acceptable if the individuals have strong affection for one another. It is even more acceptable if the relationship involves yet greater commitment, particularly engagement to be married. Remnants of the double standard remain, however. It still seems to be more acceptable for men than for women to engage in premarital sex.

Although the standard for premarital sex seems to have shifted toward more permissiveness, Hyde (1982) notes there is no evidence to suggest that promiscuity is running rampant in the younger generation. Rather

Figure 17–7.

Percentage of respondents who agree that premarital sex is acceptable for the man (left) and for the woman (right), based on the strength of the relationship commitment. (Based on data from Hunt, 1974, p. 116.)

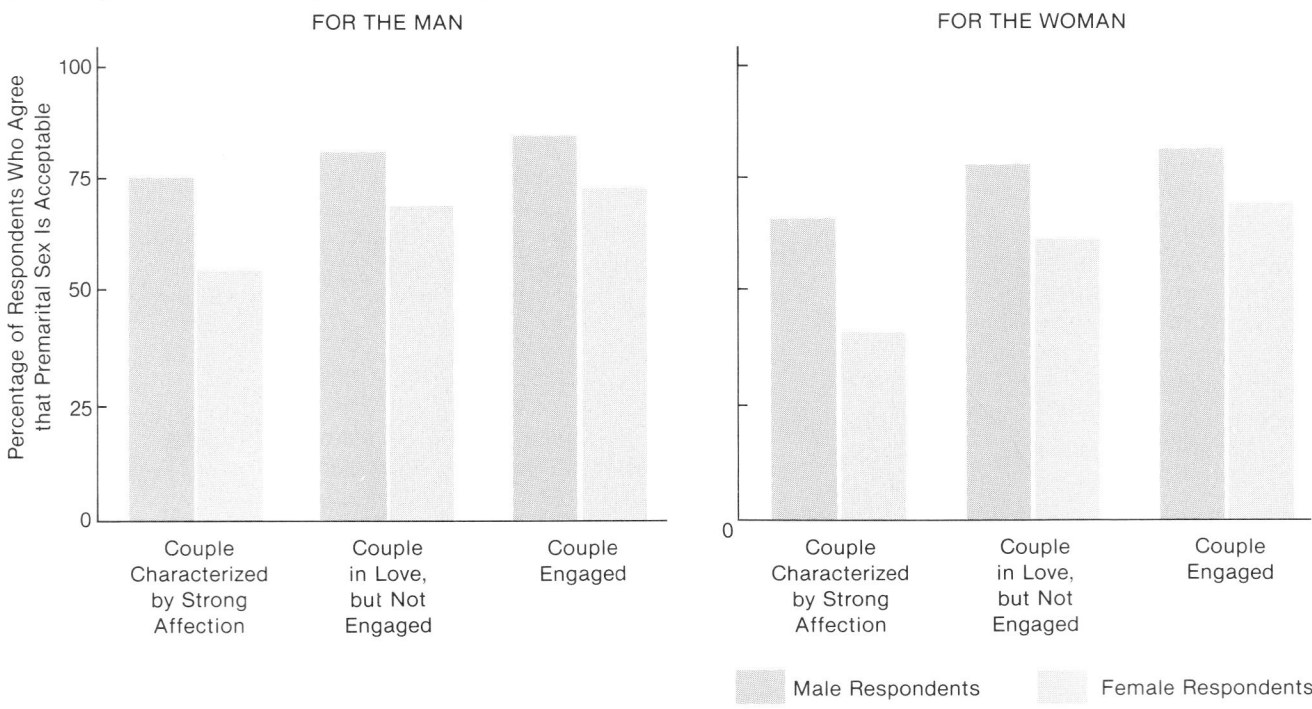

ALFRED C. KINSEY (1894–1956)

Alfred C. Kinsey is one of the most famous investigators of human sexuality as well as one of the greatest contributors to this field. Raised in a religious, middle-class family, Kinsey received his undergraduate training in psychology and his doctorate in biology. His academic career began in 1920 at Indiana University where he accepted the position of assistant professor of zoology.

In the 1930s, Kinsey's research interest changed from the behavior of the gall wasp to the sexual behavior of the human. The change came while Kinsey was teaching a course on marital problems and arose from his realization that little scientific knowledge existed on the subject of human sexuality. His extensive surveys brought human sexuality into the public consciousness at a time when frankness and openness in discussing sex was not the norm (Rosen & Rosen, 1981). One of the trademarks of Kinsey's philosophy was sexual tolerance. He believed in accepting the wide range of human sexual behaviors, not judging them (Rosen & Rosen, 1981). The Institute for Sex Research, which Kinsey and his colleagues founded in 1947 at Indiana University, continues to do research today.

than being abolished, standards have simply been changed. As Hyde (1982) suggests, "This standard of permissiveness with affection is scarcely a license for casual or impersonal sex" (p. 273). In further support of her conclusion is the finding that even when premarital sex is engaged in, the number of partners is typically small. About half the women who have premarital sex do so only with one person, whom they ultimately marry. Men average about six premarital partners, which, Hyde (1982) notes, is scarcely an orgy.

Finally, it is interesting that attitudes toward extramarital sex have changed very little over the years. They have remained strongly negative.

Physiology of Sexual Behavior: Laboratory Observations of the Sexual-Response Cycle

There are clear limitations to what can be learned about human sexual behavior through self-report data. The primary concern is accuracy. Knowingly or unknowingly, survey respondents may report inaccurate information. An alternative to the use of self-reports is observation of sexual behavior under laboratory conditions. This approach is represented in the pioneering work on the physiology of sexual response by William Masters and Virginia Johnson. Masters and Johnson have recorded the physiological responses of hundreds of normal men and women as they engage in a variety of sexual activities, including masturbation and sexual intercourse. Obviously, laboratory research avoids the problem of potential distortion that occurs in self-reports. However, it also answers different questions than those addressed in surveys (Hyde, 1982). Only surveys can assess whether and how frequently a person engages in a particular sexual activity. Masters and Johnson, on the other hand, assess the body's responses to sexual stimulation, and they record information that cannot be obtained easily or accurately, if at all, through self-reports.

The observations made by Masters and Johnson (1966) led them to describe the physiological responses of sexuality as falling into four phases: excitement, plateau, orgasm, and resolution. The four-phase process, applicable to both men and women, is known as the **sexual-response cycle** (see Figure 17–8).

In the first, **excitement phase** of the cycle, an increased flow of blood to the genital area is brought on by sexual stimulation. Erection occurs in men, and vaginal lubrication and clitoral swelling occur in women.

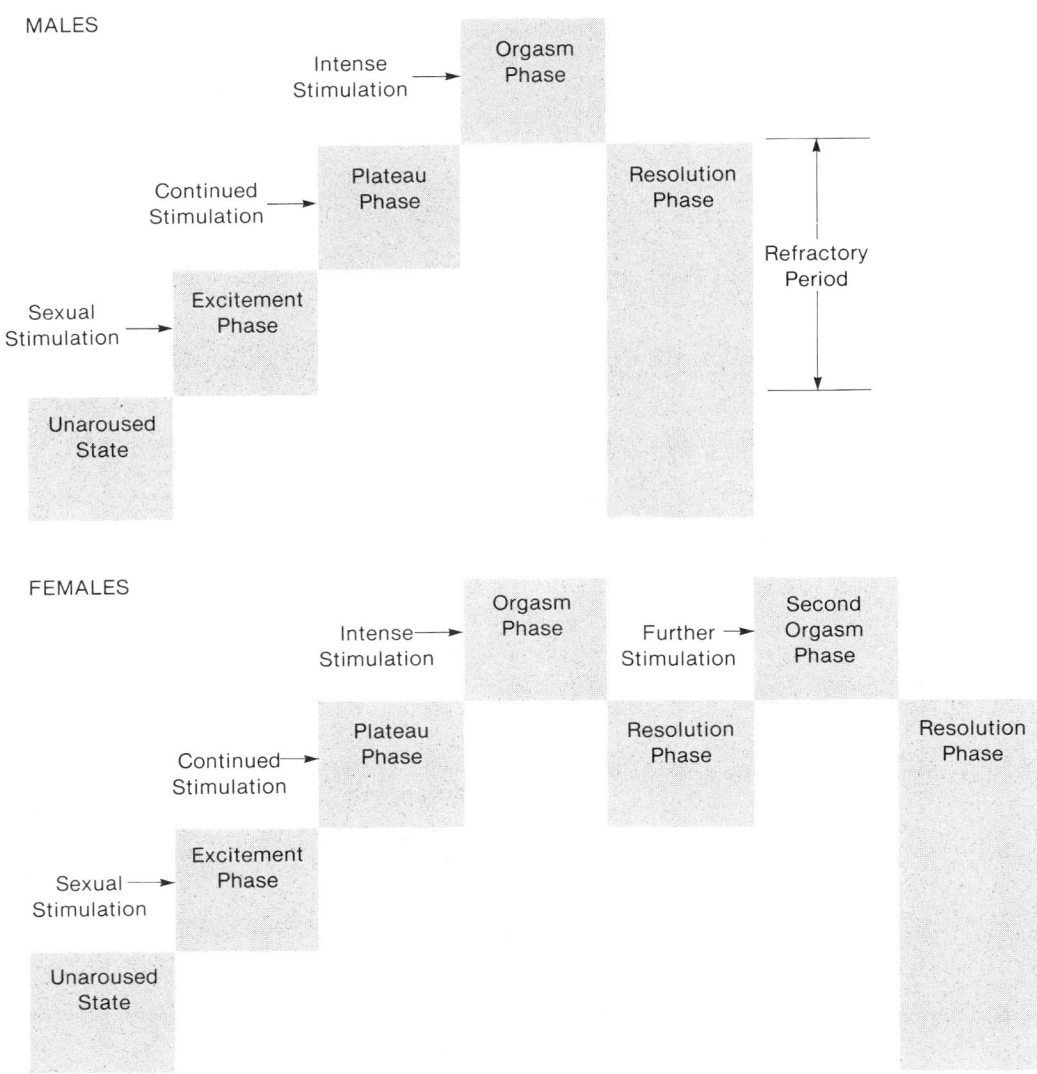

Figure 17–8.
The sexual-response cycle. (From Baron & Byrne, 1981, p. 547.)

For both men and women, there is an increase in heart rate, blood pressure, and respiration rate. The subsequent **plateau phase** involves a continuing, increasingly higher level of sexual arousal that precedes orgasm. The **orgasm phase** occurs when sexual arousal reaches a peak. Orgasm is characterized physically by involuntary contraction of muscles, especially in the genital region; the psychological experience is one of intense pleasure. Generally, this phase lasts only a few seconds. Following orgasm is the **resolution phase,** during which such body functions as heart rate and blood pressure slowly return to their prearousal state.

Few differences between men and women seem to exist with respect to the sexual-response cycle. One important difference, however, is that men undergo a **refractory period,** a period of time following orgasm when they are unresponsive to sexual stimulation. For men, the resolution phase generally continues until sexual arousal diminishes totally. For women, however, additional sexual stimulation can lead to increased sexual arousal at any time during the resolution phase. As a result, some women experience **multiple orgasms,** in which two or more successive orgasms occur prior to the end of the resolution phase.

One unfortunate result of Masters and Johnson's finding with respect to multiple orgasms is the belief by some women that they should not be satisfied with only one orgasm (Rathus & Nevid, 1983). A related problem occurs when men think that if they can't "give" women multiple orgasms, there's something wrong with them or with the women. If one sets goals or performance standards that are not met, the result may be unnecessary feelings of inadequacy or sexual incompetence. The important conclusion to draw from Masters and Johnson's finding is that multiple orgasms are possible but not necessary for sexual satisfaction.

Another interesting finding from Masters and Johnson's research has to do with the issue of clitoral orgasm (orgasm from clitoral stimulation) versus vaginal orgasm (orgasm from vaginal stimulation). Freud believed that such a distinction could be made. He suggested that clitoral orgasm is immature, the type of orgasm associated with youthful masturbation. Presumably, with greater maturity, the only appropriate (better and more mature) orgasm would be the vaginal orgasm that comes from sexual intercourse.

One direct result of Freud's distinction has been the anxiety felt by some women because the most satisfying or the only type of orgasm they could reliably achieve was the immature form. Thanks to Masters and Johnson's research, we now know that Freud's distinction is unnecessary and inappropriate. All female orgasms, however produced, occur as a result of direct or indirect stimulation of the clitoris. Because the stimulation that occurs during intercourse is usually less direct than that occurring during masturbation, it should not be surprising that many women have difficulty reaching orgasm during intercourse unless the clitoris is directly massaged (Hite, 1976). For women, masturbation seems to be the most reliable and fastest way of reaching orgasm.

Experimental Studies of Sexual Behavior

Another approach to understanding human sexuality has been to study it experimentally in the laboratory. With this approach, experimenters can manipulate any number of factors and determine whether they cause any behavior. Experimenters are limited, of course, in what they can ethically study. A further limitation of this approach is that some important and interesting issues, such as the factors causing people to develop homosexual or heterosexual preferences, simply cannot be addressed (Hyde, 1982). Despite the limitations, though, much can still be learned about human sexuality through the experimental approach.

One of the most significant issues to be experimentally investigated in recent years is pornography and its effects. **Pornography** is any written, visual, or verbal material that is considered sexually arousing. According to Myers (1983), the tolerance of pornographic materials has increased ever since the 1970 United States Commission on Obscenity and Pornography concluded that viewing such materials has no harmful effects. The Commission's conclusion, though, has not gone unchallenged.

There is no doubt that pornography does lead to both self-reported and physiologically measurable arousal in both men and women (Baron & Byrne, 1977). The effects, though, may diminish with repeated exposure. The physiological response to pornography can be just as intense as that experienced during actual sexual activity. But does this sexual excitement have subsequent effects on an individual's behavior? Of concern to many psychologists is the question of whether pornography affects aggression.

Particularly disturbing are the findings from recent research focusing on *aggressive pornography,* which involves "depictions in which physical force is used or threatened to coerce a woman to engage in sexual acts (e.g., rape)" (Malamuth & Donnerstein, 1982, p. 105). Many of the films containing such pornography depict the victim as secretly desiring sexual assault and as deriving sexual pleasure from it. Researchers have been concerned with the possible effects of viewing films that contain such pornography.

As long as rape victims are portrayed as being sexually aroused, aggressive pornography can be just as sexually arousing as depictions of mutually consenting sex—or even more so (Malamuth & Donnerstein, 1982). Depictions of rape generally lead to lower sexual arousal than do depictions of mutually consenting sex, however, if the victim is portrayed as abhorring the experience. In general, the evidence suggests that convicted rapists are not the only persons aroused by rape depictions; so too are normal college students, both male and female.

A notable finding is that men who view rape films later exhibit a much higher level of aggression toward women than do men who view nonaggressive pornographic films or neutral films (e.g., Donnerstein, 1980). One possible explanation is that seeing sexual violence lowers the man's inhibitions against displaying similar behavior (i.e., aggression toward women). Another effect of aggressive pornography is that it alters viewers' perceptions of rape and rape victims (Malamuth & Donnerstein, 1982). More specifically, men who view pornography that depicts women as enjoying rape are subsequently more likely to believe that women really do enjoy being raped than are men who view films involving consenting sex or those in which the rape victim reacts with disgust (Malamuth & Check, 1981). Zillmann and Bryant (1982) report that a loss of compassion toward rape victims also occurs after massive viewing of pornography, even when the pornography is devoid of coercion and aggression.

It appears that viewing sexual violence can have antisocial effects. One wonders, of course, of the possible role that aggressive pornography may play in rape. Especially notable is the finding that many normal men possess a proclivity to rape. Malamuth (1981) reported that about 35 percent of the sampled normal men indicated some likelihood of raping a woman if they could be assured that no one would find out and they would not be punished. Malamuth found that these men were similar to convicted rapists in several ways.

They tended to believe the rape myths (e.g., that women enjoy rape), and they were sexually aroused by depictions of rape, regardless of whether the rape victim was aroused or disgusted by the rape.

We will return to the topic of rape a little later. In addition to the issues of sex crimes and aggression, some individuals are concerned that pornography will unleash a barrage of sexual activity, including sexual acts that many consider immoral (Baron & Byrne, 1977). As Baron and Byrne point out, however, research shows that exposure to pornography has very little effect on such sexual behavior as intercourse or masturbation. Any increases in sexual behavior that do seem to occur involve only behavior that was already part of the person's sexual pattern (Cattell, Kawash, & DeYoung, 1972). Furthermore, the effects of erotic stimulation seem to be transient (Mann, Berkowitz, Sidman, Starr, & West, 1974). These data, then, offer no support for the belief that exposure to erotic materials will instigate unrestrained sexual activities.

━ APPLICATION ━

ADOLESCENT SEX AND THE PROBLEM OF CONTRACEPTION

Research in human sexuality has uncovered a fascinating array of questions; it has also helped provide solutions to some problems. One such problem is the teenage pregnancy epidemic referred to in chapter 11 (see Figure 17–9). As already indicated, the emerging sexual atmosphere in the United States seems to be one of greater tolerance and permissiveness with respect to sexual attitudes and behavior. An increase in premarital sex is part of this trend. The problem of teenage pregnancy stems not from this fact alone, however. More to the point, although many teenagers seem willing to engage in sex, they seem less willing to use contraceptive devices (Byrne, 1983). The best that many do is use the hope method of birth control—"I hope I won't get pregnant" or "I hope she won't get pregnant" (Cvetkovich & Grote, 1983). Some may not even use hope. How might this lack of contraception be explained? What solutions to the problem exist? Byrne (1983) and Fisher (1983) have offered a number

of suggestions and possible solutions. Let's have a look at their analysis of the problem.

One contributing factor to teenagers' lack of contraceptive use seems to be a lack of accurate information about sex and contraception. Many adolescents believe that contraception is unnecessary. For example, they believe that pregnancy cannot occur the first time one has sex (Byrne, 1983). Some even believe that it is impossible, or at least unlikely, for a teenager to conceive a child (Strahle, 1983). Allgeier (1983) has noted that some adolescents think that using contraception will brand them as promiscuous or that it will take the spontaneity out of sex.

The answer to eradicating informational barriers to contraception seems to lie in improved efforts to provide teenagers with the information they need to make responsible decisions about their sexual conduct (Fisher, 1983). The fact is that teenagers learn little of what they need to know, either at home or at school.

Figure 17–9.
The harsh reality of teenage pregnancy.

The popular belief that sex education and the greater use of contraceptives promote sexual promiscuity seems also to be unwarranted (Allgeier, 1983).

Emotions too play a role in contraception decisions (see, for example, Fisher, Byrne, & White, 1983). As we have seen, sex is often associated with feelings of anxiety and other negative emotions. Byrne (1983) notes that when this is the case, the individual may avoid thinking about or discussing sex and avoid planning for or using contraception (see Gerrard, 1983). As Byrne puts it, "Given all this, it is not surprising to find that, among sexually active college coeds, those who have the most negative feelings about sex are the most likely to become pregnant" (Byrne, 1983, p. 21).

Again, the solution may lie in sex education. Fisher (1983) argues that if teenagers suffer anxiety over thinking about and using contraception, it is necessary for this anxiety to be replaced with a more positive emotion. He suggests the use of systematic desensitization (see chapter 16) in alleviating anxiety about the entire contraceptive process—learning about contraception, anticipating intercourse, acquiring the contraceptive device, discussing its use, and actually using it. Although desensitization may alleviate anxiety, the use of contraceptives may also require positive feelings associated with sexual behavior. Various strategies for accomplishing this goal could be included in a sex-education program.

Finally, Byrne (1983) suggests that a contributing factor in the lack of contraceptive use is the lack of models of contraceptive behavior in the mass media. Although we are exposed to numerous scenes of sexual encounters in television and movies, rarely is there any mention of contraception. Adolescents' fantasies of sex and of how people *ought* to behave or how they *ought* to feel tend not to include fantasies of using contraception. Fantasies that do include contraception may even be anticontraception: If I bring up contraception, I'll appear too forward (Fisher, 1983).

Fisher suggests that one strategy for combating anticontraception fantasies is to have teenagers engage in discussions in which they try to clarify their values. They can consider, for example, whether it is legitimate to allow one's imagined fear of rejection to get in the way of discussing the use of contraception. Fisher further suggests the use of contraceptive models in educational films in order to promote procontraception fantasy. At the same time, Fisher notes, teens could be provided with additional models who show the le-

gitimacy of saying no and remaining a virgin. As Fisher puts it, it may not cross the minds of many adolescents that they can refuse to engage in sex and still be popular. Models legitimizing not having sex could help balance the existing tendency for media and peers to push teenagers into being sexually active. Fisher (1983) says:

> Where in our world of media hype are the with-it teenagers who dress well, play tennis, drive sports cars, date like crazy, and refrain from intercourse? In order to make abstinence a viable option, sex education must provide teens with attractive models who display successful strategies for stopping short of sexual intercourse. (p. 297)

— SEXUAL VARIATIONS, SEXUAL DYSFUNCTIONS, AND HOMOSEXUALITY —

In this section, we will focus on the forms of sexual behavior that differ from typical or conventional expressions of sexuality.

Variations in Sexual Behavior

Sexual variations are sexual behaviors that deviate from conventional norms and that are maladaptive. In our discussion, sexual variations will be grouped as follows: (1) variations in object choice, (2) variations in sexual aim, and (3) gender-identity disturbances.

— Variations in Object Choice

With respect to sexual behavior, the standard object choice in our society is a consenting adult of the opposite gender (Strong & Reynolds, 1982). Sexual variations in object choice represent a deviation from this standard. Such variations include inanimate objects (fetishism) and unwilling partners (rape).

Fetishism. Attaching sexual significance to objects that are not necessarily sexual in nature is **fetishism.** It is a sexual variation that occurs almost entirely among men. A fetish may take several forms (Hyde, 1982). In one form, the fetish object is part of the

body. It may be a sexual part, such as the breasts, or a nonsexual part, such as the feet or hair color. In any case, sexual gratification cannot be achieved without the presence of the object (e.g., large breasts or blond hair). In a second form, fetishism involves an inanimate object. Typically, the object is something associated with the body, such as clothing, shoes, or lingerie. Many fetishists collect the objects that arouse them and may even steal in order to obtain the arousing items.

Fetishes vary considerably in their extremity (Hyde, 1982). At the mild end of the continuum are those that are well within the range of normal behavior. For example, many men find objects such as lingerie sexually arousing; these objects may serve to facilitate sexual arousal during foreplay. In more extreme forms, however, the fetish object itself becomes not only necessary but sufficient for sexual gratification. In terms of what is normal and what is not, Hyde (1982) suggests that when a fetish object becomes an absolute necessity for sexual arousal and intercourse to occur, the fetish can reasonably be called abnormal or maladaptive.

Rape. An act of aggression in which one person forces another, nonconsenting person to engage in a sexual act is **rape.** Although rape victims are usually women, men are also sometimes victims—for example, in prisons (Katchadourian & Lunde, 1980). The dominant view today is that rape is an act of violence and an attempt to exert power (see, for example, Ellis & Beattie, 1983). Sexual arousal is thought to play only a minor or secondary role.

Rape is more common than most of us would like to think, and it is a crime whose occurrence is increasing. One estimate is that as many as 3.5 million rapes occur in the United States each year (Mahoney, 1983). Only a small portion of them are reported to the police. Another estimate (Mahoney, 1983) is that there are four or five times as many rapes by assailants known to the victim as there are rapes by total strangers. This goes against the stereotype that the most common form of rape involves two complete strangers. Consistent with the greater frequency of acquaintance or family-member rape, it has been found that most rapes are planned (Janda & Klenke-Hamel, 1980). This finding, in turn, is consistent with the view that rape is an act of aggression rather than a temporary loss of control over one's sexual impulses.

— Variations in Sexual Aim

Given that sexual intercourse is the standard sexual aim in our society, variations in sexual aim include behaviors not aimed at sexual intercourse (Strong & Reynolds, 1982). Included here are watching sexual activity (voyeurism), exposing one's genitals (exhibitionism), and cross dressing (transvestism).

Voyeurism. Deriving sexual pleasure from secretly watching others undress or have sexual intercourse is **voyeurism.** Excitement seems to be increased when there is the possibility of discovery. Here again we have the problem of defining what is normal and abnormal. Many individuals engage in mild forms of voyeurism. For example, many watch go-go dancers or strippers. According to Hyde (1982), voyeurism is abnormal when it replaces sexual intercourse or when it involves committing a crime in order to observe others. Voyeurs are generally male; hence the label "peeping Toms."

Exhibitionism. Exposing one's genitals to unsuspecting and unwilling strangers to attain sexual gratification is **exhibitionism** (see chapter introduction). Again, this seems to be a term applied almost exclusively to men. That is due, at least in part, to our society's attitudes toward the exposed bodies of men and

women. A man who exposes himself is much more likely to be considered deviant or abnormal, and hence reported, than is a woman who exhibits herself through revealing clothing (McCary & McCary, 1982).

Transvestism. Receiving sexual gratification by dressing in the clothing of the opposite gender is **transvestism.** Almost all transvestites are men who enjoy dressing in women's clothing (see Figure 17–10). Not all cross dressing reflects transvestism, however. We would not assume, for example, that actor Dustin Hoffman was a transvestite just because he cross-dressed for his role in the 1982 movie *Tootsie.* Also, unlike transsexuals (to be discussed shortly), transvestites have no desire to change gender. For transvestites, cross dressing alone is what produces sexual gratification (Janda & Klenke-Hamel, 1980).

Figure 17–10.
A male transvestite.

— Gender-Identity Disturbance: Transsexualism

In some cases, variations in sexual behavior involve confusion over gender identity. Transsexualism represents one such variation. As indicated earlier, transsexuals are individuals who are psychologically uncomfortable with their anatomical sex. They prefer to think of themselves as being opposite in gender to what their genitals indicate. In effect, their gender identity is at odds with their anatomy. They feel as if they are trapped in the wrong body (Masters, Johnson, & Kolodny, 1982). Most transsexuals are individuals in male bodies who prefer to think of themselves as women. The incongruity is so strong that these individuals desire to live as women and, in many cases, to alter their sexual anatomy through sex-change surgery.

Many Americans have undergone sex-change surgery since the first such operation was performed in 1953. Physicians approach this surgery very cautiously, however, because of its irreversibility. Most sex-reassignment clinics have stringent requirements for undertaking such an operation (Janda & Klenke-Hamel, 1980; Masters, Johnson, & Kolodny, 1982). One requirement is that the individual must have a lifelong history of wanting to have a body of the opposite gender. Then, during a 1-to-2-year trial period prior to surgery, the individual must prove that he or she can live satisfactorily as a person of the opposite gender. In other words, during this time, candidates must cross-dress, assume an appropriate new name, and so on.

During the trial period, the individual also receives hormone therapy that produces secondary sex characteristics of the opposite gender. The man given estrogens, for example, experiences breast growth, among other things. Assuming that satisfactory adjustment has occurred, the actual surgery transforms the individual's genitals into those of the opposite gender. Only the external genitals are altered. The man undergoing sex reassignment to become a woman will not be able to get pregnant and will not ovulate. Normal sexual relations can take place, however.

Sex reassignment is anatomical. Surgery does not necessarily end the person's troubled feelings; it does not cause a gender-identity change. The individual must still learn to be comfortable with and adjust to the new gender status (Janda & Klenke-Hamel, 1980). Whether the surgery is, in fact, helpful to those who desire it has been questioned in recent years. In 1980,

the lack of good evidence that such surgery is beneficial prompted several medical centers to discontinue it (Masters, Johnson, & Kolodny, 1982).

Homosexuality

Having sexual attraction toward or engaging in sexual behavior with a member of the same gender is **homosexuality.** Hyde (1982) concluded from the work of Kinsey and Hunt that about 75 percent of men and 85 percent of women are exclusively **heterosexual.** That is, they are sexually attracted to or engage in sexual activity with members of the opposite gender. Approximately 2 percent of men and 1 percent of women are exclusively homosexual. The remaining individuals have had both homosexual and heterosexual experiences to one degree or another.

According to DSM-III (APA, 1980), homosexuality is not considered abnormal behavior (i.e., a mental disorder) unless it causes the individual severe subjective distress and the individual wants to change. The notion that homosexuals are not by definition maladjusted and abnormal individuals has received support from a number of studies. Hooker (1957), for example, failed to find any significant differences between homosexuals and heterosexuals on a number of psychological tests. Much the same finding emerged from Bell and Weinberg's (1978) interviews with 1,500 homosexuals. These researchers concluded that as along as the individuals were satisfied and not distressed with their sexual preference, they were just as well adjusted psychologically as were heterosexuals. Furthermore, there is evidence that when homosexuals do show signs of abnormality, it is no different in type or degree from that seen in heterosexuals. It has been suggested that when homosexuals exhibit maladaptive behavior, it is not due to homosexuality per se but rather to the social stigma attached to it (Sarason & Sarason, 1980).

Although homosexuality is not generally viewed by psychologists and psychiatrists as a mental disorder, that was not always the case. Viewing it as abnormal behavior has led to considerable speculation as to its causes. Many investigators, for example, have searched for biological causes. Thus far, however, studies have failed to confirm any biological differences between homosexuals and heterosexuals. It is nevertheless true that many researchers remain convinced that there is a genetic or constitutional predisposition toward homosexuality that is then influenced by the life experiences of the individual (Katchadourian & Lunde, 1980).

Psychoanalytic studies have generally concluded that the existence of a dominant, overprotective, and overly intimate mother and a passive, unaffectionate, and hostile father can lead to homosexuality in the son (e.g., Bieber et al., 1962). Presumably, these parents inhibit the child from displaying masculine behavior and at the same time cause him to be anxious about heterosexuality.

The learning-theory position on homosexuality is that it is shaped by rewards and punishments just as heterosexuality is (Hyde, 1982). Whether one becomes predominantly heterosexual or homosexual depends, then, on one's experiences and their outcomes. Unpleasant experiences (punishment) with early heterosexual encounters, for example, may lead to homosexuality. Alternatively, early homosexual experiences that are found to be pleasant (rewarded) may also foster the development of homosexuality. The learning view is particularly advantageous in that it allows us to view homosexuality simply as learned behavior without our having to label it as abnormal.

Sexual Dysfunctions

Sexual difficulties and impairments in sexual functioning are **sexual dysfunctions.** At least half of all American marriages may be affected by some type of sexual dysfunction (McCary & McCary, 1982). In many cases, the problems become distressing enough that therapy is sought. Important contributions to our understanding of sexual dysfunctions have been made by Masters and Johnson (1970) in their book *Human Sexual Inadequacy* and by Kaplan (1974) in her book *The New Sex Therapy.*

— Sexual Dysfunction in Men

A problem experienced by some men is that of **erectile dysfunction** (a term now preferred over *impotence*), which is the inability to have or to maintain an erection. Not all cases of erectile difficulty reflect an erectile dysfunction per se. As many as 50 percent of all men have an occasional erectile problem (McCary & McCary, 1982). In distinguishing between transient problems and a true sexual dysfunction, Masters and Johnson (1970) define *erectile dysfunction* as existing when attempts at intercourse are unsuccessful approximately 25 percent of the time or more.

Erectile dysfunction typically has a psychological origin. According to Kaplan (1974), "Anticipation of being unable to perform the sexual act is perhaps the greatest immediate cause" (p. 127). In other words, the man experiences performance anxiety whereby his excessive worry over his sexual adequacy actually inhibits his performance. A single experience of erectile difficulty can turn into a chronic case of erectile dysfunction when a man starts thinking, "If it happened once, it can happen again." The goal in the treatment of this dysfunction is to reduce the man's performance anxiety by helping the couple establish an atmosphere in which the man will not feel any pressure to perform. Masters and Johnson (1970) advocate *sensate-focus* exercises, in which the man is encouraged to stop concentrating on his performance and instead to focus on the sensations experienced from the couple's "pleasuring" each other through stroking.

Another male dysfunction, **premature ejaculation,** occurs when the man ejaculates too soon for his partner to experience orgasm through intercourse. More precisely, Masters and Johnson (1970) say that ejaculation is premature if it occurs too soon for the woman to have an orgasm at least 50 percent of the time. As Hyde (1982) points out, this definition is not entirely adequate. What if the woman has difficulty reaching orgasm through intercourse? Under such circumstances, is it correct to label the man as a premature ejaculator? Presumably not. Kaplan (1974) prefers to ignore the issue of the female orgasm and instead defines *premature ejaculation* as the absence of voluntary control, regardless of how long it takes to ejaculate and whether or not the female has an orgasm. In other words, if the man can't voluntary control ejaculation, a problem exists.

Again, psychological factors such as performance anxiety are relevant. According to Kaplan (1974), it may be that the anxiety surrounding sexuality inhibits the man from perceiving the sensations that immediately precede orgasm. This in turn keeps him from learning to control ejaculation. Kaplan suggests that any effective treatment must force the man to focus on the sensations associated with intense sexual excitement. By focusing, the man will be able to learn how to exercise voluntary control over ejaculation. The technique Kaplan recommends is the Semans stop-start method. With this procedure, the woman manually stimulates the man's penis until the man feels orgasm approaching. At that point, he signals her to stop, and the process is repeated.

Retarded ejaculation is a third male dysfunction. In this case, despite having an erection, the man is unable to ejaculate into the woman's vagina. He may, however, be able to ejaculate through other forms of stimulation, such as masturbation. Psychological causes of retarded ejaculation are many (McCary & McCary, 1982). In some cases, fear of impregnating the woman or anger over her infidelity may cause the problem. To treat it, Masters and Johnson (1970) instruct the woman to stimulate the man to orgasm without vaginal penetration. Once that response is established, the woman is to stimulate the penis to just short of ejaculation and then insert it into her vagina. The idea is that once the man's emotional block against ejaculating into the vagina has been broken, less and less manual stimulation will be necessary before initiating intercourse.

— Sexual Dysfunction in Women

Women also experience sexual dysfunctions. One of these dysfunctions is **orgasmic dysfunction**—the inability to have an orgasm. (The term *orgasmic dysfunction* is preferred over *frigidity*.) In some cases, the woman has never had an orgasm (Andersen, 1983). In other cases, the woman once experienced orgasm but no longer does. In yet other cases, the woman has had orgasms on one or more occasions, but only under certain circumstances (Masters, Johnson, & Kolodny, 1982). For example, a common situation for probably the majority of dysfunctional women is the ability to have orgasms as a result of masturbation or oral or manual stimulation by the partner but not as a result of intercourse (Hyde, 1982).

There is some question as to whether this condition is really a dysfunction (Hyde, 1982). A number of studies suggest that about 10 percent of all women have never experienced orgasm during intercourse. Perhaps another 10 percent have coital orgasms on an infrequent basis (Masters, Johnson, & Kolodny, 1982). Kaplan (1974) suggests that such women do not necessarily have a problem, since she considers not having orgasms during intercourse to be well within the normal range of female sexual response. However, when a woman experiences no orgasms or infrequent or-

gasms during intercourse and is distressed by the situation, classifying the condition as a dysfunction seems warranted (Hyde, 1982; Masters, Johnson, & Kolodny, 1982).

The causes of female sexual dysfunctions are varied (see McCary & McCary, 1982). Typically, there are psychological elements to most problems. Some center on the emotions of shame, guilt, and fear. When a woman has negative feelings about sex, feelings of sexual arousal will elicit anxiety. McCary and McCary (1982) suggest that the woman's defense against this anxiety is to avoid sexual stimulation and arousal. If sexual activity itself cannot be avoided, anxiety may inhibit orgasm. Other factors involved may be the expectation of pain during coitus, a fear of letting oneself go sexually in case one is rejected or condemned, and a fear of getting pregnant.

Treatment of orgasmic dysfunction centers on teaching the woman to focus attention on the sensations associated with increasing sexual excitement rather than inhibiting them (McCary & McCary, 1982). Kaplan's (1975) suggested treatment is to have the woman first achieve orgasm by masturbation, then by clitoral stimulation by the partner, and finally by coitus (ef. McCary & McCary, 1982). Kilmann and his colleagues (Kilmann et al., 1983) found that providing couples with accurate information about sexual functioning was effective in reducing sexual anxiety and significantly increasing the woman's frequency of orgasm. The researchers suggest that open discussion of sexual matters may have reduced sexual anxiety by highlighting the normality of such activities as masturbation and oral sex. Such discussion also emphasizes that women are entitled to sexual pleasure and have the capacity for great sexual enjoyment. The result of all this may have been that the women felt more comfortable and relaxed about various sexual activities.

Another female dysfunction, called **vaginismus,** involves involuntary contraction of the muscles surrounding the vaginal entrance. These contractions can be so severe that sexual intercourse becomes impossible. Sometimes, the vaginal spasms are also exceedingly painful. According to Masters and Johnson (1970), the condition is not very common. Treatment involves extinction of the muscle spasms through teaching the woman to relax the vaginal muscles, to masturbate (finger penetration into the vagina), and then to accept manual stimulation by the partner so that pleasure will become associated with vaginal penetration. At that point, the couple is ready to begin coitus.

PREVENTING SEXUAL DYSFUNCTIONS

Many principles have emerged from the work of sex therapists and researchers. Applying them may allow individuals to prevent sexual dysfunctions. According to three noted sex therapists (Masters, Johnson, & Kolodny, 1982), the first important step is for parents to establish a family atmosphere in which children feel that they can comfortably ask questions about sex and receive appropriate and honest answers. But what about after childhood? What important principles can people keep in mind? Both Masters and his colleagues (Masters, Johnson, & Kolodny, 1982) and Hyde (1982) have offered a number of helpful suggestions. The following is a summary of their ideas:

1. Keep open the lines of communication. Don't play mind-reading games with your partner. Discuss what each of you desires and finds pleasurable.
2. Don't view sex as a performance to be evaluated and graded. Setting goals means that there is something to fail at, and feelings of failure can lead to sexual dysfunction.
3. Don't fall into the trap of thinking that there is a correct way to respond and behave sexually. Comparing yourself to others, through what you read and hear, can be informative, but don't accept such information uncritically. It may lead you to believe that you have a problem when you don't.
4. Be selective about when, where, and with whom you have sex. Anxiety and a lack of trust in one's partner make good sexual functioning difficult at best.
5. Don't ignore sexual problems when they do occur. They may get worse, and the relationship may suffer as a result. Talk the problem over with your partner, and search for a solution. If this proves ineffective, seek the help of a competent professional therapist.

SOCIETY'S REACTIONS TO THE RAPE VICTIM

On March 6, 1983, a 21-year-old woman went into a bar in New Bedford, Massachusetts, to buy cigarettes. When she tried to leave, men in the bar blocked her path. She was repeatedly raped for more than an hour by four men. The gang rape occurred while patrons of the bar cheered and applauded. No one went to the victim's aid.

This rape and ones similar to it have received considerable publicity in recent years. We can only hope that most people react to such incidents with horror and revulsion (Rosenblatt, 1983). Although these reports certainly highlight the plight of the rape victim, it is equally true that attitudes toward rape victims have not been wholeheartedly positive. When jurors and judges make decisions in rape trials, attitudes toward the rape victim and her role in the rape can have an enormous impact. Many rape victims have had to divulge their sexual history in the courtroom as attorneys tried to suggest that the victims were promiscuous and, in effect, consented to the sex act (Borgida, 1981). Police and those in the courtroom may treat the rape victim with contempt if they believe she asked for it by going to a certain place or wearing a certain style of dress. In short, the rape victim has traditionally often found herself being blamed for the rape. She becomes the one who is on trial.

There are signs that positive attitudes toward rape victims and sensitivity to their problems are on the rise. Time will tell whether this is, in fact, a developing trend. The greater sensitivity toward and positive treatment of the rape victim has been due, in part, to research by psychologists and others showing that rape victims suffer many negative consequences, both physical and psychological (Burgess & Holmstrom, 1974; Calhoun, Atkeson, & Resick, 1982; Atkeson, Calhoun, Resick, & Ellis, 1982). People are recognizing more and more that rape is a real crisis for a woman and that it may require an adjustment period of 6 months or more.

More positive attitudes toward the rape victim are shown in a number of ways. For one thing, police departments are increasingly staffed with specially trained officers (often women) who help counsel rape victims. Rape crisis centers are also becoming more common. Many legal changes are occurring as well. Because of the tendency to regard rape victims as the guilty parties, such victims have traditionally had to disprove their guilt by showing, through corroboration of testimony or through physical injury, that they resisted the rapist. In effect, they have had to convince judge and jury that they did not enjoy the rape. A few states now have or anticipate having new laws that no longer require such proof (Dowd, 1983). Also, most states have adopted laws disallowing the victim's sexual history as admissible court testimony unless attorneys can prove that it is relevant. A more positive attitude toward women is also evident in the fact that some states now have laws allowing for the charge of rape within marriage. In theory, it would appear that increased sensitivity and more positive attitudes will lead more women to press charges against the rapist, to feel less guilty, to expect less humiliation, and so on. One would also expect the conviction rate for rapists to increase. It will be of interest to observe whether these effects can be substantiated in the coming years.

Lest we paint too rosy a picture, we should note that at this point there is still considerable evidence that rape victims are viewed by many people as having desired, caused, deserved, or lied about the rape (e.g., Burt, 1980; Weidner & Griffitt, 1983). Burt (1980) concluded that many Americans believe such rape myths as: Any healthy woman can successfully resist a rapist if she really wants to. Other relevant findings indicate that a rape victim is given more responsibility for the rape if she was drunk at the time of the rape (Richardson & Campbell, 1982) and if she was physically unattractive (Seligman, Brickman, & Koulack, 1977). Rape is also judged less serious when it occurs within either a dating or an intimate context than when the rapist and victim are strang-

ers (L'Armand & Pepitone, 1982). Such factors are legally irrelevant, but people apparently consider them in their social definitions of rape. We have a long way to go in the years ahead if we are to change people's attitudes, and perceptions of rape. Will views of rape change if our society alters its traditional ways of socializing males and females?

There is evidence that those low in gender-role stereotyping have more favorable views of the rape victim (Burt, 1980; Check & Malamuth, 1983). We hope that awareness of the research findings relating to rape, such as those we have described, will be a positive force in changing and improving people's attitudes.

——— SUMMARY ———

1. Gender development begins with prenatal sexual differentiation, which is controlled by genetic and hormonal mechanisms. Hormonal influences on gender development reappear at puberty.

2. Differing socialization of males and females also contributes to the development of gender identity. Parents, peers, teachers, and the mass media all contribute to this role-learning process.

3. Males and females differ in some ways that are consistent with stereotypical gender roles, but the differences are much smaller than stereotypes would lead us to believe.

4. Some researchers have interpreted existing gender differences in terms of biology. Others believe social learning provides a better explanation.

5. Gender roles can affect sexual behavior in many ways, especially through such stereotypes as male aggressiveness and female passivity.

6. A major approach to the study of human sexual behavior has involved surveying individuals about the incidence and frequency of their sexual activities.

7. Masters and Johnson have studied the physiology of sexual response in men and women by making direct observations of sexual behavior in the laboratory. Their research shows that the physiological responses of sexuality occur in four phases: excitement, plateau, orgasm, and resolution. This process is termed the sexual response cycle.

8. Experimental work has shown that pornography leads to self-reported and physiologically measured arousal in both men and women. Aggressive pornography can lead men to more readily accept rape myths. It also leads to increased male aggression directed against women. Pornography can lead to short-term increases in sexual activities, but it increases only behaviors that are already part of the person's sexual pattern.

9. The lack of contraceptive use by teenagers is due to many factors, including a lack of accurate information regarding sex and contraception, negative emotions, and a lack of models of contraceptive behavior in the mass media.

10. Fetishism is attaching sexual significance to objects that are not necessarily sexual in nature. Rape is an act of aggression in which one person forces another nonconsenting person to engage in a sexual act.

11. Voyeurism is deriving sexual pleasure from secretly watching others undress or have sexual intercourse. Exhibitionism occurs when sexual gratification is derived from exposing one's genitals to unsuspecting and unwilling strangers. Transvestism is receiving sexual gratification by dressing in the clothing of the opposite gender.

12. Transsexualism is a variation involving a disturbance in gender identity. A transsexual is a person who is psychologically uncomfortable with his or her anatomical sex.

13. Homosexuality is having sexual attraction toward and engaging in sexual behavior with a member of the same gender. Studies of homosexuals have failed to find any significant psychological differences between them and heterosexuals.

14. Male sexual dysfunctions include erectile dysfunction, premature ejaculation, and retarded ejaculation.

Female dysfunctions include orgasmic dysfunction and vaginismus. The causes of these dysfunctions are typically (but not always) psychological in origin.

15. Prevention of sexual dysfunction can be aided by such factors as good communication between sexual partners and avoidance of goal setting.

16. In recent years, many positive changes have occurred in the attitudes toward and the treatment of rape victims. Research suggests, however, that many people still harbor negative attitudes and believe that rape victims desired or deserved rape.

— IMPORTANT TERMS AND CONCEPTS —

Gender
Primary Sexual Characteristics
Prenatal Sexual Differentiation
Gonads
Androgens
Testosterone
Estrogens
Secondary Sexual Characteristics
Gender Identity
Hermaphrodite
Transsexual
Gender Role
Masturbation
Orgasm

Petting
Coitus
Fellatio
Cunnilingus
Sexual-response Cycle
Excitement Phase
Plateau Phase
Orgasm Phase
Resolution Phase
Refractory Period
Multiple Orgasms
Pornography
Sexual Variations

Fetishism
Rape
Voyeurism
Exhibitionism
Transvestism
Homosexuality
Heterosexual
Sexual Dysfunctions
Erectile Dysfunction
Premature Ejaculation
Retarded Ejaculation
Orgasmic Dysfunction
Vaginismus

— SUGGESTIONS FOR FURTHER READING —

Byrne, D., & Fisher, W. A. (Eds.). (1983). *Adolescents, sex, and contraception*. Hillsdale, N. J.: Erlbaum. A book that deals with the problem of noncontraceptive teenage sexual behavior, the reasons for that behavior, and possible solutions to the problem.

Hunt, M. (1974). *Sexual behavior in the 1970s*. Chicago: Playboy Press. Reports on the findings of the sexual behavior survey sponsored by the Playboy Foundation.

Hyde, J. S. (1982). *Understanding human sexuality* (2nd ed.). New York: McGraw-Hill. A readable and comprehensive text covering all areas of human sexuality, including sexual anatomy and physiology, research, variations, and dysfunctions.

Masters, W. H., Johnson, V. E., & Kolodny, R. C. (1982). *Human sexuality*. Boston: Little, Brown. An excellent undergraduate text authored by pioneers in sex research and therapy.

Money, J., & Ehrhardt, A. A. (1972). *Man and woman, boy and girl*. Baltimore: Johns Hopkins University Press. A detailed account of the process of becoming male and female.

Pomeroy, W. B. (1972). *Dr. Kinsey and the Institute for Sex Research*. New York: Harper & Row. An interesting account of Kinsey, the person and the sex researcher, by one of his colleagues.

- CHAPTER 18 -

SOCIAL PSYCHOLOGY

SOCIAL PSYCHOLOGY

— CHAPTER OBJECTIVES —

To achieve the objectives of this chapter, you should be able to answer the questions listed here. You should also be able to define the important terms and concepts listed at the end of the chapter.

1. What are stereotypes? How do they affect our impressions of people?
2. How do we make attributions and form impressions? In what ways are our perceptions of others and ourselves sometimes biased?
3. What are attitudes? How are they formed? How do they change?
4. How do conformity, compliance, and obedience differ? What factors affect each?
5. What are the major theories and findings about attraction?
6. How can we explain prosocial behavior? How can we explain aggression? What determines helping in emergencies? Can aggression be controlled?

— CHAPTER OUTLINE —

Person Perception
Many processes are involved when people form judgments of others.

Appearance and Impressions
Attribution Process
Forming Impressions
Biases in Person Perception
Application: Attribution Therapy for College Students

Changing Attitudes and Influencing Behavior
Attitudes and behaviors can be influenced in many ways.

Attitude Formation and Change
Conformity
Compliance
Obedience
Application: Jumping on the Charity Bandwagon

Liking, Helping, and Hurting Others
Social psychologists study what brings people together and what drives them apart.

Attraction
Prosocial Behavior
Aggression
Application: Increasing Helpfulness and Reducing Aggression

On the Horizon: Television Violence and the Future

THIRTY-EIGHT WITNESSES

New York City, March 13, 1964: It is in the early morning hours in a middle-class area of Queens. Twenty-eight-year-old Kitty Genovese (see Figure 18–1) returns home from her job and parks her car. As she begins walking to her apartment, a man stalks her, grabs her, and stabs her with a knife. Genovese screams, "Oh, my God, he stabbed me! Please help me! Please help me!" Lights go on in some of the nearby apartments, and windows open. One man calls down, "Let that girl alone!" The attacker flees, Genovese struggles to her feet, lights go out, and no one calls the police. The assailant returns and again stabs Genovese, who is still trying to get to her apartment. She screams "I'm dying! I'm dying!" Once more, lights go on and windows are raised in many apartments. The assailant drives away. Still no one calls the police. The assailant returns a third time and makes his third, final, and fatal assault on Genovese. When police are finally summoned, they arrive within 2 minutes. The murder has taken place over a 35-minute period. As one police official puts it, "If we had been called when he first attacked, the woman might not be dead now." It is eventually determined that 38 people witnessed the murder of Kitty Genovese without calling the police (Rosenthal, 1964).

Figure 18–1.

Kitty Genovese. (NYT Pictures)

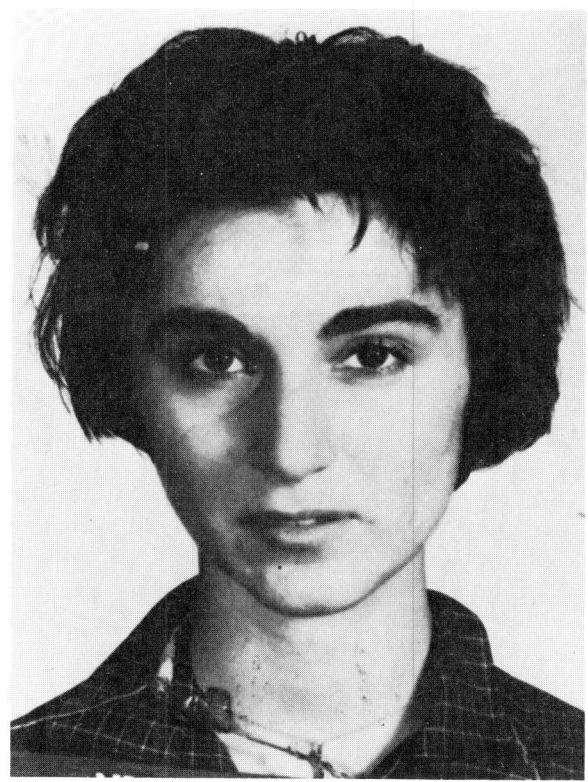

How could 38 respectable, law-abiding citizens watch a killer attack a woman three times without telephoning the police? Was the bystanders' failure to intervene due to apathy? Two social psychologists, Bibb Latané and John Darley, refused to believe it. Often, they pointed out, people do help others, even at great personal risk. Perhaps, they reasoned, the relationships among bystanders are what determine behavior in emergencies. Could it be, for instance, that bystanders are influenced by one another's presence? To find out, Latané and Darley conducted an interesting series of studies on bystander intervention. (Their research will be discussed later in the chapter.)

The inaction of the 38 witnesses to a woman's murder exemplifies the kind of phenomena that interest social psychologists. **Social psychology** is "the scientific field that studies the manner in which the behavior, feelings, or thoughts of one individual are influenced or determined by the behavior and/or characteristics of others" (Baron & Byrne, 1982, p. 6). In other words, social psychologists are interested in how we are influenced by those around us—by their affection, aggression, persuasion, or mere presence, to give but a few examples. As the definition states, we are also affected by the characteristics of others—for example, their skin color, physical attractiveness, or gender. Ultimately, even our thoughts or memories of others may influence us. That is, social influences can alter our behavior even when we are alone and thinking of others. To examine the social dimensions of behavior, let's begin with the question: How do we perceive others?

PERSON PERCEPTION

The process of making judgments about others—particularly their abilities, motives, interests, or traits—is **person perception**. Because we all have a need to make sense of the world around us, we usually do not stop at just noting what people look like or what they do. Typically, we observe some of their characteristics or actions and make judgments about what they are like in other ways. Thus, although the ideas we form about people may not always be accurate, the processes we go through to arrive at them seem to be predictable.

Consider for a moment your perceptions of someone you meet at a party. You will probably have an immediate impression of what the person is like, based on his or her appearance. Furthermore, if you are told that the person is a warm individual, you may decide that he or she has other traits as well, such as honesty and sincerity. From the person's actions, you may also infer intelligence or a liking for certain activities. In this section, we will examine some of the variables that affect such perceptions.

Appearance and Impressions

Many times, we think that we have only to look at others in order to know them. Physical appearance has a major impact on person perception, which is why billions of dollars are spent yearly on clothing, cosmetics, diets, and exercise. We are told to look our best if we want to get a job or otherwise impress the right person. In short, our judgments of others are closely tied to certain aspects of their appearance. Underlying many of these judgments are **stereotypes**—preconceived images of what most members of a particular group are like. These images are oversimplified, rigidly resistant to change, and often highly evaluative

(Oskamp, 1977). In stereotyping others, we tend to ignore their uniqueness. We assume that they are like all other members of the stereotyped group.

Stereotypes apply strongly to concepts of *physical attractiveness*. Researchers have found that physically attractive people are often evaluated more favorably than are unattractive people (Berscheid & Walster, 1974). This holds true even with nursery-school children, who believe that unattractive children aggress more than do those who are attractive. Adults also view unattractive children less favorably and consider their transgressions more serious than those of attractive children (Dion, 1972). Furthermore, attractive children are viewed as being more intelligent than unattractive children even when all the report cards are identical (cf. Berscheid & Walster, 1974).

Similar patterns hold for adults. Middlebrook (1980) summarizes the evidence this way: Attractive middle-age adults are perceived as being more pleasant, more socially at ease, of a higher occupational status, and higher in self-esteem than unattractive adults. Likewise, attractive college students are perceived as being more sensitive, poised, kind, sociable, and modest than unattractive students. They are expected to be more successful in finding good jobs, marrying well, and generally leading happy and fulfilling lives.

These findings suggest a what-is-beautiful-is-good stereotype (Dion, Berscheid, & Walster, 1972). In general, we associate good things with attractive people. It should not be surprising, then, that attractive people are treated in more positive ways than unattractive people in many situations. In one study, an essay was graded higher when it was said to have been written by an attractive person than when it was supposed to have been written by an unattractive person (Anderson & Nida, 1978). Attractive people are also often given more help than are unattractive people (Benson, Karabenick, & Lerner, 1976; Wilson, 1978), and they are responded to more honestly (Sroufe, Chaikin, Cook, & Freeman, 1977).

Surprisingly, physical attractiveness can lead to some negative perceptions as well. In a simulated (mock) trial, an unattractive defendant was judged more harshly than an attractive defendant when the crime was burglary (Sigall & Ostrove, 1975). When the crime was swindling, however, the attractive defendant was judged more harshly, presumably because she was seen as having used her beauty to her advantage. At times, attractive people may also be perceived as being vain and egotistical (Dermer & Thiel, 1975). Perhaps what is beautiful is not always good. Most of the evidence, however, points to more favorable perceptions of attractive people and more favorable treatment of them.

The Self-Fulfilling Nature of Stereotypes

Up to this point, we have side-stepped a basic question: Are stereotypes always wrong? Do physically attractive and unattractive people, for example, differ only in their beauty? The answers to these questions may surprise you. Let's have a look.

It is easy to think that once we get to know people, our stereotyped views of them, if wrong, will be easily dismissed. However, rather than falling away, stereotypes have a way of getting reinforced. We cling to our stereotypes, or at least to the kernel of truth sometimes found in them. Let's consider again the physical attractiveness stereotype. In one experiment, men anticipated having a telephone conversation with a woman they had seen in a photograph. When the woman in the photo was attractive, the men assumed that she would be humorous, poised, and socially adept. The unattractive woman, they thought, would be unsociable, awkward, serious, and socially inept. When the men were allowed to talk with the women (without actually seeing them), their behavior reflected these stereotypes. Conversing with the woman who was supposed to be attractive, the men behaved with warmth, humor, animation, and friendliness. Conversing with the supposedly unattractive woman, they were cold, reserved, and uninteresting. Furthermore, the men's behavior altered the women's behavior so that it matched the stereotypes. The women who were thought to be attractive behaved in a friendly, likable, and sociable manner. The women who were perceived as being unattractive were cool and distant (Snyder, 1982). The same thing happened when women anticipated conversing with attractive versus unattractive men (Snyder, 1982).

By behaving in accordance with our stereotypes, we produce behavioral confirmation of them (see Skrypnek & Snyder, 1982). This outcome is known as a **self-fulfilling prophecy** (see Figure 18–2). In it, persons act in accordance with the treatment they get from others, so that expected behavior actually occurs (e.g., Rosenthal & Jacobson, 1968). This is why it is difficult to shed preconceptions and stereotypes and why beauty and good traits seem to go together (Snyder, 1982). If

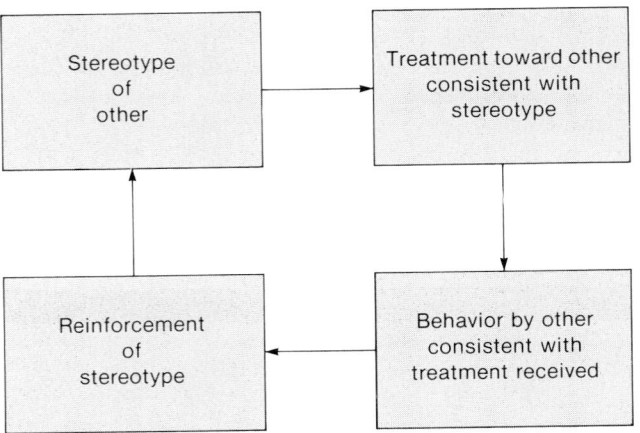

Figure 18–2.
The self-fulfilling prophecy in action. The stereotype leads one to behave in certain ways toward the stereotyped individuals. The stereotyped individuals then behave as expected in response. This in turn confirms and reinforces the original stereotype, and the process perpetuates itself.

you believe someone is friendly, sociable, and well-adjusted, the person may very well prove you right.

Although physical attractiveness and variables such as hair color, skin color, and weight all affect our impressions of others, appearance is not the only important factor. We also form impressions on the basis of others' behavior.

Attribution Process

Observing the actions of others is probably the most crucial basis for understanding what they are like. Through such observation, we infer the causes of their behavior as well as their traits, motives, and intentions. This process is known as **attribution** (Heider, 1958; Jones & Davis, 1965; Kelley, 1967, 1973). When we attribute a person's actions to some underlying stable characteristic, it allows us to understand or know the person and to predict future behavior. One of our basic goals as we make attributions is finding evidence of stable internal characteristics in the other person. How do we discover such characteristics? Consider the following question: Are you attending the college that you think is the best for you (an internal reason) or the one your parents required you to attend (an external reason)? When a given behavior is subject to strong external forces, it is difficult or impossible to infer any

personal characteristics from it. When a behavior is internally caused, however, we can gain some knowledge about what the person is really like. If you freely chose the college you are now attending, it tells us something about you.

Searching for the Internal Causes of Others' Behavior

According to Jones and Davis (1965), several key factors affect our search for internal causes. In their view, a behavior can have many effects, or consequences. As a result, the task of the perceiver is to determine which effects the actor (the person behaving) intended to create (Schneider, 1976). Such intentions help the perceiver infer something about the stable disposition or characteristics of the actor.

One important variable in this process is the social desirability of a behavior's effects. Jones and Davis assume that people typically intend their actions to have desirable effects (cf. Reeder, Henderson, & Sullivan, 1982). Consequently, behavior that has socially desirable effects reveals little about a person. For example, if you were to see someone lend a friend some class notes, you might not be especially likely to label that person as kind or altruistic (see Schneider, Hastorf, & Ellsworth, 1979). Lending notes to a friend, after all, is an expected, normal behavior. If the same person refused to lend notes to a friend, however, you might consider the person unkind or stingy. The rule seems to be that the more unusual someone's behavior, the more confident we are in attributing some characteristic to the person (Schneider, 1976). Behavior that is unpopular or contrary to what the average person does is the most revealing about what the person is like.

There is more to making attributions than simply noticing deviations from the norm. For example, you may be more confident in labeling someone as generous if the person donates $1,000 to a charity rather than $5. But a question remains: Why did the person donate the $1,000? Was it an effort to be helpful? To gain approval? To gain publicity? The perceiver's job is to determine the intended outcome.

According to Jones and Davis, a perceiver can best infer something about a person by searching for *noncommon effects*—effects or outcomes unique to the action taken. Such effects are assumed to be intended and therefore to provide information about the person. Common and noncommon effects of college choice are shown in Table 18–1 (see also Schneider,

Table 18–1.

Characteristics of various hypothetical colleges. When we know that someone has chosen one college over another, we can more confidently make an internal attribution about the person the fewer the noncommon effects or outcomes associated with the schools. For example, the only noncommon effect of choosing College A over College X is going to college in rural setting. Knowing this, we could confidently say that a person making such a choice is an outdoor person. (Adapted from Schneider, Hastorf, & Ellsworth, 1979, p. 50.)

COLLEGE A	COLLEGE B	COLLEGE C
Rural setting Coeducational Small school Private	Small town All-female Small school Private	Large city Coeducational Small school Public
COLLEGE A	**COLLEGE X**	**COLLEGE Y**
Rural setting Coeducational Small school Private	Large city Coeducational Small school Private	Small city Coeducational Small school Private

Hastorf, & Ellsworth, 1979). Imagine that someone has just decided which college to attend. As you can see from the table, there are a number of effects of attending each college. Let's say that the person chooses College A over College B and College C. An element common to all three colleges is their small size, so the perceiver can reasonably rule that out as a basis for the choice. In terms of noncommon effects, College A could be chosen over College C because of College A's rural environment or because it is a private school. It could also be chosen over College B for several different reasons. The perceiver can infer some information about the chooser, but there is still ambiguity. If the person chooses College A over College X or College Y, however, the perceiver can be more confident in attributing the decision to College A's rural environment. And this knowledge will presumably make it easier for the perceiver to attribute some characteristic to the person, such as that she is an outdoor person. The fewer the noncommon effects of a chosen behavior, the more confidently we make attributions about the person (Schneider, Hastorf, & Ellsworth, 1979).

— Distinguishing Between Internal and External Causes

Thus far, we have examined only internal attributions. Kelley's (1967, 1973) approach deals with **causal attri-**

bution—attribution in which one determines whether an actor's behavior is internally or externally caused. As stated earlier, attributing behavior to internal causes allows us to make inferences about the person's unique characteristics. Behavior attributed to external causes is not informative in this regard. Consequently, one of our tasks as perceivers is to determine whether a given act is internally or externally caused.

Suppose your friend Dave likes a particular John Denver song. Why does he like it? Is it because of some internal characteristic (he's a John Denver fan), or is it because of something about the song itself (it has a very catchy tune)? To make internal and external attributions, Kelley suggests that we use three types of information about behavior: consistency, distinctiveness, and consensus. **Consistency** refers to how stable or general the person's behavior is in time, modality, and context. Does Dave always like this song, no matter when he hears it, how he hears it, and where he hears it? **Distinctiveness** refers to whether the same behavior (liking in this instance) occurs in response to other similar stimuli as well or only this one particular stimulus. Does Dave like only this John Denver song or all John Denver songs? **Consensus** refers to how others behave in the same situation—whether only the person in question behaves in a particular way or whether other people do as well. Do other people besides Dave, for example, also like this John Denver song? To the extent that consistency is high

(Dave likes the song regardless of when, how, or where he hears it), distinctiveness is low (Dave likes all John Denver songs he hears), and consensus is low (no one else likes this John Denver song), we would be confident in attributing an internal cause for Dave's liking of the song—that he is a John Denver fan. If, on the other hand, consistency, distinctiveness, and consensus are all high, an external causal attribution would be likely. Kelley's theory is summarized in Figure 18–3. A number of researchers (e.g., Miron Zuckerman, 1978) suggest that we do indeed consider consistency, consensus, and distinctiveness when we attempt to determine the causes of others' behavior.

Forming Impressions

So far, we have seen some ways in which we gain information about others. How we take separate bits of information and combine them into a coherent picture

Figure 18–3.

A summary of Kelley's theory of causal attribution. As indicated, we usually attribute someone's behavior to external causes under conditions of high consensus, high consistency, and high distinctiveness. Conditions of low consensus, high consistency, and low distinctiveness usually lead to attributions of internal causality. (From Baron & Byrne, 1981, p. 62.)

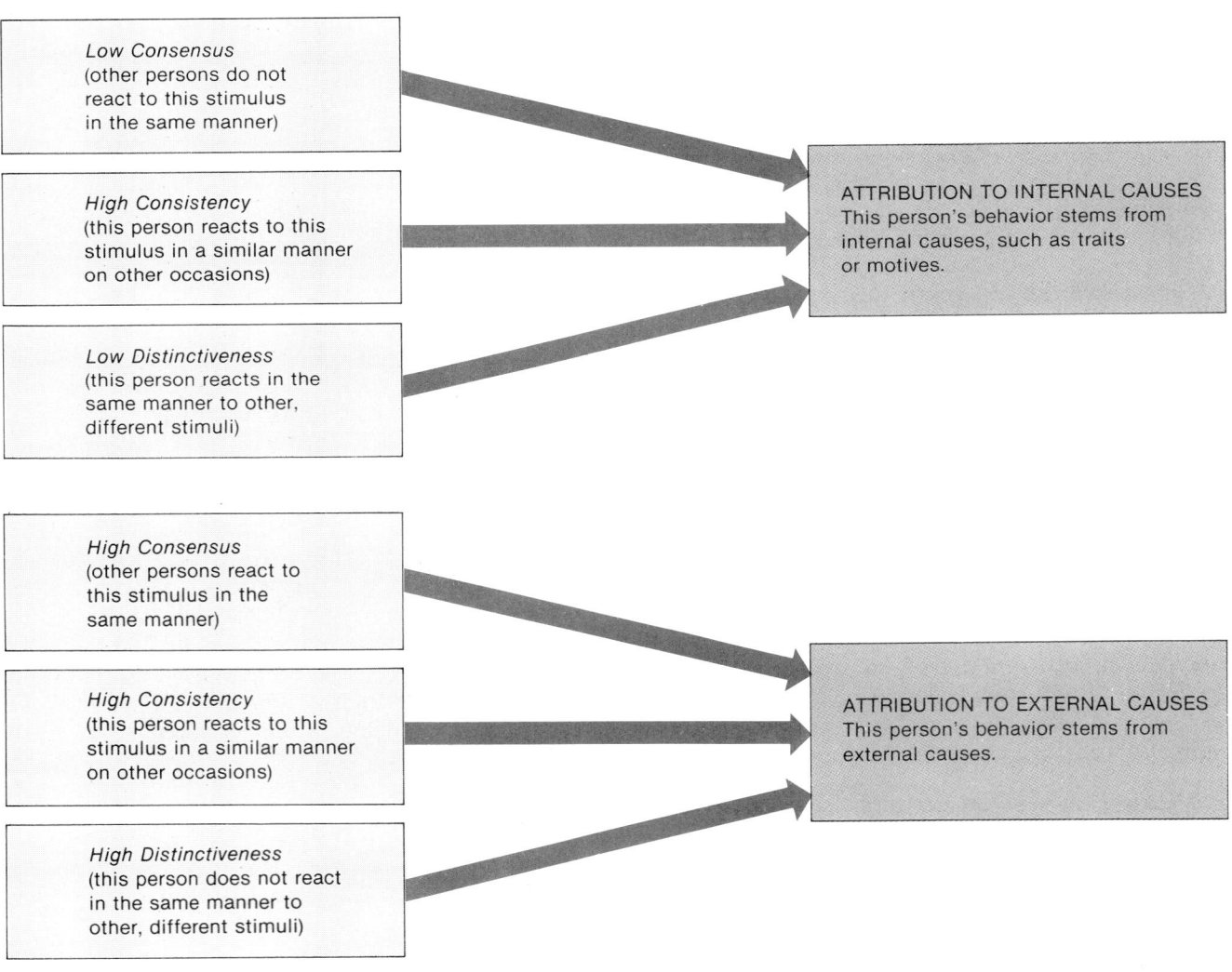

of a person is known as **impression formation.** Let's examine some issues relevant to this process.

— First Impressions

You are undoubtedly aware that first impressions can have a lasting effect. Most people are careful to look the right way, act the right way, and say the right things when first meeting someone important to them. You have probably also observed how your own first impressions affect later interpretations of others' behavior (Middlebrook, 1980). In an early study, Asch (1946, 1952) found that the order in which traits are presented to subjects affects the impressions the subjects form of a person. Specifically, being told that a person was intelligent, industrious, impulsive, critical, stubborn, and envious led to a more favorable impression than when the order of the traits was reversed. The first information presented had the greatest impact on the impression—a phenomenon commonly referred to as the *primacy effect* (which should be distinguished from the primacy effect discussed in chapter 7). When positive information (intelligent, industrious) was presented first, the person was generally seen as an able person with some shortcomings. With the negative information first, the person was seen as a problem.

According to Asch, the primacy effect occurs because early information changes the meaning of later information. If the early information is positive, the later information is viewed positively. For example, if you first learn that someone is intelligent and industrious, you may later interpret the person's being critical in a warm, constructive sense. If you begin with a negative impression (envious, stubborn), you may interpret the word *critical* as cold and ruthless.

Other explanations for the primacy effect have also been offered. It may be that once you have formed a particular impression, later contradictory information is discounted or tuned out (e.g., Anderson & Jacobson, 1965). Other evidence suggests that less attention is paid to later information after an initial impression is formed (Stewart, 1965). It is likely that all of these explanations of the primacy effect have some validity. The discounting hypothesis, however, seems to have the least supportive evidence (Schneider, Hastorf, & Ellsworth, 1979).

— Combining Information in Forming Impressions

Although the possibilities for combining information about others to form unified impressions are almost limitless, considerable research suggests that we use a special type of averaging described by the **weighted-average model** (Anderson, 1974). The model indicates that our final impression of someone is a weighted average of all the available information about the person. That is, we average the information but we put more weight, or emphasis, on some items of information than others.

We have already seen one way in which information can be weighted—the primacy effect. It is also true that each of the following kinds of information is more heavily weighted (cf. Middlebrook, 1980): highly negative traits, information from highly credible people, and information that is particularly relevant to the judgment being made, such as whether to hire someone for a job.

Biases in Person Perception

Coming to know others is a subjective process. We often think we know what a person is really like; however, it is likely that many of our impressions are faulty. This is due to the many biases inherent in person perception—for example, the physical-attractiveness stereotype. We also hold stereotypes about certain personality traits being correlated with other personality traits. This belief about traits tending to occur together is referred to as **implicit personality theory.** If we think of someone as warm, we may also assume that the person is generous. We tend to see good traits as going with other good traits and bad traits with other bad traits—a phenomenon referred to as the **halo effect.** Thus, once we form an initial impression, we assume that the person has other characteristics consistent with that impression.

A striking example of the halo effect can be seen in a study by Nisbett and Wilson (1977). Subjects watched one of two videotaped interviews with an instructor. In one tape, the instructor behaved in a warm and friendly manner; in the other, he was cold and distant. The halo effect clearly occurred for the subjects. Those who saw the cold instructor not only didn't like him, they also rated his appearance, mannerisms, and accent as being irritating; those who saw the warm instructor liked him and rated the same characteristics as being appealing. Halo effects can subtly affect decisions about people in important practical ways—for example, in job settings. Because we like someone, we may decide that the person also has the abilities or traits required for a particular job, even if someone we dislike is actually more qualified (Baron & Byrne, 1981).

Other errors in person perception also exist. We will now turn our attention to several of them. As we will see, biases can affect our perceptions of ourselves as well as others.

— Actor-Observer Difference

Interestingly, how you, the actor, explain your own behavior may differ from how an observer explains it. There is a tendency to see one's own behavior as being due to situational or external factors and others' behavior as being due to personal characteristics (Jones & Nisbett, 1971). This is known as the **actor-observer difference.** For example, a teacher may attribute a student's poor performance to laziness, a lack of intelligence, or some other internal characteristic. The student, on the other hand, may attribute the poor performance to a series of unfortunate circumstances—too many other exams to study for, outside interruptions that interfered with studying, and so on. Such actor-observer differences have been demonstrated in a number of studies (Watson, 1982).

To account for the phenomenon, it has been suggested that actors and observers have different types of information available to them (Jones & Nisbett, 1971). Actors are well aware of their past history and emotional states and are in a much better position to assess how their behavior has been influenced by the situation. Observers, in contrast, usually lack such information and are able to observe only the behavior. They may not see how the environment or situation has affected that behavior, and they may therefore attribute the behavior to internal causes. Actors and observers may also have a different focus of attention. Actors cannot directly observe their own behavior, so they tend to focus on the situational factors causing it. Observers quite naturally tend to focus on the actor's behavior and overlook situational determinants. In general, both

informational and attentional interpretations of actor-observer differences seem valid (Watson, 1982).

A recent study suggests that the actor-observer bias is alive and well in prison as well as in other settings (Saulnier & Perlman, 1981). In this study, inmates and officials at a penitentiary rated the causes of 60 prisoners' offenses. As expected, the staff made significantly more internal attributions (by saying, for example, that the offenses were due to personality or habits) than did the inmates. Attributing a criminal's behavior to lasting internal causes may heighten the feeling of hostility between inmates and staff, influence parole decisions, and decrease efforts to provide therapy for individual inmates (Saulnier & Perlman, 1981). In prisons, the actor-observer bias clearly has much practical significance.

— Self-Serving Bias

Although the actor-observer difference suggests that we emphasize situational factors in explaining our behavior, this is actually more true for our failures than for our successes. We ascribe responsibility for our negative outcomes to external factors, but we tend to take credit for our positive outcomes—a tendency known as the **self-serving bias.** Students, for example, may be willing to accept credit for their good grades (I worked hard; my ability allowed me to do well) but may ascribe low grades to a diverse range of external factors, including poor instructors and uncooperative roommates. Similarly, athletes may attribute their wins to effort or skill and their losses to bad luck or poor officiating (e.g., Lau & Russell, 1980).

The common interpretation of the self-serving bias is that it allows us to build and maintain a positive self-image. The validity of such an interpretation is supported by the finding that self-serving attributions occur even when one's test performance, evaluations, and attributions are kept private, with no public knowledge of them at all (Greenberg, Pyszczynski, & Solomon, 1982).

— APPLICATION —
ATTRIBUTION THERAPY FOR COLLEGE STUDENTS

People try to explain the behavior not only of others but of themselves. And as with other attributions, self-

attributions can be internal (behavior caused by me) or external (behavior caused by some outside factor).

In addition, behavior can be attributed to stable causes (those that are permanent and unchangeable) or to unstable causes (those that are temporary and likely to change).

The importance of the latter distinction is evident in a recent study by Wilson and Linville (1982). The researchers reasoned that college freshmen who are concerned about their academic performance may be particularly susceptible to damaging attributions regarding the stability, or permanence, of their problems. Wilson and Linville suggest that most freshmen begin college wondering if they will be able to do the work. When academic problems first arise, the students may see them as confirmation that they are unable to succeed at college. Such attributions cause additional anxiety, which makes studying more difficult. If the cycle continues, it can result in declining performance and sometimes dropping out of school.

With such problems, attribution therapy may be used to convince freshmen that their difficulties are due to unstable, nonpermanent factors. Wilson and Linville gave freshmen information indicating that, on the average, college students improve their grades from the freshman to the upperclass years. They also showed the students videotaped interviews of upperclassmen stating that their grade-point averages had, in fact, improved since their freshman year.

The effect of the therapy was striking. Those who received it were less likely than other students to leave college by the end of the sophomore year, had a greater increase than others in grade-point averages a year later, and performed better than others on sample items from the Graduate Record Exam. Thus, through an inexpensive attributional procedure, students concerned about academic performance were helped. Clearly, similar videotaped interviews with upperclassmen could be shown as part of a freshman advising program or perhaps at freshman orientations (Wilson & Linville, 1982). They would be a small price to pay for academic improvement and a reduction in dropouts.

— CHANGING ATTITUDES AND INFLUENCING BEHAVIOR —

Attitude Formation and Change

Think about the many attitudes you hold. Perhaps you believe that abortion is wrong. Maybe you oppose war. Or maybe you are in favor of the women's liberation movement. An **attitude** is a relatively enduring predisposition to feel, think, and respond in particular ways toward some object, person, group, or issue (Oskamp, 1977). Attitudes are often thought of as having three components. The *affective component* refers to emotions or feelings toward the attitude object. For example, you may say, "I do not like war." The *cognitive component* refers to thoughts or beliefs about the attitude object. You might think, for example, that war is inhumane. The *behavioral component* refers to responses or behavior toward the attitude object. You might decide not to go to war even if you are drafted.

In most situations, feelings, thoughts, and actions are highly interrelated. In fact, their consistency is what usually results in our inferring that someone holds a particular attitude. However, in practice, attitudes are typically measured by assessing what the person *believes* about some attitude object or how the person *feels* about it (e.g., good or bad). It is then assumed, at least under most circumstances, that this attitude (belief or feeling) will lead to behavior consistent with it. Research has shown, in fact, that attitudes can serve as fairly accurate predictors of behavior (Petty & Cacioppo, 1981). According to one model of the attitude-behavior relation (Fazio, Powell, & Herr, 1983), our attitudes color our perceptions of the people, events, and issues around us. Thus, we perceive these attitude objects in a manner consistent with the way we feel about them. These selective and biased perceptions then lead to behavior that is consistent with the attitude.

Of course, inconsistencies between our attitudes and behaviors do sometimes occur. In some cases, they may be due to a weak association between the attitude object and some evaluation of it (Fazio, Powell, & Herr, 1983). In other words, our attitude may simply be a very weak one. In other cases, we may display an inconsistency when we have little vested interest in the situation (Sivacek & Crano, 1982). For example, we may be in favor of some policy but not speak out in favor of it or vote for it if it will not affect us personally. In yet other situations, we may believe that we are forced to behave in a manner inconsistent with our feelings or beliefs. For example, a racially prejudiced restaurant owner might serve members of that race to avoid legal problems. In most situations, however, how we evaluate or think about some attitude object is highly consistent with how we act toward it.

— The Process of Learning Attitudes

Many theorists have argued that attitudes are learned just like behaviors are. We need only draw on the learning principles discussed in chapter 6 to see how this might be true.

Recall the process of *classical conditioning.* A previously neutral stimulus is associated with a stimulus that already elicits a response, and it comes to elicit the same response. This process can also produce attitudes. By repeatedly associating an attitude object with some stimulus that elicits positive or negative feelings, we will cause the attitude object to elicit the positive or negative feelings (Staats, 1968).

Both children and adults probably learn many attitudes through classical conditioning. A child may hear a parent utter negative words about minority-group members. Even though the child was initially neutral toward minority-group members, associating them with words that elicit negative feelings results in the minority-group members also eliciting negative feelings. The result, then, is prejudice learned through classical conditioning (Baron & Byrne, 1977).

Instrumental, or *operant, conditioning* also underlies attitude formation. The idea here is that we may hold a particular attitude because we have been rewarded for holding it (Insko & Melson, 1969). A positive attitude toward smoking marijuana, for instance, might be reinforced by approval from friends and by direct enjoyment of the experience itself. Or consider how parents continuously reinforce their children for holding what they believe to be the proper attitudes.

Finally, chapter 6 also dealt with the process of *observational learning.* Many of our attitudes may derive simply from our observation of what others say and do. Although racial bigotry may be due in part to classical conditioning, it may also be learned in part through observation of prejudiced behavior (Baron & Byrne, 1981). In fact, with respect to a given attitude such as prejudice, it is likely that all three of the processes just discussed operate at one time or another.

— Attitude Change Through Persuasion

Now that we have seen some ways in which attitudes are formed, we will examine how they can be changed by persuasive communication from parents, peers, the mass media, and so on. Clearly, some persuasive attempts are more successful than others. Indeed, a number of factors have been found to influence attitude change brought about by persuasive communication. We will examine some factors relevant to the source of the communication (who says it), the message or communication itself (what is said), and the audience or recipient of the message (who hears it).

The source. We are not equally persuaded by all people. For example, we know that the greater the credibility of the source, the greater the attitude change produced. **Credibility** refers to how believable the source is. The more of an expert and the more trustworthy the source is believed to be, the greater the perceived credibility. Research has shown that experts speaking on topics relevant to their expertise produce more attitude change than do low-expertise communicators (Hovland & Weiss, 1952; Aronson, Turner, & Carlsmith, 1963). A noted lung surgeon will probably be more effective in convincing you that smoking is bad than will a plumber because you will value the surgeon's message more highly (Mills & Harvey, 1972). Similarly, an expert on sleep will be more effective than a classical-music authority in persuading you that people need only 4 hours of sleep (Maddux & Rogers, 1980).

Low-credibility sources become more effective when they are perceived to be arguing against their own best interests (Walster, Aronson, & Abrahams, 1966). This leads them to be seen as more trustworthy, sincere, and credible. A convicted criminal arguing for greater police protection can produce more attitude change than one arguing for less police protection.

Attractiveness and similarity are also important characteristics. People generally are more easily persuaded by sources they perceive as being attractive and similar to themselves than by those who are unattractive or unlike them (Mills & Aronson, 1965; Brock, 1965).

The message. Even if the communicator is highly credible, the message itself must be effective or attitude change is unlikely. How should the communicator present the message? One relevant issue involves the use of one-sided versus two-sided arguments. *One-*

sided arguments present only the view that the communicator wants the audience to adopt; *two-sided arguments* present competing positions as well. Which is better depends on the initial view of the audience (Baron & Byrne, 1982). If the audience is initially favorable to the communicator's position, a one-sided argument is better. The audience is inclined to agree with the source, and presenting both sides only confuses the issue. If the audience is initially unfavorable to the position advocated, a two-sided argument is better, because it increases the source's credibility. The source in this case has apparently carefully weighed both sides of the issue and appears to be less biased (Baron & Byrne, 1982).

Another message factor that is commonly encountered in persuasion is fear. Fear-inducing advertisements similar to the one shown in Figure 18–4 are commonly used by a variety of organizations in an attempt to change people's attitudes toward such issues as smoking, drinking, and seat-belt use. Research on fear appeal suggests that such messages can be effective, but only when the appeal is very strong and the recipients believe that the dangers described are likely to occur and that the recommended actions will, in fact, prove effective (Baron & Byrne, 1982).

Finally, persuasion seems to be greatest when the arguments presented in favor of an issue are strong rather than weak (Cacioppo, Petty, & Morris, 1983). In any attitude-change effort, the strength of the message is a critical component.

The audience. The source may be credible and the message effective, but the message must still be accepted by the audience before attitude change can occur. What are some of the audience characteristics that might affect the relative ease or difficulty of persuasion?

One commonly held belief is that women are more easily persuaded than men. Years of social-psychological research in the laboratory have tended to support the belief, but as Eagly (1983) points out, gender differences in these studies have generally been small. What about differences in real-life settings? Eagly suggests that in work settings, families, and various task-oriented groups, men generally have higher status and more power than women. Because of this common difference in status and power, Eagly believes that large gender differences in influenceability should and do exist. Men often wield the influence; women often succumb to it. Social roles, then, are an important consid-

Horrible isn't it?

AMERICAN CANCER SOCIETY

Figure 18–4.
Do fear-inducing ads like this one affect your attitudes?

eration in Eagly's analysis. To the extent that status differences between men and women do not exist in a given situation, we will expect gender differences in persuasibility also not to exist.

Our knowledge with respect to an issue also affects how susceptible we are to a persuasive appeal. If we are relatively uninformed about the issue and therefore less confident in our attitude, we are more likely to be persuaded than if we are knowledgeable and confident. Also, if we are highly committed to an attitude or if we have made a public pronouncement of it, we are resistant to attitude change (Freedman, Sears, & Carlsmith, 1981).

Earlier we noted that the strength of the persuasive arguments greatly affects the degree of attitude change obtained. The quality of the arguments, however, has a bigger impact on persuasion for some people than others. More specifically, Cacioppo, Petty, and Morris (1983) found that the quality of arguments had an especially strong influence on those individuals who have a high rather than low *need for cognition*. These individuals more carefully scrutinize persuasive messages and tend to engage in and enjoy effortful analytic activity. In other words, some people, more than others, enjoy thinking about, analyzing, and evaluating the persuasive appeals they encounter daily. Because of this, the persuasion-enhancing effect of strong arguments and the persuasion-inhibiting effect of weak arguments will be particularly strong for these individuals. Figure 18–5 illustrates these effects with respect to subjects' attitudes toward a recommendation that student tuition be increased.

Finally, personality factors play some role in attitude change. For instance, those low in self-esteem tend to be more easily persuaded than those high in self-esteem, at least with respect to simple messages (Zellner, 1970). Presumably, individuals with low self-esteem value their opinions less highly and so are more willing to be influenced by others.

— Attitude Change Through Dissonance Reduction

Attitudes are changed not only by persuasion but also by our own behavior that is inconsistent with our attitudes. Such **attitude-discrepant behavior** is common. We may abhor violence but fight; we may dislike

Figure 18–5.
Attitudes following a persuasive communication depend on the quality of the arguments as well as a person's need for cognition. (From Cacioppo, Petty, & Morris, 1983, p. 814.)

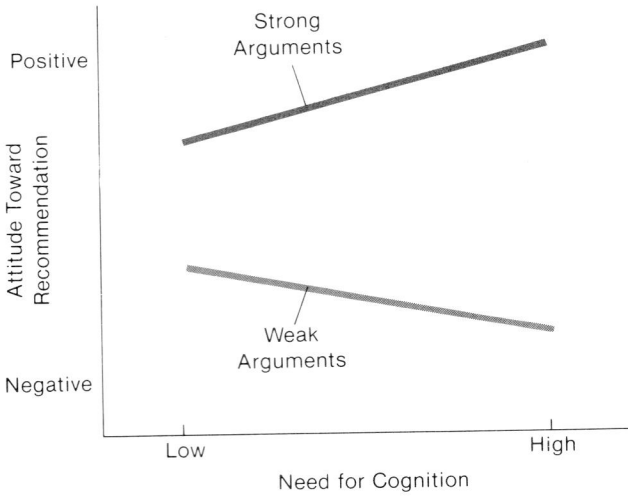

some people but be nice to them; we may believe that an advanced degree is not helpful but enroll in graduate school. When such inconsistencies occur, our attitudes tend to become consistent with our behavior.

The theory of cognitive dissonance (Festinger, 1957) helps us understand such attitude change. **Cognitive dissonance** is an unpleasant emotional state experienced when an inconsistency occurs between one's attitudes or between one's attitude and behavior. Festinger assumes that people find such inconsistencies aversive and that they are motivated to reduce them. These assumptions have received empirical support (e.g., Zanna, Higgins, & Taves, 1976; Higgins, Rhodewalt, & Zanna, 1979).

Dissonance reduction can occur in several ways. First, the importance of the dissonant or inconsistent cognitions (thoughts) may be reduced. Let's say you just bought a new car that you know is uncomfortable. Buying the car is inconsistent with knowing that it is uncomfortable. You might reduce the resulting dissonance by deciding that comfort really is not very important. You might also add consonant or consistent cognitions. You could think of good features of the car that would be consistent with buying it. Finally, you could change one of the dissonant thoughts. Many times, this means changing the attitude involved, since changing the behavior is impossible and denying that it occurred is difficult. Thus, you might decide that the car is comfortable afterall. Or, to use earlier examples, you might come to defend war if you fight in one and you might come to like those you once disliked if you behave in a pleasant manner toward them.

The simple theme here is that when we say or do something inconsistent with our attitude, dissonance results, and we try to reduce it. However, dissonance will not always be aroused whenever such inconsistencies occur. If we have good reasons, or *sufficient justification,* for behaving the way we did, little or no dissonance will be aroused. But the less justification we have for engaging in some attitude-discrepant behavior, the more dissonance we experience and the more attitude change may result from our behavior. One type of justification that may be effective in inducing us to engage in attitude-discrepant behavior is a reward. Whether the reward for such behavior is money, praise, or anything else, dissonance theory predicts that the greater the reward, the greater the justification for our behavior and the less dissonance and attitude change are generated (see Figure 18–6).

In a classic experiment testing the effects of justification, Festinger and Carlsmith (1959) gave subjects $1

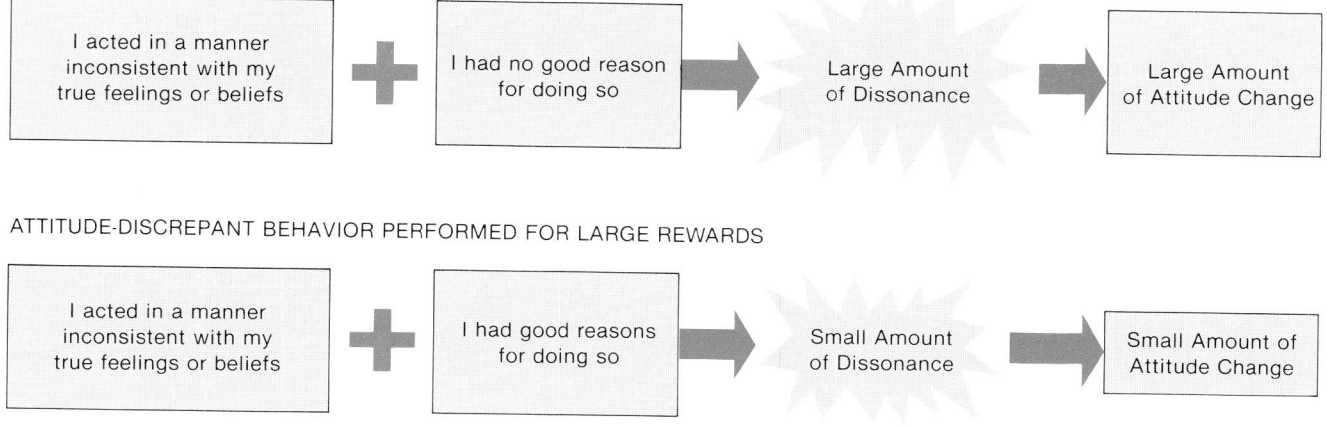

ATTITUDE-DISCREPANT BEHAVIOR PERFORMED FOR SMALL REWARDS

I acted in a manner inconsistent with my true feelings or beliefs + I had no good reason for doing so → Large Amount of Dissonance → Large Amount of Attitude Change

ATTITUDE-DISCREPANT BEHAVIOR PERFORMED FOR LARGE REWARDS

I acted in a manner inconsistent with my true feelings or beliefs + I had good reasons for doing so → Small Amount of Dissonance → Small Amount of Attitude Change

Figure 18–6.
Dissonance theory predicts that when individuals choose to engage in attitude-discrepant behavior for relatively small rewards, they will show greater attitude change than when they engage in such behavior for relatively large rewards. (From Baron & Byrne, 1981, p. 123.)

or $20 to inform another subject that the boring task in the experiment that they had just completed was actually interesting and enjoyable. As predicted by dissonance theory, the $1 subjects later reported greater liking for the task and the experiment than did the $20 subjects. The latter had sufficient justification for their behavior of telling an obvious lie and thus experienced no dissonance. The $1 subjects had little justification for telling the lie. Therefore, they experienced dissonance and reduced it by altering their attitude toward the task.

Another important justification that can reduce dissonance is a lack of choice in the behavior (Cooper & Mackie, 1983; Linder, Cooper, & Jones, 1967). Someone who detests violence but nevertheless freely chooses to join the army will experience a high level of dissonance; someone who detests violence and is drafted into the army will experience little or no dissonance. Finally, attitude-discrepant behavior results in dissonance only when the behavior leads to aversive consequences (as in the case of lying to someone) and when the aversive consequences could have been foreseen at the time the decision was made to behave in this manner (Worchel & Cooper, 1983).

Conformity

Not only attitudes are influenced by others. So is behavior—overt actions and words. Much of our behavior represents an attempt to act in accordance with **social norms**—explicit and implicit rules within a group regarding what kind of behavior is appropriate. When our behavior is consistent with these norms and like that of others in the group, we display **conformity.** Conformity occurs through the influence of others, in that others in our group define for us what is right or wrong. How we dress, how we eat, how we behave in a restaurant or church or at a movie—in effect, many of the things we do—are based on social norms. The kind of influence exerted by social norms is indirect and subtle; typically, we simply abide by unspoken rules. We usually do not even think too much about norms until someone violates them. We may be appalled at rude table manners or people's unwillingness to wait their turn in a line. Someone who does not conform to the group norms is often pressured to conform or be rejected.

— When Do We Conform?

Conformity was studied in experiments by Asch (1951, 1956), who showed that a group can exert great pressure on an individual to conform. The question Asch asked was this: Will an individual conform to the judgment of a group when the group has unanimously and incorrectly agreed on that judgment? To study this, Asch had seven to nine students participate in an experiment purportedly on visual discrimination. Only one of these students, however, was a real subject. The others (confederates) had been told by the experimenter how to respond. The students' task was to match the length of a standard line with one of three comparison lines, as illustrated in Figure 18–7. One of the three comparison lines was the same length as the standard line; the other two were not.

For each comparison, all but one of the confederates responded before the subject did. Although nothing unusual happened in 6 trials, 12 other trials presented the real subject with an interesting problem. All the confederates gave incorrect responses, as instructed by the experimenter. When it was the real subject's turn, he could conform to the group's unanimous judgment or stand alone and give the correct response (see Figure 18–8). For comparison purposes, control group subjects were tested alone and were asked to make the same judgments.

Apparently, correct judgments were not hard to make, since almost all of the control-group subjects made no errors in matching the lines. Of the experimental subjects, three-fourths of them conformed to the group's incorrect judgment on at least one trial. Indeed, the power of a majority, even when incorrect, can be great. However, Asch (1956) found that this kind of conformity is reduced when subjects can write down their responses in private rather than announce them to others. This finding suggests that at least some subjects were exhibiting *public compliance;* they doubted the group's judgment but went along to avoid appearing different. Such compliance contrasts with the *private acceptance* displayed by someone who actually changes, sincerely adopting the beliefs and behaviors of the others in the group (Wheeler, Deci, Reis, & Zuckerman, 1978).

Variations on Asch's basic procedure have been shown to affect the conformity rate. For example, if one of the confederates gives the correct responses, conformity to the incorrect majority is reduced (Morris & Miller, 1975). Research has also shown that the more

Figure 18–7.
Stimulus materials similar to those used by Asch in his conformity research. Standard line is on the left; comparison lines are on the right.

Figure 18–8.
In Asch's conformity experiment, the real subject (number 6) leans forward in the top picture to look at a pair of cards containing the lines. In the bottom picture, he shows the strain of repeatedly disagreeing with the majority. This particular subject disagreed with the majority in all 12 trials. (From Asch, 1955, p. 33.)

similar the three comparison lines are in Asch's conformity procedure, the more difficult the judgments and the greater the conformity. Or, to put it another way, "ambiguity is the mother of conformity" (Wheeler, Deci, Reis, & Zuckerman, 1978, p. 17). Some of these findings begin to suggest why people conform. It is to this issue that we now turn.

— Why Do We Conform?

Deutsch and Gerard (1955) have proposed that social influence in conformity situations is of two types, normative and informational. If we are under **normative social influence,** we conform in order to be socially accepted. If we are under **informational social influence,** we conform because we accept the information provided by others as being correct. Both types of conformity seem to occur in the Asch-type situation (Deutsch & Gerard, 1955). Although giving responses privately reduces conformity (evidence for normative conformity), some conformity still occurs (evidence for informational conformity).

The importance of informational social influence can be seen in Festinger's (1954) social-comparison theory (see chapter 9), which states that people are motivated to evaluate their opinions and abilities and that, in doing so, they often compare themselves with others. It is only through social comparisons that such evaluations can be made. Only other people, for example, can help us decide if we have correct views on abortion or homosexuality. This need for understanding and evaluating ourselves is seen as resulting in pressures to conform to the group. Agreeing with the group confirms the correctness of what one is saying or doing. Given our dependence on others for evaluating our opinions, it should not be surprising that a high degree of conformity exists in everyday life.

Compliance

A less subtle means of influencing people's behavior is to make direct requests of them. Behavior carried out in accordance with a request from someone is referred to as **compliance.** We comply with many requests each day. For instance, we may be asked to donate money to a charity, fill out a questionnaire, sign a petition, or take someone to dinner. The effectiveness of a number of techniques for obtaining compliance has been established.

One much-studied procedure is the **foot-in-the-door technique,** which involves making a small request and then a large request. The idea is that if you can get your foot in the door by getting someone to agree with an innocuous small request, the person will be more likely to agree with a large request. Salespeople have traditionally used this technique by first asking a minor, simple question and then following it with their sales pitch. Freedman and Fraser (1966) were the first to empirically demonstrate the effectiveness of the technique. In one of their studies, homemakers were asked over the telephone to answer a few questions about the kinds of soaps they used. (The first request is made sufficiently small that most people will comply with it.) Three days later, the same individuals received a large request—"to allow a survey team of five or six men to come into their homes for 2 hours to classify the household products they used" (Freedman & Fraser, 1966, p. 196). Of the subjects who agreed to the first request, over half complied with the large request. Of those who did not receive the first request, less than one-fourth complied with the large request. Many studies have replicated this finding (DeJong, 1979; Beaman, Cole, Preston, Klentz, & Steblay, 1983; Schwarzwald, Bizman, & Raz, 1983).

Robert Cialdini and his colleagues at Arizona State University have proposed that an opposite strategy may also be effective (Cialdini et al., 1975). That is, compliance to some request can be enhanced by first making a large request, which the person is likely to refuse, followed by a small request. The small favor is actually the one desired to begin with. Cialdini and colleagues (1975) have labeled this the **door-in-the-face technique,** and they have demonstrated its effectiveness on a college campus. In one study, some subjects were first asked to work as unpaid counselors to delinquents at a detention center for 2 hours a week for 2 years. As expected, none agreed to do so. Upon their refusal, they were asked to chaperone a group of delinquents on a 2-hour trip to the zoo. Compliance with this second request was greater (50 percent) than when subjects were asked only the small favor (16.7 percent). According to Cialdini and colleagues (1975), the technique works because the requester appears to back down and make a concession. Subjects then believe that they too should make a concession. Thus, greater compliance is obtained after a large request than if no previous request has been made.

Another time-honored ploy, one often used by automobile salespeople, is known as **low-balling** (Cialdini, Cacioppo, Bassett, & Miller, 1978). The general strategy in low-balling is to get a person to make a decision regarding some particular behavior. At that point, the reasons for making that decision are altered such that the behavior is now more costly to perform. Inspite of change, the individual may go through with the behavior in question. With respect to car sales, the idea is to get the customer committed to buying a car at a low price; then the salesperson talks with the manager and reports to the customer that the car cannot be sold at the low price initially quoted. The new price is often as high as or higher than the price charged by a competing dealer. Many auto dealers have apparently found this low-ball strategy to be effective in increasing their sales. Despite the fact that the ultimate offer is considerably less favorable than the initial one, the dealers know that many customers will nevertheless stay with their initial decision and proceed to buy the car.

According to Cialdini and his colleagues (Cialdini, Cacioppo, Bassett, & Miller, 1978), the success of the low-ball technique is due to a sense of *commitment* to the initial, uncoerced decision to behave in a particular way. Freely choosing to perform some behavior presumably makes a person feel responsible for the action. Commitment derives from this felt responsibility. As Cialdini and colleagues (1978) note:

> The reason we are less likely to change once committed is that reversing what we feel responsible for results in a variety of negative self-perceptions (e.g., hastiness, a lack of intelligence or judgment or appropriate caution, etc.); consequently, we will resist such change. (p. 474)

Obedience

Oftentimes, when people can't get others to do something by asking them to do it, they order them to do it. **Obedience** is behavior carried out in accordance with an order from an *authority figure*. Of all the forms of influence discussed, this is the most direct and obvious. We are taught to obey authority figures from our earliest days, and most of us do not question obeying laws and such authorities as parents, teachers, and bosses. We know that if we don't obey when told to do so by such authorities, negative ramifications may ensue.

Obedience to authority figures certainly has its place. What is troublesome, however, is obedience that is unthinking and unquestioning. Obedience is so deeply ingrained in us that we may obey even when we believe that we are being asked to do something that is unethical or immoral. We may think that we have no choice; after all, someone with authority and power over us is ordering us to do it. We have been taught, of course, that we obey such individuals. Furthermore, defiance may get us punished, fired, imprisoned, or at least diapproved of. Therefore, even when we disapprove of the orders given us, we may still obey: this type of obedience has often been termed **destructive obedience.**

Sometimes, destructive obedience takes the form of carrying out orders to inflict harm on innocent people. A vivid example is provided by the systematic slaughter of millions of innocent people in Nazi Germany from 1933 to 1945. In Milgram's (1974) words:

> Gas chambers were built, death camps were guarded, daily quotas of corpses were produced with the same efficiency as the manufacture of appliances. These inhumane policies may have originated in the mind of a single person, but they could only have been carried out on a massive scale if a very large number of people obeyed orders. (p. 1)

Milgram has studied this form of obedience in an ingenious and controversial series of laboratory experiments. His concern has been to understand when and to what extent people will obey orders. Let's examine some of his findings.

Milgram (1963) sought to assess the extent of destructive obedience with an elaborately deceptive experiment (see Figure 18–9). Subjects were ordered to administer electrical shocks to a victim, purportedly so that the experimenter could study the effects of punishment on memory. The victim was a confederate, however, and no real shocks were actually delivered. The simulated shock generator had 30 clearly labeled voltage levels, ranging from 15 to 450 volts. Labels on the switches ranged from Slight Shock (15 to 60 volts) to XXX on the final two switches. Subjects received a sample shock of 45 volts to help convince them of the authenticity of what they were doing.

Each time the victim, or learner, made a mistake on a learning task (arranged to occur at certain times), the subject was to administer a shock. He was to start with 15 volts and increase the intensity of the shock by one level each time an error was made. If a subject refused to continue, he was prodded or commanded to continue (e.g., "You have no other choice; you *must* go on"). The experiment was terminated when the subject refused to continue, despite prodding. Obedience was measured by recording the highest shock level admin-

(a)

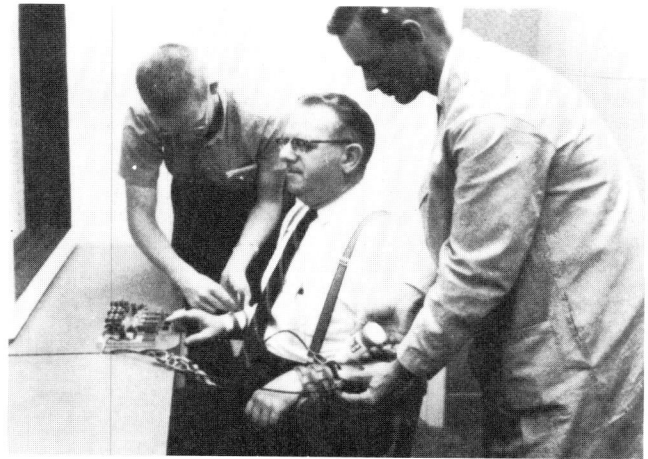
(b)

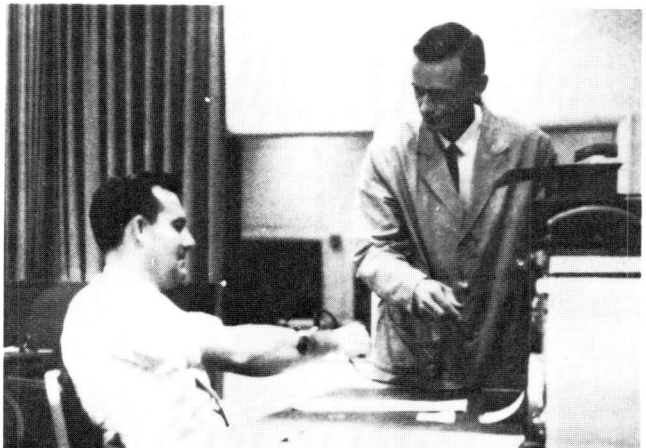
(c)

(d)

Figure 18–9.

Milgram's arrangement for studying obedience. (a) The shock generator. (b) Learner is strapped into chair and electrodes are attached to his wrists. (c) Subject, or teacher, receives sample shock. (d) Subject refuses to continue experiment. (Copyright 1965 by Stanley Milgram. From the film OBEDIENCE, distributed by The Pennsylvania State University, PCR.)

istered by the subject before he finally refused to obey.

Subjects in this study were men who ranged in age from 20 to 50 and who came from diverse occupations. They supposedly became the teachers in the experiment through a random draw, and the other subject (the confederate), a 47-year-old accountant, became the learner. In a room adjacent to the subject's, the learner was strapped into a chair and electrodes were attached to his wrists.

As the experiment proceeded, the learner remained silent until the shock level reached 300 volts. At that point, he began pounding on the wall. From that point on, he gave no more answers on the learning task. If subjects hesitated and asked what to do, they were told to treat no response as a wrong answer and to con-

tinue shocking the learner. The learner again pounded on the wall at the 315-volt level and then made no more sounds thereafter.

Most people assume that very few individuals would deliver high levels of shock to the victim. Milgram's findings were to the contrary, however. Not a single subject quit before the victim pounded on the wall, and even then only 12.5 percent refused to continue; another 10 percent refused to obey when the victim pounded on the wall on the next trial; 65 percent, though, continued to deliver shocks all the way to 450 volts.

Milgram's subjects were not callous and cold-blooded; many displayed much tension and nervousness. A few even experienced seizures. Often, those who disobeyed expressed anger about the harm being done. Apparently, harming the victim was contrary to most subjects' moral principles. Why, then, did subjects continue to shock victims to such high levels? Because they were commanded to do so. The conflict between harming the victim and disobeying the experimenter was often resolved in the direction of obeying—and harming the victim. This illustrates straightforwardly that the tendency to obey the commands of authority figures is strong. Obeying is so ingrained in us that we apparently learn to do it in blind, unthinking ways.

The high levels of obedience found by Milgram are not limited to adult men in the United States. Adults of both sexes, as well as children, in both our own and other cultures, have also been shown to be extremely obedient in the kind of setting devised by Milgram (Shanab & Yahya, 1977; Kilham & Mann, 1974).

Interestingly, Milgram and other researchers have conducted a number of variations on the basic procedure. Milgram (1965b) found that as proximity to the victim increases, obedience decreases. In the most extreme case of proximity, the subject in Milgram's experiment was required to force the victim's hand onto a shockplate. This requirement reduced obedience, but even so, almost one-third of the subjects continued to shock the victim up to the 450-volt limit. Proximity to the authority figure is also important. When the experimenter is not physically present in the room, obedience is dramatically reduced. Apparently, either closeness to the victim or distance from the authority figure make the conflict easier to resolve in favor of disobeying.

Milgram (1965a) has also found that obedience is reduced when the subject is in the presence of other "teachers" who refuse to obey the authority figure's

Figure 18–10.
The My Lai massacre, March 16, 1968. During the Vietnam War, hundreds of unarmed civilians in the village of My Lai were killed by U.S. soldiers under order of Lieutenant William Calley. Calley, in turn, claimed that he was only following superior orders.

commands. In fact, when faced with one confederate who disobeys at 150 volts and one at 210 volts, only 10 percent of the subjects obey to the final 450-volt level; of those not exposed to disobeying confederates, 65 percent continue to the final level. Obedience can also be reduced by telling subjects that they are personally responsible for the victim's welfare (Kilham & Mann, 1974). Many times, as in Milgram's studies, we are relieved of any responsibility for our actions. Putting the burden of responsibility back on us lessens our willingness to deliver harm.

In sum, obedience is a strong and pervasive tendency, but it can be counteracted. Although obedience research has been questioned on an ethical basis (Baumrind, 1964), an understanding of such an important social phenomenon seems unquestionably necessary. One need only witness Nazi Germany, the massacre of civilians in the village of My Lai during the Vietnam War (see Figure 18–10), Watergate, and other such incidents to appreciate this statement.

Gilbert (1981) has recently observed that the high level of obedience obtained by Milgram in his studies may have been due in part to the incremental shock procedure utilized. In other words, it may be easier to get someone to obey a command to deliver a 450-volt shock by having the subject gradually approach that level through 15-volt increments than if the initial command were to deliver the full 450 volts. There seems to be a clear parallel here between the incremental shock procedure and the foot-in-the-door technique discussed earlier (Gilbert, 1981). Much of the obedience that occurs in real life may be in this same kind of graduated sequence, occurring a little at a time. Such may have been the case in 1978, for example, in the tragic obedience demonstrated at Jonestown, Guyana (Osherow, 1981), where nearly 1,000 people died (cf. Gilbert, 1981). Members of the Peoples Temple settlement, under the direction of the Reverend Jim Jones, fed their children, including infants, a poison-laced liquid and then drank it themselves. More than 900 bodies were found lying together, arm in arm.

— APPLICATION —
JUMPING ON THE CHARITY BANDWAGON

As noted by Benson and Catt (1978), the public is often called on to contribute money to a wide variety of charities. Although charitable groups vary in their legitimacy, many are responsible for such important activities as helping disaster victims, financing disease research, and providing care to the handicapped and the poor (Benson & Catt, 1978). Developing effective techniques of soliciting charity donations would seem to be fruitful for these groups.

Cialdini and Schroeder (1976) have observed that requests for small favors are often readily complied with—possibly because they are difficult to decline. However, such requests also tend to produce low-level payoffs. Cialdini and Schroeder suggest a procedure for avoiding this problem. They propose that rather than directly requesting small favors, solicitors can simply legitimize such favors. The solicitor would imply that a small favor is acceptable but not necessarily desirable. This makes it difficult for the target person to refuse to help, and at the same time it makes a low level of assistance unlikely.

In order to test this idea, a door-to-door charity drive was conducted. Residents of a suburban housing area were asked to make a donation to the American Cancer Society. In one condition, the solicitor made a simple, standard request for a donation. In the other condition, the simple request was followed by the phrase "even a penny will help." This phrase presumably legitimized small donations, making it difficult for people not to give at least something. Refusing to give even a penny would appear rather selfish. It was further expected that once a person decided to donate, the amount given would be at least as large as that given by subjects hearing the standard request.

As expected, adding "even a penny will help" to a request increased the likelihood of compliance (50 percent) over a standard request (28.6 percent) without affecting the size of the individual donations. In other words, it appears that legitimizing, but not specifically requesting, trivial aid increases the likelihood of compliance and does not result in substandard assistance. That this technique could have some practical value to charitable organizations can be seen in the fact that in two experiments the "even-a-penny" request netted $90.31 in donations and the standard request produced $48.64.

A recent study by Reingen (1982) suggests that charities could also benefit from showing potential givers a list of previous contributors. In one of Reingen's experiments, half the subjects simply heard an appeal for a donation to the Heart Association. The other half heard the same appeal but also were shown a list of eight fictitious donors and their donations (which averaged 30 cents) and were given the additional comment, "As you can see, other students have given a donation already." The fictitious list apparently worked: 43 percent of the students who saw it made contributions, whereas only 25 percent of those who did not see it donated money.

— LIKING, HELPING, AND HURTING OTHERS —

Attraction

Perhaps the most basic element of human relationships is the like or dislike of other people. When describing people we know, we often indicate positive or negative feelings toward them. Such feelings indicate one's degree of attraction for another person. **Attraction** is an evaluation of another individual in a positive or negative manner, an attitude held toward another individual (Huston, 1974).

— Theories of Attraction

The two major theoretical approaches used to explain attraction are balance theory and reinforcement theory. **Balance theory** (Newcomb, 1961) emphasizes the importance of consistency among one's thoughts. The theory assumes that we like to perceive a balance (or consistency) in our network of liking relationships (such as those between ourselves, another person, and some issue). It sees balance as a pleasant state that exists when two people like each other and agree about some object of communication.

As an example of balance theory, consider the relationships, or bonds, between yourself (P), John Doe (O), and Object X (see Figure 18–11). Object X might be a thing, an issue, or another person. In any such group, an odd number of positive (+) relationships (i.e., one or three + s) will be balanced, or consistent. *Imbalance* refers to an unpleasant state in which two people like each other and disagree about some object of communication. The idea of balance theory is that everything should fit together harmoniously, or make sense. If you like John and both of you like X, the system will be balanced. Imbalance will occur if you like John but you disagree with him about X.

Since people desire balanced relationships, they should be motivated to attain them. In the example, if the relationship is imbalanced, you can change your view of X, convince John to change his view of X, or change your liking for John. Any of these changes would make the system balanced. The essence of balance theory, then, is that like or dislike of someone can come about as a function of the effort to achieve cognitive consistency.

Reinforcement approaches assume that attraction is a learned attitude or response. One such approach, labeled the **reinforcement-affect model** (Baron & Byrne, 1977; Clore & Byrne, 1974), states that our evaluations of objects or persons are based on the positive or negative emotions we associate with them. The model assumes that most stimuli in our environment are either rewarding or punishing and that we tend to approach rewarding stimuli and avoid punishing ones. Furthermore, rewarding stimuli elicit positive feelings, whereas punishing stimuli elicit negative feelings. Let's assume that a previously neutral stimulus (such as your friend John Doe) becomes associated with a rewarding stimulus. Through this simple conditioning process, John Doe will elicit positive feelings and a positive evaluation from you. If John is associated with a pun-

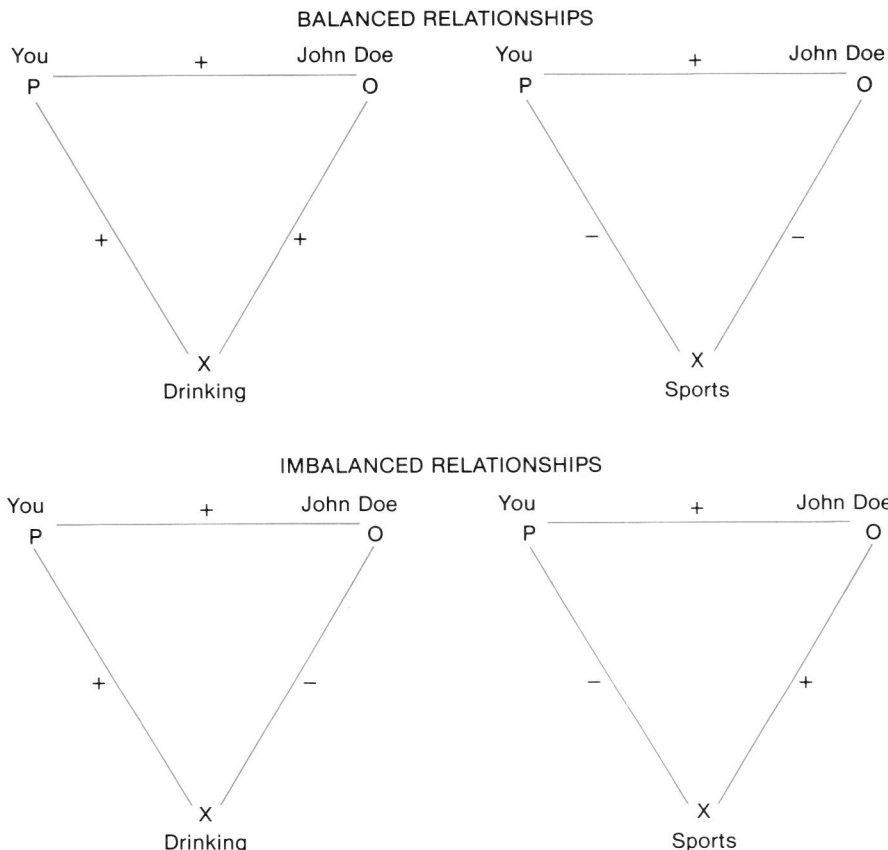

Figure 18–11.

Newcomb's conceptualization of balanced and imbalanced relationships between a person (P), a second individual (O), and some object of communication (X). The + and − signs refer to liking and disliking, respectively.

ishing stimulus, he will elicit negative feelings and dislike from you. It is true, of course, that John may be associated with a number of rewarding as well as punishing stimuli. Attraction in this case is said to increase as the proportion of rewarding stimuli increases.

— Determinants of Attraction

Although balance and reinforcement theories provide a general framework for understanding attraction, much research has focused on specific determinants of our liking for others. We will now consider several of these determinants: similarity, reciprocal liking, proximity, and affect.

Similarity. One of the strongest findings in attraction research is that as attitude similarity increases, attraction increases (Byrne, 1971; Jellison & Oliver, 1983;

Wetzel & Insko, 1982). We seem to like others who are like us. As the adage goes, birds of a feather flock together. When we first meet people and talk with them, we learn that they hold views that are similar or dissimilar to our own. Balance theory suggests that when we find that we are similar to someone, the system is balanced only when we then like the person. The reinforcement-affect model suggests that attitudinal similarity is rewarding because it is pleasant to discover that our view of the world is correct. In contrast, dissimilar attitudes are assumed to be punishing.

The model also suggests that many types of similarity, not just attitude similarity, affect attraction. Personality similarity is one such variable that has been investigated. Meyer and Pepper (1977), for example, had married couples complete personality scales that measured traits such as needs for impulsivity and affiliation. A measure of marital adjustment was also obtained. The more similar the couple in personality traits, the happier and better adjusted they seemed to be.

Reciprocal liking. Most of us find it rewarding to be liked and evaluated positively and punishing to be disliked and rejected. It has been shown that such evaluations from others are an important determinant of attraction. Byrne and Rhamey (1965) found that personal evaluations had an even stronger effect on attraction than did attitude similarity. It also seems to be the case that a positive evaluation from a physically attractive person produces greater liking than does the same evaluation from an unattractive person (Sigall & Aronson, 1969).

Proximity. We live, work, sit, and eat at various distances from other people. Numerous studies have shown that as proximity, or physical closeness, increases, attraction increases. In married-student housing units, friendships have been found to occur most often among couples who live in nearby apartments rather than in distant apartments (Festinger, Schachter, & Back, 1950). In other words, the closer the couples live to each other, the more likely they are to become friends. The proximity-attraction relationship also holds true for people with adjacent houses and adjacent seats in a classroom (Segal, 1974).

Much support exists for a simple *familiarity effect,* or frequency of exposure explanation, for the effects of proximity (Moreland & Zajonc, 1979). We like those in close proximity because we are more often exposed to them and because repeated exposure to any stimulus increases its familiarity and our attraction to it (Saegert, Swap, & Zajonc, 1973). Furthermore, increased familiarity not only leads to greater attraction, it also leads to greater perceived similarity (Moreland & Zajonc, 1982). However, one qualification is in order: If the first reaction to another person is negative, familiarity seems to breed only contempt (Swap, 1977).

Affect. The basis of the reinforcement-affect model is that many stimuli in the environment can arouse good or bad feelings. If a stimulus that produces a good or bad feeling is associated with a particular person, then that person will also elicit a good or bad feeling and like or dislike. Along these lines, it has been shown that high room temperature and humidity (Griffitt & Veitch, 1971) or bad news (Veitch & Griffitt, 1976) can decrease attraction toward a hypothetical stranger who is associated with those stimuli.

Prosocial Behavior

In the chapter introduction, we read that 38 witnesses observed the murder of Kitty Genovese, yet failed even to call the police. Incidents such as this have spurred much interest in **prosocial behavior**—voluntary acts that have positive consequences for others (Bar-Tal, 1976; Staub, 1978). Helping others can take many forms—retrieving lost objects, giving financial aid, even intervening in a life-or-death emergency. We will concentrate here on several theoretical views of helping and will then consider emergency helping in particular.

— Theories of Prosocial Behavior

Both learning and cognitive explanations of prosocial behavior have been offered. Let's first consider the learning approach.

In accord with the social-learning perspective, research indicates that prosocial acts are more likely when they are rewarded (Mussen & Eisenberg-Berg, 1977). Likewise, helping behavior decreases when it is punished—by a rude response, for example (Moss & Page, 1972). Moreover, prosocial acts are affected by expectations about being rewarded or punished. For example, we might expect approval from others for helping, or we might fear negative consequences, such as getting mugged. The inhibiting effect of unpleasant expectations was demonstrated by Pomazal and Jaccard (1976), who found that students were least likely to donate blood when they strongly believed it would cause pain, anxiety, fatigue, inconvenience, and faintness. In short, before deciding to help, we seem to consider what's in it for ourselves (Batson et al., 1978).

Also relevant from a learning perspective is the fact that we can acquire prosocial behaviors simply from observing others (Bandura, 1977b). Many studies show that helping in both children (e.g., Rushton, 1975; Grusec, 1981) and adults (e.g., Bryan & Test, 1967) is increased by altruistic models. Our observations of others help teach us how to act altruistically, show us what is appropriate behavior, and indicate to us whether helping is rewarding or punishing in a given situation.

An alternative analysis of prosocial behavior is Latané and Darley's (1970) cognitive approach, which suggests that helping or not helping in an emergency depends on one's perceptions and judgments as the emergency unfolds. We turn now to Latané and Darley's model and a discussion of emergency helping.

— Helping in Emergencies

According to Latané and Darley (1970), before a bystander helps, the person must make a series of decisions (see Figure 18–12). As we examine the decisions, imagine that you see a man lying on the street (see Figure 18–13). Will you go to his aid? To do so, you will have to work your way up the decision tree depicted in Figure 18–12.

First, you must *notice* that something is happening. Many times, we are concentrating on our own thoughts or we are hesitant to stare at someone and invade the person's privacy. If so, we may miss an important cue that a person needs help.

If we're at least aware of the situation we must then *interpret* it as an emergency. Because many emergencies are ambiguous, we are likely to be influenced by whether or not other people think it is an emergency. Latané and Darley suggest that most people want to appear poised and calm in times of distress, and they give the impression that they think nothing is wrong. Often, bystanders look to one another for a definition of what is happening; yet, at the same time, each tries to appear poised. Everyone is consequently misled into believing that the situation is not as serious as it might actually be. This is the **social-influence process,** a process whereby bystanders inhibit one an-

Figure 18–12.

Decision-tree analysis of bystander intervention in emergencies. The bystander must successfully pass each step in the decision tree before intervention will occur. (Adapted from Worchel & Cooper, 1983, p. 291.)

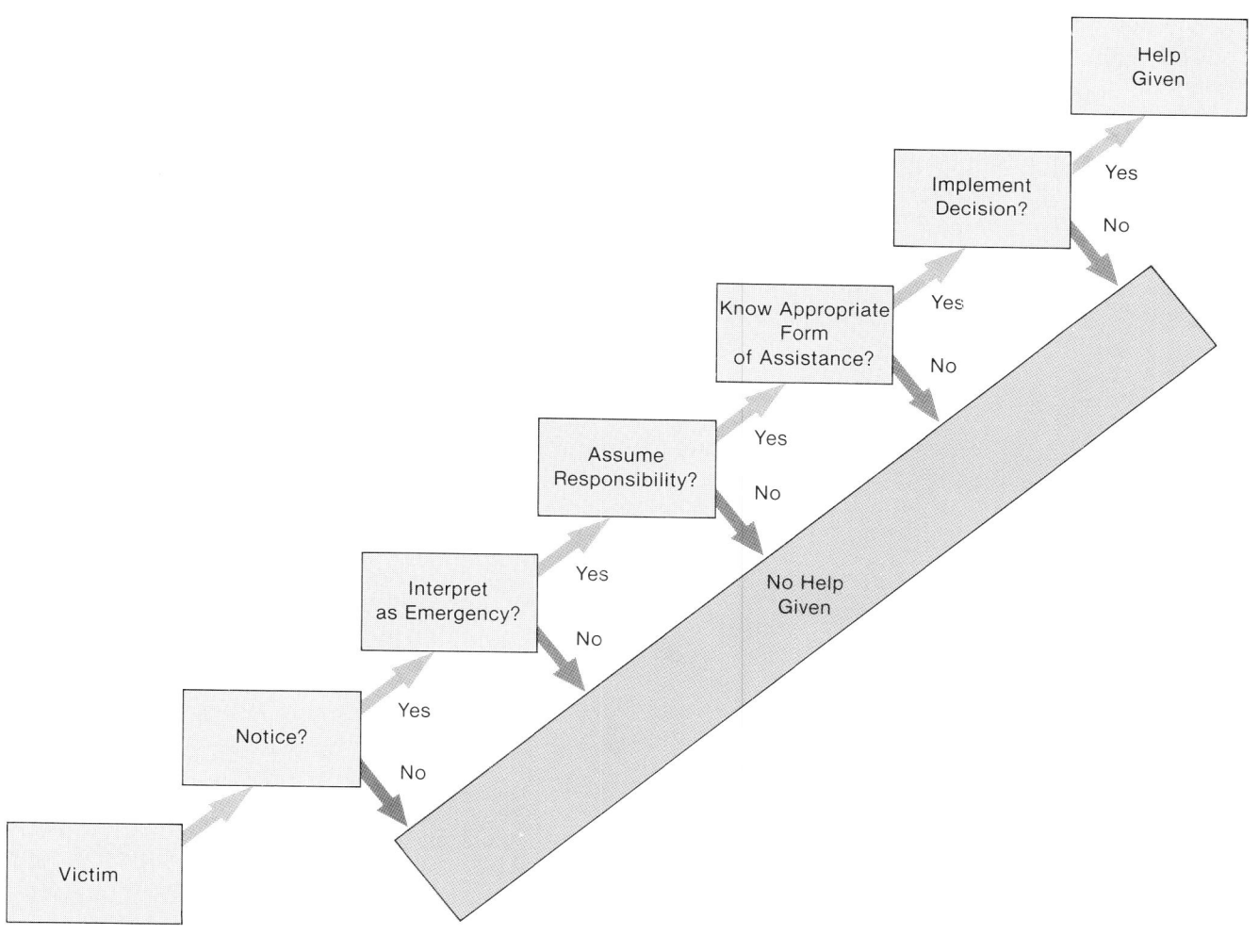

Figure 18–13.
Will anyone go to the aid of the man lying on the street? Is the man drunk? Sick? Dead? Even if the situation is interpreted as an emergency, responsibility for helping the man may be diffused among the bystanders.

other from helping through each one's lack of action or apparent concern.

Even if the situation is interpreted as an emergency, helping will not occur unless the bystander accepts *responsibility* for it. Again, the presence of others can inhibit helping. When we are with others, we can share with them the responsibility for helping and thus feel less personally responsible. We may ask, "Why me?" Latané and Darley refer to this process as **diffusion of responsibility.** When we are alone, we must accept the full burden of helping or not helping. Accepting responsibility can be affected by variables other than group size as well. For example, bystanders who believe that they are particularly qualified to help will be more likely to help than will those who do not (Clark & Word, 1974; Pantin & Carver, 1982). When in a group of other potential helpers, bystanders are especially likely to diffuse responsibility to others if they perceive that particular persons in the group have

greater ability to intervene (e.g., if they observe that a nurse is present when someone collapses on a subway platform) (Schwartz & Clausen, 1970).

If we have accepted the responsibility for helping, we must decide *how to intervene*—what mode of help to use. Will we physically intervene, call the police, or take some other action? Finally, we must *implement* our course of action and actually help.

Latané, Darley, and their colleagues have conducted several ingenious studies that directly test the influence of an important variable in their decision-making analysis: group size. We will look at one such study.

The seizure study.　Subjects in what is called the seizure study (Darley & Latané, 1968) took part in an interview over an intercom system. They were seated alone in a small room, and they believed that they were communicating with either one other person (the future victim), two others, or five others. Actually, everything was tape-recorded (except the subject's replies), so only one real subject was being tested at a time. During the taped discussion, the future victim remarked that he was prone to having seizures. Later, when he spoke again, he actually began to have a seizure. Subjects could hear the victim calling out for help, making choking sounds, and saying he was going to die. The larger the phantom group, the less likely subjects were to intervene (see Figure 18–14) and the slower their intervention was. This finding clearly demonstrated the diffusion-of-responsibility concept discussed earlier. The study situation resembles the Kitty Genovese situation in that the subjects could not see what other subjects were doing or view the expressions on their faces (thus canceling the social-influence process). They were, however, aware that others were also aware of the emergency, which is all that is necessary for diffusion of responsibility to occur.

Such studies suggest that helping or not helping is often influenced by the presence of other people and the impact they have on our thinking. Latané and Darley (1970) argue that the lack of intervention in some emergencies should not necessarily be interpreted as showing that people are apathetic and indifferent. Rather, we need to examine the social-psychological nature of the situation and the relationships between the bystanders before interpreting the event.

Other evidence on emergency helping. The influence of group size on helping has been found to be general and reliable (Latané, Nida, & Wilson, 1981; Latané & Nida, 1981). Some qualifications to the generality of the effect do exist, however. One notable finding is that group size seems to inhibit helping only among groups of strangers characterized by low cohesiveness or little attraction toward one another (Rutkowski, Gruder, & Romer, 1983). When group cohesiveness is high, group size actually seems to facilitate helping. In addition to group size, many other variables have been shown to affect emergency helping. Increasing the ambiguity of the situation (Clark & Word, 1974), increasing the negative aspects, or costs, of helping (Piliavin & Piliavin, 1972), and increasing the ease of escape from the situation (Staub & Baer, 1974) are just a few of the factors that seem to decrease helping in emergencies.

— A Case Where Someone Did Help

People are often quite willing to go to the aid of others, however. It might be fruitful to examine an actual case of helping in terms of Latané and Darley's model. On January 13, 1982, moments after take-off in Washington, D.C., a commercial jetliner hit a crowded bridge and plunged into the icy waters of the Potomac River. A 28-year-old man named Lenny Skutnik stopped and watched from the shore as rescuers tried to pull survivors out of the river. Priscilla Tirado was one of those survivors. When Tirado lost her grip on a helicopter lifeline and started to sink, Skutnik jumped into the water and pulled her to safety (see Figure 18–15). Skutnik later stated that "somebody had to go into the water." But nobody, of course, really had to go into the water.

Why did Lenny Skutnik intervene? As Dworetzky (1982) points out, in terms of Latané and Darley's model, Skutnik clearly noticed that a serious event was taking place (Step 1). As he watched the rescue efforts, he interpreted what he saw as an emergency (Step 2). If Priscilla Tirado did not receive help, she would probably drown; there was nothing ambiguous about her need for help. Nevertheless, Skutnik did not have to accept personal responsibility for helping—but he did (Step 3). It was his judgment that if he didn't res-

Figure 18–14.
In the Darley and Latané seizure study, as group size increased, the percentage of subjects helping the victim decreased. (Based on data from Darley & Latané, 1968, p. 380.)

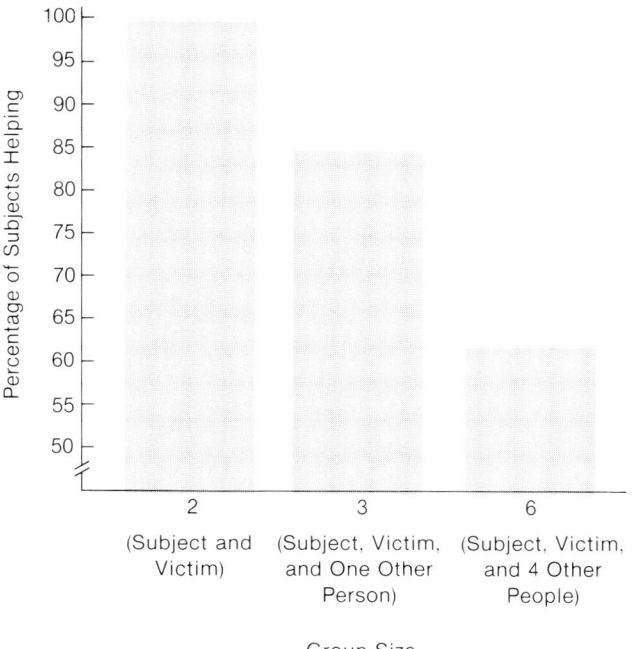

Figure 18–15.
Priscilla Tirado is saved by Lenny Skutnik.

cue the woman, she would drown. Skutnik may very well have accepted responsibility because of his belief that he was capable of making the rescue. There is evidence that diffusing responsibility to others is much less likely when we believe that the other bystanders are incapable of helping (Bickman, 1971). Skutnik's acceptance of responsibility was perhaps also affected by his **empathy,** or understanding of the victim's feelings and plight. Skutnik indicated in an interview after the rescue that he felt sorry for the victim. Research evidence, in fact, suggests that empathy for a victim can lead not only to helping, but to helping that is altruistically motivated (see chapter 9; see also Batson, O'Quin, Fultz, Vanderplas, & Isen, 1983; Davis, 1983b).

In sum, empathy combined with the other factors mentioned may have encouraged Skutnik's decision to accept responsibility for helping. The last two steps were then relatively straightforward. Skutnik had to decide how to intervene (Step 4). Since helicopter rescue efforts were not working, swimming to the victim was the only way to bring her to safety. Finally, Skutnik implemented his course of action (Step 5), plunging into the water for the dramatic rescue. Although we don't presume to know exactly why Lenny Skutnik did what he did, his actions are interpretable in terms of the Latané and Darley model.

Aggression

There is perhaps no other behavior more noticeable than **aggression**—any behavior whose intent is to inflict harm or injury on another living being. Aggression pervades our lives. Daily, we read about, hear about, or see on television murders, rapes, stabbings, riots, and other forms of aggression. We often wonder where all this aggression comes from and whether it can be controlled.

— Theories of Aggression

Social psychologists and other theorists have traditionally viewed the origins of aggression as possibly lying in instincts, frustration, and learning experiences.

Instincts. Two major theorists, Freud and Lorenz, have suggested that aggression is instinctive (Baron, 1977). As we saw in chapter 13, Freud proposed the existence of a death instinct, whose energy is directed toward the destruction of life. This aggressive energy is thought to build up over time, and unless one can find ways to release it in relatively nondestructive ways, the outcome is violence.

Lorenz (1966), an ethologist (see chapter 9), holds a similar view. For him, aggression arises from a fighting instinct that exists in many animals and humans. Lorenz believes that such an instinct has served a useful purpose and so has developed over the course of evolution. According to Lorenz, aggressive energy constantly accumulates, and aggressive acts occur because of it. Like Freud, Lorenz suggests that engaging in nondestructive aggressive actions may keep aggressive energy from building up to dangerous levels (Baron, 1977).

The problem with instinct theories is that much variability exists in aggressive behavior (Middlebrook, 1980). Some individuals are aggressive in many situations; others seldom aggress. The intensity of aggressiveness varies with individuals. People choose different ways of being aggressive. Cultures vary in their levels of aggression. In short, the usefulness of instinct theories in explaining aggression can reasonably be questioned.

Frustration. An alternate view is that aggression stems from various environmental conditions that produce frustration. Many years ago, the **frustration-aggression hypothesis** was proposed and states, in part, that frustration always leads to some form of aggression (Dollard, Doob, Miller, Mowrer, & Sears, 1939). Today, it is recognized that frustration can lead to other types of responses as well, such as apathy, helplessness, and despair. But although the original frustration-aggression hypothesis is now questioned, it is recognized that frustration can lead to aggression sometimes. We will examine this issue in more detail a little later in the chapter.

For now, we might briefly speak to the prospects of controlling aggression from the perspective of the frustration-aggression hypothesis. First, however, we should note that controlling aggression from the instinct point of view is difficult at best. The source of aggressive energy is internal and aggressive energy is always building. While frustration, in contrast, derives from external conditions, does this make it anymore benign? Berkowitz (1983) has suggested that frustration instigates aggression because it is aversive—a goal is blocked. As he observes, some amount of frustration and subsequent aggression is inevitable. All frustrations cannot be eliminated. Does this mean, then, that there is nothing that we can do to control aggression? Berkowitz's (1983) answer is no:

> Aggressive instigation need not be translated into open attacks on others. We can learn to restrain our aggressive dispositions, be led not to think of others as sources of displeasure, and turn our thoughts away from aggression-promoting ideas. (p. 1143)

That brings us to the importance of learning experiences as determinants of aggression.

A social-learning approach. Aggression can be viewed as being acquired and maintained just as other behaviors are. For example, the social-learning approach suggests that aggression that has been rewarded in the past is more likely to occur in the future than is aggression that has gone unrewarded or that has been punished. Such experiences affect one's expectations for reward and punishment with respect to any future acts of aggression. The social-learning model also recognizes that aggression is instigated by a number of social and environmental conditions, such as provocation from others (Bandura, 1973; Baron, 1977). Whether aggression does in fact occur in response to such conditions is believed to be determined by the anticipated consequences.

One simple principle involved here is that some aggression occurs simply because it has been rewarded in the past. Money, toys, candy, other desired objects, and social approval are only a few examples of rewards that have been shown to facilitate aggression in adults and children (Baron, 1977). Another principle of social-learning theory (Bandura, 1973) is that some aggression is learned through the process of modeling. We can acquire aggressive responses by watching other aggress. This modeling might occur in our physical presence or in films, on television, or in stories. The effect is particularly evident when people are seen receiving reinforcement for being aggressive (Baron, 1977). An observer might learn not only how to be aggressive but that being aggressive will be rewarded, or at least not punished.

Anecdotal evidence about observation of aggressive models leading to imitation of aggressive behavior abounds. Of course, not everyone who observes violence commits violence. It appears, though, that aggressive models can stimulate further aggressive behavior in at least some people. This point seemed all too apparent in 1982, when an unknown poisoner murdered seven people by placing cyanide in Tylenol capsules. In the month following that incident, a wave of copycat crimes plagued the nation. During that time, the Food and Drug Administration "received more than 270 reports of citizens finding chemicals, pills, poisons, needles, pins, and razor blades in everything from food to drinks and medications" (Beck, 1982).

The social-learning approach is optimistic about preventing or controlling aggression (Baron, 1977). If aggression is learned, it can be modified. If, for example, the reward of attention maintains a child's aggressive behavior, remove that attention when the child aggresses.

Determinants of Aggression

Although the three approaches described provide some general perspectives for understanding aggression, research has focused on the influence of a number of specific factors, several of which we will now consider.

Frustration and the role of aggressive cues. In its original form, the frustration-aggression hypothesis was a bold statement. As we saw earlier, however, certainly there are times when people are frustrated but not aggressive. Baron and Byrne (1981) suggest that frustration leads to aggression only when it is intense or when it is perceived as arbitrary or illegitimate by those experiencing it. (An illegitimate frustration is one without any good cause.)

Berkowitz (e.g., 1978), in a revision of the earlier frustration-aggression notion, suggests that frustration is especially likely to lead to aggression when there are **aggressive cues**—stimuli associated with aggression—in the environment. One such cue is a weapon. Berkowitz believes that the presence of weapons, such as guns, heightens the possibility of aggression in individuals who have been frustrated (e.g., Berkowitz & LePage, 1967; Berkowitz, 1981). In other words, aggressive cues contribute to the occurrence of aggression by eliciting it from us when we are frustrated and angry—and thus emotionally ready to aggress because of the aversiveness of the experience (Berkowitz, 1982).

Attack: Insult and assault. At one time or another, you have probably had the experience of being verbally attacked or insulted by someone. Perhaps you have even been physically attacked. Experiments (e.g., Ferguson, Rule, & Lindsay, 1982) have shown that physical provocation often leads to strong counterattacks. Verbal attacks can also elicit counterattacks (Wilson & Rogers, 1975), even physical retaliation. Geen (1968) has shown that verbal insult evokes even higher levels of aggression than does frustration. Verbal or physical provocation elicit strong retaliatory aggression, however, only when the provocation is seen as intentional (Dyck & Rule, 1978).

Other aversive stimulation. According to Berkowitz (1982), frustration, personal insults, and physical attacks all represent forms of aversive stimulation. The aversive quality of such stimuli leads to feelings of irritability and anger and subsequent aggressive acts. Berkowitz points out that many other stimuli can have a similar effect; among such stimuli are heat (see chapter 19), unpleasant odors, and physical pain.

Models of aggression. We see aggression occurring all around us, including on television. Bandura and his colleagues (e.g., Bandura, Ross, & Ross, 1963) were the first to examine the influence of modeled aggression. Their research has shown (among other things) that when children observe a filmed adult model aggressing against an inflated toy clown, a "Bobo doll," and then are given a chance to play with a number of toys, including the Bobo doll, they closely imitate the model. Children not exposed to the film rarely demonstrate the aggressive acts performed by the model. One conclusion, then, seems to be that children can acquire new aggressive responses simply by observing the actions of an aggressive model.

Bandura's research does not necessarily mean that violence in the mass media is partly to blame for the aggressiveness in our society (Baron, 1977). Learning aggression is different from performing it (Bandura, 1965). It is not clear from the Bobo-doll studies whether observing aggression actually encourages or facilitates later aggressive behavior. The issue is whether children, or even adults, will take what they have seen in the mass media and be motivated to then engage in an aggressive act. It is widely assumed that they will (see Figure 18–16). Slife and Rychlak (1982) recently found, however, that children in this type of research will imitate modeled aggression only when they evaluate the aggression positively. In other words, if they find the modeled aggressive acts personally distasteful, they will not be likely to imitate them even if they know how to do so.

To answer a number of criticisms of Bandura's original research, a new series of laboratory studies was performed. This series used better measures of aggression and violent films similar to, or actually taken from, movies or television (Baron, 1977). It also arranged for the context of the observed aggression to be different from the context of the performed aggression. Dozens of studies of this type have been conducted; they all suggest that movie violence and television violence do facilitate aggression in those observing it (see, e.g., Geen, 1978b). This seems to be true with both child and adult observers.

Although these laboratory studies eliminate some of the problems of the Bobo-doll studies, they have their own problems (Baron, 1977). First, the measures of aggression are often unrealistic, such as administering electric shock to other people. Second, the films are usually quite brief, unlike most movie and television aggression. Third, the brief segments don't allow the development of a plot, as most movies and television shows do. The answer to these criticisms has been a number of long-term field studies in which subjects are given a steady diet of violent or nonviolent television shows or movies over an extended period of time. Aggression in these subjects is then observed as it occurs in its natural forms in naturalistic settings. Even with these improvements in the structure of studies, the findings still point to the same conclusion. Watching movie or television aggression increases the likelihood of the observers engaging in similar aggressive actions (see, e.g., Geen, 1978b).

Support for these conclusions was bolstered in 1982 when the National Institute of Mental Health published the findings from its 2-year study, *Television and Be-*

Figure 18–16.

Does viewing violence on television cause aggressive behavior? When 15-year-old Ronald Zamora was accused of murdering an 83-year-old woman in 1977, his defense counsel argued that the boy was "not guilty by reason of insanity because of his intoxication with television." The jury did not agree.

havior: Ten Years of Scientific Progress and Implications for the Eighties (Pearl, Bouthilet, & Lazar, 1982). According to the report, there is now overwhelming evidence that excessive violence on television causes aggressive behavior in children. Further supportive evidence comes from two large-scale longitudinal field studies in Chicago (Eron, 1982). According to Eron (1982), the relationship between television violence and subsequent aggressive behavior is a circular one. Although television violence is one cause of aggressive behavior, aggressive children prefer to watch more violent television, Eron believes. Continued viewing of such programs then causes further aggression, and the cycle perpetuates itself.

A number of answers have been given to the question of why exposure to violence facilitates aggression (Baron, 1977). We have already examined one such answer—that observers may learn new ways of aggressing by watching violence. A second answer is that observation of violence reduces restraints against similar behavior. It's as though the observer says, "If they can aggress like that, so can I." A third answer is that continued exposure to violence may result in a gradual emotional desensitization to aggression and to signs of pain or suffering in others (Thomas, 1982). Observers may become used to violence, may no longer see it as an inappropriate behavior, and may no longer respond to it with physiological arousal (Thomas, Horton, Lippincott, & Drabman, 1977; Geen, 1981). All these explanations, of course, can be true, and they can operate simultaneously. We may learn to be aggressive and to feel less restrained in engaging in the act while at the same time we are gradually becoming desensitized to violence.

We should keep in mind that the effect of viewing television violence is not so strong that every viewer will leap from the chair and rush out to find a victim. But television violence certainly is one contributing factor among many in causing the aggression around us. If we assume that media violence has at least some influence and that its current level of frequency continues (see the "On the Horizon" section at the end of the chapter), can we do anything to mitigate its effects? One recent study offers a ray of hope, at least with respect to children. Over a 2-year period, a large sample of first- and third-grade children with a heavy diet of television violence were studied (Huesmann, Eron, Klein, Brice, & Fischer, 1983). Efforts were made to teach some of the children (experimental subjects) that (1) violence on television is unrealistic (people are not really getting hurt), (2) that most people don't behave in such an aggressive manner, (3) that the average person finds alternate solutions to solving conflicts, (4) that watching television violence is undesirable, and (5) that the children should not imitate the violence they see. Control-group subjects did not receive this training. The intervention proved fruitful.

For one thing, it lessened the positive relationship between violence viewing and aggressiveness in the experimental subjects. Furthermore, by the end of the second year, the experimental subjects were rated by their peers as significantly less aggressive than the control subjects. There is good reason to believe, then, that parents and others can take steps to help offset any negative effects that might otherwise occur as a result of viewing media violence. Parents might also keep in mind that at around 8 to 9 years of age children seem to be especially susceptible to the influence of television (Eron, Huesmann, Brice, Fischer, & Mermelstein, 1983).

— APPLICATION —
INCREASING HELPFULNESS AND REDUCING AGGRESSION

In thinking about the Lenny Skutnik case or others like it, you might ask yourself what you would do if you ever found yourself in a similar situation. Would you help? Why or why not? What do you think can be done to encourage more prosocial behavior in our society? Several answers are evident from our discussion. Since prosocial behavior can be affected by learning, helping behavior should be reinforced. It can be further encouraged through the modeling of prosocial acts. In other words, helping behavior can be taught through demonstrations of helpful acts—teaching through doing. Beyond this, however, we must teach people specific skills that may be needed in helping others. Lenny Skutnik needed to be able to swim well to do what he did. Unless you know how to respond in an emergency, your ability to help will be impaired.

Do you think you will be more helpful now that you are acquainted with some of the findings on prosocial behavior? If so, perhaps our society needs a more concentrated effort to make people aware of the information we have discussed. It has been found that seeing a film that explains some of the reasons for the inhibition of helping does increase people's later willingness to stop and help a victim lying on the floor (Beaman, Barnes, Klentz, & McQuirk, 1978). In addition, participating as a subject in an experiment on prosocial behavior seems to have the same effect (Schwartz & Gottlieb, 1980). Perhaps our message should be: Go out and spread the word about prosocial behavior.

Let's look at the other side of the coin now. What can you do to control aggression? First of all, to dispel one popular and mistaken notion, there is little evidence for the notion of **catharsis**—that aggression can be reduced by having people engage in safe aggressive acts or watch aggression take place. This hypothesis, consistent with the thinking of both Freud and Lorenz, suggests that hitting a punching bag, kicking the wall, watching violence on television, and similar activities will reduce anger and subsequent aggressive behavior.

If catharsis doesn't work, what does? One possibility is to teach people responses that are incompatible with aggression (Baron, 1977). Empathy is one such response. As we have seen, empathy is one's capacity for understanding what another person feels. Interestingly, Feshbach and Feshbach (cited in Myers, 1983) have found that children given special training in empathy became significantly less aggressive at school. Nonaggressive humor has also been shown to be an effective inhibitor of aggression (e.g., Baron, 1978b; Baron & Ball, 1974).

With respect to the social-learning view, we've already seen some suggestions for lessening the potential negative effects of televised violence. More generally, the social-learning view offers several useful strategies for controlling aggression—such as removing the rewards for aggression and exposing people to nonaggressive models. We'd like to address here another learning strategy for reducing aggression. It is a strategy that focuses on the issue of gender differences in aggression (see Towson & Zanna, 1982).

Eron (1980) suggests that "where we are going to have to direct massive efforts has to do with values—with what it means to be a man or masculine in our society, since the preponderance of violence is perpetrated by males or by females who are acting like males" (p. 251). Eron notes that gender differences in aggression appear to be due to differences in socialization. Males as a group are more aggressive than females. Some girls, however, are as aggressive as boys, and they seem to have been socialized like boys. Eron suggests that "just as some females can learn to be aggressive, so males can learn *not* to be aggressive" (Eron, 1980, p. 251).

What is important, of course, is what society values and expects in terms of aggressive behavior and the rewards it provides or withdraws when aggression occurs (Eron, 1980). Our society tends to discourage aggression in girls very early in life and rewards girls for engaging in nonaggressive activities. Eron contends that if we want to reduce aggression in our society, we should socialize boys like we do girls—discourage male aggression very early in life and reward other behaviors. Boys, Eron suggests, should be encouraged, as are girls, to develop positive social characteristics such as tenderness, sensitivity to feelings, nurturance, and cooperativeness, and aesthetic appreciation.

Eron concludes that "behavior that is learned can be unlearned, and aggressive behavior is no different—it, too, can be unlearned. But how much easier it would be, how much pain and suffering would be eliminated, if we arranged conditions so that aggression was not learned in the first place and all youngsters learned alternative ways of solving problems" (Eron, 1980, p. 251).

TELEVISION VIOLENCE AND THE FUTURE

Will violence on television someday be a thing of the past? Many groups in this country have called for an end to, or at least a reduction in, television violence. To cite just one example, in 1980 demonstrators protested against the Columbia Broadcasting System (CBS) for its showing of the violent movie *Exorcist II*. Protestors claimed that CBS was an accessory to murder in connection with the death of a 4-year-old Texas girl. The girl was murdered by her mother, who cut the girl's heart out after watching a similar scene in *Exorcist II*. CBS declared that there was "no clear indication that the incident was a result of a CBS program."

If social psychologists had their way, many would opt for removing televised violence, or at least reducing it. In fact, research by social psychologists on the effects of media violence may ultimately affect what you are able to watch on television. But the issues are complicated, to say the least. First, we should recognize that the role of television in the lives of most Americans is a significant one. As Singer (1983) recently put it, "We live in a society in which most people below 40 have grown up accustomed to daily viewing of several hours of television" (p. 815). Singer (1983) points out that as early as 9 months of age, children are already watching as much as 1½ hours of television everyday. By the ages of 3 to 4, the average viewing time increases to 4 hours or more a day. The following thought is a sobering one: "In general, it is clear that children spend more time in this country watching television than they ever spend in school and, very likely, in direct communication with their parents" (Singer, 1983, p. 815).

There is much to be said about television that is good (cf. Liebert, Sprafkin, & Davidson, 1982). It is an important educational medium, and a number of programs (such as *Mr. Rogers' Neighborhood*) have been shown to be beneficial for children's social and intellectual development (Singer & Singer, 1983; Wright & Huston, 1983). However, we cannot escape the fact that television is also the source of a great deal of violence. One recent study found that an average of 9 acts of physical aggression and 7.8 acts of verbal aggression occur per program hour (Williams, Zabrack, & Joy, 1982). We have three important facts in hand now: (1) We spend considerable amounts of time watching television. (2) Much violence occurs on television. (3) Such violence has been shown to influence aggression significantly. From the social psychologist's point of view, such facts are disturbing.

If televised violence can have even some influence on aggression, why does it appear so often? The basic reason is that network officials aren't convinced that televised violence is a significant cause of aggression (Rubinstein, 1983). Beyond this, the officials also usually claim that viewers enjoy watching violence (Baron & Byrne, 1982). Presumably, violence in a show makes that show more attractive and increases its ratings. But does such a link actually exist? Are the networks really giving the public what it wants and therefore serving the public interest? Not according to a study by social psychologists Diener and DeFour (1978). They found no relationship between a show's popularity and the amount of violence on the show.

Social psychologists have a challenge ahead of them to convince network executives and sponsors that televised violence can contribute to real-life aggression and that violence does not help the ratings. As Baron and Byrne (1982) observe, if the violence serves no useful purpose for the networks and if it does a disservice to society as a whole, why broadcast it? If convincing arguments are made, we may, in the coming years, see a drop in the amount of violence on television. If so, what should replace such programming? Perhaps family-oriented programming with an emphasis on constructive problem solving and prosocial behavior would predominate. What do you consider a solution to the television-violence problem? Is there a solution?

1. Social psychologists investigate the manner in which the behavior, feelings, and thoughts of individuals are influenced by the behavior or characteristics of others.

2. Person perception refers to the processes involved when we form impressions of other people—when we decide that they are characterized by certain abilities, motives, interests, or traits. Physical attractiveness is a variable that has been shown to affect impressions of others. Much of the evidence suggests a what-is-beautiful-is-good stereotype, in which the physically attractive individual is viewed and treated more favorably than is the unattractive individual.

3. The attribution process—inferring people's stable traits, motives, and intentions from their behavior—is another aspect of person perception. One attribution theory proposes that when perceivers search for these stable characteristics, they look for effects that another person intended to create. Behavior that produces either clear-cut or socially undesirable effects is thought to be the most revealing about what the actor is like. Another attribution theory suggests that in determining whether the behavior of another person was internally caused, perceivers ascertain consistency, consensus, and distinctiveness regarding the behavior.

4. Research on combining information about another person has found that perceivers use a weighted-average model, with certain variables (such as first impressions) given more weight in the final impression. Biases in person perception include the halo effect, the actor-observer difference, and the self-serving bias.

5. Attribution therapy has been used to convince students that their academic difficulties were due to unstable, nonpermanent factors. Students receiving such therapy were less likely to leave college than other students and had a greater increase in grade-point averages.

6. Attitudes are relatively enduring predispositions to feel, think, and respond in particular ways toward some object, person, group, or idea. They can be learned through classical or operant conditioning or through modeling. Attitude change often occurs through persuasion. Source, message, and audience factors affect this process. Attitudes can also change when a person engages in attitude-discrepant behavior, thus producing dissonance and a desire to reduce it. Dissonance motivates the person to bring the attitude in line with the behavior.

7. Conformity occurs when we behave in accordance with social norms. When a group's judgment is unanimous, individuals conform to the group to a high degree, even if the judgment is incorrect. Evidence exists for both normative and informational social influence.

8. Compliance occurs when behavior is performed in accordance with a request from someone. One procedure for obtaining compliance is the foot-in-the-door technique, whereby one first makes a small request and then makes a large request. Another method, the door-in-the-face technique, consists of first making a large request, then a small one. Low-balling involves first getting a person's commitment to perform a behavior, then increasing the cost of that act. All of these procedures have been shown to be effective in increasing compliance.

9. Obedience is behavior carried out in accordance with an order from an authority figure. Milgram has shown that although obedience occurs to a great extent, it can be counteracted somewhat by factors such as disobedient models, closeness to the victim, and personal responsibility for the victim.

10. There are two major theories of attraction. Balance theory explains that attraction occurs because of the desire for balanced, or consistent, relationships between ourselves, others, and objects of communication. The reinforcement-affect model explains that our attraction toward others is based on the positive emotions that get associated with those persons. Research has shown that similarity, liking from others, proximity to others, and positive affect all lead to greater attraction.

11. Legitimizing, but not specifically requesting, trivial aid ("even a penny will help") increases the likelihood of compliance and does not result in substandard assistance. Charities could also benefit from showing potential givers a list of previous contributors.

12. Prosocial behavior benefits others. Various theories have been proposed to account for such behavior. One theory is that prosocial behavior is due to learning factors. Latané and Darley have further proposed a cognitive analysis of helping in emergencies. They attribute helping or the lack of it to the perceptions and judgments made by the bystanders as the emergency unfolds. Their research has demonstrated the importance of group size in these settings. The more people present, the less likely any single bystander is to help. This occurs because of social influence—inhibition by the inaction and passiveness of other bystanders and

the diffusion of responsibility, or sharing of the burden of helping, with other bystanders.

13. Aggression is behavior aimed at harming another living being. Freud and Lorenz have suggested that aggression is instinctive. Another view is that frustration instigates aggression. A social-learning approach views aggression as being based on learning experiences and anticipated rewards and punishments and as being instigated by a number of social and environmental conditions (e.g., provocation). Research has shown that frustration, aggressive cues, attack, and other forms of aversive stimulation, as well as aggressive models can increase aggresssion.

14. Prosocial behavior can be increased by rewarding it and modeling it. Furthermore, we must teach people skills that may be needed in helping others. Making people aware of the research on prosocial behavior can also be useful.

15. In terms of controlling aggression, catharsis does not offer much hope. Teaching responses, such as empathy, that are incompatible with aggression appears more promising. The social-learning view suggests that rewards for aggression should be removed and that individuals should be exposed to nonaggressive models. Eron argues that aggression can also be reduced by socializing boys the same way we do girls.

16. Both children and adults spend considerable time watching television, the content of which is highly violent. Given that television violence has been shown to influence aggression, why is there so much of it? Network officials remain unconvinced that its effects are harmful and they often claim that viewers enjoy violence. Research suggests, however, that there is no link between a show's popularity and the amount of violence on the show.

— IMPORTANT TERMS AND CONCEPTS —

Social Psychology
Person Perception
Stereotypes
Self-fulfilling Prophecy
Attribution
Causal Attribution
Consistency
Distinctiveness
Consensus
Impression Formation
Weighted-average Model
Implicit Personality Theory
Halo Effect
Actor-observer Difference

Self-serving Bias
Attitude
Credibility
Attitude-discrepant Behavior
Cognitive Dissonance
Social Norms
Conformity
Normative Social Influence
Informational Social Influence
Compliance
Foot-in-the-door Technique
Door-in-the-face Technique
Low-balling

Obedience
Destructive Obedience
Attraction
Balance Theory
Reinforcement-affect Model
Prosocial Behavior
Social-influence Process
Diffusion of Responsibility
Empathy
Aggression
Frustration-aggression Hypothesis
Aggressive Cues
Catharsis

— SUGGESTIONS FOR FURTHER READING —

Baron, R. A. (1977). *Human aggression.* New York: Plenum Publishing. An excellent overview of research on human aggression, including social, environmental, and individual determinants of aggression and a chapter on the control of aggression.

Baron, R. A., & Byrne, D. (1984). *Social psychology: Understanding human interaction* (4th ed.). Boston: Allyn & Bacon. A comprehensive and well-written introduction to the field.

Berscheid, E., & Walster, E. (1978). *Interpersonal attraction* (2nd ed.). Reading, Mass.: Addison-Wesley. An interesting summary of theories and determinants of attraction and love by two of the leading researchers in the area.

Latané, B., & Darley, J. M. (1970). *The unresponsive bystander: Why doesn't he help?* New York: Appleton-Century-Crofts. The highly readable classic on bystander intervention.

Milgram, S. (1974). *Obedience to authority.* New York: Harper & Row. An excellent summary and analysis by Milgram of his research on obedience.

Petty, R. E., & Cacioppo, J. T. (1981). *Attitudes and persuasion: Classic and contemporary approaches.* Dubuque, Iowa: Wm. C. Brown. A thorough and up-to-date coverage of different approaches to attitudes and attitude change.

— CHAPTER 19 —

ENVIRONMENTAL PSYCHOLOGY

ENVIRONMENTAL PSYCHOLOGY

— CHAPTER OBJECTIVES —

To achieve the objectives of this chapter, you should be able to answer the questions listed here. You should also be able to define the important terms and concepts listed at the end of the chapter.

1. What are the functions of personal space and territoriality?
2. List some consequences of interacting at inappropriate distances. List the consequences of personal-space invasions.
3. How do crowding, noise, and heat affect behavior? How are these effects explained?
4. What are the psychological consequences of living in an urban environment?
5. In what ways can the environment be designed to match the needs of its users?
6. How can behavior be altered to maintain environmental quality?

— CHAPTER OUTLINE —

Spatial Behavior
People are protective of the space around them.

Personal Space
Territoriality
Application: Designing Responsive Environments

Environmental Determinants of Behavior
Behavior is influenced by a variety of environmental stressors.

Crowding
Noise
Temperature
Urban Environment
Application: Reducing Crowding Stress in a Dormitory

Environmental Design and Environmental Behavior Change
Both the environment and behavior can be manipulated to better fit them to each other.

Environmental Design
Changing Environmental Behavior
Application: Reducing Air-Conditioning Usage

On the Horizon: Crowding Research and the Future of Prisons

THE URBAN ENVIRONMENT

A few years ago, Associated Press released the following story:

HOUSTON (AP)—Not that it comes as a surprise to many residents of the Houston area who have to drive to and from work each day, or hustle down the crowded sidewalks bumping elbows and shoulders, but the people of the nation's fifth largest city are facing a massive nervous breakdown.

That's the word from the Mental Health Association of Houston and Harris County after a study of the divorce rate, the juvenile crime rate, the drug and alcohol abuse rate, in this city called the "Golden Buckle of the Sun Belt."

The Houston metropolitan area, with an estimated population of 2.2 million, is growing by 1,000 persons a week, according to the latest Chamber of Commerce figures. Traffic is a daymare, with freeways bumper to bumper each morning and afternoon. After the rush hours, the major routes resemble a drag strip on a Sunday afternoon. . .

One driver, in a recent test, drove the speed limit the 13 miles from his office to his home. He was passed by 144 cars, 23 of them blowing horns because he was moving too slowly. He passed one vehicle and it was puffing smoke from an apparent over-heated engine.

The mental health association report stated, "Fifteen percent of the entire population of Harris County, or approximately 350,000 persons, will require some form of mental health care soon."

And, the report from a team of researchers added, "the most disturbing aspect of this increasing social disintegration is its effect on our children. Our figures on child abuse, the number of children who required mental health care, juvenile crime rates, show that our children are the victims of our inability to cope. . . ."

The report concluded, "Unless the community and our public officials act on some of these urgent recommendations, the problems we are facing now in mental health care will soon become completely unmanageable." (Houston is facing, 1979)

Houston, Texas, is now the fourth largest city in the United States, and its problems continue to grow. Although we do not mean to single out Houston, its story illustrates one of the basic interests of environmental psychologists: the urban environment and its effects. Later, we will take a detailed look at these effects, but first we need to understand some terms.

Environmental psychology is the study of interrelationships between behavior and the physical environment (Holahan, 1982; Russell & Ward, 1982; Stokols, 1982). The **physical environment** is anything of a physical nature that surrounds us—a room, a city, the weather, pollution, or a work space, for example. Environmental psychologists want to know how the physical environment affects behavior and how people use and affect the environment. Some of their typical questions are: How are prisoners affected by living in crowded conditions? Does hot weather encourage riots? How should offices be designed to best meet workers' needs for privacy and personal space? What can be done behaviorally to conserve the environment? Such questions form the basis of this chapter.

Environmental psychologists have long been interested in space: how people use it, try to control it, give it meaning, and react to intruders into it. Two particularly interesting forms of such behavior are personal space and territoriality.

Personal Space

Imagine sitting alone at a table in an uncrowded library, diligently studying. Suddenly, someone takes a seat next to you, moving the chair only inches away from your own (see Figure 19–1). What would you do? If you would get up and leave, you appreciate the concept of **personal space**—an area surrounding the body that is defined by an invisible boundary, which cannot be trespassed on. The boundary may expand or contract, depending on the situation and individual needs. The particular amount of personal space required in a given situation is often referred to as a *personal-space bubble.* This bubble is portable; it goes wherever the person goes.

One function of the personal-space bubble seems to be *self-protection* (Bell, Fisher, & Loomis, 1978). Keeping a distance from others prevents excessive stimulation and intimacy while maintaining privacy. *Communication* is a second function of the personal-space bubble. By maintaining various distances between ourselves and others, we communicate the type and quality of relationship we wish to have.

— How Much Space Do You Need?

As suggested, the size of the personal-space bubble may vary by situation. That is, people are sometimes willing to let down defenses and interact with others at closer distances than usual. Sherrod (1982) has outlined several important factors in this regard. One factor is age. As people grow older, the size of their personal-space bubble increases. At about age 12, the child's personal-space zone is similar to that of adults (Aiello & Aiello, 1974). Another factor that can affect personal-space needs is anxiety. When we feel anxious, our personal-space zone increases; that is, we want to keep a greater distance from others. We also tend to keep a larger distance between ourselves and those we deem different, or abnormal. The size of our personal-space bubble is affected by our gender as well. Men tend to interact with each other at a larger distance than do women. The smallest distance is maintained by a woman and man who are acquainted. Liking also affects our personal-space bubble (see Figure 19–2);

Figure 19–1.
A personal-space invasion at the library. How would you react?

(a)

(b)

Figure 19–2.

(a) People who like each other interact at a close distance. (b) Strangers maintain a more moderate distance.

we prefer to be closer to those we like than to those we dislike (Gifford, 1982). Differing social statuses have also been found to lead to greater interpersonal distancing (cf. Hayduk, 1983). In general, the greater the similarity between individuals, the less the distance at which they interact. Similarity decreases potential threat and enhances liking.

How much space one needs can be affected greatly by past learning experiences. Some individuals learn, for example, that it is appropriate to interact at close distances, and they do not feel threatened by such closeness. They may also learn that having physical contact with others during the interaction is appropriate. Such individuals would be likely to have smaller personal space bubbles than would those who have diametrically opposed experiences. In this vein, Hall (1966) argued that North Americans have a much larger personal space zone than do Arabs. Arabs prefer to interact and communicate at distances close enough to be able to touch each other and even smell each other. North Americans tend to prefer greater distances. You can imagine the potential for misunderstandings if a North American and an Arab try to communicate without being aware of each other's differing personal-space needs.

When You Have Too Little or Too Much Space

In any situation, there is presumably an optimal amount of personal space. What happens when you interact with someone at a nonoptimal distance—either too close or too far away? If you consider the functions of personal space—protection and communication—it seems likely that such inappropriate spacing would have negative consequences.

Hall's (1966) work on **proxemics**—the study of interpersonal distancing—is relevant here. Hall suggests that interacting at an inappropriate distance (too close or too far) conveys a negative communication, resulting in negative assumptions and negative feelings about the other person. When is a particular distance inappropriate? Hall observed that North Americans tend to use four zones of personal space. **Intimate distance** (0 to 1½ feet) is reserved for intimate or close contacts involving activities such as lovemaking, comforting, protecting, and intimate conversation. **Personal distance** (1½ to 4 feet) is used for conversations between acquaintances or close friends. **Social distance** (4 to 12 feet) is used for impersonal, formal, and businesslike encounters.

Public distance (more than 12 feet) is reserved for formal public speaking, involving only one-way communication.

Albert and Dabbs (1970) tested several of Hall's ideas by varying the distance between a subject and a persuasive communicator. Subjects in the study interacted with the communicator at an appropriate distance (5 feet) or at one of two inappropriate distances (2 or 15). In support of Hall's predictions, the researchers found that the appropriate-distance condition produced greater attention to the communicator, more recall of the message, and a greater perception of the communicator's expertise. Other evidence (see, for example, Patterson & Sechrest, 1970) suggests that people have more positive feelings and greater liking for others when they interact with them at appropriate distances.

Argyle and Dean (1965) have suggested that when optimal physical distance is not maintained, individuals engage in a variety of actions to regain equilibrium. This notion is referred to as **equilibrium theory.** According to the theory, the level of immediacy, or closeness, in an interaction is affected not only by physical distance but also by such nonverbal cues as eye contact and body orientation. The smaller the distance, or the greater the eye contact, or the more direct the other's body orientation, the greater the immediacy. Argyle and Dean suggest that if immediacy is too great in one dimension, compensations will be made in others. If you are interacting too closely to someone, you may reduce eye contact to reduce immediacy. When riding in an elevator, you may have found yourself looking intently at the floor or the door to avoid looking at other riders.

— Personal-Space Invasions

Requirements for personal space are evident in the library example given earlier. Intrusions into the personal space of others are referred to as **personal-space invasions.** Reactions to such invasions have been assessed in a number of studies.

In one such study (Felipe & Sommer, 1966), subjects whose personal space was invaded as they sat outdoors were more likely to leave, or to leave sooner, than were noninvaded control subjects (see Figure 19–3). Similar flight has been noted by other investigators. For example, in a study reported by Konečni, Libuser, Morton, and Ebbesen (1975), the personal space of male and female pedestrians waiting to cross a busy intersection was invaded at distances of 1, 2, 5, and 10

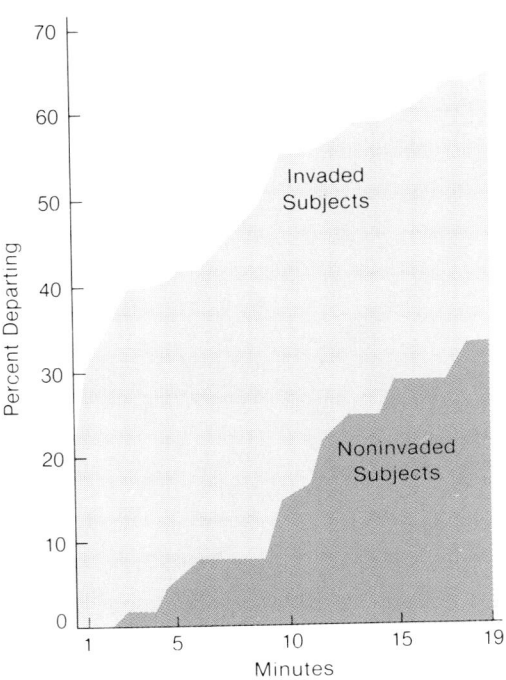

Figure 19–3.

Cumulative percentage of subjects leaving scene at various intervals after personal-space invasions or no invasions. (From *Personal Space* by Robert Sommer, © 1969 by Prentice-Hall, Inc., Englewood Cliffs, NJ 07632).

feet. The closer the personal-space invasion, the faster subjects crossed the street (see Figure 19–4). Such flight reactions seem to be based on negative impressions about the invader, who is likely to be seen as unpleasant, hostile, rude, and aggressive (Smith & Knowles, 1978). Fleeing is not the only defensive action that tends to occur in response to invasions. Invaded subjects also often shift their body orientation away from the invader, avoid eye contact, and erect physical barriers (such as books or other belongings) between themselves and the invader (Felipe & Sommer, 1966; Patterson, Mullens, & Romano, 1971).

All of these responses suggest that personal-space invasions are uncomfortable, aversive, and stressful. However, such invasions can also lead to positive reactions (Baron, 1978a). For instance, we do not generally feel uncomfortable and threatened by invasions from friends, lovers, or attractive people. The proximity of such people may actually lead to positive reactions. Storms and Thomas (1977), in fact, found that nearness increased liking for another person as long as that person behaved in a friendly manner. If the person behaved in an unfriendly manner, nearness led to decreased liking. It seems, then, that the effect of personal-space invasions depends on the actions and, perhaps, the characteristics of the invader.

Finally, there appear to be gender differences in reactions to personal-space invasions (Fisher & Byrne, 1975). Women tend to react more negatively than men to side-by-side invasions; men, on the other hand, tend to react more negatively than women to face-to-face invasions. Consistent with this finding, Fisher and Byrne (1975) also found that men sitting in a library erect barriers such as books and personal belongings so as to prevent face-to-face invasions. Women erect such barriers against adjacent invasions. The next time you are in a library, see if you can verify Fisher and Byrne's observations. You might also want to keep their findings in mind when you are trying to make a good impression on someone of the opposite sex.

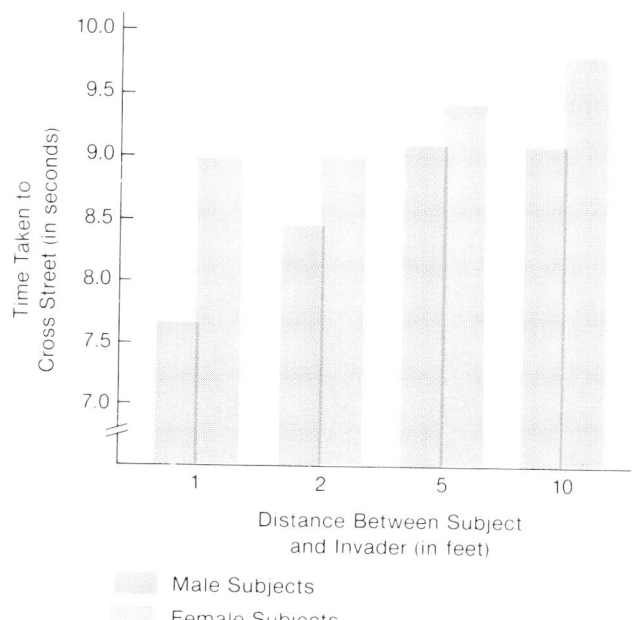

Figure 19–4.

Time taken to cross street as a function of distance from invader and sex of subject. (Based on data from Konečni, Libuser, Morton, & Ebbesen, 1975, p. 291.)

Figure 19–5.

A common example of territorial behavior.

Territoriality

Keep out! No trespassing! Do not disturb! These statements are familiar expressions of *territoriality*. **Territorial behavior** refers to acts that are carried out in an attempt to claim space and exclude other members of one's species. People put signs on their doors and fences around their houses and engage in other actions to defend spaces against intrusion by others (see Figure 19–5). Whereas personal space involves distances we maintain in interactions, territories regulate with whom we interact. Furthermore, although personal space has changing and flexible boundaries, territories often have fixed boundaries.

Territorial behavior occurs in both humans and lower animals. For lower animals, it facilitates a number of significant activities and functions, including mating, food gathering, rearing of young, and controlling aggression (Bell, Fisher, & Loomis, 1978). For humans, it regulates privacy, aids our sense of identity by specifying what belongs to us, and lends order and continuity to life.

— Types of Territories

Altman (1975) has distinguished three types of territories, according to how much control the individual has over an area. A **primary territory** is perceived as being owned, and it is used and controlled on a relatively permanent basis as a necessary, central part of everyday life. The owner of such a territory (e.g., of a home or office) has complete control over access to the area, and uninvited intrusions by others are viewed negatively.

A **secondary territory** is used regularly by an individual or group, but it is not owned, and those involved have less control over it than over a primary territory. Many different people may use such secondary territories as classrooms, local playgrounds and neighborhood bars. It is only during specified times, however, that the occupants have some control over the area.

A **public territory** is an area used only temporarily and one used by anyone, which means that it is difficult to control. The area is not owned, but occupants may nevertheless temporarily personalize it. For example, you may pick out an area at the beach as yours. But if you leave and return later to find your space occupied by someone else, there is little you can do. Usually, even with such public spaces, we tend to mark off our space with various belongings (Edney & Jordan-Edney, 1974) or through actions, such as building sand-castle walls around a chosen spot on a beach.

— Evidence for Territorial Behavior in Humans

Groups, as well as individuals, exhibit territorial behavior. Suttles (1968), for example, found that different ethnic groups in Chicago established and protected their own turfs, or territories. On the individual level, think of the many situations in which you have claimed a certain chair or area. As Altman (1975) notes, territorial behavior is evident in the home. In shared bedrooms, for example, each occupant has a separate closet (or part of one) and a separate dresser (or separate drawers). Family members also show territoriality in their unvarying mealtime seating arrangements. They all have their own places. Apart from the dining table, it is also common in many homes to find that a certain chair is reserved for the father and another for the mother. Even outside the home, in classrooms or libraries, for example, it is common for individuals to regard certain chairs or tables as theirs.

People use a variety of techniques to communicate that a certain territory is theirs. To retain a territory that we are leaving temporarily, we often place a coat over a chair or spread out our possessions. But how effective such **territorial markers** are varies according to the situation. Sommer (1969) reported that in a relatively uncrowded library, any type of marker (e.g., notebooks or newspapers) effectively prevented spatial invasions. Under crowded conditions, however, markers of a valuable and personal nature (e.g., a sports coat or textbook) were the most effective at warding off invaders. When it is difficult to use physical markers to claim a territory, actions sometimes serve the same purpose. For example, research at a game arcade found that touching the games was frequently used to claim them (Werner, Brown, & Damron, 1981).

Many, but not all, residents of houses use territorial markers, such as signs, hedges, or fences. Edney (1972) found that residents of houses with distinctive territorial markers tended to be longer-term occupants than were residents with less-distinctive markers. The longer-term occupants seemed to have a greater commitment to the territory and to be more sensitive to territorial intrusions.

Dealing with territorial intrusions. Even though we mark off our territories and even though such markers are typically effective, we nevertheless encounter occasional intrusions. What would you do if you claimed a seat at the library and, while you were temporarily away, someone occupied your seat? According to the findings of one study (Taylor & Brooks, 1980), you would tell the intruder to give the seat back.

Sommer (1980) points out that once a particular place has been claimed as a territory, people will go to great lengths to defend it. He notes that students may make others who sit at their table feel highly unwelcome. In a more extreme fashion, a gang may attack a member of a rival gang that intrudes on its territory. Defending one's territory may also take the form of swiftly removing litter left by an intruder (Worchel & Lollis, 1982). In this case, the intrusion is the contamination rather than an individual.

DESIGNING RESPONSIVE ENVIRONMENTS

Personal space and territoriality have many practical implications. Altman has proposed that both are used to regulate privacy, which he defines as "selective control of access to the self or to one's group" (Altman, 1975, p. 18). Privacy, then, refers to the fact that sometimes we want to be with others and other times we want to be alone. In line with this, Altman (1975) suggests that a general goal of environmental design should be to create **responsive environments**—environments that allow easy shifts from separateness to togetherness.

In most American homes, we usually must change rooms to change the level of privacy. We may use the family room for a high level of interaction and the bathroom, den, or bedroom for more privacy. But rather than thinking of certain places as having single functions, Altman suggests that a single space can be designed to have multiple functions. The Japanese take this approach, for example. Flexibility is built into many homes by their movable walls, which allow the same space to be used for such different purposes as eating, sleeping, and socializing.

Altman notes that what is needed is a more conscious effort on the part of environmental designers to use the concept of personal space. Questions to ask about any design are: Have gender differences in personal-space requirements been taken into account? Does the environment allow for adjustments in personal-space needs? For instance, if office chairs are in a fixed position, people who are interacting cannot change their distance or orientation (e.g., from face-to-face to side-by-side). With a more flexible arrangement, personal-space requirements could be better met.

Territorial behavior also has implications for environmental design. Recall our earlier discusssion of primary, secondary, and public territories. Altman's concern is that environments be designed so that each type of territory is recognizable and users have appropriate control over them. In Altman's view, territories function to reduce conflicts and intrusions in the course of social interaction. This is done effectively with primary territories. Homes, for example, are easily recognizable and are honored by others.

Secondary and public territories, on the other hand, are more difficult to distinguish. These types of territories need to be designed in such a way that they are accurately perceived by both users and visitors. Otherwise, Altman notes, the result will be conflict. A good example of what can happen in this regard comes from Newman's (1972) work on urban housing developments in which entranceways, play areas, and hallways were not designed for residents to have clear control and supervision over them. Because of this, the crime rate was high and the residents felt unsafe. Altman describes the situation as one "in which a secondary territory, presumably under the partial control of occupants, was actually a public territory and therefore inappropriately accessible to many people" (Altman, 1975, pp. 209–210). Territories, then, must be designed in such a way that the desired and appropriate level of control can be achieved. The same type of conflict can occur when a primary territory, such as a bedroom, is designed so that its occupants do not have a high level of control over access to the room (e.g., when one must pass through the bedroom to get to another part of the house or apartment).

In sum, environments must be designed to control social interaction and access. If the issue of privacy regulation is not respected, Altman believes, people will have to struggle against the environment to achieve desired levels of interaction.

ENVIRONMENTAL DETERMINANTS OF BEHAVIOR

In this section we will turn to a consideration of effects that the physical environment may have on us. In particular, we will look at crowding, noise, temperature, and the urban environment.

Crowding

All of us have experienced high-density environments—environments with little physical space available per person. They may be dormitory rooms, houses, elevators, or classrooms, but whatever the setting, we often consider the situation to be negative. **Crowding** is a stressful psychological state—a personal, subjective reaction to insufficient space (Stokols, 1972; Altman, 1975). **Population density,** on the other hand, is the number of people or animals per unit of space. Thus density is a physical term and crowding a psychological one. The distinction is useful when we examine the common observation that not all high-density settings are considered crowded or uncomfortable. Often, we actually seek out high-density surroundings, such as football games, parties, and concerts. However, there seems little doubt that when high density is experienced as crowding, an assortment of negative effects result.

Currently, the best-accepted view among psychologists is that crowding is experienced when a person feels a lack of personal control in the particular setting (Schmidt & Keating, 1979). According to this view, if the lack of control is not important to individuals in a given setting or if the individuals do have a sense of personal control over a high-density environment, then perceptions of crowding are lessened and negative effects are less likely (Epstein, 1981, 1982).

— Negative Effects of Crowding

If crowding is a stressful state, people who feel crowded should be subject to a number of negative consequences, among them stress-related physiological problems. Evans (1979), for example, found that crowding produces increases in heart rate and blood pressure. Physical illness also seems to be a consequence of crowding. In one study, students living in high-density dormitories made more visits to the student health center than did students living in low-density dormitories (Baron, Mandel, Adams, & Griffen, 1976). In another study, prison inmates living under high-density conditions were sick more often than were prison inmates living under low-density conditions (McCain, Cox, & Paulus, 1976).

Negative feelings should also be associated with the stress of living in a crowded environment. Such was the case in the households studied by Rohe (1982). In this study, as household density increased, satisfaction decreased; so too did the amount of time spent at home. Many negative effects on social behavior have also been uncovered. In the Rohe (1982) study, as density increased, so did the number of arguments with family members. Furthermore, there is ample evidence that crowding leads individuals to withdraw socially—to interact less with others (Baum & Greenberg, 1975; Sundstrom, 1975). Students living in crowded dormitories are less sociable and less inclined toward group activities than are students living in uncrowded dormitories (Baum & Valins, 1977).

To the extent that crowded, stressful environments produce too little privacy, too much stimulation, and too much interference with one's desired activities, social withdrawal becomes a means of coping with the environment (Altman, 1975). Given the attempts to withdraw socially, it is not surprising to find also that crowding lessens attraction toward others. Baron and his colleagues (Baron, Mandel, Adams, & Griffen, 1976), for example, found that dormitory residents living three to a room in a room that was designed for only two were less satisfied with their roommates than were residents living two to a room in rooms of similar size. There is evidence indicating that this lessened attraction may be truer of males than females (e.g., Epstein & Karlin, 1975). In general, for that matter, the stress associated with crowding seems to be greater for males, than for females (Ross, Layton, Erickson, & Schopler, 1973).

Many researchers have been concerned with the effects of crowding on task performance. Recent studies (e.g., Paulus, Annis, Seta, Schkade, & Matthews, 1976) suggest that high density can lower performance on various complex tasks. When subjects are warned, however, that crowding might cause them to feel aroused and anxious, they are able to improve their performance (Langer & Saegert, 1977; Paulus & Matthews, 1980). Apparently, being armed with such information can help lessen the impact of crowding.

— Reducing the Perception of Crowding and Its Effects

A number of variables have been shown to affect performance and the perception of crowding in high-density situations. For example, when the subjects just mentioned were warned about the effects of crowding, it apparently gave them a sense of control over the situation. The importance of control was verified by Sherrod (1974), who found that subjects showed lowered task performance after exposure to a high-density setting—unless they felt they had some control over the high-density environment. A sense of control came from the belief that they could leave the setting if they desired. Having control, then, apparently reduces the stress and aversiveness of high densities, even if the control is not exercised.

Consistent with the theory of learned helplessness (Seligman, 1975; see also chapter 6), several crowding researchers have proposed that a lack of personal control in a high-density environment leads not only to perceptions of crowding but also to a sense of helplessness. For example, Rodin (1976) compared children who lived in high-density and low-density residential conditions. In one experiment, the children could pick their own candy (as reinforcement for performing a task) or they could allow the experimenter to select the candy for them. Children from the high-density homes were less likely than the other children to try to control the selection. In a second experiment, the high-density children did less well than the other children in performing a solvable task after initial exposure to an unsolvable task (see Figure 19–6). Rodin (1976) has suggested that chronic high-density living conditions reduce one's feelings of being able to choose and control things in the home environment, which leads to a decreased expectancy of control in other situations.

Figure 19–6.

Number correct on a solvable problem after initial exposure to either solvable or unsolvable problems for low-density and high-density subjects. (From Rodin, 1976, p. 575.)

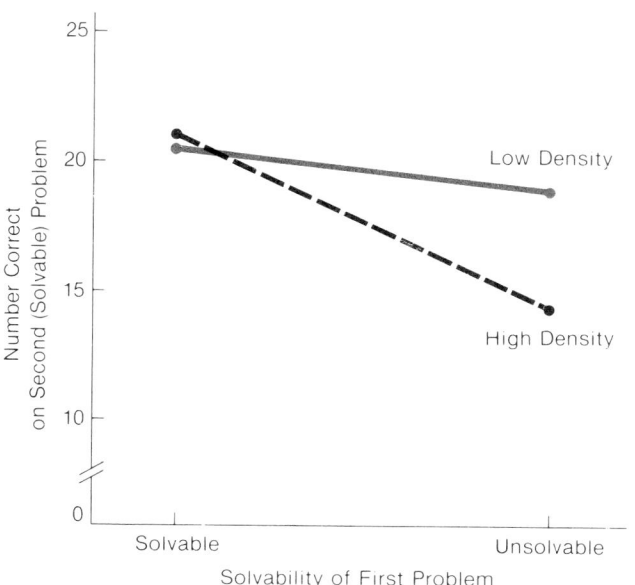

Baum and Valins (1977) noted that college dormitory residents are often faced with unwanted social interactions in public areas such as hallways and lounges. The greater the number of people using these areas, the more likely it is that unwanted interactions will occur and the more difficult it is to control them. Residents' perception of lack of control presumably should lead to their perception of crowding and to the experience of learned helplessness. Baum and Valins further reasoned that the lack of control should be more likely to occur for residents of long-corridor-style dormitories than for those of suite-style dormitories. Fewer interactions would be likely to occur in the common areas of suite-style dormitories, where residents of only three rooms share a lounge and bathroom.

The results of Baum and Valins's study showed that corridor residents in fact reported feeling more crowded than did suite residents, even though density per se was the same in both types of dormitories. In terms of evidence of helplessness, corridor residents were more likely than suite residents to state that it was useless to try to change things in the dormitory. Furthermore, when participating in a laboratory experiment, corridor residents were less likely than suite residents to seek out information about the experiment. Baum, Aiello, and Calesnick (1978) have reported similar findings from another study, as shown in Figure 19–7. Their view of crowding as the stressful loss of personal control caused by high-density conditions is a well-accepted idea among crowding researchers (cf. Baron & Rodin, 1978; Sherrod & Cohen, 1978). In support of this view is the recent finding that the perception of crowding is much greater among individuals who have a high rather than low desire for control over the events in their lives (Burger, Oakman, & Bullard, 1983). For such individuals, the perception that their control over the situation has been restricted would be particularly troubling and would lead them to perceive the setting as highly crowded.

Noise

One definition of **noise** states that it is simply unwanted sound (Kryter, 1970). Think of how often people are exposed to noise. Busy streets, industrial plants, offices, crowds, airports, and the next-door neighbor's stereo may all be sources of noise. Environmental psychologists are interested in how such noise

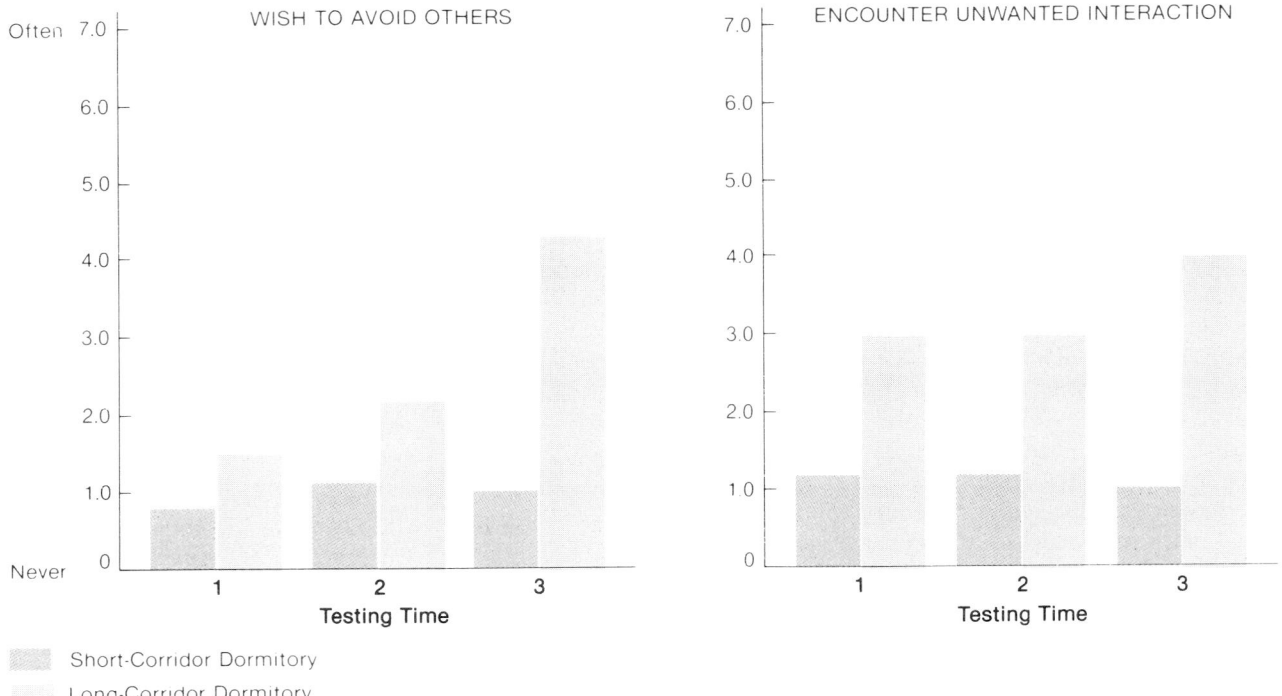

Figure 19–7.

Mean ratings over time of dormitory residents' frequency of desire to avoid others and frequency of encountering unwanted interactions as a function of long- or short-corridor living arrangements. (Based on data from Baum, Aiello, & Calesnick, 1978, p. 1008.)

affects behavior. Before we examine the effects of noise, see chapter 3 for a review of how sound is measured. The discussion there provides a basis for judging the sound levels that will be mentioned here.

— Performance Effects

Whether or not noise adversely affects task performance depends on a number of factors, such as the type of task and the predictability, controllability, and intensity of the noise. Research shows that as long as the noise is in the 90 to 110 dB (decibels) range, simple motor or mental tasks are not adversely affected (cf. Bell, Fisher, & Loomis, 1978). Unpredictable noise in this range, however, can lower performance on complex tasks, memory tasks, and tasks requiring vigilance. Such negative effects, however, are minimal when individuals perceive that they have control over the noise (Glass & Singer, 1972). Simply believing that one can have the noise stopped apparently is effective in reducing the stress, anxiety, and feeling of helpless-

ness associated with noise (Glass, Singer, & Pennebaker, 1977).

Noise also produces a variety of aftereffects. Glass, Singer, and Friedman (1969) found that subjects exposed to uncontrollable, unpredictable noise at 108 dB subsequently made more errors in a proofreading task (which requires concentration and vigilance) and were significantly less persistent in their attempts at solving unsolvable puzzles than were subjects exposed to predictable noise, controllable noise, or no noise. That is, the former showed less frustration tolerance than the latter. Again, Glass, Singer, and Pennebaker (1977) attribute such aftereffects to a sense of helplessness in individuals who are unable to control or predict the onset of noise. The more control we think we have during the noise, the better we will do on subsequent tasks, even though we may not actually exercise the control (Sherrod, Hage, Halpern, & Moore, 1977).

Noise also affects task performance in real-world environments. For example, Cohen and his colleagues (Cohen, Evans, Krantz, & Stokols, 1980) studied children whose schools are located in the flight path adjacent to the Los Angeles International Airport. In comparison to children whose schools are not in the flight path, these children had higher blood pressure, performed more poorly on tasks, gave up sooner on frustrating puzzles, and were more bothered by noise. The noise seemed to affect the children in much the same way that crowding affects people. In both cases, the stressor seems to induce a sense of helplessness. A follow-up investigation of the children whose schools were in the flight path (Cohen, Evans, Krantz, Stokols, & Kelley, 1981) revealed that a year later the children still had not adapted to the noise. In general, there is little evidence that people ever adapt to community noise (Weinstein, 1982). In other words, even with the passing of time, the noise is still attended to, still causes negative effects, and is still perceived as annoying.

— Social Effects

Recent research also indicates that noise can affect such social behaviors as aggression and helping. Donnerstein and Wilson (1976), for example, found that unpredictable and uncontrollable bursts of noise increased the aggression of angry subjects, but not of nonangry subjects (see Figure 19–8). Similar results occurred for aggression following exposure to noise. However, subjects given the perception of control over the noise were no more aggressive than were subjects not exposed to noise. Other studies also support the finding that noise can facilitate aggression in angry individuals (e.g., Geen, 1978a).

Noise can also decrease helping responses. A common interpretation of this finding is in terms of attention. Generally, a person will ignore less-important stimuli and attend to the task at hand (cf. Cohen & Weinstein, 1981, 1982). Bell and colleagues (1978) noted that "since noise reduces the attention paid to less important stimuli, if social cues that someone needs help are less important than cues associated with a more important task, then noise should make us less aware of signs of distress" (p. 114). Let's look at some relevant evidence.

In an experiment by Mathews and Canon (1975), subjects in a residential setting were exposed to someone—a confederate of the experimenters—dropping books from several boxes he was carrying. In some cases, background noise was created by a lawnmower running loudly in the adjacent yard; in other cases, the lawnmower was inoperative, leaving only the average

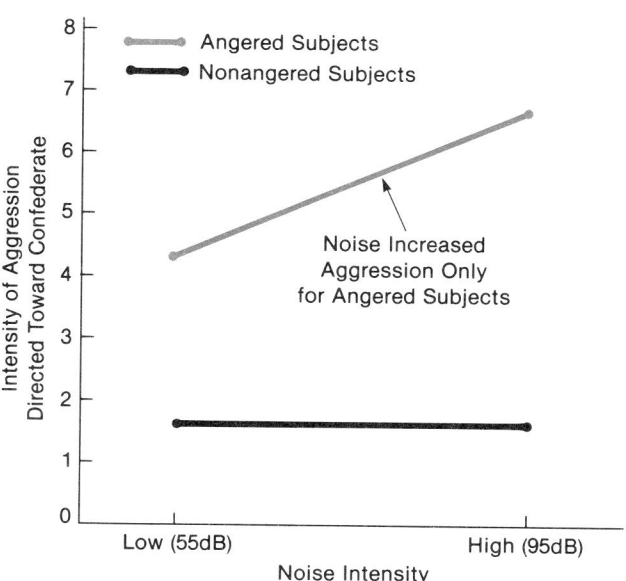

Figure 19–8.

Aggression (shock intensity) as a function of noise intensity and anger. (From Donnerstein & Wilson, 1976, p. 777.)

ambient noise level. Also, cues as to the legitimacy of the confederate's need were manipulated by having him wear or not wear a cast on his right arm. Over all, 50 percent of the subjects helped in the low-noise condition, but only 12.5 percent helped in the high-noise condition. The presence of a cast also significantly increased helping—in the low-noise condition. In this case, 80 percent of the subjects helped when the confederate wore a cast, and only 20 percent helped when he did not. Helping remained infrequent in the high-noise condition in both the presence and absence of the cast (see Figure 19–9). Apparently, not only does noise decrease helping, it also lessens attention to peripheral cues, such as the confederate's cast (cf. Page, 1977).

Temperature

The weather, particularly the temperature, is often blamed for many social ills. Erma Bombeck (1980), in her newspaper column, once mused that "hot weather makes you mean." Perhaps your own experiences verify that when you're hot, you're often irritable, uncom-

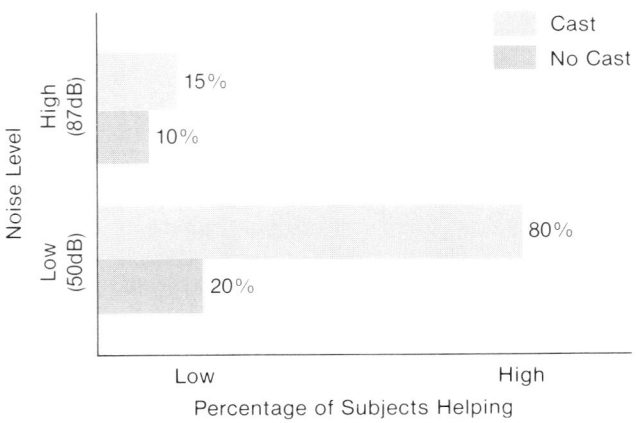

Figure 19–9.
Percentage of subjects helping as a function of noise level and presence or absence of cast. (Based on data from Mathews & Canon, 1975, p. 574.)

fortable, and on edge. Environmental psychologists have been interested in assessing the effects of high temperatures on such social behaviors as attraction and aggression. Since relatively little attention has been given to the effects of cold (Bell, 1981), we will confine our discussion to the effects of heat.

If we do feel irritable and grouchy when we're hot, it seems reasonable that if we are with others, we may like them less or may be more than ordinarily aggressive toward them. With regard to attraction, Griffitt (1970) exposed subjects either to comfortable, cool conditions or to hot conditions (temperatures in the high 90s or higher). Subjects were asked to indicate their degree of liking for an anonymous stranger on the basis of the stranger's responses on a questionnaire. Over all, subjects indicated greater liking for the person when they were in the pleasant, cool environment than when they were in the hot, aversive environment. To understand this effect, think back to Clore and Byrne's (1974) reinforcement-affect model of attraction (discussed in chapter 18). To the extent that heat elicits negative affect, it should also decrease attraction toward people associated with the negative affect.

In the Griffitt (1970) study, the stranger was not in the room with the subject. This is important, because other research (cf. Bell, 1981) has found that heat does not reduce attraction toward a person who is in the room with the subject, sharing the stress of the aversive environment. The positive effects of the shared suffering may counteract the otherwise negative effects

that heat would have. In summary, then, heat may adversely affect attraction toward total strangers but may have minimal effects on attraction in cases where the other person has been continuously present in the aversive environment (Bell, 1981).

Turning now to the issue of aggression, we find that heat and aggression are not as clearly linked as the phrases *hot under the collar* or *the long, hot summer* might suggest (Baron, 1977). Still, many of the riots that occurred during the summer in the late 1960s and early 1970s were attributed at least in part to the high temperatures. Presumably, increased irritability and short tempers would be enough to trigger outbursts of violence.

Although this seems reasonable, the available data suggest that high temperatures do not necessarily facilitate aggression. Instead, they may actually reduce it. Baron (1977) has proposed that the relationship between temperature and aggression is curvilinear; that is, aggression first increases, then declines, as heat increases. Baron assumes that increased temperatures lead to increased negative feelings, or negative affect. He also assumes that there is a curvilinear relationship between negative affect (whether generated by heat, negative personal evaluations, or whatever) and aggression (see Figure 19–10). Presumably, negative affect increases one's general irritability and, up to some point, increases one's willingness to be aggres-

Figure 19–10.
Hypothesized curvilinear relationship between negative affect and aggression. (From Baron, 1977, p. 146.)

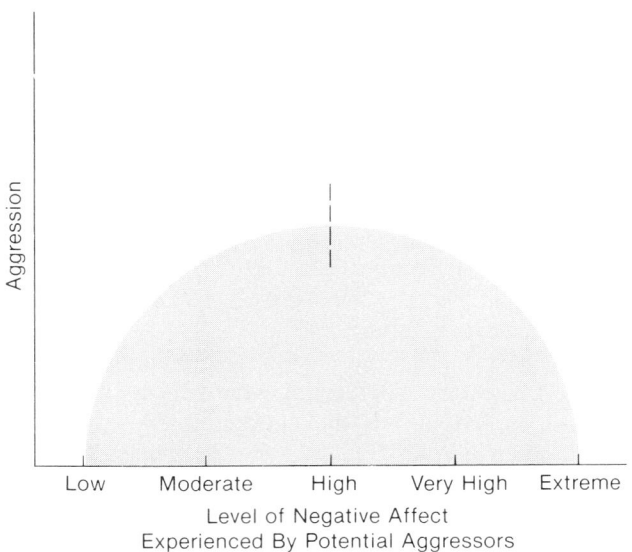

sive. Beyond this point, however, increases in negative affect make one so miserable that other responses, such as leaving the scene or trying to reduce the discomfort, take precedence over aggression.

Let's return to the earlier statement that riots have often been attributed to high temperatures. Baron and Ransberger (1978) have shown that riots are actually more likely to occur during moderate rather than high temperatures (see Figure 19–11). Consistent with a curvilinear relationship, riots are most likely to occur when temperatures are in the mid 80s. Their frequency drops off considerably beyond that point. However, Carlsmith and Anderson (1979) have presented evidence that the probability of riots increases with an increase in temperature (at least through the temperature range of 91 to 95°F). Clearly, more research is necessary to untangle the precise relationship between heat, rioting, and aggression. It is likely that at some point the probability of a riot does decrease with increased heat because of lethargy, flight from the tion, and so on (Bell & Greene, 1982). The exact temperature at which this happens may simply be higher than that documented by Baron and Ransberger (1978). (See Carlsmith & Anderson, 1979; Cotton, 1981.)

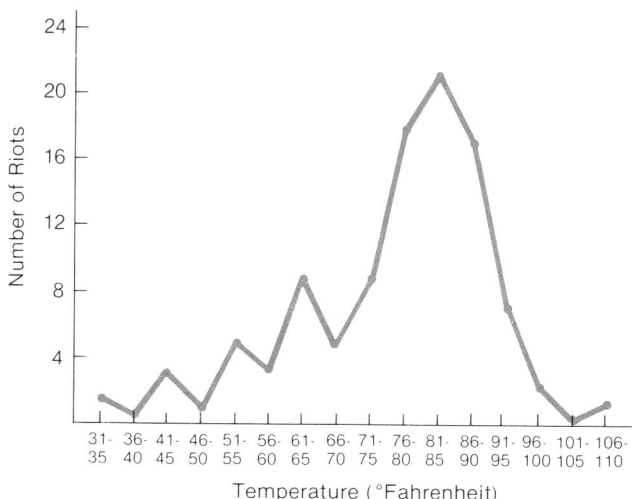

Figure 19–11.
Frequency of riots as a function of ambient temperature. (From Baron & Ransberger, 1978, p. 354.)

Urban Environment

We return now to the topic with which we began—the urban environment. In this section, we will consider whether cities are indeed breeding grounds of social ills. As we examine the urban environment, consider the fact that over 56 million Americans live in cities of 100,000 or more (Krupat, 1980).

The city clearly presents a contrast to the rural environment. Large cities are compact and intense settings. They have more traffic, more noise, and more pollution than rural areas. Most importantly, they have more people. Milgram (1970) noted that in a New York suburb one might encounter 11,000 people within a 10-minute radius of one's office. In midtown Manhattan, on the other hand, one might encounter 220,000 people within the same radius. Although it must be acknowledged that city life is exciting and satisfying for many people (cf. Shaver & Freedman, 1976)) and that it can have many positive aspects (Geller, 1980), it nevertheless is also true that cities have been viewed as the source of a number of negative effects.

Many of the negative beliefs about cities may be inaccurate. The article in the chapter introduction stated that the city of Houston was facing a nervous breakdown. Although this may or may not be so, the available evidence suggests that the people in rural and urban areas do not differ in mental health and psychological well-being (Srole, 1972; Webb, 1978). In a survey reported by Shaver and Freedman (1976), city people did not seem to feel any more anxious or unhappy than people living in small towns or rural areas. All of this aside, it is still possible that the urban environment produces an assortment of negative social effects. We turn to that issue now.

— Social Effects

One particularly striking social effect of cities is that urban residents desire less interaction with strangers than do their rural counterparts. For example, one study (Newman & McCauley, 1977) examined eye contact as a means of assessing desire for interaction. Experimenters who encountered subjects and looked them in the eye found that return eye contact became increasingly more common as they moved from a large city to a suburb to a rural area. As another indication of urban residents' lesser desire for interaction with strangers, Milgram (1977) noted that when students approached strangers with an extended hand of friendship, about two-thirds of the small-town people returned the gesture, whereas only a little more than one-third of the city people did so.

There is also evidence of differences in helping behavior between urban and rural areas (Korte, 1981; Amato, 1983). Think about this question for a moment: If you were in need of help, would you rather be in a large city or a small town? Clearly, we often think of big cities as centers of evil, crime, and pollution, where callousness and indifference prevail. On the other hand, we often believe that small-town people have a deep-rooted concern for one another and would go to any measure to help others.

Milgram (1970) has described the problem of urban **overload,** the situation where excess stimulation from a number and variety of environmental sources impinges on residents. Milgram argues that city residents adapt to this overload by minimizing the overall level of interaction and involvement with other people. A restriction on social interaction means, of course, that city dwellers may not grant requests to do favors, may fail to treat others with courtesy, and, in general, may not make themselves available to others in need. Unless the other person is a friend, involvement in another person's needs will be given low priority.

A number of findings are consistent with Milgram's analysis. Milgram (1970) reported on a study that involved comparing the willingness of city versus town dwellers to offer aid that increased their personal vulnerability and required some trust of strangers. The behavior of interest was allowing strangers to enter one's home to use the telephone. Experimenters were much less likely to have their request granted in Manhattan than in small towns around New York City. City residents communicated mainly by shouting through closed doors and by peering through peepholes. Most town residents opened the door.

Korte and Kerr (1975) examined helping in Boston and several small towns in eastern Massachusetts. Helping was greater in nonurban than urban locations on three measures: (1) making a phone call for the experimenter, who had spent his last dime in making a "wrong-number" call to the subject; (2) returning excess change for a small purchase in stores; and (3) mailing "lost" postcards.

It appears that even a lost child is better off in smaller towns than in large urban areas. Takooshian, Haber, and Lucido (1977) had children aged 6 to 10 approach strangers on busy streets and say: "I'm lost. Can you call my house?" Such requests were made at specific locations in four cities (midtown Manhattan, the Commons in Boston, City Hall in Philadelphia, and the Loop in Chicago) and in outlying towns. Although 46 percent of the strangers approached in cities helped the children, 72 percent of those in the towns helped. There were also qualitative differences between the city and town people. Town people seemed generally sympathetic even when they did not help the child. That is, most did not bluntly refuse but rather offered excuses or suggestions while refusing. On the other hand, most city people who failed to help either curtly ignored the child or swerved, side-stepped, or nodded no. City people were also somewhat more likely than town people to refer the child to others for help (e.g., "Find a cop" or "Go into a store and call"). These results are particularly striking because the individuals were singled out and asked to give help and the emergency was clear and unambiguous.

Whether this city-town difference in helping is due to city people's adaptation to urban overload is not entirely clear. It may be that city people diffuse responsibility to a greater degree because more people are available to help in higher-density environments (see chapter 18). Milgram's overload explanation is also brought into question by Amato's (1983) finding that helping rates begin to decline when communities reach a population of about 20,000. The notion of overload has traditionally been associated with the intense stimulation of cities much larger than that. It may be, however, that residents of moderately sized cities experience a partial overload that at least approximates the urban stress experienced by residents of large cities. On the other hand, it may be that, at least for moderately sized cities, diffusion of responsibility is a better explanation than overload for the reduced helping.

REDUCING CROWDING STRESS IN A DORMITORY

One of the themes that emerges from data on environmental determinants of behavior is that crowding is stressful and can lead to a number of negative effects. Ideally, such data can be used to design less stressful residential environments. As an example, a recent study by Baum and Davis (1980) explored the usefulness of architectural intervention in high-density women's college dormitories. Three types of residential living conditions were examined (see Figure 19–12). One set of students lived along a long corridor that housed 40 students. Another setting was an altered long corridor that housed two groups of 20 each. This alteration was the intervention of interest in the study. Basically, the long-corridor floor was bisected by a three-room lounge area. Relative to the unaltered long corridor, this setup did not reduce the total number of residents on the floor, but it did reduce the number of people sharing bathroom and hallway space. A third set of students lived on a short-corridor floor, which housed one group of 20 students.

The idea of the study was to alleviate crowding architecturally. We noted earlier that a high level of unwanted interaction can lead to a perceived lack of control and a concomitant perception of crowding. The purpose of the Baum and Davis (1980) study was "to modify the group size associated with the long-corridor dormitory, increasing both the likelihood of small group formation and the ease of regulating contact with neighbors" (p. 473).

A number of measures were used to assess the effects of the various housing settings. The assessments were made from the 3rd to the 14th week of residence. The results showed that, when compared with the unaltered long-corridor floor, the altered long-corridor floor (like the short-corridor floor) "resulted in more positive interaction on the dormitory floor, more local group development, more confidence among residents in their ability to control events in the dormitory, and less withdrawal in both residential and non-residential settings" (Baum & Davis, 1980, p. 478). Thus, "architectural interventions that reduce the size of residential groupings can prevent crowding stress"

(Baum & Davis, 1980, p. 480). Clearly, more attention needs to be given to the experience and behavior associated with residential and other environments when such environments are being planned (Zimring, 1981).

Figure 19–12.

Floor plans of dormitory floors studied by Baum and Davis: (a) the long-corridor floor, (b) the short-corridor floor, and (c) the architectural intervention floor. (From Baum & Davis, 1980, p. 475.)

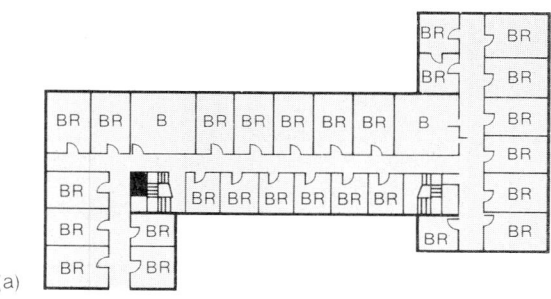

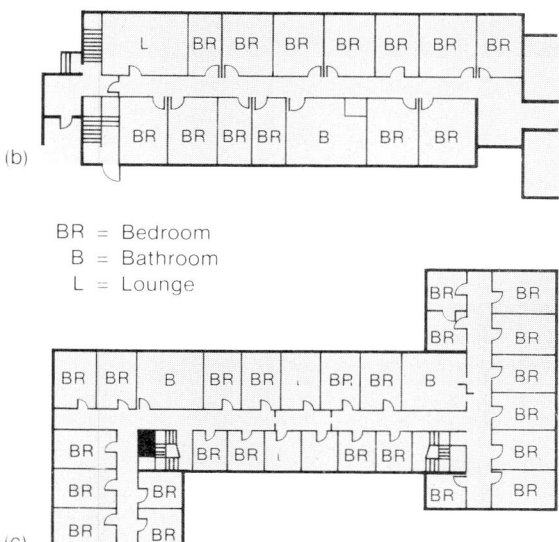

BR = Bedroom
B = Bathroom
L = Lounge

In several cases thus far, we have seen how research has implications for designing environments. In this section we will examine more closely how the environment can be designed to meet users' needs and how users' behavior can be changed to maintain environmental quality.

Environmental Design

It is not sufficient that a room or building look good. Constructed environments must also be designed with respect to their influence on behavior. Consider the effects of furniture arrangement. You may have observed that the placement of furniture can dictate the atmosphere and interactions at a party. Osmond (1957) categorized physical environments as either **sociopetal spaces** (arrangements that encourage social interaction) or **sociofugal spaces** (arrangements that reduce the level of social interaction). In accordance with such a distinction, Sommer and Ross (1958) found that altering the arrangement of furniture in a hospital geriatric ward did indeed make a difference in social interaction. They observed that the furniture was originally situated in long rows such that patients sat side-by-side or back-to-back—an obvious sociofugal arrangement. When the furniture was rearranged in groups of four chairs around each of several small tables, interactions among patients increased dramatically. Clearly, furniture arrangements affect behavior.

A good example of a setting that typically has sociofugal seating arrangements is the lounge area in airports (see Figure 19–13). Sommer (1974) has suggested that this setting inhibits comfortable conversation for airport travelers and visitors. He argues that airport seating is usually inappropriate since many travelers desire to interact with those traveling with them or spending time with them at the airport. He adds that the unsocial and uncomfortable sociofugal seating is preferred by airport managers mainly because it leads travelers to avoid such seating and to spend their money at concessions such as restaurants and cocktail lounges.

Figure 19–13.
Example of a sociofugal space (airport lounge).

The design of offices has also interested some investigators. The openness of office space has been of particular interest (e.g., Sommer, 1974). Open offices, those without walls, are associated with a high level of interaction, but they do not foster close interpersonal relationships. Workers often complain of a lack of privacy in such working environments. Following Altman's (1975) suggestions earlier in the chapter, perhaps the installation of movable wall partitions would give more flexible control of privacy.

The design of buildings to fit user needs is no less important than the design of rooms or office spaces. An often-cited example of how the design of a building can fail to match its residents' needs is the Pruitt-Igoe low-income housing complex in St. Louis. The complex, built in 1954, consisted of 43 11-story apartment buildings covering 57 acres. Despite its billing as a modern, spacious, and much-improved form of low-income housing, the Pruitt-Igoe complex soon became a center for self-destruction. Broken windows, nonworking elevators filled with human waste, vandalism, robbery, and rape became the order of the day. By 1970, only 16 of the 43 buildings remained occupied.

The entire project has now been demolished (see Figure 19–14).

The problems with the project did not seem to lie with the amount of space or the facilities. Rather, as Worchel and Cooper (1983) point out, the residents dissatisfaction arose out of the fact that the building design did not encourage interaction among neighbors and that people could not supervise their children once the children were outside the apartments (see Yancey, 1971). Another problem noted by Worchel and Cooper (1983) is something we have already addressed—the problem of too much indefensible (that is, public) territory. In contrast, **defensible space** is "physical space that is characterized by a high level of social responsibility and personal safety" (Holahan, 1982, p. 330).

The Pruitt-Igoe project was definitely lacking in defensible space. Residents of the project did not take personal responsibility for protecting the semipublic space between apartments (e.g., the stairwells) and between buildings (e.g., alleyways). Had they been able to use and patrol this space as part of their daily routine, unlawful activities would have been lessened and

Figure 19–14.

Part of the Pruitt-Igoe project being demolished in 1972.

the residents' safety would have been enhanced. But the design of the buildings did not foster such use or surveillance. It seems, then, that part of the answer to reducing urban crime may lie in designing physical settings that encourage people to use them, to personalize them, and to take responsibility for them (Holahan, 1982). (See Wise, 1982, for a different perspective on how to reduce crime through environmental design.)

According to Newman (1972), the central characteristic of defensible space is that residents have natural surveillance of the setting. That is, they are easily able to observe the public areas of the setting while they are going about their daily business. Given such surveillance, crime becomes less likely (cf. Holahan, 1982).

Changing Environmental Behavior

Environment-damaging behaviors create serious problems. How can we get people to avoid littering? To use sidewalks rather than trampling the grass? To conserve energy by car-pooling, driving less, buying smaller cars, and using less gas and electricity? Two approaches that have had some success in modifying environmental behaviors are reinforcement techniques and prompts (cf. Bell, Fisher, & Loomis, 1978).

— Reinforcement Techniques

As chapter 6 showed, reinforcement can increase the frequency of a behavior. Positive reinforcement has, in fact, been used in a number of settings to increase constructive environmental behavior. In one relevant study (Clark, Burgess, & Hendee, 1972), children were rewarded with Smokey the Bear patches and forest ranger badges for cleaning up litter at a campground. The reinforcers were small and inexpensive, but they proved effective in motivating the children to pick up the litter. Much the same result occurred when children in another study were rewarded with free snacks at a local fast-food restaurant for helping pick up litter in the community (McNees, Schnelle, Gendrich, Thomas, & Beagle, 1979).

Another positive-reinforcement approach to litter control, one that perhaps would be more effective with adults, is the marked-item technique (Bell, Fisher, & Loomis, 1978). With this technique (see, for example, Hayes, Johnson, & Cone, 1975), experimenters place specially marked items among the litter already present. Individuals are then informed that some litter items are marked in an undetectable manner and that if they pick up one of the marked items, they will be awarded a valuable prize. Such a technique has proved effective in getting people to clean up the environment. Imagine the savings in tax dollars every year if such reinforcement strategies could be implemented on a larger scale.

Energy conservation is another area in which positive reinforcement has been used (Cook & Berrenberg, 1981). Monetary reinforcers, in particular, have been the focus of several studies. Foxx and Hake (1977) offered college students money for reducing the mileage driven in their private automobiles over a 4-week period. The students rewarded for less driving significantly reduced their mileage. The mileage for unrewarded control subjects did not change. Furthermore, a study by Everett, Hayward, and Myers (1974) on the use of a campus bus system showed that such monetary reinforcers need not be large.

A particularly troublesome problem for energy conservation is master-metered apartments (Wodarski, 1982). In many apartment complexes, electricity is metered at a single point for all residents rather than at individual apartments (cf. Holahan, 1982). Energy consumption in such complexes can be as high as 25 percent greater than in individually metered apartments (McClelland—cited in Holahan, 1982). Several studies have shown that monetary-reward programs can be effective in reducing energy consumption in master-metered apartment complexes. McClelland and Cook (1980), for example, rewarded apartment dwellers in a family-housing complex with a monetary award every 2 weeks for 12 weeks if they used less natural gas than the residents of other apartments who were participating in the contest. The reduction in natural gas consumption over the 12-week period was 6.6 percent.

Are incentive systems practical and cost-effective? In a master-metered complex, the answer is certainly yes. In this situation, it is the owner of the complex who pays the energy bill, not the individual apartment dwellers. The energy saved by paying the apartment dwellers to conserve can actually exceed the cost of the incentives (Holahan, 1982). In one study (Walker, 1979), $200 a month in incentive payments saved $320 in electricity. Thus the complex saved money by spending it.

For complexes without master meters, it is not clear whether this type of incentive system has much applicability. Utility companies are not likely to adopt such a system (e.g., giving a rebate for reduced energy consumption), since to do so would reduce their profits (Cone & Hayes, 1980). If utility companies don't provide the incentive to conserve, who will? Probably no one. This doesn't mean that financial incentives can't be used in other ways, though. For example, they can take the form of tax credits on the purchase and installation of items that aid in conservation, such as insulation (Cook & Berrenberg, 1981). Monetary reinforcement isn't the only way of getting people to conserve energy, however. Many areas of society could get involved in promoting energy conservation if the expense were not prohibitive. We now turn to a strategy that is indeed inexpensive.

An approach that is related to the positive-reinforcement procedure is known as **feedback;** it involves informing people about their performance. Much of the conservation work with feedback has dealt with energy conservation in the home (Seligman, Becker, & Darley, 1981). For example, Seligman and Darley (1977) conducted a study of homeowners who either received feedback or did not. Four times a week over a 1-month period, feedback subjects were provided with information about their level of energy use. Control subjects did not receive such feedback. Those in the feedback group used 10.5 percent less electricity than did those in the control group. Apparently, feedback can serve as a positive reinforcement for using less energy.

Even more effective than feedback on one's own energy usage is feedback that compares one's usage to the average usage of other comparable homes in the area (Pallak, Cook, & Sullivan, 1980). Importantly, investigators also found that reductions in energy use that occurred from feedback persisted even after the feedback was withdrawn.

— Prompts

Cues that convey messages are **prompts.** They represent another method of inducing environmentally constructive behavior or discouraging environmentally destructive behavior (Bell, Fisher, & Loomis, 1978). Signs such as "keep off the grass" and "do not litter" are common prompts (see Figure 19–15).

In research, prompts have been studied not only with regard to lawn trampling and littering but also with regard to energy conservation and recycling. Although prompts are usually in written or spoken form, they also may take the form of a model's actions or the condition of the environment (Bell, Fisher, & Loomis,

Figure 19–15.

An example of a common prompt.

1978). Whatever the form, though, a message is conveyed. Presumably, when prompts work, they do so because they make a particular norm salient in that situation. That is, the norm is vividly brought to people's attention. When you see a "no littering" sign, for example, you are essentially being reminded of what is right and wrong behavior.

In one study dealing with walking on lawns, Hayes and Cone (1977) put up signs reading "University Mini-Park—Please Don't Trample the Grass." The signs significantly reduced lawn walking. Similarly, "please don't litter" signs have reduced littering in such settings as supermarkets, dormitories, and even a football stadium (see, for example, Geller, Witmer, & Tuso, 1977). Delprato (1977) even used a simple poster to successfully induce users of men's restrooms to turn off the lights when they left.

As indicated, the state of the environment can also serve as a prompt. This makes sense if you think about the condition of the environment as conveying a message about what kind of behavior is appropriate or inappropriate in that setting (see Figure 19–16). A spotless environment, for example, indicates a clearly existing anti-littering norm. It's almost as though there were an anti-littering sign posted. In several experi-

Figure 19–16.
Unsightly litter is a common scene. It is also an expensive problem.

ments, Krauss, Freedman, and Whitcup (1978) have shown that littering begets more littering. In one of their studies, subjects were given some tissues for wiping away a solvent after they had their palm prints taken. The experimenter then left the subjects in a waiting room that had no trash receptacle and that was either littered with trash or completely unlittered. When subjects later left the room, would they leave the used tissues there or take them? The cleanliness of the environment made a difference: 30 percent of the subjects exposed to the littered environment left the tissues; only 6.7 percent of the subjects exposed to the clean environment did so.

In attempting to solve the problem of littering, Krauss and colleagues (1978) suggest that "by diverting money from ineffectual media campaigns to street cleaning, government might reduce the rate of littering substantially" (p. 122). In a similar vein, Reiter and Samuel (1980) found that a parking garage floor free of litter prompted much less littering than a garage floor that was already littered. Thus it may be that the least expensive and most effortless way to control litter is to clean it up regularly (Holahan, 1982).

— APPLICATION —
REDUCING AIR-CONDITIONING USAGE

Psychological solutions to many environmental problems do exist. In this section, we will see how two psychologists, Becker and Seligman (1978), demonstrated that mechanical feedback could be applied to home energy consumption. Psychological intervention by mechanical means is not a new idea, but it is particularly useful in a residential environment.

Becker and Seligman believed that feedback could be presented to people living in air-conditioned homes through a signaling device informing them that, by simply opening windows, they could be comfortable without air conditioning. The problem is that peo-

ple often use their air conditioners when they could be comfortable with the windows open and the air conditioners turned off. Awareness of cooler outside temperatures is often reduced in a tightly shut home. Thus people don't know that they can turn off the air conditioner and still be cool.

To remedy the problem, Becker and Seligman installed a cool-weather signaling device in the homes of a number of people. The device was a blue light bulb mounted on the side of a wall phone and visible from the kitchen and adjacent family room. The bulb was connected to the air conditioner and to a thermostat installed on the outside wall of the house. If the air conditioner was on and the outside air temperature was below 68° F, the blue light blinked repeatedly. Turning off the air conditioner was the only way to stop the light from blinking. As long as the outside temperature was above 68 °F, the blue light did not come on, whether the air conditioner was on or off.

When Becker and Seligman assessed energy consumption over about a month's time, they found that homeowners with the signaling device used 15.7 percent less electricity than did those without such a device. The psychologists noted that the device would pay for itself in about 2 years.

One clear advantage of the mechanical device over simply being given information periodically (the typical feedback approach) is that people know at all times whether energy is being wasted. Thus adjustments in energy consumption can be made immediately.

It is worth noting that Becker and Seligman have dealt with a very significant type of energy use. Heating and cooling account for the greatest share of home energy consumption, so anything that can be done to reduce such energy usage is important. Some researchers, however, have questioned whether mechanical devices used as prompts or as feedback are effective over long time periods (Jensen, 1981). Additional research will be necessary before a final verdict is available.

Psychologists will undoubtedly continue to seek similar means of applying their knowledge. In the final analysis, though, they must also understand how to convince people to take advantage of energy-conservation processes and products (Darley & Beniger, 1981; Yates & Aronson, 1983). That in itself is a behavior problem that must be overcome if psychologists are going to apply their knowledge outside research settings.

CROWDING RESEARCH AND THE FUTURE OF PRISONS

Perhaps one of the most dramatic and important future applications of crowding research will be in the area of prison policy. Research on crowding, including crowding in prisons, is already affecting decision making about prison conditions. We suspect that this will be a much-discussed and much-debated issue in the years to come.

We have already seen some of the negative effects of crowding, so let's consider the specific effects on prisoners. We noted earlier that crowding in prisons leads to increased illness. It has also been shown to produce heightened negative affect, higher death rates among inmates over 45 years of age, increased rates of psychiatric commitment, and increased physiological symptoms of stress, including elevated blood pressure (Paulus, 1980; Paulus, McCain, & Cox, 1978; Paulus, Cox, McCain, & Chandler, 1975; Sommer, 1980). Any humane and responsible society is, of course, concerned about such effects on prisoners' physical and mental health. Other documented effects of crowded prisons are increased disciplinary problems and rule violations (Sommer, 1980). It seems to be generally believed that crowding is at least one factor in prison riots (Andersen, 1982).

Psychological research relevant to such concerns is, and will continue to be, important in the ongoing debates about prisons. In 1981, a federally funded study concluded that the ideal prison for avoiding the problems we have referred to would house about 500 inmates in single rooms or cubicles (Sniffen, 1981). The study also found that inmates' tolerance of crowded conditions does not improve over time and that inmates' moodiness increases. The study noted that in dormitory prisons, problems could be reduced by subdividing open spaces into smaller units or, ideally, individual cubicles.

Findings of this sort are contributing to policies being made by government and justice officials. Crowding is definitely a problem in the prison system. In at least 30 states, prisons are under orders to end unconstitutionally cruel conditions and prac-

tices, including the condition of too many prisoners in too little space (Andersen, 1982). The basic federal requirement is that each prisoner have a cell of at least bathroom size—60 square feet. However, only about a fifth of the prison inmates in the United States have such cells.

The future will likely bring continued efforts to improve prison conditions, and these efforts are likely to affect all of us in one way or another. The costs involved will be enormous. The answer to overcrowding in many cases may be to simply stop admitting new prisoners. As reform efforts continue, some resistance will occur and unpopular decisions may be made. When a judge in Texas ordered that each convict have at least 40 square feet of cell space, officials at one point simply stopped admitting new prisoners rather than defy the judge's order. In appealing a 1981 federal court order to house each inmate in a separate cell, Illinois officials estimated that it would take $400 million in new construction to meet that standard. Several states have laws that provide for releasing inmates automatically when crowded conditions become excessive. Early release may become quite common in the future. Crowding has led Illinois prison officials to lower their standards for giving meritorious good time (time off the sentence for good behavior) to inmates (Andersen, 1982).

Officials recognize that they can't go on forever building more and more prisons. However, prison populations in many states are rapidly growing. Part of the reason is the concern today with law and order and law enforcement. People are tired of high crime rates, lack of convictions, short sentences, and easy paroles. Such concerns, of course, will only contribute to prison crowding. The answer, according to some prison officials, may be to develop an effective and selective system for determining who goes to prison and for how long (Andersen, 1982). The available space may dictate decisions that we haven't had to make in the past.

— SUMMARY —

1. Environmental psychology is the study of the interrelationships between behavior and the physical environment. Its goal is to know not only how the physical environment affects our behavior but also how we use and affect our environment.

2. Personal space is an area surrounding the body that is defined as having an invisible boundary, which cannot be trespassed on. The amount of space required depends on the person and the situation. Age, gender, attraction, social status, similarity, and culture are among the factors influencing a person's space requirements.

3. Research has shown that interactions at inappropriate distances and personal-space invasions elicit negative feelings and negative attributions about the other person.

4. Territorial behavior refers to attempts to stake out and protect space against other members of one's own species. Territories regulate who one will interact with. Primary, secondary, and public territories can be distinguished.

5. The more central to one's life a territory is and the more control that can be exerted over it, the safer and the more useful the space is considered to be. Territorial behavior has been demonstrated to occur in settings ranging from Chicago's South Side to dining tables, classrooms, and libraries.

6. It has been suggested that the concepts of personal space and territoriality have implications for environmental design. Individuals' privacy needs need to be considered in creating environments that are responsive to the changing and differing desires for separateness and togetherness.

7. Crowding can be thought of as a stressful psychological state, a personal subjective reaction to too little space. It is experienced when a person senses a lack of personal control in the particular setting. Among the negative effects of crowding are increased physiological arousal and illness, dissatisfaction or negative feelings, withdrawal from interpersonal relations, lessened attraction toward those in the crowded setting, and poorer performance on some tasks.

8. Perception of crowding seems to be lessened by a sense of perceived control over the high-density situation. Without such control, feelings of learned helplessness set in; they lead to negative effects in both children and adults.

9. High-intensity noise does not adversely affect performance on simple motor and mental tasks. However, unpredictable high-intensity noise can cause lowered performance on complex tasks unless the individual has perceived control over the noise. With such control, negative effects are lessened.

10. Noise can also produce negative aftereffects, but again they are lessened by increases in perceived control over the noise. Socially, noise has been shown to increase aggression and reduce helping. Perceived control over the noise also lessens these negative effects.

11. High, uncomfortable temperatures seem to decrease attraction toward others unless those others have shared suffering in the hot environment. Much of the evidence on heat and aggression suggests a curvilinear relationship. Heat produces increases in negative affect, causing aggression to increase until a point is reached at which aggression is less likely and other responses, such as escape, are more likely.

12. The urban environment has long been viewed as the source of a number of negative effects. There is no indication, however, that people in rural and urban areas differ in mental health. City dwellers seem to be just as happy and satisfied as those living in small towns or rural areas.

13. There are rural-urban differences in social behavior, however. For example, urban residents desire less interaction with strangers than do rural residents. Urban residents are also less trustful of and less helpful to others than are rural dwellers. Whether these effects are due to overload, diffusion of responsibility, or other factors is not entirely clear.

14. Crowding stress in a dormitory has been reduced through architectural intervention that reduces the size of residential groupings.

15. Efforts have been made by environmental psychologists to understand how the design of environmental settings can affect users' behavior. A change from sociofugal spaces to sociopetal spaces can greatly alter social interaction. Buildings designed without attention to social behavior can fail to meet users' needs.

16. Some environmental psychologists have been concerned with how environmental behavior can be changed to make it more constructive. It has been shown that positive reinforcement is effective in getting both children and adults to pick up litter. Monetary reinforcers have been successfully applied in a variety of settings as a means of getting people to conserve energy. Giving feedback about energy consumption has also been used to significantly reduce

energy use. Prompts, such as signs, have also proved successful in fostering environmentally constructive behavior.

17. Mechanical feedback can be applied to home energy consumption. Homeowners with a cool-weather signaling device used significantly less energy than did those without such a device.

18. Crowding in prisons continues to be a problem. Many efforts are being made to provide every prisoner with a personal cell, but currently only about a fifth of the inmates in the United States have their own cells. Building more prisons is costly, and the prison population is growing rapidly; these factors compound the already existing problems.

▬ IMPORTANT TERMS AND CONCEPTS ▬

Environmental Psychology
Physical Environment
Personal Space
Proxemics
Intimate Distance
Personal Distance
Social Distance
Public Distance
Equilibrium Theory

Personal-space Invasions
Territorial Behavior
Primary Territory
Secondary Territory
Public Territory
Territorial Markers
Responsive Environments
Crowding

Population Density
Noise
Overload
Sociopetal Spaces
Sociofugal Spaces
Defensible Space
Feedback
Prompts

▬ SUGGESTIONS FOR FURTHER READING ▬

Altman, I. (1975). *The environment and social behavior.* Monterey, CA: Brooks/Cole. An excellent integration of the topics of privacy, personal space, territoriality, and crowding.

Cone, J. D., & Hayes, S. C. (1980). *Environmental problems/behavioral solutions.* Monterey, CA: Brooks/Cole. A very readable analysis of environmental problems such as litter, energy conservation, and recycling and some behavioral solutions to them.

Evans, G. W. (Ed.). (1982). *Environmental stress.* Cambridge: Cambridge University Press. Up-to-date analyses of problem areas in environmental psychology, including noise, temperature, air pollution, crowding, and designed environments.

Freedman, J. L. (1975). *Crowding and behavior.* San Francisco: W. H. Freeman. An interesting analysis of the crowding literature from the perspective that crowding does not generally seem harmful to people.

Glass, D. C., & Singer, J. E. (1972). *Urban stress.* New York: Academic Press. Mainly a presentation of the authors' research on noise, including much theoretical discussion about the effects of perceived control.

Holahan, C. J. (1982). *Environmental psychology.* New York: Random House. A good overview of all the topics covered in this chapter and more; a nice mixture of theories, findings, and applications to environmental planning.

APPLIED PSYCHOLOGY

APPLIED PSYCHOLOGY

— CHAPTER OBJECTIVES —

To achieve the objectives of this chapter, you should be able to answer the questions listed here. You should also be able to define the important terms and concepts listed at the end of the chapter.

1. What services are offered by vocational psychologists?
2. If you were doing career counseling, what steps would you take to help your client improve decision making capabilities?
3. How do professionals in industrial and organizational settings achieve the goals of personnel selection?
4. How has psychology been applied to advertising and the study of consumer behavior?
5. How has psychology been applied to medicine and law?
6. Describe the use of psychological tests in educational settings. What are the arguments for and against their use?

— CHAPTER OUTLINE —

Vocational Psychology

Counseling psychologists help people improve their capabilities for career decision making.

Vocational Choice
Career Development
Career Counseling
Application: Assessing Vocational Interests

Psychology in Industrial and Organizational Settings

As a science of human behavior, psychology is well equipped to solve problems that arise in industrial and organizational settings.

Personnel Selection
Personnel Development
Application: Consumer Psychology and the Psychology of Advertising

Psychology in Other Professions

Psychologists also help solve problems that face other professions, such as medicine, law, and education.

Psychology and Medicine
Psychology and Law
Psychology and Education
Application: Educational and Psychological Testing

On the Horizon: The Future of Admissions Testing

UNEMPLOYMENT—A NATIONAL CRISIS

Love and work, Sigmund Freud said, tell us who we are and why we exist. If Freud was right, the early 1980s have been a time of self-doubt and depression for the many millions of unemployed adults in the United States. (Paraphrased from Fisher & Cunningham, 1983, p. 2.)

Cycles of unemployment wax and wane, but their problems have a disturbing predictability. In the early 1980s, for example, the city of Detroit was stricken with severe unemployment. Detroit's human-service agencies, their own staffs depleted, struggled to help the thousands of emotional casualties of prolonged joblessness. At the height of the problem, the local 24-hour crisis hotline responded to one or two active suicide calls a night. At the same time, counselors reported a dramatic rise in calls for help from families threatened by suicide, homicide, child abuse, spouse abuse, and other kinds of violence. The incidence of alcohol abuse and marital crises increased dramatically, as did the number of children receiving psychiatric treatment. School children suffered falling grades, crying spells, and sudden outbursts of aggression. The common element in many of these problems was the family's sorrow over loss of a job and fears about the future. (Paraphrased from Cordes, 1983, p. 3.)

If recent history is any guide, the psychological impact of unemployment will be a recurring problem. Nonetheless, as never before, mental health professionals are creating programs specifically designed to aid the unemployed and their families (cf. Liem & Rayman, 1982).

Such programs exemplify one facet of the growing field of **applied psychology**—the branch of psychology concerned with solving real-life problems (Anastasi, 1979). This chapter will explore some of the functions performed by applied psychologists. It will begin with **vocational psychology,** the specialty area concerned with vocational choice and adjustment to work. The discussion will encompass the nature of vocational choices, the course of career development, and the importance of vocational counseling.

The chapter will also portray applied psychology's rapid growth and the expanding role of applied psychologists. The majority of the members of the American Psychological Association work in such applied settings as business, industry, hospitals, clinics, schools, community agencies, rehabilitation centers, correctional institutions, and government agencies (Stapp & Fulcher, 1981; 1983).

The chapter will survey some of the major areas of application in vocational psychology, in industrial and organizational settings, and in such professions as medicine, law, and education.

— VOCATIONAL PSYCHOLOGY —

Vocational Choice

Vocational choice, work adjustment, and unemployment are issues inseparable from personality development and life adjustment in general (Anastasi, 1979; Lofquist & Dawis, 1969). In selecting our work—making our *vocational choice*—we choose a way of life and largely determine our social status. Truck driver, hairdresser, nurse—these are three of the more than 20,000 occupations to choose from. Whatever the choice, occupation often determines income and lifestyle, including the neighborhood one lives in, the car one drives, and the vacations one takes. As noted by Anastasi (1979), occupation determines the distribution of work and leisure—summers off for teachers, the month of August off for psychiatrists, alternating blocks of work and time off for airline personnel and long-distance truck drivers. And occupation can limit where one lives—a rural setting for the farmer, an urban metropolis for the factory worker. Some occupations create special difficulties. For example, much has been written about the problems of the spouses of politicians, physicians, and career military officers. Also, interests and values that clash with the characteristics of one's occupation can create disruptive conflicts, thus making vocational choice an important developmental task.

It has been said that if you find the right job, it won't be work. This adage was coined by D. P. Campbell in *If You Don't Know Where You Are Going, You'll Probably End Up Somewhere Else* (Campbell, 1974). The book is intended to convince readers that vocational choice is a significant life decision.

Career Development

Vocational-counseling research suggests that career decisions are made over a period of many years. (For review, see Fretz & Leong, 1982.) This research implies a process of **career development**—the adjustment to work that takes place throughout one's work life. To describe this process, Super (1957) and Super and Hall (1978) analyzed several stages of career development.

Stage 1, the *growth* stage, extends from birth to about 14 years of age. During this period, the individual develops a concept of self and begins to try on occupational roles in play and fantasy. These roles frequently include law officer, fire fighter, nurse, and doctor. It is only later that the individual begins to recognize and consider interests, abilities, job requirements, and opportunities.

Stage 2 is the period of *exploration,* extending from age 14 to early adulthood. During this stage, initial educational decisions are made, career goals are examined, and formal work-role tryouts (part-time and temporary jobs) are begun.

Stage 3 is the period of *establishment.* The trial and error of Stage 2 is followed by a tendency to settle

down, stabilize, and advance in a chosen field of work.

Stage 4, which extends beyond middle age, is the period of *maintenance,* a time for maintaining satisfactory occupational performance. This stage leads finally to Stage 5, *occupational decline,* the period of reduced job activities and, finally, retirement.

In career development, as in other forms of human development, any system of stages is likely to be oversimplified. Nonetheless, conceptualizing career development as an extended process implies the importance of career counseling for people of all ages, whether employed or unemployed.

Career Counseling

As noted by Anastasi (1979):

The value of life-span counseling is now widely recognized. Such counseling is needed to help children keep up with the developmental tasks of their age level in preparation for later occupational choices and to guide adolescents and young adults through their career explorations and successive approximations. Following entry into the world of work, other decisions must be made about specific jobs within one's chosen field and about job changes to improve job satisfaction, to facilitate career advancement, or for any number of individual reasons. (p. 445)

The field of **career counseling** is concerned principally with vocational choice. *Career counselors* help both the young and the old make career decisions (Tittle, 1982). Rather than making the decisions themselves, career counselors try to improve each client's decision-making capabilities by providing information about alternate courses of action. Since effective career decisions require knowledge about occupations, abilities, and interests, we will consider each area separately.

— Occupations

Occupations may be classified by level, field, and enterprise (Super, 1957). *Level* is defined by such variables as income, social status, prestige, educational requirements, degree of authority, freedom and independence of action, and amount of decision-making responsibility. *Field* is defined by the type of activity performed. Bricklayers and carpenters work at the same level but in different fields. *Enterprise* is defined by the work setting. Jobs in the same field and at the same level may appeal to persons having different types of interests. Consider, for example, three psychologists—the first employed by a hospital, the second by a university research laboratory, and the third by the military.

One role of career counselors is to acquaint clients with available occupations. Another is to help clients determine which occupation they are best suited for—especially with respect to field and enterprise.

Abilities and Worker Requirements

As noted in chapter 12, people in different occupations differ significantly in average performance on tests of general cognitive ability. Therefore, it is helpful for the career counselor to have information about clients' *aptitudes* and *abilities*. One of the most widely used tests in counseling is the Differential Aptitude Test (DAT) (Zytowski & Warman, 1982). The DAT provides a profile of scores in eight areas: verbal reasoning, numerical ability, abstract reasoning, clerical speed and accuracy, mechanical reasoning, space relations, spelling, and language usage. Data about such abilities and aptitudes also can be obtained from a variety of other sources, including standardized achievement-test scores recorded in the client's school files. Although such tests have limitations, they often prove useful for both counselor and client.

Vocational Interests

In addition to obtaining information about clients' abilities, the career counselor attempts to find out about *vocational interests*. Data from an interest test can be of greater value than aptitude data in making career decisions. For instance, a client who has above-average aptitude-test scores presumably is capable of performing adequately in numerous occupations. The client may have an interest in only one of them, however.

Trends in Career Counseling

One study reviewed by Zytowski and Warman (1982) surveyed 372 college and university counseling services and found at least 158 different tests and inventories in use. Zytowski and Warman themselves surveyed 198 counseling agencies and confirmed that the use of tests in counseling is increasing. They found that the Strong-Campbell Interest Inventory (described in the following application section) topped the list of tests in frequency of use. The Differential Aptitude Test ranked 17 in frequency, which indicates that its popularity has held for more than 25 years. Throughout the 1970s and early 1980s, vocational psychologists have been refining their batteries of tests. Old tests are abandoned or updated and new ones developed (Miller, 1982), all in an attempt to help people improve their capabilities in making career decisions.

— APPLICATION —
ASSESSING VOCATIONAL INTERESTS

Even brief conversations with people who dislike their work should be sufficient to demonstrate the importance of vocational interests. The **Strong-Campbell Interest Inventory (SCII)** measures such interests. Like other inventories of its type, the SCII is a self-report inventory. It records clients' likes and dislikes, or relative preferences, for many kinds of activities, people, and objects. The SCII has been standardized on people engaged in more than 125 occupations. High scores in a given occupational area indicate that the client's interests resemble those of people employed in that occupation. Thus, SCII scores reflect interests, not abilities. For example, scores indicating

that a client likes the way engineers spend their time do not mean that the client has the mathematical skills needed in engineering.

The Strong-Campbell Interest Inventory is based on a theory of vocational choice developed by Holland (1973). According to the theory, everyone can be described in terms of one or more of six occupational-interest themes. The theory assumes that each type of person seeks a different type of work environment. A listing of the occupational themes and interests is provided in Table 20–1. Let's consider a description, based on Holland's theory, of each of the six themes. See if you can find yourself in the descriptions.

Table 20–1.

Occupational Themes and Basic Interest Scales on the Strong-Campbell Interest Inventory.

Realistic Theme	**Social Theme**
Agriculture	Teaching
Nature	Social service
Adventure	Athletics
Military activities	Domestic arts
Mechanical activities	Religious activities
Investigative Theme	**Enterprising Theme**
Science	Public speaking
Mathematics	Law/politics
Medical science	Merchandising
Medical service	Sales
Artistic Theme	Business management
Music/dramatics	**Conventional Theme**
Art	Office practices
Writing	

— R-Theme

The term *realistic* has been used to characterize people with high scores on the R-Theme. Such people are rugged, practical, and physically strong, and they have difficulty expressing themselves in words. They like to work outdoors, and they like to work with things, especially tools and large machines, more than with ideas or people. They prefer the types of work performed by mechanics, construction workers, fish and wildlife managers, and laboratory technicians, as well as work in some engineering specialties, some military jobs, agriculture, and the skilled trades.

— I-Theme

The term *investigative* is used to characterize high scorers on the I-Theme. Such people are task-oriented and like working with ideas more than with things or people. They enjoy solving abstract problems, want to understand the physical world, and do not like highly structured work settings. Often, they are creative thinkers, especially in scientific areas. They prefer the types of work performed by design engineers, biologists, social scientists, laboratory researchers, physicists, and technical writers.

— A-Theme

The term *artistic* is used to describe high scorers on the A-Theme. These people are artistically inclined and like to work on activities that require self-expression. They tend to be original and creative thinkers who enjoy working alone (as do high scorers on the I-Theme). They are usually less assertive than I-Theme high scorers about their opinions and capabilities, and they are more sensitive and emotional. They prefer the types of work performed by artists, authors, cartoonists, composers, singers, actors, and poets.

— S-Theme

The term *social* is used to characterize high scorers on the S-Theme. These people tend to be social, outgoing, concerned about the welfare of others, and able to get along well with others. They like attention and enjoy being at the centers of groups. They prefer to work with people rather than with things or ideas, and they have little interest in machinery and in exerting themselves physically. They prefer the types of work performed by school superintendents, clinical psychologists, high-school teachers, and marriage counselors.

— E-Theme

The term *enterprising* is used to characterize high scorers on the E-Theme. Such people have a great talent with words, which they enjoy putting to use in selling, leading, and dominating. They are impatient with precision work and with work that requires being alone for long periods. They enjoy power, status, and material wealth. They prefer the types of work performed by persons in sales, business executives, realtors, and politicians.

— C-Theme

The term *conventional* is used to characterize high scorers on the C-Theme. These people tend to prefer highly structured work settings. They enjoy office work and fit well into large organizations, but they do not seek leadership positions. They like unambiguous work environments and a well-established chain of command; they dislike problems that require physical skills or intense relationships with others. They prefer the types of work performed by bank examiners, bank tellers, tax experts, statisticians, computer operators, and inventory controllers.

If you are undecided about a career, these themes may help clarify your thinking. Identifying where your interests lie is a valuable first step in making a career choice. If you would like to assess your interests formally, the SCII or a similar instrument can be administered by a career counselor. (This service is often available on college campuses.) If you are interested in learning more about careers in psychology, write to the Publications Sales Department of the American Psychological Association, 1200 Seventeenth Street NW, Washington, DC 20036. Request the APA *Careers in Psychology* booklet.

PSYCHOLOGY IN INDUSTRIAL AND ORGANIZATIONAL SETTINGS

One of the fastest growing applied areas in psychology, **industrial-organizational psychology,** is concerned with behavior in the world of work. Psychologists in this field are especially interested in employee selection and placement, employee training and development, personnel research, employee motivation improvement, organization culture, organization development, and work environment design (cf. Dunnette, 1976). In this section we will focus on two aspects of the study of people in work settings—personnel selection and personnel development. Applied psychologists are also interested in the behavior of people who consume products and services. In the application at the end of this section we will examine consumer psychology and the psychology of advertising.

Personnel Selection

Many years ago, Hollingworth (1929—cited in Dunnette & Kirchner, 1965) asked sales managers to interview 57 applicants for a sales job and to rank them with respect to their apparent job capabilities. The interviewers disagreed substantially. For example, one applicant was ranked 1st by one manager and 57th by another. The results clearly demonstrated differing managerial standards and the complexity of **personnel selection**—the art and science of choosing the best person for a given job.

The managers studied by Hollingworth differed in their judgments for several reasons. Two such reasons have to do with job characteristics and person characteristics.

Job Characteristics

The study of job characteristics is the first step in successful personnel selection. To choose the best person for a given job, psychologists carry out a **job analysis,** in which they identify the duties required of the employee and the behaviors necessary for successful job performance (Dunnette, 1966). As noted by Dunnette and Kirchner (1965), a job analysis that stops with a simple description of job duties is incomplete. It must also identify specific behaviors that lead to either success or failure on the job. Such behaviors provide a base from which to develop selection and classification systems (Dunnette & Borman, 1979).

Person Characteristics

After a careful analysis, the psychologist has a good idea of the type of person who would most likely succeed in a particular job. The next step is to identify the applicants most qualified to meet specific job requirements. Various lists of desirable managerial traits, gleaned from many studies by Campbell, Dunnette, Lawler, and Weick (1970), suggest a number of personal qualities necessary for managerial effectiveness. (See Table 20–2 for a sample.)

More recently, Harry Levinson (1980) identified 20 personality dimensions that may be useful in choosing top executives:

– Capacity to abstract. Can conceptualize, organize, and integrate data into a coherent frame of reference.
– Tolerance for ambiguity. Can stand confusion until things become clear.
– Intelligence. Can abstract and can be practical as well.
– Judgment. Knows when to act.
– Authority. Feels comfortable in boss's role.
– Activity. Has vigorous orientation to problems and needs of organization.
– Achievement. Is oriented toward organization's success rather than personal aggrandizement.

Table 20–2.

Some personal qualities said to be necessary for managerial effectiveness. (After Campbell, Dunnette, Lawler, & Weick, 1970.)

Able to sustain defeat
Alert
Ambitious—achievement oriented
Assertive
Capable of good judgment
Competitive
Concrete
Creative
Decisive
Dedicated
Dynamic
Emotionally stable
Energetic
Extroverted
Fearful of failure
Group-oriented
Honest
Intelligent
Mentally healthy
Optimistic and confident
Pragmatic
Predictable
Reality-oriented
Self-controlled
Tolerant of frustration

– Sensitivity. Can perceive others' feelings.
– Involvement. Sees self as participating member of organization.
– Maturity. Has good relationships with authority figures.
– Interdependence. Accepts appropriate dependence needs of others and of self.
– Articulateness. Makes a good impression.
– Stamina. Has physical as well as mental energy.
– Adaptability. Manages stress well.
– Sense of humor. Doesn't take self too seriously.
– Vision. Is clear about progression of personal life and career as well as of direction organization should go.
– Perserverance. Is able to see a task through regardless of the difficulties encountered.

– Personal organization. Has good sense of time.
– Integrity. Has well-established value system, which has been tested in various ways in the past.
– Social responsibility. Appreciates the need to assume leadership.

Studies comparing successful top executives with those who reached a plateau late in their careers, were fired, or were forced to retire early have been particularly illuminating. Such a study was conducted by McCall and Lombardo (1983) at the Center for Creative Leadership in Greensboro, North Carolina. When the researchers compared 21 "derailed executives" with 20 "arrivers" (those who became top executives), they found the two groups astonishingly alike. Each of the 41 executives possessed remarkable strengths, and each had one or more significant weaknesses. The weaknesses were arranged in 10 categories: (1) insensitivity to others (abrasive, intimidating, bullying style); (2) coldness, aloofness, arrogance; (3) betrayal of trust; (4) overambitiousness (thinking of the next job, playing politics); (5) specific performance problems with the business; (6) overmangement (inability to delegate authority or build a team); (7) inability to staff effectively; (8) inability to think strategically; (9) inability to adapt to a boss with a different style; and (10) overdependence on advocate or mentor.

The most glaring difference between the two groups of top executives studied by McCall and Lombardo was the ability—or inability—to understand other people's perspectives. Insensitivity to others was the most often cited reason for derailment. Only 25 percent of the detailed executives were described as having a special ability with people; for arrivers the figure was 75 percent. This was never the sole reason for derailment, however. Most often, the derailment was attributed to a combination of weaknesses. The lesson to be drawn from these findings was summarized by McCall and Lombardo (1983):

> As we came to realize, executives, like the rest of us, are a patchwork of strengths and weaknesses. The reasons that some executives ultimately derailed and others made it all the way up the ladder confirm what we all know but have hesitated to admit: There is no one best way to succeed (or even to fail). (p. 31)

Ultimately, lists of person characteristics must be translated into recommendations about the selection of job applicants. Ideally, selections should rest on measurable characteristics that are clearly related to job performance. Good selection decisions are made possible through the wise use of reliable and valid psychological tests of personality, interests, and ability.

— Prediction

Persons making personnel-selection decisions must demonstrate the predictive accuracy of their assessments. That is, what are the odds of job success for persons with various test scores? Such odds can be presented most easily in the form of *expectancy charts* (Dunnette & Kirchner, 1965). Consider Figure 20–1, which charts the predictive accuracy of a battery of tests administered to thousands of pilot trainees during World War II. Standardized scores from the test battery, which ranged from 1 to 9, were combined into an overall index, the Pilot Aptitude Score. As demonstrated in Figure 20–1, about 90 percent of all trainees with high aptitude scores (7, 8, and 9) successfully completed pilot training, whereas fewer than 40 percent with low scores (1, 2 and 3) did so.

The selection of pilots for training during World War II was a great success for applied psychology. Before the program began, plane crashes during training were common. Psychologists were called on to construct tests that would predict which candidates would most

likely succeed in pilot training—before they operated any aircraft. The selection program increased the percentage of candidates who successfully completed pilot training from 25 percent to over 85 percent. This improvement led to a great savings in government airplanes, student pilots, and flight instructors.

— Assessment Centers

The most favored procedure for matching jobs and people is the **assessment-center approach,** developed for the selection of specialized military personnel during World War II. The approach has since been adopted by many large industrial corporations, including American Telephone and Telegraph (AT&T), International Business Machines (IBM), and Standard Oil Company of America, as well as by government agencies and the armed services (cf. Bray, Campbell, & Grant, 1974; Ritchie & Moses, 1983; Tziner & Dolan, 1982).

Typically, a small number of candidates for the same type of job are brought to an assessment center, where they undergo evaluation for two or three days. Multiple assessment procedures and multiple assessors are used to predict the candidates' likelihood of success. For example, in addition to taking ability tests and filling out personality and interest inventories, candidates undergo structured interviews and a variety of job-related *situational tests*. The situational tests, which are a distinctive feature of the assessment-center approach to personnel selection, may include job simulations, role playing, group problem solving, business games, and peer ratings of performance on these tasks.

One illustrative longitudinal investigation, called the Management Progress Study, was initiated by Douglas Bray and his associates at AT&T in 1956 (Bray et al., 1974). This ongoing study led to the use of assessment centers to select supervisors, managers, marketing personnel, and other specialists. As Bray (1982) noted, "Perhaps the most significant single finding from the Management Progress Study is that success as a manager is highly predictable" (p. 183). In general, assessment-center staff predictions regarding recent appointees to first-level management positions were quite accurate with respect to such criteria as salary growth and subsequent advancement—more accurate than predictions made using test scores alone. The interviews and situational tests contributed significantly to the overall evaluation. Information concerning motivational and personality factors was of special importance in predicting managerial success. As noted by Bray (1982), "It is clear that the most promising man-

Figure 20–1.

Relationship between aptitude scores of pilots and percent of individuals completing pilot training.

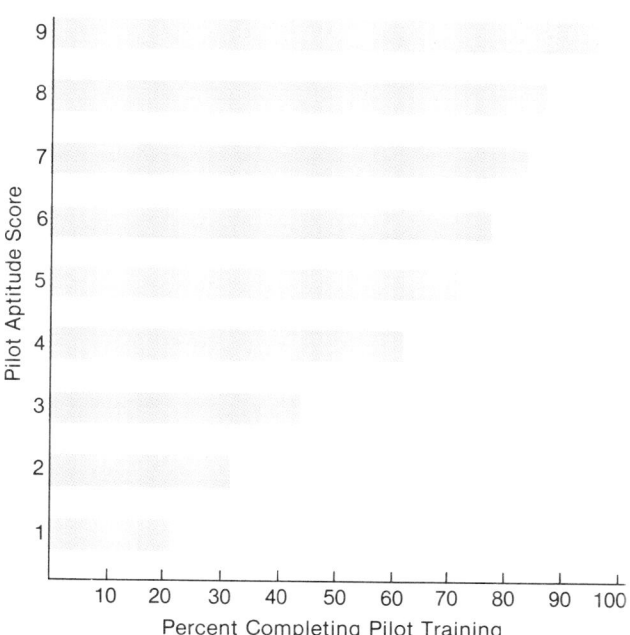

agers are those who want to lead and advance, who reject dependency on others, who are self-confident and optimistic, energetic and work oriented" (p. 186). Let's take a closer look at how professional careers develop within organizations.

Personnel Development

Dalton, Thompson, and Price (1977) described four **stages of professional careers**—apprentice, colleague, mentor, and sponsor. Each stage involves different developmental tasks, relationships, and psychological adjustments (see Figure 20–2).

In Stage I, an individual works as an *apprentice* under the direction of others, helping and learning from one or more mentors. In Stage II, the individual demonstrates competence as a contributing member, or *colleague,* of the profession. In Stage III, the individual becomes an advisor and role model, or *mentor,* for other, younger members of the profession. Finally, in Stage IV, the successful individual assumes the role of *sponsor* and provides judgment for shaping the direction of the organization.

Figure 20–2.

Four career stages. (After Dalton, Thompson, & Price, 1977.)

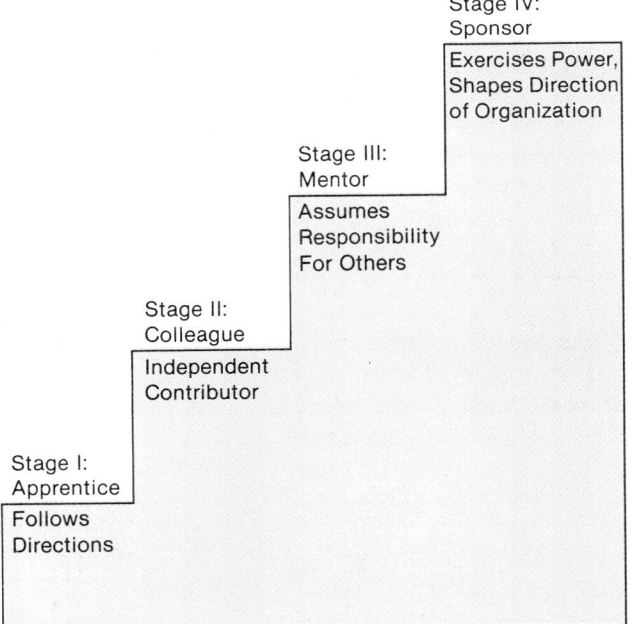

The four stages were identified from interviews with 550 employees who were professionally trained. Included were scientists, engineers, accountants, and university professors. The study's most relevant finding was that distinct differences between high performers and low performers could be found at each stage. Thus, in Stage I, the person who attempts to escape apprenticeship too quickly will likely fail to learn enough from more experienced professionals. More importantly, apprentices who undertake sole responsibility for work they are not prepared to do may acquire a lasting reputation for mediocre performance. Consequently, the effective Stage I person performs routine and detailed assignments in exchange for the learning experience and the sponsorship of a mentor. A good mentor often becomes a model for the Stage I person. "These and other benefits suggest that finding a good mentor should be a key agenda item for any professional entering an organization. Providing the opportunity to find such a mentor is an equally important responsibility of higher-ups in the organization" (Dalton et al., 1977, p. 25).

The interviews by Dalton and colleagues suggest that successful transition into Stage II involves developing a reputation as a competent professional with a specialty. During Stage II, peer relationships are of paramount importance. As dependence on a mentor declines, the high-performance Stage II person establishes close ties with competent colleagues in the same area of specialization. In contrast: "Many people remain in Stage II throughout their careers, making substantial contributions to the organization and experiencing a high degree of professional satisfaction. However, the probability that they will continue to receive above-average [performance] ratings diminishes over time, if they do not move beyond this stage" (Dalton et al., 1977, p. 28).

Dalton and colleagues refer to Stage III as the mentor stage of career development because individuals in this stage take increased responsibility for influencing, guiding, directing, and developing others. The Stage III person takes on more work responsibility, which requires more assistance from others in the detail work to develop the Stage III person's ideas. Thus, the central shift that occurs in the transition from Stage II to Stage III appears to be from learning to take care of oneself to learning to take responsibility for the development of others.

Some of the professionals studied moved beyond Stage III to a fourth stage of career development. Individuals in this stage influence and shape the organization's development and direction. Such influence is exercised in several ways: identifying goals, directing resources toward specific goals, and developing new ideas, products, markets, or services that lead the organization into new areas of activity.

> Because these functions are so critical to the growth and survival of the organization, those who fulfill them are highly valued, and only those persons whose judgment and skill have been proved in the past are trusted to play these roles. Stage IV people have gained credibility by their demonstrated ability to read the environment accurately and respond appropriately. (Dalton et al., 1977, p. 32)

Stage IV individuals in the Dalton sample fulfilled one or more of three roles: manager, internal entrepreneur, and idea innovator. The Stage IV *manager* does not supervise people directly but instead formulates organizational policy and initiates broad programs. The *entrepreneurial role* is played by Stage IV managers who influence the organization's direction, often by successfully bringing together the people, money, and resources necessary for achieving goals. *Idea innovators* often work apart from other Stage IV managers and entrepreneurs but are responsible for developing significant breakthroughs or innovative ideas. Additionally, the development of key people within the organization is a common role played by all Stage IV persons.

This conceptualization of professional career stages suggests that *mentoring relationships* are important for several reasons. The mentor serves as a model and guide to the apprentice, showing the apprentice how to cope with the work environment and encouraging the person's progress. Furthermore, the mentor serves to match the needs of the individual with those of the organization. For such reasons, the mentoring concept has attracted increasing attention by researchers in industrial and organizational settings.

In the book *The Seasons of a Man's Life* (only men were studied), psychologist Daniel Levinson and his colleagues at Yale University (Levinson, Darrow, Klein, Levinson, & McKee, 1978) described the results of a study of 40 business executives, novelists, and factory workers. Levinson concluded that the presence or absence of a mentoring relationship is an important element of people's lives during their 20s and 30s. The absence of a mentor was found to be associated with various developmental impairments and with problems in midlife. Within this context, the word **mentor** means "advisor, teacher, protector" (Levinson, Darrow, Klein, Levinson, & McKee, 1976, p. 23); or "a rabbi, a sponsor, a patron" (Hennig & Jardim, 1977, p. 41). According to Levinson and colleagues (1978) the most crucial function of a mentor is to support, foster, and facilitate the young adult's career development by believing in the person and promoting the person's professional advancement.

Levinson's insights have helped propel a growing interest in the psychology of mentoring. (See, for example, Alleman & Newman, 1982.) Some empirical support can already be found in studies of managers. Collins and Scott (1978) have argued, on the basis of interview data, that all managers who make it have a mentor. Similarly, in a survey of 1,250 prominent executives conducted by Roche (1979), nearly two-thirds of all respondents reported having had a mentor.

Top executives who have had a mentor differ in a number of ways from top executives who have not. Executives who have had a mentor earn more money at an earlier age, are better educated on the average, derive more pleasure from their work, and report higher satisfaction with their career progress. Finally, executives who once had mentors are more likely to become mentors themselves.

Mentor relationships appear to be as important for women as for men. For example, among the 28 women executives surveyed by Roche (1979), all those responding had a mentor. Similarly, Hennig found that all of the 25 high-level women executives she studied reported having had a strong relationship with a mentor (Hennig & Jardim, 1977). Kanter's (1977) study, *Men and Women of the Corporation*, supports the notion that mentors are integral to the informal network of organizations and that having a mentor is as important for women as for men.

Journalist Gail Sheehy (1976a) identified the mentor connection as the secret link in the successful woman's life. However, she recognized that fewer mentors are available for women than for men, female mentors being particularly scarce in such traditionally male professions as management, science, medicine, engineering, and architecture. Whereas only 1 in 50 of the men in Roche's (1979) study had a female mentor, 7 in 10 of the women had male mentors. Actually, the majority of available mentors for women are men, and this may be a major limiting factor in the career development of women (Epstein, 1971; Shapiro, Haseltine, & Rowe, 1978; Sheehy, 1976a, 1976b).

The implications are clear. Organizations would be wise to explicitly recognize the four stages of professional development in their training programs and internal structure. Organizational changes that foster mentoring relationships should be encouraged.

— APPLICATION —

CONSUMER PSYCHOLOGY AND THE PSYCHOLOGY OF ADVERTISING

Consumer psychology is the scientific study of consumer behavior. Consumer behavior encompasses the acquisition, use, and disposition of products, services, and ideas (Jacoby, 1976). The **psychology of advertising,** a major area of interest for consumer psychologists, is a field of study that attempts to determine how advertising motivates consumers and why consumers choose and use particular products and services. Two broad focuses of advertising research are the characteristics of ads and the characteristics of consumers.

— Characteristics of Ads

Much past and current advertising research in the psychology of advertising concerns the effect on consumer behavior of various characteristics of ads, such as size, repetition, color, position, and illustration. A summary of research findings relevant to these issues follows. (For reviews, see Anastasi, 1979; Starch, 1966.)

The larger the *size* of ads, the greater their readership. In one survey, for example, the percentage of magazine readers who recognized various ads was determined. Nearly two times more consumers noticed full-page ads than half-page ads. In fact, ad size has been found by some investigators to exceed any other single variable in accounting for readership (cf. Starch, 1966).

Repetition of an ad also is related to readership. Advertisers are obviously aware of the benefits of repetition. Some commercials appear so often that their messages may become part of the consumer's daily speech: "Orange juice isn't just for breakfast any more" provide just one example. The results of many studies suggest that when all other factors are controlled, the greater the repetition of an ad, the larger the audience and the more positive its reactions to it.

Simply running more ads is not necessarily productive, however. For example, Campbell Soup's advertising researchers discovered that increasing the number of television commercials was not productive, but using commercials that introduced new reasons (for example, nutritional) for eating soup did pay off (Poindexter, 1983).

Color ads are now common in magazines and newspapers. A study by Rudolph (1947—cited in Anastasi, 1979), analyzed ad readership for one magazine. Two-color ads (one color plus black) had about 1 percent higher readership than black-and-white ads of the same size. Four-color ads, however, averaged 54 percent higher than black-and-white ads in readership.

Advertisers have long known that color conveys emotional messages to consumers, and they routinely use *color psychology* to manipulate consumer behavior. Thus, detergent boxes tend to have designs in bold primary colors on pure white backgrounds to foster an image of strength and cleanliness. White on cans of light beer supposedly connotes few calories. And some brands of low-tar and low-nicotine cigarettes have labels with large white areas and light-colored letters to convey a feeling of purity (Toufexis, 1983).

Ad *position* within magazines and newspapers has been studied extensively. Ads appearing inside the front cover and on the back cover have a readership advantage of 30 to 64 percent over ads that appear on inside pages. The specific location of ads on inside pages seems to make little difference, however.

Illustrations serve to highlight the message of ads. They may be used to gain the consumer's attention and to facilitate comprehension and retention of the message. Ads showing illustrations of people tend to have a higher readership than those showing illustrations of products alone. Sexy illustrations attract attention; at the same time, however, they may distract consumers from the sponsor's message.

To summarize, advertisers have learned much from studies of successful ads. Such ads tend to be large, colorful, and strategically positioned in space and time (for example, on magazine covers and during prime-time television-viewing hours), and they are repeated often. Successful ads also make wise use of illustrations to get the message across.

Characteristics of Consumers

Advertisements attempt to link products with consumer preferences and needs (Anastasi, 1979). Thus, consumer psychologists have attempted to understand consumer needs—from basic physiological drives to acquired needs for approval, status, and achievement. Consumer research has also focused on opinions and attitudes of consumers and on how they might be changed (see chapter 18). Over the years, psychologists have developed sophisticated survey methods for assessing consumer behavior. Opinion surveys and other types of consumer research have resulted in a large body of data relevant to consumer behavior. These data provide information about what typical consumers like and dislike about specific products, which characteristics of products lead to a change of brands, and how particular products are used. Information about consumer behavior is useful to advertising psychologists, who are concerned with what motivates consumers and why consumers choose and use particular products and services.

Conclusion

More than $40 billion is spent on advertising each year in the United States. Does the deluge of ads actually benefit advertisers and their clients? Much attention is currently focused on this and related questions. On one hand, it can be argued that consumers will not purchase a product if they do not know it exists, which suggests the value of advertising. Among products that are advertised, however, findings are inconsistent. Some studies show that advertising increases sales; other studies show the reverse. Where positive effects are found, they are generally small.

This conclusion may be somewhat reassuring if you have ever felt manipulated by advertising. Nevertheless, making intelligent purchases remains a challenging and complex task. And although the task may be aided somewhat by such publications as *Consumer Reports,* you should be aware of the variables in advertising effectiveness. Such an awareness may help you strike a balance between the informative and the manipulative aspects of advertisements.

— PSYCHOLOGY IN OTHER PROFESSIONS —

Psychology and Medicine

As noted in chapter 1, the American Psychological Association has a newly established division—health psychology. Three terms—behavioral medicine, behavioral health, and health psychology—are used interchangeably by many psychologists to refer to this emerging area. Matarazzo (1980) proposed that the term **behavioral health** be used to refer to the new interdisciplinary specialty concerned with health maintenance and the prevention of illness. Let's examine some of the contributions psychologists have made to the diagnosis and prevention of health problems.

Diagnosis

To an increasing extent, physicians are relying on nonphysician specialists to improve the accuracy of diagnoses. For example, computers are being used to aid in and refine medical diagnoses. Computers allow the physician to integrate large amounts of information relevant to patients' medical histories. With such information, computers can match patient symptoms, medical histories, and present problems with appropriate diagnoses and treatments. These applications parallel the use of computers in many areas of psychology (Anastasi, 1979).

One of the most significant contributions to medical diagnosis by psychologists, especially in the area of psychiatry, has been the development of the Minnesota Multiphasic Personality Inventory (MMPI), which is now the most thoroughly researched and widely used structured personality test (see chapter 13). It has been used as an employment screening and selection device in government and industry, as a research instrument in a variety of areas, and as a clinical-assessment instrument for the diagnosis of mental disorders. More research has been conducted on the MMPI than on any other existing personality test. It is estimated, for example, that it has stimulated more than 6,000 publications. There are more than 50 translations of the MMPI, in at least 19 languages (Butcher, 1969). In 1977, Starke Hathaway, the University of Minnesota psychologist who was chiefly responsible for the construction and development of the MMPI, received the Distinguished Contribution Award for Applications in Psychology. Hathaway's contributions to psychiatric diagnosis and to the development of medical psychology clearly qualify him as one of the discipline's great pioneers.

— Prevention of Health Problems

Psychologists interested in the new and rapidly growing application of psychology to medicine have tackled only a limited number of health problems so far. In addition to developing such diagnostic tools as the MMPI, psychologists have begun to apply behavioral principles to the treatment of medical disorders. You may recall the chapter 14 discussion of various therapies for treating patients with such psychosomatic illnesses as high blood pressure and migraine headaches. Potentially more important will be the prevention of such dysfunctions as lung cancer, heart disease, and drug and alcohol abuse (Matarazzo, 1982).

How can behavioral-health psychologists help healthy children and adults remain healthy? Cigarette smoking is one of several areas in which psychologists are making a contribution. National polls repeatedly show that the majority of regular cigarette smokers in the United States (27 million adult men, 25 million adult women, and 3 million teenagers in 1979) would like to quit smoking but have not. Nonetheless, since the development of the massive national education program that followed the United States Surgeon General's 1964 report on smoking, some 30 million Americans have stopped smoking. Moreover, studies show that the percentage of adult men and teenage boys and girls who are current smokers is decreasing (cf. Matarazzo, 1982).

The fact that so many people have stopped smoking provides evidence that the efforts of psychologists and various health experts have a good chance of success. One troubling statistic, however, is a reported increase in recent years in the percentage of adult female smokers. The decreased percentage of adult male smokers and the increased percentage of female smokers is regarded by the National Cancer Society as reflecting a shift from men to women as the targets of advertising by cigarette companies. Skillfully crafted slogans, such as "You've come a long way, baby," have strong but subtle appeal to some women. As noted by Matarazzo (1982), the Virginia Slims brand name, artfully takes advantage of the increasingly well documented finding that quitting smoking is associated with weight gain.

Another troubling finding is that for both boys and girls, age 12 is the time of greatest susceptibility to becoming a regular cigarette smoker. A surge of research by behavioral-health experts has focused on why children begin to smoke and the special problems of preventing them from beginning. Studies in this new field of applied psychology have shown that the numbers of new smokers among sixth- and seventh-graders can be reduced as much as 50 percent by educational programs employing knowledge currently available to experimental, social, educational, and clinical psychologists (Matarazzo, 1982).

Recent years have seen the emergence of a new sense of individual responsibility for maintaining health and preventing illness. An increasing number of Americans choose life-styles and behaviors designed to promote and maintain good health. Routine schedules of exercise are a way of life for many, and jogging has become a national pastime. (See Figure 20–3.) Never before has the American public been as aware of the importance of good nutrition. Salt, sugar, and high-cholesterol foods have been removed from the tables of many families. It is common to see "you are what you eat" posters in elementary-school cafeterias. Junk-food vending machines are being gradually removed or replaced. In numbers that are increasing annually, Americans have fastened their seatbelts for safety, given up cigarettes and other potentially health-impairing substances, and improved their diet. These are examples of a few areas of present and future interest to behavioral-health specialists.

Figure 20–3.
Jogging has become a national pastime.

Psychology and Law

Forensic psychology is concerned with applying psychological knowledge and principles to law and the judicial process. Like many other fields of applied psychology, forensic psychology has grown rapidly since the 1960s (cf. Loftus & Monahan, 1980; Monahan, 1980). Today, psychologists play a variety of roles in the criminal-justice system, some of which are discussed in this section.

One of the first areas in which psychological services were utilized by police departments was in developing and evaluating selection procedures. Many police agencies throughout the country now have pro-grams for assessing applicant qualifications (e.g., Dunnette & Motowidlo, 1975). Police-officer selection procedures use many of the techniques that assessment centers use. In addition to assessment and selection, psychologists in police departments are increasingly involved in training. Their responsibilities range from designing training curriculums to conducting training programs for preservice and inservice police-department personnel. In some instances, psychologists are retained by police departments to counsel officers exposed to emotional trauma or those showing signs of ongoing stress-induced problems.

Correctional psychologists deal with problems of juvenile delinquency and crime. Correctional programs at the community, county, and state levels often enlist the interdisciplinary services of psychologists, social workers, and psychiatrists, who work as diagnostic teams and set up treatment programs for offenders.

There is an obvious need in the judicial process for objective knowledge about human behavior. *Court psychologists* are involved in an expanding variety of roles, centering on the diagnostic evaluation of individuals. They use a variety of testing and interviewing techniques (Anastasi, 1979). For example, court psychologists are trained to identify the personal characteristics of offenders that would lead to conclusions about the individuals' motives, attitudes, and potential for benefiting from rehabilitation, education, or job placement in the community. As described in chapter 5, psychologists have used hypnosis in criminal cases. One such instance is illustrated by the case of the Hillside Strangler, a man accused of committing numerous

brutal murders in the Los Angeles area in 1977–78. The defendant pleaded not guilty by reason of insanity. Psychologist John Watkins of the University of Montana claimed to have discovered, through hypnosis, that the defendant suffered from multiple personalities (see chapters 13 and 15). One of these personalities emerged during hypnosis, identified 10 of the 13 victims, and admitted killing them (Murderous personality, 1979). (The controversial insanity plea has been tested more recently in the case of John Hinckley, Jr., who tried to assassinate President Reagan in 1981; see Figure 20–4.)

There are a variety of other areas in which psychology is being applied to law. As described in previous chapters, eyewitness testimony (chapter 7), lie detection (chapter 9), jury selection (chapter 13), and personality assessment in the courtroom (chapter 13) have all had an impact on legal practice.

Figure 20–4.
John Hinckley, Jr.

Psychology and Education

Psychologists concerned with the educational issues to be discussed in the remainder of this chapter may have training in one or more specialty areas. Two such areas are school psychology and educational psychology.

School psychology is a specialty that combines education with clinical and counseling psychology (Anastasi, 1979). *School psychologists* work as consultants for educational administrators and teachers and as counselors for students. Their responsibilities include any or all of the following: (1) administering aptitude, achievement, and vocational-interest tests; (2) counseling students who have academic, emotional, or other types of problems; and (3) working with administrators and teachers to ensure smooth transition for students from one grade to another and from high school to college or work.

Educational psychology is the application of psychology to education. In contrast to school psychologists, *educational psychologists* most often have specialty areas either in the psychology of learning (see chapter 6) or in measurement and psychological test development (see chapter 12). Unlike school psychologists, who work primarily within schools, educational psychologists are most likely to be involved in teacher-training or research. They work at universities in departments of education or educational psychology or in organizations devoted to educational research (Anastasi, 1979).

During the 1950s, psychologists trained in learning theory began to apply the principles of learning to school instruction. Today, *instructional psychology* is a major area in educational psychology (Gagné & Dick, 1983). Among the most visible outcomes of research in instructional psychology are the learning–based instructional systems increasingly used by teachers and educators. Two such systems are *programmed instruction* and *computer-assisted instruction*. Since they were discussed in chapter 6, there is no need to elaborate on them. Instead, we will now turn our attention to testing—perhaps the most controversial issue in educational psychology today.

— APPLICATION —

EDUCATIONAL AND PSYCHOLOGICAL TESTING

No other application of psychology can match the contribution made by psychological testing to understanding and predicting human behavior (Dunnette & Kirchner, 1965). Testing permeates nearly every area of applied psychology. Standardized educational and psychological tests are widely used to aid in selecting, classifying, assigning, and promoting students, employees, and military personnel. In industry, tests are used for personnel selection and placement, as described earlier in this chapter. In the armed forces, tests are used to determine the occupational specialties of recruits. Tests are used by vocational counselors. It is the rare school that does not use standardized testing to evaluate incoming students beyond the elementary level.

During our lifetimes, each of us will likely be affected by test scores. The scores we obtain on standardized achievement tests follow us from one institution to another throughout our educational career. Test scores play a major role in determining access to jobs. Testing, however, is under fire; it is the target of recent attacks in books, magazines, and the daily press. In the United States, the debate over testing has reached far beyond the workplace or classroom into Congress and the Supreme Court. We cannot discuss all the areas in which testing is now routine. Instead, we will focus on some of the issues and controversies surrounding the use of tests in education.

— Admissions Testing

Selecting the applicants most likely to succeed in educational programs and colleges is the focus of **admissions testing.** Today, about half of all high-school graduates engage in the yearly ritual of completing college-admission applications. Those seeking admission to top universities must have performed well in high school. In addition, many applicants will be required to present further evidence of their likelihood of success, usually in the form of recommendations from sponsors, performance in interviews, and, almost always, scores on an admissions test. Tougher standards are required for entrance to a graduate school or professional school (law or medicine, for example).

Policies governing admissions have not always been as rigorous as they are today. For instance, in 1841, the student body at the University of Michigan totaled seven, and the admissions process was much less complex. Clear-cut policies for admission were evident a century before that, however, in the regulations of the College of New Jersey (later to become Princeton University), which read:

> None may expect to be admitted into the College but such as being examined by the President and Tutors, shall be found able to render Virgil and Tully's orations into English and to turn English into true and grammatical Latin: and be so well acquainted with the Greek as to render any part of the four Evangelists in that language into Latin or English and to give the grammatical construction of the words. (Quoted in Westoff, 1980, p. 2.)

For better or worse, admissions procedures today are dramatically different from those of the 1700s. Today, a College Entrance Examination Board (created during the early 1900s) oversees the placement of students in more than 3,000 colleges annually and contracts with the Educational Testing Service (ETS) in Princeton, New Jersey, for assistance in developing and administering admissions tests. Among other services, ETS is responsible for developing, administering, scoring, and interpreting test results in the United States and 156 other countries (Educational Testing Service, 1980a). Among its more than 300 testing programs are the Graduate Record Exam (GRE) the Graduate Management Admission Test (GMAT), the Law School Admission Test (LSAT), and the Multi-State Bar Exam.

Table 20–3 shows the number of students at various educational levels in the United States who took admissions tests during 1978–79 as part of several major ETS programs. Although it appears that testing is here to stay, during the last decade a multiplicity of forces have brought about changes in the admissions process. Nowhere were these forces more evident than in the courtrooms of our nation.

— The Case of Larry P. v. Wilson Riles

Perhaps you have read newspaper reports of the court case *Larry P. v. Wilson Riles*. This case concerns a lawsuit in which Federal District Judge Robert F. Peckham

Table 20–3.

The approximate number of individuals who took tests developed by the Educational Testing Service (ETS) during 1978–79.

TESTING PROGRAM	CANDIDATE VOLUME, 1978–79
Elementary and Secondary Level	
Cooperative Tests and Services	1,600,000
Educational Records Bureau	148,500
Secondary School Admission Test	45,000
College Level	
Admissions Testing Program	1,570,000
Advanced Placement Program	106,000
College-Level Examination Program	138,000
National Teacher Examinations	55,000
Preliminary Scholastic Aptitude Test/National Merit Scholarship Qualifying Test	1,257,000
Test of English as a Foreign Language	228,000
Graduate and Professional Level	
Graduate Management Admission Test	186,000
Graduate Record Examinations	311,000
Graduate School Foreign Language Tests	4,500
Law School Admission Test	111,000

of California decided to bar the use of intelligence tests in the assignment of children to classes for the educable mentally retarded (EMR). Larry P. was one of five black children who the plaintiffs maintained were improperly admitted to special EMR classes. Wilson Riles, then Superintendent of Public Instruction in California, was named as defendant. Testimony filling more than 10,000 transcript pages documented support for the central issue in the case—that there was a higher percentage of blacks than whites in California EMR classes.

At the time the case was filed, blacks accounted for 27.5 percent of the total school population in San Francisco but 66 percent of the EMR population. No dispute existed about the figures; the issue addressed by the court was the difficult and complex one about the cause of black overrepresentation in EMR classes. The plaintiffs charged that the overrepresentation of blacks was due to the IQ tests used for assigning students to special classes; they claimed that the tests were culturally biased against the black minority. The defense attorney, Joanne Condas, argued that the tests were not biased, that black and white students in California are part of the same culture, and that IQ tests predict school grades and achievement equally well for blacks and whites (Condas, 1980).

One expert witness for the defense, Lloyd Humphreys, a professor of psychology at the University of Illinois, believes that Judge Peckham's decision to bar the use of intelligence tests in California was based on a superficial analysis of the principal issues in the case, the substance of which was either neglected or avoided (Humphreys, 1980). Other psychologists and educators vehemently disagree with Humphreys's assessment. Thus, although the legal system today may be poorly designed to untangle complex technical matters (such as the relative influence of heredity and environment on racial IQ differences—see chapter 12), there is little doubt that the case of *Larry P. v. Wilson Riles* will have a lasting and profound effect on national educational policy and the use of tests in making educational-placement decisions.

— Nader's Raid on Testing

On January 3, 1980, Ralph Nader and his associates released a 554-page report that severely criticized admissions testing and the Educational Testing Service for its development and administration of admissions tests such as the Scholastic Aptitude Test (SAT) (Nairn, 1980—cited in Educational Testing Service 1980b).

The report charged that admissions tests have undue influence on admissions to institutions of higher education and that the tests have little value in predicting future performance. Psychologists at ETS described Nader's effort as a determined, well-organized, and well-financed campaign to eliminate rather than improve standardized testing. Turnbull (1980) criticized Nader's complaint that the major tests administered for ETS constitute respectable fraud. He argued that Nader's charges are based on falsely attributed quotations that have been taken out of context and on material that is dated and wrong in its conclusions.

An Educational Testing Service paper rebutting Nader's report (Educational Testing Service, 1980b), further argues that the report arrives at its conclusions by misrepresenting the purposes and uses of the tests and by distorting or ignoring the results of research. A more recent rebuttal to Nader's raid on the testing industry has questioned whether the criticism against the use of the SAT is in the best interest of the consumer.

> The widely publicized argument that the SAT is no better than chance in predicting college performance is based on a misunderstanding of basic statistics. Extensive evidence suggests that the SAT, in combination with high school grades, is a very good predictor of college success for students from different ethnic groups and income levels. The suggestion that the use of SAT scores is a play by the rich to deny opportunity to low income students is not well supported by a variety of validity studies. Although legislation stemming from the Nader investigation of the Educational Testing Service purports to protect consumers, it may actually work against them. (Kaplan, 1982, p. 15)

— The Bakke Case

Reverse discrimination, demonstrated by the case of Allan Bakke, is one example of test legislation working against the consumer. In order to meet the guidelines set forth by the Equal Employment Opportunity Commission (EEOC) and affirmative-action legislation (legislation passed to ensure equal representation of minority groups), some universities have instituted quotas that give preference for admission to members of minority groups. It has been argued that the use of traditional admissions criteria, such as grades and aptitude-test scores, can result in the admission of a smaller-than-desirable proportion of minority students. If it does, then a university is justified, the argument says, in reserving openings for minority-group members—regardless of the presence of better-qualified majority-group applicants who would be refused admission.

The Regents of the University of California adopted this practice for admissions to their medical school, refusing admission to a well-qualified white student, Allan Bakke, and giving preference to a number of less-qualified minority students. Bakke's grade-point average (3.51) and test scores were superior to those of minority students who were admitted under the special admissions procedure. In the combined numerical ranking by the admissions committee, Bakke scored 20 to 30 points higher than did the minority students admitted. In a classic court case over the use of test scores as a criterion for admission, Bakke sued the university. Ruling in Bakke's favor, the Supreme Court rejected the notion that racial discrimination may be more easily justified against one race than another, even if the race discriminated against is the majority rather than the minority.

THE FUTURE OF ADMISSIONS TESTING

The antitest movement spawned by Ralph Nader and his associates is certain to affect admissions testing in the future. Numerous states have already adopted legislation that will curtail the use of admissions tests. For example, the New York State Standardized Testing Act, which became effective January 1, 1980, requires questions and answers on all college, graduate, and professional-school admissions tests, as well as research on the validity of the tests, to be filed with the state within 30 days after the scores are reported to the students. The state's truth-in-testing law provides test-takers with the opportunity to obtain, upon request, a copy of the questions and correct answers.

Requiring testing companies such as ETS to make test items public will force continual redevelopment of the test material. The quality of tests is likely to suffer as a result, and the costs of taking admissions tests can be expected to increase because of the expense of continually creating and testing new items. In the years ahead, students may have to pay a higher fee to take tests that are less valid than before the requirements were issued (Kaplan, 1982).

In addition to the antitesting movement and the public's growing concern over the misuse of educational and psychological tests, other factors are likely to influence the future of admissions testing. One of the biggest challenges will be to maintain an appropriate emphasis on educational values as colleges adjust to economic difficulties and enrollment changes. During the 1960s, undergraduate enrollment across the nation doubled, to 4 million; total enrollment in undergraduate, graduate, and professional education rose to more than 8.5 million. Reduced birthrates, however, will result in decreasing numbers of college-age students throughout the 1980s and 1990s. Between 1980 and 1990, the decrease in the college-age population in the United States will be about 15 percent. There are expected to be 1.7 million fewer 18-to-21-year-olds in 1985 than in 1980. By 1995, the college-age population will drop to 13 million, a 25 percent decline from the 1979 peak of 17 million (Westoff, 1980).

Shrinking college enrollment during the next decade presents a major problem for higher education in the United States. According to psychologists at ETS, one solution to the problem may be to invest more thought and energy in the admissions process. Determining the best fit between the college and the individual is really a problem in *personnel selection* (described earlier in this chapter). Selection, or admissions, programs in the future will aim for those applicants most likely to stay on for four years—and graduate. Only half the women and 61 percent of the men who entered college as freshmen in 1971 were seniors in 1974 (Westoff, 1980). Although some students who drop out of college return later, the picture is clear.

With admissions procedures for better fitting the college and the individual, thousands of potential dropouts may stay on to obtain a degree. Which admissions practices would be changed? ETS Senior Vice-President Winton H. Manning has formulated a list of Principles of Good Practice in Admissions (Westoff, 1980):

1. Selection criteria used by institutions should represent a reasonably broad array of qualities rather than relying solely upon a single index of competence derived from ability [admissions] tests and grades.
2. Whatever admissions criteria are used, the educational institution should routinely allow applicants to demonstrate that there may be areas not covered by these particular criteria and standards.
3. Upon request, a rejected applicant should be given a statement of the reason(s) for his or her rejection, and a means of appeal. (p. 24)

We are likely to see increasing efforts to implement such ideas. This means that admissions officers will be giving more careful consideration in the fu-

ture to the whole person rather than considering test scores and grades alone. Although a single best way of matching the individual with the institution will probably never exist, we can expect the development of a new variety of alternatives designed to maximize each student's chances for obtaining a form of personalized assessment that will be sensitive to personal qualities, abilities, and needs.

Testing has been scrutinized by the public since its large-scale introduction more than 6 decades ago; however, recent public concern about admissions testing has forced psychologists to continually re-evaluate their methods. This process has stimulated the development of more scientifically justifiable tests (Kaplan, 1982). In the area of admissions testing, a fresh, more imaginative approach is taking over (Westoff, 1980; Willingham & Breland, 1982).

— SUMMARY —

1. Career, or vocational, counseling represents a major area of application for counseling psychologists.

2. The applications of psychology to industry and organizations are far-ranging. Two such applications are personnel psychology, with its emphasis on personnel selection and development, and consumer psychology, which includes the psychology of advertising.

3. Personnel selection is the art and science of choosing the best person for a given job. Psychologists have studied job characteristics and person characteristics in order to predict job performance.

4. People are a valued resource. Psychologists have devoted much attention to personnel development. Training programs are now widespread for personnel at all organizational levels.

5. Psychologists interested in the new and rapidly growing application of psychology to medicine have tackled only a limited number of potential health problems so far. Behavioral medicine and behavioral health are psychological application areas that ultimately could lead to the prevention of many diseases and disorders.

6. Forensic psychologists work in a variety of jobs within the court system and correctional institutions. A growing number of psychologists have turned their research programs in directions that will have direct application to problems in law.

7. Educational psychology is the application of psychological principles to education. Educational psychologists, like industrial-organizational psychologists, use psychological tests in a variety of areas, including admission and placement of students.

— IMPORTANT TERMS AND CONCEPTS —

Applied Psychology
Vocational Psychology
Career Development
Career Counseling
Strong-Campbell Interest Inventory
Industrial-Organizational Psychology

Personnel Selection
Job Analysis
Assessment-Center Approach
Stages of Professional Careers
Mentor
Consumer Psychology

Psychology of Advertising
Behavioral Health
Forensic Psychology
School Psychology
Educational Psychology
Admissions Testing

— SUGGESTIONS FOR FURTHER READING —

Anastasi, A. (1979). *Fields of applied psychology* (2nd ed.). New York: McGraw-Hill. A thorough introduction to the many fields of applied psychology; includes a discussion of the areas discussed in this chapter as well as several others.

Campbell, D. P. (1974). *If you don't know where you are going, you'll probably end up somewhere else.* Niles, Illinois: Argus Communications. An easy-to-read guide to factors and strategies that should be considered before making career decisions.

Dunnette, M. D. (1966). *Personnel selection and placement.* Belmont, CA: Wadsworth. This paperback is about how people differ from each other and how these differences may be measured and taken into account in personnel selection and job placement.

Dunnette, M. D. (Ed.). (1976). *Handbook of industrial and organizational psychology.* Chicago: Rand McNally. Perhaps the most energetic book in the field of industrial and organizational psychology; consists of numerous contributed chapters by experts in the field.

McCormick, E. J., and Sanders, M. S. (1982). *Human factors in engineering and design* (5th ed.). New York: McGraw-Hill. Covers a topic not discussed in this chapter—human factors; includes consideration of human capabilities and values in the development and refinement of products, equipment, facilities, and environment.

Schulz, D. P. (1979). *Psychology in use: An introduction to applied psychology.* New York: Macmillan. A broad introduction to the use of psychological principles and findings in applied settings. This text extends beyond the present chapter in several areas.

— APPENDIX —

STATISTICS

Like other scientists, psychologists are interested in the measurement, description, and explanation of observable phenomena. **Measurement** involves assigning numerical values to observations. As we will see, once measurements are made, psychologists rely on *statistics* to summarize and interpret the measurements (which are also called *data*). **Descriptive statistics** are used to summarize data; **inferential statistics** are used to interpret data. In this appendix, we will examine the uses and misuses of descriptive and inferential statistics.

As an illustration of the use of statistics, let's con-sider a hypothetical example. A student enrolled in a developmental-psychology course is required to describe a specific behavior of children in a day-care center. The student chooses to describe the smiling behavior of a group of 5-year-olds. From behind a one-way mirror, the student observes the children at play and records the frequency of smiling behavior for each child in the group during a 60-minute period. With these measurements in hand, the student must now write a report, using descriptive and inferential statistics to summarize and interpret the data on smiling.

— DESCRIPTIVE STATISTICS —

Frequency Distributions

To report the data, the student could simply list each individual score. Doing so, however, would not lend itself easily to a summarization of the data. Instead, to present the data in summary form, the student creates a **frequency distribution,** in which all possible scores are listed along with their frequency of occurrence (see Table A–1). The student also depicts the data graphically, with all possible smiling values on the horizontal axis and the frequency of each smiling score on the vertical axis. A graph that uses vertical bars to represent frequency is called a **histogram.**

As shown in Figure A–1, the children observed by the student smiled between 4 and 14 times during the 60-minute period. The resulting frequency distribution is called a **frequency polygon,** if lines are used to connect points at the center of each smiling-score category. The area under the "curve" at each category still represents score frequency, as in the histogram in Figure A–1. The frequency distributions used in the re-

Table A–1.

Frequency distribution of smiling scores.

SMILING SCORE (X)	FREQUENCY
4	1
5	1
6	2
7	4
8	6
9	8
10	6
11	4
12	2
13	1
14	1

Figure A–1.

Histogram of the smiling data, depicting number of smiles per 60-minute period on the horizontal axis and frequency of smiling scores on the vertical axis.

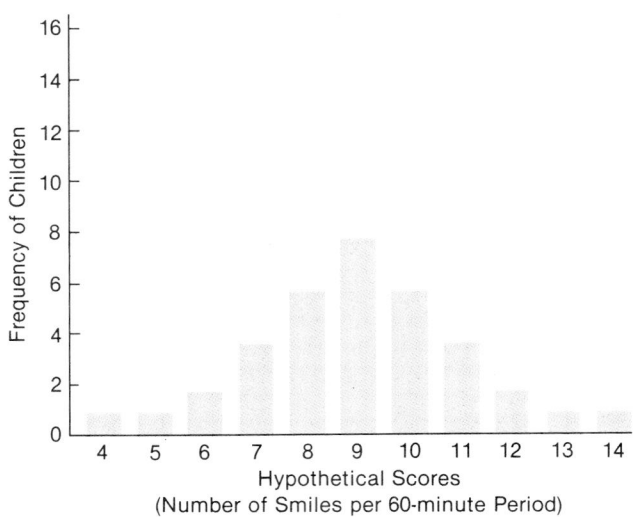

mainder of this appendix will be shown as frequency polygons.

Measures of Central Tendency

Although a graphic presentation of the smiling data provides a picture of the distribution of smiling scores, it does not quantify important characteristics of the distribution. As we will see, every distribution can be described in part by several statistics that represent the distribution's **central tendency,** the area of the distribution where most scores cluster. Three such descriptive statistics are the mean, the median, and the mode.

— The Mean

The **mean** is the measure of central tendency that indicates the average score in the distribution. The mean score, or average, is obtained by adding up all the scores and dividing the total by the number of scores. Our hypothetical student's computations, provided in Table A–2, indicate that the smiling score 9 is the mean of the distribution.

A word of caution regarding the use of the mean. Because the mean takes the value of all scores into account, it is sensitive to extreme scores. As an example of this problem, consider the statement that professional athletes earn an average yearly salary of about $350,000. An examination of the individual salaries of professional athletes, however, reveals that most athletes earn between $10,000 and $50,000 and a few earn in excess of $1 million per year. Because a few extreme values may unduly influence the arithmetic average, the mean may not always be the most appropriate statistic for expressing central tendency.

— The Median

Another measure of central tendency is the **median,** the score that divides the distribution in half. The median score in a distribution of scores is the middle score. To find the median score in the distribution of scores shown in Table A–2, we would line up each of the smiling scores in rank order. Then we would select the smiling score above and below which equal numbers of scores can be found. From the data presented in Table A–2, we can see that there are 14 scores below and 14 scores above the score of 9; thus, 9 is the median, or midpoint, of the distribution. Unlike the

Table A–2.

Computation of the mean($\overline{X}$) of the smiling data. In this example, the mean is obtained by summing the product of each score times its frequency and dividing by the total number of scores.

SMILING SCORE (X)	FREQUENCY	SCORE TIMES FREQUENCY
4	1	4
5	1	5
6	2	12
7	4	28
8	6	48
9	8	72
10	6	60
11	4	44
12	2	24
13	1	13
14	1	14

$$N = 36 \text{ scores} \qquad \sum X = 324$$

Mean, denoted by $\overline{X}$, is equal to:

$$\overline{X} = \frac{\sum X}{N}, \text{ where } \sum \text{ is the symbol for summation}$$

$$\overline{X} = \frac{324}{36}$$

$$\overline{X} = 9.0$$

mean, the median is not biased by extreme scores in the distribution.

— The Mode

A third measure of central tendency is the **mode,** the most frequently occurring score in a frequency distribution. As shown in Figure A–1, a smiling score of 9 occurs most frequently and is therefore the mode of that distribution. Like the median, the mode is uninfluenced by extreme scores. However, because a distribution can have more than one mode, the mode tends not to be the most accurate measure of central tendency; consequently, it is the least frequently used measure.

— Distribution Shapes: Normal and Skewed

Psychologists require information about the shapes of the distributions they work with because distribution shape often dictates the statistic used to describe central tendency. A symmetrical, bell-shaped distribution, such as the one obtained with the smiling data, is often referred to as a **normal probability distribution.**

Many phenomena studied by psychologists, such as IQ-test scores, assume a normal-distribution shape. As shown in Figure A–2, with a normal distribution, one

Figure A–2.

(a) A normal distribution. (b) A skewed-right distribution. (c) A skewed-left distribution. Note the relative ordering of the mean, median, and mode in each distribution.

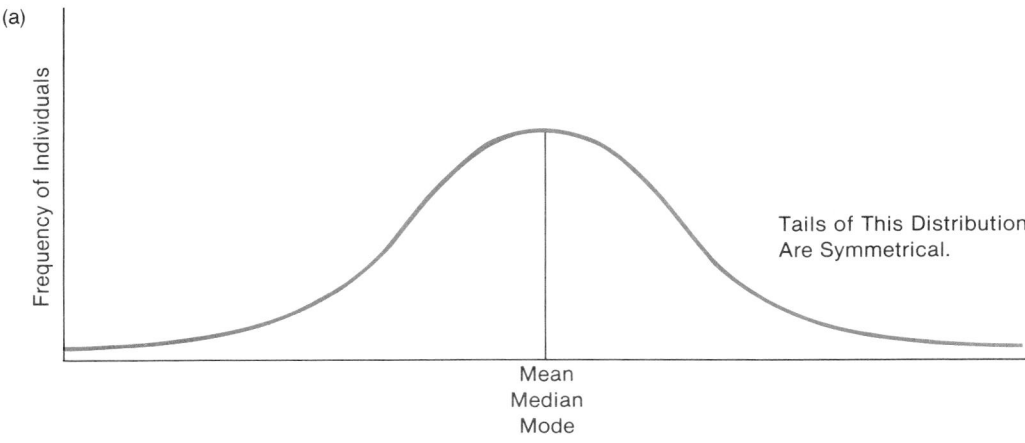

(a)

Frequency of Individuals

Tails of This Distribution Are Symmetrical.

Mean
Median
Mode

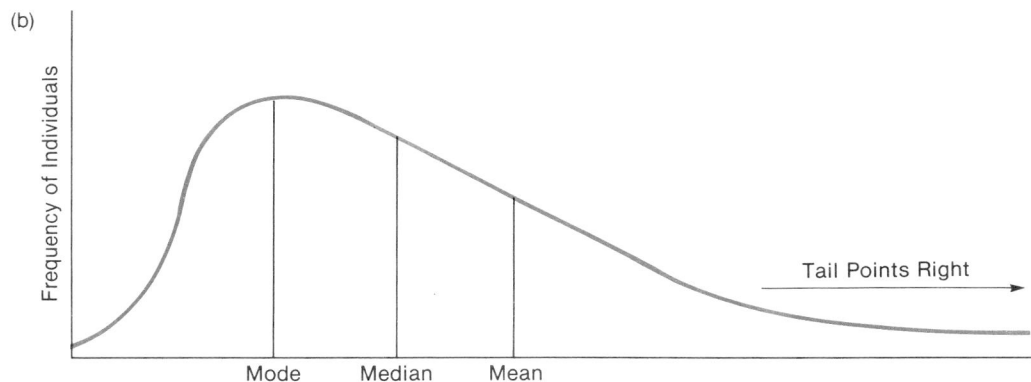

(b)

Frequency of Individuals

Tail Points Right

Mode   Median   Mean

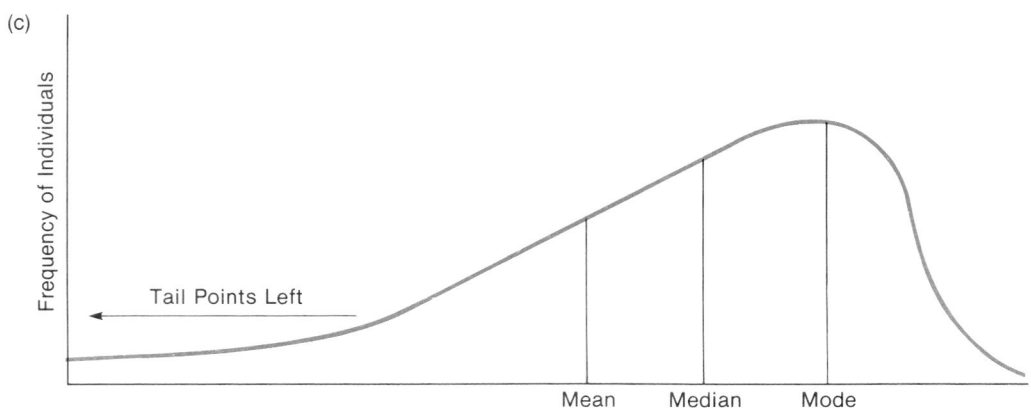

(c)

Frequency of Individuals

Tail Points Left

Mean   Median   Mode

need not be concerned about which of the measures best represents central tendency, because all three are identical. In our student's data distribution, the same smiling score, 9, is the mean, median, and mode.

In a **skewed distribution,** most of the scores cluster not at the center of the distribution but rather at one end, or tail, of it. The term *skewed-right* refers to a distribution in which most scores cluster at the left end of the distribution, with few scores found at the right tail; the term *skewed-left* refers to the opposite case (see Figure A–2). When a distribution is highly skewed, the median, or middle score, is the most meaningful index of central tendency.

Measures of Variability

As shown in Figure A–3, two frequency distributions may have identical means, but the individual scores may be spread around the mean in different patterns, yielding distributions of different shapes. Thus, measures of the **variability,** or dispersion, of scores are required to fully describe a distribution.

— The Range

The simplest index of variability is the **range,** a statistic defined as the difference between the lowest score and the highest score of a distribution. Thus, in our example, the range of smiling scores is 10 (14 minus 4). Although the range is easily computed, it yields little information on the dispersion of scores between the extremes. For example, as indicated in Figure A–3, two frequency distributions may possess identical ranges but obviously different variabilities. What is required, then, is a measure of variability that takes into account every score in the distribution.

Figure A–3.

Two hypothetical distributions having equal means but different amounts of variation around the mean.

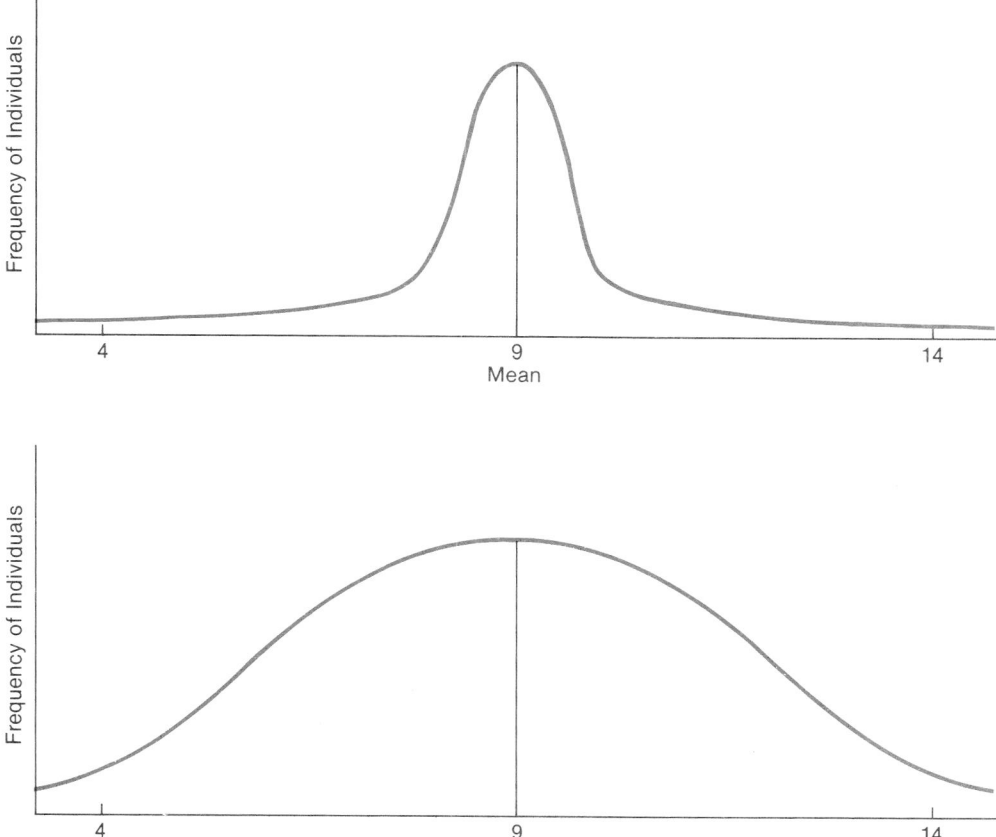

Table A–3.

Computation of the variance (S^2) and standard deviation (S) of the smiling data. The variance is obtained by summing the deviation scores and dividing by the number of scores. The standard deviation is the square root of the variance.

SMILING SCORE (X)	DEVIATION SCORE ($X - \bar{X}$)	SQUARED DEVIATION SCORE ($X - \bar{X}$)^2
4	−5	25
5	−4	16
6	−3	9
6	−3	9
7	−2	4
7	−2	4
7	−2	4
7	−2	4
8	−1	1
8	−1	1
8	−1	1
8	−1	1
8	−1	1
8	−1	1
9	0	0
9	0	0
9	0	0
9	0	0
9	0	0
9	0	0
9	0	0
9	0	0
10	1	1
10	1	1
10	1	1
10	1	1
10	1	1
10	1	1
11	2	4
11	2	4
11	2	4
11	2	4
12	3	9
12	3	9
13	4	16
14	5	25

$$\text{Variance} = S^2 = \sum \frac{(X - \bar{X})^2}{N - 1} \qquad \text{Standard deviation} = S = \sqrt{\frac{\sum(X - \bar{X})^2}{N - 1}}$$

Where: X = Each score
$\bar{X}$ = Mean of all scores (9.0)
N = Number of scores (36)

$\sum(X - \bar{X})^2 = 162$

$S^2 = \dfrac{162}{35} = 4.6$

$S = \sqrt{S^2}$
$S = \sqrt{4.6} = 2.1$

The Deviation Score

An alternate method of assessing variability involves finding the difference between each score and the mean. Such differences are known as *deviation scores.* One might assume that an index of variability can be obtained simply by calculating all the deviation scores for a distribution, summing them, and then dividing by the number of scores to get an average deviation score. Unfortunately, the deviation score is of little use by itself, because the sum of all deviation scores will always be 0.

Variance and Standard Deviation

The **variance** is the average of squared deviation scores. Remember that adding all the deviation scores yields a value of 0. To avoid this problem (created by the minus signs of deviation scores below the mean), each deviation score can be squared. The variance is then obtained, as shown in Table A–3, by adding each of the squared deviation scores and dividing by the number of scores minus 1. The variance statistic tells us the average *squared* difference from the mean. The **standard deviation,** calculated by finding the square root of the variance, provides a measure of the average difference from the mean.

Both the variance and the standard deviation measure the dispersion of scores around the mean; the smaller the dispersion or variability of scores in a distribution, the smaller the variance and standard deviation, and vice versa. In practice, we are usually interested in the standard deviation because this statistic allows us to make decisions regarding the relative standing of scores within a distribution (as we will see in the next section).

Measures of Relative Standing

Having completed the calculations of the mean (9.0) and the standard deviation (2.1) of the data on smiling provided in Table A–3, we may now better describe the distribution. Most of the smiling scores are found at the center of the distribution, and the data assume the shape of a normal curve. When a distribution is normal, certain proportions of the scores are always found within certain limits around the mean. For example, 68 percent of all the scores can be found between +1 and −1 standard deviations from the mean. That is, as illustrated in Figure A–4, 34 percent lie

Figure A–4.

Normal distribution illustrating the proportion of scores that can be expected to be found within certain standard deviations above and below the mean. The horizontal axes below the figure depict the raw scores, standard deviations, Z-scores, and percentiles and illustrate the relationship between these measures.

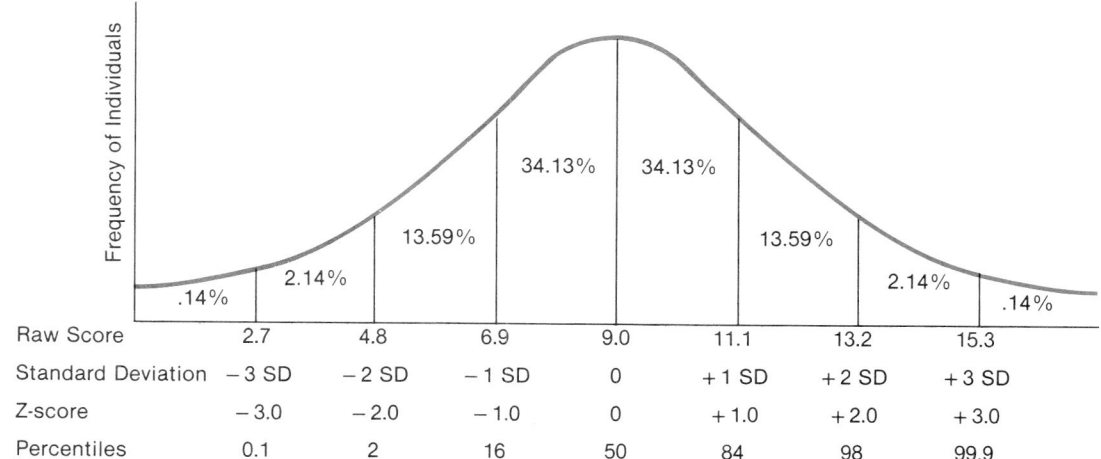

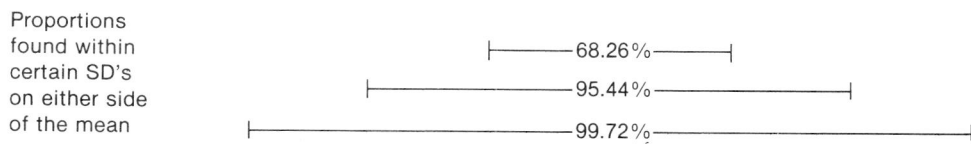

within 1 standard deviation above the mean, and 34 percent lie within 1 standard deviation below the mean. About 95 percent of all the scores can be found between +2 and -2 standard deviations, and 99 percent can be found within 3 standard deviations on either side of the mean. These proportions are characteristic of all normal distributions.

Percentiles, defined as the proportion of scores equal to or less than a particular score, are readily derived from a normal distribution. If we wish to determine the relative standing of a child with a smiling score of 9, we can look at Figure A–4 and see that a score of 9 lies at the 50th percentile. (It should be noted that the median score, which in this case is also 9, is at the 50th percentile because half the scores lie below the median.) Percentiles derived from a normal curve allow us to determine where a particular score stands relative to other scores in the distribution.

Percentiles are useful for comparing scores not only within a distribution but also between distributions. For example, we may wish to compare smiling scores with IQ-test scores for the same children. IQ-test scores are normally distributed, with a mean of 100 and a standard deviation of 15 points (see chapter 12). Thus, we have two distributions with different means and standard deviations.

Fortunately, the **Z-score** statistic can be used to *standardize* scores in different distributions, thus permitting meaningful comparisons of the relative standing of scores in two different distributions. This statistic is obtained by subtracting from a person's score (X) the mean of the distribution ($\overline{X}$). This value is then divided by the standard deviation of the distribution. Thus:

$$Z = \frac{X - \overline{X}}{\text{Standard deviation}}$$

We can now calculate a given child's relative standing in the two distributions—smiling scores and IQ-test scores.

We can compare the child's performance in the two distributions using Z-scores, because the Z-scores provide a common scale for comparison. Percentiles can be derived from the Z-score distribution, as shown in Figure A–4. The concept of relative standing, using percentiles and Z-scores, is important because psychologists seek to understand relationships between variables.

Correlation Coefficient

Referring again to smiling and IQ-test scores, we might wish to determine the relationship between these two variables. Are low values of smiling behavior associated with low values of IQ? Are high values of smiling behavior associated with high values of IQ? One way to examine this relationship is to plot each child's score on both variables. Such a scatter plot is shown in Figure A–5. Frequency of smiling behavior and IQ-test scores are plotted for each of the 36 children in our hypothetical example. Inspection of this figure suggests that there is a relationship between smiling and IQ.

A graphic presentation of these data, however, does not quantify either the magnitude or the direction of the relationship. The **correlation coefficient** (see chapter 1) is a statistic used to quantify the relationship between two variables. A correlation coefficient is typically denoted by the symbol r_{xy}, where x and y refer to values of two different variables, and can be calculated using the equation provided in Table A–4.

The correlation coefficient may range from -1.00 through 0.00 to +1.00. It is a statistic that indicates both the direction and the magnitude of the relationship between two variables. When the relationship is

Figure A–5.

A scatter plot showing a positive correlation between IQ-test scores and smiling for 36 subjects in our hypothetical example.

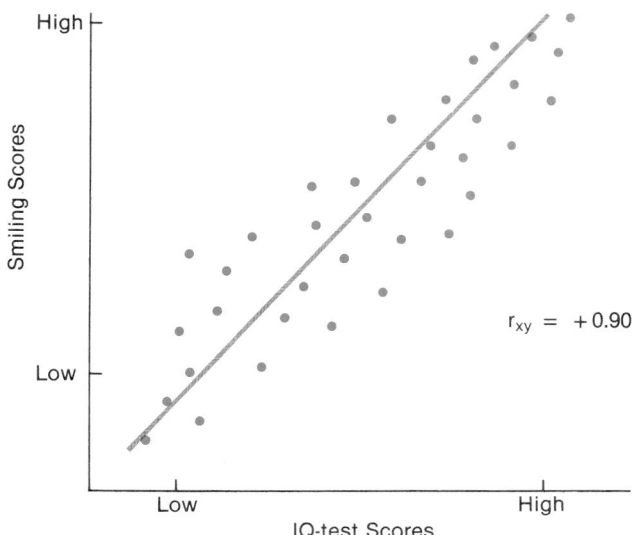

Table A–4.

Computation of the correlation coefficient between frequency of smiling and IQ-test scores for the 36 subjects in the hypothetical example.

SUBJECT NUMBER	SMILING SCORE (X)	IQ-TEST SCORE (Y)	X^2	Y^2	XY
1	4	95	16	9025	380
2	5	97	25	9409	485
3	6	99	36	9801	594
4	6	98	36	9604	588
5	7	100	49	10000	700
6	7	97	49	9409	679
7	7	100	49	10000	700
8	7	101	49	10201	707
9	8	105	64	11025	840
10	8	99	64	9801	792
11	8	102	64	10404	816
12	8	102	64	10404	816
13	8	105	64	11025	840
14	8	105	64	11025	840
15	9	102	81	10404	918
16	9	100	81	10000	900
17	9	106	81	11236	954
18	9	107	81	11449	963
19	9	107	81	11449	963
20	9	109	81	11881	981
21	9	103	81	10609	927
22	9	110	81	12100	990
23	10	110	100	12100	1100
24	10	112	100	12544	1120
25	10	112	100	12544	1120
26	10	115	100	13225	1150
27	10	115	100	13225	1150
28	10	112	100	12544	1120
29	11	110	121	12100	1210
30	11	105	121	11025	1155
31	11	115	121	13225	1265
32	11	118	121	13924	1298
33	12	119	144	14161	1428
34	12	117	144	13689	1404
35	13	120	169	14400	1560
36	14	120	196	14400	1680
N = 36	$\sum X = 324$	$\sum Y = 3849$	$\sum X^2 = 3078$	$\sum Y^2 = 413{,}367$	$\sum XY = 35{,}133$

Formula for calculating r_{xy}:

$$r_{xy} = \frac{\sum XY - \frac{(\sum X)(\sum Y)}{N}}{\sqrt{\left[\sum X^2 - \frac{(\sum X)^2}{N}\right]\left[\sum Y^2 - \frac{(\sum Y)^2}{N}\right]}} = \frac{35133 - \frac{(324)(3849)}{36}}{\sqrt{\left[3078 - \frac{(324)^2}{36}\right]\left[413367 - \frac{(3849)^2}{36}\right]}} = \frac{492}{547} = +\ 0.90$$

positive, as is the case for the hypothetical smiling and IQ-test data shown in Figure A–5, low values on one variable are associated with low values on the other variable. Similarly, high values on one variable are associated with high values on the other variable. That the relationship is positive is indicated by a line sloping upward from left to right. The magnitude of the correlation is indicated by how close the data points are to a straight line. If the correlation is perfectly positive (i.e., +1.00), all the data points will lie on a straight line. As the data points diverge from a straight line, the correlation coefficient approaches 0. This situation is illustrated by the hypothetical data shown in Figure A–6, where ear size and grade-point average are shown to be uncorrelated.

As noted, correlation coefficients can assume negative values, indicating an inverse relationship between two variables. This situation is illustrated in Figure A–7, where student evaluations of an instructor are shown to be negatively correlated with the amount of material learned during a semester. Note that a negative correlation is indicated by a line sloping down from left to right. Although the relationship is not perfect (i.e., –1.00), the size of the coefficient suggests that there is a strong inverse relationship between these variables. That is, the greater the learning, the lower the ratings of the instructor, and vice versa.

In summary, the correlation coefficient is a statistic that indicates the direction (either positive or negative)

and the magnitude (between –1.00 and +1.00) of a relationship between two variables.

Correlation and Causation

The interpretation of a correlation between two variables requires considerable care. Students often mistakenly assume that because two variables are highly correlated, they are also causally related. Or, to put it another way, it is often assumed that a high correlation means that one of the variables causes the other. One cannot assume causality between the variables, however, because the correlation may be the result of a third, unmeasured variable. For example, it is often mentioned in introductory statistics texts that the number of births in small European villages is positively correlated with the number of chimneys in each village. Similarly, the number of churches in most cities is positively correlated with the number of bars in the cities. Although such correlations are large, one can hardly assume that chimneys cause births or that churches cause bars. It is more likely that these correlations are the result of a third factor, such as the size of the town. With larger towns, one might expect to see more chimneys, births, churches, and bars.

On a positive note, a substantial correlation coefficient observed between two variables may prompt a researcher to experimentally manipulate the variables.

Figure A–6.

A scatter plot showing that measures of ear size and grade-point average are uncorrelated.

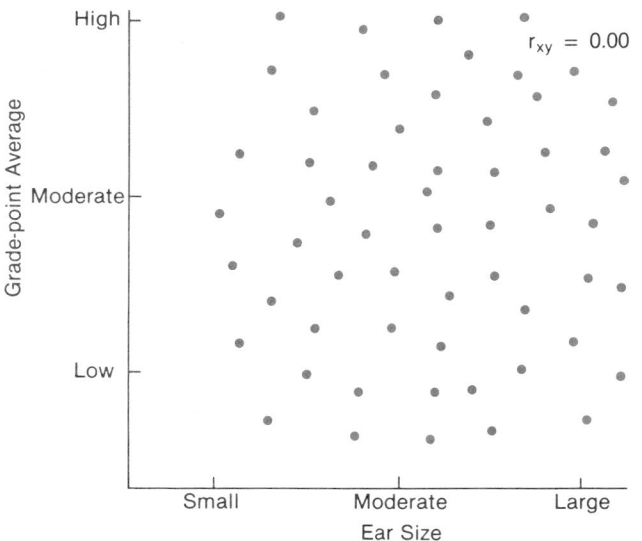

Figure A–7.

A scatter plot showing a negative correlation between student evaluations of an instructor and the amount of material learned by each student during a semester.

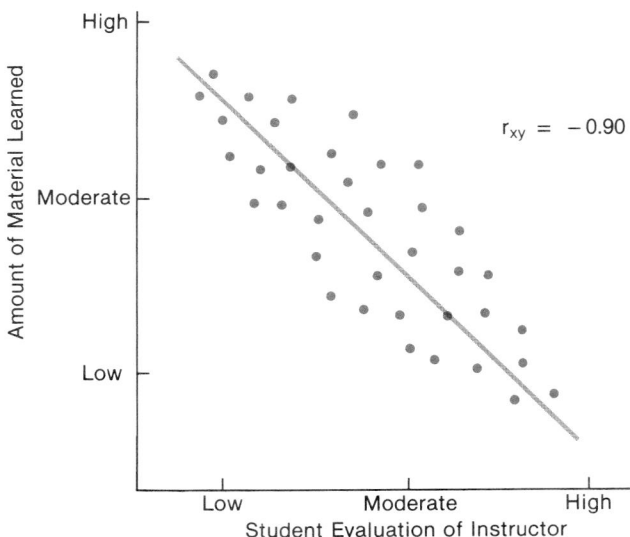

If systematic changes in one of the variables, now employed as an independent variable, result in systematic and significant changes in the other variable (the dependent variable), then one can conclude that a causal relationship exists between the variables. (See chapter 1 for further discussion of this issue.)

— Correlation and Prediction

If there is a strong relationship between two variables, our knowledge of a person's score on one of the variables allows us to predict, with some accuracy, the person's score on the other variable. Circus barkers, for example, have long known about the strong positive correlation between height and weight. (Generally, taller people weigh more than shorter people.) Thus, a barker is able to guess a person's weight by first estimating the person's height.

Psychologists make use of the predictive capacity of correlations in many settings. For example, it is known that achievement-test scores are positively correlated with college grade-point averages. Given this relationship, a counselor may estimate future college grades from a person's score on the SAT (Scholastic Aptitude Test). (See chapters 12 and 20.) The predictive power of a test score, however, is only as good as the magnitude of the correlation between two variables. If the correlation is strong, prediction is good. If the correlation is weak or nonexistent, prediction is poor. Because SAT scores and grade-point averages are not perfectly correlated, the predictive power of the SAT is less than perfect.

— INFERENTIAL STATISTICS —

Descriptive statistics are useful because they provide a means to summarize and describe data in a clear and understandable fashion. Inferential statistics are used to interpret data and to draw inferences or conclusions from data obtained in small samples.

as the size of the sample becomes larger, the sample becomes more representative, and so sampling error is decreased. The sampling procedure must also be *random;* that is, every member of the population must have an equal chance of being a member of the sample (see chapter 1).

Sampling

Our hypothetical student was required only to describe the frequency of smiling in a small sample of children. The obtained results, however, could also be used to estimate the distribution of smiling frequency in all 5-year-olds—the **population**—of which the sample studied is only a small part. **Sampling** techniques are used to estimate a population distribution and its characteristics (for example, its mean and standard deviation) from a small sample of the population.

Samples used to estimate population values must be *representative* of the population. If a sample is not representative, *sampling errors*—differences between the sample estimates and the actual population values—will occur. To accurately estimate the frequency distribution of smiling in all children, we must also study a large sample. A sample of only five children would be unlikely to represent the entire population. In general,

Significance

Tests of statistical significance are used when experimenters wish to determine if observed differences between two groups are due to chance factors (such as sampling errors). As an example, let's return to the data on smiling. Assume that we wish to find out if there is a difference in smiling frequency between a group of children whose parents are divorced and a group of children whose parents are still married. Assume also that we find that children with divorced parents show a mean smiling frequency of 7.0 whereas children from intact families show a mean smiling frequency of 11.0. Our question is: Is the 4-point difference between groups significant?

A result (or difference) is said to be **statistically significant** if the obtained difference could be expected, by chance, to occur only 5 percent or less of the time. In other words, only 5 percent of the time would a difference of the observed magnitude occur if only chance factors were operating to produce differences between groups. Using tests of significance (the descriptions of which are beyond the scope of this appendix), we may find that the difference in smiling frequency between children from divorced and nondivorced backgrounds is statistically significant. If so, we could conclude that children with divorced parents do in fact smile significantly less than children from intact families.

DECEPTION WITH STATISTICS

The purpose of statistics is to summarize and interpret data. A particular statistic, such as the mean or standard deviation, is simply a number that represents some property of the data. The interpretation of a statistic is independent of its computation; that is, one may arrive at a number that represents some property of the data, but the number itself does not automatically provide an interpretation of the data. The correct interpretation of a statistic requires consideration as to where and how the data were obtained, how the statistic was computed, and how the data were presented. To conclude this appendix, let's briefly consider some of the ways we may deceive ourselves and others at each stage of processing data.

Data Acquisition

In computer science, the saying "garbage in, garbage out" refers to the fact that computers only analyze data; they do not verify that the data are correct. This concept is applicable to the statistical process as well. Statistics only manipulate numbers; they do not verify that the numbers are correct.

Accurate interpretation of data also requires information on the sampling procedure used and the characteristics of the subjects studied. Consider the following commercial: "Seventy-five percent of dentists surveyed recommend Bleech toothpaste." This statistical statement suggests that Bleech toothpaste is preferred by most dentists and implies that it is a superior product. To evaluate the statement, however, we need more information. If we find that only four dentists were questioned, we will not take the statement seriously. Moreover, if we find that the surveyed dentists are employees of or stockholders in the company that

makes Bleech toothpaste, we may doubt the truth of the commercial.

Using the Appropriate Statistic

When a statistic is used to support some conclusion, it is essential that the proper statistic be employed. As noted earlier, three measures of central tendency—the mean, the median, and the mode—may have different values if the data form a skewed distribution. Thus, one measure of central tendency may be used to support a conclusion, but a different conclusion would be drawn if an alternate measure of central tendency were used. Such was the case in our earlier example of professional athletes' salaries. The owner of a team may wish to argue that athletes are overpaid. If so, the owner might likely select the mean of $350,000 as the index of player salaries, thereby justifying a refusal to raise salaries. In contrast, the representative of the players' union might select either the median or the mode as the index of salary. Because many players are paid only $10,000 to $50,000 per year, either measure could be used to justify a raise in player salaries. Thus, one needs information on the distribution shape in order to evaluate statistical statements.

Misleading Presentation

How data are presented can be an important determinant of how they are viewed. Data presentation can be misleading in several respects. First, data can be graphically presented so as to emphasize or deemphasize

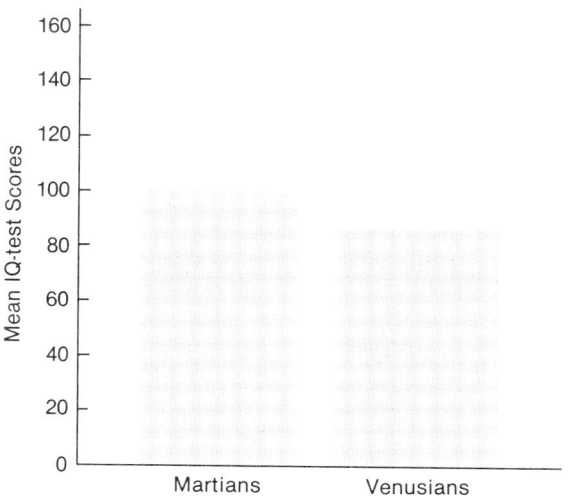

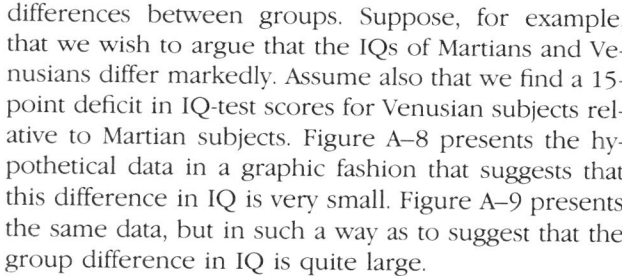

Figure A–8.

A graphic presentation of a hypothetical 15-point difference in IQs between Martians and Venusians. The vertical axis is drawn so as to deemphasize this difference.

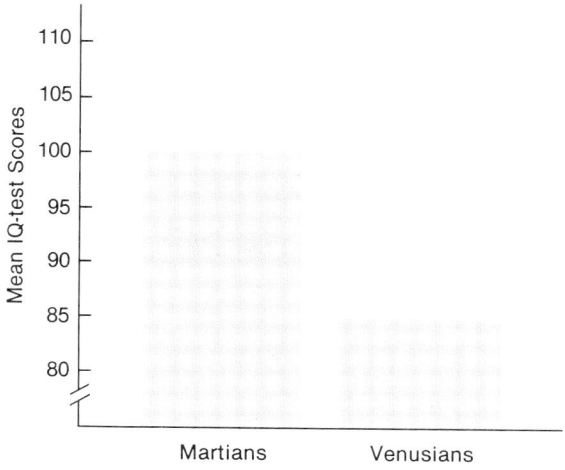

Figure A–9.

The same 15-point difference in IQ as shown in Figure A–8, but with the vertical axis drawn so as to emphasize the difference in IQs.

differences between groups. Suppose, for example, that we wish to argue that the IQs of Martians and Venusians differ markedly. Assume also that we find a 15-point deficit in IQ-test scores for Venusian subjects relative to Martian subjects. Figure A–8 presents the hypothetical data in a graphic fashion that suggests that this difference in IQ is very small. Figure A–9 presents the same data, but in such a way as to suggest that the group difference in IQ is quite large.

In Figure A–8, the entire range of possible IQ-test scores (0 to 160 points) is given on the vertical axis, whereas in Figure A–9 a smaller IQ range is presented. The effect of the latter procedure is to magnify the difference between groups. Thus, one must always consider the way in which data are presented within a graph when making a judgment about the differences depicted.

There is a second manner in which data presenta-

tion may be misleading. Often, data are presented without information about whether differences in the data are statistically significant. At the same time, it may be implied that differences are, in fact, significant. For example, a television commercial may depict five brands of pain relievers. The viewer is informed that four of the brands contain only 250 milligrams of a particular pain reliever, whereas the fifth contains 500 milligrams. The implication is that the fifth brand produces greater pain relief because it contains more of the pain reliever. Yet, nowhere within the commercial will one find a statement indicating that the greater amount of pain reliever in the fifth brand produces a statistically significant difference in pain relief. Psychologists attempt to avoid such criticisms by using descriptive and inferential statistics, which are used to summarize and interpret their data.

SUMMARY

1. Psychologists use statistics to summarize and interpret data. Descriptive statistics are used to describe and summarize data; inferential statistics are used to interpret data and to relate data obtained in small samples to larger populations.

2. Frequency distributions graphically and visually present the frequency of any given data point.

3. Quantification of data in a distribution can be accomplished using measures of central tendency. Three such measures are the mean (the arithmetic average), the median (the score that divides a distribution of scores in half), and the mode (the most frequently occurring score). The mean, median, and mode are the same value in a normal, bell-shaped distribution, but they are different values in a skewed distribution.

4. A frequency distribution can be further described through an assessment of the variability, or dispersion, of the scores. Measures of variability include the range, variance, and standard deviation.

5. The range is the difference between the lowest and highest scores in a distribution. The variance is computed by finding the deviation of each score from the mean, squaring those values, and adding them. The standard deviation is the square root of the variance.

6. The standard deviation is particularly useful in that it allows comparison of the relative standing of scores within a distribution or between distributions. In a normal distribution, known proportions of the scores are always found within certain limits of the mean.

7. A correlation coefficient quantifies the relationship between two variables. Correlation coefficients vary in direction (positive or negative) and magnitude (0 to + 1 or − 1). The greater the magnitude of a correlation, the greater the capacity to predict the value of one variable when given the value of the other.

8. In inferential statistics, there is a concern with whether a distribution of scores obtained from a sample is a good estimate of the distribution that would be obtained from the whole population of values. Issues of sampling, sampling errors, and randomness are important. Researchers are also concerned with whether observed experimental outcomes are statistically significant, as established by tests of significance.

9. Statistics may be misleading. For example, a sample may not represent the entire population and data can be presented so as to make a trivial difference look large.

IMPORTANT TERMS AND CONCEPTS

Measurement
Descriptive Statistics
Inferential Statistics
Frequency Distribution
Histogram
Frequency Polygon
Central Tendency
Mean

Median
Mode
Normal Probability Distribution
Skewed Distribution
Variability
Range
Variance

Standard Deviation
Percentiles
Z-Score
Correlation Coefficient
Population
Sampling
Statistically Significant

Ablation   The removal of a particular part of the brain.

Abnormal Behavior   Any behavior that has undesirable consequences for the individual or others; it is behavior that impairs optimal functioning, causes personal distress, disrupts daily functioning, or causes others distress or harm.

Absolute Threshold   The minimum stimulus intensity required to produce a sensation.

Accommodation   The process of changing existing mental structures to make them correspond with new information (chapter 11).

Accommodation   The changes in lens shape that the eye makes to focus objects at various distances (chapter 4).

Achievement Tests   Tests designed to measure what individuals have learned in the past.

Acquired Motives   Motives that are thought to be based on learning and experience.

Actor-observer Difference   The tendency to see one's own behavior as caused by situational or external factors and others' behaviors as caused by personal characteristics.

Acupuncture   The pain-blocking technique that involves the insertion of tiny needles into certain regions of the body and that is believed to reduce pain by triggering the release of endorphins or enkephalins in the brain.

Adaptive Behavior   The various duties and social roles appropriate to each age.

Admissions Testing   A procedure used to select the applicants most likely to succeed in educational programs and colleges.

Adolescence   The stage of development that spans the teenage years. (In Latin adolescence means "growing into maturity.")

Adrenal Glands   Glands of the endocrine system that are located above the kidneys and that secrete various hormones, including sex hormones and hormones that help the body cope with stress.

Affective Disorder   A category of mental disorders involving a major disturbance of mood or emotions.

AFP Screening   A prenatal screening procedure for detecting birth defects that involves measuring the amount of the chemical alphafetoprotein (AFP) in the pregnant woman's blood.

Afterimages   Sensory impressions that persist after removal of the stimulus that caused them.

Aggression   Any behavior whose intent is to inflict harm or injury on another living being.

Aggressive Cues   Stimuli associated with aggression, such as weapons.

Agoraphobia   A marked fear of open spaces and unfamiliar settings.

Algorithms   Problem-solving methods that, if correctly applied, guarantee a solution, even if we do not understand how they work.

Ambiguous Sentences   Sentences that have more than one plausible deep structure.

Amniocentesis   A procedure for drawing amniotic fluid from a pregnant woman's womb and analyzing fetal cells to detect genetic and chromosomal abnormalities.

Anal Stage   The psychosexual stage, usually occurring during the 2nd year of life, in which the libido changes its focus from the oral to the anal region.

Androgens   Male hormones.

Anorexia Nervosa   An eating disorder involving self-starvation and severe weight loss.

Anoxia   A lack of oxygen that may damage brain cells and that may occur if the newborn fails to breathe normally after the mother ceases to supply oxygen.

Anterograde Amnesia A type of forgetting in which memory for new events is impaired but older information is recalled normally.

Antidepressants The class of drugs used in the treatment of depression.

Antimanics The class of drugs used in treating the mania associated with bipolar disorder.

Anxiety An emotion that accompanies stress and that is characterized by unpleasant feelings of apprehension.

Anxiety Disorders A category of mental disorders in which the central feature is either high anxiety or the disruptive consequences of trying to avoid it or defend against it.

Anxiolytics The class of drugs used to treat such chronic problems as mild anxiety and tension.

Aphasias Language disorders caused by brain injuries, such as from gunshot wounds or strokes.

Apparent Motion Movement perceived without the physical motion of objects.

Applied Psychology The branch of psychology concerned with solving real-life problems.

Approach-Approach Conflict The type of conflict in which a person is motivated to approach each of two (or more) equally desirable alternatives when only one can be chosen.

Approach-avoidance Conflict The type of conflict in which a person is motivated to both approach and avoid the same goal.

Aptitude Tests Tests designed to measure the capacity to learn particular skills or subject matter.

Arousal Theory A motivation theory that proposes that individuals seek an optimal level of arousal.

Artificial Intelligence The science whose goal is to program computers to behave intelligently, such as in conversing with human beings, playing chess, and solving problems.

Assertion Training The behavioral therapy technique by which the therapist attempts to increase the client's ability to express both negative and positive feelings and to do so in an honest, socially appropriate manner.

Assessment-center Approach The most favored procedure for matching jobs with personnel, developed for the selection of specialized military personnel during World War II and involving the use of multiple assessment procedures and multiple assessors to predict job candidates' likelihood of success.

Assimilation The process of modifying new information to make it fit existing schemata, or knowledge.

Association Areas Portions of each of the lobes of the cerebral cortex involved in thinking and problem solving and responsible for organizing, storing, processing, and integrating information from the senses.

Attachment The term used to refer to the early love bond that develops between infant and care-giver.

Attention The process that allows us to selectively focus on some stimuli and filter out others.

Attitude A relatively enduring predisposition to feel, think, and respond in particular ways toward some object, person, group, or issue.

Attitude-discrepant Behavior Behavior inconsistent with one's attitudes.

Attraction An evaluation of another individual in a positive or negative manner; an attitude held toward another individual.

Attribution The process of inferring the causes of others' behavior as well as their traits, motives, and intentions.

Audition The sense of hearing, which is the product of mechanical energy, or pressure changes in the molecules of air.

Auditory Cortex The area of the temporal lobe of the cerebral cortex that is specialized for receiving and responding to sound stimuli.

Authoritarianism The personality trait typified by resistance to change, prejudice, a hostile attitude toward those who have violated the conventional values of society, and submission to authority.

Autistic Savants Children who display a curious combination of retardation and genius. Autism is the term applied to children who are noncommunicative and often totally self-absorbed and who escape reality through daydreams or fantasy. Savant is a French term that means "a person of exceptional learning."

Autokinetic Movement Movement perceived in the absence of real movement that results from signals provided by muscles that surround the eye and by tiny, uncontrollable head movements.

Autonomic Nervous System The part of the peripheral nervous system that controls body functions normally considered to be automatic, or involuntary, such as the heartbeat and the operations of the smooth muscles of the stomach, the intestines, blood vessels, and various other internal organs.

Autoshaping The term used to refer to learning that appears to occur automatically, without prior shaping or reinforcement.

Aversive Conditioning The behavioral therapy technique that attempts to establish negative feelings in response to a stimulus that now elicits positive feelings that are socially inappropriate.

Avoidance-avoidance Conflict The type of conflict in which a person is motivated to avoid each of two (or more) equally unattractive choices when one of them must be chosen.

Avoidance Training Learning to make a particular response that prevents the onset of an aversive stimulus.

Axons Fibers that extend from the cell body of a neuron; their function is to transmit messages to other neurons or to the muscles and body organs.

Babbling The unsystematic use of a wide variety of speechlike sounds, observed in infants at about 6 months of age.

Balance Theory   The theory of attraction that emphasizes the importance of consistency among one's thoughts.

Behavior Modification   A technique used to modify or control undesirable behaviors.

Behavioral Adaptive Theory   The theory that sleep patterns of each species were shaped over hundreds of years by environmental pressures.

Behavioral Approach   The approach to personality that focuses on behavior and on the environmental conditions that influence it.

Behavioral Health   A term used to refer to the new interdisciplinary specialty concerned with health maintenance and the prevention of illness.

Behavioral Model of Abnormality   An approach to abnormality in which maladaptive behavior is attributed to faulty learning processes.

Behavioral Specificity   The idea that behavior changes to fit the circumstances.

Behavioral States   Levels of alertness and consciousness that characterize newborns.

Behavioral Therapies   Therapeutic approaches that attempt to alter problem behaviors directly, through the use of scientific principles of learning.

Behaviorism   School of psychology emphasizing the study of behaviors that can be observed and measured using objective experimental procedures.

Binocular Depth Cues   Depth cues that require the use of both eyes.

Binocular Disparity   The difference in retinal images formed by near and far objects; the binocular disparity of distant objects is less than that of near objects, their angles being different.

Biofeedback   A technique whereby information about normally imperceptible body functions is routed back to the individual in an easily perceived form.

Biological Model of Abnormality (Medical Model)   An approach to abnormality in which abnormal behavior is viewed as resulting from some organic or biological impairment.

Biological Motives   Motives related to survival of the individual or the species.

Biological Rhythm Theory   The theory that sleep represents a natural rhythm governed by the body's biological clock.

Bipolar Disorder   A persistent mood disturbance in which both depressive and manic symptoms are prominent.

Birth Defect   An abnormality of structure, function, or metabolism that may have either genetic or environmental causes, or, in a majority of cases, both.

Blind Spot   An area of the retina that contains neither rods nor cones and is insensitive to light.

Brain   A soft, convoluted (folded) mass of neural tissue located within the skull.

Brightness   The term used to refer to how light or bright a color appears; determined by light-wave amplitude, or intensity.

Broca's Aphasia   An aphasia that results from injury to the anterior, or front, part of the brain; victims have difficulty speaking but they have no difficulty comprehending either spoken or written language. Also known as anterior aphasia.

Bulimia   An eating disorder characterized by intense, recurrent episodes of excessive eating (binge-eating) followed by depression, self-deprecating thoughts, and weight-reducing efforts.

Career Counseling   The specialty area of applied psychology concerned with helping people, young and old, make career decisions.

Career Development   The process of adjustment to work that takes place throughout one's work life.

Case-history Approach   One of the oldest, although perhaps the weakest, methods for investigating psychological phenomena, which involves looking into a person's past in an attempt to reconstruct life events.

Catatonic Schizophrenia   A type of schizophrenia in which the major symptom is a disturbance in motor activity, either of an excited or a stuporous type.

Catecholamine Hypothesis   The theory that depression results from low levels of catecholamines while mania results from an excess of them.

Catharsis   The reduction of anger and subsequent aggressive behavior that results from engaging in safe aggressive acts or from watching aggression take place.

Causal Attribution   A process of determining whether an actor's behavior is internally or externally caused.

Central Nervous System   The part of the nervous system that consists of the brain and spinal cord.

Central Tendency   The area in a distribution of scores where most scores cluster.

Cerebellum   The part of the hindbrain that governs body balance and coordination.

Cerebral Specialization of Function   The idea that certain higher mental faculties, such as language, depend on specialized regions in the brain.

Cerebrum   The largest portion of the forebrain, consisting of two cerebral hemispheres (the right and the left divisions) and the cerebral cortex, or outer layer.

Chain of Behavior   A series of responses in which each response produces a reinforcer, which then serves as the cue (or discriminative stimulus) for the next response in the chain.

Chemical Senses   The senses of smell and taste; chemical substances provide the physical stimulus for each.

Chemical Therapy   The form of medical therapy involving the use of drugs in treating maladaptive behavior.

Chunk   Any meaningful unit of information, such as a letter, number, word, or phrase.

Ciliary Muscles   Muscles attached to the lens of the eye that relax or contract to change the shape and thickness of the lens, thereby contributing to focus control.

Circadian Rhythms A term from the Latin *circa diem,* meaning "about a day," that refers to daily cycles, such as the cyclical pattern of waking and sleeping.

Classical (Respondent) Conditioning A basic form of learning that takes place when a neutral stimulus is paired with a stimulus that elicits a reflex response. If this pairing is repeated, the previously neutral stimulus will also begin to elicit the response.

Client-centered Therapy Carl Rogers's therapeutic approach that aims to establish a warm, accepting, and non-judgmental atmosphere in which individuals can begin to explore their true feelings and desires rather than denying them.

Clustering The tendency to organize or group items during recall; also called subjective organization.

Cognition A term that comes from the Latin word meaning "coming to know." Cognitive development is the process by which infants come to know their world and acquire knowledge.

Cognitive Appraisals Evaluations made of the events in one's environment.

Cognitive Approach The approach to personality concerned with how thoughts and beliefs affect people's behavior.

Cognitive-behavioral Approach The approach to personality that emphasizes the study of covert as well as overt behaviors.

Cognitive-behavioral Therapies Therapeutic approaches that focus primarily on techniques that directly alter an individual's cognitions.

Cognitive-consistency Theories Theories of motivation that maintain that people have a need for consistency in their thoughts.

Cognitive Dissonance An unpleasant emotional state experienced when an inconsistency occurs between one's attitudes or between one's attitude and behavior.

Cognitive Learning Learning that involves intellectual (cognitive) processes, such as thinking, reasoning, and remembering, that intervene between the stimulus and the response.

Cognitive Model of Abnormality An approach to abnormality in which maladaptive behavior is attributed to faulty thought processes.

Cognitive Theories Theories of motivation that assume that individuals are motivated to evaluate the consistency or accuracy of their knowledge about the world or themselves.

Cognitive Therapy Beck's therapeutic approach, which emphasizes the importance of undoing negative thinking and faulty reasoning in overcoming emotional disorders.

Coitus Sexual intercourse.

Compensation The defense mechanism that involves counteracting an undesirable characteristic that makes a person feel anxious and inadequate by exaggerating an opposing trait.

Compliance Behavior carried out in accordance with a request from someone.

Compulsion A repetitive behavior that an individual feels compelled to perform to prevent intolerable anxiety.

Concept A verbal or nonverbal symbol representing a class or group of objects or events having common properties.

Conception The beginning of human development, when a female's egg cell (or ovum) and a male's sperm cell are united.

Concordance Rate The degree of similarity between related individuals on some characteristic or mental disorder.

Concrete Operational Stage The Piagetian stage of cognitive development that spans the 7th through 12th years of life, during which time thought becomes logical, but only when applied to concrete objects and situations.

Conditioned Response Any response elicited by a conditioned stimulus. The term conditioned means that the stimulus-response association is learned.

Conditioned (Secondary) Reinforcing Stimuli (S^r) Reinforcers (or reinforcing stimuli) that are learned and reinforce because of their prior association with a primary reinforcing stimulus.

Conditioned Stimulus (CS) Any stimulus that elicits a conditioned response. The term conditioned means that the stimulus-response association is learned.

Cones One of two main types of photoreceptive cells (or photoreceptors) in the human retina and the retinas of most vertebrates, named for their distinctive shape.

Conflict A condition in which an individual has incompatible or opposing goals.

Conformity Behavior in accordance with established social norms.

Conjunctive Rule The type of rule for combining conceptual attributes that is based on *and* relationships; the rule states that both Attribute A and Attribute B must be present to define the concept.

Conscious The level of consciousness that contains thoughts and memories of which we are fully aware at any given moment.

Consciousness The immediate awareness of both the external environment and internal events, such as thoughts, fantasies, and daydreams.

Consensus In Kelley's theory, whether only the actor behaves in a particular way or whether other people do as well.

Conservation The ability to recognize that an object's amount, length, number, volume, and area remain the same despite changes in the object's appearance.

Consistency In Kelley's theory, the stability or generality of a person's behavior in time, modality, and context.

Consolidation A process by which a memory becomes durable and solidified in long-term memory.

Construct Validation A type of validation that demonstrates the extent to which a test is capable of measuring a psychological trait, or construct, such as human intelligence.

Consumer Psychology The specialty area of applied psychology concerned with the scientific study of consumer behavior, which, broadly defined, encompasses the acquisition, use, and disposition of products and services.

Content Analysis A procedure in which verbal behavior from an interview can be quantified by the establishment of categories of verbal content that can be reliably rated by scorers.

Content Validation A type of validation that involves examining a test's content (the test items) to determine whether the test fairly represents the abilities being measured.

Context The setting in which an object appears.

Continuous Nonreinforcement Schedules Schedules of reinforcement in which each response emitted receives no reinforcement.

Continuous Reinforcement Schedules Schedules of reinforcement in which each response emitted is reinforced.

Contour The boundary between a figure and its ground.

Control Group Participants in an experiment who are not exposed to manipulation of the independent variable.

Conventional Stages of Moral Development The second two stages of six stages of moral development proposed by Kohlberg, during which the child develops an awareness of authority and an appreciation for maintaining the social order for its own sake.

Convergence The way the eyes look inward and outward to focus on near and far objects.

Convergent Thinking An ability to narrow the possibilities, to converge on and choose the one best solution to a problem.

Conversion Disorder A mental disorder in which the central feature is a loss or alteration in physical functioning that has no physical basis and is not under voluntary control.

Cornea The eye's transparent outer surface and initial focusing device.

Corpus Callosum The bundle of nerve fibers that connects the right and left cerebral hemispheres and provides a pathway for communication between them.

Correlation Coefficient A mathematical expression of the degree of relationship between two variables.

Correlational-research Approach A systematic way of investigating relationships among variables.

Counterconditioning The conditioning strategy in behavioral therapy in which one response to a stimulus is substituted for another.

Covert Sensitization A behavioral therapy technique in which clients imagine highly aversive events in order to reduce the attraction of troublesome behaviors.

Creativity A quality of thought that leads to novel and unexpected problem solving.

Credibility The believability of a communicator; the greater the expertise and trustworthiness of a source, the greater the credibility.

Cretinism A condition that results from an insufficiency of the thyroid gland hormone thyroxine and that is associated with severe mental retardation.

Criterion-related Validation A type of validation that involves determining how well a test predicts some specific behavior.

Critical Periods Periods of development, sometimes referred to as sensitive periods or optimal periods, when the organization of certain behaviors is most easily affected by environmental events.

Cross-sectional Research Designs A type of study in which individuals of various ages, representing a cross section of the population, are tested at the same time.

Crowding A stressful psychological state—a personal, subjective reaction to insufficient space.

Cultural-familial Retardation The term used to describe the approximately 75 percent of all cases of mental retardation that are not due to some known biological disorder. Such cases are thought to be related to cultural disadvantage or to factors related to family environment, or both.

Cunnilingus Oral stimulation of the female genitals.

Dark Adaptation An increased sensitivity to light that occurs during exposure to darkness.

Decay Theory A theory of forgetting that states that memory traces in the brain fade or decay from disuse.

Deep Structure The underlying meaning of a sentence.

Defense Mechanisms Unconscious psychological processes used by people to protect themselves against anxiety through distorting reality.

Defensible Space Physical space that is characterized by a high level of social responsibility and personal safety.

Delusions Thoughts that have no basis in reality.

Dendrites Short fibers that branch out around the cell body of a neuron; their function is to receive messages from other neurons and carry them to the cell body.

Denial The defense mechanism whereby people pretend that some unpleasant reality does not exist.

Dependent Variables (DVs) The variables of interest to the investigator, which may or may not change when the independent variable is manipulated; variations in the dependent variable are assumed to be caused by manipulations of the independent variable; synonymous with behavioral *effects*.

Depth Perception The ability to judge accurately how far objects are from us or from each other.

Destructive Obedience Obedience carried out despite one's disapproval of the orders.

Descriptive Statistics Statistics used to summarize and describe data.

Developmental Psychology The scientific study of the determinants of human growth and development, the underlying processes of change, and the hows and whys of alterations in behavior.

Developmental Quotient (DQ) An index of the infant's level of development that is based on motor development, adaptive skills, language use, and personal-social development.

Developmental Tasks Behavior skills that characterize different stages of development.

Deviation IQ An IQ defined by one's relative standing among others of the same age.

Dichotic-listening Technique The technique for studying brain function that involves testing a subject's recall of different auditory information presented simultaneously to each ear.

Differential Reinforcement In operant conditioning, the process by which a discrimination is established by reinforcing some responses but not others.

Diffusion of Responsibility The process of sharing with others the responsibility for helping.

Discriminative Stimuls (S^D) The stimulus that is present before a reinforced response is made and that sets the occasion for reinforcement.

Disjunctive Rule The type of rule for combining conceptual attributes that uses the logical relation *or;* the rule states that a concept is defined if either Attribute A or Attribute B is present.

Disorganized Schizophrenia A type of schizophrenia characterized by marked incoherence and flat, incongruous, or silly affect.

Displacement The process by which the addition to memory of a new item of information results in the loss of an old item. Displacement seems to be the major cause of forgetting in short-term memory.

Display Rules Norms regarding the expected management of facial appearance.

Dissociative Disorders A category of mental disorders involving a separation or alteration between an individual and his or her normal consciousness, identity, or motor behavior.

Distinctiveness In Kelley's theory, an actor's behavior occurring either in response to only one particular stimulus or in response to other, similar stimuli as well.

Divergent Thinking An ability that involves examining alternate solutions to a problem or coming up with new solutions.

Door-in-the-face-technique A compliance strategy in which one first makes a large request (that is refused) and then a small request.

Dopamine Hypothesis A biochemical theory which attributes schizophrenia to an excess of the neurotransmitter dopamine.

Double Approach-avoidance Conflict The type of conflict in which a person is motivated to both approach and avoid two different goals.

Double-bind Pattern A family pattern in which parents present their children incompatible and contradictory messages.

Down's Syndrome A chromosomal abnormality that in a majority of cases is associated with having three, instead of two, chromosomes in group 21 and that retards mental development.

Drives Psychological tensions that are produced by needs and that motivate organisms to reduce those needs.

DSM-III The most widely used system for classifying abnormal behavior; it is a set of guidelines for categorizing disorders on the basis of symptoms or behaviors.

Dual Memory Theory The theory that short-term memory and long-term memory are two distinct systems.

Early Adulthood The period of development that extends from 18 to 35 years of age.

Early Childhood The stage of development that extends from 18 months of age to the beginning of the school years, or roughly age 5.

Echoic Store The sensory memory for auditory information.

Educational Psychology The specialty area of applied psychology concerned with the application of psychological knowledge and principles to education.

Effectance Motivation The motive to strive for competence in dealing with our surroundings.

Ego The part of the personality that is attuned to the demands and opportunities of objective reality.

Elaborative Rehearsal A type of rehearsal in which information is processed in some meaningful way through such strategies as embellishment, elaboration, and organization.

Electrical Stimulation of the Brain (ESB) The technique used to study brain functioning that involves inserting into the brain a tiny electrode through which a weak electric current is passed. Specific brain sites can be activated, and any resulting behavior can then be observed.

Electroconvulsive Therapy (ECT) The form of medical therapy in which a brief electric current is passed through the brain as a method of treating depression.

Electroencephalogram (EEG) The continuous recordings of electrical activity from neurons in the cerebral cortex that underlie electrodes placed on the scalp.

Electromyogram (EMG) A recording of muscle activity obtained from surface electrodes that are placed on the skin.

Electrooculogram (EOG) A recording of eye movements obtained from surface electrodes that are placed near the eyes.

Emotion A feeling accompanied by internal body reactions and observable expressions.

Empathy An understanding of another person's feelings and plight.

Empiricism The view that experience is the source of all knowledge.

Encoding The process by which information is put into memory in a form that can be further processed.

Endocrine System The body system that consists of numerous glands, located in different parts of the body, that release chemicals into the bloodstream.

Energy Conservation Theory The theory that sleep

serves as a restorative period each day—a time when organisms are forced to conserve energy.

Environmental Psychology The study of interrelationships between behavior and the physical environment.

Epilepsy A disorder caused by abnormal activity of neurons in the brain.

Equilibrium Theory A theory of interpersonal distancing that states that when optimal physical distance is not maintained, individuals engage in a variety of actions to regain equilibrium, such as altering distance, eye contact, or body orientation.

Erectile Dysfunction The inability to have or maintain an erection.

Escape Training Learning to make a particular response that leads to the withdrawal of an aversive stimulus.

Estrogens Female hormones.

Ethologists Those who study the behavior of animals in their natural habitat.

Evoked-potential Technique The recording of the brain's electrical activity in response to a specific stimulus, such as a tone, a light, or a word.

Excitement Phase The first phase of the sexual-response cycle, involving increased blood flow to the genital area.

Exhibitionism A sexual variation involving sexual gratification that is derived from exposing the genitals to unsuspecting and unwilling strangers.

Expectancies Anticipations about the consequences of various actions.

Experimental Group Participants in an experiment who are exposed to manipulation of the independent variable.

Experimental-research Approach A method of investigating psychological phenomena that allows the investigator to exercise precise control over conditions that might affect observed or measured relationships among variables.

Extinction The process by which conditioned responses may be weakened or eliminated.

Extraneous Variables Variables that are not under the control of the experimenter but that may cause variations in the dependent variable.

Extrasensory Perception The term used to describe perceptions that purportedly do not depend on normal sensory input or stimulation of one or another of the senses.

Extroversion The personality trait characterized by sociability, outgoingness, and impulsiveness.

Facial-feedback Hypothesis The hypothesis that facial expressions regulate emotional experiences.

Family Configuration The theory that family size, birth order, and sibling spacing, have a major influence on intellectual development.

Family Interaction Model of Abnormality An approach to abnormality which holds that abnormal behavior results from faulty or disturbed relationships among family members.

Family Therapy The therapeutic approach in which family members are treated as a group rather than individually.

Fear of Success A learned motive to avoid success for fear of its negative consequences.

Feature Detectors Cells in the visual system, particularly in the visual cortex of the brain, that specialize in detecting specific features, or patterns, of visual stimulation.

Feedback Information provided to people about their performance.

Fellatio Oral stimulation of the male genitals.

Fetal Alcohol Syndrome A condition in newborn infants that is associated with chronic, heavy drinking by pregnant women and that is characterized by symptoms such as retarded physical and mental development, premature birth, congenital eye and ear problems, and sleep disturbances.

Fetishism A sexual variation involving the attachment of sexual significance to objects that are not necessarily sexual in nature.

Fixation The permanent investment of a portion of the libido in a particular psychosexual stage because of too much or too little gratification during that stage.

Fixed-interval (FI) Schedules Schedules of reinforcement in which the first response that occurs after a fixed time period is reinforced.

Fixed-ratio (FR) Schedules Schedules of reinforcement in which the first response that occurs after a fixed number is reinforced.

Foot-in-the-door-technique A compliance strategy in which one first makes a small request (which is agreed to) and then a large request.

Forebrain The largest of the three major divisions of the human brain, consisting of numerous structures, such as the cerebrum, the limbic system, the hypothalamus, and the thalamus.

Forensic Psychology The specialty area of applied psychology concerned with applying psychological knowledge and principles to law and the judicial process.

Formal Operational Stage The Piagetian stage of cognitive development that extends from 12 years of age into adulthood and is characterized by abstract thought.

Fovea A tiny depression roughly at the center of the retina where the cones are heavily concentrated.

Free Association The technique of psychoanalysis in which a patient is told to say anything that comes to mind.

Free Recall A type of recall in which an individual is asked to recall items of information in any order.

Frequency Distribution A way of summarizing data in which all possible scores are listed along with their frequency of occurrence.

Frequency Polygon A graph used to illustrate a distribution of scores. Lines are used to connect points at the center of each response category. The area under the curve at each category represents score frequency, as in the histogram.

Frequency Theory of Pitch The theory that states that pitch is determined by the rate (rather than the place) at which receptor cells are stimulated.

Frustration The blocking of any goal-directed behavior.

Frustration-aggression Hypothesis A hypothesis that states in part that frustration always leads to some form of aggression.

Functional Analysis of Behavior The analysis of cause-effect, or functional, relationships between behavior and the environment.

Functional Fixity The tendency to perceive objects as having only the uses for which they were originally designed; the result is interference with problem solving anytime a new and creative use of a common object is required.

Functionalism School of psychology emphasizing the study of those aspects of the mind, such as learning and intelligence, that help organisms adapt to the environment.

Gender The state of being male or female.

Gender Identity One's personal sense of maleness or femaleness.

Gender Role Our society's expectations about how individuals of a particular gender are to behave.

General Adaptation Syndrome (GAS) The nonvarying pattern of physical reactions to a stressor, consisting of three stages—alarm reaction, resistance, and exhaustion.

Generalized Anxiety Disorder A mental disorder in which the individual displays a chronically high level of anxiety but is unaware of its source.

Generalized Expectancies Expectancies that are applied broadly across a wide range of situations and that are, in a sense, like learned traits.

Genetic Counseling A form of counseling aimed at helping people cope with and prevent the occurrence of genetic abnormalities.

Genital Stage The psychosexual stage, beginning with adolescence, in which the libido is focused on the genitals and the individual's sexual instincts are expressed in a desire for biological reproduction.

Genius A term used to denote intellectual giftedness. Current definitions emphasize that for a person to be classified as genius there must be evidence of public achievement, the person's ideas must solve some practical problem, and there must be widespread agreement among qualified peers that the person is a genius.

Genotype The unique set of genes inherited or transmitted from parents to offspring.

Gestalt Psychology The school of psychology emphasizing that perception depends on the brain's tendency to organize pieces of sensory information into wholes whose significance differs from the mere sum of the parts. Gestalt is a German word that means "pattern," and the Gestalt psychologists studied perception in terms of patterns, or the whole perception.

Gestalt Therapy Perls's therapeutic approach, which attempts to deal with problems by helping clients achieve awareness of all their experiences and needs.

Giftedness A term reserved for the most intellectually capable individuals in the general population.

Glucostatic Theory A theory of hunger and eating that postulates that the hypothalamus regulates eating by monitoring glucose levels.

Goal Gradients Concept useful in describing the strength of one's tendency to approach (approach gradient) or avoid (avoidance gradient) some goal object at various distances from the goal.

Gonads The reproductive glands.

Grammar The rules of syntax in conjunction with rules relating to phonemes and morphemes.

Grammatical Morphemes Inflections plus the less informative words, such as articles, auxiliary verbs, conjunctions, and prepositions.

Group Therapy The therapeutic approach in which several people are treated simultaneously.

Habituation A simple form of learning in which an organism changes its behavior by ceasing to respond to a repeated stimulus.

Hallucinations Sensory experiences in the absence of any external stimulation.

Hallucinogens A class of drugs that produce alterations in perception, thinking, and emotion. Sometimes referred to as psychedelics. Examples of hallucinogenic drugs are LSD, PCP, marijuana, and hashish.

Halo Effect The tendency to see good traits as going with other good traits and bad traits as going with other bad traits.

Hardiness A personality structure characterized by a belief in the control of events, a feeling of commitment to activities, and the anticipation of change as a challenge.

Hemorrhaging The breaking of blood vessels in the brain; may be caused by excessive pressure on the head of the fetus during prolonged labor and delivery.

Heritability A statistical measure of the contribution of heredity to observed variations of a trait, such as height or IQ, for a given population in a certain environment.

Hermaphrodite A person in whom there have been abnormalities in prenatal development and differentiation that have caused an inconsistency in the various criteria for defining gender.

Heterosexual A person who is sexually attracted to or engages in sexual activity with members of the opposite gender.

Heuristics Rules of thumb, or educated guesses, with respect to the best ways of solving a problem; they increase our chances of success, but they do not guarantee a solution.

Hierarchy of Needs Maslow's postulated needs, ranging from the basic biological motives to the ultimate motive of self-actualization.

Hindbrain A major division of the brain, which is believed to have evolved first and which is involved in controlling digestion, blood flow, and breathing—functions considered to be automatic and necessary for survival.

Histogram A graph that uses vertical bars to represent frequency of scores in a distribution.

Holophrases Single words that, uttered by a child, communicate an entire idea, thought, or sentence.

Homeostasis An optimal physiological balance that the body attempts to maintain.

Homosexuality Having sexual attraction toward or engaging in sexual behavior with a member of the same gender.

Hormones Chemicals produced in the glands of the endocrine system that travel through the bloodstream and affect a wide range of physiological activities and behaviors.

Hospices Centers established for the care of people who are terminally ill.

Hue The name given to a particular color—for example, red, green, yellow, or blue—and determined by a light wave's length.

Human Behavioral Genetics The field of study that examines the contribution of heredity to behavior.

Humanistic Approach The approach to personality that emphasizes human virtues and aspirations, conscious experience, free will, and the fulfillment of personal potential.

Humanistic Model of Abnormality An approach to abnormality in which psychological disorders are believed to arise from interference with the basic human tendencies to strive for personal growth and fulfill one's potential.

Hyperphagia Extreme overeating caused by damage to the ventromedial hypothalamus (VMH).

Hypertension Chronically high blood pressure.

Hypersomnia A sleep disorder that most often involves complaints of sleeping too much or of excessive daytime sleepiness (EDS) and continuous fatigue.

Hypnosis An altered state of awareness (sometimes called a trance) that is induced by suggestions made by another person (the hypnotist) or by subjects themselves (in self-hypnosis).

Hypochondriasis A mental disorder characterized by a preoccupation with the fear of having a serious disease.

Hypothalamus The part of the limbic system involved in regulating hunger, rage, thirst, sleep, and sex.

Hypotheses Tentative explanations used to account for observed phenomena.

Iconic Store The sensory memory for visual information.

Id The part of the personality from which the instincts and instinctual energy are derived.

Illicit Drugs Drugs that are legally or socially prohibited, often because of their undesirable or dangerous side-effects.

Illusion A distortion in perception that contradicts objective reality.

Imagery A mental representation of something that is not physically present.

Implicit Personality Theory One's beliefs about which personality traits tend to occur together.

Impression Formation The process of taking separate bits of information and combining them into a coherent picture of a person.

Imprinting According to ethologists, the instinctive act of animals becoming socially "attached" to and following the first moving object they see shortly after birth.

Incentives External objects or stimuli to which organisms are attracted and which therefore motivate behavior.

Incubation The period in which a problem solver does not actively work on an unsolved problem that was begun earlier.

Independent Variables (IVs) The variables that the investigator manipulates, independent of other controlled variables, in order to determine effects of the manipulation; synonymous with *causes* of some behavioral effect.

Induced Movement. Movement perceived in the absence of real movement that results when a small object is projected on a larger, movable background.

Industrial-organizational Psychology A specialty area of applied psychology concerned with behavior in the world of work.

Infancy The stage of development that extends from the end of the neonatal period (1 month of age) to 18 months of age.

Inferential Statistics Statistics used to interpret data and to draw inferences or conclusions from data obtained in small samples.

Inflections Grammatical markers, such as *s* for plural, *ed* or *ing* for verb endings, and the possessive markers, which are added to words to change their meaning.

Information-processing Model A model of memory that suggests that, much like the operation of a computer, information is first put into memory (encoding), then stored (storage), and later recovered (retrieval).

Informational Social Influence Conformity carried out because of acceptance of the information provided by others.

Innateness Hypothesis The view that children have a genetic potential for creating and understanding language.

Insight Learning Learning that results from a sudden perception or grasp of a problem that leads to a solution.

Insomnia A prevalent sleep disorder that refers to sleeping too little or being unable to fall asleep.

Instability The personality trait characterized by moodiness, touchiness, anxiety, and restlessness.

Instinct An innate, unlearned, goal-directed, species-specific behavior.

Intelligence The capacity of the individual to act purposefully, to think rationally, and to deal effectively with the environment. According to Binet's definition, the essential activities of intelligence are to judge well, to comprehend well, and to reason well.

Intelligence Quotient (IQ) An index of intelligence based on the relationship between mental age (MA) and chronological age (CA).

Interactionism The study of both individual differences and situation variables and of how they interact.

Interneurons Nerve fibers that connect and integrate the activities of sensory and motor neurons. Also called association neurons.

Interpretation The psychoanalytic strategy of identifying for patients their defenses and their repressed conflicts and wishes.

Intimate Distance A distance (0 to 1½ feet) reserved for intimate or close contacts with others.

Intrinsic Motivation Motivation to perform activities for their own sake, not for extrinsic (external) rewards.

Introversion The personality trait characterized by quietness, reservation, and introspection.

Iris A colored muscle that surrounds the pupil and dilates or contracts the pupil in response to changes in light intensity.

Job Analysis The first step in successful personnel selection—identifying the duties required of the employee and the employee behaviors necessary for successful job performance.

Keyword Method A mnemonic device that uses imagery and is especially useful in learning foreign language vocabularies. In this context, one first finds a keyword—a part of the foreign word that sounds like an English word—and then uses imagery in making a connection between the keyword and its English equivalent.

Kinesthesis The sense that provides information about body movement.

Language An arbitrary system of symbols that allows individuals to understand and communicate an infinite variety of messages.

Late Childhood The stage of development that extends from the end of the early childhood period to the beginning of the teenage years.

Latency Period The phase following the resolution of the Oedipus complex, beginning at around age 5 and ending at puberty, in which there is repression of sexual impulses.

Latent Learning Learning that is not immediately revealed by any obvious change in behavior.

Later Maturity The period of development that extends from 65 years of age to death.

Law of Classical (Respondent) Conditioning The law stating that when two stimuli are paired, and one elicits a reflex response, a new reflex is created in which the previously neutral stimulus comes to elicit the original reflex response.

Law of Instrumental (Operant) Conditioning The law stating that if an operant response (R) is followed by a reinforcing stimulus (S^R) (sometimes also called a reinforcer or a reward), then the probability of the response occurring again is increased.

Learned Helplessness A phenomenon resulting from exposure to aversive stimuli that cannot be controlled and leading to failure to respond appropriately in a new situation.

Learning Any relatively permanent change in behavior that can be attributed to experience or practice.

Lens An elastic structure that allows the eye to change focus and maintain clear images of objects at various distances.

Lesch-Nyhan Syndrome A genetic disorder that affects mostly males and that is characterized by spastic movements, abnormal posture, difficulty with speech, and self-destructive behavior.

Lesion An intentional injury of a particular area of the brain.

Levels-of-processing View A conceptualization of memory as one system with multiple levels of processing; in it, memory is said to be a function of how deeply and elaborately information is processed.

Libido Energy from the life instincts, according to Freud.

Licit Drugs Drugs that are legal and sanctioned by a particular culture.

Limbic System An interconnected series of brain structures involved in emotional behavior, sexual behavior, aggression, and memory formation.

Linguistic Relativity Hypothesis The view that language affects how people think and how they perceive the world.

Locus of Control A generalized expectancy referring to whether an individual believes in internal control (that reinforcements are due to one's own behavior or characteristics) or in external control (that reinforcements are due to luck, chance, fate, or powerful others).

Long-Term Memory The largest part of the memory system, storing virtually an unlimited amount of information for indefinite periods, from only a few minutes to several decades or more.

Longitudinal Research Designs A type of study in which the same individuals are periodically retested.

Loudness The psychological experience that accompanies variations in sound-wave amplitude.

Low-balling A compliance strategy in which one gets a person to make a decision to engage in some particular behavior; the person then sticks with that decision even if the reasons for making the decision are changed.

Maintenance Rehearsal A type of rehearsal in which information is simply repeated (same as Rehearsal).

Major Depressive Disorder A persistent and pronounced dysphoric mood state.

Marital Therapy The form of family therapy involving treatment for couples having marital problems.

Masturbation Self-stimulation of the genitals.

Mean The measure of central tendency that indicates the average score in the distribution.

Means-end Analysis The type of heuristic, or problem-solving, strategy that involves taking only those steps that will reduce the difference between the given state and the desired state or goal.

Measurement The assignment of numerical values to observations.

Median The measure of central tendency that divides a distribution of scores in half.

Medical Therapies Therapeutic approaches that involve some type of physical treatment or manipulation of the body for the purpose of treating maladaptive behavior.

Meditation A self-regulation technique used for achieving control over mental and physiological processes.

Medulla The portion of the hindbrain responsible for regulating heartbeat, breathing, body temperature, digestion, blood pressure, and swallowing.

Mental Retardation Significantly subaverage intellectual functioning existing concurrently with deficits in adaptive behavior and manifested during the developmental period.

Mentor A term that refers to an adviser, teacher, or sponsor—someone who facilitates the young adult's career development by believing in the person and promoting the person's professional advancement.

Method of Loci A mnemonic device that involves the use of imagery in associating new information with a series of specific physical locations (or loci) that are already firmly established in memory.

Microelectrodes Thin electrodes, usually made of glass or wire, that can be inserted into the cell body of a neuron to measure the electrical activity of a single nerve cell.

Midbrain A major division of the human brain, which contains densely packed neurons that are involved primarily in controlling eye movements and relaying visual and auditory information to higher brain centers.

Middle Age The period of development that extends from 35 to 65 years of age.

Migraine Headaches Intense, recurrent headaches that are characterized by a deep, throbbing pain.

Mnemonic Devices Memory-aiding techniques that help us organize new material by relating it to existing, well-learned information.

Mode The measure of central tendency that indicates the most frequently occurring score in a frequency distribution.

Monocular Depth Cues Depth cues that require the use of only one eye.

Moral Internalization Learning to conform to rules in situations that raise impulses to transgress and that lack surveillance and social sanctions.

Morphemes The smallest meaningful units in a language, including words, prefixes, and suffixes.

Motion Parallax The tendency, when you move through space, as in walking or riding in an automobile, or when you move your head, for the images of nearby objects to appear to move farther than do the images of more distant objects.

Motivated Forgetting Forgetting something because we want to.

Motivation Any force acting on or within an organism that initiates and directs behavior as well as governing its intensity.

Motor Cortex The area of the frontal lobe of the cerebral cortex that controls voluntary movements of the body.

Motor Development Active movement skills that develop during the first year and a half of life.

Motor Neurons Nerve fibers that carry nerve impulses from the brain and spinal cord to the muscles, glands, and other parts of the body. Also called efferent neurons.

Multiple Orgasms Two or more successive orgasms occurring prior to the end of the resolution phase.

Multiple Personality A mental disorder involving the presence of two or more distinct personalities within an individual.

Narcolepsy A sleep disorder characterized by excessive daytime drowsiness (hypersomnia) and cataplexy, a loss of muscle control.

Narcotic Drugs A class of drugs that numb the senses and with prolonged use become addictive. They produce an intoxication euphoria that is heightened when the drug is injected into the bloodstream. Examples of narcotic drugs are opium, morphine, and heroin.

Narrative-chaining Method A mnemonic device in which the strategy is to make up a story that links the items to be remembered.

Natural Selection Darwin's contribution to the theory of evolution, which states that individuals differ in various characteristics, that such differences are determined in part by heredity, and that whenever characteristics are associated with differences in fitness (that is, the relative success of offspring in surviving to reproduce), the characteristics of the more fit individuals will increasingly occur in succeeding generations.

Naturalistic Observation Observation that takes place in natural, real-life settings.

Need for Achievement (_n_ Ach) An acquired motive characterized by the need to strive for success and excellence.

Need for Affiliation (_n_ Aff) An acquired motive characterized by a desire for social contact.

Needs Any physiological deviations from homeostatic balance.

Negative Reinforcers (S^R, S^{r-}) Stimuli whose withdrawal or removal is reinforcing.

Neonatal Period The stage of development that encompasses the first month of life.

Nerve Impulse Electrical activity that travels along the axon when the cell body is stimulated.

Nerves Bundled groups of axons that conduct neural impulses from one part of the body to another.

Nervous System A cellular network that processes input from the sense organs (the eyes, for example) and regulates information flow to the muscles and body organs.

Neuroleptics The class of drugs used in the treatment and control of extreme psychological disturbances, such as schizophrenia.

Neurons Individual nerve cells—the basic units of the nervous system—that specialize in transmitting and receiving information.

Neurotransmitters Chemicals that are released from the terminal buttons of one neuron and diffuse across the synapse and activate another neuron.

Night Terrors Terrifying nighttime episodes that usually occur early in the night, during NREM Stage 4 sleep; the

sleeper is generally unable to remember them upon awakening.

Nightmares Bad dreams that generally occur toward morning during REM sleep; the sleeper generally is able to remember such dreams upon awakening.

Noise Unwanted sound.

Nonconscious The level of consciousness that includes processes such as hormone changes or electrical brain activity, which are not normally part of our awareness.

Nonnaturalistic Observation Observation that takes place in contrived or controlled settings, such as laboratories, hospitals, or schools.

Normal Probability Distribution A symmetrical, bell-shaped curve that, although a mathematical ideal, provides a good description of many physical and psychological characteristics. Measured height and IQ are examples. In a large group of individuals, a few obtain very high or very low height or IQ values and the majority score in the average range.

Normative Social Influence Conformity carried out in order to be socially accepted.

NREM Sleep One of two distinctly different states of sleep, called non-rapid-eye-movement sleep, in which dreams rarely occur.

Obedience Behavior carried out in accordance with an order from an authority figure.

Obesity A condition in which body weight exceeds the ideal weight for one's height by 20 percent or more.

Object Permanence An awareness that objects and people continue to exist even when they are not directly perceived.

Observational Learning Learning that is accomplished without reinforcement by observing the behavior of others.

Obsession A recurrent, persistent idea, thought, or impulse that one thinks of involuntarily.

Obsessive-compulsive Disorder A mental disorder in which individuals feel compelled to think something they do not want to think about or to engage in some act they do not want to perform.

Oedipus Complex (Electra Complex) An unconscious longing for affection and sexual contact with the parent of the oppostie sex and a desire to eliminate the parent of the same sex.

Olfaction The sense of smell, which provides information about chemical substances in the surrounding air.

Opponent-process Theory The theory of human color vision that assumes the existence of three color receptor systems (instead of three cone types), each containing photoreceptive cells that are activated by light waves of different lengths.

Optic Chiasm The point at which the optic nerves from both eyes meet and cross.

Oral Stage The psychosexual stage, occurring during the 1st year of life, in which the sexual instinct seeks sexual expression through oral stimulation.

Organic Retardation The term used to describe the approximately 25 percent of all cases of mental retardation that are due to some known biological defect, most commonly chromosomal and genetic abnormalities.

Orgasm Climax of sexual arousal; the pleasurable release of sexual tension.

Orgasm Phase The third phase of the sexual-response cycle, occurring when sexual arousal reaches a peak.

Orgasmic Dysfunction The inability to have an orgasm.

Osmosis A process in which water diffuses from the body cells because of increased sodium, or salt, concentration in the surrounding fluid.

Overgeneralization A type of thinking, characteristic of depressed individuals, in which a general conclusion about one's ability or worth is reached on the basis of only one event.

Overload The situation where excess stimulation from a number and variety of environmental sources impinges on urban dwellers.

Overregularization The tendency for children to take grammatical rules they have discovered and inappropriately generalize them to instances where they do not apply.

Paranoid Schizophrenia A type of schizophrenia in which the primary disturbance is in thought patterns.

Parasympathetic System The part of the autonomic nervous system most active during periods when the body is relaxed.

Partial Reinforcement Effect The phenomenon of behaviors maintained on partial reinforcement schedules showing much greater persistence, or resistance to extinction, than those maintained by continuous reinforcement.

Partial Reinforcement Schedules Schedules of reinforcement in which reinforcement occurs intermittently—that is, following some responses but not others.

Peptic Ulcer A hole, or lesion, in the lining of the stomach or duodenum.

Perceived Control The belief that one has the ability to influence the aversiveness of an event.

Percentiles A measure of relative standing that indicates the proportion of scores equal to or less than a particular score.

Perception The term used to describe the brain's interpretation of sensory information.

Perceptual Learning The ability to extract information from stimuli in the environment as a result of practice, training, or experience.

Period of the Embryo A period of prenatal development, also called the embryo phase, that lasts for approximately 6 weeks following implantation of the zygote in the uterine wall.

Period of the Fetus A period of prenatal development that lasts from the end of the 8th week of pregnancy until birth and that is marked by the development of bone cells.

Period of the Ovum A period of prenatal development, also called the egg phase or germinal period, that lasts from fertilization until the zygote is firmly implanted in the uterine wall.

Peripheral Nervous System The part of the nervous system that consists of all neural tissue that connects the brain and spinal cord with other parts of the body.

Person Perception The process of making judgments about others—particularly their abilities, motives, interests, or traits.

Personal Constructs Expectations that guide behavior, predict events, and define reality for a person.

Personal Distance A distance (1½ to 4 feet) used for conversations between acquaintances or close friends.

Personal Space An area surrounding the body that is defined by an invisible boundary, which cannot be trespassed on.

Personal-space Invasions Intrusions into the personal space of others.

Personality The personal characteristics that account for consistent and enduring patterns of response to various situations.

Personality Disorders A category of mental disorders characterized by inflexible and maladaptive patterns of relating to and interacting with others.

Personnel Selection The art and science of choosing the best person for a given job.

PET Scanning Technique The technique used to study brain functioning that involves injecting a subject with a radioactive substance and monitoring its action within the brain.

Petting Physical, sexual contact between individuals that does not include sexual intercourse.

Phallic Stage The psychosexual stage, occurring between 3 and 5 years of age, in which pleasure presumably comes from masturbation, sex play, and other genital stimulation.

Phenotype The outward, visible expression of traits affected by the genes.

Phenylketonuria (PKU) A defect in enzyme production capable of causing mental retardation.

Phobia An irrational, persistent fear of some specific object, activity, or situation in which no real danger exists or the danger is unrealistically magnified.

Phonemes The basic sounds of any language.

Physical Dependence The state in which bodily processes are modified so that continued use of a drug is required to prevent uncomfortable withdrawal symptoms.

Physical Environment Anything of a physical nature that surrounds us—a room, a city, the weather, pollution, or a work space, for example.

Physical Primary Colors Red, green, and blue—called the physical primaries because it is possible to create all the colors of the visual spectrum by mixing red, green, and blue wavelengths of light in different proportions.

Pitch The psychological experience that accompanies variations in sound-wave frequency.

Pituitary Gland The master gland of the endocrine system, which is located at the base of the brain and controls the other glands.

Place Theory of Pitch The theory of pitch assumes that different areas of the basilar membrane are responsive to particular sound frequencies.

Placebo Effect Any improvement in a client that is due to the elements of hope and expectation of improvement rather than to specific therapeutic procedures.

Planning Process The type of heuristic, or problem-solving, strategy that entails simplifying a problem by ignoring some of the details surrounding it.

Plateau Phase The second phase of the sexual-response cycle, involving a continuing and increasingly higher level of sexual arousal.

Polygraph An instrument that measures a number of body changes associated with emotion; also known as the lie detector.

Population The entire group of those subjects to be studied from which smaller samples are selected for study.

Population Density The number of people or animals per unit of space.

Pornography Any written, visual, or verbal material that is considered sexually arousing.

Positive Reinforcers (S^{R+}, S^{r+}) Stimuli whose presentation is reinforcing.

Postconventional Stages of Moral Development The third two stages of six stages of moral development proposed by Kohlberg, during which moral thought and judgment reaches its most advanced form.

Preconscious The level of consciousness that includes information (such as memories of the first day of college) that may be brought to awareness but that otherwise remains out of consciousness.

Preconventional Stages of Moral Development The first two stages of six stages of moral development proposed by Kohlberg, during which the child develops a sense of good and bad.

Prelinguistic Stage The first stage of language development, encompassing approximately the first 10 to 12 months of life, when language skills do not yet exist; development in this stage progresses through phases of crying, cooing, and babbling.

Premature Ejaculation A sexual dysfunction occurring when a man ejaculates too soon for his partner to experience orgasm through intercourse.

Prematurity Defined medically by preterm birth (gestational age of 37 weeks or less) and by low birth weight (less than 2,500 grams).

Prenatal Period The 9 months of growth that precede birth.

Prenatal Sexual Differentiation The process that leads to specific physical differences between males and females.

Preoperational Stage The Piagetian stage of cognitive development that spans the 2nd through 7th years of life and is so called because thought operations are not yet logical.

Preparedness The principle that some responses are easily learned because they reflect innate (unlearned) predispositions to respond in particular ways (such as a pigeon's pecking for food).

Primacy Effect A phenomenon whereby after learning a list of items and then recalling them in any order, a person recalls the items toward the first part of the list better than those at the middle but not quite as well as those at the end.

Primary Sexual Characteristics The sexual and reproductive organs.

Primary Territory A territory that is perceived as being owned and that is used and controlled on a relatively permanent basis as a necessary, central part of everyday life.

Principle of Aerial Perspective The tendency for clearly seen objects to appear closer than they actually are and unclear objects to appear farther away than they actually are.

Principle of Closure The tendency to perceive a complete object even though parts of it may be obscured or missing.

Principle of Continuation The tendency for lines and contours to be seen as following the smoothest path.

Principle of Figure and Ground The fact that most seen objects tend to stand out from a background of one kind or another.

Principle of Interposition The principle that, when one object obstructs the view of another object, generally the object that is entirely in view will appear to be the closer of the two.

Principle of Light and Shadow The principle that, when light creates shadows on objects, the shadowed, darker areas will appear farther away and the lighted surfaces will appear closer.

Principle of Linear Perspective The tendency for parallel lines to appear to converge in the distance and distant objects to appear to be closer together than near objects.

Principle of Perceptual Grouping The tendency to perceive stimuli as meaningful wholes or patterns.

Principle of Proximity The tendency for objects or stimuli that are near each other to appear to be grouped together.

Principle of Relative Size The tendency for objects in the background of the visual field to appear farther away and thus smaller.

Principle of Shape Constancy The tendency for an object's apparent physical shape to remain unchanged even though the object's image on the retina changes shape as the viewing angle varies.

Principle of Similarity The tendency for objects or stimuli of like appearance to be grouped together.

Principle of Size Constancy The tendency for an object's perceived size to remain constant regardless of the object's distance from the observer.

Principle of Texture Gradients The tendency for the texture of near objects in the visual field to appear to be coarse and detailed and the texture of distant objects to appear finer and less detailed.

Proactive Interference A type of forgetting in which something previously learned interferes with the ability to recall newly learned material.

Programmed Instruction A procedure that provides the student with immediate feedback, and therefore reinforcement, for each response that is to be learned. Subject matter to be learned can be programmed in a book or on a computer.

Progressive Relaxation A self-regulation technique that involves learning how to alternately tense and relax body muscles.

Project Head Start An education and day-care program for preschool disadvantaged children.

Projection The defense mechanism in which people project their own unacceptable thoughts or behavior onto other people or blame them for their own faults.

Projective Techniques Personality-assessment devices developed to probe unconscious impulses and attitudes.

Prompts Cues that convey messages.

Prosocial Behavior Voluntary acts that have positive consequences for others.

Proxemics The study of interpersonal distancing.

Psychoanalysis Freud's therapeutic approach aimed at helping patients gain insight into and become aware of the nature of their unconscious conflicts and impulses.

Psychoanalytic Model of Abnormality An approach to abnormality in which mental disorders are thought to represent substitute expressions of repressed unconscious impulses.

Psychoanalytic Theory The first modern personality theory, developed by Sigmund Freud and known for its emphasis on unconscious motives, instincts for sex and aggression, and early-childhood experiences as forces that direct and influence behavior.

Psychodrama The therapeutic approach in which individuals gain insight into their problems by acting out their feelings with respect to emotionally significant events or situations as if they were in a play.

Psychogenic Amnesia A mental disorder involving extensive but selective memory losses.

Psychogenic Fugue A mental disorder involving a sudden move away from home and work with the assumption of a new identity and no memory for one's former identity.

Psychological Dependence The compulsive use of a drug to produce pleasure or avoid emotional discomfort.

Psychology The science of human and animal behavior.

Psychology of Advertising A major area of interest for consumer psychologists and the field of study that attempts to determine how advertising motivates consumers and why consumers choose and use particular products and services.

Psychometric Tests A quantitative means for measuring

psychological variables such as intelligence, attitudes, interests, and abilities.

Psychophysics One of the original areas of study in psychology, the goal of which is to relate characteristics of physical stimuli to characteristics of the sensations they produce.

Psychosocial Development The lifelong changes in the individual's psychological and social interactions with others and with society as a whole.

Psychosomatic Disorders Organic disorders that develop in response to stress and anxiety.

Psychosurgery Any form of surgery in which part of the brain is removed or made nonfunctional for the purpose of treating severe psychological disorders, such as schizophrenia or severe depression.

Psychotherapy The process in which therapist and client communicate in an attempt to alter the client's disordered feelings, beliefs, or actions.

Puberty The biologically determined phase of adolescence when sexual maturation becomes apparent; also referred to as pubescence.

Public Distance A distance (more than 12 feet) reserved for formal public speaking, involving only one-way communication.

Public Territory An area used only temporarily and one used by anyone, which means that it is difficult to control.

Punishment A procedure in which an aversive (negative) event is presented or a positive event is removed following an operant response and in which, at least temporarily, the frequency of the response that is being punished is reduced.

Pupil An aperture, or adjustable opening, located between the cornea and the lens of the eye.

Randomization A procedure for minimizing the effects of extraneous variables that is accomplished by random assignment of subjects to experimental and control groups.

Range The measure of variability that indicates the difference between the lowest score and the highest score of a distribution.

Rape An act of aggression in which one person forces another, nonconsenting person to engage in a sexual act.

Rate of Responding A measure of operant conditioning found by dividing the number of responses by a constant unit of time.

Rational-emotive Therapy (RET) Ellis's therapeutic approach, which attempts to help clients shed their irrational beliefs so that they can behave logically and rationally and experience appropriate and adaptive emotions.

Rationalism The view that the source of all knowledge is the intellect, which is present at birth.

Rationalization The defense mechanism that involves finding "logical" and acceptable reasons to justify behavior.

Reaction Formation The defense mechanism wherein people substitute in awareness a socially acceptable desire opposite to one that is socially unacceptable.

Reaction Range The range of outcomes (phenotypes) that depends on the quality of the environment in which traits develop.

Real Motion A change in an object's position in space.

Recall One of the ways in which retrieval from long-term memory is measured; it involves reproducing information and is usually guided by retrieval cues.

Recency Effect A phenomenon whereby after learning a list of items and then recalling them in any order, a person recalls best those items toward the end of the list.

Reciprocal Determinism The notion that although people are influenced by their environment, they also influence the environment by choosing how to behave.

Recognition One of the ways in which retrieval from long-term memory is measured; it involves the correct identification of some specific item of information and the rejection of other alternatives.

Refabrication The building of a memory from bits and pieces of truth.

Reflex An unlearned reaction made in response to a specific stimulus.

Refractory Period A period of time following orgasm when men are unresponsive to further sexual stimulation.

Regression The defense mechanism in which long-outgrown behaviors are used to lessen a threat or anxiety.

Rehearsal The conscious repetition of information. Rehearsal maintains information in short-term memory and also helps transfer it to long-term memory.

Reinforcement Events or consequences that strengthen responses that precede them.

Reinforcement-affect Model The theory of attraction that states that our evaluations of other objects or persons are based on the positive or negative emotions associated with those objects or persons.

Relational Concepts Concepts in which classification is based on how an object is related to something else on some attribute dimension.

REM Sleep One of two distinctly different states of sleep, called rapid-eye-movement sleep, in which dreams commonly occur.

Repression The defense mechanism whereby people keep out of consciousness threatening and unacceptable thoughts.

Research Design A detailed plan that includes specification of the research procedures to be followed, the subjects to be studied, the hypotheses to be tested, the ways in which the data will be analyzed, and the conclusions that can be reasonably drawn from the data obtained.

Resistances Efforts on the part of the unconscious to repress sensitive topics and keep them from becoming conscious.

Resolution Phase The fourth, and final, phase of the sexual-response cycle, involving the slow return of body functions to their prearoused state.

Respondent (Reflex) Behavior Human and animal responses that are elicited (drawn out) by stimuli in the environment.

Response Sets　Consistent tendencies to respond one way or another to statements in self-report inventories.

Responsive Environments　Environments that allow easy shifts from separateness to togetherness.

Retarded Ejaculation　A sexual dysfunction occurring when a man, despite having an erection, is unable to ejaculate into the woman's vagina.

Reticular Activating System　The brain structure that extends through the midbrain and sends nerve fibers into the forebrain and that is involved in arousal, attention, and the sleep-waking cycle.

Retina　The photosensitive surface at the back of the eye that is made up of light-sensitive photoreceptive cells (or photoreceptors).

Retrieval　The process by which stored information in memory is used.

Retrieval Cues　Anything (a sight, a smell, or a word, for example) that helps us check different parts of long-term memory while searching for a particular item of information.

Retrieval Failure　A hypothesis of forgetting that assumes that "forgotten" information is temporarily inaccessible because an appropriate retrieval cue is lacking.

Retroactive Interference　A type of forgetting in which learning additional information interferes with recall of information learned earlier.

Retrograde Amnesia　A type of forgetting; the forgotten information is what was learned immediately prior to some disrupting insult to the brain (e.g., electroconvulsive therapy or a severe blow to the head) or a mentally shocking event.

Rods　One of two main types of photoreceptive cells (or photoreceptors) in the human retina and the retinas of most vertebrates, named for their distinctive shape.

Sampling　Techniques used to estimate a population distribution and its characteristics (for example, its mean and standard deviation) from a small sample of the population.

Satiation　The learning principle that states that a reinforcer is no longer reinforcing when it occurs with such a high regularity or frequency that it is no longer associated with a state of deprivation.

Saturation　The term used to refer to a color's degree of purity; determined by the complexity of the light wave.

Science　The observation, identification, description, experimental investigation, and theoretical explanation of natural phenomena; in Latin, science means "knowledge".

Scientific Method　A method used to advance knowledge that involves conducting observations and experiments and interpreting the information obtained from them.

Schizophrenic Disorders　A group of mental disorders involving disturbances in thought and perceptual processes, inappropriate affect or emotion, disturbances in motor activity, a withdrawal from social relationships, and a loss of contact with reality.

School Psychology　The specialty area of applied psychol-

ogy that combines education with clinical and counseling psychology.

Secondary Sexual Characteristics　Changes occurring at puberty that signal readiness for reproduction.

Secondary Territory　A territory used regularly by some individual or group but not owned; controlled only while occupied during specified times.

Sedative Drugs　A class of drugs that have a calming or tranquilizing effect and act as general depressants on the central nervous system. Examples of sedative drugs are barbiturates and alcohol.

Self-actualization　A psychological state characterized by wholeness, full-functioning, and the expression of all of one's capacities.

Self-concept　An image of who one is, should be, and might like to be.

Self-control　A type of behavior modification used by individuals to modify and control their own behavior.

Self-efficacy　The perceived ability to cope with specific situations.

Self-fulfilling Prophecy　Behavioral confirmation of a stereotype, produced when a person acts in accordance with the treatment received.

Self-regulation　Our ability to exercise influence over our own behavior.

Self-reinforcement　The process of reinforcing oneself for attaining personal goals and standards.

Self-serving Bias　The tendency to take credit for our positive outcomes and to deny responsibility for our negative outcomes.

Sensation　The response of a sensory system to physical stimuli.

Sensorimotor Stage　The Piagetian stage of cognitive development that encompasses the first 2 years of life, during which time the infant acquires knowledge mainly through sensory perception and motor action.

Sensory Memory　The first information storage area for memory; here, information fades quickly unless it is transferred to short-term memory.

Sensory Neurons　Nerve fibers that carry nerve impulses from the sense organs to the spinal cord and brain. Also called afferent neurons.

Serotonin Hypothesis　The theory that depression results from low levels of the neurotransmitter serotonin.

Set　The tendency to approach a problem the same way each time, using familiar or habitual types of solutions.

Set-point Theory　A theory of hunger and eating that postulates that the body has a normal weight, or set-point, which the hypothalamus works to maintain by monitoring stored fat.

Sexual Dysfunctions　Sexual difficulties and impairments in sexual functioning.

Sexual-response Cycle　A four-phase process for the biological responses of sexuality; the phases are excitement, plateau, orgasm, and resolution.

Sexual Variations   Sexual behaviors that deviate from conventional norms and that are maladaptive in nature.

Shaping   A technique for changing behavior in which a desired behavior is achieved by reinforcing successive approximations to the final behavior rather than directly reinforcing the desired response itself.

Short-term Memory   The part of memory that holds the contents of our attention.

Signal Detection Theory   A theory of psychophysical relationships that abandons the idea of an absolute threshold and focuses on measuring subjects' ability to detect stimuli when the stimuli are presented against background noise.

Simple Phobia   A persistent, irrational fear of any object or situation that is not a case of agoraphobia or social phobia.

Skewed Distribution   A frequency distribution in which most of the scores cluster not at the center of the distribution but rather at one end, or tail, of it.

Skin Senses   The senses that produce a broad range of sensations, all of which provide (through the skin) information to the organism about physical stimuli in the environment. The sensations include touch, tickling, pressure, pain, itchiness, warmth, cold, and vibration.

Sleep Apnea   A sleep disorder that involves an inability to breathe and sleep at the same time.

Social-comparison Theory   A theory of motivation that suggests that when objective yardsticks are unavailable, people evaluate their opinions and abilities by comparing them with those of other people.

Social Distance   A distance (4 to 12 feet) used for impersonal, formal, and businesslike encounters.

Social Drift Hypothesis   The hypothesis that schizophrenia is negatively related to social class because the disorder causes one to lose a job, family, and good housing, such that at the time of admission for treatment, the person's socioeconomic status is lower class.

Social-influence Process   A process whereby bystanders inhibit one another from helping because of each one's lack of action or apparent concern.

Social Norms   Explicit and implicit rules within a group regarding what kind of behavior is appropriate.

Social Phobia   A persistent, irrational fear of situations in which the individual may be scrutinized by others.

Social Psychology   The study of how the behavior, feelings, or thoughts of one individual are influenced or determined by the behavior or characteristics of others.

Socialization   The process by which individuals acquire behaviors, beliefs, standards, and motives that are valued by families, peers, and the larger community.

Sociocultural Model of Abnormality   An approach to abnormality which views the causes of abnormal behavior as lying in the larger society, rather than the individual or family.

Socioeconomic Status (SES)   A measure of social standing based on a person's income, education, and occupation.

Sociofugal Spaces   Physical arrangements that reduce the level of social interaction.

Sociopetal Spaces   Physical arrangements that encourage social interaction.

Somatic Nervous System   The part of the peripheral nervous system that consists of sensory neurons that lead to the spinal cord and brain from receptors in the sense organs and of motor neurons that lead from the brain and spinal cord to the skeletal muscles that move the body.

Somatoform Disorders   A category of mental disorders in which physical symptoms exist but without any known organic or physiological basis.

Somatosensory Cortex   The area of the parietal lobe of the cerebral cortex that is involved in the senses of touch, heat, cold, pain, and body movement.

Somnambulism   Sleepwalking that generally occurs during NREM sleep and that may accompany night terrors but not nightmares.

Spinal Cord   The portion of the central nervous system that connects the brain to various parts of the peripheral nervous system.

Split-brain Technique   The surgical technique that involves severing the cerebral hemispheres—used as a last resort to reduce the frequency and severity of epileptic seizures.

Spontaneous Recovery   The spontaneous, although brief, recurrence of a response following extinction.

Stability   The personality trait characterized by carefreeness, even-temperedness, and reliability.

Stage Theory of Cognitive Development   Piaget's theory that all children proceed through stages of cognitive development in the same order and that the skills of one stage are impossible to master without first having mastered the skills of the preceding stage.

Stages of Professional Careers   According to one theory of professional career development, there are four stages—apprentice, colleague, mentor, and sponsor—that involve different developmental tasks, relationships, and psychological adjustments.

Standard Deviation   A measure of variability that indicates the average difference from the mean of all scores in a frequency distribution; it is obtained by finding the square root of the variance.

Standardization   The administration of a test to a large standardization, or norm group, which represents the population in which the test is to be used.

Statistically Significant   A result or difference is said to be statistically significant if the obtained difference could be expected, by chance, to occur only 5 percent or less of the time.

Stereoscopic Vision   Vision that involves the use of both eyes.

Stereotypes   Preconceived images of what most members of a particular group are like.

Stimulant Drugs   A class of drugs that stimulate or arouse the central nervous system. Examples of stimulant drugs are caffeine, nicotine, amphetamines, methedrine, and cocaine.

Stimulus Discrimination The ability to make distinctions among stimuli and to respond in a specific way to a specific stimulus.

Stimulus Generalization A phenomenon that may occur in both respondent and operant conditioning and that involves the tendency for stimuli other than the one originally conditioned to evoke the conditioned response.

Stimulus-seeking Motives Motives that have as their goal the seeking of stimulation, that do not appear to be directly tied to physiological needs, and that do not seem to be learned.

Storage The process that holds information in memory or, more technically, the persistence of information in memory.

Stress A physical and psychological condition experienced whenever environmental demands are placed on an organism.

Stressors Demands on a person that induce stress.

Stroboscopic Movement Movement that is perceived between two stationary lights in the absence of real movement and that results when one light is flashed on and off and, after a brief lapse in time, the other light is flashed on and off.

Strong-Campbell Interest Inventory (SCII) A standardized self-report inventory designed to measure vocational interests and aid in occupational decision making.

Structuralism School of psychology emphasizing the study of how the elements of human consciousness form the structure of the mind.

Sudden Infant Death Syndrome (SIDS) a sleep disorder in infants that is thought to result from apnea, at least in some cases. Also known as crib death.

Superego The part of the personality that represents the cultural values adopted by the child through the process of identification with the parents.

Superstitious Behavior Responses that increase in probability not because they cause a reinforcing consequence but because they accidentally precede reinforcement.

Surface Structure The words of a sentence and their organization within the sentence.

Sympathetic System The part of the autonomic nervous system that plays a dominant role in preparing the body during times of emergency or stress.

Symptom Substitution The notion that if symptoms are eliminated without their cause being removed, the individual will merely express the problem or conflict in other ways.

Synapse The tiny junction between the terminal buttons of one neuron's axons and another neuron's dendrites or cell body.

Synaptic Transmission The electrochemical process by which neurons communicate with one another.

Syntax The rules for combining words into sentences.

Tachistoscopic Technique The technique for studying brain function that involves testing a subject's recall of visual information presented simultaneously to each eye.

Taste The sense that provides information about chemical substances entering the organism's digestive system.

Telegraphic Speech The descriptive term for children's earliest sentences, which are short and simple, much like those in a telegram.

Temperament The newborn's predispositions in mood and behavior.

Tension Headaches Headaches characterized by a sensation of tightness or pressure and a dull but steady pain around the entire head.

Territorial Behavior Acts that are carried out in an attempt to claim space and exclude other members of one's species.

Territorial Markers Items such as personal possessions that are used to communicate to others that a territory is being occupied and to ward off invasions.

Test Reliability The consistency of scores obtained when the same people take the same test on different occasions.

Test Validity The extent to which a test measures what it claims to measure.

Testosterone The most important androgen (male hormone).

Thalamus The part of the limbic system that is responsible for relaying nerve impulses from the sense organs to the cerebral cortex.

Thinking An inherent ability to mentally manipulate symbols and concepts in order to organize information, make plans, solve problems, and make decisions.

Timbre The psychological experience that accompanies variations in sound-wave complexity.

Tip-of-the-Tongue (or TOT) Phenomenon A feeling that although one can't remember some fact, it is on the "tip of the tongue" and, with the right retrieval cue, will surface.

Token Economy The behavioral therapy procedure by which tokens are used to reinforce adaptive behaviors, usually within an institutional setting.

Tolerance The need for larger and more frequent doses of a drug to produce the desired effect; occurs after repeated use of the drug.

Trait Approach The approach to personality that views the subject in terms of how people differ.

Traits Relatively enduring characteristics of individuals that remain fairly stable over the life-span.

Transduction The process by which physical energy such as electromagnetic (light) energy is translated into electrical energy in the form of nerve impulses.

Transference The process in psychoanalysis in which patients display attitudes toward and feelings for the therapist that are similar to those aimed at important people earlier in their lives.

Transformation Rules Syntactic rules that explain how a single underlying meaning can be expressed in different surface forms.

Transsexual A person who is psychologically uncomfortable with the anatomical sex.

Transvestism   A sexual variation involving sexual gratification from dressing in the clothing of the opposite gender.

Trichromatic Theory   The theory of human color vision that states that color vision is produced by three types of retinal cone cells, each differentially sensitive to the physical primary colors red, blue, and green. Also called three-color theory.

Type A Behavior Pattern   A personality characteristic marked by an excessive competitive drive, a strong need to achieve success, aggressiveness, impatience, and a sense of time urgency.

Ultrasound   A prenatal screening procedure that involves the use of mechanical energy in the form of sound waves, which are applied to the mother's abdomen.

Unconditional Positive Regard   A totally accepting and nonjudgmental attitude toward anything the client feels and expresses.

Unconditioned (Primary) Reinforcing Stimuli (S^R)   Reinforcers (or reinforcing stimuli) that have the ability to reinforce without prior learning.

Unconditioned Response (UCR)   Any response elicited by an unconditioned stimulus. The term unconditioned means "not learned."

Unconditioned Stimulus (UCS)   Any stimulus that elicits an unconditioned response. The term unconditioned means "not learned."

Unconscious   The level of consciousness that contains memories, feelings, and thoughts that are difficult to bring to awareness but that may become available through dreams, hypnosis, and other special means.

Undifferentiated Schizophrenia   A type of schizophrenia in which an individual is definitely schizophrenic but does not meet the criteria for the other types of schizophrenia or meets the criteria for more than one of them.

Unobtrusive Observation   Observation that makes use of data that the observed subjects need not be aware of.

Vaginismus   An involuntary contraction of the muscles surrounding the vaginal entrance.

Variability   In a frequency distribution, the dispersion of scores spread around the mean.

Variable   Any phenomenon that can be quantified and therefore measured in some way.

Variable-interval (VI) Schedules   Schedules of reinforcement in which responses are reinforced after time periods that vary in length.

Variable-ratio (VR) Schedules   Schedules of reinforcement in which the ratio of responses to reinforcers varies.

Variance   A measure of variability that indicates the average of squared deviation scores (deviation scores are obtained by finding the difference between each score and the mean).

Vestibular Sense   The sense that governs body orientation and position in three-dimensional space with respect to gravity.

Vicarious Extinction   The process of learning vicariously that no aversive consequences occur as a result of a feared action.

Visual Acuity   The ability (served best by the foveal cones) to form fine, sharply-focused images of objects.

Visual Cortex   The area of the occipital lobe of the cerebral cortex that is highly specialized for receiving and responding to visual stimuli.

Visual Spectrum   The portion of the electromagnetic spectrum, consisting of light waves of various lengths, to which the human visual system responds.

Visual System   All parts of the nervous system that process information from the eyes.

Vocational Psychology   The specialty area of applied psychology concerned with vocational choice and adjustment to work.

Volley Theory of Pitch   The theory of pitch that assumes that nerve impulse frequencies above 1,000 per second are generated by groups of neurons, each firing in turn.

Voyeurism   A sexual variation involving sexual pleasure derived from secretly watching others undress or have sexual intercourse.

Weighted-average Model   A model of impression formation that says that our final impression of someone is a weighted average of all the available information about that person.

Wernicke's Aphasia   An aphasia that results from injury to the posterior, or back, part of the brain; victims speak fluently and grammatically, but their speech lacks meaning and their comprehension of speech is seriously impaired. Also known as posterior aphasia.

Working Backward   The type of heuristic, or problem-solving, strategy that involves working from the desired state or goal toward the existing state.

Yerkes-Dodson Law   A principle that states that the more difficult a task is, the lower the optimal level of arousal for performance efficiency.

Z-score   A statistic used to standardize scores, thus permitting meaningful comparisons of the relative standing of scores in two different distributions.

— REFERENCES —

A ban on hypnosis. (1982, March 22). *Newsweek,* p. 57.

Abel, E. L. (1980). Fetal alcohol syndrome: Behavioral teratology. *Psychological Bulletin, 87,* 29–50.

Abramov, I., Gordon, J., Hendrickson, A., Hainline, L., Dobson, V., & LaBossiere, E. (1982). The retina of the newborn human infant. *Science, 217,* 265–267.

Abrams, R. (1976). Psychopharmacology and convulsive therapy. In B. B. Wolman (Ed.), *The therapist's handbook: Treatment methods of mental disorders* (pp. 18–45). New York: Van Nostrand Reinhold.

Abramson, L. Y., Garber, J., & Seligman, M. E. P. (1980). Learned helplessness in humans: An attributional analysis. In J. Garber & M. E. P. Seligman (Eds.), *Human helplessness: Theory and applications* (pp. 3–34). New York: Academic Press.

Abramson, L. Y., Seligman, M. E. P., & Teasdale, J. D. (1978). Learned helplessness in humans: Critique and reformulation. *Journal of Abnormal Psychology, 87,* 49–74.

Abramson, P. R., & Mosher, D. L. (1975). Development of a measure of negative attitudes toward masturbation. *Journal of Consulting and Clinical Psychology, 43,* 485–490.

Adamson, R. E. (1952). Functional fixedness as related to problem solving: A repetition of three experiments. *Journal of Experimental Psychology, 44,* 288–291.

Adler, A. (1927). *The practice and theory of individual psychology.* New York: Harcourt, Brace, & World.

Adler, A. (1930). Individual psychology. In C. Murchison (Ed.), *Psychologies of 1930* (pp. 395–405). Worcester, MA: Clark University Press.

Adorno, T. W., Frenkel-Brunswick, E., Levinson, D. J., & Sanford, R. N. (1950). *The authoritarian personality.* New York: Harper & Row.

Aiello, J. R., & Aiello, T. D. (1974). The development of personal space: Proxemic behavior of children 6 through 16. *Human Ecology, 2,* 177–189.

Ainsworth, M. D. S., Blehar, M. C., Waters, E., & Wall, S. (1978). *Patterns of attachment: A psychological study of the strange situation.* Hillsdale, NJ: Erlbaum.

Albert, R. S. (1975). Toward a behavioral definition of genius. *American Psychologist, 30,* 140–151.

Albert, S., & Dabbs, J. M., Jr. (1970). Physical distance and persuasion. *Journal of Personality and Social Psychology, 15,* 265–270.

Alexander, T., Roodin, P., & Gorman, B. (1980). *Developmental psychology.* New York: D. Van Nostrand.

Alleman, E., & Newman, I. (1982). *Mentoring relationships in organizations: An empirical study.* Paper presented at the 90th annual convention of the American Psychological Association, Washington, DC.

Allgeier, E. R. (1983). Ideological barriers to contraception. In D. Byrne & W. A. Fisher (Eds.), *Adolescents, sex, and contraception* (pp. 171–205). Hillsdale, NJ: Erlbaum.

Altman, I. (1975). *The environment and social behavior.* Belmont, CA: Brooks/Cole.

Amato, P. R. (1983). Helping behavior in urban and rural environments: Field studies based on taxonomic organization of helping episodes. *Journal of Personality and Social Psychology, 45,* 571–586.

American Psychiatric Association. (1980). *Diagnostic and statistical manual of mental disorders* (3rd ed.). Washington, DC: Author.

Anastasi, A. (1979). *Fields of applied psychology* (2nd ed.). New York: McGraw-Hill.

Anastasi, A. (1983). Evolving trait concepts. *American Psychologist, 38,* 175–184.

Andersen, B. L. (1983). Primary orgasmic dysfunction: Diagnostic considerations and review of treatment. *Psychological Bulletin, 93,* 105–136.

Andersen, K. (1982, September 13). What are prisons for? *Time,* pp. 38–41.

Anderson, J. K., Parenté, F. J., & Gordon, C. (1981). A forecast of the future for the mental health profession. *American Psychologist, 36,* 848–855.

Anderson, J. R. (1980). *Cognitive psychology and its implications.* San Francisco: W. H. Freeman.

Anderson, J. R. (1983). Retrieval of information from long-term memory. *Science, 220,* 25–30.

Anderson, N. H. (1974). Cognitive algebra: Integration theory applied to social attribution. In L. Berkowitz (Ed.), *Advances in experimental social psychology* (Vol. 7, pp. 1–101). New York: Academic Press.

Anderson, N. H., & Jacobson, A. (1965). Effect of stimulus inconsistency and discounting instructions in personality impression formation. *Journal of Personality and Social Psychology, 2,* 531–539.

Anderson, R., & Nida, S. A. (1978). Effect of physical attractiveness on opposite- and same-sex evaluations. *Journal of Personality, 46,* 401–413.

Andrews, L. B. (1982, March). Mind control in the courtroom. *Psychology Today,* pp. 66–68, 70, 73.

Aneshensel, C. S., & Stone, J. D. (1982). Stress and depression—A test of the buffering model of social support. *Archives of General Psychiatry, 39,* 1392–1396.

Anisman, H., & Zacharko, R. M. (1982). Depression: The predisposing influence of stress. *The Behavioral and Brain Sciences, 5,* 89–137.

Anyan, W. R., & Schowalter, J. E. (1983). A comprehensive approach to anorexia nervosa. *The Journal of The American Academy of Child Psychiatry, 22,* 122–127.

APA (1980). See American Psychiatric Association.

Ardrey, R. (1966). *The territorial imperative.* New York: Atheneum.

Arkes, H. R., & Garske, J. P. (1982). *Psychological theories of motivation* (2nd ed.). Monterey, CA: Brooks/Cole.

Aronson, E., Turner, J., & Carlsmith, J. M. (1963). Communicator credibility and communicator discrepancy as determinants of opinion change. *Journal of Abnormal and Social Psychology, 67,* 31–36.

Argyle, M., & Dean, J. (1965). Eye-contact, distance, and affiliation. *Sociometry, 28,* 289–304.

Asch, S. E. (1946). Forming impressions of personality. *Journal of Abnormal and Social Psychology, 41,* 258–290.

Asch, S. E. (1951). Effects of group pressure upon the modification and distortion of judgments. In H. Guetzkow (Ed.), *Groups, leadership, and men* (pp. 177–190). Pittsburgh, PA: Carnegie Press.

Asch, S. E. (1952). *Social psychology.* New York: Prentice-Hall.

Asch, S. E. (1955, November). Opinions and social pressures. *Scientific American,* pp. 31–35.

Asch, S. E. (1956). Studies of independence and conformity: A minority of one against a unanimous majority. *Psychological Monographs, 70* (9, Whole No. 416).

Aserinsky, E., & Kleitman, N. (1953). Regularly occurring periods of eye motility, and concomitant phenomena, during sleep. *Science, 118,* 273–274.

Asher, J. (1983, February 25). Mapping mental illness: From brain scans to blood tests. *NIMH Science Reporter,* pp. 1–8.

Atkeson, B. M., Calhoun, K. S., Resick, P. A., & Ellis, E. M. (1982). Victims of rape: Repeated assessment of depressive symptoms. *Journal of Consulting and Clinical Psychology, 50,* 96–102.

Atkinson, R. C. (1974). Teaching children to read using a computer. *American Psychologist, 29,* 169–178.

Atkinson, R. C. (1975). Mnemotechnics in second-language learning. *American Psychologist, 30,* 821–828.

Atkinson, R. C., & Shiffrin, R. M. (1971, August). The control of short-term memory. *Scientific American,* pp. 82–90.

Atwater, E. (1983). *Psychology of adjustment* (2nd ed.). Englewood Cliffs, NJ: Prentice-Hall.

Axelrod, S., & Apsche, J. (Eds.). (1983). *The effects of punishment on behavior.* New York: Academic Press.

Ayllon, T. (1963). Intensive treatment of psychotic behavior by stimulus satiation and food reinforcement. *Behaviour Research and Therapy, 1,* 53–61.

Ayllon, T., & Azrin, N. H. (1965). The measurement and reinforcement of behavior of psychotics. *Journal of the Experimental Analysis of Behavior, 8,* 357–383.

Ayllon, T., Haughton, E., & Hughes, H. B. (1965). Interpretation of symptoms: Fact or fiction. *Behavior Research and Therapy, 3,* 1–7.

Bachrach, A. J., Erwin, W. J., & Mohr, J. P. (1965). The control of eating behavior in an anorexic by operant conditioning techniques. In L. P. Ullmann & L. Krasner (Eds.), *Case studies in behavior modification* (pp. 153–163). New York: Holt, Rinehart and Winston.

Bach-y-Rita, P. (1972). *Brain mechanisms in sensory substitution.* New York: Academic Press.

Baird, J. C. (1982). The moon illusion: II. A reference theory. *Journal of Experimental Psychology: General, 111,* 304–315.

Baird, J. C., & Wagner, M. (1982). The moon illusion: I. How high is the sky? *Journal of Experimental Psychology: General, 111,* 296–303.

Baltes, P. B. (1968). Longitudinal and cross-sectional sequences in the study of age and generation effects. *Human Development, 11,* 145–171.

Baltes, P. B., & Schaie, K. W. (1976). On the plasticity of intelligence in adulthood and old age: Where Horn and Donaldson fail. *American Psychologist, 31,* 720–725.

Bandura, A. (1965). Vicarious processes: A case of no-trial learning. In L. Berkowitz (Ed.), *Advances in experimental social psychology* (Vol. 2, pp. 1–55). New York: Academic Press.

Bandura, A. (1969). *Principles of behavior modification.* New York: Holt, Rinehart and Winston.

Bandura, A. (1973). *Aggression: A social learning analysis.* Englewood Cliffs, NJ: Prentice-Hall.

Bandura, A. (1977a). Self-efficacy: Toward a unifying theory of behavioral change. *Psychological Review, 84,* 191–215.

Bandura, A. (1977b). *Social learning theory.* Englewood Cliffs, NJ: Prentice-Hall.

Bandura, A. (1978). The self system in reciprocal determinism. *American Psychologist, 33,* 344–358.

Bandura, A. (1982). Self-efficacy mechanism in human agency. *American Psychologist, 37,* 122–147.

Bandura, A., Adams, N. E., & Beyer, J. (1977). Cognitive processes mediating behavioral change. *Journal of Personality and Social Psychology, 35,* 125–139.

Bandura, A., Blanchard, E. B., & Ritter, B. (1969). Relative efficacy of desensitization and modeling approaches for inducing behavioral, affective, and attitudinal changes. *Journal of Personality and Social Psychology, 13,* 173–199.

Bandura, A., & Cervone, D. (1983). Self-evaluative and self-efficacy mechanisms governing the motivational effects of goal systems. *Journal of Personality and Social Psychology, 45,* 1017–1028.

Bandura, A., Ross, D., & Ross, S. A. (1963). Imitation of film-mediated aggressive models. *Journal of Abnormal and Social Psychology, 66,* 3–11.

Barber, T. X., Spanos, N. P., & Chaves, J. F. (1974). *Hypnosis, imagination, and human potentialities.* Elmsford, NY: Pergamon.

Barker, R. G. (1968). *Ecological psychology: Concepts and methods for studying the environment of human behavior.* Stanford, CA: Stanford University Press.

Barnard, C. P., & Corrales, R. G. (1979). *The theory and technique of family therapy.* Springfield, IL: Charles C Thomas.

Baron, R. A. (1977). *Human aggression.* New York: Plenum Publishing.

Baron, R. A. (1978a). Invasions of personal space and helping: Mediating effects of invader's apparent need. *Journal of Experimental Social Psychology, 14,* 304–312.

Baron, R. A. (1978b). The aggression-inhibiting influence of sexual humor. *Journal of Personality and Social Psychology, 36,* 189–197.

Baron, R. A., & Ball, R. L. (1974). The aggression-inhibiting influence of nonhostile humor. *Journal of Experimental Social Psychology, 10,* 23–33.

Baron, R. A., & Byrne, D. (1977). *Social psychology: Understanding human interaction* (2nd ed.). Boston: Allyn & Bacon.

Baron, R. A. & Byrne, D. (1981). *Social psychology: Understanding human interaction* (3rd ed.). Boston: Allyn & Bacon.

Baron, R. A., & Byrne, D. (1982). *Exploring social psychology* (2nd ed.). Boston: Allyn & Bacon.

Baron, R. A., & Ransberger, V. M. (1978). Ambient temperature and the occurrence of collective violence: The "long, hot summer" revisited. *Journal of Personality and Social Psychology, 36,* 351–360.

Baron, R. M., Mandel, D. R., Adams, C. A., & Griffen, L. M. (1976). Effects of social density in university residential environments. *Journal of Personality and Social Psychology, 34,* 434–446.

Baron, R. M., & Rodin, J. (1978). Perceived control and crowding stress. In A. Baum, J. E. Singer & S. Valins (Eds.), *Advances in environmental psychology* (Vol. 1, pp. 145–190). Hillsdale, NJ: Erlbaum.

Barron, F., & Harrington, D. M. (1981). Creativity, intelligence, and personality. *Annual Review of Psychology, 32,* 439–476.

Barsky, A. J., & Klerman, G. L. (1983). Overview: Hypochondriasis, bodily complaints, and somatic styles. *The American Journal of Psychiatry, 140,* 273–283.

Bar-Tal, D. (1976). *Prosocial behavior: Theory and research.* New York: Halsted Press.

Bartlett, F. C. (1932). *Remembering: A study in experimental and social psychology.* Cambridge: Cambridge University Press.

Bateson, G. (1960). Minimal requirements for a theory of schizophrenia. *Archives of General Psychiatry, 2,* 477–491.

Batson, C. D., Cochran, P. J., Biederman, M. F., Blosser, J. L., Ryan, M. J., & Vogt, B. (1978). Failure to help when in a hurry: Callousness or conflict? *Personality and Social Psychology Bulletin, 4,* 97–101.

Batson, C. D., O'Quin, K., Fultz, J., Vanderplas, M., & Isen, A. M. (1983). Influence of self-reported distress and empathy on egoistic versus altruistic motivation to help. *Journal of Personality and Social Psychology, 45,* 706–718.

Batson, C. D., & Coke, J. S. (1981). Empathy: A source of altruistic motivation for helping: In J. P. Rushton & R. M. Sorrentino (Eds.), *Altruism and helping behavior: Social, personality, and developmental perspectives* (pp. 167–187). Hillsdale, NJ: Erlbaum.

Baucom, D. H., & Aiken, P. A. (1981). Effect of depressed mood on eating among obese and nonobese dieting and nondieting persons. *Journal of Personality and Social Psychology, 41,* 577–585.

Baum, A., Aiello, J. R., & Calesnick, L. E. (1978). Crowding and personal control: Social density and the development of learned helplessness. *Journal of Personality and Social Psychology, 36,* 1000–1011.

Baum, A., & Davis, G. E. (1980). Reducing the stress of high-density living: An architectural intervention. *Journal of Personality and Social Psychology, 38,* 471–481.

Baum, A., Fleming, R., & Singer, J. E. (1982). Stress at Three Mile Island: Applying psychological impact analysis. In L. Bickman (Ed.), *Applied Social Psychology Annual (Vol. 3,* pp. 217–248). Beverly Hills, CA: Sage Publications.

Baum, A., & Greenberg, C. I. (1975). Waiting for a crowd: The behaviorial and perceptual effects of anticipated crowding. *Journal of Personality and Social Psychology, 32,* 671–679.

Baum, A., & Valins, S. (1977). *Architecture and social behavior: Psychological studies in social density.* Hillsdale, NJ: Erlbaum.

Baumrind, D. (1964). Some thoughts on ethics of research: After reading Milgram's "Behavioral study of obedience." *American Psychologist, 19,* 421–423.

Baumrind, D. (1967). Child care practices anteceding three patterns of preschool behavior. *Genetic Psychology Monographs, 75,* 43–88.

Baumrind, D. (1968). Authoritarian vs. authoritative parental control. *Adolescence, 3,* 255–272.

Bavelas, J. B. (1978). *Personality: Current theory and research.* Monterey, CA: Brooks/Cole.

Bayley, N., & Schaefer, E. S. (1964). Correlations of maternal and child behaviors with the development of mental abilities: Data from the Berkeley Growth Study. *Monographs of the Society for Research in Child Development, 29,* No. 6, (Serial No. 97).

Beach, B. H. (1980, September 8). Blood, sweat and tears. *Time,* p. 44.

Beaman, A. L., Barnes, P. J., Klentz, B., & McQuirk, B. (1978). Increasing helping rates through information dissemination: Teaching pays. *Personality and Social Psychology Bulletin, 4,* 406–411.

Beaman, A. L., Cole, C. M., Preston, M., Klentz, B., & Steblay, N. M. (1983). Fifteen years of foot-in-the-door research: A meta-analysis. *Personality and Social Psychology Bulletin, 9,* 181–196.

Beck, A. T. (1976). *Cognitive therapy and the emotional disorders.* New York: International Universities Press.

Beck, A. T., Rush, A. J., Shaw, B. F., & Emery, G. (1979). *Cognitive therapy of depression.* New York: Guilford Press.

Beck, A. T. (1967). *Depression: Causes and treatment.* Philadelphia: University of Pennsylvania Press.

Beck, A. T., & Harrison, R. P. (1982). Stress, neurochemical substrates, and depression: Concomitants are not necessarily causes. *The Behavioral and Brain Sciences, 5,* 101–102.

Beck, M. (1982, November 8). The Tylenol letter. *Newsweek,* p. 32.

Beck, R. C. (1983). *Motivation: Theories and principles* (2nd ed.). Englewood Cliffs, NJ: Prentice-Hall.

Becker, L. J., & Seligman, C. (1978). Reducing air conditioning waste by signalling it is cool outside. *Personality and Social Psychology Bulletin, 4,* 412–415.

Bee, H. L., & Mitchell, S. K. (1980). *The developing person: A life-span approach.* New York: Harper & Row.

Begley, S., Carey, J., & Grant, D. (1982, July 26). Do animals really think? *Newsweek,* p. 70.

Bekerian, D. A., & Bowers, J. M. (1983). Eyewitness testimony: Were we misled? *Journal of Experimental Psychology: Learning, Memory, and Cognition, 9,* 139–145.

Békésy, G. V. (1960). *Experiments in hearing.* New York: McGraw-Hill. (Translated and edited by E. G. Wever.)

Békésy, G. V. (1972). The ear. In *Physiological psychology: Readings from Scientific American.* (pp. 232–242). San Francisco: W. H. Freeman.

Bell, A. P., & Weinberg, M. S. (1978). *Homosexualities.* New York: Simon & Schuster.

Bell, P. A. (1981). Physiological, comfort, performance, and social effects of heat stress. *Journal of Social Issues, 37,* 71–94.

Bell, P. A., Fisher, J. D. & Loomis, R. J. (1978). *Environmental psychology.* Philadelphia: W. B. Saunders.

Bell, P. A., & Greene, T. C. (1982). Thermal stress: Physiological, comfort, performance, and social effects of hot and cold environments. In G. W. Evans (Ed.), *Environmental stress* (pp. 75–104). Cambridge: Cambridge University Press.

Bell, R. Q. (1979). Parent, child, and reciprocal influences. *American Psychologist, 34,* 821–826.

Bell, S. M., & Ainsworth, M. D. S. (1972). Infant crying and maternal responsiveness. *Child Development, 43,* 1171–1190.

Belmont, L., & Marolla, F. A. (1973). Birth order, family size, and intelligence. *Science, 182,* 1096–1101.

Bemis, K. M. (1978). Current approaches to the etiology and treatment of anorexia nervosa. *Psychological Bulletin, 85,* 593–617.

Benbow, C. P., & Stanley, J. C. (1982). Consequences in high school and college of sex differences in mathematical reasoning ability: A longitudinal perspective. *American Educational Research Journal, 19,* 598–622.

Benjamin, L. T., Jr., & Bruce, D. (1982). From bottle-fed chimp to bottlenose dolphin: A contemporary appraisal of Winthrop Kellogg. *The Psychological Record, 32,* 461–482.

Bennett, W., & Gurin, J. (1982). *The dieter's dilemma.* New York: Basic Books.

Benson, H. (1975). *The relaxation response.* New York: Avon Books.

Benson, P. L., & Catt, V. L. (1978). Soliciting charity contributions: The parlance of asking for money. *Journal of Applied Social Psychology, 8,* 84–95.

Benson, P. L. Karabenick, S. A., & Lerner, R. M. (1976). Pretty pleases: The effects of physical attractiveness, race, and sex on receiving help. *Journal of Experimental Social Psychology, 12,* 409–415.

Berbaum, M. L., & Moreland, R. L. (1980). Intellectual development within the family: A new application of the confluence model. *Developmental Psychology, 16,* 506–515.

Berger, R. J. (1969). The sleep and dream cycle. In A. Kales (Ed.), *Sleep: Physiology and pathology* (pp. 17–32). Philadelphia: Lippincott.

Bergin, A. E., & Lambert, J. J. (1978). The evaluation of therapeutic outcomes. In S. L. Garfield & A. E. Bergin (Eds.), *Handbook of psychotherapy and behavior change: An empirical analysis* (2nd ed., pp. 139–189). New York: Wiley.

Berko, J. (1958). The child's learning of English morphology. *Word, 14,* 150–177.

Berkowitz, L. (1978). Whatever happened to the frustration-aggression hypothesis? *American Behavioral Scientist, 21,* 691–708.

Berkowitz, L. (1981, June). How guns control us. *Psychology Today,* pp. 11–12.

Berkowitz, L. (1982). Aversive conditions as stimuli to aggression. In L. Berkowitz (Ed.), *Advances in experimental social psychology* (Vol. 15, pp. 249–288). New York: Academic Press.

Berkowitz, L. (1983). Aversively stimulated aggression: Some parallels and differences in research with animals and humans. *American Psychologist, 38,* 1135–1144.

Berkowitz, L., & LePage, A. (1967). Weapons as aggression-eliciting stimuli. *Journal of Personality and Social Psychology, 7,* 202–207.

Berlyne, D. E. (1958a). The influence of complexity and novelty in visual figures on orienting responses. *Journal of Experimental Psychology, 55,* 289–296.

Berlyne, D. E. (1958b). The influence of the albedo and complexity of stimuli on visual fixation in the human infant. *British Journal of Psychology, 49,* 315–318.

Bermant, G. (1975, May). The notion of conspiracy is not tasty to Americans. *Psychology Today,* pp. 60–61, 63, 65–67.

Bernstein, D. A., & Nietzel, M. T. (1980). *Introduction to clinical psychology.* New York: McGraw-Hill.

Berscheid, E., & Walster, E. (1974). Physical attractiveness. In L. Berkowitz (Ed.), *Advances in experimental social psychology* (Vol. 7, pp. 157–215). New York: Academic Press.

Bickman, L. (1971). The effect of another bystander's ability to help on bystander's intervention in an emergency. *Journal of Experimental Social Psychology, 7,* 367–379.

Bieber, I., Dain, J. H., Dince, P. R., Drellich, M. G., Grand, H. G., Gundlach, R. H., Kraemer, M. W., Rifkin, A. H., Wilbur, C. B., & Bieber, T. B. (1962). *Homosexuality: A psychoanalytic study.* New York: Basic Books.

Bigge, M. (1964). *Learning theories for teachers.* New York: Harper & Row.

Biller, H. B. (1982). Fatherhood: Implications for child and adult development. In B. B. Wolman (Ed.), *Handbook of developmental psychology* (pp. 702–725). Englewood Cliffs, NJ: Prentice-Hall.

Billings, A. G., & Moos, R. H. (1982). Psychosocial theory and research on depression: An integrative framework and review. *Clinical Psychology Review, 2,* 213–237.

Binet, A., & Simon, T. (1979). The development of intelligence in children. In L. Willerman & R. G. Turner (Eds.), *Readings about individual and group differences* (pp. 10–18). San Francisco: W. H. Freeman. (Original work published 1905)

Bingham, R. (1982, April). On the life of Mr. Darwin. *Science 82,* pp. 34–39.

Biran, M., & Wilson, G. T. (1981). Treatment of phobic disorders using cognitive and exposure methods: A self-efficacy analysis. *Journal of Consulting and Clinical Psychology, 49,* 886–899.

Birch, H. G. (1945). The relation of previous experience to insightful problem solving. *Journal of Comparative Psychology, 38,* 367–383.

Birren, J. E., Cunningham, W. R., & Yamamoto, K. (1983). Psychology of adult development and aging. *Annual Review of Psychology, 34,* 543–575.

Blakemore, C., & Cooper, G. F. (1970). Development of the brain depends on the visual environment. *Nature, 228,* 477–478.

Blanchard, E. B., & Andrasik, F. (1982). Psychological assessment and treatment of headache: Recent developments and emerging issues. *Journal of Consulting and Clinical Psychology, 50,* 859–879.

Block, J. (1965). *The challenge of response sets.* New York: Appleton-Century-Crofts.

Blois, M. S. (1980). Clinical judgment and computers. *New England Journal of Medicine, 303,* 192–197.

Blois, M. S. (1983). Conceptual issues in computer-aided diagnosis and the hierarchical nature of medical knowledge. *The Journal of Medicine and Philosophy, 8,* 29–50.

Bloom, L. (1973). *One word at a time.* The Hague: Mouton.

Bloom, F. (1983, September). PI conversation: Floyd Bloom. *Psychology Today,* pp. 49–55.

Blusztajn, J. K., & Wurtman, R. J. (1983). Choline and cholinergic neurons. *Science, 221,* 614–620.

Boersma, K., Den Hengst, S., Dekker, J., & Emmelkamp, P. M. G. (1976). Exposure and response prevention in the natural environment: A comparison with obsessive-compulsive patients. *Behaviour Research and Therapy, 14,* 12–24.

Bolles, R. C. (1975). *Theory of motivation* (2nd ed.). New York: Harper & Row.

Bombeck, E. (1980, August 26). Hot weather makes you really mean. *Bryan-College Station Eagle,* p. 7A.

Boom times on the psychic frontier. (1974, March 4). *Time,* pp. 65–72.

Borgida, E. (1981). Legal reform of rape laws. In L. Bickman (Ed.), *Applied social psychology annual* (Vol. 2, pp. 211–241). Beverly Hills, CA: Sage Publications.

Bouchard, T. J., Jr. (1983). Twins—Nature's twice-told tale. *Yearbook of science and the future* (pp. 66–81). Chicago: Encyclopedia Britannica.

Bouchard, T. J., Jr., Heston, L., Eckert, E., Keyes, M., & Resnick, S. (1981). The Minnesota study of twins reared apart: Project description and sample results in the developmental domain. In L. Gedda, P. Parisi, & W. E. Nance (Eds.), *Twin research 3: Part B. Intelligence, personality, and development* (pp. 227–233). New York: Alan R. Liss.

Bouchard, T. J., Jr., & McGue, M. (1981). Familial studies of intelligence: A review. *Science, 212,* 1055–1059.

Bourne, L. E., Jr. (1970). Knowing and using concepts. *Psychological Review, 77,* 546–556.

Bourne, L. E., Jr., Dominowski, R. L., & Loftus, E. F. (1979). *Cognitive processes.* Englewood Cliffs, NJ: Prentice-Hall.

Bower, G. H. (1981). Mood and memory. *American Psychologist, 36,* 129–148.

Bower, G. H., & Clark, M. C. (1969). Narrative stories as mediators for serial learning. *Psychonomic Science, 14,* 181–182.

Bower, G. H., & Gilligan, S. G. (1979). Remembering information related to one's self. *Journal of Research in Personality, 13,* 420–432.

Bower, G. H., & Hilgard, E. R. (1980). *Theories of learning* (5th ed.). Englewood Cliffs, NJ: Prentice-Hall.

Bowlby, J. (1958). The nature of the child's tie to his mother. *International Journal of Psycho-Analysis. 39,* 350–373.

Bowlby, J. (1969). *Attachment and loss: Vol. I. Attachment.* New York: Basic Books.

Bowlby, J. (1973). *Attachment and loss: Vol. II. Separation: Anxiety and anger.* New York: Basic Books.

Brain healing. (1983, August 8). *Time,* p. 59.

Brackbill, Y., & Nichols, P. L. (1982). A test of the confluence model of intellectual development. *Developmental Psychology, 18,* 192–198.

Bradshaw, G. L., & Anderson, J. R. (1982). Elaborative encoding as an explanation of levels of processing. *Journal of Verbal Learning and Verbal Behavior, 21,* 165–174.

Bray, D. W. (1982). The assessment center and the study of lives. *American Psychologist, 37,* 180–189.

Bray, D. W., Campbell, R. J., & Grant, D. L. (1974). *Formative years in business: A long-term AT&T study of managerial lives.* New York: Wiley.

Brazelton, T. B. (1973). *Neonatal behavioral assessment scale.* Philadelphia: Lippincott.

Brazelton, T. B. (1979). *Infants and mothers: Differences in development.* New York: Dell Publishing.

Brecher, E. M. (1972). *Licit and illicit drugs.* Boston: Little, Brown.

Brehm, J. W. (1966). *A theory of psychological reactance.* New York: Academic Press.

Breland, K., & Breland, M. (1966). *Animal behavior.* New York: Macmillan.

Brennecke, J. H., & Amick, R. G. (1978). *Readings in psychology and human experience* (2nd ed.). Encino, CA: Glencoe Publishing.

Bresler, D. E., Ellison, G., & Zamenhof, S. (1975). Learning deficits in rats with malnourished grandmothers. *Developmental Psychobiology, 8,* 315–323.

Breuning, S. E., & Poling, A. D. (1982). Pharmacotherapy. In J. L. Matson & R. P. Barrett (Eds.), *Psychopathology in the mentally retarded* (pp. 195–251). New York: Grune & Stratton.

Brock, T. C. (1965). Communicator-recipient similarity and decision-change. *Journal of Personality and Social Psychology, 1,* 650–654.

Brody, J. E. (1982, September 16). Subliminal perception raging. *Enid (Oklahoma) Morning News,* p. E–12. (Reprinted from *New York Times.*)

Broverman, I. K., Vogel, S. R., Broverman, D. M., Clarkson, F. E., & Rosenkrantz, P. S. (1972). Sex-role stereotypes: A current appraisal. *Journal of Social Issues, 28,* 59–79.

Browman, C. P., Sampson, M. G., Gujavarty, K. S., & Mitler, M. M. (1982, August). The drowsy crowd. *Psychology Today,* pp. 35–38.

Brown, J. S., & Burton, R. R. (1978). Diagnostic models for procedural bugs in basic mathematical skills. *Cognitive Science, 2,* 155–192.

Brown, P. L., & Jenkins, H. M. (1968). Auto-shaping of the pigeon's key-peck. *Journal of the Experimental Analysis of Behavior, 11,* 1–8.

Brown, R. (1965). *Social psychology.* New York: Free Press.

Brown, R. (1973). *A first language: The early stages.* Cambridge, MA: Harvard University Press.

Brown, R., & McNeill, D. (1966). The "tip of the tongue" phenomenon. *Journal of Verbal Learning and Verbal Behavior, 5,* 325–337.

Brownell, K. D., (1982). Obesity: Understanding and treating a serious, prevalent, and refractory disorder. *Journal of Consulting and Clinical Psychology, 50,* 820–840.

Brunson, B. I., & Matthews, K. A. (1981). The Type A coronary-prone behavior pattern and reactions to uncontrollable stress: An analysis of performance strategies, affect, and attributions during failure. *Journal of Personality and Social Psychology, 40,* 906–918.

Bryan, J. H., & Test, M. A. (1967). Models and helping: Naturalistic studies in aiding behavior. *Journal of Personality and Social Psychology, 6,* 400–407.

Bryden, M. P. (1982). *Laterality: Functional asymmetry in the intact brain.* New York: Academic Press.

Buchsbaum, M. S., Mirsky, A. F., DeLisi, L. E. et al. (1984). The Genain quadruplets: Electrophysiologic, position emission, and x-ray tomographic studies. *Psychiatry Research,* in press.

Buck, R. (1976). *Human motivation and emotion.* New York: Wiley.

Buck, R. (1980). Nonverbal behavior and the theory of emotion: The facial feedback hypothesis. *Journal of Personality and Social Psychology, 38,* 811–824.

Buckhout, R. (1974, December). Eyewitness testimony. *Scientific American,* pp. 23–31.

Bullough, V. L. (1981). Age at menarche: A misunderstanding. *Science, 213,* 365–366.

Burke, D. M., & Light, L. L. (1981). Memory and aging: The role of retrieval processes. *Psychological Bulletin, 90,* 513–546.

Burger, J. M., & Arkin, R. M. (1980). Prediction, control, and learned helplessness. *Journal of Personality and Social Psychology, 38,* 482–491.

Burger, J. M., Oakman, J. A., & Bullard, N. G. (1983). Desire for control and the perception of crowding. *Personality and Social Psychology Bulletin, 9,* 475–480.

Burgess, A. W., & Holmstrom, L. L. (1974). Rape trauma syndrome. *American Journal of Psychiatry, 131,* 981–986.

Burt, M. R. (1980). Cultural myths and supports for rape. *Journal of Personality and Social Psychology, 38,* 217–230.

Butcher, J. N. (Ed.). (1969). *MMPI: Research developments and clinical applications.* New York: McGraw-Hill.

Byrne, D. (1971). *The attraction paradigm.* New York: Academic Press.

Byrne, D. (1974). *An introduction to personality: Research, theory, and applications* (2nd ed.). Englewood Cliffs, NJ: Prentice-Hall.

Byrne, D. (1983). Sex without contraception. In D. Byrne & W. A. Fisher (Eds.), *Adolescents, sex, and contraception* (pp. 3–31). Hillsdale, NJ: Erlbaum.

Byrne, D., & Kelley, K. (1981). *An introduction to personality* (3rd ed.). Englewood Cliffs, NJ: Prentice-Hall.

Byrne, D., & Rhamey, R. (1965). Magnitude of positive and negative reinforcements as a determinant of attraction. *Journal of Personality and Social Psychology, 2,* 884–889.

Cacioppo, J. T., Petty, R. E., & Morris, K. J. (1983). Effects of need for cognition on message evaluation, recall, and persuasion. *Journal of Personality and Social Psychology, 45,* 805–818.

Calhoun, J. F. (1977). *Abnormal psychology* (2nd ed.). New York: Random House.

Calhoun, K. S., Atkeson, B. M., & Resick, P. A. (1982). A longitudinal examination of fear reactions in victims of rape. *Journal of Counseling Psychology, 29,* 655–661.

Calhoun, L. G., Selby, J. W., & Selby, L. E. (1982). The psychological aftermath of suicide: An analysis of current evidence. *Clinical Psychology Review, 2,* 409–420.

Campbell, A. M. G., Evans, M., Thomson, J. L., & Williams, M. J. (1971). Cerebral atrophy in young cannabis smokers. Lancet, 2. 1219–1224.

Campbell, D. P. (1974). *If you don't know where you're going, you'll probably end up somewhere else.* Niles, IL: Argus Communications.

Campbell, J. P., Dunnette, M D., Lawler, E. E., & Weick, K. E. (1970). *Managerial behavior, performance, and effectiveness.* New York: McGraw-Hill.

Campbell, J. B., & Hawley, C. W. (1982). Study habits and Eysenck's theory of extraversion-introversion. *Journal of Research in Personality, 16,* 139–146.

Campos, J. J., Svejda, M. J., Campos, R. G., & Bertenthal, B. (1982). The emergence of self-produced locomotion: Its importance for psychological development in infancy. In D. Bricker (Ed.), *Intervention with at-risk and handicapped infants: From research to application* (pp. 195–216). Baltimore, MD: University Park Press.

Cannell, C. F., & Kahn, R. L. (1968). Interviewing. In G. Lindzey & E. Aronson (Eds.), *The handbook of social psychology: Vol. 2. Research methods* (2nd ed., pp. 526–595). Reading, MA: Addison-Wesley.

Cannon, D. S., & Baker, T. B. (1981). Emetic and electric shock alcohol aversion therapy: Assessment of conditioning. *Journal of Consulting and Clinical Psychology, 49,* 20–33.

Cannon, D. S., Baker, T. B., & Wehl, C. K. (1981). Emetic and electric shock alcohol aversion therapy: Six- and twelve-month follow-up. *Journal of Consulting and Clinical Psychology, 49,* 360–368.

Cannon, W. B. (1918). The physiological basis of thirst. *Proceedings of the Royal Society of London, 90B,* 283–301.

Cannon, W. B. (1927). The James-Lange theory of emotions: A critical examination and an alternative theory. *American Journal of Psychology, 39,* 106–124.

Caputo, D., & Mandell, W. (1970). Consequences of low birth weight. *Developmental Psychology, 3,* 363–383.

Carlson, C. R., White, D. K., & Turkat, I. D. (1982). Night terrors: A clinical and empirical review. *Clinical Psychology Review, 2,* 455–468.

Carlson, N. R. (1981). *Physiology of behavior* (2nd ed.). Boston: Allyn & Bacon.

Carlsmith, J. M., & Anderson, C. A. (1979). Ambient temperature and the occurrence of collective violence: A new analysis. *Journal of Personality and Social Psychology, 37,* 337–344.

Carmichael, L., Hogan, H. P., & Walter, A. A. (1932). An experimental study of the effect of language on the reproduction of visually perceived form. *Journal of Experimental Psychology, 15,* 73–86.

Carrol, E. N., Zuckerman, M., & Vogel, W. H. (1982). A test of the optimal level of arousal theory of sensation seeking. *Journal of Personality and Social Psychology, 42,* 572–575.

Carroll, J. L., & Rest, J. R. (1982). Moral development. In B. B. Wolman (Ed.), *Handbook of developmental psychology* (pp. 434–451). Englewood Cliffs, NJ: Prentice-Hall.

Carver, C. S., & Glass, D. C. (1978). Coronary-prone behavior pattern and interpersonal aggression. *Journal of Personality and Social Psychology, 36,* 361–366.

Casper, R. C. (1983). On the emergence of bulimia nervosa as a syndrome: A historical view. *International Journal of Eating Disorders, 2,* 3–16.

Cates, W., Jr. (1982). Legal abortion: The public health record. *Science, 215,* 1586–1590.

Cattell, R. B. (1950). *Personality: A systematic theoretical and factual study.* New York: McGraw-Hill.

Cattell, R. B. (1965). *The scientific analysis of personality.* Baltimore: Penguin.

Cattell, R. B., Kawash, G. F., & DeYoung, G. E. (1972). Validation of objective measures of ergic tension: Response of the sex erg to visual stimulation. *Journal of Experimental Research in Personality, 6,* 76–83.

Cautela, J. R. (1967). Covert sensitization. *Psychological Reports, 20,* 459–468.

Chafetz, M. E. (1979, May–June). Alcohol and alcoholism. *American Scientist,* pp. 293–299.

Chambless, D. L. (1982). Characteristics of agoraphobics. In D. L. Chambless & A. J. Goldstein (Eds.), *Agoraphobia: Multiple perspectives on theory and treatment* (pp. 1–18). New York: Wiley.

Chance, P. (1982, January). Your child's self-esteem. *Parents Magazine,* pp. 54–59.

Chaplin, J. P., & Krawiec, T. S. (1979). *Systems and theories of psychology* (4th ed.). New York: Holt, Rinehart and Winston.

Check, J. V. P., & Malamuth, N. M. (1983). Sex role stereotyping and reactions to depictions of stranger versus acquaintance rape. *Journal of Personality and Social Psychology, 45,* 344–356.

Chedd, G. (1981, January–February). Who shall be born? *Science 81,* pp. 32–41.

Cheek, J. M., & Busch, C. M. (1981). The influence of shyness on loneliness in a new situation. *Personality and Social Psychology Bulletin, 7,* 572–577.

Chomsky, N. (1957). *Syntactic structures.* The Hague: Mouton.

Chomsky, N. (1965). *Aspects of the theory of syntax.* Cambridge, MA: M.I.T. Press.

Christensen, L. B. (1980). *Experimental methodology* (2nd ed.). Boston: Allyn & Bacon.

Chumlea, W. C. (1982). Physical growth in adolescence. In B. B. Wolman (Ed.), *Handbook of developmental psychology* (pp. 471–485). Englewood Cliffs, NJ: Prentice-Hall.

Cialdini, R. B., Cacioppo, J. T., Bassett, R., & Miller, J. A. (1978). Low-ball procedure for producing compliance: Commitment then cost. *Journal of Personality and Social Psychology, 36,* 463–476.

Cialdini, R. B., & Schroeder, D. A. (1976). Increasing compliance by legitimizing paltry contributions: When even a penny helps. *Journal of Personality and Social Psychology, 34,* 599–604.

Cialdini, R. B., Vincent, J. E., Lewis, S. K., Catalan, J., Wheeler, D., & Darby, B. L. (1975). Reciprocal concessions procedure for inducing compliance: The door-in-the-face technique. *Journal of Personality and Social Psychology, 31,* 206–215.

Clark, D. M., & Teasdale, J. D. (1982). Diurnal variation in clinical depression and accessibility of memories of positive and negative experiences. *Journal of Abnormal Psychology, 91,* 87–95.

Clark, E. V., & Hecht, B. F. (1983). Comprehension, production, and language acquisition. *Annual Review of Psychology, 34,* 325–349.

Clark, H. H., & Clark, E. V. (1977). *Psychology and language.* New York: Harcourt Brace Jovanovich.

Clark, M., Gosnell, M., Shapiro, D., & Hager, M. (1981, July 13). The mystery of sleep. *Newsweek,* pp. 48–55.

Clark, M., & Lindsay, J. J. (1981, November 23). Brady's brave comeback. *Newsweek,* p. 104.

Clark, R. D., III, & Word, L. E. (1974). Where is the apathetic bystander? Situational characteristics of the emergency. *Journal of Personality and Social Psychology, 29,* 279–287.

Clark, R. N., Burgess, R. L., & Hendee, J. C. (1972). The development of antilitter behavior in a forest campground. *Journal of Applied Behavior Analysis, 5,* 1–5.

Clarke-Stewart, A., & Koch, J. B. (1983). *Children: Development through adolescence.* New York: Wiley.

Clingempeel, W. G., & Reppucci, N. D. (1982). Joint custody after divorce: Major issues and goals for research. *Psychological Bulletin, 91,* 102–127.

Clore, G. L., & Byrne, D. (1974). A reinforcement-affect model of attraction. In T. L. Huston (Ed.), *Foundations of interpersonal attraction* (pp. 143–170). New York: Academic Press.

Cofer, C. N. (1972). *Motivation and emotion.* Glenview, IL: Scott, Foresman.

Cohen, S. (1980). Aftereffects of stress on human performance and social behavior: A review of research and theory. *Psychological Bulletin, 88,* 82–108.

Cohen, S., Evans, G. W., Krantz, D. S., & Stokols, D. S. (1980). Physiological, motivational, and cognitive effects of aircraft noise on children: Moving from the laboratory to the field. *American Psychologist, 35,* 231–243.

Cohen, S., Evans, G. W., Krantz, D. S., Stokols, D. S., & Kelly, S. (1981). Aircraft noise and children: Longitudinal and cross-sectional evidence on adaptation to noise and the effectiveness of noise abatement. *Journal of Personality and Social Psychology, 40,* 331–345.

Cohen, S., & Weinstein, N. (1981). Nonauditory effects of noise on behavior and health. *Journal of Social Issues, 37,* 36–70.

Cohen, S., & Weinstein, N. (1982). Nonauditory effects of noise on behavior and health. In G. Evans (Ed.), *Environmental stress* (pp. 45–74). Cambridge: Cambridge University Press.

Colby, A., Kohlberg, L., Gibbs, J., & Lieberman, M. (1983). A longitudinal study of moral judgment. *Monographs of the Society for Research in Child Development, 48,* (1–2, Serial No. 200).

Cole, J. O. (1964). Phenothiazine treatment in acute schizophrenia: Effectiveness. *Archives of General Psychiatry, 10,* 246–261.

Coleman, J. C. (1979). *Contemporary psychology and effective behavior* (4th ed.). Glenview, IL: Scott, Foresman.

Coleman, J. C., Butcher, J. N., & Carson, R. C. (1980). *Abnormal psychology and modern life* (6th ed.). Glenview, IL: Scott, Foresman.

Collins, E. G. C., & Scott, P. (1978, July–August). Everyone who makes it has a mentor. *Harvard Business Review,* pp. 89–101.

Colombo, J. (1982). The critical period concept: Research, methodology, and theoretical issues. *Psychological Bulletin, 91,* 260–275.

Condas, J. (1980). Personal reflections on the *Larry P.* trial and its aftermath. *School Psychology Review, 9,* 154–158.

Condry, J., & Dyer, S. (1976). Fear of success: Attribution of cause to the victim. *Journal of Social Issues, 32,* 63–83.

Cone, J. D., & Hayes, S. C. (1980). *Environmental problems/behavioral solutions.* Monterey, CA: Brooks/Cole.

Conger, J. J. (1977). *Adolescence and youth: Psychological development in a changing world.* (2nd ed.). New York: Harper & Row.

Conger, J. J. (1979). *Adolescence: Generation under pressure.* New York: Harper & Row.

Conger, J. J. (1981). Freedom and commitment: Families, youth, and social change. *American Psychologist, 36,* 1475–1484.

Conger, J. J., & Petersen, A. C. (1983). *Adolescence and youth: Psychological development in a changing world* (3rd ed.). New York: Harper & Row.

Conrad, R. (1964). Acoustic confusions in immediate memory. *British Journal of Psychology, 55,* 75–84.

Cook, S. W., & Berrenberg, J. L. (1981). Approaches to encouraging conservation behavior: A review and conceptual framework. *Journal of Social Issues, 37,* 73–107.

Coon, D. (1983). *Introduction to psychology: Exploration and application* (3rd ed.). St. Paul, MN: West.

Cooper, C. L. (1982). Psychosocial stress and cancer. *Bulletin of the British Psychological Society, 35,* 456–459.

Cooper, J., & Mackie, D. (1983). Cognitive dissonance in an intergroup context. *Journal of Personality and Social Psychology, 44,* 536–544.

Cordes, C. (1983, January). A ravaged city copes with the human toll. *APA Monitor,* pp. 3, 17.

Coren, S., & Porac, C. (1977). Fifty centuries of right-handedness: The historical record. *Science, 198,* 631–632.

Corballis, M. C. (1980). Laterality and myth. *American Psychologist, 35,* 284–295.

Cornsweet, T. N. (1970). *Visual perception.* New York: Academic Press.

Costello, C. G. (1982). Fears and phobias in women: A community study. *Journal of Abnormal Psychology, 91,* 280–286.

Cotman, C. W., & McGaugh, J. L. (1980). *Behavioral neuroscience.* New York: Academic Press.

Cotton, J. L. (1981, May). *Ambient temperature and violent crime.* Paper presented at the meeting of the Midwestern Psychological Association, Detroit, MI.

Cowart, B. J. (1981). Development of task perception in humans: Sensitivity and preference throughout the life span. *Psychological Bulletin, 90,* 43–73.

Coyne, J. C., & Lazarus, R. S. (1980). Cognitive style, stress perception, and coping. In I. L. Kutash & L. B. Schlesinger (Eds.), *Handbook on stress and anxiety* (pp. 144–158). San Francisco: Jossey-Bass.

Craighead, E., Kazdin, A. E., & Mahoney, M. J. (1981). *Behavior modification: Principles, issues, and applications* (2nd ed.). Boston: Houghton Mifflin.

Craik, F. I. M. (1979). Human memory. *Annual Review of Psychology, 30,* 63–102.

Craik, F. I. M., & Lockhart, R. S. (1972). Levels of processing: A framework for memory research. *Journal of Verbal Learning and Verbal Behavior, 11,* 671–684.

Craik, F. I. M., & Tulving, E. (1975). Depth of processing and the retention of words in episodic memory. *Journal of Experimental Psychology: General, 104,* 268–294.

Crawford, J. W. (1982). Mother-infant interaction in premature and full-term infants. *Child Development, 53,* 957–962.

Cross, D. G., Sheehan, P. W., & Khan, J. A. (1982). Short- and long-term follow-up of clients receiving insight-oriented therapy and behavior therapy. *Journal of Consulting and Clinical Psychology, 50,* 103–112.

Crouse, B. B., & Mehrabian, A. (1977). Affiliation of opposite-sexed strangers. *Journal of Research in Personality, 11,* 38–47.

Cunningham, A. M. (1982, October). Is there a seismograph for stress? *Psychology Today,* pp. 46–50, 52.

Cunningham, M. R. (1981). Sociobiology as a supplementary paradigm for social psychological research. In L. Wheeler

(Ed.), *Review of personality and social psychology* (Vol. 2, pp. 69–106). Beverly Hills, CA: Sage Publications.

Cunningham, S. (1983a, January). Bill sparks hope for hospice care. *APA Monitor,* p. 22.

Cunningham, S. (1983c, March). Superior court restarts electroshock in Berkeley. *APA Monitor,* p. 17.

Cunningham, S. (1983b, June). Psychological factors rejected in TMI case. *APA Monitor,* p. 8.

Curie-Cohen, M., Luttrell, L., & Shapiro, S. (1979). Current practice of artificial insemination by donor in the United States. *The New England Journal of Medicine, 300,* 585–590.

Curtiss, S. (1977). *Genie: A psycholinguistic study of a modern-day "wild-child."* New York: Academic Press.

Cutrona, C. E. (1982). Nonpsychotic postpartum depression: A review of recent research. *Clinical Psychology Review, 2,* 487–504.

Cvetkovich, G., & Grote, B. (1983). Adolescent development and teenage fertility. In D. Byrne & W. A. Fisher (Eds.), *Adolescents, sex, and contraception* (pp. 109–123). Hillsdale, NJ: Erlbaum.

Dalton, G. W., Thompson, P. H., & Price, R. I. (1977). The four stages of professional careers—A new look at performance by professionals. *Organizational Dynamics, 6,* 19–42.

Darian-Smith, I., Sugitani, M., Heywood, J., Karita, K., & Goodwin, A. (1982). Touching textured surfaces: Cells in somatosensory cortex respond both to finger movement and to surface features. *Science, 218,* 906–909.

Darley, C. F., Tinklenberg, J. R., Roth, W. T., Hollister, L. E., & Atkinson, R. C. (1973). Influence of marihuana on storage and retrieval processes in memory. *Memory and Cognition, 1,* 196–200.

Darley, J. M., & Beniger, J. R. (1981). Diffusion of energy-conserving information. *Journal of Social Issues, 37,* 150–171.

Darley, J. M., & Latané, B. (1968). Bystander intervention in emergencies: Diffusion of responsibility. *Journal of Personality and Social Psychology, 8,* 377–383.

Darlington, R. B., Royce, J. M., Snipper, A. S., Murray, H. W., & Lazar, I. (1980). Preschool programs and later school competence of children from low-income families. *Science, 208,* 202–204.

Darwin, C. (1967). *On the origin of species by means of natural selection, or the preservation of favoured races in the struggle for life.* New York: Modern Library. (Original work published 1859)

Davis, M. H. (1983a). Empathic concern and the muscular dystrophy telethon: Empathy as a multidimensional construct. *Personality and Social Psychology Bulletin, 9,* 223–229.

Davis, M. H. (1983b). The effects of dispositional empathy on emotional reactions of helping: A multidimensional approach. *Journal of Personality, 51,* 167–184.

Davidson, L. M., Baum, A., & Collins, D. L. (1982). Stress and control-related problems at Three Mile Island. *Journal of*

Applied Social Psychology, 12, 349–359.

Davison, G. C., & Neale, J. M. (1982). *Abnormal psychology: An experimental clinical approach* (3rd ed.). New York: Wiley.

Deaux, K. (1976). *The behavior of men and women.* Monterey, CA: Brooks/Cole.

deCharms, R. (1968). *Personal causation: The internal affective determinants of behavior.* New York: Academic Press.

Deci, E. L. (1975). *Intrinsic motivation.* New York: Plenum Publishing.

Deci, E. L., Betley, G., Kahle, J., Abrams, L., & Porac, J. (1981). When trying to win: Competition and intrinsic motivation. *Personality and Social Psychology Bulletin, 7,* 79–83.

Deci, E. L., & Ryan, R. M. (1980). The empirical exploration of intrinsic motivational processes. In L. Berkowitz (Ed.), *Advances in experimental social psychology* (Vol. 13 pp. 39–80). New York: Academic Press.

Deese, J. (1972). *Psychology as science and art.* New York: Harcourt Brace Jovanovich, Inc.

DeJong, W. (1979). An examination of self-perception mediation of the foot-in-the-door effect. *Journal of Personality and Social Psychology, 37,* 2221–2239.

Delgado, J. M. R. (1963). Cerebral heterostimulation in a monkey colony. *Science, 141,* 161–163.

Delis, D. C., Knight, R. T., & Simpson, G. (1983). Reversed hemispheric organization in a left-hander. *Neuropsychologia, 21,* 13–24.

DeLongis, A., Coyne, J. C., Dakof, G., Folkman, S., & Lazarus, R. S. (1982). Relationship of daily hassles, uplifts, and major life events to health status. *Health Psychology, 1,* 119–136.

Delprato, D. J. (1977). Prompting electrical energy conservation in commercial users. *Environment and Behavior, 9,* 433–440.

Dement, W. C. (1960). The effect of dream deprivation. *Science, 131,* 1705–1707.

Dement, W. C. (1976). *Some must watch while some must sleep.* New York: W. W. Norton.

Dement, W. C. (1979). Normal sleep and sleep disorders. In G. Usdin & J. M. Lewis (Eds.), *Psychiatry in general medical practice* (pp. 415–434). New York: McGraw-Hill.

Dempsey, D., & Zimbardo, P. G. (1978). *Psychology and you.* Glenview, IL: Scott, Foresman.

Derlega, V. J., & Janda, L. H. (1978). *Personal adjustment: The psychology of everyday life.* Morristown, NJ: General Learning Press.

Dermer, M., & Thiel, D. L. (1975). When beauty may fail. *Journal of Personality and Social Psychology, 31,* 1168–1176.

Deutsch, M., & Gerard, H. B. (1955). A study of normative and informational social influence upon individual judgment. *Journal of Abnormal and Social Psychology, 51,* 629–636.

Deutsch, S. I., & Davis, K. L. (1983). Schizophrenia: A reivew of diagnostic and biological issues: 2. Biological issues. *Hospital and Community Psychiatry, 34.* 423–437.

DeValois, R. L., & DeValois, K. K. (1980). Spatial vision. *Annual Review of Psychology, 31,* 309–341.

de Villiers, J. G., & de Villiers, P. A. (1973). A cross-sectional study of the acquisition of grammatical morphemes in child speech. *Journal of Psycholinguistic Research, 2,* 267–278.

Diaconis, P. (1978). Statistical problems in ESP research. *Science, 201,* 131–136.

Diamond, E. L. (1982). The role of anger and hostility in essential hypertension and coronary heart disease. *Psychological Bulletin, 92,* 410–433.

Diener, E., & DeFour, D. (1978). Does television violence enhance program popularity? *Journal of Personality and Social Psychology, 36,* 333–341.

Dion, K. K. (1972). Physical attractiveness and evaluations of children's transgressions. *Journal of Personality and Social Psychology, 24,* 207–213.

Dion, K. K., Berscheid, E., & Walster, E. (1972). What is beautiful is good. *Journal of Personality and Social Psychology, 24,* 285–290.

Doherty, W. J., & Ryder, R. G. (1979). Locus of control, interpersonal trust, and assertive behavior among newlyweds. *Journal of Personality and Social Psychology, 37,* 2212–2220.

Dollard, J., Doob, L., Miller, N., Mowrer, O. H., & Sears, R. R. (1939). *Frustration and aggression.* New Haven, CT: Yale University Press.

Dominguez, R. A. (1983). Evaluating the effectiveness of the new antidepressants. *Hospital and Community Psychiatry, 34,* 405–408.

Donnerstein, E. (1980). Aggressive erotica and violence against women. *Journal of Personality and Social Psychology, 39,* 269–277.

Donnerstein, E., & Wilson, D. W. (1976). Effects of noise and perceived control on ongoing and subsequent aggressive behavior. *Journal of Personality and Social Psychology, 34,* 774–781.

Dowd, M. (1983, Sept. 5). Rape: The sexual weapon. *Time,* pp. 27–29.

DuBois, P. M. (1980). *The hospice way of death.* New York: Human Science Press.

Duke, M., & Nowicki, S., Jr. (1979). *Abnormal psychology: Perspectives on being different.* Monterey, CA: Brooks/Cole.

Duncker, K. (1945). On problem solving. *Psychological Monographs, 58* (5, Whole No. 270).

Dunkle, T. (1982, April). The sound of silence. *Science 82,* pp. 30–33.

Dunner, D. L., & Somervill, J. W. (1977). Medical treatments. In D. C. Rimm & J. W. Somervill (Eds.), *Abnormal psychology* (pp. 591–614). New York: Academic Press.

Dunnette, M. D. (1966). *Personnel selection and placement.* Belmont, CA: Wadsworth Publishing.

Dunnette, M. D. (Ed.). (1976). *Handbook of industrial and organizational psychology.* Chicago: Rand McNally.

Dunnette, M. D., & Borman, W. C. (1979). Personnel selection and classification systems. *Annual Review of Psychol-*

ogy, 30, 477–525.

Dunnette, M. D., & Kirchner, W. K. (1965). *Psychology applied to industry*. New York: Appleton-Century-Crofts.

Dunnette, M. D., & Motowidlo, S. J. (1975, June). *Development of a personnel assessment and career assessment system for police officers in patrol, investigative, supervisory, and command positions: Final report*. Minneapolis, MN: Personnel Decisions.

Dush, D. M., Hirt, M. L., & Schroeder, H. (1983). Self-statement modification with adults: A meta-analysis. *Psychological Bulletin, 94*, 408–422.

Dworetzky, J. P. (1982). *Psychology*. St. Paul, MN: West.

Dworetzky, J. P. (1981). *Introduction to child development*. St. Paul, MN: West.

Dyck, R., & Rule B. G. (1978). Effect on retaliation of causal attributions concerning attack. *Journal of Personality and Social Psychology, 36*, 521–529.

Dyke, C. V., & Byck, R. (1982, March). Cocaine. *Scientific American*, pp. 128–141.

Eagly, A. H. (1983). Gender and social influence: A social psychological analysis. *American Psychologist, 38*, 971–981.

Earn, B. M. (1982). Intrinsic motivation as a function of extrinsic financial rewards and subjects' locus of control. *Journal of Personality, 50*, 360–373.

Edelman, M. W. (1981). Who is for children? *American Psychologist, 36*, 109–116.

Edney, J. J. (1972). Property, possession, and permanence: A field study in human territoriality. *Journal of Applied Social Psychology, 3*, 275–282.

Edney, J. J., & Jordan-Edney, N. L. (1974). Territorial spacing on a beach. *Sociometry, 37*, 92–104.

Educational Testing Service. (1980a). *In fact*. Princeton, NJ: Author.

Educational Testing Service. (1980b) *Test use and validity: A response to charges in the Nader/Nairn report on ETS*. Princeton, NJ: Educational Testing Service.

Eisdorfer, C. (1983). Conceptual models of aging: The challenge of a new frontier. *American Psychologist, 38*, 197–202.

Ekman, P. (1973). Cross cultural studies of facial expression. In P. Ekman (Ed.), *Darwin and facial expression* (pp. 169–229). New York: Academic Press.

Ekman, P., & Friesen, W. V. (1975). *Unmasking the face*. Englewood Cliffs, NJ: Prentice-Hall.

Ekman, P., Friesen, W. V., & Ancoli, S. (1980). Facial signs of emotional experience. *Journal of Personality and Social Psychology, 39*, 1125–1134.

Elite sperm bank announces April birth of first child. (1982, May 26). *Texas A&M University Battalion*, p. 5.

Ellis, A., & Harper, R. A. (1975). *A new guide to rational living*. Englewood Cliffs, NJ: Prentice-Hall.

Ellis, E. (1977). Rational-emotive psychotherapy. In W. S. Sahakian (Ed.), *Psychotherapy and counseling: Techniques in intervention* (pp. 272–285). Chicago: Rand McNally.

Ellis, H. C. (1972). *Fundamentals of human learning and cognition*. Dubuque, IA: Wm. C. Brown.

Ellis, H. C., Bennett, T. L., Daniel, T. C., & Rickert, E. J. (1979). *Psychology of learning and memory*. Monterey, CA: Brooks/Cole.

Ellis, L., & Beattie, C. (1983). The feminist explanation for rape—An empirical test. *The Journal of Sex Research, 19*, 74–93.

Emde, R. N., Gaensbauer, T. J., & Harmon, R. J. (1976). Emotional expression in infancy: A biobehavioral study [Monograph 1]. *Psychological Issues, 10*, 1–198.

Emde, R. N., & Harmon, R. J., (Eds.). (1982). *The development of attachment and affiliative systems*. New York: Plenum Press.

Emery, R. E. (1982). Interparental conflict and the children of discord and divorce. *Psychological Bulletin, 92*, 310–330.

Engel, B. T., Glasgow, M. S., & Gaarder, K. R. (1983). Behavioral treatment of high blood pressure: III. Follow-up results and treatment recommendations. *Psychosomatic Medicine, 45*, 23–30.

Epstein, C. F. (1971). *Woman's place*. Berkeley: University of California Press.

Epstein, Y. M. (1981). Crowding stress and human behavior. *Journal of Social Issues, 37*, 126–144.

Epstein, Y. M. (1982). Crowding stress and human behavior. In G. W. Evans (Ed.), *Environmental stress* (pp. 133–150). Cambridge: Cambridge University Press.

Epstein, Y. M., & Karlin, R. A. (1975). Effects of acute experimental crowding. *Journal of Applied Social Psychology, 5*, 34–53.

Ericsson, K. A., Chase, W. G., & Faloon, S. (1980). Acquisition of a memory skill. *Science, 208*, 1181–1182.

Erikson, E. H. (1963). *Childhood and society* (2nd ed.) . New York: W. W. Norton.

Erikson, E. H. (1968). *Identity: Youth and crisis*. New York: W. W. Norton.

Eron, L. D. (1980). Prescription for reduction of aggression. *American Psychologist, 35*, 244–252.

Eron, L. D. (1982). Parent-child interaction, television violence, and aggression of children. *American Psychologist, 37*, 197–211.

Eron, L. D., Huesmann, L. R., Brice, P., Fischer, P., & Mermelstein, R. (1983). Age trends in the development of aggression, sex typing, and related telvision habits. *Developmental Psychology, 19*, 71–77.

Etaugh, C. (1980). Effects of nonmaternal care on children: Research evidence and popular views. *American Psychologist, 35*, 309–319.

Ethical principles of psychologists (1981). *American Psychologist, 36*, 633–638.

Etzioni, A. (1974, September). On the scientific manipulation of juries. *Human Behavior*, pp. 10–11.

Evans, G. W. (1979). Behavioral and physiological consequences of crowding in humans. *Journal of Applied Social Psychology, 9*, 27–46.

Evans, R. I. (1976). *The making of psychology*. New York: Knopf.

Evarts, E. V. (1979). Brain mechanisms of movement. In *The brain: A Scientific American book* (pp. 98–106). San Francisco: W. H. Freeman.

Everett, P. B., Hayward, S. C., & Myers, A. W. (1974). The effects of a token reinforcement procedure on bus ridership. *Journal of Applied Behavior Analysis, 1,* 1–9.

Eysenck, H. J. (1970). *The structure of human personality* (3rd ed.). London: Methuen.

Eysenck, H. J. (1975). *The inequality of man.* San Diego: Edits Publishers.

Eysenck, H. J. (1965). *Crime and personality.* New York: Houghton Mifflin.

Eysenck, H. J., & Rachman, S. (1965). *The causes and cures of neurosis.* San Diego, CA: Robert R. Knapp.

Fairchild, L., & Erwin, W. M. (1977). Physical punishment by parent figures as a model of aggressive behavior in children. *Journal of Genetic Psychology, 130,* 279–284.

Falk, J. L., Schuster, C. R., Bigelow, G. E., & Woods, J. H. (1982). Progress and needs in the experimental analysis of drug and alcohol dependence. *American Psychologist, 37,* 1124–1127.

Fancher, R. E. (1979) *Pioneers of psychology.* New York: W. W. Norton.

Fantz, R. L. (1958). Pattern vision in young infants. *Psychological Record, 8,* 43–47.

Fantz, R. L., Fagan, J. F., & Miranda, S. B. (1975). Early visual selectivity. In L. B. Cohen & P. Salapatek (Eds.), *Infant perception: From sensation to cognition* (Vol. 1, pp. 249–345). New York: Academic Press.

Fazio, R. H. (1981). On the self-perception explanation of the overjustification effect: The role of the salience of initial attitude. *Journal of Experimental Social Psychology, 17,* 417–426

Fazio, R. H., Cooper, M., Dayson, K., & Johnson, M. (1981). Control and the coronary-prone behavior pattern: Responses to multiple situational demands. *Personality and Social Psychology Bulletin, 7,* 97–102.

Fazio, R. H., Powell, M. C., & Herr, P. M. (1983). Toward a process model of the attitude-behavior relation: Accessing one's attitude upon mere observation of the attitude object. *Journal of Personality and Social Psychology, 44,* 723–735.

Fehr, L. A. (1983). *Introduction to personality.* New York: Macmillan.

Feighner, J. P. (1983). The new generation of antidepressants. *The Journal of Clinical Psychiatry, 44,* 49–55.

Felipe, H., & Sommer, R. (1966). Invasions of personal space. *Social Problems, 14,* 206–214.

Ferguson, T. J., Rule, B. G., & Lindsay, R. C. L. (1982). The effects of caffeine and provocation on aggression. *Journal of Research in Personality, 16,* 60–71.

Ferster, C. B., & Skinner, B. F. (1957). *Schedules of reinforcement.* New York: Appleton-Century-Crofts.

Feshbach, S., & Weiner, B. (1982). *Personality.* Lexington, MA: D. C. Heath.

Festinger, L. (1950). Informal social communication. *Psychological Review, 57,* 271–282.

Festinger, L. (1954). A theory of social comparison processes. *Human Relations, 7,* 117–140.

Festinger, L., (1957). *A theory of cognitive dissonance.* Stanford, CA: Stanford University Press.

Festinger, L., & Carlsmith, J. M. (1959). Cognitive consequences of forced compliance. *Journal of Abnormal and Social Psychology, 58,* 203–210.

Festinger, L., Schachter, S., & Back, K. (1950). *Social pressures in informal groups: A study of human factors in housing.* New York: Harper & Row.

Field, T. M., Woodson, R., Greenberg, R., & Cohen, D. (1982). Discrimination and imitation of facial expressions by neonates. *Science, 218,* 179–181.

Fincher, J. (1982, August). Before their time. *Science 82,* pp. 78–88.

Findley, M. J., & Cooper, H. M. (1983). Locus of control and academic achievement: A literature review. *Journal of Personality and Social Psychology, 44,* 419–427.

Fish, B., Karabenick, S., & Heath, M. (1978). The effects of observation on emotional arousal and affiliation. *Journal of Experimental Social Psychology, 14,* 256–265.

Fisher, J. D., & Byrne, D. (1975). Too close for comfort: Sex differences in response to invasions of personal space. *Journal of Personality and Social Psychology, 32,* 15–21.

Fisher, K., & Cunningham, S. (1983, January). The dilemma: Problem grows, support shrinks. *APA Monitor,* p. 2.

Fisher, S., & Greenberg, R. P. (1977). *The scientific credibility of Freud's theories and therapy.* New York: Basic Books.

Fisher, W. A. (1983). Adolescent contraception: Summary and recommendations. In D. Byrne & W. A. Fisher (Eds.), *Adolescents, sex, and contraception* (pp. 273–300). Hillsdale, NJ: Erlbaum.

Fisher, W. A., Byrne, D., & White, L. A. (1983). Emotional barriers to contraception. In D. Byrne & W. A. Fisher (Eds.), *Adolescents, sex, and contraception* (pp. 207–239). Hillsdale, NJ: Erlbaum.

Flavell, J. H. (1977). *Cognitive development.* Englewood Cliffs, NJ: Prentice-Hall.

Fleece, L., O'Brien, T., & Drabman, R. (1982). Suppression of biting behavior via contingent application of an aversive tasting liquid. *Journal of Clinical Child Psychology, 11,* 163–166.

Fleming, R., Baum, A., Gisriel, M. M., & Gatchel, R. J. (1982). Mediating influences of social support on stress at Three Mile Island. *Journal of Human Stress, 8,* 14–23.

Foss, D. J., & Hakes, D. T. (1978). *Psycholinguistics: An introduction to the psychology of language.* Englewood Cliffs, NJ.: Prentice-Hall.

Foss, G. L. (1982). Artificial insemination by donor: A review of 12 years' experience. *Journal of Biosocial Science, 14,* 253–262.

Foulkes, D. (1966). *The psychology of sleep.* New York: Scribner's.

Foulkes, D. (1978, December). Dreams of innocence. *Psychology Today*, pp. 78–88.

Fouts, R. S., & Rigby, R. L. (1977). Man-chimpanzee communication. In T. A. Sebeok (Eds.), *How animals communicate* (pp. 1034–1054). Bloomington: Indiana University Press.

Fox, L. H. (1981). Identification of the academically gifted. *American Psychologist, 36*, 1103–1111.

Foxx, R. M., & Hake, D. F. (1977). Gasoline conservation: A procedure for measuring and reducing the driving of college students. *Journal of Applied Behavior Analysis, 10*, 61–74.

Frank, J. D. (1973). *Persuasion and healing: A comparative study of psychotherapy*. Baltimore: Johns Hopkins University Press.

Franken, R. E. (1982). *Human motivation*. Monterey, CA: Brooks/Cole.

Frederiksen, N., Ward, W. C., & Carlson, S. B. (1980). Can multiple-choice tests measure creativity? *Findings, 6*, 1–4.

Freedman, J. L., & Fraser, S. C. (1966). Compliance without pressure: The foot-in-the-door technique. *Journal of Personality and Social Psychology, 4*, 195–202.

Freedman, J. L., Sears, D. O., & Carlsmith, J. M. (1981). *Social psychology* (4th ed.). Englewood Cliffs, NJ: Prentice-Hall.

Fretz, B. R., & Leong, F. T. L. (1982). Vocational behavior and career development, 1981: A review. *Journal of Vocational Behavior, 21*, 123–163.

Fretz, B. R., & Stang, D. J. (1982). *Preparing for graduate study in psychology: Not for seniors only*. Washington, DC: American Psychological Association.

Freud, S. (1913). *The interpretation of dreams* (3rd ed.). New York: Macmillan.

Freud, S. (1938). *An outline of psychoanalysis*. London: Hogarth Press.

Freud, S. (1952). *A general introduction to psychoanalysis* (J. Riviere, Trans.). New York: Washington Square Press. (Original work published 1924)

Freud, S. (1955). Beyond the pleasure principle. In J. Strachey (Ed. and Trans.), *The standard edition of the complete psychological works of Sigmund Freud* (Vol. 18, pp. 7–64). London: Hogarth Press. (Original work published 1920)

Freud, S. (1964). *New introductory lectures on psychoanalysis* (J. Strachey, Trans.). New York: W. W. Norton. (Original work published 1933)

Freud, S. (1974). *Cocaine papers* (R. Byck, Ed.). New York: New American Library. (Original work published 1885)

Friedman, M., & Rosenman, R. H. (1974). *Type A behavior and your heart*. New York: Knopf.

Friedman, S. L., & Sigman, M. (Eds.). (1981). *Preterm birth and psychological development*. New York: Academic Press.

Fromer, M. J. (1983, January). Motion sickness: All in your head? *Psychology Today*, p. 65.

Fuchs, F. (1980, June). Genetic amniocentesis. *Scientific American*, pp. 47–53.

Fuller, J. J., & Simmel, E. C. (Eds.) (1983). *Behavior genetics*. Hillsdale, NJ: Erlbaum.

Gagné, R. M., & Dick, W. (1983). Instructional psychology. *Annual Review of Psychology, 34*, 261–295.

Galanter, E. (1962). Contemporary psychophysics. In R. Brown (Ed.), *New directions in psychology* (Vol. 1, pp. 87–156). New York: Holt, Rinehart and Winston.

Galbraith, R. C. (1982). Sibling spacing and intellectual development: A closer look at the confluence models. *Developmental Psychology, 18*, 151–173.

Gallatin, J. (1982). *Abnormal psychology: Concepts, issues, trends*. New York: Macmillan.

Galton, F. (1869). *Hereditary genius: An inquiry into its laws and consequences*. New York: Macmillan.

Galton, F. (1883). *Inquiries into human faculty and its development*. New York: Macmillan.

Gardner, G. T. (1978). Effects of federal human subjects regulations on data obtained in environmental stressor research. *Journal of Personality and Social Psychology, 36*, 628–634.

Gardner, L. I. (1973). Deprivation dwarfism. In *The nature and nurture of behavior: Readings from Scientific American* (pp. 101–107). San Francisco: W. H. Freeman.

Gardner, M. (1981). *Science: Good, bad, and bogus*. Buffalo, NY: Prometheus Books.

Gardner, M. (1983, August). Illusions of the third dimension. *Psychology Today*, pp. 62–67.

Gardner, R. A., & Gardner, B. T. (1969). Teaching sign language to a chimpanzee. *Science, 165*, 664–672.

Garfield, E. (1983, April 11). The dilemma of prolongevity research—must we age before we die, or if we don't, will we? *Current Contents*, No. 15, 5–18.

Garfield, S. L. (1981). Psychotherapy: A 40-year appraisal. *American Psychologist, 36*, 174–183.

Garfield, S. L. (1983). Effectiveness of psychotherapy: The perennial controversy. *Professional Psychology, 14*, 35–43.

Garfinkel, P. (1983, September). The best 'Jewish mother' in the world. *Psychology Today*, pp. 56–60.

Gastorf, J. W. (1980). Time urgency of the Tye A behavior pattern. *Journal of Consulting and Clinical Psychology, 48*, 299.

Gatchel, R. J., & Mears, F. G. (1982). *Personality: Theory, assessment, and research*. New York: St. Martin's Press.

Gazzaniga, M. S. (1970). *The bisected brain*. New York: Appleton-Century-Crofts.

Gazzaniga, M. S. (1983). Right hemisphere language following brain bisection: A 20-year perspective. *American Psychologist, 38*, 525–537.

Geen, R. G. (1968). Effects of frustration, attack, and prior training in aggressiveness upon aggressive behavior. *Journal of Personality and Social Psychology, 9*, 316–321.

Geen, R. G. (1976). *Personality: The skein of behavior*. Saint Louis, MO: C. V. Mosby.

Geen, R. G. (1978a). Effects of attack and uncontrollable

noise on aggression. *Journal of Research in Personality, 12,* 15–29.

Geen, R. G. (1978b). Some effects of observing violence upon the behavior of the observer. In B. A. Maher (Ed.), *Progress in experimental personality research* (Vol. 8). New York: Academic Press.

Geen, R. G. (1981). Behavioral and physiological reactions to observed violence: Effects of prior exposure to aggressive stimuli. *Journal of Personality and Social Psychology, 40,* 868–875.

Geer, J. H. (1965). The development of a scale to measure fear. *Behaviour Research and Therapy, 3,* 45–53.

Geiselman, R. E., Bjork, R. A., & Fishmen, D. L. (1983). Disrupted retrieval in directed forgetting: A link with posthypnotic amnesia. *Journal of Experimental Psychology: General, 112,* 58–72.

Geldard, F. A. (1972). *The human senses* (2nd ed.). New York: Wiley.

Geller, D. M (1980). Responses to urban stimuli: A balanced approach. *Journal of Social Issues, 36,* 86–100.

Geller, E. S., Witmer, J. F., & Tuso, M. A. (1977). Environmental interventions for litter control. *Journal of Applied Psychology, 62,* 344–351.

Gelman, D. (1981, May 18). Just how the sexes differ. *Newsweek,* pp. 72–75, 78, 81, 83.

Gelman, R. (1969). Conservation acquisition: A problem of learning to attend to relevant attributes. *Journal of Experimental Child Psychology, 7,* 167–187.

Gerrard, M. (1983). Sex, sex guilt, and contraceptive use. *Journal of Personality and Social Psychology, 42,* 153–158.

Geschwind, N. (1979). Specializations of the human brain. In *The brain: A Scientific American book* (pp. 108–117). San Francisco: W. H. Freeman.

Gesell, A., Halverson, H. M., Thompson, H., Ilg, F. L., Castner, B. M., Ames, L. B., & Amatruda, C. S. (1940). *The first five years of life: A guide to the study of the preschool child.* New York: Harper & Brothers.

Getts, A. G., & Hill, H. F. (1982). Sudden infant death syndrome: Incidence at various altitudes. *Developmental Medicine and Child Neurology, 24,* 61–68.

Gibson, E. J., & Walk, R. D. (1973). The "visual cliff." In *The nature and nurture of behavior: Readings from Scientific American* (pp. 19–26). San Francisco: W. H. Freeman.

Gibson, J. J. (1966). *The senses considered as perceptual systems.* Boston: Houghton Mifflin.

Gifford, R. (1982). Projected interpersonal distance and orientation choices: Personality, sex, and social situation. *Social Psychology Quarterly, 45,* 145–152.

Gilberstadt, H., & Duker, J. (1965). *A handbook for clinical and actuarial MMPI interpretation.* Philadelphia: W. B. Saunders.

Gilbert, S. J. (1981). Another look at the Milgram obedience studies: The role of the gradated series of shocks. *Personality and Social Psychology Bulletin, 7,* 690–695.

Glasgow, M. S., Gaarder, K. R., & Engel, B. T. (1982). Behavioral treatment of high blood pressure: II. Acute and sustained effects of relaxation and systolic blood pressure biofeedback. *Pyschosomatic Medicine, 44,* 155–170.

Glass, D. C. (1977). *Behavior patterns, stress, and coronary disease.* New York: Wiley.

Glass, D. C., & Singer, J. E. (1972). *Urban stress.* New York: Academic Press.

Glass, D. C., Singer, J. E., & Friedman, L. N. (1969). Psychic cost of adaptation to an environmental stressor. *Journal of Personality and Social Psychology, 12,* 200–210.

Glass, D. C., Singer, J. E., & Pennebaker, J. W. (1977). Behavioral and physiological effects of uncontrollable environmental events. In D. S. Stokols (Ed.), *Perspectives on environment and behavior: Theory, research, and applications* (pp. 131–151). New York: Plenum Publishing.

Glenberg, A. M., Bradley, M. M., Kraus, T. A., & Renzaglia, G. J. (1983). Studies of the long-term recency effect: Support for a contextually guided retrieval hypothesis. *Journal of Experimental Psychology: Learning, Memory, and Cognition, 9,* 231–255.

Glover, J. A., Plake, B. S., & Zimmer, J. W. (1982). Distinctiveness of encoding and memory for learning tasks. *Journal of Educational Psychology, 74,* 189–198.

Glucksberg, S., & Danks, J. H. (1975). *Experimental psycholinguistics: An introduction.* Hillsdale, NJ: Erlbaum.

Goldband, S. (1980). Stimulus specificity of physiological response to stress and the Type A coronary-prone behavior pattern. *Journal of Personality and Social Psychology, 39,* 670–679.

Goldfried, M. R., & Robins, C. (1982). On the facilitation of self-efficacy. *Cognitive Therapy and Research, 6,* 361–380.

Goldin-Meadow, S., & Feldman, H. (1977). The development of language-like communication without a language model. *Science, 197,* 401–403.

Goldstein, E. B. (1980). *Sensation and perception.* Belmont, CA: Wadsworth.

Goleman, D. (1978, November). Special abilities of the sexes: Do they begin in the brain? *Psychology Today,* pp. 48–49, 51, 53–56, 59, 120.

Goleman, D. (1982, March). Staying up: The rebellion against sleep's gentle tyranny. *Psychology Today,* pp. 24–35.

Goodall, J. (1971). *In the shadow of man.* Boston: Houghton Mifflin.

Goodstein, L. D., & Calhoun, J. F. (1982). *Understanding abnormal behavior: Description, explanation, management.* Reading, MA: Addison-Wesley.

Goodstein, L. D., & Lanyon, R. I. (1979). *Adjustment, behavior, and personality* (2nd ed.). Readings, MA: Addison-Wesley.

Gottesman, I. I. (1963). Genetic aspects of intelligent behavior. In N. Ellis (Ed.), *Handbook of mental deficiency: Psychological theory and research.* (pp.253–296). New York: McGraw-Hill.

Gottesman, I. I., & Shields, J. (1976). A critical review of recent adoption, twin, and family studies of schizophrenia: Behavioral genetics perspectives. *Schizophrenia Bulletin, 2,* 360–398.

Gottschalk, C. A. (1983). Vulnerability to stress. *American Journal of Psychotherapy, 37,* 5–23.

Gottschalk, C. A., Welch, W. D., & Weiss, J. (1983). Vulnerability and immune response: An overview. *Psychotherapy and Psychosomatics, 39,* 23–35.

Green, D. M., & Birdsall, T. G. (1978). Detection and recognition. *Psychological Review, 85,* 192–206.

Greenberg, J., Pyszczynski, T., & Solomon, S. (1982). The self-serving attributional bias: Beyond self-presentation. *Journal of Experimental Social Psychology, 18,* 56–67.

Greene, E., Flynn, M. S., & Loftus, E. F. (1982). Introducing resistance to misleading information. *Journal of Verbal Learning and Verbal Behavior, 21,* 207–219.

Greene, J. (1982, September). The gambling trap. *Psychology Today,* pp. 50–55.

Greene, R. L. (1980). *The MMPI: An interpretive manual.* New York: Grune & Stratton.

Greenough, W. T., & Green, E. J. (1981). Experience and the changing brain. In J. L. McGaug, J G. March, & S. B. Kiesler (Eds.), *Aging: Biology and behavior* (pp. 159–200). New York: Academic Press.

Gregory, R. L. (1977). *Eye and brain* (3rd ed.). New York: McGraw-Hill.

Greif, E. B., & Ulman, K. J. (1982). The psychological impact of menarche on early adolescent females: A review of the literature. *Child Development, 53,* 1413–1430.

Griffitt, W. (1970). Environmental effects on interpersonal affective behavior: Ambient effective temperature and attraction. *Journal of Personality and Social Psychology, 15,* 240–244.

Griffitt, W., & Veitch, R. (1971). Hot and crowded: Influences of population density and temperature on interpersonal affective behavior. *Journal of Personality and Social Psychology, 17,* 92–98.

Grossman, H. J. (Ed.). (1977). *Manual on terminology and classification in mental retardation.* Washington, DC: American Association on Mental Deficiency.

Grossman, H. J. (Ed.). (1981). *Manual on terminology and classification in mental retardation* (rev. ed.). Washington, DC: American Association on Mental Retardation.

Grotevant, H. D., Scarr, S., & Weinberg, R. A. (1977). Intellectual development in family constellations with adopted and natural children: A test of the Zajonc and Markus model. *Child Development, 48,* 1699–1703.

Grusec, J. E. (1981). Socialization processes and the development of altruism. In J. P. Rushton & R. M. Sorrentino (Eds.), *Altruism and helping behavior: Social, personality, and developmental perspectives* (pp. 65–90). Hillsdale, NJ: Erlbaum.

Guilford, J. P. (1959). *Personality.* New York: McGraw-Hill.

Gurman, A. S., & Kniskern, D. P. (1978). Research on marital and family therapy: Progress, perspective, and prospect. In S. L. Garfield & A. E. Bergin (Eds.), *Handbook of psychotherapy and behavior change: An empirical analysis* (2nd ed., pp. 817–901). New York: Wiley.

Haber, R. N. (1978). Visual perception. *Annual Review of Psychology, 29,* 31–59.

Haith, M. M. (1980). *Rules that babies look by: The organization of newborn visual activity.* Hillsdale, NJ: Erlbaum.

Haith, M. M., & Goodman, G. S. (1982). Eye-movement control in newborns in darkness and in unstructured light. *Child Development, 53,* 974–977.

Hall, C. S., Domhoff, G. W., Blick, K. A. & Weesner, K. E. (1982). The dreams of college men and women in 1950 and 1980: A comparison of dream contents and sex differences. *Sleep, 5,* 188–194.

Hall, C. S., & Van de Castle, R. L. (1966). *The content analysis of dreams.* New York: Appleton-Century-Crofts.

Hall, E. (1983, June). A conversation with Erik Erikson. *Psychology Today,* pp. 22–30.

Hall, E., Perlmutter, M., & Lamb, M. E. (1982). *Child psychology today.* New York: Random House.

Hall, E. T. (1966). *The hidden dimension.* New York: Doubleday.

Hall, G. S. (1904). *Adolescence: Its psychology and its relations to physiology, anthropology, sociology, sex, crime, religion, and education.* (Vol. 1). New York: Appleton.

Hall, J. F. (1983). Recall versus recognition: A methodological note. *Journal of Experimental Psychology: Learning, Memory, and Cognition, 9,* 346–349.

Halmi, K. A. (1983). Psychosomatic illness review; 6. Anorexia nervosa and bulimia. *Psychosomatics, 24,* 111–132.

Hamer, B. (1982, July–August). All in the family. *Science 82,* pp. 88–89.

Hamilton, E. W., & Abramson, L. Y. (1983). Cognitive patterns and major depressive disorder: A longitudinal study in a hospital setting. *Journal of Abnormal Psychology, 92,* 173–184.

Hansel, C. E. M. (1980). *ESP and parapsychology: A critical reevaluation.* Buffalo, NY: Prometheus Books.

Hardyck, C., & Petrinovich, L. F. (1977). Left-handedness. *Psychological Bulletin, 84,* 385–404.

Harlow, H. F. (1958). The nature of love. *American Psychologist, 13,* 673–685.

Harlow, H. F. (1971). *Learning to love.* San Francisco: Albion.

Harlow, H. F. (1973). Love in infant monkeys. In *The nature and nurture of behavior: Readings from Scientific American* (pp. 94–100). San Francisco: Freeman.

Harper, G. (1983). Varieties of parenting failure in anorexia nervosa: Protection and parentectomy, revisited. *Journal of the American Academy of Child Psychiatry, 22,* 134–139.

Harrell, T. W. (1972). High earning MBAs. *Personnel Psychology, 25,* 523–530.

Harrell, T. W., & Harrell, M. S. (1945). Army general classification test scores for civilian occupations. *Educational and Psychological Measurement, 5,* 229–239.

Harris, B. (1979). Whatever happened to little Albert? *Ameri-*

can *Psychologist, 34,* 151–160.

Hartmann, E. L. (1973). *The functions of sleep.* New Haven, CT: Yale University Press.

Hartmann, E. L. (1981, April). The strangest sleep disorder. *Psychology Today,* pp. 14–18.

Hathaway, S. R., & Monachesi, E. D. (1952). The Minnesota Multiphasic Personality Inventory in the study of juvenile delinquents. *American Sociological Review, 17,* 704–710.

Havighurst, R. J. (1972). *Developmental tasks and education* (3rd ed.). New York: David McKay.

Hayduk, L. A. (1983). Personal space: Where we now stand. *Psychological Bulletin, 94,* 293–335.

Hayes, K. J., & Hayes, C. (1951). The intellectual development of a homeraised chimpanzee. *Proceedings of the American Philosophical Society, 95,* 105–109.

Hayes, S. C., & Cone, J. D. (1977). Reducing residential electrical energy use: Payments, information, and feedback. *Journal of Applied Behavior Analysis, 10,* 425–435.

Hayes, S. C., Johnson, V. S., & Cone, J. D. (1975). The marked item technique: A practical procedure for litter control. *Journal of Applied Behavior Analysis, 8,* 381–386.

Haygood, R. C., & Bourne, L. E., Jr. (1965). Attribute- and rule-learning aspects of conceptual behavior. *Psychological Review, 72,* 175–195.

Haywood, H. C., Meyers, C. E., & Switzky, H. N. (1982). Mental retardation. *Annual Review of Psychology, 33,* 309–342.

Hazen, N. L., & Durrett, M. E. (1982). Relationship of security of attachment to exploration and cognitive mapping abilities in 2-year-olds. *Developmental Psychology, 18,* 751–759.

Hebb, D. O. (1955). Drives and the C.N.S. (conceptual nervous system). *Psychological Review, 62,* 243–254.

Hechinger, N. (1981, March). Seeing without eyes. *Science 81,* pp. 38–43.

Heider, F. (1958). *The psychology of interpersonal relations.* New York: Wiley.

Held, R., & Hein, A. (1963). Movement-produced stimulation in the development of visually-guided behavior. *Journal of Comparative and Physiological Psychology, 56,* 872–876.

Helmreich, R. L., Beane, W. E., Lucker, G. W., & Spence, J. T. (1978). Achievement motivation and scientific attainment. *Personality and Social Psychology Bulletin, 4,* 222–226.

Helmreich, R. L., & Spence, J. T. (1978). The Work and Family Orientation Questionnaire: An objective instrument to assess components of achievement motivation and attitudes toward family and career. *JSAS Catalog of Selected Documents in Psychology, 8,* 35. (Ms. No. 1677.)

Helmreich, R. L., Spence, J. T., Beane, W. E., Lucker, G. W., & Matthews, K. A. (1980). Making it in academic psychology: Demographic and personality correlates of attainment. *Journal of Personality and Social Psychology, 39,* 896–908.

Henderson, N. D. (1982). Human behavior genetics. *Annual Review of Psychology, 33,* 403–440.

Hendren, R. L. (1983). Depression in anorexia nervosa. *Journal of the American Academy of Child Psychiatry, 22,* 59–62.

Hennig, M., & Jardim, A. (1977). *The managerial woman.* Garden City, NY: Anchor Press.

Herman, C. P., & Mack, D. (1975). Restrained and unrestrained eating. *Journal of Personality, 43,* 647–660.

Heron, W. (1957, January). The pathology of boredom. *Scientific American,* pp. 52–56.

Herrnstein R. J. (1973). *I.Q. in the meritocracy.* Boston: Little, Brown.

Herron, J. (ed.). (1979). *Neuropsychology of left-handedness.* He's a college grad—at 12. (1982, May 17) *Denver Post,* p.8A New York: Academic Press.

Hetherington, E. M. (1979). Divorce: A child's perspective. *American Psychologist, 34,* 851–858.

Hetherington, E. M. (n.d.). Divorce—It's family conflict that hurts children. *Science for families: T.V. Newsfeature Project.* Boys Town, NB: Boys Town Center for the Study of Youth Development.

Hetherington, E. M., Cox, M., & Cox, R. (1982). Effects of divorce on parents and children. In M. E. Lamb (Ed.), *Nontraditional familes: Parenting and child development* (pp. 233–288). Hillsdale, NJ: Erlbaum.

Hibscher, J. A., & Herman, C. P. (1977). Obesity, dieting, and the expression of "obese" characteristics. *Journal of Comparative and Physiological Psychology, 91,* 374–380.

Higgins, E. T., Rhodewalt, F., & Zanna, M. P. (1979). Dissonance motivation: Its nature, persistence, and reinstatement. *Journal of Experimental Social Psychology, 15,* 16–34.

Hilgard, E.R. (Ed.). (1978). *American psychology in historical perspective.* Washington, D.C.: American Psychological Association.

Hilgard, E. R. (1980). Consciousness in contemporary psychology. *Annual Review of Psychology, 31,* 1–26.

Hilgard, E. R. (1982). Hypnotic susceptibility and implications for measurement. *The International Journal of Clinical and Experimental Hypnosis, 30,* 394–403.

Hilgard, E. R., Atkinson, R. L., & Atkinson, R. C. (1979). *Introduction to psychology* (7th ed.). New York: Harcourt Brace Jovanovich.

Hilgard, E. R., & Bower, G. H. (1975). *Theories of learning* (4th ed.). Englewood Cliffs, NJ: Prentice-Hall.

Hilgard, E. R., & Hilgard, J. R. (1975). *Hypnosis in the relief of pain.* Los Altos, CA; Kaufmann.

Hillyard, S. A., & Kutas, M. (1983). Electrophysiology of cognitive processing. *Annual Review of Psychology, 34,* 33–61.

Hirsch, H. V. B., & Spinelli, D. N. (1970). Visual experience modifies distribution of horizontally and vertically oriented receptive fields in cats. *Science, 168,* 869-871.

Hirsch, H. V. B., & Spinelli, D. N. (1971). Modification of the distribution of receptive field orientation in cats by selective visual exposure during development. *Experimental Brain Research, 12,* 509–527.

Hirst, W. (1982). The amnesic syndrome: Descriptions and explanations. *Psychological Bulletin, 91,* 435–460.

Hite, S. (1976). *The Hite report.* New York: Macmillan.

Hochberg, J. E. (1978). *Perception* (2nd ed.). Englewood Cliffs, NJ: Prentice-Hall.

Hochman, G. (1976, November 14). Inside the mind of a brilliant child. *Houston Post,* pp. 4, 6.

Hodges, W., & Cooper, M. (1981). Head Start and follow through: Influences on intellectual development. *Journal of Special Education, 15,* 221–238.

Hoff-Ginsberg, E., & Shatz, M. (1982). Linguistic input and the child's acquisition of language. *Psychological Bulletin, 92,* 3–26.

Hoffman, J. W., Benson, H., Arns, P. A., Stainbrook, G. L., Landsberg, L., Young, J. B., & Gill, A. (1982). Reduced sympathetic nervous system responsivity associated with the relaxation response. *Science, 215,* 190–192.

Hoffman, L. W. (1974). Effects of maternal employment on the child: A review of the research. *Developmental Psychology, 10,* 204–228.

Hoffman, L. W. (1979). Maternal employment: 1979. *American Psychologist, 34,* 859–865.

Hoffman, M. L. (1975). Moral internalization, parental power and the nature of parent-child interaction. *Developmental Psychology, 11,* 228–239.

Hoffman, M. L. (1979). Development of moral thought, feeling, and behavior. *American Psychologist, 34,* 958–966.

Holahan, C. J. (1982). *Environmental psychology.* New York: Random House.

Holland, J. L. (1973). *Making vocational choices: A theory of careers.* Englewood Cliffs, NJ: Prentice-Hall.

Holland, M. K. (1975). *Using psychology: Principles of behavior and your life.* Boston: Little, Brown.

Hollon, S., & Beck, A. T. (1978). Psychotherapy and drug therapy: Comparisons and combinations. In S. L. Garfield & A. E. Bergin (Eds.), *Handbook of psychotherapy and behavior change: An empirical analysis* (2nd ed., pp. 437–490). New York: Wiley.

Holmes, D. L., Nagy, J. N., Slaymaker, F., Sosnowski, R. J., Prinz, S. M., & Pasternak, J. F. (1982). Early influences of prematurity, illness, and prolonged hospitalization on infant behavior. *Developmental Psychology, 18,* 744–750.

Holmes, T. H., & Masuda, M. (1974). Life changes and illness susceptibility. In B. S. Dohrenwend & B. P. Dohrenwend (Eds.), *Stressful life events: Their nature and effects* (pp. 45–72). New York: Wiley.

Holmes, T. H., & Rahe, R. H. (1967). The Social Readjustment Rating Scale. *Journal of Psychosomatic Research, 11,* 213–218.

Hooker, E. (1957). The adjustment of the male overt homosexual. *Journal of Projective Techniques, 21,* 18–31.

Horn, J. L. (1982). The aging of human abilities. In B. B. Wolman (Ed.), *Handbook of developmental psychology* (pp. 847–870). Englewood Cliffs, NJ: Prentice-Hall.

Horner, M. S. (1972). Toward an understanding of achievement-related conflicts in women. *Journal of Social Issues, 28,* 157–176.

Horvath, F. S. (1977). The effect of selected variables on interpretation of polygraph records. *Journal of Applied Psychology, 62,* 127–136.

Householder, J., Hatcher, R., Burns, W., & Chasnoff, I. (1982). Infants born to narcotic-addicted mothers. *Psychological Bulletin, 92,* 453–468.

Houston is facing nervous disorder, mental study says. (1979, May 1). *Bryan-College Station Eagle,* p. 1A.

Houston, B. K. (1983). Psychophysiological responsivity and the Type A behavior pattern. *Journal of Research in Personality, 17,* 22–39.

Houston, J. P. (1981). *Fundamentals of learning and memory* (2nd ed.). New York: Academic Press.

Hovland, C. I., & Weiss, W. (1952). The influence of source credibility on communication effectiveness. *Public Opinion Quarterly, 15,* 635–650.

Howard, D. V. (1983). *Cognitive psychology: Memory, language, and thought.* New York: Macmillan.

Hubel, D. H. (1972). The visual cortex of the brain. In *Perception: Mechanisms and models: Readings from Scientific American* (pp. 148–156). San Francisco: W. H. Freeman.

Hubel, D. H. (1979). The brain. In *The brain: A Scientific American book* (pp. 2–11). San Francisco: W. H. Freeman.

Hubel, D. H., & Wiesel, T. N. (1959). Receptive fields of single neurones in the cat's striate cortex. *Journal of Physiology, 148,* 574–591.

Hubel, D. H., & Wiesel, T. N. (1979). Brain mechanisms of vision. In *The brain: A Scientific American book* (pp. 84–96). San Francisco: W. H. Freeman.

Hubert, N. C., Wachs, T. D., Peters-Martin, P., & Gandour, M. J. (1982). The study of early temperament: Measurement and conceptual issues. *Child Development, 53,* 571–600.

Hudspeth, A. J. (1983, January). The hair cells of the inner ear. *Scientific American,* pp. 54–64.

Huesmann, L. R., Eron, L. D., Klein, R., Brice, P., & Fischer, P. (1983). Mitigating the imitation of aggressive behaviors by changing children's attitudes about media violence. *Journal of Personality and Social Psychology, 44,* 889–910.

Hull, C. L. (1943). *Principles of behavior: An introduction to behavior theory.* New York: Appleton-Century-Crofts.

Hulse, S. H., Egeth, H., & Deese, J. (1980). *The psychology of learning* (5th ed.). New York: McGraw-Hill.

Humphreys, L. (1980, April). Larry P.: Asking the wrong question? *APA Monitor,* p. 12.

Hunt, J. M. (1979). Psychological development: Early experience. *Annual Review of Psychology, 30,* 103–143.

Hunt, M. (1974). *Sexual behavior in the 1970s.* Chicago: Playboy Press.

Hurlock E. B. (1980). *Developmental psychology: A life-span approach* (5th ed.). New York: McGraw-Hill.

Hurvich, L., & Jameson, D. (1957). An opponent-process theory of color vision. *Psychological Review, 64,* 384–404.

Huston, T. L. (1974). A perspective on interpersonal attraction. In T. L. Huston (Ed.), *Foundations of interpersonal attraction* (pp. 3–28). New York: Academic Press.

Hyde, J. S. (1981). How large are cognitive gender differences? *American Psychologist, 36,* 892–901.

Hyde, J. S. (1982). *Understanding human sexuality* (2nd ed.). New York: McGraw-Hill.

Inglis, J., & Lawson, J. S. (1981). Sex differences in the effects of unilateral brain damage on intelligence. *Science, 212,* 693–695.

Insko, C. A., & Melson, W. H. (1969). Verbal reinforcement of attitude in laboratory and nonlaboratory contexts. *Journal of Personality, 37,* 25–40.

International encyclopedia of the social sciences: Biographical supplement (Vol. 18). (1976). London: Macmillan and Free Press.

Isaacs, W., Thomas, J., & Goldiamond, I. (1960). Application of operant conditioning to reinstate verbal behavior in psychotics. *Journal of Speech and Hearing Disorders, 25,* 8–12.

Isen, A. M., & Shalker, T. E. (1982). The effect of feeling state on evaluation of positive, neutral, and negative stimuli: When you "accentuate the positive," do you "eliminate the negative"? *Social Psychology Quarterly, 45,* 58–63.

Ittelson, W. H. (1952). *The Ames demonstration in perception.* Princeton, NJ: Princeton University Press.

Iversen, L. L. (1979). The chemistry of the brain. In *The brain: A Scientific American book* (pp. 70–81). San Francisco: W. H. Freeman.

Izard, C. E. (1977). *Human emotions.* New York: Plenum Publishing.

Jacobs, T. J., & Charles, E. (1980). Life events and the occurrence of cancer in children. *Psychosomatic Medicine, 42,* 11–24.

Jacobson, E. (1938). *Progressive relaxation.* Chicago: University of Chicago Press.

Jacoby, J. (1976). Consumer psychology: An octennium. *Annual Review of Psychology, 27,* 331–358.

James, W. (1884). What is an emotion? *Mind, 9,* 188–205.

Janda, L. H., & Klenke-Hamel, K. E. (1980). *Human sexuality.* New York: Van Nostrand.

Jarvik, L. F., Eisdorfer, C., & Blum, J. E. (Eds.). (1973). *Intellectual functioning in adults: Psychological and biological influences.* New York: Springer Publishing.

Jellison, J. M., & Oliver, D. F. (1983). Attitude similarity and attraction: An impression management approach. *Personality and Social Psychology Bulletin, 9,* 111–115.

Jensen, A. R. (1969). How much can we boost IQ and scholastic achievement? *Harvard Educational Review, 39,* 1–123.

Jensen, A. R. (1973). *Educability and group differences.* New York: Harper & Row.

Jensen, A. R. (1980). *Bias in mental testing.* New York: Free Press.

Jensen, A. R. (1981). *Straight talk about mental tests.* New York: Free Press.

Jensen, T. D. (1981, April). *Promoting energy conservation: A review of psychological strategies.* Paper presented at the meeting of the Southwestern Psychological Association, Houston, TX.

Jevning, R. (1981). Circulation and metabolism during the practice of the transcendental meditation technique. In *Consciousness, Physiology, and Longevity Colloquium* (abstracts of proceedings). Fairfield, IA: Maharishi International University Press.

Joffe, L. S., & Vaughn, B. E. (1982). Infant-mother attachment: Theory, assessment, and implications for development. In B. B. Wolman (Ed.), *Handbook of developmental psychology* (pp. 190–207). Englewood Cliffs, NJ: Prentice-Hall.

Johmann, C. (1983, August). Sex and the split-brain. *Omni,* pp. 26, 113.

Johnson, J. H., & Sarason, I. G. (1979). Recent developments in research on life stress. In V. Hamilton & D. M. Warburton (Eds.), *Human stress and cognition: An information processing approach* (pp. 205–233). New York: Wiley.

Johnston, J. M. (1972). Punishment of human behavior. *American Psychologist, 27,* 1033–1054.

Johnson, P. E. (1983). What kind of expert should a system be? *The Journal of Medicine and Philosophy, 8,* 77–97.

Johnson, P. B. (1981). Achievement motivation and success: Does the end justify the means? *Journal of Personality and Social Psychology, 40,* 374–375.

Jones, B. F., & Hall, J. W. (1982). School applications of the mnemonic keyword method as a study strategy by eighth graders. *Journal of Educational Psychology, 74,* 230–237.

Jones, E. E., & Davis, K. E. (1965). From acts to dispositions: The attribution process in person perception. In L. Berkowitz (Ed.), *Advances in experimental social psychology* (Vol. 2, pp. 219–266). New York: Academic Press.

Jones, E. E., & Nisbett, R. E. (1971). *The actor and the observer: Divergent perceptions of the causes of behavior.* Morristown, NJ: General Learning Press.

Jones K. L., & Smith, D. W. (1973). Recognition of the fetal alcohol syndrome in early infancy. *Lancet, 2,* 999–1001.

Jones, M. C., & Mussen, P. H. (1958). Self-conceptions, motivations, and interpersonal attitudes of early- and late-maturing girls. *Child Development, 29,* 491–501.

Jones, W. H. (1982). Loneliness and social behavior. In L. A. Peplau & D. Perlman (Eds.), *Loneliness: A sourcebook of current theory, research and therapy* (pp. 238–252). New York: Wiley.

Jones, W. H., Hobbs, S. A., & Hockenbury, D. (1982). Loneliness and social skills deficits. *Journal of Personality and Social Psychology, 42,* 682–689.

Kagan, J., Kearsley, R. B., & Zelazo, P. R. (1978). *Infancy: Its place in human development.* Cambridge, MA: Harvard University Press.

Kagan, J., & Klein, R. E. (1973). Cross-cultural perspectives on early development. *American Psychologist, 28,* 947–961.

Kalat, J. W. (1981). *Biological psychology.* Belmont, CA: Wadsworth.

Kanizsa, G. (1976, April). Subjective contours. *Scientific*

American, pp. 48–52.

Kanter, R. M. (1977). *Men and women of the corporation.* New York: Basic Books.

Kaplan, B. J. (1972). Malnutrition and mental deficiency. *Psychological Bulletin, 78,* 321–334.

Kaplan, H. S. (1974). *The new sex therapy.* New York: Brunner/Mazel.

Kaplan, H. S. (1975). *The illustrated manual of sex therapy.* New York: Quadrangle.

Kaplan, R. M. (1982). Nader's raid on the testing industry: Is it in the best interest of the consumer? *American Psychologist, 37,* 15–23.

Kappes, B. M. (1983). Sequence effects of relaxation training, EMG, and temperature biofeedback on anxiety, symptom report, and self-concept. *Journal of Clinical Psychology, 39,* 203–207.

Karnes, M. B. (1973). Evaluation and implications of research with young handicapped and low-income children. In J. C. Stanley (Ed.), *Compensatory education for children, ages 2 to 8* (pp. 109–144). Baltimore: Johns Hopkins University Press.

Kasschau, R. A., Johnson, M. M., & Russo, N. F. (1975). *Careers in psychology.* Washington, DC: American Psychological Association.

Katchadourian, H. A., & Lunde, D. T. (1980). *Fundamentals of human sexuality* (3rd ed.). New York: Holt, Rinehart and Winston.

Kaufman, L., & Rock, I. (1962). The moon illusion: I. *Science, 136,* 953–961.

Kazdin, A. E. (1975). *Behavior modification in applied settings.* Homewood, IL: Dorsey Press.

Kazdin, A. E. (1981). Behavior modification in education: Contributions and limitations. *Developmental Review, 1,* 34–57.

Kazdin, A. E. (1982). Symptom substitution, generalization, and response covariation: Implications for psychotherapy outcome. *Psychological Bulletin, 91,* 349-365.

Keesey, R. E., & Powley, T. L. (1975). Hypothalamic regulation of body weight. *American Scientist, 63,* 558–565.

Kelley, H. H. (1967). Attribution theory in social psychology. In D. Levine (Ed.), *Nebraska symposium on motivation* (Vol. 15, pp. 192–238). Lincoln: University of Nebraska Press.

Kelley, H. H. (1973). The processes of causal attribution. *American Psychologist, 28,* 107–128.

Kellogg, W. N., & Kellogg, C. A. (1933). *The ape and the child.* New York: McGraw-Hill.

Kelly, G. A. (1955). *The psychology of personal constructs.* New York: W. W. Norton.

Kelwala, S., Stanley, M., & Gershon, S. (1983). History of antidepressants, successes and failures. *The Journal of Clinical Psychiatry, 44,* 40–48.

Kendler, H. H. (1974). *Basic psychology* (3rd ed.). Menlo Park, CA: W. A. Benjamin.

Kennedy, W. A. (1965). School phobia: Rapid treatment of fifty cases. *Journal of Abnormal Psychology, 70,* 285–289.

Kesey, K. (1962). *One flew over the cuckoo's nest.* New York: Viking.

Kiester, E. (1980, May–June). Images of the night. *Science 80,* pp. 36–43.

Kihlstrom, J. F. (1983). Instructed forgetting: Hypnotic and nonhypnotic. *Journal of Experimental Psychology: General, 112,* 73–79.

Kilham, W., & Mann, L. (1974). Level of destructive obedience as a function of transmitter and executant roles in the Milgram obedience paradigm. *Journal of Personality and Social Psychology, 29,* 696–702.

Kilmann, P. R., Mills, K. H., Bella, B., Caid, C., Davidson, E., Drose, G., & Wanlass, R. (1983). The effects of sex education on women with secondary orgasmic dysfunction. *Journal of Sex and Marital Therapy, 9,* 79–87.

Kimble, G. A., Garmezy, N, & Zigler, E. (1980). *Principles of general psychology* (5th ed.). New York: Wiley.

Kimura, D. (1961). Cerebral dominance and the perception of verbal stimuli. *Canadian Journal of Psychology, 15,* 166–171.

Kimura, D. (1966). Dual functional asymmetry of the brain in visual perception. *Neuropsychologia, 4,* 275–285.

Kimura, D. (1967). Functional asymmetry of the brain in dichotic listening. *Cortex, 3,* 163–178.

Kinsey, A. C., Pomeroy, W. B., & Martin, C. E. (1948). *Sexual behavior in the human male.* Philadelphia : W. B. Saunders.

Kinsey, A. C., Pomeroy, W. B., Martin, C. E., & Gebhard, P. H. (1953). *Sexual behavior in the human female.* Philadelphia: W. B. Saunders.

Kinsey, A. C., Pomeroy, W. B., & Martin, C. E. (1948). *Sexual behavior in the human male.* Philadelphia: W. B. Saunders.

Kirby, D. A., & Lamberth, J. (1974). *The lawyers' dilemma: The behavior of authoritarian jurors.* Unpublished manuscript.

Kirkland, K., & Hollandsworth, J. G., Jr. (1980). Effective test taking: Skills-acquisition versus anxiety-reduction techniques. *Journal of Consulting and Clinical Psychology, 48,* 431–439.

Kirschenbaum, D. S., & Tomarken, A. J. (1982). Some antecedents of regulatory eating by restrained and unrestrained eaters. *Journal of Abnormal Psychology, 91,* 326–336.

Klatzky, R. L. (1980). *Human memory: Structures and processes* (2nd ed.). San Francisco: W. H. Freeman.

Klaus, M. H., & Kennell, J. H. (1982). *Parent-infant bonding.* St. Louis, MO: C. V. Mosby.

Klein, D. F. (1982). Medication in the treatment of panic attacks and phobic states. *Psychopharmacology Bulletin, 18,* 85–90.

Klein, D. F., Zitrin, C. M., & Woerner, M. G. (1977). Imipramine and phobia. *Psychopharmacology Bulletin, 13,* 24–27.

Klein, D. F., Zitrin, C. M., Woerner, M. G., & Ross, D. C. (1983). Treatment of phobias: 2. Behavior therapy and supportive psychotherapy—Are there any specific ingredients?

Archives of General Psychiatry, 40, 139–152.

Klerman, G. L. (1983). Psychotherapies and somatic therapies in affective disorders. *The Psychiatric Clinics of North America, 6,* 85–104.

Knapp, T. W. (1982). Treating migraine by training in temporal artery vasoconstriction and/or cognitive behavioral coping: A one-year follow-up. *Journal of Psychosomatic Research, 26,* 551–557.

Knittle, J. L. (1975). Early influences on development of adipose tissue. In G. A. Bray (Ed.), *Obesity in perspective.* Washington, DC: U.S. Government Printing Office.

Knittle, J. L., & Hirsch, J. (1968). Effect of early nutrition on the development of rat epididymal fat pads: Cellularity and metabolism. *Journal of Clinical Investigation, 47,* 2091.

Knobloch, H., & Pasamanick, B. (Eds.). (1974). *Gesell and Amatruda's developmental diagnosis: The evaluation and management of normal and abnormal neuropsychologic development in infancy and early childhood* (3rd ed.). New York: Harper & Row.

Kobasa, S. C. (1979). Stressful life events, personality, and health: An inquiry into hardiness. *Journal of Personality and Social Psychology, 37,* 1–11.

Kobasa, S. C. (1982). Commitment and coping in stress resistance among lawyers. *Journal of Personality and Social Psychology, 42,* 707–717.

Kobasa, S. C., Maddi, S. R., & Kahn, S. (1982). Hardiness and health: A prospective study. *Journal of Personality and Social Psychology, 42,* 168–177.

Kobasa, S. C., Maddi, S. R., & Puccetti, M. C. (1982). Personality and exercise as buffers in the stress-illness relationship. *Journal of Behavioral Medicine, 5,* 391–404.

Kobasa, S. C., Maddi, S. R., & Zola, M. A. (1983). Type A and hardiness. *Journal of Behavioral Medicine, 6,* 41–51.

Köhler, W. (1925). *The mentality of apes.* New York: Harcourt, Brace.

Kolata, G. B. (1981). Clues to the cause of senile dementia. *Science, 211,* 1032–1033.

Konečni, V. J., Libuser, L., Morton, M., & Ebbesen, E. B. (1975). Effects of a violation of personal space on escape and helping responses. *Journal of Experimental Social Psychology, 11,* 288–299.

Konner, M. (1982, September). She and he. *Science 82,* pp. 54–61.

Kopp, C. B., & Parmelee, A. H. (1979). Prenatal and perinatal influences on infant behavior. In J. D. Osofsky (Ed.), *Handbook of infant development* (pp. 29–75). New York: Wiley-Interscience.

Koops, B. L., & Harmon, R. L. (1980). Studies on long-term outcome in newborns with birth weights under 1500 grams. In B. Camp (Ed.), *Advances in behavioral pediatrics* (pp. 1–28). Greenwich, CT: JAI Press.

Korte, C. (1981). Constraints on helping behavior in an urban environment. In J. P. Rushton & R. M. Sorrentino (Eds.), *Altruism and helping behavior: Social, personality, and developmental perspectives* (pp. 315–330). Hillsdale, NJ: Erlbaum.

Korte, C., & Kerr, N. (1975). Response to altruistic opportunities under urban and rural conditions. *Journal of Social Psychology, 95,* 183–184.

Krauss, R. M., Freedman, J. L., & Whitcup, M. (1978). Field and laboratory studies of littering. *Journal of Experimental Social Psychology, 14,* 109–122.

Krebs, D., & Gillmore, J. (1982). The relationship among the first stages of cognitive development, role-taking abilities, and moral development. *Child Development, 53,* 877–886.

Kripke, D. F., & Simons, R. N. (1976). Average sleep, insomnia, and sleeping pill use. *Sleep Research, 5,* 110.

Krupat, E. (1980). Social psychology and urban behavior. *Journal of Social Issues, 36,* 1–8.

Kryter, K. D. (1970). *The effects of noise on man.* New York: Academic Press.

Kübler-Ross, E. (1969). *On death and dying.* New York: Macmillan.

Kübler-Ross, E. (1974). *Questions and answers on death and dying.* New York: Macmillan.

Kubovy, M., & Pomerantz, J. R. (Eds.). (1982). *Perceptual organization.* Hillsdale, NJ: Erlbaum.

Kuczaj, S. A. (1978). Children's judgments of grammatical and ungrammatical irregular past-tense verbs. *Child Development, 49,* 319–326.

Kuczaj, S. A. (1983). "I mell a kunk!"—Evidence that children have more complex representations of word pronunciations which they simplify. *Journal of Psycholinguistic Research, 12,* 69–73.

Kunda, Z., & Schwartz, S. H. (1983). Undermining intrinsic moral motivation: External reward and self-presentation. *Journal of Personality and Social Psychology, 45,* 763–771.

Labbe, R., Firl, A., Jr., Mufson, E. J., & Stein, D. G. (1983). Fetal brain transplants: Reduction of cognitive deficits in rats with frontal cortex lesions. *Science, 221,* 470–472.

Lacoste-Utamsing, C., & Holloway, R. L. (1981). Sexual dimorphism in the human corpus callosum. *Science, 216,* 1431–1432.

LaFrance, M., & Mayo, C. (1978). *Moving bodies: Nonverbal communication in social relationships.* Monterey, CA: Brooks/Cole.

Lahey, B. B., & Ciminero, A. R. (1980). *Maladaptive behavior: An introduction to abnormal psychology.* Glenview, IL: Scott, Foresman.

Laird, J. D. (1974). Self-attribution of emotion: The effects of expressive behavior on the quality of emotional experience. *Journal of Personality and Social Psychology, 29,* 475–486.

Lamb, M. E. (1979). Paternal influences and the father's role. *American Psychologist, 34,* 938–943.

Lamb, M. E. (Ed.). (1981). *The role of the father in child development* (2nd ed.). New York: Wiley.

Lamberth, J., Rappaport, H., & Rappaport, M. (1978). *Personality: An introduction.* New York: Knopf.

Lammens, L., & d'Ydewalle, G. (1983). Encoding questions

and word retrieval. *American Journal of Psychology, 96,* 3–16.

Landis, D. (1980, October). A scan for mental illness. *Discover,* pp. 26–28.

Landman, J. T., & Dawes, R. M. (1982). Psychotherapy outcome: Smith and Glass' conclusions stand up under scrutiny. *American Psychologist, 37,* 504–516.

Lange, C. (1922). *The emotions.* Baltimore: Williams & Wilkins. (Original work published 1885)

Langer, E. J., & Saegert, S. (1977). Crowding and cognitive control. *Journal of Personality and Social Psychology, 35,* 175–182.

Larkin, J. H., McDermott, J., Simon, D. P., & Simon, H. A. (1980). Expert and novice performance in solving physics problems. *Science, 208,* 1335–1342.

L'Armand, K., & Pepitone, A. (1982). Judgments of rape: A study of victim-rapist relationship and victim sexual history. *Personality and Social Psychology Bulletin, 8,* 134–139.

Latané, B., & Darley, J. M. (1970). *The unresponsive bystander: Why doesn't he help?* New York: Appleton-Century Crofts.

Latané, B., & Nida, S. A. (1981). Ten years of research on group size and helping. *Psychological Bulletin, 89,* 308–324.

Latané, B., Nida, S. A., & Wilson, D. W. (1981). The effects of group size on helping behavior. In J. P. Rushton & R. M. Sorrentino (Eds.), *Altruism and helping behavior: Social, personality, and developmental perspectives* (pp. 287–313). Hillsdale, NJ: Erlbaum.

Lau, R. R. (1982). Origins of health locus of control beliefs. *Journal of Personality and Social Psychology, 42,* 322–334.

Lau, R. R., & Russell, D. (1980). Attributions in the sports pages. *Journal of Personality and Social Psychology, 39,* 29–38.

Lazar, I., & Darlington, R. (1982). Lasting effects of early education: A report from the consortium for longitudinal studies. *Monographs of the Society for Research in Child Development, 47,* (2–3, Serial No. 195).

Lazarus, A. A. (1976). *Multimodal behavior therapy.* New York: Springer.

Lazarus, R. S. (1981, July). Little hassles can be hazardous to health. *Psychology Today,* pp. 58–62.

Lazarus, R. S. (1968). Emotions and adaptation: Conceptual and empirical relations. In W. J. Arnold (Ed.), *Nebraska symposium on motivation* (pp. 175–270). Lincoln: University of Nebraska Press.

Lazarus, R. S. (1982). Thoughts on the relations between emotion and cognition. *American Psychologist, 37,* 1019–1024.

Leavy, R. L (1983). Social support and psychological disorder: A review. *Journal of Community Psychology, 11,* 3–21.

Lecker, S. (1976). Family therapies. In B. B. Wolman (Ed.), *The therapist's handbook: Treatment methods of mental disorders* (pp. 184–198). New York: Van Nostrand Rein-

hold.

Lenneberg, E. H. (1967). *Biological foundations of language.* New York: Wiley.

Leo, J. (1980, September 29). From mollusks to moppets: Jean Piaget, 1896–1980. *Time,* p. 55.

Lerner, I. M., & Libby, W. J. (1976). *Heredity, evolution, and society.* San Francisco: W. H. Freeman.

Lerner, R. M., & Hultsch, D. F. (1983). *Human development: A life-span perspective.* New York: McGraw-Hill.

Lerner, R. M., & Spanier, G. B. (1980). *Adolescent development: A life-span perspective.* New York: McGraw-Hill.

Levenkron, J. C., Cohen, J. D., Mueller, H. S., & Fisher, E. B., Jr. (1983). Modifying the Type A coronary-prone behavior pattern. *Journal of Consulting and Clinical Psychology, 51,* 192–204.

Levin, J. R., Shriberg, L. K., Miller, G. E., McCormick, C. B., & Levin, B. B. (1980). The keyword method in the classroom: How to remember the states and their capitals. *Elementary School Journal, 80,* 185–191.

Levine, F. J., & Tapp, J. L. (1982). Eyewitness identification: Problems and pitfalls. In V. J. Konečni & E. B. Ebbesen (Eds.), *The criminal justice system: A social-psychological analysis* (pp. 99–127). San Francisco: W. H. Freeman.

Levinson, D. J., Darrow, C. M., Klein, E. B., Levinson, M. H., & McKee, B. (1976). Periods in the adult development of men: Ages 18 to 45. *Counseling Psychologist, 6,* 21–25.

Levinson, D. J., Darrow, C. M., Klein, E. B., Levinson, M. H., & McKee, B. (1978). *The seasons of a man's life.* New York: Knopf.

Levinson, H. (1980, July–August). Criteria for choosing chief executives. *Harvard Business Review,* pp. 113–120.

Levy, J. (1983a). Is cerebral asymmetry of function a dynamic process? Implications for specifying degree of lateral differentiation. *Neuropsychologia, 21,* 3–11.

Levy, J. (1983b). Language, cognition, and the right hemisphere: A response to Gazzaniga. *American Psychologist, 38,* 538–541.

Lewinsohn, P. M., Muñoz, R. F., Youngren, M. A., & Zeiss, A. M. (1978). *Control your depression.* Englewood Cliffs, NJ: Prentice-Hall.

Lichtenstein, E. (1980). *Psychotherapy: Approaches and applications.* Monterey, CA: Brooks/Cole.

Liebert, R. M., & Spiegler, M. D. (1982). *Personality: Strategies and issues* (4th ed.). Homewood, IL: Dorsey Press.

Liebert, R. M., Sprafkin, J. W., & Davidson, E. S. (1982). *The early window: Effects of television on children and youth.* New York: Pergamon Press.

Liebman, R., Sargent, J., & Silver, M. (1983). A family systems orientation to the treatment of anorexia nervosa. *The Journal of the American Academy of Child Psychiatry, 22,* 128–133.

Liebowitz, M. R., & Klein, D. F. (1981). Differential diagnosis and treatment of panic attacks and phobic states. *Annual Review of Medicine, 32,* 583–599.

Liem, R., & Rayman, P. (1982). Health and social costs of unemployment: Research and policy considerations. *Ameri-*

can *Psychologist, 37,* 1116–1123.

Little, L. M., & Curran, J. P. (1978). Covert sensitization: A clinical procedure in need of some explanations. *Psychological Bulletin, 85,* 513–531.

Linder, D. E., Cooper, J., & Jones, E. E. (1967). Decision freedom as a determinant of the role of incentive magnitude in attitude change. *Journal of Personality and Social Psychology, 6,* 245–254.

Lindsley, D. B. (1952). Psychological phenomena and the electroencephalogram. *Electroencephalography and Clinical Neurophysiology, 4,* 443–456.

Linnoila, M., Karoum, F., Rosenthal, N., & Potter, W. Z. (1983). Electroconvulsive treatment and lithium carbonate. *Archives of General Psychiatry, 40,* 677–680.

Loeb, M. (1979, July 30). The strength of sampson. *Time,* p. 62.

Loehlin, J. C., Lindzey, G., & Spuhler, J. N. (1975). *Race differences in intelligence.* San Francisco: W. H. Freeman.

Lofquist, L. H., & Dawis, R. V. (1969). *Adjustment to work: A psychological view of man's problems in a work-oriented society.* New York: Appleton-Century-Crofts.

Loftus, E. F. (1975). Leading questions and the eyewitness report. *Cognitive Psychology, 7,* 560–572.

Loftus, E. F. (1977). Shifting human color memory. *Memory & Cognition, 5,* 696–699.

Loftus, E. F. (1979). *Eyewitness testimony.* Cambridge, MA: Harvard University Press.

Loftus, E. F. (1980). *Memory.* Reading, MA: Addison-Wesley.

Loftus, E. F. (1982). Memory and its distortions. In A. G. Kraut (Ed.), *The G. Stanley Hall Lecture Series* (Vol. 2, pp. 123–154). Washington, D.C.: American Psychological Association.

Loftus, E. F. (1983a). Silence is not golden. *American Psychologist, 38,* 564–572.

Loftus, E. F. (1983b). Whose shadow is crooked? *American Psychologist, 38,* 576–577.

Loftus, E. F., & Burns, T. E. (1982). Mental shock can produce retrograde amnesia. *Memory & Cognition, 10,* 318–323.

Loftus, E. F., & Loftus, G. R. (1980). On the permanence of stored information in the human memory. *American Psychologist, 35,* 409–420.

Loftus, E. F., Miller, D. G., & Burns, H. J. (1978). Semantic integration of verbal information into a visual memory. *Journal of Experimental Psychology: Human Learning and Memory, 4,* 19–31.

Loftus, E. F., & Monahan, J. (1980). Trial by data: Psychological research as legal evidence. *American Psychologist, 35,* 270–283.

Loftus, E. F., & Palmer, J. C. (1974). Reconstruction of automobile destruction: An example of the interaction between language and memory. *Journal of Verbal Learning and Verbal Behavior, 13,* 585–589.

Loftus, G. R., & Loftus, E. F. (1976). *Human memory: The processing of information.* Hillsdale, NJ: Erlbaum.

Lorenz, K. (1952). *King Solomon's ring.* New York: T.Y. Crowell.

Lorenz, K. (1966). *On aggression* (M.K. Wilson, Trans.). New York: Harcourt, Brace.

Lorenz, K. Z.; & Leyhausen, P. (Eds.). (1973). *Motivation of human and animal behavior: An ethological view* (B. A. Tonkin, Trans.). New York: Van Nostrand. (Original work published 1939).

Luborsky, L., Graff, H., Pulver, S., & Curtis, H. (1973). Clinical-quantitative examination of consensus on the concept of transference. *Archives of General Psychiatry, 29,* 69–75.

Luborsky, L., Singer, B., & Luborsky, L. (1975). Comparative studies of psychotherapies: Is it true that "Everyone has won and all must have prizes?" *Archives of General Psychiatry, 32,* 995–1008.

Luchins, A. S. (1942). Mechanization in problem solving. *Psychological Monographs, 54* (6, Whole No. 248).

Luria, A. R. (1968). *The mind of a mnemonist* (L. Solotaroff, Trans.). New York: Basic Books.

Lustman, P. J., & Sowa, C. J. (1983). Comparative efficacy of biofeedback and stress inoculation for stress reduction. *Journal of Clinical Psychology, 39,* 191–197.

Lykken, D. T. (1981). *A tremor in the blood.* New York: McGraw-Hill.

Lynn, R. (1982). IQ in Japan and the United States shows a growing disparity. *Nature, 297,* 222–223.

Maccoby, E. E. (1980). *Social development: Psychological growth and the parent-child relationship.* New York: Harcourt Brace Jovanovich.

Maccoby, E. E., & Jacklin, C. N. (1974). *Psychology of sex differences.* Stanford, CA: Stanford University Press.

MacKinnon, D. W. (1965). The nature and nurture of creative talent. In A. Anastasi (Ed.), *Individual differences* (pp. 282–295). New York: Wiley.

MacNichol, E. F., Jr. (1964, December). Three-pigment color vision. *Scientific American,* pp. 48–56.

Maddi, S. R., Hoover, M., & Kobasa, S. C. (1982). Alienation and exploratory behavior. *Journal of Personality and Social Psychology, 42,* 884–890.

Maddux, J. E., & Rogers, R. W. (1980). Effects of source expertness, physical attractiveness, and supporting arguments on persuasion: A case of brains over beauty. *Journal of Personality and Social Psychology, 89,* 235–244.

Magnusson, D., & Endler, H. S. (Eds.). (1977). *Personality at the crossroads: Current issues in interactional psychology.* Hillsdale, NJ: Erlbaum.

Maharishi Mahesh Yogi. (1963). *The science of being and the art of living.* New York: Signet Books.

Maharishi Mahesh Yogi. (1978). *Enlightenment and invincibility.* West Germany: MERU Press.

Mahoney, E. R. (1983). *Human sexuality.* New York: McGraw-Hill.

Mahoney, M. J. (1980). *Abnormal psychology: Perspectives on human variance.* San Francisco: Harper & Row.

Mahoney, M. J., & Mahoney, K. (1976). *Permanent weight control.* New York: W. W. Norton.

Maier, S.F., & Seligman, M. E. P. (1976). Learned helplessness: Theory and evidence. *Journal of Experimental Psychology:*

General, 105, 3–46.

Malamuth, N. M. (1981). Rape proclivity among males. *Journal of Social Issues, 37,* 138–157.

Malamuth, N. M., & Check, J. V. P. (1981). The effects of media exposure on acceptance of violence against women: A field experiment. *Journal of Research in Personality, 15,* 436–446.

Malamuth, N. M., & Donnerstein, E. (1982). The effects of aggressive-pornographic mass media stimuli. In L. Berkowitz (Ed.), *Advances in experimental social psychology* (Vol. 15, pp. 103–136). New York: Academic Press.

Maloney, M. J., & Klykylo, W. M. (1983). An overview of anorexia nervosa, bulimia, and obesity in children and adolescents. *Journal of the American Academy of Child Psychiatry, 22,* 99–107.

Mann, J., Berkowitz, L., Sidman, J., Starr, S., & West, S. (1974). Satiation of the transient stimulating effect of erotic films. *Journal of Personality and Social Psychology, 30,* 729–735.

Marks, D., & Kammann, R., (1980). *The psychology of the psychic.* Buffalo, NY: Prometheus Books.

Marshall, G. D., & Zimbardo, P. G. (1979). Affective consequences of inadequately explained physiological arousal. *Journal of Personality and Social Psychology, 37,* 970–988.

Marshall, W. A., & Tanner, J. M. (1969). Variations in pattern of pubertal changes in girls. *Archives of Disease in Childhood, 44,* 291–303.

Marshall, W. A., & Tanner, J. M. (1970). Variations in the pattern of pubertal changes in boys. *Archives of Disease in Childhood, 45,* 13–23.

Martin, R. A., & Poland, E. Y. (1980). *Learning to change: A self-management approach to adjustment.* New York: McGraw-Hill.

Marx, J. L. (1981). Caffeine's stimulatory effects explained. *Science, 211,* 1408–1409.

Maslach, C. (1979). Negative emotional biasing of unexplained arousal. *Journal of Personality and Social Psychology, 37,* 953–969.

Maslow, A. H. (1970). *Motivation and personality* (2nd ed.). New York: Harper & Row.

Maslow, A. H. (1971). *The farther reaches of human nature.* New York: Viking Press.

Massey, R. F. (1981). *Personality Theories: Comparisons and syntheses.* New York: Van Nostrand.

Masters, W. H., & Johnson, V. E. (1966). *Human sexual response.* Boston: Little, Brown.

Masters, W. H., & Johnson, V. E. (1970). *Human sexual inadequacy.* Boston: Little, Brown.

Masters, W. H., Johnson, V. E., & Kolodny, R. C. (1982). *Human sexuality.* Boston: Little, Brown.

Matarazzo, J. D. (1980). Behavioral health and behavioral medicine: Frontiers for a new health psychology. *American Psychologist, 35,* 807–817.

Matarazzo, J. D. (1982). Behavioral health's challenge to academic, scientific, and professional psychology. *American Psychologist, 37,* 1–14.

Matas, L., Arend, R. A., & Sroufe, L. A. (1978). Continuity of adaptation in the second year: The relationship between quality of attachment and later competence. *Child Development, 49,* 547–556.

Mathews, K. E., Jr., & Canon, L. K. (1975). Environmental noise level as a determinant of helping behavior. *Journal of Personality and Social Psychology, 32,* 571–577.

Matlin, M. (1983). *Cognition.* New York: Holt, Rinehart and Winston.

Matthews, J. R. (1983, May). Students need skills, advice to find jobs. *APA Monitor,* p. 35.

Matthews, K. A. (1982). Psychological perspectives on the Type A behavior pattern. *Psychological Bulletin, 91,* 293–323.

Matthews, K. A., Scheier, M. F., Brunson, B. I., & Carducci, B. (1980). Attention, unpredictability, and reports of physical symptoms: Eliminating the benefits of predictability. *Journal of Personality and Social Psychology, 38,* 525–537.

Maugh, T. H. (1982). Marijuana "justifies serious concern." *Science, 215,* 1488–1489.

Maupin, E. W. (1965). Individual differences in response to a Zen meditation exercise. *Journal of Consulting Psychology, 29,* 139–145.

Maurer, D., & Salapatek, P. (1976). Developmental changes in the scanning of faces by young infants. *Child Development, 47,* 523–527.

McCain, G., Cox, V. C., & Paulus, P. B. (1976). The relationship between illness complaints and degree of crowding in a prison environment. *Environment and Behavior, 8,* 283–290.

McCall, M. W., Jr., & Lombardo, M. M. (1983, February). What makes a top executive? *Psychology Today,* pp. 26–31.

McCary, J. L., & McCary, S. P. (1982). *McCary's human sexuality* (4th ed.). Belmont, CA: Wadsworth.

McClelland, D. C. (1973). Testing for competence rather than for "intelligence." *American Psychologist, 28,* 1–14.

McClelland, D. C., Atkinson, J. W., Clark, R. A. & Lowell, E. L. (1953). *The achievement motive.* Englewood Cliffs, NJ: Prentice-Hall.

McClelland, D. C., & Pilon, D. A. (1983). Sources of adult motives in patterns of parent behavior in early childhood. *Journal of Personality and Social Psychology, 44,* 564–574.

McClelland, L., & Cook, S. W. (1980). Promoting energy conservation in master-metered apartments through group financial incentives. *Journal of Applied Social Psychology, 10,* 20–31.

McClenon, J. (1982). A survey of elite scientists: Their attitudes toward ESP and parapsychology. *The Journal of Parapsychology, 46,* 127–152.

McCloskey, M., & Egeth, H. E. (1983a). Eyewitness identification: What can a psychologist tell a jury? *American Psychologist, 38,* 550–563.

McCloskey, M., & Egeth, H. E. (1983b). A time to speak, or a time to keep silence? *American Psychologist, 38,* 573–575.

McDougall, W. (1908). *An introduction to social psychology.* London: Methuen.

McFadden, D., & Wightman, F. L. (1983). Audition: Some relations between normal and pathological hearing. *Annual Review of Psychology, 34,* 95–128.

McGaugh, J. L. (1983a). Hormonal influences on memory. *Annual Review of Psychology, 34,* 297–323.

McGaugh, J. L. (1983b). Preserving the presence of the past: Hormonal influences on memory storage. *American Psychologist, 38,* 161–174.

McGee, M. G. (1979a). Human spatial abilities: Psychometric studies and environmental, genetic, hormonal, and neurological influences. *Psychological Bulletin, 86,* 889–918.

McGee, M. G. (1979b). *Human spatial abilities: Sources of sex differences.* New York: Praeger.

McGee, M. G., & Cozad, T. W. (1980). Population genetic analysis of human hand preference: Evidence for generation differences, familial resemblance, and maternal effects. *Behavior Genetics, 10,* 263–275.

McGee, M. G., Cozad, T. W., & Pate, J. C. (1982, August 23–27). *Spatial abilities in normal adolescents.* Paper presented at the 90th annual meeting of the American Psychological Association, Washington, DC.

McGlone, J. (1980). Sex differences in human brain asymmetry: A critical review. *The Behavioral and Brain Sciences, 3,* 215–263.

McKay, H., Sinisterra, L., McKay, A., Gomez, H., & Lloreda, P. (1978). Improving cognitive ability in chronically deprived children. *Science, 200,* 270–278.

McKee, S. P., McCann, J. J., & Benton, J. L. (1977). Color vision from rod and long-wave cone interactions: Conditions in which rods contribute to multicolored images. *Vision Research, 17,* 175–185.

McMorrow, M. J., & Foxx, R. M. (1983). Nicotine's role in smoking: An analysis of nicotine regulation. *Psychological Bulletin, 93,* 302–327.

McMullin, E. (1983a). Introduction. *The Journal of Medicine and Philosophy, 8,* 3–4.

McMullin, E. (1983b). Diagnosis by computer. *The Journal of Medicine and Philosophy, 8,* 5–28.

McNeill, D. (1970). *The acquisition of language: The study of developmental psycholinguistics.* New York: Harper & Row.

McNeil, E. B. (1967). *The quiet furies.* Englewood Cliffs, NJ: Prentice-Hall.

McNees, M. P., Schnelle, J. F., Gendrich, J., Thomas, M. M., & Beagle, G. (1979). McDonald's litter hunt: A community litter control system for youth. *Environment and Behavior, 11,* 131–138.

Meichenbaum, D. H. (1969). The effects of instructions and reinforcement on thinking and language behavior of schizophrenics. *Behaviour Research and Therapy, 7,* 101–114.

Meltzoff, A. N., & Moore, M. K. (1977). Imitation of facial and manual gestures by human neonates. *Science, 198,* 75–78.

Meltzoff, A. N., & Moore, M. K. (1983). Newborn infants imitate adult facial gestures. *Child Development, 54,* 702–709.

Mervis, J. (1983, February). In leak hubbub, DoD skirts issue: Do polygraphs lie? *APA Monitor,* p. 28.

Metalsky, G. I., Abramson, L. Y., Seligman M. E. P., Semmel, A., & Peterson, C. (1982). Attributional styles and life events in the classroom: Vulnerability and invulnerability to depressive mood reactions. *Journal of Personality and Social Psychology, 43,* 612–617.

Meyer, A. (1982, June). Do lie detectors lie? *Science 82,* pp. 24–27.

Meyer, J. P., & Pepper, S. (1977). Need compatibility and marital adjustment in young married couples. *Journal of Personality and Social Psychology, 35,* 331–342.

Middlebrook, P. N. (1980). *Social psychology and modern life* (2nd ed.). New York: Knopf.

Milgram, S. (1963). Behavioral study of obedience. *Journal of Abnormal and Social Psychology, 67,* 371–378.

Milgram, S. (1965a). Liberating effects of group pressure. *Journal of Personality and Social Psychology, 1,* 127–134.

Milgram, S. (1965b). Some conditions of obedience and disobedience to authority. *Human Relations, 18,* 57–76.

Milgram, S. (1970). The experience of living in cities. *Science, 167,* 1461–1464, 1468.

Milgram, S. (1974). *Obedience to authority.* New York: Harper & Row.

Milgram, S. (1977). *The individual in a social world: Essays and experiments.* Reading, MA: Addison-Wesley.

Miller, G. A. (1956). The magical number seven, plus or minus two: Some limits on our capacity for processing information. *Psychological Review, 63,* 81–97.

Miller, G. A. (1981). *Language and speech.* San Francisco: W. H. Freeman.

Miller, G. A. (1969). Psychology as a means of promoting human welfare. *American Psychologist, 24,* 1063–1075.

Miller, J. V. (1982). 1970s trends in assessing career counseling, guidance, and education. *Measurement and Evaluation in Guidance, 15,* 142–146.

Miller, L. L., & Branconnier, R. J. (1983). Cannabis: Effects on memory and the cholinergic limbic system. *Psychological Bulletin, 93,* 441–456.

Miller, N. E. (1944). Experimental studies of conflict. In J. M. Hunt (Ed.), *Personality and the behavior disorders* (pp. 431–465). New York: Ronald Press.

Miller, N. E. (1978). Biofeedback and visceral learning. *Annual Review of Psychology, 29,* 373–404.

Miller, N. E., & DiCara, L. V. (1967). Instrumental learning of heart rate changes in curarized rats: Shaping and specificity to discriminative stimulus. *Journal of Comparative and Physiological Psychology, 63,* 12–19.

Miller, P. H. (1983). *Theories of developmental psychology.* San Francisco: W. H. Freeman.

Miller, R. C., & Berman, J. S. (1983). The efficacy of cognitive behavior therapies: A quantitative review of the research evidence. *Psychological Bulletin, 94,* 39–53.

Mills, J., & Aronson, E. (1965). Opinion change as a function of communicator's attractivness and desire to influence. *Journal of Personality and Social Psychology, 1,* 173–177.

Mills, J., & Harvey, J. (1972). Opinion change as a function of when information about the communicator is received and whether he is attractive or expert. *Journal of Personality and Social Psychology, 21,* 52–55.

Milner, B., Corkin, S., & Teuber, H. L. (1968). Further analysis of the hippocampal amnesic syndrome: 14-year follow-up study of H. M. *Neuropsychologia, 6,* 215–234.

Milner, B., Taylor, L. B., & Sperry, R. W. (1968). Lateralized suppression of dichotically-presented digits after commissural section in man. *Science, 161,* 184–185.

Mintz, N. E. (1982). Bulimia: A new perspective. *Clinical Social Work Journal, 10,* 284–302.

Mirsky, A. F. (1983, November 22). Personal communication.

Mirsky, A. F. (1984, January 13). Personal communication

Mischel, W. (1961). Delay of gratification, need for achievement, and acquiescence in another culture. *Journal of Abnormal and Social Psychology, 62,* 543–552.

Mischel, W. (1968). *Personality and assessment.* New York: Wiley.

Mischel, W. (1973). Toward a cognitive social learning reconceptualization of personality. *Psychological Review, 80,* 252–283.

Mischel, W. (1974). Processes in delay of gratification. In L. Berkowitz (Ed.), *Advances in experimental social psychology* (Vol. 7, pp. 249–292). New York: Academic Press.

Mischel, W. (1981). *Introduction to personality* (3rd ed.). New York: Holt, Rinehart and Winston.

Mischel, W., & Ebbesen, E. B. (1970). Attention in delay of gratification. *Journal of Personality and Social Psychology, 16,* 329–337.

Moates, D. R., & Schumacher, G. M. (1980). *An introduction to cognitive psychology.* Belmont, CA: Wadsworth.

Moerk, E. L. (1983). A behavioral analysis of controversial topics in first language acquisition: Reinforcements, corrections, modeling, input frequencies, and the three-term contingency pattern. *Journal of Psycholinguistic Research, 12,* 129–156.

Mohs, M. (1982, September). I.Q. *Discover,* pp. 18–24.

Monahan, J. (Ed.). (1980). *Who is the client?* Washington, DC: American Psychological Association.

Money, J. (1977). Human hermaphroditism. In F. A. Beach (Ed.), *Human sexuality in four perspectives.* Baltimore: Johns Hopkins University Press.

Money, J., & Ehrhardt, A. A. (1972). *Man and woman: Boy and girl.* Baltimore: Johns Hopkins University Press.

Monroe, S. M. (1982). Life events assessment: Current practices, emerging trends. *Clinical Psychology Review, 2,* 435–454.

Moreland, J. R., Schwebel, A. I., Beck, S., & Wells, R. (1982). Parents as therapists: A review of the behavior therapy parent training literature—1975 to 1981. *Behavior Modification, 6,* 250–276.

Moreland, R. L., & Zajonc, R. B. (1979). Exposure effects may not depend on stimulus recognition. *Journal of Personality and Social Psychology, 37,* 1085–1089.

Moreland, R. L., & Zajonc, R. B. (1982). Exposure effects in person perception: Familiarity, similarity, and attraction. *Journal of Experimental Social Psychology, 18,* 395–415.

Morgan, A. H., & Hilgard, J. R. (1979a). The Stanford hypnotic clinical scale for adults. *American Journal of Clinical Hypnosis, 21,* 134–147.

Morgan, A. H., & Hilgard, J. R. (1979b). The Stanford hypnotic clinical scale for children. *American Journal of Clinical Hypnosis, 21,* 148–169.

Morganthau, T., Coppola, V., Pate, J. L., Abramson, P., Shannon, E., & Foote, D. (1982, October 25). Guns, grass—and money. *Newsweek,* pp. 36–43.

Morris, S. (1981, July). Brainbuster: Omni's new I.Q. test. *Omni,* pp. 96–98.

Morris, W. N., & Miller, R. S. (1975). The effects of consensus-breaking and consensus-preempting partners on reduction of conformity. *Journal of Experimental Social Psychology, 11,* 215–223.

Morrison, A. R. (1983, April). A window on the sleeping brain. *Scientific American,* pp. 94–102.

Moskowitz, B. A. (1978, November). The acquisition of language. *Scientific American,* pp. 92–108.

Moss, M. K., & Page, R. A. (1972). Reinforcement and helping behavior. *Journal of Applied Social Psychology, 2,* 360–371.

Mowrer, O. H., & Mowrer, W. M. (1938). Enuresis—A method for its study and treatment. *American Journal of Orthopsychiatry, 8,* 436–459.

Munsinger, H. (1983). *Principles of abnormal psychology.* New York: Macmillan.

Murderous personality. (1979, May 7). *Time,* p. 26.

Murray, H. A. (1938). *Explorations in personality.* New York: Oxford University Press.

Mussen, P., & Eisenberg-Berg, N. (1977). *Roots of caring, sharing, and helping: The development of prosocial behavior in children.* San Francisco: W. H. Freeman.

Mussen, P. H., Conger, J. J. & Kagan, J. (1979). *Child development and personality* (5th ed.). New York: Harper & Row.

Mussen, P. H., Conger, J. J., & Kagan, J. (1980). *Essentials of child development and personality* (5th ed.). New York: Harper & Row.

Mussen, P. H., Conger, J. J., Kagan, J., & Huston, A. C. (1984). *Child development and personality* (6th ed.). New York: Harper & Row.

Myers, D. G. (1983). *Social psychology,* New York: McGraw-Hill.

Naeye, R. L. (1980, April). Sudden infant death. *Scientific American,* pp. 56–62.

Nash, S. C. (1979). Sex role as a mediator of intellectual functioning. In M. A. Wittig & A. C. Petersen (Eds.), *Sex-related differences in cognitive functioning* (pp. 263–302). New York: Academic Press.

Nass, G. D., Libby, R. W. & Fisher, M. P. (1981). *Sexual choices: An introduction to human sexuality.* Belmont, CA: Wadsworth.

Natale, M., & Hantas, M. (1982). Effect of temporary mood

states on selective memory about the self. *Journal of Personality and Social Psychology, 42,* 927–934.

Nation, J. R., & Woods, D. J. (1980). Persistence: The role of partial reinforcement in psychotherapy. *Journal of Experimental Psychology: General, 109,* 175–207.

Nebes, R. D. (1974). Hemispheric specialization in commissurotomized man. *Psychological Bulletin, 81,* 1–14.

Nebes, R. D., & Sperry, R. W. (1971). Hemispheric deconnection syndrome with cerebral birth injury in the dominant arm area. *Neuropsychologia, 9,* 247.

Neisser, U., & Weene, P. (1962). Hierarchies in concept attainment. *Journal of Experimental Psychology, 64,* 640–645.

Nekanda-Trepka, C. J. S., Bishop, S., & Blackburn, I. M. (1983). Hopelessness and depression. *British Journal of Clinical Psychology, 22,* 49–60.

Nelson, K. (1973). Structure and strategy in learning to talk. *Monographs of the Society for Research in Child Development, 38* (1–2, Serial No. 149).

Nelson, T. O., & Rothbart, R. (1972). Acoustic savings for items forgotten from long-term memory. *Journal of Experimental Psychology, 93,* 357–360.

Neugarten, B. (1982, August 26). *Successful aging.* Paper presented at the 90th annual convention of the American Psychological Association, Washington, DC.

Newcomb, T. M. (1961). *The acquaintance process.* New York: Holt, Rinehart and Winston.

Newcombe, F., & Ratcliff, G. (1973). Handedness, speech lateralization and ability. *Neuropsychologia, 11,* 399–407.

Newman, B. M. (1982). Mid-life development. In B. B. Wolman (Ed.), *Handbook of developmental psychology* (pp. 617–635). Englewood Cliffs, NJ: Prentice-Hall.

Newman, J., & McCauley, C. (1977). Eye contact with strangers in city, suburb, and small town. *Environment and Behavior, 9,* 547–558.

Newman, O. (1972). *Defensible space: Crime prevention through urban design.* New York: Macmillan.

Newman, R. S., & Hirt, M. (1983). The psychoanalytic theory of depression: Symptoms as a function of aggressive wishes and level of field articulation. *Journal of Abnormal Psychology, 92,* 42–48.

Newton, B. W. (1983). The use of hypnosis in the treatment of cancer patients. *Hypnosis, 25,* 92–103.

Nickerson, R. S., & Adams, M. J. (1979). Long-term memory for a common object. *Cognitive Psychology, 11,* 287–307.

Nisbett, R. E. (1972). Hunger, obesity, and the ventromedial hypothalamus. *Psychological Review, 79,* 433–453.

Nisbett, R. E., & Wilson, T. D. (1977). The halo effect: Evidence for the unconscious alteration of judgments. *Journal of Personality and Social Psychology, 35,* 250–256.

Norman, D. A. (1976). *Memory and attention: An introduction to human information processing* (2nd ed.). New York: Wiley.

Nolte, J. (1981). *The human brain: An introduction to its functional anatomy.* St. Louis, MO: C. V. Mosby.

Nye, I. (n.d.). The effects of working mothers on children.

Science for Families: T.V. Newsfeature Project. Boys Town, NB: Boys Town Center for the Study of Youth Development.

Oakes, R. T. (1980, Winter). Marijuana and economic due process: A transition from prohibition to regulation. *Contemporary Drug Problems,* pp. 401–435.

O'Connell, P. (1977). *Facts '78.* White Plains, NY: National Foundation/March of Dimes.

O'Hara, M. W., Rehm, L. P., and Campbell, S. B. (1982). Predicting depressive symptomatology: Cognitive-behavioral models and postpartum depression. *Journal of Abnormal Psychology, 91,* 457–461.

Olds, J. (1972). Pleasure centers in the brain. In *Physiological psychology: Readings from Scientific American* (pp. 294–299). San Francisco: W. H. Freeman.

Olds, J., & Milner, P. (1954). Positive reinforcement produced by electrical stimulation of septal area and other regions of rat brain. *Journal of Comparative and Physiological Psychology, 47,* 419–427.

Oliveros, J. C., Jandali, M. K., Timsit-Berthier, M., Remy, R., Benghezal, A., Audibert, A., & Moeglen, J. M. (1978). Vasopressin in amnesia [Letter to the editor]. *The Lancet, 1,* 42.

Olton, D. S. (1979). Mazes, maps, and memory. *American Psychologist, 34,* 583–596.

Orme-Johnson, D., Dillbeck, M. C., Wallace, R. K., & Landrith, G. S. (1982). Inter-subject EEG coherence: Is consciousness a field? *International Journal of Neuroscience, 16,* 203–209.

Orwell, G. (1949). *1984.* New York: Harcourt, Brace.

Osherow, N. (1981). Making sense of the nonsensical: An analysis of Jonestown. In E. Aronson (Ed.), *Readings about the social animal* (3rd ed., pp. 69–88). San Francisco: W. H. Freeman.

Oskamp, S. (1977). *Attitudes and opinions.* Englewood Cliffs, NJ: Prentice-Hall.

Osmond, H. (1957). Function as the basis of psychiatric ward design. *Mental Hospitals, 8,* 23–29.

Osofsky, J. D., & Connors, K. (1979). Mother-infant interaction: An integrative view of a complex system. In J. D. Osofsky (Ed.), *Handbook of infant development* (pp. 519–548). New York: Wiley-Interscience.

Page, E. B., & Grandon, G. M. (1979). Family configuration and mental ability: Two theories contrasted with U.S. data. *American Educational Research Journal, 16,* 257–272.

Page, R. A. (1977). Noise and helping behavior. *Environment and Behavior, 9,* 311–335.

Pallak, M. S., Cook, D. A., & Sullivan, J. J. (1980). Commitment and energy conservation. In L. Bickman (Ed.), *Applied Social Psychology Annual* (Vol. 1, pp. 235–253). Beverly Hills, CA: Sage Publications.

Pantin, H. M., & Carver, C. S. (1982). Induced competence and the bystander effect. *Journal of Applied Social Psychology, 12,* 100–111.

Parke, R. D. (1974). Rules, roles, and resistance to deviation: Recent advances in punishment, discipline, and self-control. In A. D. Pick (Ed.), *Minnesota symposium on child psychology* (Vol. 8, pp. 111–143). Minneapolis: University of Minnesota Press.

Parke, R. D., & Asher, S. R. (1983). Social and personality development. *Annual Review of Psychology, 34,* 465–509.

Parrott, A. (1978). Erikson's developmental chart. In J. H. Brenneke & R. G. Amick (Eds.), *Readings in psychology and human experience* (2nd ed.): Encino, CA: Glencoe.

Parsons, J. E., Adler, T. F., & Kaczala, C. M. (1982). Socialization of achievement attitudes and beliefs: Parental influences. *Child Development, 53,* 310–321.

Patrusky, B. (1981, July–August). Why do we cry tears? *Science 81,* p. 104.

Patterson, C. H. (1980). *Theories of counseling and psychotherapy* (3rd ed.). New York: Harper & Row.

Patterson, F. (1978, October). Conversations with a gorilla. *National Geographic,* pp. 438–465.

Patterson, M. L., Mullens, S., & Romano, J. (1971). Compensatory reactions to spatial intrusion. *Sociometry, 34,* 114–121.

Patterson, M. L., & Sechrest, L. B. (1970). Interpersonal distance and impression formation. *Journal of Personality, 38,* 161–166.

Paul, G. L. (1966). *Insight versus desensitization in psychotherapy.* Stanford, CA: Stanford University Press.

Paul, G. L., & Lentz, R. J. (1977). *Psychosocial treatment of chronic mental patients: Milieu versus social-learning programs.* Cambridge, MA: Harvard University Press.

Paulus, P. B. (1980). Crowding. In P. B. Paulus (Ed.), *Psychology of group influence.* Hillsdale, NJ: Erlbaum.

Paulus, P. B., Annis, A. B., Seta, J. J., Schkade, J. K., & Matthews, R. W. (1976). Density does affect task performance. *Journal of Personality and Social Psychology, 34,* 248–253.

Paulus, P. B., Cox, V., McCain, G., & Chandler, J. (1975). Some effects of crowding in a prison environment. *Journal of Applied Social Psychology, 5,* 86–91.

Paulus, P. B., & Matthews, R. W. (1980). When density affects task performance. *Personality and Social Psychology Bulletin, 6,* 119–124.

Paulus, P. B., McCain, G., & Cox, V. C. (1978). Death rates, psychiatric commitments, blood pressure, and perceived crowding as a function of institutional crowding. *Environmental Psychology and Nonverbal Behavior, 3,* 107–116.

Pavlov, I. P. (1927). *Conditioned reflexes* (G. V. Anrep, Trans.). London: Oxford University Press.

Pearl, D., Bouthilet, L., & Lazar, J. (Eds.). (1982). *Television and behavior: Ten years of scientific progress and implications for the eighties* (Vols 1 & 2). Washington, D.C.: U.S. Government Printing Office

Pearson, K. (1914). *The life, letters, and labours of Francis Galton.* Cambridge: Cambridge University Press.

Penfield, W., & Perot, P. (1963). The brain's record of auditory and visual experience: A final summary and discussion. *Brain, 86,* 595–696.

Peplau, L. A. (1982). Interpersonal attraction. In D. Sherrod, *Social psychology* (pp. 194–229). New York: Random House.

Peplau, L. A., & Perlman, D. (1982). Perspectives on loneliness. In L. A. Peplau & D. Perlman (Eds.), *Loneliness: A sourcebook of current theory, research and therapy* (pp. 1–18). New York: Wiley.

Perls, F. S. (1969). *Gestalt therapy verbatim.* Lafayette, CA: Real People Press.

Perls, F. S. (1973). *The Gestalt approach and eyewitness to therapy.* Palo Alto, CA: Science and Behavior Books.

Pervin, L. A. (1963). The need to predict and control under conditions of threat. *Journal of Personality, 31,* 570–587.

Pervin, L. A. (1980). *Personality: Theory, assessment, and research* (3rd ed.). New York: Wiley.

Pervin, L. A., & Lewis, M. (Eds.). (1978). *Perspectives in interactional psychology.* New York: Plenum Publishing.

Peterson, J. M., & Lansky, L. M. (1974). Left-handedness among architects: Some facts and speculation. *Perceptual and Motor Skills, 38,* 547–550.

Petri, H. L. (1981). *Motivation: Theory and research.* Belmont, CA: Wadsworth.

Petty, R. E., & Cacioppo, J. T. (1981). *Attitudes and persuasion: Classic and contemporary approaches.* Dubuque, IA: Wm. C. Brown.

Phares, E. J. (1976). *Locus of control in personality.* Morristown, NJ: General Learning Press.

Phares, E. J. (1978). Locus of control. In H. London & J. E. Exner, Jr. (Eds.). *Dimensions of personality* (pp. 263–304). New York: Wiley.

Piaget, J. (1952). *The origins of intelligence in children* (2nd ed.). (M. Cook, Trans.). New York: International Universities Press. (Original work published 1936)

Piliavin, J. A., & Piliavin, I. (1972). Effects of blood on reactions to a victim. *Journal of Personality and Social Psychology, 23,* 353–361.

Pittman, T. S., Emery, J., & Boggiano, A. K. (1982). Intrinsic and extrinsic motivational orientations: Reward-induced changes in preference for complexity. *Journal of Personality and Social Psychology, 42,* 789–797.

Plomin, R. (1983). Developmental behavioral genetics. *Child Development, 54,* 253–259.

Plomin, R., DeFries, J. C., & McClearn, G. E. (1980). *Behavioral genetics.* San Francisco: W. H. Freeman.

Plotnik, R., & Mollenauer, S. (1978). *Brain and behavior: An introduction to physiological psychology.* San Francisco: Canfield Press.

Poindexter, J. (1983, May). Shaping the consumer. *Psychology Today,* pp. 64–68.

Pomazal, R. J., & Jaccard, J. J. (1976). An informational approach to altruistic behavior. *Journal of Personality and Social Psychology, 33,* 317–326.

Popp, G. E., & Muhs, W. F. (1982). Fear of success and women employees. *Human Relations, 35,* 511–519.

Posner, M. I. (1973). *Cognition: An introduction.* Glenview, IL: Scott, Foresman.

Posner, M. I., & Keele, S. W. (1967). Decay of visual information from a single letter. *Science, 158,* 137–139.

Potegal, M. (Ed.). (1982). *Spatial abilities: Development and physiological foundations.* New York: Academic Press.

Powledge, T. M. (1983, July). The importance of being twins. *Psychology Today,* pp. 20–27.

Premack, A. J., & Premack, D. (1972, October). Teaching language to an ape. *Scientific American,* pp. 92–99.

Premack, D. (1971). Language in chimpanzee? *Science, 172,* 808–822.

Pressley, M., Levin, J. R., & Delaney, H. D. (1982). The mnemonic keyword method. *Review of Educational Research, 52,* 61–91.

Prochaska, J. O., & Norcross, J. C. (1982). The future of psychotherapy: A Delphi poll. *Professional Psychology, 13,* 620–627.

Procidano, M. E., & Heller, K. (1983). Measures of perceived social support from friends and from family: Three validation studies. *American Journal of Community Psychology, 11,* 1–24.

President's Commission on Mental Health, National Institute of Mental Health. (1978). *Task panel reports.* (Vol. 4). Washington, DC: U.S. Government Printing Office.

Puthoff, H. E., & Targ, R. (1974). Experiments with Uri Geller. In C. Panati (Ed.), *The Geller Papers* (pp. 61–66). Boston: Houghton Mifflin.

Qualls, P. J., & Sheehan, P. W. (1981). Electromyograph biofeedback as a relaxation technique: A critical appraisal and reassessment. *Psychological Bulletin, 90,* 21–42.

Quattrochi-Tubin, S., & Jason, L. A. (1983). The influence of introversion-extraversion on activity choice and satisfaction among the elderly. *Personality and Individual Differences, 4,* 17–22.

Rabiner, C. J., & Klein, D. F. (1969). Imipramine treatment of school phobia. *Comprehensive Psychiatry, 10,* 387–390.

Rachman, S., Marks, I. M., & Hodgson, R. (1973). The treatment of obsessive-compulsive neurotics by modelling and flooding in vivo. *Behaviour Research and Therapy, 11,* 463–471.

Raczynski, J. M., Thompson, J. K., & Sturgis, E. T. (1982). An evaluation of biofeedback assessment and training paradigms. *Clinical Psychology Review, 2,* 337–348.

Ragosta, M. (1979). *Taking a long, hard look at CAI.* Princeton, NJ: Educational Testing Service.

Randi, J. (1980). *Flim flam!* New York: Lippincott and Crowell.

Raps, C. S., Peterson, C., Reinhard, K. E., Abramson, L. Y., & Seligman, M. E. P. (1982). Attributional style among depressed patients. *Journal of Abnormal Psychology, 91,* 102–108.

Rathus, S. A., & Nevid, J. S. (1983). *Adjustment and growth: The challenges of life* (2nd ed.). New York: Holt, Rinehart and Winston.

Rawlings, G., Reynolds, E. O. R., Stewart, A., & Strang, L. B. (1971). Changing prognosis for infants of very low birth weight. *Lancet, 1,* 516–519.

Ray, O. S. (1983). *Drugs, society and human behavior* (3rd ed.). St. Louis: C. V. Mosby.

Read any good records lately? (1982, January 4). *Time,* p. 84.

Reed, S. (1980). *Counseling in medical genetics* (3rd ed.). New York: Alan R. Liss.

Reed, S. K. (1982). *Cognition: Theory and applications.* Monterey, CA: Brooks/Cole.

Reeder, G. D., Henderson, D. J., & Sullivan, J. J. (1982). From dispositions to behaviors: The flip side of attribution. *Journal of Research in Personality, 16,* 355–375.

Rehm, L. P., & Marston, A. R. (1968). Reduction of social anxiety through modification of self-reinforcement: An instigation therapy technique. *Journal of Consulting and Clinical Psychology, 32,* 565–574.

Reingen, P. H. (1982). Test of a list procedure for inducing compliance with a request to donate money. *Journal of Applied Psychology, 67,* 110–118.

Reisenzein, R. (1983). The Schachter theory of emotion: Two decades later. *Psychological Bulletin, 94,* 239–264.

Reiss, S. (1982). Psychopathology and mental retardation: Survey of a developmental disabilities mental health program. *Mental Retardation, 20,* 128–132.

Reiss, S., Levitan, G. W., & McNally, R. J. (1982). Emotionally disturbed mentally retarded people. *American Psychologist, 37,* 361–367.

Reite, M. (1978a). Heart rate and body temperature in separated monkey infants. *Biological Psychiatry, 13,* 91–105.

Reite, M. (1978b). Loss of your mother is more than loss of your mother. *American Journal of Psychiatry, 135,* 370–371.

.Reiter, S. M., & Samuel, W. (1980). Littering as a function of prior litter and the presence or absence of prohibitive signs. *Journal of Applied Social Psychology, 10,* 45–55.

Reitman, J. S. (1974). Without surreptitious rehearsal, information in short-term memory decays. *Journal of Verbal Learning and Verbal Behavior, 13,* 365–377.

Rescorla, R. A. (1967). Pavlovian conditioning and its proper control procedures. *Psychological Review, 74,* 71–80.

Rescorla, R. A., & Holland, P. C. (1982). Behavioral studies of associative learning in animals. *Annual Review of Psychology, 33,* 265–308.

Rest, J. (1972). *Opinions about social problems.* Minneapolis, MN: James Rest.

Restak, R. (1982, May). Islands of genius. *Science 82,* pp. 62–67.

Restle, F. (1970). Moon illusion explained on the basis of relative size. *Science, 167,* 1092–1096.

Reynolds, G. S. (1975). *A primer of operant conditioning.* Glenview, IL: Scott, Foresman.

Rhodewalt, F., & Davison, J., Jr. (1983). Reactance and the coronary-prone behavior pattern: The role of self-attribution in responses to reduced behavioral freedom. *Journal of Personality and Social Psychology, 44,* 220–228.

Rice, B. (1981, December). Call-in therapy: Reach out and shrink someone. *Psychology Today,* pp. 39, 41, 44, 87–88, 91.

Rice, K. M., & Blanchard, E. B. (1982). Biofeedback in the treatment of anxiety disorders. *Clinical Psychology Review,*

2, 557–577.

Richardson, D., & Campbell, J. L. (1982). Alcohol and rape: The effect of alcohol on attributions of blame for rape. *Personality and Social Psychology Bulletin, 8,* 468–476.

Ridley, M., & Dawkins, R. (1981). The natural selection of altruism. In J. P. Rushton & R. M. Sorrentino (Eds.), *Altruism and helping behavior: Social, personality, and developmental perspectives* (pp. 19–39). Hillsdale, NJ: Erlbaum.

Riesen, A. H. (1947). The development of visual perception in man and chimpanzee. *Science, 106,* 107–108.

Rimland, B. (1978, August). Inside the mind of the autistic savant. *Psychology Today,* pp. 69–70, 73–74, 77–80.

Rimm, D. C. (1977). Behavior therapy. In D. C. Rimm & J. W. Somervill (Eds.), *Abnormal psychology* (pp. 455–480). New York: Academic Press.

Rimm, D. C., & Masters, J. C. (1979). *Behavior therapy: Techniques and empirical findings* (2nd ed.). New York: Academic Press.

Rimm, D. C., & Somervill, J. W. (1977). *Abnormal psychology.* New York: Academic Press.

Riskind, J. H., & Gotay, C. C. (1982). Physical posture: Could it have regulatory or feedback effects on motivation and emotion? *Motivation and Emotion, 6,* 273–298.

Riskind, J. H., & Wilson, D. W. (1982). Interpersonal attraction for the competitive person: Unscrambling the competition paradox. *Journal of Applied Social Psychology, 12,* 444–452.

Ritchie, R. J., & Moses, J. L. (1983). Assessment center correlates of women's advancement into middle management: A 7-year longitudinal analysis. *Journal of Applied Psychology, 68,* 227–231.

Robinson, F. P. (1970). *Effective study* (4th ed.). New York: Harper & Row.

Roche, G. R. (1979, January–February). Much ado about mentors. *Harvard Business Review,* pp. 14–16, 20, 24, 26–28.

Rodgers, J. E. (1982, June). The malleable memory of eyewitnesses. *Science 82,* pp. 32–35.

Rodin, J. (1976). Density, perceived choice, and response to controllable and uncontrollable outcomes. *Journal of Experimental Social Psychology, 12,* 564–578.

Rodin, J. (1981). Current status of the internal-external hypothesis for obesity: What went wrong? *American Psychologist, 36,* 361–372.

Rogers, C. R. (1951). *Client-centered therapy.* Boston: Houghton Mifflin.

Rogers, C. R. (1959). A theory of therapy, personality, and interpersonal relationships, as developed in the client-centered framework. In S. Koch (Ed.), *Psychology: A study of a science* (Vol. 3, pp. 184–256). New York: McGraw-Hill.

Rogers, C. R. (1961). *On becoming a person.* Boston: Houghton Mifflin.

Rohe, W. M. (1982). The response to density in residential settings: The mediating effects of social and personal variables. *Journal of Applied Social Psychology, 12,* 292–303.

Roper, G., Rachman, S., & Marks, I. M. (1975). Passive and participant modeling in exposure treatment of obsessive-compulsive neurotics. *Behaviour Research and Therapy, 13,* 271–279.

Rosch, E. (1974). Linguistic relativity. In A. Silverstein (Ed.), *Human communication: Theoretical perspectives* (pp. 95–121). New York: Halsted Press.

Rosch, E. (1978). Principles of categorization. In E. Rosch & B. Lloyd (Eds.), *Cognition and categorization* (pp. 27–48). Hillsdale, NJ: Erlbaum.

Rosen, R., & Rosen, L. R. (1981). *Human sexuality.* New York: Knopf.

Rosenblatt, R. (1983, April 18). The male response to rape. *Time,* p. 98.

Rosenfield, D., Folger, R., & Adelman, H. F. (1980). When rewards reflect competence: A qualification of the overjustification effect. *Journal of Personality and Social Psychology, 39,* 368–376.

Rosenthal, A. M. (1964). *Thirty-eight witnesses.* New York: McGraw-Hill.

Rosenthal, R., & Jacobson, L. F. (1968, April). Teacher expectations for the disadvantaged. *Scientific American,* pp. 19–23.

Rosenthal, T., & Bandura, A. (1978). Psychological modeling: Theory and practice. In S. L. Garfield & A. E. Bergin (Eds.), *Handbook of psychotherapy and behavior change: An empirical analysis* (2nd ed., pp. 621–658). New York: Wiley.

Rosenzweig, M. R., Bennett, E. L., & Diamond, M. C. (1973). Brain changes in response to experience. In *The nature and nurture of behavior: Readings from Scientific American* (pp. 117–124). San Francisco: W. H. Freeman.

Ross, A. O. (1980). *Psychological disorders of children.* New York: McGraw-Hill.

Ross, M., Layton, B., Erickson, B., & Schopler, J. (1973). Affect, facial regard, and reactions to crowding. *Journal of Personality and Social Psychology, 28,* 69–76.

Ross, R. J., Cole, M., Thompson, J. S., & Kim, K. H. (1983). Boxers—Computed tomography, EEG, and neurological evaluation. *Journal of the American Medical Association, 249,* 211–213.

Rothbaum, F., Weisz, J. R., & Snyder, S. S. (1982). Changing the world and changing the self: A two-process model of perceived control. *Journal of Personality and Social Psychology, 42,* 5–37.

Rotter, J. B. (1954). *Social learning and clinical psychology.* Englewood Cliffs, NJ: Prentice-Hall.

Rotter, J. B. (1966). Generalized expectancies for internal versus external control of reinforcement. *Psychological Monographs, 80* (1, Whole No. 609).

Rotter, J. B., Chance, J. E., & Phares, E. J. (1972). *Applications of a social learning theory of personality.* New York: Holt, Rinehart and Winston.

Rotter, J. B., & Hochreich, D. J. (1975). *Personality.* Glenview, IL: Scott, Foresman.

Rubenstein, R., & Newman, R. (1954). The living out of "future" experiences under hypnosis. *Science, 119,* 472–473.

Rubin, D. C., & Olson, M. J. (1980). Recall of semantic domains. *Memory & Cognition, 8,* 354–366.

Rubinstein, E. A. (1983). Television and behavior: Research conclusions of the 1982 NIMH report and their policy implications. *American Psychologist, 38,* 820–825.

Rubinstein, J., & Slife, B. D. (Eds.). (1982). *Taking sides: Clashing views on controversial psychological issues* (2nd ed.). Guilford, CT: Dushkin.

Rumbaugh, D. M. (Ed.). (1977). *Language learning by a chimpanzee: The Lana project.* New York: Academic Press.

Rundus, D., Loftus, G. R., & Atkinson, R. C. (1970). Immediate free recall and three-week delayed recognition. *Journal of Verbal Learning and Verbal Behavior, 9,* 684–688.

Rush, A. J. (1983). Cognitive therapy of depression: Rationale, techniques, and efficacy. *The Psychiatric Clinics of North America, 6,* 105–128.

Rush, A. J., Beck, A. T., Kovacs, M., & Hollon, S. D. (1977). Comparative efficacy of cognitive therapy and pharmacotherapy in the treatment of depressed outpatients. *Cognitive Therapy and Research, 1,* 17–39.

Rushton, J. P. (1975). Generosity in children: Immediate and long-term effects of modeling, preaching, and moral judgment. *Journal of Personality and Social Psychology, 31,* 459–466.

Russell, J. A., & Ward, L. M. (1982). Environmental psychology. *Annual Review of Psychology, 33,* 651–688.

Rutkowski, G. K., Gruder, C. L., & Romer, D. (1983). Group cohesiveness, social norms, and bystander intervention. *Journal of Personality and Social Psychology, 44,* 545–552.

Rychlak, J. F. (1981). *Introduction to personality and psychotherapy* (2nd ed). Boston: Houghton Mifflin.

Ryckman, R. M. (1982). *Theories of personality* (2nd ed.). Monterey, CA: Brooks/Cole.

Saegert, S. C., Swap, W., & Zajonc, R. B. (1973). Exposure, context, and interpersonal attraction. *Journal of Personality and Social Psychology, 25,* 234–242.

Saks, M. J. (1976, January). Social scientists can't rig juries. *Psychology Today,* pp. 48–50, 55–57.

Salamy, J. G. (1976). Sleep: Some concepts and constructs. In R. L. Williams & I. Karacan (Eds.), *Pharmacology of sleep* (pp. 53–82). New York: Wiley.

Salapatek, P. (1975). Pattern perception in early infancy. In L. B. Cohen and P. Salapatek (Eds.), *Infant perception: From sensation to cognition* (Vol. 1, pp. 133–248). New York: Academic Press.

Salk, L. (1982, June). How boredom affects infants and children. *A letter from Dr. Lee Salk* (Vol. 1, No. 4), pp. 1–8.

Salzinger, S., Kaplan, S., & Artemyeff, C. (1983). Mothers' personal social networks and child maltreatment. *Journal of Abnormal Psychology, 92,* 68–76.

Samelson, F. (1980). J. B. Watson's Little Albert, Cyril Burt's twins, and the need for a critical science. *American Psychologist, 35,* 619–625.

Sanders, D. (1978). *The relationship of attitude variables and explanations of perceived and actual career attainment in male and female business persons.* Unpublished doctoral dissertation, University of Texas at Austin.

Sanders, G. S., & Simmons, W. L. (1983). Use of hypnosis to enhance eyewitness accuracy: Does it work? *Journal of Applied Psychology, 68,* 70–77.

Santrock, J. W. (1983). *Life-span development.* Dubuque, IA: Wm. C. Brown.

Sarason, I. G. (1981). Test anxiety, stress, and social support. *Journal of Personality, 49,* 101–114.

Sarason, I. G., Levine, H. M., Basham, R. B., & Sarason, B. R. (1983). Assessing social support: The Social Support Questionnaire. *Journal of Personality and Social Psychology, 44,* 127–139.

Sarason, I. G., & Sarason, B. R. (1980). *Abnormal psychology* (3rd ed.). Englewood Cliffs, NJ: Prentice-Hall.

Sarason, I. G., Smith, R. E., & Diener, E. (1975). Personality research: Components of variance attributable to the person and the situation. *Journal of Personality and Social Psychology, 32,* 199–204.

Saulnier, K., & Perlman, D. (1981). The actor-observer bias is alive and well in prison: A sequel to Wells. *Personality and Social Psychology Bulletin, 7,* 559–564.

Scarr, S. (1981). *Race, social class, and individual differences in I.Q.* Hillsdale, NJ: Erlbaum.

Scarr, S., & Weinberg, R. A. (1976). IQ test performance of black children adopted by white families. *American Psychologist, 31,* 726–739.

Scarr-Salapatek, S., & Williams, M. L. (1973). The effects of early stimulation on low birth weight infants. *Child Development, 44,* 94–101.

Schachter, S. (1959). *The psychology of affiliation.* Stanford, CA: Stanford University Press.

Schachter, S. (1964). The interaction of cognitive and physiological determinants of emotional state. In L. Berkowitz (Ed.), *Advances in experimental social psychology* (Vol. 1, pp. 49–80). New York: Academic Press.

Schachter, S. (1982). Recidivism and self-cure of smoking and obesity. *American Psychologist, 37,* 436–444.

Schachter, S., & Singer, J. E. (1962). Cognitive, social, and physiological determinants of emotional states. *Psychological Review, 69,* 379–399.

Schachter, S., & Singer, J. E. (1979). Comments on the Maslach and Marshall-Zimbardo experiments. *Journal of Personality and Social Psychology, 37,* 989–995.

Schacter, D. L. (1983). Feeling of knowing in episodic memory. *Journal of Experimental Psychology: Learning, Memory, and Cognition, 9,* 39–54.

Schaeffer, J., Andrysiak, T., & Ungerleider, J. T. (1981). Cognition and long-term use of ganja (cannabis). *Science, 213,* 465–466.

Schaffer, H. R., & Emerson, P. E. (1964). The development of social attachments in infancy. *Monographs of the Society for Research in Child Development, 3 29,* No. 3, (Serial No. 94).

Schaffer, N. D. (1982). Multidimensional measures of therapist behavior as predictors of outcome. *Psychological Bulletin, 92,* 670–681.

Schell, R. E., & Hall, E. (1983). *Developmental psychology to-*

day (4th ed.). New York: Random House.

Schlaadt, R. G., & Shannon, P. T. (1982). *Drugs of choice: Current perspectives on drug use.* Englewood Cliffs, NJ: Prentice-Hall.

Schlesser, M. A., & Altshuler, K. Z. (1983). The genetics of affective disorder—Data, theory, and clinical application. *Hospital and Community Psychiatry, 34,* 415–422.

Schmidt, D. E., & Keating, J. P. (1979). Human crowding and personal control: An integration of the research. *Psychological Bulletin, 86,* 680–700.

Schneider, D. J. (1976). *Social psychology.* Reading, MA: Addison-Wesley.

Schneider, D. J., Hastorf, A. H., & Ellsworth, P. C. (1979). *Person perception* (2nd ed.). Reading, MA: Addison-Wesley.

Schreiner, T. (1983, June 6). How old are we: *USA Today,* p. 1A.

Schulman, J., Shaver, P., Colman, R., Emrich, B., & Christie, R. (1973, May). Recipe for a jury. *Psychology Today,* pp. 37–44, 77, 79–84.

Schultz, D. (1981a). *A history of modern psychology* (3rd ed.). New York: Academic Press.

Schultz, D. (1981b). *Theories of personality* (2nd ed.). Monterey, CA: Brooks/Cole.

Schwartz, S. H. & Clausen, G. T. (1970). Responsibility, norms and helping in an emergency. *Journal of Personality and Social Psychology, 16,* 299–310.

Schwartz, S. H., & Gottlieb, A. (1980). Participation in a bystander intervention experiment and subsequent everyday helping: Ethical considerations. *Journal of Experimental Social Psychology, 16,* 161–171.

Schwarzwald, J., Bizman, A., & Raz, M. (1983). The foot-in-the-door paradigm: Effects of second request size on donation probability and donor generosity. *Personality and Social Psychology Bulletin, 9,* 443–450.

Sears, R. R. (1977). Sources of life satisfactions in the Terman gifted men. *American Psychologist, 32,* 119–129.

Sebeok, T. A., & Umiker-Sebeok, J. (1979, November). Performing animals: Secrets of the trade. *Psychology Today,* pp. 78–82, 91.

Secret voices: Messages that manipulate. (1979, September 10). *Time,* p. 71.

Seeman, M. (1963). Alienation and social learning in a reformatory. *American Journal of Sociology, 69,* 270–284.

Segal, M. W. (1974). Alphabet and attraction: An unobtrusive measure of the effect of propinquity in a field setting. *Journal of Personality and Social Psychology, 30,* 654–657.

Seligman, C., Becker, L. J., & Darley, J. M. (1981). Encouraging residential energy conservation through feedback. In A. Baum & J. E. Singer (Eds.), *Advances in environmental psychology* (Vol. 3). Hillsdale, NJ: Erlbaum.

Seligman, C., Brickman, J., & Koulack, D. (1977). Rape and physical attractiveness: Assigning responsibility to victims. *Journal of Personality, 45,* 554–563.

Seligman, C., & Darley, J. M. (1977). Feedback as a means of decreasing residential energy consumption. *Journal of Applied Psychology, 62,* 363–368.

Seligman, M. E. P. (1968). Chronic fear produced by unpredictable electric shock. *Journal of Comparative and Physiological Psychology, 66,* 402–411.

Seligman, M. E. P. (1970). On the generality of the laws of learning. *Psychological Review, 77,* 406–418.

Seligman, M. E. P. (1975). *Helplessness: On depression, development, and death.* San Francisco: W. H. Freeman.

Seligmann, J. (1983, March 7). A deadly feast and famine. *Newsweek,* pp. 59–60.

Selye, H. (1974). *Stress without distress.* New York: Lippincott & Crowell.

Selye. H. (1976). *The stress of life* (rev. ed.). New York: McGraw-Hill.

Selye, H. (1980). The stress concept today. In I. L. Kutash & L. B. Schlesinger (Eds.), *Handbook of stress and anxiety* (pp. 127–143). San Francisco: Jossey-Bass.

Sergent, J. (1983). Role of input in visual hemispheric asymmetries. *Psychological Bulletin, 93,* 481–512.

Shanab, M. E., & Yahya, K. A. (1977). A behavioral study of obedience in children. *Journal of Personality and Social Psychology, 35,* 530–536.

Shapiro, D. A., & Shapiro, D. (1982). Meta-analysis of comparative therapy outcome studies: A replication and refinement. *Psychological Bulletin, 92,* 581–604.

Shapiro, D. H. (1982). Overview: Clinical and physiological comparison of meditation with other self-control strategies. *American Journal of Psychiatry, 139,* 267–274.

Shapiro, E. C., Haseltine, F. P., & Rowe, M. P. (1978). Moving up: Role models, mentors, and the "patron system." *Sloan Management Review, 19,* 51–58.

Shaver, P., & Freedman, J. L. (1976, August). Happiness. *Psychology Today,* pp. 26–29, 31–32, 75.

Shaver, P., & Klinnert, M. (1982). Schachter's theories of affiliation and emotion: Implications of developmental research. In L. Wheeler (Ed.), *Review of personality and social psychology* (Vol. 3, pp. 37–72). Beverly Hills, CA: Sage Publications.

Shaver, P., & Rubenstein, C. (1980). Childhood attachment experience and adult loneliness. In L. Wheeler (Ed.), *Review of personality and social psychology: Vol. 1* (pp. 42–73). Beverly Hills, CA: Sage Publications.

Shean, G. (1978). *Schizophrenia: An introduction to research and theory.* Cambridge, MA: Winthrop Publishing.

Sheehan, P. W., & Tilden, J. (1983). Effects of suggestibility and hypnosis on accurate and distorted retrieval from memory. *Journal of Experimental Psychology: Learning, Memory, and Cognition, 9,* 283–293.

Sheehy, G. (1976a, April). The mentor connection: The secret link in the successful woman's life. *New York Magazine,* pp. 33–39.

Sheehy, G. (1976b). *Passages: Predictable crises of adult life.* New York: Dutton.

Sherrod, D. R. (1974). Crowding, perceived control, and behavioral aftereffects. *Journal of Applied Social Psychology, 4,* 171–186.

Sherrod, D. R. (1982). The physical environment and social behavior. In D. Sherrod, *Social psychology* (pp. 378–414). New York: Random House.

Sherrod, D. R., & Cohen, S. (1978). Density, personal control, and design. In S. Kaplan & R. Kaplan (Eds.), *Humanscape: Environments for people* (pp. 331–338). North Scituate, MA: Duxbury Press.

Sherrod, D. R., & Downs, R. (1974). Environmental determinants of altruism: The effects of stimulus overload and perceived control on helping. *Journal of Experimental Social Psychology, 10,* 468–479.

Sherrod, D. R., Hage, J. N., Halpern, P. L., & Moore, B. S. (1977). Effects of personal causation and perceived control on responses to an aversive environment: The more control the better. *Journal of Experimental Social Psychology, 13,* 14–27.

Shorey, H. H. (1977). Pheromones. In T. A. Sebeok (Ed.), *How animals communicate* (pp. 137–163). Bloomington: Indiana University Press.

Shriberg, L. K., Levin, J. R., McCormick, C. B., & Pressley, M. (1982). Learning about "famous" people via the keyword method. *Journal of Educational Psychology, 74,* 238–247.

Shucard, D. W., Cummins, K. R., & McGee, M. G. (1984). Event-related brain potentials differentiate normal and disabled readers. *Brain and Language 21* 318–334.

Shucard, D. W., Shucard, J. C. & Thomas, D. G. (1977). Auditory evoked potentials as probes of hemispheric differences in cognition processing. *Science, 197,* 1295–1298.

Shucard, J. L., Shucard, D. W., Cummins, K. R., & Campos, J. J. (1981). Auditory evoked potentials and sex related differences in brain development. *Brain and Language, 13,* 91–102.

Shulman, H. G. (1972). Semantic confusion errors in short-term memory. *Journal of Verbal Learning and Verbal Behavior, 11,* 221–227.

Siegel, M., & Pallak, M. S. (1983, May). PT and APA: A perfect marriage. *APA Monitor,* p. 5.

Siegel, R. K. (1982). Cocaine and sexual dysfunction: The curse of mama coca. *Journal of Psychoactive Drugs, 14,* 71–74.

Siegler, R. S. (1983). Five generalizations about cognitive development. *American Psychologist, 38,* 263–277.

Sigall, H., & Aronson, E. (1969). Liking for an exaluator as a function of her physical attractiveness and nature of the evaluations. *Journal of Experimental Social Psychology, 5,* 93–100.

Sigall, H., & Ostrove, N. (1975). Beautiful but dangerous: Effects of offender attractiveness and nature of the crime on juridic judgment. *Journal of Personality and Social Psychology, 31,* 410–414.

Silverman, L. H. (1976). Psychoanalytic theory: The reports of my death are greatly exaggerated. *American Psychologist, 31,* 621–637.

Silverman, L. H., & Fishel, A. K., (1981). The Oedipus Complex: Studies in adult male behavior. In L. Wheeler (Ed.), *Review of personality and social psychology* (Vol. 2, pp. 43–67). Beverly Hills, CA: Sage Publications.

Silverman, R. E. (1982). *Psychology* (4th ed.). Englewood Cliffs, NJ: Prentice-Hall.

Simkins, L. (1982). Biofeedback: Clinically valid or oversold? *The Psychological Record, 32,* 3–17.

Simonds, J. F., & Parraga, H. (1982). Prevalence of sleep disorders and sleep behaviors in children and adolescents. *Journal of the American Academy of Child Psychiatry, 21,* 383–388.

Simpson, E. L. (1974). Moral development research: A case study of scientific cultural bias. *Human Development, 17,* 81–106.

Singer, D. G. (1983). A time to reexamine the role of television in our lives. *American Psychologist, 38,* 815–816.

Singer, J. L., & Singer, D. G. (1983). Psychologists look at television: Cognitive, developmental, personality, and social policy implications. *American Psychologist, 38,* 826–834.

Singular, S. (1982, October). A memory for all seasonings. *Psychology Today,* pp. 54–61, 63.

Sivacek, J., & Crano, W. D. (1982). Vested interest as a moderator of attitude-behavior consistency. *Journal of Personality and Social Psychology, 43,* 210–221.

Skinner, B. F. (1938). *The behavior of organisms.* New York: Appleton-Century-Crofts.

Skinner, B. F. (1948a). "Superstition" in the pigeon. *Journal of Experimental Psychology, 38,* 168–172.

Skinner, B. F. (1948b). *Walden two.* New York: Macmillan.

Skinner, B. F. (1953). *Science and human behavior.* New York: Free Press.

Skinner, B. F. (1957). *Verbal behavior.* Englewood Cliffs, NJ: Prentice-Hall.

Skinner, B. F. (1971). *Beyond freedom and dignity.* New York: Knopf.

Skinner, B. F. (1972). *Cumulative record* (3rd ed.). New York: Appleton-Century-Crofts.

Skinner, B. F. (1974). *About behaviorism.* New York: Knopf.

Skinner, B. F. (1979, March). My experience with the baby-tender. *Psychology Today,* pp. 29–40.

Skinner, B. F. (1982, August). *Why are we not acting to save the world?* Paper presented at the 90th annual convention of the American Psychological Association, Washington, DC.

Sklar, L. S., & Anisman, H. (1981). Stress and cancer. *Psychological Bulletin, 89,* 369–406.

Skrypnek, B. J., & Snyder, M. (1982). On the self-perpetuating nature of stereotypes about women and men. *Journal of Experimental Social Psychology, 18,* 277–291.

Slamecka, N. J. (1960). Retroactive inhibition of connected discourse as a function of practice level. *Journal of Experimental Psychology, 59,* 104–108.

Slater, E., & Shields, J. (1969). Genetical aspects of anxiety. In M. H. Lader (Ed.), *Studies of anxiety.* Ashford, England: Headley Brothers.

Slife, B. D., & Rychlak, J. F. (1982). Role of affective assessment in modeling aggressive behavior. *Journal of Personality and Social Psychology, 43,* 861–868.

Sloane, R. B., Staples, F. R., Cristol, A. N., Yorkston, N. J., & Whipple, K. (1975). *Psychotherapy versus behavior therapy.* Cambridge, MA: Harvard University Press.

Slobin, D. I. (1972, July). Children and language: They learn the same way all around the world. *Psychology Today,* pp. 71–74, 82.

Slobin, D. I. (1979). *Psycholinguistics* (2nd ed.). Glenview, IL: Scott, Foresman.

Smith, B. D., & Vetter, H. J. (1982). *Theoretical approaches to personality.* Englewood Cliffs, NJ: Prentice-Hall.

Smith, E. E. (1983). Memory. In R. L. Atkinson, R. C. Atkinson, & E. R. Hilgard, *Introduction to psychology* (8th ed., pp. 220–251). New York: Harcourt Brace Jovanovich.

Smith, M. E. (1926). An investigation of the development of the sentence and the extent of vocabulary in young children. *University of Iowa studies in child welfare, 3* (5).

Smith, M. L., & Glass, G. V. (1977). Meta-analysis of psychotherapy outcome studies. *American Psychologist, 32,* 752–760.

Smith, R. J., & Knowles, E. S. (1978). Attributional consequences of personal space invasions. *Personality and Social Psychology Bulletin, 4,* 429–433.

Smith, S. (1973). *ESP and hypnosis.* New York: Macmillan.

Smith, S. M. (1979). Remembering in and out of context. *Journal of Experimental Psychology: Human Learning and Memory, 5,* 460–471.

Smith, S. M. (1982). Enhancement of recall using multiple environmental contexts during learning. *Memory & Cognition, 10,* 405–412.

Smith, S. M., Glenberg, A., & Bjork, R. A. (1978). Environmental context and human memory. *Memory & Cognition, 6,* 342–353.

Smith, T. W. (1982). Irrational beliefs in the cause and treatment of emotional distress: A critical review of the rational-emotive model. *Clinical Psychology Review, 2,* 505–522.

Sniffen, M. J. (1981, August 24). Prison double-celling harmful, new study says, *Bryan-College Station Eagle,* pp. 1A, 4A.

Snyder, M. (1982, July). Self-fulfilling stereotypes. *Psychology Today,* pp. 60, 65, 67–68.

Snyder, M., & White, P. (1982). Moods and memories: Elation, depression, and the remembering of the events of one's life. *Journal of Personality, 50,* 149–167.

Snyder, S. H. (1982). Wonders of the brain. In *On the brink of tomorrow: Frontiers of Science* (pp. 172–192). Washington, DC: National Geographic Society

Solano, C. H., Batten, P. G., & Parish, E. A. (1982). Loneliness and patterns of self-disclosure. *Journal of Personality and Social Psychology, 43,* 524–531.

Sommer, R. (1969). *Personal space: The behavioral basis of design.* Englewood Cliffs, NJ: Prentice-Hall.

Sommer, R. (1974). *Tight spaces: Hard architecture and how to humanize it.* Englewood Cliffs, NJ: Prentice-Hall.

Sommer, R. (1980). The environment and human behavior. In P. N. Middlebrook, *Social Psychology and modern life* (2nd ed, pp. 461–497). New York: Knopf.

Sommer, R., & Ross, H. (1958). Social interaction on a geriatrics ward. *International Journal of Social Psychiatry, 4,* 128–133.

Sontag, L. W., & Wallace, R. F. (1935). The effect of cigarette smoking during pregnancy upon the fetal heart rate. *American Journal of Obstetrics and Gynecology, 29,* 77–83.

Soul of a hero. (1983, January 3). *Time,* p. 53.

Spector, P. E. (1982). Behavior in organizations as a function of employee's locus of control. *Psychological Bulletin, 91,* 482–497.

Speisman, J., Lazarus, R., Mordkoff, A., & Davison, L. (1964). Experimental reduction of stress based on ego-defense theory. *Journal of Abnormal and Social Psychology, 68,* 367–380.

Spence, J. T., & Helmreich, R. L. (1978). *Masculinity and feminity: Their psychological dimensions, correlates, and antecedents.* Austin: University of Texas Press.

Sperry, R. W. (1982). Some effects of disconnecting the cerebral hemispheres. Science, 217, 1223–1226.

Spiegel, H., & Spiegel, D. (1978). *Trance and treatment: Clinical uses of hypnosis.* New York: Basic Books.

Spiegler, M. D. (1983). *Contemporary behavioral therapy.* Palo Alto, CA: Mayfield Publishing.

Spitz, R. A. (1945). Hospitalization: An inquiry into the genesis of psychiatric conditions in early childhood. *Psychoanalytic Study of the Child, 1,* 53–74.

Spitz, R. A. (1950). Anxiety in infancy: A study of its manifestations in the first year of life. *International Journal of Psycho-Analysis, 31,* 138–143.

Srole, L. (1972). Urbanization and mental health: Some reformulations. *American Scientist, 60,* 576–583.

Sroufe, R., Chaikin, A., Cook, R., & Freeman, V. (1977). The effects of physical attractiveness on honesty: A socially desirable response. *Personality and Social Psychology Bulletin, 3,* 59–62.

Staats, A. W. (1968). Social behaviorism and human motivation: Principles of the attitude-reinforcer-discriminative system. In A. G. Greenwald, T. C. Brock, & T. M. Ostrom (Eds.), *Psychological foundations of attitudes* (pp. 33–66). New York: Academic Press.

Stanley, J. C. (1976). Test better finder of great math talent than teachers are. *American Psychologist, 31,* 313–314.

Stanley, J. C., Keating, D. P., & Fox, L. H. (Eds.). (1974). *Mathematical talent: Discovery, description and development.* Baltimore: Johns Hopkins University Press.

Stanton, M. D., Mintz, J., & Franklin, R. M. (1976). Drug flashbacks: II. Some additional findings. *International Journal of Addictions, 11,* 53–59.

Stapp, J., & Fulcher, R. (1981). The employment of APA members. *American Psychologist, 36,* 1263–1314.

Stapp, J. & Fulcher, R. (1983). The employment of APA members: 1982. *American Psychologist, 38,* 1298–1320.

Starch, D. (1966). *Measuring advertising readership and results.* New York: McGraw-Hill.

Staub, E. (1978). *Positive social behavior and morality: Social and personal influences.* New York: Academic Press.

Staub, E., & Baer, R. S., Jr. (1974). Stimulus characteristics of a sufferer and difficulty of escape as determinants of helping. *Journal of Personality and Social Psychology, 30,* 279–284.

Stechler, G., & Halton, A. (1982). Prenatal influences on human development. In B. B. Wolman (Ed.), *Handbook of developmental psychology* (pp. 175–189). Englewood Cliffs, NJ: Prentice-Hall.

Steinbach, A. (1982, October 24). The real Eve. *Denver Post,* pp. 6, 22–24.

Stengel, R. (1982, May 17). Calling "Dr. SUMEX." *Time,* p. 71.

Stern, G. S., McCants, T. R., & Pettine, P. W. (1982). Stress and illness: Controllable and uncontrollable life events' relative contributions. *Personality and Social Psychology Bulletin, 8,* 140–145.

Stern, R. S., Lipsedge, M. A., & Marks, I. M. (1973). Thought-stopping of neutral and obsessive thoughts: A controlled trial. *Behaviour Research and Therapy, 11,* 659–662.

Sternberg, S. (1966). High-speed scanning in human memory. *Science, 153,* 652–654.

Sternberg, S. (1969). Memory-scanning: Mental processes revealed by reaction-time experiments. *American Scientist, 57,* 421–457.

Stevens, C. F. (1979). The neuron. In *The brain: A Scientific American book* (pp. 15–25). San Francisco: W. H. Freeman.

Stewart, A. J., & Salt, P. (1981). Life stress, life-styles, depression, and illness in adult women. *Journal of Personality and Social Psychology, 40,* 1063–1069.

Stewart, R. (1965). Effects of continuous responding on the order effect in personality impression formation. *Journal of Personality and Social Psychology, 1,* 161–165.

Stine, G. J. (1977). *Biosocial genetics.* New York: Macmillan.

Strickland, B. R. (1977). Internal-external control of reinforcement. In T. Blass (Ed.), *Personality variables in social behavior* (pp. 219–279). Hillsdale, NJ: Earlbaum.

Stokols, D. S. (1972). On the distinction between density and crowding: Some implications for future research. *Psychological Review, 79,* 275–277.

Stokols, D. S. (1982). Environmental psychology: A coming of age. In A. G. Kraut (Ed.), *The G. Stanley Hall Lecture Series* (Vol. 2, pp. 159–205). Washington, DC: American Psychological Association.

Storms, M. D., & Thomas, G. C. (1977). Reactions to physical closeness. *Journal of Personality and Social Psychology, 35,* 412–418.

Strahle, W. M. (1983). A model of premarital coitus and contraceptive behavior among female adolescents. *Archives of Sexual Behavior, 12,* 67–94.

Strong, B., & Reynolds, R. (1982). *Understanding our sexuality.* St. Paul, MN: West.

Stuart, R. B. (1980). *Helping couples change: A social learning approach to marital therapy.* New York: Guilford.

Sue, D., Sue, D. W., & Sue, S. (1981). *Understanding abnormal behavior.* Boston: Houghton Mifflin.

Suinn, R. M. (1976, December). How to break the vicious cycle of stress. *Psychology Today,* pp. 59–60.

Suinn, R. M. (1982). Intervention with Type A behaviors. *Journal of Consulting and Clinical Psychology, 50,* 933–949.

Sundstrom, E. (1975). An experimental study of crowding: Effects of room size, intrusion, and goal-blocking on nonverbal behaviors, self-disclosure, and self-reported stress. *Journal of Personality and Social Psychology, 32,* 645–654.

Suttles, G. D. (1968). *The social order of the slum.* Chicago: University of Chicago Press.

Super, D., & Super, C. (1978). *Opportunities in psychology.* Skokie, Il: National Textbook.

Super, D. E. (1957). *The psychology of careers.* New York: Harper & Row.

Super, D. E., & Hall, D. T. (1978). Career development: Exploration and planning. *Annual Review of Psychology, 29,* 333–372.

Superkids? A sperm bank for nobelists. (1980, March 10). *Time,* p. 49.

Swann, W. B., Jr., & Miller, L. C. (1982). Why never forgetting a face matters: Visual imagery and social memory. *Journal of Personality and Social Psychology, 43,* 475–480.

Swap, W. C. (1977). Interpersonal attraction and repeated exposure to rewarders and punishers. *Personality and Social Psychology Bulletin, 3,* 248–251.

Takahashi, J. S., & Zatz, M. (1982). Regulation of circadian rhythmicity. *Science, 217,* 1104–1111.

Takooshian, H., Haber, S., & Lucido, D. J. (1977, February). Who wouldn't help a lost child? You, maybe. *Psychology Today,* pp. 67–68, 88.

Tapp, J. L. (1981). Psychologists and the law: Who needs whom? In L. Bickman (Ed.), *Applied social psychology annual* (Vol. 2, pp. 263–289). Beverly Hills, CA: Sage Publications.

Tart, C. T. (1975). *States of consciousness.* New York: E. P. Dutton.

Taylor, R. B., & Brooks, D. K. (1980). Temporary territories? Responses to intrusions in a public setting. *Population and Environment, 3,* 135–144.

Teitelbaum, P., & Epstein, A. N. (1962). The lateral hypothalamic syndrome. *Psychological Review, 69,* 74–90.

Terman, L. M. (1916). *The measurement of intelligence.* Boston: Houghton Mifflin.

Terman, L., M., & Merrill, M. A. (1960). *Stanford-Binet intelligence scale.* Boston: Houghton Mifflin.

Terman, L. M., & Merrill, M. A. (1973). *Stanford-Binet intelligence scale: Manual for the third revision.* Boston: Houghton Mifflin.

Terman, L. M., & Oden, M. H. (1959). *Genetic studies of genius: Vol. 5. The gifted group at mid-life.* Stanford, CA: Stanford University Press.

Terr, L. C. (1982). Psychic trauma in children: Observations following the Chowchilla school-bus kidnapping. In S. Chase & A. Thomas (Eds.), *Annual progress in child psychiatry and child development, 1982* (pp. 384–396). New York: Brunner/Mazel.

Terrace, H. S. (1979). *Nim.* New York: Knopf.

The trials of hypnosis. (1981, October 19). *Newsweek,* p. 96.

Terrace, H. S. (1982, March). Can animals think? *New Society,* pp. 339–342.

Terrace, H. S., Petitto, L. A., Sanders, R. J., & Bever, T. G. (1979). Can an ape create a sentence? *Science, 206,* 891–902.

The trials of hypnosis. (1981, October 19). *Newsweek,* p. 96.

Thigpen, C. H., & Cleckley, H. M. (1957). *The three faces of Eve.* New York: McGraw-Hill.

Thomas, A. (1982). Current trends in developmental theory. In S. Chess & A. Thomas (Eds.), *Annual progress in child psychiatry and child development* (pp. 7–45). New York: Brunner/Mazel.

Thomas, A., Chess, S., & Birch, H. G. (1968). *Temperament and behavior disorders in children.* New York: New York University Press.

Thomas, M. H. (1982). Physiological arousal, exposure to a relatively lengthy aggressive film, and aggressive behavior. *Journal of Research in Personality, 16,* 72–81.

Thomas, M. H., Horton, R. W., Lippincott, E. C., & Drabman, R. S. (1977). Desensitization to portrayals of real-life aggression as a function of exposure to television violence. *Journal of Personality and Social Psychology, 35,* 450–458.

Thompson, A. P. (1983). Extramarital sex: A review of the research literature. *The Journal of Sex Research, 19,* 1–22.

Thompson, J. K., Jarvie, G. J., Lahey, B. B. & Cureton, K. J. (1982). Exercise and obesity: Etiology, physiology, and intervention. *Psychological Bulletin, 91,* 55–79.

Thompson, S. C. (1981). Will it hurt less if I can control it? A complex answer to a simple question. *Psychological Bulletin, 90,* 89–101.

Thorndike, E. L. (1911). Animal intelligence. New York: Macmillan.

Thurstone, L. L. (1938). Primary mental abilities. *Psychometric Monographs, No. 1.* Chicago: University of Chicago Press.

Tinbergen, N. (1951). *The study of instinct.* London: Oxford University Press.

Tittle, C. K. (1982). Career counseling in contemporary U.S. high schools: An addendum to Rehberg and Hotchkiss. *Educational Researcher, 11,* 12–18.

Tolman, E. G. (1932). *Purposive behavior in animals and men.* New York: Appleton-Century-Crofts.

Tolman, E. C. (1948). Cognitive maps in rats and men. *Psychological Review, 55,* 189–208.

Torrance, P. (1962). *Guiding creative talent.* Englewood Cliffs, NJ: Prentice-Hall.

Torrance, P. (1965). Current research on the nature of creative talent. In A. Anastasi (Ed.), *Individual differences* (pp. 266–281). New York: Wiley.

Toufexis, A. (1981, September 14). A brainy marvel called PET. *Time,* p. 74.

Toufexis, A. (1983). The bluing of America. *Time,* p. 62.

Towson, S. M. J., and Zanna, M. P. (1982). Toward a situational analysis of gender differences in aggression. *Sex Roles, 8,* 903–914.

Tramontana, M. G. (1980). Critical review of research on psychotherapy outcome with adolescents: 1967–1977. *Psychological Bulletin, 88,* 429–450.

Trotter, R. J. (1983, August). Baby face. *Psychology Today,* pp. 14–20.

Tulving, E. (1962). Subjective organization in free-recall of "unrelated" words. *Psychological Review, 69,* 344–354.

Tulving, E., & Pearlstone, Z. (1966). Availability versus accessibility of information in memory for words. *Journal of Verbal Learning and Verbal Behavior, 5,* 381–391.

Tumblin, A., & Gholson, B. (1981). Hypothesis theory and the development of conceptual learning. *Psychological Bulletin, 90,* 102–124.

Turkington, C. (1983, April). Drugs found to block dopamine receptors. *APA Monitor,* p. 11.

Turnbull, W. (1980, Spring). ETS to professionals: "Don't stand aside from the debate." *ETS Examiner,* p. 1.

Turner, J. S., & Helms, D. B. (1983). *Lifespan development* (2nd ed.). New York: Holt, Rinehart and Winston.

Tyler, L. E. (1965). *The psychology of human differences* (3rd ed.). New York: Appleton-Century-Crofts.

Tziner, A., & Dolan, S. (1982). Validity of an assessment center for identifying future female officers in the military. *Journal of Applied Psychology, 67,* 728–736.

Underwood, B. J. (1957). Inferference and forgetting. *Psychological Review, 64,* 49–60.

Valenstein, E. S. (1973). *Brain control.* New York: Wiley.

Vallerand, R. J. (1983). The effects of differential amounts of positive verbal feedback on the intrinsic motivation of male hockey players. *Journal of Sport Psychology, 5,* 100–107.

Van Boxel, J. A. (1981). Aging and the immune response. In *Consciousness, Physiology, and Longevity Colloquium* (abstracts of proceedings). Fairfield, IA: Maharishi International University Press.

Veitch, R., & Griffitt, W. (1976). Good news, bad news: Affective and interpersonal effects. *Journal of Applied Social Psychology, 6,* 69–75.

Velandia, W., Grandon, G. M., & Page, E. B. (1978). Family size, birth order, and intelligence in a large South American sample. *American Educational Research Journal, 15,* 399–416.

Viscott, D. S. (1972). *The making of a psychiatrist.* Greenwich, CT: Fawcett.

Wadden, T. A., & Anderton, C. H. (1982). The clinical use of hypnosis. *Psychological Bulletin, 91,* 215–243.

Wadsworth, B. J. (1979). *Piaget's theory of cognitive development: An introduction for students of psychology and education* (2nd ed.). New York: Longman.

Waid, W. M., & Orne, M. T. (1982). The physiological detection of deception. *American Scientist, 70,* 402–409.

Wald, G. (1972). Eye and camera. In *Perception: Mechanisms, and models: Readings from Scientific American.* (pp. 95–103). San Francisco: W. H. Freeman.

Walker, J. M. (1979). Energy demand behavior in a master-metered apartment complex: An experimental analysis. *Journal of Applied Psychology, 64,* 190–196.

Wallace, R. K., & Benson, H. (1972,). The physiology of meditation. *Scientific American,* pp. 84–90.

Wallace, R. K., Dillbeck, M., Jacobe, E., & Harrington, B. (1982). The effects of the transcendental meditation and TM-Sidhi program on the aging process. *International Journal of Neuroscience, 16,* 53–58.

Wallis, C. (1983, June 6). Stress: Can we cope? *Time,* pp. 48–54.

Wallis, C. (1983, July 11). Slow, steady and heartbreaking. *Time,* p. 56.

Wallston, K. A., Smith, R. A., King, J. E., Forsberg, P. R., Wallston, B. S., and Nagy, V. T. (1983). Expectancies about control over health: Relationship to desire for control of health care. *Personality and Social Psychology Bulletin, 9,* 377–386.

Walster, E., Aronson, E., & Abrahams, D. (1966). On increasing the persuasiveness of low prestige communicator. *Journal of Experimental Social Psychology, 2,* 325–342.

Ward, J. A., & Hetzel, H. R. (1980). *Biology: Today and tomorrow.* St. Paul, MN: West.

Watkins, L. R., & Mayer, D. J. (1982). Organization of endogenous opiate and nonopiate pain control systems. *Science, 216,* 1185–1192.

Watson, D. (1982). The actor and the observer: How are their perceptions of causality divergent? *Psychological Bulletin, 92,* 682–700.

Watson, D. L., Tharp, R. G., & Krisberg, J. (1972). Case study in self-modification: Suppression of inflammatory scratching while awake and asleep. *Journal of Behavior Therapy and Experimental Psychiatry, 3,* 213–215.

Watson, J. B. (1928). *Psychological care of infant and child.* New York: W. W. Norton.

Watson, J. B. (1913). Psychology as the behaviorist views it. *Psychological Review, 20,* 158–177.

Watson, J. B., & Rayner, R. (1920). Conditioned emotional reactions. *Journal of Experimental Psychology, 3,* 1–14.

Webb, E. J., Campbell, D. T., Schwartz, R. D., & Sechrest, L. (1966). *Unobtrusive measures: Non-reactive research in the social sciences.* Chicago: Rand McNally.

Webb, S. D. (1978). Mental health in rural and urban environments. *Ekistics, 266,* 37–42.

Webb, W. B. (1975). *Sleep: The gentle tyrant.* Englewood Cliffs, NJ: Prentice-Hall.

Webb, W. B., & Cartwright, R. D. (1978). Sleep and dreams. *Annual Review of Psychology, 29,* 223–252.

Webb, W. B., & Friel, J. (1971). Sleep stage and personality characteristics of "natural" long and short sleepers. *Science, 171,* 587–588.

Wechsler, D. (1955). *Manual for the Wechsler Adult Intelligence Scale.* New York: Psychological Corporation.

Wechsler, D. (1958). *The measurement and appraisal of adult intelligence* (4th ed.). Baltimore: Williams & Wilkins.

Wechsler, D. (1981). *WAIS-R manual: Wechsler Adult Intelligence Scale—revised.* New York: Psychological Corporation.

Weidner, G., & Griffitt, W. (1983). Rape: A sexual stigma? *Journal of Personality, 51,* 152–166.

Weiner, B. (1980). *Human motivation.* New York: Holt, Rinehart and Winston.

Weingartner, H., Adefris, W., Eich, J. E., & Murphy, D. L. (1976). Encoding-imagery specificity in alcohol state-dependent learning. *Journal of Experimental Psychology: Human Learning and Memory, 2,* 83–87.

Weingartner, H., Gold, P., Ballenger, J. C., Smallberg, S. A., Summers, R., Rubinow, D. R., Post, R. M., & Goodwin, F. K. (1981). Effects of vasopressin on human memory functions. *Science, 211,* 601–603.

Weinstein, N. D. (1982). Community noise problems: Evidence against adaptation. *Journal of Environmental Psychology, 2,* 87–97.

Weiss, J. M. (1972, June). Psychological factors in stress and disease. *Scientific American,* pp. 104–113.

Weissman, M. M., Prusoff, B. A., DiMascio, A., Neu, C., Goklaney, M., & Klerman, G. L. (1979). The efficacy of drugs and psychotherapy in the treatment of acute depressive episodes. *American Journal of Psychiatry, 136,* 555–558.

Wender, P. H. (1971). *Minimal brain dysfunction in children.* New York: Wiley.

Werner, C. M., Brown, B. B., & Damron, G. (1981). Territorial marking in a game arcade. *Journal of Personality and Social Psychology, 41,* 1094–1104.

Werner, C. M., Kagehiro, D. K., & Strube, M. J. (1982). Conviction proneness and the authoritarian juror: Inability to disregard information or attitudinal bias? *Journal of Applied Psychology, 67,* 629–636.

Wertheimer, M. (1938). Laws of organization in perceptual forms. In W. D. Ellis (Ed.), *A sourcebook of Gestalt psychology.* London: Routledge & Kegan Paul. (Original work published 1923)

Wertheimer, M., Barclay, A. G., Cook, S. W., Kiesler, C. A., Koch, S., Riegel, K. F., Rorer, L. G., Senders, V. L., Smith, M. B., & Sperling, S. E. (1978). Psychology and the future. *American Psychologist, 33,* 631–647.

Wessells, M. G. (1982). *Cognitive psychology.* New York: Harper & Row.

Westoff, L. A. (1980). *A new era in admissions.* Princeton, NJ: Educational Testing Service.

Wetzel, C. G., & Insko, C. A. (1982). The similarity-attraction relationship: Is there an ideal one? *Journal of Experimen-*

tal Social Psychology, 18, 253–276.

Wheeler, L., Deci, E. L., Reis, H. T., & Zuckerman, M. (1978). *Interpersonal influence* (2nd ed). Boston, MA: Allyn & Bacon.

White, K. R. (1982). The relation between socioeconomic status and academic achievement. *Psychological Bulletin, 91,* 461–481.

White, R. W. (1959). Motivation reconsidered: The concept of competence. *Psychological Review, 66,* 297–333.

Whorf, B. L. (1956). Science and linguistics. In J. B. Carroll (Ed.), *Language, thought, and reality: Selected writings of Benjamin Lee Whorf* (pp. 207–219). Cambridge, MA: M.I.T. Press.

Wickelgren, W. A. (1965). Acoustic similarity and intrusion errors in short-term memory. *Journal of Experimental Psychology, 70,* 102–108.

Wicks, J. D., & Howe, K. S. (1983). *Fundamentals of ultrasonographic technique.* Chicago: Year Book Medical Publishers.

Willems, E. P. (1974). Behavioral technology and behavioral ecology. *Journal of Applied Behavior Analysis, 7,* 151–165.

Willerman, L. (1979). *The psychology of individual and group differences.* San Francisco: W. H. Freeman.

Williams, M. D., & Hollan, J. D. (1981). The process of retrieval from very long-term memory. *Cognitive Science, 5,* 87–119.

Williams, R. B., Jr., Lane, J. D., Kuhn, C. M., Melosh, W., White, A. D., & Schanberg, S. M. (1982). Type A behavior and elevated physiological and neuroendocrine responses to cognitive tasks. *Science, 218,* 483–485.

Williams, R. L., & Long, J. D. (1983). *Toward a self-managed life style* (3rd ed.). Boston: Houghton Mifflin.

Williams, T. M., Zabrack, M. L., & Joy, L. A. (1982). The portrayal of aggression on North American television. *Journal of Applied Social Psychology, 12,* 360–380.

Willingham, W. W., & Breland, H. M. (1982). *Personal qualities and college admissions.* Princeton, NJ: College Board Publications.

Wilson, D. W. (1978). Helping behavior and physical attractiveness: *Journal of Social Psychology, 104,* 313–314.

Wilson, E. O. (1972, September). Animal communication. *Scientific American,* pp. 53–60.

Wilson, E. O. (1975). *Sociobiology: The new synthesis.* Cambridge, MA: Harvard University Press.

Wilson, L., & Rogers, R. W. (1975). The fire this time: Effects of race of target, insult, and potential retaliation on black aggression. *Journal of Personality and Social Psychology, 32,* 857–864.

Wilson, T. D., & Lassiter, G. D. (1982). Increasing intrinsic interest with superfluous extrinsic constraints. *Journal of Personality and Social Psychology, 82,* 811–819.

Wilson, T. D., & Linville, P. W. (1982). Improving the academic performance of college freshmen: Attribution therapy revisited. *Journal of Personality and Social Psychology, 42,* 367–376,

Wingfield, A., & Byrnes, D. L. (1981). *The psychology of human memory.* New York: Academic Press.

Winick, M., (1976). *Malnutrition and brain development.* New York: Oxford University Press.

Winick, M. (Ed.). (1979). *Human nutrition: A comprehensive treatise: Vol. 1. Pre- and postnatal development.* New York: Plenum Press.

Wise, E. H., & Haynes, S. N. (1983). Cognitive treatment of test anxiety: Rational restructuring versus attentional training. *Cognitive Therapy and Research, 7,* 69–78.

Wise, J. (1982, September). A gentle deterrent to vandalism. *Psychology Today,* pp. 31–32, 34, 36, 38.

Wissler, C. (1901). *The correlation of mental and physical tests.* New York: Columbia University Press.

Wittig, M. A., & Petersen, A. C. (Eds.). (1979). *Sex-related differences in cognitive functioning.* New York: Academic Press.

Wodarski, J. S. (1982). National and state appeals for energy conservation: A behavioral analysis of effects. *Behavioral Engineering, 1,* 119–130.

Wolf, S. (1982). Peptic ulcer. *Psychosomatics, 23,* 1101–1108.

Wolfe, J. M. (1983, February). Hidden visual processes. *Scientific American,* pp. 94–103.

Wolpe, J. (1958). *Psychotherapy by reciprocal inhibition.* Stanford, CA: Stanford University Press.

Worchel, S., & Cooper, J. (1983). *Understanding social psychology* (3rd ed.). Homewood, IL: Dorsey Press.

Worchel, S., & Lollis, M. (1982). Reactions to territorial contamination as a function of culture. *Personality and Social Psychology Bulletin, 8,* 370–375.

Wright, J. C., & Huston, A. C. (1983). A matter of form: Potentials of television for young viewers. *American Psychologist, 38,* 835–843.

Wright, T. L., Holman, T., Steele, W. G., & Silverstein, G. (1980). Locus of control and mastery in a reformatory: A field study of defensive externality. *Journal of Personality and Social Psychology, 38,* 1005–1013.

Wurtman, R. J. (1982, April). Nutrients that modify brain function. *Scientific American,* pp. 50–59.

Yancey, W. L. (1971). Architecture, interaction, and social control. *Environment and Behavior, 3,* 3–21.

Yarmey, A. D. (1973). I recognize your face but I can't remember your name: Further evidence on the tip-of-the-tongue phenomenon. *Memory & Cognition, 1,* 287–290.

Yarnold, P. R., & Grimm, L. G. (1982). Time urgency among coronary-prone individuals. *Journal of Abnormal Psychology, 91,* 175–177.

Yates, S. M., & Aronson, E. (1983). A social psychological perspective on energy conservation in residential buildings. *American Psychologist, 38,* 435–444.

Young, P. (1983, August). A conversation with Richard Jed Wyatt. *Psychology Today,* pp. 30–41.

Yu, V. C. (1983). Conceptual obstacles in computerized medical diagnosis. *The Journal of Medicine and Philosophy, 8,* 67–76.

Zajonc, R. B. (1975, January). Birth order and intelligence: Dumber by the dozen. *Psychology Today,* pp. 37–43.

REFERENCES ∎

631

Zajonc, R. B. (1983). Validating the confluence model. *Psychological Bulletin, 93,* 457–480.

Zajonc, R. B., & Markus, G. B. (1975). Birth order and intellectual development. *Psychological Review, 82,* 74–88.

Zanna, M. P. Higgins, E. T., & Taves, P. A. (1976). Is dissonance phenomenologically aversive? *Journal of Experimental Social Psychology, 12,* 530–538.

Zarifian, E., & Rigal, F. (1983). New antidepressants and trends in the pharmacotherapy of depressive disorders. *The Psychiatric Clinics of North America, 6,* 129–140.

Zellner, M. (1970). Self-esteem, reception, and influenceability. *Journal of Personality and Social Psychology, 15,* 87–93.

Zigler, E. (1967). Familial mental retardation: A continuing dilemma. *Science, 155,* 292–298.

Zigler, E. Abelson, W. D., Trickett, P. K., & Seitz, V. (1982). Is an intervention program necessary in order to improve economically disadvantaged children's IQ scores? *Child Development, 53,* 340–348.

Zigler, E., & Muenchow, S. (1983). Infant day care and infant-care leaves: A policy vacuum. *American Psychologist, 38,* 91–94.

Zigler, E., & Valentine, J. (Eds.). (1979). *Project Head Start: A legacy of the war on poverty.* New York: Free Press.

Zillmann, D., & Bryant, J. (1982). Pornography, sexual callousness, and the trivialization of rape. *Journal of Communication, 32,* 10–21.

Zimring, C. M. (1981). Stress and the designed environment. *Journal of Social Issues, 37,* 145–171.

Zitrin, C. M., Klein, D. F., Woerner, M. G., & Ross, D. C. (1983). Treatment of phobias: 1. Comparison of imipramine hydrochloride and placebo. *Archives of General Psychiatry, 40,* 125–138.

Zuckerman, Miron (1978). Use of consensus information in prediction of behavior. *Journal of Experimental Social Psychology, 14,* 163–171.

Zuckerman, Marvin (1978a, February). The search for high sensation. *Psychology Today,* pp. 38–40, 43, 46, 96–97.

Zuckerman, Marvin (1978b). Sensation seeking. In H. London & J. E. Exner, Jr. (Eds.), *Dimensions of personality* (pp. 487–559). New York: Wiley.

Zuckerman, Marvin (1979). *Sensation seeking: Beyond the optimal level of arousal.* Hillsdale, NJ: Erlbaum.

Zuckerman, Marvin (1983). Sensation seeking and sports. *Personality and Individual Differences, 4,* 285–292.

Zuckerman, Marvin, Buchsbaum, M. S., & Murphy, D. L. (1980). Sensation-seeking and its biological correlates. *Psychological Bulletin, 88,* 187–214.

Zuckerman, Marvin, & Neeb, M. (1980). Demographic influences in sensation seeking and expressions of sensation seeking in religion, smoking and driving habits. *Personality and Individual Differences, 1,* 197–206.

Zuckerman, Miron, Klorman, R., Larrance, D. T., & Spiegel, N. H. (1981). Facial, autonomic, and subjective components of emotion: The facial feedback hypothesis versus the externalizer-internalizer distinction. *Journal of Personality and Social Psychology, 41,* 929–944.

Zuckerman, Miron, & Wheeler, L. (1975). To dispel fantasies about the fantasy-based measure of fear of success. *Psychological Bulletin, 82,* 932–946.

Zytowski, D. G., & Warman, R. E. (1982). The changing use of tests in counseling. *Measurement and Evaluation in Guidance, 15,* 147–152.

– NAME INDEX –

Beck, R. C., 222, 228, 230, 241
Beck, S., 154
Becker, L. J., 531–533
Bee, H. L., 196–198, 201, 205
Begley, S., 155, 403
Bekerian, D. A., 184
Békésy, George von, 64, 65, 68
Bell, A. P., 468
Bell, Alexander Graham, 66
Bell, P. A., 514, 517, 522–525, 530, 531
Bell, R. Q., 279
Bell, S. M., 269
Bella, B., 470
Belmont, Lillian, 324
Bemis, K. M., 244
Benbow, C. P., 322
Benghezal, A., 189
Beniger, J. R., 533
Benjamin, L. T., Jr., 202
Bennett, E. L., 97
Bennett, T. L., 206
Bennett, W., 229, 230
Benson, H., 125, 126
Benson, P. L., 479, 495
Benton, J. L., 57
Berbaum, M. L., 324
Berger, R. J., 114
Bergin, A. E., 440, 441
Berko, J., 197, 198
Berkowitz, L., 464, 503, 504
Berlyne, D. E., 232
Berman, J. S., 431, 441
Bermant, G., 358
Bernstein, D. A., 420, 425, 444
Berrenberg, J. L., 530, 531
Berscheid, E., 479
Bertenthal, B., 95, 96
Betley, G., 226
Bever, T. G., 202–203
Beyer, J., 426
Bickman, L., 502
Bieber, I., 469
Bieber, T. B., 469
Biederman, M. F 498
Bigelow, G. E., 118
Bigge, M. L., 157
Biller, H. B., 282
Billings, A. G., 403
Binet, Alfred, 275, 301–303, 307
Bingham, R., 318
Biran, M., 426
Birch, H. G., 157, 257
Birdsall, T. G., 54
Birren, J. E., 292
Bishop, S., 404
Bizman, A., 491
Bjork, R. A., 180–182
Blackburn, I. M., 404
Blakemore, C., 96
Blanchard, E. B., 374, 375, 426, 427
Blehar, M. C., 278, 280

Bleuler, Eugene, 404–405
Blick, K. A., 115
Block, J., 354
Blois, M. S., 215
Bloom, F., 48
Bloom, L., 199
Blosser, J. L., 498
Blum, J. E., 307
Blusztajn, J. K., 35
Boersma, K., 397
Boggiano, A. K., 232
Bolles, R. C., 223
Bombeck, E., 523
Borgida, E., 472
Borman, W. C., 543
Bouchard, Thomas J., Jr., 319, 320
Bourne, L. E., Jr., 203, 207–212
Bouthilet, L., 505
Bower, G. H., 136, 148, 181, 185–187
Bowers, J. M., 184
Bowlby, J., 278, 378
Bowlby, T., 222
Brackbill, Y., 324
Bradley, M. M., 174
Bradshaw, G. L., 175
Brady, James, 38
Braille, Louis, 72
Branconnier, R. J., 8
Bray, Douglas W., 545–546
Brazelton, T. B., 255, 257
Brecher, E. M., 119
Brehm, J. W., 377
Breland, H. M., 558
Breland, Keller, 151
Breland, Marion, 151
Bresler, D. E., 253
Breuning, S. E., 435–437
Brice, P., 506
Brickman, J., 472
Broca, Paul, 204
Brock, T., 486
Brody, J. E., 55
Brooks, D. K., 518
Broverman, D. M., 455, 456
Broverman, I. K., 455, 456
Browman, C. P., 117
Brown, H. B., 518
Brown, J. S., 215
Brown, P. L., 151
Brown, R., 181, 195, 198
Brownell, K. D., 228, 230
Bruce, D., 202
Bruner, J. S., 175
Brunson, B. I., 376, 379
Bryan, J. H., 498
Bryant, J., 464
Bryden, M. P., 40, 43
Buchsbaum, M. S., 233, 412
Buck, R., 224, 233, 238
Buckhout, R., 175, 176
Bullard, N. G., 521

Bullough, V. L., 284–285
Burger, J. M., 376, 521
Burgess, A. W., 472
Burgess, R. L., 530
Burke, D. M., 189
Burns, H. J., 176–178
Burns, T. E., 173, 174
Burns, W., 254
Burt, M. R., 472, 473
Burton, R. R., 215
Busch, C. M., 368
Butcher, J. N., 390, 391, 394–396, 398, 400, 402, 407–409, 411, 550
Byck, R., 118, 122
Byrne, D., 231, 234–236, 335, 342, 358, 378, 379, 462–465, 478, 482, 484, 486, 487, 489, 496–498, 503, 508, 517, 524
Byrnes, D. L., 166, 167, 179, 187

Cacioppo, J. T., 485, 487, 488, 492
Caid, C., 470
Calesnick, L. E., 521, 522
Calhoun, J. F., 5, 390, 398–399, 401–403, 406, 408–411
Calhoun, K. S., 472
Calhoun, L. G., 411
Callahan, Daniel, 328
Calley, William, 494
Campbell, A. M. G., 9
Campbell, D. P., 540
Campbell, D. T., 6
Campbell, J. B., 341
Campbell, J. L., 472
Campbell, J. P., 543
Campbell, R. J., 545
Campbell, S. B., 401
Campos, Joseph J., 44, 95, 96
Campos, R. G., 95, 96
Cannell, C. F., 183
Cannon, D. S., 425
Cannon, W. B., 230, 237
Canon, L. K., 523, 524
Caputo, D. V., 261
Carducci, B., 376
Carey, J., 155
Carlsmith, J. M., 486–489, 525
Carlson, C. R., 115
Carlson, N. R., 36
Carlson, S. B., 315
Carmichael, L., 204
Carrol, E. N., 233
Carroll, J. L., 288
Carrow, Stimson, 79
Carson, R. C., 390, 391, 394–396, 398, 400, 402, 407–409, 411
Cartwright, R. D., 111
Carver, C. S., 378, 500
Cash, Johnny, 121
Casper, R. C., 244
Castner, B. M., 307
Catalan, J., 491

Cates, W., Jr., 263
Catt, V. L., 495
Cattell, James McKeen, 11, 302
Cattell, Raymond B., 340–341, 352–353, 464
Cautela, J. R., 417
Cervone, D., 347
Chafetz, M. E., 120
Chaiken, A., 479
Chambless, D. L., 395
Chance, J. E., 347
Chance, P., 269
Chandler, J., 534
Chaplin, J. P., 11
Charles, E., 373
Chase, W. G., 169
Chasnoff, I., 254
Chaves, J. F., 109
Check, J. V. P., 464, 473
Chedd, G., 249, 262, 264
Cheek, J. M., 368
Chess, S., 257
Chomsky, Noam, 200–202
Christensen, L. B., 5
Christie, R., 358
Chumlea, W. C., 285
Cialdini, Robert B., 491, 492, 495
Ciminero, A. R., 442
Clark, D. M., 181
Clark, E. V., 197, 208
Clark, H. H., 208
Clark, M., 38, 116, 117
Clark, M. C., 185
Clark, R. A., 234
Clark, R. D., III, 500, 501
Clark, R. N., 530
Clarke-Stewart, A., 196
Clarkson, F. E., 455, 456
Clausen, G. T., 500
Cleckley, H. M., 333
Clingempeel, W. G., 282
Clore, G. L., 496, 524
Clouser, Ronald, 165, 166
Cochran, P. J., 498
Cofer, C. N., 222, 231
Cohen, D., 255
Cohen, J., 120
Cohen, J. D., 382
Cohen, S., 376, 521–523
Cohen, Sidney, 119
Coke, J. S., 221
Colby, A., 288, 289
Cole, C. M., 491
Cole, J. O., 441
Cole, M., 38
Coleman, J. C., 365, 369, 372, 373, 377, 380,
    390, 391, 394–396, 398, 400, 402, 407–409,
    411
Collins, D. L., 382–383
Collins, E. G. C., 547
Colman, R., 358
Colombo, J., 201

Condas, Joanne, 555
Condry, J., 235
Cone, J. D., 530, 531
Conger, J. J., 249, 254, 256, 260, 261, 276,
    280, 284–288, 290–292
Connors, K., 257
Conrad, John, 185
Conrad, R., 170
Cook, D. A., 531
Cook, R., 479
Cook S. W., 19, 530, 531
Coolahan, James A., 357
Coon, D., 30, 46, 114, 120, 187, 274
Cooper, C. L., 373
Cooper, G. F., 96
Cooper, H. M., 349
Cooper, J., 489, 499
Cooper, M., 325, 379
Coppola, V., 123
Cordes, C., 539
Coren, S., 44
Corkin, S., 174
Corballis, M. C., 45
Cornsweet, T. N., 58
Corrales, R. G., 432
Costello, C. G., 396
Cotman, C. W., 118–121, 123
Cotton, J. L., 525
Cowart, B. J., 255
Cox, M., 282
Cox, R., 282
Cox, V. C., 520, 534
Coyne, J. C., 365, 376
Cozad, T. W., 44, 322
Craighead, E., 154
Craik, F. I. M., 171, 174, 175
Crano, W. D., 485
Crawford, J. W., 261
Cristol, A. H., 420, 428
Cross, D. G., 440–442
Crouse, B. B., 234
Cummins, K. R., 40, 44
Cunningham, A. M., 383, 384
Cunningham, M. R., 223
Cunningham, S., 296, 384, 437, 539
Cunningham, W. R., 292
Cureton, K. J., 230
Curie-Cohen, M., 328
Curran, J. P., 425
Curtis, H. A., 420
Curtiss, S., 195
Cutrona, C. E., 401
Cvetkovich, G., 464

Dabbs, J. M., Jr., 516
Dain, J. H., 469
Dali, Salvador, 111–112
Dalton, G. W., 546–547
Dakof, G., 365
Damron, G., 518
Daniel, T. C., 206

Danks, J. H., 197
Darby, B. L., 491
Darian-Smith, I., 36
Darley, C. F., 9, 10
Darley, John M., 478, 498–501, 531, 533
Darlington, R. B., 326
Darrow, C. M., 547
Darwin, C., 314, 317–318
Davidson, E., 470
Davidson, E. S., 508
Davidson, L. M., 382–383
Davis, G. E., 527
Davis, K. E., 480
Davis, K. L., 408
Davis, M. H., 221, 502
Davis, R. V., 539
Davison, G. C., 394, 396, 397, 400, 403, 411,
    423, 424
Davison, J., Jr., 379
Davison, L., 376
Dawes, R. M., 440, 441
Dawkins, R., 223
Dayson, K., 379
Dean, J., 516
Deaux, K., 235, 455
deCharms, R., 377
Deci, Edward L., 226, 232, 491
Deese, J., 136, 339
DeFour, D., 508
DeFries, J. C., 317, 318
DeJong, W., 491
Dekker, J., 397
Delaney, H. D., 186
Delgado, J. M. R., 39
Delis, D. C., 45
DeLise, L. E., 412
DeLongis, A., 365
Delprato, D. J., 531
Dement, William C., 110–114, 116, 117
Dempsey, D., 295
Den Hengst, S., 397
Derlega, V. J., 369, 380
Dermer, M., 479
Descartes, René, 72
Deutsch, M., 491
Deutsch, S. I., 408
DeValois, K. K., 60
DeValois, R. L., 60
de Villiers, J. G., 199
de Villiers, P. A., 199
DeYoung, G. E., 464
Diaconis, P., 100
Diamond, E. L. 373
Diamond, M. C., 97
DiCara, L. V., 143
Dick, W., 551
Diener, E., 348, 508
Dillbeck, M. C., 127
DiMascio, A., 442
Dince, P. R., 469
Dion, K. K., 479

Dobson, V., 93
Doherty, W. J., 349
Dolan, S., 545
Dollard, J., 503
Domhoff, G. W., 115
Dominguez, R. A., 436
Dominowski, R. L., 203, 209–212
Donnerstein, E., 377, 463, 464, 523
Doob, L., 503
Dowd, M., 472
Down, John Langdon, 259
Downs, R., 377
Drabman, R. S., 426, 505
Drellich, M. G., 469
Drose, G., 470
DuBois, P. M., 296
Duke, M., 421, 422, 424, 435, 436
Duker, J., 353
Duncker, K., 212–213
Dunkle, T., 66
Dunner, D. L., 439, 442
Dunnette, M. D., 543, 545, 551, 553
Durrett, M. E., 280
Dush, D. M., 441
Dworetzky, J. P., 45–46, 58, 196, 199, 501
Dyck, R., 504
d'Ydewalle, G., 175
Dyer, S., 235
Dyke, C. V., 118, 122

Eagly, A. H., 487
Earn, B. M., 226
Ebbesen, E. B., 371, 516, 517
Eckert, E., 319
Edelman, M. W., 281, 288
Edison, Thomas, 112
Edney, J. J., 518
Egeth, H. E., 136, 178
Ehrhardt, A. A., 454
Eich, J. E., 181
Eisdorfer, C., 295, 307
Eisenberg-Berg, N., 223, 498
Ekman, P., 238–240
Elliott, T. R., 34
Ellis, Albert, 395, 428–429
Ellis, E. M., 472
Ellis, H. C., 187, 195, 204, 206–208
Ellis, L., 467
Ellison, G., 253
Ellsworth, P. C., 480–481, 483
Emde, R. N., 277, 278
Emerson, P. E., 280
Emery, G., 405, 430
Emery, J., 232
Emery, R. E., 281
Emmelkamp, P. M. G., 397
Emrich, B., 358
Endler, H. S., 348
Engel, B. T., 374
Englemann, 324
Epstein, A. N., 37

Epstein, C. F., 548
Epstein, Y. M., 520
Erickson, B., 520
Ericsson, K. A., 169
Erikson, Erik H., 275–276. 287, 291–294, 338, 339
Eron, L. D., 505–507
Erwin, W. J., 425
Erwin, W. M., 158
Etaugh, C., 281
Evans, G. W., 520, 522–523
Evans, M., 9
Evans, R. I., 421
Evarts, E. V., 35
Everett, P. B., 530
Eysenck, H. J., 340, 341

Fagan, J. F., 94
Fairchild, L., 158
Falk, J. L., 118
Faloon, S., 169
Fancher, R. E., 11, 135, 339
Fantz, R. L., 94, 232
Fazio, R. H., 226, 379, 485
Fehr, L. A., 352–354
Feighner, J. P. 436
Feldman, H., 201
Felipe, H., 516
Ferguson, T. J., 504
Feshbach, S., 350, 352, 353, 357
Festinger, L., 224, 488–489, 491, 498
Field, Tiffany M., 255, 256
Fincher, J., 261
Findley, M. J., 349
Firl, A., Jr., 47
Fischer, P., 506
Fish, B., 234
Fishel, A. K., 339
Fisher, E. B., Jr., 382
Fisher, J. D., 514, 517, 522, 523, 530, 531
Fisher, K., 539
Fisher, S., 420
Fisher M. P., 451
Fisher, W. A., 464–466
Fishman, D. L., 182
Flavell, J. H., 271
Fleece, L., 426
Fleming, R., 382, 384
Flynn, M. S., 177
Folger, R., 226
Folkman, S., 365
Foote, D., 123
Forsberg, P. R., 350
Foss, D. J., 201
Foss, G. L., 328
Foulkes, D., 114
Fouts, R. S., 202
Fox, L. H., 317
Foxx, R. M., 121, 530
Frank, J. D., 440
Franken, R. E., 244

Franklin, R. M., 123
Fraser, S. C., 491
Frederick II, 276
Fredericksen, N., 315
Freedman, J. L., 487, 491, 525, 532
Freeman, V., 479
Frenkel-Brunswick, E., 358
Fretz, B. R., 16, 540
Freud, Anna, 292
Freud, Sigmund, 108, 114, 122, 182, 184, 222, 292, 335–340, 350, 379, 392, 419–420, 463, 502, 539
Frey, Max von, 71
Friedman, L. N., 522
Friedman, M. 378, 379
Friedman, S. L., 261
Friel, J., 110
Friesen, W. V., 238–240
Fromer, M. J., 72
Fuchs, F., 262
Fulcher, R., 15, 539
Fuller, J. J., 317
Fultz, J., 502

Gaarder, K. R., 374
Gaensbauer, T. J., 278
Gagné, R. M., 551
Galanter, E., 54
Galbraith, R. C., 324
Gallatin, J., 420
Galton, Francis, 302, 313–315, 318
Gandour, M. J., 257
Garber, J., 404
Gardner, B. T., 202
Gardner, G. T., 377
Gardner, L. I., 276
Gardner, M., 84, 101
Gardner, R. A., 202
Gardner, Randy, 111
Garfield, E., 127
Garfield, S. L., 441, 444
Garfinkel, P., 322
Garmezy, N., 119, 123, 283
Garske, J. P., 222, 223, 227, 228, 230
Gastorf, J. W., 379
Gatchel, R. J., 354, 355, 384
Gazzaniga, M. S., 25, 41, 42
Gebhard, P. H., 7, 458
Geen, R. G., 341, 377, 504, 505, 523
Geer, J. H., 355
Geiselman, R. E., 182
Geldard, F. A., 54
Geller, D. M., 525
Geller, E. S., 531
Geller, Uri, 100
Gelman, D., 43
Gelman, R., 274
Genain, Hester, 389–390, 412
Genain, Iris, 389–390, 412
Genain, Myra, 389–390, 412
Genain, Nora, 389–390, 412

Gendrich, J., 530
Genovese, Kitty, 477, 498, 501
Gerard, H. B., 491
Gerrard, M., 455
Gershon, S., 436
Geschwind, N., 41, 204, 205
Gesell, A., 307
Getts, A. G., 117
Gholson, B., 206
Gibbs, J., 288, 289
Gibson, Eleanor J., 94–95
Gibson, J. J., 93
Gifford, R., 515
Gilberstadt, H., 353
Gilbert, S. J., 495
Gill, A., 125
Gilligan, S., G., 187
Gillmore, J., 288
Gisriel, M. M., 384
Glasgow, M. S., 374
Glass, D. C., 378, 379, 522
Glass, G. V., 440, 441
Glenberg, A. M., 174, 180, 181
Glover, J. A., 175
Glucksberg, S., 197
Goklaney, M., 442
Gold, P., 189
Goldband, S., 379
Goldfried, M. R., 427
Goldiamond, I., 150–151, 425
Goldin-Meadow, S., 201
Goldstein, E. B., 54, 64, 68, 70, 71, 73, 74, 83, 86, 87, 92, 98
Goleman, D., 43, 110, 112
Gomez, H., 326
Goodall, Jane, 6
Goodman, G. S., 255
Goodstein, L. D., 369, 380, 390, 398–399, 401–403, 406, 408–411
Goodwin, A., 36
Goodwin, F. K., 189
Gordon, C., 444
Gordon, J., 93
Gorman, B., 196–198
Gosnell, M., 116, 117
Gotay, C. C., 237
Gottesman, Irving, I., 318, 408
Gottlieb, A., 506
Gottschalk, C. A., 373
Graff, H., 420
Graham, Robert K., 328
Grand, H. G., 469
Grandon, G. M., 324
Grant, D., 155
Grant, D. L., 545
Grant, Toni, 443
Green, D. M., 54
Green, E. J., 98
Greenberg, C. I., 520
Greenberg, J., 484
Greenberg, R., 255

Greenberg, R. P., 420
Greene, E., 177
Greene, J., 133
Greene, R. L., 353
Greene, T. C., 525
Greenough, W. T., 98
Gregory, R. L., 84, 90–92, 98
Grief, E. B., 284, 286
Griffen, L. M., 520
Griffitt, W., 472, 498, 524
Grimm, L. G., 379
Grossman, H. J., 308
Grote, B., 464
Grotevant, H. D., 324
Gruder, C. L., 501
Grusec, J. E., 498
Guilford, J. P., 315, 316
Gujavarty, K. S., 117
Gundlach, R. H., 469
Gurin, J., 229, 230
Gurman, A. S., 433

Haber, R. N., 84
Haber, S., 526
Hage, J. N., 522
Hager, M., 116, 117
Haggard, Merle, 400–401
Hainline, L., 93
Haith, M. M., 93, 255
Hake, D. F., 530
Hakes, D. T., 201
Hall, C. S., 115
Hall, D. T., 540
Hall, E., 200, 250, 257, 271, 272, 276, 292
Hall, E. T., 515, 516
Hall, G. Stanley, 284
Hall, J. F., 173
Hall, J. W., 186
Halmi, K. A., 244, 245
Halpern, P. L., 522
Halton, A., 251, 253, 254
Halverson, H. M., 307
Hamer, B., 389, 412
Hamilton, E. W., 404
Hansel, C. E. M., 100
Hantas, M., 181
Hardyck, C., 45
Harlow, H. F., 279–280
Harmon, R. J., 277, 278
Harmon, R. L., 261
Harper, G., 245
Harper, R. A., 395, 429
Harrell, M. S., 321
Harrell, T. W., 321, 353
Harrington, B., 127
Harrington, D. M., 316
Harris, B., 137
Harrison, R. P., 403
Hartmann, E. L., 110, 115
Harvey, J., 486
Haseltine, F. P., 548

Hastorf, A. H., 480–481, 483
Hatcher, R., 254
Hathaway, S. R., 353, 550
Haughton, E., 409
Havighurst, R. J., 270, 291
Hawley, C. W., 341
Hayward, S. C., 530
Hayduk, L. A., 515
Hayes, C., 202
Hayes, K. J., 202
Hayes, S. C., 530, 531
Haygood, R. C., 207
Haywood, H. C., 312
Hazen, N. L., 280
Heath, M., 234
Hebb, D. O., 241
Hechinger, N., 72, 74, 80
Hecht, B. F., 197
Heider, F., 480
Hein, Alan, 96, 97
Held, Richard, 96, 97
Heller, K., 378
Helmholtz, Hermann von, 62, 68
Helmreich, R. L., 235
Helms, D. B., 205
Hendee, J. C., 530
Henderson, D. J., 480
Henderson, N. D., 317
Hendren, R. L., 244
Hendrickson, A., 93
Hennig, M., 547
Hering, Ewald, 62
Herman, C. P., 229
Heron, W., 232
Herr, P. M., 485
Herrnstein, R. J., 321
Herron, J., 45
Heston, L., 319
Hetherington, E. M., 282, 283
Hetzel, H. R., 451, 452
Heywood, J., 36
Hibscher, J. A., 229
Higgins, E. T., 288
Hilgard, Ernest R., 19, 108–110, 136, 148, 186
Hilgard, J. R., 110
Hill, H. F., 117
Hillyard, S. A., 40
Hinckley, John W., Jr., 552
Hirsch, J., 229
Hirsch, H. V. B., 96
Hirst, W., 174
Hirt, M., 403, 441
Hite, S., 463
Hobbs, S. A., 368
Hochberg, J. E., 79
Hochman, G., 317
Hochreich, D. J., 335, 336, 338
Hockenbury, D., 368
Hodges, W., 325
Hodgson, R., 397
Hoff-Ginsberg, E., 205

Hoffman, Dustin, 467
Hoffman, J. W., 125
Hoffman, L. W., 281
Hoffman, Martin L., 290
Hogan, H. P., 204
Holahan, C. J., 370, 513, 529, 530, 532
Hollan, J. D., 187
Holland, J. L., 541
Holland, M. K., 272, 274
Holland, P. C., 136
Hollandsworth, J. G., Jr., 241
Hollingworth, 543
Holloway, R. L., 44
Holman, T., 349
Holmes, D. L., 261
Holmes, T. H., 370, 373
Holmstrom, L. L., 472
Hooker, E., 468
Hoover, M., 232
Horn, J. L., 307
Horner, M. S., 235
Horton, R. W., 505
Horvath, F. S., 243
Householder, J., 254
Houston, B. K., 379
Houston, J. P., 167, 171, 172, 179, 180, 206–208, 211
Hovland, C. I., 486
Howard, D. V., 200
Howe, K. S., 262
Hubel, D. H., 29, 59–61, 96
Hubert, N. C., 257
Hudspeth, A. J., 68
Huesmann, L. R., 506
Hughes, H. B., 409
Hull, Clark, L., 223
Hulse, S. H., 136
Hultsch, D. F., 201
Humphreys, Lloyd, 555
Hunt, J. M., 278
Hunt, M., 459–460
Hurlock, E. B., 271, 286, 291, 292
Hurvich, L.M., 62
Huston, A. C., 508
Huston, T. L., 496
Hyde, J. S., 231, 322, 450, 458–461, 463, 466–471

Ilg, F. L., 307
Inglis, J., 43
Insko, C. A., 497
Isaacs, W., 150–151, 425
Isen, A. M., 239, 502
Ittelson, W. H., 87
Iversen, L. L., 34
Izard, Carroll E., 221, 236, 238–239, 241

Jaccard, J. J., 498
Jacklin, C. N., 322, 455, 456
Jacobe, E., 127
Jacobs, T. J., 373
Jacobson, A., 483

Jacobson, E., 126, 374, 423
Jacobson, L. F., 479
Jacoby, J., 548
James, Henry, 12
James, Richard, 313
James, William, 10-12, 93, 237, 255
Jameson, D., 62
Janda, L. H., 369, 380, 467, 468
Jandali, M. K., 189
Janis, I. J., 371
Jardim, A., 547
Jarvie, G. J., 230
Jarvik, L. F., 307
Jason, L. A., 342
Jellison, J. M., 497
Jenkins, H. M., 151
Jensen, Arthur R., 320–321
Jensen, T. D., 533
Jevning, R., 127
Joffe, L. S., 278
Johmann, C., 43
Johnson, J. H., 370, 373
Johnson, M., 379
Johnson, M. M., 4
Johnson, P. B., 235
Johnson, P. E., 215
Johnson, V. E., 451, 452, 454, 461–463, 468–471
Johnson, V. S., 530
Johnston, J. M., 153
Jones, B. F., 186
Jones, E. E., 480, 484, 489
Jones, Reverend Jim, 495
Jones, K. L., 254
Jones, M. C., 286
Jones, W. H., 368
Jordan-Edney, N. L., 518
Joy, L. A., 508

Kaczala, C. M., 457
Kagan, Jerome, 249, 254, 256, 260, 261, 276, 281, 284
Kagehiro, D. K., 359
Kahle, J., 226
Kahn, R. L., 183
Kahn, S., 378
Kalat, J. W., 34, 39, 46
Kales, Anthony, 116
Kammann, R., 101
Kanizsa, G., 82, 83
Kanter, R. M., 547
Kaplan, B. J., 253
Kaplan, H. S., 469–470
Kaplan, R. M., 555, 557, 558
Kaplan, S., 378
Kappes, B. M., 374
Karabenick, S. A., 234, 479
Karita, K., 36
Karlin, R. A., 520
Karnes, M. B., 324, 325
Karoum, F., 436, 437
Kasschau, R. A., 4

Katchadourian, H. A., 467, 469
Kaufman, Lloyd, 89
Kawash, G. F., 464
Kazdin, A. E., 150–151, 154, 155, 159, 428
Kearsley, R. B., 281
Keating, D. P., 317
Keating, J. P., 520
Keele, S. W., 170
Keesey, R. E., 228
Kelley, H. H., 480–482
Kelley, K., 234, 235, 335, 342
Kellogg, C. A., 202
Kellogg, W. N., 202
Kelly, George A., 344, 354
Kelly, S., 523
Kelwala, S., 436
Kendler, H. H., 146, 149
Kennedy, W. A., 142
Kennell, J. H., 277
Kerr, N., 526
Kesey, Ken, 438
Keyes, M., 319
Khan, J. A., 440–442
Kiesler, C. A., 19
Kiester, E., 114
Kihlstrom, J. F., 182
Kilham, W., 494, 495
Kilmann, P. R., 470
Kim, K. H., 38
Kimble, G. A., 119, 123, 283
Kimura, D., 43
King, J. E., 350
King, Richard, 107
Kinsey, Alfred C., 7, 458–461
Kirby, D. A., 359
Kirchner, W. K., 543, 545, 553
Kirkland, K., 241
Kirschenbaum, D. S., 230
Klatzky, R. L., 167, 168
Klaus, M. H., 277
Klein, D. F., 427, 436, 441
Klein, E. B., 547
Klein, R., 506
Klein, R. E., 256
Kleitman, N., 114
Klenke-Hamel, K. E., 467, 468
Klentz, B., 491, 506
Klerman, G. L., 398, 441, 442
Klinnert, M., 234
Klorman, R., 239
Klykylo, W. M., 228, 244, 245
Knapp, T. W., 374
Knight, R. T., 45
Kniskern, D. P., 433
Knittle, J. L., 229
Knobloch, H., 256, 307
Kobasa, S. C., 232, 378, 379
Koch, J. B., 196
Koch, S., 19
Koffka, Kurt, 80
Kohlberg, L., 288–289
Köhler, Wolfgang, 80, 156–157

Kolata, G. B., 35
Kolodny, R. C., 451, 452, 454, 468, 470, 471
Konečni, V. J., 516, 517
Konner, M., 43
Koops, B. L., 261
Kopp, C. B., 261
Korte, C., 526
Koulack, D., 468
Kovacs, M., 442
Kraemer, M. W., 469
Krantz, D. S., 522–523
Kraus, T. A., 174
Krauss, R. M., 532
Krawiec, T. S., 11
Krebs, D., 288
Kripke, D. F., 116
Krisberg, J., 154–155
Krupat, E., 525
Kryter, K. D., 521
Kübler-Ross, E., 295–296
Kubovy, M., 80
Kuczaj, S. A., 196, 199
Kuhn, C. M., 379
Kunda, Z., 226
Kutas, M., 40

Labbe, R., 47
LaBossiere, E., 93
Lacoste-Utamsing, C., 44
LaFrance, M., 237
Lahey, B. B., 230, 442
Laird, J. D., 238
Lamb, M. E., 250, 257, 271, 272, 276, 282
Lambert, J. J., 440, 441
Lamberth, J., 357, 359
Lammens, L., 175
Landers, Ann, 396, 449
Landis, D., 412
Landman, J. T., 440, 441
Landrith, G. S., 127
Landsberg, L., 125
Lane, J. D., 379
Langdon, Kevin, 307
Lange, C., 237
Langer, E. J., 520
Lansky, L. M., 45
Lanyon, R. E., 369, 380
Larkin, J. H., 209
L'Armand, K., 473
Larrance, D. T., 239
Lassiter, G. D., 226–227
Latané, Bibb, 478, 498–501
Lau, R. R., 350, 484
Lawler, E. E., 543
Lawson, J. S., 43
Layton, B., 520
Lazar, I., 326
Lazar, J., 505
Lazarus, A. A., 417
Lazarus, Richard S., 238, 365, 376
Leavy, R. L., 378
Lecker, S., 432

Lenneberg, E. H., 196, 201
Lentz, R. J., 427
Leo, J., 275
Leong, F. T. L., 540
LePage, A., 504
Lerner, I. M., 259
Lerner, R. M., 201, 285, 479
Levenkron, J. C., 382
Levin, B. B., 186
Levin, J. R., 186, 196.
Levine, F. J., 176
Levine, H. M., 377
Levinson, D. J., 358, 547
Levinson, Harry, 543–544
Levinson, M. H., 547
Levitan, G. W., 312
Levy, J., 41, 43
Lewinsohn, P. M., 403–404
Lewis, James, 319
Lewis, M., 348
Lewis, S. K., 491
Leyhausen, P., 276
Libby, R. W., 451
Libby, W. J., 259
Libuser, L., 516, 517
Lichtenstein, E., 420, 422, 427, 428, 439, 440
Lieberman, M., 288, 289
Liebert, R. M., 336, 337, 343, 345, 348, 351, 353, 355, 357, 427, 508
Liebman, R., 245
Liebowitz, M. R., 436
Liem, R., 539
Light, L. L., 189
Linder, D. E., 489
Lindsay, J. J., 38
Lindsay, R. C. L., 504
Lindsley, D. B., 241
Lindzey, G., 321
Linnoila, M., 436, 437
Lintgen, Arthur, 79
Linville, P. W., 485
Lippincott, E. C., 505
Lipsedge, M. A., 397
Little, L. M., 425
Lloreda, P., 326
Lockhart, R. S., 171, 174
Loeb, M., 326
Loehlin, J. C., 321
Lofquist, L. H., 539
Loftus, Elizabeth F., 110, 167–169, 171–180, 182–186, 189, 203, 209–212, 551
Loftus, G. R., 110, 167–169, 171–173, 175, 176, 178–180, 183, 184
Lollis, M., 518
Lombardo, M. M., 544
Long, J. D., 374
Loomis, R. J., 514, 517, 522, 523, 530, 531
Lorenz, Konrad, 222, 276, 502
Lowell, E. L., 234
Luborsky, L., 440
Luborsky, Lester, 420, 440
Luchins, A. S., 212

Lucido, D. J., 526
Lucker, G. W., 235
Lunde, D. T., 467, 469
Luo, Jay, 313
Luria, A. R., 185
Lustman, P. J., 375
Luttrell, L., 328
Lykken, D. T., 242, 243
Lynn, Richard, 322

Maccoby, E. E., 276, 322, 455, 456
Mack, D., 229
Mackie, D., 489
MacKinnon, Donald W., 316
MacNichol, E. F., Jr., 62
Maddi, S. R., 232, 378, 379
Maddux, J. E., 486
Magnusson, D., 348
Maharishi Mahesh Yogi, 125, 127
Mahoney, E. R., 458, 467
Mahoney, K., 229
Mahoney, M. J., 154, 229, 420
Maier, Steven F., 152–153
Malamuth, N. M., 463, 464, 473
Maloney, M. J., 228, 244, 245
Mandel, D. R., 520
Mandell, W., 261
Mann, J., 464
Mann, L., 494, 495
Manning, Winton H., 557
Marks, D., 101
Marks, I. M., 397
Marolla, Francis A., 324
Marshall, G. D., 238
Marshall, W. A., 284, 285
Martin, C. E., 7, 458
Martin, R. A., 374, 375
Marx, J. L., 118
Maslach, C., 238
Maslow, Abraham H., 224–226, 342, 343, 392
Massey, R. F., 225
Masters, J. C., 424, 427, 429, 431
Masters, W. H., 451, 452, 454, 461–463, 468–471
Masuda, M., 370, 373
Matarazzo, J. D., 549, 550
Matas, L., 280
Mathews, K. E., Jr., 523, 524
Matlin, M., 169–170, 185, 207
Matthews, J. R., 15
Matthews, K. A., 235, 378, 379
Matthews, R. W., 520
Maugh, T. H., 124
Maupin, E. W., 126
Maurer, D., 94
Mayer, D. J., 35
Mayo, C., 237
McCain, G., 520, 534
McCall, M. W., Jr., 544
McCann, J. J., 57
McCants, T. R., 370
McCary, J. L., 449, 459, 467, 469, 470

Rowe, M. P., 548
Royce, J. M., 326
Rubenstein, C., 366–368
Rubenstein, R., 184
Rubin, D. C., 172
Rubinow, D. R., 189
Rubinstein, E. A., 508
Rubinstein, J., 203
Rule, B. G., 504
Rumbaugh, D. M., 202
Rundus, D., 171
Rush, A. J., 405, 430, 431, 442
Rushton, J. P., 498
Russell, D., 484
Russell, J. A., 513
Russo, N. F., 4
Rutkowski, G. K., 501
Ryan, M. J., 498
Ryan, R. M., 226
Rychlak, J. F., 339, 421, 504
Ryckman, R. M., 338
Ryder, R. G., 349

Saegert, S., 498, 520
Saks, M. J., 358, 359
Salamy, J. G., 113
Salapatek, Phillip, 94
Salk, Lee, 269
Salt, P., 374
Salzinger, S., 378
Samelson, F., 137
Sampson, M. G., 117
Samuel, W., 532
Sanders, D., 235
Sanders, G. S., 184
Sanders, R. J., 202–203
Sanford, R. N., 358
Santrock, J. W., 196
Sarason, B. R., 377, 390, 391, 394, 396,
    398–400, 404, 406, 408, 468
Sarason, I. G., 348, 370, 373, 377, 378, 390,
    391, 394, 396, 398–400, 404, 406, 408, 468
Sardler, Joseph, 38
Sargent, J., 245
Saulnier, K., 484
Scarr, S., 321, 322, 324
Scarr-Salapatek, S., 261
Schachter, Stanley, 230, 234, 237–238, 444,
    498
Schacter, D. L., 182
Schaefer, E. S., 307
Schaeffer, J., 8–9, 117
Schaffer, H. R., 380
Schaffer, N. D., 441
Schaie, K. W., 307
Schanberg, S. M., 379
Scheier, M. F., 376
Schell, R. E., 200
Schkade, J. K., 520
Schlaadt, R. G., 117
Schlesser, M. A., 403

Schmidt, D. E., 520
Schnair, David, 221
Schneider, D. J., 480–481, 483
Schnelle, J. F., 530
Schopler, J., 520
Schowalter, J. E., 245
Schreiner, T., 295
Schroeder, D. A., 495
Schroeder, H., 441
Schulman, J., 358
Schultz, D., 225, 339, 340, 342, 344
Schumacher, G. M., 208, 212–214
Schuster, C. R., 118
Schwartz, R. D., 6
Schwartz, S. H., 226, 500, 506
Schwarzwald, J., 491
Schwebel, A. I., 154
Scott, P., 547
Sears, D. O., 487
Sears, R. R., 315, 503
Sebeok, T. A., 203
Sechrest, L. B., 6, 516
Seeman, M., 349
Segal, M. W., 498
Seitz, V., 325
Selby, J. W., 411
Selby, L. E., 411
Seligman, C., 472, 531–533
Seligman, M. E. P., 151–153, 376, 377, 404,
    521
Seligmann, J., 37
Selye, H., 365, 372
Semmel, A., 404
Senders, V. L., 19
Sergent, J., 41
Seta, J. J., 520
Shalker, T. E., 239
Shanab, M. E., 494
Shannon, E., 123
Shannon, P. T., 117
Shapiro, D., 116, 117
Shapiro, D. A., 440, 441
Shapiro, D. H., 124
Shapiro, Diana, 440, 441
Shapiro, E. C., 548
Shapiro, S., 328
Shatz, M., 205
Shaver, P., 234, 358, 366–368, 525
Shaw, B. F., 405, 430
Shean, G., 405
Sheehan, P. W., 184, 374, 440–442
Sheehy, Gail, 547, 548
Sherrod, D. R., 377, 514, 520–522
Shibuya, Kenichi, 322
Shields, J., 395, 408
Shiffrin, R. M., 167, 170, 171
Shorey, H. H., 231
Shriberg, L. K., 186
Shucard, David W., 40, 44
Shucard, J. L., 40, 44
Shulman, H. G., 170

Sidman, J., 464
Siegel, M., 18–20
Siegel, R. K., 123
Siegler, R. S., 273
Sigall, H., 498
Sigman, M., 261
Silver, M., 245
Silverman, L. H., 339
Silverman, R. E., 83
Silverstein, G., 349
Simkins, L., 143, 373
Simmel, E. C., 317
Simmons, W. L., 184
Simon, D. P., 209
Simon, H. A., 209
Simon, Théodore, 275, 302–303
Simonds, J. F., 115
Simons, R. N., 116
Simpson, E. L., 289
Simpson, G., 45
Singer, B., 440
Singer, D. G., 508
Singer, J. E., 237–238, 377, 382, 522
Singer, J. L., 508
Singular, S., 185
Sinisterra, L., 326
Sivacek, J., 485
Sizemore, Chris, 333, 400
Skinner, B. F., 138–141, 144, 145, 154, 159,
    160, 200, 346, 348
Sklar, L. S., 373
Skrypnek, B. J., 479
Skutnick, Lenny, 501–502, 506
Slamecka, N. J., 180
Slater, E., 395
Slaymaker, F., 261
Slife, B. D., 203, 504
Sloane, R. B., 420, 428
Slobin, D. I., 198, 204, 205
Smallberg, S. A., 189
Smith, B. D., 343, 344
Smith, D. W., 254
Smith, E. E., 170
Smith, M. B., 19
Smith, M. E., 497
Smith, M. L., 440, 441
Smith, R. A., 350
Smith, R. E., 348
Smiht, S., 109
Smith, S. M., 180, 181
Smith, T. W., 431
Sniffen, M. J., 534
Snipper, A. S., 326
Snyder, M., 181, 479
Snyder, S. H., 26, 29, 34, 38, 118
Snyder, S. S., 376
Solano, C. H., 368
Solomon, S., 484
Somervill, J. W., 372, 373, 408, 409, 439, 442
Sommer, R., 516, 518, 528, 529, 534
Sontag, L. W., 254

Sorrentino, R. P., 149
Sosnowski, R. J., 261
Sowa, C. J., 375
Spanier, G. B., 285
Spanos, N. P., 109
Spearman, C., 302
Spector, P. E., 349
Speisman, J., 376
Spence, J. T., 235
Sperling, S. E., 19
Sperry, Roger W., 41–43
Spiegel, D., 110
Spiegel, H., 110
Spiegel, N. H., 239
Spiegler, M. D., 336, 337, 343, 345, 348, 351,
    353, 355, 357, 423, 425, 427, 428, 434
Spinelli, D. N., 96
Spitz, R. A., 278
Sprafkin, J. N., 508
Springer, James, 319
Spuhler, J. N., 321
Srole, L., 525
Sroufe, L. A., 280
Sroufe, R., 479
Staats, A. W., 486
Stainbrook, G. L., 125
Stang, D. J., 16
Stanley, Julian C., 317, 322
Stanley, M., 436
Stanton, M. D., 123
Staples, F. R., 420, 428
Stapp, J., 15, 539
Starch, D., 548
Starr, S., 464
Staub, E., 498, 501
Steblay, N. M., 491
Stechler, G., 251, 253, 254
Steele, W. G., 349
Stein, D. G., 47
Steinbach, A., 334
Stengel, R., 215
Stern, G. S., 370
Stern, R. S., 397
Sternberg, S., 170–171
Stevens, C. F., 27
Stewart, A., 261
Stewart, A. J., 374
Stewart, R., 483
Stiley, Joseph, 502
Stine, G. J., 259, 262, 263
Stokols, D. S., 513, 520, 522–523
Stone, J. D., 377
Storms, M. D., 516
Strahle, W. M., 464
Strang, B., 458, 466
Strickland, B. R., 349, 350
Strong, L. B., 261
Strube, M. J., 359
Stuart, R. B., 432–433
Sturgis, E. T., 376
Sue, D., 393, 395, 397–399, 410

Sue, D. W., 393, 395, 397–399, 410
Sugitani, M., 36
Suinn, Richard M., 381–382
Sullivan, J. J., 480, 531
Summers, R., 189
Sundstrom, E., 520
Super, C., 15
Super, D. E., 15, 540
Suttles, G. D., 518
Svejda, M. J., 95, 96
Swann, W. B., Jr., 185
Swap, W. C., 498
Switzky, H. N., 312

Takahashi, J. S., 111
Takooshian, H., 526
Tanner, J. M., 284, 285
Tapp, J. L., 176, 358
Targ, R., 100
Tart, C. T., 109
Taves, P. A., 488
Taylor, L., 43
Taylor, R. B., 518
Teasdale, J. D., 181, 404
Teitelbaum, P., 37
Terman, Louis M., 303, 304, 306, 313, 315
Terr, L. C., 107
Terrace, H. S., 138, 156, 202–203
Test, M. A., 498
Teuber, H. L., 174
Tharp, R. G., 154–155
Thiel, D. L., 479
Thigpen, C. H., 333
Thomas, Alexander, 257, 271
Thomas, D.G., 40
Thomas, G. C., 516
Thomas, J., 150–151, 425
Thomas, M. H., 505
Thomas, M. M., 530
Thompson, A. P., 460
Thompson, H., 307
Thompson, J. K., 230, 376
Thompson, J. S., 38
Thompson, P. H., 546–547
Thompson, S. C., 376, 377
Thomson, J. L., 9
Thorndike, E. L., 138
Thurstone, L. L., 302
Tilden, J., 184
Timsit-Berthier, M., 189
Tinbergen, N., 222
Tirado, Priscilla, 501–502
Tittle, C. K., 540
Tolman, Edward C., 155–156
Tomarken, A. J., 230
Torrance, P., 317
Toufexis, A., 412, 548
Towson, S. M. J., 507
Tramonta, M. G., 440
Trickett, P. K., 325
Tripp, Peter, 111

Trotter, R. J., 239
Tulving, E., 172–175, 180
Tumblin, A., 206
Turkat, I. D., 115
Turkington, C., 436
Turnbull, W., 555
Turner, J. A., 486
Turner, J. S., 205
Tuso, M. A., 531
Tyler, L. E., 306, 321
Tziner, A., 545

Ulman, K. J., 284, 286
Umiker-Sebeok, J., 203
Underwood, B. J., 178–179
Ungerleider, J. T., 8–9, 124

Valenstein, E. S., 438
Valentine, J., 326
Valins, S., 520, 521
Vallerand, R. J., 226
Van Boxel, J. A., 127
Van de Castle, R. L., 115
Vanderplas, M., 502
Vaughn, B. E., 278
Veitch, R., 498
Velandia, W., 324
Vetter, H. J., 343, 344
Vincent, J. E., 491
Viscott, D. S., 398–399
Vogel, S. R., 455, 456
Vogel, W. H., 233
Vogt, B., 498

Wachs, T. D., 257
Wadden, T. A., 110
Wadsworth, B. J., 271
Wagner, M., 88
Waid, W. M., 243
Wald, George, 56–58, 62
Walk, Richard D., 94–95
Walker, J. M., 530
Wall, S., 278, 280
Wallace, R. F., 254
Wallace, R. K., 125, 127
Wallis, C., 143, 295
Wallston, B. S., 350
Wallston, K. A., 350
Walster, E., 479, 486
Walter, A. A., 204
Wanlass, R., 470
Ward, J. A., 451, 452
Ward, L. M., 513
Ward, W. C., 315
Warman, R. E., 541
Waters, E., 278, 280
Watkins, John, 552
Watkins, L. R., 35
Watson, D., 484
Watson, D. L., 154–155
Watson, John B., 11–12, 136–137, 283

— SUBJECT INDEX —

in children, 504–508
effects on, 503–508
    of frustration, 502–504
    of instincts, 222, 502, 503
    of mass-media violence, 504–506, 508
    of models, 503–507
    of noise, 523
    of pornography, 463–464
    of social learning, 503
    of temperature, 524–525
gender differences in, 456, 507
reducing, 39, 426, 506–507
theories of, 222, 502–503
Aggressive cues, 503–504
Aggressive pronography, 463–464
Aggressors, identification with, 338
Aging, self-regulation techniques affecting, 127
Agoraphobia, 395–396
Air-conditioning usage, reducing, 532–533
Alarm reaction stage of general adaptation syndrome, 372
Alcohol:
    addiction to, 120, 417, 425
    effects of, 58, 120–121, 254
Algorithms in problem solving, 211
All-or-none law of action potentials, 27
Alphafetoprotein (AFP) screening for birth defects, 262
Altered state(s) of consciousness:
    drug-induced, 117–124
    meditation as, 124–127
    sleep as, 110–117
Alternate-forms method of determining test reliability, 304
Alternate-response training in self-control, 154–155
Alternative-treatment groups in therapy evaluation, 440
Altruistic motivation, 221, 223
Alzheimer's disease, 35, 189
Ambiguous sentences, 200
Ambivalent-attachment infants, 280
American Association of Mental Deficiency (AAMD), 308
American Psychiatric Association (APA) abnormal-behavior categories, 391
American Psychological Association (APA):
    divisions in, 12, 13
    ethical guidelines of, 8, 443
    growth of, 19
    journals of, 18
American Sign Language (ASL) used by chimpanzees, 202
Ames room illusion, 87–88
Amnesia, types of, 173–174, 189, 399–400
Amniocentesis in birth-defect screening, 262, 263
Amphetamine psychosis, 121
Amphetamines, 121, 408

Amplitude. *See* Intensity
Ampulla of ears, 71
Amygdala, function of, 38
Anagrams, solving, 209–211
Anal-aggressive personality, 338
Anal-retentive personality, 338
Anal stage of psychosexual development, 337–338
Androgens, 231, 452, 454. *See also* Sex hormones
Animal magnetism (Mesmer), 108–109. *See also* Hypnosis
Anorexia nervosa, 37, 244–245, 432
Anoxia during birth, 260–261
Anterior aphasia (Broca's aphasia), 204, 205
Anterograde amnesia, 174
Anticonvulsant drugs, 41
Antidepressant drugs, 435, 436, 439, 442
Antidiuretic hormone (ADH; vasopressin), 33, 189, 230, 231
Antimanic drugs, 435–437, 439, 442
Antisocial personality, 410–411
Anxiety. *See also* Stress
    castration, 338
    about contraception, 465
    defined, 366
    emotional components of, 236
    intrapsychic conflicts in, 336
    performance, in sexual dysfunctions, 469–470
    and personal-space needs, 514
    verbal behavior expressing, 237
Anxiety-arousing stimuli, 423–424. *See also* Aversive stimuli
Anxiety disorders, 394–395
Anxiolytic drugs, 435, 436, 442
APA. *See* American Psychiatric Association (APA) abnormal behavior categories; American Psychological Association (APA)
Aperiodic complex sound waves, 65
Aperture control in eyes, 56
Aphasias, 204–205
Apnea during sleep, 116–117
Apparent distance theory about moon illusion, 89
Apparent motion, 91–92
Appearance, impressions of, 478–480
Applied psychology, 12–15, 539–558
Applied research, 4
Apprenticeship stage of careers, 546
Approach-approach conflict, 369
Approach-avoidance conflict, 368–369, 398
Aptitude tests, 304, 305, 308, 317, 541, 555, 571
Arcuate fasciculus, 204, 205
Arguments in persuasion, 486–488
Army Alpha and Beta intelligence (IQ) tests, 304
Army General Classification Test, 321

Arousal. *See* Emotional arousal; Physiological arousal, emotion affecting; Sexual arousal
Arousal theory of motivation, 224
Artificial insemination in intelligence engineering, 328
Artificial intelligence in problem solving, 215. *See also* Computer-assisted instruction (CAI); Computers
Artistic people in Strong-Campbell Interest Inventory, 542
Assertiveness training, 424–425
Assessment centers in personnel selection, 545–546
Assimilation in cognitive development, 271
Association areas in cerebral cortex, 37
Association neurons (interneurons), 32
Associative, stimulus-response approaches to learning, 133. *See also* Classical conditioning; Operant conditioning
Associativity rule in cognitive development, 274
A-Theme in Strong-Campbell Interest Inventory, 542
Attachment-in-the-making phase of attachment, 278
Attachment of infants (bonding), 222, 276–280
Attacks, aggression evoked by, 504
Attention and perception, 99
Attention-placebo groups in therapy evaluation, 440
Attitude-discrepant behavior, 488–489
Attitudes:
    and behaviors, 485–486, 488–489
    changing, 486–489
    components of, 485
    defined, 485
    formation of, 485–486
    similarity of, in attraction, 497, 498
Attraction, effects on, 496–498, 514–517, 520, 524
Attractiveness, impressions of, 479
Attribution process in person perception, 480–482
Attribution therapy for students, 484–485
Audible spectrum, 65
Audition, defined, 65. *See also* Hearing
Auditory canal, 67
Auditory codes in memory, 170, 172, 174–175. *See also* Acoustic sensory memory (echoic store)
Auditory cortex of brain, 36
Auditory hallucinations, 406
Auditory nerve, 68
Auditory system, 64–69. *See also* Ears, structure and function of; Hearing
Auditory techniques for studying brain function, 40, 43
Authoritarianism, 290, 358

Authoritarianism scales in jury selection, 358–359
Authoritative parents, 290
Authority figures in obedience, 492–495
Autistic savants, 301
Autokinetic movement, 92
Autonomic nervous system, 32, 33, 236, 410
Autonomy versus doubt in psychosocial development, 275, 294
Autoshaping of behavior, 151
Aversive conditioning, 417, 425, 444
Aversive control of behavior, 151–153. *See also* Punishment
Aversive stimuli, 376, 504
Avoidance-avoidance conflict, 369
Avoidance training, 152
Avoidant infants, 280
Avoidant personality, 410
Awake states of newborns and infants, 257
Axons of neurons, 26–28, 59

Babbling in language development, 196
Babies. *See* Infants; Newborns
Baby-tender of Skinner, 139
Backward conditioning, 136
Bakke court case, 555–556
Balance theory of attraction, 496, 497
Barbiturates, 119–120
Basal metabolism rate, obesity affecting, 230
Baseline measures for experimental control, 10
Basic research, 4
Basilar membrane of ear, 68
Bedwetting (enuresis), 117, 142
Behavior:
    and attitudes, 485–486, 488–489
    biological foundations of, 25–48
    and brain functioning, 35–46
    and brain neurotransmitters, 34–35
    chains of, 148–151
    compliance in, 490–492
    conformity in, 489–491
    consensus in, 481–482
    consequences of, expectancies about, 346, 356
    consistency in, 481–482
    control of. *See also* Control
        aversive, 151–153. *See also* Punishment
        electrical stimulation of the brain in, 45
        external and internal, 347, 349–350
        self-. *See* Self-control
        stimulus, 147–151
    distinctiveness of, 481–482
    functional analysis of, 346
    influences on, 486–496, 498–502
        emotions as, 239, 241
        external, 481–482, 484–485
        extrinsic, 226–227
        internal, 480–482, 484–485
    motivation of. *See* Motivation; Motives

observation of, types of, 6. *See also* Observations
patterns of, Type A and Type B, 378–379
rehearsal of, in assertiveness training, 424–425
self-regulation of, 347, 348. *See also* Self-regulation, of consciousness
self-reinforcement of, 154, 347
shaping of, 148–151, 200–201, 425
types of. *See specific entries, for example:* Abnormal behavior; Covert behavior; Sexual behavior
Behavioral adaptive theory of sleep, 110–111
Behavioral approach to personality, 344–348, 355–357
Behavioral genetics, 317–322
Behavioral-health psychologists, 15, 549–551
Behavioral model of abnormality, 392, 393
    on affective disorders, 403–404
    on aggression, 503–507
    on conversion disorder, 399
    on dissociative disorders, 400
    on generalized anxiety disorder, 395
    on homosexuality, 469
    on hypochondriasis, 398
    on obsessive-compulsive disorders, 398
    on phobias, 396
    on schizophrenia, 408–409
Behavioral modification (therapy), 154–155, 159, 417, 422–431, 444. *See also* Self-control
Behavioral specificity, 345
Behavioral states of newborns and infants, 257
Behavioral techniques for studying brain function, 40–41
Behavioral technology, trends in, 159–160
Behaviorism school of psychology, 11–12
Belongingness needs, 225
Benzodiazepine drugs, 435, 436
Bereavement counseling, 296
Bereiter-Engelmann group, 324, 325
Berkeley Growth Study, 307
Biases. *See also* Racial discrimination
    in person perception, 483–484
    in placement of educable mentally retarded, 554–555
Binet-Simon intelligence (IQ) test, 303, 307. *See also* Stanford-Binet Intelligence Test
Binocular depth cues, 84
Binocular disparity in retinal images, 84
Biochemical theories of schizophrenia, 408
Biofeedback, 143, 374–376
Biological aging, self-regulation techniques affecting, 127
Biological changes during adolescence, 284–286
Biological constraints on shaping learned behaviors, 151
Biological death, 295

Biological differences of males and females, 450–454, 456. *See also* Gender differences
Biological foundations of behavior, 25–48
Biological maturation, 270, 284–286
Biological (medical) model of abnormality, 392
    on affective disorders, 403
    on generalized anxiety disorder, 394–395
    on homosexuality, 468–469
    on hypochondriasis, 398
    on personality disorders, 410
    on schizophrenic disorders, 408
Biological motives for behavior, 227–232. *See also* Sociobiology
Biological rhythm theory of sleep, 111
Bipolar cells of retinas, 58
Bipolar disorder, 401–403
    drug treatment for, 435–437, 439, 442
Birth complications, 258, 260–264
Birth defects, 254, 258–260, 262, 263, 313, 328
Blacks:
    discrimination against, in intelligence (IQ) tests, 554–555
    quotas for, in college admissions, 555–556
    and whites, intelligence quotient (IQ) differences of, 321–322
Blastocysts, 251
Blindness. *See also* Vision, defects in; Visual deprivation
    color, 62–64, color plate Figure 3–13
    night, and vitamin A, 58
    recovery from, perceptual problems in, 98
    and "seeing" with skin senses, 72–74
Blind spot of eyes, 56, 57
Blood pressure, high, 373–375
Bobo-doll aggression study, 504
Bodies. *See also entries beginning with* Physiological
    emotion affecting, 236, 239, 241
    emotion expressed by, 236–243
Body senses, 71–72
Body-weight fluctuations, 227–230. *See also* Eating disorders
Bonding (attachment) of infants, 222, 276–280
Borderline personality, 410
Botulin, paralysis caused by, 35
Braille reading, 72–73
Brains. *See also* Nervous system
    damage to, 38, 45, 204–205, 260–261. *See also* Mental disorders, diagnosis of; Mental retardation
    development of, 29
    and ears, connections of, 68
    in eating behavior, 227–229
    electrical stimulation of, 39, 45–46, 183
    electroconvulsive (electroshock) therapy on, 173, 189, 437–438, 442

and eyes, connections of, 58–60
functioning of, and behavior, 35–46
gender differences in, 43–44, 322, 323, 457
implants in, 47–48
lesions in, 37–38, 43. *See also* surgery on, *below*
neurotransmitters of, 34–35, 40, 47–48
opiates of, 35, 46
in sensory system, 53, 80
structure of, 29–31, 35–37
surgery on, 25, 41–43, 45, 438, 442
visual deprivation affecting, 96–98
Brain wave activity during sleep stages, 113
Brightness, determination of, 61
Broca's aphasia (anterior aphasia), 204, 205
Bruxism (teeth-grinding), 117
Bulimia, 37, 244. *See also* Anorexia nervosa
Butyrophenone drugs, 435, 436
Bystander intervention in emergencies, 477–478, 499–502

Caffeine as stimulant, 121
CAI (computer-assisted instruction), 159, 160, 553
California Personality Inventory, 316
California Psychological Inventory (CPI), 353–354
Camouflage in form perception, 82
Cancer and life stresses, 373
Career counseling, 540–543, 553
Career-development stages, 540, 546–548
Care-givers. *See* Fathers; Mothers; Parents
Case-history approach to research, 5–6
Castration anxiety, 338
Cataplexy in narcolepsy, 117
Catatonic schizophrenia, 406, 407
Catecholamines, 244, 403, 436
Catharsis in aggression reduction, 506
Causal attribution in person perception, 481–482, 484–485
Causation and correlation, 570–571
Cell bodies of neurons (dendrites), 26–28
Cell division (mitosis) of zygotes, 251
Cells:
    parts of, 26–28
    types of. *See specific entries, for example:* Fat cells in obesity; Neurons; Receptor cells
Central nervous system, 29–32
    drugs affecting, 117–124. *See also* Drugs
Central tendency, measures of, 563–565
Cerebellum, 31
Cerebral cortex, 29–30, 35–37
Cerebral hemispheres:
    damage to, 38. *See also* Split-brain surgery
    specialization of function in, 41–45
    structure of, 29–30
    studying, techniques for, 40–41
Cerebral palsy, 261
Cerebrum, 29–30

Chains of behavior, 148–151
Charities, collection techniques for, 495–496
Chemical control of memory, 189–190
Chemical energy turned into taste or smell sensations, 69
Chemical senses, 69–71. *See also* Smell; Taste
Chemical therapy (drug therapy), 435–437, 439, 441–442
Childhood:
    developmental tasks of, 270–271
    development during, 270–284, 294
        cognitive, 271–275, 324–326
        language, 196–200, 205–206
        psychosexual, 336–338
        psychosocial, 275–276, 294
    early and late, 270
Child-rearing trends, 283–284, 290
Children. *See also* Families; Fathers; Infants; Mothers; Newborns; Parents; Prenatal period of development
    adopted, intelligence (IQ) studies of, 319–320
    aggression of, 504–508
    effects on:
        of family and social change, 280–283
        of noise, 523
        of punishment, 153, 158
    in environmental enrichment programs, 324–326
    gender-role learning by, 456–457
    language acquisition by, 200–201. *See also* Childhood, development during, language
    personalities of, 257
    and parents, relationships of, 283–284, 409
    physically attractive, 479
    schizophrenic, 409
    in single-parent families, 281–283
    sleep behaviors in, 115
    stimulus seeking by, 232
Chimpanzee language acquisition, 202–203
Choline in acetylcholine synthesis, 35
Chromosomal abnormalities, 259–260, 262, 313, 328. *See also* Genetic abnormalities
Chromosomes:
    defined, 251
    X and Y, 450–454
Chunks of information, 168–169
Cigarette smoking, 254, 550. *See also* Nicotine as stimulant
Ciliary muscles of eyes, 56
Cinema. *See* Movies
Circadian rhythms in sleep theory, 111
Circumstantial use of drugs, 118
Clairvoyance, 100
Classical conditioning, 133–137, 141–142. *See also* Reflex behaviors
    in attitude formation, 486
    in behavioral model of abnormality, 392
    law of, 135
    and operant conditioning, interaction of,

142–155. *See also* Operant conditioning
    in schizophrenia, 408
Classically conditioned responses, 136, 141
Classification systems for abnormal behavior, 390–392
Claustrophobia, 396
Clear-cut attachment phase of attachment, 278
Clearness, principle of, 84, 86, 87
Client-centered therapy (Rogers), 420–422, 444
Clinical observations:
    of brain damage, 38
    of brain lesions, 43
Clinical psychology, 14
Clitoral orgasm, 463
Closure, principle of, 81, 82
Clustering in information retrieval, 172
Cocaine, 121–123
Cochlea and cochlear fluid, 68
Cognition. *See also* Thinking
    defined, 271
    emotion influencing, 239
    need for, in persuasibility, 488
Cognitive ability. *See* Intelligence; *entries beginning with* Intellectual; Intelligence
Cognitive appraisals of stress, 376
Cognitive-appraisal theory of emotion (Lazarus), 238
Cognitive approaches:
    to behavior, 498–502. *See also* Cognitive model of abnormality
    to learning, 133, 155–158
    to personality, 344, 354–355
Cognitive-behavioral approach to personality, 345–348
Cognitive-behavioral therapies, 428–431, 444
Cognitive component of attitudes, 485
Cognitive-consistency theories of motivation, 224
Cognitive development (Piaget), 271–275. *See also* Thinking
Cognitive dissonance, reducing, 488–489
Cognitive maps in latent learning, 156
Cognitive model of abnormality, 392, 393
    on affective disorders, 404, 405
    on generalized anxiety disorder, 395
    on obsessive-compulsive disorders, 398
    on phobic disorders, 396
Cognitive motivation theories, 224
Cognitive-physiological theory of emotion (Schachter), 237–238
Cognitive social-learning theory (Mischel), 347–348
Cognitive therapy (Beck), 430–431
Coitus, 459–460
    problems in, 469–471
Colleague stage of careers, 546
Colleges, admissions testing for, 553–558. *See also* Students

Color(s):
  dimensions of, 60–61
  physical primary, 62
Color blindness, 62–64, color plate Figure
    3–13
Color vision, 60–63
Combinativity rule in cognitive development,
    274
Communication and personal space, 514–516
Community psychology, 14
Community stress checks, 383–384
Compensation in coping with stress, 380
Competence and control motivation theories,
    224–227
Complex cells in visual cortex, 59–60
Complexity:
  of light waves, 61
  of sound waves, 65–67
  in stimulus seeking, 232
Compliance, 490–492, 495–496. See also
    Conformity; Obedience
Compulsions, defined, 396. See also
    Obsessive-compulsive disorder
Compulsive drug use, 118
Compulsive personality, 410
Computer-assisted instruction (CAI), 159,
    160, 553
Computers:
  in medical diagnosis, 215, 549
  in problem solving, 215
Concept formation, 206–209
Conception, defined, 251
Concepts, attributes of, 206–208
Concordance rates in twin studies. See Twin
    studies on genetics versus environment
Concrete operational stage of cognitive
    development, 274
Conditioned reinforcing stimuli, 143–145
Conditioned responses (CR), 135–137
  acquisition of, 136, 140–141
  classically, 136, 141
  extinction of, 140–142, 146, 425
  operantly, 140–141
Conditioned stimuli (CS), 135–137, 143–145
Conditioning, 133–155. See also Learning
  acquisition stage of, 136
  aversive, 417, 425, 444
  classical (respondent). See Classical
      conditioning
  counter-, in behavioral therapies, 417,
      423–425
  escape and avoidance, 152
  operant (instrumental). See Operant
      conditioning
  spontaneous recovery in, 141
  and timing, 136
Cones of eyes, 56–59, 61–62
Conflict, 368–369, 398
Conformity, 489–491. See also Compliance;
    Obedience
Conjunctive rule in concept formation, 207

Conscious level of consciousness, 108
Consciousness:
  defined, 107
  levels of, 108
  modes of, 107–108
  nature of, 107–110
  self-regulation of, 124–127. See also Self-
      regulation, of behavior
  short-term memory in, 171
  states of:
    altered. See Altered state(s) of
        consciousness
    variability of, 107
    waking, 107
Consciousness-altering drugs, 117–124
Consensus in behavior, 481–482
Conservation:
  of energy, 530–533
  of substance, 273–274
Consistency:
  in behavior, 481–482
  in thoughts, need for, 224
Consolidation of memories, 173
Constructive alternativism (Kelly), 344, 354
Construct validation of tests, 305–306
Consumer psychology, 548–549
Consumer research, 549
Consumers, characteristics of, 549
Content analysis of interviews, 354
Content validation:
  of self-report inventories, 352
  of tests, 305
Context:
  in form perception, 83
  of learning, in memory retrieval, 187
Context-dependent memory, 180–181
Continuation, principle of, 81, 82
Continuous amnesia, 400
Continuous nonreinforcement schedules, 145
Continuous reinforcement schedules, 145
Contours in form perception, 82–83
Contraception in adolescence, 464–466
Contraprepared responses, 151
Control:
  of behavior. See Behavior, control of
  delusions of, in schizophrenia, 406
  locus of, 347, 349–350
  perceived, in coping with stress, 376–377
  sense of, 520–522
Control and competence theories of
    motivation, 224–227
Control groups, 7–10
Controlled research in therapy evaluation,
    439–440
Controlled variables, 9
Conventional people in Strong-Campbell
    Interest Inventory, 542
Conventional stages of moral development,
    288
Convergence in depth perception, 86–87
Convergent thinking, 315

Conversion disorder, 398–399
Corneas of eyes, 56, 58–59
Corpus callosum:
  split-brain surgery on, 25, 41–43, 45
  structure and function of, 30
Correctional psychologists, 551–552
Correlation:
  and causation, 570–571
  and prediction, 571
Correlation coefficient, 6, 318–320, 568–571
Correlation-research approach, 6–7. See also
    Nonexperimental research approaches
Cortex of brain (cerebral cortex), 29–30, 35–
    37
Counseling:
  bereavement, 296
  career, 540–543, 553
  genetic, 263–264
Counseling psychology, 14
Counselors, pastoral, 434
Counterconditioning in behavioral therapies,
    417, 423–425
Court psychologists, 552
Courtrooms, personality assessment in, 358–
    359
Covert behaviors, 345
Covert sensitization, 417, 425
CPI (California Psychological Inventory),
    353–354
CR. See Conditioned responses (CR)
Creativity, 315–317
Credibility in attitude change, 486
Cretinism 259
Criterion-related validation:
  of self-report inventories, 352
  of tests, 305
Critical periods of development, 201, 276–
    277
Cross-sectional research designs, 307
Crowding, effects of, 520–522, 527, 534
CS (conditioned stimuli), 135–137, 143–145
C-Theme in Strong-Campbell Interest
    Inventory, 542
Cues. See also Prompts in environmental-
    behavior changes
  aggressive, 503–504
  changing, in self-control, 154
  external:
    in obesity, 228–229
    in sexual arousal, 231
  retrieval, 172–173, 180
Cultural-familial retardation, 312–313
Cunnilingus, 459
Curare, paralysis caused by, 35
Curiosity:
  in creative thinking, 317
  in stimulus seeking, 232

Dark adaptation, 58
Data:
  defined, 562

empirical, 5
in statistical deception, 572–573
DAT (Differential Aptitude Test), 541
Day-care services, 281
Deafness and language development, 201, 204. *See also* American Sign Language (ASL) used by chimpanzees; Hearing
Death, dealing with, 295–296
Death instincts (Freud), 335
Decay of information, 170, 180
Decibels (dB) as sound-intensity measure, 66
Decision-tree analysis of bystander intervention in emergencies, 499–502
Deep structure of sentences, 200
Defense mechanisms in coping with stress, 379–381
Defensible space, 529–530
Delayed pairing procedure in conditioning, 136
Delays as frustration, 366, 367, 371
Delta waves, 113
Delusions:
in major depressive disorder, 402
in schizophrenia, 406–408
Dementia versus mental retardation, 312
Dendrites of neurons, 26–28
Denial in coping with stress, 379
Dependent personality, 410
Dependent variables, 7–9
Depression:
as affective disorder, 401–405
and life stresses, 373
and mania, alternating, 401–403
neurotransmitters in, 403, 436, 437
postpartum, 401
treatment of, 430–431, 435–439
verbal behavior expressing, 237
Deprivation:
dream, 114
maternal, 278–280
sensory, 232–233
sleep, 111–112
visual, 96–99
Depth perception, 84–87
illusions in, 87–91
in infants, 94–96
and visual deprivation, 96, 98, 99
Descriptive statistics, 562–571
Despair versus integrity in later maturity, 293, 294
Destructive obedience, 492–495
Development. *See specific entries, for example:* Critical periods of development; Growth and development; Moral development
Developmental complications in newborns. *See* Birth complications; Birth defects
Developmental psychology, 14, 249
Developmental quotients (DQs) of infants, 307
Developmental tasks:
of adolescence, 286–290, 294

of adulthood, 291, 292, 294
defined, 270
of infancy and childhood, 270–271, 294
Deviation IQs, 303, 307
Deviation scores, 566, 567
Diagnoses, medical, 38, 215, 389, 412, 549–550
Diagnostic and Statistical Manual of Mental Disorders (DSM-III; APA), categories in, 390
Dichotic-listening technique for studying brain function, 40
Dichromatism, 63–64
Diet:
and intellectual development, 326
during pregnancy, 253
Dieting and overeating, relationship of, 229–230. *See also* Eating disorders
Differential Aptitude Test (DAT), 541
Differential-emotions theory (Izard), 238–240
Differential reinforcement of responses, 148
Diffusion of responsibility, 500, 501, 526
Directive genetic counseling, 263
Discrete-trial procedures, 138
Discrimination:
racial. *See* Racial discrimination
stimulus, 148
Discriminative stimuli, 138
Diseases and disorders. *See specific entries, for example:* Eating disorders; Maternal diseases during pregnancy; Psychosomatic disorders
Disjunctive rule in concept formation, 207
Disorganized schizophrenia, 406
Displacement of information, 170
Display rules for facial expressions, 239, 240
Dissociative disorders, 399–400
Dissonance reduction, 488–489
Distinctiveness of behavior, 481–482
Distributed practice in memory improvement, 187
Distributions, frequency, 306, 562–571
Divergent thinking, 315, 316
Divorce affecting children, 281–282
Dizygotic (fraternal) twins, studies of. *See* Twin studies on genetics versus environment
DNA, recombinant, in brain-disorder treatment, 48
Door-in-the-face technique for compliance, 491
Dopamine, 47–48, 408, 436
Dormitories, crowding in, 521, 522, 527
Double approach-avoidance conflicts, 369
Double-bind pattern in schizophrenia, 409
Double-blind research design, 440
Doubt versus autonomy in psychosocial development, 275, 294
Down's syndrome, 259–260, 262, 313, 328
DQs (developmental quotients) of infants, 307
Dream deprivation, 114

Dreams, 113–115. *See also* Sleep
content and interpretation of, 114–115, 350, 419
Drinking, biological regulation of, 230–231. *See also* Alcohol; Oral stage of psychosexual development
Drive-reduction theory of motivation, 223
Drives, functions of, 223
Drug abuse, defined, 118
Drug-dependence insomnia, 116
Drugs:
addiction to, dependence on, and tolerance to, 118–124, 254, 417, 425
during pregnancy, 254
types of:
anticonvulsant, 41
antidepressant, 435, 436, 439, 442
antimanic, 435–437, 439, 442
anxiolytic, 435, 436, 442
consciousness-altering, 117–124
hallucinogenic (psychedelic), 123–124
licit and illicit, defined, 117
narcotic, 35, 118–119, 254
sedative, 119–121. *See also* Alcohol
stimulant, 121–123, 408. *See also* Cigarette smoking
Drug therapy, 435–437, 439, 441–442
Drug use, defined, 118
DSM-III (*Diagnostic and Statistical Manual of Mental Disorders;* APA), categories in, 390
Dual memory theory, 173–174
Dying, dealing with, 295–296. *See also* Death instincts (Freud)

Early adulthood, 291, 294
Early childhood, 270. *See also* Infants; Newborns
Ears, structure and function of, 64, 67–68, 71–72. *See also* Hearing; *entries beginning with* Acoustic; Auditory
Eating, over- and under-, biological reasons for, 37, 227–230. *See also* Oral stage of psychosexual development
Eating disorders, 37, 228–230, 244–245, 432
Echoic store (acoustic sensory memory), 168
ECT (electroconvulsive or electroshock therapy), 173, 189, 437–438, 442
EDS (excessive daytime sleepiness), 116–117
Educable mentally retarded (EMR), bias in placement of, 554–555
Education. *See also* Colleges, admissions testing for; Students
programmed and computer-assisted instruction in, 159, 160, 553
sex, for adolescents, 464–466
Educational psychology, 14, 553
Educational testing, 553–558. *See also* Achievement tests; Aptitude tests; Intelligence (IQ) tests; Psychological tests, characteristics of

Educational Testing Service (ETS), 554, 555, 557–558
EEGs (electroencephalograms), 39–40, 112–113
Effect(s):
    law of (Thorndike), 138
    noncommon, searching for, 480–481
Effectance motivation, 226
Efferent (motor) neurons, 31–32
Efficacy expectation in self-reinforcement, 347, 356
Egg cells (ova), 251
Egg phase of prenatal development, 251, 252
Egocentricity of infants, 272
Ego in psychoanalytic theory of personality, 335–337
Egoistic motivation, 221
Ejaculation problems, 469–470
Elaborative rehearsal of information, 172, 187
Electra complex, 338
Electrical shocks in obedience experiments, 492–495
Electrical stimulation of the brain (ESB), 39, 45–46, 183
Electroconvulsive (electroshock) therapy (ECT), 173, 189, 437–438, 442
Electroencephalograms (EEGs), 39–40, 112–113
Electromagnetic spectrum, 55
Electromyograms (EMGs), 112–113
Electromyographic (EMG) biofeedback, 374–375
Electrooculograms (EOGs), 112–113
Embryo, period of, in prenatal development, 251–253
Emergencies, helping in, 477–478, 499–502. See also Helping, influences on
EMG (electromyographic) biofeedback, 374–375
EMGs (electromyograms), 112–113
Emotional arousal, 224, 236–241
Emotional independence from parents, adolescent achievement of, 287
Emotional support in coping with stress, 377–378
Emotions. See also Feelings
    defined, 221
    defining, 236–237
    differentiating, 237
    effects of, 236, 239, 241
        on adolescent contraception, 465
        during pregnancy, 253–254
    measuring, polygraph tests in, 241–243
    and motivation, 236. See also Motivation; Motives
    outward expression of, 236–237
    of schizophrenics, 406
    theories about, 237–240
Empathetic understanding in client-centered therapy, 421

Empathy:
    in aggression reduction, 506
    in emergency helping, 502
Empirical data, 5
Empiricism in cognitive-development study, 271
Employment of mothers, children affected by, 281. See also entries beginning with Career; Personnel
EMR (educable mentally retarded), bias in placement of, 554–555
Encoding information in memory, 167, 170, 172, 185–186
Endocrine system, 32–34. See also Nervous system
Endorphins in pain inhibition, 35, 46
Energy:
    physical, turned into sensations, 55–60, 64–69
    psychic (Freud), 335, 336
    reaction-specific, 222
    sexual (libido), 335–337. See also Psychosexual stages of personality development
Energy conservation, positive reinforcement in, 530–533
Energy conservation theory of sleep, 110
Engineering psychology, 14
Enkephalins in pain inhibition, 35
Enriched environments and intellectual development, 318, 324–326
Enterprise as occupational classification, 540–541
Enterprising people in Strong-Campbell Interest Inventory, 542
Entrepreneurial role of managers, 547
Enuresis (bedwetting), 117, 142
Environment(s):
    in aggression, 502–503, 523–525
    behavior determined by, 519–534
    enrichment of, and intellectual development, 318, 324–326
    and genetics. See Genetics, and environment; Genetics, versus environment
    intellectual, value of (VIE), for families, 323, 324
    physical. See Physical environment
    prenatal, influences on, 253–254
    responsive, designing, 519, 528–530
    restricted, intelligence affected by, 318
    urban, 513, 525–526
Environmental behavior, 530–533
Environmental design, 519, 528–530
Environmental psychology, 15, 513–534
Environmental stimulation, vocalization affected by, 256
Environmental stressors, 370
EOGs (electrooculograms), 112–113
Epilepsy, 25, 41, 45
Epinephrine (adrenaline), 34
Equilibratory (vestibular) sense, 71–72

Equilibrium theory of personal space, 516
Erectile dysfunction (impotence), 469
Erogenous zones (Freud), 336–338
Escape training, 152
ESP (extrasensory perception), 100–101
Establishment stage of careers, 540
Esteem needs, 225. See also Self-esteem
Estrogens, 231, 452, 454. See also Sex hormones
E-Theme in Strong-Campbell Interest Inventory, 542
Ethical guidelines of American Psychological Association, 8, 443
Ethnic-racial differences in intelligence quotient (IQ), 321–322
Ethologists, instinct theory of, 222–223
ETS (Educational Testing Service), 554, 555, 557–558
Eugenics, controversy about, 318, 328
Eustachian tubes, 67
Evoked-potential technique for recording brain electrical activity, 40, 44
Excessive daytime sleepiness (EDS), 116–117
Excitatory synapses, 28
Excitement phase of sexual-response cycle, 461–462
Executives, mentor relationships of, 547–548. See also Career development stages
Exercise in weight control, 230
Exhaustion stage of general adaptation syndrome, 372
Exhibitionism, 467
Expectancies about behavior, 346, 347, 356
Expectancy charts in personnel selection, 545
Experience:
    and perceptual development, 95–98
    and personal-space needs, 515
Experimental drug use, 118
Experimental groups, 7
Experimental psychology, 14
Experimental research approach, 7–9
Exploration in stimulus seeking, 232
Exploration stage of careers, 540
External causes of behavior, 481–482, 484–485
External control of behavior, 347, 349–350
External cues:
    in obesity, 228–229
    in sexual arousal, 231
Extinction of conditioned responses, 140–142, 146, 425
Extracellular thirst, 230–231
Extramarital intercourse, 459–461
Extraneous variables, 7
Extrasensory perception (ESP), 100–101
Extrinsic reasons for behavior, 226–227
Extroverted personality type, 341–342
Eye-head system, 91
Eyes, structure and function of, 55–63, 134. See also Blindness; Vision; entries beginning with Optic; Visual

Eyewitness testimony, memory errors in, 165, 175–178, 184

Facial expressions:
  of emotion, 236–240
  innateness of, 239, 240
  newborn identification of, 255
Facial-feedback hypothesis, 238–239
Factor analysis:
  of personality types, 341
  of source traits, 340–341, 352, 353
Failures as frustration, 366
Familiarity effect in attraction, 498
Families:
  in antisocial personality development, 410
  mental retardation in, 312–313
  in schizophrenia, 509
  social changes in, children affected by, 280–283
Family configuration theory and intellectual development, 322–324
Family interaction model of abnormality, 392, 409, 410
Family studies in genetic versus environmental effects on intellectual development, 320
Family therapy, 432, 433, 444
Fantasies:
  anticontraception, 465–466
  in creative thinking, 317
Farsightedness (hyperopia), 63, 64
Fat cells in obesity, 229
Fathers:
  and children, in single-parent families, 282–283
  during children's phallic stage of psychosexual development, 338
Fear-inducing advertisements, 487
Fear of success as achievement barrier, 235. See also Phobias
Feature detectors in visual cortex, 59–60
Feedback in energy conservation, 531–533
Feelings. See also Emotions; entries beginning with Affective
  of loneliness, as frustration, 366–368
  negative, environmental causes of, 520, 524–525
  organismic, in experience evaluation, 342–343
  about others, in attraction, 498
Fellatio, 459
Female executives, mentor relationships of, 547–548. See also Gender; entries beginning with Gender
Fetal alcohol syndrome, 254
Fetishism, 466
Fetus, period of, in prenatal development, 252, 253
Field as occupational classification, 540–541
Figure and ground principle, 80, 81, 89
FI partial-reinforcement schedules (fixed-

interval), 145, 146
First impressions, forming, 483
First-letter technique of information organization, 185
First-sentences stage of language development, 198–200
First-words stage of language development, 197–198
Fixation at psychosexual stages, 337, 338
Fixed-interval (FI) partial-reinforcement schedules, 145, 146
Fixed-ratio (FR) partial-reinforcement schedules, 146
Focus control in eyes, 56
Foot-in-the-door technique for compliance, 491, 495
Forebrain, structure of, 29–31
Forensic psychology, 15, 551–552
Forgetting. See also Memory(ies); entries beginning with Memory
  in amnesia, 173–174, 189
  boxing in, 38
  electroconvulsive (electroshock) therapy in, 438
  marijuana in, 8–10
  motivated, 182–184, 335
  oxytocin in, 190
  prevention of, rehearsal in, 170, 171. See also Rehearsal, of information; Retrieval of information from memory
  theories of, 178–183
Formal operational stage of cognitive development, 274
Formal operational thought in cognitive development, 274
Form perception, 80–84, 93–94
Foveas of retinas, 56, 57
Fraternal (dizygotic) twins, studies of. See Twin studies on genetics versus environment
Free association in Freudian psychoanalysis, 419
Free recall of information, 174
Free-responding procedures, 138
Frequency:
  of sexual behavior, defined, 459
  of sound waves, 65
Frequency distributions, 306, 562–571
Frequency polygons, 562–563
Frequency theory of pitch, 68, 69
Freudian psychoanalysis, 184, 419–420, 444
Frigidity (orgasmic dysfunction), 470
Frontal lobe of brain, 35–37
FR partial-reinforcement schedules (fixed-ratio), 146
Frustration:
  coping with, 371
  sources of, 366–369
Frustration-aggression hypothesis, 502–504
Functional analysis of behavior, 346
Functional defects of newborns, 258

Functional fixity in problem solving, 212–213
Functionalism school of psychology, 11
Fundamental tone frequency, 67

Galvanic skin response (GSR), 236, 242
Gambling, 133, 146
Ganglion cells of retinas, 58
GAS (general adaptation syndrome), 372
Gender:
  development of, 450–458
  versus sex, 450. See also Sex; entries beginning with Sex; Sexual
Gender differences:
  in achievement motivation, 234, 235
  in aggression, 456, 507
  biological, 231, 284–286, 450–454, 456
  in cerebral specialization of function, 43–44. See also in spatial and verbal abilities, below
  in cigarette smoking, 550
  in crowding effects, 520
  in dream content, 115
  in intellectual development, 322, 323
  in life-stress effects, 373–374
  in mathematical ability, 457
  in personal-space needs, 514, 517
  in persuasibility, 487
  in sex hormones, 231
  in sexual dysfunctions, 469–470
  in spatial and verbal abilities, 43–44, 322, 323, 457
  in student suicide attempts, 411
Gender identity, development of, 454–455, 468
Gender roles, 317, 454–458
General adaptation syndrome (GAS), 372
Generalization gradients for stimuli, 148. See also Stimulus generalization
Generalized amnesia, 400
Generalized anxiety disorder, 394–395
Generalized expectancies (Rotter), 347
Generativity versus self-absorption during middle age, 291–292, 294
Genes, coining of term, 318
Genetic abnormalities, 259, 262, 263, 313. See also Chromosomal abnormalities
Genetically programmed behaviors, 222–223
Genetic counseling, 263–264
Genetics:
  in affective disorders, 403
  in brain-disorder treatment, 48
  coining of term, 318
  and environment:
    in growth and development, 250
    in schizophrenic disorders, 389–390, 408
  versus environment:
    in gender identity, 454, 455
    in homosexuality, 468–469
    in intellectual development, 317–328

in knowledge (cognitive) development, 271
in perception, 93
in generalized anxiety disorder, 394–395
human behavioral, 317–322
in prenatal sexual differentiation, 450–454
Genital stage of psychosexual development, 338
Genotypes, 318
Geniuses, 313, 315. *See also* Creativity; Giftedness; Intelligence
Germinal period of prenatal development, 251, 252
Gestalt psychology, perception in, 80–84
Gestalt therapy (Perls), 422, 444
Giftedness, 313–317
Glands, functions of, 32–34. *See also specific glands, for example:* Adrenal glands; Pituitary gland
Glial cells, 26
Glucoreceptors, 227–228
Glucostatic theory of eating, 227
Glycerol derivatives in drug therapy, 435, 436
Goal-corrected partnerships phase of attachment, 278
Goal gradients in approach-avoidance conflict, 368
Gonads, 34, 451–452, 454
Grammar in language development, 198–201
Grammatical morphemes, 198–199
Grandeur, delusions of, 406
Grand mal epileptic seizures, 41
Grouping (perceptual), principles of, 80–82
Groups. *See specific entries, for example:* Alternative-treatment groups in therapy evaluation; Control groups; Sizes, of groups, in emergency helping
Group therapy, 431–433, 444
Growth and development. *See also entries beginning with* Developmental
after birth, 255–262. *See also* Birth complications; Birth defects
prenatal period of, 249–254, 263–264, 450–454
Growth hormone, 34
Growth spurts, adolescent, 285
Growth stage of careers, 540
GSR (galvanic skin response), 236, 242
Guided participation as modeling adjunct, 426
Guilt versus initiative in psychosocial development, 275, 294
Gyri of brain, 30

Habituation to stimuli, 135, 255
Hair cells of ears, 68, 71
Hallucinations:
in major depressive disorder, 402
in schizophrenia, 406, 408
from sensory deprivation, 233

Hallucinogens (psychedelics), 123–124. *See also* Marijuana
Halo effect in person perception, 483–484
Handedness and cerebral specialization of function, 44–45
Hardiness and health, 378
Harmonics (overtones), 67
Hashish, 123. *See also* Marijuana
Headaches, 373–375
Head Start program, 325–326
Health:
exaggerated concern with (hypochondriasis), 398
and locus of control, 349–350
mental, and life stresses, 373. *See also* Mental disorders, diagnosis of
and personality, 378–379, 381–382
problems with:
crowding related to, 520
diagnosis of, 215, 549–550
life stresses related to, 373–374
prevention of, 550–551
responsibility for, individual, 550–551
and self-regulation techniques, 127
Health psychology, 15, 549–551
Hearing, 65–69. *See also* Deafness and language development; Ears, structure and function of; *entries beginning with* Acoustic; Auditory
Helping, influences on, 477–478, 498–502, 506–507, 520, 523, 524, 526
Helplessness, learned, 152–153, 269, 404, 521–523
Hemorrhaging in newborns, 260, 261
Heredity. *See* Genetics
Heritability, defined, 320
Hermaphroditism, 454
Heroin, 119
Heterosexuality, defined, 468
Heuristics in problem solving, 211
Hierarchy of needs (Maslow), 224–226, 343
Hindbrain, 31
Hippocampus, removal of, 174
Histograms, 562–563
Histrionic personality, 410
Holophrastic stage of language development, 197
Homeostasis, maintaining, 223, 228, 229
Homosexuality, 468–469
Hormones:
in biological development of gender, 452, 454
effects of, 32–34
during pregnancy, 253–254
specific:
catecholamines, 244, 403, 436
epinephrine (adrenaline), 34
growth, 34
norepinephrine (noradrenaline), 34
oxytocin, 33–34, 190
sex, 34, 231, 452, 454, 468

thyroxine, 259
vasopressin (antidiuretic hormone), 33, 189, 230, 231
Hospices for terminally ill, 296
Hospitalism, studies of, 278
Hue, determination of, 60–61
Humanistic approach to personality, 342–343, 354–355
Humanistic model of abnormality, 392, 393, 395
Humanistic therapies, 420–422, 444
Hunger as biological motive for behavior, 227–228
Hypercomplex cells in visual cortex, 59–60
Hyperkinesis, 261
Hyperopia (farsightedness), 63, 64
Hyperphagia, 227
Hypersomnia, 116–117
Hypertension (high blood pressure), 373–375
Hypnosis, 107–110, 183–184
Hypnotherapy, 109–110
Hypochondriasis, 398
Hypothalamus, 30, 33–34, 37, 227–230
Hypotheses:
defined, 5
testing, in concept formation, 206–207

Iconic store (visual sensory memory), 168
Idea innovators in organizations, 547
Identical (monozygotic) twins, studies of. *See* Twin studies on genetics versus environment
Identification with aggressor in psychosexual development, 338
Identity, gender, development of, 454–455, 468
Identity rule in cognitive development, 274
Id in psychoanalytic theory of personality, 335–337
I-E Scale (Locus of Control Scale), 349
Illegitimate frustration, 503
Illicit drugs, defined, 117
Illnesses. *See* Health, problems with; Mental disorders, diagnosis of; Mental health and life stresses
Illusions of size, 87–91
Image-retina system, 91
Imagery in information organization, 185–186
Imagination, emotion influencing, 239
Imbalance in relationships, 496, 497
Imitation in language acquisition, 200
Implicit personality theory, 483–484
Impotence (erectile dysfunction), 469
Impression formation, 478–480, 482–483
Imprinting in animals, 222, 276
Impulsivity, cause of, 261
Inborn errors of metabolism, 258
Incentive theory of motivation, 223

Incentives and drives, interaction of, 223. *See also* Motivation; Motives
Incidence of sexual behavior, defined, 459
Incubation stage of problem solving, 209, 212
Incus of ears, 67
Independent variables, 7–9
Individual psychology approach to personality development (Adler), 339
Induced movement, 92
Industrial-organizational psychology, 14, 543–549
Industry versus inferiority in psychosocial development, 276, 294
Infancy, defined, 270
Infants. *See also* Children; Families; Newborns; Parents; Prenatal period of development
 attachment (bonding) of, 222, 276–280
 baby-tender for (Skinner), 139
 behavioral states of, 257
 developmental quotients (DQs) of, 307
 developmental tasks of, 270–271
 development of, 270–284, 294
  cognitive, 271–275
  language, 196
  motor, 256, 257, 260–261
  perceptual, 94–96
  psychosocial, 275, 294
  self-concept, 342
 egocentricity of, 272
 emotions of, facial expressions of, 239
 intelligence quotients (IQs) of, 307
 learned helplessness of, 269
 parental responsiveness to, 269, 275, 294
 reflexes of, 255–256, 272
 schemata of, 272
 stimulus seeking by, 232
 temperament differences of, 257, 258
 vocalization of, 256
Inferential statistics, 562, 571–572
Inferiority versus industry in psychosocial development, 276, 294
Inflections in language development, 198–199
Influence in conformity, 491
Information:
 chunks of, 168–169
 displacement and decay of, 170, 180
 encoding, 167, 170, 172, 185–186
 in long-term memory. *See* Long-term memory(ies)
 organizing, 172, 184–186
 about others, in impression formation, 482–483
 recalling, 165, 173–180
 recognizing, 173
 rehearsing, 170–172, 187
 retrieving, 167, 170–173, 183–190. *See also* Retrieval failure hypothesis of forgetting

in sensory memory, 167–168
in short-term memory. *See* Short-term memory
 storing, 167–173, 183
Informational social influence in conformity, 491
Information-processing model of memory, 166–167. *See also* Memory(ies)
Inhibitory synapses, 28
Initiative versus guilt in psychosocial development, 275, 294
Innateness hypothesis of language acquisition, 201
Innateness of facial expressions, 239, 240
Innate releasing mechanisms, 222
Inner ear, 68, 71–72
Insight learning, 156–157
Insomnia, treatment for, 116
Instability-stability dimension of personality, 341–342
Instincts:
 in aggression, 502, 503
 defined, 222
 life and death (Freud), 335
Instinct theory of motivation, 222–223
Institute of Personality Assessment and Research (IPAR), 316
Instruction, programmed and computer-assisted, 159, 160, 553
Instructional psychology, 553
Instrumental behavior, 137
Instrumental conditioning. *See* Operant conditioning
Integrity versus despair in later maturity, 293, 294
Intellectual development:
 environmental enrichment in, 318, 324–326
 family configuration in, 323–324
 gender differences in, 322, 323
 genetics versus environment in, 317–328
Intellectual environment, value of (VIE), for families, 323, 324
Intelligence:
 artificial, in problem solving, 215. *See also* Computers
 defined, 302–303
 impairment of, 260–261, 263. *See also* Mental retardation
 versus intelligence quotient (IQ), 306
 over life-span, 306–307
 measurement of, 301–311, 327. *See also* Intelligence quotient (IQ) tests; Intelligence quotients (IQs)
Intelligence quotient (IQ) tests:
 bias in, court case about, 554–555
 characteristics of, 304–306
 history of, 302–303
 over life-span, 306–307
 limitations of, in creativity measurement, 315

scores on:
 in Army General Classification Test, 321
 distribution of, 306, 308, 312–313, 315
 high, 313, 315. *See also* Creativity; Geniuses; Giftedness
 in mental-retardation classification, 308
 specific:
  Binet-Simon, 303, 307
  Mensa, 307–311, 327
  Stanford-Binet, 303, 306, 308
  Wechsler, 303, 304, 306
 types of, 303–304
Intelligence quotients (IQs):
 in career counseling, 541
 computing, 303
 correlations of, studies of, 318–320
 declines in, age-related, 307
 deviation, 303, 307
 environmental enrichment programs affecting, 324–326
 and eugenics, 328
 and family configuration, 323–324
 of infants, 307
 versus intelligence, 306
 and occupational status, 321
 racial-ethnic differences in, 321–322
 and socioeconomic status, 321
 stability and change in, 307
Intensity:
 of light waves, 57, 61
 of noise, 522
 of sound waves, 65–66
Intensive drug use, 118
Interactionist approaches:
 to cognitive development, 271
 to personality, 348
Interaction with strangers in urban versus small-town areas, 525–526
Intercourse, sexual, 459–460
 problems in, 469–471
Interference theory of forgetting, 178–180
Internal causes of behavior, 480–482, 484–485
Internal control of behavior, 347, 349–350
Internalization of moral principles, 289
Interneurons (association neurons), 32
Interposition, principle of, 84–87
Interpretation in Freudian psychoanalysis, 419–420
Interviews:
 in correlational research, 6–7
 in personality assessment, 354–355
Intimacy versus isolation in early adulthood, 291, 294
Intimate-distance range of personal space, 515
Intracellular thirst, 230
Intrinsic motivation, 226–227, 232
Introspection in structuralism school of psychology, 11
Introverted personality type, 341–342

Intrusions into territories, 518, 519
Intuitive period of cognitive development, 272–273
Investigative people in Strong-Campbell Interest Inventory, 542
Involuntary reflex behavior, operant conditioning of, 142–143
Ions in neurons, 27
IPAR (Institute of Personality Assessment and Research), 316
IQs. See Intelligence quotient (IQ) tests; Intelligence quotients (IQs)
Irises of eyes, 56
Irritability of newborns, 257
Isolation versus intimacy in early adulthood, 291, 294
I-Theme in Strong-Campbell Interest Inventory, 542

James-Lange theory of emotion, 237
Japanese:
    environmental design of, 519
    intelligence quotients of, 322
Job analysis in personnel selection, 543
Judgment stage of problem solving, 212
Jury selection, personality assessment in, 358–359

Karyotype analysis, 259
Keyword method of information organization, 186
Kinesthesis, sense of, 71
Kitten carousel experiments, 96, 97
Knee-jerk reflex, 31–32

Labeling problem in classifying abnormal behavior, 391–392
Landolt rings test, 63
Language, 195–206
    acquisition of, 200–203
    defined, 195
    development of, 195–201, 205–206
    learning of, 200–201
    and thought, 203–205. See also Thinking
Language disorders from brain injuries, 204–205
Language function of brain, 43–44
Larry P. v. Wilson Riles court case, 554–555
Late childhood, 270. See also Adolescence
Latency period of psychosexual development, 338
Latent content of dreams (Freud), 114
Latent learning, 155–156
Lateral geniculate body, 63
Lateral hypothalamus (LH), 227, 228
Later maturity, 292–294
Law, psychologists in field of, 15, 551–552
LCUs (life-change units) in Social Readjustment Rating Scale, 370, 373
Learned behavior, shaping, 151

Learned helplessness, 152–153, 269, 404, 521–523
Learning. See also Conditioning; Social-learning theory
    approaches to:
        associative, stimulus-response, 133. See also Classical conditioning; Operant conditioning
        cognitive, 133, 155–158
    of attitudes, 486
    defined, 133
    habituation as form of, 135, 255
    of language, 200–201. See also Language, development of
    principles of, 142–155
    psychology of, 134–141
    spontaneous recovery in, 141
    types of:
        classical (respondent). See Classical conditioning
        insight, 156–157
        latent, 155–156
        observational, 157–158, 346–347, 408, 486
        operant (instrumental). See Operant conditioning
        perceptual, 93, 95–99
        programmed, 159, 160, 553
Learning contexts in memory retrieval, 187
Learning experience and personal-space needs, 515
Learning theory. See Behavioral model of abnormality; Behavioral modification (therapy); Self-control; Social-learning theory
Lecithin in acetylcholine synthesis, 35
Left-handedness, studies of, 44, 45
Lenses of eyes, 56, 58–59
Lesch-Nyhan syndrome, 259, 262
Lesion and ablation techniques for studying brain function, 37–38, 43. See also Split-brain surgery
Lesions, defined, 37
Level as occupational classification, 540–541
Levels-of-processing view of memory, 174–175
LH (lateral hypothalamus), 227, 228
Libido (sexual energy), 335–337. See also Psychosexual stages of personality development
Licit drugs, defined, 117
Lie detectors (polygraphs), 241–243
Life-change units (LCUs) in Social Readjustment Rating Scale, 370, 373
Life events as stressors, 369–370, 373–374
Life instincts (Freud), 335
Life-span:
    development during, 269–296
    intelligence (IQ) testing over, 306–307
Life-styles in personality development (Adler), 339

Light:
    and shadow, principle of, 86, 87
    as stimulus for vision, 55
Light adaptation, 58
Light energy turned into visual sensations, 55–60
Light waves:
    amplitude (intensity) of, 57, 61
    complexity of, 61
    height of, 57
    length of, 55, 60–62
Liking, effects on, 496–498, 514–517, 520, 524
Limbic system of brain, 30–31
Limen, defined, 53
Linear perspective, principle of, 84–87
Linguistic relativity hypothesis of language and thought, 203
Lithium carbonate drugs, 436–437
Litter, cleaning up, reinforcement strategies for, 530–532
Lobes of brain, 35–37
Lobotomies, 438. See also Split-brain surgery
Localized amnesia, 400
Loci, method of, in information organization, 185–186
Locus of control as personality dimension, 347, 349–350
Locus of Control Scale (I-E Scale), 349
Logical thought in cognitive development, 274
Loneliness as frustration, 366–368
Longevity and self-regulating techniques, 127
Longitudinal research designs, 307
Long-term memory(ies), 171–173. See also Sensory memory; Short-term memory
    encoding, 172, 185–186
    forgetting. See Forgetting
    improving, strategies for, 184–190
    recalling, 173–175
    retrieving, 172–173, 183–190
    and short-term memory, as systems, 173–175
    storing, 167–173, 183
Losses as frustration, 366
Loudness and sound-wave amplitude, 65–66
Love needs, 225
Low-balling technique for compliance, 491–492
Lysergic acid diethylamide (LSD), 123

Maintenance rehearsal of information, 171
Maintenance stage of careers, 520
Major affective disorders, 401–403
Major depressive disorder, 401–405
Major tranquilizers, 435–436, 439, 441–442
Maladaptive behavior. See Abnormal behavior
Maladaptive personality traits, 409. See also Personality disorders
Males. See Fathers; Gender; entries beginning with Gender

Malleus of ears, 67
Management Progress Study, 545
Managers, careers of, 543–547. *See also* Career development stages
Manias, 401–404
    drug treatment of, 435–437, 439, 442
Manifest content of dreams (Freud), 114
MAO (monoamine oxidase) inhibitors in drug therapy, 435, 436
Marijuana, 8–10, 123–124
Marital intercourse, 459
Marital separation, children affected by, 281–282
Marital therapy, 432–433, 444
Massed practice in memory improvement, 187
Mass-media violence, aggression related to, 504–506, 508
Masturbation, 459, 460, 463
Maternal deprivation (separation), 278–280
Maternal diseases during pregnancy, 254
Mathematical ability, gender differences in, 457
Maturation:
    during adolescence, 284–290
    biological, 270, 284–286
Maturity, later, 292–294
Mean, defined, 306, 563
Meaning in memory encoding, 170, 172, 174–175, 187
Means-end analysis of problems, 211
Measurement, defined, 562
Mechanical substitution devices for blind, 74
Median, defined, 563
Medical diagnoses, 38, 215, 389, 412, 549–550
Medical model of abnormality. *See* Biological (medical) model of abnormality
Medical therapies, 435–439. *See also* Drugs; Electroconvulsive (electroshock) therapy (ECT); Psychosurgery
    evaluation of, 440–442
Medicine and psychology, 549–551
Meditation as self-regulation technique, 124–127
Medulla of brain, 31
Memory(ies):
    consolidating, 173
    control of, psychological and chemical, 189–190
    impairment of. *See* Forgetting
    improving, strategies for, 184–190
    influences on:
        acetylcholine, 35
        concept formation, 206
        context, 187
        emotions, 239
        hypnosis, 107, 109–110
    information-processing model of, 166–167
    nature of, 166–177
    process of, 166–167

reconstructing, fallibility in, 165, 175–178, 184. *See also* Forgetting
reliability of, 165–166. *See also* Forgetting
repression of, 182–184, 335
structure of, 166–175
types of:
    context-dependent, 180–181
    long-term. *See* Long-term memory(ies)
    sensory, 167–168
    short-term. *See* Short-term memory
    state-dependent, 181
Memory codes, 167, 170, 172, 174–175. *See also* Encoding information in memory
Memory span procedure, 168
Menarche, 284–286
Mensa IQ test, 307–311, 327
Mental abilities. *See* Cognition; Intelligence; *entries beginning with* Cognitive; Intellectual; Intelligence
Mental disorders, diagnosis of, 38, 550. *See also* Abnormal behavior; *specific disorders, for example:* Anxiety disorders; Personality disorders; Schizophrenia
Mental health and life stresses, 373
Mental retardation, 258–260, 308, 312–313, 554–555. *See also* Brains, damage to; Intelligence, impairment of
Mental shock, retrograde amnesia from, 173–174
Mental tests. *See* Intelligence quotient (IQ) tests
Mentor relationships in career development, 546–548
Mentor stage of careers, 546
Mescaline, 123
Metabolism, inborn errors of, 258
Methedrine (speed), 121
Method of loci in information organization, 185–186
Microelectrodes:
    in nerve-impulse measurement, 26, 39
    in visual-cortex studies, 60, 61
Midbrain, 31
Middle age, 291–292, 294
Middle ear, 67
Migraine headaches, 373, 375
Minimal brain damage, 261
Minnesota Multiphasic Personality Inventory (MMPI), 352–354, 357, 550
Minnesota Study of Twins Reared Apart, 319
Minority groups. *See also* Blacks
    discrimination against, in intelligence (IQ) tests, 554–555
    quotas for, in college admissions, 555–556
Minor tranquilizers, 435, 436, 442
Misapplied size constancy in Müller-Lyer illusion, 90–91
Mistrust versus trust in psychosocial development, 275, 294
Mitosis (cell division) of zygotes, 251

MMPI (Minnesota Multiphasic Personality Inventory), 352–354, 357, 550
Mnemonic devices, 185–186
Mode, defined, 563
Modeling:
    in aggression, 503–507
    in behavioral therapies, 426–427
    of prosocial acts, 506
Monetary reinforcers for energy conservation, 530–531
Mongolism (Down's syndrome), 259–260, 262, 313, 328
Monkeys, infant, attachment and separation studies of, 278–280
Monoamine oxidase (MAO) inhibitors in drug therapy, 435, 436
Monochromatism, 64
Monocular depth cues, 84–87
Monozygotic (identical) twins, studies of. *See* Twin studies on genetics versus environment
Moods of newborns, 257
Mood-state-dependent memory, 181
Moon illusion, 88–89
Moral development, 288–290
Moral internalization of principles, 289
Moral Judgment Scale (Kohlberg), 289
Moro reflex of newborns and infants, 256
Morphemes in language development, 197–199
Morphine, 35, 118–119
Mothers. *See also* Children; Families; Fathers; Infants; Parents; *entries beginning with* Maternal
    during children's phallic stage of psychosexual development, 338
    schizophrenogenic, 409
    working, children affected by, 281
Motion:
    perception of, 91–92
    self-produced, in perceptual development, 96
Motion parallax in depth perception, 86
Motion pictures. *See* Movies
Motivated forgetting, 182–184, 335
Motivation, 221–235
    defined, 221
    and emotion, 236. *See also* Emotions
    theories of, 222–227
    types of:
        achievement, 234–235
        altruistic, 221, 223
        effectance, 226
        egoistic, 221
        intrinsic, 226–227, 232
        sexual, 231–232, 241
        unconscious, 335
Motives. *See also* Need(s)
    acquired, 234–235
    biological, 227–232. *See also* Sociobiology
    stimulus-seeking, 232–234

Motor actions, 272, 406
Motor cortex of brain, 36
Motor development, 256, 257, 260–261
Motor (efferent) neurons, 31–32
Movement. *See* Motion; *entries beginning with* Motion
Movies:
  movement in, 92
  specific:
    One Flew over the Cuckoo's Nest, 438
    Three Faces of Eve, The, 333–334, 400
  violence in, and aggression, 504–506, 508
Müller-Lyer illusion, 89–91
Multiple orgasms, 462–463
Multiple personality disorder, 333–334, 400, 552
Muscle relaxation, progressive, 374
Muscles:
  ciliary, of eyes, 56
  smooth and striate, 32
Myelin sheaths of neurons, 26
My Lai massacre, 494, 495
Myopia (nearsightedness), 63, 64

n Ach (need for achievement), 234–235
n Aff (need for affiliation), 234
Narcissistic personality, 410
Narcolepsy, 46, 117
Narcotic drugs, 35, 118–119, 254
Narrative-chaining method of information organization, 185
Nasal cavity, 69
Naturalistic observation, 6
Natural selection, principle of, 318
Natural sleep length, 112
Nature versus nurture phrase, introduction of, 314. *See also* Genetics, versus environment
Nearsightedness (myopia), 63, 64
Need(s). *See also* Motivation; Motives
  for achievement (*n* Ach), 234–235
  for affiliation (*n* Aff), 234
  for cognition, in persuasibility, 488
  for consistency, 224
  defined, 223
  hierarchy of (Maslow), 224–226, 343
  for personal space, 514–515
Negative afterimages of colors, 62
Negative feelings, environmental causes of, 520, 524–525. *See also* Environment(s); Loneliness as frustration
Negative reinforcement versus punishment, 152
Negative reinforcing stimuli, 144, 145
Neoanalytic approaches to psychoanalytic theory of personality, 338–339
Neologisms in schizophrenia, 406
Neonatal period, defined, 255. *See also* Newborns
Nerve(s). *See also* Neurons
  auditory, 68

composition of, 29
  olfactory, 69
  optic, 37, 58
Nerve impulses:
  defined, 26
  measurement of, microelectrodes in, 26, 39
  physical energy transduced into, 58–59, 68, 69
  transmission of, 26–29, 59. *See also* Neurotransmitters
Nervous system, 25–35. *See also* Visual system
  autonomic, 32, 33, 236, 410
  central, 29–32
  defined, 26
  organization of, 29–32
  parasympathetic, 32, 33, 236
  peripheral, 29, 32, 33
  somatic, 32
  sympathetic, 32, 33
Neural pathways for vision, 36–37
Neuroanatomy, 29
Neurobiology, 29
Neuroleptic drugs, 435–436, 439, 441–442
Neurons, 26, 31–32. *See also* Nerve impulses; Neurotransmitters
Neurophysiology, 29
Neurotransmitters:
  brain, 34–35, 40, 47–48
  defined, 28
  in depression, 403, 436, 437
  in Parkinson's disease, 47–48
  in schizophrenia, 408, 436
Neutral stimuli, 133, 135
Newborn Behavioral Assessment Scale, 257
Newborns, 255–261. *See also* Infants; Prenatal period of development
  baby-tender for (Skinner), 139
  behavioral states of, 257
  developmental and birth complications of. *See* Birth complications; Birth defects
  habituation of, 255
  motor development of, 256, 257, 260–261
  premature, 261
  reflex behaviors of, 255–256, 272
  sensory reactions of, 255
  temperament differences in, 257, 258
  vocalization of, 256
New York State Standardized Testing Act of 1980, 557
Nicotine as stimulant, 121. *See also* Cigarette smoking
Night blindness and vitamin A, 58
Nightmares, 115–116
Night terrors, 115–117
Noise. *See also* Sound energy; Sound waves
  defined, 65
  environmental, effects of, 521–523
Noncommon effects, searching for, 480–481
Nonconscious level of consciousness, 108

Nondirective genetic counseling, 263
Nonexperimental-research approaches, 5–9
Nonnaturalistic observation, 6
Non-power-assertive parents, 290
Non-rapid-eye-movement (NREM) sleep, 112–116
Norepinephrine (noradrenaline), 34
Normal (normal probability) frequency distributions, 306, 563–565
Normative social influence in conformity, 491
Norm groups in test standardization, 306
Norms, social, in conformity, 489
Noses, structure and function of, 69–70. *See also* Smell
No-treatment groups in therapy evaluation, 440
NREM (non-rapid-eye-movement) sleep, 112–116
Nutrition:
  and intellectual development, 326
  during pregnancy, 253

Obedience, 492–495. *See also* Compliance; Conformity
Obesity, 37, 228–230
Object permanence in cognitive development, 272, 273
Observational learning, 157–158, 346–347, 408, 486
Observations:
  of actions, in person perception, 480
  of behavior, types of, 6
  clinical:
    of brain damage, 38
    of brain lesions, 43
Observer-actor difference in person perception, 484
Obsessions, defined, 396
Obsessive-compulsive disorder, 396–398
Occipital lobe of brain, 35–37
Occupational-decline stage of careers, 540
Occupational status and intelligence quotient (IQ), 321
Occupational themes in Strong-Campbell Interest Inventory, 542–543
Occupations:
  choosing, 539–541. *See also entries beginning with* Career
  classifications of, 540–541
Oedipus complex, 338
Olfaction, defined, 69. *See also* Smell
Olfactory bulb, 69
Olfactory nerve tract, 69
Olfactory system, 69–70
One Flew over the Cuckoo's Nest (Kesey), 438
One-sided arguments, 486–487
Operant behavior, 137
Operant conditioning, 137–142. *See also* Reinforcement

in attitude formation, 486
in attraction, 496–498
in behavioral therapies, 425–427
and classical conditioning, interaction of, 142–155. *See also* Classical conditioning
law of, 137–138
in personality, 346
of reflex behavior, 142–143
in schizophrenia, 408
Operantly conditioned responses, 140–141
Operant responses in operant conditioning, 138
Opinion surveys in consumer research, 549. *See also* Surveys
Opiates, brain, 35, 46
Opium, 35, 118, 119
Opponent-process theory of color vision, 62–63
Optic chiasm, 37
Optic nerve, 37, 58
Optimal (critical) periods of development, 201, 276–277
Oral eroticism as phase in psychosexual development, 337
Oral sadism as phase in psychosexual development, 337
Oral stage of psychosexual development, 337, 408
Organic retardation, 312, 313. *See also* Mental retardation
Organismic feeling in evaluating experiences, 342–343
Organizational psychology, 14, 543–549
Organization of information, 172, 184–186
Organ of Corti, 68
Orgasmic dysfunction (frigidity), 470
Orgasm phase of sexual-response cycle, 462
Orgasms, 459, 462–463
Orienting reflex, 135
Osmoreceptors in hypothalamus, 230
Osmosis, water loss through, 230
Ossicles of ears, 67
Outer ear, 67
Ova (egg cells), 251
Oval window of ears, 67
Ovaries, development of, 451, 452, 454
Overeating, biological causes of, 37, 227–230. *See also* Eating disorders
Overgeneralization in depression, 404
Overload, urban, 526
Overregularization in language development, 199
Overt behaviors, 345
Overtones (harmonics), 67
Ovum, period of, in prenatal development, 251, 252
Oxygen deprivation during birth, 260–261
Oxytocin, 33–34, 190

Pain, controlling, 35, 45–46, 110, 119
Pain spots, 71

Pairing procedures in conditioning, 136
Paranoid personality, 410
Paranoid schizophrenia, 406–407
Paraplegics, reflexes in, 32
Parapsychology, 100–101
Parasympathetic nervous system, 32, 33, 236
Parenting styles, 283–284, 290
Parents. *See also* Children; Families; Fathers; Infants; Mothers; Newborns; Single-parent families
adolescent emotional independence from, 287
and children, relationships of, 283–284
in children's psychosexual development, 338
during infancy, responsiveness of, 269, 275, 294
in infant and child psychosocial development, 275–276, 293–294
and infants, attachment (bonding) of, 222, 276–280
Parietal lobe of brain, 35–37
Parkinson's disease, 47–48
Partial reinforcement effect, 146
Partial reinforcement schedules, 145–147
Passive-aggressive personality, 410
Passive consciousness, 107–108
Pastoral counselors, 434
Pathological gambling, 133
PCP (phencyclidine), 123
Peer relationships:
in adolescence, 279–280, 287–288
in career development, 546
Penis envy, 338
Peptic ulcers, 372–373
Perceived control in coping with stress, 376–377
Perceived self-efficacy, 426–427, 441
Percentiles, defined, 568
Perception:
and attention, 99
of crowding, 520–521
defined, 79
influences on:
drugs, 117–124
emotion, 239
genetics versus environment, 93
of motion, 91–92
in schizophrenia, 406
of size, 87–91
types of:
depth. *See* Depth perception
extrasensory, 100–101
form, 80–84, 93–94
person, 478–485
sensory, in cognitive development, 272
visual, 79–99
Perceptual development, 93–99
Perceptual grouping principles, 80–82
Perceptual illusions of size, 87–91
Perceptual learning, 93, 95–99
Perceptual organization in Gestalt

psychology, 80–84
Perceptual processes, 80–92
Performance, task, effects on, 241, 520, 522–523
Performance anxiety in sexual dysfunctions, 469–470
Periodic complex sound waves, 65
Periods in prenatal development, 251–253
Peripheral nervous system, 29, 32, 33
Persecution, delusions of, 406
Personal constructs in personality (Kelly), 344, 354
Personal-distance range of personal space, 515
Personality:
assessment of:
approaches to, 350–357, 550
in jury selection, 358–359
of children, 257
defined, 334
development of, psychosexual stages of (Freud), 336–338, 408
and health, 378–379, 381–382
locus of control in, 347, 349–350
multiple, 333–334, 400, 552
personal constructs in (Kelly), 344, 354
in persuasibility, 488
structure of, in psychoanalytic theory, 335–336
types of, 338, 341–342
Personality disorders, 333–334, 400, 409–411, 552
Personality psychology, 14
Personality tests, 340–341, 344, 350–354, 357, 550
Personality theories:
behavioral, 344–348, 355–357
cognitive, 344, 354–355
cognitive-behavioral, 345–348
humanistic, 342–343, 354–355
interactionist, 348
psychoanalytic, 334–340, 352
trait, 340–342, 346, 352–354, 357
Personality traits. *See also* Trait approach to personality
of creative and noncreative individuals, 316
defined, 340
in managerial selection, 543–546
similarity of, in attraction, 497–498
specific:
authoritarianism, 358
hardiness, 378
maladaptive, 409. *See also* Personality disorders
source, 340–341
surface, 340
stereotypes about, 483–484
Personal space, 514–517, 519. *See also* Environmental design
Personal-space bubbles, 514–515

Personal-space invasions, 516–517
Personnel development, 546–548
Personnel selection, 357, 543–546, 551
Person perception, 478–485
Perspective, linear, principle of, 84–87
Persuasion in attitude change, 486–488
PET (positron emission tomography)
　　scanning technique, 38, 389, 412
Petting, 459
Phallic stage of psychosexual development,
　　338
Phencyclidine (PCP), 123
Phenothiazine drugs, 435, 436, 441–442
Phenotypes, 318
Phenylketonuria (PKU), 259, 313
Pheromones, 70, 231
Phobias, 141–142, 395–396, 426–427
Phonemes in language development, 196–
　　197
Phonograph records, reading, 79
Photoreceptive cells (photoreceptors), 57–62
Photosensitivity of retinas, 56–59
Phrase structure of sentences, 199–200
Physical appearance, impressions of, 478–
　　480
Physical attacks, aggression evoked by, 504
Physical attractiveness, impressions of, 479
Physical dependence on drugs, 118–125
Physical development during adolescence,
　　284–286
Physical energy turned into sensations, 55–
　　60, 64–69
Physical environment. *See also*
　　Environment(s); *entries beginning with*
　　Environmental
　　behavior determined by, 519–534
　　defined, 513
　　stresses of, 370
Physical illness. *See* Health, problems with
Physical maturation, 270, 284–286
Physical primary colors, 62
Physical stimuli, 54
Physiological arousal, emotion affecting,
　　236–241. *See also* Sexual arousal
Physiological effects of stress, 239, 372–374
Physiological mechanisms and self-regulation
　　techniques, 127
Physiological needs, 225
Physiological psychology, 14
Physiology of sexual behavior, 461–463
Pictorial depth cues, 86
Pinna of ears, 67
Pitch, 65, 68–69
Pituitary gland, 33–34, 230, 231
PKU (phenylketonuria), 259, 313
Placebos in experimental research, 10, 440
Placenta, 251, 253
Place theory of pitch, 68, 69
Planning process as problem-solving
　　heuristic, 211
Plateau phase of sexual-response cycle, 462
Pleasure principle (id) in psychoanalytic

theory of personality, 335–337
Plot Titles Test (Guilford), 316
Pluralization rules in language development,
　　197–198
Police departments, selection procedures for,
　　551
Polygraphs (lie detectors), 241–243
Ponzo illusion, 91
Population density, 520–521. *See also*
　　Crowding; Urban environments
Population sampling, 571
Pornography, effects of, 463–464
Positive regard, unconditional, in therapy,
　　342–343, 421
Positive reinforcement. *See also*
　　Reinforcement
　　for environmental-behavior changes, 530–
　　533
　　lack of, in depression, 403–404
Positive reinforcing stimuli, 144, 145
Positron emission tomography (PET)
　　scanning technique, 38, 389, 412
Postconventional stages of moral
　　development, 288–289
Posterior aphasia (Wernicke's aphasia), 204–
　　205
Postpartum depression, 401
Posture in emotional expression, 236–237
Potassium ions in neurons, 27
Power-assertive parents, 290
Preattachment phase of attachment, 278
Precognition, 100
Preconceptual thought in cognitive
　　development, 273
Preconscious level of consciousness, 108
Preconventional stages of moral
　　development, 288
Predictability of aversive events, 376, 522
Predction:
　　and correlation, 571
　　in personnel selection, 545–546
Predictive contingency theory of
　　conditioning, 136
Pregnancy, 253–254, 288, 464, 465. *See also*
　　Conception, defined; Prenatal period of
　　development; *entries beginning with*
　　Birth
Prelinguistic stage of language development,
　　196–197
Premarital intercourse, 459–461
Premature ejaculation, 469–470
Premature newborns, 261
Prenatal environment, 253–254
Prenatal period of development, 249–254,
　　263–264, 450–454
Prenatal screening techniques for birth
　　defects, 262–264
Preoperational stage of cognitive
　　development, 272–274
Preparation stage of problem solving, 209–
　　210
Preparedness principle in shaping learned

behavior, 151
Prepared responses, 151
Pressure as stressor, 369
Pressure spots, 71
Primary effect:
　　in free recall of information, 174
　　in impression formation, 483
Primary colors, physical, 62
Primary reinforcing stimuli, 143–145
Primary sexual characteristics of males and
　　females, 450–454
Primary territory, 517–519
Prison crowding, 534
Privacy:
　　environmental design for, 519, 529
　　invasion of, personality testing as, 357
Private acceptance in conformity experiment,
　　490
Proactive interference in recall, 178–179
Problem solving, 209–215
Process schizophrenia, 405
Production stage of problem solving, 211–
　　212
Professional careers, stages of, 546–548. *See
　　also* Career development stages
Programmed instruction (learning), 159, 160,
　　553
Progressive muscle relaxation, 374
Progressive relaxation technique for self-
　　regulation, 126
Project Head Start program, 325–326
Projection in coping with stress, 380
Projective techniques in personality
　　assessment, 350–352, 357
Prompts in environmental-behavior changes,
　　531–532
Prosocial behavior, influences on, 477–478,
　　498–502, 506–507
　　negative, 520, 523, 524, 526
Prospective research design, 316, 374
Protein-deficient diets during pregnancy, 253
Protein needs and intellectual development,
　　326
Proxemics, 515
Proximity:
　　in attraction, 498
　　in perceptual grouping, principle of, 80–
　　82
Pruitt-Igoe low-income housing complex,
　　529–530
Psilocybin, 123
Psychedelics (halluncinogens), 123–124. *See
　　also* Marijuana
Psychiatric institutions, token economies in,
　　425, 427
Psychiatric social workers, training of, 434
Psychiatrists, training of, 434
Psychic energy (Freud), 335, 336
Psychoanalysis, Freudian, 184, 419–420, 444
Psychoanalysts, training of, 434
Psychoanalytic model of abnormality, 392,
　　393

on affective disorders, 403
on conversion disorder, 399
on dissociative disorders, 400
on generalized anxiety disorder, 395
on homosexuality, 469
on hypochondriasis, 398
on obsessive-compulsive disorders, 398
on phobic disorders, 396
on schizophrenic disorders, 408
Psychoanalytic theory of personality, 335–340, 350–352
Psychodrama in group therapy, 431–433
Psychogenic amnesia, 399–400
Psychogenic fugue, 400
Psychological control of memory, 189–190
Psychological death, 295
Psychological dependence on drugs, 118–125
Psychological impact statements, 384
Psychological research. *See* Research; *entries beginning with* Research
Psychological tests, characteristics of, 304–306. *See also specific entries, for example:* Achievement tests; Intelligence quotient (IQ) tests; Personality tests
Psychological therapies, 418–435, 444
    behavioral modification, 154–155, 159, 417, 422–431, 444
    cognitive-behavioral, 428–431, 444
    Freudian psychoanalytic, 184, 419–420, 444
    group, 431–433, 444
    humanistic, 420–422, 444
Psychologists:
    on radio, controversy about, 443
    training of, 434
Psychology. *See also* Individual psychology approach to personality development (Adler); Parapsychology
    as academic discipline, 4, 10–12
    careers in. *See specific entries for example:* Court psychologists; Forensic psychology; Vocational psychology
    defined, 4
    educational requirements in, 16, 19
    field of, broadness of, 3–4, 16–17
    future trends in, 19–20
    of learning, 134–141
    methods and techniques of, 14–15
    as profession, 4, 12–16
    schools of, historical, 10–12
    as science, 4–10
    specialty areas in, 12–15, 539–558
    types of. *See specific entries, for* example: Developmental psychology; Gestalt psychology, perception in; Social psychology
    workplaces in, 15
Psychometric tests in correlational research, 7. *See also specific entries, for example:* Aptitude tests; Intelligence quotient (IQ) tests

Psychometrics, focus of, 14–15
Psychophysics, findings of, 53–55
Psychosexual stages of personality development (Freud), 336–338, 408
Psychosocial development (Erikson), 275–276, 287, 291–294, 339
Psychosomatic disorders, 372–373
Psychosurgery, 25, 41–43, 45, 438, 442
Psychotherapists:
    on radio, controversy about, 443
    selecting, 433–435
Psychotherapy. *See also* Psychological therapies
    defined, 418
    trends in, 444
Puberty (pubescence) phase of adolescence, 284–285, 452, 454
Public compliance in conformity experiment, 490. *See also* Compliance
Public-distance range of personal space, 515–516
Public territory, 518, 519, 529–530
Punishment, 151–514, 158, 426
Pupillary reflex, 134
Pupils of eyes, 56
Pure tones of sound, 65
Puzzle-box experiments of Thorndike, 138

Questionnaries in correlational research, 6–7
Q-sort technique in self-concept measurement, 355

Racial discrimination:
    in college admissions quotas, 555–556
    in intelligence quotient (IQ) tests, 554–555
Racial-ethnic differences in intelligence quotients (IQs), 321–322
Radiation exposure during pregnancy, 254
Radiation techniques for studying brain function, 38, 389, 412
Radio psychologists, 443
Randomization, defined, 7, 571
Range of scores, defined, 565
Rape, 463–464, 466–467, 472–473
Rapid-eye-movement (REM) sleep, 112–116
Rate of responding, determining, 140
Rational-emotive therapy (RET; Ellis), 428–429, 431
Rationalism in cognitive development study, 471
Rationalization in coping with stress, 380
Ratio schedules of reinforcement, 146
Reaction formation in coping with stress, 380
Reaction range for phenotypes, 318
Reaction-specific energy, 222
Reactive schizophrenia, 405
Realistic people in Strong-Campbell Interest Inventory, 542
Reality principle (ego) in psychoanalytic theory of personality, 335–337

Real motion, 91–92
Recall of information, 165, 173–180. *See also* Retrieval of information from memory
Recency effect in free recall of information, 174
Receptor cells, 53, 57–62, 68–71
Reciprocal determinism (Banduara), 347
Reciprocal liking in attraction, 498
Recognition of information in long-term memory, 173, 175
Recombinant DNA in brain-disorder treatment, 48
Recording techniques for studying brain function, 39–40
Recreational use of drugs, 118
Refabrication of memories, 165, 175–178, 184
Reflex arc, 31–32
Reflex behaviors:
    of newborns and infants, 255–256, 272
    operant conditioning of, 142–143
    stimulus-response relationships in, 133–137
Reflexes, 31–32, 133–135
Refractory period of sexual-response cycle, 462
Regression:
    in coping with stress, 380, 381
    in psychoanalytic model of schizophrenia, 408
Rehearsal:
    of behavior, in assertiveness training, 424–425
    of information, 170–172, 187
Reinforced behaviors, partial versus continuous, 144–147
Reinforcement:
    in behavioral therapies, 425
    differential, of responses, 148
    negative, versus punishment, 152. *See also* Negative reinforcing stimuli; Punishment
    in operant conditioning, 138, 425
    positive. *See* Positive reinforcement
    principle of, 143–144
    in schizophrenia treatment, 408–409
    self-, 154, 347
Reinforcement-affect model of attraction, 496–498
Reinforcement schedules, 144–147
Reinforcement techniques for environmental-behavior changes, 530–533
Reinforcement theory of language acquisition, 200–201
Reinforcing stimuli (reinforcers), 138, 143–145
Relational concepts, 208
Relationships, balance in, 496, 497
Relative refractory period for neurons, 27
Relative size, principle of, 86, 87
Relative standing of distributions, 567–568

Social Readjustment Rating Scale (SRRS), 370, 373, 374
Social responsibility, adolescent development of, 288–290
Social status. *See* Socioeconomic status (SES)
Social support in coping with stress, 377–378
Social withdrawal, crowding as causing, 520
Sociobiology, 223
Sociocultural model of abnormality, 393, 409–411
Socioeconomic status (SES):
  and antisocial personality, 410–411
  and intelligence quotient (IQ), 321
  and personal-space needs, 515
  and schizophrenia, 409
Sociofugal spaces, 528
Sociopetal spaces, 528
Sodium ions in neurons, 27
Sodium-potassium pumps, 27
Somatic nervous system, 32
Somatoform disorders, 398–399
Somatosensory cortex of brain, 36
Somnambulism (sleepwalking), 116, 117
Sound energy, 64–69
Sound waves, 65–67. *See also* Noise
Source traits, 340–341, 352, 353
Spaces:
  defensible, 529–530
  personal, 514–517, 519. *See also* Environmental design
  sociofugal and sociopetal, 528
Spacial ability, gender differences in, 43–44, 322, 323, 457
Spatial behavior, 514–519. *See also* Environmental design
Species-specific behavior, 151
Speed (methedrine), 121
Sperm cells, 251
Spinal cord, 31–32
Spindles in brain waves, 113
Split-brain surgery, 25, 41–43, 45. *See also* Psychosurgery
Split-half method of determining test reliability, 304–305
Sponsor stage of careers, 546–547
Spontaneous recovery in conditioning, 141
SQ3R method of memory improvement, 188
SRRS (Social Readjustment Rating Scale), 370, 373, 374
Stability-instability dimension of personality, 341–342
Stage theory of cognitive development (Piaget), 272–275
Standard deviation of scores, 306, 566, 567
Standardization:
  of abnormal-behavior classifications, 391
  of tests, 306, 557
  Standardized Testing Act of New York (1980), 557
Standard pairing procedure in conditioning, 136

Standford-Binet Intelligence Test, 303, 306, 308. *See also* Binet-Simon intelligence (IQ) test
Stanford Hypnotic Susceptibility Scale, 109
Stapes of ears, 67
State-dependent memory, 181
Statistical significance, 9–10, 571–572
Statistics:
  deception with, 572–573
  descriptive, 563–571
  inferential, 562, 571–572
Status. *See* Occupational status; Socioeconomic status (SES)
Stereoscopic vision, 84
Stereotypes, 454–458, 478–480, 483–484
S-Theme in Strong-Campbell Interest Inventory, 542
Stickleback fish, instinct in, 222
Stilbestrol during pregnancy, 254
Stimulant drugs, 121–123, 408. *See also* Cigarette smoking
Stimulation:
  in brain-function studies, 39
  environmental, vocalization affected by, 256
  subliminal, 53–55
  visual, 55, 96–98
Stimuli:
  absolute threshold of, 54
  defined, 27
  habituation to, 135, 255
  intensity of, 27
  in nerve-impulse transmission, 27
  in reflex behavior, 133–134
  responses to. *See* Responses
  sensitivity to, measurement of, 54–55
  types of:
    anxiety-arousing, 423–424
    aversive, 376, 504
    conditioned, 135–137, 143–145
    discriminative, 138
    neutral, 133, 135
    physical, 54
    reinforcing (reinforcers), 138, 143–145
    sign, 22
    unconditioned, 135–137
Stimulus conditions (cues) in self-control, 154
Stimulus control of behavior, 147–151
Stimulus discrimination, 148
Stimulus generalization, 147–148
Stimulus-seeking motives for behavior, 232–234
Storage of information in memory, 167–173, 183
Strangers, interactions with, in urban versus small-town areas, 525–256
Strange situation procedure for studying infant attachment, 280
Stress. *See also* Anxiety coping with, 371, 374–382

defined, 366
effects of:
  mental, 398–401, 403, 411
  physiological, 239, 372–374
  during pregnancy, 254
  sources of, 365–370, 383–384, 520, 523
Stressors, types of, 365–370, 383–384
Stretch receptors in stomach wall, 228
Striate muscles, 32
Stroboscopic movement, 92
Strong-Campbell Interest Inventory (SCII), 541–543
Structural defects of newborns, 258
Structuralism school of psychology, 11
Structured interviews:
  in correlational research, 6–7
  in personality assessment, 354–355
Students. *See also* Career counseling
  admissions testing for, 553–558
  attribution therapy for, 484–485
  in crowded dormitories, 521, 522, 527
  suicides of, 411
Study of Mathematically Precocious Youth (SMPY), 317
Subjective contours in form perception, 82–83
Subjective organization (clustering) in information retrieval, 172
Subliminal stimulation, 53–55
Subtractive mixture of light waves, 62
Success, fear of, as achievement barrier, 235
Sudden death syndrome (SIDS), 117
Sufficient justification for attitude-discrepant behavior, 488–489
Suicides, 403, 411
Sulci of brain, 30
Superego in psychoanalytic theory of personality, 335–337
Superstitious behavior, 144
Surface structure of sentences, 200
Surface traits, 340
Surrogate mothers for infant monkeys, 279
Surveys:
  In consumer research, 549
  in correlational research, 6–7
  about sexual attitudes and behavior, 458–461
Sympathetic nervous system, 32, 33, 236, 237
Symptom substitution, 428
Synapses in neurons, 27–29
Synaptic cleft of neurons, 28
Synaptic vesicles of neurons, 28
Synaptic transmission of nerve impulses, 27–29. *See also* Neurotransmitters
Syntax in language development, 198–200
Systematic desensitization, 141–142, 423–424, 465

Tachistoscopic technique for studying brain function, 41

Photo Credits

Wide World. 193 © Susan Kuklie, Photo Researchers, Inc. 219 Ira Kirschenbaum, Stock, Boston. 202 Paul Fusco, Magnum Photos. 225 The Granger Collection, New York. 227 Courtesy P. Teitelbaum; from *Appetite,* Proceedings of the American Philosophical Society, Vol. 108, *6,* 464–472, 1964. 228 © Vivienne della Grotta, Photo Researchers, Inc. 232 Adapted from D. D. Berlyne, The influence of complexity and novelty in visual figures on orienting responses. *Journal of Experimental Psychology,* 1958, Vol. 55, p. 291, fig. 1. By permission of the American Psychological Association. 240 From Paul Eckman and Wallace V. Friesen: *Unmasking the face,* Copyright © 1975 by Paul Eckman and Wallace V. Friesen. Adapted with permission. 242 © Bruce Roberts, Photo Researchers, Inc. 244 Courtesy of Arnold E. Andersen, M.D. the Johns Hopkins Medical Institutions, Eating and Weight Disorders Clinic. 247 Monkmeyer Press Photo Service. 250 © Omikron, Photo Researchers, Inc. 256 From "Discrimination and Imitation of Facial Expressions by Neonates," by T. M. Field et. al. In *Science,* 1982, *218,* 179–181. Copyright © 1982 by American Association for the Advancement of Science. Reprinted by permission of the publisher and author. 258 Monkmeyer Press Photo Service. 259 © Leonard Lissen, Photo Researchers, Inc. 260 © Bruce Roberts, Photo Researchers, Inc. 261 © Ed Lettau, Photo Researchers, Inc. 262 Leonard McCombe, LIFE Magazine © Time, Inc. 267 Jim Harrison, Stock, Boston. 273 (top right & left) George Zimbel, Monkmeyer Press Photo Service. 275 The Granger Collection, New York. 276 Thomas McAvoy, LIFE Magazine © 1955, Time, Inc. 277 Jim Harrison, Stock, Boston. 279 University of Wisconsin Primate Laboratory. 282 Wayne Miller, Magnum Photos. 287 Paul Conklin, Monkmeyer Press Photo Service. 292 Historical Pictures Service, Chicago. 293 Linda Ferrar Rogers, Woodfin-Camp. 299 Mimi Forsyth, Monkmeyer Press Photo Service. 302 By courtesy of the Galton Laboratory, University College, London. 303 Nancy Hays, Monkmeyer Press Photo Service. 313 Wide World Photos. 314 The Granger Collection, New York. 319 United Press International. 333 Courtesy: The Baltimore Sun. 339 The Granger Collection, New York. 349 (left) © Ray Ellis, Photo Researchers, Inc. 349 (center) Michael Hay, Stock, Boston. 349 (right) © Suzanne Szasz, Photo Researchers, Inc. 363 Nicholas Sapiehe, Stock, Boston. 367 © A. Isaacs, Photo Researchers, Inc. 375 Robert Goldstein, Photo Researchers, Inc. 377 Magnum Photos. 381 © Van Bucher, Photo Researchers, Inc. 383 © George Gerster, Photo Researchers, Inc. 387 © Dr. Jay Weissberg, Photo Researchers, Inc. 389 Courtesy Allan F. Mirsky. 395 Owen Franken, Stock, Boston. 397 David Farr. 399 © Martin Gershem, Photo Researchers. 401 © Lynn Lennon, Photo Researchers. 407 Taurus Photos. 415 © Jan Lukas, Photo Researchers, Inc. 418 The Bettmann Archive. 419 Historical Picture Service, Chicago. 421 The Bettmann Archive. 423 © Van Bucher, Photo Researchers, Inc. 427 Courtesy Albert Bandura, Standford. 433 Freda Leinwand, Monkmeyer Press Photo Service. 437 Paul Fusco, Magnum Photos. 438 Culver Pictures 441 Jim Ritscher, Stock, Boston. 455 Wide World Photos. 457 © Suzanne Szasz, Photo Researchers, Inc. 461 Brown Brothers. 465 Fredrik D. Bodin, Stock, Boston. 467 Eric Kroll, Taurus Photos. 475 © M. Ursilla, Photo Researchers. 477 The New York Times. 487 Courtesy American Cancer Society. 490 From "Opinions and social pressure" by Solomon E. Asch, 1955, *Scientific American, 193,* p. 33. Copyright 1955 by Scientific American and William Vandivert. 494 Ron Haelerbe, LIFE Magazine © 1969, Time, Inc. 500 © Jan Lukas, Photo Researchers, Inc. 502 Courtesy of WJLA-TV, Washington, D.C. 505 Wide World Photos. 511 Herman J. Kokojan, Black Star. 514 Both photos by David Wilson. 515 (left) Chris Brown, Stock, Boston. 515 (right) Robert F. Holden, Black Star. 517 David Wilson 527 From "Reducing the stress of high-density living? An architectural intervention" by Andrew Baum and Glenn E. Davis, 1980, *Journal of Personality and Social Psychology, 38,* p. 475. Copyright 1980 by the American Psychological Association. Reprinted by permission of the authors. 528 Herman J. Kokojan, Black Star. 529 United Press International. 531 David Wilson. 532 Doug Wilson, Black Star. 537 Susan Miller. 551 Susan Miller. 552 Wide World Photos.

†

Drama
Psychology
Philosophy
Sociology
Intro. To. Higher Learning.

Mon [8]	Tues	Wed [3]	Thurs [3̶4]	Fri [3]
Philosophy Psychology Sociology Intro. Drama	Drama Psychology Philosophy Intro. To.	Psychology Sociology	Drama Philosophy	Sociology Intro. To.
Psychology Philosophy Intro to.	Drama Philosophy Sociology	Psychology Intro to.	Sociology	Drama Philosophy Intro to.
6̶ 8	7	2̶ 4	3	4̶ 5

Sun

Drama
Psychology
Sociology

3